EMPLOYMENT, HOURS, AND EARNINGS

STATES AND AREAS

13th Edition
2018

EMPLOYMENT, HOURS, AND EARNINGS

STATES AND AREAS

13th Edition
2018

Edited by Mary Meghan Ryan

Bernan Press

Lanham, MD

Published by Bernan Press
An imprint of The Rowman & Littlefield Publishing Group, Inc.
4501 Forbes Boulevard, Suite 200, Lanham, Maryland 20706
www.rowman.com
800-462-6420

6 Tinworth Street, London SE11 5AL

ISBN-13: 978-1-64143-271-9
e-ISBN-13: 978-1-64143-272-6

∞™ The paper used in this publication meets the minimum requirements of
American National Standard for Information Sciences—Permanence of
Paper for Printed Library Materials, ANSI/NISO Z39.48-1992.

Printed in the United States of America

CONTENTS

PART B: METROPOLITAN STATISTICAL AREA (MSA) DATA

APPENDIX

Bernan Press proudly presents the 13th edition of *Employment, Hours, and Earnings: States and Areas, 2018.* A special addition to Bernan Press's *Handbook of U.S. Labor Statistics: Employment, Earnings, Prices, Productivity, and Other Labor Data*, this reference is a consolidated wealth of employment information, providing monthly and annual data on hours worked and earnings made by industry across America for the years 2007 through 2017, including figures and summary information spanning years the same time period. These data, compiled by the Bureau of Labor Statistics, are presented for states and metropolitan statistical areas.

This edition features:

- Nearly 300 tables with data on employment for each state, the District of Columbia, and the nation's 75 largest metropolitan statistical areas (MSAs)

- Detailed, non-seasonally adjusted, industry data organized by month and year

- Hours and earnings data for each state, by industry

- An introduction for each state and the District of Columbia that denotes salient data and noteworthy trends, including changes in population and the civilian labor force, industry increases and declines, employment and unemployment statistics, and a chart detailing employment percentages, by industry

- Ranking of the 75 largest MSAs, including Census population estimates for 2017, unemployment rates for 2010 and 2017, and the percent change in total nonfarm employment from 2007 through 2017

- Concise technical notes that explain pertinent facts about the data, including sources, definitions, and significant changes; and provides references for further guidance

- A comprehensive appendix that details the geographical components of the 75 largest MSAs

The employment, hours, and earnings data in this publication provide a detailed and timely picture of the 50 states, the District of Columbia, and the nation's 75 largest MSAs. These data can be used to analyze key factors affecting state and local economies and to compare national cyclical trends to local-level economic activity.

This reference is an excellent source of information for analysts in both the public and private sectors. Readers who are involved in public policy can use these data to determine the health of the economy, to clearly identify which sectors are growing and which are declining, and to determine the need for federal assistance. State and local jurisdictions can use the data to determine the need for services, including training and unemployment assistance, and for planning and budgetary purposes. In addition, the data can be used to forecast tax revenue. In private industry, the data can be used by business owners to compare their business to the economy as a whole; and to identify suitable areas when making decisions about plant locations, wholesale and retail trade outlets, and for locating a particular sector base.

In this 13th edition, *Employment, Hours, and Earnings: States and Areas* presents monthly and annual average data on employment for each state, the District of Columbia, and the nation's 75 largest metropolitan statistical areas (MSAs). In addition, hours and earnings data are provided, where available, for each state. The industry data are based on the North American Industry Classification System (NAICS), which is discussed in greater detail later in these notes. The employment data are presented on a monthly and annual basis for 2007 through 2017. The hours and earnings data are available from 2013 through 2017.

The Bureau of Labor Statistics (BLS), the statistical agency within the U.S. Department of Labor, conducts the Current Employment Statistics (CES) survey to provide industry data on the employment, hours, and earnings of workers on nonfarm payrolls. The unemployment data and the civilian labor force estimates in this publication were obtained from the Local Area Unemployment Statistics (LAUS) program, which provides monthly employment and unemployment data for approximately 7,000 geographic areas including Census regions and divisions, states, counties, metropolitan areas, and many cities and towns.

The data from both the CES and LAUS are derived from federal and state cooperative collection efforts in which state employment security agencies prepare data using concepts, definitions, and technical procedures prescribed by the BLS. Although the estimation of the two data sets are based on differing methodologies (described in more detail later in this section), their inclusion together in this reference is intended to provide a broad overview of state and local labor market conditions.

THE CURRENT EMPLOYMENT STATISTICS (CES) SURVEY—EMPLOYMENT, HOURS, AND EARNINGS DATA

The CES survey is a monthly survey commonly referred to as the establishment or payroll survey that provides estimates of employment, hours, and earnings data by industry. Its estimates are derived from a sample of about 149,000 private nonfarm businesses and federal, state, and local government entities, which cover approximately 651,000 individual worksites in all 50 states, the District of Columbia, Puerto Rico, the U.S. Virgin Islands, and more than 350 metropolitan areas and divisions. These establishments are classified on the basis of their primary activity by major industry groupings in accordance with NAICS. For an establishment engaging in more than one activity, the entire establishment is included under the industry indicated as the principal activity.

More information on the exact methodology used to obtain data for employment, hours, and earnings was originally detailed in the *BLS Handbook of Methods*. The *Handbook* is updated online and can be found at www.bls.gov/opub/hom. Information on the CES survey can also be found on the BLS website at www.bls.gov/ces/cesprog.htm.

CONCEPTS

Employment is the total number of persons employed either full or part-time in nonfarm business establishments during a specific payroll period. Temporary employees are included as well as civilian government employees. Unpaid family members working in a family-owned business, domestic workers in private homes, farm employees, and self-employed persons are excluded from the CES, as well as military personnel and employees of the Central Intelligence Agency, the National Security Agency, the National Imagery and Mapping Agency, and the Defense Intelligence Agency. In addition, employees on layoff, on leave without pay, on strike for the entire pay period, or who had been hired but did not start work during the pay period are also excluded.

The reference period includes all persons who worked during or received pay for any part of the pay period that includes the 12th of the month, a standard for all federal agencies collecting employment data from business establishments. Workers who are on paid sick leave (when pay is received directly from the employer) or paid holiday or vacation, or who worked during only part of the specified pay period (because of unemployment or strike during the rest of the pay period) are counted as employed. Employees on the payroll of more than one establishment during the pay period are counted in each establishment that reports them, whether the duplication is due to turnover or dual jobholding.

Nonfarm employment includes employment in all goods-producing and service-providing industries. The goods-producing sector includes mining and logging, construction, and manufacturing, the last of which is made up of durable and nondurable goods (these breakdowns are not provided in this publication). The service-providing sector includes both private service-providing and government employment. Private service sector employment includes trade, transportation, and utilities (which is comprised of wholesale trade, retail trade, and transportation and utilities); information; financial activities; professional and business services; educational and health services; leisure and hospitality; and other services. Government employment encompasses federal-, state-, and local-level civilian employees. Subcategories of these industries are available on the BLS website at www.bls.gov/sae.

Unemployment consists of those who were not employed during the reference week but were available for work, except for temporary illness, and had made specific efforts to find employment some time during the 4-week period ending with the reference week. Persons who were waiting to be recalled to a job from which they had been laid off are classified as unemployed even if they have not been looking for another job.

The *unemployment rate* is the number of unemployed persons as a percent of the civilian labor force.

The *civilian labor force* consists of all persons classified as employed or unemployed as described above.

Hours and earnings data for each state are based on reports from industry payrolls and the corresponding hours paid for construction workers, production workers, and nonsupervisory workers. The data include workers who received pay for any part of the pay period that includes the 12th day of the month. Because not all sample respondents report production worker hours and earnings data, insufficient sample sizes preclude hours and earnings data from many sectors in many states. Therefore, the data available, and thus published, vary from state to state.

The payroll for these workers is reported before deductions of any kind, including Social Security, unemployment insurance, group health insurance, withholding taxes, retirement plans, or union dues.

Included in the payroll report of earnings is pay for all hours worked, including overtime, shift premiums, vacations, holiday, and sick-leave pay. Bonuses and commissions are excluded unless they are earned and paid regularly each pay period. Benefits, such as health insurance and contribution to a retirement fund, are also excluded.

Hours include all hours worked (including overtime hours) and hours paid for holidays, vacations, and sick leave during the pay period that includes the 12th day of the month. Average weekly hours differ from the concept of scheduled hours worked because of factors such as unpaid absenteeism, labor turnover, part-time work, and strikes, as well as fluctuations in work schedules. Average weekly hours are typically lower than scheduled hours of work.

Average hourly earnings are derived by dividing gross payrolls by total hours, reflecting the actual earnings of workers (including premium pay). They differ from wage rates, which are the amounts stipulated for a given unit of work or time. Average hourly earnings do not represent total labor costs per hour because they exclude retroactive payments and irregular bonuses, employee benefits,

and the employer's share of payroll taxes. Earnings for employees not included in the production worker or nonsupervisory categories are not reflected in the estimates in this publication.

Average weekly earnings are derived by multiplying average weekly hours by average hourly earnings.

Users should note that in the context of historical data, long-term trends in hours and earnings data also reflect structural changes, such as the changing mixes of full-time and part-time employees and highly paid and lower-wage workers within businesses and across industries.

METROPOLITAN STATISTICAL AREAS (MSAs) AND NEW ENGLAND CITY AND TOWN AREAS (NECTAs)

A metropolitan statistical area (MSA) is a core area with a large population nucleus, combined with adjacent communities that have high degrees of economic and social integration with the core area. The standard definition of a MSA is determined by the Office of Management and Budget (OMB), which updates the definition based on the decennial census and updated information provided by the Census Bureau between the censuses. Each MSA must have at least one urbanized area of 50,000 inhabitants or more.

New England city and town areas (NECTAs) are similar to MSAs, but are defined using cities and towns instead of counties in the six New England states. BLS only provides employment data on NECTAs in the New England region. Employment and Unemployment data are provided for the following NECTAs in this publication: Boston–Cambridge–Newton, MA–NH; Hartford–West Hartford–East Hartford, CT; Providence–Warwick, RI–MA; New Haven, CT; and Worcester, MA. All other areas are MSAs.

The appendix details the geographic components for each MSA and NECTA.

REVISIONS TO THE DATA

North American Industry Classification System (NAICS)

The most far-reaching revision of the CES data occurred when the industrial classification system was changed from the 60-year-old Standard Industrial Classification (SIC) system to the North American Industry Classification System (NAICS) in January 2003. The revision changed the way establishments were classified into industries in order to more accurately reflect the current composition of U.S. businesses. In March 2008, the CES state and area nonfarm payroll series was converted to the 2007 NAICS series. This resulted in relatively minor changes. In February 2012, CES updated the national payroll series to

NAICS 2012 from NAICS 2007. The CES data are now classified according to the 2017 North American Industry Classification System (NAICS).

NAICS was adopted as the standard measure of industry classification by statistical agencies in the United States, Canada, and Mexico to enhance the comparability of economic data across the North American Free Trade Association (NAFTA) trade area. Comparison between the NAICS and the old SIC are limited, however, the historical industry series from April 1995 through 2001 are available on both SIC and NAICS bases. The BLS has not updated the SIC data nor (for the most part) linked the historical SIC data with the current NAICS data.

Benchmark Revisions

Employment estimates are adjusted annually to a complete count of jobs—called benchmarks—which are primarily derived from tax reports submitted by employers covered by state unemployment laws (which cover most establishments). In this re-anchoring of sample-based employment estimates to full population counts, the original sample-based estimates are replaced with the benchmark data from the previous year. The benchmark information is used to adjust monthly estimates between the new benchmark and the preceding benchmark, thereby preserving the continuity of the series and establishing the level of employment for the new benchmark month.

Seasonal Adjustment

Over the course of a year, the size of a state's employment level undergoes sharp fluctuations because of changes in the weather, reduced or expanded production, harvests, major holidays, and the like. Because these seasonal events follow a more or less regular pattern each year, adjusting the data on a month-to-month basis may eliminate their influence on data trends. These adjustments make it easier for users to observe the cyclical and other nonseasonal movements in the data series, but it must be noted that the seasonally adjusted series are ovnly an approximation based on past experience. The seasonally adjusted data have a broader margin of error than the unadjusted data because they are subject to both sampling and other errors in the seasonal adjustment process. The data presented in this publication are not seasonally adjusted; therefore, the month-to-month variations in the data contain seasonal variations that may distort month-to-month comparisons. Data for the MSAs are also not seasonally adjusted, as the sample sizes do not allow for reliable estimates for seasonal adjustment factors.

The Local Area Unemployment Statistics (LAUS) Program

The Local Area Unemployment Statistics (LAUS) program provides monthly and annual estimates on several labor force concepts, including employment, unemployment, labor force totals, and the employment-population ratio. The unemployment data as well as the civilian labor force estimates presented in this publication are from the LAUS program. The unemployment rate is shown for each state in 2010 and 2017 along with the rank for each state. The rankings are from highest to lowest—a change from earlier editions of *Employment, Hours, and Earnings* but consistent with the most recent editions of the book. In 2017, unemployment ranged from a low of 2.4 percent in Hawaii to a high of 7.2 percent in Alaska. Therefore, Hawaii is ranked last and the Alaska is ranked first. Unemployment data are not available by industry.

The concepts and definitions underlying the LAUS program come from the Current Population Survey (CPS), the household survey conducted by the Census Bureau for the BLS. The LAUS models combine current and historical data from the CPS, Current Employment Statistics (CES), and the State Unemployment Insurance (UI) Systems. Numerous conceptual and technical differences exist between the household and establishment surveys, and estimates of monthly employment changes from these two surveys usually do not match in size or even direction. As a result, the unemployment data and the civilian labor force estimates on each state header page presented in this edition are not directly comparable to the employment data. However, this publication includes this information to provide complementary information on labor market conditions in each state and the District of Columbia. Monthly and annual data are available from the BLS on their website at www.bls.gov/lau. More information on the differences between the surveys, as well as guidance on the complex methods used to obtain the LAUS data, is provided on the BLS website at www.bls.gov/lau/laufaq.htm.

PART A

STATE DATA

ALABAMA
At a Glance

Population:
 2010 census: 4,779,736
 2017 estimate: 4,874,747

Percent change in population:
 2010–2017: 2.0%

Percent change in total nonfarm employment:
 2007–2017: -0.4%

Industry with the largest growth in employment, 2007–2017 (thousands):
 Education and health services, 28.3

Industry with the largest decline or smallest growth in employment, 2007–2017 (thousands):
 Manufacturing, -33.0

Civilian labor force:
 2010: 2,196,042
 2017: 2,168,444

Unemployment rate and rank among states (highest to lowest):
 2010: 10.5%, 9th
 2017: 4.4%, 23rd

Over-the-year change in unemployment rates:
 2015–2016: -0.2%
 2016–2017: -1.5%

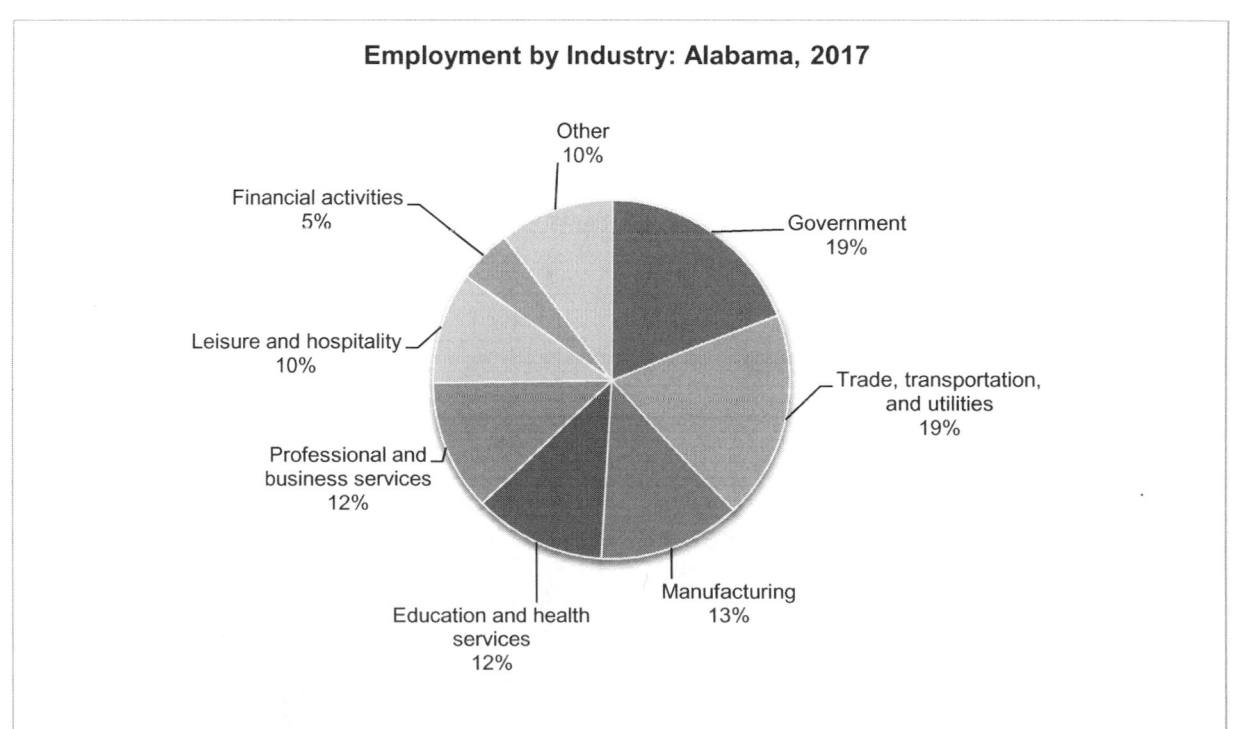

Employment by Industry: Alabama, 2017

Other 10%
Financial activities 5%
Government 19%
Leisure and hospitality 10%
Trade, transportation, and utilities 19%
Professional and business services 12%
Manufacturing 13%
Education and health services 12%

1. Employment by Industry: Alabama, 2007–2017

Industry and year	January	February	March	April	May	June	July	August	September	October	November	December	Annual average
Total Nonfarm													
2007	1,991.5	2,004.7	2,021.6	2,017.8	2,026.2	2,035.2	2,011.0	2,021.5	2,030.6	2,030.7	2,040.4	2,045.8	2,023.1
2008	2,002.9	2,012.1	2,020.3	2,025.9	2,029.8	2,029.3	2,006.1	2,008.5	2,009.6	1,999.7	1,989.4	1,983.6	2,009.8
2009	1,923.3	1,918.3	1,918.4	1,918.2	1,917.5	1,913.4	1,891.4	1,888.8	1,891.2	1,887.8	1,896.2	1,896.4	1,905.1
2010	1,858.7	1,864.4	1,879.6	1,891.4	1,907.4	1,908.6	1,889.3	1,887.6	1,891.7	1,897.4	1,904.0	1,903.4	1,890.3
2011	1,859.2	1,873.5	1,886.2	1,894.8	1,897.5	1,897.9	1,882.6	1,887.8	1,899.8	1,894.5	1,905.0	1,904.2	1,890.3
2012	1,870.7	1,882.6	1,901.3	1,909.8	1,912.7	1,917.6	1,893.7	1,904.4	1,911.1	1,913.8	1,927.0	1,925.8	1,905.9
2013	1,886.1	1,903.2	1,917.5	1,926.4	1,934.2	1,936.1	1,916.2	1,924.1	1,927.1	1,929.3	1,942.2	1,946.9	1,924.1
2014	1,906.3	1,915.3	1,929.9	1,944.2	1,950.8	1,954.1	1,935.0	1,946.0	1,952.7	1,958.9	1,966.1	1,973.8	1,944.4
2015	1,932.9	1,944.9	1,953.5	1,969.1	1,978.3	1,980.5	1,967.0	1,973.2	1,977.7	1,985.6	1,993.6	1,999.8	1,971.3
2016	1,963.1	1,974.1	1,984.1	2,000.7	2,003.0	2,003.7	1,991.5	1,997.5	2,005.3	2,004.0	2,011.6	2,013.7	1,996.0
2017	1,982.5	1,996.5	2,008.0	2,014.6	2,020.8	2,026.6	2,007.6	2,016.7	2,021.2	2,028.2	2,034.4	2,028.3	2,015.5
Total Private													
2007	1,614.2	1,624.5	1,640.2	1,636.2	1,643.8	1,652.8	1,643.0	1,649.4	1,649.5	1,646.3	1,654.5	1,659.4	1,642.8
2008	1,619.4	1,624.3	1,631.3	1,636.0	1,638.4	1,637.9	1,630.5	1,629.9	1,623.1	1,607.9	1,598.1	1,591.0	1,622.3
2009	1,536.9	1,529.4	1,528.6	1,526.4	1,525.5	1,522.3	1,516.8	1,512.0	1,505.8	1,496.9	1,504.7	1,503.7	1,517.4
2010	1,471.3	1,473.9	1,486.4	1,496.8	1,503.8	1,510.5	1,509.6	1,507.9	1,504.3	1,506.2	1,511.7	1,510.5	1,499.4
2011	1,471.6	1,483.0	1,494.7	1,503.7	1,506.8	1,510.3	1,507.6	1,513.0	1,516.1	1,508.5	1,517.6	1,518.6	1,504.3
2012	1,489.3	1,497.6	1,514.1	1,523.9	1,527.6	1,534.9	1,524.7	1,534.5	1,533.3	1,530.0	1,542.0	1,541.1	1,524.4
2013	1,506.5	1,519.3	1,531.4	1,540.8	1,549.3	1,554.6	1,543.6	1,551.3	1,549.2	1,546.5	1,557.9	1,563.6	1,542.8
2014	1,526.9	1,532.7	1,546.0	1,559.4	1,564.8	1,569.8	1,564.1	1,572.7	1,571.8	1,574.2	1,580.4	1,587.4	1,562.5
2015	1,553.7	1,563.0	1,570.7	1,585.2	1,592.9	1,596.9	1,595.4	1,598.7	1,598.0	1,603.3	1,610.3	1,616.0	1,590.3
2016	1,584.2	1,592.6	1,601.3	1,617.1	1,618.2	1,619.2	1,617.7	1,620.2	1,621.9	1,618.9	1,625.4	1,626.9	1,613.6
2017	1,600.5	1,611.8	1,621.9	1,627.7	1,632.8	1,638.7	1,631.1	1,637.3	1,635.9	1,640.0	1,645.2	1,641.0	1,630.3
Goods Producing													
2007	420.1	421.6	423.9	420.9	421.3	423.9	421.0	421.8	423.2	423.0	421.0	420.6	421.9
2008	413.2	412.5	412.1	411.1	411.2	411.1	409.0	406.0	404.6	397.1	389.8	386.1	405.3
2009	369.7	363.7	360.9	356.0	352.9	348.9	347.3	344.3	342.3	339.5	339.2	339.1	350.3
2010	332.1	331.5	334.3	336.6	338.3	339.4	338.6	337.4	336.8	335.3	333.9	331.9	335.5
2011	322.5	326.3	329.0	330.0	331.5	332.5	331.2	332.6	332.7	331.4	332.4	333.8	330.5
2012	328.5	329.9	333.3	335.1	335.5	336.9	336.7	338.2	337.9	339.0	339.0	339.6	335.8
2013	334.7	336.1	340.5	341.0	340.9	342.6	340.7	342.2	341.6	341.9	341.7	343.2	340.6
2014	338.5	339.2	341.7	342.5	344.0	345.5	345.1	346.6	347.5	348.6	348.4	349.5	344.8
2015	345.5	346.8	347.5	348.7	349.9	351.6	351.2	351.6	352.2	352.8	352.9	354.4	350.4
2016	351.4	351.2	352.8	354.6	353.7	354.6	355.1	354.3	356.4	355.0	354.6	356.2	354.2
2017	354.3	356.5	358.0	357.1	357.7	358.4	357.3	358.3	359.5	360.2	360.4	359.7	358.1
Service-Providing													
2007	1,571.4	1,583.1	1,597.7	1,596.9	1,604.9	1,611.3	1,590.0	1,599.7	1,607.4	1,607.7	1,619.4	1,625.2	1,601.2
2008	1,589.7	1,599.6	1,608.2	1,614.8	1,618.6	1,618.2	1,597.1	1,602.5	1,605.0	1,602.6	1,599.6	1,597.5	1,604.5
2009	1,553.6	1,554.6	1,557.5	1,562.2	1,564.6	1,564.5	1,544.1	1,544.5	1,548.9	1,548.3	1,557.0	1,557.3	1,554.8
2010	1,526.6	1,532.9	1,545.3	1,554.8	1,569.1	1,569.2	1,550.7	1,550.2	1,554.9	1,562.1	1,570.1	1,571.5	1,554.8
2011	1,536.7	1,547.2	1,557.2	1,564.8	1,566.0	1,565.4	1,551.4	1,555.2	1,567.1	1,563.1	1,572.6	1,570.4	1,559.8
2012	1,542.2	1,552.7	1,568.0	1,574.7	1,577.2	1,580.7	1,557.0	1,566.2	1,573.2	1,574.8	1,588.0	1,586.2	1,570.1
2013	1,551.4	1,567.1	1,577.0	1,585.4	1,593.3	1,593.5	1,575.5	1,581.9	1,585.5	1,587.4	1,600.5	1,603.7	1,583.5
2014	1,567.8	1,576.1	1,588.2	1,601.7	1,606.8	1,608.6	1,589.9	1,599.4	1,605.2	1,610.3	1,617.7	1,624.3	1,599.7
2015	1,587.4	1,598.1	1,606.0	1,620.4	1,628.4	1,628.9	1,615.8	1,621.6	1,625.5	1,632.8	1,640.7	1,645.4	1,620.9
2016	1,611.7	1,622.9	1,631.3	1,646.1	1,649.3	1,649.1	1,636.4	1,643.2	1,648.9	1,649.0	1,657.0	1,657.5	1,641.9
2017	1,628.2	1,640.0	1,650.0	1,657.5	1,663.1	1,668.2	1,650.3	1,658.4	1,661.7	1,668.0	1,674.0	1,668.6	1,657.3
Mining and Logging													
2007	12.9	13.0	13.1	12.8	12.9	12.9	12.8	12.9	12.8	12.8	12.7	12.8	12.9
2008	12.5	12.6	12.6	12.6	12.4	12.5	12.6	12.6	12.7	12.6	12.5	12.5	12.6
2009	12.2	12.2	11.9	11.8	11.7	11.8	11.8	11.6	11.7	11.7	11.7	11.6	11.8
2010	11.7	11.7	11.7	11.9	12.0	12.0	12.1	12.2	12.1	12.3	12.2	12.2	12.0
2011	12.1	12.1	12.1	12.3	12.4	12.5	12.3	12.5	12.6	12.5	12.5	12.6	12.4
2012	12.7	12.6	12.5	12.5	12.5	12.6	12.8	12.8	12.7	12.6	12.6	12.6	12.6
2013	12.3	12.3	12.4	12.1	12.2	12.3	11.9	12.0	12.0	11.9	11.9	11.9	12.1
2014	11.8	11.6	11.7	11.7	11.6	11.7	11.8	11.8	11.8	11.7	11.6	11.5	11.7
2015	11.5	11.4	11.3	11.1	11.1	11.1	11.2	11.0	10.9	10.8	10.3	10.2	11.0
2016	9.9	9.5	9.5	9.3	9.2	9.2	9.3	9.2	9.4	9.1	9.3	9.3	9.4
2017	9.6	9.7	9.7	9.7	9.7	9.7	9.7	9.8	9.9	9.8	9.9	9.8	9.8

1. Employment by Industry: Alabama, 2007–2017—*Continued*

Industry and year	January	February	March	April	May	June	July	August	September	October	November	December	Annual average
Construction													
2007	109.4	110.7	113.2	112.0	112.3	113.1	112.0	113.2	114.7	114.9	113.6	113.1	112.7
2008	109.5	110.0	110.4	110.3	110.9	110.7	110.1	109.0	108.8	105.9	103.8	102.3	108.5
2009	94.8	93.6	94.3	92.9	93.3	92.9	92.0	90.5	89.7	88.5	89.0	89.3	91.7
2010	85.4	85.4	87.4	88.2	89.1	90.2	89.3	88.2	87.8	86.8	85.1	83.5	87.2
2011	77.2	79.2	81.1	80.8	82.0	81.8	81.2	81.1	81.9	81.0	80.7	80.6	80.7
2012	76.7	77.7	79.9	80.3	79.9	80.0	79.7	80.2	80.2	80.7	80.0	79.3	79.6
2013	76.5	76.9	79.9	80.4	79.9	80.1	79.5	80.1	79.4	80.0	78.7	79.3	79.2
2014	76.2	77.4	79.0	79.4	79.9	80.3	80.3	80.9	81.1	82.0	81.1	81.0	79.9
2015	78.5	79.1	79.6	80.9	81.2	82.2	81.9	82.2	82.7	83.3	83.5	84.2	81.6
2016	82.9	82.8	84.6	85.5	84.6	84.4	84.3	83.5	84.8	84.5	83.7	84.7	84.2
2017	83.2	84.0	85.5	84.3	85.1	84.8	84.5	84.9	86.0	87.2	86.7	84.3	85.0
Manufacturing													
2007	297.8	297.9	297.6	296.1	296.1	297.9	296.2	295.7	295.7	295.3	294.7	294.7	296.3
2008	291.2	200.0	280.1	288.2	287.9	287.9	286.3	284.4	283.1	278.6	273.5	271.3	284.3
2009	262.7	257.9	254.7	251.3	247.9	244.2	243.5	242.2	240.9	239.3	238.5	238.2	246.8
2010	235.0	234.4	235.2	236.5	237.2	237.2	237.2	237.0	236.9	236.2	236.6	236.2	236.3
2011	233.2	235.0	235.8	236.9	237.1	238.2	237.7	239.0	238.2	237.9	239.2	240.6	237.4
2012	239.1	239.6	240.9	242.3	243.1	244.3	244.2	245.2	245.0	245.7	246.4	247.7	243.6
2013	245.9	246.9	248.2	248.5	248.8	250.2	249.3	250.1	250.2	250.0	251.1	252.0	249.3
2014	250.5	250.2	251.0	251.4	252.5	253.5	253.0	253.9	254.6	254.9	255.7	257.0	253.2
2015	255.5	256.3	256.6	256.7	257.6	258.3	258.1	258.4	258.6	258.7	259.1	260.0	257.8
2016	258.6	258.9	258.7	259.8	259.9	261.0	261.5	261.6	262.2	261.4	261.6	262.2	260.6
2017	261.5	262.8	262.8	263.1	262.9	263.9	263.1	263.6	263.6	263.2	263.8	265.6	263.3
Trade, Transportation, and Utilities													
2007	387.7	387.4	391.7	390.7	394.3	396.1	395.1	394.7	395.0	394.8	402.5	405.9	394.7
2008	390.6	388.7	391.0	389.5	390.1	390.3	389.5	389.7	388.3	385.8	388.9	390.1	389.4
2009	371.2	367.4	366.7	364.8	365.9	365.8	364.3	363.1	362.9	361.0	366.7	368.6	365.7
2010	356.6	355.6	358.5	359.0	360.6	361.1	360.6	360.7	359.8	363.0	368.6	371.9	361.3
2011	358.7	358.7	360.5	361.9	362.3	363.8	364.1	364.8	364.0	365.0	371.4	374.1	364.1
2012	361.8	360.2	363.4	363.6	365.4	366.3	364.2	364.6	364.2	366.1	374.7	376.5	365.9
2013	361.5	361.9	364.0	364.8	367.0	368.9	368.2	368.9	367.7	368.9	377.0	381.4	368.4
2014	367.1	365.8	368.9	370.1	370.9	372.2	372.4	372.1	371.7	372.9	381.9	385.6	372.6
2015	371.0	370.0	372.8	375.2	377.0	378.0	378.0	378.1	377.0	379.4	387.3	390.3	377.8
2016	376.6	375.9	377.5	379.3	379.9	379.9	379.7	379.0	378.8	380.0	387.0	388.9	380.2
2017	376.8	375.4	376.5	377.2	377.9	378.9	377.0	377.4	376.5	380.5	387.2	384.8	378.8
Wholesale Trade													
2007	81.3	81.6	82.1	81.9	82.3	82.8	82.2	82.2	82.4	82.5	82.3	82.4	82.2
2008	80.8	80.8	81.0	81.0	81.3	81.3	80.9	80.8	80.7	80.4	79.5	79.1	80.6
2009	77.0	76.3	75.9	75.0	74.8	74.4	73.6	73.6	73.3	73.3	73.2	72.9	74.4
2010	71.7	71.5	71.5	71.8	72.1	71.9	72.0	71.9	71.6	72.1	71.9	71.8	71.8
2011	70.9	71.3	71.5	71.8	71.9	71.9	72.3	72.5	72.4	72.9	72.7	72.9	72.1
2012	71.9	72.0	72.5	72.6	72.9	73.0	72.6	72.6	72.6	73.0	72.9	73.0	72.6
2013	72.0	72.4	72.5	72.8	73.1	72.9	73.1	73.1	73.0	73.2	73.3	73.3	72.9
2014	72.2	72.4	72.5	72.8	73.2	73.2	73.3	73.4	73.4	73.6	73.9	74.0	73.2
2015	72.8	73.0	73.3	73.8	73.8	73.8	74.1	73.9	73.9	74.2	74.1	74.0	73.7
2016	72.9	73.1	73.3	73.8	73.9	73.8	73.8	73.7	73.7	73.9	73.7	73.7	73.6
2017	72.6	72.9	73.1	73.6	73.9	74.2	73.6	73.6	73.8	74.5	74.0	73.1	73.6
Retail Trade													
2007	236.3	235.6	238.8	238.4	240.7	241.6	241.4	240.9	240.6	240.6	247.9	250.4	241.1
2008	239.0	237.4	239.6	237.6	237.7	238.1	237.1	237.1	235.9	234.5	238.9	240.5	237.8
2009	227.4	224.6	224.6	223.9	224.7	224.9	224.3	222.9	223.1	221.7	227.4	228.9	224.9
2010	219.9	219.1	221.8	221.4	222.3	222.8	221.9	222.0	221.1	224.0	229.6	232.2	223.2
2011	221.4	220.6	221.9	223.2	223.1	224.3	224.3	224.4	223.6	224.5	231.0	232.7	224.6
2012	222.4	220.1	222.1	222.1	223.5	223.9	222.5	222.4	221.8	223.4	231.8	232.7	224.1
2013	219.4	219.2	220.9	221.6	223.1	224.8	224.2	224.7	223.5	224.4	232.0	235.2	224.4
2014	223.3	222.1	224.4	225.3	225.7	226.6	226.7	226.2	225.6	226.9	235.1	237.5	227.1
2015	225.1	224.7	226.7	228.5	229.9	230.7	230.4	230.6	229.8	231.8	239.5	241.3	230.8
2016	229.7	229.4	230.8	232.2	232.5	232.5	232.3	231.7	231.3	232.7	239.7	240.1	232.9
2017	230.6	229.1	229.6	230.7	230.9	231.8	230.8	230.4	229.2	231.9	238.2	235.3	231.5

1. Employment by Industry: Alabama, 2007–2017—*Continued*

Industry and year	January	February	March	April	May	June	July	August	September	October	November	December	Annual average
Transportation and Utilities													
2007	70.1	70.2	70.8	70.4	71.3	71.7	71.5	71.6	72.0	71.7	72.3	73.1	71.4
2008	70.8	70.5	70.4	70.9	71.1	70.9	71.5	71.8	71.7	70.9	70.5	70.5	71.0
2009	66.8	66.5	66.2	65.9	66.4	66.5	66.4	66.6	66.5	66.0	66.1	66.8	66.4
2010	65.0	65.0	65.2	65.8	66.2	66.4	66.7	66.8	67.1	66.9	67.1	67.9	66.3
2011	66.4	66.8	67.1	66.9	67.3	67.6	67.5	67.9	68.0	67.6	67.7	68.5	67.4
2012	67.5	68.1	68.8	68.9	69.0	69.4	69.1	69.6	69.8	69.7	70.0	70.8	69.2
2013	70.1	70.3	70.6	70.4	70.8	71.2	70.9	71.1	71.2	71.3	71.7	72.9	71.0
2014	71.6	71.3	72.0	72.0	72.0	72.4	72.4	72.5	72.7	72.4	72.9	74.1	72.4
2015	73.1	72.3	72.8	72.9	73.3	73.5	73.5	73.6	73.3	73.4	73.7	75.0	73.4
2016	74.0	73.4	73.4	73.3	73.5	73.6	73.6	73.6	73.8	73.4	73.6	75.1	73.7
2017	73.6	73.4	73.8	72.9	73.1	72.9	72.6	73.4	73.5	74.1	75.0	76.4	73.7
Information													
2007	27.9	28.1	28.2	28.2	28.4	28.4	28.0	27.9	27.7	27.7	27.9	27.9	28.0
2008	27.4	27.3	27.3	27.3	27.3	27.1	26.9	26.8	26.4	26.2	26.2	26.3	26.9
2009	25.8	25.6	25.5	25.3	25.3	25.4	24.9	24.8	24.7	24.6	24.7	24.8	25.1
2010	24.5	24.4	24.3	24.1	24.2	24.2	24.0	23.9	23.7	23.7	23.7	23.6	24.0
2011	23.5	23.4	23.2	23.1	23.3	23.3	23.2	23.1	23.1	22.7	22.8	22.8	23.1
2012	22.9	22.9	22.9	22.8	22.8	22.8	22.7	22.6	22.5	22.2	22.4	22.4	22.7
2013	22.4	22.3	22.3	22.4	22.8	22.8	22.8	22.7	22.5	22.6	22.8	22.9	22.6
2014	22.2	22.1	22.1	22.1	22.1	22.0	22.0	21.9	21.7	21.7	21.9	21.9	22.0
2015	21.6	21.8	21.8	21.5	22.0	21.4	21.5	21.2	21.0	21.0	21.1	21.2	21.4
2016	20.7	20.7	20.6	20.8	21.0	20.9	20.8	20.7	20.5	20.7	20.9	20.8	20.8
2017	20.5	20.7	20.8	20.7	21.1	21.0	20.9	20.7	20.5	20.9	21.1	21.3	20.9
Financial Activities													
2007	99.0	99.1	99.7	99.2	99.7	100.6	100.3	100.2	100.1	99.8	100.0	100.2	99.8
2008	98.8	99.2	99.2	99.2	99.2	99.6	99.8	99.7	99.2	99.0	98.4	98.2	99.1
2009	96.9	96.6	96.6	96.6	96.9	96.9	96.4	95.8	95.0	94.3	93.7	93.6	95.8
2010	92.1	92.0	92.4	92.3	92.5	92.7	92.2	91.8	91.2	91.7	91.7	91.9	92.0
2011	91.1	91.5	91.6	92.4	93.8	93.0	93.2	92.5	93.3	92.1	92.0	91.8	92.4
2012	90.6	91.1	91.5	91.7	92.2	92.7	93.5	93.4	93.6	93.5	94.0	93.9	92.6
2013	93.2	93.3	93.8	93.7	94.0	94.5	94.7	94.9	94.2	94.6	94.8	95.0	94.2
2014	93.8	93.9	94.2	94.6	95.1	95.5	95.4	95.4	94.4	94.7	94.8	95.2	94.8
2015	94.2	94.3	94.8	95.3	95.8	96.1	96.2	95.9	95.4	95.6	95.6	95.7	95.4
2016	95.1	95.3	95.5	95.9	96.1	96.2	96.4	96.6	96.6	96.6	96.6	96.6	96.1
2017	95.5	95.7	96.0	96.1	96.5	96.9	97.1	97.2	97.7	97.3	96.4	96.4	96.6
Professional and Business Services													
2007	216.4	219.1	222.0	220.7	220.8	222.6	219.7	222.6	223.2	222.9	224.4	225.5	221.7
2008	220.8	222.2	222.9	224.4	222.7	222.7	220.6	221.1	220.7	220.3	217.4	214.7	220.9
2009	206.3	205.9	205.3	206.1	204.0	205.7	205.6	205.6	203.6	203.2	204.4	203.9	205.0
2010	200.9	202.1	204.0	206.7	207.6	211.5	213.5	212.7	212.8	213.4	214.4	214.5	209.5
2011	208.8	211.8	212.6	213.5	212.9	213.8	213.0	215.2	217.5	216.0	215.9	216.3	213.9
2012	210.9	214.3	216.6	218.0	218.8	220.1	218.0	222.3	221.6	220.2	220.5	218.9	218.4
2013	213.4	216.9	218.9	220.3	220.3	221.7	219.2	220.9	219.6	220.1	220.0	221.5	219.4
2014	216.5	217.3	219.3	222.5	223.3	224.3	224.2	227.4	226.6	228.3	228.1	228.4	223.9
2015	222.4	224.2	225.6	227.7	228.7	228.5	229.4	230.9	230.4	233.3	233.5	234.0	229.1
2016	229.1	230.7	231.9	235.4	234.9	234.3	232.7	234.5	234.1	234.9	235.5	234.8	233.6
2017	231.5	234.2	237.0	237.8	239.1	241.3	239.6	242.6	241.4	242.2	241.8	239.4	239.0
Education and Health Services													
2007	209.0	211.0	211.9	212.2	212.6	211.9	211.4	214.0	214.7	215.4	216.4	217.1	213.1
2008	212.4	214.4	215.0	215.5	216.2	214.5	214.0	215.7	216.6	217.2	216.9	216.3	215.4
2009	213.6	214.5	214.5	215.5	215.9	213.6	214.0	215.2	216.6	217.4	220.0	218.0	215.7
2010	215.8	217.8	217.3	218.8	219.0	217.7	218.8	220.0	221.3	222.0	223.1	221.5	219.4
2011	218.7	219.6	221.6	221.2	221.0	219.1	218.9	220.1	223.2	222.9	224.7	223.1	221.2
2012	221.5	222.2	223.8	224.9	222.9	222.8	219.7	222.9	225.8	225.0	228.1	228.3	224.0
2013	223.4	228.0	225.8	226.9	229.3	226.4	222.6	225.9	229.5	228.4	231.6	231.8	227.5
2014	225.1	228.6	227.4	229.8	228.9	226.9	224.1	227.3	230.8	232.5	231.3	233.8	228.9
2015	228.6	232.1	229.8	232.6	232.0	231.5	230.8	233.0	235.6	237.3	236.4	238.6	233.2
2016	233.2	236.7	235.6	237.9	237.3	236.4	237.0	239.2	241.6	241.5	240.8	242.4	238.3
2017	237.2	240.8	240.2	241.4	240.5	240.4	238.1	239.9	242.6	245.2	245.1	245.2	241.4

1. Employment by Industry: Alabama, 2007–2017—*Continued*

Industry and year	January	February	March	April	May	June	July	August	September	October	November	December	Annual average
Leisure and Hospitality													
2007	165.8	169.2	172.9	174.6	176.7	178.9	177.6	178.5	176.1	172.9	172.3	171.9	174.0
2008	166.3	169.2	172.7	177.8	180.3	181.2	179.3	179.9	176.6	171.8	170.3	169.3	174.6
2009	163.8	166.0	169.2	172.3	174.6	175.7	174.0	173.4	171.5	167.5	166.9	166.4	170.1
2010	160.3	161.0	165.9	169.5	171.4	173.0	170.9	171.0	168.8	166.5	166.5	165.5	167.5
2011	159.5	162.3	166.5	171.5	171.8	174.1	173.7	174.7	172.4	168.5	168.0	166.7	169.1
2012	163.1	166.3	170.9	176.1	178.2	180.6	177.7	178.8	176.6	172.7	172.7	171.0	173.7
2013	167.9	170.4	174.8	180.3	183.4	185.4	183.6	184.0	182.5	178.7	179.0	176.8	178.9
2014	173.1	174.8	180.4	185.6	187.9	190.4	188.3	189.6	187.0	183.6	182.3	181.4	183.7
2015	178.8	182.1	186.1	191.1	194.0	196.0	195.1	195.1	193.6	191.3	191.0	189.6	190.3
2016	186.2	190.0	194.6	199.7	202.2	203.2	202.2	202.6	200.5	197.4	197.2	194.4	197.5
2017	192.2	195.7	200.1	204.0	206.3	207.8	207.3	207.5	203.8	200.2	199.5	200.5	202.1
Other Services													
2007	88.3	89.0	89.9	89.7	90.0	90.4	89.9	89.7	89.5	89.8	90.0	90.3	89.7
2008	89.9	90.8	91.1	91.7	91.4	91.4	91.4	91.0	90.7	90.5	90.2	90.0	90.8
2009	89.6	89.7	89.9	89.8	90.0	90.3	90.3	89.8	89.2	89.4	89.1	89.3	89.7
2010	89.0	89.5	89.7	89.8	90.2	90.9	91.0	90.4	89.9	90.6	89.8	89.7	90.0
2011	88.8	89.4	89.7	90.1	90.2	90.7	90.3	90.0	89.9	89.9	90.4	90.0	90.0
2012	90.0	90.7	91.7	91.7	91.8	92.7	92.2	91.7	91.1	91.3	90.6	90.5	91.3
2013	90.0	90.4	91.3	91.4	91.6	92.3	91.8	91.8	91.6	91.3	91.0	91.0	91.3
2014	90.6	91.0	92.0	92.2	92.6	93.0	92.6	92.4	92.1	91.9	91.7	91.6	92.0
2015	91.6	91.7	92.3	93.1	93.5	93.8	93.2	92.9	92.8	92.6	92.5	92.2	92.7
2016	91.9	92.1	92.8	93.5	93.1	93.7	93.8	93.3	93.4	92.8	92.8	92.8	93.0
2017	92.5	92.8	93.3	93.4	93.7	94.0	93.8	93.7	93.9	93.5	93.7	93.7	93.5
Government													
2007	377.3	380.2	381.4	381.6	382.4	382.4	368.0	372.1	381.1	384.4	385.9	386.4	380.3
2008	383.5	387.8	389.0	389.9	391.4	391.4	375.6	378.6	386.5	391.8	391.3	392.6	387.5
2009	386.4	388.9	389.8	391.8	392.0	391.1	374.6	376.8	385.4	390.9	391.5	392.7	387.7
2010	387.4	390.5	393.2	394.6	403.6	398.1	379.7	379.7	387.4	391.2	392.3	392.9	390.9
2011	387.6	390.5	391.5	391.1	390.7	387.6	375.0	374.8	383.7	386.0	387.4	385.6	386.0
2012	381.4	385.0	387.2	385.9	385.1	382.7	369.0	369.9	377.8	383.8	385.0	384.7	381.5
2013	379.6	383.9	386.1	385.6	384.9	381.5	372.6	372.8	377.9	382.8	384.3	383.3	381.3
2014	379.4	382.6	383.9	384.8	386.0	384.3	370.9	373.3	380.9	384.7	385.7	386.4	381.9
2015	379.2	381.9	382.8	383.9	385.4	383.6	371.6	374.5	379.7	382.3	383.3	383.8	381.0
2016	378.9	381.5	382.8	383.6	384.8	384.5	373.8	377.3	383.4	385.1	386.2	386.8	382.4
2017	382.0	384.7	386.1	386.9	388.0	387.9	376.5	379.4	385.3	388.2	389.2	387.3	385.1

2. Average Weekly Hours by Selected Industry: Alabama, 2013–2017

(Not seasonally adjusted)

Industry and year	January	February	March	April	May	June	July	August	September	October	November	December	Annual average
Total Private													
2013	35.5	35.7	36.0	35.9	35.8	36.6	35.9	36.1	36.6	36.1	36.1	36.3	36.1
2014	35.0	35.1	36.0	35.6	35.5	35.8	35.4	35.6	35.5	35.2	35.6	35.5	35.5
2015	34.9	35.4	35.4	35.2	35.5	35.5	35.4	35.9	35.4	35.8	35.9	35.6	35.5
2016	35.5	35.6	35.5	35.5	35.8	35.6	35.6	35.4	35.6	36.0	35.3	35.4	35.6
2017	35.4	35.2	35.2	35.2	35.2	35.3	35.4	35.3	34.9	35.6	35.3	35.2	35.3
Goods-Producing													
2013	42.3	42.9	42.9	42.8	42.7	43.0	42.4	43.1	43.2	43.4	43.4	43.0	42.9
2014	41.4	40.2	42.6	41.9	41.9	42.0	41.8	42.5	42.4	41.8	41.7	42.1	41.9
2015	41.2	41.2	41.3	41.2	41.7	41.7	41.6	41.9	40.8	42.2	41.7	42.2	41.6
2016	41.5	41.5	41.4	41.4	42.1	42.2	41.5	41.5	42.1	42.3	41.2	41.3	41.7
2017	40.8	41.0	41.0	40.8	41.8	42.0	41.5	42.3	41.4	42.0	42.4	41.8	41.6
Construction													
2013	37.5	38.7	40.4	41.7	41.9	40.9	40.9	41.8	42.9	41.9	41.1	41.0	40.9
2014	39.5	37.7	40.1	39.8	40.6	40.8	41.3	42.3	42.2	40.3	41.4	40.9	40.6
2015	38.6	39.7	39.6	39.5	41.4	41.5	41.7	41.6	40.1	41.8	41.7	42.4	40.8
2016	41.7	41.3	40.1	41.2	41.6	41.7	41.4	40.5	41.0	41.5	40.3	39.8	41.0
2017	39.6	39.9	39.8	39.8	41.4	40.5	41.2	40.0	39.9	40.7	41.2	40.1	40.3
Manufacturing													
2013	41.8	42.5	42.3	41.9	41.7	42.3	41.7	42.4	42.3	42.9	43.1	42.7	42.3
2014	41.1	40.3	42.1	41.4	41.3	41.4	41.1	41.9	41.7	41.7	41.3	42.1	41.5
2015	41.8	41.6	41.7	41.7	41.4	41.4	41.2	41.8	41.4	42.4	41.8	42.0	41.7
2016	41.5	41.5	41.7	41.4	42.2	42.2	41.3	41.7	42.4	42.5	41.5	41.9	41.8
2017	41.3	41.4	41.5	41.2	42.1	42.8	41.7	43.4	42.2	42.7	43.0	42.7	42.2
Trade, Transportation, and Utilities													
2013	35.7	36.0	36.1	36.3	35.8	36.6	35.9	36.2	36.7	35.9	36.0	36.2	36.1
2014	35.1	35.4	35.8	35.9	35.6	35.6	35.4	35.2	35.1	34.8	34.9	35.2	35.3
2015	34.2	34.6	34.3	34.5	34.6	34.7	34.7	34.9	34.4	34.5	34.5	34.4	34.5
2016	34.1	34.3	33.9	34.0	34.0	34.1	34.3	34.0	33.7	33.8	33.5	33.9	34.0
2017	33.5	33.4	33.4	34.0	33.5	33.6	33.9	33.7	33.2	33.5	33.2	33.5	33.5
Financial Activities													
2013	37.3	37.3	36.9	37.1	37.3	38.6	37.1	36.9	38.1	36.8	37.0	37.5	37.3
2014	35.7	36.7	36.7	36.0	36.2	37.1	36.4	36.5	36.4	36.4	37.9	36.8	36.6
2015	37.0	38.1	38.4	36.8	37.2	37.2	36.9	38.3	37.2	36.9	38.6	37.3	37.5
2016	37.9	37.9	37.2	37.5	38.5	37.9	37.7	37.1	38.3	38.0	37.8	37.3	37.8
2017	39.0	38.4	38.5	38.7	38.2	38.1	38.2	38.0	37.5	38.5	37.9	38.1	38.3
Professional and Business Services													
2013	35.6	36.0	36.7	36.9	36.4	37.5	36.8	36.9	38.0	37.3	37.4	37.3	36.9
2014	35.8	36.3	36.8	36.3	36.5	37.1	36.6	37.2	36.6	36.9	37.6	37.3	36.8
2015	36.3	37.0	36.7	36.5	36.7	36.6	36.7	37.3	36.7	36.7	36.9	36.0	36.7
2016	36.3	36.4	36.5	36.7	37.0	36.5	37.0	37.1	37.1	37.7	37.0	37.0	36.9
2017	37.0	36.6	37.0	36.7	36.8	36.7	37.2	36.9	36.6	37.7	37.0	37.1	36.9
Education and Health Services													
2013	33.9	33.9	33.8	33.4	33.4	34.2	33.5	33.6	33.9	33.1	33.5	33.9	33.7
2014	33.1	33.1	33.3	32.8	32.7	33.2	32.8	33.0	32.6	32.4	33.4	32.4	32.9
2015	32.5	33.4	33.2	33.1	33.3	33.3	33.3	33.8	33.4	33.8	34.6	33.3	33.4
2016	34.0	34.0	33.8	34.0	34.2	33.9	33.9	34.2	34.4	34.8	34.5	34.2	34.2
2017	34.5	34.1	33.8	33.2	32.9	33.1	33.6	33.1	33.5	34.0	33.5	33.5	33.6
Leisure and Hospitality													
2013	25.5	26.2	26.6	26.3	26.3	27.0	26.8	26.9	26.4	26.5	26.3	26.5	26.4
2014	25.4	25.9	26.7	26.5	26.5	26.9	26.5	26.3	26.2	25.7	26.3	26.3	26.3
2015	25.7	26.5	26.6	26.9	26.9	27.3	27.1	26.7	26.0	26.2	25.8	26.1	26.5
2016	25.4	25.5	26.3	26.0	26.1	26.5	26.3	25.8	25.5	26.1	25.8	25.9	25.9
2017	25.3	25.8	26.0	25.9	25.8	26.2	26.2	25.6	25.4	25.9	25.7	25.3	25.8
Other Services													
2013	31.8	30.9	32.2	32.8	32.5	35.2	33.0	32.7	34.9	33.7	33.4	33.9	33.1
2014	31.6	31.9	32.7	32.2	31.1	32.1	30.0	30.2	32.8	32.8	32.6	31.5	31.8
2015	32.0	32.9	33.5	33.1	33.9	33.2	32.1	33.6	32.6	33.8	34.5	34.5	33.3
2016	34.1	34.5	35.2	34.9	34.6	33.9	34.2	33.8	34.1	35.0	33.5	33.5	34.3
2017	32.2	33.1	33.0	33.0	32.6	33.1	33.4	32.4	32.8	33.2	32.9	32.6	32.9

3. Average Hourly Earnings by Selected Industry: Alabama, 2013–2017

(Dollars, not seasonally adjusted)

Industry and year	January	February	March	April	May	June	July	August	September	October	November	December	Annual average
Total Private													
2013	20.25	20.27	20.23	20.10	19.96	20.08	20.03	20.11	20.34	20.17	20.09	20.46	20.17
2014	20.50	20.86	20.72	20.61	20.60	20.85	20.67	20.68	20.73	20.75	20.96	20.78	20.73
2015	21.00	21.40	21.29	20.63	20.62	20.72	20.78	20.99	21.00	21.10	21.31	21.35	21.02
2016	21.64	21.60	21.43	21.83	21.89	21.79	21.97	21.78	21.86	22.25	22.04	22.05	21.85
2017	22.47	22.32	22.24	22.75	22.44	22.20	22.56	22.45	22.87	22.97	22.78	23.05	22.59
Goods-Producing													
2013	21.93	22.05	22.25	22.01	21.75	21.92	22.00	21.84	21.96	21.98	21.96	22.37	22.00
2014	22.29	22.89	22.50	22.46	22.30	22.50	22.39	22.29	22.28	22.51	22.64	22.59	22.47
2015	22.55	22.78	22.60	22.58	22.44	22.46	22.47	22.61	22.90	22.86	23.14	23.12	22.71
2016	23.16	23.32	22.92	23.28	23.27	23.15	23.36	23.22	23.00	23.29	23.23	23.47	23.22
2017	23.60	23.42	23.51	24.06	23.81	23.59	23.83	23.59	24.19	24.30	24.22	24.36	23.88
Construction													
2013	20.16	20.60	21.27	20.63	20.45	21.08	20.99	20.79	21.23	21.57	21.33	23.05	21.11
2014	23.11	23.26	22.37	22.66	22.56	22.41	22.23	22.50	22.31	22.57	22.64	22.93	22.62
2015	23.05	22.82	22.55	22.51	22.06	22.22	22.11	22.32	22.70	22.97	23.08	22.86	22.60
2016	22.75	22.40	22.27	22.58	22.25	22.43	22.21	21.98	21.95	22.10	22.09	22.30	22.28
2017	22.14	22.56	22.30	22.13	22.40	22.27	22.39	22.69	23.05	23.23	23.47	23.54	22.69
Manufacturing													
2013	20.92	21.13	21.36	21.33	21.18	21.35	21.58	21.49	21.62	21.60	21.68	21.97	21.44
2014	22.03	22.38	22.20	22.14	22.00	22.34	22.35	22.12	22.24	22.49	22.67	22.56	22.29
2015	22.36	22.74	22.60	22.53	22.56	22.57	22.62	22.72	23.00	22.85	23.19	23.29	22.75
2016	23.36	23.71	23.18	23.57	23.64	23.44	23.86	23.72	23.41	23.82	23.74	23.97	23.62
2017	24.27	23.81	24.02	24.46	24.08	23.81	24.19	23.70	24.44	24.54	24.30	24.48	24.17
Trade, Transportation, and Utilities													
2013	18.16	18.27	18.23	17.80	17.92	18.03	17.81	17.83	18.11	18.04	17.80	18.18	18.01
2014	18.34	18.69	18.76	18.76	18.71	18.94	18.96	18.85	18.91	18.81	18.74	18.31	18.73
2015	18.92	19.09	18.99	19.13	19.04	18.88	18.99	19.16	19.32	19.17	19.17	18.87	19.06
2016	19.50	19.37	19.46	19.88	19.71	19.75	19.77	19.51	19.64	19.89	19.56	19.23	19.61
2017	19.88	19.67	19.51	19.94	19.58	19.63	19.76	19.81	20.11	20.19	19.87	19.93	19.82
Financial Activities													
2013	21.03	21.32	21.57	21.49	21.66	21.47	21.47	21.51	21.78	21.04	20.85	21.33	21.38
2014	21.01	21.57	22.02	21.74	22.16	22.10	21.89	21.77	21.86	21.89	21.92	21.59	21.80
2015	21.67	22.12	22.14	22.45	22.23	22.89	23.00	22.65	23.08	23.59	23.64	24.14	22.80
2016	24.04	23.63	24.27	25.21	25.62	24.84	25.19	24.93	25.52	26.36	25.87	25.86	25.12
2017	26.52	25.92	25.27	25.80	25.51	25.01	25.40	25.53	25.84	25.93	25.50	25.77	25.67
Professional and Business Services													
2013	23.01	23.28	23.06	23.31	23.02	23.00	23.03	23.17	23.37	22.82	22.82	23.62	23.13
2014	23.72	24.33	24.12	23.94	23.91	24.35	23.95	23.94	24.06	23.89	24.60	24.41	24.11
2015	24.74	26.08	26.09	23.40	23.62	24.17	23.99	24.65	24.70	24.70	25.06	25.38	24.71
2016	25.74	25.28	25.05	25.01	25.60	25.29	25.68	25.45	25.66	25.89	25.71	25.91	25.52
2017	26.40	26.25	26.05	26.60	26.24	26.06	26.82	26.38	26.80	26.73	26.62	27.13	26.51
Education and Health Services													
2013	20.87	20.95	20.97	20.91	20.65	20.94	20.81	20.99	21.07	21.00	20.93	20.96	20.92
2014	21.09	21.57	21.58	21.59	21.51	21.83	21.49	21.52	21.74	21.70	22.11	21.84	21.63
2015	22.16	22.14	21.83	22.04	21.91	22.06	22.17	22.16	22.19	22.49	22.69	22.88	22.23
2016	22.94	22.99	22.72	23.24	22.93	23.16	23.46	22.91	22.88	23.18	23.06	22.96	23.04
2017	23.10	23.25	23.19	24.17	24.01	23.54	23.76	23.70	23.97	24.13	23.93	24.23	23.75
Leisure and Hospitality													
2013	11.19	11.15	11.10	11.00	10.98	10.88	10.88	10.84	10.84	10.87	10.82	11.05	10.96
2014	10.99	11.09	10.94	10.91	10.85	10.86	10.75	11.00	10.79	10.86	10.90	11.03	10.91
2015	10.93	11.16	11.05	11.04	11.00	10.88	10.84	10.97	11.03	10.99	11.08	11.28	11.02
2016	11.23	11.47	11.24	11.18	11.25	11.31	11.30	11.44	11.55	11.72	11.73	11.94	11.45
2017	11.80	11.92	11.83	11.89	11.84	11.76	11.89	11.97	12.08	12.06	12.09	12.25	11.95
Other Services													
2013	19.95	19.92	19.79	19.83	19.99	20.55	19.89	20.60	20.27	20.13	20.15	20.18	20.11
2014	20.55	20.58	20.65	20.11	21.13	21.90	21.76	22.15	21.86	21.49	21.22	21.54	21.24
2015	20.87	21.18	21.52	19.99	20.06	20.23	20.05	20.28	19.72	19.54	19.25	19.12	20.14
2016	19.23	19.17	19.22	19.10	19.00	19.04	18.91	19.11	19.15	19.81	19.56	19.55	19.24
2017	20.63	20.86	20.05	20.40	19.99	19.68	19.62	19.60	20.56	21.13	21.52	21.73	20.48

4. Average Weekly Earnings by Selected Industry: Alabama, 2013–2017

(Dollars, not seasonally adjusted)

Industry and year	January	February	March	April	May	June	July	August	September	October	November	December	Annual average
Total Private													
2013	718.88	723.64	728.28	721.59	714.57	734.93	719.08	725.97	744.44	728.14	725.25	742.70	728.14
2014	717.50	732.19	745.92	733.72	731.30	746.43	731.72	736.21	735.92	730.40	746.18	737.69	735.92
2015	732.90	757.56	753.67	726.18	732.01	735.56	735.61	753.54	743.40	755.38	765.03	760.06	746.21
2016	768.22	768.96	760.77	774.97	783.66	775.72	782.13	771.01	778.22	801.00	778.01	780.57	777.86
2017	795.44	785.66	782.85	800.80	789.89	783.66	798.62	792.49	798.16	817.73	804.13	811.36	797.43
Goods-Producing													
2013	927.64	945.95	954.53	942.03	928.73	942.56	932.80	941.30	948.67	953.93	953.06	961.91	943.80
2014	922.81	920.18	958.50	941.07	934.37	945.00	935.90	947.33	944.67	940.92	944.09	951.04	941.49
2015	929.06	938.54	933.38	930.30	935.75	936.58	934.75	947.36	934.32	964.69	964.94	975.66	944.74
2016	961.14	967.78	948.89	963.79	979.67	976.93	969.44	963.63	968.30	985.17	957.08	969.31	968.27
2017	962.88	960.22	963.91	981.65	995.26	990.78	988.95	997.86	1,001.47	1,020.60	1,026.93	1,018.25	993.41
Construction													
2013	756.00	797.22	859.31	860.27	856.86	862.17	858.49	869.02	910.77	903.78	876.66	945.05	863.40
2014	912.85	876.90	897.04	901.87	915.94	914.33	918.10	951.75	941.48	909.57	937.30	937.84	918.37
2015	889.73	905.95	892.98	889.15	913.28	922.13	921.99	928.51	910.27	960.15	962.44	969.26	922.08
2016	948.68	925.12	893.03	930.30	925.60	935.33	919.49	890.19	899.95	917.15	890.23	887.54	913.48
2017	876.74	900.14	887.54	880.77	927.36	901.94	922.47	907.60	919.70	945.46	966.96	943.95	914.41
Manufacturing													
2013	874.46	898.03	903.53	893.73	883.21	903.11	899.89	911.18	914.53	926.64	934.41	938.12	906.91
2014	905.43	901.91	934.62	916.60	908.60	924.88	918.59	926.83	927.41	937.83	936.27	949.78	925.04
2015	934.65	945.98	942.42	939.50	933.98	934.40	931.94	949.70	952.20	968.84	969.34	978.18	948.68
2016	969.44	983.97	966.61	975.80	997.61	989.17	985.42	989.12	992.58	1,012.35	985.21	1,004.34	987.32
2017	1,002.35	985.73	996.83	1,007.75	1,013.77	1,019.07	1,008.72	1,028.58	1,031.37	1,047.86	1,044.90	1,045.30	1,019.97
Trade, Transportation, and Utilities													
2013	648.31	657.72	658.10	646.14	641.54	659.90	639.38	645.45	664.64	647.64	640.80	658.12	650.16
2014	643.73	661.63	671.61	673.48	666.08	674.26	671.18	663.52	663.74	654.59	654.03	644.51	661.17
2015	647.06	660.51	651.36	659.99	658.78	655.14	658.95	668.68	664.61	661.37	661.37	649.13	657.57
2016	664.95	664.39	659.69	675.92	670.14	673.48	678.11	663.34	661.87	672.28	655.26	651.90	666.74
2017	665.98	656.98	651.63	677.96	655.93	659.57	669.86	667.60	667.65	676.37	659.68	667.66	663.97
Financial Activities													
2013	784.42	795.24	795.93	797.28	807.92	828.74	796.54	793.72	829.82	774.27	771.45	799.88	797.47
2014	750.06	791.62	808.13	782.64	802.19	819.91	796.80	794.61	795.70	796.80	830.77	794.51	797.88
2015	801.79	842.77	850.18	826.16	826.96	851.51	848.70	867.50	858.58	870.47	912.50	900.42	855.00
2016	911.12	895.58	902.84	945.38	986.37	941.44	949.66	924.90	977.42	1,001.68	977.89	964.58	949.54
2017	1,034.28	995.33	972.90	998.46	974.48	952.88	970.28	970.14	969.00	998.31	966.45	981.84	983.16
Professional and Business Services													
2013	819.16	838.08	846.30	860.14	837.93	862.50	847.50	854.97	888.06	851.19	853.47	881.03	853.50
2014	849.18	883.18	887.62	869.02	872.72	903.39	876.57	890.57	880.60	881.54	924.96	910.49	887.25
2015	898.06	964.96	957.50	854.10	866.85	884.62	880.43	919.45	906.49	906.49	924.71	913.68	906.86
2016	934.36	920.19	914.33	917.87	947.20	923.09	950.16	944.20	951.99	976.05	951.27	958.67	941.69
2017	976.80	960.75	963.85	976.22	965.63	956.40	997.70	973.42	980.88	1,007.72	984.94	1,006.52	978.22
Education and Health Services													
2013	707.49	710.21	708.79	698.39	689.71	716.15	697.14	705.26	714.27	695.10	701.16	710.54	705.00
2014	698.08	713.97	718.61	708.15	703.38	724.76	704.87	710.16	708.72	703.08	738.47	707.62	711.63
2015	720.20	739.48	724.76	729.52	729.60	734.60	738.26	749.01	741.15	760.16	785.07	761.90	742.48
2016	779.96	781.66	767.94	790.16	784.21	785.12	795.29	783.52	787.07	806.66	795.57	785.23	787.97
2017	796.95	792.83	783.82	802.44	789.93	779.17	798.34	784.47	803.00	820.42	801.66	811.71	798.00
Leisure and Hospitality													
2013	285.35	292.13	295.26	289.30	288.77	293.76	291.58	291.60	286.18	288.06	284.57	292.83	289.34
2014	279.15	287.23	292.10	289.12	287.53	292.13	284.88	289.30	282.70	279.10	286.67	290.09	286.93
2015	280.90	295.74	293.93	296.98	295.90	297.02	293.76	292.90	286.78	287.94	285.86	294.41	292.03
2016	285.24	292.49	295.61	290.68	293.63	299.72	297.19	295.15	294.53	305.89	302.63	309.25	296.56
2017	298.54	307.54	307.58	307.95	305.47	308.11	311.52	306.43	306.83	312.35	310.71	309.93	308.31
Other Services													
2013	634.41	615.53	637.24	650.42	649.68	723.36	656.37	673.62	707.42	678.38	673.01	684.10	665.64
2014	649.38	656.50	675.26	647.54	657.14	702.99	652.80	668.93	717.01	704.87	691.77	678.51	675.43
2015	667.84	696.82	720.92	661.67	680.03	671.64	643.61	681.41	642.87	660.45	664.13	659.64	670.66
2016	655.74	661.37	676.54	666.59	657.40	645.46	646.72	645.92	653.02	693.35	655.26	654.93	659.93
2017	664.29	690.47	661.65	673.20	651.67	651.41	655.31	635.04	674.37	701.52	708.01	708.40	673.79

ALASKA
At a Glance

Population:
  2010 census: 710,231
  2017 estimate: 739,795

Percent change in population:
  2010–2017: 4.2%

Percent change in total nonfarm employment:
  2007–2017: 3.5%

Industry with the largest growth in employment, 2007–2017 (thousands):
  Education and health services, 11.3

Industry with the largest decline or smallest growth in employment, 2007–2017 (thousands):
  Construction, -2.5

Civilian labor force:
  2010: 361,913
  2017: 362,783

Unemployment rate and rank among states (highest to lowest):
  2010: 7.9%, 36th
  2017: 7.2%, 1st

Over-the-year change in unemployment rates:
  2015–2016: 0.4%
  2016–2017: 0.3%

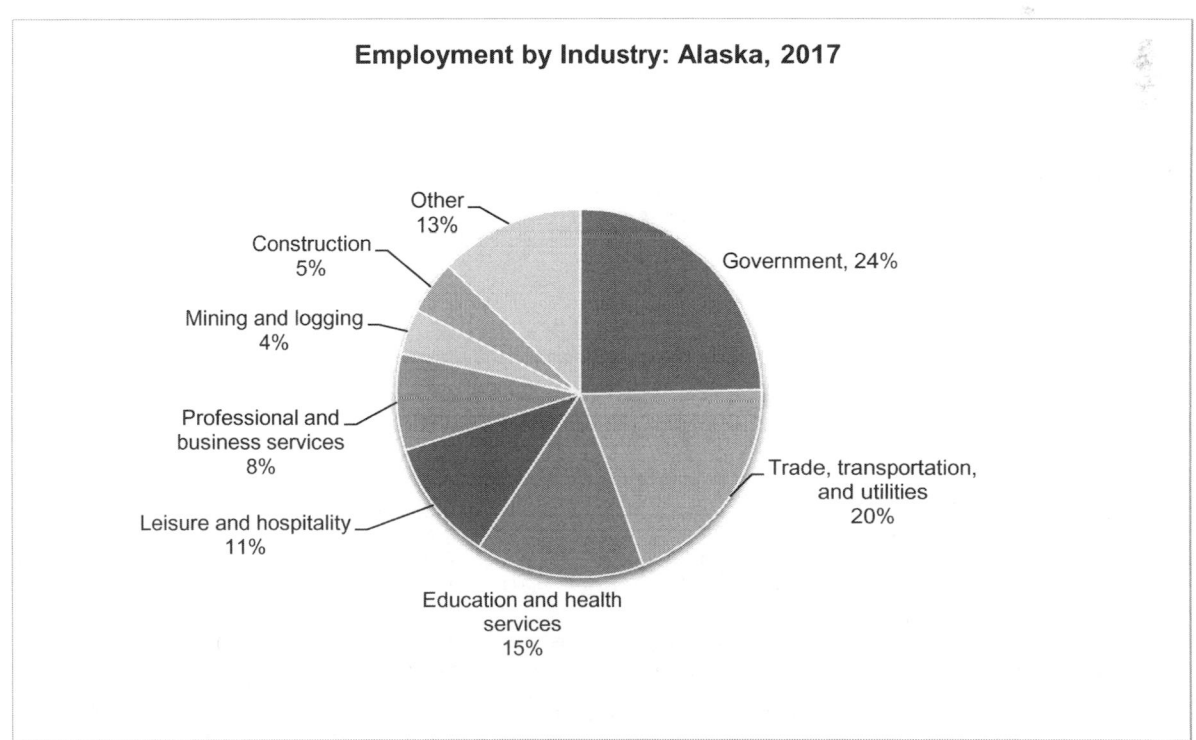

Employment by Industry: Alaska, 2017

Other 13%
Construction 5%
Mining and logging 4%
Professional and business services 8%
Leisure and hospitality 11%
Education and health services 15%
Government, 24%
Trade, transportation, and utilities 20%

1. Employment by Industry: Alaska, Selected Years, 2007–2017

(Numbers in thousands, not seasonally adjusted)

Industry and year	January	February	March	April	May	June	July	August	September	October	November	December	Annual average
Total Nonfarm													
2007	296.2	302.9	305.7	309.7	321.9	336.5	339.6	340.3	332.0	315.2	308.0	304.6	317.7
2008	300.2	306.0	308.4	312.9	327.2	341.0	346.2	345.4	337.2	319.0	311.6	309.1	322.0
2009	302.6	307.6	309.0	313.5	323.1	338.3	343.9	342.6	334.2	317.8	310.4	307.2	320.9
2010	302.9	306.9	309.4	315.5	325.8	343.7	349.6	347.9	341.4	324.7	317.4	314.1	324.9
2011	308.6	314.3	316.4	321.1	330.5	348.9	354.0	352.5	347.1	329.3	321.3	318.0	330.2
2012	312.6	320.2	322.9	326.8	337.8	354.6	358.1	357.2	349.1	336.4	325.4	321.8	335.2
2013	314.8	322.4	324.8	329.3	340.1	355.3	360.2	359.9	351.2	333.5	325.0	322.0	336.5
2014	318.6	322.9	325.5	331.2	344.0	356.5	362.4	360.3	350.6	335.1	326.3	324.2	338.1
2015	321.9	326.1	328.4	332.7	345.1	358.0	365.0	360.3	351.2	334.1	324.2	321.4	339.0
2016	317.7	322.1	323.7	329.9	340.3	351.9	358.2	354.0	342.5	328.1	318.0	316.1	333.5
2017	310.5	317.3	318.3	322.2	335.3	349.1	353.4	350.8	340.2	322.9	314.1	312.3	328.9
Total Private													
2007	217.3	221.0	223.1	226.6	238.8	256.0	263.9	263.4	250.0	232.0	225.3	222.1	236.6
2008	219.8	223.6	225.7	228.9	244.3	258.9	268.9	266.7	253.7	235.0	227.8	225.8	239.9
2009	221.0	224.0	225.3	227.9	239.6	254.0	264.5	262.4	249.2	231.8	224.9	221.8	237.2
2010	219.7	221.7	223.7	228.4	240.0	256.9	268.5	265.9	254.0	237.3	230.6	227.5	239.5
2011	224.4	228.4	230.9	234.6	245.6	263.2	274.0	272.4	260.9	242.6	235.4	232.1	245.4
2012	230.7	234.8	237	240.8	253	270.3	279	276.7	263.5	250.8	240.2	236.8	251.1
2013	233.6	238.3	240.5	244.4	255.9	271.9	282.3	281.1	267.8	250.2	241.6	239.1	253.9
2014	237.2	240.1	242.4	247.2	260.0	273.8	284.5	281.7	267.7	252.2	243.1	241.1	255.9
2015	240.4	243.2	245.3	248.7	261.1	275.5	287.3	282.1	268.4	251.5	241.6	238.9	257.0
2016	236.6	239.9	241.3	246.0	256.6	269.4	281.5	276.3	260.2	245.2	235.2	234.0	251.9
2017	229.6	235.1	236.0	239.4	251.6	267.2	277.7	273.9	258.7	241.0	232.7	231.4	247.9
Goods Producing													
2007	38.1	39.8	40.1	40.6	42.1	50.1	57.3	56.3	50.5	44.9	40.2	36.9	44.7
2008	38.6	40.8	41.3	41.2	43.9	51.4	58.6	57.2	51.4	45.2	40.2	37.9	45.6
2009	38.9	40.7	41.1	41.1	42.7	50.3	58.4	55.8	48.3	42.2	38.0	35.1	44.4
2010	37.3	38.5	39.5	39.9	42.0	50.0	58.8	56.4	50.1	43.7	39.4	36.3	44.3
2011	37.8	40.0	40.9	41.1	42.8	51.6	60.0	58.3	52.5	45.4	40.5	37.1	45.7
2012	39.7	42.2	43.4	43.6	45.6	54.2	61.3	59.3	52.3	47.4	42.2	38.7	47.5
2013	40.4	43.2	44.4	44.7	45.9	54.1	62.3	60.4	54.6	47.3	42.5	40.3	48.3
2014	43.0	44.8	45.7	47.3	47.7	55.9	63.8	60.8	53.8	47.7	43.7	41.5	49.6
2015	44.2	45.9	46.9	47.3	47.8	55.2	64.4	60.5	52.9	46.5	41.2	39.0	49.3
2016	41.0	43.2	43.7	43.2	43.0	49.7	59.0	54.1	45.5	41.3	36.4	34.4	44.5
2017	34.9	38.6	39.0	38.5	39.0	47.3	55.6	52.4	44.8	39.7	35.2	33.7	41.6
Service-Providing													
2007	258.1	263.1	265.6	269.1	279.8	286.4	282.3	284.0	281.5	270.3	267.8	267.7	273.0
2008	261.6	265.2	267.1	271.7	283.3	289.6	287.6	288.2	285.8	273.8	271.4	271.2	276.4
2009	263.7	266.9	267.9	272.4	280.4	288.0	285.5	286.8	285.9	275.6	272.4	272.1	276.5
2010	265.6	268.4	269.9	275.6	283.8	293.7	290.8	291.5	291.3	281.0	278.0	277.8	280.6
2011	270.8	274.3	275.5	280.0	287.7	297.3	294.0	294.2	294.6	283.9	280.8	280.9	284.5
2012	272.9	278	279.5	283.2	292.2	300.4	296.8	297.9	296.8	289	283.2	283.1	287.8
2013	274.4	279.2	280.4	284.6	294.2	301.2	297.9	299.5	296.6	286.2	282.5	281.7	288.2
2014	275.6	278.1	279.8	283.9	296.3	300.6	298.6	299.5	296.8	287.4	282.6	282.7	288.5
2015	277.7	280.2	281.5	285.4	297.3	302.8	300.6	299.8	298.3	287.6	283.0	282.4	289.7
2016	276.7	278.9	280.0	286.7	297.3	302.2	299.2	299.9	297.0	286.8	281.6	281.7	289.0
2017	275.6	278.7	279.3	283.7	296.3	301.8	297.8	298.4	295.4	283.2	278.9	278.6	287.3
Mining and Logging													
2007	12.5	13.0	13.1	13.3	13.4	13.9	14.2	14.4	14.4	14.3	14.1	14.2	13.7
2008	14.1	14.4	14.6	14.7	14.9	15.3	15.5	15.8	15.8	15.7	15.5	15.8	15.2
2009	15.2	15.3	15.2	15.1	15.2	15.4	15.1	15.1	14.8	14.3	14.1	14.1	14.9
2010	13.8	13.8	14.1	14.4	14.9	15.5	15.9	16.0	15.7	15.3	15.0	15.0	15.0
2011	14.4	14.6	14.8	15.0	15.2	15.8	16.2	16.2	16.1	15.9	15.6	15.8	15.5
2012	15.1	15.3	15.5	16	16.4	16.9	17.2	17.4	16.9	16.7	16.4	16.2	16.3
2013	15.8	16.3	16.7	16.6	16.8	17.3	17.3	17.4	17.1	16.5	16.4	16.5	16.7
2014	16.2	16.5	16.7	17.1	17.2	17.6	17.9	17.9	17.7	17.6	17.7	17.8	17.3
2015	17.5	17.5	17.7	17.8	17.6	17.8	17.8	17.8	17.6	17.1	16.4	16.3	17.4
2016	15.7	15.6	15.6	15.1	15.0	14.6	14.3	14.2	13.9	13.7	13.5	13.7	14.6
2017	13.1	13.1	13.1	13.0	13.1	13.4	13.5	13.5	13.2	13.0	12.7	12.6	13.1

1. Employment by Industry: Alaska, Selected Years, 2007–2017—*Continued*

(Numbers in thousands, not seasonally adjusted)

Industry and year	January	February	March	April	May	June	July	August	September	October	November	December	Annual average
Construction													
2007	14.7	15.0	15.1	16.3	18.2	20.4	20.9	21.3	20.4	19.3	16.8	15.6	17.8
2008	13.8	14.2	14.6	15.8	18.0	20.1	20.9	21.4	20.3	18.9	15.9	15.0	17.4
2009	13.2	13.5	13.9	14.7	17.0	19.0	19.8	20.1	19.0	17.9	15.6	14.6	16.5
2010	13.0	13.1	13.4	14.4	16.7	19.1	20.1	20.4	19.6	18.5	15.8	14.7	16.6
2011	12.8	13.0	13.2	14.5	16.6	18.8	19.5	19.9	19.2	18.2	15.7	14.5	16.3
2012	13.5	13.7	14.1	15	17.1	19.6	20.5	21	20	19.1	16.2	15.1	17.1
2013	13.4	13.9	14.5	15.1	16.9	19.5	20.4	21.4	20.4	18.9	16.6	15.8	17.2
2014	14.5	14.8	15.4	16.1	18.2	20.2	20.9	21.6	20.6	18.7	16.6	15.8	17.8
2015	14.9	15.3	15.9	16.9	18.5	20.2	20.9	20.8	19.5	17.9	15.9	15.0	17.6
2016	13.9	14.2	14.3	15.5	17.3	18.6	19.5	19.2	18.0	16.7	14.6	13.5	16.3
2017	12.2	12.8	13.0	13.9	15.4	17.4	18.1	18.1	17.3	15.8	14.6	14.4	15.3
Manufacturing													
2007	10.9	11.8	11.9	11.0	10.5	15.8	22.2	20.6	15.7	11.3	9.3	7.1	13.2
2008	10.7	12.2	12.1	10.7	11.0	16.0	22.2	20.0	15.3	10.6	8.8	7.1	13.1
2009	10.5	11.9	12.0	11.3	10.5	15.9	23.5	20.6	14.5	10.0	8.3	6.4	13.0
2010	10.5	11.6	12.0	11.1	10.4	15.4	22.8	20.0	14.8	9.9	8.6	6.6	12.8
2011	10.6	12.4	12.9	11.6	11.0	17.0	24.3	22.2	17.2	11.3	9.2	6.8	13.9
2012	11.1	13.2	13.8	12.6	12.1	17.7	23.6	20.9	15.4	11.6	9.6	7.4	14.1
2013	11.2	13.0	13.2	13.0	12.2	17.3	24.6	21.6	17.1	11.9	9.5	8.0	14.4
2014	12.3	13.5	13.6	14.1	12.3	18.1	25.0	21.3	15.5	11.4	9.4	7.9	14.5
2015	11.8	13.1	13.3	12.6	11.7	17.2	25.7	21.9	15.8	11.5	8.9	7.7	14.3
2016	11.4	13.4	13.8	12.6	10.7	16.5	25.2	20.7	13.6	10.9	8.3	7.2	13.7
2017	9.6	12.7	12.9	11.6	10.5	16.5	24.0	20.8	14.3	10.9	7.9	6.7	13.2
Trade, Transportation, and Utilities													
2007	59.8	59.7	60.3	61.7	65.8	68.6	69.2	69.4	66.9	62.9	62.0	62.3	64.1
2008	60.7	60.5	61.2	62.4	66.8	68.9	69.7	69.4	67.1	62.9	62.2	62.4	64.5
2009	60.0	59.4	59.9	61.3	64.8	66.8	67.7	67.9	65.9	61.7	61.2	61.1	63.1
2010	58.9	58.5	58.9	60.5	64.1	66.8	67.6	67.7	65.2	61.6	60.9	61.2	62.7
2011	58.8	58.9	59.7	60.9	64.8	67.2	68.2	68.5	66.4	62.3	61.6	61.5	63.2
2012	59.7	59.5	59.7	61.4	65.2	67.6	68.4	68.5	66.8	64.0	61.9	62.1	63.7
2013	60.0	59.7	60.0	61.4	65.7	67.8	68.5	69.3	67.2	63.2	62.3	62.4	64.0
2014	60.1	60.4	60.4	62.2	67.1	68.5	69.5	69.9	67.6	64.3	62.9	63.1	64.7
2015	61.2	61.2	61.6	63.2	67.6	69.4	70.5	70.7	68.8	65.5	64.0	63.9	65.6
2016	61.6	61.7	61.8	63.9	67.9	69.3	70.1	70.2	67.8	64.9	63.2	63.1	65.5
2017	61.0	61.0	61.0	63.0	66.7	68.7	69.5	69.4	67.1	62.6	61.4	61.4	64.4
Wholesale Trade													
2007	6.3	6.3	6.4	6.5	6.6	6.9	6.9	7.0	6.7	6.5	6.4	6.4	6.6
2008	6.3	6.3	6.3	6.4	6.6	6.8	7.0	6.9	6.6	6.3	6.2	6.2	6.5
2009	6.2	6.1	6.2	6.2	6.4	6.6	6.7	6.6	6.4	6.0	6.0	6.0	6.3
2010	5.9	5.9	6.0	6.1	6.3	6.5	6.8	6.8	6.4	6.2	6.1	6.2	6.3
2011	6.0	6.1	6.1	6.1	6.3	6.5	6.8	6.7	6.4	6.3	6.1	6.1	6.3
2012	6.0	6.0	6.0	6.2	6.3	6.5	6.6	6.6	6.6	6.4	6.4	6.5	6.3
2013	6.4	6.4	6.5	6.5	6.7	6.8	6.8	6.8	6.6	6.6	6.5	6.5	6.6
2014	6.4	6.4	6.4	6.4	6.6	6.7	6.7	6.7	6.6	6.4	6.4	6.5	6.5
2015	6.4	6.4	6.5	6.5	6.6	6.7	6.8	6.7	6.6	6.5	6.5	6.5	6.6
2016	6.4	6.4	6.4	6.4	6.5	6.6	6.6	6.6	6.5	6.3	6.3	6.3	6.4
2017	6.2	6.3	6.3	6.3	6.4	6.5	6.5	6.5	6.4	6.2	6.4	6.3	6.4
Retail Trade													
2007	34.2	33.7	34.1	34.8	36.4	37.7	38.1	37.8	36.7	35.6	35.7	36.1	35.9
2008	34.9	34.2	34.5	35.2	36.6	37.8	38.0	37.5	36.7	35.9	35.8	35.9	36.1
2009	34.2	33.5	33.7	34.6	36.0	37.0	37.3	37.2	36.5	35.4	35.5	35.5	35.5
2010	34.0	33.6	33.6	34.6	35.8	37.1	37.3	37.0	36.0	35.1	35.3	35.4	35.4
2011	33.9	33.6	33.8	34.5	35.9	37.1	37.4	37.4	36.6	35.6	35.8	35.8	35.6
2012	34.4	33.9	33.9	34.6	36.1	37.2	37.3	37.2	36.4	35.7	35.6	35.6	35.7
2013	34.2	33.7	33.8	34.5	36.0	37.2	37.5	37.9	37.1	36.0	36.1	36.2	35.9
2014	34.7	34.6	34.6	35.5	37.2	38.2	38.6	38.7	37.6	36.8	36.9	36.9	36.7
2015	35.5	35.2	35.4	36.1	37.7	38.8	39.2	39.2	38.4	37.4	37.5	37.4	37.3
2016	35.8	35.6	35.6	36.5	37.8	38.6	38.8	38.5	37.7	37.0	36.9	36.7	37.1
2017	35.4	35.1	35.0	35.8	36.9	38.0	38.1	37.8	36.9	35.0	34.7	34.7	36.1

1. Employment by Industry: Alaska, Selected Years, 2007–2017—*Continued*

(Numbers in thousands, not seasonally adjusted)

Industry and year	January	February	March	April	May	June	July	August	September	October	November	December	Annual average
Transportation and Utilities													
2007	19.3	19.7	19.8	20.4	22.8	24.0	24.2	24.6	23.5	20.8	19.9	19.8	21.6
2008	19.5	20.0	20.4	20.8	23.6	24.3	24.7	25.0	23.8	20.7	20.2	20.3	21.9
2009	19.6	19.8	20.0	20.5	22.4	23.2	23.7	24.1	23.0	20.3	19.7	19.6	21.3
2010	19.0	19.0	19.3	19.8	22.0	23.2	23.5	23.9	22.8	20.3	19.5	19.6	21.0
2011	18.9	19.2	19.8	20.3	22.6	23.6	24.0	24.4	23.4	20.4	19.7	19.6	21.3
2012	19.3	19.6	19.8	20.6	22.8	23.9	24.5	24.7	23.8	21.9	19.9	20.0	21.7
2013	19.4	19.6	19.7	20.4	23.0	23.8	24.2	24.6	23.5	20.6	19.7	19.7	21.5
2014	19.0	19.4	19.4	20.3	23.3	23.6	24.2	24.5	23.4	21.1	19.6	19.7	21.5
2015	19.3	19.6	19.7	20.6	23.3	23.9	24.5	24.8	23.8	21.6	20.0	20.0	21.8
2016	19.4	19.7	19.8	21.0	23.6	24.1	24.7	25.1	23.6	21.6	20.0	20.1	21.9
2017	19.4	19.6	19.7	20.9	23.4	24.2	24.9	25.1	23.8	21.4	20.3	20.4	21.9
Information													
2007	6.9	6.9	6.9	6.8	6.9	7.0	7.0	7.0	7.0	6.9	6.9	6.9	6.9
2008	6.8	6.9	6.9	6.9	7.1	7.1	7.1	7.1	7.1	7.0	7.0	7.0	7.0
2009	6.7	6.8	6.7	6.6	6.5	6.6	6.6	6.5	6.5	6.5	6.4	6.4	6.6
2010	6.3	6.3	6.3	6.3	6.3	6.5	6.6	6.5	6.7	7.0	6.9	6.6	6.5
2011	6.3	6.3	6.4	6.4	6.3	6.4	6.4	6.3	6.2	6.3	6.3	6.3	6.3
2012	6.2	6.2	6.2	6.2	6.3	6.3	6.3	6.2	6.1	6.2	6.1	6.2	6.2
2013	6.0	6.0	6.0	6.1	6.2	6.2	6.2	6.2	6.2	6.2	6.3	6.3	6.2
2014	6.2	6.2	6.2	6.2	6.3	6.2	6.3	6.3	6.2	6.3	6.3	6.3	6.3
2015	6.3	6.3	6.4	6.4	6.3	6.3	6.3	6.3	6.3	6.3	6.3	6.3	6.3
2016	6.2	6.3	6.2	6.4	6.4	6.4	6.4	6.3	6.3	6.1	6.1	6.1	6.3
2017	6.1	6.1	6.1	6.0	6.0	6.1	6.0	5.9	5.9	5.8	5.8	5.9	6.0
Financial Activities													
2007	12.0	12.2	12.3	12.3	12.6	13.0	12.9	13.1	12.7	12.5	12.3	12.3	12.5
2008	11.9	12.0	12.1	12.1	12.5	12.5	12.7	12.6	12.4	12.0	11.9	11.9	12.2
2009	11.8	11.8	11.8	11.9	12.1	12.4	12.6	12.6	12.2	12.3	12.2	12.1	12.2
2010	11.9	11.8	11.8	12.0	12.2	12.6	12.7	12.7	12.4	12.4	12.2	11.9	12.2
2011	11.9	12.0	12.0	12.0	12.1	12.5	12.7	12.7	12.3	12.1	12.0	11.9	12.2
2012	11.9	11.9	11.8	11.9	12.2	12.5	12.7	12.7	12.2	12.3	12.1	12.1	12.2
2013	11.8	11.9	11.8	12.0	12.1	12.7	12.9	12.8	12.2	12.2	12.0	12.0	12.2
2014	11.9	11.9	11.8	11.9	12.2	12.6	12.7	12.5	12.1	12.0	11.8	11.8	12.1
2015	11.6	11.6	11.6	11.7	12.1	12.8	13.1	12.7	12.3	12.0	12.0	11.7	12.1
2016	11.7	11.6	11.7	11.8	12.0	12.4	12.9	12.8	12.1	11.9	11.9	11.9	12.1
2017	11.5	11.7	11.6	11.8	12.0	12.5	12.6	12.6	11.9	11.7	11.7	11.6	11.9
Professional and Business Services													
2007	24.6	25.1	25.3	25.9	27.3	28.3	28.1	28.2	27.7	26.3	26.1	25.9	26.6
2008	25.6	26.1	26.2	27.1	28.6	29.6	29.8	29.8	29.1	27.9	27.4	27.5	27.9
2009	26.6	27.0	27.1	27.1	28.3	29.1	29.1	29.1	28.6	27.4	26.7	26.7	27.7
2010	26.3	26.7	26.8	27.0	28.1	29.5	29.5	29.6	29.3	28.2	27.5	27.3	28.0
2011	26.9	27.5	27.4	28.1	29.0	30.3	30.1	29.8	29.9	28.9	28.6	28.6	28.8
2012	28.0	28.6	28.8	29.1	30.2	31.4	31.5	31.4	31.2	30.1	29.3	29.2	29.9
2013	28.6	29.4	29.3	29.8	30.6	31.6	31.7	32.1	31.0	29.8	29.6	29.5	30.3
2014	28.7	28.6	29.2	29.3	30.6	31.2	31.4	31.6	31.0	30.3	29.1	29.4	30.0
2015	28.9	29.2	29.2	29.8	30.9	31.6	31.5	31.4	30.8	29.6	29.0	28.4	30.0
2016	27.6	27.7	27.7	28.7	29.3	30.0	29.8	29.8	29.1	28.0	26.9	27.5	28.5
2017	26.6	27.4	26.9	27.3	28.5	29.4	29.4	29.3	28.5	27.4	26.9	26.7	27.9
Education and Health Services													
2007	38.0	38.6	38.8	38.8	38.8	38.6	38.2	38.4	38.0	38.2	38.3	38.5	38.4
2008	38.3	38.8	39.0	39.0	39.2	39.0	39.2	39.2	39.0	39.3	39.5	39.8	39.1
2009	39.4	39.9	40.0	40.4	40.5	40.7	40.7	41.0	41.0	41.5	41.5	41.8	40.7
2010	41.7	42.1	42.2	42.8	43.0	43.1	43.3	43.2	43.5	44.0	44.1	44.4	43.1
2011	44.3	44.7	44.8	45.3	45.5	45.5	45.5	45.8	45.8	46.0	46.2	46.6	45.5
2012	46.2	46.9	46.9	47.0	47.3	47.3	46.5	46.6	46.3	47.4	47.6	47.7	47.0
2013	47.3	47.8	47.9	48.2	48.3	48.0	47.9	47.9	47.8	47.9	48.0	48.0	47.9
2014	47.4	47.7	47.8	47.9	47.8	47.6	47.6	47.6	47.4	47.6	47.6	47.6	47.6
2015	47.6	47.9	47.9	47.3	47.3	47.4	47.5	47.2	47.0	47.4	47.5	47.9	47.5
2016	47.8	48.3	48.5	48.8	48.7	48.3	48.8	48.8	48.7	48.8	48.9	49.2	48.6
2017	49.0	49.4	49.7	49.8	50.0	49.8	49.9	50.0	49.6	49.7	49.7	49.9	49.7

1. Employment by Industry: Alaska, Selected Years, 2007–2017—*Continued*

(Numbers in thousands, not seasonally adjusted)

Industry and year	January	February	March	April	May	June	July	August	September	October	November	December	Annual average
Leisure and Hospitality													
2007	26.8	27.3	27.9	29.3	33.8	39.0	39.8	39.6	35.9	29.1	28.3	28.1	32.1
2008	27.0	27.4	27.8	29.0	34.8	38.9	40.3	39.9	36.2	29.2	28.3	28.1	32.2
2009	26.5	27.1	27.5	28.1	33.1	36.5	37.7	37.8	35.1	29.0	27.7	27.5	31.1
2010	26.4	26.9	27.2	28.6	32.9	36.9	38.4	38.4	35.5	29.2	28.5	28.8	31.5
2011	27.5	28.0	28.6	29.7	33.9	38.3	39.8	39.7	36.5	30.2	29.0	28.9	32.5
2012	27.9	28.4	29.1	30.4	34.7	39.4	40.7	40.5	37.2	32.1	29.7	29.6	33.3
2013	28.4	29.1	29.8	30.8	35.6	39.9	41.2	41.0	37.5	32.4	29.7	29.5	33.7
2014	28.8	29.4	30.3	31.1	36.8	40.3	41.5	41.4	38.1	32.4	30.3	30.3	34.2
2015	29.7	30.2	30.8	31.8	37.7	41.3	42.7	42.3	39.3	33.2	30.6	30.7	35.0
2016	29.9	30.3	30.8	32.1	38.0	42.0	43.2	43.2	39.6	33.2	30.8	31.0	35.3
2017	29.8	30.1	30.9	31.9	38.1	42.0	43.5	43.2	39.7	32.9	30.9	31.3	35.4
Other Services													
2007	11.1	11.4	11.5	11.2	11.5	11.4	11.4	11.4	11.3	11.2	11.2	11.2	11.3
2008	10.9	11.1	11.2	11.2	11.4	11.5	11.5	11.5	11.4	11.5	11.3	11.2	11.3
2009	11.1	11.3	11.2	11.4	11.6	11.6	11.7	11.7	11.6	11.2	11.2	11.1	11.4
2010	10.9	10.9	11.0	11.3	11.4	11.5	11.6	11.4	11.3	11.2	11.1	11.0	11.2
2011	10.9	11.0	11.1	11.1	11.2	11.4	11.3	11.3	11.3	11.4	11.2	11.2	11.2
2012	11.1	11.1	11.1	11.2	11.5	11.6	11.6	11.5	11.4	11.3	11.3	11.2	11.3
2013	11.1	11.2	11.3	11.4	11.5	11.6	11.6	11.4	11.3	11.2	11.2	11.1	11.3
2014	11.1	11.1	11.0	11.3	11.5	11.5	11.7	11.6	11.5	11.6	11.4	11.1	11.4
2015	10.9	10.9	10.9	11.2	11.4	11.5	11.3	11.0	11.0	11.0	11.0	11.0	11.1
2016	10.8	10.8	10.9	11.1	11.3	11.3	11.3	11.1	11.1	11.0	11.0	10.8	11.0
2017	10.7	10.8	10.8	11.1	11.3	11.4	11.2	11.1	11.2	11.2	11.1	10.9	11.1
Government													
2007	78.9	81.9	82.6	83.1	83.1	80.5	75.7	76.9	82.0	83.2	82.7	82.5	81.1
2008	80.4	82.4	82.7	84.0	82.9	82.1	77.3	78.7	83.5	84.0	83.8	83.3	82.1
2009	81.6	83.6	83.7	85.6	83.5	84.3	79.4	80.2	85.0	86.0	85.5	85.4	83.7
2010	83.2	85.2	85.7	87.1	85.8	86.8	81.1	82.0	87.4	87.4	86.8	86.6	85.4
2011	84.2	85.9	85.5	86.5	84.9	85.7	80.0	80.1	86.2	86.7	85.9	85.9	84.8
2012	81.9	85.4	85.9	86.0	84.8	84.3	79.1	80.5	85.6	85.6	85.2	85.0	84.1
2013	81.2	84.1	84.3	84.9	84.2	83.4	77.9	78.8	83.4	83.3	83.4	82.9	82.7
2014	81.4	82.8	83.1	84.0	84.0	82.7	77.9	78.6	82.9	82.9	83.2	83.1	82.2
2015	81.5	82.9	83.1	84.0	84.0	82.5	77.7	78.2	82.8	82.6	82.6	82.5	82.0
2016	81.1	82.2	82.4	83.9	83.7	82.5	76.7	77.7	82.3	82.9	82.8	82.1	81.7
2017	80.9	82.2	82.3	82.8	83.7	81.9	75.7	76.9	81.5	81.9	81.4	80.9	81.0

2. Average Weekly Hours by Selected Industry: Alaska, 2013–2017

(Not seasonally adjusted)

Industry and year	January	February	March	April	May	June	July	August	September	October	November	December	Annual average
Total Private													
2013	33.7	35.6	35.3	34.4	34.6	36.4	36.7	36.5	36.0	34.7	34.1	34.5	35.3
2014	33.6	34.5	34.7	34.0	34.1	35.3	35.8	35.3	34.9	34.4	34.3	33.7	34.6
2015	34.1	35.0	35.0	34.0	34.7	35.2	35.8	36.1	34.7	34.2	34.1	33.4	34.7
2016	33.5	34.3	34.2	33.9	33.9	34.5	35.8	35.4	34.5	34.7	34.0	33.6	34.4
2017	34.7	35.1	35.1	34.7	34.6	35.7	36.7	36.3	34.8	34.7	34.3	34.1	35.1
Goods Producing													
2013	37.3	42.8	42.9	38.6	39.8	42.8	45.1	45.0	42.0	39.2	38.5	39.4	41.4
2014	37.9	39.1	40.1	37.1	37.3	37.6	41.8	40.1	39.5	38.9	36.0	37.2	38.7
2015	38.3	39.0	39.7	35.0	37.9	37.8	39.2	39.5	35.6	35.7	34.0	34.5	37.4
2016	35.0	39.1	38.9	35.7	37.3	39.2	43.6	41.3	39.3	37.0	35.3	34.0	38.3
2017	36.6	40.9	40.4	36.2	37.3	38.8	41.2	40.0	35.9	36.0	34.6	34.0	37.9
Construction													
2013	38.0	38.8	38.4	39.2	38.7	41.0	42.4	42.7	41.6	40.0	38.8	40.0	40.2
2014	39.7	39.7	39.2	39.8	37.3	39.1	39.1	40.1	39.3	39.7	35.4	37.1	38.8
2015	36.2	35.5	35.7	38.0	38.4	40.5	40.2	40.4	36.4	38.1	35.5	35.2	37.7
2016	35.3	37.1	36.8	36.9	38.3	40.5	41.7	41.7	39.8	39.3	37.6	35.6	38.6
2017	36.1	36.5	37.7	39.1	40.0	42.7	43.7	44.4	42.7	42.2	39.0	38.4	40.6
Manufacturing													
2013	36.1	53.1	52.8	37.7	40.9	44.7	50.4	49.8	40.7	33.8	33.1	32.7	43.7
2014	31.0	35.8	40.3	37.0	40.2	38.0	47.5	39.1	38.5	35.7	34.7	34.8	38.7
2015	41.0	44.5	45.8	35.0	44.3	37.3	47.1	45.0	38.2	34.0	31.5	31.8	40.8
2016	33.4	40.7	41.1	32.1	33.7	36.6	47.2	40.4	37.8	29.7	26.5	25.6	37.3
2017	34.2	46.7	42.2	29.4	30.8	32.7	37.0	34.0	22.5	21.1	24.0	22.5	32.6
Trade, Transportation, and Utilities													
2013	32.7	33.7	33.6	33.3	34.0	36.3	36.6	36.2	36.5	34.5	34.2	34.5	34.7
2014	33.9	34.1	34.5	33.9	34.3	35.9	35.3	35.2	34.8	34.0	34.4	33.3	34.5
2015	33.0	34.1	34.0	33.7	34.4	34.9	35.3	35.5	35.0	33.3	34.1	33.4	34.3
2016	33.4	33.0	33.0	33.2	34.1	34.6	35.1	35.1	33.7	34.0	33.5	33.9	33.9
2017	34.0	33.5	33.4	34.5	34.1	35.5	35.7	35.1	34.2	33.9	33.8	33.8	34.3
Professional and Business Services													
2013	35.4	36.6	35.9	35.9	35.5	36.8	36.6	36.9	36.5	36.5	35.7	36.1	36.2
2014	34.9	36.0	36.0	35.4	36.3	37.8	37.6	38.2	37.2	36.3	36.2	35.3	36.5
2015	34.8	36.6	36.9	36.9	36.6	37.9	37.8	38.7	37.6	37.6	37.3	35.0	37.0
2016	34.9	36.9	36.8	35.9	35.4	35.0	34.8	35.4	34.8	36.4	34.9	33.7	35.4
2017	35.4	36.2	36.4	36.2	35.1	35.9	36.9	36.7	34.8	35.5	34.4	34.0	35.6
Leisure and Hospitality													
2013	26.4	26.7	27.6	27.2	26.9	28.5	28.1	28.5	28.2	27.1	26.5	27.2	27.5
2014	25.7	27.4	27.6	26.7	26.4	28.7	28.9	28.8	27.7	27.2	27.4	26.5	27.5
2015	26.8	27.3	27.6	27.3	27.4	28.6	29.0	29.7	28.5	26.9	26.6	25.9	27.7
2016	25.4	25.3	25.8	25.8	26.4	27.3	28.1	28.3	25.9	25.6	24.4	24.0	26.2
2017	24.1	24.0	24.6	24.8	26.4	29.0	29.5	29.6	27.6	25.6	25.5	25.5	26.6

3. Average Hourly Earnings by Selected Industry: Alaska, 2013–2017

(Dollars, not seasonally adjusted)

Industry and year	January	February	March	April	May	June	July	August	September	October	November	December	Annual average
Total Private													
2013	26.43	26.04	26.07	26.56	26.42	26.29	26.50	26.78	27.39	27.49	27.43	27.52	26.74
2014	27.10	27.34	26.99	27.19	27.07	26.86	26.66	26.95	27.22	27.76	27.39	27.46	27.15
2015	26.93	27.02	27.41	28.11	27.87	27.75	27.85	28.09	27.90	28.51	28.63	28.60	27.89
2016	27.92	27.73	27.96	28.41	28.48	27.77	27.66	27.89	28.24	28.99	28.81	28.99	28.22
2017	28.13	27.56	27.92	28.47	27.97	27.69	27.58	27.90	28.65	29.43	29.13	29.44	28.29
Goods Producing													
2013	33.35	31.55	30.62	33.80	34.18	32.94	32.27	33.24	35.41	36.15	36.75	36.45	33.76
2014	34.49	34.51	33.39	35.62	36.56	36.07	33.24	34.21	34.48	36.15	35.38	35.66	34.89
2015	30.93	30.60	31.60	36.26	35.57	35.51	34.62	35.39	35.55	36.91	38.16	38.18	34.82
2016	32.70	32.13	32.62	35.98	37.12	33.51	31.61	33.23	34.85	37.81	37.67	38.44	34.44
2017	34.22	31.58	33.10	35.83	36.90	35.05	32.51	33.83	37.28	39.42	38.86	39.87	35.36
Construction													
2013	35.89	37.18	36.07	36.63	36.27	36.91	37.74	38.22	37.91	37.58	37.53	36.76	37.17
2014	36.13	37.06	36.41	37.28	38.17	38.46	38.96	38.44	38.42	38.41	36.25	35.73	37.62
2015	35.94	36.05	37.31	38.72	38.34	39.44	39.05	39.07	38.19	37.49	37.25	37.06	38.00
2016	36.67	37.65	37.51	38.06	38.91	40.09	40.57	40.35	39.51	38.99	38.35	37.93	38.92
2017	37.81	37.30	38.44	38.17	37.86	38.66	38.26	38.89	37.80	37.43	37.10	37.02	37.95
Manufacturing													
2013	20.46	17.31	16.29	20.22	21.44	18.92	16.79	16.97	19.49	22.25	22.19	24.10	18.78
2014	21.34	19.88	18.11	20.34	22.20	19.59	17.19	17.39	18.36	21.09	21.97	23.66	19.41
2015	17.54	16.30	17.24	20.08	20.58	19.21	17.18	19.41	20.32	23.66	25.93	26.96	19.40
2016	20.21	19.17	19.72	23.38	26.47	20.03	17.45	19.12	21.56	24.30	26.64	29.76	20.80
2017	21.15	18.40	19.52	22.61	25.34	21.84	19.83	20.10	24.45	27.80	27.59	30.11	21.72
Trade, Transportation, and Utilities													
2013	21.16	20.91	21.59	21.45	20.75	20.50	20.77	21.00	21.58	21.93	21.86	22.32	21.30
2014	22.15	22.34	22.67	22.52	21.93	21.55	21.76	22.00	22.41	22.85	22.81	22.93	22.31
2015	23.19	22.97	23.27	22.85	22.63	22.26	22.51	22.64	22.60	23.41	23.16	23.42	22.89
2016	23.44	22.90	23.79	23.53	22.98	22.53	22.59	22.56	23.56	23.81	23.74	24.13	23.27
2017	24.06	23.63	23.94	23.99	23.31	23.28	23.52	23.54	24.00	24.36	24.12	24.57	23.84
Professional and Business Services													
2013	34.64	34.22	34.25	34.48	34.79	34.82	34.81	35.34	35.33	35.19	35.28	35.25	34.87
2014	34.64	35.00	34.40	34.64	34.52	33.89	33.80	34.30	34.73	35.47	35.49	33.97	34.56
2015	34.16	33.82	33.95	34.08	34.26	33.57	33.65	34.34	33.60	34.01	34.33	34.26	34.00
2016	33.91	33.28	32.66	33.18	33.48	34.32	34.96	34.46	34.91	35.74	36.26	36.48	34.44
2017	35.25	33.88	34.19	35.07	34.14	33.22	33.58	33.44	35.02	35.31	35.55	35.92	34.51
Leisure and Hospitality													
2013	14.93	15.14	15.05	15.12	15.31	15.05	15.31	15.45	15.71	15.73	16.02	16.00	15.40
2014	16.21	16.96	16.33	16.64	16.52	16.03	16.42	16.48	16.95	16.94	16.98	17.48	16.64
2015	16.96	17.15	17.13	17.19	17.01	16.81	16.79	16.80	16.87	17.58	17.60	18.04	17.11
2016	17.94	17.80	17.56	17.45	17.46	17.29	17.45	17.36	17.31	17.52	17.67	17.79	17.52
2017	17.93	17.61	17.62	17.61	16.77	16.65	16.67	16.76	16.88	17.84	17.65	18.31	17.25

4. Average Weekly Earnings by Selected Industry: Alaska, 2013–2017

(Dollars, not seasonally adjusted)

Industry and year	January	February	March	April	May	June	July	August	September	October	November	December	Annual average
Total Private													
2013	890.69	927.02	920.27	913.66	914.13	956.96	972.55	977.47	986.04	953.90	935.36	949.44	943.92
2014	910.56	943.23	936.55	924.46	923.09	948.16	954.43	951.34	949.98	954.94	939.48	925.40	939.39
2015	918.31	945.70	959.35	955.74	967.09	976.80	997.03	1,014.05	968.13	975.04	976.28	955.24	967.78
2016	935.32	951.14	956.23	963.10	965.47	958.07	990.23	987.31	974.28	1,005.95	979.54	974.06	970.77
2017	976.11	967.36	979.99	987.91	967.76	988.53	1,012.19	1,012.77	997.02	1,021.22	999.16	1,003.90	992.98
Goods Producing													
2013	1,243.96	1,350.34	1,313.60	1,304.68	1,360.36	1,409.83	1,455.38	1,495.80	1,487.22	1,417.08	1,414.88	1,436.13	1,397.66
2014	1,307.17	1,349.34	1,338.94	1,321.50	1,363.69	1,356.23	1,389.43	1,371.82	1,361.96	1,406.24	1,273.68	1,326.55	1,350.24
2015	1,184.62	1,193.40	1,254.52	1,269.10	1,348.10	1,342.28	1,357.10	1,397.91	1,265.58	1,317.69	1,297.44	1,317.21	1,302.27
2016	1,144.50	1,256.28	1,268.92	1,284.49	1,384.58	1,313.59	1,378.20	1,372.40	1,369.61	1,398.97	1,329.75	1,306.96	1,319.05
2017	1,252.45	1,291.62	1,337.24	1,297.05	1,376.37	1,359.94	1,339.41	1,353.20	1,338.35	1,419.12	1,344.56	1,355.58	1,340.14
Construction													
2013	1,363.82	1,442.58	1,385.09	1,435.90	1,403.65	1,513.31	1,600.18	1,631.99	1,577.06	1,503.20	1,456.16	1,470.40	1,494.23
2014	1,434.36	1,471.28	1,427.27	1,483.74	1,423.74	1,503.79	1,523.34	1,541.44	1,509.91	1,524.88	1,283.25	1,325.58	1,459.66
2015	1,301.03	1,279.78	1,331.97	1,471.36	1,472.26	1,597.32	1,569.81	1,578.43	1,390.12	1,428.37	1,322.38	1,304.51	1,432.60
2016	1,294.45	1,396.82	1,380.37	1,404.41	1,490.25	1,623.65	1,691.77	1,682.60	1,572.50	1,532.31	1,441.96	1,350.31	1,502.31
2017	1,364.94	1,361.45	1,449.19	1,492.45	1,514.40	1,650.78	1,671.96	1,726.72	1,614.06	1,579.55	1,446.90	1,421.57	1,540.77
Manufacturing													
2013	738.61	919.16	860.11	762.29	876.90	845.72	846.22	845.11	793.24	752.05	734.49	788.07	820.69
2014	661.54	711.70	729.83	752.58	892.44	744.42	816.53	679.95	706.86	752.91	762.36	823.37	751.17
2015	719.14	725.35	789.59	702.80	911.69	716.53	809.18	873.45	776.22	804.44	816.80	857.33	791.52
2016	675.01	780.22	810.49	750.50	892.04	733.10	823.64	772.45	814.97	724.38	705.96	761.86	775.84
2017	723.33	859.28	823.74	664.73	780.47	714.17	733.71	683.40	550.13	586.58	662.16	677.48	708.07
Trade, Transportation, and Utilities													
2013	691.93	704.67	725.42	714.29	705.50	744.15	760.18	760.20	787.67	756.59	747.61	770.04	739.11
2014	750.89	761.79	782.12	763.43	752.20	773.65	768.13	774.40	779.87	776.90	784.66	763.57	769.70
2015	765.27	783.28	791.18	770.05	778.47	776.87	794.60	803.72	791.00	779.55	789.76	782.23	785.13
2016	782.90	755.70	785.07	781.20	783.62	779.54	792.91	791.86	793.97	809.54	795.29	818.01	788.85
2017	818.04	791.61	799.60	827.66	794.87	826.44	839.66	826.25	820.80	825.80	815.26	830.47	817.71
Professional and Business Services													
2013	1,226.26	1,252.45	1,229.58	1,237.83	1,235.05	1,281.38	1,274.05	1,304.05	1,289.55	1,284.44	1,259.50	1,272.53	1,262.29
2014	1,208.94	1,260.00	1,238.40	1,226.26	1,253.08	1,281.04	1,270.88	1,310.26	1,291.96	1,287.56	1,284.74	1,199.14	1,261.44
2015	1,188.77	1,237.81	1,252.76	1,257.55	1,253.92	1,272.30	1,271.97	1,328.96	1,263.36	1,278.78	1,280.51	1,199.10	1,258.00
2016	1,183.46	1,228.03	1,201.89	1,191.16	1,185.19	1,201.20	1,216.61	1,219.88	1,214.87	1,300.94	1,265.47	1,229.38	1,219.18
2017	1,247.85	1,226.46	1,244.52	1,269.53	1,198.31	1,192.60	1,239.10	1,227.25	1,218.70	1,253.51	1,222.92	1,221.28	1,228.56
Leisure and Hospitality													
2013	394.15	404.24	415.38	411.26	411.84	428.93	430.21	440.33	443.02	426.28	424.53	435.20	423.50
2014	416.60	464.70	450.71	444.29	436.13	460.06	474.54	474.62	469.52	460.77	465.25	463.22	457.60
2015	454.53	468.20	472.79	469.29	466.07	480.77	486.91	498.96	480.80	472.90	468.16	467.24	473.95
2016	455.68	450.34	453.05	450.21	460.94	472.02	490.35	491.29	448.33	448.51	431.15	426.96	459.02
2017	432.11	422.64	433.45	436.73	442.73	482.85	491.77	496.10	465.89	456.70	450.08	466.91	458.85

ARIZONA
At a Glance

Population:
  2010 census: 6,392,017
  2017 estimate: 7,016,270

Percent change in population:
  2010–2017: 9.8%

Percent change in total nonfarm employment:
  2007–2017: 3.5%

Industry with the largest growth in employment, 2007–2017 (thousands):
  Education and health services, 118.6

Industry with the largest decline or smallest growth in employment, 2007–2017 (thousands):
  Construction, -79.5

Civilian labor force:
  2010: 3,089,705
  2017: 3,312,720

Unemployment rate and rank among states (highest to lowest):
  2010: 10.4%, 11th
  2017: 4.9%, 10th

Over-the-year change in unemployment rates:
  2015–2016: -0.7%
  2016–2017: -0.5%

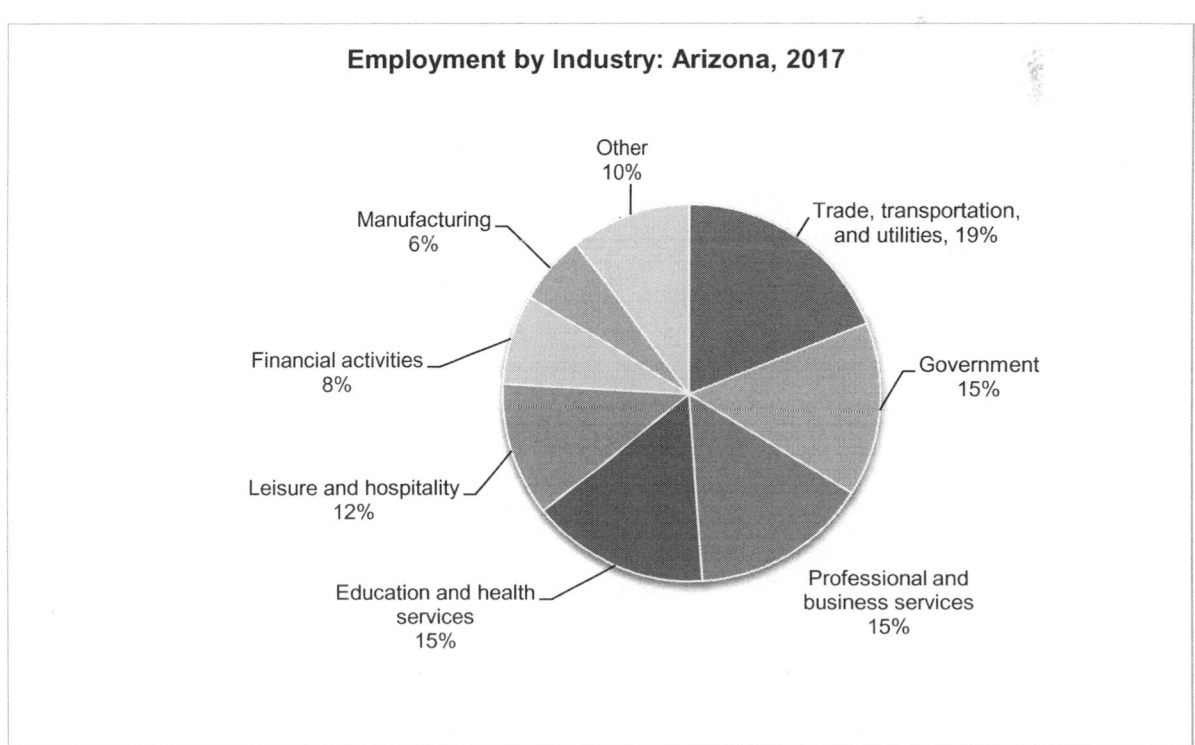

Employment by Industry: Arizona, 2017

- Other 10%
- Trade, transportation, and utilities, 19%
- Manufacturing 6%
- Government 15%
- Financial activities 8%
- Leisure and hospitality 12%
- Professional and business services 15%
- Education and health services 15%

1. Employment by Industry: Arizona, Selected Years, 2007–2017

(Numbers in thousands, not seasonally adjusted)

Industry and year	January	February	March	April	May	June	July	August	September	October	November	December	Annual average
Total Nonfarm													
2007	2,636.3	2,674.2	2,692.1	2,682.1	2,687.1	2,655.6	2,629.4	2,668.1	2,688.7	2,701.3	2,718.4	2,719.8	2,679.4
2008	2,650.5	2,673.2	2,672.3	2,661.9	2,655.0	2,605.5	2,563.4	2,601.5	2,607.4	2,600.4	2,596.9	2,581.8	2,622.5
2009	2,498.6	2,493.8	2,485.2	2,467.4	2,451.6	2,391.6	2,363.4	2,387.5	2,400.6	2,407.3	2,421.7	2,422.1	2,432.6
2010	2,366.2	2,385.2	2,396.8	2,407.1	2,413.8	2,351.8	2,326.6	2,357.2	2,373.9	2,402.3	2,423.3	2,429.9	2,386.2
2011	2,380.6	2,402.9	2,415.9	2,427.2	2,426.8	2,362.4	2,338.4	2,393.6	2,423.2	2,441.1	2,465.2	2,468.4	2,412.1
2012	2,425.9	2,449.0	2,466.8	2,468.4	2,464.6	2,423.0	2,390.1	2,448.4	2,475.4	2,494.7	2,523.4	2,531.6	2,463.4
2013	2,479.1	2,505.5	2,518.2	2,527.2	2,524.7	2,474.2	2,450.3	2,504.7	2,531.0	2,554.1	2,586.4	2,592.4	2,520.7
2014	2,536.7	2,558.6	2,567.0	2,578.0	2,565.4	2,521.8	2,497.2	2,549.8	2,575.4	2,608.6	2,638.4	2,648.2	2,570.4
2015	2,596.0	2,621.2	2,628.3	2,639.2	2,629.8	2,577.1	2,564.2	2,616.7	2,646.5	2,685.8	2,715.0	2,717.8	2,636.5
2016	2,663.5	2,693.2	2,701.6	2,717.3	2,703.9	2,646.6	2,641.2	2,690.8	2,730.4	2,754.7	2,778.2	2,782.3	2,708.6
2017	2,731.2	2,758.9	2,769.5	2,780.1	2,766.6	2,723.5	2,702.6	2,757.1	2,794.5	2,813.8	2,834.4	2,838.2	2,772.5
Total Private													
2007	2,226.5	2,248.6	2,265.2	2,255.6	2,261.2	2,264.0	2,244.3	2,256.1	2,255.6	2,264.5	2,278.5	2,280.6	2,258.4
2008	2,220.6	2,230.6	2,230.7	2,219.1	2,213.1	2,199.1	2,172.3	2,179.3	2,168.6	2,157.7	2,151.7	2,139.2	2,190.2
2009	2,068.5	2,054.1	2,047.4	2,027.3	2,018.0	1,999.8	1,981.7	1,982.5	1,973.6	1,976.8	1,990.4	1,995.0	2,009.6
2010	1,947.9	1,955.7	1,968.7	1,975.7	1,973.4	1,964.4	1,950.5	1,958.4	1,954.6	1,980.4	1,998.7	2,009.9	1,969.9
2011	1,968.9	1,980.3	1,994.0	2,003.8	2,005.0	1,993.0	1,984.1	1,998.2	2,005.8	2,020.3	2,042.7	2,052.7	2,004.1
2012	2,017.0	2,027.7	2,044.9	2,045.8	2,048.8	2,044.0	2,029.6	2,048.5	2,054.7	2,072.3	2,099.1	2,109.8	2,053.5
2013	2,066.4	2,082.4	2,096.2	2,103.7	2,105.9	2,099.0	2,090.6	2,108.8	2,111.6	2,131.2	2,163.0	2,172.3	2,110.9
2014	2,122.9	2,135.9	2,145.8	2,155.4	2,154.4	2,144.5	2,133.2	2,153.0	2,155.0	2,183.6	2,211.9	2,226.2	2,160.2
2015	2,184.2	2,197.2	2,205.2	2,215.9	2,215.3	2,206.0	2,205.3	2,222.7	2,227.6	2,260.2	2,286.7	2,295.5	2,226.8
2016	2,253.0	2,269.6	2,277.3	2,293.0	2,289.3	2,273.8	2,278.2	2,295.5	2,306.4	2,328.0	2,349.3	2,357.4	2,297.6
2017	2,318.3	2,333.0	2,343.4	2,353.4	2,350.6	2,345.1	2,336.7	2,356.2	2,368.6	2,386.5	2,405.7	2,413.7	2,359.3
Goods Producing													
2007	418.7	421.8	422.6	419.0	420.2	425.1	423.0	423.6	418.7	413.9	408.0	402.1	418.1
2008	391.4	388.8	386.7	383.0	381.5	380.1	376.1	373.4	367.0	357.7	347.2	338.5	372.6
2009	322.0	311.9	306.5	298.7	295.4	294.4	291.0	287.5	283.2	280.0	277.0	274.4	293.5
2010	267.6	267.7	268.5	270.9	271.0	272.6	272.8	272.2	270.4	272.4	271.8	271.2	270.8
2011	266.2	266.1	268.0	269.6	271.6	274.4	275.8	276.4	276.4	276.5	275.9	276.3	272.8
2012	273.5	274.7	278.3	279.3	281.5	285.5	286.8	288.7	288.5	288.9	288.8	288.5	283.6
2013	283.7	285.6	288.0	288.8	291.4	295.3	296.1	296.4	294.6	295.6	295.1	294.5	292.1
2014	292.2	294.2	294.2	295.1	295.4	296.3	295.6	295.7	293.5	295.4	295.0	295.4	294.8
2015	291.2	293.1	293.8	296.2	297.6	300.0	301.5	301.8	300.2	302.8	302.6	303.8	298.7
2016	299.9	303.1	303.8	304.9	305.5	308.8	310.1	310.3	309.3	309.0	308.9	311.0	307.1
2017	309.0	312.0	313.7	315.2	317.7	322.7	324.8	325.7	326.3	327.7	329.0	332.6	321.4
Service-Providing													
2007	2,217.6	2,252.4	2,269.5	2,263.1	2,266.9	2,230.5	2,206.4	2,244.5	2,270.0	2,287.4	2,310.4	2,317.7	2,261.4
2008	2,259.1	2,284.4	2,285.6	2,278.9	2,273.5	2,225.4	2,187.3	2,228.1	2,240.4	2,242.7	2,249.7	2,243.3	2,249.9
2009	2,176.6	2,181.9	2,178.7	2,168.7	2,156.2	2,097.2	2,072.4	2,100.0	2,117.4	2,127.3	2,144.7	2,147.7	2,139.1
2010	2,098.6	2,117.5	2,128.3	2,136.2	2,142.8	2,079.2	2,053.8	2,085.0	2,103.5	2,129.9	2,151.5	2,158.7	2,115.4
2011	2,114.4	2,136.8	2,147.9	2,157.6	2,155.2	2,088.0	2,062.6	2,117.2	2,146.8	2,164.6	2,189.3	2,192.1	2,139.4
2012	2,152.4	2,174.3	2,188.5	2,189.1	2,183.1	2,137.5	2,103.3	2,159.7	2,186.9	2,205.8	2,234.6	2,243.1	2,179.9
2013	2,195.4	2,219.9	2,230.2	2,238.4	2,233.3	2,178.9	2,154.2	2,208.3	2,236.4	2,258.5	2,291.3	2,297.9	2,228.6
2014	2,244.5	2,264.4	2,272.8	2,282.9	2,270.0	2,225.5	2,201.6	2,254.1	2,281.9	2,313.2	2,343.4	2,352.8	2,275.6
2015	2,304.8	2,328.1	2,334.5	2,343.0	2,332.2	2,277.1	2,262.7	2,314.9	2,346.3	2,383.0	2,412.4	2,414.0	2,337.8
2016	2,363.6	2,390.1	2,397.8	2,412.4	2,398.4	2,337.8	2,331.1	2,380.5	2,421.1	2,445.7	2,469.3	2,471.3	2,401.6
2017	2,422.2	2,446.9	2,455.8	2,464.9	2,448.9	2,400.8	2,377.8	2,431.4	2,468.2	2,486.1	2,505.4	2,505.6	2,451.2
Mining and Logging													
2007	10.5	10.5	10.7	10.7	10.9	11.2	11.8	12.1	12.1	12.3	12.4	12.5	11.5
2008	12.7	12.7	12.9	13.0	13.3	13.7	14.0	14.2	14.4	14.0	13.8	13.8	13.5
2009	12.6	12.1	12.1	10.9	10.6	10.7	10.7	10.8	10.7	10.8	10.8	10.8	11.1
2010	10.8	10.9	10.8	10.9	11.0	11.0	10.8	10.8	10.7	11.0	11.1	11.2	10.9
2011	11.3	11.4	11.5	11.2	11.4	11.6	11.2	11.3	11.4	12.1	12.1	12.2	11.6
2012	12.2	12.3	12.4	12.5	12.6	12.7	12.9	12.9	12.9	12.8	12.9	13.0	12.7
2013	13.0	13.1	13.1	13.3	13.3	13.6	13.6	13.5	13.2	13.2	13.0	13.0	13.2
2014	13.0	13.0	13.0	13.1	13.0	13.3	13.3	13.2	13.1	13.2	13.2	13.2	13.1
2015	12.6	12.7	12.6	12.5	12.6	12.9	12.9	12.7	12.5	12.3	12.2	12.1	12.6
2016	11.8	12.0	11.5	11.5	11.4	11.6	11.6	11.5	11.4	11.4	11.4	11.5	11.6
2017	11.3	11.4	11.4	11.6	11.6	11.8	12.0	12.0	11.9	11.8	11.8	11.6	11.7

1. Employment by Industry: Arizona, Selected Years, 2007–2017—*Continued*

(Numbers in thousands, not seasonally adjusted)

Industry and year	January	February	March	April	May	June	July	August	September	October	November	December	Annual average
Construction													
2007	226.7	227.6	228.5	226.4	227.6	231.7	228.7	229.1	225.9	221.4	215.7	210.0	224.9
2008	200.7	198.8	198.2	195.1	193.6	192.0	188.6	186.3	181.1	173.9	165.8	158.8	186.1
2009	147.3	140.4	137.4	132.7	131.0	130.8	128.2	125.3	122.0	119.3	116.5	114.0	128.7
2010	109.0	109.0	109.9	111.8	111.6	113.0	113.3	113.0	111.8	113.1	112.0	110.7	111.5
2011	106.6	106.4	107.9	109.4	110.1	112.4	113.7	113.9	113.9	113.1	112.1	111.2	110.9
2012	108.8	109.3	112.0	112.6	114.1	117.0	118.1	119.8	120.1	120.7	120.5	119.5	116.0
2013	116.2	117.6	120.0	120.9	123.1	126.1	126.5	127.4	126.4	127.2	126.9	125.9	123.7
2014	123.7	124.8	124.8	125.9	125.8	125.8	125.4	125.4	124.1	125.9	125.2	124.4	125.1
2015	122.5	123.8	124.7	126.8	127.6	128.5	129.3	129.6	129.0	131.0	130.8	130.9	127.9
2016	128.6	130.9	132.6	133.7	134.2	136.4	138.2	138.5	137.9	138.2	137.5	137.6	135.4
2017	136.8	138.5	140.8	142.0	143.8	146.7	147.7	148.4	148.7	149.8	150.4	151.1	145.4
Manufacturing													
2007	181.5	183.7	183.4	181.9	181.7	182.2	182.5	182.4	180.7	180.2	179.9	179.0	181.6
2008	178.0	177.3	175.6	174.9	174.6	174.4	173.5	172.9	171.5	169.8	167.6	165.9	173.0
2009	162.1	159.4	157.0	155.1	153.8	152.9	152.1	151.4	150.5	149.9	149.7	149.6	153.6
2010	147.8	147.8	147.8	148.2	148.4	148.6	148.7	148.4	147.9	148.3	148.7	149.3	148.3
2011	148.3	148.3	148.6	149.0	150.1	150.4	150.9	151.2	151.1	151.3	151.7	152.9	150.3
2012	152.5	153.1	153.9	154.2	154.8	155.8	155.8	156.0	155.5	155.4	155.4	156.0	154.9
2013	154.5	154.9	154.9	154.6	155.0	155.6	156.0	155.5	155.0	155.2	155.2	155.6	155.2
2014	155.5	156.4	156.4	156.1	156.6	157.2	156.9	157.1	156.3	156.3	156.6	157.8	156.6
2015	156.1	156.6	156.5	156.9	157.4	158.6	159.3	159.5	158.7	159.5	159.6	160.8	158.3
2016	159.5	160.2	159.7	159.7	159.9	160.8	160.3	160.3	160.0	159.4	160.0	161.9	160.1
2017	160.9	162.1	161.5	161.6	162.3	164.2	165.1	165.3	165.7	166.1	166.8	169.9	164.3
Trade, Transportation, and Utilities													
2007	522.0	520.8	523.2	522.7	524.0	523.8	524.2	525.2	526.0	528.8	542.4	549.2	527.7
2008	527.9	525.2	524.2	518.7	519.2	517.8	510.4	511.4	507.5	508.6	514.8	515.3	516.8
2009	495.5	487.1	484.9	479.3	478.0	474.4	471.7	471.1	469.1	468.9	478.2	482.9	478.4
2010	467.9	466.7	467.2	467.6	467.7	465.6	463.1	463.0	459.9	465.7	476.6	482.8	467.8
2011	468.0	467.5	468.9	470.7	470.7	469.8	468.3	469.4	468.3	474.6	487.9	491.3	473.0
2012	475.9	472.6	474.2	473.1	473.6	472.3	470.3	470.6	471.2	476.4	491.4	495.7	476.4
2013	475.2	473.5	473.6	474.9	476.2	476.1	476.3	478.4	479.3	484.6	499.5	506.7	481.2
2014	488.7	487.1	487.6	487.9	487.8	488.0	486.8	489.3	489.3	495.8	510.0	517.5	493.0
2015	499.0	497.9	498.7	499.4	500.2	500.8	501.2	504.2	505.9	513.3	527.3	530.3	506.5
2016	510.6	510.0	510.6	512.5	512.4	510.3	511.8	513.1	512.5	521.6	535.9	540.2	516.8
2017	521.8	519.4	518.4	519.9	520.0	520.4	519.7	521.2	521.6	525.9	540.8	540.9	524.2
Wholesale Trade													
2007	107.7	108.3	108.9	108.1	108.2	108.9	108.9	108.6	108.4	108.8	109.8	110.6	108.8
2008	108.9	109.3	109.3	108.0	108.1	107.6	106.7	106.7	106.4	106.5	106.5	106.2	107.5
2009	103.9	102.8	101.7	100.0	99.0	98.0	97.5	97.1	96.2	96.5	96.5	96.7	98.8
2010	95.2	95.5	95.6	95.5	95.4	95.0	94.5	93.9	93.1	93.5	93.9	94.2	94.6
2011	93.3	94.0	94.1	94.4	94.4	94.3	93.6	93.2	93.0	93.4	93.8	93.9	93.8
2012	93.0	93.4	93.9	93.7	93.7	93.9	93.6	93.4	93.5	93.8	94.2	94.5	93.7
2013	93.1	93.8	93.8	93.9	93.5	93.8	93.2	93.2	93.0	93.9	94.3	94.8	93.7
2014	93.3	93.7	93.9	93.5	93.7	93.3	93.1	93.1	93.0	93.0	93.2	94.1	93.4
2015	92.6	92.8	92.8	93.0	93.3	93.2	92.8	92.9	93.0	93.5	94.0	94.2	93.2
2016	93.8	94.1	93.7	94.0	94.0	93.8	94.0	93.6	93.4	94.8	95.0	95.5	94.1
2017	94.7	95.1	95.1	95.2	95.4	95.5	94.8	95.0	95.2	94.5	96.1	95.5	95.2
Retail Trade													
2007	328.5	326.6	328.5	328.4	329.0	327.7	328.6	329.4	330.1	332.9	344.9	348.7	331.9
2008	332.3	328.8	328.0	324.0	324.3	323.6	317.8	318.4	315.3	316.6	322.0	321.9	322.8
2009	306.9	300.3	299.4	297.3	297.0	294.8	293.1	292.7	292.1	292.2	301.5	304.5	297.7
2010	293.1	291.6	292.1	292.4	292.4	290.5	288.8	288.7	286.3	291.0	300.9	304.2	292.7
2011	292.9	291.4	292.4	293.7	293.3	292.1	291.9	293.2	292.3	297.4	309.6	311.1	295.9
2012	299.0	295.3	296.1	295.6	296.4	294.8	293.1	293.4	294.1	298.8	312.9	315.0	298.7
2013	297.6	295.1	295.9	297.8	298.6	298.4	299.5	301.4	302.4	305.9	319.3	324.1	303.0
2014	309.3	307.5	307.4	309.0	308.2	308.5	308.1	309.9	309.8	314.9	327.6	331.9	312.7
2015	316.5	314.7	315.3	316.8	317.0	317.7	318.1	320.6	321.8	327.7	338.8	339.8	322.1
2016	323.9	323.2	323.6	324.7	324.6	323.2	323.9	325.0	324.7	331.1	343.1	344.6	328.0
2017	330.1	327.3	326.9	328.2	328.0	328.0	328.1	328.7	328.3	332.3	344.4	342.7	331.1

1. Employment by Industry: Arizona, Selected Years, 2007–2017—*Continued*

(Numbers in thousands, not seasonally adjusted)

Industry and year	January	February	March	April	May	June	July	August	September	October	November	December	Annual average
Transportation and Utilities													
2007	85.8	85.9	85.8	86.2	86.8	87.2	86.7	87.2	87.5	87.1	87.7	89.9	87.0
2008	86.7	87.1	86.9	86.7	86.8	86.6	85.9	86.3	85.8	85.5	86.3	87.2	86.5
2009	84.7	84.0	83.8	82.0	82.0	81.6	81.1	81.3	80.8	80.2	80.2	81.7	82.0
2010	79.6	79.6	79.5	79.7	79.9	80.1	79.8	80.4	80.5	81.2	81.8	84.4	80.5
2011	81.8	82.1	82.4	82.6	83.0	83.4	82.8	83.0	83.0	83.8	84.5	86.3	83.2
2012	83.9	83.9	84.2	83.8	83.5	83.6	83.6	83.8	83.6	83.8	84.3	86.2	84.0
2013	84.5	84.6	83.9	83.2	84.1	83.9	83.6	83.8	83.9	84.8	85.9	87.8	84.5
2014	86.1	85.9	86.3	85.4	85.9	86.2	85.6	86.3	86.5	87.9	89.2	91.5	86.9
2015	89.9	90.4	90.6	89.6	89.9	89.9	90.3	90.7	91.1	92.1	94.5	96.3	91.3
2016	92.9	92.7	93.3	93.8	93.8	93.3	93.9	94.5	94.4	95.7	97.8	100.1	94.7
2017	97.0	97.0	96.4	96.5	96.6	96.9	96.8	97.5	98.1	99.1	100.3	102.7	97.9
Information													
2007	40.7	41.6	41.5	41.8	42.4	42.2	41.9	41.6	41.2	40.9	41.8	41.4	41.6
2008	40.7	41.6	42.0	41.1	42.2	41.8	40.6	40.3	40.7	39.8	40.3	40.5	41.0
2009	39.2	39.6	39.0	38.9	39.2	38.4	38.1	37.7	37.1	36.5	37.0	37.0	38.1
2010	36.5	36.7	37.0	37.0	36.9	37.3	36.4	36.2	36.0	35.7	36.3	36.7	36.6
2011	36.4	36.4	36.5	36.8	37.0	37.1	37.5	37.5	37.3	37.7	38.6	38.6	37.3
2012	38.4	38.9	39.1	39.4	40.0	39.9	40.0	40.3	39.7	39.8	40.9	41.1	39.8
2013	40.8	41.4	41.6	41.7	42.6	42.0	42.2	42.4	41.7	41.9	42.8	42.6	42.0
2014	42.5	42.5	42.9	43.3	43.8	44.0	44.4	44.2	43.3	43.7	44.0	44.4	43.6
2015	44.1	45.4	44.4	44.9	45.3	44.9	44.9	44.3	43.6	43.8	44.7	44.6	44.6
2016	44.9	45.7	45.1	45.7	46.0	45.7	45.3	44.7	44.3	44.7	44.9	44.9	45.2
2017	44.6	45.3	45.4	46.0	46.0	45.9	45.4	45.3	44.5	44.7	44.8	44.9	45.2
Financial Activities													
2007	186.8	188.4	189.1	189.1	188.9	188.5	187.9	185.6	184.5	183.3	183.1	183.9	186.6
2008	179.3	180.6	180.5	180.1	180.0	179.5	178.1	177.8	177.1	176.4	175.3	175.3	178.3
2009	171.6	171.5	171.3	170.9	171.0	170.4	170.0	170.0	168.7	168.5	168.3	169.3	170.1
2010	166.6	167.2	167.6	166.3	166.4	166.5	167.0	167.3	166.6	168.9	169.6	170.9	167.6
2011	168.3	169.2	169.9	170.5	170.4	170.9	171.5	172.1	172.0	172.7	173.4	175.4	171.4
2012	173.5	175.3	175.5	175.2	175.5	175.5	175.6	176.4	176.7	178.9	180.1	181.4	176.6
2013	179.5	182.2	182.2	183.3	184.0	184.6	184.7	185.3	185.4	188.1	189.4	190.0	184.9
2014	187.2	188.1	187.7	189.9	190.0	189.7	189.5	189.8	189.4	191.3	192.5	192.7	189.8
2015	190.7	191.9	192.4	192.4	193.1	193.4	194.5	195.4	195.6	198.0	199.3	200.8	194.8
2016	199.2	200.8	201.2	202.8	202.8	203.1	204.7	205.7	206.7	208.6	210.1	211.2	204.7
2017	210.1	210.8	211.6	212.0	212.2	213.6	214.1	215.0	215.7	216.2	218.1	217.1	213.9
Professional and Business Services													
2007	395.4	400.2	404.8	402.7	402.9	405.5	402.8	406.4	405.1	408.5	409.8	407.6	404.3
2008	395.1	398.1	396.1	393.9	390.5	387.3	383.7	385.8	382.5	380.8	376.9	374.0	387.1
2009	359.2	356.2	353.4	349.5	345.3	342.7	341.0	338.8	337.6	342.1	345.0	345.4	346.4
2010	335.0	336.4	340.1	342.5	340.5	339.3	337.1	337.9	336.8	344.3	345.7	350.4	340.5
2011	341.1	344.4	346.4	347.8	344.2	343.1	343.2	344.9	346.6	351.0	353.8	358.6	347.1
2012	348.6	350.5	353.5	354.0	353.4	355.5	354.4	358.0	358.3	363.6	369.8	373.1	357.7
2013	367.1	367.2	370.3	372.4	371.9	373.3	371.7	373.8	373.4	379.3	388.8	390.5	375.0
2014	374.3	374.2	376.2	379.1	379.3	379.7	378.6	382.8	383.6	391.8	399.2	402.9	383.5
2015	391.4	391.0	390.5	393.8	392.5	392.3	394.0	396.8	398.6	407.4	414.2	416.9	398.3
2016	405.1	406.0	406.5	411.5	408.6	405.6	411.5	413.9	417.4	420.7	422.8	423.8	412.8
2017	415.8	415.9	416.1	418.1	417.4	416.7	414.6	417.6	421.7	430.3	428.8	430.3	420.3
Education and Health Services													
2007	299.7	304.3	306.0	304.2	305.7	305.2	302.5	308.0	310.7	315.5	316.4	318.2	308.0
2008	314.0	318.6	320.1	322.1	323.5	320.9	319.5	325.1	327.8	329.8	331.9	333.6	323.9
2009	328.0	330.4	331.1	331.1	332.1	329.3	327.7	333.8	335.6	339.4	342.0	343.7	333.7
2010	339.2	340.7	342.2	342.0	343.1	339.8	337.8	344.6	346.3	351.8	353.3	353.2	344.5
2011	348.9	351.2	352.1	353.9	357.2	349.5	347.2	355.2	359.2	361.4	363.8	365.0	355.4
2012	362.0	365.1	365.9	366.1	366.3	361.6	357.1	365.4	368.5	370.7	372.9	374.4	366.3
2013	367.8	371.2	373.7	374.1	373.0	366.7	364.3	372.9	375.5	376.2	379.2	379.7	372.9
2014	374.9	377.6	378.0	379.5	379.7	374.5	372.9	381.5	384.0	389.0	391.7	393.9	381.4
2015	388.5	392.4	393.3	395.6	395.6	390.1	390.3	398.4	400.2	406.1	408.2	409.1	397.3
2016	405.6	408.3	409.0	411.5	410.6	404.3	404.1	413.0	417.8	420.6	423.4	425.4	412.8
2017	420.2	424.6	425.6	426.1	424.7	419.2	416.9	426.3	431.0	433.4	435.4	436.1	426.6

1. Employment by Industry: Arizona, Selected Years, 2007–2017—*Continued*

(Numbers in thousands, not seasonally adjusted)

Industry and year	January	February	March	April	May	June	July	August	September	October	November	December	Annual average
Leisure and Hospitality													
2007	266.8	272.9	278.4	278.1	277.9	273.0	264.0	267.7	269.9	273.9	276.2	276.9	273.0
2008	272.0	276.3	279.1	279.2	275.1	270.3	263.2	265.3	266.0	265.6	266.2	263.8	270.2
2009	257.5	261.2	264.9	264.6	262.7	255.9	249.1	250.9	250.2	250.6	252.2	251.8	256.0
2010	247.3	251.7	257.1	261.2	259.1	254.2	248.3	249.8	251.4	253.8	257.1	256.2	253.9
2011	252.1	256.5	263.0	265.3	264.6	259.0	252.7	255.5	259.2	259.8	262.7	261.5	259.3
2012	259.9	265.0	272.2	272.6	271.8	266.5	259.4	263.5	266.0	267.8	268.4	268.8	266.8
2013	266.7	273.6	279.4	280.9	279.2	273.4	268.6	273.3	275.3	278.3	280.7	280.8	275.9
2014	277.0	285.0	291.4	292.6	290.5	284.4	278.3	282.9	284.9	288.6	291.2	291.1	286.5
2015	292.1	297.2	303.6	306.0	303.0	296.7	292.0	295.4	296.9	301.6	302.7	302.6	299.2
2016	300.3	307.3	312.4	315.5	313.9	307.0	302.7	307.2	310.2	314.0	314.2	312.6	309.8
2017	309.5	316.8	324.0	327.1	323.3	317.3	312.6	316.8	319.4	320.5	320.3	322.9	319.2
Other Services													
2007	96.4	98.6	99.6	98.0	99.2	100.7	98.0	98.0	99.5	99.7	100.8	101.3	99.2
2008	100.2	101.4	102.0	101.0	101.1	101.4	100.7	100.2	100.0	99.0	99.1	98.2	100.4
2009	95.5	96.2	96.3	94.3	94.3	94.3	93.1	92.7	92.1	90.8	90.7	90.5	93.4
2010	87.8	88.6	89.0	88.2	88.7	89.1	88.0	87.4	87.2	87.8	88.3	88.5	88.2
2011	87.9	89.0	89.2	89.2	89.3	89.2	87.9	87.2	86.8	86.6	86.6	86.0	87.9
2012	85.2	85.6	86.2	86.1	86.7	87.2	86.0	85.6	85.8	86.2	86.8	86.8	86.2
2013	85.6	87.7	87.4	87.6	87.6	87.6	86.7	86.3	86.4	87.2	87.5	87.5	87.1
2014	86.1	87.2	87.8	88.0	87.9	87.9	87.1	86.8	87.0	88.0	88.3	88.3	87.5
2015	87.2	88.3	88.5	87.6	88.0	87.8	86.9	86.4	86.6	87.2	87.7	87.4	87.5
2016	87.4	88.4	88.7	88.6	89.5	89.0	88.0	87.6	88.2	88.8	89.1	88.3	88.5
2017	87.3	88.2	88.6	89.0	89.3	89.3	88.6	88.3	88.4	87.8	88.5	88.9	88.5
Government													
2007	409.8	425.6	426.9	426.5	425.9	391.6	385.1	412.0	433.1	436.8	439.9	439.2	421.0
2008	429.9	442.6	441.6	442.8	441.9	406.4	391.1	422.2	438.8	442.7	445.2	442.6	432.3
2009	430.1	439.7	437.8	440.1	433.6	391.8	381.7	405.0	427.0	430.5	431.3	427.1	423.0
2010	418.3	429.5	428.1	431.4	440.4	387.4	376.1	398.8	419.3	421.9	424.6	420.0	416.3
2011	411.7	422.6	421.9	423.4	421.8	369.4	354.3	395.4	417.4	420.8	422.5	415.7	408.1
2012	408.9	421.3	421.9	422.6	415.8	379.0	360.5	399.9	420.7	422.4	424.3	421.8	409.9
2013	412.7	423.1	422.0	423.5	418.8	375.2	359.7	395.9	419.4	422.9	423.4	420.1	409.7
2014	413.8	422.7	421.2	422.6	411.0	377.3	364.0	396.8	420.4	425.0	426.5	422.0	410.3
2015	411.8	424.0	423.1	423.3	414.5	371.1	358.9	394.0	418.9	425.6	428.3	422.3	409.7
2016	410.5	423.6	424.3	424.3	414.6	372.8	363.0	395.3	424.0	426.7	428.9	424.9	411.1
2017	412.9	425.9	426.1	426.7	416.0	378.4	365.9	400.9	425.9	427.3	428.7	424.5	413.3

2. Average Weekly Hours by Selected Industry: Arizona, 2013–2017

(Not seasonally adjusted)

Industry and year	January	February	March	April	May	June	July	August	September	October	November	December	Annual average
Total Private													
2013	34.6	34.8	34.9	34.8	34.7	35.4	34.5	34.7	34.9	34.6	34.5	35.2	34.8
2014	34.5	35.2	35.2	34.4	34.3	35.0	34.2	34.3	33.9	34.1	34.8	34.6	34.5
2015	34.4	35.1	34.9	34.7	34.6	34.8	34.6	35.1	34.4	34.4	34.6	34.3	34.7
2016	34.1	34.2	34.3	34.3	34.7	34.4	34.3	34.1	34.1	34.7	34.2	34.4	34.3
2017	34.7	34.2	34.4	35.0	34.5	34.8	35.3	34.7	34.7	35.2	34.9	34.8	34.8
Goods Producing													
2013	38.5	38.7	38.8	39.1	39.2	39.9	39.3	39.7	38.5	39.1	39.0	39.5	39.1
2014	39.3	39.1	39.5	39.1	39.0	39.0	38.9	38.4	37.8	37.8	38.4	38.3	38.7
2015	37.8	38.1	38.2	38.6	38.7	39.2	38.6	38.5	37.9	38.2	38.2	38.3	38.4
2016	37.8	37.8	38.3	38.3	39.0	38.8	38.4	38.6	38.3	38.5	37.6	38.3	38.3
2017	37.8	37.5	37.8	38.2	38.1	38.9	38.4	38.7	39.2	39.2	39.3	39.5	38.6
Construction													
2013	37.4	37.5	37.6	37.7	38.2	39.5	38.5	38.7	37.4	38.4	38.3	38.3	38.1
2014	38.6	38.2	38.1	37.7	37.5	37.8	37.5	36.6	35.6	36.1	37.0	36.4	37.3
2015	35.9	36.6	37.0	37.7	38.0	38.2	37.8	37.2	35.9	37.1	36.9	36.8	37.1
2016	36.0	36.4	36.9	37.5	38.1	38.3	37.7	37.6	37.3	37.5	36.2	36.8	37.2
2017	36.0	35.9	36.6	37.3	36.4	38.0	37.4	37.7	38.6	38.6	38.6	38.6	37.5
Manufacturing													
2013	39.5	39.6	39.7	40.3	40.1	40.2	40.0	40.6	39.4	39.6	39.5	40.4	39.9
2014	39.8	39.7	40.5	40.2	40.2	40.0	40.0	40.4	40.2	39.6	39.8	40.2	40.0
2015	39.7	39.3	39.2	39.5	39.4	40.4	39.5	39.7	39.9	39.4	39.4	39.6	39.6
2016	39.7	39.2	39.8	39.3	40.2	39.6	39.6	40.3	40.0	40.1	39.2	40.0	39.8
2017	39.9	39.3	39.2	39.2	39.9	39.8	39.5	39.8	39.8	39.8	40.1	40.6	39.8
Trade, Transportation, and Utilities													
2013	35.6	35.6	35.8	35.4	35.3	36.3	35.2	35.3	35.8	35.2	34.8	35.7	35.5
2014	34.2	35.2	35.2	34.8	34.6	35.0	34.4	34.5	34.6	34.7	35.2	35.1	34.8
2015	34.9	35.4	35.3	35.4	35.3	35.3	35.4	35.5	35.3	35.0	34.7	34.0	35.1
2016	33.8	34.1	34.1	34.5	34.6	34.4	34.5	34.1	34.2	34.8	34.5	34.7	34.4
2017	34.3	33.9	34.4	34.9	34.5	34.8	35.6	34.9	34.9	35.3	34.5	34.6	34.7
Financial Activities													
2013	38.6	38.4	38.2	38.5	38.3	38.6	37.6	38.5	38.4	38.2	38.2	39.0	38.4
2014	38.1	38.7	38.3	38.1	37.8	38.6	38.4	38.8	38.4	38.4	38.8	38.5	38.4
2015	38.7	39.1	39.0	38.9	38.6	38.8	38.8	40.0	39.2	38.9	39.4	39.2	39.1
2016	39.0	38.6	38.7	38.6	39.3	39.1	39.0	39.6	39.3	40.1	39.5	39.2	39.2
2017	40.0	39.0	39.3	39.5	39.3	39.7	40.3	39.6	39.4	39.8	39.4	39.1	39.5
Professional and Business Services													
2013	35.9	36.3	36.4	36.3	36.1	36.5	35.9	36.1	36.6	36.3	36.2	36.8	36.3
2014	35.9	36.8	36.6	35.7	35.5	36.1	35.4	35.5	35.2	35.7	36.3	36.3	35.9
2015	35.7	36.4	36.4	35.9	35.8	36.1	35.9	37.2	36.0	35.9	36.4	36.5	36.2
2016	36.4	36.5	36.8	36.9	37.5	36.9	36.7	36.8	36.6	37.3	36.4	36.5	36.8
2017	36.9	36.6	36.5	37.6	36.6	36.5	37.5	36.6	36.5	37.5	37.0	36.7	36.9
Education and Health Services													
2013	33.3	33.6	33.8	33.7	33.6	34.0	32.9	32.8	33.7	33.1	33.0	33.6	33.4
2014	33.4	34.0	33.9	33.3	33.3	34.2	33.7	33.6	33.5	33.6	34.4	33.7	33.7
2015	33.8	34.4	34.1	33.9	33.8	33.6	33.7	33.9	33.7	33.5	33.8	33.3	33.8
2016	33.4	33.5	33.3	33.0	33.4	32.8	33.0	33.2	33.2	33.5	33.6	33.4	33.3
2017	34.4	33.7	33.5	34.1	33.5	34.0	34.5	34.0	33.8	34.2	34.0	33.8	34.0
Leisure and Hospitality													
2013	25.9	26.3	26.8	26.3	26.2	26.9	26.0	25.7	26.1	26.0	26.2	26.6	26.3
2014	26.3	27.1	27.8	26.3	26.2	26.7	25.4	26.0	25.9	26.3	27.7	26.8	26.5
2015	27.1	28.2	28.2	27.2	27.2	26.9	26.4	26.6	26.0	26.2	26.5	26.2	26.9
2016	26.2	26.5	26.7	26.4	26.7	26.1	26.0	25.4	25.7	26.3	25.9	25.8	26.1
2017	26.0	25.9	26.4	26.8	26.2	25.8	26.4	25.1	25.5	26.0	26.2	26.2	26.0
Other Services													
2013	30.8	31.1	31.5	31.1	30.7	32.1	30.8	31.2	31.7	31.5	31.6	32.4	31.4
2014	31.8	33.4	33.1	32.3	31.2	32.6	31.3	31.7	31.0	31.2	30.7	30.4	31.7
2015	30.9	32.7	31.8	32.5	31.6	32.8	32.1	33.4	31.5	32.2	32.8	32.6	32.2
2016	32.8	32.8	33.2	33.3	33.2	33.1	32.7	33.3	32.7	34.2	33.7	33.7	33.2
2017	34.0	33.9	34.3	34.3	33.6	34.5	34.3	33.6	34.2	35.1	35.0	35.8	34.4

3. Average Hourly Earnings by Selected Industry: Arizona, 2013–2017

(Not seasonally adjusted)

Industry and year	January	February	March	April	May	June	July	August	September	October	November	December	Annual average
Total Private													
2013	22.74	22.73	22.57	22.85	22.79	23.05	23.01	23.17	23.45	23.08	23.22	23.29	23.00
2014	23.25	23.24	23.10	22.98	22.87	22.91	22.86	22.76	22.81	22.74	22.80	22.49	22.90
2015	22.91	23.01	23.00	23.05	22.96	22.95	23.02	23.36	23.25	23.31	23.48	23.26	23.13
2016	23.55	23.70	23.72	23.92	24.17	23.77	23.74	24.24	24.21	24.44	24.32	24.06	23.99
2017	24.71	25.03	24.69	25.26	25.00	24.74	25.44	25.62	25.56	25.84	25.58	25.56	25.26
Goods Producing													
2013	23.90	23.81	23.78	23.71	23.63	23.72	23.82	23.85	24.08	24.02	24.23	24.38	23.91
2014	24.52	24.71	24.67	24.73	24.51	24.59	24.43	24.49	24.35	24.09	24.36	24.23	24.48
2015	24.12	23.94	23.92	24.15	23.61	23.42	23.72	23.73	23.73	23.81	24.28	24.15	23.88
2016	24.25	24.13	24.49	24.43	24.44	24.63	24.74	24.88	24.90	24.78	24.72	24.80	24.60
2017	25.15	25.34	25.04	24.94	24.87	24.89	25.15	24.65	25.15	25.10	24.95	24.92	25.01
Construction													
2013	22.69	22.52	22.62	22.40	22.54	22.70	22.90	23.45	23.42	23.47	23.53	23.61	23.00
2014	24.09	24.23	24.22	24.46	24.33	24.04	24.05	24.18	23.91	23.58	24.04	23.94	24.09
2015	23.67	23.14	23.14	23.49	22.64	22.69	22.94	22.89	23.17	23.01	23.45	23.86	23.17
2016	24.39	24.05	24.51	24.44	24.60	24.73	25.10	25.65	25.55	25.26	25.47	25.72	24.97
2017	25.82	26.27	25.82	25.46	25.27	25.60	25.82	25.48	26.29	25.90	25.48	25.69	25.74
Manufacturing													
2013	24.96	24.92	24.82	24.88	24.63	24.67	24.54	24.10	24.57	24.39	24.83	25.03	24.69
2014	24.85	25.10	25.01	24.85	24.57	24.77	24.45	24.44	24.43	24.43	24.49	24.34	24.64
2015	24.38	24.62	24.60	24.67	24.59	24.13	24.50	24.57	24.28	24.57	25.06	24.38	24.53
2016	24.01	24.12	24.34	24.32	24.17	24.42	24.22	23.87	24.02	24.11	23.73	23.65	24.08
2017	24.30	24.26	24.03	24.24	24.38	24.06	24.38	23.68	23.76	24.12	24.28	24.04	24.13
Trade, Transportation, and Utilities													
2013	21.30	21.20	21.05	21.27	21.06	21.06	20.97	20.83	21.11	20.68	20.63	20.38	20.96
2014	20.61	20.79	20.87	20.49	20.58	20.66	20.66	20.53	20.69	20.68	20.47	20.25	20.60
2015	20.79	20.90	20.41	20.63	20.82	20.54	20.51	20.81	20.69	20.85	21.30	21.57	20.82
2016	22.22	22.33	22.56	22.89	23.17	22.82	22.04	22.77	22.86	23.43	23.09	22.34	22.71
2017	23.54	23.85	23.77	24.78	24.07	23.72	24.81	24.43	24.49	25.20	24.57	24.53	24.32
Financial Activities													
2013	24.14	24.64	24.81	25.19	25.79	26.64	26.52	27.51	27.94	26.39	26.84	27.38	26.16
2014	26.92	26.73	26.92	26.51	26.56	26.33	26.14	25.95	26.12	25.95	26.08	25.91	26.34
2015	25.81	26.17	26.56	26.40	26.37	26.71	26.74	27.35	26.99	27.22	27.28	27.09	26.73
2016	26.76	27.36	27.13	27.01	28.10	27.03	27.35	28.57	28.17	28.84	29.10	27.96	27.80
2017	28.55	28.78	28.25	29.07	28.68	28.37	29.01	29.77	28.85	29.74	29.76	29.49	29.03
Professional and Business Services													
2013	26.05	26.03	25.73	25.61	25.64	25.84	25.48	25.30	25.58	25.50	25.74	25.50	25.66
2014	25.10	25.35	25.19	25.16	24.99	25.28	24.94	25.06	25.18	25.29	25.52	24.04	25.09
2015	25.89	26.30	26.66	26.53	26.30	26.40	26.15	26.67	26.53	26.53	26.23	25.05	26.27
2016	25.07	25.16	25.43	25.99	26.48	25.67	26.01	26.15	26.32	26.51	26.00	25.84	25.89
2017	26.83	26.88	26.87	27.45	27.12	27.08	28.21	28.10	28.12	28.26	27.88	27.90	27.57
Education and Health Services													
2013	24.26	24.09	24.03	24.42	23.97	24.31	24.48	24.26	24.53	24.62	24.77	25.20	24.41
2014	25.08	24.90	24.61	24.88	24.64	24.33	24.65	24.47	24.57	24.48	24.67	24.98	24.69
2015	24.79	24.83	24.80	24.68	24.60	24.72	24.83	25.03	25.14	25.12	25.29	25.22	24.92
2016	25.28	25.16	25.44	25.66	25.35	25.24	25.21	25.23	25.52	25.55	25.49	26.25	25.45
2017	25.73	25.71	26.18	26.25	26.27	26.22	26.67	26.67	26.72	26.74	26.94	26.95	26.42
Leisure and Hospitality													
2013	13.54	13.51	13.46	13.43	13.50	13.33	13.36	13.38	13.65	13.52	13.52	13.64	13.49
2014	13.66	13.70	13.70	13.62	13.57	13.40	13.46	13.41	13.57	13.83	13.77	13.77	13.62
2015	14.01	14.07	13.95	13.97	14.03	13.83	13.94	14.02	14.10	14.15	14.30	14.33	14.06
2016	14.41	14.20	13.92	14.23	14.28	14.13	14.13	14.07	14.09	14.26	14.39	14.36	14.21
2017	14.98	15.09	14.94	15.00	15.13	14.82	14.69	14.82	14.80	15.14	15.20	15.79	15.04
Other Services													
2013	19.35	19.35	19.24	20.07	19.79	19.84	19.83	19.98	20.54	20.25	20.46	20.45	19.93
2014	20.87	21.11	20.20	19.70	19.29	20.14	19.72	20.09	19.23	19.02	19.40	18.92	19.82
2015	19.23	19.58	19.67	19.69	20.29	20.15	20.87	21.36	21.27	21.19	21.21	21.12	20.47
2016	21.25	21.49	21.75	21.83	22.10	21.67	22.01	22.60	22.79	22.57	23.12	22.95	22.18
2017	23.72	23.61	23.27	23.64	23.48	23.60	23.66	23.70	23.99	24.15	23.72	23.67	23.69

4. Average Weekly Earnings by Selected Industry: Arizona, 2013–2017

(Dollars, not seasonally adjusted)

	January	February	March	April	May	June	July	August	September	October	November	December	Annual average
Total Private													
2013	786.80	791.00	787.69	795.18	790.81	815.97	793.85	804.00	818.41	798.57	801.09	819.81	800.40
2014	802.13	818.05	813.12	790.51	784.44	801.85	781.81	780.67	773.26	775.43	793.44	778.15	790.05
2015	788.10	807.65	802.70	799.84	794.42	798.66	796.49	819.94	799.80	801.86	812.41	797.82	802.61
2016	803.06	810.54	813.60	820.46	838.70	817.69	814.28	826.58	825.56	848.07	831.74	827.66	822.86
2017	857.44	856.03	849.34	884.10	862.50	860.95	898.03	889.01	886.93	909.57	892.74	889.49	879.05
Goods Producing													
2013	920.15	921.45	922.66	927.06	926.30	946.43	936.13	946.85	927.08	939.18	944.97	963.01	934.88
2014	963.64	966.16	974.47	966.94	955.89	959.01	950.33	940.42	920.43	910.60	935.42	928.01	947.38
2015	911.74	912.11	913.74	932.19	913.71	918.06	915.59	913.61	899.37	909.54	927.50	924.95	916.99
2016	916.65	912.11	937.97	935.67	953.16	955.64	950.02	960.37	953.67	954.03	929.47	949.84	942.18
2017	950.67	950.25	946.51	952.71	947.55	968.22	965.76	953.96	985.88	983.92	980.54	984.34	965.39
Construction													
2013	848.61	844.50	850.51	844.48	861.03	896.65	883.96	907.52	875.91	901.25	901.20	904.26	876.30
2014	929.87	925.59	922.78	922.14	912.38	908.71	901.88	884.99	851.20	851.24	889.48	871.42	898.56
2015	849.75	846.92	856.18	885.57	860.32	866.76	867.13	851.51	831.80	853.67	865.31	878.05	859.61
2016	878.04	875.42	904.42	916.50	937.26	947.16	946.27	964.44	953.02	947.25	922.01	946.50	928.88
2017	929.52	943.09	945.01	949.66	919.83	972.80	965.67	960.60	1,014.79	999.74	983.53	991.63	965.25
Manufacturing													
2013	985.92	986.83	985.35	1,002.66	987.66	991.73	981.60	978.46	968.06	965.84	980.79	1,011.21	985.13
2014	989.03	996.47	1,012.91	998.97	987.71	990.80	978.00	987.38	982.09	967.43	974.70	978.47	985.60
2015	967.89	967.57	964.32	974.47	968.85	974.85	967.75	975.43	968.77	968.06	987.36	965.45	971.39
2016	953.20	945.50	968.73	955.78	971.63	967.03	959.11	961.96	960.80	966.81	930.22	946.00	958.38
2017	969.57	953.42	941.98	950.21	972.76	957.59	963.01	942.46	945.65	959.98	973.63	976.02	960.37
Trade, Transportation, and Utilities													
2013	758.28	754.72	753.59	752.96	743.42	764.48	738.14	735.30	755.74	727.94	717.92	727.57	744.08
2014	704.86	731.81	734.62	713.05	712.07	723.10	710.70	708.29	715.87	717.60	720.54	710.78	716.88
2015	725.57	739.86	720.47	730.30	734.95	725.06	726.05	738.76	730.36	729.75	739.11	733.38	730.78
2016	751.04	761.45	769.30	789.71	801.68	785.01	760.38	776.46	781.81	815.36	796.61	775.20	781.22
2017	807.42	808.52	817.69	864.82	830.42	825.46	883.24	852.61	854.70	889.56	847.67	848.74	843.90
Financial Activities													
2013	931.80	946.18	947.74	969.82	987.76	1,028.30	997.15	1,059.14	1,072.90	1,008.10	1,025.29	1,067.82	1,004.54
2014	1,025.65	1,034.45	1,031.04	1,010.03	1,003.97	1,016.34	1,003.78	1,006.86	1,003.01	996.48	1,011.90	997.54	1,011.46
2015	998.85	1,023.25	1,035.84	1,026.96	1,017.88	1,036.35	1,037.51	1,094.00	1,058.01	1,058.86	1,074.83	1,061.93	1,045.14
2016	1,043.64	1,056.10	1,049.93	1,042.59	1,104.33	1,056.87	1,066.65	1,131.37	1,107.08	1,156.48	1,149.45	1,096.03	1,089.76
2017	1,142.00	1,122.42	1,110.23	1,148.27	1,127.12	1,126.29	1,169.10	1,178.89	1,136.69	1,183.65	1,172.54	1,153.06	1,146.69
Professional and Business Services													
2013	935.20	944.89	936.57	929.64	925.60	943.16	914.73	913.33	936.23	925.65	931.79	938.40	931.46
2014	901.09	932.88	921.95	898.21	887.15	912.61	882.88	889.63	886.34	902.85	926.38	872.65	900.73
2015	924.27	957.32	970.42	952.43	941.54	953.04	938.79	992.12	955.08	952.43	954.77	914.33	950.97
2016	912.55	918.34	935.82	959.03	993.00	947.22	954.57	962.32	963.31	988.82	946.40	943.16	952.75
2017	990.03	983.81	980.76	1,032.12	992.59	988.42	1,057.88	1,028.46	1,026.38	1,059.75	1,031.56	1,023.93	1,017.33
Education and Health Services													
2013	807.86	809.42	812.21	822.95	805.39	826.54	805.39	795.73	826.66	814.92	817.41	846.72	815.29
2014	837.67	846.60	834.28	828.50	820.51	832.09	830.71	822.19	823.10	822.53	848.65	841.83	832.05
2015	837.90	854.15	845.68	836.65	831.48	830.59	836.77	848.52	847.22	841.52	854.80	839.83	842.30
2016	844.35	842.86	847.15	846.78	846.69	827.87	831.93	837.64	847.26	855.93	856.46	876.75	847.49
2017	885.11	866.43	877.03	895.13	880.05	891.48	920.12	906.78	903.14	914.51	915.96	910.91	898.28
Leisure and Hospitality													
2013	350.69	355.31	360.73	353.21	353.70	358.58	347.36	343.87	356.27	351.52	354.22	362.82	354.79
2014	359.26	371.27	380.86	358.21	355.53	357.78	341.88	348.66	351.46	363.73	381.43	369.04	360.93
2015	379.67	396.77	393.39	379.98	381.62	372.03	368.02	372.93	366.60	370.73	378.95	375.45	378.21
2016	377.54	376.30	371.66	375.67	381.28	368.79	367.38	357.38	362.11	375.04	372.70	370.49	370.88
2017	389.48	390.83	394.42	402.00	396.41	382.36	387.82	371.98	377.40	393.64	398.24	413.70	391.04
Other Services													
2013	595.98	601.79	606.06	624.18	607.55	636.86	610.76	623.38	651.12	637.88	646.54	662.58	625.80
2014	663.67	705.07	668.62	636.31	601.85	656.56	617.24	636.85	596.13	593.42	595.58	575.17	628.29
2015	594.21	640.27	625.51	639.93	641.16	660.92	669.93	713.42	670.01	682.32	695.69	688.51	659.13
2016	697.00	704.87	722.10	726.94	733.72	717.28	719.73	752.58	745.23	771.89	779.14	773.42	736.38
2017	806.48	800.38	798.16	810.85	788.93	814.20	811.54	796.32	820.46	847.67	830.20	847.39	814.59

ARKANSAS
At a Glance

Population:
  2010 census: 2,915,918
  2017 estimate: 3,004,279

Percent change in population:
  2010–2017: 3.0%

Percent change in total nonfarm employment:
  2007–2017: 2.9%

Industry with the largest growth in employment, 2007–2017 (thousands):
  Education and health services, 32.9

Industry with the largest decline or smallest growth in employment, 2007–2017 (thousands):
  Manufacturing, -33.5

Civilian labor force:
  2010: 1,353,338
  2017: 1,354,265

Unemployment rate and rank among states (highest to lowest):
  2010: 8.2%, 31st
  2017: 3.7%, 34th

Over-the-year change in unemployment rates:
  2015–2016: -1.1%
  2016–2017: -0.2%

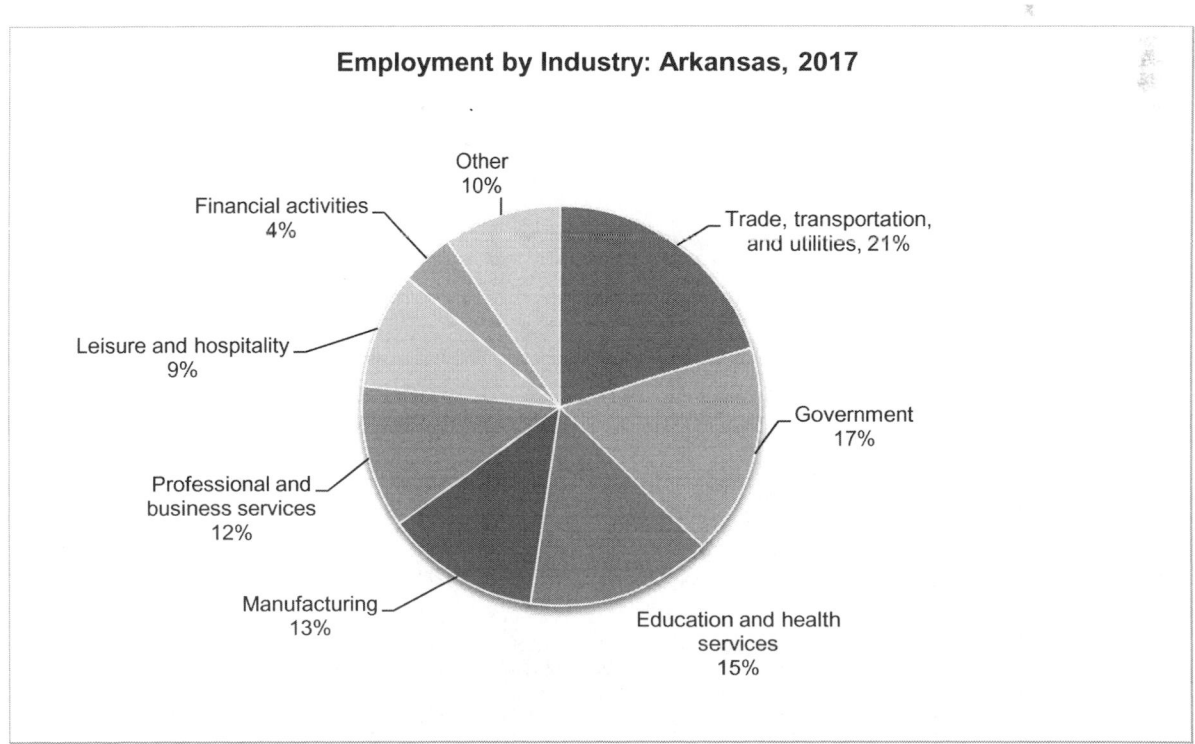

Employment by Industry: Arkansas, 2017

- Other 10%
- Financial activities 4%
- Leisure and hospitality 9%
- Professional and business services 12%
- Manufacturing 13%
- Education and health services 15%
- Government 17%
- Trade, transportation, and utilities, 21%

1. Employment by Industry: Arkansas, Selected Years, 2007–2017

(Numbers in thousands, not seasonally adjusted)

Industry and year	January	February	March	April	May	June	July	August	September	October	November	December	Annual average
Total Nonfarm													
2007	1,184.9	1,193.3	1,207.8	1,207.4	1,211.2	1,209.7	1,188.1	1,200.1	1,213.2	1,211.2	1,213.0	1,214.2	1,204.5
2008	1,190.8	1,200.0	1,207.9	1,207.9	1,212.6	1,208.4	1,189.8	1,198.4	1,211.8	1,205.4	1,200.8	1,195.9	1,202.5
2009	1,166.4	1,169.2	1,174.2	1,175.0	1,171.0	1,164.0	1,150.7	1,153.3	1,165.4	1,162.5	1,164.3	1,163.2	1,164.9
2010	1,134.9	1,138.6	1,155.1	1,164.0	1,175.0	1,177.3	1,158.2	1,162.8	1,172.6	1,171.7	1,172.4	1,173.5	1,163.0
2011	1,146.7	1,149.0	1,163.2	1,179.5	1,174.6	1,167.9	1,160.3	1,166.2	1,179.2	1,184.7	1,185.6	1,184.2	1,170.1
2012	1,158.5	1,166.8	1,178.7	1,183.2	1,186.5	1,181.8	1,160.9	1,168.6	1,181.1	1,182.0	1,183.9	1,185.6	1,176.5
2013	1,159.1	1,169.3	1,176.6	1,182.6	1,184.6	1,176.3	1,161.4	1,166.8	1,182.3	1,184.9	1,188.3	1,182.7	1,176.2
2014	1,160.9	1,171.3	1,180.5	1,189.0	1,195.1	1,188.1	1,171.3	1,180.3	1,197.5	1,200.9	1,206.4	1,208.4	1,187.5
2015	1,181.1	1,193.2	1,194.9	1,206.7	1,213.8	1,208.4	1,195.0	1,204.8	1,223.9	1,226.2	1,230.5	1,232.9	1,209.3
2016	1,204.5	1,216.4	1,224.3	1,231.5	1,232.5	1,226.0	1,212.8	1,219.8	1,237.9	1,240.6	1,242.9	1,241.9	1,227.6
2017	1,216.6	1,230.1	1,238.4	1,244.3	1,247.1	1,240.5	1,223.2	1,230.9	1,248.3	1,254.1	1,252.3	1,244.9	1,239.2
Total Private													
2007	976.8	979.7	993.2	992.9	998.0	1,001.1	994.4	1,000.0	999.3	995.3	996.0	998.1	993.7
2008	979.8	983.6	990.6	990.5	995.0	996.6	992.3	996.0	995.3	986.8	981.4	977.3	988.8
2009	952.2	949.8	953.7	953.5	950.6	949.2	948.1	947.0	948.3	940.7	941.7	940.9	948.0
2010	920.6	920.5	934.1	941.9	947.5	956.4	951.9	954.9	954.4	951.1	951.1	952.8	944.8
2011	931.6	929.5	942.0	956.8	953.0	952.5	960.7	960.5	961.6	963.1	963.1	963.6	953.2
2012	944.5	946.9	957.6	962.5	966.4	967.1	960.0	964.9	964.2	961.8	962.3	965.0	960.3
2013	945.0	950.0	956.5	962.0	965.4	963.1	961.1	963.7	966.1	967.3	970.2	965.6	961.3
2014	949.7	954.8	963.1	971.3	977.8	976.5	972.3	978.4	982.5	984.3	987.8	991.2	974.1
2015	969.9	977.4	978.5	990.0	998.0	997.9	996.5	1,003.1	1,009.1	1,009.6	1,013.4	1,016.0	996.6
2016	993.4	1,000.3	1,006.4	1,014.1	1,016.6	1,015.5	1,014.7	1,018.6	1,026.3	1,026.5	1,027.7	1,027.3	1,015.6
2017	1,008.2	1,016.3	1,023.6	1,029.0	1,032.6	1,031.0	1,025.6	1,029.9	1,034.5	1,038.8	1,036.1	1,029.5	1,027.9
Goods Producing													
2007	256.2	255.1	258.1	257.5	258.2	258.5	257.1	257.1	256.4	254.6	253.1	253.5	256.3
2008	249.7	249.5	251.2	251.0	252.2	253.2	253.1	253.4	253.1	250.5	246.4	243.8	250.6
2009	235.9	232.5	230.3	227.0	224.9	224.0	224.5	225.2	224.6	220.1	219.1	218.3	225.5
2010	213.5	212.4	216.6	219.0	220.8	224.8	223.5	223.4	222.1	220.2	219.3	219.3	219.6
2011	214.0	213.9	216.5	218.5	218.1	217.9	220.3	219.1	219.3	217.6	216.7	216.1	217.3
2012	212.7	212.7	214.9	214.7	216.1	216.6	214.9	214.8	213.9	211.2	209.7	210.0	213.5
2013	206.7	206.9	207.9	207.3	208.6	208.9	208.5	208.6	208.4	207.8	207.3	206.0	207.7
2014	205.0	204.4	205.3	207.2	209.0	209.9	210.7	211.3	212.1	212.2	211.4	212.6	209.3
2015	210.6	210.7	209.8	210.5	211.0	212.7	214.0	214.1	215.2	213.8	212.9	213.1	212.4
2016	209.6	209.7	209.8	210.3	210.4	212.5	213.1	212.5	213.3	212.6	211.6	211.8	211.4
2017	210.3	211.5	213.0	212.9	213.6	215.5	215.4	215.5	216.0	216.1	216.5	214.7	214.3
Service-Providing													
2007	928.7	938.2	949.7	949.9	953.0	951.2	931.0	943.0	956.8	956.6	959.9	960.7	948.2
2008	941.1	950.5	956.7	956.9	960.4	955.2	936.7	945.0	958.7	954.9	954.4	952.1	951.9
2009	930.5	936.7	943.9	948.0	946.1	940.0	926.2	928.1	940.8	942.4	945.2	944.9	939.4
2010	921.4	926.2	938.5	945.0	954.2	952.5	934.7	939.4	950.5	951.5	953.1	954.2	943.4
2011	932.7	935.1	946.7	961.0	956.5	950.0	940.0	947.1	959.9	967.1	968.9	968.1	952.8
2012	945.8	954.1	963.8	968.5	970.4	965.2	946.0	953.8	967.2	970.8	974.2	975.6	963.0
2013	952.4	962.4	968.7	975.3	976.0	967.4	952.9	958.2	973.9	977.1	981.0	976.7	968.5
2014	955.9	966.9	975.2	981.8	986.1	978.2	960.6	969.0	985.4	988.7	995.0	995.8	978.2
2015	970.5	982.5	985.1	996.2	1,002.8	995.7	981.0	990.7	1,008.7	1,012.4	1,017.6	1,019.8	996.9
2016	994.9	1,006.7	1,014.5	1,021.2	1,022.1	1,013.5	999.7	1,007.3	1,024.6	1,028.0	1,031.3	1,030.1	1,016.2
2017	1,006.3	1,018.6	1,025.4	1,031.4	1,033.5	1,025.0	1,007.8	1,015.4	1,032.3	1,038.0	1,035.8	1,030.2	1,025.0
Mining and Logging													
2007	8.4	8.7	9.0	9.0	9.3	9.6	9.6	9.9	10.0	9.8	9.8	9.9	9.4
2008	9.9	9.8	10.0	10.2	10.6	10.8	11.0	11.0	11.1	11.3	11.4	11.2	10.7
2009	10.6	10.5	10.5	10.3	10.1	10.2	10.4	10.4	10.3	9.9	10.0	10.0	10.3
2010	9.9	9.8	10.2	10.6	10.8	11.0	10.8	10.9	10.9	10.9	10.9	11.0	10.6
2011	10.6	10.6	10.7	10.9	10.8	11.0	11.5	11.4	11.5	11.6	11.6	11.5	11.1
2012	11.3	11.2	11.3	11.1	11.1	11.0	10.7	10.5	10.3	10.1	10.1	10.0	10.7
2013	9.6	9.6	9.6	9.5	9.6	9.6	9.7	9.6	9.5	9.3	9.2	9.0	9.5
2014	8.7	8.7	8.7	8.8	8.9	8.9	8.9	9.0	9.1	9.0	9.1	9.1	8.9
2015	8.7	8.7	8.4	8.3	8.0	8.0	8.0	7.9	7.8	7.7	7.5	7.4	8.0
2016	7.0	6.8	6.6	6.3	6.1	6.2	6.1	6.1	6.1	6.0	6.0	6.0	6.3
2017	5.8	5.9	5.8	5.8	5.9	6.0	6.0	5.9	5.9	5.8	5.8	5.8	5.9

1. Employment by Industry: Arkansas, Selected Years, 2007–2017—Continued

(Numbers in thousands, not seasonally adjusted)

Industry and year	January	February	March	April	May	June	July	August	September	October	November	December	Annual average
Construction													
2007	53.9	53.6	56.4	56.7	57.4	58.0	57.1	57.5	57.2	56.3	56.0	55.5	56.3
2008	53.4	53.8	55.1	55.7	56.6	57.3	57.8	58.5	58.2	57.4	56.0	55.0	56.2
2009	52.1	51.9	51.6	51.0	50.7	51.7	53.2	53.6	53.3	50.5	49.9	49.2	51.6
2010	46.0	45.0	47.3	48.8	49.7	51.3	51.1	50.8	50.0	48.9	47.8	47.5	48.7
2011	43.6	43.6	45.5	47.3	47.2	48.3	49.3	48.8	49.2	48.6	48.1	47.8	47.3
2012	45.6	46.1	47.5	47.6	48.6	49.4	47.7	48.3	48.5	47.3	46.1	46.0	47.4
2013	43.9	44.4	45.3	45.4	46.4	46.5	46.3	46.3	46.0	45.4	45.2	44.3	45.5
2014	43.9	43.2	43.7	45.0	46.1	46.5	46.8	47.2	47.6	47.6	47.4	47.7	46.1
2015	45.9	46.2	46.0	47.3	48.5	49.5	50.7	51.2	52.2	51.4	50.8	50.4	49.2
2016	48.3	48.6	49.2	50.3	50.5	51.5	51.6	51.1	51.5	51.1	50.1	49.6	50.3
2017	48.7	49.5	50.8	51.1	51.5	52.4	51.9	51.8	52.2	52.6	52.2	50.9	51.3
Manufacturing													
2007	193.9	192.8	192.7	191.8	191.5	190.9	190.4	189.7	189.2	188.5	187.3	188.1	190.6
2008	186.4	185.9	186.1	185.1	185.0	185.1	184.3	183.9	183.8	181.8	179.0	177.6	183.7
2009	173.2	170.1	168.2	165.7	164.1	162.1	160.9	161.2	161.0	159.7	159.2	159.1	163.7
2010	157.6	157.6	159.1	159.6	160.3	162.5	161.6	161.7	161.2	160.4	160.6	160.8	160.3
2011	159.8	159.7	160.3	160.3	160.1	158.6	159.5	158.9	158.6	157.4	157.0	156.8	158.9
2012	155.8	155.4	156.1	156.0	156.4	156.2	156.5	156.0	155.1	153.8	153.5	154.0	155.4
2013	153.2	152.9	153.0	152.4	152.6	152.8	152.5	152.7	152.9	153.1	152.9	152.7	152.8
2014	152.4	152.5	152.9	153.4	154.0	154.5	155.0	155.1	155.4	155.6	154.9	155.8	154.3
2015	156.0	155.8	155.4	154.9	154.5	155.2	155.3	155.0	155.2	154.7	154.6	155.3	155.2
2016	154.3	154.3	154.0	153.7	153.8	154.8	155.4	155.3	155.7	155.5	155.5	156.2	154.9
2017	155.8	156.1	156.4	156.0	156.2	157.1	157.5	157.8	157.9	157.7	158.5	158.0	157.1
Trade, Transportation, and Utilities													
2007	246.2	245.9	250.3	248.2	250.2	250.8	249.7	250.4	250.4	249.8	253.5	255.2	250.1
2008	247.2	246.4	248.2	247.2	248.3	248.7	247.1	247.2	246.4	244.2	245.9	246.3	246.9
2009	237.3	235.2	236.8	236.3	235.9	235.3	235.4	234.0	234.2	233.3	235.9	237.0	235.6
2010	229.7	228.7	231.6	231.9	233.6	235.7	235.6	236.1	234.8	236.6	239.6	241.4	234.6
2011	233.7	231.3	233.9	238.0	237.0	237.8	239.6	239.0	238.7	240.3	243.1	245.3	238.1
2012	238.2	237.0	239.5	240.7	241.7	242.4	241.4	241.7	241.5	241.4	245.0	246.5	241.4
2013	238.1	238.0	239.7	239.9	239.9	240.2	241.2	241.8	241.1	242.6	246.0	246.7	241.3
2014	239.2	238.6	240.6	242.7	243.7	244.8	244.5	245.7	245.8	247.0	251.4	253.4	244.8
2015	245.4	245.1	246.2	248.8	251.0	251.9	251.2	252.4	251.5	252.8	256.4	257.8	250.9
2016	249.8	249.0	250.4	250.7	251.7	252.0	252.3	252.4	252.2	252.9	256.7	257.1	252.3
2017	249.5	248.4	248.7	249.1	250.1	250.6	250.4	251.5	250.7	251.9	253.6	253.5	250.7
Wholesale Trade													
2007	47.2	47.4	48.0	48.1	48.3	48.6	48.2	48.1	47.9	48.0	48.0	48.3	48.0
2008	47.8	48.1	48.4	48.6	48.9	49.0	48.9	48.8	48.8	48.4	48.2	48.1	48.5
2009	47.0	47.0	47.2	47.2	47.3	47.2	47.0	46.7	46.3	46.3	46.1	46.1	46.8
2010	45.3	45.4	46.0	46.4	46.6	47.0	46.6	46.4	46.0	46.5	46.3	46.3	46.2
2011	45.5	45.4	45.8	46.8	46.5	46.6	47.3	47.0	46.9	47.1	46.9	47.1	46.6
2012	46.5	46.6	47.1	47.9	48.0	48.2	47.4	47.4	47.1	46.9	46.7	46.9	47.2
2013	46.5	46.7	47.1	47.2	47.2	47.1	46.9	46.7	46.4	46.6	45.8	45.7	46.7
2014	45.6	45.9	46.2	46.4	46.7	46.9	46.7	46.8	46.6	46.7	46.6	46.5	46.5
2015	46.0	46.2	46.3	46.4	46.6	46.7	46.7	46.6	46.3	46.6	46.4	46.4	46.4
2016	45.9	46.1	46.3	46.3	46.5	46.4	46.5	46.3	46.3	46.3	46.3	46.5	46.3
2017	46.1	46.4	46.8	46.7	46.9	47.0	47.1	47.1	47.0	47.0	47.0	46.4	46.8
Retail Trade													
2007	132.3	131.4	134.6	132.9	134.2	134.3	134.0	134.1	134.3	133.9	137.7	139.4	134.4
2008	133.7	132.6	133.9	132.8	133.6	134.2	133.4	133.7	132.9	131.6	133.9	135.1	133.5
2009	129.2	128.0	129.6	129.6	130.0	129.7	129.2	129.2	129.3	129.0	131.6	132.7	129.8
2010	126.7	125.6	127.5	127.7	128.9	130.1	129.8	130.1	128.9	130.4	133.5	134.8	129.5
2011	129.4	127.4	129.1	131.3	130.5	130.8	131.6	131.2	130.2	131.9	134.9	136.0	131.2
2012	130.9	129.8	131.2	131.9	132.5	132.6	132.5	132.3	132.3	132.3	136.0	136.6	132.6
2013	130.5	130.2	131.4	131.7	131.7	131.7	133.3	133.7	133.2	134.5	138.4	139.0	133.3
2014	133.1	132.2	133.4	135.2	135.5	136.3	136.0	136.6	136.2	137.4	141.4	142.4	136.3
2015	136.6	136.3	137.0	139.0	140.7	141.0	140.2	141.4	140.6	141.8	145.6	146.0	140.5
2016	140.1	139.6	140.7	141.9	142.4	142.1	142.3	142.5	141.6	142.5	146.0	145.5	142.3
2017	140.6	139.4	139.3	140.1	140.6	140.3	139.9	140.5	139.8	141.0	142.7	142.0	140.5

1. Employment by Industry: Arkansas, Selected Years, 2007–2017—*Continued*

(Numbers in thousands, not seasonally adjusted)

Industry and year	January	February	March	April	May	June	July	August	September	October	November	December	Annual average
Transportation and Utilities													
2007	66.7	67.1	67.7	67.2	67.7	67.9	67.5	68.2	68.2	67.9	67.8	67.5	67.6
2008	65.7	65.7	65.9	65.8	65.8	65.5	64.8	64.7	64.7	64.2	63.8	63.1	65.0
2009	61.1	60.2	60.0	59.5	58.6	58.4	59.2	58.1	58.6	58.1	58.2	58.2	59.0
2010	57.7	57.7	58.1	57.8	58.1	58.6	59.2	59.6	59.9	59.7	59.8	60.3	58.9
2011	58.8	58.5	59.0	59.9	60.0	60.4	60.7	60.8	61.6	61.3	61.3	62.2	60.4
2012	60.8	60.6	61.2	60.9	61.2	61.6	61.5	62.0	62.1	62.2	62.3	63.0	61.6
2013	61.1	61.1	61.2	61.0	61.0	61.4	61.0	61.4	61.5	61.5	61.8	62.0	61.3
2014	60.5	60.5	61.0	61.1	61.5	61.6	61.8	62.3	63.0	62.9	63.4	64.5	62.0
2015	62.8	62.6	62.9	63.4	63.7	64.2	64.3	64.4	64.6	64.4	64.4	65.4	63.9
2016	63.8	63.3	63.4	62.5	62.8	63.5	63.5	63.6	64.3	64.1	64.4	65.1	63.7
2017	62.8	62.6	62.6	62.3	62.6	63.3	63.4	63.9	63.9	63.9	63.9	65.1	63.4
Information													
2007	18.4	18.4	18.4	18.4	18.4	18.2	18.1	18.1	18.0	17.8	17.8	17.8	18.2
2008	17.6	17.7	17.6	17.8	17.5	17.6	17.5	17.5	17.2	17.0	16.9	16.9	17.4
2009	16.5	16.4	16.4	16.4	16.5	16.5	16.4	16.2	16.0	15.8	15.7	15.7	16.2
2010	15.3	15.4	15.5	15.4	15.5	15.8	15.3	15.2	15.2	15.1	15.1	15.1	15.3
2011	15.0	15.0	14.9	14.9	14.9	14.9	14.9	14.9	14.7	14.7	14.7	14.7	14.9
2012	14.6	14.6	14.5	14.5	14.6	14.5	14.4	14.4	14.4	14.4	14.4	14.5	14.5
2013	14.2	14.2	14.2	14.1	14.2	14.3	14.2	14.2	14.0	14.0	14.1	14.1	14.2
2014	13.8	13.8	13.7	13.7	13.7	13.6	13.7	13.6	13.3	13.3	13.4	13.4	13.6
2015	13.2	13.2	13.1	13.2	13.3	13.4	13.9	13.7	13.7	13.5	13.7	13.8	13.5
2016	13.6	13.6	13.6	13.6	13.6	13.7	13.6	13.5	13.4	13.5	13.6	13.6	13.6
2017	13.4	13.4	13.4	13.3	13.3	13.3	13.2	13.1	13.0	13.0	13.0	12.8	13.2
Financial Activities													
2007	52.4	52.4	52.6	53.1	53.3	53.7	53.7	53.6	53.4	53.2	53.1	53.3	53.2
2008	52.6	52.6	52.7	52.5	52.7	52.7	52.5	52.5	52.3	51.6	51.5	52.0	52.4
2009	51.0	50.7	50.8	50.8	50.9	51.0	50.5	50.3	50.1	49.7	49.6	49.8	50.4
2010	48.7	48.6	48.5	48.8	48.7	49.1	48.9	48.9	48.7	48.8	48.8	49.1	48.8
2011	48.2	48.0	48.2	48.7	48.4	48.6	49.0	48.7	48.3	48.7	48.7	49.0	48.5
2012	48.5	48.6	48.7	48.8	49.1	49.4	49.2	49.4	49.1	49.1	49.2	49.4	49.0
2013	48.9	49.0	49.1	49.3	49.6	49.8	49.7	50.0	49.6	49.9	49.9	49.9	49.6
2014	49.1	49.3	49.3	49.3	49.6	49.7	49.5	49.5	48.9	49.2	49.2	49.3	49.3
2015	48.8	48.8	48.8	49.2	49.6	49.9	50.1	50.5	50.2	50.8	50.9	51.2	49.9
2016	50.7	50.8	50.8	51.2	51.2	51.5	51.7	51.9	51.8	52.2	52.4	52.4	51.6
2017	52.1	52.4	52.8	53.0	53.2	53.5	53.5	53.5	52.9	53.0	53.1	53.5	53.0
Professional and Business Services													
2007	114.0	115.1	116.6	116.5	116.8	117.4	116.2	118.8	119.2	118.5	117.8	117.7	117.1
2008	115.0	117.2	117.3	117.0	117.8	117.2	116.4	117.9	118.1	117.9	116.3	115.5	117.0
2009	112.7	113.3	113.5	113.5	112.2	111.7	112.1	113.0	113.5	114.1	115.2	115.8	113.4
2010	114.1	115.0	117.3	118.6	118.5	119.4	119.5	120.2	120.5	120.1	119.5	120.1	118.6
2011	118.7	119.5	121.5	123.6	122.1	122.7	124.7	125.3	124.8	125.7	124.6	124.5	123.1
2012	121.6	122.7	124.2	125.9	125.7	125.2	125.4	125.7	125.6	126.7	126.0	126.6	125.1
2013	124.9	127.2	128.2	129.7	129.6	127.5	127.0	127.1	130.2	132.4	132.7	130.7	128.9
2014	128.0	132.3	133.8	133.8	134.3	131.9	130.7	132.3	135.3	137.6	137.8	138.0	133.8
2015	131.9	137.2	136.2	138.9	139.5	137.1	136.4	137.9	141.0	142.2	142.7	142.8	138.7
2016	136.4	141.2	142.3	144.0	143.0	140.6	140.1	141.2	144.2	145.2	144.9	144.5	142.3
2017	139.2	143.5	144.8	145.4	145.6	142.7	141.3	142.2	145.2	147.7	147.5	145.8	144.2
Education and Health Services													
2007	150.8	153.0	153.9	154.2	154.4	153.6	152.2	154.3	156.0	156.3	156.7	157.0	154.4
2008	156.8	157.7	158.5	157.5	157.6	156.3	155.3	156.9	159.3	160.0	160.0	159.7	158.0
2009	158.2	160.2	161.6	163.5	162.6	161.2	161.0	161.6	165.0	165.8	165.9	166.0	162.7
2010	163.7	164.5	165.2	165.4	165.7	164.6	163.6	165.4	168.2	168.2	168.4	168.5	166.0
2011	165.4	165.2	166.5	168.0	167.0	163.5	164.2	166.2	170.0	171.1	171.7	171.3	167.5
2012	169.5	170.0	170.8	170.3	170.1	167.4	165.6	169.5	172.0	173.5	173.5	173.4	170.5
2013	170.4	171.6	171.5	172.4	172.5	169.2	168.2	170.3	172.8	172.9	173.6	172.9	171.5
2014	170.7	171.3	171.9	172.3	172.9	169.5	168.4	170.4	173.1	173.8	174.1	174.7	171.9
2015	172.8	173.3	173.5	174.6	175.0	172.3	171.7	174.1	177.4	178.3	178.8	179.1	175.1
2016	177.9	178.7	178.8	180.3	180.5	177.8	178.4	180.5	185.7	186.7	186.9	187.2	181.6
2017	185.1	186.4	187.1	188.5	188.6	185.6	184.2	185.9	189.5	189.0	189.3	188.6	187.3

1. Employment by Industry: Arkansas, Selected Years, 2007–2017—*Continued*

(Numbers in thousands, not seasonally adjusted)

Industry and year	January	February	March	April	May	June	July	August	September	October	November	December	Annual average
Leisure and Hospitality													
2007	94.0	94.9	97.8	99.7	101.3	102.8	101.8	102.1	100.6	99.9	98.8	98.2	99.3
2008	95.9	97.3	99.5	101.7	102.9	104.4	104.0	104.3	102.7	99.9	99.0	97.5	100.8
2009	95.6	96.5	99.1	100.9	102.6	104.1	103.1	102.1	100.7	98.3	97.0	95.2	99.6
2010	93.0	93.5	96.6	99.7	101.4	103.0	101.9	102.3	101.6	99.0	97.4	96.5	98.8
2011	93.8	94.0	97.3	101.3	102.1	103.3	103.7	103.7	102.4	101.4	100.1	99.1	100.2
2012	96.6	98.3	101.6	104.0	105.3	107.1	105.4	105.9	104.3	102.2	101.3	101.4	102.8
2013	99.1	100.3	102.9	106.0	107.6	109.4	108.6	108.3	106.7	104.5	103.6	102.3	104.9
2014	101.1	102.2	105.3	108.6	110.7	112.5	110.4	111.1	109.9	107.6	106.9	106.4	107.7
2015	104.4	106.1	107.9	111.5	114.7	115.7	113.8	115.0	114.7	112.7	112.1	111.8	111.7
2016	108.9	110.8	113.8	117.0	119.0	119.3	117.3	118.6	117.5	115.5	113.8	112.7	115.4
2017	110.6	112.5	115.3	118.2	119.5	120.4	118.5	119.4	118.5	119.1	114.9	112.0	116.6
Other Services													
2007	44.8	44.9	45.5	45.3	45.4	46.1	45.6	45.6	45.3	45.2	45.2	45.4	45.4
2008	45.0	45.2	45.6	45.8	46.0	46.5	46.4	46.3	46.2	45.7	45.4	45.6	45.8
2009	45.0	45.0	45.2	45.1	45.0	45.4	45.1	44.6	44.2	43.6	43.3	43.1	44.6
2010	42.6	42.4	42.8	43.1	43.3	44.0	43.6	43.4	43.3	43.1	43.0	42.8	43.1
2011	42.8	42.6	43.2	43.8	43.4	43.8	44.3	43.6	43.4	43.6	43.5	43.6	43.5
2012	42.8	43.0	43.4	43.6	43.8	44.5	43.7	43.5	43.4	43.3	43.2	43.2	43.5
2013	42.7	42.8	43.0	43.3	43.4	43.8	43.7	43.4	43.3	43.2	43.0	43.0	43.2
2014	42.8	42.9	43.2	43.7	43.9	44.6	44.4	44.5	44.1	43.6	43.6	43.4	43.7
2015	42.8	43.0	43.0	43.3	43.9	44.9	45.4	45.4	45.4	45.5	45.9	46.4	44.6
2016	46.5	46.5	46.9	47.0	47.2	48.1	48.2	48.0	48.2	47.9	47.8	48.0	47.5
2017	48.0	48.2	48.5	48.6	48.7	49.4	49.1	48.8	48.7	49.0	48.2	48.6	48.7
Government													
2007	208.1	213.6	214.6	214.5	213.2	208.6	193.7	200.1	213.9	215.9	217.0	216.1	210.8
2008	211.0	216.4	217.3	217.4	217.6	211.8	197.5	202.4	216.5	218.6	219.4	218.6	213.7
2009	214.2	219.4	220.5	221.5	220.4	214.8	202.6	206.3	217.1	221.8	222.6	222.3	217.0
2010	214.3	218.1	221.0	222.1	227.5	220.9	206.3	207.9	218.2	220.6	221.3	220.7	218.2
2011	215.1	219.5	221.2	222.7	221.6	215.4	199.6	205.7	217.6	221.6	222.5	220.6	216.9
2012	214.0	219.9	221.1	220.7	220.1	214.7	200.9	203.7	216.9	220.2	221.6	220.6	216.2
2013	214.1	219.3	220.1	220.6	219.2	213.2	200.3	203.1	216.2	217.6	218.1	217.1	214.9
2014	211.2	216.5	217.4	217.7	217.3	211.6	199.0	201.9	215.0	216.6	218.6	217.2	213.3
2015	211.2	215.8	216.4	216.7	215.8	210.5	198.5	201.7	214.8	216.6	217.1	216.9	212.7
2016	211.1	216.1	217.9	217.4	215.9	210.5	198.1	201.2	211.6	214.1	215.2	214.6	212.0
2017	208.4	213.8	214.8	215.3	214.5	209.5	197.6	201.0	213.8	215.3	216.2	215.4	211.3

2. Average Weekly Hours by Selected Industry: Arkansas, 2013–2017

(Not seasonally adjusted)

Industry and year	January	February	March	April	May	June	July	August	September	October	November	December	Annual average
Total Private													
2013	34.0	34.4	34.6	34.5	34.7	35.7	35.0	35.2	35.7	34.8	34.9	34.9	34.9
2014	34.8	35.0	35.3	35.0	34.8	35.3	34.7	34.9	34.8	34.8	34.9	34.8	34.9
2015	34.6	34.7	34.5	34.6	34.3	34.3	34.4	34.9	34.2	34.5	34.8	34.3	34.5
2016	33.7	33.9	33.5	33.9	34.3	34.4	34.6	34.3	34.2	34.7	34.4	34.5	34.2
2017	34.5	34.4	34.5	34.8	34.6	34.9	35.0	34.8	35.0	35.4	34.9	35.1	34.8
Goods Producing													
2013	39.7	40.7	40.5	40.5	40.5	41.9	41.3	41.6	41.5	40.7	41.2	41.2	40.9
2014	40.8	41.1	41.7	41.7	40.9	41.5	39.8	41.3	41.1	41.2	40.8	41.6	41.1
2015	41.0	40.5	39.9	40.5	40.0	40.4	40.1	41.2	39.6	41.1	40.7	40.1	40.4
2016	39.9	39.9	39.0	40.6	40.5	41.6	40.8	41.6	41.0	41.4	41.0	40.9	40.7
2017	40.5	40.2	40.0	39.9	40.4	41.5	40.8	41.3	41.3	42.2	41.6	41.5	40.9
Construction													
2013	38.3	39.5	40.3	38.9	39.8	41.1	40.8	41.2	41.1	39.7	41.2	41.3	40.3
2014	39.9	40.5	42.4	40.5	39.5	40.0	41.1	42.7	39.9	40.1	39.4	40.9	40.6
2015	38.9	36.7	35.6	37.9	37.3	39.3	37.7	38.5	35.4	37.3	37.3	35.7	37.3
2016	35.7	35.8	32.7	36.5	36.9	39.1	38.3	39.6	39.2	37.8	37.4	37.9	37.3
2017	38.6	38.1	38.8	38.0	39.2	41.0	41.0	41.1	40.8	41.3	39.2	39.1	39.7
Manufacturing													
2013	39.9	40.9	40.5	41.0	40.6	42.0	41.4	41.7	41.5	41.1	41.2	41.0	41.1
2014	41.0	41.0	41.3	41.9	41.3	41.7	39.2	40.7	41.4	41.5	40.9	41.8	41.1
2015	41.4	41.4	41.1	40.8	40.6	40.4	40.6	41.6	40.9	41.2	40.8	40.8	41.0
2016	40.7	40.9	41.0	41.2	40.9	41.7	40.9	41.6	40.9	41.9	41.6	41.3	41.2
2017	40.6	40.5	40.0	40.3	40.5	41.5	40.4	41.2	41.3	42.4	42.5	42.3	41.1
Trade, Transportation, and Utilities													
2013	34.0	34.6	35.3	35.2	34.8	36.0	36.2	36.1	36.6	36.0	35.9	35.9	35.6
2014	35.8	35.8	36.8	36.2	36.1	36.5	36.2	36.1	36.1	36.0	35.8	35.9	36.1
2015	35.8	35.9	36.0	35.8	35.3	35.0	34.9	35.6	35.1	34.6	35.0	34.6	35.3
2016	34.1	34.7	34.3	34.2	35.1	35.1	35.0	34.6	34.3	34.7	33.9	34.4	34.5
2017	34.4	34.4	34.3	35.6	35.0	35.4	35.4	35.4	35.8	35.6	35.1	35.5	35.2
Financial Activities													
2013	34.7	35.4	35.0	35.1	35.3	36.6	34.4	35.5	36.2	34.8	35.5	36.5	35.4
2014	35.4	36.4	36.9	36.0	37.5	37.8	36.5	35.5	35.6	35.2	36.8	35.8	36.3
2015	36.7	37.0	37.2	35.7	35.9	35.9	36.0	36.3	35.7	35.7	37.0	36.3	36.3
2016	36.9	36.9	36.6	36.7	37.1	36.1	36.8	36.6	36.6	37.5	36.7	37.2	36.8
2017	38.2	37.3	37.3	38.5	37.7	37.1	38.3	37.5	37.1	38.5	37.3	37.6	37.7
Professional and Business Services													
2013	34.5	35.5	35.4	35.4	36.7	37.4	35.7	36.4	37.8	36.7	36.4	36.7	36.2
2014	36.3	36.2	36.3	36.2	36.1	36.5	35.9	36.4	36.4	36.3	36.7	35.6	36.2
2015	34.9	35.8	35.7	36.2	35.7	35.8	36.1	36.1	36.3	36.1	36.7	35.8	35.9
2016	35.1	35.2	34.6	35.0	35.7	35.2	35.6	34.8	34.2	34.6	34.6	34.7	34.9
2017	34.3	34.3	34.6	35.3	34.6	34.7	35.3	34.7	35.0	35.0	34.6	35.3	34.8
Education and Health Services													
2013	33.5	33.2	33.1	33.2	33.7	34.4	33.5	33.2	33.8	33.0	33.3	33.4	33.4
2014	33.1	33.2	32.8	32.9	32.9	33.3	33.4	33.5	33.5	33.4	33.5	33.5	33.2
2015	33.3	33.6	33.1	33.5	33.4	33.3	33.5	33.7	33.3	33.3	34.2	33.9	33.5
2016	33.8	33.5	33.2	33.1	33.9	33.8	34.4	33.9	34.4	34.6	35.1	35.1	34.1
2017	34.9	34.9	34.3	34.5	34.0	34.0	34.2	33.8	33.6	33.8	33.6	33.3	34.1
Leisure and Hospitality													
2013	25.1	25.7	26.4	26.3	25.6	26.9	26.4	26.3	26.3	25.7	25.3	24.1	25.9
2014	25.1	26.1	26.7	25.9	25.7	26.4	26.3	25.9	25.2	25.6	25.5	25.4	25.8
2015	25.1	25.0	24.9	24.7	25.1	25.3	25.8	25.7	25.0	25.1	25.0	25.1	25.2
2016	24.5	25.2	25.2	25.0	24.9	24.9	25.2	24.8	24.7	25.3	25.0	24.6	24.9
2017	25.1	24.5	25.2	24.6	25.3	25.4	25.5	24.9	24.9	25.7	25.2	25.4	25.1

3. Average Hourly Earnings by Selected Industry: Arkansas, 2013–2017

(Dollars, not seasonally adjusted)

Industry and year	January	February	March	April	May	June	July	August	September	October	November	December	Annual average
Total Private													
2013	19.11	19.03	19.01	19.07	19.02	19.13	19.23	19.22	19.61	19.41	19.54	19.92	19.28
2014	19.55	19.70	19.81	19.47	19.48	19.67	19.53	19.39	19.52	19.40	19.61	19.40	19.54
2015	19.39	19.44	19.61	19.38	19.44	19.29	19.40	19.61	19.51	19.59	19.72	19.69	19.51
2016	20.04	19.88	19.91	19.99	20.04	19.92	20.20	20.07	20.07	20.35	20.18	20.23	20.07
2017	20.38	20.46	20.42	20.67	20.46	20.43	20.66	20.62	20.83	20.75	20.76	20.95	20.62
Goods Producing													
2013	18.92	18.41	18.63	18.58	18.81	18.94	18.95	18.89	19.34	19.40	19.61	19.73	19.02
2014	19.45	19.47	19.62	19.15	19.36	19.50	19.75	19.55	19.62	19.59	19.93	19.66	19.55
2015	19.66	19.82	20.17	20.10	20.15	19.93	20.04	20.28	20.27	20.50	20.32	20.30	20.13
2016	20.22	20.05	20.03	20.04	20.03	19.79	19.97	19.86	20.04	20.27	20.23	20.63	20.10
2017	20.64	21.02	20.84	21.07	20.93	20.88	20.89	20.93	20.91	20.65	21.00	21.38	20.93
Construction													
2013	17.18	17.41	17.64	17.69	18.13	18.21	18.51	18.42	19.09	19.70	20.24	21.29	18.65
2014	20.35	20.35	20.08	20.15	20.61	20.68	20.46	20.14	20.22	20.39	20.66	20.33	20.37
2015	20.33	20.58	21.12	20.94	20.96	20.70	20.76	21.12	21.20	21.88	21.40	21.28	21.03
2016	21.19	21.47	21.56	21.09	20.79	20.65	20.96	21.07	21.13	21.56	21.81	21.87	21.25
2017	21.89	22.15	22.02	21.61	21.79	21.71	21.64	22.17	22.15	21.79	22.04	22.13	21.92
Manufacturing													
2013	19.33	18.60	18.80	18.71	18.87	18.99	18.88	18.83	19.28	19.19	19.31	19.13	18.99
2014	18.97	19.07	19.32	18.70	18.86	18.98	19.34	19.15	19.22	19.09	19.45	19.14	19.11
2015	19.20	19.36	19.76	19.67	19.64	19.45	19.57	19.66	19.56	19.51	19.54	19.66	19.55
2016	19.60	19.24	19.30	19.45	19.54	19.21	19.31	19.07	19.32	19.48	19.28	19.92	19.39
2017	19.67	20.19	19.96	20.43	20.17	20.17	20.24	20.18	20.12	19.98	20.41	20.97	20.21
Trade, Transportation, and Utilities													
2013	18.76	18.82	18.84	18.92	18.66	18.70	19.53	19.66	19.99	19.58	19.69	20.13	19.29
2014	19.86	19.69	20.04	19.40	19.50	19.80	19.62	19.45	19.53	19.46	19.50	18.92	19.56
2015	19.09	19.37	19.77	19.24	19.22	19.18	19.31	19.52	19.32	19.42	19.60	19.44	19.37
2016	19.75	19.46	19.64	19.54	19.49	19.30	19.52	19.66	19.60	19.77	19.68	19.42	19.57
2017	19.40	19.50	19.59	19.32	19.43	19.59	19.94	19.74	20.12	20.12	20.14	20.24	19.76
Financial Activities													
2013	23.04	23.84	23.09	23.29	23.15	23.94	23.20	22.47	22.57	21.91	23.05	24.39	23.17
2014	22.86	23.71	23.41	22.66	22.27	23.30	22.86	23.08	22.90	22.78	22.92	23.00	22.98
2015	23.30	23.18	22.82	23.62	23.68	22.60	23.08	23.06	22.95	22.72	23.49	24.02	23.21
2016	23.73	24.34	24.30	24.92	24.71	25.40	25.05	25.29	25.88	26.16	26.37	25.51	25.15
2017	26.24	26.44	25.79	26.13	25.41	26.07	26.79	26.93	27.13	27.52	26.96	26.52	26.50
Professional and Business Services													
2013	24.59	23.75	23.46	23.99	23.13	23.04	23.09	22.20	22.73	22.61	22.41	22.82	23.13
2014	22.32	22.61	22.76	22.24	22.12	22.57	21.93	21.92	21.87	21.88	22.09	22.27	22.21
2015	21.60	21.06	21.30	20.82	20.93	21.15	21.06	21.32	20.83	20.99	21.18	21.02	21.10
2016	21.20	20.93	21.03	21.36	21.78	21.55	21.63	21.36	21.41	21.74	21.12	21.19	21.36
2017	21.45	21.36	21.17	21.45	21.31	21.06	21.16	21.07	21.47	21.49	21.11	21.45	21.30
Education and Health Services													
2013	19.35	19.70	19.78	19.79	19.99	20.38	19.95	20.71	20.92	20.78	20.60	20.67	20.22
2014	20.74	21.28	21.58	21.80	21.72	21.75	21.63	21.37	21.68	21.17	21.51	21.21	21.45
2015	21.09	21.12	21.09	20.66	21.01	20.85	20.91	20.91	20.78	20.81	20.75	20.72	20.89
2016	21.13	21.33	21.40	21.71	21.43	21.59	22.24	22.12	22.03	22.54	22.28	22.65	21.89
2017	22.79	22.23	22.67	23.20	22.93	22.74	23.01	22.96	23.18	22.82	22.66	22.87	22.84
Leisure and Hospitality													
2013	10.24	10.26	10.29	10.27	10.33	10.20	10.34	10.40	10.49	10.42	10.60	10.90	10.39
2014	10.76	10.84	10.50	10.46	10.54	10.58	10.57	10.69	10.75	10.90	10.68	10.91	10.68
2015	10.92	11.02	11.21	11.15	11.05	10.92	10.92	11.26	11.50	11.42	11.60	11.69	11.22
2016	11.76	11.74	11.61	11.44	11.62	11.61	11.62	11.62	11.78	11.76	11.78	11.73	11.67
2017	11.78	12.16	12.18	12.20	12.32	12.11	12.07	12.10	12.19	12.11	12.32	12.25	12.15

4. Average Weekly Earnings by Selected Industry: Arkansas, 2013–2017

(Dollars, not seasonally adjusted)

Industry and year	January	February	March	April	May	June	July	August	September	October	November	December	Annual average
Total Private													
2013	649.74	654.63	657.75	657.92	659.99	682.94	673.05	676.54	700.08	675.47	681.95	695.21	672.87
2014	680.34	689.50	699.29	681.45	677.90	694.35	677.69	676.71	679.30	675.12	684.39	675.12	681.95
2015	670.89	674.57	676.55	670.55	666.79	661.65	667.36	684.39	667.24	675.86	686.26	675.37	673.10
2016	675.35	673.93	666.99	677.66	687.37	685.25	698.92	688.40	686.39	706.15	694.19	697.94	686.39
2017	703.11	703.82	704.49	719.32	707.92	713.01	723.10	717.58	729.05	734.55	724.52	735.35	717.58
Goods Producing													
2013	751.12	749.29	754.52	752.49	761.81	793.59	782.64	785.82	802.61	789.58	807.93	812.88	777.92
2014	793.56	800.22	818.15	798.56	791.82	809.25	786.05	807.42	806.38	807.11	813.14	817.86	803.51
2015	806.06	802.71	804.78	814.05	806.00	805.17	803.60	835.54	802.69	842.55	827.02	814.03	813.25
2016	806.78	800.00	781.17	813.62	811.22	823.26	814.78	826.18	821.64	839.18	829.43	843.77	818.07
2017	835.92	845.00	833.60	840.69	845.57	866.52	852.31	864.41	863.58	871.43	873.60	887.27	856.04
Construction													
2013	657.99	687.70	710.89	688.14	721.57	748.43	755.21	758.90	784.60	785.27	833.89	879.28	751.60
2014	811.97	824.18	851.39	816.08	814.10	827.20	840.91	859.98	806.78	817.64	814.00	831.50	827.02
2015	790.84	755.29	751.87	793.63	781.81	813.51	782.65	813.12	750.48	816.12	798.22	759.70	784.42
2016	756.48	768.63	705.01	769.79	767.15	807.42	802.77	834.37	828.30	814.97	815.69	828.87	792.63
2017	844.95	843.92	854.38	821.18	854.17	890.11	887.24	911.19	903.72	899.93	863.97	865.28	870.22
Manufacturing													
2013	771.27	760.74	761.40	767.11	766.12	797.58	781.63	785.21	800.12	788.71	795.57	784.33	780.49
2014	777.77	781.87	797.92	783.53	778.92	791.47	758.13	779.41	795.71	792.24	795.51	800.05	785.42
2015	794.88	801.50	812.14	802.54	797.38	785.78	794.54	817.86	800.00	803.81	797.23	802.13	801.55
2016	797.72	786.92	791.30	801.34	799.19	801.06	789.78	793.31	790.19	816.21	802.05	822.70	798.87
2017	798.60	817.70	798.40	823.33	816.89	837.06	817.70	831.42	830.96	847.15	867.43	887.03	830.63
Trade, Transportation, and Utilities													
2013	637.84	651.17	665.05	665.98	649.37	673.20	706.99	709.73	731.63	704.88	706.87	722.67	686.72
2014	710.99	704.90	737.47	702.28	703.95	722.70	710.24	702.15	705.03	700.56	698.10	679.23	706.12
2015	683.42	695.38	711.72	688.79	678.47	671.30	673.92	694.91	678.13	671.93	686.00	672.62	683.76
2016	673.48	675.26	673.65	668.27	684.10	677.43	683.20	680.24	672.28	686.02	667.15	668.05	675.17
2017	667.36	670.80	671.94	687.79	680.05	693.49	705.88	698.80	720.30	716.27	706.91	718.52	695.55
Financial Activities													
2013	799.49	843.94	808.15	817.48	817.20	876.20	798.08	797.69	817.03	762.47	818.28	890.24	820.22
2014	809.24	863.04	863.83	815.76	835.13	880.74	834.39	819.34	815.24	801.86	843.46	823.40	834.17
2015	855.11	857.66	848.90	843.23	850.11	811.34	830.88	837.08	819.32	811.10	869.13	871.93	842.52
2016	875.64	898.15	889.38	914.56	916.74	916.94	921.84	925.61	947.21	981.00	967.78	948.97	925.52
2017	1002.37	986.21	961.97	1006.01	957.96	967.20	1026.06	1009.88	1006.52	1059.52	1005.61	997.15	999.05
Professional and Business Services													
2013	848.36	843.13	830.48	849.25	848.87	861.70	824.31	808.08	859.19	829.79	815.72	837.49	837.31
2014	810.22	818.48	826.19	805.09	798.53	823.81	787.29	797.89	796.07	794.24	810.70	792.81	804.00
2015	753.84	753.95	760.41	753.68	747.20	757.17	760.27	769.65	756.13	757.74	777.31	752.52	757.49
2016	744.12	736.74	727.64	747.60	777.55	758.56	770.03	743.33	732.22	752.20	730.75	735.29	745.46
2017	735.74	732.65	732.48	757.19	737.33	730.78	746.95	731.13	751.45	752.15	730.41	757.19	741.24
Education and Health Services													
2013	648.23	654.04	654.72	657.03	673.66	701.07	668.33	687.57	707.10	685.74	685.98	690.38	675.35
2014	686.49	706.50	707.82	717.22	714.59	724.28	722.44	715.90	726.28	707.08	720.59	710.54	712.14
2015	702.30	709.63	698.08	692.11	701.73	694.31	700.49	704.67	691.97	692.97	709.65	702.41	699.82
2016	714.19	714.56	710.48	718.60	726.48	729.74	765.06	749.87	757.83	779.88	782.03	795.02	746.45
2017	795.37	775.83	777.58	800.40	779.62	773.16	786.94	776.05	778.85	771.32	761.38	761.57	778.84
Leisure and Hospitality													
2013	257.02	263.68	271.66	270.10	264.45	274.38	272.98	273.52	275.89	267.79	268.18	262.69	269.10
2014	270.08	282.92	280.35	270.91	270.88	279.31	277.99	276.87	270.90	279.04	272.34	277.11	275.54
2015	274.09	275.50	279.13	275.41	277.36	276.28	281.74	289.38	287.50	286.64	290.00	293.42	282.74
2016	288.12	295.85	292.57	286.00	289.34	289.09	292.82	288.18	290.97	297.53	294.50	288.56	290.58
2017	295.68	297.92	306.94	300.12	311.70	307.59	307.79	301.29	303.53	311.23	310.46	311.15	304.97

CALIFORNIA
At a Glance

Population:
  2010 census: 37,253,956
  2017 estimate: 39,536,653

Percent change in population:
  2010–2017: 6.1%

Percent change in total nonfarm employment:
  2007–2017: 8.7%

Industry with the largest growth in employment, 2007–2017 (thousands):
  Education and health services, 672.9

Industry with the largest decline or smallest growth in employment, 2007–2017 (thousands):
  Manufacturing, -159.0

Civilian labor force:
  2010: 18,336,271
  2017: 19,311,958

Unemployment rate and rank among states (highest to lowest):
  2010: 12.2%, 3rd
  2017: 4.8%, 13th

Over-the-year change in unemployment rates:
  2015–2016: -0.7%
  2016–2017: -0.7%

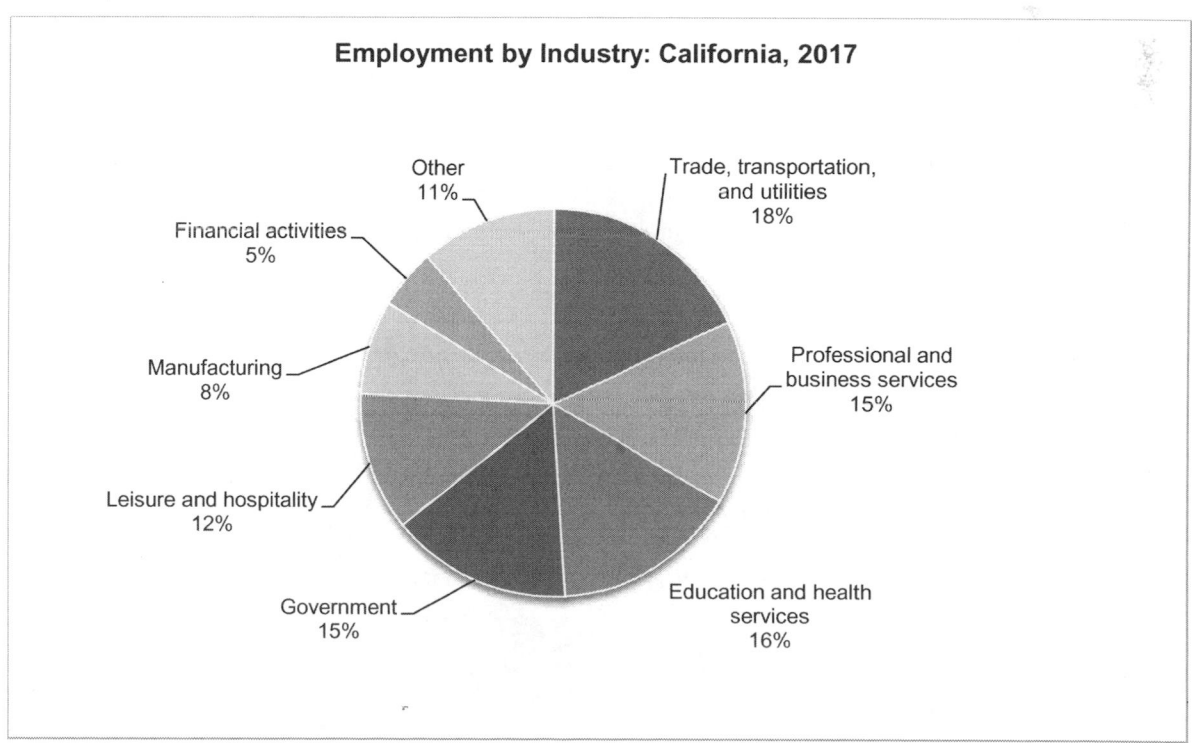

Employment by Industry: California, 2017

- Other 11%
- Financial activities 5%
- Manufacturing 8%
- Leisure and hospitality 12%
- Government 15%
- Trade, transportation, and utilities 18%
- Professional and business services 15%
- Education and health services 16%

1. Employment by Industry: California, Selected Years, 2007–2017

(Numbers in thousands, not seasonally adjusted)

Industry and year	January	February	March	April	May	June	July	August	September	October	November	December	Annual average
Total Nonfarm													
2007	15,218.5	15,330.3	15,437.2	15,389.3	15,481.1	15,555.6	15,427.3	15,437.9	15,499.4	15,539.8	15,608.2	15,651.9	15,464.7
2008	15,246.2	15,339.0	15,392.0	15,403.4	15,439.6	15,466.0	15,256.4	15,244.0	15,271.9	15,244.3	15,185.3	15,146.5	15,302.9
2009	14,691.4	14,626.7	14,604.9	14,539.6	14,548.1	14,517.4	14,226.9	14,206.1	14,224.7	14,356.0	14,378.1	14,386.7	14,442.2
2010	14,052.0	14,093.2	14,162.1	14,294.1	14,386.0	14,399.8	14,191.2	14,212.8	14,270.1	14,417.0	14,468.0	14,498.3	14,287.1
2011	14,201.0	14,284.1	14,343.4	14,408.5	14,455.8	14,474.6	14,327.2	14,373.9	14,470.4	14,578.0	14,658.3	14,681.0	14,438.0
2012	14,438.8	14,535.4	14,629.5	14,666.5	14,765.2	14,832.2	14,660.8	14,739.3	14,804.8	14,947.1	15,063.8	15,086.7	14,764.2
2013	14,798.8	14,925.1	15,003.2	15,068.2	15,150.4	15,181.7	15,035.1	15,148.3	15,203.1	15,347.4	15,484.7	15,501.4	15,154.0
2014	15,232.6	15,329.9	15,414.1	15,479.8	15,565.7	15,597.1	15,437.9	15,574.8	15,646.9	15,802.2	15,916.0	15,940.5	15,578.1
2015	15,664.0	15,758.6	15,847.2	15,920.8	16,001.8	16,040.4	15,982.4	16,079.2	16,144.2	16,332.2	16,425.4	16,449.7	16,053.8
2016	16,152.0	16,263.6	16,284.9	16,432.1	16,481.7	16,468.5	16,393.4	16,466.5	16,549.5	16,690.5	16,782.2	16,788.0	16,479.4
2017	16,457.4	16,576.3	16,665.1	16,725.4	16,821.3	16,865.0	16,721.3	16,794.0	16,857.9	17,008.5	17,119.2	17,140.0	16,812.6
Total Private													
2007	12,743.4	12,831.5	12,916.0	12,864.4	12,945.7	13,021.1	13,020.0	13,044.8	13,037.5	13,025.4	13,071.5	13,120.4	12,970.1
2008	12,735.0	12,801.8	12,837.7	12,841.2	12,867.8	12,892.6	12,831.8	12,830.2	12,797.0	12,714.9	12,642.3	12,615.4	12,784.0
2009	12,177.4	12,093.7	12,053.7	11,976.3	11,990.3	11,974.4	11,869.5	11,867.2	11,844.1	11,883.0	11,897.7	11,924.1	11,962.6
2010	11,607.8	11,633.2	11,681.9	11,767.8	11,813.9	11,868.4	11,861.0	11,902.2	11,899.6	11,969.4	12,002.8	12,055.6	11,838.6
2011	11,776.7	11,838.5	11,874.2	11,938.9	11,986.0	12,017.1	12,048.9	12,101.3	12,134.0	12,170.1	12,232.3	12,279.4	12,033.1
2012	12,056.4	12,127.1	12,201.4	12,240.8	12,331.6	12,406.4	12,409.1	12,481.9	12,487.3	12,561.3	12,657.1	12,694.6	12,387.9
2013	12,435.5	12,533.7	12,590.5	12,655.9	12,727.5	12,768.3	12,796.2	12,876.5	12,867.4	12,948.2	13,060.9	13,095.2	12,779.7
2014	12,839.7	12,914.9	12,974.2	13,028.3	13,103.1	13,145.6	13,158.7	13,265.7	13,265.9	13,351.4	13,442.1	13,480.2	13,164.2
2015	13,217.8	13,292.6	13,361.6	13,424.6	13,499.2	13,543.4	13,651.9	13,718.4	13,708.6	13,829.9	13,903.9	13,938.5	13,590.9
2016	13,661.2	13,750.6	13,744.1	13,884.8	13,921.5	13,923.7	14,011.7	14,054.9	14,057.6	14,135.0	14,206.8	14,220.1	13,964.3
2017	13,915.5	14,012.7	14,080.7	14,139.6	14,221.6	14,272.4	14,304.0	14,356.7	14,339.5	14,419.9	14,509.0	14,537.8	14,259.1
Goods Producing													
2007	2,360.3	2,372.3	2,389.3	2,376.1	2,394.4	2,422.5	2,429.2	2,433.7	2,415.0	2,381.5	2,352.4	2,330.4	2,388.1
2008	2,265.9	2,270.6	2,269.8	2,262.0	2,270.9	2,279.3	2,279.6	2,281.9	2,263.2	2,219.4	2,169.0	2,132.8	2,247.0
2009	2,047.5	1,999.2	1,983.0	1,951.4	1,950.4	1,946.6	1,927.1	1,925.5	1,908.4	1,887.9	1,869.2	1,846.0	1,936.9
2010	1,809.4	1,802.0	1,813.7	1,818.4	1,834.9	1,850.2	1,859.6	1,871.0	1,860.0	1,854.4	1,837.5	1,822.1	1,836.1
2011	1,794.9	1,801.5	1,804.6	1,821.6	1,837.8	1,854.2	1,876.2	1,890.7	1,889.0	1,876.4	1,859.8	1,848.8	1,846.3
2012	1,827.6	1,831.1	1,839.9	1,841.1	1,868.6	1,895.3	1,911.9	1,927.2	1,924.2	1,915.9	1,904.2	1,894.6	1,881.8
2013	1,869.5	1,884.0	1,892.0	1,897.9	1,913.8	1,935.8	1,957.4	1,976.9	1,971.1	1,966.9	1,959.9	1,950.1	1,931.3
2014	1,924.0	1,938.5	1,947.7	1,951.9	1,970.5	1,990.1	2,010.6	2,034.2	2,032.0	2,023.7	2,014.3	2,001.5	1,986.6
2015	1,988.8	1,999.8	2,014.1	2,024.7	2,044.5	2,067.6	2,099.3	2,117.4	2,110.1	2,107.6	2,094.8	2,087.1	2,063.0
2016	2,056.8	2,072.2	2,067.2	2,088.6	2,099.2	2,113.4	2,144.8	2,152.0	2,145.5	2,134.3	2,121.9	2,111.2	2,108.9
2017	2,065.9	2,083.5	2,102.0	2,113.2	2,134.3	2,158.2	2,176.0	2,188.9	2,187.0	2,179.8	2,168.0	2,159.1	2,143.0
Service-Providing													
2007	12,858.2	12,958.0	13,047.9	13,013.2	13,086.7	13,133.1	12,998.1	13,004.2	13,084.4	13,158.3	13,255.8	13,321.5	13,076.6
2008	12,980.3	13,068.4	13,122.2	13,141.4	13,168.7	13,186.7	12,976.8	12,962.1	13,008.7	13,024.9	13,016.3	13,013.7	13,055.9
2009	12,643.9	12,627.5	12,621.9	12,588.2	12,597.7	12,570.8	12,299.8	12,280.6	12,316.3	12,468.1	12,508.9	12,540.7	12,505.4
2010	12,242.6	12,291.2	12,348.4	12,475.7	12,551.1	12,549.6	12,331.6	12,341.8	12,410.1	12,562.6	12,630.5	12,676.2	12,451.0
2011	12,406.1	12,482.6	12,538.8	12,586.9	12,618.0	12,620.4	12,451.0	12,483.2	12,581.4	12,701.6	12,798.5	12,832.2	12,591.7
2012	12,611.2	12,704.3	12,789.6	12,825.4	12,896.6	12,936.9	12,748.9	12,812.1	12,880.6	13,031.2	13,159.6	13,192.1	12,882.4
2013	12,929.3	13,041.1	13,111.2	13,170.3	13,236.6	13,245.9	13,077.7	13,171.4	13,232.0	13,380.5	13,524.8	13,551.3	13,222.7
2014	13,308.6	13,391.4	13,466.4	13,527.9	13,595.2	13,607.0	13,427.3	13,540.6	13,614.9	13,778.5	13,901.7	13,939.0	13,591.5
2015	13,675.2	13,758.8	13,833.1	13,896.1	13,957.3	13,972.8	13,883.1	13,961.8	14,034.1	14,224.6	14,330.6	14,362.6	13,990.8
2016	14,095.2	14,191.4	14,217.7	14,343.5	14,382.5	14,355.1	14,248.6	14,314.5	14,404.0	14,556.2	14,660.3	14,676.8	14,370.5
2017	14,391.5	14,492.8	14,563.1	14,612.2	14,687.0	14,706.8	14,545.3	14,605.1	14,670.9	14,828.7	14,951.2	14,980.9	14,669.6
Mining and Logging													
2007	22.7	22.8	22.6	23.3	24.3	25.0	25.6	25.9	25.9	26.0	25.8	25.3	24.6
2008	24.5	24.9	24.9	25.8	26.5	27.0	27.7	27.8	27.7	28.0	27.3	26.5	26.6
2009	25.0	24.3	23.8	23.2	23.4	23.8	24.2	24.2	24.1	24.2	23.9	23.3	24.0
2010	22.9	22.5	22.9	23.2	24.8	25.2	25.9	25.9	26.0	25.9	25.4	24.8	24.6
2011	24.7	24.9	24.8	25.5	26.2	26.8	27.8	28.1	28.1	28.2	28.0	27.6	26.7
2012	27.3	26.9	26.9	27.0	28.1	28.9	29.6	29.8	29.3	29.2	28.9	28.2	28.3
2013	27.4	27.5	27.3	27.8	28.6	29.0	29.1	29.0	28.8	28.8	28.5	28.0	28.3
2014	27.9	27.9	27.8	28.4	29.2	29.6	30.2	30.3	30.4	30.2	30.0	29.3	29.3
2015	27.8	27.1	26.8	27.0	26.8	26.9	26.9	26.6	26.2	25.7	25.0	24.3	26.4
2016	23.5	22.9	22.2	22.0	22.4	22.8	22.7	22.3	22.1	22.1	21.9	21.4	22.4
2017	20.9	20.7	20.6	21.1	21.8	22.4	23.1	23.0	23.0	22.9	22.6	21.9	22.0

1. Employment by Industry: California, Selected Years, 2007–2017—*Continued*

(Numbers in thousands, not seasonally adjusted)

Industry and year	January	February	March	April	May	June	July	August	September	October	November	December	Annual average
Construction													
2007	874.6	879.9	894.0	890.6	903.5	917.8	918.7	919.8	905.3	886.9	868.9	850.8	892.6
2008	803.3	804.8	803.7	800.3	803.6	805.9	803.2	802.4	788.4	769.6	744.2	723.5	787.7
2009	674.4	644.7	644.1	630.4	632.2	632.3	621.7	619.6	607.6	600.2	594.2	576.2	623.1
2010	550.6	542.7	549.3	553.9	562.2	568.8	572.4	574.8	566.9	566.5	560.4	549.6	559.8
2011	532.7	535.1	534.3	545.8	554.4	562.9	578.6	584.6	584.0	580.7	575.5	567.3	561.3
2012	556.2	556.0	559.1	560.9	579.0	595.2	605.8	612.1	613.1	616.7	615.3	609.8	589.9
2013	597.6	606.6	612.7	617.8	628.0	639.9	652.5	661.5	658.0	662.1	660.1	651.9	637.4
2014	638.0	645.3	651.5	655.8	667.3	675.9	686.0	697.5	696.9	697.2	696.2	682.5	674.2
2015	681.3	687.7	698.3	707.1	719.8	732.0	749.6	759.8	755.8	767.1	765.3	757.6	731.8
2016	737.3	748.3	744.3	763.9	769.7	777.2	794.1	799.0	797.3	799.3	792.1	782.0	775.4
2017	746.5	761.1	780.6	791.8	804.8	819.3	829.8	836.1	837.8	839.7	835.1	827.0	809.1
Manufacturing													
2007	1,463.0	1,469.6	1,472.6	1,462.2	1,466.6	1,479.7	1,484.9	1,488.0	1,483.8	1,468.6	1,457.8	1,454.4	1,470.9
2008	1,438.1	1,440.9	1,441.2	1,435.9	1,440.8	1,446.3	1,448.7	1,451.7	1,447.1	1,421.8	1,397.5	1,382.8	1,432.7
2009	1,348.2	1,330.1	1,315.1	1,297.8	1,294.9	1,290.4	1,281.2	1,281.7	1,276.7	1,263.5	1,251.2	1,246.6	1,289.8
2010	1,236.0	1,236.8	1,241.5	1,241.3	1,247.9	1,256.2	1,261.4	1,270.2	1,267.1	1,262.0	1,251.7	1,247.7	1,251.7
2011	1,237.6	1,241.5	1,245.5	1,250.3	1,257.2	1,264.6	1,269.9	1,278.1	1,276.9	1,267.6	1,256.3	1,253.9	1,258.3
2012	1,244.2	1,248.3	1,253.9	1,253.1	1,261.4	1,271.2	1,276.6	1,285.4	1,281.7	1,269.9	1,260.0	1,256.7	1,263.5
2013	1,244.6	1,250.0	1,252.0	1,252.3	1,257.2	1,267.0	1,275.9	1,286.3	1,284.3	1,276.0	1,271.4	1,270.3	1,265.6
2014	1,258.2	1,265.2	1,268.3	1,267.8	1,274.0	1,284.6	1,294.5	1,306.4	1,304.8	1,296.2	1,288.1	1,289.7	1,283.2
2015	1,279.7	1,285.0	1,288.9	1,290.6	1,297.9	1,308.8	1,322.8	1,331.1	1,328.0	1,314.9	1,304.5	1,305.1	1,304.8
2016	1,296.0	1,301.1	1,300.7	1,302.7	1,307.1	1,313.4	1,328.0	1,330.7	1,326.1	1,312.9	1,307.9	1,307.8	1,311.2
2017	1,298.5	1,301.7	1,300.8	1,300.3	1,307.7	1,316.5	1,323.1	1,329.8	1,326.2	1,317.2	1,310.3	1,310.2	1,311.9
Trade, Transportation, and Utilities													
2007	2,894.9	2,870.7	2,877.5	2,863.3	2,880.4	2,891.2	2,906.1	2,910.1	2,911.6	2,922.4	2,986.2	3,030.7	2,912.1
2008	2,893.7	2,867.0	2,862.6	2,847.3	2,851.3	2,852.9	2,842.3	2,835.6	2,827.0	2,817.6	2,836.7	2,849.3	2,848.6
2009	2,712.4	2,668.5	2,646.7	2,620.7	2,628.1	2,624.4	2,603.1	2,602.5	2,609.2	2,620.6	2,664.6	2,696.0	2,641.4
2010	2,596.9	2,577.2	2,576.9	2,588.6	2,603.1	2,612.2	2,615.0	2,626.4	2,626.2	2,649.2	2,705.0	2,741.4	2,626.5
2011	2,640.2	2,624.1	2,623.4	2,639.4	2,651.5	2,658.1	2,666.8	2,679.8	2,680.4	2,699.7	2,764.4	2,792.5	2,676.7
2012	2,701.8	2,671.0	2,674.1	2,681.1	2,699.8	2,712.2	2,718.9	2,729.4	2,731.8	2,750.6	2,835.0	2,855.1	2,730.1
2013	2,748.5	2,733.1	2,730.6	2,735.8	2,754.5	2,767.3	2,777.1	2,790.0	2,783.8	2,809.0	2,895.1	2,926.5	2,787.6
2014	2,817.7	2,799.0	2,798.3	2,806.7	2,822.0	2,834.2	2,840.0	2,859.9	2,858.9	2,880.1	2,961.6	2,995.7	2,856.2
2015	2,888.1	2,866.5	2,871.2	2,876.5	2,894.3	2,899.5	2,925.4	2,941.7	2,939.7	2,965.2	3,034.3	3,056.2	2,929.9
2016	2,950.3	2,935.3	2,932.0	2,951.4	2,958.8	2,953.1	2,979.9	2,995.2	2,989.9	3,018.9	3,094.1	3,117.5	2,989.7
2017	3,019.1	2,984.8	2,986.0	3,000.9	3,011.7	3,016.7	3,025.9	3,042.3	3,038.1	3,064.8	3,149.5	3,171.7	3,042.6
Wholesale Trade													
2007	702.6	707.0	711.6	710.6	714.3	717.1	719.8	718.9	719.1	720.9	720.3	722.5	715.4
2008	710.8	712.0	713.9	710.7	710.4	709.4	705.7	703.4	700.0	696.5	689.3	684.3	703.9
2009	665.8	660.7	654.8	649.5	648.3	647.1	640.9	637.6	635.1	637.2	635.2	634.4	645.6
2010	630.0	631.4	633.0	642.0	645.5	647.5	648.6	649.2	648.8	651.1	651.4	652.1	644.2
2011	645.8	648.8	649.4	656.0	657.9	658.7	660.7	662.6	662.3	662.6	662.8	663.7	657.6
2012	658.4	661.6	664.1	667.5	672.7	675.4	676.8	679.8	679.0	681.9	683.4	684.1	673.7
2013	677.1	680.4	682.5	685.7	689.7	692.7	693.7	695.5	694.5	695.5	698.8	701.8	690.7
2014	696.0	700.5	702.0	701.9	704.7	706.5	705.9	708.3	707.7	707.1	710.4	712.0	705.3
2015	702.6	705.8	705.6	709.4	712.7	713.4	717.3	719.0	718.1	718.2	718.9	720.2	713.4
2016	711.9	714.8	712.0	717.3	718.1	716.6	721.1	722.5	720.7	718.2	718.2	719.8	717.6
2017	713.0	715.3	715.0	719.7	723.8	726.2	726.8	727.3	725.5	726.2	726.9	730.1	723.0
Retail Trade													
2007	1,693.9	1,664.7	1,668.3	1,652.2	1,661.6	1,666.5	1,674.9	1,680.6	1,676.6	1,686.5	1,749.9	1,786.0	1,688.5
2008	1,681.0	1,648.0	1,645.7	1,633.7	1,631.8	1,634.4	1,631.7	1,626.4	1,618.5	1,617.4	1,646.3	1,661.4	1,639.7
2009	1,561.5	1,527.7	1,513.8	1,497.9	1,504.8	1,502.9	1,493.2	1,495.8	1,501.5	1,511.6	1,559.4	1,588.1	1,521.5
2010	1,506.5	1,485.9	1,484.8	1,487.6	1,494.5	1,499.1	1,500.7	1,509.1	1,507.2	1,526.2	1,581.0	1,610.5	1,516.1
2011	1,530.6	1,511.4	1,509.0	1,513.6	1,520.0	1,525.1	1,531.6	1,538.9	1,538.8	1,556.3	1,620.2	1,643.2	1,544.9
2012	1,569.3	1,536.6	1,534.8	1,535.3	1,544.4	1,547.9	1,551.9	1,557.2	1,557.2	1,573.2	1,654.2	1,666.4	1,569.0
2013	1,579.5	1,558.7	1,555.1	1,556.7	1,567.0	1,575.0	1,580.0	1,587.1	1,581.5	1,603.4	1,681.0	1,703.8	1,594.1
2014	1,614.8	1,590.6	1,590.3	1,594.8	1,599.7	1,606.9	1,612.1	1,623.2	1,617.8	1,635.9	1,708.3	1,731.4	1,627.2
2015	1,647.6	1,626.1	1,625.2	1,626.6	1,636.2	1,636.9	1,650.0	1,658.0	1,654.8	1,675.1	1,735.4	1,749.4	1,660.1
2016	1,669.3	1,652.7	1,648.2	1,655.0	1,657.6	1,653.3	1,666.5	1,673.8	1,667.2	1,689.8	1,750.1	1,761.0	1,678.7
2017	1,693.1	1,664.6	1,660.0	1,668.9	1,670.2	1,670.3	1,677.6	1,684.7	1,679.9	1,700.5	1,772.5	1,781.3	1,693.6

1. Employment by Industry: California, Selected Years, 2007–2017—*Continued*

(Numbers in thousands, not seasonally adjusted)

Industry and year	January	February	March	April	May	June	July	August	September	October	November	December	Annual average
Transportation and Utilities													
2007	498.4	499.0	497.6	500.5	504.5	507.6	511.4	510.6	515.9	515.0	516.0	522.2	508.2
2008	501.9	507.0	503.0	502.9	509.1	509.1	504.9	505.8	508.5	503.7	501.1	503.6	505.1
2009	485.1	480.1	478.1	473.3	475.0	474.4	469.0	469.1	472.6	471.8	470.0	473.5	474.3
2010	460.4	459.9	459.1	459.0	463.1	465.6	465.7	468.1	470.2	471.9	472.6	478.8	466.2
2011	463.8	463.9	465.0	469.8	473.6	474.3	474.5	478.3	479.3	480.8	481.4	485.6	474.2
2012	474.1	472.8	475.2	478.3	482.7	488.9	490.2	492.4	495.6	495.5	497.4	504.6	487.3
2013	491.9	494.0	493.0	493.4	497.8	499.6	503.4	507.4	507.8	510.1	515.3	520.9	502.9
2014	506.9	507.9	506.0	510.0	517.6	520.8	522.0	528.4	533.4	537.1	542.9	552.3	523.8
2015	537.9	534.6	540.4	540.5	545.4	549.2	558.1	564.7	566.8	571.9	580.0	586.6	556.3
2016	569.1	567.8	571.8	579.1	583.1	583.2	592.3	598.9	602.0	610.9	625.8	636.7	593.4
2017	613.0	604.9	611.0	612.3	617.7	620.2	621.5	630.3	632.7	638.1	650.1	660.3	626.0
Information													
2007	464.4	472.2	474.5	465.6	471.2	474.6	472.5	476.9	475.6	465.4	471.6	479.3	472.0
2008	460.6	470.8	479.2	478.6	483.6	487.3	479.9	480.9	482.7	475.7	472.8	473.5	477.1
2009	452.3	453.3	455.7	444.2	442.2	444.0	439.5	438.9	439.5	430.4	432.9	439.8	442.7
2010	427.1	427.1	430.2	422.3	424.1	430.8	431.3	435.9	435.4	429.8	433.9	440.8	430.7
2011	433.0	433.4	434.8	430.2	429.9	432.0	433.5	435.3	431.7	433.6	431.7	435.6	432.9
2012	428.9	429.9	432.7	434.0	432.9	433.4	438.4	440.6	436.2	441.0	447.5	451.6	437.3
2013	440.5	443.5	445.4	446.1	445.9	450.6	448.7	452.2	452.0	455.7	462.4	461.8	450.4
2014	455.1	455.0	458.0	461.5	458.9	460.7	462.3	468.5	467.5	471.6	471.3	473.7	463.7
2015	466.8	475.9	479.6	480.0	480.3	488.7	489.2	492.9	493.6	501.3	504.6	504.9	488.2
2016	510.2	518.7	517.5	527.3	532.0	528.1	527.6	531.0	527.9	524.5	533.9	532.7	526.0
2017	515.4	537.2	520.6	518.9	519.3	523.4	526.7	531.4	533.6	540.0	540.1	537.9	528.7
Financial Activities													
2007	906.0	912.2	913.9	905.1	904.2	903.6	899.1	895.5	886.2	879.3	875.1	874.3	896.2
2008	856.1	857.1	855.5	848.9	847.3	845.4	843.0	839.7	832.5	827.8	822.5	821.8	841.5
2009	805.5	801.8	798.5	790.9	786.3	784.6	778.1	773.9	766.4	770.0	767.3	768.1	782.6
2010	756.2	757.3	758.9	758.4	758.3	760.6	760.5	760.3	758.5	762.3	760.7	764.9	759.7
2011	757.6	759.6	760.5	758.3	759.2	761.1	762.4	762.8	761.3	762.8	762.9	767.0	761.4
2012	760.8	764.5	768.3	766.7	769.8	773.7	776.6	777.3	774.7	778.6	779.6	783.4	772.8
2013	774.3	777.7	778.4	780.5	783.3	784.8	787.0	786.5	780.8	784.2	783.5	784.2	782.1
2014	774.5	775.3	775.3	776.7	780.3	783.3	784.4	785.2	781.3	785.3	787.4	790.4	781.6
2015	783.3	786.4	787.3	792.9	797.5	800.4	809.4	809.7	805.7	813.4	813.9	815.8	801.3
2016	809.0	811.9	811.3	819.0	820.9	820.9	829.3	829.0	825.0	827.7	828.9	830.9	822.0
2017	822.3	823.9	824.0	827.2	830.7	831.9	836.6	835.3	830.7	832.4	833.7	837.5	830.5
Professional and Business Services													
2007	2,215.0	2,242.7	2,258.6	2,246.0	2,253.3	2,271.4	2,268.8	2,278.9	2,278.3	2,293.6	2,295.1	2,298.9	2,266.7
2008	2,227.3	2,249.1	2,254.7	2,257.4	2,248.9	2,255.6	2,247.1	2,252.3	2,243.8	2,231.2	2,208.1	2,194.0	2,239.1
2009	2,111.5	2,095.3	2,079.4	2,058.7	2,048.7	2,046.1	2,033.2	2,039.2	2,029.5	2,061.2	2,066.1	2,067.1	2,061.3
2010	2,005.5	2,027.3	2,036.9	2,057.4	2,057.3	2,076.1	2,079.8	2,092.3	2,087.5	2,122.4	2,120.5	2,121.9	2,073.7
2011	2,066.2	2,089.5	2,095.8	2,104.0	2,105.9	2,115.5	2,135.1	2,148.9	2,160.0	2,175.0	2,181.7	2,187.9	2,130.5
2012	2,153.3	2,185.9	2,201.3	2,206.7	2,215.8	2,237.9	2,239.5	2,259.0	2,261.4	2,291.5	2,303.2	2,304.7	2,238.4
2013	2,255.9	2,286.3	2,298.6	2,312.3	2,316.8	2,323.6	2,341.9	2,365.0	2,363.4	2,381.5	2,394.0	2,393.3	2,336.1
2014	2,346.9	2,366.6	2,379.1	2,387.6	2,396.2	2,402.8	2,407.6	2,432.2	2,431.5	2,466.9	2,480.1	2,484.6	2,415.2
2015	2,416.3	2,429.3	2,442.9	2,446.7	2,446.6	2,457.0	2,488.5	2,503.6	2,495.8	2,537.6	2,550.9	2,556.8	2,481.0
2016	2,486.3	2,502.4	2,487.2	2,507.9	2,500.1	2,506.4	2,527.8	2,537.7	2,543.0	2,552.8	2,555.6	2,551.0	2,521.5
2017	2,497.1	2,521.4	2,538.1	2,535.5	2,550.9	2,565.4	2,578.4	2,588.8	2,583.9	2,591.9	2,598.9	2,607.4	2,563.1
Education and Health Services													
2007	1,908.6	1,942.6	1,959.3	1,953.9	1,962.6	1,951.5	1,937.5	1,940.6	1,974.7	1,999.9	2,013.2	2,019.5	1,963.7
2008	1,997.2	2,031.4	2,038.9	2,053.3	2,055.5	2,043.1	2,014.0	2,022.0	2,053.2	2,076.6	2,087.5	2,101.1	2,047.8
2009	2,071.6	2,096.8	2,108.1	2,115.1	2,120.2	2,107.3	2,079.1	2,082.9	2,106.9	2,137.7	2,140.0	2,146.6	2,109.4
2010	2,097.7	2,115.3	2,122.1	2,142.4	2,139.6	2,122.5	2,094.1	2,096.3	2,124.4	2,147.0	2,154.3	2,163.8	2,126.6
2011	2,129.5	2,155.4	2,163.4	2,168.6	2,166.5	2,146.2	2,113.7	2,119.2	2,153.6	2,178.1	2,191.2	2,205.0	2,157.5
2012	2,175.5	2,212.4	2,230.0	2,227.2	2,231.9	2,216.9	2,184.7	2,200.6	2,225.6	2,258.5	2,269.4	2,282.7	2,226.3
2013	2,258.0	2,290.9	2,302.8	2,311.6	2,313.1	2,284.0	2,257.6	2,273.2	2,297.0	2,331.0	2,346.5	2,352.1	2,301.5
2014	2,325.0	2,355.4	2,366.7	2,365.8	2,368.7	2,347.2	2,326.7	2,348.8	2,376.5	2,409.3	2,420.0	2,424.3	2,369.5
2015	2,400.4	2,430.8	2,440.9	2,449.7	2,453.6	2,431.8	2,426.0	2,437.5	2,463.8	2,501.1	2,511.1	2,517.8	2,455.4
2016	2,484.8	2,516.2	2,523.3	2,543.2	2,545.9	2,523.6	2,504.2	2,512.6	2,543.7	2,590.5	2,600.4	2,605.3	2,541.1
2017	2,576.2	2,611.4	2,628.0	2,632.8	2,639.6	2,620.2	2,608.1	2,621.1	2,644.8	2,679.0	2,687.0	2,690.4	2,636.6

1. Employment by Industry: California, Selected Years, 2007–2017—*Continued*

(Numbers in thousands, not seasonally adjusted)

Industry and year	January	February	March	April	May	June	July	August	September	October	November	December	Annual average
Leisure and Hospitality													
2007	1,495.7	1,513.1	1,533.6	1,547.2	1,568.4	1,589.5	1,592.4	1,594.3	1,578.8	1,565.9	1,561.5	1,570.5	1,559.2
2008	1,528.5	1,544.3	1,562.0	1,577.3	1,591.7	1,608.6	1,610.6	1,606.4	1,584.6	1,558.1	1,542.8	1,543.1	1,571.5
2009	1,489.1	1,490.8	1,493.5	1,503.5	1,521.6	1,528.6	1,525.6	1,521.8	1,504.0	1,490.7	1,476.0	1,481.1	1,502.2
2010	1,439.8	1,448.9	1,461.9	1,495.9	1,508.9	1,525.7	1,532.6	1,534.6	1,521.7	1,514.3	1,503.4	1,515.5	1,500.3
2011	1,475.3	1,489.7	1,505.2	1,523.1	1,539.5	1,552.9	1,563.8	1,568.2	1,559.9	1,545.2	1,542.8	1,544.8	1,534.2
2012	1,518.4	1,536.3	1,556.1	1,581.4	1,604.5	1,625.0	1,631.9	1,640.8	1,625.3	1,614.6	1,609.9	1,615.3	1,596.6
2013	1,587.9	1,610.2	1,632.3	1,656.6	1,682.3	1,702.0	1,708.5	1,713.6	1,699.9	1,696.7	1,695.0	1,704.4	1,674.1
2014	1,675.3	1,697.5	1,718.5	1,741.2	1,766.1	1,785.0	1,789.6	1,798.2	1,779.1	1,773.2	1,767.2	1,771.9	1,755.2
2015	1,742.8	1,767.1	1,786.5	1,810.0	1,834.5	1,849.9	1,864.6	1,867.9	1,852.1	1,852.4	1,844.2	1,852.3	1,827.0
2016	1,822.0	1,845.0	1,858.0	1,892.2	1,908.3	1,922.0	1,939.2	1,939.4	1,922.5	1,922.3	1,912.8	1,914.7	1,899.9
2017	1,871.8	1,895.7	1,922.0	1,947.3	1,967.6	1,986.7	1,986.5	1,983.4	1,954.5	1,962.2	1,965.6	1,971.7	1,951.3
Other Services													
2007	498.5	503.7	509.3	507.2	511.2	516.8	514.4	514.8	517.3	517.4	516.4	516.8	512.2
2008	505.7	511.5	515.0	516.4	518.6	520.4	515.3	511.4	510.0	508.5	502.9	499.8	511.3
2009	487.5	488.0	488.8	491.8	492.8	492.8	483.8	482.5	480.2	484.5	481.6	479.4	486.1
2010	475.2	478.1	481.3	484.4	487.7	490.3	488.1	485.4	485.9	490.0	487.5	485.2	484.9
2011	480.0	485.3	486.5	493.7	495.7	496.1	497.4	496.4	498.1	499.3	497.8	497.8	493.7
2012	490.1	496.0	499.0	502.6	508.3	512.0	507.2	507.0	508.1	510.6	508.3	507.2	504.7
2013	500.9	508.0	510.4	515.1	517.8	520.2	518.0	519.1	519.4	523.2	524.5	522.8	516.6
2014	521.2	527.6	530.6	536.9	540.4	542.3	537.5	538.7	539.1	541.3	540.2	538.1	536.2
2015	531.3	536.8	539.1	544.1	547.9	548.5	549.5	547.7	547.8	551.3	550.1	547.6	545.1
2016	541.8	548.9	548.6	555.2	556.3	556.2	558.9	558.0	560.1	564.0	559.2	556.8	555.3
2017	547.7	554.8	560.0	563.8	567.5	569.9	565.8	565.5	566.9	569.8	566.2	562.1	563.3
Government													
2007	2,475.1	2,498.8	2,521.2	2,524.9	2,535.4	2,534.5	2,407.3	2,393.1	2,461.9	2,514.4	2,536.7	2,531.5	2,494.6
2008	2,511.2	2,537.2	2,554.3	2,562.2	2,571.8	2,573.4	2,424.6	2,413.8	2,474.9	2,529.4	2,543.0	2,531.1	2,518.9
2009	2,514.0	2,533.0	2,551.2	2,563.3	2,557.8	2,543.0	2,357.4	2,338.9	2,380.6	2,473.0	2,480.4	2,462.6	2,479.6
2010	2,444.2	2,460.0	2,480.2	2,526.3	2,572.1	2,531.4	2,330.2	2,310.6	2,370.5	2,447.6	2,465.2	2,442.7	2,448.4
2011	2,424.3	2,445.6	2,469.2	2,469.6	2,469.8	2,457.5	2,278.3	2,272.6	2,336.4	2,407.9	2,426.0	2,401.6	2,404.9
2012	2,382.4	2,408.3	2,428.1	2,425.7	2,433.6	2,425.8	2,251.7	2,257.4	2,317.5	2,385.8	2,406.7	2,392.1	2,376.3
2013	2,363.3	2,391.4	2,412.7	2,412.3	2,422.9	2,413.4	2,238.9	2,271.8	2,335.7	2,399.2	2,423.8	2,406.2	2,374.3
2014	2,392.9	2,415.0	2,439.9	2,451.5	2,462.6	2,451.5	2,279.2	2,309.1	2,381.0	2,450.8	2,473.9	2,460.3	2,414.0
2015	2,446.2	2,466.0	2,485.6	2,496.2	2,502.6	2,497.0	2,330.5	2,360.8	2,435.6	2,502.3	2,521.5	2,511.2	2,463.0
2016	2,490.8	2,513.0	2,540.8	2,547.3	2,560.2	2,544.8	2,381.7	2,411.6	2,491.9	2,555.5	2,575.4	2,567.9	2,515.1
2017	2,541.9	2,563.6	2,584.4	2,585.8	2,599.7	2,592.6	2,417.3	2,437.3	2,518.4	2,588.6	2,610.2	2,602.2	2,553.5

2. Average Weekly Hours by Selected Industry: California, 2013–2017

(Not seasonally adjusted)

Industry and year	January	February	March	April	May	June	July	August	September	October	November	December	Annual average
Total Private													
2013	33.8	34.0	34.1	34.2	34.2	35.1	34.3	34.4	35.0	34.2	34.2	35.2	34.4
2014	33.9	34.9	34.8	34.3	34.2	35.0	34.2	34.5	34.3	34.3	35.0	34.2	34.5
2015	34.1	34.9	35.0	34.4	34.3	34.5	34.5	35.4	34.4	34.5	35.1	34.5	34.6
2016	34.2	34.3	34.1	34.3	34.9	34.3	34.4	34.4	34.3	35.0	34.1	34.2	34.4
2017	34.5	33.9	34.2	34.8	34.3	34.4	35.2	34.6	34.5	35.1	34.5	34.5	34.5
Goods Producing													
2013	38.2	38.5	38.9	38.7	38.6	39.1	38.6	38.9	39.0	39.0	38.7	39.5	38.8
2014	38.2	38.6	38.9	38.6	38.9	38.9	38.3	38.9	38.8	38.8	39.0	38.1	38.7
2015	38.5	38.8	39.1	38.8	38.6	38.9	38.9	39.6	38.2	39.3	39.2	39.3	38.9
2016	38.5	38.5	38.3	38.8	38.8	38.9	38.7	38.9	38.8	39.1	38.4	38.4	38.7
2017	37.5	37.6	38.5	38.4	38.8	39.1	39.0	39.2	39.0	39.2	38.8	39.2	38.7
Construction													
2013	35.9	36.0	36.4	37.0	36.6	37.1	36.7	37.1	36.8	36.8	36.3	37.1	36.7
2014	35.8	36.0	36.5	36.2	36.9	36.7	36.2	36.9	36.5	36.7	36.2	34.9	36.3
2015	36.5	36.6	37.1	36.9	36.5	37.2	37.1	37.7	35.0	37.8	36.9	37.2	36.9
2016	36.2	36.3	35.3	36.7	36.7	37.0	37.0	37.3	36.8	37.4	36.1	36.3	36.6
2017	34.6	35.1	37.0	36.6	37.4	37.6	37.5	37.8	37.5	37.6	37.1	37.7	37.0
Manufacturing													
2013	39.1	39.5	39.9	39.6	39.7	40.2	39.6	39.9	40.2	40.3	40.1	40.9	39.9
2014	39.5	40.1	40.2	40.0	40.2	40.3	39.7	40.2	40.3	40.2	40.8	40.4	40.2
2015	40.0	40.4	40.5	40.2	40.2	40.1	40.2	40.9	40.3	40.3	40.7	40.7	40.4
2016	40.0	39.9	40.2	40.3	40.3	40.3	39.9	40.1	40.2	40.3	40.0	39.8	40.1
2017	39.4	39.3	39.6	39.8	39.8	40.1	40.0	40.0	39.9	40.2	40.0	40.2	39.9
Trade, Transportation, and Utilities													
2013	33.6	34.1	34.4	34.6	34.9	35.7	35.0	35.2	35.6	34.7	34.5	36.3	34.9
2014	34.3	35.3	35.3	35.1	35.2	35.9	35.2	35.6	35.3	34.8	35.2	35.3	35.2
2015	34.4	35.4	35.7	35.2	35.2	35.4	35.5	36.2	35.9	35.3	35.7	35.3	35.4
2016	34.9	35.0	34.8	35.2	35.5	35.2	35.4	35.3	35.2	35.8	34.9	35.3	35.2
2017	35.2	34.9	35.0	35.9	35.5	35.5	36.4	35.7	35.6	35.9	35.7	36.2	35.6
Information													
2013	36.7	36.9	37.1	38.2	37.5	38.5	37.2	37.5	38.5	37.6	37.3	38.9	37.7
2014	37.5	38.9	38.6	37.5	37.0	38.2	36.7	36.8	36.7	36.7	37.8	37.1	37.5
2015	37.2	38.0	37.4	36.7	36.4	36.7	37.3	37.8	36.9	36.9	37.7	36.9	37.2
2016	37.7	37.0	36.9	36.9	37.6	37.1	37.1	37.0	37.3	37.5	37.1	37.0	37.2
2017	38.2	36.8	36.8	37.6	36.7	37.1	38.0	37.0	37.3	38.1	37.3	37.2	37.3
Financial Activities													
2013	36.0	36.1	36.3	36.2	36.3	37.6	36.3	36.4	37.3	36.4	36.5	38.0	36.6
2014	36.3	37.4	37.5	36.4	36.5	37.6	36.5	36.7	36.8	37.0	38.0	37.0	37.0
2015	36.8	37.8	37.8	36.9	36.9	37.0	36.8	38.0	37.0	36.8	37.8	37.0	37.2
2016	36.9	36.9	36.7	36.3	37.2	36.5	36.6	36.6	36.1	37.0	35.7	35.7	36.5
2017	36.6	35.5	35.6	36.8	35.8	36.2	37.3	36.5	36.3	37.3	36.3	36.3	36.4
Professional and Business Services													
2013	35.4	35.6	35.6	35.8	35.6	36.6	35.5	35.8	36.6	35.8	35.8	36.5	35.9
2014	35.4	36.6	36.5	35.7	35.5	36.8	35.8	36.2	35.8	36.0	37.0	35.6	36.1
2015	35.7	36.4	36.9	36.0	35.9	36.2	35.9	37.2	35.8	36.2	37.2	36.2	36.3
2016	35.7	35.9	35.7	36.0	36.8	35.8	35.9	36.0	35.9	37.0	36.0	36.0	36.1
2017	36.7	35.9	36.0	37.0	35.9	35.9	36.9	36.1	36.0	37.1	36.2	36.2	36.3
Education and Health Services													
2013	33.5	33.6	33.4	33.4	33.5	34.3	33.5	33.4	34.4	33.4	33.5	34.2	33.7
2014	33.4	34.1	33.9	33.3	33.1	33.7	33.1	33.0	33.2	33.2	34.0	33.2	33.4
2015	33.3	34.1	33.9	33.1	33.1	33.1	33.1	33.9	33.1	32.8	33.8	32.8	33.3
2016	33.2	33.0	33.2	33.3	33.9	33.1	33.2	33.2	33.3	34.1	33.4	33.3	33.4
2017	34.2	33.5	33.5	34.1	33.5	33.6	34.4	33.6	33.6	34.2	33.7	32.8	33.7
Leisure and Hospitality													
2013	25.9	26.2	26.2	26.2	26.3	27.2	26.4	26.6	26.9	26.1	26.0	26.9	26.4
2014	26.0	27.2	27.3	26.5	26.6	27.6	26.7	27.1	26.5	26.6	27.3	26.3	26.8
2015	26.3	27.4	27.4	26.7	26.7	27.0	27.0	28.0	26.8	26.8	27.3	26.6	27.0
2016	26.4	26.7	26.3	26.4	27.5	26.7	26.9	26.7	25.8	26.7	25.8	25.7	26.5
2017	26.3	25.7	25.9	26.7	26.0	26.1	26.9	26.3	26.0	26.7	25.8	26.0	26.2
Other services													
2013	30.8	30.8	31.1	31.2	30.9	32.3	31.7	31.3	31.7	30.7	31.0	31.7	31.3
2014	30.9	31.7	31.6	31.0	30.8	31.6	31.2	31.0	31.0	31.2	31.6	30.7	31.2
2015	31.0	32.2	32.4	31.5	31.5	31.6	32.1	33.3	31.6	31.8	32.1	31.6	31.9
2016	31.3	31.6	31.5	31.7	32.6	32.1	32.3	32.5	32.1	33.0	31.8	31.6	32.0
2017	31.9	31.4	32.0	32.4	31.7	32.2	32.8	32.0	31.5	32.1	31.2	31.5	31.9

3. Average Hourly Earnings by Selected Industry: California, 2013–2017

(Dollars, not seasonally adjusted)

Industry and year	January	February	March	April	May	June	July	August	September	October	November	December	Annual average
Total Private													
2013	27.03	26.99	26.86	27.32	27.24	27.46	27.23	27.14	27.52	27.26	27.27	27.42	27.23
2014	27.41	27.58	27.53	27.31	27.22	27.40	27.46	27.30	27.51	27.62	27.99	27.75	27.51
2015	28.02	28.10	28.02	27.94	27.99	27.89	27.93	28.09	27.92	28.15	28.38	28.14	28.05
2016	28.40	28.53	28.46	28.57	28.93	28.58	28.72	28.84	29.10	29.60	29.36	29.38	28.88
2017	29.80	29.71	29.54	29.97	29.73	29.64	30.14	29.87	30.22	30.63	30.22	30.22	29.98
Goods Producing													
2013	29.08	29.10	28.83	29.05	29.17	29.16	29.24	28.98	29.18	29.09	29.14	29.50	29.13
2014	29.54	29.49	29.49	29.46	29.29	29.41	29.69	29.37	29.50	29.53	29.65	29.98	29.53
2015	29.78	29.52	29.53	29.55	29.56	29.52	29.60	29.52	29.57	29.83	29.90	30.01	29.66
2016	30.08	29.87	29.90	30.00	30.38	30.27	30.42	30.52	30.68	31.07	30.94	31.39	30.46
2017	31.65	31.84	31.71	31.92	31.71	31.80	32.33	32.01	32.31	32.60	32.51	32.93	32.12
Construction													
2013	30.91	30.70	30.57	30.50	30.56	30.75	31.14	31.03	31.28	31.25	31.20	31.02	30.97
2014	31.21	31.30	31.37	31.40	31.22	31.17	31.50	31.23	31.42	31.08	31.08	31.65	31.30
2015	31.09	30.81	30.95	31.05	30.73	30.97	31.26	31.31	31.40	31.39	31.59	31.70	31.20
2016	31.67	31.58	31.54	31.43	31.96	32.00	32.41	32.40	32.65	32.74	32.53	33.20	32.19
2017	33.42	33.61	33.55	33.22	33.36	33.42	33.87	33.88	34.19	34.11	34.32	35.09	33.85
Manufacturing													
2013	27.92	28.05	27.85	28.16	28.33	28.20	28.13	27.77	27.96	27.84	27.94	28.78	28.04
2014	28.60	28.45	28.38	28.35	28.18	28.40	28.64	28.23	28.36	28.59	28.76	29.02	28.50
2015	28.94	28.68	28.60	28.60	28.78	28.57	28.50	28.35	28.44	28.77	28.75	28.87	28.65
2016	29.01	28.75	28.86	29.09	29.43	29.25	29.24	29.39	29.47	30.00	29.90	30.19	29.38
2017	30.58	30.71	30.44	31.04	30.55	30.65	31.20	30.69	30.97	31.48	31.18	31.39	30.91
Trade, Transportation, and Utilities													
2013	21.82	21.85	21.87	21.79	21.74	22.15	21.73	21.57	21.98	21.55	21.44	21.20	21.72
2014	21.70	21.80	21.73	21.49	21.38	21.53	21.54	21.52	21.85	21.94	22.18	21.45	21.68
2015	22.54	22.47	22.13	22.26	22.48	22.33	22.36	22.63	22.42	22.67	22.80	22.54	22.47
2016	22.82	23.06	22.77	23.15	23.39	23.07	23.21	23.27	23.45	24.09	23.70	23.63	23.31
2017	24.31	23.83	23.61	24.06	23.67	23.60	23.99	23.59	23.60	23.86	23.36	23.41	23.74
Information													
2013	39.76	39.75	39.99	40.30	40.39	40.30	39.77	39.87	40.79	40.71	40.45	40.97	40.26
2014	40.79	41.06	41.02	40.61	40.31	40.69	40.77	40.66	40.50	41.17	41.44	40.82	40.82
2015	41.02	41.90	41.99	42.24	42.32	41.62	41.34	42.11	41.50	41.36	41.60	41.11	41.67
2016	40.61	40.84	40.50	40.52	41.52	40.50	40.60	40.64	41.03	41.98	41.12	41.06	40.91
2017	41.84	42.02	42.20	43.36	43.15	42.78	43.01	42.72	43.88	44.97	43.63	43.47	43.10
Financial Activities													
2013	30.77	30.82	30.79	31.47	31.31	31.54	31.51	31.72	31.95	31.61	31.76	32.22	31.46
2014	32.27	32.95	33.07	32.83	32.72	33.39	33.69	33.04	33.10	33.45	34.00	33.47	33.17
2015	33.90	34.09	34.28	33.52	33.44	33.28	33.09	33.31	33.17	33.40	34.15	33.68	33.61
2016	33.60	34.39	34.05	34.25	35.44	33.62	33.87	34.83	35.52	36.30	36.23	35.46	34.80
2017	35.43	35.40	34.79	36.06	35.99	35.83	36.84	36.77	37.01	38.31	37.39	37.28	36.44
Professional and Business Services													
2013	34.12	33.76	33.53	35.37	35.31	35.90	35.13	34.74	35.28	34.70	34.78	35.21	34.83
2014	34.59	35.12	35.09	34.59	34.65	35.02	34.88	34.48	34.72	34.53	35.49	35.29	34.88
2015	35.16	35.80	35.85	35.55	35.75	35.62	35.90	36.05	35.56	35.57	36.20	35.29	35.70
2016	36.16	36.42	36.48	36.51	37.30	36.72	37.10	37.02	37.27	38.25	37.78	37.14	37.02
2017	38.19	37.88	37.68	38.39	37.83	37.58	38.37	37.86	38.38	39.14	38.43	38.54	38.20
Education and Health Services													
2013	27.65	27.72	27.53	27.63	27.51	27.66	27.86	27.92	28.12	28.01	28.07	28.36	27.84
2014	28.05	28.07	27.94	27.88	27.90	27.89	27.90	27.94	28.04	28.16	28.39	28.45	28.05
2015	28.40	28.32	28.07	28.11	28.00	28.05	28.16	28.23	28.10	28.41	28.35	28.63	28.24
2016	28.45	28.50	28.52	28.51	28.49	28.69	28.75	28.77	29.00	29.09	29.05	29.68	28.80
2017	29.25	29.37	29.40	29.67	29.68	29.71	30.06	29.81	30.23	30.30	30.31	29.98	29.82
Leisure and Hospitality													
2013	14.66	14.86	14.73	14.79	14.87	14.85	14.83	14.88	15.05	14.97	15.14	15.20	14.91
2014	15.18	15.25	15.20	15.19	15.35	15.29	15.42	15.49	15.64	15.69	15.88	15.95	15.46
2015	15.92	16.05	16.06	16.15	16.20	16.13	16.03	16.10	16.24	16.28	16.33	16.43	16.16
2016	16.73	16.80	16.88	17.06	17.12	17.11	17.12	17.21	17.09	17.10	17.12	17.33	17.06
2017	17.46	17.58	17.51	17.56	17.71	17.58	17.63	17.70	17.87	17.89	17.95	18.11	17.71
Other Services													
2013	21.82	21.51	21.73	21.74	21.71	21.70	21.48	21.84	22.23	21.83	21.95	22.50	21.84
2014	22.35	22.27	22.28	22.41	22.07	22.45	22.51	22.57	22.85	22.97	23.25	23.26	22.60
2015	23.28	23.37	23.52	23.16	23.47	23.33	22.96	23.32	23.66	23.49	23.59	23.30	23.37
2016	23.75	23.62	23.83	23.48	23.37	22.98	22.91	23.12	23.23	23.90	23.91	24.34	23.53
2017	25.19	24.99	24.74	25.37	25.25	24.86	25.70	25.85	26.22	26.50	26.32	26.30	25.61

4. Average Weekly Earnings by Selected Industry: California, 2013–2017

(Dollars, not seasonally adjusted)

Industry and year	January	February	March	April	May	June	July	August	September	October	November	December	Annual average
Total Private													
2013	913.61	917.66	915.93	934.34	931.61	963.85	933.99	933.62	963.20	932.29	932.63	965.18	936.71
2014	929.20	962.54	958.04	936.73	930.92	959.00	939.13	941.85	943.59	947.37	979.65	949.05	949.10
2015	955.48	980.69	980.70	961.14	960.06	962.21	963.59	994.39	960.45	971.18	996.14	970.83	970.53
2016	971.28	978.58	970.49	979.95	1,009.66	980.29	987.97	992.10	998.13	1,036.00	1,001.18	1,004.80	993.47
2017	1,028.10	1,007.17	1,010.27	1,042.96	1,019.74	1,019.62	1,060.93	1,033.50	1,042.59	1,075.11	1,042.59	1,042.59	1,034.31
Goods Producing													
2013	1,110.86	1,120.35	1,121.49	1,124.24	1,125.96	1,140.16	1,128.66	1,127.32	1,138.02	1,134.51	1,127.72	1,165.25	1,130.24
2014	1,128.43	1,138.31	1,147.16	1,137.16	1,139.38	1,144.05	1,137.13	1,142.49	1,144.60	1,145.76	1,156.35	1,142.24	1,142.81
2015	1,146.53	1,145.38	1,154.62	1,146.54	1,141.02	1,148.33	1,151.44	1,168.99	1,129.57	1,172.32	1,172.08	1,179.39	1,153.77
2016	1,158.08	1,150.00	1,145.17	1,164.00	1,178.74	1,177.50	1,177.25	1,187.23	1,190.38	1,214.84	1,188.10	1,205.38	1,178.80
2017	1,186.88	1,197.18	1,220.84	1,225.73	1,230.35	1,243.38	1,260.87	1,254.79	1,260.09	1,277.92	1,261.39	1,290.86	1,243.04
Construction													
2013	1,109.67	1,105.20	1,112.75	1,128.50	1,118.50	1,140.83	1,142.84	1,151.21	1,151.10	1,150.00	1,132.56	1,173.10	1,136.60
2014	1,117.32	1,126.80	1,145.01	1,136.68	1,152.02	1,143.94	1,140.30	1,152.39	1,146.83	1,140.64	1,125.10	1,104.59	1,136.19
2015	1,134.79	1,127.65	1,148.25	1,145.75	1,121.65	1,152.08	1,159.75	1,180.39	1,099.00	1,186.54	1,165.67	1,179.24	1,151.28
2016	1,146.45	1,146.35	1,113.36	1,153.48	1,172.93	1,184.00	1,199.17	1,208.52	1,201.52	1,224.48	1,174.33	1,205.16	1,178.15
2017	1,156.33	1,179.71	1,241.35	1,215.85	1,247.66	1,256.59	1,270.13	1,280.66	1,282.13	1,282.54	1,273.27	1,322.89	1,252.45
Manufacturing													
2013	1,091.67	1,107.98	1,111.22	1,115.14	1,124.70	1,133.64	1,113.95	1,108.02	1,123.99	1,121.95	1,120.39	1,156.65	1,118.80
2014	1,129.70	1,140.85	1,140.88	1,134.00	1,132.84	1,144.52	1,137.01	1,134.85	1,142.91	1,149.32	1,173.41	1,172.41	1,145.70
2015	1,157.60	1,158.67	1,158.30	1,149.72	1,156.96	1,145.66	1,145.70	1,159.52	1,146.13	1,159.43	1,170.13	1,175.01	1,157.46
2016	1,160.40	1,147.13	1,160.17	1,172.33	1,186.03	1,178.78	1,166.68	1,178.54	1,184.69	1,209.00	1,196.00	1,201.56	1,178.14
2017	1,204.85	1,206.90	1,205.42	1,235.39	1,215.89	1,229.07	1,248.00	1,227.60	1,235.70	1,265.50	1,247.20	1,261.88	1,233.31
Trade, Transportation, and Utilities													
2013	733.15	745.09	752.33	753.93	758.73	790.76	760.55	759.26	782.49	747.79	739.68	769.56	758.03
2014	744.31	769.54	767.07	754.30	752.58	772.93	758.21	766.11	771.31	763.51	780.74	757.19	763.14
2015	775.38	795.44	790.04	783.55	791.30	790.48	793.78	819.21	804.88	800.25	813.96	795.66	795.44
2016	796.42	807.10	792.40	814.88	830.35	812.06	821.63	821.43	825.44	862.42	827.13	834.14	820.51
2017	855.71	831.67	826.35	863.75	840.29	837.80	873.24	842.16	840.16	856.57	833.95	847.44	845.14
Information													
2013	1,459.19	1,466.78	1,483.63	1,539.46	1,514.63	1,551.55	1,479.44	1,495.13	1,570.42	1,530.70	1,508.79	1,593.73	1,517.80
2014	1,529.63	1,597.23	1,583.37	1,522.88	1,491.47	1,554.36	1,496.26	1,496.29	1,486.35	1,510.94	1,566.43	1,514.42	1,530.75
2015	1,525.94	1,592.20	1,570.43	1,550.21	1,540.45	1,527.45	1,541.98	1,591.76	1,531.35	1,526.18	1,568.32	1,516.96	1,550.12
2016	1,531.00	1,511.08	1,494.45	1,495.19	1,561.15	1,502.55	1,506.26	1,503.68	1,530.42	1,574.25	1,525.55	1,519.22	1,521.85
2017	1,598.29	1,546.34	1,552.96	1,630.34	1,583.61	1,587.14	1,634.38	1,580.64	1,636.72	1,713.36	1,627.40	1,617.08	1,607.63
Financial Activities													
2013	1,107.72	1,112.60	1,117.68	1,139.21	1,136.55	1,185.90	1,143.81	1,154.61	1,191.74	1,150.60	1,159.24	1,224.36	1,151.44
2014	1,171.40	1,232.33	1,240.13	1,195.01	1,194.28	1,255.46	1,229.69	1,212.57	1,218.08	1,237.65	1,292.00	1,238.39	1,227.29
2015	1,247.52	1,288.60	1,295.78	1,236.89	1,233.94	1,231.36	1,217.71	1,265.78	1,227.29	1,229.12	1,290.87	1,246.16	1,250.29
2016	1,239.84	1,268.99	1,249.64	1,243.28	1,318.37	1,227.13	1,239.64	1,274.78	1,282.27	1,343.10	1,293.41	1,265.92	1,270.20
2017	1,296.74	1,256.70	1,238.52	1,327.01	1,288.44	1,297.05	1,374.13	1,342.11	1,343.46	1,428.96	1,357.26	1,353.26	1,326.42
Professional and Business Services													
2013	1,207.85	1,201.86	1,193.67	1,266.25	1,257.04	1,313.94	1,247.12	1,243.69	1,291.25	1,242.26	1,245.12	1,285.17	1,250.40
2014	1,224.49	1,285.39	1,280.79	1,234.86	1,230.08	1,288.74	1,248.70	1,248.18	1,242.98	1,243.08	1,313.13	1,256.32	1,259.17
2015	1,255.21	1,303.12	1,322.87	1,279.80	1,283.43	1,289.44	1,288.81	1,341.06	1,273.05	1,287.63	1,346.64	1,277.50	1,295.91
2016	1,290.91	1,307.48	1,302.34	1,314.36	1,372.64	1,314.58	1,331.89	1,332.72	1,337.99	1,415.25	1,360.08	1,337.04	1,336.42
2017	1,401.57	1,359.89	1,356.48	1,420.43	1,358.10	1,349.12	1,415.85	1,366.75	1,381.68	1,452.09	1,391.17	1,395.15	1,386.66
Education and Health Services													
2013	926.28	931.39	919.50	922.84	921.59	948.74	933.31	932.53	967.33	935.53	940.35	969.91	938.21
2014	936.87	957.19	947.17	928.40	923.49	939.89	923.49	922.02	930.93	934.91	965.26	944.54	936.87
2015	945.72	965.71	951.57	930.44	926.80	928.46	932.10	957.00	930.11	931.85	958.23	939.06	940.39
2016	944.54	940.50	946.86	949.38	965.81	949.64	954.50	955.16	965.70	991.97	970.27	988.34	961.92
2017	1,000.35	983.90	984.90	1,011.75	994.28	998.26	1,034.06	1,001.62	1,015.73	1,036.26	1,021.45	983.34	1,004.93
Leisure and Hospitality													
2013	379.69	389.33	385.93	387.50	391.08	403.92	391.51	395.81	404.85	390.72	393.64	408.88	393.62
2014	394.68	414.80	414.96	402.54	408.31	422.00	411.71	419.78	414.46	417.35	433.52	419.49	414.33
2015	418.70	439.77	440.04	431.21	432.54	435.51	432.81	450.80	435.23	436.30	445.81	437.04	436.32
2016	441.67	448.56	443.94	450.38	470.80	456.84	460.53	459.51	440.92	456.57	441.70	445.38	452.09
2017	459.20	451.81	453.51	468.85	460.46	458.84	474.25	465.51	464.62	477.66	463.11	470.86	464.00
Other Services													
2013	672.06	662.51	675.80	678.29	670.84	700.91	680.92	683.59	704.69	670.18	680.45	713.25	683.59
2014	690.62	705.96	704.05	694.71	679.76	709.42	702.31	699.67	708.35	716.66	734.70	714.08	705.12
2015	721.68	752.51	762.05	729.54	739.31	737.23	737.02	776.56	747.66	746.98	757.24	736.28	745.50
2016	743.38	746.39	750.65	744.32	761.86	737.66	739.99	751.40	745.68	788.70	760.34	769.14	752.96
2017	803.56	784.69	791.68	821.99	800.43	800.49	842.96	827.20	825.93	850.65	821.18	828.45	816.96

COLORADO
At a Glance

Population:
  2010 census: 5,029,196
  2017 estimate: 5,607,154

Percent change in population:
  2010–2017: 11.5%

Percent change in total nonfarm employment:
  2007–2017: 14.1%

Industry with the largest growth in employment, 2007–2017 (thousands):
  Education and health services, 93.7

Industry with the largest decline or smallest growth in employment, 2007–2017 (thousands):
  Information, -4.7

Civilian labor force:
  2010: 2,724,417
  2017: 2,992,307

Unemployment rate and rank among states (highest to lowest):
  2010: 8.7%, 24th
  2017: 2.8%, 48th

Over-the-year change in unemployment rates:
  2015–2016: -0.6%
  2016–2017: -0.5%

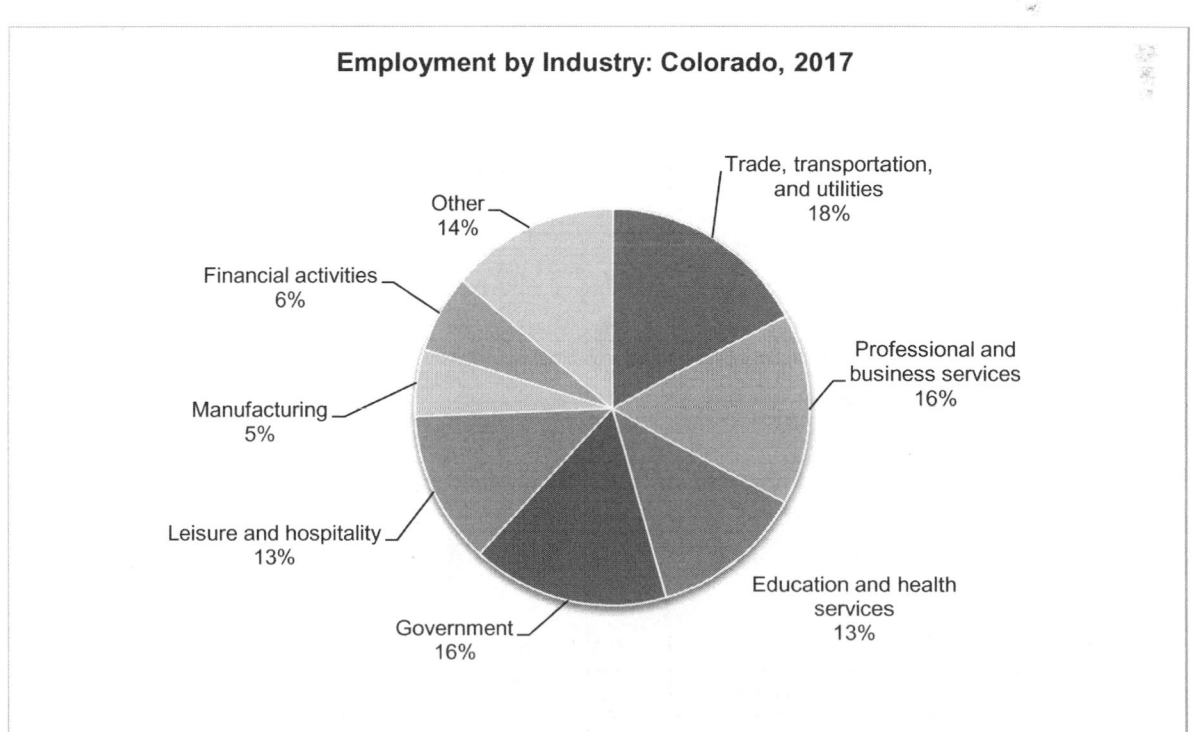

Employment by Industry: Colorado, 2017

- Trade, transportation, and utilities 18%
- Professional and business services 16%
- Education and health services 13%
- Government 16%
- Leisure and hospitality 13%
- Manufacturing 5%
- Financial activities 6%
- Other 14%

1. Employment by Industry: Colorado, Selected Years, 2007–2017

(Numbers in thousands, not seasonally adjusted)

Industry and year	January	February	March	April	May	June	July	August	September	October	November	December	Annual average
Total Nonfarm													
2007	2,262.1	2,279.9	2,305.8	2,312.5	2,327.1	2,357.7	2,341.5	2,349.8	2,351.7	2,349.9	2,358.5	2,372.3	2,330.7
2008	2,313.9	2,330.3	2,343.0	2,348.4	2,359.2	2,378.4	2,362.6	2,368.7	2,360.3	2,351.2	2,340.3	2,339.8	2,349.7
2009	2,270.5	2,261.2	2,257.2	2,247.4	2,250.1	2,258.0	2,237.2	2,234.7	2,231.3	2,230.6	2,226.3	2,233.9	2,244.9
2010	2,174.1	2,187.6	2,200.4	2,211.1	2,224.9	2,240.2	2,230.6	2,233.6	2,228.1	2,235.6	2,237.7	2,254.2	2,221.5
2011	2,202.2	2,212.7	2,228.2	2,247.3	2,252.0	2,273.9	2,262.7	2,273.5	2,279.4	2,276.9	2,284.0	2,301.0	2,257.8
2012	2,248.8	2,262.4	2,281.7	2,291.9	2,302.3	2,329.9	2,318.5	2,328.2	2,329.7	2,340.4	2,350.3	2,362.8	2,312.2
2013	2,310.2	2,331.6	2,349.0	2,357.8	2,370.6	2,395.7	2,388.7	2,402.8	2,402.6	2,408.7	2,420.8	2,434.3	2,381.1
2014	2,390.3	2,405.7	2,422.5	2,439.2	2,453.1	2,478.5	2,471.0	2,487.6	2,488.6	2,500.8	2,505.6	2,527.8	2,464.2
2015	2,482.1	2,498.8	2,509.3	2,522.4	2,531.2	2,555.9	2,551.1	2,555.6	2,557.8	2,567.8	2,576.1	2,592.2	2,541.7
2016	2,543.9	2,559.0	2,570.7	2,587.7	2,582.9	2,615.1	2,616.2	2,622.6	2,628.2	2,625.2	2,631.6	2,646.0	2,602.4
2017	2,591.6	2,613.2	2,631.5	2,640.6	2,645.7	2,676.7	2,669.8	2,676.8	2,677.5	2,683.0	2,692.0	2,704.7	2,658.6
Total Private													
2007	1,901.8	1,905.2	1,927.8	1,934.0	1,945.1	1,983.1	1,986.0	1,990.5	1,972.2	1,965.8	1,972.9	1,988.3	1,956.1
2008	1,943.2	1,947.0	1,956.7	1,961.5	1,966.6	1,996.4	1,998.0	1,998.8	1,971.8	1,955.7	1,944.3	1,946.5	1,965.5
2009	1,888.0	1,869.1	1,862.5	1,850.8	1,848.6	1,868.2	1,868.1	1,863.8	1,838.8	1,830.5	1,827.1	1,837.0	1,854.4
2010	1,791.7	1,791.7	1,800.6	1,811.0	1,813.2	1,845.7	1,856.2	1,859.6	1,835.2	1,835.3	1,836.3	1,855.6	1,827.7
2011	1,818.8	1,816.8	1,829.8	1,846.9	1,848.7	1,881.6	1,891.1	1,901.2	1,884.0	1,875.7	1,882.2	1,902.2	1,864.9
2012	1,865.0	1,866.0	1,882.1	1,891.0	1,897.9	1,935.9	1,945.4	1,950.6	1,931.5	1,937.0	1,945.0	1,961.0	1,917.4
2013	1,918.4	1,926.1	1,941.1	1,949.2	1,957.5	1,995.0	2,008.0	2,017.2	1,994.4	1,993.8	2,004.6	2,022.8	1,977.3
2014	1,991.2	1,996.2	2,010.3	2,025.8	2,034.8	2,071.7	2,086.3	2,098.5	2,078.0	2,080.9	2,083.4	2,111.2	2,055.7
2015	2,075.5	2,081.9	2,090.1	2,100.7	2,104.2	2,141.2	2,157.4	2,158.7	2,137.8	2,139.1	2,143.8	2,164.5	2,124.6
2016	2,126.3	2,130.4	2,138.7	2,152.5	2,150.8	2,190.0	2,210.2	2,211.2	2,191.1	2,187.9	2,189.2	2,206.3	2,173.7
2017	2,168.5	2,175.8	2,189.2	2,198.5	2,199.7	2,245.7	2,254.6	2,254.5	2,234.9	2,237.5	2,242.2	2,258.9	2,221.7
Goods Producing													
2007	321.2	321.8	328.7	332.4	339.7	347.4	348.5	348.5	344.6	345.3	342.6	337.0	338.1
2008	326.2	326.0	328.4	330.7	336.6	342.3	341.7	341.4	336.6	334.2	328.0	318.7	332.6
2009	300.9	293.9	289.9	284.9	285.1	287.0	285.5	282.9	278.6	276.1	272.1	265.7	283.6
2010	255.0	253.5	254.9	259.2	262.8	268.6	270.7	270.1	268.2	269.2	266.9	265.0	263.7
2011	254.8	253.6	257.4	263.8	266.3	272.6	275.5	277.4	276.0	276.8	275.2	273.1	268.5
2012	265.0	264.4	266.9	270.9	275.8	281.4	283.3	284.2	282.4	284.8	283.3	281.4	277.0
2013	273.5	275.1	278.8	281.8	288.1	294.9	297.6	300.2	298.1	300.8	301.2	299.8	290.8
2014	294.9	295.5	299.1	304.9	311.0	316.9	321.0	322.4	321.5	323.0	322.1	322.0	312.9
2015	314.0	314.1	314.4	317.0	320.0	324.7	326.6	325.5	323.5	323.8	321.9	319.7	320.4
2016	312.1	312.2	314.3	317.4	319.6	324.9	327.8	327.3	326.2	327.2	325.8	324.1	321.6
2017	317.6	319.9	324.1	327.8	330.7	338.2	340.1	340.5	338.9	339.5	341.8	340.9	333.3
Service-Providing													
2007	1,940.9	1,958.1	1,977.1	1,980.1	1,987.4	2,010.3	1,993.0	2,001.3	2,007.1	2,004.6	2,015.9	2,035.3	1,992.6
2008	1,987.7	2,004.3	2,014.6	2,017.7	2,022.6	2,036.1	2,020.9	2,027.3	2,023.7	2,017.0	2,012.3	2,021.1	2,017.1
2009	1,969.6	1,967.3	1,967.3	1,962.5	1,965.0	1,971.0	1,951.7	1,951.8	1,952.7	1,954.5	1,954.2	1,968.2	1,961.3
2010	1,919.1	1,934.1	1,945.5	1,951.9	1,962.1	1,971.6	1,959.9	1,963.5	1,959.9	1,966.4	1,970.8	1,989.2	1,957.8
2011	1,947.4	1,959.1	1,970.8	1,983.5	1,985.7	2,001.3	1,987.2	1,996.1	2,003.4	2,000.1	2,008.8	2,027.9	1,989.3
2012	1,983.8	1,998.0	2,014.8	2,021.0	2,026.5	2,048.5	2,035.2	2,044.0	2,047.3	2,055.6	2,067.0	2,081.4	2,035.3
2013	2,036.7	2,056.5	2,070.2	2,076.0	2,082.5	2,100.8	2,091.1	2,102.6	2,104.5	2,107.9	2,119.6	2,134.5	2,090.2
2014	2,095.4	2,110.2	2,123.4	2,134.3	2,142.1	2,161.6	2,150.0	2,165.2	2,167.1	2,177.8	2,183.5	2,205.8	2,151.4
2015	2,168.1	2,184.7	2,194.9	2,205.4	2,211.2	2,231.2	2,224.5	2,230.1	2,234.3	2,244.0	2,254.2	2,272.5	2,221.3
2016	2,231.8	2,246.8	2,256.4	2,270.3	2,263.3	2,290.2	2,288.4	2,295.3	2,302.0	2,298.0	2,305.8	2,321.9	2,280.9
2017	2,274.0	2,293.3	2,307.4	2,312.8	2,315.0	2,338.5	2,329.7	2,336.3	2,338.6	2,343.5	2,350.2	2,363.8	2,325.3
Mining and Logging													
2007	23.1	23.6	23.9	24.5	25.2	25.9	25.9	26.2	25.8	25.9	26.2	26.2	25.2
2008	26.4	26.7	26.8	27.5	28.0	28.6	28.9	29.2	29.2	30.0	30.2	29.9	28.5
2009	28.4	27.0	26.0	24.2	23.9	23.6	23.1	23.0	22.9	22.8	22.7	22.8	24.2
2010	22.5	22.8	23.0	23.5	23.9	24.4	25.0	25.2	25.1	25.4	25.5	26.0	24.4
2011	25.7	25.9	26.3	26.8	27.2	27.9	28.5	28.9	28.7	29.5	29.8	30.1	27.9
2012	30.0	30.2	30.3	30.2	30.4	30.7	30.7	30.6	30.1	30.1	29.9	29.9	30.3
2013	29.5	29.6	29.6	29.6	30.0	30.5	30.8	31.2	31.1	31.4	31.6	31.8	30.6
2014	31.8	32.1	32.3	32.7	33.2	33.7	34.5	35.0	35.2	35.8	36.1	36.4	34.1
2015	35.6	34.5	33.1	31.6	31.1	30.7	30.3	29.7	28.9	28.0	27.5	27.1	30.7
2016	26.0	25.4	24.6	23.7	23.3	23.1	22.8	22.9	22.9	22.9	23.0	23.4	23.7
2017	23.5	24.0	24.4	24.7	25.2	25.9	26.3	26.5	26.6	26.9	27.3	27.5	25.7

1. Employment by Industry: Colorado, Selected Years, 2007–2017—*Continued*

(Numbers in thousands, not seasonally adjusted)

Industry and year	January	February	March	April	May	June	July	August	September	October	November	December	Annual average
Construction													
2007	154.0	154.4	160.5	164.1	169.8	175.7	176.9	176.7	173.1	173.1	170.1	164.7	167.8
2008	155.4	155.6	157.9	160.0	165.0	169.6	169.5	169.2	166.0	163.4	158.5	151.3	161.8
2009	138.4	134.8	133.3	131.4	132.7	135.5	135.0	133.2	130.0	127.9	124.6	118.9	131.3
2010	110.3	108.6	109.6	112.9	115.3	119.3	120.6	119.6	118.2	118.3	115.8	113.1	115.1
2011	104.3	102.7	105.3	110.1	111.6	116.0	117.5	118.6	117.5	117.5	115.7	113.0	112.5
2012	106.5	105.4	107.4	111.0	115.1	119.2	120.5	121.4	120.5	122.4	121.1	119.4	115.8
2013	113.4	114.4	117.5	120.3	125.8	131.1	133.2	135.1	133.7	135.8	135.7	134.0	127.5
2014	130.0	130.0	133.0	137.5	142.2	146.3	148.8	149.3	148.0	148.7	146.8	146.1	142.2
2015	139.8	140.6	141.9	145.6	148.4	151.9	154.0	153.5	152.6	154.0	152.3	150.4	148.8
2016	145.0	145.2	148.0	151.9	154.2	158.8	160.9	160.8	160.3	161.1	159.7	157.1	155.3
2017	151.9	153.6	156.7	159.7	162.0	167.1	168.3	168.8	167.9	169.1	169.4	168.7	163.6
Manufacturing													
2007	144.1	143.8	144.3	143.8	144.7	145.8	145.7	145.6	145.7	146.3	146.3	146.1	145.2
2008	144.4	143.7	143.7	143.2	143.6	144.1	143.3	143.0	141.4	140.8	139.3	137.5	142.3
2009	134.1	132.1	130.6	129.3	128.5	127.9	127.4	126.7	125.7	125.4	124.8	124.0	128.0
2010	122.2	122.1	122.3	122.8	123.6	124.9	125.1	125.3	124.9	125.5	125.6	125.9	124.2
2011	124.8	125.0	125.8	126.9	127.5	128.7	129.5	129.9	129.8	129.8	129.7	130.0	128.1
2012	128.5	128.8	129.2	129.7	130.3	131.5	132.1	132.2	131.8	132.3	132.3	132.1	130.9
2013	130.6	131.1	131.7	131.9	132.3	133.3	133.6	133.9	133.3	133.6	133.9	134.0	132.8
2014	133.1	133.4	133.8	134.7	135.6	136.9	137.7	138.1	138.3	138.5	139.2	139.5	136.6
2015	138.6	139.0	139.4	139.8	140.5	142.1	142.3	142.3	142.0	141.8	142.1	142.2	141.0
2016	141.1	141.6	141.7	141.8	142.1	143.0	144.1	143.6	143.0	143.2	143.1	143.6	142.7
2017	142.2	142.3	143.0	143.4	143.5	145.2	145.5	145.2	144.4	143.5	145.1	144.7	144.0
Trade, Transportation, and Utilities													
2007	424.2	419.7	422.3	422.7	424.4	428.9	430.5	430.8	429.7	431.6	440.1	445.3	429.2
2008	430.9	426.6	428.2	427.7	427.8	431.5	431.8	431.7	427.8	426.1	428.8	432.1	429.3
2009	413.4	406.4	403.2	400.6	401.5	404.0	402.6	402.1	399.5	399.9	404.2	408.4	403.8
2010	393.0	391.0	391.6	392.8	394.6	398.5	400.0	400.5	396.6	398.7	404.5	409.6	397.6
2011	395.2	392.6	393.8	397.2	399.0	402.6	403.9	404.8	401.8	403.7	410.9	415.6	401.8
2012	402.5	399.2	401.1	402.6	405.3	409.9	411.3	411.4	409.9	413.5	422.5	427.0	409.7
2013	412.6	410.8	411.9	413.1	415.6	419.9	421.5	423.4	420.8	423.1	432.3	437.9	420.2
2014	424.1	422.4	423.5	425.4	427.9	433.6	434.3	435.6	433.3	436.3	444.5	452.4	432.8
2015	438.4	436.5	437.3	438.9	440.3	445.6	448.5	448.4	445.5	449.1	457.2	464.0	445.8
2016	448.3	445.9	446.3	448.1	449.7	453.3	456.4	456.6	453.9	456.5	464.0	470.1	454.1
2017	456.3	453.5	453.4	454.7	455.4	460.8	462.6	462.8	460.5	461.5	468.5	473.9	460.3
Wholesale Trade													
2007	97.2	97.7	98.4	98.7	99.2	100.0	99.9	100.0	99.6	100.2	100.3	100.5	99.3
2008	99.5	99.8	100.1	100.4	100.7	101.0	101.0	100.7	100.2	99.7	99.0	98.8	100.1
2009	96.7	95.7	94.7	93.8	93.6	93.4	92.8	92.4	91.7	91.7	91.3	91.4	93.3
2010	90.1	89.9	90.0	90.4	90.6	91.1	91.3	91.3	90.9	91.3	91.2	91.4	90.8
2011	90.5	90.6	91.0	91.6	91.9	92.3	92.6	92.8	92.5	92.4	92.5	92.6	91.9
2012	91.7	92.1	92.7	93.3	93.8	94.5	94.9	95.0	94.8	95.3	95.3	95.8	94.1
2013	94.6	95.1	95.5	95.9	96.2	96.9	97.0	97.2	96.8	97.2	97.5	97.7	96.5
2014	97.2	97.8	98.1	98.8	99.3	100.0	100.5	100.9	100.6	101.2	101.6	102.4	99.9
2015	101.6	102.0	102.1	102.6	103.0	103.4	104.0	104.0	103.6	104.4	104.6	104.9	103.4
2016	103.9	104.0	104.1	104.7	104.8	104.9	105.5	105.2	104.9	105.2	105.3	105.5	104.8
2017	105.0	105.3	105.7	106.0	106.3	107.1	107.4	107.5	107.2	106.7	107.0	107.4	106.6
Retail Trade													
2007	250.8	246.4	248.1	248.0	249.3	252.3	254.0	254.1	253.5	254.4	261.9	265.1	253.2
2008	253.7	250.0	251.0	250.3	250.2	253.1	253.3	253.7	251.3	250.9	253.9	255.7	252.3
2009	242.5	237.5	235.9	233.8	235.5	237.7	237.3	237.1	235.8	236.2	241.1	243.5	237.8
2010	232.4	230.3	231.0	232.6	234.2	237.3	238.8	238.9	235.7	237.0	242.4	245.3	236.3
2011	234.5	232.4	233.1	235.9	237.3	239.9	240.5	241.3	239.0	240.5	247.0	249.8	239.3
2012	239.4	235.7	237.1	238.1	240.1	243.2	243.9	243.8	242.6	244.4	252.5	255.0	243.0
2013	243.4	241.1	242.1	243.1	245.0	248.3	249.5	250.7	248.6	249.8	257.5	260.9	248.3
2014	249.5	247.3	248.4	249.6	251.0	255.2	255.4	255.8	254.1	256.2	263.1	267.4	254.4
2015	255.7	254.0	255.5	256.8	258.2	262.3	264.2	264.4	262.2	264.7	271.6	275.3	262.1
2016	263.0	261.5	262.6	263.6	265.2	268.1	270.1	270.0	267.7	269.9	276.2	278.6	268.0
2017	267.7	265.0	265.5	266.8	267.5	271.0	272.3	272.2	269.7	270.4	275.9	277.3	270.1

1. Employment by Industry: Colorado, Selected Years, 2007–2017—*Continued*

(Numbers in thousands, not seasonally adjusted)

Industry and year	January	February	March	April	May	June	July	August	September	October	November	December	Annual average
Transportation and Utilities													
2007	76.2	75.6	75.8	76.0	75.9	76.6	76.6	76.7	76.6	77.0	77.9	79.7	76.7
2008	77.7	76.8	77.1	77.0	76.9	77.4	77.5	77.3	76.3	75.5	75.9	77.6	76.9
2009	74.2	73.2	72.6	73.0	72.4	72.9	72.5	72.6	72.0	72.0	71.8	73.5	72.7
2010	70.5	70.8	70.6	69.8	69.8	70.1	69.9	70.3	70.0	70.4	70.9	72.9	70.5
2011	70.2	69.6	69.7	69.7	69.8	70.4	70.8	70.7	70.3	70.8	71.4	73.2	70.6
2012	71.4	71.4	71.3	71.2	71.4	72.2	72.5	72.6	72.5	73.8	74.7	76.2	72.6
2013	74.6	74.6	74.3	74.1	74.4	74.7	75.0	75.5	75.4	76.1	77.3	79.3	75.4
2014	77.4	77.3	77.0	77.0	77.6	78.4	78.4	78.9	78.6	78.9	79.8	82.6	78.5
2015	81.1	80.5	79.7	79.5	79.1	79.9	80.3	80.0	79.7	80.0	81.0	83.8	80.4
2016	81.4	80.4	79.6	79.8	79.7	80.3	80.8	81.4	81.3	81.4	82.5	86.0	81.2
2017	83.6	83.2	82.2	81.9	81.6	82.7	82.9	83.1	83.6	84.4	85.6	89.2	83.7
Information													
2007	74.9	75.0	75.0	75.8	76.2	77.0	76.7	76.8	76.3	77.3	77.6	77.9	76.4
2008	77.4	77.6	77.4	77.2	77.0	77.2	77.0	76.8	76.3	76.1	76.0	76.1	76.8
2009	76.7	76.2	76.0	75.4	75.0	74.8	74.5	73.9	73.5	73.5	73.6	72.9	74.7
2010	72.2	71.9	72.0	71.7	71.8	72.3	71.8	72.0	71.5	71.9	72.5	72.5	72.0
2011	72.3	72.2	71.8	71.8	71.6	71.5	71.2	71.1	70.9	70.7	70.8	70.5	71.4
2012	70.2	70.2	70.3	69.7	69.8	70.0	69.6	69.5	69.2	69.4	69.7	69.9	69.8
2013	69.5	69.7	69.7	69.4	69.6	70.2	70.3	70.3	69.7	69.5	70.1	70.1	69.8
2014	70.1	70.2	70.1	69.6	69.8	70.5	71.0	71.2	70.0	70.2	70.5	70.7	70.3
2015	70.3	70.6	70.4	70.0	70.3	70.9	71.3	71.3	70.6	70.6	71.1	71.3	70.7
2016	71.1	71.5	71.5	71.4	71.5	72.0	72.8	72.8	71.7	71.9	72.2	72.1	71.9
2017	71.3	71.6	71.4	70.9	70.7	71.6	71.5	71.6	71.1	72.8	72.8	73.6	71.7
Financial Activities													
2007	159.6	160.1	160.4	159.9	159.2	160.5	160.3	160.0	158.7	157.8	157.9	159.2	159.5
2008	157.0	157.4	157.7	156.9	156.0	156.6	156.6	155.7	154.0	153.2	152.5	153.7	155.6
2009	150.5	149.8	149.1	148.7	147.9	148.3	147.9	147.7	146.1	146.1	145.9	147.4	148.0
2010	144.9	144.6	144.7	144.2	143.2	144.2	144.7	144.7	143.6	143.7	143.6	145.7	144.3
2011	143.6	143.4	143.5	143.3	142.8	144.0	144.1	144.4	143.7	143.3	144.3	146.2	143.9
2012	144.3	144.7	145.4	145.3	145.2	146.8	147.3	147.7	146.8	147.8	148.3	150.3	146.7
2013	148.6	149.4	150.3	150.0	149.7	151.3	152.0	152.2	151.3	151.5	151.9	153.4	151.0
2014	151.5	152.0	152.2	152.5	152.4	153.6	154.7	155.1	154.1	155.0	155.7	157.8	153.9
2015	156.2	156.9	157.3	157.3	157.4	159.0	160.2	160.5	159.5	160.4	160.7	162.7	159.0
2016	161.4	161.6	161.8	162.2	162.1	163.9	165.3	165.7	164.6	165.2	165.4	166.9	163.8
2017	165.5	166.1	166.5	166.6	166.5	168.7	169.0	168.9	167.9	167.7	167.3	168.9	167.5
Professional and Business Services													
2007	333.9	335.8	340.7	346.0	350.7	356.9	356.5	358.3	357.1	355.1	352.7	353.2	349.7
2008	344.2	347.0	348.4	354.7	356.2	360.4	359.9	361.3	357.6	355.7	350.5	348.2	353.7
2009	335.8	331.9	330.9	331.8	332.6	334.3	333.5	332.4	329.4	330.2	329.5	328.9	331.8
2010	319.4	321.1	323.8	329.4	331.4	335.6	337.1	337.4	332.8	334.8	333.6	332.6	330.8
2011	328.5	330.0	330.8	338.7	341.4	344.8	346.4	348.8	346.6	346.6	347.1	347.8	341.5
2012	340.3	342.2	345.0	351.7	355.7	360.8	362.9	365.1	362.7	367.5	365.0	363.6	356.9
2013	356.3	359.5	362.8	368.0	371.5	376.6	378.7	381.2	378.1	380.4	379.2	378.5	372.6
2014	370.1	372.1	374.1	380.9	384.4	389.9	391.4	396.7	393.5	397.0	393.3	394.7	386.5
2015	386.7	388.6	389.9	394.9	397.5	401.4	404.3	405.5	402.3	404.9	402.7	401.9	398.4
2016	393.4	394.9	395.7	403.5	403.8	408.9	413.4	413.1	411.1	412.2	410.4	407.7	405.7
2017	398.5	400.6	403.2	409.6	412.1	417.6	419.7	420.1	418.2	422.3	419.4	417.3	413.2
Education and Health Services													
2007	233.2	236.2	237.8	238.2	239.3	239.5	238.1	239.9	241.1	243.2	245.1	246.5	239.8
2008	243.9	247.0	247.4	248.2	249.6	248.7	248.2	249.9	250.9	253.5	255.4	255.4	249.8
2009	253.4	255.1	255.3	255.8	256.4	255.7	255.3	256.1	256.2	258.8	259.7	260.4	256.5
2010	258.2	260.5	261.3	262.7	263.6	263.1	262.8	264.3	264.6	267.8	268.5	269.6	263.9
2011	267.2	269.2	270.6	271.7	272.3	271.5	271.1	273.4	274.8	276.3	276.9	279.4	272.9
2012	276.6	279.3	280.1	280.4	280.7	280.5	279.9	281.5	282.6	285.1	286.2	288.1	281.8
2013	280.4	282.7	283.4	284.7	285.1	283.7	283.8	286.2	286.8	289.6	291.5	292.7	285.9
2014	290.3	293.1	294.4	296.6	297.5	296.2	295.9	298.9	299.8	303.3	304.5	305.6	298.0
2015	304.7	307.5	308.8	311.4	312.3	311.9	312.5	314.0	314.6	319.2	320.7	321.3	313.2
2016	318.8	321.3	322.4	325.5	325.7	324.8	325.6	326.9	327.8	329.6	330.1	330.4	325.7
2017	327.9	330.7	332.2	333.5	334.1	333.8	332.5	333.8	334.3	336.4	337.5	335.4	333.5

1. Employment by Industry: Colorado, Selected Years, 2007–2017—*Continued*

(Numbers in thousands, not seasonally adjusted)

Industry and year	January	February	March	April	May	June	July	August	September	October	November	December	Annual average
Leisure and Hospitality													
2007	263.4	264.7	270.0	266.5	263.0	278.6	281.9	282.6	271.7	262.5	264.1	275.7	270.4
2008	269.7	271.1	274.5	271.7	268.7	283.7	286.4	285.9	273.3	262.3	259.1	268.7	272.9
2009	262.2	261.3	263.5	260.2	256.6	269.4	274.5	274.7	262.6	253.3	250.0	260.7	262.4
2010	256.7	257.0	259.9	259.3	253.7	270.1	275.7	277.2	265.6	257.4	255.0	268.6	263.0
2011	265.4	264.1	269.4	267.0	261.6	279.5	284.1	286.0	275.8	264.6	263.4	275.4	271.4
2012	272.0	271.5	278.1	275.0	269.8	289.3	293.7	294.0	281.6	272.5	274.0	284.3	279.7
2013	281.2	282.6	287.4	285.3	280.3	299.6	305.1	304.7	291.7	281.4	280.7	292.4	289.4
2014	291.7	292.4	297.9	296.3	291.8	309.3	315.3	315.4	304.2	294.0	291.0	305.5	300.4
2015	303.0	305.4	309.2	307.9	303.0	322.6	328.1	327.8	317.0	306.5	305.0	318.4	312.8
2016	316.1	317.4	320.8	318.3	312.0	334.0	339.8	339.5	327.3	316.9	313.5	327.6	323.6
2017	324.9	325.9	330.3	327.1	321.5	344.8	349.0	346.6	334.7	327.4	327.0	341.1	333.4
Other Services													
2007	91.4	91.9	92.9	92.5	92.6	94.3	93.5	93.6	93.0	93.0	92.8	93.5	92.9
2008	93.9	94.3	94.7	94.4	94.7	96.0	96.4	96.1	95.3	94.6	94.0	93.6	94.8
2009	95.1	94.5	94.6	93.4	93.5	94.7	94.3	94.0	92.9	92.6	92.1	92.6	93.7
2010	92.3	92.1	92.4	91.7	92.1	93.3	93.4	93.4	92.3	91.8	91.7	92.0	92.4
2011	91.8	91.7	92.5	93.4	93.7	95.1	94.8	95.3	94.4	93.7	93.6	94.2	93.7
2012	94.1	94.5	95.2	95.4	95.6	97.2	97.4	97.2	96.3	96.4	96.0	96.4	96.0
2013	96.3	96.3	96.8	96.9	97.6	98.8	99.0	99.0	97.9	97.5	97.7	98.0	97.7
2014	98.5	98.5	99.0	99.6	100.0	101.7	102.7	103.2	101.6	102.1	101.8	102.5	100.9
2015	102.2	102.3	102.8	103.3	103.4	105.1	105.9	105.7	104.8	104.6	104.5	105.2	104.2
2016	105.1	105.6	105.9	106.1	106.4	108.2	109.1	109.3	108.5	108.4	107.8	107.4	107.3
2017	106.5	107.5	108.1	108.3	108.7	110.2	110.2	110.2	109.3	109.9	107.9	107.8	108.7
Government													
2007	360.3	374.7	378.0	378.5	382.0	374.6	355.5	359.3	379.5	384.1	385.6	384.0	374.7
2008	370.7	383.3	386.3	386.9	392.6	382.0	364.6	369.9	388.5	395.5	396.0	393.3	384.1
2009	382.5	392.1	394.7	396.6	401.5	389.8	369.1	370.9	392.5	400.1	399.2	396.9	390.5
2010	382.4	395.9	399.8	400.1	411.7	394.5	374.4	374.0	392.9	400.3	401.4	398.6	393.8
2011	383.4	395.9	398.4	400.4	403.3	392.3	371.6	372.3	395.4	401.2	401.8	398.8	392.9
2012	383.8	396.4	399.6	400.9	404.4	394.0	373.1	377.6	398.2	403.4	405.3	401.8	394.9
2013	391.8	405.5	407.9	408.6	413.1	400.7	380.7	385.6	408.2	414.9	416.2	411.5	403.7
2014	399.1	409.5	412.2	413.4	418.3	406.8	384.7	389.1	410.6	419.9	422.2	416.6	408.5
2015	406.6	416.9	419.2	421.7	427.0	414.7	393.7	396.9	420.0	428.7	432.3	427.7	417.1
2016	417.6	428.6	432.0	435.2	432.1	425.1	406.0	411.4	437.1	437.3	442.4	439.7	428.7
2017	423.1	437.4	442.3	442.1	446.0	431.0	415.2	422.3	442.6	445.5	449.8	445.8	436.9

2. Average Weekly Hours by Selected Industry: Colorado, 2013–2017

(Not seasonally adjusted)

Industry and year	January	February	March	April	May	June	July	August	September	October	November	December	Annual average
Total Private													
2013	34.3	34.5	34.7	34.4	34.6	35.6	34.8	34.9	35.2	34.6	34.8	35.1	34.8
2014	34.2	35.0	34.9	34.1	34.1	35.2	34.5	34.5	34.3	34.4	34.4	34.1	34.5
2015	33.6	34.4	34.4	33.6	33.7	34.0	34.1	34.8	33.9	33.9	34.0	33.2	34.0
2016	33.4	33.2	33.3	33.2	33.9	33.7	33.8	33.8	33.7	34.2	33.3	33.1	33.5
2017	33.1	32.9	32.9	33.7	33.8	33.8	34.3	33.8	33.5	33.9	33.4	33.3	33.5
Goods Producing													
2013	37.5	37.6	38.0	37.7	38.6	39.6	39.1	40.0	39.2	39.4	39.1	39.6	38.8
2014	38.4	39.3	38.9	38.9	38.8	40.0	39.7	40.3	40.0	40.7	38.9	40.5	39.5
2015	39.3	40.1	40.3	39.4	39.0	40.0	40.0	40.8	39.8	40.2	40.1	40.0	39.9
2016	39.5	39.0	39.1	39.3	39.6	39.9	39.7	39.7	39.8	39.9	39.5	38.1	39.4
2017	38.7	39.0	38.8	39.7	39.6	40.7	40.3	39.9	40.2	40.1	39.9	39.4	39.7
Construction													
2013	36.8	37.0	37.6	36.7	37.7	38.9	38.7	39.6	39.0	39.3	38.9	38.4	38.3
2014	37.7	37.9	38.1	38.5	37.5	39.4	39.8	40.4	39.9	40.9	38.4	40.0	39.1
2015	37.8	38.7	39.0	38.7	37.6	39.4	39.8	40.9	39.0	40.3	39.5	39.9	39.2
2016	38.7	37.9	38.5	38.9	39.7	40.0	39.6	40.1	39.8	39.5	38.8	36.6	39.0
2017	36.7	38.0	37.5	38.1	38.1	39.8	39.1	38.7	38.9	38.5	38.4	37.6	38.3
Manufacturing													
2013	38.1	38.6	38.3	38.7	39.1	40.0	39.1	40.2	39.6	39.6	39.2	39.8	39.2
2014	39.5	40.5	39.5	39.2	40.0	40.3	39.2	39.8	39.8	40.1	40.0	39.5	39.8
2015	39.3	40.3	40.4	39.2	39.7	40.1	39.9	40.2	40.1	39.8	40.0	39.6	39.9
2016	39.8	39.5	39.4	39.6	39.3	39.3	39.5	38.9	39.5	40.0	39.7	39.6	39.5
2017	40.4	39.3	39.3	40.2	39.9	40.2	40.2	40.2	39.8	39.9	39.7	39.5	39.9
Trade, Transportation, and Utilities													
2013	34.8	35.2	35.4	35.0	35.2	36.3	35.8	35.7	35.9	35.0	35.1	35.8	35.4
2014	34.7	35.4	35.1	34.3	34.2	35.1	34.4	34.4	34.4	34.5	34.6	34.6	34.6
2015	33.7	34.6	34.5	33.4	34.0	34.2	34.5	34.7	34.5	34.2	34.3	34.0	34.2
2016	33.7	33.7	33.4	33.4	33.6	33.7	33.6	33.7	33.3	33.8	33.0	33.5	33.5
2017	33.3	33.2	32.9	33.5	32.8	33.2	33.9	33.4	33.2	33.7	33.4	33.3	33.3
Financial Activities													
2013	37.7	37.2	37.3	37.5	36.9	38.4	37.3	37.0	37.8	36.7	36.6	37.5	37.3
2014	36.6	37.2	37.5	36.3	36.2	38.3	37.1	37.0	36.9	37.1	38.6	36.9	37.1
2015	36.8	37.7	37.5	36.5	36.4	36.0	36.1	37.4	36.3	36.1	37.6	36.2	36.7
2016	36.8	36.5	36.3	36.8	37.4	37.1	36.9	36.9	37.0	37.9	37.1	36.5	36.9
2017	37.7	36.6	36.5	37.8	36.5	36.6	37.5	36.9	36.8	37.4	36.8	37.1	37.0
Professional and Business Services													
2013	36.9	37.2	37.1	36.8	37.2	38.3	36.9	37.3	37.6	37.2	37.4	37.6	37.3
2014	36.7	37.8	37.5	37.2	36.8	37.8	36.4	36.6	36.7	36.8	36.8	36.2	36.9
2015	36.2	37.0	37.2	36.5	36.6	36.6	36.6	37.2	36.2	36.2	36.2	35.1	36.5
2016	35.4	35.3	35.3	35.6	36.2	35.9	36.0	36.0	36.5	37.0	36.0	35.8	35.9
2017	35.9	35.3	35.4	36.3	35.5	36.3	36.6	35.9	35.4	35.4	35.0	35.3	35.7
Education and Health Services													
2013	32.4	32.5	32.2	32.3	32.0	32.6	31.8	31.8	32.3	31.8	32.1	32.1	32.2
2014	31.4	31.8	32.0	31.2	31.4	32.1	31.6	31.4	31.3	31.4	32.2	31.6	31.6
2015	31.3	32.0	31.9	31.1	31.1	30.9	30.6	31.4	30.7	30.6	31.4	30.5	31.1
2016	31.1	31.0	31.3	31.1	31.7	30.8	31.5	31.3	31.5	31.7	31.3	31.6	31.3
2017	32.2	31.9	31.9	32.9	32.0	32.2	32.9	32.5	31.9	32.4	32.1	31.9	32.2
Leisure and Hospitality													
2013	27.1	27.7	28.0	27.0	27.5	28.6	28.1	28.1	27.7	26.8	27.0	26.7	27.5
2014	26.6	27.3	28.1	26.1	26.5	27.9	27.9	27.9	26.8	26.4	26.0	25.7	26.9
2015	25.9	26.7	26.9	26.0	26.1	26.6	26.8	27.6	26.1	26.2	25.2	25.0	26.3
2016	25.3	25.5	25.9	24.4	26.1	26.2	26.5	26.4	25.7	26.0	24.8	25.0	25.7
2017	24.7	24.7	25.2	24.2	24.6	26.0	26.7	26.1	25.4	25.6	24.5	24.7	25.2
Other Services													
2013	34.5	34.3	34.4	33.9	33.9	34.9	33.3	33.5	34.1	33.4	33.9	34.6	34.1
2014	34.3	34.7	34.0	33.6	33.3	34.4	33.0	34.1	33.7	32.4	32.3	31.0	33.4
2015	29.8	31.0	31.1	30.1	30.4	32.2	32.3	33.6	32.5	32.7	34.2	32.8	31.9
2016	33.5	33.0	33.0	33.1	34.2	33.3	34.1	34.2	33.7	35.6	33.4	33.7	33.7
2017	33.9	33.5	33.6	35.1	33.8	34.4	36.0	35.2	35.1	36.2	35.4	35.2	34.8

3. Average Hourly Earnings by Selected Industry: Colorado, 2013–2017

(Dollars , not seasonally adjusted)

Industry and year	January	February	March	April	May	June	July	August	September	October	November	December	Annual average
Total Private													
2013	25.11	25.31	25.26	25.49	25.47	25.77	25.54	25.51	26.17	25.80	25.98	26.22	25.64
2014	26.04	26.20	26.39	26.35	26.24	26.39	26.10	26.02	26.34	26.34	26.66	26.44	26.29
2015	26.64	26.74	26.81	26.85	26.82	26.41	26.76	27.00	26.81	27.06	27.25	27.02	26.85
2016	27.41	27.47	27.31	27.42	27.31	26.79	26.62	26.60	26.76	27.24	26.97	26.95	27.07
2017	27.42	27.44	27.26	27.73	27.16	27.25	27.65	27.46	27.77	27.95	27.94	28.13	27.60
Goods Producing													
2013	26.79	27.08	27.11	27.10	27.04	27.27	27.18	27.00	27.65	27.56	27.71	28.03	27.31
2014	27.88	27.78	28.25	28.18	28.02	28.29	28.33	28.10	28.60	28.57	28.74	28.79	28.31
2015	29.10	29.28	29.42	29.57	29.54	29.43	29.88	30.08	29.96	29.96	30.19	30.13	29.72
2016	30.93	31.22	31.22	31.17	31.00	30.57	30.49	30.25	30.20	30.48	30.63	30.86	30.74
2017	30.90	31.01	30.58	30.71	30.13	29.71	29.80	29.83	30.12	30.13	30.31	30.87	30.33
Construction													
2013	24.60	25.02	24.97	24.77	25.34	25.10	25.07	25.02	25.65	26.28	26.18	26.66	25.43
2014	26.64	27.04	27.21	26.98	26.90	27.04	27.75	27.53	28.15	28.02	28.43	28.27	27.53
2015	28.06	28.64	28.22	28.44	28.21	27.83	28.04	27.75	27.61	27.78	27.73	27.41	27.96
2016	27.86	28.08	27.81	27.56	27.49	27.25	27.37	27.09	27.00	27.14	26.96	26.85	27.36
2017	26.92	26.76	26.74	27.08	26.86	26.85	26.65	26.93	27.33	27.29	27.84	28.34	27.14
Manufacturing													
2013	27.30	27.47	27.40	27.53	26.69	26.89	26.92	26.61	27.54	26.70	27.31	27.29	27.13
2014	27.42	27.28	27.68	27.42	27.35	27.84	27.20	26.73	27.18	27.27	27.23	27.60	27.35
2015	28.40	28.31	29.19	29.66	29.61	29.76	30.63	30.83	30.50	30.69	31.14	31.49	30.03
2016	32.05	31.89	32.14	32.41	32.22	32.00	31.85	31.93	31.91	32.47	32.89	33.16	32.24
2017	32.67	32.36	31.72	31.48	31.49	31.18	30.45	30.32	30.75	30.89	30.61	31.16	31.25
Trade, Transportation, and Utilities													
2013	22.81	22.57	22.46	22.71	22.87	23.23	22.80	22.71	23.48	22.72	22.96	22.93	22.86
2014	22.96	22.74	23.02	22.94	22.63	23.04	22.50	22.61	22.66	22.92	23.19	22.28	22.79
2015	22.87	22.93	23.08	23.07	22.97	22.65	22.98	23.21	23.02	23.06	22.88	22.65	22.95
2016	23.22	23.23	23.59	23.44	23.26	23.12	22.61	22.67	22.90	22.87	22.37	21.99	22.93
2017	22.31	22.14	22.29	22.31	21.66	21.28	21.81	21.61	22.15	21.88	21.77	21.92	21.93
Financial Activities													
2013	27.07	27.70	27.79	28.13	28.68	28.91	29.05	29.70	30.38	29.61	30.22	30.53	28.99
2014	29.87	31.02	31.20	30.82	31.40	31.81	31.30	31.15	30.87	30.60	30.94	30.37	30.95
2015	30.77	30.85	31.23	31.59	31.57	30.63	31.35	31.94	31.38	31.64	31.63	30.86	31.29
2016	30.82	30.69	30.76	31.12	31.53	30.38	30.43	30.55	31.07	31.84	31.64	31.18	31.00
2017	31.72	31.86	30.97	31.94	31.54	31.12	31.63	31.61	31.66	31.95	31.71	31.85	31.63
Professional and Business Services													
2013	30.60	30.99	30.94	31.14	31.04	32.01	31.82	31.50	32.07	31.57	31.61	32.40	31.49
2014	32.41	32.42	32.62	32.37	32.04	31.94	31.66	31.32	31.48	31.67	32.36	32.03	32.02
2015	32.56	32.48	32.30	32.13	31.86	31.45	32.05	32.43	32.18	32.44	33.32	33.26	32.37
2016	33.65	34.00	33.40	33.00	32.61	31.82	31.91	31.65	31.37	31.92	31.62	31.92	32.38
2017	31.19	31.53	31.32	32.26	31.65	31.54	32.40	31.95	32.10	32.72	33.04	33.60	32.11
Education and Health Services													
2013	24.12	24.14	23.94	24.00	23.73	23.75	23.73	23.70	23.70	23.60	23.60	23.63	23.80
2014	23.76	23.89	24.08	23.97	23.89	24.14	24.45	24.69	25.10	24.63	25.20	25.22	24.43
2015	24.87	25.31	25.30	25.24	25.46	25.81	26.09	25.83	25.99	26.19	26.49	26.43	25.75
2016	26.13	26.03	25.79	25.94	25.62	25.60	25.57	25.49	25.74	26.10	25.62	25.98	25.80
2017	25.77	25.88	25.76	26.05	25.89	25.93	25.89	25.89	25.72	25.91	25.90	26.22	25.90
Leisure and Hospitality													
2013	15.33	15.33	15.35	15.43	15.29	14.90	14.98	15.12	15.32	15.39	15.32	15.25	15.24
2014	15.37	15.35	15.30	15.30	15.13	14.86	14.72	14.79	15.27	15.31	15.30	15.64	15.18
2015	15.82	15.70	16.04	15.89	15.80	15.36	15.43	15.64	15.20	15.65	15.43	15.92	15.65
2016	15.86	16.14	16.18	16.26	16.39	16.18	16.32	16.44	16.63	17.14	16.74	17.03	16.44
2017	17.62	17.71	17.78	17.25	17.32	17.00	17.32	17.19	17.54	18.34	17.86	18.30	17.60
Other Services													
2013	21.21	21.80	22.10	22.19	21.79	22.02	21.52	21.42	22.18	22.55	22.96	22.78	22.04
2014	22.52	23.50	23.88	23.97	23.79	25.26	25.03	24.68	25.06	24.25	23.79	24.19	24.17
2015	23.03	23.24	23.44	23.27	23.32	22.68	23.03	23.63	23.66	24.30	24.23	23.52	23.46
2016	23.42	23.46	23.39	23.87	24.12	23.12	22.76	23.47	24.54	25.05	24.60	25.49	23.95
2017	25.39	26.35	25.94	26.92	26.38	26.61	26.88	26.16	26.48	26.17	26.83	25.90	26.34

4. Average Weekly Earnings by Selected Industry: Colorado, 2013–2017

(Dollars, not seasonally adjusted)

Industry and year	January	February	March	April	May	June	July	August	September	October	November	December	Annual average
Total Private													
2013	861.27	873.20	876.52	876.86	881.26	917.41	888.79	890.30	921.18	892.68	904.10	920.32	892.27
2014	890.57	917.00	921.01	898.54	894.78	928.93	900.45	897.69	903.46	906.10	917.10	901.60	907.01
2015	895.10	919.86	922.26	902.16	903.83	897.94	912.52	939.60	908.86	917.33	926.50	897.06	912.90
2016	915.49	912.00	909.42	910.34	925.81	902.82	899.76	899.08	901.81	931.61	898.10	892.05	906.85
2017	907.60	902.78	896.85	934.50	918.01	921.05	948.40	928.15	930.30	947.51	933.20	936.73	924.60
Goods Producing													
2013	1,004.63	1,018.21	1,030.18	1,021.67	1,043.74	1,079.89	1,062.74	1,080.00	1,083.88	1,085.86	1,083.46	1,109.99	1,059.63
2014	1,070.59	1,091.75	1,098.93	1,096.20	1,087.18	1,131.60	1,124.70	1,132.43	1,144.00	1,162.80	1,117.99	1,166.00	1,118.25
2015	1,143.63	1,174.13	1,185.63	1,165.06	1,152.06	1,177.20	1,195.20	1,227.26	1,192.41	1,204.39	1,210.62	1,205.20	1,185.83
2016	1,221.74	1,217.58	1,220.70	1,224.98	1,227.60	1,219.74	1,210.45	1,200.93	1,201.96	1,216.15	1,209.89	1,175.77	1,211.16
2017	1,195.83	1,209.39	1,186.50	1,219.19	1,193.15	1,209.20	1,200.94	1,190.22	1,210.82	1,208.21	1,209.37	1,216.28	1,204.10
Construction													
2013	905.28	925.74	938.87	909.06	955.32	979.50	970.21	990.79	1,000.35	1,032.80	1,018.40	1,023.74	973.97
2014	1,004.33	1,024.82	1,036.70	1,038.73	1,008.75	1,065.38	1,104.45	1,112.21	1,123.19	1,146.02	1,091.71	1,130.80	1,076.42
2015	1,060.67	1,108.37	1,100.58	1,100.63	1,060.70	1,096.50	1,115.99	1,134.98	1,076.79	1,119.53	1,095.34	1,093.66	1,096.03
2016	1,078.18	1,064.23	1,070.69	1,072.08	1,091.35	1,090.00	1,083.85	1,086.31	1,074.60	1,072.03	1,046.05	982.71	1,067.04
2017	987.96	1,016.88	1,002.75	1,031.75	1,023.37	1,068.63	1,042.02	1,042.19	1,063.14	1,050.67	1,069.06	1,065.58	1,039.46
Manufacturing													
2013	1,040.13	1,060.34	1,049.42	1,065.41	1,043.58	1,075.60	1,052.57	1,069.72	1,090.58	1,057.32	1,070.55	1,086.14	1,063.50
2014	1,083.09	1,104.84	1,093.36	1,074.86	1,094.00	1,121.95	1,066.24	1,063.85	1,081.76	1,093.53	1,089.20	1,090.20	1,088.53
2015	1,116.12	1,140.89	1,179.28	1,162.67	1,175.52	1,193.38	1,222.14	1,239.37	1,223.05	1,221.46	1,245.60	1,247.00	1,198.20
2016	1,275.59	1,259.66	1,266.32	1,283.44	1,266.25	1,257.60	1,258.08	1,242.08	1,260.45	1,298.80	1,305.73	1,313.14	1,273.48
2017	1,319.87	1,271.75	1,246.60	1,265.50	1,256.45	1,253.44	1,224.09	1,218.86	1,223.85	1,232.51	1,215.22	1,230.82	1,246.88
Trade, Transportation, and Utilities													
2013	793.79	794.46	795.08	794.85	805.02	843.25	816.24	810.75	842.93	795.20	805.90	820.89	809.24
2014	796.71	805.00	808.00	786.84	773.95	808.70	774.00	777.78	779.50	790.74	802.37	770.89	788.53
2015	770.72	793.38	796.26	770.54	780.98	774.63	792.81	805.39	794.19	788.65	784.78	770.10	784.89
2016	782.51	782.85	787.91	782.90	781.54	779.14	759.70	763.98	762.57	773.01	738.21	736.67	768.16
2017	742.92	735.05	733.34	747.39	710.45	706.50	739.36	721.77	735.38	737.36	727.12	729.94	730.27
Financial Activities													
2013	1,020.54	1,030.44	1,036.57	1,054.88	1,058.29	1,110.14	1,083.57	1,098.90	1,148.36	1,086.69	1,106.05	1,144.88	1,081.33
2014	1,093.24	1,153.94	1,170.00	1,118.77	1,136.68	1,218.32	1,161.23	1,152.55	1,139.10	1,135.26	1,194.28	1,120.65	1,148.25
2015	1,132.34	1,163.05	1,171.13	1,153.04	1,149.15	1,102.68	1,131.74	1,194.56	1,139.09	1,142.20	1,189.29	1,117.13	1,148.34
2016	1,134.18	1,120.19	1,116.59	1,145.22	1,179.22	1,127.10	1,122.87	1,127.30	1,149.59	1,206.74	1,173.84	1,138.07	1,143.90
2017	1,195.84	1,166.08	1,130.41	1,207.33	1,151.21	1,138.99	1,186.13	1,166.41	1,165.09	1,194.93	1,166.93	1,181.64	1,170.31
Professional and Business Services													
2013	1,129.14	1,152.83	1,147.87	1,145.95	1,154.69	1,225.98	1,174.16	1,174.95	1,205.83	1,174.40	1,182.21	1,218.24	1,174.58
2014	1,189.45	1,225.48	1,223.25	1,204.16	1,179.07	1,207.33	1,152.42	1,146.31	1,155.32	1,165.46	1,190.85	1,159.49	1,181.54
2015	1,178.67	1,201.76	1,201.56	1,172.75	1,166.08	1,151.07	1,173.03	1,206.40	1,164.92	1,174.33	1,206.18	1,167.43	1,181.51
2016	1,191.21	1,200.20	1,179.02	1,174.80	1,180.48	1,142.34	1,148.76	1,139.40	1,145.01	1,181.04	1,138.32	1,142.74	1,162.44
2017	1,119.72	1,113.01	1,108.73	1,171.04	1,123.58	1,144.90	1,185.84	1,147.01	1,136.34	1,158.29	1,156.40	1,186.08	1,146.33
Education and Health Services													
2013	781.49	784.55	770.87	775.20	759.36	774.25	754.61	753.66	765.51	750.48	757.56	758.52	766.36
2014	746.06	759.70	770.56	747.86	750.15	774.89	772.62	775.27	785.63	773.38	811.44	796.95	771.99
2015	778.43	809.92	807.07	784.96	791.81	797.53	798.35	811.06	797.89	801.41	831.79	806.12	800.83
2016	812.64	806.93	807.23	806.73	812.15	788.48	805.46	797.84	810.81	827.37	801.91	820.97	807.54
2017	829.79	825.57	821.74	857.05	828.48	834.95	851.78	841.43	820.47	839.48	831.39	836.42	833.98
Leisure and Hospitality													
2013	415.44	424.64	429.80	416.61	420.48	426.14	420.94	424.87	424.36	412.45	413.64	407.18	419.10
2014	408.84	419.06	429.93	399.33	400.95	414.59	410.69	412.64	409.24	404.18	397.80	401.95	408.34
2015	409.74	419.19	431.48	413.14	412.38	408.58	413.52	431.66	396.72	410.03	388.84	398.00	411.60
2016	401.26	411.57	419.06	396.74	427.78	423.92	432.48	434.02	427.39	445.64	415.15	425.75	422.51
2017	435.21	437.44	448.06	417.45	426.07	442.00	462.44	448.66	445.52	469.50	437.57	452.01	443.52
Other Services													
2013	731.75	747.74	760.24	752.24	738.68	768.50	716.62	717.57	756.34	753.17	778.34	788.19	751.56
2014	772.44	815.45	811.92	805.39	792.21	868.94	825.99	841.59	844.52	785.70	768.42	749.89	807.28
2015	686.29	720.44	728.98	700.43	708.93	730.30	743.87	793.97	768.95	794.61	828.67	771.46	748.37
2016	784.57	774.18	771.87	790.10	824.90	769.90	776.12	802.67	827.00	891.78	821.64	859.01	807.12
2017	860.72	882.73	871.58	944.89	891.64	915.38	967.68	920.83	929.45	947.35	949.78	911.68	916.63

CONNECTICUT
At a Glance

Population:
  2010 census: 3,574,097
  2017 estimate: 3,588,184

Percent change in population:
  2010–2017: 0.4%

Percent change in total nonfarm employment:
  2007–2017: -1.0 %

Industry with the largest growth in employment, 2007–2017 (thousands):
  Education and health services, 46.5

Industry with the largest decline or smallest growth in employment, 2007–2017 (thousands):
  Manufacturing, 28.5

Civilian labor force:
  2010: 1,911,712
  2017: 1,918,576

Unemployment rate and rank among states (highest to lowest):
  2010: 9.1%, 22nd
  2017: 4.7%, 15th

Over-the-year change in unemployment rates:
  2015–2016: -0.6%
  2016–2017: -0.4%

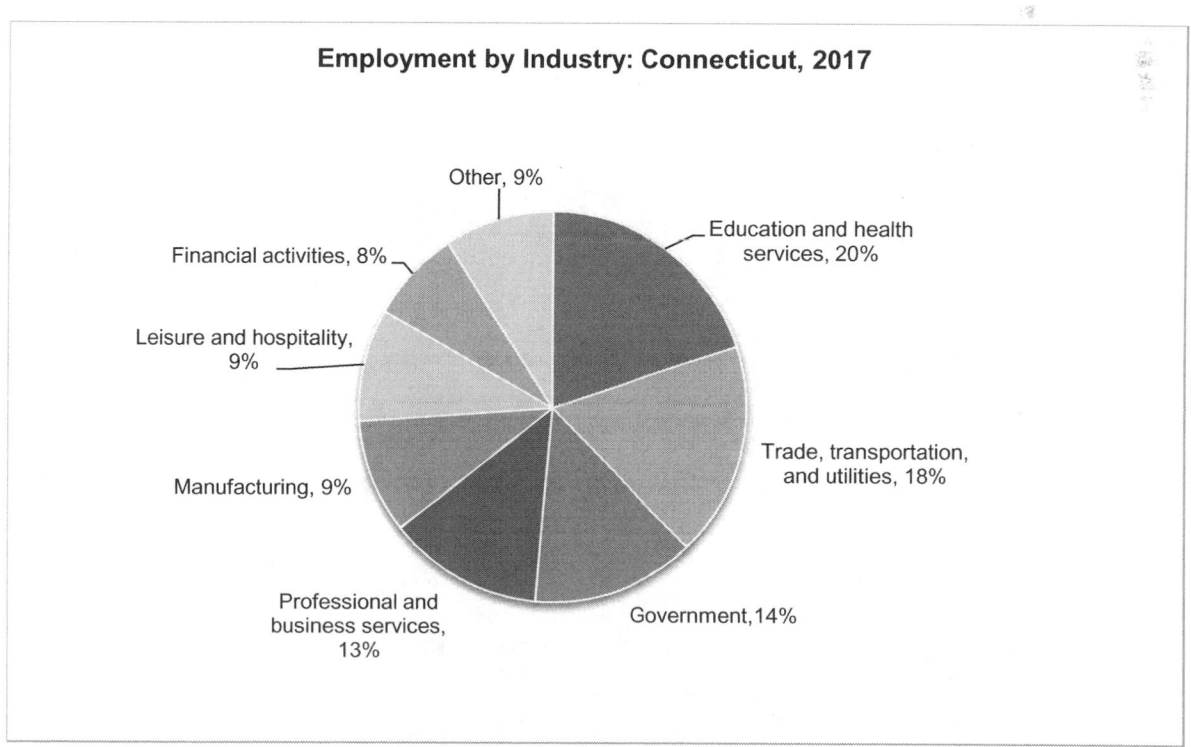

Employment by Industry: Connecticut, 2017

Other, 9%
Education and health services, 20%
Financial activities, 8%
Leisure and hospitality, 9%
Trade, transportation, and utilities, 18%
Manufacturing, 9%
Professional and business services, 13%
Government, 14%

1. Employment by Industry: Connecticut, Selected Years, 2007–2017

(Numbers in thousands, not seasonally adjusted)

Industry and year	January	February	March	April	May	June	July	August	September	October	November	December	Annual average
Total Nonfarm													
2007	1,666.6	1,668.5	1,672.0	1,689.9	1,705.7	1,720.5	1,691.5	1,690.5	1,704.4	1,714.3	1,724.3	1,731.0	1,698.3
2008	1,685.4	1,688.0	1,692.6	1,705.7	1,717.8	1,724.6	1,690.5	1,686.8	1,697.3	1,700.9	1,701.4	1,698.1	1,699.1
2009	1,639.2	1,634.8	1,626.8	1,626.8	1,639.6	1,640.6	1,608.4	1,602.7	1,617.5	1,623.0	1,628.4	1,631.4	1,626.6
2010	1,569.1	1,571.8	1,575.3	1,600.4	1,622.4	1,625.1	1,607.2	1,604.2	1,616.8	1,629.2	1,635.3	1,639.1	1,608.0
2011	1,591.5	1,597.7	1,599.8	1,627.1	1,634.1	1,637.1	1,621.4	1,615.2	1,631.1	1,636.5	1,644.6	1,650.2	1,623.9
2012	1,606.8	1,612.9	1,620.1	1,631.4	1,644.6	1,652.5	1,631.4	1,627.3	1,642.6	1,652.4	1,661.7	1,666.5	1,637.5
2013	1,617.7	1,615.8	1,626.6	1,648.9	1,661.9	1,675.1	1,653.2	1,646.0	1,653.3	1,660.8	1,672.2	1,670.2	1,650.1
2014	1,627.8	1,625.2	1,634.0	1,659.5	1,673.8	1,683.3	1,659.2	1,656.3	1,666.3	1,676.4	1,686.4	1,689.4	1,661.5
2015	1,645.9	1,642.0	1,648.8	1,669.7	1,689.2	1,700.0	1,669.2	1,664.7	1,674.2	1,689.8	1,697.8	1,698.0	1,674.1
2016	1,651.8	1,652.9	1,663.1	1,676.2	1,692.0	1,699.0	1,676.7	1,671.0	1,681.3	1,688.2	1,696.8	1,697.4	1,678.9
2017	1,657.6	1,656.6	1,661.9	1,676.3	1,692.7	1,706.8	1,676.9	1,672.5	1,681.9	1,688.0	1,696.9	1,700.2	1,680.7
Total Private													
2007	1,416.7	1,413.7	1,417.8	1,435.2	1,451.3	1,469.6	1,458.2	1,453.9	1,453.8	1,455.9	1,463.2	1,470.6	1,446.7
2008	1,430.4	1,427.9	1,433.5	1,446.3	1,457.8	1,469.9	1,454.3	1,448.1	1,444.8	1,441.0	1,439.2	1,437.6	1,444.2
2009	1,385.1	1,376.8	1,369.4	1,369.6	1,382.4	1,389.9	1,377.0	1,370.1	1,370.9	1,370.5	1,372.9	1,377.3	1,376.0
2010	1,320.9	1,319.7	1,325.0	1,350.7	1,366.0	1,378.8	1,377.0	1,372.8	1,374.0	1,379.5	1,384.1	1,388.9	1,361.5
2011	1,348.1	1,350.3	1,352.3	1,377.4	1,386.8	1,397.9	1,394.4	1,389.4	1,390.1	1,389.7	1,396.4	1,402.0	1,381.2
2012	1,366.0	1,366.1	1,373.7	1,386.1	1,400.9	1,414.4	1,406.0	1,401.7	1,402.9	1,407.9	1,414.4	1,418.8	1,396.6
2013	1,375.1	1,372.1	1,382.2	1,403.7	1,416.3	1,430.2	1,422.9	1,420.1	1,417.0	1,419.7	1,428.0	1,426.8	1,409.5
2014	1,388.3	1,383.3	1,390.8	1,414.6	1,428.2	1,440.1	1,433.3	1,429.0	1,428.0	1,433.8	1,440.8	1,445.0	1,421.3
2015	1,405.8	1,400.3	1,406.2	1,426.4	1,444.8	1,458.9	1,445.3	1,439.6	1,437.5	1,448.1	1,453.4	1,455.6	1,435.2
2016	1,413.7	1,412.2	1,421.2	1,434.6	1,447.9	1,462.6	1,456.7	1,450.4	1,448.6	1,451.6	1,457.1	1,459.1	1,443.0
2017	1,422.1	1,418.3	1,423.2	1,439.6	1,455.0	1,473.5	1,460.1	1,454.0	1,453.3	1,454.6	1,460.7	1,465.3	1,448.3
Goods Producing													
2007	252.4	250.2	252.0	255.6	258.2	262.2	261.2	261.5	259.8	258.9	258.4	256.3	257.2
2008	249.8	247.7	248.7	252.2	254.2	256.2	254.3	254.1	252.0	249.6	246.2	241.9	250.6
2009	231.1	226.5	224.6	224.5	225.6	226.9	223.9	222.8	222.1	219.9	218.3	216.4	223.6
2010	206.3	204.2	205.3	211.1	213.9	217.1	217.6	217.6	217.4	216.9	216.5	215.1	213.3
2011	208.5	208.2	209.3	213.5	216.0	219.2	219.7	219.9	218.6	217.7	217.7	215.8	215.3
2012	209.8	209.0	209.6	212.2	214.0	216.9	217.0	217.0	215.5	215.8	214.8	214.2	213.8
2013	208.8	207.9	209.0	212.8	215.7	218.1	218.8	218.3	216.8	215.9	214.9	213.1	214.2
2014	207.0	206.0	206.6	211.5	213.8	216.4	217.8	217.9	216.4	216.7	215.5	214.2	213.3
2015	208.7	207.1	208.3	213.4	216.9	219.9	219.4	219.7	218.5	218.9	217.8	216.6	215.4
2016	211.0	209.5	211.1	214.8	217.1	219.9	220.8	220.6	218.4	218.1	217.6	215.9	216.2
2017	210.5	209.7	211.1	215.3	218.6	222.7	222.7	222.6	220.6	222.8	221.7	220.6	218.2
Service-Providing													
2007	1,414.2	1,418.3	1,420.0	1,434.3	1,447.5	1,458.3	1,430.3	1,429.0	1,444.6	1,455.4	1,465.9	1,474.7	1,441.0
2008	1,435.6	1,440.3	1,443.9	1,453.5	1,463.6	1,468.4	1,436.2	1,432.7	1,445.3	1,451.3	1,455.2	1,456.2	1,448.5
2009	1,408.1	1,408.3	1,402.2	1,402.3	1,414.0	1,413.7	1,384.5	1,379.9	1,395.4	1,403.1	1,410.1	1,415.0	1,403.1
2010	1,362.8	1,367.6	1,370.0	1,389.3	1,408.5	1,408.0	1,389.6	1,386.6	1,399.4	1,412.3	1,418.8	1,424.0	1,394.7
2011	1,383.0	1,389.5	1,390.5	1,413.6	1,418.1	1,417.9	1,401.7	1,395.3	1,412.5	1,418.8	1,426.9	1,434.4	1,408.5
2012	1,397.0	1,403.9	1,410.5	1,419.2	1,430.6	1,435.6	1,414.4	1,410.3	1,427.1	1,436.6	1,446.9	1,452.3	1,423.7
2013	1,408.9	1,407.9	1,417.6	1,436.1	1,446.2	1,457.0	1,434.4	1,427.7	1,436.5	1,444.9	1,457.3	1,457.1	1,436.0
2014	1,420.8	1,419.2	1,427.4	1,448.0	1,460.0	1,466.9	1,441.4	1,438.4	1,449.9	1,459.7	1,470.9	1,475.2	1,448.2
2015	1,437.2	1,434.9	1,440.5	1,456.3	1,472.3	1,480.1	1,449.8	1,445.0	1,455.7	1,470.9	1,480.0	1,481.4	1,458.7
2016	1,440.8	1,443.4	1,452.0	1,461.4	1,474.9	1,479.1	1,455.9	1,450.4	1,462.9	1,470.1	1,479.2	1,481.5	1,462.6
2017	1,447.1	1,446.9	1,450.8	1,461.0	1,474.1	1,484.1	1,454.2	1,449.9	1,461.3	1,465.2	1,475.2	1,479.6	1,462.5
Mining and Logging													
2007	0.7	0.6	0.6	0.7	0.7	0.8	0.8	0.8	0.8	0.8	0.8	0.7	0.7
2008	0.7	0.6	0.7	0.7	0.8	0.8	0.8	0.8	0.8	0.8	0.8	0.7	0.8
2009	0.6	0.6	0.6	0.6	0.7	0.7	0.7	0.7	0.7	0.6	0.6	0.6	0.6
2010	0.5	0.5	0.5	0.6	0.6	0.6	0.6	0.6	0.6	0.6	0.6	0.6	0.6
2011	0.5	0.5	0.5	0.5	0.6	0.6	0.6	0.6	0.6	0.6	0.6	0.6	0.6
2012	0.5	0.5	0.5	0.6	0.6	0.6	0.6	0.6	0.6	0.6	0.6	0.5	0.6
2013	0.5	0.5	0.5	0.5	0.6	0.6	0.6	0.6	0.6	0.6	0.6	0.6	0.6
2014	0.5	0.4	0.4	0.5	0.6	0.6	0.6	0.6	0.6	0.6	0.6	0.6	0.6
2015	0.5	0.5	0.5	0.5	0.6	0.6	0.6	0.6	0.6	0.6	0.6	0.6	0.6
2016	0.5	0.5	0.5	0.6	0.6	0.6	0.6	0.6	0.6	0.6	0.6	0.6	0.6
2017	0.5	0.5	0.5	0.5	0.6	0.6	0.6	0.6	0.6	0.6	0.6	0.5	0.6

1. Employment by Industry: Connecticut, Selected Years, 2007–2017—*Continued*

(Numbers in thousands, not seasonally adjusted)

Industry and year	January	February	March	April	May	June	July	August	September	October	November	December	Annual average
Construction													
2007	62.6	60.7	62.4	67.1	69.7	71.9	72.7	72.9	71.9	71.7	71.0	68.8	68.6
2008	63.0	61.9	62.9	66.2	67.5	68.4	68.6	68.4	67.1	65.8	63.5	60.5	65.3
2009	53.8	52.0	51.8	53.7	55.5	56.7	56.8	56.6	56.1	55.2	54.2	52.2	54.6
2010	44.3	42.9	43.6	49.1	50.9	52.3	53.3	53.7	53.1	52.9	52.6	50.9	50.0
2011	45.6	45.2	45.9	50.1	52.1	53.8	54.7	55.0	54.5	54.1	54.2	52.0	51.4
2012	47.1	46.2	47.1	50.0	51.3	52.8	53.9	54.1	53.8	54.2	53.4	52.4	51.4
2013	47.7	46.9	48.0	52.0	54.5	55.7	56.8	57.1	56.7	56.2	55.7	53.5	53.4
2014	48.6	48.0	48.8	53.9	56.5	57.9	59.4	59.7	59.2	59.4	58.3	56.7	55.5
2015	52.0	50.7	51.5	56.4	59.4	60.7	60.8	61.3	60.7	61.7	60.7	59.3	57.9
2016	54.7	53.3	54.9	58.7	60.7	61.9	62.4	62.5	61.4	61.0	60.4	57.8	59.1
2017	53.0	52.3	53.2	57.1	59.7	61.5	61.5	61.6	61.0	62.3	59.7	56.0	58.2
Manufacturing													
2007	189.1	188.9	189.0	187.8	187.8	189.5	187.7	187.8	187.1	186.4	186.0	186.8	187.9
2008	186.1	185.2	185.1	185.3	185.9	187.0	184.9	184.9	184.1	183.0	181.9	180.7	184.5
2009	176.7	173.9	172.2	170.2	169.4	169.5	166.4	165.5	165.3	164.1	163.5	163.6	168.4
2010	161.5	160.8	161.2	161.4	162.4	164.2	163.7	163.3	163.7	163.4	163.3	163.6	162.7
2011	162.4	162.5	162.9	162.9	163.3	164.8	164.4	164.3	163.5	163.0	162.9	163.2	163.3
2012	162.2	162.3	162.0	161.6	162.1	163.5	162.5	162.3	161.1	161.0	160.8	161.3	161.9
2013	160.6	160.5	160.5	160.3	160.6	161.8	161.4	160.6	159.5	159.1	158.6	159.0	160.2
2014	157.9	157.6	157.4	157.1	156.7	157.9	157.8	157.6	156.6	156.7	156.6	156.9	157.2
2015	156.2	155.9	156.3	156.5	156.9	158.6	158.0	157.8	157.2	156.6	156.5	156.7	156.9
2016	155.8	155.7	155.7	155.5	155.8	157.4	157.8	157.5	156.4	156.5	156.6	157.5	156.5
2017	157.0	156.9	157.4	157.7	158.3	160.6	160.6	160.4	159.0	159.9	161.4	164.1	159.4
Trade, Transportation, and Utilities													
2007	307.4	301.5	302.8	302.5	307.6	311.1	304.4	302.9	306.6	308.8	316.4	323.1	307.9
2008	310.5	303.9	304.7	304.0	306.7	308.8	301.9	300.4	303.4	303.7	308.2	312.2	305.7
2009	296.1	290.1	288.1	283.4	288.9	291.1	283.6	282.5	285.8	287.5	293.0	297.6	289.0
2010	283.3	278.3	279.1	279.3	285.3	289.1	284.0	283.3	284.9	288.4	294.6	300.3	285.8
2011	286.5	283.0	283.2	287.0	288.9	291.6	285.9	285.3	287.5	289.2	295.3	301.5	288.7
2012	290.4	285.2	287.0	286.3	291.0	293.7	287.2	286.7	289.9	293.1	300.7	304.1	291.3
2013	291.4	285.6	288.3	290.7	293.5	296.6	290.6	290.7	292.9	295.9	303.1	307.5	293.9
2014	294.5	289.6	290.9	292.8	295.6	298.1	292.0	291.2	294.1	297.2	304.1	309.0	295.8
2015	295.6	290.1	291.3	292.2	297.2	300.4	292.5	291.6	295.4	299.8	307.4	311.7	297.1
2016	298.0	293.5	294.7	294.8	298.4	299.3	294.2	292.9	296.1	298.8	306.1	311.0	298.2
2017	299.1	292.9	292.7	293.3	297.7	299.7	293.3	292.3	296.7	298.1	306.2	310.8	297.7
Wholesale Trade													
2007	67.5	67.5	67.5	67.7	67.9	68.6	68.5	68.6	68.7	68.7	68.7	69.5	68.3
2008	69.2	69.1	69.5	69.4	69.8	70.0	69.4	69.1	68.9	68.7	68.6	68.4	69.2
2009	67.2	66.5	65.9	65.2	65.1	65.1	64.6	64.4	64.2	63.7	63.4	63.6	64.9
2010	61.9	61.6	61.9	62.3	62.7	63.3	63.1	63.2	62.8	62.7	63.1	63.4	62.7
2011	62.2	62.3	62.4	63.0	63.2	63.7	63.5	63.4	63.1	62.9	62.8	63.1	63.0
2012	62.5	62.5	62.7	63.0	63.3	63.7	63.3	63.1	62.8	63.3	63.1	63.1	63.0
2013	62.3	62.2	62.6	62.8	63.0	63.4	63.3	63.1	62.9	63.0	63.0	63.2	62.9
2014	62.3	62.1	62.3	62.7	63.0	63.3	63.1	62.9	62.6	62.6	62.5	62.8	62.7
2015	62.1	62.0	62.2	62.5	62.9	63.2	62.8	62.5	62.3	62.3	62.1	62.3	62.4
2016	61.7	61.9	62.1	62.6	62.8	63.1	63.0	62.9	62.7	62.3	62.3	62.7	62.5
2017	62.2	62.0	62.1	62.3	62.7	63.2	62.9	62.8	62.6	62.4	63.2	64.0	62.7
Retail Trade													
2007	191.1	185.5	186.7	186.4	190.6	192.9	190.4	190.0	188.7	190.7	198.0	202.7	191.1
2008	192.9	186.5	186.8	185.8	187.9	189.5	186.7	186.8	185.1	185.6	190.1	193.3	188.1
2009	181.2	176.3	175.2	173.9	177.1	179.5	176.5	176.8	175.9	178.0	183.7	186.9	178.4
2010	176.6	172.0	172.5	173.6	177.0	179.8	178.7	178.3	176.2	179.6	184.9	188.9	178.2
2011	179.1	175.4	175.3	178.0	179.2	180.9	179.1	179.5	177.9	179.8	185.7	190.3	180.0
2012	181.8	176.7	178.0	177.9	180.9	182.8	180.5	180.5	179.1	181.7	189.0	191.3	181.7
2013	181.8	177.1	178.0	179.8	181.9	184.1	182.4	183.2	181.0	183.8	190.4	193.4	183.1
2014	183.9	179.4	180.2	181.6	183.5	185.5	183.6	183.3	181.7	184.4	190.6	193.6	184.3
2015	184.2	179.4	180.1	180.6	184.2	186.6	183.2	183.6	182.1	185.6	191.8	194.5	184.7
2016	185.0	180.6	181.6	181.6	183.8	185.4	184.0	183.7	181.8	184.6	190.6	192.5	184.6
2017	185.5	179.9	179.6	180.9	183.0	184.4	183.0	182.5	180.4	181.2	187.3	189.6	183.1

1. Employment by Industry: Connecticut, Selected Years, 2007–2017—*Continued*

(Numbers in thousands, not seasonally adjusted)

Industry and year	January	February	March	April	May	June	July	August	September	October	November	December	Annual average
Transportation and Utilities													
2007	48.8	48.5	48.6	48.4	49.1	49.6	45.5	44.3	49.2	49.4	49.7	50.9	48.5
2008	48.4	48.3	48.4	48.8	49.0	49.3	45.8	44.5	49.4	49.4	49.5	50.5	48.4
2009	47.7	47.3	47.0	44.3	46.7	46.5	42.5	41.3	45.7	45.8	45.9	47.1	45.7
2010	44.8	44.7	44.7	43.4	45.6	46.0	42.2	41.8	45.9	46.1	46.6	48.0	45.0
2011	45.2	45.3	45.5	46.0	46.5	47.0	43.3	42.4	46.5	46.5	46.8	48.1	45.8
2012	46.1	46.0	46.3	45.4	46.8	47.2	43.4	43.1	48.0	48.1	48.6	49.7	46.6
2013	47.3	46.3	47.7	48.1	48.6	49.1	44.9	44.4	49.0	49.1	49.7	50.9	47.9
2014	48.3	48.1	48.4	48.5	49.1	49.3	45.3	45.0	49.8	50.2	51.0	52.6	48.8
2015	49.3	48.7	49.0	49.1	50.1	50.6	46.5	45.5	51.0	51.9	53.5	54.9	50.0
2016	51.3	51.0	51.0	50.6	51.8	50.8	47.2	46.3	51.6	51.9	53.2	55.8	51.0
2017	51.4	51.0	51.0	50.1	52.0	52.1	47.4	47.0	53.7	54.5	55.7	57.2	51.9
Information													
2007	37.5	37.9	37.7	38.0	39.0	38.6	38.8	38.9	39.2	39.0	38.1	38.2	38.4
2008	37.9	38.2	37.9	38.5	38.6	38.6	37.9	38.1	37.1	36.9	36.9	37.0	37.8
2009	36.4	36.3	35.5	35.1	34.6	34.5	34.3	34.0	33.3	32.7	32.8	32.3	34.3
2010	31.8	31.7	31.6	31.5	31.7	31.6	31.6	32.0	31.8	31.6	31.7	31.8	31.7
2011	31.5	31.5	31.5	31.4	31.2	31.3	31.4	31.4	31.1	31.0	31.3	31.1	31.3
2012	31.3	31.5	30.9	30.9	31.2	31.0	31.2	31.6	31.4	31.4	31.9	31.4	31.3
2013	31.5	32.3	32.0	31.6	32.2	32.3	32.4	32.4	31.8	31.8	32.1	32.1	32.0
2014	31.9	31.8	32.0	32.0	32.0	32.0	32.2	32.4	31.7	31.4	32.6	32.5	32.0
2015	32.1	32.1	32.2	32.4	32.5	32.6	32.5	32.8	32.3	32.3	32.7	32.6	32.4
2016	32.3	32.4	32.2	32.1	32.2	32.4	32.6	33.0	32.2	32.4	32.4	32.0	32.4
2017	31.7	31.9	31.7	31.7	31.6	31.7	31.5	31.6	31.3	31.0	31.0	30.6	31.4
Financial Activities													
2007	144.9	144.4	144.1	144.1	144.4	146.3	146.2	145.7	144.0	143.6	143.5	144.1	144.6
2008	143.0	143.4	144.0	143.2	143.5	145.3	144.8	144.9	142.8	141.9	142.0	142.0	143.4
2009	139.7	139.3	139.3	137.7	137.5	138.4	138.2	137.6	135.8	135.8	135.9	135.9	137.6
2010	134.0	134.1	134.5	134.0	134.3	136.2	136.7	137.0	135.2	135.2	135.5	135.8	135.2
2011	135.4	135.2	135.2	134.8	134.9	135.5	136.6	136.3	134.3	133.8	133.9	133.9	135.0
2012	132.9	132.7	132.9	132.5	133.0	134.6	134.8	134.1	132.7	132.4	132.1	132.2	133.1
2013	131.7	131.1	130.8	130.5	130.2	132.1	132.3	131.5	129.5	129.1	129.0	129.2	130.6
2014	128.1	127.7	127.5	127.4	128.3	129.7	130.3	130.0	128.7	128.9	129.0	129.3	128.7
2015	128.9	128.8	129.0	129.4	129.9	131.6	131.9	131.7	129.9	129.9	129.9	130.0	130.1
2016	129.2	128.9	129.4	129.3	129.5	131.1	131.0	130.6	129.0	128.8	128.5	128.4	129.5
2017	127.9	127.4	127.3	127.3	127.6	129.5	129.7	129.2	127.4	127.1	128.0	127.4	128.0
Professional and Business Services													
2007	203.6	204.7	205.9	210.4	212.0	215.8	211.9	212.7	212.2	212.7	213.3	215.0	210.9
2008	208.2	207.9	209.6	212.5	212.2	215.0	211.8	211.0	209.5	207.3	205.6	204.5	209.6
2009	197.1	194.5	193.3	195.2	194.5	195.6	192.7	193.4	192.7	193.5	193.7	194.8	194.3
2010	184.0	186.1	187.2	195.3	195.6	198.1	197.6	197.3	197.0	198.2	197.8	198.2	194.4
2011	192.5	194.4	194.0	201.1	200.8	202.9	202.3	201.9	202.3	203.2	204.9	205.2	200.5
2012	198.7	199.2	202.8	207.2	207.3	209.4	208.8	208.6	208.5	208.6	209.1	208.5	206.4
2013	200.8	202.9	203.5	209.0	210.0	212.6	212.1	213.6	212.5	213.0	213.5	212.6	209.7
2014	206.0	207.2	208.2	214.9	216.7	218.3	216.9	216.7	215.7	217.0	217.7	217.9	214.4
2015	212.0	213.5	213.9	219.0	220.4	222.7	220.4	219.8	218.6	220.8	221.0	220.0	218.5
2016	212.3	213.3	214.7	219.4	219.2	222.1	220.6	220.2	219.7	219.7	219.4	219.6	218.4
2017	212.6	213.1	214.9	219.1	218.8	221.8	220.2	219.4	218.9	219.0	218.0	220.0	218.0
Education and Health Services													
2007	282.1	286.6	285.2	289.3	287.5	285.9	283.8	281.3	288.5	293.0	294.7	295.4	287.8
2008	290.7	295.8	295.3	297.9	296.2	294.4	292.2	289.8	296.8	302.2	304.6	304.7	296.7
2009	299.1	304.3	301.6	302.8	301.9	299.0	298.4	296.3	302.3	306.7	307.5	308.4	302.4
2010	301.8	304.9	304.4	308.8	307.3	304.1	302.9	300.6	308.0	312.8	313.9	313.8	306.9
2011	310.1	313.0	312.5	315.8	314.7	310.9	308.8	306.7	314.0	315.8	316.9	317.2	313.0
2012	312.6	317.5	316.6	317.8	317.9	314.9	311.9	310.1	317.9	321.2	322.3	324.1	317.1
2013	315.9	318.8	319.8	323.0	321.1	318.6	315.4	314.4	321.5	324.7	327.1	324.5	320.4
2014	319.7	321.1	321.5	326.2	324.9	322.2	319.5	318.5	325.8	328.9	330.6	330.7	324.1
2015	324.8	326.2	325.3	328.5	327.8	325.8	322.2	320.0	325.5	330.4	331.6	331.5	326.6
2016	325.5	328.7	329.3	330.0	329.2	327.3	326.1	324.2	331.7	334.2	336.1	335.4	329.8
2017	330.3	333.9	333.2	335.6	335.8	333.6	328.0	327.0	334.4	339.1	340.7	340.4	334.3

1. Employment by Industry: Connecticut, Selected Years, 2007–2017—*Continued*

(Numbers in thousands, not seasonally adjusted)

Industry and year	January	February	March	April	May	June	July	August	September	October	November	December	Annual average
Leisure and Hospitality													
2007	125.4	125.2	126.5	131.4	138.5	144.4	146.4	146.0	139.5	136.1	135.0	134.5	135.7
2008	127.5	128.3	130.3	134.8	142.7	147.1	147.4	146.1	140.7	136.8	133.3	133.0	137.3
2009	124.2	124.9	125.9	129.9	138.1	142.2	143.8	141.9	137.8	133.7	131.0	130.9	133.7
2010	120.3	121.3	123.3	130.8	137.4	141.0	144.4	143.1	139.1	135.8	133.6	133.3	133.6
2011	124.3	125.7	127.1	133.6	139.7	144.8	147.9	146.4	142.3	139.5	136.6	137.1	137.1
2012	130.4	131.0	133.8	138.6	145.4	151.6	152.1	150.9	145.3	143.3	141.2	142.3	142.2
2013	134.3	132.7	137.4	144.5	151.4	156.8	157.9	156.2	150.2	147.8	146.6	145.8	146.8
2014	139.8	138.7	142.3	147.4	154.0	159.4	160.1	158.1	152.5	150.4	148.1	148.0	149.9
2015	141.1	140.0	143.1	148.4	156.1	161.2	161.4	158.5	153.3	152.1	149.1	149.1	151.1
2016	142.1	142.6	145.8	150.0	157.7	164.2	165.0	163.1	156.9	155.1	152.7	152.0	153.9
2017	146.1	145.7	148.2	152.8	159.8	167.9	168.0	165.7	158.7	153.7	150.3	151.1	155.7
Other Services													
2007	63.4	63.2	63.6	63.9	64.1	65.3	65.5	64.9	64.0	63.8	63.8	64.0	64.1
2008	62.8	62.7	63.0	63.2	63.7	64.5	64.0	63.7	62.5	62.6	62.4	62.3	63.1
2009	61.4	60.9	61.1	61.0	61.3	62.2	62.1	61.6	61.1	60.7	60.7	61.0	61.3
2010	59.4	59.1	59.6	59.9	60.5	61.6	62.2	61.9	60.6	60.6	60.5	60.6	60.5
2011	59.3	59.3	59.5	60.2	60.6	61.7	61.8	61.5	60.0	59.5	59.8	60.2	60.3
2012	59.9	60.0	60.1	60.6	61.1	62.3	63.0	62.7	61.7	62.1	62.3	62.0	61.5
2013	60.7	60.8	61.4	61.6	62.2	63.1	63.4	63.0	61.8	61.5	61.7	62.0	61.9
2014	61.3	61.2	61.8	62.4	62.9	64.0	64.5	64.2	63.1	63.3	63.2	63.4	62.9
2015	62.6	62.5	63.1	63.1	64.0	64.7	65.0	65.5	64.0	63.9	63.9	64.1	63.9
2016	63.3	63.3	64.0	64.2	64.6	66.3	66.4	65.8	64.6	64.5	64.3	64.8	64.7
2017	63.9	63.7	64.1	64.5	65.1	66.6	66.7	66.2	65.3	63.8	64.8	64.4	64.9
Government													
2007	249.9	254.8	254.2	254.7	254.4	250.9	233.3	236.6	250.6	258.4	261.1	260.4	251.6
2008	255.0	260.1	259.1	259.4	260.0	254.7	236.2	238.7	252.5	259.9	262.2	260.5	254.9
2009	254.1	258.0	257.4	257.2	257.2	250.7	231.4	232.6	246.6	252.5	255.5	254.1	250.6
2010	248.2	252.1	250.3	249.7	256.4	246.3	230.2	231.4	242.8	249.7	251.2	250.2	246.5
2011	243.4	247.4	247.5	249.7	247.3	239.2	227.0	225.8	241.0	246.8	248.2	248.2	242.6
2012	240.8	246.8	246.4	245.3	243.7	238.1	225.4	225.6	239.7	244.5	247.3	247.7	240.9
2013	242.6	243.7	244.4	245.2	245.6	244.9	230.3	225.9	236.3	241.1	244.2	243.4	240.6
2014	239.5	241.9	243.2	244.9	245.6	243.2	225.9	227.3	238.3	242.6	245.6	244.4	240.2
2015	240.1	241.7	242.6	243.3	244.4	241.1	223.9	225.1	236.7	241.7	244.4	242.4	239.0
2016	238.1	240.7	241.9	241.6	244.1	236.4	220.0	220.6	232.7	236.6	239.7	238.3	235.9
2017	235.5	238.3	238.7	236.7	237.7	233.3	216.8	218.5	228.6	233.4	236.2	234.9	232.4

2. Average Weekly Hours by Selected Industry: Connecticut, 2013–2017

(Not seasonally adjusted)

Industry and year	January	February	March	April	May	June	July	August	September	October	November	December	Annual average
Total Private													
2013	33.2	33.0	33.2	33.6	33.6	34.0	33.6	33.6	34.1	33.7	33.6	33.6	33.6
2014	33.2	32.8	33.6	33.6	33.5	33.8	33.7	33.8	33.9	33.8	34.2	33.8	33.6
2015	33.5	33.4	33.6	33.5	33.3	33.3	33.4	34.0	33.4	33.7	33.8	33.6	33.5
2016	33.2	33.1	33.2	33.4	34.0	33.6	33.6	33.6	33.9	34.2	33.7	33.7	33.6
2017	33.7	33.0	32.9	33.7	33.6	33.6	33.9	33.8	33.9	34.1	34.0	34.0	33.7
Goods-Producing													
2013	39.5	38.6	39.6	39.7	39.6	40.0	39.4	40.3	40.4	39.8	39.7	39.6	39.7
2014	39.3	37.8	39.7	39.2	39.4	39.8	39.5	39.3	39.6	39.7	40.5	39.8	39.5
2015	39.6	38.9	39.9	39.4	39.2	39.1	39.1	39.9	39.2	39.7	40.2	40.2	39.5
2016	39.8	39.2	39.7	39.7	40.9	40.6	40.3	40.1	40.6	40.3	40.2	39.4	40.1
2017	38.9	38.1	38.3	39.0	39.0	39.1	39.2	39.1	39.2	39.5	39.3	39.9	39.1
Construction													
2013	38.7	37.6	38.7	38.8	39.1	37.9	38.6	39.8	39.4	37.7	37.7	35.9	38.3
2014	36.7	34.5	36.2	36.5	37.4	37.6	38.0	38.1	38.8	38.5	39.1	37.9	37.5
2015	38.2	36.3	38.6	39.0	39.7	38.8	39.6	39.7	38.6	40.2	39.2	39.8	39.0
2016	38.6	37.2	38.4	38.4	40.2	39.5	39.0	38.8	39.9	38.8	38.7	37.0	38.7
2017	36.8	35.8	36.1	37.5	38.5	38.9	37.7	38.3	38.3	37.5	38.3	37.4	37.6
Manfacturing													
2013	39.8	38.9	39.9	40.0	39.8	40.6	39.6	40.4	40.7	40.4	40.4	40.9	40.1
2014	40.3	39.0	40.4	39.7	39.8	40.3	39.8	39.6	39.8	40.1	41.0	40.5	40.0
2015	40.1	40.0	40.6	39.8	39.1	39.3	38.9	40.0	39.6	40.2	41.3	41.0	40.0
2016	40.8	40.5	40.8	40.8	41.5	41.3	41.2	40.9	41.0	41.2	41.1	40.9	41.0
2017	40.1	39.4	39.4	39.9	39.5	39.5	40.2	39.7	39.8	40.6	39.9	40.9	39.9
Trade, Transportation, and Utilities													
2013	33.7	33.5	33.8	34.0	34.0	34.0	33.7	33.6	33.8	33.4	33.4	33.9	33.7
2014	33.1	32.2	33.0	32.9	33.0	33.2	33.5	33.5	33.7	33.1	33.3	33.5	33.2
2015	32.6	32.4	32.7	33.0	32.9	32.8	33.1	33.4	33.6	33.4	32.8	33.1	33.0
2016	32.4	32.6	32.5	32.6	33.1	33.1	32.8	32.8	33.3	33.2	32.7	33.0	32.8
2017	32.4	31.9	31.3	32.2	32.2	32.3	32.7	32.4	32.9	32.5	32.9	32.9	32.4
Financial Activities													
2013	36.6	37.3	37.2	37.1	36.9	37.7	36.5	36.7	37.9	37.1	37.2	37.9	37.2
2014	37.3	38.2	38.3	37.2	37.5	38.2	37.4	37.8	38.0	38.3	38.9	38.3	38.0
2015	38.2	39.1	39.0	38.2	38.1	38.1	37.9	39.0	37.9	38.1	39.4	37.5	38.4
2016	37.2	37.5	37.5	37.4	38.4	37.1	37.1	36.8	37.1	38.6	37.1	36.9	37.4
2017	38.0	36.5	36.5	38.2	36.9	36.7	38.0	37.0	37.0	38.0	37.0	36.9	37.2
Professional and Business Services													
2013	33.7	33.7	34.1	35.0	35.0	35.8	34.7	34.2	35.7	35.0	34.5	34.7	34.7
2014	33.7	34.2	35.0	36.0	35.5	35.9	35.8	35.4	36.0	36.3	36.4	35.5	35.5
2015	34.8	34.9	35.1	34.7	34.7	34.8	34.6	35.2	34.2	34.7	35.2	35.0	34.8
2016	34.3	34.6	34.5	34.9	35.6	35.2	35.1	34.9	34.8	35.6	34.8	34.8	34.9
2017	35.4	34.6	34.6	35.5	35.7	35.8	36.1	35.7	35.5	35.5	34.9	34.6	35.3
Education and Health Services													
2013	31.2	31.2	31.2	31.3	31.1	31.4	31.3	31.2	31.4	31.2	31.2	31.0	31.2
2014	31.3	30.9	31.2	31.2	31.2	31.3	31.4	31.7	31.4	31.4	31.4	31.2	31.3
2015	31.4	31.1	31.2	31.2	31.0	31.2	31.4	31.7	31.3	31.5	31.5	31.1	31.3
2016	31.5	31.1	31.4	31.4	31.6	31.5	31.9	31.9	32.2	32.1	32.3	32.2	31.8
2017	32.2	31.9	31.9	32.2	32.2	32.3	32.5	32.5	32.5	32.4	32.8	32.5	32.3
Leisure and Hospitality													
2013	24.5	24.4	24.9	26.0	26.2	26.3	26.8	26.8	26.7	26.1	25.7	24.8	25.8
2014	24.6	24.1	25.0	25.6	25.6	25.2	25.7	26.2	26.1	26.0	26.2	25.7	25.5
2015	25.3	25.0	25.5	26.1	26.0	25.8	26.0	26.5	25.6	26.0	25.8	25.7	25.8
2016	24.8	25.4	25.6	26.7	26.7	26.3	26.4	26.0	25.7	25.9	25.2	24.9	25.8
2017	24.6	23.8	24.0	25.0	25.4	25.4	26.1	25.7	25.7	25.9	25.9	25.9	25.3
Other Services													
2013	30.5	30.2	30.0	29.8	30.5	31.1	31.7	31.7	31.6	31.3	31.7	30.7	30.9
2014	31.0	30.0	31.0	30.7	30.9	31.2	30.5	30.5	30.2	28.9	30.2	29.9	30.4
2015	29.2	29.2	28.9	29.0	28.8	28.9	29.8	29.5	29.5	30.4	30.6	31.1	29.6
2016	30.5	30.4	30.6	31.4	30.9	30.1	30.7	31.9	32.2	31.9	31.6	31.6	31.2
2017	31.7	30.6	31.7	32.0	32.3	32.3	32.0	32.6	32.1	32.6	32.0	32.3	32.0

3. Average Hourly Earnings by Selected Industry: Connecticut, 2013–2017

(Dollars, not seasonally adjusted)

Industry and year	January	February	March	April	May	June	July	August	September	October	November	December	Annual average
Total Private													
2013	28.33	28.32	28.01	28.08	27.89	28.07	27.81	27.78	27.93	27.71	27.59	28.02	27.96
2014	27.83	28.40	28.15	27.98	27.82	28.13	27.90	27.98	28.26	28.32	28.66	28.47	28.16
2015	28.54	29.13	29.04	28.73	28.68	28.75	28.79	29.35	29.49	29.49	29.89	29.80	29.14
2016	30.28	30.32	30.10	30.52	30.71	30.04	30.18	30.39	30.38	30.95	30.57	30.66	30.43
2017	31.36	31.30	31.39	31.63	31.03	30.78	31.08	30.82	31.00	31.47	30.95	31.18	31.16
Goods-Producing													
2013	30.50	30.22	29.95	29.68	29.93	29.97	30.09	29.91	30.18	29.96	30.18	30.31	30.07
2014	30.27	30.41	30.02	30.05	30.14	30.53	30.38	30.35	30.47	30.47	30.82	30.91	30.41
2015	31.01	30.88	30.84	30.74	30.52	30.27	30.61	31.00	31.25	31.39	31.55	31.67	30.98
2016	31.87	32.22	31.94	31.90	31.89	31.60	31.50	31.20	31.10	30.90	30.55	30.56	31.43
2017	31.04	31.42	31.20	30.47	31.06	31.19	31.04	31.50	31.52	31.90	31.92	31.96	31.36
Construction													
2013	29.63	29.72	29.34	28.00	29.47	29.25	29.29	29.61	30.08	29.71	29.65	30.39	29.58
2014	29.95	30.87	30.20	30.13	30.34	30.25	31.06	31.24	30.67	31.11	30.72	31.30	30.68
2015	31.28	30.72	31.84	31.31	31.05	30.76	31.19	30.78	30.95	31.37	31.07	30.93	31.10
2016	31.29	31.18	31.20	30.86	30.51	30.44	30.57	30.69	30.83	30.85	30.62	31.17	30.83
2017	31.24	31.70	31.98	31.81	30.76	30.99	31.15	31.88	31.13	31.65	31.75	31.23	31.43
Manfacturing													
2013	30.70	30.32	30.07	29.87	30.01	30.10	30.26	29.93	30.15	29.99	30.32	30.25	30.16
2014	30.36	30.27	29.92	30.01	30.04	30.59	30.06	29.95	30.34	30.18	30.88	30.80	30.29
2015	30.93	31.23	30.60	30.67	30.32	30.09	30.38	30.92	31.23	31.28	31.60	31.81	30.93
2016	31.90	32.41	32.05	32.15	32.34	31.98	31.78	31.28	31.04	30.80	30.43	30.27	31.53
2017	30.81	31.17	30.80	30.17	30.96	31.06	30.75	31.13	31.47	31.81	31.81	32.01	31.17
Trade, Transportation, and Utilities													
2013	25.31	25.06	24.32	24.59	24.22	24.41	24.25	24.11	24.21	24.02	23.39	23.67	24.29
2014	23.52	23.89	23.41	24.03	23.70	23.84	23.88	23.64	24.12	24.15	24.21	23.85	23.86
2015	24.45	25.08	24.57	24.30	24.53	24.23	24.18	24.23	24.89	25.01	25.29	25.17	24.67
2016	26.08	26.40	26.42	27.09	26.97	26.21	26.67	26.43	26.68	27.34	26.20	25.77	26.52
2017	26.78	26.82	27.22	27.20	26.76	26.35	26.80	26.24	26.36	26.41	25.99	26.01	26.57
Financial Activities													
2013	40.95	40.74	41.71	43.33	42.66	44.08	43.50	43.44	44.62	43.44	43.17	43.93	42.97
2014	43.82	44.36	44.95	44.20	43.89	45.07	43.84	43.29	43.24	43.00	44.21	42.56	43.87
2015	42.42	43.82	44.04	43.07	43.31	43.61	44.33	46.01	44.45	44.49	44.79	44.95	44.11
2016	44.56	43.39	42.31	45.62	45.89	43.88	44.33	46.15	44.49	47.30	45.57	44.58	44.85
2017	47.54	46.31	47.21	49.68	47.12	46.06	47.10	46.75	46.33	48.17	45.94	46.04	47.03
Professional and Business Services													
2013	30.82	31.00	30.82	30.45	30.47	30.33	30.10	30.40	30.48	30.39	30.56	30.98	30.56
2014	31.42	32.51	32.25	30.98	31.10	31.61	31.20	31.77	32.23	32.33	32.22	32.52	31.84
2015	32.07	32.67	33.10	33.11	32.76	33.84	33.97	34.71	34.50	33.96	34.46	33.95	33.60
2016	35.43	35.27	35.10	34.73	35.35	34.95	34.87	34.89	35.23	35.11	35.00	36.09	35.17
2017	36.36	35.91	36.24	35.99	35.41	35.39	35.78	35.00	35.69	36.09	35.67	35.90	35.78
Education and Health Services													
2013	25.89	25.74	25.24	25.31	25.15	25.01	24.98	25.03	25.03	25.02	24.91	25.38	25.22
2014	24.73	25.07	24.86	25.01	24.84	24.84	25.08	25.31	25.25	25.37	25.59	25.91	25.16
2015	25.72	26.12	25.94	26.05	26.06	26.18	26.05	26.06	26.45	26.39	26.67	27.10	26.23
2016	27.20	27.31	27.41	27.48	27.58	27.57	27.80	28.19	28.33	28.24	28.83	28.81	27.91
2017	28.76	28.81	28.66	28.95	28.56	28.56	28.44	28.55	28.72	28.73	28.43	28.82	28.67
Leisure and Hospitality													
2013	15.59	15.70	15.59	15.41	15.37	14.99	14.89	14.74	15.13	15.15	15.15	15.32	15.23
2014	15.07	15.45	15.34	15.45	15.36	15.37	15.31	15.42	15.62	15.98	16.07	16.10	15.55
2015	16.13	16.49	16.30	16.44	16.37	16.02	15.81	15.89	15.93	16.33	16.60	16.63	16.24
2016	16.75	16.94	16.66	16.63	16.66	16.21	16.23	16.35	16.27	16.60	16.84	17.10	16.59
2017	17.20	17.52	17.49	17.61	17.63	17.06	16.96	16.94	16.99	17.22	17.35	17.80	17.30
Other Services													
2013	21.42	21.93	21.28	21.48	21.72	21.29	20.81	21.03	21.42	21.64	21.66	21.97	21.47
2014	21.97	22.56	23.32	22.72	23.01	22.37	22.17	22.15	22.49	22.14	22.51	22.46	22.49
2015	22.27	22.66	22.19	21.68	22.23	21.98	20.95	21.13	21.58	22.24	22.34	22.08	21.94
2016	22.30	22.42	22.70	22.66	23.28	22.80	22.56	22.74	23.02	23.53	23.95	24.18	23.02
2017	24.82	25.42	24.93	25.04	25.12	24.74	25.46	24.78	25.26	25.21	24.95	25.62	25.11

4. Average Weekly Earnings by Selected Industry: Connecticut, 2013–2017

(Dollars, not seasonally adjusted)

Industry and year	January	February	March	April	May	June	July	August	September	October	November	December	Annual average
Total Private													
2013	940.56	934.56	929.93	943.49	937.10	954.38	934.42	933.41	952.41	933.83	927.02	941.47	939.46
2014	923.96	931.52	945.84	940.13	931.97	950.79	940.23	945.72	958.01	957.22	980.17	962.29	946.18
2015	956.09	972.94	975.74	962.46	955.04	957.38	961.59	997.90	984.97	993.81	1,010.28	1,001.28	976.19
2016	1,005.30	1,003.59	999.32	1,019.37	1,044.14	1,009.34	1,014.05	1,021.10	1,029.88	1,058.49	1,030.21	1,033.24	1,022.45
2017	1,056.83	1,032.90	1,032.73	1,065.93	1,042.61	1,034.21	1,053.61	1,041.72	1,050.90	1,073.13	1,052.30	1,060.12	1,050.09
Goods-Producing													
2013	1,204.75	1,166.49	1,186.02	1,178.30	1,185.23	1,198.80	1,185.55	1,205.37	1,219.27	1,192.41	1,198.15	1,200.28	1,193.78
2014	1,189.61	1,149.50	1,191.79	1,177.96	1,187.52	1,215.09	1,200.01	1,192.76	1,206.61	1,209.66	1,248.21	1,230.22	1,201.20
2015	1,228.00	1,201.23	1,230.52	1,211.16	1,196.38	1,183.56	1,196.85	1,236.90	1,225.00	1,246.18	1,268.31	1,273.13	1,223.71
2016	1,268.43	1,263.02	1,268.02	1,266.43	1,304.30	1,282.96	1,269.45	1,251.12	1,262.66	1,245.27	1,228.11	1,204.06	1,260.34
2017	1,207.46	1,197.10	1,194.96	1,188.33	1,211.34	1,219.53	1,216.77	1,231.65	1,235.58	1,260.05	1,254.46	1,275.20	1,226.18
Construction													
2013	1,146.68	1,117.47	1,135.46	1,120.54	1,152.28	1,108.58	1,130.59	1,178.48	1,185.15	1,120.07	1,117.81	1,091.00	1,132.91
2014	1,099.17	1,065.02	1,093.24	1,099.75	1,134.72	1,137.40	1,180.28	1,190.24	1,190.00	1,197.74	1,201.15	1,186.27	1,150.50
2015	1,194.90	1,115.14	1,229.02	1,221.09	1,232.69	1,193.49	1,235.12	1,221.97	1,194.67	1,261.07	1,217.94	1,231.01	1,212.90
2016	1,207.79	1,159.90	1,198.08	1,185.02	1,226.50	1,202.38	1,192.23	1,190.77	1,230.12	1,196.98	1,184.99	1,153.29	1,193.12
2017	1,149.63	1,134.86	1,154.48	1,192.88	1,184.26	1,205.51	1,174.36	1,221.00	1,192.28	1,186.88	1,216.03	1,168.00	1,181.77
Manfacturing													
2013	1,221.86	1,179.45	1,199.79	1,194.80	1,194.40	1,222.06	1,198.30	1,209.17	1,227.11	1,211.60	1,224.93	1,237.23	1,209.42
2014	1,223.51	1,180.53	1,208.77	1,191.40	1,195.59	1,232.78	1,196.39	1,186.02	1,207.53	1,210.22	1,266.08	1,247.40	1,211.60
2015	1,240.29	1,249.20	1,242.36	1,220.67	1,185.51	1,182.54	1,181.78	1,236.80	1,236.71	1,257.46	1,305.08	1,304.21	1,237.20
2016	1,301.52	1,312.61	1,307.64	1,311.72	1,342.11	1,320.77	1,309.34	1,279.35	1,272.64	1,268.96	1,250.67	1,238.04	1,292.73
2017	1,235.48	1,228.10	1,213.52	1,203.78	1,222.92	1,226.87	1,236.15	1,235.86	1,252.51	1,291.49	1,269.22	1,309.21	1,243.68
Trade, Transportation, and Utilities													
2013	852.95	839.51	822.02	836.06	823.48	829.94	817.23	810.10	818.30	802.27	781.23	802.41	818.57
2014	778.51	769.26	772.53	790.59	782.10	791.49	799.98	791.94	812.84	799.37	806.19	798.98	792.15
2015	797.07	812.59	803.44	801.90	807.04	794.74	800.36	809.28	836.30	835.33	829.51	833.13	814.11
2016	844.99	860.64	858.65	883.13	892.71	867.55	874.78	866.90	888.44	907.69	856.74	850.41	869.86
2017	867.67	855.56	851.99	875.84	861.67	851.11	876.36	850.18	867.24	858.33	855.07	855.73	860.87
Financial Activities													
2013	1,498.77	1,519.60	1,551.61	1,607.54	1,574.15	1,661.82	1,587.75	1,594.25	1,691.10	1,611.62	1,605.92	1,664.95	1,598.48
2014	1,634.49	1,694.55	1,721.59	1,644.24	1,645.88	1,721.67	1,639.62	1,636.36	1,643.12	1,646.90	1,719.77	1,630.05	1,667.06
2015	1,620.44	1,713.36	1,717.56	1,645.27	1,650.11	1,661.54	1,680.11	1,794.39	1,684.66	1,695.07	1,764.73	1,685.63	1,693.82
2016	1,657.63	1,627.13	1,586.63	1,706.19	1,762.18	1,627.95	1,644.64	1,698.32	1,650.58	1,825.78	1,690.65	1,645.00	1,677.39
2017	1,806.52	1,690.32	1,723.17	1,897.78	1,738.73	1,690.40	1,789.80	1,729.75	1,714.21	1,830.46	1,699.78	1,698.88	1,749.52
Professional and Business Services													
2013	1,038.63	1,044.70	1,050.96	1,065.75	1,066.45	1,085.81	1,044.47	1,039.68	1,088.14	1,063.65	1,054.32	1,075.01	1,060.43
2014	1,058.85	1,111.84	1,128.75	1,115.28	1,104.05	1,134.80	1,116.96	1,124.66	1,160.28	1,173.58	1,172.81	1,154.46	1,130.32
2015	1,116.04	1,140.18	1,161.81	1,148.92	1,136.77	1,177.63	1,175.36	1,221.79	1,179.90	1,178.41	1,212.99	1,188.25	1,169.28
2016	1,215.25	1,220.34	1,210.95	1,212.08	1,258.46	1,230.24	1,223.94	1,217.66	1,226.00	1,249.92	1,218.00	1,255.93	1,227.43
2017	1,287.14	1,242.49	1,253.90	1,277.65	1,264.14	1,266.96	1,291.66	1,249.50	1,267.00	1,281.20	1,244.88	1,242.14	1,263.03
Education and Health Services													
2013	807.77	803.09	787.49	792.20	782.17	785.31	781.87	780.94	785.94	780.62	777.19	786.78	786.86
2014	774.05	774.66	775.63	780.31	775.01	777.49	787.51	802.33	792.85	796.62	803.53	808.39	787.51
2015	807.61	812.33	809.33	812.76	807.86	816.82	817.97	826.10	827.89	831.29	840.11	842.81	821.00
2016	856.80	849.34	860.67	862.87	871.53	868.46	886.82	899.26	912.23	906.50	931.21	927.68	887.54
2017	926.07	919.04	914.25	932.19	919.63	922.49	924.30	927.88	933.40	930.85	932.50	936.65	926.04
Leisure and Hospitality													
2013	381.96	383.08	388.19	400.66	402.69	394.24	399.05	395.03	403.97	395.42	389.36	379.94	392.93
2014	370.72	372.35	383.50	395.52	393.22	387.32	393.47	404.00	407.68	415.48	421.03	413.77	396.53
2015	408.09	412.25	415.65	429.08	425.62	413.32	411.06	421.09	407.81	424.58	428.28	427.39	418.99
2016	415.40	430.28	426.50	444.02	444.82	426.32	428.47	425.10	418.14	429.94	424.37	425.79	428.02
2017	423.12	416.98	419.76	440.25	447.80	433.32	442.66	435.36	436.64	446.00	449.37	461.02	437.69
Other Services													
2013	653.31	662.29	638.40	640.10	662.46	662.12	659.68	666.65	676.87	677.33	686.62	674.48	663.42
2014	681.07	676.80	722.92	697.50	711.01	697.94	676.19	675.58	679.20	639.85	679.80	671.55	683.70
2015	650.28	661.67	641.29	628.72	640.22	635.22	624.31	623.34	636.61	676.10	683.60	686.69	649.42
2016	680.15	681.57	694.62	711.52	719.35	686.28	692.59	725.41	741.24	750.61	756.82	764.09	718.22
2017	786.79	777.85	790.28	801.28	811.38	799.10	814.72	807.83	810.85	821.85	798.40	827.53	803.52

DELAWARE
At a Glance

Population:
  2010 census: 897,934
  2017 estimate: 961,939

Percent change in population:
  2010–2017: 7.1%

Percent change in total nonfarm employment:
  2007–2017: 3.8%

Industry with the largest growth in employment, 2007–2017 (thousands):
  Education and health services, 18.2

Industry with the largest decline or smallest growth in employment, 2007–2017 (thousands):
  Manufacturing, 7.3

Civilian labor force:
  2010: 434,419
  2017: 477,349

Unemployment rate and rank among states (highest to lowest):
  2010: 8.4%, 29th
  2017: 4.6%, 18th

Over-the-year change in unemployment rates:
  2015–2016: -0.4%
  2016–2017: 0.1%

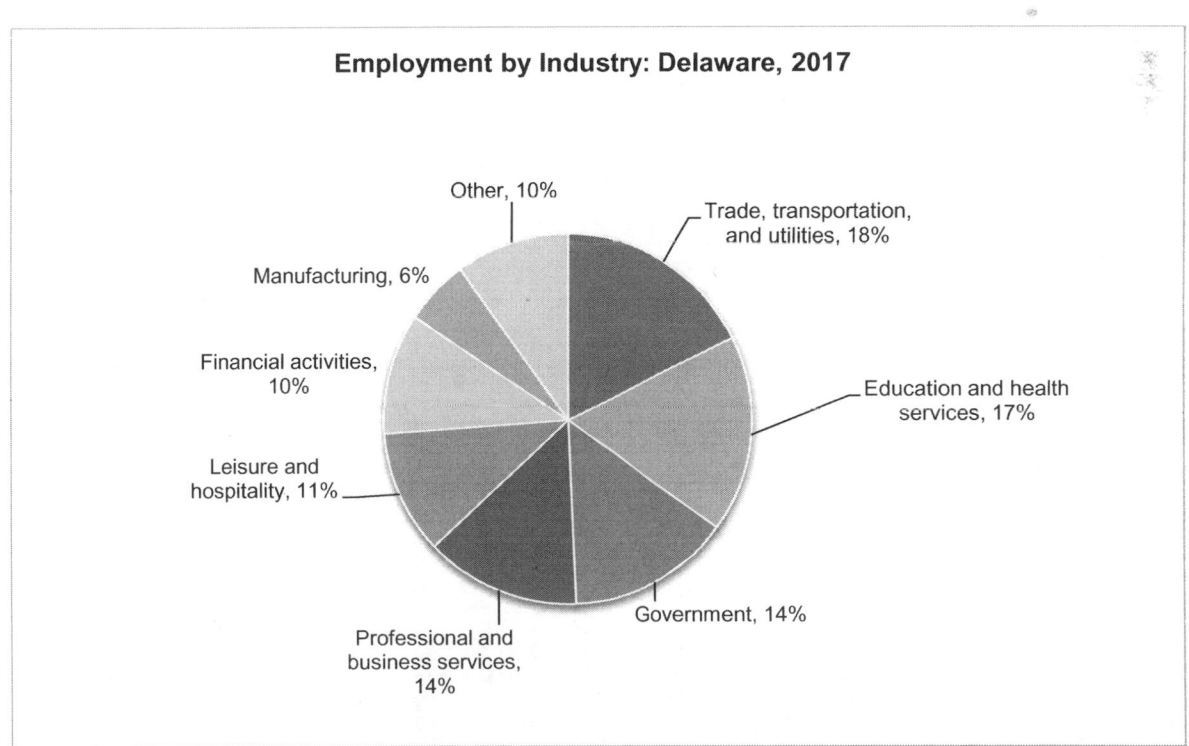

Employment by Industry: Delaware, 2017

- Other, 10%
- Trade, transportation, and utilities, 18%
- Manufacturing, 6%
- Education and health services, 17%
- Financial activities, 10%
- Leisure and hospitality, 11%
- Government, 14%
- Professional and business services, 14%

1. Employment by Industry: Delaware, Selected Years, 2007–2017

(Numbers in thousands, not seasonally adjusted)

Industry and year	January	February	March	April	May	June	July	August	September	October	November	December	Annual average
Total Nonfarm													
2007	428.8	427.7	432.9	436.8	442.4	445.9	441.8	441.2	440.3	440.6	444.4	445.8	439.1
2008	430.8	431.9	435.0	439.8	441.9	443.8	439.8	438.3	436.4	435.5	436.0	433.5	436.9
2009	415.8	414.2	415.1	416.9	422.2	421.6	416.8	415.7	415.1	416.3	415.9	414.8	416.7
2010	400.0	397.3	404.1	411.6	417.3	420.0	420.3	419.1	419.3	418.1	419.1	420.2	413.9
2011	406.7	407.8	412.0	419.6	420.4	421.6	420.6	418.6	419.7	418.3	420.0	421.0	417.2
2012	406.8	407.8	412.6	416.7	422.5	423.5	422.9	422.2	421.8	423.7	427.2	427.4	419.6
2013	412.9	415.1	419.8	425.1	430.2	432.6	432.4	432.9	432.3	434.6	439.2	436.7	428.7
2014	424.3	423.7	428.4	434.1	440.9	443.0	442.0	441.1	441.0	443.3	448.2	449.0	438.3
2015	433.8	434.1	438.6	443.3	451.3	453.6	454.4	451.3	451.6	452.6	457.3	457.0	448.2
2016	441.3	441.4	446.0	451.1	454.5	457.5	459.1	456.0	455.2	455.5	458.5	458.7	452.9
2017	446.5	446.6	450.1	453.8	456.7	460.7	460.1	457.6	457.5	460.0	460.7	458.7	455.8
Total Private													
2007	368.2	366.0	370.0	373.6	378.9	385.2	382.3	382.6	378.8	377.0	380.5	382.1	377.1
2008	368.7	369.1	371.0	375.3	377.3	382.3	379.5	378.7	373.7	371.3	372.0	369.7	374.1
2009	353.7	350.6	350.0	351.8	357.1	359.7	357.2	356.5	352.5	351.0	350.6	350.2	353.4
2010	338.0	334.3	339.3	346.3	350.9	356.6	358.8	358.8	355.6	353.3	353.9	355.0	350.1
2011	344.0	344.1	346.9	353.4	355.2	359.3	359.9	358.5	356.2	353.3	354.8	356.0	353.5
2012	344.6	343.8	347.4	351.7	357.0	361.0	362.0	362.4	358.5	358.8	362.0	362.3	356.0
2013	351.5	351.0	354.3	359.5	364.5	369.5	371.2	372.7	368.4	369.1	373.2	371.2	364.7
2014	359.8	358.2	362.1	368.0	374.5	379.6	380.2	380.7	376.3	377.3	382.0	382.9	373.5
2015	369.7	369.3	371.0	376.8	384.1	388.8	391.7	390.1	386.4	386.2	390.8	390.4	382.9
2016	376.7	376.4	379.4	383.9	387.4	393.5	395.8	394.6	389.9	388.4	390.8	391.5	387.4
2017	380.9	380.8	382.3	385.9	388.9	395.7	396.6	396.1	391.5	392.4	392.7	391.0	389.6
Goods Producing													
2007	60.3	59.0	60.1	60.6	61.5	61.9	60.9	61.4	60.5	59.9	61.0	60.4	60.6
2008	57.3	58.1	58.0	58.6	57.6	58.6	56.9	56.8	55.5	54.7	55.4	53.9	56.8
2009	50.5	48.9	48.3	48.2	48.5	48.5	47.8	47.7	46.9	47.2	46.8	46.1	48.0
2010	44.4	42.9	43.9	45.4	45.5	46.3	45.9	46.1	45.8	45.8	45.6	45.5	45.3
2011	44.0	43.9	44.7	45.8	46.0	45.8	45.7	45.0	45.0	45.2	44.7	44.5	45.0
2012	43.0	42.7	42.9	43.7	44.3	44.5	45.2	45.0	44.9	44.7	44.8	44.6	44.2
2013	43.9	43.5	43.7	44.4	44.7	45.1	45.3	45.7	45.4	46.2	45.5	44.6	44.8
2014	43.5	43.4	44.3	44.9	45.7	46.5	46.6	46.7	46.4	46.5	46.5	46.3	45.6
2015	44.8	44.8	44.8	45.9	46.6	46.9	47.3	47.4	47.7	47.0	46.5	46.4	46.3
2016	45.4	45.5	46.2	46.1	46.3	46.9	47.4	47.6	47.3	47.5	47.4	47.5	46.8
2017	46.6	46.9	47.4	47.9	47.6	48.3	48.1	47.9	48.0	48.3	48.5	48.7	47.9
Service-Providing													
2007	368.5	368.7	372.8	376.2	380.9	384.0	380.9	379.8	379.8	380.7	383.4	385.4	378.4
2008	373.5	373.8	377.0	381.2	384.3	385.2	382.9	381.5	380.9	380.8	380.6	379.6	380.1
2009	365.3	365.3	366.8	368.7	373.7	373.1	369.0	368.0	368.2	369.1	369.1	368.7	368.8
2010	355.6	354.4	360.2	366.2	371.8	373.7	374.4	373.0	373.5	372.3	373.5	374.7	368.6
2011	362.7	363.9	367.3	373.8	374.4	375.8	374.9	373.6	374.7	373.1	375.3	376.5	372.2
2012	363.8	365.1	369.7	373.0	378.2	379.0	377.7	377.2	376.9	379.0	382.4	382.8	375.4
2013	369.0	371.6	376.1	380.7	385.5	387.5	387.1	387.2	386.9	388.4	393.7	392.1	383.8
2014	380.8	380.3	384.1	389.2	395.2	396.5	395.4	394.4	394.6	396.8	401.7	402.7	392.6
2015	389.0	389.3	393.8	397.4	404.7	406.7	407.1	403.9	403.9	405.6	410.8	410.6	401.9
2016	395.9	395.9	399.8	405.0	408.2	410.6	411.7	408.4	407.9	408.0	411.1	411.2	406.1
2017	399.9	399.7	402.7	405.9	409.1	412.4	412.0	409.7	409.5	411.7	412.2	410.0	407.9
Mining, Logging, and Construction													
2007	27.2	26.0	26.8	27.4	28.0	28.2	28.1	28.0	28.0	27.3	27.5	26.9	27.5
2008	25.7	25.1	25.3	26.3	26.1	26.1	25.8	25.6	24.7	23.8	23.6	22.7	25.1
2009	20.7	19.9	20.1	20.0	20.4	20.6	20.4	20.3	19.6	19.8	19.5	19.1	20.0
2010	18.0	17.1	18.0	19.3	19.6	20.1	19.9	20.1	19.8	20.0	20.0	19.9	19.3
2011	18.7	18.6	19.3	20.2	20.1	19.9	19.6	19.1	19.2	19.3	18.9	18.8	19.3
2012	17.7	17.3	17.4	18.1	18.5	18.7	19.1	19.1	19.0	19.1	19.3	19.2	18.5
2013	18.5	18.3	18.6	19.2	19.6	19.9	20.2	20.5	20.3	20.8	20.3	19.6	19.7
2014	18.9	18.7	19.4	20.0	20.7	21.2	21.4	21.3	21.0	21.0	21.0	20.8	20.5
2015	19.4	19.4	19.5	20.4	21.1	21.1	21.6	21.6	21.9	21.5	21.0	20.8	20.8
2016	19.8	19.9	20.8	20.5	20.6	20.9	21.4	21.6	21.5	21.7	21.5	21.5	21.0
2017	20.7	20.9	21.6	22.0	21.7	22.1	22.2	22.1	22.2	22.5	22.6	22.7	21.9

1. Employment by Industry: Delaware, Selected Years, 2007–2017—*Continued*

(Numbers in thousands, not seasonally adjusted)

Industry and year	January	February	March	April	May	June	July	August	September	October	November	December	Annual average
Manufacturing													
2007	33.1	33.0	33.3	33.2	33.5	33.7	32.8	33.4	32.5	32.6	33.5	33.5	33.2
2008	31.6	33.0	32.7	32.3	31.5	32.5	31.1	31.2	30.8	30.9	31.8	31.2	31.7
2009	29.8	29.0	28.2	28.2	28.1	27.9	27.4	27.4	27.3	27.4	27.3	27.0	27.9
2010	26.4	25.8	25.9	26.1	25.9	26.2	26.0	26.0	26.0	25.8	25.6	25.6	25.9
2011	25.3	25.3	25.4	25.6	25.9	25.9	26.1	25.9	25.8	25.9	25.8	25.7	25.7
2012	25.3	25.4	25.5	25.6	25.8	25.8	26.1	25.9	25.9	25.6	25.5	25.4	25.7
2013	25.4	25.2	25.1	25.2	25.1	25.2	25.1	25.2	25.1	25.4	25.2	25.0	25.2
2014	24.6	24.7	24.9	24.9	25.0	25.3	25.2	25.4	25.4	25.5	25.5	25.5	25.2
2015	25.4	25.4	25.3	25.5	25.5	25.8	25.7	25.8	25.8	25.5	25.5	25.6	25.6
2016	25.6	25.6	25.4	25.6	25.7	26.0	26.0	26.0	25.8	25.8	25.9	26.0	25.8
2017	25.9	26.0	25.8	25.9	25.9	26.2	25.9	25.8	25.8	25.8	25.9	26.0	25.9
Trade, Transportation, and Utilities													
2007	81.9	80.6	81.1	81.3	82.9	83.9	83.8	83.7	83.2	82.0	85.2	86.1	83.0
2008	81.5	80.4	80.9	80.4	81.3	81.9	81.3	80.9	80.3	80.7	81.7	82.6	81.2
2009	76.3	74.9	74.7	74.3	75.1	75.5	75.0	74.9	74.9	74.8	76.3	76.8	75.3
2010	72.6	71.2	72.2	73.2	74.5	75.2	75.0	74.8	74.8	75.1	77.1	78.0	74.5
2011	74.0	73.4	73.7	75.1	75.3	76.1	75.6	75.5	75.4	75.3	77.7	78.5	75.5
2012	74.4	73.4	74.3	74.6	75.9	76.1	75.8	75.7	75.3	76.2	79.1	79.4	75.9
2013	75.0	74.4	75.2	76.0	76.8	77.5	77.5	78.0	78.1	79.0	81.6	82.3	77.6
2014	77.7	76.8	77.3	78.1	78.9	79.8	79.9	80.4	79.9	80.4	82.7	84.0	79.7
2015	79.2	78.8	79.1	79.9	80.7	81.3	81.8	81.9	81.5	82.7	85.4	86.0	81.5
2016	81.1	80.4	81.1	81.6	81.9	82.0	82.4	82.5	82.3	82.1	83.9	84.3	82.1
2017	80.6	79.4	79.5	79.7	80.1	80.6	80.3	81.2	81.3	81.2	83.1	83.4	80.9
Wholesale Trade													
2007	14.8	14.7	14.7	14.9	15.0	15.1	15.2	15.2	15.0	14.8	14.9	14.9	14.9
2008	14.7	14.7	14.8	14.6	14.8	14.7	14.7	14.5	14.4	14.5	14.4	14.2	14.6
2009	13.7	13.6	13.5	13.5	13.4	13.2	13.2	13.1	12.9	12.9	12.8	12.7	13.2
2010	12.4	12.5	12.5	12.6	12.6	12.5	12.6	12.5	12.6	12.4	12.4	12.4	12.5
2011	12.5	12.6	12.5	12.6	12.5	12.6	12.6	12.6	12.5	12.5	12.5	12.5	12.5
2012	12.4	12.4	12.6	12.6	12.5	12.5	12.5	12.4	12.3	12.3	12.3	12.3	12.4
2013	12.0	12.1	12.2	12.2	12.3	12.3	12.2	12.2	12.2	12.0	12.1	12.2	12.2
2014	11.9	11.8	11.9	12.0	12.1	12.2	12.0	12.0	11.9	11.9	11.9	12.0	12.0
2015	11.7	11.7	11.8	11.7	11.9	11.9	11.8	11.8	11.7	11.6	11.6	11.7	11.7
2016	11.5	11.5	11.5	11.5	11.6	11.5	11.4	11.3	11.2	11.0	11.1	11.0	11.3
2017	10.9	10.8	10.8	10.8	10.9	11.0	10.9	10.9	10.8	10.3	10.3	10.3	10.7
Retail Trade													
2007	53.1	52.1	52.7	52.8	53.9	54.9	55.1	54.9	54.2	54.1	56.5	57.2	54.3
2008	53.4	52.2	52.5	52.2	52.8	53.6	53.2	53.1	52.2	52.4	53.5	54.3	53.0
2009	49.9	48.6	48.6	48.4	49.2	49.9	50.2	50.1	49.5	49.4	51.0	51.6	49.7
2010	48.0	46.7	47.6	48.5	49.6	50.5	50.9	50.8	49.9	50.3	52.3	53.0	49.8
2011	49.2	48.5	48.9	50.1	50.3	51.1	51.3	51.4	50.4	50.2	52.5	53.1	50.6
2012	49.6	48.6	49.2	49.9	50.7	51.2	51.2	51.1	50.0	50.4	53.0	53.1	50.7
2013	49.4	48.9	49.5	50.2	50.9	51.7	52.1	52.5	51.5	52.1	54.4	54.8	51.5
2014	50.9	50.2	50.6	51.4	52.1	53.2	53.3	53.2	52.2	52.5	54.5	55.2	52.4
2015	51.5	50.9	51.1	51.9	52.5	53.4	53.7	53.5	52.6	53.4	55.8	55.8	53.0
2016	52.3	51.8	52.4	53.0	53.4	54.2	54.7	54.8	53.7	53.7	55.2	55.6	53.7
2017	52.5	52.0	52.1	52.6	53.0	53.7	53.9	53.9	52.9	52.8	54.0	54.0	53.1
Transportation and Utilities													
2007	14.0	13.8	13.7	13.6	14.0	13.9	13.5	13.6	14.0	13.9	13.8	14.0	13.8
2008	13.4	13.5	13.6	13.6	13.7	13.6	13.4	13.3	13.7	13.8	13.8	14.1	13.6
2009	12.7	12.7	12.6	12.4	12.5	12.4	11.6	11.7	12.5	12.5	12.5	12.5	12.4
2010	12.2	12.0	12.1	12.1	12.3	12.2	11.5	11.5	12.3	12.4	12.4	12.6	12.1
2011	12.3	12.3	12.3	12.4	12.5	12.4	11.7	11.5	12.5	12.6	12.7	12.9	12.3
2012	12.4	12.4	12.5	12.1	12.7	12.4	12.1	12.2	13.0	13.5	13.8	14.0	12.8
2013	13.6	13.4	13.5	13.6	13.6	13.5	13.2	13.3	14.4	14.9	15.1	15.3	14.0
2014	14.9	14.8	14.8	14.7	14.7	14.4	14.6	15.2	15.8	16.0	16.3	16.8	15.3
2015	16.0	16.2	16.2	16.3	16.3	16.0	16.3	16.6	17.2	17.7	18.0	18.5	16.8
2016	17.3	17.1	17.2	17.1	16.9	16.3	16.3	16.4	17.4	17.4	17.6	17.7	17.1
2017	17.2	16.6	16.6	16.3	16.2	15.9	15.5	16.4	17.6	18.1	18.8	19.1	17.0

1. Employment by Industry: Delaware, Selected Years, 2007–2017—Continued

(Numbers in thousands, not seasonally adjusted)

Industry and year	January	February	March	April	May	June	July	August	September	October	November	December	Annual average
Information													
2007	6.8	6.8	6.8	6.8	6.8	6.9	7.0	7.0	7.0	7.1	7.1	7.1	6.9
2008	7.0	7.1	7.1	7.1	7.1	7.2	7.0	7.1	7.0	7.0	6.9	6.8	7.0
2009	6.8	6.7	6.7	6.6	6.6	6.5	6.5	6.4	6.3	6.4	6.2	6.1	6.5
2010	5.9	5.9	6.0	6.1	6.0	6.0	6.0	5.9	6.0	5.9	5.9	5.8	6.0
2011	5.8	5.8	5.8	5.8	5.6	5.8	5.7	5.2	5.7	5.5	5.6	5.7	5.7
2012	5.6	5.6	5.6	5.5	5.5	5.5	5.4	5.5	5.3	5.3	5.3	5.3	5.5
2013	5.3	5.4	5.3	5.3	5.2	5.2	5.2	5.2	5.1	5.0	5.1	5.0	5.2
2014	5.1	4.9	4.9	4.9	5.0	4.9	4.9	5.0	4.8	4.9	4.9	4.8	4.9
2015	4.8	4.7	4.7	4.7	4.8	4.7	4.7	4.6	4.6	4.7	4.7	4.7	4.7
2016	4.6	4.6	4.6	4.6	4.3	4.7	4.7	4.7	4.7	4.6	4.6	4.7	4.6
2017	4.6	4.6	4.6	4.6	4.6	4.7	4.6	4.6	4.5	4.4	4.5	4.5	4.6
Financial Activities													
2007	44.8	44.9	44.9	45.1	45.3	45.8	45.8	45.6	45.2	45.3	45.2	45.2	45.3
2008	45.0	45.0	45.2	45.5	45.7	46.3	46.5	46.2	45.5	45.3	45.0	44.6	45.5
2009	44.3	44.0	43.9	43.8	44.2	44.4	44.6	44.3	43.9	43.4	43.1	43.0	43.9
2010	42.4	42.5	42.6	42.5	42.4	43.1	43.4	43.4	43.0	42.3	42.3	42.7	42.7
2011	42.3	42.4	42.3	42.4	42.2	42.8	43.1	42.8	42.3	41.4	41.3	41.7	42.3
2012	41.3	41.3	41.5	41.5	42.1	42.7	43.3	43.5	42.7	42.8	42.9	43.3	42.4
2013	42.9	43.2	43.3	43.3	43.5	44.2	44.7	44.7	44.1	44.0	44.3	44.5	43.9
2014	44.1	44.2	44.1	44.3	44.7	45.3	45.5	45.7	45.3	45.4	45.6	46.2	45.0
2015	45.7	46.0	46.1	46.3	46.2	46.6	47.0	47.3	47.2	46.9	47.1	46.9	46.6
2016	46.7	46.8	46.9	46.9	46.8	47.4	47.5	47.5	46.9	47.0	47.3	47.6	47.1
2017	47.3	47.4	47.5	47.4	47.7	48.5	48.6	48.6	48.1	48.0	48.0	48.0	47.9
Professional and Business Services													
2007	58.4	58.6	59.5	60.3	60.6	61.1	60.4	60.4	60.3	60.7	61.6	62.8	60.4
2008	59.7	59.5	59.5	60.4	60.0	60.1	59.7	59.5	59.1	59.1	59.6	59.6	59.7
2009	56.2	56.0	55.8	56.0	56.3	56.3	55.1	55.0	54.7	55.1	55.5	56.3	55.7
2010	53.2	53.3	53.6	54.3	54.9	55.2	55.8	55.6	55.2	55.8	55.5	56.7	54.9
2011	53.9	54.3	54.3	55.9	55.4	55.7	55.8	55.9	55.8	56.1	57.1	57.6	55.7
2012	54.9	54.6	55.2	56.1	55.9	55.9	55.9	56.2	56.0	57.0	58.5	58.6	56.2
2013	55.9	55.5	56.5	57.5	57.8	58.2	58.7	59.3	58.9	59.4	62.2	60.7	58.4
2014	58.1	57.1	57.8	59.0	59.7	60.0	60.0	59.8	59.6	60.7	64.2	63.6	60.0
2015	59.8	58.9	59.1	59.2	60.6	61.0	61.7	60.7	60.1	61.7	65.1	64.6	61.0
2016	60.5	59.6	59.7	60.6	61.1	62.7	62.8	62.1	61.1	61.7	63.3	64.2	61.6
2017	61.1	60.5	60.2	61.1	61.2	62.4	62.7	62.2	61.3	64.2	64.5	63.4	62.1
Education and Health Services													
2007	58.9	59.0	59.3	59.6	59.9	59.8	59.5	59.6	60.5	60.8	61.0	61.4	59.9
2008	61.4	62.0	61.9	62.6	62.8	62.7	62.1	62.4	62.9	63.0	63.4	63.4	62.6
2009	63.3	63.4	63.4	63.6	63.8	63.5	63.3	63.4	63.5	64.1	64.3	64.2	63.7
2010	63.7	63.6	64.2	64.8	64.9	64.5	65.1	65.4	65.2	65.3	65.5	65.5	64.8
2011	65.4	65.6	66.2	66.7	66.5	66.2	66.3	66.4	66.8	67.3	67.4	68.0	66.6
2012	67.3	67.4	67.8	68.1	68.4	68.5	68.3	68.4	69.0	69.5	69.7	70.0	68.5
2013	69.3	69.6	69.8	69.8	70.0	69.8	69.9	70.3	70.5	70.9	71.6	71.9	70.3
2014	71.4	71.6	72.1	72.4	72.8	72.4	72.3	72.5	73.0	73.6	74.1	74.3	72.7
2015	74.1	74.4	74.4	75.3	75.6	75.8	75.8	75.3	75.7	76.3	76.5	76.6	75.5
2016	76.1	76.5	76.6	76.8	77.0	76.7	76.9	76.8	77.2	77.6	77.7	77.8	77.0
2017	76.8	77.6	77.6	78.2	78.4	78.0	78.0	78.0	78.3	78.6	78.9	78.6	78.1
Leisure and Hospitality													
2007	38.0	38.2	39.2	40.8	42.9	46.4	45.8	46.0	43.3	41.5	40.5	40.1	41.9
2008	38.0	38.2	39.6	41.6	43.8	46.3	46.8	46.7	44.6	42.7	41.2	40.1	42.5
2009	37.9	38.3	38.8	40.9	43.9	46.3	46.4	46.3	44.0	41.9	40.3	39.6	42.1
2010	37.8	37.2	38.8	41.8	44.4	47.6	49.1	49.0	47.2	44.8	43.8	42.6	43.7
2011	40.5	40.6	41.8	43.6	46.0	48.5	49.3	49.3	47.0	44.4	43.0	42.0	44.7
2012	40.2	40.8	42.0	44.0	46.6	49.3	49.6	49.5	47.0	44.9	43.3	42.7	45.0
2013	41.0	41.2	42.2	44.7	48.0	50.8	51.2	50.8	47.9	46.2	44.4	43.7	46.0
2014	41.7	41.9	43.2	45.8	49.0	51.9	52.3	51.8	48.8	47.2	45.3	45.0	47.0
2015	43.0	43.3	44.5	46.9	50.8	53.5	54.6	54.1	51.0	48.3	46.9	46.6	48.6
2016	44.0	44.6	45.8	48.5	51.1	54.1	55.2	54.5	51.8	49.3	48.0	46.8	49.5
2017	45.4	45.9	46.9	48.2	50.4	54.0	55.3	54.6	51.5	48.7	46.7	45.6	49.4

1. Employment by Industry: Delaware, Selected Years, 2007–2017—*Continued*

(Numbers in thousands, not seasonally adjusted)

Industry and year	January	February	March	April	May	June	July	August	September	October	November	December	Annual average
Other Services													
2007	19.1	18.9	19.1	19.1	19.0	19.4	19.1	18.9	18.8	18.9	18.9	19.0	19.0
2008	18.8	18.8	18.8	19.1	19.0	19.2	19.2	19.1	18.8	18.8	18.8	18.7	18.9
2009	18.4	18.4	18.4	18.4	18.7	18.7	18.5	18.5	18.3	18.1	18.1	18.1	18.4
2010	18.0	17.7	18.0	18.2	18.3	18.7	18.5	18.6	18.4	18.3	18.2	18.2	18.3
2011	18.1	18.1	18.1	18.1	18.2	18.4	18.4	18.4	18.2	18.1	18.0	18.0	18.2
2012	17.9	18.0	18.1	18.2	18.3	18.5	18.5	18.6	18.3	18.4	18.4	18.4	18.3
2013	18.2	18.2	18.3	18.5	18.5	18.7	18.7	18.7	18.4	18.4	18.5	18.5	18.5
2014	18.2	18.3	18.4	18.6	18.7	18.8	18.7	18.8	18.5	18.6	18.7	18.7	18.6
2015	18.3	18.4	18.3	18.6	18.8	19.0	18.8	18.8	18.6	18.6	18.6	18.6	18.6
2016	18.3	18.4	18.5	18.8	18.9	19.0	18.9	18.9	18.6	18.6	18.6	18.6	18.7
2017	18.5	18.5	18.6	18.8	18.9	19.2	19.0	19.0	18.5	19.0	18.5	18.8	18.8
Government													
2007	60.6	61.7	62.9	63.2	63.5	60.7	59.5	58.6	61.5	63.6	63.9	63.7	62.0
2008	62.1	62.8	64.0	64.5	64.6	61.5	60.3	59.6	62.7	64.2	64.0	63.8	62.8
2009	62.1	63.6	65.1	65.1	65.1	61.9	59.6	59.2	62.6	65.3	65.3	64.6	63.3
2010	62.0	63.0	64.8	65.3	66.4	63.4	61.5	60.3	63.7	64.8	65.2	65.2	63.8
2011	62.7	63.7	65.1	66.2	65.2	62.3	60.7	60.1	63.5	65.0	65.2	65.0	63.7
2012	62.2	64.0	65.2	65.0	65.5	62.5	60.9	59.8	63.3	64.9	65.2	65.1	63.6
2013	61.4	64.1	65.5	65.6	65.7	63.1	61.2	60.2	63.9	65.5	66.0	65.5	64.0
2014	64.5	65.5	66.3	66.1	66.4	63.4	61.8	60.4	64.7	66.0	66.2	66.1	64.8
2015	64.1	64.8	67.6	66.5	67.2	64.8	62.7	61.2	65.2	66.4	66.5	66.6	65.3
2016	64.6	65.0	66.6	67.2	67.1	64.0	63.3	61.4	65.3	67.1	67.7	67.2	65.5
2017	65.6	65.8	67.8	67.9	67.8	65.0	63.5	61.5	66.0	67.6	68.0	67.7	66.2

2. Average Weekly Hours by Selected Industry: Delaware, 2013–2017

(Not seasonally adjusted)

Industry and year	January	February	March	April	May	June	July	August	September	October	November	December	Annual average
Total Private													
2013	32.0	32.4	32.7	32.4	32.4	32.9	32.5	32.9	33.0	32.2	32.4	32.8	32.5
2014	31.9	32.0	32.5	32.6	32.7	32.9	33.1	33.5	33.0	32.9	33.5	33.8	32.9
2015	33.1	33.2	33.2	33.2	33.4	33.0	33.4	33.5	33.2	32.5	32.4	33.6	33.1
2016	33.3	33.2	33.3	33.2	33.3	33.4	33.6	33.2	32.9	33.3	32.6	32.7	33.2
2017	32.3	32.1	32.2	33.1	32.3	33.4	34.0	33.5	33.1	32.9	32.8	32.8	32.9
Goods Producing													
2013	37.1	37.5	37.7	37.4	37.9	37.9	37.2	38.1	38.5	38.2	38.7	38.4	37.9
2014	38.7	38.1	38.8	38.8	39.3	39.9	40.4	40.7	40.2	39.4	38.1	38.5	39.2
2015	39.0	38.0	37.9	39.4	39.3	38.9	38.8	39.1	38.7	38.4	36.9	38.6	38.6
2016	39.1	37.7	38.7	38.2	39.0	39.4	39.8	40.0	40.5	40.3	39.2	38.9	39.2
2017	39.6	38.4	38.2	40.0	39.5	39.9	39.8	39.1	39.8	39.6	40.0	39.3	39.4
Mining, Logging, and Construction													
2013	37.6	37.6	37.8	36.8	38.1	36.5	35.7	37.2	37.9	37.2	38.5	37.5	37.4
2014	37.4	36.9	38.3	38.4	38.4	40.1	40.5	41.4	39.3	39.0	37.1	37.3	38.7
2015	36.9	36.3	36.8	38.4	36.7	37.6	36.4	37.0	36.4	36.1	34.5	37.3	36.7
2016	36.8	36.0	38.0	37.2	37.5	38.8	39.4	39.8	40.3	41.2	39.1	37.6	38.5
2017	36.8	37.2	36.3	38.3	38.0	37.8	37.8	37.3	38.6	38.6	38.4	37.7	37.7
Manufacturing													
2013	36.8	37.4	37.5	37.8	37.7	39.0	38.4	38.9	38.9	39.1	38.6	39.2	38.3
2014	39.7	38.9	39.3	39.1	40.0	39.7	40.3	40.2	40.9	39.7	38.8	39.4	39.7
2015	40.6	39.3	38.7	40.2	41.4	40.0	40.9	40.9	40.8	40.4	38.9	39.5	40.1
2016	41.0	39.2	39.1	39.1	40.3	39.9	40.1	40.1	40.6	39.4	39.2	39.9	39.8
2017	41.8	39.4	39.8	41.4	40.8	41.7	41.5	40.7	40.8	40.4	41.4	40.8	40.9
Trade, Transportation, and Utilities													
2013	31.6	32.2	32.8	32.6	32.4	32.6	32.9	32.8	32.5	32.1	32.4	33.6	32.6
2014	31.2	31.4	32.3	32.1	32.3	32.3	32.8	33.6	32.8	32.7	33.7	34.5	32.7
2015	32.4	32.7	32.9	33.2	34.2	34.0	34.1	34.2	34.6	33.1	33.4	35.2	33.7
2016	34.3	34.1	33.5	33.8	33.7	33.9	33.7	33.2	33.4	33.6	33.1	33.8	33.7
2017	33.1	32.6	32.8	33.3	33.1	33.0	33.1	32.8	33.4	33.2	32.4	33.1	33.0
Financial Activities													
2013	35.5	35.4	35.9	36.1	36.2	37.1	36.3	36.3	37.7	36.2	36.4	36.4	36.3
2014	36.1	35.8	36.2	36.1	36.4	36.7	36.3	36.7	36.7	36.9	37.8	37.8	36.6
2015	37.5	38.5	38.3	38.2	38.2	38.4	38.6	38.8	38.4	38.3	38.8	38.5	38.4
2016	38.8	38.4	38.8	38.6	39.3	39.2	38.9	38.9	39.0	39.0	39.0	39.2	38.9
2017	40.1	38.7	38.8	39.5	37.8	38.5	39.4	38.2	38.0	38.1	37.4	37.4	38.5
Professional and Business Services													
2013	34.2	35.0	35.7	35.3	35.4	36.0	33.8	35.3	36.2	34.5	34.2	35.5	35.1
2014	34.4	35.5	35.8	36.4	36.0	35.3	34.7	34.9	34.4	34.7	36.2	36.5	35.4
2015	35.8	36.8	36.9	37.1	36.4	35.2	35.1	35.3	33.7	32.9	32.5	36.0	35.3
2016	35.3	35.9	36.2	36.1	36.5	35.4	35.7	34.9	34.3	36.0	34.1	34.0	35.4
2017	31.0	32.0	31.7	33.3	31.7	32.3	33.8	33.1	31.7	30.4	30.3	30.5	31.8
Education and Health Services													
2013	32.3	32.1	32.1	32.0	31.8	32.5	31.8	32.1	32.6	31.9	31.9	31.5	32.1
2014	31.6	31.1	31.2	31.8	32.2	32.3	32.3	32.8	32.9	32.8	33.0	32.8	32.2
2015	32.6	32.5	32.1	31.7	31.9	32.3	32.3	32.0	32.1	31.7	32.0	32.4	32.1
2016	32.4	32.3	32.4	32.4	32.3	32.6	33.2	32.9	32.5	32.5	32.2	32.0	32.5
2017	32.8	32.6	32.4	32.9	32.4	32.7	32.9	33.0	32.6	33.0	32.8	32.5	32.7
Leisure and Hospitality													
2013	24.3	25.0	25.4	24.9	25.0	26.0	26.7	27.2	25.4	24.1	24.4	24.5	25.3
2014	24.1	24.1	24.7	24.8	24.5	25.2	26.2	26.2	24.9	24.4	24.8	24.9	24.9
2015	24.3	24.4	24.6	24.5	24.9	24.5	26.0	26.3	25.0	24.3	23.8	23.5	24.7
2016	23.0	23.6	23.6	23.7	23.9	25.2	25.7	25.4	24.2	23.9	23.4	23.6	24.1
2017	23.1	23.3	23.9	23.9	23.3	24.6	25.8	25.6	24.3	23.7	24.1	24.0	24.2

3. Average Hourly Earnings by Selected Industry: Delaware, 2013–2017

(Dollars, not seasonally adjusted)

Industry and year	January	February	March	April	May	June	July	August	September	October	November	December	Annual average
Total Private													
2013	22.72	22.77	22.67	22.53	22.23	21.97	21.59	21.51	22.06	21.96	21.79	21.82	22.12
2014	21.95	22.17	21.92	21.61	21.73	21.81	21.37	21.30	21.68	21.74	21.69	21.49	21.70
2015	22.07	22.53	22.56	22.27	22.12	22.08	22.11	22.67	22.87	23.34	23.62	23.27	22.63
2016	24.00	24.13	24.25	24.42	24.38	23.76	23.85	24.09	24.43	25.33	25.16	24.97	24.40
2017	25.79	25.84	25.74	26.00	25.23	26.73	26.63	26.21	26.61	26.83	26.38	26.59	26.23
Goods Producing													
2013	24.71	25.07	25.17	24.90	25.16	25.08	25.09	24.95	25.13	25.14	24.84	24.12	24.95
2014	23.96	24.27	24.49	24.18	24.66	25.08	24.78	25.04	24.94	24.88	25.39	25.01	24.74
2015	24.72	25.17	25.07	24.43	24.46	24.88	25.02	25.51	25.40	25.22	25.35	25.26	25.04
2016	25.12	25.30	25.51	25.35	25.19	25.25	25.69	25.93	25.60	25.99	26.22	25.68	25.58
2017	25.64	25.66	26.05	26.36	25.88	25.40	25.61	25.45	25.94	25.62	25.33	25.48	25.70
Mining, Logging, and Construction													
2013	29.13	29.89	29.89	29.13	29.34	29.44	29.69	28.86	29.09	29.00	28.24	26.68	29.02
2014	26.88	27.03	27.44	27.06	28.11	28.20	27.83	27.40	27.64	27.77	28.19	28.09	27.65
2015	28.19	28.67	28.51	27.70	28.27	28.35	28.60	28.86	28.07	28.05	27.83	28.02	28.26
2016	28.43	29.32	28.89	28.74	28.89	28.45	28.69	29.28	29.07	29.48	29.83	29.00	29.02
2017	28.86	28.64	29.04	29.03	28.78	27.73	27.62	27.19	28.10	27.44	26.58	27.39	28.01
Manufacturing													
2013	21.40	21.55	21.66	21.76	21.86	21.87	21.65	21.91	22.01	22.13	22.11	22.20	21.85
2014	21.85	22.30	22.25	21.92	21.92	22.45	22.18	23.00	22.79	22.55	23.18	22.64	22.42
2015	22.30	22.70	22.56	21.93	21.66	22.21	22.33	22.96	23.37	23.09	23.54	23.14	22.65
2016	22.81	22.43	22.83	22.77	22.42	22.74	23.26	23.17	22.74	22.92	23.22	23.09	22.87
2017	23.38	23.39	23.77	24.26	23.62	23.62	24.04	24.09	24.18	24.11	24.32	23.94	23.89
Trade, Transportation, and Utilities													
2013	19.18	19.23	18.94	19.25	18.88	19.00	18.74	18.58	19.00	18.88	18.45	18.49	18.88
2014	18.69	18.81	18.71	18.21	18.14	18.52	18.15	18.05	18.08	17.95	18.07	18.10	18.28
2015	19.01	18.97	18.95	18.66	18.44	18.67	18.55	18.90	18.76	19.11	19.03	19.02	18.84
2016	19.22	19.13	19.30	19.54	19.95	19.57	19.64	20.15	20.16	20.74	20.59	20.08	19.84
2017	21.00	20.82	20.94	21.60	21.06	21.64	21.47	21.10	21.50	21.89	21.23	21.51	21.32
Financial Activities													
2013	27.59	27.40	27.63	26.84	25.92	26.18	25.96	25.68	25.43	23.09	23.46	23.56	25.70
2014	23.49	23.74	23.29	22.62	23.37	24.71	24.29	24.62	25.15	25.68	27.13	26.12	24.55
2015	25.93	27.28	27.76	26.91	27.21	27.68	28.22	29.60	29.17	29.63	31.14	30.42	28.43
2016	32.14	32.82	33.01	32.24	31.53	30.30	30.67	30.54	30.24	32.35	31.34	31.24	31.53
2017	31.51	32.88	32.24	33.07	30.41	29.68	30.44	30.36	31.00	32.01	31.88	31.13	31.38
Professional and Business Services													
2013	26.49	26.84	27.07	27.31	27.26	27.12	26.52	26.81	27.64	27.51	27.75	28.13	27.22
2014	28.24	28.27	27.45	27.33	27.69	26.73	26.25	26.13	26.46	25.68	23.39	22.89	26.31
2015	24.53	24.74	24.57	24.94	24.90	24.27	24.68	26.25	26.86	26.59	25.71	23.76	25.12
2016	25.60	26.64	26.79	27.38	27.76	27.27	27.73	28.28	29.15	30.22	29.85	29.89	28.05
2017	33.72	34.43	33.95	33.11	32.16	32.12	32.80	32.21	32.71	32.72	32.62	33.17	32.97
Education and Health Services													
2013	24.03	23.94	23.82	23.48	23.11	22.88	22.95	22.78	22.94	23.28	23.14	23.22	23.30
2014	23.10	23.35	23.20	23.21	23.01	23.03	23.24	22.54	22.88	23.35	22.99	23.57	23.12
2015	23.81	23.87	24.11	24.42	24.27	24.12	24.79	24.84	25.37	26.40	25.98	26.16	24.85
2016	26.27	26.22	26.28	27.13	27.30	27.13	27.38	27.58	28.23	29.17	29.18	29.33	27.60
2017	28.44	28.49	28.05	28.27	27.75	27.45	27.13	27.32	27.35	27.77	27.15	27.75	27.74
Leisure and Hospitality													
2013	13.99	13.72	13.54	13.41	13.34	12.81	12.58	12.56	12.94	13.01	12.88	13.02	13.11
2014	13.11	13.37	13.20	13.01	13.05	13.02	12.91	13.09	13.19	13.36	13.16	13.21	13.13
2015	12.94	13.13	13.08	13.08	13.22	13.02	12.93	12.91	13.19	13.35	13.70	13.88	13.19
2016	13.63	13.62	13.74	13.57	13.46	12.95	13.06	13.46	13.89	14.02	14.03	14.19	13.61
2017	14.38	14.76	14.66	14.77	14.86	14.25	14.24	14.41	14.40	14.69	14.41	14.77	14.54

4. Average Weekly Earnings by Selected Industry: Delaware, 2013–2017

(Dollars, not seasonally adjusted)

Industry and year	January	February	March	April	May	June	July	August	September	October	November	December	Annual average
Total Private													
2013	727.04	737.75	741.31	729.97	720.25	722.81	701.68	707.68	727.98	707.11	706.00	715.70	718.90
2014	700.21	709.44	712.40	704.49	710.57	717.55	707.35	713.55	715.44	715.25	726.62	726.36	713.93
2015	730.52	748.00	748.99	739.36	738.81	728.64	738.47	759.45	759.28	758.55	765.29	781.87	749.05
2016	799.20	801.12	807.53	810.74	811.85	793.58	801.36	799.79	803.75	843.49	820.22	816.52	810.08
2017	833.02	829.46	828.83	860.60	814.93	892.78	905.42	878.04	880.79	882.71	865.26	872.15	862.97
Goods Producing													
2013	916.74	940.13	948.91	931.26	953.56	950.53	933.35	950.60	967.51	960.35	961.31	926.21	945.61
2014	927.25	924.69	950.21	938.18	969.14	1,000.69	1,001.11	1,019.13	1,002.59	980.27	967.36	962.89	969.81
2015	964.08	956.46	950.15	962.54	961.28	967.83	970.78	997.44	982.98	968.45	935.42	975.04	966.54
2016	982.19	953.81	987.24	968.37	982.41	994.85	1,022.46	1,037.20	1,036.80	1,047.40	1,027.82	998.95	1,002.74
2017	1,015.34	985.34	995.11	1,054.40	1,022.26	1,013.46	1,019.28	995.10	1,032.41	1,014.55	1,013.20	1,001.36	1,012.58
Mining, Logging, and Construction													
2013	1,095.29	1,123.86	1,129.84	1,071.98	1,117.85	1,074.56	1,059.93	1,073.59	1,102.51	1,078.80	1,087.24	1,000.50	1,085.35
2014	1,005.31	997.41	1,050.95	1,039.10	1,079.42	1,130.82	1,127.12	1,134.36	1,086.25	1,083.03	1,045.85	1,047.76	1,070.06
2015	1,040.21	1,040.72	1,049.17	1,063.68	1,037.51	1,065.96	1,041.04	1,067.82	1,021.75	1,012.61	960.14	1,045.15	1,037.14
2016	1,046.22	1,055.52	1,097.82	1,069.13	1,083.38	1,103.86	1,130.39	1,165.34	1,171.52	1,214.58	1,166.35	1,090.40	1,117.27
2017	1,062.05	1,065.41	1,054.15	1,111.85	1,093.64	1,048.19	1,044.04	1,014.19	1,084.66	1,059.18	1,020.67	1,032.60	1,055.98
Manufacturing													
2013	787.52	805.97	812.25	822.53	824.12	852.93	831.36	852.30	856.19	865.28	853.45	870.24	836.86
2014	867.45	867.47	874.43	857.07	876.80	891.27	893.85	924.60	932.11	895.24	899.38	892.02	890.07
2015	905.38	892.11	873.07	881.59	896.72	888.40	913.30	939.06	953.50	932.84	915.71	914.03	908.27
2016	935.21	879.26	892.65	890.31	903.53	907.33	932.73	929.12	923.24	903.05	910.22	921.29	910.23
2017	977.28	921.57	946.05	1,004.36	963.70	984.95	997.66	980.46	986.54	974.04	1,006.85	976.75	977.10
Trade, Transportation, and Utilities													
2013	606.09	619.21	621.23	627.55	611.71	619.40	616.55	609.42	617.50	606.05	597.78	621.26	615.49
2014	583.13	590.63	604.33	584.54	585.92	598.20	595.32	606.48	593.02	586.97	608.96	624.45	597.76
2015	615.92	620.32	623.46	619.51	630.65	634.78	632.56	646.38	649.10	632.54	635.60	669.50	634.91
2016	659.25	652.33	646.55	660.45	672.32	663.42	661.87	668.98	673.34	696.86	681.53	678.70	668.61
2017	695.10	678.73	686.83	719.28	697.09	714.12	710.66	692.08	718.10	726.75	687.85	711.98	703.56
Financial Activities													
2013	979.45	969.96	991.92	968.92	938.30	971.28	942.35	932.18	958.71	835.86	853.94	857.58	932.91
2014	847.99	849.89	843.10	816.58	850.67	906.86	881.73	903.55	923.01	947.59	1,025.51	987.34	898.53
2015	972.38	1,050.28	1,063.21	1,027.96	1,039.42	1,062.91	1,089.29	1,148.48	1,120.13	1,134.83	1,208.23	1,171.17	1,091.71
2016	1,247.03	1,260.29	1,280.79	1,244.46	1,239.13	1,187.76	1,193.06	1,188.01	1,179.36	1,261.65	1,222.26	1,224.61	1,226.52
2017	1,263.55	1,272.46	1,250.91	1,306.27	1,149.50	1,142.68	1,199.34	1,159.75	1,178.00	1,219.58	1,192.31	1,164.26	1,208.13
Professional and Business Services													
2013	905.96	939.40	966.40	964.04	965.00	976.32	896.38	946.39	1,000.57	949.10	949.05	998.62	955.42
2014	971.46	1,003.59	982.71	994.81	996.84	943.57	910.88	911.94	910.22	891.10	846.72	835.49	931.37
2015	878.17	910.43	906.63	925.27	906.36	854.30	866.27	926.63	905.18	874.81	835.58	855.36	886.74
2016	903.68	956.38	969.80	988.42	1,013.24	965.36	989.96	986.97	999.85	1,087.92	1,017.89	1,016.26	992.97
2017	1,045.32	1,101.76	1,076.22	1,102.56	1,019.47	1,037.48	1,108.64	1,066.15	1,036.91	994.69	988.39	1,011.69	1,048.45
Education and Health Services													
2013	776.17	768.47	764.62	751.36	734.90	743.60	729.81	731.24	747.84	742.63	738.17	731.43	747.93
2014	729.96	726.19	723.84	738.08	740.92	743.87	750.65	739.31	752.75	765.88	758.67	773.10	744.46
2015	776.21	775.78	773.93	774.11	774.21	779.08	800.72	794.88	814.38	836.88	831.36	847.58	797.69
2016	851.15	846.91	851.47	879.01	881.79	884.44	909.02	907.38	917.48	948.03	939.60	938.56	897.00
2017	932.83	928.77	908.82	930.08	899.10	897.62	892.58	901.56	891.61	916.41	890.52	901.88	907.10
Leisure and Hospitality													
2013	339.96	343.00	343.92	333.91	333.50	333.06	335.89	341.63	328.68	313.54	314.27	318.99	331.68
2014	315.95	322.22	326.04	322.65	319.73	328.10	338.24	342.96	328.43	325.98	326.37	328.93	326.94
2015	314.44	320.37	321.77	320.46	329.18	318.99	336.18	339.53	329.75	324.41	326.06	326.18	325.79
2016	313.49	321.43	324.26	321.61	321.69	326.34	335.64	341.88	336.14	335.08	328.30	334.88	328.00
2017	332.18	343.91	350.37	353.00	346.24	350.55	367.39	368.90	349.92	348.15	347.28	354.48	351.87

DISTRICT OF COLUMBIA
At a Glance

Population:
2010 census: 601,723
2017 estimate: 693,972

Percent change in population:
2010–2017: 15.3%

Percent change in total nonfarm employment:
2007–2017: 13.9%

Industry with the largest growth in employment, 2007–2017 (thousands):
Education and health services, 36.2

Industry with the largest decline or smallest growth in employment, 2007–2017 (thousands):
Information, -4,0

Civilian labor force:
2010: 346,065
2017: 400,894

Unemployment rate and rank among states (highest to lowest):
2010: 9.4%, 21st
2017: 6.1%, 3rd

Over-the-year change in unemployment rates:
2015–2016: -0.8%
2016–2017: 0.0%

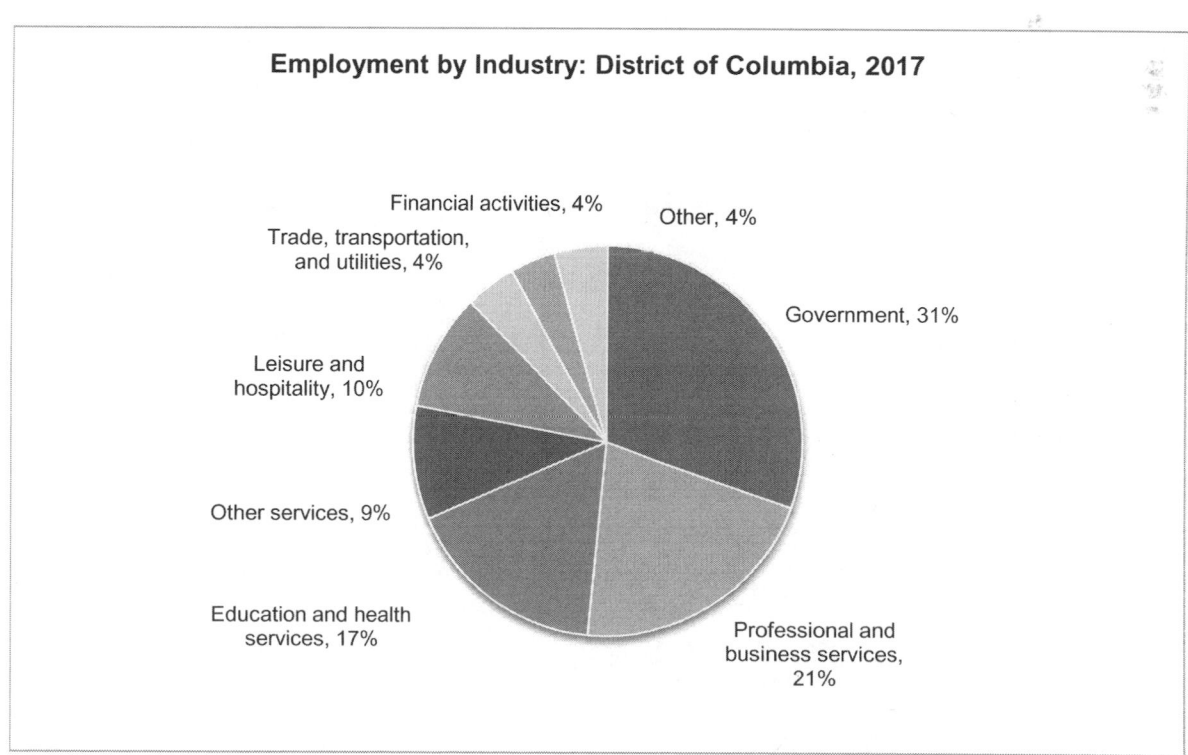

Employment by Industry: District of Columbia, 2017

Financial activities, 4%
Other, 4%
Trade, transportation, and utilities, 4%
Government, 31%
Leisure and hospitality, 10%
Other services, 9%
Education and health services, 17%
Professional and business services, 21%

1. Employment by Industry: District of Columbia, Selected Years, 2007–2017

(Numbers in thousands, not seasonally adjusted)

Industry and year	January	February	March	April	May	June	July	August	September	October	November	December	Annual average
Total Nonfarm													
2007	680.7	689.2	692.0	692.1	689.6	691.3	701.4	695.5	690.3	700.0	701.1	701.8	693.8
2008	689.0	693.6	698.2	701.2	702.7	704.1	720.0	715.9	705.1	705.9	706.0	704.5	703.9
2009	697.8	697.4	697.2	696.5	697.3	698.1	718.1	706.6	694.2	703.8	706.8	705.6	701.6
2010	698.2	695.5	703.4	713.6	715.5	715.6	732.1	707.7	711.1	717.2	718.4	717.3	712.1
2011	713.9	716.9	721.4	727.8	723.8	726.3	740.8	724.7	730.3	729.8	729.7	729.1	726.2
2012	721.9	725.1	729.8	730.8	733.9	732.8	743.0	728.9	736.1	743.9	745.7	744.7	734.7
2013	733.4	738.2	741.3	748.3	749.3	743.7	757.6	743.8	752.7	754.2	758.3	756.5	748.1
2014	739.0	743.7	747.3	752.6	754.6	749.4	759.8	744.8	758.9	762.1	763.7	763.5	753.3
2015	755.5	759.4	761.7	765.4	768.0	762.7	777.8	762.2	773.0	779.9	781.3	784.0	769.2
2016	770.2	776.7	779.7	786.3	785.3	777.8	789.0	774.0	786.5	789.5	790.7	789.4	782.9
2017	779.5	784.1	789.6	790.9	792.6	786.4	795.2	780.6	792.7	797.5	798.4	797.1	790.4
Total Private													
2007	453.8	461.4	464.9	465.2	462.3	461.3	459.8	456.9	461.6	467.3	469.0	469.5	462.8
2008	458.1	463.0	467.1	471.4	471.8	470.1	471.5	469.5	472.6	471.7	471.7	469.6	469.0
2009	463.7	463.4	463.3	462.0	462.0	459.3	458.3	454.4	455.9	463.3	465.5	465.2	461.4
2010	456.9	454.8	462.5	471.5	470.7	468.1	464.2	461.4	465.1	468.4	469.4	469.5	465.2
2011	467.0	470.5	474.6	481.7	477.3	477.8	480.1	478.1	483.6	486.1	486.5	486.1	479.1
2012	479.5	483.8	487.9	490.0	492.6	489.2	488.2	486.8	494.5	501.2	503.1	502.7	491.6
2013	493.2	498.6	501.4	508.9	509.8	503.7	507.5	506.0	513.3	514.6	518.8	516.8	507.7
2014	506.4	510.7	514.0	520.2	521.7	515.5	513.2	511.5	523.3	525.7	527.8	527.1	518.1
2015	520.0	523.4	525.6	529.4	531.4	525.5	527.2	525.8	535.5	543.0	544.1	545.1	531.3
2016	532.6	538.6	541.5	548.4	546.3	537.7	536.6	535.0	546.2	549.1	549.8	548.0	542.5
2017	538.9	544.3	548.5	552.0	552.7	545.9	544.1	542.2	553.5	558.8	559.6	558.5	549.9
Goods Producing													
2007	13.9	13.7	13.8	13.9	14.3	14.5	14.6	15.0	14.9	14.8	14.7	14.2	14.4
2008	14.4	14.5	14.5	14.1	14.5	14.6	14.6	15.0	14.5	14.6	14.5	14.2	14.5
2009	14.0	14.0	13.5	13.4	13.4	13.3	12.8	12.7	12.4	11.9	11.7	11.6	12.9
2010	11.3	10.4	11.2	11.8	11.8	11.8	12.2	12.0	11.8	12.1	12.0	12.0	11.7
2011	12.1	12.1	12.3	12.8	13.0	13.2	14.1	14.1	13.8	13.6	13.5	13.6	13.2
2012	13.5	13.8	14.1	14.5	14.7	14.9	15.0	15.0	14.9	15.2	14.9	14.8	14.6
2013	14.5	14.6	14.7	14.5	14.9	15.1	15.7	15.8	15.3	15.1	15.1	15.0	15.0
2014	14.8	14.7	14.9	15.0	15.2	15.5	15.9	15.9	15.6	15.7	15.5	15.3	15.3
2015	14.6	14.5	14.6	14.9	15.2	15.3	16.0	16.2	15.9	16.9	16.9	17.0	15.7
2016	17.0	16.7	17.1	16.9	17.0	17.2	15.9	16.0	15.9	16.5	16.3	16.4	16.6
2017	15.7	16.0	16.1	16.7	16.8	17.1	17.2	17.0	16.9	16.9	16.9	16.8	16.7
Service-Providing													
2007	666.8	675.5	678.2	678.2	675.3	676.8	686.8	680.5	675.4	685.2	686.4	687.6	679.4
2008	674.6	679.1	683.7	687.1	688.2	689.5	705.4	700.9	690.6	691.3	691.5	690.3	689.4
2009	683.8	683.4	683.7	683.1	683.9	684.8	705.3	693.9	681.8	691.9	695.1	694.0	688.7
2010	686.9	685.1	692.2	701.8	703.7	703.8	719.9	695.7	699.3	705.1	706.4	705.3	700.4
2011	701.8	704.8	709.1	715.0	710.8	713.1	726.7	710.6	716.5	716.2	716.2	715.5	713.0
2012	708.4	711.3	715.7	716.3	719.2	717.9	728.0	713.9	721.2	728.7	730.8	729.9	720.1
2013	718.9	723.6	726.6	733.8	734.4	728.6	741.9	728.0	737.4	739.1	743.2	741.5	733.1
2014	724.2	729.0	732.4	737.6	739.4	733.9	743.9	728.9	743.3	746.4	748.2	748.2	738.0
2015	740.9	744.9	747.1	750.5	752.8	747.4	761.8	746.0	757.1	763.0	764.4	767.0	753.6
2016	753.2	760.0	762.6	769.4	768.3	760.6	773.1	758.0	770.6	773.0	774.4	773.0	766.4
2017	763.8	768.1	773.5	774.2	775.8	769.3	778.0	763.6	775.8	780.6	781.5	780.3	773.7
Mining, Logging, and Construction													
2007	12.2	12.0	12.1	12.2	12.6	12.8	12.9	13.4	13.2	13.1	13.0	12.5	12.7
2008	12.7	12.8	12.8	12.6	12.9	13.0	13.1	13.5	13.1	13.2	13.1	12.8	13.0
2009	12.6	12.6	12.2	12.1	12.1	12.0	11.5	11.4	11.2	10.7	10.5	10.4	11.6
2010	10.1	9.2	10.1	10.7	10.7	10.7	11.1	11.0	10.7	11.0	11.0	11.0	10.6
2011	11.0	11.1	11.2	11.7	11.9	12.1	13.0	13.1	12.8	12.6	12.5	12.6	12.1
2012	12.5	12.8	13.0	13.5	13.7	13.9	14.0	14.0	13.9	14.2	13.9	13.8	13.6
2013	13.5	13.6	13.7	13.5	13.9	14.1	14.7	14.8	14.3	14.1	14.1	14.0	14.0
2014	13.8	13.7	13.9	14.0	14.2	14.5	14.9	14.9	14.6	14.6	14.4	14.2	14.3
2015	13.6	13.5	13.6	13.9	14.2	14.3	14.9	15.1	14.8	15.8	15.8	15.9	14.6
2016	15.8	15.5	15.9	15.7	15.8	15.9	14.7	14.8	14.7	15.3	15.1	15.2	15.4
2017	14.5	14.8	14.9	15.4	15.5	15.8	15.9	15.7	15.6	15.6	15.6	15.5	15.4

1. Employment by Industry: District of Columbia, Selected Years, 2007–2017—*Continued*

(Numbers in thousands, not seasonally adjusted)

Industry and year	January	February	March	April	May	June	July	August	September	October	November	December	Annual average
Manufacturing													
2007	1.7	1.7	1.7	1.7	1.7	1.7	1.7	1.6	1.7	1.7	1.7	1.7	1.7
2008	1.7	1.7	1.7	1.5	1.6	1.6	1.5	1.5	1.4	1.4	1.4	1.4	1.5
2009	1.4	1.4	1.3	1.3	1.3	1.3	1.3	1.3	1.2	1.2	1.2	1.2	1.3
2010	1.2	1.2	1.1	1.1	1.1	1.1	1.1	1.0	1.1	1.1	1.0	1.0	1.1
2011	1.1	1.0	1.1	1.1	1.1	1.1	1.1	1.0	1.0	1.0	1.0	1.0	1.1
2012	1.0	1.0	1.1	1.0	1.0	1.0	1.0	1.0	1.0	1.0	1.0	1.0	1.0
2013	1.0	1.0	1.0	1.0	1.0	1.0	1.0	1.0	1.0	1.0	1.0	1.0	1.0
2014	1.0	1.0	1.0	1.0	1.0	1.0	1.0	1.0	1.0	1.1	1.1	1.1	1.0
2015	1.0	1.0	1.0	1.0	1.0	1.0	1.1	1.1	1.1	1.1	1.1	1.1	1.1
2016	1.2	1.2	1.2	1.2	1.2	1.3	1.2	1.2	1.2	1.2	1.2	1.2	1.2
2017	1.2	1.2	1.2	1.3	1.3	1.3	1.3	1.3	1.3	1.3	1.3	1.3	1.3
Trade, Transportation, and Utilities													
2007	27.5	27.2	27.4	27.8	27.9	27.9	27.7	27.5	27.6	27.6	28.1	28.4	27.7
2008	27.4	27.5	27.4	27.9	27.9	28.2	28.3	27.9	28.0	27.6	28.3	28.5	27.9
2009	27.3	26.8	26.7	26.8	26.6	26.5	26.5	26.4	26.5	27.0	27.5	27.5	26.8
2010	26.9	26.1	26.9	27.4	27.4	27.6	27.4	27.2	27.2	27.6	28.1	28.2	27.3
2011	27.3	27.1	27.1	27.5	27.3	27.2	27.1	27.1	27.3	27.9	28.1	28.3	27.4
2012	27.4	27.4	27.5	27.7	28.0	28.2	28.0	28.0	28.2	28.3	29.1	29.4	28.1
2013	28.5	28.6	28.6	28.6	28.7	28.7	28.7	28.7	29.1	29.4	30.5	30.7	29.1
2014	29.5	29.5	29.8	30.5	30.5	30.7	30.3	30.5	30.7	31.2	32.1	32.1	30.6
2015	31.4	31.3	31.3	31.5	31.6	32.2	32.2	32.1	32.5	32.8	33.4	33.7	32.2
2016	32.1	32.3	32.3	32.6	32.7	33.1	32.7	32.6	32.8	33.1	33.7	33.7	32.8
2017	32.7	32.9	33.1	33.1	33.2	33.5	33.4	33.3	33.5	33.6	34.1	34.0	33.4
Wholesale Trade													
2007	4.8	4.8	4.8	4.8	4.8	4.8	4.8	4.8	4.8	4.8	4.8	4.8	4.8
2008	4.7	4.8	4.7	4.7	4.7	4.9	5.0	4.9	4.8	4.8	4.7	4.7	4.8
2009	4.7	4.6	4.6	4.6	4.6	4.6	4.6	4.5	4.5	4.6	4.6	4.6	4.6
2010	4.6	4.6	4.6	4.7	4.7	4.8	4.7	4.6	4.6	4.7	4.7	4.7	4.7
2011	4.6	4.6	4.6	4.6	4.6	4.5	4.5	4.7	4.6	4.8	4.8	4.8	4.6
2012	4.8	4.9	4.9	4.9	5.0	5.1	5.0	5.1	5.1	5.0	5.0	5.0	5.0
2013	4.9	5.0	4.9	4.8	4.8	4.8	4.9	4.8	4.9	4.8	4.9	4.9	4.9
2014	4.8	4.8	4.9	4.9	4.9	4.9	5.0	4.9	4.9	5.0	5.0	5.0	4.9
2015	5.0	5.0	5.0	4.7	4.8	4.8	4.8	4.7	4.8	4.9	4.9	4.9	4.9
2016	5.0	5.0	5.0	5.0	5.0	5.0	5.0	5.1	5.0	5.0	5.0	4.9	5.0
2017	5.0	5.0	5.0	4.9	4.9	4.9	4.9	4.9	4.9	5.0	5.1	5.1	5.0
Retail Trade													
2007	18.0	17.8	17.8	18.2	18.2	18.3	18.1	17.9	18.0	18.2	18.6	18.9	18.2
2008	18.1	18.2	18.2	18.6	18.5	18.6	18.5	18.3	18.5	18.1	18.9	19.0	18.5
2009	18.0	17.6	17.5	17.5	17.3	17.3	17.3	17.4	17.6	18.1	18.7	18.8	17.8
2010	18.3	17.5	18.1	18.4	18.4	18.5	18.4	18.3	18.3	18.6	19.1	19.3	18.4
2011	18.6	18.4	18.3	18.6	18.5	18.4	18.3	18.1	18.5	18.9	19.2	19.5	18.6
2012	18.6	18.5	18.5	18.6	18.8	18.8	18.8	18.7	18.9	19.1	20.0	20.3	19.0
2013	19.5	19.5	19.5	19.6	19.7	19.6	19.6	19.8	20.1	20.5	21.5	21.7	20.1
2014	20.7	20.6	20.7	21.3	21.2	21.3	20.9	21.1	21.4	21.7	22.6	22.7	21.4
2015	22.0	21.8	21.8	22.1	22.0	22.3	22.4	22.4	22.7	23.0	23.7	23.9	22.5
2016	22.6	22.7	22.7	22.8	22.9	23.2	22.7	22.5	22.7	23.0	23.6	23.7	22.9
2017	22.8	23.0	23.1	23.1	23.2	23.3	23.2	23.2	23.4	23.4	23.7	23.6	23.3
Transportation and Utilities													
2007	4.7	4.6	4.8	4.8	4.9	4.8	4.8	4.8	4.8	4.6	4.7	4.7	4.8
2008	4.6	4.5	4.5	4.6	4.7	4.7	4.8	4.7	4.7	4.7	4.7	4.8	4.7
2009	4.6	4.6	4.6	4.7	4.7	4.6	4.6	4.5	4.4	4.3	4.2	4.1	4.5
2010	4.0	4.0	4.2	4.3	4.3	4.3	4.3	4.3	4.3	4.3	4.3	4.2	4.2
2011	4.1	4.1	4.2	4.3	4.2	4.3	4.3	4.3	4.2	4.2	4.1	4.0	4.2
2012	4.0	4.0	4.1	4.2	4.2	4.3	4.2	4.2	4.2	4.2	4.1	4.1	4.2
2013	4.1	4.1	4.2	4.2	4.2	4.3	4.2	4.1	4.1	4.1	4.1	4.1	4.2
2014	4.0	4.1	4.2	4.3	4.4	4.5	4.4	4.4	4.4	4.5	4.5	4.4	4.4
2015	4.4	4.5	4.5	4.7	4.8	5.1	5.0	5.0	5.0	4.9	4.8	4.9	4.8
2016	4.5	4.6	4.6	4.8	4.8	4.9	5.0	5.0	5.1	5.1	5.1	5.1	4.9
2017	4.9	4.9	5.0	5.1	5.1	5.3	5.3	5.2	5.2	5.2	5.3	5.3	5.2

1. Employment by Industry: District of Columbia, Selected Years, 2007–2017—*Continued*

(Numbers in thousands, not seasonally adjusted)

Industry and year	January	February	March	April	May	June	July	August	September	October	November	December	Annual average
Information													
2007	22.4	22.5	22.4	21.8	21.8	22.2	22.5	22.3	21.4	21.3	21.3	21.3	21.9
2008	21.1	21.2	21.3	20.9	21.0	20.9	21.0	21.0	20.8	20.6	20.6	20.4	20.9
2009	19.8	19.7	19.0	19.4	19.3	19.4	19.1	18.8	18.6	18.6	18.5	18.5	19.1
2010	18.5	18.4	18.5	18.7	18.6	18.9	19.0	18.7	18.8	18.7	18.5	18.7	18.7
2011	18.3	18.5	18.6	18.8	18.5	18.7	18.4	17.9	18.2	18.0	18.0	18.2	18.3
2012	17.5	17.7	17.6	17.3	17.4	17.7	17.4	17.7	17.3	17.3	17.6	17.4	17.5
2013	17.1	17.2	17.2	16.9	17.1	17.1	17.3	17.4	16.9	16.6	16.9	16.7	17.0
2014	17.1	17.1	17.1	17.2	17.3	17.4	17.6	17.3	17.2	17.1	17.1	17.1	17.2
2015	16.6	16.7	16.7	17.1	17.2	17.3	17.4	17.3	17.2	17.5	17.5	17.6	17.2
2016	16.9	17.1	17.0	17.0	16.8	17.1	17.2	17.2	17.1	17.3	17.4	17.3	17.1
2017	17.1	17.4	17.5	17.8	18.0	18.0	18.1	18.1	18.1	18.0	18.5	18.5	17.9
Financial Activities													
2007	29.5	29.7	29.7	29.3	29.0	29.1	29.3	29.1	28.9	28.9	29.0	28.9	29.2
2008	28.3	28.4	28.3	28.4	28.3	28.4	28.2	28.2	28.2	27.8	27.8	27.6	28.2
2009	27.2	26.9	26.8	26.6	26.6	26.9	26.8	26.8	26.9	27.0	27.1	27.2	26.9
2010	26.8	26.7	27.0	27.1	27.1	27.3	26.6	26.5	26.1	27.0	27.2	27.2	26.9
2011	27.1	27.0	27.2	27.5	27.5	27.4	27.7	27.9	27.9	27.9	28.0	28.1	27.6
2012	28.1	28.1	28.1	28.1	28.1	28.3	28.1	28.0	28.0	28.2	28.3	28.2	28.1
2013	28.0	28.2	28.4	28.6	28.5	28.9	28.9	29.0	28.8	29.3	29.4	29.6	28.8
2014	29.5	29.6	29.7	29.5	29.7	30.0	30.2	30.1	29.9	29.9	30.0	30.0	29.8
2015	29.9	30.0	30.1	29.6	29.6	29.8	30.0	29.9	29.6	29.5	29.6	29.5	29.8
2016	29.5	29.5	29.7	29.9	29.9	30.0	30.3	30.3	30.2	30.1	30.0	30.1	30.0
2017	29.8	30.0	29.9	29.9	30.0	30.5	30.6	30.4	30.2	30.2	29.9	30.2	30.1
Professional and Business Services													
2007	150.7	152.3	152.8	152.6	153.5	155.4	153.1	152.7	151.7	152.3	152.9	153.3	152.8
2008	150.5	152.0	153.3	153.6	153.6	155.0	153.6	152.9	151.9	151.8	150.6	150.1	152.4
2009	149.2	148.9	148.5	146.1	146.4	148.4	148.7	147.1	145.4	147.1	147.7	148.0	147.6
2010	145.8	145.8	147.3	148.7	148.6	150.0	149.1	148.2	146.8	147.2	147.2	147.4	147.7
2011	146.7	147.4	148.4	150.4	150.5	151.8	152.7	152.1	150.2	151.8	151.5	151.0	150.4
2012	150.7	151.5	152.7	152.6	152.9	154.4	155.6	154.9	153.7	156.2	156.9	156.5	154.1
2013	153.3	154.6	154.9	155.0	154.9	156.1	157.8	157.5	156.0	156.5	157.7	156.6	155.9
2014	153.7	154.6	155.2	155.9	156.3	158.4	159.1	158.1	158.2	159.1	159.3	159.4	157.3
2015	158.2	159.3	159.5	160.0	160.8	162.8	163.5	163.1	162.0	164.5	164.3	164.2	161.9
2016	162.1	163.3	163.6	165.0	164.7	165.7	166.5	165.2	164.1	165.9	166.3	165.9	164.9
2017	164.7	165.0	165.1	165.9	165.6	168.1	168.3	166.9	165.9	167.5	167.5	167.6	166.5
Education and Health Services													
2007	97.3	101.6	102.4	101.3	96.9	92.1	92.3	91.5	97.5	102.9	103.0	103.2	98.5
2008	99.4	100.8	101.5	102.6	102.2	97.8	99.7	99.7	103.8	104.8	105.9	106.2	102.0
2009	104.9	106.0	106.6	106.8	105.3	100.3	100.9	100.2	103.4	107.9	109.1	108.9	105.0
2010	107.4	107.2	108.4	111.3	110.4	104.7	103.1	103.5	109.6	109.1	109.9	109.9	107.9
2011	112.7	113.6	114.1	114.3	110.3	108.5	109.4	108.6	115.6	115.5	115.9	116.0	112.9
2012	114.6	115.2	115.5	116.3	116.2	109.9	107.7	108.7	118.0	121.1	122.3	122.8	115.7
2013	120.5	122.3	122.7	127.1	126.6	117.9	119.7	119.4	128.3	130.3	131.3	131.2	124.8
2014	127.4	129.0	129.3	130.3	129.9	120.4	118.1	117.8	129.6	130.5	131.4	132.2	127.2
2015	129.0	130.6	130.9	132.1	131.4	121.9	122.6	122.1	133.4	137.2	137.7	138.0	130.6
2016	133.7	136.2	136.4	137.7	136.3	125.1	125.4	125.3	136.6	136.9	137.5	137.3	133.7
2017	134.6	136.6	137.2	137.2	136.6	126.5	124.7	125.1	137.4	140.0	141.1	139.0	134.7
Leisure and Hospitality													
2007	51.5	52.8	54.5	56.3	56.3	56.4	56.4	55.7	56.5	56.4	56.6	56.3	55.5
2008	53.9	55.2	56.4	59.1	59.2	59.0	59.1	58.6	59.4	58.9	58.1	56.6	57.8
2009	56.0	56.0	57.4	58.4	59.8	59.1	58.5	57.8	58.6	59.2	59.1	58.4	58.2
2010	56.1	56.1	58.6	61.7	61.4	61.4	60.5	59.6	59.6	60.9	60.4	59.7	59.7
2011	57.2	58.5	60.1	63.9	63.5	63.5	62.6	63.0	63.8	64.3	64.2	63.2	62.3
2012	60.7	62.5	64.4	66.3	67.7	67.4	66.7	66.0	66.3	66.6	65.4	64.7	65.4
2013	63.1	64.6	66.3	69.3	69.9	69.9	69.2	68.6	69.4	68.2	68.5	67.5	67.9
2014	65.4	66.5	68.3	71.6	72.4	71.7	70.5	70.6	71.2	71.4	71.4	70.2	70.1
2015	70.1	70.4	71.8	73.8	74.9	74.6	73.8	74.0	73.9	73.5	73.5	73.7	73.2
2016	70.2	72.1	73.7	77.2	76.6	76.3	74.8	74.9	76.1	75.6	74.6	73.5	74.6
2017	71.3	72.7	75.5	77.6	78.6	77.2	76.4	76.7	77.3	78.2	76.7	76.6	76.2

1. Employment by Industry: District of Columbia, Selected Years, 2007–2017—*Continued*

(Numbers in thousands, not seasonally adjusted)

Industry and year	January	February	March	April	May	June	July	August	September	October	November	December	Annual average
Other Services													
2007	61.0	61.6	61.9	62.2	62.6	63.7	63.9	63.1	63.1	63.1	63.4	63.9	62.8
2008	63.1	63.4	64.4	64.8	65.1	66.2	67.0	66.2	66.0	65.6	65.9	66.0	65.3
2009	65.3	65.1	64.8	64.5	64.6	65.4	65.0	64.6	64.1	64.6	64.8	65.1	64.8
2010	64.1	64.1	64.6	64.8	65.4	66.4	66.3	65.7	65.2	65.8	66.1	66.4	65.4
2011	65.6	66.3	66.8	66.5	66.7	67.5	68.1	67.4	66.8	67.1	67.3	67.7	67.0
2012	67.0	67.6	68.0	67.2	67.6	68.4	69.7	68.5	68.1	68.3	68.6	68.9	68.2
2013	68.2	68.5	68.6	68.9	69.2	70.0	70.2	69.6	69.5	69.2	69.4	69.5	69.2
2014	69.0	69.7	69.7	70.2	70.4	71.4	71.5	71.2	70.9	70.8	71.0	70.8	70.6
2015	70.2	70.6	70.7	70.4	70.7	71.6	71.7	71.1	71.0	71.1	71.2	71.4	71.0
2016	71.1	71.4	71.7	72.1	72.3	73.2	73.8	73.5	73.4	73.7	74.0	73.8	72.8
2017	73.0	73.7	74.1	73.8	73.9	75.0	75.4	74.7	74.2	74.4	74.9	75.8	74.4
Government													
2007	226.9	227.8	227.1	226.9	227.3	230.0	241.6	238.6	228.7	232.7	232.1	232.3	231.0
2008	230.9	230.6	231.1	229.8	230.9	234.0	248.5	246.4	232.5	234.2	234.3	234.9	234.8
2009	234.1	234.0	233.9	234.5	235.3	238.8	259.8	252.2	238.3	240.5	241.3	240.4	240.3
2010	241.3	240.7	240.9	242.1	244.8	247.5	267.9	246.3	246.0	248.8	249.0	247.8	246.9
2011	246.9	246.4	246.8	246.1	246.5	248.5	260.7	246.6	246.7	243.7	243.2	243.0	247.1
2012	242.4	241.3	241.9	240.8	241.3	243.6	254.8	242.1	241.6	242.7	242.6	242.0	243.1
2013	240.2	239.6	239.9	239.4	239.5	240.0	250.1	237.8	239.4	239.6	239.5	239.7	240.4
2014	232.6	233.0	233.3	232.4	232.9	233.9	246.6	233.3	235.6	236.4	235.9	236.4	235.2
2015	235.5	236.0	236.1	236.0	236.6	237.2	250.6	236.4	237.5	236.9	237.2	238.9	237.7
2016	237.6	238.1	238.2	237.9	239.0	240.1	252.4	239.0	240.3	240.4	240.9	241.4	240.4
2017	240.6	239.8	241.1	238.9	239.9	240.5	251.1	238.4	239.2	238.7	238.8	238.6	240.5

2. Average Weekly Hours by Selected Industry: District of Columbia, 2013–2017

(Not seasonally adjusted)

Industry and year	January	February	March	April	May	June	July	August	September	October	November	December	Annual average
Total Private													
2013	35.6	36.0	35.7	35.6	35.7	36.7	35.5	35.7	36.5	35.8	36.0	36.6	36.0
2014	35.8	36.7	36.7	36.0	36.0	36.6	36.0	36.0	35.7	35.8	36.9	35.5	36.1
2015	35.3	36.8	36.4	35.5	35.8	35.5	35.0	35.9	35.0	35.3	36.0	35.2	35.6
2016	35.2	35.3	35.4	35.6	36.4	35.6	35.4	35.3	35.4	36.3	35.4	35.4	35.6
2017	36.1	35.5	35.3	36.4	35.1	35.0	35.9	35.0	35.1	36.0	35.0	35.1	35.5
Goods-Producing													
2013	37.3	37.3	38.1	36.2	38.0	37.4	37.7	38.9	40.7	37.2	37.2	38.4	37.9
2014	39.7	37.6	40.4	39.8	38.9	39.9	41.6	38.6	40.5	38.3	37.8	40.0	39.4
2015	38.3	40.1	40.4	39.0	40.5	40.6	39.0	39.7	38.2	40.6	37.7	40.9	39.6
2016	41.3	39.9	42.3	40.2	38.4	40.9	39.5	40.0	40.7	38.5	37.8	34.4	39.5
2017	36.9	36.9	35.7	37.1	34.7	36.7	35.8	35.3	36.1	35.7	36.6	37.1	36.2
Trade, Transportation, and Utilities													
2013	37.9	36.9	36.9	37.8	37.6	37.3	36.9	36.0	36.7	36.1	35.9	36.0	36.8
2014	35.2	35.6	36.7	36.4	36.8	35.8	35.9	35.5	36.5	35.3	36.5	36.3	36.0
2015	35.4	36.6	35.9	35.7	36.0	35.7	35.3	35.1	37.3	35.9	36.2	36.3	35.9
2016	34.9	34.9	35.0	35.0	34.9	34.3	34.3	33.6	33.8	33.3	33.6	33.0	34.2
2017	33.5	32.5	32.0	33.1	32.9	32.1	32.4	31.4	32.0	31.8	32.0	31.7	32.3
Professional and Business Services													
2013	35.3	36.2	35.5	35.4	35.7	37.7	35.9	36.4	37.5	36.0	36.8	37.5	36.3
2014	37.0	38.3	38.2	37.2	37.3	37.8	36.6	37.1	36.5	36.7	37.9	36.0	37.2
2015	36.0	37.8	37.5	36.2	36.3	36.3	35.4	37.4	35.7	36.1	37.1	36.1	36.5
2016	36.1	36.2	36.1	36.3	37.3	36.3	36.4	36.3	36.4	37.6	36.0	36.6	36.5
2017	37.7	37.0	36.3	38.0	36.4	36.5	37.8	36.6	36.7	38.0	36.3	36.5	37.0
Leisure and Hospitality													
2013	30.6	31.8	31.4	31.6	30.9	30.1	30.1	29.8	30.7	30.1	30.0	29.9	30.6
2014	28.6	29.3	29.7	30.3	30.5	30.7	30.2	29.7	29.6	30.1	30.1	29.7	29.9
2015	28.2	29.1	29.9	30.2	30.7	30.0	29.0	28.7	28.2	28.8	29.0	28.5	29.2
2016	27.3	29.0	29.2	29.7	29.2	28.2	28.3	27.6	27.5	28.2	28.4	28.0	28.4
2017	27.0	27.5	29.8	28.9	28.0	26.8	26.8	27.3	26.7	27.2	27.0	27.5	27.5
Other Services													
2013	35.2	35.9	35.9	35.7	35.9	36.9	35.2	35.9	36.3	36.0	35.7	36.4	35.9
2014	35.1	36.2	36.2	35.2	35.2	36.2	35.7	35.7	35.2	35.7	37.6	35.8	35.8
2015	35.7	37.2	36.1	34.9	35.4	34.8	35.1	36.2	35.5	35.6	36.8	35.2	35.7
2016	35.6	35.2	35.1	35.7	36.6	35.5	35.0	35.2	35.6	37.0	35.7	35.6	35.6
2017	36.8	35.8	35.6	37.2	35.8	36.5	37.7	36.5	36.5	37.6	36.0	35.5	36.5

3. Average Hourly Earnings by Selected Industry: District of Columbia, 2013–2017

(Dollars, not seasonally adjusted)

Industry and year	January	February	March	April	May	June	July	August	September	October	November	December	Annual average
Total Private													
2013	37.36	38.21	37.85	37.93	37.93	38.68	37.83	37.92	38.80	38.45	38.82	39.76	38.31
2014	38.93	39.67	39.21	38.36	38.54	39.14	38.25	38.32	38.87	38.55	39.55	39.27	38.89
2015	39.61	40.49	40.52	38.94	38.19	38.30	37.65	37.97	37.38	36.07	37.36	36.88	38.28
2016	36.57	36.96	36.89	37.44	38.79	37.85	38.38	39.17	39.07	40.11	39.62	39.88	38.41
2017	41.00	39.89	40.01	39.95	39.67	39.57	41.07	40.50	40.88	41.98	41.46	41.75	40.65
Goods-Producing													
2013	33.55	34.05	33.93	32.60	32.20	31.82	32.38	32.86	32.22	32.84	33.22	33.15	32.89
2014	30.77	30.58	29.39	29.12	28.35	28.43	27.34	27.54	27.13	27.33	27.69	28.55	28.49
2015	27.87	27.93	28.78	28.09	28.01	28.19	27.61	28.60	30.33	29.24	30.66	30.33	28.84
2016	30.97	30.27	29.74	29.39	30.41	29.89	29.64	30.33	29.85	29.41	29.36	30.99	30.02
2017	30.28	30.95	31.35	30.85	31.35	31.71	31.82	32.92	32.32	32.57	33.26	33.32	31.91
Trade, Transportation, and Utilities													
2013	24.39	25.46	25.25	25.12	24.81	24.61	23.57	24.11	24.07	25.00	24.17	24.87	24.66
2014	25.72	24.76	24.06	24.19	23.57	23.42	23.15	23.10	23.11	23.58	23.75	23.53	23.81
2015	24.18	24.74	24.88	24.46	24.54	24.63	25.01	26.11	25.43	25.82	26.63	25.68	25.19
2016	26.90	26.65	27.40	27.37	27.78	27.55	27.80	28.03	27.92	26.87	26.41	26.26	27.24
2017	27.29	26.29	25.57	26.27	26.31	25.65	26.74	26.62	26.25	26.69	26.30	25.78	26.32
Professional and Business Services													
2013	45.76	47.03	46.87	46.51	46.41	47.43	46.74	46.34	48.10	47.45	48.06	49.33	47.19
2014	47.85	49.44	49.01	48.06	48.45	49.35	47.62	47.84	48.22	47.66	49.21	48.63	48.45
2015	48.54	49.33	48.95	47.45	47.73	47.54	46.49	47.38	46.84	46.49	47.75	47.30	47.65
2016	47.29	47.09	46.53	46.48	48.16	47.13	47.16	47.52	47.16	48.54	47.57	47.54	47.35
2017	48.53	46.62	46.51	45.13	44.61	44.91	47.13	46.09	46.94	48.07	48.27	49.11	46.83
Leisure and Hospitality													
2013	17.87	18.63	17.83	18.03	17.92	17.70	17.16	17.34	17.44	17.90	16.90	17.67	17.70
2014	17.83	17.44	17.38	17.15	16.69	16.98	17.06	17.35	17.74	18.09	17.80	18.26	17.47
2015	18.08	17.97	18.49	18.07	17.94	17.71	17.64	17.67	17.79	17.85	17.86	17.70	17.90
2016	16.88	16.81	17.44	17.42	17.64	17.74	17.95	17.66	18.22	18.24	18.89	19.49	17.87
2017	19.20	19.22	20.38	19.59	19.61	18.97	19.73	18.89	19.45	20.60	18.82	19.00	19.47
Other Services													
2013	40.49	40.70	40.05	41.32	41.53	41.45	40.37	40.74	41.49	40.49	41.21	42.57	41.04
2014	41.87	42.71	41.75	41.97	42.79	42.96	43.15	43.07	44.61	44.24	44.92	45.05	43.27
2015	45.35	46.56	46.83	45.39	45.09	45.26	44.73	46.26	45.50	44.42	45.68	45.38	45.54
2016	46.12	46.80	47.07	47.43	48.33	46.96	47.59	48.02	47.48	48.22	47.60	48.23	47.50
2017	49.88	48.76	49.16	50.09	49.72	49.04	50.05	49.48	50.03	50.96	49.49	49.81	49.71

4. Average Weekly Earnings by Selected Industry: District of Columbia, 2013–2017

(Dollars, not seasonally adjusted)

Industry and year	January	February	March	April	May	June	July	August	September	October	November	December	Annual average
Total Private													
2013	1,330.02	1,375.56	1,351.25	1,350.31	1,354.10	1,419.56	1,342.97	1,353.74	1,416.20	1,376.51	1,397.52	1,455.22	1,379.16
2014	1,393.69	1,455.89	1,439.01	1,380.96	1,387.44	1,432.52	1,377.00	1,379.52	1,387.66	1,380.09	1,459.40	1,394.09	1,403.93
2015	1,398.23	1,490.03	1,474.93	1,382.37	1,367.20	1,359.65	1,317.75	1,363.12	1,308.30	1,273.27	1,344.96	1,298.18	1,362.77
2016	1,287.26	1,304.69	1,305.91	1,332.86	1,411.96	1,347.46	1,358.65	1,382.70	1,383.08	1,455.99	1,402.55	1,411.75	1,367.40
2017	1,480.10	1,416.10	1,412.35	1,454.18	1,392.42	1,384.95	1,474.41	1,417.50	1,434.89	1,511.28	1,451.10	1,465.43	1,443.08
Goods-Producing													
2013	1,251.42	1,270.07	1,292.73	1,180.12	1,223.60	1,190.07	1,220.73	1,278.25	1,311.35	1,221.65	1,235.78	1,272.96	1,246.53
2014	1,221.57	1,149.81	1,187.36	1,158.98	1,102.82	1,134.36	1,137.34	1,063.04	1,098.77	1,046.74	1,046.68	1,142.00	1,122.51
2015	1,067.42	1,119.99	1,162.71	1,095.51	1,134.41	1,144.51	1,076.79	1,135.42	1,158.61	1,187.14	1,155.88	1,240.50	1,142.06
2016	1,279.06	1,207.77	1,258.00	1,181.48	1,167.74	1,222.50	1,170.78	1,213.20	1,214.90	1,132.29	1,109.81	1,066.06	1,185.79
2017	1,117.33	1,142.06	1,119.20	1,144.54	1,087.85	1,163.76	1,139.16	1,162.08	1,166.75	1,162.75	1,217.32	1,236.17	1,155.14
Trade, Transportation, and Utilities													
2013	924.38	939.47	931.73	949.54	932.86	917.95	869.73	867.96	883.37	902.50	878.47	895.32	907.12
2014	905.34	881.46	883.00	880.52	867.38	838.44	831.09	820.05	843.52	832.37	866.88	854.14	857.16
2015	855.97	905.48	893.19	873.22	883.44	879.29	882.85	916.46	948.54	926.94	964.01	932.18	904.32
2016	938.81	930.09	959.00	957.95	969.52	944.97	953.54	941.81	943.70	894.77	887.38	866.58	931.61
2017	914.22	854.43	818.24	869.54	865.60	823.37	866.38	835.87	840.00	848.74	841.60	817.23	850.14
Professional and Business Services													
2013	1,615.33	1,702.49	1,663.89	1,646.45	1,656.84	1,788.11	1,677.97	1,686.78	1,803.75	1,708.20	1,768.61	1,849.88	1,713.00
2014	1,770.45	1,893.55	1,872.18	1,787.83	1,807.19	1,865.43	1,742.89	1,774.86	1,760.03	1,749.12	1,865.06	1,750.68	1,802.34
2015	1,747.44	1,864.67	1,835.63	1,717.69	1,732.60	1,725.70	1,645.75	1,772.01	1,672.19	1,678.29	1,771.53	1,707.53	1,739.23
2016	1,707.17	1,704.66	1,679.73	1,687.22	1,796.37	1,710.82	1,716.62	1,724.98	1,716.62	1,825.10	1,712.52	1,739.96	1,728.28
2017	1,829.58	1,724.94	1,688.31	1,714.94	1,623.80	1,639.22	1,781.51	1,686.89	1,722.70	1,826.66	1,752.20	1,792.52	1,732.71
Leisure and Hospitality													
2013	546.82	592.43	559.86	569.75	553.73	532.77	516.52	516.73	535.41	538.79	507.00	528.33	541.62
2014	509.94	510.99	516.19	519.65	509.05	521.29	515.21	515.30	525.10	544.51	535.78	542.32	522.35
2015	509.86	522.93	552.85	545.71	550.76	531.30	511.56	507.13	501.68	514.08	517.94	504.45	522.68
2016	460.82	487.49	509.25	517.37	515.09	500.27	507.99	487.42	501.05	514.37	536.48	545.72	507.51
2017	518.40	528.55	607.32	566.15	549.08	508.40	528.76	515.70	519.32	560.32	508.14	522.50	535.43
Other Services													
2013	1,425.25	1,461.13	1,437.80	1,475.12	1,490.93	1,529.51	1,421.02	1,462.57	1,506.09	1,457.64	1,471.20	1,549.55	1,473.34
2014	1,469.64	1,546.10	1,511.35	1,477.34	1,506.21	1,555.15	1,540.46	1,537.60	1,570.27	1,579.37	1,688.99	1,612.79	1,549.07
2015	1,619.00	1,732.03	1,690.56	1,584.11	1,596.19	1,575.05	1,570.02	1,674.61	1,615.25	1,581.35	1,681.02	1,597.38	1,625.78
2016	1,641.87	1,647.36	1,652.16	1,693.25	1,768.88	1,667.08	1,665.65	1,690.30	1,690.29	1,784.14	1,699.32	1,716.99	1,691.00
2017	1,835.58	1,745.61	1,750.10	1,863.35	1,779.98	1,789.96	1,886.89	1,806.02	1,826.10	1,916.10	1,781.64	1,768.26	1,814.42

FLORIDA
At a Glance

Population:
 2010 census: 18,801,310
 2017 estimate: 20,984,400

Percent change in population:
 2010–2017: 11.6%

Percent change in total nonfarm employment:
 2007–2017: 7.1%

Industry with the largest growth in employment, 2007–2017 (thousands):
 Education and health services, 256.2

Industry with the largest decline or smallest growth in employment, 2007–2017 (thousands):
 Construction, -118.4

Civilian labor force:
 2010: 9,212,066
 2017: 10,100,266

Unemployment rate and rank among states (highest to lowest):
 2010: 11.1%, 6th
 2017: 4.2%, 27th

Over-the-year change in unemployment rates:
 2015–2016: -0.7%
 2016–2017: -0.6%

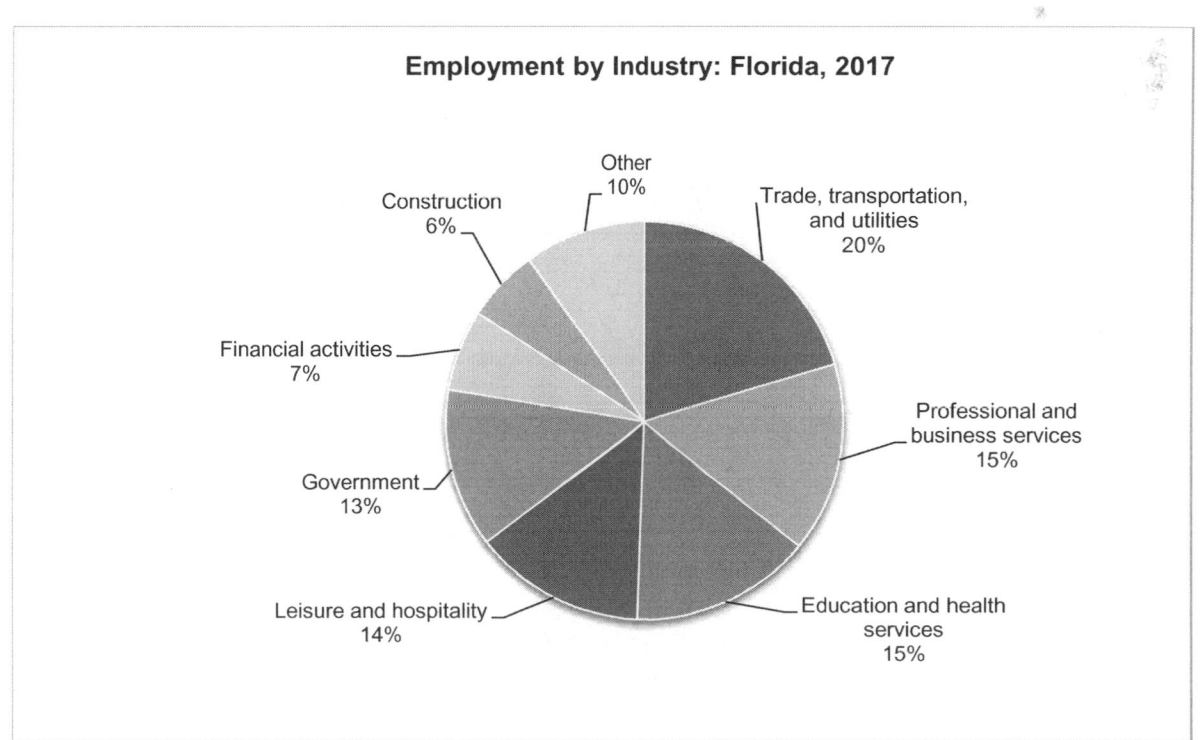

Employment by Industry: Florida, 2017

- Other 10%
- Construction 6%
- Financial activities 7%
- Government 13%
- Leisure and hospitality 14%
- Trade, transportation, and utilities 20%
- Professional and business services 15%
- Education and health services 15%

1. Employment by Industry: Florida, Selected Years, 2007–2017

(Numbers in thousands, not seasonally adjusted)

Industry and year	January	February	March	April	May	June	July	August	September	October	November	December	Annual average
Total Nonfarm													
2007	7,992.0	8,058.7	8,122.9	8,074.9	8,069.5	7,960.9	7,851.9	7,951.3	7,937.8	7,927.0	7,999.8	8,032.7	7,998.3
2008	7,851.4	7,907.3	7,928.8	7,845.1	7,813.7	7,672.5	7,562.4	7,636.9	7,608.3	7,579.6	7,586.9	7,586.1	7,714.9
2009	7,377.7	7,377.0	7,372.3	7,324.4	7,284.4	7,152.3	7,063.8	7,131.1	7,125.6	7,150.8	7,204.6	7,224.1	7,232.3
2010	7,095.1	7,145.4	7,192.6	7,213.1	7,236.5	7,115.0	7,057.8	7,143.5	7,133.1	7,196.7	7,258.2	7,286.9	7,172.8
2011	7,173.5	7,224.0	7,270.9	7,307.9	7,277.5	7,164.0	7,126.5	7,212.5	7,238.8	7,280.9	7,356.7	7,389.5	7,251.9
2012	7,283.5	7,344.9	7,404.9	7,424.1	7,414.5	7,320.7	7,266.2	7,364.8	7,379.9	7,452.2	7,540.7	7,566.0	7,396.9
2013	7,444.3	7,520.0	7,573.9	7,583.9	7,585.5	7,495.4	7,458.7	7,567.6	7,579.5	7,647.5	7,751.5	7,781.8	7,582.5
2014	7,663.4	7,735.1	7,791.4	7,820.8	7,827.5	7,728.7	7,699.5	7,812.1	7,830.3	7,918.0	8,014.1	8,057.1	7,824.8
2015	7,940.7	8,013.7	8,064.7	8,091.5	8,097.7	8,005.4	7,984.6	8,090.0	8,106.0	8,220.9	8,318.2	8,359.5	8,107.7
2016	8,236.4	8,311.7	8,357.4	8,397.2	8,386.8	8,274.2	8,275.1	8,371.1	8,408.6	8,467.8	8,567.8	8,596.2	8,387.5
2017	8,487.9	8,550.9	8,590.8	8,598.7	8,598.0	8,497.2	8,455.9	8,547.1	8,389.9	8,619.2	8,711.5	8,754.5	8,566.8
Total Private													
2007	6,868.2	6,923.6	6,982.3	6,935.7	6,933.9	6,919.9	6,810.8	6,821.2	6,799.6	6,781.4	6,848.5	6,883.3	6,875.7
2008	6,711.1	6,755.5	6,779.6	6,698.2	6,672.8	6,627.8	6,518.6	6,503.8	6,466.1	6,433.7	6,442.1	6,446.6	6,588.0
2009	6,244.6	6,237.9	6,235.4	6,181.8	6,153.9	6,116.9	6,029.6	6,017.4	6,001.6	6,022.2	6,072.8	6,098.7	6,117.7
2010	5,973.2	6,017.5	6,064.3	6,079.0	6,074.7	6,067.1	6,024.5	6,031.4	6,017.9	6,074.5	6,132.7	6,169.9	6,060.6
2011	6,058.9	6,099.7	6,148.2	6,185.1	6,167.0	6,145.5	6,114.7	6,128.9	6,146.9	6,173.7	6,249.3	6,287.8	6,158.8
2012	6,188.8	6,238.4	6,299.2	6,324.0	6,325.1	6,315.6	6,267.0	6,289.8	6,294.9	6,354.6	6,440.2	6,471.4	6,317.4
2013	6,354.1	6,420.0	6,472.5	6,484.7	6,496.3	6,492.6	6,465.0	6,496.3	6,497.7	6,554.1	6,652.8	6,689.4	6,506.3
2014	6,578.2	6,640.9	6,693.1	6,725.7	6,740.3	6,729.7	6,703.3	6,742.1	6,750.0	6,823.7	6,916.5	6,962.4	6,750.5
2015	6,853.9	6,915.2	6,963.1	6,989.6	7,003.2	6,999.6	6,980.7	7,010.6	7,016.6	7,114.7	7,210.7	7,257.3	7,026.3
2016	7,138.5	7,203.5	7,245.9	7,280.6	7,276.4	7,250.0	7,253.6	7,276.2	7,295.5	7,349.2	7,444.1	7,475.2	7,290.7
2017	7,373.4	7,422.9	7,460.2	7,471.3	7,477.7	7,464.4	7,427.3	7,448.3	7,276.6	7,492.3	7,580.9	7,626.7	7,460.2
Goods Producing													
2007	1,063.3	1,064.8	1,068.6	1,048.1	1,047.2	1,048.8	1,022.7	1,019.2	1,009.5	990.8	983.6	977.1	1,028.6
2008	945.2	944.0	938.8	915.5	911.9	908.8	886.6	880.1	872.7	852.8	838.1	823.5	893.2
2009	784.9	771.5	762.4	741.3	734.7	730.6	714.5	708.3	701.9	693.2	687.4	683.2	726.2
2010	660.6	662.1	664.5	668.6	669.1	672.4	673.1	670.7	666.2	661.3	658.4	657.0	665.3
2011	643.0	645.6	648.4	651.4	652.9	655.3	656.0	657.5	659.6	656.9	658.1	658.4	653.6
2012	649.1	651.9	657.8	657.1	661.9	667.1	665.3	670.5	672.0	673.8	677.5	677.1	665.1
2013	666.1	672.3	678.7	682.8	689.8	695.2	696.9	703.8	706.2	708.0	713.0	715.1	694.0
2014	706.1	713.3	717.0	722.5	731.0	736.5	739.0	744.4	747.1	752.4	754.0	755.8	734.9
2015	747.9	754.9	761.0	766.2	773.7	782.0	785.3	789.2	792.8	804.5	808.3	811.1	781.4
2016	804.0	813.2	818.8	826.1	831.2	837.3	842.2	844.7	850.2	852.6	858.1	860.3	836.6
2017	852.2	861.5	868.0	868.0	873.7	880.6	878.1	882.0	848.7	884.9	892.9	895.2	873.8
Service-Providing													
2007	6,928.7	6,993.9	7,054.3	7,026.8	7,022.3	6,912.1	6,829.2	6,932.1	6,928.3	6,936.2	7,016.2	7,055.6	6,969.6
2008	6,906.2	6,963.3	6,990.0	6,929.6	6,901.8	6,763.7	6,675.8	6,756.8	6,735.6	6,726.8	6,748.8	6,762.6	6,821.8
2009	6,592.8	6,605.5	6,609.9	6,583.1	6,549.7	6,421.7	6,349.3	6,422.8	6,423.7	6,457.6	6,517.2	6,540.9	6,506.2
2010	6,434.5	6,483.3	6,528.1	6,544.5	6,567.4	6,442.6	6,384.7	6,472.8	6,466.9	6,535.4	6,599.8	6,629.9	6,507.5
2011	6,530.5	6,578.4	6,622.5	6,656.5	6,624.6	6,508.7	6,470.5	6,555.0	6,579.2	6,624.0	6,698.6	6,731.1	6,598.3
2012	6,634.4	6,693.0	6,747.1	6,767.0	6,752.6	6,653.6	6,600.9	6,694.3	6,707.9	6,778.4	6,863.2	6,888.9	6,731.8
2013	6,778.2	6,847.7	6,895.2	6,901.1	6,895.7	6,800.2	6,761.8	6,863.8	6,873.3	6,939.5	7,038.5	7,066.7	6,888.5
2014	6,957.3	7,021.8	7,074.4	7,098.3	7,096.5	6,992.2	6,960.5	7,067.7	7,083.2	7,165.6	7,260.1	7,301.3	7,089.9
2015	7,192.8	7,258.8	7,303.7	7,325.3	7,324.0	7,223.4	7,199.3	7,300.8	7,313.2	7,416.4	7,509.9	7,548.4	7,326.3
2016	7,432.4	7,498.5	7,538.6	7,571.1	7,555.6	7,436.9	7,432.9	7,526.4	7,558.4	7,615.2	7,709.7	7,735.9	7,551.0
2017	7,635.7	7,689.4	7,722.8	7,730.7	7,724.3	7,616.6	7,577.8	7,665.1	7,541.2	7,734.3	7,818.6	7,859.3	7,693.0
Mining and Logging													
2007	6.7	6.8	6.7	6.8	6.8	6.9	6.6	6.7	6.6	6.6	6.7	6.7	6.7
2008	6.6	6.6	6.5	6.4	6.3	6.2	6.1	6.1	6.0	5.9	5.8	5.8	6.2
2009	5.7	5.6	5.5	5.5	5.5	5.5	5.4	5.4	5.4	5.4	5.4	5.4	5.5
2010	5.3	5.3	5.2	5.3	5.3	5.4	5.4	5.5	5.6	5.6	5.7	5.7	5.4
2011	5.7	5.7	5.7	5.7	5.7	5.7	5.6	5.6	5.6	5.6	5.6	5.6	5.7
2012	5.6	5.6	5.6	5.6	5.7	5.7	5.6	5.6	5.6	5.6	5.7	5.7	5.6
2013	5.7	5.7	5.7	5.6	5.6	5.6	5.6	5.7	5.6	5.6	5.7	5.8	5.7
2014	5.6	5.7	5.7	5.7	5.8	5.8	5.7	5.7	5.7	5.7	5.7	5.7	5.7
2015	5.7	5.8	5.8	5.8	5.9	5.9	5.9	5.8	5.8	5.8	5.8	5.8	5.8
2016	5.8	5.8	5.8	5.8	5.8	5.8	5.8	5.7	5.7	5.6	5.6	5.6	5.7
2017	5.7	5.7	5.8	5.8	5.6	5.7	5.6	5.7	5.5	5.6	5.6	5.6	5.7

1. Employment by Industry: Florida, Selected Years, 2007–2017—*Continued*

(Numbers in thousands, not seasonally adjusted)

Industry and year	January	February	March	April	May	June	July	August	September	October	November	December	Annual average
Construction													
2007	650.0	651.0	655.1	637.3	636.9	639.0	619.0	616.2	608.6	593.2	587.2	581.2	622.9
2008	554.4	553.6	550.6	531.1	528.8	527.1	511.1	506.0	501.0	486.4	475.4	465.3	515.9
2009	434.1	426.2	421.4	407.0	402.8	400.6	390.8	386.0	381.6	374.7	368.9	365.4	396.6
2010	347.5	349.2	351.5	355.1	353.8	356.1	357.8	355.7	351.6	347.3	343.3	340.4	350.8
2011	328.5	330.3	332.6	334.3	334.8	336.1	337.4	338.1	340.5	337.5	338.1	337.6	335.5
2012	328.8	330.9	335.1	334.9	338.4	343.1	342.6	347.0	349.2	350.4	352.8	352.1	342.1
2013	344.4	348.5	353.6	356.8	362.0	365.9	369.0	374.8	376.6	378.0	380.7	381.4	366.0
2014	373.7	379.4	383.1	387.6	393.9	398.7	401.5	405.8	407.9	411.3	412.1	412.7	397.3
2015	407.1	412.4	416.6	421.0	426.4	432.2	435.3	438.4	441.3	450.4	453.1	454.6	432.4
2016	449.3	456.6	460.6	467.1	471.2	475.7	479.7	482.0	487.1	489.4	492.9	494.0	475.5
2017	487.9	494.6	499.4	499.7	504.2	508.9	507.8	511.0	485.4	513.7	520.7	521.1	504.5
Manufacturing													
2007	406.6	407.0	406.8	404.0	403.5	402.0	397.1	396.3	394.3	391.0	389.7	389.2	399.0
2008	384.2	383.8	381.7	378.0	376.8	375.5	369.4	368.0	365.7	360.5	356.9	352.4	371.1
2009	345.1	339.7	335.5	328.8	326.4	324.5	318.3	316.9	314.9	313.1	313.1	312.4	324.1
2010	307.8	307.6	307.8	308.2	310.0	310.9	309.9	309.5	309.0	308.4	309.4	310.9	309.1
2011	308.8	309.6	310.1	311.4	312.4	313.5	313.0	313.8	313.5	313.8	314.4	315.2	312.5
2012	314.7	315.4	317.1	316.6	317.8	318.3	317.1	317.9	317.2	317.8	319.0	319.3	317.4
2013	316.0	318.1	319.4	320.4	322.2	323.7	322.3	323.3	324.0	324.4	326.6	327.9	322.4
2014	326.8	328.2	328.2	329.2	331.3	332.0	331.8	332.9	333.5	335.4	336.2	337.4	331.9
2015	335.1	336.7	338.6	339.4	341.4	343.9	344.1	345.0	345.7	348.3	349.4	350.7	343.2
2016	348.9	350.8	352.4	353.2	354.2	355.8	356.7	357.0	357.4	357.6	359.6	360.7	355.4
2017	358.6	361.2	362.8	362.5	363.9	366.0	364.7	365.3	357.8	365.6	366.6	368.5	363.6
Trade, Transportation, and Utilities													
2007	1,639.8	1,636.6	1,645.5	1,639.6	1,644.3	1,639.1	1,623.2	1,624.9	1,624.8	1,628.1	1,668.1	1,688.8	1,641.9
2008	1,632.7	1,628.0	1,628.8	1,610.0	1,606.7	1,595.0	1,576.9	1,574.6	1,565.6	1,562.8	1,579.8	1,594.2	1,596.3
2009	1,527.6	1,514.4	1,505.7	1,489.6	1,486.5	1,477.9	1,461.3	1,459.8	1,456.9	1,462.6	1,492.5	1,510.8	1,487.1
2010	1,464.4	1,462.9	1,467.7	1,468.8	1,470.6	1,468.9	1,457.9	1,461.3	1,456.4	1,474.0	1,508.4	1,531.0	1,474.4
2011	1,484.4	1,482.4	1,487.3	1,495.5	1,494.0	1,491.4	1,489.5	1,493.9	1,495.1	1,506.9	1,546.7	1,566.0	1,502.8
2012	1,523.0	1,520.4	1,526.8	1,527.2	1,531.6	1,528.2	1,520.1	1,522.9	1,524.6	1,537.8	1,582.4	1,599.1	1,537.0
2013	1,550.9	1,550.7	1,554.8	1,555.7	1,559.8	1,562.1	1,557.2	1,562.8	1,562.7	1,580.4	1,629.8	1,652.4	1,573.3
2014	1,597.2	1,600.0	1,604.7	1,608.8	1,611.1	1,610.3	1,605.8	1,614.6	1,615.8	1,636.4	1,688.6	1,715.4	1,625.7
2015	1,661.2	1,661.0	1,664.9	1,666.2	1,668.4	1,672.1	1,665.6	1,673.6	1,669.5	1,690.4	1,739.2	1,764.0	1,683.0
2016	1,700.0	1,700.3	1,703.1	1,707.2	1,708.6	1,704.1	1,705.6	1,709.5	1,709.3	1,722.8	1,774.0	1,794.7	1,719.9
2017	1,742.7	1,734.4	1,734.2	1,735.7	1,736.3	1,732.8	1,728.6	1,733.3	1,699.7	1,738.7	1,786.6	1,809.5	1,742.7
Wholesale Trade													
2007	360.2	362.7	363.8	362.4	363.3	363.1	359.2	359.1	358.9	359.4	360.4	362.0	361.2
2008	356.4	358.0	357.5	353.7	354.0	352.3	347.9	346.9	346.0	344.2	342.7	342.5	350.2
2009	333.5	332.3	329.3	325.7	324.8	322.2	317.9	317.0	315.5	316.2	316.9	318.3	322.5
2010	311.8	312.8	313.4	313.4	315.0	313.8	311.4	311.7	311.1	313.2	314.3	316.6	313.2
2011	309.8	311.2	312.0	313.0	312.5	311.8	310.7	310.8	311.2	312.3	313.7	316.7	312.1
2012	312.8	314.8	316.4	317.6	318.6	317.8	316.7	317.2	317.6	319.6	321.8	323.1	317.8
2013	318.3	320.1	321.2	320.5	321.5	320.7	318.6	319.4	319.9	321.4	324.0	325.4	320.9
2014	322.2	324.6	324.8	325.6	327.2	326.2	325.6	327.5	327.7	329.9	333.1	335.1	327.5
2015	331.8	332.9	333.6	333.2	334.2	334.0	333.2	334.0	334.4	337.0	338.9	340.7	334.8
2016	336.7	338.3	338.7	339.8	340.4	338.6	338.1	338.9	339.2	339.8	342.6	344.7	339.7
2017	340.9	342.4	343.3	344.1	345.6	344.8	343.8	343.8	340.6	343.8	344.8	347.8	343.8
Retail Trade													
2007	1,027.6	1,022.3	1,028.8	1,023.0	1,027.5	1,023.0	1,013.2	1,014.5	1,013.9	1,016.2	1,051.6	1,065.5	1,027.3
2008	1,023.8	1,016.9	1,017.8	1,005.1	1,002.2	995.2	984.2	982.8	976.6	975.3	992.6	1,001.4	997.8
2009	953.5	943.8	939.5	929.9	929.0	924.8	915.4	915.6	915.0	919.9	947.7	959.2	932.8
2010	926.6	923.2	926.8	928.4	929.1	929.2	921.6	924.7	921.0	934.5	964.9	979.1	934.1
2011	943.8	939.5	942.2	947.8	947.0	945.1	944.0	948.3	948.6	958.5	993.9	1,004.6	955.3
2012	972.4	966.6	970.7	970.4	973.5	970.4	964.4	966.7	967.8	977.4	1,016.6	1,026.0	978.6
2013	989.3	986.1	988.0	989.0	991.9	994.9	993.9	997.7	996.6	1,011.3	1,054.6	1,069.6	1,005.2
2014	1,025.5	1,024.5	1,027.5	1,030.6	1,030.8	1,031.1	1,027.6	1,033.2	1,033.7	1,050.1	1,094.5	1,110.7	1,043.3
2015	1,067.8	1,067.4	1,069.3	1,070.4	1,071.1	1,074.0	1,068.0	1,073.9	1,068.6	1,083.6	1,124.3	1,139.0	1,081.5
2016	1,088.4	1,087.5	1,088.7	1,091.2	1,091.8	1,089.1	1,091.0	1,094.6	1,092.6	1,103.5	1,146.1	1,156.6	1,101.8
2017	1,117.2	1,108.5	1,106.0	1,107.0	1,105.3	1,102.8	1,100.9	1,104.7	1,077.6	1,109.4	1,147.5	1,155.2	1,111.8

1. Employment by Industry: Florida, Selected Years, 2007–2017—*Continued*

(Numbers in thousands, not seasonally adjusted)

Industry and year	January	February	March	April	May	June	July	August	September	October	November	December	Annual average
Transportation and Utilities													
2007	252.0	251.6	252.9	254.2	253.5	253.0	250.8	251.3	252.0	252.5	256.1	261.3	253.4
2008	252.5	253.1	253.5	251.2	250.5	247.5	244.8	244.9	243.0	243.3	244.5	250.3	248.3
2009	240.6	238.3	236.9	234.0	232.7	230.9	228.0	227.2	226.4	226.5	227.9	233.3	231.9
2010	226.0	226.9	227.5	227.0	226.5	225.9	224.9	224.9	224.3	226.3	229.2	235.3	227.1
2011	230.8	231.7	233.1	234.7	234.5	234.5	234.8	234.8	235.3	236.1	239.1	244.7	235.3
2012	237.8	239.0	239.7	239.2	239.5	240.0	239.0	239.0	239.2	240.8	244.0	250.0	240.6
2013	243.3	244.5	245.6	246.2	246.4	246.5	244.7	245.7	246.2	247.7	251.2	257.4	247.1
2014	249.5	250.9	252.4	252.6	253.1	253.0	252.6	253.9	254.4	256.4	261.0	269.6	255.0
2015	261.6	260.7	262.0	262.6	263.1	264.1	264.4	265.7	266.5	269.8	276.0	284.3	266.7
2016	274.9	274.5	275.7	276.2	276.4	276.4	276.5	276.0	277.5	279.5	285.3	293.4	278.5
2017	284.6	283.5	284.9	284.6	285.4	285.2	283.9	284.8	281.5	285.5	294.3	306.5	287.1
Information													
2007	161.6	162.6	163.2	163.8	164.5	164.8	163.1	162.8	161.4	161.2	161.2	161.7	162.7
2008	160.1	160.6	160.4	159.1	159.3	158.8	157.9	156.6	154.3	153.8	153.4	152.4	157.2
2009	149.3	148.9	147.9	146.3	145.5	145.1	142.9	141.7	139.8	139.3	139.2	139.3	143.8
2010	137.7	137.4	138.2	137.2	137.0	137.1	136.8	136.9	136.0	136.6	137.1	136.7	137.1
2011	136.2	136.3	136.2	135.8	135.9	135.8	135.7	135.4	135.2	135.0	135.6	135.4	135.7
2012	134.1	134.0	133.9	133.8	133.6	133.4	133.4	133.0	132.0	133.9	133.9	134.0	133.6
2013	132.8	133.1	133.7	133.5	133.5	134.3	134.5	134.6	133.9	134.6	135.3	135.9	134.1
2014	135.6	136.1	136.0	136.2	136.2	137.1	136.7	135.8	135.0	135.6	136.9	136.7	136.2
2015	135.7	135.8	135.7	135.5	136.4	136.2	136.8	136.8	136.1	137.1	138.1	138.9	136.6
2016	136.3	137.2	136.7	136.8	137.5	137.3	138.1	138.3	136.5	136.8	138.6	138.5	137.4
2017	137.8	139.6	139.3	138.3	139.4	138.9	137.6	137.8	134.6	136.8	138.6	137.9	138.1
Financial Activities													
2007	550.7	554.3	556.3	554.0	554.5	555.7	552.2	550.5	547.3	545.1	546.0	547.7	551.2
2008	537.4	538.2	538.2	532.5	531.8	529.7	524.9	522.4	517.9	513.9	511.6	512.1	525.9
2009	497.7	495.7	493.9	491.3	490.6	490.0	485.7	483.7	479.3	479.6	480.0	481.2	487.4
2010	473.1	474.3	476.0	475.6	476.9	478.7	478.5	478.7	475.9	480.4	482.4	485.5	478.0
2011	478.9	480.7	483.3	484.3	484.4	484.9	487.0	488.2	489.3	490.4	491.4	495.0	486.5
2012	488.8	491.7	494.4	496.5	497.9	500.1	500.2	501.2	500.4	504.8	507.2	509.7	499.4
2013	503.2	506.0	508.7	510.0	511.1	513.8	514.1	515.1	513.9	516.7	518.9	521.0	512.7
2014	512.6	514.4	516.9	518.3	520.3	521.2	522.4	523.0	522.0	525.9	527.8	530.2	521.3
2015	525.3	527.1	529.5	530.9	532.4	533.5	535.3	536.1	534.1	539.3	541.9	543.4	534.1
2016	538.3	540.4	541.6	544.0	544.9	545.6	546.8	547.8	548.2	551.9	554.0	558.3	546.8
2017	552.9	555.5	557.5	557.8	559.1	561.5	562.4	562.5	559.7	567.1	571.9	574.9	561.9
Professional and Business Services													
2007	1,155.5	1,170.9	1,182.0	1,170.3	1,166.3	1,164.1	1,143.5	1,147.1	1,140.4	1,139.7	1,145.1	1,148.9	1,156.2
2008	1,102.2	1,117.3	1,121.4	1,104.1	1,095.9	1,088.7	1,067.6	1,066.5	1,063.5	1,059.7	1,053.6	1,052.5	1,082.8
2009	1,009.1	1,009.9	1,007.2	998.6	993.4	991.5	977.1	977.6	978.3	987.5	996.2	999.1	993.8
2010	977.9	990.0	998.0	1,000.5	1,000.5	1,005.2	1,001.7	1,007.4	1,007.7	1,022.5	1,027.3	1,033.9	1,006.1
2011	1,014.9	1,028.6	1,035.9	1,043.8	1,036.6	1,034.7	1,027.7	1,030.2	1,033.7	1,039.9	1,049.8	1,056.9	1,036.1
2012	1,034.6	1,050.4	1,061.5	1,074.8	1,073.2	1,072.9	1,065.4	1,071.8	1,072.6	1,093.8	1,105.7	1,108.6	1,073.8
2013	1,082.1	1,099.9	1,108.4	1,110.1	1,114.6	1,113.9	1,111.0	1,118.6	1,119.1	1,133.8	1,146.4	1,148.7	1,117.2
2014	1,127.8	1,140.4	1,146.5	1,155.3	1,162.2	1,158.6	1,156.9	1,168.3	1,169.6	1,188.2	1,199.9	1,205.3	1,164.9
2015	1,184.6	1,197.6	1,202.2	1,213.4	1,218.6	1,215.9	1,219.1	1,223.3	1,224.2	1,248.4	1,261.1	1,265.8	1,222.9
2016	1,250.1	1,262.4	1,270.5	1,279.1	1,276.1	1,272.7	1,280.6	1,286.7	1,288.5	1,307.2	1,316.5	1,313.2	1,283.6
2017	1,300.9	1,308.1	1,311.7	1,317.2	1,318.5	1,322.0	1,319.9	1,322.2	1,292.3	1,345.8	1,349.8	1,354.3	1,321.9
Education and Health Services													
2007	996.9	1,007.9	1,013.2	1,015.2	1,017.6	1,015.5	1,002.3	1,014.0	1,021.9	1,025.2	1,031.7	1,036.5	1,016.5
2008	1,026.7	1,036.3	1,040.8	1,038.5	1,041.2	1,034.3	1,022.7	1,030.5	1,036.8	1,042.9	1,049.9	1,054.4	1,037.9
2009	1,037.4	1,044.2	1,048.3	1,048.1	1,051.1	1,044.8	1,036.2	1,043.1	1,051.1	1,064.8	1,071.3	1,073.7	1,051.2
2010	1,059.3	1,066.7	1,071.5	1,072.8	1,074.2	1,066.5	1,057.2	1,061.3	1,066.9	1,081.0	1,086.6	1,086.2	1,070.9
2011	1,077.4	1,085.1	1,087.5	1,096.2	1,094.8	1,083.9	1,075.1	1,082.4	1,094.2	1,100.2	1,107.1	1,108.5	1,091.0
2012	1,093.8	1,101.9	1,106.3	1,112.0	1,113.0	1,104.3	1,091.8	1,103.6	1,113.0	1,119.9	1,125.0	1,126.7	1,109.3
2013	1,115.0	1,125.9	1,129.6	1,131.7	1,131.3	1,120.3	1,108.0	1,121.1	1,128.3	1,137.7	1,145.1	1,145.6	1,128.3
2014	1,134.4	1,145.3	1,148.8	1,158.4	1,159.8	1,149.6	1,140.9	1,157.2	1,166.4	1,177.9	1,184.6	1,188.1	1,159.3
2015	1,176.4	1,186.8	1,191.2	1,196.0	1,199.9	1,190.4	1,180.9	1,193.8	1,205.6	1,221.7	1,229.0	1,230.5	1,200.2
2016	1,219.8	1,229.6	1,232.3	1,243.1	1,243.4	1,229.3	1,227.7	1,239.9	1,252.9	1,263.1	1,268.9	1,274.0	1,243.7
2017	1,261.0	1,272.8	1,274.5	1,278.5	1,279.8	1,267.3	1,256.8	1,271.1	1,260.2	1,278.1	1,283.6	1,288.4	1,272.7

1. Employment by Industry: Florida, Selected Years, 2007–2017—*Continued*

(Numbers in thousands, not seasonally adjusted)

Industry and year	January	February	March	April	May	June	July	August	September	October	November	December	Annual average
Leisure and Hospitality													
2007	966.8	989.2	1,011.8	1,006.9	1,001.6	993.2	972.1	971.5	963.4	959.9	978.8	986.3	983.5
2008	973.9	995.7	1,013.7	1,005.5	993.9	982.5	959.0	951.8	938.8	934.5	945.1	949.0	970.3
2009	933.9	948.5	964.4	961.4	947.7	934.1	913.3	905.7	897.8	897.4	908.1	912.8	927.1
2010	904.2	926.1	948.7	955.0	946.8	939.1	923.0	920.1	914.9	922.2	935.4	942.6	931.5
2011	931.5	946.5	973.0	979.6	970.5	963.1	948.9	947.1	945.4	949.0	964.1	970.5	957.4
2012	967.9	988.7	1,016.9	1,019.0	1,010.8	1,006.2	990.7	987.0	980.0	988.4	1,005.0	1,011.6	997.7
2013	1,001.8	1,027.3	1,052.1	1,052.3	1,047.2	1,043.7	1,035.5	1,031.5	1,024.0	1,030.8	1,049.1	1,054.2	1,037.5
2014	1,047.5	1,070.9	1,100.0	1,102.6	1,096.1	1,093.5	1,080.3	1,076.4	1,071.3	1,081.8	1,097.5	1,102.8	1,085.1
2015	1,096.7	1,123.3	1,147.8	1,148.9	1,140.9	1,135.8	1,125.3	1,124.4	1,120.0	1,135.8	1,152.0	1,160.6	1,134.3
2016	1,147.7	1,174.7	1,194.6	1,195.3	1,186.3	1,175.6	1,166.0	1,162.9	1,162.1	1,166.3	1,183.0	1,186.4	1,175.1
2017	1,179.8	1,202.8	1,225.6	1,226.6	1,221.5	1,212.2	1,196.6	1,192.7	1,142.7	1,192.7	1,207.1	1,216.2	1,201.4
Other Services													
2007	333.6	337.3	341.7	337.0	337.9	330.7	331.7	331.2	330.9	331.4	334.0	336.3	335.2
2008	332.9	335.4	337.5	333.0	332.1	330.0	323.0	321.3	316.5	313.3	310.6	308.5	324.5
2009	304.7	304.8	305.6	305.2	304.4	302.9	298.6	297.5	296.5	297.8	298.1	298.6	301.2
2010	296.0	298.0	299.7	300.5	299.6	299.2	296.3	295.0	293.9	296.5	297.1	297.0	297.4
2011	292.6	294.5	296.6	298.5	297.9	296.4	294.8	294.2	294.4	295.4	296.5	297.1	295.7
2012	297.5	299.4	301.6	303.6	303.1	303.4	300.1	299.8	300.3	302.2	303.5	304.6	301.6
2013	302.2	304.8	306.5	308.6	309.0	309.3	307.8	308.8	309.6	312.1	315.2	316.5	309.2
2014	317.0	320.5	323.2	323.6	323.6	322.9	321.3	322.4	322.8	325.5	327.2	328.1	323.2
2015	326.1	328.7	330.8	332.5	332.9	333.7	332.4	333.4	334.3	337.5	341.1	343.0	333.9
2016	342.3	345.7	348.3	349.0	348.4	348.1	346.6	346.4	347.8	348.5	351.0	349.8	347.7
2017	346.1	348.2	349.4	349.2	349.4	349.1	347.3	346.7	338.7	348.2	350.4	350.3	347.8
Government													
2007	1,123.8	1,135.1	1,140.6	1,139.2	1,135.6	1,041.0	1,041.1	1,130.1	1,138.2	1,145.6	1,151.3	1,149.4	1,122.6
2008	1,140.3	1,151.8	1,149.2	1,146.9	1,140.9	1,044.7	1,043.8	1,133.1	1,142.2	1,145.9	1,144.8	1,139.5	1,126.9
2009	1,133.1	1,139.1	1,136.9	1,142.6	1,130.5	1,035.4	1,034.2	1,113.7	1,124.0	1,128.6	1,131.8	1,125.4	1,114.6
2010	1,121.9	1,127.9	1,128.3	1,134.1	1,161.8	1,047.9	1,033.3	1,112.1	1,115.2	1,122.2	1,125.5	1,117.0	1,112.3
2011	1,114.6	1,124.3	1,122.7	1,122.8	1,110.5	1,018.5	1,011.8	1,083.6	1,091.9	1,107.2	1,107.4	1,101.7	1,093.1
2012	1,094.7	1,106.5	1,105.7	1,100.1	1,089.4	1,005.1	999.2	1,075.0	1,085.0	1,097.6	1,100.5	1,094.6	1,079.5
2013	1,090.2	1,100.0	1,101.4	1,099.2	1,089.2	1,002.8	993.7	1,071.3	1,081.8	1,093.4	1,098.7	1,092.4	1,076.2
2014	1,085.2	1,094.2	1,098.3	1,095.1	1,087.2	999.0	996.2	1,070.0	1,080.3	1,094.3	1,097.6	1,094.7	1,074.3
2015	1,086.8	1,098.5	1,101.6	1,101.9	1,094.5	1,005.8	1,003.9	1,079.4	1,089.4	1,106.2	1,107.5	1,102.2	1,081.5
2016	1,097.9	1,108.2	1,111.5	1,116.6	1,110.4	1,024.2	1,021.5	1,094.9	1,113.1	1,118.6	1,123.7	1,121.0	1,096.8
2017	1,114.5	1,128.0	1,130.6	1,127.4	1,120.3	1,032.8	1,028.6	1,098.8	1,113.3	1,126.9	1,130.6	1,127.8	1,106.6

2. Average Weekly Hours by Selected Industry: Florida, 2013–2017

(Not seasonally adjusted)

Industry and year	January	February	March	April	May	June	July	August	September	October	November	December	Annual average
Total Private													
2013	34.1	34.5	34.5	34.3	34.2	34.5	34.2	34.4	34.5	34.2	34.3	34.6	34.4
2014	34.2	34.6	34.6	34.4	34.2	34.5	34.3	34.4	34.3	34.2	34.6	34.4	34.4
2015	34.1	34.7	34.7	34.3	34.2	34.1	34.2	34.5	33.9	34.1	34.5	34.3	34.3
2016	34.2	34.2	34.2	34.2	34.2	33.9	34.0	33.8	33.7	33.9	34.0	34.2	34.0
2017	34.4	34.3	34.3	34.6	34.1	34.1	34.5	34.2	32.7	35.1	34.9	35.0	34.3
Goods-Producing													
2013	39.6	40.1	40.3	40.1	40.1	40.2	39.6	39.9	40.2	39.9	40.1	40.7	40.1
2014	39.2	39.6	40.0	39.9	40.0	40.2	39.9	40.2	40.3	40.0	40.6	40.5	40.0
2015	39.4	39.6	40.2	39.8	39.9	40.1	39.9	40.1	38.7	40.1	40.5	40.4	39.9
2016	39.4	39.3	39.3	39.5	39.3	38.5	39.0	39.1	39.4	39.3	40.0	40.2	39.4
2017	40.2	40.2	40.1	39.6	40.0	39.8	40.2	40.5	35.3	41.1	40.9	41.2	39.9
Construction													
2013	39.1	39.0	39.6	39.5	39.3	39.3	38.9	39.3	39.4	39.2	39.2	39.6	39.3
2014	38.0	38.4	38.9	38.5	39.2	39.2	38.9	39.4	39.5	39.5	39.4	39.7	39.1
2015	38.1	38.6	39.4	38.8	39.2	39.4	39.2	39.6	38.0	40.1	40.2	40.2	39.3
2016	38.6	38.9	38.7	38.8	38.9	38.2	38.7	39.0	39.5	39.1	40.0	39.9	39.0
2017	39.8	39.8	39.8	39.0	39.5	39.0	39.8	40.0	33.9	40.0	40.1	40.1	39.3
Manufacturing													
2013	39.8	40.9	40.8	40.5	40.8	41.1	40.4	40.5	40.9	40.5	40.9	41.8	40.7
2014	40.5	40.9	41.0	41.2	40.6	41.0	40.7	40.8	41.0	40.2	41.8	41.1	40.9
2015	40.7	40.5	40.9	40.7	40.4	40.7	40.5	40.6	39.6	40.2	40.9	40.8	40.5
2016	40.5	40.0	40.1	40.3	39.9	39.5	39.9	39.8	39.8	40.1	40.5	41.0	40.1
2017	40.8	40.9	40.8	40.6	40.7	40.8	40.7	41.2	37.3	42.6	42.0	43.2	41.0
Trade, Transportation, and Utilities													
2013	32.8	33.2	33.2	32.8	33.0	33.1	32.9	32.8	32.9	32.6	32.7	33.1	32.9
2014	32.6	32.9	33.0	33.2	32.8	32.9	33.0	33.2	33.1	33.3	33.6	33.8	33.1
2015	33.2	33.8	33.6	33.5	33.5	33.2	33.2	33.3	33.4	33.3	33.4	33.5	33.4
2016	33.3	33.4	33.1	33.0	33.0	32.6	32.5	32.2	32.1	32.2	32.4	33.4	32.8
2017	33.0	33.0	33.1	33.4	32.9	32.7	33.0	32.7	32.1	34.3	34.1	34.4	33.2
Financial Activities													
2013	37.9	38.1	37.8	37.9	37.8	38.4	37.5	38.0	38.2	37.7	38.0	37.9	37.9
2014	37.4	37.5	37.6	37.0	37.2	37.9	37.2	37.1	37.6	37.4	38.4	37.7	37.5
2015	37.7	38.7	38.6	37.9	37.7	37.7	37.9	38.6	37.9	37.9	38.6	38.1	38.1
2016	37.9	38.0	37.9	37.7	38.0	37.6	37.9	37.7	38.0	38.4	37.9	38.3	37.9
2017	38.5	37.9	37.6	38.1	37.6	37.7	38.3	37.8	37.2	38.5	38.1	38.1	38.0
Professional and Business Services													
2013	35.8	36.0	36.0	36.2	35.9	36.7	36.6	36.8	37.2	36.6	36.4	36.8	36.4
2014	35.9	36.5	36.4	35.5	35.6	36.3	35.8	36.0	35.7	35.8	36.2	35.6	35.9
2015	35.0	36.0	35.8	35.6	35.7	35.7	35.6	36.3	35.4	35.6	36.0	35.6	35.7
2016	35.5	35.4	35.5	35.9	36.2	35.7	35.8	35.7	36.0	36.5	36.0	35.8	35.8
2017	36.5	36.2	36.0	36.8	36.0	36.1	36.7	36.1	34.7	36.9	36.6	36.4	36.3
Education and Health Services													
2013	34.7	34.9	34.8	34.7	34.7	34.8	34.6	34.6	34.9	34.8	35.0	34.8	34.8
2014	34.9	35.2	35.0	35.0	34.9	34.9	34.9	35.0	35.0	34.9	35.3	34.8	35.0
2015	35.1	35.1	35.2	34.8	34.8	34.7	34.8	34.9	34.6	34.5	34.9	34.5	34.8
2016	35.2	35.0	34.9	35.0	35.0	34.7	34.7	34.4	34.2	34.1	34.0	34.1	34.6
2017	34.3	34.2	33.7	34.1	34.0	33.8	34.3	34.0	34.0	34.3	34.3	34.5	34.1
Leisure and Hospitality													
2013	27.5	28.1	28.3	27.8	27.3	27.6	27.5	27.4	26.8	26.9	27.3	27.9	27.5
2014	28.1	28.9	29.3	28.7	28.2	28.4	28.4	28.2	27.5	27.6	28.2	28.1	28.3
2015	28.4	29.1	29.2	28.4	27.8	27.7	27.8	28.0	27.0	27.1	27.7	27.5	28.0
2016	27.6	28.3	28.3	28.0	27.6	27.7	27.9	27.4	26.9	26.9	27.8	27.5	27.7
2017	27.9	28.2	29.0	28.9	27.9	28.0	28.1	27.9	25.0	28.1	28.1	28.3	28.0
Other Services													
2013	33.4	33.4	33.7	33.9	33.3	33.9	33.3	33.4	33.1	32.8	32.7	33.0	33.3
2014	32.7	33.2	33.1	32.5	32.7	32.5	31.9	33.0	32.2	32.4	32.6	33.2	32.7
2015	32.7	32.7	33.1	32.4	31.9	32.5	32.4	33.0	32.7	33.2	33.3	33.4	32.8
2016	33.2	33.4	33.4	33.4	34.0	33.9	33.8	33.7	33.4	33.3	33.4	33.2	33.5
2017	33.4	33.3	33.0	33.0	32.8	33.1	33.2	33.3	30.0	32.5	32.0	33.1	32.7

3. Average Hourly Earnings by Selected Industry: Florida, 2013–2017

(Dollars, not seasonally adjusted)

Industry and year	January	February	March	April	May	June	July	August	September	October	November	December	Annual average
Total Private													
2013	21.89	21.81	21.75	21.92	21.89	22.06	21.93	21.85	22.11	22.01	22.01	22.21	21.95
2014	22.14	22.18	22.09	22.26	22.12	22.22	22.22	22.27	22.22	22.17	22.28	22.13	22.19
2015	22.32	22.53	22.45	22.42	22.51	22.41	22.55	22.80	22.80	22.81	22.98	22.88	22.63
2016	22.73	22.88	23.12	23.06	23.33	23.23	23.11	23.36	23.48	23.93	23.69	23.74	23.31
2017	23.90	23.84	23.78	24.12	23.92	23.67	24.05	23.96	24.80	24.11	24.06	24.29	24.04
Goods-Producing													
2013	23.27	22.93	22.95	23.02	22.95	22.94	23.11	23.05	23.01	22.90	22.65	22.94	22.97
2014	22.96	22.96	22.76	22.52	22.34	22.45	22.69	22.71	22.61	22.59	22.52	22.62	22.64
2015	23.01	22.92	22.95	22.93	23.03	22.90	23.12	23.43	23.36	23.23	23.41	23.18	23.13
2016	23.30	23.31	23.45	23.80	23.91	24.14	24.46	24.48	24.68	24.97	24.86	25.08	24.22
2017	25.06	24.95	24.99	25.36	25.40	25.20	25.46	25.18	26.10	24.72	24.83	25.07	25.18
Construction													
2013	22.60	22.40	22.37	22.41	22.41	22.20	22.52	22.45	22.13	22.15	21.75	22.09	22.30
2014	22.24	22.22	22.16	22.08	21.88	21.97	22.35	22.28	22.21	22.31	22.39	22.13	22.19
2015	22.44	22.41	22.48	22.68	22.66	22.64	22.75	23.07	22.93	22.89	23.31	23.33	22.81
2016	23.12	23.18	22.94	23.28	23.28	23.20	23.65	23.46	23.85	24.27	24.22	24.45	23.59
2017	24.53	24.47	24.63	24.90	25.08	24.94	25.01	24.88	25.82	24.22	24.43	24.73	24.79
Manufacturing													
2013	23.92	23.37	23.58	23.74	23.62	23.78	23.87	23.83	24.09	23.85	23.71	23.89	23.77
2014	23.78	23.81	23.44	23.03	22.92	23.06	23.17	23.29	23.15	23.02	22.69	23.30	23.22
2015	23.74	23.57	23.58	23.29	23.56	23.27	23.62	23.93	23.97	23.72	23.57	24.06	23.66
2016	24.39	24.24	24.70	24.96	25.13	25.62	25.76	26.07	26.00	26.11	25.91	26.06	25.42
2017	25.93	25.72	25.58	25.97	25.85	25.54	26.12	25.64	26.49	25.49	25.45	25.59	25.77
Trade, Transportation, and Utilities													
2013	18.83	18.75	18.81	18.93	18.78	18.88	18.87	18.74	19.16	19.09	19.18	19.17	18.93
2014	19.37	19.57	19.49	19.38	18.97	19.07	19.29	19.36	19.21	19.10	19.23	19.03	19.25
2015	19.58	19.82	19.55	19.68	20.12	20.02	20.28	20.44	20.58	20.05	20.08	20.45	20.06
2016	20.35	20.49	21.10	20.68	20.78	21.41	20.82	20.86	20.65	20.72	20.46	20.13	20.70
2017	20.60	20.55	20.66	21.10	20.89	20.87	21.24	20.75	21.84	21.10	21.30	21.34	21.02
Financial Activities													
2013	24.67	25.13	25.07	25.36	25.21	25.78	25.76	25.62	26.16	26.04	26.39	26.90	25.68
2014	26.40	26.32	26.60	26.27	26.03	26.54	26.32	26.41	26.06	26.21	26.43	26.26	26.32
2015	26.34	27.22	28.07	27.22	27.14	27.09	27.04	27.87	27.30	27.17	28.03	27.74	27.36
2016	27.17	27.72	27.78	26.86	28.09	26.83	26.87	28.48	27.75	28.76	28.82	28.37	27.80
2017	28.87	28.73	28.17	29.12	28.68	27.65	28.66	29.06	28.87	28.97	29.17	29.12	28.76
Professional and Business Services													
2013	25.32	25.48	25.43	25.56	25.48	25.85	25.18	24.92	25.33	25.07	25.13	25.60	25.36
2014	25.41	25.45	25.38	25.65	25.80	25.94	25.79	25.75	25.92	25.76	26.03	25.75	25.72
2015	25.90	26.05	26.03	25.94	25.74	25.63	25.84	26.12	26.22	26.30	26.69	26.39	26.08
2016	26.42	26.67	26.61	26.85	27.10	27.04	27.03	26.69	27.05	27.74	27.56	27.97	27.07
2017	28.04	28.03	28.14	28.50	28.06	27.95	28.46	28.40	29.59	28.79	28.27	28.62	28.40
Education and Health Services													
2013	24.85	24.63	24.57	24.83	24.90	24.99	24.90	25.01	24.89	24.82	24.68	24.88	24.83
2014	24.69	24.60	24.44	24.38	24.19	24.08	24.00	23.97	24.08	24.11	24.06	24.32	24.24
2015	24.01	24.27	24.31	24.38	24.19	24.11	24.18	24.23	24.44	24.70	24.61	24.38	24.32
2016	24.13	24.37	24.48	24.49	24.39	24.32	24.42	24.57	24.93	25.49	25.27	25.52	24.70
2017	25.40	25.42	25.40	25.59	25.53	25.24	25.41	25.49	26.01	25.72	25.72	26.18	25.59
Leisure and Hospitality													
2013	13.69	13.59	13.53	13.44	13.45	13.33	13.30	13.26	13.22	13.46	13.45	13.51	13.44
2014	13.60	13.75	13.75	13.69	13.69	13.67	13.65	13.85	13.84	14.03	14.19	14.15	13.82
2015	14.48	14.53	14.33	14.27	14.36	14.06	14.20	14.14	14.22	14.55	14.65	14.68	14.37
2016	14.72	14.82	14.89	14.95	14.95	14.80	14.85	14.91	15.15	15.49	15.47	15.61	15.05
2017	15.63	15.80	15.81	15.66	15.54	15.17	15.26	15.25	15.46	15.50	15.59	15.64	15.53
Other Services													
2013	18.67	18.73	18.53	18.80	18.80	18.99	18.94	18.83	19.03	18.86	19.18	19.33	18.89
2014	19.11	19.06	19.09	19.25	19.37	19.55	19.37	19.75	19.60	19.26	19.62	19.49	19.38
2015	19.54	19.76	19.74	19.69	19.97	20.22	20.46	20.55	20.26	20.35	20.79	20.57	20.17
2016	20.55	20.74	20.84	21.11	21.14	21.22	21.59	21.48	21.95	21.82	21.37	21.19	21.25
2017	20.81	20.76	20.73	20.67	20.37	19.93	19.98	19.95	20.69	19.96	20.15	20.60	20.38

4. Average Weekly Earnings by Selected Industry: Florida, 2013–2017

(Dollars, not seasonally adjusted)

Industry and year	January	February	March	April	May	June	July	August	September	October	November	December	Annual average
Total Private													
2013	746.45	752.45	750.38	751.86	748.64	761.07	750.01	751.64	762.80	752.74	754.94	768.47	755.08
2014	757.19	767.43	764.31	765.74	756.50	766.59	762.15	766.09	762.15	758.21	770.89	761.27	763.34
2015	761.11	781.79	779.02	769.01	769.84	764.18	771.21	786.60	772.92	777.82	792.81	784.78	776.21
2016	777.37	782.50	790.70	788.65	797.89	787.50	785.74	789.57	791.28	811.23	805.46	811.91	792.54
2017	822.16	817.71	815.65	834.55	815.67	807.15	829.73	819.43	810.96	846.26	839.69	850.15	824.57
Goods-Producing													
2013	921.49	919.49	924.89	923.10	920.30	922.19	915.16	919.70	925.00	913.71	908.27	933.66	921.10
2014	900.03	909.22	910.40	898.55	893.60	902.49	905.33	912.94	911.18	903.60	914.31	916.11	905.60
2015	906.59	907.63	922.59	912.61	918.90	918.29	922.49	939.54	904.03	931.52	948.11	936.47	922.89
2016	918.02	916.08	921.59	940.10	939.66	929.39	953.94	957.17	972.39	981.32	994.40	1,008.22	954.27
2017	1,007.41	1,002.99	1,002.10	1,004.26	1,016.00	1,002.96	1,023.49	1,019.79	921.33	1,015.99	1,015.55	1,032.88	1,004.68
Construction													
2013	886.79	876.72	885.85	885.20	880.71	874.82	876.03	882.29	871.92	868.28	852.60	874.76	876.39
2014	845.12	853.25	862.02	850.08	857.70	861.22	869.42	877.83	877.30	881.25	882.17	878.56	867.63
2015	854.96	865.03	885.71	879.98	888.27	892.02	891.80	913.57	871.34	917.89	937.06	937.87	896.43
2016	892.43	901.70	887.78	903.26	905.59	886.24	915.26	914.94	942.08	948.96	968.80	975.56	920.01
2017	976.29	973.91	980.27	971.10	990.66	972.66	995.40	995.20	875.30	968.80	979.64	991.67	974.25
Manufacturing													
2013	952.02	955.83	962.06	961.47	963.70	977.36	964.35	965.12	985.28	965.93	969.74	998.60	967.44
2014	963.09	973.83	961.04	948.84	930.55	945.46	943.02	950.23	949.15	925.40	948.44	957.63	949.70
2015	966.22	954.59	964.42	947.90	951.82	947.09	956.61	971.56	949.21	953.54	964.01	981.65	958.23
2016	987.80	969.60	990.47	1,005.89	1,002.69	1,011.99	1,027.82	1,037.59	1,034.80	1,047.01	1,049.36	1,068.46	1,019.34
2017	1,057.94	1,051.95	1,043.66	1,054.38	1,052.10	1,042.03	1,063.08	1,056.37	988.08	1,085.87	1,068.90	1,105.49	1,056.57
Trade, Transportation, and Utilities													
2013	617.62	622.50	624.49	620.90	619.74	624.93	620.82	614.67	630.36	622.33	627.19	634.53	622.80
2014	631.46	643.85	643.17	643.42	622.22	627.40	636.57	642.75	635.85	636.03	646.13	643.21	637.18
2015	650.06	669.92	656.88	659.28	674.02	664.66	673.30	680.65	687.37	667.67	670.67	685.08	670.00
2016	677.66	684.37	698.41	682.44	685.74	697.97	676.65	671.69	662.87	667.18	662.90	672.34	678.96
2017	679.80	678.15	683.85	704.74	687.28	682.45	700.92	678.53	701.06	723.73	726.33	734.10	697.86
Financial Activities													
2013	934.99	957.45	947.65	961.14	952.94	989.95	966.00	973.56	999.31	981.71	1,002.82	1,019.51	973.27
2014	987.36	987.00	1,000.16	971.99	968.32	1,005.87	979.10	979.81	979.86	980.25	1,014.91	990.00	987.00
2015	993.02	1,053.41	1,083.50	1,031.64	1,023.18	1,021.29	1,024.82	1,075.78	1,034.67	1,029.74	1,081.96	1,056.89	1,042.42
2016	1,029.74	1,053.36	1,052.86	1,012.62	1,067.42	1,008.81	1,018.37	1,073.70	1,054.50	1,104.38	1,092.28	1,086.57	1,053.62
2017	1,111.50	1,088.87	1,059.19	1,109.47	1,078.37	1,042.41	1,097.68	1,098.47	1,073.96	1,115.35	1,111.38	1,109.47	1,092.88
Professional and Business Services													
2013	906.46	917.28	915.48	925.27	914.73	948.70	921.59	917.06	942.28	917.56	914.73	942.08	923.10
2014	912.22	928.93	923.83	910.58	918.48	941.62	923.28	927.00	925.34	922.21	942.29	916.70	923.35
2015	906.50	937.80	931.87	923.46	918.92	914.99	919.90	948.16	928.19	936.28	960.84	939.48	931.06
2016	937.91	944.12	944.66	963.92	981.02	965.33	967.67	952.83	973.80	1,012.51	992.16	1,001.33	969.11
2017	1,023.46	1,014.69	1,013.04	1,048.80	1,010.16	1,009.00	1,044.48	1,025.24	1,026.77	1,062.35	1,034.68	1,041.77	1,030.92
Education and Health Services													
2013	862.30	859.59	855.04	861.60	864.03	869.65	861.54	865.35	868.66	863.74	863.80	865.82	864.08
2014	861.68	865.92	855.40	853.30	844.23	840.39	837.60	838.95	842.80	841.44	849.32	846.34	848.40
2015	842.75	851.88	855.71	848.42	841.81	836.62	841.46	845.63	845.62	852.15	858.89	841.11	846.34
2016	849.38	852.95	854.35	857.15	853.65	843.90	847.37	845.21	852.61	869.21	859.18	870.23	854.62
2017	871.22	869.36	855.98	872.62	868.02	853.11	871.56	866.66	884.34	882.20	882.20	903.21	872.62
Leisure and Hospitality													
2013	376.48	381.88	382.90	373.63	367.19	367.91	365.75	363.32	354.30	362.07	367.19	376.93	369.60
2014	382.16	397.38	402.88	392.90	386.06	388.23	387.66	390.57	380.60	387.23	400.16	397.62	391.11
2015	411.23	422.82	418.44	405.27	399.21	389.46	394.76	395.92	383.94	394.31	405.81	403.70	402.36
2016	406.27	419.41	421.39	418.60	412.62	409.96	414.32	408.53	407.54	416.68	430.07	429.28	416.89
2017	436.08	445.56	458.49	452.57	433.57	424.76	428.81	425.48	386.50	435.55	438.08	442.61	434.84
Other Services													
2013	623.58	625.58	624.46	637.32	626.04	643.76	630.70	628.92	629.89	618.61	627.19	637.89	629.04
2014	624.90	632.79	631.88	625.63	633.40	635.38	617.90	651.75	631.12	624.02	639.61	647.07	633.73
2015	638.96	646.15	653.39	637.96	637.04	657.15	662.90	678.15	662.50	675.62	692.31	687.04	661.58
2016	682.26	692.72	696.06	705.07	718.76	719.36	729.74	723.88	733.13	726.61	713.76	703.51	711.88
2017	695.05	691.31	684.09	682.11	668.14	659.68	663.34	664.34	620.70	648.70	644.80	681.86	666.43

GEORGIA
At a Glance

Population:
  2010 census: 9,687,653
  2017 estimate: 10,429,379

Percent change in population:
  2010–2017: 7.7%

Percent change in total nonfarm employment:
  2007–2017: 6.9%

Industry with the largest growth in employment, 2007–2017 (thousands):
  Construction, -37.2

Industry with the largest decline or smallest growth in employment, 2007–2017 (thousands):
  Education and health services, 122.0

Civilian labor force:
  2010: 4,696,676
  2017: 5,061,399

Unemployment rate and rank among states (highest to lowest):
  2010: 10.5%, 9th
  2017: 4.7%, 15th

Over-the-year change in unemployment rates:
  2015–2016: -0.6%
  2016–2017: -0.7%

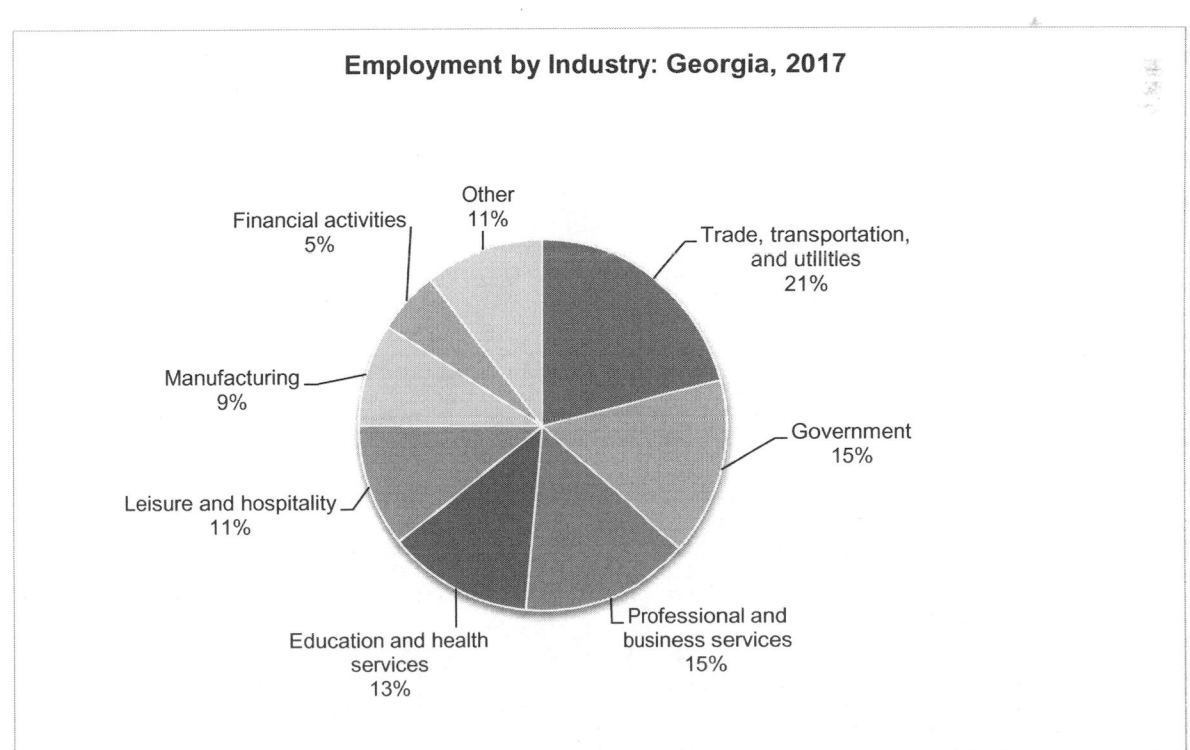

Employment by Industry: Georgia, 2017

Other 11%

Financial activities 5%

Trade, transportation, and utilities 21%

Manufacturing 9%

Government 15%

Leisure and hospitality 11%

Professional and business services 15%

Education and health services 13%

1. Employment by Industry: Georgia, Selected Years, 2007–2017

(Numbers in thousands, not seasonally adjusted)

Industry and year	January	February	March	April	May	June	July	August	September	October	November	December	Annual average
Total Nonfarm													
2006	4,115.6	4,136.0	4,151.9	4,160.9	4,179.6	4,168.6	4,137.4	4,181.3	4,174.6	4,184.0	4,204.8	4,201.2	4,166.3
2007	4,131.3	4,150.5	4,151.6	4,157.1	4,168.2	4,140.8	4,100.7	4,128.0	4,104.0	4,094.0	4,081.3	4,058.9	4,122.2
2008	3,954.1	3,943.3	3,929.1	3,931.5	3,930.3	3,898.2	3,859.0	3,870.7	3,859.8	3,868.7	3,881.7	3,872.0	3,899.9
2009	3,794.8	3,807.3	3,827.1	3,859.1	3,891.1	3,867.1	3,852.5	3,868.3	3,859.2	3,892.5	3,905.6	3,896.6	3,860.1
2010	3,804.4	3,855.8	3,876.7	3,916.8	3,926.3	3,904.4	3,885.4	3,910.4	3,909.6	3,929.3	3,948.6	3,935.1	3,900.2
2011	3,876.3	3,897.8	3,921.2	3,954.8	3,971.9	3,957.1	3,926.1	3,961.0	3,954.8	3,991.7	4,022.4	4,009.6	3,953.7
2012	3,949.7	3,977.5	3,992.9	4,026.7	4,039.6	4,023.3	4,005.5	4,043.6	4,043.2	4,078.2	4,107.1	4,101.3	4,032.4
2013	4,035.7	4,045.6	4,087.2	4,128.9	4,152.9	4,139.1	4,129.8	4,174.1	4,171.5	4,199.2	4,232.8	4,242.2	4,144.9
2014	4,161.2	4,187.9	4,208.5	4,236.1	4,261.9	4,262.1	4,242.9	4,277.3	4,281.8	4,321.4	4,344.3	4,356.6	4,261.8
2015	4,277.4	4,302.1	4,314.6	4,360.4	4,372.8	4,369.1	4,352.0	4,386.0	4,397.7	4,417.2	4,451.7	4,455.0	4,371.3
2016	4,366.8	4,392.5	4,418.9	4,442.0	4,454.6	4,461.0	4,428.1	4,467.1	4,453.9	4,500.8	4,524.6	4,515.4	4,452.1
Total Private													
2006	3,428.5	3,440.0	3,454.3	3,465.3	3,484.1	3,484.6	3,477.9	3,495.4	3,478.5	3,480.5	3,497.8	3,495.2	3,473.5
2007	3,426.7	3,435.9	3,435.4	3,442.5	3,453.1	3,437.9	3,419.4	3,422.5	3,393.9	3,373.8	3,356.3	3,337.2	3,411.2
2008	3,238.1	3,221.5	3,206.7	3,209.2	3,212.3	3,195.4	3,181.1	3,176.8	3,152.1	3,161.4	3,173.4	3,166.4	3,191.2
2009	3,093.2	3,101.2	3,118.4	3,150.4	3,169.0	3,163.8	3,174.1	3,182.1	3,169.4	3,197.5	3,208.1	3,202.3	3,160.8
2010	3,115.9	3,160.7	3,179.5	3,223.5	3,231.2	3,221.8	3,223.1	3,235.7	3,224.1	3,238.8	3,255.1	3,244.6	3,212.8
2011	3,192.7	3,209.2	3,227.4	3,260.9	3,280.2	3,274.2	3,269.4	3,286.8	3,270.2	3,300.8	3,325.5	3,318.3	3,268.0
2012	3,264.6	3,286.9	3,301.1	3,334.7	3,352.6	3,350.9	3,354.0	3,375.6	3,363.8	3,392.5	3,418.0	3,415.2	3,350.8
2013	3,362.0	3,367.3	3,405.7	3,445.2	3,468.1	3,468.0	3,478.8	3,501.3	3,490.6	3,513.9	3,542.7	3,557.0	3,466.7
2014	3,484.1	3,505.1	3,524.9	3,552.2	3,580.5	3,590.5	3,590.5	3,604.2	3,601.3	3,633.9	3,654.0	3,669.4	3,582.6
2015	3,598.2	3,616.8	3,633.1	3,673.5	3,686.8	3,690.5	3,698.8	3,708.8	3,710.6	3,726.2	3,754.6	3,763.5	3,688.5
2016	3,685.2	3,704.4	3,728.6	3,749.5	3,765.8	3,779.5	3,767.3	3,784.3	3,762.8	3,801.7	3,823.5	3,825.0	3,764.8
Goods Producing													
2006	667.6	668.5	667.8	667.3	669.0	669.2	666.2	667.2	662.3	657.7	657.3	654.0	664.5
2007	643.8	642.3	638.7	634.4	633.7	631.0	626.0	623.6	617.1	609.0	597.0	587.0	623.6
2008	567.4	558.7	552.0	544.0	540.9	534.1	525.8	522.6	518.5	514.7	512.2	508.4	533.3
2009	500.1	499.2	500.2	502.0	505.5	505.2	507.8	508.0	506.7	506.4	505.6	502.3	504.1
2010	491.3	500.6	503.8	508.0	509.1	509.8	510.6	510.7	508.0	506.9	505.7	503.3	505.7
2011	498.4	499.9	501.2	503.3	504.8	505.5	506.4	507.6	506.8	508.3	509.3	506.8	504.9
2012	502.6	505.0	507.8	508.0	510.7	512.1	514.4	516.5	516.0	517.9	520.1	519.5	512.6
2013	516.9	519.7	524.1	527.3	531.0	534.1	537.6	540.9	541.3	543.4	543.7	545.4	533.8
2014	541.7	545.6	546.3	549.3	552.9	556.2	556.8	558.0	559.4	562.1	561.9	565.3	554.6
2015	560.9	564.6	566.9	570.5	571.8	575.5	578.9	580.3	581.2	581.1	583.8	585.8	575.1
2016	580.9	584.5	586.4	585.5	588.0	592.5	591.3	592.0	591.0	597.5	600.3	601.5	591.0
Service-Providing													
2006	3,448.0	3,467.5	3,484.1	3,493.6	3,510.6	3,499.4	3,471.2	3,514.1	3,512.3	3,526.3	3,547.5	3,547.2	3,501.8
2007	3,487.5	3,508.2	3,512.9	3,522.7	3,534.5	3,509.8	3,474.7	3,504.4	3,486.9	3,485.0	3,484.3	3,471.9	3,498.6
2008	3,386.7	3,384.6	3,377.1	3,387.5	3,389.4	3,364.1	3,333.2	3,348.1	3,341.3	3,354.0	3,369.5	3,363.6	3,366.6
2009	3,294.7	3,308.1	3,326.9	3,357.1	3,385.6	3,361.9	3,344.7	3,360.3	3,352.5	3,386.1	3,400.0	3,394.3	3,356.0
2010	3,313.1	3,355.2	3,372.9	3,408.8	3,417.2	3,394.6	3,374.8	3,399.7	3,401.6	3,422.4	3,442.9	3,431.8	3,394.6
2011	3,377.9	3,397.9	3,420.0	3,451.5	3,467.1	3,451.6	3,419.7	3,453.4	3,448.0	3,483.4	3,513.1	3,502.8	3,448.9
2012	3,447.1	3,472.5	3,485.1	3,518.7	3,528.9	3,511.2	3,491.1	3,527.1	3,527.2	3,560.3	3,587.0	3,581.8	3,519.8
2013	3,518.8	3,525.9	3,563.1	3,601.6	3,621.9	3,605.0	3,592.2	3,633.2	3,630.2	3,655.8	3,689.1	3,696.8	3,611.1
2014	3,619.5	3,642.3	3,662.2	3,686.8	3,709.0	3,705.9	3,686.1	3,719.3	3,722.4	3,759.3	3,782.4	3,791.3	3,707.2
2015	3,716.5	3,737.5	3,747.7	3,789.9	3,801.0	3,793.6	3,773.1	3,805.7	3,816.5	3,836.1	3,867.9	3,869.2	3,796.2
2016	3,785.9	3,808.0	3,832.5	3,856.5	3,866.6	3,868.5	3,836.8	3,875.1	3,862.9	3,903.3	3,924.3	3,913.9	3,861.2
Mining and Logging													
2006	12.1	12.1	12.1	12.0	12.0	11.9	11.9	11.9	11.8	11.7	11.6	11.4	11.9
2007	10.8	10.6	10.5	10.5	10.4	10.3	10.3	10.3	10.3	10.3	10.2	10.1	10.4
2008	9.7	9.5	9.3	9.4	9.4	9.4	9.3	9.4	9.2	9.3	9.3	9.2	9.4
2009	9.3	9.2	9.2	9.2	9.2	9.2	9.3	9.3	9.3	9.3	9.3	9.1	9.2
2010	9.0	9.1	9.0	9.0	9.0	9.0	9.1	9.1	9.0	8.9	8.8	8.7	9.0
2011	8.6	8.7	8.5	8.6	8.6	8.6	8.7	8.7	8.5	8.7	8.7	8.6	8.6
2012	8.7	8.7	8.7	8.9	8.9	8.8	8.9	8.9	8.9	9.0	9.1	9.0	8.9
2013	9.0	8.9	9.0	8.8	8.9	8.8	9.0	9.0	9.0	9.0	9.1	9.1	9.0
2014	9.0	9.0	9.0	9.0	9.0	9.0	9.0	9.1	9.1	9.1	9.0	9.1	9.0
2015	9.3	9.3	9.4	9.4	9.2	9.4	9.4	9.5	9.5	9.4	9.5	9.5	9.4
2016	9.4	9.4	9.4	9.4	9.4	9.5	9.4	9.4	9.3	9.4	9.4	9.6	9.4

1. Employment by Industry: Georgia, Selected Years, 2007–2017—*Continued*

(Numbers in thousands, not seasonally adjusted)

Industry and year	January	February	March	April	May	June	July	August	September	October	November	December	Annual average
Construction													
2006	218.6	220.2	221.3	221.7	223.2	224.1	223.0	224.1	221.7	220.7	219.5	216.6	221.2
2007	211.1	211.4	209.9	208.7	209.5	208.1	206.9	204.5	201.2	197.4	193.0	187.7	204.1
2008	177.8	175.9	172.9	170.4	170.1	167.9	164.5	162.0	159.3	158.3	157.0	153.9	165.8
2009	148.1	148.4	148.9	150.1	151.0	150.6	152.0	151.6	150.7	150.3	149.5	145.6	149.7
2010	137.9	143.6	146.3	148.2	147.8	148.2	148.5	148.2	147.4	146.8	145.0	142.7	145.9
2011	138.3	139.3	139.9	140.9	140.9	141.2	142.7	143.5	142.7	143.6	143.5	141.3	141.5
2012	138.6	140.0	142.2	142.7	145.2	146.2	147.8	149.1	149.0	150.0	151.0	149.3	145.9
2013	147.4	149.1	151.2	153.5	155.5	157.1	159.4	160.6	160.9	162.7	161.8	162.1	156.8
2014	159.1	161.3	161.1	164.4	165.5	167.8	168.2	168.7	169.0	171.1	170.1	171.3	166.5
2015	166.9	169.5	171.1	173.4	174.8	176.9	179.8	180.0	181.1	181.2	182.1	182.2	176.6
2016	178.4	180.1	181.2	180.6	182.8	184.9	183.5	183.6	184.0	188.6	190.3	189.9	184.0
Manufacturing													
2006	436.9	436.2	434.4	433.6	433.8	433.2	431.3	431.2	428.8	425.3	426.2	426.0	431.4
2007	421.9	420.3	418.3	415.2	413.8	412.6	408.8	408.8	405.6	401.3	393.8	389.2	409.1
2008	379.9	373.3	369.8	364.2	361.4	356.8	352.0	351.2	350.0	347.1	345.9	345.3	358.1
2009	342.7	341.6	342.1	342.7	345.3	345.4	346.5	347.1	346.7	346.8	346.8	347.6	345.1
2010	344.4	347.9	348.5	350.8	352.3	352.6	353.0	353.4	351.6	351.2	351.9	351.9	350.8
2011	351.5	351.9	352.8	353.8	355.3	355.7	355.0	355.4	355.6	356.0	357.1	356.9	354.8
2012	355.3	356.3	356.9	356.4	356.6	357.1	357.7	358.5	358.1	358.9	360.0	361.2	357.8
2013	360.5	361.7	363.9	365.0	366.6	368.2	369.2	371.3	371.4	371.7	372.8	374.2	368.0
2014	373.6	375.3	376.2	375.9	378.4	379.4	379.6	380.2	381.3	381.9	382.8	384.9	379.1
2015	384.7	385.8	386.4	387.7	387.8	389.2	389.7	390.8	390.6	390.5	392.2	394.1	389.1
2016	393.1	395.0	395.8	395.5	395.8	398.1	398.4	399.0	397.7	399.5	400.6	402.0	397.5
Trade, Transportation, and Utilities													
2006	886.5	880.6	882.9	884.3	889.9	890.4	890.8	891.4	890.6	895.7	912.5	916.0	892.6
2007	889.3	885.0	886.0	882.3	883.5	879.8	879.0	878.2	873.5	870.3	874.7	875.6	879.8
2008	839.5	828.5	824.3	821.1	823.4	819.7	818.7	818.4	813.5	816.2	828.2	831.5	823.6
2009	804.0	801.5	803.1	807.0	811.8	811.1	813.6	814.7	810.5	823.6	834.8	839.6	814.6
2010	809.0	813.5	816.2	823.1	826.4	824.8	825.2	826.9	823.2	832.8	846.9	849.3	826.4
2011	827.8	824.9	827.1	832.7	838.0	834.9	835.1	836.2	832.8	843.0	861.9	863.0	838.1
2012	836.6	834.7	835.1	839.7	844.3	844.7	848.8	852.7	849.1	858.9	876.5	883.3	850.4
2013	858.5	853.6	859.0	867.6	871.9	871.8	875.0	877.6	875.7	888.8	909.5	920.2	877.4
2014	887.2	884.2	888.5	894.1	899.2	902.1	902.3	904.4	904.1	917.4	937.2	944.9	905.5
2015	914.0	911.1	914.1	917.3	920.6	920.8	922.9	922.2	922.6	930.9	953.0	962.7	926.0
2016	929.9	927.0	930.2	932.7	935.5	937.8	937.9	939.5	936.8	945.0	959.7	964.7	939.7
Wholesale Trade													
2006	216.9	217.6	217.7	219.0	219.3	219.0	219.6	219.7	219.2	220.0	220.2	219.8	219.0
2007	218.2	219.0	218.4	219.2	219.2	218.2	217.9	218.1	217.2	216.4	214.3	211.8	217.3
2008	207.0	205.0	202.3	201.4	200.4	198.6	198.4	197.7	196.1	197.3	197.3	196.4	199.8
2009	194.4	194.7	194.6	195.9	196.6	196.0	196.6	196.6	195.2	197.4	197.2	196.0	195.9
2010	194.4	195.5	195.4	197.6	198.7	197.7	198.8	199.5	198.5	200.0	200.3	199.3	198.0
2011	198.3	199.5	199.5	201.1	202.5	201.7	202.8	203.3	202.2	204.6	205.0	204.5	202.1
2012	202.4	203.4	203.1	204.3	204.9	204.7	205.1	205.3	204.1	206.6	207.6	207.1	204.9
2013	206.0	206.7	206.9	208.1	209.1	209.3	210.2	210.8	210.4	212.3	213.9	214.4	209.8
2014	212.0	213.2	214.0	214.6	215.9	216.2	217.1	217.3	216.9	219.3	219.7	219.6	216.3
2015	217.0	217.1	217.9	218.9	219.4	219.6	219.4	219.0	219.1	218.7	218.9	219.9	218.7
2016	217.4	218.5	219.2	220.5	221.0	222.4	222.6	222.6	222.7	224.1	224.3	225.7	221.8
Retail Trade													
2006	484.3	477.3	479.0	478.4	481.4	479.7	480.9	480.2	478.9	483.0	499.4	501.5	483.7
2007	479.7	474.3	475.5	471.8	472.2	469.2	469.3	468.8	465.3	464.4	471.5	473.0	471.3
2008	447.3	440.3	439.2	439.4	442.1	440.0	439.6	440.4	437.5	438.6	450.3	453.1	442.3
2009	432.7	429.8	431.2	434.0	436.7	436.1	437.3	437.9	434.4	443.1	454.2	457.6	438.8
2010	435.6	436.9	438.6	443.2	444.4	442.9	442.9	443.0	440.1	447.4	460.1	461.3	444.7
2011	444.7	440.7	442.4	445.3	448.3	446.1	446.1	446.4	444.1	451.5	468.6	467.9	449.3
2012	447.0	445.7	446.6	449.9	452.8	453.6	457.0	459.9	458.1	464.5	479.2	483.8	458.2
2013	462.4	458.2	461.5	465.5	467.8	467.4	469.0	469.7	468.3	475.2	492.9	498.2	471.3
2014	471.5	469.9	473.2	478.3	480.4	482.3	480.5	481.9	481.8	488.3	504.8	507.9	483.4
2015	484.3	482.6	485.3	487.7	489.2	488.1	489.9	489.6	489.1	495.5	512.4	514.9	492.4
2016	494.0	491.4	492.6	494.0	494.9	494.7	493.8	494.0	489.9	496.7	507.9	507.4	495.9

1. Employment by Industry: Georgia, Selected Years, 2007–2017—*Continued*

(Numbers in thousands, not seasonally adjusted)

Industry and year	January	February	March	April	May	June	July	August	September	October	November	December	Annual average
Transportation and Utilities													
2006	185.3	185.7	186.2	186.9	189.2	191.7	190.3	191.5	192.5	192.7	192.9	194.7	190.0
2007	191.4	191.7	192.1	191.3	192.1	192.4	191.8	191.3	191.0	189.5	189.2	190.8	191.2
2008	185.2	183.2	182.8	180.3	180.9	181.1	180.7	180.3	179.9	180.3	180.6	182.0	181.4
2009	176.9	177.0	177.3	177.1	178.5	179.0	179.7	180.2	180.9	183.1	183.4	186.0	179.9
2010	179.0	181.1	182.2	182.3	183.3	184.2	183.5	184.4	184.6	185.4	186.5	188.7	183.8
2011	184.8	184.7	185.2	186.3	187.2	187.1	186.2	186.5	186.5	186.9	188.3	190.6	186.7
2012	187.2	185.6	185.4	185.5	186.6	186.4	186.7	187.5	186.9	187.8	189.7	192.4	187.3
2013	190.1	188.7	190.6	194.0	195.0	195.1	195.8	197.1	197.0	201.3	202.7	207.6	196.3
2014	203.7	201.1	201.3	201.2	202.9	203.6	204.7	205.2	205.4	209.8	212.7	217.4	205.8
2015	212.7	211.4	210.9	210.7	212.0	213.1	213.6	213.6	214.4	216.7	221.7	227.9	214.9
2016	218.5	217.1	218.4	218.2	219.6	220.7	221.5	222.9	224.2	224.2	227.5	231.6	222.0
Information													
2006	108.6	108.3	108.4	106.9	107.6	107.7	107.3	107.5	107.3	106.4	107.0	107.0	107.5
2007	104.8	105.8	105.9	105.7	106.2	106.6	105.4	105.2	104.5	103.5	103.9	103.9	105.1
2008	104.5	104.3	103.7	103.6	103.4	103.1	101.8	101.4	100.9	99.9	99.9	100.6	102.3
2009	98.7	98.7	98.9	99.1	99.4	98.9	97.7	97.6	97.3	95.7	96.5	96.9	98.0
2010	96.1	96.8	96.8	97.5	97.4	96.8	97.5	97.7	97.3	97.7	99.2	97.4	97.4
2011	97.3	98.5	98.4	98.1	99.3	99.0	99.8	100.0	99.8	101.0	101.6	101.6	99.5
2012	99.3	100.3	100.5	101.6	102.3	101.5	102.2	102.5	102.5	104.4	104.3	104.5	102.2
2013	104.3	105.2	105.8	106.7	107.5	108.8	108.8	108.1	107.7	109.8	110.4	110.5	107.8
2014	107.3	108.2	108.3	109.4	111.7	111.7	113.9	112.0	110.0	114.4	115.3	115.6	111.5
2015	109.2	111.1	109.4	112.2	111.9	112.1	113.5	111.4	112.5	113.6	114.5	113.0	112.0
2016	113.2	114.9	114.9	115.9	116.5	116.2	115.3	117.8	115.1	118.5	119.4	117.0	116.2
Financial Activities													
2006	242.4	244.1	244.0	243.6	243.7	243.6	244.1	244.0	242.2	242.5	242.4	242.0	243.2
2007	238.3	239.1	238.1	238.3	238.6	237.5	237.6	236.5	234.0	234.5	231.8	231.0	236.3
2008	228.1	227.1	225.5	225.1	225.2	224.5	224.0	222.9	220.8	220.7	220.2	220.1	223.7
2009	216.6	216.4	216.3	216.6	217.9	218.2	218.3	219.1	218.4	220.6	221.3	221.9	218.5
2010	219.2	219.8	219.9	222.7	223.3	223.6	224.1	225.0	224.9	226.1	226.4	226.5	223.5
2011	225.2	225.7	226.1	226.0	226.2	226.3	227.2	227.5	226.2	228.0	229.1	228.9	226.9
2012	226.6	227.6	227.9	228.7	229.2	229.2	229.7	230.2	228.6	230.6	231.7	231.1	229.3
2013	229.4	229.7	230.1	230.7	231.6	231.7	232.2	232.8	231.1	233.0	233.3	233.4	231.6
2014	231.5	232.0	232.5	233.6	234.5	235.1	235.3	234.8	233.9	235.8	236.1	236.6	234.3
2015	235.0	235.2	235.5	236.7	238.0	238.6	240.1	240.0	239.7	240.9	241.2	241.5	238.5
2016	238.5	239.5	240.5	240.7	242.1	243.7	243.8	243.6	243.4	244.1	243.2	241.3	242.0
Professional and Business Services													
2006	547.5	552.7	558.2	556.4	559.3	561.1	559.8	567.1	565.0	566.6	567.0	572.0	561.1
2007	556.3	559.2	556.8	562.9	562.2	562.9	553.3	555.2	550.3	547.0	541.7	537.8	553.8
2008	513.1	511.2	506.5	504.7	502.3	504.7	504.6	503.7	501.5	512.4	515.6	515.9	508.0
2009	501.5	506.1	511.1	519.6	521.0	523.0	526.2	527.6	527.4	536.2	536.5	535.6	522.7
2010	515.0	528.3	532.1	542.7	540.8	541.3	541.3	545.6	546.5	547.6	549.6	548.3	539.9
2011	534.7	541.9	546.5	553.8	556.9	560.8	557.0	562.3	559.1	565.8	569.8	568.8	556.5
2012	559.0	569.0	572.4	577.8	579.8	582.7	581.8	587.2	587.3	594.2	598.0	594.8	582.0
2013	585.3	587.8	601.0	604.3	609.8	611.7	615.6	621.3	621.1	623.2	628.0	627.4	611.4
2014	612.6	620.1	624.5	624.3	631.9	634.9	635.6	639.1	640.0	645.0	643.3	645.9	633.1
2015	632.6	638.5	641.3	648.5	649.5	650.3	657.0	661.8	663.9	666.5	667.6	669.0	653.9
2016	652.2	657.5	662.7	665.2	665.9	670.7	668.4	674.2	669.4	678.0	681.4	678.0	668.6
Education and Health Services													
2006	439.8	443.7	442.6	446.7	447.6	443.4	444.2	450.7	452.2	455.8	457.2	454.8	448.2
2007	451.6	456.6	455.9	457.4	459.2	452.0	453.4	459.7	458.9	463.5	464.8	463.9	458.1
2008	461.3	463.4	461.3	464.3	466.4	459.0	459.7	465.0	462.7	469.5	471.0	469.7	464.4
2009	466.4	469.9	470.8	473.4	475.8	469.4	471.8	477.9	477.7	484.8	485.0	482.9	475.5
2010	476.0	482.9	482.6	487.2	486.4	478.3	478.5	484.9	486.1	492.0	492.2	489.8	484.7
2011	486.2	490.9	491.2	495.5	496.3	488.8	487.6	497.1	497.8	503.7	505.2	503.4	495.3
2012	501.1	505.9	506.0	510.7	511.7	504.3	501.5	510.5	511.9	517.2	520.6	518.4	510.0
2013	513.3	515.4	518.3	521.8	523.3	516.7	516.5	527.1	528.5	530.0	532.4	534.3	523.1
2014	529.4	533.3	534.4	535.5	537.6	533.2	532.5	541.0	544.3	551.3	553.2	553.5	539.9
2015	550.8	555.9	556.6	559.5	559.9	553.6	552.0	559.8	562.5	567.2	568.4	567.7	559.5
2016	560.5	564.7	567.2	568.3	570.0	564.7	562.4	570.1	571.1	578.8	581.1	583.1	570.2

1. Employment by Industry: Georgia, Selected Years, 2007–2017—*Continued*

(Numbers in thousands, not seasonally adjusted)

Industry and year	January	February	March	April	May	June	July	August	September	October	November	December	Annual average
Leisure and Hospitality													
2006	378.0	383.5	391.4	399.5	405.4	406.7	403.0	405.2	398.4	395.0	393.9	390.4	395.9
2007	383.1	387.0	393.2	400.0	407.0	404.9	402.2	402.1	395.2	386.4	383.1	379.7	393.7
2008	367.2	370.7	376.5	388.5	392.1	391.7	387.8	385.9	379.0	373.5	372.1	367.4	379.4
2009	355.0	357.9	366.2	379.0	382.7	383.4	382.8	382.6	377.7	375.7	373.9	370.5	374.0
2010	358.5	365.8	375.0	387.7	392.4	391.3	390.4	390.8	385.0	382.7	382.3	378.7	381.7
2011	372.6	375.9	385.5	398.4	404.8	404.2	401.2	402.1	395.1	397.0	394.9	393.6	393.8
2012	387.9	392.0	399.3	414.6	420.3	421.6	420.8	422.1	415.5	416.2	414.0	412.0	411.4
2013	403.6	404.7	416.1	433.1	438.4	437.7	437.3	438.5	431.5	432.1	431.6	432.1	428.1
2014	422.0	428.1	436.5	450.9	456.5	459.8	456.0	458.1	453.7	452.4	451.7	451.7	448.1
2015	441.2	445.2	453.7	471.6	477.1	479.8	475.2	475.3	471.2	468.8	469.1	467.0	466.3
2016	454.4	459.8	469.5	482.4	487.5	492.1	487.0	487.5	477.9	478.6	479.7	479.3	478.0
Other Services													
2006	158.1	158.6	159.0	160.6	161.6	162.5	162.5	162.3	160.5	160.8	160.5	159.0	160.5
2007	159.5	160.9	160.8	161.5	162.7	163.2	162.5	162.0	160.4	159.6	159.3	158.3	160.9
2008	157.0	157.6	156.9	157.9	158.6	158.6	158.7	156.9	155.2	154.5	154.2	152.8	156.6
2009	150.9	151.5	151.8	153.7	154.9	154.6	155.9	154.6	153.7	154.5	154.5	152.6	153.6
2010	150.8	153.0	153.1	154.6	155.4	155.9	155.5	154.1	153.1	153.0	152.8	151.3	153.6
2011	150.5	151.5	151.4	153.1	153.9	154.7	155.1	154.0	152.6	154.0	153.7	152.2	153.1
2012	151.5	152.4	152.1	153.6	154.3	154.8	154.8	153.9	152.9	153.1	152.8	151.6	153.2
2013	150.7	151.2	151.3	153.7	154.6	155.5	155.8	155.0	153.7	153.6	153.8	153.7	153.6
2014	152.4	153.6	153.9	155.1	156.2	157.5	158.1	156.8	155.9	155.5	155.3	155.9	155.5
2015	154.5	155.2	155.6	157.2	158.0	159.8	159.2	158.0	157.0	157.2	157.0	156.8	157.1
2016	155.6	156.5	157.2	158.8	160.3	161.8	161.2	159.6	158.1	161.2	158.7	160.1	159.1
Government													
2006	687.1	696.0	697.6	695.6	695.5	684.0	659.5	685.9	696.1	703.5	707.0	706.0	692.8
2007	704.6	714.6	716.2	714.6	715.1	702.9	681.3	705.5	710.1	720.2	725.0	721.7	711.0
2008	716.0	721.8	722.4	722.3	718.0	702.8	677.9	693.9	707.7	707.3	708.3	705.6	708.7
2009	701.6	706.1	708.7	708.7	722.1	703.3	678.4	686.2	689.8	695.0	697.5	694.3	699.3
2010	688.5	695.1	697.2	693.3	695.1	682.6	662.3	674.7	685.5	690.5	693.5	690.5	687.4
2011	683.6	688.6	693.8	693.9	691.7	682.9	656.7	674.2	684.6	690.9	696.9	691.3	685.8
2012	685.1	690.6	691.8	692.0	687.0	672.4	651.5	668.0	679.4	685.7	689.1	686.1	681.6
2013	673.7	678.3	681.5	683.7	684.8	671.1	651.0	672.8	680.9	685.3	690.1	685.2	678.2
2014	677.1	682.8	683.6	683.9	681.4	671.6	652.4	673.1	680.5	687.5	690.3	687.2	679.3
2015	679.2	685.3	681.5	686.9	686.0	678.6	653.2	677.2	687.1	691.0	697.1	691.5	682.9
2016	681.6	688.1	690.3	692.5	688.8	681.5	660.8	682.8	691.1	699.1	701.1	690.4	687.3

2. Average Weekly Hours by Selected Industry: Georgia, 2013–2017

(Not seasonally adjusted)

Industry and year	January	February	March	April	May	June	July	August	September	October	November	December	Annual average
Total Private													
2013	34.8	34.9	35.2	35.0	34.9	35.6	35.0	35.0	35.6	35.0	35.2	35.5	35.2
2014	34.6	34.0	35.8	35.2	35.2	35.8	35.2	35.4	35.3	35.1	35.6	35.2	35.2
2015	34.8	35.3	35.3	34.8	35.1	35.1	35.1	35.6	34.8	34.8	35.1	34.8	35.1
2016	34.4	34.7	34.7	34.8	35.2	34.9	34.8	34.6	34.6	35.2	34.8	34.9	34.8
2017	34.7	34.4	34.4	34.8	34.5	34.9	35.0	34.6	33.9	35.2	34.8	34.7	34.7
Goods-Producing													
2013	40.4	40.1	41.0	40.9	41.3	42.0	41.4	41.4	42.2	41.5	41.7	41.7	41.3
2014	40.2	37.4	42.1	41.3	41.3	42.0	41.8	41.9	42.0	41.4	41.9	42.2	41.3
2015	40.7	40.4	40.6	40.5	41.4	41.4	41.7	42.3	40.8	41.6	41.0	41.9	41.2
2016	40.3	40.4	41.0	40.7	41.4	41.5	40.6	40.7	41.0	41.3	41.4	41.0	40.9
2017	39.8	39.9	40.0	40.3	40.6	41.2	41.3	41.0	39.5	41.5	41.5	41.2	40.7
Construction													
2013	39.1	38.0	40.4	40.3	41.2	41.5	40.9	40.2	41.6	40.6	40.8	40.1	40.4
2014	38.6	34.9	41.6	41.6	41.8	41.9	43.0	42.7	42.6	40.9	42.2	42.4	41.2
2015	40.0	39.5	39.8	39.7	42.2	42.0	42.3	42.3	40.4	42.5	41.2	42.4	41.2
2016	40.4	40.3	41.4	40.8	41.6	41.2	41.6	40.9	41.4	40.9	41.0	39.5	40.9
2017	39.2	39.4	39.0	39.8	40.5	40.5	40.8	40.1	38.6	41.1	40.4	40.1	40.0
Manufacturing													
2013	41.2	41.2	41.2	41.2	41.3	42.2	41.6	42.1	42.4	41.9	42.2	42.5	41.7
2014	41.1	38.8	42.4	41.1	41.0	42.0	41.0	41.3	41.5	41.7	41.7	42.1	41.3
2015	41.3	41.0	41.1	41.0	40.8	40.9	41.2	42.2	40.9	40.9	40.7	41.4	41.1
2016	40.0	40.1	40.4	40.3	40.9	41.3	39.6	40.2	40.4	41.3	41.4	41.7	40.6
2017	40.1	40.0	40.3	40.4	40.6	41.6	41.4	41.5	40.1	41.7	42.2	41.8	41.0
Trade, Transportation, and Utilities													
2013	34.1	34.5	34.5	34.5	34.4	34.9	34.5	34.7	35.1	34.6	34.9	35.2	34.7
2014	34.3	33.8	35.4	35.1	35.0	35.4	35.0	35.4	35.3	34.9	35.5	35.2	35.0
2015	34.7	35.4	35.3	35.0	35.2	34.9	34.8	35.1	34.3	34.5	34.7	34.6	34.9
2016	34.2	34.6	34.1	34.3	34.6	34.3	34.3	34.2	34.1	34.5	34.2	34.4	34.3
2017	33.9	33.8	33.9	34.5	34.0	34.3	34.9	34.4	33.9	34.6	34.6	34.8	34.3
Financial Activities													
2013	36.8	36.9	36.7	36.9	36.9	38.1	37.0	37.1	38.2	36.6	36.7	38.0	37.2
2014	36.7	37.7	38.0	37.0	37.3	38.1	36.4	36.5	36.2	36.4	38.0	36.7	37.1
2015	36.6	38.1	38.1	36.9	36.9	37.3	37.1	38.6	37.4	37.1	38.9	37.6	37.6
2016	37.4	37.3	37.3	37.2	38.4	37.3	37.2	37.0	37.3	37.9	36.8	36.8	37.3
2017	38.5	37.3	36.9	38.2	36.6	36.7	38.2	36.6	36.8	38.7	37.1	36.8	37.4
Professional and Business Services													
2013	37.0	37.5	37.3	37.4	37.2	38.1	36.8	37.0	37.7	36.6	37.0	37.4	37.2
2014	35.8	36.2	37.8	36.8	36.4	37.4	36.1	36.6	36.3	36.3	37.1	36.0	36.6
2015	35.9	36.5	36.4	35.4	35.6	35.9	35.4	36.0	35.1	34.3	34.8	34.2	35.4
2016	33.6	33.9	34.3	34.8	35.3	34.8	34.8	34.9	34.6	35.8	34.6	34.8	34.7
2017	35.0	34.4	33.9	34.5	34.2	34.9	33.8	33.9	33.3	35.1	34.2	34.5	34.3
Education and Health Services													
2013	34.5	34.2	34.3	34.2	34.2	34.8	34.2	34.7	34.9	34.4	34.5	35.0	34.5
2014	34.9	34.5	35.3	34.7	34.8	35.4	34.9	35.1	35.2	35.2	35.6	34.9	35.0
2015	34.9	35.2	35.3	34.7	34.8	34.7	34.9	35.3	34.9	35.1	35.6	35.1	35.0
2016	35.3	35.2	35.3	35.1	35.3	34.9	35.2	34.6	34.7	35.6	35.5	35.7	35.2
2017	35.8	35.3	35.3	35.4	35.3	35.3	35.4	35.4	34.8	35.4	34.9	34.8	35.3
Leisure and Hospitality													
2013	25.6	26.2	26.6	26.6	26.4	26.9	26.3	26.0	26.1	26.1	26.2	26.4	26.3
2014	25.9	25.5	27.5	27.0	27.3	27.4	27.0	26.8	26.5	26.5	26.7	26.6	26.7
2015	26.2	26.8	26.7	26.8	26.8	26.7	26.5	27.0	26.4	26.7	26.6	26.4	26.6
2016	25.9	26.8	26.8	27.1	27.2	27.1	26.9	26.4	26.1	26.6	26.5	26.6	26.7
2017	26.0	26.5	26.6	26.7	26.6	26.6	26.5	26.0	25.5	26.7	26.5	26.2	26.4
Other Services													
2013	30.1	30.4	30.8	29.2	29.1	29.7	29.6	30.3	31.9	31.2	31.9	32.1	30.5
2014	31.7	31.7	32.9	32.6	32.9	34.4	34.2	33.9	33.7	32.9	33.8	33.6	33.2
2015	33.1	33.7	34.6	33.9	34.2	34.1	34.6	35.1	34.7	34.3	34.4	33.9	34.2
2016	33.3	34.6	34.0	34.5	34.2	33.8	33.7	32.9	33.0	33.2	32.9	32.6	33.6
2017	32.8	32.4	31.9	32.7	32.6	32.1	32.6	31.8	30.0	31.6	31.8	31.3	32.0

3. Average Hourly Earnings by Selected Industry: Georgia, 2013–2017

(Dollars, not seasonally adjusted)

Industry and year	January	February	March	April	May	June	July	August	September	October	November	December	Annual average
Total Private													
2013	22.21	22.40	22.15	22.26	22.18	22.44	22.34	22.45	22.77	22.61	22.71	23.06	22.47
2014	23.07	23.64	23.10	22.95	22.90	23.32	23.19	23.46	23.39	23.49	23.90	23.62	23.34
2015	23.86	24.06	23.92	23.65	23.50	23.39	23.55	23.84	23.71	24.11	24.28	24.13	23.84
2016	24.40	24.27	24.22	24.21	24.58	24.18	24.36	24.50	24.52	25.07	24.63	24.71	24.47
2017	25.53	25.20	25.11	25.58	25.15	25.86	26.37	26.31	26.64	26.68	26.15	26.33	25.92
Goods-Producing													
2013	21.86	22.16	22.00	22.08	22.22	22.53	22.47	22.42	22.51	22.39	22.50	22.85	22.34
2014	22.94	23.55	22.84	22.73	22.99	23.22	23.17	23.16	22.98	23.06	23.34	23.28	23.10
2015	23.30	23.47	23.19	23.20	23.12	23.26	23.48	23.89	23.99	24.09	24.34	24.73	23.68
2016	24.95	24.91	25.04	24.87	25.05	24.76	24.91	24.89	24.84	24.82	24.49	24.62	24.84
2017	24.75	24.59	24.42	24.42	24.28	24.31	24.50	24.22	24.60	24.37	24.48	24.47	24.45
Construction													
2013	22.47	22.91	22.39	22.21	22.49	22.54	22.48	22.59	22.01	22.51	22.46	22.88	22.57
2014	23.00	23.58	22.67	22.30	22.52	22.76	22.73	22.67	22.36	22.56	22.75	22.55	22.68
2015	22.88	23.19	23.09	23.26	23.18	22.87	23.10	23.30	23.36	23.51	24.14	23.85	23.32
2016	24.35	24.10	24.36	24.36	24.42	24.58	24.38	24.46	24.51	25.04	24.62	25.00	24.52
2017	24.57	24.84	24.84	24.73	24.35	24.95	24.99	24.87	25.40	25.07	25.58	25.39	24.97
Manufacturing													
2013	21.60	21.83	21.82	22.02	22.09	22.52	22.47	22.32	22.27	22.30	22.47	22.78	22.21
2014	22.86	23.46	22.87	22.91	23.21	23.45	23.41	23.44	23.37	23.35	23.70	23.77	23.32
2015	23.60	23.66	23.27	23.30	23.16	23.55	23.77	24.30	24.42	24.51	24.51	25.33	23.95
2016	25.33	25.39	25.36	25.19	25.44	24.88	25.27	25.22	25.10	24.67	24.42	24.42	25.05
2017	24.83	24.41	24.15	24.40	24.39	24.11	24.43	24.03	24.31	24.06	23.92	24.04	24.25
Trade, Transportation, and Utilities													
2013	20.47	20.64	20.13	20.12	20.24	20.54	20.39	20.37	20.59	20.48	20.46	20.76	20.44
2014	21.00	21.59	21.21	21.22	21.23	21.51	21.42	21.75	21.75	21.79	22.02	21.72	21.52
2015	22.44	22.26	22.25	21.94	21.68	21.43	21.56	21.48	21.49	21.58	21.33	21.30	21.72
2016	21.67	21.22	21.70	21.72	21.68	21.60	21.77	21.62	21.82	22.40	21.90	22.23	21.78
2017	23.29	22.65	22.52	22.85	22.52	22.91	23.08	23.13	23.29	22.90	22.89	22.92	22.91
Financial Activities													
2013	28.58	28.84	29.18	29.60	29.67	30.08	30.08	30.38	30.95	31.34	30.61	31.20	30.05
2014	30.71	31.89	30.69	30.78	30.56	31.07	30.90	30.46	30.17	30.14	30.54	29.72	30.64
2015	29.47	29.98	30.16	29.33	29.46	29.03	29.06	29.32	29.13	29.09	28.95	28.45	29.28
2016	28.52	29.42	28.79	28.60	30.46	29.06	29.84	31.68	30.85	32.65	32.11	32.36	30.37
2017	32.69	32.45	32.49	33.40	32.94	32.04	33.17	32.84	33.62	34.14	33.57	33.13	33.05
Professional and Business Services													
2013	25.47	25.63	25.16	25.52	25.28	25.66	25.53	25.69	26.09	25.55	26.18	26.64	25.71
2014	26.86	27.28	26.73	26.31	26.41	27.06	26.85	27.17	27.20	27.30	28.12	27.80	27.10
2015	28.29	28.97	28.63	28.06	28.02	27.76	28.16	29.01	28.56	29.18	30.09	29.60	28.69
2016	30.24	30.00	29.55	29.79	30.44	29.63	29.87	29.90	29.98	30.54	30.04	29.85	29.99
2017	31.67	30.82	30.57	31.40	30.37	32.44	34.43	33.86	34.19	33.86	32.92	33.61	32.52
Education and Health Services													
2013	23.34	23.88	23.89	23.73	23.50	23.57	23.79	24.00	24.10	24.09	24.10	23.94	23.83
2014	24.21	24.38	24.08	24.17	23.92	24.61	24.32	25.18	24.90	25.08	25.34	25.29	24.63
2015	24.94	25.05	24.90	25.14	24.83	24.98	24.91	25.02	25.06	25.86	25.52	25.50	25.15
2016	25.39	25.55	25.13	25.38	25.22	25.46	25.60	25.75	25.77	26.38	26.32	26.32	25.69
2017	26.59	26.88	27.20	27.80	27.58	27.62	27.90	28.69	29.05	29.44	27.90	28.31	27.92
Leisure and Hospitality													
2013	12.16	12.10	12.02	12.00	12.01	11.85	11.79	11.98	12.09	12.10	12.13	12.25	12.04
2014	12.02	12.11	12.08	11.94	11.95	11.73	11.74	11.91	11.96	12.05	12.42	12.37	12.02
2015	12.47	12.48	12.57	12.47	12.58	12.38	12.47	12.58	12.58	12.59	12.70	12.74	12.55
2016	12.75	12.70	12.74	12.77	12.71	12.45	12.54	12.54	12.73	12.83	12.65	12.78	12.68
2017	12.87	12.92	12.92	13.03	13.14	13.07	13.03	13.06	13.08	13.13	13.06	13.39	13.06
Other Services													
2013	18.07	18.55	18.66	19.22	19.20	18.93	18.46	18.74	18.93	19.71	19.38	19.64	18.96
2014	19.26	19.72	19.91	20.57	19.66	19.91	20.45	20.40	20.45	20.55	20.35	20.81	20.18
2015	20.76	20.86	20.58	21.14	20.99	21.03	20.91	22.00	21.56	21.61	21.60	21.59	21.22
2016	21.54	21.22	21.31	20.80	20.98	20.29	20.84	21.01	20.68	20.85	20.85	20.53	20.91
2017	20.54	21.16	20.99	20.83	20.66	20.98	20.83	21.40	21.46	21.36	21.47	21.95	21.13

4. Average Weekly Earnings by Selected Industry: Georgia, 2013–2017

(Dollars, not seasonally adjusted)

Industry and year	January	February	March	April	May	June	July	August	September	October	November	December	Annual average
Total Private													
2013	772.91	781.76	779.68	779.10	774.08	798.86	781.90	785.75	810.61	791.35	799.39	818.63	790.94
2014	798.22	803.76	826.98	807.84	806.08	834.86	816.29	830.48	825.67	824.50	850.84	831.42	821.57
2015	830.33	849.32	844.38	823.02	824.85	820.99	826.61	848.70	825.11	839.03	852.23	839.72	836.78
2016	839.36	842.17	840.43	842.51	865.22	843.88	847.73	847.70	848.39	882.46	857.12	862.38	851.56
2017	885.89	866.88	863.78	890.18	867.68	902.51	922.95	910.33	903.10	939.14	910.02	913.65	899.42
Goods-Producing													
2013	883.14	888.62	902.00	903.07	917.69	946.26	930.26	928.19	949.92	929.19	938.25	952.85	922.64
2014	922.19	880.77	961.56	938.75	949.49	975.24	968.51	970.40	965.16	954.68	977.95	982.42	954.03
2015	948.31	948.19	941.51	939.60	957.17	962.96	979.12	1,010.55	978.79	1,002.14	997.94	1,036.19	975.62
2016	1,005.49	1,006.36	1,026.64	1,012.21	1,037.07	1,027.54	1,011.35	1,013.02	1,018.44	1,025.07	1,013.89	1,009.42	1,015.96
2017	985.05	981.14	976.80	984.13	985.77	1,001.57	1,011.85	993.02	,971.70	1,011.36	1,015.92	1,008.16	995.12
Construction													
2013	878.58	870.58	904.56	895.06	926.59	935.41	919.43	908.12	953.06	913.91	916.37	917.49	911.83
2014	887.80	822.94	943.07	927.68	941.34	953.64	977.39	968.01	952.54	922.70	960.05	956.12	934.42
2015	915.20	916.01	918.98	923.42	978.20	960.54	977.13	985.59	943.74	999.18	994.57	1,011.24	960.78
2016	983.74	971.23	1,008.50	993.89	1,015.87	1,012.70	1,014.21	1,000.41	1,014.71	1,024.14	1,009.42	987.50	1,002.87
2017	963.14	978.70	968.76	984.25	986.18	1,010.48	1,019.59	997.29	980.44	1,030.38	1,033.43	1,018.14	998.80
Manufacturing													
2013	889.92	899.40	898.98	907.22	912.32	950.34	934.75	939.67	944.25	934.37	948.23	968.15	926.16
2014	939.55	910.25	969.69	941.60	951.61	984.90	959.81	968.07	969.86	973.70	988.29	1,000.72	963.12
2015	974.68	970.06	956.40	955.30	944.93	963.20	979.32	1,025.46	998.78	1,002.46	997.56	1,048.66	984.35
2016	1,013.20	1,018.14	1,024.54	1,015.16	1,040.50	1,027.54	1,000.69	1,013.84	1,014.04	1,018.87	1,010.99	1,018.31	1,017.03
2017	995.68	976.40	973.25	985.76	990.23	1,002.98	1,011.40	997.25	974.83	1,003.30	1,009.42	1,004.87	994.25
Trade, Transportation, and Utilities													
2013	698.03	712.08	694.49	694.14	696.26	716.85	703.46	706.84	722.71	708.61	714.05	730.75	709.27
2014	720.30	729.74	750.83	744.82	743.05	761.45	749.70	769.95	767.78	760.47	781.71	764.54	753.20
2015	778.67	788.00	785.43	767.90	763.14	747.91	750.29	753.95	737.11	744.51	740.15	736.98	758.03
2016	741.11	734.21	739.97	745.00	750.13	740.88	746.71	739.40	744.06	772.80	748.98	764.71	747.05
2017	789.53	765.57	763.43	788.33	765.68	785.81	805.49	795.67	789.53	792.34	791.99	797.62	785.81
Financial Activities													
2013	1,051.74	1,064.20	1,070.91	1,092.24	1,094.82	1,146.05	1,112.96	1,127.10	1,182.29	1,147.04	1,123.39	1,185.60	1,117.86
2014	1,127.06	1,202.25	1,166.22	1,138.86	1,139.89	1,183.77	1,124.76	1,111.79	1,092.15	1,097.10	1,160.52	1,090.72	1,136.74
2015	1,078.60	1,142.24	1,149.10	1,082.28	1,087.07	1,082.82	1,078.13	1,131.75	1,089.46	1,079.24	1,126.16	1,069.72	1,100.93
2016	1,066.65	1,097.37	1,073.87	1,063.92	1,169.66	1,083.94	1,110.05	1,172.16	1,150.71	1,237.44	1,181.65	1,190.85	1,132.80
2017	1,258.57	1,210.39	1,198.88	1,275.88	1,205.60	1,175.87	1,267.09	1,201.94	1,237.22	1,321.22	1,245.45	1,219.18	1,236.07
Professional and Business Services													
2013	942.39	961.13	938.47	954.45	940.42	977.65	939.50	950.53	983.59	935.13	968.66	996.34	956.41
2014	961.59	987.54	1,010.39	968.21	961.32	1,012.04	969.29	994.42	987.36	990.99	1,043.25	1,000.80	991.86
2015	1,015.61	1,057.41	1,042.13	993.32	997.51	996.58	996.86	1,044.36	1,002.46	1,000.87	1,047.13	1,012.32	1,015.63
2016	1,016.06	1,017.00	1,013.57	1,036.69	1,074.53	1,031.12	1,039.48	1,043.51	1,037.31	1,093.33	1,039.38	1,038.78	1,040.65
2017	1,108.45	1,060.21	1,036.32	1,083.30	1,038.65	1,132.16	1,163.73	1,147.85	1,138.53	1,188.49	1,125.86	1,159.55	1,115.44
Education and Health Services													
2013	805.23	816.70	819.43	811.57	803.70	820.24	813.62	832.80	841.09	828.70	831.45	837.90	822.14
2014	844.93	841.11	850.02	838.70	832.42	871.19	848.77	883.82	876.48	882.82	902.10	882.62	862.05
2015	870.41	881.76	878.97	872.36	864.08	866.81	869.36	883.21	874.59	907.69	908.51	895.05	880.25
2016	896.27	899.36	887.09	890.84	890.27	888.55	901.12	890.95	894.22	939.13	934.36	939.62	904.29
2017	951.92	948.86	960.16	984.12	973.57	974.99	987.66	1,015.63	1,010.94	1,042.18	973.71	985.19	985.58
Leisure and Hospitality													
2013	311.30	317.02	319.73	319.20	317.06	318.77	310.08	311.48	315.55	315.81	317.81	323.40	316.65
2014	311.32	308.81	332.20	322.38	326.24	321.40	316.98	319.19	316.94	319.33	331.61	329.04	320.93
2015	326.71	334.46	335.62	334.20	337.14	330.55	330.46	339.66	332.11	336.15	337.82	336.34	333.83
2016	330.23	340.36	341.43	346.07	345.71	337.40	337.33	331.06	332.25	341.28	335.23	339.95	338.56
2017	334.62	342.38	343.67	347.90	349.52	347.66	345.30	339.56	333.54	350.57	346.09	350.82	344.78
Other Services													
2013	543.91	563.92	574.73	561.22	558.72	562.22	546.42	567.82	603.87	614.95	618.22	630.44	578.28
2014	610.54	625.12	655.04	670.58	646.81	684.90	699.39	691.56	689.17	676.10	687.83	699.22	669.98
2015	687.16	702.98	712.07	716.65	717.86	717.12	723.49	772.20	748.13	741.22	743.04	731.90	725.72
2016	717.28	734.21	724.54	717.60	717.52	685.80	702.31	691.23	682.44	692.22	685.97	669.28	702.58
2017	673.71	685.58	669.58	681.14	673.52	673.46	679.06	680.52	643.80	674.98	682.75	687.04	676.16

HAWAII
At a Glance

Population:
   2010 census: 1,360,301
   2017 estimate: 1,427,538

Percent change in population:
   2010–2017: 4.9%

Percent change in total nonfarm employment:
   2007–2017: 4.4%

Industry with the largest growth in employment, 2007–2017 (thousands):
   Leisure and hospitality, 13.4

Industry with the largest decline or smallest growth in employment, 2007–2017 (thousands):
   Mining, logging, and construction, -2.7

Civilian labor force:
   2010: 647,249
   2017: 685,418

Unemployment rate and rank among states (highest to lowest):
   2010: 6.9%, 43rd
   2017: 2.4%, 51st

Over-the-year change in unemployment rates:
   2015–2016: -0.7%
   2016–2017: -0.5%

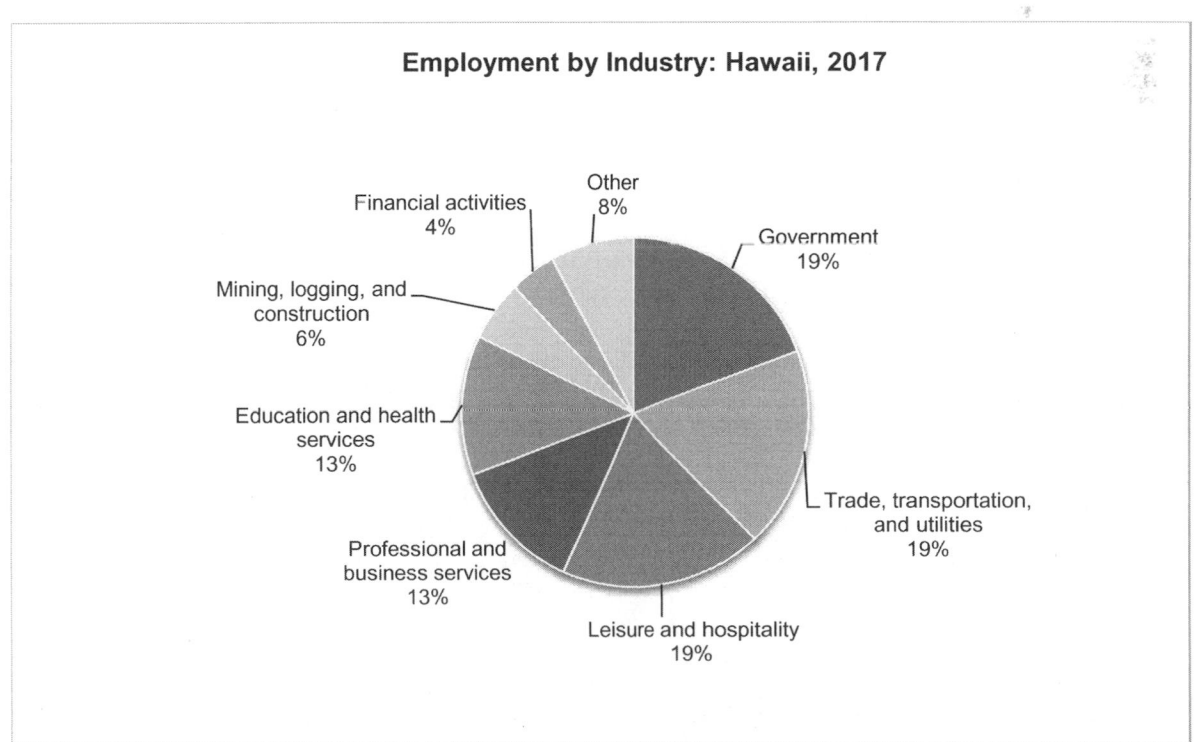

Employment by Industry: Hawaii, 2017

- Other 8%
- Government 19%
- Financial activities 4%
- Mining, logging, and construction 6%
- Education and health services 13%
- Professional and business services 13%
- Leisure and hospitality 19%
- Trade, transportation, and utilities 19%

1. Employment by Industry: Hawaii, Selected Years, 2007–2017

(Numbers in thousands, not seasonally adjusted)

Industry and year	January	February	March	April	May	June	July	August	September	October	November	December	Annual average
Total Nonfarm													
2007	615.0	622.9	626.5	618.5	627.1	630.5	618.0	619.7	624.6	626.4	632.3	637.0	624.9
2008	619.9	626.6	629.4	620.5	626.6	624.4	612.6	613.4	613.0	611.5	618.1	614.8	619.2
2009	597.6	599.3	600.6	594.8	595.0	594.3	583.0	580.7	584.3	587.0	588.6	592.5	591.5
2010	578.9	583.9	587.5	586.7	589.9	586.2	581.1	577.7	584.8	589.6	597.3	599.2	586.9
2011	580.7	592.1	595.8	592.6	593.4	591.3	587.5	584.8	593.9	597.1	603.1	608.4	593.4
2012	584.7	600.3	602.9	604.3	607.4	606.1	599.2	605.7	607.5	611.7	623.1	622.7	606.3
2013	600.2	615.8	618.7	615.7	620.6	617.6	613.7	611.7	619.7	624.1	631.0	634.4	618.6
2014	618.7	623.4	627.1	625.5	628.7	624.8	619.0	622.0	627.5	630.4	639.0	637.9	627.0
2015	627.4	632.9	636.4	635.4	637.5	635.9	630.1	633.8	636.5	642.4	648.2	654.4	637.6
2016	635.6	643.3	645.8	644.4	646.7	643.9	639.7	642.9	648.3	649.0	657.4	656.2	646.1
2017	645.5	651.8	655.6	652.0	654.0	651.5	643.6	642.9	651.8	656.2	661.4	665.5	652.7
Total Private													
2007	495.1	498.7	501.6	498.6	501.8	507.0	502.6	504.3	503.7	502.7	506.8	510.4	502.8
2008	498.5	501.4	502.4	498.7	498.7	498.5	494.2	493.1	489.7	484.5	485.1	485.9	494.2
2009	472.5	472.2	471.6	465.8	464.8	466.3	462.8	462.0	461.9	461.7	462.4	465.5	465.8
2010	456.6	458.5	460.0	459.1	460.1	460.1	460.1	461.2	462.5	464.3	466.6	471.6	461.7
2011	460.5	465.2	468.1	465.5	465.2	465.8	467.9	469.3	471.4	471.2	475.7	480.3	468.8
2012	469.6	472.8	474.6	475.8	478.4	480.2	480.5	483.1	483.8	485.2	491.1	493.8	480.7
2013	484.5	487.8	490.3	490.3	491.4	492.6	494.9	495.7	495.9	497.1	503.0	505.7	494.1
2014	494.0	495.1	498.5	497.6	499.2	498.6	499.7	501.2	502.7	503.3	507.5	511.7	500.8
2015	502.6	504.6	507.7	506.7	508.1	509.7	511.4	512.2	511.8	514.8	519.8	524.6	511.2
2016	512.7	515.4	516.8	517.8	517.6	517.7	520.9	523.2	522.9	521.3	525.5	529.1	520.1
2017	520.8	522.6	526.2	523.0	524.5	525.5	526.5	528.3	527.5	529.5	533.2	536.6	527.0
Goods Producing													
2007	52.8	53.2	53.4	53.5	54.0	54.9	54.7	55.1	55.3	55.1	55.3	55.2	54.4
2008	53.9	54.1	54.0	53.7	53.2	53.3	53.0	52.9	52.4	51.4	50.8	50.1	52.7
2009	48.0	47.1	46.6	45.5	45.4	45.3	44.9	44.3	44.1	43.6	43.2	43.1	45.1
2010	42.2	41.9	42.0	41.7	41.7	41.5	41.7	41.6	41.7	42.1	42.2	42.4	41.9
2011	40.6	41.2	41.3	41.6	41.6	42.2	42.7	42.7	43.1	42.6	42.6	42.8	42.1
2012	41.7	41.8	41.8	41.7	41.9	42.6	42.7	43.1	43.6	43.8	44.1	44.1	42.7
2013	43.2	43.5	44.0	44.0	44.6	44.5	45.0	45.1	45.2	45.0	45.5	45.5	44.6
2014	44.1	44.4	44.8	44.7	45.4	45.8	46.5	46.9	47.1	47.3	47.3	47.3	46.0
2015	46.0	46.4	47.0	47.5	48.0	48.8	49.7	50.0	50.1	51.3	51.7	52.2	49.1
2016	51.2	51.8	52.1	52.1	52.3	52.5	53.1	53.1	52.4	51.8	51.8	51.6	52.2
2017	49.8	50.2	50.6	49.9	50.2	50.6	50.4	50.5	50.2	50.9	51.6	51.6	50.5
Service-Providing													
2007	562.2	569.7	573.1	565.0	573.1	575.6	563.3	564.6	569.3	571.3	577.0	581.8	570.5
2008	566.0	572.5	575.4	566.8	573.4	571.1	559.6	560.5	560.6	560.1	567.3	564.7	566.5
2009	549.6	552.2	554.0	549.3	549.6	549.0	538.1	536.4	540.2	543.4	545.4	549.4	546.4
2010	536.7	542.0	545.5	545.0	548.2	544.7	539.4	536.1	543.1	547.5	555.1	556.8	545.0
2011	540.1	550.9	554.5	551.0	551.8	549.1	544.8	542.1	550.8	554.5	560.5	565.6	551.3
2012	543.0	558.5	561.1	562.6	565.5	563.5	556.5	562.6	563.9	567.9	579.0	578.6	563.6
2013	557.0	572.3	574.7	571.7	576.0	573.1	568.7	566.6	574.5	579.1	585.5	588.9	574.0
2014	574.6	579.0	582.3	580.8	583.3	579.0	572.5	575.1	580.4	583.1	591.7	590.6	581.0
2015	581.4	586.5	589.4	587.9	589.5	587.1	580.4	583.8	586.4	591.1	596.5	602.2	588.5
2016	584.4	591.5	593.7	592.3	594.4	591.4	586.6	589.8	595.9	597.2	605.6	604.6	594.0
2017	595.7	601.6	605.0	602.1	603.8	600.9	593.2	592.4	601.6	605.3	609.8	613.9	602.1
Mining, Logging, and Construction													
2007	37.5	37.9	38.1	38.3	38.7	39.5	39.5	39.8	40.0	40.0	40.1	39.9	39.1
2008	38.9	39.0	38.9	38.6	38.1	38.2	38.1	37.9	37.7	37.0	36.3	35.6	37.9
2009	33.9	33.2	32.7	31.8	31.7	31.7	31.4	30.7	30.4	30.1	29.7	29.6	31.4
2010	29.0	28.8	28.9	28.8	28.8	28.7	28.9	28.7	28.8	29.1	29.1	29.2	28.9
2011	27.6	28.0	28.1	28.4	28.4	29.0	29.5	29.4	29.6	29.2	29.1	29.3	28.8
2012	28.4	28.4	28.5	28.5	28.8	29.4	29.5	29.8	30.2	30.4	30.5	30.5	29.4
2013	29.8	30.1	30.5	30.7	31.2	31.0	31.4	31.5	31.5	31.3	31.6	31.7	31.0
2014	30.6	30.9	31.1	31.1	31.8	32.0	32.5	32.7	33.1	33.3	33.2	33.1	32.1
2015	32.0	32.3	33.0	33.5	34.0	34.7	35.6	35.8	36.0	37.1	37.5	37.9	35.0
2016	37.2	37.7	38.0	38.0	38.2	38.3	38.8	38.7	38.2	37.6	37.6	37.2	38.0
2017	35.9	36.1	36.4	35.8	36.0	36.3	36.2	36.2	36.0	36.9	37.4	37.5	36.4

1. Employment by Industry: Hawaii, Selected Years, 2007–2017—*Continued*

(Numbers in thousands, not seasonally adjusted)

Industry and year	January	February	March	April	May	June	July	August	September	October	November	December	Annual average
Manufacturing													
2007	15.3	15.3	15.3	15.2	15.3	15.4	15.2	15.3	15.3	15.1	15.2	15.3	15.3
2008	15.0	15.1	15.1	15.1	15.1	15.1	14.9	15.0	14.7	14.4	14.5	14.5	14.9
2009	14.1	13.9	13.9	13.7	13.7	13.6	13.5	13.6	13.7	13.5	13.5	13.5	13.7
2010	13.2	13.1	13.1	12.9	12.9	12.8	12.8	12.9	12.9	13.0	13.1	13.2	13.0
2011	13.0	13.2	13.2	13.2	13.2	13.2	13.2	13.3	13.5	13.4	13.5	13.5	13.3
2012	13.3	13.4	13.3	13.2	13.1	13.2	13.2	13.3	13.4	13.4	13.6	13.6	13.3
2013	13.4	13.4	13.5	13.3	13.4	13.5	13.6	13.6	13.7	13.7	13.9	13.8	13.6
2014	13.5	13.5	13.7	13.6	13.6	13.8	14.0	14.2	14.0	14.0	14.1	14.2	13.9
2015	14.0	14.1	14.0	14.0	14.0	14.1	14.1	14.2	14.1	14.2	14.2	14.3	14.1
2016	14.0	14.1	14.1	14.1	14.1	14.2	14.3	14.4	14.2	14.2	14.2	14.4	14.2
2017	13.9	14.1	14.2	14.1	14.2	14.3	14.2	14.3	14.2	14.0	14.2	14.1	14.2
Trade, Transportation, and Utilities													
2007	121.6	120.3	121.4	120.3	120.8	121.6	121.3	121.4	121.2	121.5	124.5	126.4	121.9
2008	122.1	120.7	120.9	118.9	118.6	118.2	117.2	117.1	116.1	115.0	115.8	116.5	118.1
2009	113.4	112.3	111.7	110.3	110.0	110.5	110.2	109.8	110.1	110.0	111.4	112.8	111.0
2010	109.7	109.1	109.0	109.2	108.9	109.3	109.7	110.2	109.8	110.4	112.1	114.0	110.1
2011	110.8	110.3	110.5	110.1	110.0	110.3	111.0	111.2	111.2	112.3	114.4	116.1	111.5
2012	113.4	112.7	113.3	113.0	113.5	114.2	114.5	114.8	114.9	115.3	118.7	119.7	114.8
2013	115.9	115.6	116.0	115.6	115.8	116.3	116.5	116.8	116.9	116.9	119.5	121.1	116.9
2014	117.1	116.2	116.5	116.3	116.5	116.8	117.4	117.1	117.2	117.9	120.5	122.7	117.7
2015	119.3	118.6	118.9	118.5	118.6	119.0	119.2	119.4	119.0	119.6	122.0	123.5	119.6
2016	119.7	119.1	119.0	118.6	118.7	118.6	119.7	120.2	120.5	120.9	123.2	125.3	120.3
2017	121.7	120.4	120.6	120.1	120.2	120.7	121.0	121.7	121.5	121.5	123.0	123.4	121.3
Wholesale Trade													
2007	18.2	18.2	18.4	18.3	18.4	18.6	18.6	18.7	18.8	18.8	19.0	19.1	18.6
2008	18.7	18.8	18.9	18.8	18.9	18.9	18.9	18.8	18.8	18.7	18.6	18.6	18.8
2009	18.2	18.1	18.0	17.9	17.8	17.8	17.8	17.7	17.8	17.7	17.7	17.8	17.9
2010	17.5	17.5	17.6	17.6	17.6	17.6	17.7	17.7	17.6	17.7	17.7	17.8	17.6
2011	17.4	17.3	17.3	17.4	17.4	17.4	17.5	17.5	17.5	17.6	17.6	17.8	17.5
2012	17.5	17.5	17.6	17.5	17.5	17.7	17.7	17.8	17.8	17.8	17.9	17.9	17.7
2013	17.7	17.7	17.8	17.7	17.7	17.7	17.7	17.7	17.7	17.6	17.7	17.7	17.7
2014	17.6	17.6	17.7	17.6	17.6	17.7	17.7	17.7	17.7	17.8	17.9	18.2	17.7
2015	17.9	17.9	17.9	17.9	17.9	18.0	18.0	18.1	18.0	17.9	17.9	18.0	18.0
2016	17.7	17.7	17.7	17.8	17.8	17.9	17.9	18.0	18.0	18.0	18.0	18.1	17.9
2017	17.9	17.8	17.9	17.8	17.8	17.9	17.8	17.9	17.9	18.0	18.1	18.1	17.9
Retail Trade													
2007	70.4	69.4	70.1	69.3	69.6	70.1	69.9	69.8	69.6	69.8	72.4	73.8	70.4
2008	70.6	69.9	70.7	69.7	69.6	70.1	70.0	69.8	69.2	68.5	69.5	70.3	69.8
2009	67.9	67.0	66.6	65.6	65.3	65.8	65.7	65.5	65.9	66.0	67.5	68.6	66.5
2010	66.0	65.4	65.3	65.3	65.0	65.5	65.7	65.8	65.5	65.8	67.5	68.9	66.0
2011	66.6	66.0	66.2	65.9	65.8	66.1	66.5	66.6	66.7	67.3	69.3	70.5	67.0
2012	68.3	67.7	67.8	67.6	68.0	68.3	68.4	68.4	68.4	68.8	71.7	72.6	68.8
2013	69.4	68.8	69.1	68.7	68.8	69.1	69.3	69.4	69.4	69.4	71.9	73.1	69.7
2014	69.6	68.7	68.8	68.7	68.8	69.3	69.7	69.4	69.6	69.9	72.1	73.6	69.9
2015	70.7	70.0	70.3	69.9	69.9	70.1	70.3	70.4	70.3	70.8	73.1	74.0	70.8
2016	70.9	70.3	70.2	69.6	69.4	69.2	70.0	70.1	70.5	70.9	72.8	74.1	70.7
2017	71.5	70.3	70.3	70.1	70.2	70.4	70.7	70.9	70.5	70.1	71.6	71.4	70.7
Transportation and Utilities													
2007	33.0	32.7	32.9	32.7	32.8	32.9	32.8	32.9	32.8	32.9	33.1	33.5	32.9
2008	32.8	32.0	31.3	30.4	30.1	29.2	28.3	28.5	28.1	27.8	27.7	27.6	29.5
2009	27.3	27.2	27.1	26.8	26.9	26.9	26.7	26.6	26.4	26.3	26.2	26.4	26.7
2010	26.2	26.2	26.1	26.3	26.3	26.2	26.3	26.7	26.7	26.9	26.9	27.3	26.5
2011	26.8	27.0	27.0	26.8	26.8	26.8	27.0	27.1	27.0	27.4	27.5	27.8	27.1
2012	27.6	27.5	27.9	27.9	28.0	28.2	28.4	28.6	28.7	28.7	29.1	29.2	28.3
2013	28.8	29.1	29.1	29.2	29.3	29.5	29.5	29.7	29.8	29.9	29.9	30.3	29.5
2014	29.9	29.9	30.0	30.0	30.1	29.8	30.0	30.0	29.9	30.2	30.5	30.9	30.1
2015	30.7	30.7	30.7	30.7	30.8	30.9	30.9	30.9	30.7	30.9	31.0	31.5	30.9
2016	31.1	31.1	31.1	31.2	31.5	31.5	31.8	32.1	32.0	32.0	32.4	33.1	31.7
2017	32.3	32.3	32.4	32.2	32.2	32.4	32.5	32.9	33.1	33.4	33.3	33.9	32.7

1. Employment by Industry: Hawaii, Selected Years, 2007–2017—*Continued*

(Numbers in thousands, not seasonally adjusted)

Industry and year	January	February	March	April	May	June	July	August	September	October	November	December	Annual average
Information													
2007	10.4	11.0	10.9	10.5	11.1	11.1	10.3	10.8	10.4	10.2	10.3	10.4	10.6
2008	9.6	10.1	10.4	10.4	10.7	11.1	9.9	9.6	9.6	9.4	9.8	10.0	10.1
2009	9.1	9.6	9.4	9.4	9.1	9.1	8.7	8.8	9.0	9.2	9.0	9.0	9.1
2010	8.9	9.7	9.9	9.5	10.7	10.0	8.8	9.4	11.1	9.8	9.4	10.3	9.8
2011	8.5	9.4	10.2	8.1	8.0	7.8	8.3	8.3	8.2	8.3	8.6	8.7	8.5
2012	8.3	8.4	8.5	8.4	8.4	7.8	8.1	8.3	8.4	8.6	9.2	8.9	8.4
2013	8.3	8.4	8.5	8.4	8.0	7.9	9.6	8.4	8.8	9.4	9.6	9.9	8.8
2014	8.3	8.4	8.5	8.3	8.8	8.1	8.2	8.7	8.8	8.5	8.7	8.7	8.5
2015	8.5	8.6	8.6	8.4	8.3	8.2	8.7	8.6	8.5	8.7	9.6	9.7	8.7
2016	8.2	8.6	8.4	8.5	9.0	8.4	8.7	9.7	9.1	8.7	9.6	8.7	8.8
2017	8.9	9.1	9.2	9.1	9.8	8.9	9.0	10.0	9.1	9.0	9.2	9.1	9.2
Financial Activities													
2007	29.9	30.0	30.2	29.9	30.0	30.2	30.2	30.1	29.9	30.0	29.9	30.1	30.0
2008	29.4	29.7	29.6	29.7	29.8	29.7	29.6	29.5	29.2	28.7	28.9	28.8	29.4
2009	27.9	27.9	27.8	27.8	27.8	27.8	27.6	27.6	27.5	27.5	27.4	27.5	27.7
2010	27.1	27.0	27.1	26.9	26.9	26.8	27.0	26.9	26.8	26.9	26.9	26.9	26.9
2011	26.5	26.5	26.6	26.6	26.5	26.5	26.7	26.7	26.6	26.5	26.8	26.8	26.6
2012	26.3	26.5	26.6	26.5	26.6	26.8	26.8	26.8	26.8	26.9	27.0	27.0	26.7
2013	26.7	26.8	27.0	27.1	27.2	27.2	27.3	27.2	27.3	27.2	27.3	27.5	27.2
2014	27.1	27.2	27.4	27.4	27.5	27.7	27.8	27.8	27.7	27.7	27.8	28.1	27.6
2015	27.7	27.9	28.1	28.1	28.2	28.3	28.3	28.2	28.0	28.0	27.9	28.3	28.1
2016	28.1	28.2	28.3	28.3	28.3	28.5	28.8	28.8	28.6	28.6	28.6	28.8	28.5
2017	28.5	28.5	28.7	28.6	28.6	28.6	28.5	28.5	28.5	28.3	28.5	28.6	28.5
Professional and Business Services													
2007	75.1	75.7	76.0	75.0	75.3	77.1	76.4	76.6	76.8	77.1	77.2	78.1	76.4
2008	75.8	76.1	76.3	76.1	75.8	75.5	75.4	75.6	75.1	74.7	74.5	75.4	75.5
2009	73.1	72.9	72.9	71.5	71.0	71.1	70.5	70.4	70.0	71.2	70.8	71.6	71.4
2010	70.2	70.6	70.9	70.9	70.8	71.2	71.9	71.8	71.9	72.5	72.8	73.5	71.6
2011	73.2	74.3	75.0	75.2	74.7	75.0	74.7	75.5	75.8	75.8	76.5	77.6	75.3
2012	75.0	75.7	76.0	76.8	77.1	77.3	76.9	77.8	77.2	77.9	78.7	79.1	77.1
2013	78.0	78.9	79.4	79.4	79.1	79.2	79.7	80.3	80.0	81.2	82.0	82.1	79.9
2014	81.2	81.4	82.1	82.3	81.9	81.9	81.5	82.1	82.2	82.1	82.7	83.3	82.1
2015	82.0	82.3	82.7	82.5	82.3	82.5	82.6	82.2	82.1	82.7	82.9	83.1	82.5
2016	81.2	81.9	81.8	82.3	81.4	81.4	81.8	82.0	81.9	81.7	82.1	82.6	81.8
2017	81.2	81.6	82.1	81.5	81.7	82.6	82.5	82.4	82.0	81.7	81.8	82.6	82.0
Education and Health Services													
2007	71.1	72.7	72.9	72.9	73.4	73.8	72.6	72.4	73.2	73.3	73.6	73.8	73.0
2008	72.5	73.7	73.9	73.8	74.2	74.7	74.0	73.8	74.4	74.7	75.2	75.5	74.2
2009	73.8	74.8	75.0	74.5	74.6	75.1	74.1	73.7	74.3	74.5	75.0	75.4	74.6
2010	74.5	75.2	75.6	75.2	75.6	75.3	74.9	74.6	74.6	75.9	75.9	76.3	75.3
2011	73.9	75.8	75.9	75.7	76.0	75.2	75.6	75.1	76.2	76.3	77.0	77.5	75.9
2012	75.0	76.4	76.1	76.7	77.4	76.8	76.7	77.2	77.9	78.1	78.3	79.1	77.1
2013	77.5	78.7	79.0	79.0	79.0	79.2	78.3	78.7	79.2	78.7	80.0	79.6	78.9
2014	77.8	78.4	79.0	79.0	79.0	78.3	78.3	78.4	79.4	79.7	80.2	80.9	79.0
2015	79.9	81.0	81.7	81.7	81.7	81.3	81.0	81.0	82.1	82.5	82.8	83.7	81.7
2016	81.6	81.9	82.9	83.2	82.7	82.3	82.5	82.2	83.5	82.9	83.1	83.7	82.7
2017	82.9	83.3	84.2	83.8	83.7	82.7	84.0	83.5	85.3	85.5	86.3	86.8	84.3
Leisure and Hospitality													
2007	108.4	109.6	110.4	110.2	110.7	111.7	110.5	111.1	110.0	108.5	108.9	109.4	110.0
2008	108.5	109.7	109.8	108.6	108.7	108.7	108.1	107.5	105.8	103.6	103.1	102.7	107.1
2009	101.2	101.4	101.8	100.9	101.0	101.5	101.0	101.5	100.8	99.7	99.6	100.2	100.9
2010	98.8	99.4	99.8	99.7	99.4	100.0	100.2	100.8	100.7	100.7	101.4	102.3	100.3
2011	101.5	101.9	102.9	102.4	102.5	102.9	103.0	103.8	104.1	103.2	103.7	104.7	103.1
2012	104.3	105.4	106.3	106.5	107.1	108.3	108.6	108.7	108.4	108.1	108.5	109.5	107.5
2013	108.6	109.5	110.0	110.3	111.1	111.8	111.9	112.5	111.7	111.9	112.4	113.2	111.2
2014	112.0	112.6	113.5	113.2	113.6	113.4	113.5	113.6	113.6	113.4	113.5	113.7	113.3
2015	112.8	113.2	113.8	113.3	114.1	114.5	115.1	116.0	115.1	115.1	115.8	117.1	114.7
2016	115.8	116.9	117.2	117.5	117.9	118.6	118.9	119.9	119.4	119.3	119.6	120.9	118.5
2017	120.4	121.8	123.0	122.3	122.6	123.5	123.4	123.9	123.1	124.9	125.0	126.6	123.4

1. Employment by Industry: Hawaii, Selected Years, 2007–2017—*Continued*

(Numbers in thousands, not seasonally adjusted)

Industry and year	January	February	March	April	May	June	July	August	September	October	November	December	Annual average
Other Services													
2007	25.8	26.2	26.4	26.3	26.5	26.6	26.6	26.8	26.9	27.0	27.1	27.0	26.6
2008	26.7	27.3	27.5	27.5	27.7	27.3	27.0	27.1	27.1	27.0	27.0	26.9	27.2
2009	26.0	26.2	26.4	25.9	25.9	25.9	25.8	25.9	26.1	26.0	26.0	25.9	26.0
2010	25.2	25.6	25.7	26.0	26.1	26.0	25.9	25.9	25.9	26.0	25.9	25.9	25.8
2011	25.5	25.8	25.7	25.8	25.9	25.9	25.9	26.0	26.2	26.2	26.1	26.1	25.9
2012	25.6	25.9	26.0	26.2	26.4	26.4	26.2	26.4	26.6	26.5	26.6	26.4	26.3
2013	26.3	26.4	26.4	26.5	26.6	26.5	26.6	26.7	26.8	26.8	26.7	26.8	26.6
2014	26.4	26.5	26.7	26.4	26.5	26.6	26.5	26.6	26.7	26.7	26.8	27.0	26.6
2015	26.4	26.6	26.9	26.7	26.9	27.1	26.8	26.8	26.9	26.9	27.1	27.0	26.8
2016	26.9	27.0	27.1	27.3	27.3	27.4	27.4	27.3	27.5	27.4	27.5	27.5	27.3
2017	27.4	27.7	27.8	27.7	27.7	27.9	27.7	27.8	27.8	27.7	27.8	27.9	27.7
Government													
2007	119.9	124.2	124.9	119.9	125.3	123.5	115.4	115.4	120.9	123.7	125.5	126.6	122.1
2008	121.4	125.2	127.0	121.8	127.9	125.9	118.4	120.3	123.3	127.0	133.0	128.9	125.0
2009	125.1	127.1	129.0	129.0	130.2	128.0	120.2	118.7	122.4	125.3	126.2	127.0	125.7
2010	122.3	125.4	127.5	127.6	129.8	126.1	121.0	116.5	122.3	125.3	130.7	127.6	125.2
2011	120.2	126.9	127.7	127.1	128.2	125.5	119.6	115.5	122.5	125.9	127.4	128.1	124.6
2012	115.1	127.5	128.3	128.5	129.0	125.9	118.7	122.6	123.7	126.5	132.0	128.9	125.6
2013	115.7	128.0	128.4	125.4	129.2	125.0	118.8	116.0	123.8	127.0	128.0	128.7	124.5
2014	124.7	128.3	128.6	127.9	129.5	126.2	119.3	120.8	124.8	127.1	131.5	126.2	126.2
2015	124.8	128.3	128.7	128.7	129.4	126.2	118.7	121.6	124.7	127.6	128.4	129.8	126.4
2016	122.9	127.9	129.0	126.6	129.1	126.2	118.8	119.7	125.4	127.7	131.9	127.1	126.0
2017	124.7	129.2	129.4	129.0	129.5	126.0	117.1	114.6	124.3	126.7	128.2	128.9	125.6

2. Average Weekly Hours by Selected Industry: Hawaii, 2013–2017

(Not seasonally adjusted)

Industry and year	January	February	March	April	May	June	July	August	September	October	November	December	Annual average
Total Private													
2013	33.0	33.1	33.1	33.2	32.9	34.1	33.2	33.0	33.8	32.9	32.6	33.7	33.2
2014	33.2	34.2	34.2	33.4	33.1	34.3	33.6	33.6	33.5	33.1	33.9	33.5	33.6
2015	33.2	34.1	34.1	33.0	33.0	32.9	33.3	34.0	32.6	32.6	33.5	33.0	33.3
2016	32.8	32.6	32.6	32.7	33.6	32.4	32.9	32.7	32.3	33.6	32.1	32.4	32.7
2017	33.7	32.6	32.3	33.8	32.6	32.8	34.1	32.7	32.8	33.6	33.0	32.9	33.1
Goods-Producing													
2013	35.3	35.2	35.7	36.3	36.4	34.8	37.3	36.5	37.1	37.3	34.5	37.2	36.2
2014	36.4	36.6	36.7	37.0	37.1	35.9	37.5	36.3	37.0	35.3	36.2	37.3	36.6
2015	36.6	36.5	36.9	37.3	37.8	35.0	36.8	36.5	34.3	36.6	35.9	38.5	36.6
2016	38.5	37.5	37.7	37.0	37.5	36.4	37.1	37.2	36.2	37.7	35.3	36.6	37.1
2017	36.6	36.7	37.1	36.4	37.2	35.2	37.9	37.2	36.5	37.3	37.5	37.0	36.9
Mining, Logging, and Construction													
2013	35.9	35.6	36.6	37.0	36.8	34.4	38.4	36.8	37.4	38.3	34.3	37.1	36.5
2014	37.0	36.8	37.1	37.5	38.3	35.8	37.9	36.5	37.1	34.2	35.0	36.8	36.7
2015	36.2	36.3	37.1	37.6	37.6	34.3	36.1	35.7	33.4	35.9	35.3	38.2	36.1
2016	38.3	37.6	37.2	37.0	37.2	36.2	36.8	37.2	35.7	37.4	34.4	36.4	36.8
2017	36.7	36.4	36.9	35.5	36.9	34.7	38.1	37.2	36.3	37.3	38.7	37.7	36.9
Manufacturing													
2013	34.1	34.4	33.8	34.6	35.6	35.6	35.2	35.9	36.5	35.0	35.4	37.4	35.3
2014	35.1	35.9	35.9	35.7	34.4	36.0	36.4	35.8	36.8	37.9	39.2	38.2	36.5
2015	37.6	37.2	36.6	36.8	38.3	36.6	38.5	38.7	36.6	38.5	37.5	39.2	37.7
2016	39.1	37.5	38.8	37.2	38.1	37.0	38.0	37.4	37.4	38.5	37.6	37.5	37.8
2017	36.2	37.7	37.7	38.7	37.9	36.4	37.6	37.1	36.7	37.2	34.4	35.1	36.9
Trade, Transportation, and Utilities													
2013	33.6	33.5	33.3	33.1	33.0	34.8	33.6	33.4	34.1	33.1	32.9	34.0	33.5
2014	33.3	34.4	34.3	33.5	33.2	34.4	33.7	33.8	33.3	33.4	34.3	34.2	33.8
2015	33.7	34.7	34.7	33.5	33.4	34.2	34.0	34.6	34.3	33.8	34.4	33.8	34.1
2016	33.8	33.6	33.5	33.6	34.0	33.5	34.1	33.6	33.5	34.8	33.4	33.7	33.7
2017	34.7	33.6	33.0	34.8	33.1	33.8	34.8	33.0	33.4	34.5	33.8	34.1	33.9
Professional and Business Services													
2013	33.8	34.5	34.1	34.7	34.4	35.5	34.1	34.0	35.5	35.1	34.5	35.5	34.7
2014	34.8	35.9	35.7	34.5	34.2	35.0	34.5	35.3	34.9	33.6	33.8	34.6	34.7
2015	34.2	34.6	34.8	34.3	33.8	33.3	33.7	34.1	33.0	33.4	35.0	34.6	34.1
2016	33.2	33.2	33.4	34.1	35.0	33.3	34.2	34.9	35.1	36.0	35.1	36.0	34.4
2017	36.5	35.0	35.3	35.8	34.9	34.3	35.7	34.7	34.7	35.0	34.6	34.5	35.1
Education and Health Services													
2013	33.4	33.1	33.3	33.5	33.3	34.4	33.8	33.3	34.2	33.3	32.9	33.0	33.5
2014	32.6	33.1	33.2	32.3	32.5	33.9	32.6	32.3	32.6	32.6	33.5	32.9	32.8
2015	31.9	32.7	31.7	31.5	31.2	31.6	31.7	32.9	31.6	31.2	32.1	31.6	31.8
2016	31.7	31.9	31.6	31.7	32.9	31.7	32.1	31.4	31.1	31.6	30.7	30.7	31.6
2017	32.5	31.7	31.5	32.7	31.8	32.0	33.0	32.1	32.5	32.8	32.1	32.4	32.3
Leisure and Hospitality													
2013	29.6	29.6	29.5	29.5	28.9	30.6	29.5	29.8	30.1	28.7	29.0	29.6	29.5
2014	30.4	31.7	31.6	30.3	29.7	31.6	30.5	30.3	29.9	29.6	31.2	29.1	30.5
2015	29.6	31.1	31.0	29.2	29.6	29.6	30.0	31.0	28.8	28.7	30.3	28.5	29.8
2016	28.8	28.8	28.3	28.8	30.5	28.9	28.9	28.8	28.3	29.9	28.4	28.4	28.9
2017	30.4	28.8	28.3	29.9	28.7	29.4	30.7	29.3	29.2	29.8	29.4	28.6	29.4

3. Average Hourly Earnings by Selected Industry: Hawaii, 2013–2017

(Dollars, not seasonally adjusted)

Industry and year	January	February	March	April	May	June	July	August	September	October	November	December	Annual average
Total Private													
2013	23.31	23.48	23.73	23.79	23.85	23.71	23.77	23.60	23.85	23.87	23.83	24.01	23.74
2014	23.98	24.02	24.13	24.08	24.29	24.34	24.43	24.51	24.62	24.57	24.60	24.40	24.33
2015	24.51	24.61	24.62	24.60	24.62	24.45	24.45	24.52	24.47	24.73	24.85	25.08	24.63
2016	25.14	25.29	25.18	25.32	25.37	25.48	25.46	25.41	25.67	25.63	25.48	25.59	25.42
2017	25.78	25.67	25.68	25.89	25.93	25.86	26.21	26.35	26.45	26.72	26.60	26.96	26.18
Goods-Producing													
2013	30.45	30.96	31.28	30.79	30.81	30.46	31.40	30.62	31.52	31.79	31.62	31.90	31.14
2014	31.59	31.68	31.82	32.25	32.78	32.10	32.76	33.49	34.26	33.13	33.13	33.25	32.71
2015	33.54	32.75	33.15	33.54	33.28	32.61	32.28	32.42	32.78	33.16	32.50	33.14	32.93
2016	32.79	32.52	32.41	33.14	32.44	33.07	32.84	33.33	33.29	33.71	33.52	33.88	33.07
2017	34.50	33.49	33.62	34.12	34.35	34.00	35.09	34.28	34.56	34.60	34.55	34.70	34.33
Mining, Logging, and Construction													
2013	35.13	35.64	35.83	35.22	35.32	35.36	35.73	35.02	35.92	36.20	36.87	36.92	35.77
2014	36.31	36.67	36.86	37.30	37.77	37.54	38.36	39.54	40.47	39.86	39.92	39.85	38.39
2015	40.19	38.91	38.97	39.11	38.98	38.11	37.23	37.43	38.14	38.41	37.28	37.98	38.37
2016	37.75	37.17	37.18	37.75	37.07	37.77	37.60	38.00	38.29	38.81	38.94	39.25	37.95
2017	39.56	38.58	38.51	39.37	39.39	38.73	39.82	39.01	39.34	39.09	38.52	38.66	39.04
Manufacturing													
2013	19.49	20.11	20.09	19.87	19.92	19.58	20.45	20.21	21.17	20.78	19.99	20.46	20.19
2014	20.30	20.00	20.00	20.10	19.83	19.55	19.26	19.23	19.47	18.77	18.89	18.47	19.46
2015	18.89	18.92	19.24	19.86	19.69	19.90	20.62	20.74	20.29	20.35	20.66	20.63	19.99
2016	19.90	20.02	20.11	20.81	20.20	20.60	20.32	20.79	20.46	20.61	20.39	20.36	20.38
2017	21.29	20.90	21.36	21.91	21.89	22.53	22.84	22.22	22.59	22.74	22.77	23.41	22.19
Trade, Transportation, and Utilities													
2013	21.68	21.87	22.25	22.43	22.60	22.36	22.31	22.50	22.89	22.67	22.68	22.83	22.43
2014	23.03	23.21	23.14	23.18	23.52	23.43	23.40	23.52	23.29	23.67	24.25	23.39	23.42
2015	23.91	24.45	24.33	24.43	24.10	23.70	23.63	24.02	23.70	23.77	24.15	24.12	24.03
2016	24.26	24.40	24.24	24.46	24.67	24.84	24.76	24.95	25.23	25.04	24.62	24.51	24.67
2017	25.22	24.87	25.20	25.63	25.55	25.60	25.41	25.63	25.81	25.96	25.39	25.68	25.50
Professional and Business Services													
2013	23.87	23.84	23.96	23.73	23.74	23.91	23.70	23.51	23.83	23.62	23.80	23.73	23.77
2014	23.75	24.00	24.52	24.32	24.35	24.74	24.47	24.70	24.76	24.25	24.01	23.44	24.28
2015	23.34	23.46	23.40	23.14	23.46	23.49	23.35	23.30	23.20	23.85	24.23	23.65	23.49
2016	23.21	24.08	23.94	24.27	25.07	25.18	25.45	25.55	26.04	25.97	25.89	26.09	25.09
2017	25.52	26.04	25.77	25.98	25.68	25.67	26.09	25.55	25.40	26.00	25.53	25.45	25.72
Education and Health Services													
2013	26.96	27.14	27.60	27.89	27.72	27.89	27.52	27.44	26.83	27.15	26.67	26.64	27.29
2014	26.11	26.04	26.11	25.64	26.01	26.27	26.54	26.54	26.67	27.01	26.98	26.95	26.41
2015	26.98	27.18	26.52	25.97	26.32	26.69	26.84	26.64	26.87	27.52	27.26	27.72	26.88
2016	27.83	27.95	27.82	27.55	26.95	26.56	26.59	26.21	26.38	26.24	26.08	26.10	26.80
2017	26.61	27.08	27.08	27.14	27.57	28.04	28.57	29.16	29.51	29.69	30.08	30.29	28.42
Leisure and Hospitality													
2013	18.04	18.15	18.15	18.19	18.20	18.05	18.08	17.76	17.96	17.87	18.05	18.54	18.09
2014	18.78	18.68	18.59	18.44	18.34	18.78	18.86	18.64	18.92	18.96	18.60	18.78	18.70
2015	19.25	19.15	19.17	18.93	19.20	19.44	19.73	19.45	19.38	19.13	19.63	19.51	19.33
2016	20.29	19.96	19.81	19.64	19.94	20.30	20.48	20.08	20.21	20.18	20.17	20.36	20.12
2017	21.17	20.95	20.75	20.94	20.78	21.06	21.21	21.21	20.92	20.90	20.92	21.39	21.02

4. Average Weekly Earnings by Selected Industry: Hawaii 2013–2017

(Dollars, not seasonally adjusted)

Industry and year	January	February	March	April	May	June	July	August	September	October	November	December	Annual average
Total Private													
2013	769.23	777.19	785.46	789.83	784.67	808.51	789.16	778.80	806.13	785.32	776.86	809.14	788.17
2014	796.14	821.48	825.25	804.27	804.00	834.86	820.85	823.54	824.77	813.27	833.94	817.40	817.49
2015	813.73	839.20	839.54	811.80	812.46	804.41	814.19	833.68	797.72	806.20	832.48	827.64	820.18
2016	824.59	824.45	820.87	827.96	852.43	825.55	837.63	830.91	829.14	861.17	817.91	829.12	831.23
2017	868.79	836.84	829.46	875.08	845.32	848.21	893.76	861.65	867.56	897.79	877.80	886.98	866.56
Goods-Producing													
2013	1,074.89	1,089.79	1,116.70	1,117.68	1,121.48	1,060.01	1,171.22	1,117.63	1,169.39	1,185.77	1,090.89	1,186.68	1,127.27
2014	1,149.88	1,159.49	1,167.79	1,193.25	1,216.14	1,152.39	1,228.50	1,215.69	1,267.62	1,169.49	1,199.31	1,240.23	1,197.19
2015	1,227.56	1,195.38	1,223.24	1,251.04	1,257.98	1,141.35	1,187.90	1,183.33	1,124.35	1,213.66	1,166.75	1,275.89	1,205.24
2016	1,262.42	1,219.50	1,221.86	1,226.18	1,216.50	1,203.75	1,218.36	1,239.88	1,205.10	1,270.87	1,183.26	1,240.01	1,226.90
2017	1,262.70	1,229.08	1,247.30	1,241.97	1,277.82	1,196.80	1,329.91	1,275.22	1,261.44	1,290.58	1,295.63	1,283.90	1,266.78
Mining, Logging, and Construction													
2013	1,261.17	1,268.78	1,311.38	1,303.14	1,299.78	1,216.38	1,372.03	1,288.74	1,343.41	1,386.46	1,264.64	1,369.73	1,305.61
2014	1,343.47	1,349.46	1,367.51	1,398.75	1,446.59	1,343.93	1,453.84	1,443.21	1,501.44	1,363.21	1,397.20	1,466.48	1,408.91
2015	1,454.88	1,412.43	1,445.79	1,470.54	1,465.65	1,307.17	1,344.00	1,336.25	1,273.88	1,378.92	1,315.98	1,450.84	1,385.16
2016	1,445.83	1,397.59	1,383.10	1,396.75	1,379.00	1,367.27	1,383.68	1,413.60	1,366.95	1,451.49	1,339.54	1,428.70	1,396.56
2017	1,451.85	1,404.31	1,421.02	1,397.64	1,453.49	1,343.93	1,517.14	1,451.17	1,428.04	1,458.06	1,490.72	1,457.48	1,440.58
Manufacturing													
2013	664.61	691.78	679.04	687.50	709.15	697.05	719.84	725.54	7.72.71	727.30	707.65	765.20	712.71
2014	712.53	718.00	718.00	717.57	682.15	703.80	701.06	688.43	716.50	711.38	740.49	705.55	710.29
2015	710.26	703.82	704.18	730.85	754.13	728.34	793.87	802.64	742.61	783.48	774.75	808.70	753.62
2016	778.09	750.75	780.27	774.13	769.62	762.20	772.16	777.55	765.20	793.49	766.66	763.50	770.36
2017	770.70	787.93	805.27	847.92	829.63	820.09	858.78	824.36	829.05	845.93	783.29	821.69	818.81
Trade, Transportation, and Utilities													
2013	728.45	732.65	740.93	742.43	745.80	778.13	749.62	751.50	780.55	750.38	746.17	776.22	751.41
2014	766.90	798.42	793.70	776.53	780.86	805.99	788.58	794.98	775.56	790.58	831.78	799.94	791.60
2015	805.77	848.42	844.25	818.41	804.94	810.54	803.42	831.09	812.91	803.43	830.76	815.26	819.42
2016	819.99	819.84	812.04	821.86	838.78	832.14	844.32	838.32	845.21	871.39	822.31	825.99	831.38
2017	875.13	835.63	831.60	891.92	845.71	865.28	884.27	845.79	862.05	895.62	858.18	875.69	864.45
Professional and Business Services													
2013	806.81	822.48	817.04	823.43	816.66	848.81	808.17	799.34	845.97	829.06	821.10	842.42	824.82
2014	826.50	861.60	875.36	839.04	832.77	865.90	844.22	871.91	864.12	814.80	811.54	811.02	842.52
2015	798.23	811.72	814.32	793.70	792.95	782.22	786.90	794.53	765.60	796.59	848.05	818.29	801.01
2016	770.57	799.46	799.60	827.61	877.45	838.49	870.39	891.70	914.00	934.92	908.74	939.24	863.10
2017	931.48	911.40	909.68	930.08	896.23	880.48	931.41	886.59	881.38	910.00	883.34	878.03	902.77
Education and Health Services													
2013	900.46	898.33	919.08	934.32	923.08	959.42	930.18	913.75	917.59	904.10	877.44	879.12	914.22
2014	851.19	861.92	866.85	828.17	845.33	890.55	865.20	857.24	869.44	880.53	903.83	886.66	866.25
2015	860.66	888.79	840.68	818.06	821.18	843.40	850.83	876.46	849.09	858.62	875.05	875.95	854.78
2016	882.21	891.61	879.11	873.34	886.66	841.95	853.54	822.99	820.42	829.18	800.66	801.27	848.78
2017	864.83	858.44	853.02	887.48	876.73	897.28	942.81	936.04	959.08	973.83	965.57	981.40	917.97
Leisure and Hospitality													
2013	533.98	537.24	535.43	536.61	525.98	552.33	533.36	529.25	540.60	512.87	523.45	548.78	533.66
2014	570.91	592.16	587.44	558.73	544.70	593.45	575.23	564.79	565.71	561.22	580.32	546.50	570.35
2015	569.80	595.57	594.27	552.76	568.32	575.42	591.90	602.95	558.14	549.03	594.79	556.04	576.03
2016	584.35	574.85	560.62	565.63	608.17	586.67	591.87	578.30	571.94	603.38	572.83	578.22	581.47
2017	643.57	603.36	587.23	626.11	596.39	619.16	651.15	621.45	610.86	622.82	615.05	611.75	617.99

IDAHO
At a Glance

Population:
  2010 census: 1,567,582
  2017 estimate: 1,716,943

Percent change in population:
  2010–2017: 9.5%

Percent change in total nonfarm employment:
  2007–2017: 9.5%

Industry with the largest growth in employment, 2007–2017 (thousands):
  Education and health services, 29.3

Industry with the largest decline or smallest growth in employment, 2007–2017 (thousands):
  Construction, -6.9

Civilian labor force:
  2010: 761,056
  2017: 833,462

Unemployment rate and rank among states (highest to lowest):
  2010: 9.0%, 23rd
  2017: 3.2%, 43rd

Over-the-year change in unemployment rates:
  2015–2016: -0.4%
  2016–2017: -0.6%

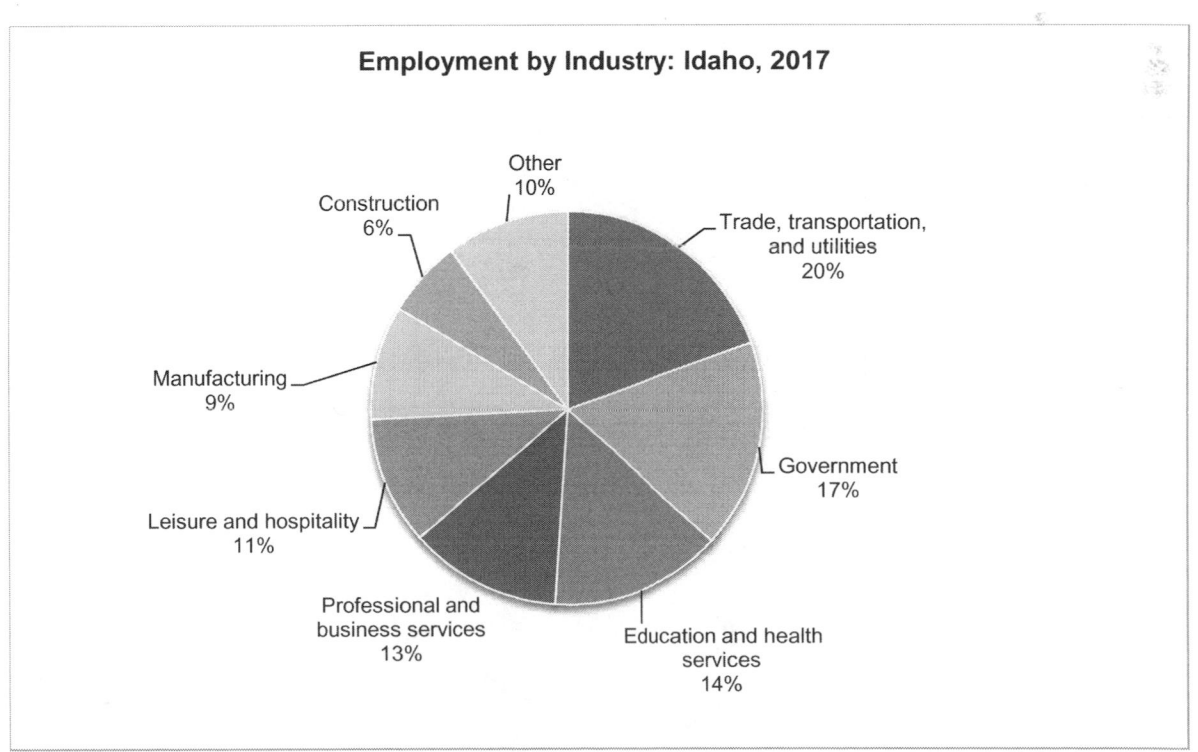

Employment by Industry: Idaho, 2017

- Other 10%
- Construction 6%
- Trade, transportation, and utilities 20%
- Manufacturing 9%
- Government 17%
- Leisure and hospitality 11%
- Professional and business services 13%
- Education and health services 14%

1. Employment by Industry: Idaho, Selected Years, 2007–2017

(Numbers in thousands, not seasonally adjusted)

Industry and year	January	February	March	April	May	June	July	August	September	October	November	December	Annual average
Total Nonfarm													
2007	627.9	635.3	642.0	649.5	659.3	668.4	661.3	665.0	666.5	661.2	660.9	657.9	654.6
2008	632.8	638.9	643.2	649.0	657.3	662.6	659.2	658.9	658.4	648.2	638.7	633.1	648.4
2009	606.3	605.0	603.7	607.2	612.2	617.7	610.4	610.4	613.4	612.4	608.0	604.8	609.3
2010	581.0	586.6	591.4	600.1	609.3	609.9	608.1	609.6	611.8	612.9	609.4	605.1	602.9
2011	585.3	591.6	594.5	605.0	611.6	615.4	616.0	617.6	623.2	621.2	620.3	618.2	610.0
2012	595.8	602.1	607.3	612.8	623.7	627.6	625.7	627.7	633.6	634.5	633.7	630.4	621.2
2013	611.4	619.0	625.1	630.1	640.5	644.0	641.2	642.1	645.4	650.2	648.3	645.0	636.9
2014	630.3	637.1	642.3	648.9	656.4	661.2	658.8	658.5	660.9	663.5	661.2	660.1	653.3
2015	645.6	651.4	658.7	663.9	673.3	678.1	678.4	675.6	681.9	683.3	681.8	680.6	671.1
2016	666.1	675.2	682.0	687.2	694.2	700.2	702.5	700.6	706.3	705.6	705.0	701.3	693.9
2017	688.4	695.1	703.5	708.4	717.7	725.9	722.1	721.1	727.1	732.2	731.1	726.9	716.6
Total Private													
2007	514.8	518.5	524.8	531.3	540.1	550.5	550.7	553.2	547.4	541.7	541.9	539.2	537.8
2008	517.4	519.4	523.1	528.6	535.6	542.4	545.4	544.7	537.8	526.7	517.2	512.0	529.2
2009	488.5	485.4	482.4	483.8	489.4	495.7	497.9	497.5	494.9	491.0	487.0	484.3	489.8
2010	466.0	467.0	470.6	477.9	483.8	489.6	495.7	497.1	493.6	493.1	490.6	486.6	484.3
2011	472.1	472.9	475.2	484.9	490.5	498.1	504.8	506.3	505.6	501.9	501.5	499.4	492.8
2012	482.5	484.3	489.1	493.7	502.9	510.6	515.4	516.9	515.2	513.6	513.4	510.6	504.0
2013	495.9	499.3	505.0	510.5	519.4	526.5	531.3	532.5	527.8	529.9	528.8	526.5	519.5
2014	515.1	517.7	521.8	528.5	535.3	543.1	547.1	547.0	542.3	542.0	540.3	540.5	535.1
2015	529.6	531.5	537.9	542.8	550.4	558.9	565.6	564.1	561.6	560.6	559.7	559.4	551.8
2016	548.7	553.5	559.2	564.9	570.6	578.9	587.1	586.1	583.5	580.8	580.9	578.5	572.7
2017	568.2	571.9	579.3	583.9	591.6	602.3	605.2	605.5	602.6	604.9	604.0	600.7	593.3
Goods Producing													
2007	117.3	118.0	119.4	121.4	124.7	127.7	128.1	127.6	125.4	122.9	121.2	118.5	122.7
2008	111.6	110.2	110.7	112.0	114.6	116.7	117.2	116.5	114.8	111.8	106.5	102.9	112.1
2009	94.1	90.9	89.7	89.8	91.8	94.0	95.1	95.1	94.4	93.8	91.1	88.1	92.3
2010	83.3	82.6	83.4	85.4	87.6	89.9	91.3	92.2	91.6	91.6	89.7	86.2	87.9
2011	82.3	82.5	83.3	85.9	88.3	90.9	92.4	93.2	92.8	93.5	92.7	90.2	89.0
2012	86.4	86.2	86.9	88.6	91.8	94.6	96.0	96.6	95.8	96.4	95.4	93.9	92.4
2013	90.6	91.4	92.9	94.1	97.4	99.7	100.7	101.3	100.4	100.8	99.4	97.4	97.2
2014	94.8	94.6	95.3	97.2	99.5	102.1	103.4	103.6	103.3	103.4	102.0	100.8	100.0
2015	97.9	98.4	100.1	102.0	104.2	106.5	107.4	107.8	106.9	107.7	106.6	105.3	104.2
2016	103.0	104.3	105.9	107.9	109.8	111.9	114.2	114.2	113.5	112.1	111.5	110.0	109.9
2017	107.3	108.3	110.7	112.4	115.0	118.1	119.1	119.6	119.0	119.7	119.6	117.9	115.6
Service-Providing													
2007	510.6	517.3	522.6	528.1	534.6	540.7	533.2	537.4	541.1	538.3	539.7	539.4	531.9
2008	521.2	528.7	532.5	537.0	542.7	545.9	542.0	542.4	543.6	536.4	532.2	530.2	536.2
2009	512.2	514.1	514.0	517.4	520.4	523.7	515.3	515.3	519.0	518.6	516.9	516.7	517.0
2010	497.7	504.0	508.0	514.7	521.7	520.0	516.8	517.4	520.2	521.3	519.7	518.9	515.0
2011	503.0	509.1	511.2	519.1	523.3	524.5	523.6	524.4	530.4	527.7	527.6	528.0	521.0
2012	509.4	515.9	520.4	524.2	531.9	533.0	529.7	531.1	537.8	538.1	538.3	536.5	528.9
2013	520.8	527.6	532.2	536.0	543.1	544.3	540.5	540.8	545.0	549.4	548.9	547.6	539.7
2014	535.5	542.5	547.0	551.7	556.9	559.1	555.4	554.9	557.6	560.1	559.2	559.3	553.3
2015	547.7	553.0	558.6	561.9	569.1	571.6	571.0	567.8	575.0	575.6	575.2	575.3	566.8
2016	563.1	570.9	576.1	579.3	584.4	588.3	588.3	586.4	592.8	593.5	593.5	591.3	584.0
2017	581.1	586.8	592.8	596.0	602.7	607.8	603.0	601.5	608.1	612.5	611.5	609.0	601.1
Mining and Logging													
2007	4.0	4.0	3.8	3.6	4.3	4.8	4.9	5.0	4.9	4.7	4.6	4.4	4.4
2008	4.1	4.1	3.7	3.5	4.0	4.5	4.8	4.8	4.6	4.4	4.1	3.9	4.2
2009	3.4	3.2	2.7	2.5	2.7	3.2	3.6	3.7	3.7	3.6	3.4	3.2	3.2
2010	3.0	2.9	2.8	2.8	3.2	3.7	3.9	4.1	4.1	4.1	3.8	3.5	3.5
2011	3.4	3.4	3.3	3.1	3.3	3.9	4.3	4.4	4.4	4.4	4.3	4.1	3.9
2012	3.9	3.8	3.4	3.2	3.7	4.3	4.5	4.5	4.4	4.2	4.0	4.0	4.0
2013	3.8	3.7	3.6	3.4	3.9	4.2	4.3	4.3	4.2	4.2	4.1	3.9	4.0
2014	3.8	3.7	3.3	3.2	3.6	4.0	4.2	4.2	4.1	4.1	3.9	3.8	3.8
2015	3.6	3.5	3.4	3.5	3.8	4.1	4.2	4.1	4.1	3.9	3.8	3.8	3.8
2016	3.6	3.6	3.3	3.4	3.8	4.0	4.2	4.2	4.1	4.1	3.9	3.9	3.8
2017	3.6	3.5	3.2	2.8	3.4	3.8	3.9	3.8	3.8	3.8	3.6	3.5	3.6

1. Employment by Industry: Idaho, Selected Years, 2007–2017—*Continued*

(Numbers in thousands, not seasonally adjusted)

Industry and year	January	February	March	April	May	June	July	August	September	October	November	December	Annual average
Construction													
2007	47.4	47.8	49.4	51.4	53.6	55.6	55.8	56.1	54.4	52.5	51.0	48.9	52.0
2008	43.3	42.1	43.2	44.8	46.9	48.2	48.5	48.2	47.1	45.0	42.2	39.8	44.9
2009	33.7	31.9	31.8	32.8	34.6	36.0	36.8	36.9	36.3	35.5	33.9	31.7	34.3
2010	28.1	27.6	28.6	30.2	31.8	32.9	33.9	34.2	33.7	32.9	31.8	29.4	31.3
2011	25.7	25.6	26.2	28.5	30.3	32.1	33.2	33.5	32.9	32.9	32.7	30.8	30.4
2012	27.5	27.3	28.0	29.4	31.3	32.8	33.9	34.2	33.8	33.8	32.9	31.8	31.4
2013	28.8	29.4	30.5	31.7	33.8	35.3	36.1	36.6	36.2	36.1	35.2	33.6	33.6
2014	31.7	31.4	32.4	34.1	35.8	37.4	38.2	38.8	38.5	38.0	37.3	36.3	35.8
2015	34.0	34.5	36.0	37.3	38.7	39.9	40.5	40.7	39.7	40.0	39.0	38.3	38.2
2016	36.3	37.2	38.7	40.5	41.9	43.2	44.6	44.6	44.4	43.6	43.1	41.5	41.6
2017	39.0	39.8	41.9	43.8	45.4	47.3	47.8	48.1	47.5	47.6	47.6	45.9	45.1
Manufacturing													
2007	65.9	66.2	66.2	66.4	66.8	67.3	67.4	66.5	66.1	65.7	65.6	65.2	66.3
2008	64.2	64.0	63.8	63.7	63.7	64.0	63.9	63.5	63.1	62.4	60.2	59.2	63.0
2009	57.0	55.8	55.2	54.5	54.5	54.8	54.7	54.5	54.4	54.7	53.8	53.2	54.8
2010	52.2	52.1	52.0	52.4	52.6	53.3	53.5	53.9	53.8	54.6	54.1	53.3	53.2
2011	53.2	53.5	53.8	54.3	54.7	54.9	54.9	55.3	55.5	56.2	55.7	55.3	54.8
2012	55.0	55.1	55.5	56.0	56.8	57.5	57.6	57.9	57.6	58.4	58.5	58.1	57.0
2013	58.0	58.3	58.8	59.0	59.7	60.2	60.3	60.4	60.0	60.5	60.1	59.9	59.6
2014	59.3	59.5	59.6	59.9	60.1	60.7	61.0	60.6	60.7	61.3	60.8	60.7	60.4
2015	60.3	60.4	60.7	61.2	61.7	62.5	62.7	63.0	63.1	63.8	63.8	63.2	62.2
2016	63.1	63.5	63.9	64.0	64.1	64.7	65.4	65.4	65.0	64.4	64.5	64.6	64.4
2017	64.7	65.0	65.6	65.8	66.2	67.0	67.4	67.7	67.7	68.3	68.4	68.5	66.9
Trade, Transportation, and Utilities													
2007	128.1	127.9	129.4	130.0	131.0	132.2	132.3	132.8	132.4	132.8	135.2	135.5	131.6
2008	130.0	129.2	129.7	130.3	131.2	131.9	132.5	132.4	130.9	130.2	130.7	130.5	130.8
2009	122.9	121.3	120.9	120.8	121.8	121.9	121.9	122.0	121.6	121.4	122.4	122.1	121.8
2010	118.0	116.8	117.4	118.8	120.0	120.5	121.2	122.3	121.0	121.8	123.0	123.1	120.3
2011	118.0	117.4	117.9	119.8	120.8	121.2	122.9	123.7	123.9	124.0	125.9	126.2	121.8
2012	121.8	121.0	122.0	122.5	124.3	125.2	126.3	126.6	126.6	127.2	129.1	128.9	125.1
2013	124.0	123.8	124.4	125.7	127.1	127.7	128.9	129.4	129.1	129.5	131.0	131.3	127.7
2014	127.4	126.6	127.5	129.1	130.2	131.2	132.0	132.3	131.7	132.5	134.4	135.1	130.8
2015	131.1	130.7	132.1	133.0	134.3	135.2	136.5	136.5	136.3	137.2	139.2	139.6	135.1
2016	134.4	134.5	135.2	136.2	136.6	137.2	138.5	139.3	139.3	139.7	141.5	141.4	137.8
2017	136.9	136.4	137.2	138.2	139.0	140.2	140.6	141.3	141.0	142.3	143.7	143.3	140.0
Wholesale Trade													
2007	25.8	26.1	26.3	26.4	26.6	26.9	26.9	26.9	27.0	26.7	26.7	26.7	26.6
2008	26.2	26.3	26.5	26.5	26.6	26.7	26.9	26.7	26.7	26.4	26.2	26.0	26.5
2009	25.2	25.0	25.0	24.9	24.9	24.9	25.1	24.6	24.7	24.6	24.4	24.2	24.8
2010	24.1	24.0	24.3	24.7	24.9	24.9	25.2	25.3	25.0	25.3	25.0	24.9	24.8
2011	24.4	24.5	24.7	25.2	25.4	25.4	25.9	25.9	25.9	26.0	25.8	25.9	25.4
2012	25.4	25.6	26.0	26.3	26.6	26.6	27.2	26.8	26.8	27.0	26.8	26.8	26.5
2013	26.6	26.9	27.0	27.3	27.4	27.5	28.2	27.6	27.7	27.7	27.5	27.5	27.4
2014	27.3	27.3	27.7	27.9	28.0	28.1	28.6	27.9	27.7	27.8	27.8	27.9	27.8
2015	27.5	27.7	27.8	27.8	27.9	28.1	28.6	28.3	28.2	28.3	28.4	28.4	28.1
2016	28.1	28.4	28.5	28.6	28.6	28.7	29.1	29.1	28.9	28.8	28.9	28.8	28.7
2017	28.3	28.6	28.8	29.0	29.2	29.3	29.3	29.4	29.3	29.8	29.4	29.6	29.2
Retail Trade													
2007	81.1	80.6	82.1	82.4	83.1	83.7	84.0	84.1	83.5	83.9	86.3	86.5	83.4
2008	82.4	81.5	82.0	82.4	83.1	83.4	83.8	83.6	82.2	81.7	82.6	82.4	82.6
2009	76.5	75.4	75.5	75.5	76.5	76.8	76.8	76.8	76.0	75.6	76.9	76.9	76.3
2010	73.4	72.4	73.1	74.0	74.9	75.2	75.5	76.0	74.9	75.3	76.7	76.6	74.8
2011	72.8	72.1	72.4	73.7	74.7	75.1	76.0	76.3	76.2	76.4	78.5	78.3	75.2
2012	75.0	74.2	74.8	75.3	76.7	77.5	78.0	78.0	77.7	78.1	80.3	79.9	77.1
2013	75.9	75.4	75.9	77.4	78.6	79.2	79.8	80.3	79.7	79.8	81.5	81.4	78.7
2014	78.0	77.3	78.0	79.3	80.4	81.4	81.5	81.7	80.9	81.5	83.4	83.5	80.6
2015	80.3	80.0	81.1	82.1	83.3	84.2	84.9	84.9	84.3	84.9	86.9	86.8	83.6
2016	82.8	82.6	83.2	84.2	84.7	85.5	86.4	86.6	86.2	86.8	88.4	87.9	85.4
2017	84.9	84.2	84.6	85.4	85.9	87.0	87.6	87.7	87.2	87.6	89.0	87.9	86.6

1. Employment by Industry: Idaho, Selected Years, 2007–2017—*Continued*

(Numbers in thousands, not seasonally adjusted)

Industry and year	January	February	March	April	May	June	July	August	September	October	November	December	Annual average
Transportation and Utilities													
2007	21.2	21.2	21.0	21.2	21.3	21.6	21.4	21.8	21.9	22.2	22.2	22.3	21.6
2008	21.4	21.4	21.2	21.4	21.5	21.8	21.8	22.1	22.0	22.1	21.9	22.1	21.7
2009	21.2	20.9	20.4	20.4	20.4	20.2	20.0	20.6	20.9	21.2	21.1	21.0	20.7
2010	20.5	20.4	20.0	20.1	20.2	20.4	20.5	21.0	21.1	21.2	21.3	21.6	20.7
2011	20.8	20.8	20.8	20.9	20.7	20.7	21.0	21.5	21.8	21.6	21.6	22.0	21.2
2012	21.4	21.2	21.2	20.9	21.0	21.1	21.1	21.8	22.1	22.1	22.0	22.2	21.5
2013	21.5	21.5	21.5	21.0	21.1	21.0	20.9	21.5	21.7	22.0	22.0	22.4	21.5
2014	22.1	22.0	21.8	21.9	21.8	21.7	21.9	22.7	23.1	23.2	23.2	23.7	22.4
2015	23.3	23.0	23.2	23.1	23.1	22.9	23.0	23.3	23.8	24.0	23.9	24.4	23.4
2016	23.5	23.5	23.5	23.4	23.3	23.0	23.0	23.6	24.2	24.1	24.2	24.7	23.7
2017	23.7	23.6	23.8	23.8	23.9	23.9	23.7	24.2	24.5	24.9	25.3	25.8	24.3
Information													
2007	10.6	10.6	10.7	10.8	10.9	11.0	10.9	11.0	10.8	10.9	11.0	11.0	10.9
2008	11.0	11.1	11.3	10.9	11.1	11.1	11.2	11.5	11.1	10.7	10.7	10.6	11.0
2009	10.4	10.5	10.3	10.0	10.0	10.1	10.0	9.8	9.7	9.7	9.8	9.8	10.0
2010	9.8	9.7	9.7	9.6	9.7	9.7	9.7	9.7	9.5	9.4	9.5	9.5	9.6
2011	9.4	9.3	9.3	9.5	9.6	9.6	9.6	9.6	9.4	9.4	9.4	9.5	9.5
2012	9.4	9.4	9.4	9.3	9.4	9.4	9.5	9.5	9.2	9.3	9.3	9.3	9.4
2013	9.1	9.1	9.3	9.4	9.4	9.4	9.4	9.4	9.1	9.2	9.4	9.3	9.3
2014	9.1	9.2	9.2	9.3	9.4	9.4	9.4	9.5	9.1	9.3	9.5	9.5	9.3
2015	9.1	9.2	9.2	9.2	9.3	9.3	9.3	9.2	9.1	9.3	9.4	9.5	9.3
2016	8.8	8.9	8.9	9.0	9.0	9.0	9.1	9.2	9.0	9.2	9.2	9.3	9.1
2017	9.0	9.0	9.0	8.9	9.0	9.1	9.1	9.0	9.0	9.1	9.1	9.2	9.0
Financial Activities													
2007	31.8	31.9	32.0	32.3	32.7	32.7	33.0	32.8	32.4	32.3	32.5	32.4	32.4
2008	31.6	31.6	31.6	31.8	31.9	32.1	32.2	32.0	31.8	31.3	30.9	31.1	31.7
2009	30.1	30.0	29.8	29.8	29.7	29.7	29.7	29.5	29.2	29.3	29.2	29.4	29.6
2010	28.7	28.6	28.7	28.9	29.1	29.2	29.7	29.5	29.2	29.4	29.4	29.6	29.2
2011	29.2	29.2	29.2	29.5	29.7	29.9	30.4	30.3	30.3	30.2	30.2	30.3	29.9
2012	29.5	29.5	29.6	30.1	30.3	30.5	30.8	30.8	30.5	30.7	30.7	30.9	30.3
2013	30.4	30.6	30.7	30.8	31.1	31.3	31.4	31.6	31.3	31.5	31.5	31.9	31.2
2014	31.8	32.2	32.4	32.5	32.7	32.8	33.4	33.1	32.9	32.7	32.8	32.8	32.7
2015	32.7	32.7	32.9	33.1	33.2	33.5	34.0	33.7	33.4	33.6	33.4	33.4	33.3
2016	33.1	33.1	33.4	33.4	33.6	34.0	34.6	34.4	34.2	34.4	34.5	34.8	34.0
2017	34.4	34.5	34.7	34.9	35.1	35.4	35.8	35.7	35.4	35.9	36.0	36.3	35.3
Professional and Business Services													
2007	78.2	79.6	80.9	83.6	84.9	86.7	85.9	87.1	86.5	85.3	84.6	83.8	83.9
2008	77.7	79.4	80.2	83.1	84.1	84.7	84.7	85.3	83.8	81.8	79.7	78.6	81.9
2009	75.1	74.9	74.1	74.9	75.7	76.5	76.5	77.0	77.1	76.7	76.1	75.7	75.9
2010	71.0	71.6	72.6	74.5	75.3	75.6	76.8	77.5	76.6	77.2	77.0	76.1	75.2
2011	73.4	73.4	73.8	75.4	76.0	77.1	78.1	79.0	78.8	77.8	77.3	76.4	76.4
2012	72.4	73.1	74.6	75.4	76.5	77.9	78.2	79.3	78.7	78.5	78.9	77.2	76.7
2013	73.8	74.6	76.3	76.8	78.3	79.9	80.1	81.1	80.3	81.4	81.4	80.8	78.7
2014	77.5	78.8	79.6	80.9	81.0	81.9	81.4	82.1	81.8	81.6	81.3	81.0	80.7
2015	78.9	78.9	79.9	80.9	81.5	82.6	83.9	84.5	84.1	82.6	82.6	81.8	81.9
2016	81.4	82.2	83.8	86.2	86.7	87.6	88.7	88.8	88.1	88.3	88.4	87.3	86.5
2017	86.0	86.6	88.1	89.6	90.9	92.2	92.1	92.5	92.0	91.8	90.3	89.7	90.2
Education and Health Services													
2007	71.4	72.2	72.5	72.6	73.0	73.5	73.0	73.5	74.0	75.4	76.3	76.3	73.6
2008	75.5	76.5	77.1	77.1	76.9	77.1	77.2	75.8	77.5	78.7	78.8	79.1	77.3
2009	78.1	79.6	79.6	80.2	80.1	80.3	80.0	79.0	81.0	82.2	82.3	82.6	80.4
2010	80.2	82.4	82.9	83.2	83.3	82.9	82.9	81.2	83.5	85.0	85.1	84.9	83.1
2011	84.7	85.3	85.5	85.8	86.1	86.1	85.1	83.6	85.9	86.8	86.9	87.3	85.8
2012	85.9	86.8	87.2	87.2	87.7	87.5	86.6	85.3	87.9	88.8	88.9	89.0	87.4
2013	88.0	89.3	89.6	90.2	90.2	89.4	89.6	88.3	89.0	91.7	92.0	92.0	89.9
2014	91.8	92.6	92.6	93.2	93.3	92.6	92.6	91.2	92.4	94.3	94.3	94.7	93.0
2015	93.9	95.0	95.6	96.2	96.1	96.1	96.3	94.2	96.5	97.9	98.3	98.5	96.2
2016	97.5	98.7	99.1	98.5	98.9	98.7	98.7	96.9	99.8	100.3	100.9	100.3	99.0
2017	100.9	102.1	103.2	102.2	102.6	102.3	101.8	100.2	102.7	105.5	105.6	105.5	102.9

1. Employment by Industry: Idaho, Selected Years, 2007–2017—*Continued*

(Numbers in thousands, not seasonally adjusted)

Industry and year	January	February	March	April	May	June	July	August	September	October	November	December	Annual average
Leisure and Hospitality													
2007	58.7	59.4	60.7	61.3	63.4	66.9	67.6	68.3	66.3	62.7	61.8	62.3	63.3
2008	60.5	61.3	61.9	62.1	64.3	66.8	68.2	68.9	66.1	61.2	59.1	58.4	63.2
2009	56.7	56.9	56.8	57.1	58.9	61.5	63.0	63.3	60.8	57.3	55.6	56.1	58.7
2010	54.2	54.3	54.9	56.6	57.8	60.6	62.3	63.2	61.2	57.8	56.1	56.5	58.0
2011	54.6	55.2	55.7	58.0	58.8	61.9	64.3	65.2	63.1	59.0	57.8	58.1	59.3
2012	56.1	57.2	58.2	59.4	61.4	63.7	65.8	66.7	64.8	61.0	59.7	60.0	61.2
2013	58.8	59.1	60.3	61.9	64.0	66.8	68.5	68.5	66.1	63.9	62.1	61.9	63.5
2014	61.0	61.8	63.0	64.0	66.6	70.1	71.4	71.7	68.0	65.5	63.5	64.1	65.9
2015	63.3	63.8	65.1	65.3	68.3	71.8	74.1	74.3	71.7	68.7	66.7	67.7	68.4
2016	67.2	68.3	69.2	69.8	71.8	76.0	78.0	78.3	75.1	72.5	70.6	71.3	72.3
2017	69.8	70.9	72.1	73.1	75.2	79.6	81.1	81.6	78.4	75.1	74.1	73.5	75.4
Other Services													
2007	18.7	18.9	19.2	19.3	19.5	19.8	19.9	20.1	19.6	19.4	19.3	19.4	19.4
2008	19.5	20.1	20.6	21.3	21.5	22.0	22.2	22.3	21.8	21.0	20.8	20.8	21.2
2009	21.1	21.3	21.2	21.2	21.4	21.7	21.7	21.8	21.1	20.6	20.5	20.5	21.2
2010	20.8	21.0	21.0	20.9	21.0	21.2	21.8	21.5	21.0	20.9	20.8	20.7	21.1
2011	20.5	20.6	20.5	21.0	21.2	21.4	22.0	21.7	21.4	21.2	21.3	21.4	21.2
2012	21.0	21.1	21.2	21.2	21.5	21.8	22.2	22.1	21.7	21.7	21.4	21.4	21.5
2013	21.2	21.4	21.5	21.6	21.9	22.3	22.7	22.9	22.5	21.9	22.0	21.9	22.0
2014	21.7	21.9	22.2	22.3	22.6	23.0	23.5	23.5	23.1	22.7	22.5	22.5	22.6
2015	22.7	22.8	23.0	23.1	23.5	23.9	24.1	23.9	23.6	23.6	23.5	23.6	23.4
2016	23.3	23.5	23.7	23.9	24.2	24.5	25.3	25.0	24.5	24.3	24.3	24.1	24.2
2017	23.9	24.1	24.3	24.6	24.8	25.4	25.6	25.6	25.1	25.5	25.6	25.3	25.0
Government													
2007	113.1	116.8	117.2	118.2	119.2	117.9	110.6	111.8	119.1	119.5	119.0	118.7	116.8
2008	115.4	119.5	120.1	120.4	121.7	120.2	113.8	114.2	120.6	121.5	121.5	121.1	119.2
2009	117.8	119.6	121.3	123.4	122.8	122.0	112.5	112.9	118.5	121.4	121.0	120.5	119.5
2010	115.0	119.6	120.8	122.2	125.5	120.3	112.4	112.5	118.2	119.8	118.8	118.5	118.6
2011	113.2	118.7	119.3	120.1	121.1	117.3	111.2	111.3	117.6	119.3	118.8	118.8	117.2
2012	113.3	117.8	118.2	119.1	120.8	117.0	110.3	110.8	118.4	120.9	120.3	119.8	117.2
2013	115.5	119.7	120.1	119.6	121.1	117.5	109.9	109.6	117.6	120.3	119.5	118.5	117.4
2014	115.2	119.4	120.5	120.4	121.1	118.1	111.7	111.5	118.6	121.5	120.9	119.6	118.2
2015	116.0	119.9	120.8	121.1	122.9	119.2	112.8	111.5	120.3	122.7	122.1	121.2	119.2
2016	117.4	121.7	122.8	122.3	123.6	121.3	115.4	114.5	122.8	124.8	124.1	122.8	121.1
2017	120.2	123.2	124.2	124.5	126.1	123.6	116.9	115.6	124.5	127.3	127.1	126.2	123.3

2. Average Weekly Hours by Selected Industry: Idaho, 2013–2017

(Not seasonally adjusted)

Industry and year	January	February	March	April	May	June	July	August	September	October	November	December	Annual average
Total Private													
2013	32.3	32.9	33.2	33.2	33.3	34.3	33.7	33.8	34.1	33.5	33.3	33.5	33.4
2014	32.5	33.5	33.5	33.0	32.9	34.1	33.3	33.9	33.5	33.3	34.0	33.3	33.4
2015	32.6	33.7	33.7	33.3	33.4	33.6	33.9	34.5	33.2	33.2	33.5	32.7	33.4
2016	32.5	32.4	32.4	32.8	33.6	33.1	33.3	33.2	32.9	33.7	32.8	32.3	32.9
2017	32.3	32.5	32.8	33.9	33.5	33.7	34.4	34.0	33.9	34.5	33.7	33.6	33.6
Goods-Producing													
2013	37.1	37.6	37.9	38.2	38.8	39.4	39.2	39.7	39.8	39.6	38.7	37.8	38.7
2014	37.6	38.9	38.7	39.3	37.9	39.0	39.0	40.0	40.1	39.4	39.2	38.8	39.0
2015	38.5	39.2	39.4	39.4	39.4	39.5	39.5	39.8	37.7	38.5	38.2	37.4	38.9
2016	37.8	37.1	37.4	38.1	38.7	38.9	38.9	39.0	38.8	39.5	38.9	37.2	38.4
2017	37.2	38.0	38.5	39.5	40.2	40.0	39.9	40.2	40.0	40.4	39.7	38.8	39.4
Construction													
2013	31.7	33.0	32.8	33.9	35.5	36.8	35.4	36.8	36.5	37.1	34.9	31.9	34.8
2014	31.7	31.2	33.0	35.3	36.0	37.0	37.5	38.4	37.8	38.2	36.8	36.1	35.9
2015	35.3	36.3	36.6	37.8	38.6	38.8	37.7	38.3	35.7	36.4	35.8	34.8	36.9
2016	35.8	35.0	35.4	36.5	37.4	38.1	37.9	38.1	38.0	37.7	37.4	35.6	37.0
2017	33.9	35.4	36.6	38.4	39.7	39.0	38.7	39.7	38.8	39.5	37.4	36.6	37.9
Manufacturing													
2013	38.9	39.4	40.0	40.0	40.1	40.4	40.6	40.8	41.1	40.9	40.7	40.3	40.3
2014	40.1	41.6	40.9	41.0	39.0	40.4	40.2	41.2	41.5	40.3	40.4	40.0	40.5
2015	39.9	40.2	40.4	39.8	39.5	39.4	40.0	40.3	38.8	39.7	39.6	39.0	39.7
2016	39.1	38.4	38.9	39.3	39.6	39.6	39.3	39.4	39.3	39.8	39.3	37.5	39.1
2017	39.0	39.2	39.5	39.7	40.1	40.4	40.3	40.3	40.7	40.9	41.2	40.2	40.1
Trade, Transportation, and Utlities													
2013	32.9	33.9	34.4	34.1	34.4	34.8	34.5	34.0	33.8	33.8	33.0	32.7	33.9
2014	32.0	32.5	32.7	32.9	33.3	34.1	33.8	34.5	34.1	34.0	34.5	33.8	33.5
2015	33.0	33.7	33.9	33.4	33.9	34.0	34.3	34.6	33.8	33.2	33.4	33.5	33.7
2016	32.3	32.4	32.5	32.8	33.6	33.2	33.2	33.0	32.8	33.3	32.4	32.6	32.8
2017	32.1	32.5	32.7	34.0	33.6	34.0	34.5	34.0	33.8	34.8	33.6	33.8	33.6
Financial Activities													
2013	34.3	35.1	34.9	35.1	34.8	36.6	34.8	35.4	37.1	35.0	36.2	38.0	35.6
2014	36.0	38.1	37.1	34.9	35.6	37.5	35.3	36.3	36.3	36.1	38.6	36.9	36.5
2015	37.2	39.6	38.4	38.6	38.1	37.9	37.8	38.8	37.1	37.6	38.8	36.9	38.0
2016	37.8	37.5	37.1	37.2	38.7	37.0	36.7	36.4	36.9	37.8	37.6	37.0	37.3
2017	38.5	37.3	37.8	39.3	38.0	37.6	39.6	38.2	38.5	39.6	38.4	38.6	38.5
Professional and Business Services													
2013	33.7	34.2	34.9	34.1	34.6	35.6	34.6	35.0	35.3	34.4	34.3	35.4	34.7
2014	34.3	35.7	35.7	35.1	35.6	36.9	35.7	36.5	36.0	36.1	37.3	36.3	35.9
2015	35.8	37.0	36.9	36.4	36.0	36.3	36.0	37.3	36.1	36.0	36.5	35.5	36.3
2016	35.3	35.5	35.6	35.6	36.1	35.6	36.3	36.0	36.3	36.6	35.7	35.1	35.8
2017	35.6	35.4	35.7	36.6	35.5	35.3	36.0	35.4	35.8	36.1	35.0	35.0	35.6
Education and Health Services													
2013	30.8	31.3	31.2	31.4	31.2	31.8	31.0	30.6	31.4	30.7	31.1	31.5	31.2
2014	30.5	31.0	31.0	30.3	30.1	31.1	29.9	30.0	29.7	29.5	30.7	30.2	30.3
2015	29.2	30.1	30.0	29.7	29.4	29.7	29.8	30.5	29.6	29.3	30.2	29.2	29.7
2016	28.9	28.6	28.8	28.9	29.6	29.4	29.7	29.7	29.5	30.4	29.6	29.5	29.4
2017	30.1	30.0	29.9	30.4	29.6	30.3	30.8	30.4	31.2	30.9	30.8	30.3	30.4
Leisure and Hospitality													
2013	21.8	22.9	23.5	23.6	23.3	25.8	25.8	26.1	26.2	24.7	24.4	25.6	24.5
2014	24.3	25.7	25.8	25.0	24.8	26.3	25.5	26.0	24.4	24.5	24.6	23.8	25.1
2015	23.1	24.6	24.7	23.4	24.0	24.7	26.2	26.6	24.7	24.6	24.8	23.9	24.7
2016	23.5	24.3	23.9	24.1	25.5	24.6	25.2	24.7	23.3	24.2	23.1	22.8	24.1
2017	21.3	21.8	22.4	23.0	23.0	23.5	24.8	24.3	22.9	23.6	22.4	22.3	23.0

3. Average Hourly Earnings by Selected Industry: Idaho, 2013–2017

(Dollars, not seasonally adjusted)

Industry and year	January	February	March	April	May	June	July	August	September	October	November	December	Annual average
Total Private													
2013	21.46	21.41	21.28	21.24	21.09	21.00	20.91	20.94	21.20	21.14	21.25	21.54	21.20
2014	21.10	21.32	21.24	21.21	21.24	21.09	21.19	21.31	21.53	21.68	21.78	21.71	21.37
2015	22.01	22.11	21.85	22.03	22.01	21.90	21.83	22.20	22.06	22.25	22.34	22.39	22.08
2016	22.60	22.52	22.45	22.71	22.49	22.08	22.09	22.16	22.32	22.49	22.41	22.44	22.39
2017	22.85	22.62	22.40	22.57	22.43	22.23	22.50	22.30	22.40	22.62	22.49	22.61	22.50
Goods-Producing													
2013	24.53	24.23	23.83	23.64	23.59	23.51	23.64	23.70	23.86	23.49	23.85	24.32	23.84
2014	22.84	22.88	22.44	22.41	22.63	22.38	23.04	22.47	22.80	22.92	23.05	23.04	22.74
2015	23.32	23.58	23.59	23.94	23.86	24.03	23.81	23.82	23.58	23.34	23.01	23.87	23.65
2016	23.47	22.92	22.72	23.02	22.63	22.46	22.17	22.08	22.24	22.30	22.45	22.53	22.57
2017	22.69	22.32	22.50	22.47	22.55	22.64	23.05	22.47	22.77	23.10	23.05	23.43	22.76
Construction													
2013	20.82	20.73	20.67	20.32	20.20	20.17	20.35	20.52	20.49	20.10	20.25	21.32	20.47
2014	20.60	21.07	20.28	19.83	20.00	20.05	19.88	19.92	20.26	20.81	21.30	21.54	20.45
2015	21.12	21.25	21.40	21.10	21.16	21.10	20.42	20.77	20.96	21.00	21.20	21.75	21.09
2016	21.42	20.53	20.92	21.32	20.79	20.86	20.69	20.69	21.37	21.41	21.82	22.12	21.16
2017	22.78	22.64	22.88	22.42	22.72	22.93	23.02	22.46	22.72	23.19	22.76	23.54	22.84
Manufacturing													
2013	25.30	24.99	24.64	24.56	24.52	24.56	24.68	24.73	24.99	24.62	24.99	25.09	24.80
2014	23.45	23.40	23.00	23.04	23.22	22.86	23.69	23.00	23.31	23.33	23.31	23.27	23.24
2015	23.72	24.06	24.11	25.00	24.93	25.31	25.41	25.30	24.90	24.49	24.17	25.07	24.71
2016	24.71	24.40	23.80	24.06	23.74	23.38	22.94	22.72	22.42	22.51	22.41	22.25	23.27
2017	22.15	21.80	21.99	22.41	22.18	22.03	22.07	21.49	21.95	22.29	22.57	22.88	22.15
Trade, Transportation, and Utilities													
2013	17.42	17.48	17.64	17.68	17.69	17.71	17.52	17.88	17.73	17.79	17.73	18.17	17.70
2014	18.16	18.49	18.88	18.35	18.81	18.65	18.46	18.57	19.05	19.48	19.23	19.32	18.80
2015	19.84	19.47	19.24	18.95	19.16	19.07	19.36	19.89	19.69	19.87	20.05	19.64	19.52
2016	19.93	19.86	19.89	19.80	19.57	19.18	19.20	19.17	19.30	19.52	18.96	18.80	19.43
2017	19.56	19.11	19.04	19.19	19.15	18.91	19.49	19.51	19.50	19.43	19.24	19.30	19.29
Financial Activities													
2013	21.02	21.32	21.14	20.97	21.04	21.04	20.95	20.83	20.48	20.34	20.70	21.22	20.92
2014	20.59	20.82	21.16	21.87	21.73	22.30	22.37	23.93	22.82	23.70	24.71	24.25	22.54
2015	25.11	26.15	25.86	26.14	26.77	25.62	25.85	27.61	25.63	25.67	26.65	25.80	26.08
2016	26.61	26.51	25.46	25.74	25.53	24.56	24.55	25.38	25.01	25.73	25.50	25.07	25.47
2017	25.86	26.37	25.30	25.06	25.31	25.46	24.87	25.44	25.54	25.58	25.22	24.83	25.40
Professional and Business Services													
2013	27.25	27.24	27.25	26.96	26.43	26.62	26.98	26.60	27.39	27.63	27.09	27.27	27.06
2014	27.24	27.90	28.13	28.96	28.64	28.50	28.47	28.70	28.71	28.52	28.47	28.44	28.40
2015	28.72	29.17	28.60	29.03	28.97	28.85	28.84	29.15	29.74	30.09	29.91	29.68	29.23
2016	30.53	31.02	30.93	31.37	30.95	30.52	30.68	31.14	30.67	30.54	30.41	30.20	30.75
2017	30.23	29.81	29.79	29.81	29.28	28.81	29.11	28.40	28.16	28.74	28.27	28.35	29.05
Education and Health Services													
2013	21.41	21.24	21.21	21.13	20.94	21.23	21.17	21.07	21.35	21.08	21.48	21.56	21.24
2014	21.42	21.82	21.30	21.22	21.18	21.40	21.99	22.06	22.17	22.03	22.17	22.65	21.78
2015	22.39	22.11	21.73	21.92	21.52	21.50	21.44	21.46	21.49	21.50	21.53	21.79	21.70
2016	21.75	21.92	22.18	22.61	22.56	22.37	22.57	22.13	22.72	22.42	22.61	23.13	22.42
2017	23.47	23.59	22.69	23.09	23.00	22.78	23.18	22.39	22.14	22.41	22.82	23.30	22.90
Leisure and Hospitality													
2013	11.44	11.46	11.51	11.51	11.74	11.34	11.31	11.26	11.72	11.76	12.03	12.28	11.61
2014	12.19	12.15	12.12	11.96	12.00	11.82	11.87	11.89	11.86	11.80	11.91	12.01	11.96
2015	12.08	12.15	12.13	12.17	11.97	11.86	11.83	11.96	11.97	11.85	11.83	12.15	11.99
2016	12.05	12.14	12.11	12.29	12.20	12.11	12.26	12.26	12.37	12.48	12.33	12.68	12.27
2017	13.19	13.04	12.97	13.00	12.93	12.70	12.99	12.94	13.06	13.20	13.00	13.24	13.02

4. Average Weekly Earnings by Selected Industry: Idaho, 2013–2017

(Dollars, not seasonally adjusted)

Industry and year	January	February	March	April	May	June	July	August	September	October	November	December	Annual average
Total Private													
2013	693.16	704.39	706.50	705.17	702.30	720.30	704.67	707.77	722.92	708.19	707.63	721.59	708.08
2014	685.75	714.22	711.54	699.93	698.80	719.17	705.63	722.41	721.26	721.94	740.52	722.94	713.76
2015	717.53	745.11	736.35	733.60	735.13	735.84	740.04	765.90	732.39	738.70	748.39	732.15	737.47
2016	734.50	729.65	727.38	744.89	755.66	730.85	735.60	735.71	734.33	757.91	735.05	724.81	736.63
2017	738.06	735.15	734.72	765.12	751.41	749.15	774.00	758.20	759.36	780.39	757.91	759.70	756.00
Goods-Producing													
2013	910.06	911.05	903.16	903.05	915.29	926.29	926.69	940.89	949.63	930.20	923.00	919.30	922.61
2014	858.78	890.03	868.43	880.71	857.68	872.82	898.56	898.80	914.28	903.05	903.56	893.95	886.86
2015	897.82	924.34	929.45	943.24	940.08	949.19	940.50	948.04	888.97	898.59	878.98	892.74	919.99
2016	887.17	850.33	849.73	877.06	875.78	873.69	862.41	861.12	862.91	880.85	873.31	838.12	866.69
2017	844.07	848.16	866.25	887.57	906.51	905.60	919.70	903.29	910.80	933.24	915.09	909.08	896.74
Construction													
2013	659.99	684.09	677.98	688.85	717.10	742.26	720.39	755.14	747.89	745.71	706.73	680.11	712.36
2014	653.02	657.38	669.24	700.00	720.00	741.85	745.50	764.93	765.83	794.94	783.84	777.59	734.16
2015	745.54	771.38	783.24	797.58	816.78	818.68	769.83	795.49	748.27	764.40	758.96	756.90	778.22
2016	766.84	718.55	740.57	778.18	777.55	794.77	784.15	788.29	812.06	807.16	816.07	787.47	782.92
2017	772.24	801.46	837.41	860.93	901.98	894.27	890.87	891.66	881.54	916.01	851.22	861.56	865.64
Manufacturing													
2013	984.17	984.61	985.60	982.40	983.25	992.22	1,002.01	1,008.98	1,027.09	1,006.96	1,017.09	1,011.13	999.44
2014	940.35	973.44	940.70	944.64	905.58	923.54	952.34	947.60	967.37	940.20	941.72	930.80	941.22
2015	946.43	967.21	974.04	995.00	984.74	997.21	1,016.40	1,019.59	966.12	972.25	957.13	977.73	980.99
2016	966.16	936.96	925.82	945.56	940.10	925.85	901.54	895.17	881.11	895.90	880.71	834.38	909.86
2017	863.85	854.56	868.61	889.68	889.42	890.01	889.42	866.05	893.37	911.66	929.88	919.78	888.22
Trade, Transportation, and Utilities													
2013	573.12	592.57	606.82	602.89	608.54	616.31	604.44	607.92	599.27	601.30	585.09	594.16	600.03
2014	581.12	600.93	617.38	603.72	626.37	635.97	623.95	640.67	649.61	662.32	663.44	653.02	629.80
2015	654.72	656.14	652.24	632.93	649.52	648.38	664.05	688.19	665.52	659.68	669.67	657.94	657.82
2016	643.74	643.46	646.43	649.44	657.55	636.78	637.44	632.61	633.04	650.02	614.30	612.88	637.30
2017	627.88	621.08	622.61	652.46	643.44	642.94	672.41	663.34	659.10	676.16	646.46	652.34	648.14
Financial Activities													
2013	720.99	748.33	737.79	736.05	732.19	770.06	729.06	737.38	759.81	711.90	749.34	806.36	744.75
2014	741.24	793.24	785.04	763.26	773.59	836.25	789.66	868.66	828.37	855.57	953.81	894.83	822.71
2015	934.09	1,035.54	993.02	1,009.00	1,019.94	971.00	977.13	1,071.27	950.87	965.19	1,034.02	952.02	991.04
2016	1,005.86	994.13	944.57	957.53	988.01	908.72	900.99	923.83	922.87	972.59	958.80	927.59	950.03
2017	995.61	983.60	956.34	984.86	961.78	957.30	984.85	971.81	983.29	1,012.97	968.45	958.44	977.90
Professional and Business Services													
2013	918.33	931.61	951.03	919.34	914.48	947.67	933.51	931.00	966.87	950.47	929.19	965.36	938.98
2014	934.33	996.03	1,004.24	1,016.50	1,019.58	1,051.65	1,016.38	1,047.55	1,033.56	1,029.57	1,061.93	1,032.37	1,019.56
2015	1,028.18	1,079.29	1,055.34	1,056.69	1,042.92	1,047.26	1,038.24	1,087.30	1,073.61	1,083.24	1,091.72	1,053.64	1,061.05
2016	1,077.71	1,101.21	1,101.11	1,116.77	1,117.30	1,086.51	1,113.68	1,121.04	1,113.32	1,117.76	1,085.64	1,060.02	1,100.85
2017	1,076.19	1,055.27	1,063.50	1,091.05	1,039.44	1,016.99	1,047.96	1,005.36	1,008.13	1,037.51	989.45	992.25	1,034.18
Education and Health Services													
2013	659.43	664.81	661.75	663.48	653.33	675.11	656.27	644.74	670.39	647.16	668.03	679.14	662.69
2014	653.31	676.42	660.30	642.97	637.52	665.54	657.50	661.80	658.45	649.89	680.62	684.03	659.93
2015	653.79	665.51	651.90	651.02	632.69	638.55	638.91	654.53	636.10	629.95	650.21	636.27	644.49
2016	628.58	626.91	638.78	653.43	667.78	657.68	670.33	657.26	670.24	681.57	669.26	682.34	659.15
2017	706.45	707.70	678.43	701.94	680.80	690.23	713.94	680.66	690.77	692.47	702.86	705.99	696.16
Leisure and Hospitality													
2013	249.39	262.43	270.49	271.64	273.54	292.57	291.80	293.89	307.06	290.47	293.53	314.37	284.45
2014	296.22	312.26	312.70	299.00	297.60	310.87	302.69	309.14	289.38	289.10	292.99	285.84	300.20
2015	279.05	298.89	299.61	284.78	287.28	292.94	309.95	318.14	295.66	291.51	293.38	290.39	296.15
2016	283.18	295.00	289.43	296.19	311.10	297.91	308.95	302.82	288.22	302.02	284.82	289.10	295.71
2017	280.95	284.27	290.53	299.00	297.39	298.45	322.15	314.44	299.07	311.52	291.20	295.25	299.46

ILLINOIS
At a Glance

Population:
  2010 census: 12,830,632
  2017 estimate: 12,802,023

Percent change in population:
  2010–2017: -0.2%

Percent change in total nonfarm employment:
  2007–2017: 1.4%

Industry with the largest growth in employment, 2007–2017 (thousands):
  Education and health services, 146.1

Industry with the largest decline or smallest growth in employment, 2007–2017 (thousands):
  Manufacturing, 98.6

Civilian labor force:
  2010: 6,625,321
  2017: 6,492,578

Unemployment rate and rank among states (highest to lowest):
  2010: 10.4%, 11th
  2017: 5.0%, 7th

Over-the-year change in unemployment rates:
  2015–2016: -0.2%
  2016–2017: -0.8%

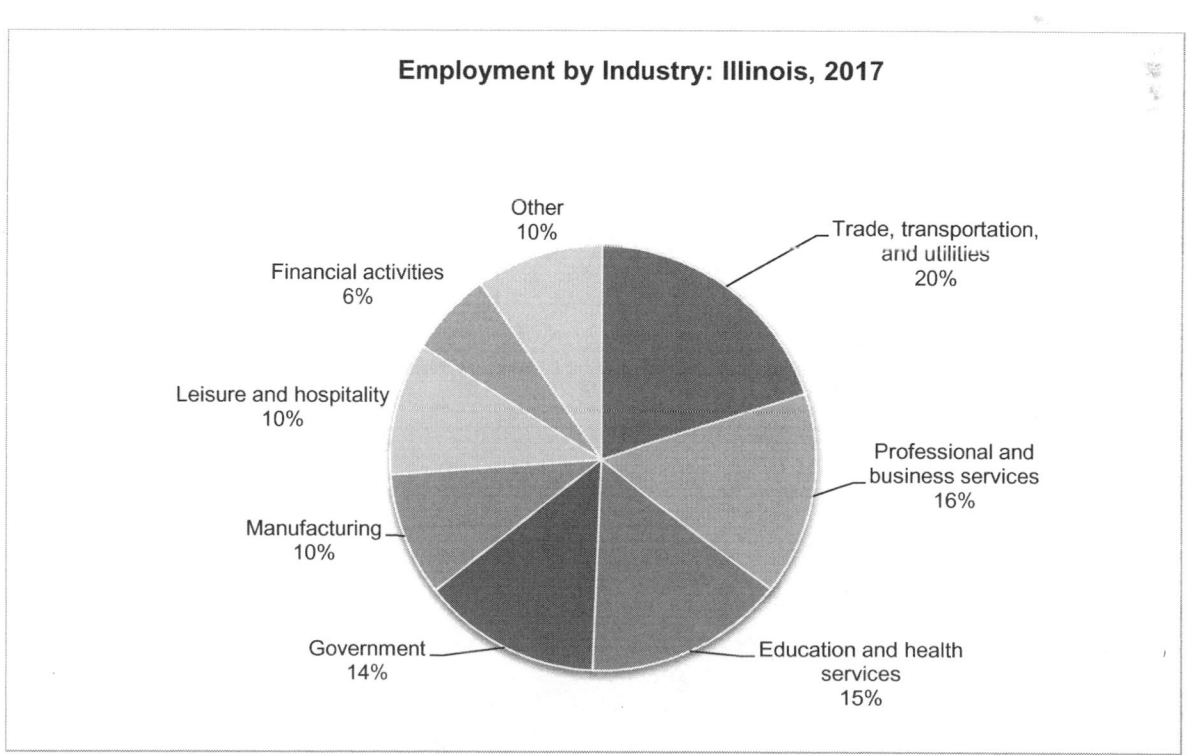

Employment by Industry: Illinois, 2017

Other 10%
Trade, transportation, and utilities 20%
Financial activities 6%
Leisure and hospitality 10%
Professional and business services 16%
Manufacturing 10%
Government 14%
Education and health services 15%

1. Employment by Industry: Illinois, Selected Years, 2007–2017

(Numbers in thousands, not seasonally adjusted)

Industry and year	January	February	March	April	May	June	July	August	September	October	November	December	Annual average
Total Nonfarm													
2007	5,841.6	5,844.1	5,902.0	5,957.9	6,016.3	6,045.9	6,005.6	6,007.8	6,017.4	6,022.6	6,043.2	6,034.2	5,978.2
2008	5,867.7	5,874.9	5,904.2	5,960.9	6,009.9	6,018.6	5,980.5	5,977.9	5,969.6	5,966.2	5,939.6	5,897.8	5,947.3
2009	5,677.5	5,659.1	5,653.1	5,670.0	5,697.7	5,690.1	5,638.1	5,622.0	5,637.5	5,646.9	5,648.3	5,628.0	5,655.7
2010	5,461.3	5,483.5	5,516.5	5,594.5	5,654.0	5,659.3	5,606.5	5,630.0	5,650.1	5,685.5	5,697.0	5,686.1	5,610.4
2011	5,525.4	5,545.6	5,590.2	5,666.7	5,701.5	5,719.2	5,691.8	5,702.1	5,727.1	5,740.7	5,751.0	5,745.8	5,675.6
2012	5,594.9	5,619.2	5,672.3	5,730.8	5,774.9	5,796.9	5,758.4	5,775.3	5,807.1	5,814.8	5,835.3	5,823.4	5,750.3
2013	5,657.3	5,688.2	5,722.3	5,770.8	5,832.0	5,849.6	5,815.4	5,832.6	5,854.3	5,866.5	5,883.4	5,880.0	5,804.4
2014	5,711.1	5,733.8	5,777.1	5,853.7	5,914.9	5,932.5	5,894.2	5,907.0	5,927.7	5,960.6	5,970.9	5,968.8	5,879.4
2015	5,789.3	5,819.1	5,852.2	5,944.8	6,010.4	6,026.2	5,996.7	5,996.5	6,019.0	6,055.5	6,056.2	6,050.7	5,968.1
2016	5,878.9	5,901.2	5,932.8	6,008.5	6,040.0	6,057.6	6,034.7	6,036.0	6,062.4	6,089.0	6,101.9	6,083.5	6,018.9
2017	5,907.3	5,936.3	5,979.9	6,034.6	6,085.2	6,122.2	6,075.4	6,083.1	6,103.6	6,147.9	6,156.3	6,117.4	6,062.4
Total Private													
2007	5,006.6	4,987.3	5,042.6	5,095.9	5,152.8	5,201.0	5,186.1	5,193.2	5,166.3	5,161.6	5,178.4	5,175.6	5,129.0
2008	5,026.1	5,010.6	5,039.2	5,093.2	5,138.7	5,167.9	5,154.3	5,159.3	5,114.5	5,096.2	5,069.3	5,031.3	5,091.7
2009	4,833.1	4,794.6	4,787.2	4,793.8	4,821.4	4,837.0	4,809.6	4,806.3	4,778.8	4,776.4	4,775.8	4,763.0	4,798.1
2010	4,617.1	4,617.1	4,650.4	4,722.7	4,768.0	4,805.1	4,788.2	4,812.6	4,800.5	4,827.0	4,837.2	4,833.4	4,756.6
2011	4,696.2	4,695.4	4,739.1	4,810.5	4,847.2	4,885.9	4,881.5	4,901.4	4,891.5	4,896.5	4,903.8	4,903.6	4,837.7
2012	4,775.7	4,779.3	4,829.3	4,884.0	4,928.3	4,970.8	4,959.7	4,981.1	4,970.0	4,969.0	4,987.1	4,980.2	4,917.9
2013	4,837.0	4,846.8	4,880.5	4,926.8	4,984.9	5,024.1	5,016.3	5,040.4	5,019.7	5,030.0	5,043.8	5,043.0	4,974.4
2014	4,900.6	4,904.9	4,945.8	5,013.5	5,072.2	5,109.5	5,095.8	5,114.9	5,092.0	5,118.1	5,128.8	5,127.3	5,052.0
2015	4,975.6	4,984.0	5,015.8	5,102.9	5,167.3	5,202.7	5,197.5	5,204.2	5,183.3	5,211.5	5,214.7	5,208.2	5,139.0
2016	5,063.6	5,068.0	5,095.1	5,169.3	5,201.9	5,230.5	5,233.5	5,242.6	5,221.7	5,250.0	5,261.5	5,236.8	5,189.5
2017	5,093.0	5,102.8	5,143.4	5,198.2	5,248.8	5,292.8	5,272.1	5,287.5	5,263.0	5,298.2	5,305.4	5,271.2	5,231.4
Goods Producing													
2007	931.2	918.6	936.6	953.0	967.3	980.6	975.6	975.8	970.8	963.8	961.1	947.5	956.8
2008	913.1	904.6	912.8	927.3	939.1	948.0	947.2	947.2	939.8	929.0	912.5	884.5	925.4
2009	831.9	818.0	813.3	807.3	805.8	808.8	804.7	804.6	800.9	793.8	783.3	766.9	803.3
2010	731.1	729.6	739.9	761.0	770.9	782.7	778.7	789.9	787.9	791.4	786.1	771.3	768.4
2011	743.6	742.6	755.1	773.2	784.1	796.7	799.5	802.2	796.1	793.4	787.9	776.7	779.3
2012	749.5	749.1	761.3	775.4	784.1	796.5	800.8	801.7	799.1	797.4	790.6	781.2	782.2
2013	752.8	753.2	759.2	768.0	783.0	794.3	796.6	798.5	794.7	793.6	791.1	778.4	780.3
2014	752.6	752.7	764.5	780.0	794.1	806.4	809.7	812.3	809.4	812.1	807.6	799.8	791.8
2015	771.3	771.4	780.6	797.9	811.2	821.7	823.1	823.3	820.4	818.9	812.7	802.7	804.6
2016	775.0	775.3	784.9	798.5	806.3	816.9	817.6	816.6	812.3	811.0	807.3	792.0	801.1
2017	762.0	766.8	777.0	797.1	809.4	822.1	821.7	822.6	820.4	823.1	822.5	811.2	804.7
Service-Providing													
2007	4,910.4	4,925.5	4,965.4	5,004.9	5,049.0	5,065.3	5,030.0	5,032.0	5,046.6	5,058.8	5,082.1	5,086.7	5,021.4
2008	4,954.6	4,970.3	4,991.4	5,033.6	5,070.8	5,070.6	5,033.3	5,030.7	5,029.8	5,037.2	5,027.1	5,013.3	5,021.9
2009	4,845.6	4,841.1	4,839.8	4,862.7	4,891.9	4,881.3	4,833.4	4,817.4	4,836.6	4,853.1	4,865.0	4,861.1	4,852.4
2010	4,730.2	4,753.9	4,776.6	4,833.5	4,883.1	4,876.6	4,827.8	4,840.1	4,862.2	4,894.1	4,910.9	4,914.8	4,842.0
2011	4,781.8	4,803.0	4,835.1	4,893.5	4,917.4	4,922.5	4,892.3	4,899.9	4,931.0	4,947.3	4,963.1	4,969.1	4,896.3
2012	4,845.4	4,870.1	4,911.0	4,955.4	4,990.8	5,000.4	4,957.6	4,973.6	5,008.0	5,017.4	5,044.7	5,042.2	4,968.1
2013	4,904.5	4,935.0	4,963.1	5,002.8	5,049.0	5,055.3	5,018.8	5,034.1	5,059.6	5,072.9	5,092.3	5,101.6	5,024.1
2014	4,958.5	4,981.1	5,012.6	5,073.7	5,120.8	5,126.1	5,084.5	5,094.7	5,118.3	5,148.5	5,163.3	5,169.0	5,087.6
2015	5,018.0	5,047.7	5,071.6	5,146.9	5,199.2	5,204.5	5,173.6	5,173.2	5,198.6	5,236.6	5,243.5	5,248.0	5,163.5
2016	5,103.9	5,125.9	5,147.9	5,210.0	5,233.7	5,240.7	5,217.1	5,219.4	5,250.1	5,278.0	5,294.6	5,291.5	5,217.7
2017	5,145.3	5,169.5	5,202.9	5,237.5	5,275.8	5,300.1	5,253.7	5,260.5	5,283.2	5,324.8	5,333.8	5,306.2	5,257.8
Mining and Logging													
2007	9.7	9.7	10.0	10.2	10.5	10.7	10.5	10.3	10.0	10.1	10.1	9.7	10.1
2008	9.3	9.3	9.6	9.5	9.9	9.9	9.9	10.1	10.0	10.0	9.9	9.8	9.8
2009	9.2	9.3	9.4	9.6	9.5	9.7	9.5	9.3	9.4	9.1	9.1	8.9	9.3
2010	8.4	8.4	8.5	9.0	9.1	9.3	9.5	9.4	9.6	9.6	9.5	9.4	9.1
2011	9.0	8.8	9.0	9.3	9.5	9.7	10.0	10.1	10.1	10.1	10.1	9.8	9.6
2012	9.6	9.6	9.9	10.3	10.3	10.4	10.6	10.6	10.4	10.2	10.2	10.0	10.2
2013	9.6	9.5	9.3	9.4	9.7	9.9	10.0	9.9	9.8	9.8	9.8	9.6	9.7
2014	9.4	9.2	9.5	9.7	10.1	10.2	10.1	10.2	10.3	10.2	10.2	10.2	9.9
2015	9.6	9.4	9.4	9.5	9.7	9.7	9.6	9.6	9.2	9.0	8.8	8.6	9.3
2016	8.2	8.0	7.9	8.0	8.1	8.2	8.0	8.2	8.1	8.1	8.2	7.8	8.1
2017	7.6	7.6	7.8	8.0	7.9	8.0	7.9	7.9	7.8	7.7	7.7	7.5	7.8

1. Employment by Industry: Illinois, Selected Years, 2007–2017—*Continued*

(Numbers in thousands, not seasonally adjusted)

Industry and year	January	February	March	April	May	June	July	August	September	October	November	December	Annual average
Construction													
2007	244.5	233.6	249.8	266.5	279.8	288.9	289.4	290.1	287.2	284.3	278.9	263.8	271.4
2008	236.3	231.2	239.2	255.3	266.9	273.2	277.3	278.8	274.7	269.7	257.8	239.1	258.3
2009	205.8	201.9	206.1	214.1	221.8	227.7	231.2	231.0	227.8	224.2	215.3	199.7	217.2
2010	172.5	169.9	178.9	196.6	203.5	210.9	206.6	215.1	213.4	213.9	207.1	190.6	198.3
2011	168.9	167.7	177.2	192.3	201.7	209.5	212.4	214.0	210.2	206.3	200.0	188.7	195.7
2012	166.0	163.9	173.0	185.0	191.8	199.2	202.5	203.1	201.7	202.1	194.8	186.0	189.1
2013	164.4	164.6	170.1	180.6	194.1	201.3	207.1	208.2	207.4	206.8	202.0	189.8	191.4
2014	168.8	168.4	177.2	192.8	204.2	212.4	217.6	219.4	218.8	220.4	215.0	205.4	201.7
2015	182.2	181.8	190.0	208.8	219.0	225.3	228.5	230.1	229.4	229.7	224.1	214.0	213.6
2016	192.3	192.2	202.1	215.7	222.5	230.8	233.0	233.3	231.7	231.9	226.7	211.7	218.7
2017	191.4	194.7	202.5	213.5	223.9	230.8	235.2	236.0	235.1	234.2	229.1	215.7	220.2
Manufacturing													
2007	677.0	675.3	676.8	676.3	677.0	681.0	675.7	675.4	673.6	669.4	672.1	674.0	675.3
2008	667.5	664.1	664.0	662.5	662.3	664.9	660.0	658.3	655.1	649.3	644.8	635.6	657.4
2009	616.9	606.8	597.8	583.6	574.5	571.4	564.0	564.3	563.7	560.5	558.9	558.3	576.7
2010	550.2	551.3	552.5	555.4	558.3	562.5	562.6	565.4	564.9	567.9	569.5	571.3	561.0
2011	565.7	566.1	568.9	571.6	572.9	577.5	577.1	578.1	575.8	577.0	577.8	578.2	573.9
2012	573.9	575.6	578.4	580.1	582.0	586.9	587.7	588.0	587.0	585.1	585.6	585.2	583.0
2013	578.8	579.1	579.8	578.0	579.2	583.1	579.5	580.4	577.5	577.0	579.3	579.0	579.2
2014	574.4	575.1	577.8	577.5	579.8	583.8	582.0	582.7	580.3	581.5	582.4	584.2	580.1
2015	579.5	580.2	581.2	579.6	582.5	586.7	585.0	583.6	581.8	580.2	579.8	580.1	581.7
2016	574.5	575.1	574.9	574.8	575.7	577.9	576.6	575.1	572.5	571.0	572.4	572.5	574.4
2017	563.0	564.5	566.7	575.6	577.6	583.3	578.6	578.7	577.5	581.2	585.7	588.0	576.7
Trade, Transportation, and Utilities													
2007	1,201.3	1,185.7	1,196.3	1,195.8	1,209.8	1,217.5	1,210.4	1,210.1	1,211.1	1,214.5	1,240.7	1,254.6	1,212.3
2008	1,210.4	1,194.0	1,199.0	1,200.1	1,209.1	1,212.2	1,203.4	1,203.1	1,198.4	1,200.2	1,210.9	1,216.9	1,204.8
2009	1,161.9	1,143.9	1,138.2	1,134.0	1,140.7	1,141.7	1,128.8	1,129.4	1,127.1	1,129.9	1,145.2	1,153.2	1,139.5
2010	1,109.4	1,099.7	1,104.1	1,113.9	1,123.5	1,128.7	1,124.1	1,127.9	1,124.7	1,133.9	1,151.9	1,165.4	1,125.6
2011	1,126.0	1,116.8	1,122.2	1,133.2	1,140.1	1,145.4	1,141.7	1,145.9	1,145.4	1,152.3	1,171.4	1,185.3	1,143.8
2012	1,141.4	1,130.5	1,138.7	1,143.4	1,152.3	1,156.1	1,153.7	1,157.0	1,155.7	1,163.2	1,188.8	1,195.1	1,156.3
2013	1,148.0	1,138.9	1,143.1	1,149.4	1,159.7	1,166.6	1,163.7	1,168.4	1,165.4	1,171.3	1,192.9	1,205.9	1,164.4
2014	1,158.8	1,147.7	1,154.6	1,163.3	1,175.8	1,183.2	1,179.0	1,183.7	1,181.8	1,190.4	1,212.9	1,225.5	1,179.7
2015	1,177.4	1,169.3	1,174.9	1,186.8	1,199.6	1,207.4	1,202.8	1,206.4	1,204.5	1,213.4	1,232.8	1,241.4	1,201.4
2016	1,193.6	1,186.6	1,190.0	1,202.5	1,207.2	1,209.7	1,208.9	1,211.0	1,206.3	1,221.8	1,241.5	1,254.6	1,211.1
2017	1,205.0	1,194.1	1,196.5	1,199.0	1,204.9	1,211.9	1,207.9	1,211.9	1,210.0	1,222.8	1,243.3	1,249.7	1,213.1
Wholesale Trade													
2007	305.9	305.5	307.6	308.8	310.7	313.8	312.8	312.1	311.7	312.9	312.9	313.8	310.7
2008	309.0	308.2	309.5	310.7	312.8	314.1	312.3	311.4	309.7	309.9	308.8	307.4	310.3
2009	299.2	296.7	295.6	293.8	293.2	293.2	290.4	289.1	287.1	287.9	287.6	287.5	291.8
2010	281.8	280.9	282.7	285.1	286.6	288.2	287.7	287.6	286.5	287.4	287.0	287.2	285.7
2011	284.3	284.3	285.9	288.6	289.7	292.0	292.2	291.8	290.8	291.5	291.2	292.1	289.5
2012	289.0	289.4	292.3	293.7	295.2	297.8	296.3	296.1	295.4	295.9	296.3	296.6	294.5
2013	293.9	294.0	295.7	297.2	299.0	301.8	300.7	299.6	298.9	299.3	299.8	300.1	298.3
2014	296.4	296.5	297.6	298.0	300.0	301.7	300.8	300.1	298.7	300.6	301.4	301.1	299.4
2015	296.9	296.2	297.8	300.3	302.7	304.6	303.6	302.4	300.8	301.3	301.3	301.1	300.8
2016	296.1	296.0	296.8	299.7	300.2	302.0	301.8	301.2	301.7	308.1	308.3	308.5	301.7
2017	301.4	301.7	302.1	303.6	305.3	308.4	307.8	309.3	311.0	311.8	314.5	313.1	307.5
Retail Trade													
2007	632.8	618.0	624.5	623.3	632.6	638.2	635.6	634.1	630.3	632.4	657.1	667.1	635.5
2008	635.6	620.4	623.0	623.4	628.0	632.2	628.8	626.7	620.4	621.9	633.7	639.1	627.8
2009	604.1	590.7	587.6	588.6	594.8	597.9	593.2	592.9	588.5	590.4	605.6	611.4	595.5
2010	580.8	572.0	574.4	579.1	585.6	591.1	589.9	590.2	583.5	590.2	607.1	617.1	588.4
2011	587.0	577.5	580.2	586.8	591.2	595.7	594.6	597.1	592.3	598.1	616.3	625.8	595.2
2012	593.0	581.9	585.4	587.0	592.3	596.7	596.2	595.7	591.5	598.4	622.1	624.8	597.1
2013	592.0	582.8	584.6	586.8	593.7	601.0	599.9	600.8	596.5	601.9	620.5	629.6	599.2
2014	594.6	584.0	587.6	594.7	601.7	608.7	607.1	607.4	603.4	609.7	628.5	636.1	605.3
2015	602.5	595.3	598.7	604.8	612.0	618.7	617.5	618.7	615.6	621.9	638.8	643.1	615.6
2016	612.0	605.6	606.9	614.5	617.5	621.0	621.0	620.8	612.2	620.2	636.6	642.6	619.2
2017	614.3	604.5	604.6	606.3	607.9	613.3	611.1	609.6	602.0	610.1	624.1	625.2	611.1

1. Employment by Industry: Illinois, Selected Years, 2007–2017—*Continued*

(Numbers in thousands, not seasonally adjusted)

Industry and year	January	February	March	April	May	June	July	August	September	October	November	December	Annual average
Transportation and Utilities													
2007	262.6	262.2	264.2	263.7	266.5	265.5	262.0	263.9	269.1	269.2	270.7	273.7	266.1
2008	265.8	265.4	266.5	266.0	268.3	265.9	262.3	265.0	268.3	268.4	268.4	270.4	266.7
2009	258.6	256.5	255.0	251.6	252.7	250.6	245.2	247.4	251.5	251.6	252.0	254.3	252.3
2010	246.8	246.8	247.0	249.7	251.3	249.4	246.5	250.1	254.7	256.3	257.8	261.1	251.5
2011	254.7	255.0	256.1	257.8	259.2	257.7	254.9	257.0	262.3	262.7	263.9	267.4	259.1
2012	259.4	259.2	261.0	262.7	264.8	261.6	261.2	265.2	268.8	268.9	270.4	273.7	264.7
2013	262.1	262.1	262.8	265.4	267.0	263.8	263.1	268.0	270.0	270.1	272.6	276.2	266.9
2014	267.8	267.2	269.4	270.6	274.1	272.8	271.1	276.2	279.7	280.1	283.0	288.3	275.0
2015	278.0	277.8	278.4	281.7	284.9	284.1	281.7	285.3	288.1	290.2	292.7	297.2	285.0
2016	285.5	285.0	286.3	288.3	289.5	286.7	286.1	289.0	292.4	293.5	296.6	303.5	290.2
2017	289.3	287.9	289.8	289.1	291.7	290.2	289.0	293.0	297.0	300.9	304.7	311.4	294.5
Information													
2007	115.3	115.7	115.7	115.7	116.2	116.9	116.9	116.8	115.6	115.5	115.7	116.0	116.0
2008	115.4	115.4	115.9	115.6	115.9	115.8	115.5	115.0	113.0	112.1	111.7	111.6	114.4
2009	109.9	108.9	108.2	107.4	107.0	106.7	105.7	105.4	104.5	104.2	103.8	104.8	106.4
2010	103.3	102.3	102.3	102.1	102.1	102.4	101.8	101.9	100.6	100.9	100.9	101.1	101.8
2011	100.6	99.9	100.1	100.4	101.0	101.3	101.6	101.4	99.8	99.8	100.4	100.5	100.6
2012	100.2	99.8	100.1	100.4	101.1	100.5	100.5	100.2	99.1	99.9	99.8	100.0	100.1
2013	99.0	98.5	98.5	99.4	100.2	100.4	99.8	99.3	98.0	97.6	98.2	98.6	99.0
2014	97.3	97.4	98.4	99.3	99.3	100.3	100.2	100.3	98.4	99.0	99.1	99.9	99.1
2015	99.4	99.4	99.3	100.7	102.1	101.6	101.0	101.1	99.5	99.9	100.4	100.7	100.4
2016	97.2	96.7	97.0	97.3	98.1	98.1	97.8	99.1	97.1	100.2	100.6	99.7	98.2
2017	98.3	98.5	98.6	97.3	98.0	97.9	96.1	97.0	94.9	95.4	96.5	96.5	97.1
Financial Activities													
2007	411.2	410.7	410.8	411.2	412.3	415.3	414.4	412.8	408.2	407.2	406.7	407.3	410.7
2008	401.4	401.4	401.5	401.3	402.1	404.1	402.4	401.9	396.7	395.6	393.7	393.8	399.7
2009	386.6	384.5	382.8	381.9	381.8	382.9	381.1	379.8	375.7	374.7	374.1	374.7	380.1
2010	369.3	368.7	368.8	370.2	371.2	373.9	373.5	373.9	370.6	372.6	372.5	373.9	371.6
2011	368.8	368.6	368.5	369.1	369.8	372.4	374.1	374.1	371.3	373.1	372.0	372.8	371.2
2012	368.7	369.3	370.1	371.8	373.4	377.1	378.0	378.6	376.2	375.7	375.4	377.2	374.3
2013	373.8	374.1	374.3	376.7	377.3	381.1	380.9	380.4	377.9	378.1	377.3	378.0	377.5
2014	373.9	373.3	373.5	373.8	375.6	378.5	379.6	380.7	376.5	377.6	376.8	378.1	376.5
2015	375.0	374.9	374.9	378.6	380.7	384.7	385.7	385.7	381.2	382.4	381.7	382.7	380.7
2016	378.7	379.1	379.4	382.1	383.0	386.3	389.0	389.3	385.7	387.6	387.1	388.1	384.6
2017	385.8	386.1	386.8	388.7	389.6	394.5	396.0	395.8	391.5	394.1	392.4	391.8	391.1
Professional and Business Services													
2007	827.3	829.6	839.2	858.5	864.5	874.8	877.0	881.8	876.8	878.6	874.4	871.0	862.8
2008	838.9	841.0	842.7	858.1	861.7	865.9	864.4	866.8	856.9	852.9	842.6	830.7	851.9
2009	789.2	779.9	772.0	777.4	779.6	781.7	779.6	780.7	775.1	781.3	782.2	778.0	779.7
2010	754.1	758.2	760.9	787.3	791.8	801.7	805.1	810.6	807.7	817.2	817.2	815.3	793.9
2011	787.1	790.5	796.6	817.8	818.0	829.2	834.9	840.2	840.4	844.4	843.6	839.2	823.5
2012	816.8	819.5	829.3	848.6	855.1	868.0	867.5	875.1	875.3	874.9	878.5	872.7	856.8
2013	839.0	846.9	853.2	868.9	879.7	890.8	893.1	902.0	898.4	908.6	909.7	906.9	883.1
2014	871.5	877.3	882.4	901.8	911.2	920.5	919.1	926.1	922.3	929.0	929.5	921.6	909.4
2015	885.7	890.6	892.4	914.8	922.6	930.8	937.4	938.2	933.2	945.6	941.7	933.7	922.2
2016	906.2	908.8	910.2	925.5	924.8	933.6	940.9	945.2	945.6	951.6	951.7	940.5	932.1
2017	907.4	910.5	918.8	932.0	940.0	954.7	951.1	955.4	952.8	958.6	958.4	942.5	940.2
Education and Health Services													
2007	764.3	772.4	776.2	777.1	778.0	774.1	768.6	770.2	779.2	787.0	791.8	792.9	777.7
2008	784.1	792.0	793.9	797.4	799.2	794.1	791.2	794.6	803.6	810.6	815.2	815.2	799.3
2009	804.7	812.4	816.2	814.3	816.1	811.2	806.6	805.1	813.4	822.3	826.3	826.8	814.6
2010	816.7	824.4	828.9	829.8	832.6	827.3	820.0	820.9	832.0	842.4	847.3	847.5	830.8
2011	836.5	844.0	849.2	847.9	848.7	843.4	834.8	836.6	850.0	856.3	859.6	862.9	847.5
2012	851.6	860.9	864.9	863.4	863.1	860.2	849.9	853.4	865.6	869.0	872.4	873.4	862.3
2013	865.5	875.3	880.2	875.2	875.6	868.1	858.1	865.2	875.3	881.5	885.6	886.9	874.4
2014	874.9	883.7	887.7	889.1	889.1	880.2	871.1	874.5	883.2	892.8	896.7	898.7	885.1
2015	884.9	891.3	895.4	901.4	904.7	896.0	890.6	891.0	900.0	910.1	913.2	913.6	899.4
2016	903.1	910.6	912.3	918.2	920.0	910.8	904.8	905.8	914.6	922.3	924.8	923.1	914.2
2017	913.3	922.5	926.7	927.7	929.5	919.0	910.0	912.2	922.4	936.6	936.8	928.8	923.8

1. Employment by Industry: Illinois, Selected Years, 2007–2017—*Continued*

(Numbers in thousands, not seasonally adjusted)

Industry and year	January	February	March	April	May	June	July	August	September	October	November	December	Annual average
Leisure and Hospitality													
2007	500.7	499.2	509.4	526.6	544.6	555.9	553.7	556.0	544.6	534.9	527.6	524.7	531.5
2008	504.7	503.5	513.1	532.8	548.8	559.7	556.7	557.6	543.9	533.3	521.1	517.0	532.7
2009	493.4	491.4	499.5	515.1	532.4	541.3	538.0	537.1	527.9	514.9	506.0	502.7	516.6
2010	482.1	483.2	492.6	511.5	527.8	538.5	536.4	538.9	530.0	520.2	513.1	509.9	515.4
2011	488.4	487.5	500.0	519.5	534.1	543.8	542.2	549.0	538.2	527.6	520.5	516.0	522.2
2012	501.0	502.9	515.8	532.4	548.4	558.3	557.1	564.0	549.3	540.1	532.7	531.3	536.1
2013	513.2	513.3	524.0	540.9	559.3	570.4	570.8	573.0	559.0	549.6	539.8	538.0	545.9
2014	524.1	524.4	534.1	554.6	572.9	583.2	580.7	583.2	569.2	565.0	554.8	551.9	558.2
2015	533.6	537.7	547.0	571.1	593.3	604.8	602.4	604.9	593.2	589.4	580.5	581.2	578.3
2016	561.1	561.5	571.0	594.1	610.3	621.5	620.9	622.2	609.6	604.1	597.7	587.4	596.8
2017	572.6	575.7	588.4	605.0	624.8	637.1	634.2	638.0	619.6	615.6	605.4	599.6	609.7
Other Services													
2007	255.3	255.4	258.4	258.0	260.1	265.9	269.5	269.7	260.0	260.1	260.4	261.6	261.2
2008	258.1	258.7	260.3	260.6	262.8	268.1	273.5	273.1	262.2	262.5	261.6	261.6	263.6
2009	255.5	255.6	257.0	256.4	258.0	262.7	265.1	264.2	254.2	255.3	254.9	255.9	257.9
2010	251.1	251.0	252.9	246.9	248.1	249.9	248.6	248.6	247.0	248.4	248.2	249.0	249.1
2011	245.2	245.5	247.4	249.4	251.4	253.7	252.7	252.0	250.3	249.6	248.4	250.2	249.7
2012	246.5	247.3	249.1	248.6	250.8	254.1	252.2	251.1	249.7	248.8	248.9	249.3	249.7
2013	245.7	246.6	248.0	248.3	250.1	252.4	253.3	253.6	251.0	249.7	249.2	250.3	249.9
2014	247.5	248.4	250.6	251.6	254.2	257.2	256.4	254.1	251.2	252.2	251.4	251.8	252.2
2015	248.3	249.4	251.3	251.6	253.1	255.7	254.5	253.6	251.3	251.8	251.7	252.2	252.0
2016	248.7	249.4	250.3	251.1	252.2	253.6	253.6	253.4	250.5	251.4	250.8	251.4	251.4
2017	248.6	248.6	250.6	251.4	252.6	255.6	255.1	254.6	251.4	252.0	250.1	251.1	251.8
Government													
2007	835.0	856.8	859.4	862.0	863.5	844.9	819.5	814.6	851.1	861.0	864.8	858.6	849.3
2008	841.6	864.3	865.0	867.7	871.2	850.7	826.2	818.6	855.1	870.0	870.3	866.5	855.6
2009	844.4	864.5	865.9	876.2	876.3	853.1	828.5	815.7	858.7	870.5	872.5	865.0	857.6
2010	844.2	866.4	866.1	871.8	886.0	854.2	818.3	817.4	849.6	858.5	859.8	852.7	853.8
2011	829.2	850.2	851.1	856.2	854.3	833.3	810.3	800.7	835.6	844.2	847.2	842.2	837.9
2012	819.2	839.9	843.0	846.8	846.6	826.1	798.7	794.2	837.1	845.8	848.2	843.2	832.4
2013	820.3	841.4	841.8	844.0	847.1	825.5	799.1	792.2	834.6	836.5	839.6	837.0	829.9
2014	810.5	828.9	831.3	840.2	842.7	823.0	798.4	792.1	835.7	842.5	842.1	841.5	827.4
2015	813.7	835.1	836.4	841.9	843.1	823.5	799.2	792.3	835.7	844.0	841.5	842.5	829.1
2016	815.3	833.2	837.7	839.2	838.1	827.1	801.2	793.4	840.7	839.0	840.4	846.7	829.3
2017	814.3	833.5	836.5	836.4	836.4	829.4	803.3	795.6	840.6	849.7	850.9	846.2	831.1

2. Average Weekly Hours by Selected Industry: Illinois, 2013–2017

(Not seasonally adjusted)

Industry and year	January	February	March	April	May	June	July	August	September	October	November	December	Annual average
Total Private													
2013	33.9	34.2	34.3	34.3	34.3	34.8	34.3	34.5	34.9	34.6	34.6	35.0	34.5
2014	34.0	34.6	34.6	34.3	34.3	34.8	34.2	34.4	34.3	34.4	34.9	34.3	34.4
2015	33.9	34.5	34.4	34.1	34.2	34.3	34.2	34.8	34.2	34.4	34.7	34.3	34.3
2016	33.9	33.8	33.9	33.9	34.3	34.2	34.1	34.0	34.2	34.6	34.1	34.0	34.1
2017	33.9	33.7	33.7	34.1	33.9	34.2	34.5	34.3	34.3	34.6	34.4	34.3	34.2
Goods-Producing													
2013	38.9	38.9	39.4	39.3	39.3	39.9	39.6	40.3	40.4	40.2	39.9	40.5	39.7
2014	39.4	39.5	39.2	39.5	39.5	39.9	39.8	40.0	39.6	39.8	40.2	40.2	39.7
2015	39.5	39.6	39.7	39.7	39.9	39.8	39.5	40.1	39.0	39.4	39.5	39.8	39.6
2016	39.3	39.0	39.3	39.4	39.7	39.9	39.6	39.5	39.6	40.0	39.9	39.1	39.5
2017	38.7	38.9	38.8	38.8	39.6	39.9	39.5	40.2	40.0	39.7	40.1	40.0	39.5
Construction													
2013	36.1	35.8	36.0	35.5	37.7	37.9	37.3	38.0	38.1	38.0	36.9	36.9	37.1
2014	35.5	36.9	36.6	37.6	37.1	38.2	38.8	38.6	37.1	37.6	38.0	37.7	37.5
2015	36.7	36.3	36.7	37.1	37.2	37.8	37.6	38.6	35.7	36.5	35.4	35.7	36.8
2016	33.8	34.3	35.0	36.2	36.3	37.0	36.9	37.2	37.2	38.1	37.7	36.3	36.4
2017	35.6	36.2	36.0	36.5	37.6	38.2	36.8	38.2	38.0	37.0	37.2	36.9	37.1
Manufacturing													
2013	40.1	40.1	40.7	40.7	40.5	41.0	40.8	41.4	41.4	41.2	41.2	41.9	40.9
2014	40.9	41.3	41.0	41.0	41.1	41.1	40.6	40.9	40.9	40.9	41.3	41.3	41.0
2015	40.6	40.8	40.9	40.8	41.1	40.8	40.4	40.8	40.6	39.5	40.2	40.6	40.6
2016	40.7	40.2	40.5	40.2	40.6	40.9	40.6	40.3	40.5	40.7	40.8	40.2	40.5
2017	39.8	39.8	39.8	39.6	40.4	40.5	40.6	41.0	40.9	41.0	41.4	41.4	40.5
Trade, Transportation, and Utilities													
2013	34.3	34.7	35.0	34.8	35.2	35.2	35.0	35.0	35.4	35.3	34.9	35.6	35.0
2014	34.4	35.0	35.1	35.0	34.9	35.4	35.0	35.0	35.1	34.9	35.3	35.1	35.0
2015	34.3	34.8	34.5	34.2	34.4	34.4	34.5	34.8	34.7	34.8	35.0	34.7	34.6
2016	34.0	34.0	34.1	34.1	34.4	34.4	34.3	34.3	34.6	34.8	34.1	34.3	34.3
2017	33.6	33.8	33.9	34.7	34.3	34.7	35.1	34.6	34.9	35.2	35.0	35.2	34.6
Information													
2013	36.6	36.7	36.8	37.0	36.9	37.5	37.4	37.2	37.7	36.6	36.5	37.2	37.0
2014	36.9	37.6	37.7	36.6	36.3	36.9	36.4	36.0	36.5	36.2	36.9	36.0	36.7
2015	36.2	36.7	36.6	36.1	35.8	36.4	36.4	36.6	35.9	35.6	36.3	35.5	36.2
2016	35.7	35.2	35.3	35.2	35.5	35.0	35.2	35.1	35.3	35.6	35.2	35.3	35.3
2017	35.8	34.5	34.9	36.1	35.2	35.2	36.1	35.6	36.3	37.4	36.7	36.3	35.8
Financial Activities													
2013	35.9	36.5	36.5	36.6	36.2	37.1	35.6	35.7	37.3	36.1	36.1	37.1	36.4
2014	36.3	37.4	37.2	36.1	36.2	37.1	35.1	35.5	35.5	35.7	36.0	34.6	36.1
2015	35.1	36.4	36.3	35.4	35.6	35.8	35.7	36.9	36.0	35.9	36.3	35.4	35.9
2016	35.4	35.5	35.4	35.6	36.6	35.9	36.1	35.8	36.1	37.3	36.2	36.3	36.0
2017	37.1	36.1	36.0	37.0	35.7	36.1	38.2	37.1	36.7	37.6	36.7	36.4	36.7
Professional and Business Services													
2013	35.7	36.0	36.0	35.9	35.7	36.5	35.6	35.8	36.4	36.1	36.2	36.6	36.0
2014	35.6	36.6	36.4	36.0	35.9	36.6	35.8	36.0	35.7	36.0	36.7	35.5	36.1
2015	35.3	36.4	35.9	35.7	35.7	36.1	35.9	36.9	35.6	36.8	37.3	36.4	36.2
2016	35.8	35.6	35.9	36.1	36.6	36.2	36.2	36.0	36.1	37.0	36.0	35.7	36.1
2017	36.3	36.0	35.6	36.0	35.9	36.2	36.2	36.1	35.9	36.5	36.0	35.8	36.0
Education and Health Services													
2013	32.7	32.7	32.6	32.5	32.6	33.1	32.9	32.6	33.0	32.6	33.0	32.8	32.8
2014	32.5	32.8	32.7	32.3	32.4	32.8	32.6	32.5	32.4	32.4	33.1	32.5	32.6
2015	32.4	32.4	32.5	32.3	32.3	32.3	32.3	32.6	32.4	32.2	32.6	32.3	32.4
2016	32.2	32.2	32.1	32.0	32.2	32.1	32.1	31.9	32.1	32.2	32.1	32.1	32.1
2017	32.4	31.8	31.7	32.0	31.6	31.7	32.2	31.9	31.8	31.9	32.1	31.9	31.9
Leisure and Hospitality													
2013	24.5	24.9	25.4	25.4	25.8	26.3	25.7	26.0	25.9	26.0	25.8	25.9	25.6
2014	24.5	25.5	25.9	25.7	26.0	25.8	25.5	25.7	25.7	25.6	25.9	25.7	25.6
2015	24.6	25.6	25.9	25.6	26.0	26.1	26.1	26.4	26.2	26.1	25.8	25.8	25.9
2016	24.9	25.3	25.4	25.5	25.9	25.7	25.7	25.7	25.5	25.8	25.7	25.1	25.5
2017	24.8	25.0	25.3	25.6	25.6	25.9	25.8	25.8	25.8	26.1	25.6	25.8	25.6
Other Services													
2013	30.8	31.0	30.8	31.3	31.4	32.4	31.7	31.9	32.2	31.4	31.7	32.5	31.6
2014	30.8	31.3	31.4	31.0	31.4	31.9	31.0	31.4	31.6	31.9	32.5	31.7	31.5
2015	32.1	32.8	33.3	32.5	32.3	32.2	32.4	33.3	32.7	32.7	33.7	32.5	32.7
2016	32.6	31.8	32.1	32.0	32.4	32.3	32.7	32.3	32.6	33.5	32.9	33.1	32.5
2017	33.1	32.8	32.4	32.8	32.4	32.5	32.9	32.4	32.1	31.9	31.6	31.7	32.4

3. Average Hourly Earnings by Selected Industry: Illinois, 2013–2017

(Dollars, not seasonally adjusted)

Industry and year	January	February	March	April	May	June	July	August	September	October	November	December	Annual average
Total Private													
2013	24.69	24.74	24.67	24.77	24.72	24.85	24.82	24.73	25.05	24.80	24.92	25.07	24.82
2014	25.05	25.33	25.41	25.24	25.25	25.33	25.25	25.42	25.47	25.51	25.89	25.64	25.40
2015	25.74	26.12	25.98	25.77	25.71	25.61	25.76	26.01	25.95	26.23	26.54	26.30	25.98
2016	26.56	26.45	26.47	26.52	26.68	26.27	26.42	26.53	26.63	26.97	26.68	26.64	26.57
2017	26.95	26.66	26.61	26.92	26.53	26.48	26.88	26.58	26.93	27.14	26.99	27.09	26.81
Goods-Producing													
2013	26.34	26.44	26.32	26.23	26.55	26.72	26.82	26.74	26.87	26.87	27.06	26.79	26.65
2014	26.44	26.48	26.53	26.72	27.05	27.34	27.62	27.86	27.91	28.11	28.08	27.99	27.36
2015	27.79	27.96	27.95	27.86	28.08	28.25	28.72	28.88	28.59	29.74	29.83	29.72	28.62
2016	28.98	28.83	28.91	29.20	29.29	29.02	29.21	29.29	29.16	29.26	28.80	28.78	29.06
2017	28.38	28.39	28.50	28.40	28.52	28.85	29.10	29.02	29.48	29.08	29.23	29.20	28.86
Construction													
2013	33.81	34.46	34.02	33.82	33.49	33.73	34.45	34.11	34.23	34.32	34.63	34.15	34.11
2014	33.66	34.27	33.98	33.87	34.03	34.32	34.50	34.80	35.56	35.54	35.57	35.90	34.72
2015	35.05	36.03	36.21	35.96	36.15	36.19	36.69	36.90	36.33	36.30	37.06	37.47	36.39
2016	36.16	36.09	36.44	36.35	36.66	36.46	36.83	36.88	37.03	37.06	36.96	37.25	36.71
2017	36.73	36.55	36.90	35.58	35.92	35.90	36.40	36.55	37.64	36.54	37.39	37.59	36.64
Manufacturing													
2013	24.60	24.52	24.42	24.28	24.47	24.47	24.28	24.23	24.41	24.38	24.65	24.68	24.45
2014	24.56	24.40	24.49	24.53	24.83	24.90	25.04	25.25	25.16	25.38	25.35	25.28	24.93
2015	25.52	25.50	25.31	25.06	25.15	25.23	25.59	25.59	25.60	26.52	26.55	26.38	25.66
2016	26.29	26.11	25.93	26.10	26.06	25.56	25.64	25.65	25.41	25.55	25.08	25.32	25.72
2017	25.19	25.14	25.08	25.29	25.10	25.45	25.71	25.37	25.56	25.68	25.58	25.75	25.41
Trade, Transportation, and Utilities													
2013	22.39	22.29	22.38	22.88	22.56	22.73	22.74	22.48	22.54	22.67	22.46	22.63	22.56
2014	22.75	23.00	23.22	23.08	23.13	23.04	22.84	22.88	22.97	22.95	23.22	22.87	23.00
2015	23.23	23.35	23.27	23.38	23.30	23.18	23.29	23.60	23.56	23.19	23.46	23.10	23.33
2016	23.55	23.24	23.29	23.53	23.72	23.41	23.50	23.43	23.60	23.86	23.64	23.37	23.51
2017	23.87	23.36	23.39	23.71	23.53	23.45	23.87	23.61	23.86	24.06	24.03	23.80	23.72
Information													
2013	28.45	28.73	28.84	29.45	29.58	30.38	29.84	29.93	30.51	30.50	30.74	30.47	29.79
2014	29.77	31.32	31.81	31.59	31.42	31.69	31.63	31.61	31.60	31.63	32.15	31.42	31.47
2015	31.23	31.92	32.24	31.57	31.80	31.38	31.63	32.46	31.68	31.93	32.31	31.93	31.84
2016	31.80	32.08	32.06	31.88	32.18	31.40	31.72	31.98	32.03	32.74	32.11	31.84	31.99
2017	33.14	32.76	32.69	33.75	32.68	33.41	34.81	32.96	33.24	34.62	33.89	34.91	33.58
Financial Activities													
2013	29.97	30.67	30.15	30.46	30.49	30.22	30.47	30.70	31.08	30.64	31.38	31.55	30.65
2014	31.73	32.63	32.47	32.38	32.42	31.84	32.02	33.09	33.29	33.14	34.67	34.16	32.81
2015	34.01	35.34	35.67	34.95	34.25	33.61	33.71	34.32	34.56	34.81	35.54	34.88	34.64
2016	36.06	36.27	36.20	36.47	37.20	35.78	36.58	37.48	37.61	38.30	37.78	37.44	36.94
2017	38.62	37.54	38.40	39.57	38.44	37.74	37.50	36.91	37.42	38.09	37.65	37.73	37.96
Professional and Business Services													
2013	28.74	28.80	28.65	28.42	28.53	28.72	28.34	28.08	28.70	27.77	28.31	28.61	28.47
2014	28.66	29.21	29.39	28.57	28.63	28.86	28.48	28.31	28.51	28.34	29.22	28.68	28.74
2015	28.98	29.91	29.49	28.91	28.79	28.60	28.70	28.89	28.91	28.59	29.27	28.94	28.99
2016	29.82	29.59	29.70	29.69	29.83	29.33	29.32	29.47	29.60	30.15	30.00	30.11	29.72
2017	30.58	30.32	30.10	30.65	29.58	29.57	30.51	29.62	30.20	30.68	30.09	30.54	30.20
Education and Health Services													
2013	24.50	24.44	24.59	24.68	24.61	24.81	24.97	24.84	25.00	25.04	25.10	25.26	24.82
2014	24.97	24.78	24.97	25.16	24.89	24.84	24.83	25.03	24.63	24.68	24.61	24.88	24.85
2015	24.61	24.63	24.64	24.52	24.61	24.61	24.54	24.57	24.76	25.64	25.65	25.56	24.87
2016	25.43	25.58	25.54	25.01	25.04	24.91	25.06	25.12	25.09	25.21	25.11	25.08	25.18
2017	25.16	25.32	24.89	25.06	25.08	24.94	25.18	25.26	25.27	25.40	25.43	25.81	25.23
Leisure and Hospitality													
2013	12.60	12.51	12.63	12.72	12.79	12.61	12.53	13.02	13.14	12.43	11.97	12.55	12.63
2014	12.58	12.82	12.77	12.88	13.02	13.18	13.27	13.38	13.54	13.73	13.94	14.09	13.28
2015	13.93	14.03	13.85	13.94	13.99	13.97	14.11	14.13	14.18	14.24	14.35	14.51	14.11
2016	14.43	14.47	14.57	14.61	14.71	14.70	14.64	14.69	14.84	15.02	15.02	15.64	14.78
2017	15.03	15.10	15.13	15.21	15.47	15.22	15.09	15.21	15.46	15.45	15.49	15.71	15.30
Other Services													
2013	23.83	23.76	23.77	23.56	23.43	23.69	23.58	23.57	24.36	24.02	23.52	24.00	23.76
2014	24.15	24.57	24.48	24.42	24.39	24.61	24.38	24.81	25.10	25.20	25.50	25.39	24.75
2015	25.35	25.64	25.15	25.06	25.22	25.09	25.04	25.64	25.40	25.85	25.97	26.48	25.53
2016	26.43	26.55	26.26	26.94	27.26	26.48	26.17	26.37	26.69	27.06	26.39	26.23	26.57
2017	26.44	25.98	26.10	26.03	25.31	25.09	25.18	25.51	26.23	26.56	26.28	26.51	25.93

4. Average Weekly Earnings by Selected Industry: Illinois, 2013–2017

(Dollars, not seasonally adjusted)

Industry and year	January	February	March	April	May	June	July	August	September	October	November	December	Annual average
Total Private													
2013	836.99	846.11	846.18	849.61	847.90	864.78	851.33	853.19	874.25	858.08	862.23	877.45	856.29
2014	851.70	876.42	879.19	865.73	866.08	881.48	863.55	874.45	873.62	877.54	903.56	879.45	873.76
2015	872.59	901.14	893.71	878.76	879.28	878.42	880.99	905.15	887.49	902.31	920.94	902.09	891.11
2016	900.38	894.01	897.33	899.03	915.12	898.43	900.92	902.02	910.75	933.16	909.79	905.76	906.04
2017	913.61	898.44	896.76	917.97	899.37	905.62	927.36	911.69	923.70	939.04	928.46	929.19	916.90
Goods-Producing													
2013	1,024.63	1,028.52	1,037.01	1,030.84	1,043.42	1,066.13	1,062.07	1,077.62	1,085.55	1,080.17	1,079.69	1,085.00	1,058.01
2014	1,041.74	1,045.96	1,039.98	1,055.44	1,068.48	1,090.87	1,099.28	1,114.40	1,105.24	1,118.78	1,128.82	1,125.20	1,086.19
2015	1,097.71	1,107.22	1,109.62	1,106.04	1,120.39	1,124.35	1,134.44	1,158.09	1,115.01	1,171.76	1,178.29	1,182.86	1,133.35
2016	1,138.91	1,124.37	1,136.16	1,150.48	1,162.81	1,157.90	1,156.72	1,156.96	1,154.74	1,170.40	1,149.12	1,125.30	1,147.87
2017	1,098.31	1,104.37	1,105.80	1,101.92	1,129.39	1,151.12	1,149.45	1,166.60	1,179.20	1,154.48	1,172.12	1,168.00	1,139.97
Construction													
2013	1,220.54	1,233.67	1,224.72	1,200.61	1,262.57	1,278.37	1,284.99	1,296.18	1,304.16	1,304.16	1,277.85	1,260.14	1,265.48
2014	1,194.93	1,264.56	1,243.67	1,273.51	1,262.51	1,311.02	1,338.60	1,343.28	1,319.28	1,336.30	1,351.66	1,353.43	1,302.00
2015	1,286.34	1,307.89	1,328.91	1,334.12	1,344.78	1,367.98	1,379.54	1,424.34	1,296.98	1,324.95	1,311.92	1,337.68	1,339.15
2016	1,222.21	1,237.89	1,275.40	1,315.87	1,330.76	1,349.02	1,359.03	1,371.94	1,377.52	1,411.99	1,393.39	1,352.18	1,336.24
2017	1,307.59	1,323.11	1,328.40	1,298.67	1,350.59	1,371.38	1,339.52	1,396.21	1,430.32	1,351.98	1,390.91	1,387.07	1,359.34
Manufacturing													
2013	986.46	983.25	993.89	988.20	991.04	1,003.27	990.62	1,003.12	1,010.57	1,004.46	1,015.58	1,034.09	1,000.01
2014	1,004.50	1,007.72	1,004.09	1,005.73	1,020.51	1,023.39	1,016.62	1,032.73	1,029.04	1,038.04	1,046.96	1,044.06	1,022.13
2015	1,036.11	1,040.40	1,035.18	1,022.45	1,033.67	1,029.38	1,033.84	1,044.07	1,039.36	1,047.54	1,067.31	1,071.03	1,041.80
2016	1,070.00	1,049.62	1,050.17	1,049.22	1,058.04	1,045.40	1,040.98	1,033.70	1,029.11	1,039.89	1,023.26	1,017.86	1,041.66
2017	1,002.56	1,000.57	998.18	1,001.48	1,014.04	1,030.73	1,043.83	1,040.17	1,045.40	1,052.88	1,059.01	1,066.05	1,029.11
Trade, Transportation, and Utilities													
2013	767.98	773.46	783.30	796.22	794.11	800.10	795.90	786.80	797.92	800.25	783.85	805.63	789.60
2014	782.60	805.00	815.02	807.80	807.24	815.62	799.40	800.80	806.25	800.96	819.67	802.74	805.00
2015	796.79	812.58	802.82	799.60	801.52	797.39	803.51	821.28	817.53	807.01	821.10	801.57	807.22
2016	800.70	790.16	794.19	802.37	815.97	805.30	806.05	803.65	816.56	830.33	806.12	801.59	806.39
2017	802.03	789.57	792.92	822.74	807.08	813.72	837.84	816.91	832.71	846.91	841.05	837.76	820.71
Information													
2013	1,041.27	1,054.39	1,061.31	1,089.65	1,091.50	1,139.25	1,116.02	1,113.40	1,150.23	1,116.30	1,122.01	1,133.48	1,102.23
2014	1,098.51	1,177.63	1,199.24	1,156.19	1,140.55	1,169.36	1,151.33	1,137.96	1,153.40	1,145.01	1,186.34	1,131.12	1,154.95
2015	1,130.53	1,171.46	1,179.98	1,139.68	1,138.44	1,142.23	1,151.33	1,188.04	1,137.31	1,136.71	1,172.85	1,133.52	1,152.61
2016	1,135.26	1,129.22	1,131.72	1,122.18	1,142.39	1,099.00	1,116.54	1,122.50	1,130.66	1,165.54	1,130.27	1,123.95	1,129.25
2017	1,186.41	1,130.22	1,140.88	1,218.38	1,150.34	1,176.03	1,256.64	1,173.38	1,206.61	1,294.79	1,243.76	1,267.23	1,202.16
Financial Activities													
2013	1,075.92	1,119.46	1,100.48	1,114.84	1,103.74	1,121.16	1,084.73	1,095.99	1,159.28	1,106.10	1,132.82	1,170.51	1,115.66
2014	1,151.80	1,220.36	1,207.88	1,168.92	1,173.60	1,181.26	1,123.90	1,174.70	1,181.80	1,183.10	1,248.12	1,181.94	1,184.44
2015	1,193.75	1,286.38	1,294.82	1,237.23	1,219.30	1,203.24	1,203.45	1,266.41	1,244.16	1,249.68	1,290.10	1,234.75	1,243.58
2016	1,276.52	1,287.59	1,281.48	1,298.33	1,361.52	1,284.50	1,320.54	1,341.78	1,357.72	1,428.59	1,367.64	1,359.07	1,329.84
2017	1,432.80	1,355.19	1,382.40	1,464.09	1,372.31	1,362.41	1,432.50	1,369.36	1,373.31	1,432.18	1,381.76	1,373.37	1,393.13
Professional and Business Services													
2013	1,026.02	1,036.80	1,031.40	1,020.28	1,018.52	1,048.28	1,008.90	1,005.26	1,044.68	1,002.50	1,024.82	1,047.13	1,024.92
2014	1,020.30	1,069.09	1,069.80	1,028.52	1,027.82	1,056.28	1,019.58	1,019.16	1,017.81	1,020.24	1,072.37	1,018.14	1,037.51
2015	1,022.99	1,088.72	1,058.69	1,032.09	1,027.80	1,032.46	1,030.33	1,066.04	1,029.20	1,052.11	1,091.77	1,053.42	1,049.44
2016	1,067.56	1,053.40	1,066.23	1,071.81	1,091.78	1,061.75	1,061.38	1,060.92	1,068.56	1,115.55	1,080.00	1,074.93	1,072.89
2017	1,110.05	1,091.52	1,071.56	1,103.40	1,061.92	1,070.43	1,104.46	1,069.28	1,084.18	1,119.82	1,083.24	1,093.33	1,087.20
Education and Health Services													
2013	801.15	799.19	801.63	802.10	802.29	821.21	821.51	809.78	825.00	816.30	828.30	828.53	814.10
2014	811.53	812.78	816.52	812.67	806.44	814.75	809.46	813.48	798.01	799.63	814.59	808.60	810.11
2015	797.36	798.01	800.80	792.00	794.90	794.90	792.64	800.98	802.22	825.61	836.19	825.59	805.79
2016	818.85	823.68	819.83	800.32	806.29	799.61	804.43	801.33	805.39	811.76	806.03	805.07	808.28
2017	815.18	805.18	789.01	801.92	792.53	790.60	810.80	805.79	803.59	810.26	816.30	823.34	804.84
Leisure and Hospitality													
2013	308.70	311.50	320.80	323.09	329.98	331.64	322.02	338.52	340.33	323.18	308.83	325.05	323.33
2014	308.21	326.91	330.74	331.02	338.52	340.04	338.39	343.87	347.98	351.49	361.05	362.11	339.97
2015	342.68	359.17	358.72	356.86	363.74	364.62	368.27	373.03	371.52	371.66	370.23	374.36	365.45
2016	359.31	366.09	370.08	372.56	380.99	377.79	376.25	377.53	378.42	387.52	386.01	392.56	376.89
2017	372.74	377.50	382.79	389.38	396.03	394.20	389.32	392.42	398.87	403.25	396.54	405.32	391.68
Other Services													
2013	733.96	736.56	732.12	737.43	735.70	767.56	747.49	751.88	784.39	754.23	745.58	780.00	750.82
2014	743.82	769.04	768.67	757.02	765.85	785.06	755.78	779.03	793.16	803.88	828.75	804.86	779.63
2015	813.74	840.99	837.50	814.45	814.61	807.90	811.30	853.81	830.58	845.30	875.19	860.60	833.52
2016	861.62	844.29	842.95	862.08	883.22	855.30	855.76	851.75	870.09	906.51	868.23	868.21	863.53
2017	875.16	852.14	845.64	853.78	820.04	815.43	828.42	826.52	841.98	847.26	830.45	840.37	840.13

INDIANA
At a Glance

Population:
  2010 census: 6,483,802
  2017 estimate: 6,666,818

Percent change in population:
  2010–2017: 2.8%

Percent change in total nonfarm employment:
  2007–2017: 3.8%

Industry with the largest growth in employment, 2007–2017 (thousands):
  Education and health services, 73.6

Industry with the largest decline or smallest growth in employment, 2007–2017 (thousands):
  Manufacturing, -18.3

Civilian labor force:
  2010: 3,175,192
  2017: 3,320,409

Unemployment rate and rank among states (highest to lowest):
  2010: 10.4%, 11th
  2017: 3.5%, 38th

Over-the-year change in unemployment rates:
  2015–2016: -0.4%
  2016–2017: -0.9%

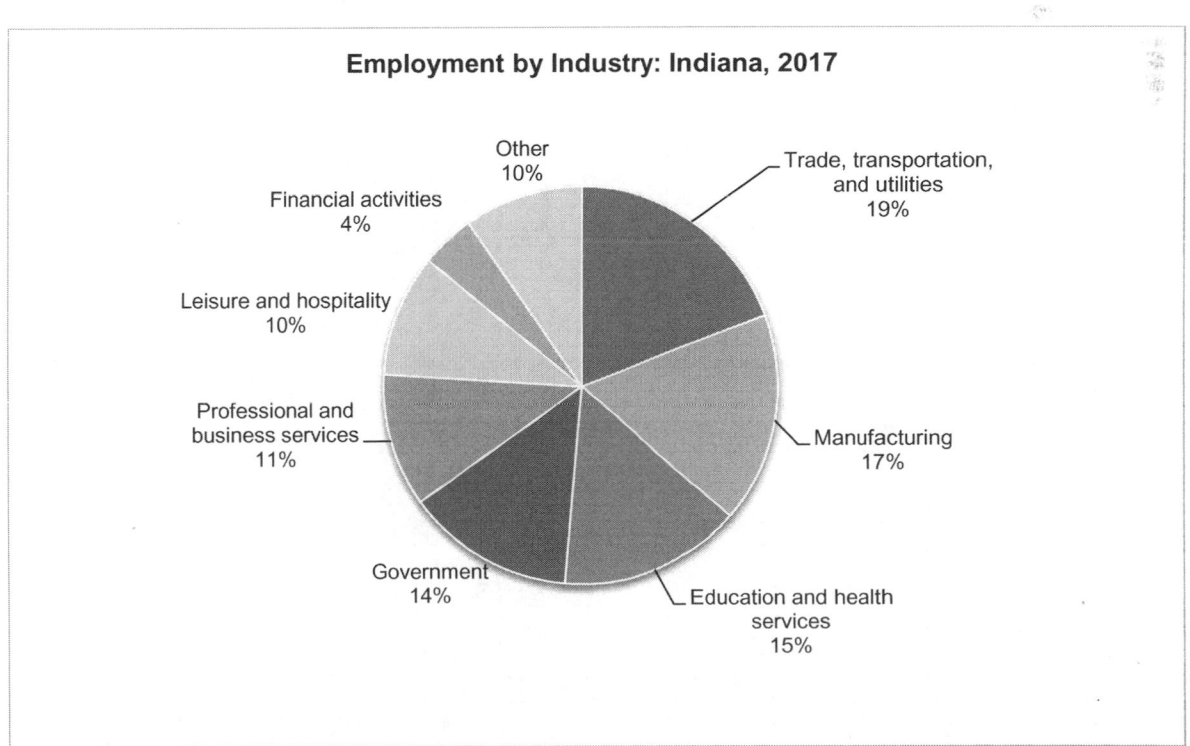

Employment by Industry: Indiana, 2017

- Other 10%
- Financial activities 4%
- Leisure and hospitality 10%
- Professional and business services 11%
- Government 14%
- Education and health services 15%
- Manufacturing 17%
- Trade, transportation, and utilities 19%

1. Employment by Industry: Indiana, Selected Years, 2007–2017

(Numbers in thousands, not seasonally adjusted)

Industry and year	January	February	March	April	May	June	July	August	September	October	November	December	Annual average
Total Nonfarm													
2007	2,927.2	2,930.3	2,971.1	2,995.0	3,016.3	3,006.5	2,955.5	2,990.5	3,024.2	3,027.8	3,032.5	3,021.6	2,991.5
2008	2,931.3	2,942.2	2,956.0	2,981.7	3,010.4	2,986.7	2,930.6	2,967.8	2,986.6	2,978.5	2,956.3	2,925.2	2,962.8
2009	2,800.2	2,792.1	2,798.0	2,805.4	2,814.6	2,772.7	2,717.9	2,761.6	2,804.4	2,812.8	2,812.9	2,804.4	2,791.4
2010	2,721.8	2,729.9	2,761.7	2,805.3	2,833.1	2,803.8	2,775.2	2,806.5	2,829.2	2,841.6	2,840.9	2,833.7	2,798.6
2011	2,765.1	2,776.3	2,808.5	2,849.4	2,873.4	2,838.1	2,808.2	2,844.4	2,889.6	2,892.3	2,893.5	2,895.6	2,844.5
2012	2,826.0	2,846.4	2,874.6	2,901.3	2,924.5	2,903.0	2,849.6	2,910.7	2,942.9	2,944.5	2,949.9	2,945.3	2,901.6
2013	2,859.8	2,887.7	2,907.4	2,934.6	2,947.6	2,932.1	2,880.6	2,950.7	2,970.7	2,978.9	3,002.6	2,997.5	2,937.5
2014	2,885.2	2,913.2	2,941.7	2,978.3	3,006.4	2,988.9	2,933.0	2,987.0	3,008.3	3,022.3	3,039.3	3,043.1	2,978.9
2015	2,954.5	2,971.0	2,993.6	3,029.9	3,056.3	3,043.5	2,990.9	3,038.5	3,065.8	3,076.4	3,090.2	3,094.0	3,033.7
2016	3,005.2	3,027.8	3,048.9	3,075.2	3,090.0	3,068.0	3,035.5	3,077.4	3,112.1	3,109.0	3,122.2	3,114.6	3,073.8
2017	3,041.8	3,058.9	3,080.6	3,099.9	3,122.3	3,114.1	3,063.8	3,110.9	3,137.1	3,146.3	3,150.0	3,133.9	3,105.0
Total Private													
2007	2,499.2	2,489.7	2,527.1	2,553.8	2,578.6	2,596.5	2,575.6	2,582.1	2,581.0	2,581.1	2,585.3	2,575.0	2,560.4
2008	2,496.5	2,493.2	2,504.5	2,531.8	2,558.5	2,563.9	2,536.0	2,544.8	2,537.9	2,524.3	2,502.0	2,474.4	2,522.3
2009	2,360.6	2,344.2	2,346.5	2,355.0	2,360.2	2,354.6	2,339.4	2,354.1	2,357.4	2,355.1	2,360.2	2,352.6	2,353.3
2010	2,281.7	2,280.7	2,312.5	2,351.7	2,372.7	2,379.3	2,382.5	2,395.0	2,389.4	2,397.8	2,397.9	2,395.6	2,361.4
2011	2,335.7	2,339.2	2,369.5	2,407.0	2,427.0	2,427.2	2,425.2	2,442.1	2,449.7	2,450.5	2,450.1	2,452.1	2,414.6
2012	2,392.5	2,406.6	2,432.5	2,461.7	2,487.7	2,495.4	2,482.9	2,497.3	2,504.2	2,503.1	2,508.8	2,509.2	2,473.5
2013	2,435.1	2,449.8	2,468.9	2,495.6	2,522.4	2,530.7	2,518.5	2,537.3	2,538.3	2,541.0	2,560.7	2,557.1	2,513.0
2014	2,468.4	2,477.6	2,503.9	2,541.2	2,573.4	2,579.5	2,561.5	2,576.6	2,576.0	2,584.7	2,600.1	2,602.5	2,553.8
2015	2,526.3	2,535.9	2,558.1	2,593.6	2,623.1	2,630.1	2,618.9	2,628.7	2,625.5	2,638.2	2,650.1	2,652.4	2,606.7
2016	2,576.5	2,590.3	2,608.9	2,639.4	2,658.2	2,661.6	2,662.8	2,667.3	2,671.7	2,672.6	2,683.4	2,677.2	2,647.5
2017	2,612.5	2,625.1	2,643.5	2,670.1	2,692.6	2,704.0	2,689.7	2,693.2	2,697.6	2,708.3	2,709.1	2,695.5	2,678.4
Goods Producing													
2007	694.3	687.3	699.5	705.6	714.0	721.4	717.6	718.6	714.4	709.6	706.9	700.1	707.4
2008	678.3	675.8	674.8	680.3	688.3	691.9	675.8	681.1	672.1	662.2	648.1	627.9	671.4
2009	588.1	577.7	570.7	569.5	561.9	562.2	561.8	567.6	566.2	563.9	563.0	558.2	567.6
2010	539.6	537.7	547.7	563.7	571.0	578.0	583.9	585.1	581.2	582.1	576.9	573.7	568.4
2011	561.3	561.3	571.6	583.1	589.9	598.2	598.6	603.6	603.6	605.1	598.8	598.0	589.4
2012	587.1	588.8	597.3	606.9	614.8	624.9	625.2	626.4	622.6	622.0	617.3	615.9	612.4
2013	600.0	604.3	608.9	616.1	622.4	631.0	627.2	631.4	627.6	628.9	628.7	624.9	621.0
2014	608.9	610.9	620.1	629.1	637.2	647.9	644.9	649.3	645.7	647.1	647.3	646.2	636.2
2015	631.3	631.2	637.6	645.2	653.4	661.5	661.0	663.1	659.4	659.2	658.9	657.0	651.6
2016	641.4	642.3	647.6	656.3	661.2	669.4	670.7	670.4	668.4	668.4	668.4	665.9	660.9
2017	655.1	657.1	663.0	670.5	677.0	686.0	684.4	683.1	683.5	680.4	678.3	675.7	674.5
Service-Providing													
2007	2,232.9	2,243.0	2,271.6	2,289.4	2,302.3	2,285.1	2,237.9	2,271.9	2,309.8	2,318.2	2,325.6	2,321.5	2,284.1
2008	2,253.0	2,266.4	2,281.2	2,301.4	2,322.1	2,294.8	2,254.8	2,286.7	2,314.5	2,316.3	2,308.2	2,297.3	2,291.4
2009	2,212.1	2,214.4	2,227.3	2,235.9	2,252.7	2,210.5	2,156.1	2,194.0	2,238.2	2,248.9	2,249.9	2,246.2	2,223.9
2010	2,182.2	2,192.2	2,214.0	2,241.6	2,262.1	2,225.8	2,191.3	2,221.4	2,248.0	2,259.5	2,264.0	2,260.0	2,230.2
2011	2,203.8	2,215.0	2,236.9	2,266.3	2,283.5	2,239.9	2,209.6	2,240.8	2,286.0	2,287.2	2,294.7	2,297.6	2,255.1
2012	2,238.9	2,257.6	2,277.3	2,294.4	2,309.7	2,278.1	2,224.4	2,284.3	2,320.3	2,322.5	2,332.6	2,329.4	2,289.1
2013	2,259.8	2,283.4	2,298.5	2,318.5	2,325.2	2,301.1	2,253.4	2,319.3	2,343.1	2,350.0	2,373.9	2,372.6	2,316.6
2014	2,276.3	2,302.3	2,321.6	2,349.2	2,369.2	2,341.0	2,288.1	2,337.7	2,362.6	2,375.2	2,392.0	2,396.9	2,342.7
2015	2,323.2	2,339.8	2,355.9	2,384.7	2,402.9	2,382.0	2,329.9	2,375.4	2,406.4	2,417.2	2,431.3	2,437.0	2,382.1
2016	2,363.8	2,385.5	2,401.3	2,418.9	2,428.8	2,398.6	2,364.8	2,407.0	2,443.7	2,440.6	2,453.8	2,448.7	2,413.0
2017	2,386.7	2,401.8	2,417.6	2,429.4	2,445.3	2,428.1	2,379.4	2,427.8	2,453.6	2,465.9	2,471.7	2,458.2	2,430.5
Mining and Logging													
2007	6.8	6.7	6.9	7.0	7.1	7.1	7.1	7.1	7.1	7.0	6.9	6.8	7.0
2008	6.4	6.4	6.5	6.7	6.8	6.9	6.8	6.9	6.9	6.9	6.8	6.7	6.7
2009	6.3	6.3	6.5	6.6	6.7	6.8	6.8	6.8	6.8	6.7	6.7	6.5	6.6
2010	6.2	6.2	6.4	6.6	6.6	6.6	6.7	6.7	6.8	6.7	6.7	6.6	6.6
2011	6.3	6.4	6.6	6.7	6.8	6.9	6.9	7.0	6.9	7.0	7.0	6.9	6.8
2012	6.8	6.8	6.9	7.0	7.1	7.1	7.1	7.1	7.0	7.0	6.9	6.8	7.0
2013	6.7	6.7	6.7	6.9	7.0	7.1	7.1	7.1	7.2	7.1	7.1	7.1	7.0
2014	6.7	6.6	6.9	7.2	7.3	7.5	7.4	7.4	7.3	7.1	7.2	7.2	7.2
2015	6.9	6.7	6.8	6.9	7.0	7.0	6.9	6.9	6.7	6.7	6.7	6.5	6.8
2016	6.2	6.3	6.2	6.3	6.3	6.3	6.3	6.3	6.3	6.1	5.9	5.9	6.2
2017	5.7	5.7	5.8	6.0	6.0	6.1	6.1	6.1	6.2	6.1	6.1	6.0	6.0

1. Employment by Industry: Indiana, Selected Years, 2007–2017—*Continued*

(Numbers in thousands, not seasonally adjusted)

Industry and year	January	February	March	April	May	June	July	August	September	October	November	December	Annual average
Construction													
2007	138.9	132.4	142.1	149.0	155.6	159.2	159.4	159.5	157.6	156.9	155.7	149.1	151.3
2008	135.5	133.2	137.6	143.6	148.7	151.8	153.2	152.0	150.0	149.2	143.3	133.7	144.3
2009	115.9	113.2	116.6	120.2	123.5	125.6	125.9	124.7	122.9	122.4	120.0	113.5	120.4
2010	100.3	98.3	104.5	115.0	118.3	121.1	126.1	124.7	121.9	123.0	120.9	114.0	115.7
2011	104.2	102.2	108.0	115.9	121.3	124.5	128.4	129.2	129.2	129.3	127.5	122.1	120.2
2012	112.4	111.2	116.9	123.8	127.4	130.9	131.9	132.0	131.5	130.8	127.4	123.7	125.0
2013	111.2	112.2	116.0	122.0	126.0	129.6	130.6	129.2	127.3	128.4	126.8	120.9	123.4
2014	108.2	107.4	113.3	120.2	124.7	129.7	131.6	130.3	128.8	129.5	128.1	124.0	123.0
2015	112.9	112.3	116.5	124.4	129.7	132.4	133.3	134.3	133.0	133.9	132.8	129.7	127.1
2016	117.1	116.5	121.0	129.8	133.3	136.8	138.3	138.3	139.1	139.8	138.4	132.7	131.8
2017	124.2	124.6	129.6	136.4	140.8	143.4	144.6	143.9	144.1	141.7	141.5	136.3	137.6
Manufacturing													
2007	548.6	548.2	550.5	549.6	551.3	555.1	551.1	552.0	549.7	545.7	544.3	544.2	549.2
2008	536.4	536.2	530.7	530.0	532.8	533.2	515.8	522.2	515.2	506.1	498.0	487.5	520.3
2009	465.9	458.2	447.6	442.7	431.7	429.8	429.1	436.1	436.5	434.8	436.3	438.2	440.6
2010	433.1	433.2	436.8	442.1	446.1	450.3	451.1	453.7	452.5	452.4	449.3	453.1	446.1
2011	450.8	452.7	457.0	460.5	461.8	466.8	463.3	467.4	467.5	468.8	464.3	469.0	462.5
2012	467.9	470.8	473.5	476.1	480.3	486.9	486.2	487.3	484.1	484.2	483.0	485.4	480.5
2013	482.1	485.4	486.2	487.2	489.4	494.3	489.5	495.1	493.1	493.4	494.8	496.9	490.6
2014	494.0	496.9	499.9	501.7	505.2	510.7	505.9	511.6	509.6	510.5	512.0	515.0	506.1
2015	511.5	512.2	514.3	513.9	516.7	522.1	520.8	521.9	519.7	518.6	519.4	520.8	517.7
2016	518.1	519.5	520.4	520.2	521.6	526.3	526.1	525.8	523.0	522.5	524.1	527.3	522.9
2017	525.2	526.8	527.6	528.1	530.2	536.5	533.7	533.1	533.2	532.6	530.7	533.4	530.9
Trade, Transportation, and Utilities													
2007	578.8	572.5	579.9	582.0	588.3	592.1	588.3	587.1	585.4	587.4	599.6	602.7	587.0
2008	576.4	571.9	574.4	577.2	583.9	584.9	582.0	583.0	578.9	578.6	582.0	582.4	579.6
2009	553.1	545.7	544.5	545.6	550.3	551.6	547.9	547.1	544.6	545.9	552.8	554.4	548.6
2010	532.3	527.1	532.3	537.6	542.5	544.9	545.5	545.3	542.1	547.9	555.9	558.4	542.7
2011	539.3	536.2	539.5	546.2	551.7	553.7	553.5	554.3	552.2	556.8	565.9	569.1	551.5
2012	549.8	546.1	550.4	554.6	561.1	564.2	562.1	561.5	561.0	564.7	577.4	579.0	561.0
2013	553.8	552.3	554.7	560.1	568.1	572.0	568.9	571.0	569.6	573.1	585.8	589.0	568.2
2014	562.7	559.9	563.4	568.0	574.5	577.1	575.5	576.2	574.1	577.1	588.5	593.3	574.2
2015	569.8	567.1	570.1	574.8	582.4	586.2	585.2	586.9	584.6	590.2	600.5	605.8	583.6
2016	586.0	584.6	587.2	590.2	594.2	595.1	596.6	595.9	595.3	596.9	607.4	610.7	595.0
2017	590.1	587.4	588.6	592.5	595.7	599.3	595.7	596.0	595.0	600.7	611.6	609.8	596.9
Wholesale Trade													
2007	122.8	122.9	124.0	124.7	125.5	126.5	127.4	126.2	125.4	125.5	125.8	125.8	125.2
2008	124.0	124.1	124.6	125.3	126.2	126.4	125.9	125.2	124.2	123.7	122.6	121.7	124.5
2009	117.9	116.8	116.2	115.4	115.7	115.5	115.4	114.1	113.1	113.3	112.9	112.8	114.9
2010	111.3	111.1	112.1	113.1	113.5	113.8	114.5	113.6	113.0	113.2	112.7	112.4	112.9
2011	112.3	112.5	113.3	114.4	115.3	116.0	116.4	115.7	115.1	115.3	115.3	115.2	114.7
2012	114.2	114.3	115.2	115.9	116.9	117.8	117.8	116.8	116.4	116.3	116.0	116.1	116.1
2013	114.3	114.8	115.6	116.4	117.4	118.2	118.1	117.4	116.7	117.0	117.1	117.1	116.7
2014	115.2	115.4	116.1	117.0	118.2	119.0	119.0	118.6	117.8	117.8	118.1	118.4	117.6
2015	117.2	117.5	118.1	118.9	119.8	120.2	119.6	119.1	118.3	118.3	118.2	118.2	118.6
2016	117.2	117.1	117.6	118.2	118.8	119.2	119.1	118.3	117.8	117.8	117.8	118.0	118.1
2017	117.3	117.7	118.1	118.7	119.4	120.8	120.4	120.2	119.5	119.2	118.4	119.2	119.1
Retail Trade													
2007	325.6	319.5	324.0	324.7	329.1	330.7	327.7	326.9	325.4	327.1	338.0	340.5	328.3
2008	321.3	316.8	317.9	319.0	323.7	324.3	323.4	323.5	321.2	321.6	326.4	327.8	322.2
2009	308.4	303.0	303.1	305.6	309.4	311.0	308.4	307.8	305.8	306.3	313.5	315.4	308.1
2010	299.7	294.9	297.8	300.9	304.4	305.9	305.6	305.3	302.0	306.8	314.5	316.9	304.6
2011	302.2	298.1	300.4	304.6	307.8	308.5	307.5	308.3	306.5	310.9	319.1	321.4	307.9
2012	306.9	302.6	305.0	307.8	312.0	313.1	311.8	311.2	310.9	314.6	326.2	326.0	312.3
2013	307.6	305.0	306.1	310.3	315.7	318.2	316.0	317.5	316.1	319.3	330.0	332.3	316.2
2014	312.0	309.6	311.5	315.0	318.8	320.3	319.1	319.7	318.0	320.8	330.4	333.0	319.0
2015	315.5	312.9	314.9	318.6	323.5	325.9	325.6	327.2	325.5	330.0	338.6	340.5	324.9
2016	324.4	324.0	325.7	329.1	331.8	332.9	333.4	332.9	332.3	334.4	342.7	344.0	332.3
2017	330.5	327.5	327.6	330.9	333.0	334.2	331.5	331.3	330.3	334.4	344.2	341.2	333.1

1. Employment by Industry: Indiana, Selected Years, 2007–2017—*Continued*

(Numbers in thousands, not seasonally adjusted)

Industry and year	January	February	March	April	May	June	July	August	September	October	November	December	Annual average
Transportation and Utilities													
2007	130.4	130.1	131.9	132.6	133.7	134.9	133.2	134.0	134.6	134.8	135.8	136.4	133.5
2008	131.1	131.0	131.9	132.9	134.0	134.2	132.7	134.3	133.5	133.3	133.0	132.9	132.9
2009	126.8	125.9	125.2	124.6	125.2	125.1	124.1	125.2	125.7	126.3	126.4	126.2	125.6
2010	121.3	121.1	122.4	123.6	124.6	125.2	125.4	126.4	127.1	127.9	128.7	129.1	125.2
2011	124.8	125.6	125.8	127.2	128.6	129.2	129.6	130.3	130.6	130.6	131.5	132.5	128.9
2012	128.7	129.2	130.2	130.9	132.2	133.3	132.5	133.5	133.7	133.8	135.2	136.9	132.5
2013	131.9	132.5	133.0	133.4	135.0	135.6	134.8	136.1	136.8	136.8	138.7	139.6	135.4
2014	135.5	134.9	135.8	136.0	137.5	137.8	137.4	137.9	138.3	138.5	140.0	141.9	137.6
2015	137.1	136.7	137.1	137.3	139.1	140.1	140.0	140.6	140.8	141.9	143.7	147.1	140.1
2016	144.4	143.5	143.9	142.9	143.6	143.0	144.1	144.7	145.2	144.7	146.9	148.7	144.6
2017	142.3	142.2	142.9	142.9	143.3	144.3	143.8	144.5	145.2	147.1	149.0	149.4	144.7
Information													
2007	39.5	39.6	39.5	39.6	40.1	40.6	40.6	40.5	39.9	39.6	39.9	40.0	40.0
2008	39.6	39.6	39.7	39.8	40.3	40.5	40.4	40.2	39.5	39.1	39.1	39.3	39.8
2009	38.6	38.4	38.1	37.8	38.1	38.4	37.8	37.6	36.8	36.4	36.5	36.7	37.6
2010	35.9	35.7	35.7	35.7	36.1	36.4	35.8	35.6	35.0	34.9	34.9	34.9	35.6
2011	34.4	34.2	34.4	34.3	34.8	35.1	35.0	35.1	35.0	35.0	35.2	35.4	34.8
2012	35.5	35.5	35.7	35.5	35.8	36.0	35.8	35.7	35.4	35.7	35.8	35.8	35.7
2013	35.7	35.6	35.8	35.8	35.8	36.1	36.3	35.9	35.5	35.5	35.6	35.8	35.8
2014	35.3	35.3	35.5	35.3	35.5	35.8	35.8	35.4	34.8	34.4	34.4	34.4	35.2
2015	34.0	33.8	33.8	33.6	33.8	34.1	34.0	33.5	33.1	32.8	33.0	33.2	33.6
2016	32.8	32.8	32.8	32.7	33.0	33.0	32.8	32.6	32.3	32.5	32.3	32.3	32.7
2017	32.4	32.2	32.5	31.9	32.1	32.0	31.4	31.0	30.4	30.6	30.2	30.3	31.4
Financial Activities													
2007	137.5	137.8	138.1	138.4	139.1	140.3	140.1	139.6	138.5	138.2	137.7	138.0	138.6
2008	135.6	135.8	136.0	136.1	136.6	137.6	137.8	137.1	135.5	134.9	134.0	134.0	135.9
2009	132.3	131.7	131.6	131.5	132.0	132.4	132.3	131.8	130.4	130.0	129.5	129.9	131.3
2010	129.9	129.4	129.7	129.7	130.4	131.7	132.3	132.2	130.9	131.6	131.3	131.7	130.9
2011	130.9	130.9	131.3	131.0	131.9	132.5	132.6	132.0	130.9	130.7	130.3	130.5	131.3
2012	129.0	128.9	129.2	129.5	130.2	131.0	130.8	130.3	129.4	129.2	129.0	129.4	129.7
2013	127.6	127.3	127.3	127.8	128.9	129.8	130.0	129.6	128.6	128.4	128.3	128.8	128.5
2014	126.2	126.2	126.4	126.7	127.8	129.0	129.2	129.3	128.8	129.0	129.4	129.5	128.1
2015	128.3	128.6	129.0	129.2	130.5	132.0	132.1	132.5	131.7	132.5	132.4	133.2	131.0
2016	131.6	131.8	132.0	132.6	133.5	134.8	135.7	135.7	134.8	135.0	134.8	135.4	134.0
2017	133.5	134.0	134.3	134.7	135.4	136.8	137.2	137.1	136.2	137.5	137.0	135.7	135.8
Professional and Business Services													
2007	276.7	277.7	284.4	290.5	293.2	294.9	291.0	296.6	296.4	296.0	294.6	292.9	290.4
2008	281.0	280.3	283.1	288.6	288.8	290.2	287.3	291.1	290.5	289.7	283.8	277.6	286.0
2009	260.4	258.6	259.2	260.1	258.8	260.1	256.8	261.8	264.2	268.8	272.2	270.3	262.6
2010	257.9	259.5	264.1	273.7	275.5	278.4	279.6	284.2	283.0	285.6	286.2	287.0	276.2
2011	276.4	277.4	283.3	289.9	288.4	288.2	288.6	293.6	296.7	297.2	297.1	296.2	289.4
2012	283.7	289.7	294.2	298.4	300.5	304.4	301.6	305.7	306.6	306.5	306.1	304.2	300.1
2013	291.8	293.2	298.2	304.0	305.2	308.4	310.0	315.4	316.5	317.3	325.8	323.7	309.1
2014	305.9	306.9	311.9	321.4	325.1	324.2	320.6	326.8	327.4	331.8	337.0	335.3	322.9
2015	318.7	317.9	321.7	331.9	333.6	334.8	333.4	334.5	332.5	336.5	340.8	339.8	331.3
2016	321.9	321.6	324.8	333.2	332.8	334.5	337.2	339.2	339.8	339.6	342.6	339.4	333.9
2017	324.3	324.9	329.4	334.3	336.2	340.1	338.3	341.7	342.0	345.3	345.4	340.5	336.9
Education and Health Services													
2007	389.2	391.4	393.6	396.5	392.2	389.8	387.3	385.5	400.2	407.5	408.7	406.5	395.7
2008	401.1	404.2	405.4	407.2	405.7	400.7	397.6	394.4	410.2	416.3	417.6	419.0	406.6
2009	409.6	412.9	416.4	416.8	415.7	402.9	400.1	405.8	419.7	422.5	423.6	423.0	414.1
2010	417.2	421.1	425.6	423.3	421.4	408.9	406.0	411.1	422.2	425.6	427.0	425.7	419.6
2011	419.6	423.6	424.6	428.9	427.3	412.2	411.8	416.3	430.4	430.4	431.1	432.3	424.0
2012	425.6	431.9	431.3	434.5	433.1	417.9	413.7	421.6	439.8	439.9	442.0	443.0	431.2
2013	434.7	442.9	442.7	441.5	439.8	426.5	422.5	429.0	441.3	442.8	445.5	443.9	437.8
2014	433.3	439.4	440.0	442.6	443.1	430.7	423.9	427.8	440.3	443.7	445.8	446.9	438.1
2015	437.9	448.3	449.5	452.8	452.3	439.9	435.4	439.6	451.8	458.2	459.8	459.2	448.7
2016	450.3	460.5	460.6	460.8	460.1	447.7	444.8	448.5	461.5	467.1	468.5	466.9	458.1
2017	459.9	468.8	468.6	470.5	471.2	460.9	458.2	460.1	472.9	479.8	481.6	479.6	469.3

1. Employment by Industry: Indiana, Selected Years, 2007–2017—*Continued*

(Numbers in thousands, not seasonally adjusted)

Industry and year	January	February	March	April	May	June	July	August	September	October	November	December	Annual average
Leisure and Hospitality													
2007	268.1	268.1	275.1	283.4	292.8	297.4	291.8	296.0	288.7	285.3	280.9	277.6	283.8
2008	267.9	268.8	273.8	284.0	294.9	297.8	295.5	298.8	293.2	285.3	280.1	277.2	284.8
2009	263.6	264.5	270.4	278.2	287.5	290.1	286.8	287.6	281.8	273.8	269.2	266.5	276.7
2010	256.3	257.7	263.5	273.4	280.9	284.8	283.1	285.9	279.8	274.8	270.5	269.1	273.3
2011	259.7	261.1	268.7	277.3	286.2	289.3	287.5	289.7	284.1	278.9	275.5	274.3	277.7
2012	266.2	269.6	277.1	284.7	293.6	297.5	294.8	297.3	291.2	286.1	282.5	282.5	285.3
2013	272.8	274.6	280.5	289.0	299.7	302.6	299.7	301.2	296.4	291.8	287.6	286.8	290.2
2014	273.8	275.7	281.9	292.9	303.8	307.2	304.5	305.7	299.7	296.6	292.7	291.7	293.9
2015	282.0	284.4	290.7	299.7	310.1	313.5	310.2	312.0	306.6	302.9	298.6	298.2	300.7
2016	288.1	291.7	298.3	307.5	316.5	319.2	317.1	317.9	312.8	306.9	303.5	300.6	306.7
2017	292.5	295.8	301.1	309.3	317.4	319.8	316.6	317.6	311.6	307.1	298.7	298.6	307.2
Other Services													
2007	115.1	115.3	117.0	117.8	118.9	120.0	118.9	118.2	117.5	117.5	117.0	117.2	117.5
2008	116.6	116.8	117.3	118.6	120.0	120.3	119.6	119.1	118.0	118.2	117.3	117.0	118.2
2009	114.9	114.7	115.6	115.5	115.9	116.8	115.9	114.8	113.7	113.8	113.4	113.6	114.9
2010	112.6	112.5	113.9	114.6	114.9	116.2	116.3	115.6	115.2	115.3	115.2	115.1	114.8
2011	114.1	114.5	116.1	116.3	116.8	118.0	117.6	117.5	116.8	116.4	116.2	116.3	116.4
2012	115.6	116.1	117.3	117.6	118.6	119.5	118.9	118.8	118.2	119.0	118.7	119.4	118.1
2013	118.7	119.6	120.8	121.3	122.5	124.3	123.9	123.8	122.8	123.2	123.4	124.2	122.4
2014	122.3	123.3	124.7	125.2	126.4	127.6	127.1	126.1	125.2	125.0	125.0	125.2	125.3
2015	124.3	124.6	125.7	126.4	127.0	128.1	127.6	126.6	125.8	125.9	126.1	126.0	126.2
2016	124.4	125.0	125.6	126.1	126.9	127.9	127.9	127.1	126.8	126.2	125.9	126.0	126.3
2017	124.7	124.9	126.0	126.4	127.6	129.1	127.9	126.6	126.0	126.9	126.3	125.3	126.5
Government													
2007	428.0	440.6	444.0	441.2	437.7	410.0	379.9	408.4	443.2	446.7	447.2	446.6	431.1
2008	434.8	449.0	451.5	449.9	451.9	422.8	394.6	423.0	448.7	454.2	454.3	450.8	440.5
2009	439.6	447.9	451.5	450.4	454.4	418.2	378.5	407.5	447.0	457.7	452.7	451.8	438.1
2010	440.1	449.2	449.2	453.6	460.4	424.5	392.7	411.5	439.8	443.8	443.0	438.1	437.2
2011	429.4	437.1	439.0	442.4	446.4	410.9	383.0	402.3	439.9	441.8	443.4	443.5	429.9
2012	433.5	439.8	442.1	439.6	436.8	407.6	366.7	413.4	438.7	441.4	441.1	436.1	428.1
2013	424.7	437.9	438.5	439.0	425.2	401.4	362.1	413.4	432.4	437.9	441.9	440.4	424.6
2014	416.8	435.6	437.8	437.1	433.0	409.4	371.5	410.4	432.3	437.6	439.2	440.6	425.1
2015	428.2	435.1	435.4	436.3	433.2	413.4	372.0	409.8	440.3	438.2	440.1	441.6	427.0
2016	428.7	437.5	440.0	435.8	431.8	406.4	372.7	410.1	440.4	436.4	438.8	437.4	426.3
2017	429.3	433.8	437.1	429.8	429.7	410.1	374.1	417.7	439.5	438.0	440.9	438.4	426.5

2. Average Weekly Hours by Selected Industry: Indiana, 2013–2017

(Not seasonally adjusted)

Industry and year	January	February	March	April	May	June	July	August	September	October	November	December	Annual average
Total Private													
2013	34.4	34.6	34.6	34.6	34.5	34.9	34.4	34.5	34.8	34.7	34.6	34.9	34.6
2014	33.7	34.6	34.9	34.6	34.8	35.3	34.8	35.1	35.0	35.0	35.4	35.4	34.9
2015	34.7	35.0	35.0	34.8	35.0	34.9	34.8	35.3	34.5	34.9	35.0	35.1	34.9
2016	34.5	34.3	34.3	34.5	34.8	34.7	34.7	34.9	34.9	35.2	35.1	34.7	34.7
2017	34.7	34.5	34.6	34.7	34.8	35.5	35.4	35.5	35.2	35.4	35.6	35.7	35.1
Goods Producing													
2013	40.9	40.9	41.0	41.2	40.3	40.9	39.6	40.4	41.3	41.0	40.9	41.6	40.8
2014	39.4	40.5	40.5	40.5	41.0	41.4	40.2	40.9	40.6	40.5	41.5	41.1	40.7
2015	40.5	40.6	40.6	40.1	40.6	40.3	39.7	40.9	39.5	40.9	41.2	41.0	40.5
2016	40.0	39.5	39.4	39.7	40.2	39.5	39.3	40.0	40.2	41.0	40.3	40.1	39.9
2017	39.9	40.1	39.8	39.9	40.8	41.5	40.9	41.7	41.1	41.5	41.4	41.3	40.8
Construction													
2013	38.4	38.5	38.2	37.7	37.7	38.8	38.5	39.3	38.9	39.4	39.3	36.8	38.5
2014	34.8	34.5	35.9	37.7	36.0	37.9	38.1	39.0	37.9	37.3	38.1	38.0	37.2
2015	36.9	36.8	36.4	37.8	38.9	39.4	38.2	39.3	35.9	38.2	37.5	37.4	37.8
2016	35.3	34.7	35.3	36.5	37.2	38.1	37.9	37.8	38.2	39.2	38.5	36.1	37.2
2017	35.8	37.2	36.7	38.1	39.6	41.1	39.9	41.1	40.2	40.4	40.2	40.6	39.3
Manufacturing													
2013	41.2	41.2	41.4	41.8	40.6	41.2	39.6	40.4	41.5	41.1	41.0	42.3	41.1
2014	40.1	41.6	41.4	40.9	42.0	41.9	40.3	40.9	40.9	40.9	42.1	41.6	41.2
2015	41.1	41.3	41.5	40.6	40.9	40.4	40.0	41.3	40.6	41.2	41.9	41.7	41.0
2016	41.0	40.6	40.4	40.5	41.0	39.9	39.7	40.8	41.0	41.7	41.0	41.5	40.8
2017	41.3	41.0	40.8	40.5	41.3	41.7	41.4	42.0	41.5	42.0	42.0	41.6	41.4
Trade, Transportation, and Utilities													
2013	33.5	33.6	33.7	33.8	34.1	34.3	34.1	34.1	34.3	34.0	33.7	34.1	33.9
2014	33.4	33.8	34.3	33.8	34.3	34.6	34.5	34.6	34.4	34.5	34.7	34.9	34.3
2015	33.7	34.5	34.7	34.5	34.9	34.5	34.9	34.8	34.7	34.4	34.4	35.0	34.6
2016	34.3	34.2	34.0	34.0	34.4	34.4	34.3	34.4	34.4	34.4	34.8	34.2	34.3
2017	34.0	33.3	33.7	34.5	34.1	34.6	34.9	34.5	34.4	34.6	35.0	35.5	34.4
Financial Activities													
2013	37.3	37.3	37.3	36.9	37.0	37.5	37.0	36.7	36.9	37.0	37.2	37.0	37.1
2014	36.5	36.7	37.0	36.5	36.9	37.3	36.4	36.6	36.4	36.4	37.2	36.6	36.7
2015	36.8	37.2	37.3	36.3	36.6	36.4	36.1	37.4	36.3	35.9	36.2	35.2	36.5
2016	36.8	35.8	35.6	36.0	36.2	35.5	36.7	36.4	36.8	37.3	36.8	37.0	36.4
2017	38.6	37.4	37.5	38.0	37.7	37.6	38.7	38.0	38.0	38.5	38.2	37.8	38.0
Professional and Business Services													
2013	34.8	35.5	35.1	35.9	36.3	36.6	35.9	35.9	35.9	35.9	35.8	35.9	35.8
2014	34.1	35.9	36.3	36.1	36.5	37.1	36.0	36.9	36.8	36.9	36.9	37.1	36.4
2015	36.2	36.3	36.2	36.0	36.2	36.0	35.7	36.4	34.7	35.4	35.3	35.5	35.8
2016	34.4	34.6	35.0	35.4	35.7	35.6	35.5	35.4	34.9	36.3	35.7	35.3	35.3
2017	35.7	35.4	35.0	35.6	35.2	35.7	35.5	35.8	35.5	35.7	35.9	36.1	35.6
Education and Health Services													
2013	33.0	32.8	32.9	32.7	32.7	32.9	32.9	32.7	33.2	32.9	33.1	33.8	33.0
2014	32.9	33.3	33.3	33.3	33.3	33.5	33.6	33.3	33.4	33.5	33.8	33.8	33.4
2015	33.5	33.7	33.7	34.0	33.9	34.0	33.9	34.1	33.9	33.7	33.9	34.0	33.9
2016	33.8	33.6	33.7	33.9	34.0	34.2	34.2	34.7	34.9	34.6	34.8	34.0	34.2
2017	33.8	33.6	34.3	33.5	33.6	34.4	34.1	34.1	33.8	33.7	34.2	34.5	34.0
Leisure and Hospitality													
2013	24.2	24.5	24.6	24.6	24.8	25.3	25.3	25.2	25.0	24.8	25.0	24.7	24.8
2014	23.3	25.0	25.2	25.2	25.2	25.8	26.0	25.9	25.5	25.4	25.4	26.1	25.4
2015	24.7	25.3	25.3	25.1	25.3	25.5	25.7	25.5	24.8	25.0	24.7	25.2	25.2
2016	24.2	24.6	24.7	24.7	24.3	24.8	25.1	24.9	24.8	24.5	24.3	23.8	24.6
2017	23.9	24.4	24.9	24.7	24.8	25.7	25.8	25.9	25.4	25.4	25.3	25.0	25.1
Other Services													
2013	28.1	28.8	28.8	28.5	28.9	29.4	29.0	29.1	28.0	28.8	28.5	28.3	28.7
2014	27.9	29.1	29.7	29.0	28.4	29.2	28.9	28.2	29.2	29.1	29.1	29.0	28.9
2015	29.2	29.1	29.8	29.6	29.5	30.5	29.8	29.7	29.5	28.6	28.9	29.6	29.5
2016	28.8	28.7	28.8	29.5	30.3	30.9	30.8	29.1	29.1	28.9	29.1	28.5	29.4
2017	29.1	28.9	29.0	29.3	28.4	29.4	29.9	29.1	29.0	29.3	29.0	28.6	29.1

3. Average Hourly Earnings by Selected Industry: Indiana, 2013–2017

(Dollars, not seasonally adjusted)

Industry and year	January	February	March	April	May	June	July	August	September	October	November	December	Annual average
Total Private													
2013	22.06	22.04	22.02	22.05	21.77	21.95	21.91	21.99	22.26	22.07	22.23	22.53	22.08
2014	22.57	22.62	22.62	22.72	22.49	22.60	22.52	22.53	22.44	22.54	22.90	22.70	22.60
2015	23.00	22.86	22.78	22.71	22.65	22.65	22.75	22.97	22.93	22.89	23.07	23.00	22.85
2016	23.32	23.24	23.16	23.45	23.41	23.20	23.40	23.36	23.60	24.09	23.85	24.15	23.52
2017	24.39	24.37	24.09	24.55	24.40	24.04	24.52	24.30	24.70	24.76	24.46	24.83	24.45
Goods Producing													
2013	24.92	24.91	24.65	24.66	24.37	24.75	24.68	24.23	24.81	24.54	24.90	25.22	24.72
2014	24.90	25.25	25.27	25.47	25.16	25.34	25.32	25.21	25.03	25.16	25.46	25.30	25.24
2015	25.30	25.29	25.36	25.13	25.03	25.17	25.23	25.50	25.42	25.26	25.65	25.40	25.31
2016	25.48	25.58	25.55	25.85	25.84	25.46	25.57	25.76	25.80	26.43	26.23	26.23	25.82
2017	26.77	26.49	26.46	27.11	26.91	26.89	27.23	26.70	26.93	27.07	26.72	27.19	26.88
Construction													
2013	28.28	28.04	28.24	28.42	27.77	27.02	26.86	26.29	26.49	26.79	26.14	25.98	27.16
2014	25.95	27.24	26.90	26.89	26.77	27.81	27.75	26.93	26.52	27.05	27.01	26.76	26.99
2015	26.94	26.83	27.31	27.13	26.33	26.58	26.70	27.19	27.05	27.33	27.07	26.88	26.94
2016	27.20	27.15	27.31	27.73	27.71	27.17	26.95	27.29	27.82	27.92	27.86	27.83	27.51
2017	27.65	27.32	27.89	28.83	29.20	29.78	29.64	29.30	29.55	29.27	29.01	28.74	28.92
Manufacturing													
2013	24.16	24.20	23.86	23.79	23.54	24.03	23.99	23.58	24.15	23.77	24.40	24.88	24.03
2014	24.50	24.70	24.80	25.04	24.70	24.58	24.40	24.55	24.44	24.46	24.88	24.77	24.65
2015	24.79	24.84	24.82	24.52	24.64	24.74	24.79	24.99	24.99	24.65	25.26	25.01	24.84
2016	25.10	25.25	25.14	25.38	25.36	24.99	25.22	25.36	25.22	26.02	25.77	25.83	25.39
2017	26.57	26.29	26.01	26.52	26.06	25.69	26.25	25.61	25.82	26.16	25.76	26.54	26.10
Trade, Transportation, and Utilities													
2013	19.59	19.76	19.96	19.64	19.48	19.75	19.83	20.07	20.14	20.12	20.26	20.47	19.93
2014	20.68	20.62	20.76	20.79	20.57	20.70	20.52	20.58	20.29	20.36	20.80	20.47	20.59
2015	20.94	20.64	20.78	20.74	20.56	20.46	20.44	20.37	20.41	20.02	20.13	20.14	20.46
2016	20.29	20.04	20.01	20.45	20.48	20.52	20.94	20.64	21.27	21.54	21.12	21.35	20.73
2017	20.80	20.76	20.47	20.40	20.16	20.63	21.13	20.91	21.47	21.58	21.10	21.53	20.92
Financial Activities													
2013	23.74	24.00	23.99	25.05	24.87	24.79	24.44	24.82	25.34	25.29	25.01	25.23	24.71
2014	25.06	24.93	24.85	25.10	24.67	24.30	24.06	24.10	23.75	23.75	23.72	23.53	24.31
2015	23.31	23.08	23.03	23.13	23.22	22.85	23.49	23.88	24.24	24.31	24.39	24.96	23.66
2016	25.33	25.59	26.00	26.30	26.23	25.82	25.64	25.37	25.91	26.66	26.50	27.36	26.06
2017	26.24	26.42	26.48	28.02	27.05	27.36	27.14	27.17	27.87	27.74	27.97	28.62	27.34
Professional and Business Services													
2013	21.10	21.29	21.17	21.13	21.05	21.29	21.65	21.97	22.23	21.86	22.21	22.48	21.64
2014	23.51	23.80	23.94	23.68	23.74	24.14	24.28	23.84	23.93	24.13	24.63	24.66	24.04
2015	25.33	25.73	25.42	24.87	24.72	24.99	25.08	25.33	25.53	25.12	25.17	25.00	25.19
2016	26.07	25.68	25.66	25.92	25.92	25.45	26.22	25.60	25.99	26.14	25.51	26.04	25.85
2017	26.96	26.48	26.23	26.58	26.28	25.97	26.64	26.25	26.17	26.11	25.69	25.89	26.26
Education and Health Services													
2013	23.89	23.74	24.11	24.25	23.92	24.11	24.08	24.47	24.24	24.06	24.01	24.30	24.10
2014	23.99	23.63	23.75	24.03	23.86	23.89	23.89	24.04	24.21	24.17	24.54	24.28	24.03
2015	24.53	24.51	24.33	24.77	24.90	24.68	25.08	25.20	24.88	25.29	25.15	25.13	24.87
2016	25.49	25.48	25.07	25.66	25.48	25.48	25.43	25.28	25.22	25.71	25.56	26.04	25.49
2017	26.88	27.19	26.36	27.16	27.54	26.23	27.34	27.11	27.51	27.32	27.03	27.48	27.10
Leisure and Hospitality													
2013	12.40	12.46	12.36	12.21	12.23	11.84	11.71	11.87	12.12	12.01	12.15	12.30	12.13
2014	12.28	12.66	12.34	12.17	12.11	12.20	12.22	12.17	12.36	12.50	12.67	12.85	12.37
2015	12.78	12.91	12.81	12.75	12.62	12.51	12.44	12.57	12.77	13.02	13.30	13.55	12.83
2016	13.34	13.50	13.27	13.25	13.29	12.94	13.01	13.28	13.51	13.63	13.79	13.88	13.38
2017	13.74	13.54	13.45	13.52	13.57	13.28	13.55	13.67	14.07	14.35	14.36	14.25	13.78
Other Services													
2013	17.79	17.63	17.56	17.32	17.05	16.84	17.23	17.20	17.60	17.52	17.52	17.99	17.43
2014	17.85	17.57	17.18	17.61	17.66	17.47	17.47	17.99	17.77	17.66	17.84	18.09	17.68
2015	17.71	17.65	17.66	17.50	17.68	17.58	17.17	17.91	18.12	18.12	18.56	18.81	17.87
2016	19.16	19.42	19.79	19.89	19.82	19.90	19.60	20.32	19.54	20.13	20.06	20.81	19.87
2017	20.93	20.92	20.92	21.30	21.10	20.39	20.60	21.72	22.06	22.54	22.31	22.62	21.45

4. Average Weekly Earnings by Selected Industry: Indiana, 2013–2017

(Dollars, not seasonally adjusted)

Industry and year	January	February	March	April	May	June	July	August	September	October	November	December	Annual average
Total Private													
2013	758.86	762.58	761.89	762.93	751.07	766.06	753.70	758.66	774.65	765.83	769.16	786.30	763.97
2014	760.61	782.65	789.44	786.11	782.65	797.78	783.70	790.80	785.40	788.90	810.66	803.58	788.74
2015	798.10	800.10	797.30	790.31	792.75	790.49	791.70	810.84	791.09	798.86	807.45	807.30	797.47
2016	804.54	797.13	794.39	809.03	814.67	805.04	811.98	815.26	823.64	847.97	837.14	838.01	816.14
2017	846.33	840.77	833.51	851.89	849.12	853.42	868.01	862.65	869.44	876.50	870.78	886.43	858.20
Goods Producing													
2013	1,019.23	1,018.82	1,010.65	1,015.99	982.11	1,012.28	977.33	978.89	1,024.65	1,006.14	1,018.41	1,049.15	1,008.58
2014	981.06	1,022.63	1,023.44	1,031.54	1,031.56	1,049.08	1,017.86	1,031.09	1,016.22	1,018.98	1,056.59	1,039.83	1,027.27
2015	1,024.65	1,026.77	1,029.62	1,007.71	1,016.22	1,014.35	1,001.63	1,042.95	1,004.09	1,033.13	1,056.78	1,041.40	1,025.06
2016	1,019.20	1,010.41	1,006.67	1,026.25	1,038.77	1,005.67	1,004.90	1,030.40	1,037.16	1,083.63	1,057.07	1,051.82	1,030.22
2017	1,068.12	1,062.25	1,053.11	1,081.69	1,097.93	1,115.94	1,113.71	1,113.39	1,106.82	1,123.41	1,106.21	1,122.95	1,096.70
Construction													
2013	1,085.95	1,079.54	1,078.77	1,071.43	1,046.93	1,048.38	1,034.11	1,033.20	1,030.46	1,055.53	1,027.30	956.06	1,045.66
2014	903.06	939.78	965.71	1,013.75	963.72	1,054.00	1,057.28	1,050.27	1,005.11	1,008.97	1,029.08	1,016.88	1,004.03
2015	994.09	987.34	994.08	1,025.51	1,024.24	1,047.25	1,019.94	1,068.57	971.10	1,044.01	1,015.13	1,005.31	1,018.33
2016	960.16	942.11	964.04	1,012.15	1,030.81	1,035.18	1,021.41	1,031.56	1,062.72	1,094.46	1,072.61	1,004.66	1,023.37
2017	989.87	1,016.30	1,023.56	1,098.42	1,156.32	1,223.96	1,182.64	1,204.23	1,187.91	1,182.51	1,166.20	1,166.84	1,136.56
Manufacturing													
2013	995.39	997.04	987.80	994.42	955.72	990.04	950.00	952.63	1,002.23	976.95	1,000.40	1,052.42	987.63
2014	982.45	1,027.52	1,026.72	1,024.14	1,037.40	1,029.90	983.32	1,004.10	999.60	1,000.41	1,047.45	1,030.43	1,015.58
2015	1,018.87	1,025.89	1,030.03	995.51	1,007.78	999.50	991.60	1,032.09	1,014.59	1,015.58	1,058.39	1,042.92	1,018.44
2016	1,029.10	1,025.15	1,015.66	1,027.89	1,039.76	997.10	1,001.23	1,034.69	1,034.02	1,085.03	1,056.57	1,071.95	1,035.91
2017	1,097.34	1,077.89	1,061.21	1,074.06	1,076.28	1,071.27	1,086.75	1,075.62	1,071.53	1,098.72	1,081.92	1,104.06	1,080.54
Trade, Transportation, and Utilities													
2013	656.27	663.94	672.65	663.83	664.27	677.43	676.20	684.39	690.80	684.08	682.76	698.03	675.63
2014	690.71	696.96	712.07	702.70	705.55	716.22	707.94	712.07	697.98	702.42	721.76	714.40	706.24
2015	705.68	712.08	721.07	715.53	717.54	705.87	713.36	708.88	708.23	688.69	692.47	704.90	707.92
2016	695.95	685.37	680.34	695.30	704.51	705.89	718.24	710.02	731.69	740.98	734.98	730.17	711.04
2017	707.20	691.31	689.84	703.80	687.46	713.80	737.44	721.40	738.57	746.67	738.50	764.32	719.65
Financial Activities													
2013	885.50	895.20	894.83	924.35	920.19	929.63	904.28	910.89	935.05	935.73	930.37	933.51	916.74
2014	914.69	914.93	919.45	916.15	910.32	906.39	875.78	882.06	864.50	864.50	882.38	861.20	892.18
2015	857.81	858.58	859.02	839.62	849.85	831.74	847.99	893.11	879.91	872.73	882.92	878.59	863.59
2016	932.14	916.12	925.60	946.80	949.53	916.61	940.99	923.47	953.49	994.42	975.20	1,012.32	948.58
2017	1,012.86	988.11	993.00	1,064.76	1,019.79	1,028.74	1,050.32	1,032.46	1,059.06	1,067.99	1,068.45	1,081.84	1,038.92
Professional and Business Services													
2013	734.28	755.80	743.07	758.57	764.12	779.21	777.24	788.72	798.06	784.77	795.12	807.03	774.71
2014	801.69	854.42	869.02	854.85	866.51	895.59	874.08	879.70	880.62	890.40	908.85	914.89	875.06
2015	916.95	934.00	920.20	895.32	894.86	899.64	895.36	922.01	885.89	889.25	888.50	887.50	901.80
2016	896.81	888.53	898.10	917.57	925.34	906.02	930.81	906.24	907.05	948.88	910.71	919.21	912.51
2017	962.47	937.39	918.05	946.25	925.06	927.13	945.72	939.75	929.04	932.13	922.27	934.63	934.86
Education and Health Services													
2013	788.37	778.67	793.22	792.98	782.18	793.22	792.23	800.17	804.77	791.57	794.73	821.34	795.30
2014	789.27	786.88	790.88	800.20	794.54	800.32	802.70	800.53	808.61	809.70	829.45	820.66	802.60
2015	821.76	825.99	819.92	842.18	844.11	839.12	850.21	859.32	843.43	852.27	852.59	854.42	843.09
2016	861.56	856.13	844.86	869.87	866.32	871.42	869.71	877.22	880.18	889.57	889.49	885.36	871.76
2017	908.54	913.58	904.15	909.86	925.34	902.31	932.29	924.45	929.84	920.68	924.43	948.06	921.40
Leisure and Hospitality													
2013	300.08	305.27	304.06	300.37	303.30	299.55	296.26	299.12	303.00	297.85	303.75	303.81	300.82
2014	286.12	316.50	310.97	306.68	305.17	314.76	317.72	315.20	315.18	317.50	321.82	335.39	314.20
2015	315.67	326.62	324.09	320.03	319.29	319.01	319.71	320.54	316.70	325.50	328.51	341.46	323.32
2016	322.83	332.10	327.77	327.28	322.95	320.91	326.55	330.67	335.05	333.94	335.10	330.34	329.15
2017	328.39	330.38	334.91	333.94	336.54	341.30	349.59	354.05	357.38	364.49	363.31	356.25	345.88
Other Services													
2013	499.90	507.74	505.73	493.62	492.75	495.10	499.67	500.52	492.80	504.58	499.32	509.12	500.24
2014	498.02	511.29	510.25	510.69	501.54	510.12	504.88	507.32	518.88	513.91	519.14	524.61	510.95
2015	517.13	513.62	526.27	518.00	521.56	536.19	511.67	531.93	534.54	518.23	536.38	556.78	527.17
2016	551.81	557.35	569.95	586.76	600.55	614.91	603.68	591.31	568.61	581.76	583.75	593.09	584.18
2017	609.06	604.59	606.68	624.09	599.24	599.47	615.94	632.05	639.74	660.42	646.99	646.93	624.20

IOWA
At a Glance

Population:
  2010 census: 3,046,355
  2017 estimate: 3,145,711

Percent change in population:
  2010–2017: 3.3%

Percent change in total nonfarm employment:
  2007–2017: 3.5%

Industry with the largest growth in employment, 2007–2017 (thousands):
  Education and health services, 28.2

Industry with the largest decline or smallest growth in employment, 2007–2017 (thousands):
  Manufacturing, -13.3

Civilian labor force:
  2010: 1,678,281
  2017: 1,678,549

Unemployment rate and rank among states (highest to lowest):
  2010: 6.0%, 47th
  2017: 3.1%, 45th

Over-the-year change in unemployment rates:
  2015–2016: -0.2%
  2016–2017: -0.5%

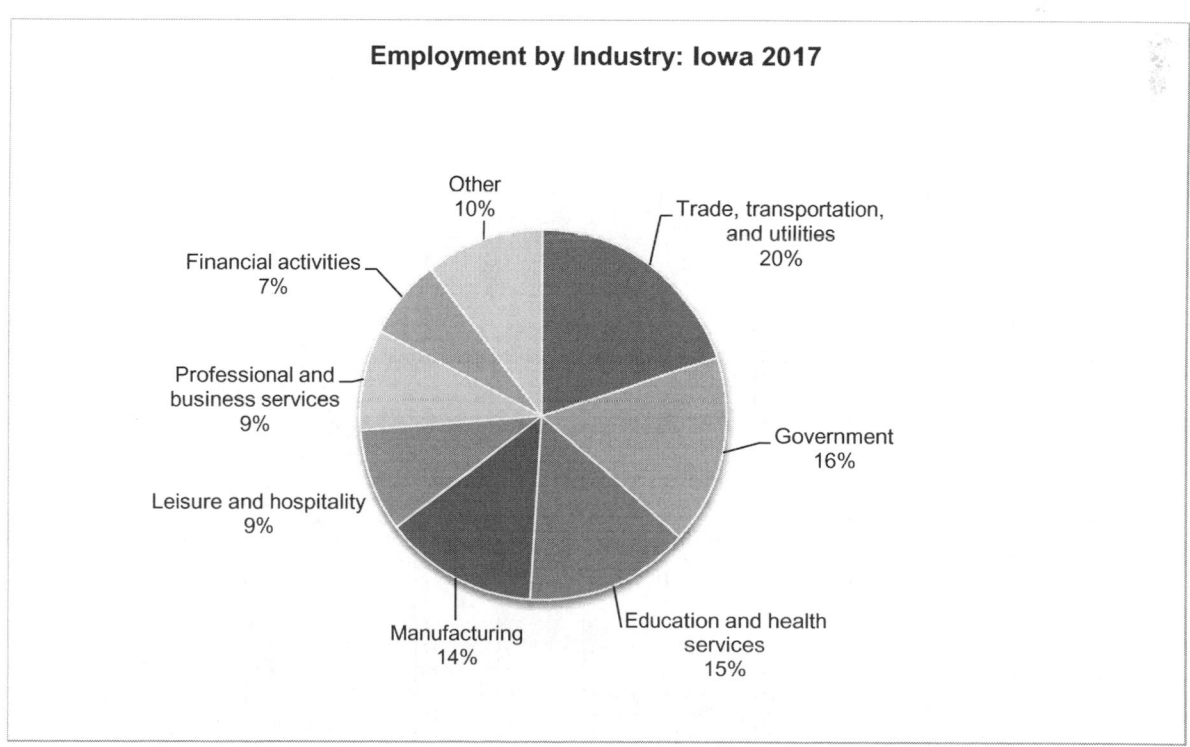

Employment by Industry: Iowa 2017

Other 10%

Trade, transportation, and utilities 20%

Financial activities 7%

Professional and business services 9%

Government 16%

Leisure and hospitality 9%

Manufacturing 14%

Education and health services 15%

1. Employment by Industry: Iowa, Selected Years, 2007–2017

(Numbers in thousands, not seasonally adjusted)

Industry and year	January	February	March	April	May	June	July	August	September	October	November	December	Annual average
Total Nonfarm													
2007	1,482.6	1,485.7	1,496.4	1,517.8	1,534.1	1,542.2	1,508.5	1,508.8	1,529.3	1,538.6	1,545.9	1,538.9	1,519.1
2008	1,496.1	1,499.9	1,509.6	1,529.6	1,546.6	1,544.7	1,515.3	1,514.8	1,534.4	1,540.8	1,535.6	1,525.3	1,524.4
2009	1,471.7	1,472.0	1,473.0	1,488.5	1,497.8	1,493.7	1,460.6	1,461.3	1,479.2	1,487.2	1,486.8	1,476.9	1,479.1
2010	1,432.2	1,437.4	1,449.8	1,477.0	1,488.9	1,486.3	1,457.4	1,455.7	1,474.3	1,490.5	1,494.0	1,487.8	1,469.3
2011	1,443.7	1,449.9	1,460.9	1,489.1	1,500.3	1,499.8	1,477.7	1,479.9	1,501.5	1,509.6	1,513.5	1,507.7	1,486.1
2012	1,467.3	1,474.5	1,488.9	1,511.0	1,524.2	1,524.1	1,500.5	1,505.2	1,519.8	1,528.8	1,533.8	1,527.4	1,508.8
2013	1,484.1	1,493.3	1,501.6	1,520.8	1,542.1	1,543.6	1,527.5	1,532.7	1,545.2	1,548.0	1,554.3	1,547.6	1,528.4
2014	1,503.9	1,512.6	1,522.6	1,548.2	1,564.3	1,564.1	1,540.5	1,545.5	1,561.7	1,566.0	1,570.0	1,565.1	1,547.0
2015	1,525.8	1,532.8	1,543.0	1,564.6	1,577.3	1,578.8	1,556.8	1,555.1	1,567.6	1,578.3	1,580.7	1,575.5	1,561.4
2016	1,535.1	1,543.4	1,554.9	1,578.9	1,585.0	1,582.2	1,566.0	1,567.8	1,581.8	1,587.9	1,588.2	1,578.5	1,570.8
2017	1,536.3	1,547.4	1,554.9	1,577.6	1,585.0	1,588.0	1,564.7	1,566.3	1,577.8	1,588.7	1,595.1	1,586.0	1,572.3
Total Private													
2007	1,235.0	1,232.0	1,242.8	1,263.8	1,277.6	1,288.7	1,279.9	1,280.3	1,279.0	1,281.7	1,287.8	1,281.8	1,269.2
2008	1,246.2	1,244.0	1,252.6	1,272.4	1,286.1	1,288.6	1,284.0	1,283.8	1,279.7	1,280.5	1,274.3	1,265.2	1,271.5
2009	1,218.6	1,213.3	1,213.3	1,227.4	1,234.7	1,235.8	1,226.3	1,227.1	1,224.8	1,226.5	1,225.4	1,217.6	1,224.2
2010	1,181.9	1,181.5	1,191.5	1,218.6	1,225.6	1,228.7	1,224.6	1,223.7	1,223.0	1,232.5	1,233.6	1,229.0	1,216.2
2011	1,194.2	1,194.4	1,204.4	1,231.2	1,241.1	1,244.5	1,241.8	1,243.6	1,247.5	1,251.8	1,254.7	1,249.5	1,233.2
2012	1,215.6	1,218.4	1,232.1	1,252.6	1,264.3	1,269.7	1,265.8	1,265.9	1,265.4	1,270.5	1,274.0	1,268.2	1,255.2
2013	1,234.0	1,236.8	1,244.6	1,263.3	1,281.3	1,287.3	1,288.8	1,290.8	1,288.3	1,288.6	1,293.4	1,287.3	1,273.7
2014	1,251.4	1,255.0	1,264.4	1,289.3	1,303.8	1,309.8	1,304.5	1,306.5	1,303.2	1,304.8	1,307.4	1,303.8	1,292.0
2015	1,271.1	1,273.3	1,283.7	1,304.9	1,316.1	1,323.2	1,320.4	1,318.1	1,312.3	1,317.0	1,317.8	1,312.9	1,305.9
2016	1,279.3	1,282.6	1,294.0	1,316.8	1,322.0	1,323.4	1,328.5	1,326.8	1,323.0	1,324.6	1,323.2	1,314.2	1,313.2
2017	1,276.7	1,284.3	1,291.5	1,313.2	1,320.5	1,326.5	1,322.8	1,320.9	1,316.9	1,322.1	1,327.6	1,320.8	1,312.0
Goods Producing													
2007	293.6	289.3	292.9	299.5	305.2	311.5	313.1	313.3	310.8	310.2	309.9	304.7	304.5
2008	293.9	290.9	293.0	301.0	307.7	311.0	312.8	312.5	308.7	305.5	300.8	292.3	302.5
2009	274.3	268.5	266.4	270.3	272.2	274.2	272.3	273.4	271.6	268.4	266.9	260.8	269.9
2010	250.0	248.5	252.1	263.7	266.4	270.5	272.3	272.1	270.7	270.7	269.6	263.8	264.2
2011	254.0	253.4	257.5	266.8	272.1	277.3	279.6	279.7	278.6	277.3	276.0	271.0	270.3
2012	261.5	260.9	266.3	275.0	280.4	285.2	286.4	286.0	283.6	283.6	281.6	278.2	277.4
2013	268.7	268.5	270.7	278.0	285.9	291.3	293.4	294.2	291.9	292.3	291.5	286.4	284.4
2014	276.3	276.3	280.2	290.8	297.2	302.3	303.2	303.3	300.4	299.5	298.5	293.9	293.5
2015	284.8	284.0	287.3	295.9	299.3	303.9	304.9	303.4	300.7	301.0	299.3	294.9	296.6
2016	284.2	282.8	289.3	296.9	299.1	303.9	306.0	306.0	303.3	301.7	298.4	292.7	297.0
2017	280.9	280.8	284.5	292.5	296.5	301.2	301.1	300.3	299.3	300.6	300.6	295.6	294.5
Service-Providing													
2007	1,189.0	1,196.4	1,203.5	1,218.3	1,228.9	1,230.7	1,195.4	1,195.5	1,218.5	1,228.4	1,236.0	1,234.2	1,214.6
2008	1,202.2	1,209.0	1,216.6	1,228.6	1,238.9	1,233.7	1,202.5	1,202.3	1,225.7	1,235.3	1,234.8	1,233.0	1,221.9
2009	1,197.4	1,203.5	1,206.6	1,218.2	1,225.6	1,219.5	1,188.3	1,187.9	1,207.6	1,218.8	1,219.9	1,216.1	1,209.1
2010	1,182.2	1,188.9	1,197.7	1,213.3	1,222.5	1,215.8	1,185.1	1,183.6	1,203.6	1,219.8	1,224.4	1,224.0	1,205.1
2011	1,189.7	1,196.5	1,203.4	1,222.3	1,228.2	1,222.5	1,198.1	1,200.2	1,222.9	1,232.3	1,237.5	1,236.7	1,215.9
2012	1,205.8	1,213.6	1,222.6	1,236.0	1,243.8	1,238.9	1,214.1	1,219.2	1,236.2	1,245.2	1,252.2	1,249.2	1,231.4
2013	1,215.4	1,224.8	1,230.9	1,242.8	1,256.2	1,252.3	1,234.1	1,238.5	1,253.3	1,255.7	1,262.8	1,261.2	1,244.0
2014	1,227.6	1,236.3	1,242.4	1,257.4	1,267.1	1,261.8	1,237.3	1,242.2	1,261.3	1,266.5	1,271.5	1,271.2	1,253.6
2015	1,241.0	1,248.8	1,255.7	1,268.7	1,278.0	1,274.9	1,251.9	1,251.7	1,266.9	1,277.3	1,281.4	1,280.6	1,264.7
2016	1,250.9	1,260.6	1,265.6	1,282.0	1,285.9	1,278.3	1,260.0	1,261.8	1,278.5	1,286.2	1,289.8	1,285.8	1,273.8
2017	1,255.4	1,266.6	1,270.4	1,285.1	1,288.5	1,286.8	1,263.6	1,266.0	1,278.5	1,288.1	1,294.5	1,290.4	1,277.8
Mining and Logging													
2007	1.8	1.7	2.0	2.1	2.2	2.3	2.3	2.3	2.3	2.3	2.3	2.1	2.1
2008	1.7	1.8	1.9	2.2	2.3	2.3	2.3	2.4	2.3	2.3	2.3	2.1	2.2
2009	1.6	1.8	2.0	2.3	2.4	2.4	2.4	2.5	2.4	2.3	2.3	2.1	2.2
2010	1.6	1.7	1.8	2.3	2.3	2.3	2.3	2.3	2.3	2.4	2.3	2.1	2.1
2011	1.7	1.8	1.8	2.2	2.3	2.4	2.4	2.4	2.4	2.4	2.3	2.2	2.2
2012	1.8	1.9	2.1	2.2	2.4	2.4	2.4	2.4	2.4	2.3	2.3	2.2	2.2
2013	1.8	1.8	2.0	2.1	2.4	2.5	2.5	2.5	2.5	2.4	2.4	2.3	2.3
2014	1.8	1.8	1.9	2.2	2.4	2.5	2.4	2.4	2.4	2.3	2.3	2.2	2.2
2015	1.8	1.9	2.1	2.3	2.4	2.5	2.5	2.5	2.4	2.3	2.2	2.1	2.3
2016	1.7	1.7	1.9	2.4	2.4	2.5	2.5	2.5	2.5	2.3	2.2	2.1	2.2
2017	1.9	2.0	2.2	2.4	2.5	2.5	2.5	2.5	2.5	2.5	2.5	2.3	2.4

1. Employment by Industry: Iowa, Selected Years, 2007–2017—*Continued*

(Numbers in thousands, not seasonally adjusted)

Industry and year	January	February	March	April	May	June	July	August	September	October	November	December	Annual average
Construction													
2007	64.0	60.7	63.4	69.5	74.6	78.4	79.0	79.4	77.9	77.7	76.6	71.4	72.7
2008	63.1	60.5	62.4	70.0	75.9	78.4	81.6	81.5	79.4	78.0	75.0	69.8	73.0
2009	58.7	57.2	58.2	64.5	67.5	69.5	70.7	70.2	68.9	68.0	66.0	60.1	65.0
2010	51.6	50.3	52.3	62.2	64.7	67.2	68.1	67.2	66.1	66.0	64.5	58.8	61.6
2011	50.6	49.6	52.1	60.8	64.5	67.4	69.0	69.3	68.6	68.3	66.8	61.4	62.4
2012	54.1	52.9	56.5	63.8	67.4	69.9	70.5	70.6	69.2	69.2	67.0	63.9	64.6
2013	56.1	55.3	56.5	63.0	69.5	72.8	74.9	75.6	74.1	74.4	73.3	67.9	67.8
2014	59.9	59.5	62.4	72.0	77.0	80.3	81.3	82.2	81.2	81.1	79.7	74.9	74.3
2015	67.2	66.8	69.3	77.8	80.2	82.8	84.2	83.9	82.7	83.6	82.4	78.0	78.2
2016	68.6	67.9	73.4	81.1	82.8	85.6	88.0	88.4	87.3	86.7	83.8	77.3	80.9
2017	66.9	66.9	69.5	75.8	78.9	81.3	81.1	80.9	79.8	80.0	78.1	70.5	75.8
Manufacturing													
2007	227.8	226.9	227.5	227.9	228.4	230.8	231.8	231.6	230.6	230.2	231.0	231.2	229.6
2008	229.1	228.6	228.7	228.8	229.5	230.3	228.9	228.6	227.0	225.2	223.5	220.4	227.4
2009	214.0	209.5	206.2	203.5	202.3	202.3	199.2	200.7	200.3	198.1	198.6	198.6	202.8
2010	196.8	196.5	198.0	199.2	199.4	201.0	201.9	202.6	202.3	202.3	202.8	202.9	200.5
2011	201.7	202.0	203.6	203.8	205.3	207.5	208.2	208.0	207.6	206.6	206.9	207.4	205.7
2012	205.6	206.1	207.7	209.0	210.6	212.9	213.5	213.0	212.0	212.1	212.3	212.1	210.6
2013	210.8	211.4	212.2	212.9	214.0	216.0	216.0	216.1	215.3	215.5	215.8	216.2	214.4
2014	214.6	215.0	215.9	216.6	217.8	219.5	219.5	218.7	216.8	216.1	216.5	216.8	217.0
2015	215.8	215.3	215.9	215.8	216.7	218.6	218.2	217.0	215.6	215.1	214.7	214.8	216.1
2016	213.9	213.2	214.0	213.4	213.9	215.8	215.5	215.1	213.5	212.7	212.4	213.3	213.9
2017	212.1	211.9	212.8	214.3	215.1	217.4	217.5	216.9	217.0	218.1	220.0	222.8	216.3
Trade, Transportation, and Utilities													
2007	305.5	302.5	304.1	306.9	310.6	312.2	310.1	308.8	307.7	309.0	314.7	315.9	309.0
2008	306.6	304.1	306.0	307.5	310.6	311.2	310.6	310.5	308.7	310.4	313.2	314.3	309.5
2009	301.9	299.3	299.7	301.8	304.2	305.0	303.8	303.3	300.4	300.8	304.8	304.7	302.5
2010	294.7	291.9	293.8	298.5	300.5	302.1	301.0	300.6	297.9	301.2	305.0	306.8	299.5
2011	295.9	294.2	296.3	300.9	304.1	305.3	304.4	304.2	302.7	305.4	310.3	312.3	303.0
2012	301.4	299.3	300.7	304.2	307.3	309.0	308.5	308.1	307.3	309.1	315.1	316.1	307.2
2013	304.6	303.0	304.8	307.8	311.4	313.2	312.7	311.9	310.4	312.3	318.0	318.9	310.8
2014	307.3	305.4	306.5	310.6	312.5	314.5	312.8	312.4	310.6	313.1	318.7	321.3	312.1
2015	310.8	309.1	310.6	313.0	315.1	317.6	316.5	315.0	312.8	315.7	320.2	321.4	314.8
2016	311.5	310.2	311.0	314.4	315.5	316.0	317.8	316.9	314.1	315.7	320.1	322.5	315.5
2017	311.5	310.1	310.6	314.1	315.2	316.6	315.8	314.9	312.5	314.6	319.6	320.5	314.7
Wholesale Trade													
2007	66.2	65.9	66.5	67.8	68.4	68.6	68.8	68.2	68.3	68.9	69.0	68.4	67.9
2008	67.3	67.2	67.8	68.7	69.8	69.6	69.8	69.2	68.5	69.4	68.7	68.2	68.7
2009	66.1	66.1	66.2	67.6	67.6	67.5	67.6	66.7	66.0	66.9	66.8	66.4	66.8
2010	64.7	64.4	64.9	67.1	66.8	66.8	66.6	66.0	65.8	66.7	66.7	66.0	66.0
2011	65.0	64.8	65.5	67.0	67.5	67.6	67.6	67.1	67.2	68.4	68.7	68.1	67.0
2012	66.8	66.9	68.0	69.1	69.4	69.6	69.3	68.7	68.8	69.1	69.3	68.5	68.6
2013	67.3	67.4	67.8	69.1	70.3	70.2	69.6	69.1	68.3	69.3	69.8	69.0	68.9
2014	67.6	67.4	67.7	69.5	69.9	70.0	69.4	68.9	68.1	69.1	69.5	68.7	68.8
2015	67.1	66.8	67.2	68.5	68.4	68.6	68.1	67.5	66.9	67.8	67.8	66.9	67.6
2016	65.8	65.7	66.4	67.5	67.4	67.3	67.3	66.6	66.5	67.0	67.1	66.4	66.8
2017	65.3	65.4	66.0	67.1	67.3	67.4	67.0	66.4	66.1	66.9	67.0	66.2	66.5
Retail Trade													
2007	178.0	175.3	175.7	177.1	179.6	180.6	179.4	178.3	177.0	177.6	182.7	184.3	178.8
2008	177.4	175.2	176.3	177.1	178.2	179.1	178.5	178.4	177.1	177.9	181.3	182.5	178.3
2009	174.7	172.5	172.8	173.8	175.9	177.3	176.3	176.3	174.0	173.8	177.6	177.6	175.2
2010	171.4	169.1	170.0	171.6	173.6	174.6	173.7	173.3	170.7	172.6	176.0	177.5	172.8
2011	170.8	169.1	170.1	172.6	174.7	175.5	175.1	175.0	173.3	174.8	179.0	180.9	174.2
2012	173.5	171.3	171.2	173.1	175.3	176.1	176.1	176.0	174.8	176.3	181.8	182.6	175.7
2013	174.6	172.8	173.8	175.6	177.3	178.7	178.9	178.6	177.8	178.8	183.3	183.9	177.8
2014	176.6	175.0	175.3	176.8	178.0	179.1	178.2	177.9	176.4	177.8	182.2	183.7	178.1
2015	177.1	175.9	176.8	178.9	180.9	182.3	181.6	180.9	179.1	181.3	185.1	186.0	180.5
2016	180.0	179.4	179.3	181.8	183.1	182.9	183.7	183.7	181.2	182.6	186.1	187.0	182.6
2017	180.6	179.4	178.9	181.3	182.0	182.6	182.2	181.8	179.9	181.1	185.0	184.1	181.6

1. Employment by Industry: Iowa, Selected Years, 2007–2017—*Continued*

(Numbers in thousands, not seasonally adjusted)

Industry and year	January	February	March	April	May	June	July	August	September	October	November	December	Annual average
Transportation and Utilities													
2007	61.3	61.3	61.9	62.0	62.6	63.0	61.9	62.3	62.4	62.5	63.0	63.2	62.3
2008	61.9	61.7	61.9	61.7	62.6	62.5	62.3	62.9	63.1	63.1	63.2	63.6	62.5
2009	61.1	60.7	60.7	60.4	60.7	60.2	59.9	60.3	60.4	60.1	60.4	60.7	60.5
2010	58.6	58.4	58.9	59.8	60.1	60.7	60.7	61.3	61.4	61.9	62.3	63.3	60.6
2011	60.1	60.3	60.7	61.3	61.9	62.2	61.7	62.1	62.2	62.2	62.6	63.3	61.7
2012	61.1	61.1	61.5	62.0	62.6	63.3	63.1	63.4	63.7	63.7	64.0	65.0	62.9
2013	62.7	62.8	63.2	63.1	63.8	64.3	64.2	64.2	64.3	64.2	64.9	66.0	64.0
2014	63.1	63.0	63.5	64.3	64.6	65.4	65.2	65.6	66.1	66.2	67.0	68.9	65.2
2015	66.6	66.4	66.6	65.6	65.8	66.7	66.8	66.6	66.8	66.6	67.3	68.5	66.7
2016	65.7	65.1	65.3	65.1	65.0	65.8	66.8	66.6	66.4	66.1	66.9	69.1	66.2
2017	65.6	65.3	65.7	65.7	65.9	66.6	66.6	66.7	66.5	66.6	67.6	70.2	66.6
Information													
2007	33.0	33.5	33.7	34.1	34.3	34.4	33.6	33.3	33.2	33.1	33.4	33.4	33.6
2008	33.2	33.5	33.5	33.8	33.9	33.6	33.0	32.6	32.3	32.3	31.9	31.7	32.9
2009	31.3	31.4	31.4	31.0	31.1	30.6	30.0	29.5	29.2	29.3	29.3	29.4	30.3
2010	29.0	29.2	29.0	29.1	29.2	28.8	28.6	28.3	27.7	28.2	28.4	28.7	28.7
2011	28.2	28.4	28.3	28.4	28.4	28.1	28.0	27.8	27.6	27.5	27.6	27.6	28.0
2012	27.2	27.4	27.6	27.3	27.2	27.1	26.8	26.6	26.3	26.5	26.8	26.5	26.9
2013	26.1	26.5	26.6	26.4	26.6	26.3	26.2	26.1	25.7	25.6	25.6	25.8	26.1
2014	25.8	25.9	26.0	26.1	26.2	26.0	25.7	25.5	25.4	25.5	25.3	25.5	25.7
2015	25.1	25.2	25.1	25.0	25.2	24.9	24.2	23.8	23.3	23.6	23.5	23.3	24.4
2016	23.1	23.0	22.8	22.7	22.8	22.7	22.8	22.7	22.4	22.2	22.2	22.1	22.6
2017	22.0	21.9	21.9	22.0	22.1	22.2	22.2	22.0	21.7	21.7	21.9	22.0	22.0
Financial Activities													
2007	101.1	101.2	101.6	101.9	102.4	103.8	103.8	103.4	102.8	103.0	103.2	103.5	102.6
2008	102.6	102.7	102.8	102.6	102.8	103.6	103.6	103.2	102.0	101.8	101.9	102.4	102.7
2009	101.7	101.4	101.4	101.8	102.2	102.9	102.8	102.7	101.6	101.6	101.6	102.3	102.0
2010	101.2	100.9	101.2	100.8	101.2	101.9	101.7	101.6	100.8	101.1	101.1	101.7	101.3
2011	100.7	100.4	100.3	100.4	100.7	101.0	101.3	101.4	100.5	100.3	100.6	101.1	100.7
2012	100.2	100.1	100.5	101.2	101.6	102.5	102.5	102.3	101.8	102.1	102.3	103.0	101.7
2013	102.5	102.4	102.6	103.2	103.6	104.3	104.4	104.3	103.6	104.0	104.3	104.5	103.6
2014	103.5	103.3	103.5	103.6	103.7	104.8	104.5	104.8	104.0	104.2	104.2	104.7	104.1
2015	104.0	104.0	104.5	104.9	105.3	106.5	106.6	106.6	106.0	106.1	106.4	107.4	105.7
2016	107.1	107.0	107.2	107.3	107.6	108.5	109.1	108.6	108.1	108.1	108.1	108.9	108.0
2017	108.0	107.9	108.0	108.4	108.8	109.8	110.2	109.9	109.0	109.0	110.1	111.7	109.2
Professional and Business Services													
2007	116.1	117.1	117.7	121.4	120.9	123.2	123.1	124.0	122.9	123.6	123.9	123.2	121.4
2008	119.6	119.9	120.4	123.5	123.6	124.8	126.2	125.7	124.5	125.2	122.4	121.3	123.1
2009	117.1	117.3	116.1	117.3	116.8	117.6	117.2	118.0	117.2	119.0	118.5	117.9	117.5
2010	115.6	116.7	117.6	121.6	121.1	122.0	123.6	124.1	123.1	125.3	125.1	124.5	121.7
2011	121.5	121.7	121.6	125.0	124.1	124.8	127.1	127.6	128.1	129.2	129.0	127.4	125.6
2012	124.8	125.8	127.4	129.8	129.4	131.3	132.5	132.3	132.0	132.3	131.4	129.7	129.9
2013	127.0	127.7	128.4	131.2	131.4	133.4	134.0	135.0	134.2	135.3	135.6	134.8	132.3
2014	131.2	132.3	131.8	136.1	136.9	138.2	138.7	139.8	138.2	139.7	138.9	137.5	136.6
2015	134.6	135.1	135.7	139.1	139.7	141.1	140.7	141.3	138.9	139.8	139.4	137.6	138.6
2016	134.4	135.2	135.1	139.5	138.5	139.2	141.4	141.1	140.2	141.2	140.4	138.4	138.7
2017	133.8	135.3	135.6	140.2	139.3	141.1	141.6	141.7	140.3	141.7	142.0	139.9	139.4
Education and Health Services													
2007	201.2	204.1	205.5	205.7	204.1	199.2	193.7	194.7	203.1	208.2	210.1	209.8	203.3
2008	206.1	208.4	209.7	210.1	208.4	202.4	197.5	197.8	206.6	213.1	214.8	214.8	207.5
2009	210.5	212.9	213.9	214.6	212.5	206.4	201.6	202.1	211.1	218.4	219.2	219.3	211.9
2010	214.2	216.3	217.8	217.6	215.0	208.4	203.0	202.7	212.4	219.7	220.6	221.0	214.1
2011	215.6	218.0	219.1	221.5	218.6	211.3	205.6	206.0	216.6	224.0	225.0	225.2	217.2
2012	219.6	222.8	224.2	223.8	221.6	214.2	208.4	209.6	218.5	225.5	226.8	226.1	220.1
2013	221.5	223.6	224.2	223.8	223.5	215.7	214.3	215.0	223.8	225.0	225.8	226.1	221.9
2014	220.3	223.5	225.7	226.5	225.1	218.2	214.8	215.3	223.7	226.6	227.1	227.5	222.9
2015	222.4	225.1	226.8	228.6	226.8	220.5	219.3	219.8	227.5	230.7	231.0	231.5	225.8
2016	227.3	231.3	232.7	234.7	232.5	223.2	221.8	222.2	230.9	234.8	235.3	234.1	230.1
2017	229.0	235.1	235.7	235.8	234.1	226.3	223.4	224.1	231.1	233.3	235.4	235.1	231.5

1. Employment by Industry: Iowa, Selected Years, 2007–2017—*Continued*

(Numbers in thousands, not seasonally adjusted)

Industry and year	January	February	March	April	May	June	July	August	September	October	November	December	Annual average
Leisure and Hospitality													
2007	127.9	127.9	130.2	136.7	142.1	145.3	144.2	144.9	140.9	136.8	134.8	133.4	137.1
2008	127.1	127.7	130.0	136.2	140.9	143.3	141.9	143.4	139.1	134.0	131.2	130.4	135.4
2009	124.6	125.2	127.0	132.9	137.8	140.6	140.3	140.7	136.6	131.9	128.2	126.2	132.7
2010	120.9	121.7	123.2	130.0	134.8	137.3	137.1	137.4	133.9	129.3	127.1	125.8	129.9
2011	122.1	122.2	124.9	131.7	136.4	139.6	138.7	139.8	136.5	131.1	129.4	127.9	131.7
2012	124.0	125.4	128.3	133.7	138.8	141.9	142.5	142.6	138.2	133.3	131.8	130.8	134.3
2013	126.4	127.9	130.0	135.3	140.7	144.5	144.9	145.2	140.4	135.5	134.1	132.2	136.4
2014	128.8	130.1	132.1	136.8	142.7	145.8	145.0	145.7	141.8	137.1	135.5	134.5	138.0
2015	130.8	132.3	134.8	139.4	145.4	148.8	148.6	148.8	144.1	140.8	138.9	137.5	140.9
2016	133.1	134.6	137.3	142.7	147.1	150.4	150.0	150.2	145.3	142.6	140.7	137.9	142.7
2017	134.5	136.1	138.0	142.9	146.8	150.8	150.0	150.0	145.5	143.6	141.0	140.0	143.3
Other Services													
2007	56.6	56.4	57.1	57.6	58.0	59.1	58.3	57.9	57.6	57.8	57.8	57.9	57.7
2008	57.1	56.8	57.2	57.7	58.2	58.7	58.4	58.1	57.8	58.2	58.1	58.0	57.9
2009	57.2	57.3	57.4	57.7	57.9	58.5	58.3	57.4	57.1	57.1	56.9	57.0	57.5
2010	56.3	56.3	56.8	57.3	57.4	57.7	57.3	56.9	56.5	57.0	56.7	56.7	56.9
2011	56.2	56.1	56.4	56.5	56.7	57.1	57.1	57.1	56.9	57.0	56.8	57.0	56.7
2012	56.9	56.7	57.1	57.6	58.0	58.5	58.2	58.4	57.7	58.1	58.2	57.8	57.8
2013	57.2	57.2	57.3	57.6	58.2	58.6	58.9	59.1	58.3	58.6	58.5	58.6	58.2
2014	58.2	58.2	58.6	58.8	59.5	60.0	59.8	59.7	59.1	59.1	59.2	59.2	59.1
2015	58.6	58.5	58.9	59.0	59.3	59.9	59.6	59.4	59.0	59.3	59.1	59.3	59.2
2016	58.6	58.5	58.6	58.6	58.9	59.5	59.6	59.1	58.7	58.3	58.0	57.6	58.7
2017	57.0	57.1	57.2	57.3	57.7	58.5	58.5	58.0	57.5	57.6	57.0	56.0	57.5
Government													
2007	247.6	253.7	253.6	254.0	256.5	253.5	228.6	228.5	250.3	256.9	258.1	257.1	249.9
2008	249.9	255.9	257.0	257.2	260.5	256.1	231.3	231.0	254.7	260.3	261.3	260.1	252.9
2009	253.1	258.7	259.7	261.1	263.1	257.9	234.3	234.2	254.4	260.7	261.4	259.3	254.8
2010	250.3	255.9	258.3	258.4	263.3	257.6	232.8	232.0	251.3	258.0	260.4	258.8	253.1
2011	249.5	255.5	256.5	257.9	259.2	255.3	235.9	236.3	254.0	257.8	258.8	258.2	252.9
2012	251.7	256.1	256.8	258.4	259.9	254.4	234.7	239.3	254.4	258.3	259.8	259.2	253.6
2013	250.1	256.5	257.0	257.5	260.8	256.3	238.7	241.9	256.9	259.4	260.9	260.3	254.7
2014	252.5	257.6	258.2	258.9	260.5	254.3	236.0	239.0	258.5	261.2	262.6	261.3	255.1
2015	254.7	259.5	259.3	259.7	261.2	255.6	236.4	237.0	255.3	261.3	262.9	262.6	255.5
2016	255.8	260.8	260.9	262.1	263.0	258.8	237.5	241.0	258.8	263.3	265.0	264.3	257.6
2017	259.6	263.1	263.4	264.4	264.5	261.5	241.9	245.4	260.9	266.6	267.5	265.2	260.3

2. Average Weekly Hours by Selected Industry: Iowa, 2013–2017

(Not seasonally adjusted)

Industry and year	January	February	March	April	May	June	July	August	September	October	November	December	Annual average
Total Private													
2013	33.7	33.9	33.8	34.0	34.4	35.1	34.5	34.7	35.1	34.7	34.7	35.0	34.5
2014	34.2	35.1	35.0	35.0	34.9	35.7	35.2	35.3	35.1	35.2	35.4	34.8	35.1
2015	34.2	34.8	34.7	34.7	34.6	34.8	34.9	35.3	34.5	34.8	34.7	34.3	34.7
2016	33.8	33.8	34.0	34.5	34.6	35.1	34.8	34.8	34.7	35.1	34.7	34.2	34.5
2017	34.1	34.0	33.8	34.6	34.2	34.6	34.6	34.4	34.4	34.6	34.7	34.3	34.4
Goods Producing													
2013	38.9	38.8	39.4	39.7	40.7	41.1	41.0	41.2	41.4	41.6	41.2	41.1	40.5
2014	40.0	40.6	40.7	41.2	41.5	42.5	42.0	42.0	41.4	42.0	41.8	41.3	41.4
2015	40.3	40.5	40.6	41.1	40.9	41.1	41.1	41.8	40.0	41.7	41.3	41.3	41.0
2016	39.3	39.9	40.6	41.5	41.2	42.9	41.8	41.8	41.8	42.2	42.7	40.6	41.4
2017	39.6	40.0	40.0	40.4	40.4	40.9	40.5	40.6	40.7	40.8	41.0	40.4	40.5
Construction													
2013	36.5	36.9	38.0	38.2	42.0	41.2	42.7	42.6	42.9	43.6	42.0	40.6	40.9
2014	38.7	38.4	39.8	42.6	42.0	43.6	43.3	43.3	41.3	43.8	41.9	40.4	41.8
2015	38.6	38.5	38.9	40.4	40.6	41.2	41.9	42.9	38.9	42.0	41.7	41.7	40.7
2016	38.1	39.3	41.8	43.8	43.2	47.3	45.1	45.2	45.2	45.5	45.3	41.4	43.6
2017	39.2	39.3	39.2	40.5	40.4	41.5	41.4	41.7	41.4	39.5	40.3	38.6	40.3
Manufacturing													
2013	40.0	39.6	40.0	40.3	40.1	41.0	40.2	40.5	40.7	40.8	40.9	41.3	40.5
2014	40.5	41.4	41.0	40.7	41.3	42.0	41.5	41.5	41.6	41.3	41.9	41.9	41.4
2015	41.1	41.4	41.4	41.6	41.2	41.2	40.9	41.4	40.7	41.7	41.2	41.2	41.2
2016	40.1	40.4	40.3	40.3	40.1	40.3	40.1	40.0	39.9	40.3	41.3	40.4	40.3
2017	39.5	40.0	40.1	40.1	40.2	40.4	39.8	39.8	40.2	41.2	40.8	40.6	40.2
Trade, Transportation, and Utilities													
2013	32.3	32.7	32.4	32.5	33.1	33.4	32.9	33.2	33.7	33.5	33.2	33.2	33.0
2014	32.8	33.2	32.8	33.1	33.2	33.7	33.2	33.1	33.1	32.7	32.8	32.0	33.0
2015	31.7	32.2	31.8	31.9	32.1	32.5	32.5	32.8	33.0	32.5	32.1	31.8	32.2
2016	31.8	31.8	31.7	32.0	32.2	32.5	32.3	32.2	32.3	32.4	31.9	32.1	32.1
2017	32.4	32.1	32.3	33.0	32.7	33.0	32.9	32.8	32.7	32.6	32.9	32.5	32.7
Financial Activities													
2013	37.7	38.0	37.8	37.9	37.9	38.9	38.1	38.4	39.1	38.1	38.2	39.2	38.3
2014	38.4	39.1	38.8	38.3	38.2	39.2	38.5	38.7	38.7	38.7	39.6	38.8	38.7
2015	38.2	39.2	39.0	38.7	38.2	38.3	38.2	38.7	38.1	38.1	39.0	37.7	38.4
2016	37.9	38.0	37.7	38.0	38.8	37.9	38.0	37.8	37.8	39.0	37.7	37.5	38.0
2017	38.2	37.1	36.8	37.6	37.2	37.6	38.0	37.6	37.5	38.4	37.8	38.0	37.7
Professional and Business Services													
2013	33.3	33.7	33.3	33.9	34.1	35.7	33.9	34.5	34.9	34.5	34.6	35.5	34.3
2014	34.5	36.9	37.3	36.5	34.7	35.9	35.2	35.5	35.3	36.2	36.7	36.0	35.9
2015	35.0	36.2	36.3	36.0	35.9	35.9	36.4	36.8	35.2	35.7	35.9	35.6	35.9
2016	34.9	34.7	34.9	35.7	35.7	35.7	35.5	35.6	35.3	36.0	34.9	34.7	35.3
2017	34.5	34.5	34.4	35.1	34.8	35.0	35.2	35.0	35.2	35.0	35.2	34.6	34.9
Education and Health Services													
2013	32.0	31.8	31.7	31.7	31.5	32.4	31.5	31.4	32.1	31.3	31.7	31.7	31.7
2014	31.3	31.4	31.5	31.6	31.5	32.4	31.9	32.0	32.1	32.0	32.2	31.8	31.8
2015	31.8	31.9	31.7	31.6	31.6	31.9	32.3	32.5	32.1	31.9	32.3	31.7	31.9
2016	32.0	31.4	31.3	31.8	32.0	32.2	32.0	32.0	32.2	32.3	32.5	32.3	32.0
2017	32.5	31.9	31.2	32.1	31.3	31.5	31.9	31.3	31.6	31.6	31.6	31.2	31.6
Leisure and Hospitality													
2013	23.9	24.3	24.5	24.2	24.8	25.5	25.0	24.8	24.6	24.2	24.5	24.6	24.6
2014	23.7	24.8	24.9	24.6	25.1	25.7	25.6	25.4	24.8	25.0	24.7	24.7	24.9
2015	23.5	24.7	24.8	24.2	24.4	24.8	25.2	25.7	24.5	24.3	24.1	23.8	24.5
2016	23.4	23.7	24.0	23.7	24.1	24.7	24.7	24.7	24.2	24.4	23.9	23.8	24.1
2017	23.7	23.9	23.7	24.3	23.8	24.5	24.5	24.1	23.7	24.2	23.9	24.0	24.0
Other Services													
2013	29.6	29.1	28.3	28.7	28.6	29.4	29.8	29.9	29.7	28.9	27.6	29.2	29.1
2014	28.2	28.5	28.7	28.6	28.6	29.9	29.4	29.4	29.6	29.4	30.0	29.9	29.2
2015	30.0	30.5	29.4	28.7	28.7	29.2	29.6	29.4	28.5	28.3	26.9	26.9	28.8
2016	26.8	25.9	26.5	25.8	27.1	28.5	28.2	28.7	28.7	28.6	29.3	29.4	27.8
2017	29.1	29.2	28.1	28.1	28.6	30.2	30.1	30.1	29.9	30.6	30.3	30.7	29.6

3. Average Hourly Earnings by Selected Industry: Iowa, 2013–2017

(Dollars, not seasonally adjusted)

Industry and year	January	February	March	April	May	June	July	August	September	October	November	December	Annual average
Total Private													
2013	21.52	21.46	21.38	21.58	21.38	21.40	21.38	21.41	21.68	21.63	21.78	22.15	21.56
2014	21.92	21.86	21.87	21.68	21.71	21.81	21.75	21.79	21.92	22.02	22.09	22.11	21.88
2015	22.10	22.28	22.35	22.48	22.57	22.31	22.37	23.01	22.99	22.94	22.51	22.67	22.55
2016	22.75	22.79	23.06	23.37	23.37	23.39	23.27	23.08	23.23	23.57	23.42	23.34	23.23
2017	23.33	23.26	23.44	23.47	23.11	23.03	23.39	23.23	23.49	23.55	23.70	24.00	23.42
Goods Producing													
2013	21.83	22.11	22.09	22.20	22.05	22.18	22.20	22.10	22.49	22.29	22.51	23.42	22.30
2014	22.88	22.96	23.00	23.02	22.78	23.03	22.92	23.29	23.35	23.52	23.73	24.15	23.22
2015	23.87	24.18	24.11	24.14	24.16	24.01	24.27	24.57	24.44	23.48	22.90	23.20	23.94
2016	23.21	23.69	24.14	24.96	25.32	26.07	25.49	25.24	25.49	25.93	25.85	25.70	25.13
2017	25.42	24.98	25.21	25.18	24.60	24.78	25.19	24.77	25.02	25.07	25.30	26.12	25.13
Construction													
2013	23.94	24.57	24.84	24.45	23.78	23.45	23.56	23.45	23.54	24.05	24.35	24.94	24.02
2014	25.03	24.97	24.76	24.86	24.43	24.42	24.35	24.59	24.91	25.27	25.54	26.05	24.92
2015	25.89	25.80	26.00	25.29	25.19	25.54	25.35	25.84	26.17	26.90	27.54	28.53	26.19
2016	28.61	29.59	29.35	29.87	29.76	31.96	31.14	30.57	30.66	30.37	30.98	30.22	30.36
2017	29.14	28.49	28.20	26.99	26.54	26.02	26.22	25.95	26.08	26.08	26.53	25.97	26.77
Manufacturing													
2013	21.06	21.22	21.08	21.33	21.29	21.62	21.48	21.39	21.93	21.42	21.63	22.78	21.53
2014	22.09	22.22	22.34	22.27	22.08	22.42	22.27	22.71	22.69	22.71	22.93	23.39	22.51
2015	23.17	23.61	23.47	23.64	23.70	23.33	23.79	23.98	23.69	24.90	24.15	23.72	23.76
2016	23.52	23.48	23.73	24.09	24.48	24.28	24.15	23.85	24.00	24.74	24.11	25.15	24.13
2017	25.12	24.66	25.01	25.50	24.61	25.04	25.33	24.74	24.98	25.01	25.10	26.53	25.14
Trade, Transportation, and Utilities													
2013	17.90	18.19	18.09	18.27	17.85	17.95	17.84	18.06	18.54	18.59	18.74	18.80	18.24
2014	18.81	18.76	18.88	18.81	18.79	18.79	18.94	19.23	19.36	19.15	19.45	19.15	19.01
2015	19.22	19.55	19.56	20.11	20.23	19.53	19.80	20.68	20.62	21.14	20.57	20.95	20.17
2016	21.28	21.00	21.19	21.48	21.03	20.80	20.89	20.78	21.19	21.33	21.13	20.93	21.08
2017	21.32	21.38	21.35	21.84	21.10	20.88	21.23	21.04	21.36	21.05	21.13	21.00	21.22
Financial Activities													
2013	29.30	28.57	28.18	28.34	29.46	29.22	29.09	28.79	28.91	28.81	28.97	28.80	28.87
2014	28.52	28.72	28.82	28.56	28.45	28.22	28.08	27.65	27.72	28.16	27.51	27.40	28.15
2015	27.61	27.28	27.79	28.13	28.19	27.87	27.77	28.15	28.16	28.42	28.73	28.73	28.07
2016	28.84	28.89	29.64	29.70	29.96	29.43	29.47	29.23	29.57	30.16	30.24	30.00	29.60
2017	30.12	30.15	30.80	30.72	30.54	30.13	30.62	30.52	30.73	30.85	31.13	31.47	30.65
Professional and Business Services													
2013	21.83	21.61	21.84	21.97	21.61	21.84	22.26	22.53	22.73	22.76	22.95	23.65	22.32
2014	23.45	22.86	23.02	22.37	23.59	24.29	23.84	23.79	23.94	23.66	24.14	23.99	23.58
2015	23.88	24.33	24.14	23.61	24.18	24.07	24.27	24.63	24.71	24.82	23.19	23.16	24.09
2016	23.48	23.61	23.76	23.98	24.29	24.49	24.75	24.40	24.51	25.07	25.09	25.84	24.45
2017	25.16	25.13	25.44	25.60	25.73	25.61	25.76	25.49	25.57	25.99	25.95	26.92	25.70
Education and Health Services													
2013	22.40	22.03	21.90	22.33	21.35	21.18	21.26	21.40	21.11	21.14	21.21	21.32	21.55
2014	21.13	20.80	20.77	20.53	20.62	20.54	20.61	20.19	20.33	20.16	20.14	20.21	20.50
2015	20.20	20.40	20.68	20.69	20.74	20.92	20.55	20.68	20.88	21.09	20.97	21.19	20.75
2016	21.01	21.06	21.23	21.10	21.00	20.98	21.13	21.00	21.20	21.39	21.13	21.14	21.12
2017	21.32	21.19	21.28	21.17	21.10	21.28	21.41	21.59	21.59	21.60	21.83	21.61	21.41
Leisure and Hospitality													
2013	12.44	12.36	12.30	12.30	12.19	11.95	11.99	12.15	12.23	12.38	12.42	12.70	12.27
2014	12.53	12.65	12.45	12.50	12.37	12.25	12.09	12.13	12.37	12.37	12.38	12.71	12.39
2015	12.72	12.61	12.30	12.43	12.47	12.19	12.22	12.49	12.46	12.60	12.79	12.95	12.51
2016	12.82	12.84	12.74	12.94	12.80	12.49	12.63	12.51	12.84	12.87	12.85	13.06	12.78
2017	12.79	13.02	12.89	12.81	12.88	12.50	12.78	12.81	13.03	13.05	13.15	13.28	12.91
Other Services													
2013	19.49	19.54	19.16	19.22	18.97	19.07	18.66	18.64	19.42	18.97	18.65	19.06	19.07
2014	19.36	19.52	19.54	19.70	19.49	19.13	19.56	19.69	19.24	20.07	20.21	20.06	19.63
2015	20.57	21.11	21.09	21.14	21.37	20.48	20.50	20.61	20.56	20.61	20.07	19.97	20.68
2016	19.82	19.38	19.45	20.05	19.82	19.27	19.40	19.49	20.26	19.80	18.91	18.62	19.52
2017	18.60	19.27	19.11	19.22	18.96	18.34	18.20	18.03	18.14	18.48	18.40	18.38	18.58

4. Average Weekly Earnings by Selected Industry: Iowa, 2013–2017

(Dollars, not seasonally adjusted)

Industry and year	January	February	March	April	May	June	July	August	September	October	November	December	Annual average
Total Private													
2013	725.22	727.49	722.64	733.72	735.47	751.14	737.61	742.93	760.97	750.56	755.77	775.25	743.82
2014	749.66	767.29	765.45	758.80	757.68	778.62	765.60	769.19	769.39	775.10	781.99	769.43	767.99
2015	755.82	775.34	775.55	780.06	780.92	776.39	780.71	812.25	793.16	798.31	781.10	777.58	782.49
2016	768.95	770.30	784.04	806.27	808.60	820.99	809.80	803.18	806.08	827.31	812.67	798.23	801.44
2017	795.55	790.84	792.27	812.06	790.36	796.84	809.29	799.11	808.06	814.83	822.39	823.20	805.65
Goods Producing													
2013	849.19	857.87	870.35	881.34	897.44	911.60	910.20	910.52	931.09	927.26	927.41	962.56	903.15
2014	915.20	932.18	936.10	948.42	945.37	978.78	962.64	978.18	966.69	987.84	991.91	997.40	961.31
2015	961.96	979.29	978.87	992.15	988.14	986.81	997.50	1,027.03	977.60	979.12	945.77	958.16	981.54
2016	912.15	945.23	980.08	1,035.84	1,043.18	1,118.40	1,065.48	1,055.03	1,065.48	1,094.25	1,103.80	1,043.42	1,040.38
2017	1,006.63	999.20	1,008.40	1,017.27	993.84	1,013.50	1,020.20	1,005.66	1,018.31	1,022.86	1,037.30	1,055.25	1,017.77
Construction													
2013	873.81	906.63	943.92	933.99	998.76	966.14	1,006.01	998.97	1,009.87	1,048.58	1,022.70	1,012.56	982.42
2014	968.66	958.85	985.45	1,059.04	1,026.06	1,064.71	1,054.36	1,064.75	1,028.78	1,106.83	1,070.13	1,052.42	1,041.66
2015	999.35	993.30	1,011.40	1,021.72	1,022.71	1,052.25	1,062.17	1,108.54	1,018.01	1,129.80	1,148.42	1,189.70	1,065.93
2016	1,090.04	1,162.89	1,226.83	1,308.31	1,285.63	1,511.71	1,404.41	1,381.76	1,385.83	1,381.84	1,403.39	1,251.11	1,323.70
2017	1,142.29	1,119.66	1,105.44	1,093.10	1,072.22	1,079.83	1,085.51	1,082.12	1,079.71	1,030.16	1,069.16	1,002.44	1,078.83
Manufacturing													
2013	842.40	840.31	843.20	859.60	853.73	886.42	863.50	866.30	892.55	873.94	884.67	940.81	871.97
2014	894.65	919.91	915.94	906.39	911.90	941.64	924.21	942.47	943.90	937.92	960.77	980.04	931.91
2015	952.29	977.45	971.66	983.42	976.44	961.20	973.01	992.77	964.18	1,038.33	994.98	977.26	978.91
2016	943.15	948.59	956.32	970.83	981.65	978.48	968.42	954.00	957.60	997.02	995.74	1,016.06	972.44
2017	992.24	986.40	1,002.90	1,022.55	989.32	1,011.62	1,008.13	984.65	1,004.20	1,030.41	1,024.08	1,077.12	1,010.63
Trade, Transportation, and Utilities													
2013	578.17	594.81	586.12	593.78	590.84	599.53	586.94	599.59	624.80	622.77	622.17	624.16	601.92
2014	616.97	622.83	619.26	622.61	623.83	633.22	628.81	636.51	640.82	626.21	637.96	612.80	627.33
2015	609.27	629.51	622.01	641.51	649.38	634.73	643.50	678.30	680.46	687.05	660.30	666.21	649.47
2016	676.70	667.80	671.72	687.36	677.17	676.00	674.75	669.12	684.44	691.09	674.05	671.85	676.67
2017	690.77	686.30	689.61	720.72	689.97	689.04	698.47	690.11	698.47	686.23	695.18	682.50	693.89
Financial Activities													
2013	1,104.61	1,085.66	1,065.20	1,074.09	1,116.53	1,136.66	1,108.33	1,105.54	1,130.38	1,097.66	1,106.65	1,128.96	1,105.72
2014	1,095.17	1,122.95	1,118.22	1,093.85	1,086.79	1,106.22	1,081.08	1,070.06	1,072.76	1,089.79	1,089.40	1,063.12	1,089.41
2015	1,054.70	1,069.38	1,083.81	1,088.63	1,076.86	1,067.42	1,060.81	1,089.41	1,072.90	1,082.80	1,120.47	1,083.12	1,077.89
2016	1,093.04	1,097.82	1,117.43	1,128.60	1,162.45	1,115.40	1,119.86	1,104.89	1,117.75	1,176.24	1,140.05	1,125.00	1,124.80
2017	1,150.58	1,118.57	1,133.44	1,155.07	1,136.09	1,132.89	1,163.56	1,147.55	1,152.38	1,184.64	1,176.71	1,195.86	1,155.51
Professional and Business Services													
2013	726.94	728.26	727.27	744.78	736.90	779.69	754.61	777.29	793.28	785.22	794.07	839.58	765.58
2014	809.03	843.53	858.65	816.51	818.57	872.01	839.17	844.55	845.08	856.49	885.94	863.64	846.52
2015	835.80	880.75	876.28	849.96	868.06	864.11	883.43	906.38	869.79	886.07	832.52	824.50	864.83
2016	819.45	819.27	829.22	856.09	867.15	874.29	878.63	868.64	865.20	902.52	875.64	896.65	863.09
2017	868.02	866.99	875.14	898.56	895.40	896.35	906.75	892.15	900.06	909.65	913.44	931.43	896.93
Education and Health Services													
2013	716.80	700.55	694.23	707.86	672.53	686.23	669.69	671.96	677.63	661.68	672.36	675.84	683.14
2014	661.37	653.12	654.26	648.75	649.53	665.50	657.46	646.08	652.59	645.12	648.51	642.68	651.90
2015	642.36	650.76	655.56	653.80	655.38	667.35	663.77	672.10	670.25	672.77	677.33	671.72	661.93
2016	672.32	661.28	664.50	670.98	672.00	675.56	676.16	672.00	682.64	690.90	686.73	682.82	675.84
2017	692.90	675.96	663.94	679.56	660.43	670.32	682.98	675.77	682.24	682.56	689.83	674.23	676.56
Leisure and Hospitality													
2013	297.32	300.35	301.35	297.66	302.31	304.73	299.75	301.32	300.86	299.60	304.29	312.42	301.84
2014	296.96	313.72	310.01	307.50	310.49	314.83	309.50	308.10	306.78	309.25	305.79	313.94	308.51
2015	298.92	311.47	305.04	300.81	304.27	302.31	307.94	320.99	305.27	306.18	308.24	308.21	306.50
2016	299.99	304.31	305.76	306.68	308.48	308.50	311.96	309.00	310.73	314.03	307.12	310.83	308.00
2017	303.12	311.18	305.49	311.28	306.54	306.25	313.11	308.72	308.81	315.81	314.29	318.72	309.84
Other Services													
2013	576.90	568.61	542.23	551.61	542.54	560.66	556.07	557.34	576.77	548.23	514.74	556.55	554.94
2014	545.95	556.32	560.80	563.42	557.41	571.99	575.06	578.89	569.50	590.06	606.30	599.79	573.20
2015	617.10	643.86	620.05	606.72	613.32	598.02	606.80	605.93	585.96	583.26	539.88	537.19	595.58
2016	531.18	501.94	515.43	517.29	537.12	549.20	547.08	559.36	581.46	566.28	554.06	547.43	542.66
2017	541.26	562.68	536.99	540.08	542.26	553.87	547.82	542.70	542.39	565.49	557.52	564.27	549.97

KANSAS
At a Glance

Population:
  2010 census: 2,853,118
  2017 estimate: 2,913,123

Percent change in population:
  2010–2017: 2.1%

Percent change in total nonfarm employment:
  2007–2017: 1.6%

Industry with the largest growth in employment, 2007–2017 (thousands):
  Professional and business services, 27.8

Industry with the largest decline or smallest growth in employment, 2007–2017 (thousands):
  Manufacturing, -23.1

Civilian labor force:
  2010: 1,500,764
  2017: 1,478,783

Unemployment rate and rank among states (highest to lowest):
  2010: 7.1%, 41st
  2017: 3.6%, 37th

Over-the-year change in unemployment rates:
  2015–2016: -0.2%
  2016–2017: -0.4%

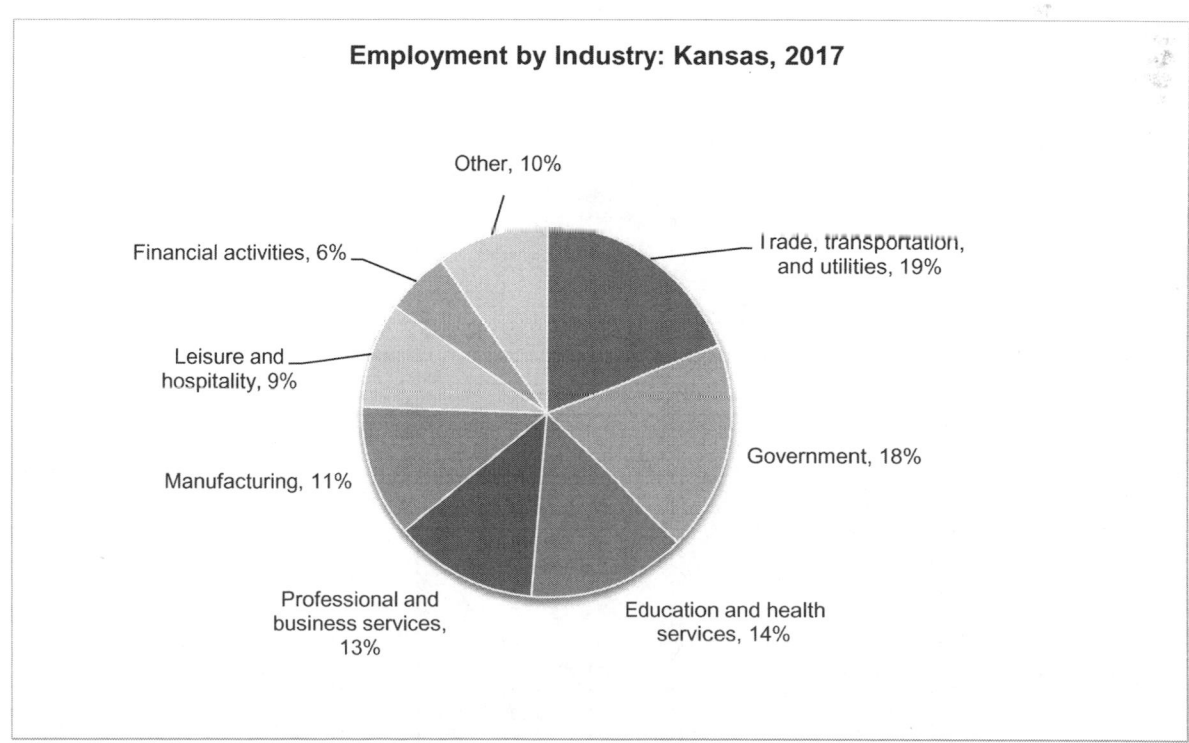

Employment by Industry: Kansas, 2017

Other, 10%
Financial activities, 6%
Trade, transportation, and utilities, 19%
Leisure and hospitality, 9%
Government, 18%
Manufacturing, 11%
Professional and business services, 13%
Education and health services, 14%

1. Employment by Industry: Kansas, Selected Years, 2007–2017

(Numbers in thousands, not seasonally adjusted)

Industry and year	January	February	March	April	May	June	July	August	September	October	November	December	Annual average
Total Nonfarm													
2007	1,342.2	1,352.8	1,373.9	1,378.7	1,388.1	1,398.6	1,370.5	1,369.2	1,392.4	1,397.9	1,405.8	1,403.2	1,381.1
2008	1,367.2	1,378.3	1,390.5	1,400.7	1,407.3	1,406.3	1,376.6	1,371.5	1,396.8	1,405.0	1,403.8	1,400.4	1,392.0
2009	1,359.6	1,357.1	1,357.3	1,357.7	1,360.8	1,350.9	1,319.8	1,314.6	1,334.7	1,340.4	1,343.3	1,339.2	1,344.6
2010	1,302.0	1,305.4	1,316.0	1,334.8	1,346.9	1,342.7	1,318.6	1,319.0	1,332.9	1,347.8	1,345.7	1,345.7	1,329.8
2011	1,315.6	1,316.9	1,326.7	1,347.4	1,353.9	1,341.0	1,325.0	1,328.3	1,348.2	1,357.5	1,359.7	1,355.0	1,339.6
2012	1,331.6	1,339.6	1,351.2	1,360.0	1,370.6	1,366.1	1,337.4	1,344.1	1,360.9	1,374.8	1,377.7	1,375.3	1,357.4
2013	1,341.8	1,353.0	1,358.9	1,375.4	1,380.7	1,374.7	1,354.0	1,359.9	1,382.6	1,391.5	1,397.5	1,395.3	1,372.1
2014	1,359.0	1,370.3	1,381.3	1,394.9	1,403.6	1,396.2	1,375.1	1,379.7	1,397.2	1,408.9	1,412.6	1,412.0	1,390.9
2015	1,374.5	1,387.3	1,392.8	1,402.6	1,410.3	1,405.7	1,384.6	1,387.1	1,404.9	1,417.0	1,419.2	1,418.0	1,400.3
2016	1,382.0	1,392.6	1,398.0	1,413.4	1,413.2	1,403.3	1,387.2	1,388.6	1,410.8	1,420.0	1,421.8	1,417.8	1,404.1
2017	1,379.9	1,395.5	1,401.0	1,402.1	1,406.1	1,399.6	1,385.9	1,389.0	1,410.1	1,422.2	1,427.7	1,424.6	1,403.6
Total Private													
2007	1,091.0	1,092.7	1,110.5	1,116.0	1,122.9	1,132.5	1,133.9	1,134.2	1,132.6	1,132.9	1,138.9	1,136.4	1,122.9
2008	1,112.9	1,115.6	1,123.9	1,134.6	1,137.1	1,145.7	1,141.7	1,136.1	1,136.1	1,137.0	1,133.9	1,129.9	1,132.0
2009	1,097.4	1,090.9	1,089.4	1,088.6	1,087.1	1,088.9	1,084.4	1,080.7	1,074.6	1,072.9	1,074.3	1,070.3	1,083.3
2010	1,042.1	1,041.9	1,048.4	1,065.9	1,070.8	1,076.0	1,076.8	1,075.7	1,070.0	1,081.2	1,081.4	1,080.8	1,067.6
2011	1,054.0	1,053.5	1,061.5	1,079.4	1,084.9	1,084.7	1,086.9	1,088.3	1,085.8	1,091.7	1,093.9	1,092.3	1,079.7
2012	1,073.9	1,076.6	1,086.7	1,095.4	1,103.0	1,110.9	1,102.8	1,104.2	1,101.9	1,108.9	1,111.4	1,111.2	1,098.9
2013	1,085.8	1,089.6	1,095.3	1,109.5	1,116.7	1,123.7	1,121.8	1,124.1	1,121.9	1,127.0	1,132.1	1,131.8	1,114.9
2014	1,104.6	1,108.1	1,117.9	1,131.3	1,140.0	1,144.1	1,141.0	1,143.3	1,137.7	1,144.1	1,147.6	1,148.6	1,134.0
2015	1,119.8	1,124.7	1,129.0	1,138.2	1,146.2	1,152.7	1,151.4	1,151.5	1,146.3	1,153.8	1,155.8	1,156.1	1,143.8
2016	1,129.3	1,131.7	1,135.2	1,149.5	1,151.0	1,151.5	1,155.0	1,153.7	1,151.4	1,156.0	1,157.9	1,154.3	1,148.0
2017	1,127.1	1,133.5	1,138.3	1,139.1	1,143.5	1,148.7	1,153.0	1,152.9	1,151.0	1,157.9	1,162.5	1,160.7	1,147.4
Goods Producing													
2007	250.7	248.9	254.9	255.4	257.3	262.0	264.0	264.2	263.3	262.3	263.1	260.8	258.9
2008	255.4	255.0	258.3	260.4	259.7	265.3	265.9	259.7	262.6	260.5	257.5	254.4	259.6
2009	243.7	240.0	237.7	234.6	231.0	231.6	230.4	229.1	225.8	224.6	222.5	218.6	230.8
2010	212.1	211.5	213.6	219.3	220.6	223.7	225.6	225.4	224.2	224.6	222.6	220.6	220.3
2011	212.2	211.5	215.5	219.5	221.0	223.2	224.9	225.1	224.3	225.8	224.5	223.4	220.9
2012	219.8	219.4	223.6	223.7	226.3	228.4	229.0	228.6	228.2	228.0	226.7	224.5	225.5
2013	219.9	220.6	222.7	226.5	228.2	230.5	230.8	231.1	230.9	231.5	231.9	230.7	227.9
2014	225.4	227.5	229.9	232.3	234.0	236.9	235.5	235.8	234.0	234.3	233.2	232.4	232.6
2015	224.5	227.7	229.3	229.0	232.3	234.1	233.7	232.4	232.4	232.4	231.7	230.7	230.9
2016	225.1	225.0	226.9	228.4	228.8	230.5	230.5	230.6	230.0	230.0	229.5	227.5	228.6
2017	223.8	225.6	227.1	226.1	227.4	230.9	230.9	229.6	230.2	230.5	231.7	229.6	228.6
Service-Providing													
2007	1,091.5	1,103.9	1,119.0	1,123.3	1,130.8	1,136.6	1,106.5	1,105.0	1,129.1	1,135.6	1,142.7	1,142.4	1,122.2
2008	1,111.8	1,123.3	1,132.2	1,140.3	1,147.6	1,141.0	1,110.7	1,111.8	1,134.2	1,144.5	1,146.3	1,146.0	1,132.5
2009	1,115.9	1,117.1	1,119.6	1,123.1	1,129.8	1,119.3	1,089.4	1,085.5	1,108.9	1,115.8	1,120.8	1,120.6	1,113.8
2010	1,089.9	1,093.9	1,102.4	1,115.5	1,126.3	1,119.0	1,093.0	1,093.6	1,108.7	1,123.2	1,123.1	1,125.1	1,109.5
2011	1,103.4	1,105.4	1,111.2	1,127.9	1,132.9	1,117.8	1,100.1	1,103.2	1,123.9	1,131.7	1,135.2	1,131.6	1,118.7
2012	1,111.8	1,120.2	1,127.6	1,136.3	1,144.3	1,137.7	1,108.4	1,115.5	1,132.7	1,146.8	1,151.0	1,150.8	1,131.9
2013	1,121.9	1,132.4	1,136.2	1,148.9	1,152.5	1,144.2	1,123.2	1,128.8	1,151.7	1,160.0	1,165.6	1,164.6	1,144.2
2014	1,133.6	1,142.8	1,151.4	1,162.6	1,169.6	1,159.3	1,139.6	1,143.9	1,163.2	1,174.6	1,179.4	1,179.6	1,158.3
2015	1,150.0	1,159.6	1,163.5	1,173.6	1,178.0	1,171.6	1,150.9	1,154.7	1,172.5	1,184.6	1,187.5	1,187.3	1,169.5
2016	1,156.9	1,167.6	1,171.1	1,185.0	1,184.4	1,172.8	1,156.7	1,158.0	1,180.8	1,190.0	1,192.3	1,190.3	1,175.5
2017	1,156.1	1,169.9	1,173.9	1,176.0	1,178.7	1,168.7	1,155.0	1,159.4	1,179.9	1,191.7	1,196.0	1,195.0	1,175.0
Mining and Logging													
2007	8.9	8.9	9.0	9.2	9.1	9.1	9.3	9.3	9.2	9.3	9.3	9.4	9.2
2008	9.4	9.4	9.5	9.6	9.6	9.7	10.0	10.2	10.1	10.0	9.9	9.8	9.8
2009	8.7	8.3	8.1	7.8	7.7	7.8	8.0	8.0	8.0	8.1	8.0	8.1	8.1
2010	7.8	7.9	8.0	8.3	8.3	8.4	8.5	8.5	8.5	8.8	8.6	8.6	8.4
2011	8.4	8.3	8.5	8.8	8.8	9.0	9.5	9.5	9.4	9.5	9.5	9.6	9.1
2012	9.5	9.5	9.6	9.6	9.8	10.0	10.3	10.3	10.1	10.5	10.5	10.5	10.0
2013	10.1	10.1	10.1	10.4	10.5	10.5	10.7	10.6	10.5	10.6	10.7	10.8	10.5
2014	10.4	10.3	10.4	10.6	10.7	10.6	10.6	10.6	10.5	10.5	10.4	10.3	10.5
2015	9.9	9.3	8.9	8.6	8.6	8.6	8.5	8.4	8.1	7.8	7.7	7.7	8.5
2016	7.2	6.9	6.8	6.7	6.8	6.8	6.9	6.9	6.8	6.7	6.8	6.7	6.8
2017	6.6	6.6	6.7	6.7	6.7	6.8	6.8	6.8	6.8	6.8	6.9	6.9	6.8

1. Employment by Industry: Kansas, Selected Years, 2007–2017—*Continued*

(Numbers in thousands, not seasonally adjusted)

Industry and year	January	February	March	April	May	June	July	August	September	October	November	December	Annual average
Construction													
2007	60.6	57.8	62.5	63.6	64.8	67.8	68.5	68.6	67.8	67.3	67.0	64.4	65.1
2008	59.9	59.0	61.8	64.5	66.3	68.2	68.5	67.9	66.3	65.1	63.8	62.2	64.5
2009	56.1	55.5	56.2	57.3	58.9	60.3	61.4	60.0	58.4	57.0	55.9	53.1	57.5
2010	47.2	46.7	49.2	53.8	54.7	56.9	58.6	58.4	57.4	57.6	55.5	53.2	54.1
2011	47.1	46.8	49.9	52.6	53.9	55.2	56.0	55.8	55.6	56.3	54.7	53.1	53.1
2012	50.5	50.4	53.9	54.8	56.2	57.8	57.6	57.2	56.7	56.2	54.9	53.5	55.0
2013	50.0	50.9	52.1	55.4	56.7	59.0	59.7	60.2	59.9	60.1	59.6	57.9	56.8
2014	55.3	54.6	57.4	59.8	61.6	62.6	63.2	62.3	61.1	61.4	59.7	58.7	59.8
2015	55.1	56.1	58.3	61.5	61.8	62.7	63.8	63.4	62.7	63.3	62.5	61.2	61.0
2016	57.3	57.2	59.8	61.2	61.6	63.5	64.0	63.4	63.1	63.2	62.3	60.3	61.4
2017	57.5	58.4	59.9	59.4	60.1	61.8	62.4	61.9	60.8	61.2	60.6	59.2	60.3
Manufacturing													
2007	181.2	182.2	183.4	182.6	183.4	185.1	186.2	186.3	186.3	185.7	186.8	187.0	184.7
2008	186.1	186.6	187.0	186.3	183.8	187.4	187.4	181.6	186.2	185.4	183.8	182.4	185.3
2009	178.9	176.2	173.4	169.5	164.4	163.5	161.0	161.1	159.4	159.5	158.6	157.4	165.2
2010	157.1	156.9	156.4	157.2	157.6	158.4	158.5	158.5	158.3	158.2	158.5	158.8	157.9
2011	156.7	156.4	157.1	158.1	158.3	159.0	159.4	159.8	159.3	160.0	160.3	160.7	158.8
2012	159.8	159.5	160.1	159.3	160.3	160.6	161.1	161.1	161.4	161.3	161.3	160.5	160.5
2013	159.8	159.6	160.5	160.7	161.0	161.0	160.4	160.3	160.5	160.8	161.6	162.0	160.7
2014	159.7	162.6	162.1	161.9	161.7	163.7	161.7	162.9	162.4	162.4	163.1	163.4	162.3
2015	159.5	162.3	162.1	158.9	161.9	162.8	161.4	160.6	161.6	161.3	161.5	161.8	161.3
2016	160.6	160.9	160.3	160.5	160.4	160.2	159.6	160.3	160.1	160.1	160.4	160.5	160.3
2017	159.7	160.6	160.5	160.0	160.6	162.3	161.7	160.9	162.6	162.5	164.2	163.5	161.6
Trade, Transportation, and Utilities													
2007	258.4	257.2	261.0	260.7	262.3	263.4	262.9	263.0	262.4	263.6	268.0	269.2	262.7
2008	260.9	259.5	260.4	260.9	261.9	263.0	263.6	262.5	261.0	262.5	265.2	266.1	262.3
2009	257.4	255.1	254.8	253.8	254.1	254.8	253.3	252.3	251.2	251.9	255.0	255.8	254.1
2010	247.3	245.8	246.9	249.8	251.3	252.5	252.1	251.8	250.3	253.6	256.9	258.3	251.4
2011	250.2	248.9	248.2	253.0	254.5	254.0	253.9	253.9	253.1	255.2	259.3	260.2	253.7
2012	252.9	251.2	252.3	253.8	255.5	257.5	254.4	254.6	254.1	256.8	260.7	261.6	255.5
2013	253.8	252.7	253.1	254.5	256.2	257.5	257.2	258.3	257.4	259.7	264.4	266.1	257.6
2014	257.0	255.2	257.9	259.8	261.4	262.2	262.1	262.8	261.2	264.0	268.3	270.6	261.9
2015	261.8	259.7	260.5	262.2	264.6	266.2	265.6	266.0	264.8	267.6	271.5	272.7	265.3
2016	264.2	263.6	263.7	266.3	267.3	267.0	268.2	267.9	266.6	269.3	273.8	275.6	267.8
2017	266.0	265.0	264.6	263.6	264.9	264.8	266.7	269.0	268.5	270.2	273.9	274.6	267.7
Wholesale Trade													
2007	58.4	58.4	59.1	58.8	59.0	60.3	60.4	59.7	59.4	60.1	60.1	60.0	59.5
2008	60.2	60.0	59.9	60.2	60.5	61.3	61.9	60.9	60.3	60.5	60.4	60.1	60.5
2009	60.2	59.9	59.9	58.4	58.2	58.9	59.0	58.0	57.6	57.5	57.3	56.9	58.5
2010	56.1	56.0	56.2	57.7	57.7	58.5	58.4	57.7	57.1	57.4	56.9	56.8	57.2
2011	56.5	56.5	56.8	57.3	57.7	58.2	58.4	57.9	57.5	57.6	57.5	57.6	57.5
2012	56.9	56.9	57.2	57.1	57.5	58.8	57.8	57.5	56.9	57.2	57.0	57.1	57.3
2013	56.9	56.8	56.8	57.1	57.4	58.2	59.5	59.0	58.4	58.9	58.9	59.0	58.1
2014	58.1	57.8	58.9	59.0	59.4	60.1	60.5	59.9	59.4	59.8	59.7	59.8	59.4
2015	59.5	59.4	59.6	59.5	60.0	60.8	60.8	60.2	59.6	60.2	60.0	59.8	60.0
2016	59.2	59.1	58.9	59.5	59.8	60.4	60.7	60.1	59.6	60.0	59.6	59.5	59.7
2017	58.8	58.8	58.9	58.9	59.4	60.2	60.6	60.1	59.6	60.4	60.5	60.5	59.7
Retail Trade													
2007	146.3	145.3	147.8	147.3	148.5	148.1	148.2	148.1	147.4	148.3	152.3	153.3	148.4
2008	146.7	145.3	146.5	146.5	147.2	147.5	147.5	147.0	146.0	145.9	148.6	149.4	147.0
2009	142.2	140.5	140.7	141.6	142.4	142.4	141.5	141.3	141.1	141.7	144.5	145.4	142.1
2010	139.4	138.0	138.7	139.9	141.1	141.2	140.7	140.4	139.2	141.2	144.5	145.5	140.8
2011	139.2	138.0	139.0	141.2	142.0	141.9	141.7	141.4	140.7	142.2	146.1	146.5	141.7
2012	141.3	139.7	140.6	141.5	142.5	143.0	142.5	142.1	141.9	143.5	147.4	147.9	142.8
2013	141.3	140.4	141.0	142.1	143.0	143.8	143.8	144.4	144.1	145.3	149.3	150.6	144.1
2014	143.8	142.6	143.7	145.3	146.1	146.6	146.5	146.6	145.4	147.2	151.1	152.3	146.4
2015	145.7	144.5	145.2	147.0	148.7	150.0	149.5	149.3	148.3	150.5	153.8	154.0	148.9
2016	148.5	148.1	148.4	149.9	150.1	149.8	150.6	149.9	148.3	150.0	153.3	153.6	150.0
2017	148.1	147.1	146.8	146.4	146.9	146.3	147.2	147.2	145.5	145.9	147.9	148.4	147.0

1. Employment by Industry: Kansas, Selected Years, 2007–2017—*Continued*

(Numbers in thousands, not seasonally adjusted)

Industry and year	January	February	March	April	May	June	July	August	September	October	November	December	Annual average
Transportation and Utilities													
2007	53.7	53.5	54.1	54.6	54.8	55.0	54.3	55.2	55.6	55.2	55.6	55.9	54.8
2008	54.0	54.2	54.0	54.2	54.2	54.2	54.2	54.6	54.7	56.1	56.2	56.6	54.8
2009	55.0	54.7	54.2	53.8	53.5	53.5	52.8	53.0	52.5	52.7	53.2	53.5	53.5
2010	51.8	51.8	52.0	52.2	52.5	52.8	53.0	53.7	54.0	55.0	55.5	56.0	53.4
2011	54.5	54.4	52.4	54.5	54.8	53.9	53.8	54.6	54.9	55.4	55.7	56.1	54.6
2012	54.7	54.6	54.5	55.2	55.5	55.7	54.1	55.0	55.3	56.1	56.3	56.6	55.3
2013	55.6	55.5	55.3	55.3	55.8	55.5	53.9	54.9	54.9	55.5	56.2	56.5	55.4
2014	55.1	54.8	55.3	55.5	55.9	55.5	55.1	56.3	56.4	57.0	57.5	58.5	56.1
2015	56.6	55.8	55.7	55.7	55.9	55.4	55.3	56.5	56.9	56.9	57.7	58.9	56.4
2016	56.5	56.4	56.4	56.9	57.4	56.8	56.9	57.9	58.7	59.3	60.9	62.5	58.1
2017	59.1	59.1	58.9	58.3	58.6	58.3	58.9	61.7	63.4	63.9	65.5	65.7	61.0
Information													
2007	39.7	39.6	39.7	39.6	39.6	39.6	39.5	39.1	38.5	38.1	38.1	38.0	39.1
2008	37.8	37.7	37.6	37.5	37.0	37.0	36.9	36.3	35.5	35.6	35.0	34.8	36.6
2009	34.1	33.8	33.7	33.9	33.4	32.9	32.5	31.8	30.9	29.0	28.8	28.8	32.0
2010	28.2	27.9	27.7	27.7	27.4	27.1	26.7	26.3	25.8	25.6	25.5	25.5	26.8
2011	25.2	25.1	25.0	24.6	23.9	23.8	23.6	23.3	22.9	22.9	22.9	22.9	23.8
2012	23.3	23	23.1	23	23	23	22.8	22.6	22.4	22.5	22.5	22.5	22.8
2013	22.1	22.1	22.0	22.1	22.1	22.2	22.5	22.5	22.2	22.2	22.3	22.5	22.2
2014	22.4	22.2	22.1	22.1	22.1	22.1	22.1	21.9	21.5	21.6	21.6	21.6	21.9
2015	21.2	21.2	21.2	21.1	21.1	21.2	21.2	21.1	20.7	20.8	20.9	21.0	21.1
2016	21.0	21.0	20.8	20.8	20.7	20.7	20.7	20.5	20.1	19.8	19.9	19.9	20.5
2017	20.0	19.8	19.7	19.6	19.6	19.4	19.2	19.0	18.8	18.8	19.3	19.5	19.4
Financial Activities													
2007	73.3	73.4	74.0	73.8	74.2	74.8	75.2	75.0	74.6	74.2	74.2	74.6	74.3
2008	73.1	73.3	73.1	73.5	73.7	74.0	73.9	73.8	73.1	73.3	73.1	73.5	73.5
2009	72.1	72.1	72.0	71.5	71.6	72.1	72.8	72.9	72.0	72.5	72.6	72.8	72.3
2010	71.7	71.6	71.4	71.9	72.3	72.4	72.5	72.4	71.7	72.7	72.7	73.1	72.2
2011	71.9	71.8	72.0	72.7	73.8	74.0	74.5	74.6	74.2	74.7	74.8	75.2	73.7
2012	74.7	75.3	75.7	76.1	76.2	76.9	77.0	76.9	76.2	76.6	77.0	77.3	76.3
2013	76.5	76.7	76.5	77.3	77.9	78.9	79.0	78.8	78.2	78.3	78.5	78.6	77.9
2014	77.4	77.3	77.5	77.6	77.9	78.3	78.4	78.6	78.1	78.5	78.6	78.9	78.1
2015	78.1	78.2	78.4	78.5	78.6	79.1	79.5	79.3	78.3	78.7	78.8	78.9	78.7
2016	79.1	78.9	78.6	79.7	79.7	79.7	80.1	80.0	79.0	79.0	78.9	78.8	79.3
2017	78.1	78.1	77.9	77.7	77.7	78.3	78.9	78.7	77.9	78.0	77.7	77.9	78.1
Professional and Business Services													
2007	142.2	143.7	145.6	147.9	148.5	149.7	151.4	152.6	152.9	152.8	154.3	153.6	149.6
2008	149.2	150.5	152.5	154.7	154.5	156.2	155.4	156.0	155.5	156.4	155.9	154.5	154.3
2009	149.3	147.8	147.3	148.1	147.4	147.6	147.4	146.7	145.8	147.2	148.4	148.5	147.6
2010	145.1	145.2	146.7	152.4	151.6	152.4	154.5	154.3	152.3	155.7	155.4	155.7	151.8
2011	152.0	152.7	154.3	157.8	156.8	155.9	157.4	158.2	158.6	159.8	160.0	158.7	156.9
2012	156.9	158.1	159.7	162.5	162.7	164.7	163.2	163.9	164.2	167.2	166.9	167.4	163.1
2013	163.7	165.3	166.9	170.7	170.2	172.5	173.4	174.3	174.5	175.0	175.8	176.3	171.6
2014	171.8	173.1	174.9	177.7	177.9	179.4	178.8	179.8	179.1	181.0	181.6	181.8	178.1
2015	175.2	175.9	176.5	178.7	178.5	179.7	180.3	180.9	179.8	181.7	181.3	181.6	179.2
2016	174.6	174.5	174.7	178.1	176.8	176.9	179.0	178.6	179.7	180.3	180.0	179.1	177.7
2017	172.3	173.0	174.2	176.3	176.0	176.6	179.9	178.9	178.4	181.5	181.9	179.8	177.4
Education and Health Services													
2007	167.6	168.8	170.1	170.7	171.0	171.3	170.0	170.4	173.0	174.3	174.5	174.8	171.4
2008	173.4	174.9	175.6	177.0	177.2	176.6	174.2	175.5	177.6	178.6	179.2	179.2	176.6
2009	178.2	179.0	179.1	179.9	180.3	179.7	178.5	178.9	180.5	181.9	182.2	182.4	180.1
2010	179.1	180.1	180.1	179.5	180.1	179.3	178.2	178.5	179.8	182.5	183.2	183.5	180.3
2011	183.8	184.2	184.3	185.9	186.3	184.4	183.2	183.8	185.2	186.5	187.0	186.9	185.1
2012	184.4	185.2	185.5	186.2	186.9	186.2	184.3	185.2	186.7	188.2	188.9	189.5	186.4
2013	186.9	187.0	187.3	188.3	188.7	187.9	185.8	186.2	187.3	188.8	189.4	189.0	187.7
2014	187.1	187.6	187.8	189.9	191.0	190.0	188.7	189.1	190.9	192.2	193.2	193.0	190.0
2015	192.0	193.2	192.9	195.1	195.1	194.0	193.4	193.4	194.1	195.9	196.4	196.4	194.3
2016	194.7	195.9	195.5	197.0	196.6	194.8	195.3	194.6	196.8	198.1	198.1	197.6	196.3
2017	195.1	196.8	196.8	196.9	196.6	196.0	195.4	195.4	196.8	198.7	199.4	199.9	197.0

1. Employment by Industry: Kansas, Selected Years, 2007–2017—*Continued*

(Numbers in thousands, not seasonally adjusted)

Industry and year	January	February	March	April	May	June	July	August	September	October	November	December	Annual average
Leisure and Hospitality													
2007	108.3	109.8	113.0	115.4	117.7	119.3	118.8	117.6	115.6	114.4	113.7	112.6	114.7
2008	110.7	111.5	113.0	116.9	119.2	120.3	118.3	118.9	117.5	116.5	114.6	114.4	116.0
2009	109.9	110.1	112.0	114.1	116.6	117.8	117.4	117.2	116.3	113.5	112.5	111.4	114.1
2010	107.1	108.2	110.3	113.4	115.8	117.4	116.3	116.2	114.9	114.2	113.4	112.5	113.3
2011	108.3	108.5	111.4	115.1	117.9	119.2	118.9	119.1	117.0	115.9	114.8	114.4	115.0
2012	112.3	114.3	116.9	120.2	122.5	124.5	122.8	123.3	120.4	119.7	119.1	118.9	119.6
2013	114.9	116.4	118.2	121.1	124.6	125.6	124.7	124.4	122.7	122.4	120.5	119.6	121.3
2014	115.6	116.7	119.0	122.7	126.8	126.8	127.0	126.9	124.6	123.6	122.4	122.1	122.9
2015	119.5	120.9	122.7	125.6	127.9	129.9	129.4	129.7	127.1	126.8	125.6	125.1	125.9
2016	121.1	122.8	124.7	128.2	130.4	131.6	130.8	131.1	128.4	128.4	126.7	125.1	127.4
2017	121.8	124.4	127.2	128.2	130.8	132.6	131.8	131.9	129.7	129.5	127.8	129.0	128.7
Other Services													
2007	50.8	51.3	52.2	52.5	52.3	52.4	52.1	52.3	52.3	53.2	53.0	52.8	52.3
2008	52.4	53.2	53.4	53.7	53.9	53.3	53.5	53.4	53.3	53.6	53.4	53.0	53.3
2009	52.7	53.0	52.8	52.7	52.7	52.4	52.1	51.8	52.1	52.3	52.3	52.0	52.4
2010	51.5	51.6	51.7	51.9	51.7	51.2	50.9	50.8	51.0	52.3	51.7	51.6	51.5
2011	50.4	50.8	50.8	50.8	50.7	50.2	50.5	50.3	50.5	50.9	50.6	50.6	50.6
2012	49.6	50.1	49.9	49.9	49.9	49.7	49.3	49.1	49.7	49.9	49.6	49.5	49.7
2013	48.0	48.8	48.6	49.0	48.8	48.6	48.4	48.5	48.7	49.1	49.3	49.0	48.7
2014	47.9	48.5	48.8	49.2	48.9	48.4	48.4	48.4	48.3	48.9	48.7	48.2	48.6
2015	47.5	47.9	47.5	48.0	48.1	48.5	48.3	48.7	49.1	49.9	49.6	49.7	48.6
2016	49.5	50.0	50.3	51.0	50.7	50.3	50.4	50.4	50.8	51.1	51.0	50.7	50.5
2017	50.0	50.8	50.8	50.7	50.5	50.1	50.2	50.4	50.7	50.7	50.8	50.4	50.5
Government													
2007	251.2	260.1	263.4	262.7	265.2	266.1	236.6	235.0	259.8	265.0	266.9	266.8	258.2
2008	254.3	262.7	266.6	266.1	270.2	260.6	234.9	235.4	260.7	268.0	269.9	270.5	260.0
2009	262.2	266.2	267.9	269.1	273.7	262.0	235.4	233.9	260.1	267.5	269.0	268.9	261.3
2010	259.9	263.5	267.6	268.9	276.1	266.7	241.8	243.3	262.9	266.6	264.3	264.9	262.2
2011	261.6	263.4	265.2	268.0	269.0	256.3	238.1	240.0	262.4	265.8	265.8	262.7	259.9
2012	257.7	263.0	264.5	264.6	267.6	255.2	234.6	239.9	259.0	265.9	266.3	264.1	258.5
2013	256.0	263.4	263.6	265.9	264.0	251.0	232.2	235.8	260.7	264.5	265.4	263.5	257.2
2014	254.4	262.2	263.4	263.6	263.6	252.1	234.1	236.4	259.5	264.8	265.0	263.4	256.9
2015	254.7	262.6	263.8	264.4	264.1	253.0	233.2	235.6	258.6	263.2	263.4	261.9	256.5
2016	252.7	260.9	262.8	263.9	262.2	251.8	232.2	234.9	259.4	264.0	263.9	263.5	256.0
2017	252.8	262.0	262.7	263.0	262.6	250.9	232.9	236.1	259.1	264.3	265.2	263.9	256.3

2. Average Weekly Hours by Selected Industry: Kansas, 2013–2017

(Not seasonally adjusted)

Industry and year	January	February	March	April	May	June	July	August	September	October	November	December	Annual average
Total Private													
2013	34.3	34.3	34.5	34.5	34.3	35.3	34.6	34.5	35.0	34.5	34.4	34.8	34.6
2014	34.0	34.4	34.8	34.4	34.4	35.0	34.6	34.7	34.6	34.5	35.2	34.5	34.6
2015	34.2	34.5	34.6	34.0	34.1	34.6	34.4	34.9	34.0	34.2	34.4	33.8	34.3
2016	33.6	33.5	33.5	33.4	33.7	34.0	33.8	33.8	33.8	34.5	33.9	33.8	33.8
2017	33.7	33.8	33.7	34.1	33.7	34.3	34.6	34.2	34.1	34.5	34.2	34.3	34.1
Goods Producing													
2013	40.4	40.4	41.2	40.9	40.5	41.6	41.5	41.5	41.7	41.9	41.6	42.0	41.3
2014	41.0	40.6	40.8	41.0	41.1	41.1	41.3	41.9	41.7	41.4	41.9	41.8	41.3
2015	40.8	40.1	40.8	40.0	39.8	40.3	40.2	40.7	39.7	40.8	40.7	40.4	40.4
2016	39.5	39.6	40.0	39.6	39.5	40.6	39.5	40.1	39.9	40.7	40.4	40.3	40.0
2017	38.4	39.6	39.7	39.8	39.9	40.4	40.4	40.8	40.7	40.7	41.3	41.8	40.3
Construction													
2013	36.7	37.6	37.4	36.9	39.2	40.1	39.4	39.2	39.5	40.3	38.9	37.9	38.6
2014	38.6	36.3	39.4	39.6	40.2	38.2	39.5	40.0	38.6	37.7	37.9	39.1	38.8
2015	38.1	37.7	39.0	36.9	36.1	37.6	37.5	40.0	36.4	38.7	38.1	36.7	37.7
2016	35.9	36.0	37.4	37.5	37.3	39.3	37.6	38.7	37.6	39.6	38.9	37.6	37.8
2017	35.5	36.4	36.8	37.1	37.0	38.6	38.6	38.7	38.3	38.4	38.4	38.1	37.7
Manufacturing													
2013	41.9	41.5	42.7	42.4	42.2	43.4	43.1	43.2	43.3	43.3	43.2	43.9	42.8
2014	41.9	42.2	42.0	42.0	42.0	43.0	42.4	43.1	43.6	43.5	44.2	43.3	42.8
2015	42.4	42.2	42.7	42.4	42.5	42.4	42.1	41.7	42.4	42.6	42.8	43.3	42.5
2016	42.1	42.2	42.1	41.5	41.3	41.7	41.1	41.2	41.6	41.5	41.5	42.1	41.7
2017	40.3	40.8	40.9	40.7	41.1	40.9	41.0	41.7	41.7	41.8	42.3	43.6	41.4
Trade, Transportation, and Utilities													
2013	34.8	34.8	34.9	34.4	34.5	35.0	34.4	34.2	34.8	34.1	34.0	34.3	34.5
2014	33.5	33.9	34.4	34.1	34.0	34.4	33.7	33.8	34.0	34.1	34.6	34.3	34.1
2015	33.4	34.5	34.5	33.9	33.8	34.2	34.4	34.8	34.2	33.8	33.9	33.4	34.1
2016	32.9	32.9	32.6	32.9	32.7	33.1	33.6	33.0	32.8	33.9	33.0	33.4	33.1
2017	33.4	33.1	33.4	33.9	33.4	34.1	34.4	33.6	33.6	33.6	33.5	33.6	33.6
Financial Activities													
2013	35.8	36.8	36.5	36.3	36.0	38.0	36.2	36.2	37.2	35.8	36.5	36.7	36.5
2014	35.5	37.0	36.9	35.9	36.2	36.4	35.8	35.5	35.3	35.0	36.7	35.3	36.0
2015	35.5	36.6	36.4	35.9	36.1	36.1	36.3	37.4	36.2	36.2	37.4	36.6	36.4
2016	36.4	36.5	36.8	37.1	37.6	36.9	37.3	37.0	36.5	37.8	36.6	36.5	36.9
2017	37.9	37.1	36.3	37.3	36.2	36.4	37.3	36.3	36.8	37.8	36.9	36.8	36.9
Professional and Business Services													
2013	34.3	35.1	34.8	35.4	35.7	37.0	35.7	36.0	36.2	36.3	36.1	36.4	35.8
2014	35.0	35.7	37.2	36.7	36.8	37.2	36.7	37.0	36.8	36.5	37.5	36.1	36.6
2015	35.9	36.4	36.8	36.3	36.5	37.0	36.3	37.0	35.8	36.2	36.1	35.6	36.3
2016	35.4	35.1	34.9	34.8	35.2	35.1	34.6	34.4	34.7	35.6	34.8	33.8	34.9
2017	34.5	34.6	34.5	34.9	34.6	35.8	35.8	35.5	35.5	36.3	36.1	36.0	35.4
Education and Health Services													
2013	31.7	31.4	31.3	31.6	31.1	32.2	31.7	31.5	32.5	31.3	31.4	32.1	31.6
2014	31.4	32.1	32.2	31.5	31.4	32.7	32.0	31.9	32.2	31.7	33.0	31.9	32.0
2015	32.4	32.7	32.5	31.9	32.1	32.4	32.4	33.1	32.4	32.2	33.0	31.7	32.4
2016	32.5	32.2	32.2	32.0	32.6	32.5	32.2	32.3	32.6	32.8	32.3	32.4	32.4
2017	32.8	32.2	31.9	32.8	31.7	31.9	32.6	31.8	31.9	32.3	31.6	31.7	32.1
Leisure and Hospitality													
2013	23.8	24.0	24.1	24.0	24.0	24.7	23.7	23.7	23.7	23.6	23.5	23.5	23.9
2014	23.0	23.3	23.6	23.3	23.6	24.5	24.1	23.6	23.3	23.4	23.2	23.2	23.5
2015	22.8	23.3	23.3	23.0	23.6	24.2	23.7	24.1	23.0	23.5	23.4	22.6	23.4
2016	22.2	22.5	23.0	22.9	22.9	23.7	23.6	23.8	23.7	23.7	23.8	23.4	23.3
2017	23.0	23.9	24.0	24.2	24.0	24.7	25.1	24.6	23.9	24.4	24.0	23.7	24.1
Other Services													
2013	31.5	29.8	29.7	29.7	29.4	31.7	31.6	31.2	31.0	29.5	29.7	30.3	30.4
2014	30.7	29.1	30.0	29.0	30.4	31.4	30.6	30.8	29.8	29.4	29.4	29.2	30.0
2015	29.6	29.2	28.2	29.3	30.2	30.6	30.5	31.3	29.2	29.7	29.5	29.3	29.7
2016	30.0	30.1	29.2	29.8	30.5	31.5	30.6	30.8	29.7	30.2	29.2	29.8	30.1
2017	29.7	30.9	30.1	29.8	30.0	31.6	32.1	31.0	30.0	30.8	30.5	29.7	30.5

3. Average Hourly Earnings by Selected Industry: Kansas, 2013–2017

(Dollars, not seasonally adjusted)

Industry and year	January	February	March	April	May	June	July	August	September	October	November	December	Annual average
Total Private													
2013	21.42	21.47	21.36	21.50	21.38	21.44	21.32	21.32	21.49	21.48	21.52	21.70	21.45
2014	21.78	22.07	22.03	21.97	21.85	21.89	21.96	22.09	22.21	22.19	22.52	22.45	22.09
2015	22.51	22.66	22.48	22.26	22.32	22.17	22.36	22.56	22.61	22.78	22.97	23.18	22.57
2016	22.98	22.90	22.71	22.99	22.80	22.46	22.69	22.80	22.92	23.17	23.03	23.05	22.88
2017	23.38	23.29	23.18	23.31	23.05	22.83	23.16	23.12	23.38	23.51	23.33	23.50	23.25
Goods Producing													
2013	21.61	21.84	21.43	21.43	21.12	21.64	21.59	21.66	22.12	22.16	22.50	22.88	21.84
2014	22.93	23.09	23.67	23.53	23.59	23.59	23.68	23.65	24.12	24.26	24.35	24.46	23.75
2015	24.31	23.94	24.09	23.41	23.84	24.01	24.14	24.38	24.33	25.11	25.17	26.02	24.40
2016	25.46	25.45	25.22	25.35	24.95	24.78	24.86	25.13	25.09	25.37	25.24	25.20	25.17
2017	25.34	25.18	24.92	24.69	24.35	24.39	24.45	24.05	24.35	24.37	24.21	24.60	24.57
Construction													
2013	23.08	23.27	21.49	21.94	22.01	22.38	22.34	22.28	22.65	23.08	23.65	23.80	22.67
2014	23.90	24.24	24.25	24.21	24.26	23.41	23.36	23.77	23.57	24.26	24.19	24.25	23.96
2015	25.03	24.40	24.25	23.34	23.56	23.79	24.03	24.56	24.76	24.42	24.35	24.33	24.23
2016	25.06	25.02	24.76	24.96	24.79	24.85	24.87	25.36	25.52	25.65	25.45	25.81	25.18
2017	26.24	26.08	25.87	25.95	25.46	25.26	25.33	25.08	25.39	25.54	25.45	25.68	25.60
Manufacturing													
2013	21.17	21.40	21.37	21.23	21.01	21.69	21.58	21.64	21.85	21.70	22.03	22.13	21.57
2014	22.26	22.36	23.14	23.17	23.20	23.61	23.86	23.51	24.37	24.16	24.37	24.50	23.56
2015	23.88	23.61	23.92	23.26	23.80	23.97	24.07	24.08	23.92	24.19	24.44	25.97	24.10
2016	24.79	24.88	24.70	24.79	24.40	24.13	24.28	24.55	24.44	24.82	24.75	24.51	24.59
2017	24.52	24.32	24.02	23.61	23.34	23.54	23.57	23.05	23.36	23.32	23.21	23.78	23.63
Trade, Transportation, and Utilities													
2013	21.11	20.94	21.00	21.03	20.62	20.82	20.55	20.51	20.44	20.47	19.98	20.09	20.63
2014	20.28	20.46	20.30	20.67	20.51	20.22	20.16	20.48	20.74	20.66	21.12	20.75	20.53
2015	21.62	21.82	21.78	22.14	21.92	21.66	21.47	21.64	21.49	21.73	21.78	21.70	21.73
2016	21.75	21.75	21.60	21.76	21.85	21.33	21.58	21.87	22.40	22.36	22.34	22.18	21.90
2017	22.84	22.49	21.81	22.22	22.16	21.78	22.21	22.09	22.31	22.38	21.89	21.47	22.13
Financial Activities													
2013	24.54	24.80	24.52	24.47	25.41	24.91	24.92	25.56	25.38	25.65	26.06	25.70	25.16
2014	26.31	26.54	26.16	26.46	26.39	28.10	28.49	28.24	27.86	27.61	28.81	27.60	27.38
2015	28.01	28.52	26.00	25.78	26.12	25.43	26.67	27.44	27.18	27.11	27.02	26.90	26.85
2016	27.01	26.75	26.63	27.64	27.52	27.13	27.64	27.47	27.74	28.41	28.26	27.98	27.52
2017	27.78	28.20	28.71	28.46	28.09	27.24	28.14	28.99	28.20	28.66	28.86	28.82	28.34
Professional and Business Services													
2013	24.29	24.13	23.83	24.16	23.81	23.72	23.57	23.46	24.05	23.72	23.66	23.60	23.83
2014	23.80	24.23	24.11	23.65	23.29	23.30	23.25	23.27	23.34	23.69	23.83	24.15	23.65
2015	23.99	24.87	24.98	24.49	24.57	24.32	24.82	25.24	25.52	25.13	25.61	25.36	24.91
2016	25.23	25.22	24.99	25.54	25.16	24.72	25.17	25.48	25.30	25.76	25.41	26.02	25.31
2017	26.62	26.74	26.96	27.30	26.57	26.17	26.67	26.50	26.67	27.09	26.84	27.71	26.82
Education and Health Services													
2013	19.76	19.95	20.05	20.60	20.85	20.90	20.88	20.91	21.04	21.15	21.33	21.52	20.75
2014	21.64	22.00	21.82	21.78	21.72	21.68	21.78	21.99	22.19	21.96	22.09	22.26	21.91
2015	21.79	21.59	21.40	21.16	21.03	20.89	20.76	20.86	21.11	21.05	21.25	21.69	21.21
2016	21.43	21.20	20.97	21.30	20.94	20.79	20.99	20.78	20.74	21.10	20.88	20.72	20.99
2017	20.81	21.11	21.00	21.39	21.47	21.45	21.59	21.55	22.16	22.12	22.12	22.28	21.59
Leisure and Hospitality													
2013	11.30	11.29	11.30	11.38	11.35	11.01	11.18	11.24	11.37	11.25	11.26	11.40	11.28
2014	11.44	11.55	11.74	11.59	11.72	11.50	11.57	11.59	11.69	11.65	11.79	12.16	11.67
2015	11.85	11.97	11.88	11.82	11.79	11.72	11.82	11.88	12.08	11.94	12.02	12.26	11.92
2016	12.13	12.07	11.96	11.92	11.95	11.74	11.91	11.85	11.99	12.10	12.31	12.40	12.02
2017	12.46	12.35	12.32	12.33	12.39	12.27	12.21	12.30	12.44	12.46	12.57	12.67	12.39
Other Services													
2013	20.76	20.50	20.84	20.69	21.22	21.31	21.46	21.35	21.07	21.08	21.12	22.11	21.13
2014	21.38	21.98	21.53	21.51	21.35	21.95	21.72	21.78	21.97	21.57	21.72	21.48	21.66
2015	21.39	21.27	21.34	20.84	20.84	21.02	20.90	20.67	20.68	21.51	21.85	21.55	21.15
2016	21.76	21.83	21.90	21.81	22.00	22.07	22.17	21.99	22.11	21.55	21.42	21.42	21.84
2017	21.44	20.72	21.27	20.93	20.99	21.45	21.04	21.16	20.96	21.19	20.80	20.86	21.07

4. Average Weekly Earnings by Selected Industry: Kansas, 2013–2017

(Dollars, not seasonally adjusted)

Industry and year	January	February	March	April	May	June	July	August	September	October	November	December	Annual average
Total Private													
2013	734.71	736.42	736.92	741.75	733.33	756.83	737.67	735.54	752.15	741.06	740.29	755.16	742.17
2014	740.52	759.21	766.64	755.77	751.64	766.15	759.82	766.52	768.47	765.56	792.70	774.53	764.31
2015	769.84	781.77	777.81	756.84	761.11	767.08	769.18	787.34	768.74	779.08	790.17	783.48	774.15
2016	772.13	767.15	760.79	767.87	768.36	763.64	766.92	770.64	774.70	799.37	780.72	779.09	773.34
2017	787.91	787.20	781.17	794.87	776.79	783.07	801.34	790.70	797.26	811.10	797.89	806.05	792.83
Goods Producing													
2013	873.04	882.34	882.92	876.49	855.36	900.22	895.99	898.89	922.40	928.50	936.00	960.96	901.99
2014	940.13	937.45	965.74	964.73	969.55	969.55	977.98	990.94	1,005.80	1,004.36	1,020.27	1,022.43	980.88
2015	991.85	959.99	982.87	936.40	948.83	967.60	970.43	992.27	965.90	1,024.49	1,024.42	1,051.21	985.76
2016	1,005.67	1,007.82	1,008.80	1,003.86	985.53	1,006.07	981.97	1,007.71	1,001.09	1,032.56	1,019.70	1,015.56	1,006.80
2017	973.06	997.13	989.32	982.66	971.57	985.36	987.78	981.24	991.05	991.86	999.87	1,028.28	990.17
Construction													
2013	847.04	874.95	803.73	809.59	862.79	897.44	880.20	873.38	894.68	930.12	919.99	902.02	875.06
2014	922.54	879.91	955.45	958.72	975.25	894.26	922.72	950.80	909.80	914.60	916.80	948.18	929.65
2015	953.64	919.88	945.75	861.25	850.52	894.50	901.13	982.40	901.26	945.05	927.74	892.91	913.47
2016	899.65	900.72	926.02	936.00	924.67	976.61	935.11	981.43	959.55	1,015.74	990.01	970.46	951.80
2017	931.52	949.31	952.02	962.75	942.02	975.04	977.74	970.60	972.44	980.74	977.28	978.41	965.12
Manufacturing													
2013	887.02	888.10	912.50	900.15	886.62	941.35	930.10	934.85	946.11	939.61	951.70	971.51	923.20
2014	932.69	943.59	971.88	973.14	974.40	1,015.23	1,011.66	1,013.28	1,062.53	1,050.96	1,077.15	1,060.85	1,008.37
2015	1,012.51	996.34	1,021.38	986.22	1,011.50	1,016.33	1,013.35	1,004.14	1,014.21	1,030.49	1,046.03	1,124.50	1,024.25
2016	1,043.66	1,049.94	1,039.87	1,028.79	1,007.72	1,006.22	997.91	1,011.46	1,016.70	1,030.03	1,027.13	1,031.87	1,025.40
2017	988.16	992.26	982.42	960.93	959.27	962.79	966.37	961.19	974.11	974.78	981.78	1,036.81	978.28
Trade, Transportation, and Utilities													
2013	734.63	728.71	732.90	723.43	711.39	728.70	706.92	701.44	711.31	698.03	679.32	689.09	711.74
2014	679.38	693.59	698.32	704.85	697.34	695.57	679.39	692.22	705.16	704.51	730.75	711.73	700.07
2015	722.11	752.79	751.41	750.55	740.90	740.77	738.57	753.07	734.96	734.47	738.34	724.78	740.99
2016	715.58	715.58	704.16	715.90	714.50	706.02	725.09	721.71	734.72	758.00	737.22	740.81	724.89
2017	762.86	744.42	728.45	753.26	740.14	742.70	764.02	742.22	749.62	751.97	733.32	721.39	743.57
Financial Activities													
2013	878.53	912.64	894.98	888.26	914.76	946.58	902.10	925.27	944.14	918.27	951.19	943.19	918.34
2014	934.01	981.98	965.30	949.91	955.32	1,022.84	1,019.94	1,002.52	983.46	966.35	1,057.33	974.28	985.68
2015	994.36	1,043.83	946.40	925.50	942.93	918.02	968.12	1,026.26	983.92	981.38	1,010.55	984.54	977.34
2016	983.16	976.38	979.98	1,025.44	1,034.75	1,001.10	1,030.97	1,016.39	1,012.51	1,073.90	1,034.32	1,021.27	1,015.49
2017	1,052.86	1,046.22	1,042.17	1,061.56	1,016.86	991.54	1,049.62	1,052.34	1,037.76	1,083.35	1,064.93	1,060.58	1,045.75
Professional and Business Services													
2013	833.15	846.96	829.28	855.26	850.02	877.64	841.45	844.56	870.61	861.04	854.13	859.04	853.11
2014	833.00	865.01	896.89	867.96	857.07	866.76	853.28	860.99	858.91	864.69	893.63	871.82	865.59
2015	861.24	905.27	919.26	888.99	896.81	899.84	900.97	933.88	913.62	909.71	924.52	902.82	904.23
2016	893.14	885.22	872.15	888.79	885.63	867.67	870.88	875.82	879.99	917.06	884.27	879.48	884.37
2017	918.39	925.20	930.12	952.77	919.32	936.89	954.79	940.75	946.79	983.37	968.92	997.56	949.43
Education and Health Services													
2013	626.39	626.43	627.57	650.96	648.44	672.98	661.90	658.67	683.80	662.00	669.76	690.79	655.70
2014	679.50	706.20	702.60	686.07	682.01	708.94	696.96	701.48	714.52	696.13	728.97	710.09	701.12
2015	706.00	705.99	695.50	675.00	675.06	676.84	672.62	690.47	683.96	677.81	701.25	687.57	687.20
2016	696.48	682.64	675.23	681.60	682.64	675.68	675.88	671.19	676.12	692.08	674.42	671.33	680.08
2017	682.57	679.74	669.90	701.59	680.60	684.26	703.83	685.29	706.90	714.48	698.99	706.28	693.04
Leisure and Hospitality													
2013	268.94	270.96	272.33	273.12	272.40	271.95	264.97	266.39	269.47	265.50	264.61	267.90	269.59
2014	263.12	269.12	277.06	270.05	276.59	281.75	278.84	273.52	272.38	272.61	273.53	282.11	274.25
2015	270.18	278.90	276.80	271.86	278.24	283.62	280.13	286.31	277.84	280.59	281.27	277.08	278.93
2016	269.29	271.58	275.08	272.97	273.66	278.24	281.08	282.03	284.16	286.77	292.98	290.16	280.07
2017	286.58	295.17	295.68	298.39	297.36	303.07	306.47	302.58	297.32	304.02	301.68	300.28	298.60
Other Services													
2013	653.94	610.90	618.95	614.49	623.87	675.53	678.14	666.12	653.17	621.86	627.26	669.93	642.35
2014	656.37	639.62	645.90	623.79	649.04	689.23	664.63	670.82	654.71	634.16	638.57	627.22	649.80
2015	633.14	621.08	601.79	610.61	629.37	643.21	637.45	646.97	603.86	638.85	644.58	631.42	628.16
2016	652.80	657.08	639.48	649.94	671.00	695.21	678.40	677.29	656.67	650.81	625.46	638.32	657.38
2017	636.77	640.25	640.23	623.71	629.70	677.82	675.38	655.96	628.80	652.65	634.40	619.54	642.64

KENTUCKY
At a Glance

Population:
  2010 census: 4,339,367
  2017 estimate: 4,454,189

Percent change in population:
  2010–2017: 2.6%

Percent change in total nonfarm employment:
  2007–2017: 3.4%

Industry with the largest growth in employment, 2007–2017 (thousands):
  Professional and business services, 28.8

Industry with the largest decline or smallest growth in employment, 2007–2017 (thousands):
  Mining and logging, -11.8

Civilian labor force:
  2010: 2,054,375
  2017: 2,052,368

Unemployment rate and rank among states (highest to lowest):
  2010: 10.2%, 16th
  2017: 4.9%, 10th

Over-the-year change in unemployment rates:
  2015–2016: -0.2%
  2016–2017: -0.2%

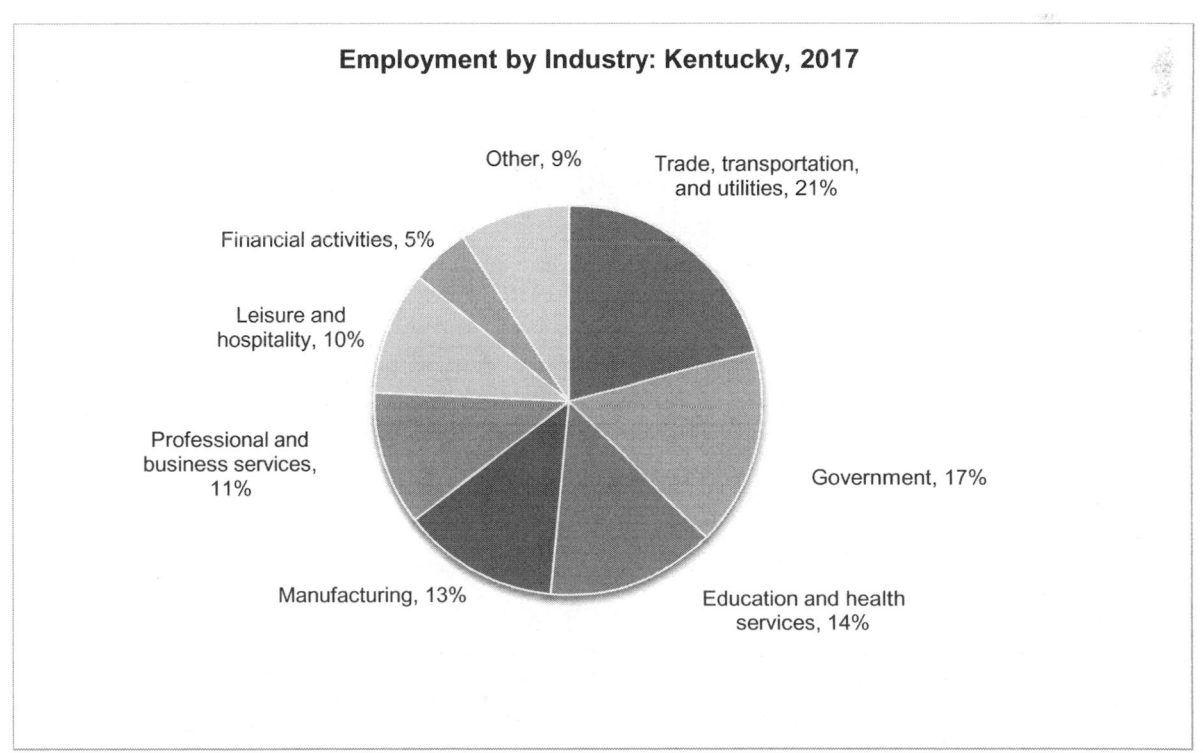

Employment by Industry: Kentucky, 2017

Other, 9%
Trade, transportation, and utilities, 21%
Financial activities, 5%
Leisure and hospitality, 10%
Professional and business services, 11%
Government, 17%
Manufacturing, 13%
Education and health services, 14%

1. Employment by Industry: Kentucky, Selected Years, 2007–2017

(Numbers in thousands, not seasonally adjusted)

Industry and year	January	February	March	April	May	June	July	August	September	October	November	December	Annual average
Total Nonfarm													
2007	1,820.6	1,820.8	1,839.9	1,855.7	1,872.5	1,876.2	1,849.6	1,859.2	1,865.2	1,865.7	1,878.3	1,877.7	1,856.8
2008	1,829.1	1,829.9	1,838.4	1,852.6	1,868.9	1,861.7	1,838.6	1,849.2	1,838.5	1,835.3	1,835.2	1,825.9	1,841.9
2009	1,755.1	1,746.5	1,752.3	1,764.6	1,769.4	1,765.4	1,748.6	1,753.9	1,758.5	1,762.5	1,770.3	1,768.1	1,759.6
2010	1,715.7	1,709.1	1,733.3	1,760.0	1,775.6	1,776.5	1,755.4	1,761.1	1,771.9	1,781.0	1,787.7	1,792.5	1,760.0
2011	1,738.8	1,744.1	1,762.1	1,783.4	1,787.1	1,792.2	1,774.0	1,792.0	1,800.6	1,801.0	1,814.3	1,814.8	1,783.7
2012	1,772.3	1,776.9	1,794.4	1,809.5	1,821.9	1,825.4	1,801.8	1,813.4	1,819.4	1,823.8	1,837.9	1,839.3	1,811.3
2013	1,791.1	1,794.7	1,809.4	1,825.7	1,837.6	1,835.2	1,817.1	1,837.2	1,842.6	1,846.4	1,863.9	1,865.1	1,830.5
2014	1,812.3	1,810.4	1,829.2	1,854.4	1,866.0	1,863.5	1,848.9	1,866.8	1,870.9	1,878.8	1,892.6	1,899.3	1,857.8
2015	1,847.6	1,844.7	1,854.4	1,876.1	1,893.4	1,893.8	1,873.3	1,888.9	1,897.0	1,906.5	1,924.2	1,928.3	1,885.7
2016	1,873.5	1,876.7	1,888.1	1,907.1	1,917.5	1,913.3	1,903.6	1,914.3	1,921.5	1,922.9	1,934.3	1,936.9	1,909.1
2017	1,886.7	1,893.8	1,905.5	1,919.4	1,928.0	1,931.1	1,911.0	1,921.6	1,930.6	1,930.7	1,943.2	1,943.1	1,920.4
Total Private													
2007	1,515.9	1,511.9	1,529.4	1,542.3	1,557.4	1,566.0	1,548.9	1,554.2	1,553.3	1,553.4	1,564.2	1,563.1	1,546.7
2008	1,519.7	1,517.0	1,524.4	1,539.1	1,554.2	1,553.1	1,541.1	1,547.1	1,531.9	1,523.2	1,522.4	1,514.0	1,532.3
2009	1,450.6	1,439.9	1,442.9	1,449.7	1,453.5	1,454.1	1,447.6	1,448.3	1,445.7	1,445.1	1,452.4	1,451.5	1,448.4
2010	1,404.3	1,394.5	1,415.7	1,439.1	1,447.3	1,454.6	1,449.8	1,454.9	1,454.3	1,460.4	1,466.0	1,472.0	1,442.7
2011	1,423.2	1,423.5	1,439.3	1,458.8	1,462.5	1,471.6	1,465.9	1,477.9	1,478.0	1,476.4	1,488.1	1,488.1	1,462.8
2012	1,450.1	1,450.2	1,465.8	1,479.0	1,492.5	1,501.9	1,493.1	1,499.5	1,496.5	1,498.4	1,511.3	1,513.0	1,487.6
2013	1,470.5	1,469.1	1,482.4	1,496.6	1,508.3	1,511.5	1,506.2	1,520.1	1,516.5	1,522.1	1,537.8	1,538.9	1,506.7
2014	1,491.7	1,488.2	1,505.1	1,526.9	1,538.6	1,541.5	1,537.6	1,547.6	1,546.2	1,554.0	1,567.4	1,575.3	1,535.0
2015	1,528.9	1,524.7	1,533.9	1,552.3	1,570.1	1,576.1	1,570.4	1,578.7	1,578.6	1,585.7	1,602.3	1,606.5	1,567.4
2016	1,557.7	1,559.5	1,568.4	1,586.8	1,596.7	1,598.9	1,600.4	1,602.9	1,603.4	1,605.9	1,615.9	1,618.7	1,592.9
2017	1,572.7	1,576.6	1,587.0	1,599.9	1,607.4	1,616.9	1,607.2	1,610.8	1,612.7	1,613.8	1,624.8	1,625.2	1,604.6
Goods Producing													
2007	358.7	356.1	358.5	363.5	366.1	369.8	362.7	364.6	367.2	362.6	365.9	361.8	363.1
2008	353.9	352.5	353.6	355.6	362.1	360.1	354.4	357.6	353.6	349.5	348.4	340.0	353.4
2009	321.4	317.5	314.6	313.5	311.4	310.3	307.4	308.0	307.7	306.0	305.1	303.0	310.5
2010	292.1	286.1	293.2	297.9	299.3	300.8	299.7	303.6	304.6	305.0	303.4	301.8	299.0
2011	292.5	293.1	296.7	301.7	302.9	307.2	302.8	308.7	309.0	308.0	309.1	307.3	303.3
2012	302.3	300.7	305.4	308.1	311.1	315.2	314.8	315.9	315.7	315.3	315.3	313.9	311.1
2013	306.5	306.1	308.7	310.7	314.2	317.1	314.1	318.2	319.3	319.6	320.0	319.2	314.5
2014	311.2	311.7	316.5	320.4	324.5	327.0	327.6	330.2	330.1	330.7	331.9	330.4	324.4
2015	323.0	322.3	323.3	325.7	331.7	333.7	332.0	336.1	336.5	336.2	335.9	335.6	331.0
2016	327.6	327.1	330.4	334.1	336.0	338.7	339.5	338.9	339.2	337.6	338.6	337.9	335.5
2017	331.1	332.1	335.3	336.9	338.2	340.9	340.7	340.5	340.3	338.5	339.0	336.1	337.5
Service-Providing													
2007	1,461.9	1,464.7	1,481.4	1,492.2	1,506.4	1,506.4	1,486.9	1,494.6	1,498.0	1,503.1	1,512.4	1,515.9	1,493.7
2008	1,475.2	1,477.4	1,484.8	1,497.0	1,506.8	1,501.6	1,484.2	1,491.6	1,484.9	1,485.8	1,486.8	1,485.9	1,488.5
2009	1,433.7	1,429.0	1,437.7	1,451.1	1,458.0	1,455.1	1,441.2	1,445.9	1,450.8	1,456.5	1,465.2	1,465.1	1,449.1
2010	1,423.6	1,423.0	1,440.1	1,462.1	1,476.3	1,475.7	1,455.7	1,457.5	1,467.3	1,476.0	1,484.3	1,490.7	1,461.0
2011	1,446.3	1,451.0	1,465.4	1,481.7	1,484.2	1,485.0	1,471.2	1,483.3	1,491.6	1,493.0	1,505.2	1,507.5	1,480.5
2012	1,470.0	1,476.2	1,489.0	1,501.4	1,510.8	1,510.2	1,487.0	1,497.5	1,503.7	1,508.5	1,522.6	1,525.4	1,500.2
2013	1,484.6	1,488.6	1,500.7	1,515.0	1,523.4	1,518.1	1,503.0	1,519.0	1,523.3	1,526.8	1,543.9	1,545.9	1,516.0
2014	1,501.1	1,498.7	1,512.7	1,534.0	1,541.5	1,536.5	1,521.3	1,536.6	1,540.8	1,548.1	1,560.7	1,568.9	1,533.4
2015	1,524.6	1,522.4	1,531.1	1,550.4	1,561.7	1,560.1	1,541.3	1,552.8	1,560.5	1,570.3	1,588.3	1,592.7	1,554.7
2016	1,545.9	1,549.6	1,557.7	1,573.0	1,581.5	1,574.6	1,564.1	1,575.4	1,582.3	1,585.3	1,595.7	1,599.0	1,573.7
2017	1,555.6	1,561.7	1,570.2	1,582.5	1,589.8	1,590.2	1,570.3	1,581.1	1,590.3	1,592.2	1,604.2	1,607.0	1,582.9
Mining and Logging													
2007	22.2	22.2	22.4	22.1	22.0	22.2	22.0	22.1	22.1	22.1	22.1	22.2	22.1
2008	22.2	22.1	22.3	22.8	23.4	23.7	24.0	24.6	24.8	25.4	25.5	25.6	23.9
2009	25.1	25.0	25.2	24.9	24.3	24.0	23.0	22.7	22.8	22.1	22.1	22.0	23.6
2010	21.3	21.3	21.5	21.8	21.9	22.3	22.2	22.4	22.5	22.4	22.5	22.7	22.1
2011	22.0	22.1	22.3	22.7	22.9	23.2	23.4	23.5	23.4	23.2	23.2	23.3	22.9
2012	23.0	22.5	22.1	21.6	21.1	21.0	20.4	19.9	19.5	18.7	18.6	18.1	20.5
2013	17.6	17.2	17.6	17.5	17.6	17.8	17.7	17.6	17.5	17.2	17.1	16.9	17.4
2014	16.2	16.1	16.3	16.4	16.7	16.8	16.7	16.8	16.7	16.7	16.6	16.5	16.5
2015	15.3	15.1	14.6	14.4	14.4	14.3	14.0	13.7	13.5	13.3	12.8	12.4	14.0
2016	11.6	11.1	11.0	10.5	10.4	10.4	10.2	10.1	10.1	10.2	10.3	10.3	10.5
2017	10.1	10.2	10.4	10.5	10.5	10.5	10.4	10.4	10.3	10.2	10.3	10.3	10.3

1. Employment by Industry: Kentucky, Selected Years, 2007–2017—*Continued*

(Numbers in thousands, not seasonally adjusted)

Industry and year	January	February	March	April	May	June	July	August	September	October	November	December	Annual average
Construction													
2007	77.4	75.5	80.9	84.3	86.5	88.3	88.7	89.1	88.9	89.3	88.4	85.8	85.3
2008	79.1	77.8	79.6	84.0	87.8	88.4	88.8	88.7	87.7	86.4	83.9	81.0	84.4
2009	72.7	71.1	71.9	73.3	74.4	75.4	76.1	75.5	75.1	75.3	74.1	71.9	73.9
2010	63.6	61.5	64.7	68.2	68.7	69.2	71.1	70.6	70.1	70.6	69.3	66.7	67.9
2011	60.4	60.7	63.7	67.5	69.0	71.3	70.9	71.3	70.6	69.5	69.4	67.3	67.6
2012	62.2	62.3	64.3	66.9	68.4	69.9	70.1	70.0	69.7	69.0	68.5	66.5	67.3
2013	61.4	61.5	63.5	65.7	68.3	70.0	71.1	71.4	71.9	71.7	71.3	69.4	68.1
2014	64.1	64.1	68.4	71.3	73.8	75.3	75.9	76.1	76.7	77.2	76.8	74.4	72.8
2015	69.1	68.8	70.0	74.5	76.5	77.7	80.0	79.0	79.0	79.3	78.3	77.1	75.8
2016	71.3	70.7	73.2	76.8	78.0	79.4	79.8	78.9	79.2	78.4	78.2	76.7	76.7
2017	71.5	72.0	74.9	76.2	77.6	79.5	80.2	80.1	80.3	79.2	78.1	75.3	77.1
Manufacturing													
2007	259.1	258.4	255.2	257.1	257.6	259.3	252.0	253.4	256.2	251.2	255.4	253.0	255.7
2008	252.6	252.6	251.7	248.8	250.9	248.0	241.6	244.3	241.1	237.7	239.0	233.4	245.1
2009	223.6	221.4	217.5	215.3	212.7	210.9	208.3	209.8	209.8	208.6	208.9	209.1	213.0
2010	207.2	203.3	207.0	207.9	208.7	209.3	206.4	210.6	212.0	212.0	211.6	212.4	209.0
2011	210.1	210.3	210.7	211.5	211.0	212.7	208.5	213.9	215.0	215.3	216.5	216.7	212.7
2012	217.1	215.9	219.0	219.6	221.6	224.3	224.3	226.0	226.5	227.6	228.2	229.3	223.3
2013	227.5	227.4	227.6	227.5	228.3	229.3	225.3	229.2	229.9	230.7	231.6	232.9	228.9
2014	230.9	231.5	231.8	232.7	234.0	234.9	235.0	237.3	236.7	236.8	238.5	239.5	235.0
2015	238.6	238.4	238.7	236.8	240.8	241.7	238.0	243.4	244.0	243.6	244.8	246.1	241.2
2016	244.7	245.3	246.2	246.8	247.6	248.9	249.5	249.9	249.9	249.0	250.1	250.9	248.2
2017	249.5	249.9	250.0	250.2	250.1	250.9	250.1	250.0	249.7	249.1	250.6	250.5	250.1
Trade, Transportation, and Utilities													
2007	381.6	378.7	383.8	383.5	387.0	388.9	385.5	385.5	385.8	388.2	395.0	397.2	386.7
2008	381.7	378.3	379.4	381.0	383.7	384.0	381.8	382.8	378.7	378.2	383.7	386.9	381.7
2009	366.7	360.7	360.9	361.3	363.5	364.2	361.9	361.6	361.2	361.6	368.1	371.3	363.6
2010	355.5	352.8	355.8	358.2	360.7	362.0	361.2	362.0	360.6	364.7	371.0	376.0	361.7
2011	359.6	357.7	360.8	362.9	364.1	366.2	365.8	367.1	366.1	368.1	377.3	380.5	366.4
2012	364.8	362.9	365.8	367.3	370.1	371.4	369.5	370.2	370.0	370.0	377.9	380.6	370.0
2013	365.3	363.3	365.8	366.8	369.4	370.9	369.7	371.8	371.2	372.6	381.5	386.4	371.2
2014	370.0	367.7	370.7	372.8	376.2	377.8	376.5	379.1	378.7	381.2	389.6	396.8	378.1
2015	381.2	378.4	380.6	382.7	386.5	388.1	386.7	389.0	388.3	390.5	398.4	402.8	387.8
2016	390.6	389.6	391.8	393.8	396.1	395.7	398.1	398.9	397.7	398.8	407.2	413.0	397.6
2017	395.7	394.0	395.5	397.0	399.7	400.9	399.5	401.2	402.3	405.2	412.5	416.5	401.7
Wholesale Trade													
2007	76.6	76.6	77.2	77.2	77.2	77.6	77.0	76.9	77.0	76.8	76.9	77.2	77.0
2008	76.5	76.6	76.6	76.4	76.6	76.9	76.5	76.4	75.8	75.9	75.9	75.7	76.3
2009	73.9	72.9	72.6	72.4	72.5	72.3	72.1	71.8	71.7	71.7	72.2	72.6	72.4
2010	71.4	71.1	71.4	71.2	71.6	71.9	72.0	71.8	71.7	72.0	72.1	72.2	71.7
2011	71.0	71.4	71.7	71.4	71.6	72.0	72.5	72.6	72.5	72.4	72.5	72.8	72.0
2012	71.9	72.0	72.2	72.4	72.7	72.9	72.8	73.2	73.2	73.1	73.3	73.5	72.8
2013	73.2	73.2	73.6	73.6	73.7	74.2	74.0	74.2	74.2	73.7	73.9	74.2	73.8
2014	73.6	73.6	74.1	74.1	74.5	74.4	74.1	74.3	74.2	73.8	74.1	74.7	74.1
2015	73.9	73.7	73.8	73.8	74.7	75.0	74.8	75.1	75.1	74.8	75.1	75.6	74.6
2016	75.1	75.0	75.3	75.3	75.7	75.8	75.8	75.5	75.3	74.9	75.2	75.9	75.4
2017	75.1	75.5	75.8	76.6	77.0	77.2	76.7	76.5	76.2	76.6	75.9	75.7	76.2
Retail Trade													
2007	211.0	208.5	212.3	212.0	214.8	214.8	213.6	212.8	212.2	212.7	219.0	220.4	213.7
2008	210.4	208.1	209.8	210.1	211.5	211.8	210.9	211.2	208.7	208.3	212.6	214.0	210.6
2009	202.2	198.4	199.0	200.8	202.5	203.0	201.7	200.8	200.3	200.7	205.5	206.8	201.8
2010	197.0	195.2	197.6	199.5	201.1	200.7	200.5	200.7	198.8	201.7	205.9	207.6	200.5
2011	198.3	196.2	198.3	200.7	201.3	201.5	200.6	201.1	199.2	201.2	207.0	208.7	201.2
2012	199.8	197.3	199.7	201.3	203.5	204.1	202.8	202.4	201.8	202.8	209.0	209.6	202.8
2013	199.7	198.1	199.6	200.9	202.8	203.5	203.0	203.6	202.4	203.9	210.1	212.4	203.3
2014	200.9	199.4	200.9	203.3	204.9	205.8	204.7	205.7	204.2	205.8	212.0	215.3	205.2
2015	205.4	204.1	206.0	208.0	210.2	211.2	209.7	210.3	209.1	210.3	216.2	218.5	209.9
2016	210.1	210.1	211.7	214.1	215.3	214.5	215.4	215.6	214.1	216.0	221.7	222.9	215.1
2017	214.0	211.9	212.5	214.0	215.4	215.3	214.1	214.5	214.5	215.6	220.7	220.3	215.2

1. Employment by Industry: Kentucky, Selected Years, 2007–2017—*Continued*

(Numbers in thousands, not seasonally adjusted)

Industry and year	January	February	March	April	May	June	July	August	September	October	November	December	Annual average
Transportation and Utilities													
2007	94.0	93.6	94.3	94.3	95.0	96.5	94.9	95.8	96.6	98.7	99.1	99.6	96.0
2008	94.8	93.6	93.0	94.5	95.6	95.3	94.4	95.2	94.2	94.0	95.2	97.2	94.8
2009	90.6	89.4	89.3	88.1	88.5	88.9	88.1	89.0	89.2	89.2	90.4	91.9	89.4
2010	87.1	86.5	86.8	87.5	88.0	89.4	88.7	89.5	90.1	91.0	93.0	96.2	89.5
2011	90.3	90.1	90.8	90.8	91.2	92.7	92.7	93.4	94.4	94.5	97.8	99.0	93.1
2012	93.1	93.6	93.9	93.6	93.9	94.4	93.9	94.6	95.0	94.1	95.6	97.5	94.4
2013	92.4	92.0	92.6	92.3	92.9	93.2	92.7	94.0	94.6	95.0	97.5	99.8	94.1
2014	95.5	94.7	95.7	95.4	96.8	97.6	97.7	99.1	100.3	101.6	103.5	106.8	98.7
2015	101.9	100.6	100.8	100.9	101.6	101.9	102.2	103.6	104.1	105.4	107.1	108.7	103.2
2016	105.4	104.5	104.8	104.4	105.1	105.4	106.9	107.8	108.3	107.9	110.3	114.2	107.1
2017	106.6	106.6	107.2	106.4	107.3	108.4	108.7	110.2	111.6	113.0	115.9	120.5	110.2
Information													
2007	28.4	28.3	28.4	28.7	29.1	29.3	29.1	28.9	28.8	28.6	28.9	29.0	28.8
2008	28.5	28.4	28.4	28.2	28.4	28.7	28.3	28.2	27.7	27.1	27.2	26.8	28.0
2009	26.4	26.2	26.0	25.8	25.7	25.6	25.4	25.3	25.0	25.0	25.0	25.1	25.5
2010	24.5	24.4	24.5	24.5	24.7	24.8	24.4	24.5	24.4	24.5	24.9	25.7	24.7
2011	25.3	25.1	25.0	24.9	24.9	24.9	24.9	24.9	24.6	24.7	25.1	25.2	25.0
2012	24.9	24.8	24.5	24.5	24.6	24.5	24.5	24.4	24.1	24.1	24.4	24.4	24.5
2013	24.3	24.2	24.3	24.1	24.2	24.2	24.1	24.2	23.8	23.8	23.9	23.9	24.1
2014	24.1	23.9	23.9	23.7	23.8	23.9	23.7	23.8	23.5	23.6	23.5	23.3	23.7
2015	23.1	23.0	22.9	22.6	22.7	22.8	22.8	22.7	22.4	22.4	22.7	22.6	22.7
2016	22.6	22.7	22.7	22.6	22.8	23.0	23.1	23.3	23.2	23.0	23.0	23.1	22.9
2017	22.6	22.6	22.7	22.7	22.9	22.9	22.9	22.7	22.6	22.6	22.6	22.7	22.7
Financial Activities													
2007	90.2	90.2	90.3	90.8	91.1	91.8	91.9	91.8	91.2	91.4	91.5	92.1	91.2
2008	91.6	92.3	92.3	92.0	92.3	92.0	92.2	92.0	91.0	90.6	90.9	90.9	91.7
2009	89.5	88.9	88.7	88.8	89.0	88.8	88.7	88.2	87.5	87.5	87.1	87.4	88.3
2010	86.3	85.8	85.9	86.1	86.1	86.3	86.1	85.6	84.9	84.9	84.8	85.4	85.7
2011	84.2	84.4	84.6	84.1	84.2	84.8	85.1	85.4	85.5	85.3	85.3	85.9	84.9
2012	85.3	85.3	85.6	85.6	86.0	86.9	87.3	87.4	87.6	87.4	87.8	88.2	86.7
2013	87.7	87.6	88.0	88.0	88.4	88.9	89.4	89.8	89.5	89.0	89.2	89.6	88.8
2014	88.8	88.5	88.6	89.0	89.7	90.1	90.7	90.9	90.8	91.0	91.5	92.2	90.2
2015	91.1	91.1	91.3	91.1	91.7	92.4	92.7	92.8	92.5	92.5	93.0	93.2	92.1
2016	92.4	92.6	92.5	92.7	93.2	93.6	93.9	93.7	93.6	93.8	93.8	94.7	93.4
2017	93.1	93.1	93.3	93.3	93.6	94.2	93.4	93.5	93.3	92.3	92.8	93.3	93.3
Professional and Business Services													
2007	180.3	180.3	182.9	183.7	185.3	186.0	183.8	185.7	185.3	188.5	190.6	193.1	185.5
2008	183.8	183.1	183.6	185.7	185.8	187.3	184.9	185.6	183.8	182.8	181.4	181.6	184.1
2009	171.0	170.1	169.2	169.3	168.3	169.1	170.6	172.5	172.8	176.2	180.4	182.0	172.6
2010	174.2	172.2	174.7	180.0	180.4	183.1	182.7	183.1	183.8	184.7	186.6	191.4	181.4
2011	181.4	180.7	182.8	186.5	185.2	187.0	188.0	191.6	192.0	192.7	194.6	197.3	188.3
2012	188.2	187.3	188.8	191.3	192.3	194.8	193.2	196.3	195.6	198.6	202.8	205.9	194.6
2013	195.1	193.6	195.4	198.9	200.1	200.8	199.9	205.8	204.6	209.1	216.7	217.9	203.2
2014	206.4	202.2	205.9	210.1	211.9	210.8	210.3	213.5	212.7	217.4	224.6	227.2	212.8
2015	213.5	209.3	210.9	213.8	216.2	218.0	216.7	218.5	218.3	221.3	228.6	231.9	218.1
2016	216.5	213.6	211.5	214.6	215.3	214.5	213.2	214.4	216.2	218.9	222.7	222.4	216.2
2017	213.2	210.5	210.0	211.1	210.9	213.6	211.9	213.7	215.7	217.5	220.9	222.9	214.3
Education and Health Services													
2007	241.2	242.0	243.1	242.9	243.7	243.2	241.9	242.8	244.1	245.6	245.7	245.8	243.5
2008	243.6	244.0	245.0	247.5	247.7	246.2	245.5	247.1	248.3	250.0	250.3	250.2	247.1
2009	246.9	246.9	248.1	249.7	249.9	248.9	247.6	249.2	250.8	252.4	253.0	252.9	249.7
2010	249.7	250.6	252.5	253.7	254.3	253.3	253.1	253.8	255.9	257.5	258.1	258.0	254.2
2011	255.0	255.6	256.4	257.5	257.2	255.8	255.4	256.7	259.5	259.8	259.9	258.7	257.3
2012	256.9	258.7	259.6	259.4	259.7	259.6	257.9	259.2	260.5	261.7	262.4	262.4	259.8
2013	259.0	260.5	261.4	261.7	261.0	258.5	259.0	260.6	261.5	263.2	263.0	261.9	260.9
2014	258.6	260.1	259.8	260.9	259.2	257.9	256.3	258.2	261.5	263.5	261.1	262.9	260.0
2015	259.4	261.6	262.1	263.6	263.1	261.7	260.7	261.8	265.3	269.1	268.9	269.6	263.9
2016	264.0	267.5	267.2	266.6	266.5	266.0	265.9	267.5	270.6	272.7	271.6	272.7	268.2
2017	267.9	271.7	271.4	273.2	271.4	272.2	269.5	270.8	273.5	274.6	274.1	275.0	272.1

1. Employment by Industry: Kentucky, Selected Years, 2007–2017—*Continued*

(Numbers in thousands, not seasonally adjusted)

Industry and year	January	February	March	April	May	June	July	August	September	October	November	December	Annual average
Leisure and Hospitality													
2007	160.9	161.7	166.9	173.5	178.8	180.2	178.3	179.1	175.2	172.8	171.1	168.5	172.3
2008	162.1	163.7	166.9	174.0	178.6	179.2	179.7	179.7	175.5	171.4	167.4	165.1	171.9
2009	158.3	158.9	164.4	170.8	175.2	176.1	175.4	173.1	170.9	167.0	164.7	160.9	168.0
2010	154.2	155.2	160.5	169.7	172.7	175.0	173.4	173.4	171.6	170.0	168.4	165.0	167.4
2011	157.5	159.1	164.6	173.4	176.2	177.6	175.8	175.8	173.9	170.6	170.0	166.4	170.1
2012	161.3	164.2	169.2	176.1	182.3	182.9	179.8	180.5	177.8	176.3	175.8	172.7	174.9
2013	168.4	169.3	173.8	181.2	185.8	185.8	185.3	185.0	182.2	180.9	179.6	176.1	179.5
2014	169.8	171.0	176.0	185.9	188.9	189.8	188.6	188.0	185.1	183.5	181.3	179.3	182.3
2015	175.0	176.3	179.4	189.4	194.1	194.7	194.7	193.4	191.3	189.9	190.0	186.5	187.9
2016	180.1	182.0	187.3	196.7	200.7	201.4	201.0	200.5	197.5	194.8	193.7	189.5	193.8
2017	184.4	187.3	192.8	199.7	204.3	205.5	203.4	202.4	199.2	197.1	195.6	191.4	196.9
Other Services													
2007	74.6	74.6	75.5	75.7	76.3	76.0	75.7	75.0	75.7	75.7	75.5	75.6	75.6
2008	74.5	74.7	75.2	75.1	75.6	75.6	74.3	74.1	73.3	73.6	73.1	72.5	74.3
2009	70.4	70.7	71.0	70.5	70.5	71.1	70.6	70.4	69.8	69.4	69.0	68.9	70.2
2010	67.8	67.4	68.6	69.0	69.1	69.3	69.2	68.9	68.5	69.1	68.8	68.7	68.7
2011	67.7	67.8	68.4	67.8	67.8	68.1	68.1	67.7	67.4	67.2	66.8	66.8	67.6
2012	66.4	66.3	66.9	66.7	66.4	66.6	66.1	65.6	65.2	65.0	64.9	64.9	65.9
2013	64.2	64.5	65.0	65.2	65.2	65.3	64.7	64.7	64.4	63.9	63.9	63.9	64.6
2014	62.8	63.1	63.7	64.1	64.4	64.2	63.9	63.9	63.8	63.1	63.9	63.2	63.7
2015	62.6	62.7	63.4	63.4	64.1	64.7	64.1	64.4	64.0	63.8	64.8	64.3	63.9
2016	63.9	64.4	65.0	65.7	66.1	66.0	65.7	65.7	65.4	66.3	65.3	65.4	65.4
2017	64.7	65.3	66.0	66.0	66.4	66.7	65.9	66.0	65.8	66.0	67.3	67.3	66.1
Government													
2007	304.7	308.9	310.5	313.4	315.1	310.2	300.7	305.0	311.9	312.3	314.1	314.6	310.1
2008	309.4	312.9	314.0	313.5	314.7	308.6	297.5	302.1	306.6	312.1	312.8	311.9	309.7
2009	304.5	306.6	309.4	314.9	315.9	311.3	301.0	305.6	312.8	317.4	317.9	316.6	311.2
2010	311.4	314.6	317.6	320.9	328.3	321.9	305.6	306.2	317.6	320.6	321.7	320.5	317.2
2011	315.6	320.6	322.8	324.6	324.6	320.6	308.1	314.1	322.6	324.6	326.2	326.7	320.9
2012	322.2	326.7	328.6	330.5	329.4	323.5	308.7	313.9	322.9	325.4	326.6	326.3	323.7
2013	320.6	325.6	327.0	329.1	329.3	323.7	310.9	317.1	326.1	324.3	326.1	326.2	323.8
2014	320.6	322.2	324.1	327.5	327.4	322.0	311.3	319.2	324.7	324.8	325.2	324.0	322.8
2015	318.7	320.0	320.5	323.8	323.3	317.7	302.9	310.2	318.4	320.8	321.9	321.8	318.3
2016	315.8	317.2	319.7	320.3	320.8	314.4	303.2	311.4	318.1	317.0	318.4	318.2	316.2
2017	314.0	317.2	318.5	319.5	320.6	314.2	303.8	310.8	317.9	316.9	318.4	317.9	315.8

2. Average Weekly Hours by Selected Industry: Kentucky, 2013–2017

(Not seasonally adjusted)

Industry and year	January	February	March	April	May	June	July	August	September	October	November	December	Annual average
Total Private													
2013	34.4	34.6	34.6	34.5	34.4	34.9	34.7	34.7	34.9	34.9	34.9	35.3	34.7
2014	33.7	34.6	34.6	34.6	34.8	35.2	34.8	34.9	35.0	35.0	35.5	35.6	34.9
2015	34.9	34.4	35.0	35.1	35.2	35.5	35.4	35.7	35.3	35.5	35.7	35.8	35.3
2016	34.8	34.8	35.1	35.1	35.0	35.5	35.2	35.0	35.1	35.4	35.3	35.4	35.1
2017	35.3	34.9	34.8	34.9	34.6	35.1	35.3	35.3	35.1	35.3	35.0	35.2	35.1
Goods Producing													
2013	40.5	40.5	40.1	40.1	40.0	40.5	40.5	40.5	40.5	40.7	40.8	40.9	40.5
2014	38.6	39.4	39.7	39.7	40.0	40.6	40.4	40.8	40.6	40.7	41.5	41.9	40.3
2015	41.1	39.8	40.5	40.9	41.4	41.6	41.0	41.8	40.8	41.2	41.2	42.0	41.1
2016	40.1	39.6	39.9	40.2	40.0	41.2	40.1	40.6	40.9	40.7	41.2	40.9	40.5
2017	40.6	40.3	40.1	40.1	40.2	40.8	41.1	41.4	40.8	41.4	40.8	41.4	40.8
Construction													
2013	36.4	36.9	36.4	37.8	36.9	37.9	39.4	39.1	38.7	39.8	39.9	38.0	38.2
2014	34.9	34.6	35.9	36.3	36.9	37.5	38.0	38.8	37.9	36.1	38.2	38.6	37.1
2015	38.1	36.7	36.9	37.8	39.6	39.8	39.8	40.4	38.1	41.1	39.7	40.5	39.1
2016	38.4	36.5	38.4	39.5	38.1	39.8	38.5	38.7	38.9	38.8	38.8	38.4	38.6
2017	38.4	38.5	38.4	38.6	38.3	40.0	41.3	40.7	39.4	40.5	39.1	39.3	39.4
Manufacturing													
2013	40.6	40.6	40.7	40.3	40.5	40.9	40.3	40.6	40.6	40.6	40.7	41.2	40.6
2014	39.8	41.1	41.0	40.8	40.9	41.6	41.1	41.3	41.3	41.8	42.3	42.6	41.3
2015	41.2	39.9	40.8	41.2	41.4	41.8	40.9	41.7	41.2	41.2	41.7	42.5	41.3
2016	40.7	41.2	41.0	40.9	41.1	41.9	40.7	41.3	41.6	41.5	42.2	41.8	41.3
2017	41.2	40.8	40.6	40.6	40.9	41.0	40.9	41.5	41.2	41.4	41.1	41.9	41.1
Trade, Transportation, and Utilities													
2013	34.6	34.8	34.9	35.0	35.1	35.2	35.2	35.5	35.5	35.3	35.2	35.6	35.2
2014	33.8	34.7	34.7	34.7	35.5	35.4	35.0	34.9	35.4	35.2	35.9	36.2	35.1
2015	34.7	34.7	35.3	35.7	35.9	36.0	35.8	36.2	36.0	35.9	36.2	36.3	35.7
2016	34.6	35.2	35.0	34.8	34.7	35.2	35.4	34.5	34.2	34.6	34.0	34.5	34.7
2017	33.6	33.5	33.7	33.9	33.7	33.7	33.9	33.8	33.7	33.5	33.5	33.8	33.7
Financial Activities													
2013	36.7	36.1	36.4	36.7	36.0	37.2	36.4	36.5	37.5	36.4	36.1	37.0	36.6
2014	36.0	37.0	36.6	36.1	36.5	37.6	36.4	36.2	36.5	36.6	37.2	36.1	36.6
2015	35.9	36.0	36.9	36.0	36.3	36.7	36.7	37.1	36.6	37.2	37.6	37.0	36.7
2016	36.6	35.8	35.9	36.3	36.9	36.7	36.3	36.3	36.0	36.6	35.8	35.3	36.2
2017	36.3	35.6	35.8	36.9	35.8	36.4	37.1	36.7	37.1	38.2	37.4	37.6	36.7
Professional and Business Services													
2013	32.9	33.8	33.9	33.4	33.3	34.7	34.2	34.0	34.1	34.8	34.5	36.4	34.2
2014	34.8	36.7	36.4	36.9	36.3	36.7	35.4	35.9	35.8	35.7	35.9	36.2	36.1
2015	35.7	35.6	35.8	36.1	36.0	36.1	36.4	36.5	35.8	36.3	36.5	36.4	36.1
2016	36.1	36.2	36.8	36.5	36.6	37.4	36.9	37.2	37.1	37.7	37.3	37.6	37.0
2017	37.5	37.1	36.8	36.7	36.0	36.7	37.0	36.4	36.6	36.8	36.5	36.1	36.7
Education and Health Services													
2013	34.0	33.8	33.9	33.9	33.8	34.2	33.9	34.1	34.3	34.3	34.5	34.4	34.1
2014	33.7	34.2	34.0	34.2	34.0	34.4	34.3	34.4	34.5	34.6	35.0	34.8	34.3
2015	34.7	34.2	34.6	34.5	34.5	34.7	35.0	35.2	35.0	34.9	35.3	34.8	34.8
2016	34.5	34.6	34.8	35.0	35.0	34.6	34.4	34.1	34.4	34.7	34.7	34.6	34.6
2017	35.4	34.6	34.6	34.8	34.4	34.9	35.0	34.2	34.1	34.1	34.4	34.3	34.6
Leisure and Hospitality													
2013	24.2	24.7	24.9	25.0	25.0	25.3	25.2	25.0	24.9	25.0	24.9	24.8	24.9
2014	24.4	25.3	25.6	25.7	25.4	26.0	25.6	25.3	25.2	25.2	25.1	25.2	25.3
2015	24.2	23.8	24.7	24.8	24.3	24.9	24.9	24.9	24.6	25.1	24.9	25.4	24.7
2016	24.1	24.3	25.0	25.2	25.0	25.5	25.7	25.5	25.6	25.8	25.8	25.9	25.3
2017	25.6	25.3	25.5	25.6	25.5	26.4	26.8	26.6	26.2	26.4	26.0	26.3	26.0

3. Average Hourly Earnings by Selected Industry: Kentucky, 2013–2017

(Dollars, not seasonally adjusted)

Industry and year	January	February	March	April	May	June	July	August	September	October	November	December	Annual average
Total Private													
2013	20.42	20.27	20.21	20.32	20.04	19.99	20.06	19.99	20.10	20.03	20.14	20.29	20.15
2014	20.36	20.60	20.63	20.40	20.23	20.32	20.46	20.50	20.35	20.51	20.87	21.13	20.53
2015	21.21	21.26	21.17	21.13	21.08	20.97	21.16	21.14	21.08	20.90	20.94	20.98	21.08
2016	21.25	21.06	21.13	21.27	21.16	21.10	21.24	21.14	21.24	21.55	21.34	21.58	21.26
2017	21.92	21.74	21.76	22.01	21.87	21.67	21.94	21.74	21.86	21.82	21.73	21.80	21.82
Goods Producing													
2013	21.27	21.18	20.85	21.12	21.09	21.30	21.32	21.30	21.56	21.64	21.77	21.85	21.36
2014	21.33	21.35	21.33	21.55	21.29	21.36	21.51	21.72	21.88	22.10	22.34	23.43	21.78
2015	22.71	22.71	22.75	22.94	22.78	22.68	23.10	22.72	22.62	22.73	22.93	22.97	22.80
2016	22.77	22.75	22.80	22.97	23.13	23.02	23.16	22.85	22.76	23.04	22.86	23.32	22.95
2017	23.42	23.24	23.14	23.37	23.41	23.47	23.36	23.25	23.20	23.18	22.99	23.03	23.25
Construction													
2013	21.26	21.67	21.13	21.58	21.18	21.15	21.26	20.96	20.76	21.19	21.43	21.15	21.22
2014	21.33	21.08	20.74	21.08	20.85	20.70	21.55	21.99	22.12	22.63	22.77	23.31	21.72
2015	23.11	23.46	23.61	23.73	23.50	23.72	24.63	23.99	23.45	23.42	23.90	23.92	23.72
2016	24.03	24.71	24.05	24.29	24.97	24.94	24.15	24.12	23.63	24.36	23.87	23.91	24.25
2017	23.67	24.23	24.54	24.88	24.88	25.27	25.03	25.15	25.43	25.40	25.44	25.97	25.01
Manufacturing													
2013	20.40	20.29	20.08	20.24	20.34	20.67	20.63	20.69	20.92	20.94	21.10	21.24	20.63
2014	21.27	21.56	21.62	21.75	21.43	21.54	21.42	21.46	21.54	21.74	21.91	23.27	21.72
2015	22.24	22.15	22.17	22.38	22.19	21.89	22.13	21.80	21.94	21.96	22.04	22.03	22.07
2016	21.66	21.50	21.74	21.93	21.96	21.74	22.32	21.91	22.04	22.14	22.11	22.78	21.99
2017	23.00	22.50	22.20	22.40	22.40	22.32	22.33	21.99	22.12	22.04	21.81	21.77	22.24
Trade, Transportation, and Utilities													
2013	17.96	17.89	18.09	18.08	18.08	18.33	18.36	18.57	18.55	18.66	18.68	19.33	18.39
2014	19.55	19.54	19.77	19.50	19.58	19.75	19.76	19.63	19.61	19.71	19.70	19.59	19.64
2015	20.04	20.00	19.89	20.10	20.01	20.18	20.09	20.25	20.17	20.08	20.03	19.89	20.06
2016	20.70	20.30	20.44	20.48	19.95	20.05	20.39	20.40	20.50	20.79	20.29	20.46	20.40
2017	20.95	20.68	20.77	21.16	21.05	21.04	21.17	21.01	21.24	20.91	20.85	20.74	20.96
Financial Activities													
2013	22.76	22.95	22.72	22.74	22.55	22.61	22.59	22.82	22.32	22.68	22.47	22.26	22.62
2014	22.25	22.63	22.65	21.93	22.10	22.47	22.36	22.37	22.08	22.12	22.46	22.17	22.30
2015	22.31	22.68	22.44	22.92	22.25	22.34	22.69	23.16	22.86	23.11	23.07	23.14	22.75
2016	23.44	24.08	23.95	23.71	23.58	23.25	23.64	23.34	23.86	24.66	24.39	25.02	23.91
2017	26.03	26.09	26.19	26.78	26.04	26.28	27.22	26.47	26.64	26.90	27.19	27.34	26.60
Professional and Business Services													
2013	20.77	21.03	21.33	21.24	20.74	20.62	20.84	20.51	20.65	20.40	20.19	19.86	20.66
2014	20.65	20.64	21.26	20.90	20.76	20.90	20.87	20.46	20.81	20.64	20.66	20.34	20.74
2015	20.84	21.33	21.54	21.09	21.24	21.28	21.88	22.29	22.16	22.19	22.33	22.21	21.71
2016	22.82	22.57	22.66	22.65	23.07	22.71	22.48	22.02	21.95	22.25	22.20	22.13	22.45
2017	22.89	23.16	23.19	23.65	23.51	23.02	23.51	23.50	23.32	23.28	23.15	23.52	23.31
Education and Health Services													
2013	25.65	25.04	24.98	24.85	24.09	23.90	24.04	23.72	23.59	23.10	23.41	23.25	24.13
2014	23.20	23.50	23.28	23.36	22.93	22.85	23.31	23.13	23.34	23.32	23.77	24.10	23.34
2015	24.34	24.18	24.02	23.65	23.87	23.48	23.47	23.12	23.26	23.29	22.89	23.22	23.56
2016	23.08	22.71	22.75	22.41	22.10	22.27	22.56	22.66	22.70	22.96	22.88	22.99	22.67
2017	22.84	22.70	22.75	22.62	22.66	22.39	22.89	22.51	22.55	22.68	22.52	22.54	22.64
Leisure and Hospitality													
2013	10.41	10.46	10.28	10.31	10.33	10.29	10.27	10.41	10.48	10.58	10.47	10.65	10.41
2014	10.62	10.80	10.79	10.75	10.77	10.75	10.72	11.01	11.08	11.20	11.26	11.39	10.93
2015	11.37	11.55	11.36	11.41	11.33	11.19	11.31	11.44	11.34	11.47	11.51	11.58	11.40
2016	11.46	11.55	11.59	11.53	11.69	11.55	11.48	11.59	11.70	11.82	11.76	12.01	11.65
2017	11.95	12.12	12.20	12.10	12.18	11.90	12.04	12.11	12.29	12.44	12.40	12.69	12.20

4. Average Weekly Earnings by Selected Industry: Kentucky, 2013–2017

(Dollars, not seasonally adjusted)

Industry and year	January	February	March	April	May	June	July	August	September	October	November	December	Annual average
Total Private													
2013	702.45	701.34	699.27	701.04	689.38	697.65	696.08	693.65	701.49	699.05	702.89	716.24	699.21
2014	686.13	712.76	713.80	705.84	704.00	715.26	712.01	715.45	712.25	717.85	740.89	752.23	716.50
2015	740.23	731.34	740.95	741.66	742.02	744.44	749.06	754.70	744.12	741.95	747.56	751.08	744.12
2016	739.50	732.89	741.66	746.58	740.60	749.05	747.65	739.90	745.52	762.87	753.30	763.93	746.23
2017	773.78	758.73	757.25	768.15	756.70	760.62	774.48	767.42	767.29	770.25	760.55	767.36	765.88
Goods Producing													
2013	861.44	857.79	836.09	846.91	843.60	862.65	863.46	862.65	873.18	880.75	888.22	893.67	865.08
2014	823.34	841.19	846.80	855.54	851.60	867.22	869.00	886.18	888.33	899.47	927.11	981.72	877.73
2015	933.38	903.86	921.38	938.25	943.09	943.49	947.10	949.70	922.90	936.48	944.72	964.74	937.08
2016	913.08	900.90	909.72	923.39	925.20	948.42	928.72	927.71	930.88	937.73	941.83	953.79	929.48
2017	950.85	936.57	927.91	937.14	941.08	957.58	960.10	962.55	946.56	959.65	937.99	953.44	948.60
Construction													
2013	773.86	799.62	769.13	815.72	781.54	801.59	837.64	819.54	803.41	843.36	855.06	803.70	810.60
2014	744.42	729.37	744.57	765.20	769.37	776.25	818.90	853.21	838.35	816.94	869.81	899.77	805.81
2015	880.49	860.98	871.21	896.99	930.60	944.06	980.27	969.20	893.45	962.56	948.83	968.76	927.45
2016	922.75	901.92	923.52	959.46	951.36	992.61	929.78	933.44	919.21	945.17	926.16	918.14	936.05
2017	908.93	932.86	942.34	960.37	952.90	1,010.80	1,033.74	1,023.61	1,001.94	1,028.70	994.70	1,020.62	985.39
Manufacturing													
2013	828.24	823.77	817.26	815.67	823.77	845.40	831.39	840.01	849.35	850.16	858.77	875.09	837.58
2014	846.55	886.12	886.42	887.40	876.49	896.06	880.36	886.30	889.60	908.73	926.79	991.30	897.04
2015	916.29	883.79	904.54	922.06	918.67	915.00	905.12	909.06	903.93	904.75	919.07	936.28	911.49
2016	881.56	885.80	891.34	896.94	902.56	910.91	908.42	904.88	916.86	918.81	933.04	952.20	908.19
2017	947.60	918.00	901.32	909.44	916.16	915.12	913.30	912.59	911.34	912.46	896.39	912.16	914.06
Trade, Transportation, and Utilities													
2013	621.42	622.57	631.34	632.80	634.61	645.22	646.27	659.24	658.53	658.70	657.54	688.15	647.33
2014	660.79	678.04	686.02	676.65	695.09	699.15	691.60	685.09	694.19	693.79	707.23	709.16	689.36
2015	695.39	694.00	702.12	717.57	718.36	726.48	719.22	733.05	726.12	720.87	725.09	722.01	716.14
2016	716.22	714.56	715.40	712.70	692.27	705.76	721.81	703.80	701.10	719.33	689.86	705.87	707.88
2017	703.92	692.78	699.95	717.32	709.39	709.05	717.66	710.14	715.79	700.49	698.48	701.01	706.35
Financial Activities													
2013	835.29	828.50	827.01	834.56	811.80	841.09	822.28	832.93	837.00	825.55	811.17	823.62	827.89
2014	801.00	837.31	828.99	791.67	806.65	844.87	813.90	809.79	805.92	809.59	835.51	800.34	816.18
2015	800.93	816.48	828.04	825.12	807.68	819.88	832.72	859.24	836.68	859.69	867.43	856.18	834.93
2016	857.90	862.06	859.81	860.67	870.10	853.28	858.13	847.24	858.96	902.56	873.16	883.21	865.54
2017	944.89	928.80	937.60	988.18	932.23	956.59	1,009.86	971.45	988.34	1,027.58	1,016.91	1,027.98	976.22
Professional and Business Services													
2013	683.33	710.81	723.09	709.42	690.64	715.51	712.73	697.34	704.17	709.92	696.56	722.90	706.57
2014	718.62	757.49	773.86	771.21	753.59	767.03	738.80	734.51	745.00	736.85	741.69	736.31	748.71
2015	743.99	759.35	771.13	761.35	764.64	768.21	796.43	813.59	793.33	805.50	815.05	808.44	783.73
2016	823.80	817.03	833.89	826.73	844.36	849.35	829.51	819.14	814.35	838.83	828.06	832.09	830.65
2017	858.38	859.24	853.39	867.96	846.36	844.83	869.87	855.40	853.51	856.70	844.98	849.07	855.48
Education and Health Services													
2013	872.10	846.35	846.82	842.42	814.24	817.38	814.96	808.85	809.14	792.33	807.65	799.80	822.83
2014	781.84	803.70	791.52	798.91	779.62	786.04	799.53	795.67	805.23	806.87	831.95	838.68	800.56
2015	844.60	826.96	831.09	815.93	823.52	814.76	821.45	813.82	814.10	812.82	808.02	808.06	819.89
2016	796.26	785.77	791.70	784.35	773.50	770.54	776.06	772.71	780.88	796.71	793.94	795.45	784.38
2017	808.54	785.42	787.15	787.18	779.50	781.41	801.15	769.84	768.96	773.39	774.69	773.12	783.34
Leisure and Hospitality													
2013	251.92	258.36	255.97	257.75	258.25	260.34	258.80	260.25	260.95	264.50	260.70	264.12	259.21
2014	259.13	273.24	276.22	276.28	273.56	279.50	274.43	278.55	279.22	282.24	282.63	287.03	276.53
2015	275.15	274.89	280.59	282.97	275.32	278.63	281.62	284.86	278.96	287.90	286.60	294.13	281.58
2016	276.19	280.67	289.75	290.56	292.25	294.53	295.04	295.55	299.52	304.96	303.41	311.06	294.75
2017	305.92	306.64	311.10	309.76	310.59	314.16	322.67	322.13	322.00	328.42	322.40	333.75	317.20

LOUISIANA
At a Glance

Population:
  2010 census: 4,533,372
  2017 estimate: 4,684,333

Percent change in population:
  2010–2016: 3.3%

Percent change in total nonfarm employment:
  2007–2017: 2.9%

Industry with the largest growth in employment, 2007–2017 (thousands):
  Education and health services, 67.1

Industry with the largest decline or smallest growth in employment, 2007–2017 (thousands):
  Government, -28.3

Civilian labor force:
  2010: 2,086,076
  2017: 2,112,320

Unemployment rate and rank among states (highest to lowest):
  2010: 8.0%, 35th
  2017: 5.1%, 5th

Over-the-year change in unemployment rates:
  2015–2016: -0.3%
  2016–2017: -0.9%

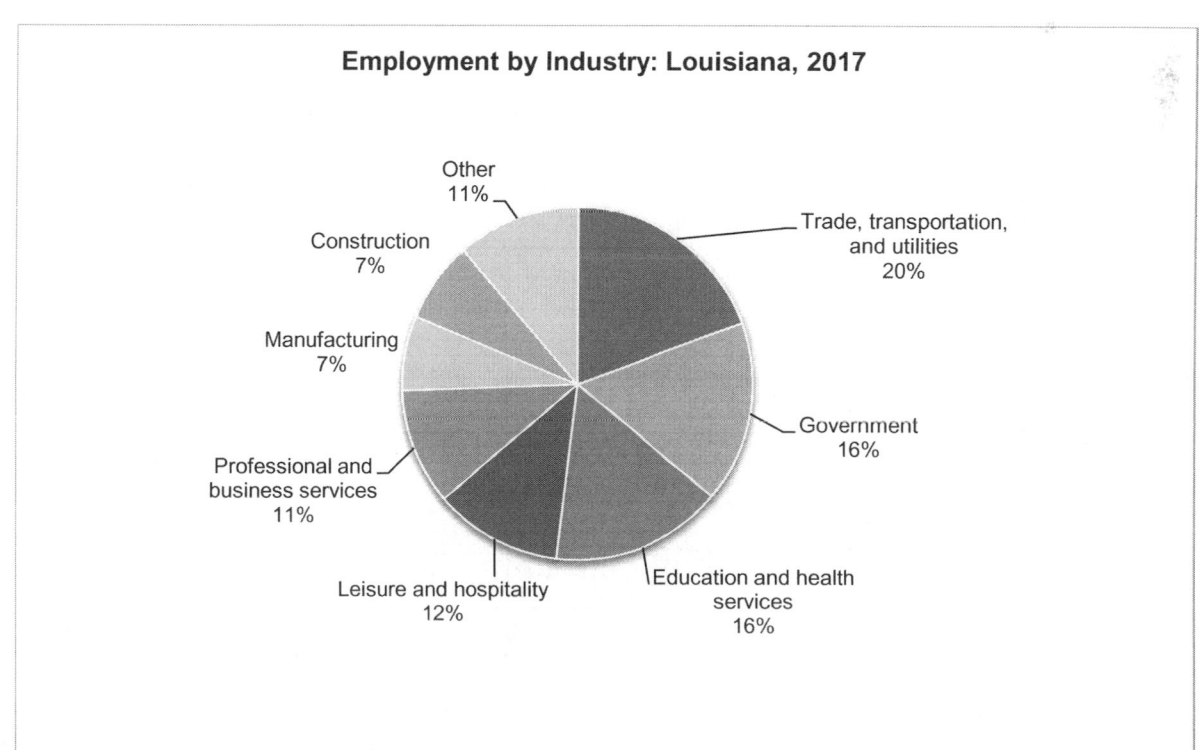

Employment by Industry: Louisiana, 2017

Other 11%

Construction 7%

Manufacturing 7%

Professional and business services 11%

Leisure and hospitality 12%

Trade, transportation, and utilities 20%

Government 16%

Education and health services 16%

1. Employment by Industry: Louisiana, Selected Years, 2007–2017

(Numbers in thousands, not seasonally adjusted)

Industry and year	January	February	March	April	May	June	July	August	September	October	November	December	Annual average
Total Nonfarm													
2007	1,876.7	1,895.6	1,915.8	1,904.8	1,911.9	1,918.0	1,894.3	1,911.6	1,922.3	1,936.9	1,947.5	1,953.9	1,915.8
2008	1,911.0	1,929.0	1,938.0	1,940.3	1,946.0	1,941.3	1,920.3	1,938.5	1,923.1	1,951.0	1,958.1	1,959.4	1,938.0
2009	1,910.8	1,918.7	1,919.0	1,910.3	1,912.7	1,897.8	1,881.7	1,886.6	1,891.6	1,895.2	1,902.3	1,896.1	1,901.9
2010	1,856.4	1,864.8	1,881.8	1,890.6	1,898.5	1,896.4	1,873.8	1,877.1	1,886.7	1,896.5	1,901.4	1,903.2	1,885.6
2011	1,872.5	1,886.7	1,898.6	1,907.5	1,909.1	1,897.3	1,888.5	1,895.7	1,910.2	1,918.3	1,925.2	1,924.6	1,902.9
2012	1,894.9	1,908.9	1,920.5	1,935.0	1,941.2	1,931.7	1,908.0	1,917.6	1,921.7	1,939.4	1,952.3	1,951.4	1,926.9
2013	1,918.4	1,937.2	1,946.2	1,953.8	1,957.2	1,953.5	1,936.1	1,950.7	1,957.2	1,974.6	1,985.5	1,976.9	1,953.9
2014	1,947.9	1,958.9	1,970.8	1,977.8	1,987.2	1,982.2	1,970.4	1,984.7	1,992.0	2,010.9	2,018.8	2,019.5	1,985.1
2015	1,983.4	1,989.4	1,990.6	1,996.9	2,001.2	1,993.7	1,982.4	1,986.6	1,988.8	2,007.9	2,008.2	2,003.0	1,994.3
2016	1,966.0	1,969.1	1,974.2	1,981.9	1,983.7	1,972.9	1,959.4	1,954.4	1,972.2	1,979.7	1,983.6	1,976.1	1,972.8
2017	1,950.3	1,967.8	1,970.3	1,974.3	1,981.3	1,973.9	1,954.2	1,961.6	1,967.2	1,982.0	1,986.7	1,982.9	1,971.0
Total Private													
2007	1,528.0	1,538.4	1,556.3	1,551.0	1,558.3	1,566.6	1,554.1	1,565.3	1,562.1	1,573.6	1,581.6	1,588.6	1,560.3
2008	1,553.8	1,563.9	1,573.6	1,573.6	1,579.2	1,580.3	1,567.0	1,579.1	1,558.1	1,579.9	1,584.5	1,588.5	1,573.5
2009	1,546.1	1,547.0	1,547.5	1,536.9	1,540.6	1,532.5	1,526.4	1,529.5	1,522.0	1,518.8	1,524.6	1,520.8	1,532.7
2010	1,489.8	1,493.5	1,508.2	1,517.5	1,520.5	1,526.2	1,521.3	1,523.8	1,525.7	1,531.4	1,535.0	1,538.6	1,519.3
2011	1,514.9	1,524.9	1,536.8	1,545.9	1,549.1	1,543.5	1,545.2	1,550.8	1,553.5	1,557.3	1,563.8	1,566.3	1,546.0
2012	1,544.9	1,554.7	1,567.1	1,580.6	1,587.9	1,584.6	1,572.3	1,580.7	1,575.7	1,588.2	1,600.3	1,600.3	1,578.1
2013	1,577.6	1,591.8	1,600.9	1,609.0	1,613.2	1,615.5	1,609.0	1,624.7	1,620.2	1,636.2	1,644.8	1,638.9	1,615.2
2014	1,617.8	1,624.5	1,637.6	1,644.9	1,654.7	1,654.0	1,654.4	1,665.5	1,661.1	1,677.0	1,683.1	1,686.9	1,655.1
2015	1,657.0	1,658.3	1,661.1	1,666.0	1,671.0	1,667.6	1,667.4	1,668.8	1,659.8	1,676.9	1,675.2	1,673.6	1,666.9
2016	1,640.9	1,640.0	1,646.1	1,652.7	1,652.7	1,647.0	1,645.8	1,639.0	1,643.1	1,647.2	1,649.0	1,644.3	1,645.7
2017	1,624.2	1,636.9	1,640.5	1,642.1	1,649.9	1,647.4	1,639.9	1,645.4	1,640.4	1,651.5	1,654.3	1,653.5	1,643.8
Goods Producing													
2007	333.1	336.4	339.6	341.0	343.5	345.7	343.1	345.1	344.4	346.6	345.9	344.7	342.4
2008	337.8	339.2	340.0	341.2	344.1	345.8	344.0	345.6	342.0	347.8	346.0	345.2	343.2
2009	336.2	333.4	331.3	326.9	327.5	325.2	323.5	321.7	318.7	317.9	316.1	312.2	324.2
2010	306.4	305.9	309.4	310.5	311.5	314.9	315.1	315.0	314.3	315.4	312.7	312.4	312.0
2011	307.6	310.5	313.8	316.6	316.4	316.3	319.4	319.1	320.4	320.3	317.7	316.2	316.2
2012	315.7	319.5	322.4	323.1	325.8	327.7	323.2	325.5	326.4	328.1	327.8	325.0	324.2
2013	320.4	325.0	328.4	328.5	330.3	333.2	332.4	333.9	334.4	338.5	336.0	331.4	331.0
2014	331.2	333.5	337.5	336.2	341.5	341.3	345.1	347.1	347.7	351.4	345.8	343.3	341.8
2015	337.8	335.7	334.3	330.8	330.1	331.1	332.9	332.4	330.9	334.7	328.4	324.3	332.0
2016	316.9	315.7	316.3	313.2	312.8	315.1	316.1	311.2	313.8	315.4	311.9	309.8	314.0
2017	309.6	313.6	315.0	315.0	317.5	319.1	319.1	319.0	316.1	316.1	314.0	312.7	315.6
Service-Providing													
2007	1,543.6	1,559.2	1,576.2	1,563.8	1,568.4	1,572.3	1,551.2	1,566.5	1,577.9	1,590.3	1,601.6	1,609.2	1,573.4
2008	1,573.2	1,589.8	1,598.0	1,599.1	1,601.9	1,595.5	1,576.3	1,592.9	1,581.1	1,603.2	1,612.1	1,614.2	1,594.8
2009	1,574.6	1,585.3	1,587.7	1,583.4	1,585.2	1,572.6	1,558.2	1,564.9	1,572.9	1,577.3	1,586.2	1,583.9	1,577.7
2010	1,550.0	1,558.9	1,572.4	1,580.1	1,587.0	1,581.5	1,558.7	1,562.1	1,572.4	1,581.1	1,588.7	1,590.8	1,573.6
2011	1,564.9	1,576.2	1,584.8	1,590.9	1,592.7	1,581.0	1,569.1	1,576.6	1,589.8	1,598.0	1,607.5	1,608.4	1,586.7
2012	1,579.2	1,589.4	1,598.1	1,611.9	1,615.4	1,604.0	1,584.8	1,592.1	1,595.3	1,611.3	1,624.5	1,626.4	1,602.7
2013	1,598.0	1,612.2	1,617.8	1,625.3	1,626.9	1,620.3	1,603.7	1,616.8	1,622.8	1,636.1	1,649.5	1,645.5	1,622.9
2014	1,616.7	1,625.4	1,633.3	1,641.6	1,645.7	1,640.9	1,625.3	1,637.6	1,644.3	1,659.5	1,673.0	1,676.2	1,643.3
2015	1,645.6	1,653.7	1,656.3	1,666.1	1,671.1	1,662.6	1,649.5	1,654.2	1,657.9	1,673.2	1,679.8	1,678.7	1,662.4
2016	1,649.1	1,653.4	1,657.9	1,668.7	1,670.9	1,657.8	1,643.3	1,643.2	1,658.4	1,664.3	1,671.7	1,666.3	1,658.8
2017	1,640.7	1,654.2	1,655.3	1,659.3	1,663.8	1,654.8	1,635.1	1,642.6	1,651.1	1,665.9	1,672.7	1,670.2	1,655.5
Mining and Logging													
2007	50.5	50.7	50.9	52.0	52.5	52.9	52.8	53.8	53.2	53.3	53.7	53.6	52.5
2008	54.7	54.5	54.8	54.9	55.2	55.8	56.2	56.3	55.7	57.2	56.8	56.5	55.7
2009	55.7	54.9	54.1	52.0	52.2	52.1	50.9	50.8	50.3	50.5	50.6	51.1	52.1
2010	50.3	51.4	51.9	52.5	53.1	53.6	53.1	53.3	52.9	53.2	52.9	53.0	52.6
2011	52.4	52.9	53.1	54.1	53.9	54.6	55.6	55.8	55.8	55.7	55.7	55.9	54.6
2012	56.9	57.7	57.4	56.1	56.6	56.5	54.8	55.1	54.5	54.7	54.7	54.2	55.8
2013	54.0	54.4	54.6	55.0	55.3	55.8	56.0	56.3	55.9	55.9	55.7	55.3	55.4
2014	55.2	55.0	55.1	54.6	55.3	55.3	55.8	55.8	55.6	55.7	55.4	55.2	55.3
2015	54.1	51.9	50.5	48.4	48.0	46.9	46.7	46.3	45.3	44.3	42.9	42.5	47.3
2016	41.6	40.4	39.4	38.2	37.4	37.2	37.3	36.6	36.3	36.1	35.5	35.6	37.6
2017	34.6	34.6	34.7	34.7	34.9	35.3	35.5	35.2	35.1	34.4	35.2	34.2	34.9

1. Employment by Industry: Louisiana, Selected Years, 2007–2017—*Continued*

(Numbers in thousands, not seasonally adjusted)

Industry and year	January	February	March	April	May	June	July	August	September	October	November	December	Annual average
Construction													
2007	129.1	130.5	132.7	132.2	133.8	134.3	132.3	133.8	133.5	134.7	133.6	132.8	132.8
2008	129.3	131.0	132.0	133.7	135.3	136.1	134.8	136.4	135.3	138.0	137.7	137.1	134.7
2009	132.7	132.9	132.7	130.8	131.9	131.1	131.6	130.3	128.3	127.9	126.9	123.5	130.1
2010	119.5	118.7	120.6	119.5	119.7	122.5	123.9	123.6	123.4	123.5	121.8	121.1	121.5
2011	118.4	120.3	122.8	124.4	123.5	122.5	123.4	122.5	123.1	122.3	120.3	118.8	121.9
2012	119.2	122.1	124.4	125.2	126.5	127.6	125.2	127.0	128.8	130.6	130.1	127.8	126.2
2013	124.5	128.4	131.1	130.6	131.1	132.3	131.4	132.2	132.8	135.6	133.6	129.7	131.1
2014	129.7	132.8	136.6	135.4	138.8	138.2	141.2	142.9	144.2	146.8	141.8	139.6	139.0
2015	136.6	137.5	138.9	138.0	137.9	139.8	141.8	142.1	142.6	147.6	143.8	140.7	140.6
2016	136.8	137.6	139.8	138.3	138.7	141.6	143.1	139.7	142.5	144.6	142.1	139.9	140.4
2017	141.4	144.8	146.1	146.0	148.1	148.5	148.7	148.8	146.7	146.7	145.2	144.2	146.3
Manufacturing													
2007	153.5	155.2	156.0	156.8	157.2	156.5	156.0	157.5	157.7	158.6	158.6	158.3	157.2
2008	153.8	153.7	153.2	152.6	153.6	153.9	153.0	152.9	151.0	152.6	151.5	151.6	152.8
2009	147.8	145.6	144.5	144.1	143.4	142.0	141.0	140.6	140.1	139.5	138.6	137.6	142.1
2010	136.6	135.8	136.9	138.5	138.7	138.8	138.1	138.1	138.0	138.7	138.0	138.3	137.9
2011	136.8	137.3	137.9	138.1	139.0	139.2	140.4	140.8	141.5	142.3	141.7	141.5	139.7
2012	139.6	139.7	140.6	141.8	142.7	143.6	143.2	143.4	143.1	142.8	143.0	143.0	142.2
2013	141.9	142.2	142.7	142.9	143.9	145.1	145.0	145.4	145.7	147.0	146.7	146.4	144.6
2014	146.3	145.7	145.8	146.2	147.4	147.8	148.1	148.4	147.9	148.9	148.6	148.5	147.5
2015	147.1	146.3	144.9	144.4	144.2	144.4	144.4	144.0	143.0	142.8	141.7	141.1	144.0
2016	138.5	137.7	137.1	136.7	136.7	136.3	135.7	134.9	135.0	134.7	134.3	134.3	136.0
2017	133.6	134.2	134.2	134.3	134.5	135.3	134.9	135.0	134.3	135.0	133.6	134.3	134.4
Trade, Transportation, and Utilities													
2007	378.9	377.9	382.4	378.8	380.3	381.3	380.6	382.3	382.7	385.8	391.9	396.2	383.3
2008	383.5	381.9	384.7	382.9	384.0	383.8	381.9	383.8	378.1	382.2	386.9	390.5	383.7
2009	375.5	373.0	373.0	369.2	369.2	369.7	369.5	368.8	367.7	365.2	370.1	371.2	370.2
2010	359.6	358.6	361.7	364.2	365.6	366.4	365.9	366.6	366.1	370.5	376.3	379.9	366.8
2011	369.8	368.9	370.7	373.1	374.0	373.1	373.9	373.9	373.1	374.6	381.3	384.2	374.2
2012	373.6	372.1	374.7	376.3	377.6	377.3	375.6	375.9	374.8	378.7	387.6	389.5	377.8
2013	378.0	376.5	379.7	380.2	380.4	381.4	380.8	382.5	383.2	384.7	391.0	395.5	382.8
2014	383.2	381.7	384.2	385.5	387.3	388.6	388.0	389.7	389.5	391.8	399.3	405.2	389.5
2015	392.2	389.5	391.2	391.8	392.7	393.0	392.1	392.6	390.3	393.5	399.0	401.5	393.3
2016	389.0	386.6	387.8	387.9	387.5	386.5	386.3	385.6	384.6	386.3	392.6	395.0	388.0
2017	383.4	381.0	381.8	381.2	381.6	381.1	379.2	380.4	378.3	378.8	383.3	384.4	381.2
Wholesale Trade													
2007	74.9	75.2	75.8	74.9	75.3	75.9	76.4	76.8	76.3	76.6	76.6	76.9	76.0
2008	75.6	75.9	76.3	75.9	76.1	76.1	75.8	76.0	75.5	75.4	75.0	75.2	75.7
2009	73.3	73.2	72.8	72.1	72.0	71.7	71.5	71.3	71.0	70.9	70.8	70.4	71.8
2010	69.2	69.4	69.9	70.2	70.5	70.6	70.6	70.8	70.6	71.3	71.2	71.2	70.5
2011	71.6	71.8	72.1	71.5	72.0	72.0	72.5	72.5	72.4	72.6	72.7	72.8	72.2
2012	71.9	72.1	72.4	72.7	72.7	72.8	72.5	72.5	72.1	72.3	72.6	72.6	72.4
2013	72.7	72.8	73.2	73.1	73.2	73.2	73.2	73.5	73.4	73.5	73.6	73.5	73.2
2014	72.4	72.6	72.9	72.9	73.4	73.4	73.3	73.5	73.7	73.6	73.6	73.8	73.3
2015	73.0	72.8	73.0	72.6	72.6	72.5	72.3	72.3	71.7	72.0	71.7	71.8	72.4
2016	71.2	71.0	70.8	70.9	70.7	70.4	70.7	70.6	70.5	70.3	69.8	70.1	70.6
2017	69.0	69.5	69.6	69.5	69.7	69.8	69.8	69.9	69.8	70.7	70.6	70.8	69.9
Retail Trade													
2007	222.3	221.2	224.8	222.6	223.6	223.6	223.2	223.4	224.3	226.6	232.6	236.1	225.4
2008	226.6	224.5	226.6	224.6	224.9	224.9	224.0	225.0	220.6	223.5	228.5	231.4	225.4
2009	220.7	219.7	220.3	219.8	220.3	221.1	221.3	220.6	220.1	217.7	222.7	223.7	220.7
2010	215.1	214.1	216.2	216.7	217.2	217.2	216.2	216.0	215.6	218.4	224.5	226.8	217.8
2011	218.7	217.7	219.2	221.2	221.4	220.6	220.1	219.5	218.6	219.9	226.4	228.1	221.0
2012	220.4	218.8	220.4	221.2	222.0	221.7	220.9	220.3	219.5	222.9	230.6	231.8	222.5
2013	221.3	219.3	221.4	221.7	221.9	223.0	222.8	223.6	224.2	225.0	231.0	233.8	224.1
2014	223.6	222.4	223.8	224.9	225.8	227.4	226.8	227.2	226.6	228.6	235.8	239.6	227.7
2015	229.3	228.5	230.4	231.1	231.9	233.0	232.4	232.8	231.3	234.5	240.6	241.9	233.1
2016	233.0	232.1	233.6	234.4	234.2	234.4	234.1	233.3	232.3	234.8	241.4	242.7	235.0
2017	233.8	231.3	231.8	231.5	231.5	231.1	229.2	229.9	228.2	228.9	232.2	232.4	231.0

1. Employment by Industry: Louisiana, Selected Years, 2007–2017—*Continued*

(Numbers in thousands, not seasonally adjusted)

Industry and year	January	February	March	April	May	June	July	August	September	October	November	December	Annual average
Transportation and Utilities													
2007	81.7	81.5	81.8	81.3	81.4	81.8	81.0	82.1	82.1	82.6	82.7	83.2	81.9
2008	81.3	81.5	81.8	82.4	83.0	82.8	82.1	82.8	82.0	83.3	83.4	83.9	82.5
2009	81.5	80.1	79.9	77.3	76.9	76.9	76.7	76.9	76.6	76.6	76.6	77.1	77.8
2010	75.3	75.1	75.6	77.3	77.9	78.6	79.1	79.8	79.9	80.8	80.6	81.9	78.5
2011	79.5	79.4	79.4	80.4	80.6	80.5	81.3	81.9	82.1	82.1	82.2	83.3	81.1
2012	81.3	81.2	81.9	82.4	82.9	82.8	82.2	83.1	83.2	83.5	84.4	85.1	82.8
2013	84.0	84.4	85.1	85.4	85.3	85.2	84.8	85.4	85.6	86.2	86.4	88.2	85.5
2014	87.2	86.7	87.5	87.7	88.1	87.8	87.9	89.0	89.2	89.6	89.9	91.8	88.5
2015	89.9	88.2	87.8	88.1	88.2	87.5	87.4	87.5	87.3	87.0	86.7	87.8	87.8
2016	84.8	83.5	83.4	82.6	82.6	81.7	81.5	81.7	81.8	81.2	81.4	82.2	82.4
2017	80.6	80.2	80.4	80.2	80.4	80.2	80.2	80.6	80.3	79.2	80.5	81.2	80.3
Information													
2007	26.5	27.5	29.6	28.7	28.5	29.0	27.9	27.4	26.2	27.0	26.7	27.1	27.7
2008	26.7	28.5	30.2	30.1	30.8	31.7	26.6	28.0	27.9	26.2	27.1	27.8	28.5
2009	24.9	25.2	25.2	24.5	24.8	24.9	24.5	24.1	23.9	24.2	25.4	24.8	24.7
2010	24.4	24.8	24.5	25.3	25.8	26.4	23.4	23.5	25.6	23.6	24.0	24.7	24.7
2011	23.4	23.5	25.1	23.7	24.6	24.0	22.9	22.9	23.0	23.6	23.5	24.2	23.7
2012	23.2	23.9	23.9	27.1	28.0	25.4	24.8	24.7	24.3	23.9	25.0	25.7	25.0
2013	25.4	26.9	26.3	27.0	27.7	28.0	25.4	25.5	24.4	26.3	27.6	25.7	26.4
2014	23.6	25.0	26.0	26.3	27.8	27.0	26.6	25.3	24.3	25.4	27.4	26.8	26.0
2015	24.8	26.6	25.5	27.5	29.0	28.1	27.5	26.2	24.9	25.1	25.8	26.2	26.4
2016	24.8	24.6	24.5	24.1	23.9	23.4	23.9	23.9	22.3	22.6	24.1	22.5	23.7
2017	21.9	24.2	23.8	24.2	25.1	22.9	22.1	22.3	21.9	22.5	22.0	21.7	22.9
Financial Activities													
2007	97.3	97.6	96.7	95.9	95.7	95.9	95.8	95.4	94.8	95.1	95.1	95.1	95.9
2008	93.7	94.1	94.4	93.9	93.9	94.2	93.6	93.3	92.5	94.3	93.3	93.2	93.7
2009	91.0	90.9	91.0	91.7	91.7	91.8	91.6	91.3	90.7	90.1	90.6	91.0	91.1
2010	90.0	90.2	90.8	90.8	91.0	91.7	92.2	92.2	91.8	92.2	92.0	92.4	91.4
2011	91.9	92.3	92.3	91.8	91.9	91.6	91.6	91.3	91.7	91.9	91.7	91.7	91.8
2012	90.8	91.2	91.6	91.4	91.5	91.6	91.4	91.4	91.1	91.7	92.4	92.7	91.6
2013	91.4	91.4	91.6	91.9	92.4	92.9	92.9	93.3	93.5	93.8	93.6	93.2	92.7
2014	92.2	92.1	92.0	92.3	92.8	93.1	93.6	94.2	94.0	94.4	94.6	94.6	93.3
2015	93.6	93.5	93.6	93.2	93.3	93.6	93.3	93.4	92.7	93.3	93.3	93.4	93.4
2016	92.4	92.4	92.3	92.7	93.0	92.4	93.3	92.9	93.2	93.4	93.0	92.8	92.8
2017	91.7	91.9	91.8	91.8	92.1	91.9	92.0	91.8	91.5	92.2	91.6	91.4	91.8
Professional and Business Services													
2007	196.9	198.8	200.8	199.6	200.1	201.4	198.6	200.8	200.8	204.6	205.1	206.1	201.1
2008	200.9	203.4	203.3	203.7	204.0	203.3	201.8	203.9	202.8	205.0	205.6	205.4	203.6
2009	197.7	198.2	197.1	193.8	193.5	192.0	190.1	190.3	188.5	190.1	190.4	190.4	192.7
2010	186.7	188.3	190.1	192.0	192.6	194.6	195.7	194.9	193.6	194.3	193.7	193.5	192.5
2011	191.3	193.8	193.8	195.3	195.4	194.9	194.6	196.4	196.6	197.7	197.7	198.0	195.5
2012	195.9	198.2	199.9	204.0	204.5	203.2	202.1	202.4	201.7	204.4	204.7	203.4	202.0
2013	200.8	206.9	205.9	205.9	205.7	205.7	205.6	207.7	205.8	210.1	211.0	210.2	206.8
2014	207.9	208.9	210.6	212.3	210.2	210.7	210.5	211.0	210.6	214.2	215.4	216.9	211.6
2015	212.1	212.9	213.7	215.4	215.0	213.5	214.6	214.9	212.4	215.9	214.5	213.0	214.0
2016	209.5	210.6	210.6	214.8	213.1	209.9	209.9	208.3	211.7	211.9	210.5	208.2	210.8
2017	206.3	209.9	209.4	208.4	209.0	208.3	209.1	209.4	209.4	216.6	218.3	217.3	211.0
Education and Health Services													
2007	241.2	243.1	244.6	246.0	245.6	245.6	243.8	248.2	249.2	251.7	253.0	253.9	247.2
2008	251.2	254.2	255.2	255.9	254.9	253.8	254.4	259.1	257.3	260.7	261.8	262.1	256.7
2009	261.0	263.4	264.1	264.9	265.5	261.0	262.3	266.4	267.3	270.2	271.0	270.8	265.7
2010	267.8	268.8	270.4	272.2	270.2	267.7	268.4	270.3	272.8	274.7	275.1	275.1	271.1
2011	272.5	274.7	275.7	277.1	276.6	273.1	273.5	276.1	279.0	281.2	282.7	282.2	277.0
2012	277.8	280.1	281.6	282.5	283.1	281.4	279.3	283.1	283.4	286.5	287.0	286.9	282.7
2013	286.7	288.5	288.8	289.1	288.7	284.9	284.4	292.1	293.1	297.5	297.8	296.7	290.7
2014	295.3	295.9	296.1	297.2	297.5	294.3	294.1	299.7	300.9	303.2	303.0	302.4	298.3
2015	301.4	301.8	301.8	304.0	304.3	301.1	300.6	304.7	305.7	309.0	309.1	309.4	304.4
2016	306.2	306.9	307.2	309.7	310.0	307.8	307.9	310.9	312.4	313.1	313.1	313.9	309.9
2017	311.6	313.3	313.2	314.4	314.8	313.0	310.0	313.9	315.4	317.8	317.2	316.5	314.3

1. Employment by Industry: Louisiana, Selected Years, 2007–2017—*Continued*

(Numbers in thousands, not seasonally adjusted)

Industry and year	January	February	March	April	May	June	July	August	September	October	November	December	Annual average
Leisure and Hospitality													
2007	186.4	188.7	193.2	192.5	195.5	198.2	195.3	196.2	193.7	192.3	193.4	194.7	193.3
2008	191.1	193.4	196.0	198.9	200.0	200.3	198.2	198.7	191.4	194.2	194.2	194.7	195.9
2009	190.7	193.4	196.1	196.3	198.5	198.2	195.2	196.0	194.1	191.4	191.3	190.6	194.3
2010	187.9	189.6	193.6	195.9	197.1	197.7	194.8	195.3	195.7	194.5	195.3	194.7	194.3
2011	192.6	195.0	198.9	201.6	203.7	203.6	202.2	203.9	202.5	201.1	202.4	203.1	200.9
2012	201.6	203.1	205.9	208.6	209.5	209.6	208.0	209.7	206.1	206.6	207.4	208.6	207.1
2013	206.6	207.6	210.7	214.8	216.1	217.1	215.4	217.6	213.7	213.3	215.7	214.3	213.6
2014	212.4	215.0	218.5	221.9	224.0	225.2	222.8	224.7	220.5	222.5	223.7	223.6	221.2
2015	221.3	224.1	226.5	228.3	231.0	231.6	230.6	229.2	227.8	230.0	230.1	230.7	228.4
2016	227.1	228.4	232.1	234.8	237.1	236.5	233.3	231.5	230.6	230.4	229.9	228.6	231.7
2017	226.2	229.4	231.7	233.4	235.8	236.7	234.5	234.7	234.2	233.6	234.2	235.3	233.3
Other Services													
2007	67.7	68.4	69.4	69.5	69.1	69.5	69.0	69.9	70.3	70.5	70.5	70.8	69.5
2008	68.9	69.2	69.8	67.0	67.5	67.4	66.5	66.7	66.1	69.5	69.6	69.6	68.2
2009	69.1	69.5	69.7	69.6	69.9	69.7	69.7	70.9	71.1	69.7	69.7	69.8	69.9
2010	67.0	67.3	67.7	66.6	66.7	66.8	65.8	66.0	65.8	66.2	65.9	65.9	66.5
2011	65.8	66.2	66.5	66.7	66.5	66.9	67.1	67.2	67.2	66.9	66.8	66.7	66.7
2012	66.3	66.6	67.1	67.6	67.9	68.4	67.9	68.0	67.9	68.3	68.4	68.5	67.7
2013	68.3	69.0	69.5	71.6	71.9	72.3	72.1	72.1	72.1	72.0	72.1	71.9	71.2
2014	72.0	72.4	72.7	73.2	73.6	73.8	73.7	73.8	73.6	74.1	73.9	74.1	73.4
2015	73.8	74.2	74.5	75.0	75.6	75.6	75.8	75.4	75.1	75.4	75.0	75.1	75.0
2016	75.0	74.8	75.3	75.5	75.3	75.4	75.1	74.7	74.5	74.1	73.9	73.5	74.8
2017	73.5	73.6	73.8	73.7	74.0	74.4	73.9	73.9	73.6	73.9	73.7	74.2	73.9
Government													
2007	348.7	357.2	359.5	353.8	353.6	351.4	340.2	346.3	360.2	363.3	365.9	365.3	355.5
2008	357.2	365.1	364.4	366.7	366.8	361.0	353.3	359.4	365.0	371.1	373.6	370.9	364.5
2009	364.7	371.7	371.5	373.4	372.1	365.3	355.3	357.1	369.6	376.4	377.7	375.3	369.2
2010	366.6	371.3	373.6	373.1	378.0	370.2	352.5	353.3	361.0	365.1	366.4	364.6	366.3
2011	357.6	361.8	361.8	361.6	360.0	353.8	343.3	344.9	356.7	361.0	361.4	358.3	356.9
2012	350.0	354.2	353.4	354.4	353.3	347.1	335.7	336.9	346.0	351.2	352.0	351.1	348.8
2013	340.8	345.4	345.3	344.8	344.0	338.0	327.1	326.0	337.0	338.4	340.7	338.0	338.8
2014	330.1	334.4	333.2	332.9	332.5	328.2	316.0	319.2	330.9	333.9	335.7	332.6	330.0
2015	326.4	331.1	329.5	330.9	330.2	326.1	315.0	317.8	329.0	331.0	333.0	329.4	327.5
2016	325.1	329.1	328.1	329.2	331.0	325.9	313.6	315.4	329.1	332.5	334.6	331.8	327.1
2017	326.1	330.9	329.8	332.2	331.4	326.5	314.3	316.2	326.8	330.5	332.4	329.4	327.2

2. Average Weekly Hours by Selected Industry: Louisiana, 2013–2017

(Not seasonally adjusted)

Industry and year	January	February	March	April	May	June	July	August	September	October	November	December	Annual average
Total Private													
2013	35.0	35.4	36.0	35.7	35.7	36.4	35.6	35.9	36.1	35.9	35.8	36.1	35.8
2014	35.5	36.2	36.5	36.0	36.1	36.4	36.1	36.4	36.2	36.4	36.8	36.6	36.3
2015	35.9	36.4	35.9	35.7	35.8	35.9	35.9	36.3	35.4	35.9	35.9	35.8	35.9
2016	35.3	35.1	34.6	35.0	35.5	35.2	35.1	34.2	34.9	35.6	35.1	35.2	35.1
2017	35.4	35.4	35.4	35.4	35.4	35.3	35.8	35.3	35.5	35.8	35.4	35.4	35.5
Goods Producing													
2013	41.1	41.9	42.8	43.3	43.2	43.5	42.8	43.9	44.0	44.5	43.7	44.2	43.2
2014	43.1	42.8	43.1	42.8	43.1	43.0	42.8	43.6	43.0	43.4	43.6	44.0	43.2
2015	42.2	42.1	40.6	41.0	41.5	41.3	41.3	41.8	40.3	42.5	42.3	42.4	41.6
2016	41.8	40.6	39.3	40.8	41.9	41.3	41.2	39.8	41.1	42.6	41.3	41.7	41.1
2017	41.7	42.4	42.4	40.7	42.5	42.0	42.6	41.7	42.8	42.3	42.0	42.1	42.1
Construction													
2013	38.6	41.2	42.6	42.4	42.1	43.5	41.7	43.0	43.6	44.0	41.9	42.1	42.2
2014	41.8	41.9	42.5	42.9	43.2	41.8	42.8	43.4	42.8	42.3	41.6	42.2	42.4
2015	40.3	40.6	38.6	40.0	40.9	41.5	41.4	41.5	38.6	41.8	41.5	42.3	40.8
2016	40.7	40.6	37.8	40.2	42.2	41.5	40.9	38.7	41.1	42.6	40.6	40.3	40.6
2017	41.4	42.1	41.5	38.5	41.9	41.2	41.4	40.6	41.4	41.4	40.5	40.9	41.1
Manufacturing													
2013	42.8	42.1	42.6	43.6	43.7	43.3	43.2	44.4	43.9	44.7	44.8	44.9	43.7
2014	43.3	42.3	42.6	42.2	42.8	43.1	42.3	42.6	42.5	44.6	45.4	45.7	43.3
2015	43.9	43.2	42.5	42.2	41.9	40.9	41.1	41.2	40.7	42.3	42.3	42.1	42.0
2016	42.0	39.9	40.1	40.9	40.6	40.4	40.2	39.4	40.2	41.3	41.0	42.1	40.7
2017	41.3	42.2	42.1	41.6	42.1	41.9	42.6	42.3	43.9	43.2	43.2	43.0	42.5
Trade, Transportation, and Utilities													
2013	35.8	35.9	36.7	36.3	36.7	37.2	36.4	36.2	36.2	35.4	35.1	35.1	36.1
2014	34.9	35.7	35.8	35.5	35.8	35.7	35.7	36.1	36.2	36.1	36.2	36.2	35.8
2015	35.6	35.9	36.1	36.2	36.4	36.1	36.3	36.6	35.9	35.4	35.9	36.1	36.0
2016	35.2	35.4	35.1	35.4	35.9	35.7	35.6	34.5	35.4	35.5	35.0	35.5	35.4
2017	35.1	35.0	35.2	35.3	35.1	34.9	35.2	35.1	35.1	35.1	35.1	35.0	35.1
Financial Activities													
2013	38.7	38.5	38.7	38.1	38.3	39.7	37.6	38.6	38.5	38.5	38.2	38.6	38.5
2014	38.4	39.2	39.3	38.3	38.1	38.6	37.3	37.6	37.5	37.3	39.2	37.9	38.2
2015	37.6	38.7	38.5	37.5	37.9	38.0	37.9	38.9	37.4	37.4	38.6	37.3	38.0
2016	37.5	37.5	37.6	36.7	37.3	37.3	36.7	36.0	36.4	37.6	36.2	36.3	36.9
2017	36.5	35.8	35.8	36.3	35.2	35.8	37.2	35.7	36.6	37.4	36.8	36.7	36.3
Professional and Business Services													
2013	37.1	37.0	37.9	36.0	36.0	37.1	35.5	35.9	36.4	36.2	36.7	36.6	36.5
2014	35.9	37.3	37.1	37.2	36.9	37.8	36.7	37.5	37.6	37.9	38.6	37.9	37.4
2015	37.6	38.2	37.6	37.2	36.9	36.9	37.0	37.8	36.6	37.2	37.7	37.6	37.4
2016	36.5	36.2	36.1	36.3	37.2	37.0	36.8	36.7	37.2	38.2	37.1	37.4	36.9
2017	37.8	37.3	36.6	37.7	37.0	37.4	38.0	37.4	37.1	38.3	37.5	37.1	37.4
Education and Health Services													
2013	33.0	32.8	32.9	33.3	33.0	33.4	33.3	33.2	33.1	32.9	33.0	33.3	33.1
2014	32.8	33.4	33.5	33.0	33.0	33.8	33.8	33.7	33.5	33.6	34.3	33.9	33.5
2015	33.9	33.9	33.7	33.5	33.3	33.7	34.1	34.1	33.9	34.0	34.2	34.0	33.9
2016	34.1	33.7	33.4	33.6	33.9	33.8	33.9	33.5	33.4	33.9	33.5	33.5	33.7
2017	34.1	33.5	33.4	33.7	33.2	33.4	34.0	33.5	33.8	34.0	33.8	34.0	33.7
Leisure and Hospitality													
2013	26.7	27.6	27.8	27.5	27.3	27.6	27.1	26.9	26.8	26.9	27.0	27.6	27.2
2014	26.8	27.5	28.5	27.7	27.6	27.6	27.3	27.1	26.9	27.7	28.0	27.9	27.5
2015	27.2	28.5	28.2	28.0	28.2	28.4	28.1	27.9	27.4	27.6	27.7	27.3	27.9
2016	26.5	27.5	27.5	27.5	27.3	26.8	26.5	25.4	26.1	26.6	27.3	26.7	26.8
2017	26.8	27.2	27.5	27.4	27.0	26.6	26.9	26.5	26.4	27.0	27.0	27.1	26.9

3. Average Hourly Earnings Selected Industry: Louisiana, 2013–2017

(Dollars, not seasonally adjusted)

Industry and year	January	February	March	April	May	June	July	August	September	October	November	December	Annual average
Total Private													
2013	21.81	21.95	21.90	22.00	21.83	22.15	21.95	21.67	22.19	22.00	22.00	22.23	21.98
2014	22.09	22.11	22.21	22.11	22.10	22.21	22.23	22.18	22.11	22.04	22.05	21.94	22.11
2015	22.12	22.15	22.31	22.26	21.98	21.94	21.93	22.24	22.15	22.31	22.55	22.38	22.19
2016	22.51	22.39	22.41	22.53	22.63	22.47	22.49	22.65	22.87	23.11	22.87	22.83	22.65
2017	23.09	23.03	23.00	22.85	22.80	22.76	23.07	22.89	23.02	23.13	23.08	23.07	22.98
Goods Producing													
2013	25.86	25.80	26.03	26.09	25.72	26.02	25.90	25.14	25.70	25.27	25.51	26.27	25.77
2014	26.21	26.71	26.72	26.73	26.65	26.64	26.60	26.55	26.20	26.01	25.86	26.18	26.42
2015	26.39	26.30	26.74	26.41	26.12	25.93	26.18	26.38	26.39	26.27	26.51	26.58	26.35
2016	26.76	26.84	27.06	26.89	26.75	26.59	26.74	26.89	27.20	27.26	26.94	26.83	26.90
2017	26.80	27.06	27.14	26.74	26.58	26.36	26.92	26.74	26.62	26.96	26.80	27.16	26.82
Construction													
2013	24.74	24.20	24.66	24.39	24.01	23.45	23.56	23.13	23.27	23.77	23.00	24.47	23.92
2014	24.14	25.03	25.05	24.65	24.92	24.80	24.39	24.61	24.25	24.54	24.41	24.78	24.63
2015	25.28	25.29	25.47	25.14	24.63	24.29	24.68	24.52	24.56	25.17	25.08	25.29	24.95
2016	25.30	25.31	25.62	25.93	25.70	25.55	25.68	25.76	26.63	26.81	26.39	26.67	25.96
2017	26.66	27.18	26.74	26.06	26.21	26.03	26.36	25.95	26.28	26.36	26.33	26.58	26.40
Manufacturing													
2013	26.13	26.40	26.46	26.84	26.38	27.05	26.84	25.85	26.29	25.45	25.66	26.33	26.30
2014	26.53	26.45	26.29	26.08	25.73	26.00	26.69	26.52	26.23	25.41	25.29	25.58	26.06
2015	25.76	25.54	26.44	26.02	25.83	25.83	25.88	26.33	26.26	25.46	25.93	25.95	25.93
2016	26.28	26.51	26.52	26.07	25.90	25.74	26.09	26.24	25.95	26.10	25.89	25.60	26.07
2017	25.45	25.71	26.04	26.16	25.84	25.54	26.27	25.84	25.86	26.29	25.93	26.33	25.94
Trade, Transportation, and Utilities													
2013	19.77	19.99	19.96	20.21	20.16	20.54	20.51	20.18	20.62	20.55	20.34	20.51	20.28
2014	20.50	20.60	20.83	20.53	20.70	21.05	21.34	21.00	21.19	20.98	20.86	20.49	20.84
2015	20.62	20.61	20.86	20.86	20.62	20.89	20.50	20.94	20.76	20.78	20.50	20.79	20.73
2016	20.72	20.37	20.13	20.37	20.40	20.30	20.04	20.30	20.39	20.24	20.02	19.82	20.26
2017	20.07	20.03	19.93	20.28	20.16	20.20	20.50	20.42	20.78	20.79	21.05	20.64	20.40
Financial Activities													
2013	20.71	20.55	20.51	21.04	21.06	21.17	21.51	21.06	21.43	21.25	21.59	21.81	21.14
2014	21.88	22.03	22.16	21.99	21.92	22.41	22.17	22.70	22.92	23.35	23.50	23.07	22.51
2015	23.63	23.89	23.97	24.67	23.98	24.12	24.53	24.92	24.85	24.96	26.12	25.40	24.59
2016	25.54	25.55	25.53	26.12	25.99	24.70	25.12	26.01	26.04	26.89	26.47	26.30	25.85
2017	27.74	26.94	28.09	27.43	26.63	25.79	26.22	26.38	26.41	26.53	26.66	26.74	26.80
Professional and Business Services													
2013	25.10	25.77	25.17	25.30	24.81	25.61	25.14	25.21	26.31	25.92	25.93	25.99	25.53
2014	25.59	25.59	25.95	25.62	25.67	25.93	25.81	25.59	25.36	25.02	25.36	25.77	25.56
2015	25.70	26.16	26.21	25.90	25.52	25.59	25.56	26.00	25.60	25.75	26.26	25.50	25.81
2016	25.55	25.48	25.72	25.24	25.59	25.43	25.48	25.14	25.40	25.93	25.68	25.98	25.55
2017	26.22	25.85	25.93	25.82	25.91	26.35	26.86	26.26	26.17	26.19	25.94	26.19	26.14
Education and Health Services													
2013	19.52	19.41	19.48	19.20	19.10	19.24	19.04	19.07	19.33	19.28	19.27	19.43	19.28
2014	19.10	19.20	19.04	18.97	18.77	18.62	18.46	18.42	18.43	18.40	18.36	18.28	18.67
2015	18.33	18.40	18.65	19.04	18.91	18.58	18.50	18.78	19.00	19.49	19.98	19.98	18.98
2016	20.04	20.29	20.66	21.33	21.67	21.77	21.83	21.92	22.30	22.59	22.83	22.77	21.67
2017	23.09	22.95	22.84	22.96	22.80	22.74	22.81	22.77	22.89	23.02	22.93	22.73	22.88
Leisure and Hospitality													
2013	12.49	12.58	12.40	12.42	12.39	12.27	12.16	12.31	12.30	12.71	12.75	12.82	12.47
2014	12.53	12.70	12.79	12.62	12.65	12.37	12.65	12.69	12.87	13.13	13.13	13.28	12.79
2015	13.29	13.12	13.07	13.06	12.96	12.87	12.87	12.88	12.98	13.16	13.16	13.31	13.06
2016	13.32	13.35	13.60	13.53	13.35	13.21	13.16	13.34	13.35	13.53	13.48	13.51	13.39
2017	13.47	13.51	13.57	13.56	13.41	13.24	13.14	13.11	13.27	13.35	13.49	13.56	13.39

4. Average Weekly Earnings Selected Industry: Louisiana, 2013–2017

(Dollars, not seasonally adjusted)

Industry and year	January	February	March	April	May	June	July	August	September	October	November	December	Annual average
Total Private													
2013	763.35	777.03	788.40	785.40	779.33	806.26	781.42	777.95	801.06	789.80	787.60	802.50	786.88
2014	784.20	800.38	810.67	795.96	797.81	808.44	802.50	807.35	800.38	802.26	811.44	803.00	802.59
2015	794.11	806.26	800.93	794.68	786.88	787.65	787.29	807.31	784.11	800.93	809.55	801.20	796.62
2016	794.60	785.89	775.39	788.55	803.37	790.94	789.40	774.63	798.16	822.72	802.74	803.62	795.02
2017	817.39	815.26	814.20	808.89	807.12	803.43	825.91	808.02	817.21	828.05	817.03	816.68	815.79
Goods Producing													
2013	1,062.85	1,081.02	1,114.08	1,129.70	1,111.10	1,131.87	1,108.52	1,103.65	1,130.80	1,124.52	1,114.79	1,161.13	1,113.26
2014	1,129.65	1,143.19	1,151.63	1,144.04	1,148.62	1,145.52	1,138.48	1,157.58	1,126.60	1,128.83	1,127.50	1,151.92	1,141.34
2015	1,113.66	1,107.23	1,085.64	1,082.81	1,083.98	1,070.91	1,081.23	1,102.68	1,063.52	1,116.48	1,121.37	1,126.99	1,096.16
2016	1,118.57	1,089.70	1,063.46	1,097.11	1,120.83	1,098.17	1,101.69	1,070.22	1,117.92	1,161.28	1,112.62	1,118.81	1,105.59
2017	1,117.56	1,147.34	1,150.74	1,088.32	1,129.65	1,107.12	1,146.79	1,115.06	1,139.34	1,140.41	1,125.60	1,143.44	1,129.12
Construction													
2013	954.96	997.04	1,050.52	1,034.14	1,010.82	1,020.08	982.45	994.59	1,014.57	1,045.88	988.84	1,030.19	1,009.42
2014	1,009.05	1,048.76	1,064.63	1,057.49	1,076.54	1,036.64	1,043.89	1,068.07	1,037.90	1,038.04	1,015.46	1,045.72	1,044.31
2015	1,018.78	1,026.77	983.14	1,005.60	1,007.37	1,008.04	1,021.75	1,017.58	948.02	1,052.11	1,040.82	1,069.77	1,017.96
2016	1,029.71	1,027.59	968.44	1,042.39	1,084.54	1,060.33	1,050.31	996.91	1,094.49	1,142.11	1,071.43	1,074.80	1,053.98
2017	1,103.72	1,144.28	1,109.71	1,003.31	1,098.20	1,072.44	1,091.30	1,053.57	1,087.99	1,091.30	1,066.37	1,087.12	1,085.04
Manufacturing													
2013	1,118.36	1,111.44	1,127.20	1,170.22	1,152.81	1,171.27	1,159.49	1,147.74	1,154.13	1,137.62	1,149.57	1,182.22	1,149.31
2014	1,148.75	1,118.84	1,119.95	1,100.58	1,101.24	1,120.60	1,128.99	1,129.75	1,114.78	1,133.29	1,148.17	1,169.01	1,128.40
2015	1,130.86	1,103.33	1,123.70	1,098.04	1,082.28	1,056.45	1,063.67	1,084.80	1,068.78	1,076.96	1,096.84	1,092.50	1,089.06
2016	1,103.76	1,057.75	1,063.45	1,066.26	1,051.54	1,039.90	1,048.82	1,033.86	1,043.19	1,077.93	1,061.49	1,077.76	1,061.05
2017	1,051.09	1,084.96	1,096.28	1,088.26	1,087.86	1,070.13	1,119.10	1,093.03	1,135.25	1,135.73	1,120.18	1,132.19	1,102.45
Trade, Transportation, and Utilities													
2013	707.77	717.64	732.53	733.62	739.87	764.09	746.56	730.52	746.44	727.47	713.93	719.90	732.11
2014	715.45	735.42	745.71	728.82	741.06	751.49	761.84	758.10	767.08	757.38	755.13	741.74	746.07
2015	734.07	739.90	753.05	755.13	750.57	754.13	744.15	766.40	745.28	735.61	735.95	750.52	746.28
2016	729.34	721.10	706.56	721.10	732.36	724.71	713.42	700.35	721.81	718.52	700.70	703.61	717.20
2017	704.46	701.05	701.54	715.88	707.62	704.98	721.60	716.74	729.38	729.73	738.86	722.40	716.04
Financial Activities													
2013	801.48	791.18	793.74	801.62	806.60	840.45	808.78	812.92	825.06	818.13	824.74	841.87	813.89
2014	840.19	863.58	870.89	842.22	835.15	865.03	826.94	853.52	859.50	870.96	921.20	874.35	859.88
2015	888.49	924.54	922.85	925.13	908.84	916.56	929.69	969.39	929.39	933.50	1,008.23	947.42	934.42
2016	957.75	958.13	959.93	958.60	969.43	921.31	921.90	936.36	947.86	1,011.06	958.21	954.69	953.87
2017	1,012.51	964.45	1,005.62	995.71	937.38	923.28	975.38	941.77	966.61	992.22	981.09	981.36	972.84
Professional and Business Services													
2013	931.21	953.49	953.94	910.80	893.16	950.13	892.47	905.04	957.68	938.30	951.63	951.23	931.85
2014	918.68	954.51	962.75	953.06	947.22	980.15	947.23	959.63	953.54	948.26	978.90	957.73	955.94
2015	966.32	999.31	985.50	963.48	941.69	944.27	945.72	982.80	936.96	957.90	990.00	958.80	965.29
2016	932.58	922.38	928.49	916.21	951.95	940.91	937.66	922.64	944.88	990.53	952.73	971.65	942.80
2017	991.12	964.21	949.04	973.41	958.67	985.49	1,020.68	982.12	970.91	1,003.08	972.75	971.65	977.64
Education and Health Services													
2013	644.16	636.65	640.89	639.36	630.30	642.62	634.03	633.12	639.82	634.31	635.91	647.02	638.17
2014	626.48	641.28	637.84	626.01	619.41	629.36	623.95	620.75	617.41	618.24	629.75	619.69	625.45
2015	621.39	623.76	628.51	637.84	629.70	626.15	630.85	640.40	644.10	662.66	683.32	679.32	643.42
2016	683.36	683.77	690.04	716.69	734.61	735.83	740.04	734.32	744.82	765.80	764.81	762.80	730.28
2017	787.37	768.83	762.86	773.75	756.96	759.52	775.54	762.80	773.68	782.68	775.03	772.82	771.06
Leisure and Hospitality													
2013	333.48	347.21	344.72	341.55	338.25	338.65	329.54	331.14	329.64	341.90	344.25	353.83	339.18
2014	335.80	349.25	364.52	349.57	349.14	341.41	345.35	343.90	346.20	363.70	367.64	370.51	351.73
2015	361.49	373.92	368.57	365.68	365.47	365.51	361.65	359.35	355.65	363.22	364.53	363.36	364.37
2016	352.98	367.13	374.00	372.08	364.46	354.03	348.74	338.84	348.44	359.90	368.00	360.72	358.85
2017	361.00	367.47	373.18	371.54	362.07	352.18	353.47	347.42	350.33	360.45	364.23	367.48	360.19

MAINE
At a Glance

Population:
  2010 census: 1,328,361
  2017 estimate: 1,335,907

Percent change in population:
  2010–2017: 0.6%

Percent change in total nonfarm employment:
  2007–2017: 0.8%

Industry with the largest growth in employment, 2007–2017 (thousands):
  Professional and business services, 11.9

Industry with the largest decline or smallest growth in employment, 2007–2017 (thousands):
  Manufacturing, 8.3

Civilian labor force:
  2010: 695,182
  2017: 700,099

Unemployment rate and rank among states (highest to lowest):
  2010: 8.1%, 32nd
  2017: 3.3%, 40th

Over-the-year change in unemployment rates:
  2015–2016: -0.6%
  2016–2017: -0.5%

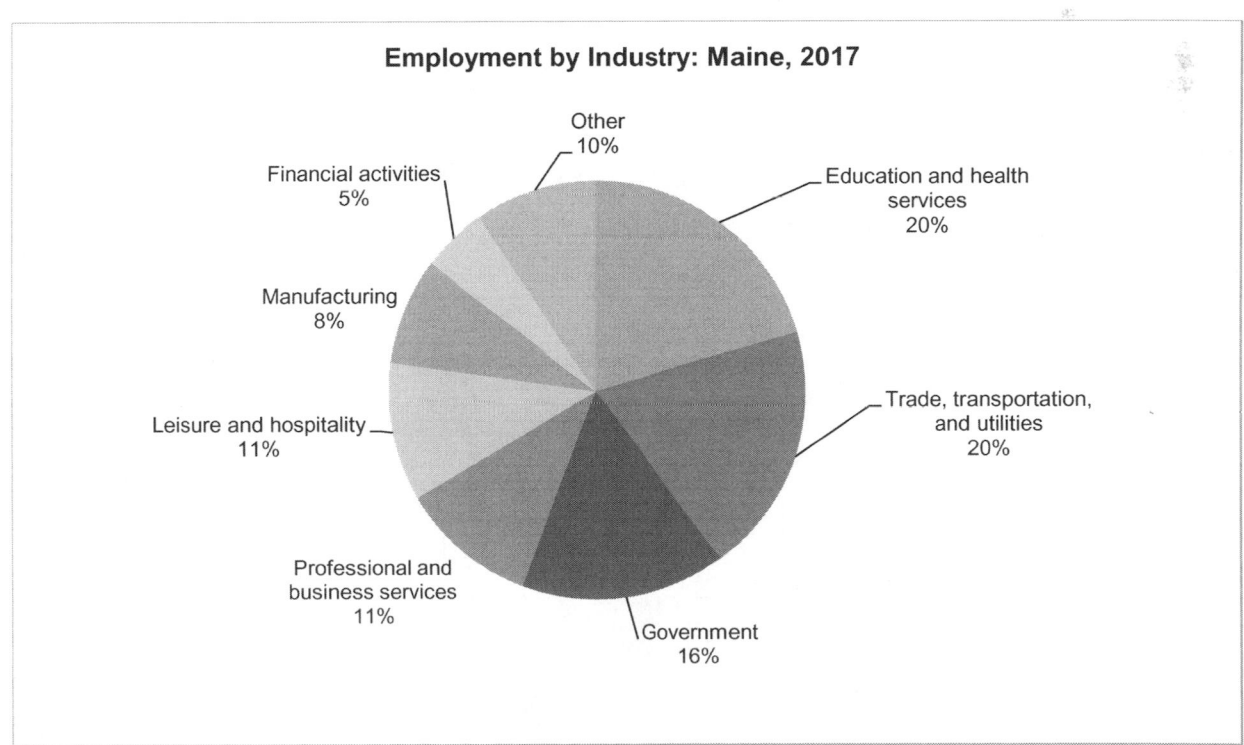

Employment by Industry: Maine, 2017

Other 10%
Financial activities 5%
Education and health services 20%
Manufacturing 8%
Trade, transportation, and utilities 20%
Leisure and hospitality 11%
Professional and business services 11%
Government 16%

1. Employment by Industry: Maine, Selected Years, 2007–2017

(Numbers in thousands, not seasonally adjusted)

Industry and year	January	February	March	April	May	June	July	August	September	October	November	December	Annual average
Total Nonfarm													
2007	596.1	596.2	599.1	604.4	618.2	632.4	629.0	629.0	628.6	627.8	626.6	625.2	617.7
2008	599.7	600.1	601.8	609.6	623.0	633.6	630.0	628.1	625.8	625.0	617.6	612.6	617.2
2009	584.1	582.5	579.9	588.4	601.9	607.6	603.9	603.9	605.3	603.8	598.6	595.8	596.3
2010	572.0	572.9	574.9	583.8	599.1	604.4	602.9	602.6	604.4	603.9	598.7	596.1	593.0
2011	572.4	574.2	575.4	582.8	594.6	605.9	608.6	608.6	608.9	606.3	601.3	597.5	594.7
2012	575.0	577.3	578.7	587.6	602.3	613.4	611.5	611.5	610.8	608.9	601.7	598.8	598.1
2013	577.8	578.1	579.8	588.9	604.5	616.2	618.0	617.1	616.4	615.0	605.4	603.3	601.7
2014	580.1	581.6	583.7	591.6	607.5	621.2	620.9	620.9	619.0	617.0	609.4	608.5	605.1
2015	586.5	585.4	588.2	598.0	613.6	626.6	628.3	627.7	624.4	621.1	614.0	613.0	610.6
2016	593.6	595.2	597.6	606.7	619.7	633.9	636.1	634.8	631.1	627.8	622.0	619.5	618.2
2017	601.7	600.6	604.8	611.0	623.8	640.1	640.0	638.6	636.5	629.7	623.9	622.1	622.7
Total Private													
2007	492.4	489.9	492.1	497.9	510.5	527.3	536.8	537.6	523.9	519.5	517.8	516.5	513.5
2008	495.8	493.6	494.4	501.9	515.1	528.4	537.9	535.8	521.4	516.8	508.8	504.1	512.8
2009	480.6	476.3	473.3	481.0	494.3	502.9	513.1	513.1	501.4	496.7	490.8	488.3	492.7
2010	468.3	466.6	467.1	476.2	489.0	499.7	511.0	511.7	501.4	497.0	491.3	488.9	489.0
2011	469.3	468.9	469.8	477.8	490.0	504.2	516.4	517.3	506.6	501.8	496.0	493.2	492.6
2012	474.0	473.5	474.5	483.8	497.4	512.4	519.6	519.5	509.2	504.4	497.3	494.5	496.7
2013	476.2	475.1	476.2	485.5	500.8	516.4	527.3	527.0	516.1	511.6	502.4	500.2	501.2
2014	480.6	480.2	481.4	489.4	505.3	520.4	530.5	530.9	518.5	513.9	506.1	505.1	505.2
2015	487.0	484.3	486.2	496.2	512.2	527.0	537.1	536.7	524.3	519.0	511.5	510.8	511.0
2016	495.0	494.0	495.5	504.5	517.7	533.3	544.5	543.1	530.1	525.0	518.2	516.9	518.2
2017	502.5	499.3	502.5	508.7	521.9	539.7	548.3	547.1	535.2	526.9	520.3	518.9	522.6
Goods Producing													
2007	89.3	87.7	88.5	89.7	92.3	95.7	96.1	96.5	95.1	95.2	95.2	93.5	92.9
2008	89.1	87.9	87.7	88.8	91.7	94.0	94.2	93.9	92.1	91.8	90.3	87.1	90.7
2009	80.9	78.6	76.8	77.6	80.1	81.3	81.9	82.0	80.9	80.8	80.0	77.6	79.9
2010	73.9	72.9	73.2	74.8	78.0	79.4	80.0	80.9	80.3	80.3	80.0	78.1	77.7
2011	74.7	73.8	74.1	75.3	77.9	80.5	81.5	82.0	81.3	81.0	80.8	79.4	78.5
2012	75.1	74.5	74.6	76.7	79.4	81.5	82.1	82.1	81.3	80.8	79.8	77.9	78.8
2013	74.1	73.5	73.6	75.2	78.3	80.7	81.9	82.2	81.3	81.2	80.4	78.4	78.4
2014	73.9	73.7	73.7	75.1	78.7	81.2	82.0	82.3	81.3	81.1	81.3	79.7	78.7
2015	75.3	74.3	74.5	76.5	79.4	81.9	83.0	83.3	82.4	82.1	82.1	80.8	79.6
2016	76.9	76.3	76.5	78.0	80.5	83.0	83.6	83.6	82.3	82.1	82.1	80.9	80.5
2017	77.7	76.9	77.5	78.6	80.7	83.5	84.2	84.5	83.9	83.1	83.7	81.6	81.3
Service-Providing													
2007	506.8	508.5	510.6	514.7	525.9	536.7	532.9	532.5	533.5	532.6	531.4	531.7	524.8
2008	510.6	512.2	514.1	520.8	531.3	539.6	535.8	534.2	533.7	533.2	527.3	525.5	526.5
2009	503.2	503.9	503.1	510.8	521.8	526.3	522.0	521.9	524.4	523.0	518.6	518.2	516.4
2010	498.1	500.0	501.7	509.0	521.1	525.0	522.9	521.7	524.1	523.6	518.7	518.0	515.3
2011	497.7	500.4	501.3	507.5	516.7	525.4	527.1	526.6	527.6	525.3	520.5	518.1	516.2
2012	499.9	502.8	504.1	510.9	522.9	531.9	529.4	529.4	529.5	528.1	521.9	520.9	519.3
2013	503.7	504.6	506.2	513.7	526.2	535.5	536.1	534.9	535.1	533.8	525.0	524.9	523.3
2014	506.2	507.9	510.0	516.5	528.8	540.0	538.9	538.6	537.7	535.9	528.1	528.8	526.5
2015	511.2	511.1	513.7	521.5	534.2	544.7	545.3	544.4	542.0	539.0	531.9	532.2	530.9
2016	516.7	518.9	521.1	528.7	539.2	550.9	552.5	551.2	548.8	545.7	539.9	538.6	537.7
2017	524.0	523.7	527.3	532.4	543.1	556.6	555.8	554.1	552.6	546.6	540.2	540.5	541.4
Mining and Logging													
2007	2.9	2.9	2.9	2.0	1.8	2.5	2.8	2.8	2.8	2.8	2.9	2.8	2.7
2008	2.8	2.8	2.8	2.1	1.8	2.3	2.6	2.6	2.6	2.8	2.8	2.8	2.6
2009	2.8	2.8	2.6	1.5	1.5	1.9	2.4	2.6	2.6	2.7	2.8	2.7	2.4
2010	2.7	2.7	2.6	1.9	2.1	2.5	2.7	2.7	2.7	2.7	2.6	2.6	2.5
2011	2.6	2.6	2.6	1.9	1.8	2.4	2.7	2.7	2.7	2.7	2.7	2.7	2.5
2012	2.6	2.6	2.5	1.8	1.9	2.4	2.6	2.7	2.7	2.7	2.6	2.6	2.5
2013	2.6	2.6	2.4	1.8	1.9	2.3	2.5	2.6	2.6	2.6	2.6	2.6	2.4
2014	2.6	2.6	2.6	2.1	1.7	2.3	2.6	2.6	2.6	2.6	2.6	2.6	2.5
2015	2.5	2.5	2.6	2.0	1.8	2.3	2.6	2.6	2.6	2.5	2.5	2.5	2.4
2016	2.4	2.5	2.3	1.7	1.7	2.3	2.4	2.4	2.4	2.4	2.4	2.4	2.3
2017	2.3	2.3	2.3	1.7	1.6	2.1	2.3	2.3	2.4	2.4	2.3	2.3	2.2

1. Employment by Industry: Maine, Selected Years, 2007–2017—*Continued*

(Numbers in thousands, not seasonally adjusted)

Industry and year	January	February	March	April	May	June	July	August	September	October	November	December	Annual average
Construction													
2007	28.1	26.9	27.4	29.1	31.4	33.0	33.2	33.3	32.8	32.7	31.9	30.3	30.8
2008	27.6	26.7	26.6	28.0	30.6	31.8	31.8	31.5	30.8	30.9	29.3	27.1	29.4
2009	24.0	22.8	22.3	23.8	26.0	26.8	27.1	27.0	26.5	26.6	25.2	23.7	25.2
2010	21.3	20.6	20.6	22.8	25.0	25.7	26.2	26.5	26.6	26.6	25.9	24.4	24.4
2011	22.0	21.3	21.4	23.2	25.3	27.0	27.7	27.7	27.6	27.6	26.9	25.6	25.3
2012	22.9	22.2	22.3	24.5	26.6	27.4	27.7	27.8	27.4	27.1	26.1	24.7	25.6
2013	22.3	21.9	21.9	23.9	26.1	27.2	27.8	28.0	27.8	27.8	26.8	25.3	25.6
2014	22.7	22.5	22.5	23.9	26.7	27.7	28.3	28.4	28.0	27.9	27.2	25.8	26.0
2015	23.3	22.7	22.7	24.5	27.2	28.4	29.0	29.0	28.4	28.5	27.9	26.9	26.5
2016	24.8	24.3	24.5	26.3	28.1	29.2	29.7	29.4	28.8	28.8	28.3	27.3	27.5
2017	25.5	24.9	25.2	26.6	28.3	29.7	30.2	30.2	29.9	29.1	29.2	27.5	28.0
Manufacturing													
2007	58.3	57.9	58.2	58.6	59.1	60.2	60.1	60.4	59.5	59.7	60.4	60.4	59.4
2008	58.7	58.4	58.3	58.7	59.3	59.9	59.8	59.8	58.7	58.1	58.2	57.2	58.8
2009	54.1	53.0	51.9	52.3	52.6	52.6	52.4	52.4	51.8	51.5	52.0	51.2	52.3
2010	49.9	49.6	50.0	50.1	50.9	51.2	51.1	51.7	51.0	51.0	51.5	51.1	50.8
2011	50.1	49.9	50.1	50.2	50.8	51.1	51.1	51.6	51.0	50.7	51.2	51.1	50.7
2012	49.6	49.7	49.8	50.4	50.9	51.7	51.8	51.6	51.2	51.0	51.1	50.6	50.8
2013	49.2	49.0	49.3	49.5	50.3	51.2	51.6	51.6	50.9	50.8	51.0	50.5	50.4
2014	48.6	48.6	48.6	49.1	50.3	51.2	51.1	51.3	50.7	50.6	51.5	51.3	50.2
2015	49.5	49.1	49.2	50.0	50.4	51.2	51.4	51.7	51.4	51.1	51.7	51.4	50.7
2016	49.7	49.5	49.7	50.0	50.7	51.5	51.5	51.8	51.1	50.9	51.4	51.2	50.8
2017	49.9	49.7	50.0	50.3	50.8	51.7	51.7	52.0	51.6	51.6	52.2	51.8	51.1
Trade, Transportation, and Utilities													
2007	123.9	120.7	121.1	121.0	123.8	127.2	129.1	129.2	126.5	127.4	131.1	132.0	126.1
2008	124.7	121.1	120.8	121.7	123.9	126.4	127.7	127.6	124.8	125.3	126.9	127.0	124.8
2009	118.8	115.4	114.3	114.9	117.6	119.6	120.9	121.3	119.3	119.4	121.6	122.4	118.8
2010	114.7	112.2	111.6	112.6	115.1	118.1	119.6	120.1	117.2	118.7	120.2	121.5	116.8
2011	114.5	112.3	111.5	112.8	114.8	118.0	119.6	120.2	118.1	119.2	121.1	121.8	117.0
2012	115.2	112.9	112.3	113.1	115.8	119.1	119.9	120.3	117.9	119.4	121.6	121.8	117.4
2013	114.4	112.0	111.5	112.8	115.8	119.6	121.7	122.2	120.0	120.6	122.5	123.4	118.0
2014	115.8	114.3	113.7	114.8	117.4	120.6	122.1	122.6	120.3	121.0	122.7	123.9	119.1
2015	116.4	114.5	114.0	115.7	118.5	121.7	123.3	123.4	120.8	121.3	122.5	123.7	119.7
2016	117.3	115.7	115.5	116.7	119.2	122.4	124.0	124.0	121.6	121.2	122.7	123.6	120.3
2017	118.0	115.4	115.5	116.3	118.7	122.3	123.9	123.9	121.3	120.8	121.9	123.1	120.1
Wholesale Trade													
2007	20.8	20.7	20.9	20.9	21.2	21.4	21.6	21.5	21.2	21.1	20.9	21.0	21.1
2008	20.7	20.5	20.5	20.5	20.8	21.1	21.3	21.2	20.9	20.8	20.5	20.5	20.8
2009	19.7	19.4	19.3	19.3	19.5	19.6	19.9	19.8	19.5	19.3	19.2	19.2	19.5
2010	18.5	18.4	18.5	18.6	18.9	19.2	19.4	19.6	19.2	19.2	19.1	19.1	19.0
2011	18.7	18.6	18.5	18.7	18.9	19.3	19.7	19.7	19.5	19.3	19.2	19.3	19.1
2012	18.9	18.8	18.8	19.1	19.4	19.9	20.1	20.0	19.7	19.7	19.5	19.5	19.5
2013	18.8	18.8	18.8	19.0	19.5	20.0	20.2	20.2	20.0	19.8	19.7	19.7	19.5
2014	19.0	18.9	19.0	19.2	19.7	20.2	20.4	20.4	20.1	20.1	19.9	19.9	19.7
2015	19.4	19.3	19.3	19.5	20.0	20.3	20.6	20.6	20.3	20.2	19.9	19.9	19.9
2016	19.4	19.3	19.3	19.5	20.0	20.3	20.6	20.5	20.2	20.0	19.7	19.6	19.9
2017	19.2	18.9	19.1	19.3	19.7	20.1	20.1	20.1	19.9	20.2	20.0	19.8	19.7
Retail Trade													
2007	84.3	81.6	82.0	82.2	84.5	87.0	88.5	88.4	85.8	86.4	89.7	90.2	85.9
2008	85.4	82.5	82.3	83.4	85.1	86.9	87.9	87.9	85.4	85.8	87.2	87.1	85.6
2009	81.3	79.0	78.2	78.8	81.1	82.9	83.9	84.4	82.7	82.9	84.4	84.8	82.0
2010	79.7	77.6	77.1	77.9	79.8	82.0	83.2	83.7	81.1	82.3	83.8	84.5	81.1
2011	79.4	77.6	77.0	78.0	79.7	81.9	83.1	83.6	81.4	82.6	84.2	84.6	81.1
2012	79.7	77.7	77.4	78.0	80.0	82.3	83.1	83.5	81.1	82.3	84.4	84.2	81.1
2013	79.0	76.8	76.4	77.4	79.6	82.3	84.2	84.5	82.2	82.8	84.3	84.7	81.2
2014	79.6	78.4	77.8	78.7	80.4	82.5	83.9	84.3	82.0	82.5	83.9	84.6	81.6
2015	79.3	77.9	77.6	78.7	80.7	83.1	84.3	84.4	82.0	82.6	83.8	84.7	81.6
2016	80.1	78.8	78.7	79.4	81.0	83.3	84.7	84.7	82.3	82.3	83.8	84.2	81.9
2017	80.2	78.2	78.2	79.0	80.4	82.8	84.5	84.4	81.8	81.6	82.3	82.8	81.4

1. Employment by Industry: Maine, Selected Years, 2007–2017—*Continued*

(Numbers in thousands, not seasonally adjusted)

Industry and year	January	February	March	April	May	June	July	August	September	October	November	December	Annual average
Transportation and Utilities													
2007	18.8	18.4	18.2	17.9	18.1	18.8	19.0	19.3	19.5	19.9	20.5	20.8	19.1
2008	18.6	18.1	18.0	17.8	18.0	18.4	18.5	18.5	18.5	18.7	19.2	19.4	18.5
2009	17.8	17.0	16.8	16.8	17.0	17.1	17.1	17.1	17.1	17.2	18.0	18.4	17.3
2010	16.5	16.2	16.0	16.1	16.4	16.9	17.0	16.9	16.9	17.2	17.3	17.9	16.8
2011	16.4	16.1	16.0	16.1	16.2	16.8	16.8	16.9	17.2	17.3	17.7	17.9	16.8
2012	16.6	16.4	16.1	16.0	16.4	16.9	16.7	16.8	17.1	17.4	17.7	18.1	16.9
2013	16.6	16.4	16.3	16.4	16.7	17.3	17.3	17.5	17.8	18.0	18.5	19.0	17.3
2014	17.2	17.0	16.9	16.9	17.3	17.9	17.8	17.9	18.2	18.4	18.9	19.4	17.8
2015	17.7	17.3	17.1	17.5	17.8	18.3	18.4	18.4	18.5	18.5	18.8	19.1	18.1
2016	17.8	17.6	17.5	17.8	18.2	18.8	18.7	18.8	19.1	18.9	19.2	19.8	18.5
2017	18.6	18.3	18.2	18.0	18.6	19.4	19.3	19.4	19.6	19.0	19.6	20.5	19.0
Information													
2007	11.2	11.4	11.4	11.4	11.3	11.3	11.3	11.2	11.0	11.1	11.1	11.1	11.2
2008	10.9	10.9	10.8	10.7	10.6	10.7	10.6	10.4	10.1	10.2	10.0	9.9	10.5
2009	9.4	9.2	9.0	9.1	9.2	9.1	9.0	8.9	8.8	8.8	8.8	8.7	9.0
2010	8.7	8.8	8.7	8.7	8.8	8.8	8.8	8.7	8.6	8.6	8.6	8.5	8.7
2011	8.4	8.3	8.3	8.3	8.3	8.3	8.3	8.3	8.1	8.1	8.1	8.1	8.2
2012	7.9	8.0	7.9	7.9	7.9	7.9	7.9	7.9	7.8	7.7	7.8	7.8	7.9
2013	7.8	7.7	7.7	7.7	7.7	7.7	7.7	7.7	7.5	7.5	7.5	7.5	7.6
2014	7.4	7.4	7.4	7.4	7.4	7.5	7.6	7.6	7.5	7.6	7.2	7.2	7.4
2015	7.3	7.3	7.5	7.6	7.7	7.9	7.9	7.8	7.6	7.7	7.8	7.7	7.7
2016	7.7	7.7	7.7	7.7	7.8	7.8	7.9	7.8	7.7	7.7	7.7	7.7	7.7
2017	7.6	7.5	7.5	7.3	7.4	7.4	7.4	7.3	7.2	7.3	7.2	7.1	7.4
Financial Activities													
2007	32.3	32.3	32.3	32.4	32.6	33.0	33.2	33.0	32.4	32.0	31.9	32.0	32.5
2008	31.6	31.7	31.7	31.9	32.2	32.5	32.7	32.6	31.7	31.5	31.4	31.2	31.9
2009	30.9	30.9	30.9	30.9	31.3	31.7	31.8	31.6	31.0	30.9	30.7	30.7	31.1
2010	30.2	30.3	30.4	30.5	30.6	31.0	31.1	31.1	30.7	30.5	30.3	30.4	30.6
2011	30.0	30.1	30.2	30.0	30.3	30.7	31.0	31.0	30.4	30.4	30.2	30.4	30.4
2012	29.9	29.8	29.8	29.9	30.2	30.6	30.9	30.8	30.2	30.0	29.8	29.9	30.2
2013	29.8	29.7	29.9	30.0	30.4	30.8	31.2	31.1	30.6	30.4	30.4	30.4	30.4
2014	29.9	29.8	29.9	30.0	30.4	30.8	31.0	31.2	30.5	30.4	30.3	30.4	30.4
2015	30.1	30.0	30.0	30.2	30.6	31.0	31.3	31.4	30.8	30.7	30.6	30.8	30.6
2016	30.5	30.5	30.6	30.8	31.2	31.6	31.9	31.9	31.3	31.1	30.8	31.0	31.1
2017	30.8	30.7	30.9	30.9	31.2	31.9	32.2	32.2	31.7	31.4	31.1	31.3	31.4
Professional and Business Services													
2007	51.8	51.7	52.0	53.7	54.7	56.1	56.2	56.4	55.5	55.9	56.1	56.0	54.7
2008	55.0	55.3	55.8	57.1	57.9	58.9	58.9	59.0	58.0	58.1	57.3	56.9	57.4
2009	55.2	54.8	54.5	55.7	56.9	57.1	57.1	57.3	56.5	56.9	56.9	56.5	56.3
2010	55.1	54.8	55.1	56.5	57.2	57.6	58.3	58.3	57.7	57.8	57.9	57.3	57.0
2011	56.0	56.3	56.4	58.0	58.8	59.8	60.3	60.6	60.1	59.8	59.7	58.6	58.7
2012	57.3	57.2	57.3	58.9	59.6	60.9	60.7	61.0	60.6	60.7	60.3	59.8	59.5
2013	58.2	58.9	58.6	60.4	61.6	62.9	63.6	63.6	63.1	62.9	62.1	61.9	61.5
2014	59.9	60.7	61.1	62.4	64.2	65.3	65.5	65.5	64.9	64.8	64.1	63.5	63.5
2015	62.0	62.7	62.7	63.7	65.9	66.6	66.7	66.6	65.6	65.7	65.1	64.7	64.8
2016	63.3	63.4	63.2	65.3	66.3	67.5	67.9	67.7	66.9	66.8	66.1	66.0	65.9
2017	64.2	64.6	64.8	65.7	67.1	68.3	68.1	67.8	67.1	67.4	67.3	67.0	66.6
Education and Health Services													
2007	114.2	116.5	116.6	116.4	116.2	115.1	114.7	115.0	115.9	117.1	117.5	117.7	116.1
2008	115.3	117.4	117.7	117.7	117.8	116.6	116.5	116.2	117.4	119.1	119.3	119.1	117.5
2009	117.2	119.0	119.1	119.6	119.4	117.4	117.4	117.2	117.9	119.7	119.8	119.8	118.6
2010	117.5	119.3	119.3	119.8	119.6	117.5	117.2	117.0	119.3	120.3	120.3	120.2	118.9
2011	117.1	119.3	119.6	120.1	119.9	118.1	118.0	118.2	120.2	122.0	122.1	122.0	119.7
2012	119.5	121.6	121.6	121.9	122.2	119.9	119.6	119.0	121.5	123.1	122.9	122.7	121.3
2013	120.6	122.4	122.4	122.9	122.2	120.2	119.9	119.7	122.5	123.6	123.4	122.7	121.9
2014	121.6	122.3	122.5	122.9	121.9	120.6	119.9	119.9	122.4	123.4	123.5	122.8	122.0
2015	122.3	122.7	123.3	123.9	123.2	122.1	121.9	121.7	124.0	124.2	124.4	124.3	123.2
2016	124.3	125.0	125.7	125.5	124.9	123.1	123.3	123.0	125.7	126.7	127.0	126.9	125.1
2017	126.7	127.2	128.0	127.8	127.3	125.8	125.6	125.3	128.0	128.9	129.4	129.6	127.5

1. Employment by Industry: Maine, Selected Years, 2007–2017—*Continued*

(Numbers in thousands, not seasonally adjusted)

Industry and year	January	February	March	April	May	June	July	August	September	October	November	December	Annual average
Leisure and Hospitality													
2007	50.3	50.3	50.8	53.6	59.6	68.7	75.6	75.8	67.4	61.0	55.2	54.5	60.2
2008	49.8	49.8	50.3	54.3	61.0	69.0	76.8	76.0	67.5	60.8	53.7	53.1	60.2
2009	48.8	49.0	49.5	53.7	60.0	66.7	74.7	74.5	67.2	60.4	53.3	52.9	59.2
2010	48.9	49.0	49.5	53.8	60.0	67.4	75.6	75.5	67.7	61.1	54.3	53.4	59.7
2011	49.3	49.5	50.3	53.6	59.9	68.5	77.1	76.6	68.4	61.3	54.2	53.1	60.2
2012	49.6	50.0	51.3	55.5	62.3	72.2	77.8	77.9	69.8	62.6	55.1	54.6	61.6
2013	51.3	50.9	52.3	56.0	63.9	73.3	79.9	79.3	70.3	64.7	55.5	55.3	62.7
2014	51.7	51.7	52.7	56.2	64.3	73.0	80.6	80.1	70.4	64.3	56.0	56.6	63.1
2015	52.9	52.3	53.5	57.5	65.5	73.9	80.8	80.5	71.7	65.8	57.6	57.2	64.1
2016	53.9	54.2	55.0	59.1	66.1	75.8	83.2	82.7	72.8	67.6	60.1	59.2	65.8
2017	56.1	55.9	57.1	60.6	67.8	78.2	84.3	83.8	74.3	66.4	58.3	57.7	66.7
Other Services													
2007	19.4	19.3	19.4	19.7	20.0	20.2	20.0	20.5	20.1	19.8	19.7	19.7	19.9
2008	19.4	19.5	19.6	19.7	20.0	20.3	20.5	20.1	19.8	20.0	19.9	19.8	19.9
2009	19.4	19.4	19.2	19.5	19.8	20.0	20.3	20.3	19.8	19.8	19.7	19.7	19.7
2010	19.3	19.3	19.3	19.5	19.7	19.9	20.4	20.1	19.9	19.7	19.7	19.5	19.7
2011	19.3	19.3	19.4	19.7	20.1	20.3	20.6	20.4	20.0	20.0	19.8	19.8	19.9
2012	19.5	19.5	19.7	19.9	20.0	20.3	20.7	20.5	20.1	20.1	20.0	20.0	20.0
2013	20.0	20.0	20.2	20.5	20.9	21.2	21.4	21.2	20.8	20.7	20.6	20.6	20.7
2014	20.4	20.3	20.4	20.6	21.0	21.4	21.8	21.7	21.2	21.3	21.0	21.0	21.0
2015	20.7	20.5	20.7	21.1	21.4	21.9	22.2	22.0	21.4	21.5	21.4	21.6	21.4
2016	21.1	21.2	21.3	21.4	21.7	22.1	22.7	22.4	21.8	21.8	21.7	21.6	21.7
2017	21.4	21.1	21.2	21.5	21.7	22.3	22.6	22.3	21.7	21.6	21.4	21.5	21.7
Government													
2007	103.7	106.3	107.0	106.5	107.7	105.1	92.2	91.4	104.7	108.3	108.8	108.7	104.2
2008	103.9	106.5	107.4	107.7	107.9	105.2	92.1	92.3	104.4	108.2	108.8	108.5	104.4
2009	103.5	106.2	106.6	107.4	107.6	104.7	90.8	90.8	103.9	107.1	107.8	107.5	103.7
2010	103.7	106.3	107.8	107.6	110.1	104.7	91.9	90.9	103.0	106.9	107.4	107.2	104.0
2011	103.1	105.3	105.6	105.0	104.6	101.7	92.2	91.3	102.3	104.5	105.3	104.3	102.1
2012	101.0	103.8	104.2	103.8	104.9	101.0	91.9	92.0	101.6	104.5	104.4	104.3	101.5
2013	101.6	103.0	103.6	103.4	103.7	99.8	90.7	90.1	100.3	103.4	103.0	103.1	100.5
2014	99.5	101.4	102.3	102.2	102.2	100.8	90.4	90.0	100.5	103.1	103.3	103.4	99.9
2015	99.5	101.1	102.0	101.8	101.4	99.6	91.2	91.0	100.1	102.1	102.5	102.2	99.5
2016	98.6	101.2	102.1	102.2	102.0	100.6	91.6	91.7	101.0	102.8	103.8	102.6	100.0
2017	99.2	101.3	102.3	102.3	101.9	100.4	91.7	91.5	101.3	102.8	103.6	103.2	100.1

2. Average Weekly Hours by Selected Industry: Maine, 2013–2017

(Not seasonally adjusted)

Industry and year	January	February	March	April	May	June	July	August	September	October	November	December	Annual average
Total Private													
2013	33.5	33.7	33.9	33.9	34.1	34.0	34.2	34.6	34.2	34.0	33.8	34.4	34.0
2014	33.6	33.8	33.7	33.8	33.9	33.9	34.3	34.3	34.2	34.1	34.1	33.9	34.0
2015	33.9	34.0	34.1	33.9	34.3	34.3	34.6	34.7	34.5	34.3	34.3	34.1	34.3
2016	33.5	33.6	33.8	33.8	34.0	33.9	34.1	34.2	34.0	34.3	34.0	33.7	33.9
2017	33.6	33.0	33.6	34.0	34.0	34.1	34.5	34.5	34.3	34.2	34.1	33.9	34.0
Goods Producing													
2013	39.5	39.6	39.8	39.7	40.1	40.1	40.0	40.6	40.1	40.5	39.6	40.7	40.0
2014	40.8	39.9	40.0	40.0	40.0	40.1	40.6	40.1	40.6	40.4	39.7	39.7	40.2
2015	40.2	39.7	40.1	40.2	41.4	41.5	41.8	41.8	40.9	41.8	41.2	41.4	41.0
2016	40.5	39.9	40.7	40.6	41.3	41.4	41.6	41.6	41.2	41.6	40.9	39.9	40.9
2017	40.5	38.7	40.0	40.6	40.9	41.3	41.2	41.6	41.4	41.2	40.7	40.3	40.7
Construction													
2013	38.1	37.8	38.4	38.4	39.4	39.0	39.0	40.3	39.0	39.4	38.7	38.4	38.9
2014	38.7	38.5	37.3	37.2	39.0	38.3	40.1	38.3	39.7	39.4	38.9	37.1	38.6
2015	37.3	37.2	37.1	38.5	40.7	41.0	41.6	40.7	39.5	40.9	40.4	40.1	39.7
2016	39.1	37.7	39.2	39.3	41.1	41.6	42.1	41.4	41.1	41.3	40.4	39.1	40.3
2017	39.6	36.7	37.9	39.4	40.2	40.8	40.3	41.6	41.6	40.8	40.4	39.4	40.0
Manufacturing													
2013	39.1	39.3	39.5	39.6	39.8	39.9	39.8	40.0	40.0	40.4	39.5	40.2	39.7
2014	40.2	39.0	39.7	40.1	39.8	40.0	39.6	40.0	39.9	39.8	38.9	39.7	39.7
2015	40.3	39.6	40.5	40.1	40.9	40.9	40.8	41.4	40.8	41.6	41.1	41.6	40.8
2016	40.5	40.3	40.9	40.8	41.1	40.9	41.2	41.5	41.1	41.6	40.7	40.0	40.9
2017	40.7	38.9	40.4	40.7	40.7	41.0	41.2	41.1	41.0	41.1	40.6	40.5	40.7
Trade, Transportation, and Utilities													
2013	31.5	32.5	32.5	32.7	32.7	33.1	33.7	34.2	33.4	33.1	32.3	33.9	33.0
2014	32.1	32.5	32.1	32.4	32.9	33.2	33.6	33.7	33.8	33.2	33.4	33.9	33.1
2015	33.1	33.8	33.4	33.1	33.7	33.4	34.3	34.2	34.8	33.7	33.5	34.1	33.8
2016	33.3	33.5	33.4	33.9	33.7	33.9	34.6	34.8	34.3	34.6	34.2	34.6	34.1
2017	33.6	32.9	33.8	33.9	34.4	34.5	35.1	34.9	34.3	34.0	34.1	34.5	34.2
Professional and Business Services													
2013	32.8	33.3	33.5	33.6	34.1	34.0	33.5	33.6	33.9	33.5	33.5	34.3	33.7
2014	32.4	33.9	33.2	33.4	33.6	33.8	33.3	33.4	33.2	33.3	33.8	33.6	33.4
2015	33.7	34.1	34.6	33.9	34.1	34.4	34.3	34.8	34.3	34.7	35.1	34.4	34.4
2016	33.2	33.6	33.9	34.4	35.0	34.3	34.2	33.7	33.5	34.8	34.2	33.9	34.1
2017	35.1	34.0	34.5	35.2	34.7	34.7	35.4	34.8	35.1	35.3	34.2	34.5	34.8
Education and Health Services													
2013	34.3	34.0	34.2	34.3	34.2	34.0	34.3	34.4	34.4	33.9	34.3	33.9	34.2
2014	34.3	33.5	33.6	33.7	33.8	33.9	34.2	34.0	34.0	33.9	34.0	33.8	33.9
2015	34.4	34.3	34.1	34.1	34.1	34.0	34.0	33.7	33.9	33.5	33.7	33.4	33.9
2016	33.1	33.3	33.1	33.0	33.0	33.1	33.1	33.5	33.6	33.3	33.3	33.1	33.2
2017	32.8	32.0	32.3	32.4	32.5	32.4	32.6	32.5	32.7	32.4	32.6	32.4	32.5
Leisure and Hospitality													
2013	25.0	25.0	25.7	25.6	25.6	25.5	27.6	28.4	26.0	26.2	25.2	24.1	26.0
2014	23.9	24.8	25.1	25.3	25.4	25.4	27.7	28.0	26.2	27.0	25.4	24.7	25.9
2015	24.5	24.3	25.1	25.2	25.6	26.2	27.3	27.9	26.4	25.8	25.3	24.4	25.8
2016	24.3	25.0	24.9	24.7	25.1	25.5	27.0	27.4	26.0	26.0	24.9	23.3	25.5
2017	24.0	23.5	25.0	25.6	25.6	26.5	27.6	28.1	26.7	26.5	25.8	24.7	26.0

3. Average Hourly Earnings by Selected Industry: Maine, 2013–2017

(Dollars, not seasonally adjusted)

Industry and year	January	February	March	April	May	June	July	August	September	October	November	December	Annual average
Total Private													
2013	21.37	21.40	21.22	21.26	20.97	20.87	20.68	20.59	20.98	20.85	21.10	20.92	21.01
2014	21.23	21.41	21.65	21.39	21.23	21.07	20.90	20.85	21.41	21.35	21.74	21.75	21.33
2015	21.93	22.00	22.11	21.94	21.67	21.46	21.42	21.54	21.82	22.01	22.20	22.24	21.85
2016	22.36	22.29	22.22	22.28	22.20	21.88	21.77	21.87	22.38	22.55	22.66	22.66	22.25
2017	23.05	23.43	23.44	23.24	23.28	22.79	22.74	22.84	23.32	23.39	23.56	23.66	23.22
Goods Producing													
2013	23.20	23.16	22.95	22.87	22.86	22.79	22.70	22.59	23.07	22.91	23.44	23.29	22.98
2014	23.43	23.58	23.37	23.23	23.40	23.26	22.81	23.13	23.23	23.26	23.63	23.63	23.33
2015	23.64	23.35	23.13	23.18	22.89	22.80	22.93	23.37	22.85	23.22	23.26	23.68	23.19
2016	23.38	23.43	23.65	23.62	23.79	23.44	23.40	23.25	23.51	23.81	24.11	24.01	23.62
2017	23.64	24.00	24.06	23.67	24.04	23.53	23.78	23.79	24.27	24.15	24.13	24.43	23.96
Construction													
2013	23.12	22.93	22.72	22.64	22.47	22.23	21.04	21.61	21.98	21.98	21.91	22.31	22.28
2014	22.65	23.02	22.75	22.61	22.36	22.14	21.44	21.93	22.03	22.43	22.46	23.16	22.38
2015	23.30	23.27	22.67	22.81	22.44	21.98	22.24	22.71	22.31	22.44	22.74	23.07	22.63
2016	23.27	23.98	23.31	23.31	23.11	23.30	23.19	22.87	23.49	23.90	23.55	23.98	23.43
2017	24.01	24.24	24.55	24.16	23.82	23.54	23.64	23.58	23.97	23.68	23.92	24.47	23.94
Manufacturing													
2012	24.15	24.27	23.97	23.73	23.81	23.87	23.91	23.85	24.31	24.09	24.92	24.39	24.11
2013	24.47	24.53	24.36	24.11	24.32	24.16	23.93	24.17	24.32	24.16	24.75	24.31	24.30
2014	24.29	23.86	23.79	23.70	23.41	23.57	23.71	24.16	23.52	24.00	23.71	24.21	23.83
2015	23.69	23.46	23.96	23.80	24.17	23.71	23.74	23.68	23.78	24.02	24.80	24.30	23.93
2016	23.69	24.17	23.96	23.73	24.51	23.92	24.25	24.21	24.76	24.76	24.57	24.73	24.28
Trade, Transportation, and Utilities													
2013	19.02	18.78	18.64	18.80	18.70	18.60	18.43	18.53	18.94	18.69	18.88	18.47	18.70
2014	18.95	19.20	19.51	19.53	19.10	19.11	19.17	18.81	19.42	19.08	19.34	19.29	19.21
2015	19.88	19.83	19.91	19.97	20.09	20.00	20.10	20.03	20.26	20.28	20.45	20.22	20.09
2016	20.87	20.59	20.49	20.38	20.29	19.98	19.86	19.84	20.13	20.08	20.12	20.02	20.21
2017	20.68	21.04	21.08	20.53	20.90	20.42	20.11	20.25	20.40	20.23	20.25	20.31	20.51
Professional and Business Services													
2013	23.10	23.14	23.10	23.31	22.60	22.96	22.80	22.55	22.72	22.61	22.87	22.51	22.85
2014	23.60	23.83	24.27	23.80	23.41	23.40	23.66	23.53	24.15	23.99	24.15	24.26	23.84
2015	24.47	24.31	24.51	24.21	23.73	23.95	24.26	24.19	24.50	24.11	24.47	24.31	24.25
2016	24.73	24.89	24.49	24.66	24.40	24.07	24.60	24.74	25.19	25.18	25.06	25.15	24.76
2017	25.72	26.34	26.61	26.11	25.71	25.75	26.06	25.85	26.26	26.09	26.48	26.84	26.15
Education and Health Services													
2013	22.08	22.16	21.96	21.97	21.63	21.75	21.90	21.83	21.38	21.23	20.88	20.88	21.64
2014	21.32	21.43	21.90	21.28	21.34	21.22	21.55	21.43	21.86	22.12	22.23	22.36	21.67
2015	22.15	22.51	23.04	22.50	22.14	21.88	21.86	22.21	22.66	23.18	23.20	23.24	22.55
2016	22.83	22.72	22.82	23.03	23.10	23.07	23.09	23.18	23.51	23.73	23.72	23.89	23.23
2017	24.49	24.82	24.89	25.16	25.20	24.83	25.18	25.37	25.58	25.77	25.86	25.94	25.26
Leisure and Hospitality													
2013	12.94	13.15	12.98	13.12	13.15	12.73	12.73	12.88	13.26	13.43	13.36	13.40	13.07
2014	13.34	13.35	13.30	13.22	13.22	13.07	13.00	13.34	13.50	13.33	13.64	13.82	13.33
2015	13.41	13.60	13.51	13.76	13.57	13.48	13.37	13.54	13.86	14.18	14.25	14.62	13.74
2016	14.36	14.15	14.12	14.36	14.26	14.05	14.03	14.27	14.72	15.06	14.85	15.22	14.43
2017	15.15	15.40	15.35	15.42	15.39	15.09	14.90	15.20	15.54	15.82	15.76	15.86	15.38

4. Average Weekly Earnings by Selected Industry: Maine, 2013–2017

(Dollars, not seasonally adjusted)

Industry and year	January	February	March	April	May	June	July	August	September	October	November	December	Annual average
Total Private													
2013	715.90	721.18	719.36	720.71	715.08	709.58	707.26	712.41	717.52	708.90	713.18	719.65	714.34
2014	713.33	723.66	729.61	722.98	719.70	714.27	716.87	715.16	732.22	728.04	741.33	737.33	725.22
2015	743.43	748.00	753.95	743.77	743.28	736.08	741.13	747.44	752.79	754.94	761.46	758.38	749.46
2016	749.06	748.94	751.04	753.06	754.80	741.73	742.36	747.95	760.92	773.47	770.44	763.64	754.28
2017	774.48	773.19	787.58	790.16	791.52	777.14	784.53	787.98	799.88	799.94	803.40	802.07	789.48
Goods Producing													
2013	916.40	917.14	913.41	907.94	916.69	913.88	908.00	917.15	925.11	927.86	928.22	947.90	919.20
2014	955.94	940.84	934.80	929.20	936.00	932.73	926.09	927.51	943.14	939.70	938.11	938.11	937.87
2015	950.33	927.00	927.51	931.84	947.65	946.20	958.47	976.87	934.57	970.60	958.31	980.35	950.79
2016	946.89	934.86	962.56	958.97	982.53	970.42	973.44	967.20	968.61	990.50	986.10	958.00	966.06
2017	957.42	928.80	962.40	961.00	983.24	971.79	979.74	989.66	1,004.78	994.98	982.09	984.53	975.17
Construction													
2013	880.87	866.75	872.45	869.38	885.32	866.97	855.66	870.88	857.22	866.01	847.92	856.70	866.69
2014	876.56	886.27	848.58	841.09	872.04	847.96	859.74	839.92	874.59	883.74	873.69	859.24	863.87
2015	869.09	865.64	841.06	878.19	913.31	901.18	925.18	924.30	881.25	917.80	918.70	925.11	898.41
2016	909.86	904.05	913.75	916.08	949.82	969.28	976.30	946.82	965.44	987.07	951.42	937.62	944.23
2017	950.80	889.61	930.45	951.90	957.56	960.43	952.69	980.93	997.15	966.14	966.37	964.12	957.60
Manufacturing													
2013	944.27	953.81	946.82	939.71	947.64	952.41	951.62	954.00	972.40	973.24	984.34	980.48	957.17
2014	983.69	956.67	967.09	966.81	967.94	966.40	947.63	966.80	970.37	961.57	962.78	965.11	964.71
2015	978.89	944.86	963.50	950.37	957.47	964.01	967.37	1,000.22	959.62	998.40	974.48	1,007.14	972.26
2016	959.45	945.44	979.96	971.04	993.39	969.74	978.09	982.72	977.36	999.23	1,009.36	972.00	978.74
2017	964.18	940.21	967.98	965.81	997.56	980.72	999.10	995.03	1,015.16	1,017.64	997.54	1,001.57	988.20
Trade, Transportation, and Utilities													
2013	599.13	610.35	605.80	614.76	611.49	615.66	621.09	633.73	632.60	618.64	609.82	626.13	617.10
2014	608.30	624.00	626.27	632.77	628.39	634.45	644.11	633.90	656.40	633.46	645.96	653.93	635.85
2015	658.03	670.25	664.99	661.01	677.03	668.00	689.43	685.03	705.05	683.44	685.08	689.50	679.04
2016	694.97	689.77	684.37	690.88	683.77	677.32	687.16	690.43	690.46	694.77	688.10	692.69	689.16
2017	694.85	692.22	712.50	695.97	718.96	704.49	705.86	706.73	699.72	687.82	690.53	700.70	701.44
Professional and Business Services													
2013	757.68	770.56	773.85	783.22	770.66	780.64	763.80	757.68	770.21	757.44	766.15	772.09	770.05
2014	764.64	807.84	805.76	794.92	786.58	790.92	787.88	785.90	801.78	798.87	816.27	815.14	796.26
2015	824.64	828.97	848.05	820.72	809.19	823.88	832.12	841.81	840.35	836.62	858.90	836.26	834.20
2016	821.04	836.30	830.21	848.30	854.00	825.60	841.32	833.74	843.87	876.26	857.05	852.59	844.32
2017	902.77	895.56	918.05	919.07	892.14	893.53	922.52	899.58	921.73	920.98	905.62	925.98	910.02
Education and Health Services													
2013	757.34	753.44	751.03	753.57	739.75	739.50	751.17	750.95	735.47	719.70	716.18	707.83	740.09
2014	731.28	717.91	735.84	717.14	721.29	719.36	737.01	728.62	743.24	749.87	755.82	755.77	734.61
2015	761.96	772.09	785.66	767.25	754.97	743.92	743.24	748.48	768.17	776.53	781.84	776.22	764.45
2016	755.67	756.58	755.34	759.99	762.30	763.62	764.28	776.53	789.94	790.21	789.88	790.76	771.24
2017	803.27	794.24	803.95	815.18	819.00	804.49	820.87	824.53	836.47	834.95	843.04	840.46	820.95
Leisure and Hospitality													
2013	323.50	328.75	333.59	335.87	336.64	324.62	351.35	365.79	344.76	351.87	336.67	322.94	339.82
2014	318.83	331.08	333.83	334.47	335.79	331.98	360.10	373.52	353.70	359.91	346.46	341.35	345.25
2015	328.55	330.48	339.10	346.75	347.39	353.18	365.00	377.77	365.90	365.84	360.53	356.73	354.49
2016	348.95	353.75	351.59	354.69	357.93	358.28	378.81	391.00	382.72	391.56	369.77	354.63	367.97
2017	363.60	361.90	383.75	394.75	393.98	399.89	411.24	427.12	414.92	419.23	406.61	391.74	399.88

MARYLAND
At a Glance

Population:
  2010 census: 5,773,552
  2017 estimate: 6,052,177

Percent change in population:
  2010–2017: 4.8%

Percent change in total nonfarm employment:
  2007–2017: 4.2%

Industry with the largest growth in employment, 2007–2017 (thousands):
  Education and health services, 87.5

Industry with the largest decline or smallest growth in employment, 2007–2017 (thousands):
  Manufacturing, -27.2

Civilian labor force:
  2010: 3,073,826
  2017: 3,219,455

Unemployment rate and rank among states (highest to lowest):
  2010: 7.7%, 38th
  2017: 4.1%, 29th

Over-the-year change in unemployment rates:
  2015–2016: -0.7%
  2016–2017: -0.3%

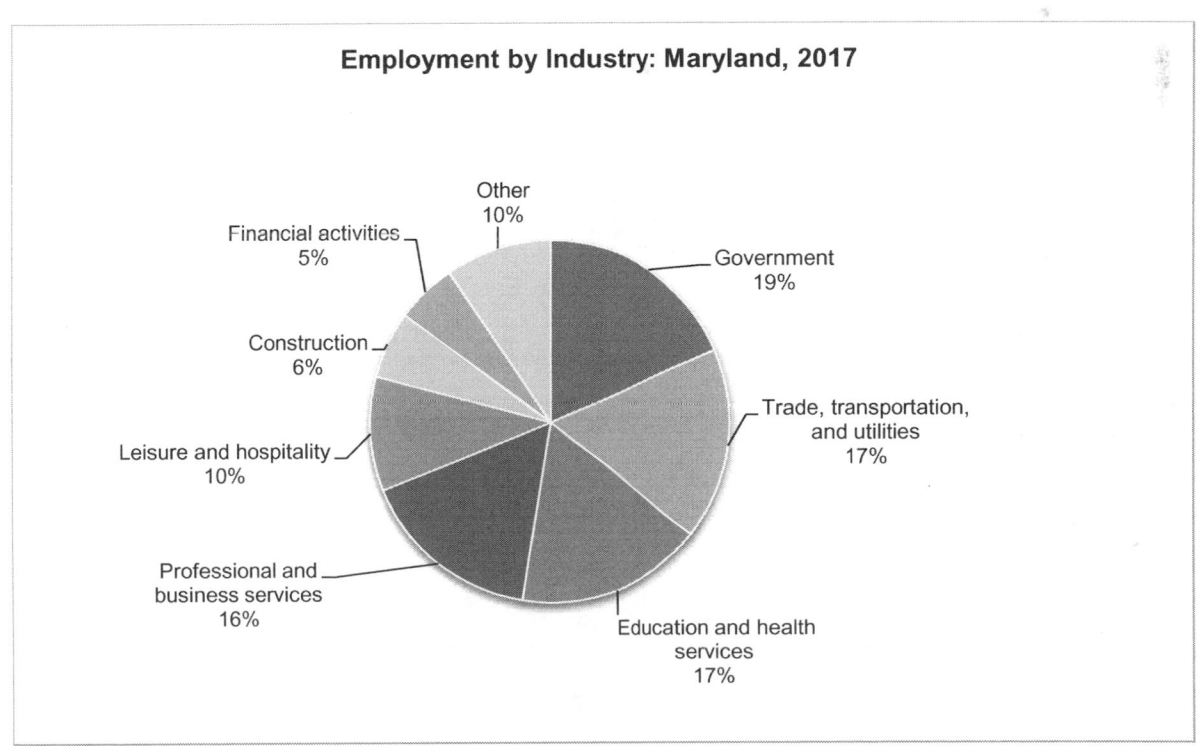

Employment by Industry: Maryland, 2017

- Other 10%
- Financial activities 5%
- Construction 6%
- Leisure and hospitality 10%
- Professional and business services 16%
- Government 19%
- Trade, transportation, and utilities 17%
- Education and health services 17%

1. Employment by Industry: Maryland, Selected Years, 2007–2017

(Numbers in thousands, not seasonally adjusted)

Industry and year	January	February	March	April	May	June	July	August	September	October	November	December	Annual average
Total Nonfarm													
2007	2,551.9	2,556.0	2,590.5	2,603.5	2,626.3	2,636.3	2,620.9	2,619.7	2,621.9	2,624.7	2,633.9	2,641.7	2,610.6
2008	2,561.7	2,573.4	2,593.3	2,613.7	2,628.3	2,628.2	2,613.0	2,608.1	2,604.2	2,605.6	2,599.7	2,595.3	2,602.0
2009	2,502.0	2,503.0	2,517.0	2,533.0	2,548.2	2,553.5	2,526.5	2,520.7	2,520.1	2,529.0	2,530.4	2,529.5	2,526.1
2010	2,450.6	2,429.0	2,487.0	2,524.3	2,548.2	2,555.4	2,535.9	2,531.9	2,535.2	2,549.0	2,552.6	2,557.3	2,521.4
2011	2,477.8	2,494.8	2,522.8	2,547.4	2,561.4	2,568.5	2,560.5	2,549.9	2,559.9	2,571.2	2,575.4	2,580.8	2,547.5
2012	2,510.3	2,526.9	2,556.0	2,571.1	2,590.0	2,601.0	2,582.3	2,581.9	2,593.1	2,601.9	2,608.1	2,613.9	2,578.0
2013	2,539.2	2,555.7	2,578.7	2,598.4	2,619.3	2,630.3	2,610.4	2,608.7	2,613.6	2,618.0	2,632.2	2,627.2	2,602.6
2014	2,549.5	2,561.2	2,584.5	2,615.3	2,642.6	2,654.1	2,628.2	2,635.7	2,642.3	2,654.1	2,664.3	2,665.6	2,624.8
2015	2,582.9	2,600.2	2,617.6	2,654.8	2,684.2	2,693.8	2,675.8	2,673.8	2,678.3	2,698.3	2,706.1	2,709.1	2,664.6
2016	2,624.3	2,635.8	2,661.4	2,695.5	2,708.7	2,715.1	2,702.5	2,703.7	2,714.7	2,722.4	2,737.7	2,739.3	2,696.8
2017	2,659.8	2,679.1	2,696.2	2,719.0	2,741.4	2,753.6	2,733.3	2,730.8	2,733.0	2,736.9	2,744.6	2,726.1	2,721.2
Total Private													
2007	2,084.5	2,076.2	2,104.5	2,117.6	2,138.6	2,164.6	2,160.6	2,159.0	2,144.5	2,134.6	2,139.5	2,147.8	2,131.0
2008	2,085.4	2,082.3	2,098.1	2,117.8	2,133.0	2,147.5	2,141.9	2,136.8	2,117.6	2,107.0	2,097.7	2,093.8	2,113.2
2009	2,019.6	2,007.0	2,015.3	2,028.8	2,044.9	2,064.9	2,051.4	2,045.6	2,031.3	2,022.3	2,022.1	2,022.0	2,031.3
2010	1,962.1	1,928.8	1,977.7	2,014.3	2,030.9	2,054.3	2,051.7	2,049.1	2,038.1	2,039.9	2,039.1	2,046.2	2,019.4
2011	1,984.8	1,985.6	2,006.8	2,033.8	2,048.5	2,068.5	2,074.4	2,069.2	2,059.0	2,056.0	2,063.2	2,068.2	2,043.2
2012	2,018.3	2,017.2	2,040.8	2,057.1	2,077.5	2,104.9	2,103.9	2,104.3	2,093.2	2,089.0	2,094.2	2,100.7	2,075.1
2013	2,045.9	2,046.6	2,065.2	2,084.4	2,106.1	2,129.3	2,129.6	2,129.0	2,113.4	2,107.8	2,118.4	2,117.1	2,099.4
2014	2,059.1	2,054.5	2,074.7	2,104.9	2,133.4	2,153.9	2,153.3	2,156.3	2,139.8	2,142.7	2,149.7	2,154.5	2,123.1
2015	2,092.3	2,093.1	2,106.9	2,142.0	2,170.9	2,190.0	2,197.2	2,194.2	2,174.3	2,187.5	2,192.4	2,195.1	2,161.3
2016	2,132.2	2,129.9	2,149.3	2,182.9	2,197.4	2,216.5	2,226.0	2,223.8	2,210.8	2,211.0	2,223.1	2,224.5	2,194.0
2017	2,164.7	2,168.0	2,181.3	2,205.0	2,226.0	2,249.9	2,253.9	2,250.9	2,232.6	2,226.7	2,231.3	2,214.6	2,217.1
Goods Producing													
2007	317.9	313.8	319.9	322.6	325.5	330.0	330.2	330.3	327.6	325.0	322.7	320.6	323.8
2008	312.2	310.6	311.9	312.7	313.0	315.4	315.0	314.5	311.2	306.8	302.3	297.0	310.2
2009	283.7	279.4	278.2	277.5	277.7	279.7	279.1	276.9	274.1	271.6	269.2	267.1	276.2
2010	256.6	246.5	255.1	262.2	264.1	267.0	268.0	267.4	265.4	263.6	262.5	260.5	261.6
2011	253.3	252.3	254.7	259.5	261.0	264.2	265.6	264.8	262.0	261.2	260.2	259.7	259.9
2012	252.1	250.1	252.3	254.9	255.7	260.3	261.6	261.2	258.7	257.8	257.5	256.7	256.6
2013	249.5	248.5	250.4	254.8	256.8	259.7	260.6	261.2	259.2	257.4	258.1	254.7	255.9
2014	247.6	246.0	248.9	254.5	257.8	261.1	261.4	262.5	260.8	260.9	261.1	259.5	256.8
2015	250.6	250.4	251.9	257.6	260.8	264.8	267.2	268.5	267.1	268.8	268.4	268.1	262.0
2016	260.1	257.9	261.8	266.5	268.5	271.2	272.9	272.8	271.7	271.5	271.3	271.3	268.1
2017	262.8	264.0	265.0	268.3	270.0	274.1	274.4	274.7	272.6	272.4	271.9	268.5	269.9
Service-Providing													
2007	2,234.0	2,242.2	2,270.6	2,280.9	2,300.8	2,306.3	2,290.7	2,289.4	2,294.3	2,299.7	2,311.2	2,321.1	2,286.8
2008	2,249.5	2,262.8	2,281.4	2,301.0	2,315.3	2,312.8	2,298.0	2,293.6	2,293.0	2,298.8	2,297.4	2,298.3	2,291.8
2009	2,218.3	2,223.6	2,238.8	2,255.5	2,270.5	2,273.8	2,247.4	2,243.8	2,246.0	2,257.4	2,261.2	2,262.4	2,249.9
2010	2,194.0	2,182.5	2,231.9	2,262.1	2,284.1	2,288.4	2,267.9	2,264.5	2,269.8	2,285.6	2,290.1	2,296.8	2,259.8
2011	2,224.5	2,242.5	2,268.1	2,287.9	2,300.4	2,304.3	2,294.9	2,285.1	2,297.9	2,310.0	2,315.2	2,321.1	2,287.7
2012	2,258.2	2,276.8	2,303.7	2,316.2	2,334.3	2,340.7	2,320.7	2,320.7	2,334.4	2,344.1	2,350.6	2,357.2	2,321.5
2013	2,289.7	2,307.2	2,328.3	2,343.6	2,362.5	2,370.6	2,349.8	2,347.5	2,354.4	2,360.6	2,374.1	2,372.5	2,346.7
2014	2,301.9	2,315.2	2,335.6	2,360.8	2,384.8	2,393.0	2,366.8	2,373.2	2,381.5	2,393.2	2,403.2	2,406.1	2,367.9
2015	2,332.3	2,349.8	2,365.7	2,397.2	2,423.4	2,429.0	2,408.6	2,405.3	2,411.2	2,429.5	2,437.7	2,441.0	2,402.6
2016	2,364.2	2,377.9	2,399.6	2,429.0	2,440.2	2,443.9	2,429.6	2,430.9	2,443.0	2,450.9	2,466.4	2,468.0	2,428.6
2017	2,397.0	2,415.1	2,431.2	2,450.7	2,471.4	2,479.5	2,458.9	2,456.1	2,460.4	2,464.5	2,472.7	2,457.6	2,451.3
Mining and Logging													
2007	1.5	1.5	1.5	1.5	1.5	1.5	1.5	1.5	1.5	1.5	1.5	1.5	1.5
2008	1.5	1.4	1.5	1.5	1.5	1.5	1.5	1.5	1.5	1.5	1.5	1.4	1.5
2009	1.4	1.4	1.4	1.4	1.4	1.4	1.4	1.4	1.4	1.4	1.3	1.3	1.4
2010	1.3	1.2	1.3	1.4	1.4	1.4	1.4	1.4	1.4	1.4	1.4	1.4	1.4
2011	1.3	1.3	1.4	1.4	1.4	1.4	1.5	1.5	1.5	1.5	1.5	1.5	1.4
2012	1.4	1.4	1.4	1.5	1.5	1.5	1.5	1.5	1.5	1.5	1.5	1.5	1.5
2013	1.3	1.3	1.4	1.4	1.4	1.4	1.4	1.5	1.5	1.4	1.4	1.4	1.4
2014	1.5	1.5	1.6	1.7	1.7	1.7	1.7	1.7	1.7	1.7	1.7	1.6	1.7
2015	1.5	1.6	1.6	1.6	1.6	1.6	1.7	1.7	1.7	1.5	1.5	1.5	1.6
2016	1.4	1.4	1.4	1.5	1.5	1.5	1.4	1.4	1.4	1.4	1.4	1.4	1.4
2017	1.3	1.3	1.3	1.3	1.3	1.3	1.3	1.3	1.3	1.3	1.3	1.2	1.3

1. Employment by Industry: Maryland, Selected Years, 2007–2017—*Continued*

(Numbers in thousands, not seasonally adjusted)

Industry and year	January	February	March	April	May	June	July	August	September	October	November	December	Annual average
Construction													
2007	182.4	178.7	184.5	187.4	190.0	193.7	194.1	194.4	192.5	190.0	187.9	185.5	188.4
2008	178.9	177.5	179.2	180.6	180.9	182.8	182.7	182.2	180.1	177.0	173.1	168.6	178.6
2009	157.4	154.9	154.4	154.7	155.1	156.8	156.9	155.2	152.8	150.5	148.3	146.1	153.6
2010	137.1	129.6	136.9	143.1	145.0	147.3	148.5	148.7	147.6	146.4	146.1	144.1	143.4
2011	136.6	136.0	138.1	142.4	143.9	146.6	148.1	147.6	146.0	145.6	145.1	144.3	143.4
2012	138.0	137.2	139.2	141.5	142.3	145.8	147.1	147.4	146.9	146.7	146.1	145.1	143.6
2013	139.4	138.6	140.5	144.8	146.7	149.1	150.2	150.8	149.9	148.6	149.0	146.0	146.1
2014	141.0	139.5	142.3	147.5	150.5	153.1	153.7	154.7	153.6	153.3	152.9	151.7	149.5
2015	144.1	143.8	145.4	150.9	153.8	156.5	158.3	159.6	158.9	160.8	160.2	159.5	154.3
2016	153.8	152.0	155.7	159.7	161.1	163.4	165.1	165.0	164.3	164.2	163.5	163.2	160.9
2017	156.3	157.2	157.7	160.5	162.0	165.3	165.9	166.1	164.6	164.8	162.4	159.6	161.9
Manufacturing													
2007	134.0	133.6	133.9	133.7	134.0	134.8	134.6	134.4	133.6	133.5	133.3	133.6	133.9
2008	131.8	131.7	131.2	130.6	130.6	131.1	130.8	130.8	129.6	128.3	127.7	127.0	130.1
2009	124.9	123.1	122.4	121.4	121.2	121.5	120.8	120.3	119.9	119.7	119.6	119.7	121.2
2010	118.2	115.7	116.9	117.7	117.7	118.3	118.1	117.3	116.4	115.6	115.0	115.0	116.8
2011	115.4	115.0	115.2	115.7	115.7	116.2	116.0	115.7	114.5	114.1	113.6	113.9	115.1
2012	112.7	111.5	111.7	111.9	111.9	113.0	113.0	112.3	110.3	109.6	109.9	110.1	111.5
2013	108.8	108.6	108.5	108.6	108.7	109.2	109.0	108.9	107.8	107.4	107.7	107.3	108.4
2014	105.1	105.0	105.0	105.3	105.6	106.3	106.0	106.1	105.5	105.9	106.5	106.2	105.7
2015	105.0	105.0	104.9	105.1	105.4	106.7	107.2	107.2	106.5	106.5	106.7	107.1	106.1
2016	104.9	104.5	104.7	105.3	105.9	106.3	106.4	106.4	106.0	105.9	106.4	106.7	105.8
2017	105.2	105.5	106.0	106.5	106.7	107.5	107.2	107.3	106.7	106.3	108.2	107.7	106.7
Trade, Transportation, and Utilities													
2007	474.8	467.3	471.8	470.2	475.4	479.0	476.2	474.4	473.1	474.6	484.5	493.2	476.2
2008	469.3	462.5	464.2	463.0	465.4	468.6	465.0	464.3	461.5	461.2	465.4	470.0	465.0
2009	445.5	437.6	436.6	436.1	438.9	441.8	436.5	436.4	436.6	436.8	445.6	449.9	439.9
2010	429.5	418.8	427.8	434.4	437.9	441.5	438.8	439.1	437.2	442.5	450.7	457.5	438.0
2011	436.8	432.1	434.9	439.3	442.2	444.9	443.5	444.5	443.8	447.0	456.8	464.0	444.2
2012	444.2	439.5	444.1	445.4	448.9	451.5	448.3	448.4	449.2	451.4	462.6	468.8	450.2
2013	446.4	440.9	443.2	444.8	449.1	452.3	451.0	451.5	450.2	452.9	464.3	471.1	451.5
2014	449.4	442.4	445.6	449.3	453.0	457.1	455.5	456.6	454.7	458.7	470.1	478.3	455.9
2015	454.9	449.2	450.9	456.5	461.3	465.9	464.3	463.8	462.8	468.7	478.3	484.9	463.5
2016	461.4	456.7	459.3	462.2	465.3	467.2	465.9	467.2	466.3	469.8	481.2	486.2	467.4
2017	464.2	457.1	458.0	461.5	464.9	468.5	466.7	466.7	465.5	467.2	477.7	480.9	466.6
Wholesale Trade													
2007	94.0	94.3	94.7	95.1	95.4	95.7	95.3	95.2	94.9	94.3	94.3	94.7	94.8
2008	93.1	93.1	93.9	93.8	94.0	94.4	93.6	93.4	92.8	92.2	91.4	90.9	93.1
2009	89.2	88.7	88.2	88.2	88.0	87.9	87.2	87.2	86.7	86.3	86.0	85.8	87.5
2010	84.2	83.7	84.6	85.5	86.1	86.3	86.0	86.0	85.1	85.8	85.8	86.0	85.4
2011	84.8	84.8	85.3	85.8	86.4	86.5	86.7	86.6	86.2	86.1	85.9	86.0	85.9
2012	84.7	85.0	85.8	86.1	86.8	87.2	86.8	86.8	86.3	86.3	86.2	86.3	86.2
2013	85.0	85.0	85.3	85.6	85.8	86.1	85.7	85.6	85.1	85.0	85.1	85.2	85.4
2014	83.9	83.8	83.8	84.3	84.9	85.1	85.1	85.1	84.5	84.6	84.7	85.4	84.6
2015	84.1	84.2	84.4	85.3	85.8	86.3	86.6	86.2	85.9	86.3	86.2	86.2	85.6
2016	85.2	85.1	85.2	85.9	86.2	86.4	86.4	86.5	86.0	86.2	86.1	86.1	85.9
2017	85.3	85.1	85.5	85.6	86.0	86.8	86.7	86.7	86.2	85.6	86.0	85.8	85.9
Retail Trade													
2007	300.2	292.5	295.9	295.2	299.1	301.5	301.0	299.7	297.5	299.6	309.4	315.3	300.6
2008	297.6	290.7	292.1	291.3	292.9	294.9	293.5	292.8	289.7	289.9	294.1	297.2	293.1
2009	279.4	273.0	272.7	272.7	275.4	277.7	275.5	275.5	274.1	275.2	283.1	286.7	276.8
2010	271.7	262.7	269.3	272.7	275.7	278.4	278.0	278.4	275.6	279.6	287.2	291.8	276.8
2011	276.4	272.2	274.1	276.8	278.5	280.8	280.1	281.1	279.2	282.5	291.2	296.5	280.8
2012	281.5	276.8	280.1	280.5	282.8	284.6	283.5	283.5	282.7	285.1	295.0	298.4	284.5
2013	281.9	277.7	279.2	280.6	283.5	285.9	286.6	287.1	284.2	286.8	296.2	300.1	285.8
2014	284.6	279.4	281.5	283.9	286.0	289.4	289.9	290.4	287.0	290.3	298.5	303.1	288.7
2015	286.6	282.0	283.4	286.8	290.0	293.3	292.1	291.9	288.9	292.8	300.4	303.6	291.0
2016	288.7	284.4	286.9	288.0	290.4	291.9	291.9	292.5	289.3	292.2	300.0	302.8	291.6
2017	288.2	282.8	283.4	285.6	287.6	289.9	289.3	289.7	286.5	288.1	296.0	296.5	288.6

1. Employment by Industry: Maryland, Selected Years, 2007–2017—*Continued*

(Numbers in thousands, not seasonally adjusted)

Industry and year	January	February	March	April	May	June	July	August	September	October	November	December	Annual average
Transportation and Utilities													
2007	80.6	80.5	81.2	79.9	80.9	81.8	79.9	79.5	80.7	80.7	80.8	83.2	80.8
2008	78.6	78.7	78.2	77.9	78.5	79.3	77.9	78.1	79.0	79.1	79.9	81.9	78.9
2009	76.9	75.9	75.7	75.2	75.5	76.2	73.8	73.7	75.8	75.3	76.5	77.4	75.7
2010	73.6	72.4	73.9	76.2	76.1	76.8	74.8	74.7	76.5	77.1	77.7	79.7	75.8
2011	75.6	75.1	75.5	76.7	77.3	77.6	76.7	76.8	78.4	78.4	79.7	81.5	77.4
2012	78.0	77.7	78.2	78.8	79.3	79.7	78.0	78.1	80.2	80.0	81.4	84.1	79.5
2013	79.5	78.2	78.7	78.6	79.8	80.3	78.7	78.8	80.9	81.1	83.0	85.8	80.3
2014	80.9	79.2	80.3	81.1	82.1	82.6	80.5	81.1	83.2	83.8	86.9	89.8	82.6
2015	84.2	83.0	83.1	84.4	85.5	86.3	85.6	85.7	88.0	89.6	91.7	95.1	86.9
2016	87.5	87.2	87.2	88.3	88.7	88.9	87.6	88.2	91.0	91.4	95.1	97.3	89.9
2017	90.7	89.2	89.1	90.3	91.3	91.8	90.7	90.3	92.8	93.5	95.7	98.6	92.0
Information													
2007	49.3	49.7	50.5	50.5	51.0	51.8	51.4	52.1	51.5	50.0	50.8	51.4	50.8
2008	50.0	50.3	50.6	50.6	50.7	50.1	49.8	49.5	49.3	48.1	49.0	48.8	49.7
2009	46.4	46.6	47.5	46.3	46.0	46.7	45.4	45.7	44.6	43.7	44.0	44.0	45.6
2010	43.2	43.6	45.0	44.8	44.7	45.5	44.1	43.1	43.9	43.4	42.3	44.2	44.0
2011	41.3	41.9	42.1	41.4	41.2	41.1	41.2	38.1	40.2	40.2	40.9	40.7	40.9
2012	39.8	39.9	39.9	38.8	39.1	40.5	40.4	40.5	40.0	39.5	39.8	40.7	39.9
2013	39.7	39.8	40.0	39.5	39.6	39.7	39.8	39.8	39.2	39.2	39.8	39.6	39.6
2014	40.2	38.8	38.8	38.6	39.6	38.7	38.9	39.9	38.3	39.3	38.9	38.9	39.1
2015	38.8	38.3	38.4	39.0	39.2	38.3	38.8	38.4	37.8	38.9	38.7	38.5	38.6
2016	37.6	37.9	37.7	38.9	36.0	39.0	38.9	38.3	38.1	37.8	38.0	38.5	38.1
2017	37.5	38.2	37.9	37.6	37.5	37.9	37.5	37.3	37.1	36.4	36.5	36.5	37.3
Financial Activities													
2007	157.1	157.2	157.4	157.0	157.6	158.6	158.5	157.9	156.4	155.5	155.0	155.5	157.0
2008	152.6	153.0	153.2	152.9	153.0	153.6	153.1	152.7	150.9	150.6	149.5	149.9	152.1
2009	146.7	146.1	145.5	145.9	146.1	146.9	146.3	145.8	144.7	144.5	144.3	144.6	145.6
2010	141.9	141.3	142.1	142.4	142.9	144.5	144.6	144.4	143.5	143.9	144.1	145.2	143.4
2011	142.3	142.6	143.0	143.3	143.3	144.1	144.2	143.5	142.6	142.7	142.3	142.7	143.1
2012	141.7	141.7	141.8	141.6	142.4	143.7	144.3	144.3	143.7	143.8	144.2	144.7	143.2
2013	143.5	143.5	143.9	144.4	145.0	146.4	147.0	146.5	145.6	145.2	145.3	145.5	145.2
2014	143.4	143.3	143.1	143.8	144.5	145.7	146.1	146.1	144.9	145.4	145.5	146.0	144.8
2015	144.4	144.7	144.8	145.4	145.7	147.0	147.0	146.6	144.6	144.9	144.6	144.5	145.4
2016	142.3	142.3	141.9	143.1	143.6	144.6	145.6	145.7	145.0	145.1	144.8	145.5	144.1
2017	143.9	144.4	144.6	144.9	145.5	147.3	148.8	148.7	147.2	146.3	146.3	145.8	146.1
Professional and Business Services													
2007	385.7	387.1	392.8	397.1	398.5	402.2	401.5	403.1	401.1	400.9	400.8	401.4	397.7
2008	390.6	391.4	394.6	400.7	401.0	402.5	402.8	403.4	400.1	398.4	395.4	392.8	397.8
2009	380.4	378.3	380.5	384.7	384.6	388.4	386.4	387.0	383.5	384.5	383.2	382.4	383.7
2010	372.5	369.3	378.5	386.9	387.5	393.1	393.0	393.5	391.5	395.4	393.0	394.3	387.4
2011	384.3	385.3	389.9	396.8	397.1	402.5	405.8	406.7	405.4	405.8	406.8	406.5	399.4
2012	396.7	397.4	403.4	406.5	409.3	413.9	414.4	417.5	415.9	416.1	417.3	415.7	410.3
2013	406.7	409.2	414.3	415.3	416.8	421.0	420.9	423.8	421.4	420.3	422.0	419.2	417.6
2014	409.3	411.6	415.5	422.5	426.0	428.9	429.6	430.7	427.4	429.1	429.1	427.7	424.0
2015	415.8	417.4	420.6	429.4	432.5	435.2	438.9	440.0	434.2	440.1	439.9	437.1	431.8
2016	426.9	427.3	430.9	440.2	440.6	444.3	447.1	449.1	444.9	445.1	445.6	442.6	440.4
2017	433.7	433.8	437.2	442.9	445.5	450.3	449.0	450.8	447.4	447.1	446.7	439.2	443.6
Education and Health Services													
2007	367.4	370.8	373.9	373.6	374.2	373.7	371.4	370.3	374.5	377.5	379.2	380.4	373.9
2008	376.6	380.0	382.2	383.8	384.2	382.8	381.9	381.0	385.9	390.4	391.7	393.2	384.5
2009	389.1	392.4	394.1	395.8	395.7	394.8	391.8	390.3	394.2	398.3	399.8	400.7	394.8
2010	396.7	393.1	400.6	402.8	402.6	400.4	399.8	397.9	402.0	405.6	407.2	407.4	401.3
2011	402.8	407.0	408.7	409.5	409.1	405.9	406.6	405.4	409.7	413.5	414.9	414.8	409.0
2012	412.2	416.2	418.2	418.9	418.8	417.4	417.1	415.4	419.5	423.2	423.4	425.3	418.8
2013	419.2	423.3	425.0	425.9	425.7	423.7	422.6	421.3	424.9	428.5	429.5	429.6	424.9
2014	422.9	425.8	428.5	429.3	430.0	429.1	428.0	427.9	431.7	434.4	436.5	437.5	430.1
2015	431.7	435.8	437.5	441.0	441.8	439.3	439.1	437.1	440.5	446.5	448.7	448.2	440.6
2016	441.6	444.5	446.7	449.8	449.4	444.8	449.0	445.7	450.5	455.6	457.3	457.6	449.4
2017	450.3	455.3	457.2	458.8	458.9	456.7	461.9	459.7	463.5	471.2	473.6	470.2	461.4

1. Employment by Industry: Maryland, Selected Years, 2007–2017—*Continued*

(Numbers in thousands, not seasonally adjusted)

Industry and year	January	February	March	April	May	June	July	August	September	October	November	December	Annual average
Leisure and Hospitality													
2007	216.7	214.7	221.4	229.5	238.6	249.9	252.0	252.5	242.5	233.5	228.7	227.3	233.9
2008	218.2	218.2	224.5	236.2	247.3	254.9	255.2	253.4	241.3	234.8	228.1	225.8	236.5
2009	213.3	212.5	218.1	227.4	240.1	249.5	249.6	248.1	238.7	228.3	221.4	218.6	230.5
2010	209.2	205.0	214.8	226.8	236.6	246.8	248.1	248.8	240.7	231.9	225.6	223.5	229.8
2011	211.8	212.1	220.4	229.9	240.5	250.6	252.7	252.2	242.7	233.5	229.2	227.6	233.6
2012	220.8	221.7	229.8	239.0	251.1	264.4	264.7	264.7	254.7	246.5	239.3	238.3	244.6
2013	232.2	232.6	239.3	248.9	261.9	274.5	275.4	273.4	261.6	254.0	248.9	247.1	254.2
2014	237.0	237.4	244.2	255.6	270.4	279.8	280.2	279.7	268.9	262.5	256.0	253.9	260.5
2015	244.8	245.8	250.7	262.5	278.0	287.0	288.7	287.0	275.4	267.8	261.9	261.8	267.6
2016	251.0	251.8	258.8	269.3	280.7	291.5	291.7	290.7	280.6	272.7	271.5	269.6	273.3
2017	260.1	262.7	268.3	277.3	289.4	299.3	299.8	298.2	285.4	272.7	264.0	260.3	278.1
Other Services													
2007	115.6	115.6	116.8	117.1	117.8	119.4	119.4	118.4	117.8	117.6	117.8	118.0	117.6
2008	115.9	116.3	116.9	117.9	118.4	119.6	119.1	118.0	117.4	116.7	116.3	116.3	117.4
2009	114.5	114.1	114.8	115.1	115.8	117.1	116.3	115.4	114.9	114.6	114.6	114.7	115.2
2010	112.5	111.2	113.8	114.0	114.6	115.5	115.3	114.9	113.9	113.8	113.7	113.6	113.9
2011	112.2	112.3	113.1	114.1	114.1	115.2	114.8	114.0	112.6	112.1	112.1	112.2	113.2
2012	110.8	110.7	111.3	112.0	112.2	113.2	113.1	112.3	111.5	110.7	110.1	110.5	111.5
2013	108.7	108.8	109.1	110.8	111.2	112.0	112.3	111.5	111.3	110.3	110.5	110.3	110.6
2014	109.3	109.2	110.1	111.3	112.1	113.5	113.6	112.9	113.1	112.4	112.5	112.7	111.9
2015	111.3	111.5	112.1	110.6	111.6	112.5	113.2	112.8	111.9	111.8	111.9	112.0	111.9
2016	111.3	111.5	112.2	112.9	113.3	113.9	114.9	114.3	113.7	113.4	113.4	113.2	113.2
2017	112.2	112.5	113.1	113.7	114.3	115.8	115.8	114.8	113.9	113.4	114.6	113.2	113.9
Government													
2007	467.4	479.8	486.0	485.9	487.7	471.7	460.3	460.7	477.4	490.1	494.4	493.9	479.6
2008	476.3	491.1	495.2	495.9	495.3	480.7	471.1	471.3	486.6	498.6	502.0	501.5	488.8
2009	482.4	496.0	501.7	504.2	503.3	488.6	475.1	475.1	488.8	506.7	508.3	507.5	494.8
2010	488.5	500.2	509.3	510.0	517.3	501.1	484.2	482.8	497.1	509.1	513.5	511.1	502.0
2011	493.0	509.2	516.0	513.6	512.9	500.0	486.1	480.7	500.9	515.2	512.2	512.6	504.4
2012	492.0	509.7	515.2	514.0	512.5	496.1	478.4	477.6	499.9	512.9	513.9	513.2	503.0
2013	493.3	509.1	513.5	514.0	513.2	501.0	480.8	479.7	500.2	510.2	513.8	510.1	503.2
2014	490.4	506.7	509.8	510.4	509.2	500.2	474.9	479.4	502.5	511.4	514.6	511.1	501.7
2015	490.6	507.1	510.7	512.8	513.3	503.8	478.6	479.6	504.0	510.8	513.7	514.0	503.3
2016	492.1	505.9	512.1	512.6	511.3	498.6	476.5	479.9	503.9	511.4	514.6	514.8	502.8
2017	495.1	511.1	514.9	514.0	515.4	503.7	479.4	479.9	500.4	510.2	513.3	511.5	504.1

2. Average Weekly Hours by Selected Industry: Maryland, 2013–2017

(Not seasonally adjusted)

Industry and year	January	February	March	April	May	June	July	August	September	October	November	December	Annual average
Total Private													
2013	33.4	33.5	33.5	33.8	33.8	34.1	34.0	34.1	34.6	33.8	34.1	34.1	33.9
2014	33.8	33.6	34.4	34.1	34.2	34.6	34.3	34.3	34.2	33.9	34.5	33.7	34.1
2015	33.3	33.9	34.1	34.1	34.3	34.3	34.5	34.7	34.5	34.6	34.6	34.3	34.3
2016	33.6	33.7	34.1	34.2	34.2	34.4	34.3	34.4	34.7	35.0	34.5	34.4	34.3
2017	34.4	34.3	34.0	34.8	34.2	34.4	34.5	34.0	34.3	34.7	34.5	34.4	34.4
Goods Producing													
2013	38.2	38.4	38.3	38.3	38.5	37.6	37.9	38.7	39.0	38.8	39.5	38.5	38.5
2014	38.5	36.3	39.2	39.6	39.6	40.4	40.5	40.1	40.0	39.1	40.0	38.8	39.3
2015	37.5	37.8	38.7	38.9	39.6	40.0	39.9	39.8	39.4	40.6	39.1	40.3	39.3
2016	38.9	38.1	39.3	39.5	38.4	39.6	39.1	39.4	39.4	39.3	38.2	37.7	38.9
2017	38.0	38.3	37.3	38.3	38.4	39.1	38.9	38.7	39.2	39.4	39.5	39.8	38.7
Mining, Logging, and Construction													
2013	37.5	37.4	36.6	37.2	37.8	36.3	37.0	38.3	38.4	37.4	38.9	37.4	37.5
2014	37.9	34.4	38.6	38.9	39.2	40.0	40.7	39.7	39.8	38.6	39.6	37.9	38.8
2015	35.9	36.7	36.9	37.8	39.2	39.5	39.4	39.0	37.6	39.9	37.7	39.9	38.3
2016	38.5	36.6	39.1	39.0	37.8	39.7	39.3	39.4	39.4	39.5	37.6	37.3	38.6
2017	37.7	37.8	36.3	38.0	37.6	38.4	38.2	37.6	37.6	37.7	38.2	38.6	37.8
Manufacturing													
2013	39.2	39.7	40.6	39.9	39.4	39.5	39.0	39.3	39.9	40.6	40.5	39.9	39.8
2014	39.3	38.9	40.0	40.6	40.3	40.9	40.1	40.6	40.3	39.8	40.5	40.0	40.1
2015	39.7	39.3	41.1	40.4	40.2	40.7	40.7	41.0	42.0	41.7	41.2	41.0	40.8
2016	39.4	40.3	39.7	40.4	39.3	39.3	38.8	39.3	39.3	39.0	39.0	38.3	39.3
2017	38.5	39.0	38.7	38.8	39.7	40.3	39.9	40.3	41.7	42.0	41.4	41.6	40.2
Trade, Transportation, and Utilities													
2013	33.2	33.3	33.5	33.2	33.5	34.1	33.9	34.0	34.0	33.0	32.8	33.0	33.5
2014	32.2	32.1	33.5	33.2	33.4	33.6	33.7	33.6	33.5	33.2	33.6	33.2	33.2
2015	32.4	32.9	33.2	33.1	33.5	33.4	34.1	33.9	34.5	33.4	33.6	33.6	33.5
2016	32.3	32.6	32.9	33.0	33.3	33.7	33.6	33.4	34.0	34.2	34.0	34.7	33.5
2017	34.2	33.8	33.5	34.2	33.8	33.9	34.3	33.7	34.2	34.7	34.6	34.0	34.1
Financial Activities													
2013	36.1	36.5	36.5	36.6	36.4	37.1	36.7	36.5	37.5	36.8	37.0	36.8	36.7
2014	37.3	37.2	37.3	36.8	36.9	37.6	37.1	37.3	37.0	37.1	37.9	37.3	37.2
2015	37.6	38.2	38.3	37.5	37.9	37.7	37.6	38.5	38.0	38.1	38.0	37.6	37.9
2016	37.7	38.1	38.3	37.8	38.6	38.5	38.6	38.3	38.0	38.6	38.0	38.3	38.2
2017	38.3	37.8	37.8	38.3	37.3	37.6	38.1	37.3	37.3	37.3	37.6	37.1	37.6
Professional and Business Services													
2013	35.4	35.3	35.3	36.3	35.7	36.1	36.3	36.6	37.1	35.8	36.3	36.5	36.1
2014	36.1	36.5	36.5	36.1	36.0	36.7	35.7	35.7	35.5	35.2	36.0	34.8	35.9
2015	34.7	35.8	35.8	35.8	35.7	35.7	35.4	36.1	35.5	36.2	36.5	35.7	35.7
2016	35.3	35.3	36.0	36.4	36.4	36.6	36.0	36.1	36.1	37.4	36.6	36.2	36.2
2017	36.4	36.3	36.2	37.8	36.6	37.4	37.1	36.9	37.0	37.8	37.1	37.1	37.0
Education and Health Services													
2013	33.0	33.3	33.0	33.3	33.3	33.9	33.3	33.1	33.5	33.2	33.2	33.1	33.3
2014	33.1	33.0	33.0	32.9	32.8	32.8	32.9	33.1	33.0	32.6	32.9	32.7	32.9
2015	32.6	33.0	32.8	32.6	32.7	32.8	33.0	32.9	32.9	33.2	33.5	32.8	32.9
2016	33.3	33.0	33.2	33.2	33.1	33.1	33.6	33.4	33.4	33.5	33.6	33.3	33.3
2017	33.2	33.0	33.0	33.3	33.1	33.0	33.4	33.2	33.1	32.8	32.7	33.1	33.1
Leisure and Hospitality													
2013	25.6	26.0	25.8	25.7	25.9	26.5	26.9	26.4	26.2	25.6	25.6	25.3	26.0
2014	24.9	24.7	25.4	25.0	25.3	25.8	26.1	26.2	25.9	25.5	25.4	25.4	25.5
2015	25.2	25.3	25.8	26.1	26.8	27.3	27.6	28.0	26.9	26.7	26.7	26.5	26.6
2016	24.9	26.0	26.0	26.1	26.1	26.1	26.4	26.3	26.2	25.8	25.6	25.3	25.9
2017	25.1	25.4	25.3	26.2	26.2	25.6	26.1	25.5	25.4	25.7	25.4	25.2	25.6
Other Services													
2013	31.8	32.4	32.5	32.8	33.3	32.5	32.5	31.8	33.5	32.2	33.1	33.4	32.7
2014	32.6	32.9	34.0	32.9	33.1	33.4	32.8	32.6	32.6	32.9	33.7	33.8	33.1
2015	32.1	33.3	33.5	33.6	34.0	33.6	33.7	32.9	32.6	32.3	32.5	32.3	33.0
2016	31.3	31.5	31.8	32.0	31.9	32.6	32.3	32.2	31.6	31.4	30.7	30.6	31.7
2017	31.1	31.6	30.5	31.5	31.4	31.7	32.5	32.1	32.6	32.2	31.6	31.8	31.7

3. Average Hourly Earnings by Selected Industry: Maryland, 2013–2017

(Dollars, not seasonally adjusted)

Industry and year	January	February	March	April	May	June	July	August	September	October	November	December	Annual average
Total Private													
2013	26.69	26.35	26.45	26.43	26.34	26.64	26.26	26.44	27.00	26.94	26.99	27.38	26.66
2014	27.42	27.82	27.41	27.28	27.09	27.29	27.15	27.19	27.46	27.18	27.50	27.45	27.35
2015	27.64	27.71	27.77	27.28	27.08	26.81	26.75	27.28	27.20	27.21	27.69	27.38	27.31
2016	27.38	27.20	27.11	27.17	27.47	26.94	27.06	27.22	27.19	27.51	27.58	27.39	27.27
2017	28.23	27.79	27.86	27.87	27.47	27.56	28.15	27.96	29.07	29.49	29.38	29.23	28.34
Goods Producing													
2013	25.37	25.06	25.51	25.61	25.71	26.23	25.95	26.24	26.23	25.79	26.04	26.69	25.87
2014	27.02	27.15	26.33	26.34	26.18	26.42	26.13	26.20	26.12	26.42	26.73	26.59	26.46
2015	26.73	26.59	26.56	26.26	26.23	26.36	26.19	26.21	26.30	26.05	26.37	26.44	26.35
2016	26.03	26.20	26.25	26.43	26.84	26.50	26.86	27.03	27.53	27.62	28.29	28.48	27.01
2017	28.80	28.84	28.95	28.88	28.74	29.03	29.59	29.03	29.63	29.51	29.77	30.02	29.24
Mining, Logging, and Construction													
2013	26.73	26.69	27.07	27.08	27.19	27.50	27.10	26.97	26.94	27.12	27.03	27.22	27.05
2014	27.30	27.78	26.86	26.86	26.71	27.07	26.68	26.83	26.92	27.53	27.17	27.30	27.07
2015	27.62	27.31	27.17	27.07	26.87	26.91	26.85	26.51	26.49	26.34	26.26	26.66	26.82
2016	26.52	26.47	26.40	26.77	26.89	26.49	27.00	27.49	27.80	27.87	28.54	28.97	27.28
2017	29.53	29.62	29.93	29.43	29.62	30.16	30.84	30.22	30.58	30.56	30.81	31.11	30.21
Manufacturing													
2013	23.68	23.08	23.67	23.77	23.77	24.63	24.43	25.24	25.28	24.07	24.71	26.00	24.36
2014	26.66	26.40	25.62	25.63	25.44	25.50	25.32	25.28	24.95	24.84	26.11	25.61	25.61
2015	25.61	25.66	25.80	25.17	25.31	25.58	25.23	25.78	26.04	25.62	26.53	26.12	25.71
2016	25.33	25.84	26.02	25.94	26.76	26.52	26.64	26.31	27.10	27.22	27.92	27.75	26.61
2017	27.72	27.71	27.58	28.05	27.47	27.35	27.72	27.31	28.30	28.05	28.31	28.50	27.85
Trade, Transportation, and Utilities													
2013	19.84	20.16	19.89	20.28	20.29	20.33	20.15	20.12	20.13	20.42	20.26	20.11	20.17
2014	20.06	20.87	20.31	20.62	20.46	20.29	20.88	20.65	21.63	21.27	21.50	22.35	20.92
2015	22.65	22.69	22.27	22.40	22.04	21.99	22.02	22.30	22.11	22.68	22.66	22.29	22.34
2016	22.96	22.86	23.08	23.45	23.31	23.14	23.59	23.70	23.86	24.08	23.98	23.49	23.47
2017	24.16	23.93	23.94	24.99	24.19	24.20	24.95	24.45	24.31	24.40	24.10	24.42	24.34
Financial Activities													
2013	31.15	31.68	31.45	31.23	31.39	31.43	32.01	32.29	32.49	32.05	32.57	32.96	31.90
2014	32.48	32.96	32.72	32.69	32.68	32.50	32.78	33.25	33.08	33.02	33.71	34.06	33.00
2015	33.76	34.57	34.96	35.50	35.58	35.11	35.45	36.52	36.66	36.36	37.73	36.82	35.75
2016	36.33	37.14	37.52	37.84	37.86	37.37	37.18	39.41	39.66	39.94	39.75	39.28	38.28
2017	40.57	40.20	39.20	39.70	38.83	38.01	37.58	38.47	36.81	37.97	37.60	37.59	38.54
Professional and Business Services													
2013	34.60	33.86	33.87	33.19	31.29	32.42	31.46	31.84	33.06	33.15	33.34	34.26	33.02
2014	34.16	34.87	34.79	33.75	33.88	34.48	34.02	34.30	34.22	33.93	34.74	34.51	34.30
2015	34.51	34.53	34.57	33.49	33.35	33.16	33.08	34.07	33.64	33.31	34.42	34.18	33.85
2016	33.31	32.58	31.83	31.87	32.68	31.67	31.99	32.31	32.64	33.25	33.51	33.88	32.63
2017	34.71	33.66	33.67	33.67	33.15	33.34	34.71	34.22	34.87	36.25	35.92	35.20	34.45
Education and Health Services													
2013	28.32	28.05	28.27	28.27	27.95	27.72	27.72	27.79	27.82	27.82	27.61	27.71	27.92
2014	27.58	27.21	27.16	26.92	26.57	26.61	26.72	26.53	26.46	26.76	26.44	26.30	26.77
2015	26.34	26.08	26.11	25.96	25.66	25.58	25.68	25.52	26.01	25.45	25.38	25.38	25.76
2016	25.28	25.20	25.22	25.42	25.52	25.36	25.54	25.30	25.47	25.33	25.11	24.95	25.31
2017	25.25	25.22	25.29	25.55	25.79	25.84	25.80	25.23	25.33	25.39	25.35	25.44	25.46
Leisure and Hospitality													
2013	13.94	14.07	13.86	13.84	14.05	13.86	13.56	13.64	14.91	14.92	14.97	15.19	14.22
2014	14.88	14.77	14.64	15.28	14.96	14.85	14.71	14.65	15.19	14.81	15.06	14.88	14.89
2015	15.08	15.10	15.23	15.48	15.95	15.18	14.82	15.04	15.06	15.32	15.09	15.16	15.21
2016	15.34	15.26	15.35	15.19	15.33	15.16	15.04	15.25	15.46	14.79	14.58	14.79	15.13
2017	15.10	15.43	15.33	15.07	15.36	15.19	14.93	15.17	15.71	14.69	14.72	15.05	15.15
Other Services													
2013	22.02	22.53	22.49	23.04	22.64	23.92	24.08	23.78	23.62	24.14	23.75	23.65	23.31
2014	24.40	23.91	23.83	24.16	24.45	24.62	24.56	25.07	25.72	25.48	25.45	25.11	24.73
2015	26.11	26.02	26.29	25.40	25.36	25.82	26.05	27.68	27.09	27.66	27.60	27.10	26.51
2016	28.24	28.31	28.86	27.82	28.49	28.00	28.10	28.42	28.98	29.92	29.22	29.24	28.63
2017	29.97	29.01	29.60	29.43	28.67	28.84	29.17	30.10	30.34	30.27	30.10	30.33	29.65

4. Average Weekly Earnings by Selected Industry: Maryland, 2013–2017

(Dollars, not seasonally adjusted)

Industry and year	January	February	March	April	May	June	July	August	September	October	November	December	Annual average
Total Private													
2013	891.45	882.73	886.08	893.33	890.29	908.42	892.84	901.60	934.20	910.57	920.36	933.66	903.77
2014	926.80	934.75	942.90	930.25	926.48	944.23	931.25	932.62	939.13	921.40	948.75	925.07	932.64
2015	920.41	939.37	946.96	930.25	928.84	919.58	922.88	946.62	938.40	941.47	958.07	939.13	936.73
2016	919.97	916.64	924.45	929.21	939.47	926.74	928.16	936.37	943.49	962.85	951.51	942.22	935.36
2017	971.11	953.20	947.24	969.88	939.47	948.06	971.18	950.64	997.10	1,023.30	1,013.61	1,005.51	974.90
Goods Producing													
2013	969.13	962.30	977.03	980.86	989.84	986.25	983.51	1,015.49	1,022.97	1,000.65	1,028.58	1,027.57	996.00
2014	1,040.27	985.55	1,032.14	1,043.06	1,036.73	1,067.37	1,058.27	1,050.62	1,044.80	1,033.02	1,069.20	1,031.69	1,039.88
2015	1,002.38	1,005.10	1,027.87	1,021.51	1,038.71	1,054.40	1,044.98	1,043.16	1,036.22	1,057.63	1,031.07	1,065.53	1,035.56
2016	1,012.57	998.22	1,031.63	1,043.99	1,030.66	1,049.40	1,050.23	1,064.98	1,084.68	1,085.47	1,080.68	1,073.70	1,050.69
2017	1,094.40	1,104.57	1,079.84	1,106.10	1,103.62	1,135.07	1,151.05	1,123.46	1,161.50	1,162.69	1,175.92	1,194.80	1,131.59
Mining, Logging, and Construction													
2013	1,002.38	998.21	990.76	1,007.38	1,027.78	998.25	1,002.70	1,032.95	1,034.50	1,014.29	1,051.47	1,018.03	1,014.38
2014	1,034.67	955.63	1,036.80	1,044.85	1,047.03	1,082.80	1,085.88	1,065.15	1,071.42	1,062.66	1,075.93	1,034.67	1,050.32
2015	991.56	1,002.28	1,002.57	1,023.25	1,053.30	1,062.95	1,057.89	1,033.89	996.02	1,050.97	990.00	1,063.73	1,027.21
2016	1,021.02	968.80	1,032.24	1,044.03	1,016.44	1,051.65	1,061.10	1,083.11	1,095.32	1,100.87	1,073.10	1,080.58	1,053.01
2017	1,113.28	1,119.64	1,086.46	1,118.34	1,113.71	1,158.14	1,178.09	1,136.27	1,149.81	1,152.11	1,176.94	1,200.85	1,141.94
Manufacturing													
2013	928.26	916.28	961.00	948.42	936.54	972.89	952.77	991.93	1,008.67	977.24	1,000.76	1,037.40	969.53
2014	1,047.74	1,026.96	1,024.80	1,040.58	1,025.23	1,042.95	1,015.33	1,026.37	1,005.49	988.63	1,057.46	1,024.40	1,026.96
2015	1,016.72	1,008.44	1,060.38	1,016.87	1,017.46	1,041.11	1,026.86	1,056.98	1,093.68	1,068.35	1,093.04	1,070.92	1,048.97
2016	998.00	1,041.35	1,032.99	1,047.98	1,051.67	1,042.24	1,033.63	1,033.98	1,065.03	1,061.58	1,088.88	1,062.83	1,045.77
2017	1,067.22	1,080.69	1,067.35	1,088.34	1,090.56	1,102.21	1,106.03	1,100.59	1,180.11	1,178.10	1,172.03	1,185.60	1,119.57
Trade, Transportation, and Utilities													
2013	658.69	671.33	666.32	673.30	679.72	693.25	683.09	684.08	684.42	673.86	664.53	663.63	675.70
2014	645.93	669.93	680.39	684.58	683.36	681.74	703.66	693.84	724.61	706.16	722.40	742.02	694.54
2015	733.86	746.50	739.36	741.44	738.34	734.47	750.88	755.97	762.80	757.51	761.38	748.94	748.39
2016	741.61	745.24	759.33	773.85	776.22	779.82	792.62	791.58	811.24	823.54	815.32	815.10	786.25
2017	826.27	808.83	801.99	854.66	817.62	820.38	855.79	823.97	831.40	846.68	833.86	830.28	829.99
Financial Activities													
2013	1,124.52	1,156.32	1,147.93	1,143.02	1,142.60	1,166.05	1,174.77	1,178.59	1,218.38	1,179.44	1,205.09	1,212.93	1,170.73
2014	1,211.50	1,226.11	1,220.46	1,202.99	1,205.89	1,222.00	1,216.14	1,240.23	1,223.96	1,225.04	1,277.61	1,270.44	1,227.60
2015	1,269.38	1,320.57	1,338.97	1,331.25	1,348.48	1,323.65	1,332.92	1,406.02	1,393.08	1,385.32	1,433.74	1,384.43	1,354.93
2016	1,369.64	1,415.03	1,437.02	1,430.35	1,461.40	1,438.75	1,435.15	1,509.40	1,507.08	1,541.68	1,510.50	1,504.42	1,462.30
2017	1,553.83	1,519.56	1,481.76	1,520.51	1,448.36	1,429.18	1,431.80	1,434.93	1,373.01	1,416.28	1,413.76	1,394.59	1,449.10
Professional and Business Services													
2013	1,224.84	1,195.26	1,195.61	1,204.80	1,117.05	1,170.36	1,142.00	1,165.34	1,226.53	1,186.77	1,210.24	1,250.49	1,192.02
2014	1,233.18	1,272.76	1,269.84	1,218.38	1,219.68	1,265.42	1,214.51	1,224.51	1,214.81	1,194.34	1,250.64	1,200.95	1,231.37
2015	1,197.50	1,236.17	1,237.61	1,198.94	1,190.60	1,183.81	1,171.03	1,229.93	1,194.22	1,205.82	1,256.33	1,220.23	1,208.45
2016	1,175.84	1,150.07	1,145.88	1,160.07	1,189.55	1,159.12	1,151.64	1,166.39	1,178.30	1,243.55	1,226.47	1,226.46	1,181.21
2017	1,263.44	1,221.86	1,218.85	1,272.73	1,213.29	1,246.92	1,287.74	1,262.72	1,290.19	1,370.25	1,332.63	1,305.92	1,274.65
Education and Health Services													
2013	934.56	934.07	932.91	941.39	930.74	939.71	923.08	919.85	931.97	923.62	916.65	917.20	929.74
2014	912.90	897.93	896.28	885.67	871.50	872.81	879.09	878.14	873.18	872.38	869.88	860.01	880.73
2015	858.68	860.64	856.41	846.30	839.08	839.02	847.44	839.61	855.73	844.94	850.23	832.46	847.50
2016	841.82	831.60	837.30	843.94	844.71	839.42	858.14	845.02	850.70	848.56	843.70	830.84	842.82
2017	838.30	832.26	834.57	850.82	853.65	852.72	861.72	837.64	838.42	832.79	828.95	842.06	842.73
Leisure and Hospitality													
2013	356.86	365.82	357.59	355.69	363.90	367.29	364.76	360.10	390.64	381.95	383.23	384.31	369.72
2014	370.51	364.82	371.86	382.00	378.49	383.13	383.93	383.83	393.42	377.66	382.52	377.95	379.70
2015	380.02	382.03	392.93	404.03	427.46	414.41	409.03	421.12	405.11	409.04	402.90	401.74	404.59
2016	381.97	396.76	399.10	396.46	400.11	395.68	397.06	401.08	405.05	381.58	373.25	374.19	391.87
2017	379.01	391.92	387.85	394.83	402.43	388.86	389.67	386.84	399.03	377.53	373.89	379.26	387.84
Other Services													
2013	700.24	729.97	730.93	755.71	753.91	777.40	782.60	756.20	791.27	777.31	786.13	789.91	762.24
2014	795.44	786.64	810.22	794.86	809.30	822.31	805.57	817.28	838.47	838.29	857.67	848.72	818.56
2015	838.13	866.47	880.72	853.44	862.24	867.55	877.89	910.67	883.13	893.42	897.00	875.33	874.83
2016	883.91	891.77	917.75	890.24	908.83	912.80	907.63	915.12	915.77	939.49	897.05	894.74	907.57
2017	932.07	916.72	902.80	927.05	900.24	914.23	948.03	966.21	989.08	974.69	951.16	964.49	939.91

MASSACHUSETTS
At a Glance

Population:
  2010 census: 6,547,629
  2017 estimate: 6,859,819

Percent change in population:
  2010–2017: 4.8%

Percent change in total nonfarm employment:
  2007–2017: 9.2%

Industry with the largest growth in employment, 2007–2017 (thousands):
  Education and health services, 151.7

Industry with the largest decline or smallest growth in employment, 2007–2017 (thousands):
  Manufacturing, 50.0

Civilian labor force:
  2010: 3,480,083
  2017: 3,657,173

Unemployment rate and rank among states (highest to lowest):
  2010: 8.3%, 30th
  2017: 3.7%, 34th

Over-the-year change in unemployment rates:
  2015–2016: -0.9%
  2016–2017: -0.2%

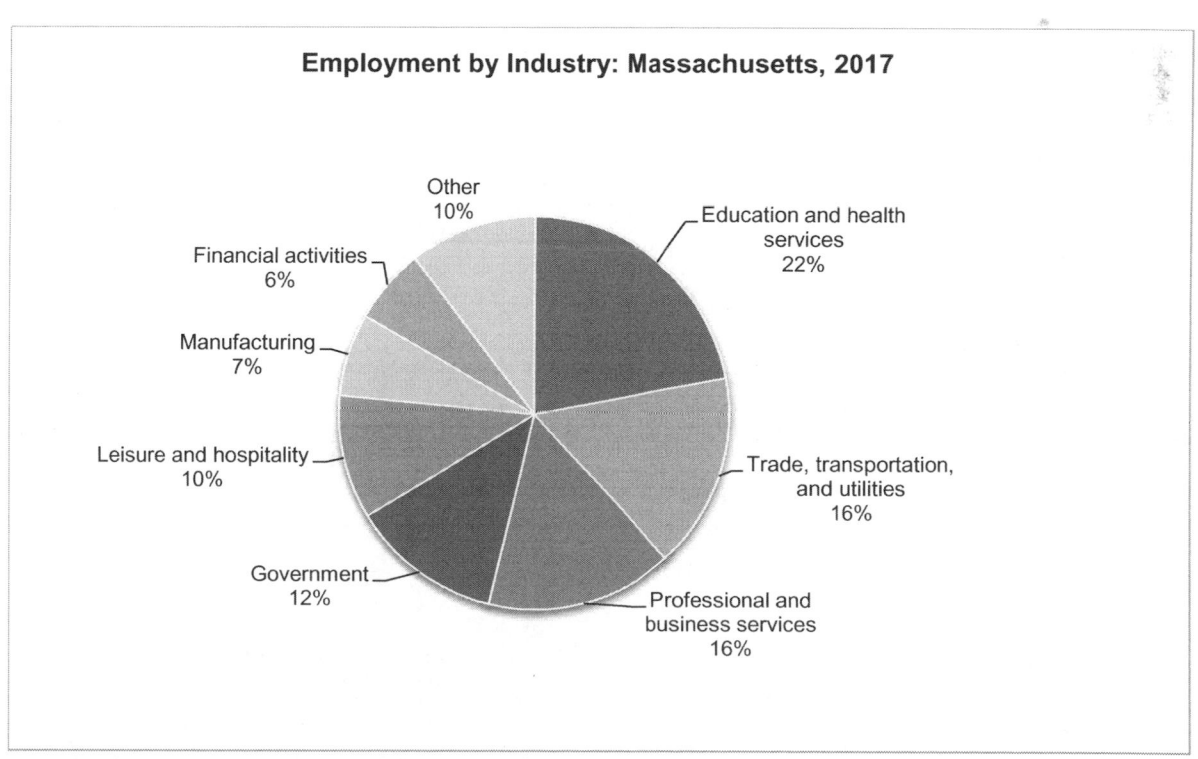

Employment by Industry: Massachusetts, 2017

- Other 10%
- Education and health services 22%
- Financial activities 6%
- Manufacturing 7%
- Trade, transportation, and utilities 16%
- Leisure and hospitality 10%
- Professional and business services 16%
- Government 12%

1. Employment by Industry: Massachusetts, Selected Years, 2007–2017

(Numbers in thousands, not seasonally adjusted)

Industry and year	January	February	March	April	May	June	July	August	September	October	November	December	Annual average
Total Nonfarm													
2007	3,221.8	3,229.7	3,244.9	3,286.9	3,321.4	3,352.0	3,319.4	3,312.7	3,331.2	3,344.2	3,351.0	3,348.4	3,305.3
2008	3,252.6	3,265.3	3,280.9	3,320.5	3,347.5	3,364.0	3,335.9	3,324.0	3,336.6	3,346.3	3,327.3	3,311.5	3,317.7
2009	3,187.8	3,187.1	3,184.0	3,215.6	3,231.7	3,239.0	3,206.5	3,191.3	3,213.2	3,228.5	3,222.3	3,224.9	3,211.0
2010	3,145.8	3,148.2	3,160.9	3,214.3	3,250.0	3,253.6	3,237.8	3,222.5	3,240.1	3,267.3	3,264.5	3,264.3	3,222.4
2011	3,166.4	3,179.1	3,194.0	3,250.8	3,271.6	3,288.7	3,283.1	3,266.7	3,294.3	3,307.7	3,304.9	3,305.0	3,259.4
2012	3,216.5	3,226.9	3,254.1	3,291.9	3,320.8	3,359.4	3,328.5	3,320.2	3,339.6	3,355.0	3,359.4	3,353.2	3,310.5
2013	3,258.6	3,273.2	3,298.4	3,353.2	3,387.6	3,417.1	3,383.8	3,378.7	3,390.0	3,412.8	3,416.0	3,414.0	3,365.3
2014	3,313.1	3,331.8	3,353.4	3,413.5	3,449.6	3,476.7	3,457.0	3,436.8	3,462.9	3,491.8	3,498.9	3,499.8	3,432.1
2015	3,384.5	3,387.6	3,417.8	3,478.5	3,523.6	3,553.2	3,537.1	3,519.1	3,518.5	3,553.1	3,557.4	3,556.6	3,498.9
2016	3,449.7	3,468.7	3,494.4	3,551.5	3,579.0	3,607.4	3,608.1	3,592.4	3,597.7	3,606.9	3,613.5	3,610.1	3,565.0
2017	3,506.7	3,520.2	3,540.1	3,590.4	3,620 6	3,665.1	3,643.0	3,629.5	3,629.2	3,654.3	3,653.4	3,645.6	3,608.2
Total Private													
2007	2,791.9	2,790.0	2,804.1	2,844.9	2,876.7	2,916.1	2,917.9	2,917.8	2,897.5	2,902.4	2,907.0	2,905.2	2,872.6
2008	2,819.3	2,820.4	2,835.3	2,873.2	2,898.8	2,925.3	2,929.5	2,924.5	2,899.0	2,899.2	2,879.1	2,864.7	2,880.7
2009	2,752.0	2,738.9	2,736.5	2,762.6	2,781.5	2,800.0	2,801.2	2,793.7	2,778.6	2,781.3	2,775.3	2,775.3	2,773.1
2010	2,707.3	2,702.0	2,713.6	2,763.0	2,789.8	2,811.6	2,832.0	2,825.0	2,803.6	2,820.5	2,814.0	2,815.1	2,783.1
2011	2,733.6	2,733.9	2,748.4	2,805.4	2,824.1	2,852.7	2,881.2	2,873.3	2,858.0	2,864.6	2,861.1	2,859.3	2,824.6
2012	2,784.8	2,783.0	2,807.1	2,845.2	2,872.5	2,920.4	2,924.8	2,922.5	2,899.3	2,908.1	2,907.8	2,903.6	2,873.3
2013	2,824.8	2,822.2	2,846.0	2,896.6	2,931.5	2,972.7	2,975.1	2,976.7	2,948.3	2,958.9	2,957.9	2,955.5	2,922.2
2014	2,869.1	2,873.7	2,894.7	2,948.9	2,986.4	3,025.7	3,039.9	3,027.6	3,008.9	3,029.0	3,029.2	3,032.4	2,980.5
2015	2,940.2	2,928.4	2,954.6	3,013.0	3,062.3	3,098.8	3,117.8	3,110.9	3,069.8	3,092.7	3,093.7	3,091.5	3,047.8
2016	3,004.9	3,009.4	3,028.4	3,087.7	3,114.9	3,153.3	3,185.8	3,178.5	3,140.0	3,143.8	3,143.0	3,143.8	3,111.1
2017	3,057.7	3,059.5	3,079.0	3,127.1	3,157.3	3,208.2	3,223.6	3,217.7	3,176.8	3,192.4	3,188.5	3,179.7	3,155.6
Goods Producing													
2007	424.4	418.8	420.4	427.6	436.7	444.4	442.7	443.9	440.9	437.2	435.1	429.4	433.5
2008	413.6	409.3	411.7	419.3	425.6	430.4	430.0	429.9	425.1	420.9	413.9	404.4	419.5
2009	380.0	371.2	367.4	371.2	373.3	376.7	375.4	373.5	370.1	367.9	365.5	361.3	371.1
2010	348.0	343.0	345.5	355.0	361.5	367.5	371.1	370.1	367.6	367.8	366.0	361.6	360.4
2011	347.3	343.5	346.1	358.0	364.3	371.3	375.4	376.1	372.5	371.1	369.1	365.6	363.4
2012	354.2	351.0	355.0	362.7	367.2	375.5	376.7	377.1	374.0	374.6	373.1	370.1	367.6
2013	357.8	355.2	357.8	366.4	374.7	381.6	383.5	384.6	381.4	380.2	378.2	374.7	373.0
2014	364.0	360.6	362.8	372.0	380.2	386.7	389.0	389.4	386.0	387.1	386.8	384.2	379.1
2015	372.5	367.5	370.4	383.0	392.1	398.7	400.6	400.7	396.0	397.2	396.1	393.7	389.0
2016	381.7	376.2	380.3	389.3	395.6	401.7	403.3	402.7	398.8	398.8	397.1	394.6	393.3
2017	381.9	378.5	380.8	389.2	395.8	403.6	407.0	407.8	404.0	405.7	407.0	404.5	397.2
Service-Providing													
2007	2,797.4	2,810.9	2,824.5	2,859.3	2,884.7	2,907.6	2,876.7	2,868.8	2,890.3	2,907.0	2,915.9	2,919.0	2,871.8
2008	2,839.0	2,856.0	2,869.2	2,901.2	2,921.9	2,933.6	2,905.9	2,894.1	2,911.5	2,925.4	2,913.4	2,907.1	2,898.2
2009	2,807.8	2,815.9	2,816.6	2,844.4	2,858.4	2,862.3	2,831.1	2,817.8	2,843.1	2,860.6	2,856.8	2,863.6	2,839.9
2010	2,797.8	2,805.2	2,815.4	2,859.3	2,888.5	2,886.1	2,866.7	2,852.4	2,872.5	2,899.5	2,898.5	2,902.7	2,862.1
2011	2,819.1	2,835.6	2,847.9	2,892.8	2,907.3	2,917.4	2,907.7	2,890.6	2,921.8	2,936.6	2,935.8	2,939.4	2,896.0
2012	2,862.3	2,875.9	2,899.1	2,929.2	2,953.6	2,983.9	2,951.8	2,943.1	2,965.6	2,980.4	2,986.3	2,983.1	2,942.9
2013	2,900.8	2,918.0	2,940.6	2,986.8	3,012.9	3,035.5	3,000.3	2,994.1	3,008.6	3,032.6	3,037.8	3,039.3	2,992.3
2014	2,949.1	2,971.2	2,990.6	3,041.5	3,069.4	3,090.0	3,068.0	3,047.4	3,076.9	3,104.7	3,112.1	3,115.6	3,053.0
2015	3,012.0	3,020.1	3,047.4	3,095.5	3,131.5	3,154.5	3,136.5	3,118.4	3,122.5	3,155.9	3,161.3	3,162.9	3,109.9
2016	3,068.0	3,092.5	3,114.1	3,162.2	3,183.4	3,205.7	3,204.8	3,189.7	3,198.9	3,208.1	3,216.4	3,215.5	3,171.6
2017	3,124.8	3,141.7	3,159.3	3,201.2	3,224.8	3,261.5	3,236.0	3,221.7	3,225.2	3,248.6	3,246.4	3,241.1	3,211.0
Mining and Logging													
2007	1.4	1.3	1.4	1.5	1.7	1.8	1.7	1.7	1.7	1.6	1.6	1.5	1.6
2008	1.2	1.2	1.2	1.4	1.5	1.5	1.5	1.4	1.4	1.4	1.4	1.3	1.4
2009	1.1	1.1	1.1	1.3	1.4	1.4	1.4	1.4	1.4	1.4	1.4	1.3	1.3
2010	1.0	1.0	1.0	1.2	1.3	1.3	1.2	1.2	1.2	1.1	1.1	1.1	1.1
2011	0.9	0.9	0.9	1.1	1.2	1.2	1.2	1.2	1.2	1.2	1.1	1.1	1.1
2012	0.9	0.8	0.9	0.9	1.0	1.0	1.0	1.0	1.0	1.0	1.0	1.0	1.0
2013	0.8	0.8	0.9	1.0	1.0	1.0	1.0	1.1	1.1	1.1	1.0	1.0	1.0
2014	0.9	0.9	0.9	1.0	1.1	1.1	1.1	1.1	1.1	1.1	1.1	1.0	1.0
2015	0.9	0.9	0.9	1.1	1.1	1.1	1.2	1.1	1.2	1.1	1.1	1.1	1.1
2016	1.0	1.0	1.0	1.1	1.2	1.2	1.2	1.2	1.2	1.2	1.1	1.1	1.1
2017	1.0	1.0	1.0	1.1	1.1	1.2	1.2	1.2	1.2	1.2	1.2	1.1	1.1

1. Employment by Industry: Massachusetts, Selected Years, 2007–2017—*Continued*

(Numbers in thousands, not seasonally adjusted)

Industry and year	January	February	March	April	May	June	July	August	September	October	November	December	Annual average
Construction													
2007	126.7	121.5	123.8	131.8	140.2	145.4	147.5	147.6	145.7	143.9	141.8	135.9	137.7
2008	123.4	120.4	123.1	130.7	136.7	139.9	142.4	141.6	138.7	136.1	131.7	124.8	132.5
2009	109.0	104.3	103.6	110.1	114.0	116.8	118.1	117.2	114.6	113.1	110.4	106.0	111.4
2010	96.1	92.3	94.5	103.3	108.7	112.8	116.3	115.5	114.0	113.2	111.5	107.3	107.1
2011	96.8	94.0	95.8	105.9	111.7	116.6	120.6	121.1	119.3	117.9	116.3	112.6	110.7
2012	103.3	100.4	103.8	111.5	115.5	120.4	123.5	123.9	122.0	122.5	121.3	118.0	115.5
2013	108.8	106.7	108.6	116.8	124.2	128.5	131.8	132.3	130.2	129.5	127.5	123.2	122.3
2014	114.8	112.3	113.9	122.8	130.4	135.0	138.0	138.1	136.5	137.1	136.3	133.1	129.0
2015	123.8	119.0	121.4	133.2	141.7	145.9	148.8	149.3	146.6	148.1	146.9	144.3	139.1
2016	134.9	130.6	134.0	143.2	148.7	152.2	154.9	154.3	152.4	152.6	151.3	148.0	146.4
2017	137.5	134.7	137.1	145.5	151.7	156.6	160.5	161.1	159.2	160.5	160.8	156.6	151.8
Manufacturing													
2007	296.3	296.0	295.2	294.3	294.8	297.2	293.5	294.0	293.5	291.7	291.7	292.0	294.2
2008	289.0	287.7	287.4	287.2	287.4	289.0	286.1	286.9	285.0	283.4	280.8	278.3	285.7
2009	269.9	265.8	262.7	259.8	257.9	258.5	255.9	254.9	254.1	253.4	253.7	254.0	258.4
2010	250.9	249.7	250.0	250.5	251.5	253.4	253.6	253.4	252.4	253.5	253.4	253.2	252.1
2011	249.6	248.6	249.4	251.0	251.4	253.5	253.6	253.8	252.0	252.0	251.7	251.9	251.5
2012	250.0	249.8	250.3	250.3	250.7	254.1	252.2	252.2	251.0	251.1	250.8	251.1	251.1
2013	248.2	247.7	248.3	248.6	249.5	252.1	250.7	251.2	250.1	249.6	249.7	250.5	249.7
2014	248.3	247.4	248.0	248.2	248.7	250.6	249.9	250.2	248.4	248.9	249.4	250.1	249.0
2015	247.8	247.6	248.1	248.7	249.3	251.7	250.6	250.3	248.2	248.0	248.1	248.3	248.9
2016	245.8	244.6	245.3	245.0	245.7	248.3	247.2	247.2	245.2	245.0	244.7	245.5	245.8
2017	243.4	242.8	242.7	242.6	243.0	245.8	245.3	245.5	243.6	244.0	245.0	246.8	244.2
Trade, Transportation, and Utilities													
2007	567.3	557.2	558.8	560.7	568.5	577.5	571.1	569.3	568.9	574.1	585.7	592.2	570.9
2008	570.9	558.9	560.2	563.1	568.8	576.1	570.2	569.2	566.8	568.6	571.7	576.7	568.4
2009	547.4	536.6	533.1	533.1	539.3	547.4	539.7	538.5	539.6	543.9	550.7	556.8	542.2
2010	537.4	528.3	528.9	535.5	541.9	548.8	545.7	545.4	541.8	548.6	555.6	565.1	543.6
2011	541.6	534.5	534.5	541.0	545.1	551.9	549.5	549.5	548.3	552.6	560.2	567.7	548.0
2012	545.9	535.7	537.8	540.6	548.4	558.4	552.8	552.6	550.7	555.5	565.8	571.1	551.3
2013	548.5	539.7	541.4	546.9	554.5	564.1	558.2	558.7	556.4	559.1	568.0	576.0	556.0
2014	555.7	548.0	549.1	554.4	561.0	569.4	563.5	553.2	563.1	568.5	578.4	587.5	562.7
2015	563.8	551.3	553.6	560.1	568.0	577.3	573.3	572.8	568.9	573.5	582.3	589.1	569.5
2016	568.1	560.3	561.4	567.3	573.2	581.9	580.1	579.3	574.3	577.5	586.5	595.2	575.4
2017	574.9	564.9	564.9	570.3	576.0	586.7	583.8	583.2	579.0	582.7	588.3	593.0	579.0
Wholesale Trade													
2007	136.7	136.4	136.9	136.9	137.5	139.1	139.1	138.9	137.8	138.4	138.3	138.5	137.9
2008	137.0	135.9	136.3	136.8	137.1	138.1	137.6	136.8	135.6	134.9	134.0	133.6	136.1
2009	130.0	128.4	127.7	127.2	127.0	127.5	126.6	125.8	124.4	124.2	123.5	123.2	126.3
2010	121.4	120.8	121.0	121.5	122.4	123.3	123.7	123.5	122.1	122.9	122.7	122.7	122.3
2011	121.0	120.8	120.6	122.0	122.1	122.4	123.2	122.6	121.1	121.2	120.8	120.8	121.6
2012	119.8	119.5	119.9	121.1	121.6	122.9	123.0	123.1	121.8	122.5	122.5	122.3	121.7
2013	121.1	121.0	121.4	122.3	122.7	123.9	124.4	124.2	123.2	123.6	123.4	123.4	122.9
2014	122.1	121.9	122.1	123.2	123.7	124.6	124.8	124.6	123.5	123.6	123.7	123.8	123.5
2015	122.2	121.4	121.6	123.2	123.8	124.9	125.5	125.2	124.1	124.4	124.3	124.4	123.8
2016	123.1	122.9	123.0	124.5	124.8	125.8	127.0	126.9	125.5	125.7	125.3	125.4	125.0
2017	124.1	124.0	124.2	124.8	125.3	126.7	127.1	126.8	125.5	126.3	126.9	127.6	125.8
Retail Trade													
2007	347.3	338.1	338.8	340.3	346.2	352.0	350.2	349.3	344.8	349.5	361.7	366.8	348.8
2008	349.8	339.5	340.0	341.8	345.8	351.1	350.4	351.1	344.7	348.0	353.0	357.3	347.7
2009	335.7	327.3	324.6	325.1	330.4	336.9	334.7	335.4	332.1	336.5	344.2	348.9	334.3
2010	334.6	326.6	327.1	331.8	335.9	340.8	341.8	342.8	336.1	341.8	349.2	356.2	338.7
2011	338.7	332.0	331.9	336.1	339.0	344.0	344.9	346.5	341.7	346.2	354.3	360.4	343.0
2012	343.3	333.8	335.1	336.4	342.3	349.3	348.1	348.6	343.1	347.0	357.6	360.8	345.5
2013	343.6	334.9	336.0	339.8	345.3	351.8	349.9	351.6	345.2	347.6	356.5	362.6	347.1
2014	347.1	339.5	339.9	343.1	347.1	352.7	351.3	342.1	347.5	352.8	361.7	367.3	349.3
2015	351.3	340.4	342.2	345.7	351.3	357.7	357.1	357.5	349.8	354.2	362.9	367.9	353.2
2016	352.5	345.3	346.2	349.3	353.2	359.3	360.1	360.6	351.7	353.8	362.2	367.6	355.2
2017	353.5	344.3	344.2	348.2	351.7	358.8	359.7	360.2	351.9	353.7	358.6	360.6	353.8

1. Employment by Industry: Massachusetts, Selected Years, 2007–2017—*Continued*

(Numbers in thousands, not seasonally adjusted)

Industry and year	January	February	March	April	May	June	July	August	September	October	November	December	Annual average
Transportation and Utilities													
2007	83.3	82.7	83.1	83.5	84.8	86.4	81.8	81.1	86.3	86.2	85.7	86.9	84.3
2008	84.1	83.5	83.9	84.5	85.9	86.9	82.2	81.3	86.5	85.7	84.7	85.8	84.6
2009	81.7	80.9	80.8	80.8	81.9	83.0	78.4	77.3	83.1	83.2	83.0	84.7	81.6
2010	81.4	80.9	80.8	82.2	83.6	84.7	80.2	79.1	83.6	83.9	83.7	86.2	82.5
2011	81.9	81.7	82.0	82.9	84.0	85.5	81.4	80.4	85.5	85.2	85.1	86.5	83.5
2012	82.8	82.4	82.8	83.1	84.5	86.2	81.7	80.9	85.8	86.0	85.7	88.0	84.2
2013	83.8	83.8	84.0	84.8	86.5	88.4	83.9	82.9	88.0	87.9	88.1	90.0	86.0
2014	86.5	86.6	87.1	88.1	90.2	92.1	87.4	86.5	92.1	92.1	93.0	96.4	89.8
2015	90.3	89.5	89.8	91.2	92.9	94.7	90.7	90.1	95.0	94.9	95.1	96.8	92.6
2016	92.5	92.1	92.2	93.5	95.2	96.8	93.0	91.8	97.1	98.0	99.0	102.2	95.3
2017	97.3	96.6	96.5	97.3	99.0	101.2	97.0	96.2	101.6	102.7	102.8	104.8	99.4
Information													
2007	86.5	86.8	87.7	88.3	88.0	89.0	89.9	90.0	90.0	88.9	88.9	89.5	88.6
2008	87.8	88.8	89.5	90.8	90.7	90.6	89.8	89.6	88.9	87.8	87.7	87.9	89.2
2009	86.9	85.6	85.7	85.3	85.2	86.0	85.3	86.2	87.1	86.1	86.2	86.0	86.0
2010	84.9	85.0	85.1	85.3	85.9	86.9	86.0	85.5	84.9	83.7	84.0	84.4	85.1
2011	83.5	83.6	84.0	84.0	84.5	85.7	87.0	83.4	85.6	85.7	85.5	85.9	84.9
2012	85.6	85.2	85.5	85.9	86.5	88.3	89.5	88.8	86.3	86.4	85.8	85.7	86.6
2013	84.9	84.9	84.9	85.4	85.9	87.5	88.0	87.8	86.6	86.1	87.9	86.4	86.4
2014	84.9	85.1	85.1	85.8	86.7	88.0	88.4	88.1	87.0	87.0	87.3	87.6	86.8
2015	87.3	87.0	87.3	87.7	87.9	89.3	89.7	89.4	88.1	88.7	88.9	89.1	88.4
2016	88.7	88.8	88.3	89.3	86.1	90.0	90.9	91.5	90.5	90.5	90.5	90.5	89.6
2017	89.7	90.8	90.6	90.9	92.1	91.9	93.0	93.6	91.9	90.4	90.8	89.8	91.3
Financial Activities													
2007	229.9	229.9	229.9	230.0	230.7	233.5	234.1	233.8	230.0	228.7	228.1	228.9	230.6
2008	226.9	226.6	226.9	227.2	227.7	230.2	231.4	230.9	227.7	226.8	225.9	226.0	227.9
2009	223.1	221.8	221.2	220.4	220.5	222.2	222.1	221.3	217.9	216.9	216.6	217.1	220.1
2010	214.6	213.9	213.6	213.7	214.8	216.5	217.8	217.6	214.8	214.4	213.9	215.0	215.1
2011	212.4	212.1	212.1	213.0	213.3	215.5	217.4	217.4	214.7	213.9	213.1	213.5	214.0
2012	211.4	211.5	211.5	211.8	212.8	215.9	216.5	216.7	213.4	213.0	212.7	213.3	213.4
2013	211.1	211.2	211.6	211.9	213.2	216.1	216.7	217.4	213.8	213.5	213.4	214.1	213.7
2014	211.6	211.4	211.6	212.6	214.3	217.1	218.1	218.0	214.7	215.0	215.1	215.8	214.6
2015	213.5	213.0	213.1	214.1	215.6	218.7	222.0	222.2	218.0	218.6	218.9	219.1	217.2
2016	217.6	217.7	217.2	218.7	219.8	222.6	225.6	225.6	221.4	220.6	220.3	221.4	220.7
2017	218.8	219.0	218.8	219.2	220.6	224.6	225.7	225.6	221.7	222.4	221.4	222.3	221.7
Professional and Business Services													
2007	461.9	463.8	467.2	480.2	484.7	492.4	490.4	492.5	487.5	488.3	489.8	489.5	482.4
2008	475.7	477.0	478.6	488.4	491.6	497.6	496.9	496.0	491.7	490.3	485.4	480.0	487.4
2009	461.5	457.1	455.1	461.1	460.1	462.8	461.6	460.5	456.8	457.0	456.0	455.4	458.8
2010	447.4	447.4	449.5	462.3	464.2	469.1	473.5	472.6	467.2	472.5	471.2	469.8	463.9
2011	460.3	461.3	461.3	477.8	478.0	484.4	489.7	488.2	485.5	488.7	488.6	486.2	479.2
2012	472.3	472.7	478.9	490.1	492.5	501.7	502.6	502.8	498.7	501.1	501.9	497.2	492.7
2013	484.8	488.0	490.5	504.2	508.0	515.4	516.9	517.6	511.4	514.1	515.3	511.8	506.5
2014	497.7	498.6	500.3	514.9	519.0	527.0	530.2	531.2	526.5	530.2	529.4	526.6	519.3
2015	512.1	512.2	515.4	530.9	537.6	545.4	549.6	549.4	541.4	547.6	547.8	543.5	536.1
2016	527.5	529.7	531.8	548.9	551.1	560.0	567.2	566.6	559.0	562.1	562.1	558.1	552.0
2017	543.9	546.2	549.5	562.3	564.6	574.2	579.3	577.8	570.2	575.8	575.4	569.4	565.7
Education and Health Services													
2007	629.3	640.6	642.4	648.2	642.0	629.2	631.6	630.1	643.2	657.3	661.4	662.2	643.1
2008	647.0	660.6	664.6	667.5	659.7	646.9	649.9	647.8	660.1	674.4	678.3	678.9	661.3
2009	663.8	675.9	679.6	682.4	674.5	660.0	661.1	662.2	674.5	686.3	690.7	691.7	675.5
2010	680.2	691.2	694.4	693.9	688.2	671.9	675.1	673.1	686.9	699.3	703.0	702.7	688.3
2011	688.2	699.5	703.4	705.3	698.8	683.2	688.4	686.0	700.4	710.0	714.6	714.5	699.4
2012	702.0	713.6	717.8	717.1	712.3	700.1	700.1	698.6	711.8	722.7	727.1	727.4	712.6
2013	713.4	721.2	726.9	731.1	726.2	714.5	712.5	709.3	719.8	732.2	735.2	736.7	723.3
2014	717.1	732.2	737.7	746.2	741.3	730.0	733.9	731.3	740.3	755.9	761.3	761.8	740.8
2015	740.9	754.2	761.1	766.6	766.4	753.2	755.0	751.3	759.9	776.1	781.4	780.3	762.2
2016	762.3	778.1	781.8	787.2	784.6	767.5	777.1	773.0	784.7	793.3	797.7	798.0	782.1
2017	779.4	793.4	798.7	801.8	798.3	787.3	787.6	784.0	794.2	801.7	806.7	804.3	794.8

1. Employment by Industry: Massachusetts, Selected Years, 2007–2017—*Continued*

(Numbers in thousands, not seasonally adjusted)

Industry and year	January	February	March	April	May	June	July	August	September	October	November	December	Annual average
Leisure and Hospitality													
2007	276.7	276.5	280.3	291.6	306.1	325.9	332.2	332.8	316.2	308.0	297.7	293.0	303.1
2008	280.1	281.3	285.1	297.7	314.4	329.6	335.2	335.8	318.7	310.8	297.0	291.9	306.5
2009	273.5	274.9	277.6	291.2	309.3	321.9	328.6	327.8	314.6	305.4	292.3	289.4	300.5
2010	279.4	278.1	280.6	299.6	314.2	328.3	337.4	336.5	322.0	316.5	302.9	299.0	307.9
2011	284.9	283.6	289.5	307.0	319.9	337.2	347.4	347.1	330.9	322.9	310.4	306.0	315.6
2012	296.1	295.9	301.5	316.3	330.8	353.8	358.2	358.6	341.2	331.8	318.3	315.4	326.5
2013	303.1	300.7	309.3	325.0	341.7	361.5	365.1	367.5	350.1	345.2	331.1	326.3	335.6
2014	311.0	310.3	318.1	331.2	350.3	369.1	376.4	376.8	357.8	352.1	337.9	335.8	343.9
2015	319.8	314.6	322.6	337.7	360.2	377.0	385.8	384.3	363.2	356.9	344.5	342.7	350.8
2016	327.8	327.4	334.4	351.8	368.0	388.6	398.0	397.1	375.8	365.4	353.8	350.7	361.6
2017	336.3	334.3	341.4	357.1	372.6	397.4	403.0	402.0	378.8	374.3	360.5	358.7	368.0
Other Services													
2007	115.9	116.4	117.4	118.3	120.0	124.2	125.9	125.4	120.8	119.9	120.3	120.5	120.4
2008	117.3	117.9	118.7	119.2	120.3	123.9	126.1	125.3	120.0	119.6	119.2	118.9	120.5
2009	115.8	115.8	116.8	117.9	119.3	123.0	124.4	123.7	118.0	117.8	117.3	117.6	119.0
2010	115.4	115.1	116.0	117.7	119.1	122.6	125.4	124.2	118.4	117.7	117.4	117.5	118.9
2011	115.4	115.8	117.5	119.3	120.2	123.5	126.4	125.6	120.1	119.7	119.6	119.9	120.3
2012	117.3	117.4	119.1	120.7	122.0	126.7	128.4	127.3	123.2	123.0	123.1	123.4	122.6
2013	121.2	121.3	123.6	125.7	127.3	132.0	134.2	133.8	128.8	128.5	128.8	129.5	127.9
2014	127.1	127.5	130.0	131.8	133.6	138.4	140.4	139.6	133.5	133.2	133.0	133.1	133.4
2015	130.3	128.6	131.1	132.9	134.5	139.2	141.8	140.8	134.3	134.1	133.8	134.0	134.6
2016	131.2	131.2	133.2	135.2	136.5	141.0	143.6	142.7	135.5	135.6	135.0	135.3	136.3
2017	132.8	132.4	134.3	136.3	137.3	142.5	144.2	143.7	137.0	139.4	138.4	137.7	138.0
Government													
2007	429.9	439.7	440.8	442.0	444.7	435.9	401.5	394.9	433.7	441.8	444.0	443.2	432.7
2008	433.3	444.9	445.6	447.3	448.7	438.7	406.4	399.5	437.6	447.1	448.2	446.8	437.0
2009	435.8	448.2	447.5	453.0	450.2	439.0	405.3	397.6	434.6	447.2	447.0	449.6	437.9
2010	438.5	446.2	447.3	451.3	460.2	442.0	405.8	397.5	436.5	446.8	450.5	449.2	439.3
2011	432.8	445.2	445.6	445.4	447.5	436.0	401.9	393.4	436.3	443.1	443.8	445.7	434.7
2012	431.7	443.9	447.0	446.7	448.3	439.0	403.7	397.7	440.3	446.9	451.6	449.6	437.2
2013	433.8	451.0	452.4	456.6	456.1	444.4	408.7	402.0	441.7	453.9	458.1	458.5	443.1
2014	444.0	458.1	458.7	464.6	463.2	451.0	417.1	409.2	454.0	462.8	469.7	467.4	451.7
2015	444.3	459.2	463.2	465.5	461.3	454.4	419.3	408.2	448.7	460.4	463.7	465.1	451.1
2016	444.8	459.3	466.0	463.8	464.1	454.1	422.3	413.9	457.7	463.1	470.5	466.3	453.8
2017	449.0	460.7	461.1	463.3	463.3	456.9	419.4	411.8	452.4	461.9	464.9	465.9	452.6

2. Average Weekly Hours by Selected Industry: Massachusetts, 2013–2017

(Not seasonally adjusted)

Industry and year	January	February	March	April	May	June	July	August	September	October	November	December	Annual average
Total Private													
2013	32.7	33.0	32.9	33.0	33.1	33.3	33.3	33.5	33.7	33.3	33.2	33.6	33.2
2014	33.0	33.1	33.3	33.2	33.2	33.4	33.2	33.4	33.4	33.3	33.7	33.4	33.3
2015	33.1	33.0	33.4	33.3	33.4	33.4	33.5	33.8	33.5	33.5	33.8	33.7	33.5
2016	33.2	33.0	33.2	33.3	33.7	33.5	33.6	33.5	33.5	33.8	33.4	33.5	33.4
2017	33.6	33.0	33.0	33.6	33.4	33.3	33.7	33.5	33.6	33.7	33.5	33.5	33.5
Goods Producing													
2013	39.3	39.2	39.3	39.3	39.5	39.6	39.2	39.8	39.8	39.9	39.4	40.0	39.5
2014	39.2	38.8	39.6	39.7	39.6	39.5	39.1	39.4	40.0	39.3	39.9	39.5	39.5
2015	39.3	38.0	39.5	39.2	39.6	39.9	39.5	39.9	38.8	39.4	39.5	40.3	39.4
2016	39.6	38.9	39.6	39.4	40.0	40.1	39.9	39.8	39.9	39.6	39.5	39.6	39.7
2017	39.7	38.2	38.4	38.9	39.1	39.3	39.1	39.4	39.6	39.2	39.7	39.4	39.2
Construction													
2013	38.0	37.1	37.3	38.0	38.6	38.2	38.0	38.9	38.3	38.2	37.3	37.7	38.0
2014	37.6	36.8	37.5	38.3	38.5	37.8	37.8	37.8	38.9	37.3	37.7	37.3	37.8
2015	37.4	35.1	37.8	37.7	38.9	39.3	38.9	39.2	37.5	38.0	37.7	39.2	38.1
2016	38.1	36.5	38.1	37.9	39.0	39.6	39.2	38.9	39.5	38.4	38.0	37.9	38.5
2017	37.8	36.5	36.3	38.0	38.1	38.5	38.0	38.6	38.7	37.9	38.7	38.5	38.0
Manufacturing													
2013	39.7	40.0	40.1	39.8	39.8	40.2	39.7	40.1	40.4	40.4	40.2	40.9	40.1
2014	39.8	39.6	40.4	40.2	40.0	40.3	39.6	40.2	40.4	40.3	41.1	40.9	40.2
2015	40.5	39.7	40.5	40.1	40.1	40.3	40.0	40.5	39.8	40.1	40.5	40.7	40.2
2016	40.2	40.0	40.3	40.1	40.4	40.3	40.3	40.4	40.2	40.4	40.5	40.6	40.3
2017	40.7	39.6	39.9	40.3	40.4	40.5	40.4	40.4	40.7	40.4	40.6	40.3	40.4
Trade, Transportation, and Utilities													
2013	32.0	32.3	32.3	32.5	32.9	32.8	33.0	33.3	33.6	33.1	32.7	33.6	32.8
2014	32.5	32.2	32.5	32.7	32.9	33.1	33.1	33.3	33.2	33.0	33.1	33.5	32.9
2015	32.4	32.1	32.7	32.9	33.1	33.3	33.5	33.1	33.1	32.9	33.3	33.6	33.0
2016	32.6	32.4	32.7	33.0	33.3	33.5	33.6	33.4	33.8	33.8	33.7	34.5	33.4
2017	33.3	32.8	32.9	33.5	33.4	33.3	33.6	33.3	33.4	33.3	33.4	33.9	33.3
Information													
2013	35.8	35.6	35.9	35.2	35.1	36.9	36.0	35.9	36.7	35.8	36.1	37.4	36.0
2014	36.4	37.1	37.5	36.2	36.3	37.7	36.5	36.7	36.7	36.7	38.1	36.4	36.9
2015	37.1	38.5	38.5	37.2	37.9	37.3	37.7	39.1	37.6	37.5	38.7	37.4	37.9
2016	38.2	38.1	38.1	38.1	39.1	37.7	37.8	38.2	38.0	39.6	38.4	37.8	38.3
2017	39.6	38.2	37.9	39.5	38.2	38.0	39.6	37.7	38.0	39.1	37.5	37.8	38.4
Financial Activities													
2013	35.4	35.9	36.0	35.9	35.8	36.8	36.1	36.2	37.1	36.2	36.2	36.9	36.2
2014	36.2	37.1	37.1	36.6	36.5	37.0	36.2	36.3	36.5	36.5	37.0	36.4	36.6
2015	36.5	37.1	37.1	36.7	36.6	36.5	36.7	37.4	36.7	36.7	37.3	36.6	36.8
2016	36.2	36.3	36.5	36.2	37.1	36.7	36.8	36.8	36.8	37.7	37.0	37.3	36.8
2017	37.9	37.5	37.2	38.0	37.3	37.1	38.0	37.1	37.5	38.1	37.8	37.8	37.6
Professional and Business Services													
2013	34.7	35.4	35.2	35.4	35.5	36.3	35.7	36.0	36.5	35.9	36.0	36.4	35.8
2014	35.8	36.3	36.3	36.0	36.1	36.6	35.9	35.8	35.8	35.8	36.8	35.6	36.1
2015	35.4	36.0	36.1	35.9	36.2	36.1	35.8	36.8	36.0	36.3	37.1	36.7	36.2
2016	36.3	35.7	36.1	36.2	37.0	36.4	36.1	36.0	35.9	36.7	35.9	35.8	36.2
2017	36.1	35.4	35.2	36.4	35.7	35.9	36.2	35.7	36.0	36.4	36.0	36.1	35.9
Education and Health Services													
2013	31.6	31.8	31.6	31.7	31.7	31.8	31.9	31.9	32.0	31.9	32.0	32.0	31.8
2014	31.8	31.8	31.6	31.6	31.5	31.8	31.6	31.6	31.8	32.0	32.0	31.9	31.8
2015	31.8	31.7	31.7	31.5	31.5	31.7	31.8	31.9	32.1	32.1	31.9	31.7	31.8
2016	31.5	31.5	31.5	31.6	31.6	31.4	31.8	31.7	31.7	31.8	31.5	31.6	31.6
2017	32.0	31.7	31.6	31.7	31.7	31.6	31.8	31.9	31.9	32.0	31.7	31.5	31.8
Leisure and Hospitality													
2013	24.8	24.6	25.1	25.4	25.6	25.5	26.4	26.3	26.0	25.4	24.8	24.4	25.4
2014	23.9	24.0	24.8	25.1	25.5	25.3	25.8	26.0	25.5	25.2	25.0	25.0	25.1
2015	24.6	24.1	25.3	25.4	26.1	25.6	26.2	26.2	25.7	25.4	25.2	25.1	25.4
2016	24.2	24.8	24.6	25.1	25.4	25.3	25.8	25.4	25.2	25.0	25.0	24.2	25.0
2017	24.0	23.9	24.5	25.3	25.4	25.5	26.0	26.2	25.7	25.4	24.8	24.5	25.1
Other Services													
2013	28.8	28.8	28.3	28.0	27.9	27.3	28.3	28.8	27.7	27.5	27.4	27.7	28.0
2014	27.4	27.9	28.3	28.3	28.2	28.0	29.3	29.7	28.9	28.9	29.1	29.0	28.6
2015	29.1	28.9	29.1	29.1	28.7	28.6	29.9	30.4	29.7	29.0	29.8	29.6	29.3
2016	29.5	28.8	28.8	28.7	28.8	28.8	30.2	30.4	29.2	29.0	28.5	28.4	29.1
2017	28.6	28.2	28.7	29.1	29.1	29.0	30.5	30.1	29.6	29.3	29.5	29.9	29.3

3. Average Hourly Earnings by Selected Industry: Massachusetts, 2013–2017

(Dollars, not seasonally adjusted)

Industry and year	January	February	March	April	May	June	July	August	September	October	November	December	Annual average
Total Private													
2013	28.74	28.96	28.86	28.79	28.60	28.83	28.58	28.63	29.18	29.07	29.23	29.49	28.91
2014	29.48	29.85	29.65	29.33	29.20	29.13	29.02	29.25	29.54	29.75	30.20	29.80	29.52
2015	30.48	30.57	30.36	30.23	30.17	29.92	29.88	30.21	30.39	30.79	31.20	30.96	30.43
2016	31.36	31.25	31.04	31.06	31.08	30.73	30.83	30.73	31.32	31.83	31.71	31.79	31.23
2017	32.26	32.27	32.15	32.29	31.71	31.62	31.89	31.52	32.08	32.46	32.63	32.60	32.12
Goods Producing													
2013	29.45	30.00	29.90	30.08	30.15	29.94	30.15	30.24	30.18	30.13	30.42	30.57	30.11
2014	30.66	30.54	30.27	30.37	30.23	30.40	31.08	30.84	30.80	30.96	30.89	31.51	30.72
2015	31.74	31.70	31.55	31.67	31.67	31.44	31.68	32.08	31.81	32.33	32.45	32.34	31.88
2016	31.90	31.95	32.16	31.95	31.95	31.95	32.16	32.16	32.27	32.34	32.01	32.29	32.09
2017	32.64	33.04	33.39	33.69	33.55	33.71	33.59	33.75	34.25	34.26	34.47	34.81	33.78
Construction													
2013	33.01	34.02	33.67	33.62	33.45	33.35	33.25	33.60	33.44	33.17	33.98	34.43	33.58
2014	35.22	34.89	34.59	34.51	33.89	34.08	34.23	34.54	34.46	34.48	35.03	35.70	34.62
2015	36.38	36.43	36.57	36.70	36.11	35.59	35.98	36.19	35.82	36.68	36.64	37.17	36.34
2016	36.52	36.39	36.69	36.53	36.74	36.59	36.61	36.64	36.56	36.44	36.41	37.14	36.61
2017	37.50	37.23	37.41	37.31	36.91	37.26	36.92	36.63	36.86	36.31	36.56	37.09	36.98
Manufacturing													
2013	27.92	28.01	28.04	28.18	28.33	28.11	28.47	28.44	28.53	28.57	28.69	28.82	28.34
2014	28.60	28.61	28.35	28.47	28.45	28.41	29.36	28.77	28.71	29.00	28.60	29.76	28.72
2015	29.41	29.51	29.16	29.12	29.18	29.03	29.11	29.57	29.44	29.60	29.80	29.31	29.35
2016	29.16	29.46	29.49	29.19	29.00	28.89	29.24	29.26	29.50	29.78	29.35	29.49	29.32
2017	29.96	30.40	30.89	31.35	31.37	31.40	31.39	31.42	32.14	32.73	32.92	33.14	31.66
Trade, Transportation, and Utilities													
2013	23.38	23.32	23.39	23.39	23.18	23.47	23.60	23.46	23.80	24.12	24.07	24.14	23.62
2014	24.89	25.05	24.99	25.11	24.81	24.68	24.83	24.36	24.57	24.84	24.94	24.36	24.78
2015	25.20	24.72	24.82	25.08	24.78	24.47	25.02	24.61	24.73	25.45	25.32	25.18	24.95
2016	26.08	25.60	25.56	25.31	25.71	25.87	25.92	26.00	26.34	26.91	26.74	26.22	26.03
2017	26.78	26.55	26.52	26.52	26.07	26.01	26.42	25.81	26.28	26.79	26.71	26.21	26.39
Information													
2013	42.17	42.65	42.51	41.72	42.38	42.48	42.90	43.79	43.24	42.90	43.41	43.51	42.82
2014	43.62	42.96	42.16	41.30	42.66	41.93	41.55	43.13	42.23	43.36	43.73	43.29	42.66
2015	45.49	45.80	45.35	45.78	45.23	45.88	44.95	43.97	45.14	45.64	46.01	46.36	45.46
2016	47.50	46.54	45.99	45.52	44.89	45.19	44.46	43.43	44.81	45.73	45.28	45.45	45.39
2017	47.10	45.62	45.55	46.24	44.67	45.10	46.53	45.59	45.00	45.89	45.54	46.69	45.80
Financial Activities													
2013	34.68	34.96	33.66	34.20	34.01	35.01	34.14	34.39	35.34	34.66	33.99	34.23	34.44
2014	34.37	35.49	35.52	36.14	36.23	34.76	35.13	35.61	36.86	36.65	37.18	36.48	35.87
2015	37.54	37.25	37.81	37.86	37.42	37.61	37.68	38.54	38.06	38.79	39.10	38.95	38.06
2016	40.10	39.78	38.90	40.22	39.90	38.42	40.26	39.47	40.03	41.05	40.92	40.25	39.95
2017	41.01	41.22	41.90	42.22	41.08	41.22	41.68	41.73	42.30	42.57	42.73	42.31	41.83
Professional and Business Services													
2013	36.54	36.48	36.61	36.46	36.29	36.51	36.37	36.09	37.01	36.88	36.86	37.58	36.64
2014	37.16	37.71	37.94	36.60	36.63	36.81	36.49	37.28	37.44	37.66	38.32	38.08	37.34
2015	38.89	39.18	39.15	38.28	38.32	37.77	37.93	38.70	38.70	38.71	39.33	38.65	38.63
2016	39.52	39.98	39.75	39.67	39.76	38.97	39.03	38.92	39.88	40.25	39.92	40.34	39.66
2017	41.61	41.20	41.20	41.25	40.43	40.05	40.57	40.10	40.23	40.72	40.67	40.04	40.66
Education and Health Services													
2013	28.34	28.49	28.74	28.54	28.34	28.64	28.32	28.61	29.03	28.63	28.99	29.02	28.64
2014	28.46	28.91	28.55	28.35	28.16	28.40	28.11	28.54	28.62	28.76	29.34	28.66	28.58
2015	28.90	28.84	28.40	28.41	28.88	28.73	28.32	28.58	29.13	29.23	29.96	29.89	28.94
2016	29.46	29.22	28.85	29.20	29.15	29.07	29.21	28.92	29.28	29.56	29.88	30.19	29.34
2017	29.42	29.74	29.20	29.38	29.00	29.22	29.44	28.97	29.65	29.98	30.48	31.07	29.63
Leisure and Hospitality													
2013	15.21	15.38	15.39	15.45	15.32	15.21	15.12	15.13	15.44	15.55	15.49	15.73	15.36
2014	15.53	15.66	15.56	15.46	15.48	15.31	15.21	15.35	15.53	15.59	15.72	15.71	15.50
2015	15.66	15.82	15.70	15.63	15.75	15.62	15.72	15.67	15.77	15.91	15.78	15.72	15.73
2016	15.77	15.88	16.06	16.01	15.89	15.88	15.87	16.22	16.65	16.82	16.96	17.30	16.27
2017	17.22	17.42	17.42	17.30	17.50	17.20	17.15	17.21	17.58	17.66	17.81	17.83	17.44
Other Services													
2013	22.48	22.64	22.13	22.04	22.14	21.91	20.93	20.91	22.06	21.94	21.71	22.27	21.92
2014	22.38	22.78	22.62	22.61	22.66	22.71	21.92	22.08	23.33	23.38	23.52	23.71	22.80
2015	23.97	24.66	24.44	24.54	24.67	24.49	23.45	23.81	25.31	25.59	25.75	26.12	24.72
2016	26.00	26.55	26.21	26.08	26.69	26.14	25.05	25.03	26.86	27.18	27.02	27.19	26.31
2017	27.62	28.04	27.85	27.95	27.86	27.16	26.41	26.32	27.74	27.31	27.53	27.51	27.42

4. Average Weekly Earnings by Selected Industry: Massachusetts, 2013–2017

(Dollars, not seasonally adjusted)

Industry and year	January	February	March	April	May	June	July	August	September	October	November	December	Annual average
Total Private													
2013	939.80	955.68	949.49	950.07	946.66	960.04	951.71	959.11	983.37	968.03	970.44	990.86	959.81
2014	972.84	988.04	987.35	973.76	969.44	972.94	963.46	976.95	986.64	990.68	1,017.74	995.32	983.02
2015	1,008.89	1,008.81	1,014.02	1,006.66	1,007.68	999.33	1,000.98	1,021.10	1,018.07	1,031.47	1,054.56	1,043.35	1,019.41
2016	1,041.15	1,031.25	1,030.53	1,034.30	1,047.40	1,029.46	1,035.89	1,029.46	1,049.22	1,075.85	1,059.11	1,064.97	1,043.08
2017	1,083.94	1,064.91	1,060.95	1,084.94	1,059.11	1,052.95	1,074.69	1,055.92	1,077.89	1,093.90	1,093.11	1,092.10	1,076.02
Goods Producing													
2013	1,157.39	1,176.00	1,175.07	1,182.14	1,190.93	1,185.62	1,181.88	1,203.55	1,201.16	1,202.19	1,198.55	1,222.80	1,189.35
2014	1,201.87	1,184.95	1,198.69	1,205.69	1,197.11	1,200.80	1,215.23	1,215.10	1,232.00	1,216.73	1,232.51	1,244.65	1,213.44
2015	1,247.38	1,204.60	1,246.23	1,241.46	1,254.13	1,254.46	1,251.36	1,279.99	1,234.23	1,273.80	1,281.78	1,303.30	1,256.07
2016	1,263.24	1,242.86	1,273.54	1,258.83	1,278.00	1,281.20	1,283.18	1,279.97	1,287.57	1,280.66	1,264.40	1,278.68	1,273.97
2017	1,295.81	1,262.13	1,282.18	1,310.54	1,311.81	1,324.80	1,313.37	1,329.75	1,356.30	1,342.99	1,368.46	1,371.51	1,324.18
Construction													
2013	1,254.38	1,262.14	1,255.89	1,277.56	1,291.17	1,273.97	1,263.50	1,307.04	1,280.75	1,267.09	1,267.45	1,298.01	1,276.04
2014	1,324.27	1,283.95	1,297.13	1,321.73	1,304.77	1,288.22	1,293.89	1,305.61	1,340.49	1,286.10	1,320.63	1,331.61	1,308.64
2015	1,360.61	1,278.69	1,382.35	1,383.59	1,404.68	1,398.69	1,399.62	1,418.65	1,343.25	1,393.84	1,381.33	1,457.06	1,384.55
2016	1,391.41	1,328.24	1,397.89	1,384.49	1,432.86	1,448.96	1,435.11	1,425.30	1,444.12	1,399.30	1,383.58	1,407.61	1,409.49
2017	1,417.50	1,358.90	1,357.98	1,417.78	1,406.27	1,434.51	1,402.96	1,413.92	1,426.48	1,376.15	1,414.87	1,427.97	1,405.24
Manufacturing													
2013	1,108.42	1,120.40	1,124.40	1,121.56	1,127.53	1,130.02	1,130.26	1,140.44	1,152.61	1,154.23	1,153.34	1,178.74	1,136.43
2014	1,138.28	1,132.96	1,145.34	1,144.49	1,138.00	1,144.92	1,162.66	1,156.55	1,159.88	1,168.70	1,175.46	1,196.73	1,154.54
2015	1,191.11	1,171.55	1,180.98	1,167.71	1,170.12	1,169.91	1,164.40	1,197.59	1,171.71	1,186.96	1,206.90	1,192.92	1,179.87
2016	1,172.23	1,178.40	1,188.45	1,170.52	1,171.60	1,164.27	1,178.37	1,182.10	1,185.90	1,203.11	1,188.68	1,197.29	1,181.60
2017	1,219.67	1,204.14	1,233.13	1,262.46	1,267.66	1,271.70	1,268.78	1,269.68	1,307.78	1,322.29	1,336.55	1,335.54	1,279.06
Trade, Transportation, and Utilities													
2013	748.16	753.24	755.50	760.18	762.62	769.82	778.80	781.22	799.68	798.37	787.09	811.10	774.74
2014	808.93	806.61	812.18	821.10	816.25	816.91	821.87	811.19	815.72	819.72	825.51	816.06	815.26
2015	816.48	793.51	811.61	825.13	820.22	814.85	838.17	814.59	818.56	837.31	843.16	846.05	823.35
2016	850.21	829.44	835.81	835.23	856.14	866.65	870.91	868.40	890.29	909.56	901.14	904.59	869.40
2017	891.77	870.84	872.51	888.42	870.74	866.13	887.71	859.47	877.75	892.11	892.11	888.52	878.79
Information													
2013	1,509.69	1,518.34	1,526.11	1,468.54	1,487.54	1,567.51	1,544.40	1,572.06	1,586.91	1,535.82	1,567.10	1,627.27	1,541.52
2014	1,587.77	1,593.82	1,581.00	1,495.06	1,548.56	1,580.76	1,516.58	1,582.87	1,549.84	1,591.31	1,666.11	1,575.76	1,574.15
2015	1,687.68	1,763.30	1,745.98	1,703.02	1,714.22	1,711.32	1,694.62	1,719.23	1,697.26	1,711.50	1,780.59	1,733.86	1,722.93
2016	1,814.50	1,773.17	1,752.22	1,734.31	1,755.20	1,703.66	1,680.59	1,659.03	1,702.78	1,810.91	1,738.75	1,718.01	1,738.44
2017	1,865.16	1,742.68	1,726.35	1,826.48	1,706.39	1,713.80	1,842.59	1,718.74	1,710.00	1,794.30	1,707.75	1,764.88	1,758.72
Financial Activities													
2013	1,227.67	1,255.06	1,211.76	1,227.78	1,217.56	1,288.37	1,232.45	1,244.92	1,311.11	1,254.69	1,230.44	1,263.09	1,246.73
2014	1,244.19	1,316.68	1,317.79	1,322.72	1,322.40	1,286.12	1,271.71	1,292.64	1,345.39	1,337.73	1,375.66	1,327.87	1,312.84
2015	1,370.21	1,381.98	1,402.75	1,389.46	1,369.57	1,372.77	1,382.86	1,441.40	1,396.80	1,423.59	1,458.43	1,425.57	1,400.61
2016	1,451.62	1,444.01	1,419.85	1,455.96	1,480.29	1,410.01	1,481.57	1,452.50	1,473.10	1,547.59	1,514.04	1,501.33	1,470.16
2017	1,554.28	1,545.75	1,558.68	1,604.36	1,532.28	1,529.26	1,583.84	1,548.18	1,586.25	1,621.92	1,615.19	1,599.32	1,572.81
Professional and Business Services													
2013	1,267.94	1,291.39	1,288.67	1,290.68	1,288.30	1,325.31	1,298.41	1,299.24	1,350.87	1,323.99	1,326.96	1,367.91	1,311.71
2014	1,330.33	1,368.87	1,377.22	1,317.60	1,322.34	1,347.25	1,309.99	1,334.62	1,340.35	1,348.23	1,410.18	1,355.65	1,347.97
2015	1,376.71	1,410.48	1,413.32	1,374.25	1,387.18	1,363.50	1,357.89	1,424.16	1,393.20	1,405.17	1,459.14	1,418.46	1,398.41
2016	1,434.58	1,427.29	1,434.98	1,436.05	1,471.12	1,418.51	1,408.98	1,401.12	1,431.69	1,477.18	1,433.13	1,444.17	1,435.69
2017	1,502.12	1,458.48	1,450.24	1,501.50	1,443.35	1,437.80	1,468.63	1,431.57	1,448.28	1,482.21	1,464.12	1,445.44	1,459.69
Education and Health Services													
2013	895.54	905.98	908.18	904.72	898.38	910.75	903.41	912.66	928.96	913.30	927.68	928.64	910.75
2014	905.03	919.34	902.18	895.86	887.04	903.12	888.28	901.86	910.12	920.32	938.88	914.25	908.84
2015	919.02	914.23	900.28	894.92	909.72	910.74	900.58	911.70	935.07	938.28	955.72	947.51	920.61
2016	927.99	920.43	908.78	922.72	921.14	912.80	928.88	916.76	928.18	940.01	941.22	954.00	927.14
2017	941.44	942.76	922.72	931.35	919.30	923.35	936.19	924.14	945.84	959.36	966.22	978.71	942.23
Leisure and Hospitality													
2013	377.21	378.35	386.29	392.43	392.19	387.86	399.17	397.92	401.44	394.97	384.15	383.81	390.14
2014	371.17	375.84	385.89	388.05	394.74	387.34	392.42	399.10	396.02	392.87	393.00	392.75	389.05
2015	385.24	381.26	397.21	397.00	411.08	399.87	411.86	410.55	405.29	404.11	397.66	394.57	399.54
2016	381.63	393.82	395.08	401.85	403.61	401.76	409.45	411.99	419.58	420.50	424.00	418.66	406.75
2017	413.28	416.34	426.79	437.69	444.50	438.60	445.90	450.90	451.81	448.56	441.69	436.84	437.74
Other Services													
2013	647.42	652.03	626.28	617.12	617.71	598.14	592.32	602.21	611.06	603.35	594.85	616.88	613.76
2014	613.21	635.56	640.15	639.86	639.01	635.88	642.26	655.78	674.24	675.68	684.43	687.59	652.08
2015	697.53	712.67	711.20	714.11	708.03	700.41	701.16	723.82	751.71	742.11	767.35	773.15	724.30
2016	767.00	764.64	754.85	748.50	768.67	752.83	756.51	760.91	784.31	788.22	770.07	772.20	765.62
2017	789.93	790.73	799.30	813.35	810.73	787.64	805.51	792.23	821.10	800.18	812.14	822.55	803.41

MICHIGAN
At a Glance

Population:
  2010 census: 9,883,640
  2017 estimate: 9,962,311

Percent change in population:
  2010–2017: 0.8%

Percent change in total nonfarm employment:
  2007–2017: 2.4%

Industry with the largest growth in employment, 2007–2017 (thousands):
  Education and health services, 74.6

Industry with the largest decline or smallest growth in employment, 2007–2017 (thousands):
  Government, -51.7

Civilian labor force:
  2010: 4,798,954
  2017: 4,883,815

Unemployment rate and rank among states (highest to lowest):
  2010: 12.6%, 2nd
  2017: 4.6%, 18th

Over-the-year change in unemployment rates:
  2015–2016: -0.4%
  2016–2017: -0.4%

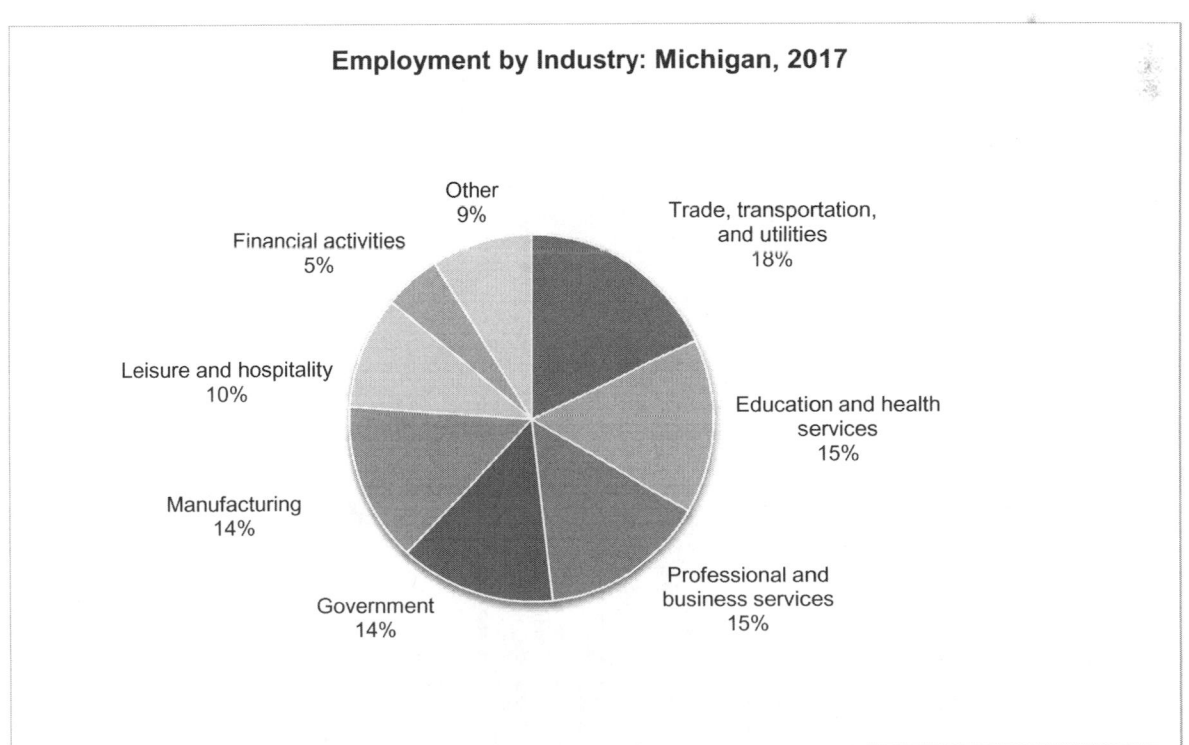

Employment by Industry: Michigan, 2017

- Other 9%
- Financial activities 5%
- Leisure and hospitality 10%
- Manufacturing 14%
- Government 14%
- Trade, transportation, and utilities 18%
- Education and health services 15%
- Professional and business services 15%

1. Employment by Industry: Michigan, Selected Years, 2007–2017

(Numbers in thousands, not seasonally adjusted)

Industry and year	January	February	March	April	May	June	July	August	September	October	November	December	Annual average
Total Nonfarm													
2007	4,185.9	4,212.6	4,233.5	4,262.1	4,325.8	4,330.4	4,214.4	4,256.5	4,302.6	4,294.3	4,306.1	4,293.1	4,268.1
2008	4,145.9	4,159.1	4,159.4	4,173.1	4,225.9	4,244.1	4,112.8	4,148.0	4,180.4	4,168.9	4,139.5	4,092.4	4,162.5
2009	3,863.9	3,882.2	3,872.4	3,896.0	3,911.2	3,882.9	3,793.8	3,818.7	3,876.7	3,896.3	3,886.8	3,869.2	3,870.8
2010	3,752.2	3,768.7	3,781.1	3,839.0	3,896.1	3,907.9	3,846.1	3,851.5	3,913.8	3,941.7	3,942.6	3,922.7	3,863.6
2011	3,832.0	3,846.9	3,874.6	3,926.4	3,972.7	3,986.1	3,931.5	3,952.7	4,012.8	4,033.9	4,038.6	4,017.4	3,952.1
2012	3,929.8	3,948.5	3,976.7	4,015.6	4,061.4	4,069.0	4,007.2	4,026.6	4,076.8	4,095.2	4,102.9	4,092.9	4,033.6
2013	4,004.4	4,029.5	4,051.5	4,068.7	4,138.6	4,149.9	4,072.5	4,106.0	4,156.7	4,181.5	4,185.7	4,169.6	4,109.6
2014	4,065.1	4,098.8	4,114.7	4,136.4	4,212.1	4,242.8	4,163.2	4,180.4	4,215.7	4,245.6	4,253.8	4,251.5	4,181.7
2015	4,141.5	4,157.6	4,173.9	4,205.8	4,274.6	4,289.8	4,225.0	4,237.3	4,275.7	4,313.1	4,316.0	4,307.5	4,243.2
2016	4,214.5	4,232.8	4,250.0	4,300.1	4,341.2	4,363.7	4,308.0	4,314.3	4,363.6	4,378.8	4,393.4	4,368.7	4,319.1
2017	4,281.6	4,297.1	4,317.0	4,349.2	4,402.2	4,429.0	4,344.1	4,366.1	4,401.9	4,423.6	4,433.2	4,410.2	4,371.3
Total Private													
2007	3,525.7	3,534.7	3,550.5	3,587.8	3,652.4	3,683.6	3,623.1	3,662.4	3,647.8	3,623.0	3,633.4	3,624.7	3,612.4
2008	3,496.7	3,493.6	3,492.5	3,504.9	3,567.9	3,602.2	3,519.8	3,549.4	3,525.6	3,498.2	3,467.8	3,430.4	3,512.4
2009	3,211.2	3,217.2	3,206.4	3,226.7	3,251.3	3,243.8	3,204.2	3,229.1	3,231.0	3,232.3	3,222.3	3,213.2	3,224.1
2010	3,110.5	3,113.3	3,125.2	3,180.5	3,239.0	3,274.3	3,261.4	3,275.5	3,283.7	3,295.6	3,294.4	3,282.6	3,228.0
2011	3,207.0	3,210.7	3,236.2	3,288.8	3,349.2	3,376.7	3,366.4	3,391.0	3,393.1	3,401.9	3,403.9	3,391.5	3,334.7
2012	3,314.0	3,320.6	3,348.4	3,388.0	3,445.5	3,472.9	3,451.7	3,470.9	3,464.5	3,472.3	3,476.6	3,475.4	3,425.1
2013	3,401.3	3,413.5	3,436.5	3,453.3	3,534.4	3,564.1	3,525.5	3,561.0	3,552.0	3,564.2	3,567.4	3,558.9	3,511.0
2014	3,468.0	3,488.0	3,503.5	3,525.1	3,612.8	3,658.0	3,617.1	3,635.0	3,616.4	3,630.3	3,636.1	3,640.7	3,585.9
2015	3,546.8	3,549.3	3,564.3	3,596.3	3,674.4	3,709.3	3,679.6	3,693.1	3,681.0	3,697.7	3,699.9	3,696.3	3,649.0
2016	3,619.1	3,622.6	3,636.0	3,686.2	3,742.9	3,776.9	3,755.9	3,762.1	3,754.4	3,759.7	3,768.9	3,751.5	3,719.7
2017	3,680.6	3,683.4	3,700.9	3,733.6	3,798.0	3,836.4	3,788.5	3,811.6	3,787.8	3,796.0	3,804.2	3,786.6	3,767.3
Goods Producing													
2007	762.0	770.2	772.9	780.1	794.3	804.6	775.6	801.2	794.6	777.7	780.8	769.6	782.0
2008	735.1	732.7	721.4	719.5	733.5	758.8	713.4	737.6	730.3	718.0	706.0	682.1	724.0
2009	588.9	599.8	594.4	593.5	583.4	578.4	577.3	594.8	596.0	597.4	588.6	580.3	589.4
2010	559.5	556.6	559.4	577.5	593.1	605.6	608.6	609.1	619.1	622.2	617.8	608.0	594.7
2011	593.0	593.5	598.8	615.1	633.0	647.4	647.4	658.4	657.7	658.3	657.8	651.7	634.3
2012	636.2	634.8	641.8	651.8	666.7	678.3	679.9	684.6	683.5	682.7	678.7	675.4	666.2
2013	658.7	659.5	664.6	668.2	689.9	702.1	695.7	710.2	709.7	711.8	709.9	698.5	689.9
2014	682.0	690.9	693.2	701.0	725.3	746.4	741.0	748.6	740.6	741.5	742.4	738.7	724.3
2015	717.4	717.0	719.1	730.0	749.2	763.4	759.9	765.6	763.8	761.6	761.1	753.7	746.8
2016	741.6	738.4	740.8	758.3	769.0	782.8	778.6	780.1	780.0	779.2	782.3	770.5	766.8
2017	760.3	759.5	762.2	773.7	789.6	802.5	788.7	802.7	795.2	797.6	795.6	787.2	784.6
Service-Providing													
2007	3423.9	3442.4	3460.6	3482.0	3531.5	3525.8	3438.8	3455.3	3508.0	3516.6	3525.3	3523.5	3486.1
2008	3410.8	3426.4	3438.0	3453.6	3492.4	3485.3	3399.4	3410.4	3450.1	3450.9	3433.5	3410.3	3438.4
2009	3275.0	3282.4	3278.0	3302.5	3327.8	3304.5	3216.5	3223.9	3280.7	3298.9	3298.2	3288.9	3281.4
2010	3192.7	3212.1	3221.7	3261.5	3303.0	3302.3	3237.5	3242.4	3294.7	3319.5	3324.8	3314.7	3268.9
2011	3239.0	3253.4	3275.8	3311.3	3339.7	3338.7	3284.1	3294.3	3355.1	3375.6	3380.8	3365.7	3317.8
2012	3293.6	3313.7	3334.9	3363.8	3394.7	3390.7	3327.3	3342	3393.3	3412.5	3424.2	3417.5	3367.4
2013	3345.7	3370.0	3386.9	3400.5	3448.7	3447.8	3376.8	3395.8	3447.0	3469.7	3475.8	3471.1	3419.7
2014	3383.1	3407.9	3421.5	3435.4	3486.8	3496.4	3422.2	3431.8	3475.1	3504.1	3511.4	3512.8	3457.4
2015	3424.1	3440.6	3454.8	3475.8	3525.4	3526.4	3465.1	3471.7	3511.9	3551.5	3554.9	3553.8	3496.3
2016	3472.9	3494.4	3509.2	3541.8	3572.2	3580.9	3529.4	3534.2	3583.6	3599.6	3611.1	3598.2	3552.3
2017	3521.3	3537.6	3554.8	3575.5	3612.6	3626.5	3555.4	3563.4	3606.7	3626.0	3637.6	3623.0	3586.7
Mining and Logging													
2007	7.2	7.2	7.0	7.3	7.8	8.2	8.2	8.1	8.0	7.9	7.7	7.4	7.7
2008	7.1	7.1	7.1	7.5	8.0	8.2	8.4	8.4	8.3	8.2	8.1	7.8	7.9
2009	6.7	6.9	6.3	6.5	6.8	7.1	7.2	7.2	7.2	7.2	7.0	6.8	6.9
2010	6.6	6.5	6.2	6.8	7.2	7.5	7.6	7.6	7.5	7.5	7.3	7.0	7.1
2011	6.7	6.7	6.7	7.0	7.5	7.8	7.9	7.9	7.8	7.9	7.8	7.6	7.4
2012	7.4	7.5	7.3	7.7	8.0	8.0	8.0	8.1	8.2	8.1	7.9	7.7	7.8
2013	7.5	7.5	7.5	7.5	8.1	8.3	8.4	8.5	8.4	8.4	8.3	8.0	8.0
2014	7.8	7.9	7.9	7.9	8.3	8.6	8.6	8.6	8.5	8.5	8.3	8.1	8.3
2015	7.7	7.6	7.5	7.5	7.8	8.0	7.7	7.7	7.7	7.7	7.7	7.4	7.7
2016	7.1	7.0	7.0	7.1	7.2	7.4	7.4	7.4	7.2	7.4	7.0	6.9	7.2
2017	6.6	6.5	6.6	7.0	7.3	7.5	7.5	7.5	7.4	7.4	7.3	7.0	7.1

1. Employment by Industry: Michigan, Selected Years, 2007–2017—*Continued*

(Numbers in thousands, not seasonally adjusted)

Industry and year	January	February	March	April	May	June	July	August	September	October	November	December	Annual average
Construction													
2007	151.1	145.6	150.1	158.4	172.0	179.3	180.8	180.8	178.2	174.7	169.1	160.0	166.7
2008	143.2	138.2	139.7	146.8	160.5	166.4	166.6	166.6	163.7	159.8	151.1	138.9	153.5
2009	119.6	116.6	115.8	124.1	133.5	136.8	137.5	136.3	133.0	132.3	127.2	118.5	127.6
2010	102.8	100.0	103.4	114.5	123.7	129.1	133.6	134.5	133.8	134.5	129.4	120.4	121.6
2011	108.0	104.9	107.4	114.5	126.1	133.9	138.9	139.6	137.6	135.7	132.3	124.6	125.3
2012	113.2	110.1	114.0	122.1	129.9	135.4	137.9	138.7	138.5	137.6	133.1	127.9	128.2
2013	118.3	115.4	117.2	121.1	135.7	140.4	144.5	145.7	144.7	145.2	140.7	133.0	133.3
2014	122.8	122.2	122.8	128.9	144.0	151.5	153.6	155.5	154.9	153.7	149.4	142.4	141.8
2015	130.6	128.6	131.4	140.5	152.0	158.4	159.1	159.6	158.4	158.8	154.5	147.3	148.3
2016	137.2	135.4	138.9	149.4	159.6	163.5	165.4	165.9	165.4	165.8	162.6	151.9	155.1
2017	143.5	142.0	145.6	154.9	166.5	172.7	174.3	175.3	173.0	175.1	169.2	161.1	162.8
Manufacturing													
2007	603.7	617.4	615.0	614.4	614.5	617.1	586.6	612.3	608.4	595.1	604.0	602.2	607.6
2008	584.8	587.4	574.6	565.2	565.0	584.2	538.4	562.6	558.3	550.0	546.8	535.4	562.7
2009	462.6	476.3	472.3	462.9	443.1	434.5	432.6	451.3	455.8	457.9	454.4	455.0	454.9
2010	450.1	450.1	449.8	456.2	462.2	469.0	467.4	467.0	477.8	480.2	481.1	480.6	466.0
2011	478.3	481.9	484.7	493.6	499.4	505.7	500.6	510.9	512.3	514.7	517.7	519.5	501.6
2012	515.6	517.2	520.5	522.0	528.8	534.9	534.0	537.8	536.8	537.0	537.7	539.8	530.2
2013	532.9	536.6	539.9	539.6	546.1	553.4	542.8	556.0	556.6	558.2	560.9	557.5	548.4
2014	551.4	560.8	562.5	564.2	573.0	586.3	578.8	584.5	577.2	579.3	584.7	588.2	574.2
2015	579.1	580.8	580.2	582.0	589.4	597.0	593.1	598.3	597.7	595.1	598.9	599.0	590.9
2016	597.3	596.0	594.9	601.8	602.2	611.9	605.8	606.8	607.4	606.0	612.7	611.7	604.5
2017	610.2	611.0	610.0	611.8	615.8	622.3	606.9	619.9	614.8	615.1	619.1	619.1	614.7
Trade, Transportation, and Utilities													
2007	779.2	770.1	772.1	777.1	789.4	794.4	789.6	791.1	787.3	787.0	800.6	806.5	787.0
2008	771.9	763.7	765.8	764.6	776.1	780.6	774.1	774.1	769.4	765.2	769.2	769.2	770.3
2009	723.6	714.0	709.8	711.6	720.4	722.6	714.3	717.3	713.0	713.1	721.3	725.4	717.2
2010	695.0	687.9	690.8	699.4	710.3	716.6	717.1	716.8	711.6	719.0	729.6	733.6	710.6
2011	704.7	698.7	700.6	709.6	720.8	727.0	728.8	728.9	725.1	729.3	742.1	746.1	721.8
2012	715.6	708.4	713.0	718.1	729.8	735.4	735.3	735.0	730.7	735.2	751.8	754.2	730.2
2013	726.2	721.7	724.9	728.4	742.1	750.2	750.8	752.0	745.8	751.3	764.6	771.3	744.1
2014	740.0	736.3	737.6	744.0	758.1	765.9	762.3	763.9	759.6	765.6	780.6	787.6	758.5
2015	756.6	750.6	752.9	759.9	772.6	779.1	774.6	775.5	771.6	776.9	791.3	797.5	771.6
2016	767.0	762.3	764.2	772.6	783.4	788.8	786.5	788.0	783.1	788.4	801.7	805.1	782.6
2017	776.8	770.1	773.4	780.1	789.0	795.5	790.8	793.1	788.0	790.6	803.9	805.3	788.1
Wholesale Trade													
2007	167.2	166.8	167.2	169.0	170.4	171.4	170.5	170.1	169.0	169.1	168.6	169.0	169.0
2008	167.0	167.1	167.7	168.5	170.0	170.6	169.1	169.0	168.1	166.9	165.3	163.8	167.8
2009	158.0	156.4	155.0	154.9	154.9	153.2	150.9	151.3	150.5	150.1	149.8	150.0	152.9
2010	146.8	147.1	147.9	149.8	151.4	152.0	152.0	152.5	151.4	152.2	152.5	152.2	150.7
2011	150.8	151.1	152.1	153.6	155.4	156.5	156.6	157.1	156.3	156.4	156.8	156.7	155.0
2012	154.9	155.4	156.4	157.9	159.8	161.0	161.2	161.2	160.3	160.6	160.4	160.9	159.2
2013	159.7	160.3	161.4	162.0	163.9	164.9	164.5	164.6	163.7	163.9	163.8	164.6	163.1
2014	163.2	163.8	164.0	165.4	167.8	169.2	168.1	168.4	166.9	166.6	167.0	167.7	166.5
2015	165.6	165.8	166.5	167.7	169.6	170.7	170.5	170.4	168.8	168.8	169.0	169.5	168.6
2016	167.5	167.9	168.1	170.2	172.0	173.0	172.8	172.4	171.1	171.2	171.4	171.4	170.8
2017	169.6	170.0	171.1	172.7	174.3	175.8	174.7	174.7	173.3	172.2	174.6	174.1	173.1
Retail Trade													
2007	486.6	476.7	478.6	481.1	490.0	492.4	492.3	490.9	488.5	489.3	503.2	507.1	489.7
2008	481.0	472.2	473.5	472.4	480.5	482.3	480.7	480.0	476.3	474.8	481.1	482.3	478.1
2009	452.6	443.3	441.4	444.7	453.2	457.1	452.0	453.5	449.3	449.9	458.8	461.2	451.4
2010	437.7	431.1	432.3	438.6	446.5	450.5	451.6	450.2	445.4	450.6	460.4	463.5	446.5
2011	439.4	433.6	434.1	440.6	447.7	451.0	452.8	451.7	448.2	452.3	464.3	467.0	448.6
2012	441.8	434.2	437.4	440.9	448.6	451.7	452.2	451.2	447.5	451.2	467.4	467.6	449.3
2013	444.4	439.1	441.0	443.5	453.0	458.5	460.8	460.5	455.5	459.8	472.0	476.0	455.3
2014	449.1	445.2	446.1	451.5	460.4	465.3	463.5	464.2	460.6	467.0	480.5	482.8	461.4
2015	457.2	453.0	454.6	458.8	467.7	471.9	468.7	470.2	466.6	471.5	483.6	486.4	467.5
2016	462.9	459.3	460.5	466.5	473.7	476.9	475.9	477.2	471.9	476.2	487.6	489.2	473.2
2017	467.5	462.2	463.6	468.0	473.4	477.0	475.5	476.0	471.2	475.1	484.1	484.1	473.1

1. Employment by Industry: Michigan, Selected Years, 2007–2017—*Continued*

(Numbers in thousands, not seasonally adjusted)

Industry and year	January	February	March	April	May	June	July	August	September	October	November	December	Annual average
Transportation and Utilities													
2007	125.4	126.6	126.3	127.0	129.0	130.6	126.8	130.1	129.8	128.6	128.8	130.4	128.3
2008	123.9	124.4	124.6	123.7	125.6	127.7	124.3	125.1	125.0	123.5	122.8	123.1	124.5
2009	113.0	114.3	113.4	112.0	112.3	112.3	111.4	112.5	113.2	113.1	112.7	114.2	112.9
2010	110.5	109.7	110.6	111.0	112.4	114.1	113.5	114.1	114.8	116.2	116.7	117.9	113.5
2011	114.5	114.0	114.4	115.4	117.7	119.5	119.4	120.1	120.6	120.6	121.0	122.4	118.3
2012	118.9	118.8	119.2	119.3	121.4	122.7	121.9	122.6	122.9	123.4	124.0	125.7	121.7
2013	122.1	122.3	122.5	122.9	125.2	126.8	125.5	126.9	126.6	127.6	128.8	130.7	125.7
2014	127.7	127.3	127.5	127.1	129.9	131.4	130.7	131.3	132.1	132.0	133.1	137.1	130.6
2015	133.8	131.8	131.8	133.4	135.3	136.5	135.4	134.9	136.2	136.6	138.7	141.6	135.5
2016	136.6	135.1	135.6	135.9	137.7	138.9	137.8	138.4	140.1	141.0	142.7	144.5	138.7
2017	139.7	137.9	138.7	139.4	141.3	142.7	140.6	142.4	143.5	143.3	145.2	147.1	141.8
Information													
2007	63.4	63.4	63.1	63.4	64.1	64.0	63.2	62.9	62.0	61.8	62.0	62.0	62.9
2008	61.2	61.2	60.5	60.0	60.6	60.9	59.9	60.2	60.2	59.0	59.5	59.1	60.2
2009	57.8	57.7	56.7	56.8	57.0	57.0	56.2	55.6	55.0	55.0	55.6	55.7	56.3
2010	54.3	54.2	53.9	54.2	54.8	55.3	54.8	57.0	56.5	54.0	54.0	54.2	54.8
2011	53.8	53.5	53.4	52.1	52.7	52.8	53.1	53.2	52.7	53.6	53.8	53.8	53.2
2012	53.4	53.2	53.1	52.9	53.2	53.2	53.6	54.2	52.9	53.2	53.5	53.6	53.3
2013	54.0	54.2	54.4	55.0	55.4	55.9	56.0	56.1	55.3	55.3	56.0	56.1	55.3
2014	56.3	56.0	56.3	57.1	57.4	58.2	59.0	58.6	57.1	57.9	58.0	57.6	57.5
2015	56.5	56.3	56.3	55.9	56.6	57.2	57.7	56.8	56.4	56.0	56.4	56.5	56.6
2016	56.7	56.5	56.7	56.9	57.5	58.1	58.5	57.9	57.4	56.8	57.4	57.1	57.3
2017	56.5	56.3	56.8	56.4	56.8	57.0	57.0	56.7	56.3	55.8	55.9	55.9	56.5
Financial Activities													
2007	209.1	209.0	208.8	209.9	211.5	213.2	213.1	211.5	208.0	207.0	206.1	206.5	209.5
2008	204.4	204.4	203.6	203.0	205.0	205.3	203.7	203.0	199.8	198.2	196.8	196.5	202.0
2009	193.1	192.6	191.4	192.4	193.5	194.3	193.2	192.6	189.8	188.4	187.8	187.5	191.4
2010	186.2	185.8	185.0	184.7	186.7	188.9	190.0	190.7	189.2	189.3	189.6	190.7	188.1
2011	190.4	190.9	191.5	191.0	192.2	194.1	195.7	196.5	194.1	193.4	193.6	194.4	193.2
2012	192.2	192.6	193.3	194.5	196.2	198.4	199.9	200.0	197.3	197.3	197.5	198.3	196.5
2013	198.5	199.1	199.5	201.0	203.3	206.4	207.1	207.3	203.4	202.8	202.8	202.8	202.8
2014	202.2	202.0	201.8	202.1	204.9	207.2	207.4	207.4	204.3	203.2	203.4	204.2	204.2
2015	202.7	202.3	202.5	204.0	207.3	210.1	210.7	210.9	208.2	208.5	208.6	209.2	207.1
2016	208.5	208.3	208.5	210.0	212.6	215.2	216.6	216.8	214.1	213.8	213.9	215.1	212.8
2017	215.4	215.3	215.1	216.5	218.4	221.9	221.2	220.6	218.1	218.5	218.0	218.6	218.1
Professional and Business Services													
2007	575.0	577.8	578.1	587.6	594.6	598.5	585.6	596.3	595.8	599.7	602.1	598.3	590.8
2008	574.5	576.3	577.5	581.2	587.6	584.0	567.5	570.9	567.8	572.0	563.5	554.2	573.1
2009	519.0	518.2	514.0	515.1	514.9	503.7	488.4	493.6	506.0	515.2	517.3	514.5	510.0
2010	498.2	504.2	504.5	516.2	523.9	527.5	517.2	524.8	536.6	546.8	548.0	541.6	524.1
2011	536.8	542.0	548.6	560.6	569.2	563.9	552.0	561.3	574.8	584.9	584.3	574.4	562.7
2012	568.4	573.9	578.3	590.1	598.9	591.5	576.1	585.4	595.0	603.4	602.7	598.8	588.5
2013	592.8	599.5	605.5	606.2	622.3	616.9	590.9	606.2	617.5	624.8	625.4	621.3	610.8
2014	604.9	611.6	614.5	615.6	631.5	631.8	610.4	616.8	625.2	636.5	635.9	634.6	622.4
2015	620.8	624.1	625.0	633.4	644.0	642.0	623.5	627.3	634.9	647.4	644.8	639.6	633.9
2016	628.5	630.8	632.2	642.5	648.8	648.7	635.2	637.6	647.5	654.6	654.9	647.9	642.4
2017	637.2	638.7	643.2	647.0	658.1	658.7	637.9	641.6	648.1	656.3	659.5	651.5	648.2
Education and Health Services													
2007	584.9	591.3	594.2	596.0	598.4	594.8	588.6	589.3	599.4	605.2	608.6	609.2	596.7
2008	600.0	605.4	607.2	607.2	610.3	606.1	600.1	600.1	607.8	613.8	616.0	614.6	607.4
2009	602.6	609.9	611.4	611.2	613.0	609.5	600.7	600.7	605.8	614.5	616.8	614.6	609.2
2010	603.6	609.4	610.9	611.9	613.8	609.6	605.3	605.6	610.3	618.9	621.8	620.8	611.8
2011	610.8	615.1	618.0	622.0	622.1	618.6	616.0	617.1	623.8	630.4	633.1	633.2	621.7
2012	623.3	630.6	632.7	632.3	632.6	630.6	624.1	626.0	631.5	638.7	641.5	642.6	632.2
2013	630.4	636.9	639.0	640.1	640.3	638.4	632.1	633.8	639.3	645.5	649.4	648.0	639.4
2014	636.5	643.5	645.4	643.4	645.6	643.3	634.0	635.6	641.1	647.1	650.0	651.6	643.1
2015	641.7	647.3	650.5	648.1	651.8	650.1	644.1	647.7	650.4	661.8	664.3	666.4	652.0
2016	654.5	660.8	662.2	664.7	667.5	663.8	659.4	660.1	666.0	671.1	673.7	674.1	664.8
2017	663.6	669.8	671.3	671.5	674.4	671.8	665.1	666.7	670.9	675.4	679.2	676.4	671.3

1. Employment by Industry: Michigan, Selected Years, 2007–2017—*Continued*

(Numbers in thousands, not seasonally adjusted)

Industry and year	January	February	March	April	May	June	July	August	September	October	November	December	Annual average
Leisure and Hospitality													
2007	379.3	379.2	386.0	398.1	422.4	433.9	429.5	431.8	423.4	408.0	397.1	395.5	407.0
2008	376.3	375.7	381.3	393.4	416.7	426.9	423.6	426.1	414.2	397.1	384.1	382.8	399.9
2009	358.8	357.2	361.1	376.8	398.1	406.0	404.2	405.1	397.0	380.9	367.8	367.1	381.7
2010	349.9	350.7	355.4	371.2	389.7	402.0	400.0	403.3	393.9	379.2	367.8	367.6	377.6
2011	353.6	352.7	359.8	372.0	391.3	403.2	404.1	406.0	397.0	384.2	372.2	370.2	380.5
2012	360.0	361.5	369.2	380.0	398.2	413.2	411.3	413.7	402.7	391.8	381.3	382.7	388.8
2013	372.3	373.7	378.3	385.0	410.4	422.0	420.4	422.8	410.5	402.5	389.5	390.9	398.2
2014	377.8	378.8	385.3	393.4	419.7	433.4	431.6	433.5	419.2	409.1	397.5	398.2	406.5
2015	386.4	386.9	392.5	399.5	425.4	438.1	439.4	439.9	427.9	417.5	405.8	405.2	413.7
2016	396.6	399.2	404.7	414.7	435.7	449.3	451.4	452.1	438.1	428.2	417.7	415.0	425.2
2017	406.2	408.5	413.2	422.1	443.1	458.1	458.0	460.3	443.2	433.1	422.9	421.5	432.5
Other Services													
2007	172.8	173.7	175.3	175.6	177.7	180.2	177.9	178.3	177.3	176.6	176.1	177.1	176.6
2008	173.3	174.2	175.2	176.0	178.1	179.6	177.5	177.4	176.1	174.9	172.7	171.9	175.6
2009	167.4	167.8	167.6	169.3	171.0	172.3	169.9	169.4	168.4	167.8	167.1	168.1	168.8
2010	163.8	164.5	165.3	165.4	166.7	168.8	168.4	168.2	166.5	166.2	165.8	166.1	166.3
2011	163.9	164.3	165.5	166.4	167.9	169.7	169.3	169.6	167.9	167.8	167.0	167.7	167.3
2012	164.9	165.6	167.0	168.3	169.9	172.3	171.5	172.0	170.9	170.0	169.6	169.8	169.3
2013	168.4	168.9	170.3	169.4	170.7	172.2	172.5	172.6	170.5	170.2	169.8	170.0	170.5
2014	168.3	168.9	169.4	168.5	170.3	171.8	171.4	170.6	169.3	169.4	168.3	168.2	169.5
2015	164.7	164.8	165.5	165.5	167.5	169.3	169.7	169.4	167.8	168.0	167.6	168.2	167.3
2016	165.7	166.3	166.7	166.5	168.4	170.2	169.7	169.5	168.2	167.6	167.3	166.7	167.7
2017	164.6	165.2	165.7	166.3	168.6	170.9	169.8	169.9	168.0	168.7	169.2	170.2	168.1
Government													
2007	660.2	677.9	683.0	674.3	673.4	646.8	591.3	594.1	654.8	671.3	672.7	668.4	655.7
2008	649.2	665.5	666.9	668.2	658.0	641.9	593.0	598.6	654.8	670.7	671.7	662.0	650.0
2009	652.7	665.0	666.0	669.3	659.9	639.1	589.6	589.6	645.7	664.0	664.5	656.0	646.8
2010	641.7	655.4	655.9	658.5	657.1	633.6	584.7	576.0	630.1	646.1	648.2	640.1	635.6
2011	625.0	636.2	638.4	637.6	623.5	609.4	565.1	561.7	619.7	632.0	634.7	625.9	617.4
2012	615.8	627.9	628.3	627.6	615.9	596.1	555.5	555.7	612.3	622.9	626.3	617.5	608.5
2013	603.1	616.0	615.0	615.4	604.2	585.8	547.0	545.0	604.7	617.3	618.3	610.7	598.5
2014	597.1	610.8	611.2	611.3	599.3	584.8	546.1	545.4	599.3	615.3	617.7	610.8	595.8
2015	594.7	608.3	609.6	609.5	600.2	580.5	545.4	544.2	594.7	615.4	616.1	611.2	594.2
2016	595.4	610.2	614.0	613.9	598.3	586.8	552.1	552.2	609.2	619.1	624.5	617.2	599.4
2017	601.0	613.7	616.1	615.6	604.2	592.6	555.6	554.5	614.1	627.6	629.0	623.6	604.0

2. Average Weekly Hours by Selected Industry: Michigan, 2013–2017

(Not seasonally adjusted)

Industry and year	January	February	March	April	May	June	July	August	September	October	November	December	Annual average
Total Private													
2013	33.6	33.8	33.9	33.8	34.2	34.8	34.3	34.6	34.7	34.3	34.3	34.7	34.2
2014	33.8	34.4	34.2	34.1	34.2	34.7	34.3	34.5	34.5	34.4	34.7	34.7	34.4
2015	34.1	34.3	34.5	34.3	34.6	34.7	34.3	34.9	34.1	34.3	34.5	34.3	34.4
2016	33.8	33.8	33.9	34.2	34.3	34.4	34.4	34.5	34.7	34.9	34.4	34.5	34.3
2017	34.4	34.4	34.4	34.6	34.8	34.9	34.8	34.9	34.9	35.0	34.6	34.7	34.7
Goods Producing													
2013	41.0	40.9	41.1	40.6	40.9	41.5	41.0	41.9	42.3	41.8	41.5	42.2	41.4
2014	40.8	41.7	41.4	41.1	41.5	41.8	40.9	41.1	41.5	41.0	41.1	42.1	41.3
2015	40.6	40.9	41.5	41.1	41.8	42.0	40.7	41.9	39.7	41.3	40.8	41.1	41.1
2016	39.9	39.7	40.1	40.7	40.4	40.9	40.3	40.6	41.1	41.5	40.7	40.8	40.6
2017	40.6	40.7	40.9	40.5	41.6	41.7	41.1	41.8	41.9	41.9	41.0	41.5	41.3
Construction													
2013	38.0	37.9	37.5	37.4	39.9	39.9	40.5	39.2	39.3	39.4	37.0	37.6	38.7
2014	36.8	37.1	36.5	37.3	37.5	39.6	38.8	38.7	39.6	38.9	37.8	38.7	38.2
2015	37.7	37.2	38.1	38.3	39.5	39.6	39.2	39.9	37.4	40.3	37.7	38.3	38.7
2016	36.6	36.5	36.8	37.8	38.4	39.3	39.8	39.4	39.4	39.9	39.1	37.8	38.5
2017	37.7	37.9	37.3	38.7	40.5	40.7	39.9	41.4	41.1	39.4	38.3	37.8	39.3
Manufacturing													
2013	41.6	41.5	41.8	41.3	41.1	41.8	41.0	42.5	43.0	42.4	42.5	43.1	42.0
2014	41.5	42.5	42.3	41.9	42.5	42.3	41.4	41.7	41.9	41.6	42.0	43.0	42.1
2015	41.3	41.8	42.3	41.8	42.4	42.7	41.1	42.5	40.4	41.7	41.8	41.9	41.8
2016	40.9	40.6	40.9	41.4	40.9	41.3	40.4	40.9	41.5	41.9	41.1	41.6	41.1
2017	41.3	41.4	41.8	40.9	41.9	42.0	41.5	41.9	42.1	42.8	42.0	42.8	41.9
Trade, Transportation, and Utilities													
2013	32.4	32.9	33.0	32.9	33.6	33.8	33.5	33.6	33.8	33.2	33.3	33.6	33.3
2014	32.9	33.2	33.2	33.2	33.3	33.8	33.8	33.9	33.7	33.5	33.8	33.8	33.5
2015	33.1	33.1	33.2	33.2	33.4	33.2	33.4	33.7	33.7	33.1	33.4	33.5	33.3
2016	32.8	32.7	32.8	33.0	33.2	33.4	33.6	33.5	34.0	34.1	33.8	34.0	33.4
2017	33.4	33.4	33.3	34.1	34.0	34.1	34.2	33.8	33.9	33.8	33.9	34.0	33.8
Information													
2013	35.1	35.6	35.0	35.4	35.8	37.3	37.5	36.7	37.9	35.9	36.0	36.6	36.2
2014	36.4	37.5	37.1	36.4	36.1	37.3	37.2	37.1	37.9	36.3	36.9	36.3	36.9
2015	36.7	36.9	37.0	36.8	36.7	37.9	37.8	37.7	37.0	35.8	36.8	36.4	37.0
2016	37.0	36.2	35.8	34.9	35.3	35.7	36.6	35.6	35.9	35.8	35.7	35.8	35.9
2017	36.9	35.8	36.3	36.1	35.6	36.2	36.7	36.3	36.0	36.5	35.8	36.2	36.2
Financial Activities													
2013	35.5	35.7	35.5	35.8	35.9	36.3	35.6	35.7	36.1	35.7	35.5	35.6	35.7
2014	35.7	36.1	36.0	35.3	35.5	36.3	35.6	35.9	35.7	36.0	36.7	35.9	35.9
2015	36.4	37.0	37.3	36.9	37.1	37.0	36.9	36.9	36.5	36.4	36.9	36.7	36.8
2016	37.0	36.8	36.8	36.7	37.3	37.0	36.8	36.8	36.6	37.1	36.7	36.9	36.9
2017	37.0	36.6	36.7	37.2	36.8	36.4	37.0	36.5	36.5	37.2	36.6	36.7	36.8
Professional and Business Services													
2013	34.9	35.5	35.6	35.9	36.2	37.8	36.6	36.4	36.8	36.4	36.4	37.1	36.3
2014	36.0	36.3	36.1	35.9	36.0	36.7	35.9	36.1	36.2	36.2	36.5	36.5	36.2
2015	35.8	36.2	36.3	35.9	36.1	36.2	35.3	36.0	35.0	35.8	36.0	35.3	35.8
2016	35.1	35.3	35.4	35.9	36.2	36.1	35.7	36.2	36.2	36.6	35.7	35.9	35.9
2017	36.1	36.0	36.1	36.4	36.2	36.2	36.2	36.0	35.9	36.6	35.9	35.9	36.1
Education and Health Services													
2013	32.4	32.4	32.3	32.1	32.2	32.7	32.3	32.4	32.7	32.3	32.6	32.9	32.4
2014	32.2	32.6	32.5	32.2	32.3	32.4	32.2	32.5	32.5	32.5	33.0	32.7	32.5
2015	32.5	32.6	32.8	32.6	32.7	32.6	32.6	32.9	32.7	32.5	33.0	32.7	32.7
2016	32.8	32.7	32.6	32.8	32.9	32.7	33.1	32.9	33.2	33.0	32.9	32.8	32.9
2017	33.0	32.9	33.0	33.1	32.8	32.9	33.0	33.1	33.3	33.2	33.2	33.1	33.1
Leisure and Hospitality													
2013	22.5	22.9	23.3	23.3	24.2	24.3	24.3	24.6	24.0	23.7	23.4	23.7	23.7
2014	22.6	23.5	23.6	23.8	23.9	24.6	24.7	24.9	24.2	23.9	23.6	23.6	23.9
2015	23.2	23.6	23.6	23.5	24.1	24.4	25.1	25.4	24.6	24.1	23.9	23.9	24.1
2016	22.9	23.4	23.5	23.9	24.4	24.7	25.3	25.6	24.9	24.6	24.3	24.0	24.3
2017	24.1	24.1	24.3	24.2	25.4	25.5	26.1	26.0	25.3	25.1	24.6	24.5	25.0
Other Services													
2013	31.0	30.8	31.1	30.9	30.9	31.2	31.0	32.2	30.8	30.1	30.2	30.4	30.9
2014	29.9	30.5	30.2	31.0	30.6	31.1	30.9	31.6	31.9	31.8	32.5	32.5	31.2
2015	32.4	32.1	32.4	31.9	32.2	32.7	32.4	33.2	32.8	32.5	32.4	31.8	32.4
2016	31.1	31.2	31.3	31.7	32.1	31.1	31.6	31.7	31.3	31.6	31.1	31.3	31.4
2017	30.6	31.3	31.1	31.5	31.4	31.8	31.2	31.5	31.3	31.3	31.3	31.4	31.3

3. Average Hourly Earnings by Selected Industry: Michigan, 2013–2017

(Dollars, not seasonally adjusted)

Industry and year	January	February	March	April	May	June	July	August	September	October	November	December	Annual average
Total Private													
2013	22.95	22.86	22.84	22.86	22.65	22.98	22.89	22.68	23.22	23.01	23.05	23.29	22.94
2014	23.52	23.70	23.83	23.69	23.46	23.50	23.30	23.29	23.58	23.61	23.85	23.63	23.58
2015	23.88	23.97	23.95	23.85	23.70	23.60	23.91	24.27	24.25	24.40	24.44	24.32	24.05
2016	24.32	24.22	24.22	24.03	24.01	23.73	23.87	23.80	23.90	24.36	24.24	24.33	24.08
2017	24.73	24.56	24.48	24.81	24.35	24.16	24.51	24.25	24.63	25.05	24.93	25.27	24.64
Goods Producing													
2013	24.94	24.68	24.63	24.57	24.66	24.74	24.87	24.56	24.84	24.60	24.65	24.79	24.71
2014	24.73	24.77	25.05	25.05	24.87	24.78	24.70	24.71	25.04	24.84	24.95	25.00	24.87
2015	25.08	25.09	25.16	25.12	24.93	24.84	24.97	25.57	25.61	25.36	25.41	25.57	25.23
2016	25.20	25.15	25.25	24.62	24.70	24.58	24.89	24.80	24.99	25.41	25.40	25.77	25.06
2017	26.05	25.80	26.00	26.43	26.05	26.13	26.41	26.06	26.23	26.33	26.01	26.55	26.17
Construction													
2013	26.03	25.99	26.03	26.07	25.82	25.45	26.20	26.07	26.07	25.90	26.11	26.77	26.04
2014	25.81	25.70	26.29	26.62	25.92	25.45	25.57	25.94	26.11	25.44	25.06	25.94	25.80
2015	25.76	25.90	26.31	26.40	26.07	25.59	25.90	26.16	26.14	26.51	26.67	27.29	26.23
2016	26.54	26.81	26.91	27.13	26.93	26.87	27.12	26.96	27.10	27.07	27.19	27.52	27.02
2017	27.49	27.34	27.84	27.38	27.43	27.28	27.54	27.77	27.84	27.51	27.27	28.06	27.56
Manufacturing													
2013	24.92	24.61	24.53	24.40	24.45	24.63	24.55	24.22	24.56	24.32	24.39	24.49	24.50
2014	24.61	24.69	24.89	24.77	24.67	24.62	24.45	24.35	24.72	24.67	24.93	24.81	24.68
2015	24.99	25.00	24.99	24.86	24.64	24.65	24.74	25.43	25.51	25.07	24.97	25.05	24.99
2016	24.85	24.76	24.85	24.03	24.14	23.98	24.28	24.21	24.42	24.96	24.91	25.33	24.56
2017	25.67	25.40	25.52	26.11	25.60	25.73	25.78	25.21	25.46	25.78	25.45	25.98	25.64
Trade, Transportation, and Utilities													
2013	20.04	20.19	20.21	20.18	19.89	20.15	20.33	20.19	20.50	20.57	20.72	20.58	20.30
2014	20.82	20.92	21.04	20.77	20.75	20.68	20.51	20.43	20.63	20.57	20.73	20.41	20.68
2015	20.62	20.64	20.46	20.46	20.43	20.47	20.71	20.96	20.96	20.81	20.91	20.53	20.66
2016	20.94	20.70	20.57	20.62	20.40	20.26	20.28	20.45	19.98	20.26	20.19	19.95	20.38
2017	20.57	20.63	20.51	20.87	20.56	20.65	21.07	21.06	21.37	21.73	21.94	22.08	21.09
Information													
2013	29.49	29.95	29.57	29.77	29.23	29.53	29.05	29.09	29.87	29.57	29.76	30.09	29.58
2014	29.81	29.81	30.74	31.05	30.97	31.06	30.51	30.56	30.89	31.27	31.12	31.42	30.77
2015	30.71	30.66	31.47	31.39	31.27	31.43	31.08	31.64	31.40	31.12	31.61	31.54	31.28
2016	32.32	32.33	31.23	31.78	32.27	30.90	30.34	31.00	30.82	31.74	32.44	31.87	31.58
2017	31.10	32.87	32.59	32.62	33.16	31.52	32.01	32.18	32.59	33.12	33.38	33.40	32.54
Financial Activities													
2013	22.87	22.60	22.90	23.04	22.71	22.68	22.42	22.56	22.83	23.31	23.31	23.56	22.90
2014	23.62	24.13	24.64	24.18	24.47	25.05	25.15	25.18	26.02	25.81	26.51	26.61	25.12
2015	26.84	27.49	27.70	27.79	27.67	27.16	27.25	27.68	27.80	27.83	28.74	28.01	27.67
2016	27.62	27.79	27.63	27.98	28.48	27.82	27.90	28.46	29.12	29.28	29.52	29.57	28.44
2017	29.81	29.40	29.04	30.03	29.21	28.63	29.08	28.46	29.50	30.03	30.00	30.56	29.48
Professional and Business Services													
2013	28.69	28.36	28.50	28.39	28.16	29.45	28.78	27.78	29.13	28.40	28.09	29.37	28.60
2014	29.99	30.72	30.90	30.65	29.84	30.21	29.67	29.47	29.30	29.52	29.95	29.17	29.94
2015	29.79	29.88	29.95	29.14	29.07	29.06	30.31	30.78	30.28	30.19	30.22	30.49	29.93
2016	30.21	30.16	30.20	29.89	29.88	29.47	29.68	29.04	29.40	30.31	29.37	29.71	29.77
2017	30.39	29.76	29.38	29.76	29.07	28.65	29.30	28.75	29.12	30.09	29.62	30.42	29.52
Education and Health Services													
2013	22.37	22.44	22.15	22.47	22.36	22.58	22.85	22.78	23.11	22.78	22.87	22.88	22.64
2014	23.08	23.01	22.98	23.02	22.95	23.10	23.23	23.35	23.61	23.48	23.64	23.47	23.24
2015	23.69	23.73	23.58	23.98	23.80	23.77	24.39	24.44	24.51	25.59	25.03	24.87	24.29
2016	24.81	24.72	24.85	24.86	24.77	24.79	25.21	24.83	24.79	25.04	25.08	25.04	24.90
2017	25.12	25.16	24.93	25.13	24.77	24.52	24.86	24.41	24.74	24.84	24.84	24.87	24.85
Leisure and Hospitality													
2013	12.01	11.81	11.77	11.74	11.68	11.59	11.63	11.68	11.84	11.86	11.97	12.18	11.81
2014	12.33	12.23	12.12	12.08	12.13	11.98	11.98	12.00	12.32	12.57	12.65	12.81	12.26
2015	12.58	12.55	12.59	12.63	12.50	12.28	12.26	12.43	12.49	12.57	12.57	12.66	12.50
2016	12.65	12.60	12.63	12.65	12.80	12.60	12.79	13.08	13.13	13.29	13.59	13.66	12.96
2017	13.61	13.67	13.87	14.04	13.92	13.68	13.99	14.11	14.32	14.50	14.50	14.43	14.06
Other Services													
2013	20.58	20.76	20.97	20.94	20.54	19.99	20.50	21.58	21.01	20.42	20.43	19.69	20.62
2014	19.87	20.14	20.10	20.52	20.05	19.81	19.89	20.13	20.08	20.38	20.51	20.39	20.16
2015	20.89	21.15	20.90	20.99	21.34	21.37	21.33	21.51	21.89	21.01	21.40	20.83	21.22
2016	20.83	20.72	20.94	20.75	21.25	20.47	20.63	21.01	20.81	20.83	21.11	21.01	20.86
2017	21.53	21.22	21.64	21.58	21.55	21.59	21.87	22.02	22.22	22.64	22.64	22.84	21.95

4. Average Weekly Earnings by Selected Industry: Michigan, 2013–2017

(Dollars, not seasonally adjusted)

Industry and year	January	February	March	April	May	June	July	August	September	October	November	December	Annual average
Total Private													
2013	771.12	772.67	774.28	772.67	774.63	799.70	785.13	784.73	805.73	789.24	790.62	808.16	784.55
2014	794.98	815.28	814.99	807.83	802.33	815.45	799.19	803.51	813.51	812.18	827.60	819.96	811.15
2015	814.31	822.17	826.28	818.06	820.02	818.92	820.11	847.02	826.93	836.92	843.18	834.18	827.32
2016	822.02	818.64	821.06	821.83	823.54	816.31	821.13	821.10	829.33	850.16	833.86	839.39	825.94
2017	850.71	844.86	842.11	858.43	847.38	843.18	852.95	846.33	859.59	876.75	862.58	876.87	855.01
Goods Producing													
2013	1,022.54	1,009.41	1,012.29	997.54	1,008.59	1,026.71	1,019.67	1,029.06	1,050.73	1,028.28	1,022.98	1,046.14	1,022.99
2014	1,008.98	1,032.91	1,037.07	1,029.56	1,032.11	1,035.80	1,010.23	1,015.58	1,039.16	1,018.44	1,025.45	1,052.50	1,027.13
2015	1,018.25	1,026.18	1,044.14	1,032.43	1,042.07	1,043.28	1,016.28	1,071.38	1,016.72	1,047.37	1,036.73	1,050.93	1,036.95
2016	1,005.48	998.46	1,012.53	1,002.03	997.88	1,005.32	1,003.07	1,006.88	1,027.09	1,054.52	1,033.78	1,051.42	1,017.44
2017	1,057.63	1,050.06	1,063.40	1,070.42	1,083.68	1,089.62	1,085.45	1,089.31	1,099.04	1,103.23	1,066.41	1,101.83	1,080.82
Construction													
2013	989.14	985.02	976.13	975.02	1,030.22	1,015.46	1,061.10	1,021.94	1,024.55	1,020.46	966.07	1,006.55	1,007.75
2014	949.81	953.47	959.59	992.93	972.00	1,007.82	992.12	1,003.88	1,033.96	989.62	947.27	1,003.88	985.56
2015	971.15	963.48	1,002.41	1,011.12	1,029.77	1,013.36	1,015.28	1,043.78	977.64	1,068.35	1,005.46	1,045.21	1,015.10
2016	971.36	978.57	990.29	1,025.51	1,034.11	1,055.99	1,079.38	1,062.22	1,067.74	1,080.09	1,063.13	1,040.26	1,040.27
2017	1,036.37	1,036.19	1,038.43	1,059.61	1,110.92	1,110.30	1,098.85	1,149.68	1,144.22	1,083.89	1,044.44	1,060.67	1,083.11
Manufacturing													
2013	1,036.67	1,021.32	1,025.35	1,007.72	1,004.90	1,029.53	1,006.55	1,029.35	1,056.08	1,031.17	1,036.58	1,055.52	1,029.00
2014	1,021.32	1,049.33	1,052.85	1,037.86	1,048.48	1,041.43	1,012.23	1,015.40	1,035.77	1,026.27	1,047.06	1,066.83	1,039.03
2015	1,032.09	1,045.00	1,057.08	1,039.15	1,044.74	1,052.56	1,016.81	1,080.78	1,030.60	1,045.42	1,043.75	1,049.60	1,044.58
2016	1,016.37	1,005.26	1,016.37	994.84	987.33	990.37	980.91	990.19	1,013.43	1,045.82	1,023.80	1,053.73	1,009.42
2017	1,060.17	1,051.56	1,066.74	1,067.90	1,072.64	1,080.66	1,069.87	1,056.30	1,071.87	1,103.38	1,068.90	1,111.94	1,074.32
Trade, Transportation, and Utilities													
2013	649.30	664.25	666.93	663.92	668.30	681.07	681.06	678.38	692.90	682.92	689.98	691.49	675.99
2014	684.98	694.54	698.53	689.56	690.98	698.98	693.24	692.58	695.23	689.10	700.67	689.86	692.78
2015	682.52	683.18	679.27	679.27	682.36	679.60	691.71	706.35	706.35	688.81	698.39	687.76	687.98
2016	686.83	676.89	674.70	680.46	677.28	676.68	681.41	685.08	679.32	690.87	682.42	678.30	680.69
2017	687.04	689.04	682.98	711.67	699.04	704.17	720.59	711.83	724.44	734.47	743.77	750.72	712.84
Information													
2013	1,035.10	1,066.22	1,034.95	1,053.86	1,046.43	1,101.47	1,089.38	1,067.60	1,132.07	1,061.56	1,071.36	1,101.29	1,070.80
2014	1,085.08	1,117.88	1,140.45	1,130.22	1,118.02	1,158.54	1,134.97	1,133.78	1,170.73	1,135.10	1,148.33	1,140.55	1,135.41
2015	1,127.06	1,131.35	1,164.39	1,155.15	1,147.61	1,191.20	1,174.82	1,192.83	1,161.80	1,114.10	1,163.25	1,148.06	1,157.36
2016	1,195.84	1,170.35	1,118.03	1,109.12	1,139.13	1,103.13	1,110.44	1,103.60	1,106.44	1,136.29	1,158.11	1,140.95	1,133.72
2017	1,147.59	1,176.75	1,183.02	1,177.58	1,180.50	1,141.02	1,174.77	1,168.13	1,173.24	1,208.88	1,195.00	1,209.08	1,177.95
Financial Activities													
2013	811.89	806.82	812.95	824.83	815.29	823.28	798.15	805.39	824.16	832.17	827.51	838.74	817.53
2014	843.23	871.09	887.04	853.55	868.69	909.32	895.34	903.96	928.91	929.16	972.92	955.30	901.81
2015	976.98	1,017.13	1,033.21	1,025.45	1,026.56	1,004.92	1,005.53	1,021.39	1,014.70	1,013.01	1,060.51	1,027.97	1,018.26
2016	1,021.94	1,022.67	1,016.78	1,026.87	1,062.30	1,029.34	1,026.72	1,047.33	1,065.79	1,086.29	1,083.38	1,091.13	1,049.44
2017	1,102.97	1,076.04	1,065.77	1,117.12	1,074.93	1,042.13	1,075.96	1,038.79	1,076.75	1,117.12	1,098.00	1,121.55	1,084.86
Professional and Business Services													
2013	1,001.28	1,006.78	1,014.60	1,019.20	1,019.39	1,113.21	1,053.35	1,011.19	1,071.98	1,033.76	1,022.48	1,089.63	1,038.18
2014	1,079.64	1,115.14	1,115.49	1,100.34	1,074.24	1,108.71	1,065.15	1,063.87	1,060.66	1,068.62	1,093.18	1,064.71	1,083.83
2015	1,066.48	1,081.66	1,087.19	1,046.13	1,049.43	1,051.97	1,069.94	1,108.08	1,059.80	1,080.80	1,087.92	1,076.30	1,071.49
2016	1,060.37	1,064.65	1,069.08	1,073.05	1,081.66	1,063.87	1,059.58	1,051.25	1,064.28	1,109.35	1,048.51	1,066.59	1,068.74
2017	1,097.08	1,071.36	1,060.62	1,083.26	1,052.33	1,037.13	1,060.66	1,035.00	1,045.41	1,101.29	1,063.36	1,092.08	1,065.67
Education and Health Services													
2013	724.79	727.06	715.45	721.29	719.99	738.37	738.06	738.07	755.70	735.79	745.56	752.75	733.54
2014	743.18	750.13	746.85	741.24	741.29	748.44	748.01	758.88	767.33	763.10	780.12	767.47	755.30
2015	769.93	773.60	773.42	781.75	778.26	774.90	795.11	804.08	801.48	831.68	825.99	813.25	794.28
2016	813.77	808.34	810.11	815.41	814.93	810.63	834.45	816.91	823.03	826.32	825.13	821.31	819.21
2017	828.96	827.76	822.69	831.80	812.46	806.71	820.38	807.97	823.84	824.69	824.69	823.20	822.54
Leisure and Hospitality													
2013	270.23	270.45	274.24	273.54	282.66	281.64	282.61	287.33	284.16	281.08	280.10	288.67	279.90
2014	278.66	287.41	286.03	287.50	289.91	294.71	295.91	298.80	298.14	300.42	298.54	302.32	293.01
2015	291.86	296.18	297.12	296.81	301.25	299.63	307.73	315.72	307.25	302.94	300.42	302.57	301.25
2016	289.69	294.84	296.81	302.34	312.32	311.22	323.59	334.85	326.94	326.93	330.24	327.84	314.93
2017	328.00	329.45	337.04	339.77	353.57	348.84	365.14	366.86	362.30	363.95	356.70	353.54	351.50
Other Services													
2013	637.98	639.41	652.17	647.05	634.69	623.69	635.50	694.88	647.11	614.64	616.99	598.58	637.16
2014	594.11	614.27	607.02	636.12	613.53	616.09	614.60	636.11	640.55	648.08	666.58	662.68	628.99
2015	676.84	678.92	677.16	669.58	687.15	698.80	691.09	714.13	717.99	682.83	693.36	662.39	687.53
2016	647.81	646.46	655.42	657.78	682.13	636.62	651.91	666.02	651.35	658.23	656.52	657.61	655.00
2017	658.82	664.19	673.00	679.77	676.67	686.56	682.34	693.63	695.49	708.63	708.63	717.18	687.04

MINNESOTA
At a Glance

Population:
  2010 census: 5,303,925
  2017 estimate: 5,576,606

Percent change in population:
  2010–2017: 5.1%

Percent change in total nonfarm employment:
  2007–2017: 5.8%

Industry with the largest growth in employment, 2007–2017 (thousands):
  Education and health services, 105.6

Industry with the largest decline or smallest growth in employment, 2007–2017 (thousands):
  Manufacturing, -23.2

Civilian labor force:
  2010: 2,938,795
  2017: 3,063,604

Unemployment rate and rank among states (highest to lowest):
  2010: 7.4%, 39th
  2017: 3.5%, 38th

Over-the-year change in unemployment rates:
  2015–2016: 0.2%
  2016–2017: -0.4%

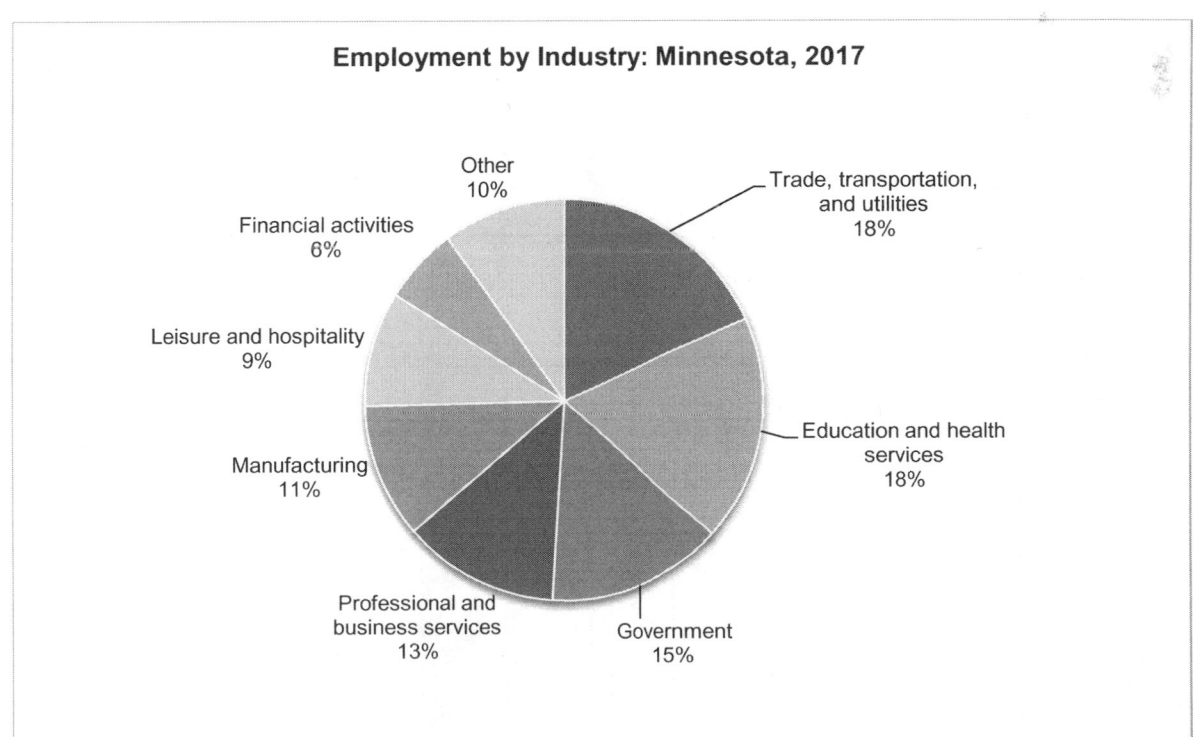

Employment by Industry: Minnesota, 2017

- Other 10%
- Financial activities 6%
- Leisure and hospitality 9%
- Manufacturing 11%
- Professional and business services 13%
- Government 15%
- Trade, transportation, and utilities 18%
- Education and health services 18%

1. Employment by Industry: Minnesota, Selected Years, 2007–2017

(Numbers in thousands, not seasonally adjusted)

Industry and year	January	February	March	April	May	June	July	August	September	October	November	December	Annual average
Total Nonfarm													
2007	2,709.4	2,709.5	2,719.8	2,743.7	2,791.6	2,821.1	2,781.9	2,783.8	2,785.9	2,796.5	2,797.3	2,786.6	2,768.9
2008	2,716.5	2,719.2	2,726.9	2,744.7	2,789.6	2,811.8	2,772.4	2,776.6	2,774.9	2,785.0	2,765.7	2,741.4	2,760.4
2009	2,651.3	2,637.6	2,629.2	2,650.2	2,680.3	2,687.3	2,647.3	2,643.8	2,635.9	2,662.4	2,654.7	2,643.7	2,652.0
2010	2,567.1	2,568.6	2,578.1	2,626.4	2,660.6	2,679.5	2,645.7	2,650.5	2,652.7	2,681.7	2,677.8	2,664.3	2,637.8
2011	2,603.3	2,609.7	2,618.7	2,667.6	2,704.6	2,723.0	2,670.5	2,701.8	2,722.3	2,728.2	2,723.4	2,714.5	2,682.3
2012	2,646.3	2,652.5	2,668.0	2,709.1	2,739.7	2,761.5	2,721.5	2,739.0	2,755.6	2,770.6	2,770.9	2,759.1	2,724.5
2013	2,698.7	2,710.5	2,718.6	2,741.7	2,789.6	2,811.2	2,766.8	2,786.8	2,803.3	2,819.5	2,814.6	2,803.0	2,772.0
2014	2,730.6	2,739.2	2,741.9	2,783.4	2,829.6	2,854.7	2,825.8	2,836.3	2,835.3	2,851.8	2,849.1	2,839.6	2,809.8
2015	2,771.0	2,781.7	2,788.2	2,837.7	2,876.2	2,896.8	2,873.3	2,877.2	2,873.9	2,896.7	2,893.1	2,881.4	2,853.9
2016	2,817.2	2,826.7	2,830.6	2,878.8	2,907.4	2,919.7	2,913.4	2,922.4	2,921.7	2,932.2	2,926.5	2,911.1	2,892.3
2017	2,866.5	2,872.9	2,880.4	2,913.4	2,944.6	2,969.8	2,947.7	2,951.6	2,953.3	2,966.5	2,956.6	2,941.5	2,930.4
Total Private													
2007	2,295.2	2,289.0	2,300.2	2,323.5	2,367.6	2,399.0	2,392.4	2,399.8	2,378.3	2,374.0	2,371.4	2,361.6	2,354.3
2008	2,299.4	2,295.3	2,302.5	2,320.8	2,361.4	2,385.3	2,380.3	2,388.0	2,361.0	2,357.7	2,335.1	2,311.4	2,341.5
2009	2,233.9	2,212.6	2,204.0	2,223.5	2,251.8	2,261.6	2,254.2	2,258.5	2,231.8	2,238.7	2,228.2	2,217.6	2,234.7
2010	2,150.4	2,145.1	2,152.7	2,200.1	2,230.0	2,253.7	2,256.4	2,267.3	2,247.9	2,259.4	2,252.0	2,239.5	2,221.2
2011	2,189.7	2,188.4	2,197.7	2,245.6	2,283.1	2,305.2	2,309.5	2,324.3	2,316.9	2,309.1	2,302.2	2,293.4	2,272.1
2012	2,236.3	2,234.5	2,249.7	2,288.4	2,319.4	2,345.0	2,345.8	2,359.8	2,347.8	2,348.5	2,344.0	2,334.8	2,312.8
2013	2,285.3	2,288.0	2,297.9	2,320.3	2,366.5	2,394.7	2,393.8	2,409.2	2,392.8	2,394.3	2,385.4	2,376.7	2,358.7
2014	2,314.6	2,314.0	2,317.2	2,356.0	2,401.9	2,431.7	2,433.4	2,446.4	2,422.7	2,423.8	2,418.2	2,411.6	2,391.0
2015	2,353.0	2,356.5	2,365.0	2,410.4	2,448.5	2,474.9	2,479.6	2,486.5	2,461.8	2,469.3	2,462.8	2,452.2	2,435.0
2016	2,396.2	2,399.6	2,403.0	2,454.4	2,482.1	2,500.0	2,518.9	2,527.7	2,506.5	2,505.0	2,497.2	2,486.0	2,473.1
2017	2,441.9	2,443.9	2,452.4	2,485.6	2,516.9	2,547.4	2,549.2	2,552.4	2,529.2	2,530.0	2,518.0	2,507.7	2,506.2
Goods Producing													
2007	452.0	446.6	449.4	454.9	471.9	485.5	485.0	486.9	479.0	474.8	468.0	456.5	467.5
2008	440.4	436.6	437.5	442.2	458.9	470.0	471.1	472.3	463.7	459.9	445.9	429.5	452.3
2009	406.2	395.5	389.5	391.1	399.1	406.7	407.8	407.9	402.8	400.3	392.6	381.3	398.4
2010	362.9	358.3	359.7	375.3	386.4	397.5	404.3	405.8	402.5	402.0	395.1	385.0	386.2
2011	372.9	371.2	373.6	386.1	399.4	411.2	417.1	420.5	416.1	414.6	407.1	397.9	399.0
2012	383.1	381.0	386.5	398.8	409.3	421.6	424.9	427.3	422.5	420.1	412.4	404.1	407.6
2013	390.0	388.8	392.6	399.1	416.0	428.5	431.5	435.7	431.4	429.2	423.3	413.0	414.9
2014	399.6	398.7	400.8	410.9	428.3	442.1	446.7	449.8	443.7	442.4	434.9	427.8	427.1
2015	413.7	413.2	416.7	431.1	442.9	455.3	460.0	460.3	453.3	451.0	443.7	434.5	439.6
2016	417.0	415.8	418.7	433.4	443.9	453.9	458.7	459.5	453.4	451.2	444.3	432.5	440.2
2017	420.7	420.9	425.1	435.0	447.8	460.3	463.4	463.7	457.1	454.4	447.5	437.6	444.5
Service-Providing													
2007	2,257.4	2,262.9	2,270.4	2,288.8	2,319.7	2,335.6	2,296.9	2,296.9	2,306.9	2,321.7	2,329.3	2,330.1	2,301.4
2008	2,276.1	2,282.6	2,289.4	2,302.5	2,330.7	2,341.8	2,301.3	2,304.3	2,311.2	2,325.1	2,319.8	2,311.9	2,308.1
2009	2,245.1	2,242.1	2,239.7	2,259.1	2,281.2	2,280.6	2,239.5	2,235.9	2,233.1	2,262.1	2,262.1	2,262.4	2,253.6
2010	2,204.2	2,210.3	2,218.4	2,251.1	2,274.2	2,282.0	2,241.4	2,244.7	2,250.2	2,279.7	2,282.7	2,279.3	2,251.5
2011	2,230.4	2,238.5	2,245.1	2,281.5	2,305.2	2,311.8	2,253.4	2,281.3	2,306.2	2,313.6	2,316.3	2,316.6	2,283.3
2012	2,263.2	2,271.5	2,281.5	2,310.3	2,330.4	2,339.9	2,296.6	2,311.7	2,333.1	2,350.5	2,358.5	2,355.0	2,316.9
2013	2,308.7	2,321.7	2,326.0	2,342.6	2,373.6	2,382.7	2,335.3	2,351.1	2,371.9	2,390.3	2,391.3	2,390.0	2,357.1
2014	2,331.0	2,340.5	2,341.1	2,372.5	2,401.3	2,412.6	2,379.1	2,386.5	2,391.6	2,409.4	2,414.2	2,411.8	2,382.6
2015	2,357.3	2,368.5	2,371.5	2,406.6	2,433.3	2,441.5	2,413.3	2,416.9	2,420.6	2,445.7	2,449.4	2,446.9	2,414.3
2016	2,400.2	2,410.9	2,411.9	2,445.4	2,463.5	2,465.8	2,454.7	2,462.9	2,468.3	2,481.0	2,482.2	2,478.6	2,452.1
2017	2,445.8	2,452.0	2,455.3	2,478.4	2,496.8	2,509.5	2,484.3	2,487.9	2,496.2	2,512.1	2,509.1	2,503.9	2,485.9
Mining and Logging													
2007	5.6	5.6	5.6	5.6	5.9	6.1	6.3	6.4	6.2	6.2	6.2	6.0	6.0
2008	5.9	5.9	5.9	5.9	6.3	6.4	6.7	6.7	6.5	6.5	6.3	6.0	6.3
2009	5.8	5.6	5.3	5.1	4.6	4.4	5.3	5.0	4.6	5.7	5.4	5.0	5.2
2010	5.3	5.4	5.4	5.7	6.0	5.6	6.5	6.5	6.4	6.5	6.3	6.0	6.0
2011	6.0	6.2	6.1	6.1	6.5	6.8	7.0	7.1	6.9	7.0	6.9	6.6	6.6
2012	6.6	6.6	6.6	6.8	7.0	7.3	7.4	7.5	7.2	7.2	7.1	6.8	7.0
2013	6.6	6.6	6.7	6.6	6.9	7.2	7.2	7.4	7.2	7.2	7.1	6.9	7.0
2014	6.6	6.7	6.7	6.8	7.1	7.3	7.6	7.6	7.4	7.5	7.4	7.1	7.2
2015	6.8	6.9	7.0	7.1	7.3	7.4	7.6	7.2	6.9	6.8	6.7	6.4	7.0
2016	5.5	5.4	5.7	5.7	6.4	6.4	6.6	6.7	6.7	6.8	6.5	6.2	6.2
2017	6.1	6.2	6.3	6.3	6.6	6.8	6.8	6.8	6.8	6.8	6.7	6.3	6.5

1. Employment by Industry: Minnesota, Selected Years, 2007–2017—*Continued*

(Numbers in thousands, not seasonally adjusted)

Industry and year	January	February	March	April	May	June	July	August	September	October	November	December	Annual average
Construction													
2007	108.0	104.0	106.5	110.3	124.9	132.6	132.7	133.4	129.2	126.7	121.6	111.3	120.1
2008	100.3	97.4	98.4	102.3	115.7	122.6	123.8	123.9	119.5	116.6	107.9	97.4	110.5
2009	82.1	79.6	79.6	86.5	97.7	102.4	103.9	103.8	102.3	100.0	95.2	87.3	93.4
2010	73.3	69.5	70.2	81.9	89.4	95.6	99.2	99.8	98.0	97.9	92.8	83.4	87.6
2011	74.2	72.7	74.5	83.3	93.6	101.1	103.8	105.6	103.8	102.5	97.3	88.8	91.8
2012	77.4	75.9	79.7	90.0	98.0	104.4	106.9	108.2	105.2	104.0	98.2	91.4	94.9
2013	80.5	80.0	82.4	88.9	102.7	110.3	113.4	116.2	114.2	112.8	107.7	98.1	100.6
2014	87.9	86.7	88.9	96.5	110.6	119.3	122.1	123.4	120.4	119.0	112.3	105.2	107.7
2015	94.4	93.9	96.3	109.3	119.2	127.0	130.2	130.6	126.6	125.1	118.6	110.8	115.2
2016	97.3	96.4	98.6	112.2	121.1	127.1	129.8	129.6	126.8	125.3	120.1	110.0	116.2
2017	100.7	100.8	104.2	113.7	124.1	131.3	133.1	133.1	129.8	127.1	122.5	114.6	119.6
Manufacturing													
2007	338.4	337.0	337.3	339.0	341.1	346.8	346.0	347.1	343.6	341.9	340.2	339.2	341.5
2008	334.2	333.3	333.2	334.0	336.9	341.0	340.6	341.7	337.7	336.8	331.7	326.1	335.6
2009	318.3	310.3	304.6	299.5	296.8	299.9	298.6	299.1	295.9	294.6	292.0	289.0	299.9
2010	284.3	283.4	284.1	287.7	291.0	296.3	298.6	299.5	298.1	297.6	296.0	295.6	292.7
2011	292.7	292.3	293.0	296.7	299.3	303.3	306.3	307.8	305.4	305.1	302.9	302.5	300.6
2012	299.1	298.5	300.2	302.0	304.3	309.9	310.6	311.6	310.1	308.9	307.1	305.9	305.7
2013	302.9	302.2	303.5	303.6	306.4	311.0	310.9	312.1	310.0	309.2	308.5	308.0	307.4
2014	305.1	305.3	305.2	307.6	310.6	315.5	317.0	318.8	315.9	315.9	315.2	315.5	312.3
2015	312.5	312.4	313.4	314.7	316.4	320.9	322.2	322.5	319.8	319.1	318.4	317.3	317.5
2016	314.2	314.0	314.4	315.5	316.4	320.4	322.3	323.2	319.9	319.1	317.7	316.3	317.8
2017	313.9	313.9	314.6	315.0	317.1	322.2	323.5	323.8	320.5	320.5	318.3	316.7	318.3
Trade, Transportation, and Utilities													
2007	523.7	518.8	519.3	523.2	530.7	534.4	529.4	529.8	528.2	531.7	539.6	543.0	529.3
2008	523.6	516.8	518.2	519.9	526.7	527.2	522.4	522.2	519.0	520.7	524.1	523.7	522.0
2009	502.9	495.2	492.5	494.1	500.0	501.2	494.7	494.5	490.6	493.0	499.6	500.5	496.6
2010	482.3	476.6	477.5	486.4	491.6	496.1	491.6	491.5	489.5	494.1	500.7	503.1	490.1
2011	484.7	480.9	482.3	492.2	499.0	500.9	499.5	500.4	500.7	502.3	509.6	513.0	497.1
2012	495.4	488.6	491.4	498.4	504.9	506.9	503.4	505.1	503.4	507.8	517.1	517.5	503.3
2013	502.3	497.0	498.2	501.4	510.7	515.3	511.5	514.8	512.8	516.3	523.7	527.2	510.9
2014	506.8	502.2	503.0	510.7	517.9	521.9	519.2	520.7	515.8	520.9	528.0	533.4	516.7
2015	514.0	509.5	510.7	519.5	526.0	530.4	527.4	528.6	524.0	529.5	536.4	539.5	524.6
2016	521.6	518.5	519.2	528.2	533.3	534.3	535.3	536.7	531.9	536.1	541.8	546.3	531.9
2017	531.9	527.6	527.3	533.3	538.3	541.5	539.3	539.1	534.6	539.3	546.7	551.5	537.5
Wholesale Trade													
2007	131.1	131.0	131.6	132.9	134.5	135.5	135.2	135.2	133.2	133.6	133.7	133.6	133.4
2008	131.7	131.5	132.1	132.8	134.3	134.9	135.0	134.9	132.9	132.6	132.1	131.2	133.0
2009	128.2	127.0	126.1	127.3	127.5	127.6	127.2	126.5	124.0	123.9	124.0	123.5	126.1
2010	120.8	120.4	120.8	123.0	123.6	124.9	125.1	124.8	123.0	124.3	124.2	123.6	123.2
2011	122.1	122.3	122.8	125.4	127.0	127.2	128.0	128.0	126.6	126.7	126.6	126.4	125.8
2012	125.2	125.2	126.2	128.6	129.5	130.7	131.1	130.5	128.9	129.3	129.4	129.4	128.7
2013	127.9	127.8	128.3	129.3	131.4	132.4	132.5	132.1	130.4	130.9	131.4	130.7	130.4
2014	128.9	129.0	129.4	130.7	132.7	133.8	133.7	133.5	131.7	132.3	132.6	132.4	131.7
2015	130.4	130.1	130.4	132.6	133.1	134.2	134.4	134.0	131.9	132.5	132.5	131.9	132.3
2016	130.0	129.9	130.2	132.5	133.2	132.9	133.7	133.4	131.5	131.5	131.3	130.9	131.8
2017	130.6	130.3	130.6	132.0	133.1	133.8	134.3	133.9	132.0	132.6	133.4	132.8	132.5
Retail Trade													
2007	299.2	293.7	294.4	296.3	301.5	304.9	302.3	302.7	299.2	301.2	309.2	311.6	301.4
2008	297.2	290.2	290.9	292.1	296.4	297.5	295.4	295.5	290.7	291.7	296.1	296.1	294.2
2009	282.8	276.8	274.8	275.9	281.3	283.6	280.4	281.6	276.1	278.0	284.1	285.3	280.1
2010	272.8	267.9	268.2	273.7	277.8	281.2	279.3	280.5	276.2	278.0	283.9	286.1	277.1
2011	272.6	268.4	269.0	275.5	280.0	282.9	282.5	284.1	281.6	282.2	289.5	292.1	280.0
2012	279.3	272.7	274.4	277.7	282.3	284.9	283.0	284.6	281.6	284.6	293.4	293.5	282.7
2013	282.0	276.5	277.4	279.6	285.4	290.3	288.8	291.1	287.5	288.5	295.0	298.5	286.7
2014	283.1	278.8	279.3	283.9	288.4	292.3	292.1	293.0	287.0	289.9	296.4	300.3	288.7
2015	286.5	282.3	283.2	287.8	293.4	297.9	296.6	298.0	292.4	295.6	301.9	304.0	293.3
2016	291.7	288.7	289.3	294.6	298.2	300.6	302.8	303.2	296.2	299.0	304.0	306.1	297.9
2017	295.6	291.8	291.8	295.7	298.7	301.9	301.7	301.7	295.1	299.2	305.9	307.3	298.9

1. Employment by Industry: Minnesota, Selected Years, 2007–2017—*Continued*

(Numbers in thousands, not seasonally adjusted)

Industry and year	January	February	March	April	May	June	July	August	September	October	November	December	Annual average
Transportation and Utilities													
2007	93.4	94.1	93.3	94.0	94.7	94.0	91.9	91.9	95.8	96.9	96.7	97.8	94.5
2008	94.7	95.1	95.2	95.0	96.0	94.8	92.0	91.8	95.4	96.4	95.9	96.4	94.9
2009	91.9	91.4	91.6	90.9	91.2	90.0	87.1	86.4	90.5	91.1	91.5	91.7	90.4
2010	88.7	88.3	88.5	89.7	90.2	90.0	87.2	86.2	90.3	91.8	92.6	93.4	89.7
2011	90.0	90.2	90.5	91.3	92.0	90.8	89.0	88.3	92.5	93.4	93.5	94.5	91.3
2012	90.9	90.7	90.8	92.1	93.1	91.3	89.3	90.0	92.9	93.9	94.3	94.6	92.0
2013	92.4	92.7	92.5	92.5	93.9	92.6	90.2	91.6	94.9	96.9	97.3	98.0	93.8
2014	94.8	94.4	94.3	96.1	96.8	95.8	93.4	94.2	97.1	98.7	99.0	100.7	96.3
2015	97.1	97.1	97.1	99.1	99.5	98.3	96.4	96.6	99.7	101.4	102.0	103.6	99.0
2016	99.9	99.9	99.7	101.1	101.9	100.8	98.8	100.1	104.2	105.6	106.5	109.3	102.3
2017	105.7	105.5	104.9	105.6	106.5	105.8	103.3	103.5	107.5	107.5	107.4	111.4	106.2
Information													
2007	57.9	57.9	58.2	58.2	58.3	58.6	58.2	58.2	57.6	57.3	57.4	57.8	58.0
2008	57.6	57.4	57.6	57.8	57.7	57.9	58.0	58.0	57.6	57.0	57.1	56.4	57.5
2009	56.1	55.9	55.7	55.1	55.2	55.3	55.6	55.5	54.9	54.7	55.0	54.8	55.3
2010	54.4	54.4	54.3	54.1	54.0	54.2	54.4	54.4	53.7	53.8	53.9	53.7	54.1
2011	53.7	53.3	53.1	53.8	53.8	54.1	54.3	54.6	54.0	53.8	53.8	53.8	53.8
2012	52.9	53.0	53.0	53.5	53.9	54.0	54.0	54.0	53.6	53.7	53.6	53.8	53.6
2013	53.1	53.2	53.1	53.1	53.3	53.3	53.8	53.6	52.8	52.7	53.0	53.1	53.2
2014	52.6	52.5	52.2	52.2	52.4	52.8	53.1	53.1	52.1	52.2	52.0	52.4	52.5
2015	51.4	51.2	51.1	51.1	51.4	51.7	52.0	52.0	51.0	50.9	51.1	50.9	51.3
2016	50.2	50.2	50.2	50.4	50.6	50.6	51.0	51.4	51.3	50.8	50.7	50.8	50.7
2017	50.4	50.3	50.3	50.4	50.4	50.6	50.6	50.9	50.0	50.4	50.5	50.3	50.4
Financial Activities													
2007	171.4	171.7	171.7	171.2	171.3	173.4	173.0	172.6	170.9	170.9	170.9	171.2	171.7
2008	168.4	168.5	168.7	168.2	168.5	169.6	170.1	169.9	167.8	167.0	166.6	167.4	168.4
2009	164.5	163.9	163.3	163.0	163.6	164.5	164.7	163.9	162.2	162.5	162.2	162.7	163.4
2010	160.5	160.2	160.0	160.4	161.0	162.7	163.1	163.4	162.1	163.4	163.3	164.4	162.0
2011	162.1	162.1	162.0	162.1	162.6	163.2	164.1	164.3	162.5	162.4	162.2	162.5	162.7
2012	162.0	162.4	162.6	163.4	164.8	166.9	167.7	168.2	167.2	168.1	168.5	169.3	165.9
2013	168.5	169.0	169.4	169.1	169.9	171.7	172.4	172.2	170.2	170.3	170.2	170.6	170.3
2014	168.8	168.3	168.4	168.9	169.9	171.8	172.2	171.8	169.6	169.7	169.6	170.3	169.9
2015	170.3	170.3	170.3	171.5	172.8	174.6	176.4	176.3	173.8	174.4	174.5	175.0	173.4
2016	173.5	173.9	173.9	175.4	175.9	177.3	179.7	179.7	177.8	178.3	178.2	178.9	176.9
2017	178.4	178.5	178.8	179.0	179.6	182.1	183.2	182.7	180.1	179.6	179.1	179.5	180.1
Professional and Business Services													
2007	325.0	326.2	328.4	331.4	334.8	339.2	339.8	343.3	339.5	339.6	338.9	337.6	335.3
2008	328.4	329.2	329.1	332.2	335.5	338.9	339.8	342.3	338.6	338.9	334.6	330.6	334.8
2009	314.6	310.4	308.2	311.9	313.5	314.3	313.9	317.7	312.5	318.5	318.1	318.4	314.3
2010	307.1	308.1	308.0	317.0	319.3	323.2	326.8	331.0	325.7	330.2	330.7	329.0	321.3
2011	322.0	322.9	324.6	333.2	335.3	338.7	343.2	347.4	346.0	347.4	346.1	344.3	337.6
2012	333.0	333.2	334.9	342.0	343.5	347.3	350.0	353.6	350.3	353.2	351.7	351.3	345.3
2013	342.1	345.3	346.3	350.1	352.9	358.2	359.4	363.3	359.5	364.4	361.5	361.1	355.3
2014	349.2	349.8	349.6	354.9	358.9	363.7	366.9	370.1	364.6	369.1	370.3	365.4	361.0
2015	354.9	356.0	355.6	364.9	368.2	369.8	372.4	373.4	367.0	374.8	374.3	370.2	366.8
2016	360.7	362.8	359.9	370.2	371.1	373.2	378.6	378.7	376.9	380.8	377.7	375.4	372.2
2017	366.1	365.3	366.1	371.5	373.1	376.1	378.3	378.8	374.7	380.1	378.0	377.0	373.8
Education and Health Services													
2007	418.0	421.1	422.9	426.1	428.1	426.3	425.6	426.0	429.4	435.1	438.4	437.6	427.9
2008	433.0	437.8	439.8	442.9	442.4	439.6	438.6	439.8	443.2	450.5	452.7	452.9	442.8
2009	448.2	452.1	453.8	458.1	457.5	450.3	448.6	448.6	448.1	458.0	458.5	458.8	453.4
2010	451.3	456.4	458.3	461.1	461.3	456.1	450.8	453.0	456.2	463.4	465.5	464.0	458.1
2011	460.8	464.6	464.7	469.7	470.3	464.6	459.7	461.9	468.7	472.2	473.6	474.1	467.1
2012	468.0	473.6	474.0	476.2	476.2	469.8	467.3	470.7	478.5	483.5	485.6	484.9	475.7
2013	481.0	486.5	486.3	490.2	490.4	483.5	480.6	483.4	489.5	494.9	497.0	495.4	488.2
2014	489.8	495.0	494.9	498.3	498.3	491.8	488.8	491.6	498.8	502.2	504.4	503.7	496.5
2015	496.6	503.3	504.1	505.3	506.3	500.3	498.8	501.0	509.1	513.0	515.2	514.2	505.6
2016	511.8	516.5	516.2	522.0	520.8	513.2	514.6	518.0	522.8	524.1	529.8	529.9	520.0
2017	525.3	531.4	531.2	535.1	534.4	530.4	527.1	528.3	535.7	538.6	542.9	541.5	533.5

1. Employment by Industry: Minnesota, Selected Years, 2007–2017—*Continued*

(Numbers in thousands, not seasonally adjusted)

Industry and year	January	February	March	April	May	June	July	August	September	October	November	December	Annual average
Leisure and Hospitality													
2007	232.1	231.9	234.0	241.6	254.8	263.3	263.6	265.1	257.0	248.1	241.3	240.5	247.8
2008	232.9	232.4	234.9	239.5	253.2	261.9	260.9	263.8	253.2	245.2	236.4	234.6	245.7
2009	226.7	224.9	225.8	234.2	246.5	252.1	252.4	254.0	245.3	237.2	228.3	227.0	237.9
2010	219.5	218.5	221.3	232.1	242.3	248.5	250.2	252.6	244.5	237.7	228.8	226.4	235.2
2011	220.8	220.4	223.8	233.7	247.5	255.9	255.1	258.3	252.7	241.1	234.6	232.3	239.7
2012	227.7	228.4	232.5	240.6	251.0	260.6	261.4	263.7	256.6	246.2	239.3	238.0	245.5
2013	233.3	232.9	235.9	241.3	256.4	266.4	267.8	269.1	261.1	252.1	243.2	243.0	250.2
2014	236.7	236.9	237.5	247.7	262.6	272.6	271.7	274.5	264.7	253.7	245.9	245.6	254.2
2015	240.3	240.8	243.6	252.8	266.4	277.0	277.1	279.3	269.9	260.9	253.1	253.0	259.5
2016	248.1	248.1	250.4	259.3	270.7	280.7	283.6	286.0	275.6	267.1	258.5	256.2	265.4
2017	254.0	255.0	257.9	265.0	276.4	288.0	289.5	291.0	280.2	270.3	256.8	254.7	269.9
Other Services													
2007	115.1	114.8	116.3	116.9	117.7	118.3	117.8	117.9	116.7	116.5	116.9	117.4	116.9
2008	115.1	116.6	116.7	118.1	118.5	120.2	119.4	119.7	117.9	118.5	117.7	116.3	117.9
2009	114.7	114.7	115.2	116.0	116.4	117.2	116.5	116.4	115.4	114.5	113.9	114.1	115.4
2010	112.4	112.6	113.6	113.7	114.1	115.4	115.2	115.6	113.7	114.8	114.0	113.9	114.1
2011	112.7	113.0	113.6	114.8	115.2	116.6	116.5	116.9	116.2	115.3	115.2	115.5	115.1
2012	114.2	114.3	114.8	115.5	115.8	117.9	117.1	117.2	115.7	115.9	115.8	115.9	115.8
2013	115.0	115.3	116.1	116.0	116.9	117.8	116.8	117.1	115.5	114.4	113.5	113.3	115.6
2014	111.1	110.6	110.8	112.4	113.6	115.0	114.8	114.8	113.4	113.6	113.1	113.0	113.0
2015	111.8	112.2	112.9	114.2	114.5	115.8	115.5	115.6	113.7	114.8	114.5	114.9	114.2
2016	113.3	113.8	114.5	115.5	115.8	116.8	117.4	117.7	116.8	116.6	116.2	116.0	115.9
2017	115.1	114.9	115.7	116.3	116.9	118.4	117.8	117.9	116.8	117.3	116.5	115.6	116.6
Government													
2007	414.2	420.5	419.6	420.2	424.0	422.1	389.5	384.0	407.6	422.5	425.9	425.0	414.6
2008	417.1	423.9	424.4	423.9	428.2	426.5	392.1	388.6	413.9	427.3	430.6	430.0	418.9
2009	417.4	425.0	425.2	426.7	428.5	425.7	393.1	385.3	404.1	423.7	426.5	426.1	417.3
2010	416.7	423.5	425.4	426.3	430.6	425.8	389.3	383.2	404.8	422.3	425.8	424.8	416.5
2011	413.6	421.3	421.0	422.0	421.5	417.8	361.0	377.5	405.4	419.1	421.2	421.1	410.2
2012	410.0	418.0	418.3	420.7	420.3	416.5	375.7	379.2	407.8	422.1	426.9	424.3	411.7
2013	413.4	422.5	420.7	421.4	423.1	416.5	373.0	377.6	410.5	425.2	429.2	426.3	413.3
2014	416.0	425.2	424.7	427.4	427.7	423.0	392.4	389.9	412.6	428.0	430.9	428.0	418.8
2015	418.0	425.2	423.2	427.3	427.7	421.9	393.7	390.7	412.1	427.4	430.3	429.2	418.9
2016	421.0	427.1	427.6	424.4	425.3	419.7	394.5	394.7	415.2	427.2	429.3	425.1	419.3
2017	424.6	429.0	428.0	427.8	427.7	422.4	398.5	399.2	424.1	436.5	438.6	433.8	424.2

2. Average Weekly Hours by Selected Industry: Minnesota, 2013–2017

(Not seasonally adjusted)

Industry and year	January	February	March	April	May	June	July	August	September	October	November	December	Annual average
Total Private													
2013	33.1	33.2	33.4	33.2	33.4	34.4	33.4	33.7	34.3	33.7	33.7	34.0	33.7
2014	33.2	33.9	34.0	33.7	34.0	34.5	34.2	34.3	34.1	34.1	34.2	33.9	34.0
2015	33.5	33.9	33.9	33.6	33.8	34.1	34.2	34.8	33.9	34.0	34.2	33.7	34.0
2016	33.5	33.4	33.5	33.7	34.3	34.3	34.1	34.1	34.1	34.5	34.2	33.9	34.0
2017	34.0	33.8	33.8	34.2	33.9	34.1	34.4	34.2	34.1	34.4	34.1	33.9	34.1
Goods Producing													
2013	39.8	39.8	40.0	40.1	40.1	41.0	40.5	41.2	41.3	41.3	40.5	40.3	40.5
2014	39.7	40.2	40.6	40.4	41.1	41.4	41.2	41.8	41.4	41.3	40.4	40.3	40.8
2015	39.2	39.3	39.2	39.1	39.7	40.1	39.6	40.4	38.9	39.5	39.3	39.1	39.5
2016	38.8	38.8	38.8	39.1	39.2	39.7	39.2	39.5	39.9	39.5	39.6	38.7	39.2
2017	38.6	39.1	39.5	39.0	39.6	39.8	39.9	40.3	40.4	39.9	39.5	39.6	39.6
Construction													
2013	38.9	38.4	38.7	38.4	39.1	41.1	40.2	41.2	41.2	41.5	39.4	37.8	39.8
2014	37.7	37.0	38.2	38.3	40.6	40.9	41.6	42.0	41.2	40.8	37.6	37.5	39.6
2015	36.3	37.0	37.0	38.2	40.2	41.6	41.2	42.1	38.6	40.3	38.8	38.1	39.3
2016	37.5	37.6	37.9	38.4	38.9	40.9	41.0	40.4	40.8	41.0	40.0	37.8	39.5
2017	37.5	38.4	38.6	38.7	40.1	40.5	40.4	41.0	40.4	40.2	38.9	38.4	39.5
Manufacturing													
2013	40.0	40.1	40.3	40.6	40.4	40.8	40.4	41.0	41.2	41.2	40.9	41.0	40.7
2014	40.2	41.0	41.1	40.7	41.0	41.3	40.6	41.4	41.3	41.3	41.3	41.0	41.0
2015	39.8	39.8	39.8	39.3	39.6	39.6	39.0	39.9	39.4	39.6	40.0	39.8	39.6
2016	39.4	39.3	39.5	39.6	39.6	39.5	38.6	39.3	39.6	38.8	39.4	39.0	39.3
2017	39.0	39.3	39.9	39.3	39.4	39.5	39.7	39.9	40.3	39.6	39.6	39.9	39.6
Trade, Transportation, and Utilities													
2013	31.9	32.3	32.6	32.4	33.2	33.6	33.2	32.9	33.6	33.0	33.0	33.7	33.0
2014	32.4	32.9	33.1	33.2	33.8	33.6	33.7	33.4	33.7	33.4	33.5	33.3	33.3
2015	32.7	33.2	32.8	32.6	32.7	33.0	33.3	33.8	33.3	32.9	33.0	32.9	33.0
2016	32.0	32.2	32.3	32.3	33.2	33.0	33.1	32.7	32.9	33.2	32.7	32.9	32.7
2017	32.3	31.7	31.8	32.4	31.9	32.2	32.8	32.4	32.2	32.0	32.6	32.8	32.3
Financial Activities													
2013	37.2	37.5	37.2	37.2	37.1	38.6	36.1	36.5	38.1	36.4	36.8	37.8	37.2
2014	37.1	37.7	37.7	36.5	36.8	37.9	36.6	37.1	36.7	36.9	37.7	36.8	37.1
2015	37.0	37.4	37.3	36.9	36.6	36.8	36.5	37.5	36.5	36.7	37.6	36.7	36.9
2016	37.3	37.2	37.0	36.9	38.0	37.4	37.2	36.8	37.2	38.1	37.2	37.3	37.3
2017	38.6	37.7	37.5	38.6	37.5	37.8	38.8	37.5	37.6	38.5	37.6	37.4	37.9
Professional and Business Services													
2013	34.8	35.4	35.5	35.1	35.0	36.5	34.3	34.8	36.3	35.1	35.3	35.7	35.3
2014	34.4	36.1	36.1	35.3	35.7	36.8	35.8	36.0	35.4	35.8	36.4	35.5	35.8
2015	35.4	36.4	36.6	35.8	36.2	36.4	36.3	37.5	35.6	36.7	37.3	35.8	36.3
2016	35.5	35.1	35.4	35.2	36.4	37.6	37.1	37.2	37.0	37.9	37.8	37.1	36.6
2017	38.0	37.6	36.8	37.7	37.2	37.5	37.4	37.1	36.8	37.7	37.1	36.2	37.3
Education and Health Services													
2013	31.1	30.9	31.0	30.8	30.8	31.2	31.0	31.2	31.3	31.1	31.1	31.3	31.1
2014	31.1	31.1	31.0	31.3	31.1	31.3	31.2	31.4	31.6	31.7	32.0	32.2	31.4
2015	32.2	32.4	32.6	32.5	32.6	32.9	33.2	33.2	33.3	33.1	33.2	33.2	32.9
2016	33.1	32.9	33.0	33.2	33.5	32.9	33.1	33.1	32.9	33.3	33.5	33.5	33.2
2017	33.9	33.6	33.6	34.1	33.7	33.7	34.0	33.9	34.1	34.6	34.2	34.2	34.0
Leisure and Hospitality													
2013	22.0	22.6	23.2	22.4	22.9	23.9	24.2	24.4	24.0	23.3	23.0	22.9	23.3
2014	22.2	23.4	23.5	23.1	23.5	24.3	24.0	24.1	23.4	23.2	23.3	22.6	23.4
2015	22.4	23.1	23.4	22.7	23.0	24.0	24.1	24.7	23.6	23.5	23.4	22.6	23.4
2016	22.8	22.7	22.8	23.0	23.5	24.0	23.6	23.7	22.6	23.3	22.4	22.0	23.1
2017	22.0	22.1	22.2	22.1	22.1	23.1	23.3	22.8	22.2	22.5	21.5	21.2	22.3
Other Services													
2013	28.4	28.7	29.5	29.2	29.5	30.1	29.1	29.5	30.0	30.2	30.5	31.5	29.7
2014	31.1	31.6	31.4	30.9	30.7	31.4	30.9	30.6	30.6	30.5	30.9	29.9	30.9
2015	30.4	31.3	30.5	30.1	30.6	30.1	31.0	31.2	29.8	29.6	30.2	29.0	30.3
2016	29.7	29.8	29.1	29.3	30.0	29.6	28.4	29.3	29.1	29.6	28.8	28.5	29.3
2017	28.0	28.1	28.2	28.8	28.8	28.8	29.0	28.3	27.9	28.8	28.0	28.7	28.5

3. Average Hourly Earnings by Selected Industry: Minnesota, 2013–2017

(Dollars, not seasonally adjusted)

Industry and year	January	February	March	April	May	June	July	August	September	October	November	December	Annual average
Total Private													
2013	25.71	25.55	25.55	25.68	25.52	25.55	25.57	25.40	25.77	25.75	25.74	25.93	25.64
2014	26.00	25.95	25.83	25.86	25.81	25.73	25.60	25.58	25.75	25.68	25.88	25.82	25.79
2015	26.08	26.08	26.32	25.98	25.79	25.71	25.80	25.98	26.00	26.39	26.32	26.36	26.06
2016	26.71	26.54	27.05	26.90	26.99	26.64	26.95	26.88	27.32	27.63	27.78	27.85	27.11
2017	28.20	28.26	28.28	28.88	28.25	27.94	28.42	28.20	28.58	28.77	28.54	28.67	28.42
Goods Producing													
2013	26.23	26.11	26.25	26.59	26.51	26.46	26.51	26.25	26.45	26.40	26.40	26.61	26.40
2014	26.72	26.44	26.58	26.68	27.07	26.83	26.85	26.68	26.91	26.64	26.28	26.47	26.68
2015	26.72	26.42	26.38	26.57	26.44	26.35	26.58	26.58	26.37	26.74	26.29	26.26	26.48
2016	26.61	26.62	26.53	27.11	27.21	27.37	28.11	27.80	28.31	28.55	28.26	28.43	27.60
2017	28.32	28.35	28.06	28.67	28.62	28.37	28.67	28.44	28.61	28.76	28.43	28.57	28.49
Construction													
2013	29.14	28.69	29.45	29.86	28.97	28.58	28.27	28.24	28.30	28.38	28.15	28.54	28.65
2014	28.70	28.78	28.58	28.63	29.75	28.73	28.92	29.18	29.89	29.74	30.02	30.21	29.30
2015	30.49	30.73	30.78	30.36	30.73	30.31	30.27	30.60	30.68	30.84	30.19	30.48	30.53
2016	30.63	30.31	30.61	30.95	31.29	31.53	31.80	31.59	32.26	32.46	32.33	32.53	31.59
2017	32.06	32.03	32.20	31.70	32.18	32.30	32.34	32.53	32.37	33.03	32.15	32.27	32.28
Manufacturing													
2013	25.28	25.34	25.23	25.44	25.55	25.55	25.70	25.32	25.57	25.50	25.59	25.81	25.49
2014	25.93	25.57	25.76	25.83	25.87	25.90	25.80	25.38	25.39	25.08	24.69	25.06	25.52
2015	25.42	24.98	24.91	25.12	24.71	24.58	24.90	24.75	24.55	24.97	24.73	24.70	24.86
2016	25.19	25.30	25.07	25.63	25.58	25.59	26.30	25.94	26.44	26.66	26.41	26.83	25.91
2017	26.91	26.90	26.44	27.31	26.92	26.44	26.86	26.44	26.82	26.78	26.77	27.04	26.80
Trade, Transportation, and Utilities													
2013	22.39	22.49	22.40	22.57	22.32	22.56	22.50	22.46	22.94	22.73	22.75	22.34	22.54
2014	22.85	22.52	22.54	23.12	22.98	22.87	22.45	22.53	22.57	22.46	22.77	22.25	22.66
2015	22.92	22.72	22.68	22.63	22.52	22.10	22.24	22.20	22.21	22.27	22.01	22.03	22.37
2016	21.96	21.79	21.69	21.93	22.01	21.76	21.56	21.46	21.74	21.77	21.62	21.18	21.70
2017	21.93	21.68	21.39	22.30	21.84	21.77	22.25	22.05	22.59	22.57	22.47	22.16	22.09
Financial Activities													
2013	32.83	33.50	33.80	33.43	33.47	33.87	34.23	34.01	33.53	33.62	33.43	33.56	33.61
2014	33.08	33.46	33.08	32.96	32.55	32.29	31.66	31.19	31.14	31.15	31.88	31.46	32.16
2015	30.88	31.59	31.64	31.79	32.24	32.39	32.43	32.27	32.20	32.59	32.98	33.45	32.21
2016	32.21	33.33	33.61	33.96	34.45	34.01	34.92	34.92	35.19	35.82	36.13	36.33	34.59
2017	35.89	37.11	35.91	36.59	36.82	36.71	37.78	36.97	37.62	38.78	37.97	38.57	37.23
Professional and Business Services													
2013	29.04	28.84	28.91	28.52	28.39	28.36	28.37	28.05	28.40	27.94	27.95	28.70	28.45
2014	28.60	28.55	28.38	28.06	27.95	28.39	28.54	28.83	29.29	28.93	29.96	30.52	28.84
2015	30.97	30.86	31.58	30.79	31.20	31.19	31.25	31.71	32.13	32.15	32.91	32.99	31.66
2016	33.72	33.25	34.54	33.06	33.41	32.70	33.47	33.18	33.40	33.79	33.79	34.47	33.56
2017	34.83	34.43	35.11	35.39	34.26	33.79	34.84	34.46	34.51	34.58	34.49	35.25	34.66
Education and Health Services													
2013	26.16	26.10	26.07	26.23	26.24	26.06	26.27	26.06	26.41	26.61	26.48	26.64	26.28
2014	26.52	26.61	26.37	26.33	26.28	25.96	26.14	26.06	26.18	26.32	26.26	26.18	26.27
2015	26.37	26.65	27.10	26.58	26.01	26.16	26.33	26.56	26.55	27.14	26.71	26.87	26.59
2016	27.04	27.23	27.57	27.79	27.74	27.18	27.31	27.14	27.39	27.66	27.47	27.77	27.44
2017	28.07	28.45	28.95	29.60	28.60	28.76	29.13	29.06	29.37	29.46	29.38	29.68	29.05
Leisure and Hospitality													
2013	13.44	13.51	13.45	13.46	13.31	13.02	13.03	12.97	13.29	13.50	13.70	13.83	13.36
2014	13.89	13.89	13.88	13.81	13.73	13.55	13.51	13.85	14.28	14.41	14.64	14.78	14.01
2015	14.66	14.87	14.89	14.88	14.51	14.55	14.62	15.12	15.23	15.37	15.48	15.50	14.97
2016	15.37	15.56	15.90	15.61	15.59	15.14	15.30	15.54	16.10	16.35	16.60	16.68	15.80
2017	16.75	16.82	16.95	16.88	16.56	16.04	16.05	16.22	16.64	16.82	17.28	17.30	16.66
Other Services													
2013	22.48	22.20	22.39	22.59	22.84	23.20	23.57	22.97	23.37	23.10	23.04	23.93	22.98
2014	23.49	22.77	22.34	22.75	23.05	23.35	23.21	23.26	23.22	23.01	22.50	23.06	23.00
2015	22.53	22.21	22.06	22.29	22.14	21.83	21.68	22.44	22.74	23.10	22.75	22.86	22.38
2016	22.55	22.36	22.77	22.48	22.57	22.35	22.57	21.98	22.39	22.51	23.03	23.34	22.57
2017	23.03	22.52	22.61	23.55	23.62	22.77	23.05	22.90	23.22	22.76	23.03	23.29	23.03

4. Average Weekly Earnings by Selected Industry: Minnesota, 2013–2017

(Dollars, not seasonally adjusted)

Industry and year	January	February	March	April	May	June	July	August	September	October	November	December	Annual average
Total Private													
2013	851.00	848.26	853.37	852.58	852.37	878.92	854.04	855.98	883.91	867.78	867.44	881.62	864.07
2014	863.20	879.71	878.22	871.48	877.54	887.69	875.52	877.39	878.08	875.69	885.10	875.30	876.86
2015	873.68	884.11	892.25	872.93	871.70	876.71	882.36	904.10	881.40	897.26	900.14	888.33	886.04
2016	894.79	886.44	906.18	906.53	925.76	913.75	919.00	916.61	931.61	953.24	950.08	944.12	921.74
2017	958.80	955.19	955.86	987.70	957.68	952.75	977.65	964.44	974.58	989.69	973.21	971.91	969.12
Goods Producing													
2013	1,043.95	1,039.18	1,050.00	1,066.26	1,063.05	1,084.86	1,073.66	1,081.50	1,092.39	1,090.32	1,069.20	1,072.38	1,069.20
2014	1,060.78	1,062.89	1,079.15	1,077.87	1,112.58	1,110.76	1,106.22	1,115.22	1,114.07	1,100.23	1,061.71	1,066.74	1,088.54
2015	1,047.42	1,038.31	1,034.10	1,038.89	1,049.67	1,056.64	1,052.57	1,073.83	1,025.79	1,056.23	1,033.20	1,026.77	1,045.96
2016	1,032.47	1,032.86	1,029.36	1,060.00	1,066.63	1,086.59	1,101.91	1,098.10	1,129.57	1,127.73	1,119.10	1,100.24	1,081.92
2017	1,093.15	1,108.49	1,108.37	1,118.13	1,133.35	1,129.13	1,143.93	1,146.13	1,155.84	1,147.52	1,122.99	1,131.37	1,128.20
Construction													
2013	1,133.55	1,101.70	1,139.72	1,146.62	1,132.73	1,174.64	1,136.45	1,163.49	1,165.96	1,177.77	1,109.11	1,078.81	1,140.27
2014	1,081.99	1,064.86	1,091.76	1,096.53	1,207.85	1,175.06	1,203.07	1,225.56	1,231.47	1,213.39	1,128.75	1,132.88	1,160.28
2015	1,106.79	1,137.01	1,138.86	1,159.75	1,235.35	1,260.90	1,247.12	1,288.26	1,184.25	1,242.85	1,171.37	1,161.29	1,199.83
2016	1,148.63	1,139.66	1,160.12	1,188.48	1,217.18	1,289.58	1,303.80	1,276.24	1,316.21	1,330.86	1,293.20	1,229.63	1,247.81
2017	1,202.25	1,229.95	1,242.92	1,226.79	1,290.42	1,308.15	1,306.54	1,333.73	1,307.75	1,327.81	1,250.64	1,239.17	1,275.06
Manufacturing													
2013	1,011.20	1,016.13	1,016.77	1,032.86	1,032.22	1,042.44	1,038.28	1,038.12	1,053.48	1,050.60	1,046.63	1,058.21	1,037.44
2014	1,042.39	1,048.37	1,058.74	1,051.28	1,060.67	1,069.67	1,047.48	1,050.73	1,048.61	1,035.80	1,019.70	1,027.46	1,046.32
2015	1,011.72	994.20	991.42	987.22	978.52	973.37	971.10	987.53	967.27	988.81	989.20	983.06	984.46
2016	992.49	994.29	990.27	1,014.95	1,012.97	1,010.81	1,015.18	1,019.44	1,047.02	1,034.41	1,040.55	1,046.37	1,018.26
2017	1,049.49	1,057.17	1,054.96	1,073.28	1,060.65	1,044.38	1,066.34	1,054.96	1,080.85	1,060.49	1,060.09	1,078.90	1,061.28
Trade, Transportation, and Utilities													
2013	714.24	726.43	730.24	731.27	741.02	758.02	747.00	738.93	770.78	750.09	750.75	752.86	743.82
2014	740.34	740.91	746.07	767.58	776.72	768.43	756.57	752.50	760.61	750.16	762.80	740.93	754.58
2015	749.48	754.30	743.90	737.74	736.40	729.30	740.59	750.36	739.59	732.68	726.33	724.79	738.21
2016	702.72	701.64	700.59	708.34	730.73	718.08	713.64	701.74	715.25	722.76	706.97	696.82	709.59
2017	708.34	687.26	680.20	722.52	696.70	700.99	729.80	714.42	727.40	722.24	732.52	726.85	713.51
Financial Activities													
2013	1,221.28	1,256.25	1,257.36	1,243.60	1,241.74	1,307.38	1,235.70	1,241.37	1,277.49	1,223.77	1,230.22	1,268.57	1,250.29
2014	1,227.27	1,261.44	1,247.12	1,203.04	1,197.84	1,223.79	1,158.76	1,157.15	1,142.84	1,149.44	1,201.88	1,157.73	1,193.14
2015	1,142.56	1,181.47	1,180.17	1,173.05	1,179.98	1,191.95	1,183.70	1,210.13	1,175.30	1,196.05	1,240.05	1,227.62	1,188.55
2016	1,201.43	1,239.88	1,243.57	1,253.12	1,309.10	1,271.97	1,299.02	1,285.06	1,309.07	1,364.74	1,344.04	1,355.11	1,290.21
2017	1,385.35	1,399.05	1,346.63	1,412.37	1,380.75	1,387.64	1,465.86	1,386.38	1,414.51	1,493.03	1,427.67	1,442.52	1,411.02
Professional and Business Services													
2013	1,010.59	1,020.94	1,026.31	1,001.05	993.65	1,035.14	973.09	976.14	1,030.92	980.69	986.64	1,024.59	1,004.29
2014	983.84	1,030.66	1,024.52	990.52	997.82	1,044.75	1,021.73	1,037.88	1,036.87	1,035.69	1,090.54	1,083.46	1,032.47
2015	1,096.34	1,123.30	1,155.83	1,102.28	1,129.44	1,135.32	1,134.38	1,189.13	1,143.83	1,179.91	1,227.54	1,181.04	1,149.26
2016	1,197.06	1,167.08	1,222.72	1,163.71	1,216.12	1,229.52	1,241.74	1,234.30	1,235.80	1,280.64	1,277.26	1,278.84	1,228.30
2017	1,323.54	1,294.57	1,292.05	1,334.20	1,274.47	1,267.13	1,303.02	1,278.47	1,269.97	1,303.67	1,279.58	1,276.05	1,292.82
Education and Health Services													
2013	813.58	806.49	808.17	807.88	808.19	813.07	814.37	813.07	826.63	827.57	823.53	833.83	817.31
2014	824.77	827.57	817.47	824.13	817.31	812.55	815.57	818.28	827.29	834.34	840.32	843.00	824.88
2015	849.11	863.46	883.46	863.85	847.93	860.66	874.16	881.79	884.12	898.33	886.77	892.08	874.81
2016	895.02	895.87	909.81	922.63	929.29	894.22	903.96	898.33	901.13	921.08	920.25	930.30	911.01
2017	951.57	955.92	972.72	1,009.36	963.82	969.21	990.42	985.13	1,001.52	1,019.32	1,004.80	1,015.06	987.70
Leisure and Hospitality													
2013	295.68	305.33	312.04	301.50	304.80	311.18	315.33	316.47	318.96	314.55	315.10	316.71	311.29
2014	308.36	325.03	326.18	319.01	322.66	329.27	324.24	333.79	334.15	334.31	341.11	334.03	327.83
2015	328.38	343.50	348.43	337.78	333.73	349.20	352.34	373.46	359.43	361.20	362.23	350.30	350.30
2016	350.44	353.21	362.52	359.03	366.37	363.36	361.08	368.30	363.86	380.96	371.84	366.96	364.98
2017	368.50	371.72	376.29	373.05	365.98	370.52	373.97	369.82	369.41	378.45	371.52	366.76	371.52
Other Services													
2013	638.43	637.14	660.51	659.63	673.78	698.32	685.89	677.62	701.10	697.62	702.72	753.80	682.51
2014	730.54	719.53	701.48	702.98	707.64	733.19	717.19	711.76	710.53	701.81	695.25	689.49	710.70
2015	684.91	695.17	672.83	670.93	677.48	657.08	672.08	700.13	677.65	683.76	687.05	662.94	678.11
2016	669.74	666.33	662.61	658.66	677.10	661.56	640.99	644.01	651.55	666.30	663.26	665.19	661.30
2017	644.84	632.81	637.60	678.24	680.26	655.78	668.45	648.07	647.84	655.49	644.84	668.42	656.36

MISSISSIPPI
At a Glance

Population:
 2010 census: 2,967,297
 2017 estimate: 2,984,100

Percent change in population:
 2010–2017: 0.6%

Percent change in total nonfarm employment:
 2007–2017: -0.2%

Industry with the largest growth in employment, 2007–2017 (thousands):
 Education and health services, 18.0

Industry with the largest decline or smallest growth in employment, 2007–2017 (thousands):
 Manufacturing, -25.5

Civilian labor force:
 2010: 1,306,608
 2017: 1,280,071

Unemployment rate and rank among states (highest to lowest):
 2010: 10.4%, 11th
 2017: 5.1%, 5th

Over-the-year change in unemployment rates:
 2015–2016: -0.6%
 2016–2017: -0.7%

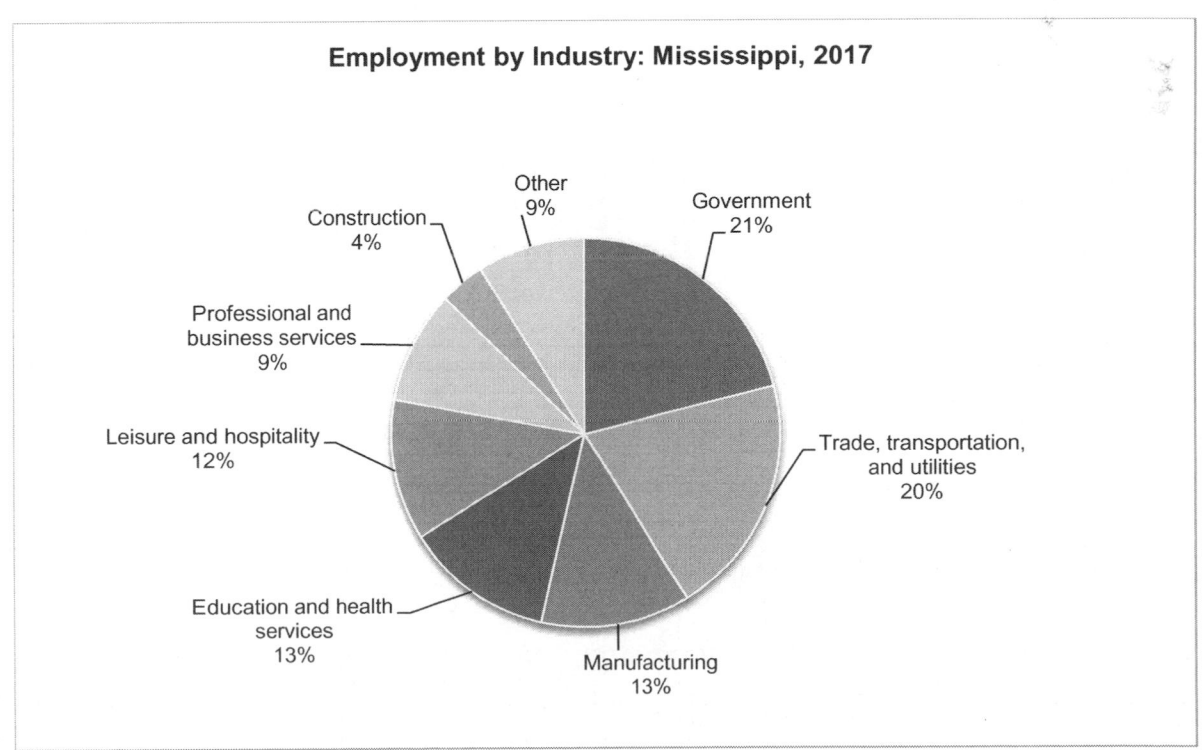

Employment by Industry: Mississippi, 2017

Other 9%
Construction 4%
Government 21%
Professional and business services 9%
Trade, transportation, and utilities 20%
Leisure and hospitality 12%
Education and health services 13%
Manufacturing 13%

1. Employment by Industry: Mississippi, Selected Years, 2007–2017

(Numbers in thousands, not seasonally adjusted)

Industry and year	January	February	March	April	May	June	July	August	September	October	November	December	Annual average
Total Nonfarm													
2007	1,139.8	1,146.4	1,150.0	1,155.5	1,157.5	1,154.0	1,138.1	1,155.0	1,163.0	1,160.5	1,166.1	1,165.3	1,154.3
2008	1,148.7	1,155.2	1,159.3	1,163.4	1,162.3	1,153.6	1,130.5	1,144.9	1,149.0	1,145.6	1,143.1	1,132.7	1,149.0
2009	1,107.9	1,107.8	1,106.8	1,105.6	1,105.5	1,098.0	1,080.6	1,088.8	1,095.6	1,091.3	1,094.0	1,089.8	1,097.6
2010	1,072.3	1,077.9	1,087.9	1,098.0	1,104.7	1,100.7	1,083.5	1,089.5	1,098.4	1,100.1	1,099.4	1,098.0	1,092.5
2011	1,078.3	1,084.0	1,094.4	1,099.9	1,100.2	1,093.7	1,078.4	1,088.8	1,099.0	1,098.9	1,101.6	1,097.6	1,092.9
2012	1,085.3	1,095.4	1,103.7	1,107.3	1,108.1	1,100.5	1,086.5	1,102.0	1,107.7	1,107.5	1,112.6	1,110.7	1,102.3
2013	1,092.7	1,104.6	1,110.1	1,114.7	1,115.2	1,110.0	1,094.1	1,108.7	1,118.5	1,118.2	1,125.1	1,123.0	1,111.2
2014	1,107.4	1,110.8	1,116.7	1,124.3	1,124.4	1,118.1	1,104.9	1,118.4	1,125.7	1,128.9	1,135.0	1,135.0	1,120.8
2015	1,113.9	1,122.8	1,124.6	1,134.3	1,138.9	1,129.7	1,120.7	1,131.1	1,140.2	1,145.9	1,150.1	1,152.1	1,133.7
2016	1,133.4	1,143.3	1,146.0	1,150.7	1,149.5	1,138.3	1,133.5	1,143.3	1,152.5	1,153.2	1,158.1	1,153.6	1,146.3
2017	1,137.6	1,147.0	1,150.7	1,154.9	1,154.5	1,147.7	1,135.7	1,146.8	1,152.9	1,161.2	1,167.9	1,167.5	1,152.0
Total Private													
2007	899.0	901.8	905.2	909.5	912.2	912.0	905.1	913.8	915.8	911.9	917.5	919.8	910.3
2008	902.9	905.8	909.5	912.6	912.9	908.1	895.6	900.7	898.8	893.5	890.6	883.3	901.2
2009	859.5	856.5	855.4	852.9	852.8	848.8	841.3	843.8	843.7	838.4	841.7	840.6	848.0
2010	823.9	826.2	834.4	845.7	849.3	849.9	844.9	847.7	850.6	849.7	850.1	849.7	843.5
2011	833.1	836.5	846.1	851.1	852.1	849.5	841.8	847.0	851.5	849.9	853.1	852.6	847.0
2012	839.9	847.0	854.4	858.5	859.5	856.6	851.2	860.3	860.7	858.6	863.6	865.0	856.3
2013	848.0	856.3	861.4	865.8	867.0	866.6	859.7	868.0	871.2	870.5	877.5	879.3	865.9
2014	864.2	864.3	869.5	876.6	877.6	875.9	870.5	878.3	879.1	881.1	888.2	891.7	876.4
2015	871.6	877.3	878.3	888.7	892.8	888.7	886.5	891.7	894.8	899.2	904.0	909.4	890.3
2016	890.8	896.6	898.8	902.9	902.8	896.7	899.0	903.8	906.1	906.4	911.6	911.1	902.2
2017	896.1	901.7	904.2	909.6	910.7	908.5	902.5	908.2	908.4	915.2	922.7	925.3	909.4
Goods Producing													
2007	239.0	238.2	235.0	239.3	238.9	238.7	236.5	237.5	238.0	236.5	236.9	237.8	237.7
2008	234.3	233.9	234.1	236.1	236.4	235.1	228.5	227.7	225.7	224.4	221.2	217.1	229.5
2009	209.3	206.5	204.8	202.8	202.8	202.2	199.9	198.6	197.4	194.3	194.3	193.9	200.6
2010	190.1	189.5	192.0	196.5	197.0	196.7	195.8	195.5	194.8	194.6	193.8	193.4	194.1
2011	190.0	190.3	193.4	193.7	195.3	195.4	193.4	193.1	193.9	193.4	192.6	192.5	193.1
2012	191.1	193.0	194.5	195.9	195.9	195.6	194.4	195.3	195.2	195.0	194.5	194.8	194.6
2013	191.5	194.0	194.5	195.8	197.9	198.7	197.4	198.1	199.0	199.7	199.2	198.7	197.0
2014	196.9	196.7	198.7	199.3	200.1	200.4	198.0	197.7	197.1	197.4	196.5	197.0	198.0
2015	193.7	195.0	194.5	195.9	197.0	197.2	196.9	196.0	196.7	196.3	195.0	195.9	195.8
2016	194.5	195.4	196.0	194.5	193.9	193.6	194.3	194.1	194.8	194.1	194.1	194.3	194.5
2017	193.0	194.1	194.2	193.9	194.1	195.3	193.8	194.4	194.6	194.1	194.2	195.2	194.2
Service-Providing													
2007	900.8	908.2	915.0	916.2	918.6	915.3	901.6	917.5	925.0	924.0	929.2	927.5	916.6
2008	914.4	921.3	925.2	927.3	925.9	918.5	902.0	917.2	923.3	921.2	921.9	915.6	919.5
2009	898.6	901.3	902.0	902.8	902.7	895.8	880.7	890.2	898.2	897.0	899.7	895.9	897.1
2010	882.2	888.4	895.9	901.5	907.7	904.0	887.7	894.0	903.6	905.5	905.6	904.6	898.4
2011	888.3	893.7	901.0	906.2	904.9	898.3	885.0	895.7	905.1	905.5	909.0	905.1	899.8
2012	894.2	902.4	909.2	911.4	912.2	904.9	892.1	906.7	912.5	912.5	918.1	915.9	907.7
2013	901.2	910.6	915.6	918.9	917.3	911.3	896.7	910.6	919.5	918.5	925.9	924.3	914.2
2014	910.5	914.1	918.0	925.0	924.3	917.7	906.9	920.7	928.6	931.5	938.5	938.0	922.8
2015	920.2	927.8	930.1	938.4	941.9	932.5	923.8	935.1	943.5	949.6	955.1	956.2	937.9
2016	938.9	947.9	950.0	956.2	955.6	944.7	939.2	949.2	957.7	959.1	964.0	959.3	951.8
2017	944.6	952.9	956.5	961.0	960.4	952.4	941.9	952.4	958.3	967.1	973.7	972.3	957.8
Mining and Logging													
2007	9.2	9.3	9.4	9.6	9.7	9.5	9.5	9.6	9.6	9.5	9.7	9.6	9.5
2008	9.4	9.1	9.2	9.4	9.5	9.5	9.4	9.5	9.5	10.0	10.0	9.8	9.5
2009	9.2	9.0	8.8	8.5	8.4	8.3	8.3	8.2	8.2	8.1	8.1	8.1	8.4
2010	8.1	8.1	8.4	8.8	8.9	8.9	8.9	9.0	9.0	9.0	8.9	8.8	8.7
2011	8.8	8.8	9.0	9.0	9.1	9.1	9.3	9.3	9.2	9.1	9.1	9.0	9.1
2012	9.0	9.1	9.2	9.3	9.3	9.3	9.4	9.4	9.4	9.2	9.3	9.2	9.3
2013	8.9	9.0	9.0	9.1	9.2	9.2	9.3	9.3	9.2	9.1	9.1	9.1	9.1
2014	9.1	8.9	9.0	9.0	9.1	9.3	9.3	9.4	9.4	9.4	9.4	9.3	9.2
2015	8.9	8.7	8.3	8.2	8.2	8.1	7.9	7.9	7.8	7.5	7.4	7.3	8.0
2016	7.2	7.1	6.9	6.7	6.8	6.8	6.8	6.9	7.0	7.0	7.0	7.0	6.9
2017	7.0	6.9	7.0	6.9	6.9	7.0	6.9	7.0	6.9	6.8	6.9	6.8	6.9

1. Employment by Industry: Mississippi, Selected Years, 2007–2017—*Continued*

(Numbers in thousands, not seasonally adjusted)

Industry and year	January	February	March	April	May	June	July	August	September	October	November	December	Annual average
Construction													
2007	56.9	56.6	58.4	58.0	58.2	58.7	58.5	59.0	59.4	59.5	60.2	61.2	58.7
2008	59.7	60.0	61.0	63.5	64.5	63.9	60.8	59.4	59.1	59.3	57.3	55.8	60.4
2009	52.5	52.1	52.1	52.0	53.1	53.9	52.3	51.3	49.8	48.4	48.3	47.4	51.1
2010	45.6	45.7	47.6	50.6	50.8	50.7	50.5	50.7	50.8	50.6	50.3	49.5	49.5
2011	46.9	47.2	49.1	49.3	50.3	50.5	49.3	48.8	49.5	49.1	48.2	47.2	48.8
2012	46.0	47.6	48.8	50.0	49.8	48.9	47.9	48.4	48.7	48.4	47.9	47.6	48.3
2013	46.2	48.6	49.3	50.3	52.2	52.9	52.6	52.5	53.0	53.2	52.0	50.5	51.1
2014	48.8	48.6	50.3	50.9	51.5	51.2	50.1	49.0	48.3	47.7	46.9	46.8	49.2
2015	44.5	45.8	45.8	46.5	46.8	46.4	47.1	46.2	46.5	46.2	45.2	45.5	46.0
2016	43.8	44.8	45.7	44.7	44.3	44.1	44.7	44.1	44.5	44.2	44.0	43.3	44.4
2017	42.4	43.0	43.4	43.5	43.3	43.6	43.4	43.5	44.0	43.5	43.1	43.1	43.3
Manufacturing													
2007	172.9	172.3	167.2	171.7	171.0	170.5	168.5	168.9	169.0	167.5	167.0	167.0	169.5
2008	165.2	164.8	163.9	163.2	162.4	161.7	158.3	158.8	157.1	155.1	153.9	151.5	159.7
2009	147.6	145.4	143.9	142.3	141.3	140.0	139.3	139.1	139.4	137.8	137.9	138.4	141.0
2010	136.4	135.7	136.0	137.1	137.3	137.1	136.4	135.8	135.0	135.0	134.6	135.1	136.0
2011	134.3	134.3	135.3	135.4	135.9	135.8	134.8	135.0	135.2	135.2	135.3	136.3	135.2
2012	136.1	136.3	136.5	136.6	136.8	137.4	137.1	137.5	137.1	137.4	137.3	138.0	137.0
2013	136.4	136.4	136.2	136.4	136.5	136.6	135.5	136.3	136.8	137.4	138.1	139.1	136.8
2014	139.0	139.2	139.4	139.4	139.5	139.9	138.6	139.3	139.4	140.3	140.2	140.9	139.6
2015	140.3	140.5	140.4	141.2	142.0	142.7	141.9	141.9	142.4	142.6	142.4	143.1	141.8
2016	143.5	143.5	143.4	143.1	142.8	142.7	142.8	143.1	143.3	142.9	143.1	144.0	143.2
2017	143.6	144.2	143.8	143.5	143.9	144.7	143.5	143.9	143.7	143.8	144.2	145.3	144.0
Trade, Transportation, and Utilities													
2007	224.2	223.3	226.1	225.7	227.2	227.7	225.6	226.7	227.0	226.9	230.6	232.4	227.0
2008	225.1	224.4	226.1	224.5	224.4	224.0	222.9	224.2	223.2	221.7	224.1	225.3	224.2
2009	216.9	215.3	214.8	213.9	214.7	214.6	213.5	213.2	213.7	213.4	216.2	217.0	214.8
2010	210.3	209.6	211.3	212.9	213.8	213.5	212.7	213.3	212.8	214.3	217.3	219.8	213.5
2011	212.5	212.2	214.2	215.1	215.3	214.6	213.8	214.6	214.2	214.4	218.5	220.7	215.0
2012	213.9	213.3	214.2	214.8	215.8	215.5	215.1	215.5	215.1	214.7	219.1	220.9	215.7
2013	213.2	212.5	213.3	214.1	215.0	216.0	216.0	217.1	217.0	217.1	222.8	225.3	216.6
2014	217.2	216.7	217.5	218.2	218.7	219.6	219.5	220.6	219.9	221.7	227.1	229.8	220.5
2015	221.5	221.1	221.2	223.8	224.7	224.9	223.8	224.8	224.7	226.7	232.0	234.7	225.3
2016	226.9	226.4	226.5	228.7	229.1	228.5	229.3	229.6	229.9	231.6	236.9	238.6	230.2
2017	230.9	229.5	229.2	229.8	229.9	230.3	230.1	230.9	230.4	232.6	236.2	239.2	231.6
Wholesale Trade													
2007	36.6	36.6	36.6	36.6	36.7	36.8	36.8	37.2	37.0	36.7	36.5	37.2	36.8
2008	36.8	36.7	36.6	36.5	36.5	36.6	36.3	36.4	36.0	36.1	35.7	36.0	36.4
2009	35.5	35.4	35.1	34.8	34.7	34.7	34.6	34.7	34.4	34.3	34.1	34.5	34.7
2010	34.0	34.0	33.0	34.2	34.2	34.3	34.2	34.6	34.2	34.3	34.1	34.7	34.2
2011	34.2	34.3	34.2	34.2	34.3	34.1	34.2	34.6	34.5	34.2	34.2	34.7	34.3
2012	34.5	34.6	34.3	34.1	34.2	34.3	34.2	34.5	34.3	33.9	33.9	34.2	34.3
2013	34.3	34.2	34.0	33.9	34.1	34.1	33.9	34.3	34.2	33.8	33.8	34.3	34.1
2014	34.0	34.2	33.8	33.9	33.9	34.0	34.0	34.4	34.1	34.0	34.0	34.6	34.1
2015	34.5	34.5	34.0	34.1	34.3	34.3	34.1	34.5	34.3	34.3	34.2	34.5	34.3
2016	34.4	34.3	33.9	33.9	34.1	34.1	34.2	34.6	34.6	34.5	34.4	34.9	34.3
2017	34.9	35	34.7	34.5	34.6	34.7	34.6	35	34.7	35.3	34.9	35.6	34.9
Retail Trade													
2007	139.9	139.2	141.5	141.0	142.0	142.5	140.5	140.7	141.0	141.2	144.8	146.1	141.7
2008	140.2	139.5	141.2	140.0	139.7	139.1	138.3	138.7	138.1	137.0	139.6	140.8	139.4
2009	133.8	132.6	132.8	132.7	133.5	133.6	132.6	131.7	132.3	132.2	135.1	135.7	133.2
2010	130.3	129.7	131.3	132.1	133.0	132.6	131.9	131.7	131.2	132.2	135.4	136.9	132.4
2011	131.2	130.8	132.4	133.4	133.5	133.1	132.4	132.3	131.7	132.4	136.3	137.7	133.1
2012	132.4	131.7	132.6	133.3	133.8	133.5	133.2	132.7	132.1	132.6	136.8	137.7	133.5
2013	130.8	130.2	131.1	131.8	132.3	133.3	133.6	133.7	133.6	133.7	138.8	140.3	133.6
2014	133.7	133.3	134.4	134.8	134.9	135.6	135.3	135.4	134.9	135.8	140.4	142.0	135.9
2015	135.5	135.3	135.7	137.6	138.1	138.3	137.5	137.6	137.3	138.5	143.0	144.4	138.2
2016	138.5	138.7	139.0	140.7	140.5	139.8	140.3	139.8	139.9	141.1	145.2	145.5	140.8
2017	140.3	139.3	139.5	140.2	140.1	140.0	139.8	139.8	139.5	140.1	142.5	143.5	140.4

1. Employment by Industry: Mississippi, Selected Years, 2007–2017—*Continued*

(Numbers in thousands, not seasonally adjusted)

Industry and year	January	February	March	April	May	June	July	August	September	October	November	December	Annual average
Transportation and Utilities													
2007	47.7	47.5	48.0	48.1	48.5	48.4	48.3	48.8	49.0	49.0	49.3	49.1	48.5
2008	48.1	48.2	48.3	48.0	48.2	48.3	48.3	49.1	49.1	48.6	48.8	48.5	48.5
2009	47.6	47.3	46.9	46.4	46.5	46.3	46.3	46.8	47.0	46.9	47.0	46.8	46.8
2010	46.0	45.9	46.1	46.6	46.6	46.6	46.6	47.0	47.4	47.8	47.8	48.2	46.9
2011	47.1	47.1	47.6	47.5	47.5	47.4	47.2	47.7	48.0	47.8	48.0	48.3	47.6
2012	47.0	47.0	47.3	47.4	47.8	47.7	47.7	48.3	48.7	48.2	48.4	49.0	47.9
2013	48.1	48.1	48.2	48.4	48.6	48.6	48.5	49.1	49.2	49.6	50.2	50.7	48.9
2014	49.5	49.2	49.3	49.5	49.9	50.0	50.2	50.8	50.9	51.9	52.7	53.2	50.6
2015	51.5	51.3	51.5	52.1	52.3	52.3	52.2	52.7	53.1	53.9	54.8	55.8	52.8
2016	54.0	53.4	53.6	54.1	54.5	54.6	54.8	55.2	55.4	56.0	57.3	58.2	55.1
2017	55.7	55.2	55.0	55.1	55.2	55.6	55.7	56.1	56.2	57.2	58.8	60.1	56.3
Information													
2007	13.2	13.3	13.3	13.3	13.3	13.5	13.6	13.5	13.4	13.3	13.5	13.5	13.4
2008	13.4	13.5	13.5	13.5	13.5	13.6	13.6	13.5	13.4	13.2	13.4	13.4	13.5
2009	13.3	13.2	13.1	13.0	12.9	12.9	12.6	12.6	12.6	12.4	12.4	12.3	12.8
2010	12.2	12.2	12.3	12.1	12.2	12.3	12.3	12.3	12.6	12.7	12.3	12.2	12.3
2011	12.0	12.0	12.0	11.9	12.0	12.1	12.1	12.1	12.1	12.1	12.2	12.4	12.1
2012	12.5	12.5	12.5	12.5	12.5	12.5	12.6	12.4	12.4	12.4	12.7	12.7	12.5
2013	12.8	12.8	12.7	12.7	12.6	12.8	12.7	12.7	12.8	12.8	12.9	13.2	12.8
2014	13.8	13.0	13.0	12.8	12.7	12.8	12.8	13.0	13.0	13.1	13.4	13.3	13.1
2015	12.8	12.8	12.7	12.5	12.8	12.7	12.7	12.5	12.6	12.7	12.7	12.8	12.7
2016	12.4	12.3	12.1	12.0	12.2	12.2	12.3	12.2	12.0	12.1	12.2	12.1	12.2
2017	11.7	11.8	11.8	11.7	11.8	11.7	11.6	11.5	11.3	11.3	11.4	11.4	11.6
Financial Activities													
2007	46.0	46.2	46.3	46.4	46.6	46.8	46.6	46.8	46.5	46.7	46.7	46.9	46.5
2008	46.5	46.5	46.7	46.5	46.6	46.6	46.5	46.4	46.2	46.5	46.3	46.5	46.5
2009	46.0	45.7	45.6	45.4	45.6	45.4	45.0	45.0	44.9	44.8	44.8	45.0	45.3
2010	44.5	44.4	44.5	44.5	44.7	44.8	44.7	44.5	44.4	44.2	44.2	44.4	44.5
2011	43.9	44.0	44.0	44.3	44.1	44.4	44.2	44.3	44.2	44.1	44.2	44.2	44.2
2012	43.9	43.9	44.0	44.1	44.3	44.3	44.3	44.4	44.2	43.9	44.0	44.0	44.1
2013	43.6	43.8	43.9	43.9	43.8	43.9	43.7	43.8	43.6	43.8	43.9	43.9	43.8
2014	43.2	43.3	43.2	43.1	43.5	43.5	43.4	43.6	43.4	43.4	43.7	43.7	43.4
2015	43.3	43.3	43.3	43.4	43.7	43.7	43.8	43.8	43.6	43.9	44.1	44.4	43.7
2016	43.8	43.9	43.8	44.1	44.1	44.1	44.3	44.3	44.1	44.2	44.2	44.2	44.1
2017	43.8	43.8	43.9	43.9	44.2	44.5	44.2	44.1	44.1	44.8	45.4	45.1	44.3
Professional and Business Services													
2007	91.0	92.3	93.4	92.4	92.2	92.3	91.9	93.2	93.9	94.0	95.0	95.8	93.1
2008	94.5	95.4	95.5	96.3	96.1	95.7	94.1	94.6	95.2	94.6	94.1	92.2	94.9
2009	89.8	89.5	89.0	87.8	87.0	86.7	85.3	86.2	85.9	86.3	87.0	87.3	87.3
2010	85.7	87.3	87.9	90.2	92.4	95.8	95.3	93.7	95.1	94.2	93.6	93.6	92.1
2011	91.9	92.8	94.2	94.9	94.4	93.8	91.8	92.9	94.0	94.2	94.5	93.5	93.6
2012	91.9	94.3	96.3	96.3	96.5	95.8	93.9	97.2	97.7	98.1	99.0	99.1	96.3
2013	97.0	100.0	100.7	100.1	99.3	98.4	95.6	98.9	98.2	98.3	99.5	101.1	98.9
2014	99.6	99.4	99.2	101.3	100.3	99.5	98.7	101.9	102.4	103.0	104.8	106.2	101.4
2015	102.2	103.4	103.2	104.9	104.7	103.4	103.6	106.5	106.8	108.7	109.9	112.2	105.8
2016	107.5	109.4	109.1	108.2	107.0	105.6	106.0	107.1	107.6	108.4	108.6	108.9	107.8
2017	105.9	107.8	108.1	108.4	107.7	106.7	104.8	106.2	106.9	109.7	112.1	113.9	108.2
Education and Health Services													
2007	124.4	125.5	126.2	126.2	126.2	123.1	122.0	126.2	128.3	128.6	128.4	127.5	126.1
2008	125.9	127.0	126.9	126.9	125.7	123.2	122.2	125.8	128.4	129.2	128.9	128.1	126.5
2009	127.0	127.7	127.9	128.3	127.3	124.4	124.6	127.7	130.5	131.3	131.5	130.7	128.2
2010	129.6	130.3	130.7	131.1	130.0	126.8	125.9	129.1	132.7	133.6	133.6	132.4	130.5
2011	131.7	132.5	132.7	133.0	131.3	128.9	127.6	130.2	134.5	134.9	134.6	133.6	132.1
2012	132.7	134.1	134.4	134.2	132.2	129.7	129.0	132.0	134.5	135.4	135.3	134.5	133.2
2013	133.4	134.7	135.0	135.7	133.6	130.4	129.3	131.6	135.7	136.1	136.2	135.1	133.9
2014	133.7	134.5	134.6	135.5	134.2	131.3	131.7	135.0	137.3	137.7	138.3	137.6	135.1
2015	136.7	137.8	138.0	138.6	138.6	134.8	134.4	136.4	139.4	140.7	140.8	139.9	138.0
2016	138.9	140.1	140.2	141.1	141.0	137.0	136.9	139.9	141.9	142.5	142.4	141.9	140.3
2017	141.8	143.6	143.8	145.0	144.4	141.2	140.7	143.4	146.1	146.2	146.8	146.7	144.1

1. Employment by Industry: Mississippi, Selected Years, 2007–2017—*Continued*

(Numbers in thousands, not seasonally adjusted)

Industry and year	January	February	March	April	May	June	July	August	September	October	November	December	Annual average
Leisure and Hospitality													
2007	120.7	122.2	123.8	125.4	126.9	128.7	127.9	129.0	127.8	125.4	125.8	125.3	125.7
2008	122.7	124.2	125.5	127.6	128.7	128.6	126.9	127.7	125.8	123.4	122.6	121.0	125.4
2009	118.1	119.6	121.1	122.4	123.3	123.3	121.3	121.7	119.9	117.5	117.2	116.2	120.1
2010	113.4	114.8	117.3	119.6	120.4	121.3	119.7	120.9	119.7	117.8	117.4	116.2	118.2
2011	113.8	115.4	118.1	120.6	121.8	122.2	121.1	122.2	121.0	119.1	118.9	118.2	119.4
2012	116.4	118.4	120.7	122.7	124.1	124.7	123.4	124.9	123.0	120.8	120.6	120.5	121.7
2013	118.2	119.9	122.5	124.7	125.9	127.0	126.0	126.9	126.0	123.9	124.2	123.3	124.0
2014	121.3	122.1	124.5	127.6	129.1	129.3	127.2	127.2	126.9	125.8	125.1	124.7	125.9
2015	122.2	124.4	125.8	129.7	131.3	131.8	131.2	131.9	131.2	130.4	129.6	129.6	129.1
2016	126.9	129.0	130.9	134.1	135.3	135.3	135.4	136.4	135.6	133.3	133.0	130.9	133.0
2017	129.1	130.9	132.8	136.5	138.1	138.1	136.9	137.4	134.6	136.2	136.3	134.1	135.1
Other Services													
2007	40.5	40.8	41.1	40.8	40.9	41.2	41.0	40.9	40.9	40.5	40.6	40.6	40.8
2008	40.5	40.9	41.2	41.2	41.5	41.3	40.9	40.8	40.9	40.5	40.0	39.7	40.8
2009	39.1	39.0	39.1	39.3	39.2	39.3	39.1	38.8	38.8	38.4	38.3	38.2	38.9
2010	38.1	38.1	38.4	38.8	38.8	38.7	38.5	38.4	38.5	38.3	37.9	37.7	38.4
2011	37.3	37.3	37.5	37.6	37.9	38.1	37.8	37.6	37.6	37.7	37.6	37.5	37.6
2012	37.5	37.5	37.8	38.0	38.2	38.5	38.5	38.6	38.6	38.3	38.4	38.5	38.2
2013	38.3	38.6	38.8	38.8	38.9	39.4	39.0	38.9	38.9	38.8	38.8	38.7	38.8
2014	38.5	38.6	38.8	38.8	39.0	39.5	39.2	39.3	39.1	39.0	39.3	39.4	39.0
2015	39.2	39.5	39.6	39.9	40.0	40.2	40.1	39.8	39.8	39.8	39.9	39.9	39.8
2016	39.9	40.1	40.2	40.2	40.2	40.4	40.5	40.2	40.2	40.2	40.2	40.2	40.2
2017	39.9	40.2	40.4	40.4	40.5	40.7	40.4	40.3	40.4	40.3	40.3	39.7	40.3
Government													
2007	240.8	244.6	244.8	246.0	245.3	242.0	233.0	241.2	247.2	248.6	248.6	245.5	244.0
2008	245.8	249.4	249.8	250.8	249.4	245.5	234.9	244.2	250.2	252.1	252.5	249.4	247.8
2009	248.4	251.3	251.4	252.7	252.7	249.2	239.3	245.0	251.9	252.9	252.3	249.2	249.7
2010	248.4	251.7	253.5	252.3	255.4	250.8	238.6	241.8	247.8	250.4	249.3	248.3	249.0
2011	245.2	247.5	248.3	248.8	248.1	244.2	236.6	241.8	247.5	249.0	248.5	245.0	245.9
2012	245.4	248.4	249.3	248.8	248.6	243.9	235.3	241.7	247.0	248.9	249.0	245.7	246.0
2013	244.7	248.3	248.7	248.9	248.2	243.4	234.4	240.7	247.3	247.7	247.6	243.7	245.3
2014	243.2	246.5	247.2	247.7	246.8	242.2	234.4	240.1	246.6	247.8	246.8	243.3	244.4
2015	242.3	245.5	246.3	245.6	246.1	241.0	234.2	239.4	245.4	246.7	246.1	242.7	243.4
2016	242.6	246.7	247.2	247.8	246.7	241.6	234.5	239.5	246.4	246.8	246.5	242.5	244.1
2017	241.5	245.3	246.5	245.3	243.8	239.2	233.2	238.6	244.5	246.0	245.2	242.2	242.6

2. Average Weekly Hours by Selected Industry: Mississippi, 2013–2017

(Not seasonally adjusted)

Industry and year	January	February	March	April	May	June	July	August	September	October	November	December	Annual average
Total Private													
2013	35.0	35.2	35.4	34.9	34.7	35.5	35.2	35.5	36.2	35.7	35.6	36.1	35.4
2014	35.5	35.6	36.0	35.5	35.5	36.1	35.7	35.9	36.0	35.7	36.0	35.6	35.8
2015	35.0	35.3	35.3	34.4	34.6	34.8	34.7	35.1	34.2	34.7	35.0	34.7	34.8
2016	34.6	34.5	34.2	34.3	34.8	34.5	34.9	34.5	34.9	35.3	34.9	34.9	34.7
2017	34.9	34.7	34.6	34.7	34.8	34.9	35.2	34.7	34.8	35.0	34.7	34.8	34.8
Goods Producing													
2013	40.7	40.4	41.6	41.1	40.3	41.4	41.0	42.0	43.1	42.2	42.2	43.3	41.6
2014	42.5	41.3	42.0	41.8	41.3	42.1	41.7	42.4	43.1	42.7	42.5	42.3	42.1
2015	41.1	40.9	41.0	39.6	40.4	40.5	40.1	41.1	39.7	41.1	41.7	41.8	40.8
2016	41.5	41.4	41.1	41.3	42.1	41.3	42.0	41.3	41.6	42.3	41.7	42.0	41.6
2017	41.2	41.4	41.0	40.0	40.9	41.5	41.7	41.0	41.5	41.4	41.6	42.0	41.3
Construction													
2013	37.4	38.3	41.5	40.6	40.1	41.2	41.0	41.3	44.6	44.9	43.2	41.1	41.3
2014	40.2	38.9	42.2	41.0	42.2	42.2	43.5	44.0	44.3	43.8	44.3	43.7	42.5
2015	40.8	40.7	40.6	36.1	38.5	37.6	38.2	38.6	36.5	40.0	40.1	40.5	39.0
2016	40.6	40.5	39.3	38.8	42.3	41.7	41.7	40.4	41.5	41.6	40.5	39.8	40.7
2017	40.4	40.5	39.5	40.3	40.5	41.4	41.1	40.0	41.2	40.9	41.2	42.0	40.8
Manufacturing													
2013	41.2	40.7	41.1	40.6	40.0	41.1	40.7	41.9	42.3	41.0	41.5	43.6	41.3
2014	42.8	41.9	42.7	42.9	41.7	42.5	41.4	42.1	42.9	42.5	42.0	42.1	42.3
2015	41.6	41.3	41.7	41.7	41.8	42.3	41.5	42.7	41.4	42.2	42.9	42.9	42.0
2016	42.3	42.3	42.3	42.7	42.5	41.6	42.6	42.2	42.0	42.9	42.5	43.2	42.4
2017	41.8	42.0	41.7	40.2	41.2	41.7	42.0	41.4	41.6	41.5	41.6	41.9	41.5
Trade, Transportation, and Utilities													
2013	34.9	35.5	35.9	35.1	35.6	36.2	36.0	36.0	36.6	35.8	35.3	35.8	35.7
2014	35.3	35.9	36.2	35.6	35.8	36.2	36.1	35.7	35.8	35.1	35.3	35.0	35.7
2015	34.3	35.1	35.2	34.5	34.9	34.7	34.6	34.7	34.2	33.9	34.1	33.7	34.5
2016	33.4	33.1	32.7	32.8	33.3	33.4	33.8	33.4	33.3	34.1	33.9	33.9	33.4
2017	33.8	33.6	34.5	34.9	34.6	34.5	34.6	34.9	34.8	35.2	34.7	35.1	34.6
Financial Activities													
2013	38.2	38.4	37.6	37.5	37.1	40.3	37.5	37.4	40.2	37.2	37.4	39.6	38.2
2014	37.8	39.2	39.2	38.3	38.1	40.0	38.5	38.6	38.2	37.3	39.2	37.4	38.5
2015	37.6	38.9	39.2	36.3	36.4	36.6	36.7	39.1	36.7	37.4	39.1	36.7	37.6
2016	37.3	36.9	36.8	37.3	38.5	36.8	37.0	36.4	36.4	37.5	36.1	35.8	36.9
2017	36.9	36.2	35.5	36.3	36.1	36.4	37.2	35.6	36.6	36.1	34.9	34.9	36.1
Professional and Business Services													
2013	34.0	34.9	35.0	33.4	33.3	34.0	33.3	34.5	34.7	34.5	35.0	35.1	34.3
2014	34.6	34.9	35.3	34.5	35.0	35.6	34.8	35.7	35.7	35.5	36.0	35.6	35.3
2015	35.1	36.3	36.2	35.3	35.4	35.6	35.6	36.7	35.1	36.1	36.1	35.8	35.8
2016	35.3	35.0	34.8	34.4	35.1	35.3	34.9	35.0	35.3	34.5	33.8	34.2	34.8
2017	34.3	34.1	33.6	33.4	34.0	33.9	34.2	33.9	33.7	34.8	34.1	34.0	34.0
Education and Health Services													
2013	33.3	33.5	32.9	33.2	33.0	33.3	33.0	33.0	33.7	33.5	33.5	33.4	33.3
2014	33.5	33.4	33.3	33.1	33.2	33.7	33.5	33.8	33.7	33.6	34.3	33.8	33.6
2015	33.7	33.9	33.5	33.6	33.3	33.1	33.4	34.1	33.6	33.7	34.0	33.5	33.6
2016	34.2	33.9	33.8	33.9	34.2	34.2	34.4	34.2	34.7	35.1	35.0	34.8	34.4
2017	34.9	34.5	34.0	34.5	34.0	34.2	34.7	34.3	34.1	34.0	34.1	33.7	34.2
Leisure and Hospitality													
2013	27.3	27.5	27.5	27.5	27.4	28.1	28.1	27.7	27.4	27.6	27.3	27.5	27.6
2014	27.0	27.5	28.3	27.5	27.6	27.6	27.5	27.4	26.9	27.3	27.1	27.3	27.4
2015	26.7	28.0	28.2	26.7	26.8	27.3	27.7	26.2	25.8	26.1	26.3	26.1	26.8
2016	26.0	26.8	26.5	26.7	27.2	26.5	27.0	26.2	26.5	26.8	26.6	26.6	26.6
2017	26.7	26.9	27.2	27.7	27.6	27.7	27.6	26.9	26.9	26.9	26.9	26.8	27.2

3. Average Hourly Earnings by Selected Industry: Mississippi, 2013–2017

(Dollars, not seasonally adjusted)

Industry and year	January	February	March	April	May	June	July	August	September	October	November	December	Annual average
Total Private													
2013	19.16	19.42	19.29	19.36	19.24	19.27	19.26	19.41	19.68	19.69	19.62	19.73	19.43
2014	19.65	19.75	19.57	19.44	19.13	19.37	19.36	19.36	19.31	19.27	19.29	19.22	19.39
2015	19.31	19.76	19.90	19.79	19.57	19.55	19.64	19.79	19.77	19.69	19.89	19.86	19.71
2016	19.87	19.69	19.66	19.95	20.05	19.94	20.08	19.96	20.03	20.28	20.05	20.09	19.97
2017	20.40	20.33	20.23	20.32	20.10	20.16	20.50	20.53	20.77	20.64	20.62	20.33	20.41
Goods Producing													
2013	20.40	20.48	20.35	20.16	20.04	20.08	20.12	20.30	20.68	21.02	20.63	20.47	20.40
2014	20.48	20.77	20.37	20.11	19.95	20.26	20.56	20.73	20.81	20.54	20.18	20.22	20.42
2015	20.14	20.41	20.84	20.87	20.65	20.68	20.83	20.77	20.75	20.79	21.08	21.41	20.77
2016	21.29	21.37	21.35	21.90	22.46	22.82	22.82	22.62	22.93	23.03	23.12	23.31	22.42
2017	23.04	22.73	22.77	22.70	22.56	22.59	22.87	22.88	22.97	22.90	22.81	22.73	22.80
Construction													
2013	20.90	21.24	21.04	21.14	20.76	20.53	20.27	20.40	20.98	21.32	21.05	21.07	20.89
2014	21.09	21.74	21.30	20.95	20.75	20.88	21.46	21.61	21.63	21.69	21.60	21.93	21.38
2015	21.63	21.42	22.27	22.19	21.72	22.45	22.12	22.08	21.95	21.89	22.13	22.47	22.02
2016	22.17	22.28	22.61	22.40	22.86	22.75	22.24	22.04	22.24	22.22	22.45	22.94	22.43
2017	22.48	22.76	22.74	22.51	22.40	22.56	22.37	22.68	22.56	22.51	22.72	23.04	22.61
Manufacturing													
2013	19.66	19.69	19.59	19.39	19.37	19.52	19.66	19.95	20.29	20.68	20.27	20.06	19.85
2014	20.06	20.23	19.91	19.63	19.54	19.87	20.04	20.30	20.40	19.97	19.53	19.48	19.91
2015	19.48	19.91	20.14	20.23	20.16	19.90	20.23	20.17	20.22	20.34	20.70	21.04	20.21
2016	20.98	21.07	20.96	21.68	22.32	22.75	22.98	22.77	23.16	23.31	23.34	23.43	22.40
2017	23.25	22.77	22.85	22.82	22.65	22.67	23.14	23.06	23.20	23.12	22.91	22.74	22.93
Trade, Transportation, and Utilities													
2013	17.18	17.45	17.47	17.80	17.65	17.68	17.83	17.77	17.87	17.94	18.04	18.44	17.77
2014	18.86	18.60	18.52	18.68	18.35	18.77	18.61	18.67	18.43	18.55	18.47	18.27	18.56
2015	18.20	18.38	18.38	18.38	17.80	18.00	18.22	18.42	18.39	18.47	18.33	18.03	18.25
2016	18.26	18.11	18.26	18.70	18.89	18.39	18.76	18.61	19.18	19.35	18.94	18.66	18.68
2017	19.41	20.01	19.62	19.86	20.06	20.05	20.20	20.69	21.05	20.79	20.58	19.77	20.18
Financial Activities													
2013	22.84	23.54	23.48	23.25	25.05	24.18	24.06	24.97	25.20	24.93	25.63	24.85	24.33
2014	24.18	24.99	25.07	24.20	23.97	23.68	23.34	23.22	22.95	23.24	24.14	23.43	23.87
2015	23.51	25.13	25.02	24.54	24.43	24.83	24.83	25.03	25.31	25.21	26.29	26.40	25.05
2016	25.13	26.34	25.77	25.53	25.35	24.71	24.61	24.57	23.98	24.29	23.97	23.61	24.83
2017	24.13	24.26	23.96	23.50	22.28	22.03	22.27	22.16	22.48	22.51	22.13	22.37	22.84
Professional and Business Services													
2013	20.92	21.49	21.44	22.34	22.08	22.19	22.19	21.81	22.37	22.06	22.00	22.49	21.95
2014	21.81	22.09	22.12	21.99	21.79	21.92	21.84	21.60	21.30	21.35	21.86	21.70	21.78
2015	21.78	22.61	22.73	22.30	22.12	21.56	21.55	21.82	21.74	21.39	21.60	20.84	21.83
2016	20.89	20.95	20.64	20.76	20.85	20.41	20.48	20.09	20.05	21.05	21.02	21.39	20.71
2017	21.35	21.30	21.19	21.52	20.85	21.16	21.27	20.97	21.33	21.03	21.07	20.49	21.12
Education and Health Services													
2013	19.65	19.88	19.87	20.09	19.74	20.02	20.02	20.21	20.14	20.14	19.82	19.90	19.96
2014	19.82	19.75	19.72	19.77	19.44	19.50	19.52	19.49	19.58	19.57	19.37	19.57	19.59
2015	19.95	20.13	20.24	20.41	20.38	20.45	20.75	20.80	20.86	20.78	20.74	21.02	20.54
2016	21.03	21.12	21.18	21.20	21.07	21.15	21.38	21.29	20.99	20.93	20.28	20.27	20.99
2017	20.38	20.55	20.59	20.90	20.74	20.95	21.26	20.83	20.93	20.99	21.22	21.34	20.89
Leisure and Hospitality													
2013	12.48	12.62	12.29	12.04	11.96	11.89	11.95	12.13	12.07	12.07	12.06	12.15	12.14
2014	12.17	12.24	11.98	11.81	11.76	11.78	11.80	11.86	11.73	11.85	11.80	11.80	11.88
2015	11.99	11.98	12.05	11.76	11.79	11.71	11.79	11.75	11.80	11.58	11.70	11.67	11.80
2016	11.89	11.91	11.91	12.05	12.00	11.63	11.73	11.74	11.87	11.93	11.80	11.80	11.85
2017	11.65	11.85	11.90	12.12	12.15	12.14	12.12	12.11	12.12	12.26	12.17	12.09	12.06

4. Average Weekly Earnings by Selected Industry: Mississippi, 2013–2017

(Dollars, not seasonally adjusted)

Industry and year	January	February	March	April	May	June	July	August	September	October	November	December	Annual average
Total Private													
2013	670.60	683.58	682.87	675.66	667.63	684.09	677.95	689.06	712.42	702.93	698.47	712.25	687.82
2014	697.58	703.10	704.52	690.12	679.12	699.26	691.15	695.02	695.16	687.94	694.44	684.23	694.16
2015	675.85	697.53	702.47	680.78	677.12	680.34	681.51	694.63	676.13	683.24	696.15	689.14	685.91
2016	687.50	679.31	672.37	684.29	697.74	687.93	700.79	688.62	699.05	715.88	699.75	701.14	692.96
2017	711.96	705.45	699.96	705.10	699.48	703.58	721.60	712.39	722.80	722.40	715.51	707.48	710.27
Goods Producing													
2013	830.28	827.39	846.56	828.58	807.61	831.31	824.92	852.60	891.31	887.04	870.59	886.35	848.64
2014	870.40	857.80	855.54	840.60	823.94	852.95	857.35	878.95	896.91	877.06	857.65	855.31	859.68
2015	827.75	834.77	854.44	826.45	834.26	837.54	835.28	853.65	823.78	854.47	879.04	894.94	847.42
2016	883.54	884.72	877.49	904.47	945.57	942.47	958.44	934.21	953.89	974.17	964.10	979.02	932.67
2017	949.25	941.02	933.57	908.00	922.70	937.49	953.68	938.08	953.26	948.06	948.90	954.66	941.64
Construction													
2013	781.66	813.49	873.16	858.28	832.48	845.84	831.07	842.52	935.71	957.27	909.36	865.98	862.76
2014	847.82	845.69	898.86	858.95	875.65	881.14	933.51	950.84	958.21	950.02	956.88	958.34	908.65
2015	882.50	871.79	904.16	801.06	836.22	844.12	844.98	852.29	801.18	875.60	887.41	910.04	858.78
2016	900.10	902.34	888.57	869.12	966.98	948.68	927.41	890.42	922.96	924.35	909.23	913.01	912.90
2017	908.19	921.78	898.23	907.15	907.20	933.98	919.41	907.20	929.47	920.66	936.06	967.68	922.49
Manufacturing													
2013	809.99	801.38	805.15	787.23	774.80	802.27	800.16	835.91	858.27	847.88	841.21	874.62	819.81
2014	858.57	847.64	850.16	842.13	814.82	844.48	829.66	854.63	875.16	848.73	820.26	820.11	842.19
2015	810.37	822.28	839.84	843.59	842.69	841.77	839.55	861.26	837.11	858.35	888.03	902.62	848.82
2016	887.45	891.26	886.61	925.74	948.60	946.40	978.95	960.89	972.72	1,000.00	991.95	1,012.18	949.76
2017	971.85	956.34	952.85	917.36	933.18	945.34	971.88	954.68	965.12	959.48	953.06	952.81	951.60
Trade, Transportation, and Utilities													
2013	599.58	619.48	627.17	624.78	628.34	640.02	641.88	639.72	654.04	642.25	636.81	660.15	634.39
2014	665.76	667.74	670.42	665.01	656.93	679.47	671.82	666.52	659.79	651.11	651.99	639.45	662.59
2015	624.26	645.14	646.98	634.11	621.22	624.60	630.41	639.17	628.94	626.13	625.05	607.61	629.63
2016	609.88	599.44	597.10	613.36	629.04	614.23	634.09	621.57	638.69	659.84	642.07	632.57	623.91
2017	656.06	672.34	676.89	693.11	694.08	691.73	698.92	722.08	732.54	731.81	714.13	693.93	698.23
Financial Activities													
2013	872.49	903.94	882.85	871.88	929.36	974.45	902.25	933.88	1,013.04	927.40	958.56	984.06	929.41
2014	914.00	979.61	982.74	926.86	913.26	947.20	898.59	896.29	876.69	866.85	946.29	876.28	919.00
2015	883.98	977.56	980.78	890.80	889.25	908.78	911.26	978.67	928.88	942.85	1,027.94	968.88	941.88
2016	937.35	971.95	948.34	952.27	975.98	909.33	910.57	894.35	872.87	910.88	865.32	845.24	916.23
2017	890.40	878.21	850.58	853.05	804.31	801.89	828.44	788.90	822.77	812.61	772.34	780.71	824.52
Professional and Business Services													
2013	711.28	750.00	750.40	746.16	735.26	754.46	738.93	752.45	776.24	761.07	770.00	789.40	752.89
2014	754.63	770.94	780.84	758.66	762.65	780.35	760.03	771.12	760.41	757.93	786.96	772.52	768.83
2015	764.48	820.74	822.83	787.19	783.05	767.54	767.18	800.79	763.07	772.18	779.76	746.07	781.51
2016	737.42	733.25	718.27	714.14	731.84	720.47	714.75	703.15	707.77	726.23	710.48	731.54	720.71
2017	732.31	726.33	711.98	718.77	708.90	717.32	727.43	710.88	718.82	731.84	718.49	696.66	718.08
Education and Health Services													
2013	654.35	665.98	653.72	666.99	651.42	666.67	660.66	666.93	678.72	674.69	663.97	664.66	664.67
2014	663.97	659.65	656.68	654.39	645.41	657.15	653.92	658.76	659.85	657.55	664.39	661.47	658.22
2015	672.32	682.41	678.04	685.78	678.65	676.90	693.05	709.28	700.90	700.29	705.16	704.17	690.14
2016	719.23	715.97	715.88	718.68	720.59	723.33	735.47	728.12	728.35	734.64	709.80	705.40	722.06
2017	711.26	708.98	700.06	721.05	705.16	716.49	737.72	714.47	713.71	713.66	723.60	719.16	714.44
Leisure and Hospitality													
2013	340.70	347.05	337.98	331.10	327.70	334.11	335.80	336.00	330.72	333.13	329.24	334.13	335.06
2014	328.59	336.60	339.03	324.78	324.58	325.13	324.50	324.96	315.54	323.51	319.78	322.14	325.51
2015	320.13	335.44	339.81	313.99	315.97	319.68	326.58	307.85	304.44	302.24	307.71	304.59	316.24
2016	309.14	319.19	315.62	321.74	326.40	308.20	316.71	307.59	314.56	319.72	313.88	313.88	315.21
2017	311.06	318.77	323.68	335.72	335.34	336.28	334.51	325.76	326.03	329.79	327.37	324.01	328.03

MISSOURI
At a Glance

Population:
  2010 census: 5,988,927
  2017 estimate: 6,113,532

Percent change in population:
  2010–2017: 2.1%

Percent change in total nonfarm employment:
  2007–2017: 2.5%

Industry with the largest growth in employment, 2007–2017 (thousands):
  Education and health services, 77.8

Industry with the largest decline or smallest growth in employment, 2007–2017 (thousands):
  Manufacturing, -37.3

Civilian labor force:
  2010: 3,056,484
  2017: 3,050,713

Unemployment rate and rank among states (highest to lowest):
  2010: 9.6%, 19th
  2017: 3.8%, 32nd

Over-the-year change in unemployment rates:
  2015–2016: -0.4%
  2016–2017: -0.8%

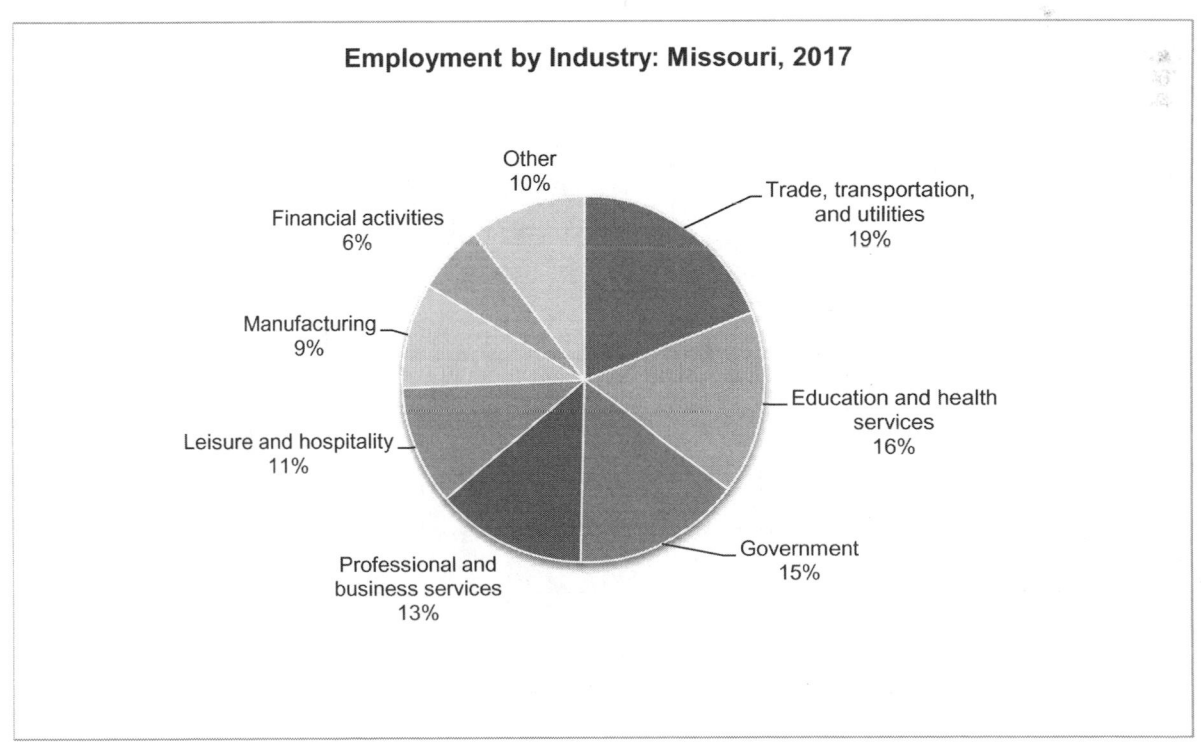

Employment by Industry: Missouri, 2017

- Other 10%
- Financial activities 6%
- Manufacturing 9%
- Leisure and hospitality 11%
- Professional and business services 13%
- Government 15%
- Education and health services 16%
- Trade, transportation, and utilities 19%

1. Employment by Industry: Missouri, Selected Years, 2007–2017

(Numbers in thousands, not seasonally adjusted)

Industry and year	January	February	March	April	May	June	July	August	September	October	November	December	Annual average
Total Nonfarm													
2007	2,731.9	2,744.6	2,788.3	2,806.5	2,827.5	2,828.7	2,771.2	2,789.1	2,818.5	2,818.7	2,825.9	2,822.3	2,797.8
2008	2,751.5	2,764.9	2,786.1	2,813.8	2,832.7	2,832.5	2,772.8	2,784.2	2,807.4	2,805.1	2,791.4	2,776.4	2,793.2
2009	2,686.0	2,684.2	2,698.0	2,714.4	2,721.7	2,714.8	2,656.0	2,664.2	2,687.7	2,687.4	2,684.0	2,678.2	2,689.7
2010	2,596.9	2,609.1	2,639.3	2,672.6	2,691.3	2,681.4	2,631.0	2,658.7	2,675.9	2,683.9	2,682.8	2,677.4	2,658.4
2011	2,606.7	2,612.3	2,646.6	2,687.0	2,698.2	2,689.4	2,646.4	2,654.3	2,685.0	2,690.2	2,692.9	2,691.3	2,666.7
2012	2,625.3	2,637.0	2,667.3	2,693.4	2,710.5	2,707.2	2,658.5	2,675.2	2,699.4	2,713.3	2,719.0	2,716.7	2,685.2
2013	2,646.5	2,664.9	2,685.4	2,720.5	2,739.7	2,733.5	2,685.0	2,703.4	2,727.6	2,742.7	2,744.4	2,738.5	2,711.0
2014	2,660.7	2,681.0	2,703.6	2,752.6	2,771.0	2,760.7	2,716.3	2,736.0	2,753.9	2,776.8	2,779.0	2,778.7	2,739.2
2015	2,717.6	2,735.4	2,754.0	2,803.8	2,825.8	2,822.1	2,784.4	2,792.2	2,814.1	2,835.1	2,840.1	2,839.2	2,797.0
2016	2,768.3	2,784.6	2,807.9	2,853.0	2,860.7	2,863.3	2,821.2	2,834.9	2,860.5	2,872.5	2,871.4	2,864.2	2,838.5
2017	2,802.6	2,826.2	2,843.3	2,877.2	2,888.3	2,897.4	2,849.3	2,859.3	2,883.0	2,897.3	2,905.1	2,894.8	2,868.7
Total Private													
2007	2,295.3	2,298.2	2,339.2	2,356.0	2,375.1	2,390.6	2,373.9	2,384.9	2,375.6	2,366.8	2,371.2	2,368.9	2,358.0
2008	2,310.0	2,311.7	2,331.6	2,356.8	2,374.1	2,385.6	2,369.9	2,372.0	2,358.5	2,345.9	2,330.7	2,316.4	2,346.9
2009	2,237.1	2,226.6	2,238.1	2,247.8	2,255.2	2,261.6	2,246.8	2,248.9	2,231.5	2,223.5	2,220.5	2,216.1	2,237.8
2010	2,147.0	2,149.8	2,176.8	2,209.6	2,220.3	2,234.8	2,232.8	2,238.6	2,227.9	2,232.5	2,230.3	2,227.4	2,210.7
2011	2,164.1	2,164.5	2,196.5	2,233.1	2,243.1	2,253.3	2,252.4	2,253.0	2,244.2	2,243.0	2,243.5	2,242.4	2,227.8
2012	2,188.4	2,189.9	2,218.0	2,241.8	2,258.4	2,272.1	2,266.3	2,270.8	2,258.1	2,264.8	2,269.5	2,268.4	2,247.2
2013	2,209.9	2,218.4	2,236.6	2,269.8	2,289.0	2,300.2	2,296.3	2,303.9	2,291.5	2,299.0	2,299.4	2,294.8	2,275.7
2014	2,229.9	2,240.2	2,261.3	2,306.5	2,323.6	2,330.2	2,329.1	2,337.6	2,319.0	2,334.7	2,336.3	2,337.7	2,307.2
2015	2,285.1	2,290.8	2,307.2	2,357.5	2,377.9	2,386.5	2,392.5	2,392.0	2,378.6	2,394.6	2,397.8	2,396.9	2,363.1
2016	2,337.3	2,346.3	2,366.5	2,410.7	2,416.4	2,427.2	2,427.5	2,431.7	2,420.4	2,427.0	2,425.8	2,418.7	2,404.6
2017	2,368.6	2,384.9	2,400.8	2,433.0	2,442.4	2,458.3	2,453.5	2,456.4	2,444.3	2,453.3	2,460.4	2,451.4	2,433.9
Goods Producing													
2007	446.7	443.8	455.0	456.9	461.7	465.9	459.5	464.1	461.5	457.0	455.2	450.6	456.5
2008	437.2	435.9	437.8	441.6	446.5	449.5	445.0	443.2	440.3	434.2	426.1	416.8	437.8
2009	395.0	389.6	389.6	385.9	382.8	384.4	382.7	378.5	374.5	369.4	365.7	359.6	379.8
2010	344.1	342.1	349.2	355.4	356.6	362.5	361.9	363.7	361.8	362.8	360.1	357.2	356.5
2011	342.1	341.1	349.1	356.0	359.2	364.4	366.4	363.6	364.0	361.4	358.9	357.3	357.0
2012	349.9	349.1	355.6	359.1	361.6	366.7	366.9	367.3	364.2	363.2	361.0	359.4	360.3
2013	350.5	352.3	354.7	360.7	365.9	371.4	370.3	372.2	370.6	369.9	367.6	363.8	364.2
2014	352.7	355.8	362.3	367.9	372.3	376.3	377.2	378.4	376.7	377.2	376.0	375.4	370.7
2015	366.7	367.2	371.6	377.5	381.3	385.4	386.6	385.8	384.6	385.0	383.6	384.1	380.0
2016	375.3	375.6	380.6	387.2	388.0	394.0	393.8	394.0	392.9	393.6	392.5	391.1	388.2
2017	382.3	385.3	386.9	390.6	393.3	399.5	398.9	398.7	397.3	397.3	398.1	396.2	393.7
Service-Providing													
2007	2,285.2	2,300.8	2,333.3	2,349.6	2,365.8	2,362.8	2,311.7	2,325.0	2,357.0	2,361.7	2,370.7	2,371.7	2,341.3
2008	2,314.3	2,329.0	2,348.3	2,372.2	2,386.2	2,383.0	2,327.8	2,341.0	2,367.1	2,370.9	2,365.3	2,359.6	2,355.4
2009	2,291.0	2,294.6	2,308.4	2,328.5	2,338.9	2,330.4	2,273.3	2,285.7	2,313.2	2,318.0	2,318.3	2,318.6	2,309.9
2010	2,252.8	2,267.0	2,290.1	2,317.2	2,334.7	2,318.9	2,269.1	2,295.0	2,314.1	2,321.1	2,322.7	2,320.2	2,301.9
2011	2,264.6	2,271.2	2,297.5	2,331.0	2,339.0	2,325.0	2,280.0	2,290.7	2,321.0	2,328.8	2,334.0	2,334.0	2,309.7
2012	2,275.4	2,287.9	2,311.7	2,334.3	2,348.9	2,340.5	2,291.6	2,307.9	2,335.2	2,350.1	2,358.0	2,357.3	2,324.9
2013	2,296.0	2,312.6	2,330.7	2,359.8	2,373.8	2,362.1	2,314.7	2,331.2	2,357.0	2,372.8	2,376.8	2,374.7	2,346.9
2014	2,308.0	2,325.2	2,341.3	2,384.7	2,398.7	2,384.4	2,339.1	2,357.6	2,377.2	2,399.6	2,403.0	2,403.3	2,368.5
2015	2,350.9	2,368.2	2,382.4	2,426.3	2,444.5	2,436.7	2,397.8	2,406.4	2,429.5	2,450.1	2,456.5	2,455.1	2,417.0
2016	2,393.0	2,409.0	2,427.3	2,465.8	2,472.7	2,469.3	2,427.4	2,440.9	2,467.6	2,478.9	2,478.9	2,473.1	2,450.3
2017	2,420.3	2,440.9	2,456.4	2,486.6	2,495.0	2,497.9	2,450.4	2,460.6	2,485.7	2,500.0	2,507.0	2,498.6	2,475.0
Mining and Logging													
2007	5.1	5.0	5.2	5.2	5.2	5.4	5.7	6.2	6.1	6.0	6.0	5.7	5.6
2008	5.4	5.2	5.1	5.0	4.9	5.0	5.1	5.3	5.4	5.4	4.9	4.7	5.1
2009	4.4	4.3	4.3	4.3	4.2	4.3	4.3	4.4	4.3	4.3	4.2	4.1	4.3
2010	3.8	3.9	4.1	4.3	4.3	4.4	4.4	4.4	4.3	4.3	4.3	4.2	4.2
2011	3.9	3.8	4.2	4.3	4.3	4.4	4.4	4.4	4.4	4.3	4.3	4.1	4.2
2012	3.9	3.9	4.1	4.2	4.2	4.3	4.2	4.2	4.2	4.2	4.1	4.1	4.1
2013	3.8	3.9	3.9	4.1	4.2	4.2	4.3	4.3	4.2	4.1	4.1	3.9	4.1
2014	3.6	3.7	3.9	4.1	4.1	4.2	4.2	4.2	4.3	4.2	4.2	4.1	4.1
2015	4.0	4.0	4.1	4.2	4.2	4.1	4.1	4.2	4.2	4.1	4.1	4.0	4.1
2016	4.0	3.9	4.0	4.1	4.1	4.2	4.2	4.1	4.1	4.1	4.1	4.1	4.1
2017	4.0	4.1	4.1	4.2	4.2	4.2	4.3	4.3	4.3	4.3	4.3	4.3	4.2

1. Employment by Industry: Missouri, Selected Years, 2007–2017—*Continued*

(Numbers in thousands, not seasonally adjusted)

Industry and year	January	February	March	April	May	June	July	August	September	October	November	December	Annual average
Construction													
2007	138.2	133.1	143.4	146.4	150.7	155.2	154.7	154.9	152.0	150.2	147.7	143.0	147.5
2008	136.0	132.5	137.4	140.4	144.3	146.6	147.3	147.2	143.9	141.0	136.8	130.7	140.3
2009	117.9	116.7	119.0	119.7	121.6	123.4	124.4	121.8	119.3	116.2	114.2	108.9	118.6
2010	97.7	95.6	101.0	106.7	106.8	110.7	112.1	111.4	110.2	109.9	107.6	104.1	106.2
2011	91.6	90.5	96.9	102.8	105.2	108.4	110.4	109.7	108.6	107.3	104.9	102.8	103.3
2012	96.1	94.9	99.7	102.6	105.6	108.4	109.2	109.6	108.2	107.3	105.8	104.7	104.3
2013	96.8	97.5	99.4	104.1	108.6	112.5	114.5	113.8	113.2	113.0	110.9	107.2	107.6
2014	100.7	99.1	105.4	108.9	111.6	114.0	115.9	115.7	114.6	114.2	112.6	111.5	110.4
2015	104.1	104.1	107.5	112.8	115.1	117.3	119.0	119.4	118.4	119.5	118.3	117.8	114.4
2016	111.1	110.1	114.5	120.4	121.1	124.8	125.3	125.3	124.8	124.9	123.7	122.0	120.7
2017	115.5	116.7	118.6	121.5	123.7	127.3	127.5	127.3	126.3	127.5	126.1	122.0	123.3
Manufacturing													
2007	303.4	305.7	306.4	305.3	305.8	305.3	299.1	303.0	303.4	300.8	301.5	301.9	303.5
2008	295.8	298.2	295.3	296.2	297.3	297.9	292.6	290.7	291.0	287.8	284.4	281.4	292.4
2009	272.7	268.6	266.3	261.9	257.0	256.7	254.0	252.3	250.9	248.9	247.3	246.6	256.9
2010	242.6	242.6	244.1	244.4	245.5	247.4	245.4	247.9	247.3	248.6	248.2	248.9	246.1
2011	246.6	246.8	248.0	248.9	249.7	251.6	251.6	249.5	251.0	249.8	249.7	250.4	249.5
2012	249.9	250.3	251.8	252.3	251.8	254.0	253.5	253.5	251.8	251.7	251.1	250.6	251.9
2013	249.9	250.9	251.4	252.5	253.1	254.7	251.5	254.1	253.2	252.8	252.6	252.7	252.5
2014	248.4	253.0	253.0	254.9	256.6	258.1	257.1	258.5	257.8	258.8	259.2	259.8	256.3
2015	258.6	259.1	260.0	260.5	262.0	264.0	263.5	262.2	262.0	261.4	261.2	262.3	261.4
2016	260.2	261.6	262.1	262.7	262.8	265.0	264.3	264.6	264.0	264.6	264.7	265.0	263.5
2017	262.8	264.5	264.2	264.9	265.4	268.0	267.1	267.1	266.7	265.5	267.7	269.9	266.2
Trade, Transportation, and Utilities													
2007	542.1	538.4	546.0	546.5	550.2	549.9	545.7	546.0	547.3	548.8	559.4	562.1	548.5
2008	542.4	537.1	540.4	542.7	545.7	546.0	542.0	542.1	540.9	540.2	544.2	545.1	542.4
2009	522.6	516.9	516.8	517.9	520.0	519.8	515.8	517.1	516.7	517.4	523.4	525.2	519.1
2010	506.4	502.3	506.7	510.6	514.4	515.1	512.5	514.4	511.9	514.0	521.4	524.9	512.9
2011	506.9	503.5	507.9	515.3	516.8	516.5	513.5	514.2	513.2	514.3	522.9	526.2	514.3
2012	507.6	502.7	506.2	509.1	513.2	513.6	511.1	512.5	512.2	514.9	525.3	527.5	513.0
2013	507.1	503.0	505.3	511.5	515.3	517.0	515.5	517.8	516.3	520.3	530.5	534.8	516.2
2014	513.5	510.1	513.7	519.2	523.0	525.3	522.5	524.7	523.1	526.8	536.5	541.5	523.3
2015	522.7	519.1	521.7	534.9	539.8	541.4	540.6	541.0	539.1	544.1	552.7	556.7	537.8
2016	537.3	535.5	538.0	543.2	545.7	544.9	545.2	545.6	543.1	546.4	555.3	558.8	544.9
2017	541.4	539.0	540.8	544.4	545.7	546.3	544.6	545.0	543.4	546.7	554.6	555.7	545.6
Wholesale Trade													
2007	123.0	123.7	124.8	124.6	124.9	125.9	125.5	125.5	125.2	125.3	125.6	126.1	125.0
2008	124.7	124.6	125.2	125.6	125.7	126.3	125.9	125.7	125.0	124.5	123.6	123.4	125.0
2009	120.5	119.8	119.2	118.9	118.4	118.6	118.0	117.5	116.6	117.2	116.6	117.1	118.2
2010	115.2	115.1	115.9	116.4	116.7	116.9	116.6	116.1	115.5	115.9	115.6	116.1	116.0
2011	114.2	114.3	115.1	116.4	116.4	117.1	117.1	116.6	116.2	116.4	116.5	117.2	116.1
2012	116.0	116.2	117.0	117.5	117.9	118.6	118.2	118.2	117.8	117.6	117.7	118.0	117.6
2013	115.9	116.3	116.8	118.4	119.0	119.5	119.3	119.3	118.9	119.6	119.8	120.5	118.6
2014	118.6	119.0	119.6	120.2	120.9	121.4	121.2	121.1	120.2	120.2	120.1	120.6	120.3
2015	119.0	118.9	119.1	120.0	120.6	121.1	121.8	120.8	119.6	120.1	119.8	120.3	120.1
2016	119.0	119.1	119.3	120.4	120.6	121.2	121.9	120.7	119.7	119.8	120.0	120.4	120.2
2017	119.6	120.0	120.4	121.3	121.5	122.5	122.2	121.7	121.6	121.8	121.2	121.1	121.2
Retail Trade													
2007	312.9	308.6	314.0	315.4	317.9	318.2	315.4	314.4	314.3	315.9	325.5	327.2	316.6
2008	312.7	307.3	309.6	311.2	313.5	314.7	311.8	311.3	309.6	310.1	315.2	316.4	312.0
2009	300.5	296.3	297.4	298.6	301.1	302.6	300.3	300.9	300.6	301.1	307.8	309.3	301.4
2010	294.9	291.5	294.5	296.1	299.1	301.0	299.9	300.2	297.6	299.4	306.8	309.2	299.2
2011	295.9	292.3	295.4	300.1	301.9	302.8	301.3	301.5	300.2	301.6	310.2	312.2	301.3
2012	298.2	294.1	296.8	298.8	301.6	302.3	301.3	300.4	299.9	302.3	312.3	313.0	301.8
2013	297.3	293.2	294.6	298.1	300.9	303.1	302.0	302.5	300.8	303.9	313.0	315.7	302.1
2014	299.4	296.0	298.6	302.6	305.0	307.7	306.1	306.2	304.8	307.9	317.1	320.0	306.0
2015	304.4	301.7	304.0	308.3	311.5	313.7	312.3	312.5	310.7	315.0	322.9	324.8	311.8
2016	309.8	308.4	310.2	314.1	315.9	316.0	316.5	316.3	314.0	316.4	324.4	325.7	315.6
2017	311.7	309.1	310.2	312.4	313.3	314.4	314.0	313.2	310.8	313.2	320.3	320.1	313.6

1. Employment by Industry: Missouri, Selected Years, 2007–2017—*Continued*

(Numbers in thousands, not seasonally adjusted)

Industry and year	January	February	March	April	May	June	July	August	September	October	November	December	Annual average
Transportation and Utilities													
2007	106.2	106.1	107.2	106.5	107.4	105.8	104.8	106.1	107.8	107.6	108.3	108.8	106.9
2008	105.0	105.2	105.6	105.9	106.5	105.0	104.3	105.1	106.3	105.6	105.4	105.3	105.4
2009	101.6	100.8	100.2	100.4	100.5	98.6	97.5	98.7	99.5	99.1	99.0	98.8	99.6
2010	96.3	95.7	96.3	98.1	98.6	97.2	96.0	98.1	98.8	98.7	99.0	99.6	97.7
2011	96.8	96.9	97.4	98.8	98.5	96.6	95.1	96.1	96.8	96.3	96.2	96.8	96.9
2012	93.4	92.4	92.4	92.8	93.7	92.7	91.6	93.9	94.5	95.0	95.3	96.5	93.7
2013	93.9	93.5	93.9	95.0	95.4	94.4	94.2	96.0	96.6	96.8	97.7	98.6	95.5
2014	95.5	95.1	95.5	96.4	97.1	96.2	95.2	97.4	98.1	98.7	99.3	100.9	97.1
2015	99.3	98.5	98.6	106.6	107.7	106.6	106.5	107.7	108.8	109.0	110.0	111.6	105.9
2016	108.5	108.0	108.5	108.7	109.2	107.7	106.8	108.6	109.4	110.2	110.9	112.7	109.1
2017	110.1	109.9	110.2	110.7	110.9	109.4	108.4	110.1	111.0	111.7	113.1	114.5	110.8
Information													
2007	62.2	62.4	62.9	62.6	63.1	63.7	63.4	63.6	63.7	64.0	64.4	64.6	63.4
2008	64.3	64.0	64.2	63.8	64.4	64.9	64.6	64.5	64.1	64.2	64.0	64.5	64.3
2009	64.0	64.0	63.7	64.4	64.5	64.9	63.6	63.6	63.2	61.1	61.0	61.4	63.3
2010	58.9	58.6	58.8	61.3	61.0	61.4	60.5	60.5	60.3	60.2	60.1	60.0	60.1
2011	58.5	58.3	58.2	59.2	59.5	59.7	60.0	59.8	59.8	59.4	59.4	59.4	59.3
2012	58.7	58.4	58.3	58.4	58.7	58.7	59.0	58.7	58.4	58.1	58.0	58.0	58.5
2013	57.5	57.8	57.9	57.4	57.7	57.9	57.6	57.4	57.0	57.2	57.2	57.4	57.5
2014	56.5	56.5	56.7	56.6	56.6	56.8	56.6	56.1	55.5	55.0	54.9	54.8	56.1
2015	54.5	54.3	54.2	54.3	54.6	54.8	54.9	54.3	53.6	53.4	53.5	53.9	54.2
2016	53.0	53.0	53.0	52.2	52.5	52.5	52.3	52.1	51.8	51.8	51.6	51.7	52.3
2017	51.2	51.1	51.2	51.4	51.6	51.8	51.8	51.5	51.3	51.3	51.7	51.5	51.5
Financial Activities													
2007	164.5	164.9	165.6	165.3	166.2	167.6	167.8	167.6	166.2	166.2	165.6	166.0	166.1
2008	165.3	165.6	165.3	165.3	166.2	166.8	167.3	167.3	165.8	165.7	165.3	165.1	165.9
2009	163.8	163.4	163.8	163.9	164.2	164.9	163.9	163.6	161.7	162.4	161.7	161.6	163.2
2010	160.9	160.8	161.1	162.1	162.6	163.6	163.7	162.9	161.9	162.5	162.5	162.3	162.2
2011	159.8	160.1	160.3	160.8	161.1	161.4	162.3	162.6	161.7	162.7	162.9	163.0	161.6
2012	161.4	162.1	162.8	162.6	163.3	164.0	164.5	164.7	163.5	164.6	164.9	164.5	163.6
2013	161.9	162.3	162.4	164.0	164.4	165.1	166.1	165.6	164.4	164.6	164.6	164.2	164.1
2014	162.2	162.4	162.2	164.0	164.9	165.5	166.2	166.2	164.6	165.1	165.1	165.4	164.5
2015	163.9	164.1	164.3	165.7	166.9	168.0	169.0	168.6	167.0	167.6	167.9	168.1	166.8
2016	166.5	167.0	167.2	168.3	169.0	170.1	170.8	170.7	169.9	169.9	170.3	170.8	169.2
2017	170.2	170.8	171.5	172.3	173.6	175.3	175.2	175.0	173.7	173.8	172.6	173.5	173.1
Professional and Business Services													
2007	324.3	325.5	331.5	334.1	333.9	337.5	336.6	338.7	336.9	336.4	336.7	337.8	334.2
2008	331.8	333.9	337.7	343.9	340.8	342.5	340.6	341.1	339.0	335.9	332.2	329.6	337.4
2009	318.4	316.5	316.1	316.1	313.7	314.4	312.2	313.1	310.4	311.5	312.3	313.5	314.0
2010	306.5	309.4	312.4	318.9	317.0	319.3	321.6	323.0	321.0	323.4	322.6	323.6	318.2
2011	318.0	319.7	324.5	330.6	328.8	330.7	329.1	329.3	329.3	330.5	331.0	332.1	327.8
2012	325.2	326.5	331.3	335.5	335.5	338.4	336.7	337.4	336.6	339.6	341.3	341.5	335.5
2013	332.2	336.2	341.0	345.1	345.8	348.2	348.2	350.5	348.5	351.7	352.0	352.3	346.0
2014	340.8	343.9	347.0	355.2	355.3	356.7	356.0	359.2	357.6	362.2	362.9	364.2	355.1
2015	354.0	357.2	360.9	367.8	368.3	368.4	371.2	372.4	371.6	376.9	378.0	378.1	368.7
2016	366.0	370.1	372.9	381.5	379.1	380.0	380.1	382.5	381.7	382.8	381.7	378.7	378.1
2017	369.5	373.9	377.9	383.8	381.5	385.3	384.9	386.7	386.0	390.5	395.4	392.5	384.0
Education and Health Services													
2007	379.2	384.1	386.2	387.5	387.5	385.8	385.6	386.7	390.9	392.7	394.1	395.1	388.0
2008	388.5	393.6	393.8	396.2	395.7	394.7	394.7	395.8	399.4	404.1	405.5	406.2	397.4
2009	399.9	403.3	404.2	405.2	405.5	403.4	403.8	405.5	409.0	412.8	414.1	415.0	406.8
2010	406.9	411.0	412.3	414.7	414.9	412.7	412.3	413.1	417.7	422.5	424.0	424.1	415.5
2011	419.3	422.8	424.3	425.5	423.7	419.8	419.6	420.3	424.1	426.2	427.6	426.9	423.3
2012	422.2	425.9	425.9	426.3	426.0	423.0	423.4	425.4	428.4	431.9	432.5	433.4	427.0
2013	427.7	433.0	431.3	436.6	434.4	428.6	429.2	430.1	431.9	437.5	437.9	435.2	432.8
2014	429.7	435.5	432.3	440.2	437.9	431.9	434.3	435.1	436.1	443.8	444.7	441.9	437.0
2015	441.6	444.9	442.0	450.1	448.5	443.9	447.4	446.9	447.2	454.8	455.5	451.3	447.8
2016	448.1	452.1	451.0	458.0	455.3	450.2	454.6	455.1	457.8	464.1	464.2	461.3	456.0
2017	458.2	464.7	462.2	468.7	467.3	461.5	463.9	464.3	466.6	471.1	472.7	468.8	465.8

1. Employment by Industry: Missouri, Selected Years, 2007–2017—*Continued*

(Numbers in thousands, not seasonally adjusted)

Industry and year	January	February	March	April	May	June	July	August	September	October	November	December	Annual average
Leisure and Hospitality													
2007	257.7	260.1	271.7	282.6	291.3	298.3	293.9	297.2	288.9	281.8	276.0	272.9	281.0
2008	260.5	261.3	271.4	282.1	293.0	298.5	293.3	295.8	287.4	280.0	273.2	269.6	280.5
2009	255.2	254.6	265.1	275.6	285.4	290.1	285.4	288.9	278.4	271.6	265.3	262.8	273.2
2010	248.2	250.3	260.5	274.4	281.3	286.9	286.9	287.9	281.2	274.5	267.3	263.2	271.9
2011	248.7	248.2	260.1	271.2	279.3	285.4	286.0	288.0	277.8	274.1	266.6	263.4	270.7
2012	251.0	252.5	264.2	276.0	284.6	291.4	288.6	289.2	280.1	277.6	271.6	269.3	274.7
2013	258.7	259.0	268.7	281.3	291.8	297.3	295.1	296.0	289.6	284.9	277.1	274.7	281.2
2014	263.3	264.3	274.3	289.4	298.8	302.3	301.0	303.0	291.5	290.8	282.8	280.8	286.9
2015	269.0	270.8	278.6	292.4	303.1	308.1	306.6	307.3	300.7	297.4	291.4	289.3	292.9
2016	276.7	278.4	288.4	303.4	309.6	317.0	312.5	314.1	306.5	301.7	293.7	290.4	299.4
2017	280.7	285.0	294.7	304.8	312.0	319.9	316.3	317.8	309.5	306.4	299.2	296.8	303.6
Other Services													
2007	118.6	119.0	120.3	120.5	121.7	121.9	121.4	121.0	120.2	119.9	119.8	119.8	120.3
2008	120.0	120.3	121.0	121.2	121.8	122.7	122.4	122.2	121.6	121.6	120.2	119.5	121.2
2009	118.2	118.3	118.8	118.8	119.1	119.7	119.4	118.6	117.6	117.3	117.0	117.0	118.3
2010	115.1	115.3	115.8	112.2	112.5	113.3	113.4	113.1	112.1	112.6	112.3	112.1	113.3
2011	110.8	110.8	112.1	114.5	114.7	115.4	115.5	115.2	114.3	114.4	114.2	114.1	113.8
2012	112.4	112.7	113.7	114.8	115.5	116.3	116.1	115.6	114.7	114.9	114.9	114.8	114.7
2013	114.3	114.8	115.3	113.2	113.7	114.7	114.3	114.3	113.2	112.9	112.5	112.4	113.8
2014	111.2	111.7	112.8	114.0	114.8	115.4	115.3	114.9	113.9	113.8	113.4	113.7	113.7
2015	112.7	113.2	113.9	114.8	115.4	116.5	116.2	115.7	114.8	115.4	115.2	115.4	114.9
2016	114.4	114.6	115.4	116.9	117.2	118.5	118.2	117.6	116.7	116.7	116.5	115.9	116.6
2017	115.1	115.1	115.6	117.0	117.4	118.7	117.9	117.4	116.5	116.2	116.1	116.4	116.6
Government													
2007	436.6	446.4	449.1	450.5	452.4	438.1	397.3	404.2	442.9	451.9	454.7	453.4	439.8
2008	441.5	453.2	454.5	457.0	458.6	446.9	402.9	412.2	448.9	459.2	460.7	460.0	446.3
2009	448.9	457.6	459.9	466.6	466.5	453.2	409.2	415.3	456.2	463.9	463.5	462.1	451.9
2010	449.9	459.3	462.5	463.0	471.0	446.6	398.2	420.1	448.0	451.4	452.5	450.0	447.7
2011	442.6	447.8	450.1	453.9	455.1	436.1	394.0	401.3	440.8	447.2	449.4	448.9	438.9
2012	436.9	447.1	449.3	451.6	452.1	435.1	392.2	404.4	441.3	448.5	449.5	448.3	438.0
2013	436.6	446.5	448.8	450.7	450.7	433.3	388.7	399.5	436.1	443.7	445.0	443.7	435.3
2014	430.8	440.8	442.3	446.1	447.4	430.5	387.2	398.4	434.9	442.1	442.7	441.0	432.0
2015	432.5	444.6	446.8	446.3	447.9	435.6	391.9	400.2	435.5	440.5	442.3	442.3	433.9
2016	431.0	438.3	441.4	442.3	444.3	436.1	393.7	403.2	440.1	445.5	445.6	445.5	433.9
2017	434.0	441.3	442.5	444.2	445.9	439.1	395.8	402.9	438.7	444.0	444.7	443.4	434.7

2. Average Weekly Hours by Selected Industry: Missouri, 2013–2017

(Not seasonally adjusted)

Industry and year	January	February	March	April	May	June	July	August	September	October	November	December	Annual average
Total Private													
2013	34.1	34.3	34.3	34.2	34.3	35.2	34.4	34.6	34.9	34.2	34.1	34.4	34.4
2014	33.6	34.3	34.5	34.1	34.1	34.6	34.3	34.2	34.0	33.8	34.5	34.2	34.2
2015	33.7	34.2	34.2	34.0	33.5	33.7	33.7	34.4	33.6	33.8	34.0	33.7	33.9
2016	33.4	33.3	33.3	33.7	33.7	33.3	33.3	33.2	33.3	33.9	33.1	33.0	33.4
2017	33.1	33.1	33.3	34.0	33.6	33.7	34.1	33.7	33.5	33.8	33.2	33.1	33.5
Goods Producing													
2013	39.0	39.4	39.7	39.1	39.4	40.2	39.3	39.5	39.9	39.7	38.7	38.6	39.4
2014	37.9	38.1	38.5	38.9	39.2	39.4	39.5	39.6	38.4	38.5	39.2	40.0	38.9
2015	38.8	39.1	38.6	39.0	39.0	39.7	39.2	40.0	38.2	39.6	38.7	39.5	39.1
2016	38.7	39.1	39.3	39.6	39.4	39.8	39.7	39.7	39.9	40.3	39.0	39.2	39.5
2017	38.4	39.5	39.4	39.2	39.7	40.0	40.3	40.5	40.5	40.4	39.6	40.0	39.8
Construction													
2013	35.9	37.1	37.7	36.2	37.2	37.9	37.0	37.8	37.8	37.5	34.9	34.4	36.8
2014	34.0	33.1	35.0	35.2	35.5	36.0	37.5	37.3	36.5	35.0	35.9	37.4	35.8
2015	36.4	35.6	36.1	36.3	35.9	37.6	36.7	38.0	34.9	38.2	35.5	38.2	36.6
2016	36.0	36.5	36.5	36.4	35.8	37.9	37.0	36.9	37.4	38.3	35.6	36.9	36.8
2017	34.4	36.4	35.9	36.1	36.4	36.9	37.3	36.6	37.2	37.2	35.7	35.4	36.3
Manufacturing													
2013	40.2	40.3	40.6	40.5	40.6	41.4	40.5	40.4	41.1	40.9	40.7	40.9	40.7
2014	39.9	40.6	40.3	40.8	41.1	41.1	40.4	40.7	39.3	40.3	40.9	41.3	40.6
2015	39.9	40.7	39.7	40.2	40.4	40.8	40.5	41.0	39.9	40.6	40.7	40.3	40.4
2016	40.2	40.5	40.8	41.3	41.3	40.8	41.1	41.1	41.2	41.4	40.8	40.5	40.9
2017	40.6	41.2	41.1	40.7	41.3	41.5	41.8	42.7	42.3	42.1	41.6	42.2	41.6
Trade, Transportation, and Utilities													
2013	34.7	34.7	34.4	34.7	34.9	35.1	34.8	34.9	34.8	34.4	34.3	34.4	34.7
2014	33.3	34.0	34.5	34.2	33.8	34.1	33.8	33.6	33.9	33.6	33.8	34.2	33.9
2015	33.1	33.6	33.5	33.6	33.4	33.9	33.8	34.2	34.1	34.1	34.2	34.2	33.8
2016	33.4	33.4	33.2	33.7	33.7	34.1	33.7	33.7	33.9	34.4	33.6	33.2	33.7
2017	32.8	33.0	33.6	34.3	33.6	33.6	33.6	33.3	33.3	33.2	32.8	32.5	33.3
Financial Activities													
2013	36.8	37.2	37.3	37.1	36.9	38.3	37.0	37.9	38.1	37.1	36.8	37.5	37.3
2014	36.8	38.0	37.8	36.8	36.7	37.1	36.0	36.1	36.0	35.9	37.6	36.5	36.8
2015	36.5	37.6	37.6	36.9	36.8	36.8	37.1	37.8	36.5	36.2	37.2	36.2	36.9
2016	36.0	35.3	35.7	36.3	37.0	34.4	34.8	34.7	34.4	35.3	34.6	34.7	35.3
2017	36.3	35.3	34.8	36.7	35.8	35.5	36.6	35.7	35.6	36.8	35.5	35.6	35.8
Professional and Business Services													
2013	35.5	36.3	35.8	36.1	35.6	37.1	35.2	36.5	37.1	35.8	35.8	36.4	36.1
2014	35.8	36.8	36.6	36.8	36.6	37.5	36.7	36.8	36.4	36.1	37.1	35.8	36.6
2015	35.8	36.7	36.5	36.1	35.5	35.6	35.4	37.0	35.7	36.2	36.3	35.4	36.0
2016	35.2	34.9	35.0	35.7	35.9	35.6	35.9	35.5	35.4	36.4	35.7	35.5	35.6
2017	36.2	35.3	35.2	36.6	35.2	36.0	36.0	36.0	35.0	34.9	34.3	34.0	35.4
Education and Health Services													
2013	32.6	32.5	32.5	32.5	32.3	33.5	32.9	32.7	33.3	32.5	32.7	32.9	32.7
2014	32.3	32.5	32.8	32.1	32.2	33.2	32.8	32.6	32.6	32.5	33.6	32.7	32.7
2015	32.8	33.1	33.1	32.8	33.0	32.3	33.0	33.5	33.2	32.3	33.9	33.0	33.0
2016	33.5	32.6	32.6	32.6	33.1	32.6	32.7	32.6	32.9	33.2	32.7	32.7	32.8
2017	33.8	33.2	32.8	33.6	32.6	32.7	33.4	32.5	32.7	33.3	32.7	32.5	33.0
Leisure and Hospitality													
2013	24.2	25.0	25.4	25.1	25.5	26.2	25.9	25.5	25.5	25.6	25.2	24.8	25.3
2014	24.0	25.0	25.4	24.9	25.1	25.8	26.1	25.9	25.5	25.5	25.6	25.5	25.4
2015	24.8	25.8	26.4	25.9	25.1	25.8	25.7	25.7	25.3	25.4	25.1	24.7	25.5
2016	24.6	24.9	25.2	25.3	24.9	24.6	25.0	24.8	24.0	24.2	24.0	23.2	24.6
2017	22.5	23.4	23.9	24.0	24.6	25.2	25.6	24.9	24.7	24.9	24.5	24.5	24.4

3. Average Hourly Earnings by Selected Industry: Missouri, 2012–2016

(Dollars, not seasonally adjusted)

Industry and year	January	February	March	April	May	June	July	August	September	October	November	December	Annual average
Total Private													
2013	21.78	22.00	21.76	21.73	21.70	21.77	21.63	21.81	22.04	21.82	22.16	22.22	21.87
2014	22.12	22.28	22.22	22.11	21.93	21.97	21.74	21.78	21.83	21.91	22.17	21.90	22.00
2015	22.07	22.21	22.16	21.99	22.19	22.00	22.00	22.08	22.09	22.04	22.21	22.13	22.10
2016	22.25	22.17	22.24	22.16	22.33	22.19	22.42	22.32	22.85	23.11	23.24	23.25	22.55
2017	23.94	23.49	23.60	23.91	23.57	23.52	24.02	23.78	24.20	24.33	24.35	24.26	23.92
Goods Producing													
2013	24.10	24.22	24.46	24.50	24.61	24.89	25.04	25.43	25.76	25.45	26.35	26.05	25.08
2014	25.92	25.88	25.95	25.62	25.74	25.50	25.86	25.87	25.97	26.28	26.41	26.33	25.95
2015	26.24	25.53	25.78	25.28	25.30	25.21	25.46	25.83	26.33	25.91	26.00	26.39	25.77
2016	25.93	25.85	26.62	26.18	26.51	26.36	26.65	26.68	27.00	27.37	27.55	27.21	26.67
2017	26.99	27.25	27.44	27.81	27.54	27.66	28.15	28.07	28.30	28.18	28.01	27.96	27.79
Construction													
2013	27.62	27.59	27.55	27.77	27.60	27.91	28.29	28.41	28.17	27.96	27.75	26.87	27.81
2014	26.51	26.36	26.36	26.44	26.95	26.51	27.16	26.92	27.18	27.44	27.95	27.88	27.00
2015	27.61	27.66	28.07	27.73	28.07	27.77	28.15	28.17	28.41	28.42	28.20	28.48	28.07
2016	27.38	26.97	27.40	27.53	28.17	27.64	28.04	28.53	29.14	29.30	28.81	29.03	28.19
2017	28.20	28.82	29.02	29.10	28.85	28.97	29.29	29.58	29.35	29.59	29.27	29.31	29.13
Manufacturing													
2013	22.83	22.93	23.28	23.25	23.40	23.62	23.59	24.01	24.63	24.29	24.73	24.96	23.80
2014	25.03	25.13	25.23	24.78	24.80	24.67	24.91	25.05	25.10	25.53	25.51	25.46	25.10
2015	25.50	24.51	24.69	24.10	24.00	23.98	24.19	24.72	24.95	24.65	24.96	25.01	24.60
2016	25.07	25.13	26.07	25.36	25.62	25.61	25.88	25.64	25.79	26.28	26.82	26.19	25.79
2017	26.31	26.42	26.68	27.18	26.96	27.09	27.66	27.48	27.93	27.67	27.58	27.51	27.21
Trade, Transportation, and Utilities													
2013	19.95	20.47	20.15	20.12	20.04	20.09	19.74	19.91	20.33	19.88	20.01	20.13	20.07
2014	20.47	20.62	20.70	20.91	20.51	20.53	20.18	19.99	19.90	19.81	19.95	19.19	20.22
2015	19.72	19.88	19.85	19.83	19.87	19.46	19.56	19.60	19.61	19.61	19.58	19.29	19.65
2016	19.71	19.41	19.50	19.63	19.59	19.98	19.62	20.12	20.20	20.64	20.38	20.75	19.97
2017	22.44	21.11	21.21	21.55	21.18	21.27	21.63	21.33	21.71	21.93	21.79	21.83	21.58
Financial Activities													
2013	26.13	27.95	26.49	26.44	26.63	26.38	25.99	26.46	26.05	25.75	26.98	27.25	26.54
2014	26.64	27.25	26.76	26.61	26.43	26.38	26.11	26.33	26.10	26.04	26.69	26.32	26.48
2015	26.55	27.08	26.90	26.61	26.61	26.17	25.87	26.15	26.14	26.01	26.51	26.24	26.40
2016	27.20	27.07	26.81	27.16	27.20	26.93	28.04	27.38	28.34	28.24	29.85	29.12	27.77
2017	30.12	28.33	28.99	29.10	28.77	29.02	30.43	29.65	30.36	30.48	30.84	31.20	29.78
Professional and Business Services													
2013	25.92	25.78	25.69	25.43	25.59	25.87	25.85	25.69	25.93	25.60	25.72	25.30	25.70
2014	25.17	25.41	25.22	24.78	24.84	25.21	24.82	24.82	25.10	25.34	25.71	25.42	25.15
2015	25.80	26.52	26.55	26.28	26.35	26.24	26.34	26.86	26.95	26.80	27.33	26.96	26.59
2016	27.55	27.61	27.05	26.91	27.10	26.68	26.99	26.87	27.17	27.51	27.49	27.76	27.22
2017	28.99	29.10	29.05	29.34	28.88	28.58	29.48	28.97	29.55	29.69	28.87	29.11	29.13
Education and Health Services													
2013	19.71	19.57	19.48	19.60	19.51	19.52	19.46	19.43	19.54	19.48	19.38	19.55	19.52
2014	19.18	19.27	19.17	19.09	18.77	18.38	18.33	18.51	18.49	18.51	18.49	18.56	18.73
2015	18.52	18.72	18.75	18.82	18.64	18.98	18.99	18.36	18.09	18.12	18.18	18.32	18.54
2016	18.09	18.34	18.70	18.83	19.17	19.13	19.31	19.29	19.67	19.53	19.96	19.87	19.16
2017	19.73	19.90	20.03	20.16	20.00	19.98	19.83	19.57	19.67	19.62	19.41	19.41	19.78
Leisure and Hospitality													
2013	12.52	12.49	12.41	12.46	12.16	11.99	12.09	12.23	12.49	12.50	12.59	12.68	12.37
2014	12.74	12.66	12.82	12.66	12.48	12.44	12.35	12.42	12.68	12.66	12.83	13.09	12.65
2015	12.95	13.04	12.96	12.96	13.28	13.09	13.07	13.09	13.11	13.34	13.23	13.42	13.13
2016	13.33	13.51	13.35	13.51	13.46	13.27	13.40	13.36	13.75	13.72	13.57	13.90	13.51
2017	13.99	13.93	14.10	13.93	13.75	13.75	13.79	13.91	14.27	14.21	14.39	14.60	14.05

4. Average Weekly Earnings by Selected Industry: Missouri, 2013–2017

(Dollars, not seasonally adjusted)

Industry and year	January	February	March	April	May	June	July	August	September	October	November	December	Annual average
Total Private													
2013	742.70	754.60	746.37	743.17	744.31	766.30	744.07	754.63	769.20	746.24	755.66	764.37	752.33
2014	743.23	764.20	766.59	753.95	747.81	760.16	745.68	744.88	742.22	740.56	764.87	748.98	752.40
2015	743.76	759.58	757.87	747.66	743.37	741.40	741.40	759.55	742.22	744.95	755.14	745.78	749.19
2016	743.15	738.26	740.59	746.79	752.52	738.93	746.59	741.02	760.91	783.43	769.24	767.25	753.17
2017	792.41	777.52	785.88	812.94	791.95	792.62	819.08	801.39	810.70	822.35	808.42	803.01	801.32
Goods Producing													
2013	939.90	954.27	971.06	957.95	969.63	1,000.58	984.07	1,004.49	1,027.82	1,010.37	1,019.75	1,005.53	988.15
2014	982.37	986.03	999.08	996.62	1,009.01	1,004.70	1,021.47	1,024.45	997.25	1,011.78	1,035.27	1,053.20	1,009.46
2015	1,018.11	998.22	995.11	985.92	986.70	1,000.84	998.03	1,033.20	1,005.81	1,026.04	1,006.20	1,042.41	1,007.61
2016	1,003.49	1,010.74	1,046.17	1,036.73	1,044.49	1,049.13	1,058.01	1,059.20	1,077.30	1,103.01	1,074.45	1,066.63	1,053.47
2017	1,036.42	1,076.38	1,081.14	1,090.15	1,093.34	1,106.40	1,134.45	1,136.84	1,146.15	1,138.47	1,109.20	1,118.40	1,106.04
Construction													
2013	991.56	1,023.59	1,038.64	1,005.27	1,026.72	1,057.79	1,046.73	1,073.90	1,064.83	1,048.50	968.48	924.33	1,023.41
2014	901.34	872.52	922.60	930.69	956.73	954.36	1,018.50	1,004.12	992.07	960.40	1,003.41	1,042.71	966.60
2015	1,005.00	984.70	1,013.33	1,006.60	1,007.71	1,044.15	1,033.11	1,070.46	991.51	1,085.64	1,001.10	1,087.94	1,027.36
2016	985.68	984.41	1,000.10	1,002.09	1,008.49	1,047.56	1,037.48	1,052.76	1,089.84	1,122.19	1,025.64	1,071.21	1,037.39
2017	970.08	1,049.05	1,041.82	1,050.51	1,050.14	1,068.99	1,092.52	1,082.63	1,091.82	1,100.75	1,044.94	1,037.57	1,057.42
Manufacturing													
2013	917.77	924.08	945.17	941.63	950.04	977.87	955.40	970.00	1,012.29	993.46	1,006.51	1,020.86	968.66
2014	998.70	1,020.28	1,016.77	1,011.02	1,019.28	1,013.94	1,006.36	1,019.54	986.43	1,028.86	1,043.36	1,051.50	1,019.06
2015	1,017.45	997.56	980.19	968.82	969.60	978.38	979.70	1,013.52	995.51	1,000.79	1,015.87	1,007.90	993.84
2016	1,007.81	1,017.77	1,063.66	1,047.37	1,058.11	1,044.89	1,063.67	1,053.80	1,062.55	1,087.99	1,094.26	1,060.70	1,054.81
2017	1,068.19	1,088.50	1,096.55	1,106.23	1,113.45	1,124.24	1,156.19	1,173.40	1,181.44	1,164.91	1,147.33	1,160.92	1,131.94
Trade, Transportation, and Utilities													
2013	692.27	710.31	693.16	698.16	699.40	705.16	686.95	694.86	707.48	683.87	686.34	692.47	696.43
2014	681.65	701.08	714.15	715.12	693.24	700.07	682.08	671.66	674.61	665.62	674.31	656.30	685.46
2015	652.73	667.97	664.98	666.29	663.66	659.69	661.13	670.32	668.70	668.70	669.64	659.72	664.17
2016	658.31	648.29	647.40	661.53	660.18	681.32	661.19	678.04	684.78	710.02	684.77	688.90	672.99
2017	736.03	696.63	712.66	739.17	711.65	714.67	726.77	710.29	722.94	728.08	714.71	709.48	718.61
Financial Activities													
2013	961.58	1,039.74	988.08	980.92	982.65	1,010.35	961.63	1,002.83	992.51	955.33	992.86	1,021.88	989.94
2014	980.35	1,035.50	1,011.53	979.25	969.98	978.70	939.96	950.51	939.60	934.84	1,003.54	960.68	974.46
2015	969.08	1,018.21	1,011.44	981.91	979.25	963.06	959.78	988.47	954.11	941.56	986.17	949.89	974.16
2016	979.20	955.57	957.12	985.91	1,006.40	926.39	975.79	950.09	974.90	996.87	1,032.81	1,010.46	980.28
2017	1,093.36	1,000.05	1,008.85	1,067.97	1,029.97	1,030.21	1,113.74	1,058.51	1,080.82	1,121.66	1,094.82	1,110.72	1,066.12
Professional and Business Services													
2013	920.16	935.81	919.70	918.02	911.00	959.78	909.92	937.69	962.00	916.48	920.78	920.92	927.77
2014	901.09	935.09	923.05	911.90	909.14	945.38	910.89	913.38	913.64	914.77	953.84	910.04	920.49
2015	923.64	973.28	969.08	948.71	935.43	934.14	932.44	993.82	962.12	970.16	992.08	954.38	957.24
2016	969.76	963.59	946.75	960.69	972.89	949.81	968.94	953.89	961.82	1,001.36	981.39	985.48	969.03
2017	1,049.44	1,027.23	1,022.56	1,073.84	1,016.58	1,028.88	1,061.28	1,042.92	1,034.25	1,036.18	990.24	989.74	1,031.20
Education and Health Services													
2013	642.55	636.03	633.10	637.00	630.17	653.92	640.23	635.36	650.68	633.10	633.73	643.20	638.30
2014	619.51	626.28	628.78	612.79	604.39	610.22	601.22	603.43	602.77	601.58	621.26	606.91	612.47
2015	607.46	619.63	620.63	617.30	615.12	613.05	626.67	615.06	600.59	585.28	616.30	604.56	611.82
2016	606.02	597.88	609.62	613.86	634.53	623.64	631.44	628.85	647.14	648.40	652.69	649.75	628.45
2017	666.87	660.68	656.98	677.38	652.00	653.35	662.32	636.03	643.21	653.35	634.71	630.83	652.74
Leisure and Hospitality													
2013	302.98	312.25	315.21	312.75	310.08	314.14	313.13	311.87	318.50	320.00	317.27	314.46	312.96
2014	305.76	316.50	325.63	315.23	313.25	320.95	322.34	321.68	323.34	322.83	328.45	333.80	321.31
2015	321.16	336.43	342.14	335.66	333.33	337.72	335.90	336.41	331.68	338.84	332.07	331.47	334.82
2016	327.92	336.40	336.42	341.80	335.15	326.44	335.00	331.33	330.00	332.02	325.68	322.48	332.35
2017	314.78	325.96	336.99	334.32	338.25	346.50	353.02	346.36	352.47	353.83	352.56	357.70	342.82

MONTANA
At a Glance

Population:
  2010 census: 989,415
  2017 estimate: 1,050,493

Percent change in population:
  2010–2017: 6.2%

Percent change in total nonfarm employment:
  2007–2017: 6.3%

Industry with the largest growth in employment, 2007–2017 (thousands):
  Education and health services, 17.7

Industry with the largest decline or smallest growth in employment, 2007–2017 (thousands):
  Construction, -4.6

Civilian labor force:
  2010: 500,525
  2017: 525,453

Unemployment rate and rank among states (highest to lowest):
  2010: 7.3%, 40th
  2017: 4.0%, 31st

Over-the-year change in unemployment rates:
  2015–2016: -0.1%
  2016–2017: -0.1%

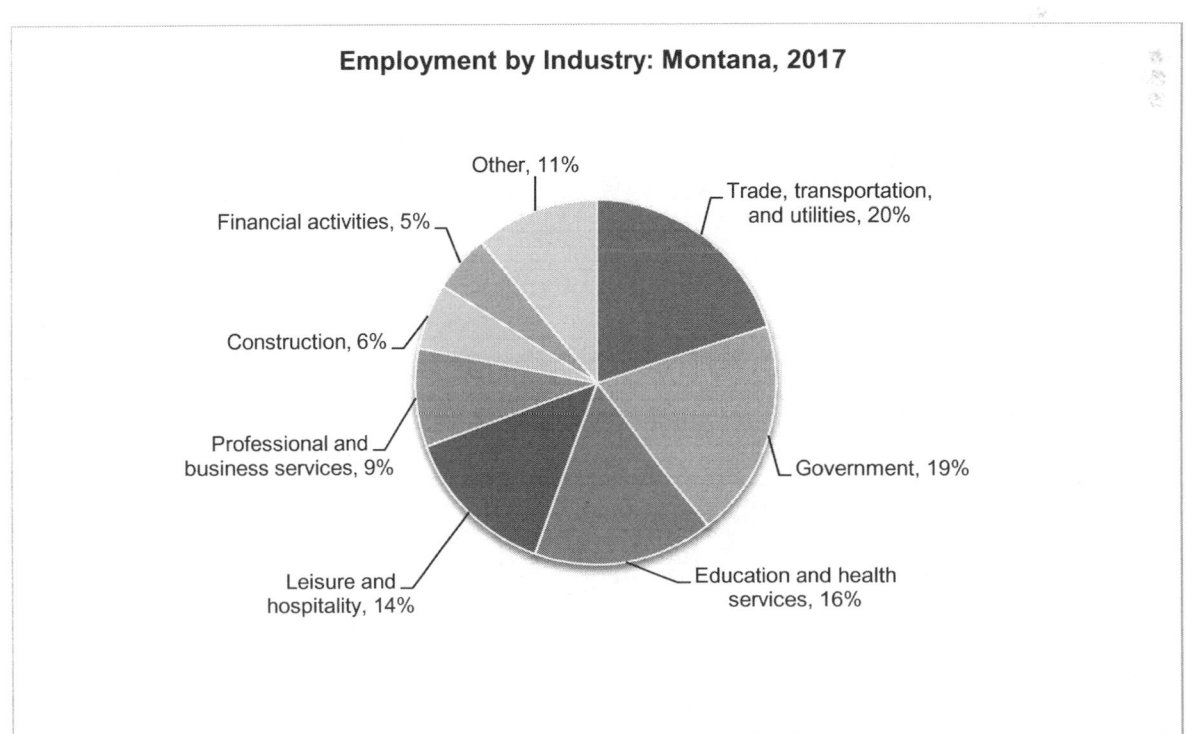

Employment by Industry: Montana, 2017

- Other, 11%
- Trade, transportation, and utilities, 20%
- Financial activities, 5%
- Government, 19%
- Construction, 6%
- Professional and business services, 9%
- Education and health services, 16%
- Leisure and hospitality, 14%

1. Employment by Industry: Montana, Selected Years, 2007–2017

(Numbers in thousands, not seasonally adjusted)

Industry and year	January	February	March	April	May	June	July	August	September	October	November	December	Annual average
Total Nonfarm													
2007	426.2	429.3	435.7	439.1	446.9	453.3	452.1	452.9	449.4	449.6	447.1	447.1	444.1
2008	432.7	435.5	439.2	441.4	449.8	454.0	452.4	453.3	450.3	447.1	442.5	439.8	444.8
2009	420.0	420.0	419.7	425.5	431.4	438.3	435.4	435.6	433.6	431.9	428.7	426.8	428.9
2010	413.3	413.9	418.5	423.7	432.3	437.3	436.7	437.4	435.5	433.0	428.2	427.5	428.1
2011	413.7	415.7	419.8	425.7	433.4	438.5	437.3	440.3	441.2	438.2	434.7	434.7	431.1
2012	422.8	423.9	427.9	434.5	443.7	448.5	448.3	450.2	449.9	447.0	443.0	443.6	440.3
2013	432.2	435.4	438.7	444.6	452.5	456.7	454.1	457.0	455.7	454.7	450.9	450.9	448.6
2014	437.8	441.2	442.6	449.1	456.2	462.0	461.4	462.5	460.3	457.3	452.6	454.7	453.1
2015	444.9	448.9	452.8	458.7	464.5	469.2	468.8	469.5	468.1	468.4	464.7	465.9	462.0
2016	452.4	455.6	459.2	465.2	471.1	476.2	474.1	475.2	474.6	471.5	469.3	468.7	467.8
2017	457.6	459.6	463.5	469.2	476.3	481.6	479.1	480.0	478.3	476.0	471.7	473.5	472.2
Total Private													
2007	340.5	341.3	346.7	351.0	357.6	366.3	368.6	370.0	363.8	359.5	357.5	358.4	356.8
2008	347.3	347.6	350.7	353.3	359.0	365.9	368.7	369.3	362.3	355.9	350.7	349.7	356.7
2009	333.2	331.1	330.1	335.2	339.5	348.0	350.1	349.7	344.5	339.2	336.1	334.5	339.3
2010	323.1	322.6	325.4	331.1	336.2	344.3	348.0	348.8	343.9	339.8	335.3	334.9	336.1
2011	324.3	324.7	327.8	333.9	340.2	347.7	352.9	354.5	350.4	347.0	343.9	344.1	341.0
2012	334.1	334.3	337.5	344.2	351.3	359.4	362.1	364.6	359.6	356.0	352.0	353.1	350.7
2013	341.9	343.9	346.8	353.2	360.4	367.5	370.3	372.2	366.3	363.0	359.7	361.1	358.9
2014	349.7	349.8	350.9	357.8	364.1	372.3	375.8	377.0	370.0	365.6	360.8	363.8	363.1
2015	356.4	357.9	360.9	366.4	371.6	379.6	383.6	383.9	377.5	375.4	372.4	373.9	371.6
2016	363.6	364.7	367.1	372.8	377.3	384.6	388.4	388.7	383.1	378.6	376.3	376.3	376.8
2017	367.4	368.5	371.8	377.2	383.5	390.9	392.4	392.9	386.0	382.3	378.5	381.0	381.0
Goods Producing													
2007	56.1	55.8	57.8	59.8	62.2	64.4	64.3	64.9	63.2	63.0	61.8	59.8	61.1
2008	55.6	55.1	56.0	57.0	59.1	60.5	61.4	61.2	59.5	58.8	56.5	53.8	57.9
2009	47.8	46.1	45.1	47.3	48.6	50.5	50.9	51.1	50.0	49.8	48.3	45.7	48.4
2010	42.2	41.6	42.4	44.9	46.7	48.3	49.5	50.0	49.5	49.8	47.9	45.1	46.5
2011	41.6	41.6	42.5	45.4	47.3	49.3	50.9	51.7	51.4	51.5	49.9	48.1	47.6
2012	44.8	44.5	45.4	48.5	50.5	52.0	52.8	53.5	53.3	53.5	51.7	50.6	50.1
2013	46.3	46.8	47.7	50.4	53.7	54.3	54.5	55.1	54.3	54.6	53.5	51.7	51.9
2014	48.1	47.7	48.5	51.1	53.6	56.0	56.7	56.6	55.3	56.0	53.5	53.0	53.0
2015	49.8	50.0	50.7	52.3	54.3	56.2	57.1	56.8	55.4	56.0	54.3	53.0	53.8
2016	49.4	49.5	50.2	52.5	54.2	55.8	56.2	56.4	55.3	55.3	54.8	52.8	53.5
2017	49.6	50.3	51.3	53.6	56.1	57.3	57.3	57.2	56.1	56.5	54.7	53.8	54.5
Service-Providing													
2007	370.1	373.5	377.9	379.3	384.7	388.9	387.8	388.0	386.2	386.6	385.3	387.3	383.0
2008	377.1	380.4	383.2	384.4	390.7	393.5	391.0	392.1	390.8	388.3	386.0	386.0	387.0
2009	372.2	373.9	374.6	378.2	382.8	387.8	384.5	384.5	383.6	382.1	380.4	381.1	380.5
2010	371.1	372.3	376.1	378.8	385.6	389.0	387.2	387.4	386.0	383.2	380.3	382.4	381.6
2011	372.1	374.1	377.3	380.3	386.1	389.2	386.4	388.6	389.8	386.7	384.8	386.6	383.5
2012	378.0	379.4	382.5	386.0	393.2	396.5	395.5	396.7	396.6	393.5	391.3	393.0	390.2
2013	385.9	388.6	391.0	394.2	398.8	402.4	399.6	401.9	401.4	400.1	397.4	399.2	396.7
2014	389.7	393.5	394.1	398.0	402.6	406.0	404.7	405.9	405.0	401.3	399.1	401.7	400.1
2015	395.1	398.9	402.1	406.4	410.2	413.0	411.7	412.7	412.7	412.4	410.4	412.9	408.2
2016	403.0	406.1	409.0	412.7	416.9	420.4	417.9	418.8	419.3	416.2	414.5	415.9	414.2
2017	408.0	409.3	412.2	415.6	420.2	424.3	421.8	422.8	422.2	419.5	417.0	419.7	417.7
Mining and Logging													
2007	8.1	8.1	8.3	8.1	8.2	8.6	8.7	8.7	8.4	8.4	8.3	8.3	8.4
2008	7.9	7.9	7.9	7.8	8.0	8.4	8.6	8.8	8.8	8.8	8.8	8.4	8.3
2009	7.7	7.1	6.9	6.8	6.8	6.9	7.2	7.2	7.0	7.1	7.0	7.0	7.1
2010	6.9	6.9	7.0	7.1	7.3	7.5	7.7	7.9	7.8	7.8	7.7	7.5	7.4
2011	7.4	7.5	7.6	7.6	7.8	8.0	8.5	8.8	8.6	8.7	8.8	8.7	8.2
2012	8.7	8.8	8.7	8.8	9.0	9.4	9.7	9.9	9.7	9.8	9.7	9.8	9.3
2013	9.1	9.3	9.3	9.2	9.5	9.7	9.6	9.7	9.6	9.4	9.5	9.4	9.4
2014	8.9	8.8	8.7	8.7	9.0	9.2	9.4	9.5	9.4	9.5	9.3	9.2	9.1
2015	8.8	8.6	8.4	8.1	8.2	8.4	8.4	8.3	8.0	7.9	7.7	7.5	8.2
2016	7.1	7.0	6.8	6.9	7.0	7.1	7.0	7.0	6.9	6.9	6.9	6.8	7.0
2017	6.7	6.7	6.6	6.6	6.7	7.0	7.1	7.2	7.0	7.1	7.0	6.9	6.9

1. Employment by Industry: Montana, Selected Years, 2007–2017—*Continued*

(Numbers in thousands, not seasonally adjusted)

Industry and year	January	February	March	April	May	June	July	August	September	October	November	December	Annual average
Construction													
2007	27.8	27.6	29.1	31.5	33.7	35.1	35.0	35.6	34.4	34.0	32.8	30.9	32.3
2008	27.6	27.2	28.1	29.1	30.8	31.7	32.5	32.2	31.0	30.1	28.3	26.3	29.6
2009	22.1	21.5	21.2	23.2	24.3	26.0	26.3	26.5	25.8	25.2	24.0	21.5	24.0
2010	18.9	18.4	19.3	21.7	23.1	24.3	25.2	25.4	25.1	25.2	23.3	20.8	22.6
2011	17.9	17.8	18.5	21.3	22.9	24.5	25.5	25.9	25.9	25.6	24.0	22.1	22.7
2012	19.3	19.0	20.0	22.5	24.0	24.9	25.2	25.6	25.7	25.4	23.7	22.4	23.1
2013	19.6	19.8	20.7	23.2	26.0	26.1	26.2	26.7	26.1	26.2	24.9	23.2	24.1
2014	20.8	20.5	21.5	23.8	25.8	27.7	28.1	27.9	26.9	27.2	25.2	24.6	25.0
2015	22.4	22.7	23.7	25.4	27.2	28.6	29.3	29.1	28.1	28.5	27.1	25.9	26.5
2016	23.1	23.3	24.3	26.4	27.9	29.2	29.5	29.6	28.7	28.5	27.9	26.1	27.0
2017	23.5	24.1	25.1	27.4	29.6	30.3	30.1	29.9	29.0	29.2	27.3	26.5	27.7
Manufacturing													
2007	20.2	20.1	20.4	20.2	20.3	20.7	20.6	20.6	20.4	20.6	20.7	20.6	20.5
2008	20.1	20.0	20.0	20.1	20.3	20.4	20.3	20.2	19.7	19.9	19.4	19.1	20.0
2009	18.0	17.5	17.0	17.3	17.5	17.6	17.4	17.4	17.2	17.5	17.3	17.2	17.4
2010	16.4	16.3	16.1	16.1	16.3	16.5	16.6	16.7	16.6	16.8	16.9	16.8	16.5
2011	16.3	16.3	16.4	16.5	16.6	16.8	16.9	17.0	16.9	17.2	17.1	17.3	16.8
2012	16.8	16.7	16.7	17.2	17.5	17.7	17.9	18.0	17.9	18.3	18.3	18.4	17.6
2013	17.6	17.7	17.7	18.0	18.2	18.5	18.7	18.7	18.6	19.0	19.1	19.1	18.4
2014	18.4	18.4	18.3	18.6	18.8	19.1	19.2	19.2	19.0	19.3	19.0	19.2	18.9
2015	18.6	18.7	18.6	18.8	18.9	19.2	19.4	19.4	19.3	19.6	19.5	19.6	19.1
2016	19.2	19.2	19.1	19.2	19.3	19.5	19.7	19.8	19.7	19.9	20.0	19.9	19.5
2017	19.4	19.5	19.6	19.6	19.8	20.0	20.1	20.1	20.1	20.2	20.4	20.4	19.9
Trade, Transportation, and Utilities													
2007	88.8	88.6	89.4	89.8	91.4	92.0	92.9	92.5	92.2	92.5	93.9	94.6	91.6
2008	91.0	90.1	90.6	90.8	91.4	92.1	91.9	92.1	91.4	90.9	91.1	91.4	91.2
2009	86.9	85.7	85.1	86.2	87.1	88.0	87.9	87.9	87.2	86.7	87.3	87.7	87.0
2010	84.3	83.6	84.1	85.0	86.0	86.9	86.7	86.8	86.0	85.9	86.5	87.2	85.8
2011	84.1	83.6	83.7	85.0	86.2	87.2	87.5	87.8	87.1	87.2	88.3	88.9	86.4
2012	85.9	85.5	85.9	87.0	88.6	89.9	89.8	90.2	89.8	90.2	91.2	91.8	88.8
2013	88.4	88.2	88.6	90.0	91.6	92.3	92.2	92.7	91.8	92.3	93.3	94.3	91.3
2014	90.8	90.3	90.2	91.3	92.8	93.7	93.6	93.9	93.2	93.1	94.3	95.3	92.7
2015	92.3	91.9	92.5	93.6	94.5	95.3	95.4	95.5	94.8	95.4	96.6	97.2	94.6
2016	93.8	93.2	93.7	94.4	95.5	95.9	95.7	95.9	95.2	94.7	95.3	95.7	94.9
2017	93.1	92.6	92.9	93.8	94.8	95.3	95.3	95.6	94.9	94.4	94.9	95.9	94.5
Wholesale Trade													
2007	16.4	16.6	16.7	16.8	17.1	17.1	17.3	17.1	17.1	17.0	17.0	17.1	16.9
2008	16.5	16.5	16.7	16.8	16.9	17.0	16.9	16.9	16.7	16.6	16.5	16.5	16.7
2009	16.0	15.9	15.8	16.1	16.1	16.2	16.2	16.0	15.8	15.7	15.7	15.7	15.9
2010	15.3	15.3	15.5	15.7	15.7	15.8	15.8	15.8	15.6	15.5	15.5	15.5	15.6
2011	15.2	15.2	15.3	15.6	15.8	15.9	16.0	16.0	15.9	15.9	15.9	16.0	15.7
2012	15.8	15.8	16.1	16.3	16.4	16.6	16.6	16.7	16.6	16.6	16.5	16.5	16.4
2013	16.5	16.6	16.9	17.1	17.3	17.3	17.2	17.2	17.0	16.9	16.9	17.0	17.0
2014	16.6	16.6	16.7	16.9	17.1	17.2	17.2	17.2	17.0	16.9	17.0	17.1	17.0
2015	17.1	17.1	17.3	17.6	17.6	17.7	17.8	17.7	17.4	17.5	17.6	17.6	17.5
2016	17.2	17.2	17.4	17.4	17.4	17.5	17.5	17.5	17.2	17.1	17.2	17.1	17.3
2017	16.9	17.0	17.1	17.2	17.4	17.4	17.4	17.4	17.1	17.2	17.3	17.2	17.2
Retail Trade													
2007	56.5	56.0	56.7	56.9	58.0	58.8	59.5	59.4	58.9	59.1	60.5	60.9	58.4
2008	58.7	57.9	58.1	58.1	58.7	59.3	59.5	59.6	58.7	58.4	58.7	58.8	58.7
2009	55.5	54.5	54.1	54.7	55.5	56.4	56.6	56.7	55.8	55.3	56.0	56.1	55.6
2010	53.7	53.0	53.2	53.9	54.7	55.6	55.5	55.6	54.6	54.7	55.3	55.6	54.6
2011	53.2	52.7	52.8	53.7	54.5	55.3	55.7	55.8	55.1	55.1	56.1	56.3	54.7
2012	53.9	53.3	53.4	54.1	55.3	56.2	56.3	56.2	55.6	56.0	57.1	57.2	55.4
2013	54.1	53.6	53.7	55.0	56.0	56.8	57.2	57.3	56.4	57.0	57.9	58.3	56.1
2014	55.6	55.2	55.1	56.2	57.3	58.1	58.4	58.5	57.6	57.8	58.8	59.1	57.3
2015	56.8	56.5	56.9	57.9	58.8	59.5	59.7	59.8	59.0	59.4	60.4	60.5	58.8
2016	58.3	57.8	58.1	59.0	59.8	60.4	60.3	60.3	59.7	59.3	59.9	59.9	59.4
2017	58.1	57.5	57.7	58.5	59.2	59.8	60.1	60.2	59.5	58.8	59.6	59.8	59.1

1. Employment by Industry: Montana, Selected Years, 2007–2017—*Continued*

(Numbers in thousands, not seasonally adjusted)

Industry and year	January	February	March	April	May	June	July	August	September	October	November	December	Annual average
Transportation and Utilities													
2007	15.9	16.0	16.0	16.1	16.3	16.1	16.1	16.0	16.2	16.4	16.4	16.6	16.2
2008	15.8	15.7	15.8	15.9	15.8	15.8	15.5	15.6	16.0	15.9	15.9	16.1	15.8
2009	15.4	15.3	15.2	15.4	15.5	15.4	15.1	15.2	15.6	15.7	15.6	15.9	15.4
2010	15.3	15.3	15.4	15.4	15.6	15.5	15.4	15.4	15.8	15.7	15.7	16.1	15.6
2011	15.7	15.7	15.6	15.7	15.9	16.0	15.8	16.0	16.1	16.2	16.3	16.6	16.0
2012	16.2	16.4	16.4	16.6	16.9	17.1	16.9	17.3	17.6	17.6	17.6	18.1	17.1
2013	17.8	18.0	18.0	17.9	18.3	18.2	17.8	18.2	18.4	18.4	18.5	19.0	18.2
2014	18.6	18.5	18.4	18.2	18.4	18.4	18.0	18.2	18.6	18.4	18.5	19.1	18.4
2015	18.4	18.3	18.3	18.1	18.1	18.1	17.9	18.0	18.4	18.5	18.6	19.1	18.3
2016	18.3	18.2	18.2	18.0	18.3	18.0	17.9	18.1	18.3	18.3	18.2	18.7	18.2
2017	18.1	18.1	18.1	18.1	18.2	18.1	17.8	18.0	18.3	18.4	18.0	18.9	18.2
Information													
2007	7.4	7.5	7.5	7.5	7.6	7.6	7.6	7.7	7.6	7.5	7.6	7.6	7.6
2008	7.6	7.6	7.6	7.7	7.7	7.8	7.7	7.7	7.8	7.7	7.7	7.8	7.7
2009	7.5	7.6	7.5	7.4	7.5	7.6	7.5	7.4	7.4	7.3	7.3	7.3	7.4
2010	7.3	7.4	7.4	7.3	7.3	7.5	7.4	7.3	7.2	7.2	7.2	7.2	7.3
2011	7.1	7.2	7.2	7.2	7.2	7.3	7.3	7.3	7.2	7.2	7.2	7.1	7.2
2012	6.9	7.0	6.9	6.8	6.9	6.9	6.9	7.0	6.9	6.9	7.0	7.0	6.9
2013	6.8	7.0	6.9	6.8	6.9	6.8	6.8	6.8	6.7	6.7	6.7	6.7	6.8
2014	6.5	6.5	6.4	6.4	6.4	6.4	6.4	6.4	6.4	6.3	6.3	6.3	6.4
2015	6.3	6.4	6.3	6.3	6.4	6.4	6.4	6.4	6.4	6.4	6.5	6.4	6.4
2016	6.3	6.4	6.3	6.3	6.3	6.3	6.3	6.3	6.3	6.4	6.5	6.4	6.3
2017	6.4	6.3	6.3	6.3	6.3	6.3	6.5	6.6	6.5	6.4	6.5	6.4	6.4
Financial Activities													
2007	21.4	21.4	21.6	21.5	21.7	21.9	22.0	22.1	21.8	21.9	21.8	22.2	21.8
2008	21.7	21.7	21.7	21.8	21.8	22.1	22.1	22.2	21.7	21.8	21.7	21.7	21.8
2009	21.1	21.0	21.0	21.1	21.3	21.6	21.8	21.8	21.6	21.6	21.6	22.0	21.5
2010	21.0	21.0	21.1	21.0	21.1	21.4	21.5	21.4	21.1	21.2	20.9	21.2	21.2
2011	20.7	20.7	20.8	20.7	20.8	21.2	21.4	21.3	21.2	21.6	21.6	21.9	21.2
2012	20.9	20.9	20.9	21.0	21.3	21.7	21.9	22.0	21.9	21.9	21.8	22.2	21.5
2013	21.6	21.7	21.8	22.2	22.3	22.6	23.0	23.2	22.9	23.2	23.1	23.4	22.6
2014	22.9	23.1	23.1	23.3	23.4	23.7	24.0	24.0	23.6	23.6	23.5	23.8	23.5
2015	23.4	23.4	23.5	23.4	23.6	23.9	24.1	24.2	23.9	24.0	23.9	24.3	23.8
2016	23.8	23.8	23.8	23.8	23.9	24.3	24.5	24.5	24.2	24.3	24.2	24.4	24.1
2017	24.0	23.9	24.1	24.1	24.3	24.6	24.8	24.7	24.5	24.5	24.6	25.0	24.4
Professional and Business Services													
2007	38.1	38.5	39.3	40.3	41.0	42.1	42.0	42.5	41.2	41.5	40.8	40.3	40.6
2008	39.1	39.6	39.7	40.8	41.6	41.8	42.2	42.2	40.9	40.4	39.5	39.3	40.6
2009	37.9	37.7	37.9	38.7	38.8	39.5	39.9	39.6	38.9	38.9	39.0	38.0	38.7
2010	37.1	37.4	37.7	38.9	39.2	40.0	40.6	40.6	39.8	40.5	39.7	39.7	39.3
2011	38.6	38.8	39.3	40.4	40.8	41.3	41.8	41.9	40.9	40.5	40.1	39.4	40.3
2012	38.7	38.8	39.4	40.7	41.1	41.6	41.9	41.8	40.6	40.5	39.8	39.4	40.4
2013	37.9	38.1	38.4	39.5	39.9	40.7	41.3	40.8	39.9	39.8	39.2	38.9	39.5
2014	37.5	38.0	38.1	39.1	39.7	40.4	40.9	41.2	40.2	39.5	38.5	38.4	39.3
2015	38.5	38.9	39.3	40.4	40.4	41.3	42.0	41.9	40.9	40.6	39.9	39.8	40.3
2016	38.8	39.2	39.7	40.6	40.8	41.2	42.0	41.8	40.8	40.6	40.2	40.0	40.5
2017	39.2	39.5	40.0	40.7	41.5	42.1	42.4	42.4	41.3	41.9	40.8	40.8	41.1
Education and Health Services													
2007	58.2	58.7	59.0	58.9	59.0	58.5	57.6	58.0	59.3	59.4	59.5	60.0	58.8
2008	60.0	60.6	60.9	60.9	61.0	60.3	59.6	60.2	61.3	61.7	62.0	62.5	60.9
2009	61.7	62.3	62.3	62.5	62.4	62.3	61.4	61.6	62.5	63.2	63.4	63.8	62.5
2010	63.1	63.3	63.5	63.9	63.9	63.8	63.1	63.2	64.0	64.3	64.5	64.6	63.8
2011	63.9	64.2	64.3	64.2	64.7	64.5	63.9	64.5	65.6	66.4	66.5	67.1	65.0
2012	66.8	67.2	67.3	67.5	67.9	67.3	66.6	67.2	67.7	68.1	68.4	68.8	67.6
2013	68.3	68.6	68.8	68.9	69.1	68.8	68.0	68.6	69.5	69.9	70.1	70.3	69.1
2014	69.7	69.9	70.1	70.9	70.7	70.1	69.1	69.4	70.0	70.5	70.8	71.2	70.2
2015	70.7	71.1	71.4	72.2	72.2	71.8	71.0	71.4	72.3	73.1	73.5	73.6	72.0
2016	73.7	74.2	74.4	74.4	74.3	74.1	73.9	74.2	75.3	75.5	75.8	76.0	74.7
2017	76.2	76.5	76.8	76.8	77.0	76.4	75.6	75.9	76.5	76.6	76.6	77.2	76.5

1. Employment by Industry: Montana, Selected Years, 2007–2017—*Continued*

(Numbers in thousands, not seasonally adjusted)

Industry and year	January	February	March	April	May	June	July	August	September	October	November	December	Annual average
Leisure and Hospitality													
2007	53.7	54.0	54.9	55.9	57.5	62.3	65.0	65.2	61.4	56.5	54.9	56.7	58.2
2008	55.2	55.6	56.6	56.7	58.8	63.5	66.1	66.1	62.2	57.0	54.7	55.9	59.0
2009	53.5	53.7	54.2	55.0	56.7	61.3	63.5	63.4	59.9	54.7	52.3	53.1	56.8
2010	51.5	51.7	52.4	53.4	55.2	59.4	62.4	62.8	59.6	54.2	52.0	53.3	55.7
2011	51.9	52.1	53.3	54.2	56.2	59.8	62.9	63.0	60.0	55.6	53.4	54.5	56.4
2012	53.4	53.5	54.7	55.4	57.5	62.3	64.6	65.2	61.7	57.1	54.6	55.9	58.0
2013	55.4	56.1	57.1	57.8	59.1	64.1	66.7	67.1	63.5	58.6	55.9	57.9	59.9
2014	56.8	56.8	57.1	58.0	59.6	64.3	67.1	67.6	63.7	58.6	56.1	58.4	60.3
2015	57.7	58.4	59.3	60.2	62.1	66.5	69.4	69.6	65.8	61.7	59.5	61.4	62.6
2016	59.9	60.5	61.0	62.6	64.0	68.5	71.3	71.1	67.4	63.1	60.9	62.5	64.4
2017	60.8	61.1	62.0	63.4	64.8	70.1	71.8	71.8	67.6	63.7	61.8	63.2	65.2
Other Services													
2007	16.8	16.8	17.2	17.3	17.2	17.5	17.2	17.1	17.1	17.2	17.2	17.2	17.2
2008	17.1	17.3	17.6	17.6	17.6	17.8	17.7	17.6	17.5	17.6	17.5	17.3	17.5
2009	16.8	17.0	17.0	17.0	17.1	17.2	17.2	16.9	17.0	17.0	16.9	16.9	17.0
2010	16.6	16.6	16.8	16.7	16.8	17.0	16.8	16.7	16.7	16.7	16.6	16.6	16.7
2011	16.4	16.5	16.7	16.8	17.0	17.1	17.2	17.0	17.0	17.0	16.9	17.1	16.9
2012	16.7	16.9	17.0	17.3	17.5	17.7	17.6	17.7	17.7	17.8	17.5	17.4	17.4
2013	17.2	17.4	17.5	17.6	17.8	17.9	17.8	17.9	17.7	17.9	17.9	17.9	17.7
2014	17.4	17.5	17.4	17.7	17.9	17.7	18.0	17.9	17.6	18.0	17.8	17.4	17.7
2015	17.7	17.8	17.9	18.0	18.1	18.2	18.2	18.1	18.0	18.2	18.2	18.2	18.1
2016	17.9	17.9	18.0	18.2	18.3	18.5	18.5	18.5	18.6	18.7	18.6	18.5	18.4
2017	18.1	18.3	18.4	18.5	18.7	18.8	18.7	18.7	18.6	18.3	18.6	18.7	18.5
Government													
2007	85.7	88.0	89.0	88.1	89.3	87.0	83.5	82.9	85.6	90.1	89.6	88.7	87.3
2008	85.4	87.9	88.5	88.1	90.8	88.1	83.7	84.0	88.0	91.2	91.8	90.1	88.1
2009	86.8	88.9	89.6	90.3	91.9	90.3	85.3	85.9	89.1	92.7	92.6	92.3	89.6
2010	90.2	91.3	93.1	92.6	96.1	93.0	88.7	88.6	91.6	93.2	92.9	92.6	92.0
2011	89.4	91.0	92.0	91.8	93.2	90.8	84.4	85.8	90.8	91.2	90.8	90.6	90.2
2012	88.7	89.6	90.4	90.3	92.4	89.1	86.2	85.6	90.3	91.0	91.0	90.5	89.6
2013	90.3	91.5	91.9	91.4	92.1	89.2	83.8	84.8	89.4	91.7	91.2	89.8	89.8
2014	88.1	91.4	91.7	91.3	92.1	89.7	85.6	85.5	90.3	91.7	91.8	90.9	90.0
2015	88.5	91.0	91.9	92.3	92.9	89.6	85.2	85.6	90.6	93.0	92.3	92.0	90.4
2016	88.8	90.9	92.1	92.4	93.8	91.6	85.7	86.5	91.5	92.9	93.0	92.4	91.0
2017	90.2	91.1	91.7	92.0	92.8	90.7	86.7	87.1	92.3	93.7	93.2	92.5	91.2

2. Average Weekly Hours by Selected Industry: Montana, 2013–2017

(Not seasonally adjusted)

Industry and year	January	February	March	April	May	June	July	August	September	October	November	December	Annual average
Total Private													
2013	32.7	33.2	33.0	33.1	33.3	34.1	33.3	33.6	33.9	33.3	33.0	33.3	33.3
2014	32.2	32.9	32.8	32.4	32.7	33.7	33.0	33.1	32.8	32.7	33.0	32.3	32.8
2015	32.1	32.7	32.5	32.0	32.5	32.7	32.9	33.5	32.7	32.5	33.0	32.3	32.6
2016	32.2	32.3	32.3	32.4	33.0	33.1	33.2	33.4	32.8	33.3	32.6	32.4	32.7
2017	32.6	32.1	32.1	33.0	32.7	33.3	33.7	33.4	32.8	33.3	32.5	32.5	32.9
Goods Producing													
2013	36.2	37.0	37.0	37.4	38.4	39.4	38.1	38.4	38.5	38.0	37.3	37.1	37.8
2014	36.3	37.0	37.2	37.6	38.4	39.4	38.2	37.5	38.2	38.6	37.2	37.4	37.8
2015	36.1	36.8	36.8	37.1	38.2	38.5	38.0	38.2	36.8	37.3	37.7	37.7	37.4
2016	36.2	37.2	37.3	37.8	38.0	38.7	38.5	38.5	38.4	38.1	37.5	35.8	37.7
2017	35.4	35.6	35.1	36.6	37.0	38.0	37.3	37.5	36.6	37.5	35.8	36.3	36.6
Construction													
2013	32.4	34.3	35.1	35.7	37.6	39.4	37.3	38.5	38.5	38.3	36.0	35.8	36.8
2014	34.5	35.6	35.4	36.4	38.4	39.0	37.8	37.0	38.1	38.8	37.0	37.3	37.2
2015	35.5	36.0	36.5	37.4	39.1	38.8	38.1	38.4	36.8	37.4	37.3	37.8	37.5
2016	35.9	36.5	36.6	37.6	37.6	39.1	38.1	38.5	37.9	37.2	37.5	35.5	37.4
2017	34.5	35.8	35.9	36.9	37.9	39.7	38.3	38.2	36.7	38.5	35.7	36.1	37.1
Trade, Transportation, and Utilities													
2013	34.0	34.4	34.1	34.3	34.4	35.5	34.6	34.8	34.7	33.4	32.9	33.4	34.2
2014	32.3	33.1	33.0	32.5	32.9	33.6	33.5	33.4	33.2	32.9	33.2	33.0	33.1
2015	32.8	33.1	32.8	32.3	32.7	33.2	33.4	34.4	33.5	33.1	33.4	32.9	33.1
2016	32.6	32.8	32.5	32.4	32.9	32.8	32.9	33.1	32.7	33.1	32.4	32.9	32.8
2017	32.4	31.7	32.0	33.1	32.6	33.3	33.8	33.7	32.9	33.4	32.9	32.9	32.9
Financial Activities													
2013	37.3	37.7	37.6	37.6	37.6	38.9	37.3	37.8	38.6	38.2	38.3	38.8	38.0
2014	37.3	38.2	38.0	36.5	36.8	37.7	35.7	36.1	35.8	35.7	37.2	35.0	36.6
2015	35.3	36.1	36.0	34.9	35.3	35.0	35.4	36.3	35.6	35.5	36.8	35.1	35.6
2016	35.9	35.4	35.3	35.6	35.6	35.5	35.5	35.5	35.5	35.8	35.5	35.4	35.5
2017	36.0	36.1	36.0	37.1	36.2	36.2	36.2	35.9	36.4	35.9	36.2	36.3	36.2
Professional and Business Services													
2013	32.6	33.8	34.1	34.0	34.3	35.5	33.4	34.5	34.4	34.1	33.9	33.6	34.0
2014	32.7	33.8	33.6	33.5	33.6	34.9	33.1	34.4	34.6	34.1	35.0	34.3	34.0
2015	34.2	34.8	34.2	33.6	34.5	34.4	34.1	34.9	34.6	33.7	34.8	33.9	34.3
2016	34.4	34.6	35.4	35.0	35.9	35.6	35.7	36.2	34.2	35.4	34.6	34.2	35.1
2017	34.8	33.7	32.7	34.2	33.4	33.4	34.6	34.1	34.2	34.5	33.1	33.2	33.8
Education and Health Services													
2013	33.4	33.4	33.5	33.5	33.1	33.0	33.4	33.4	34.1	33.9	33.8	34.5	33.6
2014	33.7	33.8	33.6	33.2	33.3	34.0	33.6	33.6	33.3	33.3	34.0	33.5	33.6
2015	33.6	34.1	34.0	33.7	33.6	33.6	33.8	34.0	33.9	33.8	34.1	33.7	33.8
2016	33.5	33.5	33.5	33.8	33.9	33.9	33.7	34.2	34.3	34.8	34.6	34.5	34.0
2017	35.1	34.7	34.9	35.3	34.6	35.0	35.4	34.8	34.8	35.2	35.1	34.5	34.9
Leisure and Hospitality													
2013	22.7	23.7	23.2	22.7	23.4	25.1	24.8	24.8	24.5	23.5	22.9	23.2	23.8
2014	22.2	23.5	23.7	22.7	23.4	25.2	25.4	25.5	24.1	23.5	24.0	22.6	23.9
2015	22.5	23.8	23.4	22.4	23.3	24.1	25.4	25.9	24.0	23.4	23.5	22.4	23.7
2016	22.8	22.6	22.7	22.7	24.6	25.1	25.9	25.6	24.3	24.6	22.9	22.8	24.0
2017	23.7	23.3	23.7	23.2	23.2	24.6	26.0	25.6	24.1	24.4	23.0	23.3	24.1

3. Average Hourly Earnings by Selected Industry: Montana, 2013–2017

(Dollars, not seasonally adjusted)

Industry and year	January	February	March	April	May	June	July	August	September	October	November	December	Annual average
Total Private													
2013	21.20	21.37	20.87	21.02	20.79	20.82	20.86	20.63	20.99	20.95	20.98	21.16	20.96
2014	21.23	21.53	21.26	21.35	21.33	21.30	21.25	21.13	21.46	21.82	21.68	21.74	21.42
2015	21.81	22.10	21.73	21.78	21.90	21.81	21.78	22.29	22.13	22.25	22.65	22.37	22.05
2016	22.17	22.38	21.98	22.37	22.44	22.13	22.27	22.11	22.58	22.79	22.67	22.72	22.38
2017	23.05	22.72	22.72	23.06	22.96	22.75	23.03	22.90	23.34	23.54	23.49	23.63	23.10
Goods Producing													
2013	23.83	23.87	23.04	23.70	23.83	23.93	23.21	23.16	22.88	22.78	22.97	23.20	23.36
2014	23.11	23.22	23.28	23.47	23.60	24.10	23.31	23.36	23.25	23.34	23.85	24.13	23.51
2015	23.79	23.75	23.83	24.51	24.70	24.58	24.20	24.95	25.38	25.05	24.97	24.30	24.52
2016	24.02	23.86	23.67	24.13	24.43	24.70	24.18	23.63	24.18	24.11	24.18	24.22	24.12
2017	24.33	23.87	24.27	24.10	24.17	24.57	24.72	25.10	25.30	25.66	25.82	25.99	24.84
Construction													
2013	24.33	23.58	23.49	23.84	24.52	24.75	23.67	23.66	23.46	23.55	24.07	24.32	23.94
2014	24.18	24.56	24.56	24.88	25.06	25.84	24.25	24.43	23.98	24.13	24.74	25.20	24.66
2015	24.30	24.32	24.22	24.59	25.27	24.99	24.19	25.09	25.46	25.43	25.28	25.28	24.90
2016	25.32	25.15	24.69	25.14	25.47	25.80	24.60	24.64	24.81	24.81	24.39	24.73	24.96
2017	24.61	25.06	24.68	24.51	24.88	25.62	24.96	25.54	25.60	26.32	26.03	26.12	25.35
Trade, Transportation, and Utilities													
2013	20.94	20.81	20.49	20.54	20.25	20.26	20.15	20.03	20.10	19.89	19.86	19.84	20.26
2014	19.89	19.69	20.01	19.84	20.04	19.73	19.66	19.72	19.98	19.95	20.16	19.97	19.89
2015	20.13	20.02	19.93	19.98	19.76	19.95	20.12	20.05	20.20	19.97	19.99	19.78	19.99
2016	20.76	20.64	20.48	20.91	21.02	20.80	21.05	20.57	20.95	20.59	20.14	19.85	20.65
2017	20.40	20.48	20.27	20.71	20.70	20.52	20.92	20.63	21.04	21.11	20.81	20.75	20.70
Financial Activities													
2013	22.09	22.11	22.09	21.90	21.50	21.75	21.52	21.47	21.82	22.15	22.31	22.00	21.89
2014	22.46	22.80	22.54	22.30	21.98	23.02	23.26	22.92	23.52	23.35	23.74	23.56	22.95
2015	23.20	23.38	24.10	24.08	24.23	24.29	24.27	25.07	24.98	24.98	25.34	25.12	24.43
2016	25.00	25.33	26.19	26.13	26.26	25.52	26.01	25.78	26.23	26.64	26.41	26.18	25.97
2017	26.71	25.12	25.12	25.58	25.14	25.02	25.19	25.15	25.52	25.33	25.19	25.35	25.37
Professional and Business Services													
2013	22.80	22.68	22.57	22.45	22.14	22.29	22.41	22.29	23.86	23.11	23.40	24.15	22.84
2014	23.80	23.72	23.80	23.33	23.22	23.20	23.17	22.87	23.43	23.33	23.80	23.57	23.43
2015	23.62	23.96	23.78	23.29	23.06	22.85	23.08	22.86	23.36	24.11	24.24	24.56	23.55
2016	24.32	24.01	24.16	24.46	24.83	23.91	23.46	23.51	25.19	25.66	25.55	25.99	24.57
2017	26.10	25.59	25.80	25.90	25.75	25.71	25.85	25.49	26.23	26.21	26.93	27.00	26.04
Education and Health Services													
2013	22.33	23.26	22.04	22.27	21.83	22.16	23.10	22.26	22.44	22.43	21.98	22.47	22.38
2014	22.86	24.26	22.94	23.34	23.16	23.27	24.01	23.52	23.89	23.83	23.24	23.63	23.49
2015	24.19	25.26	23.74	23.59	24.22	24.20	24.38	25.83	24.06	24.13	25.48	24.96	24.51
2016	24.38	25.89	24.13	24.42	24.47	24.40	25.21	25.47	25.30	25.66	25.74	26.08	25.11
2017	26.35	25.88	25.76	26.43	26.17	26.02	26.97	26.45	26.69	26.81	26.50	27.13	26.43
Leisure and Hospitality													
2013	12.35	12.26	12.23	12.09	12.04	11.77	11.92	11.88	12.07	12.14	12.08	12.30	12.08
2014	12.32	12.41	12.36	12.45	12.27	12.02	12.12	12.29	12.45	12.42	12.36	12.63	12.33
2015	12.79	13.00	12.97	13.03	13.14	13.02	13.01	13.13	13.22	13.41	13.43	13.44	13.13
2016	13.53	13.85	13.67	13.87	13.80	13.68	13.91	13.79	13.87	13.99	13.87	14.04	13.82
2017	14.14	14.11	14.05	14.30	14.00	13.76	13.96	13.92	14.09	14.41	14.18	14.23	14.09

4. Average Weekly Earnings by Selected Industry: Montana, 2013–2017

(Dollars, not seasonally adjusted)

Industry and year	January	February	March	April	May	June	July	August	September	October	November	December	Annual average
Total Private													
2013	693.24	709.48	688.71	695.76	692.31	709.96	694.64	693.17	711.56	697.64	692.34	704.63	697.97
2014	683.61	708.34	697.33	691.74	697.49	717.81	701.25	699.40	703.89	713.51	715.44	702.20	702.58
2015	700.10	722.67	706.23	696.96	711.75	713.19	716.56	746.72	723.65	723.13	747.45	722.55	718.83
2016	713.87	722.87	709.95	724.79	740.52	732.50	739.36	738.47	740.62	758.91	739.04	736.13	731.83
2017	751.43	729.31	729.31	760.98	750.79	757.58	776.11	764.86	765.55	783.88	763.43	767.98	759.99
Goods Producing													
2013	862.65	883.19	852.48	886.38	915.07	942.84	884.30	889.34	880.88	865.64	856.78	860.72	883.01
2014	838.89	859.14	866.02	882.47	906.24	949.54	890.44	876.00	888.15	900.92	887.22	902.46	888.68
2015	858.82	874.00	876.94	909.32	943.54	946.33	919.60	953.09	933.98	934.37	941.37	916.11	917.05
2016	869.52	887.59	882.89	912.11	928.34	955.89	930.93	909.76	928.51	918.59	906.75	867.08	909.32
2017	861.28	849.77	851.88	882.06	894.29	933.66	922.06	941.25	925.98	962.25	924.36	943.44	909.14
Construction													
2013	788.29	808.79	824.50	851.09	921.95	975.15	882.89	910.91	903.21	901.97	866.52	870.66	880.99
2014	834.21	874.34	869.42	905.63	962.30	1,007.76	916.65	903.91	913.64	936.24	915.38	939.96	917.35
2015	862.65	875.52	884.03	919.67	988.06	969.61	921.64	963.46	936.93	951.08	942.94	955.58	933.75
2016	908.99	917.98	903.65	945.26	957.67	1,008.78	937.26	948.64	940.30	922.93	914.63	877.92	933.50
2017	849.05	897.15	886.01	904.42	942.95	1,017.11	955.97	975.63	939.52	1,013.32	929.27	942.93	940.49
Trade, Transportation, and Utilities													
2013	711.96	715.86	698.71	704.52	696.60	719.23	697.19	697.04	697.47	664.33	653.39	662.66	692.89
2014	642.45	651.74	660.33	644.80	659.32	662.93	658.61	658.65	663.34	656.36	669.31	659.01	658.36
2015	660.26	662.66	653.70	645.35	646.15	662.34	672.01	689.72	676.70	661.01	667.67	650.76	661.67
2016	676.78	676.99	665.60	677.48	691.56	682.24	692.55	680.87	685.07	681.53	652.54	653.07	677.32
2017	660.96	649.22	648.64	685.50	674.82	683.32	707.10	695.23	692.22	705.07	684.65	682.68	681.03
Financial Activities													
2013	823.96	833.55	830.58	823.44	808.40	846.08	802.70	811.57	842.25	846.13	854.47	853.60	831.82
2014	837.76	870.96	856.52	813.95	808.86	867.85	830.38	827.41	842.02	833.60	883.13	824.60	839.97
2015	818.96	844.02	867.60	840.39	855.32	850.15	859.16	910.04	889.29	886.79	932.51	881.71	869.71
2016	897.50	896.68	924.51	930.23	934.86	905.96	923.36	915.19	931.17	953.71	937.56	926.77	921.94
2017	961.56	906.83	904.32	949.02	910.07	905.72	911.88	902.89	928.93	909.35	911.88	920.21	918.39
Professional and Business Services													
2013	743.28	766.58	769.64	763.30	759.40	791.30	748.49	769.01	820.78	788.05	793.26	811.44	776.56
2014	778.26	801.74	799.68	781.56	780.19	809.68	766.93	786.73	810.68	795.55	833.00	808.45	796.62
2015	807.80	833.81	813.28	782.54	795.57	786.04	787.03	797.81	808.26	812.51	843.55	832.58	807.77
2016	836.61	830.75	855.26	856.10	891.40	851.20	837.52	851.06	861.50	908.36	884.03	888.86	862.41
2017	908.28	862.38	843.66	885.78	860.05	858.71	894.41	869.21	897.07	904.25	891.38	896.40	880.15
Education and Health Services													
2013	745.82	776.88	738.34	746.05	722.57	731.28	771.54	743.48	765.20	760.38	742.92	775.22	751.97
2014	770.38	819.99	770.78	774.89	771.23	791.18	806.74	790.27	795.54	793.54	790.16	791.61	789.26
2015	812.78	861.37	807.16	794.98	813.79	813.12	824.04	878.22	815.63	815.59	868.87	841.15	828.44
2016	816.73	867.32	808.36	825.40	829.53	827.16	849.58	871.07	867.79	892.97	890.60	899.76	853.74
2017	924.89	898.04	899.02	932.98	905.48	910.70	954.74	920.46	928.81	943.71	930.15	935.99	922.41
Leisure and Hospitality													
2013	280.35	290.56	283.74	274.44	281.74	295.43	295.62	294.62	295.72	285.29	276.63	285.36	287.50
2014	273.50	291.64	292.93	282.62	287.12	302.90	307.85	313.40	300.05	291.87	296.64	285.44	294.69
2015	287.78	309.40	303.50	291.87	306.16	313.78	330.45	340.07	317.28	313.79	315.61	301.06	311.18
2016	308.48	313.01	310.31	314.85	339.48	343.37	360.27	353.02	337.04	344.15	317.62	320.11	331.68
2017	335.12	328.76	332.99	331.76	324.80	338.50	362.96	356.35	339.57	351.60	326.14	331.56	339.57

NEBRASKA
At a Glance

Population:
  2010 census: 1,826,341
  2017 estimate: 1,920,076

Percent change in population:
  2010–2017: 5.1%

Percent change in total nonfarm employment:
  2007–2017: 5.8%

Industry with the largest growth in employment, 2007–2017 (thousands):
  Education and health services, 21.2

Industry with the largest decline or smallest growth in employment, 2007–2017 (thousands):
  Manufacturing, -3.3

Civilian labor force:
  2010: 993,398
  2017: 1,007,011

Unemployment rate and rank among states (highest to lowest):
  2010: 4.6%, 50th
  2017: 2.9%, 47th

Over the-year change in unemployment rates:
  2015–2016: 0.1%
  2016–2017: -0.2%

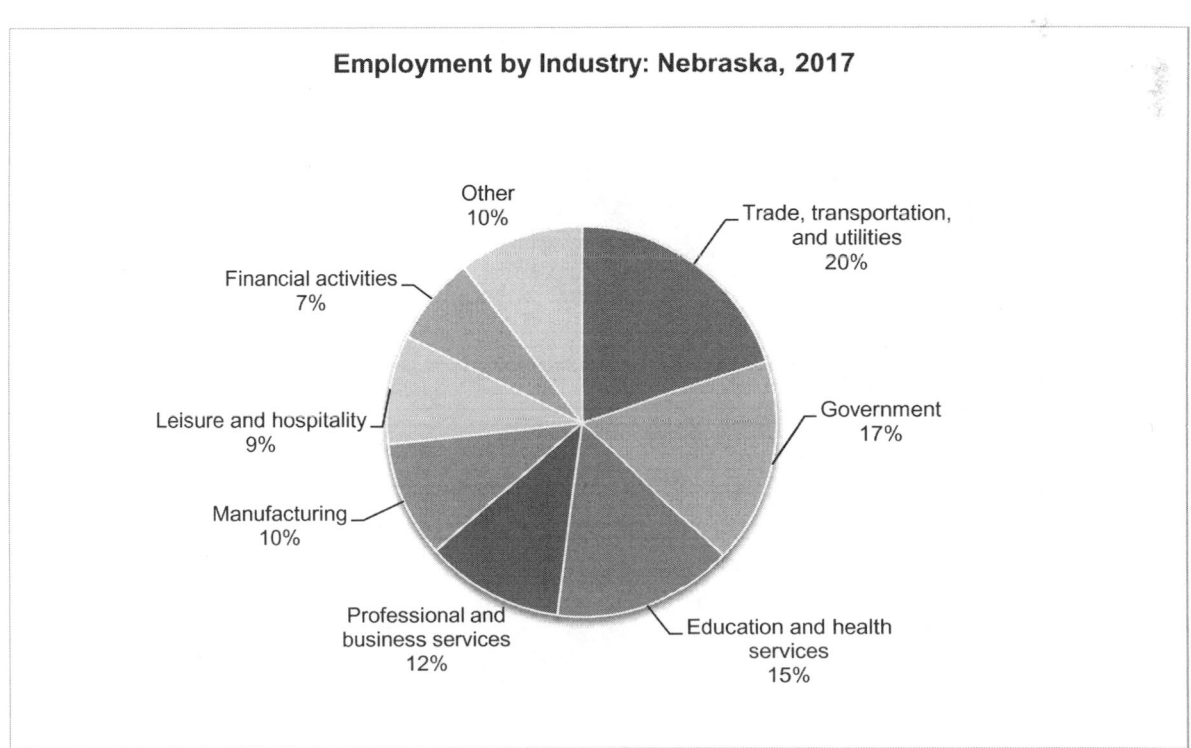

Employment by Industry: Nebraska, 2017

Other 10%
Trade, transportation, and utilities 20%
Financial activities 7%
Government 17%
Leisure and hospitality 9%
Manufacturing 10%
Professional and business services 12%
Education and health services 15%

1. Employment by Industry: Nebraska, Selected Years, 2007–2017

(Numbers in thousands, not seasonally adjusted)

Industry and year	January	February	March	April	May	June	July	August	September	October	November	December	Annual average
Total Nonfarm													
2007	936.4	939.5	946.3	956.4	968.5	974.0	961.4	965.4	969.9	972.5	975.4	973.5	961.6
2008	953.4	954.9	961.2	969.6	979.8	979.4	966.6	969.4	972.5	978.2	975.9	972.0	969.4
2009	944.7	943.9	946.3	951.5	959.6	957.5	948.3	946.7	948.7	952.0	952.0	945.8	949.8
2010	921.7	924.9	931.1	944.4	954.6	956.6	947.0	947.8	948.0	955.7	954.8	953.8	945.0
2011	928.6	931.7	939.1	953.5	960.8	959.8	950.3	952.9	957.4	964.4	966.8	965.7	952.6
2012	944.9	947.7	957.5	967.5	977.9	976.9	966.9	969.2	973.6	979.1	981.5	981.6	968.7
2013	955.6	959.7	965.7	975.8	989.2	987.6	978.0	982.4	986.5	992.8	995.7	994.8	980.3
2014	970.9	975.6	981.4	991.9	1,002.7	1,000.1	989.7	992.7	996.6	1,002.8	1,003.0	1,005.6	992.8
2015	980.8	985.8	993.0	1,005.3	1,014.1	1,014.1	1,006.5	1,009.1	1,011.7	1,018.5	1,019.0	1,020.2	1,006.5
2016	992.6	996.1	1,005.9	1,016.1	1,024.3	1,022.7	1,015.6	1,015.8	1,022.5	1,024.8	1,023.8	1,020.5	1,015.1
2017	998.4	1,004.3	1,010.8	1,019.4	1,026.7	1,026.0	1,013.9	1,017.1	1,019.5	1,023.6	1,027.0	1,024.8	1,017.6
Total Private													
2007	774.7	776.2	782.6	792.2	801.5	808.3	808.5	811.3	807.7	807.7	810.1	809.4	799.2
2008	790.5	791.6	797.6	804.1	811.8	813.7	811.2	813.6	808.4	810.6	808.0	804.7	805.5
2009	779.0	775.9	777.6	780.8	787.1	787.7	784.8	784.5	780.7	781.1	780.3	775.9	781.3
2010	754.7	755.4	759.7	772.4	779.3	784.5	784.6	785.3	780.2	783.8	782.8	782.6	775.4
2011	761.3	762.2	769.3	782.1	788.6	791.8	791.2	792.1	790.8	793.1	795.4	795.1	784.4
2012	777.8	778.0	787.7	796.6	804.4	809.8	807.1	807.8	805.4	808.1	809.9	810.9	800.3
2013	788.5	790.2	796.1	805.1	815.1	818.8	817.5	820.8	818.1	820.5	823.2	823.3	811.4
2014	802.8	804.7	810.5	820.7	828.4	831.5	829.4	830.9	826.4	829.5	829.7	833.0	823.1
2015	812.6	814.8	821.3	831.6	838.9	843.6	843.7	844.9	841.1	843.5	844.0	845.9	835.5
2016	822.4	823.4	832.0	840.8	846.9	849.2	850.6	851.6	848.1	848.2	847.2	844.9	842.1
2017	826.7	830.5	836.4	844.0	849.6	852.6	850.8	851.8	847.2	847.9	851.1	850.3	844.9
Goods Producing													
2007	144.7	144.4	146.6	149.7	152.1	155.0	156.7	156.9	155.8	155.0	153.9	151.7	151.9
2008	147.4	147.2	149.0	151.9	154.1	155.2	155.2	155.2	153.2	152.6	150.1	146.6	151.5
2009	140.2	138.8	139.0	140.7	142.8	143.6	144.1	143.4	142.4	140.6	139.0	135.2	140.8
2010	128.9	128.9	129.4	133.8	135.7	138.1	138.0	137.5	136.6	136.2	135.4	133.3	134.3
2011	128.7	128.4	130.7	134.1	136.0	137.8	138.1	137.4	137.0	137.0	137.2	135.9	134.9
2012	132.5	131.6	134.1	136.5	139.0	141.4	141.3	141.4	140.8	140.9	140.5	139.7	138.3
2013	134.8	135.5	136.6	139.9	143.2	145.2	145.3	145.5	145.0	144.3	143.9	141.6	141.7
2014	138.1	138.1	139.6	144.3	146.1	148.1	148.5	148.6	147.3	147.6	146.1	145.7	144.8
2015	141.0	141.7	143.8	147.2	148.8	150.2	150.6	150.6	149.6	149.6	148.7	147.5	147.4
2016	143.0	142.8	145.7	148.0	149.7	151.4	151.7	151.6	150.7	150.4	149.4	147.4	148.5
2017	143.8	145.0	147.0	149.5	151.1	153.0	153.0	152.9	152.1	151.0	151.7	149.1	149.9
Service-Providing													
2007	791.7	795.1	799.7	806.7	816.4	819.0	804.7	808.5	814.1	817.5	821.5	821.8	809.7
2008	806.0	807.7	812.2	817.7	825.7	824.2	811.4	814.2	819.3	825.6	825.8	825.4	817.9
2009	804.5	805.1	807.3	810.8	816.8	813.9	804.2	803.3	806.3	811.4	813.0	810.6	808.9
2010	792.8	796.0	801.7	810.6	818.9	818.5	809.0	810.3	811.4	819.5	819.4	820.5	810.7
2011	799.9	803.3	808.4	819.4	824.8	822.0	812.2	815.5	820.4	827.4	829.6	829.8	817.7
2012	812.4	816.1	823.4	831.0	838.9	835.5	825.6	827.8	832.8	838.2	841.0	841.9	830.4
2013	820.8	824.2	829.1	835.9	846.0	842.4	832.7	836.9	841.5	848.5	851.8	853.2	838.6
2014	832.8	837.5	841.8	847.6	856.6	852.0	841.2	844.1	849.3	855.2	856.9	859.9	847.9
2015	839.8	844.1	849.2	858.1	865.3	863.9	855.9	858.5	862.1	868.9	870.3	872.7	859.1
2016	849.6	853.3	860.2	868.1	874.6	871.3	863.9	864.2	871.8	874.4	874.4	873.1	866.6
2017	854.6	859.3	863.8	869.9	875.6	873.0	860.9	864.2	867.4	872.6	875.3	875.7	867.7
Mining and Logging													
2007	0.8	0.7	0.9	0.9	0.9	0.9	1.1	1.0	1.0	0.9	1.1	0.9	0.9
2008	0.8	0.9	1.0	1.0	1.1	1.1	1.0	1.1	1.0	1.0	1.0	0.9	1.0
2009	0.8	0.9	0.9	1.0	1.0	1.0	1.0	1.0	1.0	1.0	1.0	0.9	1.0
2010	0.8	0.8	0.8	0.9	1.0	1.0	1.0	1.0	1.0	1.0	1.0	0.9	0.9
2011	0.9	0.9	0.9	1.0	1.1	1.1	1.1	1.1	1.1	1.1	1.1	1.0	1.0
2012	1.0	1.0	1.1	1.1	1.2	1.2	1.2	1.4	1.2	1.2	1.1	1.1	1.2
2013	0.9	1.0	1.0	1.1	1.1	1.1	1.1	1.1	1.1	1.1	1.1	1.0	1.1
2014	1.1	1.0	1.1	1.2	1.2	1.2	1.2	1.2	1.1	1.2	1.2	1.1	1.2
2015	1.0	1.0	1.1	1.2	1.1	1.1	1.1	1.1	1.1	1.1	1.0	1.0	1.1
2016	0.9	0.9	1.0	1.0	1.0	1.0	1.0	1.0	1.0	1.0	1.0	1.0	1.0
2017	0.9	0.9	1.0	1.1	1.1	1.1	1.1	1.1	1.1	1.1	1.1	1.0	1.1

1. Employment by Industry: Nebraska, Selected Years, 2007–2017—*Continued*

(Numbers in thousands, not seasonally adjusted)

Industry and year	January	February	March	April	May	June	July	August	September	October	November	December	Annual average
Construction													
2007	43.9	43.3	45.3	48.2	50.0	52.1	53.6	54.0	53.1	52.3	50.6	48.3	49.6
2008	44.7	44.1	45.7	48.9	50.8	52.0	52.5	52.3	51.3	50.7	48.9	47.1	49.1
2009	42.6	42.2	43.3	45.9	48.2	49.5	50.9	50.4	49.5	48.0	46.2	42.9	46.6
2010	37.6	37.3	37.7	41.5	42.9	44.9	44.8	44.5	43.6	43.2	42.0	39.8	41.7
2011	36.0	35.6	37.4	40.2	41.6	42.9	43.1	42.8	42.3	42.2	41.5	39.9	40.5
2012	37.7	36.9	38.9	41.3	43.2	44.6	44.4	44.6	44.1	44.5	43.6	42.5	42.2
2013	38.8	38.9	39.9	42.8	45.6	47.1	47.7	47.7	47.0	46.3	45.4	43.3	44.2
2014	40.4	40.1	41.7	45.8	47.6	49.2	49.7	49.3	48.5	48.9	47.2	46.6	46.3
2015	42.9	43.3	45.1	48.6	50.3	51.6	52.2	51.9	51.2	51.2	50.3	49.0	49.0
2016	45.4	45.3	47.7	50.4	51.9	53.6	53.7	53.5	52.8	52.5	51.3	49.0	50.6
2017	46.1	46.8	48.5	50.8	52.1	53.7	53.8	53.5	52.9	51.5	51.0	48.5	50.8
Manufacturing													
2007	100.0	100.4	100.4	100.6	101.2	102.0	102.0	101.9	101.7	101.8	102.2	102.5	101.4
2008	101.9	102.2	102.3	102.0	102.2	102.1	101.7	101.8	100.9	100.9	100.2	98.6	101.4
2009	96.8	95.7	94.8	93.8	93.6	93.1	92.2	92.0	91.9	91.6	91.8	91.4	93.2
2010	90.5	90.8	90.9	91.4	91.8	92.2	92.2	92.0	92.0	92.0	92.4	92.6	91.7
2011	91.8	91.9	92.4	92.9	93.3	93.8	93.9	93.5	93.6	93.7	94.6	95.0	93.4
2012	93.8	93.7	94.1	94.1	94.6	95.6	95.7	95.4	95.5	95.2	95.8	96.1	95.0
2013	95.1	95.6	95.7	96.0	96.5	97.0	96.5	96.7	96.9	96.9	97.4	97.3	96.5
2014	96.6	97.0	96.8	97.3	97.3	97.7	97.6	98.1	97.7	97.5	97.7	98.0	97.4
2015	97.1	97.4	97.6	97.4	97.4	97.5	97.3	97.6	97.3	97.3	97.4	97.5	97.4
2016	96.7	96.6	97.0	96.6	96.8	96.8	97.0	97.1	96.9	96.9	97.1	97.4	96.9
2017	96.8	97.3	97.5	97.6	97.9	98.2	98.1	98.3	98.1	98.4	99.6	99.6	98.1
Trade, Transportation, and Utilities													
2007	200.9	199.9	201.1	202.4	205.0	205.4	204.9	205.3	205.1	205.9	209.5	211.1	204.7
2008	203.9	202.2	203.7	203.3	205.4	205.5	203.9	204.4	203.5	206.4	208.6	210.0	205.1
2009	200.6	198.1	198.1	197.4	198.8	198.1	196.6	196.5	195.8	197.6	199.8	200.5	198.2
2010	192.8	191.4	192.5	194.6	196.3	196.3	195.7	195.6	194.5	197.5	200.1	202.6	195.8
2011	193.8	192.7	193.8	196.4	197.6	197.8	197.6	198.4	198.1	199.3	203.2	204.8	197.8
2012	197.2	195.2	196.5	198.4	200.0	200.2	199.3	198.9	198.9	200.7	204.8	206.8	199.7
2013	198.1	196.4	197.4	198.7	201.1	201.6	201.1	201.6	200.8	202.4	206.7	209.6	201.3
2014	201.2	199.7	200.4	202.4	204.4	204.7	203.8	204.5	203.3	205.2	209.0	212.4	204.3
2015	203.2	202.5	203.1	205.2	207.0	208.1	206.9	207.3	205.7	207.5	210.8	212.9	206.7
2016	203.0	201.9	202.4	203.8	204.9	204.8	204.6	204.1	202.9	204.0	206.7	207.8	204.2
2017	200.6	200.0	200.4	202.0	203.3	202.9	201.9	202.3	201.2	203.5	207.0	208.2	202.8
Wholesale Trade													
2007	39.9	39.8	40.2	40.8	41.2	41.7	41.7	41.2	41.2	41.5	41.6	41.8	41.1
2008	41.2	41.2	41.5	41.9	42.5	42.8	42.5	42.1	41.9	42.3	42.1	42.1	42.0
2009	41.2	40.9	41.0	41.2	41.5	41.6	41.5	41.0	40.8	41.4	41.2	41.3	41.2
2010	39.9	39.8	40.1	40.9	41.2	41.4	41.2	40.7	40.4	40.7	40.4	40.5	40.6
2011	39.8	39.8	40.1	40.7	41.1	41.3	41.3	41.0	40.9	41.1	41.2	41.3	40.8
2012	40.6	40.5	41.0	41.5	41.8	42.1	41.8	41.4	41.1	41.3	41.3	41.6	41.3
2013	40.9	40.9	41.3	41.8	42.5	42.7	42.6	42.1	41.8	42.1	42.2	42.6	42.0
2014	42.2	41.9	42.4	43.0	43.5	43.8	43.7	43.2	42.6	42.6	42.5	42.8	42.9
2015	41.8	41.7	42.0	42.6	43.0	43.2	43.0	42.6	42.0	42.1	42.1	42.1	42.4
2016	41.6	41.3	41.6	42.0	42.3	42.5	42.5	41.9	41.4	41.3	41.1	41.0	41.7
2017	40.4	40.4	40.6	41.1	41.5	41.7	41.5	41.0	40.6	40.9	40.7	40.5	40.9
Retail Trade													
2007	105.6	104.5	105.2	106.1	107.9	107.7	107.2	107.5	106.9	107.7	110.9	112.4	107.5
2008	107.3	105.7	106.5	105.9	106.8	106.9	106.0	106.1	105.4	107.1	109.5	110.9	107.0
2009	105.0	103.2	103.3	103.5	104.6	104.4	103.7	103.9	103.2	104.1	106.6	106.8	104.4
2010	102.4	101.2	101.9	102.8	104.1	104.2	103.7	103.6	102.5	104.7	107.1	108.5	103.9
2011	102.8	101.9	102.4	103.9	104.6	104.6	104.3	104.8	104.2	105.2	108.7	109.7	104.8
2012	104.1	102.4	103.1	104.2	105.2	105.3	104.9	104.7	104.6	106.3	109.8	110.5	105.4
2013	104.3	103.3	103.9	104.6	105.7	106.1	106.0	106.3	105.8	107.1	110.8	112.2	106.3
2014	106.3	105.2	105.3	106.8	108.0	108.2	108.0	108.4	107.6	109.0	111.8	113.3	108.2
2015	107.9	107.3	107.6	108.6	109.5	110.3	109.7	109.9	108.7	110.2	113.1	114.1	109.7
2016	108.8	108.4	108.5	109.9	110.6	110.5	110.6	110.4	109.4	110.5	113.0	113.4	110.3
2017	108.5	107.8	108.0	109.0	109.4	109.1	108.6	109.0	108.0	108.5	111.7	112.4	109.2

1. Employment by Industry: Nebraska, Selected Years, 2007–2017—*Continued*

(Numbers in thousands, not seasonally adjusted)

Industry and year	January	February	March	April	May	June	July	August	September	October	November	December	Annual average
Transportation and Utilities													
2007	55.4	55.6	55.7	55.5	55.9	56.0	56.0	56.6	57.0	56.7	57.0	56.9	56.2
2008	55.4	55.3	55.7	55.5	56.1	55.8	55.4	56.2	56.2	57.0	57.0	57.0	56.1
2009	54.4	54.0	53.8	52.7	52.7	52.1	51.4	51.6	51.8	52.1	52.0	52.4	52.6
2010	50.5	50.4	50.5	50.9	51.0	50.7	50.8	51.3	51.6	52.1	52.6	53.6	51.3
2011	51.2	51.0	51.3	51.8	51.9	51.9	52.0	52.6	53.0	53.0	53.3	53.8	52.2
2012	52.5	52.3	52.4	52.7	53.0	52.8	52.6	52.8	53.2	53.1	53.7	54.7	53.0
2013	52.9	52.2	52.2	52.3	52.9	52.8	52.5	53.2	53.2	53.2	53.7	54.8	53.0
2014	52.7	52.6	52.7	52.6	52.9	52.7	52.1	52.9	53.1	53.6	54.7	56.3	53.2
2015	53.5	53.5	53.5	54.0	54.5	54.6	54.2	54.8	55.0	55.2	55.6	56.7	54.6
2016	52.6	52.2	52.3	51.9	52.0	51.8	51.5	51.8	52.1	52.2	52.6	53.4	52.2
2017	51.7	51.8	51.8	51.9	52.4	52.1	51.8	52.3	52.6	54.1	54.6	55.3	52.7
Information													
2007	19.5	19.5	19.5	19.8	19.7	20.0	20.0	20.0	19.8	19.8	19.9	19.8	19.8
2008	19.6	19.6	19.5	19.5	19.2	19.2	19.1	18.9	18.6	18.6	18.6	18.6	19.1
2009	18.2	18.2	18.1	17.9	17.8	18.0	18.0	17.9	17.8	17.7	17.8	17.9	17.9
2010	17.7	17.6	17.5	17.4	17.5	17.6	17.5	17.5	17.4	17.4	17.5	17.6	17.5
2011	17.4	17.5	17.4	17.3	17.3	17.5	17.8	17.7	17.7	17.7	17.8	17.8	17.6
2012	17.7	17.8	17.8	17.8	17.7	17.8	17.7	17.8	17.7	17.7	17.8	17.8	17.8
2013	17.7	17.8	17.8	17.7	17.7	17.7	17.7	17.7	17.7	17.8	17.8	17.8	17.7
2014	17.8	17.7	17.6	17.6	17.6	17.7	17.7	17.8	17.8	17.8	18.0	18.0	17.8
2015	17.9	18.0	18.0	18.1	18.2	18.3	18.4	18.5	18.3	18.5	18.5	18.6	18.3
2016	18.5	18.5	18.4	18.5	18.3	18.3	18.4	18.4	18.5	18.5	18.5	18.6	18.5
2017	18.4	18.4	18.3	18.5	18.3	18.3	18.1	18.0	17.9	18.1	18.0	17.9	18.2
Financial Activities													
2007	67.7	68.2	68.4	68.4	69.1	69.4	69.4	69.1	68.7	68.6	68.6	68.8	68.7
2008	68.5	68.9	69.0	69.0	69.3	69.7	69.7	69.6	69.0	69.2	69.1	69.5	69.2
2009	68.6	68.8	68.8	68.4	68.5	68.7	68.4	68.4	67.9	68.1	68.2	68.5	68.4
2010	68.0	68.1	68.3	68.4	68.6	69.3	69.5	69.6	69.1	69.4	69.4	69.6	68.9
2011	69.3	69.2	69.4	69.9	70.1	70.4	70.4	70.4	70.3	70.4	70.6	71.0	70.1
2012	70.3	70.2	70.4	70.7	71.0	71.4	71.4	71.3	71.0	71.2	71.4	71.8	71.0
2013	71.0	71.2	71.2	71.2	71.6	72.0	72.1	72.0	71.7	71.8	72.0	72.1	71.7
2014	71.9	71.9	72.0	71.7	71.8	72.3	72.4	72.0	71.7	71.7	71.8	71.7	71.9
2015	71.1	70.9	70.9	71.3	71.6	72.1	72.4	72.3	72.0	72.5	72.6	73.1	71.9
2016	72.5	72.6	72.7	73.0	73.1	73.5	73.9	73.9	73.3	73.3	73.4	73.6	73.2
2017	73.2	73.3	73.4	73.6	73.7	74.4	74.5	74.5	74.2	74.1	74.1	74.5	74.0
Professional and Business Services													
2007	100.1	100.8	101.6	102.7	103.3	105.2	105.3	105.7	105.0	104.7	105.3	105.9	103.8
2008	103.3	103.9	104.7	106.1	106.3	106.7	106.2	106.2	106.0	106.1	104.8	103.7	105.3
2009	100.5	100.1	99.7	100.3	100.0	100.8	99.9	99.5	98.5	99.6	98.8	98.7	99.7
2010	97.0	97.1	97.4	100.0	100.2	101.4	102.4	102.1	102.1	102.7	101.9	102.2	100.5
2011	98.9	99.5	100.2	102.2	102.3	103.1	104.2	104.3	105.0	105.1	104.6	104.5	102.8
2012	103.2	104.1	104.6	106.0	106.4	108.4	108.4	107.9	108.0	108.1	107.7	107.5	106.7
2013	105.4	105.8	106.6	108.1	108.8	110.1	110.4	110.6	110.7	112.3	112.1	112.5	109.5
2014	109.2	110.5	111.2	112.5	112.9	113.7	113.7	113.4	113.2	113.6	113.5	113.7	112.6
2015	112.2	113.0	113.8	116.0	116.1	117.6	117.9	117.3	117.2	117.0	116.7	116.5	115.9
2016	114.2	114.7	115.9	118.4	118.6	119.2	119.1	119.2	118.7	118.2	117.6	117.8	117.6
2017	114.9	115.1	116.2	117.4	117.1	118.2	118.7	118.1	118.2	118.3	117.6	117.9	117.3
Education and Health Services													
2007	129.9	131.3	131.5	132.2	132.8	132.6	132.2	133.5	134.6	135.4	136.1	136.3	133.2
2008	134.7	136.5	136.6	136.7	137.3	136.0	136.2	137.7	138.5	138.8	139.8	139.7	137.4
2009	137.8	138.6	138.5	138.5	138.7	137.0	137.0	137.5	139.0	140.1	140.7	140.7	138.7
2010	138.7	140.1	140.4	140.5	140.9	140.3	140.2	140.9	140.8	141.8	141.9	142.0	140.7
2011	141.1	141.9	142.2	143.1	143.5	142.2	141.3	142.0	143.0	144.7	145.1	145.2	142.9
2012	143.2	144.5	146.1	145.9	146.0	144.8	144.2	145.5	146.6	147.8	148.0	148.2	145.9
2013	145.5	146.6	147.3	147.8	147.8	146.0	145.5	146.5	147.0	148.0	148.2	148.3	147.0
2014	145.7	147.3	148.5	148.5	148.6	146.7	146.1	147.2	148.0	149.4	149.3	149.8	147.9
2015	147.7	148.4	149.0	149.1	149.3	147.6	148.5	149.5	150.7	152.2	152.4	152.8	149.8
2016	150.0	151.2	152.6	151.9	152.8	151.2	152.3	153.2	154.5	155.3	155.3	154.7	152.9
2017	153.2	154.7	155.2	154.4	155.2	152.8	152.5	153.1	154.1	155.6	155.7	155.9	154.4

1. Employment by Industry: Nebraska, Selected Years, 2007–2017—*Continued*

(Numbers in thousands, not seasonally adjusted)

Industry and year	January	February	March	April	May	June	July	August	September	October	November	December	Annual average
Leisure and Hospitality													
2007	77.7	77.8	79.2	82.1	84.4	85.6	85.1	86.1	84.1	83.3	81.8	80.8	82.3
2008	78.5	78.5	80.1	82.4	84.7	85.8	85.6	86.4	84.6	83.1	81.4	80.8	82.7
2009	77.8	77.9	79.9	81.7	84.3	84.9	84.2	84.7	82.8	80.9	79.2	77.6	81.3
2010	75.3	75.8	77.3	80.7	83.0	84.3	84.1	85.1	83.1	82.2	80.1	78.7	80.8
2011	76.1	76.8	79.0	82.4	85.0	86.1	85.1	85.5	83.4	82.6	80.7	79.6	81.9
2012	77.7	78.5	81.7	84.7	87.4	88.6	87.8	88.1	85.6	85.0	83.0	82.4	84.2
2013	79.8	80.5	82.2	84.7	87.8	88.9	88.4	89.9	88.4	87.4	86.1	84.9	85.8
2014	82.7	83.2	84.8	86.8	89.9	90.8	90.1	90.6	88.4	87.3	85.1	84.8	87.0
2015	82.9	83.5	85.8	87.6	90.6	92.3	91.7	92.4	90.9	89.3	87.5	87.5	88.5
2016	84.8	85.3	87.8	90.4	92.7	93.8	93.7	94.5	92.8	91.6	89.4	88.3	90.4
2017	86.3	87.6	89.3	91.7	94.0	95.9	95.2	96.1	92.9	90.8	90.3	90.4	91.7
Other Services													
2007	34.2	34.3	34.7	34.9	35.1	35.1	34.9	34.7	34.6	35.0	35.0	35.0	34.8
2008	34.6	34.8	35.0	35.2	35.5	35.6	35.3	35.2	35.0	35.8	35.6	35.8	35.3
2009	35.3	35.4	35.5	35.9	36.2	36.6	36.6	36.6	36.5	36.5	36.8	36.8	36.2
2010	36.3	36.4	36.9	37.0	37.1	37.2	37.2	37.0	36.6	36.6	36.5	36.6	36.8
2011	36.0	36.2	36.6	36.7	36.8	36.9	36.7	36.4	36.3	36.3	36.2	36.3	36.5
2012	36.0	36.1	36.5	36.6	36.9	37.2	37.0	36.9	36.8	36.7	36.7	36.7	36.7
2013	36.2	36.4	37.0	37.0	37.1	37.3	37.0	37.0	36.8	36.5	36.4	36.5	36.8
2014	36.2	36.3	36.4	36.9	37.1	37.5	37.1	36.8	36.7	36.9	36.9	36.9	36.8
2015	36.6	36.8	36.9	37.1	37.3	37.4	37.3	37.0	36.7	36.9	36.8	37.0	37.0
2016	36.4	36.4	36.5	36.8	36.8	37.0	36.9	36.7	36.7	36.9	36.9	36.7	36.7
2017	36.3	36.4	36.6	36.9	36.9	37.1	36.9	36.8	36.6	36.5	36.7	36.4	36.7
Government													
2007	161.7	163.3	163.7	164.2	167.0	165.7	152.9	154.1	162.2	164.8	165.3	164.1	162.4
2008	162.9	163.3	163.6	165.5	168.0	165.7	155.4	155.8	164.1	167.6	167.9	167.3	163.9
2009	165.7	168.0	168.7	170.7	172.5	169.8	163.5	162.2	168.0	170.9	171.7	169.9	168.5
2010	167.0	169.5	171.4	172.0	175.3	172.1	162.4	162.5	167.8	171.9	172.0	171.2	169.6
2011	167.3	169.5	169.8	171.4	172.2	168.0	159.1	160.8	166.6	171.3	171.4	170.6	168.2
2012	167.1	169.7	169.8	170.9	173.5	167.1	159.8	161.4	168.2	171.0	171.6	170.7	168.4
2013	167.1	169.5	169.6	170.7	174.1	168.8	160.5	161.6	168.4	172.3	172.5	171.5	168.9
2014	168.1	170.9	170.9	171.2	174.3	168.6	160.3	161.8	170.2	173.3	173.3	172.6	169.6
2015	168.2	171.0	171.7	173.7	175.2	170.5	162.8	164.2	170.6	175.0	175.0	174.3	171.0
2016	170.2	172.7	173.9	175.3	177.4	173.5	165.0	164.2	174.4	176.6	176.6	175.6	173.0
2017	171.7	173.8	174.4	175.4	177.1	173.4	163.1	165.3	172.3	175.7	175.9	174.5	172.7

2. Average Weekly Hours by Selected Industry: Nebraska, 2013–2017

(Not seasonally adjusted)

Industry and year	January	February	March	April	May	June	July	August	September	October	November	December	Annual average
Total Private													
2013...............	33.5	33.9	33.9	33.9	34.3	35.2	34.3	34.3	34.6	34.1	33.9	34.1	34.2
2014...............	33.4	33.8	34.1	33.8	34.1	35.0	34.4	34.4	34.0	34.1	34.3	33.9	34.1
2015...............	33.6	34.3	34.2	33.8	33.9	34.4	34.3	34.9	33.9	34.3	34.2	33.8	34.1
2016...............	33.4	33.3	33.4	33.9	34.1	34.2	34.0	34.1	33.8	34.5	33.6	33.6	33.8
2017...............	33.9	33.6	33.8	34.3	33.8	34.3	34.6	34.2	34.3	34.6	34.2	34.2	34.2
Goods-Producing													
2013...............	39.4	39.9	39.8	39.8	40.6	41.4	40.7	40.7	40.8	40.9	40.4	40.5	40.4
2014...............	40.0	39.5	40.3	40.5	41.3	41.6	41.2	41.3	40.7	40.8	40.1	40.7	40.7
2015...............	40.0	41.0	40.4	40.5	40.9	41.2	41.3	42.3	40.4	41.7	40.3	40.4	40.9
2016...............	40.2	39.4	40.0	42.1	40.6	41.9	41.9	42.5	40.5	41.2	39.9	39.5	40.8
2017...............	39.8	40.3	41.0	41.1	40.5	40.7	41.0	41.3	41.7	40.8	40.9	41.2	40.9
Mining, Logging, and Construction													
2013...............	38.5	38.4	37.7	38.7	40.9	42.1	41.6	40.0	40.5	40.4	39.0	38.4	39.8
2014...............	37.4	36.2	39.1	40.0	41.3	42.0	41.5	41.5	40.1	41.4	38.6	39.5	40.0
2015...............	37.6	39.7	40.2	39.3	39.2	41.1	42.0	43.0	41.6	42.5	40.6	40.4	40.7
2016...............	38.3	38.5	39.6	42.9	40.5	42.0	42.6	42.7	38.2	39.7	38.5	36.4	40.1
2017...............	35.8	36.6	37.3	39.4	38.8	40.1	40.1	41.3	41.1	39.8	40.8	40.3	39.4
Manufacturing													
2013...............	39.8	40.6	40.6	40.3	40.5	41.0	40.3	41.0	40.9	41.1	41.1	41.4	40.7
2014...............	41.2	40.9	40.8	40.8	41.3	41.4	41.0	41.2	41.0	40.6	40.8	41.3	41.0
2015...............	41.1	41.6	40.5	41.1	41.8	41.2	40.9	41.9	39.7	41.4	40.1	40.4	41.0
2016...............	41.1	39.8	40.2	41.7	40.7	41.8	41.4	42.3	41.8	42.1	40.6	41.1	41.2
2017...............	41.7	42.1	42.8	42.0	41.4	41.1	41.5	41.3	42.0	41.4	40.9	41.6	41.6
Trade, Transportation, and Utilities													
2013...............	33.9	34.4	34.5	34.3	34.9	35.3	34.6	34.6	34.8	34.2	33.6	34.0	34.4
2014...............	33.4	33.7	34.1	34.2	34.5	35.1	34.8	34.3	33.8	34.1	33.8	33.9	34.1
2015...............	33.1	33.7	33.8	33.7	33.5	34.3	34.0	34.2	33.4	33.9	33.5	33.6	33.7
2016...............	32.5	32.7	32.8	33.1	33.6	33.4	33.6	33.2	33.1	33.5	32.6	32.7	33.1
2017...............	32.3	32.0	32.1	32.8	32.4	32.9	32.5	32.3	32.7	32.8	32.8	32.6	32.5
Financial Activities													
2013...............	36.6	37.0	36.8	36.9	36.9	38.6	37.1	37.5	38.4	37.0	37.7	38.6	37.4
2014...............	37.3	38.5	38.6	37.7	37.7	39.4	38.0	38.0	37.9	38.0	39.5	37.8	38.2
2015...............	38.1	39.2	38.9	38.0	37.9	38.1	38.0	39.7	38.0	38.2	39.0	38.1	38.4
2016...............	37.9	38.1	38.0	38.4	39.2	38.5	37.9	38.4	38.0	39.0	38.0	38.4	38.3
2017...............	39.7	38.4	38.1	39.0	37.7	38.3	39.0	37.9	38.3	38.7	38.0	38.4	38.5
Professional and Business Services													
2013...............	34.2	34.9	34.9	34.9	35.4	36.3	34.7	35.1	35.1	34.8	34.9	34.7	35.0
2014...............	34.0	35.1	35.1	34.5	34.9	36.4	35.5	36.1	35.6	36.2	36.5	36.3	35.5
2015...............	35.7	36.4	36.2	35.7	35.5	36.0	35.4	36.3	35.5	35.9	36.4	35.1	35.8
2016...............	35.1	34.9	35.0	35.3	35.4	35.1	34.9	35.1	35.2	36.0	34.6	34.5	35.1
2017...............	34.8	34.2	34.5	35.5	35.1	35.5	36.0	35.4	35.0	36.1	36.1	35.3	35.3
Education and Health Services													
2013...............	31.5	31.7	31.9	32.2	32.1	33.1	32.1	32.0	32.8	32.2	31.9	32.3	32.2
2014...............	31.6	32.0	32.0	31.8	31.8	32.9	32.5	32.4	32.3	31.9	32.6	31.7	32.1
2015...............	31.2	31.8	31.9	31.4	31.6	32.3	32.4	32.3	32.2	31.8	32.3	31.1	31.9
2016...............	30.9	30.7	30.9	31.0	31.4	31.1	31.0	30.9	30.9	31.6	30.7	30.7	31.0
2017...............	31.1	30.8	31.2	31.9	31.3	31.6	32.1	31.7	31.7	32.3	31.6	31.7	31.6
Leisure and Hospitality													
2013...............	21.7	22.2	22.2	21.5	22.0	23.4	22.7	22.7	22.3	21.9	22.1	22.0	22.2
2014...............	21.0	22.0	22.4	21.9	22.1	23.6	22.6	23.1	22.7	22.7	22.6	22.0	22.4
2015...............	22.2	22.8	23.0	22.0	22.8	23.9	23.2	23.4	22.5	22.8	22.8	22.9	22.9
2016...............	22.3	22.3	22.5	22.5	22.9	23.5	22.9	22.5	22.9	23.0	22.7	22.0	22.7
2017...............	22.3	22.4	22.3	22.1	22.1	23.6	23.6	23.2	22.7	23.2	22.8	22.7	22.8

3. Average Hourly Earnings by Selected Industry: Nebraska, 2013–2017

(Dollars, not seasonally adjusted)

Industry and year	January	February	March	April	May	June	July	August	September	October	November	December	Annual average
Total Private													
2013	21.09	21.09	21.13	21.05	20.66	20.72	20.63	20.74	20.99	20.84	21.03	21.12	20.92
2014	21.18	21.23	21.35	21.26	21.16	21.21	21.24	21.33	21.38	21.51	21.66	21.74	21.36
2015	21.98	22.03	22.08	21.85	21.91	21.72	21.93	22.50	22.60	22.34	22.65	22.51	22.18
2016	22.76	22.88	22.84	22.94	23.04	22.78	23.02	22.97	23.19	23.37	23.04	22.94	22.98
2017	23.83	23.57	23.80	24.20	24.05	23.78	24.13	23.95	24.20	24.54	24.62	24.63	24.11
Goods-Producing													
2013	20.18	20.09	20.23	20.06	19.95	19.88	20.02	20.35	20.32	20.24	20.38	20.27	20.16
2014	20.34	19.91	20.10	20.36	20.33	20.33	20.55	20.59	20.46	20.61	20.75	21.02	20.45
2015	21.10	21.13	21.03	21.05	21.30	21.22	21.44	21.86	22.44	21.67	21.75	21.33	21.45
2016	21.36	21.83	22.10	22.13	21.74	21.66	22.00	21.84	21.88	21.98	21.80	22.27	21.88
2017	22.43	22.36	22.50	22.67	22.66	22.81	23.03	23.14	23.36	23.49	23.79	24.09	23.04
Mining, Logging, and Construction													
2013	21.43	21.55	21.60	21.25	20.96	20.45	20.86	21.33	21.24	21.62	21.61	21.75	21.28
2014	21.74	22.13	22.12	22.16	21.78	21.74	21.32	21.60	21.41	21.35	21.31	21.90	21.69
2015	22.15	21.99	21.62	21.80	21.79	21.71	22.24	22.89	23.84	22.81	22.40	21.81	22.28
2016	22.16	23.33	23.32	23.77	22.81	22.48	23.00	22.77	22.70	22.74	22.55	23.25	22.91
2017	22.98	23.27	23.30	22.52	22.76	22.77	22.78	23.42	23.66	23.76	23.95	24.69	23.32
Manufacturing													
2013	19.68	19.51	19.69	19.54	19.46	19.59	19.58	19.87	19.87	19.57	19.82	19.65	19.65
2014	19.79	19.08	19.25	19.51	19.61	19.60	20.14	20.06	19.99	20.22	20.48	20.61	19.86
2015	20.67	20.75	20.75	20.69	21.06	20.96	20.99	21.29	21.65	21.04	21.41	21.09	21.03
2016	21.00	21.14	21.50	21.23	21.16	21.19	21.42	21.31	21.46	21.58	21.42	21.82	21.35
2017	22.20	21.97	22.15	22.74	22.61	22.83	23.17	22.98	23.20	23.35	23.70	23.80	22.89
Trade, Transportation, and Utilities													
2013	18.44	18.75	18.68	18.56	18.28	18.33	18.16	18.20	18.31	18.29	18.48	18.47	18.41
2014	19.13	19.17	19.51	19.37	19.37	19.24	19.36	19.81	19.65	19.82	19.91	19.50	19.49
2015	19.69	19.64	19.51	19.42	19.41	19.20	19.34	20.00	19.70	19.59	19.68	19.50	19.56
2016	20.09	20.36	20.14	20.13	20.61	20.36	20.61	20.55	20.69	20.71	20.38	19.96	20.38
2017	21.21	20.90	21.03	21.48	21.52	21.31	21.69	21.41	21.66	21.87	21.99	21.91	21.50
Financial Activities													
2013	24.51	24.85	25.07	25.19	25.50	25.83	25.23	25.46	26.04	25.63	25.75	27.02	25.52
2014	26.45	27.14	27.12	26.58	26.53	26.97	26.17	26.34	26.09	26.10	26.84	26.81	26.60
2015	26.78	27.58	27.75	27.93	27.73	27.32	27.24	28.34	28.05	28.11	29.02	28.39	27.86
2016	28.88	28.34	28.86	29.64	29.83	29.08	29.26	29.50	29.63	30.17	29.80	29.91	29.41
2017	30.51	29.78	30.43	31.54	30.41	29.72	30.41	29.79	29.89	30.37	30.03	30.06	30.25
Professional and Business Services													
2013	26.22	25.92	25.82	25.96	25.07	25.60	25.58	25.27	25.60	25.47	25.67	25.86	25.66
2014	25.04	25.21	25.46	25.45	25.45	25.61	25.62	25.62	25.70	25.72	25.98	25.99	25.58
2015	26.65	26.25	26.69	26.42	26.63	26.53	26.69	26.69	26.84	26.46	26.94	27.01	26.65
2016	26.85	26.95	26.78	27.00	27.16	27.02	27.30	27.01	27.13	27.48	26.78	26.03	26.96
2017	27.49	27.07	27.79	28.34	28.29	27.82	28.26	27.95	28.26	28.77	29.09	28.80	28.17
Education and Health Services													
2013	21.39	21.20	21.40	21.31	21.25	21.24	21.37	21.57	21.78	21.65	21.96	22.06	21.52
2014	22.36	22.01	21.89	21.93	21.70	21.58	21.79	21.64	22.07	22.07	21.68	22.08	21.90
2015	22.22	22.28	22.33	22.27	22.30	22.13	22.43	22.73	22.87	22.56	22.46	22.52	22.43
2016	22.68	22.45	22.24	22.15	22.10	22.32	22.25	22.14	22.70	22.24	22.26	22.14	22.30
2017	22.91	22.86	23.07	23.34	23.43	23.41	23.69	23.74	24.31	24.58	24.96	24.92	23.78
Leisure and Hospitality													
2013	12.00	12.03	11.98	11.98	11.80	11.61	11.46	11.48	11.70	11.63	11.66	11.65	11.74
2014	11.72	11.80	11.94	11.91	11.96	11.85	11.84	11.78	11.86	12.11	12.13	12.27	11.93
2015	12.33	12.27	12.28	12.30	12.37	12.23	12.41	12.67	12.84	12.88	13.07	13.28	12.58
2016	13.34	13.68	13.33	13.53	13.42	13.13	13.25	13.28	13.33	13.31	13.35	13.59	13.37
2017	13.78	13.73	13.53	13.53	13.48	13.35	13.36	13.41	13.40	13.45	13.51	13.54	13.50

4. Average Weekly Earnings by Selected Industry: Nebraska, 2013–2017

(Dollars, not seasonally adjusted)

Industry and year	January	February	March	April	May	June	July	August	September	October	November	December	Annual average
Total Private													
2013	706.52	714.95	716.31	713.60	708.64	729.34	707.61	711.38	726.25	710.64	712.92	720.19	715.46
2014	707.41	717.57	728.04	718.59	721.56	742.35	730.66	733.75	726.92	733.49	742.94	736.99	728.38
2015	738.53	755.63	755.14	738.53	742.75	747.17	752.20	785.25	766.14	766.26	774.63	760.84	756.34
2016	760.18	761.90	762.86	777.67	785.66	779.08	782.68	783.28	783.82	806.27	774.14	770.78	776.72
2017	807.84	791.95	804.44	830.06	812.89	815.65	834.90	819.09	830.06	849.08	842.00	842.35	824.56
Goods-Producing													
2013	795.09	801.59	805.15	798.39	809.97	823.03	814.81	828.25	829.06	827.82	823.35	820.94	814.46
2014	813.60	786.45	810.03	824.58	839.63	845.73	846.66	850.37	832.72	840.89	832.08	855.51	832.32
2015	844.00	866.33	849.61	852.53	871.17	874.26	885.47	924.68	906.58	903.64	876.53	861.73	877.31
2016	858.67	860.10	884.00	931.67	882.64	907.55	921.80	928.20	886.14	905.58	869.82	879.67	892.70
2017	892.71	901.11	922.50	931.74	917.73	928.37	944.23	955.68	974.11	958.39	973.01	992.51	942.34
Mining, Logging, and Construction													
2013	825.06	827.52	814.32	822.38	857.26	860.95	867.78	853.20	860.22	873.45	842.79	835.20	846.94
2014	813.08	801.11	864.89	886.40	899.51	913.08	884.78	896.40	858.54	883.89	822.57	865.05	867.60
2015	832.84	873.00	869.12	856.74	854.17	892.28	934.08	984.27	991.74	969.43	909.44	881.12	906.80
2016	848.73	898.21	923.47	1,019.73	923.81	944.16	979.80	972.28	867.14	902.78	868.18	846.30	918.69
2017	822.68	851.68	869.09	887.29	883.09	913.08	913.48	967.25	972.43	945.65	977.16	995.01	918.81
Manufacturing													
2013	783.26	792.11	799.41	787.46	788.13	803.19	789.07	814.67	812.68	804.33	814.60	813.51	799.76
2014	815.35	780.37	785.40	796.01	809.89	811.44	825.74	826.47	819.59	820.93	835.58	851.19	814.26
2015	849.54	863.20	840.38	850.36	880.31	863.55	858.49	892.05	859.51	871.06	858.54	852.04	862.23
2016	863.10	841.37	864.30	885.29	861.21	885.74	886.79	901.41	897.03	908.52	869.65	896.80	879.62
2017	925.74	924.94	948.02	955.08	936.05	938.31	961.56	949.07	974.40	966.69	969.33	990.08	952.22
Trade, Transportation, and Utilities													
2013	625.12	645.00	644.46	636.61	637.97	647.05	628.34	629.72	637.19	625.52	620.93	627.98	633.30
2014	638.94	646.03	665.29	662.45	668.27	675.32	673.73	679.48	664.17	675.86	672.96	661.05	664.61
2015	651.74	661.87	659.44	654.45	650.24	658.56	657.56	684.00	657.98	664.10	659.28	655.20	659.17
2016	652.93	665.77	660.59	666.30	692.50	680.02	692.50	682.26	684.84	693.79	664.39	652.69	674.58
2017	685.08	668.80	675.06	704.54	697.25	701.10	704.93	691.54	708.28	717.34	721.27	714.27	698.75
Financial Activities													
2013	897.07	919.45	922.58	929.51	940.95	997.04	936.03	954.75	999.94	948.31	970.78	1,042.97	954.45
2014	986.59	1,044.89	1,046.83	1,002.07	1,000.18	1,062.62	994.46	1,000.92	988.81	991.80	1,060.18	1,013.42	1,016.12
2015	1,020.32	1,081.14	1,079.48	1,061.34	1,050.97	1,040.89	1,035.12	1,125.10	1,065.90	1,073.80	1,131.78	1,081.66	1,069.82
2016	1,094.55	1,079.75	1,096.68	1,138.18	1,169.34	1,119.58	1,108.95	1,132.80	1,125.94	1,176.63	1,132.40	1,148.54	1,126.40
2017	1,211.25	1,143.55	1,159.38	1,230.06	1,146.46	1,138.28	1,185.99	1,129.04	1,144.79	1,175.32	1,141.14	1,154.30	1,164.63
Professional and Business Services													
2013	896.72	904.61	901.12	906.00	887.48	929.28	887.63	886.98	898.56	886.36	895.88	897.34	898.10
2014	851.36	884.87	893.65	878.03	888.21	932.20	909.51	924.88	914.92	931.06	948.27	943.44	908.09
2015	951.41	955.50	966.18	943.19	945.37	955.08	944.83	968.85	952.82	949.91	980.62	948.05	954.07
2016	942.44	940.56	937.30	953.10	961.46	948.40	952.77	948.05	954.98	989.28	926.59	898.04	946.30
2017	956.65	925.79	958.76	1,006.07	992.98	987.61	1,017.36	989.43	989.10	1,038.60	1,050.15	1,016.64	994.40
Education and Health Services													
2013	673.79	672.04	682.66	686.18	682.13	703.04	685.98	690.24	714.38	697.13	700.52	712.54	692.94
2014	706.58	704.32	700.48	697.37	690.06	709.98	708.18	701.14	712.86	704.03	706.77	699.94	702.99
2015	693.26	708.50	712.33	699.28	704.68	714.80	726.73	734.18	736.41	717.41	725.46	700.37	715.52
2016	700.81	689.22	687.22	686.65	693.94	694.15	689.75	684.13	701.43	702.78	683.38	679.70	691.30
2017	712.50	704.09	719.78	744.55	733.36	739.76	760.45	752.56	770.63	793.93	788.74	789.96	751.45
Leisure and Hospitality													
2013	260.40	267.07	265.96	257.57	259.60	271.67	260.14	260.60	260.91	254.70	257.69	256.30	260.63
2014	246.12	259.60	267.46	260.83	264.32	279.66	267.58	272.12	269.22	274.90	274.14	269.94	267.23
2015	273.73	279.76	282.44	270.60	282.04	292.30	287.91	296.48	288.90	293.66	298.00	304.11	288.08
2016	297.48	305.06	299.93	304.43	307.32	308.56	303.43	298.80	305.26	306.13	303.05	298.98	303.50
2017	307.29	307.55	301.72	299.01	297.91	315.06	315.30	311.11	304.18	312.04	308.03	307.36	307.80

NEVADA
At a Glance

Population:
  2010 census: 2,700,551
  2017 estimate: 2,998,039

Percent change in population:
  2010–2017: 11.0%

Percent change in total nonfarm employment:
  2007–2017: 3.8%

Industry with the largest growth in employment, 2007–2017 (thousands):
  Education and health services, 40.5

Industry with the largest decline or smallest growth in employment, 2007–2017 (thousands):
  Construction, -50.3

Civilian labor force:
  2010: 1,358,578
  2017: 1,462,955

Unemployment rate and rank among states (highest to lowest):
  2010: 13.5%, 1st
  2017: 5.0%, 7th

Over-the-year change in unemployment rates:
  2015–2016: -1.1%
  2016–2017: -0.7%

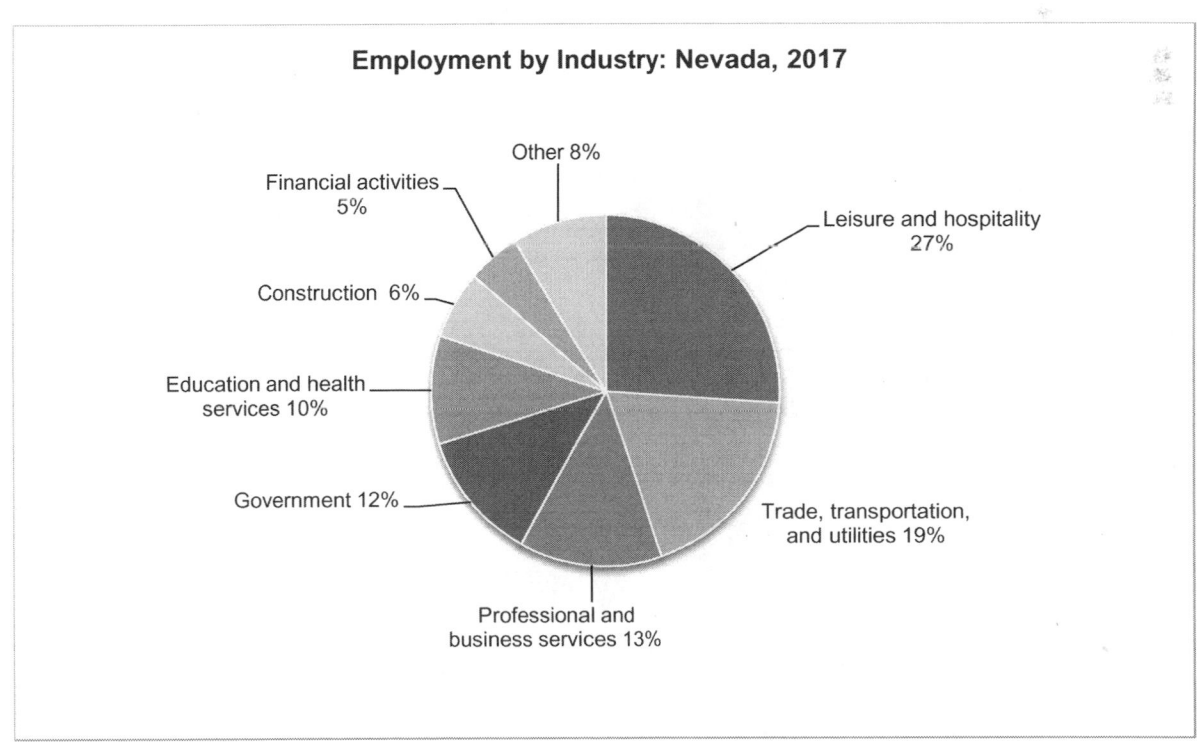

Employment by Industry: Nevada, 2017

- Other 8%
- Financial activities 5%
- Construction 6%
- Education and health services 10%
- Government 12%
- Professional and business services 13%
- Leisure and hospitality 27%
- Trade, transportation, and utilities 19%

1. Employment by Industry: Nevada, Selected Years, 2007–2017

(Numbers in thousands, not seasonally adjusted)

Industry and year	January	February	March	April	May	June	July	August	September	October	November	December	Annual average
Total Nonfarm													
2007	1,268.2	1,283.3	1,290.9	1,294.5	1,303.8	1,302.1	1,287.2	1,288.1	1,292.3	1,297.7	1,301.0	1,300.4	1,292.5
2008	1,269.1	1,272.9	1,275.8	1,281.0	1,286.2	1,279.5	1,265.2	1,260.6	1,261.7	1,252.5	1,238.1	1,221.1	1,263.6
2009	1,180.8	1,171.7	1,163.2	1,158.5	1,155.9	1,147.6	1,133.4	1,128.1	1,135.5	1,135.4	1,134.5	1,134.0	1,148.2
2010	1,104.3	1,105.8	1,108.8	1,121.0	1,128.3	1,124.0	1,116.7	1,114.0	1,116.0	1,124.1	1,125.8	1,124.7	1,117.8
2011	1,106.9	1,109.4	1,114.6	1,126.6	1,130.4	1,128.7	1,122.8	1,122.2	1,132.4	1,138.1	1,139.3	1,136.8	1,125.7
2012	1,120.2	1,123.5	1,131.0	1,139.5	1,148.1	1,150.0	1,139.4	1,145.4	1,153.6	1,160.6	1,165.5	1,160.5	1,144.8
2013	1,144.8	1,148.8	1,158.4	1,168.2	1,176.4	1,179.0	1,171.0	1,178.8	1,182.9	1,189.6	1,198.0	1,195.2	1,174.3
2014	1,180.1	1,186.5	1,198.0	1,208.5	1,219.2	1,216.1	1,208.9	1,220.4	1,229.7	1,239.7	1,243.5	1,244.1	1,216.2
2015	1,227.8	1,233.0	1,241.5	1,253.0	1,259.4	1,256.3	1,249.8	1,259.3	1,268.7	1,281.1	1,287.5	1,288.8	1,258.9
2016	1,264.1	1,271.3	1,279.9	1,292.5	1,296.2	1,295.6	1,299.3	1,302.9	1,316.2	1,320.1	1,325.5	1,323.6	1,298.9
2017	1,306.9	1,314.9	1,329.5	1,330.4	1,342.8	1,342.3	1,337.9	1,342.1	1,354.5	1,362.2	1,362.4	1,365.9	1,341.0
Total Private													
2007	1,117.8	1,126.4	1,133.4	1,135.4	1,144.2	1,147.4	1,140.0	1,142.1	1,136.8	1,137.0	1,139.4	1,138.1	1,136.5
2008	1,112.8	1,110.6	1,112.6	1,116.7	1,121.2	1,119.7	1,111.7	1,108.3	1,100.8	1,086.8	1,072.2	1,055.6	1,102.4
2009	1,022.5	1,009.5	1,001.0	996.6	994.7	991.7	983.7	979.9	979.2	977.3	976.7	976.7	990.8
2010	952.0	948.8	951.0	963.1	967.1	970.3	969.1	969.2	964.1	970.6	971.9	970.9	964.0
2011	955.8	954.8	960.2	971.9	976.1	981.1	980.5	979.8	983.8	987.5	988.5	985.1	975.4
2012	973.2	973.3	979.2	987.7	995.8	1,002.5	996.9	1,003.2	1,003.8	1,008.9	1,013.0	1,007.2	995.4
2013	995.3	996.9	1,005.3	1,015.1	1,022.8	1,029.6	1,028.5	1,033.3	1,031.8	1,036.6	1,043.8	1,039.8	1,023.2
2014	1,029.1	1,032.7	1,042.8	1,053.6	1,063.5	1,067.2	1,064.9	1,075.2	1,076.0	1,084.6	1,087.7	1,087.5	1,063.7
2015	1,075.2	1,077.5	1,084.6	1,096.2	1,102.3	1,103.9	1,103.3	1,111.7	1,112.3	1,124.7	1,129.2	1,129.0	1,104.2
2016	1,109.3	1,113.1	1,119.8	1,133.5	1,136.6	1,143.7	1,148.1	1,151.2	1,156.5	1,160.1	1,164.0	1,160.9	1,141.4
2017	1,150.3	1,153.1	1,166.5	1,169.7	1,180.8	1,185.7	1,184.0	1,185.9	1,189.9	1,195.3	1,195.5	1,198.7	1,179.6
Goods Producing													
2007	191.9	193.5	196.9	197.1	200.2	200.8	199.7	200.5	197.1	193.9	191.1	187.8	195.9
2008	179.8	179.9	179.3	179.7	181.6	182.5	182.8	181.2	177.6	173.1	165.6	158.5	176.8
2009	149.4	144.9	141.6	138.5	134.4	133.2	131.3	129.7	127.6	126.1	122.4	117.3	133.0
2010	108.6	107.1	107.1	109.7	110.6	111.5	111.3	111.3	109.6	110.1	109.0	107.1	109.4
2011	102.7	102.7	101.3	102.7	103.8	105.4	106.4	106.8	106.4	106.5	105.2	104.0	104.5
2012	100.8	100.6	101.8	103.4	105.5	107.7	108.6	110.4	110.3	110.5	110.2	109.5	106.6
2013	106.6	107.5	108.8	110.7	111.3	113.4	114.2	116.0	115.6	116.2	116.1	114.5	112.6
2014	113.7	113.9	114.9	116.3	118.2	119.4	121.2	122.5	122.4	123.1	122.7	122.2	119.2
2015	120.9	121.6	121.8	123.3	125.3	126.4	127.1	129.2	129.2	131.4	131.2	131.4	126.6
2016	128.5	128.8	129.2	130.5	131.2	133.2	135.0	135.6	136.0	136.9	136.8	137.1	133.2
2017	135.6	137.7	141.0	142.3	144.8	147.1	147.6	148.0	149.3	150.0	150.1	151.3	145.4
Service-Providing													
2007	1,076.3	1,089.8	1,094.0	1,097.4	1,103.6	1,101.3	1,087.5	1,087.6	1,095.2	1,103.8	1,109.9	1,112.6	1,096.6
2008	1,089.3	1,093.0	1,096.5	1,101.3	1,104.6	1,097.0	1,082.4	1,079.4	1,084.1	1,079.4	1,072.5	1,062.6	1,086.8
2009	1,031.4	1,026.8	1,021.6	1,020.0	1,021.5	1,014.4	1,002.1	998.4	1,007.9	1,009.3	1,012.1	1,016.7	1,015.2
2010	995.7	998.7	1,001.7	1,011.3	1,017.7	1,012.5	1,005.4	1,002.7	1,006.4	1,014.0	1,016.8	1,017.6	1,008.4
2011	1,004.2	1,006.7	1,013.3	1,023.9	1,026.6	1,023.3	1,016.4	1,015.4	1,026.0	1,031.6	1,034.1	1,032.8	1,021.2
2012	1,019.4	1,022.9	1,029.2	1,036.1	1,042.6	1,042.3	1,030.8	1,035.0	1,043.3	1,050.1	1,055.3	1,051.0	1,038.2
2013	1,038.2	1,041.3	1,049.6	1,057.5	1,065.1	1,065.6	1,056.8	1,062.8	1,067.3	1,073.4	1,081.9	1,080.7	1,061.7
2014	1,066.4	1,072.6	1,083.1	1,092.2	1,101.0	1,096.7	1,087.7	1,097.9	1,107.3	1,116.6	1,120.8	1,121.9	1,097.0
2015	1,106.9	1,111.4	1,119.7	1,129.7	1,134.1	1,129.9	1,122.7	1,130.1	1,139.5	1,149.7	1,156.3	1,157.4	1,132.3
2016	1,135.6	1,142.5	1,150.7	1,162.0	1,165.0	1,162.4	1,164.3	1,167.3	1,180.2	1,183.2	1,188.7	1,186.5	1,165.7
2017	1,171.3	1,177.2	1,188.5	1,188.1	1,198.0	1,195.2	1,190.3	1,194.1	1,205.2	1,212.2	1,212.3	1,214.6	1,195.6
Mining and Logging													
2007	11.8	11.7	11.9	11.9	12.0	12.3	12.3	12.4	12.1	11.9	12.0	11.9	12.0
2008	11.9	11.9	11.9	11.9	12.0	12.2	12.5	12.6	12.5	12.2	12.2	12.0	12.2
2009	11.6	11.5	11.5	11.4	11.5	11.9	11.9	11.9	11.7	11.7	11.6	11.6	11.7
2010	11.5	11.5	11.7	11.7	12.0	12.4	12.7	12.7	12.4	12.4	12.7	12.8	12.2
2011	12.8	13.0	13.2	13.4	13.7	14.3	14.6	14.6	14.5	14.5	14.6	14.7	14.0
2012	14.4	14.6	15.0	15.2	15.4	15.8	16.1	16.1	15.9	15.7	15.6	15.6	15.5
2013	15.4	15.5	15.4	15.3	15.3	15.4	15.7	15.6	15.0	14.8	14.8	14.7	15.2
2014	14.4	14.1	14.2	14.2	14.3	14.5	14.6	14.6	14.4	14.6	14.7	14.7	14.4
2015	14.3	14.3	14.3	14.4	14.4	14.5	14.6	14.5	14.0	13.9	13.7	13.6	14.2
2016	13.4	13.3	13.3	13.6	13.7	13.8	14.0	14.0	13.8	13.9	14.0	14.0	13.7
2017	13.9	13.9	13.9	13.9	14.0	14.2	14.5	14.5	14.4	14.3	14.4	14.3	14.2

1. Employment by Industry: Nevada, Selected Years, 2007–2017—*Continued*

(Numbers in thousands, not seasonally adjusted)

Industry and year	January	February	March	April	May	June	July	August	September	October	November	December	Annual average
Construction													
2007	130.3	132.0	134.7	134.7	137.5	137.6	136.7	137.5	134.6	132.1	129.4	126.7	133.7
2008	118.9	119.2	118.7	119.0	120.6	121.2	121.3	119.8	117.0	113.3	107.1	101.3	116.5
2009	94.4	91.2	88.6	86.2	82.7	81.5	79.8	78.5	76.7	75.4	71.9	67.0	81.2
2010	59.3	57.9	57.7	60.0	60.6	60.9	60.5	60.6	59.2	59.9	58.5	56.4	59.3
2011	52.4	52.1	50.2	51.3	51.9	52.6	53.3	53.5	53.1	53.1	51.9	50.6	52.2
2012	48.0	47.6	48.1	49.3	51.0	52.4	52.9	54.6	54.8	55.2	55.1	54.4	52.0
2013	51.9	52.4	53.6	55.3	55.6	57.2	57.8	59.5	59.6	60.3	60.1	58.6	56.8
2014	58.1	58.6	59.5	61.0	62.5	63.3	64.9	66.3	66.4	66.9	66.3	65.8	63.3
2015	65.1	65.7	65.8	67.2	69.0	69.7	70.4	72.5	72.9	74.9	74.6	74.8	70.2
2016	72.4	72.5	72.9	73.9	74.3	75.9	77.1	77.6	78.2	78.6	78.3	78.1	75.8
2017	77.1	78.8	81.5	82.3	84.2	85.6	84.5	84.4	85.2	85.6	85.5	86.5	83.4
Manufacturing													
2007	49.8	49.8	50.3	50.5	50.7	50.9	50.7	50.6	50.4	49.9	49.7	49.2	50.2
2008	49.0	48.8	48.7	48.8	49.0	49.1	49.0	48.8	48.1	47.6	46.3	45.2	48.2
2009	43.4	42.2	41.5	40.9	40.2	39.8	39.6	39.3	39.2	39.0	38.9	38.7	40.2
2010	37.8	37.7	37.7	38.0	38.0	38.2	38.1	38.0	38.0	37.8	37.8	37.9	37.9
2011	37.5	37.6	37.9	38.0	38.2	38.5	38.5	38.7	38.8	38.9	38.7	38.7	38.3
2012	38.4	38.4	38.7	38.9	39.1	39.5	39.6	39.7	39.6	39.6	39.5	39.5	39.2
2013	39.3	39.6	39.8	40.1	40.4	40.8	40.7	40.9	41.0	41.1	41.2	41.2	40.5
2014	41.2	41.2	41.2	41.1	41.4	41.6	41.7	41.6	41.6	41.6	41.7	41.7	41.5
2015	41.5	41.6	41.7	41.7	41.9	42.2	42.1	42.2	42.3	42.6	42.9	43.0	42.1
2016	42.7	43.0	43.0	43.0	43.2	43.5	43.9	44.0	44.0	44.4	44.5	45.0	43.7
2017	44.6	45.0	45.6	46.1	46.6	47.3	48.6	49.1	49.7	50.1	50.2	50.5	47.8
Trade, Transportation, and Utilities													
2007	228.6	227.5	228.8	229.6	231.1	232.1	231.6	232.8	232.9	234.1	239.7	242.6	232.6
2008	233.7	231.3	231.8	231.3	231.3	231.6	232.2	232.3	231.2	230.2	231.2	230.1	231.5
2009	219.2	215.0	213.5	211.8	211.8	212.1	211.5	211.0	211.4	212.2	215.9	217.0	213.5
2010	208.6	206.3	206.4	207.2	208.2	209.1	209.9	210.2	209.8	211.8	216.0	217.5	210.1
2011	209.0	207.4	208.0	209.5	210.5	211.2	212.2	212.9	213.3	215.5	221.2	222.0	212.7
2012	215.0	212.7	213.9	214.9	216.1	217.1	217.1	217.7	218.4	219.9	226.8	226.7	218.0
2013	218.2	216.2	215.8	216.7	219.6	220.8	221.7	222.5	223.1	225.3	231.9	233.5	222.1
2014	225.0	223.7	225.0	226.4	227.9	228.6	229.0	230.4	231.3	234.6	240.7	242.8	230.5
2015	234.7	232.9	233.9	235.1	236.5	237.0	237.1	238.0	238.9	241.6	247.1	248.4	238.4
2016	237.5	236.8	237.3	238.9	239.8	240.1	241.2	242.5	243.3	245.4	252.4	252.8	242.3
2017	245.3	243.6	243.5	244.4	245.7	246.9	247.4	248.4	249.7	252.1	260.3	263.2	249.2
Wholesale Trade													
2007	38.9	39.1	39.3	39.3	39.4	39.6	39.5	39.6	39.5	39.4	39.4	39.4	39.4
2008	39.0	39.1	39.1	39.1	39.2	39.2	39.2	39.1	38.9	38.5	37.9	37.4	38.8
2009	36.5	36.0	35.6	35.0	34.7	34.4	34.2	34.0	33.7	33.6	33.4	33.3	34.5
2010	32.7	32.6	32.7	32.9	33.1	33.1	33.0	33.0	32.9	33.1	32.9	33.0	32.9
2011	32.5	32.6	32.7	32.7	32.8	32.9	32.9	32.8	32.7	32.7	32.7	32.7	32.7
2012	32.3	32.3	32.5	32.5	32.6	32.7	32.8	32.7	32.6	32.7	32.7	32.8	32.6
2013	32.3	32.4	32.5	32.7	32.9	33.0	33.2	33.3	33.3	33.3	33.5	33.6	33.0
2014	33.3	33.5	33.6	33.7	33.8	33.8	34.1	34.1	34.2	34.2	34.2	34.4	33.9
2015	34.1	34.1	34.3	34.3	34.4	34.5	34.5	34.4	34.5	34.6	34.6	34.7	34.4
2016	34.1	34.2	34.0	34.3	34.4	34.4	34.6	34.7	34.8	34.9	35.1	35.2	34.6
2017	35.1	35.3	35.4	35.7	36.1	36.4	36.4	36.4	36.4	36.2	36.8	37.4	36.1
Retail Trade													
2007	136.4	135.5	136.2	136.8	137.8	138.1	138.2	138.7	138.4	139.0	144.0	146.3	138.8
2008	139.4	137.3	137.7	137.3	136.9	137.2	137.4	137.4	136.8	136.5	138.2	137.9	137.5
2009	130.1	126.9	126.1	125.2	125.5	126.0	125.9	125.7	126.6	127.5	131.3	132.3	127.4
2010	125.4	123.4	123.6	124.2	124.7	125.3	126.0	126.3	126.0	127.7	131.8	132.7	126.4
2011	126.0	124.3	124.7	125.4	126.2	126.5	127.0	127.6	127.7	129.4	134.7	135.1	127.9
2012	129.7	127.7	128.6	129.1	129.9	130.5	130.2	130.7	131.2	132.3	138.9	138.4	131.4
2013	131.6	129.8	130.0	130.7	132.3	133.1	133.6	134.3	134.4	136.0	141.7	142.9	134.2
2014	135.6	133.9	134.5	135.3	136.3	136.8	137.0	138.0	138.5	141.5	146.9	148.1	138.5
2015	140.9	139.4	140.4	141.3	142.1	142.3	142.3	143.0	142.8	145.0	149.6	149.9	143.3
2016	141.6	140.8	141.2	141.9	142.3	142.5	142.8	143.7	143.8	145.7	151.4	150.9	144.1
2017	144.6	143.0	142.7	143.4	144.3	144.5	144.5	144.8	145.1	146.5	152.5	152.9	145.7

1. Employment by Industry: Nevada, Selected Years, 2007–2017—*Continued*

(Numbers in thousands, not seasonally adjusted)

Industry and year	January	February	March	April	May	June	July	August	September	October	November	December	Annual average
Transportation and Utilities													
2007	53.3	52.9	53.3	53.5	53.9	54.4	53.9	54.5	55.0	55.7	56.3	56.9	54.5
2008	55.3	54.9	55.0	54.9	55.2	55.2	55.6	55.8	55.5	55.2	55.1	54.8	55.2
2009	52.6	52.1	51.8	51.6	51.6	51.7	51.4	51.3	51.1	51.1	51.2	51.4	51.6
2010	50.5	50.3	50.1	50.1	50.4	50.7	50.9	50.9	50.9	51.0	51.3	51.8	50.7
2011	50.5	50.5	50.6	51.4	51.5	51.8	52.3	52.5	52.9	53.4	53.8	54.2	52.1
2012	53.0	52.7	52.8	53.3	53.6	53.9	54.1	54.3	54.6	54.9	55.2	55.5	54.0
2013	54.3	54.0	53.3	53.3	54.4	54.7	54.9	54.9	55.4	56.0	56.7	57.0	54.9
2014	56.1	56.3	56.9	57.4	57.8	58.0	57.9	58.3	58.6	58.9	59.6	60.3	58.0
2015	59.7	59.4	59.2	59.5	60.0	60.2	60.3	60.6	61.6	62.0	62.9	63.8	60.8
2016	61.8	61.8	62.1	62.7	63.1	63.2	63.8	64.1	64.7	64.8	65.9	66.7	63.7
2017	65.6	65.3	65.4	65.3	65.3	66.0	66.5	67.2	68.2	69.4	71.0	72.9	67.3
Information													
2007	15.3	15.8	15.6	15.7	16.0	15.8	15.2	15.6	15.2	15.5	15.6	15.3	15.6
2008	15.2	15.2	15.1	15.4	15.9	15.2	14.8	14.8	14.5	14.9	14.4	14.1	15.0
2009	13.5	13.6	13.6	13.0	13.2	13.1	13.1	13.2	12.8	12.8	12.9	12.9	13.1
2010	12.3	12.4	12.3	12.6	12.6	12.5	12.8	12.5	12.3	12.4	12.6	12.5	12.5
2011	12.4	12.3	12.4	12.6	12.7	12.7	12.5	12.4	12.6	13.0	12.3	12.8	12.6
2012	12.2	12.3	12.5	12.3	12.6	12.6	12.3	12.7	12.7	13.3	14.4	12.9	12.7
2013	12.0	12.3	12.5	12.7	13.0	13.9	13.1	12.9	12.9	13.0	13.3	13.1	12.9
2014	12.7	13.0	12.7	13.9	14.8	15.4	13.4	13.4	13.5	13.5	14.1	13.7	13.7
2015	13.3	13.8	13.5	13.8	13.8	14.1	13.6	13.9	13.5	14.0	14.8	14.2	13.9
2016	14.2	14.4	13.8	14.9	14.6	14.8	14.7	14.0	14.1	14.3	14.0	14.0	14.3
2017	14.4	14.2	14.2	15.0	15.2	15.7	14.6	14.8	14.4	14.5	14.5	14.4	14.7
Financial Activities													
2007	65.0	65.1	65.5	65.0	65.3	65.4	64.7	64.5	64.4	63.9	63.4	63.5	64.6
2008	62.2	62.3	62.4	62.2	62.0	61.9	61.5	61.0	60.8	60.5	59.9	59.3	61.3
2009	57.3	57.0	56.6	56.3	55.8	55.8	54.7	54.8	54.2	54.2	53.8	53.6	55.3
2010	52.9	52.5	52.5	53.3	53.0	52.9	53.0	52.7	52.5	53.1	52.8	53.0	52.9
2011	52.4	52.1	52.1	52.5	52.4	52.6	52.7	52.3	52.7	52.9	52.7	53.0	52.5
2012	52.6	52.7	53.0	53.9	54.2	54.6	54.5	54.8	54.9	55.7	55.7	55.8	54.4
2013	55.4	56.1	56.7	56.6	57.0	57.0	56.5	56.5	56.4	56.8	57.1	57.3	56.6
2014	56.1	56.2	56.3	56.3	57.0	56.9	56.7	57.2	57.4	58.1	58.3	58.5	57.1
2015	57.9	58.4	58.5	59.4	60.0	59.9	60.3	60.4	60.5	61.7	61.7	62.4	60.1
2016	61.5	61.7	62.0	62.4	62.9	62.7	63.0	63.2	63.3	63.6	63.7	63.9	62.8
2017	63.5	64.2	64.1	64.3	65.1	64.9	65.5	65.6	65.6	66.2	65.9	65.8	65.1
Professional and Business Services													
2007	158.4	161.3	159.6	160.3	160.4	159.7	156.9	158.5	156.8	159.8	159.2	157.4	159.0
2008	156.5	155.2	155.4	156.0	156.8	154.4	150.7	150.7	151.0	147.6	146.1	143.3	152.0
2009	141.7	139.3	137.1	134.9	135.3	134.1	130.7	131.4	133.8	133.9	136.1	136.6	135.4
2010	134.8	133.2	133.4	135.3	135.8	136.2	134.8	137.0	134.9	137.6	138.0	137.9	135.7
2011	138.6	137.0	137.4	138.9	138.6	139.5	138.7	139.2	141.3	142.9	142.7	141.8	139.7
2012	144.5	143.6	142.3	143.4	144.0	145.4	141.7	145.4	146.2	147.8	147.4	145.2	144.7
2013	148.8	147.1	148.7	150.2	151.2	150.2	147.7	150.7	148.8	151.5	152.7	151.4	149.9
2014	152.9	152.7	154.0	155.0	155.6	155.7	153.1	157.0	157.1	162.1	161.5	160.9	156.5
2015	163.4	161.5	162.7	165.9	165.8	164.5	163.7	167.8	167.7	172.4	173.3	173.3	166.8
2016	172.0	170.4	172.2	175.2	174.0	176.3	175.8	176.8	179.6	181.8	180.6	177.8	176.0
2017	180.6	177.8	182.0	179.4	181.5	182.3	181.0	181.0	182.4	184.3	180.9	181.8	181.3
Education and Health Services													
2007	90.7	92.2	92.6	92.2	92.9	92.9	92.6	92.9	93.4	94.2	94.5	94.2	92.9
2008	94.2	95.3	95.6	96.8	97.0	96.9	96.7	96.8	97.1	97.9	98.2	98.2	96.7
2009	97.1	97.4	97.4	97.8	98.1	98.2	98.3	98.5	98.5	100.3	100.2	100.2	98.5
2010	99.7	100.1	100.6	101.5	101.7	101.4	101.1	101.1	101.4	103.0	103.3	103.6	101.5
2011	103.1	104.0	104.7	105.3	105.3	105.5	104.9	105.4	105.9	106.5	107.1	107.5	105.4
2012	106.9	107.8	108.1	108.6	109.1	108.6	107.4	108.7	108.5	109.1	109.2	109.6	108.5
2013	108.7	110.1	110.6	111.0	111.4	111.4	111.0	111.8	112.3	113.1	113.5	113.4	111.5
2014	112.6	113.8	114.4	114.8	115.2	115.5	115.2	116.0	116.4	117.8	118.0	118.3	115.7
2015	117.0	118.1	118.8	119.6	119.8	120.3	120.5	121.5	122.3	124.2	124.2	124.7	120.9
2016	123.5	124.8	125.1	126.0	126.5	126.6	127.1	128.1	128.8	130.1	130.7	131.4	127.4
2017	129.7	131.0	131.8	132.5	133.2	133.1	132.1	133.9	134.8	135.0	136.6	137.5	133.4

1. Employment by Industry: Nevada, Selected Years, 2007–2017—*Continued*

(Numbers in thousands, not seasonally adjusted)

Industry and year	January	February	March	April	May	June	July	August	September	October	November	December	Annual average
Leisure and Hospitality													
2007	332.7	335.7	338.4	339.4	341.8	343.6	342.3	340.2	340.0	338.9	339.0	340.1	339.3
2008	334.6	334.9	336.2	338.7	339.4	340.0	336.1	334.4	331.6	326.1	321.0	317.0	332.5
2009	310.6	308.9	307.6	310.4	311.9	310.9	310.0	307.2	306.9	304.4	302.2	306.1	308.1
2010	302.5	304.5	305.7	310.5	312.1	313.6	312.8	311.2	310.6	309.6	307.9	307.3	309.0
2011	306.0	307.5	312.4	317.9	320.1	321.3	320.1	318.0	319.0	317.9	315.1	311.7	315.6
2012	309.1	311.4	315.0	318.2	320.8	322.6	321.5	319.6	319.0	318.4	316.2	314.7	317.2
2013	313.3	315.0	319.3	323.7	325.4	328.7	330.0	328.6	328.6	326.6	325.0	322.5	323.9
2014	322.1	325.2	330.8	335.4	338.8	339.6	340.1	342.6	341.9	339.0	336.6	335.6	335.6
2015	332.8	335.8	339.7	342.9	344.5	344.6	343.9	343.7	343.3	342.4	339.8	337.3	340.9
2016	334.7	338.0	341.2	346.1	347.8	350.0	350.6	350.3	350.1	346.1	344.9	343.9	345.3
2017	341.5	344.8	349.7	350.9	354.2	354.2	353.8	352.6	352.1	351.3	345.7	343.5	349.5
Other Services													
2007	35.2	35.3	36.0	36.1	36.5	37.1	37.0	37.1	37.0	36.7	36.9	37.2	36.5
2008	36.6	36.5	36.8	36.6	37.2	37.2	36.9	37.1	37.0	36.5	35.8	35.1	36.6
2009	33.7	33.4	33.6	33.9	34.2	34.3	34.1	34.1	34.0	33.4	33.2	33.0	33.7
2010	32.6	32.7	33.0	33.0	33.1	33.1	33.4	33.2	33.0	33.0	32.3	32.0	32.9
2011	31.6	31.8	31.9	32.5	32.7	32.9	33.0	32.8	32.6	32.3	32.2	32.3	32.4
2012	32.1	32.2	32.6	33.0	33.5	33.9	33.8	33.9	33.8	34.2	33.1	32.8	33.2
2013	32.3	32.6	32.9	33.5	33.9	34.2	34.3	34.3	34.1	34.1	34.2	34.1	33.7
2014	34.0	34.2	34.7	35.5	36.0	36.1	36.2	36.1	36.0	36.4	35.8	35.5	35.5
2015	35.2	35.4	35.7	36.2	36.6	37.1	37.1	37.2	36.9	37.0	37.1	37.3	36.6
2016	37.4	38.2	39.0	39.5	39.8	40.0	40.7	40.7	41.3	41.9	40.9	40.0	40.0
2017	39.7	39.8	40.2	40.9	41.1	41.5	41.9	41.6	41.6	41.9	41.5	41.2	41.1
Government													
2007	150.4	156.9	157.5	159.1	159.6	154.7	147.2	146.0	155.5	160.7	161.6	162.3	156.0
2008	156.3	162.3	163.2	164.3	165.0	159.8	153.5	152.3	160.9	165.7	165.9	165.5	161.2
2009	158.3	162.2	162.2	161.9	161.2	155.9	149.7	148.2	156.3	158.1	157.8	157.3	157.4
2010	152.3	157.0	157.8	157.9	161.2	153.7	147.6	144.8	151.9	153.5	153.9	153.8	153.8
2011	151.1	154.6	154.4	154.7	154.3	147.6	142.3	142.4	148.6	150.6	150.8	151.7	150.3
2012	147.0	150.2	151.8	151.8	152.3	147.5	142.5	142.2	149.8	151.7	152.5	153.3	149.4
2013	149.5	151.9	153.1	153.1	153.6	149.4	142.5	145.5	151.1	153.0	154.2	155.4	151.0
2014	151.0	153.8	155.2	154.9	155.7	148.9	144.0	145.2	153.7	155.1	155.8	156.6	152.5
2015	152.6	155.5	156.9	156.8	157.1	152.4	146.5	147.6	156.4	156.4	158.3	159.8	154.7
2016	154.8	158.2	160.1	159.0	159.6	151.9	151.2	151.7	159.7	160.0	161.5	162.7	157.5
2017	156.6	161.8	163.0	160.7	162.0	156.6	153.9	156.2	164.6	166.9	166.9	167.2	161.4

2. Average Weekly Hours by Selected Industry: Nevada, 2013–2017

(Not seasonally adjusted)

Industry and year	January	February	March	April	May	June	July	August	September	October	November	December	Annual average
Total Private													
2013	33.5	33.3	33.5	33.3	33.3	33.8	33.4	33.6	33.7	33.6	33.3	33.6	33.5
2014	33.1	33.3	33.5	33.3	33.2	33.7	33.5	33.8	33.6	33.4	33.6	33.2	33.4
2015	33.2	33.5	33.6	33.4	33.5	33.6	33.7	34.1	33.8	33.6	33.9	33.4	33.6
2016	33.2	33.3	33.3	33.6	34.1	34.0	34.2	34.4	34.1	34.5	33.8	34.1	33.9
2017	34.1	33.5	33.9	34.3	34.1	34.2	34.6	34.3	34.1	34.5	34.0	33.9	34.1
Goods-Producing													
2013	36.8	35.8	36.6	37.3	37.6	38.2	37.7	38.7	38.0	38.5	38.5	39.0	37.8
2014	39.0	38.2	38.0	37.7	37.8	38.4	38.1	38.6	38.1	38.6	37.6	38.4	38.2
2015	37.7	37.7	38.7	38.7	38.4	38.8	38.1	38.3	38.0	38.5	38.1	38.2	38.3
2016	38.2	37.9	38.2	38.5	39.4	38.9	38.4	39.0	38.9	38.9	37.5	38.2	38.5
2017	37.2	37.5	37.9	37.5	38.4	38.7	39.2	39.2	38.7	39.1	38.4	39.1	38.4
Construction													
2013	35.0	33.7	34.6	35.3	35.6	37.6	37.1	38.0	36.9	37.3	37.5	37.3	36.4
2014	36.7	36.4	36.4	35.6	35.4	36.0	36.1	36.9	36.7	37.3	36.0	36.8	36.4
2015	36.0	36.5	37.6	37.5	37.1	37.8	37.0	37.2	37.2	38.1	36.5	36.0	37.0
2016	36.3	36.6	36.7	36.9	37.6	36.5	35.7	36.5	36.4	36.6	35.0	36.1	36.4
2017	34.5	34.4	35.3	35.0	36.0	35.8	36.2	36.4	36.1	36.9	36.5	37.0	35.9
Trade, Transportation, and Utilities													
2013	33.5	33.8	34.1	33.8	34.0	34.4	34.2	34.1	34.1	33.6	33.0	33.7	33.9
2014	32.5	33.1	33.7	33.6	33.4	34.0	34.1	34.5	34.2	34.2	34.4	34.4	33.8
2015	33.9	34.5	35.5	34.6	35.2	35.4	35.6	35.9	36.3	35.7	36.6	36.0	35.4
2016	35.2	35.0	35.2	35.4	35.9	36.3	35.8	35.5	35.7	35.8	34.9	35.7	35.5
2017	35.4	35.0	35.3	36.1	35.6	35.8	36.2	35.5	35.4	35.3	35.1	35.0	35.5
Financial Activities													
2013	39.6	39.3	39.5	39.1	39.4	39.9	38.6	38.3	38.8	38.0	38.4	38.7	39.0
2014	38.4	38.5	38.7	38.1	38.1	38.6	37.9	37.5	37.0	37.3	38.6	36.9	38.0
2015	37.1	37.6	37.7	37.7	37.9	37.0	37.4	37.8	38.3	37.3	37.5	36.7	37.5
2016	37.0	37.1	36.5	37.6	38.1	37.7	38.3	37.6	37.3	36.6	36.7	37.5	37.3
2017	38.2	36.9	37.2	38.3	38.1	38.4	38.7	38.1	37.6	38.0	37.8	37.2	37.9
Professional and Business Services													
2013	34.9	34.6	34.4	34.4	34.6	35.6	34.8	35.5	36.0	35.4	35.3	35.2	35.1
2014	34.7	35.0	34.5	34.4	34.3	35.4	34.8	35.2	34.8	34.8	35.6	35.0	34.9
2015	34.9	35.2	33.9	34.3	34.1	34.3	34.6	35.8	34.0	34.1	34.2	33.9	34.4
2016	33.3	33.9	33.4	34.1	34.5	34.3	34.3	35.2	34.4	35.9	34.7	34.9	34.4
2017	35.4	34.7	34.8	35.5	35.0	35.5	35.4	35.3	34.9	35.8	34.9	34.8	35.2
Leisure and Hospitality													
2013	29.8	29.7	30.0	29.7	29.6	29.9	29.8	30.0	29.8	30.3	29.8	29.5	29.8
2014	29.9	30.2	30.6	30.2	30.0	30.5	30.3	30.6	30.4	30.1	30.1	29.3	30.2
2015	29.8	30.1	30.2	29.9	30.1	30.2	30.5	30.4	30.0	29.7	29.9	29.4	30.0
2016	29.3	29.3	29.6	29.3	29.3	29.5	30.0	30.4	30.1	30.5	29.9	29.4	29.7
2017	29.9	29.5	30.0	30.1	30.1	29.8	30.0	29.9	29.7	29.7	29.3	28.6	29.7

3. Average Hourly Earnings by Selected Industry: Nevada, 2013–2017

(Dollars, not seasonally adjusted)

Industry and year	January	February	March	April	May	June	July	August	September	October	November	December	Annual average
Total Private													
2013	20.07	20.08	20.14	20.13	20.05	20.23	20.00	20.13	20.35	20.18	20.48	20.65	20.21
2014	20.85	20.89	20.79	20.86	20.75	20.87	20.72	20.83	20.91	21.03	21.45	21.41	20.95
2015	21.61	21.88	21.95	21.85	21.78	21.73	21.87	22.12	22.11	22.16	22.24	22.08	21.95
2016	22.28	22.26	22.20	22.22	22.25	22.07	21.88	22.05	22.02	22.20	22.16	22.20	22.15
2017	22.70	22.51	22.47	22.48	22.33	22.33	22.42	22.50	22.51	22.67	22.65	22.71	22.52
Goods-Producing													
2013	23.99	24.23	24.87	24.33	24.82	24.88	25.02	24.72	25.08	24.66	25.06	25.11	24.74
2014	25.43	25.81	25.51	25.72	25.06	25.75	25.76	25.53	25.63	25.62	25.67	26.03	25.63
2015	26.10	26.41	26.43	26.52	26.11	26.14	26.78	26.76	27.13	27.16	26.97	27.11	26.64
2016	27.24	27.31	27.14	27.55	27.34	27.41	27.42	27.11	27.49	27.08	27.37	27.15	27.30
2017	27.94	27.65	27.44	27.23	27.42	27.55	27.73	27.91	28.18	28.45	27.95	28.27	27.82
Construction													
2013	27.25	27.54	27.28	25.95	26.34	26.16	25.80	25.45	25.56	25.17	25.53	25.90	26.10
2014	26.43	27.60	26.78	27.39	26.82	27.84	27.40	27.24	26.68	26.46	26.69	27.01	27.02
2015	26.21	26.40	26.64	26.71	27.16	27.06	28.25	28.26	28.40	28.36	28.00	28.08	27.50
2016	28.11	28.47	27.95	28.14	27.77	27.79	27.79	27.84	27.42	27.25	27.51	27.26	27.77
2017	28.52	28.26	27.81	27.43	27.77	27.65	27.84	28.11	28.24	28.70	28.13	28.67	28.10
Trade, Transportation, and Utilities													
2013	18.86	18.81	19.02	19.31	18.76	18.85	18.47	18.42	18.70	18.93	19.05	18.90	18.84
2014	19.54	19.61	19.27	19.78	19.41	19.26	19.21	19.19	19.41	19.37	19.62	19.41	19.42
2015	19.82	19.93	19.89	19.92	19.79	19.55	19.53	19.45	19.67	19.57	19.65	19.34	19.67
2016	20.01	19.85	20.13	20.22	20.05	19.84	20.00	20.05	20.06	20.46	20.20	20.18	20.09
2017	20.64	20.76	20.46	20.50	19.97	20.06	20.06	19.90	19.70	19.80	19.41	19.67	20.07
Financial Activities													
2013	21.28	21.58	21.74	21.62	22.40	23.03	22.35	22.52	21.55	21.62	21.85	21.57	21.93
2014	21.18	21.31	21.38	21.04	21.28	22.11	21.85	22.01	21.26	21.85	22.17	21.75	21.60
2015	22.19	22.69	22.96	23.49	23.85	23.89	26.20	26.57	26.11	26.33	25.98	26.49	24.76
2016	26.28	25.48	25.20	24.69	26.01	25.34	24.82	25.32	24.94	25.58	24.94	25.56	25.34
2017	24.89	25.53	25.84	25.94	25.60	25.89	26.01	26.24	26.40	26.33	26.34	26.18	25.94
Professional and Business Services													
2013	22.34	22.86	22.64	22.88	22.71	22.93	23.25	23.40	23.85	23.62	24.31	25.02	23.33
2014	24.78	24.37	24.32	24.38	24.28	24.22	23.82	23.94	23.72	23.32	23.61	23.39	24.00
2015	23.63	24.54	24.77	24.12	24.24	24.14	24.30	24.55	24.03	24.31	24.48	23.90	24.25
2016	24.46	24.90	24.59	24.09	24.05	23.73	23.93	23.81	23.60	24.27	24.09	24.18	24.13
2017	24.74	24.40	24.44	24.52	24.76	24.05	24.55	24.74	24.53	24.65	24.84	25.24	24.62
Leisure and Hospitality													
2013	14.71	14.58	14.52	14.46	14.37	14.42	14.55	14.75	15.06	14.82	15.03	15.08	14.70
2014	15.52	15.48	15.53	15.51	15.55	15.45	15.45	15.50	15.86	15.93	16.16	16.26	15.68
2015	16.58	16.28	16.13	15.97	16.20	15.94	15.91	16.06	16.29	16.35	16.64	16.49	16.23
2016	16.61	16.75	16.88	16.77	16.89	17.10	16.72	16.91	17.12	16.95	17.09	16.86	16.89
2017	17.45	17.31	17.35	17.42	17.17	17.30	17.09	17.17	17.42	17.20	17.28	17.14	17.27

4. Average Weekly Earnings by Selected Industry: Nevada, 2013–2017

(Dollars, not seasonally adjusted)

Industry and year	January	February	March	April	May	June	July	August	September	October	November	December	Annual average
Total Private													
2013	672.35	668.66	674.69	670.33	667.67	683.77	668.00	676.37	685.80	678.05	681.98	693.84	677.04
2014	690.14	695.64	696.47	694.64	688.90	703.32	694.12	704.05	702.58	702.40	720.72	710.81	699.73
2015	717.45	732.98	737.52	729.79	729.63	730.13	737.02	754.29	747.32	744.58	753.94	737.47	737.52
2016	739.70	741.26	739.26	746.59	758.73	750.38	748.30	758.52	750.88	765.90	749.01	757.02	750.89
2017	774.07	754.09	761.73	771.06	761.45	763.69	775.73	771.75	767.59	782.12	770.10	769.87	767.93
Goods-Producing													
2013	882.83	867.43	910.24	907.51	933.23	950.42	943.25	956.66	953.04	949.41	964.81	979.29	935.17
2014	991.77	985.94	969.38	969.64	947.27	988.80	981.46	985.46	976.50	988.93	965.19	999.55	979.07
2015	983.97	995.66	1,022.84	1,026.32	1,002.62	1,014.23	1,020.32	1,024.91	1,030.94	1,045.66	1,027.56	1,035.60	1,020.31
2016	1,040.57	1,035.05	1,036.75	1,060.68	1,077.20	1,066.25	1,052.93	1,057.29	1,069.36	1,053.41	1,026.38	1,037.13	1,051.05
2017	1,039.37	1,036.88	1,039.98	1,021.13	1,052.93	1,066.19	1,087.02	1,094.07	1,090.57	1,112.40	1,073.28	1,105.36	1,068.29
Construction													
2013	953.75	928.10	943.89	916.04	937.70	983.62	957.18	967.10	943.16	938.84	957.38	966.07	950.04
2014	969.98	1,004.64	974.79	975.08	949.43	1,002.24	989.14	1,005.16	979.16	986.96	960.84	993.97	983.53
2015	943.56	963.60	1,001.66	1,001.63	1,007.64	1,022.87	1,045.25	1,051.27	1,056.48	1,080.52	1,022.00	1,010.88	1,017.50
2016	1,020.39	1,042.00	1,025.77	1,038.37	1,044.15	1,014.34	992.10	1,016.16	998.09	997.35	962.85	984.09	1,010.83
2017	983.94	972.14	981.69	960.05	999.72	989.87	1,007.81	1,023.20	1,019.46	1,059.03	1,026.75	1,060.79	1,008.79
Trade, Transportation, and Utilities													
2013	631.81	635.78	648.58	652.68	637.84	648.44	631.67	628.12	637.67	636.05	628.65	636.93	638.68
2014	635.05	649.09	649.40	664.61	648.29	654.84	655.06	662.06	663.82	662.45	674.93	667.70	656.40
2015	671.90	687.59	706.10	689.23	696.61	692.07	695.27	698.26	714.02	698.65	719.19	696.24	696.32
2016	704.35	694.75	708.58	715.79	719.80	720.19	716.00	711.78	716.14	732.47	704.98	720.43	713.20
2017	730.66	726.60	722.24	740.05	710.93	718.15	726.17	706.45	697.38	698.94	681.29	688.45	712.49
Financial Activities													
2013	842.69	848.09	858.73	845.34	882.56	918.90	862.71	862.52	836.14	821.56	839.04	834.76	855.27
2014	813.31	820.44	827.41	801.62	810.77	853.45	828.12	825.38	786.62	815.01	855.76	802.58	820.80
2015	823.25	853.14	865.59	885.57	903.92	883.93	979.88	1,004.35	1,000.01	982.11	974.25	972.18	928.50
2016	972.36	945.31	919.80	928.34	990.98	955.32	950.61	952.03	930.26	936.23	915.30	958.50	945.18
2017	950.80	942.06	961.25	993.50	975.36	994.18	1,006.59	999.74	992.64	1,000.54	995.65	973.90	983.13
Professional and Business Services													
2013	779.67	790.96	778.82	787.07	785.77	816.31	809.10	830.70	858.60	836.15	858.14	880.70	818.88
2014	859.87	852.95	839.04	838.67	832.80	857.39	828.94	842.69	825.46	811.54	840.52	818.65	837.60
2015	824.69	863.81	839.70	827.32	826.58	828.00	840.78	878.89	817.02	828.97	837.22	810.21	834.20
2016	814.52	844.11	821.31	821.47	829.73	813.94	820.80	838.11	811.84	871.29	835.92	843.88	830.07
2017	875.80	846.68	850.51	870.46	866.60	853.78	869.07	873.32	856.10	882.47	866.92	878.35	866.62
Leisure and Hospitality													
2013	438.36	433.03	435.60	429.46	425.35	431.16	433.59	442.50	448.79	449.05	447.89	444.86	438.06
2014	464.05	467.50	475.22	468.40	466.50	471.23	468.14	474.30	482.14	479.49	486.42	476.42	473.54
2015	494.08	490.03	487.13	477.50	487.62	481.39	485.26	488.22	488.70	485.60	497.54	484.81	486.90
2016	487.55	490.78	499.65	491.36	494.88	504.45	501.60	514.06	515.31	516.98	510.99	495.68	501.63
2017	521.76	510.65	520.50	524.34	516.82	515.54	512.70	513.38	517.37	510.84	506.30	490.20	512.92

NEW HAMPSHIRE
At a Glance

Population:
  2010 census: 1,316,470
  2017 estimate: 1,342,795

Percent change in population:
  2010–2017: 2.0%

Percent change in total nonfarm employment:
  2007–2017: 4.3%

Industry with the largest growth in employment, 2007–2017 (thousands):
  Education and health services, 18.9

Industry with the largest decline or smallest growth in employment, 2007–2017 (thousands):
  Manufacturing, -8.4

Civilian labor force:
  2010: 738,257
  2017: 746,549

Unemployment rate and rank among states (highest to lowest):
  2010: 5.8%, 48th
  2017: 2.7%, 49th

Over-the year change in unemployment rates:
  2015–2016: -0.5%
  2016–2017: -0.2%

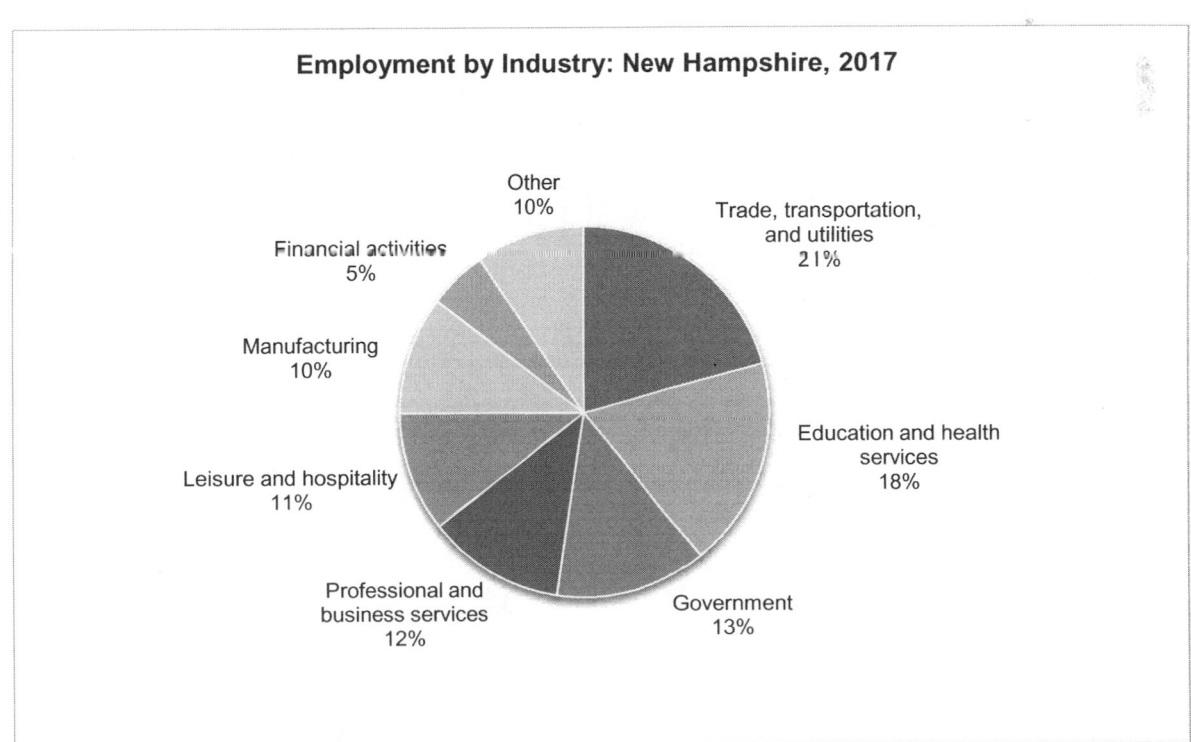

Employment by Industry: New Hampshire, 2017

- Other 10%
- Financial activities 5%
- Manufacturing 10%
- Leisure and hospitality 11%
- Professional and business services 12%
- Government 13%
- Education and health services 18%
- Trade, transportation, and utilities 21%

1. Employment by Industry: New Hampshire, Selected Years, 2007–2017

(Numbers in thousands, not seasonally adjusted)

Industry and year	January	February	March	April	May	June	July	August	September	October	November	December	Annual average
Total Nonfarm													
2007	632.4	634.9	636.8	639.8	649.9	657.4	651.3	650.6	653.6	652.2	653.1	657.1	647.4
2008	639.3	639.1	640.4	643.8	653.0	658.4	652.2	652.8	654.8	653.5	649.6	648.7	648.8
2009	627.2	624.5	621.5	623.2	632.4	635.0	623.8	624.2	629.7	630.5	627.5	630.5	627.5
2010	608.6	611.6	614.4	618.6	628.7	632.0	624.2	624.1	629.4	630.6	629.2	633.2	623.7
2011	612.8	615.8	618.0	623.5	629.8	633.5	627.3	626.5	633.6	633.9	634.5	637.0	627.2
2012	619.1	619.6	623.2	626.6	634.3	641.4	635.4	637.3	641.0	641.0	640.2	642.3	633.5
2013	623.9	626.8	627.2	632.2	641.9	646.5	639.6	642.0	642.0	646.1	645.9	649.5	638.6
2014	630.4	633.7	634.1	639.6	647.1	654.7	649.1	643.4	651.3	654.5	653.2	657.0	645.7
2015	639.3	640.2	643.3	648.2	659.0	664.6	660.0	658.8	660.8	665.3	665.7	668.9	656.2
2016	652.4	656.8	656.7	662.6	669.1	674.7	672.1	672.2	675.7	675.4	675.3	678.2	668.4
2017	661.3	662.7	664.6	668.5	675.7	684.0	678.6	678.7	678.1	683.7	683.6	681.6	675.1
Total Private													
2007	540.3	538.5	540.1	543.3	553.8	566.5	569.3	569.5	559.3	554.5	555.3	559.1	554.1
2008	545.6	542.0	542.1	546.0	555.3	565.2	569.0	568.8	557.2	553.8	548.5	547.7	553.4
2009	530.9	525.4	522.0	523.7	532.4	539.2	540.1	540.3	532.8	529.9	526.1	529.1	531.0
2010	513.4	511.3	512.9	518.4	527.1	537.3	541.3	541.7	533.5	532.4	530.1	534.3	527.8
2011	520.8	519.0	520.9	527.6	533.3	543.5	548.9	549.5	541.4	538.7	538.3	540.6	535.2
2012	527.8	525.1	527.8	531.8	539.7	553.5	555.4	557.7	547.6	545.9	544.4	545.7	541.9
2013	533.7	532.3	533.3	538.3	547.8	558.5	562.5	563.5	552.0	551.6	551.3	554.1	548.2
2014	540.8	540.0	540.0	545.5	555.1	566.0	570.1	564.4	559.2	559.7	557.6	561.3	555.0
2015	549.4	546.9	548.8	554.1	565.3	576.4	581.4	581.2	570.1	571.5	570.9	574.0	565.8
2016	563.2	562.1	562.4	568.3	576.1	587.1	593.8	593.1	583.3	581.5	580.3	583.3	577.9
2017	573.0	569.7	570.4	574.8	582.3	596.7	600.5	599.0	586.8	590.5	590.0	587.5	585.1
Goods Producing													
2007	104.1	102.9	103.4	105.0	107.2	108.4	108.2	108.6	107.2	106.9	106.5	105.4	106.2
2008	102.2	101.3	101.6	102.6	104.0	105.2	105.2	105.5	103.8	103.2	101.6	99.2	103.0
2009	94.1	92.1	90.6	91.3	92.2	92.3	91.4	92.1	91.7	91.4	89.6	88.4	91.4
2010	84.5	83.7	84.3	86.6	88.4	89.4	90.1	90.7	90.0	90.3	89.7	89.1	88.1
2011	86.2	85.7	86.6	88.9	89.9	91.0	91.6	91.9	91.2	90.9	90.6	89.7	89.5
2012	86.7	86.0	86.7	88.6	89.4	90.6	90.7	91.0	90.6	90.5	89.5	88.7	89.1
2013	86.5	86.0	86.4	88.1	89.8	91.2	91.2	91.5	90.7	91.0	91.0	90.3	89.5
2014	87.8	87.5	87.8	89.8	91.1	92.3	92.4	92.7	91.6	91.6	91.6	91.3	90.6
2015	89.2	88.3	88.5	90.7	92.5	94.1	94.7	94.8	94.3	94.7	94.1	93.9	92.5
2016	92.1	91.4	91.6	93.6	94.8	96.1	96.7	96.6	95.7	95.8	95.8	95.5	94.6
2017	93.8	93.5	94.1	95.2	96.4	97.9	98.5	98.3	97.7	98.8	98.8	97.7	96.7
Service-Providing													
2007	528.3	532.0	533.4	534.8	542.7	549.0	543.1	542.0	546.4	545.3	546.6	551.7	541.3
2008	537.1	537.8	538.8	541.2	549.0	553.2	547.0	547.3	551.0	550.3	548.0	549.5	545.9
2009	533.1	532.4	530.9	531.9	540.2	542.7	532.4	532.1	538.0	539.1	537.9	542.1	536.1
2010	524.1	527.9	530.1	532.0	540.3	542.6	534.1	533.4	539.4	540.3	539.5	544.1	535.7
2011	526.6	530.1	531.4	534.6	539.9	542.5	535.7	534.6	542.4	543.0	543.9	547.3	537.7
2012	532.4	533.6	536.5	538.0	544.9	550.8	544.7	546.3	550.4	550.5	550.7	553.6	544.4
2013	537.4	540.8	540.8	544.1	552.1	555.3	548.4	550.5	551.3	555.1	554.9	559.2	549.2
2014	542.6	546.2	546.3	549.8	556.0	562.4	556.7	550.7	559.7	562.9	561.6	565.7	555.1
2015	550.1	551.9	554.8	557.5	566.5	570.5	565.3	564.0	566.5	570.6	571.6	575.0	563.7
2016	560.3	565.4	565.1	569.0	574.3	578.6	575.4	575.6	580.0	579.6	579.5	582.7	573.8
2017	567.5	569.2	570.5	573.3	579.3	586.1	580.1	580.4	580.4	584.9	584.8	583.9	578.4
Mining and Logging													
2007	1.0	1.0	1.0	1.1	1.1	1.2	1.2	1.2	1.2	1.2	1.2	1.1	1.1
2008	1.0	1.0	1.0	1.0	1.0	1.1	1.1	1.1	1.1	1.1	1.0	0.9	1.0
2009	0.8	0.8	0.8	0.8	0.9	1.0	1.0	1.0	1.0	1.0	1.0	0.9	0.9
2010	0.8	0.8	0.8	0.9	0.9	1.0	1.0	1.0	1.0	0.9	0.9	0.9	0.9
2011	0.8	0.8	0.8	0.8	0.9	0.9	1.0	1.0	1.0	1.0	1.0	0.9	0.9
2012	0.8	0.8	0.8	0.9	0.9	1.0	1.0	1.0	1.0	1.0	0.9	0.9	0.9
2013	0.8	0.8	0.8	0.9	0.9	1.0	1.0	1.0	1.0	1.0	1.0	1.0	0.9
2014	0.9	0.9	0.9	0.9	1.0	1.0	1.0	1.1	1.1	1.1	1.0	1.0	1.0
2015	0.9	0.9	0.9	0.9	0.9	1.0	1.0	1.0	1.0	1.0	1.0	1.0	1.0
2016	0.9	0.9	0.9	0.9	1.0	1.0	1.1	1.1	1.0	1.0	1.0	1.0	1.0
2017	0.9	0.9	0.9	0.9	0.9	1.0	1.0	1.0	1.0	1.0	1.0	0.9	1.0

1. Employment by Industry: New Hampshire, Selected Years, 2007–2017—*Continued*

(Numbers in thousands, not seasonally adjusted)

Industry and year	January	February	March	April	May	June	July	August	September	October	November	December	Annual average
Construction													
2007	25.6	24.6	24.8	26.2	28.4	29.1	29.5	29.4	28.7	28.2	27.8	26.6	27.4
2008	24.2	23.6	23.9	25.5	26.7	27.3	28.2	28.0	27.2	27.0	26.0	24.5	26.0
2009	21.5	20.6	20.3	21.6	22.9	23.4	23.7	23.9	24.3	24.1	22.9	21.9	22.6
2010	18.9	18.2	18.6	20.4	21.7	22.2	23.0	23.2	22.9	23.1	22.6	21.7	21.4
2011	19.6	19.1	19.7	21.7	22.5	23.1	23.6	23.6	23.5	23.5	23.2	22.4	22.1
2012	20.0	19.5	20.1	21.8	22.6	23.2	23.5	23.7	23.7	23.6	22.8	21.9	22.2
2013	20.3	19.8	20.2	21.7	23.2	23.8	23.8	23.9	23.7	23.6	23.5	22.7	22.5
2014	20.8	20.6	20.9	22.7	23.7	24.2	24.7	24.7	24.2	24.3	24.2	23.5	23.2
2015	21.8	21.1	21.2	22.9	24.5	25.2	25.7	25.8	25.9	26.2	25.5	25.1	24.2
2016	23.6	23.0	23.3	25.0	25.8	26.4	27.0	26.8	26.6	26.6	26.3	25.6	25.5
2017	24.4	24.2	24.6	25.8	26.7	27.4	27.8	27.8	27.6	27.8	28.0	26.8	26.6
Manufacturing													
2007	77.5	77.3	77.0	77.7	77.7	78.1	77.5	78.0	77.3	77.5	77.5	77.7	77.6
2008	77.0	76.7	76.7	76.1	76.3	76.8	75.9	76.4	75.5	75.1	74.6	73.8	75.9
2009	71.8	70.7	69.5	68.9	68.4	67.9	66.7	67.2	66.4	66.3	65.7	65.6	67.9
2010	64.8	64.7	64.9	65.3	65.8	66.2	66.1	66.5	66.1	66.3	66.2	66.5	65.8
2011	65.8	65.8	66.1	66.4	66.5	67.0	67.0	67.3	66.7	66.4	66.4	66.4	66.5
2012	65.9	65.7	65.8	65.9	65.9	66.4	66.2	66.3	65.9	65.9	65.8	65.9	66.0
2013	65.4	65.4	65.4	65.5	65.7	66.4	66.4	66.6	66.0	66.4	66.5	66.6	66.0
2014	66.1	66.0	66.0	66.2	66.4	67.1	66.7	66.9	66.3	66.2	66.4	66.8	66.4
2015	66.5	66.3	66.4	66.9	67.1	67.9	68.0	68.0	67.4	67.5	67.6	67.8	67.3
2016	67.6	67.5	67.4	67.7	68.0	68.7	68.6	68.7	68.1	68.2	68.5	68.9	68.2
2017	68.5	68.4	68.6	68.5	68.8	69.5	69.7	69.5	69.1	70.0	69.8	70.0	69.2
Trade, Transportation, and Utilities													
2007	141.5	138.0	138.5	138.9	140.9	142.9	142.6	142.0	139.7	140.5	144.2	146.5	141.4
2008	140.9	137.6	137.4	137.2	139.4	141.4	141.0	140.8	138.6	139.8	141.4	142.7	139.9
2009	136.1	132.8	131.6	131.7	134.0	135.4	133.6	133.2	132.5	133.2	135.5	137.3	133.9
2010	131.5	129.2	129.3	130.1	132.3	134.3	133.6	133.5	131.8	133.5	136.2	138.8	132.8
2011	132.7	130.3	130.5	131.7	133.1	135.1	134.4	134.4	133.7	134.7	137.3	140.0	134.0
2012	134.4	131.8	132.4	132.7	134.4	137.9	137.0	137.3	135.5	136.0	139.6	140.8	135.8
2013	134.8	132.5	132.9	134.3	136.3	138.2	137.6	137.6	135.8	136.3	139.4	141.7	136.5
2014	135.7	133.6	133.7	134.3	136.3	138.2	137.6	131.5	137.1	138.0	140.8	143.0	136.7
2015	136.9	134.1	134.3	135.2	137.3	139.3	138.4	138.7	137.2	138.3	141.4	143.6	137.9
2016	138.4	136.7	136.7	137.7	139.5	141.0	140.8	140.9	139.7	140.4	143.2	145.5	140.0
2017	140.0	137.2	136.9	138.0	139.2	141.5	141.1	141.0	139.3	141.2	144.0	144.6	140.3
Wholesale Trade													
2007	28.2	28.0	28.2	28.3	28.4	28.5	28.5	28.4	28.2	28.1	28.1	28.1	28.3
2008	28.0	27.9	27.9	28.1	28.3	28.4	28.4	28.3	28.0	28.0	27.8	27.6	28.1
2009	27.1	26.7	26.5	26.6	26.7	26.6	26.4	26.4	26.1	26.2	26.1	26.1	26.5
2010	25.6	25.6	25.6	25.7	25.9	26.0	26.1	26.1	25.8	26.0	26.1	26.0	25.9
2011	25.8	25.9	26.0	26.1	26.3	26.3	26.4	26.3	26.2	26.3	26.2	26.4	26.2
2012	26.3	26.2	26.3	26.5	26.6	26.9	26.9	26.9	26.8	26.7	26.7	26.7	26.6
2013	26.4	26.4	26.5	26.6	26.8	27.0	27.0	27.0	26.8	26.7	26.8	26.9	26.7
2014	26.7	26.7	26.8	26.9	27.2	27.3	27.4	27.5	27.3	27.3	27.4	27.5	27.2
2015	27.2	27.1	27.2	27.4	27.6	27.8	27.7	27.7	27.5	27.6	27.7	27.7	27.5
2016	27.6	27.5	27.5	27.7	27.8	27.9	28.0	28.0	27.9	27.8	27.9	28.0	27.8
2017	27.7	27.6	27.7	27.8	28.0	28.3	28.3	28.3	28.0	28.1	28.2	28.2	28.0
Retail Trade													
2007	98.0	94.9	95.1	95.3	97.0	98.6	98.8	98.4	95.8	96.9	100.9	102.5	97.7
2008	97.9	95.0	94.8	94.3	95.8	97.6	97.7	97.6	95.3	96.6	98.6	99.6	96.7
2009	94.4	91.6	90.7	90.8	92.7	93.9	93.4	93.2	91.7	92.3	94.8	96.1	93.0
2010	91.7	89.4	89.5	90.2	91.8	93.4	93.6	93.6	91.2	92.5	95.1	97.2	92.4
2011	92.3	90.0	90.0	90.9	91.8	93.6	93.7	93.9	92.4	93.4	96.2	98.2	93.0
2012	93.6	91.2	91.5	91.6	92.9	95.8	95.8	95.8	93.5	94.2	97.9	98.5	94.4
2013	93.7	91.5	91.7	92.9	94.4	95.9	96.1	96.0	93.7	94.5	97.4	99.1	94.7
2014	94.3	92.2	92.1	92.7	94.0	95.5	95.7	89.4	94.3	95.2	97.8	99.4	94.4
2015	94.6	92.1	92.2	92.9	94.3	95.8	95.7	95.9	93.8	94.8	97.8	99.5	95.0
2016	95.0	93.5	93.5	94.0	95.3	96.6	97.1	97.3	95.2	96.0	98.5	99.8	96.0
2017	96.1	93.4	93.1	93.9	94.8	96.5	96.6	96.6	94.5	96.1	98.6	98.6	95.7

1. Employment by Industry: New Hampshire, Selected Years, 2007–2017—*Continued*

(Numbers in thousands, not seasonally adjusted)

Industry and year	January	February	March	April	May	June	July	August	September	October	November	December	Annual average
Transportation and Utilities													
2007	15.3	15.1	15.2	15.3	15.5	15.8	15.3	15.2	15.7	15.5	15.2	15.9	15.4
2008	15.0	14.7	14.7	14.8	15.3	15.4	14.9	14.9	15.3	15.2	15.0	15.5	15.1
2009	14.6	14.5	14.4	14.3	14.6	14.9	13.8	13.6	14.7	14.7	14.6	15.1	14.5
2010	14.2	14.2	14.2	14.2	14.6	14.9	13.9	13.8	14.8	15.0	15.0	15.6	14.5
2011	14.6	14.4	14.5	14.7	15.0	15.2	14.3	14.2	15.1	15.0	14.9	15.4	14.8
2012	14.5	14.4	14.6	14.6	14.9	15.2	14.3	14.6	15.2	15.1	15.0	15.6	14.8
2013	14.7	14.6	14.7	14.8	15.1	15.3	14.5	14.6	15.3	15.1	15.2	15.7	15.0
2014	14.7	14.7	14.8	14.7	15.1	15.4	14.5	14.6	15.5	15.5	15.6	16.1	15.1
2015	15.1	14.9	14.9	14.9	15.4	15.7	15.0	15.1	15.9	15.9	15.9	16.4	15.4
2016	15.8	15.7	15.7	16.0	16.4	16.5	15.7	15.6	16.6	16.6	16.8	17.7	16.3
2017	16.2	16.2	16.1	16.3	16.4	16.7	16.2	16.1	16.8	17.0	17.2	17.8	16.6
Information													
2007	12.3	12.2	12.1	12.3	12.3	12.5	12.6	12.8	12.4	12.4	12.5	12.5	12.4
2008	12.7	12.6	12.5	12.6	12.6	12.8	12.8	12.8	12.5	12.5	12.5	12.5	12.6
2009	12.5	12.4	12.3	12.7	12.6	12.5	12.4	12.3	12.2	12.1	12.0	12.0	12.3
2010	11.8	11.7	11.6	11.5	11.4	11.5	11.4	11.3	11.1	11.1	11.0	11.0	11.4
2011	11.0	10.9	11.0	11.1	11.2	11.4	11.6	11.6	11.6	11.6	11.8	11.8	11.4
2012	11.8	11.8	12.0	12.0	12.1	12.1	12.2	12.2	12.0	12.0	12.0	12.1	12.0
2013	11.9	11.8	11.8	11.9	11.8	12.0	12.0	12.0	11.8	11.7	11.8	11.9	11.9
2014	12.0	12.0	12.0	12.1	12.1	12.2	12.3	12.3	12.2	12.3	12.0	11.9	12.1
2015	12.1	12.1	12.5	12.6	12.6	12.7	12.8	12.7	12.4	12.5	12.6	12.6	12.5
2016	12.6	12.5	12.5	12.5	12.5	12.5	12.7	12.6	12.4	12.5	12.4	12.6	12.5
2017	12.6	12.4	12.4	12.4	12.7	12.9	12.9	12.8	12.5	12.5	12.5	12.5	12.6
Financial Activities													
2007	38.1	38.1	38.2	38.1	38.4	38.8	39.1	39.1	38.4	38.1	38.2	38.4	38.4
2008	38.0	38.0	38.0	38.1	38.2	38.6	38.6	38.5	37.8	37.8	37.6	37.7	38.1
2009	37.3	36.9	36.7	36.7	36.8	37.2	36.9	36.5	36.1	35.9	35.8	35.7	36.5
2010	35.5	35.0	35.1	35.0	34.9	35.2	35.3	35.0	34.5	34.4	34.2	34.3	34.9
2011	33.9	33.6	33.6	33.7	33.5	33.8	33.9	33.8	33.6	33.4	33.4	33.3	33.6
2012	33.1	33.1	33.2	33.3	33.6	34.3	34.3	34.5	34.0	34.1	33.9	33.9	33.8
2013	33.6	33.6	33.6	33.7	34.0	34.4	34.6	34.7	34.0	34.0	33.9	34.0	34.0
2014	33.5	33.4	33.5	33.5	33.7	34.1	34.3	34.3	33.6	33.5	33.3	33.4	33.7
2015	33.1	33.1	33.1	33.2	33.5	33.9	34.5	34.7	34.2	34.2	34.2	34.2	33.8
2016	34.2	34.2	34.2	34.5	34.5	35.2	35.5	35.5	34.9	34.8	34.6	34.6	34.7
2017	34.8	34.7	34.6	34.4	34.6	35.2	35.3	35.3	34.8	35.2	34.9	35.0	34.9
Professional and Business Services													
2007	62.4	63.2	63.1	64.7	65.6	66.6	66.5	67.1	66.3	66.6	66.5	67.3	65.5
2008	65.4	65.0	64.8	67.3	67.7	67.9	67.3	67.5	67.0	66.4	65.8	64.6	66.4
2009	63.2	62.2	61.6	62.5	62.6	63.1	63.0	62.9	62.6	63.2	63.6	63.6	62.8
2010	61.4	61.5	61.8	64.3	64.7	65.2	65.5	65.7	64.9	66.0	66.3	65.8	64.4
2011	64.6	64.6	64.5	66.9	66.9	68.0	68.1	68.3	68.0	68.3	69.4	68.5	67.2
2012	66.8	66.3	66.9	68.7	69.3	70.1	69.8	70.8	70.2	70.6	70.9	70.2	69.2
2013	68.6	69.4	69.0	70.4	71.7	72.4	73.1	73.2	72.5	73.2	74.1	73.8	71.8
2014	72.6	72.7	72.2	74.4	75.5	76.4	76.9	77.5	76.1	76.9	77.1	77.0	75.4
2015	75.1	76.1	75.8	77.5	78.5	79.7	80.0	80.4	79.7	80.3	80.6	80.1	78.7
2016	77.9	78.0	77.8	79.9	80.2	81.2	81.6	81.6	81.0	81.3	81.2	80.9	80.2
2017	79.1	79.4	79.5	81.4	81.9	83.5	83.5	83.4	82.4	82.0	82.4	81.4	81.7
Education and Health Services													
2007	101.9	104.1	104.5	104.6	104.7	104.9	103.7	103.5	105.7	106.0	106.6	106.9	104.8
2008	105.4	106.6	107.4	107.7	108.1	107.5	107.6	107.2	109.1	109.9	110.4	111.0	108.2
2009	109.4	110.8	111.1	111.0	111.2	110.1	109.5	109.4	111.1	111.8	112.1	112.7	110.9
2010	111.0	112.2	112.8	112.5	112.6	112.0	111.1	110.8	112.7	113.1	113.5	113.9	112.4
2011	112.5	113.9	114.5	114.2	114.1	113.0	112.3	112.0	113.7	114.6	114.4	114.7	113.7
2012	113.9	114.9	115.0	114.7	114.6	114.2	113.0	113.2	114.7	115.3	115.7	116.3	114.6
2013	115.3	116.2	116.4	115.4	115.3	114.6	113.6	113.9	115.0	115.8	116.2	116.4	115.3
2014	114.6	115.9	116.0	116.1	115.7	115.5	114.6	114.4	115.7	116.9	117.3	117.5	115.9
2015	117.0	117.5	118.1	118.1	118.3	117.6	116.9	116.3	117.4	119.2	120.2	120.6	118.1
2016	119.7	120.6	121.3	121.6	121.8	120.9	120.8	120.4	122.1	123.1	123.5	124.0	121.7
2017	123.3	123.6	123.5	123.7	123.6	123.5	122.5	121.9	123.0	125.2	125.7	125.1	123.7

1. Employment by Industry: New Hampshire, Selected Years, 2007–2017—*Continued*

(Numbers in thousands, not seasonally adjusted)

Industry and year	January	February	March	April	May	June	July	August	September	October	November	December	Annual average
Leisure and Hospitality													
2007	59.2	59.1	59.2	58.7	63.3	70.3	74.2	74.1	67.9	62.3	59.2	60.4	64.0
2008	59.4	59.5	59.1	59.2	63.7	69.8	74.4	74.3	66.6	62.5	57.9	58.8	63.8
2009	57.5	57.5	57.3	56.9	61.8	67.2	71.9	72.3	65.6	61.4	56.7	58.4	62.0
2010	56.9	57.2	57.1	57.4	61.5	67.9	72.2	72.6	66.8	62.2	57.4	59.5	62.4
2011	58.0	58.1	58.0	58.9	62.1	68.2	73.7	74.1	66.8	62.6	58.8	60.0	63.3
2012	58.7	58.9	59.2	59.3	63.5	71.0	75.0	75.2	67.7	64.4	60.0	61.0	64.5
2013	60.4	60.3	60.6	61.6	65.8	72.2	76.7	76.8	68.9	66.5	61.8	62.8	66.2
2014	61.5	61.8	61.7	61.9	67.0	73.2	77.7	77.5	69.2	67.0	62.1	64.0	67.1
2015	62.8	62.5	63.1	63.3	68.6	74.8	79.6	79.2	70.9	68.4	63.8	64.9	68.5
2016	64.4	64.8	64.5	64.6	68.7	75.7	80.6	80.5	73.1	69.1	65.3	66.2	69.8
2017	65.6	65.1	65.5	65.7	69.8	77.3	81.8	81.5	73.0	71.4	66.9	67.0	70.9
Other Services													
2007	20.8	20.9	21.1	21.0	21.4	22.1	22.4	22.3	21.7	21.7	21.6	21.7	21.6
2008	21.6	21.4	21.3	21.3	21.6	22.0	22.1	22.2	21.8	21.7	21.3	21.2	21.6
2009	20.8	20.7	20.8	20.9	21.2	21.4	21.4	21.6	21.0	20.9	20.8	21.0	21.0
2010	20.8	20.8	20.9	21.0	21.3	21.8	22.1	22.1	21.7	21.8	21.8	21.9	21.5
2011	21.9	21.9	22.2	22.2	22.5	23.0	23.3	23.4	22.8	22.6	22.6	22.6	22.6
2012	22.4	22.3	22.4	22.5	22.8	23.3	23.4	23.5	22.9	23.0	22.8	22.7	22.8
2013	22.6	22.5	22.6	22.9	23.1	23.5	23.7	23.8	23.3	23.1	23.1	23.2	23.1
2014	23.1	23.1	23.1	23.4	23.7	24.1	24.3	24.2	23.7	23.5	23.4	23.2	23.6
2015	23.2	23.2	23.4	23.5	24.0	24.3	24.5	24.4	24.0	23.9	24.0	24.1	23.9
2016	23.9	23.9	23.8	23.9	24.1	24.5	25.1	25.0	24.4	24.5	24.3	24.0	24.3
2017	23.8	23.8	23.9	24.0	24.1	24.9	24.9	24.8	24.1	24.2	24.8	24.2	24.3
Government													
2007	92.1	96.4	96.7	96.5	96.1	90.9	82.0	81.1	94.3	97.7	97.8	98.0	93.3
2008	93.7	97.1	98.3	97.8	97.7	93.2	83.2	84.0	97.6	99.7	101.1	101.0	95.4
2009	96.3	99.1	99.5	99.5	100.0	95.8	83.7	83.9	96.9	100.6	101.4	101.4	96.5
2010	95.2	100.3	101.5	100.2	101.6	94.7	82.9	82.4	95.9	98.2	99.1	98.9	95.9
2011	92.0	96.8	97.1	95.9	96.5	90.0	78.4	77.0	92.2	95.2	96.2	96.4	92.0
2012	91.3	94.5	95.4	94.8	94.6	87.9	80.0	79.6	93.4	95.1	95.8	96.6	91.6
2013	90.2	94.5	93.9	93.9	94.1	88.0	77.1	78.5	90.0	94.5	94.6	95.4	90.4
2014	89.6	93.7	94.1	94.1	92.0	88.7	79.0	79.0	92.1	94.8	95.6	95.7	90.7
2015	89.9	93.3	94.5	94.1	93.7	88.2	78.6	77.6	90.7	93.8	94.8	94.9	90.3
2016	89.2	94.7	94.3	94.3	93.0	87.6	78.3	79.1	92.4	93.9	95.0	94.9	90.6
2017	88.3	93.0	94.2	93.7	93.4	87.3	78.1	79.7	91.3	93.2	93.6	94.1	90.0

2. Average Weekly Hours by Selected Industry: New Hampshire, 2013–2017

(Not seasonally adjusted)

Industry and year	January	February	March	April	May	June	July	August	September	October	November	December	Annual average
Total Private													
2013	32.9	33.0	33.2	33.6	33.5	33.5	33.6	33.9	33.9	33.8	33.5	33.5	33.5
2014	33.2	32.9	33.1	33.3	33.4	33.4	33.4	33.5	33.5	33.5	33.7	33.3	33.4
2015	32.9	32.9	33.5	33.6	33.7	33.5	33.9	34.2	33.7	33.8	33.9	33.7	33.6
2016	33.3	33.2	33.1	33.6	34.0	33.7	34.0	34.0	34.2	34.5	34.1	34.0	33.8
2017	33.9	33.4	33.5	34.4	34.3	34.1	34.2	34.3	34.1	33.8	33.8	33.6	34.0
Goods-Producing													
2013	39.4	39.5	39.8	39.5	39.8	39.9	39.7	40.0	40.4	40.1	39.8	40.3	39.9
2014	39.6	39.0	39.1	39.2	40.1	40.2	39.7	39.5	39.9	39.4	39.7	39.5	39.6
2015	38.9	38.7	39.4	39.1	39.2	39.2	39.5	39.5	38.5	38.9	39.5	39.6	39.2
2016	39.5	38.8	38.8	39.2	40.0	39.8	39.7	39.7	40.0	40.0	39.4	38.4	39.4
2017	38.8	37.3	37.7	38.6	39.1	39.0	38.5	39.4	39.8	39.7	40.2	39.8	39.0
Manufacturing													
2013	40.3	40.0	40.5	40.0	40.3	40.9	40.7	40.5	41.3	41.1	41.1	41.8	40.7
2014	41.1	40.7	40.8	40.5	40.9	41.3	40.5	40.2	40.9	40.4	41.0	40.9	40.8
2015	40.7	40.4	40.6	40.2	40.0	40.3	40.2	40.1	39.4	39.4	40.2	40.4	40.2
2016	40.3	39.5	39.6	39.8	40.6	40.4	40.1	39.9	40.4	40.2	40.1	39.7	40.0
2017	40.2	38.6	38.8	39.2	40.0	40.3	39.7	40.8	41.2	41.3	41.3	41.4	40.2
Trade, Transportation, and Utilities													
2013	32.4	32.5	32.9	33.1	33.3	33.2	33.6	33.7	33.8	33.3	32.3	32.8	33.1
2014	32.4	32.0	32.4	32.4	32.9	32.8	32.8	33.0	33.0	32.6	32.7	32.5	32.6
2015	31.8	32.1	32.9	33.0	33.5	33.4	33.9	34.2	34.4	33.9	33.9	34.0	33.4
2016	33.0	33.0	32.8	33.3	33.7	33.5	33.8	33.6	33.7	33.8	33.6	34.5	33.5
2017	33.4	33.0	32.8	34.3	34.1	33.6	34.0	33.9	33.5	33.4	33.4	33.7	33.6
Professional and Business Services													
2013	35.5	35.1	35.0	36.0	35.9	35.6	34.9	35.2	35.9	36.1	36.2	36.5	35.7
2014	36.4	35.6	35.9	36.5	36.2	36.1	35.9	35.8	36.0	36.2	36.4	35.8	36.1
2015	35.0	35.2	35.6	35.4	36.3	36.1	35.7	36.0	35.4	35.7	36.3	35.8	35.7
2016	34.4	34.9	35.2	35.9	36.8	35.7	35.5	35.6	36.7	37.7	37.3	37.4	36.1
2017	37.6	36.7	36.8	38.8	38.4	37.8	37.8	37.7	37.6	36.3	36.0	35.7	37.3
Education and Health Services													
2013	32.7	33.0	32.9	33.3	33.2	33.1	33.2	33.4	33.3	33.5	33.6	33.4	33.2
2014	33.0	32.6	32.6	32.5	32.8	32.9	32.6	32.8	33.0	33.0	33.0	32.5	32.8
2015	32.6	32.3	32.7	32.8	32.4	32.7	32.7	32.7	32.0	32.2	32.0	31.7	32.4
2016	31.9	31.6	31.4	31.6	31.6	31.5	31.9	32.2	32.9	31.9	32.0	31.9	31.9
2017	31.8	31.4	31.6	31.7	31.5	31.3	31.4	31.4	31.7	31.3	31.3	31.3	31.5
Leisure and Hospitality													
2013	22.3	22.6	23.1	24.0	23.1	24.2	25.2	25.8	23.4	23.3	22.6	21.9	23.5
2014	21.8	22.3	22.6	23.1	22.5	23.1	25.2	25.8	23.6	24.1	24.1	23.5	23.5
2015	22.9	22.9	23.7	24.3	24.3	23.9	25.8	26.2	25.4	25.2	24.7	24.3	24.5
2016	23.7	24.1	24.1	24.9	24.8	25.3	26.2	26.7	25.4	25.7	24.8	24.3	25.1
2017	24.4	23.5	24.1	24.5	25.2	26.0	26.9	27.0	25.0	24.8	24.7	23.8	25.1

3. Average Hourly Earnings by Selected Industry: New Hampshire, 2013–2017

(Dollars, not seasonally adjusted)

Industry and year	January	February	March	April	May	June	July	August	September	October	November	December	Annual average
Total Private													
2013	24.30	24.35	24.31	24.62	24.22	24.13	23.79	23.83	24.47	24.40	24.72	24.59	24.31
2014	24.36	24.60	24.60	24.57	24.33	24.18	23.91	23.83	24.39	24.33	24.44	24.41	24.33
2015	24.61	24.92	24.82	25.09	24.93	24.63	24.52	24.52	24.86	25.21	25.45	25.27	24.90
2016	25.88	25.85	25.66	25.62	25.38	25.11	25.07	25.43	25.85	26.35	26.16	26.23	25.72
2017	26.70	26.75	26.68	26.65	25.98	25.83	25.55	25.65	26.37	26.49	26.36	26.67	26.30
Goods-Producing													
2013	25.75	26.00	25.65	26.14	25.65	25.66	25.41	25.58	25.90	25.90	26.25	26.27	25.85
2014	26.26	26.52	26.53	26.59	26.39	26.41	26.45	26.44	26.62	26.69	26.35	26.16	26.45
2015	26.19	26.60	26.51	26.66	26.64	26.26	26.39	26.28	26.86	27.12	26.61	26.98	26.59
2016	27.52	26.95	26.57	26.58	26.36	26.49	26.62	27.06	27.02	27.21	27.07	27.65	26.92
2017	26.95	27.01	27.27	27.19	26.50	26.56	26.15	26.18	26.25	26.42	26.34	26.46	26.59
Manufacturing													
2013	25.96	25.88	25.79	26.31	25.50	25.76	25.33	25.33	25.58	25.48	25.78	25.76	25.71
2014	25.74	25.95	26.07	25.95	25.52	25.73	25.77	25.93	25.91	26.20	25.99	25.58	25.86
2015	25.75	26.18	26.02	26.40	26.33	25.98	26.01	25.74	26.58	26.65	26.24	26.77	26.22
2016	27.28	26.70	26.54	26.71	26.46	26.84	27.07	27.42	26.86	27.36	27.02	27.48	26.98
2017	26.80	26.90	26.41	26.41	25.47	25.92	25.70	25.70	25.72	25.80	25.50	25.71	25.99
Trade, Transportation, and Utilities													
2013	21.57	21.46	20.92	21.18	20.91	21.02	20.84	20.87	21.38	21.19	21.33	20.86	21.12
2014	20.86	21.26	21.62	21.29	21.09	21.22	21.00	21.16	20.98	21.14	21.39	21.52	21.21
2015	21.72	22.14	21.53	21.81	22.02	21.65	21.80	22.16	22.46	22.79	23.01	22.24	22.12
2016	22.58	22.07	22.09	21.95	22.04	21.53	21.67	21.85	22.02	22.57	22.27	22.04	22.06
2017	22.70	22.49	22.43	22.80	22.19	22.00	22.05	22.19	22.63	22.68	22.25	22.38	22.40
Professional and Business Services													
2013	29.16	28.78	29.24	29.22	28.75	28.94	28.56	28.97	28.73	28.68	28.80	29.26	28.92
2014	28.42	28.93	28.86	28.27	28.96	28.61	28.24	28.16	28.38	28.27	27.98	28.55	28.46
2015	28.99	28.54	28.55	28.40	27.91	28.08	28.31	27.29	27.61	28.30	28.47	28.28	28.22
2016	29.88	30.65	30.55	29.66	28.54	28.39	29.18	29.30	29.63	30.57	30.43	30.42	29.76
2017	31.75	31.89	31.69	30.43	30.21	30.94	30.39	30.04	30.72	31.13	31.00	31.48	30.95
Education and Health Services													
2013	25.59	25.61	26.18	26.73	26.71	26.76	26.96	27.03	27.11	27.04	26.98	26.85	26.63
2014	26.82	26.76	26.39	26.28	26.00	25.90	25.99	25.68	26.36	26.06	25.78	26.00	26.17
2015	25.91	26.34	26.51	27.49	27.64	27.22	27.31	27.16	27.73	27.77	27.74	28.19	27.25
2016	28.41	28.48	28.40	28.45	28.07	27.90	28.20	28.27	28.28	28.57	28.66	28.83	28.38
2017	28.89	29.44	29.29	29.54	29.06	29.34	29.62	29.66	29.47	29.61	29.78	30.08	29.48
Leisure and Hospitality													
2013	13.53	13.92	13.60	13.64	13.69	13.50	12.99	13.07	13.82	14.09	14.17	14.11	13.64
2014	13.74	13.92	13.74	13.94	13.83	13.40	13.07	12.83	13.78	13.86	13.69	13.96	13.61
2015	13.75	14.06	13.92	14.09	13.78	13.44	13.26	13.55	14.06	14.30	14.51	14.54	13.91
2016	14.45	14.66	14.47	14.64	14.60	14.25	13.96	14.24	14.86	14.97	14.89	14.95	14.56
2017	14.70	14.91	14.93	15.05	14.94	14.51	14.17	14.27	14.75	15.02	15.11	15.05	14.75

4. Average Weekly Earnings by Selected Industry: New Hampshire, 2013–2017

(Dollars, not seasonally adjusted)

Industry and year	January	February	March	April	May	June	July	August	September	October	November	December	Annual average
Total Private													
2013	799.47	803.55	807.09	827.23	811.37	808.36	799.34	807.84	829.53	824.72	828.12	823.77	814.39
2014	808.75	809.34	814.26	818.18	812.62	807.61	798.59	798.31	817.07	815.06	823.63	812.85	812.62
2015	809.67	819.87	831.47	843.02	840.14	825.11	831.23	838.58	837.78	852.10	862.76	851.60	836.64
2016	861.80	858.22	849.35	860.83	862.92	846.21	852.38	864.62	884.07	909.08	892.06	891.82	869.34
2017	905.13	893.45	893.78	916.76	891.11	880.80	873.81	879.80	899.22	895.36	890.97	896.11	894.20
Goods-Producing													
2013	1,014.55	1,027.00	1,020.87	1,032.53	1,020.87	1,023.83	1,008.78	1,023.20	1,046.36	1,038.59	1,044.75	1,058.68	1,031.42
2014	1,039.90	1,034.28	1,037.32	1,042.33	1,058.24	1,061.68	1,050.07	1,044.38	1,062.14	1,051.59	1,046.10	1,033.32	1,047.42
2015	1,018.79	1,029.42	1,044.49	1,042.41	1,044.29	1,029.39	1,042.41	1,038.06	1,034.11	1,054.97	1,051.10	1,068.41	1,042.33
2016	1,087.04	1,045.66	1,030.92	1,041.94	1,054.40	1,054.30	1,056.81	1,074.28	1,080.80	1,088.40	1,066.56	1,061.76	1,060.65
2017	1,045.66	1,007.47	1,028.08	1,049.53	1,036.15	1,035.84	1,006.78	1,031.49	1,044.75	1,048.87	1,058.87	1,053.11	1,037.01
Manufacturing													
2013	1,046.19	1,035.20	1,044.50	1,052.40	1,031.28	1,053.58	1,030.93	1,025.87	1,056.45	1,047.23	1,059.56	1,076.77	1,046.40
2014	1,057.91	1,056.17	1,063.66	1,050.98	1,043.77	1,062.65	1,043.69	1,042.39	1,059.72	1,058.48	1,065.59	1,046.22	1,055.09
2015	1,048.03	1,057.67	1,056.41	1,061.28	1,053.20	1,046.99	1,045.60	1,032.17	1,047.25	1,050.01	1,054.85	1,081.51	1,054.04
2016	1,099.38	1,054.65	1,050.98	1,063.06	1,074.28	1,084.34	1,085.51	1,094.06	1,085.14	1,099.87	1,083.50	1,090.96	1,079.20
2017	1,077.36	1,038.34	1,024.71	1,035.27	1,018.80	1,044.58	1,020.29	1,048.56	1,059.66	1,065.54	1,053.15	1,064.39	1,044.80
Trade, Transportation, and Utilities													
2013	698.87	697.45	688.27	701.06	696.30	697.86	700.22	703.32	722.64	705.63	688.96	684.21	699.07
2014	675.86	680.32	700.49	689.80	693.86	696.02	688.80	698.28	692.34	689.16	699.45	699.40	691.45
2015	690.70	710.69	708.34	719.73	737.67	723.11	739.02	757.87	772.62	772.58	780.04	756.16	738.81
2016	745.14	728.31	724.55	730.94	742.75	721.26	732.45	734.16	742.07	762.87	748.27	760.38	739.01
2017	758.18	742.17	735.70	782.04	756.68	739.20	749.70	752.24	758.11	757.51	743.15	754.21	752.64
Professional and Business Services													
2013	1,035.18	1,010.18	1,023.40	1,051.92	1,032.13	1,030.26	996.74	1,019.74	1,031.41	1,035.35	1,042.56	1,067.99	1,032.44
2014	1,034.49	1,029.91	1,036.07	1,031.86	1,048.35	1,032.82	1,013.82	1,008.13	1,021.68	1,023.37	1,018.47	1,022.09	1,027.41
2015	1,014.65	1,004.61	1,016.38	1,005.36	1,013.13	1,013.69	1,010.67	982.44	977.39	1,010.31	1,033.46	1,012.42	1,007.45
2016	1,027.87	1,069.69	1,075.36	1,064.79	1,050.27	1,013.52	1,035.89	1,043.08	1,087.42	1,152.49	1,135.04	1,137.71	1,074.34
2017	1,193.80	1,170.36	1,166.19	1,180.68	1,160.06	1,169.53	1,148.74	1,132.51	1,155.07	1,130.02	1,116.00	1,123.84	1,154.44
Education and Health Services													
2013	836.79	845.13	861.32	890.11	886.77	885.76	895.07	902.80	902.76	905.84	906.53	896.79	884.12
2014	885.06	872.38	860.31	854.10	852.80	852.11	847.27	842.30	869.88	859.98	850.74	845.00	858.38
2015	844.67	850.78	866.88	901.67	895.54	890.09	893.04	888.13	887.36	894.19	887.68	893.62	882.90
2016	906.28	899.97	891.76	899.02	887.01	878.85	899.58	910.29	930.41	911.38	917.12	919.68	905.32
2017	918.70	924.42	925.56	936.42	915.39	918.34	930.07	931.32	934.20	926.79	932.11	941.50	928.62
Leisure and Hospitality													
2013	301.72	314.59	314.16	327.36	316.24	326.70	327.35	337.21	323.39	328.30	320.24	309.01	320.54
2014	299.53	310.42	310.52	322.01	311.18	309.54	329.36	331.01	325.21	334.03	329.93	328.06	319.84
2015	314.88	321.97	329.90	342.39	334.85	321.22	342.11	355.01	357.12	360.36	358.40	353.32	340.80
2016	342.47	353.31	348.73	364.54	362.08	360.53	365.75	380.21	377.44	384.73	369.27	363.29	365.46
2017	358.68	350.39	359.81	368.73	376.49	377.26	381.17	385.29	368.75	372.50	373.22	358.19	370.23

NEW JERSEY
At a Glance

Population:
  2010 census: 8,791,894
  2017 estimate: 9,005,644

Percent change in population:
  2010–2017: 2.4%

Percent change in total nonfarm employment:
  2007–2017: 1.2%

Industry with the largest growth in employment, 2007–2017 (thousands):
  Education and health services, 114.5

Industry with the largest decline or smallest growth in employment, 2007–2017 (thousands):
  Manufacturing, -63.8

Civilian labor force:
  2010: 4,555,330
  2017: 4,518,832

Unemployment rate and rank among states (highest to lowest):
  2010: 9.5%, 20th
  2017: 4.6%, 18th

Over-the-year change in unemployment rates:
  2015–2016: -0.8%
  2016–2017: -0.4%

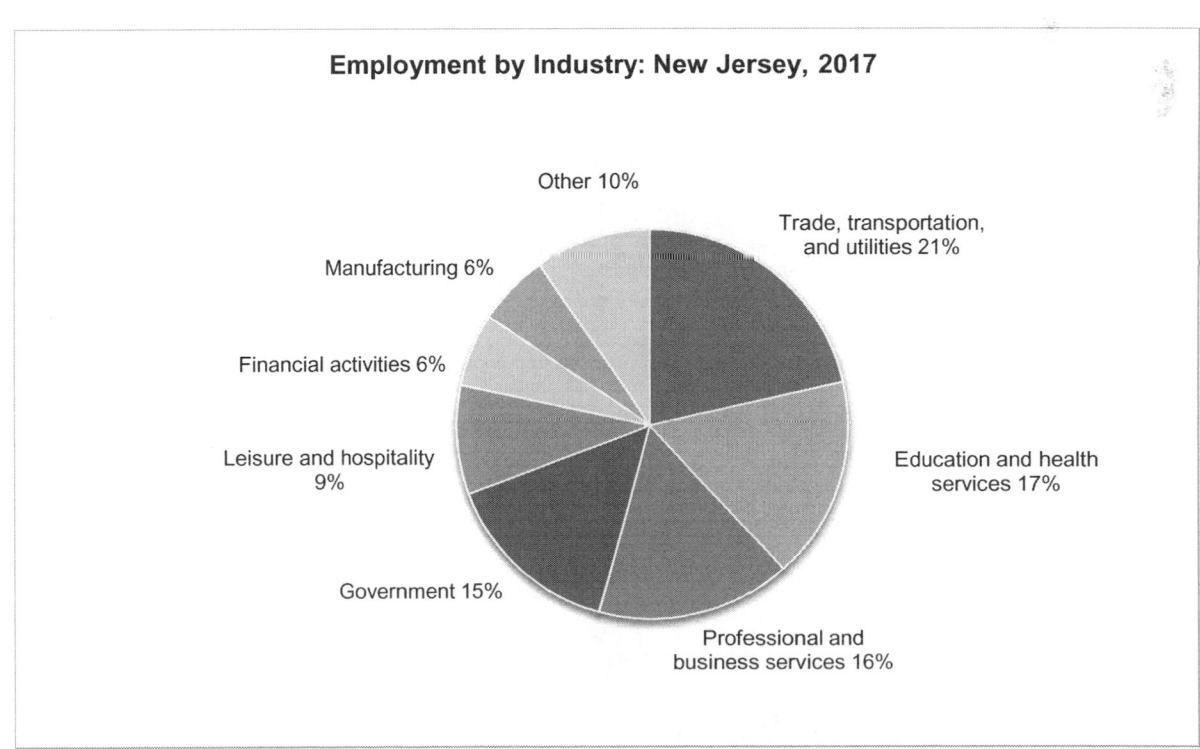

Employment by Industry: New Jersey, 2017

Other 10%

Trade, transportation, and utilities 21%

Manufacturing 6%

Financial activities 6%

Leisure and hospitality 9%

Education and health services 17%

Government 15%

Professional and business services 16%

1. Employment by Industry: New Jersey, Selected Years, 2007–2017

(Numbers in thousands, not seasonally adjusted)

Industry and year	January	February	March	April	May	June	July	August	September	October	November	December	Annual average
Total Nonfarm													
2007	3,996.3	3,991.9	4,024.8	4,053.2	4,104.3	4,156.8	4,098.8	4,083.3	4,074.5	4,101.1	4,115.6	4,125.4	4,077.2
2008	4,013.5	4,016.0	4,041.7	4,060.9	4,091.9	4,136.0	4,070.2	4,041.3	4,036.6	4,034.0	4,024.3	4,015.5	4,048.5
2009	3,880.3	3,869.0	3,874.3	3,889.9	3,929.1	3,963.6	3,893.2	3,872.0	3,877.6	3,882.8	3,894.9	3,903.6	3,894.2
2010	3,774.9	3,767.1	3,797.6	3,848.6	3,893.7	3,936.8	3,865.8	3,840.7	3,842.2	3,861.7	3,874.5	3,880.3	3,848.7
2011	3,754.3	3,764.2	3,793.6	3,836.9	3,866.8	3,916.7	3,862.5	3,838.9	3,863.0	3,876.4	3,895.6	3,903.1	3,847.7
2012	3,794.1	3,811.7	3,849.2	3,862.6	3,910.0	3,971.9	3,896.0	3,886.8	3,909.0	3,922.4	3,924.8	3,949.5	3,890.7
2013	3,837.1	3,854.0	3,887.2	3,907.2	3,948.5	4,008.2	3,945.7	3,939.2	3,953.1	3,965.5	3,989.5	3,989.1	3,935.4
2014	3,860.8	3,862.3	3,894.5	3,950.0	3,997.0	4,044.9	3,985.0	3,969.4	3,986.4	4,003.1	4,025.2	4,036.6	3,967.9
2015	3,899.5	3,906.9	3,939.1	3,980.8	4,033.5	4,082.1	4,029.1	4,015.9	4,030.1	4,060.7	4,083.9	4,090.1	4,012.6
2016	3,954.5	3,968.2	4,005.3	4,048.0	4,084.0	4,143.0	4,095.3	4,078.6	4,100.7	4,115.8	4,139.2	4,149.5	4,073.5
2017	4,021.5	4,036.3	4,059.3	4,095.2	4,152.0	4,219.8	4,141.5	4,128.3	4,146.3	4,160.3	4,182.3	4,186.1	4,127.4
Total Private													
2007	3,348.7	3,332.9	3,362.6	3,391.5	3,444.0	3,493.9	3,480.4	3,471.8	3,442.3	3,443.0	3,452.2	3,462.1	3,427.1
2008	3,362.3	3,354.0	3,377.2	3,397.3	3,428.2	3,471.3	3,444.3	3,431.3	3,401.6	3,377.6	3,362.9	3,354.5	3,396.9
2009	3,228.0	3,206.7	3,208.6	3,222.7	3,261.7	3,296.3	3,265.4	3,255.4	3,237.8	3,222.2	3,228.1	3,238.0	3,239.2
2010	3,124.7	3,110.0	3,137.5	3,186.8	3,221.8	3,270.4	3,245.9	3,242.5	3,227.3	3,227.6	3,233.9	3,243.6	3,206.0
2011	3,134.3	3,132.5	3,159.7	3,200.4	3,234.4	3,285.5	3,270.8	3,261.9	3,256.7	3,245.7	3,259.7	3,270.0	3,226.0
2012	3,178.0	3,182.3	3,215.3	3,232.4	3,283.1	3,340.9	3,308.3	3,310.4	3,303.7	3,292.9	3,294.2	3,318.8	3,271.7
2013	3,217.1	3,219.6	3,252.5	3,283.0	3,327.6	3,383.2	3,360.8	3,361.4	3,348.9	3,335.5	3,355.9	3,357.8	3,316.9
2014	3,245.0	3,233.8	3,265.0	3,312.4	3,365.7	3,414.1	3,395.1	3,389.9	3,379.5	3,375.8	3,392.2	3,406.0	3,347.9
2015	3,288.5	3,282.6	3,313.0	3,351.6	3,408.4	3,457.2	3,445.2	3,438.8	3,428.9	3,438.6	3,455.3	3,464.9	3,397.8
2016	3,345.6	3,345.8	3,378.0	3,421.6	3,459.1	3,519.6	3,511.3	3,503.9	3,496.7	3,493.6	3,512.2	3,525.5	3,459.4
2017	3,411.0	3,412.2	3,433.1	3,470.5	3,529.3	3,594.2	3,556.8	3,552.1	3,543.0	3,536.6	3,552.1	3,559.7	3,512.6
Goods Producing													
2007	474.5	467.6	472.9	481.0	486.7	491.8	490.5	490.7	487.4	485.5	482.3	477.2	482.3
2008	460.1	456.7	460.8	466.4	469.0	472.2	468.9	468.1	464.3	458.7	451.5	441.7	461.5
2009	411.3	404.0	402.9	402.9	405.4	406.4	402.3	401.1	397.5	395.4	392.8	389.8	401.0
2010	372.3	368.3	372.5	382.0	386.5	389.9	389.6	388.9	387.8	387.7	387.4	382.7	383.0
2011	364.3	362.0	368.4	376.3	380.2	384.8	385.4	386.6	384.3	383.2	382.4	379.0	378.1
2012	365.1	363.2	366.2	369.8	372.8	376.8	375.5	376.8	376.0	376.2	376.1	376.9	372.6
2013	363.9	362.5	367.2	374.5	378.5	382.8	382.8	385.3	384.5	385.3	385.0	379.2	377.6
2014	365.5	362.1	367.6	378.6	384.7	388.1	389.6	390.6	390.5	389.7	388.6	385.8	381.8
2015	372.1	368.7	372.7	383.3	389.9	394.9	397.1	397.4	395.3	397.9	397.1	396.0	388.5
2016	383.7	381.3	387.4	393.6	398.0	402.8	404.4	404.5	401.7	403.2	402.6	400.3	397.0
2017	386.3	387.3	389.7	397.6	404.1	409.3	409.3	409.8	407.7	405.9	403.4	400.2	400.9
Service-Providing													
2007	3,521.8	3,524.3	3,551.9	3,572.2	3,617.6	3,665.0	3,608.3	3,592.6	3,587.1	3,615.6	3,633.3	3,648.2	3,594.8
2008	3,553.4	3,559.3	3,580.9	3,594.5	3,622.9	3,663.8	3,601.3	3,573.2	3,572.3	3,575.3	3,572.8	3,573.8	3,587.0
2009	3,469.0	3,465.0	3,471.4	3,487.0	3,523.7	3,557.2	3,490.9	3,470.9	3,480.1	3,487.4	3,502.1	3,513.8	3,493.2
2010	3,402.6	3,398.8	3,425.1	3,466.6	3,507.2	3,546.9	3,476.2	3,451.8	3,454.4	3,474.0	3,487.1	3,497.6	3,465.7
2011	3,390.0	3,402.2	3,425.2	3,460.6	3,486.6	3,531.9	3,477.1	3,452.3	3,478.7	3,493.2	3,513.2	3,524.1	3,469.6
2012	3,429.0	3,448.5	3,483.0	3,492.8	3,537.2	3,595.1	3,520.5	3,510.0	3,533.0	3,546.2	3,548.7	3,572.6	3,518.1
2013	3,473.2	3,491.5	3,520.0	3,532.7	3,570.0	3,625.4	3,562.9	3,553.9	3,568.6	3,580.2	3,604.5	3,609.9	3,557.7
2014	3,495.3	3,500.2	3,526.9	3,571.4	3,612.3	3,656.8	3,595.4	3,578.8	3,595.9	3,613.4	3,636.6	3,650.8	3,586.2
2015	3,527.4	3,538.2	3,566.4	3,597.5	3,643.6	3,687.2	3,632.0	3,618.5	3,634.8	3,662.8	3,686.8	3,694.1	3,624.1
2016	3,570.8	3,586.9	3,617.9	3,654.4	3,686.0	3,740.2	3,690.9	3,674.1	3,699.0	3,712.6	3,736.6	3,749.2	3,676.6
2017	3,635.2	3,649.0	3,669.6	3,697.6	3,747.9	3,810.5	3,732.2	3,718.5	3,738.6	3,754.4	3,778.9	3,785.9	3,726.5
Mining and Logging													
2007	1.6	1.5	1.6	1.7	1.7	1.7	1.7	1.7	1.7	1.7	1.7	1.7	1.7
2008	1.6	1.5	1.6	1.6	1.7	1.7	1.7	1.7	1.7	1.7	1.7	1.6	1.7
2009	1.4	1.4	1.4	1.4	1.5	1.5	1.5	1.6	1.6	1.6	1.5	1.5	1.5
2010	1.2	1.3	1.3	1.4	1.4	1.4	1.4	1.4	1.4	1.4	1.4	1.4	1.4
2011	1.2	1.2	1.2	1.3	1.3	1.4	1.3	1.3	1.3	1.3	1.3	1.3	1.3
2012	1.2	1.2	1.2	1.3	1.3	1.3	1.3	1.3	1.3	1.3	1.3	1.3	1.3
2013	1.2	1.1	1.2	1.3	1.3	1.4	1.4	1.4	1.4	1.4	1.4	1.4	1.3
2014	1.3	1.3	1.4	1.4	1.5	1.5	1.5	1.5	1.4	1.4	1.5	1.5	1.4
2015	1.4	1.4	1.3	1.4	1.4	1.4	1.4	1.4	1.4	1.5	1.4	1.4	1.4
2016	1.3	1.3	1.3	1.3	1.4	1.4	1.4	1.3	1.3	1.3	1.3	1.3	1.3
2017	1.2	1.2	1.3	1.3	1.3	1.3	1.3	1.3	1.4	1.4	1.4	1.3	1.3

1. Employment by Industry: New Jersey, Selected Years, 2007–2017—*Continued*

(Numbers in thousands, not seasonally adjusted)

Industry and year	January	February	March	April	May	June	July	August	September	October	November	December	Annual average
Construction													
2007	161.2	155.4	160.7	169.9	175.7	179.5	179.6	181.0	179.1	178.1	175.5	171.5	172.3
2008	158.7	156.7	160.1	165.4	168.8	171.1	171.1	170.8	168.5	166.2	161.4	154.9	164.5
2009	137.2	134.1	135.7	139.0	141.9	143.0	142.7	142.5	139.8	138.1	136.3	133.4	138.6
2010	119.8	116.7	120.8	129.2	132.4	134.2	135.2	134.8	133.7	134.2	133.9	128.8	129.5
2011	114.2	112.4	118.3	126.9	130.9	134.3	137.2	138.3	137.4	137.5	137.2	134.2	129.9
2012	123.6	122.1	123.3	127.9	129.8	132.5	133.3	134.4	133.7	134.3	134.7	135.3	130.4
2013	125.8	124.6	128.0	135.8	139.2	141.6	142.6	144.4	143.6	144.1	143.5	137.6	137.6
2014	127.6	124.4	129.2	138.1	143.3	145.3	148.1	149.2	149.8	149.6	148.7	145.7	141.6
2015	134.7	132.0	135.4	145.7	150.5	153.1	155.3	155.7	153.6	156.2	155.2	152.8	148.4
2016	143.0	140.3	145.3	152.0	155.3	157.8	159.7	159.8	157.8	158.7	157.7	154.8	153.5
2017	143.8	144.6	146.6	153.9	158.4	161.2	161.2	162.1	160.9	158.6	156.9	151.7	155.0
Manufacturing													
2007	311.7	310.7	310.6	309.4	309.3	310.6	309.2	308.0	306.6	305.7	305.1	304.0	308.4
2008	299.8	298.5	299.1	299.4	298.5	299.4	296.1	295.6	294.1	290.8	288.4	285.2	295.4
2009	272.7	268.5	265.8	262.5	262.0	261.9	258.1	257.0	256.1	255.7	255.0	254.9	260.9
2010	251.3	250.3	250.4	251.4	252.7	254.3	253.0	252.7	252.7	252.1	252.1	252.5	252.1
2011	248.9	248.4	248.9	248.1	248.0	249.1	246.9	247.0	245.6	244.4	243.9	243.5	246.9
2012	240.3	239.9	241.7	240.6	241.7	243.0	240.9	241.1	241.0	240.6	240.1	240.3	240.9
2013	236.9	236.8	238.0	237.4	238.0	239.8	238.8	239.5	239.5	239.8	240.1	240.2	238.7
2014	236.6	236.4	237.0	239.1	239.9	241.3	240.0	239.9	239.3	238.7	238.4	238.6	238.8
2015	236.0	235.3	236.0	236.2	238.0	240.4	240.4	240.3	240.3	240.2	240.5	241.8	238.8
2016	239.4	239.7	240.8	240.3	241.3	243.6	243.3	243.4	242.6	243.2	243.6	244.2	242.1
2017	241.3	241.5	241.8	242.4	244.4	246.8	246.8	246.4	245.4	245.9	245.1	247.2	244.6
Trade, Transportation, and Utilities													
2007	871.3	856.3	860.6	860.9	873.3	884.3	873.1	868.9	869.6	874.2	890.8	905.2	874.0
2008	868.3	855.9	858.5	855.9	863.9	872.2	860.8	856.9	856.4	856.5	862.7	869.7	861.5
2009	828.8	816.2	812.8	808.2	817.8	825.6	813.1	808.9	813.0	814.0	827.3	838.3	818.7
2010	801.1	789.4	792.0	799.7	807.2	817.4	808.5	807.9	807.8	814.4	827.3	841.2	809.5
2011	806.0	798.9	801.6	805.9	811.5	821.8	814.2	813.8	815.3	819.1	835.9	848.6	816.1
2012	817.0	807.7	812.4	809.2	822.4	833.0	820.7	818.5	821.5	824.4	839.9	851.8	823.2
2013	816.8	808.1	812.0	815.1	824.0	835.9	828.3	827.7	828.9	833.4	852.7	862.3	828.8
2014	826.0	815.9	821.1	826.0	836.5	847.0	839.6	839.4	840.3	845.1	864.6	878.0	840.0
2015	840.3	831.0	835.0	840.4	852.2	864.3	856.5	856.0	856.7	862.9	880.5	888.1	855.3
2016	852.5	845.6	849.1	854.3	862.7	870.6	866.9	865.8	868.0	875.8	896.6	907.8	868.0
2017	872.4	862.1	862.6	867.0	876.9	890.3	883.7	884.1	887.2	893.3	910.9	919.8	884.2
Wholesale Trade													
2007	231.9	229.9	231.9	232.0	232.9	234.8	233.6	233.2	232.1	232.5	232.2	232.6	232.5
2008	229.2	230.2	230.5	229.8	231.3	232.2	230.9	229.7	228.4	227.3	225.5	224.5	229.1
2009	220.8	220.5	219.1	218.6	218.5	219.0	216.7	215.4	214.6	214.4	214.3	214.6	217.2
2010	209.3	207.9	207.9	208.9	209.2	210.5	210.0	209.4	208.9	209.0	209.3	209.4	209.1
2011	206.8	208.3	209.4	210.6	211.6	213.1	213.6	213.8	212.4	212.4	212.8	214.4	211.6
2012	211.9	212.5	213.7	213.3	214.4	216.3	215.3	215.1	214.8	214.1	214.6	215.1	214.3
2013	212.2	212.2	213.0	213.4	214.4	216.2	216.0	216.0	215.3	215.1	215.5	215.6	214.6
2014	212.3	212.9	214.0	214.7	216.3	217.9	217.5	217.2	217.1	216.7	217.6	218.5	216.1
2015	215.1	214.8	215.8	216.4	217.6	219.1	218.9	218.7	217.5	217.4	217.6	218.3	217.3
2016	214.7	214.9	215.7	216.2	217.2	218.3	218.7	218.6	217.7	217.7	218.1	218.7	217.2
2017	215.6	215.5	216.0	216.8	217.7	219.7	219.2	219.2	218.6	219.2	218.1	217.5	217.8
Retail Trade													
2007	464.8	452.7	454.2	455.5	463.4	470.9	469.1	466.6	459.7	463.3	479.3	489.9	465.8
2008	463.7	450.0	451.3	449.7	455.3	462.5	460.5	458.3	452.2	454.5	462.4	469.5	457.5
2009	439.4	427.9	426.7	425.0	432.7	439.2	436.5	435.7	432.6	434.9	447.0	456.1	436.1
2010	430.7	421.1	423.7	427.5	434.1	441.9	440.6	441.3	434.5	440.3	451.6	461.9	437.4
2011	435.8	427.7	428.7	431.8	435.6	443.3	442.2	442.5	437.5	440.8	455.1	464.1	440.4
2012	441.3	430.9	433.8	433.3	441.0	448.3	444.7	444.2	439.6	443.0	457.3	465.3	443.6
2013	439.8	431.4	433.6	435.9	442.8	452.2	451.5	452.1	446.7	450.5	466.5	473.5	448.0
2014	446.7	438.1	441.4	444.8	451.4	459.1	459.2	459.1	452.8	456.4	471.0	480.2	455.0
2015	452.6	444.4	446.7	450.0	458.2	466.8	464.5	465.4	459.9	463.2	477.1	480.9	460.8
2016	455.4	448.1	450.1	453.3	458.8	464.9	464.8	465.4	459.2	461.8	475.8	482.9	461.7
2017	459.0	450.5	450.7	453.4	458.9	467.4	465.9	466.0	459.7	463.4	474.9	477.9	462.3

1. Employment by Industry: New Jersey, Selected Years, 2007–2017—*Continued*

(Numbers in thousands, not seasonally adjusted)

Industry and year	January	February	March	April	May	June	July	August	September	October	November	December	Annual average
Transportation and Utilities													
2007	174.6	173.7	174.5	173.4	177.0	178.6	170.4	169.1	177.8	178.4	179.3	182.7	175.8
2008	175.4	175.7	176.7	176.4	177.3	177.5	169.4	168.9	175.8	174.7	174.8	175.7	174.9
2009	168.6	167.8	167.0	164.6	166.6	167.4	159.9	157.8	165.8	164.7	166.0	167.6	165.3
2010	161.1	160.4	160.4	163.3	163.9	165.0	157.9	157.2	164.4	165.1	166.4	169.9	162.9
2011	163.4	162.9	163.5	163.5	164.3	165.4	158.4	157.5	165.4	165.9	168.0	170.1	164.0
2012	163.8	164.3	164.9	162.6	167.0	168.4	160.7	159.2	167.1	167.3	168.0	171.4	165.4
2013	164.8	164.5	165.4	165.8	166.8	167.5	160.8	159.6	166.9	167.8	170.7	173.2	166.2
2014	167.0	164.9	165.7	166.5	168.8	170.0	162.9	163.1	170.4	172.0	176.0	179.3	168.9
2015	172.6	171.8	172.5	174.0	176.4	178.4	173.1	171.9	179.3	182.3	185.8	188.9	177.3
2016	182.4	182.6	183.3	184.8	186.7	187.4	183.4	181.8	191.1	196.3	202.7	206.2	189.1
2017	197.8	196.1	195.9	196.8	200.3	203.2	198.6	198.9	208.9	210.7	217.9	224.4	204.1
Information													
2007	95.2	95.9	96.3	95.5	95.3	95.5	95.3	96.0	94.2	92.8	93.1	92.7	94.8
2008	92.5	93.0	93.0	91.6	91.0	91.5	89.8	89.6	88.4	87.1	87.0	86.5	90.1
2009	85.2	84.6	84.8	83.2	83.5	83.6	82.7	83.3	81.8	80.7	80.7	81.1	82.9
2010	79.1	78.9	79.1	78.1	78.0	78.9	77.4	77.5	77.3	77.0	75.2	77.6	77.8
2011	74.1	73.9	74.0	74.9	75.1	76.2	77.5	71.5	77.2	74.9	75.1	75.1	75.0
2012	75.3	75.7	76.2	75.1	75.2	75.7	76.3	76.1	75.5	74.6	74.6	74.7	75.4
2013	73.4	73.7	73.3	73.4	73.6	74.3	74.4	74.6	73.1	73.3	73.9	73.6	73.7
2014	72.8	72.7	73.0	73.8	74.1	74.4	74.3	74.3	73.6	73.0	72.4	72.9	73.4
2015	72.5	72.2	72.1	72.0	72.9	73.8	73.4	73.0	72.3	72.4	72.8	72.9	72.7
2016	71.3	71.4	71.1	71.8	67.6	72.2	73.2	72.4	71.8	71.0	71.4	72.4	71.5
2017	70.8	72.0	71.4	70.6	71.0	72.2	70.4	70.5	70.2	69.5	70.4	69.9	70.7
Financial Activities													
2007	272.5	271.8	271.8	272.3	273.5	276.1	277.3	276.4	272.1	271.3	271.3	271.2	273.1
2008	269.3	269.2	269.6	268.9	269.6	271.4	270.8	270.0	265.6	262.9	261.8	261.1	267.5
2009	255.8	255.0	253.9	254.3	254.4	255.4	254.6	253.2	250.8	249.0	248.6	248.8	252.8
2010	247.4	247.0	247.4	247.6	248.0	251.1	250.7	250.6	248.7	247.6	247.6	248.2	248.5
2011	245.5	245.4	245.7	245.8	246.6	249.4	248.9	248.9	246.7	244.0	244.2	244.6	246.3
2012	243.0	243.0	244.1	245.2	246.8	250.2	249.5	249.6	247.3	246.7	246.7	248.5	246.7
2013	249.6	249.9	250.5	249.8	250.4	252.9	252.6	251.9	249.2	247.3	246.2	246.5	249.7
2014	241.9	241.0	241.2	241.5	242.9	245.3	245.7	245.2	242.9	242.0	242.7	243.4	243.0
2015	240.1	240.3	241.3	241.8	243.2	245.8	246.5	246.2	243.8	243.3	243.2	244.1	243.3
2016	240.6	240.2	240.2	241.5	242.9	246.0	248.3	248.3	246.1	246.1	245.7	246.8	244.4
2017	244.8	245.5	246.8	247.5	249.3	253.1	253.3	253.0	250.7	247.7	247.2	246.8	248.8
Professional and Business Services													
2007	591.6	592.9	602.0	613.2	619.4	629.4	630.9	633.6	629.2	630.5	631.8	629.8	619.5
2008	609.1	610.4	616.2	622.3	623.4	629.9	628.9	629.5	623.7	618.3	614.4	608.8	619.6
2009	588.6	583.7	583.5	590.7	591.7	596.9	593.3	593.9	590.9	589.5	589.4	587.8	590.0
2010	565.2	567.6	574.9	588.1	591.7	601.7	598.3	600.8	599.4	601.2	602.3	601.6	591.1
2011	584.5	585.5	591.5	602.1	605.2	614.2	613.5	615.7	615.8	617.7	619.3	616.4	606.8
2012	595.5	599.2	607.3	614.7	620.8	630.8	625.0	631.8	633.6	631.9	636.8	637.9	622.1
2013	610.5	613.7	622.7	626.6	634.1	643.3	640.3	644.8	643.1	639.2	642.4	641.5	633.5
2014	616.1	617.2	619.4	631.1	637.2	644.0	641.4	643.4	644.6	648.7	652.9	653.7	637.5
2015	624.5	626.6	633.9	642.1	647.8	653.2	653.3	655.5	657.3	665.5	668.0	666.7	649.5
2016	635.2	637.4	644.8	658.4	662.0	672.2	669.8	671.3	674.3	672.1	676.4	678.9	662.7
2017	646.3	647.9	652.7	660.0	670.7	681.7	669.7	670.0	672.0	672.3	676.8	673.4	666.1
Education and Health Services													
2007	570.9	576.0	580.5	577.3	585.3	580.7	574.7	571.6	577.7	587.1	585.9	590.0	579.8
2008	583.2	588.2	591.0	590.8	592.5	593.3	584.1	582.0	588.4	593.6	595.7	600.2	590.3
2009	589.7	594.9	597.5	598.1	600.9	601.6	590.0	588.1	595.2	603.1	605.8	610.4	597.9
2010	599.0	600.4	604.3	604.2	605.2	603.5	592.2	589.2	596.7	606.2	607.9	607.5	601.4
2011	598.4	603.6	607.5	607.8	609.6	609.1	597.9	594.9	606.4	611.9	614.9	619.1	606.8
2012	611.0	619.4	624.3	620.9	626.3	625.3	611.2	609.4	621.3	628.7	626.8	632.6	621.4
2013	623.6	630.1	635.6	637.3	640.6	637.0	624.0	622.1	633.8	640.7	646.3	646.3	634.8
2014	633.5	636.5	644.1	647.6	652.5	650.6	639.6	635.8	648.8	656.2	660.4	664.3	647.5
2015	649.9	655.0	660.8	660.5	664.2	662.7	649.7	645.5	658.5	667.6	671.6	673.7	660.0
2016	663.0	668.4	673.7	674.5	676.2	675.7	664.5	660.9	678.7	687.0	688.5	689.8	675.1
2017	682.3	687.6	692.5	694.7	698.9	696.6	678.9	675.3	694.0	707.5	709.1	713.7	694.3

1. Employment by Industry: New Jersey, Selected Years, 2007–2017—*Continued*

(Numbers in thousands, not seasonally adjusted)

Industry and year	January	February	March	April	May	June	July	August	September	October	November	December	Annual average
Leisure and Hospitality													
2007	313.2	312.8	318.2	328.0	345.6	367.9	371.9	369.2	349.7	337.9	333.4	332.1	340.0
2008	317.3	317.9	325.0	336.2	352.2	371.7	373.4	368.9	351.7	337.7	327.5	324.4	342.0
2009	309.1	308.3	313.0	323.8	344.8	361.3	365.7	363.7	348.7	330.3	323.1	321.6	334.5
2010	303.4	302.0	309.6	326.7	343.4	362.7	365.7	364.5	349.7	333.1	325.9	323.5	334.2
2011	303.7	305.2	311.7	326.9	344.2	364.1	368.7	367.1	350.5	334.2	327.4	325.8	335.8
2012	311.1	314.0	323.2	334.6	353.8	379.9	382.2	381.2	363.8	346.3	329.9	331.6	346.0
2013	317.8	319.6	328.2	341.5	360.3	386.4	388.7	386.2	370.5	350.9	343.8	342.3	353.0
2014	325.7	325.0	333.4	346.9	368.8	391.9	393.2	390.7	370.8	353.6	343.1	339.8	356.9
2015	324.0	324.1	331.0	345.0	369.3	389.8	397.3	395.0	377.5	360.9	353.3	354.2	360.1
2016	332.6	334.6	343.6	357.2	378.0	404.5	409.9	407.2	385.9	367.3	359.5	357.2	369.8
2017	338.9	340.8	347.6	361.4	384.5	412.9	415.3	414.0	388.7	368.3	361.7	363.3	374.8
Other Services													
2007	159.5	159.6	160.3	163.3	164.9	168.2	166.7	165.4	162.4	163.7	163.6	163.9	163.5
2008	162.5	162.7	163.1	165.2	166.6	169.1	167.6	166.3	163.1	162.8	162.3	162.1	164.5
2009	159.5	160.0	160.2	161.5	163.2	165.5	163.7	163.2	159.9	160.2	160.4	160.2	161.5
2010	157.2	156.4	157.7	160.4	161.8	165.2	163.5	163.1	159.9	160.4	160.3	161.3	160.6
2011	157.8	158.0	159.3	160.7	162.0	165.9	164.7	163.4	160.5	160.7	160.5	161.4	161.2
2012	160.0	160.1	161.6	162.9	165.0	169.2	167.9	167.0	164.7	164.1	163.4	164.8	164.2
2013	161.5	162.0	163.0	164.8	166.1	170.6	169.7	168.8	165.8	165.4	165.6	166.1	165.8
2014	163.5	163.4	165.2	166.9	169.0	172.8	171.7	170.5	168.0	167.5	167.5	168.1	167.8
2015	165.1	164.7	166.2	166.5	168.9	172.7	171.4	170.2	167.5	168.1	168.8	169.2	168.3
2016	166.7	166.9	168.1	170.3	171.7	175.6	174.3	173.5	170.2	171.1	171.5	172.3	171.0
2017	169.2	169.0	169.8	171.7	173.9	178.1	176.2	175.4	172.5	172.1	172.6	172.6	172.8
Government													
2007	647.6	659.0	662.2	661.7	660.3	662.9	618.4	611.5	632.2	658.1	663.4	663.3	650.1
2008	651.2	662.0	664.5	663.6	663.7	664.7	625.9	610.0	635.0	656.4	661.4	661.0	651.6
2009	652.3	662.3	665.7	667.2	667.4	667.3	627.8	616.6	639.8	660.6	666.8	665.6	655.0
2010	650.2	657.1	660.1	661.8	671.9	666.4	619.9	598.2	614.9	634.1	640.6	636.7	642.7
2011	620.0	631.7	633.9	636.5	632.4	631.2	591.7	577.0	606.3	630.7	635.9	633.1	621.7
2012	616.1	629.4	633.9	630.2	626.9	631.0	587.7	576.4	605.3	629.5	630.6	630.7	619.0
2013	620.0	634.4	634.7	624.2	620.9	625.0	584.9	577.8	604.2	630.0	633.6	631.3	618.4
2014	615.8	628.5	629.5	637.6	631.3	630.8	589.9	579.5	606.9	627.3	633.0	630.6	620.1
2015	611.0	624.3	626.1	629.2	625.1	624.9	583.9	577.1	601.2	622.1	628.6	625.2	614.9
2016	608.9	622.4	627.3	626.4	624.9	623.4	584.0	574.7	604.0	622.2	627.0	624.0	614.1
2017	610.5	624.1	626.2	624.7	622.7	625.6	584.7	576.2	603.3	623.7	630.2	626.4	614.9

2. Average Weekly Hours by Selected Industry: New Jersey, 2013–2017

(Not seasonally adjusted)

Industry and year	January	February	March	April	May	June	July	August	September	October	November	December	Annual average
Total Private													
2013	33.3	33.4	33.6	33.4	33.6	33.8	33.5	33.5	34.0	33.6	33.6	33.8	33.6
2014	33.4	33.0	33.8	33.6	33.6	33.9	33.8	33.8	33.8	33.6	33.9	33.8	33.7
2015	33.2	33.5	33.7	33.7	33.7	33.7	33.9	34.2	33.9	33.9	34.0	34.0	33.8
2016	33.6	33.6	33.5	33.8	34.0	33.9	34.1	33.9	34.8	35.1	34.5	34.7	34.1
2017	34.4	33.8	33.7	34.5	34.0	33.8	34.1	33.8	33.9	34.1	34.0	34.0	34.0
Goods-Producing													
2013	38.5	38.2	38.5	38.4	38.9	38.6	38.4	38.5	38.8	38.7	39.4	39.3	38.7
2014	38.5	37.1	39.1	38.8	38.9	39.1	38.8	38.5	39.0	38.6	38.5	39.3	38.7
2015	38.3	37.9	38.8	38.6	38.7	38.9	38.6	38.6	38.1	39.0	38.6	39.1	38.6
2016	38.4	38.2	38.5	38.8	38.5	39.1	39.2	38.9	38.9	39.3	38.7	39.1	38.8
2017	37.9	37.4	37.3	38.5	38.7	38.8	38.5	38.9	39.0	39.0	39.1	39.1	38.5
Construction													
2013	35.9	35.5	35.7	35.4	36.5	35.9	36.5	36.3	36.4	36.5	37.3	36.0	36.2
2014	36.3	34.4	38.1	37.9	38.1	37.7	37.9	37.6	38.5	37.7	36.9	38.1	37.5
2015	37.1	36.6	38.1	37.8	38.5	38.3	37.9	37.6	37.1	39.1	37.2	38.1	37.8
2016	37.2	37.1	38.0	38.5	38.5	39.1	39.3	38.8	38.0	38.9	37.8	38.2	38.3
2017	37.6	37.1	36.7	37.8	36.5	37.0	37.3	37.4	37.1	36.9	36.7	37.3	37.1
Manufacturing													
2013	39.7	39.4	39.7	39.7	40.0	39.9	39.3	39.7	40.1	39.9	40.6	40.9	39.9
2014	39.6	38.5	39.7	39.3	39.3	39.9	39.3	39.0	39.3	39.3	39.4	40.0	39.4
2015	38.9	38.5	39.1	39.0	38.7	39.2	39.0	39.1	38.6	38.9	39.4	39.7	39.0
2016	39.1	38.8	38.8	38.9	38.4	39.0	39.0	38.9	39.4	39.4	39.3	39.6	39.0
2017	37.9	37.4	37.6	38.8	40.1	40.0	39.4	40.0	40.3	40.5	40.8	40.5	39.5
Trade, Transportation, and Utilities													
2013	33.3	33.6	34.0	33.9	34.1	34.2	34.3	34.0	34.6	34.0	33.8	34.2	34.0
2014	33.8	33.2	34.1	34.2	34.0	33.9	34.2	34.2	34.3	33.9	34.0	34.4	34.0
2015	33.4	33.6	33.8	34.0	34.2	34.0	34.3	34.5	34.7	34.0	34.3	34.2	34.1
2016	33.4	33.6	33.7	33.9	34.4	34.3	34.6	34.4	34.6	34.7	34.5	35.3	34.3
2017	34.3	33.9	33.8	34.8	34.7	34.8	35.0	34.7	35.1	34.9	35.1	35.2	34.7
Financial Activities													
2013	36.1	36.2	36.1	35.6	35.5	37.0	35.4	35.9	36.9	35.5	35.3	36.7	36.0
2014	35.6	37.1	36.4	36.1	36.0	37.0	35.7	36.2	36.2	36.5	37.0	36.3	36.3
2015	36.3	37.0	37.3	36.6	36.5	36.6	37.0	37.4	36.5	36.8	37.4	36.9	36.9
2016	37.1	37.2	37.2	37.0	38.0	37.0	36.8	37.2	37.1	38.0	36.8	36.7	37.2
2017	38.1	36.7	36.7	38.0	36.8	36.7	37.4	36.4	36.8	38.1	37.1	37.2	37.2
Professional and Business Services													
2013	35.2	35.9	36.3	36.1	36.2	36.8	35.8	35.9	36.7	35.9	36.2	36.0	36.1
2014	35.6	34.9	35.8	35.6	35.9	36.7	35.9	36.0	35.7	35.5	36.1	35.4	35.8
2015	35.2	36.0	35.8	35.5	35.5	35.4	35.4	35.8	35.1	35.7	35.5	35.9	35.6
2016	35.7	35.6	35.6	36.1	36.1	35.7	35.7	35.6	35.9	36.4	35.7	35.5	35.8
2017	35.7	34.7	34.8	35.8	34.9	35.1	35.3	34.9	34.9	35.7	35.3	35.1	35.2
Education and Health Services													
2013	31.2	31.2	31.0	30.6	30.7	31.0	30.9	30.6	30.8	30.6	30.7	30.5	30.8
2014	30.7	30.5	30.9	30.9	30.7	30.8	31.0	31.0	31.1	31.0	31.2	31.3	30.9
2015	31.2	31.4	31.5	31.4	31.6	31.6	31.7	31.9	31.7	31.7	31.9	31.6	31.6
2016	32.0	31.7	31.7	31.8	32.0	32.0	31.9	31.8	31.9	32.1	31.9	31.9	31.9
2017	32.2	31.9	31.7	32.1	31.9	32.2	32.3	32.0	32.1	32.3	32.3	32.6	32.1
Leisure and Hospitality													
2013	25.4	25.7	26.0	26.1	26.5	26.6	27.0	27.4	27.3	26.9	27.0	26.8	26.6
2014	26.4	26.0	27.0	26.9	27.3	27.4	28.1	28.2	27.3	27.1	26.9	26.4	27.1
2015	26.0	26.1	26.2	26.9	26.7	26.6	27.4	27.7	27.1	26.8	26.8	26.5	26.8
2016	26.1	26.8	26.6	26.8	26.8	26.6	27.6	27.6	28.1	27.9	27.6	27.0	27.1
2017	26.8	26.5	26.6	27.5	27.0	26.4	27.2	26.9	26.4	26.4	26.1	25.8	26.6
Other Services													
2013	31.8	31.1	31.8	31.3	30.7	31.2	31.2	31.9	30.7	30.1	29.7	30.2	31.0
2014	29.1	29.3	29.5	28.8	29.4	29.7	30.0	29.9	29.8	29.3	29.9	29.5	29.5
2015	29.1	29.1	29.2	28.8	29.2	29.3	30.0	30.9	29.8	30.1	30.3	30.1	29.7
2016	29.7	29.5	28.9	29.8	30.1	30.2	31.1	30.6	30.6	30.5	30.4	30.7	30.2
2017	31.0	30.3	29.7	30.3	29.5	29.2	30.4	29.5	29.3	29.8	30.1	30.3	29.9

3. Average Hourly Earnings by Selected Industry: New Jersey, 2013–2017

(Dollars, not seasonally adjusted)

Industry and year	January	February	March	April	May	June	July	August	September	October	November	December	Annual average
Total Private													
2013	26.83	26.87	26.76	27.07	26.69	26.93	26.42	26.43	27.03	26.85	26.84	26.85	26.80
2014	26.66	27.10	27.09	26.80	26.63	26.74	26.62	26.64	27.02	27.04	27.42	27.15	26.91
2015	27.68	28.13	28.13	27.55	27.61	27.59	27.46	27.72	27.79	27.82	28.12	27.73	27.78
2016	27.82	27.99	27.99	28.07	28.27	27.77	27.75	27.93	28.19	28.72	28.37	28.43	28.11
2017	29.18	28.51	28.23	28.63	29.64	29.38	29.36	29.20	29.44	29.87	29.44	29.16	29.18
Goods-Producing													
2013	28.87	28.76	28.75	29.16	28.83	28.99	28.67	28.86	28.95	28.54	28.24	27.42	28.67
2014	27.60	27.62	28.21	28.49	28.49	28.86	29.32	29.29	29.65	29.49	29.86	30.05	28.93
2015	29.58	29.95	30.01	29.99	30.21	29.98	30.08	29.95	29.98	30.05	30.25	30.12	30.02
2016	30.04	29.95	30.01	30.47	30.98	30.69	30.63	30.66	30.67	31.05	30.75	31.24	30.60
2017	31.53	31.22	31.54	31.60	31.01	31.18	31.47	31.04	31.09	31.05	30.73	31.69	31.26
Construction													
2013	34.55	34.67	34.84	35.30	34.79	33.98	33.58	33.83	33.81	33.38	33.46	33.24	34.05
2014	32.65	32.95	33.61	33.98	34.02	34.46	35.15	35.30	36.19	35.86	36.12	36.08	34.78
2015	35.07	35.75	35.60	35.46	35.54	35.68	35.49	34.91	34.78	34.60	34.67	34.08	35.12
2016	34.29	34.67	34.78	34.41	34.72	34.05	34.37	34.31	34.91	35.30	34.91	35.44	34.68
2017	35.40	35.74	36.61	36.35	35.45	35.88	35.74	35.30	35.45	35.44	34.68	35.82	35.65
Manufacturing													
2013	25.63	25.60	25.54	25.85	25.75	26.16	25.89	26.18	26.19	25.80	25.42	25.83	25.82
2014	26.24	26.15	26.42	26.41	26.22	26.52	26.61	26.51	26.50	26.38	26.50	26.84	26.44
2015	26.74	27.12	27.19	27.01	27.18	26.86	27.10	27.18	27.28	27.39	27.77	27.87	27.23
2016	27.69	27.37	27.23	28.13	28.67	28.60	28.22	28.24	27.93	28.42	28.15	28.58	28.11
2017	29.12	28.48	28.52	28.69	28.23	28.08	28.55	28.27	28.22	28.20	28.22	28.94	28.45
Trade, Transportation, and Utilities													
2013	22.79	23.02	23.09	23.61	23.02	23.09	23.07	22.92	23.27	23.17	23.09	22.93	23.09
2014	23.53	23.75	23.55	23.52	23.38	23.15	23.39	23.53	23.72	23.72	23.94	23.42	23.55
2015	24.25	24.62	24.50	23.99	24.24	24.38	24.52	24.89	25.01	24.92	24.84	23.67	24.49
2016	23.91	24.09	24.18	24.18	24.26	24.34	24.61	24.67	25.00	25.11	24.97	24.71	24.51
2017	26.21	26.42	25.02	24.88	25.40	24.79	25.46	25.64	25.82	26.00	25.65	25.43	25.56
Financial Activities													
2013	36.33	35.95	35.57	36.13	35.50	36.72	34.32	34.13	34.39	34.14	34.11	33.57	35.08
2014	33.07	33.54	34.08	32.45	33.12	33.67	33.61	33.52	34.17	34.07	35.05	34.18	33.72
2015	34.93	36.13	36.41	35.37	35.72	35.67	35.42	36.17	35.94	35.64	36.77	35.91	35.84
2016	36.20	36.52	36.67	36.72	38.45	36.55	37.54	38.90	38.79	40.29	39.64	38.58	37.92
2017	38.60	38.21	37.79	39.34	38.38	38.55	38.60	39.06	38.77	40.17	39.90	39.95	38.95
Professional and Business Services													
2013	33.14	33.26	33.06	33.05	32.79	33.10	32.63	32.93	33.90	33.40	33.57	34.19	33.25
2014	32.92	34.33	33.96	33.24	32.63	32.94	32.32	32.14	32.45	32.52	33.15	32.78	32.94
2015	31.70	32.59	32.70	31.66	31.63	31.78	31.88	32.47	32.61	32.29	32.60	31.62	32.13
2016	32.71	32.87	33.05	33.15	33.21	32.48	32.27	32.40	32.22	33.00	32.45	32.78	32.71
2017	33.70	31.08	31.44	32.75	33.64	33.26	34.27	33.76	33.98	34.97	34.06	34.58	33.47
Education and Health Services													
2013	25.77	25.73	25.75	26.18	25.92	26.11	25.96	25.55	25.81	25.76	25.92	26.08	25.88
2014	25.37	25.44	25.32	25.46	25.67	25.83	25.89	26.08	26.24	26.03	26.23	26.31	25.83
2015	26.95	27.08	27.12	27.10	27.41	27.66	27.66	27.65	27.46	27.69	27.92	28.10	27.49
2016	27.33	27.59	27.34	27.50	27.26	27.14	27.10	27.01	27.36	27.34	27.10	27.38	27.29
2017	27.28	27.28	27.11	27.15	27.05	26.87	27.01	26.93	27.01	27.09	27.10	27.22	27.09
Leisure and Hospitality													
2013	14.00	14.12	13.91	14.10	14.18	14.15	13.96	13.97	13.99	14.18	14.19	14.54	14.11
2014	14.54	14.49	14.53	14.67	14.67	14.55	14.39	14.33	14.69	14.76	14.83	15.06	14.62
2015	15.01	15.10	14.93	14.91	15.05	14.89	14.71	14.65	14.86	14.89	14.90	14.98	14.90
2016	14.96	14.87	14.87	14.88	14.95	14.89	14.77	14.74	15.17	15.48	15.37	15.52	15.04
2017	15.71	15.64	15.62	15.96	15.89	16.78	16.44	16.47	16.78	16.76	16.71	16.93	16.32
Other Services													
2013	22.26	22.71	21.76	22.17	22.58	22.38	21.61	21.61	22.78	22.76	22.46	23.22	22.35
2014	23.32	23.17	23.27	23.02	22.72	22.65	22.60	22.32	23.24	23.04	22.88	22.76	22.91
2015	22.61	22.34	22.47	22.48	21.72	21.71	21.12	20.99	21.77	22.02	22.61	22.56	22.02
2016	22.34	23.65	23.54	23.74	23.63	23.23	22.55	22.38	23.48	24.17	23.74	24.08	23.38
2017	25.91	26.00	25.74	25.85	25.72	25.55	23.94	23.75	25.45	25.16	25.19	25.55	25.31

4. Average Weekly Earnings by Selected Industry: New Jersey, 2013–2017

(Dollars, not seasonally adjusted)

Industry and year	January	February	March	April	May	June	July	August	September	October	November	December	Annual average
Total Private													
2013	893.44	897.46	899.14	904.14	896.78	910.23	885.07	885.41	919.02	902.16	901.82	907.53	900.48
2014	890.44	894.30	915.64	900.48	894.77	906.49	899.76	900.43	913.28	908.54	929.54	917.67	906.87
2015	918.98	942.36	947.98	928.44	930.46	929.78	930.89	948.02	942.08	943.10	956.08	942.82	938.96
2016	934.75	940.46	937.67	948.77	961.18	941.40	946.28	946.83	981.01	1,008.07	978.77	986.52	958.55
2017	1,003.79	963.64	951.35	987.74	1,007.76	993.04	1,001.18	986.96	998.02	1,018.57	1,000.96	991.44	992.12
Goods-Producing													
2013	1,111.50	1,098.63	1,106.88	1,119.74	1,121.49	1,119.01	1,100.93	1,111.11	1,123.26	1,104.50	1,112.66	1,077.61	1,109.53
2014	1,062.60	1,024.70	1,103.01	1,105.41	1,108.26	1,128.43	1,137.62	1,127.67	1,156.35	1,138.31	1,149.61	1,180.97	1,119.59
2015	1,132.91	1,135.11	1,164.39	1,157.61	1,169.13	1,166.22	1,161.09	1,156.07	1,142.24	1,171.95	1,167.65	1,177.69	1,158.77
2016	1,153.54	1,144.09	1,155.39	1,182.24	1,192.73	1,199.98	1,200.70	1,192.67	1,193.06	1,220.27	1,190.03	1,221.48	1,187.28
2017	1,194.99	1,167.63	1,176.44	1,216.60	1,200.09	1,209.78	1,211.60	1,207.46	1,212.51	1,210.95	1,201.54	1,239.08	1,203.51
Construction													
2013	1,240.35	1,230.79	1,243.79	1,249.62	1,251.59	1,219.88	1,225.67	1,228.03	1,230.68	1,218.37	1,248.06	1,196.64	1,232.61
2014	1,185.20	1,133.48	1,280.54	1,287.84	1,296.16	1,299.14	1,332.19	1,327.28	1,393.32	1,351.92	1,332.83	1,374.65	1,304.25
2015	1,301.10	1,308.45	1,356.36	1,340.39	1,368.29	1,366.54	1,345.07	1,312.62	1,290.34	1,352.86	1,289.72	1,298.45	1,327.54
2016	1,275.59	1,286.26	1,321.64	1,324.79	1,336.72	1,331.36	1,350.74	1,331.23	1,326.58	1,373.17	1,319.60	1,353.81	1,328.24
2017	1,331.04	1,325.95	1,343.59	1,374.03	1,293.93	1,327.56	1,333.10	1,320.22	1,315.20	1,307.74	1,272.76	1,336.09	1,322.62
Manufacturing													
2013	1,017.51	1,008.64	1,013.94	1,026.25	1,030.00	1,043.78	1,017.48	1,039.35	1,050.22	1,029.42	1,032.05	1,056.45	1,030.22
2014	1,039.10	1,006.78	1,048.87	1,037.91	1,030.45	1,058.15	1,045.77	1,033.89	1,041.45	1,036.73	1,044.10	1,073.60	1,041.74
2015	1,040.19	1,044.12	1,063.13	1,053.39	1,051.87	1,052.91	1,056.90	1,062.74	1,053.01	1,065.47	1,094.14	1,106.44	1,061.97
2016	1,082.68	1,061.96	1,056.52	1,094.26	1,100.93	1,115.40	1,100.58	1,098.54	1,100.44	1,119.75	1,106.30	1,131.77	1,096.29
2017	1,103.65	1,065.15	1,072.35	1,113.17	1,132.02	1,123.20	1,124.87	1,130.80	1,137.27	1,142.10	1,151.38	1,172.07	1,123.78
Trade, Transportation, and Utilities													
2013	758.91	773.47	785.06	800.38	784.98	789.68	791.30	779.28	805.14	787.78	780.44	784.21	785.06
2014	795.31	788.50	803.06	804.38	794.92	784.79	799.94	804.73	813.60	804.11	813.96	805.65	800.70
2015	809.95	827.23	828.10	815.66	829.01	828.92	841.04	858.71	867.85	847.28	852.01	809.51	835.11
2016	798.59	809.42	814.87	819.70	834.54	834.86	851.51	848.65	865.00	871.32	861.47	872.26	840.69
2017	899.00	895.64	845.68	865.82	881.38	862.69	891.10	889.71	906.28	907.40	900.32	895.14	886.93
Financial Activities													
2013	1,311.51	1,301.39	1,284.08	1,286.23	1,260.25	1,358.64	1,214.93	1,225.27	1,268.99	1,211.97	1,204.08	1,232.02	1,262.88
2014	1,177.29	1,244.33	1,240.51	1,171.45	1,192.32	1,245.79	1,199.88	1,213.42	1,236.95	1,243.56	1,296.85	1,240.73	1,224.04
2015	1,267.96	1,336.81	1,358.09	1,294.54	1,303.78	1,305.52	1,310.54	1,352.76	1,311.81	1,311.55	1,375.20	1,325.08	1,322.50
2016	1,343.02	1,358.54	1,364.12	1,358.64	1,461.10	1,352.35	1,381.47	1,447.08	1,439.11	1,531.02	1,458.75	1,415.89	1,410.62
2017	1,470.66	1,402.31	1,386.89	1,494.92	1,412.38	1,414.79	1,443.64	1,421.78	1,426.74	1,530.48	1,480.29	1,486.14	1,448.94
Professional and Business Services													
2013	1,166.53	1,194.03	1,200.08	1,193.11	1,187.00	1,218.08	1,168.15	1,182.19	1,244.13	1,199.06	1,215.23	1,230.84	1,200.33
2014	1,171.95	1,198.12	1,215.77	1,183.34	1,171.42	1,208.90	1,160.29	1,157.04	1,158.47	1,154.46	1,196.72	1,160.41	1,179.25
2015	1,115.84	1,173.24	1,170.66	1,123.93	1,122.87	1,125.01	1,128.55	1,162.43	1,144.61	1,152.75	1,157.30	1,135.16	1,143.83
2016	1,167.75	1,170.17	1,176.58	1,196.72	1,198.88	1,159.54	1,152.04	1,153.44	1,156.70	1,201.20	1,158.47	1,163.69	1,171.02
2017	1,203.09	1,078.48	1,094.11	1,172.45	1,174.04	1,167.43	1,209.73	1,178.22	1,185.90	1,248.43	1,202.32	1,213.76	1,178.14
Education and Health Services													
2013	804.02	802.78	798.25	801.11	795.74	809.41	802.16	781.83	794.95	788.26	795.74	795.44	797.10
2014	778.86	775.92	782.39	786.71	788.07	795.56	802.59	808.48	816.06	806.93	818.38	823.50	798.15
2015	840.84	850.31	854.28	850.94	866.16	874.06	876.82	882.04	870.48	877.77	890.65	887.96	868.68
2016	874.56	874.60	866.68	874.50	872.32	868.48	864.49	858.92	872.78	877.61	864.49	873.42	870.55
2017	878.42	870.23	859.39	871.52	862.90	865.21	872.42	861.76	867.02	875.01	875.33	887.37	869.59
Leisure and Hospitality													
2013	355.60	362.88	361.66	368.01	375.77	376.39	376.92	382.78	381.93	381.44	383.13	389.67	375.33
2014	383.86	376.74	392.31	394.62	400.49	398.67	404.36	404.11	401.04	400.00	398.93	397.58	396.20
2015	390.26	394.11	391.17	401.08	401.84	396.07	403.05	405.81	402.71	399.05	399.32	396.97	399.32
2016	390.46	398.52	395.54	398.78	400.66	396.07	407.65	406.82	426.28	431.89	424.21	419.04	407.58
2017	421.03	414.46	415.49	438.90	429.03	442.99	447.17	443.04	442.99	442.46	436.13	436.79	434.11
Other Services													
2013	707.87	706.28	691.97	693.92	693.21	698.26	674.23	689.36	699.35	685.08	667.06	701.24	692.85
2014	678.61	678.88	686.47	662.98	667.97	672.71	678.00	667.37	692.55	675.07	684.11	671.42	675.85
2015	657.95	650.09	656.12	647.42	634.22	636.10	633.60	648.59	648.75	662.80	685.08	679.06	653.99
2016	663.50	697.68	680.31	707.45	711.26	701.55	701.31	684.83	718.49	737.19	721.70	739.26	706.08
2017	803.21	787.80	764.48	783.26	758.74	746.06	727.78	700.63	745.69	749.77	758.22	774.17	756.77

NEW MEXICO
At a Glance

Population:
  2010 census: 2,059,179
  2017 estimate: 2,088,070

Percent change in population:
  2010–2017: 1.4%

Percent change in total nonfarm employment:
  2007–2017: -1.6%

Industry with the largest growth in employment, 2007–2017 (thousands):
  Education and health services, 27.6

Industry with the largest decline or smallest growth in employment, 2007–2017 (thousands):
  Manufacturing, -10.6

Civilian labor force:
  2010: 936,088
  2017: 929,567

Unemployment rate and rank among states (highest to lowest):
  2010: 8.1%, 32nd
  2017: 6.2%, 2nd

Over-the-year change in unemployment rates:
  2015–2016: 0.2%
  2016–2017: -0.5%

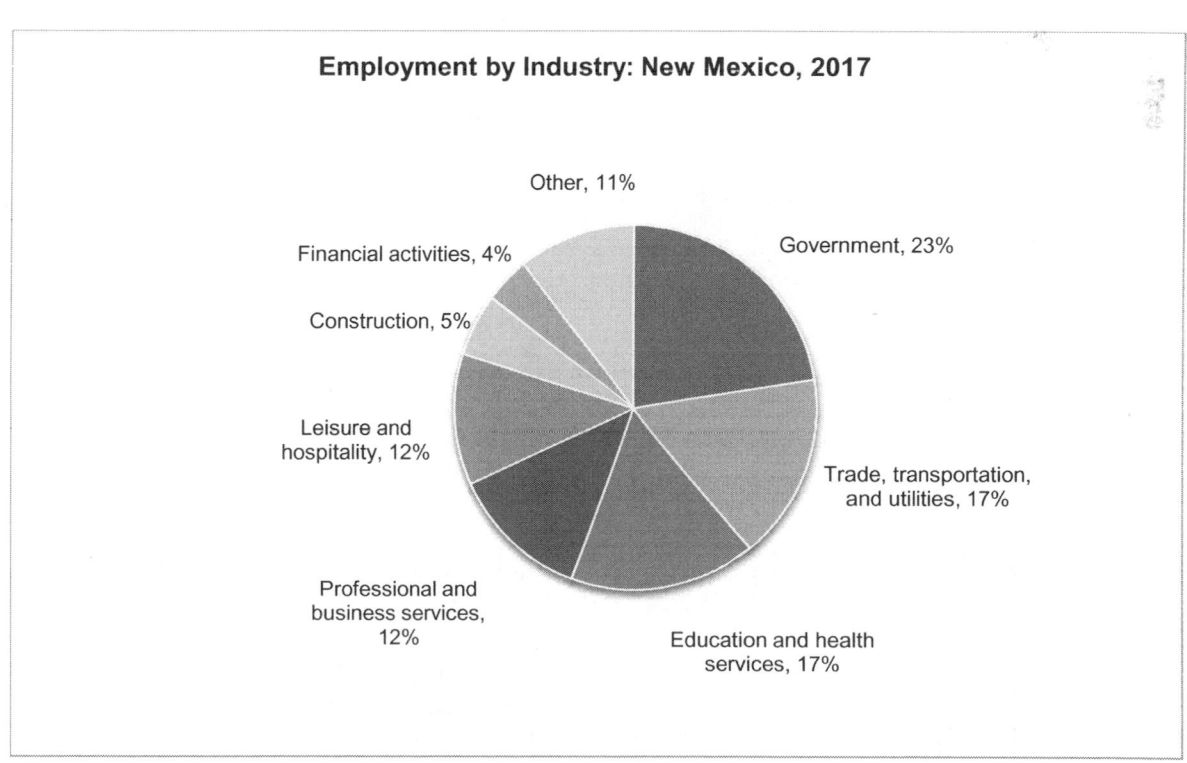

Employment by Industry: New Mexico, 2017

Other, 11%
Government, 23%
Financial activities, 4%
Construction, 5%
Leisure and hospitality, 12%
Trade, transportation, and utilities, 17%
Professional and business services, 12%
Education and health services, 17%

1. Employment by Industry: New Mexico, Selected Years, 2007–2017

(Numbers in thousands, not seasonally adjusted)

Industry and year	January	February	March	April	May	June	July	August	September	October	November	December	Annual average
Total Nonfarm													
2007	824.4	833.9	842.3	840.2	845.6	845.9	837.8	843.2	850.2	851.9	853.9	855.3	843.7
2008	834.0	843.3	847.5	848.8	852.8	850.2	841.7	846.8	854.7	852.2	847.2	842.4	846.8
2009	816.9	818.2	816.7	816.1	817.0	811.8	803.5	807.7	812.6	811.3	808.8	808.4	812.4
2010	789.4	795.8	801.0	807.1	810.5	808.2	801.0	802.7	803.6	807.9	806.3	807.3	803.4
2011	787.9	795.8	800.1	806.5	806.9	804.3	798.1	801.2	807.4	806.5	805.8	805.8	802.2
2012	786.6	796.0	801.4	804.1	806.4	803.8	795.5	801.2	807.6	819.1	818.7	816.0	804.7
2013	799.8	805.9	807.8	815.6	819.1	805.7	801.6	810.7	813.9	819.9	820.4	820.0	811.7
2014	805.9	810.0	811.5	819.1	825.6	812.1	812.1	821.6	824.5	833.3	833.2	833.4	820.2
2015	818.0	823.0	824.7	829.5	830.5	820.5	816.2	825.7	827.8	834.8	835.1	831.6	826.5
2016	818.4	826.5	825.3	832.6	832.9	821.1	817.5	826.6	832.1	832.4	833.1	833.5	827.7
2017	818.5	824.7	827.9	833.0	832.8	825.6	818.6	829.2	834.1	837.6	842.8	840.9	830.5
Total Private													
2007	633.8	637.9	644.6	643.4	648.9	653.2	651.3	655.5	653.9	653.7	654.7	655.9	648.9
2008	640.8	644.6	647.8	649.3	652.4	654.5	652.4	656.3	654.9	650.8	645.3	640.8	649.2
2009	621.2	617.3	615.0	613.5	614.8	614.4	612.5	615.7	613.6	609.7	606.8	606.6	613.4
2010	595.0	595.2	597.7	602.0	603.7	607.9	608.0	610.0	606.4	606.6	605.4	607.2	603.8
2011	595.4	597.4	600.6	607.1	608.7	611.9	613.3	614.9	613.0	610.0	609.6	608.5	607.5
2012	598.4	601.1	605.4	608.7	610.6	614.9	613.1	616.0	614.0	622.7	622.1	620.0	612.3
2013	609.8	610.9	611.7	619.1	622.0	621.0	623.0	626.7	621.7	625.7	626.4	626.2	620.4
2014	616.9	616.2	617.3	624.5	629.8	628.0	632.0	636.1	631.6	638.6	638.1	638.5	629.0
2015	628.9	629.0	629.7	636.5	638.7	637.5	640.8	642.7	637.3	642.8	641.8	639.7	637.1
2016	631.2	633.6	631.6	638.4	639.9	637.9	642.6	643.9	641.5	641.3	640.7	642.3	638.7
2017	633.9	634.4	636.8	641.9	643.7	646.0	647.4	649.0	645.9	647.0	651.2	650.4	644.0
Goods Producing													
2007	112.5	113.1	114.4	114.5	115.9	117.6	117.2	118.1	117.0	117.1	115.8	114.9	115.7
2008	112.0	112.5	113.1	114.2	114.9	115.9	115.1	116.6	115.9	114.3	111.6	108.3	113.7
2009	102.2	99.6	97.4	95.9	95.3	95.5	95.0	95.6	94.0	93.9	92.1	90.7	95.6
2010	88.7	88.2	88.3	89.9	90.7	91.7	92.6	93.3	93.1	93.8	92.6	91.9	91.2
2011	89.5	89.3	91.1	92.4	93.1	94.2	95.1	96.0	95.7	95.3	94.4	93.3	93.3
2012	91.4	91.8	92.7	93.3	94.2	95.7	95.6	96.5	96.1	98.9	97.2	96.1	95.0
2013	94.1	94.7	95.0	96.3	96.8	97.6	98.2	99.6	98.9	100.2	99.2	97.5	97.3
2014	96.5	95.6	95.8	96.9	98.0	98.6	100.0	100.4	99.8	102.3	100.9	100.5	98.8
2015	98.9	97.6	96.7	97.2	96.8	96.9	97.7	97.5	96.5	97.3	95.5	94.3	96.9
2016	91.9	91.4	90.3	90.3	89.7	89.7	89.5	89.5	89.6	90.1	89.1	89.0	90.0
2017	88.5	89.2	90.1	91.3	92.0	93.1	94.1	94.1	94.6	95.8	96.1	95.4	92.9
Service-Providing													
2007	711.9	720.8	727.9	725.7	729.7	728.3	720.6	725.1	733.2	734.8	738.1	740.4	728.0
2008	722.0	730.8	734.4	734.6	737.9	734.3	726.6	730.2	738.8	737.9	735.6	734.1	733.1
2009	714.7	718.6	719.3	720.2	721.7	716.3	708.5	712.1	718.6	717.4	716.7	717.7	716.8
2010	700.7	707.6	712.7	717.2	719.8	716.5	708.4	709.4	710.5	714.1	713.7	715.4	712.2
2011	698.4	706.5	709.0	714.1	713.8	710.1	703.0	705.2	711.7	711.2	711.4	712.5	708.9
2012	695.2	704.2	708.7	710.8	712.2	708.1	699.9	704.7	711.5	720.2	721.5	719.9	709.7
2013	705.7	711.2	712.8	719.3	722.3	708.1	703.4	711.1	715.0	719.7	721.2	722.5	714.4
2014	709.4	714.4	715.7	722.2	727.6	713.5	712.1	721.2	724.7	731.0	732.3	732.9	721.4
2015	719.1	725.4	728.0	732.3	733.7	723.6	718.5	728.2	731.3	737.5	739.6	737.3	729.5
2016	726.5	735.1	735.0	742.3	743.2	731.4	728.0	737.1	742.5	742.3	744.0	744.5	737.7
2017	730.0	735.5	737.8	741.7	740.8	732.5	724.5	735.1	739.5	741.8	746.7	745.5	737.6
Mining and Logging													
2007	19.3	19.0	19.1	19.2	19.4	19.7	19.9	20.0	19.6	19.7	19.9	19.9	19.6
2008	19.8	19.8	20.0	20.6	21.0	21.3	21.5	22.1	22.1	22.1	21.9	21.3	21.1
2009	19.9	19.1	18.3	17.8	17.5	17.5	17.5	17.5	17.1	17.3	17.5	17.5	17.9
2010	17.4	17.6	17.6	17.9	18.3	18.7	18.9	18.9	18.8	19.2	19.3	19.6	18.5
2011	19.7	20.0	20.2	20.6	21.0	21.4	21.7	22.1	22.3	22.6	22.9	23.2	21.5
2012	23.2	23.4	23.3	23.5	23.8	24.2	24.4	24.5	24.6	25.1	24.9	24.9	24.2
2013	25.2	25.4	25.5	25.8	26.0	26.2	26.4	26.5	26.2	26.4	26.7	26.6	26.1
2014	26.8	26.9	27.2	27.6	27.7	28.0	28.2	28.1	28.2	28.9	29.0	29.0	28.0
2015	28.9	28.1	27.0	26.3	25.7	25.4	25.4	25.3	24.7	24.1	23.4	22.9	25.6
2016	22.1	21.2	20.5	20.0	19.6	19.5	19.2	19.0	19.0	19.1	19.2	19.3	19.8
2017	19.6	20.0	20.2	20.5	20.6	20.9	21.3	21.0	21.4	21.3	21.3	21.1	20.8

1. Employment by Industry: New Mexico, Selected Years, 2007–2017—*Continued*

(Numbers in thousands, not seasonally adjusted)

Industry and year	January	February	March	April	May	June	July	August	September	October	November	December	Annual average
Construction													
2007	56.0	56.8	58.1	58.6	59.6	60.8	60.2	60.5	59.9	60.6	59.7	59.0	59.2
2008	57.0	57.5	58.1	58.5	58.6	59.1	58.0	58.3	57.6	57.2	55.7	53.6	57.4
2009	50.7	49.6	48.9	48.1	48.1	48.1	47.7	47.9	46.9	46.6	45.4	44.0	47.7
2010	42.7	42.2	42.3	43.4	43.5	43.9	44.6	44.6	44.3	44.4	43.9	43.0	43.6
2011	40.9	40.5	41.9	42.7	43.0	43.4	43.8	43.4	42.7	42.2	41.6	40.5	42.2
2012	38.9	39.2	40.2	40.5	40.9	41.8	41.5	41.6	41.1	43.2	42.5	41.8	41.1
2013	40.1	40.5	40.9	41.6	41.8	42.2	42.6	43.2	43.0	44.2	43.8	42.4	42.2
2014	41.7	40.9	40.9	41.4	42.4	42.8	43.6	43.6	43.1	45.1	44.1	43.7	42.8
2015	42.3	42.1	42.2	43.5	43.5	43.7	44.3	43.9	43.7	44.8	44.4	43.7	43.5
2016	42.9	43.3	43.1	43.5	43.1	43.2	43.5	43.4	43.4	43.9	43.5	43.4	43.4
2017	42.8	43.3	44.1	45.0	45.5	45.9	46.2	46.3	46.4	47.4	47.9	47.3	45.7
Manufacturing													
2007	37.2	37.3	37.2	36.7	36.9	37.1	37.1	37.6	37.5	36.8	36.2	36.0	37.0
2008	35.2	35.2	35.0	35.1	35.3	35.5	35.6	36.2	36.2	35.0	34.0	33.4	35.1
2009	31.6	30.9	30.2	30.0	29.7	29.9	29.8	30.2	30.0	30.0	29.2	29.2	30.1
2010	28.6	28.4	28.4	28.6	28.9	29.1	29.1	29.8	30.0	30.2	29.4	29.3	29.2
2011	28.9	28.8	29.0	29.1	29.1	29.4	29.6	30.5	30.7	30.5	29.9	29.6	29.6
2012	29.3	29.2	29.2	29.3	29.5	29.7	29.7	30.4	30.4	30.6	29.8	29.4	29.7
2013	28.8	28.8	28.6	28.9	29.0	29.2	29.2	29.9	29.6	29.6	28.7	28.5	29.1
2014	28.0	27.8	27.7	27.9	27.9	27.8	28.2	28.7	28.5	28.3	27.8	27.8	28.0
2015	27.7	27.4	27.5	27.4	27.6	27.8	28.0	28.3	28.1	28.4	27.7	27.7	27.8
2016	26.9	26.9	26.7	26.8	27.0	27.0	26.8	27.1	27.2	27.1	26.4	26.3	26.9
2017	26.1	25.9	25.8	25.8	25.9	26.3	26.6	26.8	26.8	27.1	26.9	27.0	26.4
Trade, Transportation, and Utilities													
2007	142.3	141.8	143.2	142.4	144.1	143.8	144.3	145.2	145.0	146.3	149.1	150.5	144.8
2008	145.8	145.1	145.8	144.9	145.0	144.3	144.1	144.5	143.7	143.3	143.7	144.2	144.5
2009	138.7	136.5	136.3	134.8	135.3	135.2	134.7	135.1	135.0	134.8	135.7	136.6	135.7
2010	132.0	131.0	131.8	132.0	132.6	132.7	133.0	133.7	132.5	133.6	135.2	136.2	133.0
2011	131.9	131.0	131.3	132.7	133.5	133.4	133.1	133.6	133.6	134.8	137.0	137.6	133.6
2012	134.0	133.3	133.9	134.2	134.9	135.0	135.0	135.2	135.3	137.4	139.4	139.9	135.6
2013	135.3	134.5	134.2	135.3	136.0	136.2	137.1	137.7	136.5	138.1	140.1	141.1	136.8
2014	136.5	136.0	135.9	137.1	137.6	137.3	138.3	138.7	138.4	139.8	141.4	142.5	138.3
2015	138.5	138.0	138.2	139.0	139.7	138.9	139.5	139.9	139.1	140.4	142.0	142.5	139.6
2016	138.3	137.3	137.2	138.5	138.5	137.7	138.8	139.0	138.3	139.1	141.0	140.9	138.7
2017	136.9	135.6	135.4	135.8	136.1	136.1	136.5	136.8	135.8	136.0	138.8	139.5	136.6
Wholesale Trade													
2007	23.4	23.4	23.4	23.5	23.6	23.9	24.1	24.0	23.9	24.1	24.1	24.2	23.8
2008	23.9	23.8	23.8	23.9	23.9	23.9	23.9	23.8	23.4	23.3	23.0	22.7	23.6
2009	22.3	22.1	22.0	21.7	21.7	22.0	21.8	21.6	21.5	21.7	21.6	21.8	21.8
2010	21.5	21.5	21.6	21.7	21.7	21.9	21.8	21.6	21.2	21.2	21.0	21.0	21.5
2011	20.7	20.6	20.7	20.8	21.1	21.3	21.4	21.3	21.2	21.1	21.0	21.0	21.0
2012	20.8	21.0	21.2	21.2	21.4	21.7	21.8	21.6	21.5	21.7	21.6	21.7	21.4
2013	21.3	21.4	21.4	21.5	21.6	21.8	21.8	21.9	21.5	21.6	21.5	21.5	21.6
2014	21.3	21.5	21.4	21.5	21.7	21.7	21.8	21.9	21.8	21.8	21.6	21.7	21.6
2015	21.4	21.3	21.4	21.5	21.6	21.7	21.7	21.7	21.5	21.7	21.5	21.6	21.6
2016	21.5	21.5	21.4	21.6	21.4	21.4	21.5	21.4	21.2	21.2	21.2	21.1	21.4
2017	20.9	20.9	21.0	20.9	21.1	21.2	21.4	21.3	21.0	21.0	21.4	21.4	21.1
Retail Trade													
2007	94.2	93.6	95.0	94.2	95.6	95.7	96.2	96.3	95.8	96.6	99.3	100.2	96.1
2008	96.5	96.1	96.7	96.1	96.0	96.5	96.6	96.5	96.0	95.9	96.7	97.3	96.4
2009	92.7	90.9	91.1	90.5	90.8	91.4	91.4	91.7	91.7	91.2	92.2	92.7	91.5
2010	88.9	88.0	88.7	88.7	89.2	89.6	89.8	90.3	89.2	90.1	91.9	92.6	89.8
2011	89.0	88.1	88.5	89.6	90.0	89.9	89.6	89.9	89.8	90.8	93.1	93.4	90.1
2012	90.2	89.2	89.5	89.9	90.2	90.3	90.3	90.3	90.4	91.9	94.0	94.2	90.9
2013	90.4	89.6	89.5	90.5	90.9	91.3	92.1	92.3	91.4	92.7	94.9	95.5	91.8
2014	91.5	90.8	91.0	91.8	91.8	92.0	92.7	92.7	92.2	93.3	95.1	95.6	92.5
2015	92.5	92.0	92.1	92.8	93.4	92.9	93.4	93.6	93.1	94.0	95.8	95.9	93.5
2016	92.3	91.5	91.7	92.8	92.9	92.6	93.3	93.2	92.6	93.5	95.3	94.8	93.0
2017	91.8	90.5	90.2	90.7	90.7	91.0	91.0	91.1	90.2	90.3	92.2	92.6	91.0

1. Employment by Industry: New Mexico, Selected Years, 2007–2017—*Continued*

(Numbers in thousands, not seasonally adjusted)

Industry and year	January	February	March	April	May	June	July	August	September	October	November	December	Annual average
Transportation and Utilities													
2007	24.7	24.8	24.8	24.7	24.9	24.2	24.0	24.9	25.3	25.6	25.7	26.1	25.0
2008	25.4	25.2	25.3	24.9	25.1	23.9	23.6	24.2	24.3	24.1	24.0	24.2	24.5
2009	23.7	23.5	23.2	22.6	22.8	21.8	21.5	21.8	21.8	21.9	21.9	22.1	22.4
2010	21.6	21.5	21.5	21.6	21.7	21.2	21.4	21.8	22.1	22.3	22.3	22.6	21.8
2011	22.2	22.3	22.1	22.3	22.4	22.2	22.1	22.4	22.6	22.9	22.9	23.2	22.5
2012	23.0	23.1	23.2	23.1	23.3	23.0	22.9	23.3	23.4	23.8	23.8	24.0	23.3
2013	23.6	23.5	23.3	23.3	23.5	23.1	23.2	23.5	23.6	23.8	23.7	24.1	23.5
2014	23.7	23.7	23.5	23.8	24.1	23.6	23.8	24.1	24.4	24.7	24.7	25.2	24.1
2015	24.6	24.7	24.7	24.7	24.7	24.3	24.4	24.6	24.5	24.7	24.7	25.0	24.6
2016	24.5	24.3	24.1	24.1	24.2	23.7	24.0	24.4	24.5	24.4	24.5	25.0	24.3
2017	24.2	24.2	24.2	24.2	24.3	23.9	24.1	24.4	24.6	24.7	25.2	25.5	24.5
Information													
2007	14.5	15.5	15.8	14.4	14.8	16.3	15.3	16.5	17.4	16.8	17.1	17.1	16.0
2008	15.6	16.3	16.1	15.1	15.4	16.2	16.0	15.8	16.5	16.3	16.3	15.6	15.9
2009	14.0	14.4	14.3	14.5	14.8	15.1	14.6	15.0	15.5	15.0	15.0	14.4	14.7
2010	14.2	14.6	14.7	15.3	14.7	15.0	13.8	14.1	14.1	13.7	14.0	14.3	14.4
2011	13.8	13.4	13.6	14.4	14.6	14.3	13.6	13.1	12.4	12.6	13.0	12.6	13.5
2012	13.2	13.7	14.3	13.9	13.6	13.1	13.3	14.0	13.2	13.0	14.0	13.1	13.5
2013	13.1	13.6	12.9	13.6	14.2	13.6	13.2	12.8	12.3	12.4	12.6	12.3	13.1
2014	11.6	12.0	12.2	12.3	12.8	12.7	12.4	12.8	11.9	12.5	13.2	13.0	12.5
2015	11.7	12.2	12.6	13.0	13.5	13.0	13.0	13.7	12.6	12.5	12.7	11.9	12.7
2016	11.5	12.8	12.3	13.4	12.9	12.7	13.3	13.2	13.2	13.3	13.8	13.6	13.0
2017	12.9	11.9	12.3	13.1	12.4	13.0	12.4	12.6	11.6	11.6	11.8	11.5	12.3
Financial Activities													
2007	34.9	35.0	35.3	35.1	35.2	35.4	35.5	35.5	35.2	35.2	35.1	35.3	35.2
2008	34.7	34.8	34.8	34.7	34.7	34.8	34.9	34.8	34.7	34.4	34.1	34.3	34.6
2009	33.7	33.5	33.2	33.8	33.9	33.7	33.7	33.6	33.5	33.9	33.5	33.8	33.7
2010	33.3	33.1	33.3	32.9	33.7	33.0	33.0	32.9	32.6	32.7	32.7	33.0	33.0
2011	32.5	32.4	32.4	32.6	32.5	32.5	32.7	32.6	32.5	32.5	32.5	32.7	32.5
2012	32.3	32.5	32.7	32.6	32.6	32.8	32.9	32.8	32.6	33.3	33.3	33.3	32.8
2013	33.0	32.9	32.9	33.0	33.0	33.0	33.2	33.2	33.1	33.3	33.6	33.8	33.2
2014	33.1	33.1	33.2	33.2	33.2	33.2	33.4	33.3	33.0	33.3	33.3	33.4	33.2
2015	33.2	33.2	33.2	33.2	33.3	33.2	33.4	33.3	32.9	33.4	33.4	33.7	33.3
2016	33.5	33.6	33.4	33.6	33.6	33.5	33.5	33.5	33.3	33.5	33.6	33.7	33.5
2017	33.6	33.6	33.6	33.7	33.7	33.8	34.1	34.0	33.8	34.3	34.7	34.9	34.0
Professional and Business Services													
2007	106.3	107.6	108.3	108.3	108.7	109.3	109.5	110.3	109.2	108.6	108.4	108.2	108.6
2008	106.5	107.5	107.4	108.1	108.5	109.0	109.2	110.3	109.7	109.1	107.5	107.0	108.3
2009	104.1	103.4	102.4	102.4	102.0	102.4	102.8	103.5	102.7	101.8	101.1	101.1	102.5
2010	99.3	99.6	99.1	100.3	99.5	100.6	101.1	101.4	101.0	101.1	100.5	100.7	100.4
2011	98.8	101.0	99.6	100.3	99.9	100.4	101.4	101.2	101.5	99.7	99.0	98.6	100.1
2012	96.5	96.7	97.2	98.5	97.8	99.1	97.9	98.1	98.2	99.2	99.2	98.2	98.1
2013	98.0	98.3	98.1	99.5	99.3	98.9	99.7	99.9	98.8	99.3	98.8	99.0	99.0
2014	98.1	98.0	97.5	99.5	99.3	98.8	99.9	100.6	98.9	99.6	99.3	99.7	99.1
2015	98.4	98.5	98.4	99.3	99.1	99.5	100.7	100.9	99.7	100.7	100.4	100.4	99.7
2016	99.1	99.5	99.3	100.7	100.6	101.2	103.1	103.0	102.8	102.2	101.9	102.3	101.3
2017	102.0	102.8	102.8	104.2	103.7	104.5	105.6	105.8	105.5	104.8	105.7	104.7	104.3
Education and Health Services													
2007	110.1	110.9	111.8	112.4	112.8	109.2	107.9	108.6	112.0	113.2	113.8	114.2	111.4
2008	112.6	114.1	114.8	115.8	116.3	113.0	111.9	113.2	116.9	117.8	118.3	118.7	115.3
2009	117.8	118.9	119.4	119.3	119.6	115.6	114.6	115.9	119.3	119.5	120.0	119.9	118.3
2010	119.3	119.9	120.4	120.1	120.1	117.8	117.1	117.0	120.2	120.8	121.4	121.6	119.6
2011	120.5	121.0	121.6	122.2	122.2	119.4	119.3	119.9	122.9	123.0	123.1	122.6	121.5
2012	121.8	122.9	122.8	122.9	122.9	120.5	120.1	120.2	123.3	124.5	124.8	125.0	122.6
2013	123.9	124.2	124.7	125.6	125.6	121.6	120.0	121.6	125.0	125.9	126.7	126.4	124.3
2014	126.1	126.7	126.7	127.5	128.1	124.0	123.4	125.5	129.4	131.1	131.4	131.3	127.6
2015	131.0	131.8	132.0	133.4	134.0	130.7	129.6	131.2	134.9	137.1	137.7	136.4	133.3
2016	137.3	138.4	138.0	139.4	139.4	135.2	134.5	136.6	139.3	140.0	139.4	140.4	138.2
2017	139.3	140.1	139.9	140.1	140.0	136.3	134.8	136.5	139.1	140.3	140.7	140.3	139.0

1. Employment by Industry: New Mexico, Selected Years, 2007–2017—*Continued*

(Numbers in thousands, not seasonally adjusted)

Industry and year	January	February	March	April	May	June	July	August	September	October	November	December	Annual average
Leisure and Hospitality													
2007	84.9	85.3	86.9	87.6	88.4	90.2	90.3	90.6	89.2	87.5	86.5	86.7	87.8
2008	84.9	85.1	86.5	87.2	87.9	89.0	89.1	89.4	87.8	85.7	84.3	83.9	86.7
2009	82.4	82.5	83.5	84.5	85.4	86.2	86.5	86.8	85.3	82.9	81.5	82.1	84.1
2010	80.7	81.1	82.4	83.8	84.6	86.2	86.1	86.3	84.9	83.3	81.8	82.4	83.6
2011	81.4	82.0	83.5	84.9	85.2	86.4	86.5	87.3	86.2	84.7	83.3	83.8	84.6
2012	82.0	82.6	84.0	85.4	86.6	88.4	88.3	89.4	87.3	87.9	86.1	86.4	86.2
2013	84.9	85.1	86.2	88.1	89.1	90.0	91.4	91.9	89.3	88.8	87.8	88.6	88.4
2014	87.7	87.3	88.4	90.2	92.5	92.9	93.9	94.4	91.9	91.6	90.5	90.2	91.0
2015	89.7	89.9	90.9	93.6	94.3	94.9	96.2	95.8	93.5	93.5	92.4	93.0	93.1
2016	92.3	93.0	93.5	94.6	97.0	97.5	99.1	98.8	96.8	95.1	94.0	94.8	95.5
2017	93.4	93.6	95.0	95.6	97.3	98.5	99.1	99.0	97.3	96.1	95.4	96.3	96.4
Other Services													
2007	28.3	28.7	28.9	28.7	29.0	31.4	31.3	30.7	28.9	29.0	28.9	29.0	29.4
2008	28.7	29.2	29.3	29.3	29.7	32.3	32.1	31.7	29.7	29.9	29.5	28.8	30.0
2009	28.3	28.5	28.5	28.3	28.5	30.7	30.6	30.2	28.3	27.9	27.9	28.0	28.8
2010	27.5	27.7	27.7	27.7	27.8	30.9	31.3	31.3	28.0	27.6	27.2	27.1	28.5
2011	27.0	27.3	27.5	27.6	27.7	31.3	31.6	31.2	28.2	27.4	27.3	27.3	28.5
2012	27.2	27.6	27.8	27.9	28.0	30.3	30.0	29.8	28.0	28.5	28.1	28.0	28.4
2013	27.5	27.6	27.7	27.7	28.0	30.1	30.2	30.0	27.8	27.7	27.6	27.5	28.3
2014	27.3	27.5	27.6	27.8	28.3	30.5	30.7	30.4	28.3	28.4	28.1	27.9	28.6
2015	27.5	27.8	27.7	27.8	28.0	30.4	30.7	30.4	28.1	27.9	27.7	27.5	28.5
2016	27.3	27.6	27.6	27.9	28.2	30.4	30.8	30.3	28.2	28.0	27.9	27.6	28.5
2017	27.3	27.6	27.7	28.1	28.5	30.7	30.8	30.2	28.2	28.1	28.0	27.8	28.6
Government													
2007	190.6	196.0	197.7	196.8	196.7	192.7	186.5	187.7	196.3	198.2	199.2	199.4	194.8
2008	193.2	198.7	199.7	199.5	200.4	195.7	189.3	190.5	199.8	201.4	201.9	201.6	197.6
2009	195.7	200.9	201.7	202.6	202.2	197.4	191.0	192.0	199.0	201.6	202.0	201.8	199.0
2010	194.4	200.6	203.3	205.1	206.8	200.3	193.0	192.7	197.2	201.3	200.9	200.1	199.6
2011	192.5	198.4	199.5	199.4	198.2	192.4	184.8	186.3	194.4	196.5	196.2	197.3	194.7
2012	188.2	194.9	196.0	195.4	195.8	188.9	182.4	185.2	193.6	196.4	196.6	196.0	192.5
2013	190.0	195.0	196.1	196.5	197.1	184.7	178.6	184.0	192.2	194.2	194.0	193.8	191.4
2014	189.0	193.8	194.2	194.6	195.8	184.1	180.1	185.5	192.9	194.7	195.1	194.9	191.2
2015	189.1	194.0	195.0	193.0	191.8	183.0	175.4	183.0	190.5	192.0	193.3	191.9	189.3
2016	187.2	192.9	193.7	194.2	193.0	183.2	174.9	182.7	190.6	191.1	192.4	191.2	188.9
2017	184.6	190.3	191.1	191.1	189.1	179.6	171.2	180.2	188.2	190.6	191.6	190.5	186.5

2. Average Weekly Hours by Selected Industry: New Mexico, 2013–2017

(Not seasonally adjusted)

Industry and year	January	February	March	April	May	June	July	August	September	October	November	December	Annual average
Total Private													
2013	34.0	34.3	34.3	34.7	34.9	35.4	34.9	35.2	35.2	35.0	34.9	35.0	34.8
2014	34.4	34.7	35.1	34.7	34.8	35.2	34.7	34.7	34.5	34.5	34.9	34.6	34.7
2015	33.9	34.3	34.3	33.9	33.9	34.1	34.3	34.9	34.2	34.2	34.3	34.0	34.2
2016	33.4	33.5	33.3	33.5	33.7	33.4	33.5	33.6	33.4	33.9	33.4	33.2	33.5
2017	33.5	33.2	33.2	33.9	33.7	34.0	34.0	33.6	33.4	34.1	33.7	33.7	33.7
Goods-Producing													
2013	40.8	41.9	41.6	43.1	43.4	43.3	43.0	45.0	43.4	44.1	43.9	41.9	43.0
2014	42.2	42.1	42.9	42.9	42.1	42.2	40.9	41.2	40.2	40.6	40.5	40.2	41.5
2015	38.9	39.5	39.2	39.9	39.7	39.7	39.7	40.9	39.5	40.8	41.3	41.1	40.0
2016	39.9	39.9	39.6	40.2	39.8	40.0	40.0	40.6	40.2	40.7	40.1	40.3	40.1
2017	40.0	39.1	39.3	38.9	39.8	40.2	39.3	39.6	39.5	39.8	40.1	40.4	39.7
Construction													
2013	37.0	38.9	38.4	39.6	40.5	40.7	39.0	41.4	39.3	40.9	41.1	39.0	39.7
2014	39.0	38.4	39.4	40.0	39.9	40.7	39.1	39.6	38.1	38.5	38.5	38.1	39.1
2015	35.6	37.0	36.1	37.3	37.2	37.3	38.1	39.2	36.3	38.2	38.8	38.1	37.4
2016	37.7	38.2	38.1	38.7	37.7	38.5	38.5	39.2	38.8	39.9	39.1	39.2	38.6
2017	39.3	37.9	38.2	37.7	39.2	39.5	38.6	39.1	38.3	38.8	39.3	39.4	38.8
Trade, Transportation, and Utilities													
2013	34.8	34.8	35.0	35.6	35.5	35.6	35.1	35.0	35.1	34.9	34.3	34.8	35.0
2014	34.1	34.7	35.2	34.6	34.9	35.3	34.9	34.7	34.6	35.0	35.0	35.0	34.8
2015	34.1	34.3	34.7	34.1	34.4	34.6	34.6	35.0	34.8	34.3	33.8	34.3	34.4
2016	33.2	33.3	32.4	33.0	33.6	33.0	33.7	33.8	33.9	33.9	33.5	33.3	33.4
2017	32.5	32.9	32.9	33.2	33.1	33.8	34.1	33.6	33.8	34.3	33.5	33.8	33.5
Professional and Business Services													
2013	34.8	35.0	35.2	35.7	35.7	36.2	35.6	36.1	36.1	36.0	35.8	36.9	35.8
2014	36.2	36.6	36.5	36.3	36.5	36.6	35.5	36.2	35.9	35.6	36.7	35.7	36.2
2015	35.4	35.5	35.6	35.0	34.7	35.0	34.9	35.7	35.2	35.8	36.2	35.1	35.3
2016	35.3	35.4	35.1	35.1	35.2	34.6	35.0	35.4	34.7	35.6	34.6	34.2	35.0
2017	34.9	34.8	34.7	36.4	35.9	35.8	36.0	35.4	35.4	36.1	35.6	35.7	35.6
Education and Health Services													
2013	33.2	33.0	32.8	32.7	32.9	33.2	32.8	32.9	33.2	32.7	33.4	33.4	33.0
2014	32.9	32.7	32.9	32.4	32.9	33.2	33.7	33.3	33.5	33.4	34.0	34.6	33.3
2015	33.9	34.1	33.9	33.6	33.6	34.0	33.3	33.7	33.6	33.2	33.5	33.5	33.7
2016	32.8	32.5	32.6	32.3	32.7	32.5	32.2	32.0	31.8	32.2	32.3	32.2	32.3
2017	33.0	32.1	31.8	32.6	32.5	32.5	32.7	32.3	32.4	32.6	32.2	32.2	32.4
Leisure and Hospitality													
2013	26.3	26.4	27.2	26.8	27.3	27.8	27.6	27.1	26.8	27.4	26.9	27.1	27.1
2014	25.9	26.7	27.5	26.0	26.7	27.3	27.4	27.2	26.6	26.0	26.2	25.7	26.6
2015	25.1	26.0	26.0	25.0	25.4	26.0	26.5	26.9	26.0	26.1	25.8	25.7	25.9
2016	25.4	25.8	26.4	26.0	26.7	26.8	26.5	26.8	26.5	26.9	26.0	25.7	26.3
2017	26.1	26.0	27.0	27.1	26.9	26.8	27.1	26.5	25.6	26.7	25.6	25.6	26.4

3. Average Hourly Earnings by Selected Industry: New Mexico, 2013–2017

(Dollars, not seasonally adjusted)

Industry and year	January	February	March	April	May	June	July	August	September	October	November	December	Annual average
Total Private													
2013	19.86	19.88	19.96	20.08	19.99	20.08	19.94	20.08	20.47	20.60	20.62	20.63	20.19
2014	20.34	20.44	20.45	20.52	20.57	20.70	20.50	20.40	20.44	20.54	20.47	20.48	20.49
2015	20.62	20.65	20.67	20.48	20.52	20.21	20.23	20.32	20.48	20.45	20.57	20.41	20.47
2016	20.59	20.65	20.48	20.46	20.38	20.32	20.44	20.48	20.71	20.94	20.83	20.93	20.60
2017	20.99	20.95	20.91	21.26	21.08	20.86	21.37	21.26	21.37	21.39	21.52	21.57	21.21
Goods-Producing													
2013	23.42	22.86	22.54	22.79	22.76	22.91	22.54	22.35	22.69	23.63	24.53	24.33	23.11
2014	23.84	23.95	23.54	23.55	23.78	23.53	23.52	23.59	23.83	23.64	23.74	23.81	23.69
2015	24.03	23.89	23.89	23.42	23.93	23.50	23.89	23.88	24.11	23.63	23.82	23.62	23.80
2016	23.73	23.47	23.21	22.71	22.17	22.47	22.46	22.39	22.61	22.54	22.96	22.54	22.77
2017	22.56	22.95	22.80	22.65	22.68	22.74	23.16	23.27	23.19	23.15	23.44	23.06	22.98
Construction													
2013	21.22	20.35	20.41	20.57	20.33	20.47	20.48	20.10	20.57	20.47	20.92	21.12	20.58
2014	21.38	21.24	21.08	21.42	21.54	21.23	21.44	21.44	21.53	20.96	21.06	20.73	21.25
2015	21.14	21.14	21.29	20.94	21.38	20.68	20.60	20.94	20.98	20.67	20.74	20.86	20.94
2016	21.11	20.99	21.24	20.62	20.61	20.94	20.93	21.16	21.54	21.52	22.02	21.60	21.19
2017	21.61	22.08	21.89	21.66	21.98	22.18	22.47	22.74	22.61	22.59	22.96	22.86	22.32
Trade, Transportation, and Utilities													
2013	18.47	18.60	18.87	18.88	18.55	18.64	18.50	18.32	18.86	18.75	18.78	18.75	18.66
2014	18.77	18.66	18.57	18.35	18.32	18.23	18.24	17.89	17.73	17.58	17.46	16.94	18.05
2015	17.50	17.41	17.35	17.45	17.15	16.62	16.58	17.26	16.81	16.53	16.91	16.40	16.99
2016	16.58	16.53	16.74	16.45	16.65	16.66	16.73	17.13	17.39	17.61	17.58	17.57	16.97
2017	17.78	17.75	17.71	18.46	18.21	18.25	18.83	18.58	18.76	19.09	18.89	19.13	18.46
Professional and Business Services													
2013	25.26	25.45	25.40	25.03	25.48	25.66	25.65	25.69	26.34	25.84	25.50	26.02	25.61
2014	25.80	26.05	26.26	26.08	25.72	25.99	25.80	26.03	26.21	26.14	26.00	26.16	26.02
2015	26.26	26.47	26.38	26.29	26.58	26.31	26.18	26.30	26.27	26.46	26.32	26.59	26.37
2016	27.15	27.09	26.49	26.75	27.03	27.16	27.26	27.37	27.45	27.91	27.68	27.77	27.26
2017	28.29	28.38	28.37	29.12	28.65	27.80	28.69	28.46	28.04	28.02	28.12	27.99	28.33
Education and Health Services													
2013	18.60	18.89	19.29	19.32	19.54	19.24	19.07	20.05	20.09	20.53	20.32	20.54	19.63
2014	20.38	20.63	20.75	21.37	21.28	21.61	21.52	21.18	21.23	21.51	20.99	21.19	21.14
2015	20.79	20.88	21.01	20.44	20.33	20.13	20.45	20.53	20.74	20.67	20.65	20.59	20.60
2016	20.31	20.74	20.55	20.79	20.60	20.24	20.28	20.39	20.47	20.86	20.40	21.14	20.57
2017	20.55	20.48	20.48	20.35	20.34	20.31	20.56	20.52	20.50	20.43	20.65	21.05	20.52
Leisure and Hospitality													
2013	11.57	11.67	11.59	11.58	11.63	11.87	12.06	12.13	11.87	11.62	11.69	11.97	11.78
2014	12.13	12.06	12.11	11.97	12.04	12.38	12.63	12.52	12.14	12.38	12.43	12.59	12.29
2015	12.41	12.73	12.72	12.49	12.79	12.70	13.06	12.84	13.05	13.08	13.03	13.17	12.84
2016	13.29	13.40	13.31	13.18	13.11	13.58	13.99	13.70	13.52	13.51	13.22	13.30	13.43
2017	13.09	13.03	13.08	12.84	12.82	13.18	13.31	13.39	13.23	13.14	13.32	13.42	13.15

4. Average Weekly Earnings by Selected Industry: New Mexico, 2013–2017

(Dollars, not seasonally adjusted)

Industry and year	January	February	March	April	May	June	July	August	September	October	November	December	Annual average
Total Private													
2013	675.24	681.88	684.63	696.78	697.65	710.83	695.91	706.82	720.54	721.00	719.64	722.05	702.61
2014	699.70	709.27	717.80	712.04	715.84	728.64	711.35	707.88	705.18	708.63	714.40	708.61	711.00
2015	699.02	708.30	708.98	694.27	695.63	689.16	693.89	709.17	700.42	699.39	705.55	693.94	700.07
2016	687.71	691.78	681.98	685.41	686.81	678.69	684.74	688.13	691.71	709.87	695.72	694.88	690.10
2017	703.17	695.54	694.21	720.71	710.40	709.24	726.58	714.34	713.76	729.40	725.22	726.91	714.78
Goods-Producing													
2013	955.54	957.83	937.66	982.25	987.78	992.00	969.22	1,005.75	984.75	1,042.08	1,076.87	1,019.43	993.73
2014	1,006.05	1,008.30	1,009.87	1,010.30	1,001.14	992.97	961.97	971.91	957.97	959.78	961.47	957.16	983.14
2015	934.77	943.66	936.49	934.46	950.02	932.95	948.43	976.69	952.35	964.10	983.77	970.78	952.00
2016	946.83	936.45	919.12	912.94	882.37	898.80	898.40	909.03	908.92	917.38	920.70	908.36	913.08
2017	902.40	897.35	896.04	881.09	902.66	914.15	910.19	921.49	916.01	921.37	939.94	931.62	912.31
Construction													
2013	785.14	791.62	783.74	814.57	823.37	833.13	798.72	832.14	808.40	837.22	859.81	823.68	817.03
2014	833.82	815.62	830.55	856.80	859.45	864.06	838.30	849.02	820.29	806.96	810.81	789.81	830.88
2015	752.58	782.18	768.57	781.06	795.34	771.36	784.86	820.85	761.57	789.59	804.71	794.77	783.16
2016	795.85	801.82	809.24	797.99	777.00	806.19	805.81	829.47	835.75	858.65	860.98	846.72	817.93
2017	849.27	836.83	836.20	816.58	861.62	876.11	867.34	889.13	865.96	876.49	902.33	900.68	866.02
Trade, Transportation, and Utilities													
2013	642.76	647.28	660.45	672.13	658.53	663.58	649.35	641.20	661.99	654.38	644.15	652.50	653.10
2014	640.06	647.50	653.66	634.91	639.37	643.52	636.58	620.78	613.46	615.30	611.10	592.90	628.14
2015	596.75	597.16	602.05	595.05	589.96	575.05	573.67	604.10	584.99	566.98	571.56	562.52	584.46
2016	550.46	550.45	542.38	542.85	559.44	549.78	563.80	578.99	589.52	596.98	588.93	585.08	566.80
2017	577.85	583.98	582.66	612.87	602.75	616.85	642.10	624.29	634.09	654.79	632.82	646.59	618.41
Professional and Business Services													
2013	879.05	890.75	894.08	893.57	909.64	928.89	913.14	927.41	950.87	930.24	912.90	960.14	916.84
2014	933.96	953.43	958.49	946.70	938.78	951.23	915.90	942.29	940.94	930.58	954.20	933.91	941.92
2015	929.60	939.69	939.13	920.15	922.33	920.85	913.68	938.91	924.70	947.27	952.78	933.31	930.86
2016	958.40	958.99	929.80	938.93	951.46	939.74	954.10	968.90	952.52	993.60	957.73	949.73	954.10
2017	987.32	987.62	984.44	1,059.97	1,028.54	995.24	1,032.84	1,007.48	992.62	1,011.52	1,001.07	999.24	1,008.55
Education and Health Services													
2013	617.52	623.37	632.71	631.76	642.87	638.77	625.50	659.65	666.99	671.33	678.69	686.04	647.79
2014	670.50	674.60	682.68	692.39	700.11	717.45	725.22	705.29	711.21	718.43	713.66	733.17	703.96
2015	704.78	712.01	712.24	686.78	683.09	684.42	680.99	691.86	696.86	686.24	691.78	689.77	694.22
2016	666.17	674.05	669.93	671.52	673.62	657.80	653.02	652.48	650.95	671.69	658.92	680.71	664.41
2017	678.15	657.41	651.26	663.41	661.05	660.08	672.31	662.80	664.20	666.02	664.93	677.81	664.85
Leisure and Hospitality													
2013	304.29	308.09	315.25	310.34	317.50	329.99	332.86	328.72	318.12	318.39	314.46	324.39	319.24
2014	314.17	322.00	333.03	311.22	321.47	337.97	346.06	340.54	322.92	321.88	325.67	323.56	326.91
2015	311.49	330.98	330.72	312.25	324.87	330.20	346.09	345.40	339.30	341.39	336.17	338.47	332.56
2016	337.57	345.72	351.38	342.68	350.04	363.94	370.74	367.16	358.28	363.42	343.72	341.81	353.21
2017	341.65	338.78	353.16	347.96	344.86	353.22	360.70	354.84	338.69	350.84	340.99	343.55	347.16

NEW YORK
At a Glance

Population:
  2010 census: 19,378,102
  2017 estimate: 19,849,399

Percent change in population:
  2010–2017: 2.4%

Percent change in total nonfarm employment:
  2007–2017: 9.1%

Industry with the largest growth in employment, 2007–2017 (thousands):
  Education and health services, 421.3

Industry with the largest decline or smallest growth in employment, 2007–2017 (thousands):
  Manufacturing, -105.7

Civilian labor force:
  2010: 9,595,362
  2017: 9,704,695

Unemployment rate and rank among states (highest to lowest):
  2010: 8.6%, 27th
  2017: 4.7%, 15th

Over-the-year change in unemployment rates:
  2015–2016: -0.5%
  2016–2017: -0.1%

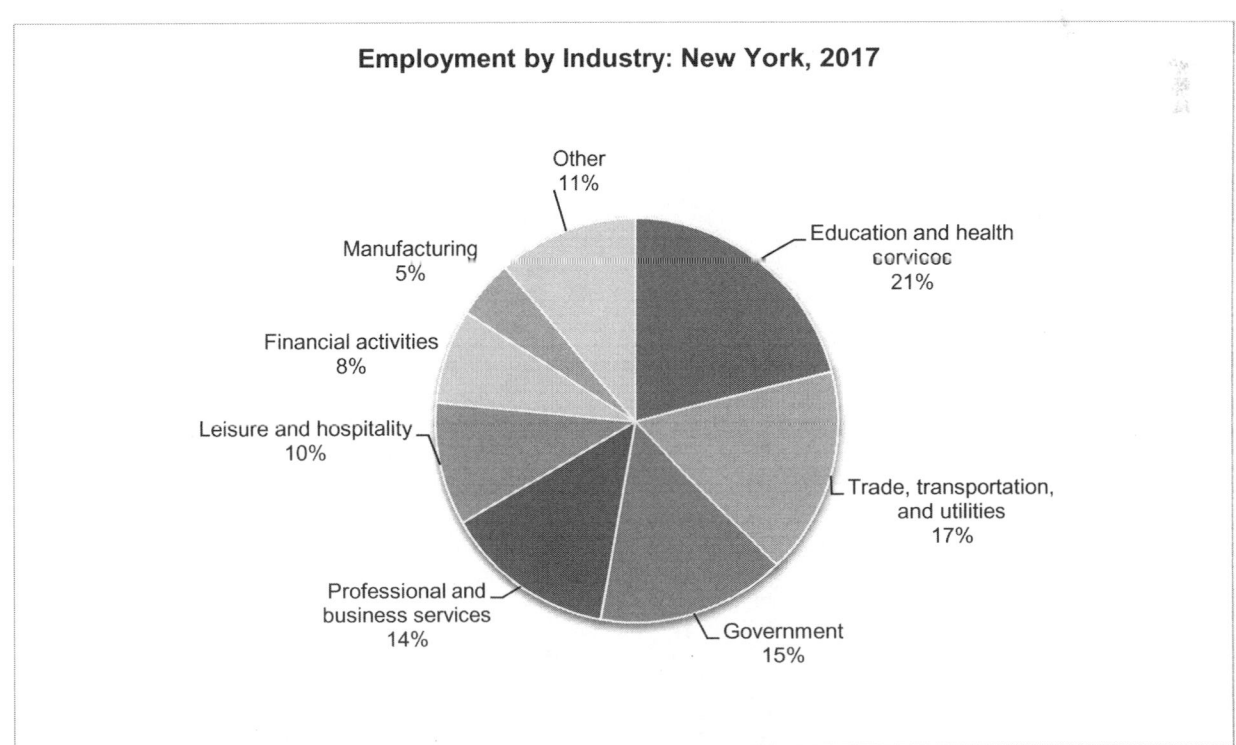

Employment by Industry: New York, 2017

- Other 11%
- Manufacturing 5%
- Financial activities 8%
- Leisure and hospitality 10%
- Professional and business services 14%
- Education and health services 21%
- Trade, transportation, and utilities 17%
- Government 15%

1. Employment by Industry: New York, Selected Years, 2007–2017

(Numbers in thousands, not seasonally adjusted)

Industry and year	January	February	March	April	May	June	July	August	September	October	November	December	Annual average
Total Nonfarm													
2007	8,518.3	8,556.8	8,613.3	8,648.8	8,746.2	8,811.2	8,717.5	8,687.4	8,724.2	8,827.4	8,873.2	8,906.5	8,719.2
2008	8,620.7	8,664.6	8,705.0	8,770.7	8,834.1	8,876.3	8,804.0	8,765.6	8,780.1	8,840.9	8,836.5	8,830.4	8,777.4
2009	8,490.2	8,507.2	8,509.2	8,515.3	8,578.3	8,587.2	8,542.3	8,494.0	8,489.0	8,569.1	8,590.6	8,608.0	8,540.0
2010	8,324.0	8,372.4	8,428.1	8,542.0	8,625.7	8,627.3	8,526.1	8,487.2	8,533.1	8,661.5	8,696.7	8,707.0	8,544.3
2011	8,440.6	8,503.4	8,548.1	8,664.3	8,695.6	8,717.7	8,669.2	8,636.7	8,690.9	8,788.2	8,826.8	8,844.8	8,668.9
2012	8,566.9	8,648.6	8,703.5	8,762.1	8,841.9	8,857.4	8,765.5	8,754.4	8,803.0	8,928.5	8,928.9	8,980.7	8,795.1
2013	8,668.3	8,744.7	8,802.7	8,897.1	8,952.0	8,974.7	8,920.9	8,897.3	8,954.5	9,081.6	9,128.4	9,137.5	8,930.0
2014	8,803.9	8,892.7	8,945.4	9,041.9	9,125.3	9,159.1	9,106.6	9,090.9	9,118.0	9,246.0	9,290.9	9,309.3	9,094.2
2015	8,989.7	9,060.9	9,106.9	9,200.7	9,295.2	9,325.7	9,286.4	9,255.8	9,271.4	9,415.5	9,458.1	9,467.5	9,261.2
2016	9,146.2	9,226.1	9,286.4	9,390.6	9,415.3	9,459.4	9,424.5	9,394.8	9,419.2	9,525.9	9,566.9	9,578.6	9,402.8
2017	9,272.6	9,362.2	9,398.5	9,470.2	9,554.1	9,606.7	9,535.3	9,512.5	9,534.9	9,624.5	9,666.6	9,660.9	9,516.6
Total Private													
2007	7,028.8	7,047.8	7,102.2	7,139.5	7,228.5	7,294.2	7,250.9	7,237.1	7,249.3	7,314.6	7,350.4	7,375.3	7,218.2
2008	7,125.3	7,148.7	7,185.2	7,240.9	7,300.5	7,342.9	7,304.7	7,294.5	7,292.4	7,314.7	7,301.4	7,291.3	7,261.9
2009	6,983.1	6,975.7	6,974.9	6,977.4	7,035.7	7,056.2	7,011.1	6,990.3	7,013.7	7,045.1	7,058.3	7,074.0	7,016.3
2010	6,823.1	6,847.9	6,898.5	7,005.9	7,048.1	7,073.2	7,053.5	7,046.3	7,070.0	7,154.9	7,180.9	7,195.1	7,033.1
2011	6,965.0	7,005.9	7,047.9	7,157.5	7,193.9	7,228.1	7,216.1	7,194.9	7,241.2	7,300.5	7,334.2	7,354.0	7,186.6
2012	7,122.4	7,171.0	7,223.0	7,281.9	7,357.9	7,386.6	7,340.2	7,346.9	7,376.0	7,461.8	7,461.6	7,507.6	7,336.4
2013	7,242.0	7,287.3	7,342.6	7,437.5	7,486.5	7,521.4	7,506.3	7,498.6	7,543.9	7,627.8	7,667.8	7,678.3	7,486.7
2014	7,396.5	7,450.0	7,498.1	7,589.8	7,672.1	7,714.7	7,698.6	7,696.3	7,707.2	7,796.7	7,833.2	7,852.6	7,658.8
2015	7,580.2	7,620.4	7,661.1	7,753.3	7,840.0	7,878.5	7,874.2	7,856.4	7,852.5	7,963.3	7,995.1	8,003.9	7,823.2
2016	7,725.9	7,777.3	7,830.2	7,930.7	7,956.4	8,007.8	8,006.7	7,988.3	7,991.2	8,067.3	8,101.6	8,109.1	7,957.7
2017	7,843.6	7,905.1	7,937.4	8,007.2	8,090.9	8,151.2	8,114.0	8,103.6	8,106.4	8,162.4	8,197.3	8,189.8	8,067.4
Goods Producing													
2007	877.1	867.8	877.5	894.1	915.9	931.2	928.8	933.1	928.8	929.1	924.1	912.2	910.0
2008	876.4	869.9	876.3	891.0	908.4	919.2	920.7	924.7	916.4	910.0	892.8	868.0	897.8
2009	815.2	801.0	798.7	803.1	812.8	817.7	818.2	817.8	810.0	803.9	793.4	777.9	805.8
2010	737.3	729.9	739.5	762.1	773.0	783.6	789.2	793.9	789.3	786.2	779.9	764.4	769.0
2011	729.1	726.6	736.4	757.7	774.0	787.9	796.5	802.1	796.5	793.4	787.9	776.2	772.0
2012	746.5	743.1	752.7	767.4	780.2	794.3	797.9	801.1	796.6	796.1	787.2	783.8	778.9
2013	754.9	749.5	757.5	776.2	792.0	801.3	806.9	811.9	806.0	808.8	803.2	790.0	788.2
2014	757.6	751.2	762.2	784.1	804.3	818.6	826.1	830.0	824.9	827.6	822.8	812.0	801.8
2015	777.0	770.4	782.1	806.4	826.8	839.4	846.6	848.7	841.7	846.9	842.1	831.9	821.7
2016	799.9	795.0	807.0	825.1	837.6	848.3	854.7	856.4	849.7	850.4	844.1	829.9	833.2
2017	802.0	801.3	807.3	825.1	840.0	852.5	855.9	857.0	851.5	849.4	844.4	829.5	834.7
Service-Providing													
2007	7,641.2	7,689.0	7,735.8	7,754.7	7,830.3	7,880.0	7,788.7	7,754.3	7,795.4	7,898.3	7,949.1	7,994.3	7,809.3
2008	7,744.3	7,794.7	7,828.7	7,879.7	7,925.7	7,957.1	7,883.3	7,840.9	7,863.7	7,930.9	7,943.7	7,962.4	7,879.6
2009	7,675.0	7,706.2	7,710.5	7,712.2	7,765.5	7,769.5	7,724.1	7,676.2	7,679.0	7,765.2	7,797.2	7,830.1	7,734.2
2010	7,586.7	7,642.5	7,688.6	7,779.9	7,852.7	7,843.7	7,736.9	7,693.3	7,743.8	7,875.3	7,916.8	7,942.6	7,775.2
2011	7,711.5	7,776.8	7,811.7	7,906.6	7,921.6	7,929.8	7,872.7	7,834.6	7,894.4	7,994.8	8,038.9	8,068.6	7,896.8
2012	7,820.4	7,905.5	7,950.8	7,994.7	8,061.7	8,063.1	7,967.6	7,953.3	8,006.4	8,132.4	8,141.7	8,196.9	8,016.2
2013	7,913.4	7,995.2	8,045.2	8,120.9	8,160.0	8,173.4	8,114.0	8,085.4	8,148.5	8,272.8	8,325.2	8,347.5	8,141.8
2014	8,046.3	8,141.5	8,183.2	8,257.8	8,321.0	8,340.5	8,280.5	8,260.9	8,293.1	8,418.4	8,468.1	8,497.3	8,292.4
2015	8,212.7	8,290.5	8,324.8	8,394.3	8,468.4	8,486.3	8,439.8	8,407.1	8,429.7	8,568.6	8,616.0	8,635.6	8,439.5
2016	8,346.3	8,431.1	8,479.4	8,565.5	8,577.7	8,611.1	8,569.8	8,538.4	8,569.5	8,675.5	8,722.8	8,748.7	8,569.7
2017	8,470.6	8,560.9	8,591.2	8,645.1	8,714.1	8,754.2	8,679.4	8,655.5	8,683.4	8,775.1	8,822.2	8,831.4	8,681.9
Mining and Logging													
2007	5.2	5.3	5.5	5.9	6.4	6.7	6.8	6.7	6.7	6.7	6.6	6.2	6.2
2008	5.3	5.2	5.5	6.0	6.6	6.9	7.1	7.0	6.9	6.8	6.3	5.8	6.3
2009	4.8	4.8	4.9	5.2	5.6	5.8	5.9	5.8	5.7	5.7	5.6	5.2	5.4
2010	4.4	4.5	4.7	5.3	5.6	5.7	5.7	5.8	5.8	5.6	5.5	5.1	5.3
2011	4.3	4.4	4.5	5.1	5.4	5.6	5.7	5.8	5.8	5.8	5.6	5.4	5.3
2012	4.5	4.6	4.9	5.3	5.5	5.6	5.7	5.6	5.6	5.6	5.3	5.0	5.3
2013	4.3	4.3	4.5	5.0	5.4	5.3	5.3	5.3	5.4	5.5	5.3	5.0	5.1
2014	4.4	4.5	4.6	5.0	5.4	5.6	5.7	5.7	5.6	5.7	5.5	5.2	5.2
2015	4.6	4.6	4.7	5.1	5.5	5.7	5.8	5.7	5.7	5.6	5.5	5.3	5.3
2016	4.4	4.5	4.7	5.0	5.3	5.5	5.5	5.5	5.4	5.2	5.2	4.8	5.1
2017	4.2	4.4	4.5	4.8	5.1	5.2	5.4	5.4	5.4	5.3	5.2	4.9	5.0

1. Employment by Industry: New York, Selected Years, 2007–2017—*Continued*

(Numbers in thousands, not seasonally adjusted)

Industry and year	January	February	March	April	May	June	July	August	September	October	November	December	Annual average
Construction													
2007	318.8	310.5	318.8	336.9	355.9	367.7	370.5	374.2	371.7	373.1	369.5	358.8	352.2
2008	334.9	330.1	335.9	351.3	366.3	373.1	379.8	383.3	377.3	374.5	363.6	345.8	359.7
2009	310.8	305.3	307.9	318.0	329.7	335.7	342.3	342.6	335.5	331.3	324.5	310.5	324.5
2010	280.1	273.2	281.2	302.4	310.7	317.5	325.5	329.4	324.2	320.1	315.1	300.3	306.6
2011	273.4	270.6	278.9	296.0	310.0	319.5	329.7	333.6	328.7	325.8	321.2	310.1	308.1
2012	288.0	283.9	291.6	305.4	315.0	324.9	330.4	333.1	328.7	328.8	323.4	319.9	314.4
2013	299.0	294.3	300.6	316.4	330.0	336.2	344.1	347.4	342.7	345.5	340.3	327.5	327.0
2014	304.1	298.2	308.3	328.6	346.1	355.7	365.0	367.5	363.9	366.3	361.7	351.1	343.0
2015	323.7	316.6	326.1	349.1	366.9	375.1	382.0	384.5	378.9	383.4	379.5	370.0	361.3
2016	345.6	340.3	350.9	369.9	381.6	388.6	395.5	398.0	393.3	393.2	388.7	375.6	376.8
2017	355.4	353.7	358.3	374.9	387.9	396.2	401.7	403.0	399.1	398.6	395.3	381.1	383.8
Manufacturing													
2007	553.1	552.0	553.2	551.3	553.6	556.8	551.5	552.2	550.4	549.3	548.0	547.2	551.6
2008	536.2	534.6	534.9	533.7	535.5	539.2	533.8	534.4	532.2	528.7	522.9	516.4	531.9
2009	499.6	490.9	485.9	479.9	477.5	476.2	470.0	469.4	468.8	466.9	463.3	462.2	475.9
2010	452.8	452.2	453.6	454.4	456.7	460.4	458.0	458.7	459.3	460.5	459.3	459.0	457.1
2011	451.4	451.6	453.0	456.6	458.6	462.8	461.1	462.7	462.0	461.8	461.1	460.7	458.6
2012	454.0	454.6	456.2	456.7	459.7	463.8	461.8	462.4	462.3	461.7	458.5	458.9	459.2
2013	451.6	450.9	452.4	454.8	456.6	459.8	457.5	459.2	457.9	457.8	457.6	457.5	456.1
2014	449.1	448.5	449.3	450.5	452.8	457.3	455.4	456.8	455.4	455.6	455.6	455.7	453.5
2015	448.7	449.2	451.3	452.2	454.4	458.6	458.8	458.5	457.1	457.9	457.1	456.6	455.0
2016	449.9	450.2	451.4	450.2	450.7	454.2	453.7	452.9	451.0	452.0	450.2	449.5	451.3
2017	442.4	443.2	444.5	445.4	447.0	451.1	448.8	448.6	447.0	445.5	443.9	443.5	445.9
Trade, Transportation, and Utilities													
2007	1,512.1	1,488.4	1,495.3	1,493.7	1,516.7	1,537.5	1,516.6	1,509.2	1,520.9	1,534.7	1,568.8	1,592.5	1,523.9
2008	1,525.1	1,501.1	1,506.4	1,507.7	1,519.7	1,535.7	1,514.1	1,511.3	1,520.2	1,524.9	1,540.2	1,555.9	1,521.9
2009	1,470.4	1,446.7	1,440.4	1,432.1	1,449.9	1,464.3	1,441.6	1,440.2	1,449.9	1,458.9	1,483.2	1,503.8	1,456.8
2010	1,437.3	1,418.2	1,425.2	1,441.8	1,455.1	1,474.3	1,456.2	1,457.0	1,464.8	1,482.2	1,507.3	1,527.0	1,462.2
2011	1,466.6	1,449.4	1,451.9	1,463.9	1,476.5	1,496.0	1,476.6	1,480.6	1,490.6	1,503.1	1,533.7	1,556.8	1,487.1
2012	1,496.6	1,476.5	1,481.3	1,483.8	1,505.4	1,522.6	1,494.4	1,499.4	1,510.7	1,525.6	1,555.1	1,576.7	1,510.7
2013	1,504.2	1,481.1	1,491.7	1,502.9	1,518.9	1,539.6	1,525.0	1,522.5	1,535.4	1,550.2	1,587.7	1,606.6	1,530.5
2014	1,534.3	1,516.3	1,520.9	1,532.5	1,548.1	1,566.4	1,550.3	1,550.3	1,559.3	1,576.9	1,610.2	1,630.6	1,558.0
2015	1,558.9	1,538.9	1,540.2	1,547.4	1,567.3	1,584.5	1,565.4	1,563.8	1,570.7	1,584.1	1,616.2	1,631.4	1,572.4
2016	1,561.1	1,544.5	1,547.0	1,557.6	1,565.0	1,580.1	1,561.9	1,558.7	1,567.4	1,582.9	1,613.5	1,631.4	1,572.6
2017	1,566.2	1,543.8	1,544.6	1,549.7	1,569.1	1,583.9	1,564.2	1,561.3	1,569.5	1,583.2	1,616.7	1,629.6	1,573.5
Wholesale Trade													
2007	352.0	351.8	353.1	353.0	354.9	358.0	356.9	355.9	354.9	357.4	357.2	358.7	355.3
2008	351.3	351.0	351.4	351.3	352.0	353.8	352.3	351.2	350.0	348.9	347.2	346.0	350.5
2009	337.4	334.1	332.3	328.9	329.0	329.7	326.7	326.2	324.8	324.6	324.5	325.3	328.6
2010	318.6	318.1	319.9	322.0	323.9	326.5	327.2	327.1	326.5	328.2	329.2	330.3	324.8
2011	324.6	324.1	325.7	328.3	330.1	332.6	332.8	333.2	331.9	332.7	332.7	334.3	330.3
2012	329.4	330.1	331.3	332.5	334.0	336.4	335.4	334.9	333.1	335.2	334.6	336.6	333.6
2013	330.9	331.0	331.8	333.6	335.1	338.5	338.5	338.0	336.6	336.8	337.8	339.1	335.6
2014	334.0	333.6	334.0	336.3	338.2	340.5	340.8	340.7	339.1	340.4	341.8	343.0	338.5
2015	337.7	337.2	338.0	338.5	340.7	343.3	343.8	343.2	341.0	342.4	342.8	344.1	341.1
2016	337.6	337.8	337.5	337.8	338.6	340.6	340.6	339.9	337.7	338.3	338.8	339.9	338.8
2017	333.8	334.2	334.8	335.9	338.0	340.8	340.9	340.4	339.1	340.3	342.2	343.6	338.7
Retail Trade													
2007	889.1	866.1	870.7	869.9	885.2	899.7	894.9	891.6	887.9	897.6	930.6	948.7	894.3
2008	899.6	876.8	880.4	879.7	888.2	899.9	896.0	895.4	891.0	897.7	914.2	926.3	895.4
2009	865.2	846.3	843.2	839.4	854.0	867.0	860.9	861.7	860.2	868.8	891.3	906.8	863.7
2010	859.5	843.2	847.4	856.5	866.0	881.0	877.3	879.1	872.2	886.6	908.4	923.3	875.0
2011	877.6	862.9	863.1	873.1	881.3	895.5	892.5	896.8	892.1	904.2	931.8	948.9	893.3
2012	905.2	885.2	887.5	890.9	904.7	916.5	911.8	912.5	908.6	921.1	949.5	961.7	912.9
2013	908.6	892.4	896.1	903.0	914.9	929.8	929.0	930.2	925.8	937.8	971.0	984.1	926.9
2014	927.3	912.1	914.2	921.1	930.7	945.2	942.6	945.0	938.7	952.6	980.4	993.5	942.0
2015	939.5	922.6	922.8	927.7	940.6	952.6	947.7	947.6	941.1	951.5	979.0	986.0	946.6
2016	936.6	921.6	922.6	930.7	936.3	947.1	944.9	944.5	937.7	950.8	976.6	985.7	944.6
2017	940.0	919.4	918.1	926.1	936.0	945.3	941.0	939.6	931.2	941.2	969.2	972.8	940.0

1. Employment by Industry: New York, Selected Years, 2007–2017—*Continued*

(Numbers in thousands, not seasonally adjusted)

Industry and year	January	February	March	April	May	June	July	August	September	October	November	December	Annual average
Transportation and Utilities													
2007	271.0	270.5	271.5	270.8	276.6	279.8	264.8	261.7	278.1	279.7	281.0	285.1	274.2
2008	274.2	273.3	274.6	276.7	279.5	282.0	265.8	264.7	279.2	278.3	278.8	283.6	275.9
2009	267.8	266.3	264.9	263.8	266.9	267.6	254.0	252.3	264.9	265.5	267.4	271.7	264.4
2010	259.2	256.9	257.9	263.3	265.2	266.8	251.7	250.8	266.1	267.4	269.7	273.4	262.4
2011	264.4	262.4	263.1	262.5	265.1	267.9	251.3	250.6	266.6	266.2	269.2	273.6	263.6
2012	262.0	261.2	262.5	260.4	266.7	269.7	247.2	252.0	269.0	269.3	271.0	278.4	264.1
2013	264.7	257.7	263.8	266.3	268.9	271.3	257.5	254.3	273.0	275.6	278.9	283.4	268.0
2014	273.0	270.6	272.7	275.1	279.2	280.7	266.9	264.6	281.5	283.9	288.0	294.1	277.5
2015	281.7	279.1	279.4	281.2	286.0	288.6	273.9	273.0	288.6	290.2	294.4	301.3	284.8
2016	286.9	285.1	286.9	289.1	290.1	292.4	276.4	274.3	292.0	293.8	298.1	305.8	289.2
2017	292.4	290.2	291.7	287.7	295.1	297.8	282.3	281.3	299.2	301.7	305.3	313.2	294.8
Information													
2007	265.5	267.1	267.5	267.2	269.9	272.5	271.1	271.7	270.3	268.8	271.1	272.4	269.6
2008	265.7	267.6	268.1	266.7	269.5	272.8	270.7	271.5	271.0	269.8	270.7	272.0	269.7
2009	263.2	261.1	261.7	260.4	260.7	260.7	259.4	258.2	257.0	256.0	256.5	257.1	259.3
2010	249.1	249.2	250.7	250.0	251.5	253.1	254.4	254.7	253.6	255.6	256.4	258.4	253.1
2011	251.2	252.0	253.3	255.6	256.1	257.5	258.5	243.2	258.0	257.0	258.0	259.3	255.0
2012	254.3	255.2	255.9	257.9	260.0	261.7	259.4	259.1	258.0	259.5	260.4	260.7	258.5
2013	252.8	254.2	255.7	257.7	259.5	262.0	261.7	263.1	262.4	264.4	266.1	266.7	260.5
2014	258.8	262.0	262.8	261.2	261.8	265.8	263.9	264.9	262.7	265.8	265.8	267.9	263.6
2015	260.4	261.8	262.0	261.4	262.3	264.5	267.0	265.5	264.5	268.9	269.9	270.9	264.9
2016	260.8	261.8	263.5	265.4	253.8	267.5	272.3	271.3	269.4	271.1	272.0	273.4	266.9
2017	262.9	266.4	267.4	265.5	267.0	271.0	269.9	271.8	271.3	270.3	271.4	270.3	268.8
Financial Activities													
2007	722.7	724.0	726.0	724.7	725.6	737.6	740.9	738.7	728.9	731.4	732.9	735.5	730.7
2008	722.9	722.6	723.2	720.5	720.5	728.1	730.2	729.3	715.2	711.2	708.1	708.3	720.0
2009	692.5	687.2	683.5	677.4	676.0	678.6	678.6	675.4	668.9	667.0	665.5	668.1	676.6
2010	656.8	657.6	659.6	664.5	665.7	675.0	678.4	678.4	671.2	671.9	673.6	678.1	669.2
2011	672.2	673.0	674.3	677.1	678.3	688.3	692.9	694.2	684.5	683.4	683.6	686.6	682.4
2012	677.3	679.1	678.9	678.9	679.2	688.7	691.4	690.5	680.4	683.0	682.8	687.6	683.2
2013	672.1	673.9	674.7	676.4	676.4	686.5	691.6	690.2	680.9	683.1	686.3	690.4	681.9
2014	680.4	682.2	683.5	684.3	688.3	700.2	704.9	704.6	694.7	696.1	697.7	703.1	693.3
2015	693.0	694.2	695.6	697.3	700.0	711.1	717.3	716.6	705.7	709.5	710.1	713.4	705.3
2016	706.1	706.6	707.7	707.3	709.1	719.3	724.1	723.8	710.3	711.0	712.7	717.2	712.9
2017	706.0	707.6	708.6	708.9	711.7	724.9	727.9	727.9	716.7	719.4	717.5	721.9	716.6
Professional and Business Services													
2007	1,097.9	1,103.2	1,115.0	1,123.0	1,130.2	1,150.3	1,150.1	1,152.9	1,140.4	1,152.8	1,157.0	1,162.7	1,136.3
2008	1,126.8	1,133.4	1,140.0	1,154.7	1,155.6	1,170.4	1,171.7	1,169.3	1,156.2	1,154.6	1,149.2	1,144.7	1,152.2
2009	1,096.2	1,091.9	1,091.1	1,091.8	1,090.2	1,100.3	1,096.0	1,090.8	1,084.4	1,087.6	1,090.3	1,092.3	1,091.9
2010	1,059.3	1,065.0	1,072.5	1,096.2	1,096.5	1,111.1	1,115.5	1,114.8	1,104.9	1,116.8	1,118.9	1,120.1	1,099.3
2011	1,092.1	1,097.9	1,106.3	1,129.9	1,130.3	1,148.4	1,154.4	1,153.0	1,148.6	1,149.7	1,156.2	1,156.4	1,135.3
2012	1,126.4	1,132.5	1,143.4	1,159.4	1,165.1	1,183.1	1,183.6	1,186.3	1,179.1	1,192.7	1,195.9	1,198.5	1,170.5
2013	1,161.3	1,167.8	1,176.5	1,193.7	1,197.6	1,213.7	1,219.4	1,218.3	1,208.5	1,220.6	1,223.6	1,223.8	1,202.1
2014	1,183.5	1,191.9	1,197.1	1,219.5	1,228.2	1,242.1	1,249.5	1,250.1	1,239.2	1,250.6	1,257.1	1,258.1	1,230.6
2015	1,222.4	1,229.3	1,233.0	1,255.4	1,265.3	1,283.0	1,289.7	1,287.4	1,273.7	1,288.9	1,291.4	1,288.5	1,267.3
2016	1,251.7	1,257.4	1,266.2	1,285.8	1,288.0	1,305.3	1,314.3	1,312.2	1,304.3	1,311.9	1,316.0	1,312.3	1,293.8
2017	1,273.9	1,283.4	1,287.9	1,304.3	1,314.0	1,335.3	1,339.4	1,336.2	1,328.9	1,331.2	1,336.3	1,335.7	1,317.2
Education and Health Services													
2007	1,556.6	1,589.8	1,600.8	1,598.1	1,590.7	1,557.5	1,529.8	1,522.2	1,579.4	1,621.6	1,628.3	1,631.8	1,583.9
2008	1,584.4	1,621.6	1,628.4	1,631.8	1,623.0	1,591.0	1,560.3	1,555.3	1,611.4	1,649.5	1,661.9	1,668.1	1,615.6
2009	1,621.7	1,658.9	1,664.2	1,662.7	1,654.2	1,621.5	1,593.3	1,587.5	1,641.3	1,683.3	1,694.7	1,701.3	1,648.7
2010	1,656.0	1,693.3	1,704.2	1,710.7	1,694.3	1,640.9	1,607.4	1,595.6	1,659.4	1,722.7	1,737.2	1,740.7	1,680.2
2011	1,689.1	1,731.9	1,738.7	1,752.9	1,726.8	1,668.3	1,644.1	1,633.5	1,695.9	1,755.7	1,765.9	1,771.0	1,714.5
2012	1,718.3	1,764.6	1,775.8	1,778.5	1,768.5	1,704.7	1,675.7	1,672.6	1,740.5	1,799.6	1,800.4	1,812.8	1,751.0
2013	1,758.5	1,808.7	1,820.0	1,832.0	1,802.2	1,745.5	1,718.8	1,715.9	1,799.6	1,849.2	1,862.3	1,863.6	1,798.0
2014	1,797.3	1,847.9	1,860.5	1,868.6	1,853.8	1,807.8	1,781.7	1,781.2	1,837.3	1,892.3	1,906.6	1,908.4	1,845.3
2015	1,847.4	1,894.8	1,905.0	1,913.8	1,897.8	1,850.9	1,828.5	1,821.6	1,869.2	1,943.2	1,959.3	1,963.0	1,891.2
2016	1,898.2	1,950.9	1,962.5	1,977.3	1,959.2	1,913.4	1,889.6	1,884.4	1,937.2	1,997.6	2,012.8	2,017.9	1,950.1
2017	1,954.0	2,011.0	2,019.7	2,030.0	2,019.5	1,979.6	1,942.1	1,939.0	1,995.3	2,046.8	2,066.7	2,059.2	2,005.2

1. Employment by Industry: New York, Selected Years, 2007–2017—*Continued*

(Numbers in thousands, not seasonally adjusted)

Industry and year	January	February	March	April	May	June	July	August	September	October	November	December	Annual average
Leisure and Hospitality													
2007	640.9	649.8	659.8	677.3	713.5	739.7	750.3	748.2	719.4	711.0	702.0	700.9	701.1
2008	662.3	669.8	678.2	701.8	733.7	754.4	767.4	765.0	734.9	724.7	708.8	704.8	717.2
2009	662.2	666.1	671.2	686.6	725.2	745.5	757.8	756.5	739.7	723.5	709.1	707.3	712.6
2010	670.4	677.4	687.3	717.8	746.5	768.6	784.3	784.9	762.6	751.1	739.1	736.9	735.6
2011	701.2	709.8	719.9	747.9	776.5	804.9	817.7	815.1	792.9	782.9	773.1	770.4	767.7
2012	731.7	747.2	759.1	778.5	817.8	846.5	856.0	858.1	830.5	821.6	797.7	803.3	804.0
2013	761.1	773.2	786.0	814.4	852.6	883.0	893.7	887.9	864.7	860.6	846.8	844.7	839.1
2014	799.4	811.0	821.8	846.3	890.1	915.3	924.1	918.5	894.1	887.9	872.3	871.1	871.0
2015	826.7	835.6	846.1	872.1	916.7	938.4	954.2	948.1	924.9	914.4	898.1	895.8	897.6
2016	847.3	857.7	871.4	902.3	931.0	960.3	976.7	970.3	942.8	929.2	917.1	914.3	918.4
2017	872.8	885.4	894.5	912.8	954.6	986.0	998.7	996.7	960.8	948.0	928.7	926.5	938.8
Other Services													
2007	356.0	357.7	360.3	361.4	366.0	367.9	363.3	361.1	361.2	365.2	366.2	367.3	362.8
2008	361.7	362.7	364.6	366.7	370.1	371.3	369.6	368.1	367.1	370.0	369.7	369.5	367.6
2009	361.7	362.8	364.1	363.3	366.7	367.6	366.2	363.9	362.5	364.9	365.6	366.2	364.6
2010	356.9	357.3	359.5	362.8	365.5	366.6	368.1	367.0	364.2	368.4	368.5	369.5	364.5
2011	363.5	365.3	367.1	372.5	375.4	376.8	375.4	373.2	374.2	375.3	375.8	377.3	372.7
2012	371.3	372.8	375.9	377.5	381.7	385.0	381.8	379.8	380.2	383.7	382.1	384.2	379.7
2013	377.1	378.9	380.5	384.2	387.3	389.8	389.2	388.8	386.4	390.9	391.8	392.5	386.5
2014	385.2	387.5	389.3	393.3	397.5	398.5	398.1	396.7	395.0	399.5	400.7	401.4	395.2
2015	394.4	395.4	397.1	399.5	403.8	406.7	405.5	404.7	402.1	407.4	408.0	409.0	402.8
2016	400.8	403.4	404.9	409.9	412.7	413.6	413.1	411.2	410.1	413.2	413.4	412.7	409.9
2017	405.8	406.2	407.4	410.9	415.0	418.0	415.9	413.7	412.4	414.1	415.6	417.1	412.7
Government													
2007	1,489.5	1,509.0	1,511.1	1,509.3	1,517.7	1,517.0	1,466.6	1,450.3	1,474.9	1,512.8	1,522.8	1,531.2	1,501.0
2008	1,495.4	1,515.9	1,519.8	1,529.8	1,533.6	1,533.4	1,499.3	1,471.1	1,487.7	1,526.2	1,535.1	1,539.1	1,515.5
2009	1,507.1	1,531.5	1,534.3	1,537.9	1,542.6	1,531.0	1,531.2	1,503.7	1,475.3	1,524.0	1,532.3	1,534.0	1,523.7
2010	1,500.9	1,524.5	1,529.6	1,536.1	1,577.6	1,554.1	1,472.6	1,440.9	1,463.1	1,506.6	1,515.8	1,511.9	1,511.1
2011	1,475.6	1,497.5	1,500.2	1,506.8	1,501.7	1,489.6	1,453.1	1,441.8	1,449.7	1,487.7	1,492.6	1,490.8	1,482.3
2012	1,444.5	1,477.6	1,480.5	1,480.2	1,484.0	1,470.8	1,425.3	1,407.5	1,427.0	1,466.7	1,467.3	1,473.1	1,458.7
2013	1,426.3	1,457.4	1,460.1	1,459.6	1,465.5	1,453.3	1,414.6	1,398.7	1,410.6	1,453.8	1,460.6	1,459.2	1,443.3
2014	1,407.4	1,442.7	1,447.3	1,452.1	1,453.2	1,444.4	1,408.0	1,394.6	1,410.8	1,449.3	1,457.7	1,456.7	1,435.4
2015	1,409.5	1,440.5	1,445.8	1,447.4	1,455.2	1,447.2	1,412.2	1,399.4	1,418.9	1,452.2	1,463.0	1,463.6	1,437.9
2016	1,420.3	1,448.8	1,456.2	1,459.9	1,458.9	1,451.6	1,417.8	1,406.5	1,428.0	1,458.6	1,465.3	1,469.5	1,445.1
2017	1,429.0	1,457.1	1,461.1	1,463.0	1,463.2	1,455.5	1,421.3	1,408.9	1,428.5	1,462.1	1,469.3	1,471.1	1,449.2

2. Average Weekly Hours by Selected Industry: New York, 2013–2017

(Not seasonally adjusted)

Industry and year	January	February	March	April	May	June	July	August	September	October	November	December	Annual average
Total Private													
2013	33.5	33.5	33.6	33.6	33.6	34.2	33.9	34.0	34.1	33.7	33.7	33.9	33.8
2014	33.4	33.6	33.8	33.6	33.6	34.0	33.8	33.9	33.8	33.6	34.0	33.7	33.7
2015	33.5	33.7	33.8	33.5	33.7	33.7	33.8	34.2	33.7	33.7	34.0	33.7	33.7
2016	33.4	33.2	33.2	33.3	33.6	33.5	33.7	33.8	33.6	33.7	33.4	33.5	33.5
2017	33.5	33.1	32.8	33.5	33.3	33.5	33.8	33.5	33.4	33.7	33.4	33.4	33.4
Goods-Producing													
2013	38.2	37.7	37.6	38.0	38.1	38.1	38.4	38.4	38.7	38.5	38.3	38.4	38.2
2014	38.1	37.4	37.9	38.3	38.7	38.6	38.7	38.9	39.1	38.7	38.8	38.9	38.5
2015	38.7	38.0	38.8	38.9	39.3	39.1	39.1	39.0	38.2	38.9	38.8	39.0	38.8
2016	38.5	37.7	38.7	38.5	38.7	38.8	38.7	38.4	38.5	38.2	37.8	37.8	38.4
2017	37.4	36.9	36.4	37.8	38.2	38.4	38.0	38.3	38.7	38.6	38.5	38.4	38.0
Construction													
2013	37.0	35.5	35.4	36.6	36.9	36.2	37.5	36.7	37.2	36.7	36.7	36.1	36.6
2014	36.0	34.7	35.4	36.2	36.6	36.3	37.0	37.3	37.5	36.6	36.7	36.5	36.5
2015	36.6	35.6	37.1	37.5	38.6	38.2	38.6	38.5	37.3	38.1	37.8	38.3	37.7
2016	37.5	35.9	38.0	37.6	37.9	38.1	37.9	37.7	37.9	37.0	36.4	36.7	37.4
2017	36.0	35.2	34.7	36.5	37.1	37.3	37.0	37.5	37.7	37.4	37.1	37.3	36.8
Manufacturing													
2013	38.8	38.8	38.8	38.6	38.7	39.2	38.7	39.3	39.5	39.4	39.2	39.6	39.1
2014	39.1	39.0	39.3	39.5	40.0	40.1	39.8	40.0	40.2	40.3	40.3	40.6	39.9
2015	40.1	39.6	39.9	39.7	39.7	39.7	39.3	39.2	38.7	39.3	39.4	39.4	39.5
2016	39.2	38.9	39.1	39.1	39.3	39.3	39.3	38.9	38.9	39.2	39.0	38.8	39.1
2017	38.6	38.3	37.9	38.4	38.7	38.8	38.3	38.5	39.1	39.3	39.4	39.2	38.7
Trade, Transportation, and Utilities													
2013	34.2	34.3	34.6	34.6	34.7	35.0	34.8	34.8	34.6	34.2	34.2	34.5	34.5
2014	33.7	33.8	34.2	34.2	34.2	34.4	34.5	34.5	34.6	34.2	34.5	34.6	34.3
2015	34.0	34.2	34.2	34.0	34.1	33.9	34.1	34.4	34.6	34.1	34.5	34.0	34.2
2016	33.3	33.3	33.1	33.3	33.6	33.5	33.8	34.0	34.1	33.9	33.7	34.3	33.7
2017	33.3	32.9	32.9	33.4	33.2	33.3	33.6	33.5	33.7	33.5	33.7	33.9	33.4
Information													
2013	35.3	35.1	34.9	35.2	34.8	35.8	34.9	35.0	35.3	34.9	34.8	35.0	35.1
2014	34.6	34.6	34.7	34.3	34.5	34.7	33.9	34.3	34.2	34.1	34.7	33.9	34.4
2015	34.6	35.0	34.8	34.3	34.4	34.3	34.8	35.4	34.9	35.1	35.5	34.8	34.8
2016	35.1	34.5	34.4	34.3	34.8	34.2	34.4	34.6	34.6	34.7	34.8	34.5	34.6
2017	35.3	35.3	35.0	35.2	35.8	35.7	36.0	35.2	35.5	36.3	35.6	35.9	35.6
Financial Activities													
2013	36.5	36.7	36.6	36.8	36.6	38.0	36.8	37.1	37.8	36.7	37.0	37.7	37.0
2014	36.8	37.9	38.0	36.9	37.0	37.8	37.0	37.0	36.7	36.8	37.9	36.8	37.2
2015	36.6	37.9	37.9	37.0	37.3	37.4	37.4	38.6	37.5	37.6	37.7	37.4	37.5
2016	37.3	37.0	36.8	36.4	37.1	36.4	36.7	36.7	35.8	37.1	36.8	36.6	36.7
2017	37.2	36.8	36.6	37.8	37.2	37.8	38.6	37.9	37.5	38.6	37.7	37.4	37.6
Professional and Business Services													
2013	34.4	34.8	34.8	34.7	34.7	35.8	35.0	35.0	35.8	34.8	34.8	35.2	35.0
2014	34.6	35.2	35.1	34.6	34.6	35.5	35.0	35.2	35.0	34.8	35.7	34.8	35.0
2015	34.7	35.5	35.4	34.5	34.7	34.8	34.4	35.3	34.4	34.8	35.6	34.8	34.9
2016	34.6	34.5	34.6	34.7	35.3	35.1	35.3	35.5	35.2	35.7	34.9	34.9	35.0
2017	35.4	34.8	34.4	35.3	34.6	34.7	35.3	34.6	34.3	35.0	34.3	34.2	34.7
Education and Health Services													
2013	32.4	32.3	32.2	32.1	32.1	32.5	32.5	32.4	32.4	32.3	32.3	32.4	32.3
2014	32.3	32.2	32.3	32.1	32.0	32.3	32.0	32.1	32.1	31.9	32.1	31.7	32.1
2015	31.8	31.8	31.8	31.8	31.9	32.0	32.2	32.3	32.1	31.9	32.0	31.9	32.0
2016	32.1	31.9	31.7	31.7	31.8	31.8	32.0	32.1	32.2	32.1	32.0	32.1	32.0
2017	32.3	32.1	31.7	31.8	31.9	31.9	32.0	32.0	31.8	31.9	31.8	31.8	31.9
Leisure and Hospitality													
2013	26.9	26.9	27.1	27.1	27.4	27.7	28.2	28.6	27.8	27.8	27.7	27.7	27.6
2014	27.0	27.4	27.6	27.9	28.2	28.1	28.4	28.5	27.8	28.0	28.1	28.1	27.9
2015	27.7	27.9	27.8	28.3	28.6	28.3	28.7	29.0	28.1	28.3	28.2	28.2	28.3
2016	27.2	27.7	27.8	28.1	28.3	28.4	28.7	28.9	28.5	28.4	28.2	28.1	28.2
2017	27.5	27.2	27.4	28.1	28.2	28.3	28.6	28.4	28.1	28.2	27.9	28.0	28.0
Other Services													
2013	31.1	31.4	31.5	31.6	31.8	32.2	31.8	32.2	32.6	31.3	31.0	31.6	31.7
2014	30.9	31.9	32.0	31.7	31.6	32.2	31.9	32.1	32.0	31.9	32.2	31.3	31.8
2015	31.2	31.7	31.4	31.2	31.5	30.8	31.4	32.0	31.2	31.1	31.3	30.9	31.3
2016	30.9	30.8	30.8	30.8	31.3	31.1	31.4	31.5	31.1	31.0	30.8	30.9	31.0
2017	31.0	30.3	30.1	31.0	30.5	30.9	31.4	31.0	30.8	31.3	30.8	31.2	30.9

3. Average Hourly Earnings by Selected Industry: New York, 2013–2017

(Dollars, not seasonally adjusted)

Industry and year	January	February	March	April	May	June	July	August	September	October	November	December	Annual average
Total Private													
2013	27.83	27.77	27.72	27.80	27.63	27.87	27.67	27.62	28.04	27.76	27.86	28.11	27.81
2014	28.02	28.29	28.26	28.09	27.94	28.28	27.87	27.82	28.08	28.23	28.62	28.34	28.15
2015	28.70	29.03	28.98	28.85	28.55	28.45	28.44	28.75	28.62	28.76	29.23	29.01	28.78
2016	29.25	29.49	29.25	29.11	29.20	28.71	28.99	29.37	29.18	29.63	29.34	29.28	29.23
2017	30.15	29.96	29.99	30.30	29.76	29.64	30.12	29.72	30.07	30.50	30.22	30.47	30.08
Goods-Producing													
2013	28.94	28.84	29.05	29.05	28.73	28.63	28.93	28.99	28.80	28.69	28.81	28.78	28.85
2014	29.10	28.71	28.81	29.15	29.11	28.98	29.25	29.46	29.61	29.65	29.72	29.83	29.29
2015	29.65	29.38	29.89	29.63	29.63	29.71	29.89	29.84	30.03	30.36	30.58	30.84	29.96
2016	30.34	30.17	30.65	30.71	30.66	30.37	30.65	30.84	30.80	30.81	30.69	30.75	30.62
2017	30.85	30.63	31.04	30.93	30.95	31.01	31.46	31.55	31.58	31.57	31.82	32.20	31.31
Construction													
2013	34.67	35.30	35.27	35.01	34.66	34.35	34.53	35.00	34.50	34.16	34.68	34.94	34.74
2014	35.54	35.06	35.40	35.69	35.46	34.84	34.85	35.20	35.57	35.03	35.80	35.61	35.42
2015	35.76	35.19	36.15	35.58	35.12	35.79	36.04	35.92	36.09	36.73	37.16	37.89	36.14
2016	37.27	37.25	37.77	37.39	36.60	36.31	37.10	37.14	37.11	37.22	37.01	37.10	37.10
2017	37.23	37.12	37.51	36.93	36.92	36.81	37.21	37.41	37.29	37.26	37.75	38.14	37.30
Manufacturing													
2013	25.88	25.57	25.80	25.78	25.34	25.37	25.45	25.33	25.37	25.45	25.35	25.65	25.53
2014	25.83	25.86	25.64	25.67	25.63	25.81	26.04	26.00	25.88	25.78	25.87	26.39	25.87
2015	26.13	26.19	26.20	25.89	25.76	25.42	25.35	25.19	25.46	25.37	25.40	25.67	25.67
2016	25.63	25.62	25.63	25.76	26.18	25.76	25.55	25.80	25.57	25.65	25.66	25.83	25.72
2017	25.94	25.74	26.13	26.08	25.95	26.07	26.35	26.17	26.42	26.46	26.41	26.83	26.21
Trade, Transportation, and Utilities													
2013	22.30	22.20	22.21	22.35	22.18	22.28	22.42	22.44	22.99	22.69	22.82	22.90	22.49
2014	23.06	23.32	23.41	23.50	23.27	23.34	23.18	23.07	22.96	22.89	22.53	22.40	23.07
2015	22.83	23.18	23.19	23.41	22.92	22.89	22.87	22.94	22.97	23.27	23.46	23.89	23.15
2016	23.91	24.05	23.98	23.95	23.73	23.43	23.72	24.48	23.63	23.85	23.75	23.44	23.82
2017	24.37	24.40	24.30	24.56	24.47	24.37	24.61	24.33	24.58	24.68	24.45	24.42	24.46
Information													
2013	42.07	42.16	42.51	42.59	43.06	43.73	42.61	41.86	41.99	41.62	41.72	41.74	42.30
2014	41.21	41.03	41.18	40.55	40.14	42.05	41.04	41.01	41.25	41.10	41.85	40.76	41.10
2015	39.93	40.86	41.20	41.51	40.66	40.61	40.91	41.85	41.07	40.85	41.35	40.40	40.94
2016	40.80	42.79	40.64	40.37	41.76	40.58	40.76	42.25	40.71	41.87	41.40	41.85	41.32
2017	42.87	42.47	42.14	43.84	43.80	44.19	45.13	44.01	44.82	45.36	45.94	47.36	44.35
Financial Activities													
2013	38.18	38.31	38.53	39.09	39.25	40.05	39.22	39.63	40.12	39.83	40.11	40.66	39.43
2014	40.59	41.01	41.25	41.23	41.23	42.85	41.14	40.53	41.19	41.85	43.92	42.58	41.62
2015	43.44	44.02	43.73	43.39	43.12	42.62	42.23	43.28	42.62	42.95	43.98	42.40	43.15
2016	41.99	43.81	43.18	42.29	43.65	41.74	42.00	43.74	43.17	44.62	43.38	43.61	43.10
2017	44.43	44.26	43.80	44.90	43.26	42.51	43.73	42.55	43.19	44.92	43.35	44.23	43.76
Professional and Business Services													
2013	35.29	34.96	34.50	34.57	34.34	34.69	34.27	33.83	34.23	33.83	33.81	34.44	34.39
2014	34.14	34.81	34.94	34.39	34.25	35.00	34.18	34.16	34.51	34.89	35.46	35.17	34.66
2015	35.89	36.45	36.19	35.79	35.64	35.31	35.31	35.89	35.38	35.48	36.30	35.73	35.78
2016	36.52	36.57	35.96	35.90	35.71	35.05	35.63	35.64	36.00	36.72	36.09	36.25	36.00
2017	38.13	37.27	37.50	37.95	36.75	36.66	37.45	36.55	37.29	38.34	37.76	38.00	37.47
Education and Health Services													
2013	25.10	25.08	25.08	25.06	24.98	24.93	25.11	25.08	25.38	25.12	25.17	25.19	25.11
2014	24.79	25.00	24.64	24.60	24.50	24.39	24.54	24.59	24.73	24.76	24.83	24.80	24.68
2015	25.02	25.02	24.83	25.04	24.80	24.74	24.94	24.82	24.88	24.65	24.99	24.95	24.89
2016	25.27	25.27	25.12	25.13	25.08	25.09	25.33	25.14	25.32	25.30	25.21	25.18	25.20
2017	25.48	25.53	25.78	25.75	25.55	25.59	25.80	25.73	25.98	25.75	25.84	26.00	25.73
Leisure and Hospitality													
2013	16.97	16.93	17.00	16.94	16.95	16.65	16.51	16.54	17.13	17.56	17.73	18.10	17.08
2014	17.77	17.93	17.85	17.84	17.84	17.15	16.74	16.66	17.41	17.99	18.22	18.50	17.64
2015	18.16	18.28	18.18	18.24	17.84	17.38	17.25	17.32	17.89	18.17	18.64	18.60	17.98
2016	18.77	18.83	18.92	19.23	19.25	18.80	18.63	18.98	19.49	19.70	19.76	19.67	19.17
2017	19.75	19.70	19.71	19.80	19.61	19.01	18.97	19.03	19.48	19.92	19.99	20.32	19.59
Other Services													
2013	23.63	23.93	23.72	23.78	23.57	24.32	23.80	23.69	24.43	23.90	23.85	24.18	23.90
2014	23.77	24.27	24.51	24.16	24.02	24.31	23.78	23.81	24.79	24.36	25.31	25.35	24.37
2015	25.42	26.15	26.44	26.21	26.36	26.71	26.25	26.56	27.29	26.98	27.23	27.20	26.57
2016	27.08	27.44	27.20	26.87	27.09	26.81	26.75	26.49	26.77	27.27	27.88	27.58	27.10
2017	27.94	28.37	28.04	28.08	27.65	27.05	26.96	26.98	27.12	27.14	27.20	27.15	27.47

4. Average Weekly Earnings by Selected Industry: New York, 2013–2017

(Dollars, not seasonally adjusted)

Industry and year	January	February	March	April	May	June	July	August	September	October	November	December	Annual average
Total Private													
2013	932.31	930.30	931.39	934.08	928.37	953.15	938.01	939.08	956.16	935.51	938.88	952.93	939.98
2014	935.87	950.54	955.19	943.82	938.78	961.52	942.01	943.10	949.10	948.53	973.08	955.06	948.66
2015	961.45	978.31	979.52	966.48	962.14	958.77	961.27	983.25	964.49	969.21	993.82	977.64	969.89
2016	976.95	979.07	971.10	969.36	981.12	961.79	976.96	992.71	980.45	998.53	979.96	980.88	979.21
2017	1,010.03	991.68	983.67	1,015.05	991.01	992.94	1,018.06	995.62	1,004.34	1,027.85	1,009.35	1,017.70	1,004.67
Goods-Producing													
2013	1,105.51	1,087.27	1,092.28	1,103.90	1,094.61	1,090.80	1,110.91	1,113.22	1,114.56	1,104.57	1,103.42	1,105.15	1,102.07
2014	1,108.71	1,073.75	1,091.90	1,116.45	1,126.56	1,118.63	1,131.98	1,145.99	1,157.75	1,147.46	1,153.14	1,160.39	1,127.67
2015	1,147.46	1,116.44	1,159.73	1,152.61	1,164.46	1,161.66	1,168.70	1,163.76	1,147.15	1,181.00	1,186.50	1,202.76	1,162.45
2016	1,168.09	1,137.41	1,186.16	1,182.34	1,186.54	1,178.36	1,186.16	1,184.26	1,185.80	1,176.94	1,160.08	1,162.35	1,175.81
2017	1,153.79	1,130.25	1,129.86	1,169.15	1,182.29	1,190.78	1,195.48	1,208.37	1,222.15	1,218.60	1,225.07	1,236.48	1,189.78
Construction													
2013	1,282.79	1,253.15	1,248.56	1,281.37	1,278.95	1,243.47	1,294.88	1,284.50	1,283.40	1,253.67	1,272.76	1,261.33	1,271.48
2014	1,279.44	1,216.58	1,253.16	1,291.98	1,297.84	1,264.69	1,289.45	1,315.20	1,333.88	1,311.38	1,317.16	1,300.86	1,292.83
2015	1,308.82	1,252.76	1,341.17	1,334.25	1,355.63	1,367.18	1,391.14	1,382.92	1,346.16	1,399.41	1,404.65	1,451.19	1,362.48
2016	1,397.63	1,337.28	1,435.26	1,405.86	1,387.14	1,383.41	1,406.09	1,400.18	1,406.47	1,377.14	1,347.16	1,361.57	1,387.54
2017	1,340.28	1,306.62	1,301.60	1,347.95	1,369.73	1,373.01	1,376.77	1,402.88	1,405.83	1,393.52	1,400.53	1,422.62	1,372.64
Manufacturing													
2013	1,004.14	992.12	1,001.04	995.11	980.66	994.50	984.92	995.47	1,002.12	1,002.73	993.72	1,015.74	998.22
2014	1,009.95	1,008.54	1,007.65	1,013.97	1,025.20	1,034.98	1,036.39	1,040.00	1,040.38	1,038.93	1,042.56	1,071.43	1,032.21
2015	1,047.81	1,037.12	1,045.38	1,027.83	1,022.67	1,009.17	996.26	987.45	985.30	997.04	1,006.70	1,011.40	1,013.97
2016	1,004.70	996.62	1,002.13	1,007.22	1,028.87	1,012.37	1,004.12	1,003.62	994.67	1,005.48	1,000.74	1,002.20	1,005.65
2017	1,001.28	985.84	990.33	1,001.47	1,004.27	1,011.52	1,009.21	1,007.55	1,033.02	1,039.88	1,040.55	1,051.74	1,014.33
Trade, Transportation, and Utilities													
2013	762.66	761.46	768.47	773.31	769.65	779.80	780.22	780.91	795.45	776.00	780.44	790.05	775.91
2014	777.12	788.22	800.62	803.70	795.83	802.90	799.71	795.92	794.42	782.84	777.29	775.04	791.30
2015	776.22	792.76	793.10	795.94	781.57	775.97	779.87	789.14	794.76	793.51	809.37	812.26	791.73
2016	796.20	800.87	793.74	797.54	797.33	784.91	801.74	832.32	805.78	808.52	800.38	803.99	802.73
2017	811.52	802.76	799.47	820.30	812.40	811.52	826.90	815.06	828.35	826.78	823.97	827.84	816.96
Information													
2013	1,485.07	1,479.82	1,483.60	1,499.17	1,498.49	1,565.53	1,487.09	1,465.10	1,482.25	1,452.54	1,451.86	1,460.90	1,484.73
2014	1,425.87	1,419.64	1,428.95	1,390.87	1,384.83	1,459.14	1,391.26	1,406.64	1,410.75	1,401.51	1,452.20	1,381.76	1,413.84
2015	1,381.58	1,430.10	1,433.76	1,423.79	1,398.70	1,392.92	1,423.67	1,481.49	1,433.34	1,433.84	1,467.93	1,405.92	1,424.71
2016	1,432.08	1,476.26	1,398.02	1,384.69	1,453.25	1,387.84	1,402.14	1,461.85	1,408.57	1,452.89	1,440.72	1,443.83	1,429.67
2017	1,513.31	1,499.19	1,474.90	1,543.17	1,568.04	1,577.58	1,624.68	1,549.15	1,591.11	1,646.57	1,635.46	1,700.22	1,578.86
Financial Activities													
2013	1,393.57	1,405.98	1,410.20	1,438.51	1,436.55	1,521.90	1,443.30	1,470.27	1,516.54	1,461.76	1,484.07	1,532.88	1,458.91
2014	1,493.71	1,554.28	1,567.50	1,521.39	1,525.51	1,619.73	1,522.18	1,499.61	1,511.67	1,540.08	1,664.57	1,566.94	1,548.26
2015	1,589.90	1,668.36	1,657.37	1,605.43	1,608.38	1,593.99	1,579.40	1,670.61	1,598.25	1,614.92	1,658.05	1,585.76	1,618.13
2016	1,566.23	1,620.97	1,589.02	1,539.36	1,619.42	1,519.34	1,541.40	1,605.26	1,545.49	1,655.40	1,596.38	1,596.13	1,581.77
2017	1,652.80	1,628.77	1,603.08	1,697.22	1,609.27	1,606.88	1,687.98	1,612.65	1,619.63	1,733.91	1,634.30	1,654.20	1,645.38
Professional and Business Services													
2013	1,213.98	1,216.61	1,200.60	1,199.58	1,191.60	1,241.90	1,199.45	1,184.05	1,225.43	1,177.28	1,176.59	1,212.29	1,203.65
2014	1,181.24	1,225.31	1,226.39	1,189.89	1,185.05	1,242.50	1,196.30	1,202.43	1,207.85	1,214.17	1,265.92	1,223.92	1,213.10
2015	1,245.38	1,293.98	1,281.13	1,234.76	1,236.71	1,228.79	1,214.66	1,266.92	1,217.07	1,234.70	1,292.28	1,243.40	1,248.72
2016	1,263.59	1,261.67	1,244.22	1,245.73	1,260.56	1,230.26	1,257.74	1,265.22	1,267.20	1,310.90	1,259.54	1,265.13	1,260.00
2017	1,349.80	1,297.00	1,290.00	1,339.64	1,271.55	1,272.10	1,321.99	1,264.63	1,279.05	1,341.90	1,295.17	1,299.60	1,300.21
Education and Health Services													
2013	813.24	810.08	807.58	804.43	801.86	810.23	816.08	812.59	822.31	811.38	812.99	816.16	811.05
2014	800.72	805.00	795.87	789.66	784.00	787.80	785.28	789.34	793.83	789.84	797.04	786.16	792.23
2015	795.64	795.64	789.59	796.27	791.12	791.68	803.07	801.69	798.65	786.34	799.68	795.91	796.48
2016	811.17	806.11	796.30	796.62	797.54	797.86	810.56	806.99	815.30	812.13	806.72	808.28	806.40
2017	823.00	819.51	817.23	818.85	815.05	816.32	825.60	823.36	826.16	821.43	821.71	826.80	820.79
Leisure and Hospitality													
2013	456.49	455.42	460.70	459.07	464.43	461.21	465.58	473.04	476.21	488.17	491.12	501.37	471.41
2014	479.79	491.28	492.66	497.74	503.09	481.92	475.42	474.81	484.00	503.72	511.98	519.85	492.16
2015	503.03	510.01	505.40	516.19	510.22	491.85	495.08	502.28	502.71	514.21	525.65	524.52	508.83
2016	510.54	521.59	525.98	540.36	544.78	533.92	534.68	548.52	555.47	559.48	557.23	552.73	540.59
2017	543.13	535.84	540.05	556.38	553.00	537.98	542.54	540.45	547.39	561.74	557.72	568.96	548.52
Other Services													
2013	734.89	751.40	747.18	751.45	749.53	783.10	756.84	762.82	796.42	748.07	739.35	764.09	757.63
2014	734.49	774.21	784.32	765.87	759.03	782.78	758.58	764.30	793.28	777.08	814.98	793.46	774.97
2015	793.10	828.96	830.22	817.75	830.34	822.67	824.25	849.92	851.45	839.08	852.30	840.48	831.64
2016	836.77	845.15	837.76	827.60	847.92	833.79	839.95	834.44	832.55	845.37	858.70	852.22	840.10
2017	866.14	859.61	844.00	870.48	843.33	835.85	846.54	836.38	835.30	849.48	837.76	847.08	848.82

NORTH CAROLINA
At a Glance

Population:
  2010 census: 9,535,483
  2017 estimate: 10,273,419

Percent change in population:
  2010–2017: 7.7%

Percent change in total nonfarm employment:
  2007–2017: 6.7%

Industry with the largest growth in employment, 2007–2017 (thousands):
  Professional and business services: 119.6

Industry with the largest decline or smallest growth in employment, 2007–2017 (thousands):
  Manufacturing, -71.1

Civilian labor force:
  2010: 4,616,691
  2017: 4,941,701

Unemployment rate and rank among states (highest to lowest):
  2010: 10.9%, 7th
  2017: 4.6%, 18th

Over-the-year change in unemployment rates:
  2015–2016: -0.6%
  2016–2017: -0.5%

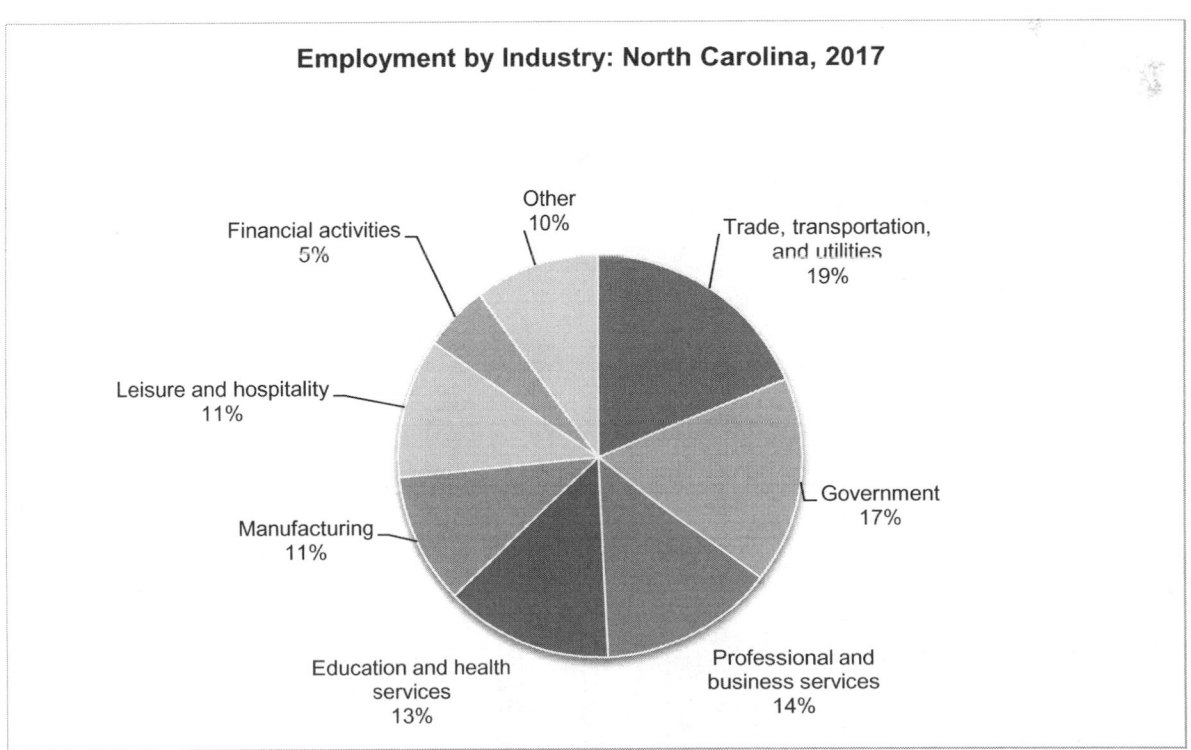

Employment by Industry: North Carolina, 2017

- Other 10%
- Financial activities 5%
- Trade, transportation, and utilities 19%
- Leisure and hospitality 11%
- Government 17%
- Manufacturing 11%
- Professional and business services 14%
- Education and health services 13%

1. Employment by Industry: North Carolina, Selected Years, 2007–2017

(Numbers in thousands, not seasonally adjusted)

Industry and year	January	February	March	April	May	June	July	August	September	October	November	December	Annual average
Total Nonfarm													
2007	4,048.4	4,070.7	4,110.8	4,120.3	4,157.9	4,161.2	4,074.5	4,153.2	4,179.5	4,182.8	4,200.7	4,203.9	4,138.7
2008	4,108.7	4,128.4	4,149.3	4,150.4	4,176.1	4,157.6	4,065.5	4,133.8	4,153.2	4,129.4	4,110.4	4,087.5	4,129.2
2009	3,945.4	3,933.8	3,927.1	3,919.6	3,934.8	3,907.8	3,816.6	3,877.4	3,900.7	3,887.7	3,891.2	3,880.4	3,901.9
2010	3,790.0	3,795.3	3,831.1	3,864.6	3,905.4	3,884.5	3,808.3	3,875.1	3,891.2	3,919.4	3,929.1	3,918.9	3,867.7
2011	3,824.5	3,859.6	3,889.5	3,921.2	3,941.0	3,926.8	3,851.2	3,923.9	3,944.5	3,958.4	3,973.3	3,968.0	3,915.2
2012	3,898.0	3,922.3	3,955.7	3,981.5	4,013.7	3,987.2	3,909.6	3,993.0	4,016.5	4,037.7	4,056.7	4,052.4	3,985.4
2013	3,964.0	3,993.7	4,022.9	4,049.9	4,076.8	4,056.1	3,983.3	4,064.3	4,090.8	4,115.0	4,131.5	4,130.4	4,056.6
2014	4,039.7	4,040.2	4,088.0	4,131.4	4,166.8	4,151.7	4,076.1	4,152.2	4,172.1	4,207.0	4,223.4	4,226.7	4,139.6
2015	4,141.5	4,164.7	4,183.7	4,221.0	4,260.6	4,251.4	4,178.8	4,246.5	4,271.9	4,309.3	4,325.0	4,330.2	4,240.4
2016	4,239.7	4,265.1	4,297.5	4,337.8	4,364.2	4,358.6	4,290.3	4,350.2	4,374.0	4,389.8	4,416.0	4,409.2	4,341.0
2017	4,319.9	4,355.7	4,376.8	4,402.3	4,436.0	4,437.3	4,362.1	4,425.1	4,433.5	4,465.4	4,480.5	4,484.6	4,414.9
Total Private													
2007	3,346.6	3,362.3	3,397.2	3,406.8	3,440.3	3,471.7	3,458.4	3,472.3	3,460.3	3,462.9	3,473.4	3,477.9	3,435.8
2008	3,391.6	3,403.6	3,419.3	3,418.7	3,439.8	3,449.1	3,435.8	3,438.3	3,412.6	3,387.1	3,363.2	3,342.3	3,408.5
2009	3,212.9	3,197.5	3,185.5	3,174.3	3,190.0	3,194.1	3,182.0	3,180.2	3,163.5	3,155.0	3,155.3	3,147.0	3,178.1
2010	3,066.8	3,066.4	3,095.9	3,123.8	3,146.4	3,166.7	3,178.6	3,185.6	3,170.6	3,186.4	3,191.2	3,184.6	3,146.9
2011	3,101.4	3,130.0	3,155.5	3,185.8	3,205.8	3,227.0	3,230.9	3,241.5	3,231.7	3,232.2	3,240.9	3,241.3	3,202.0
2012	3,178.9	3,195.2	3,225.3	3,250.1	3,279.2	3,298.2	3,298.7	3,309.0	3,298.4	3,303.4	3,316.3	3,318.1	3,272.6
2013	3,239.2	3,259.9	3,285.7	3,313.0	3,340.1	3,364.7	3,367.6	3,380.8	3,370.6	3,378.2	3,392.4	3,394.8	3,340.6
2014	3,316.9	3,312.3	3,356.9	3,395.2	3,429.0	3,452.1	3,457.2	3,469.6	3,455.3	3,473.3	3,483.6	3,493.8	3,424.6
2015	3,413.3	3,430.8	3,447.5	3,483.3	3,522.3	3,546.1	3,553.6	3,560.0	3,549.6	3,570.8	3,582.0	3,588.7	3,520.7
2016	3,513.5	3,528.6	3,553.7	3,597.5	3,620.4	3,638.3	3,647.1	3,652.9	3,639.8	3,643.7	3,663.7	3,663.0	3,613.5
2017	3,586.3	3,612.8	3,630.5	3,654.9	3,687.0	3,715.9	3,713.9	3,719.9	3,692.0	3,713.2	3,724.4	3,733.0	3,682.0
Goods Producing													
2007	797.6	797.8	801.5	796.8	799.6	807.4	801.9	804.1	802.5	799.0	797.5	795.7	800.1
2008	776.2	775.2	775.0	767.5	768.3	766.8	762.7	759.4	755.0	743.9	732.4	720.8	758.6
2009	685.1	673.9	662.2	651.9	646.9	644.8	639.3	636.8	634.5	629.8	625.5	622.7	646.1
2010	606.3	603.0	608.0	612.0	614.6	618.5	620.8	620.4	620.4	618.3	616.0	613.7	614.3
2011	597.4	603.2	608.0	610.5	614.6	617.8	618.6	619.6	619.0	615.1	614.0	613.2	612.6
2012	605.5	608.2	613.6	614.7	618.5	621.1	621.6	621.8	622.3	621.0	621.3	621.5	617.6
2013	609.8	612.4	615.5	617.5	621.2	625.9	626.2	626.1	627.0	626.9	627.0	627.3	621.9
2014	616.7	617.3	624.0	625.4	630.7	636.0	638.0	639.5	641.2	645.0	645.7	647.4	633.9
2015	639.3	642.4	645.8	649.5	655.2	659.9	661.4	662.9	662.8	665.3	664.7	666.8	656.3
2016	659.1	661.3	664.1	667.9	669.4	673.6	676.3	675.6	675.4	673.5	676.2	676.9	670.8
2017	667.1	673.2	674.9	677.3	680.3	686.8	686.7	686.7	685.6	686.3	688.3	687.1	681.7
Service-Providing													
2007	3,250.8	3,272.9	3,309.3	3,323.5	3,358.3	3,353.8	3,272.6	3,349.1	3,377.0	3,383.8	3,403.2	3,408.2	3,338.5
2008	3,332.5	3,353.2	3,374.3	3,382.9	3,407.8	3,390.8	3,302.8	3,374.4	3,398.2	3,385.5	3,378.0	3,366.7	3,370.6
2009	3,260.3	3,259.9	3,264.9	3,267.7	3,287.9	3,263.0	3,177.3	3,240.6	3,266.2	3,257.9	3,265.7	3,257.7	3,255.8
2010	3,183.7	3,192.3	3,223.1	3,252.6	3,290.8	3,266.0	3,187.5	3,254.7	3,270.8	3,301.1	3,313.1	3,305.2	3,253.4
2011	3,227.1	3,256.4	3,281.5	3,310.7	3,326.4	3,309.0	3,232.6	3,304.3	3,325.5	3,343.3	3,359.3	3,354.8	3,302.6
2012	3,292.5	3,314.1	3,342.1	3,366.8	3,395.2	3,366.1	3,288.0	3,371.2	3,394.2	3,416.7	3,435.4	3,430.9	3,367.8
2013	3,354.2	3,381.3	3,407.4	3,432.4	3,455.6	3,430.2	3,357.1	3,438.2	3,463.8	3,488.1	3,504.5	3,503.1	3,434.7
2014	3,423.0	3,422.9	3,464.0	3,506.0	3,536.1	3,515.7	3,438.1	3,512.7	3,530.9	3,562.0	3,577.7	3,579.3	3,505.7
2015	3,502.2	3,522.3	3,537.9	3,571.5	3,605.4	3,591.5	3,517.4	3,583.6	3,609.1	3,644.0	3,660.3	3,663.4	3,584.1
2016	3,580.6	3,603.8	3,633.4	3,669.9	3,694.8	3,685.0	3,614.0	3,674.6	3,698.6	3,716.3	3,739.8	3,732.3	3,670.3
2017	3,652.8	3,682.5	3,701.9	3,725.0	3,755.7	3,750.5	3,675.4	3,738.4	3,747.9	3,779.1	3,792.2	3,797.5	3,733.2
Mining and Logging													
2007	6.9	6.9	7.0	7.1	7.1	7.1	7.0	7.1	7.0	6.9	6.9	6.9	7.0
2008	6.8	6.8	6.7	6.6	6.6	6.6	6.6	6.6	6.6	6.5	6.5	6.4	6.6
2009	6.1	6.0	6.0	5.8	5.8	5.9	5.9	5.9	5.9	5.8	5.7	5.6	5.9
2010	5.6	5.5	5.6	5.6	5.6	5.6	5.8	5.7	5.7	5.7	5.6	5.6	5.6
2011	5.5	5.6	5.6	5.5	5.5	5.6	5.7	5.7	5.7	5.6	5.6	5.6	5.6
2012	5.5	5.5	5.6	5.5	5.5	5.6	5.6	5.6	5.6	5.6	5.6	5.5	5.6
2013	5.4	5.4	5.4	5.5	5.5	5.5	5.5	5.6	5.6	5.6	5.6	5.6	5.5
2014	5.4	5.4	5.5	5.5	5.5	5.6	5.6	5.6	5.6	5.5	5.5	5.5	5.5
2015	5.5	5.5	5.5	5.5	5.5	5.6	5.6	5.6	5.6	5.6	5.5	5.5	5.5
2016	5.6	5.5	5.6	5.6	5.6	5.7	5.7	5.7	5.7	5.6	5.6	5.6	5.6
2017	5.6	5.6	5.7	5.6	5.6	5.7	5.8	5.8	5.8	5.8	5.8	5.7	5.7

1. Employment by Industry: North Carolina, Selected Years, 2007–2017—*Continued*

(Numbers in thousands, not seasonally adjusted)

Industry and year	January	February	March	April	May	June	July	August	September	October	November	December	Annual average
Construction													
2007	246.5	247.0	252.0	253.7	256.0	259.8	258.6	259.2	258.4	256.6	255.0	253.0	254.7
2008	242.1	241.6	242.3	239.9	241.0	240.6	240.2	237.3	234.7	229.9	223.9	218.4	236.0
2009	202.2	199.6	197.5	193.6	193.7	194.1	193.7	191.9	189.8	186.6	183.6	182.1	192.4
2010	171.8	169.7	173.8	177.3	178.5	179.9	180.7	180.2	178.5	177.7	176.2	173.5	176.5
2011	162.5	167.2	170.7	172.9	175.2	176.8	177.7	177.7	177.1	174.8	173.7	172.8	173.3
2012	166.5	167.5	171.2	172.1	173.4	173.5	174.0	174.3	173.6	172.9	172.3	172.1	172.0
2013	165.6	166.6	169.5	172.2	174.3	175.7	176.3	176.8	176.8	176.6	176.8	175.5	173.6
2014	169.7	169.3	173.9	175.5	178.6	180.9	182.7	183.5	183.4	185.2	184.5	184.3	179.3
2015	178.4	180.1	182.3	186.1	189.8	191.7	193.4	193.9	193.6	194.8	193.7	194.2	189.3
2016	190.5	191.6	195.0	199.0	200.2	202.5	204.2	204.0	204.4	204.2	205.0	204.9	200.5
2017	198.8	202.4	204.2	206.9	208.8	211.8	211.8	211.7	211.3	212.3	211.9	211.5	208.6
Manufacturing													
2007	544.2	543.9	542.5	536.0	536.5	540.5	536.3	537.8	537.1	535.5	535.6	535.8	538.5
2008	527.3	526.8	526.0	521.0	520.7	519.6	515.9	515.5	513.7	507.5	502.0	496.0	516.0
2009	476.8	468.3	458.7	452.5	447.4	444.8	439.7	439.0	438.8	437.4	436.2	435.0	447.9
2010	428.9	427.8	428.6	429.1	430.5	433.0	434.3	434.5	436.2	434.9	434.2	434.6	432.2
2011	429.4	430.4	431.7	432.1	433.9	435.4	435.2	436.2	436.2	434.7	434.7	434.8	433.7
2012	433.5	435.2	436.8	437.1	439.6	442.0	442.0	441.9	443.1	442.5	443.4	443.9	440.1
2013	438.8	440.4	440.6	439.8	441.4	444.7	444.4	443.7	444.6	444.7	444.6	446.2	442.8
2014	441.6	442.6	444.6	444.4	446.6	449.5	449.7	450.4	452.2	454.3	455.7	457.6	449.1
2015	455.4	456.8	458.0	457.9	459.9	462.6	462.4	463.4	463.6	464.9	465.5	467.1	461.5
2016	463.0	464.2	463.5	463.3	463.6	465.4	466.4	465.9	465.3	463.7	465.6	466.4	464.7
2017	462.7	465.2	465.0	464.8	465.9	469.3	469.1	469.2	468.5	468.2	470.6	469.9	467.4
Trade, Transportation, and Utilities													
2007	765.9	762.1	770.8	770.7	777.6	780.2	779.3	779.4	776.7	780.3	795.4	802.4	778.4
2008	771.3	768.3	772.9	769.4	772.0	773.6	770.9	769.2	763.3	763.6	767.8	769.2	769.3
2009	729.7	721.3	720.4	715.9	720.7	722.5	719.2	717.9	714.0	716.1	724.1	727.2	720.8
2010	700.2	696.8	703.3	706.8	712.4	715.2	716.0	717.3	712.4	718.0	730.5	736.2	713.8
2011	709.8	710.1	715.2	720.4	724.1	726.8	730.8	731.9	728.7	733.4	746.5	753.0	727.6
2012	729.6	725.6	731.7	735.5	741.9	745.0	745.9	744.8	743.8	747.3	763.9	768.3	743.6
2013	739.3	737.8	742.6	745.6	751.6	756.2	759.0	760.5	758.1	764.6	780.9	789.5	757.1
2014	759.4	752.9	760.6	766.2	771.6	776.4	775.5	778.0	775.3	782.8	799.3	809.3	775.6
2015	776.6	775.3	780.3	786.3	792.5	798.0	798.9	799.9	797.3	805.2	820.7	828.8	796.7
2016	798.4	796.4	800.8	807.7	812.2	814.7	816.4	818.0	814.7	819.0	836.9	846.0	815.1
2017	815.5	812.4	814.6	817.3	822.2	828.1	828.3	829.4	824.3	831.8	846.0	855.3	827.1
Wholesale Trade													
2007	179.1	180.0	181.3	181.7	182.4	183.7	183.6	183.1	182.8	183.0	183.2	183.6	182.3
2008	181.3	182.1	182.8	180.8	181.4	181.3	180.4	179.8	178.4	178.3	176.7	175.2	179.9
2009	170.6	169.9	168.8	167.4	166.9	166.4	165.4	165.0	164.1	164.6	164.2	164.0	166.4
2010	161.7	162.2	163.4	164.1	164.5	164.4	165.0	165.2	164.4	165.5	166.0	166.1	164.4
2011	164.2	165.3	166.0	167.1	167.4	168.0	168.9	168.8	168.7	168.7	169.2	169.4	167.6
2012	167.6	168.5	170.0	170.9	171.9	172.3	172.6	172.7	172.5	172.6	172.8	172.7	171.4
2013	170.2	171.4	172.3	172.1	172.7	173.4	174.0	174.3	174.2	174.5	175.1	175.5	173.3
2014	173.5	173.9	175.0	175.2	175.8	176.4	176.5	177.2	176.6	177.2	177.3	177.7	176.0
2015	175.2	176.1	177.1	177.2	178.1	178.8	179.6	179.5	179.0	179.9	180.4	180.9	178.5
2016	179.0	179.8	180.6	182.0	182.3	182.6	183.3	183.2	182.6	182.7	183.2	183.6	182.1
2017	181.6	182.7	183.1	183.9	184.9	186.6	186.3	186.4	185.8	187.7	188.3	189.5	185.6
Retail Trade													
2007	456.3	452.3	458.7	458.7	464.4	465.7	465.8	466.3	464.1	468.2	482.7	488.0	465.9
2008	463.4	459.7	463.6	462.1	463.4	465.0	464.0	462.7	459.0	459.4	465.3	467.0	462.9
2009	438.4	432.4	433.2	431.8	437.1	439.0	437.9	437.4	434.4	436.5	444.7	447.0	437.5
2010	426.7	423.0	427.4	429.3	433.4	435.7	435.4	436.4	432.0	436.1	447.4	452.2	434.6
2011	430.1	428.9	432.3	435.5	438.8	440.1	442.8	443.5	439.7	444.3	456.4	460.8	441.1
2012	442.9	438.2	441.7	444.9	449.9	452.1	452.8	451.5	449.9	453.0	468.7	470.9	451.4
2013	447.5	446.1	449.0	452.1	456.6	459.8	461.8	462.0	459.4	465.0	479.2	484.8	460.3
2014	460.3	455.3	460.4	465.3	468.8	471.9	471.2	472.2	469.1	475.2	489.8	495.6	471.3
2015	470.8	469.0	472.2	476.8	481.4	485.4	485.5	486.0	483.6	489.7	502.7	506.3	484.1
2016	483.2	482.0	484.9	490.5	494.3	495.5	496.6	497.6	494.3	498.3	512.1	515.3	495.4
2017	492.9	490.2	491.7	493.4	496.1	498.9	498.9	498.7	494.0	498.1	509.7	512.5	497.9

1. Employment by Industry: North Carolina, Selected Years, 2007–2017—*Continued*

(Numbers in thousands, not seasonally adjusted)

Industry and year	January	February	March	April	May	June	July	August	September	October	November	December	Annual average
Transportation and Utilities													
2007	130.5	129.8	130.8	130.3	130.8	130.8	129.9	130.0	129.8	129.1	129.5	130.8	130.2
2008	126.6	126.5	126.5	126.5	127.2	127.3	126.5	126.7	125.9	125.9	125.8	127.0	126.5
2009	120.7	119.0	118.4	116.7	116.7	117.1	115.9	115.5	115.5	115.0	115.2	116.2	116.8
2010	111.8	111.6	112.5	113.4	114.5	115.1	115.6	115.7	116.0	116.4	117.1	117.9	114.8
2011	115.5	115.9	116.9	117.8	117.9	118.7	119.1	119.6	120.3	120.4	120.9	122.8	118.8
2012	119.1	118.9	120.0	119.7	120.1	120.6	120.5	120.6	121.4	121.7	122.4	124.7	120.8
2013	121.6	120.3	121.3	121.4	122.3	123.0	123.2	124.2	124.5	125.1	126.6	129.2	123.6
2014	125.6	123.7	125.2	125.7	127.0	128.1	127.8	128.6	129.6	130.4	132.2	136.0	128.3
2015	130.6	130.2	131.0	132.3	133.0	133.8	133.8	134.4	134.7	135.6	137.6	141.6	134.1
2016	136.2	134.6	135.3	135.2	135.6	136.6	136.5	137.2	137.8	138.0	141.6	147.1	137.6
2017	141.0	139.5	139.8	140.0	141.2	142.6	143.1	144.3	144.5	146.0	148.0	153.3	143.6
Information													
2007	72.2	72.6	72.4	72.5	72.7	73.1	73.0	72.7	72.4	72.7	72.9	72.8	72.7
2008	72.0	72.3	72.2	72.2	72.4	72.6	72.2	72.2	71.5	72.2	72.5	72.4	72.2
2009	71.3	71.1	70.6	70.4	70.3	70.1	69.6	69.1	68.5	68.6	68.8	68.7	69.8
2010	67.7	67.7	67.9	67.8	68.3	68.6	68.7	68.6	68.4	68.3	68.7	68.8	68.3
2011	67.9	67.9	67.9	68.4	68.4	68.9	69.3	69.5	69.2	69.3	69.6	69.5	68.8
2012	69.1	69.2	69.0	69.1	69.0	69.5	69.6	69.3	68.6	68.8	69.1	69.3	69.1
2013	69.2	69.5	69.4	69.2	69.9	70.1	70.6	70.6	70.0	70.7	71.5	71.9	70.2
2014	71.0	71.3	71.4	71.3	72.0	72.8	73.3	73.6	73.2	73.9	74.3	75.0	72.8
2015	74.2	74.7	74.8	74.9	76.3	76.7	77.0	76.9	76.3	76.8	77.5	77.9	76.2
2016	77.3	78.5	77.7	78.5	79.2	79.0	79.5	78.8	77.7	78.8	79.0	79.2	78.6
2017	78.2	78.6	78.6	78.7	78.6	79.0	79.2	79.2	78.3	79.6	80.0	80.7	79.1
Financial Activities													
2007	207.3	207.6	209.0	211.1	212.3	214.4	214.0	214.0	212.2	212.0	210.9	211.4	211.4
2008	210.2	211.5	212.2	213.5	213.6	215.4	214.4	214.4	211.9	211.1	209.3	209.3	212.2
2009	204.9	204.3	203.6	202.8	203.5	203.9	203.9	202.9	200.4	199.6	199.3	199.4	202.4
2010	197.1	197.4	198.1	198.3	199.0	200.7	201.5	201.8	200.5	200.5	200.4	200.5	199.7
2011	198.4	198.9	199.1	199.7	201.2	203.1	203.7	204.0	201.6	201.4	201.0	201.2	201.1
2012	198.5	199.3	200.7	201.4	202.3	204.4	204.5	204.9	203.4	204.3	204.0	204.2	202.7
2013	201.8	202.4	203.0	205.2	206.4	208.7	209.0	209.5	208.0	208.0	207.7	208.0	206.5
2014	207.2	207.2	208.2	209.1	211.0	213.2	215.1	216.0	214.7	214.3	214.3	215.1	212.2
2015	212.6	213.7	214.0	215.4	217.4	220.1	222.0	222.0	221.3	222.2	222.0	223.0	218.8
2016	220.9	221.9	222.3	223.7	225.2	227.7	229.7	230.3	228.7	229.5	229.1	230.0	226.6
2017	226.9	227.7	228.6	230.3	231.8	234.9	236.6	236.5	234.7	234.2	232.6	233.6	232.4
Professional and Business Services													
2007	476.0	483.0	488.6	493.4	497.0	504.0	501.0	505.7	507.3	509.9	507.5	507.7	498.4
2008	496.6	500.3	502.1	504.2	505.3	507.3	502.7	507.2	503.0	500.8	490.8	484.4	500.4
2009	468.9	466.2	462.0	459.7	458.2	458.7	460.0	463.2	464.9	471.2	472.7	471.8	464.8
2010	460.4	463.2	468.2	476.0	476.0	480.8	487.6	491.7	492.8	504.1	502.5	501.7	483.8
2011	489.1	498.8	502.3	508.3	507.4	512.0	514.8	519.2	522.9	524.9	524.7	524.2	512.4
2012	513.4	520.9	525.0	529.3	531.0	534.4	532.0	538.4	537.8	540.9	540.9	540.6	532.1
2013	524.8	533.9	537.8	542.6	544.0	547.3	546.8	555.0	555.8	560.2	560.1	556.7	547.1
2014	544.9	546.0	555.0	566.3	568.1	572.2	574.9	578.2	577.4	583.1	580.8	581.3	569.0
2015	567.9	573.7	574.0	582.8	586.3	589.3	592.3	597.7	598.7	604.7	604.7	601.9	589.5
2016	586.9	591.5	596.1	604.5	604.0	607.2	609.6	611.3	612.8	614.3	615.0	609.8	605.3
2017	598.0	606.0	609.1	611.9	614.1	620.9	620.1	621.7	618.9	630.4	632.0	633.1	618.0
Education and Health Services													
2007	502.3	508.7	512.3	515.0	517.7	517.4	514.6	520.4	523.5	528.1	530.9	531.9	518.6
2008	523.9	528.9	529.4	529.0	531.5	529.2	526.3	529.9	533.2	534.1	537.8	537.9	530.9
2009	532.2	536.6	536.4	537.0	538.7	536.4	532.6	535.9	537.2	539.4	541.0	539.6	536.9
2010	533.8	535.8	537.4	538.0	538.4	533.8	532.6	534.4	533.0	541.0	542.5	540.2	536.7
2011	532.3	538.5	538.7	541.3	540.8	536.6	533.1	536.1	540.6	544.8	546.7	546.0	539.6
2012	541.3	546.1	546.4	546.9	549.0	545.7	543.1	546.3	551.0	555.9	557.3	558.1	548.9
2013	550.6	556.1	557.5	557.9	558.9	555.3	554.1	557.9	562.2	564.4	565.8	565.2	558.8
2014	557.7	560.3	565.5	567.9	569.6	564.6	565.0	569.4	570.9	576.2	577.6	576.5	568.4
2015	566.6	571.8	570.9	572.1	574.2	569.4	567.7	569.2	574.2	581.9	583.5	582.7	573.7
2016	575.0	579.6	581.8	585.9	587.0	581.2	582.0	586.6	590.1	594.5	596.4	595.4	586.3
2017	590.2	597.2	596.0	598.5	600.6	594.6	593.2	597.6	598.8	605.4	607.8	608.5	599.0

1. Employment by Industry: North Carolina, Selected Years, 2007–2017—*Continued*

(Numbers in thousands, not seasonally adjusted)

Industry and year	January	February	March	April	May	June	July	August	September	October	November	December	Annual average
Leisure and Hospitality													
2007	374.2	378.0	388.2	396.0	409.8	418.7	417.1	419.0	410.6	404.0	401.3	398.9	401.3
2008	386.1	390.7	399.1	404.7	416.8	422.3	424.2	424.5	415.6	404.2	396.3	393.0	406.5
2009	375.7	378.1	384.2	391.7	406.1	411.5	411.6	410.3	402.9	391.0	385.4	380.7	394.1
2010	365.6	366.7	376.2	388.8	400.4	410.2	412.3	413.1	406.1	398.5	393.2	386.9	393.2
2011	371.1	376.4	387.3	400.3	411.7	421.4	420.2	421.7	411.9	404.9	400.4	396.2	402.0
2012	384.5	388.4	400.4	413.5	425.9	434.4	437.5	439.2	427.4	421.3	415.6	412.1	416.7
2013	400.4	403.0	413.4	428.1	440.3	451.6	453.2	453.1	442.5	437.1	432.2	430.4	432.1
2014	415.7	413.3	426.2	442.1	457.8	466.2	465.2	465.2	454.7	449.9	443.9	441.7	445.2
2015	430.3	432.9	440.7	454.2	470.5	481.7	482.1	480.4	470.0	466.2	460.5	459.3	460.7
2016	448.8	452.1	462.8	479.8	492.8	502.4	500.8	499.9	488.6	483.0	479.8	475.5	480.5
2017	461.5	468.1	478.4	489.8	507.0	517.2	516.1	516.1	499.9	494.9	487.1	483.9	493.3
Other Services													
2007	151.1	152.5	154.4	151.3	153.6	156.5	157.5	157.0	155.1	156.9	157.0	157.1	155.0
2008	155.3	156.4	156.4	158.2	159.9	161.9	162.4	161.5	159.1	157.2	156.3	155.3	158.3
2009	145.1	146.0	146.1	144.9	145.6	146.2	145.8	144.1	141.1	139.3	138.5	136.9	143.3
2010	135.7	135.8	136.8	136.1	137.3	138.9	139.1	138.3	137.0	137.7	137.4	136.6	137.2
2011	135.4	136.2	137.0	136.9	137.6	140.4	140.4	139.5	137.8	138.4	138.0	138.0	138.0
2012	137.0	137.5	138.5	139.7	141.6	143.7	144.5	144.3	144.1	143.9	144.2	144.0	141.9
2013	143.3	144.8	146.5	146.9	147.8	149.6	148.7	148.1	147.0	146.3	147.2	145.8	146.8
2014	144.3	144.0	146.0	146.9	148.2	150.3	150.2	149.7	147.9	148.1	147.7	147.5	147.6
2015	145.8	146.3	147.0	148.1	149.9	151.0	152.2	151.0	149.0	148.5	148.4	148.3	148.8
2016	147.1	147.3	148.1	149.5	150.6	152.5	152.8	152.4	151.8	151.1	151.3	150.2	150.4
2017	148.9	149.6	150.3	151.1	152.4	154.4	153.7	152.7	151.5	150.6	150.6	150.8	151.4
Government													
2007	701.8	708.4	713.6	713.5	717.6	689.5	616.1	680.9	719.2	719.9	727.3	726.0	702.8
2008	717.1	724.8	730.0	731.7	736.3	708.5	629.7	695.5	740.6	742.3	747.2	745.2	720.7
2009	732.5	736.3	741.6	745.3	744.8	713.7	634.6	697.2	737.2	732.7	735.9	733.4	723.8
2010	723.2	728.9	735.2	740.8	759.0	717.8	629.7	689.5	720.6	733.0	737.9	734.3	720.8
2011	723.1	729.6	734.0	735.4	735.2	699.8	620.3	682.4	712.8	726.2	732.4	726.7	713.2
2012	719.1	727.1	730.4	731.4	734.5	689.0	610.9	684.0	718.1	734.3	740.4	734.3	712.8
2013	724.8	733.8	737.2	736.9	736.7	691.4	615.7	683.5	720.2	736.8	739.1	735.6	716.0
2014	722.8	727.9	731.1	736.2	737.8	699.6	618.9	682.6	716.8	733.7	739.8	732.9	715.0
2015	728.2	733.9	736.2	737.7	738.3	705.3	625.2	686.5	722.3	738.5	743.0	741.5	719.7
2016	726.2	736.5	743.8	740.3	743.8	720.3	643.2	697.3	734.2	746.1	752.3	746.2	727.5
2017	733.6	742.9	746.3	747.4	749.0	721.4	648.2	705.2	741.5	752.2	756.1	751.6	733.0

2. Average Weekly Hours by Selected Industry: North Carolina, 2013–2017

(Not seasonally adjusted)

Industry and year	January	February	March	April	May	June	July	August	September	October	November	December	Annual average
Total Private													
2013	34.0	34.4	34.5	34.4	34.3	34.9	34.2	34.6	35.0	34.4	34.6	34.7	34.5
2014	34.0	33.3	35.2	34.8	34.7	35.2	34.7	34.9	34.7	34.6	35.1	34.7	34.7
2015	34.2	34.5	34.9	34.4	34.5	34.5	34.5	35.0	34.3	34.6	34.6	34.4	34.5
2016	33.8	33.8	34.1	34.3	34.5	34.4	34.5	34.4	34.4	34.6	34.5	34.3	34.3
2017	34.0	34.4	34.3	34.7	34.4	34.7	34.9	34.4	34.5	34.9	34.5	34.4	34.5
Goods-Producing													
2013	39.4	39.5	39.9	39.9	39.9	40.4	39.8	40.7	41.0	40.1	40.8	40.7	40.2
2014	40.0	38.8	42.8	42.3	42.0	42.7	41.7	42.1	41.9	41.6	42.2	41.9	41.7
2015	40.2	40.5	41.3	40.6	41.1	40.9	40.9	41.3	40.3	41.0	40.5	41.2	40.8
2016	39.8	39.7	40.8	40.8	40.8	41.0	40.7	40.6	40.9	40.6	41.4	40.5	40.6
2017	39.0	40.4	40.3	40.1	40.8	41.1	40.6	40.3	40.3	40.8	40.8	40.6	40.4
Construction													
2013	37.8	37.3	38.7	38.9	38.9	39.0	38.7	39.8	40.1	38.9	39.8	38.4	38.9
2014	38.5	35.4	41.2	40.0	40.7	41.3	40.8	40.9	40.0	40.2	40.7	40.6	40.1
2015	37.2	39.0	40.3	39.3	40.9	41.1	41.1	41.4	39.6	40.6	39.4	41.2	40.1
2016	38.8	38.1	40.9	40.3	40.3	41.3	40.8	40.0	40.6	40.4	41.1	39.0	40.1
2017	36.8	39.4	39.5	39.7	40.6	41.0	40.6	39.7	39.4	39.9	40.0	40.1	39.7
Manufacturing													
2013	40.2	40.5	40.5	40.5	40.4	41.1	40.4	41.2	41.5	40.7	41.3	41.8	40.8
2014	40.8	40.3	43.5	43.4	42.7	43.4	42.2	42.8	42.9	42.4	43.0	42.6	42.5
2015	41.7	41.3	41.8	41.3	41.3	40.9	40.8	41.3	40.7	41.1	40.9	41.0	41.2
2016	40.1	40.3	40.5	41.0	41.0	40.7	40.4	40.7	40.9	40.5	41.4	41.1	40.7
2017	40.5	41.1	40.9	40.3	41.0	41.3	40.7	40.8	40.9	41.3	41.2	40.8	40.9
Trade, Transportation, and Utilities													
2013	34.0	34.5	34.7	34.6	34.5	35.0	34.7	34.8	35.1	34.5	34.4	34.7	34.6
2014	33.9	33.1	34.8	34.5	34.4	34.7	34.4	34.3	34.2	34.1	34.2	34.3	34.2
2015	33.8	34.2	34.4	34.3	34.5	34.4	34.6	35.1	34.7	34.6	34.4	34.3	34.4
2016	33.6	34.0	34.1	34.3	34.7	34.6	34.5	34.8	34.7	34.7	34.6	34.7	34.4
2017	34.4	34.6	34.5	35.1	34.8	34.8	35.0	34.5	34.6	34.8	34.3	34.6	34.7
Information													
2013	36.1	36.3	36.1	36.5	37.1	38.9	36.5	36.7	36.8	35.7	36.9	37.2	36.7
2014	36.2	37.0	37.5	36.7	36.4	37.3	35.1	36.5	35.5	35.6	36.9	35.6	36.4
2015	35.4	36.4	36.3	35.7	35.7	36.3	36.1	36.9	36.2	35.9	36.9	35.1	36.1
2016	36.2	36.1	35.8	36.1	36.3	35.5	36.8	35.8	36.0	36.7	36.0	35.5	36.1
2017	36.6	37.0	37.5	38.0	36.4	37.7	39.4	38.2	38.1	37.6	36.4	36.6	37.5
Financial Activities													
2013	36.1	37.0	36.5	36.5	36.6	37.6	36.0	36.1	36.9	36.0	36.2	36.7	36.5
2014	36.4	36.8	36.9	36.2	36.2	37.1	36.2	36.2	36.3	36.8	37.8	36.7	36.6
2015	37.1	38.3	38.5	37.5	37.6	37.6	37.6	38.3	37.5	37.8	38.9	38.1	37.9
2016	38.2	38.2	38.4	38.5	39.2	38.6	38.7	38.3	38.3	38.9	38.0	37.9	38.4
2017	39.0	38.3	37.8	39.0	37.6	38.0	38.8	37.7	38.0	39.2	38.4	38.5	38.4
Professional and Business Services													
2013	35.7	36.2	36.1	36.2	36.4	36.9	35.8	36.6	37.2	36.4	36.5	36.5	36.4
2014	35.4	35.2	36.8	36.4	36.4	37.1	36.4	36.7	36.2	36.4	37.1	36.1	36.4
2015	35.7	36.3	36.7	36.0	36.0	36.2	35.8	36.7	35.4	36.2	36.6	35.7	36.1
2016	35.0	35.0	35.0	35.2	35.7	35.6	35.7	35.7	35.6	36.3	35.5	35.6	35.5
2017	35.5	35.5	35.6	36.1	35.8	36.2	36.5	36.0	36.2	36.7	36.1	35.5	36.0
Education and Health Services													
2013	32.9	33.0	32.8	32.8	32.7	33.4	32.7	32.7	33.2	32.8	32.8	33.0	32.9
2014	32.5	31.9	32.8	32.6	32.6	32.9	32.6	32.8	32.9	32.5	33.0	32.5	32.6
2015	32.5	32.3	32.6	32.2	32.3	32.3	32.1	32.5	32.1	32.2	32.4	32.2	32.3
2016	31.9	31.5	31.4	31.8	32.2	31.8	32.1	31.7	31.8	32.1	31.9	32.0	31.8
2017	32.2	32.1	32.0	32.5	32.3	32.3	32.7	32.3	32.6	32.9	32.5	32.5	32.4
Leisure and Hospitality													
2013	24.5	25.5	25.9	25.8	25.6	25.9	25.8	25.7	25.7	25.7	25.7	25.6	25.6
2014	25.0	24.2	26.0	25.9	25.7	26.2	26.2	26.6	26.0	26.0	26.0	26.0	25.8
2015	25.4	25.8	26.1	26.0	25.9	26.1	26.2	26.5	25.6	25.6	25.7	25.6	25.9
2016	24.7	25.4	25.9	25.8	25.9	26.0	26.3	26.2	25.9	26.0	26.2	25.7	25.8
2017	24.7	25.7	25.8	26.0	25.8	26.2	26.5	26.3	25.8	26.3	26.2	25.7	25.9
Other Services													
2013	30.9	31.1	31.3	30.7	30.3	31.3	30.5	30.8	31.9	30.9	31.4	30.8	31.0
2014	30.2	28.8	30.9	30.9	31.1	31.1	31.3	31.3	30.7	30.9	32.0	31.3	30.9
2015	31.1	31.3	31.9	30.7	31.2	30.8	31.2	31.4	30.8	30.6	30.6	29.9	31.0
2016	29.9	29.5	30.2	30.8	30.7	30.6	30.8	30.8	30.3	30.3	29.8	30.2	30.3
2017	29.4	30.4	29.8	30.9	29.3	29.7	30.4	29.8	29.0	29.6	28.9	28.9	29.7

3. Average Hourly Earnings by Selected Industry: North Carolina, 2013–2017

(Dollars, not seasonally adjusted)

Industry and year	January	February	March	April	May	June	July	August	September	October	November	December	Annual average
Total Private													
2013	21.93	21.85	21.75	21.63	21.55	21.67	21.52	21.51	21.68	21.55	21.65	21.85	21.67
2014	21.81	22.46	22.16	21.69	21.62	21.71	21.60	21.63	21.84	21.77	22.10	21.82	21.85
2015	22.04	22.35	22.03	22.04	22.10	22.03	22.13	22.54	22.35	22.48	22.84	22.66	22.30
2016	22.97	23.18	23.19	23.24	23.45	23.30	23.28	23.45	23.53	23.84	23.69	23.62	23.40
2017	24.06	23.98	24.01	24.33	23.98	23.77	24.17	23.97	24.19	24.47	24.20	24.28	24.12
Goods-Producing													
2013	21.06	20.91	20.96	20.98	20.85	20.79	20.88	20.76	20.81	20.81	20.90	21.15	20.90
2014	20.86	21.34	20.82	20.62	20.72	20.83	21.07	20.95	21.21	21.17	21.24	21.22	21.00
2015	21.56	21.55	21.36	21.50	21.49	21.38	21.26	21.43	21.42	21.46	21.70	21.84	21.50
2016	21.70	21.91	21.88	21.98	22.08	22.14	22.02	22.06	21.85	22.32	21.97	22.31	22.02
2017	22.61	22.50	22.71	22.75	22.81	22.87	23.22	22.99	23.31	23.34	23.21	23.44	22.98
Construction													
2013	21.14	21.05	20.89	20.66	20.70	20.50	20.35	20.59	20.59	20.85	20.64	21.08	20.75
2014	20.66	21.65	20.94	20.81	20.68	20.84	21.13	20.96	21.29	21.30	21.24	21.47	21.09
2015	22.33	21.80	21.71	22.02	21.73	21.90	21.69	21.92	22.23	22.48	22.74	22.77	22.11
2016	22.38	22.49	22.25	22.28	22.53	22.22	21.76	22.08	22.18	22.51	22.10	22.63	22.28
2017	23.00	22.95	23.03	22.93	22.88	23.12	23.54	23.27	23.81	23.70	23.68	23.80	23.32
Manufacturing													
2013	20.97	20.79	20.92	21.04	20.85	20.84	21.03	20.80	20.87	20.79	20.96	21.14	20.92
2014	20.90	21.24	20.81	20.57	20.77	20.85	21.07	20.95	21.22	21.09	21.28	21.13	20.99
2015	21.25	21.44	21.19	21.27	21.35	21.09	21.01	21.15	20.97	20.89	21.14	21.31	21.17
2016	21.33	21.59	21.64	21.83	21.84	22.12	22.20	22.06	21.67	22.20	21.97	22.21	21.89
2017	22.51	22.29	22.53	22.68	22.75	22.71	23.05	22.81	23.02	23.15	22.96	23.26	22.81
Trade, Transportation, and Utilities													
2013	20.92	20.70	20.72	20.70	20.54	20.82	20.82	20.71	21.07	20.90	20.85	20.96	20.81
2014	21.29	21.57	21.96	21.01	20.95	21.07	20.73	20.78	21.13	20.46	20.72	20.43	21.00
2015	20.66	21.08	20.45	20.56	20.36	20.64	20.64	21.03	21.15	21.47	21.28	20.98	20.86
2016	21.50	21.40	21.72	21.72	21.77	21.93	22.13	21.87	21.99	22.05	22.04	21.79	21.83
2017	22.15	21.79	22.38	22.72	22.34	22.17	22.52	22.13	22.52	22.64	22.28	22.13	22.31
Information													
2013	31.20	30.99	31.25	30.93	30.37	31.53	30.73	31.00	31.72	31.29	32.08	31.92	31.26
2014	31.85	33.95	32.05	31.18	31.82	32.15	32.40	32.36	33.26	33.28	34.96	33.91	32.77
2015	34.11	36.40	35.36	35.71	35.55	35.07	34.93	35.93	35.65	36.13	37.15	36.77	35.74
2016	37.31	39.39	37.23	38.48	38.62	37.86	37.85	37.70	38.66	39.52	38.41	39.28	38.36
2017	39.63	39.08	36.97	38.50	36.60	37.22	38.33	36.74	38.06	39.01	38.08	38.87	38.09
Financial Activities													
2013	27.73	28.29	27.77	27.46	28.17	28.19	28.02	28.10	27.62	27.27	27.56	27.75	27.83
2014	27.41	27.99	27.33	26.26	26.56	27.25	26.76	27.34	27.77	28.30	27.68	27.03	27.31
2015	27.14	27.56	28.88	28.23	28.88	28.66	29.24	30.33	29.66	29.93	30.87	30.11	29.15
2016	31.06	32.68	32.02	31.68	32.46	32.03	32.32	33.70	33.22	33.46	32.96	32.66	32.53
2017	33.51	34.50	33.81	34.49	33.87	33.30	34.07	34.28	34.24	34.36	33.30	32.24	33.83
Professional and Business Services													
2013	26.32	26.35	26.30	25.84	25.54	25.90	25.44	25.29	25.68	25.24	25.54	26.01	25.78
2014	25.78	27.25	27.15	26.53	26.01	26.27	26.00	25.78	26.08	26.10	26.74	26.44	26.34
2015	26.54	27.08	26.45	26.43	26.49	26.17	26.72	27.13	26.87	26.58	27.47	27.26	26.77
2016	27.71	28.00	28.57	28.56	28.69	28.39	28.32	28.29	28.64	28.88	28.58	28.48	28.43
2017	29.09	28.86	29.03	29.31	28.40	28.09	28.70	27.78	28.19	28.98	28.44	28.87	28.64
Education and Health Services													
2013	22.08	22.00	21.88	21.89	21.94	21.89	21.88	21.98	21.94	22.05	22.05	22.06	21.97
2014	22.10	22.42	22.12	22.33	22.31	22.02	22.17	22.32	21.66	21.81	22.45	22.22	22.16
2015	22.27	22.50	22.08	22.33	22.77	22.75	22.88	23.25	22.27	22.50	22.74	22.58	22.58
2016	22.70	22.65	22.68	22.87	23.45	23.10	22.69	23.55	23.54	23.85	24.44	23.78	23.28
2017	23.64	24.33	23.71	24.18	24.48	23.83	23.98	24.80	23.93	24.21	24.29	24.35	24.15
Leisure and Hospitality													
2013	13.02	12.96	12.80	12.70	12.68	12.62	12.50	12.54	12.52	12.56	12.57	12.60	12.67
2014	12.56	12.63	12.50	12.40	12.34	12.27	12.18	12.30	12.58	12.55	12.62	12.65	12.46
2015	12.63	12.43	12.33	12.38	12.43	12.34	12.23	12.38	12.44	12.63	12.64	12.88	12.47
2016	12.77	12.76	12.70	12.77	12.77	12.72	12.71	12.85	12.86	12.98	12.98	13.11	12.83
2017	13.09	12.90	12.97	13.11	13.17	13.19	13.23	13.25	13.39	13.45	13.68	13.81	13.27
Other Services													
2013	18.17	17.96	17.90	18.07	17.97	18.03	17.91	18.15	18.10	18.17	17.82	18.12	18.03
2014	17.90	18.49	17.89	17.57	17.76	17.85	17.65	17.75	18.26	18.45	18.56	17.93	18.00
2015	18.52	18.71	18.76	18.52	18.89	18.79	18.75	19.10	19.08	18.88	19.50	19.40	18.91
2016	19.68	19.72	19.65	19.83	20.19	20.08	19.93	19.97	20.40	20.54	20.83	20.67	20.13
2017	21.49	21.32	22.03	22.34	22.08	21.82	22.03	22.48	23.13	23.21	23.52	23.96	22.44

4. Average Weekly Earnings by Selected Industry: North Carolina, 2013–2017

(Dollars, not seasonally adjusted)

Industry and year	January	February	March	April	May	June	July	August	September	October	November	December	Annual average
Total Private													
2013	745.62	751.64	750.38	744.07	739.17	756.28	735.98	744.25	758.80	741.32	749.09	758.20	747.62
2014	741.54	747.92	780.03	754.81	750.21	764.19	749.52	754.89	757.85	753.24	775.71	757.15	758.20
2015	753.77	771.08	768.85	758.18	762.45	760.04	763.49	788.90	766.61	777.81	790.26	779.50	769.35
2016	776.39	783.48	790.78	797.13	809.03	801.52	803.16	806.68	809.43	824.86	817.31	810.17	802.62
2017	818.04	824.91	823.54	844.25	824.91	824.82	843.53	824.57	834.56	854.00	834.90	835.23	832.14
Goods-Producing													
2013	829.76	825.95	836.30	837.10	831.92	839.92	831.02	844.93	853.21	834.48	852.72	860.81	840.18
2014	834.40	827.99	891.10	872.23	870.24	889.44	878.62	882.00	888.70	880.67	896.33	889.12	875.70
2015	866.71	872.78	882.17	872.90	883.24	874.44	869.53	885.06	863.23	879.86	878.85	899.81	877.20
2016	863.66	869.83	892.70	896.78	900.86	907.74	896.21	895.64	893.67	906.19	909.56	903.56	894.01
2017	881.79	909.00	915.21	912.28	930.65	939.96	942.73	926.50	939.39	952.27	946.97	951.66	928.39
Construction													
2013	799.09	785.17	808.44	803.67	805.23	799.50	787.55	819.48	825.66	811.07	821.47	809.47	807.18
2014	795.41	766.41	862.73	832.40	841.68	860.69	862.10	857.26	851.60	859.48	864.47	871.68	845.71
2015	830.68	850.20	874.91	865.39	888.76	900.09	891.46	907.49	880.31	912.69	895.96	938.12	886.61
2016	868.34	856.87	910.03	897.88	907.96	917.69	887.81	883.20	900.51	909.40	908.31	882.57	893.43
2017	846.40	904.23	909.69	910.32	928.93	947.92	955.72	923.82	938.11	945.63	947.20	954.38	925.80
Manufacturing													
2013	842.99	842.00	847.26	852.12	842.34	856.52	849.61	856.96	866.11	846.15	865.65	883.65	853.54
2014	852.72	855.97	905.24	892.74	886.88	904.89	889.15	896.66	910.34	894.22	915.04	900.14	892.08
2015	886.13	885.47	885.74	878.45	881.76	862.58	857.21	873.50	853.48	858.58	864.63	873.71	872.20
2016	855.33	870.08	876.42	895.03	895.44	900.28	896.88	897.84	886.30	899.10	909.56	912.83	890.92
2017	911.66	916.12	921.48	914.00	932.75	937.92	938.14	930.65	941.52	956.10	945.95	949.01	932.93
Trade, Transportation, and Utilities													
2013	711.28	714.15	718.98	716.22	708.63	728.70	722.45	720.71	739.56	721.05	717.24	727.31	720.03
2014	721.73	713.97	764.21	724.85	720.68	731.13	713.11	712.75	722.65	697.69	708.62	700.75	718.20
2015	698.31	720.94	703.48	705.21	702.42	710.02	714.14	738.15	733.91	742.86	732.03	719.61	717.58
2016	722.40	727.60	740.65	745.00	755.42	758.78	763.49	761.08	763.05	765.14	762.58	756.11	750.95
2017	761.96	753.93	772.11	797.47	777.43	771.52	788.20	763.49	779.19	787.87	764.20	765.70	774.50
Information													
2013	1,126.32	1,124.94	1,128.13	1,128.95	1,126.73	1,226.52	1,121.65	1,137.70	1,167.30	1,117.05	1,183.75	1,187.42	1,147.24
2014	1,152.97	1,256.15	1,201.88	1,144.31	1,158.25	1,199.20	1,137.24	1,181.14	1,180.73	1,184.77	1,290.02	1,207.20	1,192.83
2015	1,207.49	1,324.96	1,283.57	1,274.85	1,269.14	1,273.04	1,260.97	1,325.82	1,290.53	1,297.07	1,370.84	1,290.63	1,290.21
2016	1,350.62	1,421.98	1,332.83	1,389.13	1,401.91	1,344.03	1,392.88	1,349.66	1,391.76	1,450.38	1,382.76	1,394.44	1,384.80
2017	1,450.46	1,445.96	1,386.38	1,463.00	1,332.24	1,403.19	1,510.20	1,403.47	1,450.09	1,466.78	1,386.11	1,422.64	1,428.38
Financial Activities													
2013	1,001.05	1,046.73	1,013.61	1,002.29	1,031.02	1,059.94	1,008.72	1,014.41	1,019.18	981.72	997.67	1,018.43	1,015.80
2014	997.72	1,030.03	1,008.48	950.61	961.47	1,010.98	968.71	989.71	1,008.05	1,041.44	1,046.30	992.00	999.55
2015	1,006.89	1,055.55	1,111.88	1,058.63	1,085.89	1,077.62	1,099.42	1,161.64	1,112.25	1,131.35	1,200.84	1,147.19	1,104.79
2016	1,186.49	1,248.38	1,229.57	1,219.68	1,272.43	1,236.36	1,250.78	1,290.71	1,272.33	1,301.59	1,252.48	1,237.81	1,249.15
2017	1,306.89	1,321.35	1,278.02	1,345.11	1,273.51	1,265.40	1,321.92	1,292.36	1,301.12	1,346.91	1,278.72	1,241.24	1,299.07
Professional and Business Services													
2013	939.62	953.87	949.43	935.41	929.66	955.71	910.75	925.61	955.30	918.74	932.21	949.37	938.39
2014	912.61	959.20	999.12	965.69	946.76	974.62	946.40	946.13	944.10	950.04	992.05	954.48	958.78
2015	947.48	983.00	970.72	951.48	953.64	947.35	956.58	995.67	951.20	962.20	1,005.40	973.18	966.40
2016	969.85	980.00	999.95	1,005.31	1,024.23	1,010.68	1,011.02	1,009.95	1,019.58	1,048.34	1,014.59	1,013.89	1,009.27
2017	1,032.70	1,024.53	1,033.47	1,058.09	1,016.72	1,016.86	1,047.55	1,000.08	1,020.48	1,063.57	1,026.68	1,024.89	1,031.04
Education and Health Services													
2013	726.43	726.00	717.66	717.99	717.44	731.13	715.48	718.75	728.41	723.24	723.24	727.98	722.81
2014	718.25	715.20	725.54	727.96	727.31	724.46	722.74	732.10	712.61	708.83	740.85	722.15	722.42
2015	723.78	726.75	719.81	719.03	735.47	734.83	734.45	755.63	714.87	724.50	736.78	727.08	729.33
2016	724.13	713.48	712.15	727.27	755.09	734.58	728.35	746.54	748.57	765.59	779.64	760.96	740.30
2017	761.21	780.99	758.72	785.85	790.70	769.71	784.15	801.04	780.12	796.51	789.43	791.38	782.46
Leisure and Hospitality													
2013	318.99	330.48	331.52	327.66	324.61	326.86	322.50	322.28	321.76	322.79	323.05	322.56	324.35
2014	314.00	305.65	325.00	321.16	317.14	321.47	319.12	327.18	327.08	326.30	328.12	328.90	321.47
2015	320.80	320.69	321.81	321.88	321.94	322.07	320.43	328.07	318.46	323.33	324.85	329.73	322.97
2016	315.42	324.10	328.93	329.47	330.74	330.72	334.27	336.67	333.07	337.48	340.08	336.93	331.01
2017	323.32	331.53	334.63	340.86	339.79	345.58	350.60	348.48	345.46	353.74	358.42	354.92	343.69
Other Services													
2013	561.45	558.56	560.27	554.75	544.49	564.34	546.26	559.02	577.39	561.45	559.55	558.10	558.93
2014	540.58	532.51	552.80	542.91	552.34	555.14	552.45	555.58	560.58	570.11	593.92	561.21	556.20
2015	575.97	585.62	598.44	568.56	589.37	578.73	585.00	599.74	587.66	577.73	596.70	580.06	586.21
2016	588.43	581.74	593.43	610.76	619.83	614.45	613.84	615.08	618.12	622.36	620.73	624.23	609.94
2017	631.81	648.13	656.49	690.31	646.94	648.05	669.71	669.90	670.77	687.02	679.73	692.44	666.47

NORTH DAKOTA
At a Glance

Population:
  2010 census: 672,591
  2017 estimate: 755,393

Percent change in population:
  2010–2017: 12.3%

Percent change in total nonfarm employment:
  2007–2017: 20.1%

Industry with the largest growth in employment, 2007–2017 (thousands):
  Education and health services, 12.2

Industry with the largest decline or smallest growth in employment, 2007–2017 (thousands):
  Manufacturing, -1.4

Civilian labor force:
  2010: 378,342
  2017: 414,399

Unemployment rate and rank among states (highest to lowest):
  2010: 3.8%, 51st
  2017: 2.6%, 50th

Over-the-year change in unemployment rates:
  2015–2016: 0.3%
  2016–2017: -0.5%

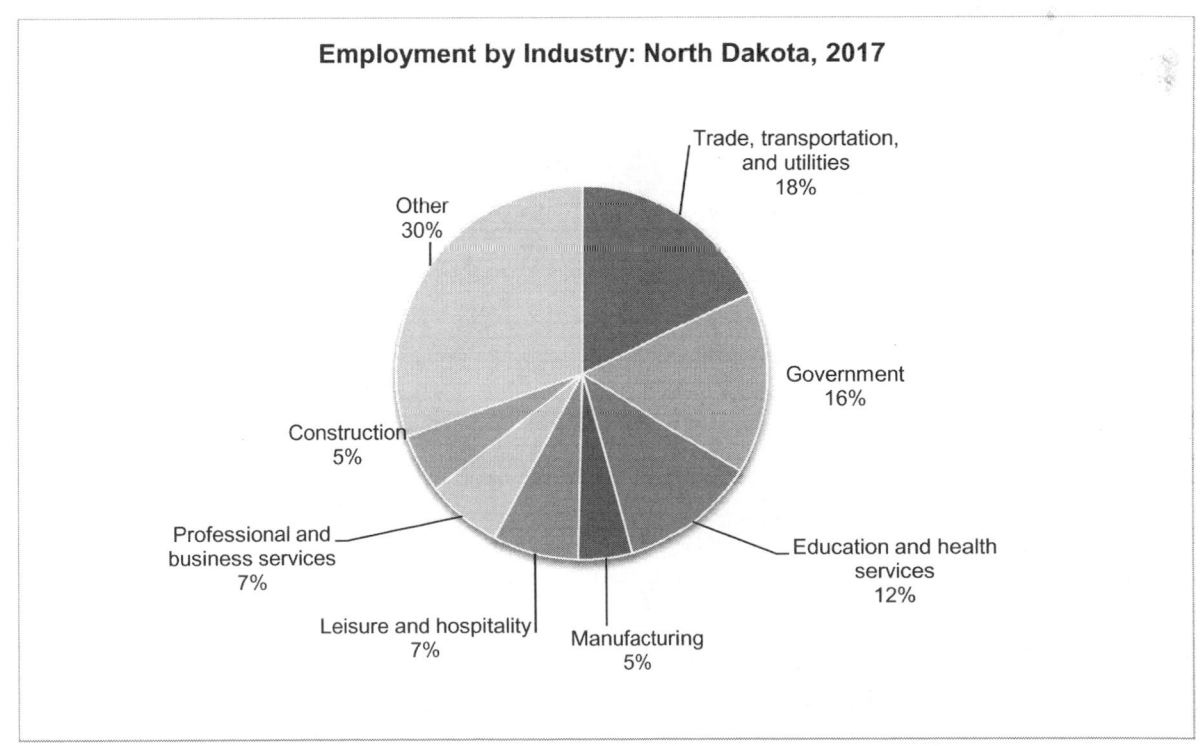

Employment by Industry: North Dakota, 2017

- Trade, transportation, and utilities 18%
- Other 30%
- Government 16%
- Construction 5%
- Professional and business services 7%
- Education and health services 12%
- Leisure and hospitality 7%
- Manufacturing 5%

1. Employment by Industry: North Dakota, Selected Years, 2007–2017

(Numbers in thousands, not seasonally adjusted)

Industry and year	January	February	March	April	May	June	July	August	September	October	November	December	Annual average
Total Nonfarm													
2007	348.5	349.6	352.6	356.2	362.7	362.7	352.9	354.2	364.2	365.8	365.8	365.6	358.4
2008	356.9	359.0	361.6	365.9	371.8	371.2	363.0	364.0	373.7	374.9	373.6	372.1	367.3
2009	358.7	359.8	360.5	362.9	370.7	371.9	361.8	362.4	372.5	374.2	372.7	372.1	366.7
2010	360.1	362.6	365.9	374.2	379.0	379.8	371.2	373.0	383.0	388.3	387.4	387.5	376.0
2011	377.5	379.1	382.7	389.2	396.0	397.8	391.8	395.4	408.2	412.2	413.6	415.2	396.6
2012	408.2	411.5	416.2	424.2	432.1	436.1	428.9	430.7	439.2	441.9	439.1	439.2	428.9
2013	428.0	431.1	433.6	436.3	446.7	449.9	441.9	444.3	454.0	456.9	457.2	453.1	444.4
2014	441.4	445.1	447.6	453.9	463.2	466.8	462.0	463.3	470.5	475.1	473.9	471.6	461.2
2015	455.6	455.2	453.7	455.5	460.0	458.7	450.7	448.6	453.2	453.8	450.7	445.9	453.5
2016	428.2	428.5	427.6	433.2	438.2	437.4	434.2	434.2	440.1	439.6	437.5	432.1	434.2
2017	421.3	422.8	424.2	431.3	436.6	437.1	430.8	430.2	435.7	436.4	431.7	427.6	430.5
Total Private													
2007	272.0	271.8	274.6	277.8	284.2	288.0	287.7	287.9	287.2	287.5	287.1	286.8	282.7
2008	279.9	280.6	283.4	287.4	292.5	296.4	296.9	297.0	296.0	295.6	294.3	292.5	291.0
2009	281.2	281.1	281.4	283.2	290.0	294.0	293.5	293.3	293.2	292.9	291.3	290.3	288.8
2010	280.7	281.6	284.0	292.1	296.1	299.8	301.0	302.5	302.5	306.1	305.2	305.1	296.4
2011	297.3	297.7	301.2	307.7	314.2	318.4	322.5	325.7	328.2	330.6	332.3	333.3	317.4
2012	328.5	330.4	335.0	342.7	350.5	356.6	358.6	360.7	358.6	359.5	356.7	356.7	349.5
2013	347.5	349.4	351.8	354.7	364.4	369.5	371.0	373.6	373.1	374.6	374.9	370.4	364.6
2014	361.3	363.3	365.7	372.3	380.9	386.7	388.3	389.9	389.7	393.1	392.0	389.2	381.0
2015	375.8	373.7	371.3	372.8	376.5	377.7	376.0	374.3	371.5	369.4	366.0	361.2	372.2
2016	345.6	343.8	342.7	348.2	352.1	354.1	357.3	357.5	356.4	354.5	352.3	346.9	351.0
2017	337.9	338.2	339.8	346.7	351.4	354.6	355.1	354.5	353.1	352.5	348.4	344.3	348.0
Goods Producing													
2007	45.9	45.3	46.4	48.2	50.9	52.9	53.7	53.6	53.2	53.1	52.1	50.4	50.5
2008	48.1	48.3	49.6	51.4	54.3	57.0	58.0	58.0	57.7	57.1	55.3	53.0	54.0
2009	47.6	47.7	47.7	48.5	51.2	53.7	54.6	54.9	54.7	54.1	52.4	50.2	51.4
2010	46.6	47.1	48.1	52.0	54.7	56.3	58.0	59.0	59.4	60.2	59.2	58.0	54.9
2011	54.9	55.0	56.5	59.9	63.4	66.0	68.7	70.4	71.6	72.8	72.8	71.4	65.3
2012	69.4	70.5	72.6	76.7	80.4	83.6	85.3	86.0	85.0	84.5	81.3	79.6	79.6
2013	76.2	76.6	77.5	79.2	84.7	87.9	88.9	90.3	89.6	89.6	88.7	84.7	84.5
2014	80.5	81.1	82.1	86.1	90.7	94.5	96.0	97.3	97.1	98.2	96.9	93.6	91.2
2015	88.1	85.3	83.2	83.4	85.1	85.8	85.3	85.2	83.4	82.1	79.1	74.9	83.4
2016	67.7	66.4	65.9	69.3	71.8	74.5	76.4	76.6	75.9	74.5	71.9	67.0	71.5
2017	63.1	63.3	64.1	68.0	71.3	73.3	74.3	74.1	73.7	72.1	69.9	66.6	69.5
Service-Providing													
2007	302.6	304.3	306.2	308.0	311.8	309.8	299.2	300.6	311.0	312.7	313.7	315.2	307.9
2008	308.8	310.7	312.0	314.5	317.5	314.2	305.0	306.0	316.0	317.8	318.3	319.1	313.3
2009	311.1	312.1	312.8	314.4	319.5	318.2	307.2	307.5	317.8	320.1	320.3	321.9	315.2
2010	313.5	315.5	317.8	322.2	324.3	323.5	313.2	314.0	323.6	328.1	328.2	329.5	321.1
2011	322.6	324.1	326.2	329.3	332.6	331.8	323.1	325.0	336.6	339.4	340.8	343.8	331.3
2012	338.8	341.0	343.6	347.5	351.7	352.5	343.6	344.7	354.2	357.4	357.8	359.6	349.4
2013	351.8	354.5	356.1	357.1	362.0	362.0	353.0	354.0	364.4	367.3	368.5	368.4	359.9
2014	360.9	364.0	365.5	367.8	372.5	372.3	366.0	366.0	373.4	376.9	377.0	378.0	370.0
2015	367.5	369.9	370.5	372.1	374.9	372.9	365.4	363.4	369.8	371.7	371.6	371.0	370.1
2016	360.5	362.1	361.7	363.9	366.4	362.9	357.8	357.6	364.2	365.1	365.6	365.1	362.7
2017	358.2	359.5	360.1	363.3	365.3	363.8	356.5	356.1	362.0	364.3	361.8	361.0	361.0
Mining and Logging													
2007	4.8	4.7	4.8	4.9	5.1	5.2	5.3	5.3	5.3	5.3	5.3	5.5	5.1
2008	5.4	5.6	5.9	6.2	6.5	6.8	6.9	7.3	7.5	7.8	8.0	7.9	6.8
2009	7.4	7.2	7.1	6.7	6.8	6.9	6.7	6.7	6.8	6.9	7.1	7.4	7.0
2010	7.6	8.3	8.8	9.4	10.0	10.6	11.2	11.7	12.1	12.5	12.7	13.2	10.7
2011	13.5	14.0	14.5	15.2	15.9	16.3	17.1	17.7	18.3	19.0	20.2	21.0	16.9
2012	21.3	22.2	23.2	23.9	24.6	25.4	26.1	26.1	25.6	25.2	24.9	24.8	24.4
2013	24.6	25.1	25.5	25.5	26.0	26.4	26.3	26.6	26.6	26.9	27.6	27.4	26.2
2014	27.5	28.0	28.3	28.9	29.4	30.0	30.3	30.9	31.2	31.8	32.0	32.0	30.0
2015	30.5	28.6	26.8	24.8	23.6	23.0	22.1	21.7	20.8	19.6	19.1	18.6	23.3
2016	17.2	16.6	15.5	15.0	14.6	14.5	14.6	14.7	14.9	15.1	15.4	15.5	15.3
2017	15.4	15.9	16.3	17.0	17.6	18.2	19.1	18.8	18.9	18.5	19.0	18.7	17.8

1. Employment by Industry: North Dakota, Selected Years, 2007–2017—*Continued*

(Numbers in thousands, not seasonally adjusted)

Industry and year	January	February	March	April	May	June	July	August	September	October	November	December	Annual average
Construction													
2007	15.6	15.3	16.1	17.7	19.9	21.2	21.8	22.0	21.6	21.4	20.4	18.6	19.3
2008	16.7	16.6	17.5	18.9	21.4	23.3	24.3	24.2	23.7	22.7	21.0	19.3	20.8
2009	16.7	16.3	16.5	17.9	20.8	23.2	24.4	24.8	24.6	23.9	22.2	20.0	20.9
2010	17.2	16.9	17.4	20.4	22.4	23.1	24.1	24.6	24.2	24.4	23.2	21.5	21.6
2011	18.5	18.1	18.9	21.1	23.8	25.7	27.6	28.8	29.2	29.4	28.1	25.8	24.6
2012	23.7	23.7	24.5	27.9	30.6	32.6	33.6	34.1	33.7	33.6	31.1	29.8	29.9
2013	27.1	26.9	27.3	28.8	33.1	35.6	36.7	37.8	37.2	36.6	35.3	31.7	32.8
2014	27.7	27.8	28.4	31.5	35.4	38.2	39.3	40.0	39.6	40.1	38.6	35.6	35.2
2015	32.2	31.4	31.1	33.1	35.8	37.1	37.7	37.8	37.0	36.9	34.5	31.3	34.7
2016	26.0	25.4	25.9	29.7	32.7	35.3	36.9	37.1	36.3	34.7	32.0	27.5	31.6
2017	23.8	23.5	23.8	26.7	28.9	30.1	30.2	30.2	29.7	28.5	25.9	22.8	27.0
Manufacturing													
2007	25.5	25.3	25.5	25.6	25.9	26.5	26.6	26.3	26.3	26.4	26.4	26.3	26.1
2008	26.0	26.1	26.2	26.3	26.4	26.9	26.8	26.5	26.5	26.6	26.3	25.8	26.4
2009	23.5	24.2	24.1	23.9	23.6	23.6	23.5	23.4	23.3	23.3	23.1	22.8	23.5
2010	21.8	21.9	21.9	22.2	22.3	22.6	22.7	22.7	23.1	23.3	23.3	23.3	22.6
2011	22.9	22.9	23.1	23.6	23.7	24.0	24.0	23.9	24.1	24.4	24.5	24.6	23.8
2012	24.4	24.6	24.9	24.9	25.2	25.6	25.6	25.8	25.7	25.7	25.3	25.0	25.2
2013	24.5	24.6	24.7	24.9	25.6	25.9	25.9	25.9	25.8	26.1	25.8	25.6	25.4
2014	25.3	25.3	25.4	25.7	25.9	26.3	26.4	26.4	26.3	26.3	26.3	26.0	26.0
2015	25.4	25.3	25.3	25.5	25.7	25.7	25.5	25.7	25.6	25.6	25.5	25.0	25.5
2016	24.5	24.4	24.5	24.6	24.5	24.7	24.9	24.8	24.7	24.7	24.5	24.0	24.6
2017	23.9	23.9	24.0	24.3	24.8	25.0	25.0	25.1	25.1	25.1	25.0	25.1	24.7
Trade, Transportation, and Utilities													
2007	75.4	75.0	75.1	75.9	77.0	76.8	76.7	76.4	76.2	77.1	78.3	78.9	76.6
2008	76.6	76.3	76.7	77.4	78.1	78.0	78.1	77.9	77.9	78.4	79.3	79.7	77.9
2009	77.0	76.5	76.6	76.9	78.5	78.5	78.2	77.8	77.8	78.7	79.8	80.1	78.0
2010	77.7	77.6	77.8	79.7	80.6	80.9	80.9	81.1	81.0	82.4	83.5	84.2	80.6
2011	82.2	82.2	82.6	84.3	85.7	86.2	86.9	87.6	88.0	89.8	91.8	93.2	86.7
2012	91.8	92.0	93.0	95.0	96.8	97.6	97.9	98.2	97.9	99.2	100.3	100.8	96.7
2013	98.3	98.4	98.7	99.5	101.6	101.9	102.1	102.8	102.8	103.5	104.9	105.4	101.7
2014	102.9	103.2	103.6	104.9	106.4	106.5	106.6	106.6	106.6	107.8	108.8	109.6	106.1
2015	106.0	105.7	105.2	105.5	105.5	104.9	104.3	102.8	102.4	102.2	102.5	102.5	104.1
2016	98.5	97.5	96.5	97.1	97.2	96.1	96.3	96.1	95.7	95.9	96.7	96.6	96.7
2017	94.2	93.9	93.7	94.8	95.4	95.2	94.9	94.6	94.5	95.0	95.5	95.8	94.8
Wholesale Trade													
2007	18.8	18.7	18.9	19.4	19.8	19.8	19.5	19.4	19.2	19.5	19.5	19.4	19.3
2008	19.1	19.2	19.4	19.9	20.3	20.2	20.2	20.1	19.9	20.0	20.0	20.0	19.9
2009	19.7	19.7	19.8	20.0	20.7	20.8	20.5	20.4	20.1	20.3	20.4	20.4	20.2
2010	20.1	20.2	20.3	21.1	21.3	21.4	21.4	21.4	21.3	21.5	21.6	21.8	21.1
2011	21.5	21.5	21.8	22.3	22.9	23.1	22.9	22.8	22.7	23.1	23.3	23.6	22.6
2012	23.5	23.7	24.2	24.9	25.5	25.7	25.6	25.6	25.4	25.5	25.7	25.8	25.1
2013	25.4	25.5	25.7	26.1	27.0	27.1	26.8	26.8	26.4	26.6	26.7	26.8	26.4
2014	26.5	26.5	26.7	27.1	27.5	27.7	27.5	27.5	27.3	27.5	27.6	27.7	27.3
2015	27.3	27.1	27.0	27.4	27.4	27.2	26.8	26.6	26.2	25.9	25.7	25.6	26.7
2016	24.9	24.7	24.6	25.0	25.0	24.6	24.5	24.4	24.0	23.9	23.9	23.8	24.4
2017	23.6	23.6	23.7	24.2	24.5	24.5	24.2	24.0	23.7	24.1	24.0	24.0	24.0
Retail Trade													
2007	42.9	42.5	42.4	42.6	43.1	43.1	43.2	42.9	42.7	43.1	44.2	44.8	43.1
2008	43.0	42.5	42.6	42.8	43.0	43.0	43.2	42.9	42.9	43.1	44.0	44.3	43.1
2009	42.4	41.9	41.9	42.0	42.7	42.7	42.8	42.6	42.7	43.2	44.2	44.4	42.8
2010	42.7	42.4	42.4	42.9	43.4	43.5	43.5	43.4	43.2	44.0	44.9	45.2	43.5
2011	43.5	43.3	43.2	43.9	44.3	44.2	44.6	44.7	44.8	45.5	47.0	47.3	44.7
2012	45.7	45.4	45.4	46.2	46.7	47.0	47.2	47.2	47.2	48.1	49.3	49.7	47.1
2013	48.0	47.8	47.7	47.8	48.5	48.6	48.9	49.3	49.5	49.9	51.0	51.4	49.0
2014	49.6	49.7	49.8	50.1	50.7	50.7	50.7	50.3	50.4	51.1	52.2	52.9	50.7
2015	50.5	50.5	50.5	50.6	50.9	50.8	50.9	50.2	50.3	50.7	51.5	51.8	50.8
2016	49.6	49.1	48.8	49.0	49.2	48.9	49.2	49.0	48.8	49.1	50.0	49.8	49.2
2017	48.1	47.7	47.4	47.6	47.8	47.7	47.7	47.5	47.3	47.4	48.2	48.2	47.7

1. Employment by Industry: North Dakota, Selected Years, 2007–2017—*Continued*

(Numbers in thousands, not seasonally adjusted)

Industry and year	January	February	March	April	May	June	July	August	September	October	November	December	Annual average
Transportation and Utilities													
2007	13.7	13.8	13.8	13.9	14.1	13.9	14.0	14.1	14.3	14.5	14.6	14.7	14.1
2008	14.5	14.6	14.7	14.7	14.8	14.8	14.7	14.9	15.1	15.3	15.3	15.4	14.9
2009	14.9	14.9	14.9	14.9	15.1	15.0	14.9	14.8	15.0	15.2	15.2	15.3	15.0
2010	14.9	15.0	15.1	15.7	15.9	16.0	16.0	16.3	16.5	16.9	17.0	17.2	16.0
2011	17.2	17.4	17.6	18.1	18.5	18.9	19.4	20.1	20.5	21.2	21.5	22.3	19.4
2012	22.6	22.9	23.4	23.9	24.6	24.9	25.1	25.4	25.3	25.6	25.3	25.3	24.5
2013	24.9	25.1	25.3	25.6	26.1	26.2	26.4	26.7	26.9	27.0	27.2	27.2	26.2
2014	26.8	27.0	27.1	27.7	28.2	28.1	28.4	28.8	28.9	29.2	29.0	29.0	28.2
2015	28.2	28.1	27.7	27.5	27.2	26.9	26.6	26.0	25.9	25.6	25.3	25.1	26.7
2016	24.0	23.7	23.1	23.1	23.0	22.6	22.6	22.7	22.9	22.9	22.8	23.0	23.0
2017	22.5	22.6	22.6	23.0	23.1	23.0	23.0	23.1	23.5	23.5	23.3	23.6	23.1
Information													
2007	7.6	7.6	7.6	7.6	7.7	7.6	7.6	7.7	7.5	7.5	7.5	7.5	7.6
2008	7.4	7.4	7.4	7.4	7.5	7.6	7.6	7.6	7.6	7.6	7.6	7.6	7.5
2009	7.7	7.7	7.6	7.5	7.5	7.5	7.5	7.5	7.4	7.3	7.3	7.3	7.5
2010	7.3	7.3	7.3	7.3	7.3	7.4	7.3	7.3	7.2	7.2	7.2	7.2	7.3
2011	7.1	7.1	7.1	7.1	7.1	7.2	7.2	7.2	7.1	7.0	7.1	7.1	7.1
2012	7.0	6.9	6.9	6.9	6.9	7.0	7.0	7.0	6.9	6.9	6.9	6.9	6.9
2013	6.9	6.8	6.7	6.7	6.8	6.9	6.9	6.9	6.8	6.8	6.8	6.8	6.8
2014	6.8	6.8	6.8	6.8	6.9	6.8	6.8	6.9	6.8	6.8	6.7	6.7	6.8
2015	6.6	6.6	6.6	6.6	6.6	6.6	6.6	6.6	6.6	6.6	6.7	6.7	6.6
2016	6.6	6.7	6.7	6.6	6.6	6.7	6.7	6.7	6.6	6.6	6.6	6.7	6.7
2017	6.6	6.6	6.5	6.5	6.5	6.5	6.5	6.5	6.5	6.4	6.4	6.5	6.5
Financial Activities													
2007	19.3	19.4	19.5	19.5	19.8	19.9	20.0	20.0	19.9	20.0	19.9	20.2	19.8
2008	19.9	20.0	20.1	20.1	20.2	20.4	20.5	20.5	20.4	20.5	20.5	20.7	20.3
2009	20.2	20.1	20.1	20.1	20.1	20.2	20.3	20.3	20.1	20.2	20.1	20.5	20.2
2010	20.1	20.1	20.1	20.4	20.5	20.7	20.7	20.8	20.7	20.8	20.8	21.2	20.6
2011	20.8	20.8	20.8	21.0	21.2	21.2	21.3	21.3	21.3	21.3	21.4	21.5	21.2
2012	21.2	21.3	21.4	21.6	21.8	22.0	22.1	22.1	22.0	22.2	22.2	22.5	21.9
2013	22.2	22.3	22.5	22.6	22.8	23.0	23.1	23.2	23.1	23.4	23.5	23.6	22.9
2014	23.5	23.6	23.6	23.8	23.9	24.1	24.2	24.4	24.2	24.6	24.6	24.8	24.1
2015	24.4	24.3	24.4	24.4	24.5	24.5	24.5	24.5	24.3	24.3	24.3	24.2	24.4
2016	24.0	24.0	23.9	23.7	23.8	23.8	24.1	24.1	24.0	24.2	24.4	24.4	24.0
2017	24.1	24.1	24.2	24.3	24.2	24.3	24.6	24.6	24.4	24.5	24.4	24.5	24.4
Professional and Business Services													
2007	28.1	28.3	28.8	29.0	29.5	29.9	29.7	29.9	30.0	29.9	29.7	29.8	29.4
2008	29.3	29.5	29.8	30.3	30.6	31.0	30.8	30.9	30.7	30.4	30.0	29.7	30.3
2009	28.8	28.8	28.7	28.7	29.2	29.7	29.3	29.2	29.8	29.0	28.8	28.5	29.0
2010	27.5	27.8	27.9	28.4	28.1	28.8	28.4	28.6	28.6	29.2	28.8	28.7	28.4
2011	28.0	28.1	28.6	29.2	29.2	29.9	30.8	31.2	31.1	31.0	30.4	30.6	29.8
2012	30.3	30.4	31.0	31.7	32.4	33.3	33.5	34.0	33.7	33.8	33.5	33.4	32.6
2013	32.6	33.2	33.3	33.7	34.1	34.7	35.2	35.2	35.1	35.2	34.9	34.2	34.3
2014	33.9	34.1	34.6	35.4	36.0	37.3	37.7	37.5	37.6	37.8	37.2	36.6	36.3
2015	35.4	35.6	35.3	35.8	36.5	37.4	37.5	37.4	37.0	36.6	35.6	35.5	36.3
2016	33.8	33.8	33.5	34.5	34.8	35.3	35.7	35.7	35.1	34.6	34.2	34.0	34.6
2017	33.4	33.3	33.5	34.4	34.8	35.6	35.5	35.5	34.8	35.0	34.3	33.6	34.5
Education and Health Services													
2007	50.0	50.1	50.3	50.3	50.6	51.2	51.0	51.2	51.3	51.4	51.4	51.7	50.9
2008	51.3	51.6	51.6	52.1	52.1	52.2	52.2	52.1	52.2	52.6	52.5	52.8	52.1
2009	52.3	52.7	52.6	52.8	53.1	53.6	53.2	53.2	53.5	54.2	53.8	54.4	53.3
2010	54.1	54.1	54.5	54.8	54.6	55.1	55.2	55.1	55.1	55.7	55.5	55.7	55.0
2011	55.6	55.6	55.8	56.0	56.1	56.1	56.1	56.1	56.6	56.6	56.8	57.1	56.2
2012	56.8	57.1	57.2	57.3	57.6	57.9	57.6	57.9	58.0	58.1	58.1	58.6	57.7
2013	58.1	58.4	58.6	58.7	58.8	58.5	58.4	58.4	58.9	59.5	59.5	59.6	58.8
2014	59.1	59.3	59.1	59.0	59.1	58.9	58.7	58.9	59.3	59.7	60.1	60.0	59.3
2015	59.5	60.0	60.1	60.1	60.3	60.1	60.0	60.1	60.5	60.6	61.2	61.2	60.3
2016	60.8	61.4	61.5	61.9	61.9	61.4	62.1	62.2	62.6	62.9	63.1	63.2	62.1
2017	62.6	62.8	63.0	63.2	63.2	63.0	62.6	62.7	63.3	63.7	63.3	63.4	63.1

1. Employment by Industry: North Dakota, Selected Years, 2007–2017—*Continued*

(Numbers in thousands, not seasonally adjusted)

Industry and year	January	February	March	April	May	June	July	August	September	October	November	December	Annual average
Leisure and Hospitality													
2007	30.7	31.1	31.7	32.1	33.5	34.4	33.9	34.1	33.9	33.3	32.9	33.0	32.9
2008	32.1	32.2	32.7	33.2	34.1	34.7	34.4	34.7	34.2	33.7	33.7	33.6	33.6
2009	32.4	32.4	32.8	33.2	34.8	35.4	35.0	35.2	34.8	34.1	33.8	33.8	34.0
2010	32.3	32.4	33.0	34.1	34.9	35.2	35.1	35.3	35.1	35.0	34.6	34.6	34.3
2011	33.4	33.5	34.2	34.5	35.8	36.3	36.0	36.4	36.8	36.3	36.3	36.7	35.5
2012	36.1	36.3	36.9	37.4	38.5	39.1	39.0	39.4	39.1	38.7	38.2	38.7	38.1
2013	37.3	37.6	38.2	38.0	39.1	40.1	40.1	40.4	40.3	40.1	40.0	39.6	39.2
2014	38.2	38.8	39.3	39.5	41.1	41.8	41.5	41.6	41.4	41.3	40.8	40.9	40.5
2015	39.1	39.4	39.6	40.3	41.2	41.6	41.2	41.3	41.0	40.6	40.3	39.9	40.5
2016	38.2	37.9	38.6	39.0	39.8	40.2	40.0	40.1	40.5	39.7	39.3	38.8	39.3
2017	37.8	38.1	38.5	38.9	39.4	40.4	40.3	40.3	39.8	39.4	38.2	37.6	39.1
Other Services													
2007	15.0	15.0	15.2	15.2	15.2	15.3	15.1	15.0	15.2	15.2	15.3	15.3	15.2
2008	15.2	15.3	15.5	15.5	15.6	15.5	15.3	15.3	15.3	15.3	15.4	15.4	15.4
2009	15.2	15.2	15.3	15.5	15.6	15.4	15.4	15.2	15.1	15.3	15.5	15.5	15.3
2010	15.1	15.2	15.3	15.4	15.4	15.4	15.4	15.3	15.4	15.6	15.6	15.5	15.4
2011	15.3	15.4	15.6	15.7	15.7	15.5	15.5	15.5	15.7	15.8	15.7	15.7	15.6
2012	15.9	15.9	16.0	16.1	16.1	16.1	16.2	16.1	16.0	16.1	16.2	16.2	16.1
2013	15.9	16.1	16.3	16.3	16.5	16.5	16.3	16.4	16.5	16.5	16.6	16.5	16.4
2014	16.4	16.4	16.6	16.8	16.8	16.8	16.8	16.7	16.7	16.9	16.9	17.0	16.7
2015	16.7	16.8	16.9	16.7	16.8	16.8	16.6	16.4	16.3	16.4	16.3	16.3	16.6
2016	16.0	16.1	16.1	16.1	16.2	16.1	16.0	16.0	16.0	16.1	16.1	16.2	16.1
2017	16.1	16.1	16.3	16.6	16.6	16.3	16.4	16.2	16.1	16.4	16.4	16.3	16.3
Government													
2007	76.5	77.8	78.0	78.4	78.5	74.7	65.2	66.3	77.0	78.3	78.7	78.8	75.7
2008	77.0	78.4	78.2	78.5	79.3	74.8	66.1	67.0	77.7	79.3	79.3	79.6	76.3
2009	77.5	78.7	79.1	79.7	80.7	77.9	68.3	69.1	79.3	81.3	81.4	81.8	77.9
2010	79.4	81.0	81.9	82.1	82.9	80.0	70.2	70.5	80.5	82.2	82.2	82.4	79.6
2011	80.2	81.4	81.5	81.5	81.8	79.4	69.3	69.7	80.0	81.6	81.3	81.9	79.1
2012	79.7	81.1	81.2	81.5	81.6	79.5	70.3	70.0	80.6	82.4	82.4	82.5	79.4
2013	80.5	81.7	81.8	81.6	82.3	80.4	70.9	70.7	80.9	82.3	82.3	82.7	79.8
2014	80.1	81.8	81.9	81.6	82.3	80.1	73.7	73.4	80.8	82.0	81.9	82.4	80.2
2015	79.8	81.5	82.4	82.7	83.5	81.0	74.7	74.3	81.7	84.4	84.7	84.7	81.3
2016	82.6	84.7	84.9	85.0	86.1	83.3	76.9	76.7	83.7	85.1	85.2	85.2	83.3
2017	83.4	84.6	84.4	84.6	85.2	82.5	75.7	75.7	82.6	83.9	83.3	83.3	82.4

2. Average Weekly Hours by Selected Industry: North Dakota, 2013–2017

(Not seasonally adjusted)

Industry and year	January	February	March	April	May	June	July	August	September	October	November	December	Annual average
Total Private													
2013	34.3	34.8	34.5	34.6	35.5	37.0	35.8	36.8	36.6	35.6	35.8	35.7	35.6
2014	34.2	35.5	35.2	35.0	35.4	36.7	36.3	36.6	36.2	36.2	36.3	35.4	35.8
2015	34.5	35.0	34.9	34.6	34.7	35.3	35.3	36.0	35.2	35.4	35.3	34.7	35.1
2016	34.1	34.1	33.7	34.2	34.9	34.7	34.8	34.9	34.6	35.1	34.2	33.8	34.4
2017	34.2	33.9	33.8	35.0	35.1	35.4	35.8	35.6	35.0	35.2	34.6	34.5	34.9
Goods-Producing													
2013	38.9	40.0	39.8	40.0	41.2	43.4	41.7	43.9	43.5	42.7	43.2	42.6	41.8
2014	40.3	41.7	42.4	41.8	43.3	44.1	45.0	44.5	45.0	44.8	43.7	43.1	43.4
2015	41.5	40.6	41.8	40.8	40.6	42.3	42.3	43.3	42.2	42.5	42.0	42.2	41.8
2016	40.0	40.4	40.5	40.6	41.4	41.5	41.2	42.6	41.9	42.8	40.6	39.1	41.1
2017	39.5	39.4	39.5	40.9	42.6	42.5	43.2	43.7	42.9	44.0	41.9	41.4	41.9
Construction													
2013	38.2	38.4	37.9	39.0	41.7	44.7	43.2	44.5	42.8	42.1	42.6	43.0	41.7
2014	39.9	39.9	40.8	41.3	45.2	46.2	47.7	46.0	46.8	46.6	42.8	43.2	44.2
2015	41.6	39.0	41.4	41.9	40.9	44.6	44.4	45.3	43.5	44.5	42.1	41.9	42.7
2016	38.6	39.9	41.0	41.9	44.1	44.2	42.9	44.1	43.9	45.0	41.5	38.6	42.4
2017	38.5	38.7	38.8	40.4	43.7	43.6	43.6	45.0	42.9	45.1	40.4	39.1	41.9
Manufacturing													
2013	38.6	40.0	40.9	41.0	40.8	42.3	40.1	43.1	42.5	41.8	41.9	39.3	41.1
2014	38.2	39.4	38.9	38.6	39.3	39.3	39.6	40.7	40.9	39.8	40.5	40.1	39.6
2015	38.2	39.1	39.4	38.6	38.6	38.9	38.9	41.0	40.6	40.5	40.2	41.1	39.6
2016	39.4	39.2	39.2	39.0	39.1	39.6	39.4	40.4	39.7	40.8	39.5	39.0	39.6
2017	38.5	38.2	38.8	39.4	40.2	39.3	40.1	39.6	39.8	39.1	38.8	38.6	39.2
Trade, Transportation, and Utilities													
2013	34.9	35.9	35.4	35.2	36.9	37.5	36.1	36.9	36.8	36.0	36.8	36.8	36.3
2014	35.1	36.5	36.2	35.8	35.7	37.5	36.5	37.1	36.3	36.6	37.0	36.3	36.4
2015	35.5	36.1	35.3	35.4	35.5	35.6	35.9	36.0	35.7	35.8	35.3	34.9	35.6
2016	34.2	34.0	33.8	34.7	35.4	35.4	35.4	34.9	34.9	34.9	34.5	34.3	34.7
2017	34.3	33.8	33.7	35.3	35.1	35.5	35.9	35.4	35.0	35.2	34.9	34.8	34.9
Financial Activities													
2013	36.2	36.3	35.9	36.4	36.2	38.1	36.5	37.1	38.7	36.9	37.3	38.0	37.0
2014	36.9	38.3	37.5	36.9	36.7	38.0	36.4	36.3	36.5	36.1	38.7	36.9	37.1
2015	36.9	37.5	36.5	35.0	34.2	34.3	34.8	36.3	34.9	35.0	37.6	35.0	35.7
2016	35.2	34.9	34.8	35.7	37.2	35.6	36.6	35.9	37.0	38.3	36.1	36.9	36.2
2017	38.3	36.6	36.9	37.3	35.2	35.9	37.1	35.8	36.2	37.1	36.5	36.6	36.6
Professional and Business Services													
2013	37.4	37.5	37.7	37.3	39.0	40.1	39.4	40.1	39.4	38.5	38.0	37.7	38.5
2014	36.0	38.9	37.5	37.6	39.2	39.9	39.0	38.9	39.1	39.3	39.0	38.0	38.5
2015	36.8	38.4	38.1	38.4	38.9	39.1	38.4	39.1	38.1	38.9	37.8	36.8	38.2
2016	36.0	36.8	35.9	36.0	37.7	37.0	36.3	36.9	37.3	38.3	37.2	37.5	36.9
2017	37.7	37.0	38.1	39.0	38.4	37.8	38.6	37.3	35.9	36.4	34.8	34.8	37.2
Education and Health Services													
2013	33.7	33.6	33.0	33.2	33.1	33.8	32.6	33.0	33.1	32.5	32.5	32.6	33.1
2014	32.2	32.3	32.0	32.2	31.6	32.7	31.5	32.1	31.9	31.6	31.8	31.6	32.0
2015	31.7	32.3	32.3	32.7	32.5	32.9	32.6	32.6	32.2	32.3	32.6	32.1	32.4
2016	32.1	32.3	31.7	31.7	31.8	31.8	32.0	31.6	31.4	31.5	31.9	31.8	31.8
2017	32.0	32.1	31.6	32.3	32.1	32.5	32.6	32.9	32.6	32.3	32.7	32.6	32.4
Leisure and Hospitality													
2013	22.0	22.5	22.9	22.8	23.4	25.1	24.6	24.4	24.1	23.2	22.7	23.2	23.4
2014	22.1	23.3	23.7	23.4	23.6	24.7	23.8	24.7	23.8	23.6	24.3	23.4	23.7
2015	22.3	23.9	23.5	22.7	23.9	24.4	24.1	25.2	23.6	23.8	24.3	24.0	23.8
2016	23.9	23.5	23.1	23.4	24.1	23.5	23.4	23.7	22.0	22.8	22.6	22.1	23.2
2017	23.3	22.8	22.9	24.0	24.8	24.8	24.5	24.4	23.2	23.3	22.5	23.0	23.6
Other Services													
2013	25.0	24.9	24.3	25.4	24.3	29.9	28.2	30.5	29.9	26.5	27.1	27.2	26.9
2014	26.4	28.7	26.8	24.4	25.0	27.4	28.7	29.3	25.4	24.7	26.3	25.2	26.6
2015	24.4	25.2	25.8	25.2	26.4	26.6	26.2	27.8	26.8	26.4	27.9	27.5	26.3
2016	28.2	27.5	27.1	29.2	29.3	27.6	28.9	28.7	29.2	29.7	28.9	28.9	28.6
2017	28.8	29.7	29.3	31.7	31.0	31.4	32.9	31.5	31.7	32.5	31.9	31.2	31.1

3. Average Hourly Earnings by Selected Industry: North Dakota, 2013–2017

(Dollars, not seasonally adjusted)

Industry and year	January	February	March	April	May	June	July	August	September	October	November	December	Annual average
Total Private													
2013	23.63	23.64	23.58	23.69	23.51	23.82	23.74	23.69	24.08	24.07	24.35	24.70	23.88
2014	24.89	25.07	24.91	24.95	24.78	24.69	24.76	24.59	24.98	24.94	24.92	24.97	24.87
2015	25.07	24.95	25.13	25.38	25.22	24.85	25.26	25.54	25.44	25.64	25.55	25.40	25.29
2016	26.25	25.68	25.66	25.89	25.94	25.40	25.62	25.70	25.78	26.01	25.64	25.72	25.77
2017	25.69	25.55	25.60	26.05	25.97	26.03	26.23	26.14	26.31	26.40	26.43	26.25	26.06
Goods-Producing													
2013	25.98	25.95	26.17	26.01	25.86	26.46	26.00	26.15	26.19	26.34	27.21	28.20	26.40
2014	27.87	27.98	28.27	27.66	27.38	27.23	27.12	27.04	27.43	27.49	27.43	27.78	27.53
2015	27.45	27.37	27.80	27.60	27.37	27.07	27.41	27.73	27.38	27.85	27.53	27.29	27.49
2016	27.74	27.47	27.87	28.07	27.89	27.28	27.40	27.74	27.75	28.18	27.58	27.98	27.74
2017	28.31	27.90	27.99	28.60	28.56	28.43	28.63	28.73	28.65	28.81	28.36	28.51	28.48
Construction													
2013	26.64	27.23	27.48	27.48	27.25	28.05	26.86	26.92	27.36	27.15	27.80	29.03	27.45
2014	28.80	28.81	29.39	28.91	27.89	27.62	27.86	27.64	28.18	27.98	28.17	29.23	28.28
2015	29.75	28.66	29.18	28.44	28.38	28.14	28.11	28.76	27.87	28.70	27.96	28.31	28.50
2016	28.26	28.12	28.54	28.41	27.86	27.31	27.47	28.37	28.13	28.71	27.70	28.32	28.08
2017	28.61	28.50	28.74	28.91	28.91	29.11	29.64	29.39	29.27	29.34	28.55	28.84	29.03
Manufacturing													
2013	22.97	22.38	22.44	22.27	22.25	22.41	22.17	22.28	22.45	22.55	22.57	23.91	22.55
2014	23.33	23.39	23.57	23.06	23.07	22.90	22.74	22.96	23.04	23.25	22.80	22.55	23.05
2015	21.33	21.46	21.73	22.04	22.11	21.41	22.04	22.13	22.42	22.86	22.95	22.43	22.08
2016	23.27	23.23	23.54	23.56	23.68	23.57	23.48	23.55	23.86	24.31	24.21	24.55	23.73
2017	24.61	24.02	24.15	25.35	25.15	24.19	24.28	24.29	24.56	24.67	24.94	24.63	24.57
Trade, Transportation, and Utilities													
2013	23.13	23.06	22.75	23.54	22.85	23.43	23.13	22.88	23.64	23.46	23.19	23.54	23.22
2014	24.37	25.39	24.88	24.73	24.90	24.86	24.67	24.44	24.95	24.61	24.97	24.58	24.78
2015	25.36	25.01	24.99	25.47	25.09	24.98	25.16	25.34	25.42	25.32	25.07	25.01	25.19
2016	25.54	25.13	24.98	25.37	25.32	24.91	25.11	24.58	24.88	25.26	25.02	25.03	25.10
2017	25.34	25.70	25.80	26.60	26.13	26.19	26.47	25.87	25.95	25.97	25.95	25.71	25.98
Financial Activities													
2013	22.80	22.91	22.74	22.28	22.49	22.29	22.08	22.24	22.67	22.82	23.37	23.84	22.72
2014	24.58	24.65	23.54	24.21	24.00	23.98	24.44	23.95	23.43	23.65	23.22	23.47	23.92
2015	24.06	24.42	25.35	25.91	26.45	26.08	27.55	27.42	25.65	26.99	27.24	26.80	26.15
2016	26.68	26.37	26.13	26.74	27.07	26.43	27.01	28.03	27.61	28.54	27.70	28.30	27.24
2017	29.90	28.50	28.47	29.35	29.99	29.70	30.87	31.10	31.43	31.26	30.79	30.88	30.19
Professional and Business Services													
2013	28.21	28.12	27.95	27.66	27.46	28.18	27.81	27.69	29.35	29.23	29.57	29.91	28.43
2014	29.59	28.94	28.88	28.81	28.37	27.84	27.53	27.94	28.36	28.30	28.26	28.55	28.42
2015	28.00	28.06	28.12	28.68	28.83	28.00	28.82	29.30	29.43	29.17	29.50	29.24	28.77
2016	28.63	27.54	28.08	28.86	29.29	27.96	28.59	28.86	29.33	29.95	29.09	29.50	28.82
2017	26.97	27.35	27.30	27.01	27.07	27.87	27.14	27.95	28.24	28.64	28.98	29.73	27.83
Education and Health Services													
2013	23.39	23.33	23.17	23.06	23.07	22.79	23.66	23.38	23.28	23.40	23.44	23.33	23.27
2014	23.49	23.44	23.50	24.08	23.56	23.58	23.96	23.86	24.29	24.03	24.18	24.41	23.86
2015	24.27	24.41	24.17	24.44	24.46	24.21	24.45	24.90	25.42	25.43	25.59	25.70	24.79
2016	25.90	25.39	25.21	25.11	25.22	24.88	24.86	25.21	25.16	25.05	25.20	24.77	25.16
2017	24.71	24.69	24.87	24.62	24.71	24.94	25.01	24.93	25.22	25.37	25.59	25.43	25.01
Leisure and Hospitality													
2013	12.53	12.81	12.72	12.79	12.88	12.57	12.66	12.62	12.90	12.79	12.85	13.05	12.76
2014	13.10	13.06	13.15	13.36	13.22	13.15	13.34	13.22	13.57	13.77	13.77	13.92	13.39
2015	14.16	14.06	14.15	14.28	14.14	13.99	14.06	14.13	14.35	14.40	14.43	14.50	14.22
2016	14.20	14.40	14.41	14.51	14.51	14.49	14.58	14.53	14.76	14.83	14.86	15.02	14.59
2017	15.61	15.01	15.03	15.51	15.46	15.08	15.03	15.08	15.20	15.20	15.30	15.37	15.24
Other Services													
2013	18.18	20.20	20.53	21.10	20.48	20.92	21.77	21.83	22.75	22.41	22.49	22.63	21.34
2014	23.31	22.06	22.44	23.47	22.57	22.79	22.76	22.23	23.26	23.72	22.81	22.41	22.80
2015	22.88	23.10	23.43	23.04	22.85	22.91	23.37	23.22	22.78	23.03	23.54	23.48	23.14
2016	22.30	22.99	22.92	22.42	23.22	22.50	23.67	23.71	23.78	22.65	22.77	23.00	23.00
2017	21.68	21.36	21.34	22.20	22.37	22.42	22.91	22.92	23.20	23.27	22.80	22.27	22.42

4. Average Weekly Earnings by Selected Industry: North Dakota, 2013–2017

(Dollars, not seasonally adjusted)

Industry and year	January	February	March	April	May	June	July	August	September	October	November	December	Annual average
Total Private													
2013	810.51	822.67	813.51	819.67	834.61	881.34	849.89	871.79	881.33	856.89	871.73	881.79	850.13
2014	851.24	889.99	876.83	873.25	877.21	906.12	898.79	899.99	904.28	902.83	904.60	883.94	890.35
2015	864.92	873.25	877.04	878.15	875.13	877.21	891.68	919.44	895.49	907.66	901.92	881.38	887.68
2016	895.13	875.69	864.74	885.44	905.31	881.38	891.58	896.93	891.99	912.95	876.89	869.34	886.49
2017	878.60	866.15	865.28	911.75	911.55	921.46	939.03	930.58	920.85	929.28	914.48	905.63	909.49
Goods-Producing													
2013	1,010.62	1,038.00	1,041.57	1,040.40	1,065.43	1,148.36	1,084.20	1,147.99	1,139.27	1,124.72	1,175.47	1,201.32	1,103.52
2014	1,123.16	1,166.77	1,198.65	1,156.19	1,185.55	1,200.84	1,220.40	1,203.28	1,234.35	1,231.55	1,198.69	1,197.32	1,194.80
2015	1,139.18	1,111.22	1,162.04	1,126.08	1,111.22	1,145.06	1,159.44	1,200.71	1,155.44	1,183.63	1,156.26	1,151.64	1,149.08
2016	1,109.60	1,109.79	1,128.74	1,139.64	1,154.65	1,132.12	1,128.88	1,181.72	1,162.73	1,206.10	1,119.75	1,094.02	1,140.11
2017	1,118.25	1,099.26	1,105.61	1,169.74	1,216.66	1,208.28	1,236.82	1,255.50	1,229.09	1,267.64	1,188.28	1,180.31	1,193.31
Construction													
2013	1,017.65	1,045.63	1,041.49	1,071.72	1,136.33	1,253.84	1,160.35	1,197.94	1,171.01	1,143.02	1,184.28	1,248.29	1,144.67
2014	1,149.12	1,149.52	1,199.11	1,193.98	1,260.63	1,276.04	1,328.92	1,271.44	1,318.82	1,303.87	1,205.68	1,262.74	1,249.98
2015	1,237.60	1,117.74	1,208.05	1,191.64	1,160.74	1,255.04	1,248.08	1,302.83	1,212.35	1,277.15	1,177.12	1,186.19	1,216.95
2016	1,090.84	1,121.99	1,170.14	1,190.38	1,228.63	1,207.10	1,178.46	1,251.12	1,234.91	1,291.95	1,149.55	1,093.15	1,190.59
2017	1,101.49	1,102.95	1,115.11	1,167.96	1,263.37	1,269.20	1,292.30	1,322.55	1,255.68	1,323.23	1,153.42	1,127.64	1,216.36
Manufacturing													
2013	886.64	895.20	917.80	913.07	907.80	947.94	889.02	960.27	954.13	942.59	945.68	939.66	926.81
2014	891.21	921.57	916.87	890.12	906.65	899.97	900.50	934.47	942.34	925.35	923.40	904.26	912.78
2015	814.81	839.09	856.16	850.74	853.45	832.85	857.36	907.33	910.25	925.83	922.59	921.87	874.37
2016	916.84	910.62	922.77	918.84	925.89	933.37	925.11	951.42	947.24	991.85	956.30	957.45	939.71
2017	947.49	917.56	937.02	998.79	1,011.03	950.67	973.63	961.88	977.49	964.60	967.67	950.72	963.14
Trade, Transportation, and Utilities													
2013	807.24	827.85	805.35	828.61	843.17	878.63	834.99	844.27	869.95	844.56	853.39	866.27	842.89
2014	855.39	926.74	900.66	885.33	888.93	932.25	900.46	906.72	905.69	900.73	923.89	892.25	901.99
2015	900.28	902.86	882.15	901.64	890.70	889.29	903.24	912.24	907.49	906.46	884.97	872.85	896.76
2016	873.47	854.42	844.32	880.34	896.33	881.81	888.89	857.84	868.31	881.57	863.19	858.53	870.97
2017	869.16	868.66	869.46	938.98	917.16	929.75	950.27	915.80	908.25	914.14	905.66	894.71	906.70
Financial Activities													
2013	825.36	831.63	816.37	810.99	814.14	849.25	805.92	825.10	877.33	842.06	871.70	905.92	840.64
2014	907.00	944.10	882.75	893.35	880.80	911.24	889.62	869.39	855.20	853.77	898.61	866.04	887.43
2015	887.81	915.75	925.28	906.85	904.59	894.54	958.74	995.35	895.19	944.65	1,024.22	938.00	933.56
2016	939.14	920.31	909.32	954.62	1,007.00	940.91	988.57	1,006.28	1,021.57	1,093.08	999.97	1,044.27	986.09
2017	1,145.17	1,043.10	1,050.54	1,094.76	1,055.65	1,066.23	1,145.28	1,113.38	1,137.77	1,159.75	1,123.84	1,130.21	1,104.95
Professional and Business Services													
2013	1,055.05	1,054.50	1,053.72	1,031.72	1,070.94	1,130.02	1,095.71	1,110.37	1,156.39	1,125.36	1,123.66	1,127.61	1,094.56
2014	1,065.24	1,125.77	1,083.00	1,083.26	1,112.10	1,110.82	1,073.67	1,086.87	1,108.88	1,112.19	1,102.14	1,084.90	1,094.17
2015	1,030.40	1,077.50	1,071.37	1,101.31	1,121.49	1,094.80	1,106.69	1,145.63	1,121.28	1,134.71	1,115.10	1,076.03	1,099.01
2016	1,030.68	1,013.47	1,008.07	1,038.96	1,104.23	1,034.52	1,037.82	1,064.93	1,094.01	1,147.09	1,082.15	1,106.25	1,063.46
2017	1,016.77	1,011.95	1,040.13	1,053.39	1,039.49	1,053.49	1,047.60	1,042.54	1,013.82	1,042.50	1,008.50	1,034.60	1,035.28
Education and Health Services													
2013	788.24	783.89	764.61	765.59	763.62	770.30	771.32	771.54	770.57	760.50	761.80	760.56	770.24
2014	756.38	757.11	752.00	775.38	744.50	771.07	754.74	765.91	774.85	759.35	768.92	771.36	763.52
2015	769.36	788.44	780.69	799.19	794.95	796.51	797.07	811.74	818.52	821.39	834.23	824.97	803.20
2016	831.39	820.10	799.16	795.99	802.00	791.18	795.52	796.64	790.02	789.08	803.88	787.69	800.09
2017	790.72	792.55	785.89	795.23	793.19	810.55	815.33	820.20	822.17	819.45	836.79	829.02	810.32
Leisure and Hospitality													
2013	275.66	288.23	291.29	291.61	301.39	315.51	311.44	307.93	310.89	296.73	291.70	302.76	298.58
2014	289.51	304.30	311.66	312.62	311.99	324.81	317.49	326.53	322.97	324.97	334.61	325.73	317.34
2015	315.77	336.03	332.53	324.16	337.95	341.36	338.85	356.08	338.66	342.72	350.65	348.00	338.44
2016	339.38	338.40	332.87	339.53	349.69	340.52	341.17	344.36	324.72	338.12	335.84	331.94	338.49
2017	363.71	342.23	344.19	372.24	383.41	373.98	368.24	367.95	352.64	354.16	344.25	353.51	359.66
Other Services													
2013	454.50	502.98	498.88	535.94	497.66	625.51	613.91	665.82	680.23	593.87	609.48	615.54	574.05
2014	615.38	633.12	601.39	572.67	564.25	624.45	653.21	651.34	590.80	585.88	599.90	564.73	606.48
2015	558.27	582.12	604.49	580.61	603.24	609.41	612.29	645.52	610.50	607.99	656.77	645.70	608.58
2016	628.86	632.23	621.13	654.66	680.35	621.00	684.06	680.48	694.38	672.71	658.05	664.70	657.80
2017	624.38	634.39	625.26	703.74	693.47	703.99	753.74	721.98	735.44	756.28	727.32	694.82	697.26

OHIO
At a Glance

Population:
  2010 census: 11,536,504
  2017 estimate: 11,658,609

Percent change in population:
  2010–2017: 1.1%

Percent change in total nonfarm employment:
  2007–2017: 1.8%

Industry with the largest growth in employment, 2007–2017 (thousands):
  Education and health services, 135.9

Industry with the largest decline or smallest growth in employment, 2007–2017 (thousands):
  Manufacturing, -84.9

Civilian labor force:
  2010: 5,846,886
  2017: 5,780,021

Unemployment rate and rank among states (highest to lowest):
  2010: 10.3%, 15th
  2017: 5.0%, 7th

Over-the-year change in unemployment rates:
  2015–2016: 0.1%
  2016–2017: 0.0%

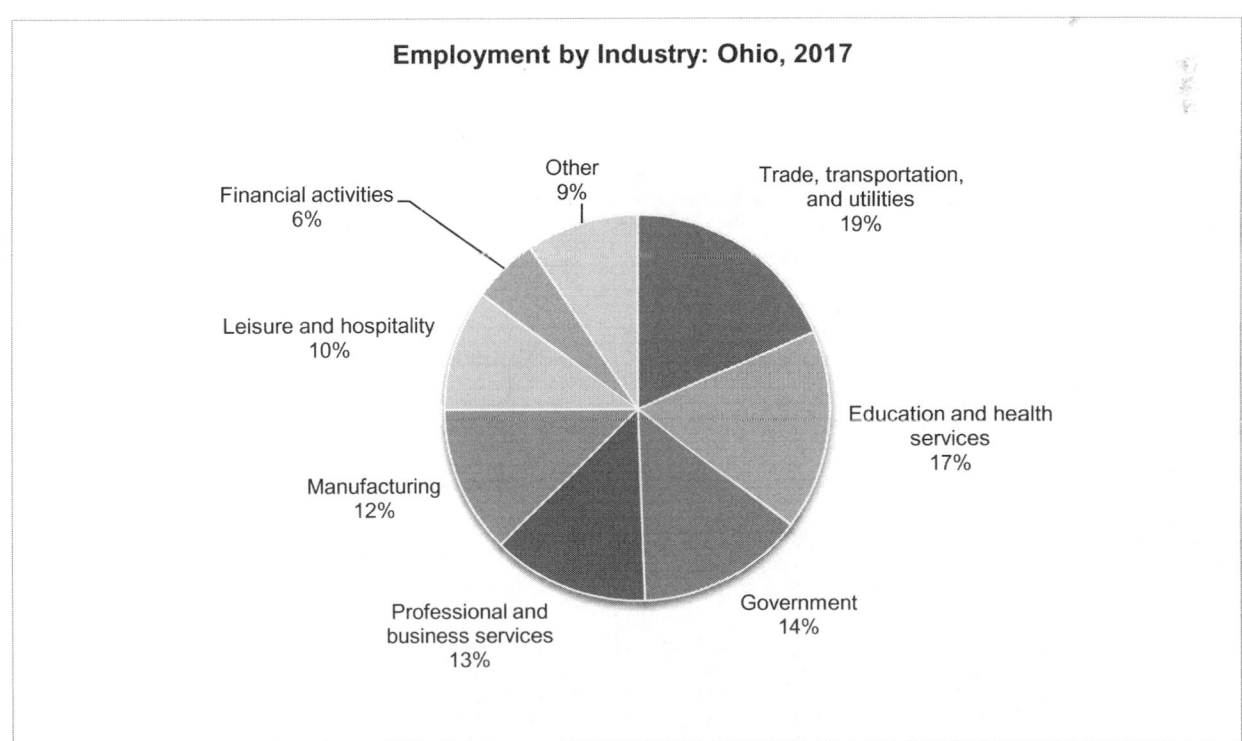

Employment by Industry: Ohio, 2017

- Other 9%
- Trade, transportation, and utilities 19%
- Financial activities 6%
- Education and health services 17%
- Leisure and hospitality 10%
- Government 14%
- Manufacturing 12%
- Professional and business services 13%

1. Employment by Industry: Ohio, Selected Years, 2007–2017

(Numbers in thousands, not seasonally adjusted)

Industry and year	January	February	March	April	May	June	July	August	September	October	November	December	Annual average
Total Nonfarm													
2007	5,323.2	5,319.8	5,367.9	5,416.3	5,473.7	5,492.7	5,423.3	5,437.7	5,451.3	5,464.3	5,482.0	5,471.5	5,427.0
2008	5,315.9	5,325.1	5,324.9	5,383.9	5,434.4	5,427.8	5,368.1	5,371.8	5,375.7	5,370.1	5,340.7	5,302.7	5,361.8
2009	5,099.5	5,084.2	5,078.2	5,093.4	5,118.8	5,091.6	5,036.3	5,033.6	5,053.6	5,066.7	5,063.3	5,050.5	5,072.5
2010	4,905.0	4,910.6	4,945.2	5,022.9	5,080.7	5,076.9	5,043.7	5,047.4	5,069.4	5,106.6	5,116.5	5,106.8	5,036.0
2011	4,959.4	4,981.3	5,015.2	5,092.4	5,133.0	5,131.8	5,128.2	5,145.3	5,158.9	5,173.0	5,192.6	5,184.6	5,108.0
2012	5,050.8	5,082.5	5,129.9	5,189.0	5,247.2	5,248.7	5,210.5	5,223.8	5,232.8	5,265.6	5,276.1	5,263.9	5,201.7
2013	5,113.7	5,142.8	5,171.7	5,248.9	5,317.3	5,303.6	5,275.7	5,297.0	5,303.8	5,330.9	5,355.1	5,341.1	5,266.8
2014	5,180.3	5,204.0	5,238.5	5,319.3	5,391.3	5,379.1	5,348.5	5,378.7	5,385.1	5,423.5	5,442.4	5,437.9	5,344.1
2015	5,273.5	5,295.7	5,322.5	5,402.9	5,474.0	5,460.6	5,445.8	5,456.5	5,453.3	5,493.8	5,505.1	5,498.8	5,423.5
2016	5,347.1	5,369.2	5,401.3	5,479.6	5,522.1	5,504.1	5,496.6	5,501.8	5,514.5	5,541.3	5,560.4	5,534.9	5,481.1
2017	5,404.8	5,427.1	5,455.5	5,517.6	5,568.6	5,567.5	5,542.7	5,556.2	5,555.2	5,578.3	5,576.4	5,560.6	5,525.9
Total Private													
2007	4,529.4	4,512.1	4,556.5	4,605.3	4,658.9	4,696.0	4,665.7	4,681.8	4,661.0	4,653.9	4,667.4	4,663.5	4,629.3
2008	4,521.6	4,512.8	4,514.2	4,572.1	4,617.7	4,633.4	4,611.5	4,616.4	4,585.6	4,557.5	4,523.1	4,493.8	4,563.3
2009	4,306.2	4,275.9	4,269.4	4,282.2	4,306.4	4,302.7	4,287.3	4,287.8	4,271.2	4,263.3	4,258.3	4,254.8	4,280.5
2010	4,121.7	4,115.0	4,147.2	4,220.5	4,260.7	4,288.6	4,300.8	4,310.1	4,298.2	4,311.3	4,317.7	4,312.0	4,250.3
2011	4,188.0	4,195.3	4,226.7	4,303.8	4,345.2	4,366.0	4,382.6	4,400.9	4,386.0	4,388.2	4,405.6	4,404.4	4,332.7
2012	4,290.1	4,301.5	4,344.9	4,401.0	4,452.4	4,486.0	4,468.5	4,482.8	4,462.3	4,480.3	4,489.4	4,483.1	4,428.5
2013	4,353.9	4,366.4	4,395.5	4,467.4	4,531.8	4,557.3	4,546.4	4,566.2	4,538.9	4,553.6	4,572.0	4,567.2	4,501.4
2014	4,430.5	4,434.3	4,467.5	4,539.8	4,605.3	4,628.5	4,622.5	4,645.7	4,611.0	4,638.6	4,655.2	4,655.9	4,577.9
2015	4,518.4	4,519.2	4,546.1	4,618.4	4,687.8	4,705.8	4,706.8	4,715.0	4,681.5	4,705.6	4,715.3	4,714.5	4,652.9
2016	4,588.9	4,591.3	4,622.8	4,686.5	4,733.5	4,748.8	4,757.0	4,759.2	4,733.4	4,744.9	4,759.9	4,746.3	4,706.0
2017	4,626.8	4,635.1	4,662.5	4,721.5	4,775.7	4,807.3	4,795.7	4,805.4	4,768.3	4,782.2	4,775.7	4,768.4	4,743.7
Goods Producing													
2007	990.8	982.6	994.1	1,003.9	1,017.9	1,029.3	1,016.8	1,027.4	1,020.1	1,010.0	1,007.6	997.3	1,008.2
2008	962.5	958.2	953.0	964.7	976.6	986.4	978.3	979.1	971.8	960.9	940.8	916.2	962.4
2009	855.7	842.7	833.3	826.7	824.5	820.1	815.2	820.2	816.3	813.4	804.0	798.1	822.5
2010	765.5	761.2	768.7	788.1	801.6	812.9	818.6	822.1	819.8	822.2	819.5	810.3	800.9
2011	785.4	784.3	794.1	811.1	821.7	833.7	843.4	851.7	848.7	849.1	849.2	842.7	826.3
2012	818.1	818.7	828.4	841.2	852.7	864.9	862.7	867.2	863.0	860.1	858.6	851.8	849.0
2013	828.7	828.6	834.8	847.8	863.9	875.9	873.9	881.9	878.3	878.7	878.3	868.3	861.6
2014	845.1	844.4	854.4	870.8	888.3	901.0	900.7	908.9	904.3	906.4	905.6	897.5	885.6
2015	871.7	870.0	875.6	892.4	908.7	917.3	916.3	920.0	913.9	914.2	911.3	905.1	901.4
2016	880.0	878.6	886.1	898.2	907.6	916.8	916.9	916.1	910.7	910.2	908.7	899.9	902.5
2017	880.8	881.0	890.6	905.5	921.8	936.2	930.6	934.2	926.6	928.1	924.0	914.5	914.5
Service-Providing													
2007	4,332.4	4,337.2	4,373.8	4,412.4	4,455.8	4,463.4	4,406.5	4,410.3	4,431.2	4,454.3	4,474.4	4,474.2	4,418.8
2008	4,353.4	4,366.9	4,371.9	4,419.2	4,457.8	4,441.4	4,389.8	4,392.7	4,403.9	4,409.2	4,399.9	4,386.5	4,399.4
2009	4,243.8	4,241.5	4,244.9	4,266.7	4,294.3	4,271.5	4,221.1	4,213.4	4,237.3	4,253.3	4,259.3	4,252.4	4,250.0
2010	4,139.5	4,149.4	4,176.5	4,234.8	4,279.1	4,264.0	4,225.1	4,225.3	4,249.6	4,284.4	4,297.0	4,296.5	4,235.1
2011	4,174.0	4,197.0	4,221.1	4,281.3	4,311.3	4,298.1	4,284.8	4,293.6	4,310.2	4,323.9	4,343.4	4,341.9	4,281.7
2012	4,232.7	4,263.8	4,301.5	4,347.8	4,394.5	4,383.8	4,347.8	4,356.6	4,369.8	4,405.5	4,417.5	4,412.1	4,352.8
2013	4,285.0	4,314.2	4,336.9	4,401.1	4,453.4	4,427.7	4,401.8	4,415.1	4,425.5	4,452.2	4,476.8	4,472.8	4,405.2
2014	4,335.2	4,359.6	4,384.1	4,448.5	4,503.0	4,478.1	4,447.8	4,469.8	4,480.8	4,517.1	4,536.8	4,540.4	4,458.4
2015	4,401.8	4,425.7	4,446.9	4,510.5	4,565.3	4,543.3	4,529.5	4,536.5	4,539.4	4,579.6	4,593.8	4,593.7	4,522.2
2016	4,467.1	4,490.6	4,515.2	4,581.4	4,614.5	4,587.3	4,579.7	4,585.7	4,603.8	4,631.1	4,651.7	4,635.0	4,578.6
2017	4,524.0	4,546.1	4,564.9	4,612.1	4,646.8	4,631.3	4,612.1	4,622.0	4,628.6	4,650.2	4,652.4	4,646.1	4,611.4
Mining and Logging													
2007	11.3	11.0	11.2	11.6	11.8	11.9	12.0	12.1	11.9	11.8	11.9	11.7	11.7
2008	11.3	11.2	11.1	11.5	11.9	12.0	12.4	12.5	12.4	12.5	12.5	12.1	12.0
2009	11.6	11.4	11.5	11.8	12.0	12.0	12.1	12.0	11.8	11.6	11.5	11.3	11.7
2010	10.5	10.5	10.5	11.2	11.4	11.5	11.7	11.6	11.7	11.6	11.5	11.3	11.3
2011	10.7	10.7	10.9	11.2	11.3	11.4	11.6	11.7	11.7	11.7	11.6	11.4	11.3
2012	11.0	10.8	11.0	11.4	11.6	11.7	11.8	11.7	11.6	11.5	11.6	11.4	11.4
2013	11.3	11.3	11.8	12.2	12.5	12.5	12.7	12.9	12.9	13.5	13.5	13.3	12.5
2014	13.1	13.3	13.7	14.2	14.6	14.9	15.4	15.8	15.7	15.8	15.9	15.8	14.9
2015	15.2	14.8	14.7	14.5	14.6	14.3	14.1	14.0	13.8	13.3	13.0	12.6	14.1
2016	11.6	11.2	11.3	11.3	11.2	11.2	11.1	11.2	11.0	11.4	11.4	11.2	11.3
2017	10.4	10.6	11.0	11.2	11.3	11.4	11.7	11.9	11.9	12.1	12.0	11.5	11.4

1. Employment by Industry: Ohio, Selected Years, 2007–2017—*Continued*

(Numbers in thousands, not seasonally adjusted)

Industry and year	January	February	March	April	May	June	July	August	September	October	November	December	Annual average
Construction													
2007	204.3	195.6	206.1	219.2	231.3	238.7	239.7	240.2	237.2	235.9	230.7	218.6	224.8
2008	196.4	192.2	194.6	208.3	218.3	223.7	226.0	225.9	221.3	219.6	210.8	196.8	211.2
2009	173.5	168.9	172.0	175.8	185.9	190.9	193.9	192.1	187.1	185.4	179.3	168.8	181.1
2010	147.4	142.8	149.6	162.8	170.2	176.7	183.1	183.4	181.0	182.5	178.6	167.9	168.8
2011	150.1	147.9	154.2	167.0	175.1	183.0	190.7	193.6	192.6	190.8	187.7	180.8	176.1
2012	162.9	160.3	165.8	176.1	184.0	189.6	191.9	192.4	191.1	191.5	187.3	179.9	181.1
2013	163.0	161.7	166.0	176.2	188.5	195.5	198.7	201.0	199.7	200.2	196.6	185.1	186.0
2014	169.1	166.6	174.9	188.0	199.9	207.3	211.0	211.9	209.5	209.4	205.1	195.6	195.7
2015	175.9	173.9	179.2	193.5	205.4	210.8	213.7	214.8	212.6	213.5	209.9	202.5	200.5
2016	185.6	184.5	191.9	203.6	211.6	217.9	218.2	217.0	214.8	214.6	212.0	201.9	206.1
2017	187.6	189.6	197.3	213.0	225.7	233.0	232.4	232.3	229.0	228.5	220.2	206.5	216.3
Manufacturing													
2007	775.2	776.0	776.8	773.1	774.8	778.7	765.1	775.1	771.0	762.3	765.0	767.0	771.7
2008	754.8	754.8	747.3	744.9	746.4	750.7	739.9	740.7	738.1	728.8	717.5	707.3	739.3
2009	670.6	662.4	649.8	639.1	626.6	617.2	609.2	616.1	617.4	616.4	613.2	618.0	629.7
2010	607.6	607.9	608.6	614.1	620.0	624.7	623.8	627.1	627.1	628.1	629.4	631.1	620.8
2011	624.6	625.7	629.0	632.9	635.3	639.3	641.1	646.4	644.4	646.6	649.9	650.5	638.8
2012	644.2	647.6	651.6	653.7	657.1	663.6	659.0	663.1	660.3	657.1	659.7	660.5	656.5
2013	654.4	655.6	657.0	659.4	662.9	667.9	662.5	668.0	665.7	665.0	668.2	669.9	663.0
2014	662.9	664.5	665.8	668.6	673.8	678.8	674.3	681.2	679.1	681.2	684.6	686.1	675.1
2015	680.6	681.3	681.7	684.4	688.7	692.2	688.5	691.2	687.5	687.4	688.4	690.0	686.8
2016	682.8	682.9	682.9	683.3	684.8	687.7	687.6	687.9	684.9	684.2	685.3	686.8	685.1
2017	682.8	680.8	682.3	681.3	684.8	691.8	686.5	690.0	685.7	687.5	691.8	696.5	686.8
Trade, Transportation, and Utilities													
2007	1,038.2	1,024.4	1,033.4	1,038.4	1,050.1	1,054.4	1,052.1	1,050.7	1,046.8	1,052.8	1,076.2	1,087.6	1,050.4
2008	1,038.3	1,024.0	1,025.2	1,031.8	1,039.6	1,039.9	1,036.3	1,036.9	1,028.0	1,027.7	1,035.2	1,040.7	1,033.6
2009	985.3	969.7	966.0	963.2	968.3	967.4	962.5	959.8	953.0	957.0	971.3	979.1	966.9
2010	934.1	924.3	929.5	937.3	945.6	949.9	948.9	949.9	943.7	954.2	970.4	980.5	947.4
2011	936.5	931.0	934.2	947.0	953.1	957.5	959.3	962.2	957.3	966.8	987.4	997.6	957.5
2012	956.4	949.5	956.7	961.7	971.9	975.4	971.2	972.1	968.6	979.1	1,001.6	1,007.4	972.6
2013	964.1	956.2	960.3	968.0	980.0	984.7	982.6	984.4	978.6	988.8	1,013.0	1,022.3	981.9
2014	975.0	968.2	971.3	981.6	992.7	996.9	994.4	998.4	992.8	1,006.5	1,029.6	1,041.5	995.7
2015	996.5	989.0	993.0	1,001.1	1,012.1	1,014.5	1,012.9	1,014.7	1,008.1	1,019.4	1,041.8	1,052.1	1,012.9
2016	1,009.7	1,002.5	1,005.4	1,010.9	1,019.2	1,019.7	1,019.7	1,022.4	1,016.4	1,026.6	1,050.5	1,061.6	1,022.1
2017	1,016.6	1,007.6	1,008.9	1,015.0	1,022.6	1,025.4	1,024.5	1,025.9	1,018.7	1,028.2	1,045.7	1,051.2	1,024.2
Wholesale Trade													
2007	236.5	236.1	237.1	237.7	239.1	240.3	240.2	239.6	237.8	238.0	237.9	238.5	238.2
2008	235.5	235.2	235.2	236.8	238.2	238.8	238.5	238.0	235.7	235.1	233.1	231.7	236.0
2009	226.8	224.6	223.3	221.7	221.1	220.7	220.2	219.0	217.0	216.9	216.6	216.7	220.4
2010	213.3	213.1	213.6	214.9	215.5	216.5	217.2	216.9	215.1	215.5	215.1	214.8	215.1
2011	212.7	213.1	213.8	216.2	217.6	218.8	220.4	220.8	219.8	220.8	221.0	221.6	218.1
2012	220.0	220.8	221.9	222.7	224.2	225.9	225.7	225.7	224.2	225.1	225.4	225.7	223.9
2013	222.9	223.1	223.9	225.4	227.3	228.2	228.5	228.6	227.2	228.5	229.4	230.0	226.9
2014	227.1	228.3	229.4	230.3	233.0	234.0	234.7	234.6	233.3	234.1	234.8	235.9	232.5
2015	232.3	233.1	234.3	234.5	236.3	236.9	237.0	236.5	234.1	235.0	235.6	235.8	235.1
2016	233.4	233.5	234.0	234.0	235.3	235.9	236.2	236.1	234.3	234.3	234.5	235.2	234.7
2017	232.6	233.2	233.7	234.7	236.4	238.1	238.0	238.0	236.3	238.3	238.3	237.2	236.2
Retail Trade													
2007	594.7	583.3	590.4	592.8	601.0	602.6	601.2	598.7	595.2	599.2	619.1	627.5	600.5
2008	592.2	579.7	581.1	585.5	590.8	592.2	591.2	591.0	584.9	586.0	595.8	603.5	589.5
2009	563.3	552.4	552.2	554.7	561.0	561.6	558.4	557.3	553.5	556.6	570.8	577.6	560.0
2010	543.0	534.9	539.1	544.4	550.4	552.7	552.0	552.5	547.4	555.9	571.2	579.1	551.9
2011	544.0	538.5	540.6	549.2	552.6	555.2	555.1	556.1	550.7	558.5	576.8	583.8	555.1
2012	551.0	543.4	549.0	552.7	559.1	560.0	556.5	556.3	553.8	561.7	581.4	583.9	559.1
2013	552.7	545.5	548.6	554.3	562.3	564.9	563.2	563.8	559.2	566.7	585.9	591.8	563.2
2014	555.1	549.0	550.6	558.9	564.2	566.7	563.8	566.0	560.7	571.4	589.6	594.9	565.9
2015	561.0	555.2	557.7	563.6	570.3	571.6	569.9	570.8	565.9	573.6	591.5	597.1	570.7
2016	567.8	562.7	564.5	569.1	574.5	574.5	573.9	575.5	570.1	578.2	596.9	603.8	576.0
2017	573.1	565.1	566.1	570.7	574.8	575.3	575.3	575.4	569.0	574.3	585.9	588.6	574.5

1. Employment by Industry: Ohio, Selected Years, 2007–2017—*Continued*

(Numbers in thousands, not seasonally adjusted)

Industry and year	January	February	March	April	May	June	July	August	September	October	November	December	Annual average
Transportation and Utilities													
2007	207.0	205.0	205.9	207.9	210.0	211.5	210.7	212.4	213.8	215.6	219.2	221.6	211.7
2008	210.6	209.1	208.9	209.5	210.6	208.9	206.6	207.9	207.4	206.6	206.3	205.5	208.2
2009	195.2	192.7	190.5	186.8	186.2	185.1	183.9	183.5	182.5	183.5	183.9	184.8	186.6
2010	177.8	176.3	176.8	178.0	179.7	180.7	179.7	180.5	181.2	182.8	184.1	186.6	180.4
2011	179.8	179.4	179.8	181.6	182.9	183.5	183.8	185.3	186.8	187.5	189.6	192.2	184.4
2012	185.4	185.3	185.8	186.3	188.6	189.5	189.0	190.1	190.6	192.3	194.8	197.8	189.6
2013	188.5	187.6	187.8	188.3	190.4	191.6	190.9	192.0	192.2	193.6	197.7	200.5	191.8
2014	192.8	190.9	191.3	192.4	195.5	196.2	195.9	197.8	198.8	201.0	205.2	210.7	197.4
2015	203.2	200.7	201.0	203.0	205.5	206.0	206.0	207.4	208.1	210.8	214.7	219.2	207.1
2016	208.5	206.3	206.9	207.8	209.4	209.3	209.6	210.8	212.0	214.1	219.1	222.6	211.4
2017	210.9	209.3	209.1	209.6	211.4	212.0	211.2	212.5	213.4	215.6	221.5	225.4	213.5
Information													
2007	87.3	87.4	87.0	87.8	88.4	88.9	88.8	88.5	87.3	86.9	87.1	87.4	87.7
2008	86.3	86.2	86.1	86.4	86.4	86.4	86.5	86.4	84.8	84.5	84.9	84.8	85.8
2009	83.6	83.1	82.2	81.2	81.3	81.1	80.9	80.4	79.1	78.5	78.7	79.0	80.8
2010	78.5	78.1	77.9	77.4	77.6	77.5	77.9	77.9	77.0	76.8	77.1	77.2	77.6
2011	76.1	75.8	75.3	75.9	76.3	76.4	76.8	76.7	76.2	75.8	76.1	76.0	76.1
2012	75.0	74.8	74.7	74.6	75.0	75.4	75.5	75.0	74.5	74.8	75.1	75.4	75.0
2013	74.9	75.3	75.5	75.5	75.5	75.9	76.0	75.7	74.8	74.5	74.3	74.7	75.2
2014	73.0	73.0	73.0	73.2	73.1	72.8	72.8	72.6	71.3	70.9	71.5	72.1	72.4
2015	70.7	71.1	71.0	71.6	71.7	72.1	72.0	72.0	71.2	71.6	72.1	72.5	71.6
2016	71.4	71.5	71.5	71.5	71.8	72.2	72.5	72.4	72.0	71.7	72.3	72.1	71.9
2017	71.4	71.5	71.1	71.5	71.8	71.8	72.1	72.0	71.3	71.3	71.4	71.7	71.6
Financial Activities													
2007	301.5	301.2	300.0	301.8	302.3	301.7	301.5	301.0	297.9	297.1	295.5	295.8	299.8
2008	292.1	291.6	291.3	291.4	292.1	292.5	291.7	291.2	288.3	287.4	286.9	286.8	290.3
2009	282.9	281.5	280.8	280.4	281.1	281.7	281.5	280.1	277.8	277.2	277.2	277.0	279.9
2010	274.4	273.9	273.6	274.9	275.8	277.3	278.9	278.8	277.1	278.2	278.6	279.3	276.7
2011	277.4	277.5	277.4	277.9	278.6	278.8	278.9	278.7	277.8	277.4	277.5	277.7	278.0
2012	275.7	275.6	276.3	277.9	279.6	281.5	282.5	282.3	280.4	281.6	282.7	282.8	279.9
2013	279.5	280.1	280.1	282.7	284.6	286.7	287.2	287.3	285.2	285.4	286.2	286.3	284.3
2014	283.7	284.5	284.9	285.3	288.1	289.9	290.3	291.2	288.5	289.3	290.6	290.7	288.1
2015	288.4	289.0	289.0	290.5	293.3	295.4	296.2	296.8	293.9	295.8	296.0	296.1	293.4
2016	294.5	295.7	296.0	298.2	299.7	301.4	303.6	303.7	302.1	303.3	303.8	304.6	300.6
2017	302.3	302.8	303.0	304.4	306.2	308.4	308.8	309.0	307.3	307.4	308.0	310.4	306.5
Professional and Business Services													
2007	646.3	647.8	654.6	665.4	668.5	678.0	675.4	679.1	677.4	681.5	682.0	680.1	669.7
2008	661.8	663.4	663.2	674.6	675.2	678.5	679.5	681.4	675.5	670.2	661.7	654.0	669.9
2009	627.2	620.5	615.5	618.4	617.0	616.1	615.3	617.8	615.5	617.6	619.9	616.0	618.1
2010	597.8	599.7	604.6	623.2	624.1	631.7	636.0	641.0	638.2	644.0	645.1	643.4	627.4
2011	626.3	629.9	636.0	651.5	650.4	654.2	660.7	665.4	664.3	666.7	668.9	668.4	653.6
2012	650.5	654.4	660.6	672.5	674.9	679.7	680.1	685.6	682.6	690.9	690.1	685.7	675.6
2013	659.1	664.3	669.1	687.4	692.9	696.9	695.4	703.1	701.0	706.8	709.7	708.6	691.2
2014	685.6	687.8	691.8	707.5	711.5	713.9	716.7	723.4	717.1	724.8	727.8	724.6	711.0
2015	698.3	696.2	699.2	713.0	719.7	722.6	726.8	729.1	720.6	732.8	731.0	726.0	717.9
2016	704.5	704.3	708.8	726.0	727.0	729.7	735.1	735.1	732.5	735.7	736.1	728.0	725.2
2017	707.4	708.4	709.8	721.6	725.5	730.9	729.9	732.4	726.2	732.1	724.9	717.4	722.2
Education and Health Services													
2007	778.8	784.1	788.4	791.3	790.4	783.8	779.4	782.6	800.3	807.8	812.7	812.8	792.7
2008	802.6	810.2	811.3	813.8	812.0	802.4	797.9	800.8	817.6	825.2	828.5	828.5	812.6
2009	817.2	824.2	825.9	828.0	825.3	815.5	813.8	815.4	831.0	840.2	843.0	842.9	826.9
2010	832.0	837.6	840.8	841.7	837.5	825.7	825.0	826.4	843.5	852.2	854.4	852.1	839.1
2011	839.8	847.9	848.8	854.3	856.1	841.8	838.3	839.5	853.1	860.7	862.8	863.2	850.5
2012	854.2	862.4	864.0	867.3	867.2	858.8	849.4	853.3	864.5	874.5	876.2	874.6	863.9
2013	863.4	874.1	873.5	879.7	880.3	870.4	867.5	872.1	877.9	888.2	893.4	891.6	877.7
2014	876.5	883.7	885.8	890.9	891.6	880.2	877.0	881.5	888.7	900.2	903.8	903.5	888.6
2015	889.2	896.9	898.3	904.4	907.2	896.7	895.4	898.3	905.9	914.8	918.5	919.1	903.7
2016	905.7	913.6	916.3	920.3	921.4	909.2	908.7	912.5	921.9	928.3	930.1	927.5	918.0
2017	916.8	925.4	927.9	931.2	931.8	922.4	920.4	923.5	930.6	937.0	939.3	937.3	928.6

1. Employment by Industry: Ohio, Selected Years, 2007–2017—*Continued*

(Numbers in thousands, not seasonally adjusted)

Industry and year	January	February	March	April	May	June	July	August	September	October	November	December	Annual average
Leisure and Hospitality													
2007	468.3	466.4	478.4	495.9	519.4	535.5	529.3	530.9	512.5	498.5	487.6	483.9	500.6
2008	462.6	463.3	467.8	491.8	516.6	527.1	522.3	522.2	503.7	485.8	471.1	469.6	492.0
2009	445.5	445.2	455.9	474.4	497.9	509.7	507.8	505.4	491.8	472.8	458.9	457.0	476.9
2010	436.7	437.3	448.5	472.0	492.3	505.5	506.7	506.1	492.6	476.8	466.2	462.4	475.3
2011	442.6	444.6	455.6	479.5	500.9	514.4	515.0	517.1	500.8	484.0	476.1	471.2	483.5
2012	454.0	459.2	474.2	495.0	518.5	535.0	532.0	533.3	516.4	505.9	492.7	492.7	500.7
2013	474.1	477.2	490.3	512.9	540.1	551.5	550.0	548.6	532.3	521.6	508.2	506.9	517.8
2014	485.8	486.8	499.4	522.0	548.9	560.7	558.2	557.7	538.8	529.3	516.0	514.9	526.5
2015	495.5	498.1	509.7	532.8	560.8	571.3	571.2	569.5	556.1	544.0	532.5	531.3	539.4
2016	513.0	514.6	526.8	547.8	571.6	583.4	583.9	581.1	563.7	553.8	543.6	539.0	551.9
2017	519.2	525.3	536.9	556.8	578.6	592.6	590.6	590.5	572.7	560.9	546.2	548.6	559.9
Other Services													
2007	218.2	218.2	220.6	220.8	221.9	224.4	222.4	221.6	218.7	219.3	218.7	218.6	220.3
2008	215.4	215.9	216.3	217.6	219.2	220.2	219.0	218.4	215.9	215.8	214.0	213.2	216.7
2009	208.8	209.0	209.8	209.9	211.0	211.1	210.3	208.7	206.7	206.6	205.3	205.7	208.6
2010	202.7	202.9	203.6	205.9	206.2	208.1	208.8	207.9	206.3	206.9	206.4	206.8	206.0
2011	203.9	204.3	205.3	206.6	208.1	209.2	210.2	209.6	207.8	207.7	207.6	207.6	207.3
2012	206.2	206.9	210.0	210.8	212.6	215.3	215.1	214.0	212.3	213.4	212.4	212.7	211.8
2013	210.1	210.6	211.9	213.4	214.5	215.3	213.8	213.1	210.8	209.6	208.9	208.5	211.7
2014	205.8	205.9	206.9	208.5	211.1	213.1	212.4	212.0	209.5	211.2	210.3	211.1	209.8
2015	208.1	208.9	210.3	212.6	214.3	215.9	216.0	214.6	211.8	213.0	212.1	212.3	212.5
2016	210.1	210.5	211.9	213.6	215.2	216.4	216.6	215.9	214.1	215.3	214.8	213.6	214.0
2017	212.3	213.1	214.3	215.5	217.4	219.6	218.8	217.9	214.9	217.2	216.2	217.3	216.2
Government													
2007	793.8	807.7	811.4	811.0	814.8	796.7	757.6	755.9	790.3	810.4	814.6	808.0	797.7
2008	794.3	812.3	810.7	811.8	816.7	794.4	756.6	755.4	790.1	812.6	817.6	808.9	798.5
2009	793.3	808.3	808.8	811.2	812.4	788.9	749.0	745.8	782.4	803.4	805.0	795.7	792.0
2010	783.3	795.6	798.0	802.4	820.0	788.3	742.9	737.3	771.2	795.3	798.8	794.8	785.7
2011	771.4	786.0	788.5	788.6	787.8	765.8	745.6	744.4	772.9	784.8	787.0	780.2	775.3
2012	760.7	781.0	785.0	788.0	794.8	762.7	742.0	741.0	770.5	785.3	786.7	780.8	773.2
2013	759.8	776.4	776.2	781.5	785.5	746.3	729.3	730.8	764.9	777.3	783.1	773.9	765.4
2014	749.8	769.7	771.0	779.5	786.0	750.6	726.0	733.0	774.1	784.9	787.2	782.0	766.2
2015	755.1	776.5	776.4	784.5	786.2	754.8	739.0	741.5	771.8	788.2	789.8	784.3	770.7
2016	758.2	777.9	778.5	793.1	788.6	755.3	739.6	742.6	781.1	796.4	800.5	788.6	775.0
2017	778.0	792.0	793.0	796.1	792.9	760.2	747.0	750.8	786.9	796.1	800.7	792.2	782.2

2. Average Weekly Hours by Selected Industry: Ohio, 2013–2017

(Not seasonally adjusted)

Industry and year	January	February	March	April	May	June	July	August	September	October	November	December	Annual average
Total Private													
2013	34.1	34.2	34.2	34.2	34.1	34.4	33.9	34.2	34.5	34.0	34.1	34.3	34.2
2014	33.3	34.1	34.1	34.0	34.6	34.4	34.1	34.3	34.3	34.3	34.6	34.5	34.2
2015	33.8	34.1	34.3	34.0	34.1	34.3	34.1	34.6	34.1	34.4	34.6	34.4	34.2
2016	34.0	34.0	34.1	34.2	34.4	34.3	34.3	34.3	34.4	34.7	34.4	34.4	34.3
2017	34.3	34.1	34.1	34.3	34.3	34.4	34.4	34.3	34.4	34.7	34.4	34.4	34.4
Goods-Producing													
2013	40.3	40.4	40.5	40.4	40.7	40.9	40.0	41.0	41.1	40.9	41.4	41.3	40.7
2014	39.8	40.8	40.8	41.0	40.9	41.3	40.6	41.1	41.3	41.3	41.3	41.4	41.0
2015	40.3	40.3	40.6	40.4	40.6	40.8	40.0	40.7	39.8	41.0	40.5	40.5	40.5
2016	39.8	39.8	40.1	40.3	40.3	40.5	40.4	40.5	40.9	41.0	40.9	40.5	40.4
2017	39.9	40.0	39.8	40.0	40.6	41.0	40.4	41.1	40.8	41.1	40.9	40.8	40.5
Construction													
2013	38.1	38.0	38.1	38.8	39.4	39.6	39.2	40.9	39.9	40.7	40.1	38.8	39.4
2014	37.3	38.4	38.0	39.0	38.5	39.7	39.4	39.4	40.1	39.1	38.3	38.1	38.8
2015	36.9	37.5	37.7	38.4	39.2	39.0	39.2	40.0	37.9	40.3	38.0	38.7	38.6
2016	36.8	37.2	37.8	38.7	37.9	39.6	39.6	39.2	39.6	39.7	39.4	37.9	38.7
2017	36.6	37.5	36.8	38.3	39.4	40.6	38.9	40.4	40.0	39.1	38.9	37.8	38.8
Manufacturing													
2013	41.1	41.2	41.2	41.0	41.3	41.6	40.5	41.3	41.7	41.2	41.9	42.0	41.3
2014	40.5	41.3	41.4	41.4	41.4	41.5	40.7	41.4	41.5	41.8	42.0	42.1	41.4
2015	41.1	40.9	41.2	40.8	40.8	41.1	40.1	40.7	40.5	41.1	41.2	41.0	40.9
2016	40.6	40.5	40.7	40.7	41.0	40.8	40.7	41.0	41.4	41.6	41.7	41.6	41.0
2017	41.3	41.0	41.0	40.7	41.2	41.3	41.2	41.4	41.1	41.8	41.7	41.9	41.3
Trade, Transportation, and Utilities													
2013	34.4	34.6	34.6	34.8	34.9	34.8	34.6	34.8	35.1	34.6	34.3	34.9	34.7
2014	33.9	34.4	34.3	34.1	34.5	34.6	34.7	34.7	34.8	34.6	34.8	34.8	34.5
2015	33.8	34.3	34.4	34.5	34.8	34.7	34.8	35.2	35.1	34.8	35.1	35.2	34.7
2016	34.2	34.4	34.2	34.7	34.9	35.0	34.9	34.8	34.8	34.8	34.6	35.3	34.7
2017	34.6	34.2	34.5	34.9	34.7	34.7	34.9	34.8	34.9	35.0	34.7	35.1	34.8
Financial Activities													
2013	37.1	36.9	37.2	36.8	36.7	37.9	36.2	35.9	37.4	35.8	36.0	37.4	36.8
2014	36.5	37.7	37.3	36.8	36.9	37.4	36.6	37.0	36.8	36.7	38.1	36.4	37.0
2015	36.7	37.8	38.6	37.3	37.3	36.7	36.6	37.4	36.3	36.6	37.2	36.2	37.1
2016	36.3	35.7	35.3	35.8	36.8	35.8	36.4	35.8	35.8	37.0	36.0	35.9	36.1
2017	37.2	36.1	36.3	37.0	36.2	36.5	36.6	35.8	36.2	36.9	36.2	36.1	36.4
Professional and Business Services													
2013	35.6	35.9	36.1	36.4	36.2	36.6	35.9	36.2	36.5	36.0	36.4	36.5	36.2
2014	35.2	36.3	36.4	36.1	35.7	36.5	35.5	35.5	35.8	35.6	35.9	35.7	35.8
2015	34.8	35.7	35.9	35.4	35.3	35.4	35.2	35.8	35.1	35.8	36.3	35.9	35.6
2016	35.4	35.4	35.6	35.6	36.0	35.2	34.7	35.1	35.4	36.0	35.3	35.3	35.4
2017	35.7	35.5	35.4	35.9	35.8	35.7	36.0	35.8	36.0	36.6	35.8	35.8	35.8
Education and Health Services													
2013	32.2	32.1	32.0	31.9	31.5	31.7	31.5	31.6	31.9	31.4	31.4	31.6	31.7
2014	31.1	31.3	31.3	31.2	31.0	30.4	30.6	30.7	30.9	31.1	31.8	31.7	31.1
2015	31.7	31.6	31.8	31.8	32.0	32.2	32.2	32.5	32.5	32.4	32.8	32.5	32.2
2016	32.7	32.2	32.4	32.4	32.5	32.4	32.4	32.5	32.5	32.7	32.8	32.5	32.5
2017	32.5	32.4	32.4	32.6	32.5	32.3	32.3	32.4	32.6	32.8	33.0	32.9	32.6
Leisure and Hospitality													
2013	23.3	24.0	24.0	24.0	24.2	24.3	24.2	24.4	23.7	23.4	23.3	23.1	23.8
2014	22.1	23.3	23.5	23.5	23.9	24.5	24.3	24.6	24.0	24.0	24.0	24.1	23.8
2015	23.1	23.8	24.0	23.7	24.2	24.5	24.8	24.9	24.1	24.4	24.4	24.6	24.2
2016	23.7	24.2	24.1	23.8	24.1	24.7	24.8	24.6	23.9	24.3	24.1	23.6	24.2
2017	23.5	23.8	24.1	23.7	24.0	24.5	24.5	24.3	23.7	24.0	23.8	23.8	24.0
Other Services													
2013	27.8	28.1	28.1	28.6	28.9	29.2	28.8	29.0	29.6	29.4	29.7	30.1	28.9
2014	29.4	30.6	30.7	29.9	30.1	29.9	29.5	29.6	29.8	30.1	30.4	30.1	30.0
2015	30.1	30.3	31.1	30.6	30.5	31.0	30.8	31.8	30.3	30.2	30.8	31.0	30.7
2016	30.8	30.9	31.9	32.3	32.1	31.7	32.2	32.4	32.7	32.7	32.2	32.6	32.0
2017	32.0	32.4	32.1	33.1	32.3	32.3	32.3	32.2	32.3	33.0	32.4	31.8	32.3

3. Average Hourly Earnings by Selected Industry: Ohio, 2013–2017

(Dollars, not seasonally adjusted)

Industry and year	January	February	March	April	May	June	July	August	September	October	November	December	Annual average
Total Private													
2013	22.40	22.32	22.17	22.18	22.01	22.19	22.11	22.08	22.44	22.25	22.34	22.45	22.24
2014	22.40	22.53	22.46	22.35	21.68	21.83	21.80	21.92	22.20	22.14	22.36	22.29	22.16
2015	22.51	22.63	22.67	22.57	22.48	22.38	22.51	22.80	22.90	22.76	22.98	22.93	22.68
2016	23.12	23.10	23.08	23.39	23.41	23.15	23.33	23.23	23.55	23.86	23.70	23.86	23.40
2017	24.08	23.88	23.91	24.01	23.75	23.70	24.19	23.94	24.17	24.30	24.23	24.35	24.04
Goods-Producing													
2013	24.04	23.89	23.80	23.79	23.87	23.86	24.07	24.16	24.28	24.12	24.20	24.66	24.07
2014	24.59	24.68	24.70	24.68	24.41	24.57	24.69	24.70	24.89	24.82	24.74	24.72	24.68
2015	24.56	24.51	24.65	24.67	24.66	24.61	24.90	24.99	25.00	24.75	24.78	25.10	24.77
2016	24.96	25.04	25.30	25.60	25.71	25.67	25.90	25.78	25.88	26.11	26.19	26.28	25.71
2017	26.11	26.09	26.21	26.41	26.39	26.49	26.74	26.55	26.98	27.00	27.03	27.06	26.60
Construction													
2013	26.13	26.18	26.01	25.67	25.43	25.23	25.49	25.66	25.68	25.60	25.45	25.98	25.69
2014	25.50	26.10	26.23	26.12	25.87	26.03	26.31	26.16	26.85	26.43	25.94	26.03	26.15
2015	25.75	25.55	25.97	26.03	26.56	26.33	26.87	26.91	27.05	26.77	26.68	26.94	26.49
2016	26.82	26.86	26.93	27.42	27.48	27.24	26.93	26.90	26.92	27.19	27.11	26.83	27.06
2017	26.81	26.84	27.32	26.88	27.76	27.75	27.71	27.95	28.35	28.47	27.89	27.40	27.64
Manufacturing													
2013	23.70	23.50	23.40	23.46	23.58	23.60	23.81	23.89	24.02	23.84	23.97	24.32	23.76
2014	24.36	24.36	24.36	24.33	24.06	24.21	24.25	24.33	24.34	24.38	24.46	24.43	24.32
2015	24.34	24.30	24.38	24.37	24.18	24.19	24.34	24.44	24.49	24.17	24.31	24.62	24.34
2016	24.56	24.66	24.98	25.15	25.25	25.26	25.66	25.49	25.70	25.89	26.01	26.26	25.41
2017	26.01	25.95	25.92	26.32	25.87	25.98	26.36	25.91	26.36	26.36	26.67	26.93	26.22
Trade, Transportation, and Utilities													
2013	20.48	20.45	20.43	20.51	20.23	20.56	20.39	20.17	20.60	20.16	20.28	20.08	20.36
2014	20.32	20.74	20.91	20.97	20.53	20.60	20.29	20.53	20.79	20.62	20.75	20.64	20.64
2015	21.00	21.19	21.35	21.34	21.16	21.16	21.32	21.56	21.67	21.69	21.76	21.35	21.38
2016	21.88	21.77	21.95	22.33	22.07	21.95	22.14	22.04	22.34	22.69	22.31	22.14	22.14
2017	22.79	22.51	22.73	23.07	22.73	22.73	22.93	22.59	22.55	22.63	22.43	22.40	22.67
Financial Activities													
2013	27.90	27.10	27.00	27.62	27.52	27.45	27.56	27.53	27.79	27.90	27.88	27.64	27.57
2014	27.90	27.41	27.19	27.08	26.75	26.75	27.08	26.92	27.23	27.31	27.47	27.26	27.19
2015	27.39	27.93	27.47	27.15	26.78	26.46	26.55	27.58	27.39	26.87	26.76	26.87	27.10
2016	26.89	27.21	27.78	27.92	28.23	28.36	28.09	28.52	29.35	30.34	30.20	30.63	28.64
2017	30.80	30.81	30.84	30.78	30.18	29.92	29.90	29.76	30.15	30.06	29.56	29.87	30.22
Professional and Business Services													
2013	25.94	25.72	25.46	25.44	25.13	25.58	25.30	25.42	25.89	25.63	25.61	26.00	25.59
2014	25.57	25.80	25.49	25.03	24.81	24.99	24.78	24.76	24.62	24.38	25.14	25.00	25.03
2015	25.39	25.71	25.71	25.44	25.40	25.21	25.40	25.98	25.93	25.81	26.49	26.23	25.73
2016	27.03	27.07	26.71	26.93	27.06	26.66	26.93	26.87	26.82	27.07	26.86	27.11	26.93
2017	27.34	27.11	27.31	27.22	26.60	26.83	27.48	26.89	27.17	27.69	27.75	27.94	27.28
Education and Health Services													
2013	21.19	21.50	21.29	21.34	21.27	21.47	21.38	21.26	21.58	21.65	21.67	21.72	21.44
2014	21.56	21.61	21.57	21.60	21.59	21.69	21.84	22.13	22.54	22.42	22.61	22.69	21.99
2015	23.02	22.88	22.78	22.61	22.57	22.41	22.30	22.43	22.67	22.36	22.46	22.70	22.60
2016	22.48	22.25	22.20	22.51	22.83	22.26	22.22	21.94	22.41	22.55	22.31	22.61	22.38
2017	22.84	22.61	22.53	22.60	22.50	22.14	22.66	22.49	22.63	22.65	22.65	22.85	22.60
Leisure and Hospitality													
2013	12.10	12.20	12.14	12.17	12.11	12.06	12.12	12.09	12.35	12.46	12.57	12.69	12.25
2014	12.80	12.75	12.65	12.63	12.53	12.29	12.29	12.21	12.36	12.39	12.42	12.56	12.48
2015	12.69	12.64	12.61	12.68	12.46	12.41	12.34	12.40	12.51	12.50	12.58	12.79	12.54
2016	12.73	12.75	12.81	13.01	13.00	12.67	12.78	12.86	13.07	13.30	13.34	13.53	12.98
2017	13.51	13.57	13.53	13.47	13.54	13.20	13.25	13.41	13.51	13.50	13.52	13.69	13.47
Other Services													
2013	19.34	19.38	19.36	19.06	19.02	18.95	19.07	19.08	19.17	19.08	19.44	19.49	19.20
2014	19.22	19.43	19.33	18.92	19.15	19.35	19.46	19.52	19.84	20.30	20.28	20.36	19.60
2015	20.25	20.77	20.79	20.71	21.00	20.81	21.15	21.34	21.76	21.03	21.49	21.29	21.04
2016	21.08	20.81	20.44	20.75	20.82	20.85	21.24	21.04	21.17	21.20	21.41	21.51	21.03
2017	21.85	21.69	21.52	21.56	21.69	21.49	21.82	21.76	21.64	21.61	21.54	21.46	21.64

4. Average Weekly Earnings by Selected Industry: Ohio, 2013–2017

(Dollars, not seasonally adjusted)

Industry and year	January	February	March	April	May	June	July	August	September	October	November	December	Annual average
Total Private													
2013	763.84	763.34	758.21	758.56	750.54	763.34	749.53	755.14	774.18	756.50	761.79	770.04	760.61
2014	745.92	768.27	765.89	759.90	750.13	750.95	743.38	751.86	761.46	759.40	773.66	769.01	757.87
2015	760.84	771.68	777.58	767.38	766.57	767.63	767.59	788.88	780.89	782.94	795.11	788.79	775.66
2016	786.08	785.40	787.03	799.94	805.30	794.05	800.22	796.79	810.12	827.94	815.28	820.78	802.62
2017	825.94	814.31	815.33	823.54	814.63	815.28	832.14	821.14	831.45	843.21	833.51	837.64	826.98
Goods-Producing													
2013	968.81	965.16	963.90	961.12	971.51	975.87	962.80	990.56	997.91	986.51	1001.88	1018.46	979.65
2014	978.68	1006.94	1007.76	1011.88	998.37	1014.74	1002.41	1015.17	1027.96	1025.07	1021.76	1023.41	1011.88
2015	989.77	987.75	1000.79	996.67	1001.20	1004.09	996.00	1017.09	995.00	1014.75	1003.59	1016.55	1003.19
2016	993.41	996.59	1014.53	1031.68	1036.11	1039.64	1046.36	1044.09	1058.49	1070.51	1071.17	1064.34	1038.68
2017	1041.79	1043.60	1043.16	1056.40	1071.43	1086.09	1080.30	1091.21	1100.78	1109.70	1105.53	1104.05	1077.30
Construction													
2013	995.55	994.84	990.98	996.00	1001.94	999.11	999.21	1049.49	1024.63	1041.92	1020.55	1008.02	1012.19
2014	951.15	1002.24	996.74	1018.68	996.00	1033.39	1036.61	1030.70	1076.69	1033.41	993.50	991.74	1014.62
2015	950.18	958.13	979.07	999.55	1041.15	1026.87	1053.30	1076.40	1025.20	1078.83	1013.84	1042.58	1022.51
2016	986.98	999.19	1017.95	1061.15	1041.49	1078.70	1066.43	1054.48	1066.03	1079.44	1068.13	1016.86	1047.22
2017	981.25	1006.50	1005.38	1029.50	1093.74	1126.65	1077.92	1129.18	1134.00	1113.18	1084.92	1035.72	1072.43
Manufacturing													
2013	974.07	968.20	964.08	961.86	973.85	981.76	964.31	986.66	1001.63	982.21	1004.34	1021.44	981.29
2014	986.58	1006.07	1008.50	1007.26	996.08	1004.72	986.98	1007.26	1010.11	1019.08	1027.32	1028.50	1006.85
2015	1000.37	993.87	1004.46	994.30	986.54	994.21	976.03	994.71	991.85	993.39	1001.57	1009.42	995.51
2016	997.14	998.73	1016.69	1023.61	1035.25	1030.61	1044.36	1045.09	1063.98	1077.02	1084.62	1092.42	1041.81
2017	1074.21	1063.95	1062.72	1071.22	1065.84	1072.97	1086.03	1072.67	1083.40	1101.85	1112.14	1128.37	1082.89
Trade, Transportation, and Utilities													
2013	704.51	707.57	706.88	713.75	706.03	715.49	705.49	701.92	723.06	697.54	695.60	700.79	706.49
2014	688.85	713.46	717.21	715.08	708.29	712.76	704.06	712.39	723.49	713.45	722.10	718.27	712.08
2015	709.80	726.82	734.44	736.23	736.37	734.25	741.94	758.91	760.62	754.81	763.78	751.52	741.89
2016	748.30	748.89	750.69	774.85	770.24	768.25	772.69	766.99	777.43	789.61	771.93	781.54	768.26
2017	788.53	769.84	784.19	805.14	788.73	788.73	800.26	786.13	787.00	792.05	778.32	786.24	788.92
Financial Activities													
2013	1035.09	999.99	1004.40	1016.42	1009.98	1040.36	997.67	988.33	1039.35	998.82	1003.68	1033.74	1014.58
2014	1018.35	1033.36	1014.19	996.54	987.08	1000.45	991.13	996.04	1002.06	1002.28	1046.61	992.26	1006.03
2015	1005.21	1055.75	1060.34	1012.70	998.89	971.08	971.73	1031.49	994.26	983.44	995.47	972.69	1005.41
2016	976.11	971.40	980.63	999.54	1038.86	1015.29	1022.48	1021.02	1050.73	1122.58	1087.20	1099.62	1033.90
2017	1145.76	1112.24	1119.49	1138.86	1092.52	1092.08	1094.34	1065.41	1091.43	1109.21	1070.07	1078.31	1100.01
Professional and Business Services													
2013	923.46	923.35	919.11	926.02	909.71	936.23	908.27	920.20	944.99	922.68	932.20	949.00	926.36
2014	900.06	936.54	927.84	903.58	885.72	912.14	879.69	878.98	881.40	867.93	902.53	892.50	896.07
2015	883.57	917.85	922.99	900.58	896.62	892.43	894.08	930.08	910.14	924.00	961.59	941.66	915.99
2016	956.86	958.28	950.88	958.71	974.16	938.43	934.47	943.14	949.43	974.52	948.16	956.98	953.32
2017	976.04	962.41	966.77	977.20	952.28	957.83	989.28	962.66	978.12	1013.45	993.45	1000.25	976.62
Education and Health Services													
2013	682.32	690.15	681.28	680.75	670.01	680.60	673.47	671.82	688.40	679.81	680.44	686.35	679.65
2014	670.52	676.39	675.14	673.92	669.29	659.38	668.30	679.39	696.49	697.26	719.00	719.27	683.89
2015	729.73	723.01	724.40	719.00	722.24	721.60	718.06	728.98	736.78	724.46	736.69	737.75	727.72
2016	735.10	716.45	719.28	729.32	741.98	721.22	719.93	713.05	728.33	737.39	731.77	734.83	727.35
2017	742.30	732.56	729.97	736.76	731.25	715.12	731.92	728.68	737.74	742.92	747.45	751.77	736.76
Leisure and Hospitality													
2013	281.93	292.80	291.36	292.08	293.06	293.06	293.30	295.00	292.70	291.56	292.88	293.14	291.55
2014	282.88	297.08	297.28	296.81	299.47	301.11	298.65	300.37	296.64	297.36	298.08	302.70	297.02
2015	293.14	300.83	302.64	300.52	301.53	304.05	306.03	308.76	301.49	305.00	306.95	314.63	303.47
2016	301.70	308.55	308.72	309.64	313.30	312.95	316.94	316.36	312.37	323.19	321.49	319.31	314.12
2017	317.49	322.97	326.07	319.24	324.96	323.40	324.63	325.86	320.19	324.00	321.78	325.82	323.28
Other Services													
2013	537.65	544.58	544.02	545.12	549.68	553.34	549.22	553.32	567.43	560.95	577.37	586.65	554.88
2014	565.07	594.56	593.43	565.71	576.42	578.57	574.07	577.79	591.23	611.03	616.51	612.84	588.00
2015	609.53	629.33	646.57	633.73	640.50	645.11	651.42	678.61	659.33	635.11	661.89	659.99	645.93
2016	649.26	643.03	652.04	670.23	668.32	660.95	683.93	681.70	692.26	693.24	689.40	701.23	672.96
2017	699.20	702.76	690.79	713.64	700.59	694.13	704.79	700.67	698.97	713.13	697.90	682.43	698.97

OKLAHOMA
At a Glance

Population:
  2010 census: 3,751,351
  2017 estimate: 3,930,864

Percent change in population:
  2010–2017: 4.8%

Percent change in total nonfarm employment:
  2007–2017: 4.2%

Industry with the largest growth in employment, 2007–2017 (thousands):
  Leisure and hospitality, 30.1

Industry with the largest decline or smallest growth in employment, 2007–2017 (thousands):
  Manufacturing, -23.2

Civilian labor force:
  2010: 1,768,284
  2017: 1,834,312

Unemployment rate and rank among states (highest to lowest):
  2010: 6.8%, 44th
  2017: 4.3%, 24th

Over-the-year change in unemployment rates:
  2015–2016: 0.4%
  2016–2017: -0.5%

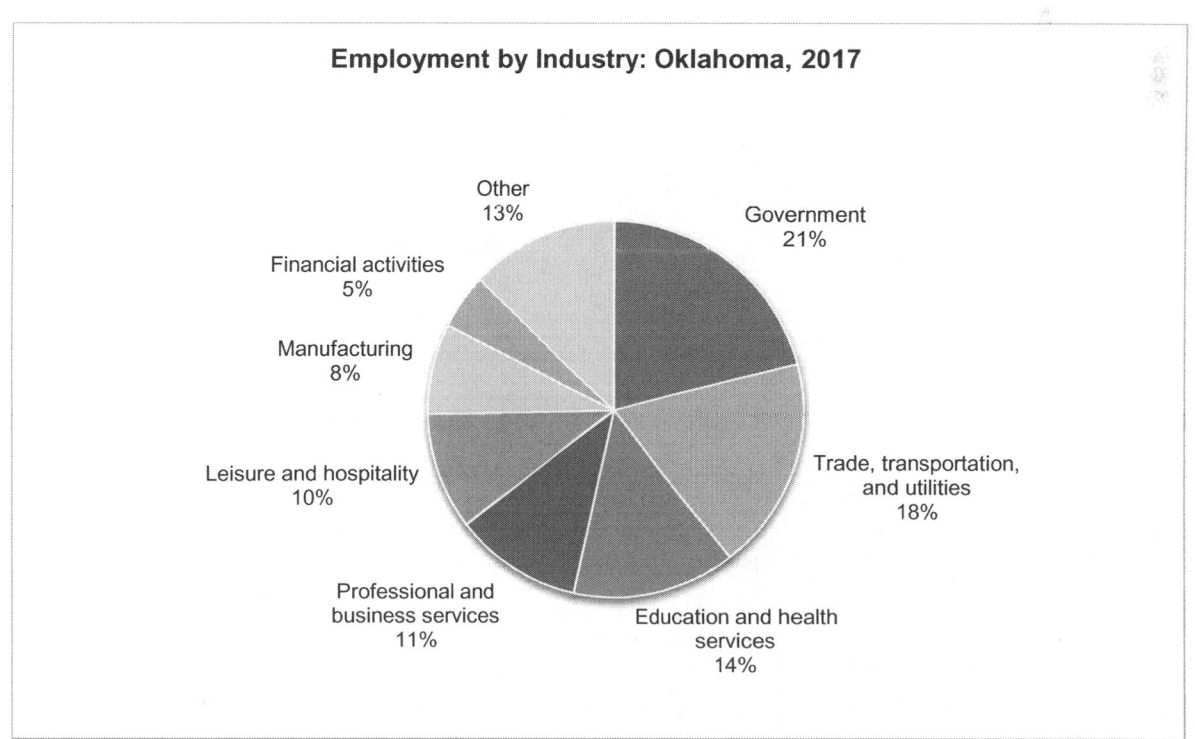

Employment by Industry: Oklahoma, 2017

Other 13%
Government 21%
Financial activities 5%
Manufacturing 8%
Trade, transportation, and utilities 18%
Leisure and hospitality 10%
Professional and business services 11%
Education and health services 14%

1. Employment by Industry: Oklahoma, Selected Years, 2007–2017

(Numbers in thousands, not seasonally adjusted)

Industry and year	January	February	March	April	May	June	July	August	September	October	November	December	Annual average
Total Nonfarm													
2007	1,554.5	1,569.5	1,590.6	1,589.0	1,599.8	1,598.9	1,579.0	1,594.9	1,607.9	1,613.9	1,622.5	1,618.0	1,594.9
2008	1,592.1	1,607.0	1,618.3	1,622.3	1,632.3	1,618.1	1,603.7	1,615.3	1,627.1	1,629.2	1,629.1	1,627.1	1,618.5
2009	1,581.2	1,582.2	1,585.2	1,580.0	1,579.9	1,568.2	1,550.5	1,550.7	1,557.5	1,558.2	1,559.7	1,557.8	1,567.6
2010	1,521.6	1,528.6	1,543.8	1,557.2	1,569.6	1,564.1	1,549.9	1,550.8	1,558.2	1,571.7	1,576.2	1,580.3	1,556.0
2011	1,541.9	1,541.5	1,565.1	1,580.7	1,584.5	1,578.4	1,564.9	1,573.2	1,594.6	1,597.8	1,602.3	1,607.4	1,577.7
2012	1,575.0	1,590.0	1,602.7	1,614.6	1,622.8	1,617.4	1,595.7	1,608.5	1,621.1	1,634.2	1,642.5	1,644.4	1,614.1
2013	1,600.8	1,614.5	1,626.1	1,634.3	1,645.8	1,636.8	1,621.0	1,633.5	1,645.7	1,650.5	1,659.9	1,654.5	1,635.3
2014	1,623.1	1,633.5	1,643.5	1,652.9	1,662.5	1,654.4	1,642.0	1,653.9	1,664.8	1,675.7	1,683.1	1,687.8	1,656.4
2015	1,654.9	1,662.9	1,664.7	1,671.8	1,675.5	1,666.6	1,654.7	1,659.2	1,669.2	1,676.3	1,680.3	1,679.0	1,667.9
2016	1,642.5	1,652.3	1,653.8	1,660.5	1,659.0	1,646.5	1,635.1	1,644.4	1,657.6	1,658.7	1,664.6	1,665.1	1,653.3
2017	1,624.6	1,638.8	1,650.6	1,657.9	1,663.7	1,660.6	1,647.4	1,655.6	1,673.0	1,687.1	1,693.9	1,691.0	1,662.0
Total Private													
2007	1,224.0	1,232.3	1,251.6	1,251.4	1,260.2	1,271.1	1,266.6	1,275.1	1,270.8	1,272.3	1,279.8	1,277.1	1,261.0
2008	1,262.5	1,269.9	1,279.5	1,280.7	1,287.4	1,289.9	1,286.8	1,291.0	1,286.9	1,281.4	1,280.3	1,278.2	1,281.2
2009	1,241.0	1,235.1	1,235.1	1,227.8	1,225.6	1,227.2	1,216.4	1,213.0	1,207.1	1,200.6	1,201.8	1,200.7	1,219.3
2010	1,175.3	1,176.7	1,189.0	1,202.2	1,208.7	1,215.6	1,213.5	1,217.1	1,215.3	1,221.5	1,225.6	1,229.3	1,207.5
2011	1,200.6	1,195.3	1,216.9	1,230.8	1,234.5	1,240.3	1,241.1	1,245.9	1,248.3	1,247.3	1,250.9	1,254.0	1,233.8
2012	1,232.2	1,239.6	1,250.7	1,262.5	1,269.9	1,277.6	1,268.3	1,274.5	1,272.8	1,279.9	1,286.4	1,289.0	1,267.0
2013	1,255.3	1,261.0	1,271.4	1,279.1	1,289.2	1,294.7	1,291.9	1,299.0	1,297.6	1,296.5	1,304.1	1,300.6	1,286.7
2014	1,278.5	1,281.5	1,290.5	1,299.8	1,307.2	1,312.6	1,312.9	1,318.8	1,316.4	1,319.8	1,326.4	1,332.3	1,308.1
2015	1,308.2	1,308.6	1,310.1	1,315.7	1,317.7	1,322.4	1,323.1	1,322.0	1,317.3	1,317.1	1,319.8	1,319.0	1,316.8
2016	1,291.6	1,294.0	1,294.1	1,300.8	1,300.0	1,300.7	1,301.9	1,305.3	1,304.4	1,303.6	1,308.2	1,308.5	1,301.1
2017	1,278.1	1,285.1	1,294.9	1,302.7	1,307.9	1,317.8	1,316.9	1,319.8	1,322.1	1,329.8	1,335.4	1,333.1	1,312.0
Goods Producing													
2007	260.9	261.4	265.2	265.1	267.0	271.6	272.2	274.1	272.0	273.6	275.4	274.9	269.5
2008	272.6	274.0	275.9	277.1	279.3	281.2	281.7	282.0	280.4	278.1	275.4	273.4	277.6
2009	264.1	258.5	253.9	246.6	243.4	242.3	238.4	235.6	232.6	230.1	228.5	227.7	241.8
2010	224.2	224.0	226.8	230.4	232.6	235.7	237.1	238.0	237.9	241.1	241.0	242.9	234.3
2011	238.1	237.4	242.5	246.6	248.0	251.7	253.5	254.4	255.6	256.7	257.1	258.3	250.0
2012	255.3	256.7	259.6	261.3	263.7	267.2	266.4	267.2	266.7	269.9	270.8	271.1	264.7
2013	264.8	266.0	268.0	268.3	270.8	274.2	273.2	274.8	274.1	275.0	274.8	274.2	271.5
2014	269.6	270.5	272.0	272.2	274.4	276.7	278.7	281.3	280.8	282.4	282.7	283.9	277.1
2015	279.4	278.2	274.7	270.4	268.2	269.0	269.6	268.0	266.0	263.6	260.9	259.3	268.9
2016	255.2	254.8	251.6	250.0	249.1	249.4	249.6	249.3	249.7	248.5	247.7	248.6	250.3
2017	244.5	246.6	248.0	248.3	250.8	255.0	255.5	256.2	257.4	258.7	259.8	259.1	253.3
Service-Providing													
2007	1,293.6	1,308.1	1,325.4	1,323.9	1,332.8	1,327.3	1,306.8	1,320.8	1,335.9	1,340.3	1,347.1	1,343.1	1,325.4
2008	1,319.5	1,333.0	1,342.4	1,345.2	1,353.0	1,336.9	1,322.0	1,333.3	1,346.7	1,351.1	1,353.7	1,353.7	1,340.9
2009	1,317.1	1,323.7	1,331.3	1,333.4	1,336.5	1,325.9	1,312.1	1,315.1	1,324.9	1,328.1	1,331.2	1,330.1	1,325.8
2010	1,297.4	1,304.6	1,317.0	1,326.8	1,337.0	1,328.4	1,312.8	1,312.8	1,320.3	1,330.6	1,335.2	1,337.4	1,321.7
2011	1,303.8	1,304.1	1,322.6	1,334.1	1,336.5	1,326.7	1,311.4	1,318.8	1,339.0	1,341.1	1,345.2	1,349.1	1,327.7
2012	1,319.7	1,333.3	1,343.1	1,353.3	1,359.1	1,350.2	1,329.3	1,341.3	1,354.4	1,364.3	1,371.7	1,373.3	1,349.4
2013	1,336.0	1,348.5	1,358.1	1,366.0	1,375.0	1,362.6	1,347.8	1,358.7	1,371.6	1,375.5	1,385.1	1,380.3	1,363.8
2014	1,353.5	1,363.0	1,371.5	1,380.7	1,388.1	1,377.7	1,363.3	1,372.6	1,384.0	1,393.3	1,400.4	1,403.9	1,379.3
2015	1,375.5	1,384.7	1,390.0	1,401.4	1,407.3	1,397.6	1,385.1	1,391.2	1,403.2	1,412.7	1,419.4	1,419.7	1,399.0
2016	1,387.3	1,397.5	1,402.2	1,410.5	1,409.9	1,397.1	1,385.5	1,395.1	1,407.9	1,410.2	1,416.9	1,416.5	1,403.1
2017	1,380.1	1,392.2	1,402.6	1,409.6	1,412.9	1,405.6	1,391.9	1,399.4	1,415.6	1,428.4	1,434.1	1,431.9	1,408.7
Mining, Logging, and Construction													
2007	111.9	112.0	115.1	115.0	116.1	119.5	119.7	121.5	120.1	121.6	122.7	121.7	118.1
2008	121.4	122.4	124.2	125.5	127.8	129.7	131.0	131.7	131.2	130.7	129.1	127.5	127.7
2009	122.0	119.8	118.1	114.2	112.8	113.3	111.8	110.4	108.5	106.9	105.9	105.5	112.4
2010	103.4	103.2	105.6	108.2	109.8	112.1	113.0	113.8	113.8	116.2	115.3	116.4	110.9
2011	112.6	111.7	115.6	118.0	118.9	121.6	122.4	123.0	123.7	124.4	124.3	124.9	120.1
2012	122.4	123.2	125.2	126.4	128.3	130.6	130.4	130.8	130.2	132.6	133.7	133.5	128.9
2013	128.6	129.7	131.4	132.0	134.3	136.9	135.9	137.7	137.5	138.2	137.8	137.0	134.8
2014	133.2	133.2	134.5	134.1	135.4	136.7	138.3	140.9	140.3	141.4	141.2	141.5	137.6
2015	138.5	137.1	134.6	131.6	130.1	131.5	132.5	132.0	130.7	129.5	127.5	125.9	131.8
2016	123.3	122.5	121.0	120.6	120.1	121.0	121.7	121.8	122.4	122.1	120.8	121.1	121.5
2017	119.1	120.0	121.5	121.4	123.0	126.4	126.8	127.4	128.5	129.0	129.3	129.7	125.2

1. Employment by Industry: Oklahoma, Selected Years, 2007–2017—*Continued*

(Numbers in thousands, not seasonally adjusted)

Industry and year	January	February	March	April	May	June	July	August	September	October	November	December	Annual average
Manufacturing													
2007	149.0	149.4	150.1	150.1	150.9	152.1	152.5	152.6	151.9	152.0	152.7	153.2	151.4
2008	151.2	151.6	151.7	151.6	151.5	151.5	150.7	150.3	149.2	147.4	146.3	145.9	149.9
2009	142.1	138.7	135.8	132.4	130.6	129.0	126.6	125.2	124.1	123.2	122.6	122.2	129.4
2010	120.8	120.8	121.2	122.2	122.8	123.6	124.1	124.2	124.1	124.9	125.7	126.5	123.4
2011	125.5	125.7	126.9	128.6	129.1	130.1	131.1	131.4	131.9	132.3	132.8	133.4	129.9
2012	132.9	133.5	134.4	134.9	135.4	136.6	136.0	136.4	136.5	137.3	137.1	137.6	135.7
2013	136.2	136.3	136.6	136.3	136.5	137.3	137.3	137.1	136.6	136.8	137.0	137.2	136.8
2014	136.4	137.3	137.5	138.1	139.0	140.0	140.4	140.4	140.5	141.0	141.5	142.4	139.5
2015	140.9	141.1	140.1	138.8	138.1	137.5	137.1	136.0	135.3	134.1	133.4	133.4	137.2
2016	131.9	132.3	130.6	129.4	129.0	128.4	127.9	127.5	127.3	126.4	126.9	127.5	128.8
2017	125.4	126.6	126.5	126.9	127.8	128.6	128.7	128.8	128.9	129.7	130.5	129.4	128.2
Trade, Transportation, and Utilities													
2007	282.6	282.4	288.1	285.0	287.1	288.0	286.5	287.1	286.2	287.6	292.9	293.9	287.3
2008	285.6	285.0	287.7	287.6	288.7	289.2	289.1	289.8	289.1	289.7	293.2	294.8	289.1
2009	283.9	282.0	282.6	282.2	282.7	282.3	279.7	279.3	278.3	277.7	281.1	282.4	281.2
2010	272.6	271.2	273.8	275.2	277.1	278.3	277.7	277.6	275.5	277.9	282.7	285.0	277.1
2011	275.6	273.9	278.2	280.9	281.6	282.3	282.2	283.7	283.3	284.5	289.4	291.7	282.3
2012	284.1	283.0	285.8	287.5	289.5	290.7	289.2	289.3	289.2	292.2	298.0	300.4	289.9
2013	287.1	287.2	289.2	291.2	293.4	294.8	294.7	296.0	295.8	296.9	303.1	305.6	294.6
2014	296.4	295.5	297.2	297.8	299.5	301.4	300.5	301.4	301.2	303.3	308.8	313.0	301.3
2015	302.1	301.7	303.0	304.6	306.0	307.6	306.6	306.3	305.7	308.5	314.3	317.0	307.0
2016	303.7	302.9	303.9	305.7	305.8	305.4	304.4	305.5	304.3	305.9	313.2	312.7	306.1
2017	300.9	299.0	299.5	300.3	301.1	301.8	301.9	302.4	302.6	305.4	311.0	312.6	303.2
Wholesale Trade													
2007	56.9	57.1	57.9	57.8	58.1	58.9	58.1	57.7	57.5	58.0	58.2	58.2	57.9
2008	57.7	57.6	57.8	57.6	58.0	58.4	58.1	57.8	57.6	57.6	57.6	57.4	57.8
2009	56.5	56.3	56.0	55.6	55.1	54.9	54.4	53.8	53.4	53.5	53.2	53.2	54.7
2010	52.6	52.7	53.0	53.5	53.9	54.4	54.1	54.0	54.0	54.6	54.9	54.9	53.9
2011	54.2	54.4	55.3	55.4	55.5	55.8	56.0	55.9	55.9	56.1	56.0	56.2	55.6
2012	55.9	56.4	57.0	57.4	57.9	58.2	57.7	57.7	57.6	58.2	58.4	58.8	57.6
2013	57.8	58.0	58.3	58.4	58.8	59.2	58.9	58.9	58.9	59.0	59.3	59.4	58.7
2014	59.4	59.4	59.8	59.8	60.2	60.7	60.3	60.5	60.5	61.0	61.1	61.4	60.3
2015	60.5	60.7	60.6	60.3	60.1	60.5	60.1	59.6	59.3	59.3	59.2	59.4	60.0
2016	58.3	58.5	58.4	58.6	58.5	58.4	58.2	58.1	57.9	57.6	57.8	57.8	58.2
2017	57.2	57.3	57.7	57.7	58.1	58.7	58.4	58.4	58.4	58.4	58.1	58.8	58.1
Retail Trade													
2007	167.8	167.1	171.7	169.5	171.0	170.7	169.9	170.9	170.5	171.6	176.7	177.3	171.2
2008	170.7	170.3	172.6	172.1	172.5	172.3	172.3	173.1	172.5	172.9	176.4	177.7	173.0
2009	169.8	168.4	169.4	169.3	170.6	170.4	168.9	169.4	169.2	168.3	171.9	172.8	169.9
2010	166.0	164.5	166.7	167.4	168.7	169.3	168.9	169.0	166.8	168.7	172.9	174.3	168.6
2011	167.2	165.3	168.2	170.1	170.4	170.1	169.6	170.9	170.4	171.1	175.8	177.0	170.5
2012	170.3	168.6	170.6	171.7	172.7	173.1	172.2	172.1	172.1	174.1	179.4	180.9	173.2
2013	170.0	169.3	170.8	172.3	173.9	174.5	174.6	175.8	175.8	176.9	182.3	184.3	175.0
2014	175.6	174.9	175.4	176.5	177.5	178.5	178.2	178.8	178.7	179.8	184.5	187.4	178.8
2015	178.9	179.0	180.1	181.6	182.8	183.7	182.9	183.3	182.9	184.2	188.5	190.2	183.2
2016	181.4	181.3	182.6	183.8	184.1	183.9	183.0	183.7	182.4	183.1	188.3	187.6	183.8
2017	179.4	177.7	177.6	178.5	178.5	178.5	178.2	178.4	177.4	179.2	183.0	183.5	179.2
Transportation and Utilities													
2007	57.9	58.2	58.5	57.7	58.0	58.4	58.5	58.5	58.2	58.0	58.0	58.4	58.2
2008	57.2	57.1	57.3	57.9	58.2	58.5	58.7	58.9	59.0	59.2	59.2	59.7	58.4
2009	57.6	57.3	57.2	57.3	57.0	57.0	56.4	56.1	55.7	55.9	56.0	56.4	56.7
2010	54.0	54.0	54.1	54.3	54.5	54.6	54.7	54.6	54.7	54.6	54.9	55.8	54.6
2011	54.2	54.2	54.7	55.4	55.7	56.4	56.6	56.9	57.0	57.3	57.6	58.5	56.2
2012	57.9	58.0	58.2	58.4	58.9	59.4	59.3	59.5	59.5	59.9	60.2	60.7	59.2
2013	59.3	59.9	60.1	60.5	60.7	61.1	61.2	61.3	61.1	61.0	61.5	61.9	60.8
2014	61.4	61.2	62.0	61.5	61.8	62.2	62.0	62.1	62.0	62.5	63.2	64.2	62.2
2015	62.7	62.0	62.3	62.7	63.1	63.4	63.6	63.4	63.5	65.0	66.6	67.4	63.8
2016	64.0	63.1	62.9	63.3	63.2	63.1	63.2	63.7	64.0	65.2	67.1	67.3	64.2
2017	64.3	64.0	64.2	64.1	64.5	64.6	65.3	65.6	66.8	67.8	69.9	70.3	66.0

1. Employment by Industry: Oklahoma, Selected Years, 2007–2017—*Continued*

(Numbers in thousands, not seasonally adjusted)

Industry and year	January	February	March	April	May	June	July	August	September	October	November	December	Annual average
Information													
2007	29.2	29.0	28.6	28.6	28.8	28.8	28.8	28.8	28.6	28.8	28.9	29.0	28.8
2008	28.7	28.9	28.8	29.0	29.1	29.0	29.1	28.8	28.4	28.2	28.2	28.2	28.7
2009	27.8	27.8	27.7	27.5	27.4	27.2	27.0	26.5	25.9	25.7	25.6	25.5	26.8
2010	25.1	24.8	24.5	24.7	24.6	24.3	24.4	24.0	23.8	23.6	23.7	23.7	24.3
2011	23.3	23.1	22.9	23.0	23.1	23.1	23.2	23.1	22.8	22.9	23.0	23.0	23.0
2012	22.8	22.7	22.7	22.6	22.6	22.5	22.6	22.3	22.1	22.2	22.2	22.3	22.5
2013	21.8	21.7	21.6	21.9	22.0	22.1	22.0	21.8	21.5	21.7	21.8	21.7	21.8
2014	21.4	21.3	21.3	21.3	21.3	21.3	21.5	21.2	21.1	20.8	20.9	21.2	21.2
2015	20.8	20.9	21.0	20.9	21.3	21.3	21.2	21.1	21.1	21.4	21.7	21.8	21.2
2016	21.2	21.4	21.3	21.2	21.3	21.4	21.3	21.1	20.9	20.9	21.0	21.3	21.2
2017	20.9	20.9	20.9	20.8	20.8	20.6	20.4	20.2	19.9	20.0	20.1	20.1	20.5
Financial Activities													
2007	79.8	80.3	80.6	79.5	79.7	80.2	80.2	80.3	80.0	80.2	80.2	80.4	80.1
2008	80.4	80.4	80.6	80.6	81.1	81.2	81.5	81.1	80.9	80.6	80.6	81.0	80.8
2009	79.6	79.3	79.4	79.9	80.0	80.2	80.1	79.8	79.1	78.9	78.9	79.1	79.5
2010	78.1	78.1	78.1	78.1	78.4	78.6	78.2	78.2	77.7	77.8	77.9	78.3	78.1
2011	77.0	76.8	77.3	77.6	77.5	77.8	77.8	78.1	77.7	77.8	77.8	78.1	77.6
2012	77.2	77.6	77.6	77.8	78.2	78.6	78.5	78.5	78.0	78.3	78.4	79.0	78.1
2013	78.1	78.4	78.4	78.3	78.9	79.1	79.3	79.2	78.9	79.0	79.5	79.6	78.9
2014	78.6	78.8	78.9	79.1	79.4	79.8	80.0	80.0	79.4	79.5	80.0	80.4	79.5
2015	79.5	79.4	79.3	79.4	79.8	79.7	80.0	79.6	79.2	79.3	79.2	79.5	79.5
2016	78.6	78.6	78.3	78.4	78.6	78.7	79.0	78.9	78.6	78.8	78.8	79.4	78.7
2017	77.8	78.0	78.3	78.5	78.7	79.1	79.5	79.5	79.6	79.9	79.9	80.0	79.1
Professional and Business Services													
2007	176.6	179.4	182.6	183.2	184.2	185.8	184.8	187.7	187.3	186.9	187.3	186.8	184.4
2008	184.2	186.5	187.3	187.5	187.1	187.2	185.5	187.0	186.3	184.8	183.6	181.4	185.7
2009	173.0	173.2	172.1	169.9	168.6	169.6	168.0	168.1	168.2	168.7	168.7	169.1	169.8
2010	165.0	166.2	168.1	170.7	171.1	173.2	174.5	175.3	175.2	176.7	176.3	175.8	172.3
2011	171.3	170.5	173.7	176.5	176.0	176.3	177.3	178.0	178.4	178.5	177.1	177.1	175.9
2012	172.9	176.3	177.0	178.6	179.0	181.3	180.0	182.2	181.1	182.8	182.6	180.6	179.5
2013	176.2	177.5	180.0	180.1	181.2	182.1	182.2	183.5	182.9	183.4	184.1	181.8	181.3
2014	179.2	180.2	182.1	184.3	185.0	185.6	185.8	186.3	184.9	186.6	187.2	186.3	184.5
2015	184.4	183.3	183.8	184.9	184.5	184.6	185.6	185.3	183.2	184.4	183.6	183.2	184.2
2016	179.5	179.7	179.2	181.5	180.9	181.8	182.0	182.7	182.9	183.5	182.3	182.1	181.5
2017	178.3	180.5	182.6	184.2	184.6	187.2	187.4	188.3	188.4	188.0	187.7	187.0	185.4
Education and Health Services													
2007	204.0	205.8	207.2	209.7	210.2	210.9	209.5	211.2	212.4	213.5	213.6	213.1	210.1
2008	211.6	213.8	214.4	214.9	215.5	213.7	213.0	214.7	215.6	216.1	216.9	216.9	214.8
2009	215.4	215.7	216.7	217.3	217.8	218.5	218.5	219.5	220.4	220.7	221.3	221.1	218.6
2010	219.0	219.7	220.5	221.8	221.7	221.1	219.9	221.1	222.5	224.1	224.4	224.7	221.7
2011	220.5	219.6	221.6	222.5	222.9	222.7	222.0	223.3	225.2	225.3	225.7	226.1	223.1
2012	223.3	224.4	225.1	226.4	226.6	225.8	223.4	225.8	227.4	228.2	228.8	229.6	226.2
2013	226.3	227.2	227.8	227.9	228.1	226.9	225.5	227.1	228.6	229.0	229.5	228.4	227.7
2014	226.2	226.8	227.3	228.5	228.3	227.5	226.4	227.6	228.7	229.4	229.9	230.4	228.1
2015	228.5	229.1	229.4	230.9	231.0	230.6	230.8	231.8	233.9	234.2	234.6	234.1	231.6
2016	232.7	233.5	233.6	233.9	233.3	231.8	232.4	233.4	235.0	235.2	235.2	235.3	233.8
2017	231.3	232.7	233.2	234.5	234.7	234.2	233.5	234.4	236.1	237.3	236.9	237.1	234.7
Leisure and Hospitality													
2007	129.4	131.9	136.6	137.2	139.8	141.3	140.8	142.1	140.6	138.7	138.5	136.3	137.8
2008	136.8	138.2	141.3	140.2	142.7	144.2	142.9	143.6	142.7	140.3	139.4	139.7	141.0
2009	135.3	136.7	140.5	142.5	143.6	144.7	142.7	142.7	141.3	138.0	136.9	135.4	140.0
2010	131.5	132.8	136.8	140.6	142.2	142.9	141.1	142.1	142.0	139.7	139.1	138.5	139.1
2011	135.3	134.6	140.6	144.6	146.3	147.0	146.2	147.0	147.0	143.7	142.9	142.0	143.1
2012	139.4	141.4	145.3	148.8	150.6	151.5	148.8	150.1	149.7	147.9	147.5	148.0	147.4
2013	143.7	145.5	148.7	151.9	155.0	155.1	154.7	156.5	156.1	152.4	152.2	150.4	151.9
2014	148.7	149.9	152.9	157.2	159.0	159.4	158.8	160.3	159.6	156.9	156.1	156.1	156.2
2015	152.8	154.9	157.0	162.3	164.4	166.5	165.5	166.9	165.4	163.2	163.0	161.7	162.0
2016	158.3	160.4	163.5	166.9	167.3	167.7	168.2	169.4	167.8	165.6	164.5	163.3	165.2
2017	158.8	160.9	165.1	168.7	169.3	171.3	170.2	170.8	170.0	171.3	170.6	168.2	167.9

1. Employment by Industry: Oklahoma, Selected Years, 2007–2017—*Continued*

(Numbers in thousands, not seasonally adjusted)

Industry and year	January	February	March	April	May	June	July	August	September	October	November	December	Annual average
Other Services													
2007	61.5	62.1	62.7	63.1	63.4	64.5	63.8	63.8	63.7	63.0	63.0	62.7	63.1
2008	62.6	63.1	63.5	63.8	63.9	64.2	64.0	64.0	63.5	63.6	63.0	62.8	63.5
2009	61.9	61.9	62.2	61.9	62.1	62.4	62.0	61.5	61.3	60.8	60.8	60.4	61.6
2010	59.8	59.9	60.4	60.7	61.0	61.5	60.6	60.8	60.7	60.6	60.5	60.4	60.6
2011	59.5	59.4	60.1	59.1	59.1	59.4	58.9	58.3	58.3	57.9	57.9	57.7	58.8
2012	57.2	57.5	57.6	59.5	59.7	60.0	59.4	59.1	58.6	58.4	58.1	58.0	58.6
2013	57.3	57.5	57.7	59.5	59.8	60.4	60.3	60.1	59.7	59.1	59.1	58.9	59.1
2014	58.4	58.5	58.8	59.4	60.3	60.9	61.2	60.7	60.7	60.9	60.8	61.0	60.1
2015	60.7	61.1	61.9	62.3	62.5	63.1	63.8	63.0	62.8	62.5	62.5	62.4	62.4
2016	62.4	62.7	62.7	63.2	63.7	64.5	65.0	65.0	65.2	65.2	65.5	65.8	64.2
2017	65.6	66.5	67.3	67.4	67.9	68.6	68.5	68.0	68.1	69.2	69.4	69.0	68.0
Government													
2007	330.5	337.7	339.0	337.6	339.6	327.8	312.4	319.8	337.1	341.6	342.7	340.9	333.9
2008	329.6	337.1	338.8	341.6	344.9	328.2	316.9	324.3	340.2	347.8	348.8	348.9	337.3
2009	340.2	347.1	350.1	352.2	354.3	341.0	334.1	337.7	350.4	357.6	357.9	357.1	348.3
2010	346.3	351.9	354.8	355.0	360.9	348.5	336.4	333.7	342.9	350.2	350.6	351.0	348.5
2011	341.3	346.2	348.2	349.9	350.0	338.1	323.8	327.3	346.3	350.5	351.4	353.4	343.9
2012	342.8	350.4	352.0	352.1	352.9	339.8	327.4	334.0	348.3	354.3	356.1	355.4	347.1
2013	345.5	353.5	354.7	355.2	356.6	342.1	329.1	334.5	348.1	354.0	355.8	353.9	348.6
2014	344.6	352.0	353.0	353.1	355.3	341.8	329.1	335.1	348.4	355.9	356.7	355.5	348.4
2015	346.7	354.3	354.6	356.1	357.8	344.2	331.6	337.2	351.9	359.2	360.5	360.0	351.2
2016	350.9	358.3	359.7	359.7	359.0	345.8	333.2	339.1	353.2	355.1	356.4	356.6	352.3
2017	346.5	353.7	355.7	355.2	355.8	342.8	330.5	335.8	350.9	357.3	358.5	357.9	350.1

2. Average Weekly Hours by Selected Industry: Oklahoma, 2013–2017

(Not seasonally adjusted)

Industry and year	January	February	March	April	May	June	July	August	September	October	November	December	Annual average
Total Private													
2013	34.6	34.8	35.1	34.8	34.9	35.9	34.8	35.2	35.6	34.9	35.0	35.3	35.1
2014	35.0	35.4	35.5	35.2	35.0	35.6	35.0	35.3	35.1	34.8	35.4	35.1	35.2
2015	34.6	35.0	35.1	34.4	34.2	34.8	34.4	35.2	34.3	34.7	35.1	35.0	34.7
2016	34.9	34.8	34.5	34.6	35.1	35.0	35.2	35.0	35.1	35.7	35.0	35.1	35.0
2017	35.3	35.3	35.3	35.8	35.2	35.5	36.1	35.5	35.4	35.9	35.3	35.4	35.5
Goods-Producing													
2013	40.8	40.7	40.9	39.8	40.0	41.0	39.5	40.2	41.0	40.5	40.8	40.9	40.5
2014	40.5	40.3	41.3	41.0	41.1	41.0	40.7	41.9	41.2	40.5	41.1	41.6	41.0
2015	40.7	40.4	40.2	39.9	39.3	40.7	40.0	40.9	39.5	40.9	41.3	41.2	40.4
2016	40.7	40.3	39.9	40.6	41.1	41.2	41.3	41.2	41.3	41.9	40.8	40.8	40.9
2017	40.3	40.9	41.1	41.5	41.4	41.1	41.6	41.1	41.0	41.9	41.3	41.8	41.3
Construction													
2013	40.2	40.7	41.4	39.9	40.8	41.9	39.5	39.7	41.6	41.4	41.3	40.3	40.7
2014	40.4	40.6	42.8	43.0	42.7	42.1	41.8	44.3	42.3	40.1	40.4	40.2	41.7
2015	40.3	40.7	40.6	41.0	39.5	41.3	41.1	41.7	39.8	41.9	42.7	42.2	41.1
2016	42.3	42.3	41.2	42.8	43.1	43.3	43.5	42.4	42.5	43.1	41.1	42.0	42.5
2017	41.2	42.4	42.0	42.3	42.3	42.8	43.7	42.7	41.0	43.3	42.0	42.4	42.3
Manufacturing													
2013	40.6	40.3	40.5	39.1	40.0	40.6	39.8	40.7	40.8	40.5	41.0	41.3	40.4
2014	40.5	40.1	40.8	40.5	40.8	40.8	40.5	40.8	40.4	40.8	41.7	41.9	40.8
2015	40.6	39.8	39.5	38.8	38.8	39.9	38.7	40.0	38.9	40.3	40.4	40.6	39.7
2016	39.8	39.0	39.3	39.3	39.8	39.9	40.1	40.9	40.5	40.8	40.1	39.4	39.9
2017	39.0	39.1	39.8	39.6	39.9	39.2	39.2	39.3	40.4	40.2	40.5	41.0	39.8
Trade, Transportation, and Utilities													
2013	33.7	34.2	34.6	34.3	34.3	35.3	34.8	34.8	35.2	34.7	34.7	34.5	34.6
2014	34.6	35.2	35.1	35.2	35.2	35.6	34.9	35.1	35.3	34.6	35.2	35.2	35.1
2015	34.7	35.3	35.5	34.9	35.1	35.2	35.3	36.1	35.1	34.7	34.8	35.2	35.2
2016	34.7	35.0	34.8	34.9	35.1	35.3	35.0	34.8	35.1	35.4	34.4	34.9	34.9
2017	35.3	35.3	35.7	36.5	35.8	36.4	36.5	35.9	35.6	35.8	35.0	34.9	35.7
Financial Activities													
2013	35.9	36.5	36.5	36.5	36.1	37.1	36.1	36.1	37.3	35.9	36.1	37.2	36.4
2014	36.6	37.4	37.4	36.0	36.0	37.4	36.1	35.7	35.7	35.2	36.6	35.8	36.3
2015	35.7	36.6	37.0	36.1	35.7	36.0	35.5	37.2	36.4	35.9	37.1	36.2	36.3
2016	35.6	35.5	35.8	36.0	37.1	35.4	35.8	35.5	36.6	36.9	35.6	35.6	36.0
2017	37.3	37.9	37.0	38.1	36.1	37.1	37.9	36.2	35.9	38.0	36.0	35.9	36.9
Professional and Business Services													
2013	35.0	35.3	36.2	36.2	36.2	37.6	36.4	36.8	37.7	36.7	36.5	36.8	36.5
2014	36.2	37.0	36.8	36.4	35.8	37.1	35.8	35.7	35.7	35.2	36.2	35.4	36.1
2015	35.0	35.8	35.7	35.3	34.6	35.2	34.4	35.0	33.5	34.8	35.4	35.1	35.0
2016	35.7	35.2	35.4	35.6	36.1	35.7	36.4	35.6	36.0	36.7	36.3	36.3	35.9
2017	37.0	36.4	36.5	36.8	36.3	36.5	37.1	36.6	37.0	37.4	36.6	36.4	36.7
Education and Health Services													
2013	33.8	33.8	33.7	33.6	33.7	34.6	33.7	33.8	34.3	33.5	33.7	33.8	33.8
2014	34.0	34.0	33.6	33.5	33.5	33.9	33.7	33.6	33.3	33.5	33.8	33.3	33.6
2015	33.2	33.4	33.3	32.7	33.2	33.4	33.9	34.4	33.6	33.8	34.4	33.7	33.6
2016	34.0	33.3	32.9	33.1	33.6	33.7	34.3	34.2	34.3	34.8	34.4	34.4	33.9
2017	35.1	34.5	34.3	35.1	34.2	34.3	35.5	34.5	34.7	35.0	34.8	34.7	34.7
Leisure and Hospitality													
2013	25.6	26.3	26.6	26.8	26.4	27.3	26.3	26.5	26.3	26.1	25.9	25.7	26.3
2014	25.7	26.0	26.4	26.0	25.3	26.5	25.6	26.0	25.6	25.9	26.2	26.0	25.9
2015	25.2	26.0	26.3	25.8	25.6	26.5	25.9	26.5	26.4	26.0	26.2	26.3	26.1
2016	25.3	26.5	26.2	26.0	26.8	26.5	26.7	26.8	26.0	26.7	26.5	26.2	26.4
2017	25.0	26.0	26.3	26.7	26.4	26.6	26.7	26.2	26.2	26.3	26.1	26.1	26.2

3. Average Hourly Earnings by Selected Industry: Oklahoma, 2013–2017

(Dollars, not seasonally adjusted)

Industry and year	January	February	March	April	May	June	July	August	September	October	November	December	Annual average
Total Private													
2013	21.19	21.12	21.02	21.10	21.12	21.21	21.10	21.22	21.34	21.40	21.32	21.52	21.22
2014	21.14	21.51	21.37	21.45	21.43	21.51	21.38	21.52	21.62	21.72	22.05	21.65	21.53
2015	21.84	21.94	21.90	21.78	21.79	21.62	21.66	21.81	21.83	21.81	21.98	21.66	21.80
2016	21.67	21.83	21.87	21.89	21.97	21.79	22.08	21.93	22.21	22.36	22.29	22.33	22.02
2017	22.60	22.60	22.63	22.91	22.74	22.64	23.04	22.92	23.06	23.13	22.95	23.02	22.86
Goods-Producing													
2013	22.38	22.63	22.47	22.62	23.01	23.03	22.88	23.18	23.25	23.08	22.86	23.14	22.88
2014	21.96	22.57	22.71	23.14	23.25	23.54	23.23	23.26	23.67	23.57	23.99	23.44	23.20
2015	23.78	23.94	24.16	23.82	24.01	23.80	23.88	24.01	24.24	24.10	24.32	24.16	24.02
2016	23.63	24.04	24.02	23.76	24.26	24.14	24.20	24.33	24.36	24.58	24.59	24.66	24.21
2017	24.50	24.51	24.77	25.12	25.20	25.09	25.42	25.52	25.62	25.92	25.33	25.60	25.23
Construction													
2013	20.51	20.68	20.87	20.79	21.45	20.99	21.09	20.70	21.10	21.01	20.83	21.12	20.94
2014	20.91	21.40	20.99	21.15	21.47	21.35	21.36	20.93	21.32	21.37	21.61	21.30	21.26
2015	21.56	21.61	21.51	21.35	21.77	21.35	21.23	21.36	21.81	21.81	21.79	22.08	21.60
2016	21.15	21.26	21.81	21.33	21.86	21.68	22.18	21.98	22.26	22.06	22.27	22.10	21.83
2017	21.82	22.05	22.02	22.12	22.79	22.64	22.55	22.92	23.08	23.38	22.79	23.00	22.61
Manufacturing													
2013	20.02	20.30	20.19	20.72	20.78	21.04	20.94	21.18	21.25	20.95	21.00	21.42	20.82
2014	21.11	21.39	21.45	21.63	21.53	21.76	21.48	21.85	22.19	22.15	22.49	22.22	21.78
2015	22.51	22.69	23.00	22.89	23.08	23.16	23.53	23.74	23.95	23.76	24.15	23.82	23.35
2016	23.56	24.00	23.61	23.71	24.07	24.11	23.67	23.82	23.70	24.12	23.55	23.74	23.81
2017	23.35	23.58	23.53	23.99	23.88	23.64	24.24	24.29	24.33	24.59	24.13	24.24	23.99
Trade, Transportation, and Utilities													
2013	21.07	20.52	20.37	20.31	20.67	20.55	20.07	20.05	20.10	19.94	19.76	19.41	20.23
2014	19.84	19.68	19.70	19.54	19.25	19.27	19.43	19.72	19.81	19.90	20.17	19.68	19.67
2015	19.90	19.77	19.58	19.60	20.01	19.61	19.82	19.91	19.76	19.96	20.17	19.53	19.80
2016	19.70	19.85	20.25	20.30	20.50	20.61	21.18	20.72	20.82	20.84	21.08	20.90	20.57
2017	21.23	20.78	20.98	21.36	21.40	21.19	21.90	21.65	21.96	22.05	21.72	21.83	21.51
Financial Activities													
2013	23.15	23.59	23.71	23.54	23.71	24.08	23.36	23.56	24.19	23.89	24.00	24.15	23.75
2014	24.13	24.41	24.18	24.20	24.04	24.17	23.82	24.00	23.81	23.92	24.02	23.87	24.05
2015	24.18	24.62	24.34	24.74	24.73	25.02	24.91	25.62	25.14	25.70	25.84	25.86	25.06
2016	25.34	25.80	25.37	25.67	25.98	25.70	25.78	26.06	27.04	27.05	26.97	26.63	26.12
2017	27.10	27.28	26.99	27.07	26.94	26.27	27.14	26.25	25.72	25.52	25.71	25.34	26.45
Professional and Business Services													
2013	21.60	22.10	21.69	21.54	21.27	21.78	21.52	21.88	22.21	22.39	22.71	23.30	22.01
2014	22.89	23.44	23.23	23.09	23.18	23.60	23.37	23.82	23.99	24.32	24.61	24.23	23.65
2015	24.56	24.76	24.66	24.11	23.99	23.89	23.89	24.03	24.15	23.80	24.10	23.80	24.15
2016	23.89	23.69	23.36	23.27	23.14	22.75	22.63	22.58	22.69	23.02	22.90	23.18	23.09
2017	23.40	23.22	23.14	23.01	22.36	22.26	22.43	22.40	22.61	22.99	23.15	23.44	22.86
Education and Health Services													
2013	21.81	21.54	21.63	22.07	21.73	21.75	22.41	22.50	22.34	22.27	22.19	22.55	22.07
2014	22.50	23.10	22.57	22.96	22.86	22.86	23.01	22.85	22.95	23.26	23.67	23.23	22.99
2015	23.05	23.37	23.30	23.67	23.26	23.10	23.14	23.12	23.11	22.85	22.85	22.46	23.10
2016	22.59	23.13	23.44	23.72	23.23	22.99	23.61	23.11	23.73	23.69	23.33	23.33	23.33
2017	23.33	23.37	23.61	24.26	24.09	24.31	24.45	24.45	24.54	24.33	24.28	24.13	24.10
Leisure and Hospitality													
2013	10.73	10.72	10.79	10.85	10.84	10.67	10.69	10.77	10.89	10.81	10.91	11.13	10.82
2014	10.70	11.11	10.99	11.02	11.24	10.94	10.97	11.12	11.18	11.21	11.53	11.54	11.13
2015	11.57	11.65	11.68	11.64	11.69	11.64	11.67	11.78	12.02	12.06	12.18	12.23	11.82
2016	12.46	12.46	12.50	12.53	12.61	12.30	12.52	12.48	12.51	12.74	12.67	12.75	12.54
2017	13.07	12.91	12.83	12.82	12.84	12.72	12.58	12.63	12.74	12.64	12.66	12.72	12.76

4. Average Weekly Earnings by Selected Industry: Oklahoma, 2013–2017

(Dollars, not seasonally adjusted)

Industry and year	January	February	March	April	May	June	July	August	September	October	November	December	Annual average
Total Private													
2013	733.17	734.98	737.80	734.28	737.09	761.44	734.28	746.94	759.70	746.86	746.20	759.66	744.82
2014	739.90	761.45	758.64	755.04	750.05	765.76	748.30	759.66	758.86	755.86	780.57	759.92	757.86
2015	755.66	767.90	768.69	749.23	745.22	752.38	745.10	767.71	748.77	756.81	771.50	758.10	756.46
2016	756.28	759.68	754.52	757.39	771.15	762.65	777.22	767.55	779.57	798.25	780.15	783.78	770.70
2017	797.78	797.78	798.84	820.18	800.45	803.72	831.74	813.66	816.32	830.37	810.14	814.91	811.53
Goods-Producing													
2013	913.10	921.04	919.02	900.28	920.40	944.23	903.76	931.84	953.25	934.74	932.69	946.43	926.64
2014	889.38	909.57	937.92	948.74	955.58	965.14	945.46	974.59	975.20	954.59	985.99	975.10	951.20
2015	967.85	967.18	971.23	950.42	943.59	968.66	955.20	982.01	957.48	985.69	1,004.42	995.39	970.41
2016	961.74	968.81	958.40	964.66	997.09	994.57	999.46	1,002.40	1,006.07	1,029.90	1,003.27	1,006.13	990.19
2017	987.35	1,002.46	1,018.05	1,042.48	1,043.28	1,031.20	1,057.47	1,048.87	1,050.42	1,086.05	1,046.13	1,070.08	1,042.00
Construction													
2013	825.71	841.68	864.02	829.52	875.16	879.48	833.06	821.79	877.76	869.81	860.28	851.14	852.26
2014	844.76	868.84	898.37	909.45	916.77	898.84	892.85	927.20	901.84	856.94	873.04	856.26	886.54
2015	868.87	879.53	873.31	875.35	859.92	881.76	872.55	890.71	868.04	913.84	930.43	931.78	887.76
2016	894.65	899.30	898.57	912.92	942.17	938.74	964.83	931.95	946.05	950.79	915.30	928.20	927.78
2017	898.98	934.92	924.84	935.68	964.02	968.99	985.44	978.68	946.28	1,012.35	957.18	975.20	956.40
Manufacturing													
2013	812.81	818.09	817.70	810.15	831.20	854.22	833.41	862.03	867.00	848.48	861.00	884.65	841.13
2014	854.96	857.74	875.16	876.02	878.42	887.81	869.94	891.48	896.48	903.72	937.83	931.02	888.62
2015	913.91	903.06	908.50	888.13	895.50	924.08	910.61	949.60	931.66	957.53	975.66	967.09	927.00
2016	937.69	936.00	927.87	931.80	957.99	961.99	949.17	974.24	959.85	984.10	944.36	935.36	950.02
2017	910.65	921.98	936.49	950.00	952.81	926.69	950.21	954.60	982.93	988.52	977.27	993.84	954.80
Trade, Transportation, and Utilities													
2013	710.06	701.78	704.80	696.63	708.98	725.42	698.44	697.74	707.52	691.92	685.67	669.65	699.96
2014	686.46	692.74	691.47	687.81	677.60	686.01	678.11	692.17	699.29	688.54	709.98	692.74	690.42
2015	690.53	697.88	695.09	684.04	702.35	690.27	699.65	718.75	693.58	692.61	701.92	687.46	696.96
2016	683.59	694.75	704.70	708.47	719.55	727.53	741.30	721.06	730.78	737.74	725.15	729.41	717.89
2017	749.42	733.53	748.99	779.64	766.12	771.32	799.35	777.24	781.78	789.39	760.20	761.87	767.91
Financial Activities													
2013	831.09	861.04	865.42	859.21	855.93	893.37	843.30	850.52	902.29	857.65	866.40	898.38	864.50
2014	883.16	912.93	904.33	871.20	865.44	903.96	859.90	856.80	850.02	841.98	879.13	854.55	873.02
2015	863.23	901.09	900.58	893.11	882.86	900.72	884.31	953.06	915.10	922.63	958.66	936.13	909.68
2016	902.10	915.90	908.25	924.12	963.86	909.78	922.92	925.13	989.66	998.15	960.13	948.03	940.32
2017	1,010.83	1,033.91	998.63	1,031.37	972.53	974.62	1,028.61	950.25	923.35	969.76	925.56	909.71	976.01
Professional and Business Services													
2013	756.00	780.13	785.18	779.75	769.97	818.93	783.33	805.18	837.32	821.71	828.92	857.44	803.37
2014	828.62	867.28	854.86	840.48	829.84	875.56	836.65	850.37	856.44	856.06	890.88	857.74	853.77
2015	859.60	886.41	880.36	851.08	830.05	840.93	821.82	841.05	809.03	828.24	853.14	835.38	845.25
2016	852.87	833.89	826.94	828.41	835.35	812.18	823.73	803.85	816.84	844.83	831.27	841.43	828.93
2017	865.80	845.21	844.61	846.77	811.67	812.49	832.15	819.84	836.57	859.83	847.29	853.22	838.96
Education and Health Services													
2013	737.18	728.05	728.93	741.55	732.30	752.55	755.22	760.50	766.26	746.05	747.80	762.19	745.97
2014	765.00	785.40	758.35	769.16	765.81	774.95	775.44	767.76	764.24	779.21	800.05	773.56	772.46
2015	765.26	780.56	775.89	774.01	772.23	771.54	784.45	795.33	776.50	772.33	786.04	756.90	776.16
2016	768.06	770.23	771.18	785.13	780.53	774.76	809.82	790.36	813.94	824.41	802.55	802.55	790.89
2017	818.88	806.27	809.82	851.53	823.88	833.83	867.98	843.53	851.54	851.55	844.94	837.31	836.27
Leisure and Hospitality													
2013	274.69	281.94	287.01	290.78	286.18	291.29	281.15	285.41	286.41	282.14	282.57	286.04	284.57
2014	274.99	288.86	290.14	286.52	284.37	289.91	280.83	289.12	286.21	290.34	302.09	300.04	288.27
2015	291.56	302.90	307.18	300.31	299.26	308.46	302.25	312.17	317.33	313.56	319.12	321.65	308.50
2016	315.24	330.19	327.50	325.78	337.95	325.95	334.28	334.46	325.26	340.16	335.76	334.05	331.06
2017	326.75	335.66	337.43	342.29	338.98	338.35	335.89	330.91	333.79	332.43	330.43	331.99	334.31

OREGON
At a Glance

Population:
  2010 census: 3,831,074
  2017 estimate: 4,142,776

Percent change in population:
  2010–2017: 8.1%

Percent change in total nonfarm employment:
  2007–2017: 8.2%

Industry with the largest growth in employment, 2007–2017 (thousands):
  Education and health services, 61.9

Industry with the largest decline or smallest growth in employment, 2007–2017 (thousands):
  Manufacturing, -14.7

Civilian labor force:
  2010: 1,984,039
  2017: 2,104,078

Unemployment rate and rank among states (highest to lowest):
  2010: 10.6%, 8th
  2017: 4.1%, 29th

Over-the-year change in unemployment rates:
  2015–2016: -0.8%
  2016–2017: -0.7%

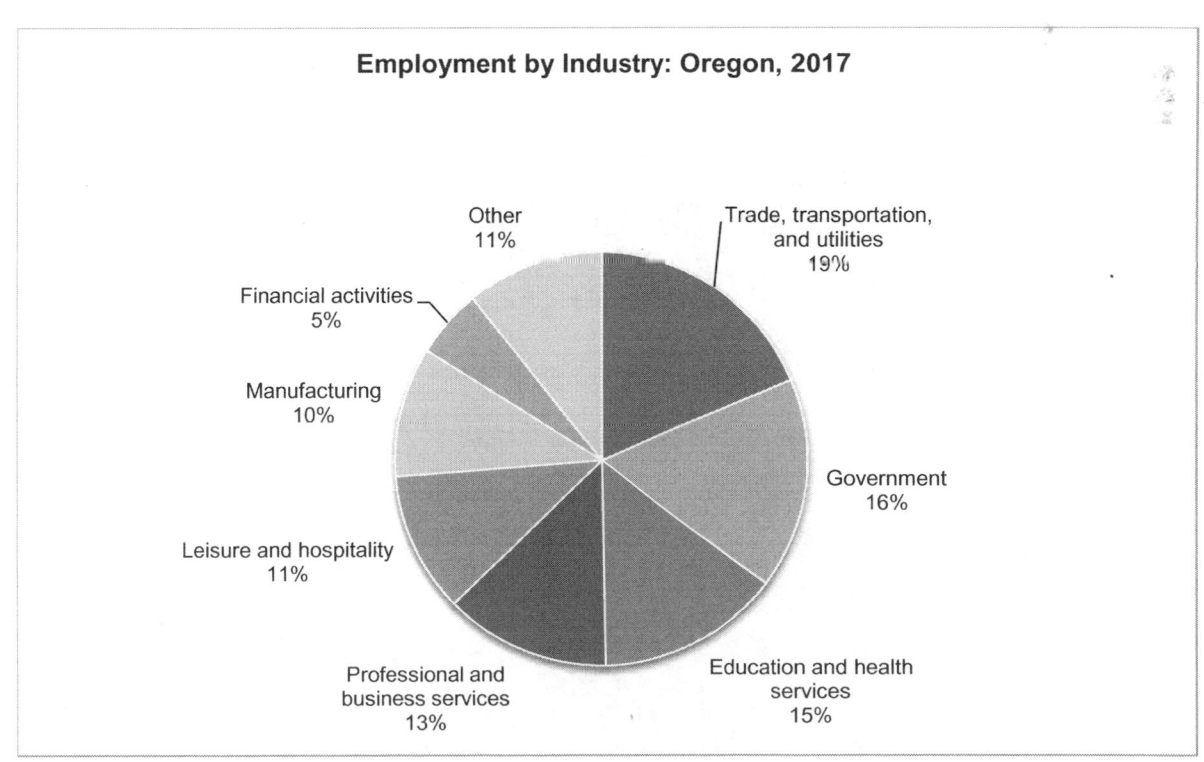

Employment by Industry: Oregon, 2017

- Other 11%
- Trade, transportation, and utilities 19%
- Financial activities 5%
- Manufacturing 10%
- Government 16%
- Leisure and hospitality 11%
- Professional and business services 13%
- Education and health services 15%

1. Employment by Industry: Oregon, Selected Years, 2007–2017

(Numbers in thousands, not seasonally adjusted)

Industry and year	January	February	March	April	May	June	July	August	September	October	November	December	Annual average
Total Nonfarm													
2007	1,687.9	1,704.2	1,717.4	1,720.7	1,736.0	1,748.6	1,722.9	1,732.1	1,740.5	1,754.7	1,755.6	1,751.4	1,731.0
2008	1,702.7	1,714.5	1,721.4	1,727.9	1,735.3	1,740.2	1,717.9	1,718.5	1,724.3	1,724.3	1,705.9	1,684.2	1,718.1
2009	1,625.7	1,620.9	1,612.9	1,614.9	1,619.8	1,623.2	1,600.5	1,595.0	1,605.6	1,614.6	1,610.1	1,603.5	1,612.2
2010	1,562.4	1,570.5	1,579.0	1,596.4	1,611.3	1,621.1	1,597.4	1,598.3	1,607.0	1,629.0	1,626.5	1,621.0	1,601.7
2011	1,583.3	1,596.1	1,603.1	1,617.9	1,624.9	1,635.0	1,611.1	1,614.9	1,628.4	1,640.9	1,642.4	1,638.9	1,619.7
2012	1,599.4	1,612.6	1,620.1	1,632.0	1,646.0	1,654.5	1,632.1	1,639.6	1,649.2	1,665.7	1,666.4	1,661.3	1,639.9
2013	1,622.4	1,639.5	1,648.0	1,664.3	1,679.8	1,686.7	1,666.2	1,674.6	1,689.5	1,704.3	1,709.3	1,705.5	1,674.2
2014	1,673.3	1,681.2	1,693.8	1,710.2	1,724.8	1,734.5	1,714.1	1,722.7	1,738.1	1,753.5	1,758.3	1,759.2	1,722.0
2015	1,725.5	1,740.8	1,750.6	1,771.9	1,786.3	1,797.7	1,776.5	1,781.4	1,794.6	1,813.3	1,817.0	1,817.4	1,781.1
2016	1,782.4	1,801.7	1,811.5	1,828.1	1,837.7	1,846.9	1,825.2	1,832.9	1,846.9	1,861.5	1,867.8	1,860.5	1,833.6
2017	1,814.8	1,842.5	1,853.9	1,869.6	1,879.4	1,891.4	1,866.9	1,871.3	1,881.6	1,898.4	1,898.1	1,904.0	1,872.7
Total Private													
2007	1,401.3	1,412.1	1,423.2	1,426.4	1,436.8	1,448.1	1,454.1	1,464.0	1,462.0	1,458.1	1,455.6	1,453.3	1,441.3
2008	1,407.9	1,414.4	1,419.4	1,425.5	1,429.6	1,433.4	1,438.1	1,440.2	1,436.0	1,420.0	1,397.9	1,379.0	1,420.1
2009	1,324.7	1,315.0	1,306.2	1,307.2	1,309.6	1,314.3	1,319.6	1,317.3	1,320.8	1,312.0	1,305.2	1,301.2	1,312.8
2010	1,263.7	1,267.1	1,274.1	1,288.9	1,296.4	1,306.6	1,316.0	1,320.6	1,323.4	1,326.1	1,320.3	1,319.5	1,301.9
2011	1,283.8	1,292.6	1,299.3	1,313.4	1,318.0	1,327.8	1,339.2	1,345.4	1,349.4	1,343.7	1,342.5	1,341.9	1,324.8
2012	1,306.9	1,314.9	1,321.7	1,334.2	1,344.5	1,353.3	1,363.5	1,372.3	1,371.1	1,370.2	1,368.2	1,366.4	1,348.9
2013	1,332.6	1,344.0	1,352.4	1,368.8	1,381.0	1,388.8	1,401.7	1,410.7	1,412.5	1,410.0	1,411.5	1,409.3	1,385.3
2014	1,380.7	1,384.3	1,396.1	1,410.9	1,422.2	1,431.4	1,442.7	1,451.6	1,454.8	1,452.0	1,453.7	1,456.0	1,428.0
2015	1,425.8	1,436.4	1,444.8	1,462.0	1,473.3	1,484.1	1,499.1	1,505.2	1,506.6	1,506.4	1,506.8	1,507.9	1,479.9
2016	1,476.9	1,491.0	1,499.1	1,515.1	1,521.9	1,530.1	1,541.1	1,550.6	1,550.9	1,548.0	1,550.8	1,546.6	1,526.8
2017	1,507.9	1,527.5	1,536.5	1,552.6	1,559.8	1,571.2	1,580.0	1,586.4	1,584.0	1,585.2	1,583.1	1,590.0	1,563.7
Goods Producing													
2007	309.5	311.0	312.7	311.9	315.2	319.7	325.4	328.7	325.2	321.8	315.7	311.0	317.3
2008	300.8	300.4	299.4	299.3	300.2	302.1	305.7	306.1	301.9	296.0	284.4	274.4	297.6
2009	259.5	251.9	247.0	245.0	244.7	247.6	252.8	251.6	250.5	246.6	239.3	235.4	247.7
2010	228.8	227.8	229.1	232.0	234.9	239.3	246.0	247.3	246.8	245.8	239.9	236.0	237.8
2011	230.5	232.5	234.2	238.2	240.6	244.8	251.1	254.6	253.2	250.2	246.5	243.9	243.4
2012	237.9	238.9	239.5	242.1	246.7	251.0	257.2	260.5	256.9	255.5	249.6	246.2	248.5
2013	241.7	243.8	245.6	249.7	253.9	258.2	264.4	266.9	265.5	265.0	261.4	258.8	256.2
2014	256.3	256.0	258.4	261.6	265.4	269.0	274.3	276.6	275.1	272.4	269.3	267.9	266.9
2015	264.8	266.1	268.0	270.8	274.3	279.0	285.3	286.2	284.8	283.2	279.8	278.2	276.7
2016	274.5	277.5	279.1	281.6	284.5	287.6	291.7	294.6	292.0	291.0	288.1	285.5	285.6
2017	278.2	282.3	284.9	289.0	292.5	297.4	302.1	304.3	301.2	300.2	294.1	295.1	293.4
Service-Providing													
2007	1,378.4	1,393.2	1,404.7	1,408.8	1,420.8	1,428.9	1,397.5	1,403.4	1,415.3	1,432.9	1,439.9	1,440.4	1,413.7
2008	1,401.9	1,414.1	1,422.0	1,428.6	1,435.1	1,438.1	1,412.2	1,412.4	1,422.4	1,428.3	1,421.5	1,409.8	1,420.5
2009	1,366.2	1,369.0	1,365.9	1,369.9	1,375.1	1,375.6	1,347.7	1,343.4	1,355.1	1,368.0	1,370.8	1,368.1	1,364.6
2010	1,333.6	1,342.7	1,349.9	1,364.4	1,376.4	1,381.8	1,351.4	1,351.0	1,360.2	1,383.2	1,386.6	1,385.0	1,363.9
2011	1,352.8	1,363.6	1,368.9	1,379.7	1,384.3	1,390.2	1,360.0	1,360.3	1,375.2	1,390.7	1,395.9	1,395.0	1,376.4
2012	1,361.5	1,373.7	1,380.6	1,389.9	1,399.3	1,403.5	1,374.9	1,379.1	1,392.3	1,410.2	1,416.8	1,415.1	1,391.4
2013	1,380.7	1,395.7	1,402.4	1,414.6	1,425.9	1,428.5	1,401.8	1,407.7	1,424.0	1,439.3	1,447.9	1,446.7	1,417.9
2014	1,417.0	1,425.2	1,435.4	1,448.6	1,459.4	1,465.5	1,439.8	1,446.1	1,463.0	1,481.1	1,489.0	1,491.3	1,455.1
2015	1,460.7	1,474.7	1,482.6	1,501.1	1,512.0	1,518.7	1,491.2	1,495.2	1,509.8	1,530.1	1,537.2	1,539.2	1,504.4
2016	1,507.9	1,524.2	1,532.4	1,546.5	1,553.2	1,559.3	1,533.5	1,538.3	1,554.9	1,570.5	1,579.7	1,575.0	1,548.0
2017	1,536.6	1,560.2	1,569.0	1,580.6	1,586.9	1,594.0	1,564.8	1,567.0	1,580.4	1,598.2	1,604.0	1,608.9	1,579.2
Mining and Logging													
2007	8.5	8.7	8.7	8.9	9.1	9.4	9.5	9.5	9.3	9.1	8.9	8.5	9.0
2008	8.1	8.1	8.0	8.0	8.2	8.5	8.8	9.0	8.9	8.7	8.4	7.8	8.4
2009	6.8	6.7	6.4	6.4	6.3	6.5	6.7	6.7	6.7	6.6	6.3	6.0	6.5
2010	5.8	5.8	5.9	6.1	6.2	6.6	6.9	6.9	6.8	6.6	6.3	6.1	6.3
2011	5.9	6.1	6.1	6.2	6.4	6.6	7.0	7.1	7.2	7.1	7.0	6.9	6.6
2012	6.3	6.4	6.3	6.4	6.7	7.0	7.1	7.3	7.1	7.2	7.0	6.9	6.8
2013	6.5	6.6	6.6	6.8	7.1	7.3	7.5	7.6	7.5	7.4	7.3	7.1	7.1
2014	7.0	7.0	6.9	7.0	7.1	7.3	7.5	7.6	7.4	7.3	7.3	7.1	7.2
2015	7.0	7.0	7.0	7.0	7.3	7.4	7.5	7.3	7.3	7.4	7.2	7.1	7.2
2016	7.0	7.0	6.9	6.9	7.2	7.2	7.3	7.4	7.3	7.2	7.1	7.0	7.1
2017	6.6	6.7	6.6	6.8	6.9	7.1	7.2	7.3	7.1	7.1	7.1	6.9	7.0

1. Employment by Industry: Oregon, Selected Years, 2007–2017—*Continued*

(Numbers in thousands, not seasonally adjusted)

Industry and year	January	February	March	April	May	June	July	August	September	October	November	December	Annual average
Construction													
2007	97.4	98.9	100.5	101.5	104.2	105.8	109.4	110.8	109.2	107.4	104.5	101.3	104.2
2008	94.4	94.3	94.2	94.7	95.8	96.9	98.7	98.6	96.9	93.1	87.9	83.4	94.1
2009	76.9	74.2	72.6	72.4	73.1	75.0	77.1	77.1	76.3	74.4	70.5	68.1	74.0
2010	63.4	62.7	63.4	65.0	66.6	68.4	71.8	72.6	72.1	71.5	68.1	66.1	67.6
2011	62.1	62.9	63.6	66.4	67.8	70.0	72.4	73.5	73.6	72.2	70.2	68.6	68.6
2012	65.0	65.4	65.4	67.1	69.6	70.9	73.9	75.7	74.0	73.1	70.0	67.9	69.8
2013	64.9	66.2	67.9	70.6	73.6	75.2	78.4	79.8	79.2	79.6	78.2	76.3	74.2
2014	74.9	74.5	76.3	78.2	80.5	81.6	83.9	84.8	84.2	82.2	80.4	79.2	80.1
2015	77.3	77.7	78.7	80.0	81.7	83.8	86.6	87.8	87.2	87.8	85.9	84.6	83.3
2016	82.1	84.5	85.5	88.0	89.7	91.2	93.8	95.4	95.0	94.8	93.4	91.6	90.4
2017	87.2	90.2	92.1	94.6	96.8	99.1	101.8	103.4	102.3	101.5	98.3	97.8	97.1
Manufacturing													
2007	203.6	203.4	203.5	201.5	201.9	204.5	206.5	208.4	206.7	205.3	202.3	201.2	204.1
2008	198.3	198.0	197.2	196.6	196.2	196.7	198.2	198.5	196.1	194.2	188.1	183.2	195.1
2009	175.8	171.0	168.0	166.2	165.3	166.1	169.0	167.8	167.5	165.6	162.5	161.3	167.2
2010	159.6	159.3	159.8	160.9	162.1	164.3	167.3	167.8	167.9	167.7	165.5	163.8	163.8
2011	162.5	163.5	164.5	165.6	166.4	168.2	171.7	174.0	172.4	170.9	169.3	168.4	168.1
2012	166.6	167.1	167.8	168.6	170.4	173.1	176.2	177.5	175.8	175.2	172.6	171.4	171.9
2013	170.3	171.0	171.1	172.3	173.2	175.7	178.5	179.5	178.8	178.0	175.9	175.4	175.0
2014	174.4	174.5	175.2	176.4	177.8	180.1	182.9	184.2	183.5	182.9	181.6	181.6	179.6
2015	180.5	181.4	182.3	183.8	185.3	187.8	191.2	191.1	190.3	188.0	186.7	186.5	186.2
2016	185.4	186.0	186.7	186.7	187.6	189.2	190.6	191.8	189.7	189.0	187.6	186.9	188.1
2017	184.4	185.4	186.2	187.6	188.8	191.2	193.1	193.6	191.8	191.6	188.7	190.4	189.4
Trade, Transportation, and Utilities													
2007	330.3	328.2	329.7	330.2	332.2	335.0	336.1	337.9	339.3	339.8	346.6	348.7	336.2
2008	332.7	330.4	330.8	330.9	331.1	331.8	332.8	333.1	332.7	331.0	330.9	330.1	331.5
2009	313.2	308.4	305.4	304.4	305.8	305.9	306.2	306.3	307.6	306.4	309.3	311.5	307.5
2010	298.4	296.0	296.4	298.9	300.3	302.2	304.1	305.6	306.5	308.3	312.6	315.8	303.8
2011	302.2	300.2	300.5	302.9	304.6	306.5	307.9	308.7	309.9	310.7	316.3	318.4	307.4
2012	305.7	303.4	304.2	306.0	309.1	311.6	311.6	313.3	314.1	315.5	321.8	323.8	311.7
2013	311.6	310.9	311.3	313.9	316.9	318.3	320.3	322.8	323.9	324.4	330.5	332.4	319.8
2014	320.7	318.1	318.6	320.8	323.9	325.7	327.8	330.2	330.9	332.7	338.8	342.5	327.6
2015	329.6	328.0	329.2	331.4	334.2	336.8	338.3	340.4	340.9	342.0	346.8	349.9	337.3
2016	336.6	335.5	336.4	338.1	339.7	341.7	343.9	346.7	346.3	347.0	354.2	355.7	343.5
2017	345.1	343.7	344.1	345.7	347.4	349.0	350.3	352.0	351.9	352.5	359.3	362.4	350.3
Wholesale Trade													
2007	74.9	75.4	75.3	75.1	75.2	75.5	76.1	75.8	75.6	75.9	75.8	75.5	75.5
2008	74.5	75.1	75.2	74.9	75.1	75.1	75.7	75.3	75.2	75.1	74.2	73.3	74.9
2009	71.6	71.1	70.3	69.9	69.9	69.5	69.5	68.9	68.6	68.1	67.6	67.3	69.4
2010	66.1	66.2	66.0	66.8	67.1	67.0	67.6	67.4	67.7	67.9	67.5	67.4	67.1
2011	66.3	66.8	66.9	67.5	67.8	67.9	68.2	68.4	68.2	68.5	68.1	67.9	67.7
2012	66.8	67.4	67.7	68.4	69.1	68.9	69.4	69.7	69.6	69.8	69.6	69.4	68.8
2013	69.9	70.5	70.4	70.9	71.3	71.2	72.1	72.3	72.3	72.2	72.4	72.3	71.5
2014	71.7	71.9	71.9	71.9	72.0	72.3	72.9	73.0	73.1	73.3	73.2	73.4	72.6
2015	72.6	73.0	73.0	73.1	73.5	73.7	74.3	74.8	74.9	74.8	75.1	75.2	74.0
2016	74.2	74.7	74.9	75.2	75.0	75.3	75.8	76.3	76.0	75.9	76.0	76.1	75.5
2017	75.4	76.0	76.0	76.4	76.8	76.8	76.8	77.0	77.0	76.2	76.5	76.7	76.5
Retail Trade													
2007	197.5	194.8	196.2	196.8	198.5	200.2	201.9	203.5	203.8	203.8	210.3	211.9	201.6
2008	199.3	196.2	196.6	196.5	196.4	197.2	198.6	198.8	198.0	196.8	198.9	198.9	197.7
2009	186.1	182.6	181.0	180.9	182.1	182.8	184.0	184.4	184.8	184.7	188.6	190.4	184.4
2010	180.5	178.3	178.8	180.0	181.0	182.6	184.6	185.9	185.4	186.9	191.9	194.2	184.2
2011	183.1	180.7	180.8	182.3	183.4	184.9	186.5	186.9	187.0	187.7	193.3	194.7	185.9
2012	185.1	182.1	182.4	183.7	185.8	188.0	188.9	189.7	189.3	190.7	196.9	198.0	188.4
2013	187.6	185.9	186.2	188.0	190.5	191.7	194.0	195.6	195.5	196.0	201.6	202.6	192.9
2014	192.5	189.7	190.5	192.4	195.0	196.3	198.7	200.1	200.0	201.1	206.8	208.5	197.6
2015	198.0	196.3	197.3	199.8	201.9	203.2	205.6	206.9	206.3	207.0	210.9	212.1	203.8
2016	202.2	201.2	201.7	202.7	204.2	205.8	208.1	209.7	208.7	209.6	214.5	214.4	206.9
2017	207.1	205.7	206.0	207.4	208.3	209.6	211.6	212.4	211.9	212.6	218.4	219.5	210.9

1. Employment by Industry: Oregon, Selected Years, 2007–2017—*Continued*

(Numbers in thousands, not seasonally adjusted)

Industry and year	January	February	March	April	May	June	July	August	September	October	November	December	Annual average
Transportation and Utilities													
2007	57.9	58.0	58.2	58.3	58.5	59.3	58.1	58.6	59.9	60.1	60.5	61.3	59.1
2008	58.9	59.1	59.0	59.5	59.6	59.5	58.5	59.0	59.5	59.1	57.8	57.9	59.0
2009	55.5	54.7	54.1	53.6	53.8	53.6	52.7	53.0	54.2	53.6	53.1	53.8	53.8
2010	51.8	51.5	51.6	52.1	52.2	52.6	51.9	52.3	53.4	53.5	53.2	54.2	52.5
2011	52.8	52.7	52.8	53.1	53.4	53.7	53.2	53.4	54.7	54.5	54.9	55.8	53.8
2012	53.8	53.9	54.1	53.9	54.2	54.7	53.3	53.9	55.2	55.0	55.3	56.4	54.5
2013	54.1	54.5	54.7	55.0	55.1	55.4	54.2	54.9	56.1	56.2	56.5	57.5	55.4
2014	56.5	56.5	56.2	56.5	56.9	57.1	56.2	57.1	57.8	58.3	58.8	60.6	57.4
2015	59.0	58.7	58.9	58.5	58.8	59.9	58.4	58.7	59.7	60.2	60.8	62.6	59.5
2016	60.2	59.6	59.8	60.2	60.5	60.6	60.0	60.7	61.6	61.5	63.7	65.2	61.1
2017	62.6	62.0	62.1	61.9	62.3	62.6	61.9	62.6	63.0	63.7	64.4	66.2	62.9
Information													
2007	34.6	35.0	35.5	35.6	35.9	36.2	35.7	35.9	35.7	35.5	35.9	36.9	35.7
2008	35.8	36.0	36.0	35.6	35.8	36.0	35.3	35.4	35.1	34.5	34.2	33.9	35.3
2009	33.0	33.1	33.0	32.5	32.9	33.9	32.8	32.7	32.2	31.7	32.3	32.5	32.7
2010	31.3	31.4	31.6	31.5	31.9	32.3	31.6	32.0	31.8	31.5	31.9	31.9	31.7
2011	31.5	31.6	32.0	31.8	31.6	31.6	31.8	31.9	31.7	31.5	31.6	31.6	31.7
2012	31.2	31.3	31.9	32.3	32.1	32.5	32.7	32.5	32.1	32.4	32.5	32.3	32.2
2013	32.0	32.1	32.2	32.2	32.0	31.9	32.0	32.3	32.5	32.6	32.7	32.7	32.3
2014	31.7	31.8	32.2	32.3	31.6	31.8	32.2	32.4	32.5	32.5	32.6	32.7	32.2
2015	32.1	32.4	32.5	32.7	32.5	32.7	33.5	33.8	33.4	32.9	33.2	33.3	32.9
2016	32.7	33.2	33.3	33.2	33.6	33.5	33.2	33.7	34.6	34.0	34.0	33.8	33.6
2017	33.6	34.1	33.8	34.8	34.3	34.3	34.0	34.4	34.4	34.6	34.4	34.0	34.2
Financial Activities													
2007	105.8	106.5	107.1	106.4	106.8	107.4	107.9	107.5	105.8	105.6	105.1	105.3	106.4
2008	102.5	102.8	102.6	102.9	102.8	102.5	102.5	102.4	101.2	100.7	99.7	99.5	101.8
2009	96.4	96.2	95.7	95.7	95.5	95.3	96.1	96.0	95.3	95.6	94.9	95.2	95.7
2010	92.4	92.1	92.1	93.1	93.2	93.8	94.2	94.1	93.5	93.4	92.8	93.5	93.2
2011	91.3	91.7	91.4	91.7	91.8	92.4	92.6	92.3	91.5	91.3	90.8	91.3	91.7
2012	89.4	89.6	89.3	89.9	89.9	90.2	91.6	91.7	91.0	91.1	90.9	91.1	90.5
2013	89.7	89.9	90.0	91.0	91.4	91.6	93.0	92.9	92.5	92.4	92.1	92.2	91.6
2014	90.5	90.2	90.3	91.2	92.1	92.7	93.6	93.9	93.6	93.5	93.4	94.0	92.4
2015	92.7	92.8	92.7	93.9	94.6	94.8	96.1	96.3	95.6	96.1	95.7	96.2	94.8
2016	94.4	94.3	94.2	95.7	96.3	96.9	98.3	98.9	98.2	98.2	98.3	98.7	96.9
2017	97.2	97.5	98.0	98.4	99.1	99.8	101.2	101.3	100.7	100.9	100.7	101.3	99.7
Professional and Business Services													
2007	195.7	198.2	200.5	201.4	201.9	204.2	204.5	206.6	205.6	205.9	203.4	202.6	202.5
2008	196.9	199.4	200.8	203.0	203.4	204.1	206.2	207.2	205.3	202.4	197.7	194.3	201.7
2009	187.9	186.6	185.0	186.0	184.9	185.8	187.1	186.1	186.1	185.7	185.2	185.2	186.0
2010	179.7	181.8	183.4	187.4	187.6	189.0	191.7	192.8	192.1	193.4	192.3	192.1	188.6
2011	186.5	188.6	190.2	193.5	193.0	194.7	199.0	199.7	200.0	199.3	198.8	198.9	195.2
2012	194.9	196.8	197.8	200.3	200.6	202.4	204.9	206.4	204.9	205.3	205.3	205.7	202.1
2013	199.0	201.1	203.5	206.7	207.7	209.9	213.8	215.4	214.3	214.0	213.7	214.4	209.5
2014	209.6	211.5	213.9	217.1	218.0	220.5	223.3	225.6	225.3	224.6	224.1	224.1	219.8
2015	218.9	220.8	222.6	226.8	227.8	229.5	232.8	234.2	233.7	235.0	234.4	234.8	229.3
2016	230.1	232.7	234.3	238.1	237.7	239.4	241.9	243.0	241.4	241.5	240.7	239.5	238.4
2017	234.1	238.2	239.7	242.5	242.1	244.9	246.4	247.0	245.5	246.8	244.2	245.2	243.1
Education and Health Services													
2007	205.4	210.4	211.5	211.9	211.7	208.4	204.3	205.3	211.4	216.2	217.0	217.0	210.9
2008	212.8	217.8	218.8	219.9	219.1	216.3	212.9	213.3	219.8	223.7	224.3	224.4	218.6
2009	218.8	222.8	223.2	224.4	223.5	220.2	216.5	216.5	223.3	227.1	228.0	227.3	222.6
2010	224.0	227.5	228.6	229.3	228.5	225.1	221.2	221.3	227.9	233.2	234.3	234.0	227.9
2011	229.8	233.4	234.6	235.1	233.8	230.1	225.8	226.4	233.4	237.5	238.7	238.1	233.1
2012	232.5	237.6	238.8	239.6	237.7	232.8	228.9	230.0	236.9	240.7	242.0	241.8	236.6
2013	236.9	242.3	242.7	244.1	243.0	237.8	233.4	234.7	241.6	246.2	247.3	246.5	241.4
2014	242.6	246.4	248.3	249.0	247.2	243.5	239.7	240.2	248.2	252.5	254.2	254.3	247.2
2015	249.9	255.6	256.0	258.1	256.5	252.9	249.7	250.6	258.0	262.3	264.2	263.4	256.4
2016	259.6	265.1	265.7	266.8	264.5	260.1	257.5	259.8	267.3	271.4	272.9	272.0	265.2
2017	265.6	273.3	274.4	275.0	273.6	268.9	265.2	266.7	274.1	277.7	279.7	279.7	272.8

1. Employment by Industry: Oregon, Selected Years, 2007–2017—*Continued*

(Numbers in thousands, not seasonally adjusted)

Industry and year	January	February	March	April	May	June	July	August	September	October	November	December	Annual average
Leisure and Hospitality													
2007	161.5	163.2	166.2	169.0	172.4	176.1	179.8	181.4	178.4	172.5	171.2	171.1	171.9
2008	166.6	167.2	170.2	172.8	175.5	178.9	181.6	181.7	178.6	171.1	167.0	163.3	172.9
2009	158.1	158.1	159.2	161.4	164.2	167.7	170.0	170.2	168.0	161.7	159.1	157.3	162.9
2010	153.2	154.4	156.5	160.3	163.1	167.4	170.2	170.9	167.9	163.6	160.2	160.0	162.3
2011	156.2	158.3	159.9	163.4	165.6	170.5	173.8	174.6	172.3	166.2	163.0	162.9	165.6
2012	159.1	160.7	163.4	166.7	170.4	174.9	178.7	180.1	177.6	171.9	168.9	168.5	170.1
2013	164.9	166.6	169.5	173.4	177.6	182.7	186.2	187.0	183.8	177.4	175.6	174.5	176.6
2014	171.6	172.5	176.1	180.2	184.5	188.3	192.1	193.0	189.4	184.0	181.7	181.1	182.9
2015	178.9	181.2	184.1	187.9	192.5	197.4	201.7	202.1	198.8	193.1	190.8	190.0	191.5
2016	187.4	190.2	193.2	197.7	201.3	206.3	210.3	209.3	206.4	200.1	198.0	197.6	199.8
2017	193.0	196.0	198.9	204.0	207.2	213.0	216.7	216.4	212.4	208.0	205.3	206.8	206.5
Other Services													
2007	58.5	59.6	60.0	60.0	60.7	61.1	60.4	60.7	60.6	60.8	60.7	60.7	60.3
2008	59.8	60.4	60.8	61.1	61.7	61.7	61.1	61.0	61.4	60.6	59.7	59.1	60.7
2009	57.8	57.9	57.7	57.8	58.1	57.9	58.1	57.9	57.8	57.2	57.1	56.8	57.7
2010	55.9	56.1	56.4	56.4	56.9	57.5	57.0	56.6	56.9	56.9	56.3	56.2	56.6
2011	55.8	56.3	56.5	56.8	57.0	57.2	57.2	57.2	57.4	57.0	56.8	56.8	56.8
2012	56.2	56.6	56.8	57.3	58.0	57.9	57.9	57.8	57.6	57.8	57.2	57.0	57.3
2013	56.8	57.3	57.6	57.8	58.5	58.4	58.6	58.7	58.4	58.0	58.2	57.8	58.0
2014	57.7	57.8	58.3	58.7	59.5	59.9	59.7	59.7	59.8	59.8	59.6	59.4	59.2
2015	58.9	59.5	59.7	60.4	60.9	61.0	61.7	61.6	61.4	61.8	61.9	62.1	60.9
2016	61.6	62.5	62.9	63.9	64.3	64.6	64.3	64.6	64.7	64.8	64.6	63.8	63.9
2017	61.1	62.4	62.7	63.2	63.6	63.9	64.1	64.3	63.8	64.5	65.4	65.5	63.7
Government													
2007	286.6	292.1	294.2	294.3	299.2	300.5	268.8	268.1	278.5	296.6	300.0	298.1	289.8
2008	294.8	300.1	302.0	302.4	305.7	306.8	279.8	278.3	288.3	304.3	308.0	305.2	298.0
2009	301.0	305.9	306.7	307.7	310.2	308.9	280.9	277.7	284.8	302.6	304.9	302.3	299.5
2010	298.7	303.4	304.9	307.5	314.9	314.5	281.4	277.7	283.6	302.9	306.2	301.5	299.8
2011	299.5	303.5	303.8	304.5	306.9	307.2	271.9	269.5	279.0	297.2	299.9	297.0	295.0
2012	292.5	297.7	298.4	297.8	301.5	301.2	268.6	267.3	278.1	295.5	298.2	294.9	291.0
2013	289.8	295.5	295.6	295.5	298.8	297.9	264.5	263.9	277.0	294.3	297.8	296.2	288.9
2014	292.6	296.9	297.7	299.3	302.6	303.1	271.4	271.1	283.3	301.5	304.6	303.2	293.9
2015	299.7	304.4	305.8	309.9	313.0	313.6	277.4	276.2	288.0	306.9	310.2	309.5	301.2
2016	305.5	310.7	312.4	313.0	315.8	316.8	284.1	282.3	296.0	313.5	317.0	313.9	306.8
2017	306.9	315.0	317.4	317.0	319.6	320.2	286.9	284.9	297.6	313.2	315.0	314.0	309.0

2. Average Weekly Hours by Selected Industry: Oregon, 2013–2017

(Not seasonally adjusted)

Industry and year	January	February	March	April	May	June	July	August	September	October	November	December	Annual average
Total Private													
2013	32.8	33.6	33.5	33.6	33.6	34.7	33.4	33.9	34.7	33.6	33.5	34.0	33.7
2014	32.9	33.8	34.3	33.7	33.6	34.7	33.7	34.1	33.9	33.7	34.4	33.4	33.9
2015	33.3	34.6	34.4	33.6	33.7	34.0	34.0	35.0	33.8	33.7	34.5	33.5	34.0
2016	33.4	33.7	33.5	33.9	34.7	34.2	34.4	34.4	34.3	35.1	34.0	33.3	34.1
2017	33.5	34.0	33.7	34.9	33.7	34.0	34.7	34.1	34.2	34.9	33.8	33.8	34.1
Goods-Producing													
2013	37.8	39.0	39.0	39.4	39.1	40.1	38.5	39.5	40.0	39.5	39.3	39.1	39.2
2014	38.2	38.2	39.3	38.8	38.9	39.5	38.7	39.3	39.7	39.5	39.6	39.0	39.1
2015	38.9	39.7	39.4	38.8	38.6	39.2	39.2	39.6	38.1	38.7	38.9	38.5	39.0
2016	38.0	38.0	38.1	38.4	39.2	38.9	38.7	38.9	39.3	39.4	38.6	37.3	38.6
2017	36.8	38.6	38.6	39.3	38.7	39.3	39.5	39.4	39.5	39.9	38.8	38.5	38.9
Construction													
2013	34.2	35.7	36.2	36.7	36.7	37.2	37.3	38.1	38.5	37.8	36.5	36.0	36.8
2014	35.7	34.7	36.2	36.0	36.5	37.1	36.7	38.1	38.0	37.2	36.6	36.2	36.6
2015	36.4	36.9	36.3	36.3	35.7	37.2	37.2	37.5	35.2	36.4	35.7	35.4	36.3
2016	35.6	35.6	35.6	36.9	36.8	37.5	37.2	37.6	37.6	37.2	36.3	35.0	36.6
2017	33.8	37.0	37.4	37.9	37.5	38.8	39.1	38.9	38.9	39.0	37.1	37.3	37.8
Manufacturing													
2013	39.0	39.9	39.9	40.2	39.9	40.8	38.7	39.6	40.2	39.7	40.1	40.2	39.9
2014	38.9	39.4	40.4	39.8	39.8	40.4	39.4	39.6	40.4	40.3	40.8	40.3	40.0
2015	40.0	40.5	40.4	39.5	39.5	39.8	39.7	40.3	39.2	39.3	40.1	39.8	39.8
2016	39.0	38.9	39.1	39.0	40.2	39.4	39.2	39.3	39.9	40.4	39.7	39.2	39.4
2017	39.1	39.8	39.7	40.4	39.7	39.8	40.1	39.9	40.1	40.5	39.8	39.3	39.9
Trade, Transportation, and Utilities													
2013	33.2	33.9	34.2	34.2	34.4	35.4	34.7	35.0	35.3	34.4	34.3	34.7	34.5
2014	33.7	34.6	35.0	34.6	34.8	35.5	35.1	35.2	34.8	34.1	34.7	34.2	34.7
2015	33.5	35.1	35.1	34.4	34.9	34.9	35.0	35.8	35.4	34.7	35.5	34.5	34.9
2016	34.2	34.5	34.7	35.4	35.9	35.3	35.6	35.5	35.4	36.1	34.9	34.8	35.2
2017	34.3	34.6	34.5	36.0	34.9	34.9	35.7	35.1	35.1	35.9	34.5	34.7	35.0
Financial Activities													
2013	36.0	36.3	36.1	36.0	36.1	38.2	36.2	36.3	38.5	35.9	36.6	37.9	36.7
2014	35.7	37.1	36.9	35.1	35.1	37.6	35.6	36.0	36.0	35.5	37.6	35.8	36.2
2015	35.7	37.1	36.5	35.6	35.3	35.4	35.4	36.9	36.2	36.2	37.0	36.4	36.1
2016	37.0	36.6	36.7	36.6	38.2	37.0	37.5	37.2	38.5	39.8	38.3	37.9	37.6
2017	38.4	37.7	38.7	38.0	37.1	37.4	38.1	37.4	38.3	37.7	36.7	36.8	37.7
Professional and Business Services													
2013	33.9	34.8	34.7	35.0	34.6	35.9	34.1	34.6	35.8	34.8	34.9	35.2	34.9
2014	34.2	35.6	35.8	35.0	34.5	36.2	35.2	35.2	35.1	35.1	35.5	34.5	35.2
2015	34.2	35.5	35.3	34.6	34.4	35.2	35.0	36.0	34.4	34.7	35.8	34.4	35.0
2016	34.5	35.0	34.5	35.0	35.9	35.0	35.0	35.0	34.7	36.3	35.2	34.1	35.0
2017	35.0	35.5	35.2	36.9	35.5	35.9	36.7	35.7	35.9	37.1	36.2	36.2	36.0
Education and Health Services													
2013	31.5	32.2	31.5	31.5	31.2	32.2	30.7	31.2	32.0	31.0	31.5	31.8	31.5
2014	31.3	32.5	32.3	31.6	31.4	32.6	31.0	31.7	31.9	31.7	33.0	32.2	31.9
2015	32.1	33.5	33.1	32.4	32.6	32.6	32.4	33.7	32.9	32.9	34.0	33.2	33.0
2016	33.3	33.2	32.8	33.2	33.8	34.1	34.2	34.1	33.1	34.2	33.3	32.7	33.5
2017	33.4	33.3	32.7	33.9	32.5	32.5	33.3	33.0	32.7	33.3	32.5	32.9	33.0
Leisure and Hospitality													
2013	23.9	24.9	24.9	24.9	25.1	26.8	25.5	26.2	26.9	24.5	24.0	25.1	25.3
2014	23.4	24.5	25.8	24.9	24.8	26.4	25.1	26.3	25.2	24.9	25.7	24.2	25.1
2015	24.1	25.8	25.8	24.8	25.1	25.6	26.1	27.4	25.5	25.0	25.5	24.3	25.4
2016	24.0	25.0	24.3	24.8	25.7	25.1	25.9	26.6	25.8	26.3	24.7	24.2	25.2
2017	24.5	24.8	24.7	26.1	24.9	25.4	26.6	26.0	25.3	25.9	24.6	24.6	25.3
Other Services													
2013	28.5	29.3	29.1	28.9	29.3	30.3	29.5	30.0	30.0	29.1	29.0	29.7	29.4
2014	29.1	29.2	30.2	29.8	30.0	30.7	29.6	29.9	29.3	28.7	29.8	27.7	29.5
2015	28.4	30.1	28.9	28.5	28.6	29.1	29.0	29.8	28.2	28.3	28.8	26.7	28.7
2016	27.0	27.7	27.4	27.8	29.4	28.0	28.8	28.7	28.1	29.8	28.4	27.7	28.2
2017	28.4	29.0	28.3	30.0	28.9	29.0	30.5	28.9	29.3	30.1	28.7	28.8	29.2

3. Average Hourly Earnings by Selected Industry: Oregon, 2013–2017

(Dollars, not seasonally adjusted)

Industry and year	January	February	March	April	May	June	July	August	September	October	November	December	Annual average
Total Private													
2013	22.41	22.41	22.31	22.39	22.27	22.37	22.34	22.34	22.65	22.68	22.83	23.21	22.52
2014	23.09	23.05	22.86	22.80	22.84	22.83	22.77	22.61	22.88	22.92	23.10	23.14	22.91
2015	23.36	23.33	23.38	23.32	23.36	23.28	23.32	23.43	23.57	23.78	24.01	24.12	23.53
2016	24.29	24.35	24.23	24.62	24.66	24.39	24.56	24.53	25.00	25.24	25.20	25.54	24.72
2017	26.01	25.56	25.50	25.64	25.21	25.30	25.55	25.49	25.79	25.93	25.82	26.06	25.65
Goods-Producing													
2013	24.05	23.95	23.96	24.08	23.98	23.95	24.03	24.05	24.26	24.28	24.17	24.59	24.12
2014	24.44	24.31	24.14	24.28	24.13	24.28	24.27	24.02	24.18	24.11	24.28	24.27	24.22
2015	24.32	24.17	24.25	24.36	24.21	24.39	24.49	24.49	24.41	24.71	24.78	25.12	24.48
2016	25.20	25.16	25.13	25.36	25.45	25.29	25.43	25.45	25.74	25.76	25.82	26.19	25.50
2017	26.19	25.94	25.93	26.06	26.36	26.23	26.29	26.03	26.45	26.56	26.28	26.61	26.25
Construction													
2013	27.86	27.79	28.30	28.55	28.71	27.91	27.90	28.04	28.00	28.12	27.92	28.76	28.11
2014	28.65	28.67	28.51	28.48	28.35	28.19	28.26	27.91	28.30	28.00	27.95	28.23	28.28
2015	28.29	28.00	28.29	28.23	28.15	28.33	28.67	28.75	28.61	28.78	28.80	29.84	28.57
2016	29.57	29.23	29.35	29.51	29.68	29.39	29.61	29.88	29.85	29.91	30.19	30.08	29.70
2017	30.65	30.21	29.98	30.21	30.58	30.05	30.40	30.22	30.71	30.51	30.38	30.81	30.39
Manufacturing													
2013	22.74	22.54	22.42	22.49	22.49	22.49	22.55	22.46	22.78	22.75	22.75	23.08	22.63
2014	22.86	22.76	22.68	22.73	22.55	22.84	22.84	22.54	22.59	22.69	22.98	22.83	22.74
2015	22.86	22.81	22.78	22.97	22.77	22.81	22.75	22.65	22.68	22.94	23.07	23.10	22.85
2016	23.29	23.38	23.28	23.42	23.54	23.34	23.46	23.26	23.77	23.78	23.69	24.40	23.55
2017	24.19	23.88	23.92	24.03	24.25	24.27	24.16	23.86	24.16	24.51	24.25	24.41	24.16
Trade, Transportation, and Utilities													
2013	20.25	20.23	20.21	20.08	20.03	20.11	20.02	20.01	20.07	19.89	19.92	20.13	20.08
2014	20.28	20.19	19.85	19.82	19.76	19.84	19.80	19.37	19.48	19.64	19.70	19.44	19.76
2015	19.93	19.73	19.82	19.67	19.74	19.71	19.91	19.73	19.69	19.82	19.88	19.78	19.78
2016	20.31	20.29	20.36	21.25	21.65	21.23	21.84	21.74	21.98	22.32	22.21	22.21	21.47
2017	23.05	22.34	22.51	22.52	22.17	22.72	22.85	22.49	22.43	22.90	22.22	22.32	22.54
Financial Activities													
2013	24.36	24.23	23.78	24.42	24.25	24.63	24.60	24.22	24.97	24.86	24.74	25.01	24.51
2014	24.46	24.29	24.21	24.11	24.70	25.40	25.72	26.19	26.00	26.34	26.37	27.44	25.45
2015	27.39	27.90	27.92	27.74	27.87	27.95	27.48	27.98	27.59	27.81	28.00	28.45	27.84
2016	27.41	28.20	28.29	29.73	28.25	27.64	28.00	27.92	28.63	29.02	28.66	28.45	28.36
2017	29.35	28.64	28.52	30.17	28.70	29.81	30.58	31.71	31.24	31.35	31.43	31.70	30.27
Professional and Business Services													
2013	25.23	25.44	25.25	25.38	25.38	25.72	25.36	25.29	25.87	25.75	26.18	26.72	25.64
2014	26.44	26.85	27.03	26.55	26.44	26.78	26.25	26.25	26.36	26.06	26.17	25.96	26.43
2015	26.22	26.18	26.38	26.41	26.64	26.16	26.26	26.37	26.72	26.91	27.56	27.41	26.61
2016	27.57	27.85	27.73	27.80	27.97	27.71	27.33	27.49	28.20	28.54	28.12	29.03	27.95
2017	29.62	29.18	29.01	29.26	28.66	28.57	29.31	29.06	30.03	30.24	30.35	30.48	29.49
Education and Health Services													
2013	23.03	23.00	23.21	23.39	23.24	23.71	24.19	24.44	24.59	24.53	24.86	25.18	23.95
2014	24.84	24.72	24.67	24.86	24.90	24.87	25.30	25.30	25.46	25.65	25.82	25.98	25.20
2015	26.26	26.22	26.19	26.49	26.70	26.76	27.30	27.45	27.66	27.60	27.81	27.76	27.03
2016	27.92	27.99	27.97	28.20	28.04	28.09	28.60	28.41	29.11	29.15	29.05	29.44	28.50
2017	29.58	29.27	29.10	29.14	29.05	29.16	29.21	29.54	29.36	29.31	29.26	29.69	29.31
Leisure and Hospitality													
2013	13.63	13.55	13.43	13.48	13.44	13.31	13.26	13.34	13.46	13.70	13.76	13.96	13.52
2014	14.14	14.10	14.03	13.87	13.98	13.83	13.66	13.68	13.86	13.72	13.79	14.12	13.89
2015	14.03	14.10	14.01	14.27	14.20	13.97	13.93	14.02	14.40	14.58	14.63	14.70	14.23
2016	14.62	14.69	14.76	14.76	14.89	14.91	15.06	15.03	15.10	15.23	15.19	15.38	14.97
2017	15.36	15.31	15.44	15.54	15.53	15.38	15.70	15.62	15.79	15.91	16.08	16.23	15.66
Other Services													
2013	20.16	20.36	20.38	20.40	20.32	20.42	20.19	20.35	20.94	20.73	21.07	21.40	20.56
2014	20.86	20.82	20.34	20.35	20.25	20.14	20.31	20.19	20.53	20.58	21.20	21.80	20.60
2015	21.44	21.27	21.49	21.67	21.61	21.81	21.51	21.98	22.04	22.10	22.20	22.40	21.79
2016	22.47	21.96	22.13	22.23	21.98	22.27	22.15	22.34	22.75	22.53	22.35	22.73	22.32
2017	22.83	22.53	22.24	22.10	21.81	22.11	21.91	21.69	21.90	21.98	22.14	22.82	22.17

4. Average Weekly Earnings by Selected Industry: Oregon, 2013–2017

(Dollars, not seasonally adjusted)

Industry and year	January	February	March	April	May	June	July	August	September	October	November	December	Annual average
Total Private													
2013	735.05	752.98	747.39	752.30	748.27	776.24	746.16	757.33	785.96	762.05	764.81	789.14	758.92
2014	759.66	779.09	784.10	768.36	767.42	792.20	767.35	771.00	775.63	772.40	794.64	772.88	776.65
2015	777.89	807.22	804.27	783.55	787.23	791.52	792.88	820.05	796.67	801.39	828.35	808.02	800.02
2016	811.29	820.60	811.71	834.62	855.70	834.14	844.86	843.83	857.50	885.92	856.80	850.48	842.95
2017	871.34	869.04	859.35	894.84	849.58	860.20	886.59	869.21	882.02	904.96	872.72	880.83	874.67
Goods-Producing													
2013	909.09	934.05	934.44	948.75	937.62	960.40	925.16	949.98	970.40	959.06	949.88	961.47	945.50
2014	933.61	928.64	948.70	942.06	938.66	959.06	939.25	943.99	959.95	952.35	961.49	946.53	947.00
2015	946.05	959.55	955.45	945.17	934.51	956.09	960.01	969.80	930.02	956.28	963.94	967.12	954.72
2016	957.60	956.08	957.45	973.82	997.64	983.78	984.14	990.01	1,011.58	1,014.94	996.65	976.89	984.30
2017	963.79	1,001.28	1,000.90	1,024.16	1,020.13	1,030.84	1,038.46	1,025.58	1,044.78	1,059.74	1,019.66	1,024.49	1,021.13
Construction													
2013	952.81	992.10	1,024.46	1,047.79	1,035.31	1,038.25	1,040.67	1,068.32	1,078.00	1,062.94	1,019.08	1,035.36	1,034.45
2014	1,022.81	994.85	1,032.06	1,025.28	1,034.78	1,045.85	1,037.14	1,063.37	1,075.40	1,041.60	1,022.97	1,021.93	1,035.05
2015	1,029.76	1,033.20	1,026.93	1,024.75	1,004.96	1,053.88	1,066.52	1,078.13	1,007.07	1,047.59	1,028.16	1,056.34	1,037.09
2016	1,052.69	1,040.59	1,044.86	1,088.92	1,092.22	1,102.13	1,101.49	1,123.49	1,122.36	1,112.65	1,095.90	1,052.80	1,087.02
2017	1,035.97	1,117.77	1,121.25	1,144.96	1,146.75	1,165.94	1,188.64	1,175.56	1,194.62	1,189.89	1,127.10	1,149.21	1,148.74
Manufacturing													
2013	886.86	899.35	894.56	904.10	897.35	917.59	872.69	889.42	915.76	903.18	912.28	927.82	902.94
2014	889.25	896.74	916.27	904.65	897.49	922.74	899.90	892.58	912.64	914.41	937.58	920.05	909.60
2015	914.40	923.81	920.31	907.32	899.42	907.84	903.18	912.80	889.06	901.54	925.11	919.38	909.43
2016	908.31	909.48	910.25	913.38	946.31	919.60	919.63	914.12	948.42	960.71	940.49	956.48	927.87
2017	945.83	950.42	949.62	970.81	962.73	965.95	968.82	952.01	968.82	992.66	965.15	959.31	963.98
Trade, Transportation, and Utilities													
2013	672.30	685.80	691.18	686.74	689.03	711.89	694.69	700.35	708.47	684.22	683.26	698.51	692.76
2014	683.44	698.57	694.75	685.77	687.65	704.32	694.98	681.82	677.90	669.72	683.59	664.85	685.67
2015	667.66	692.52	695.68	676.65	688.93	687.88	696.85	706.33	697.03	687.75	705.74	682.41	690.32
2016	694.60	700.01	706.49	752.25	777.24	749.42	777.50	771.77	778.09	805.75	775.13	772.91	755.74
2017	790.62	772.96	776.60	810.72	773.73	792.93	815.75	789.40	787.29	822.11	766.59	774.50	788.90
Financial Activities													
2013	876.96	879.55	858.46	879.12	875.43	940.87	890.52	879.19	961.35	892.47	905.48	947.88	899.52
2014	873.22	901.16	893.35	846.26	866.97	955.04	915.63	942.84	936.00	935.07	991.51	982.35	921.29
2015	977.82	1,035.09	1,019.08	987.54	983.81	989.43	972.79	1,032.46	998.76	1,006.72	1,036.00	1,035.58	1,005.02
2016	1,014.17	1,032.12	1,038.24	1,088.12	1,079.15	1,022.68	1,050.00	1,038.62	1,102.26	1,155.00	1,097.68	1,078.26	1,066.34
2017	1,127.04	1,079.73	1,103.72	1,146.46	1,064.77	1,114.89	1,165.10	1,185.95	1,196.49	1,181.90	1,153.48	1,166.56	1,141.18
Professional and Business Services													
2013	855.30	885.31	876.18	888.30	878.15	923.35	864.78	875.03	926.15	896.10	913.68	940.54	894.84
2014	904.25	955.86	967.67	929.25	912.18	969.44	924.00	924.00	925.24	914.71	929.04	895.62	930.34
2015	896.72	929.39	931.21	913.79	916.42	920.83	919.10	949.32	919.17	933.78	986.65	942.90	931.35
2016	951.17	974.75	956.69	973.00	1,004.12	969.85	956.55	962.15	978.54	1,036.00	989.82	989.92	978.25
2017	1,036.70	1,035.89	1,021.15	1,079.69	1,017.43	1,025.66	1,075.68	1,037.44	1,078.08	1,121.90	1,098.67	1,103.38	1,061.64
Education and Health Services													
2013	725.45	740.60	731.12	736.79	725.09	763.46	742.63	762.53	786.88	760.43	783.09	800.72	754.43
2014	777.49	803.40	796.84	785.58	781.86	810.76	784.30	802.01	812.17	813.11	852.06	836.56	803.88
2015	842.95	878.37	866.89	858.28	870.42	872.38	884.52	925.07	910.01	908.04	945.54	921.63	891.99
2016	929.74	929.27	917.42	936.24	947.75	957.87	978.12	968.78	963.54	996.93	967.37	962.69	954.75
2017	987.97	974.69	951.57	987.85	944.13	947.70	972.69	974.82	960.07	976.02	950.95	976.80	967.23
Leisure and Hospitality													
2013	325.76	337.40	334.41	335.65	337.34	356.71	338.13	349.51	362.07	335.65	330.24	350.40	342.06
2014	330.88	345.45	361.97	345.36	346.70	365.11	342.87	359.78	349.27	341.63	354.40	341.70	348.64
2015	338.12	363.78	361.46	353.90	356.42	357.63	363.57	384.15	367.20	364.50	373.07	357.21	361.44
2016	350.88	367.25	358.67	366.05	382.67	374.24	390.05	399.80	389.58	400.55	375.19	372.20	377.24
2017	376.32	379.69	381.37	405.59	386.70	390.65	417.62	406.12	399.49	412.07	395.57	399.26	396.20
Other Services													
2013	574.56	596.55	593.06	589.56	595.38	618.73	595.61	610.50	628.20	603.24	611.03	635.58	604.46
2014	607.03	607.94	614.27	606.43	607.50	618.30	601.18	603.68	601.53	590.65	631.76	603.86	607.70
2015	608.90	640.23	621.06	617.60	618.05	634.67	623.79	655.00	621.53	625.43	639.36	598.08	625.37
2016	606.69	608.29	606.36	617.99	646.21	623.56	637.92	641.16	639.28	671.39	634.74	629.62	629.42
2017	648.37	653.37	629.39	663.00	630.31	641.19	668.26	626.84	641.67	661.60	635.42	657.22	647.36

PENNSYLVANIA
At a Glance

Population:
  2010 census: 12,702,379
  2017 estimate: 12,805,537

Percent change in population:
  2010–2017: 0.8%

Percent change in total nonfarm employment:
  2007–2017: 2.5%

Industry with the largest growth in employment, 2007–2017 (thousands):
  Education and health services, 178.0

Industry with the largest decline or smallest growth in employment, 2007–2017 (thousands):
  Manufacturing, -97.6

Civilian labor force:
  2010: 6,380,949
  2017: 6,427,370

Unemployment rate and rank among states (highest to lowest):
  2010: 8.5%, 28th
  2017: 4.9%, 10th

Over-the-year change in unemployment rates:
  2015–2016: 0.1%
  2016–2017: -0.5%

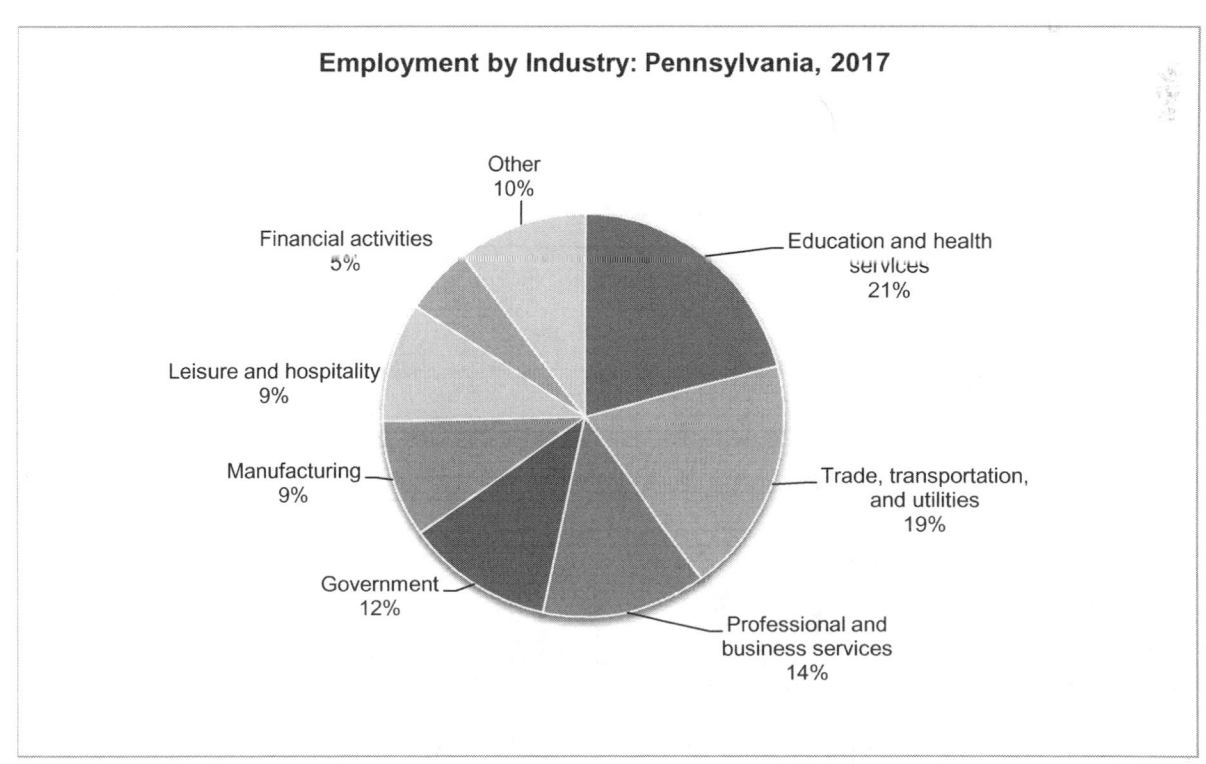

Employment by Industry: Pennsylvania, 2017

Other 10%

Financial activities 5%

Education and health services 21%

Leisure and hospitality 9%

Manufacturing 9%

Trade, transportation, and utilities 19%

Government 12%

Professional and business services 14%

1. Employment by Industry: Pennsylvania, Selected Years, 2007–2017

(Numbers in thousands, not seasonally adjusted)

Industry and year	January	February	March	April	May	June	July	August	September	October	November	December	Annual average
Total Nonfarm													
2007	5,680.0	5,691.3	5,742.6	5,793.8	5,838.5	5,854.1	5,785.8	5,777.4	5,819.3	5,861.7	5,875.9	5,866.0	5,798.9
2008	5,712.8	5,733.0	5,761.4	5,827.6	5,862.8	5,856.5	5,784.2	5,778.0	5,820.2	5,846.0	5,823.7	5,795.4	5,800.1
2009	5,601.5	5,605.4	5,604.9	5,635.1	5,661.0	5,642.2	5,568.8	5,550.1	5,598.7	5,646.5	5,651.5	5,633.6	5,616.6
2010	5,472.3	5,483.6	5,540.9	5,622.3	5,677.7	5,673.0	5,605.4	5,601.3	5,650.6	5,703.3	5,722.2	5,711.8	5,622.0
2011	5,555.1	5,587.4	5,630.7	5,700.1	5,730.2	5,729.4	5,654.4	5,648.0	5,713.1	5,748.2	5,772.3	5,758.5	5,685.6
2012	5,600.7	5,647.5	5,701.8	5,741.7	5,774.0	5,759.9	5,687.3	5,687.9	5,748.6	5,780.6	5,797.9	5,781.7	5,725.8
2013	5,619.9	5,664.2	5,702.3	5,745.5	5,784.4	5,771.0	5,705.9	5,710.6	5,765.6	5,797.2	5,819.3	5,801.0	5,740.6
2014	5,648.9	5,669.5	5,717.1	5,788.1	5,830.7	5,825.7	5,757.6	5,765.7	5,824.3	5,869.7	5,888.5	5,879.4	5,788.8
2015	5,709.2	5,736.9	5,761.0	5,835.6	5,878.4	5,869.6	5,811.3	5,811.9	5,866.4	5,909.8	5,926.0	5,914.1	5,835.9
2016	5,755.1	5,786.4	5,828.7	5,895.2	5,913.9	5,893.0	5,861.4	5,855.7	5,928.4	5,956.6	5,972.9	5,957.1	5,883.7
2017	5,811.5	5,850.0	5,871.8	5,945.6	5,978.5	5,962.2	5,918.9	5,921.1	5,986.6	6,022.7	6,039.7	6,037.8	5,945.5
Total Private													
2007	4,928.0	4,920.0	4,968.0	5,018.4	5,067.2	5,102.0	5,087.4	5,082.0	5,069.5	5,091.4	5,100.3	5,094.9	5,044.1
2008	4,959.3	4,960.9	4,986.0	5,049.3	5,091.6	5,101.1	5,086.6	5,077.8	5,057.6	5,063.3	5,036.7	5,015.0	5,040.4
2009	4,840.9	4,824.1	4,821.4	4,844.7	4,880.0	4,877.7	4,855.1	4,842.6	4,830.8	4,858.7	4,857.8	4,846.6	4,848.4
2010	4,711.8	4,701.9	4,753.1	4,828.9	4,875.8	4,893.7	4,890.7	4,892.6	4,886.6	4,919.8	4,932.7	4,929.5	4,851.4
2011	4,792.9	4,808.1	4,849.7	4,918.8	4,959.6	4,977.3	4,965.7	4,964.2	4,972.8	4,992.4	5,009.5	5,000.1	4,934.3
2012	4,870.3	4,893.4	4,946.3	4,986.6	5,021.5	5,036.3	5,014.3	5,013.5	5,018.6	5,036.0	5,049.0	5,036.8	4,993.6
2013	4,897.6	4,922.7	4,960.9	5,003.1	5,040.8	5,060.8	5,044.8	5,045.3	5,047.9	5,065.8	5,081.2	5,067.4	5,019.9
2014	4,936.2	4,941.3	4,988.5	5,057.0	5,106.0	5,119.0	5,101.4	5,107.6	5,112.5	5,144.3	5,159.2	5,155.2	5,077.4
2015	5,009.0	5,017.2	5,040.7	5,110.3	5,159.7	5,170.9	5,158.1	5,155.3	5,158.9	5,192.8	5,203.5	5,197.4	5,131.2
2016	5,058.5	5,070.8	5,110.2	5,176.2	5,201.6	5,200.0	5,206.2	5,200.5	5,217.3	5,237.5	5,248.9	5,237.7	5,180.5
2017	5,114.9	5,133.3	5,153.6	5,225.7	5,264.7	5,269.3	5,261.6	5,261.8	5,276.7	5,306.7	5,318.5	5,323.1	5,242.5
Goods Producing													
2007	921.6	906.3	922.3	936.3	948.6	962.4	962.3	961.6	955.0	953.3	945.3	932.7	942.3
2008	909.8	901.6	909.1	922.8	934.5	942.9	940.6	939.1	929.7	921.8	905.2	885.3	920.2
2009	844.3	827.6	822.3	823.9	824.8	827.5	823.2	820.6	815.5	814.6	806.2	793.0	820.3
2010	765.9	758.3	772.8	796.2	806.9	817.8	822.4	822.5	818.2	817.7	815.1	803.6	801.5
2011	780.4	777.7	792.2	810.4	822.5	834.6	841.1	842.7	839.0	839.6	836.5	826.5	820.3
2012	804.8	804.5	814.9	825.1	832.0	844.2	844.8	844.2	841.0	838.0	829.2	819.1	828.5
2013	797.2	795.9	805.4	818.2	829.2	839.6	841.4	842.5	839.2	837.3	830.6	815.9	824.4
2014	798.3	794.6	807.1	825.9	839.6	850.4	854.4	855.1	850.1	851.1	846.8	836.4	834.2
2015	813.6	808.3	814.3	833.1	845.5	854.8	857.0	855.6	849.1	845.8	838.0	827.3	836.9
2016	803.4	796.1	807.0	820.1	827.6	836.7	839.7	838.1	832.2	832.2	827.5	818.6	823.3
2017	801.2	801.6	809.1	828.8	842.5	854.5	856.6	855.9	850.3	848.7	846.6	842.7	836.5
Service-Providing													
2007	4,758.4	4,785.0	4,820.3	4,857.5	4,889.9	4,891.7	4,823.5	4,815.8	4,864.3	4,908.4	4,930.6	4,933.3	4,856.6
2008	4,803.0	4,831.4	4,852.3	4,904.8	4,928.3	4,913.6	4,843.6	4,838.9	4,890.5	4,924.2	4,918.5	4,910.1	4,879.9
2009	4,757.2	4,777.8	4,782.6	4,811.2	4,836.2	4,814.7	4,745.6	4,729.5	4,783.2	4,831.9	4,845.3	4,840.6	4,796.3
2010	4,706.4	4,725.3	4,768.1	4,826.1	4,870.8	4,855.2	4,783.0	4,778.8	4,832.4	4,885.6	4,907.1	4,908.2	4,820.6
2011	4,774.7	4,809.7	4,838.5	4,889.7	4,907.7	4,894.8	4,813.3	4,805.3	4,874.1	4,908.6	4,935.8	4,932.0	4,865.4
2012	4,795.9	4,843.0	4,886.9	4,916.6	4,942.0	4,915.7	4,842.5	4,843.7	4,907.6	4,942.6	4,968.7	4,962.6	4,897.3
2013	4,822.7	4,868.3	4,896.9	4,927.3	4,955.2	4,931.4	4,864.5	4,868.1	4,926.4	4,959.9	4,988.7	4,985.1	4,916.2
2014	4,850.6	4,874.9	4,910.0	4,962.2	4,991.1	4,975.3	4,903.2	4,910.6	4,974.2	5,018.6	5,041.7	5,043.0	4,954.6
2015	4,895.6	4,928.6	4,946.7	5,002.5	5,032.9	5,014.8	4,954.3	4,956.3	5,017.3	5,064.0	5,088.0	5,086.8	4,999.0
2016	4,951.7	4,990.3	5,021.7	5,075.1	5,086.3	5,056.3	5,021.7	5,017.6	5,096.2	5,124.4	5,145.4	5,138.5	5,060.4
2017	5,010.3	5,048.4	5,062.7	5,116.8	5,136.0	5,107.7	5,062.3	5,065.2	5,136.3	5,174.0	5,193.1	5,195.1	5,109.0
Mining and Logging													
2007	19.9	19.8	20.2	20.8	21.2	21.7	21.9	21.9	21.6	21.5	21.4	21.0	21.1
2008	20.6	20.5	20.9	21.6	22.2	22.8	22.9	23.1	23.1	23.4	23.3	22.5	22.2
2009	21.8	21.5	21.2	21.7	21.9	22.4	22.6	22.6	22.7	22.9	23.1	22.7	22.3
2010	22.4	22.8	23.6	25.3	26.0	26.8	27.5	27.9	28.6	28.9	29.6	29.4	26.6
2011	29.4	30.2	30.8	32.0	32.9	34.0	34.6	35.1	35.5	36.2	37.0	37.3	33.8
2012	36.9	37.7	37.9	37.7	37.8	37.9	37.4	37.0	36.6	36.3	35.9	35.3	37.0
2013	34.7	34.8	35.4	35.8	36.3	36.6	36.6	36.3	36.2	36.5	36.2	36.0	36.0
2014	35.4	35.6	36.0	36.9	37.5	38.0	38.5	38.8	38.8	38.9	39.0	38.9	37.7
2015	38.2	36.8	36.3	35.4	35.1	35.0	34.2	33.1	32.0	31.0	30.1	29.4	33.9
2016	27.3	26.2	25.8	25.1	24.9	24.5	24.3	24.2	24.2	24.2	24.3	24.3	24.9
2017	24.1	24.6	25.1	25.7	26.4	26.9	27.3	27.5	27.6	27.5	27.8	27.6	26.5

1. Employment by Industry: Pennsylvania, Selected Years, 2007–2017—*Continued*

(Numbers in thousands, not seasonally adjusted)

Industry and year	January	February	March	April	May	June	July	August	September	October	November	December	Annual average
Construction													
2007	241.8	232.9	243.9	257.2	267.8	275.8	277.9	278.5	275.8	274.1	266.2	253.6	262.1
2008	238.8	233.7	240.0	254.8	263.9	268.9	269.8	269.3	264.2	260.4	250.0	236.4	254.2
2009	214.9	211.2	215.3	223.9	229.9	233.6	234.7	233.6	230.0	229.2	221.3	209.8	224.0
2010	190.5	184.6	195.4	214.2	221.3	226.4	230.3	230.2	226.9	225.8	222.2	211.0	214.9
2011	193.6	191.3	202.3	216.4	224.7	231.5	236.2	237.1	235.4	236.1	232.3	221.3	221.5
2012	204.7	204.3	212.4	221.6	226.6	233.5	235.1	235.6	236.1	235.1	227.8	218.5	224.3
2013	201.9	201.2	209.2	220.3	228.8	233.8	236.8	238.9	237.7	235.3	228.4	213.7	223.8
2014	201.4	198.3	207.6	225.0	234.8	240.5	244.1	244.5	243.2	243.7	237.9	226.1	228.9
2015	209.3	205.8	211.5	230.0	240.4	246.6	249.5	251.5	249.8	250.3	244.7	234.8	235.4
2016	218.2	213.2	223.3	237.3	243.3	248.4	252.3	251.9	250.3	249.8	245.1	234.6	239.0
2017	221.1	220.9	225.9	243.0	254.7	261.6	263.5	263.6	261.0	259.7	256.9	250.9	248.6
Manufacturing													
2007	659.9	653.6	658.2	658.3	659.0	664.0	662.5	661.2	657.6	657.7	657.7	658.1	659.1
2008	650.4	647.4	648.2	646.4	648.4	651.2	647.9	646.7	642.4	638.0	631.9	626.4	643.8
2009	607.6	594.9	585.8	578.3	573.0	571.5	565.9	564.4	562.8	562.5	561.8	560.5	574.1
2010	553.0	550.9	553.8	556.7	559.6	564.6	564.6	564.4	562.7	563.0	563.3	563.2	560.0
2011	557.4	556.2	559.1	562.0	564.9	569.1	570.3	570.5	568.1	567.3	567.2	567.9	565.0
2012	563.2	562.5	564.6	565.8	567.6	572.8	572.3	571.6	568.3	566.6	565.5	565.3	567.2
2013	560.6	559.9	560.8	562.1	564.1	569.7	568.0	567.3	565.3	565.5	566.0	566.2	564.6
2014	561.5	560.7	563.5	564.0	567.3	571.9	571.8	571.8	568.1	568.5	569.9	571.4	567.5
2015	566.1	565.7	566.5	567.7	570.0	573.2	573.3	571.0	567.3	564.5	563.2	563.1	567.6
2016	557.9	556.7	557.9	557.7	559.4	563.8	563.1	562.0	557.7	558.2	558.1	559.7	559.4
2017	556.0	556.1	558.1	560.1	561.4	566.0	565.8	564.8	561.7	561.5	561.9	564.2	561.5
Trade, Transportation, and Utilities													
2007	1,128.0	1,108.0	1,116.4	1,120.3	1,131.6	1,134.6	1,123.9	1,121.1	1,124.8	1,134.3	1,159.2	1,171.6	1,131.2
2008	1,130.6	1,111.3	1,115.4	1,119.0	1,127.8	1,127.3	1,114.6	1,112.4	1,116.4	1,123.6	1,133.2	1,143.4	1,122.9
2009	1,090.4	1,074.2	1,069.6	1,069.1	1,079.8	1,079.1	1,062.9	1,061.8	1,068.4	1,078.8	1,097.0	1,107.3	1,078.2
2010	1,065.8	1,047.6	1,057.7	1,064.6	1,076.8	1,081.5	1,068.6	1,069.9	1,074.9	1,088.0	1,107.2	1,122.6	1,077.1
2011	1,080.5	1,069.7	1,072.9	1,082.1	1,089.6	1,089.4	1,078.5	1,079.2	1,085.9	1,095.1	1,117.2	1,130.0	1,089.2
2012	1,088.1	1,076.7	1,085.5	1,088.4	1,097.9	1,097.6	1,086.9	1,087.8	1,093.5	1,103.3	1,129.6	1,138.3	1,097.8
2013	1,092.7	1,082.2	1,086.6	1,089.7	1,098.3	1,100.2	1,087.1	1,090.6	1,094.8	1,104.0	1,127.7	1,139.7	1,099.5
2014	1,095.6	1,082.5	1,089.6	1,096.9	1,108.5	1,113.2	1,098.4	1,102.0	1,108.5	1,120.2	1,143.4	1,158.1	1,109.7
2015	1,112.2	1,098.5	1,102.7	1,109.7	1,121.8	1,126.0	1,113.2	1,114.4	1,118.9	1,128.6	1,151.2	1,165.4	1,121.9
2016	1,119.8	1,108.3	1,112.5	1,118.0	1,126.8	1,125.0	1,117.4	1,117.3	1,123.2	1,131.9	1,155.1	1,169.8	1,127.1
2017	1,126.4	1,112.1	1,110.0	1,117.7	1,123.6	1,122.9	1,113.5	1,115.0	1,123.7	1,132.7	1,151.5	1,166.7	1,126.3
Wholesale Trade													
2007	236.5	235.6	237.2	238.3	239.3	241.2	241.5	240.7	239.2	239.7	240.6	240.8	239.2
2008	237.8	237.7	238.4	239.3	240.5	241.2	241.2	240.3	238.1	237.7	235.6	234.5	238.5
2009	230.0	228.0	227.1	226.3	226.7	226.8	225.5	224.7	223.0	223.1	222.6	222.7	225.5
2010	219.5	210.3	210.7	221.0	222.6	222.7	224.0	224.2	222.6	223.5	223.3	223.5	222.2
2011	221.3	221.2	222.2	223.7	224.5	225.0	225.0	224.7	223.4	223.6	223.3	223.4	223.4
2012	220.8	221.0	222.4	222.9	223.9	225.4	224.4	223.9	222.7	222.5	222.2	222.9	222.9
2013	220.1	220.2	221.3	221.8	222.8	223.6	223.2	223.1	222.3	221.7	221.9	222.4	222.0
2014	219.8	219.6	220.3	221.2	222.9	224.7	225.0	225.1	223.7	224.4	224.9	225.4	223.1
2015	222.8	222.5	222.9	223.5	224.5	225.1	225.2	224.8	222.5	222.4	221.9	221.6	223.3
2016	218.9	218.1	218.2	219.1	219.9	220.1	220.6	220.0	218.4	218.4	218.4	218.6	219.1
2017	216.8	216.7	217.0	217.8	219.1	220.4	220.6	220.2	219.1	219.1	220.3	220.4	219.0
Retail Trade													
2007	651.7	633.7	638.7	640.5	649.0	651.5	650.9	649.0	642.3	651.3	673.8	683.5	651.3
2008	652.3	633.9	637.2	638.1	644.2	645.5	642.5	641.1	634.8	641.8	653.3	662.8	644.0
2009	623.7	611.2	608.8	609.2	618.8	620.9	617.5	617.5	612.2	620.7	638.2	645.7	620.4
2010	616.1	600.1	607.3	611.5	619.8	623.6	621.4	621.9	614.4	624.9	642.7	653.1	621.4
2011	621.3	610.3	611.6	617.9	623.2	624.8	623.6	625.3	618.6	626.7	646.7	655.7	625.5
2012	625.5	613.2	618.8	621.0	627.9	630.6	629.3	630.7	623.6	632.1	656.7	660.7	630.8
2013	626.5	616.2	618.3	620.7	626.8	631.4	629.2	630.7	623.1	631.4	651.7	660.0	630.5
2014	626.0	614.0	618.4	623.2	630.5	635.1	631.5	633.2	625.9	633.9	653.3	662.1	632.3
2015	628.4	616.4	618.9	623.2	631.9	636.9	634.4	634.5	626.3	633.9	652.9	659.6	633.1
2016	628.7	619.4	622.2	626.4	632.4	635.1	635.4	635.2	625.5	631.9	649.3	656.1	633.1
2017	628.7	616.6	614.8	620.3	622.2	625.7	624.1	623.7	616.6	622.7	636.0	642.2	624.5

1. Employment by Industry: Pennsylvania, Selected Years, 2007–2017—*Continued*

(Numbers in thousands, not seasonally adjusted)

Industry and year	January	February	March	April	May	June	July	August	September	October	November	December	Annual average
Transportation and Utilities													
2007	239.8	238.7	240.5	241.5	243.3	241.9	231.5	231.4	243.3	243.3	244.8	247.3	240.6
2008	240.5	239.7	239.8	241.6	243.1	240.6	230.9	231.0	243.5	244.1	244.3	246.1	240.4
2009	236.7	235.0	233.7	233.6	234.3	231.4	219.9	219.6	233.2	235.0	236.2	238.9	232.3
2010	230.2	229.2	230.7	232.1	234.4	234.2	223.2	223.8	237.9	239.6	241.2	246.0	233.5
2011	237.9	238.2	239.1	240.5	241.9	239.6	229.9	229.2	243.9	244.8	247.2	250.9	240.3
2012	241.8	242.5	244.3	244.5	246.1	241.6	233.2	233.2	247.2	248.7	250.7	254.7	244.0
2013	246.1	245.8	247.0	247.2	248.7	245.2	234.7	236.8	249.4	250.9	254.1	257.3	246.9
2014	249.8	248.9	250.9	252.5	255.1	253.4	241.9	243.7	258.9	261.9	265.2	270.6	254.4
2015	261.0	259.6	260.9	263.0	265.4	269.8	253.6	255.1	270.1	272.3	276.4	284.2	265.5
2016	272.2	270.8	272.1	272.5	274.5	269.8	261.4	262.1	279.3	281.6	287.4	295.1	274.9
2017	280.9	278.8	278.2	279.6	282.3	276.8	268.8	271.1	288.0	290.9	295.2	304.1	282.9
Information													
2007	106.8	106.5	106.4	106.6	107.3	109.0	108.1	108.0	108.1	107.0	107.6	108.9	107.5
2008	107.2	106.8	106.5	108.1	108.3	107.8	106.2	105.3	103.9	103.7	103.4	103.2	105.9
2009	101.6	101.0	100.8	100.5	100.3	100.4	99.8	98.7	97.9	98.5	97.8	98.2	99.6
2010	94.1	93.3	93.3	93.3	93.6	94.7	94.7	93.6	93.3	91.5	91.8	92.0	93.3
2011	90.6	90.6	90.7	91.4	92.0	92.5	92.1	87.6	91.2	91.7	92.5	90.6	91.1
2012	89.9	89.4	90.4	89.9	91.1	90.9	90.8	91.2	90.2	89.7	90.6	89.9	90.3
2013	88.8	88.4	88.3	87.8	88.0	88.0	88.1	87.7	86.5	87.7	87.0	87.1	87.8
2014	85.0	84.8	85.0	85.9	85.6	86.0	86.2	85.8	85.1	84.9	85.0	85.6	85.4
2015	83.6	83.9	84.4	84.3	85.0	85.9	85.9	86.3	85.2	84.9	84.7	85.1	84.9
2016	83.6	83.6	83.8	84.6	81.1	86.0	86.2	86.0	84.6	84.8	84.4	84.1	84.4
2017	83.0	83.5	82.8	83.2	83.9	85.0	84.1	84.3	82.2	81.0	81.2	82.1	83.0
Financial Activities													
2007	330.4	330.4	330.6	331.0	332.3	335.9	337.2	336.4	332.5	331.8	332.3	332.3	332.8
2008	328.2	328.7	329.3	329.9	331.1	333.7	334.2	333.6	328.5	327.0	326.5	326.6	329.8
2009	321.5	320.4	319.9	319.3	319.9	321.3	321.0	319.0	315.4	314.8	314.1	314.0	318.4
2010	311.4	310.2	310.8	310.5	311.9	313.2	313.0	312.5	308.8	309.5	309.5	310.0	310.9
2011	308.1	307.0	307.2	307.4	308.3	310.5	311.1	311.1	308.2	307.9	308.1	308.7	308.6
2012	306.7	306.7	307.4	307.3	309.0	312.2	312.6	312.4	309.5	309.4	310.0	310.5	309.5
2013	308.7	309.5	309.9	311.1	312.5	315.8	316.6	316.9	313.5	313.9	314.5	315.1	313.2
2014	312.6	312.9	313.3	313.3	315.3	318.0	318.7	318.6	315.0	314.9	315.1	316.1	315.3
2015	312.8	313.5	313.5	314.0	316.1	319.2	320.0	320.0	316.2	316.2	316.4	316.7	316.2
2016	314.4	314.3	314.2	314.9	316.3	319.4	320.4	320.6	317.7	317.4	317.8	318.8	317.2
2017	316.5	317.7	318.3	318.6	320.6	324.2	324.9	324.7	321.8	321.1	322.4	323.3	321.2
Professional and Business Services													
2007	679.9	681.6	688.1	701.8	706.3	716.3	715.2	717.4	713.7	715.8	716.8	715.8	705.7
2008	695.7	695.5	699.7	713.3	714.8	719.0	720.0	721.0	713.8	713.1	706.8	699.5	709.4
2009	675.9	671.1	669.7	674.4	673.5	675.8	672.8	674.3	670.5	679.5	680.9	679.3	674.8
2010	661.4	662.9	669.3	686.8	689.0	694.8	696.0	698.7	696.4	705.3	709.1	709.0	689.9
2011	690.8	692.7	699.1	714.2	717.4	722.6	721.6	724.9	725.7	730.2	732.6	729.5	716.8
2012	709.5	712.3	721.2	731.8	734.7	739.6	737.6	739.0	738.5	744.5	746.2	742.5	733.1
2013	723.1	729.3	736.3	746.2	749.3	755.5	755.9	757.7	752.0	757.1	760.2	753.8	748.0
2014	734.5	736.8	742.9	758.4	763.7	767.2	765.9	769.5	766.9	774.2	781.1	777.7	761.6
2015	755.4	757.1	759.3	774.1	779.3	782.3	783.2	783.4	782.3	797.1	801.7	799.0	779.5
2016	773.1	773.5	778.9	794.7	794.8	794.9	797.9	795.9	800.7	806.7	807.7	803.1	793.5
2017	783.0	781.2	784.5	798.9	803.2	803.6	803.1	803.7	807.2	814.8	814.2	809.6	800.6
Education and Health Services													
2007	1,045.8	1,069.6	1,074.9	1,076.2	1,068.5	1,050.5	1,048.0	1,045.6	1,070.0	1,093.4	1,094.8	1,089.9	1,068.9
2008	1,068.0	1,096.6	1,096.6	1,103.8	1,093.6	1,074.4	1,073.4	1,072.4	1,097.0	1,118.4	1,122.7	1,119.8	1,094.7
2009	1,097.9	1,121.6	1,120.4	1,123.6	1,114.1	1,094.0	1,092.7	1,086.4	1,108.2	1,130.8	1,135.4	1,129.6	1,112.9
2010	1,107.9	1,128.8	1,132.2	1,136.0	1,129.7	1,108.6	1,106.3	1,102.5	1,126.9	1,151.5	1,154.1	1,149.6	1,127.8
2011	1,123.3	1,150.7	1,153.0	1,154.1	1,146.0	1,125.8	1,118.8	1,115.7	1,145.4	1,163.4	1,168.6	1,163.6	1,144.0
2012	1,138.3	1,167.4	1,173.0	1,172.1	1,160.0	1,134.0	1,126.0	1,120.8	1,156.8	1,175.5	1,179.0	1,172.1	1,156.3
2013	1,145.9	1,175.2	1,177.2	1,175.7	1,160.3	1,138.4	1,131.6	1,126.7	1,165.7	1,182.8	1,191.0	1,181.8	1,162.7
2014	1,159.3	1,181.6	1,186.8	1,195.4	1,181.2	1,156.5	1,151.0	1,146.2	1,185.7	1,204.9	1,210.4	1,201.2	1,180.0
2015	1,174.6	1,198.4	1,197.9	1,206.1	1,191.7	1,165.4	1,161.6	1,155.8	1,194.0	1,215.8	1,220.6	1,213.3	1,191.3
2016	1,193.2	1,220.4	1,223.0	1,232.8	1,218.9	1,186.5	1,187.6	1,184.5	1,228.7	1,244.3	1,249.4	1,241.4	1,217.6
2017	1,219.5	1,249.6	1,250.8	1,256.9	1,245.3	1,213.5	1,213.2	1,210.0	1,255.8	1,277.7	1,287.9	1,282.4	1,246.9

1. Employment by Industry: Pennsylvania, Selected Years, 2007–2017—*Continued*

(Numbers in thousands, not seasonally adjusted)

Industry and year	January	February	March	April	May	June	July	August	September	October	November	December	Annual average
Leisure and Hospitality													
2007	463.0	464.8	474.9	490.6	515.5	533.5	532.3	533.6	510.5	501.2	489.6	489.4	499.9
2008	468.5	469.5	478.2	498.6	525.8	537.7	538.8	536.7	513.5	501.7	485.9	485.0	503.3
2009	461.4	460.2	469.5	484.8	515.9	525.6	528.7	529.7	506.9	493.4	478.5	477.0	494.3
2010	459.4	456.1	469.6	492.9	516.8	529.2	535.1	538.7	517.5	505.2	494.7	491.9	500.6
2011	471.4	471.2	484.4	506.7	529.9	544.3	544.8	546.4	524.5	511.6	501.4	498.2	511.2
2012	482.6	485.4	500.5	518.0	541.2	558.6	557.2	561.2	535.9	523.1	512.8	512.9	524.1
2013	492.7	493.6	507.3	523.4	549.8	565.9	568.3	567.7	544.1	531.7	518.8	522.6	532.2
2014	501.8	499.2	511.9	529.6	557.7	569.7	568.9	573.0	547.9	540.7	524.3	526.7	537.6
2015	506.2	506.3	515.5	535.8	564.3	577.9	577.9	581.4	558.9	549.4	535.9	534.4	545.3
2016	516.9	519.6	533.3	552.1	575.3	587.5	592.3	594.2	569.8	558.5	546.4	542.6	557.4
2017	528.0	530.3	539.5	561.5	583.0	599.7	600.7	603.4	576.0	569.9	554.0	553.7	566.6
Other Services													
2007	252.5	252.8	254.4	255.0	257.1	259.8	260.4	258.3	254.9	254.6	254.7	254.3	255.8
2008	251.3	250.9	251.2	253.8	255.7	258.3	258.8	257.3	254.8	254.0	253.0	252.2	254.3
2009	247.9	248.0	249.2	249.1	251.7	254.0	254.0	252.1	248.0	248.3	247.9	248.2	249.9
2010	245.9	244.7	247.4	248.6	251.1	253.9	254.6	254.2	250.6	251.1	251.2	250.8	250.3
2011	247.8	248.5	250.2	252.5	253.9	257.6	257.7	256.6	252.9	252.9	252.6	253.0	253.0
2012	250.4	251.0	253.4	254.0	255.6	259.2	258.4	256.9	253.2	252.5	251.6	251.5	254.0
2013	248.5	248.6	249.9	251.0	253.4	257.4	255.8	255.5	252.1	251.3	251.4	251.4	252.2
2014	249.1	248.9	251.9	251.6	254.4	258.0	257.9	257.4	253.3	253.4	253.1	253.4	253.5
2015	250.6	251.2	253.1	253.2	256.0	259.4	259.3	258.4	254.3	255.0	255.0	256.2	255.1
2016	254.1	255.0	257.5	259.0	260.8	264.0	264.7	263.9	260.4	261.7	260.6	259.3	260.1
2017	257.3	257.3	258.6	260.1	262.6	265.9	265.5	264.8	259.7	260.8	260.7	262.6	261.3
Government													
2007	752.0	771.3	774.6	775.4	771.3	752.1	698.4	695.4	749.8	770.3	775.6	771.1	754.8
2008	753.5	772.1	775.4	778.3	771.2	755.4	697.6	700.2	762.6	782.7	787.0	780.4	759.7
2009	760.6	781.3	783.5	790.4	781.0	764.5	713.7	707.5	767.9	787.8	793.7	787.0	768.2
2010	760.5	781.7	787.8	793.4	801.9	779.3	714.7	708.7	764.0	783.5	789.5	782.3	770.6
2011	762.2	779.3	781.0	781.3	770.6	752.1	688.7	683.8	740.3	755.8	762.8	758.4	751.4
2012	730.4	754.1	755.5	755.1	752.5	723.6	673.0	674.4	730.0	744.6	748.9	744.9	732.3
2013	722.3	741.5	741.4	742.4	743.6	710.2	661.1	665.3	717.7	731.4	738.1	733.6	720.7
2014	712.7	728.2	728.6	731.1	724.7	706.7	656.2	658.1	711.8	725.4	729.3	724.2	711.4
2015	700.2	719.7	720.3	725.3	718.7	698.7	653.2	656.6	707.5	717.0	722.5	716.7	704.7
2016	696.6	715.6	718.5	719.0	712.3	693.0	655.2	655.2	711.1	719.1	724.0	719.4	703.3
2017	696.6	716.7	718.2	719.9	713.8	692.9	657.3	659.3	709.9	716.0	721.2	714.7	703.0

2. Average Weekly Hours by Selected Industry: Pennsylvania, 2013–2017

(Not seasonally adjusted)

Industry and year	January	February	March	April	May	June	July	August	September	October	November	December	Annual average
Total Private													
2013	32.9	33.1	33.2	33.3	33.3	33.6	33.6	33.6	33.9	33.6	33.8	33.6	33.5
2014	33.1	33.1	33.8	33.7	33.8	34.0	33.9	33.8	33.8	33.8	34.2	33.8	33.7
2015	33.4	33.7	33.8	33.8	34.0	34.1	34.0	34.3	33.8	34.1	34.3	34.2	34.0
2016	33.7	33.6	33.6	33.7	33.9	33.8	33.8	33.8	33.8	34.1	33.8	33.8	33.8
2017	33.7	33.5	33.1	33.9	33.8	33.9	34.0	33.9	34.1	34.1	34.1	33.9	33.8
Goods-Producing													
2013	38.5	38.7	39.1	39.2	39.2	39.2	39.2	39.3	39.5	39.3	39.5	39.0	39.1
2014	39.0	38.0	39.6	39.6	39.7	40.1	39.7	39.5	39.8	39.9	40.0	39.3	39.5
2015	38.8	39.3	39.6	39.9	40.2	40.7	40.3	40.3	39.6	40.5	40.1	40.3	40.0
2016	39.6	39.0	39.5	39.7	39.9	40.1	39.8	40.2	40.0	40.3	40.3	40.0	39.9
2017	40.1	39.5	38.5	39.6	40.3	40.4	40.0	39.9	40.4	40.1	40.6	40.1	40.0
Construction													
2013	37.4	37.5	38.2	39.1	38.9	38.2	38.7	38.9	39.4	38.6	39.3	37.9	38.5
2014	37.8	37.7	38.8	39.4	39.7	40.2	39.7	38.5	39.6	39.3	39.8	38.0	39.1
2015	37.3	38.3	39.4	40.6	41.7	42.5	42.2	42.0	39.6	41.0	39.4	39.5	40.4
2016	38.5	37.5	39.4	39.5	40.0	40.2	40.2	39.9	40.1	40.7	40.0	38.7	39.6
2017	38.4	37.5	36.5	38.5	39.3	40.1	39.3	39.0	39.4	38.4	38.9	37.9	38.6
Manufacturing													
2013	39.4	39.5	39.6	39.4	39.5	39.7	39.5	39.6	39.7	39.8	39.8	39.7	39.6
2014	39.6	38.3	40.0	39.8	39.8	40.1	39.8	40.1	40.0	40.3	40.3	40.2	39.9
2015	39.7	39.9	39.9	39.8	39.7	40.0	39.6	39.7	39.7	40.0	40.2	40.4	39.9
2016	39.8	39.4	39.5	39.8	39.9	40.0	39.5	40.3	40.0	40.2	40.6	40.8	40.0
2017	41.0	40.7	39.6	40.3	40.9	40.7	40.3	40.4	41.0	40.9	41.3	41.1	40.7
Trade, Transportation, and Utilities													
2013	32.7	33.1	33.4	33.5	33.6	33.7	34.0	34.1	34.3	33.8	34.0	33.8	33.7
2014	33.3	32.8	33.8	33.8	34.0	34.0	34.2	34.1	34.3	34.0	34.3	34.3	33.9
2015	33.5	33.7	33.8	33.8	34.3	34.3	34.2	34.5	34.4	34.2	34.5	34.8	34.2
2016	33.9	34.0	33.9	33.9	34.1	34.1	34.1	34.2	34.5	34.4	34.1	34.7	34.2
2017	34.0	33.7	33.4	34.5	34.4	34.5	34.9	34.8	35.0	34.7	35.0	35.0	34.5
Information													
2013	31.5	30.8	31.7	31.4	31.7	32.6	32.3	32.6	33.3	32.9	34.3	32.2	32.3
2014	30.7	32.9	31.7	30.3	31.3	33.3	32.2	32.3	32.2	32.0	33.5	32.5	32.1
2015	32.4	34.4	34.0	33.5	33.5	33.1	33.5	34.0	33.0	33.6	33.5	32.6	33.4
2016	32.9	32.7	32.2	32.6	32.5	32.2	32.5	32.1	32.2	32.1	32.1	31.5	32.3
2017	30.9	31.7	31.3	32.0	30.7	30.6	31.5	30.9	30.6	30.9	30.6	30.7	31.0
Financial Activities													
2013	36.2	36.7	37.0	36.9	36.6	37.1	36.4	36.4	37.0	36.5	36.5	37.0	36.7
2014	36.2	36.8	36.9	36.8	36.8	37.1	36.6	36.6	36.8	36.9	37.4	36.8	36.8
2015	37.1	37.5	37.7	37.3	37.3	37.2	36.8	37.5	36.9	36.9	37.6	36.9	37.2
2016	37.0	37.0	37.0	37.2	37.4	36.9	37.3	37.3	37.2	37.5	37.5	37.3	37.2
2017	37.9	37.5	37.2	38.0	37.6	37.2	37.6	37.1	37.0	37.7	37.1	36.9	37.4
Professional and Business Services													
2013	35.8	35.8	35.9	36.1	36.1	36.7	36.3	36.2	36.9	36.3	36.4	36.5	36.3
2014	35.5	36.1	36.5	36.3	36.3	36.5	35.7	35.6	35.4	35.6	36.4	35.7	36.0
2015	34.9	35.5	35.7	35.5	35.8	35.8	35.8	36.4	35.2	35.9	36.5	36.0	35.8
2016	35.7	35.4	35.6	35.6	36.3	35.8	35.8	35.7	35.5	36.6	35.8	35.6	35.8
2017	35.4	35.3	34.8	36.0	35.6	35.5	36.0	35.6	35.8	36.1	35.5	35.4	35.6
Education and Health Services													
2013	31.4	31.6	31.4	31.5	31.5	31.9	31.8	31.7	32.1	31.9	32.1	32.1	31.8
2014	31.9	31.8	32.3	32.2	32.2	32.5	32.5	32.4	32.3	32.4	32.8	32.5	32.3
2015	32.7	32.5	32.6	32.5	32.6	32.5	32.7	32.7	32.6	32.6	33.0	32.9	32.7
2016	32.9	32.6	32.6	32.6	32.7	32.7	32.7	32.5	32.7	32.6	32.4	32.5	32.6
2017	32.5	32.2	32.1	32.4	32.5	32.5	32.4	32.4	32.6	32.5	32.4	32.4	32.4
Leisure and Hospitality													
2013	23.6	24.3	24.3	24.4	24.6	25.0	25.2	25.3	25.0	24.9	25.0	24.4	24.7
2014	24.0	24.4	24.9	25.0	25.3	25.3	25.5	25.4	24.8	25.0	24.9	24.6	24.9
2015	24.2	24.6	24.6	24.9	25.1	25.1	25.0	25.6	24.7	25.1	24.8	24.6	24.9
2016	23.3	24.3	24.2	24.3	24.6	24.6	24.7	24.7	24.4	24.6	24.3	23.9	24.3
2017	24.1	24.3	24.0	24.8	24.6	24.9	24.9	24.9	24.7	25.1	25.0	25.0	24.7
Other Services													
2013	28.5	28.6	28.2	28.5	28.0	28.4	28.6	28.8	29.0	28.6	28.4	28.3	28.5
2014	27.9	28.2	29.0	28.8	28.6	28.8	29.4	29.6	29.2	29.1	29.7	29.1	29.0
2015	29.4	29.3	29.4	29.1	29.2	29.1	29.9	30.3	30.0	30.0	30.1	29.6	29.6
2016	29.4	29.3	29.1	28.7	29.4	29.1	28.8	29.4	28.7	28.8	28.5	28.3	29.0
2017	28.6	28.4	28.1	29.4	28.5	28.7	29.6	29.0	29.0	28.8	29.0	28.9	28.8

3. Average Hourly Earnings by Selected Industry: Pennsylvania, 2013–2017

(Dollars, not seasonally adjusted)

Industry and year	January	February	March	April	May	June	July	August	September	October	November	December	Annual average
Total Private													
2013	23.11	23.18	23.19	23.24	23.15	23.21	23.12	23.15	23.43	23.36	23.45	23.73	23.28
2014	23.79	24.10	23.87	23.75	23.57	23.72	23.55	23.55	23.67	23.58	23.80	23.75	23.72
2015	23.94	24.09	24.22	24.10	24.04	24.07	24.12	24.26	24.36	24.34	24.58	24.41	24.21
2016	24.67	24.57	24.48	24.50	24.50	24.40	24.60	24.53	24.77	25.03	24.94	25.01	24.67
2017	25.18	25.02	25.06	25.20	24.85	24.85	24.97	24.89	25.15	25.34	25.14	25.44	25.09
Goods-Producing													
2013	24.86	25.07	25.09	25.12	25.18	25.10	25.18	25.19	25.28	25.26	25.22	25.48	25.17
2014	25.23	25.70	25.40	25.40	25.04	25.17	25.12	25.21	25.20	25.13	25.31	25.33	25.27
2015	25.26	25.21	25.41	25.38	25.67	25.72	25.89	25.99	25.92	25.95	25.86	25.56	25.66
2016	25.60	25.60	25.61	25.64	25.79	26.07	26.57	26.39	26.52	26.71	26.47	26.67	26.14
2017	26.70	26.61	26.78	27.09	26.70	26.93	26.92	26.95	27.08	27.00	26.78	27.22	26.90
Construction													
2013	27.08	27.32	27.37	27.41	27.30	27.27	27.77	27.65	27.84	28.16	27.56	28.11	27.58
2014	27.81	28.48	28.10	27.86	27.24	27.54	27.84	28.28	28.14	27.99	28.30	28.87	28.03
2015	28.83	29.09	29.14	28.76	29.32	28.91	29.20	29.31	29.33	29.52	29.52	29.72	29.23
2016	29.73	30.11	29.80	29.56	29.79	29.99	30.68	30.27	29.88	30.20	29.48	30.03	29.97
2017	29.99	30.18	30.44	30.01	30.04	30.72	30.01	29.89	30.07	29.89	29.60	30.15	30.08
Manufacturing													
2013	23.96	24.20	24.16	24.13	24.20	24.09	23.88	23.97	24.04	23.87	24.10	24.34	24.08
2014	24.15	24.57	24.29	24.31	24.01	24.05	23.81	23.83	23.88	23.88	23.98	23.92	24.05
2015	23.92	23.76	23.91	23.89	23.96	24.03	24.12	24.19	24.23	24.13	24.12	24.03	24.02
2016	24.21	24.09	24.03	24.08	24.14	24.38	24.65	24.47	24.86	24.98	25.02	25.17	24.51
2017	25.27	25.14	25.25	25.72	25.25	25.24	25.57	25.63	25.76	25.76	25.60	26.01	25.52
Trade, Transportation, and Utilities													
2013	19.78	19.86	20.03	20.23	20.21	20.23	20.19	20.19	20.37	20.10	20.13	20.18	20.13
2014	20.54	20.78	20.36	20.33	20.14	20.47	20.40	20.45	20.47	20.38	20.47	20.36	20.43
2015	20.88	20.78	21.36	21.41	21.21	21.09	21.04	21.13	21.11	21.05	21.04	20.75	21.07
2016	21.43	21.43	21.07	21.08	20.99	20.97	21.09	20.94	21.09	21.33	21.20	20.81	21.12
2017	21.31	21.25	21.35	21.49	21.09	21.40	21.35	21.21	21.45	21.62	21.41	21.74	21.39
Information													
2013	23.80	24.12	24.71	25.01	24.96	25.89	26.11	26.30	26.94	27.35	28.16	27.54	25.93
2014	27.33	27.71	28.60	28.28	27.81	28.58	28.06	27.40	28.35	28.21	29.29	29.89	28.22
2015	28.60	29.72	29.85	29.47	29.65	29.69	29.58	29.47	29.29	29.81	30.21	29.89	29.61
2016	29.75	29.68	29.59	30.36	30.12	30.54	30.53	30.46	30.74	31.10	31.21	31.99	30.50
2017	31.70	31.27	31.10	32.27	31.66	30.80	31.20	31.56	32.15	32.14	32.48	32.77	31.75
Financial Activities													
2013	30.20	30.24	30.12	30.54	30.37	30.55	30.50	30.50	30.48	30.20	30.61	30.88	30.43
2014	31.17	31.27	31.14	30.96	30.79	30.93	30.79	30.73	30.99	30.90	31.50	31.33	31.04
2015	31.38	31.86	31.62	31.74	31.50	31.44	31.35	32.25	31.99	32.06	32.79	33.51	31.96
2016	33.01	33.12	32.53	33.42	34.03	33.43	33.68	34.40	34.84	35.31	34.91	35.19	34.08
2017	34.95	34.54	34.42	34.16	33.36	33.00	33.43	33.03	33.25	33.86	33.41	34.23	33.80
Professional and Business Services													
2013	28.83	29.15	28.98	28.77	28.75	29.12	28.49	28.64	29.06	28.89	29.10	29.82	28.97
2014	29.79	30.64	30.66	30.18	30.13	30.44	29.99	30.06	29.99	29.45	29.96	30.26	30.13
2015	30.72	31.16	31.11	30.50	30.53	30.81	30.92	31.13	31.31	31.25	31.92	31.49	31.08
2016	32.11	31.98	31.91	31.84	31.88	31.73	31.79	31.76	31.94	32.30	32.17	32.65	32.01
2017	33.00	32.45	32.56	32.47	31.91	31.79	32.14	31.93	32.25	32.46	32.18	32.54	32.30
Education and Health Services													
2013	22.20	22.06	22.01	22.08	21.90	21.91	22.12	22.13	22.32	22.35	22.34	22.52	22.16
2014	22.58	22.46	22.25	22.37	22.46	22.38	22.44	22.35	22.50	22.54	22.51	22.41	22.44
2015	22.40	22.58	22.48	22.48	22.46	22.57	22.73	22.81	23.15	22.84	23.11	23.10	22.73
2016	23.03	22.90	22.77	22.93	22.83	22.69	22.88	22.74	22.98	23.02	23.10	23.14	22.92
2017	23.11	23.13	23.00	23.28	23.16	23.19	23.45	23.39	23.61	23.78	23.72	23.84	23.39
Leisure and Hospitality													
2013	13.56	13.53	13.63	13.60	13.61	13.50	13.46	13.56	14.06	14.24	14.37	14.85	13.83
2014	14.64	14.71	14.59	14.47	14.34	14.19	14.03	13.98	14.16	14.19	14.16	14.07	14.28
2015	13.92	13.92	13.82	13.91	13.75	13.66	13.47	13.44	13.71	13.79	13.87	13.91	13.76
2016	13.81	13.82	13.84	13.83	13.85	13.72	13.71	13.81	14.08	14.24	14.34	14.60	13.97
2017	14.51	14.62	14.69	14.74	14.92	14.56	14.41	14.51	14.87	15.07	15.08	15.21	14.76
Other Services													
2013	20.15	20.19	20.36	20.10	20.13	19.77	19.48	19.36	20.04	20.05	20.18	20.73	20.04
2014	20.88	21.07	21.06	20.53	20.26	20.26	19.74	19.73	20.26	20.53	20.56	20.67	20.45
2015	20.82	20.73	21.19	21.00	20.80	20.56	20.34	20.28	20.65	20.83	20.74	21.11	20.75
2016	21.00	20.93	20.87	20.58	20.40	19.81	19.82	19.56	20.19	20.17	20.40	20.79	20.37
2017	20.73	20.46	20.88	21.00	21.05	20.81	20.45	20.95	21.06	21.54	21.41	21.81	21.01

4. Average Weekly Earnings by Selected Industry: Pennsylvania, 2013–2017

(Dollars, not seasonally adjusted)

Industry and year	January	February	March	April	May	June	July	August	September	October	November	December	Annual average
Total Private													
2013	760.32	767.26	769.91	773.89	770.90	779.86	776.83	777.84	794.28	784.90	792.61	797.33	779.88
2014	787.45	797.71	806.81	800.38	796.67	806.48	798.35	795.99	800.05	797.00	813.96	802.75	799.36
2015	799.60	811.83	818.64	814.58	817.36	820.79	820.08	832.12	823.37	829.99	843.09	834.82	823.14
2016	831.38	825.55	822.53	825.65	830.55	824.72	831.48	829.11	837.23	853.52	842.97	845.34	833.85
2017	848.57	838.17	829.49	854.28	839.93	842.42	848.98	843.77	857.62	864.09	857.27	862.42	848.04
Goods-Producing													
2013	957.11	970.21	981.02	984.70	987.06	983.92	987.06	989.97	998.56	992.72	996.19	993.72	984.15
2014	983.97	976.60	1,005.84	1,005.84	994.09	1,009.32	997.26	995.80	1,002.96	1,002.69	1,012.40	995.47	998.17
2015	980.09	990.75	1,006.24	1,012.66	1,031.93	1,046.80	1,043.37	1,047.40	1,026.43	1,050.98	1,036.99	1,030.07	1,026.40
2016	1,013.76	998.40	1,011.60	1,017.91	1,029.02	1,045.41	1,057.49	1,060.88	1,060.80	1,076.41	1,066.74	1,066.80	1,042.99
2017	1,070.67	1,051.10	1,031.03	1,072.76	1,076.01	1,087.97	1,076.80	1,075.31	1,094.03	1,082.70	1,087.27	1,091.52	1,076.00
Construction													
2013	1,012.79	1,024.50	1,045.53	1,071.73	1,061.97	1,041.71	1,074.70	1,075.59	1,096.90	1,086.98	1,083.11	1,065.37	1,061.83
2014	1,051.22	1,073.70	1,090.28	1,097.68	1,081.43	1,107.11	1,105.25	1,088.78	1,114.34	1,100.01	1,126.34	1,097.06	1,095.97
2015	1,075.36	1,114.15	1,148.12	1,167.66	1,222.64	1,228.68	1,232.24	1,231.02	1,161.47	1,210.32	1,163.09	1,173.94	1,180.89
2016	1,144.61	1,129.13	1,174.12	1,167.62	1,191.60	1,205.60	1,233.34	1,207.77	1,198.19	1,229.14	1,179.20	1,162.16	1,186.81
2017	1,151.62	1,131.75	1,111.06	1,155.39	1,180.57	1,231.87	1,179.39	1,165.71	1,184.76	1,147.78	1,151.44	1,142.69	1,161.09
Manufacturing													
2013	944.02	955.90	956.74	950.72	955.90	956.37	943.26	949.21	954.39	950.03	959.18	966.30	953.57
2014	956.34	941.03	971.60	967.54	955.60	964.41	947.64	955.58	955.20	962.36	966.39	961.58	959.60
2015	949.62	948.02	954.01	950.82	951.21	961.20	955.15	960.34	961.93	965.20	969.62	970.81	958.40
2016	963.56	949.15	949.19	958.38	963.19	975.20	973.68	986.14	994.40	1,004.20	1,015.81	1,026.94	980.40
2017	1,036.07	1,023.20	999.90	1,036.52	1,032.73	1,027.27	1,030.47	1,035.45	1,056.16	1,053.58	1,057.28	1,069.01	1,038.66
Trade, Transportation, and Utilities													
2013	646.81	657.37	669.00	677.71	679.06	681.75	686.46	688.48	698.69	679.38	684.42	682.08	678.38
2014	683.98	681.58	688.17	687.15	684.76	695.98	697.68	697.35	702.12	692.92	702.12	698.35	692.58
2015	699.48	700.29	721.97	723.66	727.50	723.39	719.57	728.99	726.18	719.91	725.88	722.10	720.59
2016	726.48	728.62	714.27	714.61	715.76	715.08	719.17	716.15	727.61	733.75	722.92	722.11	722.30
2017	724.54	716.13	713.09	741.41	725.50	738.30	745.12	738.11	750.75	750.21	749.35	760.90	737.96
Information													
2013	749.70	742.90	783.31	785.31	791.23	844.01	843.35	857.38	897.10	899.82	965.89	886.79	837.54
2014	839.03	911.66	906.62	856.88	870.45	951.71	903.53	885.02	912.87	902.72	981.22	940.88	905.86
2015	926.64	1,022.37	1,014.90	987.25	993.28	982.74	990.93	1,001.98	966.57	1,001.62	1,012.04	974.41	988.97
2016	978.78	970.54	952.80	989.74	978.90	983.39	992.23	977.77	989.83	998.31	1,001.84	1,007.69	985.15
2017	979.53	991.26	973.43	1,032.64	971.96	942.48	982.80	975.20	983.79	993.13	993.89	1,006.04	984.25
Financial Activities													
2013	1,093.24	1,109.81	1,114.44	1,126.93	1,111.54	1,133.41	1,110.20	1,110.20	1,127.76	1,102.30	1,117.27	1,142.56	1,116.78
2014	1,128.35	1,150.74	1,149.07	1,139.33	1,133.07	1,147.50	1,126.91	1,124.72	1,140.43	1,140.21	1,178.10	1,152.94	1,142.27
2015	1,164.20	1,194.75	1,192.07	1,183.90	1,174.95	1,169.57	1,153.68	1,209.38	1,180.43	1,183.01	1,232.90	1,236.52	1,188.91
2016	1,222.48	1,225.81	1,240.61	1,243.22	1,272.72	1,233.57	1,256.26	1,283.12	1,296.05	1,324.13	1,309.13	1,312.59	1,267.78
2017	1,324.61	1,295.25	1,280.42	1,298.08	1,254.34	1,227.60	1,256.97	1,225.41	1,230.25	1,276.52	1,239.51	1,263.09	1,264.12
Professional and Business Services													
2013	1,032.11	1,043.57	1,040.38	1,038.60	1,037.88	1,068.70	1,034.19	1,036.77	1,072.31	1,048.71	1,059.24	1,088.43	1,051.61
2014	1,057.55	1,106.10	1,119.09	1,095.53	1,093.72	1,111.06	1,070.64	1,070.14	1,061.65	1,048.42	1,090.54	1,080.28	1,084.68
2015	1,072.13	1,106.18	1,110.63	1,082.75	1,092.97	1,103.00	1,106.94	1,133.13	1,102.11	1,121.88	1,165.08	1,133.64	1,112.66
2016	1,146.33	1,132.09	1,136.00	1,133.50	1,157.24	1,135.93	1,138.08	1,133.83	1,133.87	1,182.18	1,151.69	1,162.34	1,145.96
2017	1,168.20	1,145.49	1,133.09	1,168.92	1,136.00	1,128.55	1,157.04	1,136.71	1,154.55	1,171.81	1,142.39	1,151.92	1,149.88
Education and Health Services													
2013	697.08	697.10	691.11	695.52	689.85	698.93	703.42	701.52	716.47	712.97	717.11	722.89	704.69
2014	720.30	714.23	718.68	720.31	723.21	727.35	729.30	724.14	726.75	730.30	738.33	728.33	724.81
2015	732.48	733.85	732.85	730.60	732.20	733.53	743.27	745.89	754.69	744.58	762.30	759.99	743.27
2016	757.69	746.54	742.30	747.52	746.54	741.96	748.18	739.05	751.45	750.45	748.44	752.05	747.19
2017	751.08	744.79	738.30	754.27	752.70	753.68	759.78	757.84	769.69	772.85	768.53	772.42	757.84
Leisure and Hospitality													
2013	320.02	328.78	331.21	331.84	334.81	337.50	339.19	343.07	351.50	354.58	359.25	362.34	341.60
2014	351.36	358.92	363.29	361.75	362.80	359.01	357.77	355.09	351.17	354.75	352.58	346.12	355.57
2015	336.86	342.43	339.97	346.36	345.13	342.87	336.75	344.06	338.64	346.13	343.98	342.19	342.62
2016	321.77	335.83	334.93	336.07	340.71	337.51	338.64	341.11	343.55	350.30	348.46	348.94	339.47
2017	349.69	355.27	352.56	365.55	367.03	362.54	358.81	361.30	367.29	378.26	377.00	380.25	364.57
Other Services													
2013	574.28	577.43	574.15	572.85	563.64	561.47	557.13	557.57	581.16	573.43	573.11	586.66	571.14
2014	582.55	594.17	610.74	591.26	579.44	583.49	580.36	584.01	591.59	597.42	610.63	601.50	593.05
2015	612.11	607.39	622.99	611.10	607.36	598.30	608.17	614.48	619.50	624.90	624.27	624.86	614.20
2016	617.40	613.25	607.32	590.65	599.76	576.47	570.82	575.06	579.45	580.90	581.40	588.36	590.73
2017	592.88	581.06	586.73	617.40	599.93	597.25	605.32	607.55	610.74	620.35	620.89	630.31	605.09

RHODE ISLAND
At a Glance

Population:
  2010 census: 1,052,567
  2017 estimate: 1,059,639

Percent change in population:
  2010–2017: 0.7%

Percent change in total nonfarm employment:
  2007–2017: 0.5%

Industry with the largest growth in employment, 2007–2017 (thousands):
  Professional and business services, 11.5

Industry with the largest decline or smallest growth in employment, 2007–2017 (thousands):
  Manufacturing, -10.2

Civilian labor force:
  2010: 566,704
  2017: 554,658

Unemployment rate and rank among states (highest to lowest):
  2010: 11.2%, 4th
  2017: 4.5%, 22nd

Over-the-year change in unemployment rates:
  2015–2016: -0.8%
  2016–2017: -0.7%

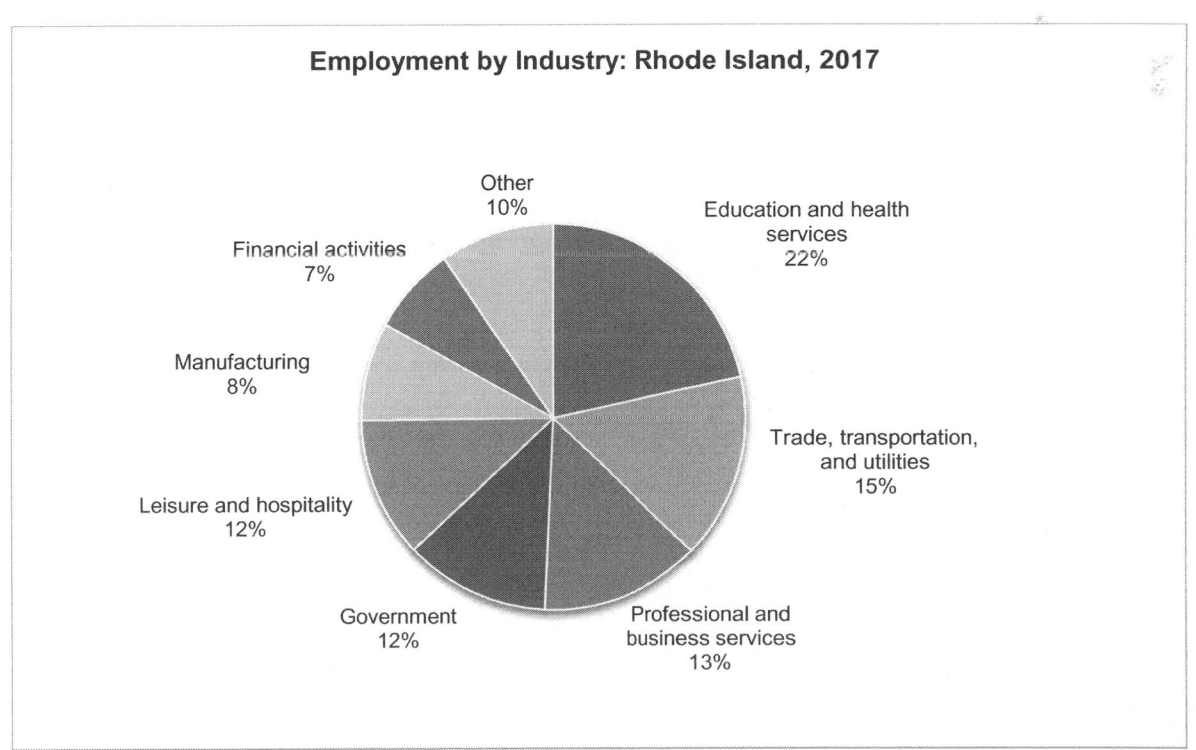

Employment by Industry: Rhode Island, 2017

- Other 10%
- Education and health services 22%
- Financial activities 7%
- Trade, transportation, and utilities 15%
- Manufacturing 8%
- Leisure and hospitality 12%
- Government 12%
- Professional and business services 13%

1. Employment by Industry: Rhode Island, Selected Years, 2007–2017

(Numbers in thousands, not seasonally adjusted)

Industry and year	January	February	March	April	May	June	July	August	September	October	November	December	Annual average
Total Nonfarm													
2007	481.0	482.8	485.2	492.4	498.9	500.7	491.9	492.0	495.3	495.1	494.1	492.5	491.8
2008	473.5	475.5	477.4	484.0	489.2	489.5	479.2	480.2	484.4	482.7	479.9	476.2	481.0
2009	454.3	455.4	454.8	458.8	465.2	465.3	456.2	456.2	461.5	463.2	462.4	460.3	459.5
2010	443.6	445.6	449.1	455.9	463.5	463.7	459.3	460.1	463.9	464.0	464.6	462.3	458.0
2011	444.6	447.8	450.8	460.2	465.8	467.9	461.6	461.2	466.1	467.4	467.3	465.0	460.5
2012	449.0	454.1	457.2	463.3	470.2	472.2	464.3	466.5	472.9	472.2	471.2	471.9	465.4
2013	455.1	457.4	461.3	467.9	475.2	478.9	472.6	473.4	478.3	480.6	479.2	477.1	471.4
2014	460.8	464.1	466.2	476.4	484.1	485.6	480.3	480.1	486.0	486.9	486.9	486.7	478.7
2015	469.9	468.4	472.4	483.3	491.5	492.4	488.0	486.3	491.6	493.7	493.9	493.1	485.4
2016	475.0	478.0	481.8	488.9	493.8	496.5	492.1	490.9	494.4	496.3	495.6	493.6	489.7
2017	477.5	481.1	482.9	491.0	497.7	502.4	496.4	496.6	499.5	502.6	502.4	499.0	494.1
Total Private													
2007	415.8	417.4	419.9	427.1	432.9	435.8	430.4	430.8	431.4	430.4	429.3	427.5	427.4
2008	408.9	411.0	412.5	419.2	423.7	425.0	419.0	420.7	422.0	419.6	415.9	412.5	417.5
2009	391.3	392.1	391.6	395.4	401.5	402.3	398.4	398.7	400.2	400.4	399.4	397.5	397.4
2010	381.3	383.3	386.4	393.2	398.7	400.6	400.8	401.9	403.4	402.4	402.5	400.4	396.2
2011	383.2	386.4	389.0	398.4	403.8	406.3	405.0	404.4	406.2	406.4	406.1	403.8	399.9
2012	388.4	393.2	396.2	402.1	408.4	411.7	408.1	409.9	413.2	411.4	410.1	410.8	405.3
2013	394.6	396.9	400.3	407.1	413.5	418.1	415.5	416.6	418.5	419.5	418.1	415.8	411.2
2014	400.2	403.6	405.4	415.4	422.1	424.3	423.1	423.4	425.7	425.8	425.3	425.5	418.3
2015	409.0	407.5	411.5	422.2	429.8	431.6	431.1	429.9	432.0	432.9	432.9	431.9	425.2
2016	414.3	417.1	420.7	428.0	432.4	435.6	434.6	433.9	434.4	435.0	434.1	432.2	429.4
2017	416.6	420.1	421.7	429.9	436.0	441.0	439.0	439.6	439.0	440.9	440.6	437.2	433.5
Goods Producing													
2007	72.6	71.6	71.9	73.0	74.2	74.8	72.7	74.3	74.1	73.8	73.1	71.7	73.2
2008	68.4	67.4	67.9	69.3	70.2	70.8	68.4	70.0	69.8	68.5	67.2	65.5	68.6
2009	60.9	59.0	58.5	59.3	59.7	59.9	58.7	59.5	59.2	59.1	58.5	57.5	59.2
2010	54.2	53.7	54.0	55.5	56.8	57.7	57.1	58.2	57.9	57.9	57.8	56.8	56.5
2011	54.0	53.4	53.9	55.6	56.5	57.4	56.9	57.4	57.0	56.9	56.8	56.1	56.0
2012	53.4	53.2	54.0	55.3	55.9	57.1	56.2	57.2	56.9	57.1	56.9	56.6	55.8
2013	53.9	53.2	54.2	55.5	56.6	57.4	56.5	57.8	57.8	57.8	57.9	57.2	56.3
2014	54.8	54.4	54.8	56.9	58.3	59.0	58.5	58.9	58.8	58.9	58.8	58.4	57.5
2015	56.1	55.0	55.5	57.5	58.7	59.4	59.3	59.7	59.5	59.7	59.9	59.5	58.3
2016	56.7	56.2	56.9	58.3	59.2	59.9	59.6	59.9	59.5	59.8	59.5	59.0	58.7
2017	56.7	56.5	56.7	58.5	59.2	60.0	59.7	60.3	59.9	59.9	61.4	60.8	59.1
Service-Providing													
2007	408.4	411.2	413.3	419.4	424.7	425.9	419.2	417.7	421.2	421.3	421.0	420.8	418.7
2008	405.1	408.1	409.5	414.7	419.0	418.7	410.8	410.2	414.6	414.2	412.7	410.7	412.4
2009	393.4	396.4	396.3	399.5	405.5	405.4	397.5	396.7	402.3	404.1	403.9	402.8	400.3
2010	389.4	391.9	395.1	400.4	406.7	406.0	402.2	401.9	406.0	406.1	406.8	405.5	401.5
2011	390.6	394.4	396.9	404.6	409.3	410.5	404.7	403.8	409.1	410.5	410.5	408.9	404.5
2012	395.6	400.9	403.2	408.0	414.3	415.1	408.1	409.3	416.0	415.1	414.3	415.3	409.6
2013	401.2	404.2	407.1	412.4	418.6	421.5	416.1	415.6	420.5	422.8	421.3	419.9	415.1
2014	406.0	409.7	411.4	419.5	425.8	426.6	421.8	421.2	427.2	428.0	428.1	428.3	421.1
2015	413.8	413.4	416.9	425.8	432.8	433.0	428.7	426.6	432.1	434.0	434.0	433.6	427.1
2016	418.3	421.8	424.9	430.6	434.6	436.6	432.5	431.0	434.9	436.5	436.1	434.6	431.0
2017	420.8	424.6	426.2	432.5	438.5	442.4	436.7	436.3	439.6	442.7	441.0	438.2	435.0
Mining and Logging													
2007	0.2	0.2	0.2	0.3	0.3	0.3	0.3	0.3	0.3	0.3	0.3	0.2	0.3
2008	0.2	0.2	0.2	0.2	0.3	0.3	0.3	0.3	0.3	0.3	0.3	0.2	0.3
2009	0.2	0.1	0.2	0.2	0.2	0.2	0.2	0.2	0.2	0.2	0.2	0.2	0.2
2010	0.1	0.1	0.1	0.2	0.2	0.2	0.2	0.2	0.2	0.2	0.2	0.2	0.2
2011	0.1	0.1	0.1	0.2	0.2	0.2	0.2	0.2	0.2	0.2	0.2	0.2	0.2
2012	0.1	0.1	0.2	0.2	0.2	0.2	0.2	0.2	0.2	0.2	0.2	0.2	0.2
2013	0.2	0.1	0.2	0.2	0.2	0.2	0.2	0.2	0.2	0.2	0.2	0.2	0.2
2014	0.1	0.1	0.2	0.2	0.2	0.2	0.3	0.2	0.2	0.2	0.2	0.2	0.2
2015	0.2	0.2	0.2	0.2	0.2	0.2	0.2	0.2	0.2	0.2	0.2	0.2	0.2
2016	0.2	0.2	0.2	0.2	0.2	0.2	0.2	0.2	0.2	0.2	0.2	0.2	0.2
2017	0.2	0.2	0.2	0.2	0.2	0.2	0.2	0.2	0.2	0.2	0.2	0.2	0.2

1. Employment by Industry: Rhode Island, Selected Years, 2007–2017—*Continued*

(Numbers in thousands, not seasonally adjusted)

Industry and year	January	February	March	April	May	June	July	August	September	October	November	December	Annual average
Construction													
2007	21.0	19.9	20.4	21.6	22.8	23.4	23.6	23.4	23.0	22.8	22.5	21.4	22.2
2008	18.8	18.3	18.7	20.3	21.3	21.9	22.0	21.9	21.7	20.9	20.2	19.0	20.4
2009	16.4	15.9	15.9	17.1	17.8	18.0	18.2	18.2	17.8	17.6	17.1	16.3	17.2
2010	13.9	13.5	13.9	15.5	16.4	16.9	17.3	17.5	17.0	16.9	16.7	15.8	15.9
2011	13.6	13.0	13.4	15.0	15.9	16.6	17.2	17.1	16.8	16.8	16.8	16.2	15.7
2012	14.3	13.8	14.5	15.7	16.1	16.9	17.2	17.1	16.8	16.8	16.7	16.3	16.0
2013	14.1	13.7	14.3	15.5	16.5	16.9	17.3	17.4	17.3	17.2	17.0	16.2	16.1
2014	14.4	14.0	14.3	16.0	17.1	17.5	17.8	17.7	17.5	17.5	17.3	16.8	16.5
2015	14.8	14.0	14.4	16.2	17.3	17.8	18.3	18.3	18.2	18.3	18.3	17.9	17.0
2016	16.0	15.5	16.1	17.6	18.5	18.9	19.3	19.4	19.2	19.3	18.9	18.2	18.1
2017	16.4	16.2	16.3	17.9	18.7	19.2	19.5	19.6	19.3	19.2	20.0	18.9	18.4
Manufacturing													
2007	51.4	51.5	51.3	51.1	51.1	51.1	48.8	50.6	50.8	50.7	50.3	50.1	50.7
2008	49.4	48.9	49.0	48.8	48.6	48.6	46.1	47.8	47.8	47.3	46.7	46.3	47.9
2009	44.3	43.0	42.4	42.0	41.7	41.7	40.3	41.1	41.2	41.3	41.2	41.0	41.8
2010	40.2	40.1	40.0	39.8	40.2	40.6	39.6	40.5	40.7	40.8	40.9	40.8	40.4
2011	40.3	40.3	40.4	40.4	40.4	40.6	39.5	40.1	40.0	39.9	39.8	39.7	40.1
2012	39.0	39.3	39.3	39.4	39.6	40.0	38.8	39.9	39.9	40.1	40.0	40.1	39.6
2013	39.6	39.4	39.7	39.8	39.9	40.3	39.0	40.2	40.3	40.4	40.7	40.8	40.0
2014	40.3	40.3	40.3	40.7	41.0	41.3	40.4	41.0	41.1	41.2	41.3	41.4	40.9
2015	41.1	40.8	40.9	41.1	41.2	41.4	40.8	41.2	41.1	41.2	41.4	41.4	41.1
2016	40.5	40.5	40.6	40.5	40.5	40.8	40.1	40.3	40.1	40.3	40.4	40.6	40.4
2017	40.1	40.1	40.2	40.4	40.3	40.6	40.0	40.5	40.4	40.5	41.2	41.7	40.5
Trade, Transportation, and Utilities													
2007	79.1	78.0	78.2	78.9	79.8	80.7	79.8	79.6	79.7	79.8	81.2	82.2	79.8
2008	77.8	76.7	76.6	77.0	77.4	78.3	77.2	77.3	77.3	77.4	77.6	78.0	77.4
2009	73.8	72.8	72.4	71.8	73.1	73.7	72.8	72.6	73.3	73.5	74.4	75.0	73.3
2010	72.0	71.5	71.9	71.4	71.8	72.9	72.3	72.4	73.0	73.5	74.5	75.2	72.7
2011	72.2	71.7	71.9	72.8	73.7	74.4	73.5	73.7	74.5	74.9	76.2	77.1	73.9
2012	73.8	73.1	73.3	73.6	74.6	75.6	74.1	74.2	74.9	75.2	76.4	76.8	74.6
2013	72.7	72.2	72.0	72.7	73.8	74.6	73.9	74.0	74.4	75.1	76.3	77.2	74.1
2014	73.5	73.1	73.0	73.8	74.7	75.7	74.7	75.1	75.5	76.1	77.4	78.8	75.1
2015	75.1	74.2	74.1	75.2	76.1	77.2	76.2	76.2	76.9	77.0	78.5	79.6	76.4
2016	75.6	75.0	75.1	75.4	76.2	76.8	75.9	76.1	76.5	76.8	78.3	79.1	76.4
2017	75.5	75.0	74.7	75.9	76.8	77.4	76.5	76.5	77.2	77.2	77.9	78.1	76.6
Wholesale Trade													
2007	17.0	16.9	16.9	17.2	17.3	17.4	17.4	17.3	17.1	17.2	17.3	17.4	17.2
2008	16.9	16.9	16.9	16.9	17.0	17.1	17.0	16.9	16.9	16.9	16.8	16.7	16.9
2009	16.3	16.2	16.1	16.0	16.0	16.1	15.9	15.9	15.9	16.0	15.9	16.0	16.0
2010	15.6	15.6	15.7	15.6	15.9	16.0	15.9	16.0	16.0	16.0	16.0	16.1	15.9
2011	15.8	15.8	15.9	16.1	16.3	16.5	16.5	16.6	16.7	16.7	16.8	16.9	16.4
2012	16.7	16.8	16.9	16.8	17.0	17.1	17.0	17.0	16.9	16.9	16.9	16.8	16.9
2013	16.5	16.4	16.5	16.5	16.7	16.7	16.7	16.8	16.7	16.8	16.9	16.9	16.7
2014	16.6	16.7	16.7	16.6	16.8	16.9	16.9	17.0	16.9	17.0	17.0	17.1	16.9
2015	16.9	16.9	16.8	16.9	17.0	17.1	17.0	17.0	16.9	16.7	16.9	16.9	16.9
2016	16.5	16.5	16.5	16.7	16.7	16.7	16.6	16.7	16.6	16.5	16.6	16.7	16.6
2017	16.4	16.4	16.4	16.5	16.6	16.6	16.6	16.6	16.5	16.6	16.5	15.9	16.5
Retail Trade													
2007	51.3	50.5	50.7	50.7	51.3	51.9	51.7	51.6	51.1	51.2	52.5	53.2	51.5
2008	50.1	49.1	49.0	49.1	49.3	49.9	49.6	49.6	49.1	49.5	50.0	50.2	49.5
2009	47.3	46.5	46.3	45.9	46.9	47.3	47.3	47.0	46.9	47.2	48.1	48.5	47.1
2010	46.5	46.0	46.3	45.6	45.6	46.3	46.5	46.6	46.2	46.7	47.7	48.0	46.5
2011	46.0	45.5	45.6	46.1	46.6	46.9	46.8	47.1	46.7	47.2	48.4	48.8	46.8
2012	46.4	45.7	45.8	46.1	46.7	47.3	46.9	46.9	46.8	47.2	48.3	48.5	46.9
2013	45.8	45.3	45.0	45.5	46.2	46.8	46.9	46.8	46.5	47.1	48.1	48.6	46.6
2014	46.2	45.8	45.6	46.4	47.0	47.5	47.4	47.5	47.2	47.7	48.8	49.6	47.2
2015	47.0	46.4	46.4	47.1	47.6	48.5	48.4	48.4	48.2	48.5	49.7	50.3	48.0
2016	47.8	47.3	47.4	47.4	47.9	48.3	48.4	48.5	48.1	48.5	49.7	49.9	48.3
2017	47.7	47.2	47.0	48.0	48.6	48.9	48.8	48.9	48.6	48.6	49.1	49.4	48.4

1. Employment by Industry: Rhode Island, Selected Years, 2007–2017—*Continued*

(Numbers in thousands, not seasonally adjusted)

Industry and year	January	February	March	April	May	June	July	August	September	October	November	December	Annual average
Transportation and Utilities													
2007	10.8	10.6	10.6	11.0	11.2	11.4	10.7	10.7	11.5	11.4	11.4	11.6	11.1
2008	10.8	10.7	10.7	11.0	11.1	11.3	10.6	10.8	11.3	11.0	10.8	11.1	10.9
2009	10.2	10.1	10.0	9.9	10.2	10.3	9.6	9.7	10.5	10.3	10.4	10.5	10.1
2010	9.9	9.9	9.9	10.2	10.3	10.6	9.9	9.8	10.8	10.8	10.8	11.1	10.3
2011	10.4	10.4	10.4	10.6	10.8	11.0	10.2	10.0	11.1	11.0	11.0	11.4	10.7
2012	10.7	10.6	10.6	10.7	10.9	11.2	10.2	10.3	11.2	11.1	11.2	11.5	10.9
2013	10.4	10.5	10.5	10.7	10.9	11.1	10.3	10.4	11.2	11.2	11.3	11.7	10.9
2014	10.7	10.6	10.7	10.8	10.9	11.3	10.4	10.6	11.4	11.4	11.6	12.1	11.0
2015	11.2	10.9	10.9	11.2	11.5	11.6	10.8	10.8	11.8	11.8	11.9	12.4	11.4
2016	11.3	11.2	11.2	11.3	11.6	11.8	10.9	10.9	11.8	11.8	12.0	12.5	11.5
2017	11.4	11.4	11.3	11.4	11.6	11.9	11.1	11.0	12.1	12.0	12.3	12.8	11.7
Information													
2007	9.6	9.5	9.6	9.6	9.7	9.7	9.7	9.8	9.7	9.6	9.9	9.9	9.7
2008	9.7	10.0	10.0	9.9	9.7	10.0	9.4	9.7	9.5	9.7	9.3	9.2	9.7
2009	9.2	9.1	9.0	9.0	9.0	8.9	8.6	8.6	8.5	8.3	8.5	8.5	8.8
2010	8.4	8.4	8.6	8.4	8.3	8.3	8.4	8.7	8.8	8.6	8.7	8.6	8.5
2011	8.2	8.2	8.3	8.8	8.9	8.8	8.6	7.8	8.4	8.2	8.3	8.5	8.4
2012	8.1	8.2	8.2	8.0	7.8	8.0	7.7	7.8	7.6	7.6	7.5	7.6	7.8
2013	7.5	7.6	7.4	7.2	7.4	7.4	7.2	7.3	7.1	7.1	7.2	7.2	7.3
2014	7.3	7.1	7.0	7.1	7.2	7.1	7.1	7.3	7.1	7.0	7.0	7.1	7.1
2015	6.8	6.7	6.8	6.9	6.9	6.7	6.8	6.7	6.8	6.9	6.2	6.1	6.7
2016	6.0	6.1	6.0	6.2	5.4	6.2	6.3	6.1	6.2	6.1	6.1	6.2	6.1
2017	6.2	6.3	6.2	6.2	6.2	6.3	6.1	6.1	6.1	6.0	6.1	6.1	6.2
Financial Activities													
2007	36.1	36.2	36.1	36.2	36.3	36.2	35.9	35.6	35.5	35.0	35.0	34.9	35.8
2008	34.5	34.6	34.4	34.3	34.4	34.4	34.5	34.5	34.6	33.5	33.5	33.5	34.2
2009	33.1	33.1	32.8	32.6	32.8	33.0	32.7	32.4	32.1	32.1	32.3	32.2	32.6
2010	31.7	31.7	31.9	31.8	32.0	32.2	32.3	32.2	32.3	32.5	32.6	32.7	32.2
2011	32.1	32.2	32.3	32.4	32.4	32.9	32.5	32.6	32.6	32.6	32.9	32.8	32.5
2012	32.6	32.8	33.0	33.0	33.4	33.6	33.5	33.5	33.6	33.6	33.6	33.7	33.3
2013	33.4	33.6	33.9	33.9	34.0	34.2	34.3	34.1	34.0	34.0	33.9	34.2	34.0
2014	33.8	33.8	33.8	34.1	34.2	34.4	34.5	34.3	34.3	34.2	34.2	34.3	34.2
2015	34.0	34.1	34.4	34.6	34.9	35.1	34.9	34.8	35.1	35.7	36.1	36.2	35.0
2016	35.3	35.5	35.6	35.5	35.5	35.8	35.8	35.7	35.6	35.7	35.8	35.8	35.6
2017	35.5	35.6	35.6	35.7	35.9	36.3	36.1	36.3	36.2	36.6	36.3	36.5	36.1
Professional and Business Services													
2007	54.3	54.0	54.3	56.4	56.9	58.0	56.8	56.8	56.6	56.2	56.0	55.7	56.0
2008	53.2	52.9	53.1	55.2	55.3	56.2	55.4	55.5	55.9	55.5	54.8	53.6	54.7
2009	51.1	51.0	51.1	52.5	52.7	53.5	53.0	53.2	53.4	53.3	53.2	52.5	52.5
2010	50.1	50.2	51.1	54.0	54.2	54.9	54.4	54.5	54.6	54.8	54.6	53.6	53.4
2011	51.5	51.8	52.2	54.2	54.6	55.2	54.9	55.3	55.7	55.9	55.7	54.5	54.3
2012	52.8	53.1	54.1	56.1	56.6	57.5	56.9	57.2	57.2	57.1	57.2	57.1	56.1
2013	55.0	55.6	56.1	58.4	59.0	60.3	59.6	60.2	60.3	60.7	60.3	59.7	58.8
2014	57.0	57.7	57.9	60.5	61.2	61.8	61.7	62.3	62.4	63.0	63.0	62.9	61.0
2015	60.0	59.9	60.7	63.7	64.7	65.0	65.0	64.9	64.7	65.1	65.5	65.2	63.7
2016	62.9	63.1	63.7	65.6	66.0	66.6	66.6	66.9	67.0	67.3	67.1	66.6	65.8
2017	64.2	64.8	64.9	66.9	67.2	68.2	68.7	68.8	68.4	70.0	69.3	68.6	67.5
Education and Health Services													
2007	96.0	99.4	100.3	100.4	100.3	96.1	94.6	94.4	98.2	100.3	101.0	100.4	98.5
2008	97.0	100.5	101.3	101.1	100.8	96.3	94.8	95.0	98.5	101.1	101.5	101.5	99.1
2009	97.8	101.1	101.5	101.3	101.0	97.2	96.0	95.8	99.5	102.4	103.1	102.7	100.0
2010	99.8	102.2	102.9	102.8	102.8	98.1	97.8	97.8	101.6	103.1	103.8	104.1	101.4
2011	99.7	102.8	103.7	104.4	104.3	99.7	98.8	98.3	101.7	104.7	104.9	104.2	102.3
2012	100.7	104.7	104.9	104.1	104.6	100.0	98.7	99.0	104.7	105.8	105.6	106.4	103.3
2013	103.3	105.5	106.3	105.7	105.5	102.2	100.9	100.5	105.0	107.2	107.5	105.8	104.6
2014	103.4	105.9	106.5	107.2	106.7	102.4	101.7	101.1	106.0	107.6	108.1	107.9	105.4
2015	104.4	105.8	106.9	107.7	106.9	103.3	102.6	101.7	106.1	108.2	108.5	107.9	105.8
2016	104.2	107.1	108.0	108.4	108.2	103.1	102.3	101.8	105.7	108.0	108.1	107.5	106.0
2017	104.2	106.8	108.2	108.3	108.3	104.8	103.2	102.8	106.8	109.5	110.2	109.6	106.9

1. Employment by Industry: Rhode Island, Selected Years, 2007–2017—*Continued*

(Numbers in thousands, not seasonally adjusted)

Industry and year	January	February	March	April	May	June	July	August	September	October	November	December	Annual average
Leisure and Hospitality													
2007	45.5	46.0	46.7	49.6	52.4	56.4	57.1	56.7	54.6	52.6	50.0	49.5	51.4
2008	45.9	46.4	46.7	49.7	53.0	55.8	55.9	55.5	53.7	51.2	49.4	48.7	51.0
2009	43.6	44.1	44.4	46.8	51.0	53.6	53.8	54.0	52.3	49.5	47.2	47.0	48.9
2010	43.6	44.0	44.4	47.6	50.8	54.3	55.5	55.2	53.1	50.0	48.3	47.3	49.5
2011	44.0	44.6	45.0	48.1	51.1	55.0	56.1	55.8	53.8	50.9	48.9	48.2	50.1
2012	45.2	46.2	46.8	49.8	53.1	56.9	57.6	57.6	55.4	52.5	50.4	49.9	51.8
2013	46.8	47.2	48.2	51.3	54.6	58.9	59.6	59.5	57.3	55.1	52.5	51.9	53.6
2014	48.4	49.4	50.1	53.3	56.9	60.4	61.0	60.6	58.6	56.3	54.0	53.2	55.2
2015	50.2	49.6	50.6	54.0	58.5	61.4	62.2	62.0	59.9	57.4	55.2	54.5	56.3
2016	51.1	51.6	52.7	55.7	58.8	63.4	63.9	63.4	60.9	58.4	56.2	55.0	57.6
2017	51.9	52.6	53.0	55.7	59.5	64.4	64.7	64.9	61.4	58.7	56.4	54.7	58.2
Other Services													
2007	22.6	22.7	22.8	23.0	23.3	23.9	23.8	23.6	23.0	23.1	23.1	23.2	23.2
2008	22.4	22.5	22.5	22.7	22.9	23.2	23.4	23.2	22.7	22.7	22.6	22.5	22.8
2009	21.8	21.9	21.9	22.1	22.2	22.5	22.8	22.6	21.9	22.2	22.2	22.1	22.2
2010	21.5	21.6	21.6	21.7	22.0	22.2	23.0	22.9	22.1	22.0	22.2	22.1	22.1
2011	21.5	21.7	21.7	22.1	22.3	22.9	23.7	23.5	22.5	22.3	22.4	22.4	22.4
2012	21.8	21.9	21.9	22.2	22.4	23.0	23.4	23.4	22.9	22.5	22.5	22.7	22.6
2013	22.0	22.0	22.2	22.4	22.6	23.1	23.5	23.2	22.6	22.5	22.5	22.6	22.6
2014	22.0	22.2	22.3	22.5	22.9	23.5	23.9	23.8	23.0	22.7	22.8	22.9	22.9
2015	22.4	22.2	22.5	22.6	23.1	23.5	24.1	23.9	23.0	22.9	23.0	22.9	23.0
2016	22.5	22.5	22.7	22.9	23.1	23.8	24.2	24.0	23.0	22.9	23.0	23.0	23.1
2017	22.4	22.5	22.4	22.7	22.9	23.6	24.0	23.9	23.0	23.0	23.0	22.8	23.0
Government													
2007	65.2	65.4	65.3	65.3	66.0	64.9	61.5	61.2	63.9	64.7	64.8	65.0	64.4
2008	64.6	64.5	64.9	64.8	65.5	64.5	60.2	59.5	62.4	63.1	64.0	63.7	63.5
2009	63.0	63.3	63.2	63.4	63.7	63.0	57.8	57.5	61.3	62.8	63.0	62.8	62.1
2010	62.3	62.3	62.7	62.7	64.8	63.1	58.5	58.2	60.5	61.6	62.1	61.9	61.7
2011	61.4	61.4	61.8	61.8	62.0	61.6	56.6	56.8	59.9	61.0	61.2	61.2	60.6
2012	60.6	60.9	61.0	61.2	61.8	60.5	56.2	56.6	59.7	60.8	61.1	61.1	60.1
2013	60.5	60.5	61.0	60.8	61.7	60.8	57.1	56.8	59.8	61.1	61.1	61.3	60.2
2014	60.6	60.5	60.8	61.0	62.0	61.3	57.2	56.7	60.3	61.1	61.6	61.2	60.4
2015	60.9	60.9	60.9	61.1	61.7	60.8	56.9	56.4	59.6	60.8	61.0	61.2	60.2
2016	60.7	60.9	61.1	60.9	61.4	60.9	57.5	57.0	60.0	61.3	61.5	61.4	60.4
2017	60.9	61.0	61.2	61.1	61.7	61.4	57.4	57.0	60.5	61.7	61.8	61.8	60.6

2. Average Weekly Hours by Selected Industry: Rhode Island, 2013–2017

(Not seasonally adjusted)

Industry and year	January	February	March	April	May	June	July	August	September	October	November	December	Annual average
Total Private													
2013	32.7	32.5	32.9	33.0	33.1	33.1	33.2	33.0	33.1	32.7	32.8	32.9	32.9
2014	32.7	32.6	32.8	33.0	33.0	33.3	33.3	33.0	33.0	33.0	33.1	33.1	33.0
2015	32.8	32.5	32.9	32.9	33.1	33.6	33.6	33.5	33.3	32.9	33.1	32.9	33.1
2016	32.5	32.4	32.5	32.5	32.9	33.0	33.0	33.0	32.8	32.4	32.3	32.7	32.7
2017	32.6	31.7	32.0	33.0	32.9	32.9	33.2	33.2	33.1	33.1	33.3	33.5	32.9
Goods-Producing													
2013	38.7	38.3	38.8	39.2	39.3	39.6	39.3	38.7	39.6	38.7	38.6	38.9	39.0
2014	38.7	38.3	38.9	39.4	38.9	39.3	38.2	38.0	38.3	38.6	38.3	39.1	38.7
2015	38.2	37.7	38.7	38.1	37.4	38.0	37.7	37.1	37.7	37.0	37.4	38.9	37.8
2016	37.9	37.6	38.4	38.0	38.4	38.8	38.4	38.2	38.2	38.1	38.2	38.8	38.3
2017	38.1	37.3	37.1	38.0	37.6	37.4	37.2	37.9	37.7	37.2	37.6	38.3	37.6
Construction													
2013	35.2	34.4	36.1	37.0	37.0	36.7	37.1	36.3	37.1	37.4	36.5	36.4	36.5
2014	38.4	36.7	38.0	38.9	38.8	38.8	37.4	36.2	36.5	36.4	36.1	36.6	37.4
2015	36.7	35.6	37.5	36.6	35.5	36.0	35.6	34.6	34.6	33.7	35.4	36.4	35.6
2016	35.8	33.8	36.2	35.1	36.5	37.1	36.7	36.1	35.6	35.9	35.9	35.6	35.9
2017	35.5	34.9	33.8	36.1	35.9	35.1	33.8	34.0	33.4	31.8	32.4	32.3	34.0
Manufacturing													
2013	39.4	39.1	39.1	39.3	39.5	40.1	39.5	39.0	40.0	40.1	40.2	40.5	39.7
2014	39.3	39.3	39.6	39.8	39.1	39.8	38.8	39.0	39.3	39.6	39.3	40.2	39.4
2015	38.9	38.5	39.2	38.8	38.3	38.9	38.6	38.1	39.0	38.4	38.2	39.9	38.7
2016	38.7	39.1	39.3	39.2	39.1	39.4	39.0	39.1	39.4	39.1	39.2	40.2	39.3
2017	39.2	38.3	38.4	38.7	38.3	38.4	38.9	39.2	39.4	39.7	40.0	41.2	39.1
Trade, Transportation, and Utilities													
2013	33.4	33.4	34.6	34.6	34.6	34.2	34.7	34.5	34.1	34.1	34.2	34.4	34.2
2014	33.3	33.1	33.4	34.4	34.3	34.2	34.4	34.4	34.4	33.8	33.7	33.9	34.0
2015	32.4	31.8	32.6	32.4	32.6	32.8	32.9	32.9	33.1	32.7	32.6	32.3	32.6
2016	31.2	31.2	31.0	31.5	31.8	32.1	32.6	32.3	32.3	32.3	32.2	32.7	31.9
2017	32.2	31.4	32.3	33.5	33.4	33.4	34.0	33.6	33.7	33.5	33.8	34.1	33.2
Professional and Business Services													
2013	35.8	35.5	35.0	35.0	35.0	34.6	34.5	34.1	34.5	33.7	33.6	33.3	34.5
2014	33.7	33.7	34.0	34.4	34.1	34.5	34.5	33.8	34.4	34.2	34.6	34.7	34.2
2015	34.8	34.7	35.3	35.3	36.4	36.1	36.1	35.8	35.1	35.3	35.7	34.8	35.5
2016	35.4	34.8	35.3	35.7	35.9	36.1	35.3	35.8	35.5	34.8	34.6	35.1	35.3
2017	35.1	34.6	34.6	35.2	35.8	35.8	35.2	35.5	35.8	35.3	35.5	35.2	35.3
Education and Health Services													
2013	30.3	30.1	30.2	30.4	30.7	30.5	31.0	31.2	30.9	31.1	31.3	31.3	30.7
2014	31.2	31.0	31.2	31.2	31.4	31.7	32.1	31.9	31.9	32.4	32.3	32.1	31.7
2015	32.2	32.0	32.2	32.1	32.1	32.0	32.0	32.5	32.2	31.8	32.1	31.3	32.0
2016	31.5	31.1	31.2	30.9	31.5	31.1	31.5	31.7	31.9	32.1	31.9	32.0	31.5
2017	32.5	32.2	32.2	32.8	32.8	33.0	32.7	32.1	32.6	33.0	33.1	33.2	32.7
Leisure and Hospitality													
2013	24.1	24.1	25.1	25.2	25.5	25.7	26.7	26.7	25.7	25.5	25.6	24.8	25.4
2014	25.2	24.9	25.6	25.4	25.4	25.5	26.7	26.5	25.1	24.3	23.9	23.7	25.2
2015	23.9	23.3	24.0	25.0	25.6	27.1	28.0	27.7	26.7	25.4	25.2	24.6	25.6
2016	23.4	24.0	23.8	23.8	24.6	25.0	25.3	25.4	24.3	23.9	24.0	23.7	24.3
2017	23.2	21.9	22.8	24.3	24.1	24.1	25.0	25.3	24.2	24.2	24.1	24.1	24.0

3. Average Hourly Earnings by Selected Industry: Rhode Island, 2013–2017

(Dollars, not seasonally adjusted)

Industry and year	January	February	March	April	May	June	July	August	September	October	November	December	Annual average
Total Private													
2013	25.66	25.76	25.62	25.56	25.29	25.06	25.13	25.07	25.40	25.37	25.45	25.70	25.42
2014	25.79	25.68	25.53	25.28	24.99	25.00	24.58	24.62	24.74	24.92	25.13	24.98	25.10
2015	25.24	25.59	25.48	25.15	25.02	24.13	24.26	24.31	24.68	25.14	25.36	25.09	24.94
2016	25.91	26.05	25.66	26.14	25.99	25.70	25.54	25.88	25.90	26.34	26.51	26.24	25.99
2017	26.88	27.01	26.81	26.91	26.72	26.49	26.63	26.67	27.08	27.32	27.42	27.65	26.97
Goods-Producing													
2013	25.22	25.35	25.64	25.60	25.51	25.54	26.01	26.28	26.17	27.00	27.25	26.71	26.04
2014	27.51	27.33	27.36	27.13	27.03	27.26	27.42	26.88	26.96	27.20	27.41	27.53	27.25
2015	27.27	27.32	26.89	26.39	26.12	25.33	25.58	25.38	25.33	25.44	25.90	25.39	26.01
2016	25.30	24.83	24.99	25.05	25.04	25.11	25.01	25.12	25.15	25.17	25.19	24.98	25.08
2017	25.30	25.10	25.25	25.08	25.19	25.37	25.44	25.08	25.46	25.05	25.28	25.68	25.28
Construction													
2013	29.26	29.25	28.93	28.96	28.87	29.08	29.24	29.60	29.35	29.66	29.86	30.21	29.37
2014	29.32	29.94	29.38	29.22	29.13	29.75	28.51	28.84	28.78	28.62	28.81	29.48	29.13
2015	29.25	29.70	29.25	28.52	29.11	27.78	27.57	27.72	28.82	28.60	28.89	28.83	28.63
2016	28.20	28.38	28.81	29.17	29.33	28.92	28.96	29.31	29.41	28.90	28.54	28.63	28.90
2017	29.19	28.68	28.91	28.19	28.90	28.66	28.67	28.72	29.86	29.82	30.31	31.26	29.25
Manufacturing													
2013	24.10	24.29	24.68	24.58	24.45	24.42	24.93	25.15	25.08	25.21	25.60	25.27	24.82
2014	26.65	26.24	26.44	26.05	25.94	25.97	26.72	25.81	25.65	26.05	26.33	26.23	26.17
2015	25.94	26.01	25.43	25.20	24.77	24.20	24.59	24.32	23.86	24.12	24.57	23.97	24.74
2016	24.13	23.61	23.58	23.54	23.40	23.65	23.42	23.39	23.41	23.62	23.78	23.52	23.59
2017	23.74	23.74	23.85	23.60	23.43	23.78	23.91	23.14	23.50	23.36	23.37	23.32	23.56
Trade, Transportation, and Utilities													
2013	21.16	21.24	21.50	21.52	21.27	21.23	21.35	21.38	21.19	20.91	21.32	20.92	21.25
2014	21.37	21.32	21.17	20.95	20.40	20.69	20.45	20.68	20.47	20.48	20.67	20.23	20.73
2015	20.48	20.31	20.09	19.66	20.01	19.88	20.02	20.01	20.23	20.66	20.55	19.70	20.13
2016	20.46	20.71	20.56	20.78	20.76	21.00	20.73	21.35	21.26	21.89	22.52	21.68	21.16
2017	22.21	22.49	23.36	23.24	23.43	23.67	23.60	23.84	24.29	24.65	24.81	24.70	23.71
Professional and Business Services													
2013	30.63	30.52	30.42	30.01	30.10	29.15	29.71	29.44	29.42	29.56	29.60	30.32	29.90
2014	30.17	30.23	29.92	29.41	28.86	28.82	27.96	28.65	28.17	28.71	29.47	29.74	29.16
2015	30.40	31.09	30.94	29.84	29.73	29.29	29.50	29.88	29.78	29.91	29.83	29.22	29.93
2016	30.03	30.15	29.79	30.14	30.11	30.05	30.12	30.32	30.95	31.26	31.47	31.33	30.48
2017	32.01	31.85	31.77	31.88	31.25	31.15	31.69	31.55	31.76	31.92	31.64	32.33	31.73
Education and Health Services													
2013	23.55	23.36	23.30	23.16	22.83	23.02	23.18	22.99	23.35	23.04	22.93	23.47	23.18
2014	22.75	22.99	23.13	23.21	23.35	23.38	23.61	23.66	23.67	23.66	23.42	23.22	23.34
2015	23.06	23.65	23.91	24.25	24.65	24.75	25.23	25.03	25.75	26.38	26.86	27.16	25.06
2016	27.53	27.86	27.35	27.55	27.65	27.78	27.98	27.66	27.75	28.39	28.22	28.22	27.83
2017	29.12	28.95	28.86	29.46	30.03	29.95	30.36	30.71	31.07	31.34	31.02	31.75	30.23
Leisure and Hospitality													
2013	13.87	14.19	14.03	14.06	14.14	13.88	13.77	13.67	14.08	14.22	14.03	14.23	14.00
2014	13.83	13.68	13.62	13.67	13.71	13.55	13.65	13.81	13.80	14.10	14.07	14.04	13.79
2015	14.40	14.58	14.66	14.49	14.39	13.99	14.27	14.50	14.84	15.25	15.02	15.42	14.63
2016	15.60	15.83	15.75	15.83	15.82	15.50	15.57	15.66	15.82	15.89	15.90	16.13	15.77
2017	16.16	16.53	16.34	16.23	16.02	16.12	16.17	15.95	16.22	16.20	16.18	16.28	16.19

4. Average Weekly Earnings by Selected Industry: Rhode Island, 2013–2017

(Dollars, not seasonally adjusted)

Industry and year	January	February	March	April	May	June	July	August	September	October	November	December	Annual average
Total Private													
2013	839.08	837.20	842.90	843.48	837.10	829.49	834.32	827.31	840.74	829.60	834.76	845.53	836.32
2014	843.33	837.17	837.38	834.24	824.67	832.50	818.51	812.46	816.42	822.36	831.80	826.84	828.30
2015	827.87	831.68	838.29	827.44	828.16	810.77	815.14	814.39	821.84	827.11	839.42	825.46	825.51
2016	842.08	844.02	833.95	849.55	855.07	848.10	842.82	854.04	849.52	853.42	856.27	858.05	849.87
2017	876.29	856.22	857.92	888.03	879.09	871.52	884.12	885.44	896.35	904.29	913.09	926.28	887.31
Goods-Producing													
2013	976.01	970.91	994.83	1,003.52	1,002.54	1,011.38	1,022.19	1,017.04	1,036.33	1,044.90	1,051.85	1,039.02	1,015.56
2014	1,064.64	1,046.74	1,064.30	1,068.92	1,051.47	1,071.32	1,047.44	1,021.44	1,032.57	1,049.92	1,049.80	1,076.42	1,054.58
2015	1,041.71	1,029.96	1,040.64	1,005.46	976.89	962.54	964.37	941.60	954.94	941.28	968.66	987.67	983.18
2016	958.87	933.61	959.62	951.90	961.54	974.27	960.38	959.58	960.73	958.98	962.26	969.22	960.56
2017	963.93	936.23	936.78	953.04	947.14	948.84	946.37	950.53	959.84	931.86	950.53	983.54	950.53
Construction													
2013	1,029.95	1,006.20	1,044.37	1,071.52	1,068.19	1,067.24	1,084.80	1,074.48	1,088.89	1,109.28	1,089.89	1,099.64	1,072.01
2014	1,125.89	1,098.80	1,116.44	1,136.66	1,130.24	1,154.30	1,066.27	1,044.01	1,050.47	1,041.77	1,040.04	1,078.97	1,089.46
2015	1,073.48	1,057.32	1,096.88	1,043.83	1,033.41	1,000.08	981.49	959.11	997.17	963.82	1,022.71	1,049.41	1,019.23
2016	1,009.56	959.24	1,042.92	1,023.87	1,070.55	1,072.93	1,062.83	1,058.09	1,047.00	1,037.51	1,024.59	1,019.23	1,037.51
2017	1,036.25	1,000.93	977.16	1,017.66	1,037.51	1,005.97	969.05	976.48	997.32	948.28	982.04	1,009.70	994.84
Manufacturing													
2013	949.54	949.74	964.99	965.99	965.78	979.24	984.74	980.85	1,003.20	1,010.92	1,029.12	1,023.44	985.35
2014	1,047.35	1,031.23	1,047.02	1,036.79	1,014.25	1,033.61	1,036.74	1,006.59	1,008.05	1,031.58	1,034.77	1,054.45	1,031.10
2015	1,009.07	1,001.39	996.86	977.76	948.69	941.38	949.17	926.59	930.54	926.21	938.57	956.40	957.44
2016	933.83	923.15	926.69	922.77	914.94	931.81	913.38	914.55	922.35	923.54	932.18	945.50	927.09
2017	930.61	909.24	915.84	913.32	897.37	913.15	930.10	907.09	925.90	927.39	934.80	960.78	921.20
Trade, Transportation, and Utilities													
2013	706.74	709.42	743.90	744.59	735.94	726.07	740.85	737.61	722.58	713.03	729.14	719.65	726.75
2014	711.62	705.69	707.08	720.68	699.72	707.60	703.48	711.39	704.17	692.22	696.58	685.80	704.82
2015	663.55	645.86	654.93	636.98	652.33	652.06	658.66	658.33	669.61	675.58	669.93	636.31	656.24
2016	638.35	646.15	637.36	654.57	660.17	674.10	675.80	689.61	686.70	707.05	725.14	708.94	675.00
2017	715.16	706.19	754.53	778.54	782.56	790.58	802.40	801.02	818.57	825.78	838.58	842.27	787.17
Professional and Business Services													
2013	1,096.55	1,083.46	1,064.70	1,050.35	1,053.50	1,008.59	1,025.00	1,003.90	1,014.99	996.17	994.56	1,009.66	1,031.55
2014	1,016.73	1,018.75	1,017.28	1,011.70	984.13	994.29	964.62	968.37	969.05	981.88	1,019.66	1,031.98	997.27
2015	1,057.92	1,078.82	1,092.18	1,053.35	1,082.17	1,057.37	1,064.95	1,069.70	1,045.28	1,055.82	1,064.93	1,016.86	1,062.52
2016	1,063.06	1,049.22	1,051.59	1,076.00	1,080.95	1,084.81	1,063.24	1,085.46	1,098.73	1,087.85	1,088.86	1,099.68	1,075.94
2017	1,123.55	1,102.01	1,099.24	1,122.18	1,118.75	1,115.17	1,115.49	1,120.03	1,137.01	1,126.78	1,123.22	1,138.02	1,120.07
Education and Health Services													
2013	713.57	703.14	703.66	704.06	700.88	702.11	718.58	717.29	721.52	716.54	717.71	734.61	711.63
2014	709.80	712.69	721.66	724.15	733.19	741.15	757.88	754.75	755.07	766.58	756.47	745.36	739.88
2015	742.53	756.80	769.90	778.43	791.27	792.00	807.36	813.48	829.15	838.88	862.21	850.11	801.92
2016	867.20	866.45	853.32	851.30	870.98	863.96	881.37	876.82	885.23	911.32	900.22	903.04	876.65
2017	946.40	932.19	929.29	966.29	984.98	988.35	992.77	985.79	1,012.88	1,034.22	1,026.76	1,054.10	988.52
Leisure and Hospitality													
2013	334.27	341.98	352.15	354.31	360.57	356.72	367.66	364.99	361.86	362.61	359.17	352.90	355.60
2014	348.52	340.63	348.67	347.22	348.23	345.53	364.46	365.97	346.38	342.63	336.27	332.75	347.51
2015	344.16	339.71	351.84	362.25	368.38	379.13	399.56	401.65	396.23	387.35	378.50	379.33	374.53
2016	365.04	379.92	374.85	376.75	389.17	387.50	393.92	397.76	384.43	379.77	381.60	382.28	383.21
2017	374.91	362.01	372.55	394.39	386.08	388.49	404.25	403.54	392.52	392.04	389.94	392.35	388.56

SOUTH CAROLINA
At a Glance

Population:
  2010 census: 4,625,364
  2017 estimate: 5,024,369

Percent change in population:
  2010–2017: 8.6%

Percent change in total nonfarm employment:
  2007–2017: 7.5%

Industry with the largest growth in employment, 2007–2017 (thousands):
  Education and health services, 50.6

Industry with the largest decline or smallest growth in employment, 2007–2017 (thousands):
  Construction, -24.3

Civilian labor force:
  2010: 2,155,668
  2017: 2,312,651

Unemployment rate and rank among states (highest to lowest):
  2010: 11.2%, 4th
  2017: 4.3%, 24th

Over-the-year change in unemployment rates:
  2015–2016: -1.0%
  2016–2017: -0.7%

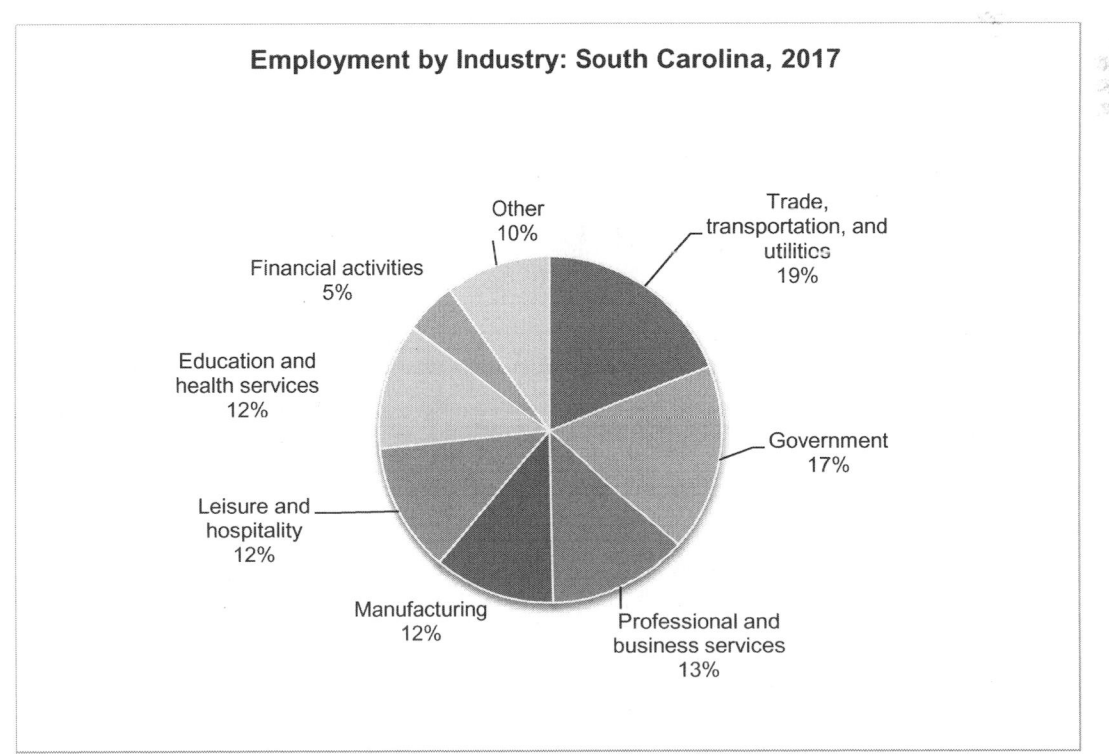

Employment by Industry: South Carolina, 2017

- Other 10%
- Trade, transportation, and utilities 19%
- Financial activities 5%
- Education and health services 12%
- Government 17%
- Leisure and hospitality 12%
- Manufacturing 12%
- Professional and business services 13%

1. Employment by Industry: South Carolina, Selected Years, 2007–2017

(Numbers in thousands, not seasonally adjusted)

Industry and year	January	February	March	April	May	June	July	August	September	October	November	December	Annual average
Total Nonfarm													
2007	1,903.2	1,914.8	1,938.4	1,946.2	1,959.2	1,966.2	1,939.0	1,948.6	1,955.7	1,953.7	1,958.7	1,956.5	1,945.0
2008	1,916.5	1,927.8	1,942.9	1,946.6	1,960.3	1,953.1	1,918.6	1,919.7	1,923.3	1,912.4	1,904.9	1,888.7	1,926.2
2009	1,826.3	1,822.4	1,826.6	1,830.4	1,834.8	1,825.8	1,802.6	1,803.8	1,801.1	1,800.6	1,802.5	1,795.5	1,814.4
2010	1,760.2	1,771.2	1,789.6	1,816.4	1,837.4	1,832.4	1,816.7	1,820.9	1,817.8	1,822.1	1,826.1	1,825.2	1,811.3
2011	1,779.3	1,799.0	1,819.5	1,842.5	1,851.3	1,850.8	1,833.7	1,839.6	1,841.1	1,840.6	1,847.4	1,846.1	1,832.6
2012	1,813.6	1,830.0	1,851.6	1,865.8	1,877.6	1,882.0	1,859.9	1,866.9	1,870.3	1,874.8	1,890.9	1,887.4	1,864.2
2013	1,844.4	1,860.5	1,878.2	1,897.1	1,911.6	1,917.3	1,899.8	1,906.2	1,912.8	1,919.0	1,932.7	1,933.1	1,901.1
2014	1,891.7	1,898.8	1,928.8	1,951.2	1,966.6	1,967.9	1,945.7	1,953.4	1,961.0	1,972.6	1,987.9	1,989.9	1,951.3
2015	1,944.7	1,960.1	1,979.2	1,998.3	2,016.7	2,021.3	2,008.5	2,014.6	2,016.5	2,031.1	2,042.8	2,046.2	2,006.7
2016	1,996.9	2,014.4	2,032.7	2,056.3	2,067.5	2,068.3	2,058.3	2,062.7	2,067.7	2,062.3	2,083.8	2,084.9	2,054.7
2017	2,045.7	2,063.4	2,079.7	2,089.4	2,102.1	2,109.2	2,093.5	2,093.3	2,085.1	2,102.1	2,114.3	2,114.5	2,091.0
Total Private													
2007	1,559.2	1,568.1	1,589.2	1,598.5	1,610.9	1,623.1	1,612.9	1,614.2	1,606.1	1,599.7	1,601.4	1,600.1	1,598.6
2008	1,563.3	1,570.7	1,584.6	1,587.4	1,599.0	1,598.0	1,583.3	1,582.4	1,565.5	1,549.9	1,539.8	1,524.6	1,570.7
2009	1,469.7	1,463.2	1,466.7	1,468.8	1,473.9	1,472.0	1,463.3	1,460.1	1,448.0	1,442.4	1,442.8	1,436.4	1,458.9
2010	1,405.7	1,413.1	1,429.5	1,455.7	1,466.8	1,474.1	1,475.0	1,476.0	1,466.7	1,468.1	1,471.3	1,471.1	1,456.1
2011	1,430.2	1,446.7	1,465.9	1,488.7	1,498.7	1,503.5	1,501.2	1,503.9	1,492.9	1,489.3	1,494.9	1,494.2	1,484.2
2012	1,466.0	1,477.0	1,497.3	1,511.6	1,523.1	1,531.1	1,523.7	1,529.0	1,518.1	1,517.9	1,529.9	1,528.7	1,512.8
2013	1,492.4	1,504.0	1,520.1	1,538.2	1,553.6	1,565.2	1,562.3	1,567.2	1,560.0	1,561.6	1,573.7	1,575.1	1,547.8
2014	1,538.5	1,541.6	1,570.1	1,591.5	1,606.6	1,613.8	1,606.3	1,610.4	1,603.5	1,610.5	1,624.9	1,626.7	1,595.4
2015	1,587.2	1,598.0	1,616.2	1,634.2	1,652.6	1,663.3	1,664.1	1,666.5	1,654.8	1,665.8	1,676.1	1,678.5	1,646.4
2016	1,635.9	1,649.5	1,665.9	1,688.8	1,700.7	1,706.5	1,708.5	1,710.2	1,703.0	1,695.6	1,715.6	1,715.4	1,691.3
2017	1,682.4	1,696.5	1,710.7	1,720.3	1,733.2	1,745.2	1,740.4	1,737.7	1,718.0	1,731.1	1,742.4	1,742.6	1,725.0
Goods Producing													
2007	377.9	378.8	381.8	380.2	381.5	383.7	380.1	379.5	378.3	374.9	373.9	373.4	378.7
2008	367.3	365.7	366.0	361.1	361.7	360.3	356.2	354.1	351.3	345.8	341.7	336.3	355.6
2009	325.5	320.0	316.0	309.3	306.3	304.8	299.7	297.6	296.1	293.1	292.5	291.6	304.4
2010	286.2	286.0	287.4	290.0	291.4	292.4	292.2	291.6	291.4	291.2	291.6	293.0	290.4
2011	287.3	291.0	294.2	295.9	297.0	298.4	298.0	298.5	298.2	298.0	298.8	299.7	296.3
2012	296.5	298.6	300.9	300.5	302.1	302.8	301.1	302.3	302.1	302.6	303.4	304.2	301.4
2013	302.0	303.5	306.1	306.4	308.1	309.2	308.2	309.3	310.0	310.1	311.5	312.5	308.1
2014	309.9	310.1	313.0	314.6	317.0	318.5	317.5	317.3	318.1	319.8	321.1	322.8	316.6
2015	320.4	322.2	323.6	324.1	326.2	329.0	327.7	328.0	329.1	329.5	331.0	331.8	326.9
2016	330.2	331.6	333.1	334.0	335.5	337.6	339.0	338.7	340.1	338.4	341.1	343.0	336.9
2017	341.1	343.2	344.4	344.4	346.6	349.1	348.5	344.7	344.4	344.4	347.7	350.2	345.7
Service-Providing													
2007	1,525.3	1,536.0	1,556.6	1,566.0	1,577.7	1,582.5	1,558.9	1,569.1	1,577.4	1,578.8	1,584.8	1,583.1	1,566.4
2008	1,549.2	1,562.1	1,576.9	1,585.5	1,598.6	1,592.8	1,562.4	1,565.6	1,572.0	1,566.6	1,563.2	1,552.4	1,570.6
2009	1,500.8	1,502.4	1,510.6	1,521.1	1,528.5	1,521.0	1,502.9	1,506.2	1,505.0	1,507.5	1,510.0	1,503.9	1,510.0
2010	1,474.0	1,485.2	1,502.2	1,526.4	1,546.0	1,540.0	1,524.5	1,529.3	1,526.4	1,530.9	1,534.5	1,532.2	1,521.0
2011	1,492.0	1,508.0	1,525.3	1,546.6	1,554.3	1,552.4	1,535.7	1,541.1	1,542.9	1,542.6	1,548.6	1,546.4	1,536.3
2012	1,517.1	1,531.4	1,550.7	1,565.3	1,575.5	1,579.2	1,558.8	1,564.6	1,568.2	1,572.2	1,587.5	1,583.2	1,562.8
2013	1,542.4	1,557.0	1,572.1	1,590.7	1,603.5	1,608.1	1,591.6	1,596.9	1,602.8	1,608.9	1,621.2	1,620.6	1,593.0
2014	1,581.8	1,588.7	1,615.8	1,636.6	1,649.6	1,649.4	1,628.2	1,636.1	1,642.9	1,652.8	1,666.8	1,667.1	1,634.7
2015	1,624.3	1,637.9	1,655.6	1,674.2	1,690.5	1,692.3	1,680.8	1,686.6	1,687.4	1,701.6	1,711.8	1,714.4	1,679.8
2016	1,666.7	1,682.8	1,699.6	1,722.3	1,732.0	1,730.7	1,719.3	1,724.0	1,727.6	1,723.9	1,742.7	1,741.9	1,717.8
2017	1,704.6	1,720.2	1,735.3	1,745.0	1,755.5	1,760.1	1,745.0	1,748.6	1,740.7	1,757.7	1,766.6	1,764.3	1,745.3
Mining and Logging													
2007	4.7	4.7	4.7	4.6	4.6	4.7	4.6	4.6	4.6	4.6	4.6	4.6	4.6
2008	4.5	4.5	4.5	4.4	4.4	4.3	4.3	4.3	4.3	4.3	4.3	4.3	4.4
2009	4.2	4.1	4.1	4.1	4.1	4.1	4.1	4.1	4.1	4.0	4.0	4.0	4.1
2010	4.0	4.0	4.0	4.0	4.0	4.0	4.0	4.0	4.0	4.0	3.9	3.9	4.0
2011	3.9	3.9	4.0	4.0	4.0	4.0	3.9	3.9	3.9	3.9	3.9	3.9	3.9
2012	3.9	3.9	3.9	3.9	3.9	3.9	3.8	3.8	3.8	3.8	3.8	3.8	3.9
2013	3.8	3.8	3.8	3.8	3.8	3.8	3.8	3.8	3.8	3.8	3.8	3.9	3.8
2014	3.8	3.7	3.8	3.8	3.9	3.9	3.9	3.9	3.9	3.9	3.9	3.9	3.9
2015	3.9	3.9	3.9	3.9	3.9	4.0	4.0	4.1	4.1	4.0	4.0	4.0	4.0
2016	4.0	4.1	4.1	4.1	4.2	4.2	4.2	4.2	4.3	4.2	4.2	4.3	4.2
2017	4.2	4.2	4.3	4.3	4.3	4.3	4.3	4.3	4.2	4.2	4.3	4.2	4.3

1. Employment by Industry: South Carolina, Selected Years, 2007–2017—*Continued*

(Numbers in thousands, not seasonally adjusted)

Industry and year	January	February	March	April	May	June	July	August	September	October	November	December	Annual average
Construction													
2007	124.3	124.5	126.8	125.9	126.7	127.8	126.8	126.9	125.7	123.0	121.9	120.9	125.1
2008	116.4	115.8	116.1	112.6	112.8	112.7	110.1	109.2	107.5	104.6	102.3	99.6	110.0
2009	94.7	92.6	92.6	89.8	89.4	89.0	87.1	85.6	84.3	82.9	82.0	81.5	87.6
2010	77.8	77.3	78.5	80.4	81.0	81.5	81.6	80.7	80.2	79.9	79.6	79.0	79.8
2011	74.5	76.1	77.3	77.9	78.6	78.8	78.5	78.3	78.0	78.0	78.0	77.6	77.6
2012	75.8	77.0	78.3	77.5	78.6	79.3	79.0	79.5	79.3	79.2	79.1	79.2	78.5
2013	78.0	77.8	79.6	80.1	81.0	81.6	82.0	82.2	82.3	82.0	82.7	83.1	81.0
2014	81.5	81.6	82.9	83.5	84.7	85.4	85.2	85.7	85.4	86.0	86.4	87.0	84.6
2015	85.5	86.1	87.3	87.7	89.1	90.5	90.2	90.2	90.6	91.9	92.3	92.9	89.5
2016	91.8	92.8	94.4	95.1	96.1	97.8	98.7	99.2	99.2	99.1	100.2	100.5	97.1
2017	99.0	99.8	100.3	100.7	102.1	103.1	103.0	99.6	98.5	100.7	100.9	102.4	100.8
Manufacturing													
2007	248.9	249.6	250.3	249.7	250.2	251.2	240.7	240.0	240.0	247.3	247.4	247.0	248.9
2008	246.4	245.4	245.4	244.1	244.5	243.3	241.8	240.6	239.5	236.9	235.1	232.4	241.3
2009	226.6	223.3	219.3	215.4	212.8	211.7	208.5	207.9	207.7	206.2	206.5	206.1	212.7
2010	204.4	204.7	204.9	205.6	206.4	206.9	206.6	206.9	207.2	207.3	208.1	210.1	206.6
2011	208.9	211.0	212.9	214.0	214.4	215.6	215.6	216.3	216.3	216.1	216.9	218.2	214.7
2012	216.8	217.7	218.7	219.1	219.6	219.6	218.3	219.0	219.0	219.6	220.5	221.2	219.1
2013	220.2	221.9	222.7	222.5	223.3	223.8	222.4	223.3	223.9	224.3	225.0	225.5	223.2
2014	224.6	224.8	226.3	227.3	228.4	229.2	228.4	227.7	228.8	229.9	230.8	231.9	228.2
2015	231.0	232.2	232.4	232.5	233.2	234.5	233.5	233.7	234.4	233.6	234.7	234.9	233.4
2016	234.4	234.7	234.6	234.8	235.2	235.6	236.1	235.3	236.6	235.1	236.7	238.2	235.6
2017	237.9	239.2	239.8	239.4	240.2	241.7	241.2	240.8	241.7	239.5	242.5	243.6	240.6
Trade, Transportation, and Utilities													
2007	370.1	369.4	374.9	374.8	377.8	380.0	379.5	379.0	378.2	379.5	385.9	388.9	378.2
2008	375.5	374.4	377.1	375.9	375.8	376.0	374.0	373.2	370.5	368.5	370.5	371.2	373.6
2009	353.0	348.4	348.6	349.4	350.9	351.3	348.9	348.3	346.0	345.0	349.1	350.6	349.1
2010	339.0	337.9	341.5	343.6	345.8	347.4	347.2	347.8	345.3	347.7	353.1	355.8	346.0
2011	341.7	342.5	345.0	348.4	349.9	351.9	351.6	351.5	349.0	350.5	355.9	358.4	349.7
2012	347.5	346.4	349.5	351.1	353.8	356.0	355.4	355.3	354.1	356.5	364.6	365.7	354.7
2013	351.4	351.3	354.8	356.9	360.0	363.7	364.7	365.7	363.4	366.6	373.3	377.0	362.4
2014	363.4	361.7	366.1	369.0	372.4	376.0	374.3	374.9	373.3	376.6	384.5	388.5	373.4
2015	373.5	373.3	376.6	380.6	384.2	387.8	388.6	389.0	385.0	388.6	395.7	398.5	385.1
2016	385.3	386.1	387.6	390.7	393.6	395.0	396.2	396.0	393.9	393.7	402.5	405.4	393.8
2017	392.6	392.1	393.6	394.0	396.1	398.3	398.1	398.4	394.2	395.4	405.1	407.1	397.1
Wholesale Trade													
2007	70.7	71.1	71.8	71.9	71.9	72.4	72.1	71.9	71.9	72.2	72.1	72.5	71.9
2008	71.9	72.4	72.6	72.3	72.4	72.5	72.3	72.2	71.9	72.0	71.5	70.8	72.1
2009	68.5	67.8	67.2	67.0	66.8	66.2	65.7	65.6	65.0	65.1	65.0	64.8	66.2
2010	64.0	64.0	64.2	64.5	64.7	64.7	64.7	64.8	64.2	64.4	64.4	64.3	64.4
2011	63.4	64.1	64.2	64.5	64.6	64.7	64.7	64.7	64.5	64.4	64.4	64.7	64.4
2012	64.9	65.3	65.6	65.6	65.8	66.3	65.9	65.9	65.6	65.7	65.7	65.8	65.7
2013	65.5	65.8	66.2	66.4	66.7	67.0	66.6	66.9	66.6	66.6	66.9	67.0	66.5
2014	67.1	67.3	67.6	67.5	68.0	68.5	68.1	68.3	68.3	69.1	69.3	69.3	68.2
2015	69.5	69.8	70.3	70.5	70.8	70.9	70.6	70.7	70.5	71.0	71.1	71.5	70.6
2016	71.1	71.4	71.5	71.8	71.9	72.0	72.0	72.0	71.8	71.6	72.0	72.3	71.8
2017	71.7	72.1	72.4	72.1	72.5	73.0	72.9	72.9	72.2	72.5	72.9	72.7	72.5
Retail Trade													
2007	234.5	232.8	237.3	236.9	239.4	240.7	241.0	240.3	239.5	240.1	246.0	248.0	239.7
2008	237.7	235.8	238.6	237.5	237.5	237.8	236.6	235.7	234.1	231.6	234.3	235.4	236.1
2009	222.4	219.2	220.2	221.9	223.7	224.6	223.9	223.3	221.6	221.0	225.8	226.8	222.9
2010	217.5	216.4	219.1	220.7	222.5	223.6	223.1	223.5	221.6	223.3	228.3	230.5	222.5
2011	219.1	219.2	221.2	224.4	225.2	226.3	226.3	225.7	223.4	224.3	229.1	230.5	224.6
2012	221.2	219.7	222.3	223.7	225.7	226.8	226.9	226.5	225.4	227.0	234.5	234.5	226.2
2013	222.7	222.1	224.8	227.0	229.3	231.9	233.0	233.4	231.5	234.3	240.0	242.2	231.0
2014	230.3	228.9	232.3	233.9	235.8	238.2	237.3	237.1	235.4	237.2	243.7	246.1	236.4
2015	233.3	232.8	235.3	238.4	241.0	244.2	244.7	244.7	241.5	244.4	251.0	252.1	242.0
2016	241.0	241.6	242.8	245.2	247.1	247.5	248.1	247.6	245.6	245.0	252.4	253.3	246.4
2017	244.2	243.3	244.2	245.4	246.8	247.9	247.2	247.1	243.1	244.2	252.0	251.6	246.4

1. Employment by Industry: South Carolina, Selected Years, 2007–2017—*Continued*

(Numbers in thousands, not seasonally adjusted)

Industry and year	January	February	March	April	May	June	July	August	September	October	November	December	Annual average
Transportation and Utilities													
2007	64.9	65.5	65.8	66.0	66.5	66.9	66.4	66.8	66.8	67.2	67.8	68.4	66.6
2008	65.9	66.2	65.9	66.1	65.9	65.7	65.1	65.3	64.5	64.9	64.7	65.0	65.4
2009	62.1	61.4	61.2	60.5	60.4	60.5	59.3	59.4	59.4	58.9	58.3	59.0	60.0
2010	57.5	57.5	58.2	58.4	58.6	59.1	59.4	59.5	59.5	60.0	60.4	61.0	59.1
2011	59.2	59.2	59.6	59.5	60.1	60.9	60.6	61.1	61.1	61.8	62.4	63.2	60.7
2012	61.4	61.4	61.6	61.8	62.3	62.9	62.6	62.9	63.1	63.8	64.4	65.4	62.8
2013	63.2	63.4	63.8	63.5	64.0	64.8	65.1	65.4	65.3	65.7	66.4	67.8	64.9
2014	66.0	65.5	66.2	67.6	68.6	69.3	68.9	69.5	69.6	70.3	71.5	73.1	68.8
2015	70.7	70.7	71.0	71.7	72.4	72.7	73.3	73.6	73.0	73.2	73.6	74.9	72.6
2016	73.2	73.1	73.3	73.7	74.6	75.5	76.1	76.4	76.5	77.1	78.1	79.8	75.6
2017	76.7	76.7	77.0	76.5	76.8	77.4	78.0	78.4	78.9	78.7	80.2	82.8	78.2
Information													
2007	27.1	27.2	27.4	27.6	27.9	28.5	28.7	28.5	28.0	28.1	28.2	28.4	28.0
2008	28.1	28.2	28.2	28.6	28.8	29.0	29.1	28.9	28.4	28.2	28.2	28.4	28.5
2009	27.9	27.7	27.9	27.5	27.4	27.4	27.6	26.9	26.5	26.5	26.4	26.3	27.2
2010	26.3	26.3	26.3	25.5	25.6	26.0	26.3	25.7	25.4	25.5	25.7	26.1	25.9
2011	26.0	25.7	25.9	25.7	25.7	25.8	25.8	25.7	25.3	26.0	26.1	26.1	25.8
2012	25.5	25.8	25.6	25.7	26.0	26.1	25.8	25.6	25.4	25.6	25.9	26.3	25.8
2013	26.1	26.4	26.4	26.7	26.7	26.5	26.6	26.3	26.2	26.2	26.4	26.4	26.4
2014	26.0	26.0	26.1	26.4	26.5	26.5	26.5	26.3	26.1	26.4	27.0	27.0	26.4
2015	26.6	26.6	26.6	26.6	26.9	26.8	27.0	26.9	26.7	26.8	27.8	27.3	26.9
2016	26.9	26.9	27.0	27.7	27.3	27.2	27.1	27.0	26.9	27.2	27.4	27.8	27.2
2017	27.3	27.5	27.7	27.4	27.7	27.8	27.4	27.4	27.3	27.8	27.9	28.0	27.6
Financial Activities													
2007	99.1	99.1	100.0	100.4	101.2	102.2	101.9	101.9	101.2	101.2	101.2	101.6	100.9
2008	100.2	101.0	101.3	101.2	101.7	102.6	101.9	101.7	100.2	99.7	99.1	99.0	100.8
2009	96.7	96.6	96.6	96.4	96.8	97.0	97.2	96.5	95.0	93.8	93.3	93.0	95.7
2010	91.6	91.5	91.9	92.3	92.8	93.4	93.6	93.1	91.7	91.7	91.5	91.2	92.2
2011	89.9	89.8	90.1	90.9	91.7	92.2	92.6	92.6	91.7	91.7	92.0	92.0	91.4
2012	91.3	91.7	92.2	93.4	93.8	94.9	94.8	95.1	94.3	94.1	94.4	94.9	93.7
2013	93.4	94.0	94.8	95.6	96.4	97.3	97.5	97.7	96.6	96.4	96.4	96.5	96.1
2014	95.0	95.1	95.6	96.7	97.1	97.9	97.6	97.8	96.6	96.3	96.4	96.6	96.6
2015	95.5	95.7	96.1	97.0	97.7	98.7	98.8	99.0	98.1	98.7	98.9	99.3	97.8
2016	98.2	98.7	99.5	100.5	101.1	101.6	101.9	102.0	100.9	101.3	101.7	101.4	100.7
2017	100.2	100.5	101.2	101.4	102.1	103.2	103.3	103.5	102.4	102.0	101.7	101.0	101.9
Professional and Business Services													
2007	220.9	223.6	225.2	227.0	228.5	230.0	226.7	229.2	229.2	227.9	227.5	226.5	226.9
2008	220.7	223.3	224.6	225.3	227.5	225.5	221.2	223.5	220.7	218.6	216.6	210.6	221.5
2009	201.0	199.9	200.2	199.2	199.0	198.2	198.5	199.9	199.5	203.8	205.3	203.5	200.7
2010	200.0	202.8	205.5	214.4	216.0	218.0	219.2	221.2	221.0	222.6	223.1	223.0	215.6
2011	217.8	222.0	225.1	230.1	230.4	230.8	231.1	233.1	231.7	230.6	231.4	231.5	228.8
2012	227.4	230.3	234.0	237.2	238.5	239.6	236.7	239.1	236.0	235.6	239.7	240.0	236.2
2013	232.9	234.8	236.2	238.5	241.2	243.4	242.1	243.7	244.1	245.7	251.2	251.7	242.1
2014	242.9	244.0	250.8	252.9	255.3	254.5	253.1	255.0	255.5	257.2	264.0	263.2	254.0
2015	251.6	253.4	255.7	258.0	262.2	262.8	263.9	265.1	265.0	270.1	272.0	274.4	262.9
2016	259.2	262.9	263.7	270.1	270.3	269.8	269.3	270.8	271.6	272.7	278.3	277.0	269.6
2017	270.2	273.5	274.5	275.0	276.6	278.9	277.6	277.5	275.5	280.5	282.5	279.8	276.8
Education and Health Services													
2007	190.9	193.2	194.2	194.8	195.3	194.8	194.7	195.7	197.9	198.5	199.2	199.1	195.7
2008	198.2	200.5	201.4	200.4	201.8	200.6	199.7	201.0	202.9	203.9	204.3	203.8	201.5
2009	201.2	202.9	202.8	203.6	204.2	202.4	202.5	204.0	204.5	206.1	207.1	206.3	204.0
2010	206.1	208.2	208.4	210.1	210.6	208.5	208.5	209.9	210.6	213.2	213.6	213.4	210.1
2011	209.8	212.8	213.3	214.1	214.0	211.9	210.9	211.9	213.9	214.7	215.3	214.8	213.1
2012	212.7	214.9	215.3	214.6	215.0	212.6	211.9	213.4	216.3	217.8	218.4	218.1	215.1
2013	214.6	217.5	217.6	218.1	218.9	217.0	216.2	218.3	220.1	222.2	223.4	223.3	218.9
2014	221.4	222.9	224.5	227.4	227.3	225.2	224.7	227.0	228.8	231.5	232.5	232.5	227.1
2015	229.3	231.9	232.7	233.6	234.6	232.9	232.3	234.8	236.0	238.2	239.4	239.1	234.6
2016	235.8	238.4	239.6	240.4	241.0	238.8	239.1	241.3	243.8	243.4	244.7	244.6	240.9
2017	241.7	245.0	245.7	245.9	246.2	244.5	243.4	245.6	246.0	250.6	250.7	250.4	246.3

1. Employment by Industry: South Carolina, Selected Years, 2007–2017—*Continued*

(Numbers in thousands, not seasonally adjusted)

Industry and year	January	February	March	April	May	June	July	August	September	October	November	December	Annual average
Leisure and Hospitality													
2007	199.8	203.0	211.3	219.4	224.1	229.3	227.9	227.4	220.9	217.9	214.0	210.6	217.1
2008	203.1	207.2	214.7	223.2	229.3	231.5	229.0	228.0	219.9	214.0	208.5	204.8	217.8
2009	195.0	198.1	204.8	213.5	219.1	220.8	219.1	217.7	211.2	205.1	200.5	196.7	208.5
2010	189.1	192.7	200.1	211.0	215.6	219.2	219.3	218.3	212.7	207.5	204.2	200.3	207.5
2011	190.2	195.0	203.7	214.7	221.0	223.5	222.1	222.1	214.8	209.9	207.6	204.1	210.7
2012	197.4	201.4	210.8	220.1	224.4	229.2	228.1	228.5	220.5	216.1	213.7	209.8	216.7
2013	202.6	206.8	213.5	225.1	231.1	236.3	235.6	234.6	227.7	222.8	220.7	216.7	222.8
2014	209.7	211.4	222.1	232.6	238.5	242.4	240.2	239.6	232.8	230.2	226.8	223.7	229.2
2015	218.3	222.5	231.3	240.7	246.6	250.9	251.6	249.7	241.3	239.9	237.3	234.0	238.7
2016	227.0	231.3	241.1	250.8	257.1	261.5	260.8	259.4	250.7	244.2	244.8	241.0	247.5
2017	234.8	240.1	248.2	256.7	262.2	267.7	266.6	265.3	253.2	253.0	249.4	248.3	253.8
Other Services													
2007	73.4	73.8	74.4	74.3	74.6	74.6	73.4	73.0	72.4	71.7	71.5	71.0	73.2
2008	70.2	70.4	71.3	71.7	72.4	72.5	72.2	72.0	71.6	71.2	70.9	70.5	71.4
2009	69.4	69.6	69.8	69.9	70.2	70.1	69.8	69.2	69.2	69.0	68.6	68.4	69.4
2010	67.4	67.7	68.4	68.8	69.0	69.2	68.7	68.4	68.6	68.7	68.5	68.3	68.5
2011	67.5	67.9	68.6	68.9	69.0	69.0	69.1	68.5	68.3	67.9	67.8	67.6	68.3
2012	67.7	67.9	69.0	69.0	69.5	69.9	69.9	69.7	69.4	69.6	69.8	69.7	69.3
2013	69.4	69.7	70.7	70.9	71.2	71.8	71.4	71.6	71.9	71.6	70.8	71.0	71.0
2014	70.2	70.4	71.9	71.9	72.5	72.8	72.4	72.5	72.3	72.5	72.6	72.4	72.0
2015	72.0	72.4	73.6	73.6	74.2	74.4	74.2	74.0	73.6	74.0	74.0	74.1	73.7
2016	73.3	73.6	74.3	74.6	74.8	75.0	75.1	75.0	75.1	74.7	75.1	75.2	74.7
2017	74.5	74.6	75.4	75.5	75.7	75.7	75.5	75.3	75.0	77.4	77.4	77.8	75.8
Government													
2007	344.0	346.7	349.2	347.7	348.3	343.1	326.1	334.4	349.6	354.0	357.3	356.4	346.4
2008	353.2	357.1	358.3	359.2	361.3	355.1	335.3	337.3	357.8	362.5	365.1	364.1	355.5
2009	356.6	359.2	359.9	361.6	360.9	353.8	339.3	343.7	353.1	358.2	359.7	359.1	355.4
2010	354.5	358.1	360.1	360.7	370.6	358.3	341.7	344.9	351.1	354.0	354.8	354.1	355.2
2011	349.1	352.3	353.6	353.8	352.6	347.3	332.5	335.7	348.2	351.3	352.5	351.9	348.4
2012	347.6	353.0	354.3	354.2	354.5	350.9	336.2	337.9	352.2	356.9	361.0	358.7	351.5
2013	352.0	356.5	358.1	358.9	358.0	352.1	337.5	339.0	352.8	357.4	359.0	358.0	353.3
2014	353.2	357.2	358.7	359.7	360.0	354.1	339.4	343.0	357.5	362.1	363.0	363.2	355.9
2015	357.5	362.1	363.0	364.1	364.1	358.0	344.4	348.1	361.7	365.3	366.7	367.7	360.2
2016	361.0	364.9	366.8	367.5	366.8	361.8	349.8	352.5	364.7	366.7	368.2	369.5	363.4
2017	363.3	366.9	369.0	369.1	368.9	364.0	353.1	355.6	367.1	371.0	371.9	371.9	366.0

2. Average Weekly Hours by Selected Industry: South Carolina, 2013–2017

(Not seasonally adjusted)

Industry and year	January	February	March	April	May	June	July	August	September	October	November	December	Annual average
Total Private													
2013	34.5	34.6	34.9	35.0	34.8	35.1	34.6	34.9	35.3	34.8	34.7	35.0	34.9
2014	34.6	33.4	34.7	34.5	34.5	34.9	34.6	34.6	34.5	34.3	34.7	34.6	34.5
2015	34.3	34.6	34.7	34.6	34.7	34.8	34.7	35.2	34.3	34.6	34.8	34.6	34.7
2016	34.4	34.4	34.6	34.6	34.8	34.6	34.4	34.4	34.4	34.2	34.5	34.5	34.5
2017	34.4	34.4	34.5	34.7	34.6	34.9	34.8	34.8	34.0	34.8	34.7	34.7	34.6
Goods-Producing													
2013	40.4	40.3	40.7	41.0	41.1	41.3	39.8	41.2	41.5	41.5	41.4	41.6	41.0
2014	41.3	38.6	39.4	39.2	40.0	40.4	39.7	40.1	40.1	39.7	40.6	40.4	40.0
2015	40.0	40.1	40.4	40.8	41.2	41.1	41.2	41.1	40.7	41.3	41.0	41.3	40.9
2016	40.7	40.8	42.0	41.4	41.7	41.7	40.3	40.5	41.0	40.7	41.1	41.1	41.1
2017	40.1	41.1	41.1	40.8	41.4	42.0	41.0	41.3	41.2	42.1	42.3	42.6	41.4
Construction													
2013	39.8	38.3	40.3	40.1	40.9	40.7	39.3	39.6	40.1	40.2	40.6	40.0	40.0
2014	40.3	35.8	39.3	38.3	39.5	39.6	39.0	39.0	38.6	38.3	39.1	39.3	38.9
2015	38.1	38.5	39.4	38.9	39.7	39.7	39.5	39.7	38.8	40.5	39.7	39.9	39.4
2016	38.8	39.1	40.6	39.3	40.5	40.7	40.0	39.9	39.6	39.7	40.2	39.6	39.8
2017	39.0	39.2	39.6	38.9	40.0	40.4	40.3	40.0	38.4	40.3	41.0	40.4	39.8
Manufacturing													
2013	40.4	40.9	40.7	41.2	41.0	41.4	39.9	41.6	41.9	41.9	41.6	42.1	41.2
2014	41.6	39.5	40.9	40.7	41.3	41.6	40.7	41.2	41.3	40.8	41.6	41.2	41.0
2015	41.2	41.1	41.1	41.9	42.0	41.9	42.1	41.8	41.7	41.6	41.7	42.0	41.7
2016	41.6	41.5	42.5	42.3	42.2	42.1	40.3	40.7	41.7	41.3	41.6	41.9	41.6
2017	40.6	41.7	41.6	41.6	41.9	42.6	41.2	41.8	42.5	43.0	43.0	43.8	42.1
Trade, Transportation, and Utilities													
2013	33.5	33.8	34.2	34.3	34.5	34.5	34.6	34.7	34.5	34.1	34.1	34.8	34.3
2014	34.0	33.0	33.8	33.9	34.1	34.5	34.5	34.3	34.7	34.3	35.0	35.0	34.3
2015	34.4	34.7	35.3	35.0	35.2	35.2	34.9	35.5	34.5	34.6	34.8	34.5	34.9
2016	34.4	34.3	34.0	34.3	34.3	34.1	34.3	34.4	34.5	33.7	33.7	34.0	34.2
2017	33.9	33.6	33.8	34.3	34.3	34.4	34.4	34.4	33.5	34.0	34.0	34.2	34.1
Financial Activities													
2013	37.0	37.5	37.4	37.2	37.2	38.4	37.9	37.7	39.2	38.1	38.0	38.5	37.8
2014	37.6	38.1	38.3	37.2	37.2	38.1	37.1	37.4	37.2	36.8	37.7	36.7	37.5
2015	36.7	37.7	37.4	36.8	36.7	37.0	37.2	38.0	36.9	37.1	38.2	37.0	37.2
2016	37.1	37.3	37.2	36.9	37.8	36.9	36.9	36.4	36.3	37.4	36.6	36.8	37.0
2017	37.7	36.7	36.6	37.6	36.6	36.8	37.6	36.7	36.7	37.9	37.2	37.4	37.1
Professional and Business Services													
2013	36.9	36.7	37.1	37.2	37.1	37.6	36.6	36.7	38.1	36.8	37.2	37.6	37.1
2014	36.9	35.3	38.0	37.8	37.9	38.2	37.6	37.8	37.5	37.5	37.8	37.2	37.5
2015	36.7	37.1	36.6	36.4	36.5	36.5	36.1	36.9	35.8	36.2	37.3	36.9	36.6
2016	36.1	36.5	36.1	36.4	36.8	36.2	35.8	36.1	36.0	36.3	36.6	36.6	36.3
2017	36.5	36.0	36.2	36.6	36.4	36.4	36.3	36.7	35.1	36.4	36.3	36.1	36.2
Education and Health Services													
2013	34.1	34.1	34.3	34.2	33.8	34.0	33.5	33.4	33.6	33.5	33.3	32.9	33.7
2014	32.6	31.9	32.7	32.4	32.3	32.1	32.5	32.6	32.4	32.6	32.9	33.1	32.5
2015	33.2	33.4	33.3	32.8	32.8	32.6	32.7	33.6	32.8	33.0	33.3	33.0	33.0
2016	32.9	32.5	32.8	32.8	33.0	32.6	32.7	32.6	32.6	32.6	32.8	32.7	32.7
2017	32.6	32.8	32.6	32.7	32.9	32.5	32.8	32.8	32.6	32.5	32.4	32.6	32.6
Leisure and Hospitality													
2013	25.0	25.4	26.1	26.2	25.9	26.4	26.6	26.9	25.8	25.5	25.1	25.0	25.8
2014	24.9	24.6	26.1	26.4	25.8	26.3	26.6	26.2	25.2	25.4	24.9	24.9	25.6
2015	24.6	25.1	25.7	26.0	25.8	26.4	26.7	26.6	25.2	25.0	25.0	24.7	25.6
2016	24.6	24.8	25.4	25.8	25.9	26.7	26.9	26.3	25.6	24.8	25.2	24.8	25.6
2017	24.5	24.9	25.5	26.1	25.4	26.4	26.9	26.4	24.8	25.9	25.6	25.1	25.6
Other Services													
2013	34.0	32.6	33.3	33.7	33.1	32.9	31.8	31.6	32.3	31.6	31.3	31.5	32.5
2014	31.2	28.9	31.0	31.4	31.0	30.3	31.1	30.9	31.1	31.2	30.5	30.6	30.8
2015	29.9	30.0	31.3	31.5	31.9	31.5	31.7	31.1	31.1	31.3	31.1	32.4	31.2
2016	32.7	33.1	33.1	34.4	33.2	33.6	34.4	33.9	34.7	34.5	33.8	33.8	33.8
2017	34.3	34.7	34.3	34.9	33.8	33.5	33.9	32.8	33.2	33.3	32.5	32.5	33.6

3. Average Hourly Earnings by Selected Industry: South Carolina, 2013–2017

(Dollars, not seasonally adjusted)

Industry and year	January	February	March	April	May	June	July	August	September	October	November	December	Annual average
Total Private													
2013	20.27	20.57	20.72	20.23	20.15	20.34	20.26	20.40	20.64	20.69	20.92	21.05	20.52
2014	21.06	21.73	21.19	20.80	20.68	20.78	20.64	20.76	21.01	21.07	21.47	21.39	21.05
2015	21.70	21.36	21.75	21.22	21.03	20.99	21.26	21.29	21.50	21.53	21.80	21.67	21.42
2016	21.87	21.79	22.17	21.93	21.87	22.07	21.93	21.95	22.24	22.53	22.49	22.46	22.11
2017	23.08	22.74	23.12	22.80	22.44	22.44	22.87	22.68	23.12	23.16	23.09	23.21	22.90
Goods-Producing													
2013	20.96	20.72	20.85	20.92	20.89	21.14	21.25	21.36	21.69	21.67	21.97	22.24	21.31
2014	22.19	22.97	22.30	22.20	21.87	22.07	22.25	22.19	22.26	22.23	22.48	22.85	22.32
2015	22.67	22.68	22.69	22.52	22.29	22.42	22.69	22.84	22.96	23.13	23.36	23.37	22.80
2016	23.39	23.33	23.55	23.47	23.47	23.59	24.20	24.04	24.33	24.02	24.08	24.27	23.81
2017	24.55	24.06	24.09	24.02	23.54	23.65	24.08	24.02	24.06	24.21	24.44	24.64	24.11
Construction													
2013	19.90	20.38	20.76	20.22	19.99	20.11	19.81	19.90	19.99	19.91	19.86	20.20	20.08
2014	20.14	21.09	20.38	19.98	20.10	20.40	20.55	20.72	20.95	20.97	20.90	20.74	20.57
2015	20.54	20.58	20.81	20.62	20.41	20.55	20.74	20.92	21.05	21.28	21.39	21.65	20.89
2016	21.68	21.72	22.15	21.79	21.76	21.98	22.60	22.57	23.08	23.16	22.98	22.76	22.37
2017	22.97	22.65	23.15	22.75	22.34	22.60	22.97	23.14	23.34	23.09	23.08	23.94	23.00
Manufacturing													
2013	21.37	20.84	21.06	21.33	21.37	21.66	21.95	22.02	22.43	22.43	22.78	23.00	21.86
2014	23.00	23.76	23.16	23.18	22.66	22.82	23.02	22.83	22.82	22.77	23.15	23.75	23.07
2015	23.56	23.57	23.50	23.35	23.11	23.26	23.59	23.75	23.86	24.03	24.34	24.25	23.68
2016	24.25	24.13	24.22	24.30	24.32	24.41	25.02	24.75	24.90	24.40	24.62	24.99	24.52
2017	25.33	24.87	24.60	24.72	24.22	24.25	24.70	24.50	24.43	24.79	25.15	24.91	24.70
Trade, Transportation, and Utilities													
2013	19.01	19.05	19.47	19.06	19.07	19.33	19.34	19.37	19.82	19.80	19.98	19.92	19.44
2014	20.39	20.89	20.87	19.57	19.37	19.60	19.14	19.50	19.73	20.02	20.12	19.57	19.89
2015	20.07	19.59	20.46	19.68	19.66	19.75	19.93	20.04	20.04	20.29	20.60	20.31	20.04
2016	20.53	20.27	21.07	20.38	20.40	20.11	20.37	20.13	20.33	20.69	20.69	20.57	20.46
2017	21.02	20.97	21.57	21.73	21.33	21.36	21.57	21.56	21.77	21.92	21.06	21.05	21.41
Financial Activities													
2013	22.95	22.77	20.16	20.69	20.64	20.69	20.80	21.09	19.87	20.45	20.82	21.32	21.01
2014	21.90	22.68	22.76	22.57	22.52	23.19	23.28	23.25	23.79	23.82	24.66	24.11	23.21
2015	24.95	25.20	25.10	25.01	24.56	24.31	24.84	24.58	24.54	24.31	25.17	25.07	24.80
2016	25.59	24.88	25.02	25.77	25.16	24.60	24.82	25.39	25.88	26.64	26.32	26.04	25.51
2017	26.73	25.75	24.99	26.09	25.73	25.75	26.19	26.26	26.93	27.19	27.22	27.04	26.33
Professional and Business Services													
2013	22.93	23.64	23.42	23.10	22.99	23.41	22.85	22.98	23.23	23.25	23.44	23.54	23.23
2014	23.57	24.64	23.69	23.34	23.45	23.24	23.21	23.17	23.20	23.06	23.17	22.75	23.36
2015	23.75	23.84	23.91	23.66	23.40	23.38	23.92	23.13	23.18	22.86	22.87	22.35	23.34
2016	22.78	22.97	22.00	23.50	23.60	23.36	23.70	23.74	24.22	24.50	24.28	24.05	23.65
2017	24.67	25.19	25.09	25.76	25.02	25.01	25.93	24.77	25.51	25.26	25.37	25.88	25.29
Education and Health Services													
2013	22.80	22.85	22.79	22.81	22.77	23.14	23.33	23.94	23.76	23.73	24.09	24.14	23.34
2014	24.10	24.67	24.19	24.62	24.48	24.79	24.83	24.94	25.40	25.36	25.89	25.94	24.94
2015	25.97	26.01	25.60	25.88	25.54	25.49	25.79	26.10	26.71	26.14	26.48	26.32	26.01
2016	26.23	26.42	25.94	26.18	25.77	25.88	26.05	25.91	25.75	26.10	26.36	26.00	26.05
2017	25.78	25.82	25.95	25.83	25.82	26.25	26.87	26.74	26.94	26.70	26.58	26.65	26.33
Leisure and Hospitality													
2013	11.54	11.75	11.57	11.43	11.56	11.46	11.49	11.36	11.61	11.60	11.70	11.77	11.56
2014	11.64	11.99	11.73	11.86	11.88	11.80	11.80	11.78	11.87	11.97	12.09	11.87	11.86
2015	11.90	12.02	12.09	12.07	12.02	11.89	11.88	12.02	12.05	12.28	12.22	12.40	12.07
2016	12.25	12.31	12.36	12.35	12.53	12.37	12.34	12.49	12.51	12.51	12.53	12.64	12.43
2017	12.58	12.48	12.47	12.78	12.83	12.55	12.48	12.53	12.57	12.72	12.73	12.82	12.63
Other Services													
2013	16.96	17.25	16.85	16.71	16.57	16.63	16.50	16.33	16.21	16.11	16.37	16.25	16.57
2014	16.43	16.75	16.16	15.95	15.69	15.51	14.56	15.04	14.92	14.98	15.46	15.65	15.58
2015	16.09	16.22	16.11	16.22	16.06	16.11	16.23	16.35	16.20	16.37	16.67	16.70	16.28
2016	17.18	17.36	17.14	17.53	18.00	17.97	18.14	17.81	17.78	18.26	19.29	19.69	18.02
2017	20.35	20.54	20.70	21.09	21.13	21.28	21.65	21.80	22.47	22.36	22.73	22.35	21.53

4. Average Weekly Earnings by Selected Industry: South Carolina, 2013–2017

(Dollars, not seasonally adjusted)

Industry and year	January	February	March	April	May	June	July	August	September	October	November	December	Annual average
Total Private													
2013	699.32	711.72	723.13	708.05	701.22	713.93	701.00	711.96	728.59	720.01	725.92	736.75	716.15
2014	728.68	725.78	735.29	717.60	713.46	725.22	714.14	718.30	724.85	722.70	745.01	740.09	726.23
2015	744.31	739.06	754.73	734.21	729.74	730.45	737.72	749.41	737.45	744.94	758.64	749.78	743.27
2016	752.33	749.58	767.08	758.78	761.08	763.62	754.39	755.08	765.06	770.53	775.91	774.87	762.80
2017	793.95	782.26	797.64	791.16	776.42	783.16	795.88	789.26	786.08	805.97	801.22	805.39	792.34
Goods-Producing													
2013	846.78	835.02	848.60	857.72	858.58	873.08	845.75	880.03	900.14	899.31	909.56	925.18	873.71
2014	916.45	886.64	878.62	870.24	874.80	891.63	883.33	889.82	892.63	882.53	912.69	923.14	892.80
2015	906.80	909.47	916.68	918.82	918.35	921.46	934.83	938.72	934.47	955.27	957.76	965.18	932.52
2016	951.97	951.86	989.10	971.66	978.70	983.70	975.26	973.62	997.53	977.61	989.69	997.50	978.59
2017	984.46	988.87	990.10	980.02	974.56	993.30	987.28	992.03	991.27	1,019.24	1,033.81	1,049.66	998.15
Construction													
2013	792.02	780.55	836.63	810.82	817.59	818.48	778.53	788.04	801.60	800.38	806.32	808.00	803.20
2014	811.64	755.02	800.93	765.23	793.95	807.84	801.45	808.08	808.67	803.15	817.19	815.08	800.17
2015	782.57	792.33	819.91	802.12	810.28	815.84	819.23	830.52	816.74	861.84	849.18	863.84	823.07
2016	841.18	849.25	899.29	856.35	881.28	894.59	904.00	900.54	913.97	919.45	923.80	901.30	890.33
2017	895.83	887.88	916.74	884.98	893.60	913.04	925.69	925.60	896.26	930.53	946.28	967.18	915.40
Manufacturing													
2013	863.35	852.36	857.14	878.80	876.17	896.72	875.81	916.03	939.82	939.82	947.65	968.30	900.63
2014	956.80	938.52	947.24	943.43	935.86	949.31	936.91	940.60	942.47	929.02	963.04	978.50	945.87
2015	970.67	968.73	965.85	978.37	970.62	974.59	993.14	992.75	994.96	999.65	1,014.98	1,018.50	987.46
2016	1,008.80	1,001.40	1,029.35	1,027.89	1,026.30	1,027.66	1,008.31	1,007.33	1,038.33	1,007.72	1,024.19	1,047.08	1,020.03
2017	1,028.40	1,037.08	1,023.36	1,028.35	1,014.82	1,033.05	1,017.64	1,024.10	1,038.28	1,065.97	1,081.45	1,091.06	1,039.87
Trade, Transportation, and Utilities													
2013	636.84	643.89	665.87	653.76	657.92	666.89	669.16	672.14	683.79	675.18	681.32	693.22	666.79
2014	693.26	689.37	705.41	663.42	660.52	676.20	660.33	668.85	684.63	686.69	704.20	684.95	682.23
2015	690.41	679.77	722.24	688.80	692.03	695.20	695.56	711.42	691.38	702.03	716.88	700.70	699.40
2016	706.23	695.26	716.38	699.03	699.72	685.75	698.69	692.47	701.39	697.25	697.25	699.38	699.73
2017	712.58	704.59	729.07	745.34	731.62	734.78	742.01	741.66	729.30	745.28	716.04	719.91	730.08
Financial Activities													
2013	849.15	853.88	753.98	769.67	767.81	794.50	788.32	795.09	778.90	779.15	791.16	820.82	794.18
2014	823.44	864.11	871.71	839.60	837.74	883.54	863.69	869.55	884.99	876.58	929.68	884.84	870.38
2015	915.67	950.04	938.74	920.37	901.35	899.47	924.05	934.04	905.53	901.90	961.49	927.59	922.56
2016	949.39	928.02	930.74	950.91	951.05	907.74	915.86	924.20	939.44	996.34	963.31	958.27	943.87
2017	1,007.72	945.03	914.63	980.98	941.72	947.60	984.74	963.74	988.33	1,030.50	1,012.58	1,011.30	976.84
Professional and Business Services													
2013	846.12	867.59	868.88	859.32	852.93	880.22	836.31	843.37	885.06	855.60	871.97	885.10	861.83
2014	869.73	869.79	900.22	882.25	888.76	887.77	872.70	875.83	870.00	864.75	875.83	846.30	876.00
2015	871.63	884.46	875.11	861.22	854.10	853.37	863.51	853.50	829.84	827.53	853.05	824.72	854.24
2016	822.36	838.41	825.97	855.40	868.48	845.63	851.68	857.01	871.92	889.35	888.65	880.23	858.50
2017	900.46	906.84	908.26	942.82	910.73	910.36	941.26	909.06	895.40	919.46	920.93	934.27	915.50
Education and Health Services													
2013	777.48	779.19	781.70	780.10	769.63	786.76	781.56	799.60	798.34	794.96	802.20	794.21	786.56
2014	785.66	786.97	791.01	797.69	790.70	795.76	806.98	813.04	822.96	826.74	851.78	858.61	810.55
2015	862.20	868.73	852.48	848.86	837.71	830.97	843.33	876.96	876.09	862.62	881.78	868.56	858.33
2016	862.97	858.65	850.83	858.70	850.41	843.69	851.84	844.67	839.45	850.86	864.61	850.20	851.84
2017	840.43	846.90	845.97	844.64	849.48	853.13	881.34	877.07	878.24	867.75	861.19	868.79	858.36
Leisure and Hospitality													
2013	288.50	298.45	301.98	299.47	299.40	302.54	305.63	305.58	299.54	295.80	293.67	294.25	298.25
2014	289.84	294.95	306.15	313.10	306.50	310.34	313.88	308.64	299.12	304.04	301.04	295.56	303.62
2015	292.74	301.70	310.71	313.82	310.12	313.90	317.20	319.73	303.66	307.00	305.50	306.28	308.99
2016	301.35	305.29	313.94	318.63	324.53	330.28	331.95	328.49	320.26	310.25	315.76	313.47	318.21
2017	308.21	310.75	317.99	333.56	325.88	331.32	335.71	330.79	311.74	329.45	325.89	321.78	323.33
Other Services													
2013	576.64	562.35	561.11	563.13	548.47	547.13	524.70	516.03	523.58	509.08	512.38	511.88	538.53
2014	512.62	484.08	500.96	500.83	486.39	469.95	452.82	464.74	464.01	467.38	471.53	478.89	479.86
2015	481.09	486.60	504.24	510.93	512.31	507.47	514.49	508.49	503.82	512.38	518.44	541.08	507.94
2016	561.79	574.62	567.33	603.03	597.60	603.79	624.02	603.76	616.97	629.97	652.00	665.52	609.08
2017	698.01	712.74	710.01	736.04	714.19	712.88	733.94	715.04	746.00	744.59	738.73	726.38	723.41

SOUTH DAKOTA
At a Glance

Population:
2010 census: 814,180
2017 estimate: 869,666

Percent change in population:
2010–2017: 6.8%

Percent change in total nonfarm employment:
2007–2017: 6.9%

Industry with the largest growth in employment, 2007–2017 (thousands):
Education and health services, 11.9

Industry with the largest decline or smallest growth in employment, 2007–2017 (thousands):
Financial activities, -1.6

Civilian labor force:
2010: 441,339
2017: 455,175

Unemployment rate and rank among states (highest to lowest):
2010: 5.0%, 49th
2017: 3.3%, 40th

Over-the-year change in unemployment rates:
2015–2016: -0.1%
2016–2017: 0.3%

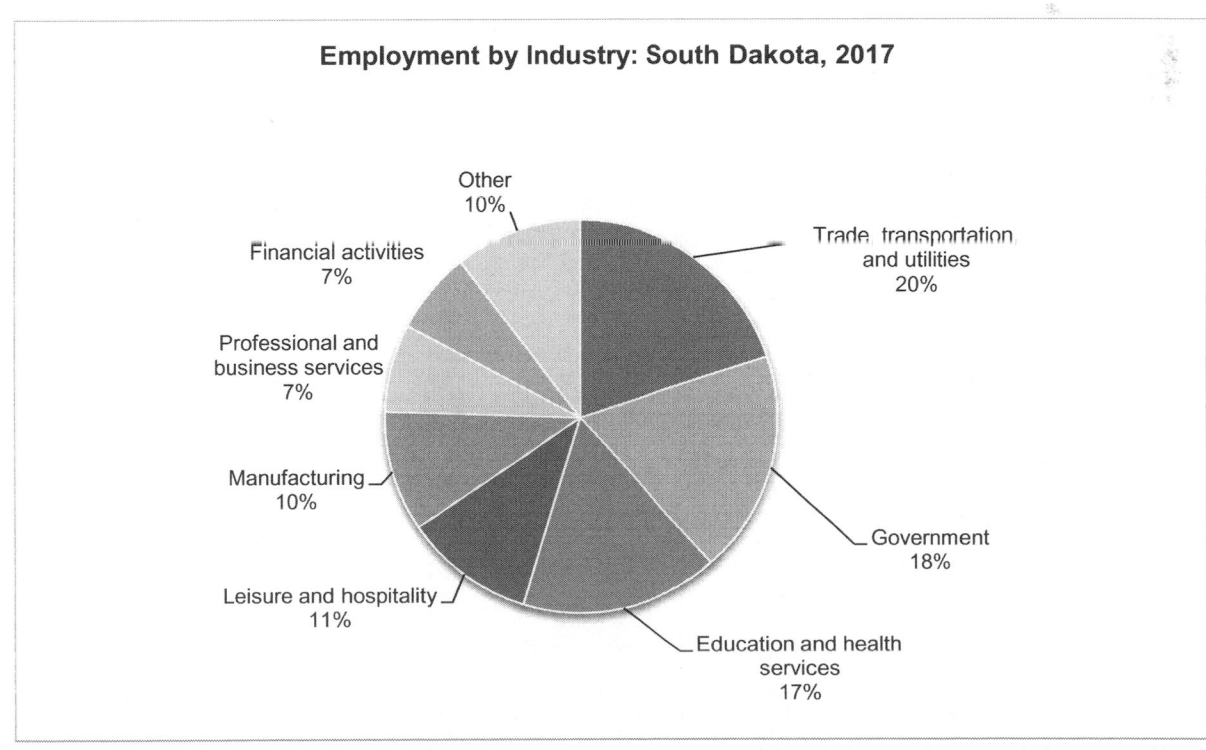

Employment by Industry: South Dakota, 2017

- Other 10%
- Financial activities 7%
- Professional and business services 7%
- Manufacturing 10%
- Leisure and hospitality 11%
- Trade, transportation and utilities 20%
- Government 18%
- Education and health services 17%

1. Employment by Industry: South Dakota, Selected Years, 2007–2017

(Numbers in thousands, not seasonally adjusted)

Industry and year	January	February	March	April	May	June	July	August	September	October	November	December	Annual average
Total Nonfarm													
2007	392.0	392.8	396.4	401.5	411.6	416.8	413.2	415.8	411.0	410.4	409.1	407.8	406.5
2008	399.6	401.1	403.5	407.1	416.6	420.9	416.6	420.2	415.2	414.7	411.6	409.7	411.4
2009	397.5	397.0	397.2	399.0	409.2	412.8	408.8	409.2	406.2	404.2	402.9	399.9	403.7
2010	388.3	389.2	392.0	399.5	407.3	413.0	409.1	411.6	407.8	408.8	407.0	405.1	403.2
2011	393.0	394.4	396.8	403.4	411.2	417.3	412.8	415.0	412.5	413.1	411.2	411.1	407.7
2012	399.9	400.7	404.8	411.3	418.9	424.6	419.2	421.0	418.7	418.1	417.4	415.6	414.2
2013	404.7	405.9	408.9	411.6	423.4	427.5	422.3	424.5	422.3	422.4	422.0	420.3	418.0
2014	410.3	411.9	414.1	419.6	429.1	434.0	429.5	431.3	429.0	428.2	426.0	425.9	424.1
2015	414.7	416.5	419.9	425.6	433.8	438.8	434.0	434.9	432.4	432.4	430.9	430.5	428.7
2016	418.5	420.5	423.3	429.6	437.0	442.2	438.6	439.4	436.9	435.7	434.6	432.5	432.4
2017	421.3	422.8	425.6	431.7	439.4	444.4	438.3	440.4	438.3	438.7	436.5	435.4	434.4
Total Private													
2007	317.8	317.0	320.6	325.7	334.0	340.0	340.6	343.0	335.7	334.0	332.5	331.5	331.0
2008	324.9	324.6	327.0	330.5	338.2	344.0	344.5	346.9	339.2	337.1	333.9	332.1	335.2
2009	321.5	319.7	319.4	320.3	328.8	334.1	333.9	334.5	328.1	325.1	323.6	321.5	325.9
2010	311.2	310.8	312.6	319.7	326.1	332.7	334.0	336.3	329.2	329.1	327.2	325.7	324.6
2011	315.4	315.4	317.7	324.0	331.4	337.3	338.5	341.5	335.2	334.3	332.5	332.2	329.6
2012	323.1	323.0	326.4	332.6	340.0	346.0	345.8	347.9	341.4	339.1	338.2	336.9	336.7
2013	327.8	327.6	330.5	333.6	344.6	350.1	349.7	351.2	344.5	343.7	343.1	341.8	340.7
2014	333.3	333.8	335.6	340.9	349.7	355.5	355.8	357.2	350.6	349.1	346.8	347.1	346.3
2015	338.0	338.6	341.5	346.9	354.1	359.9	360.0	361.3	354.3	353.4	351.7	351.4	350.9
2016	341.4	341.9	344.4	350.1	356.8	362.6	364.6	365.2	357.6	355.8	354.6	352.4	354.0
2017	343.2	343.4	345.9	351.8	358.1	363.9	363.6	365.2	358.4	357.8	355.5	354.5	355.1
Goods Producing													
2007	61.6	60.6	61.9	63.6	65.9	67.9	68.3	68.1	67.2	66.9	66.1	64.6	65.2
2008	62.7	62.3	63.2	64.8	67.5	68.8	69.1	68.8	67.6	67.2	65.9	63.4	65.9
2009	59.7	58.5	57.8	57.6	60.3	62.0	62.0	61.3	60.1	59.5	58.5	56.2	59.5
2010	53.2	52.8	53.2	56.3	57.9	60.1	61.2	61.3	60.5	60.7	59.9	58.0	57.9
2011	54.8	54.6	55.3	58.2	60.9	62.8	63.5	63.5	63.0	63.2	62.2	60.7	60.2
2012	58.4	58.2	59.2	61.5	63.3	65.0	65.1	64.9	64.0	63.6	62.9	61.4	62.3
2013	59.0	58.5	59.3	60.7	64.1	66.0	66.0	65.9	64.8	64.6	63.8	62.2	62.9
2014	59.8	59.8	60.5	62.5	65.2	67.2	67.6	67.5	66.7	66.7	65.6	64.7	64.5
2015	62.3	62.0	63.1	65.0	66.9	68.4	68.4	68.0	67.1	66.8	65.9	64.8	65.7
2016	61.8	61.6	62.7	64.6	66.6	69.4	70.0	68.9	67.6	67.1	66.2	64.6	65.9
2017	61.9	62.1	62.7	65.1	66.8	69.1	69.3	69.1	68.1	68.5	68.2	66.5	66.5
Service-Providing													
2007	330.4	332.2	334.5	337.9	345.7	348.9	344.9	347.7	343.8	343.5	343.0	343.2	341.3
2008	336.9	338.8	340.3	342.3	349.1	352.1	347.5	351.4	347.6	347.5	345.7	346.3	345.5
2009	337.8	338.5	339.4	341.4	348.9	350.8	346.8	347.9	346.1	344.7	344.4	343.7	344.2
2010	335.1	336.4	338.8	343.2	349.4	352.9	347.9	350.3	347.3	348.1	347.1	347.1	345.3
2011	338.2	339.8	341.5	345.2	350.3	354.5	349.3	351.5	349.5	349.9	349.0	350.4	347.4
2012	341.5	342.5	345.6	349.8	355.6	359.6	354.1	356.1	354.7	354.5	354.5	354.2	351.9
2013	345.7	347.4	349.6	350.9	359.3	361.5	356.3	358.6	357.5	357.8	358.2	358.1	355.1
2014	350.5	352.1	353.6	357.1	363.9	366.8	361.9	363.8	362.3	361.5	360.4	361.2	359.6
2015	352.4	354.5	356.8	360.6	366.9	370.4	365.6	366.9	365.3	365.6	365.0	365.7	363.0
2016	356.7	358.9	360.6	365.0	370.4	372.8	368.6	370.5	369.3	368.6	368.4	367.9	366.5
2017	359.4	360.7	362.9	366.6	372.6	375.3	369.0	371.3	370.2	370.2	368.3	368.9	368.0
Mining and Logging													
2007	0.8	0.8	0.8	0.9	1.0	1.1	1.1	1.1	1.0	1.0	1.0	0.9	1.0
2008	0.9	0.9	0.9	1.0	1.1	1.2	1.2	1.2	1.1	1.1	1.1	1.0	1.1
2009	0.9	0.9	0.9	0.9	1.0	1.0	1.0	1.0	1.0	0.9	0.9	0.9	0.9
2010	0.8	0.8	0.8	0.9	1.0	1.0	1.1	1.0	1.0	1.0	1.0	0.9	0.9
2011	0.8	0.8	0.8	0.9	1.0	1.1	1.1	1.1	1.1	1.0	1.0	0.9	1.0
2012	0.9	0.8	0.9	0.9	1.0	1.0	1.0	1.1	1.0	1.0	1.0	0.9	1.0
2013	0.8	0.8	0.8	0.9	1.0	1.0	1.0	1.0	1.0	0.9	0.9	0.9	0.9
2014	0.7	0.7	0.8	0.9	1.0	1.0	1.0	1.0	1.0	0.9	0.9	0.9	0.9
2015	0.8	0.8	0.8	0.9	1.0	1.0	1.0	1.0	1.0	1.0	1.0	0.9	0.9
2016	0.8	0.8	0.8	0.9	1.0	1.0	1.0	1.0	1.0	1.0	1.0	0.9	0.9
2017	0.8	0.8	0.9	1.0	1.0	1.1	1.1	1.1	1.0	1.0	1.0	0.9	1.0

1. Employment by Industry: South Dakota, Selected Years, 2007–2017—*Continued*

(Numbers in thousands, not seasonally adjusted)

Industry and year	January	February	March	April	May	June	July	August	September	October	November	December	Annual average
Construction													
2007	19.0	18.2	19.2	20.6	22.9	24.4	24.9	24.9	24.2	23.6	22.9	21.6	22.2
2008	19.7	19.1	19.6	21.2	23.5	24.4	24.7	24.6	23.7	23.2	22.2	20.6	22.2
2009	18.2	17.9	18.0	19.0	21.7	23.3	24.2	23.3	22.3	21.9	21.1	19.1	20.8
2010	16.6	16.0	16.3	19.0	20.3	22.0	22.7	22.9	22.1	22.2	21.3	19.5	20.1
2011	16.6	16.2	16.5	18.8	20.7	22.2	22.7	22.6	22.1	22.1	20.9	19.6	20.1
2012	17.6	17.1	17.9	19.7	21.0	22.2	22.2	22.1	21.3	20.8	20.1	19.1	20.1
2013	17.0	16.6	17.2	18.5	21.4	22.8	23.1	23.2	22.4	22.1	21.5	20.0	20.5
2014	18.1	17.7	18.1	19.8	22.0	23.7	23.9	23.7	23.1	22.8	21.8	20.8	21.3
2015	18.7	18.6	19.7	21.6	23.2	24.5	24.8	24.4	23.5	23.2	22.4	21.4	22.2
2016	18.9	18.8	19.8	21.6	23.3	25.8	26.6	25.7	24.7	23.9	23.1	21.5	22.8
2017	19.2	19.1	19.6	21.7	23.0	24.5	24.7	24.4	23.7	23.9	23.3	21.4	22.4
Manufacturing													
2007	41.0	41.0	41.9	42.1	42.0	42.4	42.3	42.1	42.0	42.3	42.2	42.1	42.1
2008	42.1	42.3	42.7	42.6	42.9	43.2	43.2	43.0	42.8	42.9	42.6	41.8	42.7
2009	40.6	39.7	38.9	37.7	37.6	37.7	36.8	37.0	36.8	36.7	36.5	36.2	37.7
2010	35.8	36.0	36.1	36.4	36.6	37.1	37.4	37.4	37.4	37.5	37.6	37.6	36.9
2011	37.4	37.6	38.0	38.5	39.2	39.5	39.7	39.8	39.8	40.1	40.3	40.2	39.2
2012	39.9	40.3	40.4	40.9	41.3	41.8	41.9	41.7	41.7	41.8	41.8	41.4	41.2
2013	41.2	41.1	41.3	41.3	41.7	42.2	41.9	41.7	41.4	41.6	41.4	41.3	41.5
2014	41.0	41.4	41.6	41.8	42.2	42.5	42.7	42.8	42.6	43.0	42.9	43.0	42.3
2015	42.8	42.6	42.6	42.5	42.7	42.9	42.6	42.6	42.6	42.6	42.5	42.5	42.6
2016	42.1	42.0	42.1	42.1	42.3	42.6	42.4	42.2	41.9	42.2	42.1	42.2	42.2
2017	41.9	42.2	42.2	42.4	42.8	43.5	43.5	43.6	43.4	43.6	43.9	44.2	43.1
Trade, Transportation, and Utilities													
2007	79.5	78.7	79.5	80.2	81.7	82.3	82.3	82.6	81.2	81.6	82.4	82.9	81.2
2008	81.0	80.3	80.6	81.1	82.3	83.0	83.3	83.7	82.2	82.6	82.6	83.1	82.2
2009	80.0	79.2	79.1	79.4	81.1	81.6	81.4	81.8	80.5	80.6	81.5	81.7	80.7
2010	78.8	78.1	78.6	79.7	80.9	81.7	81.6	82.0	80.4	81.2	82.0	82.3	80.6
2011	79.7	79.3	79.6	80.9	82.1	82.7	82.6	83.2	81.7	82.1	83.2	83.7	81.7
2012	81.2	80.4	81.0	82.0	83.5	84.2	83.8	84.3	83.1	83.2	84.4	84.6	83.0
2013	81.7	81.1	81.6	82.2	84.1	84.9	84.8	84.8	83.7	84.2	85.2	85.8	83.7
2014	83.5	83.3	83.6	84.5	85.8	87.0	87.4	87.6	86.0	86.3	87.1	87.8	85.8
2015	85.5	85.2	85.4	86.6	87.9	88.7	88.7	88.9	87.4	87.8	88.6	89.2	87.5
2016	86.8	86.5	86.7	87.7	88.9	89.4	89.5	89.5	87.5	87.8	88.8	88.8	88.2
2017	86.3	85.7	85.9	86.6	87.8	88.3	88.1	88.0	86.5	86.4	86.3	86.8	86.9
Wholesale Trade													
2007	18.0	17.9	18.1	18.3	18.6	18.6	18.5	18.6	18.4	18.5	18.6	18.6	18.4
2008	18.6	18.6	18.7	18.8	19.0	19.0	18.9	18.9	18.6	18.8	18.4	18.6	18.7
2009	18.1	18.1	18.1	18.2	18.6	18.5	18.5	18.5	18.1	18.4	18.4	18.3	18.3
2010	18.1	18.1	18.2	18.6	18.8	18.8	18.8	18.8	18.6	18.8	18.8	18.7	18.6
2011	18.5	18.5	18.7	18.9	19.2	19.3	19.2	19.2	18.9	19.1	19.2	19.2	19.0
2012	19.2	19.1	19.3	19.6	19.8	19.9	19.7	19.6	19.3	19.5	19.5	19.5	19.5
2013	19.4	19.3	19.6	19.8	20.3	20.4	20.3	20.0	19.8	20.0	20.2	20.2	19.9
2014	20.1	20.2	20.4	20.7	21.0	21.2	21.3	21.1	20.7	21.0	21.0	21.0	20.8
2015	20.8	20.8	21.0	21.2	21.5	21.5	21.4	21.3	21.0	21.2	21.2	21.2	21.2
2016	21.0	20.9	21.1	21.3	21.5	21.5	21.5	21.3	20.9	21.0	21.1	21.0	21.2
2017	20.7	20.6	20.9	21.0	21.3	21.4	21.2	21.1	20.7	20.7	20.4	20.4	20.9
Retail Trade													
2007	48.8	48.2	48.8	49.1	50.1	50.7	50.9	51.0	49.6	49.9	50.7	51.2	49.9
2008	49.4	48.7	48.9	49.2	50.0	50.7	51.1	51.5	50.2	50.4	50.9	51.2	50.2
2009	48.9	48.2	48.2	48.5	49.6	50.2	50.3	50.6	49.6	49.5	50.5	50.8	49.6
2010	48.5	47.9	48.2	48.7	49.5	50.2	50.3	50.6	49.1	49.7	50.5	50.9	49.5
2011	48.9	48.5	48.6	49.4	50.2	50.7	50.9	51.3	50.1	50.4	51.4	51.8	50.2
2012	49.8	49.1	49.4	50.2	51.2	51.7	51.6	52.2	51.0	51.0	52.2	52.4	51.0
2013	50.0	49.5	49.7	50.1	51.1	51.8	51.9	52.2	51.2	51.4	52.2	52.6	51.1
2014	50.7	50.3	50.4	50.9	51.6	52.6	53.0	53.2	52.0	51.9	52.8	53.3	51.9
2015	51.6	51.3	51.3	52.1	52.9	53.7	53.8	54.0	52.9	53.0	53.8	54.2	52.9
2016	52.5	52.4	52.4	53.2	54.0	54.6	54.8	54.9	53.3	53.5	54.4	54.4	53.7
2017	52.6	52.1	52.0	52.5	53.1	53.6	53.7	53.7	52.4	52.5	52.4	52.8	52.8

1. Employment by Industry: South Dakota, Selected Years, 2007–2017—*Continued*

(Numbers in thousands, not seasonally adjusted)

Industry and year	January	February	March	April	May	June	July	August	September	October	November	December	Annual average
Transportation and Utilities													
2007	12.7	12.6	12.6	12.8	13.0	13.0	12.9	13.0	13.2	13.2	13.1	13.1	12.9
2008	13.0	13.0	13.0	13.1	13.3	13.3	13.3	13.3	13.4	13.4	13.3	13.3	13.2
2009	13.0	12.9	12.8	12.7	12.9	12.9	12.6	12.7	12.8	12.7	12.6	12.6	12.8
2010	12.2	12.1	12.2	12.4	12.6	12.7	12.5	12.6	12.7	12.7	12.7	12.7	12.5
2011	12.3	12.3	12.3	12.6	12.7	12.7	12.5	12.7	12.7	12.6	12.6	12.7	12.6
2012	12.2	12.2	12.3	12.2	12.5	12.6	12.5	12.5	12.8	12.7	12.7	12.7	12.5
2013	12.3	12.3	12.3	12.3	12.7	12.7	12.6	12.6	12.7	12.8	12.8	13.0	12.6
2014	12.7	12.8	12.8	12.9	13.2	13.2	13.1	13.3	13.3	13.4	13.3	13.5	13.1
2015	13.1	13.1	13.1	13.3	13.5	13.5	13.5	13.6	13.5	13.6	13.6	13.8	13.4
2016	13.3	13.2	13.2	13.2	13.4	13.3	13.2	13.3	13.3	13.3	13.3	13.4	13.3
2017	13.0	13.0	13.0	13.1	13.4	13.3	13.2	13.2	13.4	13.2	13.5	13.6	13.2
Information													
2007	7.0	7.1	7.0	7.3	7.4	7.5	7.1	7.2	7.0	7.0	7.0	7.0	7.1
2008	7.0	7.0	6.9	6.8	6.9	7.0	7.0	7.1	6.9	6.9	6.9	6.9	6.9
2009	6.8	6.8	6.7	6.6	6.8	6.7	6.7	6.7	6.7	6.7	6.7	6.7	6.7
2010	6.6	6.6	6.5	6.5	6.5	6.6	6.6	6.6	6.5	6.4	6.5	6.5	6.5
2011	6.4	6.4	6.4	6.3	6.4	6.5	6.5	6.5	6.4	6.4	6.3	6.3	6.4
2012	6.2	6.3	6.2	6.2	6.3	6.3	6.3	6.3	6.1	6.1	6.1	6.1	6.2
2013	6.0	6.0	6.0	6.0	6.1	6.1	6.1	6.2	6.0	5.9	6.0	6.0	6.0
2014	6.0	6.0	6.0	6.0	6.1	6.2	6.2	6.1	6.0	5.9	5.9	5.9	6.0
2015	5.8	5.8	5.8	5.9	5.9	5.9	5.9	6.0	5.8	5.8	5.8	5.9	5.9
2016	5.8	5.8	5.8	5.8	5.8	5.9	5.8	5.8	5.7	5.7	5.7	5.7	5.8
2017	5.8	5.7	5.7	5.6	5.8	5.8	5.8	5.7	5.7	5.7	5.7	5.7	5.7
Financial Activities													
2007	30.2	30.4	30.7	30.6	30.8	31.3	31.3	31.2	31.1	31.2	31.2	31.2	30.9
2008	31.0	31.0	31.3	30.9	31.2	31.5	31.4	31.1	31.0	30.6	30.6	30.7	31.0
2009	30.7	30.8	30.9	30.7	30.6	30.9	30.6	30.3	30.0	29.9	29.8	29.9	30.4
2010	29.3	29.1	28.9	28.8	28.9	29.0	29.0	28.9	28.5	28.6	28.6	28.7	28.9
2011	28.3	28.3	28.3	28.1	28.1	28.3	28.1	28.1	27.9	27.9	27.9	28.2	28.1
2012	27.9	27.9	28.1	28.3	28.6	29.0	29.0	29.0	28.8	28.8	29.0	29.2	28.6
2013	29.1	29.3	29.4	29.4	29.7	30.1	30.0	30.0	29.8	29.8	30.0	30.1	29.7
2014	29.6	29.6	29.6	29.7	29.9	30.0	30.0	29.9	29.6	29.6	29.6	29.7	29.7
2015	29.4	29.3	29.4	29.4	29.6	29.9	30.1	29.9	29.7	29.7	29.7	29.8	29.7
2016	29.1	29.0	29.0	29.1	29.4	29.4	29.6	29.6	29.4	29.3	29.3	29.5	29.3
2017	29.0	28.9	29.0	29.1	29.3	29.5	29.5	29.5	29.3	29.2	29.2	29.5	29.3
Professional and Business Services													
2007	26.0	26.4	26.6	27.4	28.0	28.5	28.5	28.6	27.9	27.6	27.5	27.8	27.6
2008	27.4	27.6	27.8	28.2	28.2	28.6	28.5	28.8	28.1	27.8	27.7	27.8	28.0
2009	27.1	27.0	26.7	26.7	27.0	27.2	27.2	27.1	26.6	26.5	26.5	26.6	26.9
2010	26.2	26.4	26.6	27.6	27.6	27.9	28.2	28.2	27.7	28.1	27.8	28.0	27.5
2011	27.4	27.6	27.8	28.6	28.8	29.1	29.4	29.3	29.0	29.1	29.0	29.3	28.7
2012	28.3	28.4	28.7	29.1	29.2	29.6	29.9	30.0	29.5	29.3	29.2	29.1	29.2
2013	28.5	28.6	28.8	29.1	29.7	29.9	29.9	29.9	29.4	30.2	30.2	30.2	29.5
2014	29.5	29.5	29.4	30.4	30.8	31.1	31.1	30.9	30.3	30.4	30.3	30.3	30.3
2015	29.7	29.7	30.0	30.5	30.7	31.1	31.4	31.2	30.6	30.9	30.9	30.9	30.6
2016	30.2	30.4	30.4	31.2	31.4	31.8	32.0	31.7	31.2	31.3	31.4	31.5	31.2
2017	30.6	30.6	30.9	31.2	31.4	31.8	31.6	31.6	31.2	31.4	31.1	31.6	31.3
Education and Health Services													
2007	58.9	59.1	59.5	59.8	60.1	59.8	59.6	59.9	60.5	60.9	61.2	61.3	60.1
2008	61.2	61.5	61.7	61.6	62.0	61.9	61.4	61.9	62.2	62.7	63.0	63.4	62.0
2009	62.6	62.7	62.9	63.0	63.2	63.2	62.7	62.6	63.1	63.7	64.1	64.5	63.2
2010	63.5	63.8	64.1	64.2	64.6	64.5	64.3	64.1	64.5	65.0	65.2	65.6	64.5
2011	64.5	64.7	65.0	64.9	65.5	65.4	64.9	65.2	65.3	65.9	66.2	66.5	65.3
2012	65.6	65.9	66.3	67.1	67.5	67.6	66.9	66.9	67.3	67.6	68.0	68.1	67.1
2013	67.2	67.7	68.0	68.0	68.7	68.1	67.6	67.6	67.8	68.1	68.4	68.6	68.0
2014	67.7	68.1	68.3	68.4	68.9	68.6	68.0	67.9	68.1	68.4	68.5	69.0	68.3
2015	67.9	68.5	69.0	69.2	69.6	69.4	68.5	68.5	69.1	69.7	69.8	70.1	69.1
2016	69.1	69.6	70.0	70.1	70.5	69.9	69.8	70.0	70.6	70.8	71.2	71.5	70.3
2017	70.4	70.8	71.4	71.9	72.0	71.7	71.4	71.6	72.2	72.8	73.8	73.5	72.0

1. Employment by Industry: South Dakota, Selected Years, 2007–2017—*Continued*

(Numbers in thousands, not seasonally adjusted)

Industry and year	January	February	March	April	May	June	July	August	September	October	November	December	Annual average
Leisure and Hospitality													
2007	39.0	39.1	39.7	41.1	44.2	46.7	47.5	49.5	45.0	43.1	41.5	41.0	43.1
2008	39.1	39.3	39.9	41.3	44.1	47.1	47.6	49.3	45.2	43.3	41.4	41.0	43.2
2009	39.0	39.1	39.8	40.7	44.0	46.6	47.4	48.9	45.5	42.6	41.0	40.3	42.9
2010	38.2	38.6	39.2	41.0	44.0	47.0	47.1	49.4	45.4	43.5	41.7	41.1	43.0
2011	38.9	39.2	39.8	41.4	43.9	46.5	47.5	49.6	46.2	43.9	42.0	41.7	43.4
2012	39.8	40.2	41.1	42.5	45.5	48.0	48.4	50.2	46.6	44.5	42.6	42.4	44.3
2013	40.4	40.5	41.4	42.1	45.8	48.5	48.8	50.5	46.9	44.9	43.4	42.9	44.7
2014	41.3	41.6	42.3	43.3	46.7	48.9	49.0	50.9	47.8	45.8	43.8	43.6	45.4
2015	41.5	42.1	42.8	44.1	47.2	49.8	50.2	52.1	48.4	46.4	44.8	44.4	46.2
2016	42.5	42.8	43.5	45.1	47.6	49.8	50.8	52.7	49.0	47.2	45.5	44.4	46.7
2017	42.9	43.3	43.9	45.7	48.2	50.4	50.7	52.6	48.7	46.8	44.3	44.2	46.8
Other Services													
2007	15.6	15.6	15.7	15.7	15.9	16.0	16.0	15.9	15.8	15.7	15.6	15.7	15.8
2008	15.5	15.6	15.6	15.8	16.0	16.1	16.2	16.2	16.0	16.0	15.8	15.8	15.9
2009	15.6	15.6	15.5	15.6	15.8	15.9	15.9	15.8	15.6	15.6	15.5	15.6	15.7
2010	15.4	15.4	15.5	15.6	15.7	15.9	16.0	15.8	15.7	15.6	15.5	15.5	15.6
2011	15.4	15.3	15.5	15.6	15.7	16.0	16.0	16.1	15.7	15.8	15.7	15.8	15.7
2012	15.7	15.7	15.8	15.9	16.1	16.3	16.4	16.3	16.0	16.0	16.0	16.0	16.0
2013	15.9	15.9	16.0	16.1	16.4	16.5	16.5	16.3	16.1	16.0	16.1	16.0	16.2
2014	15.9	15.9	15.9	16.1	16.3	16.5	16.5	16.4	16.1	16.0	16.0	16.1	16.1
2015	15.9	16.0	16.0	16.2	16.3	16.7	16.8	16.7	16.2	16.3	16.2	16.3	16.3
2016	16.1	16.2	16.3	16.5	16.6	17.0	17.1	17.0	16.6	16.6	16.5	16.4	16.6
2017	16.3	16.3	16.4	16.6	16.8	17.3	17.2	17.1	16.7	17.0	16.9	16.7	16.8
Government													
2007	74.2	75.8	75.8	75.8	77.6	76.8	72.6	72.8	75.3	76.4	76.6	76.3	75.5
2008	74.7	76.5	76.5	76.6	78.4	76.9	72.1	73.3	76.0	77.6	77.7	77.6	76.2
2009	76.0	77.3	77.8	78.7	80.4	78.7	74.9	74.7	78.1	79.1	79.3	78.4	77.8
2010	77.1	78.4	79.4	79.8	81.2	80.3	75.1	75.3	78.6	79.7	79.8	79.4	78.7
2011	77.6	79.0	79.1	79.4	79.8	80.0	74.3	73.5	77.3	78.8	78.7	78.9	78.0
2012	76.8	77.7	78.4	78.7	78.9	78.6	73.4	73.1	77.3	79.0	79.2	78.7	77.5
2013	76.9	78.3	78.4	78.0	78.8	77.4	72.6	73.3	77.8	78.7	78.9	78.5	77.3
2014	77.0	78.1	78.5	78.7	79.4	78.5	73.7	74.1	78.4	79.1	79.2	78.8	77.8
2015	76.7	77.9	78.4	78.7	79.7	78.9	74.0	73.6	78.1	79.0	79.2	79.1	77.8
2016	77.1	78.6	78.9	79.5	80.2	79.6	74.0	74.2	79.3	79.9	80.0	80.1	78.5
2017	78.1	79.4	79.7	79.9	81.3	80.5	74.7	75.2	79.9	80.9	81.0	80.9	79.3

2. Average Weekly Hours by Selected Industry: South Dakota, 2013–2017

(Not seasonally adjusted)

Industry and year	January	February	March	April	May	June	July	August	September	October	November	December	Annual average
Total Private													
2013	33.9	33.9	34.0	33.2	34.3	35.5	34.6	35.1	35.3	34.4	34.6	34.8	34.5
2014	33.7	34.5	34.6	34.1	34.5	35.1	34.4	34.6	34.2	34.3	34.3	34.0	34.4
2015	33.5	34.2	34.0	33.8	33.7	34.2	34.3	34.7	33.9	34.1	34.4	33.5	34.0
2016	33.6	33.4	33.6	33.9	34.5	34.6	34.4	34.1	34.1	34.5	34.0	33.1	34.0
2017	33.7	33.2	33.3	33.9	34.0	34.0	34.3	33.8	33.6	34.0	33.5	33.1	33.7
Goods-Producing													
2013	38.7	39.5	39.9	38.4	40.3	41.7	41.6	42.2	42.7	41.4	41.8	40.8	40.8
2014	39.8	40.6	40.3	40.8	41.4	40.8	40.4	40.7	40.3	40.9	39.9	39.9	40.5
2015	38.6	39.5	39.5	39.6	39.9	40.2	41.1	41.2	40.2	40.7	40.8	39.7	40.1
2016	39.9	39.5	39.7	40.8	41.3	41.2	41.5	41.6	41.2	42.0	41.7	39.5	40.8
2017	40.7	39.5	39.8	40.5	42.0	42.1	41.5	41.3	40.8	41.4	41.0	40.6	41.0
Mining, Logging, and Construction													
2013	38.0	38.7	37.8	35.8	40.7	42.6	42.1	43.1	43.5	41.0	41.4	37.2	40.4
2014	36.1	38.7	38.1	40.9	41.2	39.8	40.5	39.6	38.5	38.4	37.9	37.4	39.0
2015	36.5	36.9	37.8	38.1	38.3	40.0	41.4	41.3	40.4	41.2	39.6	37.9	39.3
2016	37.6	37.8	38.4	39.8	40.0	40.5	41.1	41.5	41.2	42.7	41.2	37.8	40.1
2017	37.8	38.5	37.8	38.9	42.1	42.3	42.3	41.6	41.3	42.3	40.7	39.9	40.6
Manufacturing													
2013	38.9	39.7	40.8	39.6	40.2	41.3	41.1	41.5	42.2	41.7	42.1	42.6	41.0
2014	41.5	41.5	41.3	40.7	41.4	41.3	40.4	41.3	41.4	42.2	41.1	41.3	41.3
2015	39.6	40.5	40.2	40.3	40.9	40.2	40.9	41.1	40.1	40.5	41.4	40.6	40.5
2016	40.9	40.2	40.3	41.3	42.1	41.6	41.6	41.6	41.1	41.6	42.0	40.6	41.2
2017	42.1	40.0	40.7	41.4	41.9	42.0	41.1	41.2	40.4	40.9	41.1	41.0	41.2
Trade, Transportation, and Utilities													
2013	32.7	33.0	33.0	32.4	34.3	34.9	34.2	34.3	33.9	33.9	33.5	33.2	33.6
2014	32.9	33.0	33.2	33.7	34.6	35.0	34.3	34.5	34.0	34.5	34.5	34.2	34.0
2015	33.6	34.3	34.2	33.9	34.1	34.5	34.3	34.7	34.0	33.8	34.2	33.1	34.1
2016	32.9	32.8	33.0	33.1	34.0	34.1	33.8	33.3	33.6	33.7	33.2	32.5	33.3
2017	32.8	32.5	32.5	33.4	33.8	34.0	34.4	33.7	33.7	33.7	33.1	32.9	33.4
Professional and Business Services													
2013	37.1	37.0	36.8	36.1	36.7	38.1	36.8	37.4	37.3	36.3	37.1	37.0	37.0
2014	35.6	37.1	36.5	35.9	35.8	36.1	34.9	35.2	35.0	34.9	35.7	35.6	35.7
2015	35.8	37.3	36.9	36.9	36.2	37.0	36.3	37.0	36.3	36.3	36.6	35.5	36.5
2016	35.9	36.1	36.2	36.7	38.0	37.4	36.6	36.8	36.9	37.6	36.8	35.8	36.8
2017	36.5	36.8	36.3	36.3	35.6	35.4	35.5	35.1	35.7	35.9	35.2	35.0	35.8
Education and Health Services													
2013	32.8	33.0	33.1	33.0	32.8	33.7	32.2	32.2	32.5	31.6	32.3	32.7	32.7
2014	31.2	32.3	32.9	31.4	31.2	32.8	31.7	32.8	32.3	31.7	32.3	32.2	32.1
2015	32.3	32.7	32.4	32.2	31.7	32.0	31.8	32.7	32.3	32.4	33.1	32.6	32.3
2016	32.7	32.2	32.1	32.1	32.0	32.1	32.3	31.9	32.1	32.5	31.7	31.8	32.1
2017	31.9	31.4	31.3	31.9	31.2	31.4	32.3	30.9	31.3	32.0	31.1	31.1	31.5
Leisure and Hospitality													
2013	23.6	24.0	23.8	22.9	23.9	25.5	25.9	25.6	25.0	23.9	23.3	23.5	24.3
2014	22.5	23.7	24.0	23.0	23.4	25.6	25.3	25.1	24.2	24.0	23.7	23.3	24.0
2015	22.6	24.0	23.9	23.1	23.4	25.0	25.5	26.1	24.5	24.1	24.2	23.5	24.2
2016	23.6	23.7	24.1	24.1	25.0	25.4	25.5	26.1	24.7	24.8	23.3	23.1	24.5
2017	23.9	23.7	23.9	24.3	24.0	25.6	26.1	25.9	24.5	23.9	22.9	22.7	24.3

3. Average Hourly Earnings by Selected Industry: South Dakota, 2013–2017

(Dollars, not seasonally adjusted)

Industry and year	January	February	March	April	May	June	July	August	September	October	November	December	Annual average
Total Private													
2013	19.40	19.61	19.42	19.89	19.56	19.40	19.41	19.52	19.89	19.54	19.75	20.05	19.62
2014	20.00	20.13	20.10	20.17	20.15	19.87	19.89	19.94	20.22	20.45	20.61	20.57	20.17
2015	20.94	20.93	20.88	20.91	20.99	20.72	20.68	20.79	21.04	21.32	21.23	21.39	20.98
2016	21.34	21.18	21.18	21.41	21.28	20.80	21.15	21.13	21.60	21.74	21.72	21.95	21.37
2017	22.13	22.21	22.04	22.10	21.83	21.56	21.67	21.66	22.02	22.13	21.98	22.20	21.95
Goods-Producing													
2013	19.42	19.68	19.34	19.54	19.35	19.13	19.17	19.13	19.61	19.58	19.56	19.95	19.45
2014	19.97	20.29	20.01	20.14	20.42	20.35	20.42	20.59	20.74	21.04	20.88	20.95	20.49
2015	21.85	21.77	21.60	21.63	21.49	21.55	21.31	21.58	21.54	21.96	21.78	22.05	21.67
2016	21.52	21.20	21.52	21.57	21.56	21.59	22.06	21.66	22.11	22.13	21.94	22.51	21.79
2017	22.84	22.61	22.67	22.49	22.65	22.36	22.29	22.29	22.30	22.31	22.03	22.39	22.43
Mining, Logging, and Construction													
2013	20.06	20.27	19.85	20.12	19.65	19.41	19.11	19.44	19.90	20.05	20.02	20.35	19.92
2014	20.99	21.28	21.15	20.98	21.27	20.38	20.90	21.42	21.99	22.52	22.11	22.03	21.34
2015	22.56	22.54	22.65	22.71	22.25	22.55	22.18	22.49	22.40	22.77	22.68	23.18	22.57
2016	22.83	22.89	22.82	22.74	22.96	22.82	23.02	22.89	23.13	23.59	23.31	24.30	23.11
2017	24.64	24.47	24.46	24.26	24.27	23.80	24.08	23.82	23.68	23.83	23.63	24.34	24.07
Manufacturing													
2013	19.15	19.44	19.13	19.29	19.19	18.96	19.21	18.95	19.40	19.32	19.32	19.78	19.26
2014	19.56	19.88	19.53	19.73	19.95	20.33	20.14	20.13	20.09	20.30	20.77	20.46	20.08
2015	21.55	21.45	21.12	21.09	21.09	20.96	20.78	21.04	21.04	21.49	21.31	21.50	21.20
2016	20.95	20.46	20.92	20.96	20.79	20.84	21.44	20.88	21.48	21.24	21.17	21.63	21.06
2017	22.07	21.76	21.86	21.60	21.74	21.51	21.20	21.39	21.49	21.42	21.15	21.43	21.55
Trade, Transportation, and Utilities													
2013	19.60	19.51	19.27	19.75	19.42	19.06	18.69	18.64	18.83	19.01	19.30	19.03	19.17
2014	19.26	19.43	19.32	19.55	19.65	19.32	19.39	19.36	19.42	19.50	19.87	19.91	19.50
2015	19.77	19.56	19.50	19.40	19.91	19.75	19.87	19.91	20.17	20.19	20.04	20.09	19.85
2016	20.14	19.96	19.82	20.38	20.47	19.70	20.15	20.24	20.42	20.53	20.62	20.69	20.26
2017	20.86	21.08	20.66	20.88	20.48	20.35	20.68	21.10	21.14	21.44	21.51	21.54	20.97
Professional and Business Services													
2013	23.15	23.47	23.43	23.74	23.76	23.55	23.65	23.37	24.22	23.84	24.47	24.26	23.75
2014	24.55	24.28	24.61	24.36	24.13	23.65	23.78	23.12	24.02	24.17	24.33	24.47	24.12
2015	24.42	24.43	24.69	24.68	24.23	24.05	24.57	24.73	24.80	24.96	24.98	24.64	24.60
2016	24.28	23.89	24.19	24.49	24.11	24.44	24.97	25.02	25.66	26.00	25.88	26.34	24.95
2017	26.09	26.48	26.85	27.00	27.18	27.18	27.32	26.87	27.27	26.88	26.99	27.05	26.93
Education and Health Services													
2013	18.20	18.51	18.63	19.53	18.94	19.36	19.76	20.52	20.48	20.59	20.43	20.47	19.61
2014	20.60	20.65	20.88	20.75	20.81	20.61	20.74	21.40	21.30	21.54	21.64	21.46	21.03
2015	21.81	22.31	22.08	22.12	22.42	22.04	22.08	22.42	22.73	22.99	22.76	22.81	22.38
2016	23.80	23.73	23.04	23.03	22.90	22.82	23.25	23.21	23.66	23.79	23.56	23.41	23.36
2017	23.68	23.44	23.14	22.90	22.47	22.32	22.18	22.12	22.36	22.17	22.11	22.24	22.59
Leisure and Hospitality													
2013	11.97	12.09	11.89	11.93	11.70	11.41	11.46	11.48	11.80	12.09	12.23	12.44	11.85
2014	12.50	12.39	12.50	12.45	12.26	11.97	11.88	11.98	12.32	12.52	12.56	12.76	12.32
2015	13.10	13.01	13.10	13.15	12.88	12.33	12.52	12.63	12.88	12.99	13.14	13.04	12.87
2016	13.27	13.16	13.27	13.25	13.18	12.91	13.04	13.05	13.52	13.40	13.51	13.52	13.25
2017	13.63	13.65	13.65	13.66	13.69	13.33	13.47	13.49	13.82	14.10	14.02	14.28	13.71

4. Average Weekly Earnings by Selected Industry: South Dakota, 2013–2017

(Dollars, not seasonally adjusted)

Industry and year	January	February	March	April	May	June	July	August	September	October	November	December	Annual average
Total Private													
2013	657.66	664.78	660.28	660.35	670.91	688.70	671.59	685.15	702.12	672.18	683.35	697.74	676.89
2014	674.00	694.49	695.46	687.80	695.18	697.44	684.22	689.92	691.52	701.44	706.92	699.38	693.85
2015	701.49	715.81	709.92	706.76	707.36	708.62	709.32	721.41	713.26	727.01	730.31	716.57	713.32
2016	717.02	707.41	711.65	725.80	734.16	719.68	727.56	720.53	736.56	750.03	738.48	726.55	726.58
2017	745.78	737.37	733.93	749.19	742.22	733.04	743.28	732.11	739.87	752.42	736.33	734.82	739.72
Goods-Producing													
2013	751.55	777.36	771.67	750.34	779.81	797.72	797.47	807.29	837.35	810.61	817.61	813.96	793.56
2014	794.81	823.77	806.40	821.71	845.39	830.28	824.97	838.01	835.82	860.54	833.11	835.91	829.85
2015	843.41	859.92	853.20	856.55	857.45	866.31	875.84	889.10	865.91	893.77	888.62	875.39	868.97
2016	858.65	837.40	854.34	880.06	890.43	889.51	915.49	901.06	910.93	929.46	914.90	889.15	889.03
2017	929.59	893.10	902.27	910.85	951.30	941.36	925.04	920.58	909.84	923.63	903.23	909.03	919.63
Mining, Logging, and Construction													
2013	762.28	784.45	750.33	720.30	799.76	826.87	804.53	837.86	868.26	822.05	828.83	757.02	800.73
2014	757.74	823.54	805.82	858.08	876.32	811.12	846.45	848.23	846.62	864.77	800.07	823.92	832.26
2015	823.44	831.73	856.17	865.25	852.18	902.00	918.25	928.84	904.96	938.12	898.13	878.52	887.00
2016	858.41	865.24	876.29	905.05	918.40	924.21	946.12	949.94	952.96	1,007.29	960.37	918.54	926.71
2017	931.39	942.10	924.59	943.71	1,021.77	1,006.74	1,018.58	990.91	977.98	1,008.01	961.74	971.17	977.24
Manufacturing													
2013	744.94	771.77	780.50	763.88	771.44	783.05	789.53	786.43	818.68	805.64	813.37	842.63	789.66
2014	811.74	825.02	806.59	803.01	825.93	839.63	813.66	831.37	831.73	856.66	853.65	845.00	829.30
2015	853.38	868.73	849.02	849.93	862.58	842.59	849.90	864.74	843.70	870.35	882.23	872.90	858.60
2016	856.86	822.49	843.08	865.65	875.26	866.94	891.90	868.61	882.83	883.58	889.14	878.18	867.67
2017	929.15	870.40	889.70	894.24	910.91	903.42	871.32	881.27	868.20	876.08	869.27	878.63	887.86
Trade, Transportation, and Utilities													
2013	640.92	643.83	635.91	639.90	666.11	665.19	639.20	639.35	638.34	644.44	646.55	631.80	644.11
2014	633.65	641.19	641.42	658.84	679.89	676.20	665.08	667.92	660.28	672.75	685.52	680.92	663.00
2015	664.27	670.91	666.90	657.66	678.93	681.38	681.54	690.88	685.78	682.42	685.37	664.98	676.89
2016	662.61	654.69	654.06	674.58	695.98	671.77	681.07	673.99	686.11	691.86	684.58	672.43	674.66
2017	684.21	685.10	671.45	697.39	692.22	691.90	711.39	711.07	712.42	722.53	711.98	708.67	700.40
Professional and Business Services													
2013	858.87	868.39	862.22	857.01	871.99	897.26	870.32	874.04	903.41	865.39	907.84	897.62	878.75
2014	873.98	900.79	898.27	874.52	863.85	853.77	829.92	813.82	840.70	843.53	868.58	871.13	861.08
2015	874.24	911.24	911.06	910.69	877.13	889.85	891.89	915.01	900.24	906.05	914.27	874.72	897.90
2016	871.65	862.43	875.68	898.78	916.18	914.06	913.90	920.74	946.85	977.60	952.38	942.97	918.16
2017	952.29	974.46	974.66	980.10	967.61	962.17	969.86	943.14	973.54	964.99	950.05	946.75	964.09
Education and Health Services													
2013	596.96	610.83	616.65	644.49	621.23	652.43	636.27	660.74	665.60	650.64	659.89	669.37	641.25
2014	642.72	667.00	686.95	651.55	649.27	676.01	657.46	701.92	687.99	682.82	698.97	691.01	675.06
2015	704.46	729.54	715.39	712.26	710.71	705.28	702.14	733.13	734.18	744.88	753.36	743.61	722.87
2016	778.26	764.11	739.58	739.26	734.72	732.52	750.98	740.40	759.49	773.18	746.85	744.44	749.86
2017	755.39	736.02	724.28	730.51	701.06	700.85	716.41	683.51	699.87	709.44	687.62	691.66	711.59
Leisure and Hospitality													
2013	282.49	290.16	282.98	273.20	279.63	290.96	296.81	293.89	295.00	288.95	284.96	292.34	287.96
2014	281.25	293.64	300.00	286.35	286.88	306.43	300.56	300.70	298.14	300.48	297.67	297.31	295.68
2015	296.06	312.24	313.09	303.77	301.39	308.25	319.26	329.64	315.56	313.06	317.99	306.44	311.45
2016	313.17	311.89	319.81	319.33	329.50	327.91	332.52	340.61	333.94	332.32	314.78	312.31	324.63
2017	325.76	323.51	326.24	331.94	328.56	341.25	351.57	349.39	338.59	336.99	321.06	324.16	333.15

TENNESSEE
At a Glance

Population:
  2010 census: 6,346,105
  2017 estimate: 6,715,984

Percent change in population:
  2010–2017: 5.8%

Percent change in total nonfarm employment:
  2007–2017: 7.6%

Industry with the largest growth in employment, 2007–2017 (thousands):
  Education and health services, 79.7

Industry with the largest decline or smallest growth in employment, 2007–2017 (thousands):
  Manufacturing, -31.2

Civilian labor force:
  2010: 3,090,795
  2017: 3,198,767

Unemployment rate and rank among states (highest to lowest):
  2010: 9.7%, 18th
  2017: 3.7%, 34th

Over-the-year change in unemployment rates:
  2015–2016: -0.9%
  2016–2017: -1.0%

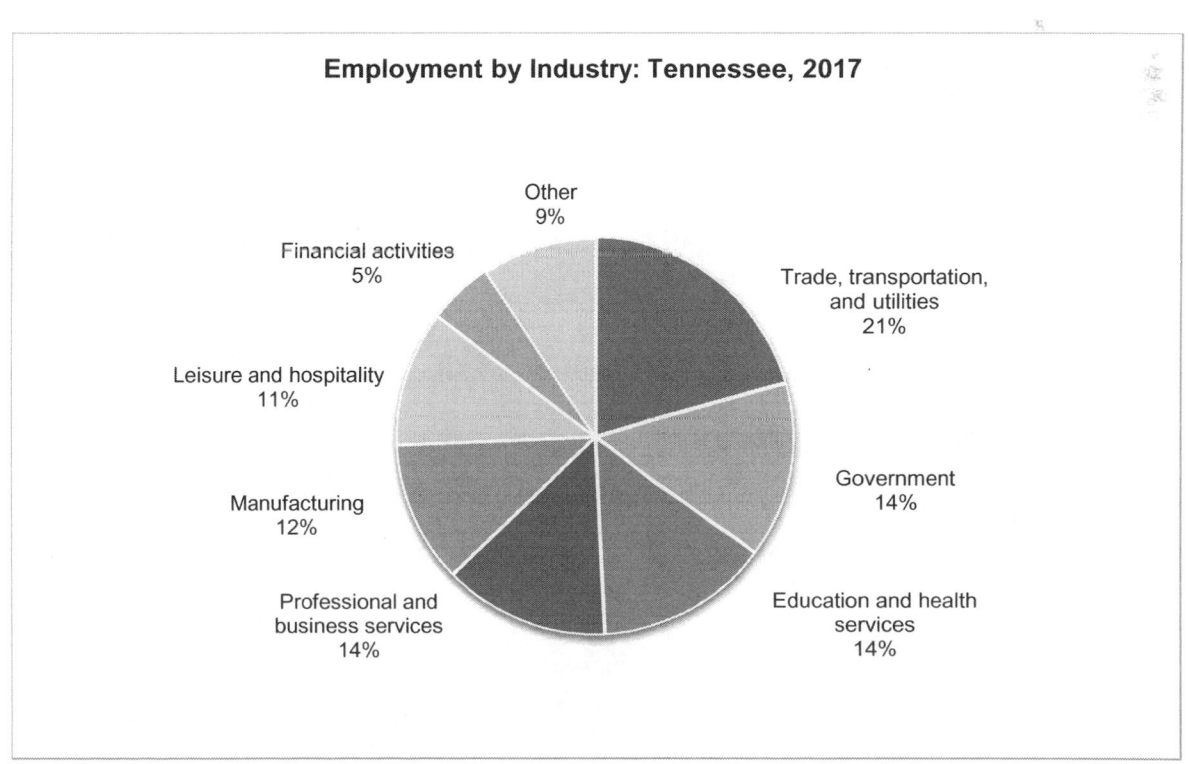

Employment by Industry: Tennessee, 2017

Other 9%
Financial activities 5%
Leisure and hospitality 11%
Manufacturing 12%
Professional and business services 14%
Trade, transportation, and utilities 21%
Government 14%
Education and health services 14%

1. Employment by Industry: Tennessee, Selected Years, 2007–2017

(Numbers in thousands, not seasonally adjusted)

Industry and year	January	February	March	April	May	June	July	August	September	October	November	December	Annual average
Total Nonfarm													
2007	2,744.8	2,753.7	2,784.0	2,787.8	2,799.3	2,797.9	2,782.5	2,811.1	2,821.7	2,815.8	2,833.6	2,836.4	2,797.4
2008	2,762.5	2,771.9	2,790.0	2,797.0	2,805.5	2,784.3	2,758.6	2,779.0	2,779.4	2,766.1	2,758.6	2,745.2	2,774.8
2009	2,647.6	2,636.8	2,634.7	2,629.8	2,630.4	2,599.4	2,582.8	2,600.0	2,609.8	2,616.3	2,629.1	2,622.1	2,619.9
2010	2,557.0	2,562.4	2,585.0	2,614.8	2,637.9	2,613.3	2,600.4	2,619.5	2,635.4	2,645.6	2,657.0	2,655.4	2,615.3
2011	2,587.6	2,609.5	2,632.3	2,660.8	2,669.3	2,646.1	2,642.9	2,670.7	2,688.3	2,697.2	2,716.7	2,715.6	2,661.4
2012	2,649.0	2,667.5	2,699.1	2,715.7	2,725.1	2,705.7	2,687.8	2,714.7	2,734.1	2,745.4	2,766.5	2,769.0	2,715.0
2013	2,691.0	2,711.0	2,733.3	2,757.7	2,767.0	2,744.8	2,729.1	2,758.4	2,778.5	2,796.0	2,825.7	2,827.9	2,760.0
2014	2,752.6	2,764.7	2,791.4	2,815.2	2,824.9	2,800.5	2,792.3	2,825.4	2,847.7	2,863.5	2,890.6	2,897.3	2,822.2
2015	2,820.8	2,831.7	2,845.5	2,881.1	2,895.4	2,875.3	2,872.3	2,895.6	2,922.1	2,945.4	2,967.0	2,974.2	2,893.9
2016	2,898.1	2,914.4	2,937.9	2,963.1	2,963.2	2,944.9	2,940.7	2,968.0	2,997.9	3,003.2	3,025.4	3,028.8	2,965.5
2017	2,947.4	2,973.5	2,987.0	3,009 0	3,011.1	2,993.8	2,982.9	3,007.3	3,033.1	3,047.8	3,066.3	3,061.3	3,010.0
Total Private													
2007	2,329.4	2,333.9	2,361.5	2,367.8	2,378.8	2,395.7	2,385.0	2,399.5	2,396.9	2,387.2	2,403.1	2,408.3	2,378.9
2008	2,340.6	2,344.6	2,360.5	2,366.5	2,374.5	2,381.5	2,355.4	2,362.8	2,351.7	2,330.0	2,321.4	2,309.4	2,349.9
2009	2,222.3	2,206.7	2,202.8	2,196.4	2,197.7	2,198.2	2,180.5	2,185.4	2,180.5	2,178.5	2,190.4	2,186.7	2,193.8
2010	2,128.6	2,129.8	2,150.6	2,176.2	2,190.4	2,202.0	2,193.6	2,200.6	2,199.3	2,207.3	2,218.1	2,219.6	2,184.7
2011	2,158.5	2,175.3	2,196.8	2,225.8	2,236.3	2,246.0	2,246.9	2,256.2	2,258.8	2,263.7	2,282.3	2,284.0	2,235.9
2012	2,226.7	2,237.2	2,265.7	2,282.9	2,298.2	2,310.2	2,295.4	2,310.0	2,309.0	2,314.1	2,333.3	2,336.8	2,293.3
2013	2,272.9	2,283.9	2,304.6	2,320.7	2,335.3	2,346.9	2,335.4	2,351.9	2,351.4	2,361.4	2,390.9	2,393.5	2,337.4
2014	2,329.5	2,333.4	2,358.4	2,381.1	2,395.1	2,404.4	2,398.2	2,417.8	2,418.0	2,428.0	2,451.6	2,460.0	2,398.0
2015	2,395.4	2,399.0	2,412.9	2,447.3	2,465.9	2,478.1	2,477.6	2,486.8	2,489.9	2,507.2	2,528.5	2,537.1	2,468.8
2016	2,472.6	2,479.9	2,498.9	2,527.2	2,533.2	2,546.3	2,545.0	2,554.4	2,560.4	2,562.3	2,581.1	2,588.0	2,537.4
2017	2,520.6	2,535.7	2,548.4	2,569.7	2,577.0	2,591.7	2,583.5	2,592.8	2,594.0	2,604.4	2,621.0	2,620.0	2,579.9
Goods Producing													
2007	517.7	517.4	522.1	519.9	518.2	521.9	517.2	519.3	518.5	515.4	513.6	512.2	517.8
2008	502.1	502.2	503.5	501.8	502.9	503.9	494.6	496.3	491.5	482.8	473.2	465.0	493.3
2009	443.7	435.5	430.9	423.1	418.3	415.0	413.5	413.9	413.2	409.6	408.2	403.8	419.1
2010	393.3	391.5	396.3	402.6	404.6	409.4	408.2	409.8	409.8	408.7	407.7	406.4	404.0
2011	397.3	400.6	405.0	409.6	412.0	416.7	417.8	418.6	419.8	420.7	421.4	417.7	413.1
2012	409.8	412.0	417.3	419.8	422.7	427.0	425.0	428.3	427.4	426.2	426.3	425.1	422.2
2013	417.0	419.1	422.0	423.0	425.8	428.5	427.0	429.8	430.2	431.4	431.9	430.6	426.4
2014	424.6	426.2	429.5	431.9	435.0	436.5	436.4	440.5	440.4	441.2	443.4	444.3	435.8
2015	438.2	439.7	440.0	445.7	449.9	452.6	452.4	454.5	456.1	457.5	457.2	457.9	450.1
2016	452.4	453.2	457.3	459.8	461.7	465.7	466.4	467.0	467.9	467.0	467.9	469.5	463.0
2017	463.6	467.2	469.3	472.0	473.0	475.7	475.1	476.2	475.6	475.3	477.6	474.0	472.9
Service-Providing													
2007	2,227.1	2,236.3	2,261.9	2,267.9	2,281.1	2,276.0	2,265.3	2,291.8	2,303.2	2,300.4	2,320.0	2,324.2	2,279.6
2008	2,260.4	2,269.7	2,286.5	2,295.2	2,302.6	2,280.4	2,264.0	2,282.7	2,287.9	2,283.3	2,285.4	2,280.2	2,281.5
2009	2,203.9	2,201.3	2,203.8	2,206.7	2,212.1	2,184.4	2,169.3	2,186.1	2,196.6	2,206.7	2,220.9	2,218.3	2,200.8
2010	2,163.7	2,170.9	2,188.7	2,212.2	2,233.3	2,203.9	2,192.2	2,209.7	2,225.6	2,236.9	2,249.3	2,249.0	2,211.3
2011	2,190.3	2,208.9	2,227.3	2,251.2	2,257.3	2,229.4	2,225.1	2,252.1	2,268.5	2,276.5	2,295.3	2,297.9	2,248.3
2012	2,239.2	2,255.5	2,281.8	2,295.9	2,302.4	2,278.7	2,262.8	2,286.4	2,306.7	2,319.2	2,340.2	2,343.9	2,292.7
2013	2,274.0	2,291.9	2,311.3	2,334.7	2,341.2	2,316.3	2,302.1	2,328.6	2,348.3	2,364.6	2,393.8	2,397.3	2,333.7
2014	2,328.0	2,338.5	2,361.9	2,383.3	2,389.9	2,364.0	2,355.9	2,384.9	2,407.3	2,422.3	2,447.2	2,453.0	2,386.4
2015	2,382.6	2,392.0	2,405.5	2,435.4	2,445.5	2,422.7	2,419.9	2,441.1	2,466.0	2,487.9	2,509.8	2,516.3	2,443.7
2016	2,445.7	2,461.2	2,480.6	2,503.3	2,501.5	2,479.2	2,474.3	2,501.0	2,530.0	2,536.2	2,557.5	2,559.3	2,502.5
2017	2,483.8	2,506.3	2,517.7	2,537.0	2,538.1	2,518.1	2,507.8	2,531.1	2,557.5	2,572.5	2,588.7	2,587.3	2,537.2
Mining and Logging													
2007	4.8	4.9	5.0	4.9	5.0	5.0	4.8	4.8	4.8	4.8	4.9	4.9	4.9
2008	4.8	4.8	4.8	4.8	4.9	4.9	4.8	4.9	4.8	4.7	4.5	4.4	4.8
2009	4.3	4.0	3.9	4.0	4.0	4.0	4.1	4.1	4.0	4.0	4.1	4.1	4.1
2010	4.0	4.1	4.2	4.4	4.4	4.5	4.5	4.5	4.5	4.4	4.4	4.4	4.4
2011	4.1	4.2	4.4	4.4	4.4	4.6	4.5	4.6	4.5	4.4	4.4	4.4	4.4
2012	4.2	4.2	4.3	4.3	4.3	4.3	4.2	4.2	4.3	4.3	4.3	4.3	4.3
2013	4.2	4.3	4.4	4.4	4.4	4.4	4.3	4.4	4.3	4.3	4.2	4.2	4.3
2014	4.2	4.2	4.3	4.4	4.4	4.4	4.4	4.5	4.5	4.5	4.4	4.4	4.4
2015	4.3	4.4	4.4	4.6	4.6	4.5	4.5	4.5	4.5	4.5	4.4	4.4	4.5
2016	4.3	4.3	4.0	4.0	4.0	4.0	4.0	4.0	4.0	3.9	4.0	4.0	4.0
2017	4.0	4.0	4.0	4.1	4.2	4.2	4.2	4.2	4.2	4.1	4.1	4.1	4.1

1. Employment by Industry: Tennessee, Selected Years, 2007–2017—*Continued*

(Numbers in thousands, not seasonally adjusted)

Industry and year	January	February	March	April	May	June	July	August	September	October	November	December	Annual average
Construction													
2007	125.0	125.2	130.0	131.5	133.6	136.4	135.6	136.7	136.7	136.1	135.0	133.6	133.0
2008	128.0	127.8	129.1	129.4	130.8	131.4	129.8	129.8	128.2	125.5	122.6	118.9	127.6
2009	108.9	107.1	107.5	106.4	106.1	107.1	106.6	106.0	106.1	104.2	103.0	100.8	105.8
2010	93.6	92.7	95.8	100.4	101.2	103.8	104.0	104.3	104.3	104.5	102.8	101.4	100.7
2011	93.8	95.6	98.8	102.6	103.8	106.6	107.6	108.5	109.8	109.4	108.4	106.3	104.3
2012	100.0	100.6	103.4	103.5	105.0	106.6	106.3	107.3	107.6	106.1	105.2	103.6	104.6
2013	97.9	99.3	100.8	102.2	104.3	105.5	105.5	105.9	106.1	106.4	105.6	103.8	103.6
2014	99.4	100.0	102.7	105.2	107.4	107.3	108.0	108.9	108.9	109.6	110.6	110.2	106.5
2015	105.7	106.4	106.8	110.6	113.1	114.4	115.4	115.3	116.2	117.4	116.1	114.9	112.7
2016	110.1	109.6	112.1	113.6	114.2	116.3	117.1	117.1	118.1	117.6	117.5	117.1	115.0
2017	113.6	115.5	117.4	119.2	120.4	121.5	121.9	122.5	122.7	121.5	122.6	120.3	119.9
Manufacturing													
2007	387.9	387.3	387.1	383.5	379.6	380.5	376.8	377.8	377.0	374.5	373.7	373.7	380.0
2008	369.3	369.6	369.6	367.6	367.2	367.6	360.0	361.6	358.5	352.6	346.1	341.7	361.0
2009	330.5	324.4	319.5	312.7	308.2	303.9	302.8	303.8	303.1	301.4	301.1	298.9	309.2
2010	295.7	294.7	296.3	297.8	299.0	301.1	299.7	301.0	301.0	299.8	300.5	300.6	298.9
2011	299.4	300.8	301.8	302.6	303.8	305.5	305.7	305.5	305.5	306.9	308.6	307.0	304.4
2012	305.6	307.2	309.6	312.0	313.4	316.1	314.5	316.8	315.5	315.8	316.8	317.2	313.4
2013	314.9	315.5	316.8	316.4	317.1	318.6	317.2	319.5	319.8	320.7	322.1	322.6	318.4
2014	321.0	322.0	322.5	322.3	323.2	324.8	324.0	327.1	327.0	327.1	328.4	329.7	324.9
2015	328.2	328.9	328.8	330.5	332.2	333.7	332.5	334.7	335.4	335.6	336.7	338.6	333.0
2016	338.0	339.3	341.2	342.2	343.5	345.4	345.3	345.9	345.8	345.5	346.4	348.4	343.9
2017	346.0	347.7	347.9	348.7	348.4	350.0	349.0	349.5	348.7	349.7	350.9	349.6	348.8
Trade, Transportation, and Utilities													
2007	603.8	600.6	607.1	606.3	609.1	609.6	606.8	609.5	610.3	611.2	623.5	628.4	610.5
2008	605.4	602.4	606.1	602.9	602.5	601.5	598.3	599.3	596.7	591.7	596.4	598.1	600.1
2009	571.7	564.4	561.8	557.0	557.7	557.1	553.8	555.1	553.1	554.2	562.0	565.8	559.5
2010	546.5	543.9	547.4	550.4	552.5	554.2	554.7	556.1	554.5	558.8	568.5	573.2	555.1
2011	550.4	550.2	553.9	559.9	561.7	563.4	562.9	564.3	563.9	568.4	579.7	583.7	563.5
2012	564.9	561.5	568.0	570.4	573.3	574.0	572.4	574.2	575.8	578.6	591.7	595.3	575.0
2013	572.5	571.0	572.6	575.3	577.7	579.8	579.4	580.6	579.0	583.5	597.5	603.3	581.0
2014	577.5	575.8	580.1	583.9	585.5	588.0	588.3	590.8	590.8	595.8	608.8	613.2	589.9
2015	589.2	585.8	588.1	594.3	597.9	600.3	603.0	604.3	603.2	610.2	622.2	628.3	602.2
2016	607.2	605.7	608.0	613.0	613.7	615.0	617.2	617.9	617.1	620.9	634.1	637.3	617.3
2017	614.5	612.5	612.8	616.1	617.4	619.7	619.9	622.7	622.4	624.2	634.8	635.5	621.0
Wholesale Trade													
2007	131.0	131.4	132.3	132.7	133.0	133.4	133.1	133.3	133.8	134.0	133.7	133.9	133.0
2008	132.5	132.9	133.1	132.8	133.1	132.5	131.8	131.9	131.7	130.5	129.3	128.2	131.7
2009	124.9	123.9	123.0	122.0	121.4	121.0	119.8	119.3	118.6	118.7	118.3	118.1	120.8
2010	116.6	116.5	117.2	117.2	117.3	117.2	116.9	116.8	116.3	116.6	116.5	116.3	116.8
2011	115.4	116.0	116.5	117.5	118.1	118.4	118.4	118.5	118.6	118.7	119.2	119.2	117.9
2012	118.1	118.9	119.6	120.1	120.8	121.1	120.7	121.1	120.9	121.2	121.2	121.2	120.4
2013	119.4	119.7	120.4	120.7	121.0	121.3	121.0	121.2	121.0	120.8	121.2	121.1	120.7
2014	119.5	119.6	120.1	120.1	120.7	120.8	120.4	120.3	120.7	120.1	120.4	120.8	120.3
2015	119.3	119.5	119.5	119.6	120.1	120.2	120.2	120.2	120.2	120.3	120.4	120.5	120.0
2016	119.0	118.8	118.9	118.8	119.0	119.3	119.6	119.9	119.9	119.8	120.1	120.6	119.5
2017	119.5	120.1	120.3	120.7	121.3	121.8	121.5	121.8	122.0	121.6	121.3	121.6	121.1
Retail Trade													
2007	327.1	323.5	328.3	327.1	329.0	329.1	327.3	328.0	328.3	330.0	342.3	346.5	330.5
2008	328.7	325.9	329.6	326.5	325.5	325.2	323.6	323.6	321.3	320.4	325.9	327.6	325.3
2009	310.6	305.9	305.1	303.7	305.1	305.4	304.5	305.5	304.2	305.1	313.1	316.2	307.0
2010	301.9	299.7	302.2	304.6	306.0	307.0	306.0	306.8	304.0	307.5	316.1	319.0	306.7
2011	303.3	302.1	304.5	307.5	308.1	309.0	308.7	308.9	307.6	309.6	319.1	321.8	309.2
2012	308.2	304.6	309.2	310.7	312.1	312.6	311.7	311.2	310.4	313.4	324.5	325.5	312.8
2013	309.7	307.5	308.8	310.2	312.4	313.7	314.1	314.3	313.3	317.0	327.3	330.9	314.9
2014	314.3	312.5	314.9	317.4	318.5	320.3	320.6	321.0	319.8	322.4	332.6	335.4	320.8
2015	317.8	315.4	317.4	321.9	323.8	325.2	325.1	326.0	324.3	329.2	338.3	341.1	325.5
2016	327.2	326.7	328.7	332.1	332.5	332.7	333.6	333.6	332.6	335.1	344.7	346.2	333.8
2017	333.2	331.1	331.6	333.8	334.1	334.8	334.5	335.0	333.5	334.5	341.7	339.5	334.8

1. Employment by Industry: Tennessee, Selected Years, 2007–2017—*Continued*

(Numbers in thousands, not seasonally adjusted)

Industry and year	January	February	March	April	May	June	July	August	September	October	November	December	Annual average
Transportation and Utilities													
2007	145.7	145.7	146.5	146.5	147.1	147.1	146.4	148.2	148.2	147.2	147.5	148.0	147.0
2008	144.2	143.6	143.4	143.6	143.9	143.8	142.9	143.8	143.7	140.8	141.2	142.3	143.1
2009	136.2	134.6	133.7	131.3	131.2	130.7	129.5	130.3	130.3	130.4	130.6	131.5	131.7
2010	128.0	127.7	128.0	128.6	129.2	130.0	131.8	132.5	134.2	134.7	135.9	137.9	131.5
2011	131.7	132.1	132.9	134.9	135.5	136.0	135.8	136.9	137.7	140.1	141.4	142.7	136.5
2012	138.6	138.0	139.2	139.6	140.4	140.3	140.0	141.9	144.5	144.0	146.0	148.6	141.8
2013	143.4	143.8	143.4	144.4	144.3	144.8	144.3	145.1	144.7	145.7	149.0	151.3	145.4
2014	143.7	143.7	145.1	146.4	146.3	146.9	147.3	149.5	150.3	153.3	155.8	157.0	148.8
2015	152.1	150.9	151.2	152.8	154.0	154.9	157.7	158.1	158.7	160.7	163.5	166.7	156.8
2016	161.0	160.2	160.4	162.1	162.2	163.0	164.0	164.4	164.6	166.0	169.3	170.5	164.0
2017	161.8	161.3	160.9	161.6	162.0	163.1	163.9	165.9	166.9	168.1	171.8	174.4	165.1
Information													
2007	49.1	49.3	49.2	49.6	50.1	50.4	50.7	50.6	50.6	50.6	51.2	51.8	50.3
2008	51.0	51.0	51.2	50.9	51.1	51.2	50.7	50.3	49.9	49.7	49.5	49.7	50.5
2009	49.1	48.8	48.3	47.6	47.3	46.8	46.2	46.1	45.8	45.5	45.9	45.7	46.9
2010	45.4	46.3	45.5	44.8	44.7	44.8	44.7	44.3	44.3	44.9	45.1	45.3	45.0
2011	44.3	44.1	44.1	44.1	44.1	43.9	43.7	43.9	43.3	43.0	43.3	43.2	43.8
2012	42.8	43.1	42.9	43.2	43.9	43.9	42.7	42.9	42.4	43.1	43.4	44.1	43.2
2013	43.5	43.8	44.0	43.8	44.3	44.8	44.2	44.2	43.6	43.8	44.4	44.3	44.1
2014	43.6	43.7	43.8	43.9	43.9	43.9	43.8	43.9	43.5	43.5	43.9	43.9	43.8
2015	43.3	43.5	43.5	43.9	44.2	44.7	44.6	44.8	44.4	44.6	45.5	45.6	44.4
2016	44.9	45.4	44.6	45.4	45.0	46.5	44.8	44.9	45.5	45.3	46.3	45.5	45.3
2017	45.1	45.8	45.3	45.2	45.7	47.3	45.5	45.5	45.2	45.1	46.2	45.7	45.6
Financial Activities													
2007	142.0	142.8	143.8	143.8	145.0	146.1	145.8	146.0	145.5	145.2	145.6	146.3	144.8
2008	144.5	144.9	145.2	145.1	145.6	146.3	145.8	145.7	144.9	144.3	144.1	144.0	145.0
2009	141.8	141.6	141.1	141.1	141.5	141.2	140.3	140.6	139.6	139.1	139.4	139.6	140.6
2010	137.7	137.6	137.5	138.6	138.5	137.9	137.5	137.3	135.9	135.6	135.7	135.6	137.1
2011	134.8	134.7	134.7	136.2	136.9	136.8	137.3	137.6	137.1	137.1	137.6	137.7	136.5
2012	136.4	136.9	137.0	137.0	137.5	137.5	137.5	137.4	136.7	136.8	137.1	137.5	137.1
2013	136.0	135.9	136.2	137.4	138.1	138.8	140.0	140.3	140.0	140.6	141.5	141.9	138.9
2014	141.0	141.6	142.3	143.2	144.0	144.4	145.1	145.3	145.1	145.6	145.8	146.4	144.2
2015	145.4	145.8	145.9	146.5	147.3	148.2	148.8	149.1	148.6	149.6	150.1	151.0	148.0
2016	149.3	149.8	150.1	151.5	152.5	153.4	154.1	154.8	155.0	155.0	155.5	156.1	153.1
2017	154.8	156.0	156.6	157.3	158.0	159.2	159.1	159.4	158.8	159.7	159.2	159.6	158.1
Professional and Business Services													
2007	311.3	313.1	316.5	318.5	319.8	323.1	322.4	327.0	329.1	328.7	333.2	334.2	323.1
2008	318.6	319.8	321.7	325.5	324.6	327.9	318.3	321.7	322.6	321.8	319.9	316.6	321.6
2009	298.3	297.3	294.6	291.5	291.5	291.1	285.0	289.8	291.8	297.7	302.3	301.5	294.4
2010	291.9	294.2	297.6	300.5	308.2	306.8	301.5	305.4	308.2	311.9	314.4	315.2	304.7
2011	305.3	312.2	316.5	320.1	319.8	320.9	321.4	326.4	328.5	331.9	336.9	339.4	323.3
2012	323.8	328.1	332.0	335.4	338.5	340.9	335.3	341.4	342.9	346.3	351.7	352.4	339.1
2013	338.2	341.6	345.3	347.3	350.0	352.1	346.3	356.2	358.9	363.8	377.0	377.6	354.5
2014	361.4	360.2	363.8	370.5	374.0	375.0	370.3	379.9	380.6	385.5	393.4	397.5	376.0
2015	378.6	378.4	381.7	387.2	390.2	393.2	391.0	395.6	397.3	404.4	411.5	412.7	393.5
2016	394.1	394.3	396.9	402.6	402.2	403.8	401.4	406.6	408.8	410.9	413.1	417.3	404.3
2017	397.0	399.1	399.9	403.6	403.7	407.0	406.1	407.6	409.5	412.4	414.0	419.2	406.6
Education and Health Services													
2007	344.9	347.9	349.7	349.6	350.3	350.1	351.7	354.5	357.3	356.2	356.6	357.5	352.2
2008	353.4	355.6	356.8	358.9	359.6	359.2	359.5	362.3	364.8	366.5	367.8	368.6	361.1
2009	363.2	364.4	364.5	367.5	366.9	367.5	366.9	367.2	370.4	371.5	372.4	372.9	367.9
2010	368.1	370.0	371.9	375.7	373.5	372.2	373.7	375.2	379.0	382.3	383.0	383.1	375.6
2011	377.7	381.6	382.4	386.2	385.8	382.4	383.5	385.2	390.1	391.8	392.9	392.6	386.0
2012	389.0	392.9	395.0	395.2	393.9	392.1	391.3	394.4	399.5	400.7	401.6	401.6	395.6
2013	396.5	400.5	402.1	402.2	400.9	397.5	394.9	397.7	403.1	405.0	406.3	406.0	401.1
2014	401.2	404.0	406.1	405.3	403.3	400.4	400.0	403.3	409.5	411.7	412.1	412.4	405.8
2015	408.2	410.9	412.7	414.3	412.7	409.2	409.9	412.1	418.7	420.8	422.4	423.0	414.6
2016	416.4	420.8	422.4	423.4	422.1	417.9	419.0	422.5	428.5	430.6	431.7	431.2	423.9
2017	424.5	430.7	431.5	432.2	430.0	426.0	424.4	427.8	434.4	439.4	441.7	440.2	431.9

1. Employment by Industry: Tennessee, Selected Years, 2007–2017—*Continued*

(Numbers in thousands, not seasonally adjusted)

Industry and year	January	February	March	April	May	June	July	August	September	October	November	December	Annual average
Leisure and Hospitality													
2007	258.9	260.5	268.9	276.2	281.2	288.3	285.9	288.2	281.7	276.0	275.5	274.1	276.3
2008	262.4	264.3	270.7	276.6	282.2	285.1	283.1	282.5	277.4	269.3	267.2	264.4	273.8
2009	253.2	253.0	259.1	266.0	271.8	275.5	271.8	270.6	265.4	259.7	258.8	256.9	263.5
2010	247.2	247.4	254.5	263.7	267.7	274.2	270.9	270.3	265.8	262.7	261.3	258.0	262.0
2011	249.0	251.5	259.0	268.2	273.7	278.0	276.8	277.0	273.8	268.8	268.2	267.4	267.6
2012	258.2	260.1	269.6	277.8	283.4	288.5	285.3	286.6	279.9	278.2	277.4	277.0	276.8
2013	266.2	268.3	277.8	285.8	292.0	297.6	296.4	296.7	290.7	287.8	286.7	284.9	285.9
2014	276.0	277.2	286.8	296.3	302.4	308.5	307.0	307.9	302.2	298.8	298.1	296.4	296.5
2015	287.4	289.2	294.8	307.9	315.0	320.1	318.5	317.9	313.1	311.4	310.8	309.8	308.0
2016	300.4	301.9	309.8	320.7	324.7	331.6	329.8	329.2	325.9	321.2	320.6	319.2	319.6
2017	310.1	312.5	320.1	329.4	334.7	340.9	338.2	339.0	333.6	334.4	332.9	331.6	329.8
Other Services													
2007	101.7	102.3	104.2	103.9	105.1	106.2	104.5	104.4	103.9	103.9	103.0	103.0	104.0
2008	103.2	104.4	105.3	104.8	106.0	106.4	105.1	104.7	103.9	103.9	103.3	103.0	104.5
2009	101.3	101.7	102.5	102.6	102.7	104.0	103.0	102.1	101.2	101.2	101.4	100.5	102.0
2010	98.5	98.9	99.9	99.9	100.7	102.5	102.4	102.2	101.8	102.4	102.4	102.8	101.2
2011	99.7	100.4	101.2	101.5	102.3	103.9	103.5	103.2	102.3	102.0	102.3	102.3	102.1
2012	101.8	102.6	103.9	104.1	105.0	106.3	105.9	104.8	104.4	104.2	104.1	103.8	104.2
2013	103.0	103.7	104.6	105.9	106.5	107.8	107.2	106.4	105.9	105.5	105.6	104.9	105.6
2014	104.2	104.7	106.0	106.1	107.0	107.7	107.3	106.2	105.9	105.9	106.1	105.9	106.1
2015	105.1	105.7	106.2	107.5	108.7	109.8	109.4	108.5	108.5	108.7	108.8	108.8	108.0
2016	107.9	108.8	109.8	110.8	111.3	112.4	112.3	111.5	111.7	111.4	111.9	111.9	111.0
2017	111.0	111.9	112.9	113.9	114.5	115.9	115.2	114.6	114.5	113.9	114.6	114.2	113.9
Government													
2007	415.4	419.8	422.5	420.0	420.5	402.2	397.5	411.6	424.8	428.6	430.5	428.1	418.5
2008	421.9	427.3	429.5	430.5	431.0	402.8	403.2	416.2	427.7	436.1	437.2	435.8	424.9
2009	425.3	430.1	431.9	433.4	432.7	401.2	402.3	414.6	429.3	437.8	438.7	435.4	426.1
2010	428.4	432.6	434.4	438.6	447.5	411.3	406.8	418.9	436.1	438.3	438.9	435.8	430.6
2011	429.1	434.2	435.5	435.0	433.0	400.1	396.0	414.5	429.5	433.5	434.4	431.6	425.5
2012	422.3	430.3	433.4	432.8	426.9	395.5	392.4	404.7	425.1	431.3	433.2	432.2	421.7
2013	418.1	427.1	428.7	437.0	431.7	397.9	393.7	406.5	427.1	434.6	434.8	434.4	422.6
2014	423.1	431.3	433.0	434.1	429.8	396.1	394.1	407.6	429.7	435.5	439.0	437.3	424.2
2015	425.4	432.7	432.6	433.8	429.5	397.2	394.7	408.8	432.2	438.2	438.5	437.1	425.1
2016	425.5	434.5	439.0	435.9	430.0	398.6	395.7	413.6	437.5	440.9	444.3	440.8	428.0
2017	426.8	437.8	438.6	439.3	434.1	402.1	399.4	414.5	439.1	443.4	445.3	441.3	430.1

2. Average Weekly Hours by Selected Industry: Tennessee, 2013–2017

(Not seasonally adjusted)

Industry and year	January	February	March	April	May	June	July	August	September	October	November	December	Annual average
Total Private													
2013	34.7	35.2	35.2	35.2	35.2	35.9	35.2	35.4	35.7	35.3	35.3	35.7	35.3
2014	34.8	35.0	35.6	35.2	35.3	35.7	35.2	35.4	35.1	34.9	35.6	35.4	35.3
2015	34.7	34.7	35.2	35.0	35.1	35.3	35.2	35.8	35.0	35.2	35.5	35.6	35.2
2016	35.1	35.1	35.3	35.4	35.8	35.6	35.5	35.5	35.4	35.8	35.5	35.6	35.5
2017	35.7	35.4	35.3	35.5	35.4	35.6	35.6	35.2	35.2	35.4	35.3	35.5	35.4
Goods-Producing													
2013	39.6	40.4	40.6	40.6	40.4	41.0	40.4	41.3	41.4	41.3	41.2	41.1	40.8
2014	40.2	39.8	41.5	41.1	41.5	41.6	40.8	41.5	41.3	40.3	41.8	41.8	41.1
2015	40.8	40.1	41.3	41.1	41.2	41.4	41.0	41.6	40.8	41.4	41.8	42.3	41.2
2016	41.5	40.9	41.7	42.0	42.5	42.4	42.3	42.8	42.9	42.5	43.2	43.2	42.3
2017	42.3	42.1	42.2	41.6	42.3	42.5	41.7	41.6	41.6	41.3	42.0	42.5	42.0
Mining, Logging, and Construction													
2013	37.9	39.0	40.0	40.7	40.9	40.9	41.1	41.7	41.0	41.8	41.4	40.0	40.5
2014	39.1	38.5	41.3	40.4	41.3	41.2	41.7	41.4	40.8	39.2	41.1	40.0	40.5
2015	37.7	37.5	37.5	38.4	40.2	40.2	40.3	39.8	38.4	40.2	39.7	40.5	39.2
2016	39.6	37.0	38.6	39.5	40.5	40.6	40.2	40.7	40.3	40.6	40.3	40.1	39.9
2017	38.9	39.5	39.5	40.4	40.8	41.3	42.0	41.1	40.8	41.5	42.0	41.8	40.8
Manufacturing													
2013	40.2	40.9	40.8	40.6	40.3	41.1	40.1	41.2	41.6	41.2	41.1	41.5	40.9
2014	40.6	40.2	41.5	41.4	41.5	41.7	40.5	41.5	41.5	40.7	42.1	42.4	41.3
2015	41.8	40.9	42.6	42.0	41.5	41.8	41.2	42.3	41.6	41.8	42.6	43.0	41.9
2016	42.1	42.2	42.7	42.8	43.2	43.1	43.0	43.5	43.8	43.1	44.2	44.3	43.2
2017	43.5	43.0	43.1	42.0	42.9	42.9	41.6	41.8	41.9	41.2	42.0	42.7	42.4
Trade, Transportation, and Utilities													
2013	34.2	34.7	34.7	34.6	35.0	35.3	35.3	35.4	35.4	35.1	35.1	35.3	35.0
2014	33.9	34.2	34.9	34.6	34.7	34.8	34.7	34.7	34.4	34.5	34.8	35.0	34.6
2015	34.0	33.9	34.8	34.6	34.6	34.8	34.7	34.9	34.7	34.3	34.6	35.0	34.6
2016	34.4	34.3	34.4	34.6	34.8	34.9	34.7	34.5	34.6	34.9	34.4	34.8	34.6
2017	34.6	34.2	34.1	34.4	34.3	34.4	34.4	34.3	34.4	34.4	34.3	34.8	34.4
Information													
2013	37.5	36.7	36.8	36.8	37.4	38.2	37.7	37.1	37.7	36.6	36.5	37.4	37.2
2014	36.8	38.0	38.5	37.9	37.7	38.0	37.2	37.6	37.4	37.9	38.4	36.5	37.7
2015	36.6	37.2	37.8	36.8	36.5	36.4	36.0	37.6	36.5	36.4	36.6	35.9	36.7
2016	35.1	35.5	35.9	37.1	37.0	36.1	36.5	36.5	37.0	37.2	36.4	37.0	36.4
2017	38.2	36.3	37.0	38.5	37.7	37.5	39.0	37.4	37.8	37.8	36.2	36.9	37.5
Financial Activities													
2013	37.3	37.2	37.2	36.8	37.2	38.6	37.0	37.0	38.2	37.5	37.0	38.9	37.5
2014	37.9	39.0	39.6	38.3	38.5	39.8	38.4	38.2	38.4	38.3	39.1	37.8	38.6
2015	37.4	38.4	38.7	37.8	37.6	37.6	37.6	38.1	37.1	37.0	37.5	37.0	37.6
2016	37.1	37.0	36.7	36.7	37.3	36.9	37.0	37.0	36.3	37.5	36.9	37.1	37.0
2017	37.9	37.4	37.2	38.1	37.2	37.5	38.7	37.5	37.7	38.7	38.0	38.1	37.8
Professional and Business Services													
2013	36.2	37.0	36.5	36.7	36.3	37.4	36.1	36.5	37.0	36.4	36.4	36.9	36.6
2014	36.0	36.1	36.2	36.2	36.4	36.6	35.9	35.9	35.7	35.2	35.9	35.6	36.0
2015	35.0	35.7	35.0	35.1	35.6	36.0	35.8	37.3	35.7	36.3	36.9	37.0	36.0
2016	36.5	36.3	36.5	36.7	37.3	36.9	36.7	36.6	36.4	37.4	36.5	36.5	36.7
2017	36.3	36.2	36.0	36.1	36.4	37.0	37.0	36.4	36.4	37.2	36.7	36.3	36.5
Education and Health Services													
2013	34.7	35.1	34.8	34.8	34.9	35.2	34.4	34.3	34.7	34.0	34.5	34.8	34.7
2014	34.5	34.5	34.7	34.2	34.1	34.5	34.3	34.5	34.4	34.2	34.9	34.7	34.5
2015	34.6	34.5	34.5	34.4	34.5	34.5	34.7	35.2	34.9	34.7	35.2	34.8	34.7
2016	34.9	34.9	34.9	34.7	35.1	34.8	34.9	34.8	35.0	34.9	34.8	34.8	34.9
2017	35.7	35.1	35.1	35.2	34.8	35.0	35.3	34.6	34.6	34.3	34.2	34.4	34.9
Leisure and Hospitality													
2013	25.2	25.9	26.3	26.5	26.5	27.3	26.9	26.9	26.8	26.8	26.6	26.7	26.6
2014	26.3	26.7	27.6	27.3	27.0	27.9	27.8	27.5	27.0	27.1	27.2	26.5	27.2
2015	25.9	25.9	26.6	27.0	26.7	27.3	27.2	27.1	26.5	26.9	26.7	26.6	26.7
2016	26.0	26.5	26.8	26.8	27.0	27.2	27.0	26.9	26.4	27.1	26.8	26.2	26.7
2017	26.3	26.7	26.7	27.4	26.8	27.4	27.3	26.7	26.5	27.1	26.7	26.5	26.8
Other Services													
2013	32.9	33.1	33.2	33.4	33.6	34.6	33.8	33.4	34.4	33.7	32.9	34.1	33.6
2014	32.4	32.9	32.5	32.3	32.4	33.3	32.8	33.4	32.4	32.5	32.6	32.9	32.7
2015	32.2	32.8	32.7	32.6	33.0	33.0	33.0	33.8	32.3	32.8	32.7	32.8	32.8
2016	31.7	31.9	32.2	32.7	33.0	32.2	32.4	32.1	31.8	32.2	32.1	32.7	32.2
2017	33.0	32.8	32.8	32.9	32.3	31.6	32.5	32.4	32.8	33.4	33.3	33.9	32.8

3. Average Hourly Earnings by Selected Industry: Tennessee, 2013–2017

(Dollars, not seasonally adjusted)

Industry and year	January	February	March	April	May	June	July	August	September	October	November	December	Annual average
Total Private													
2013	20.15	20.31	20.40	20.22	20.04	20.17	20.24	20.05	20.34	20.28	20.51	20.72	20.29
2014	20.75	20.96	20.79	20.76	20.75	20.79	20.67	20.73	20.73	20.68	20.89	20.46	20.75
2015	20.72	20.97	20.80	20.69	20.64	20.67	20.89	20.93	21.00	21.08	21.23	21.14	20.90
2016	21.46	21.33	21.34	21.37	21.66	21.53	21.78	21.71	22.09	22.28	22.20	22.65	21.79
2017	22.81	22.62	22.38	22.68	22.42	22.35	22.69	22.56	22.83	22.68	22.79	22.92	22.65
Goods-Producing													
2013	20.62	20.59	20.64	20.56	20.54	20.55	20.89	20.83	20.98	20.98	21.14	21.24	20.80
2014	21.18	21.42	20.98	21.01	20.88	21.20	21.34	21.10	21.03	21.05	21.26	21.19	21.14
2015	21.22	21.23	21.35	21.34	21.48	21.54	22.08	21.55	21.97	21.91	22.04	22.36	21.68
2016	22.55	22.52	22.47	22.59	22.98	23.02	23.40	23.25	23.85	23.63	23.96	24.42	23.24
2017	24.05	23.76	23.55	23.54	23.53	23.60	23.98	23.75	24.16	23.76	23.89	24.18	23.81
Mining, Logging, and Construction													
2013	21.24	21.53	21.46	21.04	20.93	20.89	21.02	20.98	21.36	21.53	21.31	22.06	21.27
2014	21.99	22.51	22.08	21.97	21.30	21.58	21.99	21.69	21.66	21.70	21.64	21.72	21.81
2015	21.92	22.10	22.48	22.08	22.01	22.45	22.44	22.19	22.49	22.67	23.16	23.49	22.47
2016	23.27	22.96	23.35	22.99	23.22	22.90	23.17	23.07	22.98	23.38	23.38	24.26	23.25
2017	24.07	23.88	23.94	24.20	24.09	23.98	24.26	24.04	24.38	24.10	24.75	24.69	24.21
Manufacturing													
2013	20.43	20.30	20.37	20.40	20.40	20.43	20.84	20.78	20.85	20.79	21.08	20.98	20.64
2014	20.93	21.08	20.61	20.69	20.74	21.07	21.11	20.90	20.82	20.83	21.13	21.02	20.91
2015	21.01	20.96	21.01	21.11	21.30	21.23	21.95	21.34	21.80	21.64	21.67	21.99	21.42
2016	22.32	22.39	22.20	22.46	22.90	23.06	23.48	23.31	24.13	23.71	24.15	24.47	23.23
2017	24.04	23.72	23.42	23.31	23.34	23.47	23.88	23.65	24.08	23.64	23.58	24.00	23.68
Trade, Transportation, and Utilities													
2013	18.47	18.75	19.15	19.11	18.57	18.84	19.00	18.47	18.82	18.68	18.51	18.82	18.76
2014	19.01	19.17	19.42	19.31	19.07	19.29	18.97	18.96	18.96	18.98	19.00	18.84	19.08
2015	19.37	19.37	19.12	19.41	19.07	19.20	19.25	19.05	19.10	19.11	19.13	18.90	19.17
2016	19.20	18.96	19.11	19.29	19.87	19.52	19.83	19.87	20.07	20.32	19.86	20.28	19.69
2017	20.57	20.43	20.35	20.66	20.43	20.30	20.62	20.47	20.58	20.47	20.33	20.44	20.47
Information													
2013	24.59	25.24	25.49	24.86	25.26	25.10	25.47	25.53	26.10	25.39	25.60	25.88	25.38
2014	25.82	25.16	25.26	24.72	24.64	25.57	25.54	25.70	25.74	26.10	26.44	26.49	25.60
2015	26.99	27.37	26.73	26.16	26.19	26.37	26.84	27.38	27.28	27.93	28.57	28.64	27.21
2016	29.31	28.68	27.81	27.90	28.79	28.22	28.84	28.57	29.12	30.02	29.91	30.98	29.02
2017	31.32	32.32	31.28	32.55	31.83	31.37	31.85	31.15	30.99	30.96	31.78	31.27	31.56
Financial Activities													
2013	23.51	24.23	23.70	24.26	24.00	24.37	23.84	23.46	23.31	23.08	23.66	23.98	23.78
2014	24.51	24.67	24.30	25.62	24.52	24.49	24.31	24.57	24.51	24.12	24.86	24.48	24.58
2015	25.06	25.85	25.30	25.39	25.69	25.63	25.94	27.07	25.84	26.12	26.47	26.29	25.89
2016	26.49	26.50	25.99	26.42	27.04	26.54	26.60	25.94	26.36	26.75	26.68	26.43	26.48
2017	27.06	27.55	26.61	27.82	27.18	27.18	27.72	27.82	27.97	28.57	28.64	28.30	27.71
Professional and Business Services													
2013	24.14	24.13	24.51	23.71	23.75	24.12	24.40	23.83	24.61	24.61	25.60	25.93	24.46
2014	25.64	26.12	25.88	25.46	26.49	26.24	25.90	25.90	25.80	25.40	25.65	23.54	25.66
2015	23.68	24.34	24.55	23.83	23.77	23.69	23.89	24.31	24.53	24.45	24.77	24.28	24.18
2016	24.91	24.90	25.35	24.79	24.94	25.17	25.29	25.10	25.83	26.23	26.02	26.91	25.46
2017	27.42	27.23	26.99	27.83	27.04	26.83	27.43	27.07	27.45	27.31	27.41	27.52	27.29
Education and Health Services													
2013	20.96	21.21	21.21	21.00	20.89	20.90	20.86	21.04	21.06	21.06	21.01	21.04	21.02
2014	21.00	21.23	21.15	21.27	21.27	21.20	21.18	21.38	21.42	21.50	21.45	21.49	21.30
2015	21.70	21.94	21.61	21.64	21.62	21.75	21.87	21.91	21.83	22.25	22.21	22.07	21.87
2016	22.53	22.23	22.22	22.49	22.36	22.36	22.59	22.45	22.45	22.69	22.67	23.12	22.51
2017	23.29	22.76	22.60	22.77	22.48	22.60	22.55	22.67	22.75	22.28	22.69	22.83	22.69
Leisure and Hospitality													
2013	12.03	11.96	11.85	11.81	11.75	11.66	11.59	11.52	11.55	11.62	11.59	11.75	11.72
2014	11.67	11.72	11.63	11.47	11.49	11.41	11.52	11.58	11.59	11.65	11.61	11.76	11.59
2015	11.77	11.94	11.87	11.87	11.89	12.02	12.15	12.13	12.35	12.33	12.36	12.38	12.09
2016	12.19	12.36	12.24	12.18	12.20	12.22	12.41	12.57	12.74	12.83	13.06	12.99	12.50
2017	12.88	13.08	12.97	12.90	13.06	12.87	13.00	13.31	13.67	13.72	13.92	14.13	13.29
Other Services													
2013	18.81	18.92	18.92	19.17	19.26	19.16	19.00	19.21	19.26	19.24	19.63	19.52	19.18
2014	20.00	20.35	20.18	19.67	19.19	19.21	19.52	20.14	19.91	20.02	21.29	20.24	19.97
2015	20.23	20.35	20.11	19.83	19.46	19.28	19.31	19.13	19.37	19.20	19.43	19.64	19.60
2016	19.52	19.56	19.51	19.57	19.85	19.34	19.18	19.55	19.64	19.98	19.61	19.83	19.60
2017	20.41	19.77	19.89	20.10	19.86	19.91	20.49	19.88	20.28	20.66	20.47	20.67	20.20

4. Average Weekly Earnings by Selected Industry: Tennessee, 2013–2017

(Dollars, not seasonally adjusted)

Industry and year	January	February	March	April	May	June	July	August	September	October	November	December	Annual average
Total Private													
2013	699.21	714.91	718.08	711.74	705.41	724.10	712.45	709.77	726.14	715.88	724.00	739.70	716.24
2014	722.10	733.60	740.12	730.75	732.48	742.20	727.58	733.84	727.62	721.73	743.68	724.28	732.48
2015	718.98	727.66	732.16	724.15	724.46	729.65	735.33	749.29	735.00	742.02	753.67	752.58	735.68
2016	753.25	748.68	753.30	756.50	775.43	766.47	773.19	770.71	781.99	797.62	788.10	806.34	773.55
2017	814.32	800.75	790.01	805.14	793.67	795.66	807.76	794.11	803.62	802.87	804.49	813.66	801.81
Goods-Producing													
2013	816.55	831.84	837.98	834.74	829.82	842.55	843.96	860.28	868.57	866.47	870.97	872.96	848.64
2014	851.44	852.52	870.67	863.51	866.52	881.92	870.67	875.65	868.54	848.32	888.67	885.74	868.85
2015	865.78	851.32	881.76	877.07	884.98	891.76	905.28	896.48	896.38	907.07	921.27	945.83	893.22
2016	935.83	921.07	937.00	948.78	976.65	976.05	989.82	995.10	1,023.17	1,004.28	1,035.07	1,054.94	983.05
2017	1,017.32	1,000.30	993.81	979.26	995.32	1,003.00	999.97	988.00	1,005.06	981.29	1,003.38	1,027.65	1,000.02
Mining, Logging, and Construction													
2013	805.00	839.67	858.40	856.33	856.04	854.40	863.92	874.87	875.76	899.95	882.23	882.40	861.44
2014	859.81	866.64	911.90	887.59	879.69	889.10	916.98	897.97	883.73	850.64	889.40	868.80	883.31
2015	826.38	828.75	843.00	847.87	884.80	902.49	904.33	883.16	863.62	911.33	919.45	951.35	880.82
2016	921.49	849.52	901.31	908.11	940.41	929.74	931.43	938.95	926.09	949.23	942.21	972.83	927.68
2017	936.32	943.26	945.63	977.68	982.87	990.37	1,018.92	988.04	994.70	1,000.15	1,039.50	1,032.04	987.77
Manufacturing													
2013	821.29	830.27	831.10	828.24	822.12	839.67	835.68	856.14	867.36	856.55	866.39	870.67	844.18
2014	849.76	847.42	855.32	856.57	860.71	878.62	854.96	867.35	864.03	847.78	889.57	891.25	863.58
2015	878.22	857.26	895.03	886.62	883.95	887.41	904.34	902.68	906.88	904.55	923.14	945.57	897.50
2016	939.67	944.86	947.94	961.29	989.28	993.89	1,009.64	1,013.99	1,056.89	1,021.90	1,067.43	1,084.02	1,003.54
2017	1,045.74	1,019.96	1,009.40	979.02	1,001.29	1,006.86	993.41	988.57	1,008.95	973.97	990.36	1,024.80	1,004.03
Trade, Transportation, and Utilities													
2013	631.67	650.63	664.51	661.21	649.95	665.05	670.70	653.84	666.23	655.67	649.70	664.35	656.60
2014	644.44	655.61	677.76	668.13	661.73	671.29	658.26	657.91	652.22	654.81	661.20	659.40	660.17
2015	658.58	656.64	665.38	671.59	659.82	668.16	667.98	664.85	662.77	655.47	661.90	661.50	663.28
2016	660.48	650.33	657.38	667.43	691.48	681.25	688.10	685.52	694.42	709.17	683.18	705.74	681.27
2017	711.72	698.71	693.94	710.70	700.75	698.32	709.33	702.12	707.95	704.17	697.32	711.31	704.17
Information													
2013	922.13	926.31	938.03	914.85	944.72	958.82	960.22	947.16	983.97	929.27	934.40	967.91	944.14
2014	950.18	956.08	972.51	936.89	928.93	971.66	950.09	966.32	962.68	989.19	1,015.30	966.89	965.12
2015	987.83	1,018.16	1,010.39	962.69	955.94	959.87	966.24	1,029.49	995.72	1,016.65	1,045.66	1,028.18	998.61
2016	1,028.78	1,018.14	998.38	1,035.09	1,065.23	1,018.74	1,052.66	1,042.81	1,077.44	1,116.74	1,088.72	1,146.26	1,056.33
2017	1,196.42	1,173.22	1,157.36	1,253.18	1,199.99	1,176.38	1,242.15	1,165.01	1,171.42	1,170.29	1,150.44	1,153.86	1,183.50
Financial Activities													
2013	876.92	901.36	881.64	892.77	892.80	940.68	882.08	868.02	890.44	865.50	875.42	932.82	891.75
2014	928.93	962.13	962.28	981.25	944.02	974.70	933.50	938.57	941.18	923.80	972.03	925.34	948.79
2015	937.24	992.64	979.11	959.74	965.94	963.69	975.34	1,031.37	958.66	966.44	992.63	972.73	973.46
2016	982.78	980.50	953.83	969.61	1,008.59	979.33	984.20	959.78	956.87	1,003.13	984.49	980.55	979.76
2017	1,025.57	1,030.37	989.89	1,059.94	1,011.10	1,019.25	1,072.76	1,043.25	1,054.47	1,105.66	1,088.32	1,078.23	1,047.44
Professional and Business Services													
2013	873.87	892.81	894.62	870.16	862.13	902.09	880.84	869.80	910.57	895.80	931.84	956.82	895.24
2014	923.04	942.93	936.86	921.65	964.24	960.38	929.81	929.81	921.06	894.08	920.84	838.02	923.76
2015	828.80	868.94	859.25	836.43	846.21	852.84	855.26	906.76	875.72	887.54	914.01	898.36	870.48
2016	909.22	903.87	925.28	909.79	930.26	928.77	928.14	918.66	940.21	981.00	949.73	982.22	934.38
2017	995.35	985.73	971.64	1,004.66	984.26	992.71	1,014.91	985.35	999.18	1,015.93	1,005.95	998.98	996.09
Education and Health Services													
2013	727.31	744.47	738.11	730.80	729.06	735.68	717.58	721.67	730.78	716.04	724.85	732.19	729.39
2014	724.50	732.44	733.91	727.43	725.31	731.40	726.47	737.61	736.85	735.30	748.61	745.70	734.85
2015	750.82	756.93	745.55	744.42	745.89	750.38	758.89	771.23	761.87	772.08	781.79	768.04	758.89
2016	786.30	775.83	775.48	780.40	784.84	778.13	788.39	781.26	785.75	791.88	788.92	804.58	785.60
2017	831.45	798.88	793.26	801.50	782.30	791.00	796.02	784.38	787.15	764.20	776.00	785.35	791.88
Leisure and Hospitality													
2013	303.16	309.76	311.66	312.97	311.38	318.32	311.77	309.89	309.54	311.42	308.29	313.73	311.75
2014	306.92	312.92	320.99	313.13	310.23	318.34	320.26	318.45	312.93	315.72	315.79	311.64	315.25
2015	304.84	309.25	315.74	320.49	317.46	328.15	330.48	328.72	327.28	331.68	330.01	329.31	322.80
2016	316.94	327.54	328.03	326.42	329.40	332.38	335.07	338.13	336.34	347.69	350.01	340.34	333.75
2017	338.74	349.24	346.30	353.46	350.01	352.64	354.90	355.38	362.26	371.81	371.66	374.45	356.17
Other Services													
2013	618.85	626.25	628.14	640.28	647.14	662.94	642.20	641.61	662.54	648.39	645.83	665.63	644.45
2014	648.00	669.52	655.85	635.34	621.76	639.69	640.26	672.68	645.08	650.65	694.05	665.90	653.02
2015	651.41	667.48	657.60	646.46	642.18	636.24	637.23	646.59	625.65	629.76	635.36	644.19	642.88
2016	618.78	623.96	628.22	639.94	655.05	622.75	621.43	627.56	624.55	643.36	629.48	648.44	631.12
2017	673.53	648.46	652.39	661.29	641.48	629.16	665.93	644.11	665.18	690.04	681.65	700.71	662.56

TEXAS
At a Glance

Population:
2010 census: 25,145,561
2017 estimate: 28,304,596

Percent change in population:
2010–2017: 12.6%

Percent change in total nonfarm employment:
2007–2017: 17.2%

Industry with the largest growth in employment, 2007–2017 (thousands):
Education and health services, 411.1

Industry with the largest decline or smallest growth in employment, 2007–2017 (thousands):
Manufacturing, -88.1

Civilian labor force:
2010: 12,241,970
2017: 13,538,385

Unemployment rate and rank among states (highest to lowest):
2010: 8.1%, 32nd
2017: 4.3%, 24th

Over-the-year change in unemployment rates:
2015–2016: 0.2%
2016–2017: -0.3%

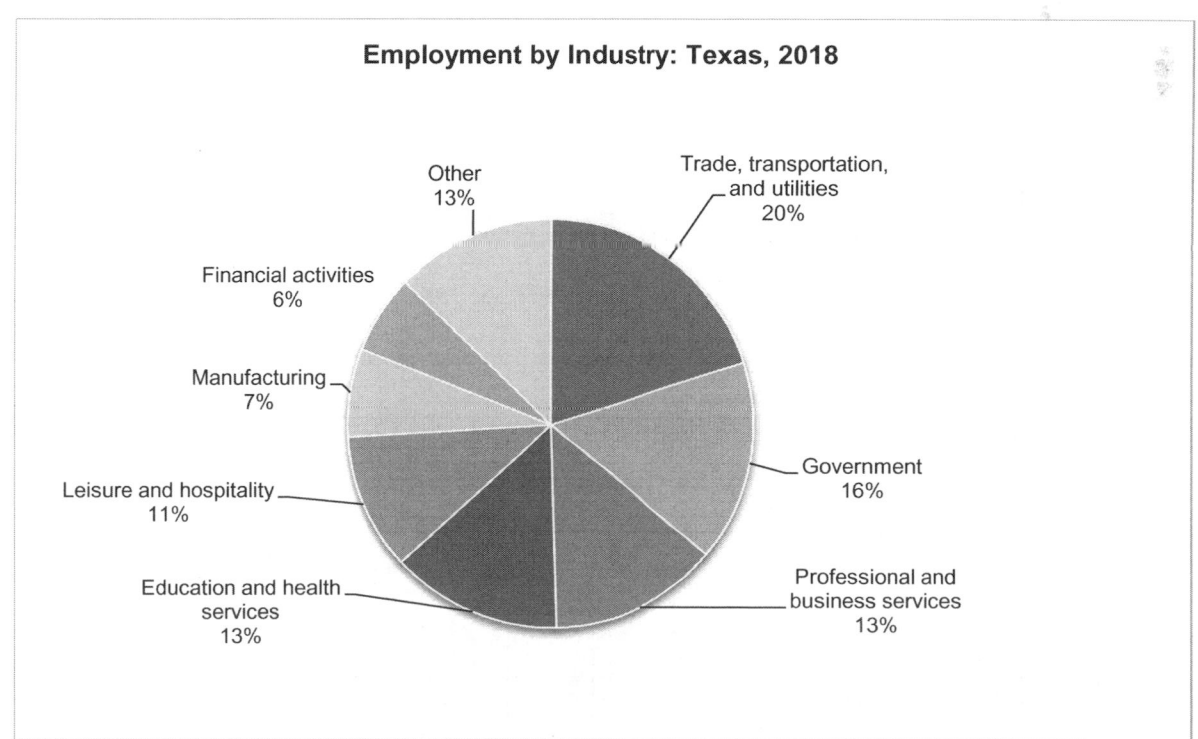

Employment by Industry: Texas, 2018

Other 13%

Trade, transportation, and utilities 20%

Financial activities 6%

Manufacturing 7%

Leisure and hospitality 11%

Education and health services 13%

Government 16%

Professional and business services 13%

1. Employment by Industry: Texas, Selected Years, 2007–2017

(Numbers in thousands, not seasonally adjusted)

Industry and year	January	February	March	April	May	June	July	August	September	October	November	December	Annual average
Total Nonfarm													
2007	10,148.9	10,243.4	10,340.7	10,369.6	10,435.8	10,482.3	10,381.6	10,436.3	10,488.2	10,547.0	10,614.7	10,649.6	10,428.2
2008	10,478.6	10,567.7	10,613.7	10,641.2	10,695.8	10,705.6	10,604.6	10,646.5	10,640.9	10,696.4	10,714.6	10,703.2	10,642.4
2009	10,443.7	10,432.3	10,429.3	10,386.3	10,394.5	10,369.5	10,229.1	10,224.0	10,246.4	10,290.1	10,317.5	10,330.7	10,341.1
2010	10,155.8	10,208.9	10,299.0	10,346.5	10,435.9	10,440.7	10,323.0	10,351.4	10,392.0	10,475.5	10,518.4	10,546.5	10,374.5
2011	10,361.3	10,420.2	10,517.3	10,588.1	10,623.1	10,658.7	10,575.9	10,611.7	10,666.3	10,693.1	10,751.8	10,782.9	10,604.2
2012	10,620.1	10,712.5	10,799.6	10,850.3	10,918.4	10,965.0	10,866.7	10,931.2	10,975.8	11,046.1	11,130.2	11,157.3	10,914.4
2013	10,942.1	11,072.5	11,142.6	11,186.9	11,240.2	11,284.1	11,205.5	11,252.3	11,297.5	11,361.3	11,450.2	11,458.7	11,241.2
2014	11,273.8	11,368.4	11,441.6	11,520.8	11,592.9	11,636.3	11,558.4	11,606.0	11,650.7	11,760.3	11,836.3	11,879.1	11,593.7
2015	11,672.4	11,749.0	11,771.3	11,820.2	11,871.4	11,911.0	11,841.7	11,860.5	11,885.4	11,967.1	12,010.3	12,031.1	11,866.0
2016	11,831.0	11,909.0	11,923.5	11,987.3	12,018.1	12,027.3	11,972.9	11,994.2	12,042.6	12,098.0	12,164.8	12,177.3	12,012.2
2017	11,990.6	12,083.1	12,142.4	12,170.9	12,231.4	12,275.6	12,173.8	12,198.4	12,219.4	12,352.5	12,432.0	12,435.6	12,225.5
Total Private													
2007	8,394.5	8,464.2	8,553.7	8,589.2	8,645.1	8,732.2	8,718.3	8,759.0	8,730.6	8,746.0	8,801.5	8,839.3	8,664.5
2008	8,678.0	8,742.6	8,779.1	8,819.4	8,862.0	8,908.1	8,893.1	8,921.8	8,839.8	8,854.9	8,856.8	8,849.0	8,833.7
2009	8,599.5	8,567.7	8,556.4	8,510.7	8,511.0	8,523.6	8,475.8	8,469.2	8,410.9	8,398.8	8,416.3	8,435.8	8,489.6
2010	8,278.9	8,307.1	8,383.1	8,425.4	8,471.8	8,529.5	8,520.9	8,553.0	8,529.3	8,565.0	8,599.9	8,639.9	8,483.7
2011	8,476.5	8,518.1	8,613.3	8,689.8	8,721.6	8,792.4	8,803.3	8,850.6	8,848.4	8,846.0	8,900.2	8,940.7	8,750.1
2012	8,797.0	8,860.2	8,942.4	8,999.5	9,061.3	9,145.1	9,120.2	9,189.3	9,168.0	9,195.6	9,271.6	9,298.1	9,087.4
2013	9,113.1	9,210.5	9,274.2	9,323.9	9,372.1	9,448.7	9,439.7	9,495.2	9,469.1	9,491.5	9,569.2	9,584.0	9,399.3
2014	9,419.6	9,489.3	9,556.0	9,641.6	9,707.0	9,779.8	9,775.8	9,833.5	9,808.7	9,870.3	9,934.6	9,979.1	9,732.9
2015	9,799.7	9,849.5	9,868.3	9,922.0	9,965.8	10,029.1	10,033.2	10,056.8	10,013.3	10,051.9	10,082.9	10,102.7	9,981.3
2016	9,925.3	9,978.4	9,986.7	10,051.1	10,072.5	10,106.0	10,124.0	10,151.6	10,130.0	10,151.5	10,204.5	10,214.7	10,091.4
2017	10,059.5	10,119.9	10,171.6	10,204.5	10,260.3	10,334.0	10,311.5	10,345.6	10,303.4	10,393.7	10,462.3	10,466.9	10,286.1
Goods Producing													
2007	1,738.7	1,756.4	1,772.8	1,778.1	1,789.5	1,813.3	1,806.3	1,814.7	1,813.0	1,819.1	1,823.7	1,825.0	1,795.9
2008	1,804.2	1,822.4	1,827.4	1,830.6	1,839.7	1,848.3	1,845.2	1,850.2	1,840.7	1,842.9	1,829.8	1,810.9	1,832.7
2009	1,755.4	1,731.7	1,705.0	1,666.0	1,650.2	1,637.9	1,619.4	1,613.1	1,599.2	1,586.7	1,576.5	1,573.6	1,642.9
2010	1,558.1	1,557.7	1,570.2	1,574.3	1,581.0	1,591.4	1,599.5	1,605.2	1,603.0	1,606.5	1,602.5	1,604.1	1,587.8
2011	1,583.4	1,595.3	1,610.6	1,619.0	1,625.2	1,645.2	1,659.0	1,669.0	1,674.2	1,674.7	1,676.4	1,679.8	1,642.7
2012	1,668.4	1,683.8	1,699.0	1,708.2	1,718.0	1,734.6	1,736.7	1,748.0	1,746.9	1,754.0	1,753.3	1,751.6	1,725.2
2013	1,732.3	1,754.6	1,763.9	1,766.9	1,771.5	1,786.3	1,787.1	1,795.9	1,791.7	1,793.5	1,796.6	1,794.4	1,777.9
2014	1,781.4	1,801.0	1,809.5	1,828.0	1,842.5	1,855.3	1,863.4	1,874.9	1,874.7	1,886.7	1,890.1	1,895.3	1,850.2
2015	1,871.7	1,869.5	1,855.1	1,840.2	1,837.1	1,843.2	1,837.8	1,833.8	1,819.3	1,816.1	1,802.5	1,796.6	1,835.2
2016	1,774.4	1,777.4	1,765.5	1,764.6	1,758.5	1,760.8	1,761.6	1,757.9	1,755.8	1,755.9	1,747.9	1,746.3	1,760.6
2017	1,734.7	1,754.4	1,765.3	1,766.7	1,780.2	1,799.2	1,797.5	1,800.5	1,799.5	1,814.4	1,818.7	1,820.6	1,787.6
Service-Providing													
2007	8,410.2	8,487.0	8,567.9	8,591.5	8,646.3	8,669.0	8,575.3	8,621.6	8,675.2	8,727.9	8,791.0	8,824.6	8,632.3
2008	8,674.4	8,745.3	8,786.3	8,810.6	8,856.1	8,857.3	8,759.4	8,796.3	8,800.2	8,853.5	8,884.8	8,892.3	8,809.7
2009	8,688.3	8,700.6	8,724.3	8,720.3	8,744.3	8,731.6	8,609.7	8,610.9	8,647.2	8,703.4	8,741.0	8,757.1	8,698.2
2010	8,597.7	8,651.2	8,728.8	8,772.2	8,854.9	8,849.3	8,723.5	8,746.2	8,789.0	8,869.0	8,915.9	8,942.4	8,786.7
2011	8,777.9	8,824.9	8,906.7	8,969.1	8,997.9	9,013.5	8,916.9	8,942.7	8,992.1	9,018.4	9,075.4	9,103.1	8,961.6
2012	8,951.7	9,028.7	9,100.6	9,142.1	9,200.4	9,230.4	9,130.0	9,183.2	9,228.9	9,292.1	9,376.9	9,405.7	9,189.2
2013	9,209.8	9,317.9	9,378.7	9,420.0	9,468.7	9,497.8	9,418.4	9,456.4	9,505.8	9,567.8	9,653.6	9,664.3	9,463.3
2014	9,492.4	9,567.4	9,632.1	9,692.8	9,750.4	9,781.0	9,695.0	9,731.1	9,776.0	9,873.6	9,946.2	9,983.8	9,743.5
2015	9,800.7	9,879.5	9,916.2	9,980.0	10,034.3	10,067.8	10,003.9	10,026.7	10,066.1	10,151.0	10,207.8	10,234.5	10,030.7
2016	10,056.6	10,131.6	10,158.0	10,222.7	10,259.6	10,266.5	10,211.3	10,236.3	10,286.8	10,342.1	10,416.9	10,431.0	10,251.6
2017	10,255.9	10,328.7	10,377.1	10,404.2	10,451.2	10,476.4	10,376.3	10,397.9	10,419.9	10,538.1	10,613.3	10,615.0	10,437.8
Mining and Logging													
2007	198.6	200.3	202.4	203.5	205.2	209.1	211.0	212.9	212.2	214.4	216.1	218.0	208.6
2008	218.8	221.8	223.0	224.6	226.7	230.9	233.5	235.8	236.0	239.0	238.0	236.1	230.4
2009	228.0	221.8	215.7	205.5	200.5	197.7	195.6	194.0	192.3	191.1	191.6	193.3	202.3
2010	193.5	195.7	197.8	200.8	203.3	207.1	208.8	211.0	211.8	214.0	215.1	217.8	206.4
2011	218.3	220.9	223.9	227.6	229.9	235.7	240.7	244.6	246.6	250.9	253.1	256.6	237.4
2012	257.0	260.3	263.5	265.8	268.0	271.9	275.0	276.1	275.4	277.9	278.8	280.4	270.8
2013	279.0	281.4	282.9	285.0	286.6	290.1	292.2	293.9	293.2	293.7	294.7	295.7	289.0
2014	296.7	299.5	301.0	304.1	306.9	311.0	315.0	317.9	317.8	320.2	321.7	322.1	311.2
2015	314.6	302.4	292.5	280.4	273.9	271.8	266.7	263.7	257.6	252.5	247.5	245.5	272.4
2016	235.1	229.4	223.0	215.8	211.4	209.4	207.5	206.5	204.8	205.7	204.9	206.2	213.3
2017	208.8	212.6	214.2	216.7	220.1	223.2	225.2	226.6	227.4	228.8	230.2	231.2	222.1

1. Employment by Industry: Texas, Selected Years, 2007–2017—*Continued*

(Numbers in thousands, not seasonally adjusted)

Industry and year	January	February	March	April	May	June	July	August	September	October	November	December	Annual average
Construction													
2007	609.2	622.2	635.2	637.7	644.9	657.9	652.2	658.7	659.4	665.3	668.5	666.3	648.1
2008	653.8	667.0	672.5	675.3	679.8	681.8	678.0	681.4	676.6	680.2	671.7	661.4	673.3
2009	634.0	627.8	620.5	606.9	603.8	602.1	595.6	591.0	582.0	576.2	569.3	565.0	597.9
2010	554.6	552.4	560.6	563.9	565.0	568.1	572.2	573.6	570.8	569.8	562.7	559.4	564.4
2011	543.5	549.4	557.6	559.0	560.1	567.3	571.6	574.7	576.5	572.2	569.0	565.5	563.9
2012	557.0	564.4	573.1	576.4	584.0	589.7	585.7	594.5	594.8	600.7	597.9	593.2	584.3
2013	583.0	599.1	606.6	607.5	611.4	618.1	617.6	623.7	622.4	623.9	623.7	619.7	613.1
2014	614.6	625.2	632.0	642.5	650.8	654.3	657.6	664.0	665.4	671.5	670.3	670.3	651.5
2015	662.1	673.2	673.1	675.1	680.9	688.0	691.4	694.0	691.2	697.3	690.8	688.5	683.8
2016	683.8	692.0	691.0	701.4	701.5	704.2	707.3	706.3	708.4	710.5	702.2	696.8	700.5
2017	688.4	699.5	707.0	705.4	713.6	720.6	716.1	716.0	715.9	730.4	731.6	729.7	714.5
Manufacturing													
2007	930.9	933.9	935.2	936.9	939.4	946.3	943.1	943.1	941.4	939.4	939.1	940.7	939.1
2008	931.6	933.6	931.9	930.7	933.2	935.6	933.7	933.0	928.1	923.7	920.1	913.4	929.1
2009	893.4	882.1	868.8	853.6	845.9	838.1	828.2	828.1	824.9	819.4	815.6	815.3	842.8
2010	810.0	809.6	811.8	809.6	812.7	816.2	818.5	820.6	820.4	822.7	824.7	826.9	817.0
2011	821.6	825.0	829.1	832.4	835.2	842.2	846.7	849.7	851.1	851.6	854.3	857.7	841.4
2012	854.4	859.1	862.4	866.0	866.0	873.0	876.0	877.4	876.7	875.4	876.6	878.0	870.1
2013	870.3	874.1	874.4	874.4	873.5	878.1	877.3	878.3	876.1	875.9	878.2	879.0	875.8
2014	870.1	876.3	876.5	881.4	884.8	890.0	890.8	893.0	891.5	895.0	898.1	902.9	887.5
2015	895.0	893.9	889.5	884.7	882.3	883.4	879.7	876.1	870.5	866.3	864.2	862.6	879.0
2016	855.5	856.0	851.5	847.4	845.6	847.2	846.8	845.1	842.6	839.7	840.8	843.3	846.8
2017	837.5	842.3	844.1	844.6	846.5	855.4	856.2	857.9	856.2	855.2	856.9	859.7	851.0
Trade, Transportation, and Utilities													
2007	2,062.6	2,054.9	2,075.4	2,075.3	2,085.8	2,097.7	2,101.1	2,112.0	2,109.1	2,121.2	2,162.1	2,189.2	2,103.9
2008	2,120.4	2,114.9	2,122.6	2,118.1	2,123.7	2,132.7	2,134.5	2,147.6	2,127.4	2,132.6	2,156.5	2,172.8	2,133.7
2009	2,088.5	2,063.1	2,060.9	2,045.1	2,043.4	2,041.6	2,034.3	2,040.2	2,031.8	2,031.9	2,054.6	2,076.2	2,051.0
2010	2,009.9	1,999.3	2,013.7	2,017.6	2,028.0	2,037.0	2,038.0	2,049.9	2,042.6	2,057.0	2,091.1	2,118.9	2,041.9
2011	2,053.4	2,044.6	2,060.8	2,077.4	2,083.3	2,092.3	2,098.0	2,113.8	2,106.2	2,117.8	2,157.8	2,186.3	2,099.3
2012	2,123.2	2,115.4	2,126.7	2,135.5	2,149.3	2,163.1	2,165.0	2,179.9	2,171.5	2,185.7	2,239.3	2,258.5	2,167.8
2013	2,186.9	2,185.5	2,191.0	2,202.7	2,212.7	2,226.2	2,229.7	2,247.0	2,241.1	2,256.1	2,306.8	2,331.2	2,234.7
2014	2,262.1	2,255.2	2,261.4	2,272.0	2,282.7	2,299.6	2,303.1	2,320.3	2,315.3	2,337.2	2,387.2	2,421.5	2,309.8
2015	2,348.3	2,342.3	2,347.5	2,358.3	2,371.3	2,383.7	2,385.7	2,397.5	2,391.2	2,406.9	2,447.4	2,472.5	2,387.7
2016	2,397.5	2,390.4	2,390.6	2,399.4	2,401.1	2,409.7	2,416.8	2,427.2	2,417.2	2,435.9	2,488.5	2,508.8	2,423.6
2017	2,436.1	2,419.7	2,418.7	2,424.4	2,431.2	2,444.7	2,445.1	2,460.6	2,444.9	2,469.0	2,514.6	2,530.9	2,453.3
Wholesale Trade													
2007	495.4	498.7	502.0	503.8	506.7	511.8	511.9	513.8	513.8	517.0	518.0	521.0	509.5
2008	515.9	518.4	518.6	519.9	521.4	523.6	522.6	523.2	520.4	520.0	518.1	517.0	519.9
2009	506.6	501.6	498.2	492.8	491.1	489.6	487.5	486.2	483.8	483.6	482.0	483.0	490.5
2010	480.4	480.7	482.0	483.9	486.3	489.1	490.1	491.1	490.9	491.9	492.7	494.8	487.8
2011	491.3	494.5	497.4	501.7	505.1	508.1	509.6	511.7	513.7	515.3	516.6	519.9	507.1
2012	517.1	520.9	524.6	526.1	531.3	535.6	535.1	537.3	537.0	538.1	540.2	543.0	532.2
2013	539.5	543.6	546.1	545.9	548.1	551.4	552.1	553.7	553.7	556.1	558.5	560.0	550.7
2014	556.0	559.7	561.3	562.7	566.3	570.8	572.3	576.0	576.4	579.7	581.8	584.8	570.7
2015	581.4	583.4	583.6	582.8	583.8	585.3	585.1	585.7	583.8	581.1	580.2	579.7	583.0
2016	580.3	581.3	579.4	579.9	579.3	580.2	581.0	581.1	580.4	578.2	578.9	580.5	580.0
2017	577.0	579.3	581.2	584.1	587.2	592.1	590.9	593.0	592.0	593.5	592.8	598.3	588.5
Retail Trade													
2007	1,142.7	1,130.2	1,143.9	1,142.7	1,148.2	1,152.1	1,156.7	1,162.5	1,158.1	1,167.1	1,206.2	1,224.2	1,161.2
2008	1,170.9	1,161.0	1,168.4	1,161.6	1,162.7	1,168.1	1,170.7	1,180.0	1,164.1	1,171.0	1,196.6	1,209.8	1,173.7
2009	1,151.5	1,136.0	1,137.2	1,132.0	1,133.2	1,133.7	1,131.0	1,138.5	1,132.3	1,133.0	1,156.7	1,171.1	1,140.5
2010	1,118.5	1,107.9	1,118.6	1,119.6	1,125.8	1,129.9	1,128.4	1,137.4	1,128.7	1,141.3	1,172.7	1,192.2	1,135.1
2011	1,138.7	1,125.9	1,136.3	1,146.5	1,147.9	1,152.9	1,154.0	1,165.2	1,153.2	1,164.5	1,200.7	1,217.6	1,158.6
2012	1,167.3	1,153.3	1,157.5	1,164.2	1,170.4	1,176.5	1,179.2	1,188.4	1,180.0	1,193.4	1,240.8	1,250.9	1,185.2
2013	1,191.6	1,186.2	1,187.2	1,197.1	1,203.0	1,210.8	1,215.3	1,228.0	1,220.8	1,232.4	1,275.9	1,292.0	1,220.0
2014	1,236.2	1,229.0	1,231.3	1,236.8	1,239.3	1,249.0	1,250.8	1,259.4	1,251.4	1,264.0	1,305.6	1,323.5	1,256.4
2015	1,265.9	1,262.4	1,266.5	1,276.4	1,285.5	1,294.6	1,296.4	1,304.2	1,298.8	1,312.6	1,345.7	1,358.7	1,297.3
2016	1,303.2	1,298.0	1,300.3	1,307.9	1,309.2	1,313.7	1,318.4	1,326.9	1,312.6	1,330.0	1,370.8	1,379.1	1,322.5
2017	1,326.0	1,311.4	1,309.4	1,313.6	1,314.7	1,319.5	1,318.9	1,326.3	1,309.9	1,328.2	1,367.2	1,370.9	1,326.3

1. Employment by Industry: Texas, Selected Years, 2007–2017—*Continued*

(Numbers in thousands, not seasonally adjusted)

Industry and year	January	February	March	April	May	June	July	August	September	October	November	December	Annual average
Transportation and Utilities													
2007	424.5	426.0	429.5	428.8	430.9	433.8	432.5	435.7	437.2	437.1	437.9	444.0	433.2
2008	433.6	435.5	435.6	436.6	439.6	441.0	441.2	444.4	442.9	441.6	441.8	446.0	440.0
2009	430.4	425.5	425.5	420.3	419.1	418.3	415.8	415.5	415.7	415.3	415.9	422.1	420.0
2010	411.0	410.7	413.1	414.1	415.9	418.0	419.5	421.4	423.0	423.8	425.7	431.9	419.0
2011	423.4	424.2	427.1	429.2	430.3	431.3	434.4	436.9	439.3	438.0	440.5	448.8	433.6
2012	438.8	441.2	444.6	445.2	447.6	451.0	450.7	454.2	454.5	454.2	458.3	464.6	450.4
2013	455.8	455.7	457.7	459.7	461.6	464.0	462.3	465.3	466.6	467.6	472.4	479.2	464.0
2014	469.9	466.5	468.8	472.5	477.1	479.8	480.0	482.7	487.5	493.5	499.8	513.2	482.8
2015	501.0	496.5	497.4	499.1	502.0	503.8	504.2	507.6	508.6	513.2	521.5	534.1	507.4
2016	514.0	511.1	510.9	511.6	512.6	515.8	517.4	519.2	524.2	527.7	538.8	549.2	521.0
2017	533.1	529.0	528.1	526.7	529.3	533.1	535.3	541.3	543.0	547.3	554.6	561.7	538.5
Information													
2007	218.9	220.2	220.2	219.5	221.4	221.8	221.3	221.6	219.8	219.4	220.5	220.4	220.4
2008	218.4	218.6	218.6	217.7	218.7	218.7	217.6	216.7	213.8	213.3	213.7	213.7	216.6
2009	210.7	209.6	208.6	206.5	205.5	204.7	202.6	200.9	198.3	198.2	198.6	199.0	203.6
2010	196.2	195.2	195.3	195.8	195.6	196.8	194.9	194.8	193.2	193.1	194.4	194.6	195.0
2011	193.9	193.5	193.9	194.2	195.1	195.8	196.9	195.9	194.6	194.5	195.7	196.3	195.0
2012	195.7	195.4	195.9	196.0	196.5	197.7	197.4	196.8	195.4	195.9	198.1	198.3	196.6
2013	196.2	196.6	197.5	198.8	200.2	201.7	202.1	202.2	199.9	200.9	203.3	204.2	200.3
2014	200.9	200.7	200.7	201.6	201.5	202.7	202.7	201.6	199.3	199.0	200.5	201.8	201.1
2015	197.7	197.3	197.4	199.4	200.5	201.3	201.9	201.4	198.8	199.1	201.1	202.6	199.9
2016	199.7	199.8	199.1	202.1	202.6	203.8	204.2	203.2	201.4	200.6	201.6	203.0	201.8
2017	201.0	201.5	202.9	202.6	202.2	203.3	203.8	202.7	200.3	199.8	199.9	201.3	201.8
Financial Activities													
2007	633.7	636.8	639.8	640.1	643.6	648.1	648.3	649.7	646.4	645.6	646.7	648.4	643.9
2008	641.7	645.2	644.7	647.8	650.6	652.9	652.4	651.7	646.9	644.3	642.4	643.2	647.0
2009	632.9	632.4	630.9	628.8	629.2	629.9	629.1	627.6	624.0	622.8	622.9	624.6	627.9
2010	618.2	619.9	621.5	621.0	623.7	626.7	626.8	627.0	624.9	629.3	631.3	634.2	625.4
2011	628.9	631.4	634.4	636.1	637.4	641.2	643.9	644.9	645.6	647.1	647.8	651.2	640.8
2012	646.9	650.0	652.6	654.2	657.6	663.0	664.3	666.3	665.7	670.4	672.5	675.5	661.6
2013	668.3	672.9	675.6	677.0	679.8	685.2	689.0	690.5	689.1	691.4	693.5	694.2	683.9
2014	686.7	689.4	690.8	692.8	696.0	700.6	703.3	706.1	704.3	709.6	710.9	713.7	700.4
2015	707.3	709.7	710.8	712.7	715.6	720.5	723.0	724.0	722.4	725.3	726.2	727.6	718.8
2016	723.5	725.4	724.8	728.3	730.9	733.7	738.7	740.0	738.8	741.9	744.4	747.2	734.8
2017	741.4	744.3	745.8	747.9	751.1	757.6	761.0	762.3	763.3	766.6	767.4	766.8	756.3
Professional and Business Services													
2007	1,255.2	1,273.3	1,287.3	1,292.2	1,297.0	1,312.0	1,311.6	1,324.0	1,324.0	1,330.3	1,334.3	1,340.1	1,306.8
2008	1,318.8	1,332.6	1,336.3	1,344.2	1,345.3	1,351.0	1,347.7	1,357.4	1,344.9	1,351.3	1,342.4	1,333.4	1,342.1
2009	1,286.2	1,278.3	1,272.5	1,260.6	1,255.3	1,256.9	1,247.5	1,246.9	1,239.2	1,249.0	1,255.3	1,255.5	1,258.6
2010	1,237.2	1,246.8	1,259.4	1,270.3	1,271.7	1,281.9	1,285.7	1,294.1	1,294.8	1,308.0	1,311.1	1,317.2	1,281.5
2011	1,294.5	1,308.2	1,324.4	1,340.5	1,337.2	1,348.5	1,351.6	1,364.2	1,369.9	1,368.5	1,374.6	1,379.9	1,346.8
2012	1,360.3	1,376.9	1,392.1	1,403.0	1,409.7	1,420.7	1,418.2	1,439.2	1,437.2	1,444.3	1,455.7	1,452.8	1,417.5
2013	1,422.1	1,443.5	1,455.6	1,460.1	1,463.0	1,475.9	1,477.7	1,493.7	1,496.2	1,505.4	1,516.0	1,513.1	1,476.9
2014	1,484.6	1,501.2	1,515.5	1,534.0	1,540.4	1,549.4	1,553.5	1,570.3	1,568.8	1,587.0	1,592.3	1,592.2	1,549.1
2015	1,567.2	1,577.6	1,578.4	1,588.5	1,586.7	1,594.9	1,606.1	1,613.5	1,609.7	1,629.6	1,631.6	1,630.6	1,601.2
2016	1,601.0	1,612.0	1,610.8	1,626.8	1,620.1	1,623.8	1,638.0	1,645.8	1,648.1	1,656.1	1,659.8	1,649.3	1,632.6
2017	1,629.6	1,643.7	1,650.4	1,652.4	1,654.6	1,666.2	1,668.8	1,675.7	1,683.2	1,697.1	1,705.7	1,702.3	1,669.1
Education and Health Services													
2007	1,223.0	1,238.1	1,246.4	1,247.4	1,252.8	1,252.5	1,252.2	1,261.4	1,268.7	1,270.1	1,275.1	1,276.6	1,255.4
2008	1,260.0	1,274.5	1,275.2	1,280.9	1,288.3	1,284.2	1,284.2	1,293.4	1,298.2	1,306.6	1,311.3	1,316.7	1,289.5
2009	1,298.4	1,308.5	1,314.7	1,325.0	1,332.6	1,332.7	1,337.8	1,344.2	1,350.9	1,361.8	1,363.8	1,366.2	1,336.4
2010	1,351.2	1,362.0	1,371.2	1,376.3	1,382.1	1,380.4	1,375.6	1,383.4	1,390.5	1,398.0	1,399.5	1,401.8	1,381.0
2011	1,384.5	1,390.4	1,398.5	1,408.2	1,411.5	1,409.2	1,409.2	1,418.8	1,430.3	1,430.6	1,434.5	1,437.9	1,413.6
2012	1,417.6	1,430.2	1,436.4	1,436.0	1,441.8	1,440.7	1,433.2	1,450.3	1,459.8	1,466.1	1,471.5	1,476.0	1,446.6
2013	1,452.6	1,470.9	1,476.8	1,481.2	1,484.9	1,479.4	1,475.0	1,490.6	1,497.2	1,504.6	1,509.9	1,508.7	1,486.0
2014	1,489.1	1,502.0	1,505.9	1,513.9	1,520.5	1,513.8	1,509.1	1,524.6	1,531.3	1,543.4	1,549.8	1,552.3	1,521.3
2015	1,537.2	1,552.3	1,555.5	1,569.5	1,575.9	1,569.8	1,571.1	1,584.4	1,590.0	1,600.5	1,606.4	1,608.2	1,576.7
2016	1,589.5	1,604.8	1,606.3	1,614.7	1,620.4	1,610.1	1,616.5	1,634.1	1,643.4	1,649.1	1,654.0	1,656.9	1,625.0
2017	1,642.8	1,658.3	1,661.2	1,664.7	1,670.7	1,666.1	1,652.9	1,667.3	1,667.8	1,681.3	1,683.7	1,680.9	1,666.5

1. Employment by Industry: Texas, Selected Years, 2007–2017—*Continued*

(Numbers in thousands, not seasonally adjusted)

Industry and year	January	February	March	April	May	June	July	August	September	October	November	December	Annual average
Leisure and Hospitality													
2007	919.8	937.3	960.9	980.6	996.6	1,013.0	1,007.7	1,008.7	991.8	982.7	980.8	982.6	980.2
2008	961.6	977.8	995.7	1,014.8	1,028.8	1,039.2	1,032.4	1,028.8	1,004.9	999.4	996.4	996.3	1,006.3
2009	971.2	984.8	1,003.7	1,014.6	1,029.4	1,040.3	1,029.2	1,025.7	1,008.3	990.2	985.3	983.6	1,005.5
2010	956.3	971.8	994.5	1,007.9	1,025.1	1,036.5	1,025.3	1,027.0	1,018.5	1,011.8	1,009.5	1,009.2	1,007.8
2011	983.4	996.8	1,028.7	1,045.8	1,061.4	1,074.3	1,061.4	1,064.2	1,055.5	1,043.0	1,042.9	1,039.9	1,041.4
2012	1,017.9	1,038.1	1,065.8	1,084.5	1,103.3	1,123.1	1,106.3	1,112.3	1,104.3	1,091.7	1,093.1	1,097.7	1,086.5
2013	1,072.2	1,097.9	1,122.3	1,140.9	1,160.4	1,177.2	1,165.1	1,165.1	1,153.3	1,140.6	1,142.0	1,139.3	1,139.7
2014	1,119.0	1,138.8	1,168.5	1,188.9	1,208.6	1,228.3	1,214.6	1,213.1	1,203.8	1,194.0	1,190.3	1,190.8	1,188.2
2015	1,165.7	1,191.6	1,212.2	1,237.8	1,259.3	1,279.4	1,272.4	1,271.6	1,262.7	1,253.8	1,249.3	1,248.1	1,242.0
2016	1,227.9	1,252.1	1,272.5	1,294.4	1,311.7	1,327.3	1,316.1	1,315.0	1,302.2	1,288.5	1,285.8	1,282.3	1,289.7
2017	1,260.7	1,278.8	1,304.8	1,318.6	1,338.8	1,356.2	1,349.1	1,346.5	1,319.5	1,338.0	1,342.7	1,337.3	1,324.3
Other Services													
2007	342.6	347.2	350.9	356.0	358.4	373.8	369.8	366.9	357.8	357.6	358.5	357.0	358.0
2008	352.9	356.6	358.6	365.3	366.9	381.1	379.1	376.0	363.0	364.5	364.3	362.0	365.9
2009	356.2	359.3	360.1	364.1	365.4	379.6	375.9	370.6	359.2	358.2	359.3	357.1	363.8
2010	351.8	354.4	357.3	362.2	364.6	378.8	375.1	371.6	361.8	361.3	360.5	359.9	363.3
2011	354.5	357.9	362.0	368.6	370.5	385.9	383.3	379.8	372.1	369.8	370.5	369.4	370.4
2012	367.0	370.4	373.9	382.1	385.1	402.2	399.1	396.5	387.2	387.5	388.1	387.7	385.6
2013	382.5	388.6	391.5	396.3	399.6	416.8	414.0	410.2	400.6	399.0	401.1	398.9	399.9
2014	395.8	401.0	403.7	410.4	414.8	430.1	426.1	422.6	411.2	413.4	413.5	411.5	412.8
2015	404.6	409.2	411.4	415.6	419.4	436.3	435.2	430.6	419.2	420.6	418.4	416.5	419.8
2016	411.8	416.5	417.1	420.8	427.2	436.8	432.1	428.4	423.1	423.5	422.5	420.9	423.4
2017	413.2	419.2	422.5	427.2	431.5	440.7	433.3	430.0	424.9	427.5	429.6	426.8	427.2
Government													
2007	1,754.4	1,779.2	1,787.0	1,780.4	1,790.7	1,750.1	1,663.3	1,677.3	1,757.6	1,801.0	1,813.2	1,810.3	1,763.7
2008	1,800.6	1,825.1	1,834.6	1,821.8	1,833.8	1,797.5	1,711.5	1,724.7	1,801.1	1,841.5	1,857.8	1,854.2	1,808.7
2009	1,844.2	1,864.6	1,872.9	1,875.6	1,883.5	1,845.9	1,753.3	1,754.8	1,835.5	1,891.3	1,901.2	1,894.9	1,851.5
2010	1,876.9	1,901.8	1,915.9	1,921.1	1,964.1	1,911.2	1,802.1	1,798.4	1,862.7	1,910.5	1,918.5	1,906.6	1,890.8
2011	1,884.8	1,902.1	1,904.0	1,898.3	1,901.5	1,866.3	1,772.6	1,761.1	1,817.9	1,847.1	1,851.6	1,842.2	1,854.1
2012	1,823.1	1,852.3	1,857.2	1,850.8	1,857.1	1,819.9	1,746.5	1,741.9	1,807.8	1,850.5	1,858.6	1,859.2	1,827.1
2013	1,829.0	1,862.0	1,868.4	1,863.0	1,868.1	1,835.4	1,765.8	1,757.1	1,828.4	1,869.8	1,881.0	1,874.7	1,841.9
2014	1,854.2	1,879.1	1,885.6	1,879.2	1,885.9	1,856.5	1,782.6	1,772.5	1,842.0	1,890.0	1,901.7	1,900.0	1,860.8
2015	1,872.7	1,899.5	1,903.0	1,898.2	1,905.6	1,881.9	1,808.5	1,803.7	1,872.1	1,915.2	1,927.4	1,928.4	1,884.7
2016	1,905.7	1,930.6	1,936.8	1,936.2	1,945.6	1,921.3	1,848.9	1,842.6	1,912.6	1,946.5	1,960.3	1,962.6	1,920.8
2017	1,931.1	1,963.2	1,970.8	1,966.4	1,971.1	1,941.6	1,862.3	1,852.8	1,916.0	1,958.8	1,969.7	1,968.7	1,939.4

2. Average Weekly Hours by Selected Industry: Texas, 2013–2017

(Not seasonally adjusted)

Industry and year	January	February	March	April	May	June	July	August	September	October	November	December	Annual average
Total Private													
2013	35.6	36.3	36.4	36.2	36.1	36.9	36.2	36.3	36.7	36.1	36.1	36.5	36.3
2014	36.0	36.7	36.8	36.3	36.2	36.9	36.4	36.7	36.4	36.4	36.9	36.6	36.5
2015	36.1	36.8	36.5	36.0	35.9	36.2	36.2	36.6	35.4	35.7	36.4	35.9	36.1
2016	35.7	35.7	35.2	35.5	36.2	35.8	35.7	35.7	35.7	36.3	35.5	35.7	35.7
2017	35.9	35.4	35.5	35.7	35.6	35.8	36.3	35.8	36.1	36.5	36.0	35.9	35.9
Goods-Producing													
2013	40.5	42.4	42.9	42.4	42.3	43.0	42.8	42.9	43.1	43.2	43.2	42.8	42.6
2014	43.1	43.3	43.5	43.4	43.0	43.5	43.2	43.7	43.4	43.4	43.0	43.4	43.3
2015	42.7	42.7	41.5	41.9	41.4	42.8	42.7	42.8	40.7	42.3	42.4	42.5	42.2
2016	41.9	41.9	40.1	41.9	42.6	42.5	42.3	42.3	42.5	43.0	41.8	42.3	42.1
2017	41.9	41.8	42.0	41.3	42.9	42.9	43.2	42.3	43.8	43.8	43.0	42.9	42.7
Construction													
2013	42.4	44.7	45.6	44.3	43.9	44.8	44.1	44.2	44.0	44.0	43.8	42.4	44.0
2014	43.1	42.3	43.0	43.2	42.1	43.0	43.7	44.3	43.4	43.8	43.2	43.8	43.3
2015	43.1	43.4	40.9	42.2	41.0	43.3	42.9	43.0	39.7	42.1	42.2	42.4	42.2
2016	42.0	41.8	39.1	41.9	43.0	43.3	43.1	43.2	43.4	43.9	42.4	42.6	42.5
2017	42.2	42.1	42.0	40.2	42.8	42.8	43.0	42.2	43.8	43.8	43.1	42.7	42.6
Manufacturing													
2013	40.9	41.9	42.1	42.0	41.7	42.0	42.2	42.4	42.7	42.9	42.9	43.1	42.2
2014	43.1	43.8	43.7	43.3	43.4	43.6	42.5	42.9	42.9	42.6	42.0	42.4	43.0
2015	41.6	41.5	41.4	41.3	41.3	41.4	41.5	41.3	40.6	41.5	41.3	41.6	41.4
2016	41.0	41.5	40.9	41.5	41.7	41.6	41.2	41.1	41.5	41.6	40.7	41.7	41.3
2017	40.7	40.7	41.1	41.2	41.9	42.2	42.2	41.2	42.6	42.3	42.0	41.8	41.7
Trade, Transportation, and Utilities													
2013	37.0	37.4	37.6	37.4	37.2	37.6	37.2	37.2	37.3	36.7	36.6	37.2	37.2
2014	36.2	36.8	37.0	36.3	36.4	36.9	36.6	36.8	36.4	36.5	36.9	36.7	36.6
2015	35.8	36.7	36.6	35.9	36.0	36.0	36.3	36.6	35.9	35.9	36.4	36.2	36.2
2016	35.6	35.7	35.4	35.5	35.8	35.9	35.8	35.6	35.9	35.9	35.5	35.9	35.7
2017	35.4	35.4	35.3	36.0	35.7	35.9	36.3	35.9	36.0	36.3	36.0	36.0	35.9
Financial Activities													
2013	38.5	38.4	38.4	38.4	38.1	39.4	37.7	37.7	39.0	37.5	37.8	38.9	38.3
2014	37.5	38.5	38.3	37.4	37.2	38.6	37.7	37.6	37.7	37.8	39.5	38.0	38.0
2015	38.2	39.7	39.6	38.4	38.3	38.4	38.7	39.9	38.2	38.4	39.8	38.4	38.8
2016	38.8	38.7	38.5	38.7	40.0	38.4	38.5	38.5	38.4	40.0	38.5	38.4	38.8
2017	39.9	38.3	38.3	39.3	37.9	38.1	39.4	38.2	38.2	39.3	38.3	38.3	38.6
Professional and Business Services													
2013	37.2	37.6	37.8	37.7	37.5	38.3	37.2	37.6	37.9	36.9	37.3	37.9	37.6
2014	37.0	38.0	37.8	37.2	37.2	38.1	37.4	37.8	37.4	37.6	38.4	37.7	37.6
2015	36.9	37.9	37.9	37.3	37.2	37.5	37.4	37.6	36.3	36.8	37.6	36.9	37.3
2016	36.6	36.6	36.4	36.6	37.7	37.1	36.9	37.0	36.7	37.8	36.6	36.8	36.9
2017	37.5	36.8	36.7	37.6	37.2	37.3	37.9	37.2	37.1	37.7	36.8	36.5	37.2
Education and Health Services													
2013	33.4	33.7	33.2	33.1	33.3	34.1	33.0	33.2	33.9	32.9	33.0	33.7	33.4
2014	33.0	33.8	33.3	32.8	32.8	33.7	33.1	33.1	33.1	33.0	33.7	32.8	33.2
2015	32.8	33.3	33.0	33.0	32.6	32.6	32.6	33.3	32.5	32.4	33.3	32.5	32.8
2016	32.9	32.6	32.4	32.6	32.9	32.7	32.4	32.5	32.8	33.0	32.6	32.7	32.7
2017	33.6	32.5	32.3	31.9	31.6	31.7	32.4	31.8	32.2	32.7	32.6	32.5	32.3
Leisure and Hospitality													
2013	27.2	28.3	28.7	27.8	28.1	28.8	28.0	28.1	27.7	27.6	27.7	27.8	28.0
2014	27.5	28.2	29.1	28.1	28.1	28.6	28.0	28.5	27.6	27.9	28.3	28.2	28.2
2015	27.6	28.7	29.0	28.2	28.1	28.4	28.4	28.7	27.6	27.8	28.3	28.1	28.2
2016	27.8	28.4	28.4	28.0	28.7	28.6	28.6	28.6	28.1	28.8	28.5	28.1	28.4
2017	28.0	27.8	28.4	28.4	27.9	28.2	28.3	28.0	27.9	28.3	27.9	28.0	28.1
Other Services													
2013	33.8	34.8	34.7	34.2	34.1	34.2	33.1	33.1	33.4	32.7	32.9	33.9	33.7
2014	32.6	33.7	33.5	33.7	33.0	33.5	32.9	33.0	32.7	32.6	33.3	33.5	33.2
2015	32.8	34.1	33.3	32.6	32.7	32.2	32.3	33.6	32.5	32.6	34.0	33.8	33.0
2016	33.3	34.0	34.0	34.0	34.7	34.0	34.1	33.7	33.3	33.9	33.4	33.7	33.8
2017	33.9	33.3	33.6	32.8	33.2	32.9	32.9	33.3	33.0	34.0	33.3	33.2	33.3

3. Average Hourly Earnings by Selected Industry: Texas, 2013–2017

(Dollars, not seasonally adjusted)

Industry and year	January	February	March	April	May	June	July	August	September	October	November	December	Annual average
Total Private													
2013	22.73	22.69	22.61	22.82	22.73	22.88	22.79	22.79	23.15	23.11	23.20	23.43	22.91
2014	23.46	23.76	23.72	23.64	23.74	23.85	23.69	23.69	23.87	24.16	24.40	24.24	23.86
2015	24.46	24.66	24.57	24.39	24.36	24.25	24.21	24.59	24.44	24.56	24.67	24.42	24.46
2016	24.57	24.42	24.51	24.43	24.66	24.31	24.39	24.42	24.59	25.04	24.79	24.85	24.58
2017	25.34	25.16	25.12	25.60	25.24	25.02	25.54	25.20	25.45	25.79	25.57	25.66	25.39
Goods-Producing													
2013	24.44	24.08	23.94	24.13	24.12	24.15	24.31	24.35	24.63	24.61	24.56	24.98	24.36
2014	25.01	25.27	25.25	25.19	25.43	25.63	25.50	25.51	25.84	26.61	26.81	26.99	25.76
2015	26.90	27.16	27.34	27.07	27.10	26.82	26.63	26.96	26.96	26.94	27.16	27.18	27.02
2016	26.90	26.75	27.38	27.21	27.68	27.35	27.36	27.26	27.46	27.73	27.78	27.72	27.38
2017	27.90	27.55	27.61	27.83	27.61	27.53	28.01	27.77	27.94	28.31	28.29	28.75	27.93
Construction													
2013	22.04	22.55	22.13	22.12	22.20	22.22	22.31	22.50	22.00	22.71	22.70	23.41	22.50
2014	23.25	23.63	23.47	23.17	23.41	23.51	23.38	23.52	23.78	24.12	24.56	24.55	23.71
2015	24.75	25.05	25.22	25.02	25.25	24.95	24.43	24.82	24.65	24.80	24.99	25.05	24.91
2016	25.47	25.24	25.94	25.55	25.72	25.53	25.18	25.32	25.38	25.33	25.54	25.43	25.46
2017	25.38	25.15	25.23	25.23	25.47	25.72	26.19	26.18	26.37	26.76	26.72	27.29	25.99
Manufacturing													
2013	24.34	24.17	24.30	24.62	24.55	24.59	24.76	24.62	24.96	25.02	24.94	25.08	24.67
2014	25.29	25.33	25.53	25.58	25.89	26.13	26.05	25.97	26.31	26.37	26.38	26.81	25.97
2015	26.76	27.05	27.19	27.21	26.98	26.97	27.03	27.39	27.52	27.47	27.59	27.70	27.23
2016	27.80	27.61	28.04	28.23	28.80	28.37	28.75	28.40	28.58	29.00	29.01	28.75	28.44
2017	29.00	28.56	28.60	28.98	28.45	27.87	28.36	28.13	28.29	28.54	28.57	28.91	28.52
Trade, Transportation, and Utilities													
2013	21.62	21.35	21.39	21.69	21.25	21.63	21.25	21.26	21.70	21.24	21.10	21.06	21.38
2014	21.16	21.32	21.66	21.65	21.50	21.60	21.35	21.25	21.38	21.56	21.77	21.86	21.51
2015	22.11	22.41	22.34	22.47	22.29	22.29	22.34	22.70	22.62	22.54	22.35	22.26	22.39
2016	22.68	22.58	22.98	22.72	22.71	22.42	22.30	22.20	22.24	22.70	22.23	22.26	22.50
2017	22.91	22.47	22.27	22.76	22.27	22.04	22.48	22.05	22.41	22.68	22.46	22.33	22.43
Financial Activities													
2013	24.24	24.87	24.66	24.93	25.03	25.37	25.35	25.10	25.53	25.44	25.66	26.07	25.19
2014	25.74	26.25	26.62	26.26	26.48	26.95	26.44	26.52	26.61	27.00	27.69	27.10	26.65
2015	27.59	28.17	28.53	28.37	28.27	28.14	28.17	28.87	28.27	28.37	28.96	28.62	28.37
2016	29.00	28.80	28.97	28.77	29.34	28.57	29.06	29.04	29.11	30.18	29.76	29.80	29.21
2017	30.24	29.91	30.17	30.65	29.58	29.14	29.76	29.85	29.84	30.51	29.94	30.07	29.97
Professional and Business Services													
2013	26.39	26.37	26.33	26.24	26.41	26.63	26.30	26.42	26.92	26.60	26.77	27.29	26.56
2014	27.58	28.15	28.10	27.75	28.13	28.34	28.15	28.38	28.40	28.36	28.75	28.19	28.20
2015	28.66	28.98	28.53	28.20	28.21	28.29	28.49	29.27	28.86	28.91	29.29	28.83	28.71
2016	29.37	29.37	29.23	29.06	29.38	28.92	29.12	28.78	29.04	29.81	29.38	29.24	29.23
2017	30.04	29.67	29.81	30.44	29.71	29.43	30.10	29.28	29.66	30.17	29.78	29.82	29.83
Education and Health Services													
2013	23.51	23.79	23.78	23.82	23.70	23.53	23.95	23.77	23.66	24.19	24.31	24.14	23.85
2014	24.18	24.22	24.01	24.07	24.12	23.87	24.16	24.05	24.00	24.40	24.18	24.15	24.12
2015	24.31	24.43	24.51	24.15	24.31	24.15	24.22	24.29	24.26	24.71	24.57	24.58	24.38
2016	24.54	24.49	24.16	24.18	24.11	24.14	24.12	24.41	24.33	24.27	24.33	24.50	24.30
2017	24.55	25.33	25.21	25.27	25.66	25.37	25.47	25.69	25.57	25.59	25.88	25.70	25.44
Leisure and Hospitality													
2013	11.92	11.82	11.77	11.86	11.91	11.78	11.74	11.89	12.06	12.09	12.11	12.42	11.95
2014	12.25	12.40	12.23	12.27	12.38	12.36	12.29	12.32	12.55	12.62	12.65	12.74	12.42
2015	12.68	12.85	12.64	12.74	12.80	12.63	12.51	12.62	12.72	12.80	12.83	12.92	12.73
2016	12.88	12.92	12.86	12.88	12.89	12.73	12.76	12.76	12.89	12.97	12.99	13.23	12.90
2017	13.04	13.09	12.92	12.95	13.02	12.85	12.84	12.95	13.10	13.13	13.10	13.47	13.04
Other Services													
2013	21.43	21.58	21.66	21.65	21.42	21.51	20.62	20.44	20.78	20.84	20.59	20.69	21.10
2014	20.54	20.89	21.04	21.41	20.99	20.91	20.55	20.82	21.22	21.02	21.24	20.94	20.96
2015	21.21	20.86	20.98	20.55	20.40	20.09	19.61	19.62	19.49	19.47	19.40	19.31	20.07
2016	19.62	19.53	19.45	19.41	19.26	19.17	18.89	19.39	19.59	19.98	19.62	19.98	19.49
2017	20.42	20.48	20.49	21.19	20.61	20.91	21.25	21.04	21.33	21.91	21.49	21.83	21.08

4. Average Weekly Earnings by Selected Industry: Texas, 2013–2017

(Dollars, not seasonally adjusted)

Industry and year	January	February	March	April	May	June	July	August	September	October	November	December	Annual average
Total Private													
2013	809.19	823.65	823.00	826.08	820.55	844.27	825.00	827.28	849.61	834.27	837.52	855.20	831.63
2014	844.56	871.99	872.90	858.13	859.39	880.07	862.32	869.42	868.87	879.42	900.36	887.18	870.89
2015	883.01	907.49	896.81	878.04	874.52	877.85	876.40	899.99	865.18	876.79	897.99	876.68	883.01
2016	877.15	871.79	862.75	867.27	892.69	870.30	870.72	871.79	877.86	908.95	880.05	887.15	877.51
2017	909.71	890.66	891.76	913.92	898.54	895.72	927.10	902.16	918.75	941.34	920.52	921.19	911.50
Goods-Producing													
2013	989.82	1,020.99	1,027.03	1,023.11	1,020.28	1,038.45	1,040.47	1,044.62	1,061.55	1,063.15	1,060.99	1,069.14	1,037.74
2014	1,077.93	1,094.19	1,098.38	1,093.25	1,093.49	1,114.91	1,101.60	1,114.79	1,121.46	1,154.87	1,152.83	1,171.37	1,115.41
2015	1,148.63	1,159.73	1,134.61	1,134.23	1,121.94	1,147.90	1,137.10	1,153.89	1,097.27	1,139.56	1,151.58	1,155.15	1,140.24
2016	1,127.11	1,120.83	1,097.94	1,140.10	1,179.17	1,162.38	1,157.33	1,153.10	1,167.05	1,192.39	1,161.20	1,172.56	1,152.70
2017	1,169.01	1,151.59	1,159.62	1,149.38	1,184.47	1,181.04	1,210.03	1,174.67	1,223.77	1,239.98	1,216.47	1,233.38	1,192.61
Construction													
2013	972.66	1,007.99	1,009.13	979.92	977.21	995.46	983.87	998.48	1,003.20	999.24	997.76	992.58	992.64
2014	1,002.08	999.55	1,009.21	1,000.94	985.56	1,010.93	1,021.71	1,041.94	1,032.05	1,056.46	1,060.99	1,075.29	1,026.64
2015	1,066.73	1,087.17	1,031.50	1,055.84	1,035.25	1,080.34	1,048.05	1,067.26	978.61	1,044.08	1,054.58	1,062.12	1,051.20
2016	1,069.74	1,055.03	1,014.25	1,070.55	1,105.96	1,105.45	1,085.26	1,093.82	1,101.49	1,111.99	1,082.90	1,083.32	1,082.05
2017	1,071.04	1,058.82	1,059.66	1,014.25	1,090.12	1,100.82	1,126.17	1,104.80	1,155.01	1,172.09	1,151.63	1,165.28	1,107.17
Manufacturing													
2013	995.51	1,012.72	1,023.03	1,034.04	1,023.74	1,032.78	1,044.87	1,043.89	1,065.79	1,073.36	1,069.93	1,080.95	1,041.07
2014	1,090.00	1,109.45	1,115.66	1,107.61	1,123.63	1,139.27	1,107.13	1,114.11	1,128.70	1,123.36	1,107.96	1,136.74	1,116.71
2015	1,113.22	1,122.58	1,125.67	1,123.77	1,114.27	1,116.56	1,121.75	1,131.21	1,117.31	1,140.01	1,139.47	1,152.32	1,127.32
2016	1,139.80	1,145.82	1,146.84	1,171.55	1,200.96	1,180.19	1,184.50	1,167.24	1,186.07	1,206.40	1,180.71	1,198.88	1,174.57
2017	1,180.30	1,162.39	1,175.46	1,193.98	1,192.06	1,176.11	1,196.79	1,158.96	1,205.15	1,207.24	1,199.94	1,208.44	1,189.28
Trade, Transportation, and Utilities													
2013	799.94	798.49	804.26	811.21	790.50	813.29	790.50	790.87	809.41	779.51	772.26	783.43	795.34
2014	765.99	784.58	801.42	785.90	782.60	797.04	781.41	782.00	778.23	786.94	803.31	802.26	787.27
2015	791.54	822.45	817.64	806.67	802.44	802.44	810.94	830.82	812.06	809.19	813.54	805.81	810.52
2016	807.41	806.11	813.49	806.56	813.02	804.88	798.34	790.32	798.42	814.93	789.17	799.13	803.25
2017	811.01	795.44	786.13	819.36	795.04	791.24	816.02	791.60	806.76	823.28	808.56	803.88	805.24
Financial Activities													
2013	933.24	955.01	946.94	957.31	953.64	999.58	955.70	946.27	995.67	954.00	969.95	1,014.12	964.78
2014	965.25	1,010.63	1,019.55	982.12	985.06	1,040.27	996.79	997.15	1,003.20	1,020.60	1,093.76	1,029.80	1,012.70
2015	1,053.94	1,118.35	1,129.79	1,089.41	1,082.74	1,080.58	1,090.18	1,151.91	1,079.91	1,089.41	1,152.61	1,099.01	1,100.76
2016	1,125.20	1,114.56	1,115.35	1,113.40	1,173.60	1,097.09	1,118.81	1,118.04	1,117.82	1,207.20	1,145.76	1,144.32	1,133.35
2017	1,206.58	1,145.55	1,155.51	1,204.55	1,121.08	1,110.23	1,172.54	1,140.27	1,139.89	1,199.04	1,146.70	1,151.68	1,156.84
Professional and Business Services													
2013	981.71	991.51	995.27	989.25	990.38	1,019.93	978.36	993.39	1,020.27	981.54	998.52	1,034.29	998.66
2014	1,020.46	1,069.70	1,062.18	1,032.30	1,046.44	1,079.75	1,052.81	1,072.76	1,062.16	1,066.34	1,104.00	1,062.76	1,060.32
2015	1,057.55	1,098.34	1,081.29	1,051.86	1,049.41	1,060.88	1,065.53	1,100.55	1,047.62	1,063.89	1,101.30	1,063.83	1,070.88
2016	1,074.94	1,074.94	1,063.97	1,063.60	1,107.63	1,072.93	1,074.53	1,064.86	1,065.77	1,126.82	1,075.31	1,076.03	1,078.59
2017	1,126.50	1,091.86	1,094.03	1,144.54	1,105.21	1,097.74	1,140.79	1,089.22	1,100.39	1,137.41	1,095.90	1,088.43	1,109.68
Education and Health Services													
2013	785.23	801.72	789.50	788.44	789.21	802.37	790.35	789.16	802.07	795.85	802.23	813.52	796.59
2014	797.94	818.64	799.53	789.50	791.14	804.42	799.70	796.06	794.40	805.20	814.87	792.12	800.78
2015	797.37	813.52	808.83	796.95	792.51	787.29	789.57	808.86	788.45	800.60	818.18	798.85	799.66
2016	807.37	798.37	782.78	788.27	793.22	789.38	781.49	793.33	798.02	800.91	793.16	801.15	794.61
2017	824.88	823.23	814.28	806.11	810.86	804.23	825.23	816.94	823.35	836.79	843.69	835.25	821.71
Leisure and Hospitality													
2013	324.22	334.51	337.80	329.71	334.67	339.26	328.72	334.11	334.06	333.68	335.45	345.28	334.60
2014	336.88	349.68	355.89	344.79	347.88	353.50	344.12	351.12	346.38	352.10	358.00	359.27	350.24
2015	349.97	368.80	366.56	359.27	359.68	358.69	355.28	362.19	351.07	355.84	363.09	363.05	358.99
2016	358.06	366.93	365.22	360.64	369.94	364.08	364.94	364.94	362.21	373.54	370.22	371.76	366.36
2017	365.12	363.90	366.93	367.78	363.26	362.37	363.37	362.60	365.49	371.58	365.49	377.16	366.42
Other Services													
2013	724.33	750.98	751.60	740.43	730.42	735.64	682.52	676.56	694.05	681.47	677.41	701.39	711.07
2014	669.60	703.99	704.84	721.52	692.67	700.49	676.10	687.06	693.89	685.25	707.29	701.49	695.87
2015	695.69	711.33	698.63	669.93	667.08	646.90	633.40	659.23	633.43	634.72	659.60	652.68	662.31
2016	653.35	664.02	661.30	659.94	668.32	651.78	644.15	653.44	652.35	677.32	655.31	673.33	658.76
2017	692.24	681.98	688.46	695.03	684.25	687.94	699.13	700.63	703.89	744.94	715.62	724.76	701.96

UTAH
At a Glance

Population:
  2010 census: 2,763,885
  2017 estimate: 3,101,833

Percent change in population:
  2010–2017: 12.2%

Percent change in total nonfarm employment:
  2007–2017: 17.1%

Industry with the largest growth in employment, 2007–2017 (thousands):
  Education and health services, 58.5

Industry with the largest decline or smallest growth in employment, 2007–2017 (thousands):
  Construction, -6.2

Civilian labor force:
  2010: 1,356,097
  2017: 1,560,846

Unemployment rate and rank among states (highest to lowest):
  2010: 7.8%, 37th
  2017: 3.2%, 43rd

Over-the-year change in unemployment rates:
  2015–2016: -0.2%
  2016–2017: -0.2%

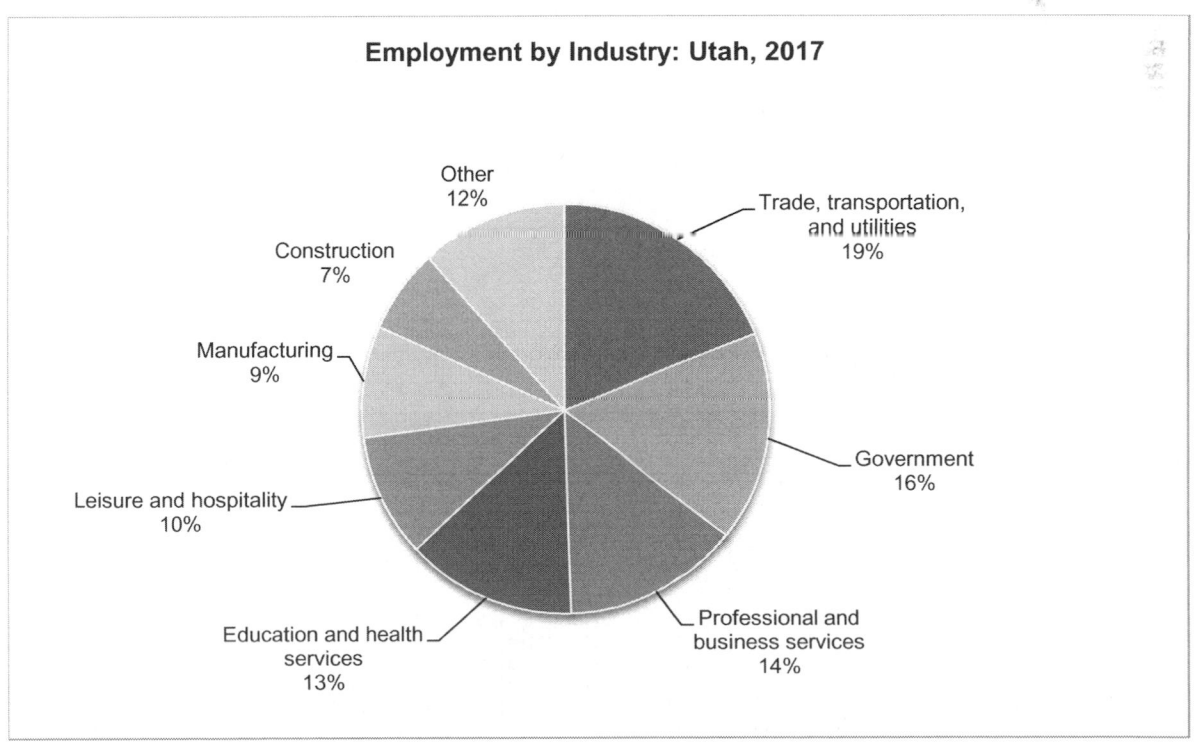

Employment by Industry: Utah, 2017

- Other 12%
- Trade, transportation, and utilities 19%
- Construction 7%
- Manufacturing 9%
- Government 16%
- Leisure and hospitality 10%
- Professional and business services 14%
- Education and health services 13%

1. Employment by Industry: Utah, Selected Years, 2007–2017

(Numbers in thousands, not seasonally adjusted)

Industry and year	January	February	March	April	May	June	July	August	September	October	November	December	Annual average
Total Nonfarm													
2007	1,219.2	1,226.7	1,238.5	1,247.0	1,250.3	1,261.9	1,244.6	1,256.2	1,266.5	1,270.5	1,276.6	1,281.0	1,253.3
2008	1,244.5	1,248.0	1,253.3	1,259.1	1,256.6	1,261.4	1,242.8	1,252.3	1,261.4	1,254.9	1,249.1	1,246.7	1,252.5
2009	1,203.3	1,197.0	1,195.9	1,194.1	1,189.7	1,190.4	1,168.5	1,174.5	1,187.3	1,187.8	1,187.5	1,190.0	1,188.8
2010	1,159.6	1,159.9	1,168.9	1,182.2	1,183.9	1,187.1	1,171.8	1,179.0	1,193.0	1,198.2	1,201.4	1,204.7	1,182.5
2011	1,177.0	1,182.2	1,190.7	1,204.8	1,203.0	1,209.7	1,197.0	1,207.7	1,224.2	1,227.3	1,231.6	1,236.9	1,207.7
2012	1,212.1	1,218.7	1,229.1	1,246.4	1,251.3	1,257.5	1,237.0	1,249.1	1,265.0	1,272.3	1,281.7	1,283.8	1,250.3
2013	1,257.6	1,265.1	1,274.4	1,286.5	1,287.9	1,291.3	1,279.0	1,287.4	1,300.9	1,312.1	1,320.2	1,323.4	1,290.5
2014	1,293.7	1,301.2	1,309.6	1,320.8	1,323.8	1,327.9	1,312.1	1,325.0	1,342.2	1,352.6	1,358.8	1,364.1	1,327.7
2015	1,340.9	1,350.6	1,361.2	1,368.1	1,372.4	1,378.3	1,366.7	1,376.0	1,394.2	1,406.0	1,410.9	1,416.1	1,378.5
2016	1,388.1	1,399.6	1,409.9	1,420.3	1,421.1	1,426.6	1,418.0	1,426.0	1,446.7	1,452.6	1,455.2	1,455.9	1,426.7
2017	1,432.0	1,442.1	1,453.8	1,461.4	1,464.1	1,473.8	1,453.6	1,463.1	1,482.7	1,490.9	1,499.6	1,500.4	1,468.1
Total Private													
2007	1,013.2	1,018.7	1,029.8	1,037.0	1,040.8	1,052.3	1,052.3	1,060.2	1,057.9	1,059.5	1,064.7	1,070.0	1,046.4
2008	1,034.4	1,035.9	1,040.3	1,044.7	1,042.3	1,047.8	1,046.5	1,051.3	1,046.7	1,038.0	1,031.6	1,030.1	1,040.8
2009	988.9	980.7	979.4	974.9	971.2	973.8	969.7	971.6	970.7	968.8	968.5	971.8	974.2
2010	943.4	942.2	950.2	961.2	959.2	966.5	969.6	973.1	973.3	975.9	979.2	983.8	964.8
2011	958.1	961.0	968.0	980.6	978.4	987.0	992.4	999.1	1,001.9	1,003.0	1,007.6	1,013.4	987.5
2012	989.6	994.3	1,004.1	1,017.9	1,023.3	1,031.3	1,029.3	1,039.2	1,040.2	1,044.0	1,053.6	1,057.5	1,027.0
2013	1,033.0	1,038.7	1,047.8	1,057.9	1,057.4	1,063.7	1,069.0	1,076.0	1,073.6	1,081.0	1,089.5	1,093.4	1,065.1
2014	1,066.2	1,071.0	1,078.9	1,085.5	1,086.4	1,094.1	1,097.4	1,108.6	1,110.0	1,117.6	1,124.1	1,130.2	1,097.5
2015	1,108.9	1,115.6	1,125.1	1,131.2	1,133.7	1,143.9	1,149.7	1,157.8	1,159.1	1,167.6	1,173.2	1,178.5	1,145.4
2016	1,153.7	1,161.6	1,170.5	1,178.1	1,177.0	1,186.5	1,195.0	1,202.2	1,204.1	1,206.7	1,209.3	1,210.9	1,188.0
2017	1,190.1	1,196.6	1,207.6	1,213.6	1,214.0	1,227.5	1,228.7	1,235.9	1,237.6	1,242.3	1,250.9	1,252.1	1,224.7
Goods Producing													
2007	231.6	232.8	236.7	239.8	243.9	248.6	248.5	250.3	248.2	247.9	244.7	241.6	242.9
2008	231.0	228.9	229.8	230.1	231.7	233.6	233.1	233.0	230.5	226.7	221.5	215.8	228.8
2009	202.1	196.4	194.8	192.3	194.2	195.5	195.3	195.1	193.7	192.9	190.4	187.7	194.2
2010	180.2	178.4	179.6	183.3	186.0	188.3	190.0	191.5	191.6	191.8	190.6	188.4	186.6
2011	181.4	181.2	182.9	186.4	188.3	191.8	195.9	197.5	196.7	196.0	195.3	193.4	190.6
2012	188.6	189.5	191.8	195.0	199.6	202.1	202.6	204.4	203.2	203.0	202.3	201.2	198.6
2013	195.6	195.9	198.7	201.8	204.9	207.1	209.1	210.3	208.8	208.7	208.1	206.2	204.6
2014	201.9	202.7	205.3	208.0	211.9	214.0	214.9	216.2	215.7	216.7	216.1	214.9	211.5
2015	210.3	210.8	213.1	215.3	218.1	220.9	222.8	223.4	222.6	224.5	223.7	223.0	219.0
2016	217.5	218.9	221.6	224.3	226.1	227.8	230.1	230.6	229.9	229.9	229.6	227.6	226.2
2017	223.6	225.6	229.7	231.4	235.0	239.2	239.5	240.0	239.5	240.5	240.9	238.9	235.3
Service-Providing													
2007	987.6	993.9	1,001.8	1,007.2	1,006.4	1,013.3	996.1	1,005.9	1,018.3	1,022.6	1,031.9	1,039.4	1,010.4
2008	1,013.5	1,019.1	1,023.5	1,029.0	1,024.9	1,027.8	1,009.7	1,019.3	1,030.9	1,028.2	1,027.6	1,030.9	1,023.7
2009	1,001.2	1,000.6	1,001.1	1,001.8	995.5	994.9	973.2	979.4	993.6	994.9	997.1	1,002.3	994.6
2010	979.4	981.5	989.3	998.9	997.9	998.8	981.8	987.5	1,001.4	1,006.4	1,010.8	1,016.3	995.8
2011	995.6	1,001.0	1,007.8	1,018.4	1,014.7	1,017.9	1,001.1	1,010.2	1,027.5	1,031.3	1,036.3	1,043.5	1,017.1
2012	1,023.5	1,029.2	1,037.3	1,051.4	1,051.7	1,055.4	1,034.4	1,044.7	1,061.8	1,069.3	1,079.4	1,082.6	1,051.7
2013	1,062.0	1,069.2	1,075.7	1,084.7	1,083.0	1,084.2	1,069.9	1,077.1	1,092.1	1,103.4	1,112.1	1,117.2	1,085.9
2014	1,091.8	1,098.5	1,104.3	1,112.8	1,111.9	1,113.9	1,097.2	1,108.8	1,126.5	1,135.9	1,142.7	1,149.2	1,116.1
2015	1,130.6	1,139.8	1,148.1	1,152.8	1,154.3	1,157.4	1,143.9	1,152.6	1,171.6	1,181.5	1,187.2	1,193.1	1,159.4
2016	1,170.6	1,180.7	1,188.3	1,196.0	1,195.0	1,198.8	1,187.9	1,195.4	1,216.8	1,222.7	1,225.6	1,228.3	1,200.5
2017	1,208.4	1,216.5	1,224.1	1,230.0	1,229.1	1,234.6	1,214.1	1,223.1	1,243.2	1,250.4	1,258.7	1,261.5	1,232.8
Mining and Logging													
2007	10.6	10.6	10.8	10.9	11.1	11.2	11.3	11.4	11.1	11.4	11.4	11.4	11.1
2008	11.4	11.4	11.5	11.8	12.3	12.6	12.8	13.4	13.5	13.6	13.5	13.2	12.6
2009	12.1	11.8	11.5	10.9	10.6	10.6	10.5	10.3	10.3	10.1	10.1	10.0	10.7
2010	9.8	9.8	10.0	10.2	10.4	10.6	10.6	10.8	10.8	11.0	11.0	11.0	10.5
2011	10.8	10.9	11.1	11.3	11.4	11.7	12.0	12.1	12.3	12.3	12.2	12.2	11.7
2012	12.1	12.3	12.5	12.6	12.8	12.8	12.8	12.9	12.8	12.7	12.6	12.4	12.6
2013	12.1	12.0	12.1	12.2	12.3	12.4	12.4	12.4	12.4	12.2	12.2	12.1	12.2
2014	11.9	11.9	12.0	12.1	12.3	12.4	12.4	12.5	12.4	12.5	12.3	12.1	12.2
2015	11.7	11.1	10.9	10.6	10.6	10.5	10.4	10.3	10.1	10.0	9.8	9.5	10.5
2016	9.1	8.8	8.8	8.7	8.6	8.5	8.6	8.6	8.4	8.3	8.2	8.1	8.6
2017	8.1	8.2	8.4	8.5	8.6	8.8	8.9	8.8	8.6	8.6	8.5	8.3	8.5

1. Employment by Industry: Utah, Selected Years, 2007–2017—*Continued*

(Numbers in thousands, not seasonally adjusted)

Industry and year	January	February	March	April	May	June	July	August	September	October	November	December	Annual average
Construction													
2007	96.0	96.5	99.3	102.1	105.2	108.6	108.3	109.7	108.0	107.2	103.2	99.7	103.7
2008	91.2	89.3	90.3	91.1	92.6	94.0	93.6	93.9	92.0	89.1	85.3	81.7	90.3
2009	72.1	69.3	69.1	68.4	70.9	72.0	72.5	72.6	71.9	71.2	69.2	66.4	70.5
2010	60.5	59.3	60.4	62.6	64.9	66.2	67.4	68.4	68.8	69.1	67.6	65.1	65.0
2011	59.4	58.8	60.0	62.5	64.0	66.5	69.3	70.5	69.7	68.8	68.0	66.0	65.3
2012	62.1	62.6	64.2	66.8	70.2	71.9	72.2	73.6	72.6	72.3	71.6	70.5	69.2
2013	66.2	66.6	68.8	71.3	74.0	75.6	77.3	78.1	77.1	77.0	76.3	74.1	73.5
2014	70.9	71.4	73.7	76.1	78.9	80.4	81.5	82.4	82.0	82.9	82.2	80.8	78.6
2015	76.8	77.7	79.8	82.0	84.0	86.3	87.9	88.6	88.2	89.3	88.6	88.2	84.8
2016	84.2	85.4	88.0	90.7	92.4	93.7	94.8	95.3	94.4	94.3	93.9	91.5	91.6
2017	88.4	89.5	92.9	94.2	97.0	100.2	101.0	101.6	101.3	102.1	102.0	99.4	97.5
Manufacturing													
2007	125.0	125.7	126.6	126.8	127.6	128.8	128.9	129.2	129.1	129.3	130.1	130.5	128.1
2008	128.4	128.2	128.0	127.2	126.8	127.0	126.7	125.7	125.0	124.0	122.7	120.9	125.9
2009	117.9	115.3	114.2	113.0	112.7	112.9	112.3	112.2	111.5	111.6	111.1	111.3	113.0
2010	109.9	109.3	109.2	110.5	110.7	111.5	112.0	112.3	112.0	111.7	112.0	112.3	111.1
2011	111.2	111.5	111.8	112.6	112.9	113.6	114.6	114.9	114.7	114.9	115.1	115.2	113.6
2012	114.4	114.6	115.1	115.6	116.6	117.4	117.6	117.9	117.8	118.0	118.1	118.3	116.8
2013	117.3	117.3	117.8	118.3	118.6	119.1	119.4	119.8	119.3	119.5	119.6	120.0	118.8
2014	119.1	119.4	119.6	119.8	120.7	121.2	121.0	121.3	121.3	121.3	121.6	122.0	120.7
2015	121.8	122.0	122.4	122.7	123.5	124.1	124.5	124.5	124.3	125.2	125.3	125.3	123.8
2016	124.2	124.7	124.8	124.9	125.1	125.6	126.7	126.7	127.1	127.3	127.5	128.0	126.1
2017	127.1	127.9	128.4	128.7	129.4	130.2	129.6	129.6	129.6	129.8	130.4	131.2	129.3
Trade, Transportation, and Utilities													
2007	240.4	239.9	241.8	241.8	243.4	244.3	245.2	246.8	247.0	248.1	253.5	256.4	245.7
2008	246.9	245.5	246.3	247.0	247.8	248.8	248.2	249.1	248.0	247.5	250.1	251.0	248.0
2009	238.6	236.0	235.1	233.2	233.9	233.6	231.6	231.8	231.8	231.8	235.4	237.1	234.2
2010	226.3	225.0	225.9	226.8	227.8	228.5	228.6	229.8	228.9	230.1	234.8	236.7	229.1
2011	227.5	226.5	227.8	230.8	231.6	232.6	233.5	234.7	234.5	235.7	241.3	243.3	233.3
2012	234.9	233.9	235.6	237.8	239.7	241.2	240.9	241.7	242.0	243.5	250.6	251.3	241.1
2013	242.0	241.2	241.6	243.1	244.8	245.5	246.8	247.8	246.4	249.3	254.9	257.0	246.7
2014	246.6	246.0	247.0	248.5	250.4	251.6	251.6	253.6	253.6	256.5	262.7	265.2	252.8
2015	256.8	257.0	258.2	258.8	260.5	261.0	262.7	264.6	264.1	266.3	271.8	274.4	263.0
2016	265.0	265.3	267.3	267.5	269.1	270.1	271.1	272.6	272.6	273.6	279.4	281.8	271.3
2017	272.7	271.8	273.2	274.5	275.0	276.9	278.2	279.2	278.7	281.2	286.6	288.6	278.1
Wholesale Trade													
2007	46.2	46.4	46.6	46.6	47.2	47.5	47.6	47.9	47.8	48.0	48.2	48.5	47.4
2008	47.7	47.8	48.0	48.2	48.5	48.6	48.5	48.6	48.5	48.2	47.9	48.0	48.2
2009	46.6	46.4	46.0	45.3	45.1	45.0	44.7	44.6	44.5	44.5	44.3	44.4	45.1
2010	43.6	43.4	43.6	43.9	44.3	44.3	44.5	44.6	44.5	44.7	44.9	45.3	44.3
2011	44.8	45.1	45.4	45.7	46.0	46.2	46.3	46.5	46.4	46.5	46.7	46.8	46.0
2012	46.4	46.6	46.9	47.1	47.4	47.5	47.4	47.6	47.5	47.6	47.6	47.7	47.3
2013	47.6	47.7	47.7	48.1	48.2	48.2	48.3	48.3	48.1	48.0	48.2	48.3	48.1
2014	47.6	47.8	47.8	48.2	48.5	48.5	48.7	48.9	48.7	49.3	49.5	49.7	48.6
2015	49.0	49.3	49.4	49.7	50.1	50.1	50.2	50.2	49.9	49.8	49.8	49.9	49.8
2016	49.4	49.7	49.6	49.6	49.8	49.8	50.0	50.1	50.0	50.0	50.1	50.2	49.9
2017	49.8	50.0	50.2	50.4	50.8	51.1	51.2	51.2	51.0	50.9	51.1	51.2	50.7
Retail Trade													
2007	144.3	143.4	144.7	144.8	145.6	145.9	146.5	147.5	147.3	147.8	152.7	154.5	147.1
2008	148.3	146.7	147.2	147.5	148.1	149.1	148.6	149.3	148.3	148.2	151.1	151.8	148.7
2009	142.0	140.2	140.2	139.5	140.5	140.7	139.1	139.7	139.8	139.9	143.7	144.9	140.9
2010	136.4	135.2	135.7	136.3	136.9	137.2	136.9	137.6	136.7	137.5	141.4	142.1	137.5
2011	134.8	133.6	134.4	136.8	137.3	137.7	138.5	139.3	139.0	140.3	145.2	146.2	138.6
2012	139.1	138.0	139.1	140.4	141.7	142.9	143.4	143.7	143.6	145.0	151.7	151.5	143.3
2013	143.4	142.6	143.2	145.1	146.4	147.0	147.8	148.7	147.6	149.4	154.2	155.2	147.6
2014	147.3	146.7	147.5	148.6	149.9	150.6	151.3	152.7	152.4	154.1	159.0	160.5	151.7
2015	153.0	152.8	153.5	155.2	156.3	156.7	157.5	159.0	158.6	160.4	165.7	166.9	158.0
2016	159.6	159.7	161.5	161.6	162.6	163.8	164.2	165.3	165.0	166.1	170.9	171.7	164.3
2017	164.1	163.4	164.1	165.3	165.4	166.5	167.6	168.6	167.6	170.2	174.4	175.2	167.7

1. Employment by Industry: Utah, Selected Years, 2007–2017—*Continued*

(Numbers in thousands, not seasonally adjusted)

Industry and year	January	February	March	April	May	June	July	August	September	October	November	December	Annual average
Transportation and Utilities													
2007	49.9	50.1	50.5	50.4	50.6	50.9	51.1	51.4	51.9	52.3	52.6	53.4	51.3
2008	50.9	51.0	51.1	51.3	51.2	51.1	51.1	51.3	51.2	51.1	51.1	51.2	51.1
2009	50.0	49.4	48.9	48.4	48.3	47.9	47.8	47.5	47.5	47.4	47.4	47.8	48.2
2010	46.3	46.4	46.6	46.6	46.6	47.0	47.2	47.6	47.7	47.9	48.5	49.3	47.3
2011	47.9	47.8	48.0	48.3	48.3	48.7	48.7	48.9	49.1	48.9	49.4	50.3	48.7
2012	49.4	49.3	49.6	50.3	50.6	50.8	50.1	50.4	50.9	50.9	51.3	52.1	50.5
2013	51.0	50.9	50.7	49.9	50.2	50.3	50.7	50.8	50.7	51.9	52.5	53.5	51.1
2014	51.7	51.5	51.7	51.7	52.0	52.5	51.6	52.0	52.5	53.1	54.2	55.0	52.5
2015	54.8	54.9	55.3	53.9	54.1	54.2	55.0	55.4	55.6	56.1	56.3	57.6	55.3
2016	56.0	55.9	56.2	56.3	56.7	56.5	56.9	57.2	57.6	57.5	58.4	59.9	57.1
2017	58.8	58.4	58.9	58.8	58.8	59.3	59.4	59.4	60.1	60.1	61.1	62.2	59.6
Information													
2007	32.0	32.0	32.2	30.9	31.1	31.0	30.9	31.0	30.4	30.4	30.5	30.5	31.1
2008	29.8	30.5	30.6	30.9	31.4	31.5	31.1	31.1	30.8	30.5	30.7	30.8	30.8
2009	29.9	30.0	29.9	29.5	29.8	29.9	29.5	29.3	29.0	29.0	29.4	29.7	29.6
2010	28.7	28.9	29.3	29.4	29.3	29.4	29.3	29.0	29.0	29.0	29.8	29.9	29.3
2011	28.9	29.2	29.2	29.2	29.5	29.6	29.6	29.8	29.6	29.8	30.7	30.8	29.7
2012	30.2	30.5	30.6	32.0	32.7	32.7	31.3	31.5	31.1	31.3	32.3	32.5	31.6
2013	33.2	33.3	33.3	32.0	32.3	32.4	32.5	32.8	32.2	32.2	33.2	33.4	32.7
2014	32.6	32.9	33.1	32.8	32.9	33.0	33.1	33.7	33.0	33.1	33.5	33.7	33.1
2015	32.9	33.3	33.5	33.6	34.1	34.4	34.8	35.3	34.9	35.4	36.2	36.2	34.6
2016	35.7	36.6	36.2	36.3	36.6	37.0	37.7	38.4	37.5	37.8	37.9	38.0	37.1
2017	38.0	38.7	38.3	38.1	38.3	38.7	38.1	38.8	38.3	39.0	39.4	39.4	38.6
Financial Activities													
2007	73.7	74.4	74.6	75.0	75.2	75.6	75.6	75.7	75.2	75.7	75.9	76.6	75.3
2008	74.2	74.9	74.6	74.3	74.3	74.2	74.1	74.1	73.4	73.1	72.9	73.8	74.0
2009	72.5	72.5	72.4	71.7	71.4	71.2	70.3	70.3	69.8	69.7	69.6	70.5	71.0
2010	68.5	67.9	68.1	67.8	67.6	67.7	67.6	67.9	67.7	68.2	68.3	68.8	68.0
2011	67.4	67.6	67.7	68.0	67.8	68.2	68.2	68.4	68.0	68.4	68.5	69.3	68.1
2012	67.9	68.2	68.2	68.6	68.6	69.2	69.5	70.3	70.1	70.6	71.0	71.9	69.5
2013	70.6	71.1	71.3	71.8	71.8	72.8	73.6	74.1	73.6	73.7	74.1	74.8	72.8
2014	73.2	73.7	73.3	73.4	73.5	74.2	75.6	76.4	75.8	76.4	76.9	77.5	75.0
2015	77.1	77.6	77.9	78.0	78.2	78.7	79.4	79.6	79.4	80.0	80.2	80.9	78.9
2016	80.1	80.7	80.6	80.7	81.1	81.6	82.5	83.0	82.5	83.1	83.1	83.6	81.9
2017	82.7	83.0	82.9	83.1	83.6	84.5	84.2	84.7	84.1	84.8	85.4	85.3	84.0
Professional and Business Services													
2007	153.5	154.5	156.4	160.0	163.0	164.7	164.1	165.8	165.0	167.0	168.2	167.8	162.5
2008	159.0	159.8	160.6	162.2	164.2	164.4	164.4	165.8	164.6	162.6	160.0	158.9	162.2
2009	150.5	149.6	148.8	149.1	149.5	149.4	149.0	149.0	148.9	149.9	148.9	149.0	149.3
2010	144.2	145.0	147.9	150.9	152.8	154.3	155.4	155.0	154.4	156.1	156.1	156.5	152.4
2011	151.8	153.2	155.0	157.7	158.5	159.3	160.4	161.6	162.2	164.8	165.0	164.9	159.5
2012	158.9	160.7	162.7	165.4	167.4	168.5	168.9	171.5	171.1	173.9	174.2	173.7	168.1
2013	168.0	170.1	172.2	175.5	176.0	176.1	178.0	179.4	179.7	183.8	185.4	184.9	177.4
2014	178.8	178.7	179.8	181.6	183.0	184.0	184.9	187.8	188.3	191.1	191.3	192.3	185.1
2015	185.8	186.6	188.7	191.3	193.1	195.1	196.4	197.7	197.3	199.7	200.9	200.8	194.5
2016	195.1	195.4	197.2	199.7	200.7	202.1	204.9	206.3	205.0	206.7	205.6	204.5	201.9
2017	199.6	199.4	201.1	203.5	205.0	206.7	208.9	210.3	210.1	210.0	210.2	207.2	206.0
Education and Health Services													
2007	137.7	139.1	139.8	140.5	136.7	136.6	135.7	137.7	142.6	144.1	145.2	146.1	140.2
2008	145.0	146.3	146.8	147.2	143.1	142.6	141.7	143.4	148.7	150.4	151.7	152.1	146.6
2009	150.4	150.9	151.7	151.5	147.5	146.8	146.0	147.6	152.6	154.5	155.7	155.7	150.9
2010	154.6	155.3	156.0	156.4	152.1	151.4	150.7	151.7	157.1	158.6	158.9	158.4	155.1
2011	157.6	158.8	159.0	159.7	155.9	155.1	153.5	155.1	160.9	162.5	163.2	163.4	158.7
2012	162.2	163.2	164.0	165.7	161.6	161.0	158.9	161.4	166.8	168.9	170.3	170.4	164.5
2013	169.4	170.9	171.5	172.9	168.1	166.5	164.6	166.8	172.0	174.8	176.0	175.5	170.8
2014	173.2	175.1	176.0	174.4	170.8	169.1	168.0	170.2	175.9	178.4	180.3	179.7	174.3
2015	179.9	181.8	182.4	182.5	179.6	178.6	176.7	179.4	186.6	189.5	190.7	189.8	183.1
2016	189.0	190.8	191.2	192.0	187.8	186.8	185.2	187.6	196.0	197.4	198.6	197.1	191.6
2017	196.5	198.5	199.4	200.6	195.6	193.6	191.5	194.3	201.6	203.2	205.2	204.0	198.7

1. Employment by Industry: Utah, Selected Years, 2007–2017—*Continued*

(Numbers in thousands, not seasonally adjusted)

Industry and year	January	February	March	April	May	June	July	August	September	October	November	December	Annual average
Leisure and Hospitality													
2007	109.9	111.2	113.3	113.8	111.6	115.2	115.7	116.0	113.6	110.6	111.1	115.4	113.1
2008	113.7	114.9	116.3	117.4	114.2	116.8	117.3	117.7	114.9	112.2	109.9	112.9	114.9
2009	111.0	111.3	112.6	113.5	110.7	112.9	113.0	113.6	111.1	107.4	105.7	108.7	111.0
2010	107.8	108.5	109.8	113.1	110.0	113.0	113.4	113.9	111.2	108.7	107.4	111.8	110.7
2011	110.5	111.2	113.0	115.1	112.7	116.0	116.4	116.9	115.4	111.5	109.4	114.1	113.5
2012	113.1	114.3	116.8	118.8	118.7	121.3	121.5	122.6	120.5	117.4	117.5	120.9	118.6
2013	119.0	120.5	123.1	124.2	122.3	126.6	127.2	127.6	124.5	122.1	121.3	125.2	123.6
2014	123.6	125.2	127.3	129.5	126.5	130.2	130.8	132.3	129.9	127.8	125.6	129.2	128.2
2015	128.1	130.1	132.6	133.3	131.7	136.1	137.4	138.3	135.6	133.5	130.9	134.6	133.5
2016	132.9	135.2	137.5	138.6	136.5	141.3	143.1	143.3	140.9	138.7	135.8	139.0	138.6
2017	137.8	140.2	143.2	142.4	141.2	146.6	146.8	147.5	145.1	142.8	143.5	148.9	143.8
Other Services													
2007	34.4	34.8	35.0	35.2	35.9	36.3	36.6	36.9	35.9	35.7	35.6	35.6	35.7
2008	34.8	35.1	35.3	35.4	35.6	35.9	36.6	37.1	35.8	35.0	34.8	34.8	35.5
2009	33.9	34.0	34.1	34.1	34.2	34.5	35.0	34.9	33.8	33.6	33.4	33.4	34.1
2010	33.1	33.2	33.6	33.5	33.6	33.9	34.6	34.3	33.4	33.4	33.3	33.3	33.6
2011	33.0	33.3	33.4	33.7	34.1	34.4	34.9	35.1	34.6	34.3	34.2	34.2	34.1
2012	33.8	34.0	34.4	34.6	35.0	35.3	35.7	35.8	35.4	35.4	35.4	35.6	35.0
2013	35.2	35.7	36.1	36.6	37.2	36.7	37.2	37.2	36.4	36.4	36.5	36.4	36.5
2014	36.3	36.7	37.1	37.3	37.4	38.0	38.5	38.4	37.8	37.6	37.7	37.7	37.5
2015	38.0	38.4	38.7	38.4	38.4	39.1	39.5	39.5	38.6	38.7	38.8	38.8	38.7
2016	38.4	38.7	38.9	39.0	39.1	39.8	40.4	40.4	39.7	39.5	39.3	39.3	39.4
2017	39.2	39.4	39.8	40.0	40.3	41.3	41.5	41.1	40.2	40.8	39.7	39.8	40.3
Government													
2007	206.0	208.0	208.7	210.0	209.5	209.6	192.3	196.0	208.6	211.0	211.9	211.0	206.9
2008	210.1	212.1	213.0	214.4	214.3	213.6	196.3	201.0	214.7	216.9	217.5	216.6	211.7
2009	214.4	216.3	216.5	219.2	218.5	216.6	198.8	202.9	216.6	219.0	219.0	218.2	214.7
2010	216.2	217.7	218.7	221.0	224.7	220.6	202.2	205.9	219.7	222.3	222.2	220.9	217.7
2011	218.9	221.2	222.7	224.2	224.6	222.7	204.6	208.6	222.3	224.3	224.0	223.5	220.1
2012	222.5	224.4	225.0	228.5	228.0	226.2	207.7	209.9	224.8	228.3	228.1	226.3	223.3
2013	224.6	226.4	226.6	228.6	230.5	227.6	210.0	211.4	227.3	231.1	230.7	230.0	225.4
2014	227.5	230.2	230.7	235.3	237.4	233.8	214.7	216.4	232.2	235.0	234.7	233.9	230.2
2015	232.0	235.0	236.1	236.9	238.7	234.4	217.0	218.2	235.1	238.4	237.7	237.6	233.1
2016	234.4	238.0	239.4	242.2	244.1	240.1	223.0	223.8	242.6	245.9	245.9	245.0	238.7
2017	241.9	245.5	246.2	247.8	250.1	246.3	224.9	227.2	245.1	248.6	248.7	248.3	243.4

2. Average Weekly Hours by Selected Industry: Utah, 2013–2017

(Not seasonally adjusted)

Industry and year	January	February	March	April	May	June	July	August	September	October	November	December	Annual average
Total Private													
2013	34.6	34.9	34.8	34.5	35.1	35.7	34.7	35.1	35.5	34.7	34.8	35.3	35.0
2014	34.8	35.5	35.7	34.8	35.1	35.9	35.2	35.4	35.2	35.3	35.6	34.7	35.2
2015	34.4	35.3	35.1	34.2	34.7	34.9	34.8	35.4	34.4	34.8	34.9	34.3	34.8
2016	34.0	34.2	34.3	34.4	35.3	34.8	34.8	34.9	34.5	35.4	34.8	34.8	34.7
2017	35.1	34.8	34.6	35.4	35.1	35.2	35.8	35.5	35.0	35.6	34.7	34.7	35.1
Goods-Producing													
2013	39.2	39.3	39.1	39.4	39.9	39.9	39.6	40.2	40.1	39.7	40.4	40.1	39.7
2014	39.3	39.2	40.0	40.2	39.9	40.3	39.9	39.7	39.6	40.2	39.3	38.8	39.7
2015	37.6	38.4	38.5	38.1	38.5	38.3	37.9	38.4	36.8	38.1	37.7	37.5	38.0
2016	36.3	37.0	37.7	38.0	38.0	38.1	37.6	38.0	37.8	38.6	38.1	38.1	37.8
2017	37.1	37.8	37.5	38.6	39.1	39.1	38.5	39.6	39.1	39.6	39.2	38.6	38.7
Construction													
2013	37.2	38.4	38.0	39.2	39.4	39.5	39.3	40.0	39.8	40.0	39.8	39.1	39.2
2014	38.3	38.1	39.4	40.1	39.7	40.1	39.7	39.9	39.5	40.5	39.1	38.3	39.4
2015	36.6	37.3	37.4	36.8	37.8	38.2	38.3	38.3	36.0	38.9	38.8	37.6	37.7
2016	35.1	35.9	37.2	38.1	37.7	37.9	37.9	38.4	38.2	38.8	37.8	36.7	37.5
2017	36.2	36.9	36.9	38.7	39.6	39.8	39.7	40.2	39.3	40.3	39.2	38.2	38.8
Manufacturing													
2013	39.1	39.8	39.7	39.5	40.2	40.1	39.7	40.2	40.2	39.3	40.4	40.4	39.9
2014	39.4	39.4	39.8	39.8	39.7	40.0	39.8	39.4	39.5	39.6	39.8	39.5	39.6
2015	38.6	39.3	39.4	39.2	39.3	38.6	38.3	39.1	37.9	38.1	37.3	37.6	38.6
2016	37.3	37.8	38.1	38.2	38.4	38.4	37.5	37.8	37.6	38.6	38.3	39.0	38.1
2017	37.6	38.5	37.9	38.6	38.7	38.7	37.6	39.2	38.8	39.1	39.1	38.6	38.5
Trade, Transportation, and Utilities													
2013	32.9	33.3	33.3	33.3	33.5	34.3	33.5	33.6	33.7	32.7	33.0	33.5	33.4
2014	32.9	34.2	34.5	33.6	34.8	34.9	34.3	34.5	34.3	33.9	34.8	34.1	34.2
2015	33.4	34.1	33.8	33.8	34.0	34.0	34.1	34.3	33.0	33.0	33.1	33.1	33.6
2016	32.2	32.8	32.5	33.0	33.8	33.3	33.4	33.6	32.8	33.9	32.8	33.7	33.2
2017	34.2	33.6	33.9	34.9	34.0	34.4	35.2	34.4	34.2	34.3	33.6	34.1	34.2
Information													
2013	31.1	31.7	32.4	32.1	32.6	34.3	31.9	31.4	33.4	32.1	32.7	34.0	32.5
2014	32.0	34.4	34.9	32.9	33.3	35.2	33.1	33.2	33.2	33.6	35.5	34.4	33.8
2015	34.8	36.0	36.0	34.5	34.6	34.5	34.6	36.3	33.6	34.3	35.9	34.5	35.0
2016	35.7	34.1	34.3	34.7	35.8	34.2	33.9	33.9	33.3	35.0	36.8	37.2	34.9
2017	38.6	36.5	36.5	37.0	36.7	34.8	36.4	34.7	34.0	36.4	34.4	34.6	35.9
Financial Activities													
2013	35.1	35.3	35.8	35.5	35.8	36.9	35.8	36.2	37.0	36.0	36.1	37.0	36.0
2014	36.5	36.2	36.9	35.7	35.7	36.9	36.2	36.4	36.3	36.4	37.7	36.1	36.4
2015	36.6	37.1	37.4	36.4	36.4	36.5	37.0	37.5	36.6	37.3	38.4	37.2	37.0
2016	37.6	37.2	37.2	37.3	38.0	37.5	37.1	37.4	37.3	38.2	37.6	37.8	37.5
2017	38.7	37.8	37.7	38.8	38.0	38.1	38.7	38.1	38.2	38.7	37.9	37.6	38.2
Professional and Business Services													
2013	34.5	35.0	35.1	34.7	35.0	36.1	34.3	35.0	35.7	35.0	34.9	35.6	35.1
2014	34.4	36.2	36.2	35.3	34.7	35.2	33.8	34.8	34.9	35.3	35.8	34.9	35.1
2015	34.0	35.2	35.5	34.7	35.0	35.7	35.1	36.2	35.3	35.2	35.7	35.1	35.2
2016	34.3	34.4	34.1	34.4	35.7	34.9	35.1	35.0	34.7	35.8	34.5	33.4	34.7
2017	34.4	33.9	33.8	35.4	35.0	35.3	36.2	36.2	35.5	36.7	35.2	35.7	35.3
Education and Health Services													
2013	39.3	38.9	38.5	37.9	38.4	38.5	37.8	38.1	38.7	37.9	37.9	38.3	38.3
2014	38.5	38.7	38.1	36.9	37.0	37.6	37.4	37.4	37.5	37.2	37.8	37.4	37.6
2015	37.7	38.1	37.1	35.9	36.1	36.8	37.1	37.3	37.4	37.7	38.2	37.7	37.3
2016	38.2	37.9	38.2	38.2	39.3	38.3	38.6	38.9	38.3	39.0	39.2	39.4	38.6
2017	39.4	39.7	39.1	38.6	38.9	38.7	39.0	38.8	38.1	38.5	38.5	38.6	38.8
Leisure and Hospitality													
2013	23.8	25.0	24.8	24.2	24.8	26.5	25.3	25.8	25.8	24.8	23.9	25.5	25.0
2014	25.5	26.2	26.1	24.6	25.0	26.6	26.1	26.6	25.5	25.3	24.7	24.0	25.5
2015	25.4	26.7	26.6	24.4	25.6	26.3	26.3	27.2	25.9	25.9	24.8	24.5	25.8
2016	25.2	25.7	25.3	24.2	25.5	25.8	25.3	25.1	24.3	25.4	23.9	24.3	25.0
2017	25.1	24.4	24.3	24.5	23.7	24.8	26.0	24.8	23.8	24.2	22.5	23.0	24.3

3. Average Hourly Earnings by Selected Industry: Utah, 2013–2017

(Dollars, not seasonally adjusted)

Industry and year	January	February	March	April	May	June	July	August	September	October	November	December	Annual average
Total Private													
2013	22.38	22.47	22.57	23.17	22.82	23.28	22.96	22.85	23.19	23.14	23.70	23.42	23.00
2014	23.40	23.54	23.59	23.66	23.35	23.40	23.47	23.47	23.56	23.59	24.34	23.66	23.59
2015	24.00	24.08	24.13	24.14	23.90	23.81	24.04	24.25	24.36	24.18	24.93	24.20	24.17
2016	24.45	24.24	24.11	24.43	24.40	24.17	24.27	24.16	24.75	24.66	25.04	24.37	24.42
2017	24.80	24.41	24.60	25.30	24.80	24.95	25.31	24.96	25.38	25.67	25.84	25.46	25.13
Goods-Producing													
2013	24.03	23.96	24.02	24.06	23.59	23.59	23.37	23.32	23.46	23.54	23.45	23.99	23.69
2014	23.91	23.86	23.86	24.02	24.24	24.04	24.01	24.10	24.17	24.38	23.84	24.04	24.04
2015	24.16	24.14	24.64	24.66	24.49	24.66	24.86	25.04	25.60	25.86	26.37	26.13	25.06
2016	26.21	26.00	26.03	26.07	26.49	26.16	26.04	26.08	26.26	26.31	26.44	26.42	26.21
2017	26.51	26.44	26.85	26.85	26.59	26.71	27.44	27.13	27.34	27.67	27.46	27.89	27.09
Construction													
2013	24.83	25.33	25.28	25.01	24.50	24.06	24.05	23.71	23.47	23.36	23.30	23.83	24.18
2014	23.99	24.06	24.07	24.01	24.04	23.93	24.04	24.18	24.09	24.30	24.06	24.58	24.12
2015	24.38	24.38	24.70	24.68	24.54	24.52	24.24	24.50	24.91	24.91	24.74	24.88	24.62
2016	25.46	24.94	24.74	24.67	25.52	25.14	25.26	25.24	25.35	25.38	25.07	25.35	25.18
2017	25.46	25.32	25.60	25.38	25.18	25.41	25.72	25.52	26.14	26.34	26.22	26.94	25.78
Manufacturing													
2013	22.29	21.92	22.16	22.50	22.04	22.31	22.00	22.10	22.52	22.67	22.54	23.08	22.35
2014	22.84	22.97	22.83	23.16	23.50	23.18	23.13	23.23	23.50	23.69	23.35	23.39	23.23
2015	23.69	23.69	24.27	24.34	24.16	24.37	24.83	24.83	25.48	25.59	26.10	25.54	24.74
2016	25.59	25.60	25.82	25.97	26.20	25.94	25.76	25.82	26.07	26.23	26.61	26.31	26.00
2017	26.44	26.50	27.00	27.23	27.00	26.94	27.71	26.97	26.97	27.35	27.18	27.47	27.07
Trade, Transportation, and Utilities													
2013	21.19	21.34	21.87	22.98	22.48	22.89	22.53	22.32	22.63	22.34	22.25	22.46	22.28
2014	22.25	23.05	23.32	23.66	22.10	22.59	23.05	23.26	22.79	22.92	23.21	22.81	22.92
2015	23.53	23.84	23.65	23.81	23.01	22.72	23.04	23.47	23.15	23.33	23.19	22.55	23.27
2016	23.15	22.87	21.92	22.75	22.57	22.34	22.77	22.20	22.80	23.00	22.49	22.19	22.58
2017	22.63	22.53	22.20	22.47	21.64	22.13	22.61	22.62	22.70	22.97	22.43	22.47	22.45
Information													
2013	26.75	26.66	28.45	29.70	28.17	32.22	28.63	28.47	29.81	29.23	29.40	29.69	28.96
2014	29.18	29.61	29.48	29.30	29.72	30.22	30.54	29.83	30.39	32.14	32.33	32.18	30.43
2015	32.88	31.90	32.62	32.38	31.37	32.12	32.43	32.69	32.75	33.18	33.78	33.63	32.66
2016	33.86	34.24	34.16	33.71	34.13	34.08	33.99	33.84	33.63	34.20	33.41	32.57	33.80
2017	33.73	32.12	32.65	34.50	33.76	35.50	34.00	33.29	34.82	35.28	35.41	34.92	34.15
Financial Activities													
2013	25.73	26.25	25.85	26.76	26.07	26.81	26.62	26.60	27.11	26.65	27.05	27.66	26.61
2014	28.06	28.02	27.75	27.50	27.81	27.71	27.20	27.38	27.14	26.36	27.31	26.93	27.42
2015	27.24	28.01	27.84	27.86	27.70	27.03	26.99	27.89	27.82	27.61	28.58	28.12	27.73
2016	27.99	28.77	29.33	28.94	28.70	28.25	28.19	28.34	28.78	29.46	29.58	28.90	28.77
2017	29.66	29.93	29.64	30.26	29.44	29.04	29.40	27.86	27.30	28.12	27.44	27.06	28.76
Professional and Business Services													
2013	26.76	26.98	26.82	27.28	27.23	27.79	27.79	27.76	28.77	28.50	28.65	29.38	27.84
2014	28.92	29.28	29.19	29.22	29.31	29.49	29.16	28.82	29.22	28.86	29.68	29.32	29.21
2015	29.32	29.65	29.40	28.51	28.48	28.05	28.13	28.94	28.82	29.16	30.14	30.13	29.06
2016	30.93	30.83	30.66	30.43	30.25	30.15	29.85	30.12	30.42	30.30	30.54	30.46	30.40
2017	31.08	30.35	30.75	32.04	31.10	31.29	31.82	31.19	32.23	31.72	31.58	31.81	31.43
Education and Health Services													
2013	21.29	21.34	21.45	22.05	21.60	22.48	21.74	21.57	21.76	21.76	23.97	21.67	21.89
2014	22.06	21.79	21.56	21.50	20.87	20.86	21.22	21.21	21.44	21.45	23.90	21.65	21.64
2015	22.33	22.28	22.27	22.48	22.62	22.84	23.31	22.91	22.99	22.89	25.22	23.28	22.97
2016	23.39	23.13	22.85	23.23	22.90	23.18	23.15	23.07	24.26	23.68	25.39	23.63	23.50
2017	24.20	23.31	23.67	24.07	23.42	24.16	24.34	23.87	25.39	24.07	26.08	24.59	24.27
Leisure and Hospitality													
2013	12.76	12.94	12.93	12.65	12.44	12.30	12.35	12.44	12.65	12.57	12.72	12.76	12.62
2014	12.88	12.97	13.22	12.55	12.55	12.46	12.60	12.74	12.88	13.09	13.15	13.33	12.86
2015	13.41	13.61	13.58	13.30	13.29	13.15	13.32	13.49	13.48	13.56	13.44	13.70	13.44
2016	13.83	13.93	13.90	13.65	13.50	13.19	13.32	13.14	13.35	13.26	13.43	13.84	13.52
2017	14.12	14.08	14.33	13.94	13.99	13.77	13.91	14.10	14.31	14.53	14.57	14.75	14.19

4. Average Weekly Earnings by Selected Industry: Utah, 2013–2017

(Dollars, not seasonally adjusted)

Industry and year	January	February	March	April	May	June	July	August	September	October	November	December	Annual average
Total Private													
2013	774.35	784.20	785.44	799.37	800.98	831.10	796.71	802.04	823.25	802.96	824.76	826.73	805.00
2014	814.32	835.67	842.16	823.37	819.59	840.06	826.14	830.84	829.31	832.73	866.50	821.00	830.37
2015	825.60	850.02	846.96	825.59	829.33	830.97	836.59	858.45	837.98	841.46	870.06	830.06	841.12
2016	831.30	829.01	826.97	840.39	861.32	841.12	844.60	843.18	853.88	872.96	871.39	848.08	847.37
2017	870.48	849.47	851.16	895.62	870.48	878.24	906.10	886.08	888.30	913.85	896.65	883.46	882.06
Goods-Producing													
2013	941.98	941.63	939.18	947.96	941.24	941.24	925.45	937.46	940.75	934.54	947.38	962.00	940.49
2014	939.66	935.31	954.40	965.60	967.18	968.81	958.00	956.77	957.13	980.08	936.91	932.75	954.39
2015	908.42	926.98	948.64	939.55	942.87	944.48	942.19	961.54	942.08	985.27	994.15	979.88	952.28
2016	951.42	962.00	981.33	990.66	1,006.62	996.70	979.10	991.04	992.63	1,015.57	1,007.36	1,006.60	990.74
2017	983.52	999.43	1,006.88	1,036.41	1,039.67	1,044.36	1,056.44	1,074.35	1,068.99	1,095.73	1,076.43	1,076.55	1,048.38
Construction													
2013	923.68	972.67	960.64	980.39	965.30	950.37	945.17	948.40	934.11	934.40	927.34	931.75	947.86
2014	918.82	916.69	948.36	962.80	954.39	959.59	954.39	964.78	951.56	984.15	940.75	941.41	950.33
2015	892.31	909.37	923.78	908.22	927.61	936.66	928.39	938.35	896.76	969.00	959.91	935.49	928.17
2016	893.65	895.35	920.33	939.93	962.10	952.81	957.35	969.22	968.37	984.74	947.65	930.35	944.25
2017	921.65	934.31	944.64	982.21	997.13	1,011.32	1,021.08	1,025.90	1,027.30	1,061.50	1,027.82	1,029.11	1,000.26
Manufacturing													
2013	871.54	872.42	879.75	888.75	886.01	894.63	873.40	888.42	905.30	890.93	910.62	932.43	891.77
2014	899.90	905.02	908.63	921.77	932.95	927.20	920.57	915.26	928.25	938.12	929.33	923.91	919.91
2015	914.43	931.02	956.24	954.13	949.49	940.68	950.99	970.85	965.69	974.98	973.53	960.30	954.96
2016	954.51	967.68	983.74	992.05	1,006.08	996.10	966.00	976.00	980.23	1,012.48	1,019.16	1,026.09	990.60
2017	994.14	1,020.25	1,023.30	1,051.08	1,044.90	1,042.58	1,041.90	1,057.22	1,046.44	1,069.39	1,062.74	1,060.34	1,042.20
Trade, Transportation, and Utilities													
2013	697.15	710.62	728.27	765.23	753.08	785.13	754.76	749.95	762.63	730.52	734.25	752.41	744.15
2014	732.03	788.31	804.54	794.98	769.08	788.39	790.62	802.47	781.70	776.99	807.71	777.82	783.86
2015	785.90	812.94	799.37	804.78	782.34	772.48	785.66	805.02	763.95	769.89	767.59	746.41	781.87
2016	745.43	750.14	712.40	750.75	762.87	743.92	760.52	745.92	747.84	779.70	737.67	747.80	749.66
2017	773.95	757.01	752.58	784.20	735.76	761.27	795.87	778.13	776.34	787.87	753.65	766.23	767.79
Information													
2013	831.93	845.12	921.78	953.37	918.34	1,105.15	913.30	893.96	995.65	938.28	961.38	1,009.46	941.20
2014	933.76	1,018.58	1,028.85	963.97	989.68	1,063.74	1,010.87	990.36	1,008.95	1,079.90	1,147.72	1,106.99	1,028.53
2015	1,144.22	1,148.40	1,174.32	1,117.11	1,085.40	1,108.14	1,122.08	1,186.65	1,100.40	1,138.07	1,212.70	1,160.24	1,143.10
2016	1,208.80	1,167.58	1,171.69	1,169.74	1,221.85	1,165.54	1,152.26	1,147.18	1,119.88	1,197.00	1,229.49	1,211.60	1,179.62
2017	1,301.98	1,172.38	1,191.73	1,276.50	1,238.99	1,235.40	1,237.60	1,155.16	1,183.88	1,284.19	1,218.10	1,208.23	1,225.99
Financial Activities													
2013	903.12	926.63	925.43	949.98	933.31	989.29	953.00	962.92	1,003.07	959.40	976.51	1,023.42	957.96
2014	1,024.19	1,014.32	1,023.98	981.75	992.82	1,022.50	984.64	996.63	985.18	959.50	1,029.59	972.17	998.09
2015	996.98	1,039.17	1,041.22	1,014.10	1,008.28	986.60	998.63	1,045.88	1,018.21	1,029.85	1,097.47	1,046.06	1,026.01
2016	1,052.42	1,070.24	1,091.08	1,079.46	1,090.60	1,059.38	1,045.85	1,059.92	1,073.49	1,125.37	1,112.21	1,092.42	1,078.88
2017	1,147.84	1,131.35	1,117.43	1,174.09	1,118.72	1,106.42	1,137.78	1,061.47	1,042.86	1,088.24	1,039.98	1,017.46	1,098.63
Profesional and Business Services													
2013	923.22	944.30	941.38	946.62	953.05	1,003.22	953.20	971.60	1,027.09	997.50	999.89	1,045.93	977.18
2014	994.85	1,059.94	1,056.68	1,031.47	1,017.06	1,038.05	985.61	1,002.94	1,019.78	1,018.76	1,062.54	1,023.27	1,025.27
2015	996.88	1,043.68	1,043.70	989.30	996.80	1,001.39	987.36	1,047.63	1,017.35	1,026.43	1,076.00	1,057.56	1,022.91
2016	1,060.90	1,060.55	1,045.51	1,046.79	1,079.93	1,052.24	1,047.74	1,054.20	1,055.57	1,084.74	1,053.63	1,017.36	1,054.88
2017	1,069.15	1,028.87	1,039.35	1,134.22	1,088.50	1,104.54	1,151.88	1,129.08	1,144.17	1,164.12	1,111.62	1,135.62	1,109.48
Education and Health Services													
2013	836.70	830.13	825.83	835.70	829.44	865.48	821.77	821.82	842.11	824.70	908.46	829.96	838.39
2014	849.31	843.27	821.44	793.35	772.19	784.34	793.63	793.25	804.00	797.94	903.42	809.71	813.66
2015	841.84	848.87	826.22	807.03	816.58	840.51	864.80	854.54	859.83	862.95	963.40	877.66	856.78
2016	893.50	876.63	872.87	887.39	899.97	887.79	893.59	897.42	929.16	923.52	995.29	931.02	907.10
2017	953.48	925.41	925.50	929.10	911.04	934.99	949.26	926.16	967.36	926.70	1,004.08	949.17	941.68
Leisure and Hospitality													
2013	303.69	323.50	320.66	306.13	308.51	325.95	312.46	320.95	326.37	311.74	304.01	325.38	315.50
2014	328.44	339.81	345.04	308.73	313.75	331.44	328.86	338.88	328.44	331.18	324.81	319.92	327.93
2015	340.61	363.39	361.23	324.52	340.22	345.85	350.32	366.93	349.13	351.20	333.31	335.65	346.75
2016	348.52	358.00	351.67	330.33	344.25	340.30	337.00	329.81	324.41	336.80	320.98	336.31	338.00
2017	354.41	343.55	348.22	341.53	331.56	341.50	361.66	349.68	340.58	351.63	327.83	339.25	344.82

VERMONT
At a Glance

Population:
  2010 census: 625,741
  2017 estimate: 623,657

Percent change in population:
  2010–2017: -0.3%

Percent change in total nonfarm employment:
  2007–2017: 1.8%

Industry with the largest growth in employment, 2007–2017 (thousands):
  Education and health services, 8.3

Industry with the largest decline or smallest growth in employment, 2007–2017 (thousands):
  Manufacturing, 6.5

Civilian labor force:
  2010: 359,402
  2017: 344,760

Unemployment rate and rank among states (highest to lowest):
  2010: 6.1%, 46th
  2017: 3.0%, 46th

Over-the-year change in unemployment rates:
  2015–2016: -0.4%
  2016–2017: -0.2%

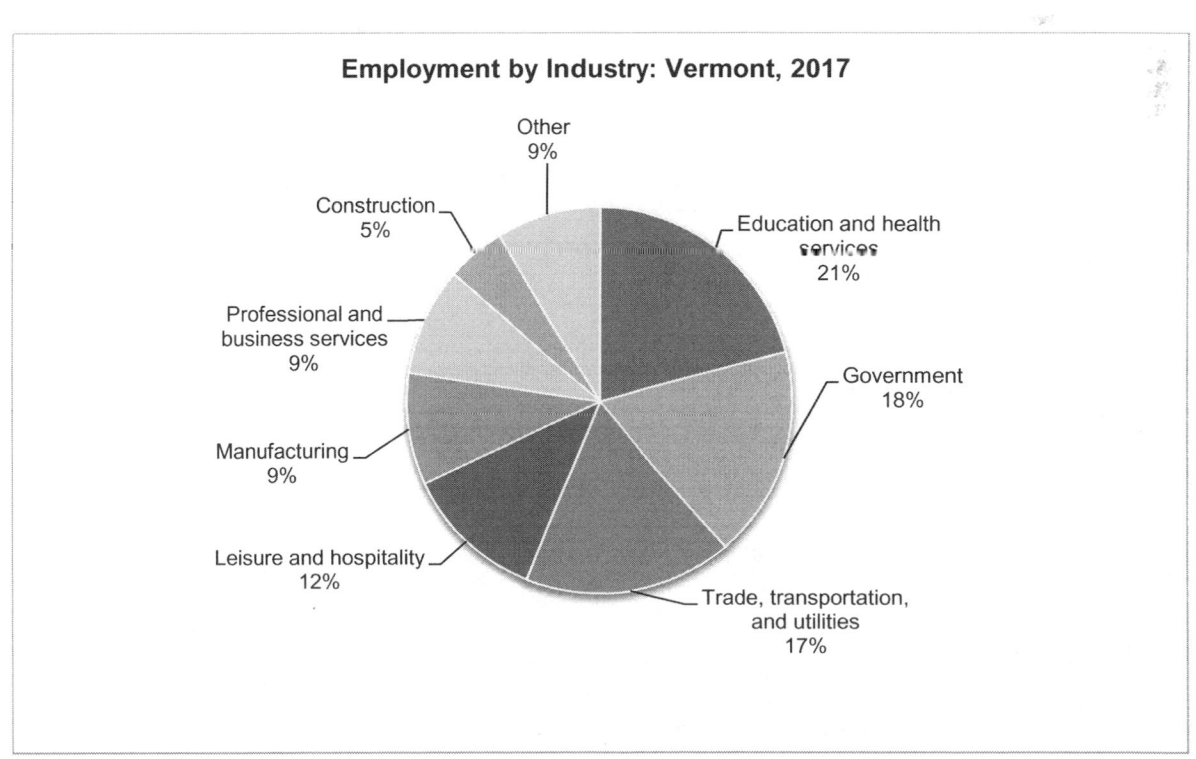

Employment by Industry: Vermont, 2017

- Other 9%
- Construction 5%
- Professional and business services 9%
- Manufacturing 9%
- Leisure and hospitality 12%
- Education and health services 21%
- Government 18%
- Trade, transportation, and utilities 17%

1. Employment by Industry: Vermont, Selected Years, 2007–2017

(Numbers in thousands, not seasonally adjusted)

Industry and year	January	February	March	April	May	June	July	August	September	October	November	December	Annual average
Total Nonfarm													
2007	306.2	307.2	306.8	303.3	308.2	311.6	303.7	303.5	310.8	312.1	311.3	315.5	308.4
2008	307.0	308.4	306.6	304.5	308.6	309.0	301.7	301.5	309.2	311.9	307.9	310.3	307.2
2009	299.0	300.9	297.3	293.8	297.7	297.3	290.1	290.8	297.5	301.6	298.4	302.4	297.2
2010	293.6	296.1	295.2	295.6	297.5	297.5	293.9	294.2	299.7	305.3	301.5	305.6	298.0
2011	297.0	299.9	298.5	295.9	299.1	300.6	294.7	297.8	303.2	306.8	304.5	310.4	300.7
2012	300.8	303.0	303.5	299.1	304.0	304.8	299.9	302.2	307.6	308.3	307.9	312.5	304.5
2013	303.5	304.9	305.6	303.5	304.9	306.9	300.0	304.1	308.2	311.5	311.0	315.1	306.6
2014	306.7	308.4	307.9	304.4	308.3	310.5	304.7	308.4	311.6	313.9	313.3	317.3	309.6
2015	310.5	311.1	310.5	308.7	311.3	313.7	308.1	308.8	313.9	316.0	314.5	318.4	312.1
2016	310.3	312.3	310.8	308.9	311.6	314.2	311.5	310.9	315.6	316.9	315.5	319.5	313.2
2017	311.8	311.7	312.5	310.5	311.7	317.0	310.2	311.8	315.8	318.6	317.5	319.5	314.1
Total Private													
2007	251.4	250.8	250.4	247.3	252.0	257.9	259.4	259.4	256.2	255.6	254.7	258.7	254.5
2008	251.5	252.0	250.3	248.2	252.4	255.6	257.1	256.9	254.3	254.6	250.3	252.9	253.0
2009	244.0	243.9	240.7	236.3	240.0	243.2	245.2	245.8	242.8	243.9	240.8	245.5	242.7
2010	238.3	239.1	237.6	238.1	238.7	242.7	249.4	247.7	245.0	247.8	244.0	248.4	243.1
2011	241.8	242.9	241.5	238.8	241.5	246.4	250.2	250.8	248.0	249.1	246.7	252.3	245.8
2012	245.4	245.6	246.0	241.4	246.0	251.3	254.7	254.9	251.4	250.6	249.8	254.5	249.3
2013	247.3	247.6	248.0	245.6	247.9	253.2	254.9	255.8	252.2	253.2	252.6	256.9	251.3
2014	250.2	250.5	250.1	246.1	250.9	255.9	258.2	259.4	254.7	255.3	254.6	259.2	253.8
2015	253.5	253.0	252.5	250.5	254.0	258.9	261.4	260.5	257.3	257.8	256.3	260.6	256.4
2016	254.1	254.5	252.9	251.0	254.4	259.4	263.1	262.2	258.8	258.5	256.8	261.7	257.3
2017	255.9	254.1	254.8	252.7	255.6	262.2	263.3	263.1	259.0	260.0	258.8	261.3	258.4
Goods Producing													
2007	51.7	50.8	50.9	51.9	54.6	55.7	55.9	55.7	54.7	54.4	53.6	52.7	53.6
2008	50.0	49.6	49.2	50.1	52.2	53.4	53.9	53.5	52.9	52.7	51.4	49.2	51.5
2009	45.6	44.7	43.7	44.2	45.6	46.4	46.9	47.4	46.8	46.7	45.9	44.8	45.7
2010	41.9	41.7	41.6	43.8	45.5	46.1	47.1	47.0	46.4	46.7	45.9	44.7	44.9
2011	42.4	42.5	42.0	43.4	45.4	47.1	48.1	48.4	48.1	48.7	47.8	47.2	45.9
2012	44.3	44.0	44.4	45.8	47.4	48.4	48.9	48.7	48.3	48.0	47.3	46.7	46.9
2013	44.2	44.2	44.4	45.1	46.9	48.0	48.3	48.2	47.8	47.8	47.5	46.9	46.6
2014	44.3	44.3	44.1	44.6	46.9	48.2	48.9	48.9	48.0	48.0	47.6	47.3	46.8
2015	44.4	44.4	44.2	45.4	47.4	48.3	48.8	48.7	48.2	47.9	47.4	46.8	46.8
2016	44.2	43.8	43.6	45.2	46.6	47.7	48.0	47.8	47.1	47.1	46.4	45.7	46.1
2017	43.5	42.8	43.1	44.1	45.9	47.0	47.1	47.1	46.5	46.5	46.1	44.9	45.4
Service-Providing													
2007	254.5	256.4	255.9	251.4	253.6	255.9	247.8	247.8	256.1	257.7	257.7	262.8	254.8
2008	257.0	258.8	257.4	254.4	256.4	255.6	247.8	248.0	256.3	259.2	256.5	261.1	255.7
2009	253.4	256.2	253.6	249.6	252.1	250.9	243.2	243.4	250.7	254.9	252.5	257.6	251.5
2010	251.7	254.4	253.6	251.8	252.0	251.4	246.8	247.2	253.3	258.6	255.6	260.9	253.1
2011	254.6	257.4	256.5	252.5	253.7	253.5	246.6	249.4	255.1	258.1	256.7	263.2	254.8
2012	256.5	259.0	259.1	253.3	256.6	256.4	251.0	253.5	259.3	260.3	260.6	265.8	257.6
2013	259.3	260.7	261.2	258.4	258.0	258.9	251.7	255.9	260.4	263.7	263.5	268.2	260.0
2014	262.4	264.1	263.8	259.8	261.4	262.3	255.8	259.5	263.6	265.9	265.7	270.0	262.9
2015	266.1	266.7	266.3	263.3	263.9	265.4	259.3	260.1	265.7	268.1	267.1	271.6	265.3
2016	266.1	268.5	267.2	263.7	265.0	266.5	263.5	263.1	268.5	269.8	269.1	273.8	267.1
2017	268.3	268.9	269.4	266.4	265.8	270.0	263.1	264.7	269.3	272.1	271.4	274.6	268.7
Mining and Logging													
2007	0.8	0.8	0.8	0.8	0.9	0.9	0.9	0.9	0.9	0.8	0.8	0.8	0.8
2008	0.8	0.8	0.8	0.8	0.9	0.9	0.9	0.9	0.9	0.9	0.9	0.8	0.9
2009	0.7	0.7	0.7	0.8	0.8	0.8	0.8	0.8	0.8	0.8	0.8	0.7	0.8
2010	0.7	0.7	0.7	0.7	0.8	0.8	0.8	0.8	0.8	0.8	0.8	0.7	0.8
2011	0.7	0.7	0.7	0.7	0.8	0.8	0.8	0.8	0.8	0.8	0.8	0.8	0.8
2012	0.7	0.7	0.7	0.8	0.8	0.8	0.9	0.9	0.9	0.9	0.8	0.8	0.8
2013	0.7	0.7	0.7	0.7	0.8	0.8	0.8	0.8	0.8	0.8	0.8	0.8	0.8
2014	0.7	0.7	0.7	0.7	0.8	0.8	0.9	0.9	0.8	0.8	0.8	0.8	0.8
2015	0.7	0.8	0.8	0.8	0.8	0.9	0.9	0.9	0.9	0.9	0.8	0.8	0.8
2016	0.8	0.7	0.7	0.8	0.8	0.9	0.9	0.9	0.8	0.9	0.8	0.8	0.8
2017	0.7	0.7	0.7	0.7	0.8	0.8	0.8	0.8	0.8	0.8	0.8	0.8	0.8

1. Employment by Industry: Vermont, Selected Years, 2007–2017—*Continued*

(Numbers in thousands, not seasonally adjusted)

Industry and year	January	February	March	April	May	June	July	August	September	October	November	December	Annual average
Construction													
2007	15.1	14.2	14.4	15.3	17.7	18.5	18.8	18.7	18.1	17.8	17.0	16.0	16.8
2008	14.1	13.5	13.3	14.2	16.2	17.1	17.5	17.3	16.9	16.9	15.9	14.3	15.6
2009	12.3	11.6	11.4	12.4	14.0	14.9	15.3	15.6	15.2	15.1	14.4	13.2	13.8
2010	11.4	10.9	10.9	12.8	14.2	14.4	15.2	15.2	14.9	15.0	14.3	13.1	13.5
2011	11.5	11.1	11.0	12.2	13.8	15.0	15.9	16.0	16.0	16.4	15.5	14.5	14.1
2012	12.5	11.9	12.1	13.4	14.6	15.4	15.9	15.8	15.4	15.2	14.6	13.6	14.2
2013	12.1	11.7	12.0	12.7	14.3	15.0	15.4	15.6	15.5	15.5	15.1	14.2	14.1
2014	12.7	12.3	12.4	13.0	14.9	15.9	16.5	16.5	16.2	16.2	15.7	15.0	14.8
2015	13.2	12.8	12.8	13.9	15.7	16.3	16.8	16.7	16.4	16.2	15.8	15.1	15.1
2016	13.4	13.0	13.2	14.6	15.9	16.6	17.0	16.8	16.5	16.2	15.7	14.8	15.3
2017	13.5	13.0	13.1	14.1	15.6	16.4	16.6	16.6	16.3	16.3	15.8	14.8	15.2
Manufacturing													
2007	35.8	35.8	35.7	35.8	36.0	36.3	36.2	36.1	35.7	35.8	35.8	35.9	35.9
2008	35.1	35.3	35.1	35.1	35.1	35.4	35.5	35.3	35.1	34.9	34.6	34.1	35.1
2009	32.6	32.4	31.6	31.0	30.8	30.8	30.8	31.0	30.8	30.8	30.7	30.9	31.2
2010	29.8	30.1	30.0	30.3	30.5	30.9	31.1	31.0	30.7	30.9	30.8	30.9	30.6
2011	30.2	30.7	30.3	30.5	30.8	31.3	31.4	31.6	31.3	31.5	31.5	31.9	31.1
2012	31.1	31.4	31.6	31.6	32.0	32.2	32.1	32.0	32.0	31.9	31.9	32.3	31.8
2013	31.4	31.8	31.7	31.7	31.8	32.2	32.1	31.8	31.5	31.5	31.6	31.9	31.8
2014	30.9	31.3	31.0	30.9	31.2	31.5	31.5	31.5	31.0	31.0	31.1	31.5	31.2
2015	30.5	30.8	30.6	30.7	30.9	31.1	31.1	31.1	30.9	30.8	30.8	30.9	30.9
2016	30.0	30.1	29.7	29.8	29.9	30.2	30.1	30.1	29.8	30.0	29.9	30.1	30.0
2017	29.3	29.1	29.3	29.3	29.5	29.8	29.7	29.7	29.4	29.4	29.5	29.3	29.4
Trade, Transportation, and Utilities													
2007	59.2	58.4	58.0	57.8	58.9	59.7	59.3	59.0	58.9	59.9	61.2	61.8	59.3
2008	59.0	58.7	58.1	58.2	59.1	59.6	58.8	58.9	58.3	58.9	59.3	59.8	58.9
2009	56.5	56.1	55.1	55.0	56.0	56.5	55.8	56.0	55.5	56.3	56.8	57.8	56.1
2010	54.8	54.5	54.0	54.7	54.9	55.7	56.6	56.4	56.0	57.2	57.7	58.4	55.9
2011	55.6	55.3	54.9	54.8	55.3	56.0	55.8	55.9	55.5	56.3	57.0	57.9	55.9
2012	54.7	54.4	54.1	54.4	55.1	56.0	55.8	55.8	55.6	55.8	56.7	57.6	55.5
2013	54.8	54.3	54.3	54.3	55.0	56.0	55.5	55.7	55.4	56.0	56.8	57.7	55.5
2014	54.9	54.4	54.5	54.4	55.5	56.1	55.8	55.9	55.5	56.2	57.3	58.1	55.7
2015	55.4	54.7	54.6	54.5	55.2	56.1	55.6	55.4	55.0	55.7	56.4	57.4	55.5
2016	55.1	54.6	54.6	54.9	55.5	55.9	55.7	55.7	55.4	55.6	56.5	57.3	55.6
2017	55.2	54.1	54.2	54.5	55.0	55.8	55.1	55.2	54.7	55.1	55.7	56.4	55.1
Wholesale Trade													
2007	10.4	10.3	10.3	10.3	10.4	10.4	10.4	10.4	10.4	10.4	10.5	10.5	10.4
2008	10.2	10.2	10.3	10.3	10.3	10.3	10.2	10.2	10.1	10.0	10.0	9.9	10.2
2009	9.8	9.7	9.7	9.7	9.7	9.7	9.6	9.6	9.5	9.5	9.5	9.5	9.6
2010	9.2	9.2	9.2	9.3	9.3	9.4	9.6	9.6	9.5	9.7	9.7	9.6	9.4
2011	9.4	9.4	9.4	9.4	9.4	9.4	9.6	9.6	9.5	9.5	9.5	9.3	9.5
2012	9.1	9.1	9.1	9.2	9.2	9.3	9.3	9.3	9.2	9.2	9.3	9.2	9.2
2013	9.0	9.0	9.0	9.0	9.1	9.3	9.3	9.3	9.2	9.2	9.2	9.3	9.2
2014	9.1	9.0	9.2	9.1	9.3	9.3	9.3	9.4	9.3	9.3	9.4	9.4	9.3
2015	9.3	9.2	9.2	9.2	9.3	9.4	9.4	9.4	9.3	9.3	9.3	9.3	9.3
2016	9.3	9.3	9.3	9.5	9.6	9.6	9.5	9.5	9.4	9.3	9.4	9.3	9.4
2017	9.3	9.1	9.2	9.2	9.3	9.4	9.4	9.4	9.3	9.3	9.3	9.3	9.3
Retail Trade													
2007	40.0	39.4	39.1	39.0	39.7	40.4	40.5	40.2	39.6	40.4	41.5	42.0	40.2
2008	40.1	39.9	39.3	39.4	40.0	40.4	40.2	40.2	39.4	40.1	40.4	40.8	40.0
2009	38.3	38.0	37.2	37.2	38.0	38.5	38.2	38.3	37.6	38.2	38.6	39.3	38.1
2010	37.3	37.0	36.5	37.2	37.2	37.8	38.6	38.4	37.7	38.6	39.1	39.5	37.9
2011	37.5	37.3	36.9	37.0	37.4	37.9	38.0	38.2	37.2	37.8	38.4	39.3	37.7
2012	37.1	36.9	36.6	36.7	37.3	38.0	38.3	38.2	37.6	37.7	38.5	39.1	37.7
2013	37.1	36.8	36.6	36.9	37.4	38.1	38.1	38.2	37.9	37.9	38.5	39.2	37.7
2014	37.3	37.0	36.9	37.0	37.6	38.2	38.4	38.4	37.6	38.2	39.0	39.5	37.9
2015	37.7	37.3	37.2	37.2	37.7	38.3	38.4	38.2	37.4	38.0	38.6	39.2	37.9
2016	37.7	37.4	37.3	37.5	37.8	38.4	38.7	38.6	37.9	38.1	38.8	39.3	38.1
2017	37.9	37.1	37.1	37.4	37.7	38.3	38.1	38.1	37.4	37.9	38.3	38.7	37.8

1. Employment by Industry: Vermont, Selected Years, 2007–2017—*Continued*

(Numbers in thousands, not seasonally adjusted)

Industry and year	January	February	March	April	May	June	July	August	September	October	November	December	Annual average
Transportation and Utilities													
2007	8.8	8.7	8.6	8.5	8.8	8.9	8.4	8.4	8.9	9.1	9.2	9.3	8.8
2008	8.7	8.6	8.5	8.5	8.8	8.9	8.4	8.5	8.8	8.8	8.9	9.1	8.7
2009	8.4	8.4	8.2	8.1	8.3	8.3	8.0	8.1	8.4	8.6	8.7	9.0	8.4
2010	8.3	8.3	8.3	8.2	8.4	8.5	8.4	8.4	8.8	8.9	8.9	9.3	8.6
2011	8.7	8.6	8.6	8.4	8.5	8.7	8.2	8.1	8.8	9.0	9.1	9.3	8.7
2012	8.5	8.4	8.4	8.5	8.6	8.7	8.2	8.3	8.8	8.9	8.9	9.3	8.6
2013	8.7	8.5	8.7	8.4	8.5	8.6	8.1	8.2	8.7	8.9	9.1	9.2	8.6
2014	8.5	8.4	8.4	8.3	8.6	8.6	8.1	8.1	8.6	8.7	8.9	9.2	8.5
2015	8.4	8.2	8.2	8.1	8.2	8.4	7.8	7.8	8.3	8.4	8.5	8.9	8.3
2016	8.1	7.9	8.0	7.9	8.1	7.9	7.5	7.6	8.1	8.2	8.3	8.7	8.0
2017	8.0	7.9	7.9	7.9	8.0	8.1	7.6	7.7	8.0	7.9	8.1	8.4	8.0
Information													
2007	6.0	5.9	5.9	5.9	5.9	5.9	6.0	6.0	5.9	5.8	5.8	5.8	5.9
2008	5.8	5.8	5.8	5.8	5.8	5.7	5.8	5.8	5.8	5.7	5.7	5.7	5.8
2009	5.6	5.6	5.6	5.6	5.5	5.6	5.5	5.5	5.4	5.4	5.4	5.4	5.5
2010	5.4	5.4	5.4	5.4	5.4	5.4	5.3	5.3	5.3	5.3	5.3	5.3	5.4
2011	5.2	5.3	5.2	5.0	4.9	5.0	4.9	4.9	4.8	4.8	4.8	4.8	5.0
2012	4.7	4.7	4.7	4.6	4.7	4.7	4.7	4.7	4.7	4.7	4.7	4.8	4.7
2013	4.7	4.7	4.7	4.7	4.7	4.8	4.7	4.8	4.7	4.7	4.8	4.8	4.7
2014	4.8	4.8	4.9	4.8	4.8	4.9	4.8	4.8	4.8	4.8	4.4	4.4	4.8
2015	4.5	4.5	4.7	4.7	4.7	4.7	4.7	4.7	4.6	4.7	4.7	4.7	4.7
2016	4.6	4.6	4.7	4.6	4.7	4.6	4.6	4.6	4.7	4.6	4.6	4.6	4.6
2017	4.6	4.6	4.6	4.5	4.5	4.6	4.4	4.4	4.4	4.4	4.3	4.3	4.5
Financial Activities													
2007	13.2	13.1	13.2	13.1	13.2	13.4	13.4	13.3	13.1	13.0	13.0	13.0	13.2
2008	12.8	12.8	12.8	12.8	12.9	13.0	13.1	13.0	12.8	12.7	12.6	12.7	12.8
2009	12.5	12.4	12.4	12.2	12.4	12.5	12.6	12.5	12.3	12.3	12.2	12.2	12.4
2010	12.1	12.1	12.0	12.1	12.0	12.3	12.4	12.4	12.1	12.2	12.1	12.2	12.2
2011	12.1	12.0	12.0	11.9	12.0	12.3	12.3	12.3	12.1	12.1	12.0	12.1	12.1
2012	12.0	11.9	12.0	11.8	12.1	12.2	12.3	12.2	12.0	11.9	11.9	12.0	12.0
2013	11.8	11.8	11.8	11.8	12.1	12.3	12.3	12.3	12.1	12.1	12.0	12.1	12.0
2014	12.0	11.9	11.8	11.9	12.1	12.3	12.4	12.4	12.2	12.2	12.1	12.1	12.1
2015	12.0	12.0	11.8	11.9	12.1	12.2	12.3	12.3	12.0	12.1	11.9	11.9	12.0
2016	11.9	11.9	11.8	11.9	12.0	12.2	12.2	12.2	12.0	12.0	11.9	12.1	12.0
2017	11.9	11.9	11.9	11.9	12.0	12.2	12.3	12.3	12.0	12.2	12.1	12.3	12.1
Professional and Business Services													
2007	21.2	21.3	21.6	22.1	22.6	23.1	23.1	23.2	22.9	22.8	22.5	22.7	22.4
2008	21.8	21.9	21.7	22.4	23.3	23.5	23.5	23.3	23.1	23.3	22.7	22.4	22.7
2009	21.3	21.3	21.1	21.8	22.4	22.8	22.9	23.0	22.4	22.9	22.9	22.6	22.3
2010	21.8	21.8	22.0	23.1	23.2	23.6	24.3	24.4	24.1	24.4	24.0	23.6	23.4
2011	23.0	23.2	23.4	24.1	24.9	25.4	25.7	25.9	25.9	25.9	25.6	25.5	24.9
2012	24.6	24.8	25.1	26.0	26.2	26.9	26.9	27.0	26.5	26.4	26.1	26.0	26.0
2013	25.0	25.1	25.5	26.2	26.8	27.2	27.1	27.1	26.8	26.7	26.5	26.3	26.4
2014	25.2	25.4	25.6	26.0	26.9	27.5	27.5	27.4	27.1	27.2	26.9	26.7	26.6
2015	25.8	25.9	25.9	27.1	27.9	28.6	28.3	28.5	28.0	28.2	27.8	27.4	27.5
2016	26.3	26.5	26.6	27.5	27.9	28.6	29.0	29.1	28.5	28.5	27.9	27.8	27.9
2017	26.9	26.9	27.2	28.2	28.9	29.6	29.4	29.4	28.8	29.1	28.5	27.7	28.4
Education and Health Services													
2007	55.7	56.7	56.8	57.1	57.0	57.1	57.1	56.8	58.1	58.0	58.6	58.4	57.3
2008	57.3	58.2	58.6	58.7	59.1	58.0	58.3	58.2	59.3	59.6	59.5	59.6	58.7
2009	58.0	59.5	59.8	59.5	60.0	59.0	59.4	58.8	59.4	59.5	59.1	59.2	59.3
2010	58.1	59.0	59.2	59.7	58.9	58.2	59.5	58.5	59.4	60.0	59.5	59.7	59.1
2011	58.5	59.7	59.8	59.9	59.5	58.5	59.5	59.1	59.8	59.7	59.8	60.1	59.5
2012	59.5	60.2	60.8	60.4	60.2	59.6	61.0	61.0	60.7	61.5	61.4	61.8	60.7
2013	60.7	61.3	61.9	61.6	61.3	60.8	61.9	61.7	61.5	62.3	62.5	62.5	61.7
2014	61.9	61.9	62.3	62.1	62.1	62.0	62.6	62.5	62.2	62.9	63.0	63.3	62.4
2015	62.9	62.8	63.2	63.2	63.5	63.0	64.2	63.0	63.2	63.8	64.0	64.6	63.5
2016	63.7	64.1	64.2	64.7	64.4	63.6	65.0	64.1	64.4	64.9	65.1	65.6	64.5
2017	64.5	64.6	65.5	65.4	65.4	65.4	66.0	65.3	65.5	66.4	66.3	66.3	65.6

1. Employment by Industry: Vermont, Selected Years, 2007–2017—*Continued*

(Numbers in thousands, not seasonally adjusted)

Industry and year	January	February	March	April	May	June	July	August	September	October	November	December	Annual average
Leisure and Hospitality													
2007	34.6	34.8	34.2	29.7	29.9	32.9	34.5	35.3	32.7	31.7	30.1	34.3	32.9
2008	35.1	35.3	34.4	30.4	30.1	32.4	33.8	34.4	32.3	31.9	29.4	33.8	32.8
2009	35.0	34.8	33.6	28.5	28.5	30.6	32.3	32.9	31.3	31.0	28.8	33.7	31.8
2010	34.5	34.9	33.7	29.4	29.0	31.5	34.0	33.6	31.7	32.0	29.7	34.7	32.4
2011	35.3	35.2	34.5	29.8	29.5	32.0	33.7	34.2	31.7	31.5	29.7	34.6	32.6
2012	35.6	35.6	34.8	28.5	30.3	33.4	34.9	35.3	33.5	32.2	31.7	35.6	33.5
2013	36.3	36.4	35.6	31.9	31.1	33.8	34.8	35.7	33.7	33.5	32.5	36.5	34.3
2014	37.2	37.8	36.9	32.3	32.4	34.5	35.7	37.0	34.6	33.8	33.1	37.0	35.2
2015	38.4	38.7	37.9	33.5	33.0	35.5	36.9	37.4	35.9	35.0	33.8	37.4	36.1
2016	38.1	38.7	37.1	31.8	32.8	36.2	38.0	38.1	36.3	35.4	34.2	38.4	36.3
2017	39.4	39.3	38.3	34.1	33.7	37.3	38.7	39.1	36.9	36.1	35.7	39.2	37.3
Other Services													
2007	9.8	9.8	9.8	9.7	9.9	10.1	10.1	10.1	9.9	10.0	9.9	10.0	9.9
2008	9.7	9.7	9.7	9.8	9.9	10.0	9.9	9.8	9.8	9.8	9.7	9.7	9.8
2009	9.5	9.5	9.4	9.5	9.6	9.8	9.8	9.7	9.7	9.8	9.7	9.8	9.7
2010	9.7	9.7	9.7	9.9	9.8	9.9	10.2	10.1	10.0	10.0	9.8	9.8	9.9
2011	9.7	9.7	9.7	9.9	10.0	10.1	10.2	10.1	10.1	10.1	10.0	10.1	10.0
2012	10.0	10.0	10.1	9.9	10.0	10.1	10.2	10.2	10.1	10.1	10.0	10.0	10.1
2013	9.8	9.8	9.8	10.0	10.0	10.3	10.3	10.3	10.2	10.1	10.0	10.1	10.1
2014	9.9	10.0	10.0	10.0	10.2	10.4	10.5	10.5	10.3	10.2	10.2	10.3	10.2
2015	10.1	10.0	10.2	10.2	10.2	10.5	10.6	10.5	10.4	10.4	10.3	10.4	10.3
2016	10.2	10.3	10.3	10.4	10.5	10.6	10.6	10.6	10.4	10.4	10.2	10.2	10.4
2017	9.9	9.9	10.0	10.0	10.2	10.3	10.3	10.3	10.2	10.2	10.1	10.2	10.1
Government													
2007	54.8	56.4	56.4	56.0	56.2	53.7	44.3	44.1	54.6	56.5	56.6	56.8	53.9
2008	55.5	56.4	56.3	56.3	56.2	53.4	44.6	44.6	54.9	57.3	57.6	57.4	54.2
2009	55.0	57.0	56.6	57.5	57.7	54.1	44.9	45.0	54.7	57.7	57.6	56.9	54.6
2010	55.3	57.0	57.6	57.5	58.8	54.8	44.5	46.5	54.7	57.5	57.5	57.2	54.9
2011	55.2	57.0	57.0	57.1	57.6	54.2	44.5	47.0	55.2	57.7	57.8	58.1	54.9
2012	55.4	57.4	57.5	57.7	58.0	53.5	45.2	47.3	56.2	57.7	58.1	58.0	55.2
2013	56.2	57.3	57.6	57.9	57.0	53.7	45.1	48.3	56.0	58.3	58.4	58.2	55.3
2014	56.5	57.9	57.8	58.3	57.4	54.6	46.5	49.0	56.9	58.6	58.7	58.1	55.9
2015	57.0	58.1	58.0	58.2	57.3	54.8	46.7	48.3	56.6	58.2	58.2	57.8	55.8
2016	56.2	57.8	57.9	57.9	57.2	54.8	48.4	48.7	56.8	58.4	58.7	57.8	55.9
2017	55.9	57.6	57.7	57.8	56.1	54.8	46.9	48.7	56.8	58.6	58.7	58.2	55.7

2. Average Weekly Hours by Selected Industry: Vermont, 2013–2017

(Not seasonally adjusted)

Industry and year	January	February	March	April	May	June	July	August	September	October	November	December	Annual average
Total Private													
2013	33.2	33.5	33.5	33.4	34.1	34.1	34.1	34.3	34.2	34.0	33.6	33.6	33.8
2014	33.0	33.0	32.9	33.5	33.7	33.8	33.8	33.6	33.8	33.7	33.5	32.8	33.4
2015	32.9	33.0	33.0	33.1	33.5	33.5	33.8	33.8	33.5	33.6	33.3	32.9	33.3
2016	33.0	32.9	32.9	33.3	33.8	33.7	34.0	33.8	33.8	33.7	33.3	32.6	33.4
2017	33.4	32.9	32.6	33.4	33.6	33.7	34.2	33.9	33.8	33.8	33.3	32.9	33.5
Goods-Producing													
2013	38.0	38.2	38.3	38.4	39.3	39.0	39.0	39.3	39.1	39.1	38.6	38.9	38.8
2014	38.0	37.7	37.4	38.9	39.0	38.7	39.1	38.7	38.8	38.3	38.4	37.5	38.4
2015	37.3	37.0	37.4	37.5	37.9	37.8	37.9	37.9	37.0	37.8	38.0	38.2	37.6
2016	37.9	37.2	37.4	38.0	38.0	38.2	38.1	37.9	38.0	38.0	37.8	37.8	37.9
2017	38.5	37.9	37.4	38.2	38.4	38.5	38.7	38.2	38.5	38.8	38.3	37.2	38.2
Construction													
2013	37.1	37.5	37.1	37.5	39.9	38.7	39.6	39.8	39.5	39.9	38.4	38.1	38.7
2014	36.7	35.8	35.6	37.8	39.8	39.2	40.5	39.7	39.9	38.7	39.2	36.7	38.4
2015	35.9	35.4	36.4	36.5	37.1	37.1	37.9	37.6	36.7	37.7	37.4	38.2	37.1
2016	37.4	36.4	36.3	37.5	38.3	38.1	38.2	37.8	38.6	38.6	37.9	37.1	37.7
2017	37.5	36.4	35.7	37.0	38.5	38.9	39.1	38.5	38.8	38.5	37.6	36.8	37.8
Manufacturing													
2013	38.6	38.6	38.9	38.8	38.9	39.3	38.6	39.0	38.9	38.7	38.8	39.5	38.9
2014	38.8	38.8	38.4	39.5	38.6	38.4	38.2	38.1	38.2	38.2	37.9	38.0	38.4
2015	38.1	37.9	37.9	38.0	38.3	38.1	37.8	38.0	37.1	37.8	38.3	38.1	37.9
2016	38.1	37.6	38.0	38.1	37.6	38.1	37.8	37.8	37.4	37.4	37.5	38.0	37.8
2017	38.9	38.6	38.2	38.7	38.3	38.2	38.4	38.0	38.3	38.9	38.7	37.5	38.4
Trade, Transportation, and Utilities													
2013	32.5	33.0	33.3	33.3	33.8	33.6	33.8	33.8	34.0	33.4	32.8	33.7	33.4
2014	32.9	32.2	32.8	33.1	33.4	33.4	33.2	33.3	33.3	33.5	33.6	33.5	33.2
2015	33.4	33.2	33.6	33.2	33.6	33.6	34.0	33.9	33.9	34.0	34.0	33.6	33.7
2016	33.8	33.1	33.2	33.5	33.8	33.5	33.7	33.6	33.6	33.3	33.0	32.9	33.4
2017	33.0	32.5	32.3	33.1	33.2	33.2	33.6	33.2	33.1	32.9	33.2	33.0	33.0
Professional and Business Services													
2013	35.8	35.5	35.4	35.6	36.1	36.5	35.6	36.0	36.6	35.9	36.4	36.5	36.0
2014	35.3	35.1	35.2	34.9	35.3	35.4	35.3	35.6	35.7	35.3	35.9	35.2	35.4
2015	34.3	35.5	35.2	34.6	34.5	35.4	35.2	35.4	34.9	35.0	35.0	34.5	35.0
2016	34.5	34.8	35.0	35.4	36.0	35.7	35.2	35.0	35.1	35.6	35.0	34.4	35.1
2017	35.3	33.5	33.3	34.5	33.5	33.7	33.9	34.8	33.8	33.6	33.3	32.7	33.8
Education and Health Services													
2013	33.0	33.1	32.7	32.6	32.6	32.9	33.0	33.1	33.3	32.9	32.8	32.9	32.9
2014	33.1	33.0	32.9	32.9	32.8	33.0	33.2	32.9	33.2	33.1	33.2	33.0	33.0
2015	33.2	33.5	33.4	33.1	33.2	33.3	33.5	33.6	33.6	33.4	33.7	33.5	33.4
2016	33.7	33.6	33.6	33.5	33.7	33.6	33.9	33.8	34.2	33.6	33.7	33.2	33.7
2017	34.1	33.5	33.4	33.5	33.4	34.3	34.4	34.2	33.9	33.9	34.0	34.3	33.9
Leisure and Hospitality													
2013	25.7	25.9	26.1	25.0	26.5	26.9	27.6	27.9	26.4	26.7	25.2	24.4	26.2
2014	24.5	25.7	25.0	24.4	25.7	26.1	26.4	26.2	25.6	25.8	23.7	23.4	25.2
2015	24.6	25.4	24.4	24.9	25.7	25.9	26.4	26.5	25.8	25.9	23.3	23.4	25.2
2016	24.3	25.1	23.7	23.5	24.5	25.4	26.6	26.5	25.5	25.9	24.2	23.4	24.9
2017	24.9	25.5	24.1	24.3	25.7	26.3	27.1	27.1	25.9	26.4	23.6	23.9	25.4

3. Average Hourly Earnings by Selected Industry: Vermont, 2013–2017

(Dollars, not seasonally adjusted)

Industry and year	January	February	March	April	May	June	July	August	September	October	November	December	Annual average
Total Private													
2013	22.73	22.68	22.69	22.87	22.72	22.72	22.53	22.58	22.91	23.03	22.91	22.85	22.77
2014	23.08	23.07	23.11	23.15	22.88	23.11	22.85	23.02	23.36	23.43	23.57	23.41	23.17
2015	23.57	23.67	23.88	24.14	24.13	23.96	23.93	23.99	24.12	24.12	24.57	24.67	24.06
2016	24.64	24.40	24.31	24.46	24.40	24.06	23.95	23.85	24.33	24.58	24.67	24.54	24.34
2017	24.42	24.25	24.23	24.60	24.41	24.04	24.14	24.24	24.54	24.70	24.76	24.82	24.43
Goods-Producing													
2013	22.72	22.57	22.51	22.47	21.88	21.95	21.95	21.81	21.88	21.89	21.76	22.02	22.10
2014	22.12	22.23	22.41	22.47	22.21	22.30	22.26	22.33	22.40	22.34	22.43	22.88	22.36
2015	22.83	23.02	23.36	23.53	23.42	23.35	23.49	23.43	23.75	23.56	23.80	24.22	23.49
2016	24.19	24.25	24.25	24.03	24.13	24.08	23.97	23.99	24.16	24.18	24.48	24.64	24.19
2017	24.24	24.15	24.15	24.23	24.08	24.13	23.92	24.29	24.57	24.50	24.67	25.43	24.36
Construction													
2013	22.58	22.76	22.55	22.51	21.58	21.67	21.66	21.57	21.81	21.63	21.02	21.82	21.94
2014	22.29	22.92	22.91	22.98	21.67	22.02	21.80	22.19	22.28	22.45	22.52	23.07	22.38
2015	23.01	23.56	23.59	23.75	23.08	22.93	23.01	22.72	22.80	22.76	22.90	23.02	23.06
2016	22.99	23.61	23.41	23.25	23.12	22.97	22.94	22.54	23.08	23.30	23.75	23.75	23.21
2017	23.52	23.57	23.83	23.69	22.87	22.90	22.79	23.55	23.90	24.06	24.74	25.38	23.71
Manufacturing													
2013	22.81	22.49	22.51	22.47	22.09	22.15	22.18	22.00	21.94	22.08	21.75	22.18	22.22
2014	22.11	21.99	22.28	22.28	22.48	22.43	22.51	22.36	22.45	22.27	22.39	22.81	22.36
2015	22.78	22.78	23.30	23.34	23.56	23.59	23.81	23.88	24.41	24.13	24.44	25.10	23.76
2016	25.06	24.71	24.81	24.55	24.89	24.91	25.05	25.28	25.17	25.03	25.20	25.38	25.00
2017	24.89	24.71	24.58	24.73	24.90	24.98	24.80	24.89	25.13	24.91	24.73	25.57	24.90
Trade, Transportation, and Utilities													
2013	18.41	18.47	18.54	18.56	18.69	18.72	18.78	18.80	19.39	19.27	18.94	18.88	18.79
2014	19.02	18.75	19.04	19.07	18.97	19.07	19.07	19.29	19.40	19.13	19.42	19.59	19.16
2015	19.80	19.62	19.68	19.91	20.04	20.11	20.12	20.12	20.45	20.16	20.38	21.14	20.13
2016	21.01	20.54	20.54	20.63	20.66	20.45	20.55	20.63	20.64	20.70	20.79	20.79	20.66
2017	21.32	21.17	20.94	21.06	21.00	20.78	20.96	21.15	21.24	21.20	21.33	21.22	21.11
Professional and Business Services													
2013	30.50	30.70	30.96	30.44	30.73	30.62	30.11	31.07	30.96	31.07	31.06	31.45	30.81
2014	31.68	31.86	31.28	30.87	30.49	30.38	30.32	30.08	30.35	30.43	30.83	30.68	30.75
2015	30.95	31.45	31.60	31.37	30.93	30.08	31.02	31.02	30.69	30.51	31.02	31.04	30.96
2016	31.34	30.69	30.12	30.06	29.89	29.48	29.91	29.05	30.02	30.19	29.91	30.11	30.05
2017	30.06	31.16	30.89	31.41	30.40	30.04	30.56	30.04	29.96	29.92	29.76	30.71	30.40
Education and Health Services													
2013	23.95	23.98	24.10	24.49	24.43	24.80	24.69	24.55	25.04	25.79	25.24	25.13	24.69
2014	25.30	25.21	25.02	24.94	24.85	25.54	24.99	25.55	26.47	26.95	26.73	26.54	25.68
2015	27.01	27.25	27.50	27.52	27.33	27.19	26.92	26.89	27.03	27.64	28.29	28.76	27.45
2016	28.78	28.28	27.93	27.90	27.74	27.30	27.05	26.83	27.62	28.02	28.24	28.35	27.84
2017	27.39	27.09	27.09	27.00	27.25	26.39	26.43	26.42	26.90	27.11	27.14	26.98	26.93
Leisure and Hospitality													
2013	14.44	14.63	14.37	14.47	14.45	14.35	14.19	14.21	14.80	15.14	15.07	15.09	14.59
2014	15.18	15.18	15.02	15.38	15.23	15.09	15.24	15.37	15.45	15.76	15.59	15.31	15.31
2015	15.25	15.32	15.35	15.94	15.83	15.99	15.78	16.13	16.34	16.40	16.38	16.03	15.88
2016	15.92	16.04	16.20	16.38	16.42	16.08	16.03	16.15	16.75	17.09	17.02	16.45	16.37
2017	16.35	16.55	16.71	16.99	16.98	16.77	16.64	16.78	17.31	17.79	17.38	16.84	16.91

4. Average Weekly Earnings by Selected Industry: Vermont, 2013–2017

(Dollars, not seasonally adjusted)

Industry and year	January	February	March	April	May	June	July	August	September	October	November	December	Annual average
Total Private													
2013	754.64	759.78	760.12	763.86	774.75	774.75	768.27	774.49	783.52	783.02	769.78	767.76	769.63
2014	761.64	761.31	760.32	775.53	771.06	781.12	772.33	773.47	789.57	789.59	789.60	767.85	773.88
2015	775.45	781.11	788.04	799.03	808.36	802.66	808.83	810.86	808.02	810.43	818.18	811.64	801.20
2016	813.12	802.76	799.80	814.52	824.72	810.82	814.30	806.13	822.35	828.35	821.51	800.00	812.96
2017	815.63	797.83	789.90	821.64	820.18	810.15	825.59	821.74	829.45	834.86	824.51	816.58	818.41
Goods-Producing													
2013	863.36	862.17	862.13	862.85	859.88	856.05	856.05	857.13	855.51	855.90	839.94	856.58	857.48
2014	840.56	838.07	838.13	874.08	866.19	863.01	870.37	864.17	855.62	861.31	858.00	858.62	858.62
2015	851.56	851.74	873.66	882.38	887.62	882.63	890.27	888.00	878.75	890.57	904.40	925.20	883.22
2016	916.80	902.10	906.95	913.14	916.94	919.86	913.26	909.22	918.08	918.84	925.34	931.39	916.80
2017	933.24	915.29	903.21	925.59	924.67	929.01	925.70	927.88	945.95	950.60	944.86	946.00	930.55
Construction													
2013	837.72	853.50	836.61	844.13	861.04	838.63	857.74	858.49	861.50	863.04	837.89	831.34	849.08
2014	818.04	820.54	815.60	868.64	862.47	863.18	882.90	880.94	888.97	868.82	882.78	846.67	859.39
2015	826.06	834.02	858.68	866.88	856.27	850.70	872.08	854.27	836.76	858.05	856.46	879.36	855.53
2016	859.83	859.40	849.78	871.88	885.50	875.16	876.31	852.01	890.89	899.38	900.13	881.13	875.02
2017	882.00	857.95	850.73	876.53	880.50	890.81	891.09	906.68	927.32	926.31	930.22	933.98	896.24
Manufacturing													
2013	880.47	868.11	875.64	871.84	859.30	870.50	856.15	858.00	853.47	854.50	843.90	876.11	864.36
2014	857.87	853.21	855.55	880.06	867.73	861.31	859.88	851.92	857.59	850.71	848.58	866.78	858.62
2015	867.92	863.36	883.07	886.92	902.35	898.78	900.02	907.44	905.61	912.11	936.05	956.31	900.50
2016	954.79	929.10	942.78	935.36	935.86	949.07	946.89	955.58	941.36	936.12	945.00	964.44	945.00
2017	968.22	953.81	938.96	957.05	953.67	954.24	952.32	945.82	962.48	969.00	957.05	958.88	956.16
Trade, Transportation, and Utilities													
2013	598.33	609.51	617.38	618.05	631.72	628.99	634.76	635.44	659.26	643.62	621.23	636.26	627.59
2014	625.76	603.75	624.51	631.22	633.60	636.94	633.12	642.36	642.36	640.86	652.51	656.27	636.11
2015	661.32	651.38	661.25	661.01	673.34	675.70	684.08	682.07	693.26	685.44	692.92	710.30	678.38
2016	710.14	679.87	681.93	691.11	698.31	685.08	692.54	693.17	693.50	689.31	686.07	683.99	690.04
2017	703.56	688.03	676.36	697.09	697.20	689.90	704.26	702.18	703.04	697.48	708.16	700.26	696.63
Professional and Business Services													
2013	1,091.90	1,089.85	1,095.98	1,083.66	1,109.35	1,117.63	1,071.92	1,118.52	1,133.14	1,115.41	1,130.58	1,147.93	1,109.16
2014	1,118.30	1,118.29	1,101.06	1,077.36	1,076.30	1,075.45	1,070.30	1,070.85	1,083.50	1,074.18	1,106.80	1,079.94	1,088.55
2015	1,061.59	1,116.48	1,112.32	1,085.40	1,067.09	1,064.83	1,091.90	1,098.11	1,071.08	1,067.85	1,085.70	1,070.88	1,083.60
2016	1,081.23	1,068.01	1,054.20	1,064.12	1,076.04	1,052.44	1,052.83	1,016.75	1,053.70	1,074.76	1,046.85	1,035.78	1,054.76
2017	1,061.12	1,043.86	1,028.64	1,083.65	1,018.40	1,012.35	1,035.98	1,045.39	1,012.65	1,005.31	991.01	1,004.22	1,027.52
Education and Health Services													
2013	790.35	793.74	788.07	798.37	796.42	815.92	814.77	812.61	833.83	848.49	827.87	826.78	812.30
2014	837.43	831.93	823.16	820.53	815.08	842.82	829.67	840.60	878.80	892.05	887.44	875.82	847.44
2015	896.73	912.88	918.50	910.91	907.36	905.43	901.82	903.50	908.21	923.18	953.37	963.46	916.83
2016	969.89	950.21	938.45	934.65	934.84	919.97	917.00	906.85	944.95	941.81	951.69	941.22	938.21
2017	934.00	907.52	904.81	904.50	910.15	905.18	909.19	903.56	911.91	919.03	922.76	925.41	912.93
Leisure and Hospitality													
2013	371.11	378.92	375.06	361.75	382.93	386.02	391.64	396.46	390.72	404.24	379.76	368.20	382.26
2014	371.91	390.13	375.50	375.27	391.41	393.85	402.34	402.69	395.52	406.61	369.48	358.25	385.81
2015	375.15	389.13	374.54	396.91	406.83	414.14	416.59	421.57	427.45	424.76	381.65	375.10	400.18
2016	386.86	402.60	383.94	384.93	402.29	408.43	426.40	427.98	427.13	442.63	411.88	384.93	407.61
2017	407.12	422.03	402.71	412.86	436.39	441.05	450.94	454.74	448.33	469.66	410.17	402.48	429.51

VIRGINIA
At a Glance

Population:
  2010 census: 8,001,024
  2017 estimate: 8,470,020

Percent change in population:
  2010–2017: 5.9%

Percent change in total nonfarm employment:
  2007–2017: 4.8%

Industry with the largest growth in employment, 2007–2017 (thousands):
  Education and health services, 101.4

Industry with the largest decline or smallest growth in employment, 2007–2017 (thousands):
  Construction, -46.6

Civilian labor force:
  2010: 4,157,658
  2017: 4,307,753

Unemployment rate and rank among states (highest to lowest):
  2010: 7.1%, 41st
  2017: 3.8%, 32nd

Over the year change in unemployment rates:
  2015–2016: -0.4%
  2016–2017: -0.3%

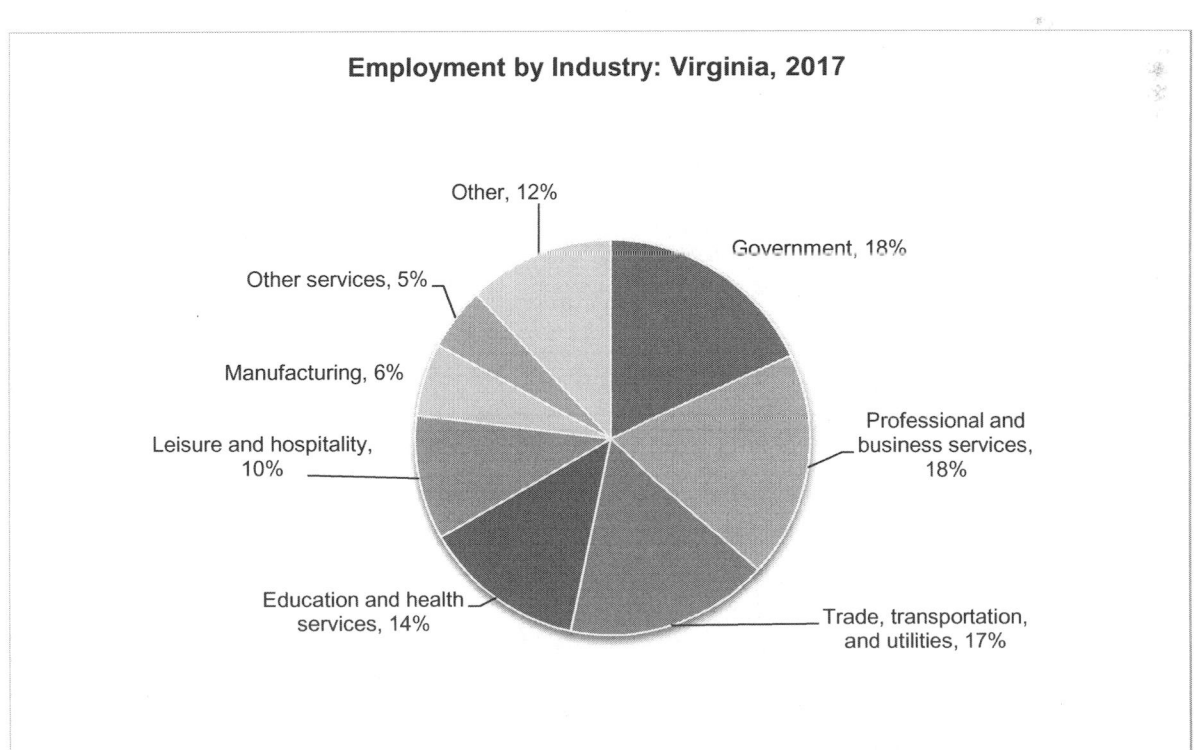

Employment by Industry: Virginia, 2017

Other, 12%
Government, 18%
Other services, 5%
Professional and business services, 18%
Manufacturing, 6%
Leisure and hospitality, 10%
Education and health services, 14%
Trade, transportation, and utilities, 17%

1. Employment by Industry: Virginia, Selected Years, 2007–2017

(Numbers in thousands, not seasonally adjusted)

Industry and year	January	February	March	April	May	June	July	August	September	October	November	December	Annual average
Total Nonfarm													
2007	3,703.7	3,709.7	3,741.1	3,757.2	3,781.9	3,813.0	3,781.7	3,774.1	3,777.4	3,784.3	3,802.7	3,807.0	3,769.5
2008	3,727.1	3,735.7	3,756.6	3,780.6	3,797.9	3,818.8	3,786.3	3,781.0	3,773.7	3,776.9	3,771.2	3,762.6	3,772.4
2009	3,649.5	3,638.3	3,645.0	3,654.9	3,673.3	3,686.1	3,640.8	3,631.6	3,632.0	3,644.9	3,655.6	3,652.9	3,650.4
2010	3,562.7	3,547.9	3,590.4	3,646.3	3,677.6	3,694.9	3,662.8	3,651.8	3,661.3	3,681.7	3,691.7	3,692.2	3,646.8
2011	3,611.5	3,629.5	3,656.2	3,692.3	3,697.4	3,717.1	3,701.1	3,694.1	3,715.7	3,723.7	3,740.5	3,734.4	3,692.8
2012	3,659.2	3,676.4	3,704.0	3,728.1	3,738.5	3,758.9	3,724.6	3,737.8	3,750.9	3,773.0	3,790.2	3,788.3	3,735.8
2013	3,700.5	3,720.2	3,740.9	3,764.0	3,770.3	3,785.2	3,761.7	3,765.6	3,770.5	3,776.8	3,801.9	3,789.8	3,762.3
2014	3,710.4	3,710.6	3,736.8	3,783.9	3,801.6	3,814.6	3,787.4	3,792.6	3,798.9	3,811.2	3,828.8	3,824.6	3,783.5
2015	3,758.3	3,766.5	3,780.1	3,841.5	3,860.9	3,878.1	3,877.5	3,877.2	3,888.5	3,915.2	3,934.4	3,930.4	3,859.1
2016	3,835.9	3,851.0	3,876.7	3,915.7	3,916.9	3,936.8	3,917.2	3,918.8	3,933.9	3,945.9	3,964.5	3,956.4	3,914.1
2017	3,874.4	3,900.9	3,917.6	3,951.3	3,960.3	3,987.6	3,958.3	3,955.4	3,964.9	3,977.7	3,986.5	3,976.6	3,951.0
Total Private													
2007	3,024.5	3,021.7	3,051.6	3,065.3	3,093.0	3,125.6	3,119.3	3,118.7	3,099.6	3,095.7	3,105.3	3,113.0	3,086.1
2008	3,040.0	3,038.1	3,054.7	3,080.2	3,098.3	3,121.4	3,114.9	3,110.6	3,083.0	3,071.0	3,059.0	3,052.3	3,077.0
2009	2,951.9	2,933.0	2,935.3	2,942.9	2,962.8	2,978.0	2,968.4	2,961.0	2,936.8	2,935.9	2,937.8	2,940.4	2,948.7
2010	2,860.6	2,840.8	2,877.3	2,927.6	2,951.6	2,973.7	2,983.1	2,980.2	2,957.8	2,970.1	2,975.8	2,977.9	2,939.7
2011	2,905.2	2,910.9	2,934.2	2,969.2	2,979.8	3,002.1	3,018.1	3,014.9	3,002.4	2,999.9	3,011.4	3,006.3	2,979.5
2012	2,947.8	2,953.6	2,979.5	3,004.3	3,019.5	3,042.9	3,047.2	3,057.5	3,040.2	3,050.8	3,062.6	3,061.5	3,022.3
2013	2,990.7	2,998.0	3,017.5	3,038.6	3,049.2	3,070.2	3,077.2	3,084.6	3,061.3	3,060.4	3,080.0	3,069.5	3,049.8
2014	3,004.0	2,995.8	3,019.5	3,062.8	3,084.1	3,103.2	3,103.0	3,109.8	3,087.4	3,094.7	3,107.2	3,103.3	3,072.9
2015	3,051.9	3,047.8	3,062.8	3,119.9	3,143.6	3,165.6	3,193.2	3,196.2	3,178.9	3,195.4	3,210.1	3,206.9	3,147.7
2016	3,129.5	3,131.7	3,153.6	3,190.3	3,197.3	3,222.1	3,228.7	3,233.3	3,218.5	3,224.1	3,237.6	3,230.3	3,199.8
2017	3,163.0	3,176.6	3,192.6	3,223.9	3,237.9	3,268.0	3,268.1	3,268.2	3,246.5	3,254.7	3,259.1	3,250.7	3,234.1
Goods Producing													
2007	526.8	525.1	529.8	531.2	532.9	537.0	534.0	533.2	529.3	524.1	521.0	518.3	528.6
2008	504.5	500.1	500.4	505.0	504.4	506.5	504.8	503.2	498.7	493.7	486.3	478.9	498.9
2009	456.4	446.7	443.8	441.3	440.0	441.0	440.3	438.5	435.9	434.3	430.7	429.4	439.9
2010	414.1	407.8	415.2	424.5	428.1	429.3	431.6	430.5	429.0	428.0	425.8	423.0	423.9
2011	409.7	410.3	414.1	418.9	421.0	424.4	428.5	427.8	424.7	422.8	421.6	420.2	420.3
2012	411.4	410.8	414.6	416.4	418.3	421.7	424.9	424.5	422.7	421.5	420.3	419.5	418.9
2013	409.4	410.2	412.7	415.6	417.8	422.0	423.2	423.4	421.1	419.2	419.6	417.4	417.6
2014	408.7	407.5	411.6	418.1	421.6	425.1	424.8	425.3	424.2	424.0	423.5	421.4	419.7
2015	413.4	412.6	415.4	425.4	429.0	432.0	435.3	435.0	433.1	433.4	432.3	431.3	427.4
2016	420.4	418.6	422.1	425.9	427.9	431.7	432.9	432.3	432.4	434.6	433.9	432.1	428.7
2017	423.1	425.3	428.7	433.4	435.8	440.2	440.0	440.3	439.0	439.5	439.9	440.1	435.4
Service-Providing													
2007	3,176.9	3,184.6	3,211.3	3,226.0	3,249.0	3,276.0	3,247.7	3,240.9	3,248.1	3,260.2	3,281.7	3,288.7	3,240.9
2008	3,222.6	3,235.6	3,256.2	3,275.6	3,293.5	3,312.3	3,281.5	3,277.8	3,275.0	3,283.2	3,284.9	3,283.7	3,273.5
2009	3,193.1	3,191.6	3,201.2	3,213.6	3,233.3	3,245.1	3,200.5	3,193.1	3,196.1	3,210.6	3,224.9	3,223.5	3,210.6
2010	3,148.6	3,140.1	3,175.2	3,221.8	3,249.5	3,265.6	3,231.2	3,221.3	3,232.3	3,253.7	3,265.9	3,269.2	3,222.9
2011	3,201.8	3,219.2	3,242.1	3,273.4	3,276.4	3,292.7	3,272.6	3,266.3	3,291.0	3,300.9	3,318.9	3,314.2	3,272.5
2012	3,247.8	3,265.6	3,289.4	3,311.7	3,320.2	3,337.2	3,299.7	3,313.3	3,328.2	3,351.5	3,369.9	3,368.8	3,316.9
2013	3,291.1	3,310.0	3,328.2	3,348.4	3,352.5	3,363.2	3,338.5	3,342.2	3,349.4	3,357.6	3,382.3	3,372.4	3,344.7
2014	3,301.7	3,303.1	3,325.2	3,365.8	3,380.0	3,389.5	3,362.6	3,367.3	3,374.7	3,387.2	3,405.3	3,403.2	3,363.8
2015	3,344.9	3,353.9	3,364.7	3,416.1	3,431.9	3,446.1	3,442.2	3,442.2	3,455.4	3,481.8	3,502.1	3,499.1	3,431.7
2016	3,415.5	3,432.4	3,454.6	3,489.8	3,489.0	3,505.1	3,484.3	3,486.5	3,501.5	3,511.3	3,530.6	3,524.3	3,485.4
2017	3,451.3	3,475.6	3,488.9	3,517.9	3,524.5	3,547.4	3,518.3	3,515.1	3,525.9	3,538.2	3,546.6	3,536.5	3,515.5
Mining and Logging													
2007	11.3	11.2	11.4	10.7	10.8	10.8	11.0	11.0	10.6	10.7	10.6	10.8	10.9
2008	10.6	10.9	10.8	10.9	11.0	11.1	11.2	11.2	11.3	11.5	11.5	11.4	11.1
2009	10.8	10.5	10.4	10.2	10.1	10.1	10.0	10.1	10.1	10.2	10.2	10.2	10.2
2010	9.9	9.8	10.0	10.3	10.3	10.4	10.5	10.6	10.6	10.7	10.7	10.6	10.4
2011	10.7	10.6	10.7	10.7	10.8	10.9	11.0	11.1	11.2	11.1	11.2	11.2	10.9
2012	11.1	11.1	11.1	11.0	11.0	11.1	11.0	11.0	10.8	10.3	10.5	10.4	10.9
2013	10.2	10.1	10.1	10.1	10.1	10.2	9.8	9.8	9.7	9.9	9.8	9.9	10.0
2014	9.7	9.7	9.8	9.7	9.6	9.7	9.5	9.4	9.4	9.3	9.3	9.3	9.5
2015	9.4	9.3	9.2	9.2	9.1	9.0	9.1	9.1	8.8	8.6	8.5	8.5	9.0
2016	8.0	8.0	8.0	7.7	7.7	7.7	7.8	7.7	7.8	7.9	7.9	8.0	7.9
2017	7.9	8.0	8.0	7.9	8.0	8.0	8.0	8.1	8.1	8.1	8.3	8.2	8.1

1. Employment by Industry: Virginia, Selected Years, 2007–2017—*Continued*

(Numbers in thousands, not seasonally adjusted)

Industry and year	January	February	March	April	May	June	July	August	September	October	November	December	Annual average
Construction													
2007	236.1	233.3	237.6	240.9	243.3	246.0	244.9	245.2	242.6	238.7	236.1	233.6	239.9
2008	223.7	222.0	223.9	226.2	226.8	228.6	228.3	227.1	223.8	220.4	214.9	209.6	222.9
2009	195.4	190.8	190.2	190.6	191.1	192.4	192.9	192.2	189.9	188.4	185.6	184.0	190.3
2010	173.9	168.6	175.5	184.1	186.4	187.6	190.2	189.4	187.9	186.4	185.0	181.7	183.1
2011	171.7	171.9	174.5	178.1	179.5	181.4	184.3	183.7	180.8	179.7	178.5	177.3	178.5
2012	169.7	169.0	172.3	174.8	177.1	180.4	181.4	181.0	179.2	179.2	177.9	176.9	176.6
2013	169.6	170.3	172.7	175.6	177.4	180.4	181.7	182.1	180.5	178.3	178.4	175.5	176.9
2014	169.4	168.5	171.7	177.3	179.8	182.1	182.5	183.1	182.1	182.3	181.8	179.4	178.3
2015	173.3	172.9	175.2	183.6	186.8	188.5	190.9	190.7	189.1	189.9	188.7	187.7	184.8
2016	180.1	179.0	182.4	187.1	188.6	191.2	191.7	191.2	191.2	193.3	192.5	190.6	188.2
2017	183.9	185.1	187.8	191.6	194.2	197.4	197.0	197.3	196.5	197.0	196.9	195.3	193.3
Manufacturing													
2007	279.4	280.6	280.8	279.6	278.8	280.2	278.1	277.0	276.1	274.7	274.3	273.9	277.8
2008	270.2	267.2	265.7	267.9	266.6	266.8	265.3	264.9	263.6	261.8	259.9	257.9	264.8
2009	250.2	245.4	243.2	240.5	238.8	238.5	237.4	236.2	235.9	235.7	234.9	235.2	239.3
2010	230.3	229.4	229.7	230.1	231.4	231.3	230.9	230.5	230.5	230.9	230.1	230.7	230.5
2011	227.3	227.8	228.9	230.1	230.7	232.1	233.2	233.0	232.7	232.0	231.9	231.7	231.0
2012	230.6	230.7	231.2	230.6	230.2	230.2	232.5	232.5	232.7	232.0	231.9	232.2	231.4
2013	229.6	229.8	229.9	229.9	230.3	231.4	231.7	231.5	230.9	231.0	231.4	232.0	230.8
2014	229.6	229.3	230.1	231.1	232.2	233.3	232.8	232.8	232.7	232.4	232.4	232.7	231.8
2015	230.7	230.4	231.0	232.6	233.1	234.5	235.3	235.2	235.2	234.9	235.1	235.1	233.6
2016	232.3	231.6	231.7	231.1	231.6	232.8	233.4	233.4	233.4	233.4	233.5	233.5	232.6
2017	231.3	232.2	232.9	233.9	233.6	234.8	235.0	234.9	234.4	234.4	234.7	236.6	234.1
Trade, Transportation, and Utilities													
2007	663.5	654.2	658.5	657.6	664.4	668.4	668.2	667.2	665.7	669.1	686.2	694.4	668.1
2008	663.4	653.3	655.3	654.2	658.0	661.5	660.0	659.4	655.7	654.8	663.8	669.7	659.1
2009	633.3	622.3	619.7	618.1	623.6	624.9	620.9	619.8	617.9	620.1	631.9	638.8	624.3
2010	611.2	601.0	607.0	614.2	620.3	623.6	622.6	623.6	618.6	625.9	638.2	647.3	621.1
2011	619.6	614.5	616.8	623.1	626.3	629.1	629.4	630.5	626.6	630.2	644.6	653.1	628.7
2012	626.8	619.9	623.9	625.7	631.5	633.2	631.0	631.2	629.1	636.3	652.4	660.8	633.5
2013	626.8	620.9	623.0	626.5	631.2	635.1	635.7	636.6	633.3	638.3	653.7	661.3	635.2
2014	632.6	625.4	629.1	634.1	638.7	642.5	641.8	642.9	639.5	644.6	659.5	668.0	641.6
2015	640.0	633.5	634.9	642.0	648.1	652.5	658.2	659.2	656.3	660.9	675.5	681.5	653.6
2016	652.9	647.7	650.5	655.5	659.9	663.3	661.2	662.2	658.0	662.6	678.7	683.7	661.4
2017	657.0	650.5	651.5	655.8	660.0	664.8	663.4	663.4	660.1	664.4	674.8	682.9	662.4
Wholesale Trade													
2007	120.0	120.4	121.1	120.7	121.2	121.8	121.2	121.4	120.9	120.7	120.6	121.0	120.9
2008	119.6	119.7	119.7	120.0	120.4	120.6	120.3	120.1	119.2	119.0	118.1	117.6	119.5
2009	115.4	114.7	114.2	113.8	113.6	113.1	112.2	112.0	111.1	110.6	110.2	110.2	112.6
2010	107.9	107.6	108.2	109.5	110.0	110.2	110.7	110.9	110.5	111.2	111.5	111.7	110.0
2011	110.6	110.7	111.1	111.7	111.8	112.1	112.3	112.1	111.2	110.9	111.0	111.2	111.4
2012	110.0	110.3	110.9	111.1	111.7	112.1	112.0	112.2	111.7	111.7	111.8	111.8	111.4
2013	110.6	110.8	111.2	110.9	111.0	111.2	111.0	111.0	110.5	110.5	110.5	110.7	110.8
2014	109.7	109.7	110.2	110.5	111.2	111.3	111.3	111.3	110.7	110.5	110.7	110.9	110.7
2015	109.4	109.3	109.4	109.9	110.3	110.7	111.7	111.5	111.2	111.3	111.5	111.6	110.7
2016	110.0	109.8	110.1	110.9	111.2	111.3	111.2	111.2	110.9	111.1	111.2	111.5	110.9
2017	109.9	110.3	110.6	111.0	111.6	112.2	111.8	112.0	111.5	112.3	111.0	111.9	111.3
Retail Trade													
2007	425.5	416.2	419.2	418.7	424.3	426.4	426.5	425.4	424.4	428.1	444.5	450.3	427.5
2008	425.9	415.8	418.1	415.8	418.5	421.0	420.0	419.2	417.1	417.4	426.7	431.5	420.6
2009	403.5	394.4	392.8	392.4	397.4	399.0	396.2	395.6	394.3	397.3	408.6	414.0	398.8
2010	393.1	383.8	388.5	393.3	398.0	400.0	398.3	398.9	394.4	400.0	410.9	417.9	398.1
2011	396.1	391.4	392.9	397.8	400.3	402.0	401.2	402.2	399.8	403.8	417.4	423.9	402.4
2012	403.4	395.9	399.3	400.0	403.9	404.5	402.4	402.3	400.9	407.6	423.2	429.0	406.0
2013	401.2	396.3	397.5	400.8	404.6	407.4	407.5	408.1	405.5	410.2	423.9	428.7	407.6
2014	405.6	400.1	402.5	406.5	409.0	411.5	410.4	410.7	407.4	412.2	424.4	429.5	410.8
2015	407.6	402.4	403.8	408.6	413.0	415.8	417.7	418.5	416.1	420.1	432.0	434.6	415.9
2016	413.5	409.6	411.9	415.0	418.3	420.4	419.1	420.1	416.1	420.2	432.8	434.7	419.3
2017	415.9	409.9	410.9	413.9	416.4	419.9	418.8	418.1	414.3	417.1	427.2	429.5	417.7

1. Employment by Industry: Virginia, Selected Years, 2007–2017—*Continued*

(Numbers in thousands, not seasonally adjusted)

Industry and year	January	February	March	April	May	June	July	August	September	October	November	December	Annual average
Transportation and Utilities													
2007	118.0	117.6	118.2	118.2	118.9	120.2	120.5	120.4	120.4	120.3	121.1	123.1	119.7
2008	117.9	117.8	117.5	118.4	119.1	119.9	119.7	120.1	119.4	118.4	119.0	120.6	119.0
2009	114.4	113.2	112.7	111.9	112.6	112.8	112.5	112.2	112.5	112.2	113.1	114.6	112.9
2010	110.2	109.6	110.3	111.4	112.3	113.4	113.6	113.8	113.7	114.7	115.8	117.7	113.0
2011	112.9	112.4	112.8	113.6	114.2	115.0	115.9	116.2	115.6	115.5	116.2	118.0	114.9
2012	113.4	113.7	113.7	114.6	115.9	116.6	116.6	116.7	116.5	117.0	117.4	120.0	116.0
2013	115.0	113.8	114.3	114.8	115.6	116.5	117.2	117.5	117.3	117.6	119.3	121.9	116.7
2014	117.3	115.6	116.4	117.1	118.5	119.7	120.1	120.9	121.4	121.9	124.4	127.6	120.1
2015	123.0	121.8	121.7	123.5	124.8	126.0	128.8	129.2	129.0	129.5	132.0	135.3	127.1
2016	129.4	128.3	128.5	129.6	130.4	131.6	130.9	130.9	131.0	131.3	134.7	137.5	131.2
2017	131.2	130.3	130.0	130.9	132.0	132.7	132.8	133.3	134.3	135.0	136.6	141.5	133.4
Information													
2007	91.9	91.3	90.7	90.5	91.0	90.9	90.3	89.8	89.7	89.6	89.7	89.5	90.4
2008	88.7	88.7	88.5	88.1	88.2	88.4	88.0	87.5	86.4	85.6	85.4	84.9	87.4
2009	84.0	83.8	83.1	82.1	81.9	81.8	81.1	80.1	79.1	79.0	78.7	78.5	81.1
2010	77.4	76.7	76.7	75.7	75.7	76.0	75.8	75.8	75.5	75.5	75.5	75.7	76.0
2011	74.7	74.5	74.6	74.0	74.2	74.4	74.8	70.1	73.5	72.7	73.3	74.1	73.7
2012	71.3	72.0	72.6	71.1	71.8	72.8	71.6	72.9	70.3	70.5	72.1	70.9	71.7
2013	70.3	72.1	72.0	71.1	71.2	71.5	71.6	72.8	70.6	71.1	72.6	71.4	71.5
2014	72.2	70.8	71.0	70.9	72.4	71.3	71.5	72.4	70.4	70.8	70.1	70.0	71.2
2015	70.0	69.5	69.2	69.4	70.0	69.8	70.5	69.8	68.9	69.4	69.2	69.2	69.6
2016	68.5	68.8	67.9	68.5	66.1	69.1	69.2	68.8	68.5	67.5	67.5	68.3	68.2
2017	67.8	68.4	68.3	67.8	68.1	68.5	68.0	67.7	67.4	66.8	67.0	67.8	67.8
Financial Activities													
2007	193.7	193.9	194.7	194.0	195.1	196.6	196.0	195.1	193.0	191.3	190.2	190.3	193.7
2008	189.3	189.5	189.6	189.1	189.1	190.5	191.1	190.1	187.7	186.7	185.5	185.6	188.7
2009	182.1	181.1	181.1	181.0	180.6	181.6	181.0	180.8	178.4	177.4	177.0	177.5	180.0
2010	176.3	175.6	176.4	177.4	178.3	180.8	181.7	181.6	179.9	180.1	180.2	180.7	179.1
2011	178.4	178.6	179.0	180.9	182.0	183.7	185.4	185.4	184.2	183.8	184.2	185.3	182.6
2012	183.2	184.0	184.8	186.8	187.3	189.6	190.7	190.8	189.9	190.3	190.7	191.4	188.3
2013	189.2	189.7	190.4	191.4	192.1	193.9	194.8	194.6	193.0	193.4	193.6	193.9	192.5
2014	190.8	191.1	191.7	192.5	193.5	195.6	196.3	196.0	194.5	194.7	195.1	195.7	194.0
2015	194.1	194.8	195.2	195.9	197.3	198.9	200.2	200.0	198.5	199.1	199.1	199.6	197.7
2016	197.5	197.5	198.1	199.5	200.7	202.2	202.9	203.3	201.5	202.3	202.8	203.6	201.0
2017	201.2	202.0	202.3	203.4	205.1	207.5	208.4	208.1	206.6	206.0	205.9	206.5	205.3
Professional and Business Services													
2007	628.4	631.9	638.2	642.1	643.6	650.6	650.9	653.7	649.9	655.0	655.3	656.4	646.3
2008	644.9	647.3	650.3	656.4	657.0	662.5	663.2	665.6	661.1	662.0	658.3	655.8	657.0
2009	640.3	639.0	639.2	638.0	636.7	639.7	639.5	640.8	636.9	642.4	644.6	643.7	640.1
2010	631.2	631.1	636.0	648.7	648.4	652.4	657.5	658.3	655.1	661.7	662.5	661.7	650.4
2011	652.7	655.3	659.5	665.5	663.9	666.2	672.6	674.7	673.7	675.3	677.2	673.1	667.5
2012	664.4	666.9	671.0	675.8	675.7	679.1	681.9	685.4	682.0	687.7	686.6	685.1	678.5
2013	675.2	677.7	679.9	682.5	681.0	683.4	683.8	686.0	679.7	680.5	685.8	680.2	681.3
2014	668.7	668.4	670.8	681.1	683.2	685.1	687.1	688.1	682.4	688.0	693.0	690.2	682.2
2015	681.2	680.4	681.9	696.9	700.4	703.6	709.6	709.9	705.9	717.1	721.8	720.0	702.4
2016	700.3	702.7	705.0	712.2	711.0	715.8	719.4	722.1	719.5	723.8	726.3	725.6	715.3
2017	710.2	716.2	717.3	724.5	726.6	734.2	735.7	736.8	732.5	737.9	736.9	733.7	728.5
Education and Health Services													
2007	415.8	418.7	421.5	424.1	426.6	427.7	425.2	426.8	433.4	437.2	439.7	441.8	428.2
2008	436.9	442.9	444.2	448.8	449.5	448.3	443.9	444.5	450.4	453.9	455.0	455.6	447.8
2009	450.6	452.8	454.1	456.4	458.3	456.1	453.8	453.1	455.4	458.6	460.2	460.8	455.9
2010	454.8	454.6	458.5	462.1	463.2	460.3	462.6	461.4	464.3	471.4	472.8	471.4	463.1
2011	467.2	470.2	472.0	472.0	464.9	462.1	464.0	465.6	473.7	476.6	478.0	469.4	469.6
2012	473.7	477.0	478.8	480.8	473.3	472.1	472.3	478.1	486.2	491.5	493.1	487.5	480.4
2013	488.5	492.9	495.3	494.8	485.9	482.0	482.7	488.0	495.6	498.4	500.6	492.5	491.4
2014	494.1	495.2	497.0	502.3	494.2	491.0	490.7	495.0	501.8	505.6	506.2	499.5	497.7
2015	504.6	506.6	507.7	515.1	507.3	504.6	508.9	513.2	520.6	526.5	528.5	522.4	513.8
2016	523.8	526.2	527.8	529.5	520.6	515.7	517.1	521.5	530.8	532.9	533.1	525.2	525.4
2017	527.6	531.1	531.8	533.7	525.0	522.0	521.3	524.6	531.6	537.6	538.6	530.5	529.6

1. Employment by Industry: Virginia, Selected Years, 2007–2017—*Continued*

(Numbers in thousands, not seasonally adjusted)

Industry and year	January	February	March	April	May	June	July	August	September	October	November	December	Annual average
Leisure and Hospitality													
2007	322.3	323.9	333.7	341.0	353.3	367.0	367.2	366.3	353.1	343.2	337.0	335.4	345.3
2008	327.2	329.7	339.2	349.7	362.1	372.7	372.9	369.6	354.3	344.6	336.2	333.6	349.3
2009	320.2	321.9	328.4	339.7	355.0	364.9	364.0	361.1	348.3	339.0	330.3	327.2	341.7
2010	313.3	312.5	323.8	339.8	351.6	364.2	364.5	363.0	351.2	342.7	336.4	334.0	341.4
2011	319.9	323.5	333.0	346.9	359.2	371.8	372.0	370.7	357.4	350.0	344.0	342.4	349.2
2012	330.2	335.2	344.8	355.2	368.3	379.5	379.3	380.4	367.2	359.4	354.2	353.3	358.9
2013	340.4	342.9	351.7	363.2	375.4	386.1	387.9	387.0	373.6	365.3	360.0	358.9	366.0
2014	345.1	345.4	354.7	368.9	384.2	394.1	392.7	392.1	378.5	371.6	364.8	363.8	371.3
2015	354.7	356.4	363.0	380.0	394.6	405.5	410.3	409.4	397.8	390.9	385.4	384.9	386.1
2016	370.6	374.3	384.8	398.5	409.8	421.0	421.8	420.1	406.5	398.5	393.6	390.9	399.2
2017	376.9	383.4	391.8	403.7	414.9	425.9	425.3	423.0	406.7	399.5	391.9	386.3	402.4
Other Services													
2007	182.1	182.7	184.5	184.8	186.1	187.4	187.5	186.6	185.5	186.2	186.2	186.9	185.5
2008	185.1	186.6	187.2	188.9	190.0	191.0	191.0	190.7	188.7	189.7	188.5	188.2	188.8
2009	185.0	185.4	185.9	186.3	186.7	188.0	187.8	186.8	184.9	185.1	184.4	184.5	185.9
2010	182.3	181.5	183.7	185.2	186.0	187.1	186.8	186.0	184.2	184.8	184.4	184.1	184.7
2011	183.0	184.0	185.2	187.9	188.3	190.4	191.4	190.1	188.6	188.5	188.5	188.7	187.9
2012	186.8	187.8	189.0	192.5	193.3	194.9	195.5	194.2	192.8	193.6	193.2	193.0	192.2
2013	190.9	191.6	192.5	193.5	194.6	196.2	197.5	196.2	194.4	194.2	194.1	193.9	194.1
2014	191.8	192.0	193.6	194.9	196.3	198.5	198.1	198.0	196.1	195.4	195.0	194.7	195.4
2015	193.9	194.0	195.5	195.2	196.9	198.7	200.2	199.7	197.8	198.1	198.3	198.0	197.2
2016	195.5	195.9	197.4	200.7	201.3	203.3	204.2	203.0	201.3	201.9	201.7	200.9	200.6
2017	199.2	199.7	200.9	201.6	202.4	204.9	206.0	204.3	202.6	203.0	204.1	202.9	202.6
Government													
2007	679.2	688.0	689.5	691.9	688.9	687.4	662.4	655.4	677.8	688.6	697.4	694.0	683.4
2008	687.1	697.6	701.9	700.4	699.6	697.4	671.4	670.4	690.7	705.9	712.2	710.3	695.4
2009	697.6	705.3	709.7	712.0	710.5	708.1	672.4	670.6	695.2	709.0	717.8	712.5	701.7
2010	702.1	707.1	713.1	718.7	726.0	721.2	679.7	671.6	703.5	711.6	715.9	714.3	707.1
2011	706.3	718.6	722.0	723.1	717.6	715.0	683.0	679.2	713.3	723.8	729.1	728.1	713.3
2012	711.4	722.8	724.5	723.8	719.0	716.0	677.4	680.3	710.7	722.2	727.6	726.8	713.5
2013	709.8	722.2	723.4	725.4	721.1	715.0	684.5	681.0	709.2	716.4	721.9	720.3	712.5
2014	706.4	714.8	717.3	721.1	717.5	711.4	684.4	682.8	711.5	716.5	721.6	721.3	710.6
2015	706.4	718.7	717.3	721.6	717.3	712.5	684.3	681.0	709.6	719.8	724.3	723.5	711.4
2016	706.4	719.3	723.1	725.4	719.6	714.7	688.5	685.5	715.4	721.8	726.9	726.1	714.4
2017	711.4	724.3	725.0	727.4	722.4	719.6	690.2	687.2	718.4	723.0	727.4	725.9	716.9

2. Average Weekly Hours by Selected Industry: Virginia, 2013–2017

(Not seasonally adjusted)

Industry and year	January	February	March	April	May	June	July	August	September	October	November	December	Annual average
Total Private													
2013	34.1	34.5	34.5	34.7	34.6	34.9	34.5	34.6	34.9	33.9	34.3	34.6	34.5
2014	34.0	33.9	34.7	34.8	34.8	35.2	34.6	34.7	34.8	34.9	35.5	34.9	34.7
2015	34.5	35.1	35.3	35.3	35.3	35.1	35.1	35.6	35.0	35.0	35.4	35.0	35.1
2016	34.7	34.7	34.8	34.9	35.1	34.9	34.9	35.1	35.1	35.3	34.9	34.8	34.9
2017	34.7	34.5	34.2	34.7	34.2	34.5	34.9	34.3	34.6	34.9	34.7	34.8	34.6
Goods-Producing													
2013	38.2	38.5	38.4	39.3	39.3	38.7	39.0	40.1	40.2	38.4	40.3	38.5	39.1
2014	37.5	36.1	39.1	39.7	40.2	40.0	39.6	40.1	39.8	39.6	40.1	39.6	39.3
2015	38.7	38.8	39.3	40.0	40.6	40.6	40.0	40.5	39.8	40.4	40.1	40.4	39.9
2016	39.9	38.3	39.1	39.5	38.7	39.4	39.6	39.7	39.4	39.4	39.2	39.0	39.3
2017	38.7	37.4	36.7	37.3	37.2	38.4	38.6	37.8	38.5	38.7	39.2	39.4	38.2
Construction													
2013	37.2	37.3	37.1	38.9	38.5	38.1	38.1	39.6	39.9	37.1	40.1	37.4	38.3
2014	36.2	34.5	38.2	38.8	39.4	39.2	38.7	38.6	37.5	37.8	38.3	37.4	37.9
2015	35.5	36.6	37.5	38.4	39.7	39.8	38.8	39.1	37.3	38.7	37.8	38.0	38.1
2016	37.4	35.6	37.3	38.1	37.2	38.7	39.1	39.1	39.0	39.2	38.4	37.5	38.1
2017	36.5	38.0	36.4	38.5	37.4	39.0	39.1	37.9	38.8	38.6	39.0	39.6	38.3
Manufacturing													
2013	39.2	39.7	39.8	39.7	40.2	39.5	40.1	40.7	40.9	40.1	40.6	40.8	40.1
2014	40.0	38.8	41.2	41.5	41.7	41.3	41.0	41.6	42.0	41.3	41.9	41.8	41.2
2015	41.7	41.0	41.0	41.6	41.5	41.4	41.1	41.9	42.5	41.7	42.3	42.8	41.7
2016	42.1	40.6	40.7	40.7	39.9	39.9	40.0	40.1	39.7	39.4	39.7	40.3	40.3
2017	40.6	41.3	40.9	39.8	40.1	40.5	40.5	40.0	40.3	40.7	41.0	40.7	40.5
Trade, Transportation, and Utilities													
2013	33.6	34.1	34.1	34.2	34.3	34.5	34.6	34.6	34.9	33.8	33.9	34.3	34.2
2014	33.5	33.4	33.9	34.0	34.0	34.1	33.7	33.8	34.0	33.6	34.2	34.5	33.9
2015	33.7	33.7	33.8	33.9	34.4	34.0	34.3	34.3	34.3	34.0	34.0	34.2	34.1
2016	33.2	33.4	33.2	33.3	33.4	33.5	33.7	33.9	34.0	33.6	33.1	33.8	33.5
2017	32.9	33.1	33.3	33.7	33.4	33.1	33.5	33.3	33.6	33.2	33.3	33.5	33.3
Financial Activities													
2013	38.6	38.6	38.6	38.1	37.7	38.7	37.5	37.4	37.4	36.7	36.8	37.5	37.8
2014	36.8	37.2	36.8	36.5	36.4	37.6	36.6	36.9	37.0	37.3	39.0	37.7	37.2
2015	37.8	39.1	39.1	38.5	38.9	38.6	38.7	40.4	40.0	39.5	40.5	39.4	39.2
2016	39.6	39.5	39.0	38.2	38.3	37.9	38.2	39.2	38.8	39.7	39.2	38.5	38.8
2017	39.5	38.7	38.2	38.5	38.1	38.1	38.5	38.1	38.0	38.3	38.2	38.0	38.3
Professional and Business Services													
2013	35.7	36.3	36.2	36.2	36.2	37.3	36.4	36.3	36.9	35.4	35.9	36.9	36.3
2014	35.9	36.3	36.7	36.5	36.7	37.2	36.2	36.6	36.4	37.0	38.1	36.8	36.7
2015	36.4	37.4	37.7	37.2	37.2	36.9	36.8	37.9	36.6	36.6	37.9	37.3	37.2
2016	36.9	37.0	37.2	37.7	38.2	37.5	37.2	37.4	37.5	38.2	37.4	37.2	37.5
2017	37.7	37.5	37.1	38.0	36.8	37.8	38.0	37.4	37.9	38.4	37.7	37.5	37.7
Education and Health Services													
2013	34.1	34.0	34.0	33.9	33.9	34.2	33.9	33.8	34.1	33.8	33.8	34.1	34.0
2014	33.9	33.7	33.9	34.2	34.1	34.6	34.2	33.9	34.3	34.1	34.5	34.1	34.1
2015	34.2	34.6	34.3	34.2	34.2	34.2	34.1	34.5	34.2	34.3	34.7	33.7	34.3
2016	34.6	34.5	34.6	34.7	35.1	34.8	34.6	34.7	34.7	34.8	34.4	34.4	34.7
2017	34.6	34.0	33.8	34.1	33.9	33.7	34.0	33.4	33.9	34.1	33.6	34.0	33.9
Leisure and Hospitality													
2013	26.6	27.1	27.0	27.5	27.1	27.1	26.7	26.5	26.1	25.9	26.0	25.9	26.6
2014	25.5	25.5	26.5	26.9	26.8	27.0	26.9	26.7	26.5	26.3	26.5	25.9	26.4
2015	25.3	25.4	26.2	26.6	26.6	26.5	26.8	27.1	26.1	26.1	26.2	25.8	26.2
2016	24.7	25.6	25.9	26.3	26.4	26.4	26.7	26.5	26.4	26.8	26.7	26.2	26.2
2017	25.6	26.2	26.3	26.2	25.7	26.2	27.0	26.5	25.9	26.2	25.9	25.9	26.1
Other Services													
2013	31.4	32.1	31.9	32.7	32.4	32.6	32.4	31.5	32.7	31.7	31.4	32.8	32.1
2014	31.8	32.0	32.5	32.4	32.6	32.9	32.2	31.6	32.2	32.3	32.6	32.4	32.3
2015	32.4	32.4	32.5	32.5	31.9	32.7	32.7	32.4	31.8	32.1	32.8	32.4	32.4
2016	32.5	32.5	32.7	32.2	32.9	32.4	32.2	32.3	32.2	33.0	32.0	32.4	32.4
2017	32.6	32.2	32.1	33.1	32.0	32.0	32.6	31.7	31.4	32.6	31.8	32.5	32.2

3. Average Hourly Earnings by Selected Industry: Virginia, 2013–2017

(Dollars, not seasonally adjusted)

Industry and year	January	February	March	April	May	June	July	August	September	October	November	December	Annual average
Total Private													
2013	25.13	25.07	25.25	25.05	25.04	25.28	24.96	24.98	25.50	25.25	25.32	25.90	25.23
2014	25.82	25.29	25.60	25.18	25.04	25.27	25.02	25.18	25.25	25.32	25.64	25.47	25.34
2015	25.79	26.30	26.23	26.04	25.94	25.79	25.81	26.34	26.26	26.36	26.55	26.26	26.14
2016	26.64	26.63	26.71	26.89	27.20	26.76	27.03	26.64	27.08	27.55	27.13	27.29	26.96
2017	27.97	27.73	27.55	28.08	27.45	27.01	27.52	27.22	27.48	27.73	27.39	27.75	27.57
Goods-Producing													
2013	22.34	22.49	22.82	22.60	22.56	22.90	22.79	22.73	22.77	22.84	22.76	23.11	22.73
2014	23.35	23.75	23.06	23.20	23.16	23.22	23.19	23.11	23.19	23.41	23.60	23.47	23.30
2015	23.52	23.61	23.55	23.50	23.39	23.29	23.46	23.36	23.73	23.72	23.75	23.66	23.54
2016	23.96	24.19	24.06	24.35	24.42	24.60	24.98	24.82	24.98	25.08	24.77	24.78	24.59
2017	25.12	24.66	24.88	25.02	24.89	24.88	24.98	25.00	25.14	24.92	24.74	25.22	24.96
Construction													
2013	22.71	23.14	23.56	23.35	23.43	23.55	23.64	23.89	23.88	23.94	23.57	24.39	23.60
2014	24.82	25.23	23.99	24.29	24.25	23.95	23.88	24.08	24.15	24.07	24.04	24.20	24.23
2015	24.30	24.67	24.44	24.14	24.24	24.03	24.27	24.13	24.28	24.66	24.89	24.99	24.42
2016	25.47	25.76	25.69	26.02	25.82	25.88	26.04	26.12	26.13	26.17	25.92	25.87	25.92
2017	26.40	25.62	26.23	25.89	26.18	26.06	26.19	26.24	26.48	26.01	25.88	26.44	26.14
Manufacturing													
2013	22.03	21.87	22.10	21.80	21.63	22.12	21.88	21.44	21.44	21.62	21.77	21.81	21.79
2014	21.90	22.30	22.01	21.98	21.93	22.32	22.34	22.08	22.18	22.37	22.72	22.39	22.21
2015	22.47	22.36	22.40	22.69	22.37	22.36	22.49	22.43	22.60	22.20	22.12	21.92	22.37
2016	22.30	22.59	22.20	22.56	22.86	23.15	23.71	23.36	23.70	23.85	23.76	23.84	23.15
2017	24.09	23.76	23.54	24.15	23.65	23.72	23.83	23.83	23.86	23.88	23.73	24.06	23.84
Trade, Transportation, and Utilities													
2013	20.07	19.76	19.72	19.68	19.76	20.16	19.72	19.92	19.97	19.90	19.82	20.02	19.88
2014	19.76	20.70	20.15	20.15	20.33	20.35	20.36	20.24	20.20	20.01	20.05	19.34	20.13
2015	19.76	20.46	20.21	20.56	20.20	20.36	20.36	20.83	20.29	20.87	20.31	20.00	20.35
2016	20.71	20.04	20.35	21.24	20.87	20.95	21.47	20.98	21.34	21.77	21.30	21.37	21.04
2017	21.88	21.13	20.74	21.28	20.66	20.75	21.14	20.74	21.01	21.26	21.15	21.26	21.08
Financial Activities													
2013	26.15	26.55	26.91	27.21	26.72	26.65	27.22	26.82	27.04	26.54	26.56	27.24	26.80
2014	26.43	26.43	27.07	26.40	26.15	26.78	26.33	26.44	26.41	25.96	25.99	26.44	26.37
2015	25.79	26.29	26.33	26.53	26.69	26.74	26.70	27.10	26.53	26.71	27.13	26.73	26.61
2016	26.41	26.58	26.56	27.27	28.00	26.85	27.38	26.45	28.31	28.79	28.47	28.76	27.49
2017	28.74	28.91	28.59	29.43	29.06	29.50	30.20	29.36	30.09	30.39	29.67	30.11	29.51
Professional and Business Services													
2013	35.29	35.06	35.42	35.20	34.81	34.89	34.12	34.07	34.92	34.49	34.49	35.46	34.85
2014	34.86	35.71	35.33	34.29	33.87	34.33	33.81	33.88	33.65	33.84	34.58	34.28	34.36
2015	35.19	35.87	35.49	34.82	34.81	34.56	34.87	35.55	35.50	36.06	36.36	35.50	35.39
2016	35.73	35.99	36.12	36.07	37.03	36.08	36.44	36.25	36.31	37.10	36.56	37.49	36.44
2017	38.45	37.70	37.72	38.20	37.68	36.74	37.55	37.36	37.57	37.54	36.93	37.69	37.59
Education and Health Services													
2013	23.66	23.84	24.49	24.04	24.47	24.62	24.57	24.59	24.91	24.35	24.52	24.92	24.41
2014	24.32	24.86	24.37	24.23	24.17	24.27	24.36	24.64	24.84	24.56	24.62	25.29	24.54
2015	24.77	25.02	25.40	25.50	25.72	25.85	25.45	25.98	26.22	26.04	26.00	26.94	25.75
2016	25.70	25.96	26.14	25.62	26.02	25.97	26.31	26.17	26.51	26.90	27.06	27.04	26.28
2017	27.56	27.73	27.61	27.72	27.50	27.28	27.80	27.38	27.44	27.76	27.66	27.73	27.60
Leisure and Hospitality													
2013	12.98	12.95	12.84	12.72	12.79	12.78	12.74	12.76	12.90	12.98	13.02	13.22	12.88
2014	13.09	13.35	13.11	13.11	13.08	13.13	12.84	12.88	13.13	13.24	13.21	13.30	13.12
2015	13.32	13.44	13.39	13.34	13.27	13.06	12.93	12.83	13.12	13.27	13.34	13.40	13.22
2016	13.48	13.37	13.29	13.38	13.60	13.21	13.18	13.12	13.31	13.57	13.57	13.94	13.41
2017	13.93	13.80	14.01	14.21	14.25	13.76	13.80	13.77	13.87	14.00	14.13	14.27	13.98
Other Services													
2013	25.43	25.63	26.00	25.24	25.41	25.39	24.95	24.74	25.78	25.51	26.14	25.90	25.51
2014	25.81	25.88	25.89	25.78	25.61	25.68	25.24	25.10	25.12	25.42	25.61	26.17	25.61
2015	26.23	25.79	26.22	25.80	26.37	25.91	25.82	26.21	26.64	26.62	27.15	27.37	26.34
2016	27.75	27.29	27.49	27.52	27.64	27.66	26.75	26.71	27.47	27.70	27.35	27.35	27.39
2017	27.95	27.58	27.52	27.95	27.79	27.50	27.82	27.79	27.69	28.19	27.68	27.47	27.75

4. Average Weekly Earnings by Selected Industry: Virginia, 2013–2017

(Dollars, not seasonally adjusted)

Industry and year	January	February	March	April	May	June	July	August	September	October	November	December	Annual average
Total Private													
2013	856.93	864.92	871.13	869.24	866.38	882.27	861.12	864.31	889.95	855.98	868.48	896.14	870.44
2014	877.88	857.33	888.32	876.26	871.39	889.50	865.69	873.75	878.70	883.67	910.22	888.90	879.30
2015	889.76	923.13	925.92	919.21	915.68	905.23	905.93	937.70	919.10	922.60	939.87	919.10	917.51
2016	924.41	924.06	929.51	938.46	954.72	933.92	943.35	935.06	950.51	972.52	946.84	949.69	940.90
2017	970.56	956.69	942.21	974.38	938.79	931.85	960.45	933.65	950.81	967.78	950.43	965.70	953.92
Goods-Producing													
2013	853.39	865.87	876.29	888.18	886.61	886.23	888.81	911.47	915.35	877.06	917.23	889.74	888.74
2014	875.63	857.38	901.65	921.04	931.03	928.80	918.32	926.71	922.96	927.04	946.36	929.41	915.69
2015	910.22	916.07	925.52	940.00	949.63	945.57	938.40	946.08	944.45	958.29	952.38	955.86	939.25
2016	956.00	926.48	940.75	961.83	945.05	969.24	989.21	985.35	984.21	988.15	970.98	966.42	966.39
2017	972.14	922.28	913.10	933.25	925.91	955.39	964.23	945.00	967.89	964.40	969.81	993.67	953.47
Construction													
2013	844.81	863.12	874.08	908.32	902.06	897.26	900.68	946.04	952.81	888.17	945.16	912.19	903.88
2014	898.48	870.44	916.42	942.45	955.45	938.84	924.16	929.49	905.63	909.85	920.73	905.08	918.32
2015	862.65	902.92	916.50	926.98	962.33	956.39	941.68	943.48	905.64	954.34	940.84	949.62	930.40
2016	952.58	917.06	958.24	991.36	960.50	1,001.56	1,018.16	1,021.29	1,019.07	1,025.86	995.33	970.13	987.55
2017	963.60	973.56	954.77	996.77	979.13	1,016.34	1,024.03	994.50	1,027.42	1,003.99	1,009.32	1,047.02	1,001.16
Manufacturing													
2013	863.58	868.24	879.58	865.46	869.53	873.74	877.39	872.61	876.90	866.96	883.86	889.85	873.78
2014	876.00	865.24	906.81	912.17	914.48	921.82	915.94	918.53	931.56	923.88	951.97	935.90	915.05
2015	937.00	916.76	918.40	943.90	928.36	925.70	924.34	939.82	960.50	925.74	935.68	938.18	932.83
2016	938.83	917.15	903.54	918.19	912.11	923.69	948.40	936.74	940.89	939.69	943.27	960.75	932.95
2017	978.05	981.29	962.79	961.17	948.37	960.66	965.12	953.20	961.56	971.92	972.93	979.24	965.52
Trade, Transportation, and Utilities													
2013	674.35	673.82	672.45	673.06	677.77	695.52	682.31	689.23	696.95	672.62	671.90	686.69	679.90
2014	661.96	691.38	683.09	685.10	691.22	693.94	686.13	684.11	686.80	672.34	685.71	667.23	682.41
2015	665.91	689.50	683.10	696.98	694.88	692.24	698.35	714.47	695.95	709.58	690.54	684.00	693.94
2016	687.57	669.34	675.62	707.29	697.06	701.83	723.54	711.22	725.56	731.47	705.03	722.31	704.84
2017	719.85	699.40	690.64	717.14	690.04	686.83	708.19	690.64	705.94	705.83	704.30	712.21	701.96
Financial Activities													
2013	1,009.39	1,024.83	1,038.73	1,036.70	1,007.34	1,031.36	1,020.75	1,003.07	1,011.30	974.02	977.41	1,021.50	1,013.04
2014	972.62	983.20	996.18	963.60	951.86	1,006.93	963.68	975.64	977.17	968.31	1,013.61	981.33	980.96
2015	974.86	1,027.94	1,029.50	1,021.41	1,038.24	1,032.16	1,033.29	1,094.84	1,061.20	1,055.05	1,098.77	1,053.16	1,043.11
2016	1,045.84	1,049.91	1,035.84	1,041.71	1,072.40	1,017.62	1,045.92	1,036.84	1,098.43	1,142.96	1,116.02	1,107.26	1,066.61
2017	1,135.23	1,118.82	1,092.14	1,133.06	1,107.19	1,123.95	1,162.70	1,118.62	1,143.42	1,163.94	1,133.39	1,144.18	1,130.23
Professional and Business Services													
2013	1,259.85	1,272.68	1,282.20	1,274.24	1,260.12	1,301.40	1,241.97	1,236.74	1,288.55	1,220.95	1,238.19	1,308.47	1,265.06
2014	1,251.47	1,296.27	1,296.61	1,251.59	1,243.03	1,277.08	1,223.92	1,240.01	1,224.86	1,252.08	1,317.50	1,261.50	1,261.01
2015	1,280.92	1,341.54	1,337.97	1,295.30	1,294.93	1,275.26	1,283.22	1,347.35	1,299.30	1,319.80	1,378.04	1,324.15	1,316.51
2016	1,318.44	1,331.63	1,343.66	1,359.84	1,414.55	1,353.00	1,355.57	1,355.75	1,361.63	1,417.22	1,367.34	1,394.63	1,366.50
2017	1,449.57	1,413.75	1,399.41	1,451.60	1,386.62	1,388.77	1,426.90	1,397.26	1,423.90	1,441.54	1,392.26	1,413.38	1,417.14
Education and Health Services													
2013	806.81	810.56	832.66	814.96	829.53	842.00	832.92	831.14	849.43	823.03	828.78	849.77	829.94
2014	824.45	837.78	826.14	828.67	824.20	839.74	833.11	835.30	852.01	837.50	849.39	862.39	836.81
2015	847.13	865.69	871.22	872.10	879.62	884.07	867.85	896.31	896.72	893.17	902.20	907.88	883.23
2016	889.22	895.62	904.44	889.01	913.30	903.76	910.33	908.10	919.90	936.12	930.86	930.18	911.92
2017	953.58	942.82	933.22	945.25	932.25	919.34	945.20	914.49	930.22	946.62	929.38	942.82	935.64
Leisure and Hospitality													
2013	345.27	350.95	346.68	349.80	346.61	346.34	340.16	338.14	336.69	336.18	338.52	342.40	342.61
2014	333.80	340.43	347.42	352.66	350.54	354.51	345.40	343.90	347.95	348.21	350.07	344.47	346.37
2015	337.00	341.38	350.82	354.84	352.98	346.09	346.52	347.69	342.43	346.35	349.51	345.72	346.36
2016	332.96	342.27	344.21	351.89	359.04	348.74	351.91	347.68	351.38	363.68	362.32	365.23	351.34
2017	356.61	361.56	368.46	372.30	366.23	360.51	372.60	364.91	359.23	366.80	365.97	369.59	364.88
Other Services													
2013	798.50	822.72	829.40	825.35	823.28	827.71	808.38	779.31	843.01	808.67	820.80	849.52	818.87
2014	820.76	828.16	841.43	835.27	834.89	844.87	812.73	793.16	808.86	821.07	834.89	847.91	827.20
2015	849.85	835.60	852.15	838.50	841.20	847.26	844.31	849.20	847.15	854.50	890.52	886.79	853.42
2016	901.88	886.93	898.92	886.14	909.36	896.18	861.35	862.73	884.53	914.10	875.20	886.14	887.44
2017	911.17	888.08	883.39	925.15	889.28	880.00	906.93	880.94	869.47	918.99	880.22	892.78	893.55

WASHINGTON
At a Glance

Population:
  2010 census: 6,724,540
  2017 estimate: 7,405,743

Percent change in population:
  2010–2017: 10.1%

Percent change in total nonfarm employment:
  2007–2017: 12.0%

Industry with the largest growth in employment, 2007–2017 (thousands):
  Education and health services, 94.8

Industry with the largest decline or smallest growth in employment, 2007–2017 (thousands):
  Manufacturing, -9.4

Civilian labor force:
  2010: 3,511,326
  2017: 3,724,722

Unemployment rate and rank among states (highest to lowest):
  2010: 10.0%, 17th
  2017: 4.8%, 13th

Over-the-year change in unemployment rates:
  2015–2016: -0.4%
  2016–2017: -0.5%

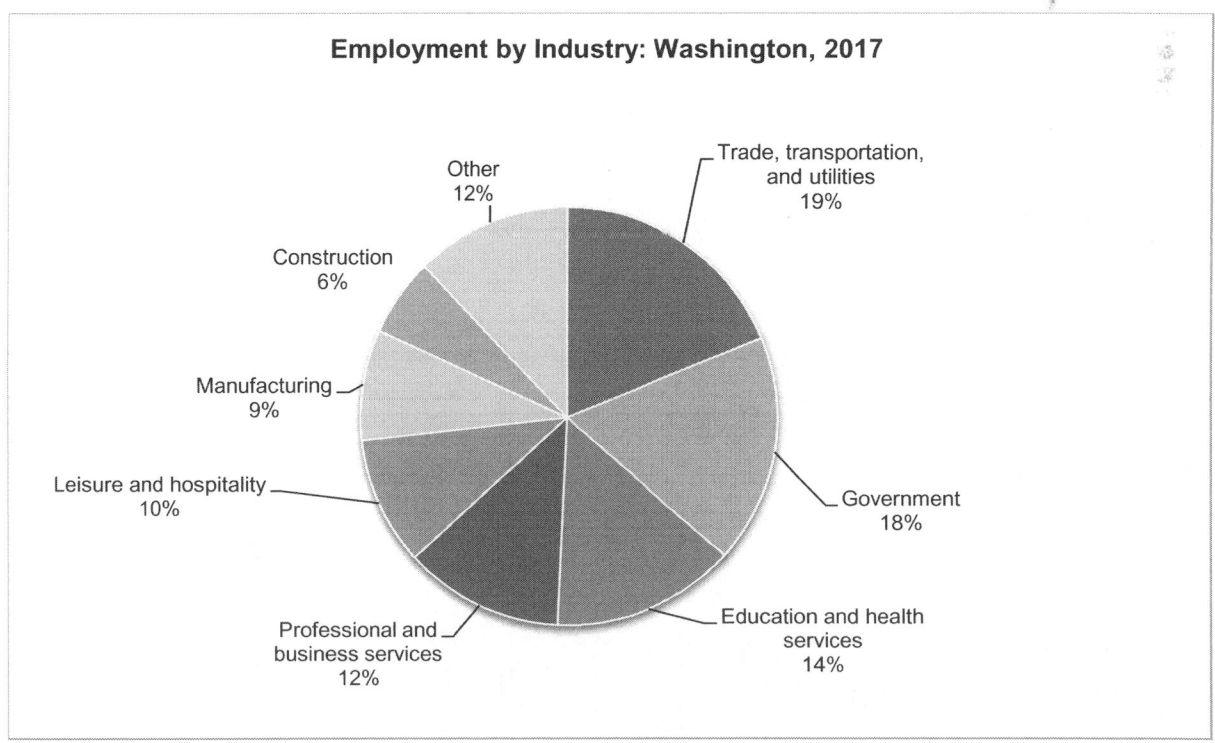

Employment by Industry: Washington, 2017

- Other 12%
- Trade, transportation, and utilities 19%
- Construction 6%
- Manufacturing 9%
- Leisure and hospitality 10%
- Professional and business services 12%
- Education and health services 14%
- Government 18%

1. Employment by Industry: Washington, Selected Years, 2007–2017

(Numbers in thousands, not seasonally adjusted)

Industry and year	January	February	March	April	May	June	July	August	September	October	November	December	Annual average
Total Nonfarm													
2007	2,878.3	2,908.6	2,926.4	2,944.5	2,973.8	3,000.4	2,978.7	2,979.4	2,995.6	3,005.8	3,019.0	3,009.7	2,968.4
2008	2,951.3	2,971.0	2,983.5	2,994.4	3,015.6	3,028.4	3,013.6	3,009.2	3,015.1	2,990.4	2,993.1	2,960.3	2,993.8
2009	2,885.9	2,879.6	2,871.3	2,867.5	2,880.7	2,881.0	2,858.2	2,836.7	2,850.6	2,860.1	2,849.4	2,832.3	2,862.8
2010	2,777.4	2,785.1	2,801.9	2,827.4	2,853.6	2,860.0	2,847.7	2,829.1	2,849.5	2,872.4	2,870.3	2,859.1	2,836.1
2011	2,807.5	2,820.5	2,832.4	2,862.7	2,880.5	2,893.4	2,889.3	2,878.0	2,895.8	2,905.6	2,908.3	2,895.6	2,872.5
2012	2,840.1	2,854.8	2,876.7	2,897.8	2,926.5	2,945.9	2,932.2	2,928.2	2,943.6	2,964.7	2,969.4	2,955.1	2,919.6
2013	2,906.8	2,924.4	2,938.9	2,960.6	2,990.0	3,001.5	2,992.8	2,994.4	3,011.7	3,027.0	3,033.4	3,023.8	2,983.8
2014	2,985.7	2,992.6	3,010.5	3,026.7	3,051.7	3,069.5	3,073.9	3,076.1	3,093.9	3,101.4	3,106.7	3,108.2	3,058.1
2015	3,063.0	3,075.4	3,097.6	3,124.1	3,149.8	3,174.2	3,165.3	3,161.4	3,180.8	3,186.4	3,192.4	3,190.0	3,146.7
2016	3,154.5	3,173.2	3,191.6	3,226.0	3,251.0	3,268.1	3,263.2	3,259.6	3,285.1	3,282.3	3,291.4	3,288.0	3,244.5
2017	3,234.5	3,252.1	3,277.5	3,300.1	3,331.3	3,355.8	3,343.3	3,334.2	3,355.1	3,374.0	3,381.2	3,370.8	3,325.8
Total Private													
2007	2,347.6	2,371.0	2,389.6	2,404.8	2,431.8	2,458.9	2,461.2	2,474.9	2,473.8	2,464.6	2,469.6	2,467.2	2,434.6
2008	2,410.0	2,421.3	2,434.3	2,444.5	2,462.8	2,475.2	2,482.6	2,489.7	2,481.3	2,434.5	2,428.9	2,405.0	2,447.5
2009	2,334.2	2,323.3	2,312.7	2,302.5	2,315.8	2,325.5	2,325.7	2,322.7	2,320.3	2,304.1	2,289.7	2,282.4	2,313.2
2010	2,226.0	2,230.0	2,245.2	2,266.2	2,281.2	2,299.5	2,312.0	2,313.7	2,319.2	2,318.3	2,312.0	2,310.6	2,286.2
2011	2,257.9	2,267.4	2,278.9	2,307.1	2,323.4	2,344.0	2,360.2	2,367.3	2,372.4	2,357.6	2,357.3	2,354.3	2,329.0
2012	2,297.6	2,309.1	2,328.1	2,346.8	2,374.1	2,399.3	2,406.2	2,419.4	2,418.3	2,415.1	2,415.7	2,411.3	2,378.4
2013	2,360.9	2,374.4	2,388.1	2,407.4	2,435.5	2,453.6	2,467.5	2,482.9	2,482.9	2,476.7	2,478.9	2,477.4	2,440.5
2014	2,436.3	2,439.9	2,455.2	2,468.4	2,491.7	2,515.4	2,539.0	2,554.4	2,553.1	2,540.3	2,543.7	2,551.8	2,507.4
2015	2,503.3	2,512.0	2,531.0	2,553.7	2,577.6	2,607.6	2,618.8	2,628.3	2,626.5	2,615.9	2,618.4	2,623.3	2,584.7
2016	2,582.4	2,596.7	2,613.4	2,644.2	2,664.7	2,690.5	2,703.2	2,713.5	2,716.8	2,695.8	2,700.9	2,704.3	2,668.9
2017	2,652.2	2,665.1	2,687.3	2,706.3	2,733.4	2,764.6	2,768.4	2,778.1	2,778.5	2,777.1	2,780.9	2,778.5	2,739.2
Goods Producing													
2007	484.5	490.4	494.5	499.8	508.0	518.5	522.5	526.8	525.9	521.8	515.4	508.1	509.7
2008	496.9	498.7	500.4	500.6	505.4	509.3	513.6	515.6	511.2	479.7	487.0	471.7	499.2
2009	451.0	444.4	436.5	430.8	431.7	433.8	434.9	434.5	432.0	424.8	412.8	404.5	431.0
2010	393.4	392.5	394.1	397.4	401.4	406.8	414.4	416.7	417.9	415.2	406.9	400.3	404.8
2011	390.5	393.3	396.0	401.7	406.8	413.7	421.7	426.3	428.5	424.5	417.9	412.0	411.1
2012	402.0	403.8	409.2	413.5	420.1	429.2	435.9	441.8	441.5	440.7	435.6	430.2	425.3
2013	422.4	425.9	429.2	431.9	438.6	445.5	452.0	457.0	456.9	453.1	447.4	441.6	441.8
2014	436.4	436.5	441.0	442.9	448.7	456.3	465.5	469.8	469.5	466.2	461.9	461.1	454.7
2015	455.9	456.9	461.3	464.6	469.3	476.9	483.2	483.9	482.2	478.7	473.3	471.2	471.5
2016	466.7	470.2	472.7	478.3	482.5	487.4	494.0	494.7	494.0	488.1	484.0	481.1	482.8
2017	473.2	476.1	481.0	484.6	489.1	497.5	498.3	499.5	499.5	497.8	491.7	489.7	489.8
Service-Providing													
2007	2,393.8	2,418.2	2,431.9	2,444.7	2,465.8	2,481.9	2,456.2	2,452.6	2,469.7	2,484.0	2,503.6	2,501.6	2,458.7
2008	2,454.4	2,472.3	2,483.1	2,493.8	2,510.2	2,519.1	2,500.0	2,493.6	2,503.9	2,510.7	2,506.1	2,488.6	2,494.7
2009	2,434.9	2,435.2	2,434.8	2,436.7	2,449.0	2,447.2	2,423.3	2,402.2	2,418.6	2,435.3	2,436.6	2,427.8	2,431.8
2010	2,384.0	2,392.6	2,407.8	2,430.0	2,452.2	2,453.2	2,433.3	2,412.4	2,431.6	2,457.2	2,463.4	2,458.8	2,431.4
2011	2,417.0	2,427.2	2,436.4	2,461.0	2,473.7	2,479.7	2,467.6	2,451.7	2,467.3	2,481.1	2,490.4	2,483.6	2,461.4
2012	2,438.1	2,451.0	2,467.5	2,484.3	2,506.4	2,516.7	2,496.3	2,486.4	2,502.1	2,524.0	2,533.8	2,524.9	2,494.3
2013	2,484.4	2,498.5	2,509.7	2,528.7	2,551.4	2,556.0	2,540.8	2,537.4	2,554.8	2,573.9	2,586.0	2,582.2	2,542.0
2014	2,549.3	2,556.1	2,569.5	2,583.8	2,603.0	2,613.2	2,608.4	2,606.3	2,624.4	2,635.2	2,644.8	2,647.1	2,603.4
2015	2,607.1	2,618.5	2,636.3	2,659.5	2,680.5	2,697.3	2,682.1	2,677.5	2,698.6	2,707.7	2,719.1	2,718.8	2,675.3
2016	2,687.8	2,703.0	2,718.9	2,747.7	2,768.5	2,780.7	2,769.2	2,764.9	2,791.1	2,794.2	2,807.4	2,806.9	2,761.7
2017	2,761.3	2,776.0	2,796.5	2,815.5	2,842.2	2,858.3	2,845.0	2,834.7	2,855.6	2,876.2	2,889.5	2,881.1	2,836.0
Mining and Logging													
2007	8.4	7.9	7.6	7.9	8.2	8.5	8.5	8.4	8.3	8.3	8.0	7.9	8.2
2008	7.4	7.4	7.3	7.3	7.5	7.6	7.9	7.9	7.8	7.8	7.4	7.2	7.5
2009	6.5	6.4	5.8	5.6	5.8	6.2	6.3	6.3	6.3	6.1	5.7	5.5	6.0
2010	5.4	5.5	5.5	5.6	5.9	6.1	6.2	6.3	6.3	6.2	5.9	5.7	5.9
2011	5.6	5.7	5.7	5.7	5.8	6.1	6.2	6.3	6.2	6.3	6.1	6.0	6.0
2012	5.7	5.6	5.6	5.6	5.7	6.0	6.1	6.2	6.2	6.2	6.0	5.9	5.9
2013	5.7	5.8	5.8	5.8	6.0	6.2	6.3	6.4	6.4	6.4	6.3	6.2	6.1
2014	6.0	6.1	6.1	5.9	6.1	6.2	6.4	6.5	6.4	6.4	6.3	6.3	6.2
2015	6.3	6.3	6.2	6.2	6.3	6.4	6.5	6.4	6.3	6.5	6.3	6.3	6.3
2016	6.1	6.2	6.0	6.1	6.3	6.4	6.5	6.5	6.5	6.4	6.2	6.1	6.3
2017	5.9	6.0	5.9	6.0	6.2	6.4	6.3	6.3	6.3	6.2	6.1	6.0	6.1

1. Employment by Industry: Washington, Selected Years, 2007–2017—*Continued*

(Numbers in thousands, not seasonally adjusted)

Industry and year	January	February	March	April	May	June	July	August	September	October	November	December	Annual average
Construction													
2007	190.3	194.4	199.6	203.5	210.2	215.3	216.5	220.4	218.0	214.6	210.3	205.2	208.2
2008	196.6	197.3	200.3	201.6	204.6	206.9	209.1	210.1	206.5	200.9	190.6	181.1	200.5
2009	168.4	163.7	162.4	159.9	161.8	162.8	162.6	162.3	160.6	156.7	148.9	143.3	159.5
2010	134.7	133.9	135.5	137.2	140.0	142.2	146.8	148.6	147.7	146.2	140.4	135.2	140.7
2011	127.2	127.8	129.3	132.8	136.3	139.3	142.5	144.5	144.5	142.0	137.2	133.4	136.4
2012	125.5	126.9	130.2	133.7	137.6	141.6	144.7	148.1	147.4	147.5	144.2	141.5	139.1
2013	135.2	137.4	139.9	143.0	147.6	150.8	155.2	159.0	158.7	157.1	154.1	149.8	149.0
2014	146.8	146.3	150.4	151.6	155.7	160.0	165.5	169.2	169.5	168.3	166.4	165.8	159.6
2015	162.3	163.3	166.2	169.9	173.5	176.4	179.8	180.3	179.1	178.2	175.3	174.3	173.2
2016	171.7	174.6	177.6	182.3	185.4	188.5	193.0	195.1	195.4	193.1	191.8	190.4	186.6
2017	184.8	187.7	192.2	195.1	199.4	204.2	205.2	207.3	207.7	207.8	204.0	201.7	199.8
Manufacturing													
2007	285.8	288.1	287.3	288.4	289.6	294.7	297.5	298.0	299.6	298.9	297.1	295.0	293.3
2008	292.9	294.0	292.8	291.7	293.3	294.8	296.6	297.6	296.9	271.0	289.0	283.4	291.2
2009	276.1	274.3	268.3	265.3	264.1	264.8	266.0	265.9	265.1	262.0	258.2	255.7	265.5
2010	253.3	253.1	253.1	254.6	255.5	258.5	261.4	261.8	263.9	262.8	260.6	259.4	258.2
2011	257.7	259.8	261.0	263.2	264.7	268.3	273.0	275.5	277.8	276.2	274.6	272.6	268.7
2012	270.8	271.3	273.4	274.2	276.8	281.6	285.1	287.5	287.9	287.0	285.4	282.8	280.3
2013	281.5	282.7	283.5	283.1	285.0	288.5	290.5	291.6	291.8	289.6	287.0	285.6	286.7
2014	283.6	284.1	284.5	285.4	286.9	290.1	293.6	294.1	293.6	291.5	289.2	289.0	288.8
2015	287.3	287.3	288.9	288.5	289.5	294.1	296.9	297.2	296.8	294.0	291.7	290.6	291.9
2016	288.9	289.4	289.1	289.9	290.8	292.5	294.5	293.1	292.1	288.6	286.0	284.6	290.0
2017	282.5	282.4	282.9	283.5	283.5	286.9	286.8	285.9	285.5	283.8	281.6	282.0	283.9
Trade, Transportation, and Utilities													
2007	540.1	538.7	541.5	543.6	548.5	553.7	555.3	557.0	555.8	557.9	570.0	573.1	552.9
2008	552.0	547.8	549.3	549.1	552.1	554.1	556.6	557.0	553.8	553.2	554.6	555.3	552.9
2009	530.7	522.6	518.4	515.2	519.0	520.3	522.3	521.3	520.9	520.3	525.1	527.4	522.0
2010	507.2	503.5	505.8	510.0	513.5	517.2	519.0	518.7	518.1	522.2	529.4	533.3	516.5
2011	512.2	509.5	511.8	515.4	519.9	524.4	529.9	530.8	529.9	530.6	539.4	542.1	524.7
2012	521.6	518.5	521.3	523.5	530.8	537.2	540.3	541.9	540.8	543.3	552.8	554.6	535.6
2013	535.1	533.2	534.0	537.3	545.1	549.6	554.0	557.2	556.1	560.3	570.7	574.2	550.6
2014	555.1	551.4	552.5	555.4	561.7	568.0	573.6	577.6	577.1	578.2	588.6	593.6	569.4
2015	572.8	570.4	574.2	577.1	583.1	590.0	591.9	595.1	594.1	594.1	604.2	607.9	587.9
2016	587.4	585.7	589.2	594.9	600.9	609.3	612.8	614.7	612.9	614.3	625.1	629.0	606.4
2017	609.9	606.4	610.1	614.2	620.9	628.2	633.1	634.6	634.2	636.4	647.4	646.6	626.8
Wholesale Trade													
2007	125.9	126.6	127.3	128.0	128.9	130.3	130.7	130.6	130.2	131.2	131.4	130.9	129.3
2008	129.0	129.6	130.0	130.1	130.7	130.7	131.4	130.8	130.7	131.3	129.4	127.7	130.1
2009	125.6	124.7	123.8	122.7	122.7	122.8	122.9	121.9	121.6	122.5	121.2	120.1	122.7
2010	110.0	110.4	110.9	120.3	120.6	120.0	121.0	120.6	120.4	121.4	121.3	120.1	120.2
2011	119.0	119.4	120.1	120.7	121.9	122.3	123.1	122.8	122.6	123.3	123.1	122.2	121.7
2012	121.0	121.4	122.1	122.8	123.9	124.9	125.1	125.6	125.0	125.8	125.5	124.9	124.0
2013	123.4	124.6	125.0	125.6	126.3	127.2	128.1	128.2	128.2	129.0	128.9	128.0	126.9
2014	127.1	127.5	127.7	128.0	128.9	129.9	131.8	131.8	131.9	131.8	131.6	131.2	129.9
2015	129.6	130.1	130.6	131.2	131.8	133.1	133.1	133.3	133.0	132.7	132.7	132.6	132.0
2016	130.5	131.0	131.4	132.4	132.7	133.5	133.9	134.0	133.8	133.5	133.5	133.4	132.8
2017	131.8	132.4	132.8	133.6	134.3	135.3	135.8	135.2	135.6	135.8	136.2	135.4	134.5
Retail Trade													
2007	321.2	318.9	320.3	321.1	324.4	326.8	328.8	329.7	328.3	329.6	341.9	344.4	328.0
2008	328.7	323.5	324.8	324.3	325.7	327.2	328.8	329.7	326.6	326.3	330.6	332.2	327.4
2009	312.3	307.1	305.0	303.4	306.6	307.7	309.0	309.6	308.7	308.5	315.1	317.6	309.2
2010	303.0	299.4	300.7	302.8	305.4	308.0	308.7	309.2	308.0	311.0	319.0	322.7	308.2
2011	306.3	303.3	303.8	306.0	308.9	312.1	314.1	315.6	314.0	316.3	325.2	327.4	312.8
2012	311.3	307.6	309.2	310.5	315.1	319.1	321.8	322.6	321.7	324.2	334.0	335.3	319.4
2013	320.2	317.0	317.9	320.5	326.2	329.4	332.2	334.4	332.8	336.1	346.0	349.3	330.2
2014	333.1	329.6	330.7	332.4	336.5	340.8	344.1	347.0	345.8	347.5	357.8	360.8	342.2
2015	344.4	342.0	344.9	347.7	351.9	355.7	357.2	360.1	359.2	359.2	368.0	369.4	355.0
2016	355.3	353.7	356.3	360.6	365.2	371.0	373.6	375.0	372.8	375.5	385.0	386.0	369.2
2017	373.0	369.5	372.2	375.2	380.1	385.2	390.0	391.8	390.8	391.3	400.7	399.1	384.9

1. Employment by Industry: Washington, Selected Years, 2007–2017—*Continued*

(Numbers in thousands, not seasonally adjusted)

Industry and year	January	February	March	April	May	June	July	August	September	October	November	December	Annual average
Transportation and Utilities													
2007	93.0	93.2	93.9	94.5	95.2	96.6	95.8	96.7	97.3	97.1	96.7	97.8	95.7
2008	94.3	94.7	94.5	94.7	95.7	96.2	96.4	96.5	96.5	95.6	94.6	95.4	95.4
2009	92.8	90.8	89.6	89.1	89.7	89.8	90.4	89.8	90.6	89.3	88.8	89.7	90.0
2010	86.2	85.7	86.2	86.9	87.5	88.4	89.3	88.9	89.7	89.8	89.1	90.5	88.2
2011	86.9	86.8	87.9	88.7	89.1	90.0	92.7	92.4	93.3	91.0	91.1	92.5	90.2
2012	89.3	89.5	90.0	90.2	91.8	93.2	93.4	93.7	94.1	93.3	93.3	94.4	92.2
2013	91.5	91.6	91.1	91.2	92.6	93.0	93.7	94.6	95.1	95.2	95.8	96.9	93.5
2014	94.9	94.3	94.1	95.0	96.3	97.3	97.7	98.8	99.4	98.9	99.2	101.6	97.3
2015	98.8	98.3	98.7	98.2	99.4	101.2	101.6	101.7	101.9	102.2	103.5	105.9	101.0
2016	101.6	101.0	101.5	101.9	103.0	104.8	105.3	105.7	106.3	105.3	106.6	109.6	104.4
2017	105.1	104.5	105.1	105.4	106.5	107.7	107.3	107.6	107.8	109.3	110.5	112.1	107.4
Information													
2007	100.4	101.3	101.0	101.5	102.4	103.5	103.7	104.0	103.3	102.0	103.1	103.3	102.5
2008	102.7	103.8	104.0	104.2	104.9	106.0	107.2	107.9	106.8	105.9	107.0	107.0	105.6
2009	104.9	105.4	105.0	103.7	104.2	104.5	104.8	104.2	102.9	102.2	102.5	102.4	103.9
2010	102.2	102.4	102.3	101.7	102.5	103.6	103.8	104.2	103.7	102.8	103.3	103.8	103.0
2011	102.8	103.4	103.1	103.3	103.6	104.7	105.7	106.0	104.9	104.0	104.5	104.3	104.2
2012	104.0	104.4	104.0	103.8	104.6	105.9	106.0	106.0	104.5	103.9	104.5	105.0	104.7
2013	104.1	104.8	104.5	104.8	105.7	106.5	107.9	108.4	107.2	106.5	107.3	107.4	106.3
2014	107.0	107.2	107.3	107.8	108.8	110.7	112.4	113.2	112.2	110.4	110.8	110.6	109.9
2015	110.1	111.1	111.3	111.4	112.6	114.5	116.5	117.6	116.9	116.2	117.2	117.6	114.4
2016	117.0	118.0	118.4	119.2	120.0	122.7	124.0	124.8	124.2	122.9	123.7	123.9	121.6
2017	123.2	123.7	124.2	123.9	125.0	127.4	128.2	129.2	128.5	127.8	128.5	129.3	126.6
Financial Activities													
2007	156.4	156.9	157.5	158.0	158.3	159.3	159.2	159.1	157.2	156.5	156.7	156.5	157.6
2008	155.0	155.2	155.1	154.8	155.7	155.4	154.6	154.7	153.1	151.5	150.5	149.6	153.8
2009	146.8	146.4	144.8	144.5	144.5	145.1	144.1	143.5	142.4	140.8	139.8	139.6	143.5
2010	137.4	137.0	137.2	137.7	137.6	138.2	139.1	139.2	138.7	138.4	138.0	138.5	138.1
2011	136.8	136.9	137.0	137.7	137.6	138.7	139.2	139.4	139.2	138.1	138.4	138.5	138.1
2012	137.0	137.7	138.3	139.0	140.1	140.9	142.2	142.1	141.1	140.9	141.0	141.3	140.1
2013	140.8	141.2	141.9	142.4	143.5	144.4	145.7	145.8	144.9	144.6	144.5	145.0	143.7
2014	143.5	143.7	144.1	144.6	144.3	145.4	146.7	147.2	146.2	145.8	145.7	146.3	145.3
2015	145.4	145.8	145.9	146.8	147.6	148.5	149.5	149.7	148.9	147.8	147.7	147.9	147.6
2016	147.4	147.5	148.0	148.8	149.8	150.8	152.7	152.9	152.2	151.0	150.9	151.4	150.3
2017	149.8	150.8	151.4	151.2	152.7	153.9	154.1	155.5	154.9	155.4	156.2	155.9	153.5
Professional and Business Services													
2007	329.7	335.8	340.2	341.0	343.7	347.8	349.1	351.5	351.5	350.0	349.4	350.0	345.0
2008	340.8	344.4	347.3	351.4	352.7	354.2	355.7	355.9	354.3	350.6	343.0	338.1	349.0
2009	330.3	327.8	326.1	323.8	323.1	325.5	325.5	324.4	324.4	324.4	322.0	322.0	324.9
2010	313.6	315.7	319.6	323.8	324.4	327.8	332.7	331.4	333.0	335.0	333.3	334.0	327.0
2011	326.7	329.9	332.3	339.4	339.3	341.7	346.1	345.7	347.5	345.3	344.8	344.0	340.2
2012	335.9	339.2	341.9	347.2	349.9	354.1	353.6	357.4	357.9	359.4	358.4	356.2	350.9
2013	349.7	352.8	355.2	360.0	361.4	363.9	365.1	369.4	370.5	370.0	367.6	366.6	362.7
2014	360.3	361.5	364.7	366.8	368.2	371.9	378.2	381.3	382.3	382.7	381.5	382.2	373.5
2015	373.7	375.6	379.7	386.0	387.5	392.3	394.7	397.7	399.0	397.2	396.6	397.2	389.8
2016	389.7	391.9	395.3	400.8	402.0	406.1	407.9	411.1	413.6	409.2	408.2	406.7	403.5
2017	399.8	402.8	406.8	410.1	413.8	417.7	419.5	421.7	422.0	424.7	424.6	421.5	415.4
Education and Health Services													
2007	371.5	377.4	379.7	380.4	382.9	379.5	373.3	374.7	382.1	388.8	391.0	390.4	381.0
2008	385.8	391.3	392.4	394.3	396.5	393.3	389.2	391.1	397.9	404.6	405.9	405.0	395.6
2009	403.2	408.1	410.6	411.3	413.6	410.4	405.2	405.7	412.9	419.9	421.9	422.4	412.1
2010	418.2	423.1	425.1	426.6	427.5	424.1	417.9	417.0	423.8	431.0	432.2	430.8	424.8
2011	427.7	431.4	432.9	433.1	433.2	430.3	425.3	424.5	430.3	435.2	436.7	436.2	431.4
2012	429.3	434.2	436.5	436.1	437.3	433.5	426.7	426.6	431.8	437.0	438.6	437.5	433.8
2013	431.8	437.5	438.4	438.6	439.2	433.6	429.4	428.8	435.5	442.3	444.0	443.8	436.9
2014	440.7	446.1	445.8	445.6	446.6	441.7	438.3	437.3	442.9	446.4	447.8	448.7	444.0
2015	442.9	447.5	448.2	449.9	449.7	447.6	441.5	440.7	447.0	454.1	455.9	456.6	448.5
2016	455.6	461.3	462.7	465.3	465.7	462.4	455.6	457.2	464.7	468.6	471.0	472.0	463.5
2017	465.8	472.1	474.1	474.5	476.0	473.6	468.2	471.1	478.3	483.0	487.1	486.3	475.8

1. Employment by Industry: Washington, Selected Years, 2007–2017—*Continued*

(Numbers in thousands, not seasonally adjusted)

Industry and year	January	February	March	April	May	June	July	August	September	October	November	December	Annual average
Leisure and Hospitality													
2007	263.0	266.8	270.6	276.0	282.6	289.9	291.6	294.9	292.1	282.2	278.4	280.2	280.7
2008	271.9	274.1	278.6	282.8	287.3	293.8	295.7	297.6	295.3	281.5	274.1	272.4	283.8
2009	261.8	262.6	264.6	266.7	272.8	278.5	281.2	281.8	278.9	266.5	261.1	259.8	269.7
2010	251.4	252.8	257.5	264.7	269.3	275.3	277.6	279.0	277.8	267.6	262.7	263.8	266.6
2011	256.2	257.1	259.6	268.8	274.3	280.4	281.7	284.1	282.8	270.9	267.2	268.4	271.0
2012	260.5	263.0	267.4	273.3	280.1	286.3	288.5	290.9	289.0	278.6	274.1	276.1	277.3
2013	269.0	270.4	275.4	282.2	290.6	298.0	300.0	302.9	299.7	288.1	285.4	287.3	287.4
2014	282.4	282.3	287.4	292.8	299.8	306.5	308.1	311.8	308.3	296.7	293.6	295.1	297.1
2015	290.2	292.0	296.5	303.3	312.2	321.3	324.2	326.5	322.9	313.0	308.9	310.3	310.1
2016	304.4	307.3	311.4	319.6	325.4	332.3	336.7	338.3	336.9	324.1	320.3	322.3	323.3
2017	314.1	315.9	321.3	329.0	335.7	344.3	344.6	344.9	340.9	332.0	324.7	329.5	331.4
Other Services													
2007	102.0	103.7	104.6	104.5	105.4	106.7	106.5	106.9	105.9	105.4	105.6	105.6	105.2
2008	104.9	106.0	107.2	107.3	108.2	109.1	110.0	109.9	108.9	107.5	106.8	105.9	107.6
2009	105.5	106.0	106.7	106.5	106.9	107.4	107.7	107.3	105.9	105.2	104.5	104.3	106.2
2010	102.6	103.0	103.6	104.3	105.0	106.5	107.5	107.5	106.2	106.1	106.2	106.1	105.4
2011	105.0	105.9	106.2	107.7	108.7	110.1	110.6	110.5	109.3	109.0	108.4	108.8	108.4
2012	107.3	108.3	109.5	110.4	111.2	112.2	113.0	112.7	111.7	111.3	110.7	110.4	110.7
2013	108.0	108.6	109.5	110.2	111.4	112.1	113.4	113.4	112.1	111.8	112.0	111.5	111.2
2014	110.9	111.2	112.4	112.5	113.6	114.9	116.2	116.2	114.6	113.9	113.8	114.2	113.7
2015	112.3	112.7	113.9	114.6	115.6	116.5	117.3	117.1	115.5	114.8	114.6	114.6	115.0
2016	114.2	114.8	115.7	117.3	118.4	119.5	119.5	119.8	118.3	117.6	117.7	117.9	117.6
2017	116.4	117.3	118.4	118.8	120.2	122.0	121.7	121.6	120.2	120.0	120.7	119.7	119.8
Government													
2007	530.7	537.6	536.8	539.7	542.0	541.5	517.5	504.5	521.8	541.2	549.4	542.5	533.8
2008	541.3	549.7	549.2	549.9	552.8	553.2	531.0	519.5	533.8	555.9	564.2	555.3	546.3
2009	551.7	556.3	558.6	565.0	564.9	555.5	532.5	514.0	530.3	556.0	559.7	549.9	549.5
2010	551.4	555.1	556.7	561.2	572.4	560.5	535.7	515.4	530.3	554.1	558.3	548.5	550.0
2011	549.6	553.1	553.5	555.6	557.1	549.4	529.1	510.7	523.4	548.0	551.0	541.3	543.5
2012	542.5	545.7	548.6	551.0	552.4	546.6	526.0	508.8	525.3	549.6	553.7	543.8	541.2
2013	545.9	550.0	550.8	553.2	554.5	547.9	525.3	511.5	528.8	550.3	554.5	546.4	543.3
2014	549.4	552.7	555.3	558.3	560.0	554.1	534.9	521.7	540.8	561.1	563.0	556.4	550.6
2015	559.7	563.4	566.6	570.4	572.2	566.6	546.5	533.1	554.3	570.5	574.0	566.7	562.0
2016	572.1	576.5	578.2	581.8	586.3	577.6	560.0	546.1	568.3	586.5	590.5	583.7	575.6
2017	582.3	587.0	590.2	593.8	597.9	591.2	574.9	556.1	576.6	596.9	600.3	592.3	586.6

2. Average Weekly Hours by Selected Industry: Washington, 2013–2017

(Not seasonally adjusted)

Industry and year	January	February	March	April	May	June	July	August	September	October	November	December	Annual average
Total Private													
2013	33.6	34.2	34.1	34.1	34.0	35.2	34.0	34.4	35.1	34.0	34.0	34.7	34.3
2014	33.4	34.7	34.8	33.9	34.0	34.9	34.0	34.3	34.1	33.9	34.9	33.9	34.2
2015	33.6	34.7	34.7	34.0	34.0	34.2	34.3	35.3	34.3	34.3	35.1	34.0	34.4
2016	34.0	34.2	34.1	34.4	35.2	34.5	34.6	34.9	34.6	35.4	34.5	34.4	34.6
2017	34.9	34.2	34.3	35.4	34.5	34.6	35.5	34.8	34.6	35.5	34.5	34.6	34.8
Goods-Producing													
2013	39.6	39.9	40.1	40.0	39.8	40.2	39.5	40.2	40.0	39.9	39.9	39.8	39.9
2014	39.2	39.5	39.7	39.4	39.5	39.9	39.3	39.8	40.0	40.1	40.3	39.9	39.7
2015	39.5	39.8	39.8	39.6	39.8	40.1	39.9	40.3	39.2	40.1	39.9	39.5	39.8
2016	39.2	39.2	39.4	39.5	39.9	39.5	39.5	39.6	39.5	39.8	39.5	39.2	39.5
2017	38.7	38.5	39.1	39.5	39.5	39.7	39.6	39.9	39.7	40.4	39.6	39.8	39.5
Construction													
2013	34.8	35.7	36.3	36.4	36.4	37.4	36.4	38.0	37.7	37.2	36.7	36.2	36.6
2014	36.3	36.1	36.6	36.9	37.0	37.9	37.8	38.3	38.5	38.1	38.2	37.8	37.5
2015	37.8	38.1	37.9	37.9	38.1	38.5	38.3	38.8	36.3	37.9	37.5	36.7	37.8
2016	36.6	36.9	37.2	37.5	38.2	37.6	37.6	38.1	37.7	37.4	37.4	36.9	37.4
2017	36.0	35.7	36.8	37.4	37.8	38.3	38.4	38.5	38.0	38.8	37.5	37.5	37.6
Manufacturing													
2013	41.2	41.3	41.5	41.3	41.0	41.2	40.6	41.0	40.9	41.1	41.3	41.4	41.1
2014	40.4	40.8	40.9	40.4	40.5	40.7	40.0	40.5	40.8	41.1	41.4	41.0	40.7
2015	40.4	40.7	40.8	40.6	40.7	41.0	40.8	41.1	40.7	41.2	41.1	40.9	40.8
2016	40.5	40.3	40.4	40.4	40.6	40.3	40.3	40.2	40.3	41.0	40.6	40.4	40.4
2017	40.1	39.9	40.2	40.5	40.4	40.4	40.3	40.7	40.7	41.3	40.8	41.1	40.5
Trade, Transportation, and Utilities													
2013	34.0	34.7	34.6	34.3	34.6	35.7	34.9	35.1	35.6	34.4	34.3	34.9	34.8
2014	33.5	35.0	35.1	34.5	34.7	35.5	34.9	35.1	35.0	34.4	35.6	34.8	34.8
2015	34.2	35.3	35.3	34.7	35.2	35.2	35.2	36.4	35.9	35.1	36.0	35.0	35.3
2016	34.9	35.4	35.2	35.9	36.6	35.6	35.8	35.9	35.7	36.3	35.3	35.9	35.7
2017	35.5	35.2	35.0	36.0	35.5	35.6	36.3	35.6	35.6	36.0	35.2	35.3	35.6
Information													
2013	37.9	38.3	38.2	38.4	38.3	40.9	37.9	37.6	40.7	39.2	39.2	42.1	39.1
2014	38.8	42.0	41.6	38.6	38.4	41.6	38.4	38.3	39.4	38.4	41.6	38.4	39.6
2015	38.1	41.3	41.3	38.3	38.2	38.2	38.2	41.0	37.9	37.9	41.2	37.7	39.1
2016	38.1	38.0	38.0	38.2	41.0	38.0	38.6	37.9	37.8	41.0	38.2	37.3	38.5
2017	41.2	37.7	37.7	40.8	37.9	38.1	41.4	37.9	37.9	41.4	37.8	38.6	39.0
Financial Activities													
2013	34.8	35.6	35.1	35.0	34.6	36.2	34.5	34.8	35.8	34.2	34.5	35.7	35.1
2014	34.6	36.3	36.2	35.0	35.1	35.9	34.4	34.8	34.8	34.7	36.0	34.9	35.2
2015	35.0	36.6	36.6	35.3	35.1	35.2	35.0	36.7	35.1	35.4	37.1	35.7	35.7
2016	35.7	35.9	35.7	36.0	37.1	36.0	35.4	35.8	35.7	37.0	35.7	35.3	35.9
2017	36.8	35.7	35.4	37.1	35.4	35.8	36.6	35.3	35.7	36.7	35.4	35.3	35.9
Professional and Business Services													
2013	35.1	35.8	35.6	36.0	35.7	37.0	35.3	36.0	36.9	35.6	35.4	36.0	35.9
2014	34.7	36.4	36.6	35.8	35.7	36.7	35.4	35.7	35.7	35.7	36.6	35.3	35.9
2015	35.0	36.4	36.4	35.5	35.3	35.5	35.2	36.5	35.6	35.7	36.5	35.2	35.7
2016	35.4	35.8	35.7	36.0	36.9	35.9	35.8	36.0	35.7	36.6	35.7	35.6	35.9
2017	36.3	35.6	35.8	36.9	35.6	35.7	36.8	35.8	35.8	36.9	36.0	35.7	36.1
Education and Health Services													
2013	31.6	31.8	31.6	31.7	31.6	32.8	31.7	31.8	33.0	31.9	32.1	32.6	32.0
2014	31.7	32.8	32.8	31.8	32.0	32.7	31.7	31.9	32.0	32.0	33.2	32.4	32.3
2015	32.5	33.4	33.1	32.4	32.3	32.5	32.9	33.7	33.1	32.9	33.8	32.5	32.9
2016	33.1	32.6	32.5	32.6	33.4	33.8	34.1	34.6	34.3	34.7	34.0	33.9	33.6
2017	34.9	34.0	33.9	34.7	33.9	34.0	34.9	34.6	34.2	35.1	34.2	34.3	34.4
Leisure and Hospitality													
2013	24.1	25.1	25.0	25.0	25.1	26.3	25.1	26.0	26.2	24.7	24.4	25.4	25.2
2014	24.1	25.3	25.2	24.4	24.2	25.4	25.1	25.7	24.7	23.8	24.7	23.7	24.7
2015	22.8	24.2	24.3	24.0	24.0	24.5	25.0	26.3	24.8	24.6	25.1	24.1	24.5
2016	23.8	24.3	24.2	24.5	25.5	24.7	25.1	25.6	25.1	25.6	24.6	24.2	24.8
2017	25.0	24.6	24.7	26.2	25.1	25.2	26.5	25.8	25.1	25.6	24.8	24.7	25.3
Other Services													
2013	30.0	30.9	30.7	30.5	31.1	32.2	30.8	31.4	32.5	30.7	31.2	32.2	31.2
2014	30.5	31.3	31.7	30.5	30.4	31.3	30.6	30.6	28.2	28.1	29.3	27.6	30.0
2015	28.1	29.8	29.4	28.5	28.6	28.8	29.0	29.7	27.7	27.5	28.8	27.7	28.6
2016	27.9	28.7	28.6	28.8	29.6	28.3	28.7	29.6	28.2	29.2	28.2	28.2	28.7
2017	28.8	28.5	28.4	29.9	28.4	28.4	29.9	29.6	28.6	29.2	28.2	28.8	28.9

3. Average Hourly Earnings by Selected Industry: Washington, 2012–2016

(Dollars, not seasonally adjusted)

Industry and year	January	February	March	April	May	June	July	August	September	October	November	December	Annual average
Total Private													
2013	27.66	27.77	27.76	27.72	27.51	27.66	27.44	27.33	27.80	27.80	27.93	28.00	27.70
2014	28.15	28.25	28.31	28.22	28.14	28.35	28.21	28.19	28.72	28.68	29.12	29.07	28.45
2015	29.50	29.54	29.53	29.38	29.38	29.16	29.13	29.45	29.80	30.00	30.39	30.28	29.63
2016	30.39	30.33	30.31	30.25	30.37	29.98	30.03	29.82	30.44	30.85	30.59	30.65	30.33
2017	31.41	31.15	31.07	31.48	31.04	30.98	31.36	31.07	31.59	31.84	31.71	31.91	31.39
Goods-Producing													
2013	31.58	31.65	31.65	31.66	31.52	31.47	31.38	31.39	31.49	31.72	31.96	32.53	31.67
2014	32.49	32.30	32.70	32.68	32.66	32.69	32.52	32.42	32.53	32.50	32.44	32.66	32.55
2015	32.48	32.61	32.90	32.82	32.80	32.73	32.46	32.58	32.80	32.71	32.80	33.37	32.75
2016	33.06	33.24	33.62	33.58	33.48	33.40	33.36	33.55	33.78	33.69	33.95	34.21	33.58
2017	34.42	34.51	34.75	34.62	34.47	34.62	34.71	34.72	35.18	35.22	35.64	35.80	34.89
Construction													
2013	29.72	30.10	30.17	30.03	30.20	30.11	29.44	29.78	29.50	29.50	30.03	30.09	29.88
2014	30.29	30.42	30.32	30.34	30.60	31.04	30.82	31.11	31.52	31.49	31.60	31.56	30.96
2015	31.32	31.52	31.27	31.41	31.50	31.91	31.60	31.75	31.79	31.55	31.62	32.16	31.62
2016	31.46	31.64	31.99	31.71	31.61	31.74	31.98	32.31	32.56	32.66	32.85	32.79	32.12
2017	32.97	33.17	33.23	32.74	32.70	32.81	32.67	33.06	33.35	33.75	33.89	33.83	33.19
Manufacturing													
2013	32.19	32.19	32.17	32.26	32.04	32.03	32.16	32.08	32.32	32.59	32.74	33.49	32.36
2014	33.40	33.10	33.70	33.67	33.56	33.46	33.32	33.05	33.03	32.97	32.84	33.19	33.27
2015	33.07	33.18	33.71	33.54	33.48	33.17	32.94	33.06	33.30	33.32	33.40	33.83	33.33
2016	33.68	33.93	34.32	34.46	34.39	34.23	34.02	34.17	34.42	34.24	34.52	34.93	34.27
2017	35.15	35.20	35.56	35.63	35.43	35.67	35.88	35.69	36.22	36.09	36.62	36.87	35.84
Trade, Transportation, and Utilities													
2013	22.37	22.55	22.72	22.75	22.56	22.77	22.48	22.37	22.75	22.36	22.32	21.58	22.46
2014	22.72	23.05	23.01	23.10	23.06	23.33	22.99	23.37	23.57	23.52	24.28	23.66	23.32
2015	24.56	24.55	24.50	24.75	24.71	24.69	24.83	25.43	26.31	26.59	26.81	26.36	25.36
2016	26.61	26.28	26.16	26.17	26.08	25.60	25.56	25.16	25.30	25.70	25.17	24.86	25.71
2017	25.91	25.36	25.21	26.02	25.47	25.54	25.99	25.38	25.44	25.63	25.31	25.35	25.55
Information													
2013	52.39	52.50	52.88	52.62	53.12	53.45	52.50	52.61	56.23	54.25	54.04	54.89	53.49
2014	54.64	55.19	55.57	55.46	55.22	55.28	54.61	54.69	59.33	54.28	54.85	54.77	55.33
2015	56.22	55.92	56.27	55.88	56.36	55.97	55.96	57.74	59.72	58.88	60.42	58.73	57.37
2016	59.11	59.24	58.79	58.37	59.88	58.56	58.15	58.81	61.33	61.91	61.09	60.85	59.70
2017	60.62	60.80	61.14	62.89	61.31	60.42	60.14	59.94	63.81	61.84	61.89	61.49	61.36
Financial Activities													
2013	28.70	29.28	29.34	28.77	28.54	28.45	28.88	28.27	28.34	28.54	28.75	28.54	28.70
2014	28.76	28.62	28.90	28.44	28.43	28.64	28.61	28.38	28.60	28.54	29.15	28.54	28.64
2015	29.21	29.15	29.33	29.40	29.82	28.67	29.83	29.37	28.81	29.39	28.97	28.65	29.22
2016	29.62	29.36	29.47	30.18	30.54	30.61	31.12	31.33	32.05	32.68	32.25	32.86	31.02
2017	33.88	32.51	32.40	33.13	32.57	32.63	32.52	32.97	33.18	33.98	34.02	34.14	33.25
Professional and Business Services													
2013	32.42	32.79	32.57	32.48	32.17	32.67	31.87	31.66	32.29	32.48	32.72	32.86	32.41
2014	32.88	32.95	32.70	32.49	32.35	32.56	32.60	32.29	32.51	32.78	33.40	33.23	32.73
2015	33.71	33.92	33.65	33.27	33.38	33.06	32.95	32.83	32.74	33.13	33.69	33.78	33.34
2016	33.84	33.99	33.93	33.50	33.80	33.53	33.61	33.20	33.76	34.54	34.04	34.33	33.84
2017	35.45	35.10	34.80	35.37	34.87	34.80	35.53	34.91	35.24	36.01	35.61	36.05	35.32
Education and Health Services													
2013	25.65	25.41	25.26	25.27	25.06	25.16	25.30	25.50	25.31	25.39	25.74	25.81	25.41
2014	25.25	25.40	25.46	25.58	25.55	25.93	26.56	26.42	26.34	27.12	27.64	28.43	26.31
2015	28.46	28.32	28.13	28.11	28.11	27.81	27.60	27.99	28.26	28.39	28.71	28.72	28.22
2016	28.42	28.46	28.09	28.25	28.06	27.52	27.84	27.44	28.76	28.79	28.79	29.03	28.29
2017	29.03	29.58	29.20	29.18	29.17	28.90	29.29	29.80	29.93	29.81	29.88	30.08	29.49
Leisure and Hospitality													
2013	14.78	14.90	14.85	14.85	14.92	14.92	14.77	14.66	14.94	15.19	15.27	15.54	14.96
2014	15.41	15.58	15.57	15.72	15.44	15.37	15.20	15.27	15.54	15.77	15.73	16.09	15.55
2015	15.95	16.04	16.15	15.98	15.97	15.91	15.80	15.85	16.01	16.12	16.16	16.48	16.03
2016	16.68	16.76	16.74	16.76	16.81	16.84	16.78	16.77	17.00	17.11	17.32	17.63	16.93
2017	17.88	18.10	18.30	18.46	18.50	18.43	18.27	18.32	18.75	18.88	19.01	19.63	18.54
Other Services													
2013	21.70	22.06	21.92	22.08	21.81	21.84	22.59	22.33	22.60	22.56	22.54	23.29	22.28
2014	22.85	21.80	21.71	21.40	21.80	21.50	20.96	21.21	22.50	22.60	23.22	23.67	22.07
2015	23.78	23.42	23.09	23.02	22.81	22.94	23.01	23.45	23.97	24.13	25.35	25.95	23.73
2016	25.95	25.49	25.75	25.95	26.30	26.03	25.98	25.48	25.90	26.42	26.18	26.61	26.00
2017	27.92	27.07	26.70	27.02	26.42	26.00	26.19	25.52	26.84	26.92	26.67	26.82	26.66

4. Average Weekly Earnings by Selected Industry: Washington, 2012–2016

(Dollars, not seasonally adjusted)

Industry and year	January	February	March	April	May	June	July	August	September	October	November	December	Annual average
Total Private													
2013	929.38	949.73	946.62	945.25	935.34	973.63	932.96	940.15	975.78	945.20	949.62	971.60	950.11
2014	940.21	980.28	985.19	956.66	956.76	989.42	959.14	966.92	979.35	972.25	1,016.29	985.47	972.99
2015	991.20	1,025.04	1,024.69	998.92	998.92	997.27	999.16	1,039.59	1,022.14	1,029.00	1,066.69	1,029.52	1,019.27
2016	1,033.26	1,037.29	1,033.57	1,040.60	1,069.02	1,034.31	1,039.04	1,040.72	1,053.22	1,092.09	1,055.36	1,054.36	1,049.42
2017	1,096.21	1,065.33	1,065.70	1,114.39	1,070.88	1,071.91	1,113.28	1,081.24	1,093.01	1,130.32	1,094.00	1,104.09	1,092.37
Goods-Producing													
2013	1,250.57	1,262.84	1,269.17	1,266.40	1,254.50	1,265.09	1,239.51	1,261.88	1,259.60	1,265.63	1,275.20	1,294.69	1,263.63
2014	1,273.61	1,275.85	1,298.19	1,287.59	1,290.07	1,304.33	1,278.04	1,290.32	1,301.20	1,303.25	1,307.33	1,303.13	1,292.24
2015	1,282.96	1,297.88	1,309.42	1,299.67	1,305.44	1,312.47	1,295.15	1,312.97	1,285.76	1,311.67	1,308.72	1,318.12	1,303.45
2016	1,295.95	1,303.01	1,324.63	1,326.41	1,335.85	1,319.30	1,317.72	1,328.58	1,334.31	1,340.86	1,341.03	1,341.03	1,326.41
2017	1,332.05	1,328.64	1,358.73	1,367.49	1,361.57	1,374.41	1,374.52	1,385.33	1,396.65	1,422.89	1,411.34	1,424.84	1,378.16
Construction													
2013	1,034.26	1,074.57	1,095.17	1,093.09	1,099.28	1,126.11	1,071.62	1,131.64	1,112.15	1,097.40	1,102.10	1,089.26	1,093.61
2014	1,099.53	1,098.16	1,109.71	1,119.55	1,132.20	1,176.42	1,165.00	1,191.51	1,213.52	1,199.77	1,207.12	1,192.97	1,161.00
2015	1,183.90	1,200.91	1,185.13	1,190.44	1,200.15	1,228.54	1,210.28	1,231.90	1,153.98	1,195.75	1,185.75	1,180.27	1,195.24
2016	1,151.44	1,167.52	1,190.03	1,189.13	1,207.50	1,193.42	1,202.45	1,231.01	1,227.51	1,221.48	1,228.59	1,209.95	1,201.29
2017	1,186.92	1,184.17	1,222.86	1,224.48	1,236.06	1,256.62	1,254.53	1,272.81	1,267.30	1,309.50	1,270.88	1,268.63	1,247.94
Manufacturing													
2013	1,326.23	1,329.45	1,335.06	1,332.34	1,313.64	1,319.64	1,305.70	1,315.28	1,321.89	1,339.45	1,352.16	1,386.49	1,330.00
2014	1,349.36	1,350.48	1,378.33	1,360.27	1,359.18	1,361.82	1,332.80	1,338.53	1,347.62	1,355.07	1,359.58	1,360.79	1,354.09
2015	1,336.03	1,350.43	1,375.37	1,361.72	1,362.64	1,359.97	1,343.95	1,358.77	1,355.31	1,372.78	1,372.74	1,383.65	1,359.86
2016	1,364.04	1,367.38	1,386.53	1,392.18	1,396.23	1,379.47	1,371.01	1,373.63	1,387.13	1,403.84	1,401.51	1,411.17	1,384.51
2017	1,409.52	1,404.48	1,429.51	1,443.02	1,431.37	1,441.07	1,445.96	1,452.58	1,474.15	1,490.52	1,494.10	1,515.36	1,451.52
Trade, Transportation, and Utilities													
2013	760.58	782.49	786.11	780.33	780.58	812.89	784.55	785.19	809.90	769.18	765.58	753.14	781.61
2014	761.12	806.75	807.65	796.95	800.18	828.22	802.35	820.29	824.95	809.09	864.37	823.37	811.54
2015	839.95	866.62	864.85	858.83	869.79	869.09	874.02	925.65	944.53	933.31	965.16	922.60	895.21
2016	928.69	930.31	920.83	939.50	954.53	911.36	915.05	903.24	903.21	932.91	888.50	892.47	917.85
2017	919.81	892.67	882.35	936.72	904.19	909.22	943.44	903.53	905.66	922.68	890.91	894.86	909.58
Information													
2013	1,985.58	2,010.75	2,020.02	2,020.61	2,034.50	2,186.11	1,989.75	1,978.14	2,288.56	2,126.60	2,118.37	2,310.87	2,091.46
2014	2,120.03	2,317.98	2,311.71	2,140.76	2,120.45	2,299.65	2,097.02	2,094.63	2,337.60	2,084.35	2,281.76	2,103.17	2,191.07
2015	2,141.98	2,309.50	2,323.95	2,140.20	2,152.95	2,138.05	2,137.67	2,367.34	2,263.39	2,231.55	2,489.30	2,214.12	2,243.17
2016	2,252.09	2,251.12	2,234.02	2,229.73	2,455.08	2,225.28	2,244.59	2,228.90	2,318.27	2,538.31	2,333.64	2,269.71	2,298.45
2017	2,497.54	2,292.16	2,304.98	2,565.91	2,323.65	2,302.00	2,489.80	2,271.73	2,418.40	2,560.18	2,339.44	2,373.51	2,393.04
Financial Activities													
2013	998.76	1,042.37	1,029.83	1,006.95	987.48	1,029.89	996.36	983.80	1,014.57	976.07	991.88	1,018.88	1,007.37
2014	995.10	1,038.91	1,046.18	995.40	997.89	1,028.18	984.18	987.62	995.28	990.34	1,049.40	996.05	1,008.13
2015	1,022.35	1,066.89	1,073.48	1,037.82	1,046.68	1,009.18	1,044.05	1,077.88	1,011.23	1,040.41	1,074.79	1,022.81	1,043.15
2016	1,057.43	1,054.02	1,052.08	1,086.48	1,133.03	1,101.96	1,101.65	1,121.61	1,144.19	1,209.16	1,151.33	1,159.96	1,113.62
2017	1,246.78	1,160.61	1,146.96	1,229.12	1,152.98	1,168.15	1,226.83	1,162.08	1,184.53	1,247.07	1,204.31	1,205.14	1,193.68
Professional and Business Services													
2013	1,137.94	1,173.88	1,159.49	1,169.28	1,148.47	1,208.79	1,125.01	1,139.76	1,191.50	1,156.29	1,158.29	1,182.96	1,163.52
2014	1,140.94	1,199.38	1,196.82	1,163.14	1,154.90	1,194.95	1,154.04	1,152.75	1,160.61	1,170.25	1,222.44	1,173.02	1,175.01
2015	1,179.85	1,234.69	1,224.86	1,181.09	1,178.31	1,173.63	1,159.84	1,198.30	1,165.54	1,182.74	1,229.69	1,189.06	1,190.24
2016	1,197.94	1,216.84	1,211.30	1,206.00	1,247.22	1,203.73	1,203.24	1,195.20	1,205.23	1,264.16	1,215.23	1,222.15	1,214.86
2017	1,286.84	1,249.56	1,245.84	1,305.15	1,241.37	1,242.36	1,307.50	1,249.78	1,261.59	1,328.77	1,281.96	1,286.99	1,275.05
Education and Health Services													
2013	810.54	808.04	798.22	801.06	791.90	825.25	802.01	810.90	835.23	809.94	826.25	841.41	813.12
2014	800.43	833.12	835.09	813.44	817.60	847.91	841.95	842.80	842.88	867.84	917.65	921.13	849.81
2015	924.95	945.89	931.10	910.76	907.95	903.83	908.04	943.26	935.41	934.03	970.40	933.40	928.44
2016	940.70	927.80	912.93	920.95	937.20	930.18	949.34	949.42	986.47	999.01	978.86	984.12	950.54
2017	1,013.15	1,005.72	989.88	1,012.55	988.86	982.60	1,022.22	1,031.08	1,023.61	1,046.33	1,021.90	1,031.74	1,014.46
Leisure and Hospitality													
2013	356.20	373.99	371.25	371.25	374.49	392.40	370.73	381.16	391.43	375.19	372.59	394.72	376.99
2014	371.38	394.17	392.36	383.57	373.65	390.40	381.52	392.44	383.84	375.33	388.53	381.33	384.09
2015	363.66	388.17	392.45	383.52	383.28	389.80	395.00	416.86	397.05	396.55	405.62	397.17	392.74
2016	396.98	407.27	405.11	410.62	428.66	415.95	421.18	429.31	426.70	438.02	426.07	426.65	419.86
2017	447.00	445.26	452.01	483.65	464.35	464.44	484.16	472.66	470.63	483.33	471.45	484.86	469.06
Other Services													
2013	651.00	681.65	672.94	673.44	678.29	703.25	695.77	701.16	734.50	692.59	703.25	749.94	695.14
2014	696.93	682.34	688.21	652.70	662.72	672.95	641.38	649.03	634.50	635.06	680.35	653.29	662.10
2015	668.22	697.92	678.85	656.07	652.37	660.67	667.29	696.47	663.97	663.58	730.08	718.82	678.68
2016	724.01	731.56	736.45	747.36	778.48	736.65	745.63	754.21	730.38	771.46	738.28	750.40	746.20
2017	804.10	771.50	758.28	807.90	750.33	738.40	783.08	755.39	767.62	786.06	752.09	772.42	770.47

WEST VIRGINIA
At a Glance

Population:
  2010 census: 1,852,994
  2017 estimate: 1,815,857

Percent change in population:
  2010–2017: -2.0%

Percent change in total nonfarm employment:
  2007–2017: -1.7%

Industry with the largest growth in employment, 2007–2017 (thousands):
  Education and health services, 16.2

Industry with the largest decline or smallest growth in employment, 2007–2017 (thousands):
  Manufacturing, -12.3

Civilian labor force:
  2010: 811,125
  2017: 778,821

Unemployment rate and rank among states (highest to lowest):
  2010: 8.7%, 24th
  2017: 5.2%, 4th

Over-the-year change in unemployment rates:
  2015–2016: -0.6%
  2016–2017: -0.9%

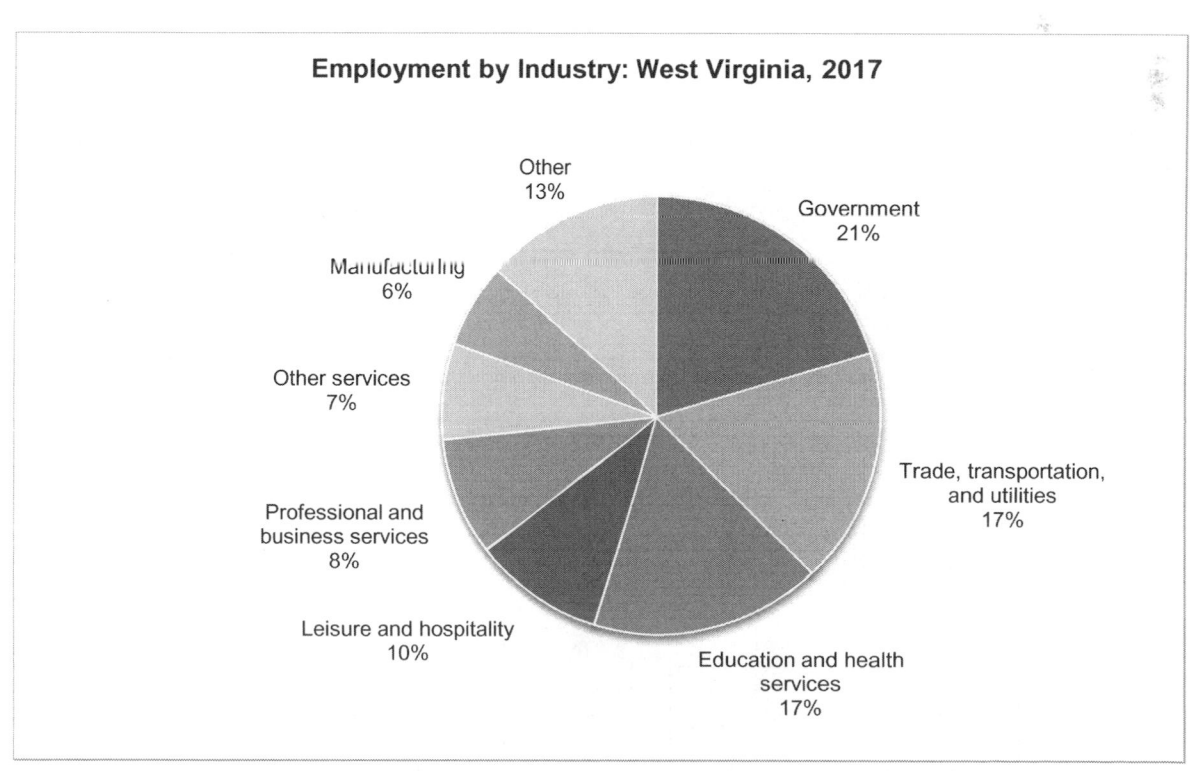

Employment by Industry: West Virginia, 2017

Other
13%

Government
21%

Manufacturing
6%

Other services
7%

Professional and
business services
8%

Leisure and hospitality
10%

Education and health
services
17%

Trade, transportation,
and utilities
17%

1. Employment by Industry: West Virginia, Selected Years, 2007–2017

(Numbers in thousands, not seasonally adjusted)

Industry and year	January	February	March	April	May	June	July	August	September	October	November	December	Annual average
Total Nonfarm													
2007	740.1	741.7	752.2	756.1	762.0	763.6	753.2	757.7	764.5	766.1	769.4	768.8	758.0
2008	746.3	750.8	755.1	760.6	777.4	762.9	759.1	761.0	768.9	770.6	770.2	768.0	762.6
2009	740.2	741.1	745.1	747.3	752.2	752.6	741.1	742.1	744.8	747.1	748.7	750.1	746.0
2010	724.7	725.8	738.0	745.6	762.9	753.3	747.9	748.3	755.0	756.7	758.7	755.2	747.7
2011	730.0	736.6	745.3	755.1	759.2	753.8	748.8	753.7	766.2	768.4	771.8	771.2	755.0
2012	748.7	754.4	762.5	768.0	782.2	763.5	755.6	758.5	770.5	771.8	772.4	771.8	765.0
2013	747.1	752.6	758.7	765.3	771.5	764.9	757.6	760.9	767.4	769.2	772.7	769.8	763.1
2014	742.2	744.6	753.1	762.8	778.4	753.5	749.4	754.7	767.0	772.6	773.4	771.5	760.3
2015	746.1	746.5	750.7	758.3	764.3	757.4	749.4	750.7	759.5	765.0	765.7	763.7	756.4
2016	735.3	736.1	744.4	749.7	759.5	743.1	737.1	739.6	750.0	752.3	763.6	751.6	746.9
2017	729.5	734.4	741.2	743.2	748.1	743.1	736.9	739.5	751.4	756.7	758.4	756.7	744.9
Total Private													
2007	597.7	595.9	604.8	608.9	613.9	619.2	615.4	618.7	619.9	619.1	621.5	621.1	613.0
2008	603.0	604.3	607.2	612.5	616.5	618.4	618.8	619.7	621.6	620.8	619.8	617.5	615.0
2009	594.9	592.2	594.1	596.9	599.7	598.6	595.4	595.8	596.3	594.8	596.0	597.2	596.0
2010	575.6	574.1	583.0	591.1	594.0	599.1	601.0	601.9	603.0	603.1	604.1	600.8	594.2
2011	583.2	585.6	591.8	600.3	604.2	606.7	608.1	611.3	611.7	612.5	615.7	615.2	603.9
2012	597.9	599.6	605.9	612.0	615.3	616.1	613.9	615.7	616.7	615.7	615.0	614.6	611.5
2013	596.6	597.7	602.6	608.9	613.7	612.8	612.4	614.4	613.7	612.7	615.8	613.2	609.5
2014	592.3	591.2	598.0	606.4	611.5	612.3	610.0	612.4	613.6	615.9	616.6	615.3	608.0
2015	596.6	593.3	597.0	603.2	608.6	607.2	604.9	605.0	605.8	607.3	607.5	606.0	603.5
2016	583.6	581.0	587.4	592.1	592.2	590.5	590.8	591.6	595.1	594.8	596.6	594.5	590.9
2017	578.0	578.1	582.5	586.5	591.2	592.6	592.0	593.4	597.4	600.2	601.0	600.2	591.1
Goods Producing													
2007	123.4	121.0	124.3	125.9	127.3	129.4	128.6	128.7	128.2	128.4	127.8	125.5	126.5
2008	120.9	119.8	121.1	124.9	126.3	127.7	128.5	129.4	130.4	132.0	130.4	127.4	126.6
2009	118.9	116.8	116.8	116.3	115.9	114.3	112.7	112.7	112.0	112.7	112.1	111.6	114.4
2010	104.7	104.0	107.5	110.8	111.6	113.6	115.2	115.8	116.3	116.5	115.6	112.2	112.0
2011	107.7	108.4	110.6	114.1	115.8	117.9	118.9	119.7	120.0	120.3	120.5	119.6	116.1
2012	115.8	115.8	117.4	119.0	119.6	121.0	119.8	119.4	119.3	119.1	116.9	115.5	118.2
2013	110.7	110.5	111.7	114.5	116.4	116.2	117.1	117.3	116.7	115.9	114.9	112.0	114.5
2014	106.9	105.9	108.4	111.7	113.6	114.2	113.9	114.4	114.8	114.8	112.5	110.1	111.8
2015	105.4	103.8	105.2	107.4	109.4	108.5	107.5	107.2	106.7	106.2	103.9	101.8	106.1
2016	95.7	94.2	96.7	98.4	97.2	97.8	98.2	98.1	98.5	98.3	97.5	96.4	97.3
2017	92.9	93.6	95.5	97.9	99.3	101.6	101.9	102.3	103.6	104.9	103.9	103.0	100.0
Service-Providing													
2007	616.7	620.7	627.9	630.2	634.7	634.2	624.6	629.0	636.3	637.7	641.6	643.3	631.4
2008	625.4	631.0	634.0	635.7	651.1	635.2	630.6	631.6	638.5	638.6	639.8	640.6	636.0
2009	621.3	624.3	628.3	631.0	636.3	638.3	628.4	629.4	632.8	634.4	636.6	638.5	631.6
2010	620.0	621.8	630.5	634.8	651.3	639.7	632.7	632.5	638.7	640.2	643.1	643.0	635.7
2011	622.3	628.2	634.7	641.0	643.4	635.9	629.9	634.0	646.2	648.1	651.3	651.6	638.9
2012	632.9	638.6	645.1	649.0	662.6	642.5	635.8	639.1	651.2	652.7	655.5	656.3	646.8
2013	636.4	642.1	647.0	650.8	655.1	648.7	640.5	643.6	650.7	653.3	657.8	657.8	648.7
2014	635.3	638.7	644.7	651.1	664.8	639.3	635.5	640.3	652.2	657.8	660.9	661.4	648.5
2015	640.7	642.7	645.5	650.9	654.9	648.9	641.9	643.5	652.8	658.8	661.8	661.9	650.4
2016	639.6	641.9	647.7	651.3	662.3	645.3	638.9	641.5	651.5	654.0	666.1	655.2	649.6
2017	636.6	640.8	645.7	645.3	648.8	641.5	635.0	637.2	647.8	651.8	654.5	653.7	644.9
Mining and Logging													
2007	28.1	27.9	27.9	28.2	28.2	28.9	28.9	29.2	28.9	28.9	29.1	29.1	28.6
2008	28.7	28.8	29.2	29.8	30.5	31.1	31.3	31.7	32.5	33.3	33.4	33.4	31.1
2009	32.7	32.0	31.8	30.9	29.9	29.3	28.5	28.5	28.4	28.5	28.5	28.9	29.8
2010	28.2	28.4	28.8	29.2	29.4	30.1	30.5	30.9	31.1	31.2	31.6	31.6	30.1
2011	31.6	32.0	32.2	32.6	32.9	33.7	33.8	34.4	34.8	35.0	35.3	35.7	33.7
2012	35.2	34.9	34.7	34.0	33.7	33.7	33.1	33.0	32.8	32.6	32.5	32.2	33.5
2013	31.6	31.6	31.7	31.9	32.1	32.3	31.9	32.0	31.6	31.6	31.4	31.1	31.7
2014	30.1	30.2	30.5	30.6	30.5	30.6	30.1	30.2	30.1	30.0	29.8	29.0	30.1
2015	28.5	27.8	27.6	27.3	27.0	26.0	25.5	24.9	24.9	24.7	24.0	23.3	26.0
2016	21.7	21.4	21.2	20.8	19.9	19.8	19.5	19.6	19.6	20.0	20.2	20.5	20.4
2017	20.5	20.9	21.2	21.2	21.5	21.8	22.0	22.1	22.0	21.9	21.6	21.8	21.5

1. Employment by Industry: West Virginia, Selected Years, 2007–2017—*Continued*

(Numbers in thousands, not seasonally adjusted)

Industry and year	January	February	March	April	May	June	July	August	September	October	November	December	Annual average
Construction													
2007	36.2	34.2	37.2	38.7	39.9	40.8	40.2	40.3	40.2	40.9	40.3	38.3	38.9
2008	34.9	34.2	35.3	38.2	39.0	39.6	40.4	41.0	41.6	42.5	41.5	38.7	38.9
2009	32.6	32.6	33.9	33.8	35.1	34.6	34.8	34.5	34.2	34.9	34.4	33.5	34.1
2010	28.3	27.5	30.3	32.8	33.0	34.0	35.0	35.1	35.8	36.0	34.6	31.1	32.8
2011	27.4	27.7	29.2	32.2	33.4	34.2	35.1	35.5	35.6	35.8	35.6	34.3	33.0
2012	31.3	31.6	33.3	35.6	36.4	37.6	37.3	37.9	38.2	37.7	35.9	34.3	35.6
2013	31.0	30.9	32.0	34.5	35.9	35.2	36.3	36.6	36.4	35.9	35.1	32.5	34.4
2014	29.1	28.4	30.3	33.4	35.1	35.4	35.6	36.1	36.8	36.9	35.0	33.2	33.8
2015	29.3	28.5	29.8	32.6	34.6	34.4	34.2	34.6	34.2	33.9	32.4	31.0	32.5
2016	27.0	26.2	28.7	30.7	30.4	30.9	31.5	31.7	32.0	31.7	30.7	29.0	30.0
2017	26.1	26.2	27.7	29.9	31.2	32.8	33.0	33.6	35.0	36.1	35.4	34.0	31.8
Manufacturing													
2007	59.1	58.9	59.2	59.0	59.2	59.7	59.5	59.2	59.1	58.6	58.4	58.1	59.0
2008	57.3	56.8	56.6	56.9	56.8	57.0	56.8	56.7	56.3	56.2	55.5	55.3	56.5
2009	53.6	52.2	51.1	51.6	50.9	50.4	49.4	49.7	49.4	49.3	49.2	49.2	50.5
2010	48.2	48.1	48.4	48.8	49.2	49.5	49.7	49.8	49.4	49.3	49.4	49.5	49.1
2011	48.7	48.7	49.2	49.3	49.5	50.0	50.0	49.8	49.6	49.5	49.6	49.6	49.5
2012	49.3	49.3	49.4	49.4	49.5	49.7	49.4	48.5	48.3	48.8	48.5	49.0	49.1
2013	48.1	48.0	48.0	48.1	48.4	48.7	48.9	48.7	48.7	48.4	48.4	48.4	48.4
2014	47.7	47.3	47.6	47.7	48.0	48.2	48.2	48.1	47.9	47.9	47.7	47.9	47.9
2015	47.6	47.5	47.8	47.5	47.8	48.1	47.8	47.7	47.6	47.6	47.5	47.5	47.7
2016	47.0	46.6	46.8	46.9	46.9	47.1	47.2	46.8	46.9	46.6	46.6	46.9	46.9
2017	46.3	46.5	46.6	46.8	46.6	47.0	46.9	46.6	46.6	46.9	46.9	47.2	46.7
Trade, Transportation, and Utilities													
2007	141.3	140.1	141.6	141.4	142.6	143.3	142.7	143.4	143.6	144.4	147.2	147.8	143.3
2008	141.7	140.8	141.5	140.9	141.4	141.9	141.7	141.5	141.5	141.0	142.6	143.3	141.7
2009	136.5	134.6	134.6	135.0	135.8	136.3	135.5	135.5	135.8	135.6	137.6	138.2	135.9
2010	132.5	131.1	132.5	133.2	134.4	134.8	134.8	134.7	134.1	135.8	138.8	139.1	134.7
2011	133.4	132.5	133.2	134.4	134.8	135.2	135.3	135.8	135.5	136.1	139.1	139.7	135.4
2012	134.4	132.9	133.8	134.0	134.7	135.0	134.9	135.4	135.6	136.4	139.7	140.2	135.6
2013	134.3	133.2	133.4	134.0	134.7	135.4	135.1	135.1	135.1	136.4	140.9	141.1	135.7
2014	133.8	132.5	132.6	133.8	134.5	135.0	134.2	134.8	134.6	136.9	140.9	141.2	135.4
2015	133.7	132.4	132.9	134.0	135.1	135.3	135.0	134.6	134.8	136.5	140.1	140.7	135.4
2016	132.7	131.4	132.2	133.1	133.2	132.7	132.7	132.9	133.4	134.0	137.9	138.4	133.7
2017	130.9	129.1	129.1	129.5	130.2	130.7	130.6	130.7	131.7	133.3	137.1	137.3	131.7
Wholesale Trade													
2007	24.8	24.7	24.9	24.8	24.8	24.9	25.0	25.1	25.2	25.5	25.6	25.7	25.1
2008	24.5	24.5	24.6	24.6	24.8	24.8	24.6	24.6	24.7	24.5	24.4	24.4	24.6
2009	23.8	23.5	23.5	23.4	23.5	23.4	23.3	23.1	23.1	23.0	22.9	22.8	23.3
2010	22.4	22.5	22.5	22.7	22.7	22.0	23.0	22.9	23.0	23.3	23.4	23.3	22.9
2011	22.7	22.6	22.9	23.1	23.2	23.2	23.2	23.3	23.3	23.4	23.6	23.7	23.2
2012	23.1	22.9	23.2	23.1	23.1	23.1	23.0	23.0	23.2	23.4	23.7	23.5	23.2
2013	22.8	22.7	22.6	22.7	22.7	22.8	22.8	22.9	22.9	22.8	22.9	22.9	22.8
2014	22.4	22.4	22.4	22.5	22.6	22.6	22.7	22.7	22.8	22.9	23.0	22.9	22.7
2015	22.4	22.3	22.4	22.4	22.4	22.4	22.3	22.2	22.0	22.2	22.1	22.0	22.3
2016	21.3	21.1	21.1	21.2	21.2	21.0	21.3	21.2	21.1	21.1	21.1	21.1	21.2
2017	20.5	20.5	20.5	20.6	20.6	20.9	20.8	20.7	20.6	21.1	21.3	21.5	20.8
Retail Trade													
2007	90.0	89.0	90.2	89.9	90.8	91.2	90.7	91.2	91.2	91.9	94.5	94.9	91.3
2008	90.4	89.4	90.1	89.1	89.3	89.6	89.6	89.4	89.3	89.1	90.9	91.5	89.8
2009	86.4	84.8	85.0	85.6	86.4	87.0	86.6	86.8	87.1	87.2	89.4	90.0	86.9
2010	85.3	84.0	84.9	85.4	86.3	86.5	86.5	86.5	85.9	87.2	90.1	90.2	86.6
2011	85.7	84.8	85.3	86.5	86.8	87.1	87.1	87.5	87.1	87.6	90.4	90.7	87.2
2012	86.7	85.4	86.1	86.4	87.1	87.3	87.4	87.8	87.6	88.2	91.1	91.4	87.7
2013	86.9	85.9	86.2	86.7	87.3	87.8	87.5	87.2	87.1	87.9	90.5	91.0	87.7
2014	86.2	85.2	85.4	86.4	86.9	87.2	86.4	86.9	86.3	86.5	89.3	89.7	86.9
2015	85.4	84.6	85.0	86.0	86.8	86.8	87.0	86.9	86.9	87.6	89.8	90.1	86.9
2016	85.9	85.5	86.1	86.8	87.1	86.8	86.6	86.8	86.8	86.7	89.0	89.0	86.9
2017	85.2	83.7	83.8	84.0	84.5	84.4	84.6	84.5	84.6	84.9	86.3	85.8	84.7

1. Employment by Industry: West Virginia, Selected Years, 2007–2017—*Continued*

(Numbers in thousands, not seasonally adjusted)

Industry and year	January	February	March	April	May	June	July	August	September	October	November	December	Annual average
Transportation and Utilities													
2007	26.5	26.4	26.5	26.7	27.0	27.2	27.0	27.1	27.2	27.0	27.1	27.2	26.9
2008	26.8	26.9	26.8	27.2	27.3	27.5	27.5	27.5	27.5	27.4	27.3	27.4	27.3
2009	26.3	26.3	26.1	26.0	25.9	25.9	25.6	25.6	25.6	25.4	25.3	25.4	25.8
2010	24.8	24.8	25.1	25.1	25.4	25.5	25.3	25.3	25.2	25.3	25.3	25.6	25.2
2011	25.0	25.1	25.0	24.8	24.8	24.9	25.0	25.0	25.1	25.1	25.1	25.3	25.0
2012	24.6	24.6	24.5	24.5	24.5	24.6	24.5	24.6	24.8	24.8	24.9	25.3	24.7
2013	24.6	24.6	24.6	24.6	24.7	24.8	24.8	25.0	25.1	25.7	27.5	27.2	25.3
2014	25.2	24.9	24.8	24.9	25.0	25.2	25.1	25.2	25.5	27.5	28.6	28.6	25.9
2015	25.9	25.5	25.5	25.6	25.9	26.1	25.7	25.5	25.9	26.7	28.2	28.6	26.3
2016	25.5	24.8	25.0	25.1	24.9	24.9	24.8	24.9	25.5	26.2	27.8	28.3	25.6
2017	25.2	24.9	24.8	24.9	25.1	25.4	25.2	25.5	26.5	27.3	29.5	30.0	26.2
Information													
2007	11.3	11.3	11.2	11.3	11.4	11.5	11.6	11.5	11.5	11.4	11.4	11.5	11.4
2008	11.3	11.3	11.2	11.2	11.2	11.2	11.2	11.2	11.1	11.1	11.0	10.9	11.2
2009	10.9	10.7	10.7	10.6	10.5	10.4	10.3	10.2	10.3	10.2	10.2	10.2	10.4
2010	10.1	10.0	10.0	9.8	10.1	10.3	10.7	10.6	10.5	10.5	10.5	10.6	10.3
2011	10.4	10.4	10.4	10.3	10.2	10.2	10.2	10.2	10.0	10.0	9.9	9.9	10.2
2012	9.5	9.5	9.5	9.6	9.6	9.7	9.6	9.6	9.6	9.6	9.6	9.5	9.6
2013	9.3	9.4	9.5	9.5	9.6	9.6	9.7	9.7	9.7	9.7	9.8	9.8	9.6
2014	9.6	9.6	9.7	9.6	9.6	9.6	9.6	9.6	9.6	9.5	9.6	9.7	9.6
2015	9.6	9.6	9.7	9.7	9.8	9.7	9.7	9.7	9.6	9.7	9.7	9.7	9.7
2016	9.6	9.6	9.6	9.5	9.5	9.5	9.5	9.5	9.5	9.5	9.6	9.5	9.5
2017	9.2	8.9	8.9	8.7	8.7	8.7	8.6	8.4	8.4	8.4	8.4	8.3	8.6
Financial Activities													
2007	29.7	29.7	29.8	30.0	30.2	30.4	30.2	30.3	30.2	30.1	30.1	30.3	30.1
2008	30.0	30.0	29.9	30.1	30.0	30.1	30.1	29.9	29.8	29.8	29.8	29.8	29.9
2009	29.1	28.9	28.9	29.1	29.2	29.2	29.1	29.0	28.7	28.7	28.6	28.5	28.9
2010	28.2	28.3	28.5	28.7	28.7	28.9	28.7	28.6	28.5	28.7	28.7	28.5	28.6
2011	28.0	27.7	27.7	27.7	27.8	27.9	28.0	28.0	27.9	28.0	27.9	28.1	27.9
2012	27.7	27.8	27.9	28.1	28.2	28.3	28.3	28.5	28.4	28.2	28.2	28.4	28.2
2013	28.0	28.2	28.4	28.5	28.6	28.4	28.5	28.5	28.4	28.5	28.5	28.6	28.4
2014	28.2	28.1	28.3	28.0	28.0	28.0	27.9	27.8	27.6	27.6	27.5	27.6	27.9
2015	27.1	27.0	27.1	27.4	27.6	27.6	27.5	27.5	27.4	27.5	27.4	27.4	27.4
2016	27.1	27.1	27.2	27.0	27.1	27.0	27.0	26.9	26.8	26.8	26.8	26.9	27.0
2017	26.5	26.5	26.7	26.7	26.8	26.7	26.9	27.0	27.0	27.2	26.7	26.9	26.8
Professional and Business Services													
2007	59.1	58.8	59.7	60.7	60.7	61.1	60.9	61.4	61.2	61.1	61.4	62.4	60.7
2008	60.2	60.4	60.4	61.4	61.3	61.5	61.4	61.3	60.8	61.1	61.1	61.4	61.0
2009	60.1	60.0	59.7	60.3	60.0	60.1	59.8	60.1	60.0	60.2	60.7	61.7	60.2
2010	59.7	59.5	60.2	61.3	60.4	61.0	61.8	61.7	61.5	61.8	61.9	62.0	61.1
2011	61.3	61.9	62.5	63.4	62.8	63.2	63.7	64.2	64.4	64.6	65.2	65.2	63.5
2012	63.4	63.7	63.9	65.2	65.0	65.1	64.7	65.1	64.8	65.0	64.6	64.7	64.6
2013	63.4	63.9	64.5	65.0	65.1	65.3	65.3	65.9	65.2	64.6	65.0	64.5	64.8
2014	63.6	63.9	64.6	66.1	66.5	67.2	67.7	68.2	67.9	68.8	68.9	69.3	66.9
2015	66.9	66.5	66.5	66.9	66.7	67.2	67.4	67.9	67.0	67.4	67.2	66.9	67.0
2016	64.4	64.7	65.2	65.8	65.2	65.5	66.8	66.5	66.0	66.5	66.4	65.5	65.7
2017	64.8	65.2	65.8	66.1	66.5	67.1	67.2	67.4	67.2	66.4	66.2	66.6	66.4
Education and Health Services													
2007	110.7	112.7	113.5	113.1	113.6	112.9	112.0	112.9	115.5	116.2	116.8	116.4	113.9
2008	114.3	116.6	116.5	116.4	116.4	115.2	114.7	115.0	117.4	117.1	117.6	117.4	116.2
2009	115.0	117.0	117.7	118.5	119.0	118.0	117.7	118.1	120.4	120.7	121.2	121.4	118.7
2010	118.0	119.4	120.4	120.8	120.5	119.8	119.5	119.7	122.2	121.9	122.4	122.4	120.6
2011	119.7	121.5	122.3	123.2	123.5	121.6	121.1	122.0	124.0	124.9	125.6	125.6	122.9
2012	122.5	124.4	125.3	126.2	126.5	124.3	123.7	124.5	127.4	127.2	127.5	127.7	125.6
2013	124.3	126.1	126.5	126.5	126.9	124.4	123.4	124.4	127.1	127.3	127.8	128.2	126.1
2014	124.9	125.6	126.7	127.3	127.6	125.2	124.0	124.9	128.0	128.1	128.6	128.8	126.6
2015	127.9	128.3	128.6	129.1	129.5	126.7	125.3	126.1	129.7	130.6	131.1	131.2	128.7
2016	128.7	128.7	129.4	130.3	130.4	126.9	125.9	127.0	131.4	131.1	131.5	131.7	129.4
2017	130.1	130.5	130.7	130.6	130.8	127.0	126.2	126.9	131.0	132.2	132.5	132.3	130.1

1. Employment by Industry: West Virginia, Selected Years, 2007–2017—*Continued*

(Numbers in thousands, not seasonally adjusted)

Industry and year	January	February	March	April	May	June	July	August	September	October	November	December	Annual average
Leisure and Hospitality													
2007	67.0	66.9	69.0	70.9	72.6	74.6	74.0	75.3	74.3	72.1	71.3	71.9	71.7
2008	69.3	69.9	70.9	72.2	74.1	75.0	75.6	76.0	75.2	73.2	71.6	71.6	72.9
2009	68.8	68.7	70.3	71.3	73.4	74.5	74.8	75.1	73.9	71.4	70.2	70.2	71.9
2010	67.7	67.4	69.3	71.5	73.0	75.0	75.1	75.8	74.8	72.9	71.4	71.2	72.1
2011	68.6	68.9	70.5	72.4	74.3	75.5	75.6	76.3	74.8	73.2	72.1	72.0	72.9
2012	69.9	70.7	72.7	74.0	75.7	76.7	77.1	77.6	76.2	74.6	73.0	73.2	74.3
2013	71.7	71.5	72.9	74.3	76.3	77.4	77.2	77.4	75.6	74.5	73.2	73.6	74.6
2014	70.5	70.8	72.4	73.9	75.8	77.1	76.9	77.1	75.7	74.7	73.3	73.4	74.3
2015	71.3	71.0	72.1	74.1	75.8	77.1	77.4	77.2	76.0	74.9	73.9	74.1	74.6
2016	71.8	71.6	72.9	74.0	75.7	76.9	76.7	76.8	75.8	74.7	73.3	72.5	74.4
2017	70.3	71.0	72.3	73.4	75.1	76.7	76.8	76.9	74.9	74.4	73.0	72.5	73.9
Other Services													
2007	55.2	55.4	55.7	55.6	55.5	56.0	55.4	55.2	55.4	55.4	55.5	55.3	55.5
2008	55.3	55.5	55.7	55.4	55.8	55.8	55.6	55.4	55.4	55.5	55.7	55.7	55.6
2009	55.6	55.5	55.4	55.8	55.9	55.8	55.5	55.1	55.2	55.3	55.4	55.4	55.5
2010	54.7	54.4	54.6	55.0	55.3	55.7	55.2	55.0	55.1	55.0	54.8	54.8	55.0
2011	54.1	54.3	54.6	54.8	55.0	55.2	55.3	55.1	55.1	55.4	55.4	55.1	55.0
2012	54.7	54.8	55.4	55.9	56.0	56.0	55.8	55.6	55.4	55.6	55.5	55.4	55.5
2013	54.9	54.9	55.7	56.6	56.1	56.1	56.1	56.1	55.9	55.8	55.7	55.4	55.8
2014	54.8	54.8	55.3	56.0	55.9	56.0	55.8	55.6	55.4	55.5	55.3	55.2	55.5
2015	54.7	54.7	54.9	54.6	54.7	55.1	55.1	54.8	54.6	54.5	54.2	54.2	54.7
2016	53.6	53.7	54.2	54.0	53.9	54.2	54.0	53.9	53.7	53.9	53.6	53.6	53.9
2017	53.3	53.3	53.5	53.6	53.8	54.1	53.8	53.8	53.6	53.4	53.2	53.3	53.6
Government													
2007	142.4	145.8	147.4	147.2	148.1	144.4	137.8	139.0	144.6	147.0	147.9	147.7	144.9
2008	143.3	146.5	147.9	148.1	160.9	144.5	140.3	141.3	147.3	149.8	150.4	150.5	147.6
2009	145.3	148.9	151.0	150.4	152.5	154.0	145.7	146.3	148.5	152.3	152.7	152.9	150.0
2010	149.1	151.7	155.0	154.5	168.9	154.2	146.9	146.4	152.0	153.6	154.6	154.4	153.4
2011	146.8	151.0	153.5	154.8	155.0	147.1	140.7	142.4	154.5	155.9	156.1	156.0	151.2
2012	150.8	154.8	156.6	156.0	166.9	147.4	141.7	142.8	153.8	156.1	157.4	157.2	153.5
2013	150.5	154.9	156.1	156.4	157.8	152.1	145.2	146.5	153.7	156.5	156.9	156.6	153.6
2014	149.9	153.4	155.1	156.4	166.9	141.2	139.4	142.3	153.4	156.7	156.8	156.2	152.3
2015	149.5	153.2	153.7	155.1	155.7	150.2	144.5	145.7	153.7	157.7	158.2	157.7	152.9
2016	151.7	155.1	157.0	157.6	167.3	152.6	146.3	148.0	154.9	157.5	167.0	157.1	156.0
2017	151.5	156.3	158.7	156.7	156.9	150.5	144.9	146.1	154.0	156.5	157.4	156.5	153.8

2. Average Weekly Hours by Selected Industry: West Virginia, 2012–2016

(Not seasonally adjusted)

Industry and year	January	February	March	April	May	June	July	August	September	October	November	December	Annual average
Total Private													
2013	33.9	34.0	34.4	34.3	34.6	34.9	34.4	34.7	35.0	34.8	35.0	34.5	34.5
2014	33.9	34.0	34.4	34.6	34.6	35.3	35.3	35.3	35.3	35.1	35.2	35.0	34.8
2015	34.3	34.2	34.6	34.6	34.9	34.8	34.9	35.1	34.6	34.9	34.9	34.6	34.7
2016	34.2	34.3	34.8	35.1	34.9	35.2	35.3	35.2	35.2	35.4	35.3	35.2	35.0
2017	35.2	35.1	35.0	35.3	35.3	35.8	36.0	35.7	35.7	35.7	35.4	35.4	35.5
Goods-Producing													
2013	39.2	39.4	39.9	39.7	41.1	40.7	39.9	41.0	41.6	41.6	41.4	39.5	40.4
2014	38.7	39.4	39.8	40.3	39.9	41.8	41.7	41.8	41.6	41.4	40.4	41.4	40.7
2015	39.4	38.9	39.6	39.9	41.3	40.5	40.0	41.1	39.2	41.1	39.8	40.1	40.1
2016	39.3	39.0	40.1	40.5	39.4	40.4	39.8	40.6	40.6	41.3	41.2	40.5	40.2
2017	40.4	40.9	40.4	41.3	41.0	41.6	41.3	41.5	41.6	41.7	41.1	41.3	41.2
Mining and Logging													
2013	41.7	41.0	43.6	42.4	42.6	43.6	42.2	43.1	43.7	45.5	43.9	41.8	42.9
2014	43.7	44.0	44.3	45.6	44.3	47.0	47.0	46.9	46.4	46.3	46.2	48.9	45.9
2015	47.6	44.6	46.3	46.2	45.8	45.3	45.8	46.0	43.2	46.3	46.9	46.0	45.8
2016	45.8	44.4	46.0	46.5	45.5	43.9	44.1	46.1	46.4	48.4	46.6	44.8	45.7
2017	44.5	43.8	42.2	42.3	43.0	42.4	42.8	43.3	43.3	43.3	43.5	43.9	43.2
Construction													
2013	37.9	38.5	38.2	39.6	41.3	40.5	39.9	40.8	41.2	40.0	40.0	38.1	39.7
2014	37.6	37.3	37.7	39.1	38.0	39.7	39.8	40.0	39.3	38.6	37.0	38.0	38.6
2015	36.2	35.7	36.8	37.3	39.2	39.1	38.5	40.1	38.1	40.7	37.4	38.9	38.3
2016	37.3	36.6	38.6	38.9	38.3	41.0	40.2	40.5	40.6	40.7	40.3	38.9	39.4
2017	37.7	39.1	38.2	41.3	40.7	42.7	41.9	41.7	42.1	41.8	41.6	41.3	41.0
Manufacturing													
2013	38.4	38.9	38.5	38.0	39.9	39.0	38.5	39.8	40.6	40.3	40.7	38.9	39.3
2014	36.3	37.7	38.1	37.7	38.6	39.9	39.6	39.9	40.4	40.4	39.4	39.2	38.9
2015	36.5	37.5	37.5	38.1	40.2	39.0	37.9	39.1	37.9	38.8	37.9	37.8	38.2
2016	37.4	37.9	38.5	39.0	37.5	38.5	37.7	38.4	38.2	38.6	39.5	39.7	38.4
2017	40.1	40.7	40.8	40.7	40.3	40.5	40.1	40.6	40.4	40.7	39.7	40.2	40.4
Trade, Transportation, and Utilities													
2013	34.3	34.7	35.0	35.0	34.9	35.3	35.1	35.0	34.9	34.7	34.6	34.5	34.8
2014	33.7	33.3	33.6	34.0	34.4	34.1	34.4	34.9	34.9	34.8	35.0	34.9	34.3
2015	34.2	34.7	35.3	35.5	36.0	35.9	35.7	36.0	35.7	35.8	35.7	35.1	35.5
2016	34.4	34.8	34.9	35.2	35.1	35.1	35.4	35.4	35.5	35.6	35.6	35.9	35.2
2017	35.4	35.2	35.3	35.1	35.5	36.0	36.0	36.0	35.7	35.1	35.2	34.9	35.4
Financial Activities													
2013	34.4	34.4	35.5	36.0	35.9	37.3	35.3	36.7	37.2	37.2	37.4	37.5	36.3
2014	35.3	35.6	35.2	34.5	34.7	35.3	34.7	35.5	35.5	35.5	36.2	34.3	35.2
2015	35.5	35.9	35.8	36.1	36.1	36.6	36.0	37.0	35.6	36.2	36.6	36.1	36.1
2016	35.7	35.9	35.0	35.5	35.7	36.3	35.9	35.3	34.6	36.2	35.9	36.0	35.7
2017	36.5	35.9	35.8	36.1	35.7	35.6	36.2	35.7	35.5	36.2	35.5	35.9	35.9
Professional and Business Services													
2013	35.4	35.4	36.1	36.1	35.9	36.5	35.9	36.1	36.1	36.1	35.4	35.6	35.9
2014	34.5	34.1	34.5	34.9	35.3	36.1	36.7	36.3	36.6	36.2	36.5	35.5	35.6
2015	35.0	34.2	35.2	34.2	34.9	34.6	35.4	35.3	35.4	35.7	36.5	36.5	35.2
2016	35.5	35.5	36.1	36.4	36.6	36.7	36.6	36.5	36.5	38.0	37.2	37.4	36.6
2017	37.1	37.2	37.1	37.5	36.6	36.9	37.8	36.8	37.1	36.6	36.3	36.2	36.9
Education and Health Services													
2013	34.1	33.9	34.1	34.2	34.2	34.3	34.0	33.9	34.5	34.4	35.1	34.8	34.3
2014	34.8	34.7	35.0	34.9	34.9	35.4	35.3	35.0	35.1	34.8	35.3	35.2	35.0
2015	35.0	34.5	34.5	34.7	34.8	34.8	35.1	35.0	34.9	34.5	34.9	34.8	34.8
2016	35.0	35.0	35.3	35.5	35.7	35.9	36.3	35.7	35.7	35.6	35.3	35.5	35.5
2017	36.0	35.4	35.5	35.8	35.9	36.1	36.5	36.0	36.0	36.0	35.8	35.8	35.9
Leisure and Hospitality													
2013	25.3	26.0	26.2	25.8	26.1	26.3	26.5	26.5	26.2	26.0	26.0	25.6	26.1
2014	24.8	25.3	26.1	26.8	26.4	26.9	27.1	26.7	26.2	25.9	25.8	25.7	26.2
2015	25.0	25.2	25.8	26.0	26.3	26.7	27.0	26.8	26.4	26.4	26.5	25.9	26.2
2016	25.4	26.1	27.1	26.8	26.8	27.3	27.3	27.0	26.5	26.1	26.0	25.5	26.5
2017	25.0	25.7	25.6	25.5	25.9	26.6	26.9	27.0	26.8	26.4	26.3	26.3	26.2
Other Services													
2013	32.9	32.3	31.9	32.5	32.0	32.7	31.8	32.9	32.9	31.4	32.0	31.7	32.3
2014	31.4	30.8	32.3	31.4	31.4	32.3	32.7	33.0	31.6	32.7	33.5	32.6	32.1
2015	32.1	32.1	32.1	32.5	31.7	32.1	32.2	32.4	32.0	32.3	32.9	32.4	32.2
2016	31.6	32.4	31.9	32.5	32.7	33.3	32.1	32.2	32.9	33.8	33.6	33.2	32.7
2017	33.0	32.8	33.4	32.9	33.5	33.7	33.4	33.4	33.6	33.7	33.3	33.6	33.4

3. Average Hourly Earnings by Selected Industry: West Virginia, 2013–2017

(Dollars, not seasonally adjusted)

Industry and year	January	February	March	April	May	June	July	August	September	October	November	December	Annual average
Total Private													
2013	20.09	20.26	20.13	20.34	20.29	20.44	20.49	20.40	20.57	20.45	20.42	20.40	20.36
2014	20.61	20.78	20.55	20.59	20.41	20.41	20.56	20.46	20.57	20.60	20.50	20.45	20.54
2015	20.85	20.83	20.75	20.61	20.59	20.55	20.65	20.78	20.83	20.81	20.97	20.78	20.75
2016	21.08	21.11	20.92	20.87	20.66	20.56	20.83	20.80	21.00	21.18	21.10	21.03	20.93
2017	21.45	21.45	21.56	21.52	21.41	21.48	21.71	21.73	21.97	22.13	22.22	22.22	21.74
Goods-Producing													
2013	24.48	24.64	24.95	25.08	25.16	25.32	25.39	25.11	25.37	25.31	25.49	25.38	25.15
2014	25.49	25.18	25.26	25.18	24.94	24.94	25.03	24.78	24.82	24.67	24.66	24.83	24.97
2015	24.96	24.71	24.84	24.90	24.65	24.73	24.56	24.82	25.26	24.99	25.28	25.09	24.90
2016	25.16	24.99	25.11	25.15	25.00	25.21	25.32	25.30	25.28	25.69	25.19	25.24	25.22
2017	25.15	25.45	25.02	25.43	25.45	25.53	25.75	25.90	26.05	26.14	25.92	25.97	25.66
Mining and Logging													
2013	29.40	29.51	30.00	30.41	30.65	31.40	31.73	31.31	31.43	31.80	32.05	32.07	30.99
2014	31.84	31.22	31.04	30.76	30.58	30.32	30.08	30.09	29.78	29.29	29.10	29.22	30.26
2015	29.89	29.86	30.10	29.68	29.78	29.71	29.48	29.31	30.16	29.38	29.47	28.87	29.65
2016	29.72	29.23	29.26	28.49	28.40	28.52	27.79	28.35	28.33	28.75	27.84	28.47	28.61
2017	28.35	29.20	29.07	28.85	28.99	28.03	28.37	28.80	28.84	28.95	29.04	28.52	28.75
Construction													
2013	24.74	24.65	25.12	25.02	25.13	24.90	24.83	24.66	24.91	24.58	24.57	24.58	24.81
2014	24.25	24.00	24.56	24.65	24.35	24.55	24.76	24.57	24.43	24.38	24.55	24.93	24.51
2015	24.26	23.80	24.18	24.90	24.47	25.16	24.30	24.97	25.00	25.36	25.12	25.43	24.78
2016	24.60	24.95	25.67	26.36	25.96	26.03	26.51	25.82	25.98	26.12	25.60	25.08	25.76
2017	24.77	25.71	25.15	25.75	25.82	26.61	26.62	26.98	26.90	27.04	27.00	27.03	26.38
Manufacturing													
2013	20.79	21.24	21.05	21.18	21.30	21.14	21.27	21.04	21.49	21.06	21.57	21.30	21.21
2014	21.44	21.39	21.39	21.24	21.24	21.20	21.50	21.03	21.54	21.57	21.49	21.45	21.37
2015	21.54	21.65	21.50	21.58	21.48	21.29	21.57	21.94	22.52	21.99	22.77	22.62	21.87
2016	22.92	22.74	22.52	22.59	22.60	23.06	23.28	23.40	23.22	23.74	23.55	23.74	23.12
2017	23.77	23.50	23.04	23.61	23.46	23.51	23.79	23.63	23.97	24.03	23.48	23.89	23.64
Trade, Transportation, and Utilities													
2013	17.20	17.29	17.17	17.32	17.40	17.67	17.68	17.59	17.66	17.72	17.77	17.96	17.54
2014	18.17	18.57	18.40	18.75	18.69	18.66	18.56	18.60	18.72	18.82	18.31	17.93	18.51
2015	18.44	18.64	18.39	18.54	18.27	18.53	18.66	18.73	18.88	19.04	18.94	18.72	18.65
2016	19.23	18.85	19.42	19.78	19.40	19.42	19.77	19.49	19.80	20.07	19.78	19.45	19.54
2017	19.64	20.00	20.12	20.16	19.94	19.64	19.62	19.55	19.90	20.07	19.85	19.85	19.86
Financial Activities													
2013	17.39	17.53	17.94	18.49	18.30	18.57	18.88	19.11	19.63	19.23	18.96	20.03	18.69
2014	19.83	19.76	19.85	19.93	20.04	20.61	20.47	20.61	20.44	20.92	20.67	20.34	20.29
2015	20.37	20.39	20.20	20.95	20.60	19.83	21.86	22.73	21.84	21.28	22.27	21.35	21.15
2016	21.24	21.74	21.64	21.27	21.23	20.41	20.45	20.60	21.49	21.97	22.19	22.03	21.35
2017	22.26	21.90	22.22	22.74	22.00	21.55	22.10	22.01	22.22	22.38	23.04	22.55	22.25
Professional and Business Services													
2013	22.08	22.36	22.26	22.58	22.18	22.08	21.38	21.36	21.41	20.73	21.32	21.15	21.74
2014	21.05	21.35	21.15	21.02	20.52	20.48	20.54	20.30	20.38	20.36	20.45	20.07	20.62
2015	20.17	20.18	20.10	20.18	19.94	19.96	20.00	20.28	20.47	20.33	20.85	19.98	20.21
2016	20.23	20.31	20.08	20.41	20.48	20.46	20.82	20.89	20.87	21.16	21.12	21.56	20.71
2017	21.51	21.43	21.90	21.76	22.15	22.11	22.02	22.23	22.42	22.98	22.92	23.05	22.20
Education and Health Services													
2013	21.27	21.61	21.08	21.31	21.26	21.53	21.96	21.79	21.76	21.63	21.15	21.12	21.45
2014	21.70	22.03	21.46	21.57	21.38	21.31	21.83	21.55	21.59	21.52	21.56	21.63	21.59
2015	22.45	22.54	22.49	22.22	22.38	22.23	22.48	22.33	22.20	22.18	22.33	22.34	22.35
2016	22.83	23.10	22.16	21.70	21.58	21.36	22.05	22.05	22.18	22.06	22.21	22.12	22.11
2017	22.72	22.50	22.93	22.85	22.59	22.61	23.09	23.01	23.13	23.17	23.16	23.02	22.90
Leisure and Hospitality													
2013	10.41	10.43	10.31	10.46	10.32	10.37	10.36	10.41	10.50	10.51	10.56	10.71	10.44
2014	10.78	10.69	10.61	10.44	10.61	10.45	10.47	10.54	10.66	10.78	10.76	10.91	10.64
2015	11.24	11.27	11.30	11.17	11.09	11.10	11.07	11.14	11.28	11.36	11.29	11.42	11.22
2016	11.55	11.67	11.65	11.64	11.75	11.55	11.60	11.69	11.83	11.96	11.93	11.92	11.73
2017	11.92	11.99	11.94	11.86	12.11	11.92	12.09	12.03	12.28	12.31	12.45	12.53	12.12
Other Services													
2013	17.06	17.42	17.51	17.56	17.53	17.43	17.48	17.56	18.22	18.63	18.45	18.94	17.81
2014	19.22	20.06	20.25	20.22	20.06	20.20	20.20	20.47	20.71	21.00	20.91	21.02	20.37
2015	21.47	20.91	21.12	20.92	20.60	20.58	20.87	20.89	20.67	20.50	20.31	20.32	20.76
2016	20.41	20.63	20.67	20.57	20.19	20.09	20.60	20.81	20.69	20.29	20.62	20.33	20.49
2017	20.50	20.49	20.49	20.60	20.36	19.92	20.21	20.62	20.47	20.45	20.47	20.36	20.41

4. Average Weekly Earnings by Selected Industry: West Virginia, 2013–2017

(Dollars, not seasonally adjusted)

Industry and year	January	February	March	April	May	June	July	August	September	October	November	December	Annual average
Total Private													
2013	681.05	688.84	692.47	697.66	702.03	713.36	704.86	707.88	719.95	711.66	714.70	703.80	702.42
2014	698.68	706.52	706.92	712.41	706.19	720.47	725.77	722.24	726.12	723.06	721.60	715.75	714.79
2015	715.16	712.39	717.95	713.11	718.59	715.14	720.69	729.38	720.72	726.27	731.85	718.99	720.03
2016	720.94	724.07	728.02	732.54	721.03	723.71	735.30	732.16	739.20	749.77	744.83	740.26	732.55
2017	755.04	752.90	754.60	759.66	755.77	768.98	781.56	775.76	784.33	790.04	786.59	786.59	771.77
Goods-Producing													
2013	959.62	970.82	995.51	995.68	1,034.08	1,030.52	1,013.06	1,029.51	1,055.39	1,052.90	1,055.29	1,002.51	1,016.06
2014	986.46	992.09	1,005.35	1,014.75	995.11	1,042.49	1,043.75	1,035.80	1,032.51	1,021.34	996.26	1,027.96	1,016.28
2015	983.42	961.22	983.66	993.51	1,018.05	1,001.57	982.40	1,020.10	990.19	1,027.09	1,006.14	1,006.11	998.49
2016	988.79	974.61	1,006.91	1,018.58	985.00	1,018.48	1,007.74	1,027.18	1,026.37	1,061.00	1,037.83	1,022.22	1,013.84
2017	1,016.06	1,040.91	1,010.81	1,050.26	1,043.45	1,062.05	1,063.48	1,074.85	1,083.68	1,090.04	1,065.31	1,072.56	1,057.19
Mining and Logging													
2013	1,225.98	1,209.91	1,308.00	1,289.38	1,305.69	1,369.04	1,339.01	1,349.46	1,373.49	1,446.90	1,407.00	1,340.53	1,329.47
2014	1,391.41	1,373.68	1,375.07	1,402.66	1,354.69	1,425.04	1,413.76	1,411.22	1,381.79	1,356.13	1,344.42	1,428.86	1,388.93
2015	1,422.76	1,331.76	1,393.63	1,371.22	1,363.92	1,345.86	1,350.18	1,348.26	1,302.91	1,360.29	1,382.14	1,328.02	1,357.97
2016	1,361.18	1,297.81	1,345.96	1,324.79	1,292.20	1,252.03	1,225.54	1,306.94	1,314.51	1,391.50	1,297.34	1,275.46	1,307.48
2017	1,261.58	1,278.96	1,226.75	1,220.36	1,246.57	1,188.47	1,214.24	1,247.04	1,248.77	1,253.54	1,263.24	1,252.03	1,242.00
Construction													
2013	937.65	949.03	959.58	990.79	1,037.87	1,008.45	990.72	1,006.13	1,026.29	983.20	982.80	936.50	984.96
2014	911.80	895.20	925.91	963.82	925.30	974.64	985.45	982.80	960.10	941.07	908.35	947.34	946.09
2015	878.21	849.66	889.82	928.77	959.22	983.76	935.55	1,001.30	952.50	1,032.15	939.49	989.23	949.07
2016	917.58	913.17	990.86	1,025.40	994.27	1,067.23	1,065.70	1,045.71	1,054.79	1,063.08	1,031.68	975.61	1,014.94
2017	933.83	1,005.26	960.73	1,063.48	1,050.87	1,136.25	1,115.38	1,125.07	1,132.49	1,130.27	1,123.20	1,116.34	1,081.58
Manufacturing													
2013	798.34	826.24	810.43	804.84	849.87	824.46	818.90	837.39	872.49	848.72	877.90	828.57	833.55
2014	778.27	806.40	814.96	800.75	819.86	845.88	851.40	839.10	870.22	871.43	846.71	840.84	831.29
2015	786.21	811.88	806.25	822.20	863.50	830.31	817.50	857.85	853.51	853.21	862.98	855.04	835.43
2016	857.21	861.85	867.02	881.01	847.50	887.81	877.66	898.56	887.00	916.36	930.23	942.48	887.81
2017	953.18	956.45	940.03	960.93	945.44	952.16	953.98	959.38	968.39	978.02	932.16	960.38	955.06
Trade, Transportation, and Utilities													
2013	589.96	599.96	600.95	606.20	607.26	623.75	620.57	615.65	616.33	614.88	614.84	619.62	610.39
2014	612.33	618.38	618.24	637.50	642.94	636.31	638.46	649.14	653.33	654.94	640.85	625.76	634.89
2015	630.65	646.81	649.17	658.17	657.72	665.23	666.16	674.28	674.02	681.63	676.16	657.07	662.08
2016	661.51	655.98	677.76	696.26	680.94	681.64	699.86	689.95	702.90	714.49	704.17	698.26	687.81
2017	695.26	704.00	710.24	707.62	707.87	707.04	706.32	703.80	710.43	704.46	698.72	692.77	703.04
Financial Activities													
2013	598.22	603.03	636.87	665.64	656.97	692.66	666.46	701.34	730.24	715.36	709.10	751.13	678.45
2014	700.00	703.46	698.72	687.59	695.39	727.53	710.31	731.66	725.62	742.66	748.25	697.66	714.21
2015	723.14	732.00	723.16	756.30	743.66	725.78	786.96	841.01	777.50	770.34	815.08	770.74	763.52
2016	758.27	780.47	757.40	755.09	757.91	740.88	734.16	727.18	743.55	795.31	796.62	793.08	762.20
2017	812.49	786.21	795.48	820.91	785.40	767.18	800.02	785.76	788.81	810.16	817.92	809.55	798.78
Professional and Business Services													
2013	781.63	791.54	803.59	815.14	796.26	805.92	767.54	771.10	772.90	748.35	754.73	752.94	780.47
2014	726.23	728.04	729.68	733.60	724.36	739.33	753.82	736.89	745.91	737.03	746.43	712.49	734.07
2015	705.95	690.16	707.52	690.16	695.91	690.62	708.00	715.88	724.64	725.78	761.03	729.27	711.39
2016	718.17	721.01	724.89	742.92	749.57	750.88	762.01	762.49	761.76	804.08	785.66	806.34	757.99
2017	798.02	797.20	812.49	816.00	810.69	815.86	832.36	818.06	831.78	841.07	832.00	834.41	819.18
Education and Health Services													
2013	725.31	732.58	718.83	728.80	727.09	738.48	746.64	738.68	750.72	744.07	742.37	734.98	735.74
2014	755.16	764.44	751.10	752.79	746.16	754.37	770.60	754.25	757.81	748.90	761.07	761.38	755.65
2015	785.75	777.63	775.91	771.03	778.82	773.60	789.05	781.55	774.78	765.21	779.32	777.43	777.78
2016	799.05	808.50	782.25	770.35	770.41	766.82	800.42	787.19	791.83	785.78	783.57	785.26	784.91
2017	819.06	798.08	815.62	818.94	811.66	817.13	842.79	827.67	831.99	834.12	829.13	824.12	822.11
Leisure and Hospitality													
2013	263.37	271.18	270.12	269.87	269.35	272.73	274.54	275.87	275.10	273.26	274.56	274.18	272.48
2014	267.34	270.46	276.92	279.79	280.10	281.11	283.74	281.42	279.29	279.20	277.61	280.39	278.77
2015	281.00	284.00	291.54	290.42	291.67	296.37	298.89	298.55	297.79	299.90	299.19	295.78	293.96
2016	293.37	304.59	315.72	311.95	314.90	315.32	316.68	315.63	313.50	312.16	310.18	303.96	310.85
2017	298.00	308.14	305.66	302.43	313.65	317.07	325.22	324.81	329.10	324.98	327.44	329.54	317.54
Other Services													
2013	561.27	562.67	558.57	570.70	560.96	569.96	555.86	577.72	599.44	584.98	590.40	600.40	575.26
2014	603.51	617.85	654.08	634.91	629.88	652.46	660.54	675.51	654.44	686.70	700.49	685.25	653.88
2015	689.19	671.21	677.95	679.90	653.02	660.62	672.01	676.84	661.44	662.15	668.20	658.37	668.47
2016	644.96	668.41	659.37	668.53	660.21	669.00	661.26	670.08	680.70	685.80	692.83	674.96	670.02
2017	676.50	672.07	684.37	677.74	682.06	671.30	675.01	688.71	687.79	689.17	681.65	684.10	681.69

WISCONSIN
At a Glance

Population:
  2010 census: 5,686,986
  2017 estimate: 5,795,483

Percent change in population:
  2010–2017: 1.9%

Percent change in total nonfarm employment:
  2007–2017: 2.4%

Industry with the largest growth in employment, 2007–2017 (thousands):
  Education and health services, 57.9

Industry with the largest decline or smallest growth in employment, 2007–2017 (thousands):
  Manufacturing, -33.1

Civilian labor force:
  2010: 3,081,512
  2017: 3,151,909

Unemployment rate and rank among states (highest to lowest):
  2010: 8.7%, 24th
  2017: 3.3%, 40th

Over-the-year change in unemployment rates:
  2015–2016: -0.5%
  2016–2017: -0.7%

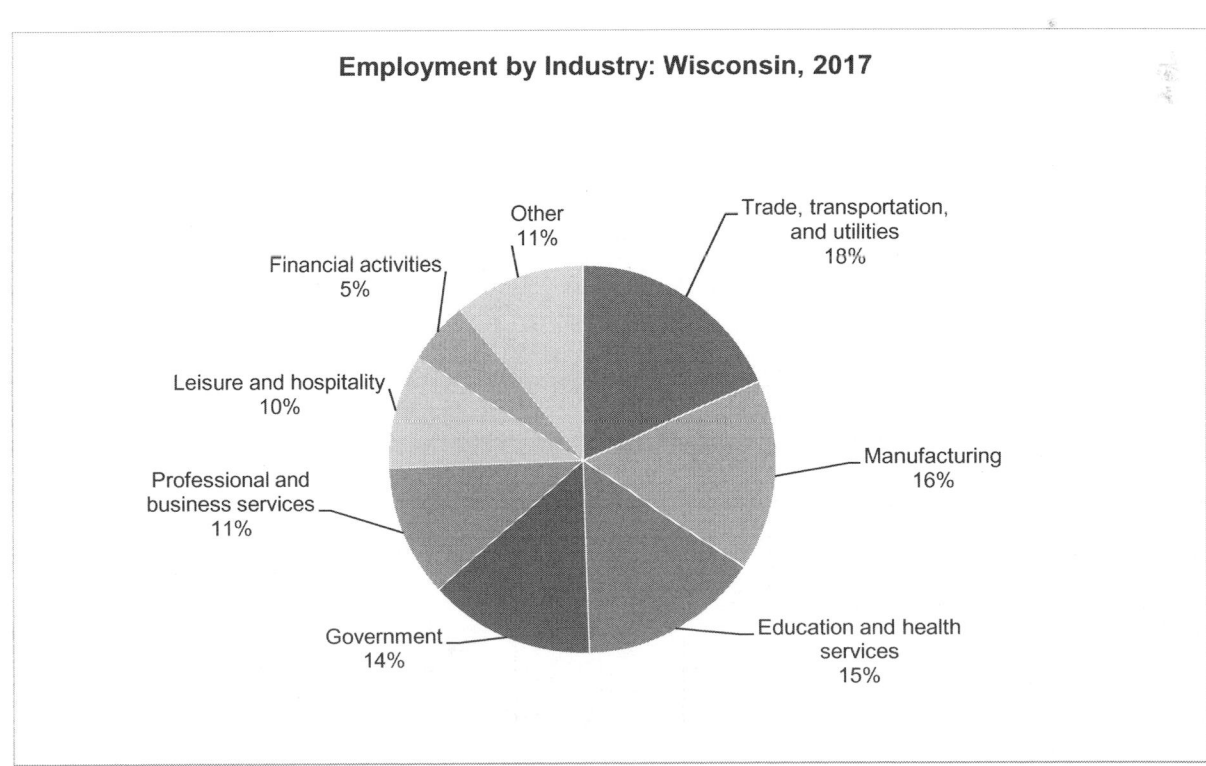

Employment by Industry: Wisconsin, 2017

- Other 11%
- Trade, transportation, and utilities 18%
- Financial activities 5%
- Leisure and hospitality 10%
- Manufacturing 16%
- Professional and business services 11%
- Government 14%
- Education and health services 15%

1. Employment by Industry: Wisconsin, Selected Years, 2007–2017

(Numbers in thousands, not seasonally adjusted)

Industry and year	January	February	March	April	May	June	July	August	September	October	November	December	Annual average
Total Nonfarm													
2007	2,806.3	2,801.8	2,821.7	2,854.0	2,895.8	2,934.1	2,897.5	2,898.8	2,899.0	2,900.1	2,901.3	2,897.6	2,875.7
2008	2,818.9	2,814.6	2,827.3	2,855.8	2,898.0	2,919.1	2,887.6	2,886.3	2,889.5	2,889.6	2,877.1	2,854.6	2,868.2
2009	2,744.6	2,731.3	2,723.6	2,735.6	2,765.0	2,775.3	2,738.5	2,732.3	2,732.0	2,744.1	2,739.8	2,731.9	2,741.2
2010	2,646.3	2,651.1	2,665.3	2,710.7	2,743.2	2,761.9	2,740.7	2,744.9	2,747.1	2,767.5	2,768.1	2,753.3	2,725.0
2011	2,676.6	2,683.6	2,699.3	2,737.1	2,766.6	2,784.3	2,770.8	2,770.9	2,782.5	2,786.0	2,785.9	2,777.5	2,751.8
2012	2,690.2	2,704.4	2,732.8	2,768.6	2,802.2	2,820.3	2,787.9	2,794.3	2,805.3	2,819.0	2,826.9	2,814.5	2,780.5
2013	2,716.8	2,746.3	2,760.2	2,779.5	2,822.3	2,844.7	2,821.1	2,830.1	2,840.8	2,849.8	2,853.3	2,847.0	2,809.3
2014	2,761.8	2,778.5	2,792.1	2,827.8	2,863.0	2,888.5	2,867.0	2,880.2	2,881.6	2,892.9	2,902.7	2,891.0	2,852.3
2015	2,805.0	2,824.4	2,838.1	2,877.4	2,905.4	2,927.3	2,910.9	2,913.0	2,915.5	2,929.6	2,928.3	2,929.0	2,892.0
2016	2,847.9	2,868.8	2,878.5	2,922.0	2,937.0	2,955.8	2,946.8	2,952.2	2,945.6	2,954.0	2,963.9	2,945.2	2,926.5
2017	2,870.4	2,890.4	2,903.0	2,934.8	2,959.4	2,983.0	2,965.6	2,961.3	2,957.0	2,979.5	2,975.4	2,957.8	2,944.8
Total Private													
2007	2,396.1	2,385.0	2,399.2	2,427.0	2,468.7	2,512.0	2,509.2	2,514.0	2,485.0	2,476.3	2,475.0	2,468.8	2,459.7
2008	2,402.2	2,392.4	2,400.1	2,426.2	2,465.5	2,496.9	2,495.2	2,499.3	2,466.5	2,457.1	2,435.7	2,418.6	2,446.3
2009	2,326.0	2,300.1	2,290.9	2,300.7	2,329.2	2,353.5	2,346.0	2,347.2	2,323.4	2,317.9	2,308.6	2,300.1	2,320.3
2010	2,231.0	2,226.0	2,237.7	2,275.3	2,305.7	2,340.5	2,350.7	2,360.6	2,335.9	2,338.7	2,334.2	2,326.8	2,305.3
2011	2,264.4	2,257.0	2,271.2	2,306.3	2,338.0	2,372.8	2,383.9	2,390.2	2,373.8	2,366.9	2,363.9	2,355.2	2,337.0
2012	2,294.3	2,293.0	2,312.9	2,341.3	2,373.5	2,411.6	2,409.6	2,415.7	2,398.6	2,396.7	2,397.2	2,391.6	2,369.7
2013	2,321.9	2,326.0	2,340.7	2,356.8	2,405.4	2,440.5	2,442.9	2,454.4	2,431.9	2,427.5	2,429.8	2,424.8	2,400.2
2014	2,356.6	2,360.4	2,373.3	2,403.1	2,445.1	2,482.8	2,486.2	2,495.8	2,471.1	2,470.3	2,471.7	2,468.2	2,440.4
2015	2,401.9	2,404.4	2,419.2	2,450.7	2,488.0	2,523.3	2,530.6	2,535.8	2,509.6	2,511.0	2,509.1	2,508.3	2,482.7
2016	2,444.8	2,449.7	2,460.3	2,494.9	2,521.8	2,552.1	2,563.5	2,565.1	2,537.5	2,533.3	2,530.7	2,521.9	2,514.6
2017	2,469.5	2,473.5	2,489.4	2,511.5	2,542.8	2,583.6	2,584.3	2,584.8	2,552.2	2,559.6	2,554.2	2,541.4	2,537.2
Goods Producing													
2007	614.4	607.4	612.2	620.8	633.6	649.2	650.1	650.0	640.9	636.2	632.3	623.2	630.9
2008	606.8	601.7	603.6	610.3	621.3	633.8	633.5	632.1	621.9	616.0	605.5	590.1	614.7
2009	561.4	546.8	538.3	536.2	540.5	546.9	546.2	545.7	541.8	536.5	531.3	521.7	541.1
2010	504.3	500.9	504.7	517.5	526.3	540.1	546.2	548.7	542.8	540.1	536.7	527.8	528.0
2011	515.0	512.5	517.3	529.2	539.9	554.4	561.0	562.0	555.3	551.6	549.2	541.3	540.7
2012	529.3	527.1	533.0	544.3	551.5	566.8	571.5	571.6	563.8	562.1	558.0	552.9	552.7
2013	539.4	537.6	541.0	545.2	559.4	573.0	577.6	579.3	570.8	569.0	566.3	558.0	559.7
2014	546.2	544.5	549.3	559.0	571.5	585.9	593.3	594.2	585.7	583.2	579.9	574.3	572.3
2015	561.8	560.2	563.4	573.3	582.2	595.1	600.2	598.6	589.3	585.9	582.4	577.2	580.8
2016	563.8	561.6	565.6	574.7	581.5	594.3	598.7	597.9	588.9	586.2	583.2	576.5	581.1
2017	566.6	566.2	571.0	580.2	588.5	603.4	608.1	607.1	597.9	597.2	594.9	589.0	589.2
Service-Providing													
2007	2,191.9	2,194.4	2,209.5	2,233.2	2,262.2	2,284.9	2,247.4	2,248.8	2,258.1	2,263.9	2,269.0	2,274.4	2,244.8
2008	2,212.1	2,212.9	2,223.7	2,245.5	2,276.7	2,285.3	2,254.1	2,254.2	2,267.6	2,273.6	2,271.6	2,264.5	2,253.5
2009	2,183.2	2,184.5	2,185.3	2,199.4	2,224.5	2,228.4	2,192.3	2,186.6	2,190.2	2,207.6	2,208.5	2,210.2	2,200.1
2010	2,142.0	2,150.2	2,160.6	2,193.2	2,216.9	2,221.8	2,194.5	2,196.2	2,204.3	2,227.4	2,231.4	2,225.5	2,197.0
2011	2,161.6	2,171.1	2,182.0	2,207.9	2,226.7	2,229.9	2,209.8	2,208.9	2,227.2	2,234.4	2,236.7	2,236.2	2,211.0
2012	2,160.9	2,177.3	2,199.8	2,224.3	2,250.7	2,253.5	2,216.4	2,222.7	2,241.5	2,256.9	2,268.9	2,261.6	2,227.9
2013	2,177.4	2,208.7	2,219.2	2,234.3	2,262.9	2,271.7	2,243.5	2,250.8	2,270.0	2,280.8	2,287.0	2,289.0	2,249.6
2014	2,215.6	2,234.0	2,242.8	2,268.8	2,291.5	2,302.6	2,273.7	2,286.0	2,295.9	2,309.7	2,322.8	2,316.7	2,280.0
2015	2,243.2	2,264.2	2,274.7	2,304.1	2,323.2	2,332.2	2,310.7	2,314.4	2,326.2	2,343.7	2,345.9	2,351.8	2,311.2
2016	2,284.1	2,307.2	2,312.9	2,347.3	2,355.5	2,361.5	2,348.1	2,354.3	2,356.7	2,367.8	2,380.7	2,368.7	2,345.4
2017	2,303.8	2,324.2	2,332.0	2,354.6	2,370.9	2,379.6	2,357.5	2,354.2	2,359.1	2,382.3	2,380.5	2,368.8	2,355.6
Mining and Logging													
2007	3.2	3.2	3.3	3.5	3.9	3.9	4.0	4.0	3.9	3.8	3.7	3.3	3.6
2008	3.0	2.9	3.0	3.1	3.5	3.7	3.7	3.8	3.7	3.6	3.5	3.1	3.4
2009	2.6	2.6	2.6	2.7	3.1	3.2	3.3	3.3	3.3	3.3	3.1	2.8	3.0
2010	2.4	2.4	2.5	2.8	3.1	3.2	3.3	3.3	3.2	3.2	3.1	2.7	2.9
2011	2.5	2.5	2.6	2.7	3.0	3.3	3.3	3.3	3.4	3.4	3.4	3.1	3.0
2012	2.9	2.9	3.1	3.4	3.6	3.7	3.8	3.8	3.8	3.7	3.6	3.4	3.5
2013	3.2	3.2	3.2	3.4	3.8	4.0	4.0	4.1	4.0	4.0	3.9	3.6	3.7
2014	3.4	3.5	3.5	3.8	4.1	4.3	4.4	4.5	4.4	4.5	4.4	4.2	4.1
2015	3.9	4.0	4.0	4.2	4.4	4.5	4.4	4.3	4.2	4.2	4.1	3.9	4.2
2016	3.5	3.5	3.6	3.7	3.9	3.9	3.9	3.9	3.8	3.9	3.8	3.6	3.8
2017	3.5	3.6	3.9	4.2	4.4	4.6	4.7	4.8	4.7	4.7	4.7	4.3	4.3

1. Employment by Industry: Wisconsin, Selected Years, 2007–2017—*Continued*

(Numbers in thousands, not seasonally adjusted)

Industry and year	January	February	March	April	May	June	July	August	September	October	November	December	Annual average
Construction													
2007	112.5	107.9	113.0	120.0	130.2	135.7	137.0	136.9	133.8	132.8	130.0	121.2	125.9
2008	108.0	104.9	106.8	113.8	123.9	127.9	129.4	129.0	125.6	124.1	118.4	108.9	118.4
2009	93.9	91.4	91.0	98.0	105.7	109.5	110.8	109.5	107.6	106.2	102.7	94.3	101.7
2010	82.1	79.9	81.6	92.1	97.1	101.7	103.6	103.9	102.1	102.3	98.5	90.0	94.6
2011	79.2	76.8	79.5	87.7	95.1	100.5	102.8	103.0	101.0	100.3	97.3	89.6	92.7
2012	79.7	78.0	81.5	90.4	95.3	100.6	101.9	102.3	100.5	101.2	98.3	93.1	93.6
2013	83.6	82.9	85.2	89.4	101.0	106.3	108.8	110.2	107.6	107.2	104.4	96.1	98.6
2014	87.1	86.2	89.1	96.2	105.2	111.7	114.1	115.1	113.0	112.5	109.4	103.1	103.6
2015	94.4	93.2	95.5	105.7	112.7	117.7	120.1	119.4	116.6	116.2	113.3	108.0	109.4
2016	98.3	98.1	101.0	109.5	114.8	119.8	122.2	122.3	119.7	119.0	116.8	109.4	112.6
2017	102.0	102.3	104.6	113.1	120.0	125.3	127.4	126.9	124.1	122.2	118.5	112.9	116.6
Manufacturing													
2007	498.7	496.3	495.9	497.3	499.5	509.6	509.1	509.1	503.2	499.6	498.6	498.7	501.3
2008	495.8	493.9	493.8	493.4	493.9	502.2	500.4	499.3	492.6	488.3	483.6	478.1	492.9
2009	464.9	452.8	444.7	435.5	431.7	434.2	432.1	432.9	430.9	427.0	425.5	424.6	436.4
2010	419.8	418.6	420.6	422.6	426.1	435.2	439.3	441.5	437.5	434.6	435.1	435.1	430.5
2011	433.3	433.2	435.2	438.8	441.8	450.6	454.9	455.7	450.9	447.9	448.5	448.6	445.0
2012	446.7	446.2	448.4	450.5	452.6	462.5	465.8	465.5	459.5	457.2	456.1	456.4	455.6
2013	452.6	451.5	452.6	452.4	454.6	462.7	464.8	465.0	459.2	457.8	458.0	458.3	457.5
2014	455.7	454.8	456.7	459.0	462.2	469.9	474.8	474.6	468.3	466.2	466.1	467.0	464.6
2015	463.5	463.0	463.9	463.4	465.1	472.9	475.7	474.9	468.5	465.5	465.0	465.3	467.2
2016	462.0	460.0	461.0	461.5	462.8	470.6	472.6	471.7	465.4	463.3	462.6	463.5	464.8
2017	461.1	460.3	462.5	462.9	464.1	473.5	476.0	475.4	469.1	470.3	471.7	471.8	468.2
Trade, Transportation, and Utilities													
2007	541.3	533.5	536.3	538.3	547.7	552.3	547.5	547.2	546.5	550.0	561.0	563.0	547.1
2008	539.9	531.4	533.2	536.6	543.2	546.3	541.6	542.1	538.8	541.5	546.4	547.7	540.7
2009	520.7	511.9	510.2	512.4	519.0	523.1	515.9	515.7	513.6	517.8	523.2	524.6	517.3
2010	501.3	494.5	496.3	501.7	507.6	512.2	508.0	508.9	507.2	514.7	521.5	524.1	508.2
2011	502.1	495.5	497.7	503.9	508.7	512.1	511.4	512.6	512.2	516.8	525.5	527.9	510.5
2012	505.5	498.6	500.6	503.3	511.2	514.8	511.6	513.1	511.8	517.3	528.9	530.5	512.3
2013	507.5	502.5	504.4	508.5	517.0	522.3	518.8	520.9	517.9	522.6	533.1	537.0	517.7
2014	513.4	509.3	511.9	517.2	524.3	529.2	526.5	527.6	524.4	528.5	539.4	542.8	524.5
2015	519.4	514.3	517.4	521.3	529.4	534.8	533.9	536.2	535.0	539.3	548.1	550.6	531.6
2016	530.3	526.9	528.5	534.6	540.0	542.5	543.1	543.0	539.2	543.1	552.2	555.3	539.9
2017	536.7	531.8	533.2	535.7	542.1	544.7	543.3	544.1	539.9	542.3	553.0	553.3	541.7
Wholesale Trade													
2007	120.8	120.6	120.9	122.0	123.1	125.0	125.2	124.4	123.2	123.1	123.5	123.8	123.0
2008	122.0	121.3	121.8	122.9	124.1	125.2	125.1	124.5	122.4	122.0	121.7	121.1	122.8
2009	118.6	117.4	116.9	116.6	117.1	117.9	117.2	116.2	114.3	114.7	114.2	114.0	116.3
2010	111.5	110.9	111.1	112.8	113.6	114.9	115.5	115.3	113.2	114.2	114.2	114.3	113.5
2011	112.7	112.4	112.9	114.5	115.6	117.0	118.1	117.6	116.3	116.6	116.7	116.9	115.6
2012	115.3	115.1	115.8	117.2	117.9	119.4	119.3	118.6	117.1	117.5	117.7	117.9	117.4
2013	117.4	117.3	117.5	118.7	120.1	121.5	121.4	121.0	119.3	119.4	119.5	119.7	119.4
2014	117.8	117.8	118.6	119.8	121.1	122.5	122.8	122.6	120.6	120.6	120.7	121.0	120.5
2015	119.9	119.6	120.2	121.8	123.1	124.7	125.1	124.8	122.9	123.6	123.8	124.0	122.8
2016	122.4	122.4	122.9	124.3	125.1	126.3	126.9	126.4	124.5	124.2	124.3	124.8	124.5
2017	123.2	123.1	123.6	124.5	125.9	127.6	127.6	127.5	125.6	125.6	126.9	124.4	125.5
Retail Trade													
2007	312.7	304.7	306.7	307.0	313.1	315.2	314.8	314.1	311.0	314.0	324.7	326.5	313.7
2008	309.4	301.6	302.9	305.0	309.0	311.1	310.3	311.1	307.0	309.8	315.8	318.1	309.3
2009	298.5	291.5	290.5	291.6	296.0	298.9	296.9	297.5	293.8	297.6	304.5	306.2	297.0
2010	289.4	283.1	284.4	286.5	290.8	293.7	292.5	293.9	290.8	296.5	303.8	306.2	292.6
2011	289.7	283.7	285.1	288.7	291.4	294.2	294.6	296.2	293.4	297.4	306.2	308.2	294.1
2012	291.3	284.7	286.0	287.4	291.9	294.8	293.9	295.7	292.6	297.4	308.8	309.6	294.5
2013	291.3	286.3	287.6	290.5	295.8	300.2	299.8	301.2	297.2	301.2	311.2	314.4	298.1
2014	296.4	292.1	293.7	297.0	301.1	304.7	304.8	305.2	300.8	304.4	314.1	316.0	302.5
2015	298.3	293.7	295.6	297.2	302.4	305.8	306.1	307.4	304.3	307.6	315.8	316.5	304.2
2016	302.8	299.4	300.5	304.2	307.5	309.8	311.5	311.3	306.1	309.7	317.6	318.8	308.3
2017	306.3	302.2	303.0	304.4	307.3	309.8	310.0	310.0	304.5	306.6	315.5	315.3	307.9

1. Employment by Industry: Wisconsin, Selected Years, 2007–2017—*Continued*

(Numbers in thousands, not seasonally adjusted)

Industry and year	January	February	March	April	May	June	July	August	September	October	November	December	Annual average
Transportation and Utilities													
2007	107.8	108.2	108.7	109.3	111.5	112.1	107.5	108.7	112.3	112.9	112.8	112.7	110.4
2008	108.5	108.5	108.5	108.7	110.1	110.0	106.2	106.5	109.4	109.7	108.9	108.5	108.6
2009	103.6	103.0	102.8	104.2	105.9	106.3	101.8	102.0	105.5	105.5	104.5	104.4	104.1
2010	100.4	100.5	100.8	102.4	103.2	103.6	100.0	99.7	103.2	104.0	103.5	103.6	102.1
2011	99.7	99.4	99.7	100.7	101.7	100.9	98.7	98.8	102.5	102.8	102.6	102.8	100.9
2012	98.9	98.8	98.8	98.7	101.4	100.6	98.4	98.8	102.1	102.4	102.4	103.0	100.4
2013	98.8	98.9	99.3	99.3	101.1	100.6	97.6	98.7	101.4	102.0	102.4	102.9	100.3
2014	99.2	99.4	99.6	100.4	102.1	102.0	98.9	99.8	103.0	103.5	104.6	105.8	101.5
2015	101.2	101.0	101.6	102.3	103.9	104.3	102.7	104.0	107.8	108.1	108.5	110.1	104.6
2016	105.1	105.1	105.1	106.1	107.4	106.4	104.7	105.3	108.6	109.2	110.3	111.7	107.1
2017	107.2	106.5	106.6	106.8	108.9	107.3	105.7	106.6	109.8	110.1	110.6	113.6	108.3
Information													
2007	49.8	49.5	49.4	49.7	49.9	50.4	50.6	50.8	50.3	50.6	50.8	50.9	50.2
2008	50.3	50.0	49.9	50.1	50.9	50.7	50.5	50.5	49.8	49.7	49.9	49.9	50.2
2009	49.1	48.9	48.3	48.0	48.1	48.1	48.1	48.0	47.4	46.9	47.4	47.6	48.0
2010	46.6	46.2	46.1	45.9	46.1	46.7	47.1	47.2	46.8	46.5	47.4	47.4	46.7
2011	46.9	46.6	46.4	46.5	46.5	46.4	47.1	47.2	46.8	46.7	47.2	47.1	46.8
2012	46.4	46.0	45.8	45.9	45.9	46.5	46.8	47.1	46.5	46.6	47.1	46.9	46.5
2013	46.9	46.7	46.5	46.7	47.1	47.2	47.7	47.9	47.1	47.4	47.8	47.9	47.2
2014	47.4	47.3	47.1	47.1	47.5	47.7	48.4	48.8	47.7	48.5	48.7	48.8	47.9
2015	48.5	48.1	47.8	48.0	48.3	48.4	49.6	50.0	49.0	49.6	49.8	49.6	48.9
2016	49.2	49.1	48.9	49.0	49.0	49.0	49.5	49.7	48.6	48.8	49.0	48.9	49.1
2017	48.7	48.4	48.1	47.7	47.7	47.8	48.0	47.9	47.0	47.3	47.0	47.4	47.8
Financial Activities													
2007	156.4	156.1	155.8	156.5	156.9	158.7	158.8	158.3	156.6	157.8	157.7	158.6	157.4
2008	157.4	157.7	157.3	158.1	159.2	160.0	160.7	160.3	157.8	157.3	157.1	157.6	158.4
2009	156.4	155.6	155.1	155.8	156.1	156.9	156.8	156.7	154.1	153.8	153.5	153.8	155.4
2010	152.1	151.7	151.9	152.0	152.2	153.2	153.5	153.2	151.5	151.5	151.3	151.9	152.2
2011	150.2	149.8	149.9	150.3	150.6	151.8	152.3	152.0	151.0	150.6	150.3	150.8	150.8
2012	150.1	149.8	150.0	150.1	150.8	152.2	152.5	152.5	150.8	150.7	150.4	150.9	150.9
2013	149.4	149.2	149.5	149.4	150.3	151.5	151.6	152.4	150.6	150.3	150.0	150.4	150.5
2014	147.9	147.8	148.2	148.9	149.7	151.5	152.0	152.3	150.8	150.0	150.0	150.9	150.0
2015	149.6	149.5	149.7	150.0	151.1	152.8	153.5	153.1	151.2	151.1	151.0	151.6	151.2
2016	150.0	149.8	150.0	150.6	151.2	153.1	154.4	154.2	152.4	152.2	152.1	152.5	151.9
2017	151.7	151.7	152.2	152.2	152.7	154.5	155.1	154.8	152.7	152.0	152.0	150.6	152.7
Professional and Business Services													
2007	268.6	270.4	272.3	279.0	281.3	287.2	286.8	289.8	287.1	287.0	286.6	287.5	282.0
2008	277.4	279.8	278.9	283.5	285.3	288.8	289.6	292.6	289.4	286.5	281.4	278.9	284.3
2009	262.9	258.6	255.6	257.9	258.6	260.4	261.5	263.1	261.5	264.9	265.5	265.8	261.4
2010	256.0	259.5	259.8	269.2	271.0	274.8	279.0	283.2	281.6	285.6	286.0	286.2	274.3
2011	277.2	277.6	280.4	283.9	284.8	290.6	291.3	293.8	294.0	294.0	293.7	291.1	287.7
2012	282.8	284.3	288.2	291.6	292.9	298.2	297.2	298.7	298.8	300.3	301.5	297.6	294.3
2013	287.6	291.3	294.8	294.7	299.6	304.6	306.6	309.1	307.5	307.6	309.0	307.7	301.7
2014	298.0	299.2	299.0	302.3	306.2	309.8	311.2	314.0	312.0	315.4	315.2	311.6	307.8
2015	302.6	303.4	304.2	310.4	312.8	316.3	320.6	323.5	319.6	322.5	321.6	321.8	314.9
2016	314.4	315.7	315.4	321.3	321.0	324.1	326.7	327.9	325.7	325.8	325.2	322.4	322.1
2017	314.2	314.8	317.9	321.7	323.7	327.4	329.6	329.8	326.3	330.9	329.4	326.5	324.4
Education and Health Services													
2007	387.6	389.8	390.7	391.2	392.7	393.5	392.3	393.5	394.7	394.5	395.2	396.2	392.7
2008	392.3	394.3	395.7	396.5	398.1	398.5	397.8	399.5	400.8	405.3	406.5	408.4	399.5
2009	403.7	405.7	407.4	405.9	406.3	406.1	404.4	405.0	405.2	408.9	409.0	409.3	406.4
2010	405.4	407.5	409.3	406.5	407.1	406.1	405.5	406.0	406.2	409.5	410.5	411.0	407.6
2011	405.2	407.5	408.4	410.4	411.6	408.2	406.9	407.4	412.8	415.9	416.7	418.1	410.8
2012	410.1	415.6	418.2	418.4	419.3	416.2	410.6	413.3	420.2	425.1	425.8	427.1	418.3
2013	416.7	423.4	424.8	425.0	425.5	422.0	416.1	419.3	425.4	429.6	430.7	431.0	424.1
2014	422.8	429.3	430.7	431.4	431.5	429.3	423.2	425.7	431.7	435.1	436.9	438.1	430.5
2015	427.6	434.8	436.7	437.0	437.6	434.8	429.4	430.6	436.5	441.4	442.9	444.8	436.2
2016	435.9	443.3	444.7	446.6	446.2	442.8	439.2	440.3	447.1	449.9	450.9	451.0	444.8
2017	443.1	450.3	451.5	452.0	450.8	450.3	443.5	445.0	451.3	457.1	456.3	455.6	450.6

1. Employment by Industry: Wisconsin, Selected Years, 2007–2017—*Continued*

(Numbers in thousands, not seasonally adjusted)

Industry and year	January	February	March	April	May	June	July	August	September	October	November	December	Annual average
Leisure and Hospitality													
2007	242.9	242.8	246.0	254.2	268.6	281.0	284.1	286.1	271.4	261.9	253.6	251.0	262.0
2008	242.2	241.1	244.2	252.7	268.3	277.9	281.2	282.2	268.7	259.6	249.2	246.1	259.5
2009	235.1	235.6	237.9	246.3	262.0	271.9	274.0	274.3	262.2	251.5	241.5	239.6	252.7
2010	230.8	230.7	233.6	245.4	258.1	268.8	273.1	275.4	262.8	253.0	244.1	241.2	251.4
2011	232.7	232.4	235.0	245.1	258.4	270.3	275.1	276.7	264.3	253.8	244.3	241.0	252.4
2012	234.4	235.4	240.4	250.2	263.9	276.5	280.2	280.6	269.0	256.6	247.8	247.6	256.9
2013	238.8	239.6	243.2	250.4	268.6	279.8	284.5	286.6	273.8	262.5	253.6	252.6	261.2
2014	242.5	243.8	246.8	255.8	271.8	284.5	286.3	287.5	273.8	264.4	256.3	255.2	264.1
2015	247.3	248.5	253.1	262.8	277.9	290.9	293.5	294.4	280.7	272.8	265.3	263.4	270.9
2016	254.3	256.4	259.2	268.6	283.1	295.1	300.1	300.5	284.8	276.7	267.6	264.5	275.9
2017	259.8	261.1	265.2	271.6	286.3	302.6	304.8	304.3	286.5	280.5	270.5	267.9	280.1
Other Services													
2007	135.1	135.5	136.5	137.3	138.0	139.7	139.0	138.3	137.5	138.3	137.8	138.4	137.6
2008	135.9	136.4	137.3	138.4	139.2	140.9	140.3	140.0	139.3	141.2	139.7	139.9	139.0
2009	136.7	137.0	138.1	138.2	138.6	140.1	139.1	138.7	137.6	137.6	137.2	137.7	138.1
2010	134.5	135.0	136.0	137.1	137.3	138.6	138.3	138.0	137.0	137.8	136.7	137.2	137.0
2011	135.1	135.1	136.1	137.0	137.5	139.0	138.8	138.5	137.4	137.5	137.0	137.9	137.2
2012	135.7	136.2	136.7	137.5	138.0	140.4	139.2	138.8	137.7	138.0	137.7	138.1	137.8
2013	135.6	135.7	136.5	136.9	137.9	139.7	139.0	138.9	138.8	138.5	139.3	140.2	138.1
2014	138.4	139.2	140.3	141.4	142.6	144.9	145.3	145.7	145.0	145.2	145.3	146.5	143.3
2015	145.1	145.6	146.9	147.9	148.7	150.2	149.9	149.4	148.3	148.4	148.0	149.3	148.1
2016	146.9	146.9	148.0	149.5	149.8	151.2	151.8	151.6	150.8	150.6	150.5	150.8	149.9
2017	148.7	149.2	150.3	150.4	151.0	152.9	151.9	151.8	150.6	152.3	151.1	151.1	150.9
Government													
2007	410.2	416.8	422.5	427.0	427.1	422.1	388.3	384.8	414.0	423.8	426.3	428.8	416.0
2008	416.7	422.2	427.2	429.6	432.5	422.2	392.4	387.0	423.0	432.5	441.4	436.0	421.9
2009	418.6	431.2	432.7	434.9	435.8	421.8	392.5	385.1	408.6	426.2	431.2	431.8	420.9
2010	415.3	425.1	427.6	435.4	437.5	421.4	390.0	384.3	411.2	428.8	433.9	426.5	419.8
2011	412.2	426.6	428.1	430.8	428.6	411.5	386.9	380.7	408.7	419.1	422.0	422.3	414.8
2012	395.9	411.4	419.9	427.3	428.7	408.7	378.3	378.6	406.7	422.3	429.7	422.9	410.9
2013	394.9	420.3	419.5	422.7	416.9	404.2	378.2	375.7	408.9	422.3	423.5	422.2	409.1
2014	405.2	418.1	418.8	424.7	417.9	405.7	380.8	384.4	410.5	422.6	431.0	422.8	411.9
2015	403.1	420.0	418.9	426.7	417.4	404.0	380.3	377.2	405.9	418.6	419.2	420.7	409.3
2016	403.1	419.1	418.2	427.1	415.2	403.7	383.3	387.1	408.1	420.7	433.2	423.3	411.8
2017	400.9	416.9	413.6	423.3	416.6	399.4	381.3	376.5	404.8	419.9	421.2	416.4	407.6

2. Average Weekly Hours by Selected Industry: Wisconsin, 2013–2017

(Not seasonally adjusted)

Industry and year	January	February	March	April	May	June	July	August	September	October	November	December	Annual average
Total Private													
2013	33.2	33.4	33.4	33.3	33.3	33.8	33.6	33.7	33.8	33.5	33.4	33.6	33.5
2014	33.0	33.8	33.9	33.5	33.7	34.2	33.9	34.0	34.1	34.0	34.1	33.8	33.8
2015	33.4	33.7	33.8	33.4	33.6	33.7	33.8	34.1	33.6	33.7	34.0	33.6	33.7
2016	33.1	33.1	33.3	33.4	33.6	33.6	33.8	33.8	33.6	34.0	33.7	33.4	33.5
2017	33.6	33.3	33.3	33.8	33.5	33.8	34.2	33.9	33.8	34.1	33.9	33.8	33.7
Goods-Producing													
2013	39.5	39.4	39.6	39.5	39.5	40.2	39.9	40.1	40.0	40.1	40.0	39.8	39.8
2014	38.9	39.6	40.0	39.8	40.4	40.8	40.6	41.0	41.3	40.9	41.0	40.8	40.4
2015	40.3	39.8	40.0	40.3	40.9	40.7	40.7	41.0	40.6	41.3	41.1	40.6	40.6
2016	39.7	39.3	39.9	40.0	40.1	40.2	40.6	40.2	40.6	40.8	41.1	40.0	40.2
2017	39.8	39.7	40.1	40.0	40.4	40.2	40.5	40.8	40.8	40.8	40.6	40.3	40.3
Construction													
2013	37.1	36.0	37.1	36.2	39.1	40.0	40.0	40.3	39.7	40.0	38.8	37.2	38.6
2014	36.3	36.7	37.5	38.6	40.5	41.1	41.0	41.2	41.0	40.4	39.7	39.0	39.6
2015	37.9	36.0	37.8	38.6	39.7	38.6	39.0	39.7	38.4	40.7	39.0	38.6	38.7
2016	37.0	37.4	38.2	39.4	39.0	40.2	40.1	40.4	40.2	40.3	40.1	37.5	39.2
2017	37.7	37.9	38.1	39.3	40.2	39.6	39.0	40.0	40.0	40.2	39.4	38.2	39.2
Manufacturing													
2013	39.8	40.1	40.1	40.2	39.5	40.1	39.7	39.9	39.9	40.0	40.2	40.3	40.0
2014	39.4	40.1	40.4	39.9	40.3	40.7	40.4	40.8	41.2	40.9	41.2	41.1	40.5
2015	40.7	40.5	40.3	40.6	41.0	41.1	41.0	41.3	40.5	40.7	41.0	40.5	40.8
2016	39.8	39.3	39.9	39.8	40.1	39.9	40.3	39.7	40.3	40.5	41.0	40.4	40.1
2017	40.1	40.0	40.4	40.0	40.2	40.2	40.7	40.8	40.9	40.9	40.9	40.8	40.5
Trade, Transportation, and Utilities													
2013	31.8	32.0	32.7	32.3	32.5	32.8	32.7	32.8	33.0	32.3	32.0	32.5	32.5
2014	31.8	32.8	32.8	32.8	33.1	33.2	33.1	33.3	33.4	33.4	33.5	33.9	33.1
2015	33.2	33.8	33.9	33.4	33.9	33.8	34.0	34.0	33.5	33.4	33.7	33.6	33.7
2016	32.3	32.3	32.3	32.9	32.9	33.2	33.3	33.2	32.9	32.9	32.4	32.6	32.8
2017	32.1	31.9	32.0	32.6	32.4	32.9	33.3	33.0	33.0	33.1	33.5	33.5	32.8
Financial Activities													
2013	36.5	36.9	36.6	36.6	36.4	37.5	36.4	36.6	37.5	36.6	36.6	38.0	36.9
2014	37.1	38.0	38.1	37.0	37.0	38.5	37.2	37.1	36.9	37.1	38.1	37.1	37.4
2015	36.7	37.6	37.9	36.5	36.5	36.3	36.0	37.8	37.1	36.8	37.9	37.2	37.0
2016	37.4	37.3	37.9	37.4	38.3	36.8	36.5	37.3	36.8	38.1	37.5	37.4	37.4
2017	37.9	36.2	36.3	37.8	36.4	37.2	37.5	37.4	36.7	37.9	37.2	37.5	37.2
Professional and Business Services													
2013	33.4	34.5	34.0	33.8	33.7	34.7	34.0	34.6	34.6	34.6	34.5	34.8	34.3
2014	34.1	35.4	35.7	34.9	34.9	35.6	34.8	34.7	34.8	35.0	35.0	34.6	35.0
2015	34.1	34.6	34.8	34.1	34.5	34.6	34.4	34.8	34.0	34.4	35.1	34.3	34.5
2016	34.2	34.9	35.0	34.6	35.1	35.2	34.9	35.1	34.9	35.6	34.8	34.6	34.9
2017	35.1	35.0	34.9	35.7	35.3	36.1	36.2	35.4	35.3	35.7	35.4	35.1	35.4
Education and Health Services													
2013	32.0	31.8	31.7	31.7	31.6	31.8	31.6	31.4	31.7	31.3	31.5	31.7	31.6
2014	31.5	31.7	31.7	31.4	31.5	31.6	31.3	31.3	31.4	31.5	31.8	31.4	31.5
2015	31.2	31.4	31.2	30.9	30.9	30.8	30.9	31.1	31.0	30.8	31.0	30.9	31.0
2016	30.9	30.8	30.8	31.1	31.6	31.2	31.5	31.3	31.2	31.5	31.3	31.4	31.2
2017	32.1	31.6	31.6	32.0	31.5	31.6	32.2	31.5	31.6	31.6	31.3	31.7	31.7
Leisure and Hospitality													
2013	21.5	22.4	22.3	21.9	22.5	23.2	23.4	23.2	22.8	22.6	22.2	22.2	22.5
2014	21.4	22.5	22.5	21.9	22.1	22.9	23.4	23.4	22.8	22.6	22.6	22.0	22.5
2015	21.8	22.5	22.4	22.1	22.0	22.7	22.9	23.2	22.1	22.0	21.8	21.8	22.3
2016	21.2	22.0	21.7	21.8	22.4	22.7	23.2	23.3	22.4	22.3	21.9	21.2	22.2
2017	21.7	22.0	22.0	21.8	21.9	22.9	23.3	22.8	22.3	22.4	21.7	21.4	22.2
Other Services													
2013	29.5	29.6	29.0	29.4	28.9	30.1	29.9	30.5	29.3	29.4	29.4	30.6	29.6
2014	30.6	30.6	30.4	29.6	29.0	30.1	29.2	29.5	29.1	28.7	27.9	28.1	29.4
2015	27.6	27.6	28.1	27.1	27.2	29.0	29.2	29.5	27.8	27.7	28.0	27.8	28.1
2016	28.3	27.7	27.4	27.7	28.0	28.5	28.7	28.6	27.8	28.5	28.4	28.3	28.2
2017	28.2	27.9	27.2	27.8	27.2	27.8	27.6	27.7	26.6	26.9	27.0	27.0	27.4

3. Average Hourly Earnings by Selected Industry: Wisconsin, 2013–2017

(Dollars, not seasonally adjusted)

Industry and year	January	February	March	April	May	June	July	August	September	October	November	December	Annual average
Total Private													
2013	23.10	23.22	23.00	23.26	23.04	22.90	22.92	22.83	23.36	23.10	23.19	23.39	23.11
2014	23.48	23.59	23.45	23.57	23.23	23.11	22.99	22.91	23.11	23.08	23.23	23.21	23.24
2015	23.57	23.60	23.54	23.52	23.40	23.09	23.11	23.25	23.38	23.60	23.69	23.81	23.46
2016	23.98	23.91	23.86	23.99	24.09	23.76	23.96	23.91	23.84	24.28	24.31	24.43	24.03
2017	24.68	24.40	24.50	24.95	24.40	24.15	24.53	24.39	24.87	25.21	25.15	25.57	24.73
Goods-Producing													
2013	23.11	23.21	23.17	23.33	23.37	23.40	23.33	23.23	23.68	23.54	23.55	23.81	23.40
2014	23.87	23.90	23.94	24.11	23.96	23.94	23.85	23.92	24.10	24.23	24.34	24.67	24.07
2015	24.44	24.53	24.61	24.73	24.62	24.38	24.48	24.55	24.48	24.66	24.63	25.08	24.60
2016	24.74	24.73	24.53	24.76	24.78	24.96	25.20	25.23	25.44	25.74	25.54	25.78	25.13
2017	25.73	25.49	25.46	25.87	25.70	25.55	25.95	25.80	26.08	26.12	26.31	26.75	25.91
Construction													
2013	25.96	25.95	26.05	26.40	25.68	25.76	26.06	25.89	26.56	26.47	26.72	27.19	26.22
2014	27.33	26.85	27.08	26.58	25.75	26.03	26.15	26.69	27.08	27.28	26.89	27.39	26.73
2015	27.37	27.26	27.77	27.99	27.91	27.67	27.64	27.82	27.36	27.65	27.72	27.91	27.68
2016	28.19	27.76	27.69	27.77	27.52	28.10	28.56	27.89	28.20	28.07	27.88	28.55	28.02
2017	27.99	27.92	28.28	27.69	28.13	28.01	28.54	28.97	28.67	28.71	28.17	29.04	28.36
Manufacturing													
2013	22.40	22.44	22.36	22.50	22.59	22.59	22.38	22.32	22.72	22.58	22.56	22.91	22.53
2014	23.03	23.18	23.18	23.43	23.36	23.24	23.13	23.10	23.27	23.39	23.66	24.02	23.33
2015	23.79	23.96	23.92	23.94	23.79	23.54	23.64	23.62	23.71	23.81	23.80	24.37	23.82
2016	23.96	24.00	23.76	23.90	24.02	23.98	24.15	24.37	24.58	25.02	24.83	25.06	24.31
2017	25.15	24.87	24.75	25.36	25.16	24.98	25.34	24.96	25.38	25.43	25.86	26.21	25.29
Trade, Transportation, and Utilities													
2013	20.38	20.49	19.82	20.31	20.06	20.03	19.85	19.94	20.31	19.92	19.75	19.58	20.03
2014	19.69	19.89	19.94	20.15	19.99	20.09	20.35	19.97	20.15	20.18	20.25	19.93	20.05
2015	20.68	20.84	20.65	20.96	20.64	20.38	20.57	20.63	20.71	20.57	20.41	20.44	20.62
2016	20.93	20.87	20.92	21.16	21.23	21.08	21.15	20.82	21.32	21.48	21.55	21.53	21.17
2017	21.68	21.43	21.53	21.93	22.12	22.07	22.23	22.23	22.79	22.84	22.35	22.63	22.16
Financial Activities													
2013	29.46	29.09	28.92	29.77	29.04	28.57	28.61	28.28	28.62	28.20	28.37	28.33	28.77
2014	28.61	29.49	28.81	29.00	28.12	28.26	28.00	28.37	28.55	28.22	28.89	29.22	28.63
2015	29.60	29.91	29.75	29.33	29.98	29.31	29.79	29.54	29.21	29.91	29.49	29.38	29.60
2016	30.43	30.25	29.98	30.22	30.22	29.31	29.82	29.81	30.36	30.24	30.24	30.33	30.10
2017	31.41	31.23	31.61	32.32	31.50	30.58	31.50	31.04	31.53	32.43	32.14	33.29	31.71
Professional and Business Services													
2013	27.61	28.58	28.35	28.58	28.79	28.92	29.95	29.66	29.75	29.28	29.49	29.51	29.06
2014	29.69	29.80	29.13	29.54	28.76	28.50	28.05	27.66	27.26	27.11	27.09	26.71	28.26
2015	27.13	26.82	26.86	26.16	25.96	25.80	25.51	25.78	26.04	26.46	26.94	26.96	26.36
2016	27.06	27.12	26.93	27.29	27.19	27.44	27.21	27.21	27.40	28.08	28.20	28.27	27.31
2017	27.39	26.86	27.39	28.34	27.68	27.86	28.35	27.79	27.98	28.52	28.33	28.19	27.90
Education and Health Services													
2013	23.76	23.53	23.50	23.56	23.44	23.18	23.09	23.15	23.90	23.47	23.80	24.39	23.57
2014	24.32	24.16	24.22	24.12	24.06	24.01	23.95	24.06	24.61	24.17	24.28	24.50	24.21
2015	24.93	24.67	24.52	24.57	24.59	24.39	24.29	24.56	24.73	24.86	25.06	25.15	24.70
2016	25.06	24.93	25.00	24.66	24.90	24.71	25.26	25.33	25.36	25.71	26.01	25.75	25.23
2017	26.00	26.21	26.03	26.17	26.11	25.90	26.12	25.83	26.11	26.42	26.53	26.67	26.18
Leisure and Hospitality													
2013	11.86	11.81	11.85	11.93	11.71	11.48	11.49	11.55	11.75	11.98	12.06	12.16	11.79
2014	12.23	12.29	12.25	12.39	12.26	11.96	11.80	12.00	12.09	12.49	12.59	12.59	12.23
2015	12.73	13.03	12.95	13.13	13.01	12.72	12.70	12.69	13.02	13.43	13.52	13.49	13.02
2016	13.43	13.59	13.58	13.68	13.49	13.02	13.08	12.99	13.50	13.84	13.73	14.00	13.47
2017	13.97	14.02	14.14	14.21	14.07	13.47	13.25	13.39	13.75	14.04	14.06	14.44	13.88
Other Services													
2013	19.79	19.95	20.08	19.77	19.71	19.42	19.19	19.11	20.53	20.89	19.77	21.02	19.94
2014	20.80	20.55	20.19	19.99	19.96	19.31	19.10	19.02	19.05	18.81	19.04	18.51	19.53
2015	19.39	19.56	19.47	19.61	19.65	19.20	19.01	19.19	19.48	18.75	19.17	19.27	19.31
2016	19.09	18.93	19.09	18.95	19.10	18.62	19.06	18.91	19.35	19.81	19.88	20.37	19.27
2017	20.52	20.77	20.39	20.35	20.08	19.36	19.80	19.84	20.37	20.71	20.14	21.02	20.28

4. Average Weekly Earnings by Selected Industry: Wisconsin, 2012–2016

(Dollars, not seasonally adjusted)

Industry and year	January	February	March	April	May	June	July	August	September	October	November	December	Annual average
Total Private													
2013	766.92	775.55	768.20	774.56	767.23	774.02	770.11	769.37	789.57	773.85	774.55	785.90	774.19
2014	774.84	797.34	794.96	789.60	782.85	790.36	779.36	778.94	788.05	784.72	792.14	784.50	785.51
2015	787.24	795.32	795.65	785.57	786.24	778.13	781.12	792.83	785.57	795.32	805.46	800.02	790.60
2016	793.74	791.42	794.54	801.27	809.42	798.34	809.85	808.16	801.02	825.52	819.25	815.96	805.01
2017	829.25	812.52	815.85	843.31	817.40	816.27	838.93	826.82	840.61	859.66	852.59	864.27	833.40
Goods-Producing													
2013	912.85	914.47	917.53	921.54	923.12	940.68	930.87	931.52	947.20	943.95	942.00	947.64	931.32
2014	928.54	946.44	957.60	959.58	967.98	976.75	968.31	980.72	995.33	991.01	997.94	1,006.54	972.43
2015	984.93	976.29	984.40	996.62	1,006.96	992.27	996.34	1,006.55	993.89	1,018.46	1,012.29	1,018.25	998.76
2016	982.18	971.89	978.75	990.40	993.68	1,003.39	1,023.12	1,014.25	1,032.86	1,050.19	1,049.69	1,031.20	1,010.23
2017	1,024.05	1,011.95	1,020.95	1,034.80	1,038.28	1,027.11	1,050.98	1,052.64	1,064.06	1,065.70	1,068.19	1,078.03	1,044.17
Construction													
2013	963.12	934.20	966.46	955.68	1,004.09	1,030.40	1,042.40	1,043.37	1,054.43	1,058.80	1,036.74	1,011.47	1,012.09
2014	992.08	985.40	1,015.50	1,025.99	1,042.88	1,069.83	1,072.15	1,099.63	1,110.28	1,102.11	1,067.53	1,068.21	1,058.51
2015	1,037.32	981.36	1,049.71	1,080.41	1,108.03	1,068.06	1,077.96	1,104.45	1,050.62	1,125.36	1,081.08	1,077.33	1,071.22
2016	1,043.03	1,038.22	1,057.76	1,094.14	1,073.28	1,129.62	1,145.26	1,126.76	1,133.64	1,131.22	1,117.99	1,070.63	1,098.38
2017	1,055.22	1,058.17	1,077.47	1,088.22	1,130.83	1,109.20	1,113.06	1,158.80	1,146.80	1,154.14	1,109.90	1,109.33	1,111.71
Manufacturing													
2013	891.52	899.84	896.64	904.50	892.31	905.86	888.49	890.57	906.53	903.20	906.91	923.27	901.20
2014	907.38	929.52	936.47	934.86	941.41	945.87	934.45	942.48	958.72	956.65	974.79	987.22	944.87
2015	968.25	970.38	963.98	971.96	975.39	967.49	969.24	975.51	960.26	969.07	975.80	986.99	971.86
2016	953.61	943.20	948.02	951.22	963.20	956.80	973.25	967.49	990.57	1,013.31	1,018.03	1,012.42	974.83
2017	1,008.52	994.80	999.90	1,014.40	1,011.43	1,004.20	1,031.34	1,018.37	1,038.04	1,040.09	1,057.67	1,069.37	1,024.25
Trade, Transportation, and Utilities													
2013	648.08	655.68	648.11	656.01	651.95	656.98	649.10	654.03	670.23	643.42	632.00	636.35	650.98
2014	626.14	652.39	654.03	660.92	661.67	666.99	673.59	665.00	673.01	674.01	678.38	675.63	663.66
2015	686.58	704.39	700.04	700.06	699.70	688.84	699.38	701.42	693.79	687.04	687.82	686.78	694.89
2016	676.04	674.10	675.72	696.16	698.47	699.86	704.30	691.22	701.43	706.69	698.22	701.88	694.38
2017	695.93	683.62	688.96	714.92	716.69	726.10	740.26	733.59	752.07	756.00	748.73	758.11	726.85
Financial Activities													
2013	1,075.29	1,073.42	1,058.47	1,089.58	1,057.06	1,071.38	1,041.40	1,035.05	1,073.25	1,032.12	1,038.34	1,076.54	1,061.61
2014	1,061.43	1,120.62	1,097.66	1,073.00	1,040.44	1,088.01	1,041.60	1,052.53	1,053.50	1,046.96	1,100.71	1,084.06	1,070.76
2015	1,086.32	1,124.62	1,127.53	1,070.55	1,094.27	1,063.95	1,072.44	1,116.61	1,083.69	1,100.69	1,117.67	1,092.94	1,095.20
2016	1,138.08	1,128.33	1,136.24	1,130.23	1,157.43	1,078.61	1,088.43	1,111.91	1,117.25	1,152.14	1,134.00	1,134.34	1,125.74
2017	1,190.44	1,130.53	1,147.44	1,221.70	1,146.60	1,137.58	1,181.25	1,160.90	1,157.15	1,229.10	1,195.61	1,248.38	1,179.61
Professional and Business Services													
2013	922.17	986.01	963.90	966.00	970.22	1,003.52	1,018.30	1,026.24	1,029.35	1,013.09	1,017.41	1,026.95	996.76
2014	1,012.43	1,054.92	1,039.94	1,030.95	1,003.72	1,014.60	976.14	959.80	948.65	948.85	948.15	924.17	989.10
2015	925.13	927.97	934.73	892.06	895.62	892.68	877.54	897.14	885.36	910.22	945.59	924.73	909.42
2016	925.45	946.49	942.55	944.23	975.43	965.89	949.63	957.18	956.26	999.65	981.36	978.14	960.10
2017	961.39	940.10	955.91	1,011.74	977.10	1,005.75	1,026.27	983.77	987.69	1,018.16	1,002.88	989.47	987.66
Education and Health Services													
2013	760.32	748.25	744.95	746.85	740.70	737.12	729.64	726.91	757.63	734.61	749.70	773.16	744.81
2014	766.08	765.87	767.77	757.37	757.89	758.72	749.64	753.08	772.75	761.36	772.10	769.30	762.62
2015	777.82	774.64	765.02	759.21	759.83	751.21	750.56	763.82	766.63	765.69	776.86	777.14	765.70
2016	774.35	767.84	770.00	766.93	786.84	770.95	795.69	792.83	791.23	809.87	814.11	808.55	787.18
2017	834.60	828.24	822.55	837.44	822.47	818.44	841.06	813.65	825.08	834.87	830.39	845.44	829.91
Leisure and Hospitality													
2013	254.99	264.54	264.26	261.27	263.48	266.34	268.87	267.96	267.90	270.75	267.73	269.95	265.28
2014	261.72	276.53	275.63	271.34	270.95	273.88	276.12	280.80	275.65	282.27	284.53	276.98	275.18
2015	277.51	293.18	290.08	290.17	286.22	288.74	290.83	294.41	287.74	295.46	294.74	294.08	290.35
2016	284.72	298.98	294.69	298.22	302.18	295.55	303.46	302.67	302.40	308.63	300.69	296.80	299.03
2017	303.15	308.44	311.08	309.78	308.13	308.46	308.73	305.29	306.63	314.50	305.10	309.02	308.14
Other Services													
2013	583.81	590.52	582.32	581.24	569.62	584.54	573.78	582.86	601.53	614.17	581.24	643.21	590.22
2014	636.48	628.83	613.78	591.70	578.84	581.23	557.72	561.09	554.36	539.85	531.22	520.13	574.18
2015	535.16	539.86	547.11	531.43	534.48	556.80	555.09	566.11	541.54	519.38	536.76	535.71	542.61
2016	540.25	524.36	523.07	524.92	534.80	530.67	547.02	540.83	537.93	564.59	564.59	576.47	543.41
2017	578.66	579.48	554.61	565.73	546.18	538.21	546.48	549.57	541.84	557.10	543.78	567.54	555.67

WYOMING
At a Glance

Population:
 2010 census: 563,626
 2017 estimate: 579,315

Percent change in population:
 2010–2017: 2.8%

Percent change in total nonfarm employment:
 2007–2017: -2.8%

Industry with the largest growth in employment, 2007–2017 (thousands):
 Education and health services, 4.3

Industry with the largest decline or smallest growth in employment, 2007–2017 (thousands):
 Mining and logging, -7.8

Civilian labor force:
 2010: 303,297
 2017: 293,347

Unemployment rate and rank among states (highest to lowest):
 2010: 6.4%, 45th
 2017: 4.2%, 27th

Over-the-year change in unemployment rates:
 2015–2016: 1.0%
 2016–2017: -1.1%

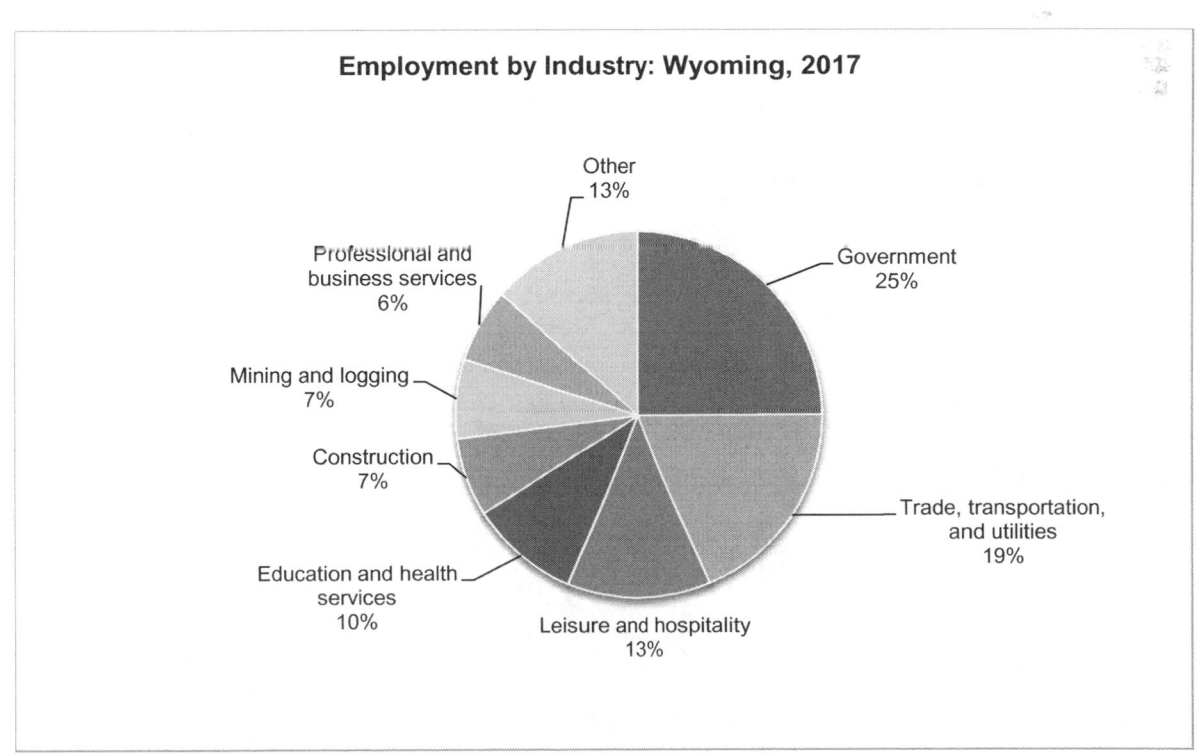

Employment by Industry: Wyoming, 2017

Other 13%
Professional and business services 6%
Mining and logging 7%
Construction 7%
Education and health services 10%
Leisure and hospitality 13%
Government 25%
Trade, transportation, and utilities 19%

1. Employment by Industry: Wyoming, Selected Years, 2006–2016

(Numbers in thousands, not seasonally adjusted)

Industry and year	January	February	March	April	May	June	July	August	September	October	November	December	Annual average
Total Nonfarm													
2007	275.9	277.7	281.1	281.3	290.0	299.2	295.5	296.0	296.9	294.7	292.6	293.4	289.5
2008	287.3	289.2	291.0	291.5	300.3	307.6	305.3	305.0	306.6	304.2	298.6	297.4	298.7
2009	287.3	285.5	285.5	283.3	290.8	294.5	289.4	288.5	291.0	285.4	280.7	280.0	286.8
2010	272.2	273.3	275.5	278.0	285.9	292.4	288.5	290.1	292.7	290.0	283.7	283.9	283.9
2011	275.6	277.2	279.5	280.6	288.1	296.1	296.1	296.8	298.4	294.7	289.5	290.9	288.6
2012	282.3	283.7	285.8	286.9	293.3	299.8	298.2	298.2	298.1	295.1	290.0	290.8	291.9
2013	282.7	283.4	285.8	286.4	294.0	302.0	300.3	299.9	298.8	296.9	291.1	292.0	292.8
2014	285.3	286.3	288.2	290.0	298.4	306.0	305.5	304.3	304.0	302.7	294.9	297.2	296.9
2015	290.0	290.2	291.2	291.6	297.0	302.2	301.8	301.0	300.4	297.8	289.5	289.8	295.2
2016	281.3	280.6	281.4	280.9	286.2	291.7	289.7	288.7	287.1	283.7	277.7	278.4	284.0
2017	272.0	273.0	274.9	275.2	283.0	289.0	288.3	288.7	287.9	284.4	278.9	280.4	281.3
Total Private													
2007	209.8	210.8	213.7	213.9	221.2	230.5	233.0	233.5	228.9	225.6	223.5	224.4	222.4
2008	219.9	220.5	221.7	222.0	228.9	237.4	241.5	241.7	237.1	233.6	228.1	226.7	229.9
2009	218.3	215.0	214.3	211.7	217.6	222.4	224.5	223.7	219.5	213.4	208.9	208.2	216.5
2010	202.1	201.7	202.8	205.9	210.9	218.6	222.6	224.3	220.9	217.2	211.3	211.5	212.5
2011	205.0	205.0	206.7	207.9	214.1	222.8	227.0	228.3	225.9	221.5	216.7	217.9	216.6
2012	211.0	210.7	212.4	214.3	219.0	226.7	228.7	229.9	225.5	221.6	216.9	217.5	219.5
2013	211.1	210.7	212.6	213.6	220.1	229.0	232.1	231.9	226.9	224.2	218.9	219.6	220.9
2014	214.7	214.5	215.6	218.1	225.4	234.4	237.1	237.1	232.7	230.5	223.3	225.3	225.7
2015	220.2	219.2	219.2	220.0	224.0	230.5	234.1	233.1	228.4	224.8	217.0	217.2	224.0
2016	210.7	208.7	208.8	208.9	212.9	219.4	222.0	220.9	215.9	212.1	206.4	206.9	212.8
2017	202.6	202.1	203.4	204.2	210.7	218.1	221.6	221.8	217.8	213.3	208.6	210.2	211.2
Goods Producing													
2007	59.7	59.4	60.6	61.7	63.8	65.8	66.3	67.0	65.9	66.5	66.9	65.6	64.1
2008	63.9	63.6	63.9	64.6	66.9	68.7	70.3	71.1	70.2	70.4	69.0	66.2	67.4
2009	61.6	59.3	58.3	57.7	59.0	58.9	59.4	59.2	58.3	57.6	56.7	55.0	58.4
2010	52.3	51.9	52.5	54.2	55.8	56.9	58.3	59.7	59.3	59.7	57.9	56.1	56.2
2011	52.9	52.7	53.2	54.5	56.5	58.5	59.9	60.7	61.3	61.6	60.7	59.4	57.7
2012	56.1	55.7	56.4	58.3	59.2	59.8	59.9	60.6	60.4	60.1	58.8	57.4	58.6
2013	55.1	54.6	55.2	56.0	58.1	59.6	60.3	60.5	59.5	60.0	59.1	58.5	58.0
2014	56.7	56.6	57.1	58.6	61.4	63.3	63.8	63.7	63.5	63.5	61.7	60.8	60.9
2015	58.3	57.4	56.7	57.1	57.3	57.3	58.2	58.2	57.5	57.4	54.9	53.1	57.0
2016	50.2	49.0	48.7	49.5	49.6	49.5	50.1	50.0	49.3	49.1	48.4	47.3	49.2
2017	45.2	45.2	45.8	47.4	48.8	49.4	50.4	50.5	50.6	50.8	49.8	48.9	48.6
Service-Providing													
2007	216.2	218.3	220.5	219.6	226.2	233.4	229.2	229.0	231.0	228.2	225.7	227.8	225.4
2008	223.4	225.6	227.1	226.9	233.4	238.9	235.0	233.9	236.4	233.8	229.6	231.2	231.3
2009	225.7	226.2	227.2	225.6	231.8	235.6	230.0	229.3	232.7	227.8	224.0	225.0	228.4
2010	219.9	221.4	223.0	223.8	230.1	235.5	230.2	230.4	233.4	230.3	225.8	227.8	227.6
2011	222.7	224.5	226.3	226.1	231.6	237.6	236.2	236.1	237.1	233.1	228.8	231.5	231.0
2012	226.2	228.0	229.4	228.6	234.1	240.0	238.3	237.6	237.7	235.0	231.2	233.4	233.3
2013	227.6	228.8	230.6	230.4	235.9	242.4	240.0	239.4	239.3	236.9	232.0	233.5	234.7
2014	228.6	229.7	231.1	231.4	237.0	242.7	241.7	240.6	240.5	239.2	233.2	236.4	236.0
2015	231.7	232.8	234.5	234.5	239.7	244.9	243.6	242.8	242.9	240.4	234.6	236.7	238.3
2016	231.1	231.6	232.7	231.4	236.6	242.2	239.6	238.7	237.8	234.6	229.3	231.1	234.7
2017	226.8	227.8	229.1	227.8	234.2	239.6	237.9	238.2	237.3	233.6	229.1	231.5	232.7
Mining and Logging													
2007	27.0	26.9	26.8	26.8	27.2	27.7	27.6	27.7	27.5	27.6	27.8	27.9	27.4
2008	28.1	28.1	28.1	28.0	28.6	29.3	29.8	30.2	30.2	30.5	30.5	30.3	29.3
2009	29.2	28.1	27.2	25.8	25.2	24.8	24.6	24.4	24.2	24.1	24.2	24.2	25.5
2010	24.0	24.0	24.1	24.2	24.6	25.1	25.6	25.9	25.8	26.1	26.3	26.5	25.2
2011	26.2	26.2	26.3	26.4	26.7	27.3	27.8	28.1	28.2	28.5	28.6	28.8	27.4
2012	28.3	28.3	28.1	27.8	27.8	28.1	27.8	27.7	27.3	27.3	27.4	27.3	27.8
2013	26.6	26.5	26.5	26.4	26.3	26.6	26.8	26.9	26.7	26.8	26.8	27.0	26.7
2014	26.9	26.8	26.9	26.9	27.0	27.4	27.6	27.8	27.7	27.8	27.9	27.9	27.4
2015	27.4	26.6	25.7	24.5	23.8	23.4	23.4	23.2	22.8	22.8	22.0	21.7	23.9
2016	21.2	20.5	19.8	19.0	18.3	18.1	18.1	18.0	18.0	18.3	18.4	18.6	18.9
2017	18.5	18.7	18.9	19.1	19.4	19.6	19.9	20.0	20.1	20.2	20.5	20.6	19.6

1. Employment by Industry: Wyoming, Selected Years, 2006–2016—*Continued*

(Numbers in thousands, not seasonally adjusted)

Industry and year	January	February	March	April	May	June	July	August	September	October	November	December	Annual average
Construction													
2007	22.4	22.4	23.6	24.9	26.5	28.0	28.6	29.2	28.3	28.6	28.7	27.4	26.6
2008	25.8	25.6	26.2	26.8	28.5	29.4	30.5	30.9	30.1	29.6	28.2	25.9	28.1
2009	22.8	22.0	22.1	23.0	24.9	25.2	25.8	25.8	25.0	24.4	23.5	21.9	23.9
2010	19.7	19.5	19.9	21.6	22.8	23.2	24.0	24.9	24.6	24.5	22.4	20.5	22.3
2011	17.9	17.8	18.3	19.3	20.9	22.1	23.0	23.3	23.8	23.5	22.5	21.0	21.1
2012	18.6	18.2	19.2	21.5	22.3	22.4	22.7	23.6	23.7	23.1	21.8	20.6	21.5
2013	19.1	18.8	19.6	20.5	22.6	23.5	23.9	24.0	23.1	23.2	22.4	21.6	21.9
2014	20.2	20.3	20.6	22.3	24.8	26.1	26.3	26.0	25.9	25.6	23.7	22.8	23.7
2015	21.0	21.0	21.5	23.1	23.8	24.2	25.0	25.2	24.9	24.7	23.1	21.7	23.3
2016	19.6	19.3	19.8	21.5	22.3	22.2	22.7	22.7	22.1	21.5	20.6	19.4	21.1
2017	17.5	17.4	17.7	19.3	20.3	20.6	21.0	20.9	20.9	20.8	19.5	18.5	19.5
Manufacturing													
2007	10.3	10.1	10.2	10.0	10.1	10.1	10.1	10.1	10.1	10.3	10.4	10.3	10.2
2008	10.0	9.9	9.6	9.8	9.8	10.0	10.0	10.0	9.9	10.3	10.3	10.0	10.0
2009	9.6	9.2	9.0	8.9	8.9	8.9	9.0	9.0	9.1	9.1	9.0	8.9	9.1
2010	8.6	8.4	8.5	8.4	8.4	8.6	8.7	8.9	8.9	9.1	9.2	9.1	8.7
2011	8.8	8.7	8.6	8.8	8.9	9.1	9.1	9.3	9.3	9.6	9.6	9.6	9.1
2012	9.2	9.2	9.1	9.0	9.1	9.3	9.4	9.3	9.4	9.7	9.6	9.5	9.3
2013	9.4	9.3	9.1	9.1	9.2	9.5	9.6	9.6	9.7	10.0	9.9	9.9	9.5
2014	9.6	9.5	9.6	9.4	9.6	9.8	9.9	9.9	9.9	10.1	10.1	10.1	9.8
2015	9.9	9.8	9.5	9.5	9.7	9.7	9.8	9.8	9.8	9.9	9.8	9.7	9.7
2016	9.4	9.2	9.1	9.0	9.0	9.2	9.3	9.3	9.2	9.3	9.4	9.3	9.2
2017	9.2	9.1	9.2	9.0	9.1	9.2	9.5	9.6	9.6	9.8	9.8	9.8	9.4
Trade, Transportation, and Utilities													
2007	53.0	53.2	53.8	53.4	54.7	56.3	56.8	56.9	56.1	55.7	56.0	56.7	55.2
2008	55.0	54.7	54.8	54.8	55.8	56.9	57.4	57.3	56.7	56.0	56.0	56.4	56.0
2009	54.1	53.5	53.3	52.8	53.5	54.5	54.5	54.4	53.6	52.5	52.4	52.6	53.5
2010	50.6	50.3	50.3	50.9	51.6	52.9	53.2	53.1	52.5	52.1	52.2	52.7	51.9
2011	50.8	50.7	51.0	51.4	52.3	53.5	54.1	54.1	53.6	52.9	53.2	53.6	52.6
2012	52.1	51.8	52.1	52.5	53.4	54.4	54.7	54.7	53.8	53.5	53.8	54.4	53.4
2013	52.3	52.2	52.5	52.6	54.0	55.2	55.7	55.7	54.5	54.4	54.6	55.1	54.1
2014	53.4	53.1	53.3	53.6	54.7	55.9	56.3	56.5	55.5	55.6	55.7	56.5	55.0
2015	55.1	54.8	55.2	55.2	55.8	57.0	57.3	57.0	55.9	55.6	55.6	56.0	55.9
2016	54.4	53.7	53.5	53.0	53.5	54.5	54.8	54.4	53.3	52.9	52.9	52.9	53.7
2017	51.4	50.9	50.9	50.8	51.7	52.9	53.5	53.6	52.6	52.1	52.7	52.9	52.2
Wholesale Trade													
2007	8.4	8.5	8.6	8.7	8.8	9.0	8.8	8.9	8.8	8.7	8.8	8.9	8.7
2008	8.8	8.8	8.9	9.0	9.2	9.2	9.2	9.2	9.2	9.2	9.2	9.2	9.1
2009	9.0	9.0	8.9	8.8	8.8	8.9	8.7	8.6	8.5	8.4	8.4	8.4	8.7
2010	8.3	8.3	8.4	8.4	8.5	8.6	8.5	8.5	8.5	8.5	8.6	8.6	8.5
2011	8.5	8.6	8.7	8.7	8.8	8.9	8.9	8.9	8.9	8.9	9.0	9.0	8.8
2012	9.0	9.0	9.1	9.3	9.3	9.3	9.2	9.2	9.1	9.1	9.1	9.2	9.2
2013	9.0	9.0	9.1	9.1	9.2	9.2	9.2	9.3	9.2	9.3	9.3	9.4	9.2
2014	9.3	9.3	9.3	9.4	9.5	9.6	9.6	9.6	9.5	9.6	9.6	9.7	9.5
2015	9.6	9.6	9.7	9.6	9.6	9.6	9.5	9.4	9.3	9.3	9.2	9.2	9.5
2016	9.1	9.0	8.9	8.7	8.6	8.4	8.4	8.3	8.2	8.1	8.1	8.1	8.5
2017	8.0	8.0	8.1	8.1	8.1	8.1	8.1	8.2	8.2	8.3	8.2	8.4	8.2
Retail Trade													
2007	30.8	30.8	31.2	30.7	31.7	32.6	33.3	33.1	32.4	32.2	32.4	32.8	32.0
2008	31.6	31.3	31.3	31.2	31.8	32.8	33.3	33.1	32.7	32.2	32.2	32.4	32.2
2009	30.7	30.1	30.1	30.0	30.7	31.4	31.7	31.6	31.0	30.3	30.2	30.3	30.7
2010	28.8	28.7	28.7	28.9	29.5	30.3	30.5	30.2	29.6	29.3	29.3	29.6	29.5
2011	28.2	27.9	28.1	28.4	29.0	29.9	30.4	30.3	29.8	29.3	29.5	29.7	29.2
2012	28.5	28.2	28.3	28.5	29.3	30.3	30.6	30.5	29.8	29.6	29.9	30.1	29.5
2013	28.5	28.3	28.5	28.6	29.7	30.7	31.1	30.9	30.0	29.8	30.0	30.2	29.7
2014	28.7	28.5	28.7	28.9	29.7	30.6	30.9	30.9	30.1	30.1	30.1	30.5	29.8
2015	29.3	29.3	29.6	30.0	30.7	31.6	32.1	31.9	31.2	31.1	31.2	31.4	30.8
2016	30.2	30.0	30.0	30.0	30.6	31.6	31.8	31.6	30.8	30.6	30.5	30.4	30.7
2017	29.3	28.8	28.7	28.7	29.6	30.6	31.1	31.0	30.1	29.4	29.9	29.5	29.7

1. Employment by Industry: Wyoming, Selected Years, 2006–2016—*Continued*

(Numbers in thousands, not seasonally adjusted)

Industry and year	January	February	March	April	May	June	July	August	September	October	November	December	Annual average
Transportation and Utilities													
2007	13.8	13.9	14.0	14.0	14.2	14.7	14.7	14.9	14.9	14.8	14.8	15.0	14.5
2008	14.6	14.6	14.6	14.6	14.8	14.9	14.9	15.0	14.8	14.6	14.6	14.8	14.7
2009	14.4	14.4	14.3	14.0	14.0	14.2	14.1	14.2	14.1	13.8	13.8	13.9	14.1
2010	13.5	13.3	13.2	13.6	13.6	14.0	14.2	14.4	14.4	14.3	14.3	14.5	13.9
2011	14.1	14.2	14.2	14.3	14.5	14.7	14.8	14.9	14.9	14.7	14.7	14.9	14.6
2012	14.6	14.6	14.7	14.7	14.8	14.8	14.9	15.0	14.9	14.8	14.8	15.1	14.8
2013	14.8	14.9	14.9	14.9	15.1	15.3	15.4	15.5	15.3	15.3	15.3	15.5	15.2
2014	15.4	15.3	15.3	15.3	15.5	15.7	15.8	16.0	15.9	15.9	16.0	16.3	15.7
2015	16.2	15.9	15.9	15.6	15.5	15.8	15.7	15.7	15.4	15.2	15.2	15.4	15.6
2016	15.1	14.7	14.6	14.3	14.3	14.5	14.6	14.5	14.3	14.2	14.3	14.4	14.5
2017	14.1	14.1	14.1	14.0	14.0	14.2	14.3	14.4	14.3	14.4	14.6	15.0	14.3
Information													
2007	4.0	4.0	4.0	4.0	4.0	4.1	4.1	4.1	4.0	4.0	4.0	4.1	4.0
2008	4.0	4.0	4.0	4.0	4.0	4.0	4.1	4.1	4.0	4.0	4.0	4.0	4.0
2009	4.0	4.0	4.0	3.9	4.0	4.0	4.0	4.0	3.9	3.9	3.9	3.9	4.0
2010	3.9	3.9	3.9	3.9	3.9	3.9	3.9	3.9	3.9	3.8	3.8	3.8	3.9
2011	3.8	3.8	3.8	3.8	3.9	3.9	3.9	3.9	3.8	3.8	3.8	3.9	3.8
2012	3.9	3.9	3.9	3.9	3.9	4.0	4.0	4.0	3.9	3.8	3.9	3.9	3.9
2013	3.8	3.8	3.8	3.7	3.8	3.8	3.8	3.8	3.8	3.8	3.8	3.8	3.8
2014	3.8	3.7	3.7	3.7	3.8	3.8	3.8	3.8	3.8	3.8	3.8	3.8	3.8
2015	3.8	3.8	3.8	3.8	3.8	3.8	3.8	3.8	3.8	3.7	3.7	3.8	3.8
2016	3.8	3.8	3.7	3.7	3.7	3.8	3.8	3.8	3.7	3.7	3.7	3.7	3.7
2017	3.7	3.7	3.7	3.7	3.7	3.7	3.7	3.7	3.7	3.6	3.6	3.6	3.7
Financial Activities													
2007	11.0	11.0	11.1	11.2	11.3	11.6	11.6	11.6	11.5	11.5	11.4	11.5	11.4
2008	11.4	11.4	11.4	11.5	11.6	11.8	11.9	11.9	11.7	11.7	11.6	11.6	11.6
2009	11.3	11.3	11.2	11.2	11.3	11.4	11.3	11.3	11.1	11.0	10.9	11.0	11.2
2010	10.7	10.7	10.7	10.8	10.9	10.9	10.9	10.8	10.7	10.8	10.7	10.8	10.8
2011	10.7	10.6	10.6	10.7	10.7	10.8	10.8	10.9	10.8	10.7	10.7	10.7	10.7
2012	10.6	10.6	10.7	10.6	10.7	10.9	10.9	11.0	10.8	10.9	10.8	10.8	10.8
2013	10.9	10.9	10.9	11.0	11.1	11.3	11.4	11.4	11.3	11.2	11.2	11.2	11.2
2014	11.0	11.0	11.0	11.0	11.2	11.4	11.4	11.5	11.4	11.4	11.3	11.4	11.3
2015	11.2	11.2	11.1	11.1	11.0	11.1	11.3	11.2	11.1	11.0	11.0	11.0	11.1
2016	10.9	10.9	10.8	10.8	10.8	11.0	11.0	10.9	10.8	10.7	10.7	10.8	10.8
2017	10.7	10.7	10.7	10.7	10.8	11.0	11.0	11.1	11.0	10.8	10.9	11.0	10.9
Professional and Business Services													
2007	16.8	17.1	17.5	17.9	18.8	19.6	19.5	19.5	19.0	18.8	18.0	17.8	18.4
2008	17.3	17.5	17.7	18.2	18.9	19.7	19.8	19.8	19.2	19.0	18.3	18.0	18.6
2009	17.3	17.0	17.0	17.1	17.6	17.9	18.0	18.0	17.5	17.2	16.7	16.3	17.3
2010	16.0	15.8	16.1	16.8	17.2	17.9	18.3	18.6	18.0	17.5	17.0	16.7	17.2
2011	16.4	16.4	16.6	17.1	17.8	18.5	18.8	19.2	18.5	18.2	17.9	17.7	17.8
2012	17.1	17.2	17.3	17.7	18.0	18.9	18.7	19.0	18.4	18.2	17.7	17.6	18.0
2013	16.9	17.0	17.2	17.8	18.3	19.0	19.1	19.0	18.5	18.5	18.3	17.7	18.1
2014	17.1	17.4	17.5	18.1	18.6	19.2	19.5	19.4	18.9	18.9	18.3	18.2	18.4
2015	17.5	17.6	17.6	18.2	18.7	19.1	19.6	19.6	19.0	18.7	18.2	17.9	18.5
2016	17.0	16.9	16.9	17.5	17.9	18.4	18.7	18.7	18.2	18.0	17.4	17.5	17.8
2017	17.1	17.1	17.2	17.7	18.1	18.6	19.0	19.1	18.7	19.1	18.6	18.7	18.3
Education and Health Services													
2007	23.0	23.2	23.3	23.0	23.3	22.9	22.8	23.0	23.7	23.8	24.1	23.9	23.3
2008	24.0	24.4	24.4	24.3	24.3	24.1	24.1	24.2	25.0	25.3	25.2	25.1	24.5
2009	25.5	25.6	25.8	25.5	25.9	25.1	25.1	25.2	25.9	26.1	26.4	26.4	25.7
2010	26.1	26.3	26.4	26.4	26.4	25.8	25.7	25.9	26.7	27.0	27.1	26.9	26.4
2011	26.9	27.2	27.4	27.0	27.1	26.1	25.8	26.1	26.9	26.9	26.6	26.9	26.7
2012	26.5	26.7	26.7	26.6	26.7	26.0	25.8	26.2	26.9	26.9	27.0	27.1	26.6
2013	26.8	26.8	27.2	27.1	27.1	26.5	26.2	26.5	27.1	27.1	27.1	27.1	26.9
2014	27.0	27.0	27.1	27.2	27.3	26.5	26.2	26.4	27.0	27.5	26.9	26.9	26.9
2015	26.9	26.9	27.0	27.3	27.4	26.6	26.5	26.6	27.4	28.0	27.4	27.7	27.1
2016	27.4	27.7	28.0	28.1	28.0	27.2	27.1	27.0	27.8	28.0	27.8	27.7	27.7
2017	27.7	27.8	27.9	27.7	27.8	27.3	26.9	26.9	27.8	28.2	27.7	27.9	27.6

1. Employment by Industry: Wyoming, Selected Years, 2006–2016—*Continued*

(Numbers in thousands, not seasonally adjusted)

Industry and year	January	February	March	April	May	June	July	August	September	October	November	December	Annual average
Leisure and Hospitality													
2007	30.5	31.0	31.3	30.5	32.6	37.4	39.1	38.6	36.0	32.6	30.4	31.9	33.5
2008	31.6	32.0	32.5	31.6	34.1	38.8	40.3	39.7	36.9	33.8	30.6	31.9	34.5
2009	31.1	30.8	31.2	30.1	32.5	36.8	38.5	38.0	35.8	31.8	28.7	29.8	32.9
2010	29.4	29.6	29.6	29.4	31.6	36.7	38.5	38.5	36.1	32.6	28.9	30.8	32.6
2011	29.8	29.8	30.2	29.3	31.7	37.1	39.1	38.9	36.7	33.1	29.6	31.5	33.1
2012	30.6	30.7	31.1	30.4	32.7	38.1	40.1	39.8	36.8	33.9	30.7	32.1	33.9
2013	31.3	31.3	31.7	31.1	33.4	39.0	40.9	40.5	38.0	34.8	31.0	32.5	34.6
2014	32.1	32.1	32.3	31.9	34.3	39.9	41.6	41.5	38.4	35.5	31.4	33.5	35.4
2015	33.2	33.2	33.4	32.9	35.5	40.8	42.5	42.0	39.2	36.0	31.8	33.3	36.2
2016	32.8	32.6	32.9	32.0	35.1	40.8	42.3	42.0	38.8	35.8	31.7	33.2	35.8
2017	33.1	33.0	33.4	32.4	35.8	40.9	42.7	42.6	39.3	34.4	30.9	32.9	36.0
Other Services													
2007	11.8	11.9	12.1	12.2	12.7	12.8	12.8	12.8	12.7	12.7	12.7	12.9	12.5
2008	12.7	12.9	13.0	13.0	13.3	13.4	13.6	13.6	13.4	13.4	13.4	13.5	13.3
2009	13.4	13.5	13.5	13.4	13.8	13.8	13.8	13.7	13.6	13.4	13.3	13.2	13.5
2010	13.1	13.2	13.3	13.5	13.5	13.6	13.8	13.8	13.7	13.7	13.7	13.7	13.6
2011	13.7	13.8	13.9	14.1	14.1	14.4	14.6	14.5	14.3	14.3	14.2	14.2	14.2
2012	14.1	14.1	14.2	14.3	14.4	14.6	14.6	14.6	14.5	14.3	14.2	14.2	14.3
2013	14.0	14.1	14.1	14.3	14.3	14.6	14.7	14.5	14.2	14.4	13.8	13.7	14.2
2014	13.6	13.6	13.6	14.0	14.1	14.4	14.5	14.3	14.2	14.3	14.2	14.2	14.1
2015	14.2	14.3	14.4	14.4	14.5	14.8	14.9	14.7	14.5	14.4	14.4	14.4	14.5
2016	14.2	14.1	14.3	14.3	14.3	14.2	14.2	14.1	14.0	13.9	13.8	13.8	14.1
2017	13.7	13.7	13.8	13.8	14.0	14.3	14.4	14.3	14.1	14.3	14.4	14.3	14.1
Government													
2007	66.1	66.9	67.4	67.4	68.8	68.7	62.5	62.5	68.0	69.1	69.1	69.0	67.1
2008	67.4	68.7	69.3	69.5	71.4	70.2	63.8	63.3	69.5	70.6	70.5	70.7	68.7
2009	69.0	70.5	71.2	71.6	73.2	72.1	64.9	64.8	71.5	72.0	71.8	71.8	70.4
2010	70.1	71.6	72.7	72.1	75.0	73.8	65.9	65.8	71.8	72.8	72.4	72.4	71.4
2011	70.6	72.2	72.8	72.7	74.0	73.3	69.1	68.5	72.5	73.2	72.8	73.0	72.1
2012	71.3	73.0	73.4	72.6	74.3	73.1	69.5	68.3	72.6	73.5	73.1	73.3	72.3
2013	71.6	72.7	73.2	72.8	73.9	73.0	68.2	68.0	71.9	72.7	72.2	72.4	71.9
2014	70.6	71.8	72.6	71.9	73.0	71.6	68.4	67.2	71.3	72.2	71.6	71.9	71.2
2015	69.8	71.0	72.0	71.6	73.0	71.7	67.7	67.9	72.0	73.0	72.5	72.6	71.2
2016	70.6	71.9	72.6	72.0	73.3	72.3	67.7	67.8	71.2	71.6	71.3	71.5	71.2
2017	69.4	70.9	71.5	71.0	72.3	70.9	66.7	66.9	70.1	71.1	70.3	70.2	70.1

2. Average Weekly Hours by Selected Industry: Wyoming, 2013–2017

(Not seasonally adjusted)

Industry and year	January	February	March	April	May	June	July	August	September	October	November	December	Annual average
Total Private													
2013	35.8	36.3	35.7	35.0	35.9	36.8	35.4	35.9	36.4	35.5	36.0	35.8	35.9
2014	34.9	36.3	35.9	35.4	35.3	36.3	35.4	36.2	35.7	35.8	35.6	35.1	35.7
2015	34.7	35.9	35.4	35.0	35.3	35.8	35.6	36.3	34.5	34.5	34.8	33.4	35.1
2016	33.5	33.4	33.3	32.1	33.1	32.9	33.3	33.7	33.4	34.1	33.2	32.5	33.2
2017	33.6	33.0	33.0	34.4	34.0	34.7	35.2	34.8	34.3	35.2	34.5	33.7	34.2
Goods-Producing													
2013	41.7	42.1	41.4	39.8	42.3	42.4	40.8	42.1	41.9	41.1	42.3	41.8	41.6
2014	40.5	41.9	41.7	42.3	41.6	42.2	40.7	42.7	41.5	42.6	40.5	41.6	41.7
2015	40.2	40.6	40.0	40.0	41.4	41.5	41.5	41.9	39.7	41.6	41.3	39.8	40.8
2016	39.2	38.4	39.4	40.0	40.4	39.8	40.0	41.4	40.8	41.5	41.2	38.7	40.1
2017	38.7	39.2	39.3	41.0	41.5	41.8	41.2	41.1	40.2	41.4	41.4	39.4	40.6
Mining and Logging													
2013	42.9	42.1	42.9	41.7	42.9	43.9	43.2	44.2	45.3	43.1	45.0	45.0	43.5
2014	45.1	46.2	45.7	45.8	44.9	44.0	43.3	45.0	44.2	45.3	44.5	46.3	45.0
2015	43.8	44.5	44.0	42.9	44.0	42.5	42.8	43.0	41.7	42.6	43.1	42.5	43.2
2016	41.7	41.5	41.4	41.5	40.0	40.5	41.7	42.9	42.6	43.7	43.1	41.6	41.9
2017	42.0	41.0	41.8	42.2	44.1	45.1	44.3	43.6	42.5	43.8	45.9	44.2	43.4
Construction													
2013	42.0	41.8	41.8	38.9	43.5	42.7	41.0	41.8	40.4	40.5	41.2	41.1	41.4
2014	38.3	39.9	39.6	40.7	40.5	42.0	40.0	42.5	41.0	42.3	39.2	40.5	40.6
2015	39.0	39.3	38.8	39.3	40.7	41.6	41.3	41.8	39.9	42.0	41.0	39.2	40.4
2016	37.7	36.7	38.6	39.1	40.5	39.3	39.3	41.2	40.3	40.5	40.4	38.3	39.3
2017	37.7	39.9	39.3	42.1	41.6	41.1	40.4	40.4	39.3	40.8	39.4	39.0	40.2
Trade, Transportation, and Utilities													
2013	36.0	36.9	36.5	35.6	36.6	36.6	35.4	35.6	36.8	36.1	36.2	36.6	36.2
2014	35.4	36.1	36.3	35.3	35.2	35.4	35.1	35.4	35.2	35.0	35.5	34.5	35.4
2015	34.9	36.1	35.7	35.0	35.0	36.0	35.6	35.8	35.2	34.6	34.6	33.8	35.2
2016	33.4	33.7	33.3	34.1	34.4	34.4	34.5	34.7	34.5	34.9	34.0	34.7	34.2
2017	35.1	33.8	34.0	35.1	34.3	34.7	35.9	34.9	34.6	35.7	35.2	35.0	34.9
Professional and Business Services													
2013	34.5	35.3	34.3	34.2	34.2	35.4	33.1	34.1	35.0	34.2	34.8	35.0	34.5
2014	34.0	35.7	34.8	34.5	34.6	36.4	36.1	36.1	35.7	35.7	35.6	35.0	35.4
2015	34.0	35.1	34.9	35.4	35.1	35.4	35.4	36.8	34.9	34.2	34.8	33.4	35.0
2016	33.5	34.4	33.9	34.6	35.2	34.8	34.4	35.4	34.5	34.6	33.9	33.3	34.4
2017	35.0	33.8	32.9	35.2	34.9	35.2	35.8	34.9	35.3	35.8	34.6	33.9	34.7
Education and Health Services													
2013	33.4	34.5	34.2	33.8	33.8	35.5	33.7	34.7	35.3	33.6	34.6	34.3	34.3
2014	33.4	35.1	34.2	33.6	33.7	34.5	33.4	32.9	33.4	33.0	33.5	33.4	33.7
2015	33.4	35.1	34.6	33.8	33.8	34.2	33.3	34.6	33.6	33.6	34.9	33.1	34.0
2016	33.9	34.2	34.2	34.3	35.4	35.4	35.3	35.0	35.2	36.2	35.2	34.7	34.9
2017	35.7	35.3	34.4	35.5	33.7	33.9	34.7	33.6	34.5	34.7	34.3	33.6	34.5
Leisure and Hospitality													
2013	23.9	24.4	24.3	24.3	24.7	27.8	27.7	27.6	27.1	25.6	24.7	24.8	25.7
2014	24.9	26.1	26.4	24.6	25.6	28.7	28.5	28.7	27.4	26.4	26.4	25.7	26.7
2015	26.1	27.4	27.2	25.9	26.7	28.6	29.5	30.2	28.3	25.2	25.0	24.5	27.2
2016	25.2	25.3	25.2	24.9	26.9	27.3	27.9	28.0	26.2	24.6	23.5	23.0	25.8
2017	24.5	24.5	24.7	23.5	24.5	27.4	28.7	28.7	26.9	25.6	24.1	24.4	25.8
Other Services													
2013	36.8	35.4	33.9	34.1	35.0	36.7	34.3	34.5	36.0	36.2	35.4	35.6	35.3
2014	35.4	35.6	35.0	35.6	33.9	35.4	35.0	34.8	34.5	33.3	32.2	30.6	34.3
2015	31.4	32.9	31.8	31.3	30.0	30.3	29.8	30.5	29.3	28.4	28.8	26.7	30.1
2016	26.2	27.0	26.4	26.4	27.2	27.2	27.7	26.8	27.1	29.0	27.1	26.7	27.1
2017	27.9	27.9	27.8	29.1	27.4	28.3	29.6	28.8	29.1	29.8	28.8	28.4	28.6

3. Average Hourly Earnings by Selected Industry: Wyoming, 2013–2017

(Dollars, not seasonally adjusted)

Industry and year	January	February	March	April	May	June	July	August	September	October	November	December	Annual average
Total Private													
2013	22.92	22.99	23.20	23.31	23.02	22.62	22.53	22.50	23.01	22.86	22.95	23.17	22.92
2014	23.32	23.25	23.40	23.38	23.28	22.71	22.62	22.91	23.34	23.27	23.49	23.29	23.18
2015	23.27	23.25	23.30	23.24	23.05	22.61	22.71	22.98	23.22	23.34	23.39	23.24	23.13
2016	23.03	23.17	23.23	23.50	23.28	22.66	22.74	22.84	23.27	23.78	23.78	23.67	23.24
2017	23.62	23.68	23.63	24.23	24.10	23.38	23.57	23.32	24.10	24.30	24.09	24.53	23.88
Goods-Producing													
2013	26.57	26.73	27.24	27.91	27.46	27.21	27.04	27.13	27.59	27.02	27.02	27.47	27.20
2014	28.19	27.71	28.00	27.83	27.83	26.93	27.19	27.26	27.88	27.68	27.89	27.69	27.66
2015	27.85	27.58	27.58	27.69	27.54	27.39	27.56	27.77	27.91	27.77	28.03	28.49	27.76
2016	28.55	28.63	28.65	28.47	28.64	27.99	27.95	28.09	28.47	28.77	28.39	28.57	28.43
2017	28.72	28.43	28.42	28.76	28.82	28.01	28.10	28.22	28.94	28.96	28.39	29.32	28.59
Mining and Logging													
2013	29.82	30.01	30.79	31.90	31.80	32.25	32.42	32.69	33.73	33.73	33.50	34.08	32.26
2014	35.13	33.85	33.93	33.72	33.83	33.37	33.82	33.75	34.85	34.04	33.71	34.20	34.02
2015	34.85	34.16	34.36	34.47	34.40	35.04	35.31	36.07	36.34	35.24	35.00	35.69	35.04
2016	36.30	35.79	35.89	35.35	35.77	35.87	34.82	34.14	35.14	35.54	34.95	35.10	35.40
2017	36.04	35.93	35.65	35.86	34.87	34.38	34.52	34.43	35.32	35.36	33.94	35.39	35.12
Construction													
2013	24.43	25.15	24.96	26.18	25.64	24.81	24.54	24.65	25.12	24.56	24.85	25.48	25.02
2014	25.54	25.45	26.19	26.24	26.34	24.96	24.99	24.98	25.30	25.31	25.32	24.99	25.44
2015	25.21	25.14	25.15	25.68	25.50	24.96	25.20	25.28	25.13	25.69	25.92	25.97	25.40
2016	25.31	25.48	25.70	25.78	26.48	25.05	25.32	26.23	25.89	26.17	25.84	26.06	25.79
2017	25.64	25.07	25.24	25.59	26.14	25.43	25.35	25.72	26.40	26.27	26.65	27.22	25.90
Trade, Transportation, and Utilities													
2013	22.82	22.59	22.73	22.95	22.58	22.53	22.12	21.94	22.48	22.16	22.05	22.06	22.41
2014	21.94	22.28	22.33	22.39	21.89	21.68	21.43	21.58	21.79	21.52	21.79	21.55	21.84
2015	21.33	21.51	21.95	21.71	21.30	21.10	21.31	21.60	20.91	20.65	20.75	20.39	21.21
2016	20.62	20.63	21.05	21.15	21.31	20.77	20.98	21.17	21.56	21.69	21.81	21.59	21.19
2017	21.96	22.04	22.03	22.68	22.21	22.07	22.41	22.01	22.18	22.20	22.08	22.19	22.17
Professional and Business Services													
2013	25.23	25.19	25.63	25.52	25.17	25.33	25.84	25.53	25.92	26.05	25.75	26.32	25.63
2014	26.07	25.80	25.92	26.16	26.05	25.68	25.88	25.88	26.39	26.67	26.81	26.98	26.26
2015	27.52	27.27	27.23	27.03	26.63	26.10	26.03	26.12	27.55	27.16	26.39	26.38	26.77
2016	25.83	25.77	25.86	26.10	25.93	25.90	25.90	26.15	26.53	27.40	27.17	27.71	26.35
2017	27.42	27.36	26.87	27.02	26.74	26.59	26.71	26.38	26.57	26.71	26.78	27.47	26.87
Education and Health Services													
2013	21.60	22.00	22.11	21.84	21.49	21.13	21.65	21.56	21.93	21.82	21.60	22.02	21.73
2014	21.91	21.65	21.68	21.30	21.36	21.15	21.34	21.43	21.86	21.45	21.97	22.17	21.61
2015	22.37	22.87	22.83	22.65	22.68	22.65	22.85	22.94	22.82	22.60	22.71	22.42	22.70
2016	22.05	22.16	21.96	21.97	22.18	21.91	22.19	22.11	22.03	22.30	21.99	22.14	22.08
2017	22.41	22.64	22.47	22.72	23.24	23.52	23.91	23.76	23.80	24.36	23.53	24.28	23.38
Leisure and Hospitality													
2013	12.47	12.45	12.43	12.28	12.23	12.09	12.49	12.18	12.49	12.53	12.64	12.72	12.41
2014	13.15	13.25	13.33	12.93	12.93	12.99	13.02	13.33	13.48	13.53	13.84	14.11	13.31
2015	14.06	14.30	14.14	13.91	13.56	13.44	13.36	13.46	13.70	13.68	13.63	13.74	13.72
2016	13.98	14.15	14.17	14.07	13.52	13.68	13.89	13.90	14.26	14.21	14.21	14.44	14.02
2017	14.98	15.10	14.89	14.69	14.33	14.22	14.33	14.43	14.86	14.73	14.76	15.10	14.67
Other Services													
2013	20.47	21.06	21.24	20.29	20.26	19.61	19.39	19.30	18.98	19.30	19.63	19.84	19.94
2014	19.47	19.65	19.57	19.26	20.04	19.78	19.06	19.21	19.39	19.13	19.17	19.26	19.42
2015	19.93	20.89	20.72	20.07	21.27	19.96	20.84	21.65	20.65	20.01	20.53	20.68	20.60
2016	20.71	20.76	20.72	20.22	21.07	20.27	20.75	21.60	21.97	22.76	22.11	22.54	21.29
2017	21.96	21.76	21.90	22.32	22.65	21.51	21.45	21.57	21.61	21.88	21.02	21.77	21.77

4. Average Weekly Earnings by Selected Industry: Wyoming, 2013–2017

(Dollars, not seasonally adjusted)

Industry and year	January	February	March	April	May	June	July	August	September	October	November	December	Annual average
Total Private													
2013	820.54	834.54	828.24	815.85	826.42	832.42	797.56	807.75	837.56	811.53	826.20	829.49	822.83
2014	813.87	843.98	840.06	827.65	821.78	824.37	800.75	829.34	833.24	833.07	836.24	817.48	827.53
2015	807.47	834.68	824.82	813.40	813.67	809.44	808.48	834.17	801.09	805.23	813.97	776.22	811.86
2016	771.51	773.88	773.56	754.35	770.57	745.51	757.24	769.71	777.22	810.90	789.50	769.28	771.57
2017	793.63	781.44	779.79	833.51	819.40	811.29	829.66	811.54	826.63	855.36	831.11	826.66	816.70
Goods-Producing													
2013	1,107.97	1,125.33	1,127.74	1,110.82	1,161.56	1,153.70	1,103.23	1,142.17	1,156.02	1,110.52	1,142.95	1,148.25	1,131.52
2014	1,141.70	1,161.05	1,167.60	1,177.21	1,157.73	1,136.45	1,106.63	1,164.00	1,157.02	1,179.17	1,129.55	1,151.90	1,153.42
2015	1,119.57	1,119.75	1,103.20	1,107.60	1,140.16	1,136.69	1,143.74	1,163.56	1,108.03	1,155.23	1,157.64	1,133.90	1,132.61
2016	1,119.16	1,099.39	1,128.81	1,138.80	1,157.06	1,114.00	1,118.00	1,162.93	1,161.58	1,193.96	1,169.67	1,105.66	1,140.04
2017	1,111.46	1,114.46	1,116.91	1,179.16	1,196.03	1,170.82	1,157.72	1,159.84	1,163.39	1,198.94	1,175.35	1,155.21	1,160.75
Mining and Logging													
2013	1,279.28	1,263.42	1,320.89	1,330.23	1,364.22	1,415.78	1,400.54	1,444.90	1,527.97	1,453.76	1,507.50	1,533.60	1,403.31
2014	1,584.36	1,563.87	1,550.60	1,544.38	1,518.97	1,468.28	1,464.41	1,518.75	1,540.37	1,542.01	1,500.10	1,583.46	1,530.90
2015	1,526.43	1,520.12	1,511.84	1,478.76	1,513.60	1,489.20	1,511.27	1,551.01	1,515.38	1,501.22	1,508.50	1,516.83	1,513.73
2016	1,513.71	1,485.29	1,485.85	1,467.03	1,430.80	1,452.74	1,451.99	1,464.61	1,496.96	1,553.10	1,506.35	1,460.16	1,483.26
2017	1,513.68	1,473.13	1,490.17	1,513.29	1,537.77	1,550.54	1,529.24	1,501.15	1,501.10	1,548.77	1,557.85	1,564.24	1,523.77
Construction													
2013	1,026.06	1,051.27	1,043.33	1,018.40	1,115.34	1,059.39	1,006.14	1,030.37	1,014.85	994.68	1,023.82	1,047.23	1,035.83
2014	978.18	1,015.46	1,037.12	1,067.97	1,066.77	1,048.32	999.60	1,061.65	1,037.30	1,070.61	992.54	1,012.10	1,032.86
2015	983.19	988.00	975.82	1,009.22	1,037.85	1,038.34	1,040.76	1,056.70	1,002.69	1,078.98	1,062.72	1,018.02	1,026.16
2016	954.19	935.12	992.02	1,008.00	1,072.44	984.47	995.08	1,080.68	1,043.37	1,059.89	1,043.94	998.10	1,013.55
2017	966.63	1,000.29	991.93	1,077.34	1,087.42	1,045.17	1,024.14	1,039.09	1,037.52	1,071.82	1,050.01	1,061.58	1,041.18
Trade, Transportation, and Utilities													
2013	821.52	833.57	829.65	817.02	826.43	824.60	783.05	781.06	827.26	799.98	798.21	807.40	811.24
2014	776.68	804.31	810.58	790.37	770.53	767.47	752.19	763.93	767.01	753.20	773.55	743.48	773.14
2015	744.42	776.51	783.62	759.85	745.50	759.60	758.64	773.28	736.03	714.49	717.95	689.18	746.59
2016	688.71	695.23	700.97	721.22	733.06	714.49	723.81	734.60	743.82	756.98	741.54	749.17	724.70
2017	770.80	744.95	749.02	796.07	761.80	765.83	804.52	768.15	767.43	792.54	777.22	776.65	773.73
Professional and Business Services													
2013	870.44	889.21	879.11	872.78	860.81	896.68	855.30	870.57	907.20	890.91	896.10	921.20	884.24
2014	886.38	921.06	902.02	902.52	901.33	934.75	934.27	952.68	952.12	952.12	954.44	944.30	929.60
2015	935.68	957.18	950.33	956.86	934.71	923.94	921.46	961.22	961.50	928.87	918.37	881.09	936.95
2016	865.31	886.49	876.65	903.06	912.74	901.32	890.96	925.71	915.29	948.04	921.06	922.74	906.44
2017	959.70	924.77	884.02	951.10	933.23	935.97	956.22	920.66	937.92	956.22	926.59	931.23	932.39
Education and Health Services													
2013	721.44	759.00	756.16	738.19	726.36	750.12	729.61	748.13	774.13	733.15	747.36	755.29	745.34
2014	731.79	759.92	741.46	715.68	719.83	729.68	712.76	705.05	730.12	707.85	736.00	740.48	728.26
2015	747.16	802.74	789.92	765.57	766.58	774.63	760.91	793.72	766.75	759.36	792.58	742.10	771.80
2016	747.50	757.87	751.03	753.57	785.17	775.61	783.31	773.85	775.46	807.26	774.05	768.26	770.59
2017	800.04	799.19	772.97	806.56	783.19	797.33	829.68	798.34	821.10	845.29	807.08	815.81	806.61
Leisure and Hospitality													
2013	298.03	303.78	302.05	298.40	302.08	336.10	345.97	336.17	338.48	320.77	312.21	315.46	318.94
2014	327.44	345.83	351.91	318.08	331.01	372.81	371.07	382.57	369.35	357.19	365.38	362.63	355.38
2015	366.97	391.82	384.61	360.27	362.05	384.38	394.12	406.49	387.71	344.74	340.75	336.63	373.18
2016	352.30	358.00	357.08	350.34	363.69	373.46	387.53	389.20	373.61	349.57	333.94	332.12	361.72
2017	367.01	369.95	367.78	345.22	351.09	389.63	411.27	414.14	399.73	377.09	355.72	368.44	378.49
Other Services													
2013	753.30	745.52	720.04	691.89	709.10	719.69	665.08	665.85	683.28	698.66	694.90	706.30	703.88
2014	689.24	699.54	684.95	685.66	679.36	700.21	667.10	668.51	668.96	637.03	617.27	589.36	666.11
2015	625.80	687.28	658.90	628.19	638.10	604.79	621.03	660.33	605.05	568.28	591.26	552.16	620.06
2016	542.60	560.52	547.01	533.81	573.10	551.34	574.78	578.88	595.39	660.04	599.18	601.82	576.96
2017	612.68	607.10	608.82	649.51	620.61	608.73	634.92	621.22	628.85	652.02	605.38	618.27	622.91

PART B

METROPOLITAN STATISTICAL AREA (MSA) DATA

METROPOLITAN STATISTICAL AREA (MSA) DATA

Part B provides employment data for the 75 largest metropolitan statistical areas (MSAs) and New England city and town areas (NECTAs) in the United States from 2007 through 2017. As mentioned in the technical notes, all employment data are for MSAs unless otherwise noted. NECTAs are similar to MSAs but are defined by cities and towns rather than counties in the New England region.

According to the 2017 estimates from the Census Bureau, New York-Newark-Jersey City, NY-NJ-PA metro area, was the largest MSA in the United States—with a population of 20,320,876. Los Angeles-Long Beach-Anaheim, CA followed with a population of 13,353,907. Although the New York area was the most populated MSA, it was not among the fastest growing among the 75 largest MSAs. The fastest growing MSAs between 2016 and 2017 was Austin–Round Rock–San Marcos, TX with a growth rate of 2.7 percent followed by Raleigh, NC and Orlando-Kissimmee-Sanford, FL with a growth rate of 2.3 percent. MSAs in the South and West typically had higher growth rates. Five MSAs among the 75 largest experienced a decline in growth.

Four of the five fastest growing MSAs in total nonfarm employment from 2007 to 2017 were located in Texas. Austin-Round Rock, TX grew the fastest at 33.7 percent, followed by Nashville-Davidson—Murfreesboro—Franklin, TN at 23.3 percent. San Antonio-New Braunfels, TX grew the third fastest at 23.0 percent followed by McAllen-Edinburg–Mission, TX at 21.0 percent and Dallas-Fort Worth–Arlington, TX at 19.7 percent. Although nonfarm employment increased in most areas during this time period, 7 of the 75 largest MSAs experienced a decrease in total nonfarm employment. Greensboro-High Point, NC experienced the largest decline dropping 3.0 percent.

According to the unemployment ratings from the Bureau of Labor Statistics, unemployment rates increased between 2016 and 2017 in 4 of the 75 largest MSAs. Birmingham-Hoover, AL Metro Area experienced the greatest decline in unemployment from 2016 to 2017 declining 1.5 percent. Unemployment rates ranged from 2.2 percent in Honolulu, HI, to a high of 9.2 percent in Bakersfield, CA. Of the MSAs with population of 1,000,000 or more, Cleveland-Elyria, OH had the highest unemployment rate at 5.7 percent followed by Buffalo-Cheektowaga-Niagara Falls, NY at 5.4 percent and Las Vegas-Henderson-Paradise, NV at 5.2 percent.

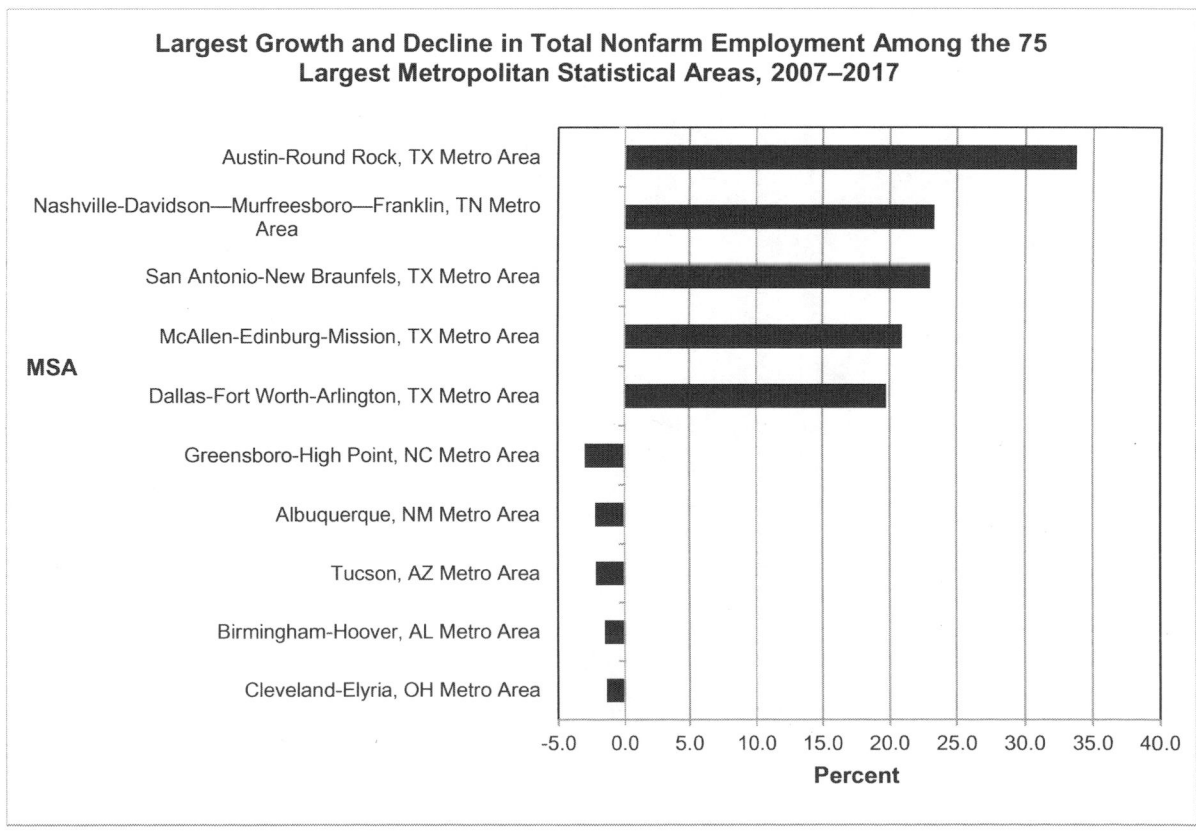

Largest Growth and Decline in Total Nonfarm Employment Among the 75 Largest Metropolitan Statistical Areas, 2007–2017

Metropolitan Statistical Areas: Rankings and Employment and Unemployment Rates

(Seventy-five largest MSAs; ranked by population)

Rank	Metropolitan statistical area	2017 Census population estimates[1]	Total nonfarm employment		Percent change in total nonfarm employment, 2007–2017	Unemployment rates	
			2007	2017		2016	2017
1	New York-Newark-Jersey City, NY-NJ-PA Metro Area	20,320,876	8,855.3	9,672.2	9.2	4.8	4.5
2	Los Angeles-Long Beach-Anaheim, CA Metro Area	13,353,907	5,772.3	6,052.2	4.8	5.0	4.4
3	Chicago-Naperville-Elgin, IL-IN-WI Metro Area	9,533,040	4,554.0	4,697.2	3.1	5.8	4.9
4	Dallas-Fort Worth-Arlington, TX Metro Area	7,399,662	3,003.6	3,596.7	19.7	3.9	3.6
5	Houston-The Woodlands-Sugar Land, TX Metro Area	6,892,427	2,585.1	3,021.3	16.9	5.3	5.0
6	Washington-Arlington-Alexandria, DC-VA-MD-WV Metro Area	6,216,589	3,008.1	3,274.1	8.8	3.9	3.7
7	Miami-Fort Lauderdale-West Palm Beach, FL Metro Area	6,158,824	2,422.9	2,629.4	8.5	4.9	4.3
8	Philadelphia-Camden-Wilmington, PA-NJ-DE-MD Metro Area	6,096,120	2,811.3	2,910.1	3.5	5.1	4.7
9	Atlanta-Sandy Springs-Roswell, GA Metro Area	5,884,736	2,460.0	2,723.7	10.7	5.1	4.5
10	Boston-Cambridge-Newton, MA-NH Metro Area	4,836,531	1,644.3	1,843.2	12.1	3.3	3.2
11	Phoenix-Mesa-Scottsdale, AZ Metro Area	4,737,270	1,917.9	2,034.1	6.1	4.6	4.2
12	San Francisco-Oakland-Hayward, CA Metro Area	4,727,357	2,075.0	2,396.4	15.5	3.8	3.3
13	Riverside-San Bernardino-Ontario, CA Metro Area	4,580,670	1,290.0	1,451.6	12.5	6.0	5.1
14	Detroit-Warren-Dearborn, MI Metro Area	4,313,002	1,962.3	2,004.3	2.1	5.3	4.4
15	Seattle-Tacoma-Bellevue, WA Metro Area	3,867,046	1,758.7	2,000.6	13.8	4.4	4.1
16	Minneapolis-St. Paul-Bloomington, MN-WI Metro Area	3,600,618	1,846.9	1,988.8	7.7	3.5	3.2
17	San Diego-Carlsbad, CA Metro Area	3,337,685	1,323.9	1,453.2	9.8	4.7	4.0
18	Tampa-St. Petersburg-Clearwater, FL Metro Area	3,091,399	1,230.6	1,321.2	7.4	4.6	3.9
19	Denver-Aurora-Lakewood, CO Metro Area	2,888,227	1,241.4	1,461.7	17.7	3.1	2.7
20	Baltimore-Columbia-Towson, MD Metro Area	2,808,175	1,315.6	1,397.5	6.2	4.6	4.3
21	St. Louis, MO-IL Metro Area	2,807,338	1,350.9	1,377.4	2.0	4.6	3.7
22	Charlotte-Concord-Gastonia, NC-SC Metro Area	2,525,305	1,023.1	1,181.5	15.5	4.8	4.3
23	Orlando-Kissimmee-Sanford, FL Metro Area	2,509,831	1,083.3	1,247.1	15.1	4.5	3.8
24	San Antonio-New Braunfels, TX Metro Area	2,473,974	844.8	1,039.3	23.0	3.8	3.5
25	Portland-Vancouver-Hillsboro, OR-WA Metro Area	2,453,168	1,043.6	1,172.9	12.4	4.6	3.9
26	Pittsburgh, PA Metro Area	2,333,367	1,146.1	1,175.4	2.6	5.6	5.0
27	Sacramento--Roseville--Arden-Arcade, CA Metro Area	2,324,884	921.1	968.5	5.1	5.3	4.5
28	Las Vegas-Henderson-Paradise, NV Metro Area	2,204,079	928.1	976.8	5.2	5.9	5.2
29	Cincinnati, OH-KY-IN Metro Area	2,179,082	1,043.8	1,093.6	4.8	4.4	4.3
30	Kansas City, MO-KS Metro Area	2,128,912	1,007.5	1,082.6	7.5	4.3	3.8
31	Austin-Round Rock, TX Metro Area	2,115,827	772.1	1,032.6	33.7	3.3	3.1
32	Columbus, OH Metro Area	2,078,725	960.8	1,083.9	12.8	4.2	4.1
33	Cleveland-Elyria, OH Metro Area	2,058,844	1,072.3	1,057.6	-1.4	5.4	5.7
34	Indianapolis-Carmel-Anderson, IN Metro Area	2,028,614	952.8	1,057.8	11.0	4.1	3.3
35	San Jose-Sunnyvale-Santa Clara, CA Metro Area	1,998,463	921.8	1,098.2	19.1	3.9	3.3
36	Nashville-Davidson--Murfreesboro--Franklin, TN Metro Area	1,903,045	794.7	980.0	23.3	3.7	2.9
37	Virginia Beach-Norfolk-Newport News, VA-NC Metro Area	1,725,246	775.5	779.9	0.6	4.7	4.2
38	Providence-Warwick, RI-MA Metro Area	1,621,122	582.8	588.9	1.0	5.1	4.5
39	Milwaukee-Waukesha-West Allis, WI Metro Area	1,576,236	861.3	866.6	0.6	4.3	3.5
40	Jacksonville, FL Metro Area	1,504,980	631.0	689.7	9.3	4.6	3.9
41	Oklahoma City, OK Metro Area	1,383,737	576.9	634.6	10.0	4.2	3.9
42	Memphis, TN-MS-AR Metro Area	1,348,260	642.0	642.2	0.0	5.2	4.3
43	Raleigh, NC Metro Area	1,335,079	516.8	616.1	19.2	4.4	4.0
44	Richmond, VA Metro Area	1,294,204	622.8	671.3	7.8	4.2	3.9
45	Louisville/Jefferson County, KY-IN Metro Area	1,293,953	612.8	666.6	8.8	4.3	4.1
46	New Orleans-Metairie, LA Metro Area	1,275,762	525.7	575.0	9.4	5.5	4.8
47	Hartford-West Hartford-East Hartford, CT Metro Area	1,210,259	566.3	572.1	1.0	5.2	4.7
48	Salt Lake City, UT Metro Area	1,203,105	615.3	716.3	16.4	3.2	3.1
49	Birmingham-Hoover, AL Metro Area	1,149,807	537.6	529.5	-1.5	5.5	4.0
50	Buffalo-Cheektowaga-Niagara Falls, NY Metro Area	1,136,856	545.7	563.9	3.3	5.1	5.4
51	Rochester, NY Metro Area	1,077,948	519.9	534.1	2.7	4.7	5.0
52	Grand Rapids-Wyoming, MI Metro Area	1,059,113	489.5	553.4	13.1	3.6	3.6
53	Tucson, AZ Metro Area	1,022,769	385.6	377.2	-2.2	5.0	4.5
54	Tulsa, OK Metro Area	990,706	435.1	448.7	3.1	5.0	4.5
55	Fresno, CA Metro Area	989,255	316.1	344.5	9.0	9.5	8.5
56	Urban Honolulu, HI Metro Area	988,650	455.4	476.5	4.6	2.8	2.2
57	Bridgeport-Stamford-Norwalk, CT Metro Area	949,921	411.9	406.5	-1.3	5.0	4.7
58	Worcester, MA-CT Metro Area	942,475	269.9	286.5	6.2	4.2	3.9
59	Omaha-Council Bluffs, NE-IA Metro Area	933,316	464.8	499.6	7.5	3.3	3.0
60	Albuquerque, NM Metro Area	910,726	398.1	389.3	-2.2	6.1	5.7

[1]Population estimates are as July 1, 2016.

Metropolitan Statistical Areas: Rankings and Employment and Unemployment Rates—*Continued*

(Seventy-five largest MSAs; ranked by population)

Rank	Metropolitan statistical area	2017 Census population estimates[1]	Total nonfarm employment		Percent change in total nonfarm employment, 2007–2017	Unemployment rates	
			2007	2017		2016	2017
61	Greenville-Anderson-Mauldin, SC Metro Area	895,923	379.6	415.4	9.4	4.5	3.8
62	Bakersfield, CA Metro Area	893,119	242.6	257.7	6.2	10.4	9.2
63	Albany-Schenectady-Troy, NY Metro Area	886,188	444.8	468.7	5.4	4.1	4.3
64	Knoxville, TN Metro Area	877,104	371.4	395.8	6.6	4.4	3.5
65	McAllen-Edinburg-Mission, TX Metro Area	860,661	213.1	257.8	21.0	7.8	7.4
66	New Haven, CT Metro Area	860,435	279.7	283.9	1.5	5.1	4.6
67	Oxnard-Thousand Oaks-Ventura, CA Metro Area	854,223	298.8	304.0	1.7	5.2	4.5
68	El Paso, TX Metro Area	844,818	274.9	312.3	13.6	4.9	4.6
69	Allentown-Bethlehem-Easton, PA-NJ Metro Area	840,550	344.8	369.5	7.2	5.2	4.9
70	Baton Rouge, LA Metro Area	834,159	374.2	406.6	8.7	5.2	4.5
71	Columbia, SC Metro Area	825,033	368.3	396.6	7.7	4.6	4.1
72	North Port-Sarasota-Bradenton, FL Metro Area	804,690	273.4	300.7	10.0	4.5	3.9
73	Dayton, OH Metro Area	803,416	392.8	389.0	-1.0	4.7	4.7
74	Charleston-North Charleston, SC Metro Area	775,831	301.3	353.4	17.3	4.3	3.6
75	Greensboro-High Point, NC Metro Area	761,184	370.0	359.0	-3.0	5.2	4.8

[1]Population estimates are as July 1, 2016.

Employment by Industry: New York-Newark-Jersey City, NY-NJ-PA, Selected Years, 2007–2017

(Numbers in thousands, not seasonally adjusted)

Industry and year	January	February	March	April	May	June	July	August	September	October	November	December	Annual average
Total Nonfarm													
2007	8,666.8	8,690.0	8,754.3	8,799.0	8,879.1	8,962.4	8,868.5	8,817.6	8,835.8	8,942.3	9,001.2	9,046.9	8,855.3
2008	8,770.0	8,796.1	8,847.0	8,897.2	8,941.7	8,994.9	8,902.5	8,845.9	8,847.5	8,900.1	8,915.2	8,915.5	8,881.1
2009	8,569.6	8,562.7	8,572.5	8,578.5	8,633.7	8,658.9	8,582.4	8,523.0	8,509.8	8,596.1	8,635.6	8,671.3	8,591.2
2010	8,377.6	8,401.9	8,471.1	8,582.1	8,659.9	8,697.4	8,579.5	8,534.4	8,562.1	8,673.8	8,719.5	8,749.0	8,584.0
2011	8,471.9	8,515.4	8,578.4	8,681.8	8,723.5	8,778.3	8,719.9	8,669.4	8,713.0	8,791.3	8,850.7	8,880.0	8,697.8
2012	8,609.5	8,674.2	8,749.3	8,791.1	8,871.0	8,928.4	8,819.2	8,792.8	8,842.0	8,936.7	8,942.2	9,018.6	8,831.3
2013	8,721.4	8,776.7	8,852.7	8,942.8	9,001.6	9,055.2	8,995.7	8,953.8	8,989.6	9,113.8	9,186.4	9,202.2	8,982.7
2014	8,884.3	8,935.7	9,010.2	9,113.6	9,195.5	9,248.2	9,192.9	9,156.3	9,182.5	9,304.1	9,376.7	9,408.9	9,167.4
2015	9,095.3	9,142.8	9,210.7	9,301.6	9,386.8	9,439.2	9,392.9	9,348.3	9,365.2	9,501.3	9,564.8	9,586.4	9,361.3
2016	9,271.5	9,327.3	9,405.9	9,496.4	9,528.6	9,600.7	9,554.7	9,508.9	9,540.7	9,633.7	9,701.2	9,731.7	9,525.1
2017	9,434.7	9,499.4	9,549.8	9,613.9	9,710.1	9,789.8	9,698.6	9,654.9	9,679.9	9,770.9	9,825.7	9,838.2	9,672.2
Total Private													
2007	7,328.5	7,339.8	7,399.4	7,446.7	7,521.0	7,596.6	7,540.5	7,516.0	7,523.9	7,593.8	7,641.0	7,680.1	7,510.6
2008	7,425.9	7,440.2	7,486.1	7,531.1	7,574.1	7,621.2	7,553.8	7,531.5	7,525.4	7,540.4	7,538.6	7,534.6	7,525.2
2009	7,219.0	7,199.5	7,203.6	7,204.7	7,258.0	7,286.4	7,208.0	7,177.5	7,198.6	7,240.8	7,269.1	7,302.8	7,230.7
2010	7,038.8	7,049.2	7,111.2	7,212.4	7,255.8	7,312.3	7,260.1	7,253.6	7,268.7	7,339.6	7,379.7	7,413.9	7,241.3
2011	7,168.2	7,194.5	7,253.5	7,349.6	7,398.4	7,452.6	7,418.0	7,391.1	7,436.5	7,476.6	7,528.7	7,563.3	7,385.9
2012	7,331.0	7,370.5	7,437.0	7,480.2	7,561.6	7,618.2	7,545.3	7,547.9	7,580.3	7,633.4	7,639.3	7,711.2	7,538.0
2013	7,448.2	7,477.2	7,548.5	7,635.9	7,695.6	7,754.0	7,724.7	7,713.6	7,734.6	7,811.1	7,876.6	7,896.3	7,693.0
2014	7,619.4	7,646.1	7,712.8	7,806.3	7,891.6	7,949.0	7,920.5	7,910.3	7,919.1	8,003.2	8,064.5	8,100.2	7,878.6
2015	7,828.7	7,851.0	7,911.7	7,995.0	8,080.3	8,135.9	8,112.7	8,092.1	8,094.8	8,198.7	8,249.4	8,273.3	8,068.6
2016	7,996.1	8,028.2	8,096.7	8,184.3	8,217.0	8,291.8	8,272.8	8,252.5	8,263.8	8,326.1	8,385.4	8,417.7	8,227.7
2017	8,153.8	8,194.6	8,239.0	8,302.9	8,400.3	8,479.3	8,413.2	8,395.5	8,403.9	8,459.7	8,504.6	8,520.5	8,372.3
Goods Producing													
2007	812.4	805.4	814.7	829.6	841.6	852.4	848.5	850.7	849.4	850.1	846.5	839.0	836.7
2008	806.9	803.8	811.0	820.9	826.6	831.3	828.2	830.0	825.3	818.1	805.9	787.2	816.3
2009	738.2	727.8	726.6	727.6	731.7	733.6	729.0	726.4	720.4	716.9	710.4	702.0	724.2
2010	663.9	658.3	668.3	687.0	691.2	697.4	697.9	699.8	697.3	695.8	694.5	685.3	686.4
2011	650.1	649.2	660.4	675.5	685.6	693.0	697.8	701.3	699.4	698.4	698.1	692.2	683.4
2012	665.1	664.0	672.4	681.0	687.5	694.7	696.3	699.4	698.0	700.0	696.8	700.1	687.9
2013	675.3	673.3	682.7	698.5	705.6	711.8	715.2	720.6	719.0	722.8	722.0	711.9	704.9
2014	682.4	677.1	689.9	708.9	720.3	728.7	735.1	737.5	736.4	739.5	739.6	732.7	719.0
2015	701.9	695.8	707.1	728.2	740.6	749.0	754.2	756.5	752.6	759.5	758.7	753.3	738.1
2016	727.3	723.1	736.3	750.0	756.7	763.8	767.9	770.5	765.9	767.8	766.7	760.7	754.7
2017	734.3	736.0	741.1	754.6	765.7	773.2	774.0	774.6	771.0	772.2	769.5	761.8	760.7
Service-Providing													
2007	7,854.4	7,884.6	7,939.6	7,969.4	8,037.5	8,110.0	8,020.0	7,966.9	7,986.4	8,092.2	8,154.7	8,207.9	8,018.6
2008	7,963.1	7,992.3	8,036.0	8,076.3	8,115.1	8,163.6	8,074.3	8,015.9	8,022.2	8,082.0	8,109.3	8,128.3	8,064.9
2009	7,831.4	7,834.9	7,845.9	7,850.9	7,902.0	7,925.3	7,853.4	7,796.6	7,789.4	7,879.2	7,925.2	7,969.3	7,867.0
2010	7,713.7	7,743.6	7,802.8	7,895.1	7,968.7	8,000.0	7,881.6	7,834.6	7,864.8	7,978.0	8,025.0	8,063.7	7,897.6
2011	7,821.8	7,866.2	7,918.0	8,006.3	8,037.9	8,085.3	8,022.1	7,968.1	8,013.6	8,092.9	8,152.6	8,187.8	8,014.4
2012	7,944.4	8,010.2	8,076.9	8,110.1	8,183.5	8,233.7	8,122.9	8,093.4	8,144.0	8,236.7	8,245.4	8,318.5	8,143.3
2013	8,046.1	8,103.4	8,170.0	8,244.3	8,296.0	8,343.4	8,280.5	8,233.2	8,270.6	8,391.0	8,464.4	8,490.3	8,277.8
2014	8,201.9	8,258.6	8,320.3	8,404.7	8,475.2	8,519.5	8,457.8	8,418.8	8,446.1	8,564.6	8,637.1	8,676.2	8,448.4
2015	8,393.4	8,447.0	8,503.6	8,573.4	8,646.2	8,690.2	8,638.7	8,591.8	8,612.6	8,741.8	8,806.1	8,833.1	8,623.2
2016	8,544.2	8,604.2	8,669.6	8,746.4	8,771.9	8,836.9	8,786.8	8,738.4	8,774.8	8,865.9	8,934.5	8,971.0	8,770.4
2017	8,700.4	8,763.4	8,808.7	8,859.3	8,944.4	9,016.6	8,924.6	8,880.3	8,908.9	8,998.7	9,056.2	9,076.4	8,911.5
Mining, Logging, and Construction													
2007	348.4	342.0	350.8	367.8	379.2	388.5	389.2	392.4	391.3	392.0	390.0	383.7	376.3
2008	359.1	356.6	363.0	374.7	381.2	384.5	387.5	389.6	385.0	381.8	373.7	360.1	374.7
2009	325.0	320.6	323.1	329.4	334.1	336.2	338.0	337.2	331.4	328.4	324.0	316.1	328.6
2010	286.4	281.0	289.4	306.7	309.9	313.7	317.3	319.3	316.7	314.7	313.4	304.0	306.0
2011	276.4	275.2	285.6	300.2	309.3	314.7	321.7	324.1	321.4	320.8	320.2	314.7	307.0
2012	293.7	291.7	298.3	308.0	312.4	317.4	321.7	324.4	321.7	323.4	322.2	324.8	313.3
2013	307.6	304.5	311.7	326.6	332.4	336.7	342.6	346.9	344.7	348.3	347.3	337.3	332.2
2014	315.2	309.9	321.8	340.9	351.1	357.3	366.0	368.1	367.6	370.6	370.3	363.7	350.2
2015	338.2	331.9	341.9	363.1	373.9	379.6	385.7	388.1	383.8	390.2	389.4	383.4	370.8
2016	362.6	357.2	369.3	384.5	390.5	395.1	400.6	403.3	400.0	400.5	399.2	392.8	388.0
2017	372.2	373.3	377.7	391.4	400.3	405.5	408.1	409.2	407.2	408.0	405.7	398.2	396.4

Employment by Industry: New York-Newark-Jersey City, NY-NJ-PA, Selected Years, 2007–2017—*Continued*

(Numbers in thousands, not seasonally adjusted)

Industry and year	January	February	March	April	May	June	July	August	September	October	November	December	Annual average
Manufacturing													
2007	464.0	463.4	463.9	461.8	462.4	463.9	459.3	458.3	458.1	458.1	456.5	455.3	460.4
2008	447.8	447.2	448.0	446.2	445.4	446.8	440.7	440.4	440.3	436.3	432.2	427.1	441.5
2009	413.2	407.2	403.5	398.2	397.6	397.4	391.0	389.2	389.0	388.5	386.4	385.9	395.6
2010	377.5	377.3	378.9	380.3	381.3	383.7	380.6	380.5	380.6	381.1	381.1	381.3	380.4
2011	373.7	374.0	374.8	375.3	376.3	378.3	376.1	377.2	378.0	377.6	377.9	377.5	376.4
2012	371.4	372.3	374.1	373.0	375.1	377.3	374.6	375.0	376.3	376.6	374.6	375.3	374.6
2013	367.7	368.8	371.0	371.9	373.2	375.1	372.6	373.7	374.3	374.5	374.7	374.6	372.7
2014	367.2	367.2	368.1	368.0	369.2	371.4	369.1	369.4	368.8	368.9	369.3	369.0	368.8
2015	363.7	363.9	365.2	365.1	366.7	369.4	368.5	368.4	368.8	369.3	369.3	369.9	367.4
2016	364.7	365.9	367.0	365.5	366.2	368.7	367.3	367.2	365.9	367.3	367.5	367.9	366.8
2017	362.1	362.7	363.4	363.2	365.4	367.7	365.9	365.4	363.8	364.2	363.8	363.6	364.3
Trade, Transportation, and Utilities													
2007	1,669.1	1,646.4	1,652.8	1,653.4	1,672.6	1,692.9	1,665.1	1,655.6	1,671.7	1,685.8	1,724.5	1,753.9	1,678.7
2008	1,679.8	1,656.0	1,662.6	1,658.9	1,668.9	1,683.3	1,656.9	1,651.7	1,663.0	1,666.7	1,685.1	1,702.1	1,669.6
2009	1,610.8	1,585.1	1,578.1	1,564.3	1,579.8	1,592.8	1,562.7	1,558.5	1,575.2	1,588.6	1,616.5	1,642.8	1,587.9
2010	1,568.1	1,549.2	1,555.3	1,570.0	1,581.3	1,600.8	1,578.5	1,577.6	1,590.2	1,608.0	1,636.3	1,663.3	1,589.9
2011	1,595.3	1,578.1	1,582.7	1,594.9	1,605.0	1,624.3	1,602.2	1,602.0	1,617.7	1,629.5	1,665.0	1,693.2	1,615.8
2012	1,630.7	1,611.0	1,618.3	1,615.4	1,636.3	1,654.5	1,619.5	1,622.6	1,639.6	1,652.4	1,684.5	1,713.7	1,641.5
2013	1,636.8	1,613.9	1,627.0	1,638.0	1,651.6	1,673.2	1,656.7	1,654.0	1,670.1	1,684.4	1,728.3	1,750.0	1,665.3
2014	1,674.4	1,653.8	1,661.4	1,669.3	1,685.2	1,703.5	1,687.0	1,686.4	1,699.2	1,716.3	1,756.7	1,783.3	1,698.0
2015	1,705.7	1,685.3	1,689.2	1,694.3	1,712.7	1,731.3	1,709.3	1,706.9	1,717.1	1,731.1	1,768.6	1,784.3	1,719.7
2016	1,711.9	1,695.2	1,698.9	1,708.2	1,716.3	1,731.0	1,713.1	1,708.7	1,720.7	1,739.3	1,778.2	1,804.2	1,727.1
2017	1,734.1	1,711.5	1,712.5	1,716.3	1,735.9	1,753.7	1,733.3	1,730.1	1,742.6	1,759.1	1,796.2	1,814.0	1,744.9
Wholesale Trade													
2007	445.8	445.9	447.0	447.4	449.2	452.6	450.3	449.6	448.8	451.7	451.2	452.9	449.4
2008	447.3	447.2	448.2	446.5	447.2	448.9	445.9	444.4	443.2	440.9	438.4	436.7	444.6
2009	425.9	421.8	419.5	415.2	414.9	415.6	410.1	408.9	407.8	409.1	409.0	410.1	414.0
2010	401.7	400.7	402.4	403.2	404.8	407.8	407.3	406.7	406.7	407.8	409.0	410.9	405.8
2011	404.2	403.4	405.4	406.8	408.0	410.9	410.5	410.7	409.3	409.9	410.1	413.1	408.5
2012	409.1	410.2	412.0	411.7	413.1	416.2	413.8	413.3	412.2	413.4	413.4	415.9	412.9
2013	408.8	409.2	410.4	412.7	414.2	418.1	418.2	417.8	416.8	417.4	418.8	420.1	415.2
2014	413.1	413.5	414.8	416.4	418.3	420.6	421.2	420.6	419.7	420.6	422.7	424.1	418.8
2015	417.5	417.6	419.1	419.6	421.5	424.5	424.7	424.1	422.2	423.1	424.0	424.9	421.9
2016	417.9	418.3	418.6	418.1	418.6	420.5	420.5	419.9	418.1	418.4	419.3	421.2	419.1
2017	414.3	414.8	415.4	416.2	418.4	422.2	421.9	421.4	420.3	419.5	420.9	421.9	418.9
Retail Trade													
2007	894.0	871.9	875.6	877.2	888.2	902.0	895.8	890.7	887.6	897.0	934.1	956.3	897.5
2008	902.1	878.7	882.0	879.1	886.3	896.8	892.1	889.8	885.3	893.0	912.6	927.2	893.8
2009	863.0	843.0	839.9	834.0	845.9	857.4	850.3	850.6	851.2	862.0	887.1	908.0	857.7
2010	855.7	839.9	843.9	855.3	863.6	877.7	873.5	874.5	869.4	884.5	908.8	928.1	872.9
2011	877.4	862.9	864.0	872.7	879.6	892.9	889.4	890.7	889.2	900.1	930.7	951.5	891.8
2012	905.1	884.7	888.5	890.4	902.3	914.4	906.7	906.7	905.9	917.5	947.5	965.8	911.3
2013	911.1	895.4	900.5	906.6	916.8	932.5	931.2	932.6	929.9	941.4	979.0	994.8	931.0
2014	936.5	919.9	924.0	930.1	939.5	953.2	951.1	953.0	948.8	961.5	993.4	1,011.7	951.9
2015	952.1	934.5	935.9	938.7	950.8	963.3	957.0	956.5	951.4	961.0	991.5	998.6	957.6
2016	948.0	932.1	933.7	940.0	946.3	957.5	955.2	954.1	947.8	960.2	991.1	1,006.3	956.0
2017	957.1	936.9	936.2	942.1	951.5	961.6	956.7	954.7	947.4	960.4	988.7	995.9	957.4
Transportation and Utilities													
2007	329.3	328.6	330.2	328.8	335.2	338.3	319.0	315.3	335.3	337.1	339.2	344.7	331.8
2008	330.4	330.1	332.4	333.3	335.4	337.6	318.9	317.5	334.5	332.8	334.1	338.2	331.3
2009	321.9	320.3	318.7	315.1	319.0	319.8	302.3	299.0	316.2	317.5	320.4	324.7	316.2
2010	310.7	308.6	309.0	311.5	312.9	315.3	297.7	296.4	314.1	315.7	318.5	324.3	311.2
2011	313.7	311.8	313.3	315.4	317.4	320.5	302.3	300.6	319.2	319.5	324.2	328.6	315.5
2012	316.5	316.1	317.8	313.3	320.9	323.9	299.0	302.6	321.5	321.5	323.6	332.0	317.4
2013	316.9	309.3	316.1	318.7	320.6	322.6	307.3	303.6	323.4	325.6	330.5	335.1	319.1
2014	324.8	320.4	322.6	322.8	327.4	329.7	314.7	312.8	330.7	334.2	340.6	347.5	327.4
2015	336.1	333.2	334.2	336.0	340.4	343.5	327.6	326.3	343.5	347.0	353.1	360.8	340.1
2016	346.0	344.8	346.6	350.1	351.4	353.0	337.4	334.7	354.8	360.7	367.8	376.7	352.0
2017	362.7	359.8	360.9	358.0	366.0	369.9	354.7	354.0	374.9	379.2	386.6	396.2	368.6

Employment by Industry: New York-Newark-Jersey City, NY-NJ-PA, Selected Years, 2007–2017—*Continued*

(Numbers in thousands, not seasonally adjusted)

Industry and year	January	February	March	April	May	June	July	August	September	October	November	December	Annual average
Information													
2007	284.9	286.8	287.1	286.9	288.8	291.3	290.0	290.5	289.5	288.0	289.9	291.4	288.8
2008	286.0	288.2	288.3	286.6	288.0	290.8	287.3	288.0	287.6	285.8	286.1	286.8	287.5
2009	279.0	277.1	278.0	278.7	278.7	278.6	277.1	276.0	275.1	274.0	274.4	275.0	276.8
2010	267.6	267.8	268.9	268.9	270.1	272.1	272.2	272.6	272.2	274.1	273.6	277.8	271.5
2011	269.0	270.0	271.8	274.4	274.8	276.4	278.2	261.3	277.7	275.4	276.8	278.8	273.7
2012	273.9	275.2	276.7	277.0	278.7	280.7	278.1	277.8	276.2	277.9	278.8	279.2	277.5
2013	271.4	273.2	274.5	276.2	278.3	281.1	280.6	283.3	281.1	282.6	286.0	285.1	279.5
2014	277.1	280.0	281.0	279.7	280.6	284.1	282.4	283.7	281.1	283.4	283.1	285.6	281.8
2015	278.6	280.1	280.7	279.3	280.4	283.3	285.3	283.7	282.7	286.8	288.3	289.1	283.2
2016	278.5	279.5	281.0	282.9	269.9	285.1	290.5	289.3	287.2	288.6	289.6	291.2	284.4
2017	280.7	284.8	285.7	283.5	285.2	289.4	287.4	289.2	289.2	288.6	290.2	288.3	286.9
Financial Activities													
2007	798.5	799.9	801.6	801.3	801.9	813.3	816.9	814.1	804.7	806.5	808.0	810.0	806.4
2008	798.9	799.5	799.5	797.4	797.0	804.2	805.8	803.9	790.3	785.6	781.6	781.5	795.4
2009	764.4	758.9	754.9	749.6	747.3	749.4	748.2	744.5	738.9	736.8	735.6	737.8	747.2
2010	726.3	727.1	729.3	729.9	731.1	740.7	742.9	743.8	738.0	737.3	739.5	743.9	735.8
2011	734.5	735.6	736.7	738.9	740.6	750.9	754.0	755.1	746.5	743.5	744.0	746.7	743.9
2012	737.2	739.5	740.7	739.4	740.2	749.5	750.4	749.1	740.4	741.9	741.3	746.9	743.0
2013	733.3	735.4	736.0	736.1	736.5	746.7	750.7	750.1	741.5	743.1	745.9	749.6	742.1
2014	738.8	740.4	742.3	742.5	745.9	757.7	761.2	760.3	751.0	751.5	753.6	758.9	750.3
2015	747.4	748.6	750.0	751.1	753.6	765.1	771.5	771.3	761.2	764.3	765.2	769.1	759.9
2016	760.3	760.7	761.9	761.3	763.6	774.1	779.3	779.3	766.6	767.1	768.9	773.7	768.1
2017	763.3	765.8	768.2	768.5	772.0	785.4	788.0	788.3	777.8	780.7	779.3	781.8	776.6
Professional and Business Services													
2007	1,289.1	1,294.2	1,309.9	1,323.0	1,332.5	1,353.7	1,356.9	1,361.2	1,350.9	1,363.7	1,369.3	1,373.6	1,339.8
2008	1,327.8	1,333.3	1,342.6	1,356.1	1,357.7	1,370.9	1,369.9	1,367.2	1,355.3	1,350.3	1,345.1	1,338.4	1,351.2
2009	1,279.8	1,273.1	1,271.7	1,273.3	1,273.4	1,281.8	1,274.8	1,269.9	1,264.8	1,268.4	1,272.5	1,275.8	1,273.3
2010	1,233.3	1,240.0	1,251.6	1,277.8	1,281.8	1,299.4	1,295.8	1,297.9	1,292.8	1,304.4	1,309.8	1,312.5	1,283.1
2011	1,277.1	1,282.1	1,294.8	1,317.2	1,321.0	1,339.7	1,343.6	1,345.3	1,342.5	1,347.4	1,356.6	1,356.3	1,327.0
2012	1,312.1	1,320.8	1,336.5	1,352.3	1,362.5	1,381.0	1,377.2	1,386.6	1,384.3	1,393.5	1,400.8	1,407.9	1,368.0
2013	1,354.8	1,360.7	1,374.7	1,388.8	1,396.8	1,415.0	1,420.5	1,423.9	1,415.2	1,423.4	1,429.3	1,431.2	1,402.9
2014	1,380.4	1,388.7	1,395.2	1,422.4	1,432.7	1,447.9	1,455.4	1,457.0	1,447.2	1,460.0	1,468.4	1,471.0	1,435.5
2015	1,426.3	1,434.2	1,445.3	1,468.2	1,477.1	1,494.6	1,499.8	1,500.3	1,491.7	1,509.7	1,514.3	1,513.1	1,481.2
2016	1,463.9	1,471.6	1,485.6	1,506.0	1,510.9	1,530.7	1,535.5	1,537.8	1,534.0	1,537.7	1,545.6	1,546.0	1,517.1
2017	1,495.5	1,504.3	1,511.6	1,528.1	1,543.7	1,566.9	1,561.8	1,559.7	1,556.0	1,560.8	1,564.6	1,563.5	1,543.0
Education and Health Services													
2007	1,482.9	1,508.9	1,520.6	1,516.8	1,516.6	1,495.7	1,467.8	1,456.7	1,492.8	1,537.8	1,543.0	1,550.7	1,507.5
2008	1,511.5	1,539.5	1,548.6	1,551.5	1,548.7	1,529.0	1,494.6	1,488.3	1,523.9	1,563.2	1,574.8	1,582.7	1,538.0
2009	1,542.5	1,570.8	1,578.0	1,578.3	1,576.8	1,557.4	1,523.3	1,516.4	1,550.4	1,595.8	1,606.4	1,615.4	1,567.6
2010	1,574.6	1,601.0	1,614.2	1,618.4	1,613.1	1,586.8	1,554.5	1,546.5	1,582.0	1,627.3	1,639.9	1,642.9	1,600.1
2011	1,601.4	1,632.4	1,644.0	1,649.8	1,645.7	1,611.1	1,580.8	1,572.3	1,616.5	1,652.1	1,662.5	1,670.1	1,628.2
2012	1,626.6	1,662.8	1,676.5	1,676.4	1,680.8	1,648.2	1,613.8	1,605.7	1,655.8	1,689.6	1,685.4	1,700.0	1,660.1
2013	1,656.8	1,692.6	1,706.1	1,719.6	1,715.3	1,676.7	1,648.4	1,638.8	1,684.1	1,736.5	1,751.2	1,754.0	1,698.3
2014	1,700.1	1,732.4	1,750.5	1,760.9	1,761.6	1,730.2	1,704.4	1,699.1	1,739.3	1,791.4	1,808.4	1,814.4	1,749.4
2015	1,762.2	1,796.8	1,812.0	1,820.8	1,817.8	1,783.7	1,755.6	1,744.9	1,782.7	1,845.9	1,862.5	1,869.0	1,804.5
2016	1,816.4	1,853.3	1,867.4	1,878.0	1,872.1	1,841.9	1,814.2	1,805.4	1,853.7	1,901.9	1,916.8	1,923.7	1,862.1
2017	1,875.9	1,916.6	1,929.4	1,937.1	1,938.5	1,911.8	1,869.1	1,860.0	1,909.0	1,956.4	1,974.9	1,979.7	1,921.5
Leisure and Hospitality													
2007	623.8	628.7	640.6	661.6	688.5	714.4	719.0	714.1	692.4	685.9	682.0	682.6	677.8
2008	644.9	649.0	660.9	684.6	709.0	730.7	733.4	727.1	706.6	696.4	686.0	682.2	692.6
2009	640.2	641.6	650.5	666.8	700.5	720.2	723.7	718.8	709.5	693.8	685.3	685.1	686.3
2010	645.6	646.7	661.8	694.3	718.0	742.3	747.3	746.1	729.6	721.4	714.7	715.4	706.9
2011	675.2	679.9	693.8	724.1	747.6	774.6	780.7	776.1	759.0	751.2	746.2	744.5	737.7
2012	708.4	719.1	734.6	754.4	786.7	815.0	818.9	817.7	797.1	787.0	762.7	770.8	772.7
2013	735.4	741.8	759.3	787.9	818.3	850.8	855.7	847.3	830.5	822.8	817.0	816.9	807.0
2014	775.2	780.8	797.0	822.3	860.1	887.7	888.3	881.2	861.5	854.6	846.5	844.9	841.7
2015	804.5	807.5	822.7	846.7	886.5	912.2	922.4	915.1	895.4	886.5	875.7	878.0	871.1
2016	828.1	832.7	851.6	878.7	905.6	939.5	948.8	940.4	916.3	901.5	896.8	895.2	894.6
2017	854.8	860.3	873.8	894.4	934.5	968.6	973.2	969.8	935.9	917.9	904.6	904.6	916.0

Employment by Industry: New York-Newark-Jersey City, NY-NJ-PA, Selected Years, 2007–2017—*Continued*

(Numbers in thousands, not seasonally adjusted)

Industry and year	January	February	March	April	May	June	July	August	September	October	November	December	Annual average
Other Services													
2007	367.8	369.5	372.1	374.1	378.5	382.9	376.3	373.1	372.5	376.0	377.8	378.9	375.0
2008	370.1	370.9	372.6	375.1	378.2	381.0	377.7	375.3	373.4	374.3	374.0	373.7	374.7
2009	364.1	365.1	365.8	366.1	369.8	372.6	369.2	367.0	364.3	366.5	368.0	368.9	367.3
2010	359.4	359.1	361.8	366.1	369.2	372.8	371.0	369.3	366.6	371.3	371.4	372.8	367.6
2011	365.6	367.2	369.3	374.8	378.1	382.6	380.7	377.7	377.2	379.1	379.5	381.5	376.1
2012	377.0	378.1	381.3	384.3	388.9	394.6	391.1	389.0	388.9	391.1	389.0	392.6	387.2
2013	384.4	386.3	388.2	390.8	393.2	398.7	396.9	395.6	393.1	395.5	396.9	397.6	393.1
2014	391.0	392.9	395.5	400.3	405.2	409.2	406.7	405.1	403.4	406.5	408.2	409.4	402.8
2015	402.1	402.7	404.7	406.4	411.6	416.7	414.6	413.4	411.4	414.9	416.1	417.4	411.0
2016	409.7	412.1	414.0	419.2	421.9	425.7	423.5	421.1	419.4	422.2	422.8	423.0	419.6
2017	415.2	415.3	416.7	420.4	424.8	430.3	426.4	423.8	422.4	424.0	425.3	426.8	422.6
Government													
2007	1,338.3	1,350.2	1,354.9	1,352.3	1,358.1	1,365.8	1,328.0	1,301.6	1,311.9	1,348.5	1,360.2	1,366.8	1,344.7
2008	1,344.1	1,355.9	1,360.9	1,366.1	1,367.6	1,373.7	1,348.7	1,314.4	1,322.1	1,359.7	1,376.6	1,380.9	1,355.9
2009	1,350.6	1,363.2	1,368.9	1,373.8	1,375.7	1,372.5	1,374.4	1,345.5	1,311.2	1,355.3	1,366.5	1,368.5	1,360.5
2010	1,338.8	1,352.7	1,359.9	1,369.7	1,404.1	1,385.0	1,319.4	1,280.8	1,293.4	1,334.2	1,339.8	1,335.1	1,342.8
2011	1,303.7	1,320.9	1,324.9	1,332.2	1,325.1	1,325.7	1,301.9	1,278.3	1,276.5	1,314.7	1,322.0	1,316.7	1,311.9
2012	1,278.5	1,303.7	1,312.3	1,310.9	1,309.4	1,310.2	1,273.9	1,244.9	1,261.7	1,303.3	1,302.9	1,307.4	1,293.3
2013	1,273.2	1,299.5	1,304.2	1,306.9	1,306.0	1,301.2	1,271.0	1,240.2	1,255.0	1,302.7	1,309.8	1,305.9	1,289.6
2014	1,264.9	1,289.6	1,297.4	1,307.3	1,303.9	1,299.2	1,272.4	1,246.0	1,263.4	1,300.9	1,312.2	1,308.7	1,288.8
2015	1,266.6	1,291.8	1,299.0	1,306.6	1,306.5	1,303.3	1,280.2	1,256.2	1,270.4	1,302.6	1,315.4	1,313.1	1,292.6
2016	1,275.4	1,299.1	1,309.2	1,312.1	1,311.6	1,308.9	1,281.9	1,256.4	1,276.9	1,307.6	1,315.8	1,314.0	1,297.4
2017	1,280.9	1,304.8	1,310.8	1,311.0	1,309.8	1,310.5	1,285.4	1,259.4	1,276.0	1,311.2	1,321.1	1,317.7	1,299.9

Employment by Industry: Los Angeles-Long Beach-Anaheim, CA, Selected Years, 2007–2017

(Numbers in thousands, not seasonally adjusted)

Industry and year	January	February	March	April	May	June	July	August	September	October	November	December	Annual average
Total Nonfarm													
2007	5,709.8	5,747.9	5,782.7	5,761.0	5,773.0	5,791.4	5,746.0	5,735.0	5,768.3	5,793.2	5,816.5	5,842.9	5,772.3
2008	5,687.3	5,722.7	5,744.2	5,747.4	5,749.7	5,746.0	5,682.9	5,655.4	5,674.9	5,683.3	5,660.1	5,647.0	5,700.1
2009	5,476.7	5,456.6	5,451.8	5,407.2	5,400.9	5,382.7	5,283.8	5,247.9	5,265.8	5,319.3	5,325.5	5,339.2	5,363.1
2010	5,231.6	5,241.9	5,263.1	5,298.5	5,322.2	5,318.9	5,248.5	5,237.1	5,265.3	5,329.2	5,349.9	5,371.7	5,289.8
2011	5,270.5	5,296.6	5,316.2	5,320.2	5,330.2	5,331.6	5,282.6	5,278.6	5,322.9	5,364.6	5,400.5	5,423.3	5,328.2
2012	5,327.2	5,365.1	5,400.5	5,439.9	5,466.9	5,475.9	5,416.3	5,428.6	5,463.9	5,513.5	5,569.5	5,589.8	5,454.8
2013	5,457.9	5,502.1	5,522.4	5,549.5	5,570.1	5,574.2	5,521.1	5,549.3	5,576.1	5,633.1	5,689.6	5,705.0	5,570.9
2014	5,594.4	5,622.1	5,646.0	5,655.7	5,679.5	5,672.0	5,609.5	5,657.0	5,691.8	5,746.7	5,790.8	5,808.6	5,681.2
2015	5,697.7	5,740.6	5,764.4	5,783.2	5,797.7	5,803.0	5,779.5	5,800.4	5,840.6	5,924.3	5,958.1	5,971.7	5,821.8
2016	5,874.5	5,916.5	5,916.7	5,967.1	5,978.9	5,946.7	5,920.9	5,936.2	5,977.0	6,037.7	6,076.7	6,088.4	5,969.8
2017	5,948.0	5,993.4	6,011.0	6,023.7	6,049.6	6,049.2	6,008.6	6,027.9	6,072.1	6,121.5	6,152.5	6,169.0	6,052.2
Total Private													
2007	4,958.2	4,990.1	5,018.8	4,998.2	5,008.0	5,026.2	5,013.4	5,015.2	5,026.4	5,031.5	5,046.9	5,074.1	5,017.3
2008	4,924.6	4,952.0	4,968.8	4,971.2	4,969.7	4,967.7	4,942.8	4,927.2	4,927.7	4,914.8	4,885.2	4,875.5	4,935.6
2009	4,709.6	4,685.9	4,675.8	4,629.6	4,625.8	4,608.7	4,556.1	4,543.5	4,554.2	4,571.2	4,575.3	4,591.9	4,610.6
2010	4,490.5	4,498.1	4,514.4	4,541.6	4,551.4	4,561.8	4,547.6	4,560.3	4,571.0	4,601.7	4,616.3	4,641.0	4,558.0
2011	4,545.7	4,568.8	4,581.8	4,587.0	4,596.0	4,597.0	4,604.5	4,616.1	4,635.2	4,648.8	4,676.3	4,703.7	4,613.4
2012	4,617.7	4,646.6	4,676.2	4,718.0	4,742.4	4,752.7	4,748.2	4,768.8	4,779.4	4,810.0	4,859.6	4,881.5	4,750.1
2013	4,759.7	4,794.8	4,808.5	4,838.4	4,856.7	4,861.1	4,859.4	4,884.2	4,890.9	4,927.9	4,976.9	4,993.0	4,871.0
2014	4,892.1	4,914.8	4,928.8	4,937.4	4,956.1	4,953.4	4,943.9	4,982.8	4,991.6	5,027.2	5,063.8	5,081.5	4,972.8
2015	4,978.7	5,013.9	5,031.9	5,046.8	5,064.0	5,067.1	5,092.8	5,113.7	5,124.2	5,185.6	5,215.4	5,228.3	5,096.9
2016	5,141.9	5,175.7	5,170.3	5,219.7	5,228.4	5,206.1	5,225.3	5,239.7	5,248.5	5,289.1	5,323.5	5,334.0	5,233.5
2017	5,203.2	5,241.9	5,253.0	5,266.4	5,287.8	5,287.2	5,305.8	5,324.9	5,337.7	5,366.9	5,391.2	5,408.9	5,306.2
Goods Producing													
2007	895.8	901.5	905.8	902.0	903.4	909.7	905.5	903.4	899.1	893.5	886.6	882.4	899.1
2008	867.2	868.9	868.2	865.9	864.5	863.6	859.8	856.9	851.5	841.1	828.0	816.8	854.4
2009	791.6	777.5	770.4	757.5	753.8	749.3	735.4	729.7	724.5	719.5	716.1	710.8	744.7
2010	701.5	700.0	702.6	704.6	707.5	710.9	709.8	710.1	706.9	707.3	705.8	703.5	705.9
2011	694.0	695.7	699.3	701.9	705.7	708.3	712.4	713.4	712.1	708.7	708.8	707.5	705.7
2012	703.1	705.2	708.7	711.5	715.0	720.5	723.2	723.7	723.2	722.6	724.2	723.3	717.0
2013	716.7	722.6	723.7	724.4	727.1	732.2	734.5	737.1	735.6	737.2	738.7	737.1	730.6
2014	725.6	731.5	732.6	728.8	732.5	734.3	734.9	738.7	737.5	737.1	737.5	735.9	733.9
2015	733.3	735.0	737.3	738.4	741.8	745.6	751.9	754.5	751.6	754.6	754.6	754.1	746.1
2016	745.6	750.1	748.2	751.1	751.5	750.5	755.1	755.3	754.2	753.2	752.8	752.4	751.7
2017	738.9	743.4	747.4	747.9	750.5	754.2	755.8	757.8	755.6	754.3	753.5	753.6	751.1
Service-Providing													
2007	4,814.0	4,846.4	4,876.9	4,859.0	4,869.6	4,881.7	4,840.5	4,831.6	4,869.2	4,899.7	4,929.9	4,960.5	4,873.3
2008	4,820.1	4,853.8	4,876.0	4,881.5	4,885.2	4,882.4	4,823.1	4,798.5	4,823.4	4,842.2	4,832.1	4,830.2	4,845.7
2009	4,685.1	4,679.1	4,681.4	4,649.7	4,647.1	4,633.4	4,548.4	4,518.2	4,541.3	4,599.8	4,609.4	4,628.4	4,618.4
2010	4,530.1	4,541.9	4,560.5	4,593.9	4,614.7	4,608.0	4,538.7	4,527.0	4,558.4	4,621.9	4,644.1	4,668.2	4,584.0
2011	4,576.5	4,600.9	4,616.9	4,618.3	4,624.5	4,623.3	4,570.2	4,565.2	4,610.8	4,655.9	4,691.7	4,715.8	4,622.5
2012	4,624.1	4,659.9	4,691.8	4,728.4	4,751.9	4,755.4	4,693.1	4,704.9	4,740.7	4,790.9	4,845.3	4,866.5	4,737.7
2013	4,741.2	4,779.5	4,798.7	4,825.1	4,843.0	4,842.0	4,786.6	4,812.2	4,840.5	4,895.9	4,950.9	4,967.9	4,840.3
2014	4,868.8	4,890.6	4,913.4	4,926.9	4,947.0	4,937.7	4,874.6	4,918.3	4,954.3	5,009.6	5,053.3	5,072.7	4,947.3
2015	4,964.4	5,005.6	5,027.1	5,044.8	5,055.9	5,057.4	5,027.6	5,045.9	5,089.0	5,169.7	5,203.5	5,217.6	5,075.7
2016	5,128.9	5,166.4	5,168.5	5,216.0	5,227.4	5,196.2	5,165.8	5,180.9	5,222.8	5,284.5	5,323.9	5,336.0	5,218.1
2017	5,209.1	5,250.0	5,263.6	5,275.8	5,299.1	5,295.0	5,252.8	5,270.1	5,316.5	5,367.2	5,399.0	5,415.4	5,301.1
Mining and Logging													
2007	3.8	3.9	3.9	3.8	3.7	3.8	3.8	3.7	3.8	3.7	3.8	3.7	3.8
2008	3.9	3.9	3.9	3.8	3.8	3.9	3.9	3.9	3.8	3.9	3.9	3.9	3.9
2009	3.8	3.7	3.6	3.6	3.6	3.6	3.5	3.5	3.5	3.5	3.6	3.5	3.6
2010	3.5	3.6	3.6	3.5	3.5	3.5	3.5	3.5	3.4	3.5	3.5	3.5	3.5
2011	3.4	3.4	3.4	3.5	3.5	3.5	3.5	3.5	3.5	3.6	3.7	3.7	3.5
2012	3.7	3.7	3.7	3.7	3.7	3.7	3.8	3.8	3.8	3.8	3.8	4.0	3.8
2013	4.0	4.0	3.9	4.0	4.0	4.0	4.0	4.1	4.0	4.0	4.0	4.0	4.0
2014	3.9	3.9	3.8	3.8	3.9	3.9	3.8	3.8	3.8	3.9	3.8	3.8	3.8
2015	3.8	3.7	3.7	3.6	3.5	3.5	3.5	3.4	3.4	3.4	3.4	3.3	3.5
2016	3.3	3.2	3.1	3.1	3.0	3.0	3.1	3.1	3.0	3.1	3.0	3.0	3.1
2017	2.9	2.9	2.9	2.9	3.0	3.0	2.9	2.9	2.9	2.9	2.9	2.9	2.9

Employment by Industry: Los Angeles-Long Beach-Anaheim, CA, Selected Years, 2007–2017—*Continued*

(Numbers in thousands, not seasonally adjusted)

Industry and year	January	February	March	April	May	June	July	August	September	October	November	December	Annual average
Construction													
2007	255.2	257.9	261.6	260.1	261.9	265.8	266.7	266.1	263.8	260.6	255.6	252.7	260.7
2008	242.9	243.3	243.6	241.4	240.6	239.3	237.9	238.0	234.7	230.5	224.9	220.1	236.4
2009	209.1	202.1	201.3	195.9	195.2	193.6	188.3	187.7	185.0	182.8	180.9	176.5	191.5
2010	171.3	169.6	170.9	172.5	173.4	174.1	173.7	174.6	172.8	173.4	173.2	171.2	172.6
2011	167.2	167.8	169.4	171.1	173.5	175.2	178.1	179.8	179.3	177.3	177.3	175.6	174.3
2012	173.8	173.8	175.1	175.0	177.5	181.0	183.7	184.7	184.8	184.9	186.0	185.3	180.5
2013	183.6	185.9	187.4	188.2	190.5	193.9	195.9	198.0	197.0	199.1	199.1	197.3	193.0
2014	193.4	196.2	198.0	197.2	200.2	201.2	202.3	205.8	205.6	206.7	207.5	204.9	201.6
2015	205.6	206.4	209.4	211.0	213.5	216.5	221.4	224.6	223.2	227.6	227.9	226.7	217.8
2016	223.5	226.0	225.7	229.4	230.2	230.3	234.4	235.6	235.1	236.2	234.9	233.7	231.3
2017	224.4	229.4	233.8	236.6	238.4	241.2	244.0	246.3	245.7	246.0	243.8	242.9	239.4
Manufacturing													
2007	636.8	639.7	640.3	638.1	637.8	640.1	635.0	633.6	631.5	629.2	627.2	626.0	634.6
2008	620.4	621.7	620.7	620.7	620.1	620.4	618.0	615.0	613.0	606.7	599.2	592.8	614.1
2009	578.7	571.7	565.5	558.0	555.0	552.1	543.6	538.5	536.0	533.2	531.6	530.8	549.6
2010	526.7	526.8	528.1	528.6	530.6	533.3	532.6	532.0	530.7	530.4	529.1	528.8	529.8
2011	523.4	524.5	526.5	527.3	528.7	529.6	530.8	530.1	529.3	527.8	527.8	528.2	527.8
2012	525.6	527.7	529.9	532.8	533.8	535.8	535.7	535.2	534.6	533.9	534.4	534.0	532.8
2013	529.1	532.7	532.4	532.2	532.6	534.3	534.6	535.0	534.6	534.1	535.6	535.8	533.6
2014	528.3	531.4	530.8	527.8	528.4	529.2	528.8	529.1	528.1	526.5	526.2	527.2	528.5
2015	523.9	524.9	524.2	523.8	524.8	525.6	527.0	526.5	525.0	523.6	523.3	524.1	524.7
2016	518.8	520.9	519.4	518.6	518.3	517.2	517.6	516.6	516.1	513.9	514.9	515.7	517.3
2017	511.6	511.1	510.7	508.4	509.1	510.0	508.9	508.6	507.0	505.4	506.8	507.8	508.8
Trade, Transportation, and Utilities													
2007	1,092.9	1,084.1	1,081.9	1,081.6	1,083.4	1,087.7	1,093.1	1,092.3	1,093.4	1,101.3	1,123.0	1,142.3	1,096.4
2008	1,094.5	1,085.9	1,081.6	1,077.9	1,077.1	1,077.6	1,074.1	1,068.5	1,064.1	1,065.7	1,069.8	1,074.7	1,076.0
2009	1,028.3	1,011.6	1,003.2	990.1	990.2	986.5	975.0	974.1	977.0	982.5	996.1	1,008.9	993.6
2010	978.7	972.6	971.1	976.7	981.8	983.6	981.7	984.5	982.6	991.1	1,008.7	1,022.1	986.3
2011	989.5	985.8	983.3	987.4	990.0	991.5	993.6	997.5	996.5	1,000.9	1,023.9	1,037.2	998.1
2012	1,006.1	995.5	997.0	1,004.0	1,008.6	1,012.3	1,012.0	1,014.4	1,015.3	1,020.9	1,052.1	1,061.2	1,016.6
2013	1,025.6	1,019.6	1,015.9	1,018.0	1,023.7	1,027.1	1,028.7	1,032.5	1,029.7	1,038.9	1,070.1	1,081.5	1,034.3
2014	1,045.7	1,037.7	1,035.2	1,037.4	1,042.3	1,046.2	1,047.3	1,052.9	1,053.2	1,062.4	1,092.1	1,104.9	1,054.8
2015	1,067.9	1,059.3	1,062.0	1,058.8	1,063.6	1,064.9	1,071.0	1,075.6	1,074.9	1,083.6	1,108.8	1,117.0	1,075.6
2016	1,083.1	1,074.1	1,073.2	1,078.9	1,080.9	1,078.0	1,087.1	1,090.6	1,088.0	1,093.3	1,117.7	1,128.6	1,089.5
2017	1,097.9	1,082.6	1,087.2	1,090.9	1,092.7	1,093.8	1,097.6	1,100.2	1,100.4	1,109.2	1,131.0	1,138.9	1,101.9
Wholesale Trade													
2007	311.7	313.2	314.6	314.1	314.0	314.5	314.7	314.2	314.6	315.9	315.6	317.4	314.5
2008	314.5	315.2	315.6	315.2	313.6	313.4	311.3	309.4	308.5	307.3	304.3	303.0	310.9
2009	295.9	293.6	291.2	287.5	285.9	285.1	280.4	279.0	277.9	279.3	278.1	279.2	284.4
2010	277.5	278.0	278.7	280.6	281.8	282.0	281.6	281.7	281.4	283.3	283.2	283.9	281.1
2011	281.0	281.9	281.7	283.1	283.5	283.4	282.9	283.4	283.6	283.7	283.7	285.0	283.1
2012	282.2	283.1	283.9	288.2	289.5	290.2	289.8	291.0	290.7	292.3	293.7	295.5	289.2
2013	293.2	294.6	295.9	296.9	297.6	298.8	298.2	298.7	298.2	299.9	301.3	303.4	298.1
2014	300.0	301.6	301.9	301.0	301.9	302.3	302.6	304.3	304.5	305.3	306.9	307.8	303.3
2015	303.6	305.1	305.1	305.4	305.9	306.0	307.2	307.5	306.5	307.6	308.4	308.8	306.4
2016	304.9	305.7	304.0	306.4	306.5	305.2	307.4	307.4	306.6	305.8	306.2	306.9	306.1
2017	303.4	304.1	305.2	306.3	307.6	308.0	306.6	306.6	306.4	307.5	308.0	309.0	306.6
Retail Trade													
2007	587.6	577.2	576.7	573.7	575.7	579.4	583.2	585.3	583.2	589.2	610.9	626.6	587.4
2008	588.9	577.3	575.9	571.6	570.1	570.9	568.4	565.0	563.9	565.3	574.1	580.0	572.6
2009	547.1	535.1	529.6	523.1	524.5	523.1	518.8	520.0	522.7	526.1	540.8	551.2	530.2
2010	526.2	519.2	517.9	521.1	522.3	523.3	523.3	525.4	523.7	528.4	546.3	556.9	527.8
2011	532.0	525.4	524.4	525.2	527.2	528.9	531.6	533.8	533.5	537.4	559.6	569.5	535.7
2012	545.0	534.0	533.5	533.5	536.3	537.9	538.6	540.5	540.9	545.3	574.4	579.1	544.9
2013	548.6	540.8	538.7	539.8	542.4	544.8	545.3	547.6	545.9	552.8	580.3	588.2	551.3
2014	558.4	548.8	547.8	550.2	552.0	555.1	555.7	559.0	557.8	564.1	590.5	599.0	561.5
2015	570.5	562.3	560.9	559.0	561.8	562.5	565.8	568.7	567.7	573.9	595.2	600.7	570.8
2016	574.3	566.4	564.7	566.1	566.9	565.1	568.7	570.8	568.7	575.9	596.6	602.0	573.9
2017	579.4	568.0	566.2	568.3	568.0	568.4	570.6	572.5	571.9	577.8	597.8	601.5	575.9

Employment by Industry: Los Angeles-Long Beach-Anaheim, CA, Selected Years, 2007–2017—*Continued*

(Numbers in thousands, not seasonally adjusted)

Industry and year	January	February	March	April	May	June	July	August	September	October	November	December	Annual average
Transportation and Utilities													
2007	193.6	193.7	190.6	193.8	193.7	193.8	195.2	192.8	195.6	196.2	196.5	198.3	194.5
2008	191.1	193.4	190.1	191.1	193.4	193.3	194.4	194.1	191.7	193.1	191.4	191.7	192.4
2009	185.3	182.9	182.4	179.5	179.8	178.3	175.8	175.1	176.4	177.1	177.2	178.5	179.0
2010	175.0	175.4	174.5	175.0	177.7	178.3	176.8	177.4	177.5	179.4	179.2	181.3	177.3
2011	176.5	178.5	177.2	179.1	179.3	179.2	179.1	180.3	179.4	179.8	180.6	182.7	179.3
2012	178.9	178.4	179.6	182.3	182.8	184.2	183.6	182.9	183.7	183.3	184.0	186.6	182.5
2013	183.8	184.2	181.3	181.3	183.7	183.5	185.2	186.2	185.6	186.2	188.5	189.9	185.0
2014	187.3	187.3	185.5	186.2	188.4	188.8	189.0	189.6	190.9	193.0	194.7	198.1	189.9
2015	193.8	191.9	196.0	194.4	195.9	196.4	198.0	199.4	200.7	202.1	205.2	207.5	198.4
2016	203.9	202.0	204.5	206.4	207.5	207.7	211.0	212.4	212.7	211.6	214.9	219.7	209.5
2017	215.1	210.5	215.8	216.3	217.1	217.4	220.4	221.1	222.1	223.9	225.2	228.4	719.4
Information													
2007	235.1	241.6	249.3	238.0	241.5	243.8	240.6	244.6	244.9	234.0	238.5	245.1	241.4
2008	227.1	235.3	243.8	243.0	247.0	249.3	240.5	241.8	245.8	241.0	237.0	238.2	240.8
2009	219.0	222.2	225.8	218.2	217.1	219.7	215.7	217.0	221.4	212.9	215.7	223.2	219.0
2010	212.3	212.9	216.5	211.0	211.8	215.6	215.9	220.9	222.9	216.7	219.3	225.6	216.8
2011	219.6	219.0	220.1	216.0	214.8	214.7	214.2	216.6	214.8	216.0	213.5	216.9	216.4
2012	210.9	211.5	213.5	217.4	214.3	211.7	215.5	218.0	214.8	218.9	223.3	226.5	216.4
2013	217.7	219.4	221.0	220.9	219.6	221.2	217.2	221.0	223.1	225.6	229.2	228.1	222.0
2014	223.4	221.4	223.1	225.5	221.2	219.5	217.8	223.7	224.9	227.4	225.9	226.4	223.4
2015	219.7	228.1	230.9	229.7	228.0	231.8	228.6	232.9	235.7	242.5	244.9	243.1	233.0
2016	249.6	256.3	255.2	263.4	266.1	257.2	251.8	255.1	252.9	250.2	255.5	253.9	255.6
2017	237.9	258.7	239.9	237.8	237.5	234.7	232.5	236.7	244.4	247.1	247.3	246.2	241.7
Financial Activities													
2007	380.1	381.2	381.5	377.7	375.4	373.2	371.6	369.5	364.9	363.7	361.1	359.1	371.6
2008	353.8	353.7	352.8	350.7	349.5	348.4	346.9	345.0	341.6	339.4	337.6	337.5	346.4
2009	332.4	329.9	329.3	326.5	324.2	323.6	321.0	319.1	316.2	317.0	315.9	317.1	322.7
2010	312.2	312.6	313.3	313.7	313.5	314.8	315.3	315.2	314.8	315.7	315.9	318.3	314.6
2011	314.3	314.7	315.3	313.0	313.3	314.5	315.0	315.4	314.4	315.6	315.4	317.6	314.9
2012	313.4	314.7	316.1	318.2	319.5	321.2	322.5	323.0	322.7	324.2	325.2	327.5	320.7
2013	323.8	325.0	325.4	326.0	326.6	327.1	327.7	326.8	324.3	326.5	326.7	326.9	326.1
2014	321.6	322.2	321.9	322.6	324.3	325.6	324.9	325.6	324.0	326.1	328.2	330.0	324.8
2015	324.9	326.6	327.0	328.2	330.0	330.8	333.9	334.5	333.1	336.3	336.2	337.6	331.6
2016	333.0	334.3	333.7	336.3	337.0	336.5	339.4	339.1	337.4	339.6	340.4	342.0	337.4
2017	337.5	337.8	337.5	338.3	340.1	340.6	342.6	341.7	340.0	339.8	341.2	343.9	340.1
Professional and Business Services													
2007	859.7	868.7	874.4	864.1	864.4	871.4	867.9	872.7	874.3	876.7	875.9	878.8	870.8
2008	842.1	850.9	853.3	851.3	846.4	845.9	842.5	841.4	837.1	833.8	822.6	816.9	840.4
2009	785.4	780.7	775.3	762.7	758.5	755.4	744.9	745.8	744.7	755.9	756.3	755.7	760.1
2010	744.9	750.4	752.3	758.3	758.1	762.8	759.7	764.6	763.1	783.3	781.5	782.0	763.4
2011	763.9	771.9	773.5	770.8	771.2	775.2	780.8	783.5	789.6	795.3	797.6	802.0	781.3
2012	783.5	797.1	805.9	812.4	816.9	823.1	821.4	827.0	830.5	841.1	849.2	852.0	821.7
2013	824.3	834.9	838.5	842.5	844.9	846.0	850.3	859.4	860.2	868.8	877.8	878.0	852.1
2014	858.5	862.8	865.6	862.9	863.6	863.0	862.7	870.3	868.9	876.3	881.2	883.5	868.3
2015	860.5	867.6	869.2	873.4	871.7	873.2	881.0	883.4	882.9	900.0	901.3	900.9	880.4
2016	884.8	892.6	885.6	893.4	890.5	891.5	899.8	902.5	906.0	915.1	921.1	918.2	900.1
2017	889.8	897.9	900.9	899.4	903.3	907.3	922.4	926.3	929.7	931.7	933.5	939.1	915.1
Education and Health Services													
2007	754.8	767.9	772.7	773.4	773.3	765.0	759.4	759.2	779.0	789.4	793.3	795.2	773.6
2008	785.6	798.4	802.2	806.5	805.8	798.1	794.2	795.5	815.9	826.3	831.5	834.0	807.8
2009	819.0	832.3	837.1	839.1	839.3	830.5	823.3	821.8	837.7	849.2	849.5	850.1	835.7
2010	832.4	840.0	843.5	846.9	842.5	831.5	820.7	822.8	840.3	848.9	852.0	853.8	839.6
2011	841.4	853.3	856.8	854.9	851.9	840.0	829.0	830.6	846.9	857.4	862.2	867.1	849.3
2012	854.9	870.8	874.9	879.6	881.2	870.8	860.3	868.0	879.2	889.1	892.9	896.6	876.5
2013	870.1	882.4	886.1	896.9	894.2	879.3	870.3	877.3	888.4	899.5	903.7	908.6	888.1
2014	894.9	907.5	911.1	912.3	912.2	899.5	890.1	901.9	915.6	928.2	931.7	932.5	911.5
2015	917.5	932.4	934.6	937.2	938.3	925.0	923.0	930.0	945.1	960.5	965.8	969.0	939.9
2016	953.5	966.1	968.5	975.5	975.3	963.0	954.8	958.6	972.7	994.3	998.9	1,002.1	973.6
2017	988.7	1,001.2	1,007.0	1,007.9	1,010.7	998.2	997.5	1,003.1	1,016.2	1,027.1	1,030.0	1,031.9	1,010.0

Employment by Industry: Los Angeles-Long Beach-Anaheim, CA, Selected Years, 2007–2017—*Continued*

(Numbers in thousands, not seasonally adjusted)

Industry and year	January	February	March	April	May	June	July	August	September	October	November	December	Annual average
Leisure and Hospitality													
2007	549.6	552.5	559.2	567.3	571.9	578.9	580.8	579.3	575.0	576.5	572.9	575.7	570.0
2008	562.0	565.6	572.4	580.7	584.1	589.6	591.4	587.3	580.3	575.8	569.0	568.8	577.3
2009	550.4	548.5	550.9	553.9	560.7	561.5	562.0	558.8	555.4	554.2	547.0	547.7	554.3
2010	532.7	534.2	538.5	550.9	555.9	561.4	564.3	563.6	560.4	558.0	553.5	557.1	552.5
2011	546.6	550.4	554.8	563.5	568.9	572.3	578.3	578.9	578.8	572.9	573.4	573.2	567.7
2012	565.4	569.4	576.4	589.3	599.4	605.0	606.4	608.3	605.7	603.8	604.0	606.2	594.9
2013	595.5	602.5	608.5	618.5	628.8	635.8	639.3	638.6	636.9	638.3	637.2	639.6	626.6
2014	630.1	636.9	643.4	650.3	661.4	665.5	668.5	671.5	668.2	669.9	667.7	669.1	658.5
2015	659.0	667.1	672.3	681.9	689.9	695.4	702.8	703.2	700.1	705.9	701.6	705.4	690.4
2016	693.7	700.6	704.9	717.6	723.2	726.5	732.9	734.6	731.8	735.9	730.8	731.3	722.0
2017	712.3	717.9	728.8	738.9	747.1	752.1	752.6	754.5	745.9	752.5	750.4	752.1	742.1
Other Services													
2007	190.2	192.6	194.0	194.1	194.7	196.5	194.5	194.2	195.8	196.4	195.6	195.5	194.5
2008	192.3	193.3	194.5	195.2	195.3	195.2	193.4	190.8	191.4	191.7	189.7	188.6	192.6
2009	183.5	183.2	183.8	181.6	182.0	182.2	178.8	177.2	177.3	180.0	178.7	178.4	180.6
2010	175.8	175.4	176.6	179.5	180.3	181.2	180.2	178.6	180.0	180.7	179.6	178.6	178.9
2011	176.4	178.0	178.7	179.5	180.2	180.5	181.2	180.2	182.1	182.0	181.5	182.2	180.2
2012	180.4	182.4	183.7	185.6	187.5	188.1	186.9	186.4	188.0	189.4	188.7	188.2	186.3
2013	186.0	188.4	189.4	191.2	191.8	192.4	191.4	191.5	192.7	193.1	193.5	193.2	191.1
2014	192.3	194.8	195.9	197.6	198.6	199.8	197.7	198.2	199.3	199.8	199.5	199.2	197.7
2015	195.9	197.8	198.6	199.2	200.7	200.4	200.6	199.6	200.8	202.2	202.2	201.2	199.9
2016	198.6	201.6	201.0	203.5	203.9	202.9	204.4	203.9	205.5	207.5	206.3	205.5	203.7
2017	200.2	202.4	204.3	205.3	205.9	206.3	204.8	204.6	205.5	205.2	204.3	203.2	204.3
Government													
2007	751.6	757.8	763.9	762.8	765.0	765.2	732.6	719.8	741.9	761.7	769.6	768.8	755.1
2008	762.7	770.7	775.4	776.2	780.0	778.3	740.1	728.2	747.2	768.5	774.9	771.5	764.5
2009	767.1	770.7	776.0	777.6	775.1	774.0	727.7	704.4	711.6	748.1	750.2	747.3	752.5
2010	741.1	743.8	748.7	756.9	770.8	757.1	700.9	676.8	694.3	727.5	733.6	730.7	731.9
2011	724.8	727.8	734.4	733.2	734.2	734.6	678.1	662.5	687.7	715.8	724.2	719.6	714.7
2012	709.5	718.5	724.3	721.9	724.5	723.2	668.1	659.8	684.5	703.5	709.9	708.3	704.7
2013	698.2	707.3	713.9	711.1	713.4	713.1	661.7	665.1	685.2	705.2	712.7	712.0	699.9
2014	702.3	707.3	717.2	718.3	723.4	718.6	665.6	674.2	700.2	719.5	727.0	727.1	708.4
2015	719.0	726.7	732.5	736.4	733.7	735.9	686.7	686.7	716.4	738.7	742.7	743.4	724.9
2016	732.6	740.8	746.4	747.4	750.5	740.6	695.6	696.5	728.5	748.6	753.2	754.4	736.3
2017	744.8	751.5	758.0	757.3	761.8	762.0	702.8	703.0	734.4	754.6	761.3	760.1	746.0

Employment by Industry: Chicago-Naperville-Elgin, IL-IN-WI, Selected Years, 2007–2017

(Numbers in thousands, not seasonally adjusted)

Industry and year	January	February	March	April	May	June	July	August	September	October	November	December	Annual average
Total Nonfarm													
2007	4,449.9	4,448.1	4,487.9	4,529.4	4,577.9	4,611.0	4,584.2	4,584.9	4,579.4	4,588.8	4,604.1	4,601.8	4,554.0
2008	4,470.2	4,467.8	4,488.1	4,533.7	4,572.9	4,589.3	4,563.5	4,558.8	4,536.4	4,533.7	4,511.4	4,480.3	4,525.5
2009	4,313.2	4,291.5	4,283.1	4,292.3	4,317.7	4,321.8	4,280.9	4,267.7	4,265.4	4,276.6	4,278.0	4,263.8	4,287.7
2010	4,136.8	4,145.5	4,166.6	4,219.7	4,274.4	4,288.3	4,245.4	4,254.3	4,263.5	4,298.0	4,310.1	4,301.2	4,242.0
2011	4,181.2	4,191.0	4,222.4	4,280.8	4,313.8	4,339.4	4,324.2	4,332.4	4,346.7	4,358.7	4,372.3	4,363.1	4,302.2
2012	4,250.1	4,261.5	4,296.2	4,343.4	4,385.8	4,417.8	4,391.0	4,403.6	4,417.2	4,427.3	4,446.8	4,441.0	4,373.5
2013	4,313.7	4,335.2	4,363.9	4,400.5	4,457.0	4,489.9	4,462.5	4,477.0	4,480.8	4,494.3	4,511.5	4,513.3	4,441.6
2014	4,373.6	4,387.8	4,420.3	4,474.4	4,531.1	4,560.6	4,533.7	4,541.9	4,539.3	4,568.7	4,580.4	4,583.5	4,507.9
2015	4,448.4	4,464.1	4,492.7	4,559.5	4,618.5	4,649.1	4,629.7	4,628.6	4,629.4	4,661.6	4,667.4	4,673.1	4,593.5
2016	4,540.5	4,550.0	4,575.4	4,634.5	4,668.6	4,703.2	4,695.3	4,692.4	4,691.0	4,712.5	4,724.4	4,715.1	4,658.6
2017	4,583.7	4,597.3	4,631.8	4,664.2	4,714.9	4,757.4	4,722.5	4,726.0	4,724.0	4,754.6	4,758.6	4,730.9	4,697.2
Total Private													
2007	3,892.9	3,880.5	3,917.8	3,957.9	4,003.9	4,040.1	4,030.4	4,033.7	4,015.4	4,020.8	4,034.1	4,035.4	3,988.6
2008	3,911.2	3,898.9	3,916.5	3,960.6	3,994.2	4,014.9	4,004.5	4,003.6	3,968.1	3,958.2	3,935.7	3,907.9	3,956.2
2009	3,751.6	3,723.0	3,711.6	3,716.6	3,738.2	3,748.5	3,726.1	3,719.0	3,699.3	3,700.7	3,701.8	3,693.3	3,719.1
2010	3,575.6	3,576.8	3,597.4	3,645.9	3,683.0	3,711.0	3,696.9	3,712.2	3,706.0	3,732.4	3,743.1	3,742.2	3,676.9
2011	3,632.4	3,634.4	3,663.6	3,719.9	3,750.0	3,782.9	3,781.2	3,796.3	3,794.3	3,802.0	3,813.2	3,809.1	3,748.3
2012	3,707.5	3,709.9	3,741.5	3,787.9	3,826.6	3,862.8	3,853.8	3,869.2	3,867.5	3,872.5	3,890.7	3,888.5	3,823.2
2013	3,772.8	3,784.6	3,810.9	3,847.4	3,898.7	3,934.2	3,926.3	3,941.0	3,931.2	3,944.5	3,959.1	3,962.0	3,892.7
2014	3,839.0	3,845.2	3,874.1	3,925.9	3,975.7	4,009.8	3,998.0	4,008.9	3,991.5	4,016.9	4,029.0	4,031.7	3,962.1
2015	3,911.0	3,917.1	3,943.3	4,007.3	4,060.5	4,094.6	4,092.8	4,094.8	4,080.3	4,107.3	4,115.4	4,119.2	4,045.3
2016	4,002.2	4,005.0	4,025.5	4,084.9	4,115.1	4,145.4	4,153.7	4,155.4	4,136.8	4,162.9	4,173.5	4,157.1	4,109.8
2017	4,045.4	4,051.6	4,082.4	4,117.2	4,162.5	4,200.1	4,182.9	4,191.3	4,171.3	4,195.3	4,198.3	4,173.0	4,147.6
Goods Producing													
2007	682.3	673.6	686.0	697.8	706.9	716.3	712.8	712.3	710.4	708.9	704.4	696.0	700.6
2008	667.2	660.6	666.3	677.2	685.2	689.9	688.2	688.1	682.1	675.9	662.5	642.7	673.8
2009	601.9	593.3	588.6	586.2	585.4	588.1	582.1	581.4	577.4	573.8	567.1	555.3	581.7
2010	528.0	526.8	533.5	546.6	554.2	560.5	556.0	565.5	563.1	567.3	563.7	553.3	551.5
2011	533.2	531.8	540.5	554.4	563.1	569.9	572.5	574.2	570.5	569.5	566.6	557.5	558.6
2012	538.2	536.8	545.2	555.7	562.8	571.2	573.9	575.0	573.8	571.4	567.4	562.0	561.1
2013	539.9	540.9	546.6	552.9	563.7	571.7	572.4	573.7	570.9	571.6	569.9	560.8	561.3
2014	538.7	540.5	547.9	559.2	569.6	578.6	580.5	581.0	579.1	583.2	581.8	576.1	568.0
2015	555.1	554.4	563.0	574.4	583.8	592.9	593.7	593.5	592.2	592.6	591.0	583.8	580.9
2016	562.7	564.1	572.3	586.4	592.4	599.9	600.8	599.7	596.5	597.9	595.6	583.1	587.6
2017	564.3	566.5	574.0	584.1	593.8	602.0	601.1	601.0	599.4	600.4	600.1	593.1	590.0
Service-Providing													
2007	3,767.6	3,774.5	3,801.9	3,831.6	3,871.0	3,894.7	3,871.4	3,872.6	3,869.0	3,879.9	3,899.7	3,905.8	3,853.3
2008	3,803.0	3,807.2	3,821.8	3,856.5	3,887.7	3,899.4	3,875.3	3,870.7	3,854.3	3,857.8	3,848.9	3,837.6	3,851.7
2009	3,711.3	3,698.2	3,694.5	3,706.1	3,732.3	3,733.7	3,698.8	3,686.3	3,688.0	3,702.8	3,710.9	3,708.5	3,706.0
2010	3,608.8	3,618.7	3,633.1	3,673.1	3,720.2	3,727.8	3,689.4	3,688.8	3,700.4	3,730.7	3,746.4	3,747.9	3,690.4
2011	3,648.0	3,659.2	3,681.9	3,726.4	3,750.7	3,769.5	3,751.7	3,758.2	3,776.2	3,789.2	3,805.7	3,805.6	3,743.5
2012	3,711.9	3,724.7	3,751.0	3,787.7	3,823.0	3,846.6	3,817.1	3,828.6	3,843.4	3,855.9	3,879.4	3,879.0	3,812.4
2013	3,773.8	3,794.3	3,817.3	3,847.6	3,893.3	3,918.2	3,890.1	3,903.3	3,909.9	3,922.7	3,941.6	3,952.5	3,880.4
2014	3,834.9	3,847.3	3,872.4	3,915.2	3,961.5	3,982.0	3,953.2	3,960.9	3,960.2	3,985.5	3,998.6	4,007.4	3,939.9
2015	3,893.3	3,909.7	3,929.7	3,985.1	4,034.7	4,056.2	4,036.0	4,035.1	4,037.2	4,069.0	4,076.4	4,089.3	4,012.6
2016	3,977.8	3,985.9	4,003.1	4,048.1	4,076.2	4,103.3	4,094.5	4,092.7	4,094.5	4,114.6	4,128.8	4,132.0	4,071.0
2017	4,019.4	4,030.8	4,057.8	4,080.1	4,121.1	4,155.4	4,121.4	4,125.0	4,124.6	4,154.2	4,158.5	4,137.8	4,107.2
Mining and Logging													
2007	2.3	2.1	2.4	2.3	2.4	2.4	2.4	2.4	2.3	2.3	2.3	2.1	2.3
2008	1.9	1.8	1.9	2.1	2.1	2.2	2.2	2.2	2.1	2.0	1.9	1.8	2.0
2009	1.5	1.5	1.7	1.8	1.8	1.8	1.8	1.8	1.8	1.7	1.7	1.5	1.7
2010	1.2	1.2	1.3	1.5	1.5	1.6	1.6	1.6	1.7	1.6	1.6	1.5	1.5
2011	1.2	1.2	1.3	1.5	1.5	1.5	1.6	1.5	1.5	1.5	1.5	1.3	1.4
2012	1.2	1.2	1.2	1.3	1.4	1.5	1.5	1.5	1.5	1.5	1.5	1.3	1.4
2013	1.2	1.2	1.2	1.3	1.6	1.6	1.5	1.5	1.5	1.5	1.6	1.3	1.4
2014	1.2	1.2	1.2	1.4	1.5	1.6	1.6	1.6	1.6	1.6	1.6	1.6	1.5
2015	1.3	1.3	1.5	1.6	1.6	1.5	1.5	1.6	1.6	1.6	1.7	1.7	1.5
2016	1.4	1.5	1.6	1.6	1.6	1.6	1.6	1.6	1.6	1.6	1.6	1.5	1.6
2017	1.3	1.3	1.4	1.6	1.6	1.7	1.6	1.7	1.6	1.6	1.6	1.5	1.5

Employment by Industry: Chicago-Naperville-Elgin, IL-IN-WI, Selected Years, 2007–2017—*Continued*

(Numbers in thousands, not seasonally adjusted)

Industry and year	January	February	March	April	May	June	July	August	September	October	November	December	Annual average
Construction													
2007	196.3	188.3	199.4	211.9	220.9	227.1	227.3	227.2	225.5	224.2	221.0	210.7	215.0
2008	188.1	184.6	189.7	201.1	209.3	212.7	215.2	215.9	212.3	209.3	199.9	185.6	202.0
2009	157.4	155.6	157.0	163.4	167.2	170.8	171.0	170.9	167.6	166.2	161.0	149.6	163.1
2010	128.1	126.6	132.3	144.1	149.7	153.7	150.0	157.5	155.4	157.2	152.9	141.9	145.8
2011	125.7	124.2	130.5	142.2	150.1	154.3	157.7	159.5	157.3	155.8	153.2	144.3	146.2
2012	128.6	126.7	133.3	142.7	148.4	154.0	157.4	158.4	158.4	158.0	153.5	146.9	147.2
2013	129.9	130.5	135.5	143.1	152.7	157.4	160.2	160.6	160.0	160.7	157.9	148.7	149.8
2014	130.6	132.1	137.7	148.8	157.7	163.8	167.1	167.6	166.9	169.7	166.9	160.0	155.7
2015	141.9	141.5	148.6	161.1	168.5	173.2	174.9	175.2	174.7	176.7	174.7	166.5	164.8
2016	149.1	149.5	156.7	169.1	174.2	179.7	182.2	182.3	181.6	183.4	179.9	167.0	171.2
2017	151.8	152.9	159.0	168.4	176.8	180.7	182.2	182.8	183.0	182.6	179.4	171.4	172.6
Manufacturing													
2007	483.7	483.2	484.2	483.6	483.6	486.8	483.1	482.7	482.6	482.4	481.1	483.2	483.4
2008	477.2	474.2	474.7	474.0	473.8	475.0	470.8	470.0	467.7	464.6	460.7	455.3	469.8
2009	443.0	436.2	429.9	421.0	416.4	415.5	409.3	408.7	408.0	405.9	404.4	404.2	416.9
2010	398.7	399.0	399.9	401.0	403.0	405.2	404.4	406.4	406.0	408.5	409.2	409.9	404.3
2011	406.3	406.4	408.7	410.7	411.5	414.1	413.2	413.2	411.7	412.2	411.9	411.9	411.0
2012	408.4	408.9	410.7	411.7	413.0	415.7	415.0	415.1	413.9	411.9	412.4	413.8	412.5
2013	408.8	409.2	409.9	408.5	409.4	412.7	410.7	411.6	409.4	409.4	410.4	410.8	410.1
2014	406.9	407.2	409.0	409.0	410.4	413.2	411.8	411.8	410.6	411.9	413.3	414.5	410.8
2015	411.9	411.6	412.9	411.7	413.7	418.2	417.3	416.7	415.9	414.3	414.6	415.6	414.5
2016	412.2	413.1	414.0	415.7	416.6	418.6	417.0	415.8	413.3	412.9	414.1	414.6	414.8
2017	411.2	412.3	413.6	414.1	415.4	419.6	417.3	416.5	414.8	416.2	419.1	420.2	415.9
Trade, Transportation, and Utilities													
2007	923.6	911.6	917.9	916.0	926.5	933.7	928.1	928.0	927.0	931.3	953.6	965.7	930.3
2008	931.2	917.9	920.3	920.5	927.3	930.3	923.3	922.4	917.2	918.5	926.8	931.5	923.9
2009	889.6	875.1	869.8	863.4	868.2	869.3	859.4	859.1	855.2	858.0	868.9	876.4	867.7
2010	842.7	834.9	837.5	843.4	851.0	856.4	853.1	855.3	852.4	861.3	876.8	888.4	854.4
2011	857.1	848.9	851.8	860.3	866.0	872.0	869.2	873.3	873.5	879.6	896.1	907.1	871.2
2012	874.1	864.1	869.1	871.8	879.4	884.5	883.5	885.7	884.9	892.2	913.8	919.8	885.2
2013	884.1	875.9	879.3	883.9	893.3	900.9	898.2	901.5	898.2	903.9	922.1	934.6	898.0
2014	895.1	885.8	891.3	896.0	905.8	913.4	910.1	912.6	910.9	918.0	937.0	948.9	910.4
2015	910.7	904.2	908.4	916.3	927.1	935.9	934.2	935.6	935.2	942.1	959.1	968.6	931.5
2016	930.2	924.0	926.7	934.8	939.5	944.1	944.7	945.6	940.6	953.6	969.9	983.6	944.8
2017	944.4	935.2	937.1	938.2	943.7	951.4	946.9	949.0	946.7	955.6	973.9	980.3	950.2
Wholesale Trade													
2007	247.8	247.7	248.8	248.9	250.2	252.5	252.0	251.3	250.6	251.7	252.0	253.5	250.6
2008	250.4	249.8	250.4	250.8	252.0	252.9	251.0	250.5	249.2	248.6	247.7	247.0	250.0
2009	241.3	239.0	237.7	235.2	234.2	233.8	231.1	230.6	228.6	229.1	228.3	228.8	233.1
2010	225.6	225.0	226.2	227.6	228.9	230.1	230.2	230.4	228.8	229.9	230.1	230.8	228.6
2011	229.0	229.1	229.9	231.5	232.3	234.2	234.3	234.4	233.4	233.6	233.9	235.4	232.6
2012	233.9	233.8	235.1	236.2	237.3	239.4	238.9	238.8	238.1	238.6	239.3	240.0	237.5
2013	237.9	238.0	239.4	240.4	241.5	244.1	243.7	243.2	242.6	242.3	242.9	244.2	241.7
2014	240.2	240.7	241.5	241.1	242.5	243.6	242.9	242.5	241.2	242.5	243.0	244.1	242.2
2015	241.3	241.0	242.1	244.1	246.2	247.8	247.5	246.8	245.3	245.4	246.3	247.2	245.1
2016	242.1	242.3	242.7	244.5	245.1	246.8	247.0	246.8	245.8	250.8	251.3	252.3	246.5
2017	247.1	247.6	247.8	248.6	250.4	253.0	252.2	253.7	254.8	254.6	257.9	258.7	252.2
Retail Trade													
2007	474.5	462.6	466.7	465.6	472.5	478.0	475.8	475.3	471.3	474.2	495.0	502.9	476.2
2008	477.9	465.2	466.3	466.4	470.2	474.2	471.8	469.7	463.5	465.8	475.3	479.7	470.5
2009	452.6	441.8	439.1	437.2	442.1	445.1	441.9	441.5	436.9	439.2	450.9	456.4	443.7
2010	431.7	424.4	425.6	428.2	433.1	437.8	436.9	437.0	432.3	438.6	452.7	460.9	436.6
2011	437.0	428.7	430.2	435.1	438.7	443.3	442.3	444.7	442.0	447.7	463.0	470.5	443.6
2012	444.5	434.9	437.3	437.1	441.7	446.2	445.8	445.8	442.8	449.0	468.7	471.3	447.1
2013	445.6	437.1	438.5	439.7	446.7	453.2	451.6	452.3	448.6	454.4	470.1	478.8	451.4
2014	450.0	440.7	443.7	447.5	453.0	459.6	458.8	458.5	455.5	461.3	476.7	483.1	457.4
2015	456.0	449.7	452.3	455.6	461.5	468.1	467.2	466.7	464.8	470.0	484.2	488.1	465.4
2016	463.9	457.5	459.3	463.7	466.4	471.1	471.2	470.4	464.1	470.6	483.5	489.6	469.3
2017	467.0	458.9	458.8	460.1	461.4	466.6	464.3	462.4	456.1	462.4	475.4	476.3	464.1

Employment by Industry: Chicago-Naperville-Elgin, IL-IN-WI, Selected Years, 2007–2017—*Continued*

(Numbers in thousands, not seasonally adjusted)

Industry and year	January	February	March	April	May	June	July	August	September	October	November	December	Annual average
Transportation and Utilities													
2007	201.3	201.3	202.4	201.5	203.8	203.2	200.3	201.4	205.1	205.4	206.6	209.3	203.5
2008	202.9	202.9	203.6	203.3	205.1	203.2	200.5	202.2	204.5	204.1	203.8	204.8	203.4
2009	195.7	194.3	193.0	191.0	191.9	190.4	186.4	187.0	189.7	189.7	189.7	191.2	190.8
2010	185.4	185.5	185.7	187.6	189.0	188.5	186.0	187.9	191.3	192.8	194.0	196.7	189.2
2011	191.1	191.1	191.7	193.7	195.0	194.5	192.6	194.2	198.1	198.3	199.2	201.2	195.1
2012	195.7	195.4	196.7	198.5	200.4	198.9	198.8	201.1	204.0	204.6	205.8	208.5	200.7
2013	200.6	200.8	201.4	203.8	205.1	203.6	202.9	206.0	207.0	207.2	209.1	211.6	204.9
2014	204.9	204.4	206.1	207.4	210.3	210.2	208.4	211.6	214.2	214.2	217.3	221.7	210.9
2015	213.4	213.5	214.0	216.6	219.4	220.0	219.5	222.1	225.1	226.7	228.6	233.3	221.0
2016	224.2	224.2	224.7	226.6	228.0	226.2	226.5	228.4	230.7	232.2	235.1	241.7	229.0
2017	230.3	228.7	230.5	229.5	231.9	231.8	230.4	232.9	235.8	238.6	240.6	245.3	233.9
Information													
2007	90.4	90.8	90.5	90.5	90.8	91.3	91.6	91.7	91.0	91.0	91.0	91.1	91.0
2008	90.7	90.9	90.9	90.8	91.1	91.0	90.9	90.7	89.0	88.4	88.0	87.9	90.0
2009	86.7	85.8	84.8	84.1	83.9	83.8	83.4	83.2	82.7	82.4	82.1	82.2	83.8
2010	81.5	80.8	80.5	80.4	80.5	80.9	80.8	80.6	79.8	80.2	80.1	79.9	80.5
2011	79.5	79.3	79.1	79.4	79.8	80.5	81.3	81.0	80.1	80.3	80.7	80.6	80.1
2012	80.6	80.4	80.3	80.9	81.5	81.3	81.3	80.9	80.5	81.2	81.2	81.1	80.9
2013	80.0	80.0	79.6	80.2	81.0	81.4	81.2	80.7	79.8	79.5	79.9	80.0	80.3
2014	78.7	78.9	79.5	80.0	80.2	81.2	81.3	81.2	79.8	80.1	80.1	80.3	80.1
2015	79.7	79.5	78.9	80.5	81.4	80.9	81.0	80.9	79.7	79.7	79.9	79.9	80.2
2016	78.5	78.0	78.1	78.2	79.0	79.3	79.3	80.2	79.0	82.0	82.3	81.3	79.6
2017	80.6	80.6	80.6	79.4	80.1	80.2	78.9	79.5	77.8	77.9	77.8	78.2	79.3
Financial Activities													
2007	330.2	329.9	329.7	329.8	330.4	332.6	331.4	330.2	326.0	325.2	324.4	324.6	328.7
2008	319.0	319.0	318.9	318.5	318.8	320.4	318.8	318.1	313.9	312.7	311.0	310.9	316.7
2009	304.7	302.8	301.1	300.2	299.8	300.5	298.9	297.9	294.8	293.9	293.3	293.8	298.5
2010	289.2	288.8	288.8	288.3	288.5	290.5	289.7	289.3	286.4	287.6	287.1	287.5	288.5
2011	283.5	283.1	283.1	283.3	283.8	286.4	287.8	287.9	285.9	286.8	286.5	286.7	285.4
2012	283.6	284.0	284.3	285.2	286.4	289.4	290.3	290.7	288.7	288.2	287.9	288.9	287.3
2013	286.3	286.6	286.3	287.2	287.9	291.6	291.6	291.0	289.4	289.9	289.3	290.0	288.9
2014	286.7	286.1	286.0	286.6	288.6	291.4	292.2	293.2	290.0	290.8	290.3	291.4	289.4
2015	289.1	289.0	289.1	290.9	293.1	296.9	298.0	298.3	294.7	296.4	295.9	297.0	294.0
2016	293.9	294.5	294.8	296.4	297.5	300.4	303.1	303.5	300.4	301.8	301.4	302.2	299.2
2017	299.8	300.0	300.8	301.4	302.8	307.0	308.8	308.6	305.3	305.8	304.3	304.8	304.1
Professional and Business Services													
2007	711.5	714.0	721.1	739.1	744.9	753.2	754.1	760.1	755.0	757.8	755.4	752.9	743.3
2008	723.5	725.1	724.8	739.3	743.2	746.5	744.5	747.7	739.4	736.9	727.3	717.6	734.7
2009	681.8	674.0	666.8	672.2	675.3	677.3	675.3	676.5	672.1	676.9	677.6	674.0	675.0
2010	652.5	655.3	656.4	676.7	681.1	690.1	692.2	697.5	695.7	703.7	703.4	701.6	683.9
2011	677.3	681.3	685.8	704.3	705.0	715.1	719.6	724.9	724.9	728.5	728.9	722.8	709.9
2012	702.9	704.7	712.0	730.2	737.6	748.9	748.0	755.9	757.5	759.1	762.4	758.0	739.8
2013	731.3	737.7	743.6	757.1	769.5	779.6	782.6	790.4	789.0	798.2	800.1	798.0	773.1
2014	763.6	768.7	773.2	788.9	798.6	807.3	805.5	810.9	807.1	815.2	815.3	808.8	796.9
2015	778.6	781.8	783.5	802.0	810.2	817.6	825.4	824.3	820.3	830.8	828.1	825.4	810.7
2016	799.5	799.7	799.6	812.2	813.0	822.2	830.3	833.0	831.8	835.9	836.7	827.0	820.1
2017	797.3	799.2	805.5	816.1	824.7	837.9	834.1	838.2	836.3	842.3	840.2	827.6	825.0
Education and Health Services													
2007	576.9	584.3	587.0	588.0	590.4	585.6	581.4	578.9	589.4	597.5	601.1	601.3	588.5
2008	594.6	601.6	602.7	606.1	606.4	602.5	600.1	599.0	608.5	616.3	620.9	620.5	606.6
2009	611.5	619.1	620.9	620.6	621.0	614.2	611.4	607.8	617.7	626.6	630.3	630.2	619.3
2010	621.5	629.7	632.8	634.5	636.4	629.9	624.2	621.8	633.3	643.4	648.1	648.5	633.7
2011	640.1	648.2	651.1	650.7	650.6	644.8	638.1	637.5	652.5	659.3	662.2	664.5	650.0
2012	652.5	662.7	663.4	665.4	665.0	659.9	651.6	651.3	666.1	671.1	674.4	674.8	663.2
2013	664.0	675.9	677.9	676.1	676.7	668.9	658.9	662.0	674.6	680.8	684.7	685.1	673.8
2014	676.2	684.7	686.5	690.3	691.3	682.7	675.3	677.9	686.1	693.7	697.1	699.3	686.8
2015	688.3	695.9	699.7	704.2	707.0	698.4	692.7	692.3	700.8	710.7	712.8	712.8	701.3
2016	704.6	712.1	713.6	718.0	719.4	711.5	707.1	706.3	714.9	722.2	723.8	722.6	714.7
2017	714.3	723.7	726.8	727.9	729.0	718.5	712.4	713.0	722.8	735.5	734.6	727.1	723.8

Employment by Industry: Chicago-Naperville-Elgin, IL-IN-WI, Selected Years, 2007–2017—*Continued*

(Numbers in thousands, not seasonally adjusted)

Industry and year	January	February	March	April	May	June	July	August	September	October	November	December	Annual average
Leisure and Hospitality													
2007	383.4	381.8	388.6	400.6	416.0	426.6	425.9	427.3	418.1	411.2	405.8	404.4	407.5
2008	388.5	386.7	394.3	409.8	422.3	431.9	430.8	429.9	418.3	410.0	400.1	397.5	410.0
2009	381.0	378.4	384.0	395.2	408.6	416.9	414.5	412.8	406.0	394.8	388.1	386.3	397.2
2010	369.5	369.9	376.3	389.8	403.9	413.4	412.6	414.0	408.2	400.5	395.1	393.7	395.6
2011	375.6	375.0	383.9	398.5	410.9	421.4	420.7	426.1	416.8	408.6	403.4	400.0	403.4
2012	388.2	389.3	398.0	410.3	423.9	434.6	433.7	439.1	426.4	420.6	414.5	414.5	416.1
2013	400.3	399.9	408.8	420.5	435.9	447.4	447.1	447.2	436.8	429.4	422.2	421.6	426.4
2014	410.0	409.6	417.2	432.0	446.6	457.4	455.5	456.8	445.5	442.3	434.1	433.2	436.7
2015	418.5	420.5	427.6	445.9	463.7	475.2	472.0	474.6	464.1	461.1	454.5	457.1	452.9
2016	440.6	440.1	447.0	464.7	479.5	491.5	492.0	491.2	479.6	475.2	469.9	462.7	469.5
2017	452.0	453.6	463.0	475.1	492.3	504.8	502.9	504.4	487.9	482.6	474.2	467.7	480.0
Other Services													
2007	194.0	194.5	197.0	196.1	198.0	200.8	205.1	205.2	198.5	197.9	198.4	199.4	198.8
2008	196.5	197.1	198.3	198.4	199.9	202.4	207.9	207.7	199.7	199.5	199.1	199.3	200.5
2009	194.4	194.5	195.6	194.7	196.0	198.4	201.1	200.3	193.4	194.3	194.4	195.1	196.0
2010	190.7	190.6	191.6	186.2	187.4	189.3	188.3	188.2	187.1	188.4	188.8	189.3	188.8
2011	186.1	186.8	188.3	189.0	190.8	192.8	192.0	191.4	190.1	189.4	188.8	189.9	189.6
2012	187.4	187.9	189.2	188.4	190.0	193.0	191.5	190.6	189.6	188.7	189.1	189.4	189.6
2013	186.9	187.7	188.8	189.5	190.7	192.7	194.3	194.5	192.5	191.2	190.9	191.9	191.0
2014	190.0	190.9	192.5	192.9	195.0	197.8	197.6	195.3	193.0	193.6	193.3	193.7	193.8
2015	191.0	191.8	193.1	193.1	194.2	196.8	195.8	195.3	193.3	193.9	194.1	194.6	193.9
2016	192.2	192.5	193.4	194.2	194.8	196.5	196.4	195.9	194.0	194.3	193.9	194.6	194.4
2017	192.7	192.8	194.6	195.0	196.1	198.3	197.8	197.6	195.1	195.2	193.2	194.2	195.2
Government													
2007	557.0	567.6	570.1	571.5	574.0	570.9	553.8	551.2	564.0	568.0	570.0	566.4	565.4
2008	559.0	568.9	571.6	573.1	578.7	574.4	559.0	555.2	568.3	575.5	575.7	572.4	569.3
2009	561.6	568.5	571.5	575.7	579.5	573.3	554.8	548.7	566.1	575.9	576.2	570.5	568.5
2010	561.2	568.7	569.2	573.8	591.4	577.3	548.5	542.1	557.5	565.6	567.0	559.0	565.1
2011	548.8	556.6	558.8	560.9	563.8	556.5	543.0	536.1	552.4	556.7	559.1	554.0	553.9
2012	542.6	551.6	554.7	555.5	559.2	555.0	537.2	534.4	549.7	554.8	556.1	552.5	550.3
2013	540.9	550.6	553.0	553.1	558.3	555.7	536.2	536.0	549.6	549.8	552.4	551.3	548.9
2014	534.6	542.6	546.2	548.5	555.4	550.8	535.7	533.0	547.8	551.8	551.4	551.8	545.8
2015	537.4	547.0	549.4	552.2	558.0	554.5	536.9	533.8	549.1	554.3	552.0	553.9	548.2
2016	538.3	545.0	549.9	549.6	553.5	557.8	541.6	537.0	554.2	549.6	550.9	558.0	548.8
2017	538.3	545.7	549.4	547.0	552.4	557.3	539.6	534.7	552.7	559.3	560.3	557.9	549.6

Employment by Industry: Dallas-Fort Worth-Arlington, TX, Selected Years, 2007–2017

(Numbers in thousands, not seasonally adjusted)

Industry and year	January	February	March	April	May	June	July	August	September	October	November	December	Annual average
Total Nonfarm													
2007	2,921.5	2,951.0	2,979.5	2,985.8	3,002.8	3,018.4	2,991.7	3,010.7	3,020.5	3,038.7	3,057.0	3,065.7	3,003.6
2008	3,007.5	3,030.5	3,041.6	3,047.0	3,065.9	3,066.1	3,040.7	3,046.2	3,042.3	3,046.7	3,039.4	3,036.3	3,042.5
2009	2,955.2	2,949.7	2,947.3	2,940.6	2,945.2	2,937.5	2,907.9	2,908.6	2,904.0	2,917.3	2,920.8	2,924.9	2,929.9
2010	2,867.4	2,878.4	2,902.2	2,914.6	2,939.5	2,948.4	2,923.9	2,930.7	2,934.2	2,962.7	2,970.8	2,981.1	2,929.5
2011	2,927.2	2,941.1	2,969.0	2,992.1	3,004.3	3,019.2	3,004.6	3,015.4	3,026.7	3,034.9	3,047.6	3,055.1	3,003.1
2012	3,003.6	3,026.6	3,049.8	3,065.0	3,082.3	3,098.8	3,070.6	3,090.5	3,098.6	3,115.8	3,139.5	3,146.8	3,082.3
2013	3,078.1	3,107.7	3,127.6	3,144.2	3,165.9	3,185.9	3,169.9	3,189.6	3,199.1	3,213.7	3,240.7	3,242.4	3,172.1
2014	3,184.8	3,210.0	3,231.9	3,255.7	3,278.3	3,298.2	3,279.7	3,297.9	3,306.4	3,335.5	3,358.8	3,374.4	3,284.3
2015	3,319.3	3,341.9	3,347.4	3,373.3	3,394.7	3,413.8	3,403.5	3,414.8	3,418.5	3,445.2	3,459.4	3,472.0	3,400.3
2016	3,421.4	3,446.7	3,453.7	3,481.9	3,497.7	3,507.4	3,498.1	3,512.5	3,526.9	3,543.1	3,568.9	3,577.5	3,503.0
2017	3,522.0	3,543.1	3,555.6	3,568.0	3,585.5	3,606.8	3,585.8	3,601.1	3,611.3	3,643.4	3,671.0	3,666.8	3,596.7
Total Private													
2007	2,543.9	2,566.8	2,594.2	2,602.3	2,616.5	2,641.3	2,633.5	2,648.4	2,640.4	2,647.6	2,663.9	2,674.2	2,622.8
2008	2,620.1	2,635.9	2,645.4	2,651.2	2,667.5	2,676.5	2,667.0	2,670.6	2,651.3	2,644.0	2,634.6	2,631.4	2,649.6
2009	2,557.3	2,544.9	2,541.6	2,535.0	2,538.0	2,540.7	2,528.2	2,528.9	2,510.6	2,510.0	2,512.3	2,520.2	2,530.6
2010	2,466.7	2,470.8	2,493.0	2,505.5	2,518.8	2,536.8	2,534.3	2,544.6	2,537.9	2,553.0	2,560.5	2,571.9	2,524.5
2011	2,522.9	2,532.6	2,559.9	2,581.2	2,592.0	2,613.5	2,617.7	2,630.6	2,629.7	2,631.8	2,644.4	2,653.7	2,600.8
2012	2,607.9	2,625.8	2,648.4	2,663.7	2,678.7	2,704.1	2,692.8	2,712.2	2,704.1	2,712.5	2,735.9	2,742.0	2,685.7
2013	2,680.4	2,703.8	2,722.2	2,738.1	2,758.9	2,785.1	2,784.1	2,803.2	2,799.7	2,805.1	2,829.9	2,831.6	2,770.2
2014	2,781.2	2,799.4	2,819.1	2,842.7	2,863.3	2,890.6	2,889.6	2,906.0	2,900.7	2,919.4	2,940.7	2,955.6	2,875.7
2015	2,907.3	2,923.1	2,928.4	2,954.3	2,973.9	2,998.1	3,006.1	3,016.5	3,005.1	3,022.6	3,034.1	3,045.1	2,984.6
2016	3,000.5	3,020.3	3,026.1	3,053.8	3,067.3	3,083.8	3,091.9	3,104.0	3,102.2	3,112.8	3,135.9	3,142.7	3,078.4
2017	3,094.0	3,107.7	3,118.2	3,130.7	3,146.8	3,176.2	3,173.4	3,187.3	3,182.1	3,201.7	3,226.0	3,221.3	3,163.8
Goods Producing													
2007	479.0	484.3	489.5	487.9	489.8	496.1	492.6	494.8	495.5	492.3	492.8	493.5	490.7
2008	486.6	491.4	493.1	490.7	492.9	495.3	493.0	493.7	491.2	487.0	480.9	477.2	489.4
2009	462.4	457.3	452.4	445.1	440.8	437.1	430.4	431.2	425.9	418.5	415.4	414.0	435.9
2010	408.7	406.1	409.8	411.5	413.6	417.9	418.6	419.7	417.9	416.8	416.0	416.4	414.4
2011	409.1	411.2	415.3	417.5	419.1	424.4	427.3	428.6	427.7	425.9	426.4	426.9	421.6
2012	423.1	426.7	429.6	430.9	431.2	436.5	439.1	440.5	439.4	438.2	439.2	439.4	434.5
2013	433.3	436.2	439.6	439.7	442.2	446.6	448.0	449.4	448.4	445.5	446.2	444.2	443.3
2014	440.3	445.3	447.8	451.8	455.4	458.9	460.8	461.7	460.9	461.9	463.2	465.1	456.1
2015	460.9	462.2	460.0	462.1	463.0	466.6	468.2	467.4	464.5	464.1	463.0	462.4	463.7
2016	460.8	464.0	463.5	467.3	467.2	470.8	473.2	473.5	472.6	472.1	472.2	473.4	469.2
2017	471.1	475.8	478.4	479.7	481.9	489.5	489.1	488.9	488.2	490.4	490.6	486.5	484.2
Service-Providing													
2007	2,442.5	2,466.7	2,490.0	2,497.9	2,513.0	2,522.3	2,499.1	2,515.9	2,525.0	2,546.4	2,564.2	2,572.2	2,512.9
2008	2,520.9	2,539.1	2,548.5	2,556.3	2,573.0	2,570.8	2,547.7	2,552.5	2,551.1	2,559.7	2,558.5	2,559.1	2,553.1
2009	2,492.8	2,492.4	2,494.9	2,495.5	2,504.4	2,500.4	2,477.5	2,477.4	2,478.1	2,498.8	2,505.4	2,510.9	2,494.0
2010	2,458.7	2,472.3	2,492.4	2,503.1	2,525.9	2,530.5	2,505.3	2,511.0	2,516.3	2,545.9	2,554.8	2,564.7	2,515.1
2011	2,518.1	2,529.9	2,553.7	2,574.6	2,585.2	2,594.8	2,577.3	2,586.8	2,599.0	2,609.0	2,621.2	2,628.2	2,581.5
2012	2,580.5	2,599.9	2,620.2	2,634.1	2,651.1	2,662.3	2,631.5	2,650.0	2,659.2	2,677.6	2,700.3	2,707.4	2,647.8
2013	2,644.8	2,671.5	2,688.0	2,704.5	2,723.7	2,739.3	2,721.9	2,740.2	2,750.7	2,768.2	2,794.5	2,798.2	2,728.8
2014	2,744.5	2,764.7	2,784.6	2,803.9	2,822.9	2,839.3	2,818.9	2,836.2	2,845.5	2,873.6	2,895.6	2,909.3	2,828.3
2015	2,858.4	2,879.7	2,887.4	2,911.2	2,931.7	2,947.2	2,935.3	2,947.4	2,954.0	2,981.1	2,996.4	3,009.6	2,936.6
2016	2,960.6	2,982.7	2,990.2	3,014.6	3,030.5	3,036.6	3,024.9	3,039.0	3,054.3	3,071.0	3,096.7	3,104.1	3,033.8
2017	3,050.9	3,067.3	3,077.2	3,088.3	3,103.6	3,117.3	3,096.7	3,112.2	3,123.1	3,153.0	3,180.4	3,180.3	3,112.5
Mining, Logging, and Construction													
2007	181.0	184.5	189.1	189.1	190.5	195.1	193.0	196.1	197.4	196.6	197.8	197.9	192.3
2008	194.1	198.5	201.2	200.3	202.0	204.6	202.8	203.5	202.2	199.6	195.7	193.4	199.8
2009	184.6	182.7	180.8	176.9	175.3	175.3	172.9	171.1	166.9	161.6	160.0	159.2	172.3
2010	155.1	154.1	157.4	158.8	159.8	162.4	163.4	164.1	162.8	161.9	160.8	160.6	160.1
2011	156.1	157.2	160.0	161.2	162.1	165.1	167.1	168.1	167.0	165.3	165.5	165.9	163.4
2012	163.7	166.0	168.3	169.5	172.4	175.6	175.6	176.9	176.1	175.7	176.6	176.3	172.7
2013	172.6	174.9	177.6	178.2	180.4	183.3	185.4	187.0	186.7	184.7	185.2	183.5	181.6
2014	183.6	184.9	187.2	190.3	193.1	195.6	197.2	197.9	197.9	198.7	199.1	199.4	193.7
2015	197.0	197.7	196.1	197.9	198.3	200.9	201.9	201.5	199.8	200.6	199.5	198.9	199.2
2016	197.9	200.0	199.6	203.7	203.2	205.4	206.6	207.1	207.1	206.6	206.0	206.1	204.1
2017	205.3	208.1	210.3	211.1	212.9	217.0	216.8	216.4	216.2	216.6	215.6	211.9	213.2

Employment by Industry: Dallas-Fort Worth-Arlington, TX, Selected Years, 2007–2017—*Continued*

(Numbers in thousands, not seasonally adjusted)

Industry and year	January	February	March	April	May	June	July	August	September	October	November	December	Annual average
Manufacturing													
2007	298.0	299.8	300.4	298.8	299.3	301.0	299.6	298.7	298.1	295.7	295.0	295.6	298.3
2008	292.5	292.9	291.9	290.4	290.9	290.7	290.2	290.2	289.0	287.4	285.2	283.8	289.6
2009	277.8	274.6	271.6	268.2	265.5	261.8	257.5	260.1	259.0	256.9	255.4	254.8	263.6
2010	253.6	252.0	252.4	252.7	253.8	255.5	255.2	255.6	255.1	254.9	255.2	255.8	254.3
2011	253.0	254.0	255.3	256.3	257.0	259.3	260.2	260.5	260.7	260.6	260.9	261.0	258.2
2012	259.4	260.7	261.3	261.4	258.8	260.9	263.5	263.6	263.3	262.5	262.6	263.1	261.8
2013	260.7	261.3	262.0	261.5	261.8	263.3	262.6	262.4	261.7	260.8	261.0	260.7	261.7
2014	256.7	260.4	260.1	261.5	262.3	263.3	263.6	263.8	263.0	263.2	264.1	265.7	262.3
2015	263.9	264.5	263.9	264.2	264.7	265.7	266.3	265.9	264.7	263.5	263.5	263.5	264.5
2016	262.9	264.0	263.9	263.6	264.0	265.4	266.6	266.4	265.5	265.5	266.2	267.3	265.1
2017	265.8	267.7	268.1	268.6	269.0	272.5	272.3	272.5	272.0	273.8	275.0	274.6	271.0
Trade, Transportation, and Utilities													
2007	631.8	629.8	635.2	634.3	636.3	639.9	640.3	642.3	641.1	646.3	658.6	665.7	641.8
2008	645.4	642.9	644.9	642.4	644.1	645.4	644.7	647.8	642.7	642.3	646.7	651.3	645.1
2009	627.4	619.2	617.9	612.0	611.7	609.6	607.9	608.3	605.8	606.4	612.7	619.2	613.2
2010	599.6	596.1	600.9	601.7	605.2	607.4	607.2	609.9	607.7	612.7	622.9	629.3	608.4
2011	610.0	607.8	612.5	617.4	618.9	621.3	622.9	627.6	626.3	629.5	640.3	647.6	623.5
2012	628.4	626.7	630.4	631.4	635.4	639.6	639.7	644.3	641.8	645.4	661.2	666.6	640.9
2013	643.7	642.9	644.5	647.6	651.5	656.4	657.1	663.2	661.6	667.4	684.0	690.4	659.2
2014	667.3	664.8	668.4	670.5	675.3	681.9	683.4	689.2	689.0	696.9	712.9	724.8	685.4
2015	704.8	703.5	705.2	710.3	715.8	721.8	724.1	729.3	728.1	734.9	747.5	757.1	723.5
2016	734.3	733.2	733.5	737.5	739.6	744.0	747.5	752.0	750.5	758.7	777.4	786.5	749.6
2017	762.3	755.4	754.4	755.8	758.0	765.6	767.0	774.6	772.6	778.1	792.2	796.0	769.3
Wholesale Trade													
2007	176.9	178.3	179.2	179.2	179.9	181.4	181.3	181.7	181.7	183.8	184.7	185.1	181.1
2008	183.1	183.8	183.7	183.4	183.6	183.6	182.8	182.8	181.8	181.2	180.6	180.1	182.5
2009	176.6	175.6	174.0	172.0	171.5	170.3	169.6	168.9	168.2	167.6	166.8	167.3	170.7
2010	165.4	165.3	166.0	165.6	166.5	166.9	167.5	167.7	167.4	168.1	168.3	168.9	167.0
2011	167.2	168.5	169.0	169.8	170.8	171.5	171.4	172.0	172.2	172.6	172.9	173.9	171.0
2012	172.2	173.5	174.5	175.2	176.5	177.6	177.6	178.3	178.1	177.7	178.6	179.4	176.6
2013	177.8	178.8	179.4	179.8	180.6	181.6	181.6	182.1	181.7	183.0	184.2	184.8	181.3
2014	182.2	183.2	184.1	184.2	185.0	186.4	187.3	188.3	188.2	189.2	189.5	190.2	186.5
2015	190.3	191.5	191.8	192.1	193.2	194.2	194.9	195.4	194.9	193.7	193.3	193.1	193.2
2016	195.5	196.6	196.1	196.7	196.9	197.6	198.4	198.9	198.2	197.6	197.8	198.4	197.4
2017	197.0	197.2	197.0	197.5	198.6	200.5	200.2	201.3	201.0	200.0	198.9	200.2	199.1
Retail Trade													
2007	312.7	308.8	312.4	311.7	312.3	313.6	314.8	315.6	313.7	316.7	328.0	333.4	316.1
2008	318.2	314.9	317.1	314.2	315.2	316.6	317.2	318.9	314.6	315.8	321.0	324.9	317.4
2009	308.3	303.2	303.5	301.3	301.9	301.6	301.1	302.6	300.6	302.3	309.0	313.9	304.1
2010	300.0	296.8	300.1	301.8	304.0	305.1	304.0	306.1	303.6	307.6	316.5	321.6	305.6
2011	305.9	301.8	305.0	308.7	309.1	310.7	312.2	315.7	313.0	316.7	326.4	331.3	313.0
2012	316.3	312.3	314.0	314.4	316.1	318.1	318.0	320.7	317.8	322.0	335.5	337.6	320.2
2013	321.1	319.1	319.3	321.4	323.4	326.2	326.6	331.2	329.5	333.4	346.9	350.6	329.1
2014	333.4	330.5	332.1	333.2	334.7	338.3	338.5	341.6	339.2	343.9	356.9	362.9	340.4
2015	346.7	345.1	345.6	349.1	351.6	354.9	356.2	358.4	356.6	362.1	372.0	377.1	356.3
2016	358.9	357.0	357.4	360.3	360.9	362.6	365.1	367.6	363.2	369.4	381.5	385.9	365.8
2017	369.7	364.9	364.8	366.4	366.7	370.1	370.8	373.7	369.8	374.6	388.1	388.0	372.3
Transportation and Utilities													
2007	142.2	142.7	143.6	143.4	144.1	144.9	144.2	145.0	145.7	145.8	145.9	147.2	144.6
2008	144.1	144.2	144.1	144.8	145.3	145.2	144.7	146.1	146.3	145.3	145.1	146.3	145.1
2009	142.5	140.4	140.4	138.7	138.3	137.7	137.2	136.8	137.0	136.5	136.9	138.0	138.4
2010	134.2	134.0	134.8	134.3	134.7	135.4	135.7	136.1	136.7	137.0	138.1	138.8	135.8
2011	136.9	137.5	138.5	138.9	139.0	139.1	139.3	139.9	141.1	140.2	141.0	142.4	139.5
2012	139.9	140.9	141.9	141.8	142.8	143.9	144.1	145.3	145.9	145.7	147.1	149.6	144.1
2013	144.8	145.0	145.8	146.4	147.5	148.6	148.9	149.9	150.4	151.0	152.9	155.0	148.9
2014	151.7	151.1	152.2	153.1	155.6	157.2	157.6	159.3	161.6	163.8	166.5	171.7	158.5
2015	167.8	166.9	167.8	169.1	171.0	172.7	173.0	175.5	176.6	179.1	182.2	186.9	174.1
2016	179.9	179.6	180.0	180.5	181.8	183.8	184.0	185.5	189.1	191.7	198.1	202.2	186.4
2017	195.6	193.3	192.6	191.9	192.7	195.0	196.0	199.6	201.8	203.5	205.2	207.8	197.9

Employment by Industry: Dallas-Fort Worth-Arlington, TX, Selected Years, 2007–2017—*Continued*

(Numbers in thousands, not seasonally adjusted)

Industry and year	January	February	March	April	May	June	July	August	September	October	November	December	Annual average
Information													
2007	89.3	89.9	90.1	89.6	90.2	90.3	90.8	91.6	91.1	91.3	91.8	91.6	90.6
2008	90.5	90.6	90.7	90.3	90.2	90.0	89.7	89.3	88.0	87.4	87.7	87.7	89.3
2009	86.8	86.2	85.6	85.0	84.8	84.6	83.7	83.0	82.2	82.3	82.4	82.7	84.1
2010	81.2	80.7	80.8	81.3	81.0	81.6	81.0	81.0	80.3	80.0	80.3	80.3	80.8
2011	80.4	80.2	80.2	80.0	80.3	80.5	80.8	80.4	79.9	80.2	80.5	80.7	80.3
2012	79.5	79.4	79.3	79.5	79.5	79.9	79.3	79.0	78.6	79.1	80.1	80.0	79.4
2013	79.6	79.9	79.8	80.2	80.9	81.2	81.5	81.7	80.7	81.2	81.8	82.2	80.9
2014	81.8	81.6	81.3	81.5	81.9	82.4	82.2	81.8	80.8	80.1	80.5	80.7	81.4
2015	79.5	79.3	79.5	80.0	80.2	80.3	81.3	81.4	80.5	80.5	81.1	82.0	80.5
2016	81.1	81.3	81.2	82.6	82.5	83.1	83.6	83.7	83.2	82.5	83.0	83.4	82.6
2017	83.2	83.4	84.3	83.5	83.2	83.7	84.0	83.6	82.6	82.6	83.2	84.2	83.5
Financial Activities													
2007	234.2	235.2	236.7	237.5	238.4	240.4	239.7	240.8	239.7	239.0	239.2	239.7	238.4
2008	236.9	237.9	238.1	239.6	240.7	241.3	239.8	239.5	237.7	236.6	235.3	234.9	238.2
2009	231.8	231.8	231.4	233.8	234.5	234.6	234.0	234.0	232.6	232.4	232.9	233.9	233.1
2010	231.7	232.3	232.9	232.9	233.6	234.3	235.1	235.3	234.9	236.4	236.7	238.1	234.5
2011	237.0	237.8	239.0	238.9	238.9	240.7	241.8	242.5	242.6	243.4	244.0	245.7	241.0
2012	243.8	245.3	246.5	247.2	248.4	250.6	250.5	250.7	250.8	252.5	253.7	255.2	249.6
2013	253.1	255.0	256.8	256.9	258.6	261.0	262.8	263.3	262.7	263.0	263.8	264.3	260.1
2014	261.6	262.5	263.1	264.1	264.0	265.9	267.8	268.4	267.5	269.6	270.0	270.7	266.3
2015	268.9	269.9	270.3	271.2	272.1	273.9	275.3	275.7	275.8	276.1	276.8	277.4	273.6
2016	277.3	278.4	278.7	280.4	281.8	282.7	284.5	285.1	285.6	286.9	288.0	289.1	283.2
2017	286.7	288.3	289.5	291.3	292.7	295.3	296.7	297.3	299.8	296.8	296.4	295.5	293.9
Professional and Business Services													
2007	437.4	443.9	448.7	451.0	451.9	457.4	456.2	462.5	463.4	468.1	470.3	473.2	457.0
2008	460.0	462.7	464.6	466.2	468.3	470.2	468.0	470.3	466.6	465.7	461.7	456.3	465.1
2009	437.9	433.8	431.2	428.7	429.1	430.6	430.0	431.0	427.8	432.7	434.6	434.0	431.8
2010	424.3	427.1	430.6	436.0	436.8	440.1	442.0	446.5	448.5	453.1	454.7	456.4	441.3
2011	447.5	451.4	456.4	462.1	461.9	465.6	467.1	471.7	474.3	474.7	477.1	476.3	465.5
2012	468.0	473.5	478.7	483.3	486.9	489.8	484.9	493.8	492.9	497.7	502.6	498.1	487.5
2013	485.8	492.0	495.3	497.3	500.6	505.8	506.4	513.9	517.0	520.6	524.9	522.3	506.8
2014	512.8	518.4	522.7	529.4	532.6	536.2	537.8	543.6	544.1	549.5	552.8	552.0	536.0
2015	545.3	548.7	548.9	553.8	555.3	557.2	561.9	564.8	562.8	571.3	571.7	571.3	559.4
2016	564.4	569.1	567.7	574.6	575.4	577.7	582.9	587.2	588.4	590.8	594.3	589.3	580.2
2017	581.2	585.6	584.3	585.8	588.1	589.9	592.1	595.5	596.5	600.3	604.6	602.3	592.2
Education and Health Services													
2007	305.4	310.6	313.7	314.8	316.3	316.1	315.8	319.0	321.3	322.9	324.6	325.1	317.1
2008	321.2	326.2	327.0	327.5	330.3	328.1	329.0	331.1	333.2	334.6	336.0	338.4	330.2
2009	333.6	336.4	339.3	341.3	343.3	342.8	344.8	347.0	349.7	353.3	353.5	355.1	345.0
2010	347.7	350.7	354.2	356.5	358.0	356.9	356.2	358.6	360.3	363.7	363.9	365.7	357.7
2011	360.8	361.8	365.7	368.2	369.8	369.7	369.6	371.6	375.2	375.4	376.0	378.0	370.2
2012	372.4	375.9	378.2	378.2	378.4	377.5	376.1	379.3	381.0	381.8	382.6	384.0	378.8
2013	376.8	381.5	383.0	385.6	387.1	385.6	384.2	388.7	391.0	392.6	394.6	395.0	387.1
2014	390.1	394.0	395.7	396.3	398.3	397.5	395.7	400.7	403.0	405.7	408.1	409.7	399.6
2015	403.5	407.7	408.6	412.5	415.8	414.9	414.7	418.3	419.2	422.2	424.1	425.6	415.6
2016	420.7	424.7	425.6	426.8	428.9	426.0	426.2	430.1	432.9	434.3	435.7	436.5	429.0
2017	434.4	438.9	440.2	441.3	442.7	442.5	439.2	443.1	445.0	446.6	452.6	450.4	443.1
Leisure and Hospitality													
2007	261.6	265.7	271.8	280.0	284.6	286.8	286.1	286.8	281.0	282.1	281.4	281.1	279.1
2008	275.0	278.5	281.7	289.0	293.6	294.6	292.6	289.9	285.5	285.2	281.7	281.8	285.8
2009	274.3	276.2	280.0	285.3	288.9	292.2	289.4	288.0	283.5	281.5	277.6	278.9	283.0
2010	271.5	275.0	280.4	283.1	287.1	290.6	287.0	287.8	285.3	287.1	283.3	283.4	283.5
2011	276.1	279.3	286.7	292.4	297.1	300.7	297.3	298.6	295.7	295.6	293.3	292.1	292.1
2012	285.8	290.5	297.1	304.5	308.6	314.8	308.5	311.1	309.1	306.6	305.5	308.0	304.2
2013	298.2	304.7	311.1	318.4	323.9	329.5	325.5	325.4	323.0	320.8	320.4	319.7	318.4
2014	313.0	317.7	324.7	332.5	337.5	344.3	339.0	339.0	337.4	337.1	334.8	334.7	332.6
2015	327.5	333.5	337.1	347.8	353.4	360.0	357.8	358.1	356.3	355.1	351.7	351.6	349.2
2016	345.3	351.6	357.4	365.0	370.5	374.7	370.5	370.3	368.6	367.4	364.8	364.1	364.2
2017	357.5	361.4	366.9	372.3	378.1	383.7	381.0	381.0	375.8	382.9	382.6	383.1	375.5

Employment by Industry: Dallas-Fort Worth-Arlington, TX, Selected Years, 2007–2017—*Continued*

(Numbers in thousands, not seasonally adjusted)

Industry and year	January	February	March	April	May	June	July	August	September	October	November	December	Annual average
Other Services													
2007	105.2	107.4	108.5	107.2	109.0	114.3	112.0	110.6	107.3	105.6	105.2	104.3	108.1
2008	104.5	105.7	105.3	105.5	107.4	111.6	110.2	109.0	106.4	105.2	104.6	103.8	106.6
2009	103.1	104.0	103.8	103.8	104.9	109.2	108.0	106.4	103.1	102.9	103.2	102.4	104.6
2010	102.0	102.8	103.4	102.5	103.5	108.0	107.2	105.8	103.0	103.2	102.7	102.3	103.9
2011	102.0	103.1	104.1	104.7	106.0	110.6	110.9	109.6	108.0	107.1	106.8	106.4	106.6
2012	106.9	107.8	108.6	108.7	110.3	115.4	114.7	113.5	110.5	111.2	111.0	110.7	110.8
2013	109.9	111.6	112.1	112.4	114.1	119.0	118.6	117.6	115.3	114.0	114.2	113.5	114.4
2014	114.3	115.1	115.9	116.6	118.3	123.5	122.9	121.6	118.0	118.6	118.4	117.9	118.4
2015	116.9	118.3	118.8	116.6	118.3	123.4	122.8	121.5	117.9	118.4	118.2	117.7	119.1
2016	116.6	118.0	118.5	119.6	121.4	124.8	123.5	122.1	120.4	120.1	120.5	120.4	120.5
2017	117.6	118.9	120.2	121.0	122.1	126.0	124.3	123.3	121.6	124.0	123.8	123.3	122.2
Government													
2007	377.6	384.2	385.3	383.5	386.3	377.1	358.2	362.3	380.1	391.1	393.1	391.5	380.9
2008	387.4	394.6	396.2	395.8	398.4	389.6	373.7	375.6	391.0	402.7	404.8	404.9	392.9
2009	397.9	404.8	405.7	405.6	407.2	396.8	379.7	379.7	393.4	407.3	408.5	404.7	399.3
2010	400.7	407.6	409.2	409.1	420.7	411.6	389.6	386.1	396.3	409.7	410.3	409.2	405.0
2011	404.3	408.5	409.1	410.9	412.3	405.7	386.9	384.8	397.0	403.1	403.2	401.4	402.3
2012	395.7	400.8	401.4	401.3	403.6	394.7	377.8	378.3	394.5	403.3	403.6	404.8	396.7
2013	397.7	403.9	405.4	406.1	407.0	400.8	385.8	386.4	399.4	408.6	410.8	410.8	401.9
2014	403.6	410.6	412.8	413.0	415.0	407.6	390.1	391.9	405.7	416.1	418.1	418.8	408.6
2015	412.0	418.8	419.0	419.0	420.8	415.7	397.4	398.3	413.4	422.6	425.3	426.9	415.8
2016	420.9	426.4	427.6	428.1	430.4	423.6	406.2	408.5	424.7	430.3	433.0	434.8	424.5
2017	428.0	435.4	437.4	437.3	438.7	430.6	412.4	413.8	429.2	441.7	445.0	445.5	432.9

Employment by Industry: Houston-The Woodlands-Sugar Land, TX, Selected Years, 2007–2017

(Numbers in thousands, not seasonally adjusted)

Industry and year	January	February	March	April	May	June	July	August	September	October	November	December	Annual average
Total Nonfarm													
2007	2,509.6	2,533.7	2,556.6	2,564.5	2,584.0	2,604.6	2,585.6	2,594.3	2,599.1	2,612.5	2,631.3	2,645.5	2,585.1
2008	2,594.4	2,616.5	2,626.3	2,634.6	2,647.2	2,658.7	2,645.7	2,653.5	2,631.6	2,650.2	2,664.6	2,666.8	2,640.8
2009	2,602.9	2,602.7	2,597.3	2,583.3	2,584.5	2,582.2	2,550.7	2,543.2	2,543.8	2,546.3	2,550.0	2,556.3	2,570.3
2010	2,512.1	2,526.1	2,542.6	2,557.9	2,577.4	2,581.7	2,564.9	2,568.2	2,572.7	2,585.9	2,596.6	2,606.6	2,566.1
2011	2,565.3	2,580.8	2,603.2	2,624.2	2,630.1	2,646.5	2,633.0	2,639.8	2,653.8	2,658.3	2,673.7	2,689.7	2,633.2
2012	2,648.9	2,673.7	2,698.7	2,711.9	2,733.0	2,751.4	2,735.7	2,751.1	2,763.2	2,778.1	2,797.7	2,808.5	2,737.7
2013	2,759.4	2,796.3	2,812.8	2,824.0	2,837.5	2,851.5	2,839.7	2,845.1	2,854.6	2,872.4	2,889.7	2,898.5	2,840.1
2014	2,851.8	2,881.1	2,898.3	2,916.2	2,935.5	2,947.4	2,937.0	2,946.7	2,957.8	2,984.5	3,000.2	3,015.2	2,939.3
2015	2,964.6	2,984.7	2,988.8	2,990.0	2,997.1	3,003.4	2,986.9	2,984.6	2,987.9	3,006.3	3,006.7	3,012.7	2,992.8
2016	2,971.9	2,987.3	2,987.5	2,996.4	2,999.4	2,998.7	2,983.2	2,978.7	2,987.3	2,999.0	3,007.3	3,010.5	2,992.3
2017	2,965.1	2,991.4	3,009.5	3,013.0	3,029.0	3,038.8	3,011.3	3,012.9	3,007.2	3,041.0	3,063.4	3,073.4	3,021.3
Total Private													
2007	2,155.1	2,172.3	2,194.2	2,200.2	2,218.9	2,248.8	2,244.3	2,250.7	2,239.8	2,245.5	2,260.3	2,274.2	2,225.4
2008	2,225.0	2,243.4	2,252.1	2,261.1	2,273.5	2,293.2	2,290.6	2,299.1	2,261.8	2,277.6	2,286.9	2,289.3	2,271.1
2009	2,228.3	2,223.4	2,217.1	2,199.5	2,201.2	2,206.5	2,191.1	2,186.8	2,169.1	2,159.9	2,161.3	2,168.2	2,192.7
2010	2,131.4	2,137.3	2,152.1	2,164.6	2,175.0	2,192.0	2,193.2	2,199.6	2,190.6	2,196.4	2,205.2	2,217.5	2,179.6
2011	2,179.0	2,191.1	2,212.9	2,233.4	2,241.8	2,266.3	2,269.2	2,282.3	2,281.9	2,281.3	2,296.6	2,313.6	2,254.1
2012	2,279.7	2,297.6	2,321.8	2,334.7	2,355.2	2,382.7	2,379.9	2,397.8	2,393.5	2,401.2	2,418.9	2,429.2	2,366.0
2013	2,389.5	2,417.0	2,432.7	2,442.8	2,455.5	2,477.5	2,479.5	2,491.2	2,478.2	2,487.9	2,503.0	2,512.1	2,463.9
2014	2,474.2	2,494.2	2,510.6	2,528.6	2,547.1	2,563.8	2,569.5	2,584.7	2,576.0	2,593.9	2,606.8	2,622.5	2,556.0
2015	2,580.2	2,591.8	2,594.6	2,596.8	2,603.1	2,614.8	2,614.0	2,616.1	2,600.0	2,608.6	2,606.5	2,612.4	2,603.2
2016	2,578.3	2,585.7	2,584.5	2,591.6	2,592.9	2,596.8	2,597.5	2,598.4	2,588.2	2,592.0	2,596.8	2,598.1	2,591.7
2017	2,564.6	2,580.5	2,595.7	2,600.2	2,615.1	2,630.4	2,621.5	2,628.3	2,604.2	2,629.0	2,648.1	2,657.3	2,614.6
Goods Producing													
2007	503.7	509.9	513.8	513.2	518.8	526.0	524.3	524.4	523.6	530.0	533.0	534.0	521.2
2008	523.2	530.1	530.9	533.9	536.9	539.4	539.2	541.1	538.0	544.7	543.8	539.4	536.7
2009	525.3	520.6	511.0	498.3	494.8	490.7	484.9	481.9	477.9	474.5	469.6	468.4	491.5
2010	465.5	465.6	466.9	468.2	470.2	472.7	474.3	475.8	475.6	477.1	475.5	475.7	471.9
2011	470.0	476.0	479.1	481.8	482.6	490.6	494.9	498.7	502.3	504.5	504.8	507.0	491.0
2012	501.9	508.3	514.5	516.4	520.4	526.1	526.2	530.4	532.6	538.7	537.7	538.2	524.3
2013	533.4	543.0	544.9	546.6	547.5	552.6	551.9	553.8	551.9	554.8	554.2	555.1	549.1
2014	551.7	559.2	560.8	564.5	568.6	570.9	573.3	577.4	578.8	583.3	584.7	587.3	571.7
2015	579.5	579.3	575.2	567.8	565.4	565.2	562.1	558.7	554.3	554.4	546.2	542.4	562.5
2016	537.6	537.8	533.4	530.7	527.1	523.8	520.3	515.7	514.8	515.8	509.7	506.7	522.8
2017	503.3	509.1	512.0	510.6	514.8	516.1	512.7	514.1	513.1	514.0	519.2	520.4	513.3
Service-Providing													
2007	2,005.9	2,023.8	2,042.8	2,051.3	2,065.2	2,078.6	2,061.3	2,069.9	2,075.5	2,082.5	2,098.3	2,111.5	2,063.9
2008	2,071.2	2,086.4	2,095.4	2,100.7	2,110.3	2,119.3	2,106.5	2,112.4	2,093.6	2,105.5	2,120.8	2,127.4	2,104.1
2009	2,077.6	2,082.1	2,086.3	2,085.0	2,089.7	2,091.5	2,065.8	2,061.3	2,065.9	2,071.8	2,080.4	2,087.9	2,078.8
2010	2,046.6	2,060.5	2,075.7	2,089.7	2,107.2	2,109.0	2,090.6	2,092.4	2,097.1	2,108.8	2,121.1	2,130.9	2,094.1
2011	2,095.3	2,104.8	2,124.1	2,142.4	2,147.5	2,155.9	2,138.1	2,141.1	2,151.5	2,153.8	2,168.9	2,182.7	2,142.2
2012	2,147.0	2,165.4	2,184.2	2,195.5	2,212.6	2,225.3	2,209.5	2,220.7	2,230.6	2,239.4	2,260.0	2,270.3	2,213.4
2013	2,226.0	2,253.3	2,267.9	2,277.4	2,290.0	2,298.9	2,287.8	2,291.3	2,302.7	2,317.6	2,335.5	2,343.4	2,291.0
2014	2,300.1	2,321.9	2,337.5	2,351.7	2,366.9	2,376.5	2,363.7	2,369.3	2,379.0	2,401.2	2,415.5	2,427.9	2,367.6
2015	2,385.1	2,405.4	2,413.6	2,422.2	2,431.7	2,438.2	2,424.8	2,425.9	2,433.6	2,451.9	2,460.5	2,470.3	2,430.3
2016	2,434.3	2,449.5	2,454.1	2,465.7	2,472.3	2,474.9	2,462.9	2,463.0	2,472.5	2,483.2	2,497.6	2,503.8	2,469.5
2017	2,461.8	2,482.3	2,497.5	2,502.4	2,514.2	2,522.7	2,498.6	2,498.8	2,494.1	2,527.0	2,544.2	2,553.0	2,508.1
Mining and Logging													
2007	81.1	81.6	81.9	81.4	82.1	83.4	83.8	83.8	83.0	84.0	84.5	84.8	83.0
2008	84.0	85.0	85.1	85.8	86.6	88.6	89.3	89.8	89.5	91.0	90.8	90.6	88.0
2009	88.9	87.4	86.0	83.1	82.0	81.5	81.6	81.0	80.2	79.6	79.1	79.3	82.5
2010	79.3	79.6	79.8	81.1	81.9	83.6	83.8	84.4	84.2	84.8	85.3	85.7	82.8
2011	85.4	86.4	86.9	87.9	88.2	91.0	92.7	94.1	94.3	95.7	96.3	97.6	91.4
2012	96.4	97.2	98.3	98.9	98.9	100.3	102.1	102.1	102.1	102.9	103.2	104.1	100.5
2013	103.9	104.5	105.0	106.1	106.6	108.1	109.5	109.9	109.2	110.2	110.5	110.7	107.9
2014	109.7	110.5	110.1	110.2	110.8	111.5	112.6	112.7	112.3	111.9	112.8	113.0	111.5
2015	111.3	107.5	105.0	102.5	100.6	99.9	99.1	97.5	95.6	94.9	92.4	91.2	99.8
2016	89.5	88.0	86.1	83.5	81.7	81.1	79.3	78.6	77.3	77.4	76.0	75.7	81.2
2017	76.1	77.0	76.7	77.0	78.0	78.1	78.3	78.4	78.0	77.1	77.5	77.9	77.5

Employment by Industry: Houston-The Woodlands-Sugar Land, TX, Selected Years, 2007–2017—*Continued*

(Numbers in thousands, not seasonally adjusted)

Industry and year	January	February	March	April	May	June	July	August	September	October	November	December	Annual average
Construction													
2007	195.4	200.7	203.0	202.6	205.6	209.1	206.7	206.8	207.0	211.2	212.2	211.9	206.0
2008	203.3	208.5	208.9	209.4	209.9	208.4	206.7	208.1	205.8	210.8	209.3	205.3	207.9
2009	197.9	196.6	193.0	187.6	187.3	185.4	182.1	181.2	179.2	179.0	175.6	173.9	184.9
2010	172.2	171.5	172.4	173.2	173.9	173.9	174.5	175.0	174.9	175.2	172.4	171.0	173.3
2011	165.9	169.6	170.8	170.9	170.7	173.3	174.5	175.9	178.0	177.7	176.1	174.5	173.2
2012	171.7	175.3	178.2	178.0	180.6	181.8	179.5	183.8	184.9	190.2	188.1	186.7	181.6
2013	183.6	190.8	191.6	192.0	192.3	193.9	192.0	193.4	192.5	194.2	192.5	192.1	191.7
2014	191.5	196.9	198.3	202.2	204.4	203.7	204.0	207.5	209.4	212.4	211.1	211.8	204.4
2015	208.8	214.4	214.9	214.4	216.2	217.8	218.2	219.1	219.0	222.6	218.9	217.4	216.8
2016	216.5	219.5	219.5	222.1	222.0	220.0	219.3	216.9	218.5	220.9	216.6	213.3	218.8
2017	210.1	214.2	216.4	215.7	218.1	217.3	213.5	214.4	214.4	220.2	221.6	221.4	216.4
Manufacturing													
2007	227.2	227.6	228.9	229.2	231.1	233.5	233.8	233.8	233.6	234.8	236.3	237.3	232.3
2008	235.9	236.6	236.9	238.7	240.4	242.4	243.2	243.2	242.7	242.9	243.7	243.5	240.8
2009	238.5	236.6	232.0	227.6	225.5	223.8	221.2	219.7	218.5	215.9	214.9	215.2	224.1
2010	214.0	214.5	214.7	213.9	214.4	215.2	216.0	216.4	216.5	217.1	217.8	219.0	215.8
2011	218.7	220.0	221.4	223.0	223.7	226.3	227.7	228.7	230.0	231.1	232.4	234.9	226.5
2012	233.8	235.8	238.0	239.5	240.9	244.0	244.6	244.5	245.6	245.6	246.4	247.4	242.2
2013	245.9	247.7	248.3	248.5	248.6	250.6	250.4	250.5	250.2	250.4	251.2	252.3	249.6
2014	250.5	251.8	252.4	252.1	253.4	255.7	256.7	257.2	257.1	259.0	260.8	262.5	255.8
2015	259.4	257.4	255.3	250.9	248.6	247.5	244.8	242.1	239.7	236.9	234.9	233.8	245.9
2016	231.6	230.3	227.8	225.1	223.4	222.7	221.7	220.2	219.0	217.5	217.1	217.7	222.8
2017	217.1	217.9	218.9	217.9	218.7	220.7	220.9	221.3	220.7	216.7	220.1	221.1	219.3
Trade, Transportation, and Utilities													
2007	510.9	509.3	514.7	515.2	518.9	524.7	525.7	528.8	528.2	531.2	541.4	550.1	524.9
2008	531.6	531.3	533.9	532.7	534.6	538.8	539.6	542.9	535.4	536.6	546.8	554.2	538.2
2009	531.5	527.0	526.8	523.2	522.8	523.4	520.3	521.8	519.4	518.6	523.6	531.7	524.2
2010	514.9	512.5	515.6	516.0	517.8	521.2	521.7	524.9	522.5	525.7	534.6	544.0	522.6
2011	526.9	524.6	528.8	532.8	533.8	537.7	538.0	542.2	539.4	542.6	553.8	563.9	538.7
2012	545.4	543.4	546.6	548.5	552.9	556.8	557.3	561.6	558.5	562.3	576.3	581.9	557.6
2013	564.7	563.9	565.9	568.4	570.6	574.3	575.8	580.5	577.0	579.4	591.6	599.6	576.0
2014	584.8	582.8	584.0	585.6	588.0	591.9	593.5	598.6	595.4	600.0	612.2	621.9	594.9
2015	603.8	602.2	602.6	604.3	607.1	608.7	608.9	611.4	608.3	611.2	620.3	626.3	609.6
2016	609.0	606.6	605.8	606.0	605.7	608.0	609.0	610.3	606.3	611.3	623.1	629.7	610.9
2017	613.1	609.9	610.0	610.6	613.0	615.5	615.8	618.3	610.5	619.9	633.7	640.2	617.5
Wholesale Trade													
2007	132.4	133.9	134.9	135.2	136.1	137.5	137.7	138.5	138.7	139.2	139.5	140.2	137.0
2008	139.3	140.7	141.0	141.3	142.1	143.1	142.6	143.0	142.4	142.1	142.0	141.9	141.8
2009	138.5	138.4	137.6	135.9	135.4	135.2	133.8	133.6	133.3	133.1	132.9	133.4	135.1
2010	132.5	132.7	133.3	133.4	133.9	134.7	135.0	135.3	135.3	135.1	135.3	135.9	134.4
2011	135.7	136.5	137.4	138.5	139.3	140.3	141.0	141.8	142.6	143.0	143.8	145.0	140.4
2012	144.2	145.4	146.4	146.6	149.1	150.7	150.7	151.6	151.6	152.1	152.9	153.5	149.6
2013	152.4	153.9	154.8	154.9	155.8	157.0	157.6	158.6	159.0	159.3	160.2	160.7	157.0
2014	159.7	161.2	161.9	162.0	163.3	164.8	165.0	166.8	167.3	168.1	168.9	170.1	164.9
2015	168.9	169.9	169.9	169.2	168.7	168.6	167.9	168.2	167.3	167.3	166.8	166.6	168.3
2016	165.9	166.0	164.9	163.5	163.2	163.0	163.0	163.0	162.8	161.7	162.2	162.7	163.5
2017	161.7	162.6	163.4	164.6	165.7	167.1	165.9	166.3	165.2	166.2	165.5	168.0	165.2
Retail Trade													
2007	257.0	253.2	256.8	257.0	259.2	262.3	262.9	264.3	263.1	265.6	275.2	279.8	263.0
2008	265.8	263.4	265.8	264.5	264.8	266.8	267.3	269.8	264.3	265.6	275.4	280.2	267.8
2009	266.5	262.8	263.4	262.4	262.9	263.8	263.0	264.9	263.3	263.2	268.6	273.0	264.8
2010	260.5	258.1	260.2	260.0	261.2	263.1	262.5	264.9	262.3	265.7	274.1	279.4	264.3
2011	266.7	263.6	266.3	268.8	269.1	271.5	270.2	273.3	269.4	272.7	282.3	287.0	271.7
2012	274.2	270.6	271.6	272.8	274.6	276.4	276.8	279.6	276.9	280.4	292.0	295.4	278.4
2013	280.4	278.5	279.1	281.4	282.6	284.7	285.8	288.4	284.9	287.0	297.4	302.6	286.1
2014	290.4	288.2	288.2	288.9	289.2	291.2	292.1	294.1	290.8	292.9	302.7	307.3	293.0
2015	293.6	292.1	292.8	294.5	297.5	299.8	300.5	302.6	300.6	303.4	311.9	315.3	300.4
2016	302.8	301.4	302.1	303.1	303.6	305.5	306.0	307.9	303.6	309.0	318.8	321.6	307.1
2017	310.6	306.9	306.0	306.0	306.5	307.6	307.8	309.1	303.0	311.3	323.2	324.5	310.2

Employment by Industry: Houston-The Woodlands-Sugar Land, TX, Selected Years, 2007–2017—*Continued*

(Numbers in thousands, not seasonally adjusted)

Industry and year	January	February	March	April	May	June	July	August	September	October	November	December	Annual average
Transportation and Utilities													
2007	121.5	122.2	123.0	123.0	123.6	124.9	125.1	126.0	126.4	126.4	126.7	130.1	124.9
2008	126.5	127.2	127.1	126.9	127.7	128.9	129.7	130.1	128.7	128.9	129.4	132.1	128.6
2009	126.5	125.8	125.8	124.9	124.5	124.4	123.5	123.3	122.8	122.3	122.1	125.3	124.3
2010	121.9	121.7	122.1	122.6	122.7	123.4	124.2	124.7	124.9	124.9	125.2	128.7	123.9
2011	124.5	124.5	125.1	125.5	125.4	125.9	126.8	127.1	127.4	126.9	127.7	131.9	126.6
2012	127.0	127.4	128.6	129.1	129.2	129.7	129.8	130.4	130.0	129.8	131.4	133.0	129.6
2013	131.9	131.5	132.0	132.1	132.2	132.6	132.4	133.5	133.1	133.1	134.0	136.3	132.9
2014	134.7	133.4	133.9	134.7	135.5	135.9	136.4	137.7	137.3	139.0	140.6	144.5	137.0
2015	141.3	140.2	139.9	140.6	140.9	140.5	140.5	140.6	140.4	140.5	141.6	144.4	140.9
2016	140.3	139.2	138.8	139.4	138.9	139.5	140.0	139.4	139.9	140.6	142.1	145.4	140.3
2017	140.8	140.4	140.6	140.0	140.8	140.8	142.1	142.9	142.3	142.4	145.0	147.7	142.2
Information													
2007	37.1	37.3	37.3	37.0	37.4	37.7	37.6	37.7	37.4	37.2	37.3	37.4	37.4
2008	37.1	37.3	37.2	37.0	37.2	37.2	37.3	37.0	36.4	36.3	36.3	36.4	36.9
2009	35.7	35.7	35.6	35.1	35.0	35.0	34.6	34.3	33.8	34.0	34.0	34.0	34.7
2010	33.2	32.9	32.7	32.6	32.5	33.1	32.5	32.5	32.1	32.2	32.4	32.5	32.6
2011	32.5	32.4	32.2	32.2	32.4	32.5	32.3	32.2	32.0	31.8	31.8	31.9	32.2
2012	31.7	31.7	31.7	31.7	31.9	32.4	32.7	32.9	32.8	32.3	32.6	32.7	32.3
2013	32.2	32.4	32.7	32.7	32.9	33.4	33.4	33.4	33.0	33.5	33.6	33.7	33.1
2014	33.0	32.9	32.9	32.9	32.8	33.0	32.8	32.5	31.9	31.9	32.0	32.2	32.6
2015	32.0	32.0	32.0	32.3	32.3	32.5	32.6	32.4	31.8	31.5	31.7	32.1	32.1
2016	32.2	32.2	32.1	32.5	32.7	33.1	33.1	32.8	32.3	32.2	32.3	32.7	32.5
2017	32.3	32.2	32.5	32.5	32.5	32.6	32.6	32.2	31.2	31.2	31.4	31.9	32.1
Financial Activities													
2007	142.9	143.8	144.5	143.8	144.7	146.2	146.7	147.1	146.4	146.7	146.8	147.0	145.6
2008	145.0	146.2	145.9	145.7	146.3	146.9	146.9	147.1	145.7	144.7	144.6	144.7	145.8
2009	142.2	142.1	141.8	141.2	141.3	141.7	141.3	140.8	139.9	138.6	138.5	138.6	140.7
2010	137.3	137.4	137.7	137.5	137.6	138.4	138.4	138.5	137.5	138.2	138.5	138.9	138.0
2011	138.0	138.1	138.6	138.5	138.8	139.3	139.9	140.0	140.6	140.9	140.7	140.7	139.5
2012	139.4	140.1	140.6	141.1	141.9	143.0	143.0	143.1	142.5	143.8	143.9	144.4	142.2
2013	142.2	143.4	143.1	143.6	144.2	144.5	146.3	146.5	146.2	146.9	146.7	146.8	145.1
2014	145.1	145.9	145.8	146.6	147.6	148.3	149.0	149.5	149.0	150.2	150.1	150.6	148.1
2015	149.1	149.7	150.0	150.5	151.0	151.5	152.1	152.2	151.7	153.0	153.1	153.3	151.4
2016	153.5	153.9	153.8	154.4	154.7	155.3	156.9	157.0	156.6	157.0	157.4	157.8	155.7
2017	157.0	157.4	157.7	157.8	158.0	159.5	160.0	160.3	159.4	160.4	160.3	160.4	159.0
Professional and Business Services													
2007	376.4	380.7	384.9	388.4	390.7	396.1	396.7	397.0	394.8	395.3	395.3	396.3	391.1
2008	390.1	395.4	397.2	398.6	399.2	403.2	402.6	404.2	397.3	403.7	401.1	398.0	399.2
2009	384.3	382.2	380.2	375.9	374.5	374.7	372.8	371.2	368.8	368.6	369.5	369.4	374.3
2010	362.0	364.8	367.9	373.0	374.5	378.6	380.8	381.9	380.9	382.3	383.0	384.9	376.2
2011	379.5	383.8	388.8	395.2	395.6	401.0	403.4	406.5	406.8	405.3	406.6	410.1	398.6
2012	407.3	412.1	417.5	420.8	423.8	430.3	431.7	436.1	435.4	434.4	437.5	439.2	427.2
2013	432.2	438.2	443.5	443.6	444.5	449.6	450.5	452.8	451.0	453.8	454.8	454.8	447.4
2014	446.2	450.3	455.4	459.5	462.8	466.2	468.4	473.1	471.7	475.6	475.2	476.2	465.1
2015	469.1	471.7	471.3	472.6	471.8	475.0	476.6	477.4	474.1	477.4	475.4	476.3	474.1
2016	470.3	470.9	470.0	473.4	470.9	471.1	474.6	475.2	474.6	475.4	473.7	470.7	472.6
2017	467.2	471.7	475.6	476.4	476.9	482.5	483.2	484.4	485.2	488.8	491.9	492.8	481.4
Education and Health Services													
2007	275.0	277.4	278.9	280.0	281.4	281.0	280.4	282.3	283.3	284.3	284.9	285.4	281.2
2008	281.0	282.9	282.2	284.3	285.4	286.0	285.7	288.5	285.9	289.4	291.0	292.1	286.2
2009	288.9	291.5	292.6	294.4	296.4	297.5	298.0	300.1	300.6	302.6	303.2	303.6	297.5
2010	302.5	304.6	306.2	308.0	309.5	308.7	308.7	310.4	311.6	313.1	313.6	313.7	309.2
2011	309.8	310.9	312.3	314.1	315.0	314.6	314.4	316.2	318.4	318.5	320.6	321.5	315.5
2012	318.0	320.8	322.6	323.6	325.5	325.9	325.1	328.8	330.8	332.7	333.5	334.5	326.8
2013	330.4	334.3	335.1	336.4	338.0	337.1	337.0	341.2	342.1	345.2	346.7	345.9	339.1
2014	341.7	344.5	345.1	347.8	349.2	347.3	348.8	352.7	354.0	358.5	359.7	360.3	350.8
2015	358.0	361.6	362.8	363.9	364.8	362.8	364.4	367.5	368.8	371.5	372.4	372.6	365.9
2016	369.4	372.5	372.6	374.2	375.5	374.0	375.7	380.1	381.4	382.4	383.4	384.1	377.1
2017	379.3	382.9	383.4	384.8	386.7	385.5	383.5	386.1	383.5	386.3	384.1	383.9	384.2

Employment by Industry: Houston-The Woodlands-Sugar Land, TX, Selected Years, 2007–2017—*Continued*

(Numbers in thousands, not seasonally adjusted)

Industry and year	January	February	March	April	May	June	July	August	September	October	November	December	Annual average
Leisure and Hospitality													
2007	215.8	219.3	225.2	227.3	231.2	236.9	234.1	235.2	230.9	227.3	228.7	230.8	228.6
2008	224.8	227.4	232.5	234.3	238.6	242.1	239.5	238.9	228.9	227.7	229.4	231.0	232.9
2009	226.7	230.0	235.4	235.9	240.8	244.1	240.3	239.7	234.9	230.1	230.5	230.4	234.9
2010	224.0	226.8	232.6	235.9	238.8	241.7	238.8	239.1	236.8	234.9	235.4	235.6	235.0
2011	230.5	232.8	240.5	243.9	247.7	250.6	246.5	247.9	246.4	242.6	244.0	244.0	243.1
2012	241.4	245.7	253.1	254.8	259.9	265.1	260.7	262.3	260.7	257.5	259.1	259.7	256.7
2013	255.8	262.1	267.7	270.1	275.4	278.1	277.3	277.5	273.6	271.2	272.7	273.9	271.3
2014	269.1	274.4	282.2	285.0	290.6	294.8	292.3	290.9	287.9	286.2	286.0	287.3	285.6
2015	282.8	288.3	294.0	298.7	303.1	307.6	305.7	306.3	303.4	301.2	300.1	302.3	299.5
2016	300.0	304.4	309.6	312.6	317.6	320.7	317.8	318.0	313.5	308.4	308.8	309.0	311.7
2017	306.4	309.1	315.5	316.4	322.0	326.2	323.4	323.0	312.5	319.9	319.5	318.5	317.7
Other Services													
2007	93.3	94.6	94.9	95.3	95.8	100.2	98.8	98.2	95.2	93.5	92.9	93.2	95.5
2008	92.2	92.8	92.3	94.6	95.3	99.6	99.8	99.4	94.2	94.5	93.9	93.5	95.2
2009	93.7	94.3	93.7	95.5	95.6	99.4	98.9	97.0	93.8	92.9	92.4	92.1	94.9
2010	92.0	92.7	92.5	93.4	94.1	97.6	98.0	96.5	93.6	92.9	92.2	92.2	94.0
2011	91.8	92.5	92.6	94.9	95.9	100.0	99.8	98.6	96.0	95.1	94.3	94.5	95.5
2012	94.6	95.5	95.2	97.8	98.9	103.1	103.2	102.6	100.2	99.5	98.3	98.6	99.0
2013	98.6	99.7	99.8	101.4	102.4	106.9	107.3	105.5	103.4	103.1	102.7	102.3	102.8
2014	102.6	104.2	104.4	106.7	107.5	111.4	111.4	110.0	107.3	108.2	106.9	106.7	107.3
2015	105.9	107.0	106.7	106.7	107.6	111.5	111.6	110.2	107.6	108.4	107.3	107.1	108.1
2016	106.3	107.4	107.2	107.8	108.7	110.8	110.1	109.3	108.7	109.5	108.4	107.4	108.5
2017	106.0	108.2	109.0	111.1	111.2	112.5	110.3	109.9	108.8	108.5	108.0	109.2	109.4
Government													
2007	354.5	361.4	362.4	364.3	365.1	355.8	341.3	343.6	359.3	367.0	371.0	371.3	359.8
2008	369.4	373.1	374.2	373.5	373.7	365.5	355.1	354.4	369.8	372.6	377.7	377.5	369.7
2009	374.6	379.3	380.2	383.8	383.3	375.7	359.6	356.4	374.7	386.4	388.7	388.1	377.6
2010	380.7	388.8	390.5	393.3	402.4	389.7	371.7	368.6	382.1	389.5	391.4	389.1	386.5
2011	386.3	389.7	390.3	390.8	388.3	380.2	363.8	357.5	371.9	377.0	377.1	376.1	379.1
2012	369.2	376.1	376.9	377.2	377.8	368.7	355.8	353.3	369.7	376.9	378.8	379.3	371.6
2013	369.9	379.3	380.1	381.2	382.0	374.0	360.2	353.9	376.4	384.5	386.7	386.4	376.2
2014	377.6	386.9	387.7	387.6	388.4	383.6	367.5	362.0	381.8	390.6	393.4	392.7	383.3
2015	384.4	392.9	394.2	393.2	394.0	388.6	372.9	368.5	387.9	397.7	400.2	400.3	389.6
2016	393.6	401.6	403.0	404.8	406.5	401.9	385.7	380.3	399.1	407.0	410.5	412.4	400.5
2017	400.5	410.9	413.8	412.8	413.9	408.4	389.8	384.6	403.0	412.0	415.3	416.1	406.8

Employment by Industry: Washington-Arlington-Alexandria, DC-VA-MD-WV, Selected Years, 2007–2017

(Numbers in thousands, not seasonally adjusted)

Industry and year	January	February	March	April	May	June	July	August	September	October	November	December	Annual average
Total Nonfarm													
2007	2,959.3	2,965.5	2,989.6	2,996.0	3,014.3	3,031.6	3,019.7	3,009.3	3,005.8	3,023.3	3,036.1	3,046.9	3,008.1
2008	2,976.7	2,985.6	3,003.8	3,023.3	3,040.2	3,047.9	3,045.4	3,033.5	3,022.6	3,024.5	3,025.4	3,024.1	3,021.1
2009	2,954.9	2,953.0	2,961.7	2,962.1	2,977.5	2,988.8	2,985.7	2,966.1	2,950.7	2,971.5	2,984.4	2,986.7	2,970.3
2010	2,916.9	2,893.7	2,940.1	2,977.4	3,002.4	3,016.0	3,013.7	2,981.0	2,986.2	3,007.0	3,018.0	3,024.0	2,981.4
2011	2,964.8	2,973.9	2,996.3	3,022.4	3,023.6	3,041.6	3,048.7	3,022.5	3,039.3	3,044.5	3,055.0	3,059.4	3,024.3
2012	2,996.8	3,010.6	3,037.9	3,052.4	3,066.8	3,083.9	3,073.6	3,061.7	3,072.9	3,093.1	3,106.5	3,105.5	3,063.5
2013	3,045.2	3,058.0	3,074.1	3,089.6	3,101.9	3,107.3	3,102.5	3,087.4	3,095.9	3,099.1	3,119.7	3,112.4	3,091.1
2014	3,048.4	3,055.0	3,072.7	3,100.0	3,123.0	3,134.1	3,117.1	3,104.2	3,119.6	3,133.8	3,146.2	3,145.1	3,108.3
2015	3,095.8	3,106.6	3,114.5	3,145.5	3,168.3	3,181.3	3,181.1	3,162.1	3,176.9	3,201.3	3,215.1	3,219.2	3,164.0
2016	3,152.4	3,162.1	3,181.7	3,220.1	3,228.2	3,237.7	3,235.0	3,223.2	3,239.3	3,253.4	3,272.3	3,272.4	3,223.2
2017	3,214.7	3,233.3	3,250.6	3,269.2	3,286.9	3,300.3	3,283.1	3,266.3	3,275.4	3,292.7	3,306.2	3,310.2	3,274.1
Total Private													
2007	2,319.3	2,319.5	2,340.6	2,347.6	2,361.8	2,383.0	2,373.8	2,367.3	2,357.2	2,364.2	2,373.2	2,382.2	2,357.5
2008	2,323.3	2,324.5	2,338.7	2,362.7	2,376.0	2,386.0	2,382.4	2,373.4	2,362.1	2,354.9	2,351.7	2,348.8	2,357.0
2009	2,287.9	2,278.2	2,282.9	2,285.3	2,297.9	2,310.9	2,301.6	2,293.0	2,276.5	2,287.5	2,295.5	2,298.4	2,291.3
2010	2,237.5	2,211.7	2,251.7	2,287.6	2,301.3	2,318.8	2,312.2	2,307.9	2,297.8	2,309.9	2,317.1	2,325.2	2,289.9
2011	2,277.8	2,279.5	2,298.1	2,326.6	2,326.4	2,346.4	2,360.1	2,351.6	2,345.3	2,348.6	2,359.3	2,363.2	2,331.9
2012	2,312.4	2,318.0	2,340.1	2,357.3	2,370.9	2,390.3	2,391.3	2,393.3	2,382.7	2,393.8	2,405.8	2,405.5	2,371.8
2013	2,357.7	2,362.8	2,376.8	2,392.0	2,402.6	2,412.5	2,422.4	2,421.2	2,407.9	2,405.2	2,422.1	2,417.4	2,400.1
2014	2,371.2	2,369.3	2,385.8	2,412.8	2,431.7	2,443.8	2,443.0	2,441.0	2,430.8	2,439.6	2,449.3	2,450.5	2,422.4
2015	2,413.8	2,413.4	2,420.8	2,453.8	2,473.8	2,486.0	2,501.7	2,496.5	2,485.8	2,509.6	2,520.0	2,523.1	2,474.9
2016	2,467.0	2,470.7	2,486.6	2,520.2	2,527.4	2,539.0	2,550.0	2,546.9	2,539.6	2,549.3	2,564.1	2,564.7	2,527.1
2017	2,519.3	2,527.6	2,542.0	2,563.2	2,577.5	2,593.8	2,594.5	2,587.4	2,575.4	2,589.1	2,598.0	2,603.7	2,572.6
Goods Producing													
2007	248.1	245.0	249.0	251.3	253.1	256.3	255.6	255.8	253.2	250.6	248.3	245.7	251.0
2008	238.4	237.2	238.4	239.2	239.4	241.1	240.3	240.0	237.8	234.6	230.5	226.1	236.9
2009	214.5	211.1	209.8	209.5	209.3	209.4	209.2	208.0	205.4	202.5	200.5	198.9	207.3
2010	189.7	181.6	189.4	195.3	197.1	198.5	200.4	200.3	198.8	197.6	196.8	195.0	195.0
2011	188.5	187.8	189.6	194.0	195.6	198.3	201.6	201.0	198.1	196.6	196.2	196.3	195.3
2012	189.9	189.4	192.1	194.5	195.5	199.4	201.2	200.6	199.3	199.4	198.5	197.5	196.4
2013	191.6	191.0	192.7	195.2	197.8	200.3	201.6	202.4	200.2	198.8	199.8	197.1	197.4
2014	192.1	190.8	193.5	198.7	201.1	203.9	203.3	204.4	202.7	203.3	203.2	201.3	199.9
2015	194.1	193.9	195.0	200.7	203.5	205.8	208.5	209.2	208.0	211.2	211.8	211.2	204.4
2016	204.0	202.9	206.5	209.9	212.0	214.0	213.7	213.5	213.1	215.2	215.0	214.9	211.2
2017	207.7	209.0	210.6	213.9	215.1	218.0	218.4	218.0	217.0	217.4	214.7	214.2	214.5
Service-Providing													
2007	2,711.2	2,720.5	2,740.6	2,744.7	2,761.2	2,775.3	2,764.1	2,753.5	2,752.6	2,772.7	2,787.8	2,801.2	2,757.1
2008	2,738.3	2,748.4	2,765.4	2,784.1	2,800.8	2,806.8	2,805.1	2,793.5	2,784.8	2,789.9	2,794.9	2,798.0	2,784.2
2009	2,740.4	2,741.9	2,751.9	2,752.6	2,768.2	2,779.4	2,776.5	2,758.1	2,745.3	2,769.0	2,783.9	2,787.8	2,762.9
2010	2,727.2	2,712.1	2,750.7	2,782.1	2,805.3	2,817.5	2,813.3	2,780.7	2,787.4	2,809.4	2,821.2	2,829.0	2,786.3
2011	2,776.3	2,786.1	2,806.7	2,828.4	2,828.0	2,843.3	2,847.1	2,821.5	2,841.2	2,847.9	2,858.8	2,863.1	2,829.0
2012	2,806.9	2,821.2	2,845.8	2,857.9	2,871.3	2,884.5	2,872.4	2,861.1	2,873.6	2,893.7	2,908.0	2,908.0	2,867.0
2013	2,853.6	2,867.0	2,881.4	2,894.4	2,904.1	2,907.0	2,900.9	2,885.0	2,895.7	2,900.3	2,919.9	2,915.3	2,893.7
2014	2,856.3	2,864.2	2,879.2	2,901.3	2,921.9	2,930.2	2,913.8	2,899.8	2,916.9	2,930.5	2,943.0	2,943.8	2,908.4
2015	2,901.7	2,912.7	2,919.5	2,944.8	2,964.8	2,975.5	2,972.6	2,952.9	2,968.9	2,990.1	3,003.3	3,008.0	2,959.6
2016	2,948.4	2,959.2	2,975.2	3,010.2	3,016.2	3,023.7	3,021.3	3,009.7	3,026.2	3,038.2	3,057.3	3,057.5	3,011.9
2017	3,007.0	3,024.3	3,040.0	3,055.3	3,071.8	3,082.3	3,064.7	3,048.3	3,058.4	3,075.3	3,091.5	3,096.0	3,059.6
Mining, Logging, and Construction													
2007	183.7	180.5	184.5	187.0	188.7	191.2	190.6	190.9	188.6	186.2	184.0	181.2	186.4
2008	174.8	173.7	175.0	175.9	176.1	177.4	176.9	176.6	174.9	172.0	168.0	163.8	173.8
2009	154.4	152.1	151.2	151.4	151.4	151.8	152.1	151.1	149.2	146.4	144.4	142.5	149.8
2010	135.0	128.0	135.3	141.0	142.6	143.8	146.2	146.4	145.3	143.9	143.1	141.3	141.0
2011	135.4	135.2	137.0	141.5	143.0	145.4	148.9	148.5	146.2	144.7	144.2	143.8	142.8
2012	138.1	138.6	141.0	143.3	144.4	147.8	149.5	149.1	148.1	148.5	147.2	146.4	145.2
2013	141.1	141.0	142.6	145.0	147.4	149.7	151.0	151.8	150.2	148.3	148.8	145.9	146.9
2014	141.9	140.7	143.1	146.8	149.1	151.5	151.1	152.0	150.6	150.8	150.1	148.1	148.0
2015	142.0	141.7	142.6	147.7	150.3	152.2	154.5	155.0	154.1	157.1	157.2	156.7	150.9
2016	151.1	149.9	153.3	156.2	157.7	159.5	158.9	158.9	158.8	160.7	159.9	159.7	157.1
2017	153.5	154.6	156.0	159.2	160.3	162.9	163.2	163.0	162.3	162.5	159.6	159.5	159.7

Employment by Industry: Washington-Arlington-Alexandria, DC-VA-MD-WV, Selected Years, 2007–2017—Continued

(Numbers in thousands, not seasonally adjusted)

Industry and year	January	February	March	April	May	June	July	August	September	October	November	December	Annual average
Manufacturing													
2007	64.4	64.5	64.5	64.3	64.4	65.1	65.0	64.9	64.6	64.4	64.3	64.5	64.6
2008	63.6	63.5	63.4	63.3	63.3	63.7	63.4	63.4	62.9	62.6	62.5	62.3	63.2
2009	60.1	59.0	58.6	58.1	57.9	57.6	57.1	56.9	56.2	56.1	56.1	56.4	57.5
2010	54.7	53.6	54.1	54.3	54.5	54.7	54.2	53.9	53.5	53.7	53.7	53.7	54.1
2011	53.1	52.6	52.6	52.5	52.6	52.9	52.7	52.5	51.9	51.9	52.0	52.5	52.5
2012	51.8	50.8	51.1	51.2	51.1	51.6	51.7	51.5	51.2	50.9	51.3	51.1	51.3
2013	50.5	50.0	50.1	50.2	50.4	50.6	50.6	50.6	50.0	50.5	51.0	51.2	50.5
2014	50.2	50.1	50.4	51.9	52.0	52.4	52.2	52.4	52.1	52.5	53.1	53.2	51.9
2015	52.1	52.2	52.4	53.0	53.2	53.6	54.0	54.2	53.9	54.1	54.6	54.5	53.5
2016	52.9	53.0	53.2	53.7	54.3	54.5	54.8	54.6	54.3	54.5	55.1	55.2	54.2
2017	54.2	54.4	54.6	54.7	54.8	55.1	55.2	55.0	54.7	54.9	55.1	54.7	54.8
Trade, Transportation, and Utilities													
2007	407.2	399.6	401.9	402.5	405.9	409.6	408.2	406.2	404.1	406.2	416.8	424.9	407.8
2008	405.0	398.1	398.6	398.5	400.6	403.2	401.8	400.0	397.0	396.5	401.9	407.0	400.7
2009	385.4	378.1	377.1	374.9	378.3	380.3	378.0	377.5	376.5	379.1	387.7	393.5	380.5
2010	376.0	366.2	372.6	375.7	379.5	383.3	381.4	381.8	379.3	384.8	393.4	400.9	381.2
2011	382.5	377.6	379.2	382.8	384.3	387.0	387.5	387.5	385.4	389.5	398.4	405.4	387.3
2012	387.5	382.9	385.2	384.8	388.6	391.2	389.4	389.2	387.7	391.1	402.3	407.5	390.6
2013	388.5	383.2	385.1	386.1	389.0	391.9	392.2	392.4	390.2	393.8	404.5	411.2	392.3
2014	392.3	386.7	389.2	391.5	395.0	398.3	398.0	397.8	395.5	399.4	409.2	416.7	397.5
2015	398.5	392.3	393.1	394.9	399.6	402.8	403.9	403.6	401.6	405.7	415.2	421.5	402.7
2016	400.4	395.8	397.5	400.5	403.7	405.7	406.1	405.5	402.9	406.7	417.4	423.3	405.5
2017	404.8	399.3	400.4	402.7	405.2	408.4	407.6	407.5	404.1	406.0	414.6	421.0	406.8
Wholesale Trade													
2007	70.5	70.6	70.9	70.9	71.1	71.5	70.8	70.7	70.4	70.5	70.6	70.7	70.8
2008	70.0	70.3	70.3	70.0	70.0	70.1	69.8	69.5	68.9	68.7	68.0	67.6	69.4
2009	66.9	66.6	66.2	65.7	65.5	65.3	64.9	64.8	64.2	64.1	63.9	64.1	65.2
2010	63.1	62.8	63.1	62.8	63.0	63.1	63.0	63.0	62.6	63.0	62.8	63.1	63.0
2011	62.8	62.8	63.0	62.9	62.9	62.8	63.0	63.0	62.5	62.8	62.6	62.7	62.8
2012	62.3	62.6	62.9	62.0	62.8	63.0	63.0	63.3	63.0	63.2	63.3	63.2	62.9
2013	63.0	63.1	63.2	62.9	62.9	63.0	62.8	62.7	62.2	62.6	62.7	62.8	62.8
2014	62.0	62.0	62.3	62.0	62.4	62.4	62.4	62.4	61.9	61.6	61.6	61.6	62.1
2015	61.1	60.9	61.0	60.6	60.9	61.0	61.7	61.5	61.1	61.3	61.3	61.5	61.2
2016	61.2	61.0	60.8	61.5	61.7	61.9	62.6	62.7	62.5	62.8	62.7	62.6	62.0
2017	62.5	62.7	62.5	62.3	62.5	62.7	62.9	62.9	62.4	62.7	62.9	62.7	62.6
Retail Trade													
2007	273.7	266.0	267.6	268.5	271.2	273.6	273.1	271.1	269.4	271.7	281.7	287.2	272.9
2008	272.1	264.8	265.6	265.9	267.5	269.3	268.5	266.8	264.8	264.8	269.8	273.5	267.0
2009	256.4	250.3	249.7	248.4	251.2	252.9	251.6	251.5	250.9	254.1	262.2	266.2	253.8
2010	252.9	244.1	249.4	252.5	255.5	258.2	257.1	257.4	255.4	260.6	268.1	273.1	257.0
2011	258.4	254.2	255.2	258.5	259.8	261.9	261.5	261.7	260.7	264.2	272.8	277.7	262.2
2012	263.6	258.6	260.7	260.5	263.0	264.7	263.4	262.9	262.1	265.1	275.4	278.1	264.8
2013	263.7	259.6	260.8	262.3	264.7	266.8	267.4	267.5	266.2	269.7	278.8	282.7	267.5
2014	268.3	264.0	265.7	267.9	270.2	272.8	272.8	272.5	270.7	274.6	282.8	287.4	272.5
2015	273.8	269.5	270.3	272.1	275.5	278.1	278.3	277.9	276.7	280.8	288.7	291.5	277.8
2016	275.9	271.8	273.6	275.1	277.5	278.6	278.5	278.3	275.6	279.4	287.9	290.7	278.6
2017	277.3	272.2	273.3	275.0	276.6	278.8	277.8	277.9	274.7	276.5	283.9	286.5	277.5
Transportation and Utilities													
2007	63.0	63.0	63.4	63.1	63.6	64.5	64.3	64.4	64.3	64.0	64.5	67.0	64.1
2008	62.9	63.0	62.7	62.6	63.1	63.8	63.5	63.7	63.3	63.0	64.1	65.9	63.5
2009	62.1	61.2	61.2	60.8	61.6	62.1	61.5	61.2	61.4	60.9	61.6	63.2	61.6
2010	60.0	59.3	60.1	60.4	61.0	62.0	61.3	61.4	61.3	61.2	62.4	64.7	61.3
2011	61.3	60.6	61.0	61.4	61.6	62.3	63.0	62.8	62.2	62.5	63.0	65.0	62.2
2012	61.6	61.7	61.6	62.3	62.8	63.5	63.0	63.0	62.6	62.8	63.6	66.2	62.9
2013	61.8	60.5	61.1	60.9	61.4	62.1	62.0	62.2	61.8	61.5	63.0	65.7	62.0
2014	62.0	60.7	61.2	61.6	62.4	63.1	62.8	62.9	62.9	63.2	64.8	67.7	62.9
2015	63.6	61.9	61.8	62.2	63.2	63.7	63.9	64.2	63.8	63.6	65.2	68.5	63.8
2016	63.3	63.0	63.1	63.9	64.5	65.2	65.0	64.5	64.8	64.5	66.8	70.0	64.9
2017	65.0	64.4	64.6	65.4	66.1	66.9	66.9	66.7	67.0	66.8	67.8	71.8	66.6

Employment by Industry: Washington-Arlington-Alexandria, DC-VA-MD-WV, Selected Years, 2007–2017—Continued

(Numbers in thousands, not seasonally adjusted)

Industry and year	January	February	March	April	May	June	July	August	September	October	November	December	Annual average
Information													
2007	95.1	95.2	95.0	94.0	94.3	94.9	95.1	94.8	93.9	93.4	93.7	94.0	94.5
2008	92.6	93.0	92.9	92.7	92.5	92.4	92.1	91.6	90.8	89.7	90.0	89.2	91.6
2009	87.0	87.0	86.4	84.7	84.4	84.9	83.8	83.2	82.0	81.7	81.6	81.6	84.0
2010	80.5	80.0	80.2	79.7	79.6	80.6	80.9	80.8	81.9	81.8	81.3	83.1	80.9
2011	80.1	80.7	81.0	82.0	80.0	81.8	81.6	76.2	80.2	77.3	78.5	79.8	79.9
2012	76.1	77.3	78.1	76.3	77.1	78.8	77.9	79.1	77.0	76.8	78.4	77.3	77.5
2013	76.5	78.0	77.9	76.5	77.2	77.2	77.6	78.7	76.6	76.7	78.5	77.3	77.4
2014	79.1	77.8	77.8	77.9	79.3	78.5	78.5	79.3	77.3	78.1	77.4	77.4	78.2
2015	77.7	77.0	76.6	77.0	77.2	76.5	76.9	76.1	75.1	76.3	76.1	76.1	76.6
2016	75.0	75.4	74.4	74.7	71.8	74.7	74.9	74.5	74.2	73.7	73.8	74.2	74.3
2017	73.6	74.4	74.1	73.8	74.0	74.4	74.2	74.0	73.9	73.2	73.4	74.9	74.0
Financial Activities													
2007	159.8	160.2	160.4	159.3	159.8	160.8	160.4	159.2	157.9	156.9	156.3	156.4	159.0
2008	154.1	154.1	153.9	154.7	154.6	155.3	155.4	154.8	153.3	152.3	151.6	151.4	153.8
2009	148.6	147.8	147.2	147.0	147.3	148.3	148.1	147.7	146.6	147.0	147.0	147.5	147.5
2010	145.3	144.6	145.6	145.4	146.2	147.6	147.5	146.9	145.4	146.6	146.7	146.9	146.2
2011	144.4	144.4	144.7	145.9	146.1	146.8	147.1	146.6	145.9	146.3	146.0	146.6	145.9
2012	145.1	145.4	145.9	146.6	146.9	148.2	148.4	148.0	147.6	148.2	148.3	148.9	147.3
2013	147.7	148.0	148.7	149.0	149.3	150.7	151.2	150.9	149.6	150.3	150.5	151.0	149.7
2014	148.9	148.6	149.0	149.1	149.7	151.1	151.6	151.1	150.1	150.5	150.6	151.0	150.1
2015	150.4	150.6	150.9	150.3	151.1	152.5	153.4	152.9	151.6	152.4	152.2	152.6	151.7
2016	151.3	151.4	151.6	152.8	153.3	154.4	155.6	155.6	154.6	155.2	155.2	156.1	153.9
2017	154.8	155.4	155.7	156.2	157.4	159.0	159.3	158.7	157.5	158.1	157.3	158.6	157.3
Professional and Business Services													
2007	662.3	667.3	672.7	676.1	678.2	685.2	682.7	682.8	676.3	681.9	682.3	683.6	677.6
2008	672.2	675.4	679.0	686.7	687.0	691.4	691.8	690.6	685.7	686.5	684.8	682.9	684.5
2009	673.9	673.3	674.8	674.4	674.4	679.8	680.3	678.3	671.0	679.1	679.9	680.1	676.6
2010	667.3	666.9	674.2	684.8	685.5	691.5	689.1	687.3	681.7	688.7	688.8	689.6	683.0
2011	683.2	685.7	690.8	694.2	692.9	698.1	705.4	704.9	699.3	703.2	703.5	701.9	696.9
2012	691.6	694.5	700.7	708.1	708.4	714.9	717.2	718.5	710.4	716.2	717.0	713.9	709.3
2013	704.3	708.0	710.2	710.2	708.1	711.1	715.1	714.6	706.2	705.1	706.6	702.7	708.5
2014	693.4	696.0	697.8	704.3	706.9	711.3	715.1	713.5	706.8	711.3	711.8	710.0	706.5
2015	706.8	708.6	709.4	718.6	721.0	725.8	731.9	730.2	722.3	731.4	731.9	729.6	722.3
2016	721.3	723.9	726.7	735.6	734.6	740.0	746.1	745.6	737.9	742.0	742.4	739.8	736.3
2017	734.1	735.8	737.9	744.2	745.3	754.8	756.7	755.3	747.0	749.8	751.4	748.6	746.7
Education and Health Services													
2007	328.7	333.9	336.7	335.4	332.9	328.9	323.4	322.2	333.1	340.0	341.8	342.9	333.3
2008	336.0	339.8	341.6	344.2	345.5	340.7	337.9	337.5	346.7	349.8	351.7	353.2	343.7
2009	349.9	353.1	354.7	356.7	356.8	351.8	348.1	346.4	352.4	360.7	363.1	363.5	354.8
2010	358.3	356.3	361.9	367.0	367.2	360.7	358.3	357.7	365.6	367.2	369.2	369.2	363.2
2011	370.1	372.0	374.0	377.3	371.4	368.3	370.3	369.1	379.2	381.2	382.9	380.7	374.7
2012	379.2	382.0	383.7	385.7	383.8	377.0	375.2	377.0	389.0	393.9	395.2	394.2	384.7
2013	391.1	394.9	396.8	400.4	397.4	387.4	390.0	389.9	401.8	403.7	405.6	403.1	396.8
2014	400.1	403.2	405.2	407.6	405.8	396.1	393.5	394.3	407.9	410.5	412.5	411.8	404.0
2015	409.7	413.4	413.3	419.3	417.2	407.1	409.1	408.8	422.6	430.6	433.0	431.5	418.0
2016	426.4	430.5	431.7	436.3	432.7	419.2	420.3	420.3	433.2	436.0	437.8	435.1	430.0
2017	433.2	436.9	438.3	439.5	437.7	427.4	426.2	425.2	439.9	448.4	451.7	449.8	437.9
Leisure and Hospitality													
2007	240.9	240.2	245.9	251.6	258.9	266.9	268.2	267.5	260.7	256.7	255.0	254.7	255.6
2008	246.8	247.8	253.8	264.3	272.2	276.6	277.4	274.8	267.7	263.0	259.0	256.5	263.3
2009	247.5	246.8	251.4	257.1	265.5	272.5	271.5	269.7	262.2	258.6	256.7	253.8	259.4
2010	243.9	240.4	249.7	260.5	265.9	274.8	273.5	272.9	266.8	264.0	261.9	261.1	261.3
2011	251.5	252.7	259.4	268.8	274.3	282.8	282.2	283.2	275.5	272.8	271.4	269.8	270.4
2012	262.0	264.3	271.3	278.6	287.0	295.9	295.1	295.2	287.1	283.7	281.4	280.7	281.9
2013	274.6	275.8	281.3	289.4	297.7	306.5	306.4	304.7	296.5	290.6	289.8	288.4	291.8
2014	280.1	280.6	286.6	296.3	305.6	314.1	312.6	311.1	302.4	299.0	297.1	295.1	298.4
2015	290.4	291.2	295.6	305.4	315.3	324.9	326.2	325.0	315.4	312.2	309.9	310.7	310.2
2016	300.3	302.0	308.6	318.7	325.9	334.7	334.2	332.6	324.5	319.7	320.3	318.4	320.0
2017	308.9	312.5	319.0	326.3	335.5	342.1	341.5	339.8	329.4	328.8	325.9	326.0	328.0

Employment by Industry: Washington-Arlington-Alexandria, DC-VA-MD-WV, Selected Years, 2007–2017—Continued

(Numbers in thousands, not seasonally adjusted)

Industry and year	January	February	March	April	May	June	July	August	September	October	November	December	Annual average
Other Services													
2007	177.2	178.1	179.0	177.4	178.7	180.4	180.2	178.8	178.0	178.5	179.0	180.0	178.8
2008	178.2	179.1	180.5	182.4	184.2	185.3	185.7	184.1	183.1	182.5	182.2	182.5	182.5
2009	181.1	181.0	181.5	181.0	181.9	183.9	182.6	182.2	180.4	178.8	179.0	179.5	181.1
2010	176.5	175.7	178.1	179.2	180.3	181.8	181.1	180.2	178.3	179.2	179.1	179.4	179.1
2011	177.5	178.6	179.4	181.6	181.8	183.3	184.4	183.1	181.7	181.7	182.4	182.7	181.5
2012	181.0	182.2	183.1	182.7	183.6	184.9	186.9	185.7	184.6	184.5	184.7	185.5	184.1
2013	183.4	183.9	184.1	185.2	186.1	187.4	188.3	187.6	186.8	186.2	186.8	186.6	186.0
2014	185.2	185.6	186.7	187.4	188.3	190.5	190.4	189.5	188.1	187.5	187.5	187.2	187.8
2015	186.2	186.4	186.9	187.6	188.9	190.6	191.8	190.7	189.2	189.8	189.9	189.9	189.0
2016	188.3	188.8	189.6	191.7	193.4	196.3	199.1	199.3	199.2	200.8	202.2	202.9	196.0
2017	202.2	204.3	206.0	206.6	207.3	209.7	210.6	208.9	206.6	207.4	209.0	210.6	207.4
Government													
2007	640.0	646.0	649.0	648.4	652.5	648.6	645.9	642.0	648.6	659.1	662.9	664.7	650.6
2008	653.4	661.1	665.1	660.6	664.2	661.9	663.0	660.1	660.5	669.6	673.7	675.3	664.0
2009	667.0	674.8	678.8	676.8	679.6	677.9	684.1	673.1	674.2	684.0	688.9	688.3	679.0
2010	679.4	682.0	688.4	689.8	701.1	697.2	701.5	673.1	688.4	697.1	700.9	698.8	691.5
2011	687.0	694.4	698.2	695.8	697.2	695.2	688.6	670.9	694.0	695.9	695.7	696.2	692.4
2012	684.4	692.6	697.8	695.1	695.9	693.6	682.3	668.4	690.2	699.3	700.7	700.0	691.7
2013	687.5	695.2	697.3	697.6	699.3	694.8	680.1	666.2	688.0	693.9	697.6	695.0	691.0
2014	677.2	685.7	686.9	687.2	691.3	690.3	674.1	663.2	688.8	694.2	696.9	694.6	685.9
2015	682.0	693.2	693.7	691.7	694.5	695.3	679.4	665.6	691.1	691.7	695.1	696.1	689.1
2016	685.4	691.4	695.1	699.9	700.8	698.7	685.0	676.3	699.7	704.1	708.2	707.7	696.0
2017	695.4	705.7	708.6	706.0	709.4	706.5	688.6	678.9	700.0	703.6	708.2	706.5	701.5

Employment by Industry: Miami-Fort Lauderdale-West Palm Beach, FL, Selected Years, 2007–2017

(Numbers in thousands, not seasonally adjusted)

Industry and year	January	February	March	April	May	June	July	August	September	October	November	December	Annual average
Total Nonfarm													
2007	2,415.3	2,433.8	2,449.6	2,428.6	2,436.7	2,408.3	2,366.6	2,406.4	2,414.4	2,410.4	2,441.4	2,463.0	2,422.9
2008	2,406.3	2,420.3	2,426.5	2,397.4	2,391.5	2,347.8	2,300.5	2,325.9	2,321.7	2,315.0	2,327.2	2,335.6	2,359.6
2009	2,265.1	2,259.5	2,254.3	2,232.2	2,223.7	2,186.0	2,152.9	2,176.0	2,178.1	2,190.7	2,213.7	2,226.6	2,213.2
2010	2,180.7	2,192.4	2,200.1	2,199.2	2,207.8	2,172.4	2,150.5	2,178.9	2,181.6	2,203.2	2,229.3	2,247.1	2,195.3
2011	2,211.9	2,224.4	2,230.5	2,243.0	2,237.2	2,202.4	2,186.8	2,217.5	2,231.4	2,249.4	2,277.9	2,297.1	2,234.1
2012	2,261.3	2,274.6	2,287.1	2,288.8	2,290.4	2,259.4	2,237.6	2,267.7	2,279.7	2,306.5	2,338.3	2,350.8	2,286.9
2013	2,313.8	2,333.3	2,344.8	2,345.7	2,348.2	2,320.0	2,303.6	2,336.4	2,346.2	2,367.6	2,407.7	2,423.0	2,349.2
2014	2,383.5	2,401.6	2,413.5	2,421.1	2,425.2	2,395.7	2,380.2	2,416.7	2,429.8	2,460.2	2,498.2	2,514.1	2,428.3
2015	2,472.6	2,487.4	2,498.9	2,501.5	2,506.0	2,475.7	2,465.3	2,499.6	2,505.9	2,544.7	2,577.8	2,594.0	2,510.8
2016	2,552.8	2,571.2	2,578.5	2,590.9	2,586.7	2,550.0	2,544.8	2,573.8	2,585.7	2,605.6	2,640.0	2,653.2	2,586.1
2017	2,616.2	2,632.1	2,642.0	2,640.7	2,645.8	2,613.8	2,595.2	2,620.8	2,564.6	2,636.0	2,666.5	2,679.3	2,629.4
Total Private													
2007	2,088.8	2,105.9	2,119.4	2,098.2	2,105.5	2,106.2	2,068.8	2,078.6	2,082.8	2,080.2	2,108.8	2,129.5	2,097.7
2008	2,075.5	2,087.0	2,093.5	2,065.8	2,058.9	2,044.6	2,001.9	2,000.5	1,994.5	1,988.4	1,998.6	2,005.8	2,034.6
2009	1,937.2	1,933.2	1,927.8	1,905.2	1,898.3	1,888.7	1,858.1	1,859.4	1,859.0	1,869.7	1,891.8	1,904.9	1,894.4
2010	1,862.4	1,873.6	1,881.4	1,879.4	1,878.6	1,876.8	1,861.4	1,868.7	1,870.1	1,889.6	1,915.2	1,933.7	1,882.6
2011	1,899.8	1,910.8	1,918.4	1,931.0	1,927.1	1,918.8	1,906.3	1,914.0	1,924.9	1,939.7	1,969.7	1,988.4	1,929.1
2012	1,956.0	1,968.0	1,981.5	1,983.2	1,985.7	1,980.0	1,960.9	1,969.5	1,977.3	2,001.0	2,032.7	2,045.4	1,986.8
2013	2,010.5	2,027.1	2,038.3	2,039.5	2,042.1	2,039.7	2,025.7	2,037.8	2,042.8	2,062.5	2,100.4	2,117.5	2,048.7
2014	2,079.5	2,095.7	2,106.8	2,114.4	2,119.2	2,115.3	2,102.6	2,118.5	2,127.9	2,155.2	2,191.5	2,209.2	2,128.0
2015	2,169.5	2,182.4	2,192.6	2,194.4	2,199.1	2,194.2	2,185.7	2,199.9	2,201.9	2,236.9	2,269.8	2,287.1	2,209.5
2016	2,246.8	2,262.7	2,269.6	2,279.6	2,276.1	2,263.4	2,258.9	2,268.7	2,274.0	2,293.0	2,325.7	2,340.6	2,279.9
2017	2,303.6	2,317.3	2,325.9	2,325.5	2,330.4	2,321.6	2,305.4	2,312.1	2,251.6	2,321.3	2,350.3	2,366.7	2,319.3
Goods Producing													
2007	265.0	266.3	267.4	262.0	263.0	266.0	258.8	259.5	259.4	255.3	254.6	253.8	260.9
2008	244.4	243.3	241.9	234.8	233.4	232.4	225.3	223.9	222.0	217.6	214.1	210.9	228.7
2009	199.1	196.3	193.5	187.4	185.8	184.2	179.5	178.1	177.0	174.7	173.1	172.0	183.4
2010	164.5	165.0	164.9	164.4	165.0	165.7	165.3	165.8	165.6	165.1	164.6	164.3	165.0
2011	160.1	160.7	160.8	161.3	161.4	162.0	161.3	162.2	163.1	163.3	163.8	163.8	162.0
2012	160.9	161.5	162.5	161.5	162.7	164.1	163.1	165.5	166.2	166.6	167.7	167.6	164.2
2013	163.8	165.7	167.0	166.9	169.5	170.9	171.9	174.5	174.9	175.6	177.1	177.5	171.3
2014	174.8	177.3	178.8	179.7	182.0	183.8	184.6	186.8	188.0	189.8	190.3	190.8	183.9
2015	188.8	191.1	192.8	193.9	196.1	198.3	198.4	200.5	201.5	205.3	206.4	207.1	198.4
2016	203.9	206.2	207.3	209.1	209.9	210.6	211.8	213.4	214.5	215.0	216.8	216.7	211.3
2017	213.7	216.2	217.8	217.8	219.3	220.2	218.9	220.2	211.0	223.6	224.5	226.1	219.1
Service-Providing													
2007	2,150.3	2,167.5	2,182.2	2,166.6	2,173.7	2,142.3	2,107.8	2,146.9	2,155.0	2,155.1	2,186.8	2,209.2	2,162.0
2008	2,161.9	2,177.0	2,184.6	2,162.6	2,158.1	2,115.4	2,075.2	2,102.0	2,099.7	2,097.4	2,113.1	2,124.7	2,131.0
2009	2,066.0	2,063.2	2,060.8	2,044.8	2,037.9	2,001.8	1,973.4	1,997.9	2,001.1	2,016.0	2,040.6	2,054.6	2,029.8
2010	2,016.2	2,027.4	2,035.2	2,034.8	2,042.8	2,006.7	1,985.2	2,013.1	2,016.0	2,038.1	2,064.7	2,082.8	2,030.3
2011	2,051.8	2,063.7	2,069.7	2,081.7	2,075.8	2,040.4	2,025.5	2,055.3	2,068.3	2,086.1	2,114.1	2,133.3	2,072.1
2012	2,100.4	2,113.1	2,124.6	2,127.3	2,127.7	2,095.3	2,074.5	2,102.2	2,113.5	2,139.9	2,170.6	2,183.2	2,122.7
2013	2,150.0	2,167.6	2,177.8	2,178.8	2,178.7	2,149.1	2,131.7	2,161.9	2,171.3	2,192.0	2,230.6	2,245.5	2,177.9
2014	2,208.7	2,224.3	2,234.7	2,241.4	2,243.2	2,211.9	2,195.6	2,229.9	2,241.8	2,270.4	2,307.9	2,323.3	2,244.4
2015	2,283.8	2,296.3	2,306.1	2,307.6	2,309.9	2,277.4	2,266.9	2,299.1	2,304.4	2,339.4	2,371.4	2,386.9	2,312.4
2016	2,348.9	2,365.0	2,371.2	2,381.8	2,376.8	2,339.4	2,333.0	2,360.4	2,371.2	2,390.6	2,423.2	2,436.5	2,374.8
2017	2,402.5	2,415.9	2,424.2	2,422.9	2,426.5	2,393.6	2,376.3	2,400.6	2,353.6	2,412.4	2,442.0	2,453.2	2,410.3
Mining and Logging													
2007	0.8	0.8	0.8	0.8	0.8	0.8	0.8	0.8	0.8	0.9	0.9	0.9	0.8
2008	0.7	0.7	0.8	0.8	0.8	0.7	0.6	0.6	0.6	0.6	0.6	0.6	0.7
2009	0.6	0.6	0.5	0.5	0.5	0.5	0.5	0.5	0.5	0.5	0.5	0.5	0.6
2010	0.5	0.5	0.5	0.5	0.5	0.5	0.5	0.5	0.5	0.5	0.6	0.6	0.5
2011	0.6	0.6	0.6	0.7	0.6	0.6	0.6	0.6	0.5	0.6	0.6	0.6	0.6
2012	0.6	0.6	0.6	0.5	0.6	0.6	0.6	0.6	0.6	0.6	0.6	0.6	0.6
2013	0.6	0.6	0.6	0.6	0.6	0.5	0.6	0.6	0.6	0.6	0.6	0.6	0.6
2014	0.6	0.6	0.6	0.6	0.6	0.6	0.6	0.6	0.6	0.6	0.6	0.6	0.6
2015	0.6	0.6	0.6	0.6	0.6	0.6	0.6	0.6	0.6	0.6	0.6	0.6	0.6
2016	0.7	0.7	0.7	0.7	0.7	0.7	0.7	0.7	0.7	0.7	0.7	0.7	0.7
2017	0.7	0.7	0.7	0.7	0.7	0.7	0.7	0.7	0.7	0.7	0.7	0.7	0.7

Employment by Industry: Miami-Fort Lauderdale-West Palm Beach, FL, Selected Years, 2007–2017—*Continued*

(Numbers in thousands, not seasonally adjusted)

Industry and year	January	February	March	April	May	June	July	August	September	October	November	December	Annual average
Construction													
2007	163.6	164.4	165.4	161.4	162.1	164.6	160.1	160.3	160.1	156.3	155.1	154.1	160.6
2008	146.4	145.2	144.5	138.8	137.8	137.2	132.5	131.3	129.6	126.5	123.8	121.5	134.6
2009	112.3	110.5	109.3	105.1	104.3	103.2	100.6	99.2	98.5	96.5	94.7	93.8	102.3
2010	88.0	88.4	88.3	88.2	88.6	88.9	89.3	89.4	89.4	88.6	87.8	87.1	88.5
2011	84.1	84.5	84.7	84.7	84.4	84.7	84.7	85.1	86.1	85.8	86.0	85.8	85.1
2012	83.5	83.6	84.3	84.3	85.1	86.5	86.3	88.1	88.8	88.9	89.5	89.4	86.5
2013	87.4	88.5	89.4	89.6	91.6	92.5	93.5	95.6	96.1	96.3	96.9	97.0	92.9
2014	94.7	96.5	98.0	99.0	100.7	102.2	102.9	104.5	105.2	106.4	106.4	106.7	101.9
2015	105.2	107.0	108.1	109.2	110.6	112.3	112.8	114.2	115.2	118.0	118.7	119.0	112.5
2016	116.2	117.9	119.0	120.7	121.7	122.4	123.9	124.8	125.6	126.0	127.0	127.0	122.7
2017	125.2	127.1	128.2	128.2	129.1	129.9	129.7	130.4	123.1	132.5	133.0	133.4	129.2
Manufacturing													
2007	100.6	101.1	101.2	99.8	100.1	100.6	97.9	98.4	98.5	98.1	98.6	98.8	99.5
2008	97.3	97.4	96.6	95.2	94.8	94.5	92.2	92.0	91.8	90.5	89.7	88.8	93.4
2009	86.2	85.2	83.7	81.8	81.0	80.5	78.4	78.4	78.0	77.7	77.9	77.7	80.5
2010	76.0	76.1	76.1	75.7	75.9	76.3	75.5	75.9	75.7	76.0	76.3	76.6	76.0
2011	75.4	75.6	75.5	75.9	76.4	76.7	76.0	76.5	76.5	76.9	77.2	77.4	76.3
2012	76.8	77.3	77.6	76.7	77.0	77.0	76.2	76.8	76.8	77.1	77.6	77.6	77.0
2013	75.8	76.6	77.0	76.7	77.3	77.9	77.8	78.3	78.2	78.7	79.6	79.9	77.8
2014	79.5	80.2	80.2	80.1	80.7	81.0	81.1	81.7	82.2	82.8	83.3	83.5	81.4
2015	83.0	83.5	84.1	84.1	84.9	85.4	85.0	85.7	85.7	86.7	87.1	87.5	85.2
2016	87.0	87.6	87.6	87.7	87.5	87.5	87.2	87.9	88.2	88.3	89.1	89.0	87.9
2017	87.8	88.4	88.9	88.9	89.5	89.6	88.5	89.1	87.2	90.4	90.8	92.0	89.3
Trade, Transportation, and Utilities													
2007	547.6	546.8	549.0	545.7	549.2	549.4	543.5	545.4	545.8	547.4	561.8	570.9	550.2
2008	551.5	550.5	550.5	544.6	544.5	541.6	534.6	534.4	532.8	531.2	537.1	542.6	541.3
2009	519.9	515.8	512.6	505.0	504.3	501.8	495.7	495.8	495.0	499.1	510.4	517.7	506.1
2010	500.4	499.1	500.0	501.1	502.7	502.7	498.9	500.8	500.3	507.3	519.8	528.1	505.1
2011	511.8	511.1	512.1	515.5	515.4	515.5	515.3	517.5	519.5	525.5	538.9	546.7	520.4
2012	532.8	531.7	533.0	533.5	535.3	533.7	530.5	531.1	533.0	538.2	553.4	558.6	537.1
2013	543.9	542.7	543.9	544.2	545.7	546.9	543.6	545.7	546.7	552.8	570.4	579.3	550.5
2014	558.4	558.3	558.7	560.0	561.1	561.4	559.4	563.6	564.3	572.4	590.3	599.3	567.3
2015	581.1	578.9	580.3	579.5	580.1	581.1	578.1	580.9	578.5	586.6	602.3	610.0	584.8
2016	589.3	587.9	588.3	590.0	590.3	588.4	588.7	589.5	588.6	592.6	609.8	617.7	593.4
2017	599.2	596.0	597.0	595.9	596.9	595.9	594.7	596.0	582.8	595.5	614.1	619.0	598.6
Wholesale Trade													
2007	147.6	149.2	149.8	148.7	149.4	149.2	147.0	147.3	147.5	147.4	148.2	149.3	148.4
2008	146.7	147.6	147.7	146.7	147.1	146.1	144.0	143.8	143.8	143.0	142.8	143.0	145.2
2009	139.5	139.4	138.1	136.7	136.6	135.1	133.2	133.1	132.5	133.2	134.2	135.0	135.6
2010	132.1	132.7	132.8	132.7	133.4	132.7	131.6	131.8	131.7	132.7	133.5	134.5	132.7
2011	132.3	133.3	133.5	134.5	134.1	133.9	133.4	133.8	134.3	135.7	136.7	138.3	134.5
2012	137.0	138.1	139.0	139.4	139.8	139.1	138.3	138.3	138.7	139.5	140.5	141.6	139.1
2013	139.6	140.6	140.9	140.4	141.0	140.7	139.6	140.0	140.3	140.7	141.9	142.8	140.7
2014	141.3	142.4	142.1	142.3	142.8	142.1	141.3	142.3	142.6	143.9	145.4	146.2	142.9
2015	144.9	145.3	145.4	144.9	145.2	144.7	143.7	144.0	143.7	145.4	146.2	146.8	145.0
2016	145.4	146.1	146.1	146.6	146.7	145.7	145.2	145.2	145.1	145.5	147.1	148.0	146.1
2017	146.4	146.8	147.4	147.4	148.0	147.3	146.5	146.6	145.2	147.8	148.5	147.5	147.1
Retail Trade													
2007	305.1	302.8	303.9	302.0	304.9	304.8	301.7	303.0	303.0	304.1	315.9	321.6	306.1
2008	307.6	305.2	305.1	301.8	301.7	300.8	297.0	296.8	295.8	294.7	300.0	303.8	300.9
2009	288.0	284.6	282.9	278.5	278.7	278.1	274.9	275.3	275.8	278.6	287.7	292.9	281.3
2010	280.1	278.1	278.7	279.9	281.4	282.2	279.9	281.6	281.1	286.4	296.5	302.2	284.0
2011	290.1	287.7	288.2	290.3	290.8	290.9	291.3	293.1	294.4	298.5	309.5	314.0	294.9
2012	303.0	299.9	300.1	300.3	301.7	300.9	298.8	299.5	300.6	303.9	316.8	319.1	303.7
2013	308.7	306.1	306.7	307.4	308.5	309.6	308.4	310.1	310.3	315.1	330.1	336.1	313.1
2014	319.2	317.5	317.9	318.9	319.6	320.5	319.5	322.3	322.3	328.5	342.7	348.8	324.8
2015	334.0	331.6	332.3	331.8	332.3	333.5	331.1	333.3	330.8	335.7	348.1	352.5	335.6
2016	335.6	333.3	333.2	334.3	335.0	334.2	334.9	336.3	334.9	338.1	351.5	355.8	338.1
2017	340.8	337.3	337.0	336.2	336.5	335.9	335.6	336.6	326.0	335.2	348.3	350.4	338.0

Employment by Industry: Miami-Fort Lauderdale-West Palm Beach, FL, Selected Years, 2007–2017—*Continued*

(Numbers in thousands, not seasonally adjusted)

Industry and year	January	February	March	April	May	June	July	August	September	October	November	December	Annual average
Transportation and Utilities													
2007	94.9	94.8	95.3	95.0	94.9	95.4	94.8	95.1	95.3	95.9	97.7	100.0	95.8
2008	97.2	97.7	97.7	96.1	95.7	94.7	93.6	93.8	93.2	93.5	94.3	95.8	95.3
2009	92.4	91.8	91.6	89.8	89.0	88.6	87.6	87.4	86.7	87.3	88.5	89.8	89.2
2010	88.2	88.3	88.5	88.5	87.9	87.8	87.4	87.4	87.5	88.2	89.8	91.4	88.4
2011	89.4	90.1	90.4	90.7	90.5	90.7	90.6	90.6	90.8	91.3	92.7	94.4	91.0
2012	92.8	93.7	93.9	93.8	93.8	93.7	93.4	93.3	93.7	94.8	96.1	97.9	94.2
2013	95.6	96.0	96.3	96.4	96.2	96.6	95.6	95.6	96.1	97.0	98.4	100.4	96.7
2014	97.9	98.4	98.7	98.8	98.7	98.8	98.6	99.0	99.4	100.0	102.2	104.3	99.6
2015	102.2	102.0	102.6	102.8	102.6	102.9	103.3	103.6	104.0	105.5	108.0	110.7	104.2
2016	108.3	108.5	109.0	109.1	108.6	108.5	108.6	108.0	108.6	109.0	111.2	113.9	109.3
2017	112.0	111.9	112.6	112.3	112.4	112.7	112.6	112.8	111.6	112.5	117.3	121.1	113.5
Information													
2007	50.7	51.1	51.4	51.2	51.4	51.7	51.3	51.3	50.7	51.0	51.1	51.3	51.2
2008	50.7	50.7	50.7	50.3	50.4	50.3	49.6	49.3	48.9	48.6	48.7	48.4	49.7
2009	47.1	46.9	46.6	45.8	45.7	45.2	44.3	44.2	43.4	43.5	43.5	43.5	45.0
2010	43.1	43.1	43.5	43.4	43.6	43.7	43.6	43.8	43.5	43.9	44.0	44.1	43.6
2011	43.9	43.9	44.0	43.9	43.9	43.9	43.8	44.2	44.2	44.3	44.6	44.7	44.1
2012	44.7	44.7	45.1	45.1	45.1	44.9	45.0	45.1	44.8	45.9	45.9	46.1	45.2
2013	45.5	45.6	46.2	45.9	46.1	46.2	46.4	46.6	46.6	47.2	47.3	47.6	46.4
2014	47.3	47.5	47.2	47.5	47.5	48.2	48.1	47.7	47.6	47.8	48.5	48.5	47.8
2015	47.6	47.5	47.9	47.6	48.3	48.2	48.1	48.6	48.2	48.5	48.5	48.8	48.2
2016	48.6	49.2	49.1	49.2	49.8	49.9	49.8	50.4	49.2	49.9	50.5	50.5	49.7
2017	50.8	52.1	52.0	51.3	51.8	51.4	50.7	51.2	49.2	50.0	50.6	50.5	51.0
Financial Activities													
2007	183.3	184.3	184.4	183.2	183.0	183.3	182.0	181.7	180.7	179.9	180.9	182.2	182.4
2008	177.5	177.6	177.7	175.2	174.5	173.3	170.7	169.4	167.9	166.6	165.9	166.0	171.9
2009	160.2	159.7	159.1	157.4	157.2	156.8	154.7	154.3	153.2	154.0	154.4	155.2	156.4
2010	151.8	152.3	152.8	152.4	152.6	153.5	153.3	153.3	152.7	154.1	155.1	156.2	153.3
2011	153.4	153.9	154.3	155.6	156.0	155.7	156.2	156.7	157.0	158.3	159.0	160.3	156.4
2012	158.4	159.1	159.7	160.7	161.3	161.6	161.4	161.7	161.1	163.1	163.8	164.9	161.4
2013	162.4	162.7	163.3	163.7	163.9	164.7	164.4	164.5	164.5	166.0	166.7	167.8	164.6
2014	165.5	166.2	166.6	167.4	168.2	168.4	168.5	168.6	168.8	171.3	172.4	173.4	168.8
2015	171.5	172.4	172.6	173.0	173.5	174.0	174.6	175.0	174.1	176.2	177.0	177.7	174.3
2016	174.4	175.3	175.4	175.7	176.1	175.6	175.8	175.9	175.9	177.1	177.9	179.7	176.2
2017	178.1	178.7	179.0	178.6	179.1	179.4	179.1	179.0	178.1	177.1	179.5	181.7	179.0
Professional and Business Services													
2007	366.6	371.6	373.9	368.7	369.5	369.4	361.9	363.7	363.6	361.8	363.4	365.9	366.7
2008	354.1	358.9	360.8	356.2	353.2	350.9	344.5	344.3	343.3	343.8	343.6	344.3	349.8
2009	327.8	327.8	325.5	321.7	320.0	320.1	316.6	317.9	318.1	321.2	325.2	326.9	322.4
2010	319.6	324.2	325.9	323.8	322.1	323.1	322.8	324.7	325.1	329.3	332.4	336.8	325.8
2011	331.4	336.2	337.7	340.6	338.5	337.3	336.1	336.8	338.7	342.6	346.5	350.0	339.4
2012	341.3	345.8	348.9	350.6	350.4	351.2	349.4	350.7	352.6	361.1	366.0	368.2	353.0
2013	360.7	366.5	368.5	369.0	369.1	368.4	368.3	370.6	370.7	376.2	382.0	383.7	371.1
2014	377.1	380.7	382.6	386.3	388.1	386.7	386.6	389.9	391.5	398.5	403.5	407.0	389.9
2015	395.1	399.4	399.7	401.4	403.2	401.3	403.3	406.0	406.4	416.1	420.5	422.5	406.2
2016	415.2	419.1	419.0	422.7	421.0	418.9	420.6	424.0	423.4	431.9	435.9	434.8	423.9
2017	429.5	432.4	432.4	434.4	434.7	434.8	433.7	433.9	422.3	440.6	441.4	443.2	434.4
Education and Health Services													
2007	312.0	315.4	316.9	317.2	319.0	318.6	314.5	317.8	321.2	322.1	324.0	326.5	318.8
2008	322.6	326.1	328.0	326.3	328.0	326.6	320.9	324.0	326.1	327.3	329.0	330.0	326.2
2009	325.4	327.2	328.7	329.4	331.5	330.2	326.3	329.0	332.2	335.6	337.0	337.0	330.8
2010	332.6	334.8	335.3	335.5	337.0	335.4	331.6	332.8	335.2	338.2	340.1	340.7	335.8
2011	338.6	341.4	341.7	344.3	343.7	340.6	334.7	336.4	340.6	342.1	343.7	343.8	341.0
2012	339.2	342.3	343.8	343.2	343.1	340.4	334.6	338.6	342.0	343.7	345.3	344.8	341.8
2013	341.9	345.5	346.5	347.9	348.1	345.8	339.8	344.1	346.9	348.7	351.2	352.1	346.5
2014	349.0	352.4	353.0	355.2	355.7	353.6	349.4	354.9	358.9	361.2	362.9	364.1	355.9
2015	360.6	363.7	364.9	366.3	368.4	365.8	361.6	364.7	369.4	373.9	376.4	376.8	367.7
2016	374.3	377.0	377.7	381.4	381.7	378.2	376.0	379.2	384.3	386.9	388.7	390.7	381.3
2017	387.0	391.0	392.2	393.7	395.8	391.1	386.5	390.2	387.0	396.2	393.4	395.6	391.6

Employment by Industry: Miami-Fort Lauderdale-West Palm Beach, FL, Selected Years, 2007–2017—*Continued*

(Numbers in thousands, not seasonally adjusted)

Industry and year	January	February	March	April	May	June	July	August	September	October	November	December	Annual average
Leisure and Hospitality													
2007	255.8	261.3	265.9	262.6	262.3	259.3	250.0	252.0	253.5	252.9	261.4	265.7	258.6
2008	262.6	267.1	270.3	266.4	263.7	259.1	248.0	247.7	247.1	247.6	254.9	258.2	257.7
2009	254.4	256.3	258.6	255.5	251.4	248.3	240.1	239.5	239.5	240.5	246.4	250.2	248.4
2010	248.9	252.8	256.4	256.0	253.4	250.8	245.4	246.9	247.4	250.5	257.2	261.2	252.2
2011	259.1	261.6	265.2	266.3	264.4	260.9	255.6	256.5	257.5	258.4	266.7	272.0	262.0
2012	271.9	275.2	280.0	279.4	278.6	275.0	268.9	269.3	269.7	273.5	281.0	285.2	275.6
2013	282.9	287.8	291.7	290.2	288.2	285.2	280.2	280.7	280.8	283.2	291.8	294.8	286.5
2014	292.8	297.3	303.0	301.4	299.6	296.6	289.6	290.4	291.8	295.9	303.9	306.0	297.4
2015	305.3	308.9	313.3	311.3	308.4	304.3	301.1	303.6	302.8	308.7	315.6	320.5	308.7
2016	318.3	324.0	328.1	326.7	322.9	317.6	312.6	313.3	315.0	316.2	322.1	326.7	320.3
2017	322.8	327.4	331.7	330.0	328.9	325.4	319.1	319.4	302.2	314.2	322.4	324.9	322.4
Other Services													
2007	107.8	109.1	110.5	107.6	108.1	108.5	106.8	107.2	107.9	109.8	111.6	113.2	109.0
2008	112.1	112.8	113.6	112.0	111.2	110.4	108.3	107.5	106.4	105.7	105.3	105.4	109.2
2009	103.3	103.2	103.2	103.0	102.4	102.1	100.9	100.6	100.6	101.1	101.8	102.4	102.1
2010	101.5	102.3	102.6	102.8	102.2	101.9	100.5	100.6	100.3	101.2	102.0	102.3	101.7
2011	101.5	102.0	102.6	103.5	103.8	102.9	103.3	103.7	104.3	105.2	106.5	107.1	103.9
2012	106.8	107.7	108.5	109.2	109.2	109.1	108.0	107.5	107.9	108.9	109.6	110.0	108.5
2013	109.4	110.6	111.2	111.7	111.5	111.6	111.1	111.1	111.7	112.8	113.9	114.7	111.8
2014	114.6	116.0	116.9	116.9	117.0	116.6	116.4	116.6	117.0	118.3	119.7	120.1	117.2
2015	119.5	120.5	121.1	121.4	121.1	121.2	120.5	120.6	121.0	121.6	123.1	123.7	121.3
2016	122.8	124.0	124.7	124.8	124.4	124.2	123.6	123.0	123.1	123.4	124.0	123.8	123.8
2017	122.5	123.5	123.8	123.8	123.9	123.4	122.7	122.2	119.0	124.1	124.4	125.7	123.3
Government													
2007	326.5	327.9	330.2	330.4	331.2	302.1	297.8	327.8	331.6	330.2	332.6	333.5	325.2
2008	330.8	333.3	333.0	331.6	332.6	303.2	298.6	325.4	327.2	326.6	328.6	329.8	325.1
2009	327.9	326.3	326.5	327.0	325.4	297.3	294.8	316.6	319.1	321.0	321.9	321.7	318.8
2010	318.3	318.8	318.7	319.8	329.2	295.6	289.1	310.2	311.5	313.6	314.1	313.4	312.7
2011	312.1	313.6	312.1	312.0	310.1	283.6	280.5	303.5	306.5	309.7	308.2	308.7	305.1
2012	305.3	306.6	305.6	305.6	304.7	279.4	276.7	298.2	302.4	305.5	305.6	305.4	300.1
2013	303.3	306.2	306.5	306.2	306.1	280.3	277.9	298.6	303.4	305.1	307.3	305.5	300.5
2014	304.0	305.9	306.7	306.7	306.0	280.4	277.6	298.2	301.9	305.0	306.7	304.9	300.3
2015	303.1	305.0	306.3	307.1	306.9	281.5	279.6	299.7	304.0	307.8	308.0	306.9	301.3
2016	306.0	308.5	308.9	311.3	310.6	286.6	285.9	305.1	311.7	312.6	314.3	312.6	306.2
2017	312.6	314.8	316.1	315.2	315.4	292.2	289.8	308.7	313.0	314.7	316.2	312.6	310.1

Employment by Industry: Philadelphia-Camden-Wilmington, PA-NJ-DE-MD, Selected Years, 2007–2017

(Numbers in thousands, not seasonally adjusted)

Industry and year	January	February	March	April	May	June	July	August	September	October	November	December	Annual average
Total Nonfarm													
2007	2,765.2	2,771.0	2,790.0	2,811.3	2,825.0	2,832.5	2,802.4	2,792.5	2,806.3	2,836.4	2,851.8	2,851.7	2,811.3
2008	2,779.4	2,789.2	2,802.2	2,830.9	2,834.5	2,834.5	2,793.8	2,784.2	2,800.2	2,820.8	2,815.9	2,808.4	2,807.8
2009	2,719.3	2,719.2	2,715.4	2,726.5	2,731.9	2,725.9	2,686.2	2,670.4	2,686.8	2,721.6	2,724.8	2,720.0	2,712.3
2010	2,649.8	2,648.5	2,668.8	2,702.9	2,726.2	2,723.9	2,685.8	2,675.1	2,693.6	2,725.2	2,737.7	2,739.9	2,698.1
2011	2,664.2	2,676.1	2,697.2	2,726.8	2,727.7	2,726.3	2,687.8	2,677.6	2,706.9	2,727.7	2,741.6	2,742.6	2,708.5
2012	2,670.8	2,686.8	2,712.5	2,726.4	2,737.7	2,739.5	2,700.8	2,698.7	2,726.3	2,753.2	2,769.5	2,769.7	2,724.3
2013	2,692.1	2,710.9	2,731.0	2,752.4	2,761.2	2,764.3	2,721.9	2,719.6	2,749.1	2,773.1	2,793.8	2,786.5	2,746.3
2014	2,714.8	2,720.0	2,743.9	2,778.0	2,792.0	2,796.8	2,756.8	2,755.1	2,790.3	2,818.7	2,837.4	2,838.1	2,778.5
2015	2,755.8	2,768.4	2,783.6	2,819.4	2,838.4	2,841.9	2,803.6	2,798.5	2,828.6	2,861.1	2,877.9	2,880.0	2,821.4
2016	2,797.9	2,811.8	2,835.6	2,869.4	2,876.3	2,878.8	2,856.8	2,851.0	2,888.2	2,907.8	2,922.1	2,924.9	2,868.4
2017	2,854.8	2,867.1	2,880.6	2,908.6	2,925.2	2,923.2	2,893.4	2,892.1	2,922.7	2,947.4	2,955.7	2,950.9	2,910.1
Total Private													
2007	2,411.3	2,410.0	2,427.2	2,448.5	2,463.8	2,474.8	2,468.6	2,462.9	2,457.6	2,475.6	2,489.0	2,490.7	2,456.7
2008	2,424.6	2,428.7	2,439.8	2,467.1	2,473.1	2,475.6	2,464.5	2,455.5	2,447.8	2,455.8	2,449.6	2,442.4	2,452.0
2009	2,360.5	2,354.8	2,348.6	2,358.6	2,367.9	2,364.7	2,351.7	2,339.1	2,331.5	2,355.4	2,356.7	2,353.3	2,353.6
2010	2,291.6	2,284.3	2,302.6	2,334.7	2,352.3	2,355.9	2,350.3	2,345.5	2,344.5	2,366.7	2,375.8	2,378.0	2,340.2
2011	2,311.3	2,318.4	2,337.6	2,366.3	2,371.8	2,374.4	2,365.4	2,359.0	2,367.3	2,378.6	2,390.6	2,391.6	2,361.0
2012	2,330.0	2,338.8	2,363.3	2,377.2	2,391.1	2,397.8	2,385.3	2,384.9	2,391.6	2,407.7	2,422.3	2,422.4	2,384.4
2013	2,354.0	2,365.7	2,383.9	2,406.0	2,415.2	2,423.8	2,409.3	2,409.7	2,416.8	2,430.8	2,449.1	2,443.4	2,409.0
2014	2,379.8	2,378.2	2,400.8	2,433.8	2,449.4	2,457.5	2,444.7	2,445.8	2,457.3	2,477.3	2,494.3	2,496.8	2,443.0
2015	2,422.1	2,428.9	2,441.5	2,476.5	2,496.4	2,503.9	2,493.1	2,488.7	2,495.4	2,522.6	2,536.9	2,539.7	2,487.1
2016	2,466.3	2,474.1	2,495.1	2,529.5	2,537.4	2,544.7	2,544.5	2,539.8	2,553.5	2,567.5	2,579.6	2,583.1	2,534.6
2017	2,520.8	2,527.1	2,538.5	2,567.4	2,584.8	2,588.2	2,579.4	2,577.3	2,587.6	2,606.0	2,610.8	2,607.0	2,574.6
Goods Producing													
2007	343.2	338.6	342.8	346.9	350.4	354.2	354.4	354.8	352.3	351.9	351.3	347.7	349.0
2008	338.1	337.2	340.0	343.8	344.0	347.4	345.5	344.3	339.5	335.6	332.1	324.7	339.4
2009	309.1	303.2	301.7	301.3	300.8	301.2	299.3	298.0	294.3	294.5	291.1	288.9	298.6
2010	279.7	275.4	279.8	286.5	289.1	291.9	292.6	292.4	290.2	290.8	289.6	286.7	287.1
2011	276.2	275.0	281.0	286.8	287.6	290.1	291.2	291.4	289.5	289.6	288.1	284.6	285.9
2012	276.3	276.0	278.9	280.8	281.6	285.1	285.3	285.8	285.0	284.3	282.2	280.9	281.9
2013	273.7	273.4	277.2	281.2	282.4	285.4	285.9	287.8	286.2	286.3	285.3	279.9	282.1
2014	274.1	272.6	278.2	282.8	285.8	288.5	289.7	289.8	288.5	288.7	288.5	286.1	284.4
2015	278.0	278.2	280.6	287.9	291.4	294.1	295.5	296.1	294.9	294.3	293.0	291.5	289.6
2016	283.6	282.8	287.2	290.8	292.9	296.4	298.0	298.1	296.9	297.7	296.5	295.0	293.0
2017	288.7	289.5	290.6	296.3	299.7	301.5	301.7	301.5	299.1	299.1	297.3	295.6	296.7
Service-Providing													
2007	2,422.0	2,432.4	2,447.2	2,464.4	2,474.6	2,478.3	2,448.0	2,437.7	2,454.0	2,484.5	2,500.5	2,504.0	2,462.3
2008	2,441.3	2,452.0	2,462.2	2,487.1	2,490.5	2,487.1	2,448.3	2,439.9	2,460.7	2,485.2	2,483.8	2,483.7	2,468.5
2009	2,410.2	2,416.0	2,413.7	2,425.2	2,431.1	2,424.7	2,386.9	2,372.4	2,392.5	2,427.1	2,433.7	2,431.1	2,413.7
2010	2,370.1	2,373.1	2,389.0	2,416.4	2,437.1	2,432.0	2,393.2	2,382.7	2,403.4	2,434.4	2,448.1	2,453.2	2,411.1
2011	2,388.0	2,401.1	2,416.2	2,440.0	2,440.1	2,436.2	2,396.6	2,386.2	2,417.4	2,438.1	2,453.5	2,458.0	2,422.6
2012	2,394.5	2,410.8	2,433.6	2,445.6	2,456.1	2,454.4	2,415.5	2,412.9	2,441.3	2,468.9	2,487.3	2,488.8	2,442.5
2013	2,418.4	2,437.5	2,453.8	2,471.2	2,478.8	2,478.9	2,436.0	2,431.8	2,462.9	2,486.8	2,508.5	2,506.6	2,464.3
2014	2,440.7	2,447.4	2,465.7	2,495.2	2,506.2	2,508.3	2,467.1	2,465.3	2,501.8	2,530.0	2,548.9	2,552.0	2,494.1
2015	2,477.8	2,490.2	2,503.0	2,531.5	2,547.0	2,547.8	2,508.1	2,502.4	2,533.7	2,566.8	2,584.9	2,588.5	2,531.8
2016	2,514.3	2,529.0	2,548.4	2,578.6	2,583.4	2,582.4	2,558.8	2,552.9	2,591.3	2,610.1	2,625.6	2,629.9	2,575.4
2017	2,566.1	2,577.6	2,590.0	2,612.3	2,625.5	2,621.7	2,591.7	2,590.6	2,623.6	2,648.3	2,658.4	2,655.3	2,613.4
Mining, Logging, and Construction													
2007	121.7	117.9	121.7	126.1	128.9	131.3	132.5	133.3	132.4	131.8	129.9	125.9	127.8
2008	120.4	118.6	121.2	126.0	127.2	128.5	128.6	128.2	125.3	123.1	120.1	114.9	123.5
2009	104.6	101.9	103.2	104.3	105.1	106.2	106.8	106.3	103.7	103.7	101.0	98.6	103.8
2010	92.0	89.1	93.5	99.4	101.6	103.1	104.6	104.6	103.1	103.7	102.7	99.3	99.7
2011	90.6	90.0	95.2	100.8	101.5	103.2	104.9	105.2	104.4	104.6	103.3	99.9	100.3
2012	93.4	93.5	96.0	98.2	98.9	101.4	102.2	102.9	103.0	102.6	101.3	99.8	99.4
2013	94.3	94.1	98.1	101.5	102.4	104.3	105.4	106.9	105.8	106.0	104.7	99.3	101.9
2014	95.3	94.0	99.1	104.2	106.0	107.9	109.5	109.3	108.8	109.1	108.4	105.5	104.8
2015	99.1	99.3	101.4	108.8	111.4	113.4	114.9	115.7	115.2	115.4	114.0	112.1	110.1
2016	106.0	104.9	109.6	112.7	114.2	116.3	118.0	118.3	117.8	118.6	117.1	115.0	114.0
2017	110.3	111.1	112.0	116.7	119.4	120.0	120.1	119.9	118.9	118.4	116.8	113.8	116.5

Employment by Industry: Philadelphia-Camden-Wilmington, PA-NJ-DE-MD, 2007–2017—*Continued*

(Numbers in thousands, not seasonally adjusted)

Industry and year	January	February	March	April	May	June	July	August	September	October	November	December	Annual average
Manufacturing													
2007	221.5	220.7	221.1	220.8	221.5	222.9	221.9	221.5	219.9	220.1	221.4	221.8	221.3
2008	217.7	218.6	218.8	217.8	216.8	218.9	216.9	216.1	214.2	212.5	212.0	209.8	215.8
2009	204.5	201.3	198.5	197.0	195.7	195.0	192.5	191.7	190.6	190.8	190.1	190.3	194.8
2010	187.7	186.3	186.3	187.1	187.5	188.8	188.0	187.8	187.1	187.1	186.9	187.4	187.3
2011	185.6	185.0	185.8	186.0	186.1	186.9	186.3	186.2	185.1	185.0	184.8	184.7	185.6
2012	182.9	182.5	182.9	182.6	182.7	183.7	183.1	182.9	182.0	181.7	180.9	181.1	182.4
2013	179.4	179.3	179.1	179.7	180.0	181.1	180.5	180.9	180.4	180.3	180.6	180.6	180.2
2014	178.8	178.6	179.1	178.6	179.8	180.6	180.2	180.5	179.7	179.6	180.1	180.6	179.7
2015	178.9	178.9	179.2	179.1	180.0	180.7	180.6	180.4	179.7	178.9	179.0	179.4	179.6
2016	177.6	177.9	177.6	178.1	178.7	180.1	180.0	179.8	179.1	179.1	179.4	180.0	179.0
2017	178.4	178.4	178.6	179.6	180.3	181.5	181.6	181.6	180.2	180.7	180.5	181.8	180.3
Trade, Transportation, and Utilities													
2007	531.0	521.6	523.6	524.5	529.5	532.8	529.6	527.5	527.3	531.8	544.3	552.1	531.3
2008	532.4	522.6	524.3	525.7	528.9	529.5	523.9	522.2	522.8	527.0	530.4	536.5	527.2
2009	510.3	502.0	499.0	496.8	501.1	503.4	496.1	494.8	497.0	503.0	512.3	517.7	502.8
2010	498.0	488.9	492.3	495.4	500.5	503.2	496.9	495.7	496.8	502.2	512.1	520.8	500.2
2011	499.6	494.5	495.5	499.3	501.1	502.4	497.1	496.5	498.7	502.6	514.2	521.7	501.9
2012	501.4	496.3	499.8	499.4	505.2	505.8	501.3	501.2	502.6	507.9	521.9	526.4	505.8
2013	504.8	499.7	501.6	503.2	506.8	509.5	504.8	505.2	507.1	512.0	525.1	532.2	509.3
2014	509.4	503.6	507.1	509.4	513.5	516.7	510.5	510.9	512.0	517.2	530.7	538.0	514.9
2015	512.2	506.5	508.5	512.2	517.2	521.0	515.0	515.3	515.9	521.7	534.8	541.3	518.5
2016	516.5	511.5	513.5	516.1	519.8	521.0	518.9	518.9	520.1	524.6	537.7	544.8	522.0
2017	523.0	515.4	515.1	517.6	520.3	522.1	518.4	520.1	522.0	525.5	537.2	542.1	523.2
Wholesale Trade													
2007	128.7	128.2	129.0	130.0	130.2	131.4	131.8	131.3	130.4	130.5	131.0	131.4	130.3
2008	130.0	129.8	130.2	130.4	131.0	131.4	131.5	131.0	130.0	130.1	129.1	128.8	130.3
2009	127.2	126.2	125.8	124.9	124.7	124.6	123.5	122.8	121.8	122.0	121.7	121.8	123.9
2010	120.5	119.8	120.2	120.8	121.4	121.7	121.6	121.5	120.9	121.1	121.1	121.3	121.0
2011	120.3	120.4	121.1	121.9	122.1	122.7	123.0	123.0	122.4	122.6	122.6	123.0	122.1
2012	121.0	121.3	122.1	122.2	122.5	123.2	122.8	122.5	121.7	121.9	121.8	122.1	122.1
2013	120.5	120.6	121.2	121.5	122.1	122.6	122.0	121.5	121.7	121.2	121.5	121.9	121.5
2014	120.3	120.5	120.9	121.0	121.5	122.3	121.6	121.2	120.3	119.9	120.3	120.8	120.9
2015	118.1	117.9	118.0	118.5	119.3	119.9	119.6	119.7	118.8	118.9	118.8	119.0	118.9
2016	117.6	117.5	117.5	117.7	118.1	118.2	118.7	118.6	118.0	117.8	118.0	118.0	118.0
2017	117.8	117.4	117.7	118.4	118.8	119.6	119.3	119.3	118.8	119.0	119.4	119.5	118.8
Retail Trade													
2007	307.5	299.0	299.8	300.2	304.1	305.9	305.1	304.2	302.0	307.3	318.4	324.3	306.5
2008	308.0	298.7	300.0	300.4	302.7	303.9	301.0	300.6	298.8	302.6	307.2	312.0	303.0
2009	291.7	285.0	282.9	281.7	286.0	287.8	285.7	285.6	284.2	289.1	298.0	302.2	288.3
2010	287.0	278.9	282.1	284.0	288.1	290.1	288.3	288.0	285.0	289.8	299.1	305.1	288.8
2011	288.5	283.4	283.4	286.0	287.0	287.8	285.8	286.2	284.3	288.1	298.8	304.1	288.6
2012	289.8	284.0	286.4	287.0	291.0	291.6	290.6	291.3	288.9	292.9	305.9	308.4	292.3
2013	292.0	286.9	287.8	288.6	291.0	293.3	292.5	293.4	291.0	295.3	306.6	311.4	294.2
2014	294.0	288.7	291.1	292.6	295.4	297.7	296.5	297.2	294.5	298.8	310.0	314.4	297.6
2015	296.4	291.0	292.6	294.9	298.7	301.7	298.8	299.0	295.9	300.2	311.0	314.1	299.5
2016	297.3	292.9	294.7	296.5	299.3	300.9	301.1	301.1	296.8	300.2	309.2	312.9	300.2
2017	298.3	293.1	292.5	294.6	296.1	297.5	297.1	297.2	294.0	296.5	305.2	307.5	297.5
Transportation and Utilities													
2007	94.8	94.4	94.8	94.3	95.2	95.5	92.7	92.0	94.9	94.0	94.9	96.4	94.5
2008	94.4	94.1	94.1	94.9	95.2	94.2	91.4	90.6	94.0	94.3	94.1	95.7	93.9
2009	91.4	90.8	90.3	90.2	90.4	91.0	86.9	86.4	91.0	91.9	92.6	93.7	90.6
2010	90.5	90.2	90.0	90.6	91.0	91.4	87.0	86.2	90.9	91.3	91.9	94.4	90.5
2011	90.8	90.7	91.0	91.4	92.0	91.9	88.3	87.3	92.0	91.9	92.8	94.6	91.2
2012	90.6	91.0	91.3	90.2	91.7	91.0	87.9	87.4	92.0	93.1	94.2	95.9	91.4
2013	92.3	92.2	92.6	93.1	93.7	93.6	90.3	90.3	94.4	95.5	97.0	98.9	93.7
2014	95.1	94.4	95.1	95.8	96.6	96.7	92.4	92.5	97.2	98.5	100.4	102.8	96.5
2015	97.7	97.6	97.9	98.8	99.2	99.4	96.6	96.6	101.2	102.6	105.0	108.2	100.1
2016	101.6	101.1	101.3	101.9	102.4	101.9	99.1	99.2	105.3	106.6	110.5	113.9	103.7
2017	106.9	104.9	104.9	104.6	105.4	105.0	102.0	103.6	109.2	110.0	112.6	115.1	107.0

Employment by Industry: Philadelphia-Camden-Wilmington, PA-NJ-DE-MD, 2007–2017—*Continued*

(Numbers in thousands, not seasonally adjusted)

Industry and year	January	February	March	April	May	June	July	August	September	October	November	December	Annual average
Information													
2007	56.4	56.4	56.5	57.1	57.3	58.1	57.8	58.1	58.9	58.2	58.3	58.8	57.7
2008	57.8	57.8	57.6	57.9	57.9	57.6	57.3	57.1	56.5	56.3	56.2	56.1	57.2
2009	55.4	55.1	54.8	54.5	54.3	54.3	54.0	53.6	53.2	53.3	52.7	52.9	54.0
2010	51.8	51.4	51.7	51.9	51.8	52.4	52.2	51.8	51.9	51.1	51.0	51.3	51.7
2011	50.2	50.2	50.0	50.6	50.4	50.8	50.7	47.7	50.9	50.3	50.7	50.1	50.2
2012	49.7	49.5	49.9	49.5	49.4	49.8	49.8	50.4	49.6	49.2	50.1	49.5	49.7
2013	49.2	49.3	49.1	48.3	48.2	48.0	48.0	48.1	47.2	47.2	47.2	47.4	48.1
2014	46.5	46.4	46.2	46.4	46.3	46.6	46.6	46.6	46.3	46.4	46.4	46.8	46.5
2015	45.9	46.1	46.4	46.1	46.0	46.5	46.8	46.9	46.5	46.4	46.5	47.0	46.4
2016	46.3	46.2	46.1	46.6	44.5	47.1	47.3	47.1	46.2	46.4	46.3	46.5	46.4
2017	46.2	46.3	45.9	46.0	46.4	46.6	46.3	46.2	45.3	44.9	45.0	45.2	45.9
Financial Activities													
2007	219.6	219.6	219.6	219.9	220.0	221.7	222.8	222.1	219.7	220.0	220.0	220.4	220.5
2008	217.8	218.0	218.2	218.1	217.9	218.9	219.4	218.2	215.3	214.1	213.6	212.7	216.9
2009	210.2	209.2	208.4	208.2	208.1	208.3	207.9	206.1	204.0	203.4	202.6	202.1	206.5
2010	200.4	199.8	199.7	199.6	200.3	201.0	201.6	201.4	200.0	200.3	200.5	201.5	200.5
2011	199.6	198.9	198.9	198.9	198.8	199.7	200.6	200.1	199.2	198.7	198.4	199.3	199.3
2012	198.1	198.0	198.5	198.6	199.5	201.1	202.0	202.1	200.8	200.9	201.5	202.4	200.3
2013	201.7	202.5	202.5	202.8	202.9	204.7	205.0	204.7	202.8	202.5	202.7	203.2	203.2
2014	201.6	201.5	201.6	202.2	203.2	205.3	205.8	206.0	204.6	205.1	205.7	207.0	204.1
2015	205.3	205.9	206.3	207.0	208.0	209.9	210.9	210.3	209.0	208.9	209.5	210.2	208.4
2016	209.2	209.4	209.8	210.2	210.7	213.0	213.5	213.8	212.2	212.4	213.1	213.7	211.8
2017	212.1	212.5	212.8	213.0	213.7	216.5	216.8	217.0	215.5	215.0	215.0	215.6	214.6
Professional and Business Services													
2007	417.9	418.6	422.9	430.9	432.9	436.1	434.5	434.9	432.1	435.8	438.8	438.5	431.2
2008	425.7	425.0	429.0	435.7	436.0	437.3	434.8	434.3	431.1	431.2	428.6	425.5	431.2
2009	411.9	409.2	408.6	412.3	410.8	410.4	407.9	407.1	403.4	409.8	410.2	407.7	409.1
2010	396.7	397.6	399.8	408.2	410.0	412.1	411.4	411.7	410.2	414.5	415.8	415.4	408.6
2011	406.9	406.8	410.7	419.2	418.3	420.9	418.5	418.6	419.7	422.3	423.5	422.4	417.3
2012	410.4	411.7	416.8	421.7	423.0	426.2	424.6	425.7	427.7	432.2	433.9	431.3	423.8
2013	417.8	420.1	425.1	431.1	432.9	436.4	431.7	432.9	432.9	437.7	441.6	437.7	431.5
2014	425.4	424.3	428.1	438.6	441.2	443.6	438.5	439.8	444.1	449.2	453.2	452.2	439.9
2015	436.6	436.5	438.7	447.5	452.0	453.2	451.2	450.3	451.6	462.1	466.0	463.1	450.7
2016	447.5	447.7	452.3	460.7	462.1	464.1	464.3	461.5	465.5	467.2	469.1	470.1	461.0
2017	455.3	454.2	457.8	464.6	468.7	471.1	467.5	466.6	470.8	476.0	475.3	472.1	466.7
Education and Health Services													
2007	511.8	523.9	525.0	525.1	522.0	513.3	513.5	511.2	520.2	532.9	533.2	531.0	521.9
2008	521.3	536.6	534.3	539.6	535.0	525.4	524.4	523.8	534.6	545.7	548.5	548.5	534.8
2009	538.9	551.4	547.5	549.9	545.9	535.8	534.3	530.8	539.8	551.5	553.9	551.3	544.3
2010	542.2	551.5	551.3	553.7	551.7	540.7	539.9	537.2	546.7	560.7	561.9	559.4	549.7
2011	547.1	560.8	561.2	561.8	558.2	547.4	545.8	543.8	556.6	565.0	567.9	567.7	556.9
2012	556.7	569.3	571.8	572.7	568.5	557.2	552.8	550.1	565.8	576.3	577.7	575.8	566.2
2013	564.6	577.4	578.9	579.1	573.4	563.6	560.4	558.5	576.5	585.6	590.4	586.1	574.5
2014	576.8	586.7	588.3	594.1	588.7	578.6	576.9	575.8	593.1	602.9	606.7	603.1	589.3
2015	593.4	604.9	603.6	609.3	604.3	594.1	591.3	587.9	604.3	615.7	618.4	616.1	603.6
2016	606.0	618.1	618.9	627.5	621.9	610.1	610.0	608.4	628.4	636.3	638.3	636.4	621.7
2017	628.4	641.2	641.1	645.3	641.4	628.2	626.6	624.8	644.3	658.2	659.4	656.5	641.3
Leisure and Hospitality													
2007	211.0	210.6	215.5	222.1	228.9	234.3	232.6	231.9	225.5	223.4	221.3	220.4	223.1
2008	210.7	210.8	215.8	225.8	231.9	237.3	237.5	234.5	227.7	226.2	220.9	219.2	224.9
2009	207.2	207.1	210.6	217.7	227.8	231.5	233.0	230.3	222.7	222.6	216.7	215.4	220.2
2010	206.3	204.1	211.0	221.4	229.8	234.4	236.4	236.1	230.4	228.4	226.1	224.0	224.0
2011	213.9	214.2	221.5	230.0	237.2	241.4	240.9	240.9	233.7	231.2	229.0	226.9	230.1
2012	219.0	219.7	228.6	234.8	243.1	250.1	248.3	248.6	240.3	237.2	235.4	236.1	236.8
2013	223.6	224.5	230.2	240.2	247.8	253.8	254.0	253.4	246.7	242.2	239.9	240.5	241.4
2014	231.2	229.1	236.1	244.1	253.0	258.6	258.2	259.0	252.0	250.6	245.9	246.7	247.0
2015	235.1	235.0	240.8	249.5	259.2	265.2	263.7	263.7	256.3	256.0	250.8	252.2	252.3
2016	240.3	240.9	248.5	258.0	265.0	271.0	271.1	271.0	264.9	262.2	258.3	257.0	259.0
2017	248.2	249.4	255.8	264.2	272.9	279.1	280.0	279.3	270.7	268.4	262.4	260.0	265.9

Employment by Industry: Philadelphia-Camden-Wilmington, PA-NJ-DE-MD, 2007–2017—*Continued*

(Numbers in thousands, not seasonally adjusted)

Industry and year	January	February	March	April	May	June	July	August	September	October	November	December	Annual average
Other Services													
2007	120.4	120.7	121.3	122.0	122.8	124.3	123.4	122.4	121.6	121.6	121.8	121.8	122.0
2008	120.8	120.7	120.6	120.5	121.5	122.2	121.7	121.1	120.3	119.7	119.3	119.2	120.6
2009	117.5	117.6	118.0	117.9	119.1	119.8	119.2	118.4	117.1	117.3	117.2	117.3	118.0
2010	116.5	115.6	117.0	118.0	119.1	120.2	119.3	119.2	118.3	118.7	118.8	118.9	118.3
2011	117.8	118.0	118.8	119.7	120.2	121.7	120.6	120.0	119.0	118.9	118.8	118.9	119.4
2012	118.4	118.3	119.0	119.7	120.8	122.5	121.2	121.0	119.8	119.7	119.6	120.0	120.0
2013	118.6	118.8	119.3	120.1	120.8	122.4	119.5	119.1	117.4	117.3	116.9	116.4	118.9
2014	114.8	114.0	115.2	116.2	117.7	119.6	118.5	117.9	116.7	117.2	117.2	116.9	116.8
2015	115.6	115.8	116.6	117.0	118.3	119.9	118.7	118.2	116.9	117.5	117.9	118.3	117.6
2016	116.9	117.5	118.8	119.6	120.5	122.0	121.4	121.0	119.3	120.7	120.3	119.6	119.8
2017	118.9	118.6	119.4	120.4	121.7	123.1	122.1	121.8	119.9	118.9	119.2	119.9	120.3
Government													
2007	353.9	361.0	362.8	362.8	361.2	357.7	333.8	329.6	348.7	360.8	362.8	361.0	354.7
2008	354.8	360.5	362.4	363.8	361.4	358.9	329.3	328.7	352.4	365.0	366.3	366.0	355.8
2009	358.8	364.4	366.8	367.9	364.0	361.2	334.5	331.3	355.3	366.2	368.1	366.7	358.8
2010	358.2	364.2	366.2	368.2	373.9	368.0	335.5	329.6	349.1	358.5	361.9	361.9	357.9
2011	352.9	357.7	359.6	360.5	355.9	351.9	322.4	318.6	339.6	349.1	351.0	351.0	347.5
2012	340.8	348.0	349.2	349.2	346.6	341.7	315.5	313.8	334.7	345.5	347.2	347.3	340.0
2013	338.1	345.2	347.1	346.4	346.0	340.5	312.6	309.9	332.3	342.3	344.7	343.1	337.4
2014	335.0	341.8	343.1	344.2	342.6	339.3	312.1	309.3	333.0	341.4	343.1	341.3	335.5
2015	333.7	339.5	342.1	342.9	342.0	338.0	310.5	309.8	333.2	338.5	341.0	340.3	334.3
2016	331.6	337.7	340.5	339.9	338.9	334.1	312.3	311.2	334.7	340.3	342.5	341.8	333.8
2017	334.0	340.0	342.1	341.2	340.4	335.0	314.0	314.8	335.1	341.4	344.9	343.9	335.6

Employment by Industry: Atlanta-Sandy Springs-Roswell, GA, Selected Years, 2007–2017

(Numbers in thousands, not seasonally adjusted)

Industry and year	January	February	March	April	May	June	July	August	September	October	November	December	Annual average
Total Nonfarm													
2007	2,427.6	2,439.9	2,451.9	2,450.1	2,461.7	2,455.5	2,451.2	2,474.1	2,470.1	2,470.2	2,482.7	2,484.6	2,460.0
2008	2,439.7	2,450.9	2,452.4	2,452.7	2,460.2	2,445.1	2,421.4	2,434.9	2,419.6	2,415.6	2,409.1	2,396.8	2,433.2
2009	2,337.5	2,331.5	2,321.8	2,315.5	2,313.0	2,294.5	2,271.6	2,274.6	2,268.6	2,274.3	2,281.0	2,278.8	2,296.9
2010	2,236.3	2,243.6	2,255.7	2,272.8	2,291.2	2,282.1	2,274.8	2,280.6	2,273.0	2,295.7	2,305.0	2,301.4	2,276.0
2011	2,248.4	2,283.2	2,299.1	2,314.2	2,322.7	2,311.4	2,305.8	2,318.4	2,318.2	2,331.2	2,343.7	2,343.4	2,311.6
2012	2,304.7	2,317.2	2,332.0	2,349.8	2,363.0	2,360.3	2,343.1	2,361.1	2,353.7	2,376.3	2,397.3	2,392.7	2,354.3
2013	2,357.3	2,373.0	2,382.1	2,401.3	2,411.0	2,409.3	2,401.8	2,424.6	2,424.0	2,448.1	2,468.5	2,470.8	2,414.3
2014	2,428.2	2,431.2	2,463.0	2,483.4	2,503.1	2,501.4	2,499.8	2,525.9	2,519.9	2,542.7	2,566.2	2,574.9	2,503.3
2015	2,520.1	2,534.9	2,546.4	2,559.1	2,579.9	2,584.1	2,576.0	2,592.8	2,590.9	2,620.5	2,635.1	2,645.6	2,582.1
2016	2,602.0	2,615.6	2,622.9	2,649.9	2,661.5	2,662.5	2,658.6	2,676.0	2,681.4	2,695.3	2,717.6	2,723.9	2,663.9
2017	2,665.5	2,681.8	2,698.1	2,711.4	2,723.5	2,731.3	2,714.6	2,737.7	2,731.2	2,752.2	2,770.3	2,767.0	2,723.7
Total Private													
2007	2,097.3	2,105.5	2,116.3	2,115.6	2,128.0	2,130.2	2,132.1	2,141.1	2,132.1	2,132.9	2,143.6	2,145.7	2,126.7
2008	2,100.7	2,106.6	2,106.5	2,107.5	2,115.6	2,108.0	2,096.1	2,096.3	2,080.2	2,069.4	2,059.7	2,050.0	2,091.4
2009	1,990.9	1,981.6	1,971.1	1,965.7	1,967.2	1,958.4	1,948.6	1,943.2	1,928.9	1,935.1	1,941.7	1,940.9	1,956.1
2010	1,899.5	1,904.8	1,915.8	1,932.3	1,945.4	1,945.0	1,951.9	1,955.5	1,945.7	1,967.1	1,972.4	1,973.1	1,942.4
2011	1,923.9	1,955.2	1,969.5	1,986.6	1,994.9	1,990.4	1,994.5	2,001.6	1,996.5	2,007.8	2,017.4	2,018.8	1,988.1
2012	1,982.8	1,993.0	2,004.3	2,023.3	2,037.9	2,039.1	2,035.8	2,045.8	2,034.5	2,054.7	2,070.9	2,070.5	2,032.7
2013	2,037.0	2,050.6	2,059.4	2,076.7	2,088.9	2,093.9	2,097.7	2,112.0	2,106.2	2,126.5	2,143.6	2,147.3	2,095.0
2014	2,111.0	2,111.8	2,140.8	2,160.5	2,179.3	2,184.4	2,192.9	2,207.7	2,198.5	2,219.2	2,238.4	2,250.4	2,182.9
2015	2,198.0	2,210.1	2,221.2	2,234.0	2,256.0	2,264.9	2,266.8	2,273.2	2,267.6	2,293.7	2,305.5	2,317.8	2,259.1
2016	2,276.5	2,287.8	2,295.4	2,321.2	2,332.8	2,336.7	2,347.0	2,351.3	2,352.4	2,364.3	2,382.8	2,391.6	2,336.7
2017	2,337.0	2,349.6	2,365.4	2,378.5	2,393.0	2,403.2	2,396.9	2,409.0	2,397.1	2,413.3	2,428.8	2,430.4	2,391.9
Goods Producing													
2007	317.0	318.6	319.3	317.8	318.7	319.4	318.0	318.9	316.5	315.8	315.0	313.1	317.3
2008	307.5	307.8	306.3	302.9	302.8	301.7	298.8	296.5	293.3	289.7	284.7	279.0	297.6
2009	267.3	264.1	259.8	255.5	253.4	250.4	244.8	242.8	241.0	239.8	238.6	236.6	249.5
2010	233.9	233.9	234.1	234.8	236.4	236.9	238.5	238.3	237.5	238.5	237.7	236.0	236.4
2011	228.4	234.6	236.4	238.8	239.5	240.2	241.2	240.5	238.9	239.4	238.4	236.9	237.8
2012	233.5	234.4	234.8	235.9	236.9	237.2	238.0	238.2	238.0	239.3	239.9	238.7	237.1
2013	236.2	237.4	239.1	238.9	241.1	242.6	244.7	245.4	246.1	246.9	248.4	247.7	242.9
2014	245.6	246.7	249.2	251.2	253.5	255.5	257.1	258.6	258.9	261.3	261.0	261.8	255.0
2015	259.2	261.4	261.7	263.6	265.5	267.7	268.6	269.3	270.3	272.3	271.9	273.7	267.1
2016	271.0	273.3	274.9	276.9	278.2	279.9	282.6	283.5	284.3	284.7	285.7	286.6	280.1
2017	284.5	286.3	287.2	287.1	288.6	290.8	290.1	290.2	290.4	294.2	296.2	296.6	290.2
Service-Providing													
2007	2,110.6	2,121.3	2,132.6	2,132.3	2,143.0	2,136.1	2,133.2	2,155.2	2,153.6	2,154.4	2,167.7	2,171.5	2,142.6
2008	2,132.2	2,143.1	2,146.1	2,149.8	2,157.4	2,143.4	2,122.6	2,138.4	2,126.3	2,125.9	2,124.4	2,117.8	2,135.6
2009	2,070.2	2,067.4	2,062.0	2,060.0	2,059.6	2,044.1	2,026.8	2,031.8	2,027.6	2,034.5	2,042.4	2,042.2	2,047.4
2010	2,002.4	2,009.7	2,021.6	2,038.0	2,054.8	2,045.2	2,036.3	2,042.3	2,035.5	2,057.2	2,067.3	2,065.4	2,039.6
2011	2,020.0	2,048.6	2,062.7	2,075.4	2,083.2	2,071.2	2,064.6	2,077.9	2,079.3	2,091.8	2,105.3	2,106.5	2,073.9
2012	2,071.2	2,082.8	2,097.2	2,113.9	2,126.1	2,123.1	2,105.1	2,122.9	2,115.7	2,137.0	2,157.4	2,154.0	2,117.2
2013	2,121.1	2,135.6	2,143.0	2,162.4	2,169.9	2,166.7	2,157.1	2,179.2	2,177.9	2,201.2	2,220.1	2,223.1	2,171.4
2014	2,182.6	2,184.5	2,213.8	2,232.2	2,249.6	2,245.9	2,242.7	2,267.3	2,261.0	2,281.4	2,305.2	2,313.1	2,248.3
2015	2,260.9	2,273.5	2,284.7	2,295.5	2,314.4	2,316.4	2,307.4	2,323.5	2,320.6	2,348.2	2,363.2	2,371.9	2,315.0
2016	2,331.0	2,342.3	2,348.0	2,373.0	2,383.3	2,382.6	2,376.0	2,392.5	2,397.1	2,410.6	2,431.9	2,437.3	2,383.8
2017	2,381.0	2,395.5	2,410.9	2,424.3	2,434.9	2,440.5	2,424.5	2,447.5	2,440.8	2,458.0	2,474.1	2,470.4	2,433.5
Mining, Logging, and Construction													
2007	1.9	1.8	1.9	1.8	1.8	1.8	1.8	1.8	1.8	1.8	1.8	1.7	1.8
2008	1.6	1.6	1.6	1.5	1.4	1.4	1.3	1.3	1.3	1.3	1.3	1.3	1.4
2009	1.2	1.2	1.2	1.2	1.2	1.2	1.2	1.2	1.2	1.2	1.2	1.1	1.2
2010	1.2	1.2	1.2	1.1	1.2	1.2	1.1	1.1	1.2	1.2	1.2	1.2	1.2
2011	1.1	1.1	1.1	1.1	1.1	1.1	1.2	1.2	1.2	1.2	1.1	1.1	1.1
2012	1.0	1.1	1.1	1.0	1.1	1.0	1.0	1.1	1.0	1.0	1.0	1.0	1.0
2013	1.0	1.0	1.1	1.1	1.1	1.1	1.2	1.2	1.2	1.2	1.2	1.2	1.1
2014	1.2	1.2	1.2	1.2	1.3	1.3	1.2	1.2	1.2	1.3	1.3	1.3	1.2
2015	1.3	1.3	1.3	1.3	1.4	1.4	1.4	1.4	1.4	1.4	1.4	1.4	1.4
2016	1.5	1.5	1.5	1.5	1.5	1.5	1.6	1.6	1.6	1.6	1.6	1.6	1.6
2017	1.6	1.6	1.6	1.6	1.6	1.6	1.6	1.6	1.6	1.6	1.6	1.6	1.6

Employment by Industry: Atlanta-Sandy Springs-Roswell, GA, Selected Years, 2007–2017—*Continued*

(Numbers in thousands, not seasonally adjusted)

Industry and year	January	February	March	April	May	June	July	August	September	October	November	December	Annual average
Construction													
2007	137.3	139.0	139.9	139.4	140.2	140.7	140.2	140.9	139.5	139.4	138.7	137.0	139.4
2008	133.0	133.6	132.5	130.7	130.9	130.3	129.2	127.8	126.0	123.6	120.4	117.1	127.9
2009	110.7	109.5	107.1	105.1	104.4	102.9	99.9	98.0	96.8	96.2	95.6	93.9	101.7
2010	91.2	91.6	91.4	92.4	92.9	92.8	93.4	93.2	92.7	92.8	92.0	89.8	92.2
2011	84.3	88.4	90.0	91.7	91.6	92.0	92.3	91.9	91.3	91.4	90.1	88.6	90.3
2012	85.6	86.4	86.5	87.3	87.1	87.4	88.0	88.2	87.9	88.9	89.4	88.0	87.6
2013	85.9	87.0	88.6	88.7	90.5	91.7	93.4	94.3	94.8	95.6	96.7	95.7	91.9
2014	94.5	95.7	97.5	98.6	99.9	101.3	102.9	103.8	104.2	105.8	105.1	105.1	101.2
2015	102.9	104.5	104.4	106.7	107.4	108.8	109.0	109.5	109.8	111.3	110.4	111.2	108.0
2016	109.1	110.9	111.8	113.0	114.1	115.5	117.6	118.1	118.9	119.0	119.2	119.3	115.5
2017	116.7	118.3	118.5	119.0	120.5	122.0	121.2	121.0	121.8	124.8	126.0	125.6	121.3
Manufacturing													
2007	177.8	177.8	177.5	176.6	176.7	176.9	176.0	176.2	175.2	174.6	174.5	174.4	176.2
2008	172.9	172.6	172.2	170.7	170.5	170.0	168.3	167.4	166.0	164.8	163.0	160.6	168.3
2009	155.4	153.4	151.5	149.2	147.8	146.3	143.7	143.6	143.0	142.4	141.8	141.6	146.6
2010	141.5	141.1	141.5	141.3	142.3	142.9	144.0	144.0	143.6	144.5	144.5	145.0	143.0
2011	143.0	145.1	145.3	146.0	146.8	147.1	147.7	147.4	146.4	146.8	147.2	147.2	146.3
2012	146.9	146.9	147.2	147.6	148.7	148.8	149.0	148.9	149.1	149.4	149.5	149.7	148.5
2013	149.3	149.4	149.4	149.1	149.5	149.8	150.1	149.9	150.1	150.1	150.5	150.8	149.8
2014	149.9	149.8	150.5	151.4	152.3	152.9	153.0	153.6	153.5	154.2	154.6	155.4	152.6
2015	155.0	155.6	156.0	155.6	156.7	157.5	158.2	158.4	159.1	159.6	160.1	161.1	157.7
2016	160.4	160.9	161.6	162.4	162.6	162.9	163.4	163.8	163.8	164.1	164.9	165.7	163.0
2017	166.2	166.4	167.1	166.5	166.5	167.2	167.3	167.6	167.0	167.8	168.6	169.4	167.3
Trade, Transportation, and Utilities													
2007	567.5	563.5	564.2	564.6	567.9	568.1	568.6	568.3	568.6	570.7	581.1	585.7	569.9
2008	567.5	565.1	565.4	561.7	562.9	560.9	560.4	559.2	556.8	554.2	557.3	558.9	560.9
2009	535.8	529.6	526.3	521.8	522.3	520.9	519.1	519.2	517.0	516.1	523.7	527.6	523.3
2010	513.2	511.2	512.3	513.0	516.3	517.0	518.1	519.2	515.7	524.1	531.7	536.1	519.0
2011	515.9	519.4	521.7	525.1	527.1	526.8	527.7	528.4	526.3	531.7	540.5	543.7	527.9
2012	528.3	526.3	528.1	531.0	534.2	533.6	533.9	534.1	531.8	536.6	549.5	551.0	534.9
2013	534.1	532.7	532.6	534.2	537.4	538.3	541.2	543.5	541.8	546.9	558.8	564.8	542.2
2014	547.7	543.9	548.1	552.9	555.3	555.9	559.1	560.3	558.3	567.6	581.8	588.9	560.0
2015	569.8	567.3	569.1	570.9	574.1	575.6	576.4	577.4	575.8	584.0	596.5	602.1	578.3
2016	584.6	581.9	583.2	584.3	586.9	587.5	589.7	589.1	588.7	594.7	609.6	617.5	591.5
2017	595.0	592.9	595.7	597.4	599.4	601.5	602.5	603.5	602.3	607.7	619.2	622.9	603.3
Wholesale Trade													
2007	159.7	160.1	160.1	160.6	160.4	160.2	161.1	161.1	160.7	160.6	160.5	160.9	160.5
2008	160.2	160.7	160.4	160.1	160.2	159.6	159.9	159.7	159.1	158.1	156.8	155.6	159.2
2009	152.9	151.3	149.6	148.3	147.2	146.1	145.6	145.1	144.6	144.6	144.3	144.4	147.0
2010	143.6	144.0	144.0	144.5	145.1	144.9	145.0	145.0	143.8	145.4	145.1	144.7	144.6
2011	143.5	144.6	144.7	145.5	146.1	145.5	146.6	146.8	146.1	147.0	147.2	146.9	145.9
2012	145.8	146.7	146.8	147.3	148.2	147.8	148.8	148.8	147.4	148.5	148.8	148.6	147.8
2013	146.9	147.6	147.3	147.9	148.4	148.4	148.7	148.9	148.1	149.8	150.6	151.1	148.6
2014	150.7	151.2	151.4	151.8	152.3	152.4	153.3	153.8	153.5	154.6	155.9	156.6	153.1
2015	155.5	156.2	156.6	156.8	157.5	157.5	157.2	157.5	156.9	158.5	158.6	158.8	157.3
2016	157.0	157.2	157.7	158.3	158.9	158.7	159.1	158.8	158.5	158.2	158.3	159.1	158.3
2017	158.0	158.7	159.4	159.7	159.9	160.6	160.7	160.4	160.3	160.7	161.6	162.4	160.2
Retail Trade													
2007	281.6	276.8	277.0	276.7	278.0	277.2	277.9	277.4	277.4	279.8	289.9	292.8	280.2
2008	278.1	274.8	275.2	272.1	272.6	271.3	271.2	270.3	268.9	268.2	272.9	274.3	272.5
2009	257.1	253.7	252.3	251.1	252.2	251.8	250.5	251.2	249.4	248.9	256.4	259.1	252.8
2010	247.2	245.0	245.9	247.1	248.7	249.2	249.7	250.0	247.8	252.9	260.0	263.0	250.5
2011	248.8	249.9	251.1	253.7	254.3	254.2	254.2	254.5	253.1	257.3	265.2	267.4	255.3
2012	256.2	253.9	255.2	256.4	258.2	257.9	257.5	257.5	256.8	260.2	271.6	271.7	259.4
2013	259.2	258.1	258.6	259.8	261.8	262.8	264.5	266.3	265.7	269.2	278.8	282.6	265.6
2014	268.2	264.6	266.8	268.3	269.6	270.4	271.3	271.6	270.4	275.4	287.4	290.9	272.9
2015	274.8	273.5	275.4	277.5	279.0	280.2	279.8	280.3	279.5	283.9	294.5	296.7	281.3
2016	282.4	280.5	282.1	283.7	284.7	284.5	285.8	285.1	284.5	289.5	300.4	302.7	287.2
2017	288.6	286.7	287.7	288.7	289.4	290.0	289.6	289.6	287.1	291.8	299.2	299.6	290.7

Employment by Industry: Atlanta-Sandy Springs-Roswell, GA, Selected Years, 2007–2017—*Continued*

(Numbers in thousands, not seasonally adjusted)

Industry and year	January	February	March	April	May	June	July	August	September	October	November	December	Annual average
Transportation and Utilities													
2007	126.2	126.6	127.1	127.3	129.5	130.7	129.6	129.8	130.5	130.3	130.7	132.0	129.2
2008	129.2	129.6	129.8	129.5	130.1	130.0	129.3	129.2	128.8	127.9	127.6	129.0	129.2
2009	125.8	124.6	124.4	122.4	122.9	123.0	123.0	122.9	123.0	122.6	123.0	124.1	123.5
2010	122.4	122.2	122.4	121.4	122.5	122.9	123.4	124.2	124.1	125.8	126.6	128.4	123.9
2011	123.6	124.9	125.9	125.9	126.7	127.1	126.9	127.1	127.1	127.4	128.1	129.4	126.7
2012	126.3	125.7	126.1	127.3	127.8	127.9	127.6	127.8	127.6	127.9	129.1	130.7	127.7
2013	128.0	127.0	126.7	126.5	127.2	127.1	128.0	128.3	128.0	127.9	129.4	131.1	127.9
2014	128.8	128.1	129.9	132.8	133.4	133.1	134.5	134.9	134.4	137.6	138.5	141.4	134.0
2015	139.5	137.6	137.1	136.6	137.6	137.9	139.4	139.6	139.4	141.6	143.4	146.6	139.7
2016	145.2	144.2	143.4	142.3	143.3	144.3	144.8	145.2	145.7	147.0	150.9	155.7	146.0
2017	148.4	147.5	148.6	149.0	150.1	150.9	152.2	153.5	154.9	155.2	158.4	160.9	152.5
Information													
2007	82.0	81.8	81.8	81.1	81.6	81.6	81.3	81.4	81.5	80.5	80.9	81.0	81.4
2008	79.1	79.6	79.9	79.9	80.4	80.6	79.7	79.5	78.9	78.1	78.2	78.1	79.3
2009	79.5	79.4	79.0	78.7	78.5	78.0	77.1	76.7	76.2	75.5	75.5	75.9	77.5
2010	74.8	74.8	75.1	75.8	76.2	75.9	76.0	75.9	75.2	75.4	75.9	76.1	75.6
2011	77.5	77.6	78.0	78.2	78.1	77.4	78.2	78.4	78.1	78.6	80.1	78.3	78.2
2012	78.0	79.2	79.0	78.7	79.6	79.4	80.0	80.3	80.2	81.6	81.9	81.9	80.0
2013	80.4	81.3	81.4	82.1	82.6	81.8	82.9	83.3	83.3	85.5	85.3	85.2	82.9
2014	85.5	85.8	86.8	87.3	87.6	88.1	88.3	88.3	87.7	89.8	90.4	90.5	88.0
2015	87.6	88.4	89.1	90.0	91.9	92.1	94.3	92.1	90.6	95.0	95.8	96.1	91.9
2016	91.9	94.0	93.1	95.8	95.1	95.4	97.3	95.2	96.4	96.5	98.6	96.7	95.5
2017	96.9	98.8	98.8	99.0	99.9	99.3	97.7	100.5	98.1	99.7	100.2	99.5	99.0
Financial Activities													
2007	169.1	170.6	170.9	170.2	170.1	169.9	170.0	169.9	168.6	168.4	168.3	168.0	169.5
2008	164.3	164.8	164.3	164.0	163.9	163.2	163.2	162.2	160.4	161.0	159.4	158.7	162.5
2009	156.3	155.6	154.6	153.9	154.0	153.8	153.1	152.2	150.9	150.6	150.4	150.4	153.0
2010	148.5	148.5	148.3	148.1	148.5	148.4	148.3	148.8	148.1	149.6	149.8	150.2	148.8
2011	149.4	150.0	150.3	150.7	150.9	151.0	151.2	151.7	151.7	152.4	152.6	152.8	151.2
2012	152.7	153.2	153.6	153.6	153.4	153.7	153.9	154.0	153.0	154.5	155.5	155.6	153.9
2013	153.6	154.2	154.8	155.6	156.0	156.5	156.7	157.2	156.1	157.5	158.6	158.5	156.3
2014	156.5	156.9	157.4	157.8	158.4	159.0	159.3	159.9	158.9	160.6	160.7	160.9	158.9
2015	159.9	160.3	160.7	161.4	161.8	162.3	162.7	162.2	161.5	163.2	163.3	163.5	161.9
2016	163.4	163.5	163.5	164.6	165.7	166.3	167.8	168.0	167.7	168.7	168.9	169.2	166.4
2017	167.1	167.9	168.6	169.2	170.1	171.4	171.4	171.4	171.3	170.9	170.7	170.4	170.0
Professional and Business Services													
2007	401.2	404.7	408.4	405.1	407.3	408.8	412.6	415.8	415.1	415.3	416.6	417.5	410.7
2008	409.2	410.0	407.7	412.3	411.3	412.1	407.0	408.0	404.7	404.7	400.7	398.1	407.2
2009	380.6	378.1	375.0	373.6	372.4	373.5	375.3	372.3	370.1	378.9	380.9	381.4	376.0
2010	371.0	373.7	376.9	383.8	384.9	386.3	388.7	388.1	386.5	393.1	392.7	392.8	384.9
2011	386.3	396.7	399.9	399.9	399.4	399.7	400.8	404.0	404.7	407.3	408.2	410.0	401.4
2012	399.7	404.0	406.7	411.3	414.4	418.6	415.5	418.8	415.9	422.6	425.7	425.5	414.9
2013	418.8	426.1	427.8	431.2	431.8	435.7	434.5	438.5	438.6	445.2	448.3	447.0	435.3
2014	440.5	442.4	453.1	453.0	457.6	460.7	464.4	468.4	467.2	471.0	474.0	474.7	460.6
2015	461.7	466.3	469.0	468.2	475.1	477.8	478.2	479.8	479.4	484.6	483.1	485.1	475.7
2016	476.8	480.6	481.2	487.1	487.4	487.4	492.5	495.0	497.0	498.4	499.0	500.8	490.3
2017	487.7	491.4	494.8	496.9	497.2	501.0	500.5	503.6	500.8	503.1	504.4	501.2	498.6
Education and Health Services													
2007	239.0	241.2	241.4	242.8	242.8	240.6	241.5	245.4	246.7	249.3	250.2	250.3	244.3
2008	247.2	250.4	250.5	251.4	252.8	248.2	248.9	253.3	253.4	255.3	256.3	256.7	252.0
2009	254.7	256.1	255.1	255.8	257.2	252.5	251.5	254.9	254.3	258.5	259.4	259.2	255.8
2010	256.9	259.4	260.5	261.2	262.8	259.4	261.0	264.4	264.4	268.6	268.6	268.2	263.0
2011	263.7	267.7	268.6	273.6	273.3	268.9	269.3	273.4	275.0	278.9	279.0	279.9	272.6
2012	278.0	280.9	282.2	284.3	285.1	281.0	280.0	285.6	286.7	289.8	290.0	290.4	284.5
2013	289.7	292.4	293.0	295.4	296.0	292.2	290.6	296.4	297.7	300.8	303.0	303.3	295.9
2014	300.2	300.9	303.7	305.4	307.0	303.3	302.6	309.4	310.4	311.7	313.2	314.6	306.9
2015	312.9	314.7	315.2	316.2	317.9	315.0	313.9	319.2	320.8	326.4	328.0	328.7	319.1
2016	326.8	329.9	330.2	332.5	332.8	329.1	328.7	333.7	335.3	338.6	339.1	338.9	333.0
2017	334.2	336.9	338.6	339.8	341.2	337.7	336.8	341.8	343.1	346.5	348.4	349.2	341.2

Employment by Industry: Atlanta-Sandy Springs-Roswell, GA, Selected Years, 2007–2017—*Continued*

(Numbers in thousands, not seasonally adjusted)

Industry and year	January	February	March	April	May	June	July	August	September	October	November	December	Annual average
Leisure and Hospitality													
2007	225.1	228.4	233.2	235.8	240.7	242.5	240.6	242.0	237.3	234.8	233.7	232.9	235.6
2008	228.4	230.4	234.0	237.0	242.1	242.0	239.4	238.9	235.1	229.5	226.7	224.8	234.0
2009	217.9	219.6	222.9	227.1	230.3	230.8	229.0	227.9	224.3	220.6	219.0	216.8	223.9
2010	209.4	211.1	216.3	222.2	226.2	227.6	227.0	226.9	224.8	223.4	221.6	220.5	221.4
2011	211.2	216.1	221.4	227.8	233.4	233.3	232.9	232.4	229.4	227.2	226.3	225.7	226.4
2012	221.7	223.5	228.4	235.7	241.0	241.8	240.5	241.2	236.0	236.6	234.7	234.7	234.7
2013	231.8	233.7	238.1	245.6	249.9	252.5	253.0	253.8	249.3	250.3	247.9	248.1	246.2
2014	243.0	242.9	249.9	258.7	265.1	266.6	266.6	267.3	262.4	262.9	262.7	264.3	259.4
2015	253.3	257.2	261.6	267.8	273.2	277.2	275.0	276.2	273.0	272.4	271.4	272.5	269.2
2016	266.6	268.7	273.2	282.5	288.6	291.8	289.1	288.3	285.4	284.7	284.0	284.2	282.3
2017	274.7	277.9	283.6	289.7	296.1	300.2	297.1	297.8	291.7	290.7	290.7	290.3	290.0
Other Services													
2007	96.4	96.7	97.1	98.2	98.9	99.3	99.5	99.4	97.8	98.1	97.8	97.2	98.0
2008	97.5	98.5	98.4	98.3	99.4	99.3	98.7	98.7	97.6	96.9	96.4	95.7	98.0
2009	98.8	99.1	98.4	99.3	99.1	98.5	98.7	97.2	95.1	95.1	94.2	93.0	97.2
2010	91.8	92.2	92.3	93.4	94.1	93.5	94.3	93.9	93.5	94.4	94.4	93.2	93.4
2011	91.5	93.1	93.2	92.5	93.2	93.1	93.2	92.8	92.4	92.3	92.3	91.5	92.6
2012	90.9	91.5	91.5	92.8	93.3	93.8	94.0	93.6	92.9	93.7	93.7	92.7	92.9
2013	92.4	92.8	92.6	93.7	94.1	94.3	94.1	93.9	93.3	93.4	93.3	92.7	93.4
2014	92.0	92.3	92.6	94.2	94.8	95.3	95.5	95.5	94.7	94.3	94.6	94.7	94.2
2015	93.6	94.5	94.8	95.9	96.5	97.2	97.7	97.0	96.2	95.8	95.5	96.1	95.9
2016	95.4	95.9	96.1	97.5	98.1	99.3	99.3	98.5	97.6	98.0	97.9	97.7	97.6
2017	96.9	97.5	98.1	99.4	100.5	101.3	100.8	100.2	99.4	100.5	99.0	100.3	99.5
Government													
2007	330.3	334.4	335.6	334.5	333.7	325.3	319.1	333.0	338.0	337.3	339.1	338.9	333.3
2008	339.0	344.3	345.9	345.2	344.6	337.1	325.3	338.6	339.4	346.2	349.4	346.8	341.8
2009	346.6	349.9	350.7	349.8	345.8	336.1	323.0	331.4	339.7	339.2	339.3	337.9	340.8
2010	336.8	338.8	339.9	340.5	345.8	337.1	322.9	325.1	327.3	328.6	332.6	328.3	333.6
2011	324.5	328.0	329.6	327.6	327.8	321.0	311.3	316.8	321.7	323.4	326.3	324.6	323.6
2012	321.9	324.2	327.7	326.5	325.1	321.2	307.3	315.3	319.2	321.6	326.4	322.2	321.6
2013	320.3	322.4	322.7	324.6	322.1	315.4	304.1	312.6	317.8	321.6	324.9	323.5	319.3
2014	317.2	319.4	322.2	322.9	323.8	317.0	306.9	318.2	321.4	323.5	327.8	324.5	320.4
2015	322.1	324.8	325.2	325.1	323.9	319.2	309.2	319.6	323.3	326.8	329.6	327.8	323.1
2016	325.5	327.8	327.5	328.7	328.7	325.8	311.6	324.7	329.0	331.0	334.8	332.3	327.3
2017	328.5	332.2	332.7	332.9	330.5	328.1	317.7	328.7	334.1	338.9	341.5	336.6	331.9

Employment by Industry: Boston-Cambridge-Newton, MA-NH, Selected Years, 2007–2017

(Numbers in thousands, not seasonally adjusted)

Industry and year	January	February	March	April	May	June	July	August	September	October	November	December	Annual average
Total Nonfarm													
2007	1,607.3	1,612.2	1,618.6	1,637.3	1,645.2	1,657.3	1,646.2	1,644.1	1,650.4	1,665.4	1,673.5	1,674.5	1,644.3
2008	1,632.6	1,639.9	1,645.6	1,661.4	1,666.0	1,674.3	1,664.4	1,659.8	1,664.6	1,674.2	1,669.4	1,661.8	1,659.5
2009	1,606.3	1,604.8	1,602.1	1,613.3	1,614.3	1,614.1	1,602.8	1,594.8	1,605.5	1,618.2	1,619.4	1,620.5	1,609.7
2010	1,587.4	1,591.2	1,596.7	1,615.6	1,625.0	1,622.8	1,616.9	1,611.0	1,618.6	1,637.6	1,641.4	1,643.1	1,617.3
2011	1,601.4	1,607.0	1,615.0	1,639.0	1,642.1	1,646.0	1,649.0	1,642.9	1,655.3	1,666.9	1,671.1	1,672.4	1,642.3
2012	1,631.2	1,636.5	1,647.4	1,662.0	1,669.8	1,683.0	1,677.0	1,673.5	1,682.0	1,695.7	1,703.0	1,701.1	1,671.9
2013	1,659.9	1,664.4	1,676.8	1,701.4	1,710.3	1,721.5	1,707.3	1,705.5	1,711.5	1,728.9	1,736.8	1,734.0	1,704.9
2014	1,687.0	1,697.3	1,707.0	1,731.7	1,742.5	1,751.4	1,746.3	1,738.8	1,747.5	1,767.7	1,776.3	1,777.2	1,739.2
2015	1,726.9	1,728.0	1,743.7	1,771.6	1,785.6	1,795.4	1,792.9	1,784.3	1,781.5	1,806.1	1,812.3	1,812.7	1,778.4
2016	1,763.9	1,774.5	1,785.8	1,811.5	1,819.7	1,829.1	1,835.7	1,829.0	1,829.6	1,838.4	1,845.1	1,846.8	1,817.4
2017	1,800.0	1,807.8	1,816.5	1,838.9	1,847.6	1,864.9	1,854.4	1,847.2	1,847.3	1,865.2	1,865.9	1,862.7	1,843.2
Total Private													
2007	1,415.6	1,419.2	1,425.1	1,443.1	1,450.7	1,463.1	1,463.9	1,464.1	1,459.6	1,472.2	1,479.2	1,480.4	1,453.0
2008	1,439.2	1,444.7	1,450.1	1,465.4	1,469.9	1,478.0	1,478.2	1,475.6	1,470.5	1,478.5	1,473.0	1,465.8	1,465.7
2009	1,412.1	1,409.1	1,406.4	1,414.5	1,416.5	1,417.7	1,417.8	1,412.6	1,412.7	1,423.5	1,424.6	1,424.9	1,416.0
2010	1,393.5	1,396.2	1,401.2	1,418.9	1,423.6	1,425.0	1,431.0	1,427.7	1,426.0	1,442.4	1,444.7	1,446.8	1,423.1
2011	1,408.0	1,411.7	1,419.7	1,444.2	1,446.9	1,451.5	1,465.0	1,461.4	1,462.8	1,473.5	1,477.4	1,477.5	1,450.0
2012	1,438.7	1,442.1	1,452.2	1,468.3	1,475.9	1,489.2	1,492.9	1,491.2	1,489.9	1,502.6	1,507.8	1,506.9	1,479.8
2013	1,469.4	1,470.8	1,483.0	1,506.3	1,514.7	1,526.5	1,524.2	1,524.3	1,518.9	1,532.4	1,538.6	1,536.4	1,512.1
2014	1,492.6	1,499.7	1,509.1	1,531.7	1,542.8	1,552.5	1,559.1	1,553.7	1,551.3	1,568.9	1,574.9	1,577.1	1,542.8
2015	1,531.3	1,530.5	1,544.5	1,571.8	1,586.3	1,596.4	1,605.4	1,600.9	1,586.9	1,608.6	1,613.5	1,613.5	1,582.5
2016	1,568.2	1,576.3	1,585.0	1,612.2	1,619.5	1,629.4	1,645.6	1,642.0	1,631.0	1,639.2	1,643.7	1,646.4	1,619.9
2017	1,603.4	1,609.4	1,618.1	1,640.0	1,647.9	1,665.6	1,668.5	1,663.7	1,651.6	1,667.9	1,666.6	1,664.4	1,647.3
Goods Producing													
2007	151.7	149.6	150.6	152.5	155.8	158.8	159.1	159.5	158.3	157.3	156.7	154.6	155.4
2008	149.0	147.2	147.8	150.1	152.5	154.1	154.3	154.0	152.3	150.4	148.0	144.5	150.4
2009	136.5	133.6	132.1	133.5	133.9	134.8	134.9	134.8	133.3	132.4	131.6	130.0	133.5
2010	125.0	123.4	124.0	126.9	129.3	131.5	133.3	133.1	132.0	132.0	131.7	130.5	129.4
2011	125.2	124.2	125.2	128.5	130.4	132.6	134.5	134.4	132.2	131.6	130.7	129.8	129.9
2012	126.3	125.0	126.1	129.3	131.1	134.2	136.2	136.2	135.0	135.6	135.5	134.8	132.1
2013	130.3	129.1	130.4	133.5	136.9	139.3	140.2	140.5	139.2	138.6	137.9	137.0	136.1
2014	132.7	131.8	132.5	135.0	138.3	140.7	142.8	142.7	141.2	141.2	141.7	141.3	138.5
2015	137.5	136.0	137.2	141.3	144.4	147.3	148.0	148.0	145.7	146.6	146.3	145.5	143.7
2016	142.3	140.0	141.1	144.2	146.3	148.8	150.3	150.0	148.6	148.3	147.7	147.2	146.2
2017	142.2	140.6	140.9	143.4	145.7	148.8	150.7	151.2	149.8	150.7	150.2	149.1	146.9
Service-Providing													
2007	1,455.6	1,462.6	1,468.0	1,484.8	1,489.4	1,498.5	1,487.1	1,484.6	1,492.1	1,508.1	1,516.8	1,519.9	1,489.0
2008	1,483.6	1,492.7	1,497.8	1,511.3	1,513.5	1,520.2	1,510.1	1,505.8	1,512.3	1,523.8	1,521.4	1,517.3	1,509.2
2009	1,469.8	1,471.2	1,470.0	1,479.8	1,480.4	1,479.3	1,467.9	1,460.0	1,472.2	1,485.8	1,487.8	1,490.5	1,476.2
2010	1,462.4	1,467.8	1,472.7	1,488.7	1,495.7	1,491.3	1,483.6	1,477.9	1,486.6	1,505.6	1,509.7	1,512.6	1,487.9
2011	1,476.2	1,482.8	1,489.8	1,510.5	1,511.7	1,513.4	1,514.5	1,508.5	1,523.1	1,535.3	1,540.4	1,542.6	1,512.4
2012	1,504.9	1,511.5	1,521.3	1,532.7	1,538.7	1,548.8	1,540.8	1,537.3	1,547.0	1,560.1	1,567.5	1,566.3	1,539.7
2013	1,529.6	1,535.3	1,546.4	1,567.9	1,573.4	1,582.2	1,567.1	1,565.0	1,572.3	1,590.3	1,598.9	1,597.0	1,568.8
2014	1,554.3	1,565.5	1,574.5	1,596.7	1,604.2	1,610.7	1,603.5	1,596.1	1,606.3	1,626.5	1,634.6	1,635.9	1,600.7
2015	1,589.4	1,592.0	1,606.5	1,630.3	1,641.2	1,648.1	1,644.9	1,636.3	1,635.8	1,659.5	1,666.0	1,667.2	1,634.8
2016	1,621.6	1,634.5	1,644.7	1,667.3	1,673.4	1,680.3	1,685.4	1,679.0	1,681.0	1,690.1	1,697.4	1,699.6	1,671.2
2017	1,657.8	1,667.2	1,675.6	1,695.5	1,701.9	1,716.1	1,703.7	1,696.0	1,697.5	1,714.5	1,715.7	1,713.6	1,696.3
Mining, Logging, and Construction													
2007	57.2	55.1	56.3	58.8	61.7	64.1	65.3	65.5	64.9	64.2	63.6	61.3	61.5
2008	56.8	55.5	56.6	59.0	61.3	62.5	63.8	63.4	62.2	60.7	58.9	56.4	59.8
2009	50.3	48.4	47.9	49.7	50.8	51.6	52.4	52.2	50.9	50.2	49.1	47.3	50.1
2010	43.8	42.5	43.2	46.0	47.9	49.4	51.0	50.8	49.9	49.3	48.8	47.5	47.5
2011	43.5	42.6	43.4	46.7	48.8	50.5	52.2	52.4	51.1	50.3	49.7	48.7	48.3
2012	45.2	44.1	45.1	47.9	49.5	51.7	53.9	54.1	53.4	53.8	53.5	52.4	50.4
2013	49.1	48.3	49.3	52.2	55.1	56.8	58.3	58.5	57.6	57.1	56.3	55.2	54.5
2014	52.0	51.2	51.7	54.6	57.7	59.6	61.5	61.6	60.6	60.9	61.0	60.4	57.7
2015	57.3	55.6	56.7	60.9	63.8	65.6	66.6	66.8	65.5	66.1	65.9	65.2	63.0
2016	62.6	60.9	62.0	65.1	67.0	68.7	70.0	69.5	68.5	68.2	67.7	66.9	66.4
2017	62.3	61.0	61.9	64.6	66.6	68.6	70.3	70.8	70.0	70.9	70.5	68.8	67.2

Employment by Industry: Boston-Cambridge-Newton, MA-NH, Selected Years, 2007–2017—*Continued*

(Numbers in thousands, not seasonally adjusted)

Industry and year	January	February	March	April	May	June	July	August	September	October	November	December	Annual average
Manufacturing													
2007	94.5	94.5	94.3	93.7	94.1	94.7	93.8	94.0	93.4	93.1	93.1	93.3	93.9
2008	92.2	91.7	91.2	91.1	91.2	91.6	90.5	90.6	90.1	89.7	89.1	88.1	90.6
2009	86.2	85.2	84.2	83.8	83.1	83.2	82.5	82.6	82.4	82.2	82.5	82.7	83.4
2010	81.2	80.9	80.8	80.9	81.4	82.1	82.3	82.3	82.1	82.7	82.9	83.0	81.9
2011	81.7	81.6	81.8	81.8	81.6	82.1	82.3	82.0	81.1	81.3	81.0	81.1	81.6
2012	81.1	80.9	81.0	81.4	81.6	82.5	82.3	82.1	81.6	81.8	82.0	82.4	81.7
2013	81.2	80.8	81.1	81.3	81.8	82.5	81.9	82.0	81.6	81.5	81.6	81.8	81.6
2014	80.7	80.6	80.8	80.4	80.6	81.1	81.3	81.1	80.6	80.3	80.7	80.9	80.8
2015	80.2	80.4	80.5	80.4	80.6	81.7	81.4	81.2	80.2	80.5	80.4	80.3	80.7
2016	79.7	79.1	79.1	79.1	79.3	80.1	80.3	80.5	80.1	80.1	80.0	80.3	79.8
2017	79.9	79.6	79.0	78.8	79.1	80.2	80.4	80.4	79.8	79.8	79.7	80.3	79.8
Trade, Transportation, and Utilities													
2007	240.1	236.0	236.3	236.1	238.5	241.8	238.7	238.0	238.1	241.3	246.5	249.2	240.1
2008	241.2	236.7	236.7	238.1	239.5	242.2	239.1	238.7	238.6	240.1	241.0	243.2	239.6
2009	231.1	226.6	224.7	223.9	225.8	228.3	225.2	224.1	226.0	229.1	231.7	234.2	227.6
2010	226.8	223.4	223.5	225.7	227.7	229.6	227.8	227.1	226.6	230.0	233.0	237.0	228.2
2011	228.3	225.4	225.5	228.7	229.6	232.3	231.7	231.4	231.7	233.8	236.9	240.0	231.3
2012	231.1	226.8	227.6	228.0	230.7	233.9	231.6	231.2	231.3	234.7	239.4	241.4	232.3
2013	233.8	230.0	230.8	232.7	234.9	238.7	236.6	236.8	237.0	238.7	242.7	246.4	236.6
2014	239.0	235.7	236.1	237.5	240.0	243.1	240.3	237.5	241.0	244.4	248.8	252.3	241.3
2015	243.9	238.3	240.1	242.8	245.6	249.5	247.9	247.6	246.5	249.6	252.7	255.7	246.7
2016	247.4	243.9	244.4	247.0	249.3	253.2	251.9	251.4	250.1	250.9	254.0	258.0	250.1
2017	250.3	245.8	246.3	248.7	250.5	254.4	252.3	251.1	250.6	253.0	254.0	256.3	251.1
Wholesale Trade													
2007	61.4	61.3	61.4	61.0	61.1	61.7	61.5	61.5	60.8	61.2	61.2	61.4	61.3
2008	60.7	60.3	60.4	60.6	60.4	60.8	60.8	60.4	59.8	59.6	59.3	59.2	60.2
2009	57.6	56.7	56.3	55.8	55.5	55.7	55.4	55.0	54.4	54.8	54.5	54.3	55.5
2010	53.6	53.5	53.5	53.3	53.7	54.0	54.3	54.1	53.6	53.8	53.8	53.9	53.8
2011	53.2	53.1	53.3	53.9	53.8	53.9	54.5	54.3	53.7	53.9	53.8	53.7	53.8
2012	53.2	53.0	53.2	53.5	53.7	54.1	54.4	54.5	53.9	54.7	55.4	55.4	54.1
2013	55.1	55.0	55.2	55.6	55.5	56.0	56.6	56.6	56.2	56.5	56.5	56.5	55.9
2014	56.2	56.1	56.1	56.5	56.7	57.2	57.3	57.2	56.8	57.0	57.3	57.3	56.8
2015	56.8	56.4	56.5	57.2	57.5	58.2	59.0	58.9	58.4	58.8	59.0	59.1	58.0
2016	58.4	58.3	58.2	58.8	58.9	59.4	60.4	60.4	59.6	59.9	59.9	60.0	59.4
2017	59.5	59.3	59.4	59.3	59.5	60.1	60.3	60.0	59.5	59.9	59.8	60.9	59.8
Retail Trade													
2007	139.5	135.7	135.7	135.8	137.5	139.4	138.1	137.6	136.6	139.5	145.0	147.5	139.0
2008	141.0	137.1	136.9	137.7	138.7	140.4	139.0	139.4	138.0	140.2	142.2	144.2	139.6
2009	135.3	131.9	130.4	129.9	131.7	133.7	132.5	132.6	132.7	135.4	138.6	140.8	133.8
2010	135.2	132.1	132.2	134.0	135.0	136.3	136.0	136.2	134.5	137.7	141.0	144.2	136.2
2011	137.4	134.6	134.3	135.8	136.4	138.1	138.2	138.8	137.7	140.1	143.6	146.4	138.5
2012	139.1	135.1	135.5	135.5	137.5	139.6	138.4	138.6	137.2	140.0	144.6	145.9	138.9
2013	140.0	136.3	136.7	137.7	139.2	141.4	140.5	141.3	139.8	141.3	145.5	148.6	140.7
2014	142.4	139.3	139.3	140.3	141.8	143.8	142.6	140.7	142.1	145.5	149.6	152.1	143.3
2015	146.0	141.2	142.3	143.5	145.2	147.5	146.6	146.8	144.1	146.9	150.3	152.5	146.1
2016	146.5	143.4	143.6	144.9	146.3	148.9	148.3	148.7	145.9	147.0	150.2	153.3	147.3
2017	147.5	143.6	143.9	145.4	146.4	148.8	148.6	148.5	145.9	146.8	148.9	150.0	147.0
Transportation and Utilities													
2007	39.2	39.0	39.2	39.3	39.9	40.7	39.1	38.9	40.7	40.6	40.3	40.3	39.8
2008	39.5	39.3	39.4	39.8	40.4	41.0	39.3	38.9	40.8	40.3	39.5	39.8	39.8
2009	38.2	38.0	38.0	38.2	38.6	38.9	37.3	36.5	38.9	38.9	38.6	39.1	38.3
2010	38.0	37.8	37.8	38.4	39.0	39.3	37.5	36.8	38.5	38.5	38.2	38.9	38.2
2011	37.7	37.7	37.9	39.0	39.4	40.3	39.0	38.3	40.3	39.8	39.5	39.9	39.1
2012	38.8	38.7	38.9	39.0	39.5	40.2	38.8	38.1	40.2	40.0	39.4	40.1	39.3
2013	38.7	38.7	38.9	39.4	40.2	41.3	39.5	38.9	41.0	40.9	40.7	41.3	40.0
2014	40.4	40.3	40.7	40.7	41.5	42.1	40.4	39.6	42.1	41.9	41.9	42.9	41.2
2015	41.1	40.7	41.3	42.1	42.9	43.8	42.3	41.9	44.0	43.9	43.4	44.1	42.6
2016	42.5	42.2	42.6	43.3	44.1	44.9	43.2	42.3	44.6	44.0	43.9	44.7	43.5
2017	43.3	42.9	43.0	44.0	44.6	45.5	43.4	42.6	45.2	46.3	45.3	45.4	44.3

Employment by Industry: Boston-Cambridge-Newton, MA-NH, Selected Years, 2007–2017—*Continued*

(Numbers in thousands, not seasonally adjusted)

Industry and year	January	February	March	April	May	June	July	August	September	October	November	December	Annual average
Information													
2007	51.1	51.2	51.5	51.4	51.8	52.4	52.7	52.4	52.2	52.1	52.5	52.7	52.0
2008	52.9	53.3	53.5	53.3	53.2	53.9	54.1	54.1	53.8	53.5	53.4	53.5	53.5
2009	53.5	52.4	52.2	51.7	51.8	52.0	52.3	52.4	52.1	52.4	52.8	53.1	52.4
2010	53.6	53.5	53.5	53.8	53.9	54.5	54.1	53.9	53.3	52.9	53.1	53.3	53.6
2011	52.9	53.0	53.2	53.3	53.8	54.5	55.7	54.1	55.3	55.6	55.7	56.0	54.4
2012	53.9	53.9	53.9	54.3	54.4	55.7	56.6	55.9	54.2	54.4	54.3	54.1	54.6
2013	53.8	53.7	53.6	54.4	54.5	55.7	55.9	55.7	55.2	54.9	56.2	55.2	54.9
2014	54.3	54.5	54.6	54.9	55.2	56.1	56.2	56.2	55.6	55.8	55.9	56.1	55.5
2015	56.0	55.8	56.2	56.3	56.4	57.4	57.9	57.6	57.0	57.4	57.3	57.5	56.9
2016	57.4	57.2	57.4	58.0	56.9	58.6	59.2	59.5	58.9	59.2	59.2	59.4	58.4
2017	58.9	59.1	59.3	59.1	59.1	60.0	60.5	60.4	59.8	59.5	59.7	59.1	59.5
Financial Activities													
2007	153.3	153.2	153.1	153.3	153.5	155.4	155.4	155.7	153.6	153.5	153.4	154.2	154.0
2008	152.1	152.0	152.1	152.0	152.2	153.9	155.6	155.4	153.4	153.0	152.6	152.7	153.1
2009	151.7	150.8	150.3	149.9	149.5	150.3	149.9	149.2	147.1	146.8	146.7	146.9	149.1
2010	144.8	144.5	144.2	143.9	144.4	145.5	146.6	146.3	144.5	144.3	144.1	145.1	144.9
2011	143.4	142.8	142.6	143.0	143.5	144.6	146.1	146.3	144.7	144.0	143.8	144.2	144.1
2012	143.0	143.2	143.1	143.1	143.8	145.7	146.1	146.3	144.2	144.2	144.1	144.6	144.3
2013	143.0	143.5	143.8	143.6	144.0	145.6	146.3	146.8	144.5	144.4	144.6	145.0	144.6
2014	143.4	143.5	143.5	143.9	144.7	146.7	147.3	147.4	145.7	146.5	146.8	147.5	145.6
2015	146.2	146.2	146.1	146.4	147.2	148.9	151.9	152.4	149.5	151.0	151.4	151.8	149.1
2016	150.5	150.9	150.7	151.3	152.0	153.8	156.3	156.3	153.4	153.2	153.2	154.2	153.0
2017	152.2	152.7	152.3	152.2	153.1	155.6	155.9	155.9	153.4	153.8	152.7	152.9	153.6
Professional and Business Services													
2007	292.4	294.0	295.8	301.6	303.6	308.2	308.0	308.8	306.1	307.9	308.8	309.6	303.7
2008	303.4	304.7	305.8	308.6	309.5	312.8	312.8	311.9	309.5	309.2	306.8	303.8	308.2
2009	293.7	290.7	289.0	290.2	289.0	290.4	289.7	288.4	285.5	286.5	285.9	286.6	288.8
2010	283.2	283.6	284.4	289.3	289.3	291.7	293.6	293.2	290.1	293.2	293.2	293.5	289.9
2011	289.1	289.3	290.1	297.8	297.9	300.8	304.5	303.2	301.5	304.1	304.8	305.5	299.1
2012	297.8	298.2	300.7	306.7	307.9	313.3	315.1	315.1	313.3	316.2	317.1	316.9	309.9
2013	310.1	311.8	313.6	320.5	322.0	326.3	328.0	327.8	324.6	327.7	329.3	328.6	322.5
2014	320.7	320.7	321.4	327.8	329.8	334.0	336.4	336.4	333.3	335.6	336.2	336.0	330.7
2015	329.2	328.8	330.9	339.0	341.6	346.3	348.8	348.4	343.5	347.6	348.5	348.0	341.7
2016	338.5	340.6	342.1	350.0	350.9	356.0	361.0	360.4	355.8	358.7	359.5	359.2	352.7
2017	351.5	352.8	354.9	360.4	361.4	367.6	369.8	368.7	363.9	367.7	368.4	367.9	362.9
Education and Health Services													
2007	334.8	342.6	343.1	348.4	342.6	333.3	335.3	333.7	341.1	351.5	354.1	354.3	342.9
2008	343.6	353.1	354.7	357.5	351.5	342.9	344.7	342.9	350.4	360.7	363.3	362.9	352.4
2009	352.6	361.3	362.7	364.3	358.0	348.6	353.2	351.8	361.2	369.5	372.3	372.1	360.6
2010	362.9	372.0	373.5	371.0	364.6	352.2	355.4	353.7	364.9	373.5	376.1	375.2	366.3
2011	365.2	374.4	376.2	376.1	370.3	358.4	361.7	360.6	371.6	380.2	383.4	382.7	371.7
2012	373.4	382.4	384.1	382.5	377.2	367.0	368.1	366.9	377.6	386.0	389.0	388.5	378.6
2013	379.1	385.6	388.0	391.0	385.5	376.1	374.5	371.8	379.9	388.9	391.6	390.9	383.6
2014	378.6	390.4	392.5	397.6	392.5	382.0	385.4	382.9	390.6	401.3	404.8	404.0	391.9
2015	388.3	399.4	402.5	407.3	404.0	392.6	394.4	391.7	398.4	409.1	412.1	410.4	400.9
2016	397.1	409.5	410.6	413.8	410.4	397.8	403.4	401.0	409.5	415.9	419.4	418.4	408.9
2017	406.5	418.3	419.8	423.8	419.9	410.9	410.8	408.2	415.5	422.1	425.0	423.5	417.0
Leisure and Hospitality													
2007	134.2	134.0	135.7	140.5	144.7	151.0	152.1	153.3	149.3	147.9	146.0	144.5	144.4
2008	137.3	137.8	139.4	145.2	150.4	155.1	154.3	155.4	151.2	150.3	146.7	144.2	147.3
2009	133.6	134.2	135.5	140.9	147.9	150.9	150.5	150.3	147.8	146.8	143.6	142.0	143.7
2010	138.0	136.7	138.6	147.1	152.3	156.3	156.0	156.4	152.7	154.5	151.2	149.8	149.1
2011	142.5	140.7	144.1	152.8	157.0	162.1	163.9	164.7	161.4	159.8	157.3	154.8	155.1
2012	150.0	149.0	152.0	159.1	164.7	171.2	171.0	171.9	168.1	165.4	162.4	160.8	162.1
2013	154.8	152.6	157.1	164.4	170.4	176.9	174.7	177.1	172.7	173.5	170.5	167.7	167.7
2014	159.7	158.8	163.3	169.0	175.5	181.1	181.6	181.9	177.3	177.3	174.0	173.2	172.7
2015	165.3	161.9	165.8	172.7	180.5	185.7	187.3	186.5	179.9	180.8	178.8	178.3	177.0
2016	170.2	169.4	172.9	181.4	186.7	192.6	193.9	194.4	187.9	186.1	183.7	183.2	183.5
2017	176.2	174.4	178.1	185.4	190.6	198.5	198.1	198.1	191.0	191.0	186.6	186.8	187.9

Employment by Industry: Boston-Cambridge-Newton, MA-NH, Selected Years, 2007–2017—*Continued*

(Numbers in thousands, not seasonally adjusted)

Industry and year	January	February	March	April	May	June	July	August	September	October	November	December	Annual average
Other Services													
2007	58.0	58.6	59.0	59.3	60.2	62.2	62.6	62.7	60.9	60.7	61.2	61.3	60.6
2008	59.7	59.9	60.1	60.6	61.1	63.1	63.3	63.2	61.3	61.3	61.2	61.0	61.3
2009	59.4	59.5	59.9	60.1	60.6	62.4	62.1	61.6	59.7	60.0	60.0	60.0	60.4
2010	59.2	59.1	59.5	61.2	62.1	63.7	64.2	64.0	61.9	62.0	62.3	62.4	61.8
2011	61.4	61.9	62.8	64.0	64.4	66.2	66.9	66.7	64.4	64.4	64.8	64.5	64.4
2012	63.2	63.6	64.7	65.3	66.1	68.2	68.2	67.7	66.2	66.1	66.0	65.8	65.9
2013	64.5	64.5	65.7	66.2	66.5	67.9	68.0	67.8	65.8	65.7	65.8	65.6	66.2
2014	64.2	64.3	65.2	66.0	66.8	68.8	69.1	68.7	66.6	66.8	66.7	66.7	66.7
2015	64.9	64.1	65.7	66.0	66.6	68.7	69.2	68.7	66.4	66.5	66.4	66.3	66.6
2016	64.8	64.8	65.8	66.5	67.0	68.6	69.6	69.0	66.8	66.9	67.0	66.8	67.0
2017	65.6	65.7	66.5	67.0	67.6	69.8	70.4	70.1	67.6	70.1	70.0	68.8	68.3
Government													
2007	191.7	193.0	193.5	194.2	194.5	194.2	182.3	180.0	190.8	193.2	194.3	194.1	191.3
2008	193.4	195.2	195.5	196.0	196.1	196.3	186.2	184.2	194.1	195.7	196.4	196.0	193.8
2009	194.2	195.7	195.7	198.8	197.8	196.4	185.0	182.2	192.8	194.7	194.8	195.6	193.6
2010	193.9	195.0	195.5	196.7	201.4	197.8	185.9	183.3	192.6	195.2	196.7	196.3	194.2
2011	193.4	195.3	195.3	194.8	195.2	194.5	184.0	181.5	192.5	193.4	193.7	194.9	192.4
2012	192.5	194.4	195.2	193.7	193.9	193.8	184.1	182.3	192.1	193.1	195.2	194.2	192.0
2013	190.5	193.6	193.8	195.1	195.6	195.0	183.1	181.2	192.6	196.5	198.2	197.6	192.7
2014	194.4	197.6	197.9	200.0	199.7	198.9	187.2	185.1	196.2	198.8	201.4	200.1	196.4
2015	195.6	197.5	199.2	199.8	199.3	199.0	187.5	183.4	194.6	197.5	198.8	199.2	196.0
2016	195.7	198.2	200.8	199.3	200.2	199.7	190.1	187.0	198.6	199.2	201.4	200.4	197.6
2017	196.6	198.4	198.4	198.9	199.7	199.3	185.9	183.5	195.7	197.3	199.3	198.3	195.9

Employment by Industry: Phoenix-Mesa-Scottsdale, AZ, Selected Years, 2007–2017

(Numbers in thousands, not seasonally adjusted)

Industry and year	January	February	March	April	May	June	July	August	September	October	November	December	Annual average
Total Nonfarm													
2007	1,884.7	1,911.3	1,924.1	1,917.1	1,922.1	1,901.7	1,885.1	1,914.0	1,925.6	1,935.2	1,946.5	1,947.6	1,917.9
2008	1,900.8	1,912.8	1,909.4	1,900.5	1,893.9	1,855.1	1,822.0	1,853.1	1,857.8	1,852.3	1,849.6	1,837.2	1,870.4
2009	1,776.9	1,772.3	1,765.1	1,751.1	1,739.0	1,694.4	1,671.1	1,683.7	1,695.9	1,703.8	1,716.0	1,715.9	1,723.8
2010	1,676.9	1,689.3	1,699.5	1,704.2	1,708.8	1,664.9	1,647.2	1,670.0	1,681.5	1,705.8	1,723.0	1,728.2	1,691.6
2011	1,694.1	1,708.1	1,718.7	1,727.3	1,724.6	1,680.3	1,665.9	1,702.9	1,725.3	1,738.9	1,758.6	1,762.3	1,717.3
2012	1,732.0	1,746.5	1,759.4	1,760.6	1,758.1	1,727.4	1,707.4	1,749.5	1,768.9	1,786.1	1,809.9	1,817.7	1,760.3
2013	1,779.0	1,797.6	1,807.2	1,812.9	1,811.1	1,777.2	1,761.7	1,801.2	1,817.0	1,838.4	1,865.1	1,870.1	1,811.5
2014	1,828.0	1,842.5	1,849.6	1,855.1	1,843.3	1,814.4	1,798.1	1,840.0	1,854.4	1,881.7	1,907.0	1,917.1	1,852.6
2015	1,878.1	1,896.4	1,901.8	1,910.4	1,904.0	1,870.9	1,865.9	1,903.1	1,922.3	1,956.2	1,981.4	1,984.1	1,914.6
2016	1,944.7	1,965.7	1,972.3	1,981.8	1,970.9	1,933.5	1,933.8	1,969.4	1,994.8	2,013.2	2,033.5	2,036.4	1,979.2
2017	1,999.5	2,019.3	2,027.0	2,036.3	2,025.6	1,999.2	1,985.6	2,025.6	2,049.2	2,067.1	2,086.3	2,088.4	2,034.1
Total Private													
2007	1,653.9	1,670.8	1,682.2	1,675.5	1,679.7	1,682.2	1,668.7	1,678.3	1,679.5	1,686.9	1,695.8	1,697.0	1,679.2
2008	1,651.6	1,659.2	1,655.9	1,647.1	1,641.7	1,630.7	1,609.3	1,613.8	1,606.3	1,598.8	1,594.7	1,583.9	1,624.4
2009	1,531.5	1,520.6	1,514.3	1,500.2	1,492.0	1,477.6	1,461.3	1,460.1	1,454.2	1,459.1	1,470.8	1,473.3	1,484.6
2010	1,438.6	1,444.7	1,456.2	1,460.1	1,458.0	1,450.3	1,440.2	1,446.8	1,445.5	1,467.2	1,483.0	1,491.0	1,456.8
2011	1,460.4	1,469.3	1,480.1	1,488.1	1,485.7	1,476.9	1,473.0	1,483.4	1,490.5	1,501.1	1,519.9	1,527.9	1,488.0
2012	1,500.4	1,508.4	1,521.0	1,521.7	1,524.2	1,520.4	1,510.5	1,525.4	1,531.0	1,546.7	1,569.1	1,577.8	1,529.7
2013	1,543.9	1,557.3	1,567.7	1,572.6	1,573.9	1,569.4	1,563.2	1,577.1	1,578.7	1,597.1	1,623.7	1,631.0	1,579.6
2014	1,592.4	1,601.8	1,609.4	1,613.9	1,611.8	1,605.0	1,598.0	1,613.3	1,614.5	1,638.0	1,662.5	1,674.9	1,619.6
2015	1,643.0	1,653.1	1,659.0	1,668.0	1,668.3	1,662.8	1,664.5	1,677.5	1,682.6	1,711.3	1,735.0	1,742.2	1,680.6
2016	1,710.7	1,722.5	1,729.2	1,738.0	1,734.1	1,721.6	1,728.0	1,741.6	1,750.5	1,767.2	1,786.1	1,791.5	1,743.4
2017	1,762.1	1,773.3	1,781.3	1,789.6	1,788.0	1,782.3	1,778.0	1,794.2	1,804.2	1,820.9	1,838.8	1,844.3	1,796.4
Goods Producing													
2007	309.9	311.6	312.1	310.5	311.6	314.8	313.8	314.5	310.8	307.3	301.2	296.9	309.6
2008	288.7	286.3	283.7	280.8	279.6	277.8	274.2	272.6	267.8	261.2	253.2	246.1	272.7
2009	234.7	227.6	223.3	218.5	215.7	214.5	211.2	208.9	205.9	203.8	201.6	199.2	213.7
2010	194.2	194.2	194.7	196.1	196.0	196.9	197.0	196.8	196.0	197.5	197.0	196.5	196.1
2011	193.4	193.1	194.4	196.4	198.1	199.8	201.8	202.2	202.3	202.1	202.0	202.3	199.0
2012	200.7	201.6	204.0	205.1	206.6	209.6	210.3	212.1	212.3	212.7	212.3	211.4	208.2
2013	207.9	209.6	211.0	211.7	213.6	216.4	216.6	217.0	216.0	216.8	216.5	215.8	214.1
2014	214.5	215.9	215.9	217.4	217.9	218.2	217.9	217.8	216.5	217.8	218.3	218.6	217.2
2015	216.0	217.7	218.2	220.2	221.3	222.6	223.6	224.0	223.5	225.3	225.4	226.3	222.0
2016	224.0	226.4	226.7	227.3	227.8	230.1	231.3	231.7	230.9	230.1	230.1	231.3	229.0
2017	230.1	231.9	232.9	234.5	236.9	241.1	242.7	243.6	244.5	245.6	246.7	249.7	240.0
Service-Providing													
2007	1,574.8	1,599.7	1,612.0	1,606.6	1,610.5	1,586.9	1,571.3	1,599.5	1,614.8	1,627.9	1,645.3	1,650.7	1,608.3
2008	1,612.1	1,626.5	1,625.7	1,619.7	1,614.3	1,577.3	1,547.8	1,580.5	1,590.0	1,591.1	1,596.4	1,591.1	1,597.7
2009	1,542.2	1,544.7	1,541.8	1,532.6	1,523.3	1,479.9	1,459.9	1,474.8	1,490.0	1,500.0	1,514.4	1,516.7	1,510.0
2010	1,482.7	1,495.1	1,504.8	1,508.1	1,512.8	1,468.0	1,450.2	1,473.2	1,485.5	1,508.3	1,526.0	1,531.7	1,495.5
2011	1,500.7	1,515.0	1,524.3	1,530.9	1,526.5	1,480.5	1,464.1	1,500.7	1,523.0	1,536.8	1,556.6	1,560.0	1,518.3
2012	1,531.3	1,544.9	1,555.4	1,555.5	1,551.5	1,517.8	1,497.1	1,537.4	1,556.6	1,573.4	1,597.6	1,606.3	1,552.1
2013	1,571.1	1,588.0	1,596.2	1,601.2	1,597.5	1,560.8	1,545.1	1,584.2	1,601.0	1,621.6	1,648.6	1,654.3	1,597.5
2014	1,613.5	1,626.6	1,633.7	1,637.7	1,625.4	1,596.2	1,580.2	1,622.2	1,637.9	1,663.9	1,688.7	1,698.5	1,635.4
2015	1,662.1	1,678.7	1,683.6	1,690.2	1,682.7	1,648.3	1,642.3	1,679.1	1,698.8	1,730.9	1,756.0	1,757.8	1,692.5
2016	1,720.7	1,739.3	1,745.6	1,754.5	1,743.1	1,703.4	1,702.5	1,737.7	1,763.9	1,783.1	1,803.4	1,805.1	1,750.2
2017	1,769.4	1,787.4	1,794.1	1,801.8	1,788.7	1,758.1	1,742.9	1,782.0	1,804.7	1,821.5	1,839.6	1,838.7	1,794.1
Mining and Logging													
2007	2.9	3.0	3.1	3.0	3.0	3.1	3.4	3.4	3.4	3.5	3.5	3.5	3.2
2008	3.5	3.5	3.6	3.6	3.7	3.9	3.9	4.0	3.9	3.9	3.9	3.8	3.8
2009	3.3	3.3	3.3	3.2	3.0	3.0	2.9	2.9	2.9	3.0	3.0	3.0	3.1
2010	3.0	3.0	3.0	3.0	3.1	3.0	3.0	3.0	3.0	3.0	3.1	3.1	3.0
2011	3.2	3.2	3.2	3.1	3.2	3.2	3.2	3.2	3.2	3.4	3.4	3.4	3.2
2012	3.4	3.4	3.4	3.4	3.4	3.5	3.6	3.6	3.7	3.6	3.6	3.6	3.5
2013	3.6	3.6	3.6	3.6	3.6	3.8	3.8	3.7	3.6	3.5	3.5	3.5	3.6
2014	3.4	3.4	3.4	3.4	3.4	3.4	3.4	3.4	3.4	3.4	3.4	3.4	3.4
2015	3.4	3.4	3.4	3.3	3.4	3.4	3.5	3.4	3.3	3.2	3.2	3.2	3.3
2016	3.2	3.2	3.2	3.2	3.2	3.3	3.3	3.3	3.2	3.2	3.2	3.2	3.2
2017	3.1	3.1	3.1	3.2	3.2	3.3	3.3	3.3	3.2	3.2	3.2	3.1	3.2

Employment by Industry: Phoenix-Mesa-Scottsdale, AZ, Selected Years, 2007–2017—*Continued*

(Numbers in thousands, not seasonally adjusted)

Industry and year	January	February	March	April	May	June	July	August	September	October	November	December	Annual average
Construction													
2007	169.6	170.8	171.2	170.2	171.1	174.2	172.1	172.9	170.9	167.3	162.1	158.1	169.2
2008	151.5	149.8	148.6	145.9	144.9	143.3	140.4	139.0	135.3	130.0	123.9	118.6	139.3
2009	110.0	105.1	102.7	99.4	97.8	97.6	95.1	93.1	90.6	88.5	86.3	84.1	95.9
2010	81.1	81.3	81.8	82.7	82.2	83.1	83.2	83.1	82.3	83.4	82.6	81.5	82.4
2011	79.2	78.9	80.0	81.5	82.4	83.9	85.3	85.6	85.8	85.2	84.5	83.9	83.0
2012	82.5	83.0	84.8	85.5	86.5	88.5	89.4	90.9	91.3	91.9	91.5	90.2	88.0
2013	87.8	89.1	90.6	91.4	92.9	95.1	95.3	96.2	95.6	96.2	95.8	94.9	93.4
2014	93.8	94.4	94.4	95.7	96.0	96.1	95.9	95.6	94.7	95.9	96.0	95.8	95.4
2015	94.8	96.0	96.7	97.9	98.6	99.2	99.6	100.0	100.0	101.6	101.5	101.7	99.0
2016	100.4	102.3	103.2	103.9	104.3	105.9	107.6	107.9	107.3	107.4	106.8	107.0	105.3
2017	106.8	108.1	109.6	110.4	112.0	114.5	115.3	115.9	116.4	117.2	117.8	118.4	113.5
Manufacturing													
2007	137.4	137.8	137.8	137.3	137.5	137.5	138.3	138.2	136.5	136.5	135.6	135.3	137.1
2008	133.7	133.0	131.5	131.3	131.0	130.6	129.9	129.6	128.6	127.3	125.4	123.7	129.6
2009	121.4	119.2	117.3	115.9	114.9	113.9	113.2	112.9	112.4	112.3	112.3	112.1	114.8
2010	110.1	109.9	109.9	110.4	110.7	110.8	110.8	110.7	110.7	111.1	111.3	111.9	110.7
2011	111.0	111.0	111.2	111.8	112.5	112.7	113.3	113.4	113.3	113.5	114.1	115.0	112.7
2012	114.8	115.2	115.8	116.2	116.7	117.6	117.3	117.6	117.3	117.2	117.2	117.6	116.7
2013	116.5	116.9	116.8	116.7	117.1	117.5	117.5	117.1	116.8	117.1	117.2	117.4	117.1
2014	117.3	118.1	118.1	118.3	118.5	118.7	118.6	118.8	118.4	118.5	118.9	119.4	118.5
2015	117.8	118.3	118.1	119.0	119.3	120.0	120.5	120.6	120.2	120.5	120.7	121.4	119.7
2016	120.4	120.9	120.3	120.2	120.3	120.9	120.4	120.5	120.4	119.5	120.1	121.1	120.4
2017	120.2	120.7	120.2	120.9	121.7	123.3	124.1	124.4	124.9	125.2	125.7	128.2	123.3
Trade, Transportation, and Utilities													
2007	385.7	385.1	386.1	386.5	387.5	387.6	388.6	389.8	391.1	393.4	402.5	407.5	391.0
2008	390.9	389.2	387.7	385.4	385.5	384.3	378.3	379.0	376.4	377.0	381.3	381.3	383.0
2009	366.3	360.3	358.4	355.0	353.6	351.1	348.7	347.9	346.5	347.1	354.1	356.8	353.8
2010	345.8	345.2	345.5	345.6	345.8	343.5	341.5	341.4	339.2	343.8	351.8	356.1	345.4
2011	345.4	345.2	345.9	347.9	347.6	346.5	346.1	346.8	346.6	351.2	360.7	362.8	349.4
2012	351.3	349.0	350.2	350.5	351.2	350.0	349.0	348.8	349.7	353.9	365.1	367.7	353.0
2013	351.5	350.6	350.3	351.1	352.1	351.7	352.1	353.6	354.5	359.1	370.0	375.3	356.0
2014	361.2	360.0	360.0	360.5	360.3	360.5	360.4	362.2	362.3	367.5	378.2	383.9	364.8
2015	369.9	369.5	370.4	370.8	371.4	372.3	373.0	375.3	377.0	383.4	394.3	396.0	376.9
2016	380.8	380.6	381.2	382.5	382.3	380.9	383.1	384.0	384.2	391.7	402.7	406.1	386.7
2017	391.4	389.8	388.9	389.8	390.0	390.3	390.6	392.0	392.1	396.5	409.0	409.2	394.1
Wholesale Trade													
2007	87.5	88.0	88.4	88.6	88.8	89.4	89.9	89.8	89.7	90.0	90.1	90.2	89.2
2008	88.6	89.2	89.0	88.8	89.1	88.7	88.3	88.4	88.2	88.2	87.6	87.0	88.4
2009	85.5	84.8	84.0	83.2	82.4	81.8	81.6	81.3	80.6	80.7	80.5	80.3	82.2
2010	79.0	79.3	79.5	79.3	79.3	79.1	78.9	78.7	78.1	78.3	78.3	78.4	78.9
2011	77.6	78.2	78.2	78.6	78.6	78.5	78.3	78.1	77.8	77.9	77.9	77.9	78.1
2012	77.4	77.7	78.1	78.0	77.9	78.1	78.2	78.1	78.1	78.3	78.3	78.3	78.0
2013	77.1	77.8	77.7	77.9	77.7	77.8	77.7	77.8	77.5	78.1	78.1	78.4	77.8
2014	77.1	77.3	77.5	77.2	77.4	77.2	77.3	77.4	77.2	77.2	77.1	77.7	77.3
2015	76.3	76.4	76.5	76.8	77.0	77.0	77.0	77.3	77.4	77.6	77.8	77.8	77.1
2016	77.3	77.6	77.3	77.8	77.8	77.7	78.6	78.3	78.2	79.3	79.2	79.5	78.2
2017	78.8	79.2	79.2	79.2	79.4	79.6	79.3	79.6	79.7	79.1	80.4	80.1	79.5
Retail Trade													
2007	231.7	230.4	231.1	231.0	231.3	230.7	231.6	232.5	233.6	235.6	244.5	247.9	234.3
2008	235.2	232.5	231.4	229.2	229.1	228.6	223.5	223.9	221.8	222.8	227.1	227.5	227.7
2009	215.8	211.1	210.3	208.8	208.4	206.7	204.9	204.5	204.2	205.2	212.3	214.5	208.9
2010	206.3	205.4	205.7	206.6	206.6	204.6	203.2	203.0	201.2	205.1	212.7	215.2	206.3
2011	206.9	206.0	206.5	207.5	207.0	205.8	205.9	206.6	206.6	210.2	219.0	220.0	209.0
2012	210.5	207.9	208.4	209.2	209.9	208.7	207.3	207.2	208.0	211.8	222.7	224.0	211.3
2013	210.2	208.6	208.9	210.0	210.6	210.3	211.1	212.3	213.5	216.7	226.9	230.5	214.1
2014	219.1	217.9	217.5	218.8	218.2	218.4	218.5	219.5	219.7	223.9	233.7	237.0	221.9
2015	225.6	224.7	225.2	226.1	226.2	227.2	227.3	229.0	230.3	235.6	244.4	244.8	230.5
2016	232.2	231.7	232.1	232.5	232.4	231.4	232.0	232.7	233.1	238.4	247.8	249.3	235.5
2017	237.7	235.8	235.5	236.2	236.1	236.1	236.4	236.9	236.6	240.8	251.1	249.5	239.1

Employment by Industry: Phoenix-Mesa-Scottsdale, AZ, Selected Years, 2007–2017—*Continued*

(Numbers in thousands, not seasonally adjusted)

Industry and year	January	February	March	April	May	June	July	August	September	October	November	December	Annual average
Transportation and Utilities													
2007	66.5	66.7	66.6	66.9	67.4	67.5	67.1	67.5	67.8	67.8	67.9	69.4	67.4
2008	67.1	67.5	67.3	67.4	67.3	67.0	66.5	66.7	66.4	66.0	66.6	66.8	66.9
2009	65.0	64.4	64.1	63.0	62.8	62.6	62.2	62.1	61.7	61.2	61.3	62.0	62.7
2010	60.5	60.5	60.3	59.7	59.9	59.8	59.4	59.7	59.9	60.4	60.8	62.5	60.3
2011	60.9	61.0	61.2	61.8	62.0	62.2	61.9	62.1	62.2	63.1	63.8	64.9	62.3
2012	63.4	63.4	63.7	63.3	63.4	63.2	63.5	63.5	63.6	63.8	64.1	65.4	63.7
2013	64.2	64.2	63.7	63.2	63.8	63.6	63.3	63.5	63.5	64.3	65.0	66.4	64.1
2014	65.0	64.8	65.0	64.5	64.7	64.9	64.6	65.3	65.4	66.4	67.4	69.2	65.6
2015	68.0	68.4	68.7	67.9	68.2	68.1	68.7	69.0	69.3	70.2	72.1	73.4	69.3
2016	71.3	71.3	71.8	72.2	72.1	71.8	72.5	73.0	72.9	74.0	75.7	77.3	73.0
2017	74.9	74.8	74.2	74.4	74.5	74.6	74.9	75.5	75.8	76.6	77.5	79.6	75.6
Information													
2007	30.0	30.9	30.8	31.1	31.7	31.7	31.5	31.1	30.9	30.5	31.4	31.0	31.1
2008	30.5	31.5	31.9	31.2	32.2	32.0	30.8	30.5	31.0	30.2	30.6	30.5	31.1
2009	29.6	29.9	29.6	29.5	29.9	29.2	28.8	28.5	28.0	27.5	28.0	27.8	28.9
2010	27.2	27.5	27.7	27.8	27.6	28.0	27.2	27.1	26.9	26.7	27.2	27.6	27.4
2011	27.4	27.4	27.8	28.0	28.1	28.3	28.6	28.7	28.6	28.9	29.7	29.8	28.4
2012	29.8	30.1	30.4	30.7	31.2	31.2	31.4	31.6	31.2	31.2	32.2	32.5	31.1
2013	32.1	32.7	33.0	32.9	33.6	33.3	33.4	33.5	33.0	33.3	34.0	33.9	33.2
2014	33.8	33.8	34.3	34.6	35.0	35.4	35.7	35.6	34.8	35.2	35.4	35.7	34.9
2015	35.4	36.5	35.8	36.3	36.7	36.4	36.3	35.6	35.0	35.1	35.6	35.6	35.9
2016	36.0	36.5	36.0	36.4	36.7	36.5	36.3	35.6	35.2	35.5	35.4	35.5	36.0
2017	35.0	35.7	35.7	36.4	36.6	36.4	36.2	36.0	35.5	35.5	35.4	35.6	35.8
Financial Activities													
2007	156.0	157.2	157.8	157.2	157.4	156.9	156.2	155.4	154.6	153.5	153.4	153.6	155.8
2008	150.6	151.7	151.4	151.1	150.8	150.5	149.7	149.2	148.7	149.0	148.0	147.7	149.9
2009	144.7	144.5	144.1	143.4	143.5	142.9	142.3	142.1	141.0	140.9	140.7	141.5	142.6
2010	139.3	139.9	140.8	139.6	139.6	139.7	140.2	140.7	140.2	142.3	142.9	144.1	140.8
2011	142.1	142.9	143.7	144.4	144.3	144.7	145.3	145.8	146.0	146.4	147.1	148.8	145.1
2012	147.2	149.0	149.3	149.0	149.1	149.1	149.3	150.2	150.4	152.3	153.6	154.5	150.3
2013	153.3	155.9	156.0	156.9	157.5	158.0	158.1	158.6	158.6	160.9	162.1	162.5	158.2
2014	160.7	161.6	161.1	160.5	160.7	160.7	160.5	161.1	161.1	162.8	163.9	164.2	161.6
2015	163.1	164.5	164.9	165.2	165.8	166.4	167.4	168.4	168.6	171.0	172.5	173.7	167.6
2016	172.6	174.0	174.6	175.9	175.9	176.2	177.8	178.8	179.6	181.3	182.9	183.7	177.8
2017	182.8	183.3	184.2	184.7	184.8	185.8	186.5	187.3	187.8	188.3	190.3	188.8	186.2
Professional and Business Services													
2007	317.2	321.7	325.5	323.5	324.0	325.9	324.2	326.3	325.2	327.7	328.6	326.7	324.7
2008	315.9	318.8	316.0	314.0	311.8	308.6	305.8	307.5	305.0	303.8	301.3	298.4	308.9
2009	285.2	282.8	280.0	277.4	274.4	272.0	270.2	268.0	267.4	271.2	273.7	273.9	274.7
2010	264.8	265.8	269.5	271.9	271.0	270.3	268.4	269.2	268.6	275.0	276.6	280.3	271.0
2011	272.0	274.8	276.5	278.0	275.0	274.2	274.3	276.1	276.6	279.8	282.5	286.7	277.2
2012	277.9	279.2	281.2	282.1	282.5	284.5	283.8	286.7	286.7	291.0	296.3	299.8	286.0
2013	294.3	293.6	296.5	298.5	298.7	301.3	300.3	301.8	300.5	306.4	314.5	316.2	301.9
2014	301.3	301.0	303.0	305.7	306.0	306.8	306.7	309.6	309.4	316.6	323.5	327.3	309.7
2015	316.4	315.7	315.6	319.3	319.2	320.3	322.1	323.4	324.4	332.4	338.8	341.9	324.1
2016	332.4	332.9	333.6	337.4	335.4	332.3	337.8	339.5	341.9	344.5	346.9	347.4	338.5
2017	340.5	340.6	340.6	343.0	342.6	340.9	339.4	342.5	346.1	353.8	353.1	354.0	344.8
Education and Health Services													
2007	202.6	206.0	207.3	206.0	206.5	207.7	205.6	209.4	211.2	214.8	215.3	216.5	209.1
2008	213.9	217.4	218.2	219.5	220.5	219.5	218.5	221.8	223.8	225.0	226.3	228.1	221.0
2009	223.2	225.1	225.7	226.3	227.1	225.6	224.4	228.4	229.9	233.3	235.3	236.7	228.4
2010	234.2	235.2	236.4	236.4	237.4	235.4	234.7	239.4	241.0	245.4	246.9	245.9	239.0
2011	242.7	244.4	245.3	246.2	247.2	242.7	242.1	247.3	250.5	252.1	253.8	254.6	247.4
2012	251.8	254.2	254.8	255.0	255.2	251.8	249.0	255.2	257.3	259.2	260.8	262.2	255.5
2013	257.3	259.9	261.8	261.9	261.0	256.6	254.7	260.8	262.8	263.3	265.7	265.8	261.0
2014	263.7	265.7	266.2	267.1	266.9	263.6	262.9	269.4	271.2	274.4	276.5	278.0	268.8
2015	274.6	277.9	278.3	280.0	279.9	276.5	277.4	283.5	285.1	289.8	291.7	292.0	282.2
2016	288.6	290.6	291.4	293.1	291.7	287.4	288.1	294.8	298.8	300.7	303.2	304.3	294.4
2017	301.4	304.7	305.5	306.4	305.3	301.5	300.4	307.4	311.1	313.3	314.9	315.4	307.3

Employment by Industry: Phoenix-Mesa-Scottsdale, AZ, Selected Years, 2007–2017—*Continued*

(Numbers in thousands, not seasonally adjusted)

Industry and year	January	February	March	April	May	June	July	August	September	October	November	December	Annual average
Leisure and Hospitality													
2007	182.7	186.8	190.4	189.8	189.0	184.5	177.8	181.0	183.4	187.4	190.2	191.1	186.2
2008	188.0	190.4	192.6	191.5	187.7	184.2	178.6	180.0	180.5	180.5	181.6	180.0	184.6
2009	177.9	179.9	182.9	181.5	179.0	173.5	168.1	168.9	168.6	169.5	171.6	171.8	174.4
2010	169.2	172.4	176.9	179.0	176.5	172.2	167.8	169.2	170.8	173.2	176.7	176.4	173.4
2011	173.7	176.9	181.7	182.4	180.4	175.9	171.1	173.3	176.8	177.8	181.4	180.7	177.7
2012	180.1	183.5	188.9	187.2	185.7	181.2	175.7	179.2	181.4	184.1	185.9	186.7	183.3
2013	185.1	190.7	195.2	195.6	193.2	188.1	184.6	188.7	190.1	193.4	196.7	197.3	191.6
2014	194.2	200.0	204.7	204.1	201.1	196.1	191.0	195.1	196.4	200.1	203.1	203.8	199.1
2015	204.8	207.7	212.2	212.9	210.4	204.7	201.4	204.3	205.6	210.3	212.2	212.2	208.2
2016	211.7	216.0	219.9	219.7	217.8	212.2	208.5	212.3	214.5	217.6	218.7	217.7	215.6
2017	216.2	221.7	227.7	228.8	225.5	220.3	216.5	220.1	221.6	223.0	224.0	225.9	222.6
Other Services													
2007	69.8	71.5	72.2	70.9	72.0	73.1	71.0	70.8	72.3	72.3	73.2	73.7	71.9
2008	73.1	73.9	74.4	73.6	73.6	73.8	73.4	73.2	73.1	72.1	72.4	71.8	73.2
2009	69.9	70.5	70.3	68.6	68.8	68.8	67.6	67.4	66.9	65.8	65.8	65.6	68.0
2010	63.9	64.5	64.7	63.7	64.1	64.3	63.4	63.0	62.8	63.3	63.9	64.1	63.8
2011	63.7	64.6	64.8	64.8	65.0	64.8	63.7	63.2	63.1	62.8	62.7	62.2	63.8
2012	61.6	61.8	62.2	62.1	62.7	63.0	62.0	61.6	62.0	62.3	62.9	63.0	62.3
2013	62.4	64.3	63.9	64.0	64.2	64.0	63.4	63.1	63.2	63.9	64.2	64.2	63.7
2014	63.0	63.8	64.2	64.0	63.9	63.7	62.9	62.5	62.8	63.6	63.6	63.4	63.5
2015	62.8	63.6	63.6	63.3	63.6	63.6	63.3	63.0	63.4	64.0	64.5	64.5	63.6
2016	64.6	65.5	65.8	65.7	66.5	66.0	65.1	64.9	65.4	65.8	66.2	65.5	65.6
2017	64.7	65.6	65.8	66.0	66.3	66.0	65.7	65.3	65.5	64.9	65.4	65.7	65.6
Government													
2007	230.8	240.5	241.9	241.6	242.4	219.5	216.4	235.7	246.1	248.3	250.7	250.6	238.7
2008	249.2	253.6	253.5	253.4	252.2	224.4	212.7	239.3	251.5	253.5	254.9	253.3	246.0
2009	245.4	251.7	250.8	250.9	247.0	216.8	209.8	223.6	241.7	244.7	245.2	242.6	239.2
2010	238.3	244.6	243.3	244.1	250.8	214.6	207.0	223.2	236.0	238.6	240.0	237.2	234.8
2011	233.7	238.8	238.6	239.2	238.9	203.4	192.9	219.5	234.8	237.8	238.7	234.4	229.2
2012	231.6	238.1	238.4	238.9	233.9	207.0	196.9	224.1	237.9	239.4	240.8	239.9	230.6
2013	235.1	240.3	239.5	240.3	237.2	207.8	198.5	224.1	238.3	241.3	241.4	239.1	231.9
2014	235.6	240.7	240.2	241.2	231.5	209.4	200.1	226.7	239.9	243.7	244.5	242.2	233.0
2015	235.1	243.3	242.8	242.4	235.7	208.1	201.4	225.6	239.7	244.9	246.4	241.9	233.9
2016	234.0	243.2	243.1	243.8	236.8	211.9	205.8	227.8	244.3	246.0	247.4	244.9	235.8
2017	237.4	246.0	245.7	246.7	237.6	216.9	207.6	231.4	245.0	246.2	247.5	244.1	237.7

Employment by Industry: San Francisco-Oakland-Hayward, CA, Selected Years, 2007–2017

(Numbers in thousands, not seasonally adjusted)

Industry and year	January	February	March	April	May	June	July	August	September	October	November	December	Annual average
Total Nonfarm													
2007	2,035.6	2,052.3	2,063.8	2,057.6	2,073.9	2,082.3	2,074.2	2,076.7	2,083.0	2,089.2	2,102.8	2,108.7	2,075.0
2008	2,059.0	2,072.7	2,075.6	2,078.8	2,084.0	2,088.8	2,079.0	2,072.8	2,071.1	2,072.7	2,065.6	2,061.4	2,073.5
2009	2,001.4	1,991.8	1,984.1	1,976.8	1,973.3	1,970.7	1,945.3	1,929.1	1,935.0	1,952.7	1,954.2	1,953.4	1,964.0
2010	1,907.6	1,910.1	1,917.7	1,932.2	1,943.9	1,946.2	1,926.7	1,920.1	1,936.2	1,949.0	1,952.1	1,957.0	1,933.2
2011	1,925.0	1,933.0	1,938.6	1,957.1	1,965.5	1,968.0	1,966.4	1,970.5	1,981.1	1,994.2	2,003.2	2,008.6	1,967.6
2012	1975.5	1988.8	2000.9	2024.9	2040	2051.5	2044.7	2051.8	2056.5	2074.1	2088.5	2095.7	2041.1
2013	2,053.0	2,071.2	2,082.9	2,096.0	2,107.5	2,108.9	2,103.9	2,114.7	2,116.3	2,136.2	2,154.6	2,157.8	2,108.6
2014	2,119.0	2,135.7	2,146.1	2,161.0	2,173.9	2,180.1	2,175.1	2,185.0	2,188.5	2,206.2	2,222.9	2,230.9	2,177.0
2015	2,198.7	2,211.7	2,227.4	2,240.8	2,252.8	2,261.2	2,267.5	2,278.1	2,279.5	2,302.2	2,313.3	2,320.5	2,262.8
2016	2,286.9	2,304.9	2,310.9	2,333.2	2,338.6	2,343.9	2,348.5	2,354.1	2,359.1	2,376.3	2,387.1	2,388.5	2,344.3
2017	2,347.4	2,364.5	2,379.7	2,382.0	2,393.9	2,404.9	2,395.5	2,397.7	2,399.6	2,418.3	2,435.7	2,437.7	2,396.4
Total Private													
2007	1,716.6	1,728.9	1,738.6	1,732.5	1,746.2	1,755.8	1,760.1	1,763.5	1,761.3	1,772.4	1,783.4	1,790.0	1,754.1
2008	1,744.1	1,755.0	1,756.6	1,759.2	1,765.1	1,768.0	1,768.6	1,766.1	1,759.7	1,757.3	1,748.7	1,746.4	1,757.9
2009	1,688.4	1,676.3	1,667.2	1,658.7	1,657.2	1,654.4	1,644.9	1,641.0	1,635.3	1,646.6	1,648.1	1,651.2	1,655.8
2010	1,607.6	1,608.1	1,614.2	1,623.2	1,628.6	1,635.4	1,640.4	1,637.4	1,637.4	1,646.8	1,646.8	1,653.4	1,631.6
2011	1,624.0	1,629.3	1,632.5	1,650.4	1,658.6	1,662.8	1,676.0	1,680.2	1,688.1	1,694.5	1,702.4	1,709.9	1,667.4
2012	1679.3	1689.7	1699.1	1722.9	1737.7	1750.4	1754	1763	1764.1	1777.3	1787	1795.7	1743.4
2013	1,757.3	1,773.4	1,781.2	1,793.4	1,804.9	1,810.9	1,816.4	1,826.1	1,822.3	1,836.2	1,851.7	1,859.1	1,811.1
2014	1,820.1	1,834.6	1,843.8	1,855.4	1,867.1	1,875.4	1,880.0	1,891.3	1,889.4	1,900.5	1,913.4	1,922.3	1,874.4
2015	1,892.9	1,904.7	1,917.0	1,928.3	1,939.8	1,950.5	1,967.6	1,975.6	1,972.3	1,989.8	1,998.3	2,006.9	1,953.6
2016	1,974.6	1,990.3	1,993.2	2,014.2	2,017.8	2,026.6	2,043.6	2,046.1	2,043.5	2,054.5	2,063.0	2,065.5	2,027.7
2017	2,028.4	2,043.6	2,056.2	2,058.9	2,068.7	2,083.5	2,088.1	2,089.5	2,082.8	2,095.8	2,109.8	2,113.2	2,076.5
Goods Producing													
2007	249.4	250.0	252.5	251.8	253.7	256.5	257.1	259.0	257.6	257.1	256.4	254.4	254.6
2008	247.0	248.0	246.9	245.6	246.0	246.9	247.3	246.4	244.3	240.9	235.4	231.4	243.8
2009	222.3	215.4	213.3	209.3	208.2	208.4	207.1	207.0	205.5	205.3	204.7	201.9	209.0
2010	196.4	194.7	196.4	192.4	194.6	196.1	198.4	198.8	197.2	197.6	196.0	194.7	196.1
2011	192.4	192.2	190.4	192.9	194.8	196.7	201.8	202.8	201.7	201.7	200.7	199.6	197.3
2012	195.9	196.1	196.1	197.8	201.7	205	208	208.4	208.9	209.1	208.1	207.1	203.5
2013	203.4	205.3	206.1	206.7	208.5	211.0	213.7	215.9	215.4	216.3	216.5	214.3	211.1
2014	211.1	212.8	213.6	215.1	217.3	220.3	223.2	225.2	225.4	225.5	226.2	224.1	220.0
2015	224.9	226.1	228.5	227.1	229.5	232.4	236.9	238.8	239.1	241.0	241.1	240.0	233.8
2016	238.0	240.3	239.1	242.8	243.6	246.7	251.5	252.8	253.2	253.9	252.9	251.2	247.2
2017	247.6	249.7	252.5	251.9	255.5	258.8	263.2	263.7	263.7	263.8	263.7	261.6	258.0
Service-Providing													
2007	1,786.2	1,802.3	1,811.3	1,805.8	1,820.2	1,825.8	1,817.1	1,817.7	1,825.4	1,832.1	1,846.4	1,854.3	1,820.4
2008	1,812.0	1,824.7	1,828.7	1,833.2	1,838.0	1,841.9	1,831.7	1,826.4	1,826.8	1,831.8	1,830.2	1,830.0	1,829.6
2009	1,779.1	1,776.4	1,770.8	1,767.5	1,765.1	1,762.3	1,738.2	1,722.1	1,729.5	1,747.4	1,749.5	1,751.5	1,755.0
2010	1,711.2	1,715.4	1,721.3	1,739.8	1,749.3	1,750.1	1,728.3	1,721.3	1,739.0	1,751.4	1,756.1	1,762.3	1,737.1
2011	1,732.6	1,740.8	1,748.2	1,764.2	1,770.7	1,771.3	1,764.6	1,767.7	1,779.4	1,792.5	1,802.5	1,809.0	1,770.3
2012	1779.6	1792.7	1804.8	1827.1	1838.3	1846.5	1836.7	1843.4	1847.6	1865.0	1880.4	1888.6	1,837.6
2013	1,849.6	1,865.9	1,876.8	1,889.3	1,899.0	1,897.9	1,890.2	1,898.8	1,900.9	1,919.9	1,938.1	1,943.5	1,897.5
2014	1,907.9	1,922.9	1,932.5	1,945.9	1,956.6	1,959.8	1,951.9	1,959.8	1,963.1	1,980.7	1,996.7	2,006.8	1,957.1
2015	1,973.8	1,985.6	1,998.9	2,013.7	2,023.3	2,028.8	2,030.6	2,039.3	2,040.4	2,061.2	2,072.2	2,080.5	2,029.0
2016	2,048.9	2,064.6	2,071.8	2,090.4	2,095.0	2,097.2	2,097.0	2,101.3	2,105.9	2,122.4	2,134.2	2,137.3	2,097.2
2017	2,099.8	2,114.8	2,127.2	2,130.1	2,138.4	2,146.1	2,132.3	2,134.0	2,135.9	2,154.5	2,172.0	2,176.1	2,138.4
Mining and Logging													
2007	1.0	1.1	1.0	1.1	1.1	1.1	0.9	1.0	0.9	0.9	0.9	0.9	1.0
2008	0.9	0.9	0.9	0.9	0.9	0.9	0.9	0.9	0.9	0.9	0.9	0.9	0.9
2009	0.9	0.9	0.8	0.8	0.8	0.8	0.8	0.8	0.8	0.8	0.8	0.8	0.8
2010	0.8	0.8	0.8	0.8	0.8	0.8	0.8	0.9	0.9	0.8	0.7	0.7	0.8
2011	0.8	0.8	0.8	0.8	0.8	0.8	0.7	0.7	0.6	0.7	0.6	0.6	0.7
2012	0.6	0.6	0.6	0.6	0.6	0.6	0.6	0.7	0.6	0.6	0.6	0.6	0.6
2013	0.5	0.5	0.5	0.6	0.5	0.5	0.5	0.5	0.5	0.5	0.4	0.4	0.5
2014	0.5	0.5	0.5	0.4	0.4	0.4	0.5	0.5	0.5	0.5	0.5	0.4	0.5
2015	0.5	0.5	0.5	0.5	0.4	0.4	0.4	0.4	0.4	0.4	0.4	0.4	0.4
2016	0.5	0.5	0.4	0.5	0.5	0.5	0.5	0.5	0.5	0.5	0.5	0.5	0.5
2017	0.4	0.4	0.4	0.4	0.4	0.5	0.5	0.5	0.5	0.5	0.5	0.5	0.5

Employment by Industry: San Francisco-Oakland-Hayward, CA, Selected Years, 2007–2017—*Continued*

(Numbers in thousands, not seasonally adjusted)

Industry and year	January	February	March	April	May	June	July	August	September	October	November	December	Annual average
Construction													
2007	112.0	112.0	114.4	114.4	116.1	118.4	120.0	121.2	119.8	118.8	117.2	115.4	116.6
2008	109.8	110.3	109.3	109.0	109.7	110.4	111.1	110.7	109.3	108.2	104.0	101.3	108.6
2009	94.9	90.2	89.7	87.9	88.0	88.5	88.1	88.0	86.5	86.1	85.6	82.9	88.0
2010	77.8	76.0	77.4	77.5	79.0	80.0	81.6	81.9	80.4	80.9	79.0	77.6	79.1
2011	75.4	75.2	73.1	75.4	77.0	78.7	83.0	84.3	84.6	84.7	83.9	82.9	79.9
2012	80.2	80.4	79.8	80.8	84.2	87	89.6	90.1	90.5	91.1	90.5	89.5	86.1
2013	87.0	88.5	88.8	89.3	90.6	92.5	94.7	95.9	95.4	96.6	96.2	94.0	92.5
2014	91.6	93.1	93.3	94.3	95.9	98.0	99.9	101.2	101.0	100.3	100.3	97.8	97.2
2015	99.6	100.6	102.3	100.8	102.5	104.1	106.9	108.3	108.4	109.8	110.1	108.7	105.2
2016	106.9	108.8	107.4	110.6	111.2	112.8	116.1	116.7	117.2	118.5	117.1	114.8	113.2
2017	111.5	112.9	114.3	114.4	116.5	118.3	121.4	121.5	121.5	121.4	120.8	119.5	117.8
Manufacturing													
2007	136.4	136.9	137.1	136.3	136.5	137.0	136.2	136.8	136.9	137.4	138.3	138.1	137.0
2008	136.3	136.8	136.7	135.7	135.4	135.6	135.3	134.8	134.1	131.8	130.5	129.2	134.4
2009	126.5	124.3	122.8	120.6	119.4	119.1	118.2	118.2	118.2	118.4	118.3	118.2	120.2
2010	117.8	117.9	118.2	114.1	114.8	115.3	116.0	116.0	115.9	115.9	116.3	116.4	116.2
2011	116.2	116.2	116.5	116.7	117.0	117.2	118.1	117.8	116.5	116.3	116.2	116.1	116.7
2012	115.1	115.1	115.7	116.4	116.9	117.4	117.8	117.6	117.8	117.4	117	117	116.8
2013	115.9	116.3	116.8	116.8	117.4	118.0	118.5	119.5	119.5	119.2	119.9	119.9	118.1
2014	119.0	119.2	119.8	120.4	121.0	121.9	122.8	123.5	123.9	124.7	125.4	125.9	122.3
2015	124.8	125.0	125.7	125.8	126.6	127.9	129.6	130.1	130.3	130.8	130.6	130.9	128.2
2016	130.6	131.0	131.3	131.7	131.9	133.4	134.9	135.6	135.5	134.9	135.3	135.9	133.5
2017	135.7	136.4	137.8	137.1	138.6	140.0	141.3	141.7	141.7	141.9	142.4	141.6	139.7
Trade, Transportation, and Utilities													
2007	362.9	359.4	359.3	356.2	357.7	359.2	359.7	360.4	360.0	361.0	369.8	375.7	361.8
2008	361.3	356.9	356.1	352.7	353.3	353.5	352.7	351.5	348.6	347.9	351.1	353.2	353.2
2009	340.0	334.5	330.9	327.7	327.2	326.3	323.1	323.0	322.4	323.9	330.3	335.3	328.7
2010	321.4	317.8	317.1	317.4	318.4	319.7	318.4	318.8	317.9	319.8	326.1	331.9	320.4
2011	319.2	316.6	316.1	318.7	319.9	320.5	322.4	323.5	323.0	324.8	333.2	338.2	323.0
2012	327.7	323.6	323.9	327.2	329.4	330.9	332.3	334	333.4	336.7	347.3	352.1	333.2
2013	340.6	338.0	337.4	337.6	339.8	341.5	343.2	344.5	344.1	348.1	357.8	364.2	344.7
2014	350.8	347.5	348.1	348.3	350.0	352.0	353.7	355.8	353.7	356.7	366.0	372.6	354.6
2015	361.5	358.2	358.3	359.2	361.3	363.1	366.3	367.6	366.4	369.1	377.2	382.5	365.9
2016	371.7	370.0	369.1	371.2	371.1	371.9	376.8	378.1	376.3	379.0	387.5	393.5	376.4
2017	382.8	378.9	378.2	379.5	379.5	380.7	382.2	383.6	381.6	385.4	394.5	399.2	383.8
Wholesale Trade													
2007	75.7	76.1	76.6	75.5	76.0	76.2	75.6	75.6	75.4	75.7	75.5	75.6	75.8
2008	75.1	75.2	75.2	75.0	75.1	74.8	74.4	74.0	73.8	73.5	72.9	72.5	74.3
2009	70.6	70.1	69.3	68.9	68.6	68.2	67.5	67.2	66.5	66.7	66.6	66.4	68.1
2010	65.2	65.2	65.1	65.6	65.9	66.1	65.8	65.7	65.5	66.0	65.9	65.7	65.6
2011	65.1	65.2	65.3	66.0	66.4	66.5	67.0	67.2	67.4	67.6	68.0	68.1	66.7
2012	67.3	67.5	67.7	68.9	69.4	69.7	70.4	70.6	70.3	70.8	71	71.3	69.6
2013	71.0	71.0	71.1	71.4	71.8	72.2	72.8	72.9	73.0	73.1	73.5	74.3	72.3
2014	73.2	73.4	73.4	73.4	73.7	74.1	74.5	74.7	74.5	75.1	75.4	75.9	74.3
2015	75.7	76.0	76.1	76.3	76.7	77.0	77.8	77.7	77.5	77.9	78.0	78.3	77.1
2016	77.7	77.9	77.9	78.3	78.2	78.4	79.9	79.8	79.5	79.6	79.7	79.9	78.9
2017	79.3	79.6	79.5	79.9	80.4	80.8	81.4	81.2	80.5	80.8	80.4	81.1	80.4
Retail Trade													
2007	210.1	206.0	205.9	203.7	204.6	205.5	207.0	207.4	206.9	207.5	216.2	221.2	208.5
2008	210.0	205.3	204.7	203.1	202.7	203.7	203.7	202.9	200.6	200.5	204.2	206.2	204.0
2009	197.9	193.2	191.1	188.8	188.3	187.9	186.4	186.8	186.8	187.8	194.5	199.0	190.7
2010	188.7	185.0	184.6	185.1	186.0	186.5	186.3	186.9	185.8	187.3	193.4	197.8	187.8
2011	187.9	185.3	184.8	185.7	186.3	186.7	187.8	188.6	187.9	189.5	197.0	200.4	189.0
2012	192.5	188.3	188	189.4	190.9	191.5	192.6	193.5	193	195.3	204.7	208	194
2013	198.3	195.7	195.3	194.6	196.0	197.3	198.0	199.1	198.3	201.0	209.5	213.3	199.7
2014	203.7	199.9	200.3	200.4	201.1	202.4	203.3	204.6	202.6	204.8	213.0	216.6	204.4
2015	207.7	204.4	204.2	204.3	205.2	205.8	207.5	208.2	207.3	208.3	215.1	218.1	208.0
2016	210.1	207.8	207.0	207.5	207.5	207.6	209.5	210.0	208.5	210.1	216.5	219.4	210.1
2017	212.4	208.9	208.3	209.6	209.4	209.6	210.4	211.2	209.6	211.6	218.9	220.6	211.7

Employment by Industry: San Francisco-Oakland-Hayward, CA, Selected Years, 2007–2017—*Continued*

(Numbers in thousands, not seasonally adjusted)

Industry and year	January	February	March	April	May	June	July	August	September	October	November	December	Annual average
Transportation and Utilities													
2007	77.1	77.3	76.8	77.0	77.1	77.5	77.1	77.4	77.7	77.8	78.1	78.9	77.5
2008	76.2	76.4	76.2	74.6	75.5	75.0	74.6	74.6	74.2	73.9	74.0	74.5	75.0
2009	71.5	71.2	70.5	70.0	70.3	70.2	69.2	69.0	69.1	69.4	69.2	69.9	70.0
2010	67.5	67.6	67.4	66.7	66.5	67.1	66.3	66.2	66.6	66.5	66.8	68.4	67.0
2011	66.2	66.1	66.0	67.0	67.2	67.3	67.6	67.7	67.7	67.7	68.2	69.7	67.4
2012	67.9	67.8	68.2	68.9	69.1	69.7	69.3	69.9	70.1	70.6	71.6	72.8	69.7
2013	71.3	71.3	71.0	71.6	72.0	72.0	72.4	72.5	72.8	74.0	74.8	76.6	72.7
2014	73.9	74.2	74.4	74.5	75.2	75.5	75.9	76.5	76.6	76.8	77.6	80.1	75.9
2015	78.1	77.8	78.0	78.6	79.4	80.3	81.0	81.7	81.6	82.9	84.1	86.1	80.8
2016	83.9	84.3	84.2	85.4	85.4	85.9	87.4	88.3	88.3	89.3	91.3	94.2	87.3
2017	91.1	90.4	90.4	90.0	89.7	90.3	90.4	91.2	91.5	93.0	95.2	97.5	91.7
Information													
2007	68.3	68.5	68.5	68.4	68.8	68.8	69.1	69.1	68.6	68.3	68.2	68.2	68.6
2008	68.0	68.6	68.3	68.8	69.0	69.0	70.0	69.8	69.1	68.9	68.7	68.5	68.9
2009	67.6	66.9	66.6	65.2	65.1	65.1	65.3	64.8	64.2	64.1	64.0	64.1	65.3
2010	63.4	63.0	63.0	62.7	62.9	63.3	63.5	63.1	62.7	62.8	63.2	63.5	63.1
2011	63.7	64.1	64.7	64.9	65.6	66.4	67.2	67.6	67.5	68.1	68.7	68.9	66.5
2012	69.5	69.9	70.1	71.1	71.6	72.6	73	73.3	73.1	73.2	74	74.5	72.2
2013	72.7	73.4	73.2	73.9	74.4	75.4	76.1	76.2	75.5	76.1	77.6	77.3	75.2
2014	76.6	77.3	78.1	78.4	79.2	80.4	81.7	82.7	82.3	83.2	84.0	85.3	80.8
2015	85.2	86.2	87.2	88.4	89.5	91.5	93.0	93.7	93.3	93.8	94.4	95.0	90.9
2016	95.5	96.4	97.5	97.9	98.4	100.5	101.6	102.1	101.9	100.1	101.8	101.2	99.6
2017	101.9	102.3	103.3	102.8	103.3	106.8	108.2	108.2	107.3	107.7	108.2	108.1	105.7
Financial Activities													
2007	146.2	146.8	146.9	145.8	146.2	146.0	145.4	145.2	144.1	142.2	142.3	141.6	144.9
2008	139.1	139.1	138.9	138.0	137.9	138.2	137.2	137.0	135.7	135.4	134.2	134.1	137.1
2009	129.4	128.8	128.1	126.5	125.7	125.3	123.6	122.9	121.9	122.6	122.0	121.9	124.9
2010	121.9	122.3	122.3	122.4	122.8	122.8	123.2	123.2	123.1	122.9	122.5	123.3	122.7
2011	121.4	121.7	121.8	121.6	122.0	122.6	123.2	123.5	123.7	123.4	123.6	124.3	122.7
2012	123.6	124.4	124.8	125.5	126.1	127.1	127.3	127.7	127.2	127.9	127.7	128.5	126.5
2013	128.3	129.2	129.2	129.7	130.4	130.9	131.5	131.9	131.3	131.6	131.7	132.4	130.7
2014	130.8	131.3	131.5	131.4	132.0	132.6	133.7	133.9	133.5	133.9	134.3	134.7	132.8
2015	134.0	134.7	135.1	134.6	135.7	137.0	138.5	138.9	137.8	139.3	139.4	140.2	137.1
2016	139.3	139.8	140.0	140.8	141.2	141.8	143.3	143.0	142.2	142.2	142.5	142.7	141.6
2017	140.6	141.4	141.6	141.5	142.0	142.9	143.4	143.6	142.5	142.9	142.5	143.9	142.4
Professional and Business Services													
2007	355.6	359.5	361.6	360.3	363.1	366.5	370.5	372.5	371.6	382.4	383.8	384.9	369.4
2008	378.5	380.8	381.4	381.1	380.4	382.6	383.9	384.5	382.5	382.7	379.4	377.8	381.3
2009	367.0	364.2	361.5	357.5	354.4	355.5	354.7	354.6	351.6	357.0	356.6	356.2	357.6
2010	346.4	348.4	350.4	352.9	352.2	355.8	359.3	359.2	358.9	360.8	360.9	361.1	355.5
2011	359.6	361.8	363.7	368.1	369.0	371.8	377.2	379.2	381.6	383.5	385.2	386.5	373.9
2012	383.4	386.2	389.3	396.3	398.1	402.9	404.3	407.4	407.1	412.2	412.8	413.2	401.1
2013	407.2	410.1	412.3	416.0	415.8	418.0	421.5	424.7	421.6	425.3	427.4	428.9	419.1
2014	424.8	428.0	430.3	432.5	435.4	436.5	438.2	442.3	440.6	443.4	444.8	447.0	437.0
2015	441.3	444.1	447.2	451.5	451.2	453.7	459.8	463.0	460.3	465.4	465.7	467.1	455.9
2016	461.0	464.1	464.3	468.7	467.4	470.7	475.2	475.5	473.0	474.9	475.6	473.6	470.3
2017	468.7	472.0	474.2	474.6	475.4	480.0	481.0	481.9	479.1	482.1	487.4	485.9	478.5
Education and Health Services													
2007	260.0	266.9	269.1	267.4	268.5	267.9	264.8	263.7	267.2	271.1	273.2	274.0	267.8
2008	269.5	276.6	278.4	282.2	283.9	280.3	280.1	280.3	284.8	288.9	290.4	292.1	282.3
2009	286.2	290.4	291.5	293.2	293.3	290.0	287.2	285.4	288.9	292.3	292.8	293.9	290.4
2010	289.4	292.0	293.8	294.7	295.1	291.5	290.1	286.8	291.7	294.8	294.7	295.4	292.5
2011	291.2	294.1	294.7	295.9	295.4	290.5	288.2	287.2	293.3	296.5	297.3	298.3	293.6
2012	292.9	300	302.6	304.2	305	302.3	300.5	300.6	304.2	307	308.7	310.5	303.2
2013	303.7	311.5	314.0	314.9	316.4	312.9	309.6	309.9	312.2	316.6	318.6	319.1	313.3
2014	310.9	318.1	319.4	320.9	320.9	317.6	314.3	314.1	317.6	322.1	324.4	324.3	318.7
2015	320.0	325.2	326.4	328.0	328.6	326.8	326.6	325.8	328.9	334.5	335.8	336.6	328.6
2016	329.7	335.4	337.7	339.8	340.3	337.5	337.2	335.5	340.8	347.1	347.9	348.9	339.8
2017	341.8	348.6	351.4	349.5	350.2	347.5	344.4	343.8	347.6	354.5	356.5	356.4	349.4

Employment by Industry: San Francisco-Oakland-Hayward, CA, Selected Years, 2007–2017—*Continued*

(Numbers in thousands, not seasonally adjusted)

Industry and year	January	February	March	April	May	June	July	August	September	October	November	December	Annual average
Leisure and Hospitality													
2007	202.0	204.4	206.6	208.5	213.2	215.7	217.8	218.1	216.9	214.8	214.2	215.3	212.3
2008	207.1	210.3	211.5	215.1	218.4	221.1	220.9	220.9	219.4	216.7	214.3	214.2	215.8
2009	203.1	203.5	202.8	206.0	210.0	210.7	211.0	210.9	209.2	208.7	205.3	205.8	207.3
2010	197.9	198.7	199.7	208.0	209.2	212.3	213.6	214.4	213.3	214.2	210.4	210.5	208.5
2011	204.3	206.3	208.3	213.8	217.4	219.5	220.4	221.3	222.1	220.7	218.0	218.4	215.9
2012	212.4	214.8	216.8	224.3	228.1	231.2	230.8	233.9	232.3	232.9	230.2	231.2	226.6
2013	224.6	227.8	230.5	234.9	239.7	240.8	240.5	242.6	241.8	241.5	241.3	242.0	237.3
2014	235.1	238.6	241.4	245.9	249.2	252.8	252.4	254.5	253.6	252.8	251	251.9	248.3
2015	244.4	247.8	251.5	256.3	260.0	261.9	262.6	264.3	263.2	262.5	260.8	261.7	258.1
2016	255.9	260.4	261.5	267.6	270.2	271.3	271.8	273.1	270.6	271.2	269.1	268.7	267.6
2017	260.0	265.1	268.7	271.9	275.2	278.6	277.7	277.1	274.0	272.5	271.4	273.7	272.2
Other Services													
2007	72.2	73.4	74.1	74.1	75.0	75.2	75.7	75.5	75.3	75.5	75.5	75.9	74.8
2008	73.6	74.7	75.1	75.7	76.2	76.4	76.5	75.7	75.3	75.9	75.2	75.1	75.5
2009	72.8	72.6	72.5	73.3	73.3	73.1	72.9	72.4	71.6	72.7	72.4	72.1	72.6
2010	70.8	71.2	71.5	72.7	73.4	73.9	73.9	73.1	72.6	73.9	73.0	73.0	72.8
2011	72.2	72.5	72.8	74.5	74.5	74.8	75.6	75.1	75.2	75.8	75.7	75.7	74.5
2012	73.9	74.7	75.5	76.5	77.7	78.4	77.8	77.7	77.9	78.3	78.2	78.6	77.1
2013	76.8	78.1	78.5	79.7	79.9	80.4	80.3	80.4	80.4	80.7	80.8	80.9	79.7
2014	80.0	81.0	81.4	82.9	83.1	83.2	82.8	82.8	82.7	82.9	82.7	82.4	82.3
2015	81.6	82.4	82.8	83.2	84.0	84.1	83.9	83.5	83.3	84.2	83.9	83.8	83.4
2016	83.5	83.9	84.0	85.4	85.6	86.2	86.2	86.0	85.5	86.1	85.7	85.7	85.3
2017	85.0	85.6	86.3	87.2	87.6	88.2	88.0	87.6	87.0	86.9	85.6	84.4	86.6
Government													
2007	319.0	323.4	325.2	325.1	327.7	326.5	314.1	313.2	321.7	316.8	319.4	318.7	320.9
2008	314.9	317.7	319.0	319.6	318.9	320.8	310.4	306.7	311.4	315.4	316.9	315.0	315.6
2009	313.0	315.5	316.9	318.1	316.1	316.3	300.4	288.1	299.7	306.1	306.1	302.2	308.2
2010	300.0	302.0	303.5	309.0	315.3	310.8	286.3	282.7	298.8	302.2	305.3	303.6	301.6
2011	301.0	303.7	306.1	306.7	306.9	305.2	290.4	290.3	293.0	299.7	300.8	298.7	300.2
2012	296.2	299.1	301.8	302.0	302.3	301.1	290.7	288.8	292.4	296.8	301.5	300.0	297.7
2013	295.7	297.8	301.7	302.6	302.6	298.0	287.5	288.6	294.0	300.0	302.9	298.7	297.5
2014	298.9	301.1	302.3	305.6	306.8	304.7	295.1	293.7	299.1	305.7	309.5	308.6	302.6
2015	305.8	307.0	310.4	312.5	313.0	310.7	299.9	302.5	307.2	312.4	315.0	313.6	309.2
2016	312.3	314.6	317.7	319.0	320.8	317.3	304.9	308.0	315.6	321.8	324.1	323.0	316.6
2017	319.0	320.9	323.5	323.1	325.2	321.4	307.4	308.2	316.8	322.5	325.9	324.5	319.9

Employment by Industry: Riverside-San Bernardino-Ontario, CA, Selected Years, 2007–2017

(Numbers in thousands, not seasonally adjusted)

Industry and year	January	February	March	April	May	June	July	August	September	October	November	December	Annual average
Total Nonfarm													
2007	1,280.8	1,285.8	1,293.7	1,291.6	1,297.9	1,297.4	1,283.5	1,278.5	1,283.0	1,289.1	1,298.0	1,300.3	1,290.0
2008	1,267.9	1,267.0	1,267.4	1,265.8	1,260.8	1,257.1	1,232.8	1,229.9	1,227.9	1,232.3	1,233.2	1,227.9	1,247.5
2009	1,198.6	1,188.5	1,187.9	1,182.4	1,179.2	1,172.8	1,146.3	1,145.1	1,141.1	1,154.5	1,163.5	1,163.2	1,168.6
2010	1,142.1	1,143.0	1,149.7	1,157.6	1,161.4	1,158.0	1,131.1	1,138.3	1,139.2	1,152.9	1,166.6	1,168.6	1,150.7
2011	1,144.6	1,148.9	1,153.7	1,157.4	1,157.1	1,151.2	1,135.3	1,143.0	1,149.2	1,160.9	1,176.1	1,176.4	1,154.5
2012	1,165.1	1,167.5	1,173.1	1,183.2	1,186.6	1,185.5	1,166.4	1,176.8	1,182.0	1,201.0	1,219.0	1,216.5	1,185.2
2013	1,207.9	1,214.6	1,220.9	1,226.3	1,230.1	1,229.3	1,210.1	1,225.2	1,234.0	1,252.5	1,273.6	1,275.0	1,233.3
2014	1,257.2	1,263.6	1,271.1	1,280.0	1,282.1	1,281.2	1,265.6	1,281.4	1,292.1	1,312.5	1,340.2	1,344.4	1,289.3
2015	1,322.9	1,324.9	1,332.2	1,338.8	1,343.7	1,342.1	1,334.1	1,347.0	1,352.2	1,380.6	1,406.0	1,413.2	1,353.1
2016	1,381.9	1,380.9	1,384.8	1,396.4	1,396.4	1,390.5	1,383.8	1,393.8	1,402.1	1,424.0	1,442.9	1,445.8	1,401.9
2017	1,423.1	1,425.4	1,438.2	1,439.6	1,447.2	1,445.8	1,432.5	1,443.6	1,452.6	1,474.4	1,497.3	1,499.6	1,451.6
Total Private													
2007	1,056.1	1,060.6	1,066.1	1,063.2	1,068.7	1,068.4	1,066.2	1,065.3	1,063.8	1,060.9	1,067.6	1,068.8	1,064.6
2008	1,037.1	1,035.4	1,033.9	1,031.2	1,025.8	1,023.3	1,010.8	1,007.7	1,004.2	998.7	997.8	991.9	1,016.5
2009	963.0	953.0	950.2	941.6	938.2	933.4	920.5	916.4	914.5	918.5	925.5	925.7	933.4
2010	905.3	905.6	910.0	915.8	916.7	916.4	909.6	912.3	913.5	919.8	932.9	938.6	916.4
2011	913.3	917.3	920.3	924.0	923.5	920.4	921.3	925.2	929.2	933.0	947.0	949.6	927.0
2012	937.0	939.4	943.5	953.4	956.5	959.4	957.2	961.8	965.3	974.5	990.0	989.5	960.6
2013	981.0	987.4	992.3	997.8	1,000.5	1,001.5	999.1	1,008.6	1,013.0	1,024.9	1,044.0	1,047.5	1,008.1
2014	1,028.8	1,035.0	1,039.5	1,047.2	1,049.4	1,049.8	1,050.5	1,061.1	1,067.3	1,080.3	1,106.1	1,111.4	1,060.5
2015	1,090.5	1,091.6	1,096.1	1,102.4	1,106.5	1,107.7	1,114.7	1,121.5	1,122.6	1,143.3	1,166.4	1,174.9	1,119.9
2016	1,142.1	1,141.7	1,141.6	1,151.9	1,151.5	1,146.3	1,152.4	1,158.0	1,162.1	1,177.6	1,193.8	1,196.6	1,159.6
2017	1,173.9	1,176.1	1,186.0	1,188.5	1,193.4	1,192.6	1,194.7	1,203.1	1,206.3	1,220.6	1,241.0	1,243.5	1,201.6
Goods Producing													
2007	234.2	234.6	235.8	235.0	236.4	237.8	237.2	236.7	233.1	226.6	222.3	218.5	232.4
2008	208.9	207.2	206.8	205.0	203.8	203.5	200.5	199.4	196.0	190.2	184.9	179.5	198.8
2009	170.0	164.2	163.3	160.4	160.9	159.9	157.1	155.6	153.3	151.7	150.4	147.6	157.9
2010	144.5	143.9	144.9	146.5	147.5	147.9	146.7	147.4	146.3	145.3	145.2	144.2	145.9
2011	140.4	141.9	142.8	144.5	145.5	146.2	147.5	147.9	147.9	146.7	146.3	145.0	145.2
2012	144.0	144.7	146.0	147.1	149.6	152.1	152.9	154.4	154.2	154.6	153.8	153.1	150.5
2013	151.8	153.9	155.2	155.3	156.4	157.5	159.6	161.4	161.7	163.3	163.6	163.1	158.6
2014	163.2	164.6	165.7	166.4	168.3	169.7	172.0	174.6	174.8	174.4	174.9	173.7	170.2
2015	173.8	176.0	177.7	178.5	180.5	182.7	186.3	188.6	187.2	188.9	188.7	187.6	183.0
2016	185.7	187.1	188.2	190.5	191.2	191.9	194.2	195.2	194.3	194.1	192.6	192.6	191.5
2017	186.0	189.3	192.6	194.9	197.0	199.1	199.1	200.5	200.8	200.1	200.6	199.3	196.6
Service-Providing													
2007	1,046.6	1,051.2	1,057.9	1,056.6	1,061.5	1,059.6	1,046.3	1,041.8	1,049.9	1,062.5	1,075.7	1,081.8	1,057.6
2008	1,059.0	1,059.8	1,060.6	1,060.8	1,057.0	1,053.6	1,032.3	1,030.5	1,031.9	1,042.1	1,048.3	1,048.4	1,048.7
2009	1,028.6	1,024.3	1,024.6	1,022.0	1,018.3	1,012.9	989.2	989.5	987.8	1,002.8	1,013.1	1,015.6	1,010.7
2010	997.6	999.1	1,004.8	1,011.1	1,013.9	1,010.1	984.4	990.9	992.9	1,007.6	1,021.4	1,024.4	1,004.9
2011	1,004.2	1,007.0	1,010.9	1,012.9	1,011.6	1,005.0	987.8	995.1	1,001.3	1,014.2	1,029.8	1,031.4	1,009.3
2012	1,021.1	1,022.8	1,027.1	1,036.1	1,037.0	1,033.4	1,013.5	1,022.4	1,027.8	1,046.4	1,065.2	1,063.4	1,034.7
2013	1,056.1	1,060.7	1,065.7	1,071.0	1,073.7	1,071.8	1,050.5	1,063.8	1,072.3	1,089.2	1,110.0	1,111.9	1,074.7
2014	1,094.0	1,099.0	1,105.4	1,113.6	1,113.8	1,111.5	1,093.6	1,106.8	1,117.3	1,138.1	1,165.3	1,170.7	1,119.1
2015	1,149.1	1,148.9	1,154.5	1,160.3	1,163.2	1,159.4	1,147.8	1,158.4	1,165.0	1,191.7	1,217.3	1,225.6	1,170.1
2016	1,196.2	1,193.8	1,196.6	1,205.9	1,205.2	1,198.6	1,189.6	1,198.6	1,207.8	1,229.9	1,250.3	1,253.2	1,210.5
2017	1,237.1	1,236.1	1,245.6	1,244.7	1,250.2	1,246.7	1,233.4	1,243.1	1,251.8	1,274.3	1,296.7	1,300.3	1,255.0
Mining and Logging													
2007	1.4	1.3	1.3	1.3	1.3	1.3	1.4	1.4	1.4	1.3	1.3	1.2	1.3
2008	1.3	1.3	1.3	1.2	1.2	1.2	1.2	1.2	1.2	1.2	1.1	1.2	1.2
2009	1.2	1.2	1.2	1.2	1.2	1.2	1.1	1.1	1.1	1.1	1.1	1.0	1.1
2010	1.0	1.0	1.0	1.0	1.0	1.0	1.0	1.0	1.0	1.0	1.0	1.0	1.0
2011	1.0	1.0	1.0	1.0	1.0	1.0	1.0	1.1	1.1	1.1	1.1	1.1	1.0
2012	1.1	1.2	1.2	1.2	1.2	1.2	1.2	1.2	1.2	1.2	1.2	1.2	1.2
2013	1.2	1.2	1.2	1.2	1.2	1.2	1.2	1.2	1.2	1.2	1.2	1.2	1.2
2014	1.2	1.3	1.3	1.3	1.3	1.3	1.3	1.3	1.3	1.3	1.3	1.3	1.3
2015	1.3	1.3	1.4	1.4	1.4	1.4	1.4	1.3	1.3	1.1	1.1	1.0	1.3
2016	0.9	0.9	0.9	0.9	0.9	0.9	0.9	0.9	0.9	1.0	1.0	1.0	0.9
2017	1.0	1.0	0.9	0.9	0.9	0.9	0.9	0.9	0.9	0.9	0.9	0.9	0.9

Employment by Industry: Riverside-San Bernardino-Ontario, CA, Selected Years, 2007–2017—*Continued*

(Numbers in thousands, not seasonally adjusted)

Industry and year	January	February	March	April	May	June	July	August	September	October	November	December	Annual average
Construction													
2007	112.2	112.9	114.2	114.4	115.3	116.6	116.5	116.4	113.6	108.8	105.8	103.2	112.5
2008	95.8	94.8	95.3	94.0	93.6	93.8	92.3	92.0	89.5	85.7	82.5	79.5	90.7
2009	73.7	70.0	70.5	68.9	70.0	69.8	68.4	67.9	66.1	64.6	63.9	61.6	68.0
2010	59.0	58.5	59.8	60.5	61.2	61.3	60.4	60.7	59.7	58.8	58.8	57.7	59.7
2011	55.6	56.9	57.3	58.6	59.1	59.4	60.8	61.0	61.0	60.5	60.0	58.7	59.1
2012	58.0	58.0	58.8	59.3	61.1	63.5	64.4	65.7	65.8	66.1	65.7	65.2	62.6
2013	64.7	66.4	67.1	67.5	68.1	68.9	70.9	72.4	72.7	74.0	74.1	73.5	70.0
2014	72.9	73.6	74.5	75.1	76.3	77.2	79.3	81.4	81.2	80.4	80.3	78.8	77.6
2015	78.7	80.3	81.4	82.0	83.4	85.1	88.2	90.2	89.1	90.5	90.1	88.9	85.7
2016	87.7	88.7	89.4	91.1	91.5	92.1	93.8	94.9	94.3	94.3	92.8	92.8	92.0
2017	86.7	89.7	92.6	95.1	96.9	98.6	99.5	100.9	101.4	101.0	101.9	100.1	97.0
Manufacturing													
2007	120.6	120.4	120.3	119.3	119.8	119.9	119.3	118.9	118.1	116.5	115.2	114.1	118.5
2008	111.8	111.1	110.2	109.8	109.0	108.5	107.0	106.2	105.3	103.3	101.3	98.8	106.9
2009	95.1	93.0	91.6	90.3	89.7	88.9	87.6	86.6	86.1	86.0	85.4	85.0	88.8
2010	84.5	84.4	84.1	85.0	85.3	85.6	85.3	85.7	85.6	85.5	85.4	85.5	85.2
2011	83.8	84.0	84.5	84.9	85.4	85.8	85.7	85.8	85.8	85.1	85.2	85.2	85.1
2012	84.9	85.5	86.0	86.6	87.3	87.4	87.3	87.5	87.2	87.3	86.9	86.7	86.7
2013	85.9	86.3	86.9	86.6	87.1	87.4	87.5	87.8	87.8	88.1	88.3	88.4	87.3
2014	89.1	89.7	89.9	90.0	90.7	91.2	91.4	91.9	92.3	92.7	93.3	93.6	91.3
2015	93.8	94.4	94.9	95.1	95.7	96.2	96.7	97.1	96.8	97.3	97.5	97.7	96.1
2016	97.1	97.5	97.9	98.5	98.8	98.9	99.5	99.4	99.1	98.8	98.8	98.8	98.6
2017	98.3	98.6	99.1	98.9	99.2	99.6	98.7	98.7	98.5	98.2	97.8	98.3	98.7
Trade, Transportation, and Utilities													
2007	298.3	296.0	297.2	296.7	298.2	298.2	299.6	299.9	301.2	302.3	310.9	314.8	301.1
2008	301.3	296.5	295.2	294.0	293.7	292.5	289.4	288.6	288.0	286.3	289.7	290.3	292.1
2009	279.5	274.7	272.2	269.1	269.5	269.3	266.3	265.8	267.2	268.1	274.1	277.5	271.1
2010	268.1	265.9	266.2	266.8	268.0	268.3	267.2	267.3	268.2	271.2	279.9	283.1	270.0
2011	272.7	270.7	270.4	271.4	272.3	272.2	272.9	274.0	275.1	277.4	287.6	290.0	275.6
2012	281.8	278.4	278.9	282.4	283.9	284.5	284.8	286.6	288.1	291.7	304.6	305.3	287.6
2013	293.4	291.9	292.2	292.8	294.8	295.5	295.6	298.1	298.6	304.1	317.8	321.1	299.7
2014	306.8	305.0	304.9	307.2	308.9	309.8	309.8	314.0	316.4	321.6	335.4	339.0	314.9
2015	325.0	322.6	323.3	323.9	326.7	326.9	331.2	334.4	335.5	341.0	352.8	355.2	333.2
2016	340.5	338.7	339.0	341.3	341.3	338.8	343.2	345.7	346.6	356.5	371.4	373.6	348.1
2017	359.9	354.8	355.3	356.4	358.7	359.0	362.8	367.0	367.8	374.5	386.8	388.9	366.0
Wholesale Trade													
2007	55.4	56.0	56.3	56.4	56.6	57.0	57.2	57.3	57.5	57.6	57.7	57.8	56.9
2008	56.4	56.1	55.7	55.3	55.2	55.1	53.9	53.7	53.2	52.8	52.0	51.3	54.2
2009	50.5	49.9	49.2	48.9	48.8	48.9	48.7	48.5	48.3	48.5	48.6	48.6	49.0
2010	48.4	48.4	48.5	48.7	48.9	49.0	48.9	48.7	48.7	48.9	48.8	48.9	48.7
2011	48.5	48.8	49.0	49.0	49.1	49.1	49.3	49.3	49.4	49.5	49.5	49.5	49.2
2012	49.4	49.6	50.0	51.7	52.1	52.5	52.7	53.2	53.5	54.0	54.0	54.1	52.2
2013	54.6	55.0	55.6	55.6	56.0	56.3	56.6	57.1	57.1	57.2	57.7	58.0	56.4
2014	57.4	57.8	58.1	58.6	59.0	58.9	59.2	59.0	59.2	59.7	60.0	60.2	58.9
2015	59.7	60.0	60.1	61.3	61.7	61.4	61.9	62.2	62.4	62.8	62.7	62.8	61.6
2016	62.5	62.5	62.5	62.6	62.8	62.7	63.1	63.4	63.3	62.9	62.4	62.5	62.8
2017	62.1	62.4	62.8	63.2	63.4	63.5	63.6	64.1	64.3	64.3	64.9	65.4	63.7
Retail Trade													
2007	176.7	173.2	174.2	173.1	174.1	173.3	173.2	173.5	173.4	174.4	182.4	185.3	175.6
2008	175.2	170.8	170.3	169.2	168.7	168.1	166.7	165.8	165.3	164.7	168.7	169.6	168.6
2009	161.1	157.5	156.0	154.4	154.6	154.1	153.3	153.0	153.4	154.4	160.0	162.7	156.2
2010	154.8	153.0	153.3	153.8	154.1	153.9	153.2	153.1	153.0	155.5	163.0	165.2	155.5
2011	157.3	155.0	154.5	155.5	155.8	155.6	156.3	157.1	157.1	159.0	168.4	170.2	158.5
2012	162.6	158.9	158.4	159.8	160.0	159.3	159.6	160.0	160.1	162.3	173.8	173.3	162.3
2013	163.3	161.1	160.6	161.0	162.1	162.3	162.3	162.8	162.3	165.4	176.1	178.4	164.8
2014	167.7	165.4	165.4	166.4	166.3	166.5	166.8	167.9	167.6	170.1	180.2	182.4	169.4
2015	172.2	169.8	169.7	170.0	171.4	171.2	172.5	173.2	172.8	176.2	185.5	186.6	174.3
2016	177.2	174.9	174.9	175.5	175.6	174.4	175.9	176.6	175.9	178.8	187.8	188.7	178.0
2017	182.5	178.8	178.4	179.0	179.1	178.7	179.8	180.4	179.7	183.3	192.3	193.1	182.1

Employment by Industry: Riverside-San Bernardino-Ontario, CA, Selected Years, 2007–2017—*Continued*

(Numbers in thousands, not seasonally adjusted)

Industry and year	January	February	March	April	May	June	July	August	September	October	November	December	Annual average
Transportation and Utilities													
2007	66.2	66.8	66.7	67.2	67.5	67.9	69.2	69.1	70.3	70.3	70.8	71.7	68.6
2008	69.7	69.6	69.2	69.5	69.8	69.3	68.8	69.1	69.5	68.8	69.0	69.4	69.3
2009	67.9	67.3	67.0	65.8	66.1	66.3	64.3	64.3	65.5	65.2	65.5	66.2	66.0
2010	64.9	64.5	64.4	64.3	65.0	65.4	65.1	65.5	66.5	66.8	68.1	69.0	65.8
2011	66.9	66.9	66.9	66.9	67.4	67.5	67.3	67.6	68.6	68.9	69.7	70.3	67.9
2012	69.8	69.9	70.5	70.9	71.8	72.7	72.5	73.4	74.5	75.4	76.8	77.9	73.0
2013	75.5	75.8	76.0	76.2	76.7	76.9	76.7	78.2	79.2	81.5	84.0	84.7	78.5
2014	81.7	81.8	81.4	82.2	83.6	84.4	83.8	87.1	89.6	91.8	95.2	96.4	86.6
2015	93.1	92.8	93.5	92.6	93.6	94.3	96.8	99.0	100.3	102.0	104.6	105.8	97.4
2016	100.8	101.3	101.6	103.2	102.9	101.7	104.2	105.7	107.4	114.8	121.2	122.4	107.3
2017	115.3	113.6	114.1	114.2	116.2	116.8	119.4	122.5	123.8	126.9	129.6	130.4	120.2
Information													
2007	15.7	15.6	15.3	15.3	15.5	15.5	15.5	15.4	15.2	15.1	15.3	15.3	15.4
2008	15.3	15.4	15.2	15.1	15.1	14.8	14.7	14.6	14.3	14.2	14.3	14.1	14.8
2009	13.9	13.9	14.0	14.0	14.1	14.3	14.4	14.5	14.4	14.0	14.0	13.9	14.1
2010	14.2	14.2	14.3	14.2	14.2	14.3	14.2	14.1	13.8	13.6	13.6	13.5	14.0
2011	12.9	12.7	12.5	12.4	12.3	12.3	12.4	12.2	11.8	11.7	11.6	11.6	12.2
2012	12.0	11.9	11.8	11.7	11.7	11.8	11.8	11.6	11.5	11.5	11.6	11.7	11.7
2013	11.6	11.6	11.5	11.5	11.6	11.6	11.6	11.5	11.4	11.5	11.5	11.5	11.5
2014	11.5	11.4	11.3	11.3	11.3	11.4	11.2	11.1	11.0	11.1	11.2	11.3	11.3
2015	11.3	11.3	11.3	11.5	11.5	11.2	11.4	11.4	11.2	11.5	11.6	11.7	11.4
2016	11.5	11.4	11.4	11.6	11.7	11.6	11.7	11.5	11.4	11.2	11.3	11.3	11.5
2017	11.3	11.2	11.3	11.4	11.3	11.2	11.6	11.5	11.2	11.2	11.3	11.2	11.3
Financial Activities													
2007	50.7	50.9	51.0	50.2	49.9	49.8	49.2	49.0	48.7	47.9	47.8	47.9	49.4
2008	46.7	46.7	46.6	46.4	46.1	46.2	45.4	45.3	45.0	45.0	45.0	44.7	45.8
2009	44.3	44.1	43.8	43.1	42.2	41.9	41.4	41.1	40.8	41.3	41.2	41.2	42.2
2010	40.7	40.7	41.0	41.0	40.6	40.6	40.4	40.3	40.6	40.8	40.6	40.8	40.7
2011	40.1	40.3	40.1	40.1	39.9	39.9	39.6	39.6	39.5	39.7	39.7	39.8	39.9
2012	39.5	39.7	40.0	40.6	40.7	40.6	40.7	40.8	41.0	41.2	41.5	41.6	40.7
2013	41.2	41.4	41.4	41.7	42.0	42.0	41.9	42.0	41.9	42.1	42.2	42.2	41.8
2014	42.0	42.0	42.0	43.1	43.2	43.1	43.0	43.0	42.9	43.2	43.3	43.5	42.9
2015	43.3	43.5	43.5	43.9	44.0	43.9	44.0	44.0	43.7	44.5	44.4	44.6	43.9
2016	44.6	44.4	44.1	44.5	44.5	44.5	44.8	44.8	44.6	44.8	44.8	44.7	44.6
2017	44.3	44.2	44.1	44.7	44.6	44.3	44.2	44.3	44.1	44.8	45.1	44.8	44.5
Professional and Business Services													
2007	142.5	144.5	146.1	144.4	145.7	145.6	146.3	146.4	146.7	147.0	146.1	144.8	145.5
2008	139.9	140.7	139.5	138.0	136.4	138.7	138.4	138.4	138.2	138.1	137.4	135.2	138.2
2009	131.1	129.7	129.3	127.7	125.4	124.7	122.8	122.4	122.0	123.3	123.4	121.3	125.3
2010	118.6	119.6	120.4	121.7	122.0	122.9	123.4	124.9	124.9	127.3	127.6	128.1	123.5
2011	122.7	124.8	125.3	125.4	124.0	123.2	124.5	127.2	127.8	128.0	127.8	126.6	125.6
2012	124.5	126.5	125.7	128.0	126.7	128.0	127.1	127.5	127.0	129.7	128.3	125.8	127.1
2013	126.4	129.5	128.8	131.5	130.3	130.9	131.8	134.2	135.1	135.7	135.3	133.7	131.9
2014	130.6	133.1	133.9	136.2	134.2	134.9	136.2	137.8	139.7	144.1	151.3	152.6	138.7
2015	145.2	142.6	141.8	144.0	143.2	144.2	144.1	144.0	144.3	152.1	159.9	163.8	147.4
2016	149.4	145.8	142.3	143.2	142.0	142.4	143.3	144.2	146.7	147.5	146.2	147.1	145.0
2017	145.8	146.1	147.6	144.0	143.5	144.0	144.5	146.2	147.8	149.9	153.2	153.4	147.2
Education and Health Services													
2007	142.8	144.5	145.4	145.4	145.7	145.7	146.6	147.1	148.1	150.8	151.6	151.9	147.1
2008	150.5	153.5	154.1	155.7	155.1	154.1	152.8	153.1	154.8	158.0	158.8	159.4	155.0
2009	157.8	160.2	161.0	162.4	162.1	161.7	160.7	161.4	161.9	163.4	163.7	163.5	161.7
2010	159.7	160.9	161.1	161.6	161.3	160.3	159.1	160.0	161.1	162.4	164.2	164.5	161.4
2011	162.1	164.4	164.8	165.9	165.1	163.6	163.1	163.5	166.3	167.8	169.0	169.7	165.4
2012	169.6	171.4	172.5	172.7	172.8	172.4	170.9	171.8	174.4	177.3	178.3	179.2	173.6
2013	183.6	185.1	186.5	186.9	187.3	187.2	184.3	186.3	188.5	190.8	192.5	192.5	187.6
2014	190.4	192.4	193.3	194.5	194.1	193.2	192.2	194.4	196.0	198.3	199.2	199.7	194.8
2015	200.4	202.2	202.6	203.6	203.5	202.9	203.6	205.2	207.0	209.3	210.2	211.0	205.1
2016	209.3	211.2	211.4	214.6	214.2	212.4	211.5	213.4	215.3	219.1	220.3	218.8	214.3
2017	218.9	220.6	221.6	223.4	223.8	222.3	223.5	225.1	226.1	230.9	231.4	230.5	224.8

Employment by Industry: Riverside-San Bernardino-Ontario, CA, Selected Years, 2007–2017—*Continued*

(Numbers in thousands, not seasonally adjusted)

Industry and year	January	February	March	April	May	June	July	August	September	October	November	December	Annual average
Leisure and Hospitality													
2007	131.7	133.6	134.6	134.6	135.4	133.8	130.7	129.7	129.4	130.2	132.5	134.7	132.6
2008	133.8	134.4	134.9	134.6	133.0	131.3	128.8	127.5	127.5	127.4	128.8	130.2	131.0
2009	129.2	129.1	129.2	127.5	126.5	124.1	120.3	118.7	118.1	119.0	121.0	123.3	123.8
2010	122.4	122.9	124.1	125.2	124.2	122.9	120.2	120.1	120.6	121.1	123.6	126.1	122.8
2011	124.4	124.0	125.8	125.2	125.0	123.6	122.2	121.4	121.5	122.2	125.6	127.5	124.0
2012	126.8	127.6	129.1	130.6	130.5	129.2	128.5	128.4	128.3	128.6	131.9	133.1	129.4
2013	133.2	133.8	135.7	137.0	137.0	135.5	133.4	133.7	134.3	135.7	139.2	141.7	135.9
2014	142.2	143.9	145.3	144.8	145.8	144.3	143.2	143.0	143.4	144.9	147.8	148.8	144.8
2015	148.8	150.1	152.2	152.6	152.8	151.6	149.7	149.9	149.8	151.6	154.5	156.9	151.7
2016	157.1	158.7	160.5	161.3	161.8	159.9	159.3	158.7	158.4	159.6	162.5	164.0	160.2
2017	163.5	165.4	168.5	168.0	168.7	166.8	163.3	162.7	162.7	163.5	166.0	169.2	165.7
Other Services													
2007	40.2	40.9	40.7	41.6	41.9	42.0	41.1	41.1	41.4	41.0	41.1	40.9	41.2
2008	40.7	41.0	41.6	42.4	42.6	42.2	40.8	40.8	40.4	39.5	38.9	38.5	40.8
2009	37.2	37.1	37.4	37.4	37.5	37.5	37.5	36.9	36.8	37.7	37.7	37.4	37.3
2010	37.1	37.5	38.0	38.8	38.9	39.2	38.4	38.2	38.0	38.1	38.2	38.3	38.2
2011	38.0	38.5	38.6	39.1	39.4	39.4	39.1	39.4	39.3	39.5	39.4	39.4	39.1
2012	38.8	39.2	39.5	40.3	40.6	40.8	40.5	40.7	40.8	39.9	40.0	39.7	40.1
2013	39.8	40.2	41.0	41.1	41.1	41.3	40.9	41.4	41.5	41.7	41.9	41.7	41.1
2014	42.1	42.6	43.1	43.7	43.6	43.4	42.9	43.2	43.1	42.7	43.0	42.8	43.0
2015	42.7	43.3	43.7	44.4	44.3	44.3	44.4	44.0	43.9	44.4	44.3	44.1	44.0
2016	44.0	44.4	44.7	44.9	44.8	44.8	44.4	44.5	44.8	44.8	44.7	44.5	44.6
2017	44.2	44.5	45.0	45.7	45.8	45.9	45.7	45.8	45.8	45.7	46.6	46.2	45.6
Government													
2007	224.7	225.2	227.6	228.4	229.2	229.0	217.3	213.2	219.2	228.2	230.4	231.5	225.3
2008	230.8	231.6	233.5	234.6	235.0	233.8	222.0	222.2	223.7	233.6	235.4	236.0	231.0
2009	235.6	235.5	237.7	240.8	241.0	239.4	225.8	228.7	226.6	236.0	238.0	237.5	235.2
2010	236.8	237.4	239.7	241.8	244.7	241.6	221.5	226.0	225.7	233.1	233.7	230.0	234.3
2011	231.3	231.6	233.4	233.4	233.6	230.8	214.0	217.8	220.0	227.9	229.1	226.8	227.5
2012	228.1	228.1	229.6	229.8	230.1	226.1	209.2	215.0	216.7	226.5	229.0	227.0	224.6
2013	226.9	227.2	228.6	228.5	229.6	227.8	211.0	216.6	221.0	227.6	229.6	227.5	225.2
2014	228.4	228.6	231.6	232.8	232.7	231.4	215.1	220.3	224.8	232.2	234.1	233.0	228.8
2015	232.4	233.3	236.1	236.4	237.2	234.4	219.4	225.5	229.6	237.3	239.6	238.3	233.3
2016	239.8	239.2	243.2	244.5	244.9	244.2	231.4	235.8	240.0	246.4	249.1	249.2	242.3
2017	249.2	249.3	252.2	251.1	253.8	253.2	237.8	240.5	246.3	253.8	256.3	256.1	250.0

Employment by Industry: Detroit-Warren-Dearborn, MI, Selected Years, 2007–2017

(Numbers in thousands, not seasonally adjusted)

Industry and year	January	February	March	April	May	June	July	August	September	October	November	December	Annual average
Total Nonfarm													
2007	1,936.0	1,948.5	1,952.3	1,965.5	1,990.4	1,994.0	1,928.4	1,957.1	1,966.9	1,960.2	1,977.6	1,970.2	1,962.3
2008	1,907.7	1,909.3	1,905.0	1,908.7	1,928.9	1,937.3	1,866.8	1,887.2	1,894.1	1,893.9	1,885.6	1,866.4	1,899.2
2009	1,751.9	1,760.7	1,757.5	1,757.5	1,749.2	1,738.8	1,706.0	1,716.4	1,734.0	1,744.3	1,743.5	1,739.4	1,741.6
2010	1,694.4	1,698.5	1,701.8	1,725.9	1,750.0	1,757.9	1,723.5	1,727.4	1,750.3	1,766.9	1,770.5	1,767.5	1,736.2
2011	1,731.1	1,739.3	1,751.2	1,775.1	1,793.4	1,800.2	1,770.2	1,785.6	1,805.5	1,820.2	1,827.1	1,821.8	1,785.1
2012	1,790.7	1,797.7	1,812.2	1,817.7	1,840.4	1,849.3	1,821.6	1,834.8	1,842.8	1,855.7	1,863.8	1,862.9	1,832.5
2013	1,825.7	1,834.5	1,845.1	1,851.4	1,879.6	1,889.3	1,844.9	1,866.6	1,877.7	1,893.7	1,898.4	1,892.0	1,866.6
2014	1,847.4	1,862.4	1,871.3	1,873.0	1,904.8	1,924.5	1,892.7	1,902.1	1,904.1	1,921.5	1,932.5	1,934.5	1,897.6
2015	1,893.4	1,896.5	1,904.3	1,918.6	1,950.0	1,960.9	1,930.4	1,939.0	1,945.7	1,960.5	1,968.3	1,966.0	1,936.1
2016	1,931.2	1,932.5	1,938.6	1,962.9	1,983.2	1,996.2	1,972.9	1,975.8	1,987.9	1,996.0	2,011.7	2,001.9	1,974.2
2017	1,967.4	1,970.5	1,977.8	1,993.1	2,019.4	2,034.6	1,995.3	2,009.6	2,013.0	2,018.4	2,029.7	2,023.0	2,004.3
Total Private													
2007	1,707.5	1,716.7	1,718.2	1,732.8	1,755.0	1,762.8	1,723.5	1,753.4	1,746.7	1,734.2	1,751.1	1,745.1	1,737.3
2008	1,687.8	1,685.4	1,680.6	1,684.7	1,703.2	1,714.6	1,664.4	1,683.7	1,676.7	1,670.7	1,661.5	1,645.4	1,679.9
2009	1,535.3	1,540.3	1,536.1	1,534.5	1,527.8	1,519.8	1,508.4	1,519.1	1,522.4	1,527.5	1,526.4	1,524.7	1,526.9
2010	1,484.8	1,484.8	1,487.5	1,510.0	1,531.1	1,544.2	1,529.5	1,538.3	1,547.4	1,559.6	1,563.8	1,562.4	1,528.6
2011	1,531.9	1,535.8	1,547.6	1,571.5	1,592.4	1,600.6	1,586.9	1,603.4	1,608.0	1,619.6	1,625.5	1,622.4	1,587.1
2012	1,596.3	1,599.5	1,613.7	1,619.7	1,644.2	1,653.5	1,642.9	1,656.3	1,649.6	1,661.2	1,668.2	1,669.1	1,639.5
2013	1,637.1	1,642.4	1,653.1	1,659.9	1,690.4	1,700.3	1,672.1	1,695.3	1,691.3	1,704.3	1,708.7	1,704.1	1,679.9
2014	1,663.7	1,674.6	1,683.0	1,684.0	1,718.0	1,738.1	1,721.8	1,732.5	1,720.9	1,733.5	1,742.9	1,747.9	1,713.4
2015	1,711.4	1,710.7	1,717.6	1,731.1	1,763.2	1,775.6	1,760.9	1,771.1	1,763.1	1,773.8	1,780.4	1,779.6	1,753.2
2016	1,749.0	1,746.5	1,750.4	1,775.2	1,798.0	1,810.7	1,800.7	1,804.3	1,802.3	1,808.2	1,821.3	1,813.8	1,790.0
2017	1,783.3	1,783.8	1,789.8	1,804.8	1,831.1	1,846.4	1,821.5	1,837.2	1,825.4	1,828.6	1,839.3	1,833.5	1,818.7
Goods Producing													
2007	305.5	316.9	317.1	319.9	325.0	327.3	306.5	326.5	323.9	311.3	317.7	312.4	317.5
2008	295.3	296.7	290.7	287.6	291.4	302.9	272.7	289.8	289.1	286.0	283.3	272.0	288.1
2009	223.9	233.4	233.7	231.2	219.1	216.6	217.6	226.4	230.0	231.8	227.0	223.7	226.2
2010	217.3	215.2	215.2	222.7	228.8	234.2	232.9	231.7	240.9	242.0	240.7	237.8	230.0
2011	232.4	233.9	236.2	244.6	251.3	257.2	254.1	260.6	262.0	262.8	263.7	261.1	251.7
2012	256.9	256.0	259.1	260.0	267.4	271.4	271.2	274.1	274.2	275.1	274.4	272.5	267.7
2013	267.6	267.9	269.8	272.0	280.5	284.4	277.0	286.1	286.9	288.5	287.9	280.8	279.1
2014	274.9	280.5	282.0	278.6	290.1	301.7	297.9	302.9	299.1	301.7	304.0	303.8	293.1
2015	294.8	294.3	295.4	300.0	308.9	314.3	310.6	314.6	314.4	312.4	313.7	310.2	307.0
2016	306.0	302.6	303.0	313.4	318.7	323.0	317.6	318.8	321.5	321.3	325.2	318.6	315.8
2017	316.1	316.5	315.8	321.3	328.8	333.7	323.0	333.4	329.1	329.5	330.9	325.8	325.3
Service-Providing													
2007	1,630.5	1,631.6	1,635.2	1,645.6	1,665.4	1,666.7	1,621.9	1,630.6	1,643.0	1,648.9	1,659.9	1,657.8	1,644.8
2008	1,612.4	1,612.6	1,614.3	1,621.1	1,637.5	1,634.4	1,594.1	1,597.4	1,605.0	1,607.9	1,602.3	1,594.4	1,611.1
2009	1,528.0	1,527.3	1,523.8	1,526.3	1,530.1	1,522.2	1,488.4	1,490.0	1,504.0	1,512.5	1,516.5	1,515.7	1,515.4
2010	1,477.1	1,483.3	1,486.6	1,503.2	1,521.2	1,523.7	1,490.6	1,495.7	1,509.4	1,524.9	1,529.8	1,529.7	1,506.3
2011	1,498.7	1,505.4	1,515.0	1,530.5	1,542.1	1,543.0	1,516.1	1,525.0	1,543.5	1,557.4	1,563.4	1,559.7	1,533.3
2012	1,533.8	1,541.7	1,553.1	1,557.7	1,573.0	1,577.9	1,550.4	1,560.7	1,568.6	1,580.6	1,589.4	1,590.4	1,564.8
2013	1,558.1	1,566.6	1,575.3	1,579.4	1,599.1	1,604.9	1,567.9	1,580.5	1,590.8	1,605.2	1,610.5	1,611.2	1,587.5
2014	1,572.5	1,581.9	1,589.3	1,594.4	1,614.7	1,622.8	1,594.8	1,599.2	1,605.0	1,619.8	1,628.5	1,630.7	1,604.5
2015	1,598.6	1,602.2	1,608.9	1,618.6	1,641.1	1,646.6	1,619.8	1,624.4	1,631.3	1,648.1	1,654.6	1,655.8	1,629.2
2016	1,625.2	1,629.9	1,635.6	1,649.5	1,664.5	1,673.2	1,655.3	1,657.0	1,666.4	1,674.7	1,686.5	1,683.3	1,658.4
2017	1,651.3	1,654.0	1,662.0	1,671.8	1,690.6	1,700.9	1,672.3	1,676.2	1,683.9	1,688.9	1,698.8	1,697.2	1,679.0
Mining, Logging, and Construction													
2007	64.9	62.4	64.4	67.1	72.7	75.5	77.9	77.7	76.4	74.0	71.8	68.1	71.1
2008	61.0	58.6	58.6	61.6	66.8	68.9	69.2	68.9	67.4	66.5	63.3	57.8	64.1
2009	50.0	48.4	48.3	49.8	53.9	55.1	55.5	55.0	54.0	54.4	52.6	49.4	52.2
2010	43.9	42.6	44.3	47.9	51.6	53.7	56.2	56.8	56.2	56.6	55.3	52.3	51.5
2011	47.4	46.2	47.3	50.3	54.7	58.6	60.4	60.6	59.7	59.0	57.8	55.2	54.8
2012	51.0	49.1	50.3	52.9	56.4	59.1	59.9	60.0	60.0	59.7	58.4	55.8	56.1
2013	52.2	50.7	51.8	53.3	59.6	61.1	62.7	62.6	61.6	61.9	60.7	57.9	58.0
2014	53.1	52.6	52.9	55.3	62.2	65.5	66.3	67.9	68.0	67.7	66.1	63.4	61.8
2015	58.0	56.9	58.3	62.1	67.3	70.2	70.3	70.5	69.6	70.2	68.8	65.9	65.7
2016	61.1	60.0	61.3	65.7	70.4	71.8	72.9	73.0	72.8	72.9	71.7	66.8	68.4
2017	64.0	63.2	64.4	68.5	74.2	76.7	77.5	77.9	77.1	77.0	75.4	71.1	72.3

Employment by Industry: Detroit-Warren-Dearborn, MI, Selected Years, 2007–2017—*Continued*

(Numbers in thousands, not seasonally adjusted)

Industry and year	January	February	March	April	May	June	July	August	September	October	November	December	Annual average
Manufacturing													
2007	240.6	254.5	252.7	252.8	252.3	251.8	228.6	248.8	247.5	237.3	245.9	244.3	246.4
2008	234.3	238.1	232.1	226.0	224.6	234.0	203.5	220.9	221.7	219.5	220.0	214.2	224.1
2009	173.9	185.0	185.4	181.4	165.2	161.5	162.1	171.4	176.0	177.4	174.4	174.3	174.0
2010	173.4	172.6	170.9	174.8	177.2	180.5	176.7	174.9	184.7	185.4	185.4	185.5	178.5
2011	185.0	187.7	188.9	194.3	196.6	198.6	193.7	200.0	202.3	203.8	205.9	206.9	197.0
2012	205.9	206.9	208.8	207.1	211.0	212.3	211.3	214.1	214.2	215.4	216.0	216.7	211.6
2013	215.4	217.2	218.0	218.7	220.9	223.3	214.3	223.5	225.3	226.6	227.2	222.9	221.1
2014	221.8	227.9	229.1	223.3	227.9	236.2	231.6	235.0	231.1	234.0	237.9	240.4	231.4
2015	236.8	237.4	237.1	237.9	241.6	244.1	240.3	244.1	244.8	242.2	244.9	244.3	241.3
2016	244.9	242.6	241.7	247.7	248.3	251.2	244.7	245.8	248.7	248.4	253.5	251.8	247.4
2017	252.1	253.3	251.4	252.8	254.6	257.0	245.5	255.5	252.0	252.5	255.5	254.7	253.1
Trade, Transportation, and Utilities													
2007	366.2	361.7	361.5	362.2	366.6	366.8	362.1	365.3	364.4	366.5	375.2	378.7	366.4
2008	363.3	358.3	358.9	357.0	359.7	360.5	356.2	356.4	355.5	354.4	357.2	358.3	358.0
2009	336.6	332.7	330.1	326.0	328.1	327.4	323.4	323.8	323.8	326.1	331.5	334.8	328.7
2010	320.6	317.6	319.0	322.1	326.0	328.1	326.2	327.8	326.2	332.3	338.1	341.7	327.1
2011	328.3	325.3	326.3	329.1	333.1	334.6	333.7	334.9	334.6	337.9	345.7	348.9	334.4
2012	337.8	334.6	336.2	335.0	339.8	341.5	339.1	340.5	339.4	343.4	353.1	354.6	341.3
2013	341.1	338.6	339.3	339.4	344.7	347.7	345.9	347.8	346.1	349.5	357.3	361.8	346.6
2014	348.2	346.6	347.3	349.4	354.0	356.1	353.9	355.0	352.9	357.4	365.6	370.1	354.7
2015	355.5	352.6	353.2	354.8	359.6	361.3	358.9	359.9	357.5	361.0	369.6	373.7	359.8
2016	360.5	357.8	358.1	360.0	364.2	365.4	364.3	365.5	363.9	366.9	375.0	378.1	365.0
2017	365.8	362.5	363.2	364.6	368.1	370.4	367.7	368.9	367.5	370.7	378.3	380.3	369.0
Wholesale Trade													
2007	90.5	90.0	89.8	89.9	90.5	90.4	90.2	90.0	89.4	89.9	89.3	89.7	90.0
2008	89.2	88.8	88.9	89.0	89.3	89.2	88.7	88.5	88.2	87.7	86.7	86.0	88.4
2009	84.1	83.1	81.9	80.8	80.1	78.7	77.7	77.9	77.5	77.7	77.5	77.8	79.6
2010	76.3	76.6	76.8	77.4	78.0	78.6	78.5	79.1	78.8	79.5	79.8	80.2	78.3
2011	79.2	79.2	79.6	80.5	81.0	81.1	81.4	81.5	81.1	81.4	81.8	81.9	80.8
2012	81.6	82.0	82.3	82.2	83.1	83.5	83.3	83.6	83.2	83.6	83.6	83.9	83.0
2013	83.4	83.5	83.8	83.6	84.2	84.6	84.3	84.3	83.8	83.7	83.7	84.1	83.9
2014	83.3	83.5	83.6	83.5	84.6	85.0	84.4	84.7	84.0	84.0	84.3	84.7	84.1
2015	83.6	83.9	84.0	84.3	85.0	85.2	85.1	85.1	84.3	84.4	84.3	84.6	84.5
2016	83.7	84.1	83.8	84.5	85.2	85.5	85.2	85.5	85.1	85.4	85.4	85.8	84.9
2017	85.3	85.6	85.8	86.0	86.8	87.3	86.7	87.0	86.5	86.6	88.3	87.8	86.6
Retail Trade													
2007	212.2	207.0	207.3	207.7	210.7	210.6	209.1	210.2	209.9	212.2	220.7	223.0	211.7
2008	211.3	206.4	206.6	205.6	208.0	207.8	206.6	206.7	205.7	206.3	210.0	211.4	207.7
2009	197.5	193.4	192.3	190.9	194.5	195.9	193.2	192.7	192.1	194.3	199.8	201.7	194.9
2010	190.6	187.5	188.2	191.0	193.9	194.8	193.7	194.2	192.3	196.7	201.8	204.1	194.1
2011	192.9	190.1	190.6	192.6	194.9	195.5	195.1	195.8	195.3	198.4	205.2	207.5	196.2
2012	197.2	193.5	194.6	194.1	197.2	198.0	196.7	197.3	196.0	199.0	208.3	208.8	198.4
2013	197.3	194.4	194.9	195.4	199.2	201.3	200.9	201.9	200.4	203.0	210.0	212.7	201.0
2014	201.0	199.1	199.7	201.7	204.8	206.2	204.9	205.5	204.0	208.3	215.7	217.6	205.7
2015	205.0	203.0	203.8	204.3	207.8	208.9	207.2	208.3	206.3	209.3	216.5	218.5	208.2
2016	208.0	205.9	206.5	207.7	210.8	211.6	211.1	211.9	209.7	212.3	219.0	220.9	211.3
2017	211.2	208.5	208.9	210.1	212.1	213.3	212.3	212.6	210.9	212.8	218.1	219.3	212.5
Transportation and Utilities													
2007	63.5	64.7	64.4	64.6	65.4	65.8	62.8	65.1	65.1	64.4	65.2	66.0	64.8
2008	62.8	63.1	63.4	62.4	62.4	63.5	60.9	61.2	61.6	60.4	60.5	60.9	61.9
2009	55.0	56.2	55.9	54.3	53.5	52.8	52.5	53.2	54.2	54.1	54.2	55.3	54.3
2010	53.7	53.5	54.0	53.7	54.1	54.7	54.0	54.5	55.1	56.1	56.5	57.4	54.8
2011	56.2	56.0	56.1	56.0	57.2	58.0	57.2	57.6	58.2	58.1	58.7	59.5	57.4
2012	59.0	59.1	59.3	58.7	59.5	60.0	59.1	59.6	60.2	60.8	61.2	61.9	59.9
2013	60.4	60.7	60.6	60.4	61.3	61.8	60.7	61.6	61.9	62.8	63.6	65.0	61.7
2014	63.9	64.0	64.0	64.2	64.6	64.9	64.6	64.8	64.9	65.1	65.6	67.8	64.9
2015	66.9	65.7	65.4	66.2	66.8	67.2	66.6	66.5	66.9	67.3	68.8	70.6	67.1
2016	68.8	67.8	67.8	67.8	68.2	68.3	68.0	68.1	69.1	69.2	70.6	71.4	68.8
2017	69.3	68.4	68.5	68.5	69.2	69.8	68.7	69.3	70.1	71.3	71.9	73.2	69.9

Employment by Industry: Detroit-Warren-Dearborn, MI, Selected Years, 2007–2017—*Continued*

(Numbers in thousands, not seasonally adjusted)

Industry and year	January	February	March	April	May	June	July	August	September	October	November	December	Annual average
Information													
2007	30.1	29.9	29.7	30.0	30.3	30.2	30.0	29.9	29.6	29.6	29.7	29.6	29.9
2008	29.7	29.7	29.3	29.2	29.4	29.5	29.2	29.5	29.8	29.0	29.2	28.8	29.4
2009	28.2	28.3	27.7	27.5	27.6	27.7	27.5	27.2	27.0	27.1	27.5	27.7	27.6
2010	26.9	26.8	26.7	26.8	27.0	27.2	26.8	28.6	28.4	26.4	26.3	26.5	27.0
2011	26.4	26.1	26.1	25.8	26.0	26.0	26.1	26.2	26.0	26.7	26.7	26.6	26.2
2012	26.8	26.6	26.7	26.3	26.5	26.3	26.6	27.0	26.2	26.4	26.6	26.6	26.6
2013	26.7	26.7	26.8	27.4	27.6	27.9	27.6	27.6	27.1	27.0	27.2	27.2	27.2
2014	27.5	27.2	27.4	27.8	27.8	28.3	28.8	28.6	27.6	28.2	28.2	27.9	27.9
2015	27.2	27.0	27.0	26.8	27.3	27.7	28.3	27.7	27.6	27.3	27.5	27.1	27.4
2016	27.5	27.4	27.6	27.9	28.2	28.6	29.1	28.6	28.4	27.7	28.2	27.9	28.1
2017	27.2	27.2	27.6	27.2	27.5	27.7	27.9	27.7	27.8	27.7	27.1	27.0	27.4
Financial Activities													
2007	111.0	110.8	110.5	111.1	111.4	112.2	112.1	111.1	109.0	108.0	107.6	107.5	110.2
2008	106.8	106.7	106.2	105.8	106.7	106.7	105.9	105.0	103.5	102.7	101.9	101.6	105.0
2009	99.9	99.4	98.8	98.8	99.2	99.2	98.8	98.3	97.0	96.0	95.6	95.6	98.1
2010	95.1	94.9	94.2	93.8	95.0	96.1	96.4	96.8	95.7	96.0	96.3	96.9	95.6
2011	96.5	96.7	97.3	97.9	98.1	98.8	99.2	99.5	98.0	97.6	97.6	97.8	97.9
2012	97.3	97.6	98.1	98.1	98.9	100.3	101.4	101.9	100.1	100.4	100.8	101.7	99.7
2013	101.6	102.0	102.5	102.7	103.6	105.6	106.3	106.5	104.2	104.1	104.1	104.3	104.0
2014	103.4	103.4	103.3	103.1	104.6	106.1	106.0	106.3	104.5	104.5	104.6	105.1	104.6
2015	104.5	104.6	104.8	105.7	107.1	109.0	109.1	109.4	108.1	108.4	108.7	109.0	107.4
2016	109.1	109.3	109.4	110.3	111.6	113.6	114.1	114.1	113.0	113.1	113.3	113.8	112.1
2017	114.2	114.1	114.2	114.6	115.3	117.2	116.9	116.7	115.5	116.2	116.2	116.7	115.7
Professional and Business Services													
2007	359.0	359.1	356.4	363.3	365.0	367.2	361.6	367.7	365.7	366.2	369.2	365.0	363.8
2008	353.2	352.9	351.6	356.5	358.4	356.6	346.6	347.9	345.0	347.6	342.3	337.7	349.7
2009	316.0	314.5	310.9	309.9	305.9	301.8	299.8	301.9	305.8	307.8	308.1	307.2	307.5
2010	301.9	304.6	304.0	310.7	313.7	316.0	310.6	315.2	320.4	325.6	326.7	324.1	314.5
2011	323.1	325.4	329.3	335.3	338.8	336.9	330.3	337.3	343.1	349.5	349.8	344.4	336.9
2012	342.8	346.4	349.4	353.9	358.9	356.6	352.0	357.5	358.7	364.0	363.4	361.8	355.5
2013	357.6	360.8	364.5	365.5	373.0	372.7	358.4	368.2	371.4	376.3	375.6	373.4	368.1
2014	364.2	367.6	369.1	367.7	375.3	376.4	369.7	372.9	374.1	377.3	377.2	376.5	372.3
2015	375.5	377.1	377.7	382.3	387.9	387.5	379.7	382.4	384.9	388.6	387.2	384.6	383.0
2016	379.6	380.1	379.5	386.0	390.1	391.9	388.2	389.5	391.3	394.9	395.8	391.8	388.2
2017	385.8	386.4	388.5	391.5	396.8	398.7	391.6	394.1	394.0	393.9	394.7	391.2	392.3
Education and Health Services													
2007	272.5	275.2	276.4	275.9	277.3	277.8	273.4	273.3	277.4	278.9	280.7	280.8	276.6
2008	277.8	279.9	280.2	280.5	282.2	280.8	278.3	278.1	281.0	283.3	284.1	284.1	280.9
2009	279.8	283.0	283.9	283.3	284.7	284.2	280.2	280.5	281.6	284.6	286.4	285.6	283.2
2010	281.3	283.9	284.7	283.9	284.8	283.7	282.2	282.2	283.5	288.4	289.4	289.3	284.8
2011	285.8	287.8	288.8	291.4	291.9	290.3	289.5	289.9	291.8	294.7	295.7	296.4	291.2
2012	292.2	295.5	296.7	295.3	296.1	295.5	293.8	294.4	294.6	297.9	298.8	299.9	295.9
2013	295.4	298.2	298.8	298.3	298.8	297.9	295.2	296.0	297.7	300.3	301.2	301.2	298.3
2014	296.2	299.8	300.7	299.2	300.0	299.0	296.7	297.2	298.3	301.8	303.3	304.2	299.7
2015	299.2	301.4	302.6	301.3	303.0	302.8	301.6	304.2	302.5	309.2	309.4	310.3	304.0
2016	306.0	308.5	309.0	309.8	311.0	309.8	309.7	309.2	310.6	312.8	314.0	314.4	310.4
2017	309.7	312.1	312.6	312.5	314.1	313.7	310.4	310.8	311.1	313.6	315.0	315.0	312.6
Leisure and Hospitality													
2007	175.9	175.5	178.6	182.8	191.0	192.3	189.5	191.0	188.6	185.9	183.4	183.2	184.8
2008	175.9	175.2	177.5	181.5	187.9	189.9	187.8	189.4	185.7	181.3	178.0	177.8	182.3
2009	167.8	166.1	168.4	175.2	180.1	179.7	178.7	179.0	176.5	173.2	169.7	169.4	173.7
2010	162.8	163.0	164.9	171.8	177.1	179.9	176.6	178.8	176.0	173.2	171.1	171.0	172.2
2011	165.5	166.9	169.7	173.4	178.6	181.5	179.2	180.0	177.9	175.7	172.0	171.5	174.3
2012	168.6	168.7	172.5	175.3	180.2	184.3	181.7	183.1	179.1	177.1	174.6	175.6	176.7
2013	171.1	171.7	174.2	177.8	184.8	186.1	184.2	185.3	180.7	181.5	178.3	178.3	179.5
2014	172.9	173.0	176.5	181.5	188.9	192.7	190.8	191.7	187.1	185.2	183.1	183.5	183.9
2015	179.7	178.6	181.7	185.2	193.5	196.2	195.6	195.6	191.4	190.2	187.9	188.0	188.6
2016	185.0	185.5	188.2	192.4	198.0	201.7	201.3	202.0	197.1	195.4	193.6	193.3	194.5
2017	189.9	190.3	192.9	197.8	204.1	207.8	207.3	208.7	203.9	201.1	201.0	201.3	200.5

Employment by Industry: Detroit-Warren-Dearborn, MI, Selected Years, 2007–2017—*Continued*

(Numbers in thousands, not seasonally adjusted)

Industry and year	January	February	March	April	May	June	July	August	September	October	November	December	Annual average
Other Services													
2007	87.3	87.6	88.0	87.6	88.4	89.0	88.3	88.6	88.1	87.8	87.6	87.9	88.0
2008	85.8	86.0	86.2	86.6	87.5	87.7	87.7	87.6	87.1	86.4	85.5	85.1	86.6
2009	83.1	82.9	82.6	82.6	83.1	83.2	82.4	82.0	80.7	80.9	80.6	80.7	82.1
2010	78.9	78.8	78.8	78.2	78.7	79.0	77.8	77.2	76.3	75.7	75.2	75.1	77.5
2011	73.9	73.7	73.9	74.0	74.6	75.3	74.8	75.0	74.6	74.7	74.3	74.7	74.5
2012	73.9	74.1	75.0	75.8	76.4	77.6	77.1	77.8	77.3	76.9	76.5	76.4	76.2
2013	76.0	76.5	77.2	76.8	77.4	78.0	77.5	77.8	77.2	77.1	77.1	77.1	77.1
2014	76.4	76.5	76.7	76.7	77.3	77.8	78.0	77.9	77.3	77.4	76.9	76.8	77.1
2015	75.0	75.1	75.2	75.0	75.9	76.8	77.1	77.3	76.7	76.7	76.4	76.7	76.2
2016	75.3	75.3	75.6	75.4	76.2	76.7	76.4	76.6	76.5	76.1	76.2	75.9	76.0
2017	74.6	74.7	75.0	75.3	76.4	77.2	76.7	76.9	76.5	76.4	76.1	76.2	76.0
Government													
2007	228.5	231.8	234.1	232.7	235.4	231.2	204.9	203.7	220.2	226.0	226.5	225.1	225.0
2008	219.9	223.9	224.4	224.0	225.7	222.7	202.4	203.5	217.4	223.2	224.1	221.0	219.4
2009	216.6	220.4	221.4	223.0	221.4	219.0	197.6	197.3	211.6	216.8	217.1	214.7	214.7
2010	209.6	213.7	214.3	215.9	218.9	213.7	194.0	189.1	202.9	207.3	206.7	205.1	207.6
2011	199.2	203.5	203.6	203.6	201.0	199.6	183.3	182.2	197.5	200.6	201.6	199.4	197.9
2012	194.4	198.2	198.5	198.0	196.2	195.8	178.7	178.5	193.2	194.5	195.6	193.8	193.0
2013	188.6	192.1	192.0	191.5	189.2	189.0	172.8	171.3	186.4	189.4	189.7	187.9	186.7
2014	183.7	187.8	188.3	189.0	186.8	186.4	170.9	169.6	183.2	188.0	189.6	186.6	184.2
2015	182.0	185.8	186.7	187.5	186.8	185.3	169.5	167.9	182.6	186.7	187.9	186.4	182.9
2016	182.2	186.0	188.2	187.7	185.2	185.5	172.2	171.5	185.6	187.8	190.4	188.1	184.2
2017	184.1	186.7	188.0	188.3	188.3	188.2	173.8	172.4	187.6	189.8	190.4	189.5	185.6

Employment by Industry: Seattle-Tacoma-Bellevue, WA, Selected Years, 2007–2017

(Numbers in thousands, not seasonally adjusted)

Industry and year	January	February	March	April	May	June	July	August	September	October	November	December	Annual average
Total Nonfarm													
2007	1,707.8	1,727.8	1,735.5	1,740.8	1,757.5	1,772.6	1,765.3	1,767.1	1,770.8	1,776.5	1,791.0	1,791.2	1,758.7
2008	1,757.2	1,769.6	1,770.3	1,775.6	1,785.8	1,794.1	1,788.4	1,788.0	1,786.9	1,757.8	1,775.2	1,760.0	1,775.7
2009	1,717.0	1,710.8	1,700.9	1,691.9	1,695.7	1,696.7	1,683.1	1,668.7	1,677.4	1,675.0	1,673.4	1,670.0	1,688.4
2010	1,637.0	1,639.6	1,646.8	1,658.8	1,671.6	1,678.7	1,675.6	1,664.8	1,675.6	1,684.1	1,688.6	1,688.0	1,667.4
2011	1,656.8	1,664.7	1,669.6	1,684.4	1,693.5	1,703.8	1,705.6	1,698.6	1,706.9	1,711.9	1,719.8	1,719.3	1,694.6
2012	1,688.9	1,697.6	1,708.3	1,718.0	1,734.5	1,747.0	1,743.0	1,739.6	1,747.5	1,756.3	1,766.3	1,764.2	1,734.3
2013	1,738.0	1,747.6	1,754.1	1,764.6	1,780.7	1,790.5	1,790.3	1,790.2	1,797.0	1,803.2	1,813.2	1,814.6	1,782.0
2014	1,792.4	1,795.8	1,803.6	1,809.9	1,824.5	1,836.4	1,844.6	1,845.8	1,850.8	1,853.6	1,862.2	1,867.7	1,832.3
2015	1,842.6	1,847.7	1,859.1	1,868.5	1,882.5	1,901.3	1,902.7	1,901.8	1,910.1	1,910.6	1,918.8	1,923.1	1,889.1
2016	1,898.2	1,910.5	1,918.8	1,935.1	1,949.9	1,963.1	1,964.1	1,962.6	1,971.4	1,968.0	1,978.4	1,982.9	1,950.3
2017	1,953.8	1,961.7	1,974.3	1,981.3	1,997.4	2,014.5	2,011.1	2,008.2	2,012.9	2,024.3	2,032.2	2,035.8	2,000.6
Total Private													
2007	1,454.7	1,470.8	1,478.4	1,484.0	1,499.6	1,513.6	1,515.6	1,523.6	1,522.9	1,519.6	1,528.1	1,532.3	1,503.6
2008	1,499.3	1,506.5	1,509.0	1,514.0	1,522.6	1,529.5	1,532.2	1,536.9	1,530.9	1,493.1	1,503.9	1,494.2	1,514.3
2009	1,451.5	1,444.1	1,433.8	1,421.7	1,425.5	1,429.6	1,424.5	1,421.2	1,419.4	1,409.3	1,405.9	1,406.7	1,424.4
2010	1,372.3	1,373.4	1,380.5	1,390.4	1,397.4	1,408.1	1,415.3	1,416.4	1,417.8	1,419.4	1,421.5	1,426.3	1,403.2
2011	1,393.9	1,400.3	1,405.3	1,419.9	1,427.8	1,440.9	1,449.5	1,453.7	1,456.5	1,450.1	1,456.8	1,460.4	1,434.6
2012	1,428.5	1,436.1	1,445.2	1,454.4	1,470.3	1,485.3	1,487.2	1,495.2	1,494.8	1,493.5	1,501.5	1,504.1	1,474.7
2013	1,476.3	1,483.9	1,490.2	1,500.1	1,515.5	1,527.4	1,534.9	1,543.8	1,542.2	1,539.1	1,547.4	1,552.3	1,521.1
2014	1,528.2	1,530.6	1,537.2	1,542.3	1,556.1	1,569.7	1,584.0	1,594.1	1,590.5	1,585.2	1,592.4	1,601.0	1,567.6
2015	1,573.9	1,577.4	1,587.2	1,595.1	1,609.0	1,627.8	1,637.3	1,643.8	1,642.5	1,636.9	1,642.9	1,651.1	1,618.7
2016	1,626.2	1,634.6	1,642.7	1,657.0	1,670.0	1,685.7	1,693.4	1,700.1	1,699.7	1,688.6	1,696.5	1,703.7	1,674.9
2017	1,674.9	1,680.8	1,691.7	1,697.9	1,712.5	1,731.5	1,733.9	1,740.1	1,738.7	1,739.8	1,746.0	1,753.4	1,720.1
Goods Producing													
2007	299.3	304.6	305.7	307.4	311.9	317.4	319.8	322.3	322.0	320.0	318.9	316.0	313.8
2008	310.9	312.8	311.8	311.0	312.8	314.0	315.7	316.7	313.4	285.4	301.3	294.5	308.4
2009	283.7	280.8	274.1	269.7	268.4	268.1	267.2	266.0	263.9	259.8	255.5	251.8	267.4
2010	247.5	246.5	246.2	247.2	248.2	250.7	254.5	255.5	255.1	254.1	251.2	249.1	250.5
2011	244.8	245.9	246.9	249.3	251.6	255.6	260.1	262.0	263.5	262.0	260.4	259.9	255.2
2012	255.6	256.8	258.6	260.5	263.8	268.9	272.0	275.2	275.6	274.9	273.9	272.5	267.4
2013	269.8	271.4	272.8	273.5	276.1	279.8	282.6	282.6	284.7	282.6	280.9	279.9	278.3
2014	276.7	277.1	278.6	278.7	281.7	285.1	289.8	291.8	291.3	290.8	289.9	290.3	285.2
2015	288.2	288.8	291.1	291.3	293.4	297.3	301.1	301.4	300.9	298.8	297.0	297.2	295.5
2016	294.8	296.7	297.4	299.5	301.3	303.3	306.0	305.6	305.0	301.5	300.1	299.3	300.9
2017	295.5	296.1	297.4	298.6	299.0	303.0	302.3	302.3	302.2	302.2	300.0	300.5	299.9
Service-Providing													
2007	1,408.5	1,423.2	1,429.8	1,433.4	1,445.6	1,455.2	1,445.5	1,444.8	1,448.8	1,456.5	1,472.1	1,475.2	1,444.9
2008	1,446.3	1,456.8	1,458.5	1,464.6	1,473.0	1,480.1	1,472.7	1,471.3	1,473.5	1,472.4	1,473.9	1,465.5	1,467.4
2009	1,433.3	1,430.0	1,426.8	1,422.2	1,427.3	1,428.6	1,415.9	1,402.7	1,413.5	1,415.2	1,417.9	1,418.2	1,421.0
2010	1,389.5	1,393.1	1,400.6	1,411.6	1,423.4	1,428.0	1,421.1	1,409.3	1,420.5	1,430.0	1,437.4	1,438.9	1,417.0
2011	1,412.0	1,418.8	1,422.7	1,435.1	1,441.9	1,448.2	1,445.5	1,436.6	1,443.4	1,449.9	1,459.4	1,459.4	1,439.4
2012	1,433.3	1,440.8	1,449.7	1,457.5	1,470.7	1,478.1	1,471.0	1,464.4	1,471.9	1,481.4	1,492.4	1,491.7	1,466.9
2013	1,468.2	1,476.2	1,481.3	1,491.1	1,504.6	1,510.7	1,507.7	1,504.7	1,512.3	1,520.6	1,532.3	1,534.7	1,503.7
2014	1,515.7	1,518.7	1,525.0	1,531.2	1,542.8	1,551.3	1,554.8	1,554.0	1,559.5	1,562.8	1,572.3	1,577.4	1,547.1
2015	1,554.4	1,558.9	1,568.0	1,577.2	1,589.1	1,604.0	1,601.6	1,600.4	1,609.2	1,611.8	1,621.8	1,625.9	1,593.5
2016	1,603.4	1,613.8	1,621.4	1,635.6	1,648.6	1,659.8	1,658.1	1,657.0	1,666.4	1,666.5	1,678.3	1,683.6	1,649.4
2017	1,658.3	1,665.6	1,676.9	1,682.7	1,698.4	1,711.5	1,708.8	1,705.9	1,710.7	1,722.1	1,732.2	1,735.3	1,700.7
Mining and Logging													
2007	1.4	1.5	1.4	1.6	1.6	1.6	1.7	1.6	1.5	1.6	1.5	1.5	1.5
2008	1.3	1.4	1.4	1.4	1.4	1.4	1.4	1.4	1.4	1.4	1.3	1.3	1.4
2009	1.3	1.3	1.2	1.1	1.1	1.1	1.1	1.1	1.1	1.1	1.1	1.0	1.1
2010	1.0	1.1	1.0	1.0	1.1	1.1	1.1	1.1	1.1	1.1	1.0	1.0	1.1
2011	1.0	1.0	1.0	1.0	1.0	1.0	1.0	1.0	1.0	1.1	1.1	1.1	1.0
2012	1.0	1.0	1.0	1.0	1.0	1.0	1.0	1.1	1.0	1.1	1.0	1.0	1.0
2013	1.0	1.0	1.0	1.0	1.0	1.1	1.0	1.1	1.1	1.0	1.0	1.0	1.0
2014	1.0	1.0	1.0	1.0	1.0	1.0	1.0	1.0	1.0	1.1	1.1	1.1	1.0
2015	1.1	1.1	1.0	1.1	1.1	1.1	1.1	1.1	1.1	1.2	1.1	1.1	1.1
2016	1.0	1.0	1.0	1.1	1.1	1.1	1.1	1.1	1.1	1.1	1.1	1.1	1.1
2017	1.1	1.1	1.0	1.1	1.1	1.1	1.1	1.1	1.1	1.1	1.1	1.1	1.1

Employment by Industry: Seattle-Tacoma-Bellevue, WA, Selected Years, 2007–2017—*Continued*

(Numbers in thousands, not seasonally adjusted)

Industry and year	January	February	March	April	May	June	July	August	September	October	November	December	Annual average
Construction													
2007	114.4	117.5	119.7	121.6	124.9	128.2	128.8	131.1	130.3	128.3	126.4	124.5	124.6
2008	120.0	120.2	120.7	120.7	121.7	122.5	123.7	124.1	122.2	119.0	113.3	108.4	119.7
2009	101.2	98.8	97.0	94.8	94.8	94.9	94.7	94.0	93.1	90.6	87.0	84.3	93.8
2010	80.4	79.6	79.8	80.6	81.9	82.9	85.6	86.6	85.9	85.1	81.8	79.7	82.5
2011	75.5	75.3	75.5	76.6	78.2	80.1	82.1	83.2	83.4	82.1	79.9	79.0	79.2
2012	75.0	76.1	76.8	78.4	80.6	83.2	85.1	87.2	87.4	87.3	85.9	85.1	82.3
2013	82.4	83.8	84.5	85.7	88.0	89.9	92.6	95.0	94.5	93.7	92.5	91.1	89.5
2014	89.4	89.6	91.2	91.3	93.8	96.1	99.1	101.3	101.7	102.0	101.4	101.6	96.5
2015	99.8	100.5	102.0	103.4	105.1	107.3	109.5	109.9	109.4	109.4	108.0	108.1	106.0
2016	106.5	108.5	109.4	111.4	113.0	115.0	117.0	118.3	118.3	117.2	116.7	116.4	114.0
2017	113.8	114.9	116.5	117.3	119.0	122.0	122.2	123.2	123.7	125.4	123.9	125.0	120.6
Manufacturing													
2007	183.5	185.6	184.6	184.2	185.4	187.6	189.3	189.6	190.2	190.1	191.0	190.0	187.6
2008	189.6	191.2	189.7	188.9	189.7	190.1	190.6	191.2	189.8	165.0	186.7	184.8	187.3
2009	181.2	180.7	175.9	173.8	172.5	172.1	171.4	170.9	169.7	168.1	167.4	166.5	172.5
2010	166.1	165.8	165.4	165.6	165.2	166.7	167.8	167.8	168.1	167.9	168.4	168.4	166.9
2011	168.3	169.6	170.4	171.7	172.4	174.5	177.0	177.8	179.1	178.8	179.4	179.8	174.9
2012	179.6	179.7	180.8	181.1	182.2	184.7	185.9	186.9	187.2	186.5	187.0	186.4	184.0
2013	186.4	186.6	187.3	186.8	187.1	188.8	189.0	189.4	189.1	187.9	187.4	187.8	187.8
2014	186.3	186.5	186.4	186.4	186.9	188.0	189.7	189.5	188.6	187.7	187.4	187.6	187.6
2015	187.3	187.2	188.1	186.8	187.2	188.9	190.5	190.4	190.4	188.2	187.9	188.0	188.4
2016	187.3	187.2	187.0	187.0	187.2	187.2	187.9	186.2	185.6	183.2	182.3	181.8	185.8
2017	180.6	180.1	179.9	180.2	178.9	179.9	179.0	178.0	177.4	175.7	175.0	174.4	178.3
Trade, Transportation, and Utilities													
2007	319.9	319.4	319.9	320.5	323.3	325.7	327.2	327.8	326.2	327.1	334.7	338.6	325.9
2008	326.9	324.8	324.6	324.1	325.0	326.4	327.8	328.9	325.7	324.3	325.8	328.0	326.0
2009	313.3	308.0	305.3	302.2	303.8	304.2	304.7	304.3	303.8	302.0	305.3	308.8	305.5
2010	297.5	295.6	296.0	297.4	299.2	301.7	302.9	303.6	302.5	304.6	309.4	314.6	302.1
2011	302.2	301.0	301.9	303.2	305.6	308.5	310.9	312.0	310.7	310.7	316.7	320.2	308.6
2012	309.0	307.1	308.4	309.2	313.4	317.5	319.9	320.7	319.5	320.5	327.3	329.7	316.9
2013	319.8	317.8	318.3	319.4	324.0	327.0	330.0	332.0	330.8	332.4	339.9	343.6	327.9
2014	333.9	331.9	331.9	332.8	336.7	340.8	344.4	346.8	345.9	346.5	353.3	357.7	341.9
2015	347.3	345.3	346.8	347.2	350.8	355.5	357.0	359.0	358.3	357.8	364.3	368.9	354.9
2016	356.7	355.2	356.9	359.9	364.0	369.1	372.4	374.0	372.4	373.1	380.8	385.0	368.3
2017	375.1	372.7	374.7	375.6	380.5	385.7	389.3	391.2	390.5	392.1	398.1	399.8	385.4
Wholesale Trade													
2007	82.0	82.4	82.7	82.8	83.4	83.9	84.1	84.2	83.9	84.0	84.4	84.8	83.6
2008	83.9	84.3	84.4	84.4	84.8	85.0	84.8	85.0	84.5	83.9	83.4	83.0	84.3
2009	82.2	81.3	80.7	79.8	79.5	79.4	79.3	78.7	78.4	77.9	77.6	77.6	79.4
2010	76.5	76.8	77.0	77.2	77.3	77.4	77.5	77.5	77.2	77.3	77.5	77.5	77.2
2011	76.9	77.2	77.4	77.8	78.1	78.3	78.5	78.5	78.3	78.0	78.0	78.2	77.9
2012	77.6	77.8	78.1	78.5	78.8	79.2	79.7	80.2	79.7	79.5	79.6	79.9	79.1
2013	79.4	80.0	80.3	80.2	80.5	81.1	81.5	81.7	81.6	81.1	81.5	81.6	80.9
2014	81.3	81.6	81.5	81.2	81.6	82.1	83.0	83.2	83.3	82.7	82.9	83.2	82.3
2015	82.5	82.7	83.0	82.9	83.3	84.0	84.1	84.4	84.2	83.7	83.8	84.2	83.6
2016	83.0	83.2	83.3	83.6	83.9	84.2	84.6	84.7	84.5	84.2	84.6	84.9	84.1
2017	84.4	84.7	85.0	84.9	85.3	86.0	86.1	86.3	86.3	86.3	86.4	85.9	85.6
Retail Trade													
2007	176.2	175.1	175.0	174.9	176.7	177.8	179.3	179.6	178.5	179.4	186.7	189.3	179.0
2008	180.8	177.9	177.8	177.3	177.2	178.1	179.5	180.6	178.5	178.7	181.1	183.0	179.2
2009	170.6	167.7	166.1	164.0	165.6	166.3	166.8	167.2	166.9	166.5	170.5	173.1	167.6
2010	165.0	163.0	163.1	164.2	165.5	167.1	167.6	168.3	167.5	169.6	174.3	177.8	167.8
2011	168.3	166.6	166.5	167.0	168.9	171.0	172.2	173.3	172.0	173.4	178.9	181.3	171.6
2012	172.7	170.4	171.0	171.3	174.1	176.9	178.7	178.9	178.5	180.3	186.6	188.1	177.3
2013	180.4	178.2	178.3	179.4	182.8	184.9	187.2	188.7	187.5	189.8	196.2	199.0	186.0
2014	190.3	188.3	188.5	188.7	191.3	194.3	196.7	198.4	197.3	198.6	204.9	207.5	195.4
2015	199.6	197.7	198.8	199.6	201.9	205.0	206.0	207.7	207.2	206.7	212.3	214.4	204.7
2016	206.0	204.9	206.3	208.5	211.5	215.5	218.1	219.1	217.4	219.3	225.7	227.3	215.0
2017	220.6	218.5	219.6	220.8	224.4	228.2	231.9	233.6	232.6	233.4	239.3	240.4	228.6

Employment by Industry: Seattle-Tacoma-Bellevue, WA, Selected Years, 2007–2017—*Continued*

(Numbers in thousands, not seasonally adjusted)

Industry and year	January	February	March	April	May	June	July	August	September	October	November	December	Annual average
Transportation and Utilities													
2007	61.7	61.9	62.2	62.8	63.2	64.0	63.8	64.0	63.8	63.7	63.6	64.5	63.3
2008	62.2	62.6	62.4	62.4	63.0	63.3	63.5	63.3	62.7	61.7	61.3	62.0	62.5
2009	60.5	59.0	58.5	58.4	58.7	58.5	58.6	58.4	58.5	57.6	57.2	58.1	58.5
2010	56.0	55.8	55.9	56.0	56.4	57.2	57.8	57.8	57.8	57.7	57.6	59.3	57.1
2011	57.0	57.2	58.0	58.4	58.6	59.2	60.2	60.2	60.4	59.3	59.8	60.7	59.1
2012	58.7	58.9	59.3	59.4	60.5	61.4	61.5	61.6	61.3	60.7	61.1	61.7	60.5
2013	60.0	59.6	59.7	59.8	60.7	61.0	61.3	61.6	61.7	61.5	62.2	63.0	61.0
2014	62.3	62.0	61.9	62.9	63.8	64.4	64.7	65.2	65.3	65.2	65.5	67.0	64.2
2015	65.2	64.9	65.0	64.7	65.6	66.5	66.9	66.9	66.9	67.4	68.2	70.3	66.5
2016	67.7	67.1	67.3	67.8	68.6	69.4	69.7	70.2	70.5	69.6	70.5	72.8	69.3
2017	70.1	69.5	70.1	69.9	70.8	71.5	71.3	71.3	71.6	72.4	72.4	73.5	71.2
Information													
2007	83.3	84.3	83.9	84.3	85.1	85.9	86.1	86.4	86.0	85.1	86.2	86.4	85.3
2008	85.9	87.0	87.2	87.5	88.0	89.1	90.4	91.2	90.2	89.6	90.6	90.7	89.0
2009	88.9	89.4	89.1	87.8	88.4	88.6	88.9	88.4	87.6	87.0	87.3	87.1	88.2
2010	86.6	86.9	86.8	86.5	87.0	88.1	88.3	88.8	88.7	87.9	88.3	88.6	87.7
2011	87.2	88.0	87.7	87.8	88.0	89.1	90.1	90.4	89.6	88.9	89.2	88.9	88.7
2012	88.8	89.3	89.0	88.8	89.6	90.7	90.7	91.0	89.7	89.1	89.6	89.5	89.7
2013	89.0	89.8	89.3	89.6	90.3	91.2	92.5	93.1	92.2	91.6	92.3	92.4	91.1
2014	92.1	92.3	92.5	92.9	93.3	95.0	96.8	97.7	96.9	95.2	95.6	95.3	94.6
2015	93.8	94.7	94.8	94.8	95.7	97.4	99.5	100.5	99.7	99.6	100.4	100.5	97.6
2016	100.1	101.1	101.6	102.1	103.0	105.8	107.4	108.4	107.8	107.2	108.1	108.3	105.1
2017	107.9	108.5	109.0	108.9	109.6	111.9	113.1	113.9	113.4	112.8	113.0	113.6	111.3
Financial Activities													
2007	106.4	106.7	107.2	107.3	107.3	107.6	107.9	107.9	106.7	106.8	107.2	107.1	107.2
2008	106.0	106.0	105.8	105.4	106.0	105.8	105.3	105.3	104.3	102.9	102.6	102.0	104.8
2009	100.0	99.9	98.7	98.1	97.9	97.8	96.9	96.1	95.5	94.4	93.8	93.6	96.9
2010	91.9	91.7	91.7	92.4	92.2	92.3	92.9	92.3	92.0	91.9	91.6	91.9	92.1
2011	90.7	90.9	90.7	91.1	90.7	91.0	91.1	90.9	90.6	90.2	90.4	90.2	90.7
2012	89.0	89.3	89.5	89.7	90.3	90.7	91.5	91.3	90.9	91.0	91.3	91.5	90.5
2013	91.3	91.7	92.2	92.7	93.3	93.5	94.3	94.3	93.8	93.7	93.7	94.2	93.2
2014	93.1	93.3	93.6	93.8	94.1	94.6	95.3	95.7	95.1	95.0	95.1	95.4	94.5
2015	94.7	94.9	94.9	95.2	95.7	96.0	96.8	96.9	96.4	95.8	95.9	96.1	95.8
2016	95.5	95.8	95.9	96.3	96.7	97.0	98.2	98.4	97.8	97.1	97.2	97.5	97.0
2017	96.4	97.1	97.4	97.2	98.2	98.9	99.4	99.8	99.4	99.6	100.5	101.1	98.8
Professional and Business Services													
2007	228.0	232.3	234.7	235.2	237.1	239.7	240.6	242.6	243.0	242.4	243.2	244.1	238.6
2008	237.5	239.5	240.5	243.2	244.4	244.9	245.7	245.5	244.9	242.8	238.3	234.5	241.8
2009	228.3	226.3	224.4	221.4	220.0	221.1	219.9	219.5	219.7	218.8	218.4	219.2	221.4
2010	212.1	213.2	216.1	218.6	219.2	220.8	223.8	223.0	223.9	225.1	225.1	225.8	220.6
2011	220.3	222.5	223.9	228.0	227.9	229.3	232.5	233.1	233.9	234.3	234.7	234.6	229.6
2012	228.9	231.3	232.6	236.4	238.6	240.8	239.8	242.6	242.7	244.1	244.8	244.6	238.9
2013	240.2	242.3	242.8	245.2	247.0	249.1	249.5	251.9	252.2	252.8	253.5	253.2	248.3
2014	248.8	249.4	251.0	251.8	252.9	254.9	258.5	261.0	260.7	261.8	262.6	263.8	256.4
2015	258.4	259.1	261.5	264.0	265.6	268.5	271.0	273.3	273.8	273.6	274.6	276.3	268.3
2016	270.6	272.1	274.3	276.5	277.4	279.7	280.7	282.5	283.8	282.0	282.8	283.0	278.8
2017	278.3	279.4	281.5	282.8	284.9	286.9	288.4	289.8	289.2	291.6	291.7	290.7	286.3
Education and Health Services													
2007	203.1	205.6	207.2	207.5	208.9	206.2	202.4	203.0	206.5	211.6	212.9	212.5	207.3
2008	210.1	213.1	213.3	214.3	215.6	214.4	211.3	211.9	215.2	220.1	220.8	220.8	215.1
2009	220.5	222.8	223.8	223.8	225.3	224.2	220.4	220.5	224.1	229.7	230.6	230.7	224.7
2010	228.0	230.0	231.1	231.6	232.4	230.9	227.2	226.8	230.6	235.8	237.3	236.0	231.5
2011	235.0	237.5	238.2	238.6	238.6	237.4	234.2	233.6	236.8	240.0	242.0	240.9	237.7
2012	238.2	240.9	242.5	241.8	242.8	240.9	236.2	235.9	238.8	242.4	244.0	243.8	240.7
2013	239.7	243.5	244.1	244.8	244.7	242.0	239.2	239.1	242.7	246.5	248.1	248.1	243.5
2014	246.2	249.4	249.2	249.0	249.6	247.0	245.3	244.9	247.4	249.5	250.4	251.1	248.3
2015	248.1	250.2	250.6	251.8	251.9	251.0	247.5	247.1	250.4	254.3	255.9	256.2	251.3
2016	255.9	259.2	260.1	261.2	261.5	259.9	256.0	257.4	260.8	263.2	264.5	264.9	260.4
2017	261.9	265.4	266.5	265.7	266.6	265.4	262.0	263.5	267.0	268.9	271.3	271.8	266.3

Employment by Industry: Seattle-Tacoma-Bellevue, WA, Selected Years, 2007–2017—*Continued*

(Numbers in thousands, not seasonally adjusted)

Industry and year	January	February	March	April	May	June	July	August	September	October	November	December	Annual average
Leisure and Hospitality													
2007	153.7	155.9	157.3	159.5	163.0	167.4	168.0	169.6	169.1	163.7	161.9	164.3	162.8
2008	159.3	160.0	161.9	164.3	165.9	169.6	170.2	171.5	171.6	163.6	160.1	159.9	164.8
2009	153.3	153.3	154.4	154.9	157.8	161.3	162.0	162.1	161.5	154.8	152.6	152.9	156.7
2010	147.4	148.0	150.8	154.5	156.4	159.9	161.2	161.8	161.5	156.1	154.5	156.4	155.7
2011	150.7	151.2	152.4	157.5	160.3	164.0	163.9	165.2	165.6	158.7	158.1	160.1	159.0
2012	154.4	156.1	158.7	161.8	165.2	168.4	169.0	170.7	170.2	164.5	163.5	165.6	164.0
2013	161.2	161.6	164.5	168.3	172.8	177.0	178.1	179.5	178.1	171.7	171.1	173.2	171.4
2014	170.1	169.7	172.3	175.2	178.8	182.5	183.3	185.5	183.6	177.1	175.9	177.5	177.6
2015	174.8	175.5	177.8	181.2	185.7	191.0	192.9	194.1	192.5	186.6	184.6	185.4	185.2
2016	182.7	184.1	185.7	189.8	193.1	197.4	199.5	200.3	199.7	192.3	190.6	193.2	192.4
2017	188.7	190.1	193.1	197.0	200.7	205.4	205.3	205.5	204.0	199.7	197.8	202.8	199.2
Other Services													
2007	61.0	62.0	62.5	62.3	63.0	63.7	63.6	64.0	63.4	62.9	63.1	63.3	62.9
2008	62.7	63.3	63.9	64.2	64.9	65.3	65.8	65.9	65.6	64.4	64.4	63.8	64.5
2009	63.5	63.6	64.0	63.8	63.9	64.3	64.5	64.3	63.3	62.8	62.4	62.6	63.6
2010	61.3	61.5	61.8	62.2	62.8	63.7	64.5	64.6	63.5	63.9	64.1	63.9	63.2
2011	63.0	63.3	63.6	64.4	65.1	66.0	66.7	66.5	65.8	65.3	65.3	65.6	65.1
2012	64.6	65.3	65.9	66.2	66.6	67.4	68.1	67.8	67.4	67.0	67.1	66.9	66.7
2013	65.3	65.8	66.2	66.6	67.3	67.8	68.7	68.4	67.7	67.8	67.9	67.7	67.3
2014	67.3	67.5	68.1	68.1	69.0	69.8	70.6	70.7	69.6	69.3	69.6	69.9	69.1
2015	68.6	68.9	69.7	69.6	70.2	71.1	71.5	71.5	70.5	70.4	70.2	70.5	70.2
2016	69.9	70.4	70.8	71.7	73.0	73.5	73.2	73.5	72.4	72.2	72.4	72.5	72.1
2017	71.1	71.5	72.1	72.1	73.0	74.3	74.1	74.1	73.0	72.9	73.6	73.1	72.9
Government													
2007	253.1	257.0	257.1	256.8	257.9	259.0	249.7	243.5	247.9	256.9	262.9	258.9	255.1
2008	257.9	263.1	261.3	261.6	263.2	264.6	256.2	251.1	256.0	264.7	271.3	265.8	261.4
2009	265.5	266.7	267.1	270.2	270.2	267.1	258.6	247.5	258.0	265.7	267.5	263.3	264.0
2010	264.7	266.2	266.3	268.4	274.2	270.6	260.3	248.4	257.8	264.7	267.1	261.7	264.2
2011	262.9	264.4	264.3	264.5	265.7	262.9	256.1	244.9	250.4	261.8	263.0	258.9	260.0
2012	260.4	261.5	263.1	263.6	264.2	261.7	255.8	244.4	252.7	262.8	264.8	260.1	259.6
2013	261.7	263.7	263.9	264.5	265.2	263.1	255.4	246.4	254.8	264.1	265.8	262.3	260.9
2014	264.2	265.2	266.4	267.6	268.4	266.7	260.6	251.7	260.3	268.4	269.8	266.7	264.7
2015	268.7	270.3	271.9	273.4	273.5	273.5	265.4	258.0	267.6	273.7	275.9	272.0	270.3
2016	272.0	275.9	276.1	278.1	279.9	277.4	270.7	262.5	271.7	279.4	281.9	279.2	275.4
2017	278.9	280.9	282.6	283.4	284.9	283.0	277.2	268.1	274.2	284.5	286.2	282.4	280.5

Employment by Industry: Minneapolis-St. Paul-Bloomington, MN-WI, Selected Years, 2007–2017

(Numbers in thousands, not seasonally adjusted)

Industry and year	January	February	March	April	May	June	July	August	September	October	November	December	Annual average
Total Nonfarm													
2007	1,814.7	1,815.8	1,819.9	1,833.0	1,859.1	1,873.4	1,849.1	1,849.3	1,854.1	1,864.1	1,868.1	1,862.0	1,846.9
2008	1,816.9	1,819.3	1,823.5	1,834.0	1,857.2	1,867.9	1,847.4	1,846.6	1,847.2	1,849.7	1,839.7	1,824.5	1,839.5
2009	1,764.8	1,754.3	1,746.6	1,758.7	1,775.2	1,774.9	1,755.7	1,748.9	1,744.7	1,759.0	1,758.5	1,753.1	1,757.9
2010	1,704.4	1,704.3	1,709.4	1,744.7	1,765.6	1,773.2	1,751.8	1,752.9	1,758.7	1,777.6	1,779.5	1,774.1	1,749.7
2011	1,738.6	1,742.7	1,749.0	1,781.8	1,802.0	1,807.9	1,779.2	1,798.0	1,814.5	1,820.6	1,822.1	1,819.3	1,789.6
2012	1,776.2	1,780.4	1,789.2	1,811.6	1,829.2	1,839.8	1,813.4	1,822.3	1,838.7	1,849.4	1,852.6	1,845.5	1,820.7
2013	1,812.4	1,820.5	1,823.7	1,841.0	1,867.7	1,878.7	1,850.5	1,863.0	1,879.1	1,890.9	1,892.2	1,887.1	1,858.9
2014	1,841.9	1,846.6	1,848.4	1,873.5	1,901.5	1,915.3	1,898.2	1,904.3	1,906.3	1,918.5	1,922.1	1,918.4	1,891.3
2015	1,874.7	1,881.2	1,885.7	1,916.0	1,940.8	1,953.0	1,937.4	1,939.6	1,937.5	1,953.5	1,955.0	1,950.3	1,927.1
2016	1,908.5	1,914.3	1,915.2	1,947.7	1,963.9	1,970.1	1,970.5	1,976.0	1,976.5	1,982.8	1,984.1	1,976.4	1,957.2
2017	1,947.8	1,951.5	1,956.3	1,976.4	1,994.8	2,009.0	1,998.9	2,002.9	2,006.0	2,014.3	2,008.8	1,998.5	1,988.8
Total Private													
2007	1,568.1	1,566.1	1,570.8	1,584.2	1,607.6	1,625.6	1,620.4	1,625.8	1,610.9	1,615.3	1,617.8	1,612.8	1,602.1
2008	1,570.7	1,567.4	1,572.2	1,582.9	1,602.9	1,616.1	1,612.9	1,615.1	1,598.4	1,597.7	1,586.1	1,572.1	1,591.2
2009	1,519.6	1,503.4	1,496.2	1,508.8	1,523.8	1,526.3	1,519.5	1,518.5	1,504.2	1,512.1	1,510.2	1,505.8	1,512.4
2010	1,461.9	1,457.1	1,462.1	1,494.8	1,511.9	1,524.1	1,527.0	1,531.1	1,519.9	1,530.8	1,531.0	1,526.7	1,506.5
2011	1,496.8	1,495.1	1,502.6	1,535.2	1,554.2	1,565.6	1,570.9	1,579.5	1,579.0	1,578.0	1,579.1	1,576.9	1,551.1
2012	1,539.0	1,538.7	1,547.2	1,567.6	1,584.8	1,598.7	1,597.5	1,604.1	1,599.5	1,604.7	1,605.9	1,600.4	1,582.3
2013	1,572.3	1,574.8	1,579.0	1,593.5	1,620.3	1,636.3	1,635.7	1,645.6	1,636.8	1,641.9	1,641.4	1,638.8	1,618.0
2014	1,598.6	1,597.9	1,600.5	1,624.2	1,651.9	1,669.3	1,670.6	1,678.2	1,664.3	1,668.7	1,670.8	1,669.5	1,647.0
2015	1,630.4	1,632.5	1,638.7	1,667.2	1,692.0	1,707.1	1,709.1	1,713.3	1,695.8	1,704.6	1,705.4	1,701.6	1,683.1
2016	1,663.8	1,666.3	1,667.8	1,700.7	1,717.3	1,727.0	1,741.7	1,746.7	1,731.9	1,732.8	1,733.4	1,729.5	1,713.2
2017	1,699.6	1,700.4	1,706.6	1,727.3	1,745.7	1,763.6	1,767.0	1,770.8	1,755.1	1,757.2	1,750.6	1,744.1	1,740.7
Goods Producing													
2007	278.9	275.9	276.7	279.9	288.4	294.8	294.6	295.8	290.7	289.4	286.1	279.6	285.9
2008	269.8	267.1	267.0	269.6	277.7	283.4	283.5	283.9	278.8	276.6	268.8	259.6	273.8
2009	246.6	239.7	235.8	237.7	241.8	245.1	244.7	243.9	241.0	239.7	236.3	231.0	240.3
2010	220.9	217.5	217.8	226.7	232.2	237.7	241.4	241.5	239.4	239.3	236.5	231.8	231.9
2011	225.7	224.6	226.2	232.7	239.7	245.7	248.8	250.7	248.4	248.1	244.9	240.1	239.6
2012	231.7	231.0	234.2	240.5	245.8	252.0	254.3	255.6	252.7	252.3	248.8	244.3	245.3
2013	238.0	237.8	239.6	243.7	252.6	258.5	260.6	263.1	260.9	260.5	258.0	252.9	252.2
2014	245.7	244.9	247.0	252.3	261.6	268.7	271.0	272.7	269.3	269.7	266.4	263.3	261.1
2015	255.6	255.7	257.8	266.7	273.2	279.5	282.4	282.8	278.3	278.8	275.1	269.8	271.3
2016	260.9	260.3	262.3	271.1	276.2	281.1	284.8	284.6	281.1	280.2	276.4	269.5	274.0
2017	263.1	263.4	265.8	271.4	278.0	284.5	287.1	287.7	283.6	282.1	278.7	271.4	276.4
Service-Providing													
2007	1,535.8	1,539.9	1,543.2	1,553.1	1,570.7	1,578.6	1,554.5	1,553.5	1,563.4	1,574.7	1,582.0	1,582.4	1,561.0
2008	1,547.1	1,552.2	1,556.5	1,564.4	1,579.5	1,584.5	1,563.9	1,562.7	1,568.4	1,573.1	1,570.9	1,564.9	1,565.7
2009	1,518.2	1,514.6	1,510.8	1,521.0	1,533.4	1,529.8	1,511.0	1,505.0	1,503.7	1,519.3	1,522.2	1,522.1	1,517.6
2010	1,483.5	1,486.8	1,491.6	1,518.0	1,533.4	1,535.5	1,510.4	1,511.4	1,519.3	1,538.3	1,543.0	1,542.3	1,517.8
2011	1,512.9	1,518.1	1,522.8	1,549.1	1,562.3	1,562.2	1,530.4	1,547.3	1,566.1	1,572.5	1,577.2	1,579.2	1,550.0
2012	1,544.5	1,549.4	1,555.0	1,571.1	1,583.4	1,587.8	1,559.1	1,566.7	1,586.0	1,597.1	1,603.8	1,601.2	1,575.4
2013	1,574.4	1,582.7	1,584.1	1,597.3	1,615.1	1,620.2	1,589.9	1,599.9	1,618.2	1,630.4	1,634.2	1,634.2	1,606.7
2014	1,596.2	1,601.7	1,601.4	1,621.2	1,639.9	1,646.6	1,627.2	1,631.6	1,637.0	1,648.8	1,655.7	1,655.1	1,630.2
2015	1,619.1	1,625.5	1,627.9	1,649.3	1,667.6	1,673.5	1,655.0	1,656.8	1,659.2	1,674.7	1,679.9	1,680.5	1,655.8
2016	1,647.6	1,654.0	1,652.9	1,676.6	1,687.7	1,689.0	1,685.7	1,691.4	1,695.4	1,702.6	1,707.7	1,706.9	1,683.1
2017	1,684.7	1,688.1	1,690.5	1,705.0	1,716.8	1,724.5	1,711.8	1,715.2	1,722.4	1,732.2	1,730.1	1,727.1	1,712.4
Mining, Logging, and Construction													
2007	73.7	71.5	72.7	75.2	82.5	86.6	86.9	87.2	84.8	83.5	80.4	74.3	79.9
2008	67.7	66.3	66.7	68.6	75.6	79.3	80.2	80.1	77.6	75.4	70.0	63.9	72.6
2009	54.8	53.1	52.9	56.5	62.4	64.3	64.8	64.3	64.0	63.0	60.5	56.4	59.8
2010	48.3	45.7	45.8	52.4	56.2	59.5	61.7	61.9	60.8	60.6	58.0	53.0	55.3
2011	48.5	47.8	49.1	53.8	59.1	62.8	64.4	65.7	64.7	64.0	61.2	56.7	58.2
2012	50.4	50.0	52.3	57.7	61.7	65.4	67.1	68.0	66.6	66.0	62.8	58.7	60.6
2013	53.7	53.9	55.3	59.1	66.8	70.4	72.7	74.8	74.0	73.2	70.4	65.1	65.8
2014	59.3	58.7	60.1	64.7	72.4	76.6	78.4	79.4	77.7	77.2	73.6	70.0	70.7
2015	64.1	64.2	65.7	73.5	79.0	82.8	84.9	85.4	82.8	82.5	78.8	73.8	76.5
2016	66.5	66.2	67.7	75.8	80.5	83.4	85.1	85.1	83.8	83.0	80.0	74.0	77.6
2017	69.0	69.3	71.3	76.7	82.7	86.6	88.0	88.3	86.3	84.7	82.7	76.0	80.1

Employment by Industry: Minneapolis-St. Paul-Bloomington, MN-WI, Selected Years, 2007–2017—*Continued*

(Numbers in thousands, not seasonally adjusted)

Industry and year	January	February	March	April	May	June	July	August	September	October	November	December	Annual average
Manufacturing													
2007	205.2	204.4	204.0	204.7	205.9	208.2	207.7	208.6	205.9	205.9	205.7	205.3	206.0
2008	202.1	200.8	200.3	201.0	202.1	204.1	203.3	203.8	201.2	201.2	198.8	195.7	201.2
2009	191.8	186.6	182.9	181.2	179.4	180.8	179.9	179.6	177.0	176.7	175.8	174.6	180.5
2010	172.6	171.8	172.0	174.3	176.0	178.2	179.7	179.6	178.6	178.7	178.5	178.8	176.6
2011	177.2	176.8	177.1	178.9	180.6	182.9	184.4	185.0	183.7	184.1	183.7	183.4	181.5
2012	181.3	181.0	181.9	182.8	184.1	186.6	187.2	187.6	186.1	186.3	186.0	185.6	184.7
2013	184.3	183.9	184.3	184.6	185.8	188.1	187.9	188.3	186.9	187.3	187.6	187.8	186.4
2014	186.4	186.2	186.9	187.6	189.2	192.1	192.6	193.3	191.6	192.5	192.8	193.3	190.4
2015	191.5	191.5	192.1	193.2	194.2	196.7	197.5	197.4	195.5	196.3	196.3	196.0	194.9
2016	194.4	194.1	194.6	195.3	195.7	197.7	199.7	199.5	197.3	197.2	196.4	195.5	196.5
2017	194.1	194.1	194.5	194.7	195.3	197.9	199.1	199.4	197.3	197.4	196.0	195.4	196.3
Trade, Transportation, and Utilities													
2007	352.7	349.6	348.6	351.1	354.9	357.2	354.6	354.7	353.2	356.2	362.1	365.2	355.0
2008	352.0	346.8	347.7	347.5	350.7	350.9	347.8	347.2	344.5	345.4	348.6	348.8	348.2
2009	334.4	328.2	326.3	325.9	328.3	329.2	325.1	324.5	321.8	323.5	328.8	330.0	327.2
2010	318.7	314.7	315.5	319.8	323.0	325.9	323.6	322.8	321.7	324.6	330.3	332.9	322.8
2011	321.1	317.9	319.1	325.6	328.5	329.7	330.1	330.3	330.5	331.8	337.6	340.9	328.6
2012	329.6	324.6	326.1	329.9	333.7	335.6	332.8	333.1	331.6	334.9	342.3	343.2	333.1
2013	333.4	329.6	329.7	331.8	336.9	340.1	338.0	340.3	338.2	340.6	346.9	350.2	338.0
2014	337.8	334.5	334.7	339.2	343.2	346.2	345.1	345.9	341.8	345.2	351.5	356.2	343.4
2015	342.9	339.6	340.4	345.4	349.8	353.7	351.4	352.2	348.4	351.8	358.1	361.2	349.6
2016	349.0	346.9	347.1	352.2	355.9	356.9	358.7	359.7	355.0	357.7	363.3	368.1	355.9
2017	358.2	355.0	354.6	358.0	361.1	363.9	363.3	363.2	359.2	362.8	367.9	372.0	361.6
Wholesale Trade													
2007	97.6	97.8	97.9	98.4	99.2	100.0	100.5	100.5	98.9	98.9	98.9	99.1	99.0
2008	98.4	98.2	98.5	98.4	98.8	99.4	99.5	99.3	97.8	97.4	96.7	96.2	98.2
2009	94.5	93.4	92.6	92.6	92.4	92.8	92.7	92.0	90.1	90.2	90.3	90.2	92.0
2010	88.6	88.4	88.6	89.4	90.0	91.0	91.3	91.0	89.7	90.3	90.3	90.3	89.9
2011	89.9	89.9	90.2	91.7	92.2	92.6	93.6	93.7	92.7	92.6	92.6	92.7	92.0
2012	92.3	92.2	92.6	93.8	94.5	95.6	95.6	95.1	94.0	94.1	94.1	94.3	94.0
2013	93.8	93.8	93.9	94.2	95.0	95.9	96.1	96.0	95.0	95.0	95.2	95.2	94.9
2014	94.6	94.8	94.9	95.4	96.3	97.3	97.5	97.3	96.1	96.3	96.5	96.7	96.1
2015	95.5	95.4	95.6	96.5	96.9	98.0	98.4	98.0	96.6	96.7	96.9	96.8	96.8
2016	95.5	95.7	95.6	96.8	97.4	97.3	98.3	98.2	96.8	96.3	96.4	96.6	96.7
2017	96.3	96.2	96.3	96.6	97.3	98.1	98.8	98.5	97.2	98.1	98.5	98.3	97.5
Retail Trade													
2007	189.5	185.5	185.4	186.5	189.1	190.9	189.2	189.3	187.0	189.5	195.5	197.4	189.6
2008	187.3	182.2	182.5	182.7	185.0	185.5	184.1	183.9	180.7	181.9	185.7	185.8	183.9
2009	176.4	171.9	170.4	170.7	173.4	174.8	172.7	173.3	169.8	171.3	175.9	177.1	173.1
2010	169.0	165.6	165.9	169.1	171.3	173.3	172.1	172.6	169.8	171.6	176.4	178.3	171.3
2011	169.2	166.0	166.4	170.6	172.8	174.3	174.5	175.3	173.6	174.7	180.4	182.7	173.4
2012	174.0	169.4	170.3	172.6	175.1	176.9	175.6	176.1	173.9	176.6	183.5	183.9	175.7
2013	176.3	172.4	172.6	174.3	177.6	180.6	179.8	181.1	178.2	179.4	185.0	187.6	178.7
2014	178.2	175.1	175.2	178.1	180.8	183.4	183.4	183.9	179.5	181.9	187.6	190.6	181.5
2015	181.3	178.1	178.5	181.4	185.1	188.6	187.4	188.5	184.3	186.3	191.9	193.5	185.4
2016	185.1	183.1	183.4	186.3	188.7	190.3	192.3	192.3	186.4	188.9	193.3	195.3	188.8
2017	188.0	185.2	185.1	187.9	189.7	191.7	191.9	192.0	186.8	189.5	194.7	196.3	189.9
Transportation and Utilities													
2007	65.6	66.3	65.3	66.2	66.6	66.3	64.9	64.9	67.3	67.8	67.7	68.7	66.5
2008	66.3	66.4	66.7	66.4	66.9	66.0	64.2	64.0	66.0	66.1	66.2	66.8	66.0
2009	63.5	62.9	63.3	62.6	62.5	61.6	59.7	59.2	61.9	62.0	62.6	62.7	62.0
2010	61.1	60.7	61.0	61.3	61.7	61.6	60.2	59.2	62.2	62.7	63.6	64.3	61.6
2011	62.0	62.0	62.5	63.3	63.5	62.8	62.0	61.3	64.2	64.5	64.6	65.5	63.2
2012	63.3	63.0	63.2	63.5	64.1	63.1	61.6	61.9	63.7	64.2	64.7	65.0	63.4
2013	63.3	63.4	63.2	63.3	64.3	63.6	62.1	63.2	65.0	66.2	66.7	67.4	64.3
2014	65.0	64.6	64.6	65.7	66.1	65.5	64.2	64.7	66.2	67.0	67.4	68.9	65.8
2015	66.1	66.1	66.3	67.5	67.8	67.1	65.6	65.7	67.5	68.8	69.3	70.9	67.4
2016	68.4	68.1	68.1	69.1	69.8	69.3	68.1	69.2	71.8	72.5	73.6	76.2	70.4
2017	73.9	73.6	73.2	73.5	74.1	74.1	72.6	72.7	75.2	75.2	74.7	77.4	74.2

Employment by Industry: Minneapolis-St. Paul-Bloomington, MN-WI, Selected Years, 2007–2017—*Continued*

(Numbers in thousands, not seasonally adjusted)

Industry and year	January	February	March	April	May	June	July	August	September	October	November	December	Annual average
Information													
2007	43.1	43.2	43.3	43.4	43.5	43.7	43.6	43.7	43.2	43.2	43.1	43.4	43.4
2008	43.0	42.8	43.0	43.1	43.0	43.1	43.4	43.3	43.2	42.8	43.0	42.3	43.0
2009	41.8	41.7	41.6	41.2	41.2	41.1	41.3	41.2	40.7	40.5	40.6	40.3	41.1
2010	40.3	40.3	40.3	40.4	40.1	40.2	40.7	40.7	40.3	40.4	40.3	40.2	40.4
2011	40.6	40.2	40.0	40.7	40.6	40.8	41.3	41.6	41.2	41.1	41.0	41.1	40.9
2012	40.0	40.1	40.2	40.6	40.9	40.8	40.9	40.9	40.7	40.9	40.8	40.9	40.6
2013	40.2	40.2	40.2	40.3	40.2	40.3	40.8	40.5	40.0	39.9	40.0	40.2	40.2
2014	39.6	39.6	39.3	39.3	39.4	39.8	40.0	39.9	39.2	39.4	39.3	39.6	39.5
2015	38.7	38.5	38.5	38.4	38.5	38.8	38.9	38.9	38.1	38.0	38.1	37.9	38.4
2016	37.6	37.5	37.6	37.6	37.8	37.8	38.2	38.6	38.6	38.2	38.2	38.2	38.0
2017	38.1	38.0	38.1	38.0	37.9	38.1	38.1	38.5	37.8	37.6	37.7	37.6	38.0
Financial Activities													
2007	138.0	138.5	138.3	137.5	137.7	139.4	138.7	138.8	137.5	137.6	137.8	137.8	138.1
2008	135.7	135.8	136.0	135.6	135.6	136.5	136.9	136.5	134.9	134.2	134.0	134.5	135.5
2009	132.5	132.1	131.6	131.2	131.5	131.9	132.2	131.6	130.8	130.9	130.8	131.2	131.5
2010	129.4	129.2	129.0	129.5	130.0	131.3	131.9	132.1	131.3	132.2	132.6	133.0	131.0
2011	132.3	132.3	132.4	131.8	132.1	132.5	133.1	133.2	132.2	131.8	131.8	131.9	132.3
2012	132.6	132.9	133.0	133.5	134.2	135.6	135.6	135.6	134.7	135.6	135.7	135.9	134.6
2013	135.7	135.9	136.0	136.1	136.5	138.0	138.3	138.5	136.9	137.2	137.1	137.4	137.0
2014	136.2	136.0	136.0	135.4	135.9	137.4	137.6	137.4	135.8	136.3	136.3	136.8	136.4
2015	137.4	137.6	137.7	138.6	139.6	141.0	142.2	142.3	140.2	140.7	140.9	141.1	139.9
2016	140.0	140.4	140.3	141.4	141.8	142.9	144.7	144.8	143.7	144.2	144.2	144.6	142.8
2017	144.0	144.1	144.2	144.6	144.9	146.8	147.4	147.1	145.4	145.0	144.5	145.0	145.3
Professional and Business Services													
2007	274.6	275.8	277.3	277.8	280.1	284.1	285.1	287.7	284.5	286.9	287.1	285.7	282.2
2008	278.3	279.2	278.9	281.1	283.2	285.7	287.0	287.1	285.7	285.9	282.9	280.4	283.0
2009	267.6	263.6	261.6	264.4	265.3	266.1	265.7	267.1	263.8	269.0	269.6	269.7	266.1
2010	261.0	262.0	261.7	269.0	271.2	274.2	277.9	279.6	276.5	280.1	281.1	280.6	272.9
2011	274.5	275.0	276.6	284.2	285.5	288.5	293.5	296.0	296.2	297.7	297.9	297.9	288.6
2012	289.0	289.3	289.9	292.1	293.7	296.3	298.1	300.2	298.9	301.5	300.9	300.5	295.9
2013	293.4	296.0	296.0	297.7	299.6	303.4	304.6	306.3	304.7	308.7	307.4	307.0	302.1
2014	298.3	298.8	298.2	302.0	305.7	308.8	311.6	313.0	310.7	313.9	316.2	312.6	307.5
2015	304.8	305.8	305.3	312.5	315.2	315.9	317.9	318.0	313.8	319.3	319.6	317.9	313.8
2016	310.0	311.8	309.1	317.0	317.6	319.2	323.3	323.7	322.7	326.0	324.2	323.4	319.0
2017	316.6	315.7	316.2	319.8	321.0	322.7	324.4	325.2	322.4	326.3	324.6	322.3	321.4
Education and Health Services													
2007	248.3	250.5	251.8	254.6	255.8	254.2	252.5	253.2	254.0	258.2	260.4	259.8	254.4
2008	257.1	260.0	261.5	264.2	263.6	261.7	260.9	261.0	263.3	268.5	269.5	268.9	263.4
2009	266.1	268.7	269.5	272.4	272.3	267.3	266.4	265.5	267.0	271.9	273.0	273.2	269.4
2010	267.7	270.4	272.2	275.6	276.1	272.2	268.6	269.8	271.8	277.2	278.6	277.8	273.2
2011	276.3	278.9	279.3	284.2	283.5	279.3	276.1	277.3	282.0	285.4	286.6	287.2	281.3
2012	283.7	287.6	287.9	289.2	289.2	284.8	282.7	283.8	290.1	293.9	295.1	294.5	288.5
2013	294.1	297.8	297.6	299.9	301.2	296.7	294.5	296.3	300.1	303.7	305.4	304.9	299.4
2014	300.6	303.8	304.0	306.7	307.4	303.5	301.6	303.5	307.7	310.6	311.7	312.0	306.1
2015	306.7	310.8	311.8	312.6	314.1	310.3	308.7	310.0	314.7	317.3	318.9	318.7	312.9
2016	316.3	319.3	319.2	321.8	321.9	317.3	317.5	319.8	321.0	321.6	326.7	326.8	320.8
2017	323.3	327.4	327.7	330.7	330.6	328.6	327.2	328.2	332.5	333.9	336.0	336.0	330.2
Leisure and Hospitality													
2007	156.6	156.9	157.7	163.1	169.8	174.1	172.9	173.6	170.6	166.3	162.9	162.7	165.6
2008	157.4	157.1	158.9	162.1	169.4	173.8	172.9	174.9	169.0	165.1	160.6	159.1	165.0
2009	154.1	152.8	153.1	158.4	165.6	167.1	166.3	167.1	162.7	159.4	154.3	153.7	159.6
2010	148.5	147.4	149.3	157.2	162.7	164.8	165.0	166.5	162.6	159.7	155.0	153.9	157.7
2011	150.5	150.1	152.5	158.7	166.7	170.6	168.8	170.8	169.7	163.9	161.0	159.6	161.9
2012	155.2	155.8	158.3	163.7	168.9	173.6	173.6	175.3	172.5	167.1	164.0	162.9	165.9
2013	160.0	159.8	161.7	165.9	174.1	179.2	179.2	180.5	176.7	172.9	168.4	168.0	170.5
2014	163.1	163.1	163.8	170.6	179.2	184.2	183.0	185.0	180.2	174.0	170.0	170.1	173.9
2015	167.1	167.1	169.2	174.2	182.5	187.7	187.6	188.9	183.8	179.4	175.5	175.7	178.2
2016	172.6	172.2	173.9	180.1	186.5	191.5	193.4	194.3	189.0	184.7	180.3	179.1	183.1
2017	177.2	177.7	180.2	184.7	191.5	197.1	197.6	198.9	193.1	187.9	179.6	178.9	187.0

Employment by Industry: Minneapolis-St. Paul-Bloomington, MN-WI, Selected Years, 2007–2017—*Continued*

(Numbers in thousands, not seasonally adjusted)

Industry and year	January	February	March	April	May	June	July	August	September	October	November	December	Annual average
Other Services													
2007	75.9	75.7	77.1	76.8	77.4	78.1	78.4	78.3	77.2	77.5	78.3	78.6	77.4
2008	77.4	78.6	79.2	79.7	79.7	81.0	80.5	81.2	79.0	79.2	78.7	78.5	79.4
2009	76.5	76.6	76.7	77.6	77.8	78.5	77.8	77.6	76.4	77.2	76.8	76.7	77.2
2010	75.4	75.6	76.3	76.6	76.6	77.8	77.9	78.1	76.3	77.3	76.6	76.5	76.8
2011	75.8	76.1	76.5	77.3	77.6	78.5	79.2	79.6	78.8	78.2	78.3	78.2	77.8
2012	77.2	77.4	77.6	78.1	78.4	80.0	79.5	79.6	78.3	78.5	78.3	78.2	78.4
2013	77.5	77.7	78.2	78.1	79.2	80.1	79.7	80.1	79.3	78.4	78.2	78.2	78.7
2014	77.3	77.2	77.5	78.7	79.5	80.7	80.7	80.8	79.6	79.6	79.4	78.9	79.2
2015	77.2	77.4	78.0	78.8	79.1	80.2	80.0	80.2	78.5	79.3	79.2	79.3	78.9
2016	77.4	77.9	78.3	79.5	79.6	80.3	81.1	81.2	80.8	80.2	80.1	79.8	79.7
2017	79.1	79.1	79.8	80.1	80.7	81.9	81.9	82.0	81.1	81.6	81.6	80.9	80.8
Government													
2007	246.6	249.7	249.1	248.8	251.5	247.8	228.7	223.5	243.2	248.8	250.3	249.2	244.8
2008	246.2	251.9	251.3	251.1	254.3	251.8	234.5	231.5	248.8	252.0	253.6	252.4	248.3
2009	245.2	250.9	250.4	249.9	251.4	248.6	236.2	230.4	240.5	246.9	248.3	247.3	245.5
2010	242.5	247.2	247.3	249.9	253.7	249.1	224.8	221.8	238.8	246.8	248.5	247.4	243.2
2011	241.8	247.6	246.4	246.6	247.8	242.3	208.3	218.5	235.5	242.6	243.0	242.4	238.6
2012	237.2	241.7	242.0	244.0	244.4	241.1	215.9	218.2	239.2	244.7	246.7	245.1	238.4
2013	240.1	245.7	244.7	247.5	247.4	242.4	214.8	217.4	242.3	249.0	250.8	248.3	240.9
2014	243.3	248.7	247.9	249.3	249.6	246.0	227.6	226.1	242.0	249.8	251.3	248.9	244.2
2015	244.3	248.7	247.0	248.8	248.8	245.9	228.3	226.3	241.7	248.9	249.6	248.7	243.9
2016	244.7	248.0	247.4	247.0	246.6	243.1	228.8	229.3	244.6	250.0	250.7	246.9	243.9
2017	248.2	251.1	249.7	249.1	249.1	245.4	231.9	232.1	250.9	257.1	258.2	254.4	248.1

Employment by Industry: San Diego-Carlsbad, CA, Selected Years, 2007–2017

(Numbers in thousands, not seasonally adjusted)

Industry and year	January	February	March	April	May	June	July	August	September	October	November	December	Annual average
Total Nonfarm													
2007	1,303.3	1,311.8	1,319.6	1,317.9	1,326.5	1,335.1	1,325.9	1,326.5	1,325.8	1,324.9	1,331.5	1,337.7	1,323.9
2008	1,307.1	1,315.6	1,320.6	1,320.1	1,324.4	1,328.5	1,316.8	1,316.7	1,312.7	1,311.6	1,310.9	1,307.5	1,316.0
2009	1,270.7	1,266.5	1,264.1	1,256.2	1,257.7	1,257.0	1,234.1	1,234.2	1,229.6	1,240.5	1,246.6	1,248.2	1,250.5
2010	1,218.8	1,222.4	1,227.4	1,240.8	1,251.7	1,253.5	1,242.1	1,245.0	1,243.4	1,248.6	1,253.4	1,257.4	1,242.0
2011	1,235.1	1,242.6	1,246.3	1,249.2	1,251.9	1,255.9	1,245.5	1,248.5	1,252.9	1,258.4	1,267.7	1,270.6	1,252.1
2012	1,246.5	1,255.5	1,262.4	1,280.2	1,289.5	1,297.3	1,282.1	1,288.4	1,288.5	1,299.4	1,310.9	1,314.1	1,284.6
2013	1,289.9	1,298.3	1,305.4	1,311.1	1,316.3	1,322.5	1,311.5	1,316.3	1,317.4	1,332.9	1,344.4	1,346.7	1,317.7
2014	1,316.9	1,326.1	1,333.3	1,337.2	1,343.9	1,351.6	1,340.1	1,348.7	1,348.5	1,361.1	1,374.4	1,377.1	1,346.6
2015	1,354.5	1,360.5	1,367.3	1,373.1	1,384.1	1,387.7	1,388.0	1,391.2	1,391.3	1,407.9	1,417.9	1,418.3	1,386.8
2016	1,393.3	1,404.0	1,404.1	1,418.4	1,423.6	1,424.6	1,422.3	1,427.2	1,430.3	1,442.1	1,452.1	1,453.3	1,424.6
2017	1,427.1	1,435.8	1,439.7	1,448.4	1,453.3	1,460.7	1,450.5	1,453.1	1,452.6	1,466.1	1,477.4	1,474.0	1,453.2
Total Private													
2007	1,081.8	1,088.1	1,094.6	1,092.8	1,101.5	1,109.4	1,111.0	1,114.3	1,107.7	1,100.5	1,105.6	1,110.6	1,101.5
2008	1,082.9	1,088.1	1,091.9	1,092.3	1,095.6	1,098.4	1,100.1	1,101.4	1,092.6	1,084.8	1,082.9	1,080.1	1,090.9
2009	1,044.5	1,039.6	1,035.5	1,026.4	1,028.2	1,027.0	1,019.6	1,022.0	1,013.5	1,014.2	1,019.0	1,021.6	1,025.9
2010	994.2	996.7	1,000.0	1,006.0	1,011.0	1,015.5	1,016.5	1,021.2	1,015.8	1,016.7	1,020.1	1,025.2	1,011.6
2011	1,005.0	1,009.7	1,012.5	1,015.4	1,019.2	1,022.3	1,025.8	1,031.3	1,029.7	1,028.8	1,036.6	1,040.8	1,023.1
2012	1,019.8	1,026.1	1,031.5	1,049.4	1,058.2	1,065.2	1,064.0	1,069.4	1,065.5	1,070.0	1,078.8	1,082.9	1,056.7
2013	1,062.3	1,068.3	1,073.0	1,079.2	1,084.0	1,088.5	1,091.0	1,095.4	1,091.5	1,101.6	1,110.5	1,113.6	1,088.2
2014	1,087.6	1,093.7	1,098.9	1,102.5	1,108.7	1,113.9	1,117.8	1,125.4	1,121.4	1,127.2	1,137.8	1,141.0	1,114.7
2015	1,120.0	1,124.7	1,129.7	1,134.9	1,144.5	1,148.9	1,160.6	1,164.3	1,159.7	1,168.6	1,175.6	1,176.5	1,150.7
2016	1,154.9	1,162.9	1,161.2	1,174.7	1,178.7	1,179.2	1,191.1	1,192.9	1,190.6	1,195.3	1,203.0	1,203.9	1,182.4
2017	1,180.5	1,186.3	1,189.9	1,196.8	1,201.3	1,208.3	1,211.5	1,214.6	1,210.0	1,216.2	1,225.0	1,221.5	1,205.2
Goods Producing													
2007	190.1	190.7	191.7	190.2	191.9	193.4	192.5	191.9	189.8	187.3	186.2	185.6	190.1
2008	181.3	181.3	181.6	180.6	181.2	181.9	181.5	181.1	179.5	177.4	174.9	172.5	179.6
2009	168.4	165.7	164.4	160.8	159.7	158.7	156.9	156.2	154.1	153.4	152.8	152.4	158.6
2010	150.8	149.7	150.7	152.1	152.5	152.4	152.2	152.6	151.5	150.7	150.7	150.9	151.4
2011	150.0	150.4	150.8	151.0	151.6	152.6	152.7	153.6	153.1	153.1	152.7	152.8	152.0
2012	150.6	150.9	152.0	153.7	155.2	156.6	157.2	158.0	157.5	157.9	158.9	158.7	155.6
2013	157.1	158.0	158.5	159.4	159.5	160.7	161.7	162.5	162.0	162.6	163.5	163.6	160.8
2014	161.9	162.4	162.7	163.8	165.0	165.7	167.4	168.6	168.7	170.1	170.7	170.8	166.5
2015	169.7	170.4	172.0	172.8	174.7	176.0	178.9	180.5	180.1	180.4	180.6	181.2	176.4
2016	180.1	181.4	181.3	182.6	183.3	184.2	186.7	186.8	186.1	187.1	187.4	187.8	184.6
2017	182.9	184.7	185.8	186.9	187.3	189.2	189.9	190.6	191.4	191.0	191.2	192.0	188.6
Service-Providing													
2007	1,113.2	1,121.1	1,127.9	1,127.7	1,134.6	1,141.7	1,133.4	1,134.6	1,136.0	1,137.6	1,145.3	1,152.1	1,133.8
2008	1,125.8	1,134.3	1,139.0	1,139.5	1,143.2	1,146.6	1,135.3	1,135.6	1,133.2	1,134.2	1,136.0	1,135.0	1,136.5
2009	1,102.3	1,100.8	1,099.7	1,095.4	1,098.0	1,098.3	1,077.2	1,078.0	1,075.5	1,087.1	1,093.8	1,095.8	1,091.8
2010	1,068.0	1,072.7	1,076.7	1,088.7	1,099.2	1,101.1	1,089.9	1,092.4	1,091.9	1,097.9	1,102.7	1,106.5	1,090.6
2011	1,085.1	1,092.2	1,095.5	1,098.2	1,100.3	1,103.3	1,092.8	1,094.9	1,099.8	1,105.3	1,115.0	1,117.8	1,100.0
2012	1,095.9	1,104.6	1,110.4	1,126.5	1,134.3	1,140.7	1,124.9	1,130.4	1,131.0	1,141.5	1,152.0	1,155.4	1,129.0
2013	1,132.8	1,140.3	1,146.9	1,151.7	1,156.8	1,161.8	1,149.8	1,153.8	1,155.4	1,170.3	1,180.9	1,183.1	1,157.0
2014	1,155.0	1,163.7	1,170.6	1,173.4	1,178.9	1,185.9	1,172.7	1,180.1	1,179.8	1,191.0	1,203.7	1,206.3	1,180.1
2015	1,184.8	1,190.1	1,195.3	1,200.3	1,209.4	1,211.7	1,209.1	1,210.7	1,211.2	1,227.5	1,237.3	1,237.1	1,210.4
2016	1,213.2	1,222.6	1,222.8	1,235.8	1,240.3	1,240.4	1,235.6	1,240.4	1,244.2	1,255.0	1,264.7	1,265.5	1,240.0
2017	1,244.2	1,251.1	1,253.9	1,261.5	1,266.0	1,271.5	1,260.6	1,262.5	1,261.2	1,275.1	1,286.2	1,282.0	1,264.7
Mining and Logging													
2007	0.4	0.4	0.4	0.4	0.4	0.4	0.4	0.4	0.4	0.4	0.4	0.4	0.4
2008	0.4	0.4	0.4	0.4	0.4	0.4	0.4	0.4	0.4	0.3	0.3	0.3	0.4
2009	0.3	0.3	0.3	0.3	0.3	0.3	0.3	0.3	0.3	0.3	0.3	0.3	0.3
2010	0.3	0.3	0.4	0.3	0.4	0.4	0.4	0.4	0.4	0.4	0.4	0.4	0.4
2011	0.4	0.4	0.4	0.4	0.4	0.4	0.4	0.4	0.4	0.3	0.3	0.3	0.4
2012	0.3	0.3	0.3	0.4	0.4	0.4	0.3	0.4	0.3	0.3	0.4	0.4	0.4
2013	0.3	0.3	0.3	0.3	0.3	0.3	0.3	0.3	0.3	0.3	0.3	0.3	0.3
2014	0.4	0.4	0.3	0.4	0.4	0.4	0.4	0.4	0.4	0.4	0.4	0.4	0.4
2015	0.4	0.3	0.3	0.3	0.3	0.3	0.3	0.3	0.3	0.3	0.3	0.3	0.3
2016	0.3	0.3	0.3	0.3	0.3	0.3	0.3	0.3	0.3	0.3	0.3	0.3	0.3
2017	0.3	0.3	0.3	0.3	0.3	0.3	0.3	0.3	0.3	0.4	0.3	0.3	0.3

Employment by Industry: San Diego-Carlsbad, CA, Selected Years, 2007–2017—*Continued*

(Numbers in thousands, not seasonally adjusted)

Industry and year	January	February	March	April	May	June	July	August	September	October	November	December	Annual average
Construction													
2007	86.8	87.6	88.3	87.9	89.5	90.9	89.1	88.8	87.0	83.9	82.4	81.3	87.0
2008	78.0	78.0	77.9	77.0	77.5	77.9	77.7	77.0	75.8	73.9	72.1	70.3	76.1
2009	66.0	64.3	64.1	62.2	62.2	61.7	60.6	60.4	58.8	58.4	58.1	57.6	61.2
2010	55.8	54.8	55.2	55.8	56.2	56.2	56.2	56.3	55.4	54.6	54.5	54.2	55.4
2011	53.7	54.2	54.4	54.7	55.1	55.5	55.8	56.6	56.0	56.1	55.6	55.2	55.2
2012	54.2	54.2	55.2	56.0	57.0	58.1	57.8	58.2	58.0	58.3	58.9	58.4	57.0
2013	58.0	58.6	59.0	59.9	60.2	61.5	62.0	62.8	62.2	62.4	62.9	62.7	61.0
2014	61.4	61.7	61.9	62.2	63.1	63.3	64.5	65.4	65.4	66.1	66.3	65.8	63.9
2015	65.1	65.6	66.5	67.4	68.8	69.6	71.5	72.7	72.5	72.9	73.0	73.4	69.9
2016	72.7	73.9	73.8	74.8	75.4	75.9	77.7	78.3	77.9	78.0	78.4	78.6	76.3
2017	75.0	76.6	77.7	78.5	78.8	80.1	79.6	80.5	81.8	81.1	81.1	81.0	79.3
Manufacturing													
2007	102.9	102.7	103.0	101.9	102.0	102.1	103.0	102.7	102.4	103.0	103.4	103.9	102.8
2008	102.9	102.9	103.3	103.2	103.3	103.6	103.4	103.7	103.3	103.2	102.5	101.9	103.1
2009	102.1	101.1	100.0	98.3	97.2	96.7	96.0	95.5	95.0	94.7	94.4	94.5	97.1
2010	94.7	94.6	95.1	96.0	95.9	95.8	95.6	95.9	95.7	95.7	95.8	96.3	95.6
2011	95.9	95.8	96.0	95.9	96.1	96.7	96.5	96.6	96.7	96.7	96.8	97.3	96.4
2012	96.1	96.4	96.5	97.3	97.8	98.1	99.1	99.4	99.2	99.3	99.6	99.9	98.2
2013	98.8	99.1	99.2	99.2	99.0	98.9	99.4	99.4	99.5	99.9	100.3	100.6	99.4
2014	100.1	100.3	100.5	101.2	101.5	102.0	102.5	102.8	102.9	103.6	104.0	104.6	102.2
2015	104.2	104.5	105.2	105.1	105.6	106.1	107.1	107.5	107.3	107.2	107.3	107.5	106.2
2016	107.1	107.2	107.2	107.5	107.6	108.0	108.7	108.2	107.9	108.8	108.7	108.9	108.0
2017	107.6	107.8	107.8	108.1	108.2	108.8	110.0	109.8	109.3	109.5	109.8	110.7	109.0
Trade, Transportation, and Utilities													
2007	224.2	222.3	221.8	220.8	222.2	222.7	223.8	225.0	223.5	222.9	228.7	232.4	224.2
2008	221.5	218.9	217.9	217.9	216.9	217.0	218.3	217.3	216.3	215.4	217.9	219.2	217.9
2009	206.3	203.0	201.1	199.5	200.6	200.2	199.1	199.1	198.7	199.9	204.8	207.4	201.6
2010	197.0	195.6	194.8	196.2	197.2	198.1	199.0	199.8	199.2	200.7	206.5	209.9	199.5
2011	200.6	198.4	198.1	199.4	200.1	201.0	202.6	203.6	203.9	204.9	211.4	214.5	203.2
2012	206.8	204.5	204.2	206.7	208.3	209.1	209.3	209.7	210.0	211.9	221.0	222.7	210.4
2013	212.8	211.2	211.1	211.3	212.6	213.0	213.4	214.0	212.9	215.8	223.7	226.1	214.8
2014	216.1	214.7	213.5	213.3	214.4	215.7	216.1	216.9	216.5	218.2	226.0	228.8	217.5
2015	219.3	218.0	217.1	217.7	219.2	219.6	220.0	221.8	221.5	224.2	230.3	231.8	221.9
2016	222.3	221.7	220.1	221.9	222.1	221.4	223.6	224.6	223.4	226.9	233.8	235.4	224.8
2017	228.5	226.4	225.2	225.8	226.3	226.3	228.2	228.5	227.9	228.6	236.5	237.5	228.8
Wholesale Trade													
2007	46.6	47.1	47.2	47.1	47.6	47.6	47.9	47.8	47.6	47.3	47.5	47.4	47.4
2008	46.8	47.2	47.0	47.5	46.9	46.7	47.3	47.2	46.8	46.6	46.4	46.3	46.9
2009	44.2	44.1	43.5	43.1	43.1	42.5	42.1	41.9	41.7	42.0	42.0	42.0	42.7
2010	40.8	41.1	40.9	41.6	41.9	42.1	42.4	42.6	42.7	43.4	43.9	44.2	42.3
2011	42.9	43.2	43.2	43.5	43.6	43.6	43.7	43.9	43.9	44.2	44.3	44.4	43.7
2012	44.1	44.7	44.6	45.6	46.1	45.8	46.1	46.3	46.1	46.6	47.0	46.8	45.8
2013	46.4	47.1	46.9	46.3	46.7	46.1	45.8	45.8	45.6	46.6	46.7	46.5	46.4
2014	45.8	46.5	46.2	46.0	46.2	46.4	46.1	46.3	46.2	46.0	46.3	46.6	46.2
2015	45.5	46.4	46.0	46.3	46.5	46.3	46.9	46.8	46.8	47.5	47.6	47.5	46.7
2016	47.0	47.6	46.8	47.4	47.3	46.9	47.6	47.6	47.5	48.3	48.5	48.6	47.6
2017	48.0	48.7	47.5	47.9	48.0	47.8	48.3	48.2	48.1	48.4	48.8	48.9	48.2
Retail Trade													
2007	149.5	146.9	146.6	145.8	146.4	146.4	146.7	147.9	146.6	146.7	151.9	155.2	148.1
2008	145.7	142.3	141.7	141.5	141.0	141.3	141.9	141.1	140.5	140.2	143.0	144.2	142.0
2009	134.2	131.6	130.3	129.2	130.3	130.1	129.7	129.9	129.8	130.9	136.0	138.2	131.7
2010	130.0	128.4	127.8	128.3	128.7	129.3	129.8	130.4	129.8	130.9	136.1	138.7	130.7
2011	131.6	129.5	129.1	130.1	130.7	131.4	132.8	133.4	133.6	134.7	141.0	143.3	133.4
2012	136.4	133.4	133.0	134.2	135.0	135.6	135.5	135.8	136.2	137.9	146.3	147.4	137.2
2013	139.2	137.0	137.0	137.5	138.4	139.4	140.1	140.9	140.4	142.6	150.1	152.4	141.3
2014	143.6	141.5	140.9	140.9	141.4	142.2	142.8	143.7	143.2	145.0	152.3	154.1	144.3
2015	146.2	144.1	143.6	143.9	145.0	145.1	146.3	146.2	145.8	147.9	153.5	154.4	146.8
2016	146.4	145.3	144.5	145.6	145.7	145.1	146.0	146.8	145.7	148.3	154.6	155.6	147.5
2017	149.6	146.8	146.3	146.8	146.8	146.7	147.7	148.1	147.6	148.0	154.7	155.4	148.7

Employment by Industry: San Diego-Carlsbad, CA, Selected Years, 2007–2017—*Continued*

(Numbers in thousands, not seasonally adjusted)

Industry and year	January	February	March	April	May	June	July	August	September	October	November	December	Annual average
Transportation and Utilities													
2007	28.1	28.3	28.0	27.9	28.2	28.7	29.2	29.3	29.3	28.9	29.3	29.8	28.8
2008	29.0	29.4	29.2	28.9	29.0	29.0	29.1	29.0	29.0	28.6	28.5	28.7	29.0
2009	27.9	27.3	27.3	27.2	27.2	27.6	27.3	27.3	27.2	27.0	26.8	27.2	27.3
2010	26.2	26.1	26.1	26.3	26.6	26.7	26.8	26.8	26.7	26.4	26.5	27.0	26.5
2011	26.1	25.7	25.8	25.8	25.8	26.0	26.1	26.3	26.4	26.0	26.1	26.8	26.1
2012	26.3	26.4	26.6	26.9	27.2	27.7	27.7	27.6	27.7	27.4	27.7	28.5	27.3
2013	27.2	27.1	27.2	27.5	27.5	27.5	27.5	27.3	26.9	26.6	26.9	27.2	27.2
2014	26.7	26.7	26.4	26.4	26.8	27.1	27.2	26.9	27.1	27.2	27.4	28.1	27.0
2015	27.6	27.5	27.5	27.5	27.7	28.2	28.8	28.8	28.9	28.8	29.2	29.9	28.4
2016	28.9	28.8	28.8	28.9	29.1	29.4	30.0	30.2	30.2	30.3	30.7	31.2	29.7
2017	30.9	30.9	31.4	31.1	31.5	31.8	32.2	32.2	32.2	32.2	33.0	33.2	31.9
Information													
2007	31.6	31.7	31.5	31.4	31.2	31.2	31.3	31.3	31.0	31.2	31.4	31.6	31.4
2008	31.4	31.5	31.3	31.1	31.4	31.7	32.0	32.0	31.5	31.3	31.4	31.4	31.5
2009	30.6	30.5	30.1	29.4	28.9	28.7	28.3	27.8	26.9	26.7	26.5	26.2	28.4
2010	26.0	25.7	25.6	25.5	25.5	25.6	25.5	25.4	25.1	25.0	25.0	24.9	25.4
2011	24.8	24.8	24.7	24.6	24.6	24.5	24.7	24.7	24.8	24.8	24.7	24.8	24.7
2012	25.0	24.9	24.8	25.2	25.1	25.3	25.1	25.0	24.8	24.9	24.9	25.0	25.0
2013	24.7	24.5	24.5	24.5	24.7	24.8	24.7	24.8	24.8	24.8	25.0	25.1	24.7
2014	24.8	25.0	24.9	24.8	24.9	24.8	24.9	24.9	24.8	24.8	24.6	24.6	24.8
2015	24.1	24.1	24.1	24.2	24.3	24.2	24.5	24.4	24.0	24.1	24.1	24.2	24.2
2016	24.2	24.0	23.8	23.9	23.7	23.9	24.5	24.4	24.2	24.1	24.3	24.4	24.1
2017	24.3	24.4	24.3	24.2	24.3	24.5	24.7	24.6	24.4	24.4	24.5	24.4	24.4
Financial Activities													
2007	80.9	81.9	81.9	81.2	81.5	81.6	80.7	80.2	79.3	78.6	77.9	77.8	80.3
2008	76.3	76.7	76.6	76.6	76.3	75.9	75.4	75.0	74.1	73.7	73.2	72.9	75.2
2009	71.6	72.0	71.6	70.4	70.2	70.1	69.5	69.0	68.0	68.4	68.2	68.0	69.8
2010	66.9	67.2	67.1	67.0	66.7	66.9	67.2	67.0	66.8	67.7	67.5	67.6	67.1
2011	66.8	67.1	66.7	66.8	66.9	67.2	67.7	67.4	67.6	68.0	67.9	68.6	67.4
2012	68.0	68.2	68.5	69.4	69.5	69.9	70.6	70.6	70.1	70.5	70.9	71.2	69.8
2013	70.4	70.8	70.8	70.9	71.1	71.1	71.3	71.1	70.6	70.8	70.2	70.3	70.8
2014	69.2	69.3	69.3	68.9	69.1	69.3	70.1	70.0	69.3	69.4	69.6	69.6	69.4
2015	69.9	69.9	70.0	70.6	71.0	71.0	72.1	71.7	71.0	72.3	72.2	72.2	71.2
2016	71.3	71.5	71.3	72.3	72.6	72.7	73.6	73.6	73.2	73.7	73.5	73.6	72.7
2017	73.0	73.1	73.1	73.5	73.8	74.0	75.0	74.6	74.1	75.2	75.0	74.4	74.1
Professional and Business Services													
2007	216.2	218.6	219.6	219.9	220.2	222.2	222.9	223.9	223.2	223.2	223.0	223.1	221.3
2008	220.1	222.5	223.3	223.1	222.0	221.6	220.4	221.6	219.9	217.9	215.7	214.9	220.3
2009	209.0	207.6	205.2	203.0	202.2	201.6	201.3	201.5	199.4	201.3	202.4	203.5	203.2
2010	197.5	199.2	198.7	200.7	201.3	203.0	204.5	206.4	205.9	206.5	205.6	206.9	203.0
2011	203.0	204.5	204.9	204.2	203.0	203.3	204.5	206.2	204.7	205.0	205.7	206.4	204.6
2012	202.1	205.3	205.9	210.9	211.5	212.9	211.4	212.7	211.4	214.0	213.6	215.3	210.6
2013	212.9	215.1	215.6	215.1	215.9	216.6	218.0	218.7	218.9	223.6	224.0	224.3	218.2
2014	217.6	220.3	221.2	218.6	219.1	219.9	220.5	222.3	221.5	224.5	225.4	225.7	221.4
2015	222.1	223.6	223.5	224.0	224.7	226.0	228.5	229.3	227.6	231.9	232.7	232.0	227.2
2016	228.8	230.4	228.7	230.9	230.5	230.0	233.2	232.9	232.7	232.0	232.0	232.4	231.2
2017	229.3	231.1	231.4	230.7	230.7	231.8	234.6	235.6	234.7	237.1	237.1	238.4	233.5
Education and Health Services													
2007	139.4	140.9	142.9	143.1	144.2	143.4	142.4	143.7	145.7	146.8	147.7	149.2	144.1
2008	148.3	150.6	151.6	152.0	153.1	152.7	152.4	153.9	155.3	158.6	160.2	161.2	154.2
2009	159.6	161.3	162.7	161.9	162.8	162.3	159.2	160.9	162.7	165.2	166.8	167.9	162.8
2010	163.1	164.8	165.6	164.8	165.3	164.5	161.9	162.4	163.9	165.4	166.0	166.5	164.5
2011	165.8	167.7	168.4	167.7	168.2	167.4	165.3	165.6	167.9	168.8	170.7	170.9	167.9
2012	168.8	170.7	172.3	174.5	175.9	175.1	172.9	173.6	175.6	177.8	178.2	178.9	174.5
2013	179.1	180.6	181.9	182.6	182.2	180.3	177.2	178.2	180.0	183.3	183.7	183.4	181.0
2014	181.7	183.0	184.6	187.3	186.6	185.4	182.6	183.9	186.8	189.2	190.5	190.9	186.0
2015	189.2	189.8	191.5	192.1	192.6	191.4	190.4	191.6	193.8	195.9	196.3	197.4	192.7
2016	195.1	197.4	197.0	199.6	199.7	198.0	195.8	196.4	198.8	201.0	202.3	202.9	198.7
2017	200.8	202.8	203.7	204.7	205.2	204.9	200.9	203.3	204.8	206.9	208.6	207.2	204.5

Employment by Industry: San Diego-Carlsbad, CA, Selected Years, 2007–2017—*Continued*

(Numbers in thousands, not seasonally adjusted)

Industry and year	January	February	March	April	May	June	July	August	September	October	November	December	Annual average
Leisure and Hospitality													
2007	152.1	154.2	157.0	158.5	161.9	165.7	168.5	169.7	166.5	162.5	162.4	162.4	161.8
2008	156.6	158.7	161.1	162.9	166.1	168.2	171.0	171.4	167.7	162.4	161.5	159.9	164.0
2009	152.7	152.5	153.1	154.3	156.5	157.9	158.6	160.4	157.5	152.9	151.2	149.9	154.8
2010	147.4	148.4	150.8	154.3	156.4	158.4	159.7	161.2	157.6	154.4	152.9	152.7	154.5
2011	148.3	150.0	152.0	153.9	156.3	158.0	160.2	162.2	159.5	155.9	155.7	155.4	155.6
2012	151.3	153.3	155.1	159.7	162.8	165.9	167.9	170.5	166.7	163.2	162.2	162.2	161.7
2013	157.6	159.8	162.4	166.7	168.9	172.1	174.7	176.1	172.4	170.8	170.3	170.9	168.6
2014	166.3	168.3	171.7	174.4	177.5	180.9	183.5	186.1	180.8	178.1	178.4	178.2	177.0
2015	174.3	176.8	179.3	180.8	184.8	187.2	190.0	190.7	187.6	185.9	185.7	184.2	183.9
2016	180.0	182.5	185.5	189.2	192.2	194.3	198.5	199.0	197.1	195.5	195.3	193.2	191.9
2017	188.5	189.9	192.3	196.5	198.5	201.7	202.2	202.0	197.2	198.2	196.8	193.2	196.4
Other Services													
2007	47.3	47.8	48.2	47.7	48.4	49.2	48.9	48.6	48.7	48.0	48.3	48.5	48.3
2008	47.4	47.9	48.5	48.1	48.6	49.4	49.1	49.1	48.3	48.1	48.1	48.1	48.4
2009	46.3	47.0	47.3	47.1	47.3	47.5	46.7	47.1	46.2	46.4	46.3	46.3	46.8
2010	45.5	46.1	46.7	45.4	46.1	46.6	46.5	46.4	45.8	46.3	45.9	45.8	46.1
2011	45.7	46.8	46.9	47.8	48.5	48.3	48.1	48.0	48.2	48.3	47.8	47.4	47.7
2012	47.2	48.3	48.7	49.3	49.9	50.4	49.6	49.3	49.4	49.8	49.1	48.9	49.2
2013	47.7	48.3	48.2	48.7	49.1	49.9	50.0	50.0	49.9	49.9	50.1	49.9	49.3
2014	50.0	50.7	51.0	51.4	52.1	52.2	52.7	52.7	53.0	52.9	52.6	52.4	52.0
2015	51.4	52.1	52.2	52.7	53.2	53.5	54.2	54.3	54.1	53.9	53.7	53.5	53.2
2016	53.1	54.0	53.5	54.3	54.6	54.7	55.2	55.2	55.1	55.0	54.4	54.2	54.4
2017	53.2	53.9	54.1	54.5	55.2	55.9	56.0	55.4	55.5	54.8	55.3	54.4	54.9
Government													
2007	221.5	223.7	225.0	225.1	225.0	225.7	214.9	212.2	218.1	224.4	225.9	227.1	222.4
2008	224.2	227.5	228.7	227.8	228.8	230.1	216.7	215.3	220.1	226.8	228.0	227.4	225.1
2009	226.2	226.9	228.6	229.8	229.5	230.0	214.5	212.2	216.1	226.3	227.6	226.6	224.5
2010	224.6	225.7	227.4	234.8	240.7	238.0	225.6	223.8	227.6	231.9	233.3	232.2	230.5
2011	230.1	232.9	233.8	233.8	232.7	233.6	219.7	217.2	223.2	229.6	231.1	229.8	229.0
2012	226.7	229.4	230.9	230.8	231.3	232.1	218.1	219.0	223.0	229.4	232.1	231.2	227.8
2013	227.6	230.0	232.4	231.9	232.3	234.0	220.5	220.9	225.9	231.3	233.9	233.1	229.5
2014	229.3	232.4	234.4	234.7	235.2	237.7	222.3	223.3	227.1	233.9	236.6	236.1	231.9
2015	234.5	235.8	237.6	238.2	239.6	238.8	227.4	226.9	231.6	239.3	242.3	241.8	236.2
2016	238.4	241.1	242.9	243.7	244.9	245.4	231.2	234.3	239.7	246.8	249.1	249.4	242.2
2017	246.6	249.5	249.8	251.6	252.0	252.4	239.0	238.5	242.6	249.9	252.4	252.5	248.1

Employment by Industry: Tampa-St. Petersburg-Clearwater, FL, Selected Years, 2007–2017

(Numbers in thousands, not seasonally adjusted)

Industry and year	January	February	March	April	May	June	July	August	September	October	November	December	Annual average
Total Nonfarm													
2007	1,228.5	1,236.9	1,248.6	1,243.0	1,239.8	1,230.5	1,212.7	1,225.3	1,222.1	1,219.9	1,227.8	1,232.3	1,230.6
2008	1,207.0	1,214.9	1,219.6	1,206.3	1,201.2	1,185.3	1,168.1	1,178.5	1,173.4	1,168.1	1,167.4	1,169.2	1,188.3
2009	1,139.3	1,139.7	1,140.2	1,132.8	1,125.2	1,109.3	1,095.6	1,105.0	1,102.9	1,104.2	1,106.9	1,109.7	1,117.6
2010	1,089.8	1,098.8	1,107.3	1,106.8	1,113.0	1,100.1	1,093.0	1,103.6	1,102.0	1,113.8	1,118.7	1,123.8	1,105.9
2011	1,106.6	1,115.1	1,123.1	1,127.2	1,123.1	1,110.5	1,107.5	1,121.2	1,128.3	1,132.3	1,139.8	1,145.2	1,123.3
2012	1,132.2	1,140.7	1,148.3	1,153.0	1,152.0	1,139.9	1,132.3	1,146.7	1,146.9	1,155.2	1,165.8	1,172.0	1,148.8
2013	1,154.9	1,165.4	1,173.8	1,177.4	1,178.4	1,166.5	1,162.9	1,176.9	1,176.9	1,185.5	1,198.6	1,200.6	1,176.5
2014	1,181.9	1,190.4	1,200.2	1,208.0	1,210.8	1,198.6	1,195.2	1,209.7	1,211.7	1,221.5	1,234.2	1,239.1	1,208.4
2015	1,222.1	1,234.3	1,241.8	1,246.6	1,248.6	1,238.7	1,235.7	1,248.7	1,251.2	1,269.9	1,285.2	1,288.2	1,250.9
2016	1,270.6	1,281.5	1,287.3	1,297.8	1,295.5	1,280.7	1,281.0	1,292.0	1,298.0	1,309.7	1,321.0	1,324.3	1,295.0
2017	1,307.8	1,315.6	1,320.4	1,323.4	1,321.6	1,312.0	1,307.6	1,320.2	1,303.6	1,331.0	1,343.5	1,347.5	1,321.2
Total Private													
2007	1,076.2	1,083.5	1,094.5	1,089.2	1,087.6	1,088.2	1,071.4	1,074.1	1,068.0	1,064.5	1,072.4	1,077.3	1,078.9
2008	1,053.6	1,059.1	1,064.4	1,051.5	1,048.0	1,042.6	1,026.7	1,026.0	1,017.7	1,011.7	1,010.4	1,011.2	1,035.2
2009	983.7	981.6	982.7	974.3	969.6	963.8	950.9	950.6	947.7	947.7	950.8	954.1	963.1
2010	935.3	941.4	950.3	950.5	951.7	952.2	946.4	949.7	946.3	957.4	962.1	968.7	951.0
2011	951.7	957.7	966.0	970.9	968.6	966.2	964.9	969.5	973.2	976.9	984.7	990.1	970.0
2012	977.5	985.5	993.5	997.3	997.3	995.8	989.5	995.8	994.1	1,002.0	1,011.6	1,018.2	996.5
2013	1,000.6	1,009.9	1,018.4	1,021.9	1,025.0	1,023.4	1,020.9	1,026.0	1,024.2	1,030.8	1,043.5	1,046.2	1,024.2
2014	1,028.9	1,037.0	1,044.5	1,051.9	1,055.3	1,054.0	1,051.8	1,058.5	1,058.1	1,066.1	1,079.0	1,083.9	1,055.8
2015	1,068.3	1,078.7	1,086.5	1,090.7	1,093.4	1,094.2	1,092.1	1,096.7	1,097.6	1,112.6	1,127.4	1,132.2	1,097.5
2016	1,114.3	1,123.4	1,129.8	1,139.4	1,138.4	1,134.4	1,135.4	1,138.7	1,141.3	1,150.6	1,161.5	1,165.3	1,139.4
2017	1,150.0	1,155.2	1,160.6	1,163.6	1,164.0	1,163.7	1,161.9	1,166.6	1,147.1	1,171.5	1,184.1	1,189.1	1,164.8
Goods Producing													
2007	168.9	169.1	169.8	166.2	166.2	166.3	162.8	162.0	161.1	158.4	157.1	156.7	163.7
2008	153.3	154.0	153.8	151.3	151.0	151.0	148.4	147.2	145.4	142.3	139.8	137.4	147.9
2009	131.1	129.3	127.6	125.3	123.9	123.2	120.6	119.8	118.4	116.8	115.2	114.0	122.1
2010	110.6	110.6	110.7	110.4	111.5	111.6	111.9	111.8	110.9	110.8	110.3	110.2	110.9
2011	108.3	108.9	110.1	111.0	111.6	111.9	112.4	112.3	113.0	112.6	112.3	112.5	111.4
2012	110.7	111.7	112.5	112.8	113.6	114.6	114.2	114.9	114.1	114.6	114.9	115.0	113.6
2013	112.6	113.3	114.5	116.0	116.6	117.4	117.5	118.2	118.3	119.0	120.1	119.7	116.9
2014	117.5	118.8	119.8	120.9	122.4	123.2	123.1	123.6	123.6	123.9	123.6	123.7	122.0
2015	122.2	123.1	124.3	124.9	125.9	127.3	127.8	128.6	129.1	130.6	131.3	131.1	127.2
2016	129.9	131.2	132.6	134.1	135.0	135.7	136.1	136.3	137.2	138.1	138.1	138.3	135.2
2017	136.7	138.0	139.1	139.4	139.8	141.2	140.7	141.6	137.9	140.8	141.5	139.8	139.7
Service-Providing													
2007	1,059.6	1,067.8	1,078.8	1,076.8	1,073.6	1,064.2	1,049.9	1,063.3	1,061.0	1,061.5	1,070.7	1,075.6	1,066.9
2008	1,053.7	1,060.9	1,065.8	1,055.0	1,050.2	1,034.3	1,019.7	1,031.3	1,028.0	1,025.8	1,027.6	1,031.8	1,040.3
2009	1,008.2	1,010.4	1,012.6	1,007.5	1,001.3	986.1	975.0	985.2	984.5	987.4	991.7	995.7	995.5
2010	979.2	988.2	996.6	996.4	1,001.5	988.5	981.1	991.8	991.1	1,003.0	1,008.4	1,013.6	995.0
2011	998.3	1,006.2	1,013.0	1,016.2	1,011.5	998.6	995.1	1,008.9	1,015.3	1,019.7	1,027.5	1,032.7	1,011.9
2012	1,021.5	1,029.0	1,035.8	1,040.2	1,038.4	1,025.3	1,018.1	1,031.8	1,032.8	1,040.6	1,050.9	1,057.0	1,035.1
2013	1,042.3	1,052.1	1,059.3	1,061.4	1,061.8	1,049.1	1,045.4	1,058.7	1,058.6	1,066.5	1,078.5	1,080.9	1,059.6
2014	1,064.4	1,071.6	1,080.4	1,087.1	1,088.4	1,075.4	1,072.1	1,086.1	1,088.1	1,097.6	1,110.6	1,115.4	1,086.4
2015	1,099.9	1,111.2	1,117.5	1,121.7	1,122.7	1,111.4	1,107.9	1,120.1	1,122.1	1,139.3	1,153.9	1,157.1	1,123.7
2016	1,140.7	1,150.3	1,154.7	1,163.7	1,160.5	1,145.0	1,144.9	1,155.7	1,160.8	1,171.6	1,182.9	1,186.0	1,159.7
2017	1,171.1	1,177.6	1,181.3	1,184.0	1,181.8	1,170.8	1,166.9	1,178.6	1,165.7	1,190.2	1,202.0	1,207.7	1,181.5
Mining and Logging													
2007	0.6	0.6	0.6	0.7	0.7	0.7	0.7	0.7	0.7	0.7	0.7	0.7	0.7
2008	0.7	0.6	0.7	0.7	0.7	0.7	0.6	0.6	0.6	0.5	0.5	0.5	0.6
2009	0.5	0.5	0.5	0.5	0.5	0.5	0.5	0.5	0.5	0.5	0.5	0.5	0.5
2010	0.5	0.5	0.4	0.4	0.4	0.4	0.4	0.4	0.4	0.4	0.4	0.4	0.4
2011	0.4	0.4	0.4	0.4	0.4	0.4	0.4	0.4	0.4	0.4	0.5	0.5	0.4
2012	0.5	0.5	0.5	0.5	0.5	0.5	0.5	0.5	0.4	0.5	0.5	0.5	0.5
2013	0.4	0.4	0.5	0.5	0.4	0.4	0.5	0.4	0.4	0.4	0.4	0.4	0.4
2014	0.4	0.4	0.4	0.4	0.4	0.4	0.4	0.4	0.4	0.4	0.4	0.4	0.4
2015	0.3	0.3	0.4	0.4	0.4	0.4	0.4	0.4	0.3	0.3	0.3	0.3	0.4
2016	0.3	0.3	0.3	0.3	0.3	0.3	0.3	0.3	0.3	0.2	0.2	0.2	0.3
2017	0.3	0.3	0.3	0.3	0.2	0.3	0.2	0.2	0.2	0.2	0.2	0.2	0.2

Employment by Industry: Tampa-St. Petersburg-Clearwater, FL, Selected Years, 2007–2017—*Continued*

(Numbers in thousands, not seasonally adjusted)

Industry and year	January	February	March	April	May	June	July	August	September	October	November	December	Annual average
Construction													
2007	91.3	91.3	92.2	88.9	88.8	89.0	86.3	85.6	84.9	83.1	82.4	82.2	87.2
2008	79.2	80.0	79.8	78.0	77.8	77.9	75.8	75.1	74.1	72.1	70.5	69.1	75.8
2009	64.4	63.2	62.3	61.2	60.4	60.2	59.2	58.8	58.2	57.0	55.9	55.2	59.7
2010	52.4	52.4	52.6	52.2	52.7	52.7	53.0	52.7	52.2	52.4	51.6	51.4	52.4
2011	50.1	50.5	51.3	52.0	52.5	52.5	52.8	52.6	53.3	53.2	52.8	52.9	52.2
2012	51.3	52.0	52.6	52.8	53.5	54.4	54.0	54.5	54.5	54.7	55.0	55.1	53.7
2013	53.4	54.0	54.8	55.5	56.2	56.8	56.8	57.4	57.6	58.0	58.8	58.5	56.5
2014	56.8	57.8	58.5	59.6	60.5	61.4	61.5	61.8	61.8	61.9	61.7	61.8	60.4
2015	60.9	61.6	62.4	63.2	63.9	64.7	64.9	65.5	66.0	67.1	67.6	67.4	64.6
2016	66.5	67.6	68.3	69.4	70.1	70.5	70.7	70.9	71.7	72.7	72.4	72.5	70.3
2017	70.9	71.9	72.5	73.0	73.4	74.4	74.1	74.8	72.0	73.7	74.2	72.5	73.1
Manufacturing													
2007	77.0	77.2	77.0	76.6	76.7	76.6	75.8	75.7	75.5	74.6	74.0	73.8	75.9
2008	73.4	73.4	73.3	72.6	72.5	72.4	72.0	71.5	70.7	69.7	68.8	67.8	71.5
2009	66.2	65.6	64.8	63.6	63.0	62.5	60.9	60.5	59.7	59.3	58.8	58.3	61.9
2010	57.7	57.7	57.7	57.8	58.4	58.5	58.5	58.7	58.3	58.0	58.3	58.4	58.2
2011	57.8	58.0	58.4	58.6	58.7	59.0	59.2	59.3	59.3	59.0	59.0	59.1	58.8
2012	58.9	59.2	59.4	59.5	59.6	59.7	59.7	59.9	59.2	59.4	59.4	59.4	59.4
2013	58.8	58.9	59.2	60.0	60.0	60.2	60.2	60.4	60.3	60.6	60.9	60.8	60.0
2014	60.3	60.6	60.9	60.9	61.5	61.4	61.2	61.4	61.4	61.6	61.5	61.5	61.2
2015	61.0	61.2	61.5	61.3	61.6	62.2	62.5	62.7	62.8	63.2	63.4	63.4	62.2
2016	63.1	63.3	64.0	64.4	64.6	64.9	65.1	65.1	65.2	65.2	65.5	65.6	64.7
2017	65.5	65.8	66.3	66.1	66.2	66.5	66.4	66.6	65.7	66.9	67.1	67.1	66.4
Trade, Transportation, and Utilities													
2007	235.6	234.4	235.6	234.4	235.1	234.6	232.2	232.9	232.9	232.8	238.8	241.3	235.1
2008	233.5	232.6	232.6	229.3	229.1	227.2	224.4	223.9	222.2	222.1	224.6	226.5	227.3
2009	217.2	214.6	213.2	210.8	210.7	209.0	206.7	206.7	206.3	207.2	210.9	213.4	210.6
2010	206.6	206.5	207.3	207.6	208.7	208.7	207.5	208.1	207.9	210.5	214.7	218.7	209.4
2011	210.9	210.3	211.3	211.9	212.1	211.2	211.6	212.6	212.9	214.1	219.4	222.6	213.4
2012	217.7	217.3	216.8	217.4	218.3	217.2	216.7	217.4	217.4	218.9	225.0	227.5	219.0
2013	220.8	220.7	220.4	220.3	221.2	221.2	220.5	221.4	221.3	223.6	230.4	233.2	222.9
2014	226.8	227.5	228.0	229.4	230.1	229.9	229.3	230.4	231.3	233.6	241.8	245.8	232.0
2015	237.1	236.7	237.5	237.0	237.8	238.5	237.3	238.1	237.9	242.2	248.7	252.3	240.1
2016	245.0	245.5	245.4	246.4	246.5	244.8	245.0	245.2	245.0	247.5	255.2	257.4	247.4
2017	249.0	247.4	246.2	246.4	246.8	246.3	246.0	247.4	242.5	246.4	253.4	256.4	247.9
Wholesale Trade													
2007	54.4	54.5	54.6	54.3	54.6	54.5	53.8	54.0	53.8	54.0	54.6	54.8	54.3
2008	54.3	54.3	54.2	53.8	54.0	53.4	52.5	52.2	51.8	51.5	51.4	51.2	52.9
2009	50.0	49.4	49.1	48.4	48.3	47.5	46.7	46.6	46.4	46.6	46.5	46.7	47.7
2010	45.7	45.8	46.2	46.1	46.5	46.2	45.6	45.6	45.5	45.9	45.8	46.3	45.9
2011	45.5	45.5	45.7	45.8	46.1	45.8	46.1	46.3	46.6	46.8	47.2	47.8	46.3
2012	48.2	48.5	48.3	48.4	48.7	48.4	47.9	48.2	48.3	48.4	49.1	49.0	48.5
2013	48.9	49.0	49.1	48.7	48.9	48.6	48.4	48.7	48.6	48.9	49.5	49.6	48.9
2014	49.4	49.8	50.0	50.2	50.5	50.3	50.2	50.5	50.5	50.7	51.2	51.6	50.4
2015	50.9	50.9	51.2	51.0	51.2	50.9	51.0	51.1	51.1	51.6	51.9	52.1	51.2
2016	51.6	51.7	51.7	52.0	52.0	51.6	52.0	52.2	52.3	52.6	53.0	53.4	52.2
2017	52.6	53.0	53.0	53.2	53.4	53.3	53.3	53.5	53.0	53.3	53.1	53.2	53.2
Retail Trade													
2007	151.9	150.9	151.8	151.1	151.7	151.2	149.5	149.9	150.2	150.0	155.2	156.7	151.7
2008	151.0	150.0	150.1	147.3	146.9	145.8	144.5	144.5	143.3	143.4	146.0	147.1	146.7
2009	140.3	138.7	137.9	136.4	136.5	135.8	134.5	134.8	134.7	135.8	139.5	140.8	137.1
2010	136.1	135.9	136.4	136.6	137.1	137.6	136.9	137.5	137.4	139.3	143.4	145.8	138.3
2011	140.0	139.5	140.1	140.7	140.4	139.8	139.7	140.5	140.4	141.4	146.0	147.5	141.3
2012	143.2	142.4	142.1	142.5	143.0	142.2	142.2	142.9	142.7	144.1	149.2	150.9	144.0
2013	145.1	144.6	144.2	144.4	145.1	145.2	145.0	145.6	145.6	147.5	153.1	155.0	146.7
2014	149.5	149.6	149.7	150.8	151.0	151.0	150.5	151.3	152.1	154.0	161.2	163.5	152.9
2015	156.9	156.7	157.1	156.8	157.3	158.2	157.0	157.7	157.5	160.9	166.4	168.7	159.3
2016	162.9	163.7	163.7	164.4	164.3	163.2	162.7	162.8	162.5	164.4	170.9	172.2	164.8
2017	165.7	163.8	162.8	162.9	162.8	162.5	162.3	163.5	159.6	162.8	169.1	170.6	164.0

Employment by Industry: Tampa-St. Petersburg-Clearwater, FL, Selected Years, 2007–2017—*Continued*

(Numbers in thousands, not seasonally adjusted)

Industry and year	January	February	March	April	May	June	July	August	September	October	November	December	Annual average
Transportation and Utilities													
2007	29.3	29.0	29.2	29.0	28.8	28.9	28.9	29.0	28.9	28.8	29.0	29.8	29.1
2008	28.2	28.3	28.3	28.2	28.2	28.0	27.4	27.2	27.1	27.2	27.2	28.2	27.8
2009	26.9	26.5	26.2	26.0	25.9	25.7	25.5	25.3	25.2	24.8	24.9	25.9	25.7
2010	24.8	24.8	24.7	24.9	25.1	24.9	25.0	25.0	25.0	25.3	25.5	26.6	25.1
2011	25.4	25.3	25.5	25.4	25.6	25.6	25.8	25.8	25.9	25.9	26.2	27.3	25.8
2012	26.3	26.4	26.4	26.5	26.6	26.6	26.6	26.3	26.4	26.4	26.7	27.6	26.6
2013	26.8	27.1	27.1	27.2	27.2	27.4	27.1	27.1	27.1	27.2	27.8	28.6	27.3
2014	27.9	28.1	28.3	28.4	28.6	28.6	28.6	28.6	28.7	28.9	29.4	30.7	28.7
2015	29.3	29.1	29.2	29.2	29.3	29.4	29.3	29.3	29.3	29.7	30.4	31.5	29.6
2016	30.5	30.1	30.0	30.0	30.2	30.0	30.3	30.2	30.2	30.5	31.3	31.8	30.4
2017	30.7	30.6	30.4	30.3	30.6	30.5	30.4	30.4	29.9	30.3	31.2	32.6	30.7
Information													
2007	31.6	31.8	31.9	32.1	32.2	32.4	31.9	31.9	31.7	31.4	31.4	31.3	31.8
2008	30.9	31.1	31.0	31.0	30.9	30.7	30.3	30.0	29.5	29.6	29.3	29.0	30.3
2009	28.7	28.6	28.5	28.1	27.8	27.7	27.6	27.3	26.9	26.5	26.5	26.5	27.6
2010	26.0	26.0	26.0	25.8	25.8	25.7	25.7	25.6	25.5	25.5	25.6	25.6	25.7
2011	25.8	25.9	25.7	25.6	25.7	25.8	26.0	25.9	25.9	26.0	26.1	26.2	25.9
2012	25.8	25.7	25.7	25.7	25.6	25.8	25.7	25.6	25.6	25.9	25.9	25.9	25.7
2013	26.1	26.1	26.2	26.2	26.3	26.4	26.1	26.1	25.9	25.9	26.0	26.0	26.1
2014	25.5	25.6	25.4	25.5	25.5	25.6	25.6	25.5	25.4	25.7	25.7	25.6	25.6
2015	25.5	25.6	25.4	25.5	25.6	25.7	26.0	25.8	25.9	26.0	26.2	26.4	25.8
2016	25.6	25.6	25.5	25.3	25.4	25.5	25.9	25.7	25.5	25.3	25.6	25.6	25.5
2017	25.4	25.2	25.4	25.0	25.1	25.2	25.1	24.8	24.4	24.5	24.8	24.8	25.0
Financial Activities													
2007	103.2	104.2	104.3	104.4	104.2	104.0	103.7	102.8	102.4	102.1	102.0	101.8	103.3
2008	100.5	100.5	100.2	99.3	99.1	98.6	98.3	98.0	97.4	97.2	97.0	96.9	98.6
2009	96.0	95.3	95.0	94.4	94.2	93.7	93.0	92.6	91.8	91.1	90.7	90.8	93.2
2010	89.3	89.2	89.4	89.1	89.1	89.2	89.0	89.5	89.0	89.6	89.7	90.5	89.4
2011	89.7	89.9	90.3	90.5	90.4	90.9	91.2	92.1	93.0	93.5	93.4	94.2	91.6
2012	93.3	93.8	94.4	94.5	94.8	95.5	95.5	96.0	96.1	96.9	97.6	98.1	95.5
2013	97.6	98.4	99.0	98.8	99.2	99.8	100.2	100.5	100.1	100.3	100.9	101.3	99.7
2014	100.3	100.5	101.0	101.0	101.3	101.6	102.3	102.4	102.5	102.3	102.8	103.0	101.8
2015	102.3	102.5	102.6	102.8	103.2	103.4	104.3	104.7	104.3	105.0	106.0	106.1	103.9
2016	105.3	105.4	105.6	106.2	106.4	106.8	108.1	108.5	108.6	109.2	109.5	110.7	107.5
2017	109.9	110.4	110.6	110.6	110.7	111.3	113.0	113.0	112.8	114.0	114.8	116.2	112.3
Professional and Business Services													
2007	196.9	198.2	201.1	201.3	199.1	200.9	196.9	198.2	193.7	192.4	192.8	193.3	197.1
2008	188.0	189.1	190.6	185.9	184.0	184.4	181.9	182.1	179.7	177.0	176.2	177.2	183.0
2009	172.6	172.8	173.0	171.2	169.4	170.1	168.0	168.4	168.2	167.6	168.6	169.6	170.0
2010	167.0	169.8	172.2	172.1	172.1	174.2	173.8	175.9	174.5	178.8	179.2	180.6	174.2
2011	177.6	179.8	180.6	182.1	180.7	181.5	182.4	183.8	183.7	184.2	186.2	188.0	182.6
2012	185.8	188.4	190.3	190.9	190.3	190.0	189.8	191.6	190.2	192.9	194.7	196.3	190.9
2013	192.1	195.6	196.9	197.6	199.0	198.1	198.8	199.9	198.7	199.7	201.3	201.2	198.2
2014	198.0	200.1	200.2	201.5	202.8	202.7	203.7	206.6	205.0	208.6	211.0	211.5	204.3
2015	210.1	213.5	214.0	215.3	216.1	216.5	218.3	219.6	218.4	221.8	224.8	225.9	217.9
2016	223.6	226.0	226.9	230.0	229.5	228.7	230.1	230.4	230.2	232.7	233.8	233.5	229.6
2017	232.7	232.5	232.9	235.0	235.0	235.0	236.6	237.1	233.3	238.8	238.7	240.9	235.7
Education and Health Services													
2007	164.2	166.0	167.9	168.2	168.4	168.2	166.1	168.2	169.2	171.0	172.6	173.4	168.6
2008	171.6	172.9	174.0	173.6	173.9	172.1	170.4	171.7	172.3	173.5	174.9	175.6	173.0
2009	172.1	172.9	174.3	174.2	174.6	173.4	172.2	173.0	174.3	176.5	177.8	178.6	174.5
2010	176.4	177.3	179.3	178.5	178.1	177.2	175.8	176.1	176.8	179.5	180.4	180.6	178.0
2011	179.0	180.1	181.1	182.5	181.6	179.7	178.6	179.8	181.0	182.0	182.9	182.8	180.9
2012	180.7	182.0	182.9	183.5	183.1	182.0	179.2	181.1	182.1	183.1	183.7	184.2	182.3
2013	182.2	183.6	185.0	185.4	185.2	183.4	181.7	183.6	184.5	186.5	187.6	187.1	184.7
2014	185.1	186.3	187.6	188.4	188.5	186.8	185.5	188.0	188.8	191.0	192.1	192.4	188.4
2015	190.2	192.4	192.8	194.4	194.5	193.6	191.6	193.3	195.1	198.6	199.7	199.8	194.7
2016	196.7	197.9	198.3	200.3	199.7	197.2	196.8	198.9	200.5	203.0	203.5	204.2	199.8
2017	202.6	204.4	205.3	205.9	205.5	204.3	202.6	204.9	204.0	206.1	207.7	209.6	205.2

Employment by Industry: Tampa-St. Petersburg-Clearwater, FL, Selected Years, 2007–2017—*Continued*

(Numbers in thousands, not seasonally adjusted)

Industry and year	January	February	March	April	May	June	July	August	September	October	November	December	Annual average
Leisure and Hospitality													
2007	129.4	132.6	136.0	136.1	135.2	133.9	131.1	131.4	130.4	129.1	129.8	130.9	132.2
2008	128.0	130.6	133.7	133.5	132.0	130.5	126.1	126.4	125.2	124.8	123.8	124.1	128.2
2009	122.2	124.4	127.2	126.8	125.4	123.3	120.1	120.1	119.3	119.3	118.6	118.8	122.1
2010	117.8	120.0	123.3	124.8	124.1	123.1	120.7	121.0	120.3	120.6	120.5	120.7	121.4
2011	119.1	121.2	124.8	125.2	124.5	123.7	121.5	122.1	123.0	123.8	123.8	123.2	123.0
2012	123.1	125.9	129.8	131.3	130.4	129.5	127.5	128.3	127.5	128.5	128.4	129.7	128.3
2013	128.1	130.8	134.7	135.3	135.0	134.3	133.6	133.6	132.7	133.0	134.0	134.4	133.3
2014	132.7	134.7	138.7	141.6	141.2	140.6	138.9	138.7	138.3	137.8	138.9	138.7	138.4
2015	138.2	142.0	146.7	147.5	146.9	145.6	143.8	143.3	143.5	144.7	146.7	146.4	144.6
2016	144.0	147.4	151.0	152.3	151.0	150.5	148.5	148.5	148.7	149.0	150.0	149.8	149.2
2017	148.7	151.9	155.7	155.7	155.4	154.6	152.2	152.3	147.7	154.9	156.4	155.1	153.4
Other Services													
2007	46.4	47.2	47.9	46.5	47.2	47.9	46.7	46.7	46.6	47.3	47.9	48.6	47.2
2008	47.8	48.3	48.5	47.6	48.0	48.1	46.9	46.7	46.0	45.2	44.8	44.5	46.9
2009	43.8	43.7	43.9	43.5	43.6	43.4	42.7	42.7	42.5	42.7	42.5	42.4	43.1
2010	41.6	42.0	42.1	42.2	42.3	42.5	42.0	41.7	41.4	42.1	41.7	41.8	42.0
2011	41.3	41.6	42.1	42.1	42.0	41.5	41.2	40.9	40.7	40.7	40.6	40.6	41.3
2012	40.4	40.7	41.1	41.2	41.2	41.2	40.9	40.9	41.1	41.2	41.4	41.5	41.1
2013	41.1	41.4	41.7	42.3	42.5	42.8	42.5	42.7	42.7	42.8	43.2	43.3	42.4
2014	43.0	43.5	43.8	43.6	43.5	43.6	43.4	43.3	43.2	43.2	43.1	43.2	43.4
2015	42.7	42.9	43.2	43.3	43.4	43.6	43.0	43.3	43.4	43.7	44.0	44.2	43.4
2016	44.2	44.4	44.5	44.8	44.9	45.2	44.9	45.2	45.6	45.8	45.8	45.8	45.1
2017	45.0	45.4	45.4	45.6	45.7	45.8	45.7	45.5	44.5	46.0	46.8	46.3	45.6
Government													
2007	152.3	153.4	154.1	153.8	152.2	142.3	141.3	151.2	154.1	155.4	155.4	155.0	151.7
2008	153.4	155.8	155.2	154.8	153.2	142.7	141.4	152.5	155.7	156.4	157.0	158.0	153.0
2009	155.6	158.1	157.5	158.5	155.6	145.5	144.7	154.4	155.2	156.5	156.1	155.6	154.4
2010	154.5	157.4	157.0	156.3	161.3	147.9	146.6	153.9	155.7	156.4	156.6	155.1	154.9
2011	154.9	157.4	157.1	156.3	154.5	144.3	142.6	151.7	155.1	155.4	155.1	155.1	153.3
2012	154.7	155.2	154.8	155.7	154.7	144.1	142.8	150.9	152.8	153.2	154.2	153.8	152.2
2013	154.3	155.5	155.4	155.5	153.4	143.1	142.0	150.9	152.7	154.7	155.1	154.4	152.3
2014	153.0	153.4	155.7	156.1	155.5	144.6	143.4	151.2	153.6	155.4	155.2	155.2	152.7
2015	153.8	155.6	155.3	155.9	155.2	144.5	143.6	152.0	153.6	157.3	157.8	156.0	153.4
2016	156.3	158.1	157.5	158.4	157.1	146.3	145.6	153.3	156.7	159.1	159.5	159.0	155.6
2017	157.8	160.4	159.8	159.8	157.6	148.3	145.7	153.6	156.5	159.5	159.4	158.4	156.4

Employment by Industry: Denver-Aurora-Lakewood, CO, Selected Years, 2007–2017

(Numbers in thousands, not seasonally adjusted)

Industry and year	January	February	March	April	May	June	July	August	September	October	November	December	Annual average
Total Nonfarm													
2007	1,202.8	1,209.2	1,221.6	1,230.5	1,244.2	1,257.9	1,249.7	1,253.0	1,253.1	1,254.5	1,258.8	1,261.4	1,241.4
2008	1,231.5	1,237.5	1,244.7	1,252.5	1,262.2	1,271.9	1,262.0	1,266.1	1,259.7	1,256.5	1,251.5	1,244.7	1,253.4
2009	1,206.8	1,198.6	1,197.6	1,199.3	1,206.9	1,210.8	1,200.1	1,198.3	1,194.9	1,197.3	1,196.1	1,194.1	1,200.1
2010	1,162.4	1,167.6	1,175.0	1,186.2	1,200.0	1,207.1	1,202.9	1,203.4	1,200.0	1,206.7	1,208.2	1,207.6	1,193.9
2011	1,181.0	1,184.5	1,192.0	1,208.4	1,218.0	1,227.1	1,219.6	1,224.5	1,225.2	1,226.5	1,231.5	1,233.3	1,214.3
2012	1,208.0	1,213.3	1,225.0	1,236.8	1,249.1	1,263.0	1,256.7	1,258.8	1,260.1	1,270.0	1,276.4	1,277.1	1,249.5
2013	1,251.1	1,260.0	1,270.2	1,282.1	1,294.7	1,307.0	1,303.0	1,310.6	1,309.4	1,318.5	1,324.0	1,324.0	1,296.2
2014	1,299.6	1,305.5	1,314.3	1,330.7	1,344.5	1,355.3	1,351.3	1,363.5	1,363.0	1,373.8	1,374.9	1,380.1	1,346.4
2015	1,356.9	1,365.1	1,370.4	1,384.8	1,396.1	1,408.9	1,405.4	1,411.0	1,410.5	1,416.4	1,421.3	1,424.4	1,397.6
2016	1,399.1	1,405.5	1,411.7	1,425.9	1,431.8	1,445.3	1,444.4	1,447.5	1,445.9	1,448.8	1,451.6	1,451.3	1,434.1
2017	1,425.0	1,432.2	1,441.1	1,449.3	1,460.2	1,475.4	1,470.4	1,473.1	1,470.9	1,476.9	1,482.2	1,483.9	1,461.7
Total Private													
2007	1,038.9	1,040.2	1,051.3	1,059.8	1,072.4	1,087.1	1,086.3	1,088.7	1,081.4	1,082.0	1,085.4	1,088.4	1,071.8
2008	1,063.6	1,065.2	1,071.1	1,078.3	1,085.9	1,097.4	1,094.3	1,095.6	1,084.3	1,079.1	1,073.2	1,067.4	1,079.6
2009	1,034.0	1,022.7	1,020.3	1,021.0	1,026.6	1,033.0	1,031.1	1,028.2	1,017.7	1,017.7	1,017.2	1,016.4	1,023.8
2010	990.5	990.0	996.2	1,006.4	1,014.8	1,026.9	1,030.1	1,032.0	1,021.4	1,025.6	1,026.7	1,028.1	1,015.7
2011	1,007.1	1,005.2	1,012.0	1,027.0	1,035.1	1,046.6	1,048.0	1,053.1	1,046.6	1,046.3	1,051.0	1,053.8	1,036.0
2012	1,034.1	1,034.1	1,044.1	1,055.0	1,065.7	1,080.5	1,083.3	1,086.4	1,080.2	1,088.5	1,093.2	1,095.5	1,070.1
2013	1,074.9	1,078.0	1,087.0	1,097.5	1,109.1	1,122.9	1,127.2	1,133.5	1,123.9	1,129.8	1,135.6	1,137.6	1,113.1
2014	1,118.4	1,120.5	1,128.2	1,143.8	1,156.3	1,168.7	1,175.8	1,183.6	1,175.4	1,182.3	1,182.5	1,190.2	1,160.5
2015	1,171.4	1,175.4	1,179.9	1,192.6	1,202.1	1,216.8	1,223.0	1,225.1	1,216.2	1,221.5	1,225.3	1,229.5	1,206.6
2016	1,208.5	1,210.5	1,215.7	1,228.6	1,234.3	1,248.2	1,256.9	1,256.3	1,248.6	1,250.9	1,251.8	1,253.1	1,238.6
2017	1,230.2	1,233.1	1,240.6	1,250.3	1,259.4	1,276.9	1,279.4	1,280.2	1,272.7	1,279.1	1,283.0	1,286.2	1,264.3
Goods Producing													
2007	157.3	158.0	161.1	162.5	164.7	168.0	168.6	168.7	167.2	167.6	166.2	163.3	164.4
2008	159.7	159.7	160.9	161.5	163.0	165.6	164.9	165.0	162.8	161.7	158.1	153.9	161.4
2009	146.7	143.2	141.4	140.0	140.0	141.5	141.3	139.7	137.9	136.9	135.6	132.7	139.7
2010	127.8	127.2	128.0	129.9	131.1	133.3	134.4	133.8	132.2	132.3	131.1	130.2	130.9
2011	126.1	125.4	127.4	130.6	131.0	133.9	134.9	135.5	134.8	134.7	134.1	132.8	131.8
2012	130.0	130.0	131.7	133.5	135.5	138.6	139.4	139.9	139.5	140.7	140.2	139.3	136.5
2013	136.6	137.3	139.2	140.3	143.4	146.4	147.4	148.7	147.7	149.0	149.2	148.5	144.5
2014	146.6	147.3	149.3	152.3	154.9	157.6	159.4	160.3	160.0	160.5	160.1	160.5	155.7
2015	157.8	158.6	159.5	160.8	162.2	164.8	165.6	165.4	164.8	165.3	164.7	164.3	162.8
2016	161.5	162.1	163.8	165.0	165.5	168.1	169.0	168.6	168.2	168.7	168.0	167.6	166.3
2017	164.2	165.4	167.2	168.1	169.2	172.7	173.4	174.0	173.3	174.2	175.9	174.9	171.0
Service-Providing													
2007	1,045.5	1,051.2	1,060.5	1,068.0	1,079.5	1,089.9	1,081.1	1,084.3	1,085.9	1,086.9	1,092.6	1,098.1	1,077.0
2008	1,071.8	1,077.8	1,083.8	1,091.0	1,099.2	1,106.3	1,097.1	1,101.1	1,096.9	1,094.8	1,093.4	1,090.8	1,092.0
2009	1,060.1	1,055.4	1,056.2	1,059.3	1,066.9	1,069.3	1,058.8	1,058.6	1,057.0	1,060.4	1,060.5	1,061.4	1,060.3
2010	1,034.6	1,040.4	1,047.0	1,056.3	1,068.9	1,073.8	1,068.5	1,069.6	1,067.8	1,074.4	1,077.1	1,077.4	1,063.0
2011	1,054.9	1,059.1	1,064.6	1,077.8	1,087.0	1,093.2	1,084.7	1,089.0	1,090.4	1,091.8	1,097.4	1,100.5	1,082.5
2012	1,078.0	1,083.3	1,093.3	1,103.3	1,113.6	1,124.4	1,117.3	1,118.9	1,120.6	1,129.3	1,136.2	1,137.8	1,113.0
2013	1,114.5	1,122.7	1,131.0	1,141.8	1,151.3	1,160.6	1,155.6	1,161.9	1,161.7	1,169.5	1,174.8	1,175.5	1,151.7
2014	1,153.0	1,158.2	1,165.0	1,178.4	1,189.6	1,197.7	1,191.9	1,203.2	1,203.0	1,213.3	1,214.8	1,219.6	1,190.6
2015	1,199.1	1,206.5	1,210.9	1,224.0	1,233.9	1,244.1	1,239.8	1,245.6	1,245.7	1,251.1	1,256.6	1,260.1	1,234.8
2016	1,237.6	1,243.4	1,247.9	1,260.9	1,266.3	1,277.2	1,275.4	1,278.9	1,277.7	1,280.1	1,283.6	1,283.7	1,267.7
2017	1,260.8	1,266.8	1,273.9	1,281.2	1,291.0	1,302.7	1,297.0	1,299.1	1,297.6	1,302.7	1,306.3	1,309.0	1,290.7
Mining, Logging, and Construction													
2007	86.1	87.1	90.1	91.7	93.4	96.1	96.7	96.8	95.4	95.7	94.3	91.5	92.9
2008	88.7	89.3	90.5	91.4	92.9	95.1	94.5	94.8	93.0	92.3	89.7	86.2	91.5
2009	80.7	78.5	77.3	76.4	76.9	78.5	78.4	77.2	76.0	75.1	73.8	71.2	76.7
2010	67.5	66.9	67.6	69.4	70.0	71.7	72.7	72.1	70.7	70.8	69.6	68.7	69.8
2011	64.9	64.3	66.0	68.8	68.9	71.4	72.3	72.7	72.0	72.3	71.6	70.4	69.6
2012	68.1	67.9	69.2	70.8	72.5	75.0	75.5	76.1	75.7	76.8	76.3	75.5	73.3
2013	73.3	73.9	75.4	76.7	79.6	82.1	83.2	84.4	83.6	85.0	85.1	84.3	80.6
2014	83.0	83.5	85.3	87.7	89.9	92.1	93.5	94.2	93.9	94.2	93.4	93.5	90.4
2015	91.2	91.8	92.4	93.5	94.6	96.3	96.9	96.7	96.2	96.8	95.9	95.4	94.8
2016	92.8	93.4	95.1	96.3	96.7	98.8	99.4	99.3	99.1	99.5	99.0	98.2	97.3
2017	95.8	96.9	98.5	99.5	100.4	103.0	103.9	104.7	104.3	104.9	105.9	105.1	101.9

Employment by Industry: Denver-Aurora-Lakewood, CO, Selected Years, 2007–2017—*Continued*

(Numbers in thousands, not seasonally adjusted)

Industry and year	January	February	March	April	May	June	July	August	September	October	November	December	Annual average
Manufacturing													
2007	71.2	70.9	71.0	70.8	71.3	71.9	71.9	71.9	71.8	71.9	71.9	71.8	71.5
2008	71.0	70.4	70.4	70.1	70.1	70.5	70.4	70.2	69.8	69.4	68.4	67.7	69.9
2009	66.0	64.7	64.1	63.6	63.1	63.0	62.9	62.5	61.9	61.8	61.8	61.5	63.1
2010	60.3	60.3	60.4	60.5	61.1	61.6	61.7	61.7	61.5	61.5	61.5	61.5	61.1
2011	61.2	61.1	61.4	61.8	62.1	62.5	62.6	62.8	62.8	62.4	62.5	62.4	62.1
2012	61.9	62.1	62.5	62.7	63.0	63.6	63.9	63.8	63.8	63.9	63.9	63.8	63.2
2013	63.3	63.4	63.8	63.6	63.8	64.3	64.2	64.3	64.1	64.0	64.1	64.2	63.9
2014	63.6	63.8	64.0	64.6	65.0	65.5	65.9	66.1	66.1	66.3	66.7	67.0	65.4
2015	66.6	66.8	67.1	67.3	67.6	68.5	68.7	68.7	68.6	68.5	68.8	68.9	68.0
2016	68.7	68.7	68.7	68.7	68.8	69.3	69.6	69.3	69.1	69.2	69.0	69.4	69.0
2017	68.4	68.5	68.7	68.6	68.8	69.7	69.5	69.3	69.0	69.3	70.0	69.8	69.1
Trade, Transportation, and Utilities													
2007	242.2	239.4	240.1	241.0	242.8	244.3	244.5	244.5	243.8	245.6	251.2	253.8	244.4
2008	245.8	243.0	244.1	244.3	245.0	246.2	245.9	245.5	243.5	243.0	244.7	246.3	244.8
2009	235.7	231.7	229.8	229.0	229.8	230.6	229.5	229.2	227.8	229.2	231.8	234.1	230.7
2010	225.0	223.9	224.1	224.9	226.5	228.2	228.8	229.2	227.7	229.6	232.9	235.3	228.0
2011	226.4	224.6	225.4	227.5	228.9	230.1	230.9	231.3	230.0	231.7	236.1	238.1	230.1
2012	231.0	229.0	229.9	231.1	232.8	235.0	235.7	235.7	235.6	238.4	244.0	246.5	235.4
2013	238.2	236.8	237.7	238.5	240.5	242.1	243.0	244.5	243.4	245.0	250.3	253.2	242.8
2014	245.3	244.3	244.8	246.4	248.2	250.7	250.8	251.8	250.3	252.6	257.6	261.4	250.4
2015	253.5	252.3	252.6	253.8	254.7	257.2	258.5	258.8	257.1	259.8	264.6	268.3	257.6
2016	259.6	258.1	258.1	259.2	260.2	261.6	263.2	263.0	261.7	263.4	268.3	272.3	262.4
2017	264.4	262.6	262.5	263.3	264.3	266.7	267.1	267.4	266.1	267.2	272.1	275.7	266.6
Wholesale Trade													
2007	65.0	65.4	65.8	65.8	66.3	66.7	66.6	66.7	66.4	66.8	66.9	66.8	66.3
2008	66.5	66.7	66.8	67.0	67.2	67.4	67.4	67.1	66.8	66.4	66.1	66.0	66.8
2009	64.8	64.2	63.5	62.8	62.6	62.5	62.1	61.8	61.3	61.4	61.2	61.4	62.5
2010	60.9	60.7	60.8	60.9	61.1	61.5	61.7	61.7	61.5	61.7	61.7	61.8	61.3
2011	61.3	61.4	61.7	62.0	62.2	62.4	62.6	62.7	62.5	62.4	62.4	62.4	62.2
2012	62.0	62.2	62.6	63.0	63.2	63.7	64.0	64.1	64.0	64.3	64.3	64.7	63.5
2013	63.9	64.3	64.6	64.7	65.0	65.5	65.5	65.7	65.5	65.7	65.9	66.0	65.2
2014	65.7	66.1	66.4	66.9	67.2	67.6	68.0	68.5	68.2	68.7	69.0	69.4	67.6
2015	68.8	69.2	69.3	69.3	69.6	69.9	70.2	70.5	70.2	70.7	71.0	71.0	70.0
2016	70.6	70.7	70.7	71.1	71.0	71.0	71.5	71.3	71.3	71.3	71.4	71.5	71.1
2017	71.3	71.5	71.8	71.8	72.0	72.6	72.8	72.9	72.8	72.1	72.8	73.0	72.3
Retail Trade													
2007	126.8	124.0	124.3	124.9	126.1	127.0	127.3	127.0	126.6	127.5	132.2	133.8	127.3
2008	127.5	125.1	125.9	126.0	126.4	127.3	127.0	127.4	126.4	126.8	128.5	129.3	127.0
2009	122.2	119.5	118.6	117.9	119.2	120.1	119.5	119.5	119.0	120.2	123.2	124.3	120.3
2010	117.9	116.7	117.1	118.2	119.6	120.8	121.4	121.7	120.4	121.7	124.7	125.9	120.5
2011	119.4	117.9	118.4	119.9	121.0	121.9	122.2	122.7	121.9	123.2	127.1	128.4	122.0
2012	122.7	120.4	121.1	121.8	123.3	124.6	124.7	124.6	124.5	125.7	130.6	131.9	124.7
2013	125.3	123.6	124.0	124.7	126.3	127.5	128.3	129.2	128.3	129.3	133.6	135.4	128.0
2014	128.8	127.4	127.9	128.7	129.8	131.6	131.5	131.8	130.7	132.3	136.2	138.4	131.3
2015	131.8	130.6	131.4	132.2	133.2	135.1	135.6	135.9	134.5	136.5	140.3	142.2	134.9
2016	135.3	134.2	134.7	135.0	136.0	137.3	137.7	137.4	136.0	137.6	141.5	143.3	137.2
2017	137.0	135.3	135.6	136.5	137.0	138.3	138.4	138.4	136.8	138.1	141.4	142.4	137.9
Transportation and Utilities													
2007	50.4	50.0	50.0	50.3	50.4	50.6	50.6	50.8	50.8	51.3	52.1	53.2	50.9
2008	51.8	51.2	51.4	51.3	51.4	51.5	51.5	51.0	50.3	49.8	50.1	51.0	51.0
2009	48.7	48.0	47.7	48.3	48.0	48.0	47.9	47.9	47.5	47.6	47.4	48.4	48.0
2010	46.2	46.5	46.2	45.8	45.8	45.9	45.7	45.8	45.8	46.2	46.5	47.6	46.2
2011	45.7	45.3	45.3	45.6	45.7	45.8	46.1	45.9	45.6	46.1	46.6	47.3	45.9
2012	46.3	46.4	46.2	46.3	46.3	46.7	47.0	47.0	47.1	48.4	49.1	49.9	47.2
2013	49.0	48.9	49.1	49.1	49.2	49.1	49.2	49.6	49.6	50.0	50.8	51.8	49.6
2014	50.8	50.8	50.5	50.8	51.2	51.5	51.3	51.5	51.4	51.6	52.4	53.6	51.5
2015	52.9	52.5	51.9	52.3	51.9	52.2	52.7	52.4	52.4	52.6	53.4	55.1	52.7
2016	53.7	53.2	52.7	53.1	53.2	53.3	54.0	54.3	54.4	54.5	55.4	57.5	54.1
2017	56.1	55.8	55.1	55.0	55.3	55.8	55.9	56.1	56.5	57.0	57.9	60.3	56.4

Employment by Industry: Denver-Aurora-Lakewood, CO, Selected Years, 2007–2017—*Continued*

(Numbers in thousands, not seasonally adjusted)

Industry and year	January	February	March	April	May	June	July	August	September	October	November	December	Annual average
Information													
2007	47.2	47.4	47.4	48.1	48.3	48.7	48.5	48.3	47.7	47.8	47.9	47.9	47.9
2008	47.2	47.3	47.2	47.2	47.1	47.2	47.2	47.0	46.6	46.6	46.7	46.7	47.0
2009	46.0	45.8	45.7	45.4	45.1	45.1	44.9	44.6	44.3	44.1	44.2	44.2	45.0
2010	43.9	43.7	43.7	43.4	43.5	43.8	43.8	43.8	43.7	43.8	44.2	44.2	43.8
2011	44.0	44.0	43.6	43.9	43.8	43.8	43.6	43.6	43.5	43.4	43.5	43.4	43.7
2012	43.3	43.4	43.4	43.2	43.3	43.5	43.3	43.3	43.3	43.4	43.6	43.7	43.4
2013	43.8	44.2	44.2	44.2	44.4	44.9	45.0	44.9	44.5	44.4	44.7	44.7	44.5
2014	44.8	45.0	44.9	44.9	45.0	45.7	46.2	46.2	45.2	45.3	45.2	45.6	45.3
2015	45.6	45.9	45.9	45.8	46.0	46.4	46.7	46.6	46.1	45.8	46.1	46.3	46.1
2016	45.9	46.3	46.3	46.5	46.6	47.0	47.5	47.3	46.5	46.7	46.9	46.8	46.7
2017	46.5	46.4	46.5	46.3	46.5	47.4	47.3	47.3	47.1	48.1	48.2	48.8	47.2
Financial Activities													
2007	99.4	99.9	99.9	100.0	100.1	100.5	100.4	100.0	99.1	98.8	98.7	98.8	99.6
2008	97.5	97.7	98.1	97.8	97.6	98.0	97.9	97.3	96.4	96.0	95.5	95.6	97.1
2009	93.7	93.5	93.0	93.2	93.3	93.0	92.9	92.6	92.0	92.0	91.7	92.1	92.8
2010	90.5	90.4	90.4	90.5	90.5	90.9	91.2	91.2	90.8	91.0	90.9	91.4	90.8
2011	90.2	90.1	90.1	90.2	90.3	90.9	90.9	91.1	90.8	90.6	91.1	91.7	90.7
2012	90.7	90.8	91.3	91.5	92.0	92.8	93.0	93.4	93.2	94.1	94.1	94.9	92.7
2013	93.9	94.5	94.9	95.3	95.6	96.4	96.7	96.8	96.6	96.7	96.9	97.1	96.0
2014	95.7	96.0	96.2	96.8	97.5	97.9	98.6	99.0	98.7	99.5	99.9	100.7	98.0
2015	99.6	100.2	100.6	101.0	101.7	102.7	103.5	103.8	103.4	104.0	104.3	104.7	102.5
2016	104.2	104.3	104.5	105.0	105.4	106.3	107.0	107.0	106.7	107.2	107.4	107.7	106.1
2017	106.9	107.4	107.6	107.9	108.5	109.3	109.4	109.4	109.0	109.0	107.9	109.4	108.5
Professional and Business Services													
2007	201.6	202.7	205.5	208.3	211.1	215.3	215.3	216.9	217.0	216.1	215.3	216.8	211.8
2008	211.2	213.2	213.9	218.0	218.0	220.5	219.8	221.5	219.5	217.9	216.0	214.5	217.0
2009	207.4	204.5	204.2	204.9	205.0	205.7	204.9	204.1	202.5	202.8	203.0	202.8	204.3
2010	197.1	198.0	199.9	203.4	205.0	207.3	208.2	208.6	205.5	207.3	207.3	206.5	204.5
2011	204.2	204.4	205.1	210.5	212.4	213.8	214.3	215.9	214.8	215.1	216.7	217.0	212.0
2012	212.5	213.3	216.2	220.0	222.1	225.3	226.3	227.8	226.5	229.3	229.1	228.3	223.1
2013	223.8	225.4	227.5	230.8	232.4	235.2	236.0	237.9	235.5	237.7	237.4	237.2	233.1
2014	232.2	233.0	234.5	238.7	240.5	243.2	245.0	248.6	247.0	249.4	246.8	247.7	242.2
2015	243.4	244.7	245.6	249.1	250.9	253.1	254.5	255.7	253.7	255.5	254.4	254.4	251.3
2016	249.7	250.6	251.5	255.9	256.0	259.0	261.9	261.7	260.5	261.5	260.9	259.7	257.4
2017	254.0	255.6	257.6	261.4	262.5	266.0	267.5	267.9	267.0	269.0	269.1	266.0	263.6
Education and Health Services													
2007	124.5	126.0	126.8	127.2	127.9	127.8	127.3	127.9	128.5	129.6	130.7	131.5	128.0
2008	130.0	131.8	132.0	132.5	133.4	133.3	132.8	133.8	134.5	136.1	137.1	136.8	133.7
2009	135.7	136.8	136.9	137.3	137.7	137.7	137.5	137.9	138.1	139.5	140.3	140.7	138.0
2010	139.6	140.8	141.7	142.1	142.7	142.7	142.1	143.0	143.4	144.5	145.4	145.7	142.8
2011	144.8	145.9	146.4	147.0	147.5	147.4	146.9	148.4	148.8	150.0	150.5	151.9	148.0
2012	150.5	152.0	152.4	152.8	153.0	152.8	152.7	153.2	153.7	155.2	156.0	156.9	153.4
2013	155.8	157.2	157.7	159.1	159.1	158.8	159.2	160.4	161.1	162.8	164.1	164.6	160.0
2014	163.1	164.7	165.4	167.4	167.8	167.0	167.1	168.5	169.2	171.4	172.1	172.7	168.0
2015	172.6	174.3	174.6	176.6	176.9	176.3	176.8	177.4	177.8	180.3	181.2	181.3	177.2
2016	180.0	181.2	181.6	183.6	183.3	182.6	183.0	183.2	183.5	183.5	183.2	182.9	182.6
2017	181.3	182.2	182.9	184.0	184.6	184.3	183.8	184.3	184.6	186.1	187.2	186.5	184.3
Leisure and Hospitality													
2007	120.4	120.5	123.7	125.8	130.4	134.8	134.3	134.9	130.9	129.2	128.2	128.8	128.5
2008	124.4	124.6	126.7	129.1	133.5	137.9	136.8	136.4	132.1	129.1	126.8	125.8	130.3
2009	120.9	119.9	121.9	124.2	128.2	131.6	132.2	132.3	127.8	125.9	123.5	122.7	125.9
2010	119.5	119.1	121.4	125.3	128.2	132.9	133.6	134.3	130.6	129.8	127.4	127.4	127.5
2011	124.0	123.5	126.4	129.2	132.7	137.7	137.6	138.1	135.2	132.4	130.6	130.3	131.5
2012	127.5	127.0	130.2	133.7	137.6	142.3	142.7	142.8	138.4	137.2	136.2	136.0	136.0
2013	132.7	132.9	135.7	139.0	142.7	147.9	148.6	149.0	144.3	143.4	142.1	141.5	141.7
2014	139.2	139.0	141.8	145.4	150.1	153.7	155.1	155.4	152.0	149.9	147.5	148.5	148.1
2015	145.6	146.3	147.7	152.0	156.0	161.9	162.6	162.6	158.9	156.4	155.8	155.8	155.1
2016	153.1	153.2	155.0	158.3	161.8	167.2	168.6	168.6	164.8	163.0	160.6	160.1	161.2
2017	157.5	157.5	160.1	163.0	167.0	173.1	173.7	172.6	168.6	167.6	166.2	168.4	166.3

Employment by Industry: Denver-Aurora-Lakewood, CO, Selected Years, 2007–2017—*Continued*

(Numbers in thousands, not seasonally adjusted)

Industry and year	January	February	March	April	May	June	July	August	September	October	November	December	Annual average
Other Services													
2007	46.3	46.3	46.8	46.9	47.1	47.7	47.4	47.5	47.2	47.3	47.2	47.5	47.1
2008	47.8	47.9	48.2	47.9	48.3	48.7	49.0	49.1	48.9	48.7	48.3	47.8	48.4
2009	47.9	47.3	47.4	47.0	47.5	47.8	47.9	47.8	47.3	47.3	47.1	47.1	47.5
2010	47.1	46.9	47.0	46.9	47.3	47.8	48.0	48.1	47.5	47.3	47.5	47.4	47.4
2011	47.4	47.3	47.6	48.1	48.5	49.0	48.9	49.2	48.7	48.4	48.4	48.6	48.3
2012	48.6	48.6	49.0	49.2	49.4	50.2	50.2	50.3	50.0	50.2	50.0	49.9	49.6
2013	50.1	49.7	50.1	50.3	51.0	51.2	51.3	51.3	50.8	50.8	50.9	50.8	50.7
2014	51.5	51.2	51.3	51.9	52.3	52.9	53.6	53.8	53.0	53.7	53.3	53.1	52.6
2015	53.3	53.1	53.4	53.5	53.7	54.4	54.8	54.8	54.4	54.4	54.2	54.4	54.0
2016	54.5	54.7	54.9	55.1	55.5	56.4	56.7	56.9	56.7	56.9	56.5	56.0	55.9
2017	55.4	56.0	56.2	56.3	56.8	57.4	57.2	57.3	57.0	57.9	56.4	56.5	56.7
Government													
2007	163.9	169.0	170.3	170.7	171.8	170.8	163.4	164.3	171.7	172.5	173.4	173.0	169.6
2008	167.9	172.3	173.6	174.2	176.3	174.5	167.7	170.5	175.4	177.4	178.3	177.3	173.8
2009	172.8	175.9	177.3	178.3	180.3	177.8	169.0	170.1	177.2	179.6	178.9	177.7	176.2
2010	171.9	177.6	178.8	179.8	185.2	180.2	172.8	171.4	178.6	181.1	181.5	179.5	178.2
2011	173.9	179.3	180.0	181.4	182.9	180.5	171.6	171.4	178.6	180.2	180.5	179.5	178.3
2012	173.9	179.2	180.9	181.8	183.4	182.5	173.4	172.4	179.9	181.5	183.2	181.6	179.5
2013	176.2	182.0	183.2	184.6	185.6	184.1	175.8	177.1	185.5	188.7	188.4	186.4	183.1
2014	181.2	185.0	186.1	186.9	188.2	186.6	175.5	179.9	187.6	191.5	192.4	189.9	185.9
2015	185.5	189.7	190.5	192.2	194.0	192.1	182.4	185.9	194.3	194.9	196.0	194.9	191.0
2016	190.6	195.0	196.0	197.3	197.5	197.1	187.5	191.2	197.3	197.9	199.8	198.2	195.5
2017	194.8	199.1	200.5	199.0	200.8	198.5	191.0	192.9	198.2	197.8	199.2	197.7	197.5

Employment by Industry: Baltimore-Columbia-Towson, MD, Selected Years, 2007–2017

(Numbers in thousands, not seasonally adjusted)

Industry and year	January	February	March	April	May	June	July	August	September	October	November	December	Annual average
Total Nonfarm													
2007	1,289.1	1,290.6	1,306.7	1,313.6	1,323.4	1,326.8	1,317.3	1,317.3	1,318.9	1,322.2	1,328.6	1,332.3	1,315.6
2008	1,296.8	1,301.0	1,310.5	1,318.4	1,323.6	1,323.4	1,314.8	1,312.3	1,310.8	1,314.2	1,310.2	1,308.6	1,312.1
2009	1,264.2	1,262.0	1,266.8	1,275.0	1,281.4	1,283.3	1,266.8	1,264.0	1,267.4	1,275.8	1,276.4	1,276.8	1,271.7
2010	1,240.8	1,228.6	1,258.6	1,277.5	1,285.7	1,288.0	1,275.4	1,273.3	1,274.7	1,286.9	1,289.5	1,290.3	1,272.4
2011	1,255.3	1,263.5	1,277.4	1,294.7	1,300.3	1,302.1	1,295.5	1,294.3	1,300.8	1,308.4	1,313.7	1,316.6	1,293.6
2012	1,284.0	1,290.1	1,302.6	1,311.3	1,320.0	1,322.7	1,311.9	1,313.0	1,321.1	1,328.1	1,333.6	1,336.3	1,314.6
2013	1,303.6	1,310.5	1,322.9	1,331.1	1,340.5	1,344.2	1,333.2	1,332.2	1,337.2	1,341.7	1,349.3	1,345.5	1,332.7
2014	1,305.6	1,309.6	1,321.8	1,342.1	1,351.6	1,354.0	1,341.9	1,346.1	1,351.4	1,359.0	1,364.9	1,365.5	1,342.8
2015	1,325.5	1,331.7	1,339.7	1,360.8	1,373.6	1,374.2	1,371.7	1,370.6	1,371.1	1,386.6	1,391.8	1,394.2	1,366.0
2016	1,352.1	1,355.4	1,367.0	1,385.2	1,392.3	1,393.0	1,386.2	1,386.2	1,392.2	1,399.0	1,406.6	1,406.6	1,385.2
2017	1,365.4	1,372.5	1,380.4	1,392.9	1,404.1	1,407.8	1,403.1	1,401.6	1,404.9	1,411.1	1,417.1	1,408.5	1,397.5
Total Private													
2007	1,071.2	1,067.4	1,081.1	1,088.1	1,097.6	1,106.8	1,104.3	1,104.1	1,099.4	1,096.8	1,101.4	1,105.6	1,093.7
2008	1,077.7	1,075.8	1,083.8	1,090.5	1,095.8	1,101.3	1,098.1	1,096.1	1,087.8	1,084.6	1,080.1	1,078.2	1,087.5
2009	1,041.3	1,033.8	1,036.9	1,043.0	1,049.8	1,056.8	1,048.1	1,046.0	1,043.8	1,040.5	1,041.5	1,042.2	1,043.6
2010	1,013.4	996.2	1,022.1	1,039.2	1,045.9	1,053.4	1,049.8	1,048.7	1,045.4	1,049.8	1,050.8	1,053.9	1,039.1
2011	1,025.7	1,027.8	1,038.2	1,054.5	1,062.0	1,068.6	1,071.5	1,069.6	1,068.7	1,068.5	1,075.0	1,077.5	1,059.0
2012	1,055.4	1,054.9	1,064.6	1,074.1	1,084.3	1,094.2	1,091.2	1,093.3	1,092.5	1,091.8	1,097.3	1,100.5	1,082.8
2013	1,075.6	1,076.9	1,087.0	1,095.6	1,105.5	1,114.7	1,113.5	1,113.4	1,110.0	1,109.7	1,115.3	1,113.0	1,102.5
2014	1,081.4	1,078.9	1,089.4	1,107.6	1,119.8	1,126.8	1,125.4	1,128.4	1,124.8	1,126.5	1,130.9	1,133.2	1,114.4
2015	1,101.8	1,102.5	1,108.2	1,129.1	1,142.3	1,148.7	1,154.6	1,153.5	1,147.0	1,156.1	1,160.2	1,162.6	1,138.9
2016	1,129.7	1,128.1	1,137.1	1,154.1	1,161.3	1,167.7	1,169.8	1,170.2	1,168.1	1,169.8	1,176.5	1,175.7	1,159.0
2017	1,142.4	1,144.6	1,151.3	1,163.0	1,174.1	1,182.5	1,187.8	1,187.0	1,182.3	1,182.5	1,186.6	1,178.1	1,171.9
Goods Producing													
2007	155.6	153.7	156.2	157.1	158.6	160.5	161.1	161.1	159.7	158.0	157.4	156.6	158.0
2008	153.6	152.5	153.1	153.0	153.2	154.6	155.1	154.9	153.0	150.9	149.1	147.0	152.5
2009	140.4	138.3	137.6	137.1	137.5	138.9	138.4	137.8	136.4	135.5	134.5	133.8	137.2
2010	129.3	124.8	128.4	131.9	132.8	134.4	134.3	134.2	133.2	132.6	132.2	131.9	131.7
2011	128.7	128.1	129.4	132.0	132.8	134.2	134.9	134.4	132.9	132.4	131.9	131.6	131.9
2012	128.5	127.3	128.3	129.1	129.4	131.3	131.7	131.7	130.0	129.4	129.6	129.2	129.6
2013	125.9	125.0	125.9	127.8	128.6	130.0	130.9	131.0	130.0	129.4	129.0	127.4	128.4
2014	124.0	122.9	124.6	127.6	129.1	130.6	130.9	131.2	130.5	130.0	129.7	129.1	128.4
2015	125.3	124.6	125.5	128.1	129.8	131.7	133.2	133.7	132.9	133.3	132.7	132.6	130.3
2016	129.4	127.7	130.0	132.9	133.5	135.1	135.8	135.6	134.7	134.1	133.7	133.4	133.0
2017	129.9	130.2	130.9	132.1	133.5	135.6	136.1	136.4	135.3	134.9	135.6	133.5	133.7
Service-Providing													
2007	1,133.5	1,136.9	1,150.5	1,156.5	1,164.8	1,166.3	1,156.2	1,156.2	1,159.2	1,164.2	1,171.2	1,175.7	1,157.6
2008	1,143.2	1,148.5	1,157.4	1,165.4	1,170.4	1,168.8	1,159.7	1,157.4	1,157.8	1,163.3	1,161.1	1,161.6	1,159.6
2009	1,123.8	1,123.7	1,129.2	1,137.9	1,143.9	1,144.4	1,128.4	1,126.2	1,131.0	1,140.3	1,141.9	1,143.0	1,134.5
2010	1,111.5	1,103.8	1,130.2	1,145.6	1,152.9	1,153.6	1,141.1	1,139.1	1,141.5	1,154.3	1,157.3	1,158.4	1,140.8
2011	1,126.6	1,135.4	1,148.0	1,162.7	1,167.5	1,167.9	1,160.6	1,159.9	1,167.9	1,176.0	1,181.8	1,185.0	1,161.6
2012	1,155.5	1,162.8	1,174.3	1,182.2	1,190.6	1,191.4	1,180.2	1,181.3	1,191.1	1,198.7	1,204.0	1,207.1	1,184.9
2013	1,177.7	1,185.5	1,197.0	1,203.3	1,211.9	1,214.2	1,202.3	1,201.2	1,207.2	1,212.3	1,220.3	1,218.1	1,204.3
2014	1,181.6	1,186.7	1,197.2	1,214.5	1,222.5	1,223.4	1,211.0	1,214.9	1,220.9	1,229.0	1,235.2	1,236.4	1,214.4
2015	1,200.2	1,207.1	1,214.2	1,232.7	1,243.8	1,242.5	1,238.5	1,236.9	1,238.2	1,253.3	1,259.1	1,261.6	1,235.7
2016	1,222.7	1,227.7	1,237.0	1,252.3	1,258.8	1,257.9	1,250.4	1,250.6	1,257.5	1,264.9	1,272.9	1,273.2	1,252.2
2017	1,235.5	1,242.3	1,249.5	1,260.8	1,270.6	1,272.2	1,267.0	1,265.2	1,269.6	1,276.2	1,281.5	1,275.0	1,263.8
Mining, Logging, and Construction													
2007	83.2	81.5	83.9	84.9	86.2	87.7	88.2	88.4	87.4	86.0	85.5	84.3	85.6
2008	82.1	81.1	81.9	82.4	82.5	83.6	84.4	84.2	83.0	81.8	80.5	78.5	82.2
2009	73.2	72.0	71.6	71.7	72.2	73.4	73.5	72.9	71.7	70.8	70.0	69.2	71.9
2010	65.2	61.7	64.9	68.1	68.9	70.1	69.9	69.9	69.4	69.2	69.1	68.5	67.9
2011	64.8	64.2	65.4	67.6	68.5	69.8	70.7	70.5	69.8	69.8	69.5	69.2	68.3
2012	66.4	65.6	66.7	67.7	68.1	69.4	69.8	70.0	69.9	69.6	69.8	69.4	68.5
2013	66.9	66.1	67.1	69.3	70.2	71.4	72.3	72.5	72.1	71.9	71.9	70.4	70.2
2014	68.0	67.1	68.7	71.4	72.9	74.1	74.6	74.9	74.5	74.0	73.7	73.2	72.3
2015	69.8	69.2	70.3	73.2	74.7	76.0	77.0	77.5	77.2	77.7	77.2	76.8	74.7
2016	74.3	72.8	75.0	77.4	77.9	79.1	79.7	79.4	78.9	78.4	78.1	77.6	77.4
2017	74.8	74.8	75.2	76.2	77.6	79.2	79.7	80.0	79.3	79.7	80.1	78.0	77.9

Employment by Industry: Baltimore-Columbia-Towson, MD, Selected Years, 2007–2017—*Continued*

(Numbers in thousands, not seasonally adjusted)

Industry and year	January	February	March	April	May	June	July	August	September	October	November	December	Annual average
Manufacturing													
2007	72.4	72.2	72.3	72.2	72.4	72.8	72.9	72.7	72.3	72.0	71.9	72.3	72.4
2008	71.5	71.4	71.2	70.6	70.7	71.0	70.7	70.7	70.0	69.1	68.6	68.5	70.3
2009	67.2	66.3	66.0	65.4	65.3	65.5	64.9	64.9	64.7	64.7	64.5	64.6	65.3
2010	64.1	63.1	63.5	63.8	63.9	64.3	64.4	64.3	63.8	63.4	63.1	63.4	63.8
2011	63.9	63.9	64.0	64.4	64.3	64.4	64.2	63.9	63.1	62.6	62.4	62.4	63.6
2012	62.1	61.7	61.6	61.4	61.3	61.9	61.9	61.7	60.1	59.8	59.8	59.8	61.1
2013	59.0	58.9	58.8	58.5	58.4	58.6	58.6	58.5	57.9	57.5	57.1	57.0	58.2
2014	56.0	55.8	55.9	56.2	56.2	56.5	56.3	56.3	56.0	56.0	56.0	55.9	56.1
2015	55.5	55.4	55.2	54.9	55.1	55.7	56.2	56.2	55.7	55.6	55.5	55.8	55.6
2016	55.1	54.9	55.0	55.5	55.6	56.0	56.1	56.2	55.8	55.7	55.6	55.8	55.6
2017	55.1	55.4	55.7	55.9	55.9	56.4	56.4	56.4	56.0	55.2	55.5	55.5	55.8
Trade, Transportation, and Utilities													
2007	246.3	242.3	244.4	243.7	246.9	247.9	246.2	245.3	244.8	246.1	251.2	255.7	246.7
2008	244.1	240.4	241.4	240.2	241.2	242.4	240.5	239.9	238.6	238.8	240.4	242.7	240.9
2009	231.5	227.5	226.8	226.5	227.4	229.0	225.0	224.8	225.6	226.2	230.3	231.8	227.7
2010	221.5	216.1	220.9	224.7	225.7	226.4	224.8	224.8	224.4	228.1	231.7	235.0	225.3
2011	226.1	224.2	225.7	228.4	229.7	230.5	229.4	230.0	230.0	231.4	236.7	240.4	230.2
2012	230.6	228.1	230.0	231.2	232.8	233.3	231.5	231.5	232.8	233.9	239.6	242.4	233.1
2013	234.5	231.8	232.8	233.4	235.3	236.1	234.9	234.7	234.9	235.9	241.4	244.7	235.9
2014	233.4	229.5	231.4	233.7	235.4	237.1	235.9	236.5	236.5	239.2	245.8	249.7	237.0
2015	238.1	235.9	236.2	239.8	241.8	244.3	243.8	243.3	243.6	248.0	252.8	256.4	243.7
2016	244.8	242.4	243.4	244.6	245.6	246.4	244.7	245.4	245.8	247.3	253.1	255.0	246.5
2017	244.6	241.2	241.2	243.0	244.9	246.5	245.2	245.0	245.1	247.0	253.2	253.1	245.8
Wholesale Trade													
2007	55.9	56.0	56.0	56.2	56.4	56.5	56.4	56.3	56.1	55.8	55.8	56.1	56.1
2008	55.5	55.3	55.7	55.7	55.9	56.0	55.5	55.3	55.0	54.8	54.4	54.2	55.3
2009	53.6	53.3	52.9	52.7	52.5	52.4	51.8	51.7	51.6	51.6	51.4	51.3	52.2
2010	50.3	50.1	50.5	51.0	51.2	51.1	51.2	51.0	50.6	51.1	51.2	51.3	50.9
2011	50.9	51.1	51.3	51.7	51.9	52.0	52.0	51.9	51.6	51.4	51.4	51.5	51.6
2012	51.0	51.1	51.5	52.2	52.6	52.8	52.6	52.6	52.3	52.4	52.4	52.6	52.2
2013	51.9	52.1	52.2	52.5	52.6	52.7	52.6	52.4	52.2	51.7	51.8	51.9	52.2
2014	51.1	51.0	50.9	51.5	51.8	52.0	52.1	52.0	51.7	52.4	52.4	53.1	51.8
2015	52.3	52.3	52.2	52.8	52.9	53.2	53.4	53.1	53.0	53.5	53.4	53.5	53.0
2016	53.0	52.9	53.0	53.6	53.7	53.7	53.2	53.3	52.9	52.8	52.7	52.9	53.1
2017	52.5	52.4	52.6	52.7	53.0	53.6	53.3	53.4	53.2	53.3	53.6	53.2	53.1
Retail Trade													
2007	145.1	141.2	142.8	142.1	144.4	144.9	144.4	144.1	143.0	144.6	149.7	153.2	145.0
2008	143.8	140.3	141.1	140.6	141.0	141.8	141.0	140.7	139.0	139.6	141.7	143.4	141.2
2009	135.0	131.8	131.7	131.8	132.9	133.7	132.4	132.3	131.8	132.7	136.5	138.2	133.4
2010	130.1	125.7	129.0	130.5	131.7	132.3	131.9	132.1	130.9	133.4	137.1	139.7	132.0
2011	132.4	130.5	131.6	132.5	133.5	134.2	133.4	134.0	133.3	135.4	140.0	143.0	134.5
2012	135.1	132.5	133.9	133.9	134.9	135.1	134.5	134.5	134.5	135.7	140.5	142.3	135.6
2013	137.1	134.9	135.4	135.7	136.8	137.6	137.6	137.8	136.6	137.8	142.6	144.6	137.9
2014	136.7	134.0	135.1	136.4	137.1	138.4	138.3	138.7	137.4	139.0	143.5	146.0	138.4
2015	137.8	135.5	136.2	137.7	138.8	140.2	139.7	139.6	138.3	140.5	144.5	146.5	139.6
2016	139.7	137.4	138.5	138.3	139.1	139.9	138.9	139.4	138.2	139.1	143.0	144.7	139.7
2017	137.7	135.1	135.2	136.1	136.8	137.3	137.0	137.0	135.9	137.7	143.0	143.0	137.7
Transportation and Utilities													
2007	45.3	45.1	45.6	45.4	46.1	46.5	45.4	44.9	45.7	45.7	45.7	46.4	45.7
2008	44.8	44.8	44.6	43.9	44.3	44.6	44.0	43.9	44.6	44.4	44.3	45.1	44.4
2009	42.9	42.4	42.2	42.0	42.0	42.9	40.8	40.8	42.2	41.9	42.4	42.3	42.1
2010	41.1	40.3	41.4	43.2	42.8	43.0	41.7	41.7	42.9	43.6	43.4	44.0	42.4
2011	42.8	42.6	42.8	44.2	44.3	44.3	44.0	44.1	45.1	44.6	45.3	45.9	44.2
2012	44.5	44.5	44.6	45.1	45.3	45.4	44.4	44.4	46	45.8	46.7	47.5	45.4
2013	45.5	44.8	45.2	45.2	45.9	45.8	44.7	44.5	46.1	46.4	47.0	48.2	45.8
2014	45.6	44.5	45.4	45.8	46.5	46.7	45.5	45.8	47.4	47.8	49.9	50.6	46.8
2015	48.0	48.1	47.8	49.3	50.1	50.9	50.7	50.6	52.3	54.0	54.9	56.4	51.1
2016	52.1	52.1	51.9	52.7	52.8	52.8	52.6	52.7	54.7	55.4	57.4	57.4	53.7
2017	54.4	53.7	53.4	54.2	55.1	55.6	54.9	54.6	56.0	56.0	56.6	56.9	55.1

Employment by Industry: Baltimore-Columbia-Towson, MD, Selected Years, 2007–2017—*Continued*
(Numbers in thousands, not seasonally adjusted)

Industry and year	January	February	March	April	May	June	July	August	September	October	November	December	Annual average
Information													
2007	22.4	22.6	23.1	23.1	23.3	24.0	23.7	24.1	24.1	23.1	23.6	23.6	23.4
2008	23.1	23.1	23.4	23.2	23.3	22.9	22.7	23.0	22.8	22.1	22.4	22.3	22.9
2009	21.3	21.3	21.5	20.6	20.5	20.8	20.1	20.3	19.9	19.5	19.7	19.6	20.4
2010	19.4	19.8	21.1	20.8	20.9	21.3	20.0	19.3	19.3	18.9	18.5	19.3	19.9
2011	17.7	18.1	18.2	17.7	17.8	17.5	17.5	16.6	17.1	17.2	17.6	17.3	17.5
2012	17.1	17.1	17.1	16.7	16.7	17.2	17.2	17.2	17.1	16.8	16.9	17.6	17.1
2013	17.0	16.9	16.9	16.6	16.7	16.8	17.0	17.0	16.8	16.9	17.0	17.0	16.9
2014	16.8	16.3	16.4	16.2	16.5	16.2	16.5	16.8	16.2	16.6	16.4	16.4	16.4
2015	16.1	16.0	16.2	16.6	16.8	16.7	17.1	17.0	16.7	17.0	17.1	17.0	16.7
2016	16.3	16.5	16.6	17.3	16.7	17.7	17.6	17.5	17.2	17.2	17.3	17.5	17.1
2017	17.3	17.6	17.6	17.6	17.6	17.8	17.7	17.5	17.3	17.2	17.2	17.2	17.5
Financial Activities													
2007	80.9	80.9	81.0	81.0	81.1	81.5	81.4	81.0	80.1	79.7	79.5	79.9	80.7
2008	78.6	78.9	79.1	78.6	78.7	79.1	78.4	78.1	77.3	77.4	76.7	76.9	78.2
2009	75.2	74.9	74.6	74.6	74.4	74.7	74.0	74.0	73.6	73.6	73.8	73.8	74.3
2010	72.5	72.0	72.4	72.5	72.6	73.2	73.4	73.4	73.1	73.6	73.6	74.0	73.0
2011	73.1	73.1	73.5	73.7	73.6	73.8	73.9	73.6	73.2	73.2	73.2	73.1	73.4
2012	73.0	73.0	72.8	72.8	73.1	73.7	74.1	74.4	74.2	74.2	74.7	74.8	73.7
2013	74.4	74.4	74.5	74.9	75.2	75.9	76.2	76.1	75.8	75.6	75.8	75.8	75.4
2014	75.0	75.1	74.7	75.6	75.9	76.6	76.8	77.0	76.5	76.7	76.7	76.9	76.1
2015	76.2	76.4	76.3	76.7	76.9	77.7	78.1	78.3	77.4	77.7	78.0	78.3	77.3
2016	77.6	77.9	77.6	78.2	78.5	78.9	79.4	79.7	79.3	79.5	79.6	79.8	78.8
2017	79.4	79.5	79.8	79.9	80.2	81.2	82.9	83.0	82.4	83.1	82.4	81.8	81.3
Professional and Business Services													
2007	184.3	184.3	186.9	189.9	190.5	192.3	191.8	193.7	193.3	193.4	193.9	193.9	190.7
2008	189.2	189.4	191.2	193.5	194.3	194.6	194.8	195.4	193.4	192.2	189.7	187.5	192.1
2009	180.4	178.3	178.7	181.4	181.2	182.9	183.1	183.8	182.5	182.9	182.0	181.6	181.6
2010	176.2	173.9	178.9	182.9	183.2	186.2	185.1	186.2	185.2	187.9	187.2	187.2	183.3
2011	182.3	182.3	184.8	190.5	191.8	194.7	196.7	198.3	199.2	200.6	202.1	202.4	193.8
2012	198.1	197.9	200.2	202.4	205.0	206.8	206.4	209.8	210.1	210.2	211.9	210.9	205.8
2013	205.9	207.1	210.0	210.9	212.7	215.9	214.9	217.3	217.4	216.7	218.3	215.9	213.6
2014	210.6	211.5	213.6	218.2	220.0	221.6	221.7	222.8	221.6	221.9	221.8	221.3	218.9
2015	215.0	215.6	217.1	221.5	223.3	224.4	227.4	228.9	226.1	230.4	230.1	228.8	224.1
2016	223.6	223.1	224.4	229.2	230.6	232.5	233.0	235.2	233.9	234.2	235.3	233.4	230.7
2017	225.0	225.1	226.4	230.3	232.0	233.8	233.7	234.7	234.0	232.3	231.9	230.0	230.8
Education and Health Services													
2007	216.9	219.6	221.3	221.8	221.7	220.7	220.3	219.2	221.7	224.2	224.7	225.3	221.5
2008	223.3	225.7	226.9	228.2	227.5	226.6	226.2	225.5	229.0	231.4	232.4	233.1	228.0
2009	231.0	232.7	233.8	234.7	234.3	233.2	231.3	230.3	233.4	235.7	236.7	237.4	233.7
2010	235.2	233.4	237.8	238.9	238.6	236.8	237.1	235.4	237.9	240.5	241.5	241.4	237.9
2011	238.7	242.3	242.6	243.1	242.4	240.5	241.1	239.8	242.8	245.2	245.8	245.3	242.5
2012	243.7	246.2	247.0	247.9	247.3	246.7	246.1	245.2	247.9	250.4	250.7	252.2	247.6
2013	248.3	251.5	252.9	253.3	252.8	251.4	250.7	249.9	252.2	255.2	256.0	255.7	252.5
2014	250.9	252.9	254.2	255.0	254.8	254.0	253.2	252.9	255.7	257.2	258.5	258.9	254.9
2015	255.0	257.6	257.9	262.7	262.6	260.7	260.9	259.2	262.1	265.2	266.7	266.7	261.4
2016	261.2	263.7	265.2	266.7	266.3	263.2	265.9	263.9	267.5	271.0	272.1	272.1	266.6
2017	266.4	270.4	271.9	272.6	272.5	269.9	275.4	274.6	277.1	282.3	284.0	282.4	275.0
Leisure and Hospitality													
2007	108.7	108.0	111.5	115.4	119.0	122.7	122.4	123.0	119.3	115.9	114.5	113.9	116.2
2008	110.0	109.7	112.2	117.1	120.8	123.7	123.4	122.6	117.3	115.5	113.2	112.7	116.5
2009	106.4	105.8	108.5	112.7	118.7	121.2	120.2	119.2	116.9	111.5	108.9	108.5	113.2
2010	104.8	102.5	107.4	112.1	116.3	119.1	119.0	119.6	116.7	112.8	110.6	109.8	112.6
2011	104.5	105.0	108.8	113.4	118.1	121.1	121.9	121.1	118.5	113.7	113.0	112.4	114.3
2012	110.1	111.0	114.5	118.6	124.6	129.1	128.2	128.1	125.2	122.0	119.3	118.6	120.8
2013	115.4	115.7	119.1	123.5	128.9	132.9	133.4	132.9	128.5	126.4	124.2	123.3	125.4
2014	118.5	118.7	122.2	127.9	134.7	136.8	136.7	138.1	134.7	132.3	129.6	128.6	129.9
2015	124.7	125.1	127.6	132.2	139.3	141.1	141.9	141.3	137.0	133.7	132.0	132.2	134.0
2016	126.5	126.7	129.7	134.7	139.3	142.8	142.0	141.9	138.8	135.6	134.4	133.8	135.5
2017	129.6	130.2	132.8	136.6	142.1	145.6	144.8	144.4	139.8	135.3	130.9	130.1	136.9

Employment by Industry: Baltimore-Columbia-Towson, MD, Selected Years, 2007–2017—*Continued*

(Numbers in thousands, not seasonally adjusted)

Industry and year	January	February	March	April	May	June	July	August	September	October	November	December	Annual average
Other Services													
2007	56.1	56.0	56.7	56.1	56.5	57.2	57.4	56.7	56.4	56.4	56.6	56.7	56.6
2008	55.8	56.1	56.5	56.7	56.8	57.4	57.0	56.7	56.4	56.3	56.2	56.0	56.5
2009	55.1	55.0	55.4	55.4	55.8	56.1	56.0	55.8	55.5	55.6	55.6	55.7	55.6
2010	54.5	53.7	55.2	55.4	55.8	56.0	56.1	55.8	55.6	55.4	55.5	55.3	55.4
2011	54.6	54.7	55.2	55.7	55.8	56.3	56.1	55.8	55.0	54.8	54.7	55.0	55.3
2012	54.3	54.3	54.7	55.4	55.4	56.1	56.0	55.4	55.2	54.9	54.6	54.8	55.1
2013	54.2	54.5	54.9	55.2	55.3	55.7	55.5	54.5	54.4	53.6	53.6	53.2	54.6
2014	52.2	52.0	52.3	53.4	53.4	53.9	53.7	53.1	53.1	52.6	52.4	52.3	52.9
2015	51.4	51.3	51.4	51.5	51.8	52.1	52.2	51.8	51.2	50.8	50.8	50.6	51.4
2016	50.3	50.1	50.2	50.5	50.8	51.1	51.4	51.0	50.9	50.9	51.0	50.7	50.7
2017	50.2	50.4	50.7	50.9	51.3	52.1	52.0	51.4	51.3	50.4	51.4	50.0	51.0
Government													
2007	217.9	223.2	225.6	225.5	225.8	220.0	213.0	213.2	219.5	225.4	227.2	226.7	221.9
2008	219.1	225.2	226.7	227.9	227.8	222.1	216.7	216.2	223.0	229.6	230.1	230.4	224.6
2009	222.9	228.2	229.9	232.0	231.6	226.5	218.7	218.0	223.6	235.3	234.9	234.6	228.0
2010	227.4	232.4	236.5	238.3	239.8	234.6	225.6	224.6	229.3	237.1	238.7	236.4	233.4
2011	229.6	235.7	239.2	240.2	238.3	233.5	224.0	224.7	232.1	239.9	238.7	239.1	234.6
2012	228.6	235.2	238.0	237.2	235.7	228.5	220.7	219.7	228.6	236.3	236.3	235.8	231.7
2013	228.0	233.6	235.9	235.5	235.0	229.5	219.7	218.8	227.2	232.0	234.0	232.5	230.1
2014	224.2	230.7	232.4	234.5	231.8	227.2	216.5	217.7	226.6	232.5	234.0	232.3	228.4
2015	223.7	229.2	231.5	231.7	231.3	225.5	217.1	217.1	224.1	230.5	231.6	231.6	227.1
2016	222.4	227.3	229.9	231.1	231.0	225.3	216.4	216.0	224.1	229.2	230.1	230.9	226.1
2017	223.0	227.9	229.1	229.9	230.0	225.3	215.3	214.6	222.6	228.6	230.5	230.4	225.6

Employment by Industry: St. Louis, MO-IL, Selected Years, 2007–2017

(Numbers in thousands, not seasonally adjusted)

Industry and year	January	February	March	April	May	June	July	August	September	October	November	December	Annual average
Total Nonfarm													
2007	1,320.9	1,324.6	1,341.3	1,353.3	1,366.1	1,366.7	1,338.1	1,346.1	1,359.3	1,361.8	1,365.7	1,367.1	1,350.9
2008	1,334.0	1,340.1	1,343.5	1,355.0	1,367.8	1,371.0	1,337.7	1,345.8	1,353.0	1,347.3	1,339.6	1,333.2	1,347.3
2009	1,293.3	1,292.1	1,293.9	1,302.3	1,307.3	1,303.9	1,274.7	1,280.6	1,286.8	1,285.7	1,283.5	1,284.3	1,290.7
2010	1,256.4	1,262.0	1,273.1	1,286.1	1,294.5	1,291.4	1,268.1	1,280.4	1,286.2	1,293.9	1,292.9	1,290.8	1,281.3
2011	1,266.7	1,269.5	1,282.6	1,303.5	1,308.9	1,304.5	1,285.5	1,293.8	1,302.0	1,303.1	1,301.4	1,302.2	1,293.6
2012	1,270.0	1,275.5	1,287.9	1,300.3	1,308.5	1,304.8	1,280.7	1,290.0	1,297.6	1,304.6	1,304.9	1,306.9	1,294.3
2013	1,276.1	1,282.9	1,289.8	1,307.2	1,317.3	1,313.6	1,293.0	1,302.3	1,310.9	1,317.0	1,317.5	1,319.3	1,303.9
2014	1,281.9	1,292.0	1,301.2	1,325.7	1,333.5	1,328.9	1,309.0	1,319.5	1,325.7	1,340.4	1,339.0	1,340.2	1,319.8
2015	1,309.1	1,314.6	1,321.0	1,343.6	1,355.6	1,354.8	1,337.7	1,345.6	1,354.5	1,366.0	1,367.1	1,368.5	1,344.8
2016	1,330.6	1,339.2	1,347.1	1,368.5	1,374.3	1,374.2	1,353.3	1,362.6	1,372.7	1,382.5	1,381.5	1,378.1	1,363.7
2017	1,348.0	1,360.2	1,364.6	1,380.5	1,387.7	1,392.6	1,369.4	1,375.7	1,382.5	1,390.9	1,393.0	1,384.0	1,377.4
Total Private													
2007	1,154.1	1,154.7	1,171.3	1,182.9	1,194.6	1,201.2	1,194.1	1,195.3	1,191.0	1,190.6	1,193.3	1,195.0	1,184.8
2008	1,165.8	1,167.5	1,171.8	1,183.0	1,193.8	1,203.3	1,190.7	1,191.4	1,181.9	1,173.4	1,165.6	1,159.8	1,179.0
2009	1,122.9	1,119.4	1,120.6	1,125.1	1,129.9	1,131.5	1,125.5	1,123.3	1,113.5	1,111.4	1,109.6	1,110.5	1,120.3
2010	1,086.9	1,089.7	1,100.7	1,111.5	1,116.0	1,123.8	1,123.0	1,124.2	1,117.9	1,123.8	1,122.6	1,121.2	1,113.4
2011	1,100.3	1,101.4	1,113.8	1,133.5	1,138.2	1,142.5	1,143.6	1,143.4	1,135.0	1,135.8	1,134.1	1,134.8	1,129.7
2012	1,107.1	1,109.8	1,121.3	1,132.7	1,140.0	1,144.8	1,141.2	1,142.0	1,134.1	1,140.0	1,140.4	1,142.1	1,133.0
2013	1,115.7	1,119.5	1,125.7	1,138.5	1,148.0	1,152.8	1,153.4	1,154.2	1,147.0	1,152.0	1,152.0	1,153.6	1,142.7
2014	1,120.8	1,127.6	1,136.2	1,161.7	1,168.8	1,172.6	1,173.3	1,175.5	1,166.4	1,177.6	1,177.0	1,177.9	1,161.3
2015	1,151.8	1,153.7	1,159.9	1,182.2	1,193.2	1,197.3	1,201.1	1,200.6	1,193.9	1,202.3	1,203.7	1,204.9	1,187.1
2016	1,172.7	1,177.8	1,185.5	1,206.5	1,210.9	1,215.7	1,216.2	1,216.8	1,211.1	1,220.0	1,218.9	1,215.2	1,205.6
2017	1,190.8	1,199.8	1,204.3	1,220.5	1,227.3	1,235.1	1,233.2	1,235.4	1,226.7	1,234.2	1,237.0	1,228.5	1,222.7
Goods Producing													
2007	211.4	211.4	216.7	218.1	221.2	222.6	219.6	221.0	220.3	219.6	218.4	216.1	218.0
2008	206.7	207.5	206.3	209.1	212.4	216.5	211.7	211.6	210.8	207.3	202.3	197.8	208.3
2009	185.5	183.9	183.1	179.8	179.1	178.9	179.6	176.7	174.7	173.3	170.2	167.7	177.7
2010	161.3	160.4	163.9	166.2	166.9	170.7	170.8	170.6	170.1	171.0	169.7	168.2	167.5
2011	165.2	165.3	169.3	172.6	173.8	176.1	177.0	176.2	173.9	171.7	169.3	168.2	171.6
2012	162.0	161.7	164.3	166.6	168.6	170.8	171.4	171.3	169.4	169.2	167.4	167.0	167.5
2013	162.2	162.9	163.7	166.5	169.4	173.0	173.4	173.0	171.8	171.5	169.9	168.0	168.8
2014	161.5	163.3	166.7	170.1	172.5	175.4	176.6	176.5	176.1	176.0	174.0	173.3	171.8
2015	168.3	168.2	170.5	174.3	177.2	179.4	180.7	180.6	180.2	180.5	178.6	179.3	176.5
2016	173.9	173.4	175.9	178.8	179.8	183.2	183.1	182.7	182.3	183.3	182.6	181.7	180.1
2017	176.2	177.9	178.4	180.1	181.6	184.7	184.0	184.1	182.8	182.0	183.5	181.2	181.4
Service-Providing													
2007	1,109.5	1,113.2	1,124.6	1,135.2	1,144.9	1,144.1	1,118.5	1,125.1	1,139.0	1,142.2	1,147.3	1,151.0	1,132.9
2008	1,127.3	1,132.6	1,137.2	1,145.9	1,155.4	1,154.5	1,126.0	1,134.2	1,142.2	1,140.0	1,137.3	1,135.4	1,139.0
2009	1,107.8	1,108.2	1,110.8	1,122.5	1,128.2	1,125.0	1,095.1	1,103.9	1,112.1	1,112.4	1,113.3	1,116.6	1,113.0
2010	1,095.1	1,101.6	1,109.2	1,119.9	1,127.6	1,120.7	1,097.3	1,109.8	1,116.1	1,122.9	1,123.2	1,122.6	1,113.8
2011	1,101.5	1,104.2	1,113.3	1,130.9	1,135.1	1,128.4	1,108.5	1,117.6	1,128.1	1,131.4	1,132.1	1,134.0	1,122.1
2012	1,108.0	1,113.8	1,123.6	1,133.7	1,139.9	1,134.0	1,109.3	1,118.7	1,128.2	1,135.4	1,137.5	1,139.9	1,126.8
2013	1,113.9	1,120.0	1,126.1	1,140.7	1,147.9	1,140.6	1,119.6	1,129.3	1,139.1	1,145.5	1,147.6	1,151.3	1,135.1
2014	1,120.4	1,128.7	1,134.5	1,155.6	1,161.0	1,153.5	1,132.4	1,143.0	1,149.6	1,164.4	1,165.0	1,166.9	1,147.9
2015	1,140.8	1,146.4	1,150.5	1,169.3	1,178.4	1,175.4	1,157.0	1,165.0	1,174.3	1,185.5	1,188.5	1,189.2	1,168.4
2016	1,156.7	1,165.8	1,171.2	1,189.7	1,194.5	1,191.0	1,170.2	1,179.9	1,190.4	1,199.2	1,198.9	1,196.4	1,183.7
2017	1,171.8	1,182.3	1,186.2	1,200.4	1,206.1	1,207.9	1,185.4	1,191.6	1,199.7	1,208.9	1,209.5	1,202.8	1,196.1
Mining, Logging, and Construction													
2007	76.9	73.9	79.3	80.8	83.7	86.6	86.1	86.0	84.1	83.6	82.5	79.9	82.0
2008	75.7	73.6	76.0	77.9	79.9	82.0	82.2	82.1	80.6	77.9	74.9	71.5	77.9
2009	63.8	62.9	64.4	64.6	65.5	66.6	67.7	66.6	65.6	64.5	62.1	59.9	64.5
2010	54.9	53.9	57.1	59.2	59.5	62.2	62.5	62.2	61.8	61.8	60.4	58.4	59.5
2011	56.5	56.5	59.8	62.9	63.9	65.2	65.4	64.7	62.7	60.5	58.6	57.0	61.1
2012	51.9	51.4	53.5	55.7	57.3	58.8	59.6	60.0	59.5	58.9	57.5	56.9	56.8
2013	52.3	52.4	53.6	56.4	59.0	61.7	62.9	62.2	61.3	60.6	59.1	57.1	58.2
2014	52.9	52.1	55.8	58.3	59.8	61.4	62.5	62.5	62.4	62.2	60.5	59.6	59.2
2015	55.5	55.3	57.4	60.8	63.0	64.0	64.8	65.6	65.4	66.1	64.4	64.7	62.3
2016	60.9	59.4	62.1	65.1	66.0	68.3	68.1	68.1	68.0	68.4	67.9	66.9	65.8
2017	62.8	63.6	64.6	65.9	67.1	68.9	68.8	68.9	68.1	67.7	68.2	65.5	66.7

Employment by Industry: St. Louis, MO-IL, Selected Years, 2007–2017—*Continued*

(Numbers in thousands, not seasonally adjusted)

Industry and year	January	February	March	April	May	June	July	August	September	October	November	December	Annual average
Manufacturing													
2007	134.5	137.5	137.4	137.3	137.5	136.0	133.5	135.0	136.2	136.0	135.9	136.2	136.1
2008	131.0	133.9	130.3	131.2	132.5	134.5	129.5	129.5	130.2	129.4	127.4	126.3	130.5
2009	121.7	121.0	118.7	115.2	113.6	112.3	111.9	110.1	109.1	108.8	108.1	107.8	113.2
2010	106.4	106.5	106.8	107.0	107.4	108.5	108.3	108.4	108.3	109.2	109.3	109.8	108.0
2011	108.7	108.8	109.5	109.7	109.9	110.9	111.6	111.5	111.2	111.2	110.7	111.2	110.4
2012	110.1	110.3	110.8	110.9	111.3	112.0	111.8	111.3	109.9	110.3	109.9	110.1	110.7
2013	109.9	110.5	110.1	110.1	110.4	111.3	110.5	110.8	110.5	110.9	110.8	110.9	110.6
2014	108.6	111.2	110.9	111.8	112.7	114.0	114.1	114.0	113.7	113.8	113.5	113.7	112.7
2015	112.8	112.9	113.1	113.5	114.2	115.4	115.9	115.0	114.8	114.4	114.2	114.6	114.2
2016	113.0	114.0	113.8	113.7	113.8	114.9	115.0	114.6	114.3	114.9	114.7	114.8	114.3
2017	113.4	114.3	113.8	114.2	114.5	115.8	115.2	115.2	114.7	114.3	115.3	115.7	114.7
Trade, Transportation, and Utilities													
2007	254.4	251.3	254.4	255.6	257.9	258.5	257.1	256.3	256.7	257.7	263.8	266.5	257.5
2008	258.5	255.0	256.1	256.3	257.8	258.9	256.6	257.0	255.6	255.1	257.7	259.0	257.0
2009	248.7	245.4	244.8	244.8	245.6	245.2	242.6	243.5	242.9	242.4	246.0	247.4	244.9
2010	239.1	236.7	238.3	239.0	240.5	240.7	239.3	240.7	239.4	240.4	243.9	246.8	240.4
2011	239.9	238.2	239.5	242.2	243.3	243.2	242.4	243.2	242.1	242.5	247.1	249.3	242.7
2012	241.1	239.0	240.5	242.4	244.1	243.8	242.9	244.2	243.8	245.7	251.2	253.0	244.3
2013	242.9	240.2	240.6	243.0	244.7	245.1	244.4	245.9	245.1	247.3	252.5	255.9	245.6
2014	245.2	243.2	244.7	247.1	248.7	250.2	248.6	250.0	249.0	251.6	257.2	260.2	249.6
2015	249.7	247.2	248.5	250.3	252.3	252.9	252.8	253.8	253.0	255.2	260.1	263.1	253.2
2016	253.1	251.4	252.2	254.4	255.5	255.0	255.8	254.8	254.2	258.0	262.8	265.5	256.1
2017	256.0	254.3	254.9	256.0	256.8	257.4	257.7	258.7	259.0	261.2	264.2	264.8	258.4
Wholesale Trade													
2007	61.2	61.4	61.8	61.6	62.0	62.5	62.8	62.7	62.5	62.6	62.7	62.9	62.2
2008	62.6	62.6	62.7	63.0	63.2	63.6	63.5	63.5	63.1	62.5	62.0	61.9	62.9
2009	60.7	60.4	60.1	59.8	59.5	59.7	59.5	59.3	58.8	59.2	58.9	59.2	59.6
2010	58.5	58.4	58.8	60.6	60.6	60.5	60.2	59.8	59.5	59.5	59.3	59.5	59.6
2011	59.1	59.1	59.3	59.5	59.6	60.0	60.4	60.2	59.9	59.9	60.0	60.0	59.8
2012	59.7	59.7	60.0	60.6	61.0	61.3	61.1	61.4	60.9	61.0	61.0	61.2	60.7
2013	60.0	59.9	60.0	60.3	60.8	61.2	61.2	61.3	61.0	61.5	61.7	61.9	60.9
2014	61.0	61.1	61.4	61.7	62.0	62.5	62.6	62.7	62.1	62.2	62.4	62.5	62.0
2015	61.4	61.2	61.3	60.9	61.4	61.6	61.6	61.9	61.5	61.6	61.7	61.8	61.6
2016	61.2	61.1	60.9	61.5	61.6	61.9	62.7	61.7	62.2	64.0	64.1	64.3	62.3
2017	63.2	63.3	63.2	63.2	63.5	64.1	64.7	64.9	66.1	65.9	65.3	65.2	64.4
Retail Trade													
2007	145.1	142.1	144.3	145.5	146.8	147.7	146.3	145.2	144.8	145.7	151.4	153.3	146.5
2008	146.8	143.4	144.2	144.3	145.2	146.2	144.5	144.2	142.6	142.9	145.8	147.0	144.8
2009	139.0	136.5	136.4	137.2	138.1	138.8	137.4	137.6	136.9	137.0	140.9	141.8	138.1
2010	135.3	133.2	134.3	134.9	136.2	137.5	136.8	136.8	135.4	136.3	139.9	142.1	136.6
2011	136.6	134.8	135.6	137.6	138.3	138.9	138.6	138.4	137.0	137.5	141.9	143.4	138.2
2012	137.1	134.9	136.0	136.8	137.6	138.2	137.8	137.2	136.8	138.6	143.7	144.5	138.3
2013	137.6	135.2	135.3	137.0	138.1	139.3	138.7	138.7	137.8	139.6	144.1	146.4	139.0
2014	138.2	136.2	137.3	138.9	139.8	141.6	140.7	140.6	139.3	141.3	146.2	147.8	140.7
2015	140.2	138.2	139.3	141.0	142.1	143.6	142.8	143.3	142.1	144.3	148.3	150.0	142.9
2016	142.6	141.3	142.0	143.2	144.0	144.5	144.6	143.6	141.8	143.6	147.7	148.8	144.0
2017	142.6	140.9	141.7	142.7	143.0	143.9	143.9	143.4	141.7	143.8	146.4	145.7	143.3
Transportation and Utilities													
2007	48.1	47.8	48.3	48.5	49.1	48.3	48.0	48.4	49.4	49.4	49.7	50.3	48.8
2008	49.1	49.0	49.2	49.0	49.4	49.1	48.6	49.3	49.9	49.7	49.9	50.1	49.4
2009	49.0	48.5	48.3	47.8	48.0	46.7	45.7	46.6	47.2	46.2	46.2	46.4	47.2
2010	45.3	45.1	45.2	43.5	43.7	42.7	42.3	44.1	44.5	44.6	44.7	45.2	44.2
2011	44.2	44.3	44.6	45.1	45.4	44.3	43.4	44.6	45.2	45.1	45.2	45.9	44.8
2012	44.3	44.4	44.5	45.0	45.5	44.3	44.0	45.6	46.1	46.1	46.5	47.3	45.3
2013	45.3	45.1	45.3	45.7	45.8	44.6	44.5	45.9	46.3	46.2	46.7	47.6	45.8
2014	46.0	45.9	46.0	46.5	46.9	46.1	45.3	46.7	47.6	48.1	48.6	49.9	47.0
2015	48.1	47.8	47.9	48.4	48.8	47.7	47.4	48.6	49.4	49.3	50.1	51.3	48.7
2016	49.3	49.0	49.3	49.7	49.9	48.6	48.5	49.5	50.2	50.4	51.0	52.4	49.8
2017	50.2	50.1	50.0	50.1	50.3	49.4	49.1	50.4	51.2	51.5	52.5	53.9	50.7

Employment by Industry: St. Louis, MO-IL, Selected Years, 2007–2017—*Continued*

(Numbers in thousands, not seasonally adjusted)

Industry and year	January	February	March	April	May	June	July	August	September	October	November	December	Annual average
Information													
2007	29.7	29.6	29.7	30.0	30.3	30.5	30.3	30.3	30.2	30.6	30.8	30.8	30.2
2008	30.3	30.1	30.2	30.7	31.1	31.2	31.1	30.9	30.7	30.8	30.9	31.0	30.8
2009	30.7	30.6	30.5	30.2	30.2	30.4	30.4	30.4	30.1	29.8	29.8	30.1	30.3
2010	29.8	29.6	29.6	31.6	31.3	31.8	31.4	31.4	31.1	30.9	30.8	31.0	30.9
2011	30.4	30.3	30.1	30.9	31.1	31.3	31.6	31.5	31.3	30.9	30.8	30.8	30.9
2012	30.6	30.5	30.4	30.0	30.2	30.2	30.3	30.1	29.7	29.3	29.2	29.2	30.0
2013	29.1	29.2	29.2	29.1	29.4	29.4	29.2	29.2	28.9	28.8	28.7	28.9	29.1
2014	28.2	28.1	28.3	28.6	28.9	29.1	29.3	29.2	28.9	28.6	28.7	28.7	28.7
2015	28.6	28.6	28.6	28.7	28.8	29.0	29.0	28.9	28.5	28.4	28.4	28.6	28.7
2016	28.5	28.4	28.5	28.6	28.8	28.9	28.8	28.8	28.5	28.3	28.2	28.2	28.5
2017	28.1	27.9	27.9	28.0	28.3	28.4	28.4	28.4	28.0	27.8	27.8	27.9	28.1
Financial Activities													
2007	78.3	78.4	78.6	78.8	79.5	80.0	80.2	80.0	79.4	79.5	79.1	79.4	79.3
2008	79.8	80.0	80.1	79.6	79.6	79.7	79.2	79.5	78.7	78.1	77.9	77.8	79.2
2009	77.9	78.1	78.2	78.7	78.8	79.1	79.0	78.9	78.2	78.6	78.2	78.2	78.5
2010	78.1	78.1	78.2	79.5	79.6	80.1	81.0	80.9	80.5	81.5	81.3	81.4	80.0
2011	80.4	80.3	80.5	81.8	82.0	81.9	82.8	82.9	82.5	83.0	83.2	83.3	82.1
2012	82.7	83.0	83.6	84.2	84.4	84.8	85.0	85.1	84.8	85.7	86.0	85.9	84.6
2013	83.9	84.1	84.3	84.5	85.3	85.8	85.9	85.8	85.3	85.7	85.8	85.5	85.2
2014	84.5	84.6	84.5	84.9	85.3	85.4	85.8	85.7	85.0	85.4	85.6	85.6	85.2
2015	84.6	84.6	84.7	85.2	85.7	86.2	86.7	86.5	85.6	86.1	86.3	86.4	85.7
2016	85.1	85.1	85.2	85.4	85.7	86.0	86.3	86.3	86.0	86.5	86.4	86.7	85.9
2017	86.3	86.5	86.9	87.3	87.7	88.4	88.6	88.6	87.9	88.8	88.6	87.8	87.8
Professional and Business Services													
2007	188.4	189.0	191.6	194.1	194.2	195.0	194.3	195.0	194.6	194.6	194.2	194.5	193.3
2008	193.2	194.7	196.3	199.8	198.6	199.9	198.2	198.2	195.4	193.6	191.0	189.1	195.7
2009	183.5	183.2	181.9	184.0	183.0	183.2	181.9	181.9	180.7	180.6	180.8	181.3	182.2
2010	178.6	180.6	182.0	187.5	186.7	187.7	188.7	189.0	187.9	189.6	189.4	188.5	186.4
2011	186.7	187.5	189.5	193.7	192.3	192.4	192.2	191.6	191.0	191.3	190.9	190.4	190.8
2012	185.9	186.6	188.7	192.8	192.4	193.4	191.1	191.0	190.2	191.9	192.4	192.5	190.7
2013	189.1	190.8	193.7	197.4	197.8	198.6	199.6	200.6	199.9	201.2	201.4	202.2	197.7
2014	196.6	198.4	200.5	205.6	204.6	205.1	203.0	204.1	203.8	205.8	205.1	205.6	203.2
2015	200.2	201.5	203.0	206.5	207.5	207.1	208.4	209.1	208.6	209.6	210.2	210.4	206.8
2016	204.8	207.0	208.1	213.2	212.3	212.8	211.7	212.6	211.7	213.1	212.1	210.2	210.8
2017	206.4	208.5	210.4	213.2	212.7	214.8	214.3	215.4	214.3	216.6	216.6	213.8	213.1
Education and Health Services													
2007	202.7	205.4	206.5	207.3	207.4	206.8	206.6	206.4	209.0	210.6	211.6	212.1	207.7
2008	207.1	210.3	210.1	210.8	210.7	209.9	209.6	209.9	212.5	213.9	214.6	215.0	211.2
2009	211.7	214.0	214.2	213.6	214.1	213.0	212.6	212.9	215.4	216.9	218.7	220.7	214.8
2010	218.8	221.8	222.2	223.2	223.1	222.1	220.5	220.6	223.6	227.3	228.0	227.6	223.2
2011	225.6	228.2	228.6	230.0	229.6	227.9	227.9	228.0	231.1	233.3	234.8	234.8	230.0
2012	232.5	235.6	235.9	232.3	231.2	229.0	228.8	228.6	231.7	233.8	233.8	234.1	232.3
2013	231.3	235.0	234.1	231.0	229.0	225.7	226.1	225.8	228.0	230.5	231.0	230.1	229.8
2014	227.3	232.0	229.6	234.6	232.2	228.6	230.9	230.7	232.6	237.6	238.3	236.2	232.6
2015	236.1	238.4	236.5	242.7	240.9	238.4	240.5	239.4	240.9	246.0	246.3	244.1	240.9
2016	240.8	245.2	244.2	247.4	245.6	241.9	244.4	245.1	246.9	250.6	250.6	248.3	245.9
2017	246.5	250.9	248.6	253.6	252.6	248.6	249.8	249.9	251.4	254.8	256.7	254.7	251.5
Leisure and Hospitality													
2007	133.1	133.2	137.0	142.0	146.8	150.2	148.8	149.1	144.3	141.2	138.5	138.9	141.9
2008	134.0	133.7	136.1	139.8	146.1	149.4	146.8	147.0	141.5	137.6	134.7	134.0	140.1
2009	129.9	129.2	132.6	138.5	143.5	146.3	144.5	144.5	137.6	135.2	131.5	130.5	137.0
2010	127.3	128.5	131.9	139.1	142.5	145.0	145.7	145.4	140.5	138.0	134.3	132.5	137.6
2011	127.7	127.2	131.3	136.4	140.0	143.0	142.9	143.5	137.0	137.3	132.3	132.2	135.9
2012	127.4	128.3	132.4	139.0	143.2	146.5	145.5	145.7	139.2	139.1	135.2	135.3	138.1
2013	131.8	131.9	134.5	141.5	146.4	148.4	148.3	147.3	142.3	140.9	136.6	136.8	140.6
2014	131.7	131.9	135.2	143.5	148.9	150.4	150.6	151.2	143.9	145.6	141.4	141.4	143.0
2015	137.7	138.3	140.8	146.9	153.0	155.6	154.6	154.4	150.0	149.1	146.4	145.4	147.7
2016	139.5	140.2	144.1	150.8	154.8	158.0	156.0	156.3	152.0	150.3	146.0	144.2	149.4
2017	141.0	143.1	145.9	150.4	155.5	159.7	157.5	157.6	151.7	150.9	147.4	145.9	150.6

Employment by Industry: St. Louis, MO-IL, Selected Years, 2007–2017—*Continued*

(Numbers in thousands, not seasonally adjusted)

Industry and year	January	February	March	April	May	June	July	August	September	October	November	December	Annual average
Other Services													
2007	56.1	56.4	56.8	57.0	57.3	57.6	57.2	57.2	56.5	56.8	56.9	56.7	56.9
2008	56.2	56.2	56.6	56.9	57.5	57.8	57.5	57.3	56.7	57.0	56.5	56.1	56.9
2009	55.0	55.0	55.3	55.5	55.6	55.4	54.9	54.5	53.9	54.6	54.4	54.6	54.9
2010	53.9	54.0	54.6	45.4	45.4	45.7	45.6	45.6	44.8	45.1	45.2	45.2	47.5
2011	44.4	44.4	45.0	45.9	46.1	46.7	46.8	46.5	46.1	45.8	45.7	45.8	45.8
2012	44.9	45.1	45.5	45.4	45.9	46.3	46.2	46.0	45.3	45.3	45.2	45.1	45.5
2013	45.4	45.4	45.6	45.5	46.0	46.8	46.5	46.6	45.7	46.1	46.1	46.2	46.0
2014	45.8	46.1	46.7	47.3	47.7	48.4	48.5	48.1	47.1	47.0	46.7	46.9	47.2
2015	46.6	46.9	47.3	47.6	47.8	48.7	48.4	47.9	47.1	47.4	47.4	47.6	47.6
2016	47.0	47.1	47.3	47.9	48.4	49.9	50.1	50.2	49.5	49.9	50.2	50.4	49.0
2017	50.3	50.7	51.3	51.9	52.1	53.1	52.9	52.7	51.6	52.1	52.2	52.4	51.9
Government													
2007	166.8	169.9	170.0	170.4	171.5	165.5	144.0	150.8	168.3	171.2	172.4	172.1	166.1
2008	168.2	172.6	171.7	172.0	174.0	167.7	147.0	154.4	171.1	173.9	174.0	173.4	168.3
2009	170.4	172.7	173.3	177.2	177.4	172.4	149.2	157.3	173.3	174.3	173.9	173.8	170.4
2010	169.5	172.3	172.4	174.6	178.5	167.6	145.1	156.2	168.3	170.1	170.3	169.6	167.9
2011	166.4	168.1	168.8	170.0	170.7	162.0	141.9	150.4	167.0	167.3	167.3	167.4	163.9
2012	162.9	165.7	166.6	167.6	168.5	160.0	139.5	148.0	163.5	164.6	164.5	164.8	161.4
2013	160.4	163.4	164.1	168.7	169.3	160.8	139.6	148.1	163.9	165.0	165.5	165.7	161.2
2014	161.1	164.4	165.0	164.0	164.7	156.3	135.7	144.0	159.3	162.8	162.0	162.3	158.5
2015	157.3	160.9	161.1	161.4	162.4	157.5	136.6	145.0	160.6	163.7	163.4	163.6	157.8
2016	157.9	161.4	161.6	162.0	163.4	158.5	137.1	145.8	161.6	162.5	162.6	162.9	158.1
2017	157.2	160.4	160.3	160.0	160.4	157.5	136.2	140.3	155.8	156.7	156.0	155.5	154.7

Employment by Industry: Charlotte-Concord-Gastonia, NC-SC, Selected Years, 2007–2017

(Numbers in thousands, not seasonally adjusted)

Industry and year	January	February	March	April	May	June	July	August	September	October	November	December	Annual average
Total Nonfarm													
2007	1,000.5	1,006.5	1,017.5	1,018.0	1,026.5	1,023.0	1,000.5	1,025.0	1,031.4	1,039.6	1,043.6	1,045.4	1,023.1
2008	1,017.4	1,023.8	1,029.9	1,026.9	1,032.3	1,025.0	998.4	1,020.2	1,024.7	1,021.4	1,014.8	1,011.7	1,020.5
2009	974.4	972.5	970.8	963.6	965.5	956.6	931.0	951.1	952.2	951.6	952.8	952.5	957.9
2010	933.8	936.5	946.1	953.3	963.4	955.2	932.7	954.6	958.0	969.5	973.3	974.2	954.2
2011	952.1	962.3	970.6	976.4	980.1	975.8	955.0	979.6	983.7	989.2	996.2	997.0	976.5
2012	981.7	986.9	998.0	1,001.5	1,010.9	1,000.1	982.8	1,004.1	1,009.3	1,019.6	1,025.9	1,027.3	1,004.0
2013	1,005.8	1,012.6	1,021.0	1,026.3	1,033.6	1,024.5	1,008.0	1,028.4	1,032.6	1,046.7	1,054.1	1,057.7	1,029.3
2014	1,040.1	1,039.0	1,052.9	1,061.7	1,071.5	1,065.3	1,047.5	1,066.4	1,071.7	1,087.9	1,094.0	1,099.1	1,066.4
2015	1,078.9	1,086.2	1,092.2	1,099.4	1,112.2	1,111.6	1,093.4	1,109.1	1,113.1	1,130.2	1,136.7	1,143.2	1,108.9
2016	1,120.6	1,125.7	1,135.0	1,144.8	1,150.0	1,148.0	1,135.0	1,148.5	1,157.7	1,165.6	1,171.2	1,173.0	1,147.9
2017	1,153.3	1,159.1	1,167.6	1,172.8	1,182.9	1,184.9	1,167.0	1,183.2	1,186.5	1,203.6	1,205.8	1,211.3	1,181.5
Total Private													
2007	868.5	872.9	883.4	885.0	892.5	899.2	895.6	898.8	897.2	902.9	905.3	906.8	892.3
2008	879.7	884.6	890.0	887.0	891.8	892.5	886.1	886.7	881.6	878.5	870.4	866.7	883.0
2009	831.5	828.9	826.5	818.9	821.3	818.5	815.0	813.5	809.7	808.5	808.8	808.5	817.5
2010	789.1	790.5	798.9	805.7	811.9	815.6	815.8	818.4	818.2	823.8	826.9	827.6	811.9
2011	808.7	817.7	825.1	830.3	834.0	839.0	838.9	841.9	843.3	844.6	848.7	849.9	835.2
2012	836.8	840.7	850.4	853.3	861.8	866.4	865.0	866.5	865.6	869.6	874.5	876.3	860.6
2013	857.0	862.8	869.9	875.1	881.9	888.1	887.6	891.0	889.2	895.0	901.3	905.3	883.7
2014	890.7	889.1	902.0	909.5	918.7	924.6	924.7	927.7	927.3	935.4	940.3	945.9	919.7
2015	928.7	934.8	940.0	946.7	959.2	966.5	968.1	968.6	967.2	977.0	982.3	988.4	960.6
2016	971.2	974.9	983.0	992.8	997.4	1,001.5	1,005.6	1,006.7	1,005.0	1,011.2	1,015.5	1,017.8	998.6
2017	1,000.3	1,004.7	1,012.2	1,016.7	1,026.9	1,034.9	1,034.8	1,038.6	1,031.3	1,040.7	1,041.8	1,048.0	1,027.6
Goods Producing													
2007	188.5	188.8	189.4	186.5	186.4	189.4	187.8	188.5	188.0	186.9	186.9	186.3	187.8
2008	181.1	181.5	181.3	179.4	179.3	178.9	177.2	176.3	175.2	172.0	168.7	165.4	176.4
2009	155.0	154.2	151.9	148.0	147.0	145.9	144.9	143.6	142.8	141.3	140.7	140.4	146.3
2010	136.1	135.8	136.4	137.3	137.5	138.1	138.2	137.8	137.2	137.0	137.2	136.7	137.1
2011	132.5	134.5	135.3	136.6	137.4	138.5	139.9	140.3	140.7	140.4	140.7	140.6	138.1
2012	140.4	141.3	142.8	143.3	144.5	145.6	145.6	145.6	145.3	144.1	145.6	146.1	144.2
2013	144.6	145.8	147.3	146.9	147.1	148.4	148.6	148.7	148.4	148.3	148.7	148.9	147.6
2014	147.3	147.4	149.4	150.1	151.7	152.9	153.4	154.0	154.2	155.0	155.8	156.6	152.3
2015	155.4	156.3	157.0	158.3	159.8	161.4	162.2	162.7	163.1	163.2	163.6	164.1	160.6
2016	163.6	164.6	165.3	166.3	165.4	165.6	166.5	166.0	165.8	165.5	165.6	166.1	165.5
2017	163.6	164.6	165.1	166.7	167.7	169.5	170.0	170.0	169.5	170.5	169.8	168.8	168.0
Service-Providing													
2007	812.0	817.7	828.1	831.5	840.1	833.6	812.7	836.5	843.4	852.7	856.7	859.1	835.3
2008	836.3	842.3	848.6	847.5	853.0	846.1	821.2	843.9	849.5	849.4	846.1	846.3	844.2
2009	819.4	818.3	818.9	815.6	818.5	810.7	786.1	807.5	809.4	810.3	812.1	812.1	811.6
2010	797.7	800.7	809.7	816.0	825.9	817.1	794.5	816.8	820.8	832.5	836.1	837.5	817.1
2011	819.6	827.8	835.3	839.8	842.7	837.3	815.1	839.3	843.0	848.8	855.5	856.4	838.4
2012	841.3	845.6	855.2	858.2	866.4	854.5	837.2	858.5	864.0	875.5	880.3	881.2	859.8
2013	861.2	866.8	873.7	879.4	886.5	876.1	859.4	879.7	884.2	898.4	905.4	908.8	881.6
2014	892.8	891.6	903.5	911.6	919.8	912.4	894.1	912.4	917.5	932.9	938.2	942.5	914.1
2015	923.5	929.9	935.2	941.1	952.4	950.2	931.2	946.4	950.0	967.0	973.1	979.1	948.3
2016	957.0	961.1	969.7	978.5	984.6	982.4	968.5	982.5	991.9	1,000.1	1,005.6	1,006.9	982.4
2017	989.7	994.5	1,002.5	1,006.1	1,015.2	1,015.4	997.0	1,013.2	1,017.0	1,033.1	1,036.0	1,042.5	1,013.5
Mining, Logging, and Construction													
2007	68.6	69.1	70.2	70.9	71.1	72.2	72.5	72.7	72.3	71.8	71.1	70.5	71.1
2008	67.6	67.4	67.2	66.8	67.0	66.7	66.2	65.5	64.6	63.0	61.2	59.8	65.3
2009	55.3	54.5	53.8	52.3	52.2	52.1	51.8	51.0	50.3	49.1	48.6	48.2	51.6
2010	45.1	44.7	45.3	46.0	46.0	46.6	46.4	46.1	45.7	45.6	45.7	45.2	45.7
2011	41.7	43.4	43.8	44.7	45.1	45.5	46.1	46.0	45.9	45.6	45.5	45.2	44.9
2012	44.7	45.0	46.0	46.2	46.7	47.4	47.2	47.1	46.9	46.9	47.1	47.2	46.5
2013	46.2	46.8	48.0	48.6	48.8	49.3	49.7	50.0	50.1	50.5	50.7	50.5	49.1
2014	49.4	49.5	50.9	51.2	52.1	52.6	53.0	53.3	53.4	54.0	54.2	54.3	52.3
2015	53.1	53.4	53.8	54.6	55.7	56.4	57.1	57.2	57.8	58.1	58.1	58.2	56.1
2016	57.8	58.6	59.8	60.7	60.9	61.3	61.5	61.5	61.5	61.7	61.6	61.4	60.7
2017	59.3	60.0	60.2	61.1	61.7	62.4	62.9	62.9	63.0	63.5	63.1	62.9	61.9

Employment by Industry: Charlotte-Concord-Gastonia, NC-SC, Selected Years, 2007–2017—*Continued*

(Numbers in thousands, not seasonally adjusted)

Industry and year	January	February	March	April	May	June	July	August	September	October	November	December	Annual average
Manufacturing													
2007	119.9	119.7	119.2	115.6	115.3	117.2	115.3	115.8	115.7	115.1	115.8	115.8	116.7
2008	113.5	114.1	114.1	112.6	112.3	112.2	111.0	110.8	110.6	109.0	107.5	105.6	111.1
2009	99.7	99.7	98.1	95.7	94.8	93.8	93.1	92.6	92.5	92.2	92.1	92.2	94.7
2010	91.0	91.1	91.1	91.3	91.5	91.5	91.8	91.7	91.5	91.4	91.5	91.5	91.4
2011	90.8	91.1	91.5	91.9	92.3	93.0	93.8	94.3	94.8	94.8	95.2	95.4	93.2
2012	95.7	96.3	96.8	97.1	97.8	98.2	98.4	98.5	98.4	97.2	98.5	98.9	97.7
2013	98.4	99.0	99.3	98.3	98.3	99.1	98.9	98.7	98.3	97.8	98.0	98.4	98.5
2014	97.9	97.9	98.5	98.9	99.6	100.3	100.4	100.7	100.8	101.0	101.6	102.3	100.0
2015	102.3	102.9	103.2	103.7	104.1	105.0	105.1	105.5	105.3	105.1	105.5	105.9	104.5
2016	105.8	106.0	105.5	105.6	104.5	104.3	105.0	104.5	104.3	103.8	104.0	104.7	104.8
2017	104.3	104.6	104.9	105.6	106.0	107.1	107.1	107.1	106.5	107.0	106.7	105.9	106.1
Trade, Transportation, and Utilities													
2007	209.8	209.0	211.4	211.9	213.3	213.6	214.0	214.2	214.4	216.3	220.5	222.3	214.2
2008	214.7	213.6	215.0	213.5	213.8	213.6	211.9	211.6	210.4	210.6	211.9	212.4	212.8
2009	205.2	202.7	202.2	199.5	200.5	200.0	198.9	198.9	197.8	198.3	200.2	201.0	200.4
2010	194.5	193.5	195.2	195.5	196.9	197.2	197.3	197.9	197.1	198.8	202.2	204.0	197.5
2011	197.3	197.2	198.7	199.1	199.7	199.8	200.9	201.2	200.6	202.5	206.3	208.0	200.9
2012	202.6	201.6	203.2	204.1	205.5	206.4	206.8	206.9	206.9	208.5	213.4	214.8	206.7
2013	207.3	206.8	208.0	208.1	209.5	210.3	211.2	212.0	211.6	213.7	219.0	222.1	211.6
2014	214.8	213.0	215.3	215.4	216.9	218.4	217.9	218.6	218.9	222.0	227.6	230.5	219.1
2015	222.0	221.6	222.8	224.8	226.4	227.8	227.6	228.1	227.5	230.7	236.0	239.2	227.9
2016	231.4	231.1	231.7	232.3	233.6	233.6	235.4	236.1	236.0	238.4	244.4	248.5	236.0
2017	238.5	237.0	237.7	237.8	239.3	240.7	240.8	241.8	240.6	243.9	247.1	250.5	241.3
Wholesale Trade													
2007	54.4	54.8	55.3	55.6	55.7	55.9	56.2	56.1	56.0	56.8	56.7	56.8	55.9
2008	56.4	56.7	57.3	56.5	56.5	56.3	55.5	55.6	55.3	55.4	55.0	55.0	56.0
2009	54.0	53.9	53.3	51.9	51.5	51.1	50.7	50.4	50.0	50.2	49.9	49.8	51.4
2010	49.2	49.4	49.7	49.5	49.6	49.4	49.6	49.7	49.5	49.9	49.9	50.1	49.6
2011	49.6	49.9	50.0	49.7	49.8	49.8	50.2	50.2	50.2	50.6	50.7	50.9	50.1
2012	50.5	50.6	50.9	51.0	51.3	51.4	51.5	51.5	51.4	51.4	51.5	51.7	51.2
2013	51.0	51.4	51.6	51.6	51.7	51.8	52.1	52.4	52.3	52.7	53.1	53.4	52.1
2014	53.1	53.2	53.5	53.4	53.6	53.8	53.9	54.2	54.1	54.3	54.7	54.9	53.9
2015	54.3	54.6	55.1	55.2	55.6	55.8	56.1	56.2	56.2	56.6	56.9	57.3	55.8
2016	57.2	57.4	57.6	58.1	58.5	58.4	59.1	59.2	59.3	59.3	59.6	59.9	58.6
2017	58.9	59.5	59.7	59.7	60.1	60.5	60.2	60.2	59.9	60.7	60.8	61.4	60.1
Retail Trade													
2007	110.7	109.7	111.3	111.5	112.8	112.9	113.0	113.4	113.6	114.9	119.2	120.5	113.6
2008	114.1	112.9	113.9	112.6	112.7	112.8	112.2	111.8	111.1	111.4	113.1	113.3	112.7
2009	108.7	107.0	107.0	106.2	107.6	107.4	107.0	107.4	106.7	107.3	109.6	110.2	107.7
2010	105.5	104.4	105.5	105.8	106.8	107.1	107.0	107.7	106.9	108.1	111.2	112.6	107.4
2011	106.9	106.5	107.4	107.9	108.3	108.4	109.0	109.2	108.5	109.9	113.3	114.4	109.1
2012	110.4	109.3	110.3	111.0	112.1	112.6	112.8	112.8	112.7	114.3	118.7	119.3	113.0
2013	113.4	112.8	113.3	113.6	114.5	115.1	115.5	115.8	115.3	116.8	120.9	122.9	115.8
2014	116.6	115.2	116.5	116.7	117.4	118.1	117.8	118.0	117.7	120.2	124.5	126.2	118.7
2015	119.9	119.3	119.7	120.9	121.6	122.5	121.9	122.3	121.6	124.0	128.0	129.2	122.6
2016	123.0	123.0	123.3	123.9	124.5	124.3	125.1	125.4	125.2	127.2	130.7	131.8	125.6
2017	125.8	124.7	125.1	124.7	125.5	125.8	125.7	126.0	125.3	126.9	129.8	130.8	126.3
Transportation and Utilities													
2007	44.7	44.5	44.8	44.8	44.8	44.8	44.8	44.7	44.8	44.6	44.6	45.0	44.7
2008	44.2	44.0	43.8	44.4	44.6	44.5	44.2	44.2	44.0	43.8	43.8	44.1	44.1
2009	42.5	41.8	41.9	41.4	41.4	41.5	41.2	41.1	41.1	40.8	40.7	41.0	41.4
2010	39.8	39.7	40.0	40.2	40.5	40.7	40.7	40.5	40.7	40.8	41.1	41.3	40.5
2011	40.8	40.8	41.3	41.5	41.6	41.6	41.7	41.8	41.9	42.0	42.3	42.7	41.7
2012	41.7	41.7	42.0	42.1	42.1	42.4	42.5	42.6	42.8	42.8	43.2	43.8	42.5
2013	42.9	42.6	43.1	42.9	43.3	43.4	43.6	43.8	44.0	44.2	45.0	45.8	43.7
2014	45.1	44.6	45.3	45.3	45.9	46.5	46.2	46.4	47.1	47.5	48.4	49.4	46.5
2015	47.8	47.7	48.0	48.7	49.2	49.5	49.6	49.6	49.7	50.1	51.1	52.7	49.5
2016	51.2	50.7	50.8	50.3	50.6	50.9	51.2	51.5	51.5	51.9	54.1	56.8	51.8
2017	53.8	52.8	52.9	53.4	53.7	54.4	54.9	55.6	55.4	56.3	56.5	58.3	54.8

Employment by Industry: Charlotte-Concord-Gastonia, NC-SC, Selected Years, 2007–2017—*Continued*

(Numbers in thousands, not seasonally adjusted)

Industry and year	January	February	March	April	May	June	July	August	September	October	November	December	Annual average
Information													
2007	23.1	23.1	23.0	23.0	23.1	23.5	23.4	23.4	23.3	23.2	23.5	23.6	23.3
2008	23.0	23.2	23.3	23.2	23.3	23.4	23.3	23.3	23.2	23.5	23.5	23.6	23.3
2009	22.9	22.7	22.7	22.8	22.7	22.6	22.5	22.3	22.2	22.1	22.2	22.3	22.5
2010	22.2	22.1	22.3	22.2	22.3	22.5	22.4	22.5	22.6	22.6	22.8	22.8	22.4
2011	22.6	22.6	22.6	22.7	22.5	22.8	22.9	23.0	23.2	23.1	23.2	23.1	22.9
2012	23.0	23.1	23.2	23.1	23.1	23.3	23.4	23.3	23.2	23.1	23.2	23.2	23.2
2013	23.3	23.3	23.3	23.3	23.7	23.8	23.9	24.0	23.9	24.1	24.2	24.5	23.8
2014	24.2	24.3	24.3	24.1	24.4	24.6	24.7	24.7	24.7	25.1	25.3	25.5	24.7
2015	25.6	25.7	25.8	25.7	26.1	26.3	26.7	26.7	26.4	26.6	26.7	26.9	26.3
2016	27.1	27.1	26.9	27.2	27.3	27.6	27.6	27.5	27.3	27.5	27.7	27.8	27.4
2017	27.5	27.5	27.8	27.2	27.4	27.7	28.0	27.9	28.0	28.1	28.2	28.5	27.8
Financial Activities													
2007	81.7	82.3	82.5	82.7	83.0	83.2	82.8	82.7	82.3	82.7	82.6	82.7	82.6
2008	80.3	80.5	80.6	81.3	80.6	80.8	79.7	79.7	78.9	78.8	78.2	78.7	79.8
2009	76.9	76.7	76.5	75.7	75.8	75.3	75.0	74.5	73.5	73.5	73.5	73.6	75.0
2010	73.1	73.7	73.9	73.5	73.7	74.1	74.0	74.2	74.7	75.2	75.5	75.6	74.3
2011	75.7	76.1	76.1	75.3	75.7	76.2	75.3	75.5	75.1	75.8	76.0	76.3	75.8
2012	75.8	76.2	76.4	76.0	76.2	76.6	76.5	76.6	76.5	76.8	77.2	77.5	76.5
2013	77.1	77.4	77.1	78.0	78.2	78.6	78.8	78.7	78.5	78.8	78.9	79.0	78.3
2014	79.2	79.1	79.4	79.6	79.9	80.6	81.2	81.3	81.3	81.7	82.1	82.4	80.7
2015	82.1	82.4	82.7	82.8	83.3	84.0	84.7	84.6	84.5	85.9	86.2	86.3	84.1
2016	86.3	86.6	87.1	87.4	87.6	88.2	89.1	89.4	89.0	89.4	89.5	89.9	88.3
2017	90.1	90.3	90.5	90.6	91.0	91.9	92.4	92.7	92.3	92.7	92.6	93.7	91.7
Professional and Business Services													
2007	139.9	141.8	144.8	147.1	149.0	150.0	149.8	151.7	152.1	154.2	153.6	152.8	148.9
2008	148.3	151.0	151.9	151.7	153.2	153.5	152.0	152.5	151.8	150.6	147.1	145.3	150.7
2009	140.5	140.3	139.4	138.3	137.4	136.8	137.2	137.5	138.2	140.0	140.5	140.9	138.9
2010	137.6	138.7	141.5	143.8	144.4	145.3	146.3	147.7	148.5	151.3	151.2	151.5	145.7
2011	148.0	152.3	153.8	155.7	155.0	155.9	155.5	156.1	158.1	157.8	158.0	157.6	155.3
2012	154.8	156.4	158.3	159.0	159.9	160.6	158.5	159.5	160.3	162.5	161.3	160.7	159.3
2013	155.8	157.9	159.3	162.1	162.7	163.9	164.4	166.2	166.8	169.9	170.5	170.0	164.1
2014	168.5	169.4	172.3	175.8	176.4	177.5	177.9	178.5	179.1	181.5	181.1	182.3	176.7
2015	178.4	181.1	181.5	182.2	184.0	184.9	185.8	186.8	188.3	190.4	191.2	191.2	185.5
2016	186.7	187.7	190.3	194.0	193.9	195.3	196.8	197.3	197.7	198.8	199.2	197.9	194.6
2017	195.3	197.3	200.0	201.0	201.5	202.8	203.1	204.0	202.5	204.9	203.7	202.7	201.6
Education and Health Services													
2007	92.3	93.4	94.0	94.4	94.6	95.0	94.8	95.4	95.9	97.3	97.1	97.7	95.2
2008	95.4	96.4	96.8	96.4	96.6	96.5	96.2	97.3	97.8	99.9	100.6	101.1	97.6
2009	98.9	99.5	99.3	99.6	99.8	99.4	98.8	99.7	99.8	100.7	101.2	101.1	99.8
2010	99.7	100.4	100.4	101.7	101.8	100.9	101.1	101.7	101.8	103.5	104.0	104.1	101.8
2011	103.2	104.3	104.4	104.2	103.8	103.0	102.8	103.6	104.9	105.6	106.1	106.6	104.4
2012	105.3	106.5	106.3	105.4	105.8	105.2	104.6	105.1	106.0	108.1	108.3	108.9	106.3
2013	106.2	107.7	107.2	107.3	107.8	107.2	106.2	107.1	108.3	108.5	109.4	110.0	107.7
2014	108.3	108.8	109.5	109.3	109.9	109.1	109.1	110.1	111.1	112.4	113.1	113.4	110.3
2015	112.4	113.4	113.6	113.7	114.5	113.4	112.9	112.7	113.7	116.0	116.4	116.6	114.1
2016	115.1	115.7	116.2	117.0	116.8	115.7	116.4	116.9	118.2	119.5	119.4	119.3	117.2
2017	119.3	120.5	120.0	120.1	120.6	119.9	119.0	120.0	121.6	123.2	122.8	124.6	121.0
Leisure and Hospitality													
2007	96.7	97.6	100.8	103.0	106.3	107.3	105.9	105.8	104.3	104.5	103.3	103.4	103.2
2008	100.5	102.0	104.7	105.9	108.7	109.6	109.8	110.0	109.0	108.1	105.7	105.7	106.6
2009	98.9	99.5	101.3	102.3	105.4	105.9	105.2	104.7	103.7	101.3	99.2	98.3	102.1
2010	95.4	95.7	98.2	100.9	104.1	106.0	104.9	104.8	104.3	103.2	101.7	100.5	101.6
2011	97.0	97.9	101.2	103.6	106.6	109.2	108.1	108.6	107.4	105.9	104.9	104.1	104.5
2012	101.6	102.2	106.4	108.4	112.4	114.2	114.6	114.4	112.2	111.3	110.1	109.5	109.8
2013	107.1	107.8	110.7	112.4	116.3	119.3	117.9	117.7	115.2	115.3	113.4	114.4	114.0
2014	112.3	111.2	115.1	118.1	122.3	124.3	123.1	123.0	120.7	120.3	118.0	117.7	118.8
2015	115.9	117.1	119.3	121.3	126.7	130.3	129.6	128.4	125.5	126.0	124.0	125.8	124.2
2016	122.9	123.9	127.1	130.0	133.7	136.5	134.7	134.5	132.0	132.9	130.6	129.3	130.7
2017	126.7	128.1	131.4	133.7	139.5	142.3	141.6	142.5	137.4	137.4	136.8	137.9	136.3

Employment by Industry: Charlotte-Concord-Gastonia, NC-SC, Selected Years, 2007–2017—*Continued*

(Numbers in thousands, not seasonally adjusted)

Industry and year	January	February	March	April	May	June	July	August	September	October	November	December	Annual average
Other Services													
2007	36.5	36.9	37.5	36.4	36.8	37.2	37.1	37.1	36.9	37.8	37.8	38.0	37.2
2008	36.4	36.4	36.4	35.6	36.3	36.2	36.0	36.0	35.3	35.0	34.7	34.5	35.7
2009	33.2	33.3	33.2	32.7	32.7	32.6	32.5	32.3	31.7	31.3	31.3	30.9	32.3
2010	30.5	30.6	31.0	30.8	31.2	31.5	31.6	31.8	32.0	32.2	32.3	32.4	31.5
2011	32.4	32.8	33.0	33.1	33.3	33.6	33.5	33.6	33.3	33.5	33.5	33.6	33.3
2012	33.3	33.4	33.8	34.0	34.4	34.5	35.0	35.1	35.2	35.2	35.4	35.6	34.6
2013	35.6	36.1	37.0	37.0	36.6	36.6	36.6	36.6	36.5	36.4	37.2	36.4	36.6
2014	36.1	35.9	36.7	37.1	37.2	37.2	37.4	37.5	37.3	37.4	37.3	37.5	37.1
2015	36.9	37.2	37.3	37.9	38.4	38.4	38.6	38.6	38.2	38.2	38.2	38.3	38.0
2016	38.1	38.2	38.4	38.6	39.1	39.0	39.1	39.0	39.0	39.2	39.1	39.0	38.8
2017	39.3	39.4	39.7	39.6	39.9	40.1	39.9	39.7	39.4	40.0	40.8	41.3	39.9
Government													
2007	132.0	133.6	134.1	133.0	134.0	123.8	104.9	126.2	134.2	136.7	138.3	138.6	130.8
2008	137.7	139.2	139.9	139.9	140.5	132.5	112.3	133.5	143.1	142.9	144.4	145.0	137.6
2009	142.9	143.6	144.3	144.7	144.2	138.1	116.0	137.6	142.5	143.1	144.0	144.0	140.4
2010	144.7	146.0	147.2	147.6	151.5	139.6	116.9	136.2	139.8	145.7	146.4	146.6	142.4
2011	143.4	144.6	145.5	146.1	146.1	136.8	116.1	137.7	140.4	144.6	147.5	147.1	141.3
2012	144.9	146.2	147.6	148.2	149.1	133.7	117.8	137.6	143.7	150.0	151.4	151.0	143.4
2013	148.8	149.8	151.1	151.2	151.7	136.4	120.4	137.4	143.4	151.7	152.8	152.4	145.6
2014	149.4	149.9	150.9	152.2	152.8	140.7	122.8	138.7	144.4	152.5	153.7	153.2	146.8
2015	150.2	151.4	152.2	152.7	153.0	145.1	125.3	140.5	145.9	153.2	154.4	154.8	148.2
2016	149.4	150.8	152.0	152.0	152.6	146.5	129.4	141.8	152.7	154.4	155.7	155.2	149.4
2017	153.0	154.4	155.4	156.1	156.0	150.0	132.2	144.6	155.2	162.9	164.0	163.3	153.9

Employment by Industry: Orlando-Kissimmee-Sanford, FL, Selected Years, 2007–2017

(Numbers in thousands, not seasonally adjusted)

Industry and year	January	February	March	April	May	June	July	August	September	October	November	December	Annual average
Total Nonfarm													
2007	1,072.1	1,082.0	1,087.6	1,087.7	1,089.1	1,076.0	1,067.9	1,081.1	1,080.3	1,084.3	1,095.5	1,096.4	1,083.3
2008	1,077.6	1,087.8	1,091.3	1,080.1	1,077.6	1,060.6	1,051.2	1,059.1	1,052.5	1,048.5	1,046.4	1,044.5	1,064.8
2009	1,018.0	1,017.9	1,015.5	1,009.5	1,005.5	988.6	977.7	985.9	984.7	986.6	992.9	993.5	998.0
2010	976.2	982.4	989.9	995.9	1,000.9	989.1	984.3	994.1	989.9	998.1	1,004.4	1,005.7	992.6
2011	989.5	996.1	1,002.5	1,007.5	1,007.0	995.5	993.8	1,004.3	1,009.7	1,012.3	1,022.8	1,025.0	1,005.5
2012	1,011.2	1,021.2	1,031.0	1,030.6	1,031.2	1,021.2	1,018.0	1,029.0	1,031.5	1,043.5	1,056.3	1,056.9	1,031.8
2013	1,037.2	1,051.3	1,058.9	1,059.7	1,063.8	1,056.8	1,054.1	1,069.5	1,069.4	1,079.1	1,092.8	1,094.8	1,065.6
2014	1,082.5	1,091.5	1,100.4	1,103.0	1,109.0	1,100.6	1,098.5	1,114.2	1,113.8	1,122.1	1,134.0	1,137.7	1,108.9
2015	1,122.2	1,135.1	1,142.1	1,150.1	1,156.3	1,148.7	1,148.3	1,162.1	1,164.2	1,177.7	1,190.8	1,196.5	1,157.8
2016	1,178.4	1,189.7	1,196.5	1,203.4	1,206.6	1,195.5	1,200.2	1,213.0	1,217.6	1,224.9	1,238.4	1,242.0	1,208.9
2017	1,227.4	1,238.0	1,243.1	1,244.7	1,246.9	1,238.5	1,234.6	1,247.0	1,233.2	1,256.7	1,271.4	1,284.2	1,247.1
Total Private													
2007	955.0	963.4	968.6	968.0	969.7	967.9	962.0	961.9	960.4	965.2	976.3	978.3	966.4
2008	959.9	969.2	971.6	960.3	957.6	952.8	945.6	941.4	933.7	929.7	926.9	925.1	947.8
2009	899.7	898.6	896.1	890.2	887.9	881.9	872.4	870.4	868.3	869.5	875.2	877.0	882.3
2010	859.6	865.6	872.9	878.0	880.2	881.1	877.8	877.5	873.6	880.4	886.6	889.2	876.9
2011	873.2	878.1	884.3	890.1	890.4	889.8	889.1	889.4	893.4	894.7	904.7	907.8	890.4
2012	893.6	901.8	911.1	912.4	914.0	914.7	912.0	911.9	914.3	924.9	936.9	938.5	915.5
2013	919.5	931.9	939.1	939.8	944.8	948.9	947.0	951.1	951.5	960.5	973.6	976.3	948.7
2014	963.6	972.3	981.0	982.6	989.3	991.8	990.2	994.7	994.6	1,000.8	1,012.5	1,016.3	990.8
2015	1,001.0	1,013.1	1,019.6	1,027.4	1,034.9	1,038.3	1,037.9	1,040.2	1,043.0	1,054.4	1,067.3	1,073.6	1,037.6
2016	1,054.9	1,065.8	1,071.9	1,078.3	1,081.8	1,081.1	1,085.6	1,087.8	1,092.7	1,099.0	1,111.4	1,115.8	1,085.5
2017	1,102.0	1,111.4	1,116.2	1,117.6	1,121.1	1,123.2	1,118.1	1,121.3	1,107.7	1,130.2	1,143.8	1,156.5	1,122.4
Goods Producing													
2007	132.2	131.9	132.4	130.9	130.9	131.1	129.6	129.9	129.4	127.9	127.5	126.0	130.0
2008	121.8	121.8	121.2	118.4	117.7	116.9	115.3	114.2	113.5	110.7	108.3	106.2	115.5
2009	102.8	100.8	99.4	95.4	94.3	93.7	91.3	90.2	88.9	88.0	87.4	86.5	93.2
2010	84.7	85.1	85.7	86.1	86.2	86.9	87.0	86.4	86.0	85.4	84.6	84.3	85.7
2011	83.1	83.2	83.0	83.0	83.0	82.9	83.2	83.4	83.7	83.3	83.4	83.4	83.2
2012	82.6	83.1	83.6	82.3	83.0	83.3	84.1	84.8	85.2	85.9	86.4	85.8	84.2
2013	85.0	86.1	86.9	87.9	88.7	89.3	90.1	90.9	91.4	91.7	92.2	92.3	89.4
2014	92.0	93.1	93.3	94.1	94.8	95.5	96.1	96.9	97.3	97.8	98.0	97.5	95.5
2015	97.0	98.1	98.7	99.7	100.7	101.8	102.8	103.0	103.5	105.5	106.0	106.6	102.0
2016	106.2	107.4	107.7	108.9	109.6	110.9	112.2	112.7	113.4	112.6	113.6	113.8	110.8
2017	113.7	115.5	116.6	116.5	117.4	119.0	119.3	119.9	117.7	120.6	121.7	122.2	118.3
Service-Providing													
2007	939.9	950.1	955.2	956.8	958.2	944.9	938.3	951.2	950.9	956.4	968.0	970.4	953.4
2008	955.8	966.0	970.1	961.7	959.9	943.7	935.9	944.9	939.0	937.8	938.1	938.3	949.3
2009	915.2	917.1	916.1	914.1	911.2	894.9	886.4	895.7	895.8	898.6	905.5	907.0	904.8
2010	891.5	897.3	904.2	909.8	914.7	902.2	897.3	907.7	903.9	912.7	919.8	921.4	906.9
2011	906.4	912.9	919.5	924.5	924.0	912.6	910.6	920.9	926.0	929.0	939.4	941.6	922.3
2012	928.6	938.1	947.4	948.3	948.2	937.9	933.9	944.2	946.3	957.6	969.9	971.1	947.6
2013	952.2	965.2	972.0	971.8	975.1	967.5	964.0	978.6	978.0	987.4	1,000.6	1,002.5	976.2
2014	990.5	998.4	1,007.1	1,008.9	1,014.2	1,005.1	1,002.4	1,017.3	1,016.5	1,024.3	1,036.0	1,040.2	1,013.4
2015	1,025.2	1,037.0	1,043.4	1,050.4	1,055.6	1,046.9	1,045.5	1,059.1	1,060.7	1,072.2	1,084.8	1,089.9	1,055.9
2016	1,072.2	1,082.3	1,088.8	1,094.5	1,097.0	1,084.6	1,088.0	1,100.3	1,104.2	1,112.3	1,124.8	1,128.2	1,098.1
2017	1,113.7	1,122.5	1,126.5	1,128.2	1,129.5	1,119.5	1,115.3	1,127.1	1,115.5	1,136.1	1,149.7	1,162.0	1,128.8
Mining, Logging, and Construction													
2007	87.7	87.3	87.6	86.0	86.1	86.2	84.9	85.3	84.9	83.7	83.1	81.6	85.4
2008	78.1	78.1	77.6	74.9	74.4	73.6	72.4	71.8	71.2	68.7	66.7	65.0	72.7
2009	62.5	60.9	59.8	56.5	55.5	54.8	53.0	52.0	50.9	50.1	49.4	48.8	54.5
2010	47.4	47.9	48.2	48.5	48.1	48.7	48.4	48.1	47.7	47.2	46.3	45.8	47.7
2011	44.9	44.9	44.8	44.7	44.8	44.9	45.3	45.5	45.8	45.6	45.6	45.6	45.2
2012	44.6	45.0	45.3	44.1	44.8	45.1	46.0	47.0	47.6	48.2	48.6	48.1	46.2
2013	47.6	48.5	49.3	49.8	50.5	51.0	51.8	52.7	52.9	53.2	53.5	53.6	51.2
2014	53.3	54.2	54.5	54.8	55.3	55.8	56.2	56.9	57.3	57.7	58.0	57.3	55.9
2015	57.0	57.9	58.3	59.0	59.9	60.8	61.7	62.1	62.5	63.6	64.2	64.7	61.0
2016	64.7	65.8	65.9	66.8	67.5	68.3	69.3	69.7	70.5	69.9	70.6	70.6	68.3
2017	70.6	71.9	72.9	72.7	73.6	74.6	74.5	75.1	73.5	74.8	75.6	75.8	73.8

Employment by Industry: Orlando-Kissimmee-Sanford, FL, Selected Years, 2007–2017—*Continued*

(Numbers in thousands, not seasonally adjusted)

Industry and year	January	February	March	April	May	June	July	August	September	October	November	December	Annual average
Manufacturing													
2007	44.5	44.6	44.8	44.9	44.8	44.9	44.7	44.6	44.5	44.2	44.4	44.4	44.6
2008	43.7	43.7	43.6	43.5	43.3	43.3	42.9	42.4	42.3	42.0	41.6	41.2	42.8
2009	40.3	39.9	39.6	38.9	38.8	38.9	38.3	38.2	38.0	37.9	38.0	37.7	38.7
2010	37.3	37.2	37.5	37.6	38.1	38.2	38.6	38.3	38.3	38.2	38.3	38.5	38.0
2011	38.2	38.3	38.2	38.3	38.2	38.0	37.9	37.9	37.9	37.7	37.8	37.8	38.0
2012	38.0	38.1	38.3	38.2	38.2	38.2	38.1	37.8	37.6	37.7	37.8	37.7	38.0
2013	37.4	37.6	37.6	38.1	38.2	38.3	38.3	38.2	38.5	38.5	38.7	38.7	38.2
2014	38.7	38.9	38.8	39.3	39.5	39.7	39.9	40.0	40.0	40.1	40.0	40.2	39.6
2015	40.0	40.2	40.4	40.7	40.8	41.0	41.1	40.9	41.0	41.9	41.8	41.9	41.0
2016	41.5	41.6	41.8	42.1	42.1	42.6	42.9	43.0	42.9	42.7	43.0	43.2	42.5
2017	43.1	43.6	43.7	43.8	43.8	44.4	44.8	44.8	44.2	45.8	46.1	46.4	44.5
Trade, Transportation, and Utilities													
2007	200.7	201.2	200.9	201.2	203.1	202.9	202.4	203.5	204.1	205.1	210.1	212.6	204.0
2008	205.7	205.1	204.7	201.9	201.3	200.4	199.0	198.6	197.5	196.3	198.6	199.9	200.8
2009	191.9	190.1	188.4	186.4	185.7	184.6	183.1	183.2	182.6	182.3	186.4	188.0	186.1
2010	182.6	182.9	182.7	183.9	184.6	185.1	185.0	185.8	185.1	187.2	192.7	195.5	186.1
2011	188.8	188.4	188.7	189.3	189.7	189.6	190.5	191.5	191.4	193.5	199.9	202.0	191.9
2012	195.9	194.9	196.1	195.7	196.4	196.3	196.6	196.9	196.5	198.4	205.8	207.5	198.1
2013	200.2	199.6	200.0	200.1	201.3	202.3	203.2	204.2	204.5	206.2	214.1	216.8	204.4
2014	209.6	209.7	210.5	209.7	210.1	210.5	210.8	211.8	211.6	213.5	221.4	224.4	212.8
2015	216.3	216.3	216.7	217.4	218.3	219.6	219.6	221.2	220.7	222.4	229.8	233.6	221.0
2016	223.8	223.4	224.2	224.7	225.7	225.6	226.1	227.2	227.7	229.5	237.1	240.7	228.0
2017	232.3	230.8	231.2	231.6	232.2	232.3	231.8	232.5	230.1	232.3	240.9	243.5	233.5
Wholesale Trade													
2007	46.6	47.2	47.1	47.1	47.3	47.2	47.2	47.1	47.2	47.6	47.6	47.8	47.3
2008	47.3	48.0	47.5	46.4	46.2	46.0	45.5	45.3	45.0	44.4	44.2	43.9	45.8
2009	42.4	42.5	41.6	41.0	40.7	40.5	39.9	39.7	39.5	39.2	39.0	39.0	40.4
2010	38.4	38.9	38.7	38.7	38.8	38.5	38.1	38.1	38.0	38.2	38.1	38.1	38.4
2011	38.5	38.6	38.6	38.4	38.5	38.4	38.4	38.3	38.3	38.3	38.4	38.6	38.4
2012	38.5	38.5	38.7	38.9	38.8	38.9	39.1	39.3	39.2	39.4	39.6	39.6	39.0
2013	39.2	39.6	39.7	39.8	39.9	39.9	39.9	40.0	40.3	40.6	41.0	41.1	40.1
2014	40.7	41.1	41.3	41.4	41.7	41.8	42.1	42.3	42.4	42.6	42.7	42.9	41.9
2015	42.8	43.0	43.1	43.2	43.5	43.5	43.5	43.6	43.6	43.4	43.7	44.0	43.4
2016	43.5	43.7	43.8	44.1	44.4	44.2	43.9	44.1	44.4	44.2	44.6	44.9	44.2
2017	44.1	44.3	44.7	44.8	45.0	45.1	45.2	45.2	45.1	44.1	44.5	44.5	44.7
Retail Trade													
2007	122.6	121.8	121.7	121.5	123.0	123.2	122.6	123.3	123.2	123.8	128.4	129.8	123.7
2008	124.5	123.2	123.3	121.6	121.3	121.1	120.6	120.7	120.2	120.0	122.6	123.4	121.9
2009	117.8	116.4	115.8	114.9	114.7	114.3	113.7	114.2	113.8	113.9	118.1	119.1	115.6
2010	114.9	114.3	114.3	115.5	116.0	117.0	117.3	118.1	117.5	119.4	124.6	126.7	118.0
2011	120.8	120.3	120.2	120.9	121.2	121.2	122.1	123.1	122.9	124.6	130.5	131.7	123.3
2012	126.6	125.5	126.3	125.9	126.7	126.5	126.7	126.9	126.8	128.2	135.1	136.3	128.1
2013	130.4	129.4	129.5	129.4	130.1	130.9	132.1	132.8	132.6	134.1	141.0	143.4	133.0
2014	137.3	136.8	137.1	136.5	136.6	136.9	136.7	137.3	137.1	138.5	145.5	147.2	138.6
2015	140.3	140.1	140.4	140.6	140.7	141.4	141.3	142.5	142.0	143.2	149.2	151.2	142.7
2016	143.6	143.1	143.3	143.4	143.8	143.9	144.5	145.4	145.4	147.0	153.5	155.1	146.0
2017	149.1	147.8	147.5	147.8	147.9	148.0	147.7	148.2	146.1	149.5	156.4	157.3	149.4
Transportation and Utilities													
2007	31.5	32.2	32.1	32.6	32.8	32.5	32.6	33.1	33.7	33.7	34.1	35.0	33.0
2008	33.9	33.9	33.9	33.9	33.8	33.3	32.9	32.6	32.3	31.9	31.8	32.6	33.1
2009	31.7	31.2	31.0	30.5	30.3	29.8	29.5	29.3	29.3	29.2	29.3	29.9	30.1
2010	29.3	29.7	29.7	29.7	29.8	29.6	29.6	29.6	29.6	29.6	30.0	30.7	29.7
2011	29.5	29.5	29.9	30.0	30.0	30.0	30.0	30.1	30.2	30.6	31.0	31.7	30.2
2012	30.8	30.9	31.1	30.9	30.9	30.9	30.8	30.7	30.5	30.8	31.1	31.6	30.9
2013	30.6	30.6	30.8	30.9	31.3	31.5	31.2	31.4	31.6	31.5	32.1	32.3	31.3
2014	31.6	31.8	32.1	31.8	31.8	31.8	32.0	32.2	32.1	32.4	33.2	34.3	32.3
2015	33.2	33.2	33.2	33.6	34.1	34.7	34.8	35.1	35.1	35.8	36.9	38.4	34.8
2016	36.7	36.6	37.1	37.2	37.5	37.5	37.7	37.7	37.9	38.3	39.0	40.7	37.8
2017	39.1	38.7	39.0	39.0	39.3	39.2	38.9	39.1	38.9	38.7	40.0	41.7	39.3

Employment by Industry: Orlando-Kissimmee-Sanford, FL, Selected Years, 2007–2017—*Continued*

(Numbers in thousands, not seasonally adjusted)

Industry and year	January	February	March	April	May	June	July	August	September	October	November	December	Annual average
Information													
2007	26.1	26.3	26.8	27.1	27.3	27.2	26.9	26.7	26.5	26.5	26.4	26.5	26.7
2008	26.5	26.7	26.7	26.4	26.4	26.4	26.3	26.2	25.5	25.9	25.9	25.8	26.2
2009	25.8	25.9	25.7	25.1	25.1	25.0	24.7	24.4	24.1	23.9	23.9	23.9	24.8
2010	23.9	23.8	23.9	23.8	23.6	23.7	23.7	23.9	23.7	23.7	23.9	23.9	23.8
2011	23.8	23.9	23.9	23.9	24.0	24.0	24.2	24.1	24.1	23.9	24.2	24.1	24.0
2012	23.9	23.9	23.8	23.6	23.5	23.5	23.6	23.5	23.3	23.6	23.5	23.5	23.6
2013	23.2	23.5	23.4	23.4	23.5	23.7	23.7	23.7	23.6	23.6	23.7	23.7	23.6
2014	23.7	23.6	23.8	23.7	23.9	24.1	23.9	23.8	23.7	23.8	24.2	24.2	23.9
2015	24.3	24.3	24.2	24.1	24.2	24.2	23.9	23.7	23.5	23.8	24.0	24.0	24.0
2016	24.0	24.0	23.9	24.0	24.1	24.0	24.3	24.3	24.0	24.1	24.4	24.3	24.1
2017	24.1	24.4	24.2	24.0	24.3	24.3	23.9	24.0	23.8	24.0	24.2	24.3	24.1
Financial Activities													
2007	70.3	70.9	71.1	70.6	70.8	71.4	70.9	70.8	70.5	70.5	70.6	70.9	70.8
2008	69.9	70.2	70.3	69.7	70.2	69.8	69.6	69.6	69.0	68.6	68.5	68.6	69.5
2009	67.3	67.1	66.8	66.4	66.2	66.1	65.4	65.3	64.6	64.9	65.2	65.2	65.9
2010	64.1	64.4	64.7	64.6	65.0	65.5	65.5	65.6	65.0	65.7	65.6	65.9	65.1
2011	65.5	65.8	66.1	65.7	65.7	65.5	65.9	65.9	66.1	65.8	66.0	66.2	65.9
2012	65.9	66.3	66.7	66.7	67.0	67.2	67.4	67.4	67.3	68.0	68.4	68.5	67.2
2013	68.0	68.5	68.8	69.1	69.3	69.9	69.8	70.2	70.1	70.8	71.1	71.1	69.7
2014	70.1	70.4	70.5	70.2	70.5	70.4	70.3	70.4	70.2	70.5	70.5	70.5	70.4
2015	70.0	70.2	70.5	70.5	70.9	71.0	71.1	71.3	71.3	71.9	72.5	72.7	71.2
2016	72.7	72.9	72.9	73.0	73.1	73.1	73.1	73.3	73.0	73.9	74.1	74.4	73.3
2017	73.3	73.6	73.7	74.0	74.3	74.6	74.5	74.6	74.4	75.5	76.4	77.4	74.7
Professional and Business Services													
2007	179.2	181.7	182.3	182.5	182.4	179.3	178.6	178.0	178.3	180.5	182.3	180.8	180.5
2008	178.4	182.5	181.4	179.3	177.9	175.6	174.3	174.2	174.4	175.1	173.1	171.6	176.5
2009	166.7	166.5	165.3	164.0	165.6	163.1	160.3	161.0	163.0	163.0	165.1	164.3	164.2
2010	161.3	161.6	163.0	163.7	163.4	162.2	159.9	160.0	159.7	159.9	159.6	159.0	161.1
2011	157.4	158.8	159.4	161.7	161.8	161.5	160.5	161.4	163.6	164.0	166.1	165.8	161.8
2012	164.7	167.8	169.8	169.7	170.3	168.8	166.1	166.9	168.1	172.0	173.6	173.2	169.3
2013	169.5	173.1	174.3	174.7	176.2	176.3	173.9	175.3	175.7	178.2	180.4	179.7	175.6
2014	179.5	180.7	182.1	182.0	184.6	184.1	183.0	184.6	183.8	185.3	186.7	185.6	183.5
2015	185.3	187.7	189.7	193.6	196.1	196.1	196.8	196.1	196.7	199.5	201.0	200.4	194.9
2016	198.3	200.4	202.9	205.2	205.5	206.2	208.8	209.4	210.3	213.5	214.7	214.4	207.5
2017	215.6	218.1	218.9	218.1	219.4	220.0	217.4	216.9	212.9	225.3	225.6	226.9	219.6
Education and Health Services													
2007	109.5	110.6	111.0	111.7	112.5	112.3	111.5	112.7	113.7	114.8	115.8	116.1	112.7
2008	115.5	116.3	116.6	116.6	117.2	116.3	115.3	116.0	116.2	116.9	117.0	117.4	116.4
2009	116.0	116.8	117.8	117.7	118.1	117.9	118.0	118.3	118.8	120.2	121.1	121.4	118.5
2010	120.0	120.2	120.7	121.3	121.7	120.8	120.2	120.7	120.3	121.5	122.0	121.1	120.9
2011	121.1	121.9	122.2	123.4	123.6	122.6	122.9	123.6	124.6	124.9	125.6	125.9	123.5
2012	124.3	125.1	125.8	128.4	128.5	127.9	127.6	128.3	129.3	130.5	130.9	131.1	128.1
2013	129.7	130.9	131.4	131.4	131.6	130.6	129.2	131.3	131.6	132.6	133.4	133.3	131.4
2014	132.3	133.5	134.2	135.1	136.0	134.7	133.5	135.8	136.8	138.2	139.2	139.8	135.8
2015	139.1	140.6	141.4	142.7	143.8	142.7	141.1	143.2	144.5	146.1	146.8	146.8	143.2
2016	145.7	146.9	147.1	148.5	148.7	146.9	146.4	147.6	149.2	150.2	150.9	151.4	148.3
2017	150.6	151.4	151.5	152.2	152.2	150.4	149.5	152.0	151.1	153.2	154.1	154.7	151.9
Leisure and Hospitality													
2007	188.0	191.1	193.9	194.7	193.5	194.8	194.2	193.0	190.8	193.1	197.1	199.3	193.6
2008	196.9	201.2	205.0	203.4	202.5	203.6	202.6	200.3	195.4	194.6	194.6	195.0	199.6
2009	189.1	191.3	192.3	194.7	192.8	191.9	190.4	189.1	187.4	186.4	187.7	189.3	190.2
2010	184.7	189.2	193.6	195.7	196.8	198.0	197.7	196.6	195.5	198.6	199.9	201.4	195.6
2011	195.7	198.2	202.8	205.1	204.9	206.5	205.4	203.7	204.5	204.2	204.8	206.1	203.5
2012	202.2	206.4	210.7	211.2	210.5	212.6	211.7	209.3	209.8	211.3	213.1	213.5	210.2
2013	208.7	214.9	218.8	217.4	218.3	220.7	221.1	219.5	218.5	221.1	222.1	222.6	218.6
2014	219.2	223.9	229.0	230.1	231.4	234.6	234.9	233.5	233.0	233.2	233.8	235.4	231.0
2015	229.8	236.3	238.6	239.0	240.0	242.0	241.6	240.3	241.2	243.1	244.6	246.6	240.3
2016	240.9	247.0	248.9	249.6	250.6	250.2	250.7	249.5	251.1	251.5	252.4	252.4	249.6
2017	248.5	253.6	256.4	257.4	257.5	258.8	258.0	257.6	254.4	256.2	256.6	262.9	256.5

Employment by Industry: Orlando-Kissimmee-Sanford, FL, Selected Years, 2007–2017—*Continued*

(Numbers in thousands, not seasonally adjusted)

Industry and year	January	February	March	April	May	June	July	August	September	October	November	December	Annual average
Other Services													
2007	49.0	49.7	50.2	49.3	49.2	48.9	47.9	47.3	47.1	46.8	46.5	46.1	48.2
2008	45.2	45.4	45.7	44.6	44.4	43.8	43.2	42.3	42.2	41.6	40.9	40.6	43.3
2009	40.1	40.1	40.4	40.5	40.1	39.6	39.2	38.9	38.9	38.8	38.4	38.4	39.5
2010	38.3	38.4	38.6	38.9	38.9	38.9	38.8	38.5	38.3	38.4	38.3	38.1	38.5
2011	37.8	37.9	38.2	38.0	37.7	37.2	36.5	35.8	35.4	35.1	34.7	34.3	36.6
2012	34.1	34.3	34.6	34.8	34.8	35.1	34.9	34.8	34.8	35.2	35.2	35.4	34.8
2013	35.2	35.3	35.5	35.8	35.9	36.1	36.0	36.0	36.1	36.3	36.6	36.8	36.0
2014	37.2	37.4	37.6	37.7	38.0	37.9	37.7	37.9	38.2	38.5	38.7	38.9	38.0
2015	39.2	39.6	39.8	40.4	40.9	40.9	41.0	41.4	41.6	42.1	42.6	42.9	41.0
2016	43.3	43.8	44.3	44.4	44.5	44.2	44.0	43.8	44.0	43.7	44.2	44.4	44.1
2017	43.9	44.0	43.7	43.8	43.8	43.8	43.7	43.8	43.3	43.1	44.3	44.6	43.8
Government													
2007	117.1	118.6	119.0	119.7	119.4	108.1	105.9	119.2	119.9	119.1	119.2	118.1	116.9
2008	117.7	118.6	119.7	119.8	120.0	107.8	105.6	117.7	118.8	118.8	119.5	119.4	117.0
2009	118.3	119.3	119.4	119.3	117.6	106.7	105.3	115.5	116.4	117.1	117.7	116.5	115.8
2010	116.6	116.8	117.0	117.9	120.7	108.0	106.5	116.6	116.3	117.7	117.8	116.5	115.7
2011	116.3	118.0	118.2	117.4	116.6	105.7	104.7	114.9	116.3	117.6	118.1	117.2	115.1
2012	117.6	119.4	119.9	118.2	117.2	106.5	106.0	117.1	117.2	118.6	119.4	118.4	116.3
2013	117.7	119.4	119.8	119.9	119.0	107.9	107.1	118.4	117.9	118.6	119.2	118.5	117.0
2014	118.9	119.2	119.4	120.4	119.7	108.8	108.3	119.5	119.2	121.3	121.5	121.4	118.1
2015	121.2	122.0	122.5	122.7	121.4	110.4	110.4	121.9	121.2	123.3	123.5	122.9	120.3
2016	123.5	123.9	124.6	125.1	124.8	114.4	114.6	125.2	124.9	125.9	127.0	126.2	123.3
2017	125.4	126.6	126.9	127.1	125.8	115.3	116.5	125.7	125.5	126.5	127.6	127.7	124.7

Employment by Industry: San Antonio-New Braunfels, TX, Selected Years, 2007–2017

(Numbers in thousands, not seasonally adjusted)

Industry and year	January	February	March	April	May	June	July	August	September	October	November	December	Annual average
Total Nonfarm													
2007	818.3	829.4	835.8	839.8	847.7	850.1	844.4	847.5	851.0	852.1	858.5	862.7	844.8
2008	845.8	855.9	861.0	865.9	870.7	871.4	863.0	864.5	864.6	866.3	867.6	866.0	863.6
2009	842.5	847.3	848.4	849.9	851.9	853.0	842.8	842.2	843.2	847.7	851.6	852.6	847.8
2010	836.3	844.4	851.2	855.6	863.0	862.7	851.5	853.2	853.7	861.0	862.6	864.7	855.0
2011	849.7	856.9	865.1	870.9	874.3	875.6	871.4	873.5	876.2	877.5	880.5	883.1	871.2
2012	867.8	876.2	883.5	888.3	893.9	898.7	891.6	898.5	899.8	903.9	909.1	912.1	893.6
2013	894.8	905.9	912.0	917.6	922.6	928.6	924.4	926.6	929.1	932.4	938.4	938.9	922.6
2014	923.6	932.6	940.2	948.3	955.2	960.7	955.8	958.1	959.6	969.6	974.8	976.1	954.6
2015	962.4	972.0	975.9	981.7	988.1	991.1	987.3	988.5	992.8	999.0	1005.1	1005.5	987.5
2016	993.4	1001.7	1006.0	1011.9	1015.6	1017.6	1016.0	1018.6	1022.9	1025.8	1033.0	1034.1	1016.4
2017	1020.1	1025.9	1031.4	1033.3	1037.3	1044.2	1037.7	1039.3	1044.4	1049.8	1051.9	1056.3	1039.3
Total Private													
2007	668.2	677.0	682.9	686.6	694.1	700.4	699.4	701.7	698.3	698.5	703.5	706.7	693.1
2008	691.3	699.0	703.6	708.4	712.7	715.4	713.3	713.7	709.6	706.3	707.0	705.9	707.2
2009	683.9	686.1	686.9	686.5	689.3	692.7	688.9	688.3	683.4	683.6	687.0	688.7	687.1
2010	675.5	680.6	686.5	689.8	694.5	698.5	695.8	695.5	690.7	694.1	695.8	698.5	691.3
2011	686.5	691.2	699.9	705.5	708.8	712.7	714.9	717.2	714.9	713.6	716.9	719.4	708.5
2012	706.7	713.1	720.3	724.6	730.6	739.1	737.6	742.3	737.8	739.7	744.8	747.8	732.0
2013	732.9	741.7	747.8	752.7	758.0	766.3	766.6	768.8	766.0	766.4	772.2	773.2	759.4
2014	760.3	767.1	774.6	782.4	789.7	797.6	798.0	799.9	795.3	801.4	806.0	807.9	790.0
2015	795.6	803.4	807.5	812.8	819.1	825.7	826.8	827.6	824.3	829.1	833.5	834.2	820.0
2016	823.1	830.1	834.5	841.7	845.0	849.4	852.9	855.0	852.4	854.5	860.7	861.8	846.8
2017	848.9	853.0	858.1	860.7	864.5	874.0	872.9	873.9	872.6	876.2	877.8	882.2	867.9
Goods Producing													
2007	99.3	100.7	101.1	101.2	102.4	104.1	103.8	104.2	103.9	104.6	104.6	105.2	102.9
2008	103.7	104.5	104.9	105.1	105.6	106.2	104.9	105.0	104.1	103.4	102.5	101.1	104.3
2009	98.1	97.1	96.3	95.8	95.5	95.1	94.9	94.3	93.3	92.7	92.1	92.1	94.8
2010	91.2	90.6	90.9	91.6	91.6	91.7	91.9	91.5	90.7	91.0	90.5	90.5	91.1
2011	89.0	89.2	90.0	90.7	90.8	91.6	92.1	91.9	91.4	91.0	90.8	90.4	90.7
2012	90.0	90.4	90.7	91.4	91.8	93.0	93.4	93.8	93.4	93.7	94.0	93.9	92.5
2013	93.0	93.3	94.2	95.2	95.7	96.9	97.5	97.7	97.4	97.2	97.7	97.4	96.1
2014	96.8	97.6	98.2	99.2	100.1	101.3	101.8	102.5	102.5	104.0	104.5	104.9	101.1
2015	103.8	104.6	104.1	104.9	105.2	106.0	106.3	106.0	105.1	105.7	105.4	105.3	105.2
2016	104.5	105.1	104.8	104.7	104.6	104.7	105.7	105.6	105.6	105.1	105.1	105.3	105.1
2017	104.6	105.5	105.8	106.0	106.5	107.9	108.3	109.2	109.3	109.8	110.2	111.4	107.9
Service-Providing													
2007	719.0	728.7	734.7	738.6	745.3	746.0	740.6	743.3	747.1	747.5	753.9	757.5	741.9
2008	742.1	751.4	756.1	760.8	765.1	765.2	758.1	759.5	760.5	762.9	765.1	764.9	759.3
2009	744.4	750.2	752.1	754.1	756.4	757.9	747.9	747.9	749.9	755.0	759.5	760.5	753.0
2010	745.1	753.8	760.3	764.0	771.4	771.0	759.6	761.7	763.0	770.0	772.1	774.2	763.9
2011	760.7	767.7	775.1	780.2	783.5	784.0	779.3	781.6	784.8	786.5	789.7	792.7	780.5
2012	777.8	785.8	792.8	796.9	802.1	805.7	798.2	804.7	806.4	810.2	815.1	818.2	801.2
2013	801.8	812.6	817.8	822.4	826.9	831.7	826.9	828.9	831.7	835.2	840.7	841.5	826.5
2014	826.8	835.0	842.0	849.1	855.1	859.4	854.0	855.6	857.1	865.6	870.3	871.2	853.4
2015	858.6	867.4	871.8	876.8	882.9	885.1	881.0	882.5	887.7	893.3	899.7	900.2	882.3
2016	888.9	896.6	901.2	907.2	911.0	912.9	910.3	913.0	917.3	920.7	927.9	928.8	911.3
2017	915.5	920.4	925.6	927.3	930.8	936.3	929.4	930.1	935.1	940.0	941.7	944.9	931.4
Mining and Logging													
2007	3.0	3.1	3.1	3.1	3.2	3.2	3.3	3.4	3.4	3.5	3.5	3.6	3.3
2008	3.4	3.4	3.4	3.5	3.6	3.7	3.7	3.7	3.6	3.6	3.5	3.4	3.5
2009	3.3	3.3	3.2	3.1	3.1	3.0	3.1	3.0	3.0	3.0	3.0	3.0	3.1
2010	3.0	3.0	2.9	3.0	3.0	3.1	3.0	3.0	3.0	3.0	2.9	2.9	3.0
2011	2.9	2.9	2.9	3.0	3.0	3.1	3.3	3.3	3.3	3.4	3.4	3.5	3.2
2012	3.5	3.6	3.7	4.0	4.0	4.2	4.4	4.5	4.6	4.7	4.8	4.9	4.2
2013	5.0	5.1	5.2	5.5	5.7	5.8	6.3	6.3	6.3	6.8	6.8	6.9	6.0
2014	7.5	7.7	7.9	8.2	8.4	8.7	8.6	8.8	8.9	9.3	9.5	9.6	8.6
2015	9.4	9.4	8.9	8.8	8.6	8.6	8.6	8.4	8.0	7.9	7.8	7.8	8.5
2016	7.5	7.4	7.2	7.0	6.8	6.7	6.8	6.7	6.7	6.7	6.9	7.0	7.0
2017	6.8	7.0	7.1	7.2	7.4	7.7	7.9	8.0	7.9	8.1	8.1	8.1	7.6

Employment by Industry: San Antonio-New Braunfels, TX, Selected Years, 2007–2017—*Continued*

(Numbers in thousands, not seasonally adjusted)

Industry and year	January	February	March	April	May	June	July	August	September	October	November	December	Annual average
Construction													
2007	47.1	48.3	49.2	49.1	50.0	51.3	51.2	51.6	51.4	51.9	52.0	52.6	50.5
2008	52.1	53.2	53.7	54.1	54.5	55.0	54.3	54.6	54.2	53.8	53.1	52.1	53.7
2009	50.1	49.5	49.1	49.0	48.9	49.0	48.8	48.5	47.6	46.7	46.0	45.6	48.2
2010	45.0	44.3	44.8	45.0	44.7	44.3	44.5	44.0	43.1	43.0	42.4	42.3	44.0
2011	40.8	41.0	41.9	42.2	42.2	42.5	42.7	42.5	41.9	41.4	41.1	40.5	41.7
2012	40.3	40.5	40.7	40.6	41.1	41.9	42.2	42.6	42.2	42.3	42.3	42.1	41.6
2013	41.6	41.9	42.9	43.4	43.8	44.7	44.8	45.0	44.7	44.5	44.6	44.2	43.8
2014	43.6	44.1	44.6	45.1	45.5	46.1	46.8	47.1	47.1	47.8	48.1	48.3	46.2
2015	47.8	48.4	48.5	49.2	49.7	50.2	50.9	51.1	50.5	50.6	50.3	50.1	49.8
2016	49.9	50.3	50.3	50.3	50.4	50.6	51.1	51.1	51.0	50.8	50.2	50.2	50.5
2017	50.0	50.4	50.6	50.7	51.0	51.6	51.6	52.0	52.2	53.4	53.6	55.0	51.8
Manufacturing													
2007	49.2	49.3	48.8	49.0	49.2	49.6	49.3	49.2	49.1	49.2	49.1	49.0	49.2
2008	48.2	47.9	47.8	47.5	47.5	47.5	46.9	46.7	46.3	46.0	45.9	45.6	47.0
2009	44.7	44.3	44.0	43.7	43.5	43.1	43.0	42.8	42.7	43.0	43.1	43.5	43.5
2010	43.2	43.3	43.2	43.6	43.9	44.3	44.4	44.5	44.6	45.0	45.2	45.3	44.2
2011	45.3	45.3	45.2	45.5	45.6	46.0	46.1	46.1	46.2	46.2	46.3	46.4	45.9
2012	46.2	46.3	46.3	46.8	46.7	46.9	46.8	46.7	46.6	46.7	46.9	46.9	46.7
2013	46.4	46.3	46.1	46.3	46.2	46.4	46.4	46.4	46.4	45.9	46.3	46.3	46.3
2014	45.7	45.8	45.7	45.9	46.2	46.5	46.4	46.6	46.5	46.9	46.9	47.0	46.3
2015	46.6	46.8	46.7	46.9	46.9	47.2	46.8	46.5	46.6	47.2	47.3	47.4	46.9
2016	47.1	47.4	47.3	47.4	47.4	47.4	47.8	47.8	47.9	47.6	48.0	48.1	47.6
2017	47.8	48.1	48.1	48.1	48.1	48.6	48.8	49.2	49.2	48.3	48.5	48.3	48.4
Trade, Transportation, and Utilities													
2007	149.4	148.3	149.3	149.3	149.9	150.1	151.4	152.3	151.5	152.1	155.7	157.6	151.4
2008	151.8	151.4	152.2	151.4	151.4	151.6	152.3	153.5	152.0	152.4	154.1	154.6	152.4
2009	148.1	146.6	145.7	145.3	145.2	145.6	145.1	146.0	145.2	145.4	147.5	148.5	146.2
2010	143.5	142.4	142.9	143.5	143.9	144.1	143.8	145.1	144.0	145.5	147.7	149.4	144.7
2011	145.3	144.1	144.9	145.8	146.0	146.5	147.0	148.2	147.7	149.1	152.0	153.7	147.5
2012	149.3	148.4	148.9	149.6	150.2	151.2	151.2	152.3	152.1	153.9	158.1	159.0	152.0
2013	154.1	154.0	154.0	155.1	156.0	156.8	157.3	159.0	159.1	161.0	164.6	166.7	158.1
2014	161.9	161.6	161.9	163.1	163.6	165.0	165.4	166.5	166.8	169.2	172.8	175.0	166.1
2015	169.7	168.9	169.3	170.5	171.6	172.7	173.4	174.3	174.9	176.7	179.6	181.3	173.6
2016	175.2	175.0	175.4	176.2	177.0	178.1	178.6	179.7	179.6	181.2	185.8	186.5	179.0
2017	181.5	179.8	179.5	180.4	180.8	181.5	181.1	182.7	182.3	182.8	186.2	187.1	182.1
Wholesale Trade													
2007	29.7	29.9	30.1	30.3	30.4	30.5	30.5	30.6	30.5	30.6	30.6	30.8	30.4
2008	30.2	30.4	30.4	30.3	30.4	30.5	30.5	30.7	30.5	30.4	30.3	30.1	30.4
2009	29.8	29.7	29.5	29.5	29.5	29.5	29.0	29.0	28.9	29.2	29.2	29.1	29.3
2010	29.0	29.0	28.4	29.3	29.4	29.5	29.4	29.5	29.5	29.8	29.7	29.7	29.4
2011	29.3	29.4	29.7	29.9	30.0	30.2	30.3	30.3	30.3	30.5	30.6	30.5	30.1
2012	30.6	30.7	30.9	31.0	31.1	31.4	31.4	31.6	31.3	31.6	31.5	31.5	31.2
2013	31.8	32.1	31.8	31.7	31.9	32.1	32.0	32.2	32.3	32.2	32.4	32.4	32.1
2014	32.2	32.6	32.7	32.7	32.8	33.1	33.2	33.3	33.5	33.8	34.1	34.1	33.2
2015	34.2	34.4	34.5	34.3	34.6	34.7	34.7	34.7	34.8	34.8	34.8	34.7	34.6
2016	34.8	34.9	34.9	35.0	35.1	35.1	35.4	35.5	35.5	35.5	35.5	35.6	35.2
2017	35.6	35.8	35.9	36.0	36.1	36.2	36.0	36.0	36.1	36.1	36.5	36.0	36.0
Retail Trade													
2007	97.3	95.8	96.4	96.1	96.7	96.7	98.1	98.8	98.2	98.9	102.5	104.1	98.3
2008	99.6	99.0	99.7	99.1	98.9	99.1	99.6	100.7	99.5	100.1	101.9	102.5	100.0
2009	97.0	95.9	95.2	95.3	95.3	95.7	95.9	96.9	96.2	96.1	98.1	99.3	96.4
2010	94.7	93.8	94.6	94.3	94.6	94.7	94.5	95.7	94.5	95.6	97.8	99.3	95.3
2011	95.6	94.3	94.7	95.3	95.3	95.5	95.8	96.8	96.0	97.2	99.9	101.2	96.5
2012	97.4	96.3	96.4	96.9	97.2	97.6	97.6	98.3	98.3	99.8	103.8	104.2	98.7
2013	99.3	99.0	99.2	100.1	100.6	100.9	101.6	102.8	102.7	104.5	107.3	108.8	102.2
2014	104.4	104.0	103.9	104.7	104.7	105.7	105.8	106.5	106.6	108.1	110.9	112.1	106.5
2015	107.4	106.8	106.9	108.3	108.9	109.6	110.1	110.9	111.3	113.0	115.2	116.1	110.4
2016	111.9	111.8	112.2	112.7	113.1	113.4	113.9	115.0	114.2	115.6	118.6	118.7	114.3
2017	115.0	113.6	113.5	114.2	114.2	114.2	114.2	115.1	114.1	114.0	116.7	117.3	114.7

Employment by Industry: San Antonio-New Braunfels, TX, Selected Years, 2007–2017—*Continued*

(Numbers in thousands, not seasonally adjusted)

Industry and year	January	February	March	April	May	June	July	August	September	October	November	December	Annual average
Transportation and Utilities													
2007	22.4	22.6	22.8	22.9	22.8	22.9	22.8	22.9	22.8	22.6	22.6	22.7	22.7
2008	22.0	22.0	22.1	22.0	22.1	22.0	22.2	22.1	22.0	21.9	21.9	22.0	22.0
2009	21.3	21.0	21.0	20.5	20.4	20.4	20.2	20.1	20.1	20.1	20.2	20.1	20.5
2010	19.8	19.6	19.9	19.9	19.9	19.9	19.9	19.9	20.0	20.1	20.2	20.4	20.0
2011	20.4	20.4	20.5	20.6	20.7	20.8	20.9	21.1	21.4	21.4	21.5	22.0	21.0
2012	21.3	21.4	21.6	21.7	21.9	22.2	22.2	22.4	22.5	22.5	22.8	23.3	22.2
2013	23.0	22.9	23.0	23.3	23.5	23.8	23.7	24.0	24.1	24.3	24.9	25.5	23.8
2014	25.3	25.0	25.3	25.7	26.1	26.2	26.4	26.7	26.7	27.3	27.8	28.8	26.4
2015	28.1	27.7	27.9	27.9	28.1	28.4	28.6	28.7	28.8	28.9	29.6	30.5	28.6
2016	28.5	28.3	28.3	28.5	28.8	29.6	29.3	29.2	29.9	30.1	31.7	32.2	29.5
2017	30.9	30.4	30.1	30.2	30.5	31.1	30.9	31.6	32.1	32.7	33.0	33.8	31.4
Information													
2007	22.0	22.2	22.0	21.8	22.0	22.0	22.0	21.8	21.6	21.6	21.8	21.8	21.9
2008	21.7	21.8	22.0	21.7	21.9	21.7	21.3	21.2	21.0	21.2	21.2	21.0	21.5
2009	20.8	20.8	20.9	20.5	20.2	19.8	19.4	19.2	18.8	18.8	18.8	18.6	19.7
2010	18.5	18.6	18.9	19.5	19.3	19.0	18.7	18.5	18.3	18.1	18.3	18.4	18.7
2011	18.6	18.6	19.0	19.3	19.3	18.9	19.7	19.5	19.3	19.3	19.5	19.7	19.2
2012	19.7	19.7	20.1	20.3	20.3	20.3	20.3	20.4	20.3	20.2	20.6	20.5	20.2
2013	20.4	20.6	20.9	21.5	21.6	21.6	21.6	21.5	21.2	21.2	21.7	21.5	21.3
2014	20.8	20.8	21.0	21.6	21.7	21.5	21.6	21.4	21.4	21.4	21.5	21.8	21.4
2015	21.0	21.0	21.1	21.5	22.0	22.0	21.6	21.4	21.0	21.3	21.4	21.5	21.4
2016	21.1	21.2	21.1	21.4	21.5	21.3	21.3	20.9	20.7	21.0	20.8	21.1	21.1
2017	20.6	20.9	20.9	21.5	21.3	21.1	20.5	20.6	20.3	20.4	20.2	20.5	20.7
Financial Activities													
2007	65.1	65.7	65.5	66.3	66.8	66.7	66.7	66.5	66.2	66.4	66.5	66.7	66.3
2008	66.0	66.3	66.1	67.9	68.2	68.0	68.4	67.8	67.5	67.2	66.8	67.4	67.3
2009	65.9	66.0	65.4	65.6	65.9	66.4	66.8	66.8	66.7	66.8	66.9	67.1	66.4
2010	66.8	67.4	67.6	67.5	68.2	68.8	68.6	68.5	68.1	69.0	69.4	69.8	68.3
2011	69.2	70.0	70.4	70.6	70.8	71.2	71.9	71.5	71.2	71.5	71.5	71.9	71.0
2012	71.9	72.3	72.5	72.8	73.2	73.8	74.4	74.6	74.6	75.2	75.7	76.3	73.9
2013	75.7	76.6	77.0	77.2	77.4	78.0	78.4	78.3	78.1	78.1	78.6	78.6	77.7
2014	78.4	78.7	78.8	79.5	80.0	81.0	81.1	81.3	81.2	81.6	82.1	82.4	80.5
2015	82.5	82.7	82.7	83.1	83.6	84.4	84.8	84.8	84.7	85.5	85.9	86.2	84.2
2016	86.4	87.0	87.0	87.1	87.4	88.1	88.3	88.0	87.6	88.1	88.7	89.0	87.7
2017	88.7	89.3	89.0	88.6	88.8	89.7	89.7	89.4	89.3	90.1	90.9	90.1	89.5
Professional and Business Services													
2007	104.6	105.9	106.6	108.1	109.1	109.6	108.7	109.4	109.5	110.2	110.8	110.8	108.6
2008	110.1	111.8	111.9	112.6	112.2	112.0	109.5	109.6	110.1	108.7	108.5	107.8	110.4
2009	104.1	103.7	103.8	102.8	102.4	103.1	100.9	102.0	101.5	102.9	104.5	105.8	103.1
2010	104.3	105.2	105.5	104.5	104.0	104.5	103.0	103.4	103.1	104.2	104.3	104.3	104.2
2011	103.6	104.7	105.8	106.1	105.4	105.7	105.3	106.8	107.8	107.1	107.3	108.2	106.2
2012	106.0	107.4	108.3	108.7	109.0	109.8	110.0	112.3	112.3	112.1	112.9	114.1	110.2
2013	111.4	113.0	113.8	113.5	113.0	114.4	114.6	115.3	116.3	116.4	117.3	117.3	114.7
2014	115.3	117.3	118.1	120.4	120.5	121.2	121.4	122.5	122.1	123.6	123.9	122.8	120.8
2015	122.9	124.3	124.9	125.0	124.2	124.2	124.4	124.4	125.0	126.5	126.9	126.9	125.0
2016	127.2	127.5	128.2	129.9	128.4	128.5	130.3	131.7	132.9	133.8	133.9	133.5	130.5
2017	132.4	132.5	133.1	132.6	132.5	134.3	134.4	134.9	137.8	136.1	136.1	138.0	134.6
Education and Health Services													
2007	110.3	112.7	113.4	113.1	113.9	113.7	113.1	114.3	115.6	116.2	117.0	117.4	114.2
2008	114.4	116.5	116.5	117.2	118.2	117.1	117.0	118.1	120.4	121.6	122.1	122.9	118.5
2009	119.9	121.8	122.1	122.8	123.7	123.1	123.3	123.4	125.0	126.4	126.8	127.1	123.8
2010	125.5	127.5	128.1	128.5	129.1	129.3	128.8	129.1	130.2	131.4	131.6	131.9	129.3
2011	130.1	131.1	131.9	133.1	133.4	132.7	132.7	134.2	136.1	136.2	136.5	137.1	133.8
2012	134.7	136.3	137.1	136.8	137.6	137.7	135.3	137.0	137.2	137.7	138.2	138.7	137.0
2013	135.8	137.5	138.2	138.8	139.5	139.4	138.2	139.9	140.8	141.0	141.5	142.2	139.4
2014	140.5	142.0	142.9	143.1	144.4	144.5	144.3	145.4	145.9	146.9	147.1	147.4	144.5
2015	146.1	148.0	148.7	149.5	150.0	149.5	148.9	150.4	151.0	151.8	153.3	153.9	150.1
2016	152.1	153.6	154.8	155.4	156.3	155.1	155.2	157.0	158.5	159.5	160.9	161.3	156.6
2017	159.9	160.5	160.9	160.2	160.5	160.8	159.7	160.5	161.7	163.3	162.3	163.1	161.1

Employment by Industry: San Antonio-New Braunfels, TX, Selected Years, 2007–2017—*Continued*

(Numbers in thousands, not seasonally adjusted)

Industry and year	January	February	March	April	May	June	July	August	September	October	November	December	Annual average
Leisure and Hospitality													
2007	89.2	92.6	95.9	97.5	100.2	102.9	102.5	102.0	98.9	96.3	95.6	95.9	97.5
2008	92.8	95.4	98.3	100.6	102.9	105.4	106.2	105.2	101.9	99.7	99.6	99.3	100.6
2009	95.7	98.4	101.0	101.9	104.1	106.2	105.3	103.8	100.9	98.6	97.9	97.5	100.9
2010	94.3	97.1	100.5	102.4	105.7	107.3	107.3	106.0	103.3	102.0	101.3	101.2	102.4
2011	98.9	101.3	105.6	107.3	110.2	112.2	112.1	111.3	108.1	106.4	106.0	105.6	107.1
2012	102.4	105.6	109.2	111.6	114.8	118.0	117.7	116.9	113.3	112.3	110.5	110.8	111.9
2013	108.4	112.0	114.8	116.4	119.3	122.5	122.0	120.6	117.2	115.6	114.8	114.2	116.5
2014	111.6	113.8	118.3	120.0	123.4	125.7	125.1	123.3	119.1	118.4	117.6	117.7	119.5
2015	114.1	117.9	120.6	122.8	126.4	129.4	130.1	129.2	126.2	125.2	124.3	123.0	124.1
2016	120.9	124.5	126.9	130.2	132.4	135.3	135.9	134.6	130.5	128.8	128.0	127.8	129.7
2017	124.7	127.4	131.7	133.7	136.0	139.7	140.4	138.3	133.9	135.7	133.5	134.0	134.1
Other Services													
2007	28.3	28.9	29.1	29.3	29.8	31.3	31.2	31.2	31.1	31.1	31.5	31.3	30.3
2008	30.8	31.3	31.7	31.9	32.3	33.4	33.7	33.3	32.6	32.1	32.2	31.8	32.3
2009	31.3	31.7	31.7	31.8	32.3	33.4	33.2	32.8	32.0	32.0	32.5	32.0	32.2
2010	31.4	31.8	32.1	32.3	32.7	33.8	33.7	33.4	33.0	32.9	32.7	33.0	32.7
2011	31.8	32.2	32.3	32.6	32.9	33.9	34.1	33.8	33.3	33.0	33.3	32.8	33.0
2012	32.7	33.0	33.5	33.4	33.7	35.3	35.3	35.0	34.6	34.6	34.8	34.5	34.2
2013	34.1	34.7	34.9	35.0	35.5	36.7	37.0	36.5	35.9	35.9	36.0	35.3	35.6
2014	35.0	35.3	35.4	35.5	36.0	37.4	37.3	37.0	36.3	36.3	36.5	35.9	36.2
2015	35.5	36.0	36.1	35.5	36.1	37.5	37.3	37.1	36.4	36.4	36.7	36.1	36.4
2016	35.7	36.2	36.3	36.8	37.4	38.3	37.6	37.5	37.0	37.0	37.5	37.3	37.1
2017	36.5	37.1	37.2	37.7	38.1	39.0	38.8	38.3	38.0	38.0	38.4	38.0	37.9
Government													
2007	150.1	152.4	152.9	153.2	153.6	149.7	145.0	145.8	152.7	153.6	155.0	156.0	151.7
2008	154.5	156.9	157.4	157.5	158.0	156.0	149.7	150.8	155.0	160.0	160.6	160.1	156.4
2009	158.6	161.2	161.5	163.4	162.6	160.3	153.9	153.9	159.8	164.1	164.6	163.9	160.7
2010	160.8	163.8	164.7	165.8	168.5	164.2	155.7	157.7	163.0	166.9	166.8	166.2	163.7
2011	163.2	165.7	165.2	165.4	165.5	162.9	156.5	156.3	161.3	163.9	163.6	163.7	162.8
2012	161.1	163.1	163.2	163.7	163.3	159.6	154.0	156.2	162.0	164.2	164.3	164.3	161.6
2013	161.9	164.2	164.2	164.9	164.6	162.3	157.8	157.8	163.1	166.0	166.2	165.7	163.2
2014	163.3	165.5	165.6	165.9	165.5	163.1	157.8	158.2	164.3	168.2	168.8	168.2	164.5
2015	166.8	168.6	168.4	168.9	169.0	165.4	160.5	160.9	168.5	169.9	171.6	171.3	167.5
2016	170.3	171.6	171.5	170.2	170.6	168.2	163.1	163.6	170.5	171.3	172.3	172.3	169.6
2017	171.2	172.9	173.3	172.6	172.8	170.2	164.8	165.4	171.8	173.6	174.1	174.1	171.4

Employment by Industry: Portland-Vancouver-Hillsboro, OR-WA, Selected Years, 2007–2017

(Numbers in thousands, not seasonally adjusted)

Industry and year	January	February	March	April	May	June	July	August	September	October	November	December	Annual average
Total Nonfarm													
2007	1,020.9	1,030.7	1,037.5	1,038.1	1,045.3	1,046.7	1,038.8	1,040.1	1,046.8	1,056.7	1,061.3	1,060.2	1,043.6
2008	1,035.0	1,041.9	1,045.6	1,049.6	1,052.5	1,050.6	1,044.3	1,041.7	1,046.8	1,045.7	1,039.6	1,027.3	1,043.4
2009	997.7	994.5	989.0	988.0	988.4	984.1	973.0	969.4	973.9	981.7	981.9	979.4	983.4
2010	958.7	962.9	967.5	975.7	981.9	983.9	973.6	974.2	980.9	995.6	997.7	997.2	979.2
2011	976.9	983.7	987.5	997.8	999.6	1,000.8	994.7	995.4	1,001.6	1,011.6	1,016.0	1,016.4	998.5
2012	998.0	1,004.7	1,009.7	1,016.2	1,022.5	1,024.5	1,016.3	1,018.4	1,022.6	1,034.4	1,037.6	1,036.2	1,020.1
2013	1,013.9	1,023.8	1,028.4	1,038.5	1,045.6	1,047.9	1,040.0	1,045.6	1,051.4	1,062.6	1,068.6	1,067.1	1,044.5
2014	1,050.0	1,053.6	1,061.6	1,069.4	1,075.4	1,078.9	1,071.5	1,076.1	1,083.3	1,092.6	1,098.0	1,101.0	1,076.0
2015	1,082.9	1,091.7	1,096.9	1,104.9	1,109.4	1,113.2	1,110.2	1,113.7	1,119.1	1,130.6	1,133.9	1,136.9	1,112.0
2016	1,117.8	1,128.2	1,133.0	1,142.7	1,146.1	1,148.0	1,141.2	1,144.7	1,151.3	1,159.9	1,165.1	1,162.7	1,145.1
2017	1,137.8	1,155.4	1,163.0	1,171.4	1,175.2	1,179.4	1,172.6	1,173.9	1,179.1	1,186.2	1,188.8	1,192.4	1,172.9
Total Private													
2007	879.8	887.8	893.4	893.8	898.8	900.2	904.1	908.5	910.7	911.4	914.3	913.3	901.3
2008	889.3	894.8	897.3	901.0	902.4	900.8	903.2	903.4	904.0	896.2	887.8	876.5	896.4
2009	848.7	843.5	837.2	836.1	835.7	833.0	832.0	831.2	833.6	832.4	831.0	829.5	835.3
2010	810.1	812.9	817.1	826.1	828.5	830.6	834.0	836.9	841.4	847.2	847.3	849.3	831.8
2011	828.6	834.4	838.3	846.9	848.2	851.9	857.6	860.6	864.5	864.8	867.6	869.7	852.8
2012	851.5	856.7	861.7	868.3	873.3	876.1	879.5	883.7	885.4	888.1	889.8	889.9	875.3
2013	868.8	876.5	881.3	891.0	897.2	899.3	905.2	911.6	914.8	916.9	921.0	920.3	900.3
2014	903.7	906.1	913.5	920.3	925.0	929.7	934.4	938.8	942.7	943.1	946.5	950.1	929.5
2015	932.5	939.6	944.6	952.1	956.2	961.4	969.2	972.4	975.3	977.4	979.2	982.8	961.9
2016	965.0	973.4	977.5	986.3	988.3	991.3	996.0	1,000.8	1,003.4	1,004.0	1,007.6	1,006.0	991.6
2017	983.8	998.1	1,004.2	1,012.0	1,015.1	1,019.4	1,023.0	1,025.7	1,028.0	1,028.4	1,029.3	1,033.3	1,016.7
Goods Producing													
2007	189.4	190.5	191.7	190.8	193.0	193.9	197.3	198.6	197.4	196.3	193.9	191.8	193.7
2008	187.3	187.5	187.4	187.0	187.9	188.7	190.3	189.8	188.7	184.3	180.3	174.9	186.2
2009	169.3	165.3	162.3	160.1	159.5	159.8	160.8	160.5	159.7	158.4	154.5	153.0	160.3
2010	149.3	148.8	149.7	150.7	151.9	153.5	156.8	157.6	157.7	158.3	155.8	155.0	153.8
2011	151.7	153.0	154.4	156.4	157.9	160.3	162.9	164.1	163.7	163.4	161.9	161.5	159.3
2012	158.9	159.4	160.2	161.1	163.5	165.4	168.3	169.3	168.0	167.3	165.0	163.3	164.1
2013	161.2	162.1	163.2	165.5	167.7	169.9	172.2	173.7	173.4	173.7	172.5	171.1	168.9
2014	170.4	170.1	172.1	172.7	174.2	176.0	178.2	178.7	178.0	176.7	175.4	175.2	174.8
2015	174.0	174.6	175.6	176.5	178.0	180.3	183.2	183.7	183.2	183.7	182.0	182.0	179.7
2016	180.6	182.1	183.2	184.2	185.6	186.3	188.6	190.2	188.8	188.5	186.9	186.2	185.9
2017	182.9	185.6	187.1	189.0	191.1	193.5	195.5	196.4	195.5	195.2	192.3	193.0	191.4
Service-Providing													
2007	831.5	840.2	845.8	847.3	852.3	852.8	841.5	841.5	849.4	860.4	867.4	868.4	849.9
2008	847.7	854.4	858.2	862.6	864.6	861.9	854.0	851.9	858.1	861.4	859.3	852.4	857.2
2009	828.4	829.2	826.7	827.9	828.9	824.3	812.2	808.9	814.2	823.3	827.4	826.4	823.2
2010	809.4	814.1	817.8	825.0	830.0	830.4	816.8	816.6	823.2	837.3	841.9	842.2	825.4
2011	825.2	830.7	833.1	841.4	841.7	840.5	831.8	831.3	837.9	848.2	854.1	854.9	839.2
2012	839.1	845.3	849.5	855.1	859.0	859.1	848.0	849.1	854.6	867.1	872.6	872.9	856.0
2013	852.7	861.7	865.2	873.0	877.9	878.0	867.8	871.9	878.0	888.9	896.1	896.0	875.6
2014	879.6	883.5	889.5	896.7	901.2	902.9	893.3	897.4	905.3	915.9	922.6	925.8	901.1
2015	908.9	917.1	921.3	928.4	931.4	932.9	927.0	930.0	935.9	946.9	951.9	954.9	932.2
2016	937.2	946.1	949.8	958.5	960.5	961.7	952.6	954.5	962.5	971.4	978.2	976.5	959.1
2017	954.9	969.8	975.9	982.4	984.1	985.9	977.1	977.5	983.6	991.0	996.5	999.4	981.5
Mining and Logging													
2007	1.5	1.6	1.6	1.6	1.7	1.7	1.7	1.7	1.7	1.7	1.6	1.5	1.6
2008	1.5	1.5	1.5	1.5	1.6	1.6	1.6	1.7	1.6	1.6	1.5	1.4	1.6
2009	1.2	1.2	1.2	1.1	1.2	1.2	1.3	1.3	1.3	1.3	1.2	1.1	1.2
2010	1.0	1.0	1.1	1.0	1.1	1.1	1.1	1.1	1.1	1.1	1.1	1.0	1.1
2011	0.9	1.0	1.0	1.0	1.1	1.1	1.1	1.1	1.1	1.1	1.1	1.0	1.1
2012	0.9	0.9	0.9	0.9	1.0	1.0	1.0	1.0	1.0	1.0	1.0	1.0	1.0
2013	1.0	1.0	1.0	1.0	1.0	1.1	1.1	1.1	1.1	1.2	1.2	1.1	1.1
2014	1.1	1.1	1.1	1.2	1.2	1.2	1.2	1.3	1.3	1.2	1.2	1.2	1.2
2015	1.2	1.2	1.2	1.3	1.2	1.3	1.3	1.3	1.3	1.3	1.3	1.3	1.3
2016	1.3	1.3	1.3	1.3	1.3	1.3	1.4	1.4	1.3	1.4	1.3	1.3	1.3
2017	1.3	1.3	1.3	1.3	1.3	1.4	1.3	1.3	1.2	1.2	1.2	1.2	1.3

Employment by Industry: Portland-Vancouver-Hillsboro, OR-WA, Selected Years, 2007–2017—*Continued*

(Numbers in thousands, not seasonally adjusted)

Industry and year	January	February	March	April	May	June	July	August	September	October	November	December	Annual average
Construction													
2007	61.9	62.7	63.7	64.0	66.1	66.2	68.6	69.7	69.1	68.1	66.6	64.9	66.0
2008	61.4	61.5	61.5	61.5	62.5	63.2	63.8	63.9	63.3	61.0	57.8	54.9	61.4
2009	52.4	50.9	49.9	49.4	49.6	50.6	51.4	51.4	50.8	49.7	47.1	46.1	49.9
2010	43.2	42.8	43.4	44.1	44.8	45.6	47.8	48.4	48.3	48.1	45.8	45.3	45.6
2011	42.8	43.3	44.2	45.6	46.4	47.7	49.4	50.1	50.0	49.6	48.2	48.0	47.1
2012	46.2	46.3	46.7	47.3	49.0	49.7	51.3	52.5	51.4	50.8	48.8	47.7	49.0
2013	46.4	47.0	48.1	49.8	51.8	52.8	54.7	55.6	55.5	55.7	55.0	54.0	52.2
2014	53.6	53.2	54.7	54.9	55.8	56.7	57.7	58.0	57.2	55.8	54.8	54.3	55.6
2015	53.3	53.5	53.8	54.2	55.1	56.2	57.7	58.6	58.3	58.9	57.8	57.4	56.2
2016	56.6	57.9	58.5	60.0	61.1	61.9	63.9	65.0	64.9	64.4	63.7	63.1	61.8
2017	61.1	63.2	64.2	65.5	66.9	68.2	69.5	70.6	70.2	69.2	67.3	67.0	66.9
Manufacturing													
2007	126.0	126.2	126.4	125.2	125.2	126.0	127.0	127.2	126.6	126.5	125.7	125.4	126.1
2008	124.4	124.5	124.4	124.0	123.8	123.9	124.9	124.2	123.8	121.7	121.0	118.6	123.3
2009	115.7	113.2	111.2	109.6	108.7	108.0	108.1	107.8	107.6	107.4	106.2	105.8	109.1
2010	105.1	105.0	105.2	105.6	106.0	106.8	107.9	108.1	108.3	109.1	108.9	108.7	107.1
2011	108.0	108.7	109.2	109.8	110.4	111.5	112.4	112.9	112.6	112.7	112.6	112.5	111.1
2012	111.8	112.2	112.6	112.9	113.5	114.7	116.0	115.8	115.6	115.5	115.2	114.6	114.2
2013	113.8	114.1	114.1	114.7	114.9	116.0	116.4	117.0	116.8	116.8	116.3	116.0	115.6
2014	115.7	115.8	116.3	116.6	117.2	118.1	119.3	119.4	119.5	119.7	119.4	119.7	118.1
2015	119.5	119.9	120.6	121.0	121.7	122.8	124.2	123.8	123.6	123.5	122.9	123.3	122.2
2016	122.7	122.9	123.4	122.9	123.2	123.1	123.3	123.8	122.6	122.7	121.9	121.8	122.9
2017	120.5	121.1	121.6	122.2	122.9	123.9	124.7	124.5	124.1	124.8	123.8	124.8	123.2
Trade, Transportation, and Utilities													
2007	201.3	200.3	200.7	200.9	202.4	203.6	204.3	204.6	204.9	205.0	209.9	211.8	204.1
2008	203.4	202.0	201.7	201.7	201.9	201.8	203.0	202.9	202.3	201.2	201.7	201.5	202.1
2009	192.7	189.7	187.2	186.2	187.0	186.7	186.3	186.1	186.0	185.5	187.7	189.9	187.6
2010	183.0	181.5	181.6	182.8	183.5	184.4	185.5	185.8	185.8	187.1	190.5	192.9	185.4
2011	185.7	184.5	184.3	185.8	186.9	187.7	188.9	188.8	189.0	189.4	193.3	195.1	188.3
2012	188.2	186.8	187.2	188.5	190.4	191.9	191.7	192.2	191.9	193.0	197.9	199.9	191.6
2013	192.2	192.0	192.1	193.3	194.9	195.5	196.8	197.8	197.7	198.3	202.7	204.5	196.5
2014	198.2	196.7	196.9	197.8	199.4	200.9	202.3	203.5	203.6	204.4	208.7	211.4	202.0
2015	204.6	203.4	203.8	204.6	205.9	207.3	208.3	209.4	209.6	210.0	213.2	215.7	208.0
2016	208.7	207.6	207.6	208.4	208.9	210.5	211.3	211.9	211.8	212.2	217.3	219.2	211.3
2017	213.1	212.5	212.8	213.0	214.1	214.7	215.6	216.1	216.1	216.5	222.0	223.3	215.8
Wholesale Trade													
2007	55.2	55.7	55.6	55.7	56.0	56.0	56.3	55.9	55.5	55.7	55.6	55.6	55.7
2008	55.0	55.3	55.1	55.0	55.4	55.4	56.0	55.6	55.3	55.2	54.9	54.2	55.2
2009	53.2	53.0	52.2	52.1	52.1	51.6	51.6	51.2	50.7	50.2	49.9	49.8	51.5
2010	48.9	49.1	49.0	49.7	50.1	50.1	50.7	50.6	50.3	50.6	50.7	50.8	50.1
2011	49.9	50.3	50.1	51.1	51.6	51.5	52.0	52.0	51.6	51.8	51.7	51.7	51.3
2012	51.1	51.5	51.6	52.6	53.1	53.0	53.3	53.4	53.0	53.2	53.3	53.5	52.7
2013	52.5	53.2	53.1	53.5	53.9	53.7	54.4	54.5	54.2	54.0	54.4	54.4	53.8
2014	53.6	53.8	53.7	53.7	53.9	54.2	54.5	54.6	54.5	54.4	54.6	54.8	54.2
2015	54.2	54.7	54.6	54.8	55.0	55.1	55.6	55.7	55.6	55.4	55.7	55.9	55.2
2016	55.3	55.7	55.6	55.9	55.7	56.1	56.4	56.4	56.2	56.2	56.5	56.8	56.1
2017	56.1	56.7	56.7	56.8	57.3	57.4	57.9	57.9	57.8	57.5	57.7	58.2	57.3
Retail Trade													
2007	108.8	107.2	107.4	107.6	108.5	109.6	110.8	111.3	111.1	111.0	115.5	116.9	110.5
2008	110.8	109.0	108.9	108.5	108.3	108.5	109.8	109.7	109.1	108.1	109.8	110.1	109.2
2009	103.5	101.5	100.3	99.8	100.6	100.9	101.4	101.6	101.2	101.5	104.1	105.8	101.9
2010	100.9	99.5	99.7	99.8	100.2	100.9	102.0	102.4	101.8	102.7	106.0	107.5	102.0
2011	102.2	100.9	100.8	101.2	101.6	102.5	103.5	103.5	103.1	103.7	107.3	108.7	103.3
2012	103.6	101.8	101.8	102.4	103.5	104.8	105.3	105.5	105.0	105.8	110.1	111.3	105.1
2013	106.0	105.0	105.1	105.7	106.9	107.7	108.9	109.6	109.1	109.8	113.4	114.6	108.5
2014	109.7	108.1	108.5	109.2	110.4	111.4	113.1	113.7	113.3	113.8	117.4	118.8	112.3
2015	113.5	112.1	112.6	113.6	114.4	115.0	116.5	117.2	116.8	117.2	119.6	120.7	115.8
2016	115.7	114.8	114.9	115.1	115.7	116.8	117.9	118.1	117.5	117.9	120.7	121.3	117.2
2017	117.4	116.8	117.0	117.3	117.5	118.0	119.2	119.4	118.9	119.1	123.5	123.2	118.9

Employment by Industry: Portland-Vancouver-Hillsboro, OR-WA, Selected Years, 2007–2017—*Continued*

(Numbers in thousands, not seasonally adjusted)

Industry and year	January	February	March	April	May	June	July	August	September	October	November	December	Annual average
Transportation and Utilities													
2007	37.3	37.4	37.7	37.6	37.9	38.0	37.2	37.4	38.3	38.3	38.8	39.3	37.9
2008	37.6	37.7	37.7	38.2	38.2	37.9	37.2	37.6	37.9	37.9	37.0	37.2	37.7
2009	36.0	35.2	34.7	34.3	34.3	34.2	33.3	33.3	34.1	33.8	33.7	34.3	34.3
2010	33.2	32.9	32.9	33.3	33.2	33.4	32.8	32.8	33.7	33.8	33.8	34.6	33.4
2011	33.6	33.3	33.4	33.5	33.7	33.7	33.4	33.3	34.3	33.9	34.3	34.7	33.8
2012	33.5	33.5	33.8	33.5	33.8	34.1	33.1	33.3	33.9	34.0	34.5	35.1	33.8
2013	33.7	33.8	33.9	34.1	34.1	34.1	33.5	33.7	34.4	34.5	34.9	35.5	34.2
2014	34.9	34.8	34.7	34.9	35.1	35.3	34.7	35.2	35.8	36.2	36.7	37.8	35.5
2015	36.9	36.6	36.6	36.2	36.5	37.2	36.2	36.5	37.2	37.4	37.9	39.1	37.0
2016	37.7	37.1	37.1	37.4	37.5	37.6	37.0	37.4	38.1	38.1	40.1	41.1	38.0
2017	39.6	39.0	39.1	38.9	39.3	39.3	38.5	38.8	39.4	39.9	40.8	41.9	39.5
Information													
2007	24.3	24.7	25.0	24.9	25.2	25.0	24.9	25.2	25.0	25.0	25.2	25.3	25.0
2008	25.1	25.2	25.2	25.0	25.2	25.2	24.8	24.9	24.7	24.2	24.1	23.9	24.8
2009	23.5	23.5	23.4	23.2	23.3	24.1	23.0	23.1	22.8	22.6	22.9	22.9	23.2
2010	22.4	22.5	22.6	22.6	23.0	23.0	22.5	22.8	22.7	22.4	22.7	22.7	22.7
2011	22.7	22.7	23.0	22.8	22.6	22.5	22.7	22.9	22.6	22.5	22.7	22.7	22.7
2012	22.4	22.6	23.1	23.2	23.1	23.4	23.6	23.4	23.2	23.7	23.7	23.5	23.2
2013	23.1	23.1	23.2	23.2	23.1	23.0	23.1	23.3	23.4	23.5	23.5	23.6	23.3
2014	22.8	22.9	23.2	23.3	23.2	23.4	23.8	23.9	23.8	23.8	23.9	24.0	23.5
2015	23.4	23.7	23.8	23.7	23.9	24.0	24.6	25.0	24.6	24.3	24.5	24.8	24.2
2016	24.4	24.6	24.7	24.8	25.2	25.2	25.0	25.3	26.2	25.8	25.6	25.5	25.2
2017	25.3	25.9	25.7	26.4	25.9	25.8	25.5	25.8	25.8	25.6	25.4	25.6	25.7
Financial Activities													
2007	71.0	71.2	71.3	71.1	71.1	71.1	71.2	70.9	70.0	69.8	69.8	69.6	70.7
2008	68.9	69.0	68.7	68.8	68.8	68.4	68.4	68.2	67.5	67.2	66.7	66.2	68.1
2009	65.5	65.0	64.5	64.5	64.4	64.1	64.1	64.0	63.4	63.4	63.1	63.0	64.1
2010	62.2	61.9	61.9	62.3	62.1	62.4	62.4	62.4	62.2	62.2	62.0	62.2	62.2
2011	61.6	61.6	61.4	61.4	61.5	61.8	62.0	61.9	61.7	61.6	61.7	61.9	61.7
2012	61.6	61.7	61.7	61.9	62.0	62.1	62.8	62.9	62.6	62.7	62.7	62.9	62.3
2013	62.2	62.2	62.3	62.9	63.3	63.4	64.4	64.3	64.0	64.1	64.0	64.0	63.4
2014	63.1	62.9	62.9	63.3	63.5	64.0	64.5	64.9	64.7	65.0	65.0	65.2	64.1
2015	64.9	65.1	64.9	65.7	66.1	66.4	67.2	67.2	66.9	67.2	67.2	67.6	66.4
2016	66.6	66.5	66.4	67.3	67.6	68.0	68.8	69.3	68.9	69.3	69.5	69.5	68.1
2017	68.8	68.9	69.3	69.7	70.0	70.5	71.4	71.3	70.6	71.0	70.6	71.2	70.3
Professional and Business Services													
2007	139.4	140.8	142.4	142.8	142.6	143.9	144.2	145.8	145.7	146.1	145.2	144.4	143.6
2008	141.0	142.7	143.9	145.4	145.1	145.5	146.8	147.6	146.2	144.8	141.8	139.4	144.2
2009	134.9	133.7	132.7	133.2	131.9	132.0	132.5	132.3	131.4	132.4	132.4	132.1	132.6
2010	129.7	131.0	132.5	135.2	134.9	135.8	137.3	138.6	138.5	140.0	139.6	139.7	136.1
2011	136.1	137.6	138.8	141.0	140.9	141.9	144.3	144.9	145.4	145.4	145.5	145.9	142.3
2012	143.8	144.5	145.6	147.0	147.4	148.6	149.9	151.0	150.6	151.8	151.1	151.1	148.5
2013	147.9	149.4	151.3	153.6	154.4	155.6	158.0	159.6	159.4	160.2	160.2	160.1	155.8
2014	157.2	158.2	159.9	162.0	162.8	164.4	165.9	167.3	167.6	167.8	167.4	167.8	164.0
2015	164.4	165.9	167.6	170.1	170.7	171.7	173.7	174.4	174.2	174.9	174.3	174.3	171.4
2016	171.5	173.2	174.2	176.3	176.3	177.4	178.6	179.4	178.2	178.8	178.5	177.4	176.7
2017	174.5	177.5	178.6	180.3	180.4	182.0	182.3	182.8	182.6	183.5	181.5	181.4	180.6
Education and Health Services													
2007	125.5	129.5	130.4	130.6	129.9	126.7	124.5	124.6	129.5	133.3	134.2	133.8	129.4
2008	130.5	134.4	135.1	135.8	134.8	131.9	129.8	129.8	135.1	138.2	138.8	138.5	134.4
2009	134.5	137.8	138.1	139.0	138.4	134.9	133.0	132.9	138.8	141.4	142.3	141.5	137.7
2010	139.5	142.3	143.2	144.0	142.9	139.6	137.3	137.0	142.3	146.2	147.2	147.2	142.4
2011	144.5	147.2	147.8	148.1	146.3	143.4	140.9	141.2	146.2	149.3	150.2	149.8	146.2
2012	146.3	150.1	150.7	151.4	149.3	145.8	142.9	143.5	148.5	151.2	152.2	151.8	148.6
2013	147.7	151.8	151.9	153.3	152.2	148.3	145.4	146.6	151.6	155.3	156.3	155.7	151.3
2014	152.6	155.4	156.2	156.8	155.2	152.8	150.1	149.9	155.3	158.2	159.6	159.5	155.1
2015	156.3	160.3	160.6	161.3	159.2	156.9	155.0	154.9	160.3	163.1	164.2	163.8	159.7
2016	161.2	165.1	165.4	166.1	163.7	160.6	158.6	159.7	165.2	168.4	169.3	168.2	164.3
2017	164.1	169.9	170.9	171.0	169.2	166.1	163.7	164.6	170.3	172.5	174.7	174.3	169.3

Employment by Industry: Portland-Vancouver-Hillsboro, OR-WA, Selected Years, 2007–2017—*Continued*

(Numbers in thousands, not seasonally adjusted)

Industry and year	January	February	March	April	May	June	July	August	September	October	November	December	Annual average
Leisure and Hospitality													
2007	93.2	94.4	95.4	96.3	97.9	99.0	101.1	102.0	101.2	98.8	98.9	99.4	98.1
2008	96.3	97.0	98.1	99.8	101.0	101.5	102.5	102.7	101.7	99.0	97.6	95.8	99.4
2009	92.6	92.7	93.3	94.4	95.5	95.9	96.9	97.0	96.6	94.0	93.4	92.5	94.6
2010	90.1	90.8	91.3	94.0	95.3	96.4	97.1	97.7	97.2	95.7	94.8	94.8	94.6
2011	91.9	93.0	93.7	96.2	96.8	98.8	100.1	100.8	100.0	97.3	96.5	97.0	96.8
2012	94.6	95.5	97.0	98.6	100.4	101.9	103.3	104.4	103.8	101.5	100.6	101.0	100.2
2013	98.3	99.4	100.7	102.5	104.4	106.6	107.8	108.8	108.2	104.9	104.6	104.4	104.2
2014	102.5	102.9	104.9	106.9	108.5	109.6	111.0	112.0	111.1	108.7	108.1	108.6	107.9
2015	106.9	108.2	109.8	111.3	113.3	115.5	117.4	117.8	116.8	114.4	113.9	114.6	113.3
2016	112.0	113.7	115.1	117.6	119.1	121.2	123.1	122.8	122.0	119.0	118.6	118.6	118.6
2017	115.4	117.2	118.8	121.4	123.0	125.3	127.0	126.6	125.4	122.2	120.6	122.3	122.1
Other Services													
2007	35.7	36.4	36.5	36.4	36.7	37.0	36.6	36.8	37.0	37.1	37.2	37.2	36.7
2008	36.8	37.0	37.2	37.5	37.7	37.8	37.6	37.5	37.8	37.3	36.8	36.3	37.3
2009	35.7	35.8	35.7	35.5	35.7	35.5	35.4	35.3	34.9	34.7	34.7	34.6	35.3
2010	33.9	34.1	34.3	34.5	34.9	35.5	35.1	35.0	35.0	35.3	34.7	34.8	34.8
2011	34.4	34.8	34.9	35.2	35.3	35.5	35.8	36.0	35.9	35.9	35.8	35.8	35.4
2012	35.7	36.1	36.2	36.6	37.2	37.0	37.0	37.0	36.8	36.9	36.6	36.4	36.6
2013	36.2	36.5	36.6	36.7	37.2	37.0	37.5	37.5	37.1	36.9	37.2	36.9	36.9
2014	36.9	37.0	37.4	37.5	38.2	38.6	38.6	38.6	38.6	38.5	38.4	38.4	38.1
2015	38.0	38.4	38.5	38.9	39.1	39.3	39.8	40.0	39.7	39.8	39.9	40.0	39.3
2016	40.0	40.6	40.9	41.6	41.9	42.1	42.0	42.2	42.3	42.0	41.9	41.4	41.6
2017	39.7	40.6	41.0	41.2	41.4	41.5	42.0	42.1	41.7	41.9	42.2	42.2	41.5
Government													
2007	141.1	142.9	144.1	144.3	146.5	146.5	134.7	131.6	136.1	145.3	147.0	146.9	142.3
2008	145.7	147.1	148.3	148.6	150.1	149.8	141.1	138.3	142.8	149.5	151.8	150.8	147.0
2009	149.0	151.0	151.8	151.9	152.7	151.1	141.0	138.2	140.3	149.3	150.9	149.9	148.1
2010	148.6	150.0	150.4	149.6	153.4	153.3	139.6	137.3	139.5	148.4	150.4	147.9	147.4
2011	148.3	149.3	149.2	150.9	151.4	148.9	137.1	134.8	137.1	146.8	148.4	146.7	145.7
2012	146.5	148.0	148.0	147.9	149.2	148.4	136.8	134.7	137.2	146.3	147.8	146.3	144.8
2013	145.1	147.3	147.1	147.5	148.4	148.6	134.8	134.0	136.6	145.7	147.6	146.8	144.1
2014	146.3	147.5	148.1	149.1	150.4	149.2	137.1	137.3	140.6	149.5	151.5	150.9	146.5
2015	150.4	152.1	152.3	152.8	153.2	151.8	141.0	141.3	143.8	153.2	154.7	154.1	150.1
2016	152.8	154.8	155.5	156.4	157.8	156.7	145.2	143.9	147.9	155.9	157.5	156.7	153.4
2017	154.0	157.3	158.8	159.4	160.1	160.0	149.6	148.2	151.1	157.8	159.5	159.1	156.2

Employment by Industry: Pittsburgh, PA, Selected Years, 2007–2017

(Numbers in thousands, not seasonally adjusted)

Industry and year	January	February	March	April	May	June	July	August	September	October	November	December	Annual average
Total Nonfarm													
2007	1,120.3	1,119.9	1,132.3	1,142.0	1,156.1	1,164.4	1,147.4	1,145.0	1,151.8	1,157.8	1,159.7	1,156.7	1,146.1
2008	1,125.9	1,128.0	1,135.5	1,150.2	1,161.9	1,165.3	1,151.1	1,147.6	1,154.7	1,160.1	1,157.0	1,149.6	1,148.9
2009	1,112.5	1,111.4	1,114.3	1,123.2	1,131.4	1,132.6	1,115.9	1,111.6	1,119.3	1,124.8	1,126.8	1,124.8	1,120.7
2010	1,090.6	1,088.4	1,102.7	1,122.2	1,134.1	1,142.1	1,130.0	1,127.4	1,135.5	1,143.1	1,144.6	1,143.3	1,125.3
2011	1,116.1	1,118.0	1,128.3	1,142.7	1,152.9	1,160.3	1,144.1	1,140.1	1,153.3	1,160.4	1,162.9	1,159.8	1,144.9
2012	1,130.3	1,137.4	1,151.0	1,160.7	1,168.4	1,170.9	1,154.5	1,150.3	1,160.0	1,169.2	1,170.8	1,165.6	1,157.4
2013	1,133.7	1,140.8	1,148.1	1,158.3	1,167.8	1,169.9	1,157.1	1,152.8	1,161.7	1,167.5	1,168.1	1,164.5	1,157.5
2014	1,134.3	1,135.2	1,144.4	1,160.3	1,171.4	1,173.1	1,158.5	1,156.3	1,166.1	1,172.5	1,172.3	1,170.5	1,159.6
2015	1,139.7	1,139.8	1,145.8	1,162.0	1,172.4	1,172.2	1,162.3	1,161.0	1,167.5	1,173.0	1,175.8	1,169.8	1,161.8
2016	1,140.4	1,142.8	1,151.5	1,167.0	1,171.8	1,169.4	1,162.8	1,159.1	1,168.3	1,173.4	1,177.0	1,170.3	1,162.8
2017	1,143.7	1,151.4	1,157.9	1,174.0	1,183.1	1,181.6	1,174.1	1,172.7	1,184.7	1,190.6	1,196.6	1,193.9	1,175.4
Total Private													
2007	993.6	990.4	1,002.0	1,012.2	1,027.5	1,037.1	1,029.8	1,028.8	1,026.4	1,029.4	1,030.2	1,027.6	1,019.6
2008	1,000.5	999.3	1,006.2	1,021.1	1,033.6	1,038.7	1,032.7	1,030.5	1,028.3	1,030.3	1,026.8	1,020.6	1,022.4
2009	987.3	982.6	985.1	992.9	1,002.2	1,004.9	996.5	993.7	992.4	994.7	995.2	993.9	993.5
2010	964.9	958.8	972.1	990.8	1,000.8	1,011.0	1,009.8	1,009.6	1,008.3	1,012.9	1,014.1	1,013.2	997.2
2011	989.5	988.7	998.3	1,013.2	1,025.1	1,034.4	1,028.7	1,026.8	1,031.7	1,035.8	1,037.2	1,034.3	1,020.3
2012	1,010.8	1,013.2	1,026.5	1,036.4	1,044.2	1,049.7	1,041.9	1,038.6	1,040.0	1,046.6	1,047.1	1,042.3	1,036.4
2013	1,015.3	1,018.0	1,025.2	1,035.3	1,044.2	1,050.8	1,046.6	1,042.7	1,042.7	1,046.6	1,045.9	1,042.8	1,038.0
2014	1,016.3	1,014.9	1,023.9	1,039.2	1,050.1	1,055.2	1,049.1	1,047.7	1,048.5	1,052.5	1,051.4	1,049.8	1,041.6
2015	1,023.6	1,020.6	1,026.4	1,041.7	1,052.2	1,055.0	1,053.0	1,052.3	1,050.4	1,054.7	1,056.3	1,051.5	1,044.8
2016	1,025.5	1,024.9	1,032.7	1,048.3	1,052.7	1,053.5	1,053.0	1,050.9	1,051.2	1,055.0	1,057.9	1,051.6	1,046.4
2017	1,029.9	1,033.1	1,039.3	1,055.4	1,064.2	1,066.4	1,064.2	1,064.8	1,067.9	1,073.1	1,078.2	1,076.6	1,059.4
Goods Producing													
2007	155.7	153.3	157.5	161.1	164.8	166.8	166.3	166.0	165.4	164.9	163.1	159.2	162.0
2008	154.2	152.6	155.3	160.3	163.6	165.3	165.7	165.8	165.0	164.6	160.7	156.1	160.8
2009	148.2	146.2	146.7	148.2	148.8	149.5	148.1	147.0	146.5	146.9	145.0	141.0	146.8
2010	134.0	131.9	136.5	142.8	145.3	147.2	149.0	148.8	147.8	147.6	146.9	143.3	143.4
2011	137.7	137.7	141.7	145.9	149.2	151.9	153.6	154.0	154.3	154.7	153.3	150.4	148.7
2012	145.5	145.6	148.3	153.1	155.4	157.6	158.0	157.8	157.7	158.5	155.5	151.9	153.7
2013	146.2	146.3	148.7	152.4	155.2	156.9	157.5	157.4	156.7	156.5	153.8	150.1	153.1
2014	146.0	144.9	148.1	153.2	156.1	159.0	159.4	159.5	158.9	158.4	155.9	152.8	154.4
2015	147.4	145.8	147.7	152.8	155.5	157.7	158.9	158.8	157.5	155.7	153.5	150.1	153.5
2016	143.8	141.8	145.6	149.7	151.3	152.4	153.0	152.2	150.8	150.7	149.1	146.1	148.9
2017	141.9	142.4	144.6	150.3	154.0	157.4	158.0	158.5	158.0	157.2	157.8	156.4	153.0
Service-Providing													
2007	964.6	966.6	974.8	980.9	991.3	997.6	981.1	979.0	986.4	992.9	996.6	997.5	984.1
2008	971.7	975.4	980.2	989.9	998.3	1,000.0	985.4	981.8	989.7	995.5	996.3	993.5	988.1
2009	964.3	965.2	967.6	975.0	982.6	983.1	967.8	964.6	972.8	977.9	981.8	983.8	973.9
2010	956.6	956.5	966.2	979.4	988.8	994.9	981.0	978.6	987.7	995.5	997.7	1,000.0	981.9
2011	978.4	980.3	986.6	996.8	1,003.7	1,008.4	990.5	986.1	999.0	1,005.7	1,009.6	1,009.4	996.2
2012	984.8	991.8	1,002.7	1,007.6	1,013.0	1,013.3	996.5	992.5	1,002.3	1,010.7	1,015.3	1,013.7	1,003.7
2013	987.5	994.5	999.4	1,005.9	1,012.6	1,013.0	999.6	995.4	1,005.0	1,011.0	1,014.3	1,014.4	1,004.4
2014	988.3	990.3	996.3	1,007.1	1,015.3	1,014.1	999.1	996.8	1,007.2	1,014.1	1,016.4	1,017.7	1,005.2
2015	992.3	994.0	998.1	1,009.2	1,016.9	1,014.5	1,003.4	1,002.2	1,010.0	1,017.3	1,022.3	1,019.7	1,008.3
2016	996.6	1,001.0	1,005.9	1,017.3	1,020.5	1,017.0	1,009.8	1,006.9	1,017.5	1,022.7	1,027.9	1,024.2	1,013.9
2017	1,001.8	1,009.0	1,013.3	1,023.7	1,029.1	1,024.2	1,016.1	1,014.2	1,026.7	1,033.4	1,038.8	1,037.5	1,022.3
Mining and Logging													
2007	4.8	4.7	4.7	4.7	4.8	4.9	5.0	5.0	4.9	4.9	5.0	5.0	4.9
2008	5.0	5.0	5.0	5.1	5.3	5.5	5.5	5.6	5.6	5.7	5.7	5.7	5.4
2009	5.6	5.5	5.3	5.4	5.4	5.5	5.6	5.6	5.7	5.8	5.9	5.9	5.6
2010	5.9	6.0	6.2	6.4	6.5	6.7	6.9	7.1	7.3	7.2	7.3	7.4	6.7
2011	7.5	7.7	7.9	8.2	8.4	8.6	8.9	9.0	9.1	9.2	9.4	9.5	8.6
2012	9.6	9.6	9.7	9.8	9.9	10.0	10.0	10.1	10.1	10.1	10.1	10.1	9.9
2013	10.1	10.2	10.4	10.7	10.7	10.8	10.8	10.9	10.9	11.0	10.9	11.1	10.7
2014	11.2	11.1	11.3	11.5	11.7	11.9	12.0	12.1	12.1	12.2	12.3	12.3	11.8
2015	12.1	12.0	11.9	11.6	11.5	11.4	11.4	11.1	10.9	10.5	10.2	10.2	11.2
2016	9.9	9.4	9.1	8.7	8.7	8.6	8.5	8.5	8.5	8.6	8.7	8.8	8.8
2017	8.8	9.1	9.3	9.4	9.7	10.0	10.2	10.2	10.2	10.1	10.2	10.4	9.8

Employment by Industry: Pittsburgh, PA, Selected Years, 2007–2017—*Continued*

(Numbers in thousands, not seasonally adjusted)

Industry and year	January	February	March	April	May	June	July	August	September	October	November	December	Annual average
Construction													
2007	50.6	48.7	52.5	55.8	59.2	60.5	60.5	60.6	60.8	60.4	58.3	54.4	56.9
2008	50.6	49.2	51.6	56.7	59.4	60.4	61.0	61.4	61.1	60.9	57.8	53.9	57.0
2009	48.7	48.9	50.8	53.1	54.8	55.6	54.9	54.4	54.2	54.0	51.8	47.4	52.4
2010	41.7	40.0	44.0	49.7	51.9	52.6	53.9	53.6	52.7	52.4	51.2	47.5	49.3
2011	42.6	42.3	45.7	49.3	52.2	54.1	55.1	55.6	55.8	56.2	54.5	51.4	51.2
2012	47.1	47.2	49.6	54.1	55.8	57.1	57.4	57.0	57.4	58.3	55.1	51.8	54.0
2013	46.6	46.9	49.0	52.4	55.1	56.1	56.9	56.9	56.6	56.3	53.7	49.6	53.0
2014	46.5	45.6	48.1	53.2	55.9	58.0	58.5	58.2	58.2	57.9	55.1	51.7	53.9
2015	47.2	46.0	47.9	52.9	55.8	57.4	58.8	59.4	59.1	59.0	57.1	53.8	54.5
2016	48.6	47.4	50.6	55.2	56.7	57.3	57.9	57.4	56.9	56.7	55.0	51.5	54.3
2017	47.8	47.9	50.1	55.5	58.9	61.4	61.8	62.3	62.4	61.6	61.6	59.8	57.6
Manufacturing													
2007	100.3	99.9	100.3	100.6	100.8	101.4	100.8	100.4	99.7	99.6	99.8	99.8	100.3
2008	98.6	98.4	98.7	98.5	98.9	99.4	99.2	98.8	98.3	98.0	97.2	96.5	98.4
2009	93.9	91.8	90.6	89.7	88.6	88.4	87.6	87.0	86.6	87.1	87.3	87.7	88.9
2010	86.4	85.9	86.3	86.7	86.9	87.9	88.2	88.1	87.8	88.0	88.4	88.4	87.4
2011	87.6	87.7	88.1	88.4	88.6	89.2	89.6	89.4	89.4	89.3	89.4	89.5	88.9
2012	88.8	88.8	89.0	89.2	89.7	90.5	90.6	90.7	90.2	90.1	90.3	90.0	89.8
2013	89.5	89.2	89.3	89.3	89.4	90.0	89.8	89.6	89.2	89.2	89.2	89.4	89.4
2014	88.3	88.2	88.7	88.5	88.5	89.1	88.9	89.2	88.6	88.3	88.5	88.8	88.6
2015	88.1	87.8	87.9	88.3	88.2	88.9	88.7	88.3	87.5	86.2	86.2	86.1	87.7
2016	85.3	85.0	85.9	85.8	85.9	86.5	86.6	86.3	85.4	85.4	85.4	85.8	85.8
2017	85.3	85.4	85.2	85.4	85.4	86.0	86.0	86.0	85.4	85.5	86.0	86.2	85.7
Trade, Transportation, and Utilities													
2007	225.9	221.5	223.3	223.4	225.9	226.2	222.8	222.1	222.6	224.2	228.8	231.3	224.8
2008	223.6	220.0	220.9	221.1	223.3	223.2	219.4	218.7	220.3	222.6	225.0	227.6	222.1
2009	217.2	213.8	213.0	213.5	215.3	214.5	210.2	210.1	211.3	213.0	217.3	219.4	214.1
2010	211.6	208.0	210.1	211.6	214.0	215.3	212.2	212.5	213.8	217.0	220.8	224.2	214.3
2011	215.3	213.1	213.8	215.6	217.5	217.1	214.4	214.4	216.2	218.1	222.5	225.3	216.9
2012	217.0	214.9	216.7	216.8	218.0	217.2	213.8	212.9	214.5	216.5	221.7	223.3	216.9
2013	214.2	211.6	212.2	212.3	214.6	214.7	212.1	212.7	213.6	215.4	220.4	223.4	214.8
2014	213.7	211.0	212.0	213.5	216.3	217.4	213.2	213.4	214.8	217.0	221.6	225.2	215.8
2015	216.2	212.6	212.8	213.7	216.6	216.9	213.8	213.6	213.8	215.8	220.3	223.4	215.8
2016	213.9	211.3	211.5	212.6	214.6	213.5	211.2	210.7	211.6	213.1	217.7	220.9	213.6
2017	212.3	210.0	210.0	211.3	212.7	211.7	209.5	209.2	211.3	214.2	217.7	219.5	212.5
Wholesale Trade													
2007	49.1	48.9	49.2	49.1	49.2	49.5	49.5	49.6	49.1	49.0	49.1	49.1	49.2
2008	48.9	48.8	48.9	49.2	49.5	49.7	49.5	49.4	49.0	49.0	48.7	48.6	49.1
2009	47.8	47.4	47.1	46.9	46.9	46.7	46.3	46.1	45.8	45.6	45.5	45.5	46.5
2010	45.3	44.9	45.4	46.0	46.2	46.4	46.7	46.9	46.6	47.1	46.9	47.1	46.3
2011	46.6	46.6	46.9	47.3	47.6	47.3	47.2	47.3	46.9	47.0	46.9	46.9	47.0
2012	46.4	46.6	47.0	47.1	46.8	46.9	46.6	46.3	45.9	45.8	45.7	45.7	46.4
2013	45.0	44.8	45.0	45.0	45.2	45.4	45.4	45.4	45.1	45.1	45.0	45.3	45.1
2014	44.8	44.7	44.8	44.7	45.1	45.5	45.5	45.2	45.0	45.2	45.3	45.4	45.1
2015	44.8	44.6	44.4	44.4	44.7	44.9	45.0	44.8	44.3	44.5	44.5	44.4	44.6
2016	43.8	43.8	43.7	43.7	43.8	43.7	43.7	43.5	43.1	43.1	43.0	43.0	43.5
2017	42.4	42.7	42.7	42.7	43.0	43.2	43.2	43.1	42.8	43.0	43.1	43.5	43.0
Retail Trade													
2007	131.6	127.7	129.0	129.0	131.2	131.9	131.4	130.9	128.7	130.6	135.3	137.4	131.2
2008	130.9	127.6	128.5	128.0	129.3	129.8	129.2	128.7	127.5	129.0	131.6	133.8	129.5
2009	126.1	123.3	123.2	123.8	125.6	126.2	125.3	125.4	123.7	125.2	129.3	130.8	125.7
2010	124.7	121.8	123.1	123.7	125.6	126.6	126.5	126.6	124.6	126.7	130.4	132.6	126.1
2011	126.0	123.7	124.1	125.2	126.7	127.3	127.5	127.9	126.1	127.5	131.6	133.5	127.3
2012	127.2	124.9	126.0	126.2	127.4	128.1	127.4	127.0	125.3	127.0	132.0	132.8	127.6
2013	125.9	123.7	124.0	124.2	125.9	127.0	126.6	126.9	124.9	126.5	130.7	132.7	126.6
2014	125.2	122.9	123.7	124.6	126.5	127.7	126.7	127.1	125.0	126.5	130.3	132.7	126.6
2015	125.9	123.0	123.4	124.0	126.0	126.9	126.6	126.6	124.2	125.9	129.7	131.8	126.2
2016	125.1	123.2	123.6	124.5	126.1	126.4	126.2	126.0	123.4	124.6	128.6	130.4	125.7
2017	124.9	122.3	122.2	123.1	123.7	124.3	124.0	123.8	122.2	124.1	126.8	127.3	124.1

Employment by Industry: Pittsburgh, PA, Selected Years, 2007–2017—*Continued*

(Numbers in thousands, not seasonally adjusted)

Industry and year	January	February	March	April	May	June	July	August	September	October	November	December	Annual average
Transportation and Utilities													
2007	45.2	44.9	45.1	45.3	45.5	44.8	41.9	41.6	44.8	44.6	44.4	44.8	44.4
2008	43.8	43.6	43.5	43.9	44.5	43.7	40.7	40.6	43.8	44.6	44.7	45.2	43.6
2009	43.3	43.1	42.7	42.8	42.8	41.6	38.6	38.6	41.8	42.2	42.5	43.1	41.9
2010	41.6	41.3	41.6	41.9	42.2	42.3	39.0	39.0	42.6	43.2	43.5	44.5	41.9
2011	42.7	42.8	42.8	43.1	43.2	42.5	39.7	39.2	43.2	43.6	44.0	44.9	42.6
2012	43.4	43.4	43.7	43.5	43.8	42.2	39.8	39.6	43.3	43.7	44.0	44.8	42.9
2013	43.3	43.1	43.2	43.1	43.5	42.3	40.1	40.4	43.6	43.8	44.7	45.4	43.0
2014	43.7	43.4	43.5	44.2	44.7	44.2	41.0	41.1	44.8	45.3	46.0	47.1	44.1
2015	45.5	45.0	45.0	45.3	45.9	45.1	42.2	42.2	45.3	45.4	46.1	47.2	45.0
2016	45.0	44.3	44.2	44.4	44.7	43.4	41.3	41.2	45.1	45.4	46.1	47.5	44.4
2017	45.0	45.0	45.1	45.5	46.0	44.2	42.3	42.3	46.3	47.1	47.8	48.7	45.4
Information													
2007	22.0	21.9	22.1	21.8	21.9	22.2	21.9	21.8	21.4	21.2	21.2	21.6	21.8
2008	21.3	21.2	21.1	21.3	21.4	21.3	20.8	20.5	20.2	20.1	20.1	20.2	20.8
2009	19.9	19.8	19.8	19.9	19.8	20.0	19.8	19.5	19.3	19.7	19.6	20.3	19.8
2010	18.6	18.5	18.2	18.4	18.4	18.9	18.8	18.5	18.7	18.1	18.2	18.3	18.5
2011	18.2	18.2	18.3	18.5	18.7	18.9	18.8	17.3	18.5	18.6	18.9	18.3	18.4
2012	18.2	18.2	18.5	18.5	19.5	19.0	18.8	18.9	18.7	18.6	18.7	18.5	18.7
2013	18.6	18.2	18.2	18.1	18.3	18.3	18.7	18.6	18.6	19.7	19.0	19.1	18.6
2014	18.0	18.1	18.1	18.9	18.4	18.4	18.4	18.4	18.3	18.1	18.1	18.2	18.3
2015	17.8	18.0	18.0	18.0	18.3	18.5	18.5	18.7	18.3	18.3	18.2	18.2	18.2
2016	17.7	17.7	17.8	18.1	17.1	18.7	18.7	18.8	18.5	18.6	18.5	18.3	18.2
2017	18.1	18.5	18.1	18.5	18.8	19.2	18.7	19.1	18.6	18.4	18.5	18.6	18.6
Financial Activities													
2007	67.6	67.8	68.0	67.8	68.2	68.8	68.9	68.8	68.0	67.7	67.8	67.6	68.1
2008	66.8	67.1	67.5	67.7	68.3	69.0	68.9	68.8	67.6	67.4	67.4	67.4	67.8
2009	66.9	66.9	66.8	67.0	67.4	68.1	68.1	68.0	67.4	67.7	67.9	68.1	67.5
2010	67.6	67.4	67.7	68.0	68.4	68.9	69.0	69.0	68.2	68.3	68.3	68.5	68.3
2011	68.6	68.4	68.5	68.8	69.3	70.1	70.4	70.4	69.7	69.9	70.1	70.3	69.5
2012	69.9	70.0	70.3	70.3	70.7	71.7	71.8	71.8	71.0	71.1	71.3	71.3	70.9
2013	70.8	70.9	71.0	71.1	71.2	71.9	71.8	71.9	70.9	71.0	71.1	70.8	71.2
2014	70.9	70.7	70.5	70.3	70.8	71.2	71.3	71.0	69.9	70.0	70.1	70.1	70.6
2015	69.3	69.5	69.5	69.6	70.3	71.0	71.2	71.2	70.3	70.6	70.9	70.7	70.3
2016	70.3	70.5	70.4	70.7	71.2	71.8	72.3	72.5	71.8	72.0	72.2	72.4	71.5
2017	72.1	72.6	72.5	72.6	73.1	73.9	74.2	74.0	73.3	72.8	72.6	72.7	73.0
Professional and Business Services													
2007	148.2	149.4	151.1	154.2	155.7	159.1	158.7	159.7	158.0	158.3	159.2	159.4	155.9
2008	156.2	156.8	157.2	160.6	161.1	162.8	163.2	163.0	161.0	160.7	160.3	158.6	160.1
2009	154.3	153.7	153.3	153.9	154.7	155.3	154.3	154.3	153.4	153.9	153.8	153.9	154.1
2010	151.0	151.1	152.7	156.6	157.5	159.6	160.6	160.9	159.7	161.1	162.0	161.4	157.9
2011	159.7	160.0	161.1	164.2	165.8	167.0	167.3	167.4	167.4	169.4	169.2	168.1	165.6
2012	167.0	167.6	170.0	172.0	172.9	174.3	173.6	173.0	171.9	174.0	173.8	173.0	171.9
2013	170.6	172.2	173.7	175.4	176.5	177.4	177.5	176.7	175.1	175.7	175.1	173.9	175.0
2014	170.9	171.6	172.8	176.0	177.5	178.3	178.7	179.0	177.8	179.0	179.5	178.5	176.6
2015	176.0	176.4	177.4	180.0	181.2	181.8	182.4	181.9	180.7	183.1	183.2	181.9	180.5
2016	178.8	178.5	179.2	182.3	181.9	182.8	182.3	181.8	181.8	183.2	183.6	181.6	181.5
2017	178.5	178.4	179.2	181.8	182.4	183.1	183.2	183.2	182.8	183.1	183.3	182.8	181.8
Education and Health Services													
2007	222.6	225.4	226.5	226.4	225.2	224.0	223.3	221.9	226.9	230.7	231.2	230.4	226.2
2008	226.3	229.9	230.1	231.0	229.4	227.4	226.5	225.8	231.1	234.1	235.3	234.0	230.1
2009	231.1	232.7	233.0	234.1	232.8	231.2	230.7	228.4	233.2	235.9	236.9	236.6	233.1
2010	234.2	234.6	235.9	236.4	234.8	234.7	233.7	231.6	236.6	240.0	239.8	239.5	236.0
2011	238.2	240.0	240.6	240.5	238.6	239.1	235.9	234.4	240.3	243.1	244.1	243.2	239.8
2012	240.1	243.5	245.1	244.1	240.7	237.8	235.6	233.0	239.7	243.7	244.5	242.4	240.9
2013	239.6	243.4	243.3	243.3	238.5	237.1	235.1	231.9	239.4	242.7	244.0	242.7	240.1
2014	240.3	242.2	243.2	243.9	240.1	237.1	235.5	232.2	240.3	243.7	244.5	242.6	240.5
2015	239.6	240.9	241.2	242.5	238.6	234.0	233.4	232.2	239.5	243.5	244.3	241.7	239.3
2016	240.7	244.3	244.3	246.3	242.4	236.8	237.4	236.5	244.6	247.7	249.1	246.9	243.1
2017	245.7	249.6	250.3	251.4	248.3	241.9	242.8	241.6	250.9	254.4	257.5	254.6	249.1

Employment by Industry: Pittsburgh, PA, Selected Years, 2007–2017—*Continued*

(Numbers in thousands, not seasonally adjusted)

Industry and year	January	February	March	April	May	June	July	August	September	October	November	December	Annual average
Leisure and Hospitality													
2007	98.7	98.4	100.2	104.2	112.3	116.0	113.8	114.9	111.2	109.5	105.9	105.4	107.5
2008	100.0	99.9	102.0	106.4	113.4	116.1	114.6	114.9	110.7	108.4	105.7	104.2	108.0
2009	98.2	98.1	100.7	104.5	111.1	113.3	112.3	114.0	110.0	106.3	103.6	103.5	106.3
2010	97.6	97.3	100.3	106.2	111.0	114.2	114.1	115.9	112.5	109.7	107.1	106.9	107.7
2011	101.5	100.8	103.4	108.6	114.3	117.8	115.9	116.7	114.0	110.8	107.9	107.4	109.9
2012	102.4	102.5	106.1	109.9	115.0	119.0	117.4	118.9	114.8	112.9	110.5	110.8	111.7
2013	105.2	105.2	107.6	111.8	118.5	122.1	121.4	121.4	117.0	114.7	111.7	111.9	114.0
2014	106.3	106.1	108.5	112.8	119.8	121.9	120.0	121.8	117.2	115.2	110.9	111.4	114.3
2015	106.9	106.9	108.8	113.8	119.9	122.6	122.0	123.4	119.1	116.6	114.8	114.4	115.8
2016	109.5	110.0	112.6	116.9	122.3	124.8	125.2	126.1	120.9	118.2	116.7	114.5	118.1
2017	110.8	111.0	113.7	118.4	123.2	126.7	125.1	126.7	121.9	121.8	119.3	120.4	119.9
Other Services													
2007	52.9	52.7	53.3	53.3	53.5	54.0	54.1	53.6	52.9	52.9	53.0	52.7	53.2
2008	52.1	51.8	52.1	52.7	53.1	53.6	53.6	53.0	52.4	52.4	52.3	52.5	52.6
2009	51.5	51.4	51.8	51.8	52.3	53.0	53.0	52.4	51.3	51.3	51.1	51.1	51.8
2010	50.3	50.0	50.7	50.8	51.4	52.2	52.4	52.4	51.0	51.1	51.0	51.1	51.2
2011	50.3	50.5	50.9	51.1	51.7	52.5	52.4	52.2	51.3	51.2	51.2	51.3	51.4
2012	50.7	50.9	51.5	51.7	52.0	53.1	52.9	52.3	51.7	51.3	51.1	51.1	51.7
2013	50.1	50.2	50.5	50.9	51.4	52.4	52.5	52.1	51.4	50.9	50.8	50.9	51.2
2014	50.2	50.3	50.7	50.6	51.1	51.9	52.6	52.4	51.3	51.1	50.8	51.0	51.2
2015	50.4	50.5	51.0	51.3	51.8	52.5	52.8	52.5	51.2	51.1	51.1	51.1	51.4
2016	50.8	50.8	51.3	51.7	51.9	52.7	52.9	52.3	51.2	51.5	51.0	50.9	51.6
2017	50.5	50.6	50.9	51.1	51.7	52.5	52.7	52.5	51.1	51.2	51.5	51.6	51.5
Government													
2007	126.7	129.5	130.3	129.8	128.6	127.3	117.6	116.2	125.4	128.4	129.5	129.1	126.5
2008	125.4	128.7	129.3	129.1	128.3	126.6	118.4	117.1	126.4	129.8	130.2	129.0	126.5
2009	125.2	128.8	129.2	130.3	129.2	127.7	119.4	117.9	126.9	130.1	131.6	130.9	127.3
2010	125.7	129.6	130.6	131.4	133.3	131.1	120.2	117.8	127.2	130.2	130.5	130.1	128.1
2011	126.6	129.3	130.0	129.5	127.8	125.9	115.4	113.3	121.6	124.6	125.7	125.5	124.6
2012	119.5	124.2	124.5	124.3	124.2	121.2	112.6	111.7	120.0	122.6	123.7	123.3	121.0
2013	118.4	122.8	122.9	123.0	123.6	119.1	110.5	110.1	119.0	120.9	122.2	121.7	119.5
2014	118.0	120.3	120.5	121.1	121.3	117.9	109.4	108.6	117.6	120.0	120.9	120.7	118.0
2015	116.1	119.2	119.4	120.3	120.2	117.2	109.3	108.7	117.1	118.3	119.5	118.3	117.0
2016	114.9	117.9	118.8	118.7	119.1	115.9	109.8	108.2	117.1	118.4	119.1	118.7	116.4
2017	113.8	118.3	118.6	118.6	118.9	115.2	109.9	107.9	116.8	117.5	118.4	117.3	115.9

Employment by Industry: Sacramento—Roseville—Arden-Arcade, CA, Selected Years, 2007–2017

(Numbers in thousands, not seasonally adjusted)

Industry and year	January	February	March	April	May	June	July	August	September	October	November	December	Annual average
Total Nonfarm													
2007	909.7	913.0	920.0	917.8	924.5	928.7	923.1	923.9	923.7	920.5	923.7	924.3	921.1
2008	904.0	907.7	909.6	908.3	911.1	912.1	903.8	899.2	897.0	893.5	892.1	890.3	902.4
2009	871.3	866.2	864.8	862.3	863.3	861.1	844.0	839.0	837.4	845.2	846.0	844.1	853.7
2010	826.9	826.4	829.7	834.1	839.7	841.1	828.4	825.7	827.1	832.6	833.3	831.2	831.4
2011	819.7	822.2	823.9	827.7	829.3	831.0	822.2	826.9	831.1	835.3	839.6	837.3	828.9
2012	825.8	831.3	835.2	845.5	850.8	858.5	844.6	848.2	848.1	854.0	860.5	857.9	846.7
2013	854.1	860.1	863.7	865.9	869.8	872.9	863.3	868.4	870.4	875.9	883.8	882.7	869.3
2014	872.1	875.6	880.0	884.9	890.8	897.6	884.7	890.6	892.0	898.8	905.7	902.8	889.6
2015	896.5	898.8	905.0	909.8	914.5	920.5	918.1	920.7	921.1	931.9	937.2	939.4	917.8
2016	929.7	935.9	936.4	945.2	948.9	952.4	949.9	953.2	952.4	957.8	962.4	963.2	949.0
2017	946.5	950.7	957.3	959.5	966.6	971.3	971.1	973.3	973.1	980.2	987.0	985.9	968.5
Total Private													
2007	678.3	680.1	684.0	681.7	686.9	689.9	691.8	693.1	689.7	684.1	686.2	686.6	686.0
2008	667.0	668.8	668.8	668.3	669.1	670.2	667.7	666.9	662.5	656.0	653.2	651.4	664.2
2009	632.6	625.8	622.6	619.7	620.5	620.4	618.5	616.8	611.5	610.6	611.0	610.9	618.4
2010	595.9	594.4	596.1	597.7	599.6	604.0	605.7	606.4	603.0	602.6	602.5	605.2	601.1
2011	592.4	593.1	593.6	596.8	599.8	602.7	608.1	611.9	611.9	610.1	614.4	616.3	604.3
2012	604.1	607.4	609.0	619.0	624.2	630.8	632.2	635.3	632.1	631.8	637.4	639.1	625.2
2013	633.4	637.6	639.0	641.1	643.8	646.5	648.5	652.3	651.0	651.8	656.5	659.0	646.7
2014	646.8	648.1	651.4	654.0	659.3	664.5	666.1	670.3	668.5	667.1	672.2	674.3	661.9
2015	665.6	667.2	671.6	675.6	680.7	685.4	693.4	694.8	692.7	696.8	700.5	705.6	685.8
2016	695.7	701.4	699.8	708.6	711.3	714.4	720.8	723.4	721.1	722.1	725.5	727.3	714.3
2017	711.8	715.6	720.0	722.8	728.7	733.6	739.3	741.8	739.4	739.6	744.9	745.5	731.9
Goods Producing													
2007	107.2	107.4	108.5	108.1	110.7	112.0	111.1	112.3	110.5	107.2	104.6	101.6	108.4
2008	95.0	94.9	95.2	95.3	96.9	98.3	98.7	99.4	97.9	95.1	91.4	88.8	95.6
2009	83.2	79.8	79.2	78.3	79.2	79.9	79.0	79.0	77.8	77.2	75.3	72.9	78.4
2010	69.8	68.6	69.5	70.3	71.4	73.1	73.9	74.8	73.9	73.0	71.4	69.7	71.6
2011	67.1	67.0	66.6	68.2	69.5	70.9	72.6	74.1	74.5	74.0	72.3	70.3	70.6
2012	68.3	68.1	67.4	69.2	71.7	73.8	75.6	77.0	76.9	76.0	74.7	73.8	72.7
2013	72.4	73.5	74.2	75.5	77.2	78.5	80.0	81.9	81.8	80.9	79.6	78.6	77.8
2014	76.8	77.1	77.4	78.5	80.8	82.3	83.7	85.1	85.0	84.1	83.6	81.3	81.3
2015	80.8	81.1	82.4	83.9	85.7	87.6	89.5	90.6	90.8	91.5	90.7	89.9	87.0
2016	86.8	87.8	87.2	90.1	91.6	92.5	94.8	95.6	95.4	93.9	92.8	90.4	91.6
2017	86.9	88.0	90.2	91.6	94.4	96.5	97.6	98.7	99.4	98.6	96.8	96.4	94.6
Service-Providing													
2007	802.5	805.6	811.5	809.7	813.8	816.7	812.0	811.6	813.2	813.3	819.1	822.7	812.6
2008	809.0	812.8	814.4	813.0	814.2	813.8	805.1	799.8	799.1	798.4	800.7	801.5	806.8
2009	788.1	786.4	785.6	784.0	784.1	781.2	765.0	760.0	759.6	768.0	770.7	771.2	775.3
2010	757.1	757.8	760.2	763.8	768.3	768.0	754.5	750.9	753.2	759.6	761.9	761.5	759.7
2011	752.6	755.2	757.3	759.5	759.8	760.1	749.6	752.8	756.6	761.3	767.3	767.0	758.3
2012	757.5	763.2	767.8	776.3	779.1	784.7	769.0	771.2	771.2	778.0	785.8	784.1	774.0
2013	781.7	786.6	789.5	790.4	792.6	794.4	783.3	786.5	788.6	795.0	804.2	804.1	791.4
2014	795.3	798.5	802.6	806.4	810.0	815.3	801.0	805.5	807.0	814.7	822.1	821.5	808.3
2015	815.7	817.7	822.6	825.9	828.8	832.9	828.6	830.1	830.3	840.4	846.5	849.5	830.8
2016	842.9	848.1	849.2	855.1	857.3	859.9	855.1	857.6	857.0	863.9	869.6	872.8	857.4
2017	859.6	862.7	867.1	867.9	872.2	874.8	873.5	874.6	873.7	881.6	890.2	889.5	874.0
Mining and Logging													
2007	0.6	0.6	0.6	0.6	0.7	0.7	0.7	0.7	0.7	0.8	0.7	0.7	0.7
2008	0.6	0.6	0.6	0.7	0.7	0.7	0.7	0.7	0.7	0.7	0.6	0.6	0.7
2009	0.4	0.4	0.4	0.4	0.4	0.4	0.5	0.5	0.5	0.5	0.5	0.4	0.4
2010	0.3	0.3	0.4	0.4	0.4	0.5	0.5	0.5	0.5	0.5	0.5	0.5	0.4
2011	0.4	0.4	0.4	0.4	0.4	0.4	0.4	0.5	0.5	0.5	0.5	0.4	0.4
2012	0.4	0.4	0.4	0.3	0.4	0.4	0.4	0.4	0.4	0.4	0.4	0.4	0.4
2013	0.3	0.3	0.3	0.3	0.4	0.4	0.4	0.4	0.4	0.4	0.4	0.4	0.4
2014	0.3	0.4	0.3	0.4	0.4	0.5	0.4	0.5	0.4	0.5	0.5	0.4	0.4
2015	0.4	0.4	0.4	0.4	0.4	0.4	0.5	0.5	0.5	0.5	0.4	0.4	0.4
2016	0.4	0.4	0.4	0.4	0.4	0.4	0.5	0.5	0.5	0.5	0.5	0.4	0.4
2017	0.4	0.4	0.4	0.4	0.4	0.5	0.5	0.5	0.5	0.5	0.5	0.5	0.5

Employment by Industry: Sacramento—Roseville—Arden-Arcade, CA, Selected Years, 2007–2017—*Continued*

(Numbers in thousands, not seasonally adjusted)

Industry and year	January	February	March	April	May	June	July	August	September	October	November	December	Annual average
Construction													
2007	65.7	65.7	67.0	66.8	69.0	70.0	69.6	69.8	68.2	66.1	63.9	61.1	66.9
2008	55.2	55.3	55.5	55.7	57.2	58.5	59.2	59.0	57.6	56.2	53.6	51.2	56.2
2009	47.0	44.2	44.0	43.5	44.4	45.0	44.3	43.9	42.7	42.4	41.5	39.4	43.5
2010	37.1	36.1	36.8	37.6	38.6	40.0	40.5	40.5	39.5	39.2	38.2	36.4	38.4
2011	34.4	34.2	33.6	35.1	36.2	37.3	39.3	39.6	39.6	39.2	38.5	36.4	37.0
2012	34.8	34.6	34.0	35.5	37.7	39.4	40.7	41.4	41.2	41.4	40.6	39.8	38.4
2013	38.8	39.7	40.6	41.5	43.0	44.2	45.4	46.4	46.1	46.0	44.8	43.6	43.3
2014	42.3	42.2	42.6	43.4	45.5	46.6	47.5	48.0	47.9	47.8	47.3	45.1	45.5
2015	44.9	45.2	46.2	47.5	49.2	50.8	52.1	52.8	52.8	54.4	53.9	53.1	50.2
2016	50.2	51.2	50.5	53.7	54.9	56.1	57.8	58.2	57.9	57.5	56.7	54.6	54.9
2017	51.4	52.4	55.1	56.1	58.5	60.4	61.3	61.9	62.2	62.3	61.0	60.5	58.6
Manufacturing													
2007	40.9	41.1	40.9	40.7	41.0	41.3	40.8	41.8	41.6	40.3	40.0	39.8	40.9
2008	39.2	39.0	39.1	38.9	39.0	39.1	38.8	39.7	39.6	38.2	37.2	37.0	38.7
2009	35.8	35.2	34.8	34.4	34.4	34.5	34.2	34.6	34.6	34.3	33.3	33.1	34.4
2010	32.4	32.2	32.3	32.3	32.4	32.6	32.9	33.8	33.9	33.3	32.7	32.8	32.8
2011	32.3	32.4	32.6	32.7	32.9	33.2	32.9	34.0	34.4	34.3	33.3	33.5	33.2
2012	33.1	33.1	33.0	33.4	33.6	34.0	34.5	35.2	35.3	34.2	33.7	33.6	33.9
2013	33.3	33.5	33.3	33.7	33.8	33.9	34.2	35.1	35.3	34.5	34.4	34.6	34.1
2014	34.2	34.5	34.5	34.7	34.9	35.2	35.8	36.6	36.7	35.8	35.8	35.8	35.4
2015	35.5	35.5	35.8	36.0	36.1	36.4	36.9	37.3	37.5	36.6	36.4	36.4	36.4
2016	36.2	36.2	36.3	36.0	36.3	36.0	36.5	36.9	37.0	35.9	35.6	35.4	36.2
2017	35.1	35.2	34.7	35.1	35.5	35.6	35.8	36.3	36.7	35.8	35.3	35.4	35.5
Trade, Transportation, and Utilities													
2007	153.9	152.2	152.0	151.2	151.7	152.2	152.8	152.7	152.2	152.3	156.3	158.2	153.1
2008	150.5	148.5	148.2	147.3	147.0	147.1	146.4	145.7	144.3	143.7	145.2	145.8	146.6
2009	138.2	135.4	134.1	133.6	134.6	134.7	133.8	133.2	133.4	133.7	136.9	137.8	135.0
2010	132.4	130.3	130.3	130.9	131.5	131.6	131.9	132.5	132.1	133.4	136.1	138.1	132.6
2011	132.5	131.0	131.0	131.2	132.0	132.7	133.4	134.0	134.2	135.8	140.0	141.8	134.1
2012	135.9	134.2	134.6	136.7	137.7	138.7	138.8	139.4	139.6	140.4	145.0	146.3	138.9
2013	140.3	139.2	139.3	139.4	140.1	140.6	141.1	141.0	140.8	142.4	147.3	148.6	141.7
2014	142.1	140.7	140.9	140.7	141.3	142.1	142.7	143.5	143.0	144.0	148.6	150.6	143.4
2015	144.4	142.9	143.3	144.3	145.5	145.5	146.8	147.6	147.6	149.5	154.1	155.3	147.2
2016	149.7	148.8	148.5	149.9	150.5	150.8	152.2	152.8	152.1	153.4	158.2	158.7	152.1
2017	153.2	151.1	150.9	151.8	152.4	152.5	153.5	154.7	154.0	155.4	161.2	161.5	154.4
Wholesale Trade													
2007	28.4	28.2	28.5	28.1	28.0	28.1	27.8	27.7	27.5	27.4	27.3	27.5	27.9
2008	27.0	27.0	26.8	26.8	26.9	26.8	26.6	26.3	26.2	26.0	25.7	25.4	26.5
2009	25.0	24.7	24.5	24.4	24.6	24.6	24.1	23.7	23.5	23.6	23.5	23.1	24.1
2010	23.0	22.8	22.6	22.9	23.0	22.8	22.7	22.7	22.6	22.8	22.8	22.9	22.8
2011	22.8	22.7	22.8	23.3	23.5	23.7	23.7	23.7	23.9	24.3	24.6	24.8	23.7
2012	24.6	24.8	25.2	25.5	25.6	25.6	25.3	25.2	25.1	25.2	25.2	25.2	25.2
2013	24.9	24.9	25.0	25.0	25.0	25.1	25.1	24.8	24.8	25.1	25.1	25.0	25.0
2014	24.8	24.9	24.8	24.5	24.5	24.5	24.4	24.3	24.3	24.2	24.3	24.3	24.5
2015	24.3	24.2	24.2	24.4	24.6	24.5	24.7	24.7	24.6	25.2	25.2	25.2	24.7
2016	25.2	25.3	25.2	25.6	25.5	25.6	26.0	26.0	25.9	26.0	26.0	26.2	25.7
2017	26.1	26.2	26.2	26.3	26.4	26.5	26.9	26.9	26.8	27.1	26.8	26.8	26.6
Retail Trade													
2007	100.4	98.9	98.4	98.2	98.6	98.7	99.5	99.3	98.9	99.3	103.3	104.4	99.8
2008	98.4	96.3	96.1	95.5	95.2	95.2	94.5	94.1	92.9	92.8	94.8	95.4	95.1
2009	89.4	87.0	86.1	85.9	86.9	87.0	86.9	86.5	86.8	87.3	90.4	91.6	87.7
2010	87.2	85.6	85.7	86.4	86.9	87.1	87.6	88.1	88.0	89.0	91.7	93.2	88.0
2011	89.0	87.6	87.3	87.1	87.5	87.9	88.6	89.0	89.1	90.2	94.0	95.3	89.4
2012	90.7	88.7	88.8	89.7	90.3	90.9	91.2	91.8	91.9	92.6	97.0	97.8	91.8
2013	92.8	91.7	91.7	91.8	92.4	92.6	93.2	93.3	93.0	94.3	98.8	99.7	93.8
2014	94.5	93.1	93.4	93.3	93.6	94.2	94.7	95.2	94.7	95.8	99.8	101.1	95.3
2015	96.2	94.9	95.2	95.9	96.8	96.8	97.4	97.9	98.0	99.2	103.3	103.9	98.0
2016	99.5	98.7	98.4	99.0	99.2	99.1	99.9	100.4	99.8	101.1	105.1	105.1	100.4
2017	101.2	99.3	98.9	100.0	100.4	100.3	101.0	101.8	101.4	102.6	107.1	107.0	101.8

Employment by Industry: Sacramento—Roseville—Arden-Arcade, CA, Selected Years, 2007–2017—*Continued*

(Numbers in thousands, not seasonally adjusted)

Industry and year	January	February	March	April	May	June	July	August	September	October	November	December	Annual average
Transportation and Utilities													
2007	25.1	25.1	25.1	24.9	25.1	25.4	25.5	25.7	25.8	25.6	25.7	26.3	25.4
2008	25.1	25.2	25.3	25.0	24.9	25.1	25.3	25.3	25.2	24.9	24.7	25.0	25.1
2009	23.8	23.7	23.5	23.3	23.1	23.1	22.8	23.0	23.1	22.8	23.0	23.1	23.2
2010	22.2	21.9	22.0	21.6	21.6	21.7	21.6	21.7	21.5	21.6	21.6	22.0	21.8
2011	20.7	20.7	20.9	20.8	21.0	21.1	21.1	21.3	21.2	21.3	21.4	21.7	21.1
2012	20.6	20.7	20.6	21.5	21.8	22.2	22.3	22.4	22.6	22.6	22.8	23.3	22.0
2013	22.6	22.6	22.6	22.6	22.7	22.9	22.8	22.9	23.0	23.0	23.4	23.9	22.9
2014	22.8	22.7	22.7	22.9	23.2	23.4	23.6	24.0	24.0	24.0	24.5	25.2	23.6
2015	23.9	23.8	23.9	24.0	24.1	24.2	24.7	25.0	25.0	25.1	25.6	26.2	24.6
2016	25.0	24.8	24.9	25.3	25.8	26.1	26.3	26.4	26.4	26.3	27.1	27.4	26.0
2017	25.9	25.6	25.8	25.5	25.6	25.7	25.6	26.0	25.8	25.7	27.3	27.7	26.0
Information													
2007	20.4	20.7	20.4	20.1	20.3	20.0	20.0	20.0	19.8	19.7	19.7	19.7	20.1
2008	19.5	19.7	19.5	19.4	19.4	19.4	19.3	19.3	19.1	18.6	18.8	18.8	19.2
2009	18.9	18.8	18.6	18.1	18.3	18.2	18.4	18.3	18.1	18.0	18.0	18.0	18.3
2010	17.8	17.7	17.4	17.3	17.2	17.6	17.1	16.9	16.7	16.7	17.0	17.0	17.2
2011	16.9	16.8	16.8	16.7	16.6	16.5	16.4	16.2	15.9	15.9	15.7	15.6	16.3
2012	15.6	15.6	15.6	15.7	15.7	15.8	15.7	15.5	15.3	15.3	15.5	15.6	15.6
2013	15.3	15.3	15.0	15.1	15.0	15.0	14.9	14.7	14.4	14.2	14.2	14.1	14.8
2014	13.8	13.7	13.6	13.7	13.8	13.9	14.0	14.0	13.8	13.9	14.0	14.2	13.9
2015	14.2	14.2	14.1	14.2	14.2	14.3	14.3	14.1	14.0	14.0	13.9	14.1	14.1
2016	14.0	14.0	13.9	13.9	13.9	13.8	13.7	13.7	13.5	13.4	13.6	13.6	13.8
2017	13.4	12.7	12.6	12.5	12.5	12.4	12.5	12.5	12.3	12.2	12.2	12.2	12.5
Financial Activities													
2007	62.7	62.9	62.5	62.5	62.3	62.1	61.9	61.4	60.7	60.2	59.6	59.6	61.5
2008	58.6	58.6	58.2	58.0	57.7	57.5	57.4	56.9	56.5	55.8	55.6	55.4	57.2
2009	55.5	55.3	55.1	53.9	53.5	53.1	52.8	52.4	51.3	51.0	50.6	50.6	52.9
2010	49.8	49.5	49.5	49.0	48.7	48.8	48.3	48.1	47.8	47.5	46.5	46.5	48.3
2011	46.3	46.0	46.2	46.5	46.7	46.7	47.0	47.3	47.1	46.8	46.6	46.7	46.7
2012	47.0	47.1	47.3	47.7	47.8	48.2	48.7	48.8	48.6	48.9	48.8	49.2	48.2
2013	49.0	49.2	49.1	49.5	49.6	49.7	50.2	50.0	49.5	49.1	48.8	49.0	49.4
2014	48.6	48.4	48.2	48.1	48.4	48.8	49.0	49.1	49.1	49.6	49.6	49.9	48.9
2015	49.8	50.1	50.3	50.3	50.6	51.0	51.6	51.4	50.9	51.2	51.3	51.4	50.8
2016	51.1	51.2	51.1	51.2	51.5	51.4	52.2	52.2	52.0	52.2	52.1	52.2	51.7
2017	51.8	51.9	52.0	51.6	51.8	52.0	52.8	52.9	52.6	52.2	52.0	51.7	52.1
Professional and Business Services													
2007	108.7	110.1	110.9	111.5	111.5	112.5	113.5	113.9	113.4	113.7	113.6	114.1	112.3
2008	110.1	111.3	111.0	111.4	110.9	110.3	110.1	110.0	109.5	110.0	108.9	108.4	110.2
2009	104.0	103.3	102.4	101.4	100.1	100.1	101.4	101.2	99.7	100.8	100.4	100.3	101.3
2010	98.9	100.5	100.9	101.6	101.7	103.0	103.8	103.8	103.3	104.0	103.2	102.8	102.3
2011	100.5	102.3	101.5	102.7	102.9	103.3	105.4	106.7	106.3	106.9	107.2	107.2	104.4
2012	104.0	106.4	105.8	109.9	111.6	113.1	114.1	114.8	112.5	114.3	114.0	113.1	111.1
2013	112.2	113.8	113.0	112.7	113.0	114.1	113.8	115.6	116.2	117.2	117.1	116.6	114.6
2014	114.4	116.6	117.1	117.7	118.3	118.7	118.6	119.8	119.7	118.9	119.3	119.3	118.2
2015	116.6	117.5	117.8	118.3	118.7	119.3	121.9	122.7	121.7	122.8	122.5	123.0	120.2
2016	123.6	125.6	124.9	127.4	127.5	127.9	129.0	130.3	129.1	130.7	130.1	130.1	128.0
2017	127.1	128.7	128.9	128.5	130.2	130.8	132.4	132.9	132.1	131.4	131.5	131.1	130.5
Education and Health Services													
2007	112.1	112.4	114.0	113.9	115.2	114.3	114.6	114.5	116.2	116.5	118.3	117.9	115.0
2008	117.8	119.2	119.3	120.1	120.4	119.5	118.5	119.1	120.4	120.8	122.1	121.7	119.9
2009	121.3	121.8	121.9	122.1	122.9	121.6	120.3	120.6	121.1	122.7	122.7	122.4	121.8
2010	120.1	120.0	120.1	121.2	121.8	120.7	119.6	119.6	120.2	121.2	121.8	121.8	120.7
2011	121.1	121.2	121.7	122.5	123.0	122.0	121.2	121.8	123.0	123.2	124.3	124.4	122.5
2012	124.5	125.3	126.6	126.3	127.0	126.1	123.8	124.1	125.6	125.1	126.7	126.2	125.6
2013	129.0	130.1	130.8	131.3	132.1	129.8	128.7	129.6	130.5	131.6	132.2	132.3	130.7
2014	132.3	131.8	132.9	133.5	135.1	133.8	132.8	134.0	135.2	136.1	136.7	137.0	134.3
2015	136.9	137.4	138.6	139.7	140.5	139.5	139.5	139.5	140.6	142.5	142.7	143.6	140.1
2016	142.6	144.3	144.0	144.9	145.7	145.1	144.1	144.5	146.2	148.0	148.5	149.6	145.6
2017	147.5	149.0	150.1	151.1	151.7	151.2	151.5	152.5	153.6	155.5	156.5	156.2	152.2

Employment by Industry: Sacramento—Roseville—Arden-Arcade, CA, Selected Years, 2007–2017—*Continued*

(Numbers in thousands, not seasonally adjusted)

Industry and year	January	February	March	April	May	June	July	August	September	October	November	December	Annual average
Leisure and Hospitality													
2007	85.5	86.2	87.2	85.8	86.1	87.6	88.6	88.8	87.4	85.1	85.0	86.2	86.6
2008	87.0	87.7	88.4	87.1	86.7	88.1	87.1	86.3	84.6	82.2	81.8	83.3	85.9
2009	82.6	82.4	82.5	82.9	82.4	83.6	83.7	83.3	81.4	78.7	78.8	81.0	81.9
2010	79.5	80.2	80.6	79.3	78.9	80.7	82.4	82.1	80.4	78.5	78.6	81.7	80.2
2011	80.5	81.2	82.2	80.9	80.9	82.3	83.6	83.4	82.4	79.7	80.6	82.5	81.7
2012	80.9	82.7	83.3	84.9	83.7	85.7	86.9	86.9	85.1	83.3	84.2	86.5	84.5
2013	87.0	87.9	88.8	88.7	87.7	89.6	90.7	90.3	88.6	87.1	88.0	90.5	88.7
2014	89.8	90.4	91.6	91.6	91.0	93.9	94.5	94.2	92.1	90.1	90.1	92.0	91.8
2015	93.1	94.0	94.8	93.9	94.4	96.9	98.2	97.5	95.8	94.1	94.3	97.4	95.4
2016	97.4	98.7	99.2	99.9	99.0	100.8	102.4	102.2	100.7	98.3	98.1	101.0	99.8
2017	100.6	102.3	103.1	103.5	103.2	105.2	106.2	104.8	102.4	101.9	103.2	104.8	103.4
Other Services													
2007	27.8	28.2	28.5	28.6	29.1	29.2	29.3	29.5	29.5	29.4	29.1	29.3	29.0
2008	28.5	28.9	29.0	29.7	30.1	30.0	30.2	30.2	30.2	29.8	29.4	29.2	29.6
2009	28.9	29.0	28.8	29.4	29.5	29.2	29.1	28.8	28.7	28.5	28.3	27.9	28.8
2010	27.6	27.6	27.8	28.1	28.4	28.5	28.7	28.6	28.6	28.3	27.9	27.6	28.1
2011	27.5	27.6	27.6	28.1	28.2	28.3	28.5	28.4	28.5	27.8	27.7	27.8	28.0
2012	27.9	28.0	28.4	28.6	29.0	29.4	28.6	28.8	28.5	28.5	28.5	28.4	28.6
2013	28.2	28.6	28.8	28.9	29.1	29.2	29.1	29.2	29.2	29.3	29.3	29.3	29.0
2014	29.0	29.4	29.7	30.2	30.6	31.0	30.8	30.6	30.6	30.4	30.3	30.0	30.2
2015	29.8	30.0	30.3	31.0	31.1	31.3	31.6	31.4	31.3	31.2	31.0	30.9	30.9
2016	30.5	31.0	31.0	31.3	31.6	32.1	32.4	32.1	32.1	32.2	32.1	31.7	31.7
2017	31.3	31.9	32.2	32.2	32.5	33.0	32.8	32.8	33.0	32.4	31.5	31.6	32.3
Government													
2007	231.4	232.9	236.0	236.1	237.6	238.8	231.3	230.8	234.0	236.4	237.5	237.7	235.0
2008	237.0	238.9	240.8	240.0	242.0	241.9	236.1	232.3	234.5	237.5	238.9	238.9	238.2
2009	238.7	240.4	242.2	242.6	242.8	240.7	225.5	222.2	225.9	234.6	235.0	233.2	235.3
2010	231.0	232.0	233.6	236.4	240.1	237.1	222.7	219.3	224.1	230.0	230.8	226.0	230.3
2011	227.3	229.1	230.3	230.9	229.5	228.3	214.1	215.0	219.2	225.2	225.2	221.0	224.6
2012	221.7	223.9	226.2	226.5	226.6	227.7	212.4	212.9	216.0	222.2	223.1	218.8	221.5
2013	220.7	222.5	224.7	224.8	226.0	226.4	214.8	216.1	219.4	224.1	227.3	223.7	222.5
2014	225.3	227.5	228.6	230.9	231.5	233.1	218.6	220.3	223.5	231.7	233.5	228.5	227.8
2015	230.9	231.6	233.4	234.2	233.8	235.1	224.7	225.9	228.4	235.1	236.7	233.8	232.0
2016	234.0	234.5	236.6	236.6	237.6	238.0	229.1	229.8	231.3	235.7	236.9	235.9	234.7
2017	234.7	235.1	237.3	236.7	237.9	237.7	231.8	231.5	233.7	240.6	242.1	240.4	236.6

Employment by Industry: Las Vegas-Henderson-Paradise, NV, Selected Years, 2007–2017

(Numbers in thousands, not seasonally adjusted)

Industry and year	January	February	March	April	May	June	July	August	September	October	November	December	Annual average
Total Nonfarm													
2007	913.3	924.0	928.0	930.5	936.8	933.4	921.3	921.2	924.7	932.3	935.4	936.4	928.1
2008	919.6	921.5	923.6	926.3	929.7	923.1	910.3	906.8	910.1	903.6	893.6	880.7	912.4
2009	855.7	850.4	842.8	836.4	832.2	824.2	811.3	807.4	815.6	815.7	815.8	816.9	827.0
2010	798.3	798.7	799.4	808.2	811.7	807.8	800.6	799.4	799.8	806.4	807.9	805.5	803.6
2011	797.2	797.3	803.5	810.3	811.3	807.5	804.6	803.8	811.6	817.6	818.4	816.6	808.3
2012	808.6	810.6	815.7	822.1	827.8	826.9	818.8	822.6	830.7	837.8	842.4	838.6	825.2
2013	831.0	832.3	839.6	846.6	850.6	851.1	845.0	849.3	854.0	861.7	868.0	865.6	849.6
2014	858.5	863.1	871.5	878.1	884.8	881.0	874.4	885.2	892.9	903.1	905.5	905.6	883.6
2015	897.9	900.5	908.1	915.2	919.3	915.5	910.1	918.3	924.6	935.3	941.4	941.8	919.0
2016	926.4	930.1	937.3	946.3	947.5	946.3	946.9	950.3	961.2	964.7	969.6	966.9	949.5
2017	959.4	962.0	973.1	970.7	977.8	974.1	971.1	974.3	984.5	991.0	991.1	993.0	976.8
Total Private													
2007	819.5	826.2	829.7	830.6	836.7	837.4	829.7	831.1	827.6	831.1	833.4	834.0	830.6
2008	821.0	819.2	820.6	822.2	825.7	823.7	814.4	812.2	808.4	798.0	787.9	775.1	810.7
2009	755.1	747.9	740.4	734.6	731.4	727.7	718.2	715.7	717.4	716.6	717.3	718.8	728.4
2010	702.7	700.5	701.0	709.5	710.8	712.5	707.4	708.2	704.0	709.6	711.0	708.7	707.2
2011	702.0	700.5	706.6	713.6	715.0	717.4	715.6	714.7	718.3	723.0	723.8	721.1	714.3
2012	716.0	716.1	720.0	726.5	732.0	735.5	729.5	733.9	736.3	742.4	746.1	741.4	731.3
2013	736.6	736.9	743.4	750.1	754.2	758.4	755.5	758.2	758.8	764.8	770.2	766.9	754.5
2014	762.7	765.8	773.1	780.2	786.6	788.4	783.5	793.3	796.0	804.9	806.8	806.1	787.3
2015	800.9	802.3	808.7	815.8	820.1	819.9	817.5	824.4	825.4	836.3	840.7	839.8	821.0
2016	827.3	829.5	835.3	845.2	846.4	850.9	852.0	854.9	859.8	863.5	867.0	863.3	849.6
2017	859.7	859.5	869.6	869.4	875.5	877.7	873.7	875.1	879.4	884.5	884.7	886.3	874.6
Goods Producing													
2007	128.1	129.6	131.9	131.0	132.7	132.1	131.5	132.0	129.5	127.9	126.5	125.5	129.9
2008	121.3	121.4	120.9	120.7	121.7	122.0	121.9	120.6	118.0	114.7	109.7	104.8	118.1
2009	99.3	96.8	94.0	90.8	86.5	84.8	82.9	82.2	81.2	79.8	77.2	73.7	85.8
2010	66.8	65.3	64.6	66.8	66.7	66.3	65.2	65.0	63.6	63.0	61.7	60.1	64.6
2011	57.7	57.5	57.2	57.6	57.1	57.2	57.9	58.5	58.0	58.0	57.2	57.0	57.6
2012	54.8	54.7	55.1	55.6	56.6	57.8	58.0	59.5	60.0	60.5	61.0	61.0	57.9
2013	59.3	59.8	60.4	61.2	61.1	61.9	62.0	63.4	63.3	64.2	64.4	64.1	62.1
2014	63.7	64.2	64.4	65.3	65.8	66.0	66.9	68.6	68.9	69.6	69.4	69.6	66.9
2015	69.8	70.3	70.3	70.8	72.1	72.7	72.6	74.0	74.3	76.0	76.4	77.0	73.0
2016	75.6	75.6	75.5	75.5	75.3	76.9	77.7	78.4	78.9	79.1	79.0	79.3	77.2
2017	79.4	80.1	81.9	81.6	82.1	83.0	82.5	82.5	83.8	84.7	84.8	86.3	82.7
Service-Providing													
2007	785.2	794.4	796.1	799.5	804.1	801.3	789.8	789.2	795.2	804.4	808.9	810.9	798.3
2008	798.3	800.1	802.7	805.6	808.0	801.1	788.4	786.2	792.1	788.9	783.9	775.9	794.3
2009	756.4	753.6	748.8	745.6	745.7	739.4	728.4	725.2	734.4	735.9	738.6	743.2	741.3
2010	731.5	733.4	734.8	741.4	745.0	741.5	735.4	734.4	736.2	743.4	746.2	745.4	739.1
2011	739.5	739.8	746.3	752.7	754.2	750.3	746.7	745.3	753.6	759.6	761.2	759.6	750.7
2012	753.8	755.9	760.6	766.5	771.2	769.1	760.8	763.1	770.7	777.3	781.4	777.6	767.3
2013	771.7	772.5	779.2	785.4	789.5	789.2	783.0	785.9	790.7	797.5	803.6	801.5	787.5
2014	794.8	798.9	807.1	812.8	819.0	815.0	807.5	816.6	824.0	833.5	836.1	836.0	816.8
2015	828.1	830.2	837.8	844.4	847.2	842.8	837.5	844.3	850.3	859.3	865.0	864.8	846.0
2016	850.8	854.5	861.8	870.8	872.2	869.4	869.2	871.9	882.3	885.6	890.6	887.6	872.2
2017	880.0	881.9	891.2	889.1	895.7	891.1	888.6	891.8	900.7	906.3	906.3	906.7	894.1
Mining, Logging, and Construction													
2007	101.4	102.9	105.0	104.1	105.7	104.9	104.5	105.1	102.8	101.6	100.2	99.4	103.1
2008	95.4	95.6	95.1	94.9	95.8	96.0	96.1	95.0	92.7	89.8	85.5	81.1	92.8
2009	76.5	74.5	72.1	69.3	65.5	64.1	62.3	61.5	60.5	59.4	57.0	53.6	64.7
2010	47.1	45.8	45.2	47.1	47.1	46.7	45.7	45.7	44.2	43.6	42.2	40.7	45.1
2011	38.3	38.1	37.7	38.0	37.6	37.5	38.2	38.5	38.0	37.9	37.2	36.9	37.8
2012	35.1	35.1	35.3	35.6	36.5	37.3	37.6	39.0	39.6	40.1	40.5	40.5	37.7
2013	39.1	39.5	40.0	40.6	40.3	41.0	41.1	42.5	42.5	43.3	43.4	42.9	41.4
2014	42.7	43.3	43.5	44.3	44.7	44.9	45.8	47.4	47.7	48.2	48.0	48.2	45.7
2015	48.5	49.0	48.8	49.4	50.5	50.9	51.0	52.5	52.7	54.3	54.5	55.1	51.4
2016	53.9	53.8	53.6	53.7	53.4	54.8	55.5	56.1	56.5	56.6	56.5	56.6	55.1
2017	56.9	57.5	59.1	58.7	59.2	59.9	59.3	59.4	60.5	61.3	61.6	62.8	59.7

Employment by Industry: Las Vegas-Henderson-Paradise, NV, Selected Years, 2007–2017—*Continued*

(Numbers in thousands, not seasonally adjusted)

Industry and year	January	February	March	April	May	June	July	August	September	October	November	December	Annual average
Manufacturing													
2007	26.7	26.7	26.9	26.9	27.0	27.2	27.0	26.9	26.7	26.3	26.3	26.1	26.7
2008	25.9	25.8	25.8	25.8	25.9	26.0	25.8	25.6	25.3	24.9	24.2	23.7	25.4
2009	22.8	22.3	21.9	21.5	21.0	20.7	20.6	20.7	20.7	20.4	20.2	20.1	21.1
2010	19.7	19.5	19.4	19.7	19.6	19.6	19.5	19.3	19.4	19.4	19.5	19.4	19.5
2011	19.4	19.4	19.5	19.6	19.5	19.7	19.7	20.0	20.0	20.1	20.0	20.1	19.8
2012	19.7	19.6	19.8	20.0	20.1	20.5	20.4	20.5	20.4	20.4	20.5	20.5	20.2
2013	20.2	20.3	20.4	20.6	20.8	20.9	20.9	20.9	20.8	20.9	21.0	21.2	20.7
2014	21.0	20.9	20.9	21.0	21.1	21.1	21.1	21.2	21.2	21.4	21.4	21.4	21.1
2015	21.3	21.3	21.5	21.4	21.6	21.8	21.6	21.5	21.6	21.7	21.9	21.9	21.6
2016	21.7	21.8	21.9	21.8	21.9	22.1	22.2	22.3	22.4	22.5	22.5	22.7	22.2
2017	22.5	22.6	22.8	22.9	22.9	23.1	23.2	23.1	23.3	23.4	23.2	23.5	23.0
Trade, Transportation, and Utilities													
2007	158.4	157.7	158.4	158.8	160.0	160.7	160.0	161.0	161.0	162.1	166.6	168.9	161.1
2008	163.2	161.2	161.6	161.0	160.9	160.9	161.1	161.1	160.3	159.5	160.4	160.0	160.9
2009	152.8	150.1	149.1	147.6	147.4	147.5	146.6	146.5	147.1	148.0	151.2	152.2	148.8
2010	146.5	144.7	144.8	145.1	145.8	146.6	146.8	147.3	146.9	148.4	151.8	152.9	147.3
2011	147.1	145.7	146.1	147.5	147.8	148.4	149.1	149.6	149.8	151.9	156.2	156.7	149.7
2012	152.2	150.3	151.2	152.0	152.8	153.4	153.2	153.4	153.9	154.5	160.1	159.8	153.9
2013	154.5	152.4	151.7	152.4	154.7	155.5	156.1	156.7	157.4	158.9	164.1	165.3	156.6
2014	159.1	158.0	158.6	159.1	160.0	160.7	161.0	162.1	162.8	165.5	170.4	171.8	162.4
2015	166.0	164.6	165.7	166.5	167.5	167.7	167.8	168.6	168.9	170.7	175.2	175.6	168.7
2016	167.1	166.4	166.8	168.4	169.0	169.1	169.8	170.7	171.1	172.5	177.9	178.1	170.6
2017	172.3	170.7	170.8	171.2	172.0	172.6	172.9	174.3	174.9	176.3	183.4	185.3	174.7
Wholesale Trade													
2007	23.8	23.9	24.0	24.0	24.2	24.3	24.2	24.3	24.3	24.2	24.2	24.2	24.1
2008	24.0	24.0	24.1	23.9	24.0	24.0	24.1	24.1	24.0	23.7	23.4	23.1	23.9
2009	22.5	22.3	22.0	21.6	21.3	21.2	21.1	21.0	20.9	20.9	20.8	20.8	21.4
2010	20.4	20.3	20.4	20.4	20.5	20.6	20.5	20.5	20.4	20.6	20.5	20.5	20.5
2011	20.2	20.1	20.2	20.3	20.2	20.3	20.3	20.2	20.1	20.1	20.1	20.1	20.2
2012	19.9	19.9	20.0	20.0	20.1	20.2	20.2	20.2	20.2	20.2	20.2	20.3	20.1
2013	20.0	20.0	20.1	20.2	20.3	20.4	20.5	20.7	20.7	20.7	20.8	20.9	20.4
2014	20.7	20.9	20.9	20.8	20.9	20.9	21.1	21.1	21.1	21.2	21.2	21.3	21.0
2015	21.2	21.2	21.2	21.2	21.3	21.3	21.4	21.4	21.5	21.6	21.7	21.7	21.4
2016	21.2	21.3	21.1	21.4	21.5	21.5	21.6	21.7	21.7	21.8	21.9	22.0	21.6
2017	21.9	22.0	22.2	22.4	22.7	22.9	22.9	22.9	22.9	22.8	23.2	23.6	22.7
Retail Trade													
2007	98.7	97.8	98.1	98.5	99.2	99.5	99.4	99.9	99.6	100.2	104.1	106.2	100.1
2008	101.6	99.9	100.0	99.6	99.2	99.4	99.4	99.3	98.8	98.5	99.8	100.0	99.6
2009	94.5	92.2	91.6	90.7	90.8	91.0	90.6	90.7	91.6	92.6	95.6	96.7	92.4
2010	91.6	90.1	90.2	90.6	91.1	91.6	92.0	92.5	92.2	93.5	96.8	97.6	92.5
2011	92.7	91.3	91.5	92.2	92.7	93.0	93.4	94.0	94.2	95.9	100.1	100.6	94.3
2012	96.5	94.8	95.5	96.0	96.4	96.8	96.5	96.7	97.2	98.1	103.6	103.0	97.6
2013	98.0	96.3	96.4	96.7	97.9	98.4	98.9	99.4	99.7	101.0	105.8	106.8	99.6
2014	101.2	99.8	100.2	100.5	101.1	101.5	101.6	102.5	103.0	105.4	110.0	110.9	103.1
2015	105.2	104.0	104.7	105.4	105.8	106.0	105.9	106.6	106.4	108.1	112.1	112.1	106.9
2016	105.4	104.6	105.0	105.6	106.0	106.1	106.3	107.0	107.1	108.8	113.5	113.2	107.4
2017	107.7	106.3	106.1	106.2	107.0	107.0	106.9	107.3	107.6	108.4	114.5	114.7	108.3
Transportation and Utilities													
2007	35.9	36.0	36.3	36.3	36.6	36.9	36.4	36.8	37.1	37.7	38.3	38.5	36.9
2008	37.6	37.3	37.5	37.5	37.7	37.5	37.6	37.7	37.5	37.3	37.2	36.9	37.4
2009	35.8	35.6	35.5	35.3	35.3	35.3	34.9	34.8	34.6	34.5	34.8	34.7	35.1
2010	34.5	34.3	34.2	34.1	34.2	34.4	34.3	34.3	34.3	34.3	34.5	34.8	34.4
2011	34.2	34.3	34.4	35.0	34.9	35.1	35.4	35.4	35.5	35.9	36.0	36.0	35.2
2012	35.8	35.6	35.7	36.0	36.3	36.4	36.5	36.5	36.5	36.2	36.3	36.5	36.2
2013	36.5	36.1	35.2	35.5	36.5	36.7	36.7	36.6	37.0	37.2	37.5	37.6	36.6
2014	37.2	37.3	37.5	37.8	38.0	38.3	38.3	38.5	38.7	38.9	39.2	39.6	38.3
2015	39.6	39.4	39.8	39.9	40.4	40.4	40.5	40.6	41.0	41.0	41.4	41.8	40.5
2016	40.5	40.5	40.7	41.4	41.5	41.5	41.9	42.0	42.3	41.9	42.5	42.9	41.6
2017	42.7	42.4	42.5	42.6	42.3	42.7	43.1	44.1	44.4	45.1	45.7	47.0	43.7

Employment by Industry: Las Vegas-Henderson-Paradise, NV, Selected Years, 2007–2017—*Continued*

(Numbers in thousands, not seasonally adjusted)

Industry and year	January	February	March	April	May	June	July	August	September	October	November	December	Annual average
Information													
2007	11.3	11.6	11.3	11.4	11.6	11.5	10.9	11.3	10.9	11.4	11.4	11.1	11.3
2008	11.0	11.1	11.1	11.3	11.8	11.2	10.8	10.8	10.7	11.0	10.6	10.2	11.0
2009	9.8	9.9	10.0	9.5	9.5	9.6	9.5	9.7	9.4	9.4	9.4	9.4	9.6
2010	9.0	9.0	8.9	9.3	9.1	9.1	9.4	9.2	9.0	9.1	9.3	9.3	9.1
2011	9.2	9.0	9.1	9.4	9.4	9.4	9.2	9.1	9.5	9.8	9.1	9.6	9.3
2012	9.1	9.2	9.4	9.4	9.5	9.5	9.2	9.5	9.6	10.2	11.3	9.9	9.7
2013	9.1	9.3	9.5	9.7	9.8	10.8	10.1	9.8	9.8	9.9	10.1	10.1	9.8
2014	9.8	9.9	9.7	10.9	11.7	12.2	10.3	10.1	10.4	10.5	10.9	10.7	10.6
2015	10.3	10.7	10.6	10.5	10.5	10.9	10.2	10.4	10.2	10.6	11.3	10.9	10.6
2016	11.0	11.1	10.7	11.6	11.4	11.5	11.1	10.7	10.8	11.0	10.8	10.6	11.0
2017	11.1	10.9	10.9	11.7	11.9	12.3	11.1	11.3	11.0	11.1	11.1	11.0	11.3
Financial Activities													
2007	50.4	50.4	50.7	50.2	50.5	50.6	50.0	49.8	49.7	49.4	48.9	49.0	50.0
2008	48.0	48.1	48.2	48.0	47.9	48.0	47.5	47.1	47.0	46.9	46.4	45.9	47.4
2009	44.1	43.9	43.5	43.1	42.9	42.9	41.7	41.7	41.3	41.4	41.0	40.9	42.4
2010	40.3	39.9	40.0	40.5	40.3	40.1	40.2	39.9	39.8	40.3	40.2	40.3	40.2
2011	39.8	39.6	39.8	40.0	39.9	40.0	39.9	39.7	40.0	40.2	40.2	40.5	40.0
2012	40.2	40.3	40.6	41.4	41.7	41.9	41.8	42.0	42.2	42.8	42.8	42.9	41.7
2013	42.5	42.9	43.6	43.3	43.7	43.5	43.0	43.0	42.9	43.4	43.6	43.8	43.3
2014	42.8	42.9	43.0	43.0	43.5	43.4	43.1	43.6	43.7	44.4	44.5	44.7	43.6
2015	44.3	44.8	45.0	45.5	46.1	45.7	46.1	46.1	46.3	47.3	47.3	47.9	46.0
2016	47.3	47.5	47.7	48.3	48.6	48.3	48.4	48.6	48.8	49.1	49.2	49.3	48.4
2017	49.1	49.7	49.5	49.7	50.3	50.2	50.8	50.8	50.9	51.4	51.4	50.9	50.4
Professional and Business Services													
2007	117.0	119.6	117.6	118.0	118.0	117.0	113.7	115.4	113.9	116.4	115.4	113.2	116.3
2008	116.0	115.2	115.0	115.1	116.1	113.7	109.9	110.1	110.9	108.0	106.8	103.1	111.7
2009	105.6	103.8	101.5	99.3	99.6	98.4	94.8	95.5	97.6	97.6	99.0	98.5	99.3
2010	100.3	99.1	98.6	99.7	99.7	100.4	98.2	100.4	98.4	100.9	100.7	99.3	99.6
2011	102.7	101.1	101.5	101.9	101.6	101.8	101.1	101.2	102.8	104.2	103.8	102.7	102.2
2012	107.2	106.6	105.0	106.1	106.2	106.7	103.4	106.8	107.8	109.7	108.5	106.9	106.7
2013	111.6	110.2	111.4	112.4	112.7	111.6	108.9	111.2	110.3	113.4	113.6	111.7	111.6
2014	115.5	115.6	116.5	116.6	116.9	116.9	113.6	117.5	118.3	122.9	121.7	120.5	117.7
2015	124.7	123.1	124.3	126.6	126.2	124.5	123.5	127.1	127.0	130.9	131.2	130.4	126.6
2016	130.8	129.5	131.3	133.3	132.3	134.1	133.1	134.0	136.5	138.9	137.8	135.2	133.9
2017	139.2	136.3	139.8	136.9	138.2	138.9	137.3	137.3	138.5	139.6	136.9	137.1	138.0
Education and Health Services													
2007	61.5	62.4	62.7	62.6	63.2	63.4	63.3	63.5	64.0	64.6	64.9	64.7	63.4
2008	64.6	65.3	65.6	66.3	66.5	66.6	66.2	66.5	67.0	67.2	67.5	67.6	66.4
2009	66.4	66.9	66.9	66.9	67.3	67.5	67.4	67.7	67.7	68.8	68.9	69.0	67.6
2010	68.3	68.6	69.1	69.7	69.8	69.7	69.1	69.3	69.6	70.7	71.1	71.3	69.7
2011	70.8	71.4	71.9	72.5	72.5	72.7	72.3	72.7	73.0	73.7	74.0	74.4	72.7
2012	73.9	74.6	74.6	75.2	75.8	75.4	74.9	76.0	75.9	76.8	76.8	77.2	75.6
2013	76.7	77.8	78.3	78.8	78.9	79.0	78.9	79.5	80.0	80.5	80.9	80.9	79.2
2014	80.2	80.9	81.4	81.5	81.8	82.0	81.8	82.5	82.8	83.9	84.1	84.3	82.3
2015	83.5	84.3	84.8	85.2	85.5	86.1	86.3	87.2	87.8	89.2	89.3	89.6	86.6
2016	88.6	89.6	89.8	90.2	90.7	90.8	91.2	92.1	92.7	93.8	94.5	94.8	91.6
2017	93.7	94.7	95.2	95.7	96.2	96.3	95.5	97.1	97.9	98.0	98.6	99.2	96.5
Leisure and Hospitality													
2007	268.3	270.4	272.1	273.4	275.1	276.1	274.4	272.1	272.6	273.5	273.8	275.4	273.1
2008	271.1	271.3	272.4	274.1	274.7	275.1	271.1	269.9	268.4	265.0	261.4	258.9	269.5
2009	253.6	253.1	251.9	253.7	254.3	253.1	251.7	248.7	249.4	248.3	247.6	252.1	251.5
2010	248.9	251.2	252.0	255.1	256.0	256.9	255.0	253.5	253.2	253.6	253.1	252.6	253.4
2011	252.0	253.2	257.8	261.4	263.2	264.2	262.4	260.3	261.8	261.9	260.1	256.9	259.6
2012	255.4	257.2	260.6	263.0	265.1	266.2	264.5	262.1	262.2	262.8	261.5	259.8	261.7
2013	259.2	260.6	264.3	267.7	268.5	271.2	271.7	269.8	270.5	269.9	268.9	266.4	267.4
2014	267.2	269.8	274.6	278.4	281.1	281.3	280.8	283.0	283.1	281.7	280.0	278.9	278.3
2015	276.9	278.9	282.1	284.4	285.5	285.1	283.7	283.5	283.4	283.9	282.1	280.1	282.5
2016	278.4	280.5	283.4	287.3	288.4	289.4	289.3	289.0	289.0	286.6	286.1	285.2	286.1
2017	284.2	286.4	290.6	291.1	293.4	292.7	291.5	289.9	290.5	291.4	286.7	284.9	289.4

Employment by Industry: Las Vegas-Henderson-Paradise, NV, Selected Years, 2007–2017—*Continued*

(Numbers in thousands, not seasonally adjusted)

Industry and year	January	February	March	April	May	June	July	August	September	October	November	December	Annual average
Other Services													
2007	24.5	24.5	25.0	25.2	25.6	26.0	25.9	26.0	26.0	25.8	25.9	26.2	25.6
2008	25.8	25.6	25.8	25.7	26.1	26.2	25.9	26.1	26.1	25.7	25.1	24.6	25.7
2009	23.5	23.4	23.5	23.7	23.9	23.9	23.6	23.7	23.7	23.3	23.0	23.0	23.5
2010	22.6	22.7	23.0	23.3	23.4	23.4	23.5	23.6	23.5	23.6	23.1	22.9	23.2
2011	22.7	23.0	23.2	23.3	23.5	23.7	23.7	23.6	23.4	23.3	23.2	23.3	23.3
2012	23.2	23.2	23.5	23.8	24.3	24.6	24.5	24.6	24.7	25.1	24.1	23.9	24.1
2013	23.7	23.9	24.2	24.6	24.8	24.9	24.8	24.8	24.6	24.6	24.6	24.6	24.5
2014	24.4	24.5	24.9	25.4	25.8	25.9	26.0	25.9	26.0	26.4	25.8	25.6	25.6
2015	25.4	25.6	25.9	26.3	26.7	27.2	27.3	27.5	27.5	27.7	27.9	28.3	26.9
2016	28.5	29.3	30.1	30.6	30.7	30.8	31.4	31.4	32.0	32.5	31.7	30.8	30.8
2017	30.7	30.7	30.9	31.5	31.4	31.7	32.1	31.9	31.9	32.0	31.8	31.6	31.5
Government													
2007	93.8	97.8	98.3	99.9	100.1	96.0	91.6	90.1	97.1	101.2	102.0	102.4	97.5
2008	98.6	102.3	103.0	104.1	104.0	99.4	95.9	94.6	101.7	105.6	105.7	105.6	101.7
2009	100.6	102.5	102.4	101.8	100.8	96.5	93.1	91.7	98.2	99.1	98.5	98.1	98.6
2010	95.6	98.2	98.4	98.7	100.9	95.3	93.2	91.2	95.8	96.8	96.9	96.8	96.5
2011	95.2	96.8	96.9	96.7	96.3	90.1	89.0	89.1	93.3	94.6	94.6	95.5	94.0
2012	92.6	94.5	95.7	95.6	95.8	91.4	89.3	88.7	94.4	95.4	96.3	97.2	93.9
2013	94.4	95.4	96.2	96.5	96.4	92.7	89.5	91.1	95.2	96.9	97.8	98.7	95.1
2014	95.8	97.3	98.4	97.9	98.2	92.6	90.9	91.9	96.9	98.2	98.7	99.5	96.4
2015	97.0	98.2	99.4	99.4	99.2	95.6	92.6	93.9	99.2	99.0	100.7	102.0	98.0
2016	99.1	100.6	102.0	101.1	101.1	95.4	94.9	95.4	101.4	101.2	102.6	103.6	99.9
2017	99.7	102.5	103.5	101.3	102.3	96.4	97.4	99.2	105.1	106.5	106.4	106.7	102.3

Employment by Industry: Cincinnati, OH-KY-IN, Selected Years, 2007–2017

(Numbers in thousands, not seasonally adjusted)

Industry and year	January	February	March	April	May	June	July	August	September	October	November	December	Annual average
Total Nonfarm													
2007	1,019.5	1,020.0	1,033.0	1,042.5	1,053.9	1,052.6	1,041.0	1,047.3	1,048.3	1,052.8	1,056.0	1,058.1	1,043.8
2008	1,030.9	1,032.6	1,035.3	1,049.4	1,056.7	1,049.2	1,043.2	1,046.8	1,040.4	1,040.9	1,036.3	1,033.8	1,041.3
2009	996.6	993.3	992.7	994.9	1,000.5	992.9	982.3	988.4	987.1	988.3	989.7	989.8	991.4
2010	959.8	960.4	970.9	985.4	995.6	989.2	978.2	983.1	983.8	990.3	992.3	990.7	981.6
2011	964.9	968.3	978.1	993.4	999.9	994.6	992.3	1,000.7	1,001.6	1,003.0	1,005.6	1,004.8	992.3
2012	979.6	986.8	996.6	1,008.4	1,019.4	1,016.5	1,006.5	1,012.9	1,017.0	1,021.9	1,021.1	1,018.0	1,008.7
2013	990.9	1,000.1	1,006.9	1,026.3	1,036.5	1,031.5	1,021.4	1,031.8	1,035.2	1,038.6	1,041.5	1,036.9	1,024.8
2014	1,009.1	1,015.2	1,027.6	1,041.8	1,054.7	1,047.7	1,040.6	1,049.1	1,048.6	1,053.5	1,057.5	1,058.9	1,042.0
2015	1,030.3	1,032.3	1,041.9	1,057.7	1,070.6	1,068.8	1,063.3	1,068.2	1,068.8	1,073.5	1,077.5	1,078.5	1,061.0
2016	1,051.6	1,055.0	1,066.5	1,079.3	1,088.4	1,083.2	1,082.2	1,085.0	1,087.8	1,091.4	1,095.0	1,094.7	1,080.0
2017	1,069.2	1,075.1	1,082.8	1,093.6	1,103.5	1,104.5	1,095.6	1,100.5	1,099.8	1,100.7	1,101.4	1,096.3	1,093.6
Total Private													
2007	887.7	885.2	896.8	906.6	917.9	924.0	919.1	921.3	916.6	918.0	919.0	921.9	911.2
2008	898.7	896.1	898.8	912.7	919.7	921.1	920.0	919.5	907.6	904.6	898.0	896.3	907.8
2009	862.4	856.4	856.0	857.2	863.5	864.3	861.6	861.9	854.4	852.6	853.6	854.5	858.2
2010	827.0	825.2	834.7	848.1	855.8	860.1	858.9	859.2	853.8	857.5	857.8	856.5	849.6
2011	834.4	835.4	844.3	859.3	867.0	870.6	874.0	875.6	871.3	870.1	873.1	875.2	862.5
2012	853.7	854.7	863.3	874.8	885.3	891.8	888.4	890.7	887.3	889.5	888.2	889.2	879.7
2013	864.5	867.7	874.9	891.1	902.2	907.3	905.0	906.6	903.2	905.3	907.9	908.0	895.3
2014	882.8	883.3	895.4	908.0	920.1	923.3	922.0	924.9	917.4	921.0	925.0	927.3	912.5
2015	902.5	901.4	909.9	925.2	937.1	943.5	943.0	943.1	938.4	941.7	945.3	947.0	931.5
2016	924.0	923.9	934.3	946.3	954.4	958.2	959.8	959.0	956.1	958.4	961.7	962.2	949.9
2017	940.2	942.8	949.4	959.8	968.8	976.6	973.3	974.5	968.4	968.9	968.7	964.4	963.0
Goods Producing													
2007	167.1	166.1	169.3	171.5	173.4	174.2	173.4	173.7	172.6	171.7	170.6	169.3	171.1
2008	164.9	164.1	164.4	167.3	168.6	169.3	168.7	168.4	166.2	164.9	162.3	159.5	165.7
2009	151.2	148.9	147.7	145.9	146.4	146.2	145.2	145.7	144.2	143.7	142.8	141.4	145.8
2010	135.0	133.6	135.7	138.5	139.7	140.5	141.6	141.7	141.5	142.2	141.6	139.4	139.3
2011	135.5	135.6	137.3	140.1	141.8	143.1	144.5	144.8	144.6	144.6	144.1	143.7	141.6
2012	139.7	139.3	140.7	142.6	144.1	146.0	146.1	146.0	145.3	144.8	144.3	143.5	143.5
2013	139.4	138.9	139.3	142.3	144.8	146.5	147.3	147.1	147.4	148.0	148.1	146.8	144.7
2014	143.5	143.6	146.5	149.3	152.1	153.4	153.6	154.2	153.6	154.4	154.4	153.7	151.0
2015	149.7	149.6	150.9	154.1	156.6	158.6	158.4	159.1	158.1	159.2	159.3	158.9	156.0
2016	154.8	154.7	156.8	159.0	160.3	161.8	162.5	162.2	161.8	161.4	161.5	161.0	159.8
2017	158.3	159.2	160.6	162.0	163.9	165.5	164.9	165.5	164.7	163.9	163.7	163.3	163.0
Service-Providing													
2007	852.4	853.9	863.7	871.0	880.5	878.4	867.6	873.6	875.7	881.1	885.4	888.8	872.7
2008	866.0	868.5	870.9	882.1	888.1	879.9	874.5	878.4	874.2	876.0	874.0	874.3	875.6
2009	845.4	844.4	845.0	849.0	854.1	846.7	837.1	842.7	842.9	844.6	846.9	848.4	845.6
2010	824.8	826.8	835.2	846.9	855.9	848.7	836.6	841.4	842.3	848.1	850.7	851.3	842.4
2011	829.4	832.7	840.8	853.3	858.1	851.5	847.8	855.9	857.0	858.4	861.5	861.1	850.6
2012	839.9	847.5	855.9	865.8	875.3	870.5	860.4	866.9	871.7	877.1	876.8	874.5	865.2
2013	851.5	861.2	867.6	884.0	891.7	885.0	874.1	884.7	887.8	890.6	893.4	890.1	880.1
2014	865.6	871.6	881.1	892.5	902.6	894.3	887.0	894.9	895.0	899.1	903.1	905.2	891.0
2015	880.6	882.7	891.0	903.6	914.0	910.2	904.9	909.1	910.7	914.3	918.2	919.6	904.9
2016	896.8	900.3	909.7	920.3	928.1	921.4	919.7	922.8	926.0	930.0	933.5	933.7	920.2
2017	910.9	915.9	922.2	931.6	939.6	939.0	930.7	935.0	935.1	936.8	937.7	933.0	930.6
Mining, Logging, and Construction													
2007	47.1	45.6	47.8	50.2	51.8	52.5	52.8	52.8	52.2	52.0	51.0	49.4	50.4
2008	45.2	44.4	44.9	47.1	48.5	49.2	49.5	49.3	48.0	47.7	46.4	44.5	47.1
2009	39.8	39.0	39.2	39.0	40.5	40.7	40.8	40.9	40.0	39.7	38.9	37.7	39.7
2010	32.9	31.8	33.3	35.8	36.6	37.3	38.1	38.3	37.9	38.8	38.1	36.4	36.3
2011	33.3	33.3	34.6	36.8	37.9	38.7	39.8	40.1	39.8	39.8	39.0	38.4	37.6
2012	35.4	34.9	36.1	37.9	38.8	39.6	39.7	39.9	39.8	39.4	39.0	38.0	38.2
2013	35.2	34.8	35.4	37.3	38.7	39.7	40.2	40.5	41.0	41.1	40.6	39.1	38.6
2014	36.5	36.0	38.0	40.2	42.0	42.5	42.8	43.3	43.1	43.2	42.9	41.8	41.0
2015	38.6	38.5	39.3	41.7	43.6	44.6	44.5	45.0	44.7	45.6	45.6	44.6	43.0
2016	41.4	41.2	43.3	45.2	45.9	46.7	47.1	47.0	47.0	47.0	46.9	45.9	45.4
2017	42.9	43.4	44.6	46.3	47.8	48.7	48.6	48.9	48.9	48.9	48.4	46.7	47.0

Employment by Industry: Cincinnati, OH-KY-IN, Selected Years, 2007–2017—*Continued*

(Numbers in thousands, not seasonally adjusted)

Industry and year	January	February	March	April	May	June	July	August	September	October	November	December	Annual average
Manufacturing													
2007	120.0	120.5	121.5	121.3	121.6	121.7	120.6	120.9	120.4	119.7	119.6	119.9	120.6
2008	119.7	119.7	119.5	120.2	120.1	120.1	119.2	119.1	118.2	117.2	115.9	115.0	118.7
2009	111.4	109.9	108.5	106.9	105.9	105.5	104.4	104.8	104.2	104.0	103.9	103.7	106.1
2010	102.1	101.8	102.4	102.7	103.1	103.2	103.5	103.4	103.6	103.4	103.5	103.0	103.0
2011	102.2	102.3	102.7	103.3	103.9	104.4	104.7	104.7	104.8	104.8	105.1	105.3	104.0
2012	104.3	104.4	104.6	104.7	105.3	106.4	106.4	106.1	105.5	105.4	105.3	105.5	105.3
2013	104.2	104.1	103.9	105.0	106.1	106.8	107.1	106.6	106.4	106.9	107.5	107.7	106.0
2014	107.0	107.6	108.5	109.1	110.1	110.9	110.8	110.9	110.5	111.2	111.5	111.9	110.0
2015	111.1	111.1	111.6	112.4	113.0	114.0	113.9	114.1	113.4	113.6	113.7	114.3	113.0
2016	113.4	113.5	113.5	113.8	114.4	115.1	115.4	115.2	114.8	114.4	114.6	115.1	114.4
2017	115.4	115.8	116.0	115.7	116.1	116.8	116.3	116.6	115.8	115.0	115.3	116.6	116.0
Trade, Transportation, and Utilities													
2007	209.8	207.9	209.6	210.1	212.4	212.8	212.3	212.1	212.4	213.8	218.0	220.7	212.7
2008	211.7	209.4	209.7	210.4	211.9	211.3	210.4	210.8	209.0	208.9	210.7	212.3	210.5
2009	201.8	199.0	197.6	195.6	196.8	196.2	195.2	196.2	195.4	197.3	200.2	201.9	197.8
2010	192.8	192.1	193.1	194.1	195.7	195.8	194.2	194.2	193.3	195.8	199.8	200.9	195.2
2011	192.5	191.4	192.4	194.2	195.1	195.5	196.3	197.3	197.4	199.2	204.1	205.6	196.8
2012	196.5	195.4	196.8	197.7	200.1	200.0	199.0	199.8	199.7	201.4	205.1	205.9	199.8
2013	198.1	196.9	198.0	199.4	201.2	201.6	200.2	201.0	199.8	202.0	206.8	208.2	201.1
2014	199.5	198.7	199.6	201.0	202.5	203.3	202.4	204.0	202.4	206.0	209.7	211.7	203.4
2015	203.4	202.4	203.5	205.3	207.0	207.6	207.0	207.7	206.6	209.7	214.1	216.8	207.6
2016	208.4	207.2	208.0	209.1	210.3	210.0	210.4	211.6	211.1	213.5	217.7	219.7	211.4
2017	210.9	210.2	211.0	212.9	214.9	215.1	214.9	215.9	215.6	218.5	224.4	224.0	215.7
Wholesale Trade													
2007	60.5	60.4	60.6	60.7	60.8	61.3	61.1	61.1	61.2	61.3	61.3	61.7	61.0
2008	61.3	61.4	61.5	61.3	61.5	61.8	61.6	61.3	60.7	60.8	60.6	60.4	61.2
2009	59.1	58.6	58.0	56.4	56.3	55.8	55.7	55.4	55.0	55.2	55.2	55.4	56.3
2010	54.8	54.8	54.8	54.7	54.8	55.2	54.9	54.7	54.3	54.5	54.6	54.5	54.7
2011	54.5	54.6	54.9	55.4	55.6	55.7	56.0	56.1	56.3	56.1	56.2	56.1	55.6
2012	56.2	56.4	56.7	57.2	57.6	58.2	57.9	58.1	57.9	58.2	58.1	58.5	57.6
2013	58.6	58.8	59.1	59.2	59.5	59.7	59.6	59.5	59.4	59.1	59.4	59.4	59.3
2014	58.4	58.9	58.9	59.2	59.4	59.7	59.7	59.9	59.6	59.7	59.8	60.1	59.4
2015	59.6	59.8	60.0	60.2	60.7	61.0	60.7	60.8	60.2	60.6	60.8	61.1	60.5
2016	60.9	61.1	61.1	61.1	61.4	61.6	61.3	61.4	61.2	61.1	61.1	61.4	61.2
2017	60.8	60.8	61.0	61.2	61.6	62.1	61.8	61.8	61.4	61.5	62.7	62.5	61.6
Retail Trade													
2007	107.6	106.0	107.5	108.1	109.5	109.4	109.4	108.8	108.2	109.0	112.5	114.0	109.2
2008	108.0	105.9	106.2	107.1	108.1	107.9	107.7	107.8	106.6	106.5	108.4	109.8	107.5
2009	102.9	101.3	101.0	101.0	102.3	102.4	101.4	101.6	101.2	102.4	104.9	106.0	102.4
2010	99.5	98.9	99.9	100.8	102.0	101.5	101.4	101.2	100.4	102.2	105.4	106.1	101.6
2011	100.0	99.0	99.4	100.5	101.0	101.4	101.5	101.5	100.4	102.0	105.5	106.6	101.6
2012	100.3	99.0	100.1	100.9	102.3	102.2	101.8	101.7	101.5	103.3	107.0	107.3	102.3
2013	101.3	100.1	100.9	102.1	103.4	103.8	103.1	103.5	102.1	104.0	107.4	108.4	103.3
2014	102.2	101.1	101.6	103.0	103.9	104.4	103.9	104.5	103.2	105.9	109.0	110.0	104.4
2015	103.6	102.8	103.4	104.6	105.3	105.7	105.2	105.4	104.8	107.0	110.7	112.3	105.9
2016	105.9	104.8	105.4	106.3	106.9	106.6	107.2	107.6	107.0	109.1	112.2	112.8	107.7
2017	107.0	106.2	106.3	107.7	108.6	108.3	108.2	108.4	107.9	109.6	112.8	111.8	108.6
Transportation and Utilities													
2007	41.7	41.5	41.5	41.3	42.1	42.1	41.8	42.2	43.0	43.5	44.2	45.0	42.5
2008	42.4	42.1	42.0	42.0	42.3	41.6	41.1	41.7	41.7	41.6	41.7	42.1	41.9
2009	39.8	39.1	38.6	38.2	38.2	38.0	38.1	39.2	39.2	39.7	40.1	40.5	39.1
2010	38.5	38.4	38.4	38.6	38.9	39.1	37.9	38.3	38.6	39.1	39.8	40.3	38.8
2011	38.0	37.8	38.1	38.3	38.5	38.4	38.8	39.7	40.7	41.1	42.4	42.9	39.6
2012	40.0	40.0	40.0	39.6	40.2	39.6	39.3	40.0	40.3	39.9	40.0	40.1	39.9
2013	38.2	38.0	38.0	38.1	38.3	38.1	37.5	38.0	38.3	38.9	40.0	40.4	38.5
2014	38.9	38.7	39.1	38.8	39.2	39.2	38.8	39.6	39.6	40.4	40.9	41.6	39.6
2015	40.2	39.8	40.1	40.5	41.0	40.9	41.1	41.5	41.6	42.1	42.6	43.4	41.2
2016	41.6	41.3	41.5	41.7	42.0	41.8	41.9	42.6	42.9	43.3	44.4	45.5	42.5
2017	43.1	43.2	43.7	44.0	44.7	44.7	44.9	45.7	46.3	47.4	48.9	49.7	45.5

Employment by Industry: Cincinnati, OH-KY-IN, Selected Years, 2007–2017—*Continued*
(Numbers in thousands, not seasonally adjusted)

Industry and year	January	February	March	April	May	June	July	August	September	October	November	December	Annual average
Information													
2007	15.3	15.4	15.3	15.5	15.6	15.7	15.7	15.7	15.3	15.2	15.2	15.2	15.4
2008	15.1	15.1	15.2	15.1	15.1	15.2	15.3	15.3	15.1	15.2	15.1	15.1	15.2
2009	15.0	14.9	14.9	14.8	14.8	14.8	14.8	14.6	14.4	14.3	14.4	14.3	14.7
2010	14.2	14.0	14.0	13.9	14.0	14.0	14.2	14.2	14.1	14.0	14.1	14.0	14.1
2011	13.9	13.9	13.8	13.8	13.9	14.0	14.0	14.1	14.0	13.8	14.0	13.9	13.9
2012	13.9	13.9	13.8	13.7	13.8	13.9	13.9	13.8	13.7	14.0	14.1	14.2	13.9
2013	14.1	14.2	14.1	14.1	14.1	14.1	14.0	13.9	13.6	13.5	13.5	13.5	13.9
2014	13.3	13.3	13.4	13.6	13.7	13.5	13.6	13.7	13.4	13.3	13.5	13.7	13.5
2015	13.5	13.5	13.6	13.6	13.5	13.7	13.5	13.8	13.5	13.9	14.0	14.2	13.7
2016	14.1	14.2	14.2	14.1	14.2	14.2	14.3	14.2	14.0	14.0	14.0	14.0	14.1
2017	13.9	14.1	13.9	13.9	13.9	14.0	14.1	13.8	13.6	13.5	13.5	13.5	13.8
Financial Activities													
2007	64.3	64.5	64.6	64.7	65.1	65.4	65.7	65.4	64.9	64.7	64.5	65.0	64.9
2008	64.6	64.5	64.6	65.1	65.3	65.5	65.6	65.5	64.8	64.6	64.6	64.4	64.9
2009	63.6	63.3	63.2	63.0	63.4	63.3	63.3	62.7	62.1	62.1	62.1	61.9	62.8
2010	61.5	61.3	61.3	62.0	62.3	62.6	63.3	63.2	63.1	63.1	63.2	63.5	62.5
2011	63.3	63.3	63.3	63.2	63.4	63.5	63.2	63.2	63.0	62.9	63.1	63.4	63.2
2012	63.4	63.3	63.4	63.6	64.0	64.5	64.6	64.5	64.5	64.5	64.7	65.1	64.2
2013	64.4	64.6	64.9	65.2	65.6	66.2	66.5	66.6	66.2	66.0	66.2	66.2	65.7
2014	65.6	65.7	65.8	66.1	66.8	67.4	67.8	67.8	67.2	67.2	67.9	67.8	66.9
2015	67.4	67.6	67.7	68.1	68.8	69.5	69.8	70.1	69.6	69.9	70.1	70.3	69.1
2016	70.4	70.8	70.8	71.3	71.8	72.3	73.2	73.2	72.9	73.2	73.5	73.8	72.3
2017	73.4	73.6	73.6	73.8	74.1	74.6	74.5	74.6	73.8	73.3	73.5	74.4	73.9
Professional and Business Services													
2007	150.6	150.9	153.6	155.4	155.6	157.5	156.4	157.5	157.5	160.3	161.0	161.1	156.5
2008	157.6	157.0	157.0	159.1	158.3	159.0	160.1	160.3	158.8	159.3	157.3	156.2	158.3
2009	149.7	148.6	147.8	147.0	146.0	145.9	145.8	146.6	145.5	145.8	147.0	147.7	147.0
2010	143.6	143.6	145.2	148.2	147.9	149.4	149.4	150.1	149.6	151.4	151.3	150.8	148.4
2011	148.9	149.2	151.1	154.0	153.0	153.5	156.0	156.8	156.8	157.4	158.6	158.6	154.5
2012	156.1	155.9	157.4	160.1	160.2	161.2	161.3	163.0	163.1	163.8	162.6	162.3	160.6
2013	156.8	157.6	159.0	162.6	162.6	163.7	163.6	165.2	165.7	166.0	166.6	167.5	163.1
2014	161.7	161.4	163.4	166.1	166.2	166.0	167.0	168.4	167.9	168.2	169.9	169.9	166.3
2015	164.6	163.6	164.3	167.3	167.1	168.6	169.0	169.3	168.4	169.3	169.5	169.1	167.5
2016	164.7	163.6	165.1	168.6	167.4	167.8	168.4	169.1	169.2	170.2	170.8	170.4	167.9
2017	165.4	164.0	164.1	166.9	166.0	168.2	168.3	168.7	167.3	168.3	167.1	165.5	166.7
Education and Health Services													
2007	139.0	139.6	140.6	141.3	141.9	140.7	139.3	139.9	142.5	143.6	144.6	144.5	141.5
2008	142.9	143.8	144.5	145.7	146.1	143.6	144.0	144.2	144.9	145.8	146.4	146.2	144.8
2009	143.8	144.3	144.9	146.5	146.7	144.9	145.2	144.9	145.5	146.9	147.9	147.4	145.7
2010	144.7	145.6	146.6	148.3	148.6	146.7	146.1	146.1	147.2	148.7	149.2	149.2	147.3
2011	146.4	147.6	148.2	150.1	151.2	149.4	148.6	148.8	150.0	150.7	151.0	151.2	149.4
2012	149.4	151.0	151.6	152.5	153.3	152.0	150.3	150.8	152.8	154.1	154.7	154.5	152.3
2013	152.4	154.1	154.7	156.3	157.5	156.1	155.2	155.5	157.1	158.0	159.6	158.9	156.3
2014	157.3	158.1	159.2	159.3	160.5	158.9	158.0	158.6	159.9	160.3	161.7	161.8	159.5
2015	159.4	159.7	160.9	161.7	162.6	160.8	159.7	160.2	161.7	163.2	164.4	163.9	161.5
2016	161.5	162.6	163.9	164.2	165.0	162.5	160.9	161.3	163.2	164.0	164.8	164.4	163.2
2017	163.2	164.4	165.1	165.6	166.5	164.8	163.3	163.5	165.2	165.5	165.5	164.0	164.7
Leisure and Hospitality													
2007	99.4	98.6	100.9	105.0	110.4	113.5	112.5	113.0	108.2	105.1	101.5	102.5	105.9
2008	98.7	99.0	99.9	106.3	110.5	112.9	112.0	111.3	105.9	102.7	98.7	99.6	104.8
2009	95.0	95.1	97.3	102.0	106.7	110.2	109.2	108.6	105.1	100.2	97.3	97.7	102.0
2010	93.9	93.9	97.2	102.3	106.9	110.1	109.0	108.7	104.5	101.8	98.3	98.5	102.1
2011	94.1	94.8	98.2	103.7	108.1	111.3	111.3	110.8	106.2	102.7	99.7	100.4	103.4
2012	96.9	98.3	101.7	106.1	110.9	114.6	113.7	113.3	109.0	107.5	103.3	104.1	106.6
2013	100.1	102.0	105.2	111.3	116.4	118.9	118.2	117.5	113.9	112.5	108.1	107.9	111.0
2014	103.6	104.2	108.8	113.6	119.0	121.3	120.3	119.0	114.6	112.8	109.2	109.9	113.0
2015	106.6	107.2	110.8	116.5	122.4	125.2	125.9	123.3	121.4	116.9	114.2	113.9	117.0
2016	110.4	110.9	115.2	119.1	124.2	128.5	128.6	126.1	122.7	120.2	117.5	116.8	120.0
2017	112.9	114.8	118.1	121.7	126.1	130.6	130.0	129.4	125.2	121.7	118.1	116.4	122.1

Employment by Industry: Cincinnati, OH-KY-IN, Selected Years, 2007–2017—*Continued*

(Numbers in thousands, not seasonally adjusted)

Industry and year	January	February	March	April	May	June	July	August	September	October	November	December	Annual average
Other Services													
2007	42.2	42.2	42.9	43.1	43.5	44.2	43.8	44.0	43.2	43.6	43.6	43.6	43.3
2008	43.2	43.2	43.5	43.7	43.9	44.3	43.9	43.7	42.9	43.2	42.9	43.0	43.5
2009	42.3	42.3	42.6	42.4	42.7	42.8	42.9	42.6	42.2	42.3	41.9	42.2	42.4
2010	41.3	41.1	41.6	40.8	40.7	41.0	41.1	41.0	40.5	40.5	40.3	40.2	40.8
2011	39.8	39.6	40.0	40.2	40.5	40.3	40.1	39.8	39.3	38.8	38.5	38.4	39.6
2012	37.8	37.6	37.9	38.5	38.9	39.6	39.5	39.5	39.2	39.4	39.4	39.6	38.9
2013	39.2	39.4	39.7	39.9	40.0	40.2	40.0	39.8	39.5	39.3	39.0	39.0	39.6
2014	38.3	38.3	38.7	39.0	39.3	39.5	39.3	39.2	38.4	38.8	38.7	38.8	38.9
2015	37.9	37.8	38.2	38.6	39.1	39.5	39.7	39.6	39.1	39.6	39.7	39.9	39.1
2016	39.7	39.9	40.3	40.9	41.2	41.1	41.5	41.3	41.2	41.9	41.9	42.1	41.1
2017	42.2	42.5	43.0	43.0	43.4	43.8	43.3	43.1	43.0	44.2	42.9	43.3	43.1
Government													
2007	131.8	134.8	136.2	135.9	136.0	128.6	121.9	126.0	131.7	134.8	137.0	136.2	132.6
2008	132.2	136.5	136.5	136.7	137.0	128.1	123.2	127.3	132.8	136.3	138.3	137.5	133.5
2009	134.2	136.9	136.7	137.7	137.0	128.6	120.7	126.5	132.7	135.7	136.1	135.3	133.2
2010	132.8	135.2	136.2	137.3	139.8	129.1	119.3	123.9	130.0	132.8	134.5	134.2	132.1
2011	130.5	132.9	133.8	134.1	132.9	124.0	118.3	125.1	130.3	132.9	132.5	129.6	129.7
2012	125.9	132.1	133.3	133.6	134.1	124.7	118.1	122.2	129.7	132.4	132.9	128.8	129.0
2013	126.4	132.4	132.0	135.2	134.3	124.2	116.4	125.2	132.0	133.3	133.6	128.9	129.5
2014	126.3	131.9	132.2	133.8	134.6	124.4	118.6	124.2	131.2	132.5	132.5	131.6	129.5
2015	127.8	130.9	132.0	132.5	133.5	125.3	120.3	125.1	130.4	131.8	132.2	131.5	129.4
2016	127.6	131.1	132.2	133.0	134.0	125.0	122.4	126.0	131.7	133.0	133.3	132.5	130.2
2017	129.0	132.3	133.4	133.8	134.7	127.9	122.3	126.0	131.4	131.8	132.7	131.9	130.6

Employment by Industry: Kansas City, MO-KS, Selected Years, 2007–2017

(Numbers in thousands, not seasonally adjusted)

Industry and year	January	February	March	April	May	June	July	August	September	October	November	December	Annual average
Total Nonfarm													
2007	982.6	986.2	1,001.3	1,007.0	1,013.2	1,017.6	1,008.4	1,012.1	1,014.9	1,013.1	1,018.6	1,015.5	1,007.5
2008	996.1	998.9	1,008.4	1,019.9	1,019.5	1,022.5	1,011.3	1,010.1	1,012.7	1,013.9	1,008.5	1,003.5	1,010.4
2009	976.9	974.3	976.9	982.9	983.6	984.3	970.3	968.7	970.2	969.7	968.4	965.9	974.3
2010	940.7	943.8	952.0	971.0	977.9	978.8	958.8	959.7	970.6	975.7	975.6	975.4	965.0
2011	949.1	952.0	964.7	975.2	980.7	980.8	970.5	970.3	979.6	984.3	988.6	987.9	973.6
2012	967.2	972.4	982.8	991.4	997.2	999.1	982.8	990.5	992.4	998.3	1,001.1	997.3	989.4
2013	976.2	979.9	986.4	999.5	1,006.0	1,010.3	994.7	1,001.1	1,008.5	1,013.1	1,013.0	1,012.7	1,000.1
2014	988.1	993.8	1,004.6	1,018.2	1,026.6	1,030.7	1,016.8	1,022.1	1,025.6	1,034.5	1,037.0	1,038.2	1,019.7
2015	1,015.4	1,022.3	1,030.6	1,040.7	1,049.5	1,053.7	1,043.8	1,043.9	1,050.2	1,059.3	1,059.1	1,060.8	1,044.1
2016	1,040.9	1,045.0	1,050.8	1,067.0	1,068.2	1,070.2	1,061.4	1,066.7	1,076.7	1,081.6	1,082.9	1,081.9	1,066.1
2017	1,057.9	1,064.0	1,070.7	1,080.0	1,083.8	1,088.3	1,079.9	1,081.9	1,091.7	1,097.1	1,099.2	1,096.9	1,082.6
Total Private													
2007	837.2	837.1	850.7	854.9	861.8	867.5	865.4	870.0	866.2	863.3	867.4	866.0	859.0
2008	847.9	847.4	855.1	865.7	865.0	869.3	868.6	866.5	861.3	861.1	855.6	850.7	859.5
2009	826.1	819.5	821.9	826.3	826.3	829.6	826.9	826.0	817.8	816.5	815.5	813.5	822.2
2010	791.0	790.9	797.6	814.6	818.9	822.8	821.4	823.4	820.3	825.3	825.0	825.5	814.7
2011	800.9	801.5	811.6	821.4	827.5	829.8	831.9	833.5	831.8	835.8	839.8	839.1	825.4
2012	821.6	823.1	832.3	840.2	845.6	851.4	847.2	851.3	845.1	849.5	852.3	848.9	842.4
2013	831.6	831.7	837.5	848.3	855.3	862.7	860.7	866.0	861.0	866.4	866.4	866.3	854.5
2014	844.6	847.2	857.0	870.2	877.5	883.7	882.1	887.9	878.7	887.1	889.7	891.9	874.8
2015	869.6	874.2	881.1	890.7	899.7	906.4	908.5	907.6	901.7	911.0	910.6	913.4	897.9
2016	893.4	895.5	900.9	915.7	918.2	922.4	924.7	928.5	925.8	931.3	932.8	932.8	918.5
2017	909.3	913.1	919.4	928.2	932.6	937.9	940.1	940.8	939.4	943.7	945.6	943.7	932.8
Goods Producing													
2007	130.3	127.8	132.4	132.6	133.9	135.2	133.1	135.2	134.7	131.8	132.8	130.2	132.5
2008	126.2	125.4	128.3	129.7	128.0	129.9	130.9	129.7	128.9	128.3	126.3	123.0	127.9
2009	116.4	113.7	114.8	115.3	114.2	115.8	115.6	114.3	112.7	112.4	110.9	107.7	113.7
2010	103.3	102.9	105.1	108.5	108.9	110.6	109.7	111.7	111.3	111.4	110.2	108.8	108.5
2011	102.4	101.6	104.6	107.0	107.9	109.2	109.2	107.3	108.9	108.6	108.6	107.7	106.9
2012	104.5	104.0	106.4	107.5	107.7	109.6	109.0	109.8	109.7	109.2	108.8	106.5	107.7
2013	105.1	104.6	106.7	108.3	110.5	112.4	110.2	112.3	112.9	112.9	112.7	111.1	110.0
2014	106.5	109.1	111.7	114.3	114.9	117.1	116.2	117.9	117.0	117.7	118.0	118.1	114.9
2015	113.0	115.5	117.9	117.0	120.4	122.0	121.5	121.3	122.2	123.2	122.3	122.0	119.9
2016	118.8	119.3	122.1	125.0	125.5	127.9	126.6	128.0	127.7	127.8	127.4	126.1	125.2
2017	121.9	123.1	124.6	125.7	126.6	129.1	128.7	126.4	127.6	126.6	127.5	127.0	126.2
Service-Providing													
2007	852.3	858.4	868.9	874.4	879.3	882.4	875.3	876.9	880.2	881.3	885.8	885.3	875.0
2008	869.9	873.5	880.1	890.2	891.5	892.6	880.4	880.4	883.8	885.6	882.2	880.5	882.6
2009	860.5	860.6	862.1	867.6	869.4	868.5	854.7	854.4	857.5	857.3	857.5	858.2	860.7
2010	837.4	840.9	846.9	862.5	869.0	868.2	849.1	848.0	859.3	864.3	865.4	866.6	856.5
2011	846.7	850.4	860.1	868.2	872.8	871.6	861.3	863.0	870.7	875.7	880.0	880.2	866.7
2012	862.7	868.4	876.4	883.9	889.5	889.5	873.8	880.7	882.7	889.1	892.3	890.8	881.7
2013	871.1	875.3	879.7	891.2	895.5	897.9	884.5	888.8	895.6	900.2	900.3	901.6	890.1
2014	881.6	884.7	892.9	903.9	911.7	913.6	900.6	904.2	908.6	916.8	919.0	920.1	904.8
2015	902.4	906.8	912.7	923.7	929.1	931.7	922.3	922.6	928.0	936.1	936.8	938.8	924.3
2016	922.1	925.7	928.7	942.0	942.7	942.3	934.8	938.7	949.0	953.8	955.5	955.8	940.9
2017	936.0	940.9	946.1	954.3	957.2	959.2	951.2	955.5	964.1	970.5	971.7	969.9	956.4
Mining, Logging, and Construction													
2007	49.9	47.5	51.5	52.2	53.5	54.6	55.2	54.7	54.5	53.7	53.2	50.9	52.6
2008	47.4	46.6	49.1	50.3	51.6	52.2	52.1	51.8	50.8	50.7	49.5	46.8	49.9
2009	42.6	42.3	43.1	43.6	44.8	45.1	45.2	43.7	42.4	41.9	41.0	38.4	42.8
2010	33.8	33.5	35.7	38.8	38.8	40.1	40.8	40.8	40.2	40.4	39.5	37.9	38.4
2011	33.1	32.4	35.1	37.4	38.1	38.9	39.4	39.2	38.9	38.7	38.6	37.6	37.3
2012	35.3	34.8	36.7	38.0	39.4	40.4	40.5	40.5	40.2	40.0	39.6	39.1	38.7
2013	36.6	37.2	37.9	39.7	41.6	42.8	43.7	43.4	43.0	43.2	42.6	41.0	41.1
2014	39.0	38.4	41.0	42.6	43.9	44.7	45.9	45.1	44.3	44.5	44.4	44.4	43.2
2015	42.1	42.3	43.5	45.3	45.5	46.4	47.2	47.0	46.6	47.0	46.1	45.6	45.4
2016	43.1	43.4	45.5	47.8	48.2	50.1	50.3	50.2	50.2	50.4	49.6	48.6	48.1
2017	46.3	46.9	47.9	48.9	49.8	51.5	51.4	51.0	50.6	50.6	50.9	50.8	49.7

Employment by Industry: Kansas City, MO-KS, Selected Years, 2007–2017—*Continued*

(Numbers in thousands, not seasonally adjusted)

Industry and year	January	February	March	April	May	June	July	August	September	October	November	December	Annual average
Manufacturing													
2007	80.4	80.3	80.9	80.4	80.4	80.6	77.9	80.5	80.2	78.1	79.6	79.3	79.9
2008	78.8	78.8	79.2	79.4	76.4	77.7	78.8	77.9	78.1	77.6	76.8	76.2	78.0
2009	73.8	71.4	71.7	71.7	69.4	70.7	70.4	70.6	70.3	70.5	69.9	69.3	70.8
2010	69.5	69.4	69.4	69.7	70.1	70.5	68.9	70.9	71.1	71.0	70.7	70.9	70.2
2011	69.3	69.2	69.5	69.6	69.8	70.3	69.8	68.1	70.0	69.9	70.0	70.1	69.6
2012	69.2	69.2	69.7	69.5	68.3	69.2	68.5	69.3	69.5	69.2	69.2	67.4	69.0
2013	68.5	67.4	68.8	68.6	68.9	69.6	66.5	68.9	69.9	69.7	70.1	70.1	68.9
2014	67.5	70.7	70.7	71.7	71.0	72.4	70.3	72.8	72.7	73.2	73.6	73.7	71.7
2015	70.9	73.2	74.4	71.7	74.9	75.6	74.3	74.3	75.6	76.2	76.2	76.4	74.5
2016	75.7	75.9	76.6	77.2	77.3	77.8	76.3	77.8	77.5	77.4	77.8	77.5	77.1
2017	75.6	76.2	76.7	76.8	76.8	77.6	77.3	75.4	77.0	76.0	76.6	76.2	76.5
Trade, Transportation, and Utilities													
2007	201.8	200.9	202.9	203.0	203.9	203.8	203.6	204.3	204.7	205.3	209.4	210.9	204.5
2008	202.9	201.3	201.5	202.6	202.5	202.5	202.1	201.5	201.0	203.4	204.6	204.9	202.6
2009	196.7	194.0	193.4	193.0	192.9	192.9	191.7	191.8	190.7	191.8	194.3	194.3	193.1
2010	187.5	186.0	186.7	189.2	190.7	191.3	190.8	191.2	190.6	192.8	195.8	196.9	190.8
2011	190.0	188.9	190.3	192.3	193.4	192.9	193.0	193.8	193.3	194.8	198.6	199.7	193.4
2012	194.0	192.0	193.1	194.0	195.6	195.9	194.4	194.9	194.4	195.7	199.6	200.0	195.3
2013	193.5	192.2	192.7	194.5	195.4	196.5	196.7	197.5	196.7	199.2	203.2	204.5	196.9
2014	198.1	196.0	198.5	200.0	201.5	202.3	202.1	203.0	201.3	203.5	207.1	209.0	201.9
2015	203.0	201.6	202.2	203.8	205.9	207.3	206.5	206.4	205.5	207.9	211.3	213.3	206.2
2016	205.9	205.4	206.1	207.8	209.1	209.4	210.0	210.7	209.7	212.1	216.9	219.5	210.2
2017	211.6	210.4	210.4	211.5	212.5	213.0	213.7	215.7	215.5	216.8	220.3	221.0	214.4
Wholesale Trade													
2007	50.0	50.2	50.9	50.5	50.5	50.9	51.1	51.3	51.3	51.6	51.6	51.7	51.0
2008	51.3	51.3	51.1	51.5	51.4	51.4	51.7	51.5	51.1	52.2	51.8	51.5	51.5
2009	50.7	50.2	49.8	49.2	48.6	48.4	48.1	47.6	47.2	47.3	47.1	46.8	48.4
2010	46.4	46.4	46.5	47.8	47.9	48.0	47.9	47.7	47.4	47.6	47.5	47.4	47.4
2011	46.8	46.9	47.0	47.4	47.9	47.8	48.0	48.0	47.9	47.6	47.7	48.0	47.6
2012	47.9	47.9	48.0	48.2	48.4	48.7	48.5	48.6	48.3	48.2	48.2	48.3	48.3
2013	47.7	48.0	47.8	48.0	48.1	48.3	49.3	49.3	49.0	49.4	49.5	49.6	48.7
2014	49.2	49.1	50.0	49.9	50.2	50.5	50.5	50.4	50.1	50.4	50.2	50.4	50.1
2015	50.3	50.3	50.3	50.2	50.4	50.6	50.5	50.3	49.9	50.2	50.2	50.1	50.3
2016	49.6	49.6	49.7	50.3	50.6	50.6	51.0	50.9	50.9	51.1	51.1	51.2	50.6
2017	51.0	51.2	51.3	51.7	52.0	52.3	52.5	52.4	52.2	52.3	52.2	52.3	52.0
Retail Trade													
2007	106.3	105.4	106.5	106.9	107.6	107.8	107.4	107.2	106.6	107.5	111.1	112.4	107.7
2008	106.5	104.4	105.1	105.4	105.9	106.2	105.8	105.3	104.4	105.4	107.0	107.6	105.8
2009	102.3	100.5	100.9	101.0	101.6	102.2	101.9	102.0	101.3	102.2	104.9	105.2	102.2
2010	100.0	98.7	99.2	100.8	101.9	102.4	102.0	102.1	101.2	102.6	105.5	106.4	101.9
2011	101.3	100.0	101.1	102.5	103.1	103.3	103.3	103.5	102.6	103.9	107.4	107.8	103.3
2012	103.0	101.4	102.4	102.8	104.0	104.0	103.8	103.3	103.1	103.9	107.6	107.9	103.9
2013	102.7	101.2	101.9	103.2	103.8	104.8	104.7	104.6	104.0	105.5	108.7	110.0	104.6
2014	104.8	102.9	104.1	105.4	106.2	107.0	107.2	107.0	105.8	107.2	110.6	111.7	106.7
2015	106.4	105.1	105.8	107.3	108.8	110.3	109.9	109.5	108.3	110.2	113.0	114.0	109.1
2016	108.9	108.5	109.1	110.2	111.0	111.7	112.2	112.2	110.5	111.9	115.4	116.8	111.5
2017	111.7	110.3	110.5	111.2	111.7	112.3	112.4	112.1	110.4	111.2	113.9	114.4	111.8
Transportation and Utilities													
2007	45.5	45.3	45.5	45.6	45.8	45.1	45.1	45.8	46.8	46.2	46.7	46.8	45.9
2008	45.1	45.6	45.3	45.7	45.7	44.9	44.6	44.7	45.5	45.8	45.8	45.8	45.4
2009	43.7	43.3	42.7	42.8	42.7	42.3	41.7	42.2	42.2	42.3	42.3	42.3	42.5
2010	41.1	40.9	41.0	40.6	40.9	40.9	40.9	41.4	42.0	42.6	42.8	43.1	41.5
2011	41.9	42.0	42.2	42.4	42.4	41.8	41.7	42.3	42.8	43.3	43.5	43.9	42.5
2012	43.1	42.7	42.7	43.0	43.2	43.2	42.1	43.0	43.0	43.6	43.8	43.8	43.1
2013	43.1	43.0	43.0	43.3	43.5	43.4	42.7	43.6	43.7	44.3	45.0	44.9	43.6
2014	44.1	44.0	44.4	44.7	45.1	44.8	44.4	45.6	45.4	45.9	46.3	46.9	45.1
2015	46.3	46.2	46.2	46.3	46.7	46.4	46.1	46.6	47.3	47.5	48.1	49.2	46.9
2016	47.4	47.3	47.3	47.3	47.5	47.1	46.8	47.6	48.3	49.1	50.4	51.5	48.1
2017	48.9	48.9	48.6	48.6	48.8	48.4	48.8	51.2	52.9	53.3	54.2	54.3	50.6

Employment by Industry: Kansas City, MO-KS, Selected Years, 2007–2017—*Continued*

(Numbers in thousands, not seasonally adjusted)

Industry and year	January	February	March	April	May	June	July	August	September	October	November	December	Annual average
Information													
2007	40.0	39.9	39.8	39.7	40.0	40.0	40.4	40.2	39.9	40.3	40.3	40.4	40.1
2008	40.4	40.0	40.0	39.2	39.3	39.2	39.1	38.8	38.0	37.5	37.0	36.7	38.8
2009	36.5	36.1	35.8	35.8	35.3	34.9	34.6	34.0	33.2	30.8	30.3	30.3	34.0
2010	28.4	27.9	27.9	28.7	28.5	28.0	27.4	27.0	26.6	26.4	26.2	25.8	27.4
2011	24.7	24.6	24.5	24.6	24.6	24.6	24.6	24.6	24.6	24.5	24.6	24.8	24.6
2012	24.7	24.6	24.6	24.7	24.7	24.8	24.6	24.8	24.4	24.7	24.7	24.8	24.7
2013	24.4	24.5	24.3	24.3	24.4	24.6	24.7	24.7	24.3	24.3	24.4	24.2	24.4
2014	24.2	24.1	23.9	23.3	23.1	23.1	22.8	22.4	21.8	21.5	21.4	21.3	22.7
2015	21.0	20.8	20.9	20.9	20.8	20.7	20.9	20.6	20.2	20.0	20.1	20.1	20.6
2016	19.9	19.9	19.7	18.8	18.8	18.8	18.9	18.8	18.5	18.5	18.6	18.7	19.0
2017	18.0	18.1	18.1	18.1	18.0	18.0	17.9	17.7	17.4	17.4	17.5	17.5	17.8
Financial Activities													
2007	73.4	73.7	74.4	73.6	73.7	74.3	75.0	74.8	74.2	73.9	73.9	74.1	74.1
2008	73.1	73.4	73.3	73.7	73.7	73.4	73.6	73.2	72.2	71.8	71.2	70.8	72.8
2009	70.2	69.9	70.2	70.9	70.9	71.3	71.9	71.9	70.7	70.8	70.9	70.8	70.9
2010	70.8	71.0	71.1	71.7	72.1	72.1	71.9	71.5	71.0	71.3	71.3	71.4	71.4
2011	70.7	70.9	71.0	71.4	72.1	72.1	72.0	72.1	71.6	73.2	73.2	73.2	72.0
2012	73.6	74.1	74.4	74.5	74.5	74.8	75.1	75.1	74.4	74.6	74.8	74.6	74.5
2013	75.0	75.2	74.9	74.6	74.6	75.3	75.6	75.2	74.6	74.1	74.2	74.0	74.8
2014	73.0	73.1	73.4	73.9	74.2	74.6	74.8	75.0	74.5	74.9	74.9	75.0	74.3
2015	74.7	75.1	75.3	75.6	76.0	76.5	77.3	77.3	76.4	76.9	77.0	77.1	76.3
2016	77.9	78.1	78.1	79.1	79.2	79.4	79.8	79.6	79.1	79.1	79.1	79.0	79.0
2017	78.5	78.8	78.9	78.7	79.3	80.0	80.5	80.3	79.8	80.0	80.6	80.0	79.6
Professional and Business Services													
2007	145.9	147.0	149.1	149.5	150.9	152.4	152.4	153.9	153.9	154.3	155.3	155.5	151.7
2008	151.7	152.4	154.0	156.5	154.2	155.5	155.6	155.3	155.4	153.5	153.1	152.6	154.2
2009	149.6	148.7	148.5	148.7	147.3	147.4	146.7	146.4	145.2	145.3	146.3	147.5	147.3
2010	145.0	145.1	146.6	152.8	152.1	152.5	153.0	153.0	152.3	154.3	154.4	155.7	151.4
2011	152.4	153.5	155.4	157.7	157.6	158.0	158.6	159.5	159.7	160.3	161.7	161.2	158.0
2012	158.1	159.5	161.4	164.0	164.1	165.9	165.8	166.3	166.6	169.4	169.3	168.5	164.9
2013	163.8	165.1	166.7	170.2	169.6	171.6	171.3	172.6	171.7	173.0	173.0	173.6	170.2
2014	168.6	169.8	170.8	174.0	174.0	176.6	177.8	179.4	177.9	180.7	182.4	183.3	176.3
2015	176.1	177.5	178.9	181.6	182.0	183.7	184.8	184.7	184.0	187.1	186.4	187.1	182.8
2016	181.0	182.4	182.4	185.3	184.1	185.6	188.3	189.9	190.4	191.2	191.1	190.4	186.8
2017	183.6	184.8	186.9	190.3	189.2	191.1	193.8	193.7	193.1	196.0	198.3	196.7	191.5
Education and Health Services													
2007	114.6	115.9	116.5	117.3	117.5	117.5	117.8	118.0	118.7	119.8	120.1	119.9	117.8
2008	119.7	121.2	121.4	123.1	123.1	123.2	123.1	122.9	123.3	125.3	125.6	125.6	123.1
2009	123.5	124.3	124.6	125.9	126.0	125.9	126.8	126.5	127.4	128.8	129.2	129.3	126.5
2010	127.7	128.8	128.9	127.9	128.3	128.2	128.8	128.8	129.9	131.3	131.7	132.2	129.4
2011	130.1	131.5	132.0	131.6	131.8	130.8	131.2	132.4	133.4	135.1	135.7	135.9	132.6
2012	132.9	134.1	134.4	134.4	135.1	134.6	133.4	134.5	134.2	135.8	136.5	137.1	134.8
2013	135.0	135.8	135.1	136.9	137.9	136.7	136.5	137.4	137.3	140.2	140.4	140.3	137.5
2014	138.3	139.3	139.0	142.0	142.9	142.3	142.0	142.4	142.6	144.6	145.1	145.1	142.1
2015	144.0	145.4	144.7	146.6	146.7	146.1	147.4	147.0	146.8	148.6	149.0	148.4	146.7
2016	147.0	147.5	147.2	149.0	148.8	146.2	147.0	146.8	148.9	150.9	150.9	150.2	148.4
2017	149.4	150.7	150.6	151.6	151.8	149.5	149.7	150.1	152.1	153.6	152.9	153.2	151.3
Leisure and Hospitality													
2007	89.1	89.5	93.0	95.3	97.8	99.6	98.1	98.8	95.9	94.0	91.9	91.4	94.5
2008	89.8	89.5	92.2	96.4	99.0	100.6	99.4	100.4	97.9	96.7	93.3	92.9	95.7
2009	89.0	88.6	90.6	92.4	95.3	96.8	95.1	96.9	94.2	92.6	89.9	90.0	92.6
2010	85.0	85.8	88.0	92.1	94.5	96.1	95.6	96.2	95.0	93.9	91.5	90.8	92.0
2011	86.9	86.9	89.9	92.7	95.9	97.8	98.8	99.4	96.2	95.0	93.2	92.4	93.8
2012	90.2	91.1	94.1	97.2	100.0	102.1	101.4	102.6	98.5	97.4	96.1	94.9	97.1
2013	92.7	92.3	95.0	97.7	100.9	103.4	103.5	103.9	101.4	100.8	96.7	96.7	98.8
2014	94.7	94.5	97.9	101.7	105.5	106.5	105.1	106.7	102.7	103.1	100.0	99.3	101.5
2015	97.1	97.6	100.3	103.9	106.4	108.5	108.3	108.4	105.2	105.3	102.7	103.6	103.9
2016	101.1	101.0	103.2	107.4	109.3	111.6	110.2	111.2	108.2	108.2	105.2	105.6	106.9
2017	103.4	104.2	106.9	108.9	111.5	113.3	112.1	113.3	110.5	109.7	105.0	104.9	108.6

Employment by Industry: Kansas City, MO-KS, Selected Years, 2007–2017—*Continued*

(Numbers in thousands, not seasonally adjusted)

Industry and year	January	February	March	April	May	June	July	August	September	October	November	December	Annual average
Other Services													
2007	42.1	42.4	42.6	43.9	44.1	44.7	45.0	44.8	44.2	43.9	43.7	43.6	43.8
2008	44.1	44.2	44.4	44.5	44.7	44.9	44.9	44.7	44.6	44.6	44.5	44.2	44.5
2009	44.2	44.2	44.0	44.3	44.4	44.6	44.5	44.2	43.7	44.0	43.7	43.6	44.1
2010	43.3	43.4	43.3	43.7	43.8	44.0	44.2	44.0	43.6	43.9	43.9	43.9	43.8
2011	43.7	43.6	43.9	44.1	44.2	44.4	44.5	44.4	44.1	44.3	44.2	44.2	44.1
2012	43.6	43.7	43.9	43.9	43.9	43.7	43.5	43.3	42.9	42.7	42.5	42.5	43.3
2013	42.1	42.0	42.1	41.8	42.0	42.2	42.2	42.4	42.1	41.9	41.8	41.9	42.0
2014	41.2	41.3	41.8	41.0	41.4	41.2	41.3	41.1	40.9	41.1	40.8	40.8	41.2
2015	40.7	40.7	40.9	41.3	41.5	41.6	41.8	41.9	41.4	42.0	41.8	41.8	41.5
2016	41.8	41.9	42.1	43.3	43.4	43.5	43.9	43.5	43.3	43.5	43.6	43.3	43.1
2017	42.9	43.0	43.0	43.4	43.7	43.9	43.7	43.6	43.4	43.6	43.5	43.4	43.4
Government													
2007	145.4	149.1	150.6	152.1	151.4	150.1	143.0	142.1	148.7	149.8	151.2	149.5	148.6
2008	148.2	151.5	153.3	154.2	154.5	153.2	142.7	143.6	151.4	152.8	152.9	152.8	150.9
2009	150.8	154.8	155.0	156.6	157.3	154.7	143.4	142.7	152.4	153.2	152.9	152.4	152.2
2010	149.7	152.9	154.4	156.4	159.0	156.0	137.4	136.3	150.3	150.4	150.6	149.9	150.3
2011	148.2	150.5	153.1	153.8	153.2	151.0	138.6	136.8	147.8	148.5	148.8	148.8	148.3
2012	145.6	149.3	150.5	151.2	151.6	147.7	135.6	139.2	147.3	148.8	148.8	148.4	147.0
2013	144.6	148.2	148.9	151.2	150.7	147.6	134.0	135.1	147.5	146.7	146.6	146.4	145.6
2014	143.5	146.6	147.6	148.0	149.1	147.0	134.7	134.2	146.9	147.4	147.3	146.3	144.9
2015	145.8	148.1	149.5	150.0	149.8	147.3	135.3	136.3	148.5	148.3	148.5	147.4	146.2
2016	147.5	149.5	149.9	151.3	150.0	147.8	136.7	138.2	150.9	150.3	150.1	149.1	147.6
2017	148.6	150.9	151.3	151.8	151.2	150.4	139.8	141.1	152.3	153.4	153.6	153.2	149.8

Employment by Industry: Austin-Round Rock, TX, Selected Years, 2007–2017

(Numbers in thousands, not seasonally adjusted)

Industry and year	January	February	March	April	May	June	July	August	September	October	November	December	Annual average
Total Nonfarm													
2007	746.2	758.3	766.5	769.5	774.5	777.7	765.7	769.4	778.6	782.3	787.6	789.0	772.1
2008	778.9	787.4	789.6	791.7	795.4	795.4	782.7	786.3	795.3	795.8	798.5	795.4	791.0
2009	775.6	776.3	776.5	778.0	780.2	778.0	763.4	764.5	770.8	773.5	777.5	777.1	774.3
2010	765.8	771.5	780.2	783.4	788.6	790.9	777.8	780.7	787.1	796.6	802.1	801.9	785.6
2011	789.3	797.5	804.6	812.8	814.1	815.8	804.5	809.3	818.3	820.9	827.2	828.7	811.9
2012	819.2	825.9	832.9	837.5	842.5	847.2	835.7	841.5	852.0	859.3	869.9	869.1	844.4
2013	855.3	864.9	871.6	878.6	883.7	888.7	878.4	881.7	892.0	898.0	908.1	907.3	884.0
2014	895.3	905.9	913.4	918.5	923.0	928.3	917.7	919.7	928.1	936.6	944.4	945.7	923.1
2015	933.3	943.4	949.9	955.8	962.2	969.0	960.4	962.4	970.5	979.6	985.8	986.9	963.3
2016	975.1	984.7	988.9	995.8	998.7	1,003.3	999.2	999.3	1,007.1	1,014.7	1,019.9	1,019.7	1,000.5
2017	1,008.3	1,017.6	1,023.4	1,028.1	1,034.9	1,038.4	1,029.8	1,029.9	1,032.5	1,042.1	1,052.8	1,053.5	1,032.6
Total Private													
2007	588.1	596.7	604.0	606.9	611.2	617.8	616.7	618.9	617.9	619.2	623.5	626.5	612.3
2008	614.8	619.7	619.9	624.9	627.9	630.0	628.3	630.9	627.7	628.5	629.0	627.1	625.7
2009	606.6	604.1	603.7	603.9	605.6	605.9	604.2	605.0	599.8	601.6	603.2	604.2	604.0
2010	592.8	596.2	602.2	606.1	609.3	613.5	614.6	617.4	615.8	622.1	626.3	628.3	612.1
2011	616.8	621.5	628.5	636.2	637.8	641.3	643.6	648.8	648.9	650.9	655.8	659.1	640.8
2012	648.5	653.2	660.0	664.1	669.0	675.8	675.6	682.3	682.5	687.8	695.9	697.4	674.3
2013	682.8	689.9	696.1	702.9	707.7	714.3	714.8	720.3	720.3	725.1	733.0	734.4	711.8
2014	721.7	730.0	736.9	742.5	746.4	753.5	753.5	757.6	755.8	761.5	768.4	770.0	749.8
2015	757.5	766.2	772.4	778.1	784.1	792.2	793.9	797.8	795.7	802.3	808.0	809.1	788.1
2016	797.8	806.2	808.4	815.9	817.8	823.4	828.8	831.1	829.9	834.3	838.0	837.8	822.5
2017	826.3	834.1	839.0	844.2	849.7	855.2	857.0	859.6	856.5	864.1	873.3	875.1	852.8
Goods Producing													
2007	111.5	112.9	114.0	115.0	115.8	117.4	117.0	117.3	116.2	116.4	115.9	115.5	115.4
2008	113.3	113.8	113.4	112.9	112.9	112.9	111.9	111.1	109.5	107.4	105.6	104.0	110.7
2009	99.0	97.3	95.2	95.8	95.4	95.5	95.0	94.4	93.5	92.9	92.2	92.5	94.9
2010	90.7	90.7	91.4	92.4	92.3	93.4	94.2	95.1	94.6	95.0	94.8	94.6	93.3
2011	93.3	93.6	94.3	94.3	94.5	95.5	96.0	96.2	95.9	96.0	95.9	96.0	95.1
2012	95.3	96.3	97.1	97.5	98.3	100.1	100.6	101.5	101.2	101.2	100.8	100.7	99.2
2013	99.7	100.3	101.1	102.2	103.0	103.9	104.1	104.6	104.4	104.7	105.2	105.6	103.2
2014	104.5	105.7	106.4	106.7	107.7	109.0	109.5	109.8	109.0	108.6	108.9	109.1	107.9
2015	108.7	109.6	109.9	109.7	110.0	111.5	112.3	112.5	111.3	111.7	111.7	111.7	110.9
2016	111.5	112.6	112.7	113.4	113.8	115.0	116.5	116.5	115.6	115.9	115.8	115.8	114.6
2017	114.6	115.7	116.6	117.7	118.7	120.5	120.8	120.7	120.0	119.2	118.9	119.8	118.6
Service-Providing													
2007	634.7	645.4	652.5	654.5	658.7	660.3	648.7	652.1	662.4	665.9	671.7	673.5	656.7
2008	665.6	673.6	676.2	678.8	682.5	682.5	670.8	675.2	685.8	688.4	692.9	691.4	680.3
2009	676.6	679.0	681.3	682.2	684.8	682.5	668.4	670.1	677.3	680.6	685.3	684.6	679.4
2010	675.1	680.8	688.8	691.0	696.3	697.5	683.6	685.6	692.5	701.6	707.3	707.3	692.3
2011	696.0	703.9	710.3	718.5	719.6	720.3	708.5	713.1	722.4	724.9	731.3	732.7	716.8
2012	723.9	729.6	735.8	740.0	744.2	747.1	735.1	740.0	750.8	758.1	769.1	768.4	745.2
2013	755.6	764.6	770.5	776.4	780.7	784.8	774.3	777.1	787.6	793.3	802.9	801.7	780.8
2014	790.8	800.2	807.0	811.8	815.3	819.3	808.2	809.9	819.1	828.0	835.5	836.6	815.1
2015	824.6	833.8	840.0	846.1	852.2	857.5	848.1	849.9	859.2	867.9	874.1	875.2	852.4
2016	863.6	872.1	876.2	882.4	884.9	888.3	882.7	882.8	891.5	898.8	904.1	903.9	885.9
2017	893.7	901.9	906.8	910.4	916.2	917.9	909.0	909.2	912.5	922.9	933.9	933.7	914.0
Mining, Logging, and Construction													
2007	46.2	47.2	48.0	48.7	49.4	50.4	50.2	50.7	50.4	50.8	51.2	50.4	49.5
2008	48.5	48.9	48.8	48.8	49.0	49.1	48.5	48.4	47.7	46.5	45.4	44.5	47.8
2009	42.8	42.4	41.8	41.1	41.2	41.8	41.6	41.0	40.6	40.1	40.1	40.2	41.2
2010	38.6	38.4	39.1	40.2	40.0	40.7	41.5	42.0	41.4	41.5	41.1	40.8	40.4
2011	39.8	39.8	40.1	39.7	39.6	40.2	40.3	40.4	40.4	40.1	40.0	40.1	40.0
2012	40.0	40.5	41.2	41.6	42.1	43.2	43.4	44.0	44.0	44.0	43.8	44.0	42.7
2013	43.4	44.1	44.9	45.4	46.1	46.3	46.4	46.8	46.9	47.0	47.2	47.4	46.0
2014	46.9	47.8	48.5	49.3	50.3	51.2	51.9	52.4	52.3	52.4	52.7	52.9	50.7
2015	52.9	53.8	54.1	54.2	54.6	55.4	56.1	56.4	56.0	56.5	56.6	56.8	55.3
2016	56.4	57.3	57.5	58.0	58.2	58.8	59.9	59.9	59.7	59.9	59.8	59.8	58.8
2017	58.9	59.7	60.4	61.0	61.8	62.8	62.9	62.6	62.3	61.9	61.1	62.1	61.5

Employment by Industry: Austin-Round Rock, TX, Selected Years, 2007–2017—*Continued*

(Numbers in thousands, not seasonally adjusted)

Industry and year	January	February	March	April	May	June	July	August	September	October	November	December	Annual average
Manufacturing													
2007	65.3	65.7	66.0	66.3	66.4	67.0	66.8	66.6	65.8	65.6	64.7	65.1	65.9
2008	64.8	64.9	64.6	64.1	63.9	63.8	63.4	62.7	61.8	60.9	60.2	59.5	62.9
2009	56.2	54.9	53.4	54.7	54.2	53.7	53.4	53.4	52.9	52.8	52.1	52.3	53.7
2010	52.1	52.3	52.3	52.2	52.3	52.7	52.7	53.1	53.2	53.5	53.7	53.8	52.8
2011	53.5	53.8	54.2	54.6	54.9	55.3	55.7	55.8	55.5	55.9	55.9	55.9	55.1
2012	55.3	55.8	55.9	55.9	56.2	56.9	57.2	57.5	57.2	57.2	57.0	56.7	56.6
2013	56.3	56.2	56.2	56.8	56.9	57.6	57.7	57.8	57.5	57.7	58.0	58.2	57.2
2014	57.6	57.9	57.9	57.4	57.4	57.8	57.6	57.4	56.7	56.2	56.2	56.2	57.2
2015	55.8	55.8	55.8	55.5	55.4	56.1	56.2	56.1	55.3	55.2	55.1	54.9	55.6
2016	55.1	55.3	55.2	55.4	55.6	56.2	56.6	56.6	55.9	56.0	56.0	56.0	55.8
2017	55.7	56.0	56.2	56.7	56.9	57.7	57.9	58.1	57.7	57.3	57.8	57.7	57.1
Trade, Transportation, and Utilities													
2007	128.6	128.8	129.9	130.6	131.0	132.4	132.8	133.0	133.0	134.5	137.3	140.1	132.7
2008	135.5	135.0	134.7	135.1	135.1	135.8	136.2	137.4	136.7	137.8	139.5	140.3	136.6
2009	134.6	130.8	130.9	129.0	129.2	129.1	129.2	130.2	129.3	130.2	132.5	134.1	130.8
2010	131.1	130.1	130.7	131.6	132.1	132.5	132.7	133.8	133.5	135.0	138.4	140.6	133.5
2011	136.0	135.6	136.6	137.4	137.7	137.6	138.6	140.2	139.8	141.3	144.4	146.9	139.3
2012	142.0	141.3	141.9	142.7	143.4	144.1	144.2	145.9	145.3	146.7	151.4	153.0	145.2
2013	148.0	147.8	147.8	149.1	149.9	151.4	151.8	153.4	153.0	154.9	159.2	161.4	152.3
2014	156.3	155.8	155.6	156.2	156.5	157.5	157.5	158.5	158.2	159.9	163.9	165.9	158.5
2015	160.5	160.2	160.8	161.1	162.3	163.8	164.5	165.9	165.9	167.3	171.2	173.8	164.8
2016	168.4	168.1	168.5	169.0	169.1	170.1	171.4	172.6	172.6	174.2	178.0	180.0	171.8
2017	175.0	174.0	173.9	175.0	175.5	176.2	176.5	177.7	176.7	177.8	182.5	184.5	177.1
Wholesale Trade													
2007	36.4	36.6	36.8	36.9	37.2	38.0	37.8	37.5	37.3	37.5	37.0	38.0	37.3
2008	37.7	37.8	37.7	37.7	37.8	38.3	38.5	38.6	38.6	38.7	38.7	38.6	38.2
2009	38.2	35.3	35.4	34.5	34.4	34.3	34.8	34.6	34.4	34.4	34.5	34.6	35.0
2010	36.4	36.4	36.6	37.0	37.1	37.3	37.4	37.5	37.4	37.9	38.2	38.3	37.3
2011	38.3	38.7	38.9	39.2	39.4	39.6	39.9	40.1	40.4	41.0	41.2	41.5	39.9
2012	41.0	41.2	41.4	41.6	41.9	42.1	42.0	42.2	42.0	41.9	42.1	42.4	41.8
2013	42.6	42.9	43.1	43.2	43.0	43.7	43.8	44.1	43.9	44.4	44.5	44.7	43.7
2014	44.5	44.6	44.4	44.6	44.8	45.1	45.3	45.5	45.6	46.0	46.4	46.5	45.3
2015	46.8	47.0	47.2	47.2	47.4	47.9	48.3	48.8	48.7	48.9	49.3	49.5	48.1
2016	48.8	48.9	49.1	49.7	49.6	49.8	49.8	49.9	49.8	49.7	49.4	49.4	49.5
2017	49.9	49.9	50.1	50.9	51.0	51.4	51.6	52.0	52.1	52.7	53.0	53.9	51.5
Retail Trade													
2007	79.2	79.1	79.7	80.5	80.5	81.1	81.8	82.0	82.1	83.3	86.5	88.1	82.0
2008	84.3	83.6	83.4	84.0	83.9	84.1	84.6	85.4	84.6	85.7	87.3	88.1	84.9
2009	83.4	82.6	82.7	81.7	82.0	82.0	81.8	82.8	82.0	82.7	84.8	85.9	82.9
2010	81.9	80.9	81.2	81.8	82.1	82.4	82.7	83.5	83.0	84.1	87.0	88.6	83.3
2011	84.2	83.5	84.2	84.7	84.7	84.9	85.4	86.3	85.5	86.6	89.4	91.0	85.9
2012	87.1	86.2	86.5	87.2	87.6	88.2	88.5	89.6	89.0	90.6	94.9	95.7	89.3
2013	91.1	90.8	90.7	91.5	92.2	92.9	93.5	94.3	94.0	95.3	99.1	100.6	93.8
2014	96.3	95.9	95.9	96.1	96.2	96.8	97.1	97.6	96.9	98.1	101.5	102.6	97.6
2015	97.7	97.6	97.9	98.0	98.8	99.7	100.1	100.6	100.7	101.6	104.7	106.1	100.3
2016	102.0	102.0	102.3	102.3	102.4	102.9	103.3	104.0	103.8	104.9	108.4	109.6	104.0
2017	105.1	104.5	104.4	104.6	105.0	105.2	105.2	105.5	104.5	104.3	108.1	108.4	105.4
Transportation and Utilities													
2007	13.0	13.1	13.4	13.2	13.3	13.3	13.2	13.5	13.6	13.7	13.8	14.0	13.4
2008	13.5	13.6	13.6	13.4	13.4	13.4	13.1	13.4	13.5	13.4	13.5	13.6	13.5
2009	13.0	12.9	12.8	12.8	12.8	12.8	12.6	12.8	12.9	13.1	13.2	13.6	12.9
2010	12.8	12.8	12.9	12.8	12.9	12.8	12.6	12.8	13.1	13.0	13.2	13.7	13.0
2011	13.5	13.4	13.5	13.5	13.6	13.1	13.3	13.8	13.9	13.7	13.8	14.4	13.6
2012	13.9	13.9	14.0	13.9	13.9	13.8	13.7	14.1	14.3	14.2	14.4	14.9	14.1
2013	14.3	14.1	14.0	14.4	14.7	14.8	14.5	15.0	15.1	15.2	15.6	16.1	14.8
2014	15.5	15.3	15.3	15.5	15.5	15.6	15.1	15.4	15.7	15.8	16.0	16.8	15.6
2015	16.0	15.6	15.7	15.9	16.1	16.2	16.1	16.5	16.5	16.8	17.2	18.2	16.4
2016	17.6	17.2	17.1	17.0	17.1	17.4	18.3	18.7	19.0	19.6	20.2	21.0	18.4
2017	20.0	19.6	19.4	19.5	19.5	19.6	19.7	20.2	20.1	20.8	21.4	22.2	20.2

Employment by Industry: Austin-Round Rock, TX, Selected Years, 2007–2017—*Continued*

(Numbers in thousands, not seasonally adjusted)

Industry and year	January	February	March	April	May	June	July	August	September	October	November	December	Annual average
Information													
2007	22.3	22.5	22.5	22.6	22.7	22.6	22.0	22.0	22.0	21.9	22.2	22.1	22.3
2008	21.6	21.4	21.3	21.1	21.3	21.4	21.4	21.5	21.2	21.1	21.4	21.4	21.3
2009	20.7	20.6	20.5	20.3	20.2	19.9	19.9	19.9	19.7	19.6	19.7	19.9	20.1
2010	19.5	19.5	19.6	19.6	19.7	19.8	19.9	20.0	20.0	20.1	20.3	20.5	19.9
2011	20.1	20.2	20.3	20.4	20.6	20.8	21.2	21.3	21.4	21.4	21.8	21.9	21.0
2012	21.9	21.9	22.1	22.1	22.3	22.6	23.0	23.0	22.9	23.2	23.6	23.8	22.7
2013	23.1	23.2	23.6	23.4	23.4	23.8	24.1	24.2	24.1	24.1	24.6	24.9	23.9
2014	24.3	24.3	24.4	25.0	24.4	25.2	25.5	25.6	25.6	25.9	26.5	27.0	25.3
2015	26.6	26.6	26.8	27.3	27.4	27.9	27.7	27.9	27.9	28.1	28.8	28.8	27.7
2016	28.7	28.9	28.6	28.7	28.7	29.0	29.0	28.9	28.7	29.0	29.0	29.3	28.9
2017	29.3	29.4	29.7	29.5	29.6	30.0	30.5	30.3	30.5	30.5	30.7	30.9	30.1
Financial Activities													
2007	44.6	44.9	45.3	45.4	45.8	46.0	45.9	45.9	45.7	45.5	45.8	46.1	45.6
2008	45.3	45.7	45.7	45.9	46.0	46.2	46.2	46.2	46.0	45.7	45.8	46.0	45.9
2009	44.6	44.6	44.5	44.6	44.6	44.7	44.5	44.4	44.1	44.1	44.0	44.1	44.4
2010	43.1	43.2	43.3	43.2	43.4	43.4	43.4	43.4	43.1	43.5	43.6	43.7	43.4
2011	43.5	43.7	44.1	44.5	44.7	44.9	45.2	45.3	45.2	45.4	45.6	46.0	44.8
2012	45.7	45.9	46.2	46.3	46.7	47.1	47.0	47.4	47.4	48.0	48.1	48.3	47.0
2013	47.9	48.2	48.3	48.7	49.0	49.3	49.7	49.8	49.8	50.3	50.4	50.7	49.3
2014	50.7	51.1	51.3	51.4	51.7	52.1	52.0	52.2	51.9	52.4	52.5	53.0	51.9
2015	52.4	52.9	52.9	53.6	53.9	54.2	54.4	54.6	54.3	54.9	55.1	55.5	54.1
2016	55.1	55.5	55.8	56.0	56.2	56.7	57.3	57.7	57.4	57.7	57.8	58.3	56.8
2017	57.9	58.3	58.6	59.1	59.3	59.9	60.4	60.6	60.4	60.7	61.0	60.7	59.7
Professional and Business Services													
2007	104.1	106.3	107.8	107.3	108.3	109.8	110.1	111.4	111.4	111.8	112.3	112.3	109.4
2008	112.2	113.2	112.7	114.7	115.6	115.7	115.0	115.9	115.3	116.0	115.4	114.4	114.7
2009	111.5	111.3	111.1	111.0	111.1	111.2	109.8	110.1	108.9	110.4	110.5	109.8	110.6
2010	108.5	109.6	111.2	111.4	112.1	113.3	113.4	113.8	113.9	116.3	116.4	116.8	113.1
2011	115.8	117.4	118.8	120.3	120.0	121.2	121.6	123.0	123.8	124.1	124.7	125.5	121.4
2012	123.9	125.0	126.8	126.8	127.5	128.8	129.8	131.8	132.2	133.6	134.9	134.2	129.6
2013	131.3	133.4	135.0	137.0	137.8	139.0	140.0	142.1	142.7	143.9	145.1	144.6	139.3
2014	142.5	145.2	147.7	149.0	149.5	150.3	151.0	152.4	152.3	154.6	155.2	154.9	150.4
2015	153.3	155.6	157.5	158.4	159.3	161.0	162.6	163.4	163.4	165.7	166.3	165.0	161.0
2016	163.5	165.9	166.3	168.3	168.2	169.3	170.7	171.2	170.6	171.8	172.4	170.8	169.1
2017	168.9	171.2	172.5	173.2	174.1	175.9	176.5	177.3	177.4	181.5	184.1	183.0	176.3
Education and Health Services													
2007	73.8	75.7	76.5	76.4	77.1	76.7	77.0	77.5	78.9	79.4	79.8	80.0	77.4
2008	79.0	80.4	80.3	80.9	81.3	80.3	80.0	80.9	81.8	82.5	82.8	83.1	81.1
2009	81.0	82.3	82.9	83.5	84.0	83.1	83.3	83.9	84.0	84.9	85.2	85.3	83.6
2010	84.5	86.0	86.4	87.4	87.8	87.3	87.8	88.2	88.6	89.8	90.1	89.7	87.8
2011	88.7	89.8	90.1	92.2	92.5	91.9	92.6	94.3	95.0	95.4	96.1	95.9	92.9
2012	95.0	96.4	97.0	97.2	97.7	97.5	96.8	98.3	99.4	100.1	100.7	100.6	98.1
2013	99.7	101.3	101.3	102.4	102.6	102.0	101.3	102.7	103.4	104.3	104.9	104.4	102.5
2014	102.9	104.6	104.9	106.2	106.7	106.1	105.3	106.5	107.0	108.5	109.5	109.1	106.4
2015	107.7	109.7	109.9	111.6	112.1	111.5	110.7	112.2	112.5	113.8	114.0	113.7	111.6
2016	113.4	114.9	114.2	114.6	114.7	113.6	115.0	116.4	116.9	118.1	117.6	117.4	115.6
2017	117.9	119.7	119.6	120.6	120.9	119.3	119.4	120.9	120.6	122.2	121.4	121.1	120.3
Leisure and Hospitality													
2007	74.5	76.1	77.8	79.4	80.0	81.3	80.6	81.0	80.4	79.4	79.5	79.5	79.1
2008	78.0	79.5	80.7	82.4	83.3	84.0	83.0	83.3	82.8	83.5	83.7	82.5	82.2
2009	80.6	81.7	82.7	83.9	85.0	85.1	85.3	85.5	84.7	84.0	83.7	82.9	83.8
2010	80.7	82.1	83.9	85.3	86.6	87.4	86.4	86.6	86.5	86.8	87.2	86.9	85.5
2011	84.8	86.2	88.6	91.3	91.9	92.2	90.9	91.5	91.7	91.0	91.1	90.6	90.2
2012	88.8	90.2	92.2	94.1	95.3	96.3	94.4	94.9	95.3	95.9	97.1	97.2	94.3
2013	94.5	96.5	99.2	100.1	101.6	103.1	101.7	101.9	102.3	102.1	102.4	101.6	100.6
2014	100.3	102.6	105.1	106.4	107.8	109.6	108.6	108.9	109.3	108.8	109.3	108.6	107.1
2015	106.8	109.7	112.2	114.8	117.0	118.5	117.6	117.5	117.8	118.0	118.2	118.1	115.5
2016	115.7	118.3	119.8	122.3	122.9	124.4	123.9	123.3	124.0	123.3	123.2	122.3	122.0
2017	119.5	121.9	123.8	124.7	126.6	127.3	127.0	126.7	126.3	127.2	129.4	129.8	125.9

Employment by Industry: Austin-Round Rock, TX, Selected Years, 2007–2017—*Continued*

(Numbers in thousands, not seasonally adjusted)

Industry and year	January	February	March	April	May	June	July	August	September	October	November	December	Annual average
Other Services													
2007	28.7	29.5	30.2	30.2	30.5	31.6	31.3	30.8	30.3	30.3	30.7	30.9	30.4
2008	29.9	30.7	31.1	31.9	32.4	33.7	34.6	34.6	34.4	34.5	34.8	35.4	33.2
2009	34.6	35.5	35.9	35.8	36.1	37.3	37.2	36.6	35.6	35.5	35.4	35.6	35.9
2010	34.7	35.0	35.7	35.2	35.3	36.4	36.8	36.5	35.6	35.6	35.5	35.5	35.7
2011	34.6	35.0	35.7	35.8	35.9	37.2	37.5	37.0	36.1	36.3	36.2	36.3	36.1
2012	35.9	36.2	36.7	37.4	37.8	39.3	39.8	39.5	38.8	39.1	39.3	39.6	38.3
2013	38.6	39.2	39.8	40.0	40.4	41.8	42.1	41.6	40.6	40.8	41.2	41.2	40.6
2014	40.2	40.7	41.5	41.6	42.1	43.7	44.1	43.7	42.5	42.8	42.6	42.4	42.3
2015	41.5	41.9	42.4	41.6	42.1	43.8	44.1	43.8	42.6	42.8	42.7	42.5	42.7
2016	41.5	42.0	42.5	43.6	44.2	45.3	45.0	44.5	44.1	44.3	44.2	43.9	43.8
2017	43.2	43.9	44.3	44.4	45.0	46.1	45.9	45.4	44.6	45.0	45.3	45.3	44.9
Government													
2007	158.1	161.6	162.5	162.6	163.3	159.9	149.0	150.5	160.7	163.1	164.1	162.5	159.8
2008	164.1	167.7	169.7	166.8	167.5	165.4	154.4	155.4	167.6	167.3	169.5	168.3	165.3
2009	169.0	172.2	172.8	174.1	174.6	172.1	159.2	159.5	171.0	171.9	174.3	172.9	170.3
2010	173.0	175.3	178.0	177.3	179.3	177.4	163.2	163.3	171.3	174.5	175.8	173.6	173.5
2011	172.5	176.0	176.1	176.6	176.3	174.5	160.9	160.5	169.4	170.0	171.4	169.6	171.2
2012	170.7	172.7	172.9	173.4	173.5	171.4	160.1	159.2	169.5	171.5	174.0	171.7	170.1
2013	172.5	175.0	175.5	175.7	176.0	174.4	163.6	161.4	171.7	172.9	175.1	172.9	172.2
2014	173.6	175.9	176.5	176.0	176.6	174.8	164.2	162.1	172.3	175.1	176.0	175.7	173.2
2015	175.8	177.2	177.5	177.7	178.1	176.8	166.5	164.6	174.8	177.3	177.8	177.8	175.2
2016	177.3	178.5	180.5	179.9	180.9	179.9	170.4	168.2	177.2	180.4	181.9	181.9	178.1
2017	182.0	183.5	184.4	183.9	185.2	183.2	172.8	170.3	176.0	178.0	179.5	178.4	179.8

Employment by Industry: Columbus, OH, Selected Years, 2007–2017

(Numbers in thousands, not seasonally adjusted)

Industry and year	January	February	March	April	May	June	July	August	September	October	November	December	Annual average
Total Nonfarm													
2007	944.3	941.9	949.9	959.2	967.7	966.2	957.6	957.5	962.5	970.1	976.8	975.7	960.8
2008	948.8	950.1	950.0	960.2	966.3	960.3	955.2	955.1	956.9	963.5	961.8	957.6	957.2
2009	926.9	923.2	923.5	927.3	931.4	922.7	913.8	913.3	916.8	925.0	926.7	923.6	922.9
2010	900.0	901.5	906.8	919.3	927.3	921.3	916.0	918.7	923.3	933.8	938.1	937.8	920.3
2011	912.3	917.0	922.4	939.2	945.9	939.6	938.7	942.7	951.9	958.0	965.0	964.0	941.4
2012	941.0	947.7	952.9	961.9	971.7	969.0	960.4	963.6	973.0	987.3	994.8	993.2	968.0
2013	966.4	968.5	972.1	986.6	996.9	989.8	986.4	991.9	997.2	1,007.1	1,018.1	1,018.0	991.6
2014	987.8	990.2	993.5	1,009.9	1,021.2	1,013.9	1,012.6	1,020.2	1,025.6	1,034.9	1,044.9	1,045.6	1,016.7
2015	1,015.3	1,017.0	1,019.8	1,032.2	1,043.6	1,043.5	1,041.9	1,046.7	1,044.4	1,056.5	1,063.3	1,063.4	1,040.6
2016	1,039.2	1,042.0	1,047.5	1,056.3	1,065.2	1,063.2	1,063.2	1,068.0	1,070.2	1,080.5	1,090.2	1,086.6	1,064.3
2017	1,062.8	1,065.4	1,067.9	1,079.4	1,089.0	1,089.5	1,088.2	1,093.1	1,088.9	1,090.7	1,095.4	1,096.9	1,083.9
Total Private													
2007	778.9	774.5	781.3	790.1	797.9	802.5	800.3	801.4	797.9	801.3	806.7	806.2	794.9
2008	782.9	781.2	780.9	790.6	795.2	796.2	797.0	797.5	792.6	793.9	792.0	789.0	790.8
2009	761.9	755.5	755.0	757.3	761.1	760.2	757.9	758.3	752.8	755.5	756.8	755.5	757.3
2010	735.1	734.1	738.9	749.4	753.9	757.2	760.5	763.4	759.3	764.7	768.5	767.9	754.4
2011	748.6	751.1	755.4	769.4	775.2	776.9	782.6	785.8	786.0	790.6	796.3	796.7	776.2
2012	777.0	780.9	786.4	795.6	803.1	808.9	807.5	809.9	808.2	818.2	824.6	824.3	803.7
2013	803.2	803.2	807.0	819.5	828.6	832.0	832.3	836.0	832.7	839.7	848.6	849.1	827.7
2014	824.5	824.3	827.9	841.9	851.8	855.8	856.9	863.2	857.8	865.7	875.4	877.0	851.9
2015	849.3	848.5	851.4	862.8	873.3	879.0	880.3	882.9	875.3	885.0	891.4	891.8	872.6
2016	869.2	868.8	874.5	882.7	893.0	896.1	899.6	903.1	897.9	905.0	913.3	911.4	892.9
2017	888.4	889.2	892.1	902.4	912.8	918.3	919.6	921.3	912.4	913.1	916.5	919.0	908.8
Goods Producing													
2007	116.5	114.3	115.8	117.4	119.2	121.1	120.8	121.0	120.3	118.7	118.1	116.6	118.3
2008	112.7	111.8	111.3	112.8	114.3	115.4	115.2	115.0	114.3	112.7	110.9	108.4	112.9
2009	102.6	100.1	99.3	99.3	99.6	100.1	98.9	98.8	97.5	96.2	95.3	93.9	98.5
2010	89.8	88.9	89.8	92.1	93.6	94.8	95.6	95.8	95.5	96.0	95.6	94.2	93.5
2011	90.8	90.8	91.7	94.4	95.6	97.0	98.6	98.9	98.3	98.5	98.2	97.1	95.8
2012	94.3	94.7	95.6	97.5	99.0	100.3	101.2	101.3	100.7	100.6	100.5	99.5	98.8
2013	97.2	97.3	98.3	100.3	102.4	104.1	104.3	104.5	104.1	104.3	104.3	103.0	102.0
2014	99.5	99.3	100.7	102.9	104.9	106.0	106.8	107.0	106.3	106.4	107.1	105.2	104.3
2015	102.5	102.8	103.4	105.7	108.4	109.2	109.9	110.0	109.2	109.3	109.5	108.5	107.4
2016	104.9	105.3	107.0	108.6	110.0	111.0	111.2	111.1	110.2	110.3	110.5	109.0	109.1
2017	106.7	107.3	108.6	110.8	112.9	114.4	114.6	114.4	113.1	111.1	112.8	112.6	111.6
Service-Providing													
2007	827.8	827.6	834.1	841.8	848.5	845.1	836.8	836.5	842.2	851.4	858.7	859.1	842.5
2008	836.1	838.3	838.7	847.4	852.0	844.9	840.0	840.1	842.6	850.8	850.9	849.2	844.3
2009	824.3	823.1	824.2	828.0	831.8	822.6	814.9	814.5	819.3	828.8	831.4	829.7	824.4
2010	810.2	812.6	817.0	827.2	833.7	826.5	820.4	822.9	827.8	837.8	842.5	843.6	826.9
2011	821.5	826.2	830.7	844.8	850.3	842.6	840.1	843.8	853.6	859.5	866.8	866.9	845.6
2012	846.7	853.0	857.3	864.4	872.7	868.7	859.2	862.3	872.3	886.7	894.3	893.7	869.3
2013	869.2	871.2	873.8	886.3	894.5	885.7	882.1	887.4	893.1	902.8	913.8	915.0	889.6
2014	888.3	890.9	892.8	907.0	916.3	907.9	905.8	913.2	919.3	928.5	937.8	940.4	912.4
2015	912.8	914.2	916.4	926.5	935.2	934.3	932.0	936.7	935.2	947.2	953.8	954.9	933.3
2016	934.3	936.7	940.5	947.7	955.2	952.2	952.0	956.9	960.0	970.2	979.7	977.6	955.3
2017	956.1	958.1	959.3	968.6	976.1	975.1	973.6	978.7	975.8	979.6	982.6	984.3	972.3
Mining, Logging, and Construction													
2007	37.3	35.6	37.1	38.5	40.2	41.7	41.9	41.8	41.3	40.7	39.8	38.1	39.5
2008	35.1	34.2	34.2	36.5	37.9	38.6	38.2	38.1	37.5	37.0	35.5	33.5	36.4
2009	30.0	29.2	29.6	30.2	31.3	32.4	32.8	32.6	31.6	30.3	29.6	28.2	30.7
2010	25.5	24.6	25.4	27.5	28.8	29.7	30.5	30.6	30.5	30.7	30.1	28.6	28.5
2011	26.0	25.9	26.7	28.6	29.7	30.7	32.2	32.4	32.0	31.7	31.1	30.0	29.8
2012	27.8	27.8	28.6	30.0	31.2	32.0	32.7	32.8	32.4	32.3	31.5	30.5	30.8
2013	28.6	28.6	29.4	31.2	33.1	34.3	34.6	35.0	34.6	34.7	34.4	32.7	32.6
2014	30.5	30.2	31.7	33.5	35.1	36.3	36.5	36.6	36.2	36.1	35.6	34.3	34.4
2015	31.6	31.8	32.6	34.4	36.5	37.4	37.7	37.9	37.6	37.6	37.0	35.9	35.7
2016	33.4	33.5	35.0	37.1	38.4	39.4	39.6	39.6	39.0	38.9	38.4	37.1	37.5
2017	35.2	35.6	37.0	39.0	40.8	42.1	42.1	42.0	41.4	40.3	40.4	38.6	39.5

Employment by Industry: Columbus, OH, Selected Years, 2007–2017—*Continued*

(Numbers in thousands, not seasonally adjusted)

Industry and year	January	February	March	April	May	June	July	August	September	October	November	December	Annual average
Manufacturing													
2007	79.2	78.7	78.7	78.9	79.0	79.4	78.9	79.2	79.0	78.0	78.3	78.5	78.8
2008	77.6	77.6	77.1	76.3	76.4	76.8	77.0	76.9	76.8	75.7	75.4	74.9	76.5
2009	72.6	70.9	69.7	69.1	68.3	67.7	66.1	66.2	65.9	65.9	65.7	65.7	67.8
2010	64.3	64.3	64.4	64.6	64.8	65.1	65.1	65.2	65.0	65.3	65.5	65.6	64.9
2011	64.8	64.9	65.0	65.8	65.9	66.3	66.4	66.5	66.3	66.8	67.1	67.1	66.1
2012	66.5	66.9	67.0	67.5	67.8	68.3	68.5	68.5	68.3	68.3	69.0	69.0	68.0
2013	68.6	68.7	68.9	69.1	69.3	69.8	69.7	69.5	69.5	69.6	69.9	70.3	69.4
2014	69.0	69.1	69.0	69.4	69.8	69.7	70.3	70.4	70.1	70.3	71.5	70.9	70.0
2015	70.9	71.0	70.8	71.3	71.9	71.8	72.2	72.1	71.6	71.7	72.5	72.6	71.7
2016	71.5	71.8	72.0	71.5	71.6	71.6	71.6	71.5	71.2	71.4	72.1	71.9	71.6
2017	71.5	71.7	71.6	71.8	72.1	72.3	72.5	72.4	71.7	70.8	72.4	74.0	72.1
Trade, Transportation, and Utilities													
2007	191.3	188.0	189.2	189.7	191.8	192.0	192.5	192.6	192.8	195.6	201.6	203.6	193.4
2008	192.7	189.4	189.2	190.7	191.7	191.1	192.0	192.6	191.7	193.3	196.0	197.8	192.4
2009	185.2	181.4	180.3	180.5	181.2	180.3	179.9	180.2	179.1	180.6	184.6	186.5	181.7
2010	176.9	174.8	174.9	175.7	177.3	177.6	176.7	177.5	176.7	179.7	183.2	185.6	178.1
2011	177.9	177.5	177.4	179.9	180.6	180.7	181.5	182.2	181.5	184.4	188.7	191.4	182.0
2012	183.0	181.4	181.6	182.3	183.9	184.3	184.0	184.1	183.9	187.3	192.3	193.9	185.2
2013	184.6	182.7	182.6	183.9	185.4	186.4	187.0	187.1	186.6	189.9	195.6	197.6	187.5
2014	187.4	185.4	185.2	187.5	189.4	190.5	191.1	192.4	192.2	196.1	202.4	205.5	192.1
2015	194.9	193.1	193.1	194.2	195.5	195.9	196.5	197.0	196.1	199.6	205.0	207.3	197.4
2016	198.8	196.9	196.7	196.8	199.0	198.7	200.2	200.7	201.3	205.6	212.7	217.5	202.1
2017	206.4	203.2	203.1	204.2	205.8	206.5	207.1	207.6	205.9	207.2	212.4	215.7	207.1
Wholesale Trade													
2007	38.0	38.0	38.2	38.3	38.9	39.0	39.0	39.0	38.9	39.0	38.9	38.9	38.7
2008	39.0	39.0	39.0	39.4	39.6	39.6	39.7	39.8	39.5	39.1	38.9	38.7	39.3
2009	38.5	38.3	38.4	37.8	37.7	37.6	37.5	37.4	36.9	36.7	36.7	36.7	37.5
2010	37.0	37.2	37.1	37.4	37.6	37.7	37.5	37.6	37.3	37.4	37.4	37.2	37.4
2011	37.3	37.3	37.3	37.6	37.8	37.7	37.8	37.9	37.6	37.8	37.8	37.8	37.6
2012	38.0	38.2	38.1	38.4	38.5	38.6	38.8	38.8	38.6	38.6	38.7	38.6	38.5
2013	38.4	38.6	38.6	38.9	39.1	39.0	39.3	39.5	39.3	39.6	39.9	39.9	39.2
2014	40.3	40.7	40.9	41.1	41.5	41.5	41.7	41.7	41.6	41.5	41.8	42.0	41.4
2015	41.3	41.5	41.6	41.7	41.9	41.8	41.9	41.9	41.6	41.9	42.1	42.2	41.8
2016	41.9	42.0	42.1	41.7	42.0	41.9	42.2	42.2	41.9	42.0	41.9	41.9	42.0
2017	41.7	41.9	41.8	42.0	42.3	42.4	42.5	42.6	42.0	42.4	42.9	42.5	42.3
Retail Trade													
2007	103.9	101.6	102.6	102.9	103.8	103.5	104.0	103.8	103.4	104.6	108.8	110.5	104.5
2008	103.0	100.7	100.4	101.8	103.0	102.9	104.1	104.5	103.4	104.9	107.1	109.3	103.8
2009	100.4	98.1	97.4	98.3	99.1	98.7	98.3	98.5	97.9	99.2	102.5	104.4	99.4
2010	96.4	94.7	95.1	96.1	97.0	97.3	97.2	97.8	97.1	99.5	102.2	104.1	97.9
2011	97.4	96.9	96.9	98.6	98.8	98.9	99.7	100.2	99.4	101.4	104.7	106.9	100.0
2012	99.8	98.4	98.6	99.3	100.3	100.2	99.7	99.8	99.5	101.8	105.7	106.5	100.8
2013	100.1	98.5	98.4	99.6	100.6	101.0	101.5	101.5	101.0	103.5	107.5	108.6	101.8
2014	100.6	99.2	98.7	100.7	101.1	101.8	102.0	102.8	101.9	104.6	108.6	109.8	102.7
2015	102.2	100.9	101.0	101.5	102.3	102.3	102.7	102.8	101.8	103.4	106.8	107.6	102.9
2016	102.8	101.6	101.3	102.0	103.2	103.1	104.1	104.6	104.7	107.6	112.7	116.6	105.4
2017	109.9	107.9	108.1	108.8	109.7	109.9	110.4	110.7	108.9	109.1	111.2	114.5	109.9
Transportation and Utilities													
2007	49.4	48.4	48.4	48.5	49.1	49.5	49.5	49.8	50.5	52.0	53.9	54.2	50.3
2008	50.7	49.7	49.8	49.5	49.1	48.6	48.2	48.3	48.8	49.3	50.0	49.8	49.3
2009	46.3	45.0	44.5	44.4	44.4	44.0	44.1	44.3	44.3	44.7	45.4	45.4	44.7
2010	43.5	42.9	42.7	42.2	42.7	42.6	42.0	42.1	42.3	42.8	43.6	44.3	42.8
2011	43.2	43.3	43.2	43.7	44.0	44.1	44.0	44.1	44.5	45.2	46.2	46.7	44.4
2012	45.2	44.8	44.9	44.6	45.1	45.5	45.5	45.5	45.8	46.9	47.9	48.8	45.9
2013	46.1	45.6	45.6	45.4	45.7	46.4	46.2	46.1	46.3	46.8	48.2	49.1	46.5
2014	46.5	45.5	45.6	45.7	46.8	47.2	47.4	47.9	48.7	50.0	52.0	53.7	48.1
2015	51.4	50.7	50.5	51.0	51.3	51.8	51.9	52.3	52.7	54.3	56.1	57.5	52.6
2016	54.1	53.3	53.3	53.1	53.8	53.7	53.9	53.9	54.7	56.0	58.1	59.0	54.7
2017	54.8	53.4	53.2	53.4	53.8	54.2	54.2	54.3	55.0	55.7	58.3	58.7	54.9

Employment by Industry: Columbus, OH, Selected Years, 2007–2017—*Continued*

(Numbers in thousands, not seasonally adjusted)

Industry and year	January	February	March	April	May	June	July	August	September	October	November	December	Annual average
Information													
2007	18.8	18.9	18.8	18.9	18.9	18.9	18.9	18.7	18.4	18.1	18.1	18.1	18.6
2008	17.7	17.8	17.8	17.9	17.8	17.8	17.8	17.8	17.6	17.6	17.7	17.7	17.8
2009	17.7	17.6	17.4	17.2	17.2	17.1	17.2	17.0	16.7	16.6	16.6	16.8	17.1
2010	16.9	16.9	16.8	16.6	16.7	16.7	16.8	16.8	16.7	16.6	16.9	16.9	16.8
2011	16.7	16.7	16.6	16.9	17.0	17.0	17.1	17.1	16.8	16.8	16.9	17.0	16.9
2012	16.7	16.8	16.8	16.9	17.0	17.3	17.4	17.3	17.3	17.4	17.6	17.8	17.2
2013	18.0	18.3	18.5	18.7	18.6	18.7	18.7	18.8	18.6	18.5	18.5	18.5	18.5
2014	18.2	18.2	18.1	18.1	17.8	17.7	17.5	17.3	16.8	16.6	16.9	17.0	17.5
2015	16.6	16.8	16.8	17.1	17.0	17.2	17.0	16.9	16.8	16.8	17.0	16.9	16.9
2016	16.7	16.8	16.7	16.5	16.6	16.9	17.0	17.0	17.1	17.1	17.2	17.1	16.9
2017	16.8	17.0	16.9	17.3	17.4	17.1	17.3	17.3	17.1	17.1	17.2	17.2	17.1
Financial Activities													
2007	74.6	74.5	73.9	74.7	74.2	73.5	73.4	73.4	72.7	72.7	72.3	72.3	73.5
2008	71.7	71.9	71.7	71.5	71.6	71.5	71.1	71.2	70.8	71.0	70.6	70.7	71.3
2009	70.1	69.9	69.9	69.5	69.6	69.4	69.6	69.4	69.0	69.1	69.5	69.4	69.5
2010	68.6	68.6	68.5	69.2	69.2	69.4	69.8	69.6	69.3	69.8	69.9	70.0	69.3
2011	70.1	70.1	70.2	70.0	70.5	70.7	70.9	71.4	71.9	72.1	72.1	72.0	71.0
2012	72.3	72.5	72.9	72.9	73.5	74.0	74.2	74.3	74.0	74.3	74.8	74.9	73.7
2013	74.8	75.1	75.3	75.3	75.7	76.0	75.9	75.9	75.2	74.9	75.1	75.0	75.4
2014	75.2	75.3	75.1	75.3	76.0	76.5	76.9	77.4	77.0	77.6	78.0	78.1	76.5
2015	77.9	78.2	78.2	78.5	79.1	79.5	80.3	80.5	79.7	80.2	80.3	80.2	79.4
2016	81.2	81.5	81.5	82.2	82.6	82.6	83.1	83.4	83.0	83.5	83.9	84.2	82.7
2017	84.2	84.3	84.3	84.8	85.1	85.5	85.7	85.7	85.2	85.2	85.5	86.0	85.1
Professional and Business Services													
2007	144.3	144.5	146.3	148.9	149.5	151.4	151.4	152.0	151.6	153.3	154.1	154.6	150.2
2008	151.7	152.0	152.2	154.7	154.0	154.3	155.7	155.4	154.0	154.3	153.3	152.5	153.7
2009	149.4	147.4	146.5	146.8	146.3	145.5	145.3	146.0	144.0	145.5	145.2	143.6	146.0
2010	141.7	142.0	142.8	146.4	145.7	147.0	148.6	149.9	147.9	149.5	150.2	150.3	146.8
2011	146.2	146.6	148.0	150.4	149.9	150.7	152.8	153.7	154.2	155.5	157.2	157.5	151.9
2012	153.3	154.3	155.6	157.4	157.4	158.8	158.9	160.1	159.8	163.4	165.5	165.8	159.2
2013	160.0	159.3	159.7	163.0	164.1	165.3	166.3	167.4	167.3	170.1	173.0	174.3	165.8
2014	169.3	168.9	169.5	172.7	173.1	174.6	175.7	177.9	177.3	179.8	182.7	183.8	175.4
2015	173.7	171.5	171.8	174.5	175.1	177.0	178.3	179.0	176.6	180.9	182.2	181.3	176.8
2016	175.1	174.2	175.6	178.1	179.0	181.2	183.0	184.1	182.7	183.6	185.2	183.6	180.5
2017	177.2	176.4	176.1	177.3	179.1	181.0	180.7	181.4	180.6	182.7	182.0	180.8	179.6
Education and Health Services													
2007	109.8	110.7	111.5	112.5	112.7	111.8	111.1	111.4	113.0	114.3	115.2	114.9	112.4
2008	113.9	115.6	115.5	115.9	115.7	114.5	114.2	114.5	116.3	117.7	118.6	118.6	115.9
2009	117.7	119.2	119.4	120.0	120.1	119.3	119.4	120.0	122.2	123.9	124.4	124.8	120.9
2010	124.0	125.1	126.3	126.6	126.4	124.4	125.3	126.4	128.0	129.0	129.5	128.9	126.7
2011	128.0	129.6	129.8	132.2	132.7	129.8	130.6	131.3	134.6	135.6	136.3	136.2	132.2
2012	135.0	137.3	137.4	139.2	138.9	137.3	135.1	136.0	137.1	139.5	140.0	139.4	137.7
2013	138.6	139.7	139.1	141.4	141.6	138.8	138.0	140.1	140.7	143.3	144.4	144.4	140.8
2014	142.8	144.9	145.0	147.8	147.7	145.3	144.2	145.7	146.4	148.4	149.1	148.8	146.3
2015	148.2	149.7	149.6	151.2	152.2	151.7	150.4	151.3	151.2	152.9	153.5	153.9	151.3
2016	152.9	154.2	154.8	155.5	156.7	154.5	154.4	155.8	155.8	158.1	158.4	157.4	155.7
2017	157.6	159.2	159.6	161.7	162.1	160.9	161.6	162.2	161.6	160.9	161.5	162.0	160.9
Leisure and Hospitality													
2007	86.1	86.0	88.0	90.5	93.7	95.7	94.3	94.6	92.1	91.4	90.2	89.2	91.0
2008	86.1	86.2	86.6	90.2	93.0	94.2	93.4	93.3	90.6	89.3	87.6	86.8	89.8
2009	83.2	83.5	85.7	87.5	90.2	91.7	91.1	90.6	88.6	87.7	85.5	84.8	87.5
2010	81.6	82.1	83.9	87.0	89.2	91.2	91.2	91.1	89.3	88.0	87.3	86.1	87.3
2011	83.7	84.5	86.4	89.9	93.0	94.9	94.6	94.8	92.8	91.4	90.8	89.7	90.5
2012	86.6	87.9	90.3	92.7	96.4	99.1	98.4	99.0	97.6	96.7	95.6	94.8	94.6
2013	92.6	93.2	95.7	98.7	102.3	104.1	103.5	103.8	102.0	100.5	99.3	98.1	99.5
2014	93.9	93.9	95.7	98.8	103.6	105.3	104.5	105.2	101.8	100.7	99.3	98.8	100.1
2015	95.9	96.6	98.3	101.1	105.3	107.4	106.4	106.7	104.6	104.2	103.0	103.0	102.7
2016	99.3	99.5	101.5	103.9	107.7	109.3	109.0	109.0	106.3	105.0	103.8	102.4	104.7
2017	99.4	101.5	103.1	105.5	109.4	111.0	110.5	110.7	108.2	107.7	104.3	104.2	106.3

Employment by Industry: Columbus, OH, Selected Years, 2007–2017—*Continued*

(Numbers in thousands, not seasonally adjusted)

Industry and year	January	February	March	April	May	June	July	August	September	October	November	December	Annual average
Other Services													
2007	37.5	37.6	37.8	37.5	37.9	38.1	37.9	37.7	37.0	37.2	37.1	36.9	37.5
2008	36.4	36.5	36.6	36.9	37.1	37.4	37.6	37.7	37.3	38.0	37.3	36.5	37.1
2009	36.0	36.4	36.5	36.5	36.9	36.8	36.5	36.3	35.7	35.9	35.7	35.7	36.2
2010	35.6	35.7	35.9	35.8	35.8	36.1	36.5	36.3	35.9	36.1	35.9	35.9	36.0
2011	35.2	35.3	35.3	35.7	35.9	36.1	36.5	36.4	35.9	36.3	36.1	35.8	35.9
2012	35.8	36.0	36.2	36.7	37.0	37.8	38.3	37.8	37.8	39.0	38.3	38.2	37.4
2013	37.4	37.6	37.8	38.2	38.5	38.6	38.6	38.4	38.2	38.2	38.4	38.2	38.2
2014	38.2	38.4	38.6	38.8	39.3	39.9	40.2	40.3	40.0	40.1	39.9	39.8	39.5
2015	39.6	39.8	40.2	40.5	40.7	41.1	41.5	41.5	41.1	41.1	40.9	40.7	40.7
2016	40.3	40.4	40.7	41.1	41.4	41.9	41.7	42.0	41.5	41.8	41.6	40.2	41.2
2017	40.1	40.3	40.4	40.8	41.0	41.9	42.1	42.0	40.7	41.2	40.8	40.5	41.0
Government													
2007	165.4	167.4	168.6	169.1	169.8	163.7	157.3	156.1	164.6	168.8	170.1	169.5	165.9
2008	165.9	168.9	169.1	169.6	171.1	164.1	158.2	157.6	164.3	169.6	169.8	168.6	166.4
2009	165.0	167.7	168.5	170.0	170.3	162.5	155.9	155.0	164.0	169.5	169.9	168.1	165.5
2010	164.9	167.4	167.9	169.9	173.4	164.1	155.5	155.3	164.0	169.1	169.6	169.9	165.9
2011	163.7	165.9	167.0	169.8	170.7	162.7	156.1	156.9	165.9	167.4	168.7	167.3	165.2
2012	164.0	166.8	166.5	166.3	168.6	160.1	152.9	153.7	164.8	169.1	170.2	168.9	164.3
2013	163.2	165.3	165.1	167.1	168.3	157.8	154.1	155.9	164.5	167.4	169.5	168.9	163.9
2014	163.3	165.9	165.6	168.0	169.4	158.1	155.7	157.0	167.8	169.2	169.5	168.6	164.8
2015	166.0	168.5	168.4	169.4	170.3	164.5	161.6	163.8	169.1	171.5	171.9	171.6	168.1
2016	170.0	173.2	173.0	173.6	172.2	167.1	163.6	164.9	172.3	175.5	176.9	175.2	171.5
2017	174.4	176.2	175.8	177.0	176.2	171.2	168.6	171.8	176.5	177.6	178.9	177.9	175.2

Employment by Industry: Cleveland-Elyria, OH, Selected Years, 2007–2017

(Numbers in thousands, not seasonally adjusted)

Industry and year	January	February	March	April	May	June	July	August	September	October	November	December	Annual average
Total Nonfarm													
2007	1,052.8	1,052.7	1,061.5	1,070.4	1,080.2	1,090.2	1,075.6	1,076.9	1,073.8	1,076.5	1,079.5	1,077.4	1,072.3
2008	1,050.0	1,050.4	1,048.3	1,060.8	1,072.8	1,075.8	1,064.3	1,062.6	1,060.8	1,058.9	1,052.5	1,044.9	1,058.5
2009	1,009.2	1,006.1	1,003.4	1,004.9	1,008.6	1,006.7	995.9	992.4	994.1	995.9	997.2	994.6	1,000.8
2010	969.1	969.7	972.9	986.3	998.5	1,000.0	996.2	995.7	995.5	1,002.2	1,003.5	1,001.4	990.9
2011	971.4	977.5	981.9	998.8	1,006.2	1,008.0	1,009.0	1,011.8	1,007.3	1,009.9	1,016.6	1,015.2	1,001.1
2012	987.1	994.4	1,002.9	1,016.2	1,027.3	1,033.0	1,025.9	1,025.5	1,023.7	1,031.3	1,034.8	1,032.0	1,019.5
2013	1,002.2	1,004.8	1,009.9	1,023.9	1,037.2	1,042.7	1,033.4	1,039.9	1,032.8	1,040.5	1,044.6	1,043.5	1,029.6
2014	1,010.9	1,012.1	1,017.6	1,031.5	1,044.9	1,048.8	1,039.6	1,044.7	1,039.3	1,047.9	1,050.5	1,051.3	1,036.6
2015	1,018.6	1,022.1	1,024.5	1,041.4	1,056.9	1,058.5	1,052.9	1,054.4	1,045.8	1,055.3	1,056.6	1,057.3	1,045.4
2016	1,033.6	1,036.1	1,040.8	1,053.2	1,063.6	1,064.2	1,063.6	1,064.3	1,056.2	1,062.7	1,064.9	1,060.7	1,055.3
2017	1,033.8	1,038.3	1,042.6	1,055.2	1,066.6	1,072.3	1,065.6	1,067.4	1,060.7	1,066.4	1,061.7	1,060.1	1,057.6
Total Private													
2007	913.0	909.4	916.8	925.2	934.3	942.9	936.1	938.6	933.7	932.8	935.2	934.1	929.3
2008	908.7	906.2	904.9	916.8	926.3	928.6	924.8	924.7	920.6	915.3	908.9	902.6	915.7
2009	868.8	863.4	860.8	861.8	864.5	863.9	860.0	857.9	855.9	854.8	855.9	854.7	860.2
2010	831.4	829.3	833.0	845.8	853.9	859.0	861.7	863.6	860.5	863.3	864.5	863.3	852.4
2011	838.8	840.5	844.4	860.4	868.1	870.7	877.5	881.7	874.0	875.1	880.4	879.3	865.9
2012	855.2	858.6	866.5	879.5	889.4	896.3	894.3	895.3	889.6	895.8	899.3	897.3	884.8
2013	868.9	870.7	876.2	889.3	900.8	908.1	904.8	909.6	900.4	906.2	909.6	908.8	896.1
2014	878.9	878.6	884.1	897.1	908.4	913.7	910.2	913.7	906.0	912.3	914.8	916.2	902.8
2015	885.8	888.0	891.8	906.2	919.6	922.1	922.7	922.0	912.0	918.7	920.0	920.7	910.8
2016	899.3	900.1	904.8	915.9	924.7	926.7	930.3	929.7	921.4	925.0	926.9	923.4	919.0
2017	898.4	901.4	906.0	917.8	927.7	933.9	933.0	933.2	924.9	929.3	923.6	922.9	921.0
Goods Producing													
2007	180.8	178.8	181.1	182.9	186.4	188.5	184.2	186.8	185.5	184.8	184.4	181.9	183.8
2008	176.1	175.3	174.9	177.8	180.3	181.7	181.5	179.6	179.4	178.1	173.4	167.8	177.2
2009	158.6	156.9	154.6	152.9	151.9	151.5	149.8	149.5	149.4	148.6	149.1	147.1	151.7
2010	142.1	141.6	143.1	145.1	148.4	150.9	150.6	151.8	151.2	151.9	151.1	149.0	148.1
2011	145.2	145.2	146.4	149.7	152.0	152.9	156.3	158.4	156.2	156.8	158.4	157.3	152.9
2012	150.4	151.6	153.4	156.1	158.1	160.2	159.4	160.0	159.4	158.5	159.5	158.5	157.1
2013	153.6	153.4	154.3	156.4	158.8	160.6	158.4	161.6	160.8	160.9	161.6	158.7	158.3
2014	154.1	153.6	155.1	157.6	160.2	162.4	161.0	163.2	162.6	163.0	162.9	161.6	159.8
2015	156.3	156.2	157.3	160.2	162.2	163.4	163.1	162.7	161.0	160.8	160.2	158.9	160.2
2016	155.3	154.3	155.1	157.0	158.2	159.1	159.1	158.9	157.3	157.4	157.3	155.3	157.0
2017	152.0	152.2	153.8	155.7	157.9	160.3	161.1	160.9	159.8	162.4	161.1	158.0	157.9
Service-Providing													
2007	872.0	873.9	880.4	887.5	893.8	901.7	891.4	890.1	888.3	891.7	895.1	895.5	888.5
2008	873.9	875.1	873.4	883.0	892.5	894.1	882.8	883.0	881.4	880.8	879.1	877.1	881.4
2009	850.6	849.2	848.8	852.0	856.7	855.2	846.1	842.9	844.7	847.3	848.1	847.5	849.1
2010	827.0	828.1	829.8	841.2	850.1	849.1	845.6	843.9	844.3	850.3	852.4	852.4	842.9
2011	826.2	832.3	835.5	849.1	854.2	855.1	852.7	853.4	851.1	853.1	858.2	857.9	848.2
2012	836.7	842.8	849.5	860.1	869.2	872.8	866.5	865.5	864.3	872.8	875.3	873.5	862.4
2013	848.6	851.4	855.6	867.5	878.4	882.1	875.0	878.3	872.0	879.6	883.0	884.8	871.4
2014	856.8	858.5	862.5	873.9	884.7	886.4	878.6	881.5	876.7	884.9	887.6	889.7	876.8
2015	862.3	865.9	867.2	881.2	894.7	895.1	889.8	891.7	884.8	894.5	896.4	898.4	885.2
2016	878.3	881.8	885.7	896.2	905.4	905.1	904.5	905.4	898.9	905.3	907.6	905.4	898.3
2017	881.8	886.1	888.8	899.5	908.7	912.0	904.5	906.5	900.9	904.0	900.6	902.1	899.6
Mining, Logging, and Construction													
2007	36.6	34.9	36.6	39.6	43.0	44.4	43.9	44.2	43.5	43.3	42.4	39.9	41.0
2008	35.1	34.4	34.5	37.1	39.7	40.9	42.0	41.9	40.9	40.6	38.5	35.6	38.4
2009	30.6	29.9	30.6	31.9	34.0	35.2	35.8	35.5	34.9	34.9	33.6	31.6	33.2
2010	27.3	26.6	27.9	30.2	31.9	33.4	34.7	34.6	34.1	34.2	33.3	30.8	31.6
2011	27.6	27.2	28.1	30.3	32.1	33.6	35.8	36.3	36.2	36.1	35.7	34.4	32.8
2012	30.0	29.3	30.4	32.6	34.4	35.4	36.1	35.7	35.0	35.5	35.2	33.9	33.6
2013	30.0	29.7	30.4	32.4	34.7	35.8	36.2	36.9	36.9	38.0	37.2	34.1	34.4
2014	30.3	30.2	31.5	33.9	36.1	37.4	38.0	38.4	38.1	38.4	37.7	35.9	35.5
2015	31.7	31.3	32.3	35.4	37.1	37.9	38.2	38.2	37.6	37.7	37.3	35.7	35.9
2016	32.9	32.5	33.6	35.7	36.9	37.7	37.9	37.8	37.2	37.2	36.7	34.6	35.9
2017	31.9	32.1	33.2	35.3	37.3	38.7	39.1	39.2	38.8	39.7	37.6	34.2	36.4

Employment by Industry: Cleveland-Elyria, OH, Selected Years, 2007–2017—*Continued*

(Numbers in thousands, not seasonally adjusted)

Industry and year	January	February	March	April	May	June	July	August	September	October	November	December	Annual average
Manufacturing													
2007	144.2	143.9	144.5	143.3	143.4	144.1	140.3	142.6	142.0	141.5	142.0	142.0	142.8
2008	141.0	140.9	140.4	140.7	140.6	140.8	139.5	137.7	138.5	137.5	134.9	132.2	138.7
2009	128.0	127.0	124.0	121.0	117.9	116.3	114.0	114.0	114.5	113.7	115.5	115.5	118.5
2010	114.8	115.0	115.2	114.9	116.5	117.5	115.9	117.2	117.1	117.7	117.8	118.2	116.5
2011	117.6	118.0	118.3	119.4	119.9	119.3	120.5	122.1	120.0	120.7	122.7	122.9	120.1
2012	120.4	122.3	123.0	123.5	123.7	124.8	123.3	124.3	124.4	123.0	124.3	124.6	123.5
2013	123.6	123.7	123.9	124.0	124.1	124.8	122.2	124.7	123.9	122.9	124.4	124.6	123.9
2014	123.8	123.4	123.6	123.7	124.1	125.0	123.0	124.8	124.5	124.6	125.2	125.7	124.3
2015	124.6	124.9	125.0	124.8	125.1	125.5	124.9	124.5	123.4	123.1	122.9	123.2	124.3
2016	122.4	121.8	121.5	121.3	121.3	121.4	121.2	121.1	120.1	120.2	120.6	120.7	121.1
2017	120.1	120.1	120.6	120.4	120.6	121.6	122.0	121.7	121.0	122.7	123.5	123.8	121.5
Trade, Transportation, and Utilities													
2007	198.2	195.4	196.8	197.4	198.6	199.8	199.0	198.1	196.6	197.6	201.3	204.0	198.6
2008	196.5	193.2	192.6	193.9	195.4	195.4	194.9	195.2	192.9	192.7	193.9	195.7	194.4
2009	185.7	182.9	182.2	180.7	181.3	181.4	179.9	179.0	177.1	177.6	179.6	181.5	180.7
2010	174.3	172.3	172.6	173.6	175.0	176.4	176.8	177.3	175.5	176.9	179.5	182.1	176.0
2011	174.0	172.9	173.5	175.7	176.7	177.7	177.8	178.3	176.4	178.3	182.0	184.6	177.3
2012	177.8	176.4	177.8	179.0	181.2	181.8	181.2	180.7	179.7	181.5	185.4	187.1	180.8
2013	179.1	177.2	177.8	179.5	181.9	182.8	181.7	182.0	180.4	182.1	186.5	188.5	181.6
2014	180.3	178.8	178.8	180.7	183.1	183.9	182.4	182.9	180.7	182.7	186.8	189.2	182.5
2015	181.7	179.6	180.3	182.1	184.5	185.0	184.5	184.8	182.6	184.2	188.8	190.9	184.1
2016	184.6	183.0	183.4	183.7	185.3	185.4	184.8	185.2	182.6	183.4	186.9	189.2	184.8
2017	181.8	180.0	180.3	181.5	182.9	183.6	182.8	183.2	181.4	184.0	186.5	188.0	183.0
Wholesale Trade													
2007	55.4	55.4	55.5	55.3	55.3	55.4	55.2	54.8	54.1	53.9	53.8	53.8	54.8
2008	53.7	53.5	53.3	53.7	53.9	53.8	53.5	53.3	52.7	52.5	52.0	51.5	53.1
2009	50.6	50.0	49.5	48.9	48.7	48.4	48.0	47.7	47.2	47.1	46.9	46.6	48.3
2010	46.2	46.1	46.0	46.2	46.3	46.5	47.1	47.1	46.8	46.8	46.7	46.8	46.6
2011	47.1	47.1	47.2	47.6	47.8	48.1	48.4	48.4	47.9	48.3	48.5	48.8	47.9
2012	48.6	48.6	48.8	49.1	49.5	49.8	49.8	49.6	49.3	49.5	49.6	49.7	49.3
2013	48.9	48.8	49.0	49.2	49.5	49.8	49.5	49.5	49.2	49.9	50.1	50.3	49.5
2014	49.6	49.6	49.7	49.8	50.4	50.7	50.7	50.8	50.4	50.7	50.9	51.2	50.4
2015	50.4	50.4	50.7	50.6	51.0	51.2	51.4	51.3	50.7	50.9	51.1	51.1	50.9
2016	51.3	51.3	51.4	51.4	51.6	51.8	51.8	51.7	51.3	51.3	51.4	51.7	51.5
2017	51.2	51.2	51.4	51.4	51.7	52.2	52.4	52.4	52.1	53.4	53.0	53.0	52.1
Retail Trade													
2007	108.9	106.3	107.3	107.5	109.0	110.0	109.8	109.2	108.1	109.1	112.8	115.2	109.4
2008	108.9	106.1	105.9	106.4	107.4	107.9	107.8	108.1	106.6	106.8	108.7	110.6	107.6
2009	103.1	100.9	101.1	100.9	101.9	102.4	101.8	101.4	100.1	100.7	103.2	105.0	101.9
2010	99.1	97.3	97.7	98.4	99.6	100.5	100.4	100.7	99.3	100.6	103.4	105.5	100.2
2011	98.3	97.3	97.7	99.2	99.8	100.4	100.3	100.6	99.1	100.4	103.9	105.6	100.2
2012	100.2	98.7	99.8	100.4	101.8	102.0	101.4	100.8	100.1	101.6	104.9	106.0	101.5
2013	100.4	98.7	99.2	100.2	101.9	102.4	102.1	102.1	100.7	101.7	105.3	106.5	101.8
2014	100.3	99.0	99.1	100.4	101.8	102.3	101.4	101.6	99.9	101.4	104.7	105.9	101.5
2015	100.5	98.9	99.4	100.9	102.4	102.7	102.2	102.4	100.8	102.1	105.7	107.2	102.1
2016	102.3	100.9	101.3	101.4	102.5	102.5	102.1	102.3	100.1	101.1	104.1	105.6	102.2
2017	100.3	98.4	98.7	99.6	100.4	100.6	99.9	100.0	98.3	99.0	101.4	102.2	99.9
Transportation and Utilities													
2007	33.9	33.7	34.0	34.6	34.3	34.4	34.0	34.1	34.4	34.6	34.7	35.0	34.3
2008	33.9	33.6	33.4	33.8	34.1	33.7	33.6	33.8	33.6	33.4	33.2	33.6	33.6
2009	32.0	32.0	31.6	30.9	30.7	30.6	30.1	29.9	29.8	29.8	29.5	29.9	30.6
2010	29.0	28.9	28.9	29.0	29.1	29.4	29.3	29.5	29.4	29.5	29.4	29.8	29.3
2011	28.6	28.5	28.6	28.9	29.1	29.2	29.1	29.3	29.4	29.6	29.6	30.2	29.2
2012	29.0	29.1	29.2	29.5	29.9	30.0	30.0	30.3	30.3	30.4	30.9	31.4	30.0
2013	29.8	29.7	29.6	30.1	30.5	30.6	30.1	30.4	30.5	30.5	31.1	31.7	30.4
2014	30.4	30.2	30.0	30.5	30.9	30.9	30.3	30.5	30.4	30.6	31.2	32.1	30.7
2015	30.8	30.3	30.2	30.6	31.1	31.1	30.9	31.1	31.1	31.2	32.0	32.6	31.1
2016	31.0	30.8	30.7	30.9	31.2	31.1	30.9	31.2	31.2	31.0	31.4	31.9	31.1
2017	30.3	30.4	30.2	30.5	30.8	30.8	30.5	30.8	31.0	31.6	32.1	32.8	31.0

Employment by Industry: Cleveland-Elyria, OH, Selected Years, 2007–2017—*Continued*

(Numbers in thousands, not seasonally adjusted)

Industry and year	January	February	March	April	May	June	July	August	September	October	November	December	Annual average
Information													
2007	18.4	18.5	18.3	18.5	18.6	18.6	18.7	18.5	18.4	18.3	18.4	18.4	18.5
2008	18.2	18.0	18.0	18.0	18.0	17.9	17.8	17.7	17.2	17.2	17.3	17.3	17.7
2009	17.1	17.0	16.7	16.5	16.5	16.6	16.5	16.4	16.1	16.1	16.2	16.2	16.5
2010	16.0	15.9	15.8	15.8	15.9	15.8	15.8	15.9	15.5	15.6	15.6	15.7	15.8
2011	15.4	15.3	15.2	15.3	15.4	15.4	15.5	15.5	15.5	15.4	15.5	15.5	15.4
2012	15.5	15.3	15.3	15.3	15.3	15.4	15.5	15.4	15.2	15.2	15.3	15.2	15.3
2013	14.9	15.0	15.0	15.0	15.1	15.3	15.4	15.3	15.2	15.1	15.0	15.3	15.1
2014	14.7	14.6	14.6	14.6	14.6	14.6	14.7	14.6	14.5	14.5	14.4	14.6	14.6
2015	14.3	14.3	14.3	14.4	14.3	14.3	14.4	14.3	14.1	14.1	14.2	14.3	14.3
2016	14.0	14.0	14.0	14.0	14.1	14.2	14.2	14.3	14.1	14.0	14.2	14.0	14.1
2017	13.9	13.8	13.8	13.9	13.9	14.1	14.1	14.1	14.0	14.0	14.0	14.0	14.0
Financial Activities													
2007	73.1	73.0	72.9	72.8	72.9	72.8	72.7	72.3	71.3	71.0	70.7	70.5	72.2
2008	69.7	69.3	69.3	69.1	69.2	69.2	69.4	69.2	68.2	67.9	67.9	67.7	68.8
2009	66.9	66.5	66.2	65.9	65.9	66.1	66.1	65.8	65.3	64.9	64.9	64.9	65.8
2010	64.4	64.3	64.1	64.5	64.6	64.8	65.1	65.0	64.3	64.7	64.6	64.6	64.6
2011	64.4	64.3	64.0	64.1	63.9	63.7	63.5	63.2	62.7	62.5	62.4	62.2	63.4
2012	61.8	61.8	61.9	62.2	62.4	62.7	63.1	63.1	62.6	62.8	63.0	63.0	62.5
2013	62.4	62.5	62.4	63.1	63.2	63.9	64.3	64.7	64.2	64.6	64.8	64.9	63.8
2014	63.9	64.3	64.5	64.5	64.7	65.2	64.9	64.9	64.2	64.5	64.8	64.9	64.6
2015	64.3	64.5	64.5	65.0	65.1	65.7	65.5	65.3	64.7	65.0	65.1	64.8	65.0
2016	64.5	64.5	64.4	64.8	65.0	65.5	66.0	66.0	65.6	66.0	66.2	66.3	65.4
2017	65.9	66.0	66.1	66.2	66.5	67.0	67.2	67.2	66.6	66.6	66.5	67.3	66.6
Professional and Business Services													
2007	141.3	141.6	142.1	144.5	145.3	147.6	147.5	148.3	147.4	147.4	147.4	146.6	145.6
2008	143.5	143.5	142.9	145.5	146.9	147.8	147.9	148.8	147.2	144.6	143.0	140.4	145.2
2009	135.5	133.7	132.8	132.9	133.0	133.6	133.1	133.3	132.7	133.3	133.2	131.4	133.2
2010	127.9	127.6	128.0	132.9	133.7	135.4	136.3	136.6	136.1	136.3	136.6	136.2	133.6
2011	132.9	134.3	135.4	140.3	141.0	142.3	144.9	146.1	144.7	144.9	144.8	143.7	141.3
2012	139.3	140.4	141.9	144.2	145.5	146.9	147.9	148.4	146.1	149.1	149.0	146.3	145.4
2013	140.2	141.6	143.3	147.3	149.3	151.2	150.8	152.4	149.1	151.7	151.4	150.6	148.2
2014	145.1	145.7	146.6	150.5	151.9	152.6	152.8	154.2	151.7	153.1	152.9	151.3	150.7
2015	145.8	146.6	146.8	149.5	152.8	153.2	154.3	154.3	150.5	153.6	151.9	150.1	150.8
2016	147.2	147.6	148.3	152.7	153.8	155.1	156.9	156.5	154.9	155.6	154.8	152.4	153.0
2017	149.2	150.3	150.4	154.1	155.4	157.6	157.8	158.5	156.0	155.5	152.9	151.1	154.1
Education and Health Services													
2007	170.2	171.7	172.8	173.5	172.8	172.0	170.8	171.0	175.2	177.0	177.9	178.2	173.6
2008	175.6	177.9	177.7	178.5	177.7	176.0	173.4	174.1	179.3	182.1	182.7	182.9	178.2
2009	180.6	182.7	183.0	183.3	182.2	179.8	179.2	179.4	184.0	186.1	186.6	186.5	182.8
2010	185.4	186.7	186.8	186.5	185.5	182.7	183.1	182.6	187.2	189.0	189.5	188.8	186.2
2011	185.2	187.0	186.8	188.2	188.4	185.7	184.9	184.9	187.5	189.3	189.8	189.6	187.3
2012	187.5	190.6	190.7	192.2	192.8	191.3	189.2	189.5	193.0	195.7	195.7	194.8	191.9
2013	191.5	193.9	193.9	193.8	193.3	192.6	192.1	192.4	193.7	195.9	196.8	196.7	193.9
2014	191.4	192.7	193.3	194.0	193.7	192.4	192.0	191.7	194.0	197.2	197.8	197.8	194.0
2015	193.1	195.5	195.7	197.1	197.4	195.6	195.6	195.4	197.9	200.7	201.1	202.2	197.3
2016	198.0	200.8	201.6	201.9	201.6	199.2	199.8	200.0	202.9	204.3	204.7	204.4	201.6
2017	198.9	201.6	202.2	202.5	202.6	200.8	199.7	199.6	201.7	202.7	202.3	202.2	201.4
Leisure and Hospitality													
2007	87.6	87.0	89.0	91.6	95.5	98.7	98.3	99.0	95.2	92.8	91.2	90.5	93.0
2008	85.7	85.4	86.0	90.6	95.1	96.7	96.2	96.5	93.2	89.7	87.8	87.8	90.9
2009	82.1	81.4	82.9	87.1	91.1	92.4	92.8	92.2	89.4	86.3	84.6	85.2	87.3
2010	80.2	80.0	81.4	86.0	89.5	91.4	92.3	92.9	89.5	87.5	86.3	85.4	86.9
2011	80.8	80.7	82.3	86.3	89.9	92.2	93.4	94.3	90.6	87.4	87.2	86.3	87.6
2012	83.2	82.7	85.4	90.4	93.8	97.2	97.3	97.7	93.7	93.2	91.7	92.6	91.6
2013	87.9	88.0	90.3	94.5	99.3	101.7	102.2	101.2	97.6	96.3	93.9	94.5	95.6
2014	90.2	89.7	91.9	95.7	100.2	102.6	102.5	102.3	99.0	97.6	95.6	96.9	97.0
2015	91.4	92.2	93.8	98.2	103.2	104.6	105.2	105.2	101.7	100.7	99.1	99.6	99.6
2016	95.9	96.1	98.1	101.7	106.3	107.8	108.8	108.5	104.3	104.4	103.1	102.2	103.1
2017	97.5	98.3	100.1	104.5	108.8	110.6	110.3	109.9	106.2	104.7	100.6	103.0	104.5

Employment by Industry: Cleveland-Elyria, OH, Selected Years, 2007–2017—*Continued*

(Numbers in thousands, not seasonally adjusted)

Industry and year	January	February	March	April	May	June	July	August	September	October	November	December	Annual average
Other Services													
2007	43.4	43.4	43.8	44.0	44.2	44.9	44.9	44.6	44.1	43.9	43.9	44.0	44.1
2008	43.4	43.6	43.5	43.4	43.7	43.9	43.7	43.6	43.2	43.0	42.9	43.0	43.4
2009	42.3	42.3	42.4	42.5	42.6	42.5	42.6	42.3	41.9	41.9	41.7	41.9	42.2
2010	41.1	40.9	41.2	41.4	41.3	41.6	41.7	41.5	41.2	41.4	41.3	41.5	41.3
2011	40.9	40.8	40.8	40.8	40.8	40.8	41.2	41.0	40.4	40.5	40.3	40.1	40.7
2012	39.7	39.8	40.1	40.1	40.3	40.8	40.7	40.5	39.9	39.8	39.7	39.8	40.1
2013	39.3	39.1	39.2	39.7	39.9	40.0	39.9	40.0	39.4	39.6	39.6	39.6	39.6
2014	39.2	39.2	39.3	39.5	40.0	40.0	39.9	39.9	39.3	39.7	39.6	39.9	39.6
2015	38.9	39.1	39.1	39.7	40.1	40.3	40.1	40.0	39.5	39.6	39.6	39.9	39.7
2016	39.8	39.8	39.9	40.1	40.4	40.4	40.7	40.3	39.7	39.9	39.7	39.6	40.0
2017	39.2	39.2	39.3	39.4	39.7	39.9	40.0	39.8	39.2	39.4	39.7	39.3	39.5
Government													
2007	139.8	143.3	144.7	145.2	145.9	147.3	139.5	138.3	140.1	143.7	144.3	143.3	143.0
2008	141.3	144.2	143.4	144.0	146.5	147.2	139.5	137.9	140.2	143.6	143.6	142.3	142.8
2009	140.4	142.7	142.6	143.1	144.1	142.8	135.9	134.5	138.2	141.1	141.3	139.9	140.6
2010	137.7	140.4	139.9	140.5	144.6	141.0	134.5	132.1	135.0	138.9	139.0	138.1	138.5
2011	132.6	137.0	137.5	138.4	138.1	137.3	131.5	130.1	133.3	134.8	136.2	135.9	135.2
2012	131.9	135.8	136.4	136.7	137.9	136.7	131.6	130.2	134.1	135.5	135.5	134.7	134.8
2013	133.3	134.1	133.7	134.6	136.4	134.6	128.6	130.3	132.4	134.3	135.0	134.7	133.5
2014	132.0	133.5	133.5	134.4	136.5	135.1	129.4	131.0	133.3	135.6	135.7	135.1	133.8
2015	132.8	134.1	132.7	135.2	137.3	136.4	130.2	132.4	133.8	136.6	136.6	136.6	134.6
2016	134.3	136.0	136.0	137.3	138.9	137.5	133.3	134.6	134.8	137.7	138.0	137.3	136.3
2017	135.4	136.9	136.6	137.4	138.9	138.4	132.6	134.2	135.8	137.1	138.1	137.2	136.6

Employment by Industry: Indianapolis-Carmel-Anderson, IN, Selected Years, 2007–2017

(Numbers in thousands, not seasonally adjusted)

Industry and year	January	February	March	April	May	June	July	August	September	October	November	December	Annual average
Total Nonfarm													
2007	927.3	926.4	941.8	949.3	961.6	958.3	943.9	957.7	963.2	966.3	969.7	967.9	952.8
2008	935.4	940.7	947.5	954.0	968.1	961.0	952.2	964.5	963.0	962.6	957.3	948.7	954.6
2009	913.3	911.3	912.4	913.4	918.7	911.0	899.6	910.7	914.2	915.0	918.0	915.4	912.8
2010	889.0	889.1	898.4	912.9	921.9	916.0	907.3	918.7	916.8	925.6	927.0	924.3	912.3
2011	901.0	902.5	913.0	925.7	933.7	924.5	924.9	936.1	943.2	946.0	948.3	950.4	929.1
2012	926.7	937.0	942.6	949.3	959.5	955.8	947.7	963.4	968.2	969.3	972.8	971.8	955.3
2013	944.5	951.6	959.2	966.9	975.5	972.8	964.8	984.5	986.9	990.0	1,002.8	1,000.4	975.0
2014	963.2	966.6	977.2	987.7	1,000.5	996.2	985.1	1,002.2	1,001.3	1,005.0	1,017.5	1,018.9	993.5
2015	987.0	990.6	1,000.3	1,011.7	1,023.4	1,022.1	1,014.0	1,029.3	1,028.4	1,034.2	1,042.5	1,045.4	1,019.1
2016	1,014.7	1,020.0	1,029.2	1,037.9	1,047.7	1,042.6	1,042.0	1,054.6	1,057.0	1,052.7	1,060.8	1,057.9	1,043.1
2017	1,031.6	1,035.7	1,045.1	1,054.3	1,064.5	1,064.0	1,051.8	1,065.0	1,066.8	1,066.7	1,076.3	1,072.0	1,057.8
Total Private													
2007	802.8	798.3	812.7	821.0	831.8	836.3	830.5	836.1	833.1	835.3	837.9	835.9	826.0
2008	807.4	808.0	813.8	821.5	833.9	834.3	830.5	835.0	829.7	828.2	822.6	814.1	823.3
2009	781.9	777.1	777.7	780.7	785.0	787.6	780.9	784.1	782.9	782.5	785.8	782.9	782.4
2010	758.0	756.1	765.2	779.7	785.1	789.3	788.4	793.3	787.8	794.6	795.7	793.9	782.3
2011	771.6	772.3	782.4	795.1	802.7	802.6	807.9	812.7	815.1	816.9	819.1	820.8	801.6
2012	799.4	807.2	813.6	821.0	830.1	835.6	832.9	838.4	839.3	840.6	844.0	843.3	828.8
2013	819.6	822.9	830.0	838.2	846.5	852.9	852.7	858.4	858.5	861.4	873.0	870.8	848.7
2014	836.7	837.1	846.9	857.9	870.0	871.7	869.1	874.4	872.2	876.2	887.5	888.2	865.7
2015	858.1	860.6	869.9	881.5	892.4	897.4	896.7	901.1	897.3	904.3	911.2	913.2	890.3
2016	884.1	888.0	896.2	907.6	916.6	920.1	922.7	924.3	924.4	922.0	928.3	925.3	913.3
2017	900.0	903.3	912.2	922.4	930.6	936.8	931.9	933.9	933.6	935.8	942.3	937.8	926.7
Goods Producing													
2007	153.2	150.0	153.4	155.6	157.6	159.5	159.2	160.3	159.3	157.2	156.2	154.7	156.4
2008	150.2	149.8	150.7	151.2	153.3	154.4	153.6	153.1	150.4	148.9	145.8	141.7	150.3
2009	134.6	131.6	130.6	130.2	129.8	130.3	130.0	130.4	129.3	128.0	126.7	124.7	129.7
2010	120.5	119.4	121.6	124.5	125.8	127.6	128.1	128.0	126.7	126.2	124.8	122.6	124.7
2011	118.2	117.6	119.9	122.5	124.4	127.1	128.1	128.9	129.0	129.2	127.6	126.6	124.9
2012	124.0	123.8	125.7	128.2	130.0	132.6	133.1	133.5	131.8	131.3	129.6	128.6	129.4
2013	126.0	126.1	126.5	128.7	130.6	133.2	133.6	133.8	133.2	133.7	133.1	131.4	130.8
2014	126.6	126.0	128.2	130.3	132.0	134.6	135.7	135.7	134.9	134.3	134.1	133.2	132.1
2015	129.0	129.1	130.6	132.8	134.9	137.4	138.1	138.8	138.1	137.6	137.3	136.7	135.0
2016	132.5	132.6	134.8	137.5	139.6	142.3	142.8	142.7	142.2	142.0	141.7	140.8	139.3
2017	137.6	138.5	140.6	142.5	143.6	145.6	145.0	144.9	144.5	143.4	143.8	142.9	142.7
Service-Providing													
2007	774.1	776.4	788.4	793.7	804.0	798.8	784.7	797.4	803.9	809.1	813.5	813.2	796.4
2008	785.2	790.9	796.8	802.8	814.8	806.6	798.6	811.4	812.6	813.7	811.5	807.0	804.3
2009	778.7	779.7	781.8	783.2	788.9	780.7	769.6	780.3	784.9	787.0	791.3	790.7	783.1
2010	768.5	769.7	776.8	788.4	796.1	788.4	779.2	790.7	790.1	799.4	802.2	801.7	787.6
2011	782.8	784.9	793.1	803.2	809.3	797.4	796.8	807.2	814.2	816.8	820.7	823.8	804.2
2012	802.7	813.2	816.9	821.1	829.5	823.2	814.6	829.9	836.4	838.0	843.2	843.2	826.0
2013	818.5	825.5	832.7	838.2	844.9	839.6	831.2	850.7	853.7	856.3	869.7	869.0	844.2
2014	836.6	840.6	849.0	857.4	868.5	861.6	849.4	866.5	866.4	870.7	883.4	885.7	861.3
2015	858.0	861.5	869.7	878.9	888.5	884.7	875.9	890.5	890.3	896.6	905.2	908.7	884.0
2016	882.2	887.4	894.4	900.4	908.1	900.3	899.2	911.9	914.8	910.7	919.1	917.1	903.8
2017	894.0	897.2	904.5	911.8	920.9	918.4	906.8	920.1	922.3	923.3	932.5	929.1	915.1
Mining and Logging													
2007	0.8	0.7	0.8	0.8	0.8	0.8	0.8	0.8	0.8	0.8	0.8	0.8	0.8
2008	0.7	0.7	0.8	0.8	0.8	0.8	0.8	0.8	0.8	0.8	0.8	0.8	0.8
2009	0.7	0.7	0.7	0.8	0.8	0.8	0.8	0.8	0.8	0.7	0.7	0.7	0.8
2010	0.7	0.7	0.7	0.7	0.7	0.7	0.7	0.7	0.7	0.7	0.7	0.7	0.7
2011	0.5	0.5	0.6	0.6	0.7	0.7	0.7	0.7	0.6	0.6	0.6	0.6	0.6
2012	0.6	0.6	0.6	0.6	0.6	0.6	0.6	0.6	0.6	0.6	0.6	0.6	0.6
2013	0.6	0.6	0.6	0.6	0.6	0.6	0.6	0.6	0.6	0.6	0.6	0.6	0.6
2014	0.5	0.5	0.6	0.6	0.6	0.6	0.7	0.6	0.6	0.6	0.6	0.6	0.6
2015	0.6	0.6	0.6	0.6	0.6	0.7	0.6	0.6	0.6	0.7	0.7	0.6	0.6
2016	0.6	0.6	0.7	0.7	0.7	0.7	0.7	0.7	0.7	0.7	0.7	0.7	0.7
2017	0.6	0.7	0.7	0.7	0.7	0.7	0.7	0.7	0.7	0.7	0.7	0.7	0.7

Employment by Industry: Indianapolis-Carmel-Anderson, IN, Selected Years, 2007–2017—*Continued*

(Numbers in thousands, not seasonally adjusted)

Industry and year	January	February	March	April	May	June	July	August	September	October	November	December	Annual average
Construction													
2007	50.5	48.2	51.2	53.8	55.9	57.3	57.7	58.0	57.1	56.6	55.8	53.4	54.6
2008	49.5	49.1	50.1	51.6	53.0	53.4	54.0	53.1	52.0	50.7	49.4	46.6	51.0
2009	41.7	40.8	41.3	42.1	42.6	43.2	43.7	43.2	42.6	41.9	41.2	39.0	41.9
2010	35.5	34.5	36.4	39.3	40.5	41.8	42.4	42.2	41.2	41.2	40.4	38.2	39.5
2011	35.3	34.9	36.6	38.9	40.5	42.5	43.6	44.1	44.2	44.3	43.6	42.3	40.9
2012	39.6	39.4	40.7	42.8	44.1	45.4	45.9	45.8	44.8	44.6	43.8	42.8	43.3
2013	39.7	39.7	40.1	42.1	43.9	45.8	46.3	46.1	46.0	46.7	46.4	44.3	43.9
2014	40.0	39.4	41.0	42.9	44.0	45.9	46.5	46.3	45.9	45.3	45.2	43.8	43.9
2015	40.2	40.1	41.3	43.6	45.6	47.1	47.8	48.1	47.9	48.0	47.8	46.9	45.4
2016	43.1	43.2	45.0	47.7	49.5	51.0	51.1	50.8	50.8	51.1	50.6	49.1	48.6
2017	45.8	46.5	48.3	50.3	50.9	52.2	52.3	52.4	52.2	51.7	51.8	49.8	50.4
Manufacturing													
2007	101.9	101.1	101.4	101.0	100.9	101.4	100.7	101.5	101.4	99.8	99.6	100.5	100.9
2008	100.0	100.0	99.8	98.8	99.5	100.2	98.8	99.2	97.6	97.4	95.6	94.3	98.4
2009	92.2	90.1	88.6	87.3	86.4	86.3	85.5	86.4	85.9	85.4	84.8	85.0	87.0
2010	84.3	84.2	84.5	84.5	84.6	85.1	85.0	85.1	84.8	84.3	83.7	83.7	84.5
2011	82.4	82.2	82.7	83.0	83.2	83.9	83.8	84.1	84.2	84.3	83.4	83.7	83.4
2012	83.8	83.8	84.4	84.8	85.3	86.6	86.6	87.1	86.4	86.1	85.2	85.2	85.4
2013	85.7	85.8	85.8	86.0	86.1	86.8	86.7	87.1	86.6	86.4	86.1	86.5	86.3
2014	86.1	86.1	86.6	86.8	87.4	88.1	88.5	88.8	88.4	88.4	88.3	88.8	87.7
2015	88.2	88.4	88.7	88.6	88.7	89.6	89.7	90.1	89.6	88.9	88.8	89.2	89.0
2016	88.8	88.8	89.1	89.1	89.4	90.6	91.0	91.2	90.7	90.2	90.4	91.0	90.0
2017	91.2	91.3	91.6	91.5	92.0	92.7	92.0	91.8	91.6	91.0	91.3	92.4	91.7
Trade, Transportation, and Utilities													
2007	202.9	200.2	203.2	203.1	205.6	207.1	206.0	205.2	204.9	205.5	210.2	211.9	205.5
2008	202.5	201.1	202.3	202.6	205.6	205.9	205.0	205.5	204.3	205.1	206.4	206.8	204.4
2009	196.8	194.2	193.7	193.2	195.0	195.4	194.0	193.9	192.6	193.9	196.8	197.3	194.7
2010	190.2	188.1	189.8	191.4	193.2	194.1	194.3	194.8	193.0	195.7	199.0	200.3	193.7
2011	193.1	192.2	192.9	195.3	197.2	197.7	198.2	198.6	197.4	199.7	203.4	204.4	197.5
2012	197.3	196.4	197.6	198.8	201.4	202.7	202.1	202.0	202.2	204.4	209.0	210.3	202.0
2013	201.8	201.6	202.6	204.2	206.5	208.1	207.0	207.6	207.8	209.6	214.4	215.6	207.2
2014	206.2	205.6	206.4	207.2	209.5	210.7	210.7	210.9	210.6	211.5	215.5	217.4	210.2
2015	209.2	208.6	209.8	211.2	213.9	215.3	216.2	217.4	216.5	219.1	223.2	226.5	215.6
2016	218.5	218.1	219.1	218.9	220.6	221.0	222.7	223.0	222.9	223.2	227.5	229.1	222.1
2017	221.3	220.1	220.6	222.1	223.5	225.1	223.8	224.3	224.1	224.8	228.6	227.4	223.8
Wholesale Trade													
2007	48.6	48.6	49.0	48.9	49.1	49.5	49.9	49.4	49.2	49.2	49.5	49.6	49.2
2008	49.1	49.3	49.6	49.6	49.9	49.9	49.9	49.6	49.4	49.4	49.4	49.2	49.5
2009	47.9	47.5	47.7	46.6	46.6	46.4	46.5	46.0	45.5	45.7	45.6	45.6	46.4
2010	45.2	45.0	45.3	45.4	45.4	45.5	46.0	45.9	45.6	45.7	45.6	45.5	45.5
2011	45.7	45.9	46.0	46.4	46.8	46.8	47.0	47.0	46.8	46.9	47.0	46.9	46.6
2012	46.4	46.4	46.5	46.8	47.1	47.3	47.4	47.1	47.0	47.1	46.9	47.0	46.9
2013	46.4	46.7	47.0	47.2	47.4	47.7	47.9	47.5	47.3	47.3	47.4	47.4	47.3
2014	46.9	46.9	47.0	47.1	47.4	47.7	47.8	47.7	47.4	47.4	47.4	47.5	47.4
2015	47.2	47.3	47.4	47.6	47.8	47.8	48.1	48.1	47.8	48.1	48.1	48.3	47.8
2016	48.4	48.3	48.5	48.8	49.1	49.2	49.4	49.1	48.8	48.7	48.8	49.0	48.8
2017	49.1	49.2	49.3	49.5	49.7	50.1	50.1	50.3	49.8	48.8	48.5	48.4	49.4
Retail Trade													
2007	100.9	98.6	100.2	100.1	101.8	102.5	101.6	101.0	100.5	101.0	104.4	105.8	101.5
2008	99.0	97.5	97.8	97.8	100.0	100.2	100.2	100.3	99.6	100.3	101.4	101.8	99.7
2009	95.4	93.7	93.8	94.3	95.8	96.4	95.4	95.2	94.1	94.9	97.6	98.0	95.4
2010	93.5	91.9	92.8	93.6	95.0	95.5	95.3	95.3	93.6	95.6	98.4	99.2	95.0
2011	94.4	93.1	93.8	95.1	96.3	96.6	96.8	97.1	96.2	98.2	101.1	101.9	96.7
2012	97.2	96.2	97.2	97.8	99.4	99.7	99.0	98.7	98.7	100.4	104.2	104.3	99.4
2013	98.5	97.7	97.9	99.2	100.7	101.6	100.8	101.2	101.2	102.5	106.1	106.7	101.2
2014	100.1	99.8	100.4	101.4	103.1	103.8	103.6	103.7	103.6	104.2	107.4	108.3	103.3
2015	102.6	102.0	102.8	103.8	105.4	106.1	106.8	107.8	107.1	108.9	111.7	112.7	106.5
2016	106.9	106.9	107.7	108.2	109.4	109.8	110.5	110.6	110.4	111.3	114.1	114.6	110.0
2017	109.8	108.6	109.0	110.5	111.5	112.0	111.0	111.1	110.9	111.8	114.4	113.1	111.1

Employment by Industry: Indianapolis-Carmel-Anderson, IN, Selected Years, 2007–2017—*Continued*

(Numbers in thousands, not seasonally adjusted)

Industry and year	January	February	March	April	May	June	July	August	September	October	November	December	Annual average
Transportation and Utilities													
2007	53.4	53.0	54.0	54.1	54.7	55.1	54.5	54.8	55.2	55.3	56.3	56.5	54.7
2008	54.4	54.3	54.9	55.2	55.7	55.8	54.9	55.6	55.3	55.4	55.6	55.8	55.2
2009	53.5	53.0	52.7	52.3	52.6	52.6	52.1	52.7	53.0	53.3	53.6	53.7	52.9
2010	51.5	51.2	51.7	52.4	52.8	53.1	53.0	53.6	53.8	54.4	55.0	55.6	53.2
2011	53.0	53.2	53.1	53.8	54.1	54.3	54.4	54.5	54.4	54.6	55.3	55.6	54.2
2012	53.7	53.8	53.9	54.2	54.9	55.7	55.7	56.2	56.5	56.9	57.9	59.0	55.7
2013	56.9	57.2	57.7	57.8	58.4	58.8	58.3	58.9	59.3	59.8	60.9	61.5	58.8
2014	59.2	58.9	59.0	58.7	59.0	59.2	59.3	59.5	59.6	59.9	60.7	61.6	59.6
2015	59.4	59.3	59.6	59.8	60.7	61.4	61.3	61.5	61.6	62.1	63.4	65.5	61.3
2016	63.2	62.9	62.9	61.9	62.1	62.0	62.8	63.3	63.7	63.2	64.6	65.5	63.2
2017	62.4	62.3	62.3	62.1	62.3	63.0	62.7	62.9	63.4	64.2	65.7	65.9	63.3
Information													
2007	16.7	16.8	16.7	16.8	17.0	17.2	17.3	17.3	17.2	17.1	17.1	17.3	17.0
2008	17.3	17.3	17.3	17.3	17.5	17.6	17.6	17.5	17.2	17.0	16.9	16.9	17.3
2009	16.7	16.7	16.4	16.3	16.4	16.6	16.4	16.3	16.1	15.9	15.8	15.9	16.3
2010	15.6	15.6	15.5	15.6	15.8	16.0	15.8	15.7	15.4	15.2	15.3	15.2	15.6
2011	14.9	14.8	14.9	14.8	15.1	15.3	15.2	15.3	15.3	15.3	15.4	15.4	15.1
2012	15.8	15.9	16.0	15.9	16.1	16.3	16.2	16.2	16.1	16.4	16.4	16.4	16.1
2013	16.4	16.4	16.5	16.6	16.5	16.9	17.0	16.8	16.6	16.7	16.7	16.7	16.7
2014	16.6	16.6	16.8	16.8	17.0	17.2	17.3	17.1	16.8	16.6	16.5	16.6	16.8
2015	16.6	16.7	16.6	16.4	16.5	16.6	16.7	16.4	16.1	16.0	16.1	16.1	16.4
2016	15.9	15.9	15.9	15.9	16.0	16.1	15.9	15.8	15.6	15.7	15.6	15.6	15.8
2017	15.9	15.9	15.9	15.7	15.5	15.4	15.0	14.7	14.5	14.5	14.3	14.3	15.1
Financial Activities													
2007	63.3	63.6	63.7	64.0	64.1	64.7	65.0	64.8	64.4	64.0	63.8	63.9	64.1
2008	62.2	62.3	62.2	62.1	62.3	62.7	62.9	62.4	61.6	61.5	60.8	61.0	62.0
2009	60.4	60.3	60.2	60.1	60.1	60.2	60.2	60.0	59.3	59.2	59.0	59.2	59.9
2010	59.1	58.9	59.0	59.1	59.3	59.8	60.3	60.2	59.7	60.1	60.1	60.2	59.7
2011	59.8	59.9	60.1	60.0	60.3	60.7	60.8	60.5	60.2	60.3	60.2	60.4	60.3
2012	60.0	60.0	60.1	60.1	60.4	60.8	60.8	60.6	60.1	60.1	60.0	60.2	60.3
2013	59.7	59.6	59.6	59.9	60.4	61.1	61.1	61.0	60.6	60.7	60.8	61.0	60.5
2014	59.8	59.9	60.2	60.4	60.9	61.3	61.5	61.6	61.4	61.7	61.9	62.0	61.1
2015	61.6	61.9	62.2	62.5	63.1	63.7	63.9	64.2	63.9	64.3	64.5	64.7	63.4
2016	64.2	64.3	64.5	65.0	65.4	65.9	66.3	66.1	65.8	66.1	65.9	66.0	65.5
2017	65.4	65.6	65.6	65.7	65.9	66.5	67.0	67.6	67.3	67.9	68.5	68.3	66.8
Professional and Business Services													
2007	127.7	126.9	130.2	132.8	134.7	134.2	133.8	135.4	135.5	137.9	137.6	135.5	133.5
2008	130.6	129.9	131.0	133.4	134.2	134.6	133.9	136.0	134.7	136.3	133.8	130.1	133.2
2009	122.5	121.2	121.0	121.7	121.2	122.8	120.6	122.6	123.4	125.8	128.0	127.8	123.2
2010	119.5	118.8	120.6	125.7	125.4	126.9	127.4	129.3	127.1	130.8	131.1	131.9	126.2
2011	126.9	126.3	128.8	132.4	132.5	131.5	134.1	136.2	136.9	138.0	138.6	140.4	133.6
2012	133.1	136.8	137.0	138.6	140.1	143.0	142.4	144.9	144.7	145.2	146.4	145.2	141.5
2013	139.6	139.0	141.2	143.6	144.4	146.3	148.2	151.4	151.5	152.4	160.4	158.8	148.1
2014	149.6	147.0	149.5	154.2	156.8	155.8	154.3	158.1	158.2	161.7	169.3	168.4	156.9
2015	156.4	155.6	158.4	163.2	165.3	165.9	165.1	165.6	164.5	168.9	172.3	171.8	164.4
2016	161.6	161.2	162.6	166.7	167.7	167.9	169.0	169.7	169.6	169.2	171.7	170.2	167.3
2017	160.9	160.8	163.5	166.3	167.2	169.9	169.1	170.8	170.9	172.0	175.2	174.1	168.4
Education and Health Services													
2007	111.3	113.4	114.5	115.5	114.8	113.1	112.1	114.0	117.2	118.8	119.4	120.0	115.3
2008	116.4	118.9	119.4	120.4	120.6	118.1	117.9	118.9	123.0	124.5	125.1	125.6	120.7
2009	123.4	125.5	125.6	126.8	126.0	124.2	123.4	124.8	128.9	129.6	130.4	130.4	126.6
2010	128.9	131.0	131.5	132.5	131.4	128.8	127.5	128.9	133.1	134.5	134.8	134.5	131.5
2011	132.9	135.1	135.5	136.8	136.2	132.6	133.3	134.3	140.2	139.5	139.6	139.8	136.3
2012	138.1	141.3	141.7	141.3	140.2	136.7	135.9	137.6	143.6	143.4	143.7	144.0	140.6
2013	141.2	144.6	145.0	144.5	143.0	140.2	139.7	141.1	144.6	145.1	145.3	145.2	143.3
2014	141.5	144.2	144.7	144.7	144.2	140.9	140.0	140.6	143.8	144.2	144.7	145.0	143.2
2015	143.3	145.6	145.9	147.3	146.4	144.4	144.2	145.0	147.8	149.1	149.5	149.3	146.5
2016	147.7	150.4	150.8	152.2	152.0	150.0	149.8	150.8	154.1	153.7	154.5	153.6	151.6
2017	152.4	154.5	155.4	156.9	157.9	156.1	155.0	154.8	158.2	161.3	161.9	161.5	157.2

Employment by Industry: Indianapolis-Carmel-Anderson, IN, Selected Years, 2007–2017—*Continued*

(Numbers in thousands, not seasonally adjusted)

Industry and year	January	February	March	April	May	June	July	August	September	October	November	December	Annual average
Leisure and Hospitality													
2007	88.9	88.5	91.7	93.5	97.8	99.7	96.3	98.8	94.8	95.0	93.9	92.9	94.3
2008	89.1	89.2	91.3	94.3	99.6	99.9	98.3	100.6	98.0	94.7	93.6	92.2	95.1
2009	88.2	88.4	90.8	93.0	96.6	97.8	96.2	96.6	94.4	91.2	90.3	88.8	92.7
2010	85.6	85.8	88.1	91.7	94.7	96.0	94.9	96.6	93.3	92.5	91.0	89.8	91.7
2011	86.7	87.2	90.5	93.4	96.8	97.0	97.1	97.9	95.6	94.6	93.9	93.5	93.7
2012	91.0	92.5	94.8	97.3	100.7	101.6	100.5	101.8	99.6	98.4	97.5	97.3	97.8
2013	93.8	94.1	96.5	99.2	103.1	103.9	103.0	103.8	101.7	100.5	99.3	98.8	99.8
2014	93.8	94.7	97.4	100.7	105.4	106.2	104.8	106.1	102.7	102.6	101.7	101.9	101.5
2015	98.5	99.4	102.3	104.6	108.3	109.4	107.7	109.2	106.4	105.5	104.1	104.0	105.0
2016	100.1	101.6	104.2	106.8	110.3	111.3	110.6	110.9	109.3	107.4	106.6	105.3	107.0
2017	102.4	103.6	105.8	108.3	111.5	112.0	111.2	111.9	109.5	107.1	105.0	104.4	107.7
Other Services													
2007	38.8	38.9	39.3	39.7	40.2	40.8	40.8	40.3	39.8	39.8	39.7	39.7	39.8
2008	39.1	39.5	39.6	40.2	40.8	41.1	41.3	41.0	40.5	40.2	40.2	39.8	40.3
2009	39.3	39.2	39.4	39.4	39.9	40.3	40.1	39.5	38.9	38.9	38.8	38.8	39.4
2010	38.6	38.5	39.1	39.2	39.5	40.1	40.1	39.8	39.5	39.6	39.6	39.4	39.4
2011	39.1	39.2	39.8	39.9	40.2	40.7	41.1	41.0	40.5	40.3	40.4	40.3	40.2
2012	40.1	40.5	40.7	40.8	41.2	41.9	41.9	41.8	41.2	41.4	41.4	41.3	41.2
2013	41.1	41.5	42.1	41.5	42.0	43.2	43.1	42.9	42.5	42.7	43.0	43.3	42.4
2014	42.6	43.1	43.7	43.6	44.2	45.0	44.8	44.3	43.8	43.6	43.8	43.7	43.9
2015	43.5	43.7	44.1	43.5	44.0	44.7	44.8	44.5	44.0	43.8	44.2	44.1	44.1
2016	43.6	43.9	44.3	44.6	45.0	45.6	45.6	45.3	44.9	44.7	44.8	44.7	44.8
2017	44.1	44.3	44.8	44.9	45.5	46.2	45.8	44.9	44.6	44.8	45.0	44.9	45.0
Government													
2007	124.5	128.1	129.1	128.3	129.8	122.0	113.4	121.6	130.1	131.0	131.8	132.0	126.8
2008	128.0	132.7	133.7	132.5	134.2	126.7	121.7	129.5	133.3	134.4	134.7	134.6	131.3
2009	131.4	134.2	134.7	132.7	133.7	123.4	118.7	126.6	131.3	132.5	132.2	132.5	130.3
2010	131.0	133.0	133.2	133.2	136.8	126.7	118.9	125.4	129.0	131.0	131.3	130.4	130.0
2011	129.4	130.2	130.6	130.6	131.0	121.9	117.0	123.4	128.1	129.1	129.2	129.6	127.5
2012	127.3	129.8	129.0	128.3	129.4	120.2	114.8	125.0	128.9	128.7	128.8	128.5	126.6
2013	124.9	128.7	129.2	128.7	129.0	119.9	112.1	126.1	128.4	128.6	129.8	129.6	126.3
2014	126.5	129.5	130.3	129.8	130.5	124.5	116.0	127.8	129.1	128.8	130.0	130.7	127.8
2015	128.9	130.0	130.4	130.2	131.0	124.7	117.3	128.2	131.1	129.9	131.3	132.2	128.8
2016	130.6	132.0	133.0	130.3	131.1	122.5	119.3	130.3	132.6	130.7	132.5	132.6	129.8
2017	131.6	132.4	132.9	131.9	133.9	127.2	119.9	131.1	133.2	130.9	134.0	134.2	131.1

Employment by Industry: San Jose-Sunnyvale-Santa Clara, CA, Selected Years, 2007–2017

(Numbers in thousands, not seasonally adjusted)

Industry and year	January	February	March	April	May	June	July	August	September	October	November	December	Annual average
Total Nonfarm													
2007	902.4	908.5	914.6	911.9	919.4	927.5	926.8	925.4	924.3	930.6	934.2	935.9	921.8
2008	923.1	926.8	930.7	928.5	932.2	935.0	929.2	933.2	932.1	927.6	923.4	919.5	928.4
2009	893.8	885.4	881.7	875.9	876.1	876.1	852.8	856.5	858.9	866.2	869.4	869.0	871.8
2010	853.8	855.5	859.7	866.8	873.7	875.5	863.9	864.6	868.8	879.6	884.2	886.2	869.4
2011	872.3	877.6	881.1	885.2	888.5	894.0	884.3	888.3	894.3	903.2	905.7	908.8	890.3
2012	896.1	902.5	908.9	917.6	923.5	931.9	921.0	926.7	930.5	940.5	946.1	949.1	924.5
2013	934.9	943.2	947.9	952.9	958.9	964.9	953.8	963.3	967.1	974.7	984.6	987.9	961.2
2014	975.8	983.7	988.8	994.3	1,000.2	1,005.7	996.4	1,005.7	1,009.3	1,016.7	1,021.2	1,023.7	1,001.8
2015	1,012.5	1,017.6	1,021.8	1,029.3	1,036.3	1,043.6	1,040.2	1,045.7	1,045.3	1,058.9	1,060.6	1,061.0	1,039.4
2016	1,048.6	1,054.6	1,055.0	1,066.0	1,070.5	1,076.3	1,074.6	1,077.1	1,074.5	1,082.5	1,088.1	1,089.5	1,071.4
2017	1,073.3	1,079.9	1,085.6	1,086.5	1,093.0	1,103.0	1,100.4	1,103.4	1,099.2	1,111.9	1,119.2	1,123.0	1,098.2
Total Private													
2007	804.7	811.5	816.3	813.8	821.1	829.7	831.7	831.5	829.4	832.3	835.6	837.6	824.6
2008	824.1	828.6	831.6	830.1	833.2	836.4	835.2	838.7	834.1	828.9	825.1	821.7	830.6
2009	796.4	788.6	784.1	776.4	775.9	775.8	767.7	767.7	762.9	767.7	770.1	770.9	775.4
2010	757.8	759.3	762.1	767.4	772.8	778.9	778.9	781.1	778.9	784.2	787.2	790.1	774.9
2011	777.7	782.3	785.4	788.7	791.7	797.8	803.0	805.9	803.4	809.4	811.3	814.4	797.6
2012	804.4	809.6	814.9	823.4	829.3	837.0	839.9	843.6	840.3	847.0	852.0	855.8	833.1
2013	842.3	849.2	854.8	858.6	863.2	870.5	875.2	879.9	875.8	880.6	889.2	893.7	869.4
2014	881.3	888.1	893.0	897.4	903.2	911.5	914.1	919.6	917.1	921.5	925.3	928.5	908.4
2015	918.7	923.0	927.7	934.5	941.1	948.9	956.5	958.4	953.7	964.1	965.1	965.8	946.5
2016	955.0	960.3	959.6	970.4	974.1	980.3	989.3	988.8	981.6	986.5	990.2	991.7	977.3
2017	977.5	984.1	988.8	989.1	995.1	1,006.3	1,012.3	1,013.9	1,005.2	1,013.5	1,020.3	1,024.2	1,002.5
Goods Producing													
2007	208.7	210.3	211.1	211.3	213.1	217.0	219.7	220.2	219.4	217.9	215.9	214.5	214.9
2008	212.4	212.7	212.4	212.3	214.1	215.3	216.8	217.2	215.3	212.5	209.0	206.9	213.1
2009	200.3	196.4	194.4	191.9	190.5	190.0	188.9	188.8	187.8	186.0	185.3	183.8	190.3
2010	182.6	182.2	182.9	183.2	184.4	187.1	188.6	190.1	189.4	189.1	187.7	186.8	186.2
2011	184.8	185.3	186.0	187.9	188.8	191.2	193.5	194.6	192.9	191.3	189.2	188.9	189.5
2012	188.1	188.4	189.1	190.9	193.1	196.4	197.0	197.9	196.4	195.0	194.3	194.0	193.4
2013	190.9	191.3	192.3	193.1	194.0	196.9	199.9	201.1	200.3	197.8	198.2	198.4	196.2
2014	196.2	197.2	197.9	198.2	200.0	202.6	204.1	206.6	206.1	203.6	203.7	204.1	201.7
2015	201.9	203.4	204.6	205.9	207.4	210.5	212.7	213.8	212.5	212.6	211.2	211.1	209.0
2016	210.1	211.0	211.0	213.3	214.2	216.6	220.0	219.9	218.0	216.3	215.7	215.2	215.1
2017	213.5	213.9	211.8	212.1	213.4	216.4	218.2	218.8	218.5	220.2	221.4	222.0	216.7
Service-Providing													
2007	693.7	698.2	703.5	700.6	706.3	710.5	707.1	705.2	704.9	712.7	718.3	721.4	706.9
2008	710.7	714.1	718.3	716.2	718.1	719.7	712.4	716.0	716.8	715.1	714.4	712.6	715.4
2009	693.5	689.0	687.3	684.0	685.6	686.1	663.9	667.7	671.1	680.2	684.1	685.2	681.5
2010	671.2	673.3	676.8	683.6	689.3	688.4	675.3	674.5	679.4	690.5	696.5	699.4	683.2
2011	687.5	692.3	695.1	697.3	699.7	702.8	690.8	693.7	701.4	711.9	716.5	719.9	700.7
2012	708.0	714.1	719.8	726.7	730.4	735.5	724.0	728.8	734.1	745.5	751.8	755.1	731.2
2013	744.0	751.9	755.6	759.8	764.9	768.0	753.9	762.2	766.8	776.9	786.4	789.5	765.0
2014	779.6	786.5	790.9	796.1	800.2	803.1	792.3	799.1	803.2	813.1	817.5	819.6	800.1
2015	810.6	814.2	817.2	823.4	828.9	833.1	827.5	831.9	832.8	846.3	849.4	849.9	830.4
2016	838.5	843.6	844.0	852.7	856.3	859.7	854.6	857.2	856.5	866.2	872.4	874.3	856.3
2017	859.8	866.0	873.8	874.4	879.6	886.6	882.2	884.6	880.7	891.7	897.8	901.0	881.5
Mining and Logging													
2007	0.3	0.3	0.3	0.3	0.3	0.3	0.3	0.3	0.3	0.3	0.3	0.3	0.3
2008	0.3	0.3	0.3	0.3	0.3	0.3	0.3	0.3	0.3	0.3	0.3	0.3	0.3
2009	0.3	0.2	0.2	0.2	0.2	0.2	0.2	0.2	0.3	0.2	0.2	0.2	0.2
2010	0.2	0.2	0.2	0.2	0.2	0.2	0.2	0.2	0.2	0.2	0.2	0.2	0.2
2011	0.2	0.2	0.2	0.2	0.2	0.2	0.2	0.2	0.2	0.2	0.2	0.2	0.2
2012	0.2	0.2	0.2	0.2	0.2	0.2	0.2	0.3	0.3	0.3	0.3	0.2	0.2
2013	0.2	0.2	0.2	0.2	0.3	0.3	0.3	0.3	0.3	0.3	0.3	0.3	0.3
2014	0.3	0.3	0.3	0.3	0.3	0.3	0.3	0.3	0.3	0.3	0.3	0.3	0.3
2015	0.2	0.2	0.2	0.2	0.2	0.2	0.3	0.3	0.3	0.2	0.2	0.2	0.2
2016	0.2	0.3	0.3	0.3	0.3	0.3	0.3	0.3	0.3	0.3	0.3	0.3	0.3
2017	0.2	0.2	0.3	0.2	0.2	0.3	0.2	0.2	0.2	0.2	0.2	0.2	0.2

Employment by Industry: San Jose-Sunnyvale-Santa Clara, CA, Selected Years, 2007–2017—*Continued*

(Numbers in thousands, not seasonally adjusted)

Industry and year	January	February	March	April	May	June	July	August	September	October	November	December	Annual average
Construction													
2007	45.3	45.8	46.6	46.3	47.3	48.2	48.9	49.5	49.5	48.6	47.6	46.9	47.5
2008	44.6	44.9	44.5	44.3	44.9	45.4	45.8	46.2	45.4	44.0	42.2	41.2	44.5
2009	38.1	36.3	36.1	35.1	34.5	34.5	34.0	34.0	33.6	33.4	33.4	32.5	34.6
2010	31.5	31.0	31.3	31.9	32.3	33.1	33.6	33.5	33.3	33.0	32.2	31.8	32.4
2011	30.0	29.9	30.3	30.3	30.6	31.3	33.0	33.3	33.6	33.2	33.0	32.8	31.8
2012	32.1	32.3	32.5	33.4	34.9	35.8	36.0	36.1	35.9	36.2	36.2	36.2	34.8
2013	35.1	35.6	35.9	36.1	36.5	37.4	39.0	39.4	38.8	38.7	38.6	38.8	37.5
2014	37.5	37.7	37.8	38.1	38.6	39.7	40.9	41.4	41.4	41.2	41.1	40.7	39.7
2015	40.4	41.1	41.8	42.8	43.1	44.2	45.1	45.9	45.5	46.4	45.7	45.3	43.9
2016	45.1	45.8	45.6	47.5	48.0	48.8	50.4	50.6	50.4	49.8	48.9	48.2	48.3
2017	47.1	47.2	48.2	48.6	48.9	49.8	50.6	50.8	50.3	51.4	52.1	52.2	49.8
Manufacturing													
2007	163.1	164.2	164.2	164.7	165.5	168.5	170.5	170.4	169.6	169.0	168.0	167.3	167.1
2008	167.5	167.5	167.6	167.7	168.9	169.6	170.7	170.7	169.6	168.2	166.5	165.4	168.3
2009	161.9	159.9	158.1	156.6	155.8	155.3	154.7	154.6	153.9	152.4	151.7	151.1	155.5
2010	150.9	151.0	151.4	151.1	151.9	153.8	154.8	156.4	155.9	155.9	155.3	154.8	153.6
2011	154.6	155.2	155.5	157.4	158.0	159.7	160.3	161.1	159.1	157.9	156.0	155.9	157.6
2012	155.8	155.9	156.4	157.3	158.0	160.4	160.8	161.5	160.2	158.5	157.8	157.6	158.4
2013	155.6	155.5	156.2	156.8	157.2	159.2	160.6	161.4	161.2	158.8	159.3	159.3	158.4
2014	158.4	159.2	159.8	159.8	161.1	162.6	162.9	164.9	164.4	162.1	162.3	163.1	161.7
2015	161.3	162.1	162.6	162.9	164.1	166.1	167.3	167.6	166.7	166.0	165.3	165.6	164.8
2016	164.8	164.9	165.1	165.5	165.9	167.5	169.3	169.0	167.3	166.2	166.5	166.7	166.6
2017	166.2	166.5	163.3	163.3	164.3	166.3	167.4	167.8	168.0	168.6	169.1	169.6	166.7
Trade, Transportation, and Utilities													
2007	139.4	137.5	137.7	137.0	137.6	138.5	139.7	139.6	139.3	140.0	143.1	145.2	139.6
2008	140.2	138.6	138.8	136.8	136.9	136.6	137.1	137.2	136.3	135.9	137.2	138.0	137.5
2009	130.7	128.4	126.8	125.3	125.7	125.1	124.1	124.1	123.9	124.4	127.9	129.1	126.3
2010	124.1	122.8	122.4	122.8	123.6	124.2	124.7	125.2	124.9	125.2	129.0	131.1	125.0
2011	125.6	124.5	123.9	124.4	124.7	125.5	126.4	127.1	127.0	128.4	132.7	135.0	127.1
2012	129.4	127.7	127.2	128.4	129.0	129.9	130.9	131.3	130.7	132.1	137.4	138.9	131.1
2013	133.0	131.8	131.5	131.7	131.9	133.1	133.9	134.2	133.5	134.5	139.1	141.3	134.1
2014	135.6	134.2	134.2	135.3	135.4	136.0	136.6	137.4	136.7	136.4	140.9	142.8	136.8
2015	138.0	135.6	135.3	136.2	136.5	137.4	137.9	138.8	138.7	139.8	142.5	143.9	138.4
2016	138.4	137.5	136.4	136.8	136.8	136.9	137.8	138.8	138.1	136.9	140.3	142.6	138.1
2017	136.4	134.8	134.1	134.8	135.4	136.5	137.9	138.6	137.9	137.7	140.9	141.9	137.2
Wholesale Trade													
2007	39.1	39.4	39.4	39.1	39.4	39.9	40.1	40.1	40.2	40.8	40.6	40.9	39.9
2008	40.7	40.5	41.0	40.3	40.4	40.2	39.8	39.5	39.7	39.5	38.9	38.5	39.9
2009	37.2	36.8	36.4	36.5	36.0	35.7	35.2	35.2	34.8	35.1	35.3	35.0	35.8
2010	34.6	34.7	34.7	34.8	35.0	35.1	35.4	35.2	35.4	35.0	34.9	34.9	35.0
2011	34.6	34.6	34.3	34.0	33.9	33.8	34.0	33.9	33.7	33.8	33.7	33.9	34.0
2012	34.0	34.4	34.0	34.5	34.6	34.8	35.3	35.4	35.2	36.0	36.0	36.0	35.0
2013	36.0	36.1	36.1	36.3	36.2	36.3	36.7	36.7	36.5	36.4	36.6	36.9	36.4
2014	37.0	36.9	37.0	37.5	37.4	37.3	37.5	37.7	37.6	36.7	36.9	36.7	37.2
2015	36.6	36.3	36.2	37.3	37.5	37.8	37.4	37.6	37.9	38.0	37.0	36.8	37.2
2016	37.0	37.0	36.6	37.4	37.3	37.0	36.6	37.6	37.6	35.9	35.8	36.0	36.8
2017	35.2	35.1	34.6	35.1	35.5	35.7	36.5	36.8	36.5	35.4	35.1	34.5	35.5
Retail Trade													
2007	87.4	85.1	85.2	84.5	84.7	84.8	85.8	85.7	85.2	85.5	88.8	90.4	86.1
2008	86.3	84.7	84.4	83.2	82.9	82.7	83.9	84.2	83.1	83.0	84.9	85.8	84.1
2009	80.8	79.1	78.3	76.9	77.5	77.4	77.1	77.1	77.1	77.4	80.8	82.1	78.5
2010	77.7	76.4	76.0	76.3	76.6	77.0	77.2	77.8	77.2	78.1	82.0	83.8	78.0
2011	79.2	78.0	77.7	78.4	78.7	79.5	80.2	81.1	81.1	82.5	86.8	88.5	81.0
2012	83.1	81.1	81.0	81.5	81.9	82.3	82.7	82.8	82.3	82.9	88.1	89.2	83.2
2013	83.8	82.3	82.0	82.0	82.3	83.2	83.4	83.7	83.0	83.8	87.9	89.2	83.9
2014	84.5	83.3	83.1	83.8	83.8	84.3	84.7	85.3	84.8	85.3	89.4	90.8	85.3
2015	86.5	85.2	85.0	84.7	84.8	85.3	86.0	86.6	86.2	87.1	90.3	91.2	86.6
2016	86.4	85.6	85.0	84.5	84.5	84.6	85.7	85.7	85.0	85.3	88.1	89.2	85.8
2017	85.7	84.4	84.3	84.5	84.7	85.3	86.0	86.2	85.9	86.9	90.5	91.5	86.3

Employment by Industry: San Jose-Sunnyvale-Santa Clara, CA, Selected Years, 2007–2017—*Continued*

(Numbers in thousands, not seasonally adjusted)

Industry and year	January	February	March	April	May	June	July	August	September	October	November	December	Annual average
Transportation and Utilities													
2007	12.9	13.0	13.1	13.4	13.5	13.8	13.8	13.8	13.9	13.7	13.7	13.9	13.5
2008	13.2	13.4	13.4	13.3	13.6	13.7	13.4	13.5	13.5	13.4	13.4	13.7	13.5
2009	12.7	12.5	12.1	11.9	12.2	12.0	11.8	11.8	12.0	11.9	11.8	12.0	12.1
2010	11.8	11.7	11.7	11.7	12.0	12.1	12.1	12.2	12.3	12.1	12.1	12.4	12.0
2011	11.8	11.9	11.9	12.0	12.1	12.2	12.2	12.1	12.2	12.1	12.2	12.6	12.1
2012	12.3	12.2	12.2	12.4	12.5	12.8	12.9	13.1	13.2	13.2	13.3	13.7	12.8
2013	13.2	13.4	13.4	13.4	13.4	13.6	13.8	13.8	14.0	14.3	14.6	15.2	13.8
2014	14.1	14.0	14.1	14.0	14.2	14.4	14.4	14.4	14.3	14.4	14.6	15.3	14.4
2015	14.9	14.1	14.1	14.2	14.2	14.3	14.5	14.6	14.6	14.7	15.2	15.9	14.6
2016	15.0	14.9	14.8	14.9	15.0	15.3	15.5	15.5	15.5	15.5	15.7	16.4	17.4	15.5
2017	15.5	15.3	15.2	15.2	15.2	15.5	15.4	15.6	15.5	15.4	15.3	15.9	15.4
Information													
2007	38.8	39.4	39.7	39.3	40.1	40.9	41.4	41.7	41.5	41.7	42.3	42.6	40.8
2008	42.5	42.5	42.3	42.8	43.4	43.8	45.0	44.9	44.3	44.0	44.3	44.0	43.7
2009	44.7	43.6	43.3	42.8	43.0	43.4	44.5	44.3	43.9	44.0	44.3	44.4	43.9
2010	44.1	44.5	44.2	44.8	45.4	46.6	47.6	47.8	47.5	47.9	48.5	48.6	46.5
2011	49.2	49.7	49.8	50.0	50.4	51.9	52.7	52.7	52.1	52.2	52.2	52.5	51.3
2012	52.1	52.6	52.8	53.3	53.5	54.5	55.5	55.3	54.9	55.1	55.2	55.6	54.2
2013	56.4	56.6	57.1	57.0	57.2	58.9	60.2	60.0	59.3	60.0	60.7	61.3	58.7
2014	61.4	62.4	63.3	63.6	64.2	66.5	68.5	67.9	67.2	67.4	67.6	67.9	65.7
2015	68.5	68.4	68.6	68.8	69.1	71.5	73.1	72.0	71.1	71.5	71.7	71.8	70.5
2016	72.3	72.4	72.1	72.4	73.2	75.8	78.1	77.7	76.9	78.3	79.5	79.8	75.7
2017	80.3	81.0	81.8	81.5	82.3	86.0	88.2	89.9	87.1	87.1	87.9	88.3	85.1
Financial Activities													
2007	37.0	37.1	37.1	37.0	37.2	37.0	37.1	36.9	36.8	36.6	36.2	36.3	36.9
2008	35.3	35.5	35.1	34.9	34.8	34.5	34.3	34.0	33.8	33.4	32.7	32.8	34.3
2009	32.2	31.8	31.8	31.8	31.7	31.4	31.3	31.2	30.8	31.2	31.2	31.3	31.5
2010	30.8	30.9	31.5	30.2	30.5	30.8	30.9	31.0	30.9	31.3	31.7	31.7	31.0
2011	31.6	31.7	31.7	31.9	32.0	32.3	32.5	32.5	32.5	32.8	33.1	33.2	32.3
2012	32.7	32.6	32.9	32.9	33.2	33.4	33.5	33.4	33.3	33.6	33.7	33.6	33.2
2013	32.6	32.9	33.3	33.5	33.8	33.8	33.9	33.9	33.7	34.1	34.2	34.2	33.7
2014	33.6	33.8	34.0	34.0	34.2	34.6	34.4	34.2	34.2	34.2	34.2	34.2	34.1
2015	34.0	34.0	33.8	34.1	34.4	34.7	34.9	34.9	34.7	35.3	35.3	35.0	34.6
2016	35.0	35.1	35.1	35.4	35.4	35.5	36.0	36.0	35.8	35.9	36.1	36.2	35.6
2017	35.8	35.9	35.9	36.2	36.3	36.4	36.1	35.8	35.6	36.3	36.4	36.3	36.1
Professional and Business Services													
2007	175.1	176.6	176.6	176.0	176.4	177.0	177.5	177.1	176.9	177.6	178.5	179.2	177.0
2008	176.0	177.1	178.3	178.4	177.5	178.7	178.6	179.1	178.4	176.7	175.6	174.4	177.4
2009	166.8	164.9	163.6	159.7	158.3	158.7	157.3	157.2	156.4	157.0	157.4	158.0	159.6
2010	155.3	156.4	157.2	158.6	159.0	160.6	161.3	161.7	161.1	162.3	162.6	163.4	160.0
2011	161.5	162.6	163.7	164.1	163.6	165.0	167.6	168.3	167.7	168.0	167.7	168.2	165.7
2012	167.4	169.4	171.1	174.1	174.6	176.9	180.0	181.2	180.4	182.0	183.0	185.1	177.1
2013	182.9	185.2	186.5	186.1	186.3	188.8	192.0	194.1	192.5	193.2	195.4	197.0	190.0
2014	195.2	196.6	197.4	197.9	198.1	201.0	203.0	204.9	204.4	206.6	207.8	208.8	201.8
2015	206.8	208.0	209.1	211.6	212.6	214.2	218.4	219.2	218.0	220.3	221.2	221.3	215.1
2016	218.7	220.5	219.9	223.3	222.5	223.7	226.2	226.4	223.3	225.2	225.1	224.7	223.3
2017	220.6	222.4	226.3	226.1	226.6	229.0	231.8	232.0	228.9	229.9	229.1	228.8	227.6
Education and Health Services													
2007	109.2	112.0	113.4	111.7	113.5	114.5	112.6	112.2	112.4	116.1	117.7	117.7	113.6
2008	118.7	121.4	121.9	121.5	121.3	121.0	117.6	121.0	121.0	122.6	124.1	124.1	121.4
2009	123.4	124.9	125.1	125.0	125.7	125.2	121.7	122.1	121.1	126.1	126.3	126.6	124.4
2010	124.8	125.9	126.0	128.2	128.8	128.4	125.6	125.4	124.8	128.3	129.0	129.6	127.1
2011	128.5	130.3	130.7	129.5	130.0	129.1	125.9	126.4	126.7	131.8	133.5	133.8	129.7
2012	133.5	136.7	137.3	137.3	137.7	136.8	133.2	134.6	134.4	139.2	140.5	140.7	136.8
2013	140.4	142.7	143.5	144.1	145.1	143.8	140.5	141.9	141.8	146.1	147.9	147.6	143.8
2014	147.9	149.6	150.1	150.8	151.4	150.2	147.0	147.7	148.0	152.7	152.3	152.0	150.0
2015	153.1	154.7	155.5	156.0	157.0	156.1	154.4	154.8	154.6	159.4	159.8	159.6	156.3
2016	159.2	161.5	161.8	163.2	164.0	163.0	160.9	160.4	160.6	164.4	165.6	165.1	162.5
2017	166.2	168.9	169.8	168.3	168.9	168.7	166.8	166.2	165.8	169.6	172.3	173.2	168.7

Employment by Industry: San Jose-Sunnyvale-Santa Clara, CA, Selected Years, 2007–2017—*Continued*

(Numbers in thousands, not seasonally adjusted)

Industry and year	January	February	March	April	May	June	July	August	September	October	November	December	Annual average
Leisure and Hospitality													
2007	72.6	74.0	75.9	76.7	78.0	79.2	78.6	78.7	77.7	76.9	76.5	76.7	76.8
2008	74.3	75.6	77.3	77.9	79.3	80.6	80.5	80.2	79.5	78.3	76.9	76.3	78.1
2009	73.8	74.0	74.4	75.1	76.1	77.1	75.9	76.2	74.8	74.7	73.1	73.2	74.9
2010	71.5	71.7	72.7	75.5	76.9	76.7	76.4	76.2	76.3	75.9	74.4	74.8	74.9
2011	72.4	73.9	75.3	76.4	77.5	78.1	79.5	79.7	79.9	80.2	78.0	78.1	77.4
2012	77.1	78.0	80.1	81.7	83.2	83.9	84.6	85.0	85.4	85.1	83.1	83.2	82.5
2013	81.4	83.6	85.5	87.7	89.2	89.5	89.2	89.3	89.2	89.3	88.0	88.3	87.5
2014	85.9	88.5	90.1	91.1	93.2	93.7	93.9	94.3	94.0	93.9	92.1	92.3	91.9
2015	90.2	92.5	94.2	95.1	96.9	97.4	97.9	97.7	97.1	98.0	96.2	96.0	95.8
2016	94.7	95.3	96.4	98.6	100.3	101.1	102.3	101.6	101.0	101.3	99.8	100.1	99.4
2017	96.6	98.7	100.4	101.3	103.0	104.2	104.5	103.9	102.7	103.5	103.8	105.1	102.3
Other Services													
2007	23.9	24.6	24.8	24.8	25.2	25.6	25.1	25.1	25.4	25.5	25.4	25.4	25.1
2008	24.7	25.2	25.5	25.5	25.9	25.9	25.3	25.1	25.5	25.5	25.3	25.2	25.4
2009	24.5	24.6	24.7	24.8	24.9	24.9	24.0	23.8	24.2	24.3	24.6	24.5	24.5
2010	24.6	24.9	25.2	24.1	24.2	24.5	23.8	23.7	24.0	24.2	24.3	24.1	24.3
2011	24.1	24.3	24.3	24.5	24.7	24.7	24.9	24.6	24.6	24.7	24.9	24.7	24.6
2012	24.1	24.2	24.4	24.8	25.0	25.2	25.2	24.9	24.8	24.9	24.8	24.7	24.8
2013	24.7	25.1	25.1	25.4	25.7	25.7	25.6	25.4	25.5	25.6	25.7	25.6	25.4
2014	25.5	25.8	26.0	26.5	26.7	26.9	26.6	26.6	26.5	26.7	26.7	26.4	26.4
2015	26.2	26.4	26.6	26.8	27.2	27.1	27.2	27.2	27.0	27.2	27.2	27.1	26.9
2016	26.6	27.0	26.9	27.4	27.7	27.7	28.0	28.0	27.9	28.2	28.1	28.0	27.6
2017	28.1	28.5	28.7	28.8	29.2	29.1	28.8	28.7	28.7	29.2	28.5	28.6	28.7
Government													
2007	97.7	97.0	98.3	98.1	98.3	97.8	95.1	93.9	94.9	98.3	98.6	98.3	97.2
2008	99.0	98.2	99.1	98.4	99.0	98.6	94.0	94.5	98.0	98.7	98.3	97.8	97.8
2009	97.4	96.8	97.6	99.5	100.2	100.3	85.1	88.8	96.0	98.5	99.3	98.1	96.5
2010	96.0	96.2	97.6	99.4	100.9	96.6	85.0	83.5	89.9	95.4	97.0	96.1	94.5
2011	94.6	95.3	95.7	96.5	96.8	96.2	81.3	82.4	90.9	93.8	94.4	94.4	92.7
2012	91.7	92.9	94.0	94.2	94.2	94.9	81.1	83.1	90.2	93.5	94.1	93.3	91.4
2013	92.6	94.0	93.1	94.3	95.7	94.4	78.6	83.4	91.3	94.1	95.4	94.2	91.8
2014	94.5	95.6	95.8	96.9	97.0	94.2	82.3	86.1	92.2	95.2	95.9	95.2	93.4
2015	93.8	94.6	94.1	94.8	95.2	94.7	83.7	87.3	91.6	94.8	95.5	95.2	92.9
2016	93.6	94.3	95.4	95.6	96.4	96.0	85.3	88.3	92.9	96.0	97.9	97.8	94.1
2017	95.8	95.8	96.8	97.4	97.9	96.7	88.1	89.5	94.0	98.4	98.9	98.8	95.7

Employment by Industry: Nashville-Davidson—Murfreesboro—Franklin, TN, Selected Years, 2007–2017

(Numbers in thousands, not seasonally adjusted)

Industry and year	January	February	March	April	May	June	July	August	September	October	November	December	Annual average
Total Nonfarm													
2006	776.2	780.5	788.7	787.6	789.4	792.1	788.9	802.6	806.7	800.8	811.2	811.7	794.7
2007	786.2	792.2	795.7	796.2	801.3	794.3	785.7	793.4	797.3	793.8	793.4	791.9	793.5
2008	762.2	761.5	759.2	757.8	758.1	745.7	742.0	749.9	754.7	758.3	764.0	762.5	756.3
2009	742.4	745.0	751.5	760.2	766.7	758.3	752.5	761.1	770.6	777.3	781.9	782.2	762.5
2010	759.9	765.7	773.1	781.7	785.5	779.4	780.8	790.3	796.4	801.4	808.6	810.5	786.1
2011	791.4	798.0	808.8	811.4	815.0	810.9	806.9	818.5	824.8	830.9	839.5	841.2	816.4
2012	817.7	827.1	833.1	841.0	845.2	840.9	837.1	849.7	855.0	863.1	871.3	872.4	846.1
2013	850.9	857.7	862.3	874.6	879.6	873.3	870.5	885.4	891.5	899.8	907.1	909.8	880.2
2014	886.3	892.0	896.7	907.0	913.1	908.8	907.6	918.0	924.8	934.8	941.2	945.0	914.6
2015	923.2	929.0	936.3	944.0	945.3	942.5	943.6	953.4	962.6	966.9	974.8	977.0	949.9
2016	954.7	964.0	968.6	975.1	976.9	975.9	973.9	983.5	991.4	996.3	1000.1	999.1	980.0
Total Private													
2006	670.7	673.6	681.6	682.6	686.0	694.5	690.2	697.8	696.0	691.9	700.2	702.3	689.0
2007	678.0	682.0	685.4	686.5	690.3	693.7	685.3	687.7	685.7	681.4	680.2	677.8	684.5
2008	651.5	647.9	646.1	644.2	645.2	645.1	640.5	643.3	642.5	644.6	649.8	648.7	645.8
2009	630.9	631.6	637.7	645.7	650.4	654.2	651.1	654.0	655.5	661.7	666.7	667.4	650.6
2010	648.1	653.6	660.4	668.4	672.4	676.0	677.3	681.1	683.6	688.3	695.2	697.4	675.2
2011	680.5	685.2	695.2	698.8	704.0	709.6	706.5	711.6	714.0	719.1	726.8	728.6	706.7
2012	707.9	714.9	720.7	727.1	732.5	738.5	735.3	741.4	742.5	749.0	757.2	758.5	735.5
2013	739.5	743.7	748.2	760.6	765.5	770.0	767.8	776.1	777.8	784.7	790.1	794.3	768.2
2014	774.0	776.6	781.3	791.8	798.5	804.0	803.3	807.0	809.2	817.0	823.8	827.6	801.2
2015	809.5	812.9	818.1	827.2	830.3	836.6	837.7	840.2	844.6	849.1	856.1	858.4	835.1
2016	838.7	845.5	849.7	856.5	859.4	868.0	866.5	869.5	873.0	876.9	879.9	878.6	863.5
Goods Producing													
2006	128.6	128.5	129.7	129.1	127.4	130.4	126.9	129.4	129.6	126.1	128.2	127.9	128.5
2007	122.5	124.2	123.9	123.3	123.9	124.2	121.6	121.1	119.1	115.7	113.3	111.4	120.4
2008	105.7	104.4	103.0	101.4	100.2	97.9	99.0	99.0	98.6	97.9	97.6	95.3	100.0
2009	92.0	91.4	92.3	94.2	94.5	95.8	95.6	96.3	96.4	96.8	96.3	96.1	94.8
2010	93.4	94.2	95.7	97.7	97.8	98.8	99.0	99.3	99.9	100.5	100.5	100.9	98.1
2011	98.6	100.0	101.7	102.1	102.7	103.9	104.2	105.0	105.8	105.3	105.6	105.7	103.4
2012	104.1	105.0	105.9	106.3	107.5	108.6	108.7	109.5	109.8	110.5	110.4	110.7	108.1
2013	109.5	110.0	110.9	111.6	112.8	113.1	112.8	114.5	114.1	114.8	115.7	116.4	113.0
2014	114.6	115.5	115.5	117.4	118.7	119.3	118.7	119.4	119.8	119.6	119.5	119.2	118.1
2015	118.5	118.9	119.8	120.2	121.3	122.5	123.7	123.5	123.7	124.1	124.7	126.2	122.3
2016	124.8	125.8	126.2	127.4	127.3	128.2	128.2	128.0	128.0	127.4	127.5	124.9	127.0
Service-Providing													
2006	647.6	652.0	659.0	658.5	662.0	661.7	662.0	673.2	677.1	674.7	683.0	683.8	666.2
2007	663.7	668.0	671.8	672.9	677.4	670.1	664.1	672.3	678.2	678.1	680.1	680.5	673.1
2008	656.5	657.1	656.2	656.4	657.9	647.8	643.0	650.9	656.1	660.4	666.4	667.2	656.3
2009	650.4	653.6	659.2	666.0	672.2	662.5	656.9	664.8	674.2	680.5	685.6	686.1	667.7
2010	666.5	671.5	677.4	684.0	687.7	680.6	681.8	691.0	696.5	700.9	708.1	709.6	688.0
2011	692.8	698.0	707.1	709.3	712.3	707.0	702.7	713.5	719.0	725.6	733.9	735.5	713.1
2012	713.6	722.1	727.2	734.7	737.7	732.3	728.4	740.2	745.2	752.6	760.9	761.7	738.1
2013	741.4	747.7	751.4	763.0	766.8	760.2	757.7	770.9	777.4	785.0	791.4	793.4	767.2
2014	771.7	776.5	781.2	789.6	794.4	789.5	788.9	798.6	805.0	815.2	821.7	825.8	796.5
2015	804.7	810.1	816.5	823.8	824.0	820.0	819.9	829.9	838.9	842.8	850.1	850.8	827.6
2016	829.9	838.2	842.4	847.7	849.6	847.7	845.7	855.5	863.4	868.9	872.6	874.2	853.0
Mining, Logging, and Construction													
2006	40.2	40.7	42.3	42.6	43.3	44.5	44.3	44.7	44.7	44.3	44.0	43.5	43.3
2007	41.9	41.7	41.8	41.7	42.0	42.2	41.4	41.4	40.7	39.4	38.1	37.0	40.8
2008	34.5	33.7	33.4	32.8	32.7	32.9	32.9	32.7	32.4	31.9	31.6	31.2	32.7
2009	29.0	28.7	29.6	31.5	31.7	32.7	32.8	33.1	33.0	33.4	32.5	32.1	31.7
2010	29.5	30.1	31.3	32.8	32.9	33.8	33.7	33.9	34.2	33.8	33.5	33.1	32.7
2011	31.9	32.3	33.6	33.2	33.4	33.6	33.4	33.7	34.0	33.1	32.6	32.3	33.1
2012	31.0	31.8	32.5	33.0	33.7	34.3	34.2	34.2	34.2	34.2	33.4	33.3	33.3
2013	32.5	32.8	34.1	34.8	35.6	35.4	35.8	36.2	35.9	36.4	36.8	37.1	35.3
2014	36.2	36.8	37.2	38.7	39.7	40.1	40.4	40.0	40.3	40.3	40.1	39.3	39.1
2015	38.2	38.2	38.5	38.9	39.5	40.4	41.0	40.9	41.1	41.3	41.6	41.7	40.1
2016	40.4	41.1	41.9	42.6	43.0	43.5	43.5	43.6	43.6	43.0	43.7	41.7	42.6

Employment by Industry: Nashville-Davidson—Murfreesboro—Franklin, TN, Selected Years, 2007–2017—Continued

(Numbers in thousands, not seasonally adjusted)

Industry and year	January	February	March	April	May	June	July	August	September	October	November	December	Annual average
Manufacturing													
2006	88.4	87.8	87.4	86.5	84.1	85.9	82.6	84.7	84.9	81.8	84.2	84.4	85.2
2007	80.6	82.5	82.1	81.6	81.9	82.0	80.2	79.7	78.4	76.3	75.2	74.4	79.6
2008	71.2	70.7	69.6	68.6	67.5	65.0	66.1	66.3	66.2	66.0	66.0	64.1	67.3
2009	63.0	62.7	62.7	62.7	62.8	63.1	62.8	63.2	63.4	63.4	63.8	64.0	63.1
2010	63.9	64.1	64.4	64.9	64.9	65.0	65.3	65.4	65.7	66.7	67.0	67.8	65.4
2011	66.7	67.7	68.1	68.9	69.3	70.3	70.8	71.3	71.8	72.2	73.0	73.4	70.3
2012	73.1	73.2	73.4	73.3	73.8	74.3	74.5	75.3	75.6	76.3	77.0	77.4	74.8
2013	77.0	77.2	76.8	76.8	77.2	77.7	77.0	78.3	78.2	78.4	78.9	79.3	77.7
2014	78.4	78.7	78.3	78.7	79.0	79.2	78.3	79.4	79.5	79.3	79.4	79.9	79.0
2015	80.3	80.7	81.3	81.3	81.8	82.1	82.7	82.6	82.6	82.8	83.1	84.5	82.2
2016	84.4	84.7	84.3	84.8	84.3	84.7	84.7	84.4	84.4	84.4	83.8	83.2	84.3
Trade, Transportation, and Utilities													
2006	158.0	157.4	159.1	158.2	159.0	159.1	158.8	159.5	160.0	160.3	164.2	166.2	160.0
2007	159.7	159.5	160.6	159.6	159.7	159.7	159.9	160.2	160.1	159.9	161.9	163.4	160.4
2008	156.1	153.7	152.6	151.3	151.7	151.8	151.5	152.3	151.5	152.7	155.4	156.9	153.1
2009	150.7	149.7	150.5	151.2	151.5	152.5	152.2	153.1	152.6	154.9	158.0	159.8	153.1
2010	153.2	153.3	154.5	156.0	156.6	157.0	157.2	157.5	157.9	160.0	163.8	165.3	157.7
2011	159.3	158.4	160.3	161.0	161.9	161.9	161.7	162.4	163.1	165.2	170.1	171.1	163.0
2012	162.9	162.7	163.4	165.3	166.2	167.2	166.6	167.6	167.3	169.5	174.7	177.4	167.6
2013	167.6	167.1	168.0	170.9	171.6	172.4	172.2	173.2	173.4	176.3	180.1	182.1	172.9
2014	173.4	172.0	172.3	173.8	174.7	175.3	175.3	176.3	176.2	179.0	183.2	185.4	176.4
2015	178.5	177.4	177.6	178.8	179.0	179.8	181.1	181.5	181.8	184.7	189.4	190.9	181.7
2016	182.7	182.4	182.7	183.6	184.0	185.3	185.7	187.2	187.8	188.7	192.6	193.2	186.3
Wholesale Trade													
2006	37.0	37.2	37.6	37.6	37.8	38.0	38.0	38.1	38.5	38.5	38.7	38.7	38.0
2007	38.4	38.6	38.5	38.6	39.0	39.2	39.3	39.5	39.8	39.7	39.7	39.5	39.2
2008	38.4	38.1	37.7	37.6	37.4	37.2	37.0	37.1	37.0	37.2	37.1	37.1	37.4
2009	36.5	36.4	36.6	36.7	36.8	36.8	36.9	37.1	37.0	37.5	37.5	37.7	37.0
2010	37.4	37.6	37.9	37.9	38.1	38.3	38.3	38.4	38.7	38.9	39.2	39.4	38.3
2011	38.9	39.1	39.3	39.4	39.7	39.8	40.0	40.3	40.3	40.5	40.7	40.7	39.9
2012	40.1	40.4	40.8	41.0	41.1	41.3	41.5	41.4	41.3	41.4	41.6	41.4	41.1
2013	40.5	40.4	40.6	40.6	40.7	40.8	40.7	40.7	40.8	40.9	40.8	40.9	40.7
2014	40.0	40.1	40.0	40.0	39.9	39.9	39.9	39.9	39.9	40.2	40.1	40.0	40.0
2015	39.1	39.0	38.9	38.9	38.9	39.1	39.5	39.7	39.9	40.2	40.3	40.5	39.5
2016	40.0	40.3	40.3	40.5	40.7	40.9	41.0	41.2	41.4	41.1	41.0	40.6	40.8
Retail Trade													
2006	89.9	89.1	90.3	89.6	90.2	90.0	89.6	90.0	90.1	90.8	94.3	96.1	90.8
2007	91.1	90.8	92.0	90.7	90.3	90.0	89.9	90.1	89.6	89.4	91.6	92.5	90.7
2008	87.6	86.2	85.7	85.2	85.7	85.8	85.6	86.1	85.2	86.0	88.3	89.6	86.4
2009	85.4	84.7	85.1	85.8	85.9	86.5	86.0	86.5	85.6	86.8	89.3	90.5	86.5
2010	86.5	86.5	87.1	88.1	88.2	88.5	88.5	88.5	88.3	89.1	91.8	93.0	88.7
2011	88.9	87.7	89.0	89.1	89.3	89.2	88.7	88.5	88.2	89.2	92.5	92.8	89.4
2012	88.0	87.1	87.4	88.7	89.4	89.7	89.4	89.8	89.4	90.7	93.4	94.6	89.8
2013	90.0	89.6	90.1	92.8	93.4	93.8	93.6	93.8	93.6	94.7	97.5	98.7	93.5
2014	93.9	93.0	93.3	94.1	94.8	95.1	95.0	95.0	94.4	95.6	98.5	99.6	95.2
2015	95.4	95.1	95.5	96.1	96.3	96.7	96.9	97.0	96.8	97.6	100.5	101.5	97.1
2016	97.7	97.2	97.3	97.8	98.0	98.5	98.7	99.0	98.5	98.7	101.0	101.3	98.6
Transportation and Utilities													
2006	31.1	31.1	31.2	31.0	31.0	31.1	31.2	31.4	31.4	31.0	31.2	31.4	31.2
2007	30.2	30.1	30.1	30.3	30.4	30.5	30.7	30.6	30.7	30.8	30.6	31.4	30.5
2008	30.1	29.4	29.2	28.5	28.6	28.8	28.9	29.1	29.3	29.5	30.0	30.2	29.3
2009	28.8	28.6	28.8	28.7	28.8	29.2	29.3	29.5	30.0	30.6	31.2	31.6	29.6
2010	29.3	29.2	29.5	30.0	30.3	30.2	30.4	30.6	30.9	32.0	32.8	32.9	30.7
2011	31.5	31.6	32.0	32.5	32.9	32.9	33.0	33.6	34.6	35.5	36.9	37.6	33.7
2012	34.8	35.2	35.2	35.6	35.7	36.2	35.7	36.4	36.6	37.4	39.7	41.4	36.7
2013	37.1	37.1	37.3	37.5	37.5	37.8	37.9	38.7	39.0	40.7	41.8	42.5	38.7
2014	39.5	38.9	39.0	39.7	40.0	40.3	40.4	41.4	41.9	43.2	44.6	45.8	41.2
2015	44.0	43.3	43.2	43.8	43.8	44.0	44.7	44.8	45.1	46.9	48.6	48.9	45.1
2016	45.0	44.9	45.1	45.3	45.3	45.9	46.0	47.0	47.9	48.9	50.6	51.3	46.9

Employment by Industry: Nashville-Davidson—Murfreesboro—Franklin, TN, Selected Years, 2007–2017—*Continued*

(Numbers in thousands, not seasonally adjusted)

Industry and year	January	February	March	April	May	June	July	August	September	October	November	December	Annual average
Information													
2006	19.6	19.6	19.6	19.9	20.3	20.4	20.6	20.7	20.8	20.9	21.0	21.4	20.4
2007	21.7	21.7	21.8	21.8	21.9	21.9	21.6	21.6	21.5	21.8	21.7	21.8	21.7
2008	21.4	21.3	21.1	20.8	20.7	20.5	20.4	20.5	20.3	20.0	20.0	19.9	20.6
2009	19.9	19.9	20.0	19.9	19.8	19.9	19.8	19.5	19.5	19.8	19.8	19.8	19.8
2010	19.4	19.3	19.3	19.4	19.6	19.7	19.7	20.1	19.8	20.1	20.4	20.5	19.8
2011	20.3	20.5	20.4	20.5	21.3	21.5	20.4	20.6	20.4	20.6	20.6	20.7	20.7
2012	20.4	20.7	20.8	20.6	21.0	21.6	20.9	21.0	20.7	20.8	21.2	21.1	20.9
2013	20.5	20.5	20.6	20.6	20.7	20.7	20.6	20.5	20.4	20.6	20.6	20.5	20.6
2014	20.4	20.5	20.5	20.6	21.1	21.7	21.6	22.1	21.9	22.3	23.0	22.9	21.6
2015	22.7	22.9	22.4	22.4	22.4	23.8	22.2	22.3	23.1	23.1	23.9	22.8	22.8
2016	22.5	23.4	22.7	22.8	23.1	24.7	23.1	23.0	22.9	22.8	23.2	23.0	23.1
Financial Activities													
2006	47.7	48.1	48.3	48.5	49.0	49.2	49.0	49.0	48.7	48.7	48.6	48.8	48.6
2007	48.3	48.6	48.5	48.5	48.6	48.9	48.8	48.6	48.2	47.8	47.7	47.7	48.4
2008	47.1	47.0	46.9	47.0	47.2	47.3	47.1	47.6	47.4	47.6	47.8	48.1	47.3
2009	47.6	47.7	47.6	48.1	48.4	48.4	48.5	48.8	48.5	48.9	49.1	49.2	48.4
2010	48.4	48.5	48.5	49.3	49.8	49.5	49.7	50.0	50.0	50.2	50.5	50.4	49.6
2011	49.8	50.2	50.2	50.3	50.6	51.0	51.1	51.5	51.5	51.6	51.9	52.4	51.0
2012	52.1	52.4	52.8	53.4	53.7	53.7	54.4	54.2	54.0	54.4	54.7	54.7	53.7
2013	54.7	55.0	55.2	55.8	56.3	56.6	57.0	57.4	57.5	57.8	57.9	58.3	56.6
2014	57.9	58.3	58.6	58.9	59.2	59.6	59.9	60.0	59.9	60.5	60.7	61.1	59.6
2015	60.5	61.0	61.1	61.9	62.5	63.0	63.4	63.8	63.9	64.0	64.1	64.5	62.8
2016	63.9	64.7	65.2	65.4	65.8	66.4	66.4	66.6	66.3	66.2	66.2	66.6	65.8
Professional and Business Services													
2006	98.6	99.5	101.1	101.3	102.3	104.9	105.4	107.0	106.4	106.5	108.3	108.0	104.1
2007	101.2	101.0	101.5	102.5	103.4	105.8	100.9	102.6	104.2	104.5	104.5	102.4	102.9
2008	95.3	95.0	94.3	93.3	94.0	95.6	92.0	94.0	94.9	96.6	98.5	97.8	95.1
2009	93.9	94.7	96.0	97.9	102.3	102.2	100.6	101.3	103.1	103.1	104.9	105.1	100.4
2010	101.1	103.3	104.8	106.0	106.8	109.1	109.2	110.7	111.6	112.3	113.8	113.7	108.5
2011	109.7	111.4	114.4	114.7	116.0	118.3	117.8	119.6	120.7	122.2	123.9	123.6	117.7
2012	118.6	120.6	121.7	121.5	122.7	125.1	124.4	127.7	128.9	131.4	133.6	132.5	125.7
2013	129.1	130.1	129.7	133.3	134.5	136.9	135.3	139.6	140.1	142.3	142.7	144.2	136.5
2014	138.3	139.0	141.2	143.4	144.3	147.5	148.0	149.5	149.9	152.6	153.3	153.9	146.7
2015	149.9	150.5	151.7	154.6	154.6	156.4	155.7	156.7	157.2	158.7	158.3	158.2	155.2
2016	154.3	154.8	155.7	158.1	158.1	161.1	161.6	161.3	162.2	163.9	163.1	165.3	160.0
Education and Health Services													
2006	108.8	109.7	110.2	110.9	111.3	111.7	112.7	113.6	114.4	113.6	113.8	114.1	112.1
2007	113.0	113.8	113.8	115.4	115.6	115.8	116.3	117.0	117.8	117.8	118.2	118.7	116.1
2008	117.5	118.0	117.9	119.1	118.6	118.1	118.5	118.2	119.6	119.9	120.4	120.6	118.9
2009	119.7	120.5	121.0	122.6	121.4	120.9	122.5	122.6	124.5	125.3	125.6	125.3	122.7
2010	123.9	125.3	125.4	126.2	125.6	124.4	125.0	125.3	126.9	127.6	128.2	128.4	126.0
2011	127.6	128.8	129.3	129.6	128.5	128.3	127.9	128.8	130.9	131.1	131.7	131.4	129.5
2012	130.2	131.8	132.3	133.2	132.4	131.8	131.0	132.0	134.2	134.0	133.9	133.9	132.6
2013	133.2	134.2	134.8	136.0	135.3	134.4	134.5	135.4	137.7	138.5	138.5	138.8	135.9
2014	138.1	139.1	139.4	140.4	140.3	138.7	139.4	139.7	142.6	143.2	144.2	144.5	140.8
2015	142.1	143.7	144.5	144.9	144.8	143.2	144.3	145.3	148.2	148.3	148.9	148.8	145.6
2016	146.9	148.7	149.2	149.3	148.8	147.1	147.3	148.5	151.9	152.6	153.3	151.4	149.6
Leisure and Hospitality													
2006	78.5	79.5	81.7	83.0	84.7	86.7	85.2	86.7	84.4	83.8	84.1	84.0	83.5
2007	79.8	80.9	82.4	83.2	84.6	84.9	83.7	84.3	82.9	81.3	80.7	80.3	82.4
2008	77.2	77.0	78.4	79.9	81.2	82.0	80.4	80.5	79.5	78.7	78.9	79.1	79.4
2009	76.5	76.8	79.1	80.7	81.1	82.4	79.9	80.3	78.9	80.5	80.4	79.2	79.7
2010	75.9	76.4	78.6	80.5	82.5	83.0	83.2	84.1	83.7	83.8	83.9	84.1	81.6
2011	81.3	81.7	84.3	85.9	88.0	88.9	87.8	88.5	86.6	87.9	87.7	88.2	86.4
2012	84.3	85.9	87.7	90.4	92.3	93.3	92.4	92.7	91.2	92.0	92.1	91.9	90.5
2013	88.8	90.4	92.3	95.4	97.1	98.4	97.9	98.6	97.8	97.4	97.4	97.0	95.7
2014	94.5	95.4	96.8	100.0	102.3	103.5	102.3	102.4	101.2	102.0	102.0	102.4	100.4
2015	99.5	100.3	102.4	105.5	106.5	108.3	107.6	107.6	107.2	106.7	107.1	107.2	105.5
2016	104.2	105.9	107.9	109.6	111.6	113.8	113.1	114.0	113.0	114.9	113.1	113.5	111.2

Employment by Industry: Nashville-Davidson—Murfreesboro—Franklin, TN, Selected Years, 2007–2017— *Continued*

(Numbers in thousands, not seasonally adjusted)

Industry and year	January	February	March	April	May	June	July	August	September	October	November	December	Annual average
Other Services													
2006	30.9	31.3	31.9	31.7	32.0	32.1	31.6	31.9	31.7	32.0	32.0	31.9	31.8
2007	31.8	32.3	32.9	32.2	32.6	32.5	32.5	32.3	31.9	32.6	32.2	32.1	32.3
2008	31.2	31.5	31.9	31.4	31.6	31.9	31.6	31.2	30.7	31.2	31.2	31.0	31.4
2009	30.6	30.9	31.2	31.1	31.4	32.1	32.0	32.1	32.0	32.4	32.6	32.9	31.8
2010	32.8	33.3	33.6	33.3	33.7	34.5	34.3	34.1	33.8	33.8	34.1	34.1	33.8
2011	33.9	34.2	34.6	34.7	35.0	35.8	35.6	35.2	35.0	35.2	35.3	35.5	35.0
2012	35.3	35.8	36.1	36.4	36.7	37.2	36.9	36.7	36.4	36.4	36.6	36.3	36.4
2013	36.1	36.4	36.7	37.0	37.2	37.5	37.5	36.9	36.8	37.0	37.2	37.0	36.9
2014	36.8	36.8	37.0	37.3	37.9	38.4	38.1	37.6	37.7	37.8	37.9	38.2	37.6
2015	37.8	38.2	38.6	38.9	39.2	39.6	39.7	39.5	39.5	39.5	39.7	39.8	39.2
2016	39.4	39.8	40.1	40.3	40.7	41.4	41.1	40.9	40.9	40.4	40.9	40.7	40.6
Government													
2006	105.5	106.9	107.1	105.0	103.4	97.6	98.7	104.8	110.7	108.9	111.0	109.4	105.8
2007	108.2	110.2	110.3	109.7	111.0	100.6	100.4	105.7	111.6	112.4	113.2	114.1	109.0
2008	110.7	113.6	113.1	113.6	112.9	100.6	101.5	106.6	112.2	113.7	114.2	113.8	110.5
2009	111.5	113.4	113.8	114.5	116.3	104.1	101.4	107.1	115.1	115.6	115.2	114.8	111.9
2010	111.8	112.1	112.7	113.3	113.1	103.4	103.5	109.2	112.8	113.1	113.4	113.1	111.0
2011	110.9	112.8	113.6	112.6	111.0	101.3	100.4	106.9	110.8	111.8	112.7	112.6	109.8
2012	109.8	112.2	112.4	113.9	112.7	102.4	101.8	108.3	112.5	114.1	114.1	113.9	110.7
2013	111.4	114.0	114.1	114.0	114.1	103.3	102.7	109.3	113.7	115.1	117.0	115.5	112.0
2014	112.3	115.4	115.4	115.2	114.6	104.8	104.3	111.0	115.6	117.8	117.4	117.4	113.4
2015	113.7	116.1	118.2	116.8	115.0	105.9	105.9	113.2	118.0	117.8	118.7	118.6	114.8
2016	116.0	118.5	118.9	118.6	117.5	107.9	107.4	114.0	118.4	119.4	120.2	120.5	116.4

Employment by Industry: Virginia Beach-Norfolk-Newport News, VA-NC, Selected Years, 2007–2017

(Numbers in thousands, not seasonally adjusted)

Industry and year	January	February	March	April	May	June	July	August	September	October	November	December	Annual average
Total Nonfarm													
2007	758.1	759.5	767.6	773.0	778.6	786.7	788.4	787.2	782.1	772.8	776.4	775.6	775.5
2008	754.0	757.3	763.7	767.5	774.3	781.8	777.8	777.8	769.5	763.5	761.1	757.6	767.2
2009	737.5	736.3	739.4	742.6	747.9	753.1	744.9	745.3	740.1	741.0	739.4	739.0	742.2
2010	720.6	720.0	727.5	738.1	743.7	748.4	744.4	744.5	739.8	740.0	739.3	738.9	737.1
2011	720.9	722.5	730.6	739.8	743.1	751.1	749.4	749.1	745.5	742.8	743.5	743.5	740.2
2012	728.5	731.7	738.1	744.7	747.0	754.4	751.3	753.0	748.8	753.6	755.3	755.6	746.8
2013	740.2	742.6	748.7	755.1	758.4	765.2	763.7	765.5	758.7	758.9	760.4	760.4	756.5
2014	742.8	742.4	748.9	758.3	762.8	768.2	764.9	767.5	761.0	760.5	761.6	761.7	758.4
2015	748.1	748.7	752.3	763.6	768.0	774.0	775.2	776.7	771.7	774.4	775.8	775.4	767.0
2016	755.6	757.3	763.3	772.3	772.5	780.2	778.1	779.3	776.9	777.6	780.3	778.3	772.6
2017	760.6	768.0	772.9	781.3	782.6	791.7	787.1	787.5	783.7	782.5	781.6	779.5	779.9
Total Private													
2007	604.1	603.9	611.6	617.3	623.0	630.1	635.1	633.8	626.8	616.8	618.0	618.1	619.9
2008	598.1	599.2	605.1	610.1	616.3	622.5	622.3	622.1	612.1	604.1	599.4	597.4	609.1
2009	578.3	576.3	578.5	581.6	587.3	591.6	590.4	589.1	582.0	579.5	576.1	577.2	582.3
2010	559.9	558.4	565.2	575.2	578.6	584.1	586.9	586.5	579.0	577.9	576.8	576.8	575.4
2011	559.9	560.7	567.9	576.9	580.5	588.1	590.1	589.2	583.2	578.9	577.8	578.0	577.6
2012	565.5	567.6	574.5	581.0	583.6	590.7	592.4	593.8	587.5	590.2	590.4	591.5	584.1
2013	578.8	579.6	585.6	592.1	596.0	603.1	605.3	606.7	598.3	597.0	597.6	597.3	594.8
2014	582.8	581.6	587.7	596.8	602.2	608.2	608.1	609.8	602.0	600.9	600.8	600.7	598.5
2015	589.2	588.2	592.4	602.3	607.7	613.7	618.8	620.4	614.3	613.6	613.5	613.5	607.3
2016	597.0	596.9	602.0	611.1	612.2	619.8	621.9	622.7	617.9	616.5	617.9	616.0	612.7
2017	601.4	607.0	612.0	620.3	623.1	631.2	631.0	630.8	624.6	621.6	619.5	617.4	620.0
Goods Producing													
2007	105.8	104.7	105.6	106.7	106.9	107.5	107.4	107.4	106.9	105.1	104.9	104.4	106.1
2008	102.1	101.8	101.9	102.1	102.5	103.0	102.8	102.7	101.4	100.4	99.5	98.2	101.5
2009	94.2	93.2	92.9	92.1	91.9	92.1	92.1	91.8	91.2	91.1	90.2	90.4	91.9
2010	87.8	87.5	88.2	89.2	89.6	89.1	89.3	89.2	88.9	88.4	88.3	87.7	88.6
2011	85.6	85.6	86.5	86.4	87.0	87.5	88.1	88.2	87.7	86.7	86.7	86.5	86.9
2012	86.5	86.7	87.2	86.6	86.2	86.5	89.4	89.3	89.6	89.4	89.3	89.2	88.0
2013	87.9	88.3	88.6	88.6	88.8	89.4	90.0	90.0	89.7	89.1	89.3	89.4	89.1
2014	88.0	87.9	88.3	89.0	89.3	89.9	90.0	89.8	89.3	89.2	89.2	89.2	89.1
2015	87.9	87.7	88.0	89.3	89.5	90.1	90.9	90.5	90.0	90.2	89.7	89.4	89.4
2016	87.5	86.7	86.7	86.3	86.3	87.1	88.0	88.1	88.3	88.5	88.9	88.8	87.6
2017	87.8	88.4	88.9	89.4	89.8	90.4	90.2	90.3	90.3	90.2	90.3	90.7	89.7
Service-Providing													
2007	652.3	654.8	662.0	666.3	671.7	679.2	681.0	679.8	675.2	667.7	671.5	671.2	669.4
2008	651.9	655.5	661.8	665.4	671.8	678.8	675.0	675.1	668.1	663.1	661.6	659.4	665.6
2009	643.3	643.1	646.5	650.5	656.0	661.0	652.8	653.5	648.9	649.9	649.2	648.6	650.3
2010	632.8	632.5	639.3	648.9	654.1	659.3	655.1	655.3	650.9	651.6	651.0	651.2	648.5
2011	635.3	636.9	644.1	653.4	656.1	663.6	661.3	660.9	657.8	656.1	656.8	657.0	653.3
2012	642.0	645.0	650.9	658.1	660.8	667.9	661.9	663.7	659.2	664.2	666.0	666.4	658.8
2013	652.3	654.3	660.1	666.5	669.6	675.8	673.7	675.5	669.0	669.8	671.1	671.0	667.4
2014	654.8	654.5	660.6	669.3	673.5	678.3	674.9	677.7	671.7	671.3	672.4	672.5	669.3
2015	660.2	661.0	664.3	674.3	678.5	683.9	684.3	686.2	681.7	684.2	686.1	686.0	677.6
2016	668.1	670.6	676.6	686.0	686.2	693.1	690.1	691.2	688.6	689.1	691.4	689.5	685.0
2017	672.8	679.6	684.0	691.9	692.8	701.3	696.9	697.2	693.4	692.3	691.3	688.8	690.2
Mining, Logging, and Construction													
2007	47.9	47.8	48.5	48.6	48.7	49.1	49.6	49.6	49.1	47.7	47.4	46.8	48.4
2008	45.4	45.3	45.6	45.8	46.1	46.4	46.3	46.2	45.1	44.5	43.7	42.5	45.2
2009	39.9	39.2	39.0	38.6	38.4	38.5	38.6	38.4	37.9	37.6	36.9	37.0	38.3
2010	35.8	35.5	36.2	37.1	37.5	37.4	37.8	37.7	37.3	36.9	36.8	36.3	36.9
2011	34.8	34.9	35.1	35.5	35.6	35.7	35.6	35.5	35.0	34.6	34.5	34.4	35.1
2012	33.4	33.5	33.8	34.2	34.7	35.4	35.5	35.3	34.6	34.9	34.6	34.5	34.5
2013	33.9	34.1	34.4	34.4	34.7	35.2	35.4	35.4	35.1	34.6	34.7	34.5	34.7
2014	33.6	33.3	33.6	34.1	34.4	34.9	35.1	35.2	34.9	34.8	34.8	34.8	34.5
2015	34.1	34.1	34.4	35.6	36.0	36.4	37.1	37.0	36.6	36.9	36.8	36.8	36.0
2016	35.6	35.5	35.8	35.7	35.6	36.1	36.7	36.6	36.7	36.9	37.1	37.1	36.3
2017	36.3	36.7	37.0	37.3	37.7	38.3	37.8	38.0	37.7	37.6	37.6	37.8	37.5

Employment by Industry: Virginia Beach-Norfolk-Newport News, VA-NC, Selected Years, 2007–2017— Continued

(Numbers in thousands, not seasonally adjusted)

Industry and year	January	February	March	April	May	June	July	August	September	October	November	December	Annual average
Manufacturing													
2007	57.9	56.9	57.1	58.1	58.2	58.4	57.8	57.8	57.8	57.4	57.5	57.6	57.7
2008	56.7	56.5	56.3	56.3	56.4	56.6	56.5	56.5	56.3	55.9	55.8	55.7	56.3
2009	54.3	54.0	53.9	53.5	53.5	53.6	53.5	53.4	53.3	53.5	53.3	53.4	53.6
2010	52.0	52.0	52.0	52.1	52.1	51.7	51.5	51.5	51.6	51.5	51.5	51.4	51.7
2011	50.8	50.7	51.4	50.9	51.4	51.8	52.5	52.7	52.7	52.1	52.2	52.1	51.8
2012	53.1	53.2	53.4	52.4	51.5	51.1	53.9	54.0	55.0	54.5	54.7	54.7	53.5
2013	54.0	54.2	54.2	54.2	54.1	54.2	54.6	54.6	54.6	54.5	54.6	54.9	54.4
2014	54.4	54.6	54.7	54.9	54.9	55.0	54.9	54.6	54.4	54.4	54.4	54.4	54.6
2015	53.8	53.6	53.6	53.7	53.5	53.7	53.8	53.5	53.4	53.3	52.9	52.6	53.5
2016	51.9	51.2	50.9	50.6	50.7	51.0	51.3	51.5	51.6	51.6	51.8	51.7	51.3
2017	51.5	51.7	51.9	52.1	52.1	52.1	52.4	52.3	52.6	52.6	52.7	52.9	52.2
Trade, Transportation, and Utilities													
2007	141.5	139.7	140.5	140.0	141.3	142.5	144.5	143.8	142.1	142.3	146.8	147.0	142.7
2008	139.1	137.1	137.4	137.3	138.0	139.0	138.7	138.5	137.1	135.6	138.2	138.9	137.9
2009	130.0	127.3	127.0	127.5	129.0	129.4	128.9	128.7	127.4	128.1	130.5	131.7	128.8
2010	125.9	124.3	125.4	126.8	128.2	128.6	128.7	128.8	127.3	128.7	131.0	132.5	128.0
2011	126.4	125.3	125.8	127.2	127.6	128.5	128.0	128.1	126.7	127.3	130.1	131.6	127.7
2012	125.6	124.4	125.3	126.2	127.4	128.2	127.7	127.2	125.9	127.7	130.9	131.9	127.4
2013	125.9	124.7	125.2	126.0	127.2	128.4	129.0	129.4	128.3	129.1	132.4	133.7	128.3
2014	127.0	125.8	126.2	127.2	128.3	129.4	129.6	130.2	129.5	130.6	134.4	135.5	129.5
2015	129.3	128.3	128.5	129.2	130.6	131.7	132.7	132.8	131.6	132.3	135.9	136.9	131.7
2016	130.8	130.0	130.6	132.1	133.6	134.6	134.2	134.6	134.1	135.0	138.5	138.4	133.9
2017	132.2	131.5	131.9	132.8	133.9	135.5	134.9	135.1	134.3	134.7	136.9	137.9	134.3
Wholesale Trade													
2007	24.1	24.2	24.3	24.2	24.3	24.3	24.4	24.2	24.1	23.7	23.7	23.7	24.1
2008	23.5	23.4	23.4	23.5	23.5	23.5	23.4	23.4	23.1	22.9	22.7	22.6	23.2
2009	22.4	22.1	22.1	22.0	22.0	22.0	21.9	21.9	21.6	21.6	21.6	21.5	21.9
2010	20.9	20.7	20.8	21.1	21.1	21.1	21.1	21.2	21.1	21.1	21.1	21.1	21.0
2011	20.8	20.6	20.7	20.8	20.8	20.9	20.8	20.7	20.4	20.3	20.3	20.5	20.6
2012	20.2	20.2	20.2	20.2	20.2	20.3	20.3	20.3	20.1	20.2	20.2	20.2	20.2
2013	19.7	19.7	19.7	19.8	19.8	19.9	20.0	20.1	20.0	20.1	20.1	20.2	19.9
2014	20.0	20.0	20.0	20.0	20.2	20.0	20.0	20.1	20.0	20.0	20.2	20.3	20.1
2015	20.0	20.0	19.9	19.9	20.0	20.1	20.2	20.1	20.1	20.1	20.1	20.2	20.1
2016	19.8	19.8	19.7	19.7	19.8	19.9	19.9	19.8	19.7	19.7	19.8	19.8	19.8
2017	19.8	19.7	19.7	19.9	19.9	20.0	19.9	19.9	19.8	19.8	19.8	19.8	19.8
Retail Trade													
2007	93.1	91.2	91.7	91.3	92.4	93.2	94.7	94.6	93.2	93.6	97.9	98.2	93.8
2008	92.1	90.1	90.5	89.7	90.3	90.9	90.7	90.5	89.6	88.4	90.9	91.6	90.4
2009	84.8	82.8	82.6	83.0	84.4	84.9	84.3	84.3	83.3	83.7	85.7	86.9	84.2
2010	82.8	81.6	82.5	83.4	84.4	84.7	84.4	84.5	83.0	83.8	86.0	87.4	84.0
2011	82.6	81.9	82.3	83.4	84.2	84.9	84.6	84.7	83.5	84.1	86.7	88.0	84.2
2012	83.3	81.9	82.8	83.4	84.3	84.8	84.4	84.0	82.9	84.3	87.6	88.4	84.3
2013	83.8	83.0	83.5	84.0	84.9	85.7	85.9	86.2	85.2	85.8	88.7	89.9	85.6
2014	84.1	83.1	83.4	84.4	85.1	86.1	86.2	86.7	86.0	87.2	90.1	90.8	86.1
2015	86.0	84.9	85.3	85.9	86.9	87.6	88.0	88.2	87.2	87.5	90.6	91.1	87.4
2016	86.6	86.0	86.6	87.7	88.6	89.2	88.8	89.2	88.7	89.3	92.0	91.7	88.7
2017	87.0	86.4	86.8	87.4	88.4	89.7	89.2	89.3	88.5	88.7	91.0	91.6	88.7
Transportation and Utilities													
2007	24.3	24.3	24.5	24.5	24.6	25.0	25.4	25.0	24.8	25.0	25.2	25.1	24.8
2008	23.5	23.6	23.5	24.1	24.2	24.6	24.6	24.6	24.4	24.3	24.6	24.7	24.2
2009	22.8	22.4	22.3	22.5	22.6	22.5	22.7	22.5	22.5	22.8	23.2	23.3	22.7
2010	22.2	22.0	22.1	22.3	22.7	22.8	23.2	23.1	23.2	23.8	23.9	24.0	22.9
2011	23.0	22.8	22.8	23.0	22.6	22.7	22.6	22.7	22.8	22.9	23.1	23.1	22.8
2012	22.1	22.3	22.3	22.6	22.9	23.1	23.0	22.9	22.9	23.2	23.1	23.3	22.8
2013	22.4	22.0	22.0	22.2	22.5	22.8	23.1	23.1	23.1	23.2	23.6	23.6	22.8
2014	22.9	22.7	22.8	22.8	23.0	23.3	23.4	23.4	23.5	23.4	24.1	24.4	23.3
2015	23.3	23.4	23.3	23.4	23.7	24.0	24.5	24.5	24.3	24.7	25.2	25.6	24.2
2016	24.4	24.2	24.3	24.7	25.2	25.5	25.5	25.6	25.7	26.0	26.7	26.9	25.4
2017	25.4	25.4	25.4	25.5	25.6	25.8	25.8	25.9	26.0	26.2	26.1	26.5	25.8

Employment by Industry: Virginia Beach-Norfolk-Newport News, VA-NC, Selected Years, 2007–2017— *Continued*

(Numbers in thousands, not seasonally adjusted)

Industry and year	January	February	March	April	May	June	July	August	September	October	November	December	Annual average
Information													
2007	15.5	15.6	15.6	15.6	15.7	15.8	15.6	15.6	15.4	15.2	15.2	15.3	15.5
2008	15.3	15.2	15.1	15.0	15.2	15.2	15.0	14.9	14.5	14.2	14.0	13.9	14.8
2009	13.7	13.7	13.6	13.5	13.6	13.5	13.3	13.2	12.9	12.9	12.8	12.8	13.3
2010	12.6	12.4	12.5	12.3	12.4	12.4	12.2	12.2	12.0	11.8	11.8	11.7	12.2
2011	11.6	11.5	11.6	11.6	11.7	11.8	11.9	10.9	11.6	11.4	11.4	11.6	11.6
2012	11.6	11.6	11.7	11.7	11.8	11.8	11.5	11.7	11.3	11.4	11.6	11.6	11.6
2013	11.5	11.6	11.6	11.4	11.6	11.6	11.6	11.6	11.3	11.3	11.4	11.2	11.5
2014	11.2	10.9	10.9	10.8	11.2	11.0	11.0	11.1	10.8	10.8	10.8	10.8	10.9
2015	10.8	10.7	10.7	10.8	11.0	11.0	11.2	11.0	10.8	11.0	11.1	11.1	10.9
2016	11.3	11.3	11.1	11.4	10.7	11.5	11.4	11.2	11.0	11.0	11.0	11.2	11.2
2017	11.2	11.3	11.2	11.2	11.2	11.3	11.3	11.2	11.0	10.9	10.9	11.1	11.2
Financial Activities													
2007	40.9	41.1	41.3	41.6	41.8	42.3	42.5	42.5	41.8	41.1	40.8	40.8	41.5
2008	40.3	40.5	40.5	40.3	40.3	41.0	41.3	41.0	40.2	39.3	38.8	38.7	40.2
2009	38.2	38.1	38.0	37.9	37.9	38.4	38.1	38.0	37.1	36.3	35.9	36.0	37.5
2010	36.1	35.9	35.9	36.2	36.2	37.1	37.3	37.4	36.8	36.2	36.2	36.1	36.5
2011	36.0	36.1	36.1	36.9	37.0	37.6	37.9	37.6	37.0	36.6	36.5	36.9	36.9
2012	36.4	36.7	36.8	37.3	37.1	37.9	38.3	38.2	37.8	37.7	37.6	37.7	37.5
2013	37.1	37.1	37.2	37.8	38.0	38.6	38.7	38.5	38.0	37.7	37.7	37.8	37.9
2014	36.9	37.0	37.2	37.5	37.9	38.4	38.6	38.5	38.2	37.7	37.6	37.8	37.8
2015	37.6	37.8	37.8	37.6	37.9	38.4	38.7	38.6	38.2	37.9	37.5	37.6	38.0
2016	37.0	36.8	37.0	37.5	37.8	38.5	38.6	38.5	38.0	37.9	37.7	37.8	37.8
2017	37.0	37.2	37.2	37.4	37.9	38.7	39.0	38.9	38.8	37.9	37.3	37.1	37.9
Professional and Business Services													
2007	99.9	100.3	101.5	101.9	102.4	102.9	103.3	104.0	104.0	103.0	103.8	104.8	102.7
2008	101.7	102.5	103.6	105.0	105.1	106.4	106.1	107.0	106.3	105.1	104.0	103.8	104.7
2009	100.6	100.4	100.1	99.6	98.9	99.4	98.8	99.2	98.8	98.9	99.4	99.5	99.5
2010	96.8	96.3	96.5	97.8	96.6	97.5	98.9	99.0	98.7	98.7	98.9	99.0	97.9
2011	96.5	96.5	96.9	98.0	97.7	98.6	99.5	100.4	100.7	99.5	99.3	99.0	98.6
2012	97.6	98.2	98.6	99.3	98.7	99.7	99.6	100.4	99.9	101.5	101.4	101.7	99.7
2013	101.3	101.7	102.2	102.7	102.3	103.1	103.2	103.8	102.1	102.6	102.9	102.3	102.5
2014	101.6	102.1	103.1	104.9	104.5	105.5	105.5	106.1	104.9	105.5	104.9	104.3	104.4
2015	102.8	103.0	103.3	104.7	104.8	105.4	106.3	107.0	106.0	106.0	105.5	105.2	105.0
2016	102.2	102.9	102.5	104.1	103.1	104.4	105.4	105.9	105.4	105.5	105.7	105.2	104.4
2017	103.7	106.2	107.1	109.1	108.2	109.6	109.2	109.7	109.6	109.7	109.7	108.7	108.4
Education and Health Services													
2007	89.2	89.6	90.2	90.5	89.6	89.4	89.8	90.4	92.0	92.1	92.2	92.8	90.7
2008	90.1	90.9	91.4	91.7	90.8	90.7	90.8	91.5	92.4	93.3	93.3	93.7	91.7
2009	93.3	93.5	93.8	93.6	92.6	92.2	92.5	93.0	94.5	95.1	94.9	95.3	93.7
2010	93.4	93.8	94.7	95.0	93.9	93.3	93.7	94.1	94.7	96.5	96.8	96.9	94.7
2011	96.3	97.1	97.7	98.4	97.3	97.0	97.3	97.6	99.1	99.5	99.7	98.4	98.0
2012	98.8	99.6	99.9	100.4	99.1	99.2	98.6	99.6	101.2	102.9	103.3	102.5	100.4
2013	102.9	103.6	103.8	104.7	103.0	103.0	102.4	103.9	105.2	106.0	106.6	105.3	104.2
2014	105.1	105.3	105.3	106.2	104.7	104.1	103.8	105.0	106.0	106.4	106.4	105.3	105.3
2015	106.6	106.9	107.0	108.8	107.3	106.8	107.5	108.8	110.2	111.4	111.8	110.3	108.6
2016	110.3	110.7	111.1	111.7	109.8	109.0	109.2	109.9	111.9	112.1	112.2	110.7	110.7
2017	110.5	111.6	111.7	111.6	109.8	109.6	109.4	110.0	110.7	111.6	111.5	109.9	110.7
Leisure and Hospitality													
2007	77.2	78.5	82.3	85.2	88.7	93.5	95.9	94.7	89.7	84.4	81.0	80.2	85.9
2008	78.1	79.6	83.4	86.4	90.9	94.2	94.7	93.7	87.9	84.1	79.4	78.1	85.9
2009	74.3	75.9	78.8	83.0	88.8	91.8	91.9	90.7	86.0	82.9	78.4	77.5	83.3
2010	74.0	74.9	78.2	83.7	87.2	91.5	92.0	91.1	86.3	83.2	79.6	79.1	83.4
2011	74.0	74.9	79.1	83.6	87.2	91.8	92.0	91.0	85.3	82.9	79.3	79.3	83.4
2012	75.0	76.1	80.3	83.7	87.4	91.2	91.3	91.3	86.2	83.6	80.4	81.1	84.0
2013	76.8	77.0	81.2	84.7	88.7	92.3	93.6	93.0	87.6	85.3	81.5	81.9	85.3
2014	77.9	77.4	81.1	85.3	90.0	93.3	93.0	92.5	87.0	84.9	81.9	82.3	85.6
2015	78.9	78.5	81.5	86.3	90.6	94.0	95.2	95.4	91.6	88.8	86.0	87.0	87.8
2016	82.4	83.1	87.2	91.7	94.4	98.1	98.5	98.0	93.0	90.2	87.6	87.9	91.0
2017	83.2	84.9	87.8	92.5	95.9	99.3	100.0	98.8	93.5	90.3	86.6	85.8	91.6

Employment by Industry: Virginia Beach-Norfolk-Newport News, VA-NC, Selected Years, 2007–2017—Continued

(Numbers in thousands, not seasonally adjusted)

Industry and year	January	February	March	April	May	June	July	August	September	October	November	December	Annual average
Other Services													
2007	34.1	34.4	34.6	35.8	36.6	36.2	36.1	35.4	34.9	33.6	33.3	32.8	34.8
2008	31.4	31.6	31.8	32.3	33.5	33.0	32.9	32.8	32.3	32.1	32.2	32.1	32.3
2009	34.0	34.2	34.3	34.4	34.6	34.8	34.8	34.5	34.1	34.2	34.0	34.0	34.3
2010	33.3	33.3	33.8	34.2	34.5	34.6	34.8	34.7	34.3	34.4	34.2	33.8	34.2
2011	33.5	33.7	34.2	34.8	35.0	35.3	35.4	35.4	35.1	35.0	34.8	34.7	34.7
2012	34.0	34.3	34.7	35.8	35.9	36.2	36.0	36.1	35.6	36.0	35.9	35.8	35.5
2013	35.4	35.6	35.8	36.2	36.4	36.7	36.8	36.5	36.1	35.9	35.8	35.7	36.1
2014	35.1	35.2	35.6	35.9	36.3	36.6	36.6	36.6	36.3	35.8	35.6	35.5	35.9
2015	35.3	35.3	35.6	35.6	36.0	36.3	36.3	36.3	35.9	36.0	36.0	36.0	35.9
2016	35.5	35.4	35.8	36.3	36.5	36.6	36.6	36.5	36.2	36.3	36.3	36.0	36.2
2017	35.8	35.9	36.2	36.3	36.4	36.8	37.0	36.8	36.4	36.3	36.3	36.2	36.4
Government													
2007	154.0	155.6	156.0	155.7	155.6	156.6	153.3	153.4	155.3	156.0	158.4	157.5	155.6
2008	155.9	158.1	158.6	157.4	158.0	159.3	155.5	155.7	157.4	159.4	161.7	160.2	158.1
2009	159.2	160.0	160.9	161.0	160.6	161.5	154.5	156.2	158.1	161.5	163.3	161.8	159.9
2010	160.7	161.6	162.3	162.9	165.1	164.3	157.5	158.0	160.8	162.1	162.5	162.1	161.7
2011	161.0	161.8	162.7	162.9	162.6	163.0	159.3	159.9	162.3	163.9	165.7	165.5	162.6
2012	163.0	164.1	163.6	163.7	163.4	163.7	158.9	159.2	161.3	163.4	164.9	164.1	162.8
2013	161.4	163.0	163.1	163.0	162.4	162.1	158.4	158.8	160.4	161.9	162.8	163.1	161.7
2014	160.0	160.8	161.2	161.5	160.6	160.0	156.8	157.7	159.0	159.6	160.8	161.0	159.9
2015	158.9	160.5	159.9	161.3	160.3	160.3	156.4	156.3	157.4	160.8	162.3	161.9	159.7
2016	158.6	160.4	161.3	161.2	160.3	160.4	156.2	156.6	159.0	161.1	162.4	162.3	160.0
2017	159.2	161.0	160.9	161.0	159.5	160.5	156.1	156.7	159.1	160.9	162.1	162.1	159.9

Employment by Industry: Providence-Warwick, RI-MA NECTA, Selected Years, 2007–2017

(Numbers in thousands, not seasonally adjusted)

Industry and year	January	February	March	April	May	June	July	August	September	October	November	December	Annual average
Total Nonfarm													
2007	572.5	573.1	575.8	583.8	590.7	592.7	580.7	581.6	586.1	585.8	585.9	584.9	582.8
2008	562.5	563.8	566.2	573.8	579.6	579.4	565.9	566.4	572.3	571.1	567.8	563.8	569.4
2009	538.4	538.7	537.7	542.2	548.5	548.3	536.0	536.0	543.4	545.1	545.0	543.3	541.9
2010	524.2	526.4	530.7	538.8	547.1	547.3	540.2	541.3	546.8	549.0	550.6	548.2	540.9
2011	527.8	531.0	533.5	544.9	550.7	552.6	543.4	542.7	550.0	552.9	553.2	550.5	544.4
2012	532.9	537.0	541.0	548.4	555.7	557.1	546.9	549.4	557.0	558.1	558.4	558.7	550.1
2013	539.9	541.2	545.5	555.0	563.2	566.9	556.9	557.9	565.1	568.9	568.5	566.6	558.0
2014	548.3	550.8	554.2	565.1	573.7	574.7	566.1	566.8	575.3	578.4	579.8	579.1	567.7
2015	558.4	556.3	561.0	573.0	582.4	583.7	576.8	575.0	581.8	586.8	588.1	587.4	575.9
2016	567.0	569.9	575.1	582.5	588.3	591.3	583.4	581.8	587.2	590.6	591.5	589.9	583.2
2017	571.7	574.0	576.8	585.5	593.3	598.0	589.5	590.0	594.3	598.7	598.9	596.2	588.9
Total Private													
2007	497.8	498.2	500.8	508.9	515.2	518.0	511.0	512.2	513.0	511.7	511.6	510.3	509.1
2008	488.6	489.6	491.8	499.4	504.3	505.1	498.0	499.2	500.9	498.6	494.5	490.7	496.7
2009	466.2	466.4	465.5	469.6	475.6	476.0	470.3	470.8	473.2	473.2	472.8	471.2	470.9
2010	452.7	454.9	458.5	466.6	472.9	474.8	473.9	475.2	477.2	477.7	478.5	476.4	469.9
2011	456.8	459.9	461.8	473.3	478.9	481.2	478.4	477.6	480.7	482.2	482.3	479.5	474.4
2012	462.7	466.4	470.3	477.5	484.0	486.9	482.2	484.4	487.8	487.4	487.1	487.5	480.4
2013	469.3	471.0	474.8	484.2	491.4	496.0	491.2	493.0	495.5	497.6	497.0	494.7	488.0
2014	477.5	479.8	483.0	493.6	501.2	503.1	500.4	501.7	505.0	506.9	507.6	507.3	497.3
2015	487.2	485.2	489.8	501.5	510.3	512.4	511.2	510.2	512.4	515.5	516.7	515.7	505.7
2016	495.9	498.8	503.3	511.1	516.3	519.7	517.2	516.2	517.0	518.9	519.3	517.9	512.6
2017	500.2	502.5	504.9	513.9	521.0	526.2	523.1	524.0	523.6	526.4	526.2	523.5	518.0
Goods Producing													
2007	92.3	90.9	91.3	92.5	94.1	95.1	92.7	94.9	94.6	93.0	92.1	90.6	92.8
2008	86.2	85.1	85.6	87.4	88.6	89.1	86.5	88.1	87.5	86.0	84.1	82.1	86.4
2009	76.2	74.1	73.0	73.8	74.3	74.5	72.9	73.5	73.2	72.7	72.1	71.0	73.4
2010	67.0	66.5	67.0	69.0	70.6	71.7	71.3	72.5	72.1	72.1	72.0	70.9	70.2
2011	67.2	66.6	67.1	69.5	70.7	71.8	71.3	72.1	71.7	71.7	71.4	70.4	70.1
2012	67.3	66.9	67.7	69.4	70.2	71.5	70.6	71.7	71.4	71.5	71.2	70.9	70.0
2013	67.5	66.7	67.9	69.6	71.2	72.2	71.1	72.6	72.6	72.5	72.6	71.7	70.7
2014	68.9	68.1	68.6	71.1	72.9	73.9	73.0	74.0	73.9	73.9	73.9	73.4	72.1
2015	70.3	69.0	69.7	72.0	73.7	74.6	74.6	75.3	74.9	75.1	75.3	74.8	73.3
2016	71.4	70.8	71.8	73.4	74.6	75.5	75.1	75.6	75.0	75.2	74.9	74.0	73.9
2017	71.2	70.7	71.0	73.4	74.5	75.7	75.4	76.1	75.6	75.7	77.1	76.5	74.4
Service-Providing													
2007	480.2	482.2	484.5	491.3	496.6	497.6	488.0	486.7	491.5	492.8	493.8	494.3	490.0
2008	476.3	478.7	480.6	486.4	491.0	490.3	479.4	478.3	484.8	485.1	483.7	481.7	483.0
2009	462.2	464.6	464.7	468.4	474.2	473.8	463.1	462.5	470.2	472.4	472.9	472.3	468.4
2010	457.2	459.9	463.7	469.8	476.5	475.6	468.9	468.8	474.7	476.9	478.6	477.3	470.7
2011	460.6	464.4	466.4	475.4	480.0	480.8	472.1	470.6	478.3	481.2	481.8	480.1	474.3
2012	465.6	470.1	473.3	479.0	485.5	485.6	476.3	477.7	485.6	486.6	487.2	487.8	480.0
2013	472.4	474.5	477.6	485.4	492.0	494.7	485.8	485.3	492.5	496.4	495.9	494.9	487.3
2014	479.4	482.7	485.6	494.0	500.8	500.8	493.1	492.8	501.4	504.5	505.9	505.7	495.6
2015	488.1	487.3	491.3	501.0	508.7	509.1	502.2	499.7	506.9	511.7	512.8	512.6	502.6
2016	495.6	499.1	503.3	509.1	513.7	515.8	508.3	506.2	512.2	515.4	516.6	515.9	509.3
2017	500.5	503.3	505.8	512.1	518.8	522.3	514.1	513.9	518.7	523.0	521.8	519.7	514.5
Mining and Logging													
2007	0.3	0.2	0.2	0.3	0.3	0.3	0.3	0.3	0.3	0.3	0.3	0.3	0.3
2008	0.2	0.2	0.2	0.2	0.3	0.3	0.3	0.3	0.3	0.3	0.3	0.3	0.3
2009	0.2	0.2	0.2	0.2	0.2	0.2	0.2	0.2	0.2	0.2	0.2	0.2	0.2
2010	0.1	0.1	0.1	0.2	0.2	0.2	0.2	0.2	0.2	0.2	0.2	0.2	0.2
2011	0.1	0.1	0.1	0.2	0.2	0.2	0.2	0.2	0.2	0.2	0.2	0.2	0.2
2012	0.1	0.1	0.1	0.2	0.2	0.2	0.2	0.2	0.2	0.2	0.2	0.2	0.2
2013	0.1	0.1	0.1	0.2	0.2	0.2	0.2	0.2	0.2	0.2	0.2	0.2	0.2
2014	0.1	0.1	0.1	0.2	0.2	0.2	0.2	0.2	0.2	0.2	0.2	0.2	0.2
2015	0.2	0.2	0.2	0.2	0.2	0.2	0.2	0.2	0.2	0.2	0.2	0.2	0.2
2016	0.2	0.2	0.2	0.2	0.2	0.2	0.2	0.2	0.2	0.2	0.2	0.2	0.2
2017	0.2	0.2	0.2	0.2	0.2	0.2	0.2	0.2	0.2	0.2	0.2	0.2	0.2

Employment by Industry: Providence-Warwick, RI-MA NECTA, Selected Years, 2007–2017—*Continued*

(Numbers in thousands, not seasonally adjusted)

Industry and year	January	February	March	April	May	June	July	August	September	October	November	December	Annual average
Construction													
2007	26.0	24.6	25.2	26.7	28.3	29.1	29.6	29.5	29.0	28.4	27.9	26.6	27.6
2008	23.2	22.6	23.1	25.1	26.2	26.9	27.2	27.1	26.8	25.8	24.9	23.4	25.2
2009	20.2	19.6	19.4	20.9	21.8	21.9	22.2	22.1	21.7	21.4	20.8	19.8	21.0
2010	16.8	16.3	16.8	18.8	20.1	20.7	21.4	21.6	21.0	20.8	20.6	19.5	19.5
2011	16.6	16.0	16.4	18.5	19.7	20.5	21.2	21.1	20.8	20.8	20.7	19.8	19.3
2012	17.6	17.0	17.8	19.3	19.9	20.8	21.2	21.1	20.8	20.8	20.5	20.1	19.7
2013	17.4	16.9	17.6	19.2	20.6	21.2	21.8	21.9	21.8	21.7	21.4	20.3	20.2
2014	18.2	17.5	17.9	20.0	21.4	22.0	22.4	22.3	22.2	22.2	22.0	21.3	20.8
2015	18.7	17.7	18.2	20.3	21.8	22.4	23.1	23.2	23.0	23.1	23.1	22.7	21.4
2016	20.2	19.6	20.4	22.2	23.4	23.9	24.4	24.5	24.3	24.3	23.9	22.9	22.8
2017	20.7	20.3	20.4	22.6	23.6	24.4	24.9	25.0	24.6	24.7	25.2	23.8	23.4
Manufacturing													
2007	66.0	66.1	65.9	65.5	65.5	65.7	62.8	65.1	65.3	64.3	63.9	63.7	65.0
2008	62.8	62.3	62.3	62.1	62.1	61.9	59.0	60.7	60.4	59.9	58.9	58.4	60.9
2009	55.8	54.3	53.4	52.7	52.3	52.4	50.5	51.2	51.3	51.1	51.1	51.0	52.3
2010	50.1	50.1	50.1	50.0	50.3	50.8	49.7	50.7	50.9	51.1	51.2	51.2	50.5
2011	50.5	50.5	50.6	50.8	50.8	51.1	49.9	50.8	50.7	50.7	50.5	50.4	50.6
2012	49.6	49.8	49.8	49.9	50.1	50.5	49.2	50.4	50.4	50.5	50.5	50.6	50.1
2013	50.0	49.7	50.2	50.2	50.4	50.8	49.1	50.5	50.6	50.6	51.0	51.2	50.4
2014	50.6	50.5	50.6	50.9	51.3	51.7	50.4	51.5	51.5	51.5	51.7	51.9	51.2
2015	51.4	51.1	51.3	51.5	51.7	52.0	51.3	51.9	51.7	51.8	52.0	51.9	51.6
2016	51.0	51.0	51.2	51.0	51.0	51.4	50.5	50.9	50.5	50.7	50.8	50.9	50.9
2017	50.3	50.2	50.4	50.6	50.7	51.1	50.3	50.9	50.8	50.8	51.7	52.5	50.9
Trade, Transportation, and Utilities													
2007	102.6	100.7	101.0	101.7	102.6	103.6	102.0	101.7	102.2	102.5	104.8	106.3	102.6
2008	100.5	98.8	98.7	99.1	100.0	100.7	99.1	99.2	99.5	99.7	100.4	100.8	99.7
2009	95.4	93.9	93.4	92.6	94.2	95.1	93.2	93.2	94.4	95.0	96.5	97.3	94.5
2010	93.5	92.6	93.1	92.5	93.2	94.4	93.2	93.4	94.3	95.2	96.9	97.8	94.2
2011	93.6	93.0	92.8	94.0	95.0	95.6	94.2	94.4	95.5	96.6	98.5	99.7	95.2
2012	95.5	94.3	94.5	94.9	96.2	97.0	94.9	95.2	96.3	97.0	99.0	99.5	96.2
2013	94.6	93.7	93.7	94.6	95.7	96.6	95.0	95.3	96.2	97.2	99.1	100.3	96.0
2014	95.8	95.1	94.9	95.8	96.9	97.8	96.1	96.3	97.5	99.0	101.2	102.7	97.4
2015	98.1	96.8	96.7	97.8	98.9	99.9	98.4	98.5	99.3	100.0	102.4	103.7	99.2
2016	99.0	98.3	98.1	98.3	99.2	100.0	98.6	98.5	99.3	101.0	103.8	105.3	100.0
2017	100.5	99.3	99.0	99.8	101.1	101.8	100.7	100.5	101.6	101.9	103.1	104.2	101.1
Wholesale Trade													
2007	21.4	21.2	21.2	21.5	21.5	21.6	21.6	21.5	21.3	21.3	21.4	21.5	21.4
2008	20.9	20.9	20.9	21.0	21.1	21.2	21.1	21.0	21.0	21.0	20.9	20.6	21.0
2009	20.2	20.0	20.0	19.9	20.0	20.1	19.8	19.8	19.9	20.0	19.9	19.9	20.0
2010	19.4	19.4	19.5	19.4	19.7	19.8	19.8	19.9	19.8	19.8	19.9	19.9	19.7
2011	19.5	19.6	19.2	19.3	19.5	19.6	19.7	19.7	19.7	19.8	19.8	20.0	19.6
2012	19.9	19.9	20.0	20.0	20.2	20.3	20.2	20.2	20.1	20.1	20.1	20.0	20.1
2013	19.8	19.7	19.9	19.9	20.0	20.1	20.0	20.1	20.0	20.1	20.2	20.1	20.0
2014	19.9	19.9	19.9	19.8	20.0	20.0	20.1	20.2	20.1	20.2	20.3	20.3	20.1
2015	20.1	20.1	20.1	20.2	20.3	20.3	20.3	20.3	20.1	20.0	20.2	20.2	20.2
2016	19.8	19.8	19.8	20.0	20.0	20.0	20.0	20.0	19.9	19.8	19.9	19.9	19.9
2017	19.7	19.7	19.7	19.8	19.9	20.0	20.0	19.9	19.8	20.1	19.9	19.4	19.8
Retail Trade													
2007	68.4	67.0	67.2	67.3	68.0	68.6	68.0	67.8	67.4	67.9	70.1	71.2	68.2
2008	66.9	65.3	65.2	65.2	65.7	66.2	65.5	65.5	64.9	65.5	66.5	66.9	65.8
2009	62.9	61.7	61.3	60.7	61.9	62.5	62.1	62.0	61.9	62.6	64.1	64.8	62.4
2010	62.2	61.2	61.6	60.8	61.0	61.8	61.8	62.0	61.6	62.4	64.0	64.7	62.1
2011	61.6	60.9	61.1	61.8	62.4	62.7	62.4	62.8	62.4	63.4	65.3	65.9	62.7
2012	62.6	61.5	61.6	61.9	62.7	63.2	62.6	62.7	62.7	63.4	65.4	65.7	63.0
2013	62.1	61.2	61.0	61.6	62.4	63.0	62.7	62.8	62.6	63.5	65.2	66.0	62.8
2014	62.8	62.1	61.9	62.7	63.4	63.9	63.4	63.3	63.3	64.7	66.6	67.6	63.8
2015	64.2	63.0	63.1	63.7	64.4	65.3	65.0	65.1	64.8	65.5	67.6	68.4	65.0
2016	65.2	64.4	64.4	64.3	64.9	65.3	65.1	65.1	64.6	65.1	66.8	67.2	65.2
2017	64.2	63.1	62.9	63.9	64.7	64.9	64.7	64.7	64.3	64.5	65.1	66.0	64.4

Employment by Industry: Providence-Warwick, RI-MA NECTA, Selected Years, 2007–2017—*Continued*

(Numbers in thousands, not seasonally adjusted)

Industry and year	January	February	March	April	May	June	July	August	September	October	November	December	Annual average
Transportation and Utilities													
2007	12.8	12.5	12.6	12.9	13.1	13.4	12.4	12.4	13.5	13.3	13.3	13.6	13.0
2008	12.7	12.6	12.6	12.9	13.2	13.3	12.5	12.7	13.6	13.2	13.0	13.3	13.0
2009	12.3	12.2	12.1	12.0	12.3	12.5	11.3	11.4	12.6	12.4	12.5	12.6	12.2
2010	11.9	12.0	12.0	12.3	12.5	12.8	11.6	11.5	12.9	13.0	13.0	13.2	12.4
2011	12.5	12.5	12.5	12.9	13.1	13.3	12.1	11.9	13.4	13.4	13.4	13.8	12.9
2012	13.0	12.9	12.9	13.0	13.3	13.5	12.1	12.3	13.5	13.5	13.5	13.8	13.1
2013	12.7	12.8	12.8	13.1	13.3	13.5	12.3	12.4	13.6	13.6	13.7	14.2	13.2
2014	13.1	13.1	13.1	13.3	13.5	13.9	12.6	12.8	14.1	14.1	14.3	14.8	13.6
2015	13.8	13.7	13.5	13.9	14.2	14.3	13.1	13.1	14.4	14.5	14.6	15.1	14.0
2016	14.0	14.1	13.9	14.0	14.3	14.7	13.5	13.4	14.8	16.1	17.1	18.2	14.8
2017	16.6	16.5	16.4	16.1	16.5	16.9	16.0	15.9	17.5	17.3	18.1	18.8	16.9
Information													
2007	10.4	10.3	10.3	10.4	10.5	10.6	10.6	10.7	10.6	10.6	10.8	10.8	10.6
2008	10.7	11.0	11.0	10.8	10.9	11.1	10.6	10.9	10.6	10.8	10.5	10.4	10.8
2009	10.4	10.3	10.2	10.2	10.2	10.1	9.8	9.8	9.7	9.5	9.7	9.7	10.0
2010	9.6	9.7	9.8	9.6	9.6	9.6	9.7	10.0	10.1	9.9	9.9	9.9	9.8
2011	9.4	9.3	9.4	9.9	10.1	10.0	9.8	8.8	9.5	9.4	9.5	9.6	9.6
2012	9.3	9.3	9.4	9.2	9.0	9.2	8.9	9.0	8.8	8.8	8.8	8.8	9.0
2013	8.8	8.8	8.6	8.4	8.6	8.6	8.4	8.5	8.3	8.3	8.4	8.4	8.5
2014	8.5	8.3	8.3	8.3	8.4	8.3	8.4	8.5	8.3	8.2	8.2	8.3	8.3
2015	8.0	7.9	8.0	8.1	8.1	7.9	8.0	7.9	8.0	8.1	7.3	7.2	7.9
2016	7.2	7.3	7.2	7.4	6.5	7.4	7.5	7.3	7.4	7.3	7.3	7.3	7.3
2017	7.3	7.5	7.4	7.4	7.5	7.6	7.3	7.4	7.3	7.1	7.3	7.3	7.4
Financial Activities													
2007	39.4	39.5	39.4	39.5	39.6	39.4	39.1	38.7	38.6	38.2	38.1	38.1	39.0
2008	37.7	37.8	37.6	37.4	37.5	37.4	37.5	37.3	37.4	36.5	36.3	36.3	37.2
2009	35.9	35.8	35.6	35.4	35.5	35.6	35.3	34.9	34.6	34.7	34.9	34.8	35.3
2010	34.3	34.3	34.5	34.4	34.6	34.7	34.8	34.7	34.8	35.0	35.1	35.2	34.7
2011	34.6	34.7	34.8	34.9	34.8	35.4	35.0	35.1	35.1	35.1	35.4	35.3	35.0
2012	35.1	35.3	35.5	35.6	35.9	36.1	36.1	36.0	36.1	36.1	36.2	36.2	35.9
2013	35.9	36.2	36.4	36.4	36.4	36.6	36.7	36.5	36.3	36.4	36.4	36.6	36.4
2014	36.2	36.1	36.2	36.6	36.7	36.9	37.0	36.8	36.7	36.7	36.7	36.7	36.6
2015	36.4	36.6	36.8	37.1	37.3	37.5	37.4	37.3	37.6	38.2	38.7	38.8	37.5
2016	37.9	38.1	38.2	38.0	38.0	38.4	38.4	38.4	38.3	38.3	38.4	38.4	38.2
2017	38.1	38.2	38.2	38.4	38.6	39.0	38.9	39.0	39.0	39.4	38.8	39.1	38.7
Professional and Business Services													
2007	60.6	60.3	60.7	63.0	63.5	64.6	63.4	63.4	63.1	62.7	62.5	62.2	62.5
2008	59.5	59.0	59.3	61.6	61.4	62.5	61.7	61.9	62.3	61.8	60.8	59.6	61.0
2009	56.9	56.8	56.8	58.2	58.1	58.8	58.1	58.5	58.7	58.5	58.3	57.5	57.9
2010	54.9	55.3	56.2	59.5	59.5	60.4	60.2	60.1	60.2	60.4	60.3	59.2	58.9
2011	56.9	57.3	57.5	59.7	59.9	60.4	60.2	60.7	61.3	61.3	61.2	59.7	59.7
2012	57.8	58.1	59.2	61.3	61.7	62.5	62.1	62.5	62.3	62.3	62.4	62.1	61.2
2013	59.9	60.4	60.8	63.6	64.3	65.8	64.9	65.7	65.8	66.7	66.3	65.5	64.1
2014	62.6	63.5	63.9	66.7	67.3	68.0	67.9	68.7	68.9	69.8	69.9	69.4	67.2
2015	64.9	65.1	65.6	69.0	70.2	70.6	70.7	70.6	70.4	71.1	71.5	70.9	69.2
2016	68.5	68.6	69.2	71.5	72.0	72.7	73.0	73.3	73.4	73.6	73.5	72.9	71.9
2017	70.3	71.0	71.1	73.5	73.9	75.1	75.6	75.9	75.5	77.5	76.3	75.3	74.3
Education and Health Services													
2007	111.5	115.1	115.7	116.0	115.9	111.6	110.0	109.9	113.7	116.2	117.1	116.4	114.1
2008	113.0	116.4	117.4	117.6	116.9	112.5	111.0	110.9	114.7	117.3	117.9	117.7	115.3
2009	113.8	117.3	117.9	117.7	117.4	113.6	112.3	112.4	116.0	118.6	119.2	119.1	116.3
2010	116.0	118.6	119.6	119.4	119.6	114.9	114.2	114.4	118.3	120.3	121.0	121.1	118.1
2011	116.9	120.2	120.7	121.8	121.8	117.2	116.0	115.2	119.0	122.1	122.1	121.4	119.5
2012	118.0	121.8	122.4	121.5	122.0	117.6	116.0	116.3	122.0	123.3	123.2	124.0	120.7
2013	120.9	123.2	123.8	123.9	123.6	120.4	119.1	118.8	123.3	125.7	125.9	124.4	122.8
2014	121.9	124.1	125.1	125.6	125.1	120.8	120.2	119.7	124.5	126.5	127.0	126.9	124.0
2015	123.4	124.6	126.0	126.6	126.1	122.6	121.8	120.8	125.3	127.7	128.2	127.5	125.1
2016	123.3	126.6	127.6	127.9	127.9	122.7	121.7	121.1	125.1	127.5	127.5	127.1	125.5
2017	124.0	126.3	127.9	128.1	128.0	124.7	122.9	122.7	126.5	128.8	129.6	129.2	126.6

Employment by Industry: Providence-Warwick, RI-MA NECTA, Selected Years, 2007–2017—*Continued*

(Numbers in thousands, not seasonally adjusted)

Industry and year	January	February	March	April	May	June	July	August	September	October	November	December	Annual average
Leisure and Hospitality													
2007	54.9	55.3	56.1	59.4	62.3	65.6	65.7	65.6	63.8	62.0	59.7	59.2	60.8
2008	55.1	55.6	56.1	59.3	62.6	65.0	64.5	64.1	62.8	60.3	58.5	57.8	60.1
2009	52.4	53.0	53.3	56.2	60.2	62.4	62.4	62.5	61.4	58.6	56.6	56.2	57.9
2010	52.6	52.9	53.3	57.1	60.3	63.3	64.0	63.7	62.0	59.5	57.9	56.9	58.6
2011	53.4	53.9	54.4	58.1	60.9	64.4	64.7	64.3	62.8	60.5	58.5	57.6	59.5
2012	54.6	55.5	56.3	59.7	62.9	66.2	66.4	66.4	64.4	62.3	60.1	59.6	61.2
2013	56.1	56.4	57.7	61.2	64.8	68.3	68.1	68.0	66.2	64.3	61.7	61.1	62.8
2014	57.6	58.4	59.5	62.9	66.8	69.5	69.4	69.4	68.0	65.9	63.7	62.8	64.5
2015	59.6	58.9	60.2	64.0	68.6	71.2	71.5	71.2	69.6	68.0	65.9	65.4	66.2
2016	61.7	62.2	64.0	67.1	70.3	74.2	73.6	73.0	71.0	68.7	66.5	65.4	68.1
2017	61.9	62.6	63.3	66.1	69.9	73.9	73.3	73.6	70.7	68.5	66.5	64.5	67.9
Other Services													
2007	26.1	26.1	26.3	26.4	26.7	27.5	27.5	27.3	26.4	26.5	26.5	26.7	26.7
2008	25.9	25.9	26.1	26.2	26.4	26.8	27.1	26.8	26.1	26.2	26.0	26.0	26.3
2009	25.2	25.2	25.3	25.5	25.7	25.9	26.3	26.0	25.2	25.6	25.5	25.6	25.6
2010	24.8	25.0	25.0	25.1	25.5	25.8	26.5	26.4	25.4	25.3	25.4	25.4	25.5
2011	24.8	24.9	25.1	25.4	25.7	26.4	27.2	27.0	25.8	25.5	25.7	25.8	25.8
2012	25.1	25.2	25.3	25.9	26.1	26.8	27.2	27.3	26.5	26.1	26.2	26.4	26.2
2013	25.6	25.6	25.9	26.5	26.8	27.5	27.9	27.6	26.8	26.5	26.6	26.7	26.7
2014	26.0	26.2	26.5	26.6	27.1	27.9	28.4	28.3	27.2	26.9	27.0	27.1	27.1
2015	26.5	26.3	26.8	26.9	27.4	28.1	28.8	28.6	27.3	27.3	27.4	27.4	27.4
2016	26.9	26.9	27.2	27.5	27.8	28.8	29.3	29.0	27.5	27.3	27.4	27.5	27.8
2017	26.9	26.9	27.0	27.2	27.5	28.4	29.0	28.8	27.4	27.5	27.5	27.4	27.6
Government													
2007	74.7	74.9	75.0	74.9	75.5	74.7	69.7	69.4	73.1	74.1	74.3	74.6	73.7
2008	73.9	74.2	74.4	74.4	75.3	74.3	67.9	67.2	71.4	72.5	73.3	73.1	72.7
2009	72.2	72.3	72.2	72.6	72.9	72.3	65.7	65.2	70.2	71.9	72.2	72.1	71.0
2010	71.5	71.5	72.2	72.2	74.2	72.5	66.3	66.1	69.6	71.3	72.1	71.8	70.9
2011	71.0	71.1	71.7	71.6	71.8	71.4	65.0	65.1	69.3	70.7	70.9	71.0	70.1
2012	70.2	70.6	70.7	70.9	71.7	70.2	64.7	65.0	69.2	70.7	71.3	71.2	69.7
2013	70.6	70.2	70.7	70.8	71.8	70.9	65.7	64.9	69.6	71.3	71.5	71.9	70.0
2014	70.8	71.0	71.2	71.5	72.5	71.6	65.7	65.1	70.3	71.5	72.2	71.8	70.4
2015	71.2	71.1	71.2	71.5	72.1	71.3	65.6	64.8	69.4	71.3	71.4	71.7	70.2
2016	71.1	71.1	71.8	71.4	72.0	71.6	66.2	65.6	70.2	71.7	72.2	72.0	70.6
2017	71.5	71.5	71.9	71.6	72.3	71.8	66.4	66.0	70.7	72.3	72.7	72.7	71.0

Employment by Industry: Milwaukee-Waukesha-West Allis, WI, Selected Years, 2007–2017

(Numbers in thousands, not seasonally adjusted)

Industry and year	January	February	March	April	May	June	July	August	September	October	November	December	Annual average
Total Nonfarm													
2007	847.0	846.7	849.7	856.8	865.7	875.0	863.0	865.8	864.3	866.5	867.5	867.6	861.3
2008	847.6	846.9	850.1	857.1	864.0	869.0	859.1	858.9	859.9	860.7	856.8	851.6	856.8
2009	824.2	818.9	814.0	816.9	820.6	822.9	809.9	809.3	814.0	815.0	813.1	811.4	815.9
2010	793.3	792.8	795.5	804.2	812.0	813.5	811.0	812.7	811.0	817.9	820.1	817.5	808.5
2011	798.8	800.6	804.3	811.9	816.3	820.1	817.6	819.0	818.7	819.3	822.3	818.7	814.0
2012	799.7	803.0	809.8	815.8	825.4	828.4	821.9	824.8	826.2	830.9	835.2	832.3	821.1
2013	809.0	816.6	820.7	826.3	835.9	840.2	835.6	837.5	842.1	843.0	846.3	846.2	833.3
2014	822.2	829.1	830.9	837.2	843.9	851.8	846.2	853.7	852.5	853.7	859.5	858.1	844.9
2015	831.2	839.3	842.5	852.0	859.3	865.0	859.2	864.7	862.0	865.7	867.5	867.3	856.3
2016	845.9	852.6	854.2	864.0	866.2	869.8	865.6	870.8	867.8	868.9	871.2	868.9	863.8
2017	847.8	854.5	860.1	863.4	869.4	874.9	869.5	873.1	868.8	872.4	874.8	870.4	866.6
Total Private													
2007	756.9	755.0	757.7	764.2	772.7	781.4	778.0	780.9	772.8	774.3	775.3	774.6	770.3
2008	756.4	755.6	756.4	763.8	769.7	774.8	773.2	774.3	766.4	765.6	759.9	756.0	764.3
2009	731.0	723.9	719.1	721.6	726.0	729.3	726.3	726.7	722.5	722.0	720.0	718.2	723.9
2010	701.6	701.2	703.5	712.6	718.0	722.2	726.1	728.7	723.0	727.6	728.3	727.4	718.4
2011	709.9	707.8	712.0	720.3	725.3	729.4	730.4	732.4	730.8	732.8	733.8	729.9	724.6
2012	713.9	715.8	721.0	725.7	734.4	739.1	738.6	739.8	739.4	742.3	744.0	743.4	733.1
2013	724.3	728.5	732.6	738.3	748.2	752.9	753.8	754.1	754.7	755.3	758.4	758.6	746.6
2014	737.2	741.9	743.3	749.8	756.7	764.0	764.2	767.6	765.0	766.3	770.7	770.8	758.1
2015	748.1	751.8	755.2	763.7	771.7	778.2	776.9	780.8	775.1	778.6	780.5	779.9	770.0
2016	760.4	765.0	766.6	775.0	778.6	783.8	784.9	786.5	781.1	780.6	781.4	780.2	777.0
2017	763.1	766.8	772.4	774.9	781.8	789.2	788.8	789.4	782.8	784.0	785.9	781.9	780.1
Goods Producing													
2007	166.1	163.9	165.1	167.5	170.2	172.7	172.3	172.9	170.9	170.7	169.8	168.1	169.2
2008	164.5	163.4	163.9	165.4	167.3	168.9	167.8	168.0	165.3	164.5	162.5	159.4	165.1
2009	153.5	149.7	146.5	145.7	145.4	145.7	144.1	144.3	143.3	142.4	140.8	138.6	145.0
2010	135.2	133.6	134.0	136.7	137.9	140.4	142.2	142.9	141.5	141.7	140.8	139.1	138.8
2011	136.6	135.9	137.0	140.1	141.7	144.8	145.8	146.2	144.6	144.4	144.1	142.4	142.0
2012	139.7	139.1	140.1	142.3	143.6	146.6	147.4	147.0	145.4	145.3	144.6	143.7	143.7
2013	141.5	141.0	141.6	143.2	145.7	148.3	148.8	149.4	147.5	147.6	147.1	145.1	145.6
2014	142.6	142.4	143.5	145.4	147.6	149.9	151.9	152.3	150.8	149.9	149.9	148.6	147.9
2015	146.2	145.7	146.7	148.5	150.2	152.5	153.2	153.1	151.3	150.8	150.2	149.1	149.8
2016	146.3	145.9	146.4	148.2	149.2	151.4	152.0	152.0	150.0	149.5	149.0	147.5	149.0
2017	145.1	145.2	146.0	147.6	149.3	151.7	152.4	152.1	150.4	151.1	150.7	147.6	149.1
Service-Providing													
2007	680.9	682.8	684.6	689.3	695.5	702.3	690.7	692.9	693.4	695.8	697.7	699.5	692.1
2008	683.1	683.5	686.2	691.7	696.7	700.1	691.3	690.9	694.6	696.2	694.3	692.2	691.7
2009	670.7	669.2	667.5	671.2	675.2	677.2	665.8	665.0	670.7	672.6	672.3	672.8	670.9
2010	658.1	659.2	661.5	667.5	674.1	673.1	668.8	669.8	669.5	676.2	679.3	678.4	669.6
2011	662.2	664.7	667.3	671.8	674.6	675.3	671.8	672.8	674.1	674.9	678.2	676.3	672.0
2012	660.0	663.9	669.7	673.5	681.8	681.8	674.5	677.8	680.8	685.6	690.6	688.6	677.4
2013	667.5	675.6	679.1	683.1	690.2	691.9	686.8	688.1	694.6	695.4	699.2	701.1	687.7
2014	679.6	686.7	687.4	691.8	696.3	701.9	694.3	701.4	701.7	703.8	709.6	709.5	697.0
2015	685.0	693.6	695.8	703.5	709.1	712.5	706.0	711.6	710.7	714.9	717.3	718.2	706.5
2016	699.6	706.7	707.8	715.8	717.0	718.4	713.6	718.8	717.8	719.4	722.2	721.4	714.9
2017	702.7	709.3	714.1	715.8	720.1	723.2	717.1	721.0	718.4	721.3	724.1	722.8	717.5
Mining and Logging													
2007	0.5	0.4	0.5	0.5	0.5	0.5	0.5	0.5	0.5	0.5	0.5	0.5	0.5
2008	0.4	0.4	0.4	0.4	0.4	0.4	0.4	0.4	0.4	0.4	0.4	0.4	0.4
2009	0.3	0.3	0.3	0.4	0.4	0.4	0.4	0.4	0.4	0.4	0.4	0.3	0.4
2010	0.3	0.3	0.3	0.4	0.4	0.4	0.4	0.4	0.4	0.4	0.3	0.3	0.4
2011	0.3	0.3	0.3	0.3	0.3	0.4	0.4	0.4	0.4	0.4	0.4	0.3	0.4
2012	0.3	0.3	0.3	0.4	0.4	0.4	0.4	0.4	0.4	0.4	0.4	0.3	0.4
2013	0.3	0.3	0.3	0.4	0.4	0.4	0.4	0.4	0.4	0.4	0.4	0.4	0.4
2014	0.3	0.3	0.3	0.4	0.4	0.4	0.5	0.4	0.4	0.4	0.4	0.4	0.4
2015	0.4	0.4	0.4	0.4	0.5	0.5	0.5	0.5	0.5	0.5	0.5	0.4	0.5
2016	0.4	0.4	0.4	0.4	0.5	0.5	0.5	0.5	0.5	0.5	0.5	0.4	0.5
2017	0.4	0.4	0.4	0.4	0.4	0.5	0.5	0.5	0.5	0.5	0.5	0.4	0.5

Employment by Industry: Milwaukee-Waukesha-West Allis, WI, Selected Years, 2007–2017—*Continued*

(Numbers in thousands, not seasonally adjusted)

Industry and year	January	February	March	April	May	June	July	August	September	October	November	December	Annual average
Construction													
2007	32.2	30.8	32.6	34.1	36.4	37.8	38.2	38.2	37.4	37.1	36.5	34.3	35.5
2008	31.3	30.5	31.2	32.9	35.3	36.2	36.4	36.2	35.1	35.3	33.9	31.7	33.8
2009	27.9	27.2	27.0	28.7	30.0	30.8	31.1	30.9	30.0	29.5	28.5	26.2	29.0
2010	23.3	22.5	22.8	25.2	26.2	27.4	27.9	28.2	27.5	27.2	26.2	24.2	25.7
2011	21.6	21.0	21.6	23.8	25.2	26.4	26.7	26.8	26.4	26.2	25.6	23.6	24.6
2012	20.8	20.5	21.2	23.1	24.2	25.4	25.8	25.7	25.3	25.2	24.7	23.4	23.8
2013	21.6	21.6	22.1	23.1	25.8	26.9	27.8	28.3	27.7	27.7	27.2	25.2	25.4
2014	23.2	23.0	23.8	25.6	27.6	28.8	29.7	30.2	29.8	29.4	29.0	27.5	27.3
2015	25.3	25.0	25.7	27.7	29.3	30.4	30.9	30.9	30.2	30.2	29.7	28.6	28.7
2016	26.4	26.4	27.0	28.7	29.9	31.2	31.7	31.8	31.3	31.0	30.7	29.0	29.6
2017	27.4	27.4	28.0	29.8	31.4	32.5	33.1	33.0	32.3	31.9	31.5	28.7	30.6
Manufacturing													
2007	133.4	132.7	132.0	132.0	133.3	134.4	133.6	134.2	133.0	133.1	132.8	133.3	133.2
2008	132.8	132.5	132.3	132.1	131.6	132.3	131.0	131.4	129.8	128.8	128.2	127.3	130.8
2009	125.3	122.2	119.2	116.6	115.0	114.5	112.6	113.0	112.9	112.5	111.9	112.1	115.7
2010	111.6	110.8	110.9	111.1	111.3	112.6	113.9	114.3	113.6	114.1	114.3	114.6	112.8
2011	114.7	114.6	115.1	116.0	116.2	118.0	118.7	119.0	117.8	117.8	118.1	118.5	117.0
2012	118.6	118.3	118.6	118.8	119.0	120.8	121.2	120.9	119.7	119.7	119.5	120.0	119.6
2013	119.6	119.1	119.2	119.7	119.5	121.0	120.6	120.7	119.4	119.5	119.5	119.5	119.8
2014	119.1	119.1	119.4	119.4	119.6	120.7	121.7	121.7	120.6	120.1	120.5	120.7	120.2
2015	120.5	120.3	120.6	120.4	120.4	121.6	121.8	121.7	120.6	120.1	120.0	120.1	120.7
2016	119.5	119.1	119.0	119.1	118.8	119.7	119.8	119.7	118.2	118.0	117.8	118.1	118.9
2017	117.3	117.4	117.6	117.4	117.5	118.7	118.8	118.6	117.6	118.7	118.7	118.5	118.1
Trade, Transportation, and Utilities													
2007	156.7	154.6	154.6	154.5	156.5	157.2	155.3	155.4	155.0	155.8	158.6	159.5	156.1
2008	154.3	152.0	152.1	153.1	153.7	154.2	153.2	153.2	152.3	152.7	153.5	153.8	153.2
2009	147.4	145.0	144.2	143.4	145.0	145.9	143.3	142.9	143.4	145.3	145.8	146.2	144.8
2010	140.9	138.6	138.8	139.1	140.5	141.2	139.9	140.3	140.7	143.9	145.0	145.8	141.2
2011	140.9	139.3	140.1	140.9	141.6	141.9	141.5	141.8	142.5	144.7	146.0	146.3	142.3
2012	142.0	140.3	140.6	139.8	142.4	143.0	141.9	142.4	142.6	144.2	146.9	147.4	142.8
2013	141.8	140.7	141.0	141.7	143.6	144.5	143.2	143.3	143.4	144.3	146.8	148.2	143.5
2014	142.3	141.4	142.1	143.0	144.1	145.6	143.9	144.4	143.5	144.4	147.3	148.3	144.2
2015	143.0	141.6	141.9	142.6	144.1	144.5	144.6	145.6	144.9	146.2	148.9	149.0	144.8
2016	144.3	143.6	143.9	144.9	145.5	146.1	146.0	146.4	145.0	146.3	148.6	149.4	145.8
2017	145.3	144.0	144.4	144.2	145.8	145.7	146.0	146.8	145.2	146.1	148.0	147.4	145.7
Wholesale Trade													
2007	43.0	43.1	43.1	43.2	43.4	44.0	44.0	43.9	43.5	43.5	43.4	43.5	43.5
2008	42.8	42.9	42.9	43.0	43.0	43.1	43.2	43.1	42.5	42.1	42.2	41.8	42.7
2009	41.1	40.8	40.3	39.8	39.7	39.7	39.4	39.0	38.6	38.6	38.4	38.3	39.5
2010	37.5	37.4	37.3	37.2	37.4	37.6	37.9	37.9	37.5	37.9	37.8	37.8	37.6
2011	37.3	37.3	37.5	37.7	37.8	38.0	38.6	38.5	38.2	38.7	38.6	38.4	38.1
2012	38.1	38.2	38.4	38.5	38.7	39.0	39.0	38.9	38.5	38.7	38.7	38.8	38.6
2013	38.2	38.1	38.1	38.2	38.4	38.6	38.6	38.6	38.3	38.1	38.0	38.2	38.3
2014	37.7	37.7	37.9	38.1	38.2	38.6	38.5	38.5	38.1	38.1	38.2	38.4	38.2
2015	38.1	38.0	38.2	38.4	38.6	39.0	39.1	39.2	38.6	38.7	38.8	38.8	38.6
2016	38.4	38.5	38.6	38.5	38.6	38.8	39.0	39.0	38.5	38.4	38.4	38.6	38.6
2017	38.4	38.4	38.6	38.6	38.7	39.1	39.2	39.3	38.8	39.4	39.3	38.7	38.9
Retail Trade													
2007	83.5	81.3	81.3	80.7	82.1	82.2	81.9	81.7	80.3	81.0	83.6	84.4	82.0
2008	81.4	79.1	79.3	79.8	80.4	80.8	80.9	80.8	79.4	80.1	81.2	81.8	80.4
2009	77.7	75.7	75.6	75.4	76.5	77.4	76.8	76.8	76.2	77.8	78.6	78.9	77.0
2010	75.6	73.7	74.1	74.5	75.5	75.8	75.5	75.8	75.4	77.7	78.7	79.3	76.0
2011	75.8	74.2	74.7	75.3	75.7	76.2	76.1	76.6	76.1	77.8	79.1	79.7	76.4
2012	76.4	74.6	74.8	74.8	75.9	76.6	76.5	77.0	76.6	77.9	80.5	80.7	76.9
2013	76.8	75.8	76.0	76.7	78.0	78.8	78.7	78.8	78.2	79.2	81.4	82.4	78.4
2014	78.3	77.3	77.8	78.3	79.0	80.0	79.7	79.9	78.4	79.0	81.6	82.1	79.3
2015	78.3	77.1	77.2	77.5	78.4	79.5	79.7	80.3	79.2	80.3	82.7	82.6	79.4
2016	79.7	78.9	79.1	79.8	80.3	81.1	81.5	81.6	79.8	80.9	82.9	83.2	80.7
2017	80.8	79.4	79.5	79.7	80.4	80.9	81.3	81.5	79.6	79.7	81.5	81.1	80.5

Employment by Industry: Milwaukee-Waukesha-West Allis, WI, Selected Years, 2007–2017—*Continued*

(Numbers in thousands, not seasonally adjusted)

Industry and year	January	February	March	April	May	June	July	August	September	October	November	December	Annual average
Transportation and Utilities													
2007	30.2	30.2	30.2	30.6	31.0	31.0	29.4	29.8	31.2	31.3	31.6	31.6	30.7
2008	30.1	30.0	29.9	30.3	30.3	30.3	29.1	29.3	30.4	30.5	30.1	30.2	30.0
2009	28.6	28.5	28.3	28.2	28.8	28.8	27.1	27.1	28.6	28.9	28.8	29.0	28.4
2010	27.8	27.5	27.4	27.4	27.6	27.8	26.5	26.6	27.8	28.3	28.5	28.7	27.7
2011	27.8	27.8	27.9	27.9	28.1	27.7	26.8	26.7	28.2	28.2	28.3	28.2	27.8
2012	27.5	27.5	27.4	26.5	27.8	27.4	26.4	26.5	27.5	27.6	27.7	27.9	27.3
2013	26.8	26.8	26.9	26.8	27.2	27.1	25.9	25.9	26.9	27.0	27.4	27.6	26.9
2014	26.3	26.4	26.4	26.6	26.9	27.0	25.7	26.0	27.0	27.3	27.5	27.8	26.7
2015	26.6	26.5	26.5	26.7	27.1	27.0	25.8	26.1	27.1	27.2	27.4	27.6	26.8
2016	26.2	26.2	26.2	26.6	26.6	26.2	25.5	25.8	26.7	27.0	27.3	27.6	26.5
2017	26.1	26.2	26.3	25.9	26.7	25.7	25.5	26.0	26.8	27.0	27.2	27.6	26.4
Information													
2007	17.6	17.6	17.6	17.6	17.6	17.8	17.7	17.7	17.5	17.5	17.7	17.6	17.6
2008	17.2	17.3	17.2	17.6	17.6	17.9	17.7	17.6	17.5	17.4	17.4	17.5	17.5
2009	17.1	17.1	16.9	16.8	16.7	16.7	16.6	16.6	16.4	16.3	16.4	16.3	16.7
2010	15.8	15.7	15.7	15.7	15.6	15.8	16.0	15.9	15.7	15.4	15.9	15.8	15.8
2011	15.7	15.7	15.6	15.6	15.6	15.6	15.5	15.6	15.5	15.4	15.4	15.3	15.5
2012	15.1	15.0	14.9	14.9	14.8	15.0	15.0	15.0	14.9	15.0	15.0	14.8	15.0
2013	14.8	14.7	14.6	14.9	15.0	15.0	15.0	15.0	14.9	14.7	14.8	14.6	14.8
2014	14.4	14.5	14.5	14.5	14.5	14.5	14.7	14.6	14.4	14.5	14.6	14.6	14.5
2015	14.4	14.3	14.2	14.2	14.3	14.4	14.3	14.4	14.3	14.5	14.6	14.6	14.4
2016	14.4	14.4	14.4	14.3	14.2	14.3	14.2	14.1	13.9	13.9	13.9	13.9	14.2
2017	14.0	14.0	13.9	13.7	13.7	13.8	13.7	13.5	13.3	13.3	13.2	13.2	13.6
Financial Activities													
2007	56.4	56.5	56.2	56.6	56.8	57.3	57.3	57.0	56.3	56.7	56.9	57.1	56.8
2008	56.5	56.7	56.3	56.6	57.0	57.0	57.5	57.4	56.3	56.7	56.6	56.6	56.8
2009	56.0	55.8	55.5	56.0	55.9	55.9	56.1	56.0	54.9	55.2	55.1	54.8	55.6
2010	54.0	54.0	54.2	54.1	54.0	54.1	54.3	54.2	53.7	53.8	53.7	54.0	54.0
2011	52.9	52.8	52.9	52.9	52.9	53.3	53.2	52.9	52.7	52.5	52.5	51.9	52.8
2012	51.9	51.8	51.9	51.8	52.0	52.4	52.5	52.4	51.7	51.9	51.7	51.9	52.0
2013	51.4	51.3	51.4	51.8	51.9	52.4	53.0	52.5	52.1	52.1	51.9	52.1	52.0
2014	51.1	51.1	51.3	51.3	51.5	52.1	52.3	52.4	51.7	51.7	51.8	52.1	51.7
2015	51.7	51.5	51.7	51.9	52.1	52.7	53.0	52.7	51.7	51.5	51.3	51.6	52.0
2016	51.0	50.8	51.0	50.9	50.9	51.5	51.9	51.7	51.2	51.2	51.1	51.1	51.2
2017	51.2	51.2	51.5	51.5	51.5	51.8	52.0	52.0	51.1	50.5	50.7	50.6	51.3
Professional and Business Services													
2007	112.4	113.1	113.8	115.2	115.8	118.4	117.9	119.7	118.3	118.1	118.3	118.5	116.6
2008	115.2	116.0	114.9	116.5	116.8	118.2	118.2	119.0	118.3	116.8	114.8	113.6	116.5
2009	107.8	105.6	103.9	104.3	104.4	104.9	105.4	105.1	104.4	105.7	105.9	106.2	105.3
2010	102.5	103.8	102.8	106.4	107.0	108.5	111.0	112.5	112.0	113.4	114.4	114.6	109.1
2011	111.5	111.7	113.0	113.0	112.6	115.2	115.1	116.5	116.4	115.9	116.7	115.6	114.4
2012	113.9	114.7	116.3	116.6	117.5	119.7	119.1	120.0	121.0	121.4	121.9	120.9	118.6
2013	117.3	119.0	121.1	120.4	121.5	123.1	123.9	124.0	124.9	124.0	125.0	125.4	122.5
2014	120.6	121.8	121.2	121.4	122.9	124.2	124.3	126.2	126.0	126.7	127.3	126.3	124.1
2015	120.8	121.6	120.8	123.2	124.3	125.9	126.8	128.5	127.1	128.0	127.8	126.5	125.1
2016	124.0	124.9	124.3	126.2	125.8	127.3	128.3	129.0	128.4	127.6	127.5	127.2	126.7
2017	122.9	123.2	125.1	124.9	125.5	127.3	128.2	128.5	127.6	129.1	129.5	129.3	126.8
Education and Health Services													
2007	137.6	139.0	139.2	139.5	139.9	139.4	138.7	139.6	141.0	141.7	142.1	142.2	140.0
2008	140.1	141.5	142.1	142.5	142.8	141.7	140.8	141.6	142.5	144.8	144.9	145.3	142.6
2009	142.6	144.0	144.4	145.3	145.6	145.2	144.5	145.1	146.1	147.8	148.0	148.0	145.6
2010	146.2	147.9	148.9	148.4	148.3	146.4	146.0	145.6	145.7	147.5	147.8	147.7	147.2
2011	144.1	144.9	145.2	146.1	146.6	143.3	142.1	141.6	145.4	147.3	147.9	148.0	145.2
2012	143.1	146.4	147.9	148.8	149.1	145.8	144.3	145.2	149.0	151.7	152.0	152.4	148.0
2013	147.8	151.7	151.9	153.0	152.9	150.2	148.8	149.7	154.0	156.8	157.3	157.4	152.6
2014	153.2	157.1	157.4	158.0	157.5	155.3	154.1	155.2	159.0	161.0	162.2	162.6	157.7
2015	156.8	161.5	162.5	162.9	163.2	160.5	158.8	159.6	163.3	165.9	166.5	167.6	162.4
2016	162.0	166.5	167.0	167.9	167.4	164.8	163.4	163.7	167.8	169.0	169.6	169.2	166.5
2017	164.0	168.2	168.9	169.1	168.2	166.9	164.8	165.4	169.0	170.9	170.3	171.1	168.1

Employment by Industry: Milwaukee-Waukesha-West Allis, WI, Selected Years, 2007–2017—*Continued*

(Numbers in thousands, not seasonally adjusted)

Industry and year	January	February	March	April	May	June	July	August	September	October	November	December	Annual average
Leisure and Hospitality													
2007	69.0	69.0	69.8	71.1	74.0	76.0	76.6	76.7	72.5	71.4	69.7	69.3	72.1
2008	66.9	66.7	67.8	69.5	71.8	73.7	74.8	74.5	71.8	69.8	67.6	67.2	70.2
2009	65.2	65.3	66.1	67.8	70.3	71.6	72.6	72.7	70.1	67.4	65.8	65.6	68.4
2010	63.3	63.4	64.4	67.1	69.9	70.7	71.7	72.4	69.6	68.0	67.0	66.7	67.9
2011	65.0	64.5	65.1	68.2	70.7	71.6	73.3	74.0	70.7	69.4	68.3	67.4	69.0
2012	66.2	66.6	67.4	69.6	72.9	73.8	75.8	75.4	72.8	70.6	69.8	70.1	70.9
2013	68.2	68.6	69.3	71.1	75.2	76.5	78.1	77.4	75.2	73.4	73.0	73.1	73.3
2014	71.1	71.6	71.2	73.3	75.6	78.4	78.7	78.0	75.2	73.8	73.2	73.6	74.5
2015	70.8	71.0	72.3	75.0	77.9	80.7	79.8	80.6	76.8	76.2	75.8	75.7	76.1
2016	73.3	73.9	74.3	76.7	79.7	82.1	82.4	82.9	78.5	77.0	75.7	75.8	77.7
2017	74.8	75.1	76.5	77.6	81.2	84.7	84.6	84.0	79.5	76.2	77.1	76.6	79.0
Other Services													
2007	41.1	41.3	41.4	42.2	41.9	42.6	42.2	41.9	41.3	42.4	42.2	42.3	41.9
2008	41.7	42.0	42.1	42.6	42.7	43.2	43.2	43.0	42.4	42.9	42.6	42.6	42.6
2009	41.4	41.4	41.6	42.3	42.7	43.4	43.7	44.0	43.9	41.9	42.2	42.5	42.6
2010	43.7	44.2	44.7	45.1	44.8	45.1	45.0	44.9	44.1	43.9	43.7	43.7	44.4
2011	43.2	43.0	43.1	43.5	43.6	43.7	43.9	43.8	43.0	43.2	42.9	43.0	43.3
2012	42.0	41.9	41.9	41.9	42.1	42.8	42.6	42.4	42.0	42.2	42.1	42.2	42.2
2013	41.5	41.5	41.7	42.2	42.4	42.9	43.0	42.8	42.7	42.4	42.5	42.7	42.4
2014	41.9	42.0	42.1	42.9	43.0	44.0	44.3	44.5	44.2	44.3	44.4	44.7	43.5
2015	44.4	44.6	45.1	45.4	45.6	46.0	46.4	46.3	45.7	45.5	45.4	45.8	45.5
2016	45.1	45.0	45.3	45.9	45.9	46.3	46.7	46.7	46.3	46.1	46.0	46.1	46.0
2017	45.8	45.9	46.1	46.3	46.6	47.3	47.1	47.1	46.7	46.8	46.4	46.1	46.5
Government													
2007	90.1	91.7	92.0	92.6	93.0	93.6	85.0	84.9	91.5	92.2	92.2	93.0	91.0
2008	91.2	91.3	93.7	93.3	94.3	94.2	85.9	84.6	93.5	95.1	96.9	95.6	92.5
2009	93.2	95.0	94.9	95.3	94.6	93.6	83.6	82.6	91.5	93.0	93.1	93.2	92.0
2010	91.7	91.6	92.0	91.6	94.0	91.3	84.9	84.0	88.0	90.3	91.8	90.1	90.1
2011	88.9	92.8	92.3	91.6	91.0	90.7	87.2	86.6	87.9	86.5	88.5	88.8	89.4
2012	85.8	87.2	88.8	90.1	91.0	89.3	83.3	85.0	86.8	88.6	91.2	88.9	88.0
2013	84.7	88.1	88.1	88.0	87.7	87.3	81.8	83.4	87.4	87.7	87.9	87.6	86.6
2014	85.0	87.2	87.6	87.4	87.2	87.8	82.0	86.1	87.5	87.4	88.8	87.3	86.8
2015	83.1	87.5	87.3	88.3	87.6	86.8	82.3	83.9	86.9	87.1	87.0	87.4	86.3
2016	85.5	87.6	87.6	89.0	87.6	86.0	80.7	84.3	86.7	88.3	89.8	88.7	86.8
2017	84.7	87.7	87.7	88.5	87.6	85.7	80.7	83.7	86.0	88.4	88.9	88.5	86.5

Employment by Industry: Jacksonville, FL, Selected Years, 2007–2017

(Numbers in thousands, not seasonally adjusted)

Industry and year	January	February	March	April	May	June	July	August	September	October	November	December	Annual average
Total Nonfarm													
2007	625.5	628.8	634.7	634.0	636.2	631.0	623.5	629.9	628.9	629.7	634.7	634.9	631.0
2008	623.6	626.7	628.0	627.3	627.8	619.1	610.9	613.4	612.7	611.4	612.8	610.2	618.7
2009	592.6	592.3	591.7	588.2	587.6	580.0	574.4	576.6	575.7	579.1	582.9	582.7	583.7
2010	571.1	573.7	576.9	579.0	583.1	576.3	575.1	578.2	580.0	585.5	589.6	590.8	579.9
2011	580.4	583.9	588.5	589.8	590.0	583.0	578.7	583.3	584.9	587.6	591.2	592.8	586.2
2012	584.5	589.0	593.4	595.7	597.9	593.0	588.4	593.7	594.1	598.5	602.7	604.2	594.6
2013	592.1	599.3	603.8	605.9	607.9	604.1	603.8	609.7	610.7	614.7	620.3	623.1	608.0
2014	608.9	613.7	617.6	621.5	624.2	619.4	617.7	624.7	624.2	634.2	639.0	643.6	624.1
2015	630.0	636.9	641.4	643.8	645.8	641.5	640.9	646.8	647.1	656.1	660.8	663.5	646.2
2016	651.2	656.4	660.6	666.4	668.3	662.5	665.4	671.5	673.8	676.6	684.9	685.7	668.6
2017	675.8	680.5	683.1	688.1	691.1	685.8	685.9	692.2	684.2	697.3	705.0	707.9	689.7
Total Private													
2007	549.9	552.2	557.9	557.0	559.0	558.0	552.8	553.4	552.0	552.3	556.5	556.8	554.8
2008	546.6	548.8	550.0	549.8	550.1	546.1	539.3	537.5	535.7	534.0	534.1	532.1	542.0
2009	516.3	514.9	514.2	510.6	509.7	506.9	502.0	500.7	499.1	501.8	505.4	505.7	507.3
2010	494.1	496.2	499.5	501.1	502.7	502.2	501.5	502.2	503.1	507.8	511.3	513.0	502.9
2011	502.6	505.7	510.3	511.6	512.0	509.6	506.5	507.6	509.0	511.1	514.5	516.1	509.7
2012	509.0	512.5	516.8	520.3	522.5	521.9	517.8	519.9	519.4	522.8	527.0	528.9	519.9
2013	518.1	523.9	528.4	530.5	532.6	533.7	534.3	536.8	537.0	540.4	545.4	548.1	534.1
2014	536.1	539.1	542.8	546.3	549.2	549.2	548.0	551.5	550.0	559.4	564.0	568.2	550.3
2015	556.9	561.6	565.8	568.2	570.5	570.9	570.7	572.9	572.3	580.3	584.6	587.1	571.8
2016	576.4	580.3	584.1	589.9	591.9	590.7	593.7	596.3	597.3	600.2	608.0	608.2	593.1
2017	600.3	603.3	605.5	610.7	613.4	612.6	613.6	616.2	607.3	620.3	627.6	629.9	613.4
Goods Producing													
2007	82.7	82.6	83.5	82.5	83.6	84.5	83.9	84.0	83.1	81.6	81.5	81.2	82.9
2008	78.8	79.1	78.9	77.4	77.4	77.3	75.9	75.3	75.1	73.5	72.4	71.2	76.0
2009	68.3	67.3	66.4	63.9	62.8	62.6	61.6	61.1	60.5	59.2	58.9	58.6	62.6
2010	56.3	56.1	56.6	56.7	56.7	56.8	57.1	56.7	56.9	56.7	56.5	56.1	56.6
2011	54.2	54.1	54.7	54.9	54.8	54.9	55.4	55.6	55.3	54.9	55.2	54.9	54.9
2012	54.2	54.3	54.7	55.4	55.4	56.0	55.9	56.1	56.3	56.5	56.7	56.5	55.7
2013	56.0	56.7	57.6	57.5	57.6	58.1	58.3	58.4	58.6	58.6	59.1	59.0	58.0
2014	58.5	58.9	59.2	59.6	60.2	60.7	61.0	61.2	61.4	62.1	62.5	62.6	60.7
2015	62.5	63.2	63.9	64.2	64.5	65.1	65.0	64.9	64.7	65.7	65.8	66.1	64.6
2016	66.1	66.6	67.1	68.1	68.7	69.5	69.9	69.7	70.2	70.2	71.1	71.5	69.1
2017	71.8	72.5	72.9	73.9	74.8	75.5	75.8	76.1	73.6	75.9	76.1	75.9	74.6
Service-Providing													
2007	542.8	546.2	551.2	551.5	552.6	546.5	539.6	545.9	545.8	548.1	553.2	553.7	548.1
2008	544.8	547.6	549.1	549.9	550.4	541.8	535.0	538.1	537.6	537.9	540.4	539.0	542.6
2009	524.3	525.0	525.3	524.3	524.8	517.4	512.8	515.5	515.2	519.9	524.0	524.1	521.1
2010	514.8	517.6	520.3	522.3	526.4	519.5	518.0	521.5	523.1	528.8	533.1	534.7	523.3
2011	526.2	529.8	533.8	534.9	535.2	528.1	523.3	527.7	529.6	532.7	536.0	537.9	531.3
2012	530.3	534.7	538.7	540.3	542.5	537.0	532.5	537.6	537.8	542.0	546.0	547.7	538.9
2013	536.1	542.6	546.2	548.4	550.3	546.0	545.5	551.3	552.1	556.1	561.2	564.1	550.0
2014	550.4	554.8	558.4	561.9	564.0	558.7	556.7	563.5	562.8	572.1	576.5	581.0	563.4
2015	567.5	573.7	577.5	579.6	581.3	576.4	575.9	581.9	582.4	590.4	595.0	597.4	581.6
2016	585.1	589.8	593.5	598.3	599.6	593.0	595.5	601.8	603.6	606.4	613.8	614.2	599.6
2017	604.0	608.0	610.2	614.2	616.3	610.3	610.1	616.1	610.6	621.4	628.9	632.0	615.2
Mining and Logging													
2007	0.4	0.4	0.4	0.4	0.4	0.4	0.4	0.4	0.4	0.4	0.4	0.4	0.4
2008	0.4	0.4	0.4	0.4	0.4	0.4	0.4	0.4	0.4	0.4	0.4	0.4	0.4
2009	0.4	0.4	0.4	0.4	0.4	0.4	0.3	0.4	0.4	0.3	0.3	0.3	0.4
2010	0.3	0.3	0.3	0.3	0.3	0.4	0.3	0.3	0.3	0.4	0.4	0.4	0.3
2011	0.3	0.3	0.3	0.3	0.3	0.3	0.3	0.3	0.3	0.3	0.3	0.3	0.3
2012	0.3	0.3	0.3	0.3	0.3	0.3	0.3	0.3	0.3	0.4	0.4	0.4	0.3
2013	0.4	0.4	0.4	0.4	0.4	0.4	0.4	0.4	0.4	0.4	0.4	0.4	0.4
2014	0.4	0.4	0.4	0.4	0.4	0.4	0.4	0.4	0.4	0.4	0.4	0.4	0.4
2015	0.4	0.4	0.4	0.4	0.4	0.4	0.4	0.4	0.4	0.4	0.4	0.4	0.4
2016	0.4	0.4	0.4	0.4	0.4	0.4	0.4	0.4	0.4	0.4	0.4	0.4	0.4
2017	0.5	0.4	0.5	0.4	0.4	0.4	0.4	0.4	0.4	0.4	0.4	0.4	0.4

Employment by Industry: Jacksonville, FL, Selected Years, 2007–2017—*Continued*

(Numbers in thousands, not seasonally adjusted)

Industry and year	January	February	March	April	May	June	July	August	September	October	November	December	Annual average
Construction													
2007	49.0	48.8	49.7	49.4	50.4	51.1	50.5	50.5	49.6	48.3	48.2	47.8	49.4
2008	45.5	45.8	45.7	44.3	44.3	44.3	43.0	42.6	42.4	41.2	40.2	39.1	43.2
2009	36.6	36.3	35.7	33.9	33.3	33.2	32.5	32.0	31.6	30.6	30.3	30.1	33.0
2010	28.3	28.4	29.0	29.2	29.2	29.2	29.4	29.1	29.1	28.6	28.4	27.9	28.8
2011	26.5	26.5	27.1	27.2	27.1	27.2	27.6	27.8	27.7	27.3	27.4	27.1	27.2
2012	26.2	26.3	26.7	27.2	27.1	27.6	27.6	28.0	28.1	28.2	28.4	28.4	27.5
2013	27.7	28.4	29.2	29.2	29.3	29.7	30.1	30.3	30.6	30.7	31.1	31.0	29.8
2014	30.5	31.1	31.5	31.7	32.0	32.3	32.6	32.7	32.8	33.1	33.3	33.4	32.3
2015	33.2	33.8	34.4	34.6	34.9	35.4	35.4	35.4	35.4	36.4	36.7	37.0	35.2
2016	36.7	37.2	37.8	38.6	38.9	39.4	39.5	39.4	39.8	39.9	40.6	40.8	39.1
2017	40.8	41.2	41.5	42.4	43.2	43.7	44.1	44.5	43.2	44.9	45.0	44.6	43.3
Manufacturing													
2007	33.3	33.4	33.4	32.7	32.8	33.0	33.0	33.1	33.1	32.9	32.9	33.0	33.1
2008	32.9	32.9	32.8	32.7	32.7	32.6	32.5	32.3	32.3	31.9	31.8	31.7	32.4
2009	31.3	30.6	30.3	29.6	29.1	29.0	28.8	28.7	28.5	28.3	28.3	28.2	29.2
2010	27.7	27.4	27.3	27.2	27.2	27.2	27.4	27.3	27.5	27.7	27.7	27.8	27.5
2011	27.4	27.3	27.3	27.4	27.4	27.4	27.5	27.5	27.3	27.3	27.5	27.5	27.4
2012	27.7	27.7	27.7	27.9	28.0	28.1	28.0	27.8	27.9	27.9	27.9	27.7	27.9
2013	27.9	27.9	28.0	27.9	27.9	28.0	27.8	27.7	27.6	27.5	27.6	27.6	27.8
2014	27.6	27.4	27.3	27.5	27.8	28.0	28.0	28.1	28.2	28.6	28.8	28.8	28.0
2015	28.9	29.0	29.1	29.2	29.2	29.3	29.2	29.1	28.9	28.9	28.7	28.7	29.0
2016	29.0	29.0	28.9	29.1	29.4	29.7	30.0	29.9	30.0	29.9	30.1	30.3	29.6
2017	30.5	30.9	30.9	31.1	31.2	31.4	31.3	31.2	30.0	30.6	30.7	30.9	30.9
Trade, Transportation, and Utilities													
2007	138.0	137.6	139.1	138.9	139.3	138.7	137.9	138.1	138.1	139.1	142.4	143.3	139.2
2008	138.5	138.0	138.3	137.2	137.1	136.0	135.3	135.5	134.2	134.2	135.5	136.0	136.3
2009	130.3	128.9	128.3	126.8	126.8	126.2	125.3	125.0	124.9	125.2	127.1	128.2	126.9
2010	124.3	123.4	123.7	123.7	123.7	123.7	123.1	123.9	123.3	124.5	126.7	128.2	124.4
2011	123.0	123.2	123.9	124.2	123.6	123.7	123.7	123.9	123.4	123.4	125.9	126.7	124.1
2012	124.5	124.5	125.0	124.9	125.3	125.2	124.0	124.8	125.0	125.2	128.0	129.1	125.5
2013	125.4	125.4	126.1	127.0	127.1	127.0	127.1	127.5	127.2	128.7	131.5	133.5	127.8
2014	128.0	128.1	128.0	128.5	128.9	128.8	129.1	130.4	130.2	133.1	136.6	138.5	130.7
2015	133.4	133.5	133.4	133.3	133.8	133.9	134.1	135.5	135.3	136.1	139.2	140.5	135.2
2016	135.9	136.1	136.3	136.8	137.1	136.8	137.6	138.3	137.9	138.0	141.3	142.7	137.9
2017	139.6	139.3	139.0	140.0	139.8	139.0	139.6	140.4	140.8	142.7	146.9	148.4	141.3
Wholesale Trade													
2007	30.2	30.4	30.6	30.4	30.3	30.4	30.3	30.2	30.0	30.1	29.8	29.7	30.2
2008	29.0	29.0	29.0	28.8	28.7	28.8	28.8	28.7	28.5	28.2	28.0	27.9	28.6
2009	27.7	27.4	27.1	27.0	26.8	26.8	26.6	26.4	26.2	26.2	26.1	26.0	26.7
2010	25.7	25.5	25.4	25.5	25.6	25.7	25.8	25.9	25.7	25.6	25.5	25.5	25.6
2011	24.8	25.0	25.1	24.9	24.9	24.8	24.8	24.8	24.6	24.6	24.6	24.5	24.8
2012	24.5	24.6	24.8	24.7	24.8	24.7	24.9	24.8	24.7	24.7	24.7	24.8	24.7
2013	24.6	24.7	24.8	25.0	25.0	25.1	24.8	24.6	24.5	24.5	24.5	24.3	24.7
2014	24.0	24.1	24.1	23.8	24.0	24.0	24.0	24.0	23.9	24.2	24.2	24.2	24.0
2015	24.2	24.3	24.2	24.5	24.7	25.0	25.2	25.5	25.7	25.8	25.9	26.2	25.1
2016	25.7	26.1	26.2	25.7	25.8	25.7	25.9	25.9	25.8	25.6	25.6	25.6	25.8
2017	25.4	25.6	25.5	25.6	25.8	25.8	25.6	25.6	25.2	24.8	25.8	25.6	25.5
Retail Trade													
2007	75.5	75.0	76.2	75.7	76.2	76.0	75.7	76.0	75.7	76.2	79.2	80.2	76.5
2008	77.1	76.5	76.8	75.9	76.0	75.5	74.7	74.5	74.0	73.8	75.2	75.3	75.4
2009	70.8	70.0	70.0	69.1	69.4	69.3	68.8	68.7	68.4	68.6	70.4	71.0	69.5
2010	68.8	68.2	68.5	68.5	68.4	68.3	67.9	68.1	67.7	68.6	70.7	71.3	68.8
2011	67.9	67.8	68.3	68.4	68.5	68.8	68.7	68.9	68.7	69.0	71.3	71.8	69.0
2012	69.6	69.5	69.9	69.9	70.3	70.2	69.1	69.5	69.6	69.8	72.2	72.6	70.2
2013	70.1	69.8	70.2	70.5	70.8	71.1	71.5	71.4	71.0	72.2	75.0	75.5	71.6
2014	71.9	71.7	71.6	71.9	72.1	72.1	72.5	73.1	73.2	75.3	78.7	79.5	73.6
2015	75.4	75.3	75.3	74.6	75.0	75.2	75.3	75.8	75.2	75.7	78.3	78.8	75.8
2016	75.7	75.7	75.9	76.5	76.8	76.6	77.6	78.0	77.6	77.7	80.7	81.5	77.5
2017	79.0	78.6	78.2	78.7	78.7	78.6	79.0	79.4	80.2	82.0	84.3	85.1	80.2

Employment by Industry: Jacksonville, FL, Selected Years, 2007–2017—*Continued*

(Numbers in thousands, not seasonally adjusted)

Industry and year	January	February	March	April	May	June	July	August	September	October	November	December	Annual average
Transportation and Utilities													
2007	32.3	32.2	32.3	32.8	32.8	32.3	31.9	31.9	32.4	32.8	33.4	33.4	32.5
2008	32.4	32.5	32.5	32.5	32.4	31.7	31.8	32.3	31.7	32.2	32.3	32.8	32.3
2009	31.8	31.5	31.2	30.7	30.6	30.1	29.9	29.9	30.3	30.4	30.6	31.2	30.7
2010	29.8	29.7	29.8	29.7	29.7	29.7	29.4	29.9	29.9	30.3	30.5	31.4	30.0
2011	30.3	30.4	30.5	30.9	30.2	30.1	30.2	30.2	30.1	29.8	30.0	30.4	30.3
2012	30.4	30.4	30.3	30.3	30.2	30.3	30	30.5	30.7	30.7	31.1	31.7	30.6
2013	30.7	30.9	31.1	31.5	31.3	30.8	30.8	31.5	31.7	32.0	32.0	33.7	31.5
2014	32.1	32.3	32.3	32.8	32.8	32.7	32.6	33.3	33.1	33.6	33.7	34.8	33.0
2015	33.8	33.9	33.9	34.2	34.1	33.7	33.6	34.2	34.4	34.6	35.0	35.5	34.2
2016	34.5	34.3	34.2	34.6	34.5	34.5	34.1	34.4	34.5	34.7	35.0	35.6	34.6
2017	35.2	35.1	35.3	35.7	35.3	34.6	35.0	35.4	35.4	35.9	36.8	37.7	35.6
Information													
2007	10.1	10.1	10.2	10.2	10.2	10.3	10.2	10.2	10.2	10.1	10.0	10.0	10.2
2008	9.9	9.9	10.0	10.1	10.1	10.2	10.4	10.3	10.4	10.4	10.5	10.5	10.2
2009	10.4	10.4	10.4	10.5	10.5	10.5	10.4	10.4	10.2	10.1	10.2	10.2	10.4
2010	10.2	10.2	10.4	10.4	10.3	10.2	10.2	10.2	10.1	10.0	10.0	9.9	10.2
2011	9.7	9.6	9.6	9.7	9.7	9.6	9.6	9.6	9.5	9.5	9.6	9.5	9.6
2012	9.4	9.3	9.2	9.3	9.3	9.3	9.3	9.1	9.0	9.1	9.1	9.2	9.2
2013	9.1	9.1	9.1	9.0	9.1	9.1	9.2	9.2	9.2	9.2	9.3	9.3	9.2
2014	9.3	9.2	9.3	9.2	9.3	9.3	9.3	9.2	9.1	9.1	9.2	9.1	9.2
2015	9.1	9.2	9.2	9.1	9.2	9.2	9.4	9.4	9.3	9.4	9.5	9.5	9.3
2016	9.3	9.3	9.4	9.4	9.5	9.4	9.5	9.4	9.4	9.4	9.5	9.4	9.4
2017	9.3	9.3	9.2	9.3	9.4	9.4	9.3	9.3	9.1	9.2	9.3	9.3	9.3
Financial Activities													
2007	58.9	59.1	59.4	59.5	59.8	60.1	60.5	60.8	60.7	60.7	61.1	61.1	60.1
2008	60.7	60.7	60.8	60.7	60.5	60.3	60.0	59.6	59.1	58.6	58.0	57.9	59.7
2009	56.9	56.7	56.5	55.7	55.8	55.7	55.8	55.5	55.0	55.1	55.1	55.2	55.8
2010	54.9	55.0	55.0	54.8	55.1	55.4	55.9	55.9	55.9	56.4	56.9	57.3	55.7
2011	57.0	57.3	57.8	57.8	57.7	58.0	57.9	58.0	58.5	58.4	58.3	59.0	58.0
2012	58.6	59.2	59.5	59.5	59.8	60.0	60.1	60.1	60.2	60.8	61.2	61.4	60.0
2013	60.8	61.1	61.1	61.2	61.2	61.6	61.7	61.7	61.6	61.7	61.9	62.0	61.5
2014	61.0	60.9	61.2	61.1	61.0	60.8	61.0	60.7	60.3	60.7	60.9	60.9	60.9
2015	61.2	61.2	61.3	61.0	61.0	61.1	61.0	61.2	61.4	62.3	62.5	62.5	61.5
2016	62.5	62.9	62.9	63.4	63.8	63.9	64.1	64.4	65.1	65.4	65.8	66.5	64.2
2017	66.2	66.4	66.8	67.0	67.2	67.3	67.2	67.5	67.3	68.3	68.3	68.2	67.3
Professional and Business Services													
2007	93.8	94.0	94.6	94.2	92.7	91.0	88.8	87.9	87.4	88.2	87.6	86.8	90.6
2008	85.0	86.2	86.6	87.0	87.6	85.8	82.0	81.9	82.7	82.6	82.3	82.1	84.3
2009	79.4	80.1	79.7	79.6	79.5	79.0	77.2	77.3	78.1	80.4	81.4	82.0	79.5
2010	79.2	80.5	81.1	81.0	81.5	81.5	81.2	81.8	83.3	85.6	85.9	85.9	82.4
2011	85.3	87.2	88.0	88.0	88.7	87.5	84.8	85.2	87.3	88.8	89.7	90.0	87.5
2012	89.0	90.1	90.7	92.3	93.1	92.1	89.6	90.4	90.0	91.4	91.7	91.5	91.0
2013	89.0	90.6	92.0	92.4	93.7	93.8	94.1	95.0	95.5	97.3	97.4	97.5	94.0
2014	94.9	95.2	95.6	96.9	98.0	97.6	97.2	98.5	98.8	101.1	102.1	102.9	98.2
2015	99.3	100.3	100.6	101.5	101.6	100.4	100.3	99.4	99.1	101.7	102.1	102.0	100.7
2016	99.1	99.2	100.2	102.0	101.7	100.8	102.2	102.6	102.5	105.8	106.6	105.5	102.4
2017	103.5	103.1	103.7	104.5	104.6	105.1	105.5	105.8	103.9	108.7	108.2	107.3	105.3
Education and Health Services													
2007	76.2	77.1	77.5	77.4	77.6	77.3	77.0	77.6	78.6	78.9	79.4	79.9	77.9
2008	80.6	81.0	80.9	81.8	81.5	80.9	80.8	80.9	81.5	82.8	83.9	83.8	81.7
2009	82.5	83.2	83.5	83.3	83.4	82.9	82.6	82.9	83.7	85.2	85.9	85.6	83.7
2010	84.5	85.0	85.2	85.4	85.5	84.9	84.6	84.8	85.5	87.5	87.9	88.0	85.7
2011	87.1	87.6	87.7	87.4	87.4	86.4	86.3	86.8	88.1	89.2	89.5	89.8	87.8
2012	87.6	88.4	88.7	88.7	89.0	88.6	88.2	88.9	90.0	90.5	90.8	91.3	89.2
2013	90.0	91.4	91.4	90.8	91.0	90.7	90.0	90.6	91.3	92.1	92.7	93.0	91.3
2014	91.4	92.5	92.8	93.4	93.3	92.4	92.2	93.2	93.7	95.1	95.3	96.0	93.4
2015	95.0	95.7	96.4	96.7	96.9	96.3	96.2	97.4	98.4	100.4	100.9	101.0	97.6
2016	99.7	100.9	101.2	102.4	102.7	101.7	101.9	103.0	103.7	104.6	104.8	104.6	102.6
2017	103.4	104.7	104.8	105.3	105.5	104.4	103.9	105.0	104.4	105.5	106.2	106.2	104.9

Employment by Industry: Jacksonville, FL, Selected Years, 2007–2017—*Continued*

(Numbers in thousands, not seasonally adjusted)

Industry and year	January	February	March	April	May	June	July	August	September	October	November	December	Annual average
Leisure and Hospitality													
2007	62.6	64.0	65.5	66.7	68.1	68.1	67.0	67.6	67.0	66.7	67.4	67.4	66.5
2008	66.2	66.8	67.4	68.8	69.2	69.1	69.1	68.5	67.8	67.4	67.4	67.0	67.9
2009	65.3	65.1	66.1	67.4	67.6	66.7	66.1	65.4	63.8	63.5	63.6	62.8	65.3
2010	61.8	63.0	64.4	66.0	66.8	66.5	66.4	66.0	65.4	64.2	64.5	64.9	65.0
2011	63.8	64.1	65.8	67.1	68.0	67.7	67.1	67.2	66.0	66.3	66.1	66.3	66.3
2012	65.7	66.6	68.7	69.7	70.1	70.2	70.3	70.1	68.6	69.0	69.3	69.7	69.0
2013	67.8	69.5	70.9	72.2	72.4	72.7	73.1	73.5	72.9	71.9	72.4	72.7	71.8
2014	71.9	73.0	75.2	75.8	76.6	77.7	76.5	76.5	74.7	76.2	75.5	76.3	75.5
2015	74.5	76.4	78.7	80.0	80.7	81.8	81.3	81.6	80.6	80.9	80.7	81.4	79.9
2016	79.6	80.7	82.1	82.7	83.2	83.3	83.1	83.6	83.2	81.9	83.8	82.9	82.5
2017	81.8	83.0	84.0	85.7	86.8	86.4	86.6	86.7	83.1	84.5	87.0	89.0	85.4
Other Services													
2007	27.6	27.7	28.1	27.6	27.7	28.0	27.5	27.2	26.9	27.0	27.1	27.1	27.5
2008	26.9	27.1	27.1	26.8	26.7	26.5	25.8	25.5	24.9	24.5	24.1	23.6	25.8
2009	23.2	23.2	23.3	23.4	23.3	23.3	23.0	23.1	22.9	23.1	23.2	23.1	23.2
2010	22.9	23.0	23.1	23.1	23.1	23.2	23.0	22.9	22.7	22.9	22.9	22.7	23.0
2011	22.5	22.6	22.8	22.5	22.1	21.8	21.7	21.3	20.9	20.6	20.2	19.9	21.6
2012	20.0	20.1	20.3	20.5	20.5	20.5	20.4	20.4	20.3	20.3	20.2	20.2	20.3
2013	20.0	20.1	20.2	20.4	20.5	20.7	20.8	20.9	20.7	20.9	21.1	21.1	20.6
2014	21.1	21.3	21.5	21.8	21.9	21.9	21.7	21.8	21.8	22.0	21.9	21.9	21.7
2015	21.9	22.1	22.3	22.4	22.8	23.1	23.4	23.5	23.5	23.8	23.9	24.1	23.1
2016	24.2	24.6	24.9	25.1	25.2	25.3	25.4	25.3	25.3	24.9	25.1	25.1	25.0
2017	24.7	25.0	25.1	25.0	25.3	25.5	25.7	25.4	25.1	25.5	25.6	25.6	25.3
Government													
2007	75.6	76.6	76.8	77.0	77.2	73.0	70.7	76.5	76.9	77.4	78.2	78.1	76.2
2008	77.0	77.9	78.0	77.5	77.7	73.0	71.6	75.9	77.0	77.4	78.7	78.1	76.7
2009	76.3	77.4	77.5	77.6	77.9	73.1	72.4	75.9	76.6	77.3	77.5	77.0	76.4
2010	77.0	77.5	77.4	77.9	80.4	74.1	73.6	76.0	76.9	77.7	78.3	77.8	77.1
2011	77.8	78.2	78.2	78.2	78.0	73.4	72.2	75.7	75.9	76.5	76.7	76.7	76.5
2012	75.5	76.5	76.6	75.4	75.4	71.1	70.6	73.8	74.7	75.7	75.7	75.3	74.7
2013	74.0	75.4	75.4	75.4	75.3	70.4	69.5	72.9	73.7	74.3	74.9	75.0	73.9
2014	72.8	74.6	74.8	75.2	75.0	70.2	69.7	73.2	74.2	74.8	75.0	75.4	73.7
2015	73.1	75.3	75.6	75.6	75.3	70.6	70.2	73.9	74.8	75.8	76.2	76.4	74.4
2016	74.8	76.1	76.5	76.5	76.4	71.8	71.7	75.2	76.5	76.4	76.9	77.5	75.5
2017	75.5	77.2	77.6	77.4	77.7	73.2	72.3	76.0	76.9	77.0	77.4	78.0	76.4

Employment by Industry: Oklahoma City, OK, Selected Years, 2007–2017

(Numbers in thousands, not seasonally adjusted)

Industry and year	January	February	March	April	May	June	July	August	September	October	November	December	Annual average
Total Nonfarm													
2007	563.2	568.8	576.1	575.7	578.3	578.3	568.2	574.4	581.1	583.5	588.5	586.8	576.9
2008	573.5	579.7	583.6	585.6	588.3	583.8	575.9	580.8	589.2	589.6	591.5	590.3	584.3
2009	575.5	573.6	575.3	572.3	570.7	566.8	559.4	560.0	565.5	565.2	566.8	566.5	568.1
2010	552.5	555.3	561.7	565.9	569.5	566.5	560.3	564.4	571.3	575.7	578.3	580.7	566.8
2011	564.7	567.6	575.5	582.0	582.2	579.1	574.1	577.8	586.6	587.4	590.8	593.6	580.1
2012	579.5	586.1	592.3	595.9	597.8	595.6	584.8	590.3	597.1	602.9	606.1	606.8	594.6
2013	593.2	600.2	604.8	607.7	611.8	608.5	602.3	607.2	612.3	615.8	621.5	619.0	608.7
2014	604.7	610.0	615.0	618.7	622.1	618.9	613.8	619.2	626.0	629.7	633.1	634.9	620.5
2015	621.5	626.6	627.6	630.0	631.8	629.5	625.2	628.6	633.0	635.0	637.2	638.0	630.3
2016	623.1	628.8	629.0	633.2	632.1	627.0	622.9	627.2	632.7	631.9	634.8	635.0	629.8
2017	617.4	624.7	629.7	633.4	634.4	633.3	629.0	632.8	641.3	645.3	646.9	646.5	634.6
Total Private													
2007	446.5	449.9	456.5	456.3	458.6	462.1	459.3	462.8	462.9	462.5	466.9	466.1	459.2
2008	457.7	459.9	463.0	465.1	467.2	468.7	467.2	467.9	469.1	467.6	468.5	468.0	465.8
2009	454.9	452.8	453.2	449.9	448.0	448.9	446.4	445.2	444.3	441.0	441.9	441.8	447.4
2010	432.6	432.5	437.7	441.5	443.3	445.6	445.2	447.8	449.0	452.0	454.2	456.2	444.8
2011	445.6	444.8	451.9	458.1	458.2	459.9	459.7	462.6	463.5	462.7	465.6	467.9	458.4
2012	459.4	462.6	467.8	470.9	472.9	475.7	471.3	474.2	474.0	476.6	479.2	480.7	472.1
2013	471.7	474.2	478.2	480.6	483.9	485.8	484.8	487.5	487.8	488.8	493.6	492.0	484.1
2014	483.2	484.1	488.7	492.3	494.7	496.5	496.7	499.7	500.3	501.6	504.6	507.0	495.8
2015	498.0	498.6	499.2	501.4	502.4	505.1	505.8	507.0	505.4	504.4	506.0	507.2	503.4
2016	496.7	498.1	497.7	501.2	500.4	500.3	501.1	502.9	502.5	501.1	503.7	504.6	500.9
2017	492.0	495.0	499.2	502.9	504.0	507.7	508.1	509.7	511.9	513.1	514.3	514.4	506.0
Goods Producing													
2007	75.4	75.5	76.9	77.1	77.4	78.8	78.6	79.4	79.0	79.2	79.8	79.3	78.0
2008	78.5	79.0	79.6	80.3	81.0	82.1	82.0	82.1	81.6	81.4	80.7	79.7	80.7
2009	77.6	75.9	74.6	72.6	71.8	72.0	71.3	70.6	69.6	68.8	68.7	68.6	71.8
2010	67.6	67.1	68.1	69.1	69.7	70.6	70.9	71.4	71.6	73.1	72.8	73.6	70.5
2011	72.3	72.2	73.4	74.9	75.2	76.3	76.9	77.0	77.1	77.3	77.6	78.6	75.7
2012	77.9	78.5	79.9	80.9	81.5	83.0	82.4	82.7	82.4	83.0	83.0	83.1	81.5
2013	82.6	82.9	83.3	83.6	84.2	85.3	85.1	85.1	84.8	85.2	85.5	85.4	84.4
2014	83.9	84.1	85.3	85.6	86.6	87.7	88.2	89.0	89.2	89.7	89.8	90.2	87.4
2015	89.7	89.1	88.0	86.6	86.2	86.3	87.3	87.0	86.2	85.0	84.0	83.6	86.6
2016	82.3	82.1	80.9	80.9	80.3	80.2	80.2	79.9	79.5	79.0	79.0	79.8	80.3
2017	78.1	79.0	79.4	79.5	80.1	81.4	81.7	81.9	82.6	82.7	83.3	83.4	81.1
Service-Providing													
2007	487.8	493.3	499.2	498.6	500.9	499.5	489.6	495.0	502.1	504.3	508.7	507.5	498.9
2008	495.0	500.7	504.0	505.3	507.3	501.7	493.9	498.7	507.6	508.2	510.8	510.6	503.7
2009	497.9	497.7	500.7	499.7	498.9	494.8	488.1	489.4	495.9	496.4	498.1	497.9	496.3
2010	484.9	488.2	493.6	496.8	499.8	495.9	489.4	493.0	499.7	502.6	505.5	507.1	496.4
2011	492.4	495.4	502.1	507.1	507.0	502.8	497.2	500.8	509.5	510.1	513.2	515.0	504.4
2012	501.6	507.6	512.4	515.0	516.3	512.6	502.4	507.6	514.7	519.9	523.1	523.7	513.1
2013	510.6	517.3	521.5	524.1	527.6	523.2	517.2	522.1	527.5	530.6	536.0	533.6	524.3
2014	520.8	525.9	529.7	533.1	535.5	531.2	525.6	530.2	536.8	540.0	543.3	544.7	533.1
2015	531.8	537.5	539.6	543.4	545.6	543.2	537.9	541.6	546.8	550.0	553.2	554.4	543.8
2016	540.8	546.7	548.1	552.3	551.8	546.8	542.7	547.3	553.2	552.9	555.8	555.2	549.5
2017	539.3	545.7	550.3	553.9	554.3	551.9	547.3	550.9	558.7	562.6	563.6	563.1	553.5
Mining, Logging, and Construction													
2007	39.0	38.9	39.9	40.2	40.3	41.5	41.5	42.1	41.9	42.0	42.5	42.1	41.0
2008	41.5	42.0	42.6	43.1	43.8	44.7	44.9	44.9	44.6	44.5	44.1	43.4	43.7
2009	42.0	41.0	40.6	39.3	39.1	39.7	39.3	39.1	38.5	37.7	37.8	37.8	39.3
2010	37.0	36.6	37.6	38.4	38.9	39.7	40.1	40.4	40.4	41.6	41.1	41.7	39.5
2011	40.9	40.6	41.5	42.4	42.6	43.5	43.8	43.6	43.6	43.6	43.7	44.3	42.8
2012	43.7	44.1	45.3	46.2	46.7	47.9	47.4	47.5	47.1	47.3	47.1	47.1	46.5
2013	46.8	47.0	47.3	47.4	47.8	48.7	48.4	48.4	48.3	48.3	48.4	48.3	47.9
2014	47.2	47.0	48.2	48.5	49.3	50.1	50.7	51.3	51.4	51.7	51.7	51.8	49.9
2015	51.2	50.6	49.8	48.8	48.6	48.9	49.8	49.6	49.1	48.3	47.7	47.3	49.1
2016	46.4	46.0	45.6	46.0	45.6	45.7	45.9	45.7	45.5	45.6	45.5	46.1	45.8
2017	45.2	45.9	46.5	46.4	46.9	47.9	48.2	48.3	48.9	49.0	49.5	49.8	47.7

Employment by Industry: Oklahoma City, OK, Selected Years, 2007–2017—*Continued*

(Numbers in thousands, not seasonally adjusted)

Industry and year	January	February	March	April	May	June	July	August	September	October	November	December	Annual average
Manufacturing													
2007	36.4	36.6	37.0	36.9	37.1	37.3	37.1	37.3	37.1	37.2	37.3	37.2	37.0
2008	37.0	37.0	37.0	37.2	37.2	37.4	37.1	37.2	37.0	36.9	36.6	36.3	37.0
2009	35.6	34.9	34.0	33.3	32.7	32.3	32.0	31.5	31.1	31.1	30.9	30.8	32.5
2010	30.6	30.5	30.5	30.7	30.8	30.9	30.8	31.0	31.2	31.5	31.7	31.9	31.0
2011	31.4	31.6	31.9	32.5	32.6	32.8	33.1	33.4	33.5	33.7	33.9	34.3	32.9
2012	34.2	34.4	34.6	34.7	34.8	35.1	35.0	35.2	35.3	35.7	35.9	36.0	35.1
2013	35.8	35.9	36.0	36.2	36.4	36.6	36.7	36.7	36.5	36.9	37.1	37.1	36.5
2014	36.7	37.1	37.1	37.1	37.3	37.6	37.5	37.7	37.8	38.0	38.1	38.4	37.5
2015	38.5	38.5	38.2	37.8	37.6	37.4	37.5	37.4	37.1	36.7	36.3	36.3	37.4
2016	35.9	36.1	35.3	34.9	34.7	34.5	34.3	34.2	34.0	33.4	33.5	33.7	34.5
2017	32.9	33.1	32.9	33.1	33.2	33.5	33.5	33.6	33.7	33.7	33.8	33.6	33.4
Trade, Transportation, and Utilities													
2007	100.3	100.3	102.0	100.9	101.3	101.2	100.4	100.7	100.3	100.7	102.9	103.3	101.2
2008	100.4	99.8	100.5	99.8	99.9	100.1	100.5	100.4	100.8	100.9	102.5	102.9	100.7
2009	98.9	97.9	98.2	97.6	97.4	97.6	96.8	96.7	96.4	96.5	97.9	98.4	97.5
2010	94.8	94.4	95.5	95.8	96.5	97.2	97.4	97.6	97.1	98.3	100.2	101.6	97.2
2011	97.9	97.5	98.8	99.2	99.1	99.5	99.6	100.6	100.5	100.7	102.8	103.8	100.0
2012	100.4	100.2	101.0	101.5	102.3	102.5	102.4	102.7	103.1	104.2	106.7	107.9	102.9
2013	103.7	104.0	104.9	105.4	106.3	106.7	106.8	107.4	107.5	108.3	111.0	112.0	107.0
2014	108.3	107.5	107.9	107.8	108.3	109.0	108.8	109.4	109.8	110.4	112.7	114.5	109.5
2015	110.0	109.8	110.0	110.7	111.1	112.0	112.0	112.2	111.9	112.1	114.5	115.8	111.8
2016	110.9	110.9	111.2	111.8	111.9	111.8	111.7	112.1	112.0	112.2	114.8	115.0	112.2
2017	110.7	110.0	110.2	110.6	110.6	110.8	111.0	111.6	111.7	111.6	112.9	113.9	111.3
Wholesale Trade													
2007	21.5	21.6	21.7	21.7	21.8	21.9	21.7	21.4	21.3	21.6	21.6	21.8	21.6
2008	21.6	21.5	21.6	21.5	21.6	21.8	21.8	21.6	21.7	21.7	21.7	21.6	21.6
2009	21.2	21.1	20.9	20.7	20.4	20.4	20.4	20.3	20.2	20.4	20.2	20.2	20.5
2010	20.1	20.1	20.1	20.2	20.4	20.5	20.6	20.7	20.7	21.0	21.1	21.2	20.6
2011	21.1	21.1	21.3	21.5	21.5	21.7	21.6	21.6	21.7	21.8	21.8	21.9	21.6
2012	22.1	22.3	22.4	22.3	22.6	22.7	22.8	22.9	22.8	23.1	23.3	23.6	22.7
2013	23.6	23.7	23.8	23.7	23.9	24.1	23.9	23.9	23.9	24.0	24.2	24.2	23.9
2014	24.2	24.1	24.1	24.2	24.3	24.5	24.3	24.5	24.7	24.9	24.9	25.1	24.5
2015	24.9	24.9	24.7	24.5	24.5	24.6	24.7	24.6	24.6	24.4	24.4	24.4	24.6
2016	24.0	24.2	24.1	24.3	24.2	24.1	24.1	24.1	24.0	24.0	23.9	23.8	24.1
2017	23.6	23.8	23.9	24.0	24.1	24.1	24.1	24.3	24.3	24.3	23.9	24.0	24.0
Retail Trade													
2007	61.1	60.9	62.2	61.3	61.7	61.6	61.2	61.7	61.5	61.9	64.3	64.4	62.0
2008	62.5	62.0	62.4	61.5	61.5	61.4	61.8	61.9	62.2	62.3	63.8	64.1	62.3
2009	60.8	60.0	60.7	59.9	60.1	60.2	59.6	59.7	59.6	59.4	61.0	61.4	60.2
2010	58.6	58.2	59.1	59.2	59.7	60.1	60.1	60.2	59.6	60.6	62.3	63.0	60.1
2011	60.1	59.6	60.5	60.8	60.6	60.5	60.7	61.6	61.3	61.3	63.3	63.9	61.2
2012	60.9	60.5	61.2	61.7	61.9	62.0	61.6	61.8	62.2	63.0	65.2	65.9	62.3
2013	62.0	61.7	62.4	63.0	63.6	63.6	63.9	64.4	64.6	65.2	67.5	68.4	64.2
2014	65.0	64.6	64.7	64.9	65.0	65.4	65.5	65.8	66.0	66.3	68.4	69.4	65.9
2015	65.8	65.8	66.2	66.9	67.0	67.6	67.6	67.9	67.6	68.1	70.1	70.8	67.6
2016	67.1	67.1	67.5	67.9	68.0	67.9	67.8	68.2	68.2	68.4	70.5	70.1	68.2
2017	66.7	65.9	65.9	66.3	66.0	66.2	66.0	66.3	66.2	66.1	67.6	67.8	66.4
Transportation and Utilities													
2007	17.7	17.8	18.1	17.9	17.8	17.7	17.5	17.6	17.5	17.2	17.0	17.1	17.6
2008	16.3	16.3	16.5	16.8	16.8	16.9	16.9	16.9	16.9	16.9	17.0	17.2	16.8
2009	16.9	16.8	17.1	17.0	16.9	17.0	16.8	16.7	16.6	16.7	16.7	16.8	16.8
2010	16.1	16.1	16.3	16.4	16.4	16.6	16.7	16.7	16.8	16.7	16.8	17.4	16.6
2011	16.7	16.8	17.0	16.9	17.0	17.3	17.3	17.4	17.5	17.6	17.7	18.0	17.3
2012	17.4	17.4	17.4	17.5	17.8	17.8	18.0	18.0	18.1	18.1	18.2	18.4	17.8
2013	18.1	18.6	18.7	18.7	18.8	19.0	19.0	19.1	19.0	19.1	19.3	19.4	18.9
2014	19.1	18.8	19.1	18.7	19.0	19.1	19.0	19.1	19.1	19.2	19.4	20.0	19.1
2015	19.3	19.1	19.1	19.3	19.6	19.8	19.7	19.7	19.7	19.6	20.0	20.6	19.6
2016	19.8	19.6	19.6	19.6	19.7	19.8	19.8	19.8	19.8	19.8	20.4	21.1	19.9
2017	20.4	20.3	20.4	20.3	20.5	20.5	20.9	21.0	21.2	21.2	21.4	22.1	20.9

Employment by Industry: Oklahoma City, OK, Selected Years, 2007–2017—*Continued*

(Numbers in thousands, not seasonally adjusted)

Industry and year	January	February	March	April	May	June	July	August	September	October	November	December	Annual average
Information													
2007	13.0	12.6	12.3	12.3	12.2	12.3	12.2	12.2	12.2	12.1	12.2	12.2	12.3
2008	12.2	12.3	12.1	12.3	12.3	12.3	12.4	12.2	12.0	11.9	12.0	11.9	12.2
2009	11.8	11.6	11.6	11.5	11.4	11.3	11.1	10.9	10.6	10.4	10.3	10.2	11.1
2010	10.2	10.1	9.9	9.8	9.7	9.6	9.5	9.3	9.2	9.1	9.2	9.1	9.6
2011	9.2	9.1	8.9	9.0	9.0	9.0	9.0	8.9	8.9	9.0	9.0	9.0	9.0
2012	8.9	8.9	8.8	8.7	8.7	8.6	8.7	8.5	8.3	8.4	8.4	8.3	8.6
2013	8.1	8.1	8.0	8.2	8.2	8.2	8.2	8.2	8.2	8.2	8.4	8.3	8.2
2014	8.1	8.1	8.1	8.1	8.1	8.1	8.2	8.2	8.2	8.1	8.2	8.1	8.1
2015	8.1	8.0	8.1	8.1	8.3	8.3	8.3	8.3	8.3	8.4	8.4	8.5	8.3
2016	8.2	8.3	8.3	8.2	8.2	8.2	8.1	8.1	8.0	8.0	8.1	8.2	8.2
2017	7.8	7.8	7.8	7.8	7.8	7.7	7.6	7.5	7.5	7.5	7.6	7.6	7.7
Financial Activities													
2007	31.7	32.1	32.0	31.5	31.6	31.6	31.5	31.5	31.2	31.2	31.2	31.3	31.5
2008	31.6	31.5	31.6	31.7	32.1	32.1	32.2	32.0	31.9	31.7	31.8	31.9	31.8
2009	31.2	31.1	31.2	31.2	31.3	31.4	31.4	31.4	31.2	31.3	31.3	31.5	31.3
2010	31.1	31.1	31.2	30.9	31.0	31.0	30.9	30.9	30.7	30.9	30.9	31.2	31.0
2011	30.3	30.3	30.5	30.6	30.7	30.7	30.8	31.0	30.9	31.1	31.3	31.4	30.8
2012	31.2	31.4	31.5	31.6	31.8	32.0	31.8	31.8	31.7	31.9	32.0	32.3	31.8
2013	32.1	32.2	32.2	32.1	32.2	32.3	32.4	32.5	32.4	32.5	32.7	32.8	32.4
2014	32.5	32.7	32.8	32.9	33.1	33.2	33.3	33.3	33.2	33.3	33.5	33.9	33.1
2015	33.4	33.4	33.3	33.3	33.4	33.4	33.5	33.4	33.2	33.2	33.2	33.4	33.3
2016	32.8	33.0	32.9	32.9	32.9	33.0	33.3	33.3	33.2	33.3	33.4	33.6	33.1
2017	32.8	33.0	33.1	33.1	33.2	33.4	33.4	33.5	33.5	33.3	33.3	33.2	33.2
Professional and Business Services													
2007	74.3	75.6	76.6	76.9	77.5	78.8	77.4	78.5	79.1	78.3	79.4	79.5	77.7
2008	77.2	77.9	78.0	77.9	77.8	77.9	76.5	77.0	77.5	76.9	76.8	76.9	77.4
2009	73.6	73.7	73.5	72.4	71.1	71.4	71.2	71.0	71.9	71.0	70.7	70.8	71.9
2010	69.7	70.3	71.0	71.8	71.7	72.7	73.5	74.6	74.9	75.6	75.8	75.7	73.1
2011	73.9	73.7	74.8	76.4	76.2	75.8	76.0	76.8	76.2	76.4	76.3	76.9	75.8
2012	75.4	76.5	77.0	76.9	76.4	77.5	76.3	77.3	76.3	77.5	77.3	76.7	76.8
2013	75.7	76.2	77.5	77.4	77.4	78.0	77.5	78.0	77.6	78.4	79.2	78.0	77.6
2014	76.8	77.0	77.8	78.2	78.1	78.3	78.9	79.7	79.0	79.9	80.5	80.0	78.7
2015	78.9	78.9	78.8	79.4	79.2	79.7	79.9	80.3	79.6	80.1	80.2	80.6	79.6
2016	79.2	79.2	78.9	79.6	79.2	79.1	79.3	80.0	80.3	80.3	79.9	79.8	79.6
2017	78.0	78.3	79.3	80.5	80.2	81.6	82.6	83.0	83.3	84.1	82.8	82.7	81.4
Education and Health Services													
2007	77.1	77.8	78.4	78.8	79.0	79.1	78.7	79.4	80.3	80.9	81.2	81.1	79.3
2008	80.0	80.9	81.0	82.0	82.3	81.7	81.9	82.6	83.1	83.4	83.6	83.6	82.2
2009	83.0	82.9	83.0	82.8	82.8	82.8	82.6	82.8	83.4	82.9	83.0	82.9	82.9
2010	82.0	82.4	82.7	83.3	83.2	83.0	82.2	82.8	83.8	84.3	84.4	84.3	83.2
2011	82.6	82.6	83.5	84.1	84.2	84.3	83.8	84.5	85.5	85.4	86.0	86.0	84.4
2012	84.5	85.2	85.8	86.4	86.6	86.5	85.4	86.5	87.3	87.4	87.7	88.0	86.4
2013	86.9	87.3	87.7	87.9	88.1	87.7	86.9	87.7	88.3	88.9	89.3	88.7	88.0
2014	87.7	88.1	88.6	89.4	89.3	88.8	88.2	88.5	89.1	89.5	89.6	89.9	88.9
2015	89.2	89.7	89.9	90.5	90.5	90.4	89.9	90.3	91.2	91.6	91.6	91.5	90.5
2016	90.7	91.0	90.9	91.3	91.0	90.3	90.9	91.3	91.8	91.3	91.7	91.7	91.2
2017	89.7	90.6	91.0	92.0	91.9	91.7	91.2	91.6	92.3	93.2	93.1	93.1	91.8
Leisure and Hospitality													
2007	52.1	53.3	55.4	55.5	56.1	56.5	57.0	57.7	57.5	56.9	57.0	56.4	56.0
2008	54.7	55.1	56.6	57.2	57.8	58.3	57.6	57.5	58.1	57.4	57.2	57.3	57.1
2009	55.2	56.1	57.4	58.3	58.7	58.7	58.6	58.7	58.2	57.2	57.0	56.6	57.6
2010	54.7	54.6	56.6	58.0	58.7	58.6	58.2	58.6	59.1	58.0	58.1	57.9	57.6
2011	57.0	57.0	59.5	61.2	60.8	61.3	60.8	61.1	61.6	60.1	59.9	59.6	60.0
2012	58.6	59.3	61.2	62.1	62.8	62.7	61.7	62.4	62.8	62.4	62.3	62.6	61.7
2013	60.9	61.7	62.8	64.0	65.3	65.1	65.2	65.9	66.3	64.6	64.6	63.8	64.2
2014	63.0	63.5	64.8	66.6	67.1	67.0	66.6	67.3	67.4	66.2	65.8	65.8	65.9
2015	64.2	65.0	66.0	67.6	68.4	69.5	69.3	70.0	69.5	68.7	68.8	68.5	68.0
2016	67.2	68.0	69.1	70.5	70.6	71.0	70.8	71.5	70.9	70.3	70.0	69.5	70.0
2017	68.0	69.1	70.7	71.6	72.2	72.7	72.4	72.6	72.8	72.6	73.1	72.3	71.7

Employment by Industry: Oklahoma City, OK, Selected Years, 2007–2017—*Continued*

(Numbers in thousands, not seasonally adjusted)

Industry and year	January	February	March	April	May	June	July	August	September	October	November	December	Annual average
Other Services													
2007	22.6	22.7	22.9	23.3	23.5	23.8	23.5	23.4	23.3	23.2	23.2	23.0	23.2
2008	23.1	23.4	23.6	23.9	24.0	24.2	24.1	24.1	24.1	24.0	23.9	23.8	23.9
2009	23.6	23.6	23.7	23.5	23.5	23.7	23.4	23.1	23.0	22.9	23.0	22.8	23.3
2010	22.5	22.5	22.7	22.8	22.8	22.9	22.6	22.6	22.6	22.7	22.8	22.8	22.7
2011	22.4	22.4	22.5	22.7	23.0	23.0	22.8	22.7	22.8	22.7	22.7	22.6	22.7
2012	22.5	22.6	22.6	22.8	22.8	22.9	22.6	22.3	22.1	21.8	21.8	21.8	22.4
2013	21.7	21.8	21.8	22.0	22.2	22.5	22.7	22.7	22.7	22.7	22.9	23.0	22.4
2014	22.9	23.1	23.4	23.7	24.1	24.4	24.5	24.3	24.4	24.5	24.5	24.6	24.0
2015	24.5	24.7	25.1	25.2	25.3	25.5	25.6	25.5	25.5	25.3	25.3	25.3	25.2
2016	25.4	25.6	25.5	26.0	26.3	26.7	26.8	26.7	26.8	26.7	26.8	27.0	26.4
2017	26.9	27.2	27.7	27.8	28.0	28.4	28.2	28.0	28.2	28.1	28.2	28.2	27.9
Government													
2007	116.7	118.9	119.6	119.4	119.7	116.2	108.9	111.6	118.2	121.0	121.6	120.7	117.7
2008	115.8	119.8	120.6	120.5	121.1	115.1	108.7	112.9	120.1	122.0	123.0	122.3	118.5
2009	120.6	120.8	122.1	122.4	122.7	117.9	113.0	114.8	121.2	124.2	124.9	124.7	120.8
2010	119.9	122.8	124.0	124.4	126.2	120.9	115.1	116.6	122.3	123.7	124.1	124.5	122.0
2011	119.1	122.8	123.6	123.9	124.0	119.2	114.4	115.2	123.1	124.7	125.2	125.7	121.7
2012	120.1	123.5	124.5	125.0	124.9	119.9	113.5	116.1	123.1	126.3	126.9	126.1	122.5
2013	121.5	126.0	126.6	127.1	127.9	122.7	117.5	119.7	124.5	127.0	127.9	127.0	124.6
2014	121.5	125.9	126.3	126.4	127.4	122.4	117.1	119.5	125.7	128.1	128.5	127.9	124.7
2015	123.5	128.0	128.4	128.6	129.4	124.4	119.4	121.6	127.6	130.6	131.2	130.8	127.0
2016	126.4	130.7	131.3	132.0	131.7	126.7	121.8	124.3	130.2	130.8	131.1	130.4	129.0
2017	125.4	129.7	130.5	130.5	130.4	125.6	120.9	123.1	129.4	132.2	132.6	132.1	128.5

Employment by Industry: Memphis, TN-MS-AR, Selected Years, 2007–2017

(Numbers in thousands, not seasonally adjusted)

Industry and year	January	February	March	April	May	June	July	August	September	October	November	December	Annual average
Total Nonfarm													
2007	631.3	632.7	639.0	640.8	642.4	641.4	639.5	644.5	646.3	645.0	650.1	651.1	642.0
2008	633.6	632.4	635.1	637.9	638.7	633.5	633.7	636.2	633.7	632.2	632.5	628.7	634.0
2009	609.1	608.5	607.2	606.3	605.2	602.3	599.0	599.5	598.0	599.2	603.4	601.0	603.2
2010	584.4	586.2	591.0	591.9	597.8	592.5	588.5	591.8	589.8	596.3	599.3	598.4	592.3
2011	584.3	586.4	589.8	595.8	596.3	591.8	592.8	596.8	597.8	600.5	606.7	607.2	595.5
2012	590.6	595.1	598.4	600.5	603.1	600.8	598.7	603.9	605.7	609.6	618.0	618.9	603.6
2013	599.6	604.4	606.3	610.5	611.7	606.8	600.9	605.4	607.4	609.1	620.6	622.3	608.8
2014	604.0	605.5	609.0	617.5	617.7	613.8	609.8	617.0	617.8	622.3	630.4	633.1	616.5
2015	614.1	617.5	618.3	621.9	623.8	621.8	626.2	629.7	631.1	636.9	645.9	650.5	628.1
2016	628.8	631.5	633.2	637.4	636.0	632.1	633.6	638.4	641.2	643.9	650.6	651.8	638.2
2017	630.3	635.0	637.0	640.1	639.8	638.1	636.1	641.3	643.6	648.8	658.3	657.6	642.2
Total Private													
2007	545.0	545.6	551.9	554.2	556.7	560.2	558.5	560.1	559.9	556.6	561.4	562.7	556.1
2008	546.3	543.9	546.5	549.0	551.0	550.9	550.3	549.8	546.2	543.5	543.9	541.2	546.9
2009	523.2	521.2	519.7	518.8	517.8	518.4	514.9	514.8	511.8	511.5	515.3	513.5	516.7
2010	499.6	499.2	503.7	504.4	508.4	509.6	506.0	507.2	503.8	508.7	511.7	512.3	506.2
2011	498.9	499.5	503.1	508.9	510.6	512.2	513.5	513.8	513.0	515.2	521.0	522.5	511.0
2012	506.4	509.3	512.5	514.2	518.2	520.6	518.0	520.9	520.4	523.9	531.8	533.7	519.2
2013	515.7	518.2	520.4	523.7	527.2	528.0	522.8	524.5	524.3	525.6	536.5	539.8	525.6
2014	522.0	522.2	525.5	533.4	535.7	536.6	532.7	536.8	535.2	539.1	546.9	550.4	534.7
2015	532.4	533.3	534.2	538.6	542.9	545.7	550.1	550.6	548.9	553.5	562.4	568.4	546.8
2016	547.9	548.8	550.0	555.2	556.1	556.9	557.9	559.3	558.4	560.4	566.7	569.0	557.2
2017	548.4	551.2	553.3	556.2	557.9	560.6	558.3	560.4	558.5	563.1	572.1	573.1	559.4
Goods Producing													
2007	78.0	78.4	80.0	79.8	80.2	81.0	80.4	79.8	79.3	78.8	78.3	77.3	79.3
2008	75.9	75.4	76.2	76.8	77.3	77.4	76.7	76.8	76.2	74.7	73.7	72.5	75.8
2009	70.9	69.5	69.1	68.4	68.3	68.6	68.0	68.1	67.9	66.4	66.8	64.8	68.1
2010	62.7	63.0	64.0	64.1	64.6	65.1	65.2	65.1	64.8	63.8	64.1	63.8	64.2
2011	63.0	62.6	62.9	63.6	64.3	65.3	65.8	65.5	65.1	64.0	64.8	64.4	64.3
2012	63.4	63.5	64.1	64.8	65.5	66.3	66.2	66.5	65.3	64.7	65.4	65.0	65.1
2013	64.3	64.3	64.7	65.0	65.5	65.9	65.6	65.1	64.9	64.5	64.7	64.5	64.9
2014	64.6	64.5	64.4	65.4	66.1	65.9	66.3	66.4	66.0	66.1	66.2	66.5	65.7
2015	65.3	65.4	65.7	66.4	67.0	67.9	68.7	67.9	67.7	67.7	67.6	67.8	67.1
2016	66.8	66.6	66.4	67.5	67.7	68.1	68.7	68.0	67.5	67.1	67.2	67.4	67.4
2017	66.9	67.3	67.8	68.2	68.3	68.7	68.8	69.0	68.5	69.1	69.0	67.9	68.3
Service-Providing													
2007	553.3	554.3	559.0	561.0	562.2	560.4	559.1	564.7	567.0	566.2	571.8	573.8	562.7
2008	557.7	557.0	558.9	561.1	561.4	556.1	557.0	559.4	557.5	557.5	558.8	556.2	558.2
2009	538.2	539.0	538.1	537.9	536.9	533.7	531.0	531.4	530.1	532.8	536.6	536.2	535.2
2010	521.7	523.2	527.0	527.8	533.2	527.4	523.3	526.7	525.0	532.5	535.2	534.6	528.1
2011	521.3	523.8	526.9	532.2	532.0	526.5	527.0	531.3	532.7	536.5	541.9	542.8	531.2
2012	527.2	531.6	534.3	535.7	537.6	534.5	532.5	537.4	540.4	544.9	552.6	553.9	538.6
2013	535.3	540.1	541.6	545.5	546.2	540.9	535.3	540.3	542.5	544.6	555.9	557.8	543.8
2014	539.4	541.0	544.6	552.1	551.6	547.9	543.5	550.6	551.8	556.2	564.2	566.6	550.8
2015	548.8	552.1	552.6	555.5	556.8	553.9	557.5	561.8	563.4	569.2	578.3	582.7	561.1
2016	562.0	564.9	566.8	569.9	568.3	564.0	564.9	570.4	573.7	576.8	583.4	584.4	570.8
2017	563.4	567.7	569.2	571.9	571.5	569.4	567.3	572.3	575.1	579.7	589.3	589.7	573.9
Mining, Logging, and Construction													
2007	25.6	25.6	26.0	26.3	26.8	27.3	26.9	27.0	26.8	26.5	26.3	26.2	26.4
2008	24.5	24.5	25.0	25.5	25.7	25.8	25.2	25.1	24.7	23.8	23.4	22.9	24.7
2009	21.8	21.5	21.5	21.5	21.5	22.0	21.7	21.7	21.4	20.5	20.6	20.1	21.3
2010	19.0	18.7	19.3	19.2	19.4	19.8	19.8	19.8	19.7	19.4	19.1	18.9	19.3
2011	18.1	18.2	18.5	19.0	19.4	20.2	20.7	20.8	20.8	20.8	20.7	20.6	19.8
2012	19.5	19.5	20.0	20.4	20.9	21.4	21.3	21.5	21.3	20.8	20.6	20.5	20.6
2013	19.8	19.8	20.0	20.2	20.7	20.9	20.8	20.8	20.7	20.5	20.7	20.5	20.5
2014	20.5	20.3	19.9	21.0	21.4	21.1	21.1	21.2	21.1	21.4	21.5	21.4	21.0
2015	20.6	20.6	20.5	21.0	21.1	21.6	22.4	22.4	22.3	22.3	22.2	22.0	21.6
2016	21.2	21.0	20.9	21.5	21.5	21.8	22.4	22.0	22.1	21.9	22.0	21.9	21.7
2017	21.6	22.1	22.5	22.6	22.8	23.0	23.2	23.3	23.4	23.1	23.1	22.7	22.8

Employment by Industry: Memphis, TN-MS-AR, Selected Years, 2007–2017—*Continued*

(Numbers in thousands, not seasonally adjusted)

Industry and year	January	February	March	April	May	June	July	August	September	October	November	December	Annual average
Manufacturing													
2007	52.4	52.8	54.0	53.5	53.4	53.7	53.5	52.8	52.5	52.3	52.0	51.1	52.8
2008	51.4	50.9	51.2	51.3	51.6	51.6	51.5	51.7	51.5	50.9	50.3	49.6	51.1
2009	49.1	48.0	47.6	46.9	46.8	46.6	46.3	46.4	46.5	45.9	46.2	44.7	46.8
2010	43.7	44.3	44.7	44.9	45.2	45.3	45.4	45.3	45.1	44.4	45.0	44.9	44.9
2011	44.9	44.4	44.4	44.6	44.9	45.1	45.1	44.7	44.3	43.2	44.1	43.8	44.5
2012	43.9	44.0	44.1	44.4	44.6	44.9	44.9	45.0	44.0	43.9	44.8	44.5	44.4
2013	44.5	44.5	44.7	44.8	44.8	45.0	44.8	44.3	44.2	44.0	44.0	44.0	44.5
2014	44.1	44.2	44.5	44.4	44.7	44.8	45.2	45.2	44.9	44.7	44.7	45.1	44.7
2015	44.7	44.8	45.2	45.4	45.9	46.3	46.3	45.5	45.4	45.4	45.4	45.8	45.5
2016	45.6	45.6	45.5	46.0	46.2	46.3	46.3	46.0	45.4	45.2	45.2	45.5	45.7
2017	45.3	45.2	45.3	45.6	45.5	45.7	45.6	45.7	45.1	46.0	45.9	45.2	45.5
Trade, Transportation, and Utilities													
2007	173.6	172.8	174.1	175.0	175.8	175.9	175.6	175.6	175.9	175.1	178.3	179.4	175.6
2008	173.1	171.7	172.0	172.0	172.0	171.6	171.1	170.5	169.6	168.6	170.2	170.7	171.1
2009	164.7	163.3	162.6	161.3	161.3	160.8	160.2	159.7	159.0	158.6	160.0	161.1	161.1
2010	157.5	156.6	157.1	158.2	158.4	158.6	158.8	158.8	157.3	158.9	161.3	162.5	158.7
2011	157.2	156.6	156.9	158.6	159.1	159.4	160.1	159.7	159.9	161.8	164.4	165.5	159.9
2012	160.4	159.6	160.3	160.3	161.4	161.7	161.6	161.6	162.0	162.7	166.4	167.7	162.1
2013	162.1	161.7	161.1	162.0	162.0	162.3	162.6	161.8	161.1	162.0	165.7	167.1	162.6
2014	161.1	161.1	162.0	163.5	163.4	164.1	163.9	164.2	164.5	166.5	170.1	170.9	164.6
2015	165.1	164.0	164.2	164.8	166.0	167.0	170.4	169.0	168.7	170.6	175.7	178.3	168.7
2016	171.3	170.9	171.1	172.3	172.6	173.9	175.0	174.2	173.9	176.2	179.5	180.7	174.3
2017	173.7	173.2	172.9	173.4	173.8	174.9	176.0	175.7	175.3	176.8	182.0	183.0	175.9
Wholesale Trade													
2007	37.0	37.2	37.3	37.5	37.6	37.6	37.5	37.5	37.6	37.3	37.1	37.0	37.4
2008	36.2	36.0	35.9	36.3	36.1	35.8	35.2	35.2	35.0	34.9	34.7	34.3	35.5
2009	33.6	33.6	33.3	33.4	33.3	33.2	32.8	32.7	32.4	32.3	32.2	32.2	32.9
2010	32.0	32.0	32.0	32.8	32.7	32.8	32.7	32.8	32.5	32.6	32.8	32.8	32.5
2011	32.6	32.7	32.6	32.9	33.0	33.0	33.1	33.2	33.1	33.2	33.2	33.1	33.0
2012	33.1	33.3	33.3	33.4	33.7	33.8	33.8	33.8	33.8	33.8	33.9	33.9	33.6
2013	33.4	33.5	33.5	33.8	33.8	33.9	33.8	33.9	33.9	33.6	33.6	33.7	33.7
2014	33.2	33.4	33.6	33.6	33.7	33.8	33.6	33.6	33.7	33.5	33.7	33.9	33.6
2015	33.7	33.7	33.7	33.9	34.2	34.3	34.8	35.0	35.2	35.4	35.7	35.9	34.6
2016	35.1	35.3	35.4	35.3	35.4	35.5	35.6	35.8	35.7	35.7	35.8	36.0	35.6
2017	36.0	36.2	36.2	36.3	36.5	36.6	36.5	36.5	36.5	36.8	37.0	37.0	36.5
Retail Trade													
2007	72.1	71.1	72.0	72.3	72.6	73.0	72.8	71.9	71.9	71.8	74.9	75.7	72.7
2008	71.7	70.7	71.2	70.6	70.6	70.5	70.6	69.6	68.9	68.5	69.7	70.0	70.2
2009	66.9	66.0	65.9	65.3	65.6	65.8	65.9	65.3	64.9	65.1	67.0	67.8	66.0
2010	64.6	64.0	64.5	64.4	64.6	64.5	64.7	64.1	63.0	63.9	65.8	66.5	64.6
2011	62.5	61.8	61.9	62.6	62.7	62.6	62.8	62.2	61.9	62.7	65.3	66.0	62.9
2012	62.7	62.0	62.6	62.7	63.2	63.3	63.2	62.6	62.3	63.1	66.0	66.3	63.3
2013	63.6	63.1	63.2	63.3	63.6	63.8	64.3	64.0	63.8	64.4	67.0	68.1	64.4
2014	64.4	63.9	64.2	65.2	65.4	65.6	65.5	65.2	65.0	65.6	68.0	68.7	65.6
2015	65.0	64.3	64.6	64.8	65.3	65.8	66.5	65.9	65.2	66.5	69.6	70.4	66.2
2016	66.8	66.7	66.9	67.7	67.6	67.7	68.4	67.5	67.3	68.9	70.2	70.8	68.0
2017	67.8	67.4	67.3	67.6	67.5	67.6	67.9	67.7	67.4	68.3	70.8	70.7	68.2
Transportation and Utilities													
2007	64.5	64.5	64.8	65.2	65.6	65.3	65.3	66.2	66.4	66.0	66.3	66.7	65.6
2008	65.2	65.0	64.9	65.1	65.3	65.3	65.3	65.7	65.7	65.2	65.8	66.4	65.4
2009	64.2	63.7	63.4	62.6	62.4	61.8	61.5	61.7	61.7	61.2	60.8	61.1	62.2
2010	60.9	60.6	60.6	61.0	61.1	61.3	61.4	61.9	61.8	62.4	62.7	63.2	61.6
2011	62.1	62.1	62.4	63.1	63.4	63.8	64.2	64.3	64.9	65.9	65.9	66.4	64.0
2012	64.6	64.3	64.4	64.2	64.5	64.6	64.6	65.2	65.9	65.8	66.5	67.5	65.2
2013	65.1	65.1	64.4	64.9	64.6	64.6	64.5	63.9	63.4	64.0	65.1	65.3	64.6
2014	63.5	63.8	64.2	64.7	64.3	64.7	64.8	65.4	65.8	67.4	68.4	68.3	65.4
2015	66.4	66.0	65.9	66.1	66.5	66.9	69.1	68.1	68.3	68.7	70.4	72.0	67.9
2016	69.4	68.9	68.8	69.3	69.6	70.7	71.0	70.9	70.9	71.6	73.5	73.9	70.7
2017	69.9	69.6	69.4	69.5	69.8	70.7	71.6	71.5	71.4	71.7	74.2	75.3	71.2

Employment by Industry: Memphis, TN-MS-AR, Selected Years, 2007–2017—*Continued*

(Numbers in thousands, not seasonally adjusted)

Industry and year	January	February	March	April	May	June	July	August	September	October	November	December	Annual average
Information													
2007	7.4	7.4	7.3	7.4	7.4	7.5	7.5	7.4	7.3	7.3	7.4	7.4	7.4
2008	7.4	7.4	7.4	7.4	7.4	7.4	7.2	7.2	7.2	7.3	7.2	7.3	7.3
2009	7.2	7.1	7.0	6.9	6.9	6.8	6.8	6.7	6.7	6.6	6.6	6.6	6.8
2010	6.4	6.3	6.3	6.2	6.3	6.3	6.2	6.2	6.2	6.2	6.2	6.3	6.3
2011	6.2	6.1	6.1	6.1	6.2	6.1	6.1	6.1	6.0	6.0	6.0	6.0	6.1
2012	6.1	6.1	6.1	6.1	6.1	6.0	6.1	6.1	6.0	6.0	6.0	6.0	6.1
2013	5.9	5.9	5.9	5.9	6.0	6.1	6.0	6.0	6.0	6.0	6.1	6.1	6.0
2014	6.0	6.0	6.0	6.0	6.0	6.0	5.9	6.0	5.9	5.8	6.0	6.0	6.0
2015	5.8	5.8	5.8	5.9	5.9	5.9	5.8	5.8	5.7	5.7	5.8	5.9	5.8
2016	5.8	5.8	5.7	5.7	5.7	5.7	5.8	5.7	5.7	5.6	5.7	5.8	5.7
2017	5.7	5.7	5.7	5.6	5.7	5.7	5.7	5.6	5.6	5.5	5.6	5.6	5.6
Financial Activities													
2007	32.4	32.8	33.0	33.0	33.3	33.6	33.5	33.7	33.5	33.1	33.2	33.2	33.2
2008	32.8	32.7	33.0	32.9	33.0	32.9	32.6	32.5	32.1	32.0	31.9	31.4	32.5
2009	31.3	31.2	31.1	31.2	31.2	31.1	30.9	30.7	30.5	30.2	30.4	30.3	30.8
2010	29.7	29.6	29.5	29.2	29.1	29.0	28.9	28.8	28.5	28.2	28.0	28.1	28.9
2011	27.6	27.3	27.2	27.5	27.6	27.6	27.7	27.7	27.6	27.5	27.5	27.6	27.5
2012	27.4	27.4	27.4	27.3	27.5	27.3	27.5	27.4	27.1	27.3	27.4	27.4	27.4
2013	27.2	27.0	27.0	27.0	27.0	27.2	27.4	27.3	27.3	27.3	27.4	27.5	27.2
2014	27.1	27.1	27.1	27.4	27.6	27.6	27.6	27.6	27.4	27.5	27.5	27.5	27.4
2015	27.3	27.2	27.1	27.2	27.4	27.6	27.7	27.8	27.6	27.8	27.9	28.0	27.6
2016	27.7	27.8	27.6	27.8	27.9	28.0	28.2	28.2	28.1	28.1	28.2	28.3	28.0
2017	28.1	28.1	28.2	28.3	28.5	28.8	28.7	28.7	28.6	28.9	28.9	29.1	28.6
Professional and Business Services													
2007	80.4	80.5	81.3	82.0	81.9	81.7	82.7	84.0	85.3	85.4	87.0	87.5	83.3
2008	81.5	81.1	81.0	81.9	81.6	81.5	83.6	84.0	84.1	85.1	85.1	84.0	82.9
2009	77.9	77.9	76.9	76.1	75.0	74.5	73.7	74.8	74.6	76.7	78.0	77.7	76.2
2010	74.0	73.4	74.1	73.2	76.0	75.8	73.0	74.7	75.7	79.8	80.8	81.0	76.0
2011	77.0	78.2	79.3	80.3	80.2	79.9	80.4	81.5	81.7	84.8	86.9	87.7	81.5
2012	80.2	82.1	81.7	82.0	82.9	83.5	82.0	83.3	85.0	87.7	91.3	91.6	84.4
2013	83.6	85.1	86.1	86.5	87.9	87.6	84.0	86.9	88.1	88.7	94.9	97.3	88.1
2014	88.6	87.3	88.2	92.0	92.9	92.1	91.2	93.5	93.7	95.7	100.1	102.1	93.1
2015	94.5	94.6	94.9	95.1	96.1	96.3	96.5	98.1	98.3	99.9	103.2	105.0	97.7
2016	96.2	95.8	96.0	97.0	96.3	95.1	94.6	96.4	97.4	97.6	100.2	100.7	96.9
2017	90.9	91.4	91.5	92.1	92.2	92.8	91.6	92.3	92.6	92.8	95.7	97.0	92.7
Education and Health Services													
2007	78.9	79.2	80.1	79.8	80.3	80.2	79.9	80.8	81.2	81.2	81.4	82.2	80.4
2008	81.5	81.8	82.3	82.1	82.6	82.2	81.4	81.7	82.2	82.6	82.8	82.8	82.2
2009	81.3	82.1	82.4	83.0	82.6	82.3	81.6	81.9	82.6	83.7	84.3	84.2	82.7
2010	82.4	83.1	83.8	83.5	83.3	82.8	82.6	83.0	83.0	83.6	83.9	83.8	83.2
2011	82.5	83.0	83.5	84.3	84.1	83.6	83.8	84.5	85.6	85.8	86.2	86.1	84.4
2012	85.7	86.6	87.3	86.2	86.3	85.8	85.6	87.2	88.1	88.3	88.9	89.4	87.1
2013	88.1	89.3	89.5	89.3	89.4	88.4	87.4	88.1	89.2	89.6	90.1	90.1	89.0
2014	88.8	89.4	89.4	89.6	89.0	87.8	87.6	88.9	89.5	89.6	89.6	89.6	89.1
2015	88.3	89.5	89.6	89.7	89.2	88.4	89.1	90.5	91.3	91.7	92.2	92.6	90.2
2016	91.1	91.9	92.0	92.6	92.7	91.1	91.3	92.9	93.5	93.8	93.8	93.7	92.5
2017	92.2	93.4	93.8	94.0	93.8	92.6	91.8	93.5	94.3	96.0	97.0	96.3	94.1
Leisure and Hospitality													
2007	70.5	70.7	71.9	72.8	73.2	75.3	74.3	74.3	73.1	71.5	71.7	71.7	72.6
2008	70.1	69.8	70.5	71.7	72.5	72.8	72.7	72.1	69.9	68.3	68.1	67.5	70.5
2009	65.1	65.2	65.7	66.9	67.4	69.0	68.5	68.0	65.7	64.6	64.7	64.4	66.3
2010	62.5	62.8	64.3	65.2	66.0	67.3	66.9	66.5	64.6	64.3	63.8	63.4	64.8
2011	62.3	62.6	63.9	65.1	65.7	66.6	65.7	64.9	63.3	61.7	61.6	61.6	63.8
2012	59.7	60.4	61.7	63.4	64.2	65.4	64.6	64.6	62.8	63.1	62.4	62.6	62.9
2013	60.8	61.1	62.1	63.7	65.0	65.8	65.2	65.0	63.5	63.5	63.6	63.3	63.6
2014	62.1	62.9	64.4	65.5	66.6	68.6	65.9	66.1	64.1	63.9	63.6	63.9	64.8
2015	62.2	62.7	62.8	65.2	66.8	67.8	67.1	66.8	64.9	65.5	65.3	66.0	65.3
2016	64.3	65.2	66.2	67.3	68.1	69.5	68.8	68.5	66.9	66.8	66.8	67.1	67.1
2017	65.7	66.7	67.8	69.0	69.9	71.1	69.8	69.8	67.8	68.3	68.1	68.9	68.6

Employment by Industry: Memphis, TN-MS-AR, Selected Years, 2007–2017—*Continued*

(Numbers in thousands, not seasonally adjusted)

Industry and year	January	February	March	April	May	June	July	August	September	October	November	December	Annual average
Other Services													
2007	23.8	23.8	24.2	24.4	24.6	25.0	24.6	24.5	24.3	24.2	24.1	24.0	24.3
2008	24.0	24.0	24.1	24.2	24.6	25.1	25.0	25.0	24.9	24.9	24.9	25.0	24.6
2009	24.8	24.9	24.9	25.0	25.1	25.3	25.2	24.9	24.8	24.7	24.5	24.4	24.9
2010	24.4	24.4	24.6	24.8	24.7	24.7	24.4	24.1	23.7	23.9	23.6	23.4	24.2
2011	23.1	23.1	23.3	23.4	23.4	23.7	23.9	23.9	23.8	23.6	23.6	23.6	23.5
2012	23.5	23.6	23.9	24.1	24.3	24.6	24.4	24.2	24.1	24.1	24.0	24.0	24.1
2013	23.7	23.8	24.0	24.3	24.4	24.7	24.6	24.3	24.2	24.0	24.0	23.9	24.2
2014	23.7	23.9	24.0	24.0	24.1	24.5	24.3	24.1	24.1	24.0	23.8	23.9	24.0
2015	23.9	24.1	24.1	24.3	24.5	24.8	24.8	24.7	24.7	24.6	24.7	24.8	24.5
2016	24.7	24.8	25.0	25.0	25.1	25.5	25.5	25.4	25.4	25.2	25.3	25.3	25.2
2017	25.2	25.4	25.6	25.6	25.7	26.0	25.9	25.8	25.8	25.7	25.8	25.3	25.7
Government													
2007	86.3	87.1	87.1	86.6	85.7	81.2	81.0	84.4	86.4	88.4	88.7	88.4	85.9
2008	87.3	88.5	88.6	88.9	87.7	82.6	83.4	86.4	87.5	88.7	88.6	87.5	87.1
2009	85.9	87.3	87.5	87.5	87.4	83.9	84.1	84.7	86.2	87.7	88.1	87.5	86.5
2010	84.8	87.0	87.3	87.5	89.4	82.9	82.5	84.6	86.0	87.6	87.6	86.1	86.1
2011	85.4	86.9	86.7	86.9	85.7	79.6	79.3	83.0	84.8	85.3	85.7	84.7	84.5
2012	84.2	85.8	85.9	86.3	84.9	80.2	80.7	83.0	85.3	85.7	86.2	85.2	84.5
2013	83.9	86.2	85.9	86.8	84.5	78.8	78.1	80.9	83.1	83.5	84.1	82.5	83.2
2014	82.0	83.3	83.5	84.1	82.0	77.2	77.1	80.2	82.6	83.2	83.5	82.7	81.8
2015	81.7	84.2	84.1	83.3	80.9	76.1	76.1	79.1	82.2	83.4	83.5	82.1	81.4
2016	80.9	82.7	83.2	82.2	79.9	75.2	75.7	79.1	82.8	83.5	83.9	82.8	81.0
2017	81.9	83.8	83.7	83.9	81.9	77.5	77.8	80.9	85.1	85.7	86.2	84.5	82.7

Employment by Industry: Raleigh, NC, Selected Years, 2007–2017

(Numbers in thousands, not seasonally adjusted)

Industry and year	January	February	March	April	May	June	July	August	September	October	November	December	Annual average
Total Nonfarm													
2007	501.5	504.9	509.5	510.7	517.2	520.1	514.4	520.7	520.7	525.1	528.2	528.5	516.8
2008	518.3	520.4	521.6	521.6	525.8	523.6	520.3	524.1	523.9	524.9	522.9	520.1	522.3
2009	503.8	501.9	501.0	501.4	504.0	500.7	496.7	497.9	497.4	498.0	499.8	499.3	500.2
2010	487.7	487.9	492.2	497.6	502.3	502.2	500.7	503.2	502.8	506.8	509.1	508.2	500.1
2011	499.0	502.6	505.6	508.3	509.8	509.2	507.6	511.4	512.2	515.2	517.7	516.8	509.6
2012	512.2	514.6	518.4	522.7	525.9	526.2	524.8	529.8	528.8	531.9	535.5	534.7	525.5
2013	525.5	530.3	533.6	535.4	537.9	537.6	536.5	545.1	547.7	550.0	553.9	553.8	540.6
2014	544.2	544.1	550.1	555.1	559.5	562.2	557.5	563.8	564.7	571.6	574.9	575.0	560.2
2015	563.8	567.2	570.2	575.6	579.3	582.0	578.2	584.3	585.4	590.6	594.1	594.9	580.5
2016	585.8	588.8	591.7	597.0	599.5	601.2	598.6	602.8	603.9	608.2	612.8	611.2	600.1
2017	599.4	605.3	607.9	610.4	615.8	618.0	615.4	622.2	619.2	624.6	628.5	625.9	616.1
Total Private													
2007	411.7	414.2	418.2	419.1	424.9	429.3	427.0	430.0	428.0	432.1	434.8	435.4	425.4
2008	425.7	427.0	427.7	427.4	431.3	430.8	429.8	431.2	428.4	427.3	426.2	423.8	428.1
2009	410.3	408.2	406.6	405.3	407.9	406.8	406.8	406.7	404.1	403.8	405.6	405.7	406.5
2010	395.6	395.0	398.7	402.6	405.4	407.6	410.3	411.0	408.8	412.3	415.1	414.5	406.4
2011	406.3	409.1	411.8	414.9	416.5	419.1	421.3	422.0	420.6	422.3	425.0	426.1	417.9
2012	420.9	422.1	425.9	430.6	434.4	436.4	438.8	440.0	437.0	439.0	442.5	443.4	434.3
2013	434.0	437.4	440.4	442.7	446.5	449.5	450.8	454.9	454.3	455.0	458.7	460.3	448.7
2014	451.1	450.5	456.0	460.2	465.5	469.6	469.9	472.6	470.0	474.5	477.5	479.5	466.4
2015	469.1	471.2	474.3	479.6	485.1	489.1	490.3	492.7	489.9	494.0	497.0	499.2	486.0
2016	490.9	492.0	494.8	500.3	504.6	507.3	510.2	511.1	508.1	510.8	514.4	514.8	504.9
2017	503.9	507.6	510.0	512.6	518.8	523.2	525.9	526.4	521.2	525.0	527.9	527.3	519.2
Goods Producing													
2007	74.3	74.5	75.3	75.2	75.8	76.4	76.6	77.2	76.6	76.0	75.8	75.3	75.8
2008	73.6	73.5	73.6	72.6	72.8	72.7	72.6	72.0	71.4	69.9	68.7	67.1	71.7
2009	64.1	63.0	62.4	61.1	60.7	60.7	60.5	60.2	59.6	59.1	58.7	58.6	60.7
2010	56.8	56.5	57.1	57.3	57.9	58.3	59.1	59.2	59.0	59.0	58.9	58.4	58.1
2011	57.4	58.0	58.6	58.6	58.8	59.3	59.8	59.6	59.3	59.0	59.0	59.0	58.9
2012	58.7	59.0	59.5	59.7	60.2	60.8	61.4	61.4	61.2	61.0	61.0	61.0	60.4
2013	59.6	60.0	60.3	60.4	60.8	61.4	61.7	62.1	62.0	62.4	62.5	62.7	61.3
2014	61.8	61.9	62.9	62.7	63.6	64.5	65.3	65.6	65.5	65.5	65.5	65.4	64.2
2015	65.1	65.5	65.8	66.4	67.3	68.1	68.3	68.3	67.8	68.1	67.9	68.2	67.2
2016	67.9	68.0	68.3	68.9	69.3	70.1	70.4	70.4	70.0	70.5	70.8	70.9	69.6
2017	70.2	71.2	71.5	71.7	72.1	73.1	73.6	73.5	73.0	73.2	73.7	73.2	72.5
Service-Providing													
2007	427.2	430.4	434.2	435.5	441.4	443.7	437.8	443.5	444.1	449.1	452.4	453.2	441.0
2008	444.7	446.9	448.0	449.0	453.0	450.9	447.7	452.1	452.5	455.0	454.2	453.0	450.6
2009	439.7	438.9	438.6	440.3	443.3	440.0	436.2	437.7	437.8	438.9	441.1	440.7	439.4
2010	430.9	431.4	435.1	440.3	444.4	443.9	441.6	444.0	443.8	447.8	450.2	449.8	441.9
2011	441.6	444.6	447.0	449.7	451.0	449.9	447.8	451.8	452.9	456.2	458.7	457.8	450.8
2012	453.5	455.6	458.9	463.0	465.7	465.4	463.4	468.4	467.6	470.9	474.5	473.7	465.1
2013	465.9	470.3	473.3	475.0	477.1	476.2	474.8	483.0	485.7	487.6	491.4	491.1	479.3
2014	482.4	482.2	487.2	492.4	495.9	497.7	492.2	498.2	499.2	506.1	509.4	509.6	496.0
2015	498.7	501.7	504.4	509.2	512.0	513.9	509.9	516.0	517.6	522.5	526.2	526.7	513.2
2016	517.9	520.8	523.4	528.1	530.2	531.1	528.2	532.4	533.9	537.7	542.0	540.3	530.5
2017	529.2	534.1	536.4	538.7	543.7	544.9	541.8	548.7	546.2	551.4	554.8	552.7	543.6
Mining, Logging, and Construction													
2007	39.2	39.4	40.1	40.3	40.8	41.3	41.5	41.8	41.5	41.1	40.9	40.4	40.7
2008	39.2	39.2	39.3	38.3	38.6	38.5	38.4	38.0	37.6	36.4	35.3	34.2	37.8
2009	31.7	31.1	30.7	29.9	30.0	30.1	30.0	29.8	29.4	28.8	28.5	28.3	29.9
2010	27.0	26.8	27.3	27.7	28.1	28.4	29.0	29.1	28.9	28.9	28.6	28.1	28.2
2011	27.2	27.8	28.2	28.0	28.3	28.8	29.3	29.1	28.9	28.7	28.6	28.6	28.5
2012	28.4	28.6	29.1	29.2	29.6	30.0	30.5	30.5	30.4	30.3	30.2	30.2	29.8
2013	29.0	29.3	29.6	29.6	30.1	30.4	30.4	30.6	30.5	30.9	30.9	30.8	30.2
2014	30.1	30.0	30.9	30.9	31.5	31.9	32.5	32.6	32.4	32.3	32.0	31.8	31.6
2015	31.6	31.8	32.1	32.7	33.4	33.8	34.3	34.1	33.8	34.1	34.0	34.1	33.3
2016	33.7	33.7	34.1	34.7	35.1	35.4	35.6	35.7	35.8	36.2	36.4	36.5	35.2
2017	35.7	36.4	36.8	37.1	37.5	38.2	38.5	38.4	38.1	38.2	38.6	38.1	37.6

Employment by Industry: Raleigh, NC, Selected Years, 2007–2017—*Continued*

(Numbers in thousands, not seasonally adjusted)

Industry and year	January	February	March	April	May	June	July	August	September	October	November	December	Annual average
Manufacturing													
2007	35.1	35.1	35.2	34.9	35.0	35.1	35.1	35.4	35.1	34.9	34.9	34.9	35.1
2008	34.4	34.3	34.3	34.3	34.2	34.2	34.2	34.0	33.8	33.5	33.4	32.9	34.0
2009	32.4	31.9	31.7	31.2	30.7	30.6	30.5	30.4	30.2	30.3	30.2	30.3	30.9
2010	29.8	29.7	29.8	29.6	29.8	29.9	30.1	30.1	30.1	30.1	30.3	30.3	30.0
2011	30.2	30.2	30.4	30.6	30.5	30.5	30.5	30.5	30.4	30.3	30.4	30.4	30.4
2012	30.3	30.4	30.4	30.5	30.6	30.8	30.9	30.9	30.8	30.7	30.8	30.8	30.7
2013	30.6	30.7	30.7	30.8	30.7	31.0	31.3	31.5	31.5	31.5	31.6	31.9	31.2
2014	31.7	31.9	32.0	31.8	32.1	32.6	32.8	33.0	33.1	33.2	33.5	33.6	32.6
2015	33.5	33.7	33.7	33.7	33.9	34.3	34.0	34.2	34.0	34.0	33.9	34.1	33.9
2016	34.2	34.3	34.2	34.2	34.2	34.7	34.8	34.7	34.2	34.3	34.4	34.4	34.4
2017	34.5	34.8	34.7	34.6	34.6	34.9	35.1	35.1	34.9	35.0	35.1	35.1	34.9
Trade, Transportation, and Utilities													
2007	90.0	89.2	90.2	90.2	91.2	91.4	91.3	91.2	91.1	92.1	95.0	96.3	91.6
2008	91.9	91.5	91.9	91.8	91.8	92.0	91.6	91.7	90.9	91.5	92.3	92.8	91.8
2009	88.1	87.1	87.1	86.5	87.0	86.9	87.0	86.8	86.4	87.1	88.7	89.5	87.4
2010	86.0	85.3	85.5	86.0	86.7	86.9	87.2	87.3	86.2	87.6	89.7	91.1	87.1
2011	87.5	87.3	87.8	88.6	88.9	89.2	89.5	89.7	89.6	90.0	92.5	93.5	89.5
2012	91.4	90.6	91.3	91.0	92.0	92.2	92.4	92.1	92.0	92.6	95.1	95.7	92.4
2013	91.9	91.3	92.0	91.7	92.6	93.2	93.5	94.1	94.0	95.3	98.0	99.3	93.9
2014	96.1	95.6	96.5	97.2	98.0	98.4	98.5	99.2	98.9	100.3	103.4	105.1	98.9
2015	100.7	100.6	101.3	102.4	102.9	103.5	103.7	104.1	103.8	105.1	107.7	108.7	103.7
2016	104.8	104.8	105.5	106.5	107.4	107.6	107.8	107.9	107.6	108.3	110.7	112.6	107.6
2017	107.8	107.7	108.2	108.4	109.3	109.9	110.0	110.3	109.6	110.5	112.9	113.3	109.8
Wholesale Trade													
2007	21.9	22.0	22.2	22.1	22.2	22.2	22.3	22.2	22.2	22.1	22.2	22.2	22.2
2008	22.0	22.2	22.2	22.1	22.2	22.3	22.3	22.4	22.2	22.3	22.0	21.9	22.2
2009	21.4	21.4	21.2	21.0	20.9	20.8	20.7	20.7	20.5	20.5	20.4	20.4	20.8
2010	20.0	20.0	19.9	20.1	20.2	20.2	20.4	20.5	20.3	20.5	20.5	20.5	20.3
2011	20.7	20.7	20.7	21.1	21.3	21.4	21.8	21.9	22.1	21.8	22.1	22.1	21.5
2012	22.5	22.7	22.8	22.7	22.9	22.9	23.3	23.3	23.2	23.0	22.9	22.8	22.9
2013	22.5	22.5	22.5	22.1	22.3	22.5	22.7	22.8	22.7	22.7	22.8	22.8	22.6
2014	22.6	22.7	22.8	22.9	23.1	23.1	23.3	23.7	23.6	23.8	24.0	24.1	23.3
2015	23.9	24.0	24.1	24.2	24.1	24.3	24.5	24.5	24.5	24.6	24.6	24.6	24.3
2016	24.9	25.1	25.1	25.2	25.3	25.3	25.7	25.8	25.8	25.8	25.8	26.0	25.5
2017	25.7	25.9	26.0	26.2	26.4	26.7	26.6	26.7	26.6	27.1	27.1	27.6	26.6
Retail Trade													
2007	57.1	56.3	57.0	57.0	57.8	58.0	57.9	57.9	57.8	59.1	61.9	62.8	58.4
2008	59.3	58.8	59.1	58.9	58.8	58.9	58.6	58.5	58.0	58.5	59.7	59.9	58.9
2009	56.2	55.4	55.7	55.4	56.1	56.2	56.4	56.3	56.0	56.7	58.3	59.0	56.5
2010	56.2	55.5	55.8	55.9	56.5	56.6	56.7	56.7	56.0	57.1	59.2	60.4	56.9
2011	57.2	57.0	57.4	57.5	57.6	57.7	57.6	57.7	57.3	58.2	60.4	61.1	58.1
2012	58.8	57.9	58.4	58.3	58.9	59.0	58.9	58.7	58.7	59.5	62.0	62.4	59.3
2013	59.2	58.8	59.4	59.5	60.1	60.4	60.5	60.9	60.8	61.9	64.3	65.2	60.9
2014	61.9	61.5	62.1	62.8	63.2	63.6	63.6	63.8	63.5	64.8	67.4	68.4	63.9
2015	65.0	64.7	65.3	66.1	66.6	67.0	67.1	67.3	67.0	68.3	70.5	70.9	67.2
2016	67.4	67.3	67.9	68.8	69.4	69.5	69.4	69.4	68.9	69.7	71.9	72.9	69.4
2017	69.3	69.1	69.3	69.4	69.8	70.0	70.5	70.5	69.7	70.0	72.3	71.9	70.2
Transportation and Utilities													
2007	11.0	10.9	11.0	11.1	11.2	11.2	11.1	11.1	11.1	10.9	10.9	11.3	11.1
2008	10.6	10.5	10.6	10.8	10.8	10.8	10.7	10.8	10.7	10.7	10.6	11.0	10.7
2009	10.5	10.3	10.2	10.1	10.0	9.9	9.9	9.8	9.9	9.9	10.0	10.1	10.1
2010	9.8	9.8	9.8	10.0	10.0	10.1	10.1	10.1	9.9	10.0	10.0	10.2	10.0
2011	9.6	9.6	9.7	10.0	10.0	10.1	10.1	10.1	10.2	10.0	10.0	10.3	10.0
2012	10.1	10.0	10.1	10.0	10.2	10.3	10.2	10.1	10.1	10.1	10.2	10.5	10.2
2013	10.2	10.0	10.1	10.1	10.2	10.3	10.3	10.4	10.5	10.7	10.9	11.3	10.4
2014	11.6	11.4	11.6	11.5	11.7	11.7	11.6	11.7	11.8	11.7	12.0	12.6	11.7
2015	11.8	11.9	11.9	12.1	12.2	12.2	12.1	12.3	12.3	12.3	12.6	13.2	12.2
2016	12.5	12.4	12.5	12.5	12.7	12.8	12.7	12.7	12.9	12.8	13.0	13.7	12.8
2017	12.8	12.7	12.9	12.8	13.1	13.2	12.9	13.1	13.3	13.4	13.5	13.8	13.1

Employment by Industry: Raleigh, NC, Selected Years, 2007–2017—*Continued*

(Numbers in thousands, not seasonally adjusted)

Industry and year	January	February	March	April	May	June	July	August	September	October	November	December	Annual average
Information													
2007	16.3	16.6	16.5	16.4	16.5	16.8	16.9	16.9	16.7	16.9	16.8	16.8	16.7
2008	16.7	16.8	16.7	17.0	17.1	17.2	17.1	17.2	17.1	17.2	17.2	17.3	17.1
2009	17.1	17.0	16.9	17.0	16.8	16.9	16.9	16.8	16.7	16.8	16.8	16.8	16.9
2010	16.5	16.5	16.6	16.6	16.5	16.7	16.8	16.8	16.7	16.7	16.9	16.9	16.7
2011	16.9	17.0	17.0	17.1	17.1	17.4	17.5	17.7	17.5	17.6	17.8	17.8	17.4
2012	17.7	17.7	17.7	17.5	17.5	17.7	17.7	17.7	17.5	17.6	17.6	17.7	17.6
2013	17.7	17.8	17.8	17.8	17.9	18.0	18.2	18.2	18.0	17.9	18.1	18.2	18.0
2014	18.2	18.2	18.3	18.3	18.5	18.8	19.0	19.3	19.1	19.1	19.1	19.3	18.8
2015	19.2	19.2	19.3	19.3	19.4	19.7	19.9	20.0	20.0	20.2	20.3	20.4	19.7
2016	20.5	20.7	20.8	20.8	20.9	21.2	21.5	21.4	21.2	21.2	21.3	21.4	21.1
2017	21.2	21.4	21.4	21.6	21.7	22.0	22.2	22.1	22.0	22.2	22.4	22.4	21.9
Financial Activities													
2007	25.6	25.7	25.8	26.3	26.6	26.9	27.1	27.3	27.1	27.5	27.4	27.7	26.8
2008	26.8	27.0	27.0	27.1	27.2	27.4	27.4	27.5	27.4	27.5	27.3	27.3	27.2
2009	26.9	26.9	26.7	26.8	26.7	26.8	26.9	26.8	26.4	26.5	26.6	26.8	26.7
2010	26.4	26.4	26.4	26.3	26.4	26.4	26.6	26.6	26.8	26.7	26.9	27.0	26.6
2011	26.4	26.4	26.4	26.3	26.3	26.3	26.3	26.4	26.2	26.2	26.1	26.2	26.3
2012	25.8	26.1	26.2	26.4	26.4	26.5	26.4	26.3	26.2	26.7	26.6	26.7	26.4
2013	26.5	26.4	26.6	26.9	27.0	27.1	27.1	27.2	27.1	27.4	27.5	27.7	27.0
2014	27.2	27.3	27.3	27.5	27.7	27.9	27.9	28.0	27.9	28.2	28.2	28.5	27.8
2015	28.2	28.5	28.7	29.2	29.7	30.0	30.1	30.2	30.1	30.4	30.5	30.6	29.7
2016	30.5	30.6	30.5	30.7	30.7	30.8	31.1	31.1	30.9	31.0	31.0	30.9	30.8
2017	30.7	30.9	30.9	31.2	31.4	31.7	31.9	32.0	31.9	32.1	32.1	31.9	31.6
Professional and Business Services													
2007	87.3	88.3	89.0	89.4	89.7	91.6	89.2	89.7	89.5	92.2	90.8	90.0	89.7
2008	88.5	88.5	88.6	89.1	89.2	88.9	88.1	89.1	88.1	88.3	87.3	86.0	88.3
2009	84.1	83.3	81.9	81.8	81.8	81.7	81.7	81.8	82.1	82.8	83.5	83.4	82.5
2010	81.8	81.9	82.7	84.3	84.7	85.7	86.2	86.3	86.4	89.2	89.3	89.3	85.7
2011	87.7	88.5	88.4	89.7	90.0	91.0	91.6	91.4	92.1	92.5	92.7	92.9	90.7
2012	91.9	92.0	92.6	95.5	95.7	96.8	98.3	98.6	97.8	98.5	99.3	99.2	96.4
2013	98.0	100.5	100.9	101.0	102.0	102.0	103.0	105.2	105.3	104.8	105.2	104.5	102.7
2014	102.7	102.2	103.5	105.0	106.1	107.2	107.3	108.1	107.3	108.9	108.6	108.5	106.3
2015	105.0	105.5	106.0	106.7	107.8	108.5	108.9	109.9	109.5	110.6	110.8	110.9	108.3
2016	108.5	108.2	108.4	109.1	110.3	111.1	112.4	112.5	112.8	113.4	113.1	112.0	111.0
2017	110.1	110.7	110.6	111.3	112.8	114.8	116.2	116.3	115.1	118.0	118.6	117.9	114.4
Education and Health Services													
2007	54.9	55.8	56.2	56.6	57.0	56.5	56.1	56.9	57.5	58.5	58.7	58.8	57.0
2008	58.1	58.9	58.9	58.9	59.3	58.4	57.9	58.4	59.1	59.9	60.5	60.2	59.0
2009	59.2	59.8	59.9	60.2	60.8	59.7	59.2	60.0	60.0	60.3	60.4	60.3	60.0
2010	59.6	60.1	60.5	61.3	61.4	60.3	60.3	60.7	60.6	61.0	61.2	60.7	60.6
2011	60.7	61.5	61.6	61.1	61.3	60.6	60.5	60.8	61.0	62.2	62.3	62.1	61.3
2012	62.1	62.8	63.4	63.2	63.8	62.9	62.7	63.3	63.7	64.5	64.7	64.8	63.5
2013	63.5	64.2	64.4	64.6	64.9	64.1	64.2	65.1	65.6	65.7	65.9	65.9	64.8
2014	64.9	65.5	66.0	66.1	66.7	65.8	66.0	66.8	66.9	67.9	68.3	68.2	66.6
2015	67.5	68.1	68.3	69.0	69.4	68.8	69.0	70.0	70.1	71.1	71.3	71.5	69.5
2016	71.0	71.7	72.2	72.6	73.0	71.9	72.2	73.1	73.1	74.1	74.5	74.5	72.8
2017	73.8	74.7	74.9	75.3	76.0	74.4	75.2	76.1	75.9	75.5	75.7	75.4	75.2
Leisure and Hospitality													
2007	44.7	45.2	45.8	45.5	48.1	49.1	48.8	49.7	49.0	47.5	48.6	48.8	47.6
2008	47.6	48.0	48.5	48.5	50.9	50.9	51.3	51.5	50.8	49.4	49.5	50.1	49.8
2009	48.5	48.6	49.1	49.3	51.4	51.5	51.6	51.5	50.6	49.4	49.4	49.2	50.0
2010	47.4	47.3	48.6	49.7	50.6	51.9	52.7	52.9	52.4	50.9	51.4	50.7	50.5
2011	49.5	50.2	51.5	53.1	53.6	54.3	55.1	55.4	54.2	53.8	53.7	53.9	53.2
2012	52.5	53.0	54.2	55.9	56.9	57.5	57.7	58.1	56.1	55.8	55.9	56.5	55.8
2013	55.1	55.2	56.1	57.8	58.5	60.5	60.4	60.5	59.9	59.1	59.2	59.8	58.5
2014	58.0	57.6	58.9	60.7	61.7	63.5	62.5	62.3	61.4	61.5	61.3	61.8	60.9
2015	61.0	61.3	62.2	63.5	65.2	66.9	66.6	66.6	65.2	65.1	65.1	65.5	64.5
2016	64.1	64.4	65.3	67.7	68.9	70.3	70.1	70.0	68.1	67.7	68.5	68.5	67.8
2017	66.5	67.4	68.6	69.1	71.3	72.8	72.4	71.9	69.7	69.5	68.5	69.5	69.8

Employment by Industry: Raleigh, NC, Selected Years, 2007–2017—*Continued*

(Numbers in thousands, not seasonally adjusted)

Industry and year	January	February	March	April	May	June	July	August	September	October	November	December	Annual average
Other Services													
2007	18.6	18.9	19.4	19.5	20.0	20.6	21.0	21.1	20.5	21.4	21.7	21.7	20.4
2008	22.5	22.8	22.5	22.4	23.0	23.3	23.8	23.8	23.6	23.6	23.4	23.0	23.1
2009	22.3	22.5	22.6	22.6	22.7	22.6	23.0	22.8	22.3	21.8	21.5	21.1	22.3
2010	21.1	21.0	21.3	21.1	21.2	21.4	21.4	21.2	20.7	21.2	20.8	20.4	21.1
2011	20.2	20.2	20.5	20.4	20.5	21.0	21.0	21.0	20.7	21.0	20.9	20.7	20.7
2012	20.8	20.9	21.0	21.4	21.9	22.0	22.2	22.5	22.5	22.3	22.3	21.8	21.8
2013	21.7	22.0	22.3	22.5	22.8	23.2	22.7	22.5	22.4	22.4	22.3	22.2	22.4
2014	22.2	22.2	22.6	22.7	23.2	23.5	23.4	23.3	23.0	23.1	23.1	22.7	22.9
2015	22.4	22.5	22.7	23.1	23.4	23.6	23.8	23.6	23.4	23.4	23.4	23.4	23.2
2016	23.6	23.6	23.8	24.0	24.1	24.3	24.7	24.7	24.4	24.6	24.5	24.0	24.2
2017	23.6	23.6	23.9	24.0	24.2	24.5	24.4	24.2	24.0	24.0	24.0	23.7	24.0
Government													
2007	89.8	90.7	91.3	91.6	92.3	90.8	87.4	90.7	92.7	93.0	93.4	93.1	91.4
2008	92.6	93.4	93.9	94.2	94.5	92.8	90.5	92.9	95.5	97.6	96.7	96.3	94.2
2009	93.5	93.7	94.4	96.1	96.1	93.9	89.9	91.2	93.3	94.2	94.2	93.6	93.7
2010	92.1	92.9	93.5	95.0	96.9	94.6	90.4	92.2	94.0	94.5	94.0	93.7	93.7
2011	92.7	93.5	93.8	93.4	93.3	90.1	86.3	89.4	91.6	92.9	92.7	90.7	91.7
2012	91.3	92.5	92.5	92.1	91.5	89.8	86.0	89.8	91.8	92.9	93.0	91.3	91.2
2013	91.5	92.9	93.2	92.7	91.4	88.1	85.7	90.2	93.4	95.0	95.2	93.5	91.9
2014	93.1	93.6	94.1	94.9	94.0	92.6	87.6	91.2	94.7	97.1	97.4	95.5	93.8
2015	94.7	96.0	95.9	96.0	94.2	92.9	87.9	91.6	95.5	96.6	97.1	95.7	94.5
2016	94.9	96.8	96.9	96.7	94.9	93.9	88.4	91.7	95.8	97.4	98.4	96.4	95.2
2017	95.5	97.7	97.9	97.8	97.0	94.8	89.5	95.8	98.0	99.6	100.6	98.6	96.9

Employment by Industry: Richmond, VA, Selected Years, 2007–2017

(Numbers in thousands, not seasonally adjusted)

Industry and year	January	February	March	April	May	June	July	August	September	October	November	December	Annual average
Total Nonfarm													
2007	614.2	617.5	619.2	620.3	625.6	631.6	622.4	622.6	622.9	624.4	625.5	626.8	622.8
2008	615.9	616.9	619.3	622.8	622.5	626.0	618.4	617.5	618.5	622.3	620.9	618.5	620.0
2009	603.0	598.5	598.7	598.9	600.1	601.4	588.8	586.3	589.5	592.9	594.0	592.9	595.4
2010	581.8	579.0	585.4	593.5	599.2	600.7	593.3	590.7	591.1	595.5	596.5	596.5	591.9
2011	587.2	589.3	593.8	600.6	601.0	602.8	601.7	599.1	601.6	607.9	611.5	610.0	600.5
2012	598.3	600.4	605.4	611.2	613.6	617.9	611.5	614.4	615.3	619.9	622.9	624.6	613.0
2013	609.5	612.3	616.6	621.6	622.1	625.2	622.8	623.7	623.7	626.0	635.1	632.7	622.6
2014	621.0	618.9	624.4	631.8	636.3	638.5	634.0	635.2	634.1	637.6	644.0	644.4	633.4
2015	633.9	634.1	636.8	645.4	650.4	653.4	652.5	653.4	656.3	663.6	669.7	668.1	651.5
2016	653.1	655.1	657.8	663.8	662.9	666.6	661.7	661.5	665.1	669.2	675.0	675.7	664.0
2017	657.8	663.4	666.2	670.0	672.4	677.7	673.0	672.7	674.7	676.8	675.6	675.2	671.3
Total Private													
2007	501.1	503.2	505.9	507.1	512.9	519.7	515.4	516.7	516.5	515.6	516.3	518.4	512.4
2008	508.0	508.0	510.5	511.8	512.5	515.7	513.5	513.3	510.6	511.1	508.8	508.1	511.0
2009	491.9	486.9	486.7	486.3	488.4	489.7	484.2	481.5	481.2	481.4	481.4	481.6	485.1
2010	470.5	467.2	473.3	480.0	485.0	487.4	485.8	483.9	482.4	484.7	484.7	485.3	480.9
2011	475.8	477.1	481.4	488.0	489.8	492.1	494.6	493.1	492.3	496.2	499.1	498.1	489.8
2012	486.7	487.6	492.3	499.3	502.8	507.3	505.9	508.7	507.3	510.0	511.5	513.4	502.7
2013	499.3	501.4	505.7	509.8	512.1	515.0	516.9	518.5	515.7	516.3	524.7	522.3	513.1
2014	510.9	508.6	513.6	521.1	526.3	528.5	527.5	528.3	524.8	527.1	532.8	533.2	523.6
2015	523.4	523.2	526.3	535.0	540.9	543.9	547.1	548.3	548.2	552.5	557.9	556.8	542.0
2016	543.0	543.3	545.6	551.3	552.3	555.8	554.9	555.2	555.3	557.7	562.5	563.2	553.3
2017	547.0	551.0	553.8	557.7	561.8	567.1	565.3	565.6	564.5	564.6	562.5	561.9	560.2
Goods Producing													
2007	84.3	83.9	84.5	85.3	86.1	87.2	86.7	87.0	86.6	85.8	85.1	85.0	85.6
2008	82.5	82.1	81.8	81.7	81.2	80.9	80.5	80.3	79.2	78.8	76.7	75.5	80.1
2009	71.9	69.0	68.8	68.3	67.5	67.6	67.0	66.5	66.2	65.9	65.5	65.0	67.4
2010	62.8	61.7	62.7	64.1	64.3	64.6	65.2	64.5	64.2	64.5	64.2	63.6	63.9
2011	61.3	61.5	62.0	62.4	62.6	62.6	63.0	62.8	62.6	63.2	63.1	63.0	62.5
2012	61.1	60.6	61.6	62.7	63.2	63.7	63.7	64.2	63.9	63.7	63.6	63.5	63.0
2013	61.9	62.5	63.3	64.0	64.3	65.1	65.2	65.2	64.7	64.2	64.1	63.6	64.0
2014	62.5	62.3	63.1	64.1	64.9	65.3	65.9	66.1	65.8	65.7	65.6	65.6	64.7
2015	64.2	64.3	65.1	66.8	67.5	67.6	68.5	68.6	68.4	68.1	67.8	67.4	67.0
2016	66.3	66.6	67.1	68.0	68.4	69.0	69.5	69.2	69.3	69.6	69.3	69.0	68.4
2017	67.2	68.0	68.8	69.7	70.2	71.4	71.5	71.5	71.4	71.9	72.2	72.3	70.5
Service-Providing													
2007	529.9	533.6	534.7	535.0	539.5	544.4	535.7	535.6	536.3	538.6	540.4	541.8	537.1
2008	533.4	534.8	537.5	541.1	541.3	545.1	537.9	537.2	539.3	543.5	544.2	543.0	539.9
2009	531.1	529.5	529.9	530.6	532.6	533.8	521.8	519.8	523.3	527.0	528.5	527.9	528.0
2010	519.0	517.3	522.7	529.4	534.9	536.1	528.1	526.2	526.9	531.0	532.3	532.9	528.1
2011	525.9	527.8	531.8	538.2	538.4	540.2	538.7	536.3	539.0	544.7	548.4	547.0	538.0
2012	537.2	539.8	543.8	548.5	550.4	554.2	547.8	550.2	551.4	556.2	559.3	561.1	550.0
2013	547.6	549.8	553.3	557.6	557.8	560.1	557.6	558.5	559.0	561.8	571.0	569.1	558.6
2014	558.5	556.6	561.3	567.7	571.4	573.2	568.1	569.1	568.3	571.9	578.4	578.8	568.6
2015	569.7	569.8	571.7	578.6	582.9	585.8	584.0	584.8	587.9	595.5	601.9	600.7	584.4
2016	586.8	588.5	590.7	595.8	594.5	597.6	592.2	592.3	595.8	599.6	605.7	606.7	595.5
2017	590.6	595.4	597.4	600.3	602.2	606.3	601.5	601.2	603.3	604.9	603.4	602.9	600.8
Mining, Logging, and Construction													
2007	43.4	43.2	43.7	44.6	45.4	46.2	46.1	46.4	46.3	45.5	44.8	44.5	45.0
2008	42.4	42.1	42.2	42.2	41.9	41.9	41.9	42.0	41.0	40.8	39.4	38.6	41.4
2009	36.3	35.2	35.1	35.2	35.0	34.9	34.7	34.4	33.9	33.9	33.5	33.0	34.6
2010	31.2	30.3	31.3	32.6	32.8	32.9	33.5	33.0	32.7	33.1	33.0	32.4	32.4
2011	30.7	30.7	31.2	31.7	31.9	31.8	32.3	32.1	31.9	32.4	32.4	32.3	31.8
2012	31.0	30.6	31.4	32.3	32.7	33.0	33.2	33.6	33.4	33.2	33.2	32.9	32.5
2013	31.6	31.9	32.7	33.3	33.4	34.0	34.1	34.2	33.8	33.3	33.2	32.7	33.2
2014	31.7	31.7	32.5	33.4	34.0	34.3	34.9	34.9	34.7	34.8	34.7	34.6	33.9
2015	33.6	33.8	34.5	36.2	36.7	36.6	37.5	37.6	37.4	37.1	36.7	36.2	36.2
2016	35.2	35.3	35.7	36.5	36.9	37.3	37.7	37.5	37.6	37.9	37.7	37.2	36.9
2017	35.7	36.2	36.9	37.5	38.0	39.0	39.0	39.0	39.0	39.6	39.9	39.8	38.3

Employment by Industry: Richmond, VA, Selected Years, 2007–2017—*Continued*

(Numbers in thousands, not seasonally adjusted)

Industry and year	January	February	March	April	May	June	July	August	September	October	November	December	Annual average
Manufacturing													
2007	40.9	40.7	40.8	40.7	40.7	41.0	40.6	40.6	40.3	40.3	40.3	40.5	40.6
2008	40.1	40.0	39.6	39.5	39.3	39.0	38.6	38.3	38.2	38.0	37.3	36.9	38.7
2009	35.6	33.8	33.7	33.1	32.5	32.7	32.3	32.1	32.3	32.0	32.0	32.0	32.8
2010	31.6	31.4	31.4	31.5	31.5	31.7	31.7	31.5	31.5	31.4	31.2	31.2	31.5
2011	30.6	30.8	30.8	30.7	30.7	30.8	30.7	30.7	30.7	30.8	30.7	30.7	30.7
2012	30.1	30.0	30.2	30.4	30.5	30.7	30.5	30.6	30.5	30.5	30.4	30.6	30.4
2013	30.3	30.6	30.6	30.7	30.9	31.1	31.1	31.0	30.9	30.9	30.9	30.9	30.8
2014	30.8	30.6	30.6	30.7	30.9	31.0	31.0	31.2	31.1	30.9	30.9	31.0	30.9
2015	30.6	30.5	30.6	30.6	30.8	31.0	31.0	31.0	31.0	31.0	31.1	31.2	30.9
2016	31.1	31.3	31.4	31.5	31.5	31.7	31.8	31.7	31.7	31.7	31.6	31.8	31.6
2017	31.5	31.8	31.9	32.2	32.2	32.4	32.5	32.5	32.4	32.3	32.3	32.5	32.2
Trade, Transportation, and Utilities													
2007	113.9	112.9	113.6	113.2	114.4	115.2	115.0	115.2	115.2	115.7	118.2	119.6	115.2
2008	114.7	113.1	113.3	112.9	113.3	113.9	113.6	113.6	113.6	114.3	115.9	116.9	114.1
2009	111.2	109.3	108.6	107.6	108.0	107.9	106.9	106.7	106.1	107.3	108.9	110.2	108.2
2010	106.0	104.5	105.3	106.6	107.9	108.2	107.7	107.6	106.4	107.7	109.6	111.2	107.4
2011	107.4	106.6	107.0	108.6	108.9	109.3	109.4	109.7	108.7	110.2	112.7	114.3	109.4
2012	109.8	108.7	109.5	110.1	111.2	111.2	110.3	110.7	111.0	113.9	117.2	120.8	112.0
2013	113.0	111.9	112.1	112.6	113.4	113.8	114.0	114.4	114.0	115.4	118.6	120.1	114.4
2014	115.7	114.9	115.7	116.7	117.4	118.1	117.8	118.2	117.1	117.5	119.8	121.2	117.5
2015	117.0	115.9	116.2	117.5	118.2	119.1	120.8	121.0	120.7	121.6	124.3	125.6	119.8
2016	121.1	120.2	120.5	121.3	121.6	122.3	121.2	121.5	120.8	121.4	124.7	125.4	121.8
2017	120.4	119.1	119.1	120.2	121.2	122.0	121.6	121.7	122.2	123.0	123.7	124.8	121.6
Wholesale Trade													
2007	27.8	28.0	28.2	28.2	28.3	28.5	28.5	28.5	28.4	28.6	28.4	28.4	28.3
2008	28.2	28.3	28.3	28.3	28.2	28.3	28.4	28.3	28.1	28.0	27.8	27.6	28.2
2009	27.2	26.9	26.7	26.4	26.3	26.1	25.9	25.9	25.6	25.8	25.7	25.6	26.2
2010	25.3	25.3	25.4	25.9	26.1	26.1	26.2	26.3	26.0	26.5	26.6	26.6	26.0
2011	26.7	26.7	26.9	27.0	27.0	27.2	27.4	27.4	27.1	27.1	27.1	27.1	27.1
2012	26.9	27.0	27.3	27.7	27.9	28.1	27.9	28.1	28.0	28.0	28.1	28.1	27.8
2013	28.1	28.2	28.3	28.2	28.3	28.4	28.4	28.4	28.3	28.3	28.2	28.2	28.3
2014	27.8	27.7	27.8	28.0	28.2	28.3	28.4	28.5	28.3	28.1	28.2	28.2	28.1
2015	28.3	28.3	28.4	28.6	28.8	28.9	28.9	29.0	29.0	29.0	29.1	29.1	28.8
2016	28.6	28.5	28.7	28.7	28.7	28.6	28.6	28.6	28.5	28.5	28.6	28.7	28.6
2017	28.4	28.5	28.7	28.7	28.8	29.0	28.8	28.9	28.9	29.2	28.9	29.1	28.8
Retail Trade													
2007	67.2	66.1	66.5	66.2	67.3	67.7	67.6	67.6	67.6	68.2	70.6	71.5	67.8
2008	68.0	66.4	66.6	66.1	66.5	66.9	66.6	66.7	67.0	67.9	69.5	70.2	67.4
2009	66.0	64.6	64.2	63.8	64.2	64.4	63.6	63.5	63.3	64.2	65.7	66.7	64.5
2010	63.5	62.1	62.6	63.2	64.4	64.6	64.0	63.8	62.9	63.7	65.4	66.4	63.9
2011	63.3	62.5	62.6	63.4	63.6	63.6	63.3	63.6	62.9	64.3	66.6	67.8	64.0
2012	64.4	63.3	63.6	63.7	64.5	64.2	63.6	63.8	64.1	67.1	70.1	73.0	65.5
2013	65.6	64.5	64.4	64.9	65.5	65.6	65.7	65.9	65.5	66.9	69.7	70.3	66.2
2014	66.9	66.5	67.0	67.5	67.6	67.8	67.3	67.3	66.3	66.7	68.4	69.0	67.4
2015	65.4	64.4	64.5	65.1	65.5	66.0	66.1	66.0	65.5	66.1	68.0	68.4	65.9
2016	65.7	65.4	65.5	66.2	66.5	66.9	66.7	66.8	65.9	66.6	68.7	68.9	66.7
2017	66.2	65.3	65.5	65.9	66.5	67.0	67.3	66.7	66.0	66.4	67.2	67.3	66.4
Transportation and Utilities													
2007	18.9	18.8	18.9	18.8	18.8	19.0	18.9	19.1	19.2	18.9	19.2	19.7	19.0
2008	18.5	18.4	18.4	18.5	18.6	18.7	18.6	18.6	18.5	18.4	18.6	19.1	18.6
2009	18.0	17.8	17.7	17.4	17.5	17.4	17.4	17.3	17.2	17.3	17.5	17.9	17.5
2010	17.2	17.1	17.3	17.5	17.4	17.5	17.5	17.5	17.5	17.5	17.6	18.2	17.5
2011	17.4	17.4	17.5	18.2	18.3	18.5	18.7	18.7	18.7	18.8	19.0	19.4	18.4
2012	18.5	18.4	18.6	18.7	18.8	18.9	18.8	18.8	18.9	18.8	19.0	19.7	18.8
2013	19.3	19.2	19.4	19.5	19.6	19.8	19.9	20.1	20.2	20.2	20.7	21.6	20.0
2014	21.0	20.7	20.9	21.2	21.6	22.0	22.1	22.4	22.5	22.7	23.2	24.0	22.0
2015	23.3	23.2	23.3	23.8	23.9	24.2	25.8	26.0	26.2	26.5	27.2	28.1	25.1
2016	26.8	26.3	26.3	26.4	26.4	26.8	25.9	26.1	26.4	26.3	27.4	27.8	26.6
2017	25.8	25.3	24.9	25.6	25.9	26.0	25.5	26.1	27.3	27.4	27.6	28.4	26.3

Employment by Industry: Richmond, VA, Selected Years, 2007–2017—*Continued*

(Numbers in thousands, not seasonally adjusted)

Industry and year	January	February	March	April	May	June	July	August	September	October	November	December	Annual average
Information													
2007	11.6	11.6	11.5	11.7	11.9	11.6	11.3	11.2	11.0	10.8	10.7	10.6	11.3
2008	10.5	10.4	10.5	10.4	10.3	10.4	10.2	10.1	10.1	10.3	10.4	10.4	10.3
2009	10.4	10.4	10.3	10.3	10.3	10.3	10.1	9.8	9.7	9.6	9.6	9.6	10.0
2010	9.5	9.4	9.4	9.3	9.4	9.4	9.4	9.4	9.4	9.5	9.4	9.4	9.4
2011	9.2	9.1	9.1	8.8	8.8	8.8	8.9	7.6	8.5	9.2	9.3	9.4	8.9
2012	8.0	8.1	8.2	8.0	8.0	8.1	8.0	8.2	7.7	7.6	7.9	7.9	8.0
2013	7.7	8.0	8.0	8.4	7.9	8.0	7.8	7.9	7.7	7.7	7.9	7.9	7.9
2014	8.3	7.9	7.9	7.8	8.0	7.6	7.9	8.0	7.7	7.8	7.6	7.6	7.8
2015	7.5	7.5	7.4	7.4	7.5	7.4	7.5	7.4	7.4	7.5	7.4	7.3	7.4
2016	7.2	7.3	7.2	7.5	6.7	7.5	7.5	7.4	7.6	7.2	7.2	7.4	7.3
2017	7.1	7.3	7.4	7.3	7.5	7.5	7.4	7.4	7.7	7.6	7.6	7.7	7.5
Financial Activities													
2007	45.5	45.4	45.7	45.7	45.8	46.1	46.0	46.2	45.5	45.1	44.9	44.8	45.6
2008	44.4	44.3	44.3	43.8	43.6	43.8	44.1	44.1	43.5	43.9	43.8	43.9	44.0
2009	43.5	43.3	43.4	43.3	42.9	42.9	42.9	42.9	42.4	42.4	42.3	42.4	42.9
2010	42.0	41.9	42.2	42.3	42.5	42.8	42.6	42.7	42.3	42.6	42.6	42.8	42.4
2011	42.5	42.6	43.0	43.2	43.4	43.8	44.3	44.5	44.3	44.7	45.4	45.8	44.0
2012	45.1	45.4	45.6	46.1	46.4	46.9	47.0	47.2	47.0	47.0	47.3	47.3	46.5
2013	46.9	47.0	47.2	47.4	47.6	47.9	48.4	48.4	48.1	48.2	48.3	48.1	47.8
2014	47.9	48.2	48.2	48.4	48.5	48.8	49.0	49.1	48.7	48.9	49.4	49.6	48.7
2015	49.6	50.1	50.1	50.3	50.3	50.6	50.8	50.8	50.5	50.6	50.6	50.5	50.4
2016	49.8	49.8	49.8	50.2	50.4	50.5	50.6	50.8	50.5	50.8	51.2	51.4	50.5
2017	50.5	50.9	50.9	51.1	51.5	52.0	52.2	52.2	51.7	52.1	51.6	51.4	51.5
Professional and Business Services													
2007	96.4	97.0	97.7	97.7	97.6	99.1	98.7	98.9	99.0	99.6	99.3	99.7	98.4
2008	98.9	99.4	99.7	99.6	99.4	100.0	99.1	99.2	98.0	98.6	97.7	96.9	98.9
2009	94.7	94.2	94.0	92.4	92.1	91.6	91.3	91.0	90.7	91.3	91.6	91.8	92.2
2010	89.9	89.9	90.6	91.9	92.1	92.4	93.4	93.5	93.7	94.5	94.5	94.7	92.6
2011	94.1	94.7	95.8	96.7	96.4	96.0	96.6	96.5	96.9	97.4	98.3	96.4	96.3
2012	95.9	96.8	96.9	98.2	98.5	99.4	99.5	100.0	100.4	101.0	100.0	99.7	98.9
2013	98.4	98.8	99.3	98.9	99.3	99.3	99.7	100.7	100.4	100.9	105.4	103.9	100.4
2014	100.7	99.1	99.7	101.2	102.7	102.6	101.6	101.5	101.8	103.6	108.3	108.1	102.6
2015	105.0	103.8	104.2	106.1	108.2	109.0	108.1	108.6	110.3	113.9	118.0	118.1	109.4
2016	111.8	111.0	110.6	111.9	112.0	111.9	110.8	111.0	112.7	114.6	116.9	119.1	112.9
2017	112.6	113.6	113.2	113.2	114.5	115.3	114.3	114.2	115.2	116.0	114.6	115.8	114.4
Education and Health Services													
2007	71.8	74.2	72.8	71.5	72.9	73.5	70.9	71.4	75.5	76.8	77.7	78.5	74.0
2008	78.2	79.2	79.5	80.6	80.7	80.6	78.3	78.6	81.3	82.3	82.9	83.0	80.4
2009	81.9	82.2	82.1	82.7	83.7	83.5	80.5	80.5	83.3	84.5	85.3	85.1	82.9
2010	84.4	84.3	85.0	85.0	85.7	84.9	82.4	82.1	84.2	85.5	85.7	85.3	84.5
2011	84.7	85.2	85.3	86.1	85.1	84.7	85.6	85.8	87.0	88.0	88.4	87.1	86.1
2012	87.0	87.5	87.7	88.9	87.7	87.7	87.8	88.7	90.2	90.7	90.9	90.0	88.7
2013	89.6	90.5	90.7	91.1	90.1	89.2	89.9	90.7	92.0	92.8	93.3	92.0	91.0
2014	92.0	92.4	92.8	94.1	93.0	92.5	92.4	93.0	93.6	94.7	94.8	93.6	93.2
2015	94.3	94.8	94.9	95.9	94.8	94.2	94.8	95.5	96.6	97.5	97.6	96.5	95.6
2016	96.9	97.4	97.3	97.2	95.9	95.3	95.4	95.9	97.9	98.5	98.7	97.3	97.0
2017	97.7	98.6	98.6	98.6	97.5	97.1	96.3	97.1	98.3	97.3	96.2	96.0	97.4
Leisure and Hospitality													
2007	48.2	48.7	50.2	51.2	53.4	55.8	55.6	55.2	53.1	51.6	50.2	49.9	51.9
2008	48.6	48.9	50.7	52.7	54.8	56.6	56.2	55.4	52.6	51.5	50.0	50.1	52.3
2009	48.3	48.4	49.4	51.6	53.9	55.7	55.2	54.2	52.3	50.7	48.6	48.3	51.4
2010	46.7	46.2	48.2	51.2	53.4	55.2	55.2	54.3	52.7	50.9	49.2	48.9	51.0
2011	47.4	48.1	49.8	52.4	54.9	56.9	56.9	56.4	54.9	54.0	52.4	52.5	53.1
2012	50.6	51.3	53.3	55.2	57.4	59.7	59.1	59.0	56.7	55.5	54.0	54.1	55.5
2013	52.3	53.0	55.1	57.1	58.9	60.8	60.8	60.1	58.0	56.3	56.4	56.1	57.1
2014	53.5	53.5	55.7	58.0	60.7	62.1	61.5	61.0	59.0	58.0	56.4	56.7	58.0
2015	55.2	56.0	57.4	60.1	63.0	64.4	64.9	64.6	62.9	61.7	60.6	60.0	60.9
2016	58.7	59.7	61.6	63.2	65.3	67.0	67.2	66.8	64.4	63.2	62.2	61.5	63.4
2017	59.6	61.5	63.5	65.2	66.9	69.0	68.8	68.5	65.0	63.8	63.5	61.5	64.7

Employment by Industry: Richmond, VA, Selected Years, 2007–2017—*Continued*

(Numbers in thousands, not seasonally adjusted)

Industry and year	January	February	March	April	May	June	July	August	September	October	November	December	Annual average
Other Services													
2007	29.4	29.5	29.9	30.8	30.8	31.2	31.2	31.6	30.6	30.2	30.2	30.3	30.5
2008	30.2	30.6	30.7	30.1	29.2	29.5	31.5	32.0	32.3	31.4	31.4	31.4	30.9
2009	30.0	30.1	30.1	30.1	30.0	30.2	30.3	29.9	30.5	29.7	29.6	29.2	30.0
2010	29.2	29.3	29.9	29.6	29.7	29.9	29.9	29.8	29.5	29.5	29.5	29.4	29.6
2011	29.2	29.3	29.4	29.8	29.7	30.0	29.9	29.8	29.4	29.5	29.5	29.6	29.6
2012	29.2	29.2	29.5	30.1	30.4	30.6	30.5	30.7	30.4	30.6	30.6	30.1	30.2
2013	29.5	29.7	30.0	30.3	30.6	30.9	31.1	31.1	30.8	30.8	30.7	30.6	30.5
2014	30.3	30.3	30.5	30.8	31.1	31.5	31.4	31.4	31.1	30.9	30.9	30.8	30.9
2015	30.6	30.8	31.0	30.9	31.4	31.6	31.7	31.8	31.4	31.6	31.6	31.4	31.3
2016	31.2	31.3	31.5	32.0	32.0	32.3	32.7	32.6	32.1	32.4	32.3	32.1	32.0
2017	31.9	32.0	32.3	32.4	32.5	32.8	33.2	33.0	33.0	32.9	33.1	32.4	32.6
Government													
2007	113.1	114.3	113.3	113.2	112.7	111.9	107.0	105.9	106.4	108.8	109.2	108.4	110.4
2008	107.9	108.9	108.8	111.0	110.0	110.3	104.9	104.2	107.9	111.2	112.1	110.4	109.0
2009	111.1	111.6	112.0	112.6	111.7	111.7	104.6	104.8	108.3	111.5	112.6	111.3	110.3
2010	111.3	111.8	112.1	113.5	114.2	113.3	107.5	106.8	108.7	110.8	111.8	111.2	111.1
2011	111.4	112.2	112.4	112.6	111.2	110.7	107.1	106.0	109.3	111.7	112.4	111.9	110.7
2012	111.6	112.8	113.1	111.9	110.8	110.6	105.6	105.7	108.0	109.9	111.4	111.2	110.2
2013	110.2	110.9	110.9	111.8	110.0	110.2	105.9	105.2	108.0	109.7	110.4	110.4	109.5
2014	110.1	110.3	110.8	110.7	110.0	110.0	106.5	106.9	109.3	110.5	111.2	111.2	109.8
2015	110.5	110.9	110.5	110.4	109.5	109.5	105.4	105.1	108.1	111.1	111.8	111.3	109.5
2016	110.1	111.8	112.2	112.5	110.6	110.8	106.8	106.3	109.8	111.5	112.5	112.5	110.6
2017	110.8	112.4	112.4	112.3	110.6	110.6	107.7	107.1	110.2	112.2	113.1	113.3	111.1

Employment by Industry: Louisville/Jefferson County, KY-IN, Selected Years, 2007–2017

(Numbers in thousands, not seasonally adjusted)

Industry and year	January	February	March	April	May	June	July	August	September	October	November	December	Annual average
Total Nonfarm													
2006	599.7	600.0	603.0	611.3	619.6	623.6	611.0	614.2	616.6	615.1	620.7	618.2	612.8
2007	603.2	603.5	605.4	610.5	620.6	619.4	607.2	612.1	606.9	605.7	608.7	602.8	608.8
2008	580.0	579.1	580.8	584.6	587.1	586.4	580.1	582.3	582.5	583.7	584.9	582.6	582.8
2009	567.0	561.3	572.3	579.3	586.1	586.7	578.4	581.2	582.6	586.3	590.2	591.9	580.3
2010	572.0	574.1	579.2	584.9	587.2	589.4	580.3	587.1	588.7	589.7	594.6	592.9	585.0
2011	580.5	579.7	587.8	593.6	601.9	604.1	597.5	602.6	605.0	607.1	614.0	615.2	599.1
2012	599.2	599.7	604.6	611.2	614.9	615.9	608.1	618.1	618.2	618.9	624.7	625.2	613.2
2013	607.9	607.1	613.3	622.4	626.4	629.4	626.3	631.7	632.3	634.2	639.5	642.5	626.1
2014	627.7	627.0	631.2	635.1	644.8	646.9	637.7	645.7	646.4	650.6	657.6	660.6	642.6
2015	643.7	644.2	649.7	655.0	660.0	662.0	661.0	662.6	663.2	661.3	667.0	669.7	658.3
2016	653.2	653.5	658.0	662.3	667.2	671.2	666.2	668.3	670.6	671.6	678.4	679.1	666.6
Total Private													
2006	525.4	524.9	527.5	534.4	542.4	546.8	538.5	539.4	540.1	539.2	544.5	541.9	537.1
2007	527.2	526.6	528.2	533.4	543.0	542.3	534.6	537.4	530.2	528.5	531.4	525.9	532.4
2008	504.1	503.1	504.3	507.3	509.2	509.4	506.3	506.2	503.8	504.2	505.8	504.6	505.7
2009	489.7	483.8	493.0	498.9	504.0	506.4	502.8	504.8	504.9	508.1	512.2	514.6	501.9
2010	495.2	496.5	501.3	506.7	508.7	511.9	506.3	510.7	509.8	510.7	515.3	514.0	507.3
2011	502.2	501.1	508.7	514.5	522.7	525.8	523.3	526.1	526.3	528.0	535.0	536.4	520.8
2012	521.1	520.6	524.9	531.0	534.6	536.4	532.2	540.0	538.3	539.1	544.6	545.3	534.0
2013	529.1	528.3	533.9	542.8	547.0	550.5	550.6	553.7	552.5	554.3	559.8	563.1	547.1
2014	549.0	548.3	552.2	555.6	565.2	568.8	563.5	570.0	569.1	572.6	579.4	582.7	564.7
2015	566.5	567.1	571.4	577.5	582.7	585.7	587.2	587.6	586.5	585.5	591.0	594.0	581.9
2016	578.4	578.6	583.0	586.9	591.2	596.1	594.4	594.7	595.2	596.4	603.0	604.2	591.8
Goods Producing													
2006	106.6	105.9	104.0	108.3	109.8	111.3	105.4	106.5	109.5	105.2	108.7	105.7	107.2
2007	104.2	104.4	104.5	104.0	107.3	106.3	101.7	104.2	101.9	100.9	103.1	98.6	103.4
2008	93.3	93.4	92.2	93.1	91.9	91.7	90.2	91.2	90.6	90.2	89.4	88.4	91.3
2009	85.2	80.5	85.2	85.5	86.5	87.0	84.8	87.1	87.5	87.5	87.3	86.7	85.9
2010	83.2	83.4	84.1	85.6	86.0	87.4	84.6	88.0	88.3	88.1	88.7	87.9	86.3
2011	87.0	85.9	89.5	91.3	92.9	94.5	94.8	95.5	95.8	95.8	96.5	96.6	93.0
2012	94.4	94.3	94.8	95.8	96.5	97.5	95.0	98.6	98.4	98.1	98.4	98.2	96.7
2013	96.2	96.3	97.5	99.5	100.9	102.2	102.6	102.8	102.5	102.8	103.8	103.6	100.9
2014	102.1	101.9	102.3	101.0	105.3	106.6	103.8	107.4	107.3	107.3	107.5	107.7	105.0
2015	106.1	106.5	108.1	108.2	109.5	111.3	111.9	111.5	111.0	110.3	110.7	110.0	109.6
2016	107.7	107.8	108.5	109.6	110.4	111.4	112.7	112.3	112.2	112.6	111.6	110.5	110.6
Service-Providing													
2006	493.1	494.1	499.0	503.0	509.8	512.3	505.6	507.7	507.1	509.9	512.0	512.5	505.5
2007	499.0	499.1	500.9	506.5	513.3	513.1	505.5	507.9	505.0	504.8	505.6	504.2	505.4
2008	486.7	485.7	488.6	491.5	495.2	494.7	489.9	491.1	491.9	493.5	495.5	494.2	491.5
2009	481.8	480.8	487.1	493.8	499.6	499.7	493.6	494.1	495.1	498.8	502.9	505.2	494.4
2010	488.8	490.7	495.1	499.3	501.2	502.0	495.7	499.1	500.4	501.6	505.9	505.0	498.7
2011	493.5	493.8	498.3	502.3	509.0	509.6	502.7	507.1	509.2	511.3	517.5	518.6	506.1
2012	504.8	505.4	509.8	515.4	518.4	518.4	513.1	519.5	519.8	520.8	526.3	527.0	516.6
2013	511.7	510.8	515.8	522.9	525.5	527.2	523.7	528.9	529.8	531.4	535.7	538.9	525.2
2014	525.6	525.1	528.9	534.1	539.5	540.3	533.9	538.3	539.1	543.3	550.1	552.9	537.6
2015	537.6	537.7	541.6	546.8	550.5	550.7	549.1	551.1	552.2	551.0	556.3	559.7	548.7
2016	545.5	545.7	549.5	552.7	556.8	559.8	553.5	556.0	558.4	559.0	566.8	568.6	556.0
Mining, Logging, and Construction													
2006	29.0	28.5	30.0	31.4	32.4	33.2	33.7	33.5	33.4	33.2	33.0	32.4	32.0
2007	30.5	30.3	30.7	32.2	33.2	33.8	33.8	33.9	33.5	33.4	32.7	32.0	32.5
2008	29.7	29.0	29.0	29.3	29.2	29.3	29.4	29.3	29.1	29.2	28.4	27.3	29.0
2009	24.7	23.8	24.5	25.3	25.3	25.7	26.3	25.8	25.4	25.2	24.7	23.8	25.0
2010	21.9	21.9	22.9	23.9	24.2	25.1	25.5	25.4	25.2	24.8	24.7	24.2	24.1
2011	22.7	22.6	23.6	24.2	24.7	25.3	25.2	25.0	24.8	24.5	24.7	24.4	24.3
2012	22.7	22.5	23.2	24.1	24.7	25.4	26.1	26.1	26.0	25.7	25.7	25.4	24.8
2013	23.9	23.9	25.2	26.2	27.0	28.1	28.4	28.2	28.2	28.2	28.3	27.8	27.0
2014	26.3	26.4	26.6	27.7	28.7	29.4	30.4	29.6	29.3	29.2	28.9	28.7	28.4
2015	27.0	26.7	27.3	28.2	28.4	28.9	29.2	28.9	28.6	28.5	28.5	28.1	28.2
2016	26.6	26.8	27.5	28.2	28.7	29.5	30.5	30.0	29.8	29.7	29.0	28.5	28.7

Employment by Industry: Louisville/Jefferson County, KY-IN, Selected Years, 2007–2017—*Continued*

(Numbers in thousands, not seasonally adjusted)

Industry and year	January	February	March	April	May	June	July	August	September	October	November	December	Annual average
Manufacturing													
2006	77.6	77.4	74.0	76.9	77.4	78.1	71.7	73.0	76.1	72.0	75.7	73.3	75.3
2007	73.7	74.1	73.8	71.8	74.1	72.5	67.9	70.3	68.4	67.5	70.4	66.6	70.9
2008	63.6	64.4	63.2	63.8	62.7	62.4	60.8	61.9	61.5	61.0	61.0	61.1	62.3
2009	60.5	56.7	60.7	60.2	61.2	61.3	58.5	61.3	62.1	62.3	62.6	62.9	60.9
2010	61.3	61.5	61.2	61.7	61.8	62.3	59.1	62.6	63.1	63.3	64.0	63.7	62.1
2011	64.3	63.3	65.9	67.1	68.2	69.2	69.6	70.5	71.0	71.3	71.8	72.2	68.7
2012	71.7	71.8	71.6	71.7	71.8	72.1	68.9	72.5	72.4	72.4	72.7	72.8	71.9
2013	72.3	72.4	72.3	73.3	73.9	74.1	74.2	74.6	74.3	74.6	75.5	75.8	73.9
2014	75.8	75.5	75.7	73.3	76.6	77.2	73.4	77.8	78.0	78.1	78.6	79.0	76.6
2015	79.1	79.8	80.8	80.0	81.1	82.4	82.7	82.6	82.4	81.8	82.2	81.9	81.4
2016	81.1	81.0	81.0	81.4	81.7	81.9	82.2	82.3	82.4	82.9	82.6	82.0	81.9
Trade, Transportation, and Utilities													
2006	135.9	134.7	135.6	135.7	137.0	138.4	137.1	137.4	137.6	139.3	141.3	143.0	137.8
2007	136.3	134.4	134.2	134.6	136.1	135.8	134.6	135.1	133.1	133.0	135.3	137.5	135.0
2008	129.0	127.1	127.2	126.5	127.2	127.4	126.0	125.8	125.4	126.1	128.7	130.4	127.2
2009	124.1	122.9	124.0	125.5	126.4	127.1	127.3	127.9	127.9	129.8	132.9	136.2	127.7
2010	128.4	127.7	128.8	129.4	129.5	130.2	129.4	129.6	129.1	129.6	133.0	134.4	129.9
2011	128.2	128.0	128.6	128.7	130.1	130.8	130.4	130.5	130.7	131.5	135.0	137.3	130.8
2012	130.9	130.4	131.2	131.1	131.8	132.5	132.3	133.4	133.7	133.8	137.4	140.3	133.2
2013	133.0	132.5	133.0	133.2	134.6	135.3	135.3	136.6	137.0	138.5	141.9	145.8	136.4
2014	139.0	138.0	138.6	138.6	139.9	141.0	140.5	142.2	142.1	143.5	146.8	149.2	141.6
2015	144.7	143.7	144.1	144.7	145.7	145.8	147.1	147.5	147.4	147.7	151.5	155.8	147.1
2016	148.1	147.2	147.5	147.6	148.4	149.7	149.3	150.0	150.2	151.0	155.5	156.9	150.1
Wholesale Trade													
2006	30.0	30.1	30.2	30.0	30.0	30.1	29.9	29.9	29.9	30.0	29.8	29.9	30.0
2007	29.6	29.7	29.6	29.7	29.8	29.8	29.7	29.7	29.6	29.5	29.3	29.2	29.6
2008	28.4	28.2	28.0	27.9	27.9	27.7	27.5	27.6	27.7	27.6	27.6	27.5	27.8
2009	27.2	27.1	27.3	27.3	27.4	27.5	27.7	27.7	27.7	27.7	27.8	27.7	27.5
2010	27.5	27.6	27.8	27.7	27.7	27.8	27.9	28.0	28.0	28.0	28.0	28.1	27.8
2011	27.7	27.8	27.9	27.9	28.2	28.2	28.4	28.5	28.6	28.6	28.6	28.6	28.3
2012	28.7	28.8	28.9	28.8	28.7	28.8	28.9	29.0	29.0	28.9	29.0	29.1	28.9
2013	28.8	28.9	28.9	28.8	28.9	28.8	28.9	28.9	28.9	28.8	28.8	28.8	28.9
2014	28.7	28.7	28.8	28.7	29.0	29.0	29.1	29.3	29.3	29.3	29.4	29.6	29.1
2015	29.2	29.1	29.3	29.3	29.5	29.4	29.5	29.3	29.3	29.3	29.5	29.7	29.4
2016	29.3	29.5	29.5	30.0	30.1	30.2	30.1	30.0	29.9	29.5	29.4	29.0	29.7
Retail Trade													
2006	63.3	62.3	63.0	62.9	63.7	64.2	64.2	63.9	63.6	63.8	65.9	66.5	63.9
2007	63.2	62.3	62.8	62.3	63.1	63.1	62.9	62.9	61.8	62.0	63.5	64.1	62.8
2008	60.2	59.0	59.4	59.4	59.9	60.1	59.6	59.3	58.8	59.6	61.3	62.0	59.9
2009	58.5	57.8	58.5	58.6	59.0	59.2	59.2	59.3	58.7	59.9	61.5	62.1	59.4
2010	58.9	58.2	58.9	59.5	59.6	59.6	59.3	59.3	58.7	59.6	61.6	62.2	59.6
2011	59.6	59.1	59.6	59.8	60.5	61.0	60.8	60.7	60.5	61.5	64.2	64.3	61.0
2012	61.0	60.5	60.9	61.1	61.7	62.0	61.9	62.2	62.0	62.4	64.8	65.5	62.2
2013	61.2	61.1	61.3	61.8	62.4	62.7	62.6	63.2	62.7	63.6	65.7	67.0	62.9
2014	63.7	63.1	63.5	64.0	64.9	65.6	65.3	65.9	65.3	66.2	68.3	69.2	65.4
2015	66.0	66.1	66.3	67.0	67.4	67.4	67.7	67.6	67.2	67.9	70.2	71.1	67.7
2016	68.4	67.7	67.8	68.1	68.5	68.9	68.9	69.0	68.8	70.1	73.4	73.1	69.4
Transportation and Utilities													
2006	42.6	42.3	42.4	42.8	43.3	44.1	43.0	43.6	44.1	45.5	45.6	46.6	43.8
2007	43.5	42.4	41.8	42.6	43.2	42.9	42.0	42.5	41.7	41.5	42.5	44.2	42.6
2008	40.4	39.9	39.8	39.2	39.4	39.6	38.9	38.9	38.9	38.9	39.8	40.9	39.6
2009	38.4	38.0	38.2	39.6	40.0	40.4	40.4	40.9	41.5	42.2	43.6	46.4	40.8
2010	42.0	41.9	42.1	42.2	42.2	42.8	42.2	42.3	42.4	42.0	43.4	44.1	42.5
2011	40.9	41.1	41.1	41.0	41.4	41.6	41.2	41.3	41.6	41.4	42.2	44.4	41.6
2012	41.2	41.1	41.4	41.2	41.4	41.7	41.5	42.2	42.7	42.5	43.6	45.7	42.2
2013	43.0	42.5	42.8	42.6	43.3	43.8	43.8	44.5	45.4	46.1	47.4	50.0	44.6
2014	46.6	46.2	46.3	45.9	46.0	46.4	46.1	47.0	47.5	48.0	49.1	50.4	47.1
2015	49.5	48.5	48.5	48.4	48.8	49.0	49.9	50.6	50.9	50.5	51.8	55.0	50.1
2016	50.4	50.0	50.2	49.5	49.8	50.6	50.3	51.0	51.5	51.4	52.7	54.8	51.0

Employment by Industry: Louisville/Jefferson County, KY-IN, Selected Years, 2007–2017—*Continued*

(Numbers in thousands, not seasonally adjusted)

Industry and year	January	February	March	April	May	June	July	August	September	October	November	December	Annual average
Information													
2006	10.3	10.3	10.3	10.3	10.4	10.4	10.5	10.4	10.3	10.2	10.2	10.2	10.3
2007	10.2	10.1	10.2	10.2	10.4	10.7	10.6	10.5	10.3	10.1	10.1	10.0	10.3
2008	9.9	9.8	9.7	9.6	9.6	9.6	9.7	9.6	9.5	9.4	9.5	9.5	9.6
2009	9.3	9.2	9.3	9.3	9.3	9.3	9.3	9.3	9.2	9.1	9.2	9.3	9.3
2010	9.2	9.1	9.1	9.2	9.2	9.1	9.2	9.1	9.1	9.1	9.3	9.3	9.2
2011	9.2	9.2	9.5	9.6	9.6	9.6	9.5	9.5	9.3	9.2	9.3	9.3	9.4
2012	9.4	9.4	9.4	9.4	9.5	9.5	9.5	9.6	9.4	9.3	9.3	9.3	9.4
2013	9.4	9.4	9.5	9.4	9.4	9.4	9.3	9.3	9.1	9.2	9.3	9.2	9.3
2014	9.1	9.1	9.0	8.9	9.0	8.9	9.0	9.0	8.9	9.0	9.1	9.1	9.0
2015	9.1	9.2	9.1	9.1	9.2	9.2	9.2	9.3	9.3	9.3	9.4	9.4	9.2
2016	9.3	9.3	9.4	9.4	9.5	9.5	9.5	9.5	9.5	9.5	9.5	9.5	9.5
Financial Activities													
2006	42.7	42.7	42.8	43.0	43.0	43.3	43.4	43.3	43.0	43.2	43.2	43.1	43.1
2007	42.9	43.1	43.0	43.0	43.2	43.0	43.2	43.3	43.1	42.8	42.9	42.8	43.0
2008	42.5	42.4	42.2	42.2	42.3	42.3	42.4	42.0	41.7	41.6	41.4	41.6	42.1
2009	41.1	40.9	40.8	40.4	40.4	40.5	40.4	40.1	39.7	39.9	40.1	40.3	40.4
2010	40.1	40.2	40.3	39.7	39.8	40.0	40.0	40.2	40.5	40.4	40.5	40.7	40.2
2011	40.4	40.3	40.5	40.2	40.6	41.1	41.4	41.5	41.6	41.7	41.9	42.3	41.1
2012	42.1	42.1	42.3	42.3	42.6	42.9	43.1	43.4	43.4	43.6	43.8	44.0	43.0
2013	43.9	43.8	43.9	44.0	44.3	44.6	44.8	44.9	45.1	45.5	45.7	45.9	44.7
2014	45.6	45.6	45.7	45.3	45.5	46.0	46.0	45.9	45.8	46.0	46.1	46.4	45.8
2015	46.1	46.2	46.1	46.1	46.3	46.6	46.9	46.5	46.4	46.6	46.5	46.8	46.4
2016	46.1	45.9	45.9	45.7	45.9	46.2	45.9	45.9	45.9	45.4	45.7	45.8	45.9
Professional and Business Services													
2006	69.4	70.1	71.5	71.5	73.4	73.7	72.9	73.2	72.9	74.2	74.8	74.2	72.7
2007	70.9	71.1	71.4	72.8	74.3	75.1	73.9	73.9	73.7	73.8	73.5	71.9	73.0
2008	67.4	68.1	68.1	68.4	68.3	68.2	68.9	69.0	69.3	70.6	71.4	70.5	69.0
2009	68.6	68.6	69.4	71.2	71.7	72.3	71.8	71.6	72.7	72.7	73.6	74.2	71.5
2010	69.9	70.8	71.5	72.0	72.4	72.8	72.5	73.4	73.5	75.3	75.3	75.4	72.9
2011	72.0	71.3	72.0	73.5	74.7	74.6	73.9	75.4	76.3	77.5	79.0	78.8	74.9
2012	74.4	73.7	74.9	76.9	77.0	77.4	76.7	79.3	78.8	80.6	81.4	80.9	77.7
2013	77.4	76.2	77.8	80.0	80.9	81.1	81.3	82.9	82.4	83.5	84.6	85.1	81.1
2014	82.0	81.3	82.1	84.1	85.7	85.5	84.7	85.1	85.3	86.2	88.4	89.6	85.0
2015	83.8	83.0	83.0	84.6	85.6	85.6	85.1	85.7	86.2	86.7	88.3	88.8	85.5
2016	84.5	83.9	84.4	84.7	84.7	85.3	84.8	85.1	86.6	88.7	91.1	92.7	86.4
Education and Health Services													
2006	75.7	76.1	76.4	76.7	77.3	77.6	78.2	77.8	77.8	78.6	78.4	78.6	77.4
2007	78.2	78.1	78.2	79.3	79.4	79.4	79.3	79.5	79.3	79.8	79.7	79.8	79.2
2008	79.6	79.4	80.0	80.4	80.6	80.8	80.4	81.4	81.7	82.2	82.0	82.3	80.9
2009	81.6	81.7	82.3	82.3	82.8	82.5	82.6	82.7	83.0	83.5	83.8	83.8	82.7
2010	83.2	83.2	83.5	82.9	83.0	83.0	83.1	83.2	83.6	83.4	83.4	82.6	83.2
2011	83.3	83.4	83.6	84.0	84.2	84.4	84.0	84.3	84.6	85.1	85.5	85.7	84.3
2012	84.5	84.7	85.0	85.2	84.7	84.3	84.3	84.3	84.6	85.3	85.5	85.2	84.8
2013	84.2	84.4	84.8	85.1	84.4	84.0	84.0	84.5	85.4	85.9	85.0	85.8	84.8
2014	84.8	85.2	85.9	85.6	85.6	84.8	84.7	86.4	87.4	89.3	89.6	89.6	86.6
2015	88.3	88.8	89.2	88.7	88.7	88.2	88.8	89.3	90.2	90.6	90.8	90.9	89.4
2016	92.0	92.7	93.2	93.8	93.7	93.9	93.4	93.6	94.5	94.1	93.9	93.7	93.5
Leisure and Hospitality													
2006	56.8	57.1	58.7	60.5	62.8	63.1	62.6	62.4	60.8	60.4	59.9	58.8	60.3
2007	56.9	57.7	58.9	61.5	63.9	63.5	63.4	63.0	61.5	60.5	59.4	58.1	60.7
2008	55.8	56.3	58.3	60.6	62.8	62.7	62.3	60.9	59.7	58.7	58.0	56.5	59.4
2009	54.7	54.9	56.5	59.1	61.2	61.6	60.7	60.3	59.4	59.9	59.7	58.3	58.9
2010	55.8	56.5	58.2	62.1	63.0	63.3	61.3	61.3	60.0	59.3	59.6	58.0	59.9
2011	56.6	57.4	59.2	61.4	64.9	64.7	63.4	63.9	62.7	61.8	62.4	60.9	61.6
2012	59.8	60.3	61.5	64.4	66.6	66.3	65.5	65.6	64.5	63.2	63.7	62.3	63.6
2013	60.4	61.1	62.6	66.6	67.5	68.8	68.2	67.7	66.1	64.3	64.5	63.1	65.1
2014	62.0	62.6	63.8	67.5	69.3	70.6	69.5	68.6	67.2	66.0	66.3	65.6	66.6
2015	63.1	64.1	65.9	69.9	71.6	72.7	71.8	71.4	69.9	67.8	67.9	66.3	68.5
2016	65.0	65.9	67.8	69.8	72.1	73.5	72.3	71.7	70.0	68.4	68.5	68.0	69.4

Employment by Industry: Louisville/Jefferson County, KY-IN, Selected Years, 2007–2017—*Continued*

(Numbers in thousands, not seasonally adjusted)

Industry and year	January	February	March	April	May	June	July	August	September	October	November	December	Annual average
Other Services													
2006	28.0	28.0	28.2	28.4	28.7	29.0	28.4	28.4	28.2	28.1	28.0	28.3	28.3
2007	27.6	27.7	27.8	28.0	28.4	28.5	27.9	27.9	27.3	27.6	27.4	27.2	27.8
2008	26.6	26.6	26.6	26.5	26.5	26.7	26.4	26.3	25.9	25.4	25.4	25.4	26.2
2009	25.1	25.1	25.5	25.6	25.7	26.1	25.9	25.8	25.5	25.7	25.6	25.8	25.6
2010	25.4	25.6	25.8	25.8	25.8	26.1	26.2	25.9	25.7	25.5	25.5	25.7	25.8
2011	25.5	25.6	25.8	25.8	25.7	26.1	25.9	25.5	25.3	25.4	25.4	25.5	25.6
2012	25.6	25.7	25.8	25.9	25.9	26.0	25.8	25.8	25.5	25.2	25.1	25.1	25.6
2013	24.6	24.6	24.8	25.0	25.0	25.1	25.1	25.0	24.9	24.6	25.0	24.6	24.9
2014	24.4	24.6	24.8	24.6	24.9	25.4	25.3	25.4	25.1	25.3	25.6	25.5	25.1
2015	25.3	25.6	25.9	26.2	26.1	26.3	26.4	26.4	26.1	26.5	25.9	26.0	26.1
2016	25.7	25.9	26.3	26.3	26.5	26.6	26.5	26.6	26.3	26.7	27.2	27.1	26.5
Government													
2006	74.3	75.1	75.5	76.9	77.2	76.8	72.5	74.8	76.5	75.9	76.2	76.3	75.7
2007	76.0	76.9	77.2	77.1	77.6	77.1	72.6	74.7	76.7	77.2	77.3	76.9	76.4
2008	75.9	76.0	76.5	77.3	77.9	77.0	73.8	76.1	78.7	79.5	79.1	78.0	77.2
2009	77.3	77.5	79.3	80.4	82.1	80.3	75.6	76.4	77.7	78.2	78.0	77.3	78.3
2010	76.8	77.6	77.9	78.2	78.5	77.5	74.0	76.4	78.9	79.0	79.3	78.9	77.8
2011	78.3	78.6	79.1	79.1	79.2	78.3	74.2	76.5	78.7	79.1	79.0	78.8	78.2
2012	78.1	79.1	79.7	80.2	80.3	79.5	75.9	78.1	79.9	79.8	80.1	79.9	79.2
2013	78.8	78.8	79.4	79.6	79.4	78.9	75.7	78.0	79.8	79.9	79.7	79.4	79.0
2014	78.7	78.7	79.0	79.5	79.6	78.1	74.2	75.7	77.3	78.0	78.2	77.9	77.9
2015	77.2	77.1	78.3	77.5	77.3	76.3	73.8	75.0	76.7	75.8	76.0	75.7	76.4
2016	74.8	74.9	75.0	75.4	76.0	75.1	71.8	73.6	75.4	75.2	75.4	74.9	74.8

Employment by Industry: New Orleans-Metairie, LA, Selected Years, 2007–2017

(Numbers in thousands, not seasonally adjusted)

Industry and year	January	February	March	April	May	June	July	August	September	October	November	December	Annual average
Total Nonfarm													
2007	515.1	519.8	526.4	519.8	521.4	524.0	518.2	523.1	524.2	534.3	539.3	543.2	525.7
2008	533.1	537.0	540.9	540.0	539.6	538.9	531.8	539.1	532.0	540.6	543.3	545.4	538.5
2009	532.6	534.9	534.9	536.7	538.2	533.3	528.6	532.8	530.5	533.2	535.2	535.2	533.8
2010	525.9	528.4	532.8	535.4	535.2	534.5	527.4	528.8	532.0	535.2	539.0	541.2	533.0
2011	533.3	536.5	539.5	541.1	541.7	536.9	533.2	536.9	538.8	542.1	546.3	548.1	539.5
2012	537.2	540.5	542.9	549.4	550.8	545.1	541.0	543.5	539.7	546.8	552.0	554.0	545.2
2013	550.2	554.2	553.3	553.1	554.1	553.0	546.3	554.8	552.2	559.6	564.7	564.0	555.0
2014	554.4	559.7	563.3	563.4	565.3	567.2	562.8	567.1	564.8	571.1	578.0	578.3	566.3
2015	569.2	572.0	573.2	579.2	580.4	577.1	573.2	574.3	572.1	580.6	581.7	583.2	576.4
2016	572.8	572.8	573.8	579.2	580.8	575.8	572.4	574.5	576.3	577.8	580.6	578.1	576.2
2017	570.5	576.9	574.4	577.7	581.4	575.9	568.5	570.8	571.6	575.7	577.4	578.7	575.0
Total Private													
2007	437.1	440.8	446.7	445.4	446.6	448.8	445.1	448.9	446.7	454.5	458.8	462.4	448.5
2008	453.5	456.6	460.6	457.6	457.1	457.7	451.6	456.7	448.6	456.4	458.6	460.9	456.3
2009	449.1	450.9	451.3	451.6	453.4	450.9	445.4	447.8	445.9	447.4	449.6	450.0	449.4
2010	442.0	444.0	447.7	450.5	448.7	450.0	445.5	446.1	448.9	451.7	455.2	457.9	449.0
2011	450.9	454.1	457.4	458.8	459.6	456.8	454.8	457.1	457.5	461.3	465.4	467.6	458.4
2012	458.7	461.2	464.0	469.2	470.7	466.2	464.5	465.7	461.0	467.7	472.7	474.7	466.4
2013	472.6	476.1	475.2	475.3	476.0	476.0	472.5	481.3	477.7	484.8	489.6	488.7	478.8
2014	480.8	484.8	488.1	488.8	491.0	491.1	489.9	494.2	490.5	496.3	503.0	504.1	491.9
2015	496.0	497.6	499.4	505.0	506.3	504.0	502.7	503.0	499.1	508.3	509.2	511.1	503.5
2016	501.2	500.4	501.8	506.7	506.4	503.0	502.6	504.4	505.1	505.5	508.2	506.0	504.3
2017	499.3	504.5	502.3	503.7	507.2	503.3	498.7	500.7	500.4	503.2	504.5	506.3	502.8
Goods Producing													
2007	77.8	78.3	78.5	78.6	78.9	79.5	79.4	79.8	79.9	80.0	79.9	80.2	79.2
2008	80.0	79.5	79.4	79.8	80.3	80.6	81.1	81.4	80.7	81.7	80.9	81.2	80.6
2009	79.3	78.9	78.2	78.1	78.3	78.0	76.9	76.3	75.7	76.1	75.6	74.6	77.2
2010	72.7	72.8	73.2	73.3	73.7	74.2	73.9	73.7	73.5	74.3	73.5	73.6	73.5
2011	72.7	72.8	73.0	73.3	73.2	72.8	73.0	72.8	72.2	72.3	72.3	72.2	72.7
2012	71.2	71.3	71.5	71.0	71.6	72.0	72.2	72.1	71.9	72.0	72.1	71.4	71.7
2013	70.0	69.8	70.2	69.7	70.3	71.0	71.1	71.1	70.9	70.5	70.0	69.4	70.3
2014	68.7	69.1	69.6	69.3	69.9	69.7	69.9	69.7	69.4	69.7	69.7	70.1	69.6
2015	70.2	69.6	68.7	69.2	69.1	69.2	69.2	68.8	68.5	68.8	67.9	67.6	68.9
2016	65.5	65.1	64.9	64.8	64.4	64.5	65.0	64.4	64.6	63.9	63.7	63.3	64.5
2017	63.7	64.2	63.9	64.0	64.5	64.6	64.3	64.2	64.3	64.0	63.4	64.4	64.1
Service-Providing													
2007	437.3	441.5	447.9	441.2	442.5	444.5	438.8	443.3	444.3	454.3	459.4	463.0	446.5
2008	453.1	457.5	461.5	460.2	459.3	458.3	450.7	457.7	451.3	458.9	462.4	464.2	457.9
2009	453.3	456.0	456.7	458.6	459.9	455.3	451.7	456.5	454.8	457.1	459.6	460.6	456.7
2010	453.2	455.6	459.6	462.1	461.5	460.3	453.5	455.1	458.5	460.9	465.5	467.6	459.5
2011	460.6	463.7	466.5	467.8	468.5	464.1	460.2	464.1	466.6	469.8	474.0	475.9	466.8
2012	466.0	469.2	471.4	478.4	479.2	473.1	468.8	471.4	467.8	474.8	479.9	482.6	473.6
2013	480.2	484.4	483.1	483.4	483.8	482.0	475.2	483.7	481.3	489.1	494.7	494.6	484.6
2014	485.7	490.6	493.7	494.1	495.4	497.5	492.9	497.4	495.4	501.4	508.3	508.2	496.7
2015	499.0	502.4	504.5	510.0	511.3	507.9	504.0	505.5	503.6	511.8	513.8	515.6	507.5
2016	507.3	507.7	508.9	514.4	516.4	511.3	507.4	510.1	511.7	513.9	516.9	514.8	511.7
2017	506.8	512.7	510.5	513.7	516.9	511.3	504.2	506.6	507.3	511.7	514.0	514.3	510.8
Mining, Logging, and Construction													
2007	39.7	39.9	40.3	40.3	40.5	40.8	40.7	41.1	40.9	41.2	40.9	40.8	40.6
2008	41.1	40.7	40.6	41.3	41.4	41.5	42.0	42.4	42.3	43.0	42.3	42.3	41.7
2009	41.0	40.9	40.6	40.5	40.8	40.8	40.0	39.7	39.4	40.2	39.8	38.9	40.2
2010	37.6	37.9	38.2	37.9	38.2	38.8	38.9	38.9	38.9	39.9	39.5	39.4	38.7
2011	38.8	38.8	39.2	40.1	39.8	39.6	39.5	39.4	39.0	39.1	39.1	39.0	39.3
2012	38.4	38.7	39.1	38.8	39.2	39.5	39.6	39.6	39.8	39.9	39.9	39.2	39.3
2013	38.1	38.2	38.6	38.2	38.4	38.8	38.9	38.9	38.9	38.5	38.1	37.7	38.4
2014	37.2	37.7	38.2	38.2	38.4	38.4	38.7	38.6	38.6	38.9	39.1	39.4	38.5
2015	39.5	39.0	38.9	38.6	38.6	38.4	38.2	37.9	37.7	38.2	37.3	36.9	38.3
2016	35.5	35.0	34.9	34.6	34.2	34.3	34.8	34.4	34.5	34.0	33.8	33.1	34.4
2017	33.2	33.5	33.4	33.6	34.0	33.8	33.8	33.7	33.9	33.3	32.7	33.5	33.5

Employment by Industry: New Orleans-Metairie, LA, Selected Years, 2007–2017—*Continued*

(Numbers in thousands, not seasonally adjusted)

Industry and year	January	February	March	April	May	June	July	August	September	October	November	December	Annual average
Manufacturing													
2007	38.1	38.4	38.2	38.3	38.4	38.7	38.7	38.7	39.0	38.8	39.0	39.4	38.6
2008	38.9	38.8	38.8	38.5	38.9	39.1	39.1	39.0	38.4	38.7	38.6	38.9	38.8
2009	38.3	38.0	37.6	37.6	37.5	37.2	36.9	36.6	36.3	35.9	35.8	35.7	37.0
2010	35.1	34.9	35.0	35.4	35.5	35.4	35.0	34.8	34.6	34.4	34.0	34.2	34.9
2011	33.9	34.0	33.8	33.2	33.4	33.2	33.5	33.4	33.2	33.2	33.2	33.2	33.4
2012	32.8	32.6	32.4	32.2	32.4	32.5	32.6	32.5	32.1	32.1	32.2	32.2	32.4
2013	31.9	31.6	31.6	31.5	31.9	32.2	32.2	32.2	32.0	32.0	31.9	31.7	31.9
2014	31.5	31.4	31.4	31.1	31.5	31.3	31.2	31.1	30.8	30.8	30.6	30.7	31.1
2015	30.7	30.6	29.8	30.6	30.5	30.8	31.0	30.9	30.8	30.6	30.6	30.7	30.6
2016	30.0	30.1	30.0	30.2	30.2	30.2	30.2	30.0	30.1	29.9	29.9	30.2	30.1
2017	30.5	30.7	30.5	30.4	30.5	30.8	30.5	30.5	30.4	30.7	30.7	30.9	30.6
Trade, Transportation, and Utilities													
2007	109.0	108.6	109.7	108.9	109.1	109.4	109.1	109.3	108.6	111.3	113.8	115.5	110.2
2008	111.6	110.7	111.2	110.3	110.5	110.3	109.8	110.2	107.9	110.0	111.9	113.0	110.6
2009	108.3	107.4	107.2	106.7	106.4	106.9	105.7	105.8	105.3	104.9	106.4	107.0	106.5
2010	103.7	103.2	104.0	104.4	104.5	104.6	104.9	104.7	104.6	106.3	108.3	109.6	105.2
2011	107.9	107.4	107.5	107.7	107.9	107.7	107.8	107.6	107.3	107.9	109.9	110.7	108.1
2012	108.1	107.4	107.7	108.1	108.3	108.2	107.8	107.8	107.3	109.3	112.3	113.2	108.8
2013	111.4	110.4	111.3	110.5	110.5	110.6	110.8	111.6	111.5	112.5	114.4	116.0	111.8
2014	112.6	112.1	112.7	112.8	113.6	114.2	114.7	115.2	114.8	115.5	118.0	120.2	114.7
2015	116.2	115.3	115.8	116.2	116.6	116.8	116.6	116.6	116.1	117.1	118.8	120.1	116.9
2016	116.4	115.5	115.8	115.9	115.8	115.6	115.5	115.6	115.0	115.6	117.5	118.7	116.1
2017	114.5	113.8	113.8	113.7	113.8	113.9	112.8	113.0	112.5	112.6	114.0	115.4	113.7
Wholesale Trade													
2007	23.8	23.9	24.2	24.0	24.2	24.4	24.8	25.0	24.7	25.1	25.1	25.2	24.5
2008	24.7	24.8	24.9	24.2	24.2	24.2	24.1	24.1	23.9	24.0	24.1	24.1	24.3
2009	23.6	23.6	23.5	23.8	23.7	23.7	23.1	23.1	22.9	22.9	22.9	22.8	23.3
2010	22.2	22.3	22.3	22.3	22.4	22.5	22.4	22.4	22.3	22.5	22.6	22.6	22.4
2011	23.1	23.2	23.1	22.6	22.8	22.9	22.8	22.8	22.7	22.8	22.8	22.8	22.9
2012	22.5	22.5	22.5	22.8	22.7	22.7	22.6	22.6	22.5	22.5	22.5	22.6	22.6
2013	23.1	23.2	23.3	23.1	23.1	23.2	23.2	23.4	23.3	23.4	23.4	23.5	23.3
2014	23.4	23.5	23.5	23.4	23.4	23.5	23.6	23.6	23.6	23.6	23.7	23.8	23.6
2015	23.3	23.3	23.4	23.4	23.5	23.5	23.4	23.4	23.2	23.4	23.3	23.4	23.4
2016	23.3	23.3	23.1	23.2	23.2	23.1	23.2	23.1	22.9	22.8	22.9	22.8	23.1
2017	22.3	22.3	22.4	22.5	22.6	22.6	22.5	22.4	22.4	22.5	22.3	22.3	22.4
Retail Trade													
2007	60.1	59.6	60.3	59.7	60.0	60.0	60.0	59.6	59.5	61.1	63.4	64.7	60.7
2008	62.1	60.9	61.3	60.8	60.8	60.7	60.4	60.6	58.9	60.1	61.6	62.6	60.9
2009	59.1	58.7	58.6	58.3	58.4	58.7	58.2	58.3	58.0	57.5	58.9	59.4	58.5
2010	57.1	56.6	57.3	57.0	56.9	56.9	56.9	56.6	56.7	57.9	59.8	60.7	57.5
2011	58.7	58.4	58.6	58.9	58.8	58.6	58.7	58.4	58.0	58.8	60.6	61.1	59.0
2012	59.2	58.4	58.5	58.5	58.7	58.6	58.6	58.3	57.9	59.5	62.1	62.6	59.2
2013	60.4	59.4	59.9	59.8	60.0	60.1	60.4	60.7	60.8	61.3	63.1	64.0	60.8
2014	61.3	60.9	61.1	61.2	61.7	62.4	62.8	62.9	62.4	63.0	65.1	66.5	62.6
2015	63.5	63.0	63.4	63.5	63.8	64.2	64.0	64.0	63.5	64.4	66.1	66.8	64.2
2016	64.1	63.6	63.9	64.1	64.1	64.3	64.1	64.1	63.6	64.4	66.1	66.8	64.4
2017	63.7	63.0	63.0	62.7	62.6	62.5	62.0	62.3	61.7	62.4	63.3	64.1	62.8
Transportation and Utilities													
2007	25.1	25.1	25.2	25.2	24.9	25.0	24.3	24.7	24.4	25.1	25.3	25.6	25.0
2008	24.8	25.0	25.0	25.3	25.5	25.4	25.3	25.5	25.1	25.9	26.2	26.3	25.4
2009	25.6	25.1	25.1	24.6	24.3	24.5	24.4	24.4	24.4	24.5	24.6	24.8	24.7
2010	24.4	24.3	24.4	25.1	25.2	25.2	25.6	25.7	25.6	25.9	25.9	26.3	25.3
2011	26.1	25.8	25.8	26.2	26.3	26.2	26.3	26.4	26.6	26.3	26.5	26.8	26.3
2012	26.4	26.5	26.7	26.8	26.9	26.9	26.6	26.9	26.9	27.3	27.7	28.0	27.0
2013	27.9	27.8	28.1	27.6	27.4	27.3	27.2	27.5	27.4	27.8	27.9	28.5	27.7
2014	27.9	27.7	28.1	28.2	28.5	28.3	28.3	28.7	28.8	28.9	29.2	29.9	28.5
2015	29.4	29.0	29.0	29.3	29.3	29.1	29.2	29.2	29.4	29.3	29.4	29.9	29.3
2016	29.0	28.6	28.8	28.6	28.5	28.2	28.2	28.4	28.5	28.4	28.5	29.1	28.6
2017	28.5	28.5	28.4	28.5	28.6	28.8	28.3	28.3	28.4	27.7	28.4	29.0	28.5

Employment by Industry: New Orleans-Metairie, LA, Selected Years, 2007–2017—*Continued*

(Numbers in thousands, not seasonally adjusted)

Industry and year	January	February	March	April	May	June	July	August	September	October	November	December	Annual average
Information													
2007	7.4	8.2	10.1	9.5	9.2	9.8	8.7	8.3	7.3	7.1	7.4	7.3	8.4
2008	8.0	9.2	11.2	9.8	10.6	11.2	7.2	8.6	8.9	6.9	7.4	7.9	8.9
2009	6.0	6.4	6.6	6.3	6.7	7.1	6.4	6.4	6.4	6.0	6.4	6.2	6.4
2010	6.8	7.3	7.2	6.9	7.5	8.3	6.0	6.3	8.7	6.5	6.9	7.1	7.1
2011	6.9	6.8	8.4	7.6	8.5	8.0	6.9	6.9	7.1	7.4	7.4	8.0	7.5
2012	7.2	7.8	8.0	10.5	11.9	9.2	8.6	8.7	7.9	7.7	8.6	8.9	8.8
2013	9.1	10.1	9.2	9.6	10.2	10.5	7.6	8.3	8.0	9.6	10.6	9.1	9.3
2014	7.4	8.4	9.0	8.5	8.7	8.2	8.2	8.0	7.6	7.7	9.6	9.0	8.4
2015	6.8	8.4	8.5	9.8	10.3	9.7	9.2	8.6	8.1	9.0	9.6	9.8	9.0
2016	8.7	8.1	7.9	7.9	7.5	6.7	7.3	8.0	6.6	6.8	8.0	6.7	7.5
2017	6.5	8.3	7.6	8.1	8.7	6.6	6.4	7.2	7.0	7.2	7.0	6.9	7.3
Financial Activities													
2007	27.7	27.8	27.6	27.4	27.5	27.7	27.9	27.8	27.6	27.9	27.8	27.8	27.7
2008	27.3	27.5	27.5	27.2	27.2	27.2	26.9	26.7	26.3	26.5	26.4	26.4	26.9
2009	26.0	26.1	26.1	26.5	26.5	26.6	26.5	26.4	26.3	26.1	26.2	26.3	26.3
2010	26.0	26.0	26.1	26.1	26.4	26.3	26.3	26.2	26.1	26.4	26.5	26.5	26.2
2011	26.7	26.7	26.7	26.4	26.6	26.5	26.8	26.8	26.7	26.9	27.0	27.0	26.7
2012	26.7	26.8	26.8	26.8	26.9	27.0	26.9	26.9	26.8	27.0	27.1	27.1	26.9
2013	27.0	27.1	27.1	27.3	27.5	27.6	27.8	28.0	27.9	28.2	28.1	28.1	27.6
2014	28.0	28.2	28.3	28.6	28.7	28.9	29.0	29.1	28.9	29.1	29.3	29.3	28.8
2015	29.3	29.4	29.5	29.6	29.6	29.7	29.7	29.7	29.5	29.8	29.9	29.8	29.6
2016	29.6	29.6	29.6	30.1	30.2	30.1	30.3	30.4	30.6	30.6	30.4	30.3	30.2
2017	30.1	30.1	30.0	29.8	29.9	29.8	29.9	29.7	29.5	29.6	29.4	29.4	29.8
Professional and Business Services													
2007	67.7	68.8	69.4	68.8	69.5	69.2	67.3	68.4	68.3	70.3	70.5	70.7	69.1
2008	67.5	69.1	69.5	69.9	69.7	69.1	68.7	69.5	68.2	69.2	69.3	69.4	69.1
2009	67.2	67.9	67.7	67.9	68.2	67.7	66.5	66.3	66.2	67.8	68.0	68.5	67.5
2010	66.2	67.1	67.8	69.7	69.5	69.8	69.5	69.0	68.0	68.6	68.8	68.7	68.6
2011	67.1	68.6	68.3	68.8	68.5	68.1	67.4	68.0	68.0	69.7	69.8	69.9	68.5
2012	67.8	69.0	69.5	71.4	71.0	69.4	69.8	69.1	68.1	70.5	70.4	70.0	69.7
2013	70.3	73.6	71.7	72.0	71.7	71.6	72.2	72.6	71.9	74.0	74.1	74.4	72.5
2014	73.0	74.1	74.8	75.4	74.7	75.0	74.2	74.3	73.4	75.3	75.6	75.8	74.6
2015	74.1	74.5	75.4	77.0	76.4	75.5	75.3	75.3	73.7	75.8	75.3	75.2	75.3
2016	74.0	74.6	74.7	76.9	76.7	75.4	74.6	74.8	76.3	75.9	75.3	74.3	75.3
2017	74.4	76.4	75.5	74.8	75.7	74.9	74.6	74.3	74.4	77.5	77.1	76.9	75.5
Education and Health Services													
2007	64.3	65.0	65.6	65.9	64.7	64.5	64.4	66.2	67.4	69.2	69.8	70.0	66.4
2008	69.6	70.4	70.9	71.0	68.9	68.8	68.9	70.6	70.7	73.0	73.5	73.7	70.8
2009	74.1	74.9	75.3	75.8	76.1	73.4	73.6	75.5	75.7	77.3	77.6	77.6	75.6
2010	77.5	77.8	78.3	79.2	76.4	75.3	75.2	76.0	77.1	78.4	78.8	78.8	77.4
2011	77.5	78.6	79.1	79.8	79.1	77.4	77.5	78.6	80.2	81.4	82.1	81.7	79.4
2012	80.0	81.0	81.8	81.7	81.7	81.0	80.4	81.9	81.9	82.7	82.9	83.0	81.7
2013	84.4	84.9	84.5	84.0	83.6	82.2	81.5	85.9	86.6	88.3	88.4	88.2	85.2
2014	87.7	88.3	88.4	88.7	88.9	88.0	88.1	91.0	91.8	92.3	92.7	92.3	89.9
2015	92.3	92.7	92.9	94.2	94.4	93.3	93.2	95.1	95.7	97.8	97.7	97.8	94.8
2016	97.1	97.4	97.7	98.8	99.1	98.2	98.3	100.0	100.8	100.5	100.9	100.8	99.1
2017	99.0	99.6	99.2	100.4	100.4	99.7	97.8	99.8	100.8	100.7	101.5	100.5	100.0
Leisure and Hospitality													
2007	63.8	64.3	65.7	65.4	66.6	67.4	66.3	66.9	65.3	66.0	66.9	68.0	66.1
2008	67.5	68.0	68.6	69.3	69.4	69.9	68.8	69.4	65.8	67.5	67.4	67.6	68.3
2009	66.6	67.5	68.3	68.2	69.0	69.1	67.6	68.7	67.8	67.3	67.4	67.7	67.9
2010	67.8	68.4	69.6	70.2	70.0	70.6	69.1	69.6	70.4	70.2	71.3	72.4	70.0
2011	70.9	71.9	73.0	73.6	74.2	74.5	73.6	74.6	74.3	73.8	74.9	76.1	73.8
2012	75.8	75.9	76.5	77.4	76.9	76.9	76.3	76.8	74.8	76.1	76.9	78.6	76.6
2013	77.9	77.6	78.5	79.3	79.3	79.5	78.4	80.7	78.0	78.8	81.1	80.6	79.1
2014	80.4	81.7	82.3	82.5	83.3	83.9	82.6	83.7	81.6	83.5	84.9	84.0	82.9
2015	83.8	84.3	85.2	85.3	85.9	85.8	85.3	84.8	83.6	86.1	86.1	86.9	85.3
2016	86.1	86.4	87.4	87.9	88.4	88.2	87.2	86.8	87.0	88.0	88.1	87.8	87.4
2017	86.8	87.8	88.1	88.9	89.9	89.5	88.7	88.2	87.8	87.4	87.9	88.6	88.3

Employment by Industry: New Orleans-Metairie, LA, Selected Years, 2007–2017—*Continued*

(Numbers in thousands, not seasonally adjusted)

Industry and year	January	February	March	April	May	June	July	August	September	October	November	December	Annual average
Other Services													
2007	19.4	19.8	20.1	20.9	21.1	21.3	22.0	22.2	22.3	22.7	22.7	22.9	21.5
2008	22.0	22.2	22.3	20.3	20.5	20.6	20.2	20.3	20.1	21.6	21.8	21.7	21.1
2009	21.6	21.8	21.9	22.1	22.2	22.1	22.2	22.4	22.5	21.9	22.0	22.1	22.1
2010	21.3	21.4	21.5	20.7	20.7	20.9	20.6	20.6	20.5	21.0	21.1	21.2	21.0
2011	21.2	21.3	21.4	21.6	21.6	21.8	21.8	21.8	21.7	21.9	22.0	22.0	21.7
2012	21.9	22.0	22.2	22.3	22.4	22.5	22.5	22.4	22.3	22.4	22.4	22.5	22.3
2013	22.5	22.6	22.7	22.9	22.9	23.0	23.1	23.1	22.9	22.9	22.9	22.9	22.9
2014	23.0	22.9	23.0	23.0	23.2	23.2	23.2	23.2	23.0	23.2	23.2	23.4	23.1
2015	23.3	23.4	23.4	23.7	24.0	24.0	24.2	24.1	23.9	23.9	23.9	23.9	23.8
2016	23.8	23.7	23.8	24.4	24.3	24.3	24.4	24.4	24.2	24.2	24.3	24.1	24.2
2017	24.3	24.3	24.2	24.0	24.3	24.3	24.2	24.3	24.1	24.2	24.2	24.2	24.2
Government													
2007	78.0	79.0	79.7	74.4	74.8	75.2	73.1	74.2	77.5	79.8	80.5	80.8	77.3
2008	79.6	80.4	80.3	82.4	82.5	81.2	80.2	82.4	83.4	84.2	84.7	84.5	82.2
2009	83.5	84.0	83.6	85.1	84.8	82.4	83.2	85.0	84.6	85.8	85.6	85.2	84.4
2010	83.9	84.4	85.1	84.9	86.5	84.5	81.9	82.7	83.1	83.5	83.8	83.3	84.0
2011	82.4	82.4	82.1	82.3	82.1	80.1	78.4	79.8	81.3	80.8	80.9	80.5	81.1
2012	78.5	79.3	78.9	80.2	80.1	78.9	76.5	77.8	78.7	79.1	79.3	79.3	78.9
2013	77.6	78.1	78.1	77.8	78.1	77.0	73.8	73.5	74.5	74.8	75.1	75.3	76.1
2014	73.6	74.9	75.2	74.6	74.3	76.1	72.9	72.9	74.3	74.8	75.0	74.2	74.4
2015	73.2	74.4	73.8	74.2	74.1	73.1	70.5	71.3	73.0	72.3	72.5	72.1	72.9
2016	71.6	72.4	72.0	72.5	71.4	72.8	69.8	70.1	71.2	72.3	72.4	72.1	72.0
2017	71.2	72.4	72.1	74.0	74.2	72.6	69.8	70.1	71.2	72.5	72.9	72.4	72.1

Employment by Industry: Hartford-West Hartford-East Hartford, CT, Selected Years, 2007–2017

(Numbers in thousands, not seasonally adjusted)

Industry and year	January	February	March	April	May	June	July	August	September	October	November	December	Annual average
Total Nonfarm													
2007	556.4	558.8	560.2	565.0	568.5	571.7	562.8	560.6	568.7	571.9	576.0	575.4	566.3
2008	562.0	565.7	567.5	571.4	572.6	574.9	565.6	562.0	570.5	572.6	571.1	567.5	568.6
2009	551.1	553.7	551.2	552.3	553.5	552.3	543.0	539.9	549.3	552.1	552.7	551.6	550.2
2010	530.9	534.3	536.6	544.3	546.2	545.1	538.6	536.3	548.0	552.7	554.8	554.7	543.5
2011	539.9	543.6	544.4	551.9	550.6	549.9	544.2	539.7	551.6	553.2	553.6	555.6	548.2
2012	541.4	546.5	548.6	551.4	551.8	554.2	547.6	545.3	556.7	561.8	564.8	563.7	552.8
2013	549.0	550.4	553.3	558.7	559.9	563.3	554.4	551.2	560.5	562.5	565.9	565.2	557.9
2014	552.8	554.1	556.6	563.9	565.7	568.1	559.2	556.6	567.1	571.4	573.4	573.3	563.5
2015	559.5	560.5	562.9	569.0	572.0	574.4	564.4	561.0	570.9	574.8	576.8	575.1	568.5
2016	562.8	563.8	566.0	569.0	572.0	574.5	566.8	563.4	572.3	573.4	577.5	576.4	569.8
2017	565.1	565.8	567.7	570.9	574.0	578.1	566.3	563.4	575.1	578.0	579.6	581.3	572.1
Total Private													
2007	465.9	464.8	466.3	470.4	476.9	482.7	478.8	477.6	477.3	477.4	480.6	482.0	475.1
2008	472.3	471.4	473.2	476.3	480.6	485.4	480.8	478.2	478.8	478.1	476.7	475.3	477.3
2009	462.6	459.3	457.2	456.9	461.5	463.3	459.8	457.7	457.7	457.1	457.4	457.5	459.0
2010	443.4	442.9	444.8	452.0	456.1	459.2	457.4	456.4	458.4	460.3	462.2	463.1	454.7
2011	452.0	452.3	453.3	460.1	463.0	465.8	464.1	461.3	462.3	461.6	462.1	464.7	460.2
2012	455.5	456.0	458.4	461.9	466.4	470.2	467.6	466.5	467.3	470.0	472.3	472.2	465.4
2013	461.3	460.3	463.0	468.3	472.7	476.4	472.4	471.6	471.9	471.9	475.0	474.8	470.0
2014	464.0	463.7	465.6	473.1	477.7	480.9	477.1	476.1	477.1	478.9	480.7	481.5	474.7
2015	470.6	470.0	472.2	478.4	484.3	488.5	483.0	481.4	481.8	484.0	485.5	485.3	480.4
2016	475.1	474.4	476.3	480.0	485.3	489.6	487.5	486.0	486.1	486.5	488.8	489.3	483.7
2017	478.9	478.1	479.7	483.7	490.1	494.4	488.8	487.6	490.2	490.7	491.6	495.0	487.4
Goods Producing													
2007	85.0	84.3	84.7	86.3	87.7	88.8	88.7	88.8	87.9	87.7	87.6	86.8	87.0
2008	84.3	83.9	83.7	85.5	86.0	87.0	86.6	86.4	86.0	85.2	83.9	82.4	85.1
2009	79.8	78.2	77.2	77.2	77.5	77.7	77.3	76.8	76.9	75.7	75.2	74.6	77.0
2010	71.3	70.5	70.7	72.7	73.7	74.7	74.6	74.7	75.0	75.2	75.1	74.9	73.6
2011	72.2	72.0	72.5	73.7	74.7	76.0	76.1	75.9	75.8	75.4	75.5	75.0	74.6
2012	73.1	72.7	73.0	74.0	74.6	75.7	76.1	75.9	75.3	75.5	75.3	75.1	74.7
2013	73.0	72.6	72.7	74.1	75.4	76.1	76.6	75.9	75.5	75.0	74.8	74.3	74.7
2014	71.9	71.6	71.6	73.5	74.4	75.3	75.9	75.9	75.5	75.6	75.4	74.9	74.3
2015	72.8	72.6	73.1	75.2	76.7	77.6	77.1	77.3	77.0	76.9	76.6	76.2	75.8
2016	74.2	73.5	74.2	75.7	76.8	77.7	78.1	78.1	77.5	77.5	77.3	76.9	76.5
2017	74.9	74.8	75.4	76.7	78.2	79.7	79.7	79.5	78.9	79.6	78.2	77.9	77.8
Service-Providing													
2007	471.4	474.5	475.5	478.7	480.8	482.9	474.1	471.8	480.8	484.2	488.4	488.6	479.3
2008	477.7	481.8	483.8	485.9	486.6	487.9	479.0	475.6	484.5	487.4	487.2	485.1	483.5
2009	471.3	475.5	474.0	475.1	476.0	474.6	465.7	463.1	472.4	476.4	477.5	477.0	473.2
2010	459.6	463.8	465.9	471.6	472.5	470.4	464.0	461.6	473.0	477.5	479.7	479.8	470.0
2011	467.7	471.6	471.9	478.2	475.9	473.9	468.1	463.8	475.8	477.8	478.1	480.6	473.6
2012	468.3	473.8	475.6	477.4	477.2	478.5	471.5	469.4	481.4	486.3	489.5	488.6	478.1
2013	476.0	477.8	480.6	484.6	484.5	487.2	477.8	475.3	485.0	487.5	491.1	490.9	483.2
2014	480.9	482.5	485.0	490.4	491.3	492.8	483.3	480.7	491.6	495.8	498.0	498.4	489.2
2015	486.7	487.9	489.8	493.8	495.3	497.2	487.3	483.7	493.9	497.9	500.2	498.9	492.7
2016	488.6	490.3	491.8	493.3	495.2	496.8	488.7	485.3	494.8	495.9	500.2	499.5	493.4
2017	490.2	491.0	492.3	494.2	495.8	498.4	486.6	483.9	496.2	498.4	501.4	503.4	494.3
Mining, Logging, and Construction													
2007	20.5	19.8	20.2	21.8	23.1	23.6	23.8	23.9	23.5	23.3	23.0	22.1	22.4
2008	20.2	19.9	19.9	21.2	21.7	22.1	22.3	22.1	21.7	21.2	20.4	19.4	21.0
2009	17.6	17.0	17.0	17.8	18.5	18.9	19.2	19.2	19.0	18.5	18.3	17.7	18.2
2010	15.2	14.5	14.6	16.6	17.3	17.8	18.0	18.2	18.0	18.1	17.9	17.3	17.0
2011	15.4	15.1	15.3	16.5	17.3	18.1	18.4	18.4	18.2	18.0	18.1	17.4	17.2
2012	15.8	15.3	15.7	16.7	17.1	17.7	18.2	18.3	18.1	18.2	18.0	17.6	17.2
2013	16.0	15.8	16.0	17.3	18.5	18.9	19.4	19.4	19.3	19.3	19.1	18.4	18.1
2014	16.8	16.5	16.5	18.3	19.3	19.7	20.4	20.5	20.3	20.2	20.0	19.3	19.0
2015	17.7	17.4	17.6	19.6	20.8	21.2	21.3	21.5	21.2	21.3	21.1	20.6	20.1
2016	19.0	18.3	19.0	20.3	21.3	21.6	21.8	21.8	21.4	21.2	20.9	20.0	20.6
2017	18.2	17.9	18.3	19.4	20.6	21.1	21.2	21.1	20.9	21.3	19.8	18.4	19.9

Employment by Industry: Hartford-West Hartford-East Hartford, CT, Selected Years, 2007–2017—*Continued*

(Numbers in thousands, not seasonally adjusted)

Industry and year	January	February	March	April	May	June	July	August	September	October	November	December	Annual average
Manufacturing													
2007	64.5	64.5	64.5	64.5	64.6	65.2	64.9	64.9	64.4	64.4	64.6	64.7	64.6
2008	64.1	64.0	63.8	64.3	64.3	64.9	64.3	64.3	64.3	64.0	63.5	63.0	64.1
2009	62.2	61.2	60.2	59.4	59.0	58.8	58.1	57.6	57.9	57.2	56.9	56.9	58.8
2010	56.1	56.0	56.1	56.1	56.4	56.9	56.6	56.5	57.0	57.1	57.2	57.6	56.6
2011	56.8	56.9	57.2	57.2	57.4	57.9	57.7	57.5	57.6	57.4	57.4	57.6	57.4
2012	57.3	57.4	57.3	57.3	57.5	58.0	57.9	57.6	57.2	57.3	57.3	57.5	57.5
2013	57.0	56.8	56.7	56.8	56.9	57.2	57.2	56.5	56.2	55.7	55.7	55.9	56.6
2014	55.1	55.1	55.1	55.2	55.1	55.6	55.5	55.4	55.2	55.4	55.4	55.6	55.3
2015	55.1	55.2	55.5	55.6	55.9	56.4	55.8	55.8	55.6	55.6	55.5	55.6	55.7
2016	55.2	55.2	55.2	55.4	55.5	56.1	56.3	56.3	56.1	56.3	56.4	56.9	55.9
2017	56.7	56.9	57.1	57.3	57.6	58.6	58.5	58.4	58.0	58.3	58.4	59.5	57.9
Trade, Transportation, and Utilities													
2007	89.6	88.2	88.6	88.4	90.1	91.1	89.2	88.7	90.3	91.3	93.6	95.3	90.4
2008	91.4	90.0	90.2	90.2	90.9	91.5	89.2	88.8	90.1	90.4	91.3	92.3	90.5
2009	88.0	86.4	85.7	84.4	85.8	86.3	84.3	84.2	85.3	85.9	87.3	88.2	86.0
2010	85.0	83.8	83.8	84.1	85.4	86.3	84.8	84.4	85.0	86.1	87.8	89.3	85.5
2011	85.8	84.9	85.0	86.2	86.5	87.1	85.4	85.0	85.7	86.0	87.7	89.4	86.2
2012	86.2	85.1	85.6	85.7	87.0	87.3	85.4	85.2	86.5	87.4	89.5	90.3	86.8
2013	87.7	86.2	87.0	87.9	88.6	89.4	87.3	87.3	88.8	89.8	91.9	92.9	88.7
2014	89.2	88.0	88.2	89.1	89.7	90.3	87.9	87.4	89.3	90.1	91.7	92.7	89.5
2015	89.5	88.2	88.2	88.7	89.9	90.5	87.8	87.5	89.7	91.2	92.9	94.0	89.8
2016	90.9	89.5	89.7	89.3	90.7	90.6	88.8	88.2	89.6	90.4	92.5	94.2	90.4
2017	90.7	89.0	88.7	88.7	90.3	90.7	88.5	88.6	91.3	91.2	93.4	95.1	90.5
Wholesale Trade													
2007	19.7	19.7	19.8	19.8	20.0	20.1	20.2	20.1	20.1	20.1	20.1	20.3	20.0
2008	20.1	20.1	20.3	20.2	20.4	20.5	20.3	20.2	20.1	20.0	19.8	19.6	20.1
2009	19.4	19.2	19.1	18.9	18.8	18.9	18.8	18.8	18.6	18.5	18.4	18.5	18.8
2010	18.0	18.0	18.0	18.2	18.3	18.5	18.5	18.5	18.3	18.3	18.4	18.4	18.3
2011	18.0	18.0	18.1	18.3	18.4	18.5	18.4	18.4	18.2	18.1	18.0	18.0	18.2
2012	17.8	17.8	17.8	17.9	18.1	18.1	18.2	18.1	18.0	18.2	18.0	18.1	18.0
2013	17.9	17.9	17.9	18.0	18.1	18.2	18.1	18.1	18.0	18.1	18.0	18.1	18.0
2014	17.9	17.8	17.9	18.0	18.0	18.1	18.1	18.0	18.0	17.9	17.8	17.9	18.0
2015	17.8	17.7	17.8	18.0	18.1	18.2	18.1	18.1	18.1	18.0	17.9	18.0	18.0
2016	18.1	18.0	18.1	18.2	18.3	18.4	18.3	18.2	18.1	17.9	17.9	18.1	18.1
2017	18.0	18.0	18.0	18.1	18.3	18.4	18.3	18.2	18.2	18.1	18.3	18.4	18.2
Retail Trade													
2007	56.7	55.3	55.7	55.8	57.1	57.8	56.9	57.0	56.9	57.7	59.9	61.1	57.3
2008	58.2	56.7	56.8	56.8	57.2	57.6	56.5	56.7	56.4	56.6	57.6	58.5	57.1
2009	55.1	53.8	53.4	53.0	53.8	54.3	53.6	53.7	53.7	54.2	55.6	56.4	54.2
2010	53.7	52.5	52.6	53.0	53.6	54.4	54.1	53.9	53.4	54.4	55.8	57.2	54.1
2011	54.6	53.6	53.5	54.4	54.5	54.9	54.3	54.3	53.8	54.3	56.0	57.4	54.6
2012	55.1	54.0	54.3	54.4	55.1	55.3	54.6	54.6	54.2	54.9	57.1	57.5	55.1
2013	55.6	54.4	54.8	55.3	55.7	56.2	55.7	56.0	55.6	56.4	58.2	58.8	56.1
2014	56.3	55.2	55.3	55.9	56.4	56.8	55.9	55.7	55.6	56.3	58.0	58.5	56.3
2015	56.2	55.1	55.1	55.2	56.0	56.4	55.4	55.4	55.2	56.1	57.6	58.4	56.0
2016	55.8	54.6	54.9	54.7	55.5	55.9	55.4	55.2	54.6	55.4	57.0	57.5	55.5
2017	56.0	54.3	54.1	54.7	55.3	55.5	55.2	55.1	54.4	54.0	55.5	56.7	55.1
Transportation and Utilities													
2007	13.2	13.2	13.1	12.8	13.0	13.2	12.1	11.6	13.3	13.5	13.6	13.9	13.0
2008	13.1	13.2	13.1	13.2	13.3	13.4	12.4	11.9	13.6	13.8	13.9	14.2	13.3
2009	13.5	13.4	13.2	12.5	13.2	13.1	11.9	11.7	13.0	13.2	13.3	13.3	12.9
2010	13.3	13.3	13.2	12.9	13.5	13.4	12.2	12.0	13.3	13.4	13.6	13.7	13.2
2011	13.2	13.3	13.4	13.5	13.6	13.7	12.7	12.3	13.7	13.6	13.7	14.0	13.4
2012	13.3	13.3	13.5	13.4	13.8	13.9	12.6	12.5	14.3	14.3	14.4	14.7	13.7
2013	14.2	13.9	14.3	14.6	14.8	15.0	13.5	13.2	15.2	15.3	15.7	16.0	14.6
2014	15.0	15.0	15.0	15.2	15.3	15.4	13.9	13.7	15.7	15.9	15.9	16.3	15.2
2015	15.5	15.4	15.3	15.5	15.8	15.9	14.3	14.0	16.4	17.1	17.4	17.6	15.9
2016	17.0	16.9	16.7	16.4	16.9	16.3	15.1	14.8	16.9	17.1	17.6	18.6	16.7
2017	16.7	16.7	16.6	15.9	16.7	16.8	15.0	15.3	18.7	19.1	19.6	20.0	17.3

Employment by Industry: Hartford-West Hartford-East Hartford, CT, Selected Years, 2007–2017—*Continued*

(Numbers in thousands, not seasonally adjusted)

Industry and year	January	February	March	April	May	June	July	August	September	October	November	December	Annual average
Information													
2007	12.1	12.2	12.2	12.3	12.3	12.5	12.6	12.6	12.5	12.4	12.5	12.6	12.4
2008	12.6	12.6	12.6	12.6	12.6	12.8	12.9	12.7	12.4	12.3	12.4	12.3	12.6
2009	12.2	12.2	12.0	12.0	11.9	11.9	11.9	11.8	11.7	11.5	11.4	11.4	11.8
2010	11.3	11.2	11.2	11.2	11.2	11.2	11.3	11.4	11.4	11.4	11.5	11.5	11.3
2011	11.5	11.4	11.4	11.3	11.3	11.3	11.3	11.3	11.2	11.1	11.1	11.0	11.3
2012	11.0	11.1	10.9	11.1	11.2	11.2	11.2	11.3	11.3	11.3	11.6	11.3	11.2
2013	11.5	11.7	11.7	11.4	11.5	11.5	11.5	11.6	11.2	11.2	11.3	11.3	11.5
2014	11.2	11.3	11.5	11.5	11.4	11.5	11.6	11.7	11.5	11.3	11.6	11.7	11.5
2015	11.5	11.6	11.6	11.8	11.8	11.9	11.9	12.0	11.9	11.9	12.0	12.0	11.8
2016	11.7	11.6	11.6	11.5	11.5	11.6	11.6	11.6	11.4	11.2	11.1	11.1	11.5
2017	10.6	10.6	10.6	10.6	10.5	10.6	10.6	10.7	10.6	10.5	10.5	10.4	10.6
Financial Activities													
2007	67.8	67.3	67.1	66.8	66.9	67.7	67.4	67.3	66.6	66.3	66.3	66.4	67.0
2008	66.1	66.2	66.8	66.1	66.2	67.0	67.0	66.9	65.9	65.5	65.6	65.4	66.2
2009	64.9	64.6	64.6	64.0	64.0	64.3	63.9	63.6	62.8	62.4	62.3	62.1	63.6
2010	61.8	61.8	62.2	61.4	61.5	62.4	62.4	62.6	62.0	62.2	62.2	62.3	62.1
2011	62.2	62.0	62.2	61.8	61.8	62.3	62.5	62.3	61.7	61.6	61.4	61.5	61.9
2012	61.1	61.1	61.3	60.7	60.7	61.6	61.6	61.1	60.5	60.3	60.1	60.1	60.9
2013	60.0	59.5	59.4	59.1	58.8	59.6	59.4	58.7	57.6	56.9	56.7	56.7	58.5
2014	57.0	56.6	56.4	56.3	56.5	57.1	57.4	57.1	56.6	56.7	56.7	56.8	56.8
2015	56.7	56.6	56.7	56.8	57.0	57.9	58.1	58.0	57.3	57.2	57.5	57.4	57.3
2016	57.2	57.0	57.2	57.3	57.3	58.1	58.1	58.0	57.3	57.1	57.1	57.0	57.4
2017	56.8	56.7	56.8	56.7	56.8	57.7	57.7	57.5	56.8	56.3	56.8	56.6	56.9
Professional and Business Services													
2007	60.8	61.1	61.4	63.0	63.4	64.5	63.8	64.0	63.4	63.2	63.6	64.3	63.0
2008	63.7	64.0	64.2	64.5	65.0	65.9	65.5	65.2	64.7	64.2	63.9	63.1	64.5
2009	62.0	61.2	60.7	61.2	61.5	61.6	60.8	61.1	60.5	60.8	60.8	60.7	61.1
2010	58.3	59.1	59.0	61.4	61.6	62.0	61.8	61.6	61.5	61.9	61.8	61.6	61.0
2011	60.6	60.9	60.5	62.4	62.5	63.2	63.4	63.1	63.2	63.7	63.5	64.1	62.6
2012	62.8	63.3	63.9	65.0	65.5	66.2	66.1	66.3	66.0	66.4	66.4	66.0	65.3
2013	63.6	64.4	64.3	65.9	66.5	67.4	67.5	68.1	68.4	68.4	68.9	68.9	66.9
2014	67.6	68.5	68.7	70.3	71.5	71.9	71.2	71.2	71.0	71.7	71.9	72.0	70.6
2015	70.7	71.5	71.9	72.7	73.6	74.8	73.8	73.3	72.9	72.9	73.3	72.6	72.8
2016	70.7	71.1	71.1	72.2	72.6	73.7	73.1	73.4	73.2	73.3	73.4	73.6	72.6
2017	71.8	72.0	72.3	73.0	73.5	74.3	74.5	74.1	74.1	75.3	74.4	76.4	73.8
Education and Health Services													
2007	90.7	91.5	92.0	92.1	92.3	92.0	91.4	90.6	92.7	93.4	94.3	94.1	92.3
2008	93.7	94.1	94.5	94.9	94.8	94.9	94.5	93.7	95.8	96.9	97.5	97.6	95.2
2009	96.4	97.1	97.4	97.7	97.3	97.0	97.8	97.1	98.2	99.1	99.3	99.4	97.8
2010	98.1	98.5	99.2	99.9	99.3	98.5	97.7	97.2	99.4	100.4	101.0	101.1	99.2
2011	100.4	101.0	101.5	102.0	101.4	100.0	99.2	98.4	100.2	100.0	99.8	100.3	100.4
2012	99.4	100.4	100.8	100.7	100.4	99.6	99.2	98.8	101.2	102.3	103.0	103.5	100.8
2013	101.5	102.1	103.0	103.1	102.5	102.0	100.6	100.8	103.2	103.5	104.3	103.9	102.5
2014	102.1	102.9	103.4	104.8	104.3	103.9	102.4	103.0	105.0	105.3	105.8	105.9	104.1
2015	103.8	104.2	104.4	105.4	105.0	104.9	103.7	103.1	104.5	105.2	105.5	105.6	104.6
2016	104.3	105.0	105.1	105.1	105.0	105.3	105.8	105.4	107.1	107.2	108.2	107.5	105.9
2017	106.9	107.7	107.8	108.2	108.7	107.9	105.4	105.7	107.8	109.0	109.1	109.5	107.8
Leisure and Hospitality													
2007	39.0	39.3	39.4	40.4	43.1	44.6	44.5	44.5	42.9	41.9	41.7	41.5	41.9
2008	39.7	39.7	40.2	41.4	43.9	44.9	44.3	43.8	43.0	42.7	41.2	41.5	42.2
2009	38.7	39.2	39.2	39.9	42.9	43.9	43.5	42.8	42.0	41.3	40.8	40.7	41.2
2010	37.5	38.0	38.6	41.1	43.0	43.5	44.3	44.0	43.6	42.6	42.2	41.9	41.7
2011	39.1	39.9	39.9	42.2	44.1	44.8	45.5	44.8	44.2	43.5	42.7	43.0	42.8
2012	41.4	41.8	42.6	44.2	46.2	47.4	46.8	46.6	45.3	45.2	44.6	44.8	44.7
2013	43.0	42.7	43.7	45.9	48.3	48.9	48.3	48.2	46.4	46.4	46.3	45.9	46.2
2014	44.2	44.0	44.9	46.5	48.6	49.3	49.1	48.4	46.8	46.7	46.1	46.1	46.7
2015	44.3	44.0	44.8	46.4	48.6	49.1	48.7	47.9	46.9	47.1	46.1	45.9	46.7
2016	44.5	45.1	45.7	47.2	49.5	50.4	49.8	49.2	48.2	47.9	47.4	47.1	47.7
2017	45.5	45.6	46.3	47.9	49.9	51.1	50.2	49.5	48.6	47.4	47.5	47.5	48.1

Employment by Industry: Hartford-West Hartford-East Hartford, CT, Selected Years, 2007–2017—*Continued*

(Numbers in thousands, not seasonally adjusted)

Industry and year	January	February	March	April	May	June	July	August	September	October	November	December	Annual average
Other Services													
2007	20.9	20.9	20.9	21.1	21.1	21.5	21.2	21.1	21.0	21.2	21.0	21.0	21.1
2008	20.8	20.9	21.0	21.1	21.2	21.4	20.8	20.7	20.9	20.9	20.9	20.7	20.9
2009	20.6	20.4	20.4	20.5	20.6	20.6	20.3	20.3	20.3	20.4	20.3	20.4	20.4
2010	20.1	20.0	20.1	20.2	20.4	20.6	20.5	20.5	20.5	20.5	20.6	20.5	20.4
2011	20.2	20.2	20.3	20.5	20.7	21.1	20.7	20.5	20.3	20.3	20.4	20.4	20.5
2012	20.5	20.5	20.3	20.5	20.8	21.2	21.2	21.3	21.2	21.6	21.8	21.1	21.0
2013	21.0	21.1	21.2	20.9	21.1	21.5	21.2	21.0	20.8	20.7	20.8	20.9	21.0
2014	20.8	20.8	20.9	21.1	21.3	21.6	21.6	21.4	21.4	21.5	21.5	21.4	21.3
2015	21.3	21.3	21.5	21.4	21.7	21.8	21.9	22.3	21.6	21.6	21.6	21.6	21.6
2016	21.6	21.6	21.7	21.7	21.9	22.2	22.2	22.1	21.8	21.9	21.8	21.9	21.9
2017	21.7	21.7	21.8	21.9	22.2	22.4	22.2	22.0	22.1	21.4	21.7	21.6	21.9
Government													
2007	90.5	94.0	93.9	94.6	91.6	89.0	84.0	83.0	91.4	94.5	95.4	93.4	91.3
2008	89.7	94.3	94.3	95.1	92.0	89.5	84.8	83.8	91.7	94.5	94.4	92.2	91.4
2009	88.5	94.4	94.0	95.4	92.0	89.0	83.2	82.2	91.6	95.0	95.3	94.1	91.2
2010	87.5	91.4	91.8	92.3	90.1	85.9	81.2	79.9	89.6	92.4	92.6	91.6	88.9
2011	87.9	91.3	91.1	91.8	87.6	84.1	80.1	78.4	89.3	91.6	91.5	90.9	88.0
2012	85.9	90.5	90.2	89.5	85.4	84.0	80.0	78.8	89.4	91.8	92.5	91.5	87.5
2013	87.7	90.1	90.3	90.4	87.2	86.9	82.0	79.6	88.6	90.6	90.9	90.4	87.9
2014	88.8	90.4	91.0	90.8	88.0	87.2	82.1	80.5	90.0	92.5	92.7	91.8	88.8
2015	88.9	90.5	90.7	90.6	87.7	86.3	81.4	79.6	89.1	90.8	91.3	89.8	88.1
2016	87.7	89.4	89.7	89.0	86.7	84.9	79.3	77.4	86.2	86.9	88.7	87.1	86.1
2017	86.2	87.7	88.0	87.2	83.9	83.7	77.5	75.8	84.9	87.3	88.0	86.3	84.7

Employment by Industry: Salt Lake City, UT, Selected Years, 2007–2017

(Numbers in thousands, not seasonally adjusted)

Industry and year	January	February	March	April	May	June	July	August	September	October	November	December	Annual average
Total Nonfarm													
2007	601.1	603.8	608.2	610.6	614.4	618.9	614.6	619.0	619.1	620.3	625.2	627.8	615.3
2008	613.8	615.1	617.1	619.4	619.8	621.8	617.4	621.2	620.8	618.8	616.9	616.4	618.2
2009	595.6	592.3	590.9	588.4	588.9	588.6	582.0	583.9	586.2	587.6	588.8	591.1	588.7
2010	576.9	576.6	580.7	583.9	586.8	588.4	586.6	587.7	590.4	594.7	597.4	598.5	587.4
2011	585.5	586.9	589.9	594.7	595.1	597.8	596.2	600.2	603.8	604.7	609.2	610.6	597.9
2012	600.9	603.9	607.4	617.2	621.8	624.4	616.2	620.8	625.0	629.2	636.0	636.3	619.9
2013	625.0	628.7	632.2	636.6	637.9	639.5	634.7	638.3	641.1	648.9	654.5	655.9	639.4
2014	641.7	644.2	646.7	650.7	652.1	655.6	647.5	652.7	658.0	663.0	668.6	671.1	654.3
2015	660.3	663.6	668.3	670.0	674.2	675.6	673.9	677.0	681.5	688.5	692.8	695.6	676.8
2016	682.5	687.8	691.3	694.8	697.1	699.3	699.0	701.4	707.1	709.9	712.7	713.2	699.7
2017	702.6	705.8	708.8	711.7	714.8	719.0	711.4	715.6	720.5	724.6	730.4	730.1	716.3
Total Private													
2007	511.2	513.7	518.1	520.1	524.2	528.1	527.3	531.2	528.6	529.2	533.8	536.1	525.1
2008	522.4	523.4	525.0	527.2	527.6	529.0	528.4	531.1	527.2	524.9	522.7	522.1	525.9
2009	502.2	498.4	497.2	494.0	494.8	494.3	491.7	492.8	491.8	492.8	494.2	496.3	495.0
2010	482.6	482.4	486.5	489.0	490.2	492.8	494.6	495.3	494.3	497.8	500.5	502.4	492.4
2011	490.3	491.6	494.5	498.4	498.7	501.3	503.5	507.0	507.4	508.6	512.5	513.7	502.3
2012	504.1	506.7	510.1	518.6	523.6	526.2	522.6	527.3	527.3	530.2	537.2	538.2	522.7
2013	527.4	530.7	534.4	537.0	537.8	539.0	539.2	543.1	540.7	546.1	552.1	553.5	540.1
2014	539.5	541.2	543.5	546.2	547.2	550.4	549.5	555.4	555.4	559.4	564.9	567.2	551.7
2015	557.2	559.7	563.7	564.7	568.4	570.8	573.8	578.1	577.0	582.0	586.7	589.2	572.6
2016	578.0	581.9	584.9	586.8	588.8	591.4	596.9	600.7	599.7	600.6	603.7	603.9	593.1
2017	594.9	596.9	599.6	601.6	604.0	609.0	608.7	612.9	611.9	614.2	620.1	619.6	607.8
Goods Producing													
2007	98.9	99.1	100.6	101.7	103.6	105.7	105.6	106.7	105.5	104.5	103.7	102.3	103.2
2008	99.3	98.3	99.0	99.5	100.1	101.2	101.4	101.6	100.4	99.2	96.7	94.7	99.3
2009	88.7	86.4	86.0	85.0	86.3	86.9	87.3	87.5	87.1	86.8	86.0	85.0	86.6
2010	82.2	81.6	82.1	83.4	84.5	85.3	85.9	86.6	86.6	86.8	86.0	85.1	84.7
2011	82.9	82.6	83.2	84.2	85.2	86.4	88.5	89.3	88.8	88.6	88.3	87.3	86.3
2012	85.3	85.9	86.5	88.0	89.9	90.7	90.6	91.2	90.8	90.7	90.1	89.6	89.1
2013	87.4	87.2	88.0	89.1	89.7	90.1	89.9	90.8	90.1	89.6	89.2	88.4	89.1
2014	86.5	86.9	87.6	88.6	89.4	90.2	90.4	91.1	91.1	91.5	91.0	90.3	89.6
2015	88.5	88.8	89.9	90.7	91.7	92.7	93.5	93.6	93.5	94.2	94.0	93.9	92.1
2016	91.9	92.3	93.5	94.2	95.1	95.8	96.8	96.9	97.2	97.4	96.9	96.0	95.3
2017	94.7	95.4	96.9	97.3	99.0	100.4	100.3	100.5	100.6	101.2	101.7	101.0	99.1
Service-Providing													
2007	502.2	504.7	507.6	508.9	510.8	513.2	509.0	512.3	513.6	515.8	521.5	525.5	512.1
2008	514.5	516.8	518.1	519.9	519.7	520.6	516.0	519.6	520.4	519.6	520.2	521.7	518.9
2009	506.9	505.9	504.9	503.4	502.6	501.7	494.7	496.4	499.1	500.8	502.8	506.1	502.1
2010	494.7	495.0	498.6	500.5	502.3	503.1	500.7	501.1	503.8	507.9	511.4	513.4	502.7
2011	502.6	504.3	506.7	510.5	509.9	511.4	507.7	510.9	515.0	516.1	520.9	523.3	511.6
2012	515.6	518.0	520.9	529.2	531.9	533.7	525.6	529.6	534.2	538.5	545.9	546.7	530.8
2013	537.6	541.5	544.2	547.5	548.2	549.4	544.8	547.5	551.0	559.3	565.3	567.5	550.3
2014	555.2	557.3	559.1	562.1	562.7	565.4	557.1	561.6	566.9	571.5	577.6	580.8	564.8
2015	571.8	574.8	578.4	579.3	582.5	582.9	580.4	583.4	588.0	594.3	598.8	601.7	584.7
2016	590.6	595.5	597.8	600.6	602.0	603.5	602.2	604.5	609.9	612.5	615.8	617.2	604.3
2017	607.9	610.4	611.9	614.4	615.8	618.6	611.1	615.1	619.9	623.4	628.7	629.1	617.2
Mining, Logging, and Construction													
2007	43.1	43.0	44.1	45.1	46.7	48.1	48.0	48.7	47.8	46.8	45.8	44.4	46.0
2008	41.4	40.5	41.2	42.1	42.8	43.8	44.0	44.5	43.6	42.6	40.8	39.3	42.2
2009	34.8	33.8	33.8	33.4	34.7	35.1	35.5	35.8	35.6	35.3	34.6	33.3	34.6
2010	31.1	30.6	31.1	31.9	33.1	33.5	33.8	34.3	34.6	35.0	34.2	33.3	33.0
2011	31.1	30.8	31.4	32.1	32.8	33.8	35.2	35.7	35.3	35.1	34.8	33.7	33.5
2012	32.0	32.6	32.9	34.2	35.7	36.1	35.9	36.5	36.2	35.9	35.6	34.9	34.9
2013	33.1	33.0	33.7	34.8	35.3	35.6	35.5	36.3	35.8	35.3	35.1	34.1	34.8
2014	32.5	32.8	33.5	34.5	35.3	35.9	36.4	36.9	37.1	37.4	36.9	36.0	35.4
2015	34.3	34.6	35.4	36.0	36.6	37.3	38.0	38.0	38.1	38.5	38.3	38.1	36.9
2016	36.6	36.9	38.0	38.8	39.3	39.8	40.1	40.2	40.3	40.5	40.0	38.9	39.1
2017	37.7	38.2	39.6	39.8	41.3	42.5	42.9	43.1	43.2	43.8	43.8	42.4	41.5

Employment by Industry: Salt Lake City, UT, Selected Years, 2007–2017—*Continued*

(Numbers in thousands, not seasonally adjusted)

Industry and year	January	February	March	April	May	June	July	August	September	October	November	December	Annual average
Manufacturing													
2007	55.8	56.1	56.5	56.6	56.9	57.6	57.6	58.0	57.7	57.7	57.9	57.9	57.2
2008	57.9	57.8	57.8	57.4	57.3	57.4	57.4	57.1	56.8	56.6	55.9	55.4	57.1
2009	53.9	52.6	52.2	51.6	51.6	51.8	51.8	51.7	51.5	51.5	51.4	51.7	51.9
2010	51.1	51.0	51.0	51.5	51.4	51.8	52.1	52.3	52.0	51.8	51.8	51.8	51.6
2011	51.8	51.8	51.8	52.1	52.4	52.6	53.3	53.6	53.5	53.5	53.5	53.6	52.8
2012	53.3	53.3	53.6	53.8	54.2	54.6	54.7	54.7	54.6	54.8	54.5	54.7	54.2
2013	54.3	54.2	54.3	54.3	54.4	54.5	54.4	54.5	54.3	54.3	54.1	54.3	54.3
2014	54.0	54.1	54.1	54.1	54.1	54.3	54.0	54.2	54.0	54.1	54.1	54.3	54.1
2015	54.2	54.2	54.5	54.7	55.1	55.4	55.5	55.6	55.4	55.7	55.7	55.8	55.2
2016	55.3	55.4	55.5	55.4	55.8	56.0	56.7	56.7	56.9	56.9	56.9	57.1	56.2
2017	57.0	57.2	57.3	57.5	57.7	57.9	57.4	57.4	57.4	57.4	57.9	58.6	57.6
Trade, Transportation, and Utilities													
2007	126.0	125.4	126.3	126.1	127.1	127.7	128.0	128.9	128.7	129.2	132.1	133.9	128.3
2008	129.0	128.0	128.1	128.7	129.0	129.7	129.1	129.6	128.7	128.8	129.8	130.3	129.1
2009	124.2	122.6	121.7	120.6	120.6	120.1	119.4	119.4	119.4	119.5	121.5	122.4	121.0
2010	117.7	117.1	117.4	117.4	118.0	118.4	118.5	119.2	118.7	119.7	121.8	122.9	118.9
2011	118.6	118.2	118.8	119.9	120.0	120.7	121.1	121.7	121.8	122.1	124.9	126.1	121.2
2012	122.9	122.5	123.5	124.6	125.5	126.3	125.6	126.2	126.7	127.3	130.4	130.9	126.0
2013	127.1	126.8	126.9	126.7	127.5	127.8	128.2	128.6	127.9	129.7	132.3	133.3	128.6
2014	128.6	128.1	128.4	128.7	129.4	130.0	129.6	130.4	130.9	132.6	135.5	136.7	130.7
2015	133.2	133.2	133.6	133.5	134.3	134.3	135.5	136.7	136.4	137.9	140.4	141.9	135.9
2016	138.0	138.2	138.8	138.3	139.1	139.0	139.8	140.5	140.8	140.6	143.4	145.1	140.1
2017	140.1	139.5	140.2	140.3	140.5	141.5	142.0	142.4	142.5	144.3	147.2	148.6	142.4
Wholesale Trade													
2007	29.8	29.9	30.0	30.0	30.3	30.5	30.6	30.8	30.7	30.7	30.8	31.0	30.4
2008	30.7	30.7	30.7	31.1	31.2	31.3	31.2	31.3	31.1	30.9	30.8	30.8	31.0
2009	30.0	29.9	29.6	29.3	29.2	29.1	29.0	28.9	28.8	28.7	28.6	28.7	29.2
2010	28.2	28.1	28.3	28.4	28.7	28.7	28.9	29.0	28.8	29.0	29.1	29.3	28.7
2011	29.2	29.4	29.7	29.9	29.9	30.2	30.3	30.4	30.5	30.4	30.6	30.7	30.1
2012	30.5	30.7	30.8	30.8	31.0	31.0	30.8	30.9	30.7	30.6	30.5	30.6	30.7
2013	30.7	30.7	30.7	30.7	30.8	30.8	30.8	30.9	30.6	30.6	30.7	30.7	30.7
2014	30.2	30.3	30.2	30.3	30.5	30.6	30.7	30.7	30.7	31.0	31.1	31.3	30.6
2015	30.9	31.1	31.3	31.5	31.7	31.8	32.0	32.0	31.8	31.9	31.9	32.0	31.7
2016	31.8	32.0	32.1	31.9	32.0	32.0	32.3	32.3	32.3	32.1	32.1	32.2	32.1
2017	31.9	31.9	32.1	32.2	32.4	32.6	32.7	32.7	32.6	33.0	33.0	32.9	32.5
Retail Trade													
2007	66.0	65.3	65.9	65.8	66.3	66.5	66.7	67.2	66.8	67.0	69.5	70.7	67.0
2008	67.6	66.6	66.8	67.0	67.2	67.9	67.4	67.8	67.2	67.5	68.7	69.3	67.6
2009	64.7	63.6	63.4	63.0	63.3	63.3	62.6	63.0	63.2	63.5	65.6	66.2	63.8
2010	62.7	62.1	62.1	62.0	62.3	62.4	62.3	62.6	62.2	62.7	64.4	64.9	62.7
2011	61.4	60.8	61.0	61.6	61.8	62.0	62.2	62.6	62.6	63.3	65.5	66.2	62.6
2012	63.5	62.8	63.5	64.1	64.7	65.3	65.6	65.8	66.2	66.9	69.8	69.9	65.7
2013	66.4	66.1	66.3	66.9	67.5	67.8	68.0	68.4	68.1	68.9	71.0	71.4	68.1
2014	67.5	67.2	67.5	67.7	68.2	68.3	68.7	69.3	69.4	70.4	72.5	73.3	69.2
2015	69.9	69.6	69.5	69.8	70.3	70.2	70.6	71.4	71.2	72.0	74.4	75.1	71.2
2016	72.0	72.1	72.5	72.3	72.8	72.9	73.1	73.6	73.6	73.9	76.0	76.6	73.5
2017	72.8	72.3	72.6	72.9	72.9	73.3	73.3	73.9	73.7	74.7	76.3	77.0	73.8
Transportation and Utilities													
2007	30.2	30.2	30.4	30.3	30.5	30.7	30.7	30.9	31.2	31.5	31.8	32.2	30.9
2008	30.7	30.7	30.6	30.6	30.6	30.5	30.5	30.5	30.4	30.4	30.3	30.2	30.5
2009	29.5	29.1	28.7	28.3	28.1	27.7	27.8	27.5	27.4	27.3	27.3	27.5	28.0
2010	26.8	26.9	27.0	27.0	27.0	27.3	27.3	27.6	27.7	28.0	28.3	28.7	27.5
2011	28.0	28.0	28.1	28.4	28.3	28.5	28.6	28.7	28.7	28.4	28.8	29.2	28.5
2012	28.9	29.0	29.2	29.7	29.8	30.0	29.2	29.5	29.8	29.8	30.1	30.4	29.6
2013	30.0	30.0	29.9	29.1	29.2	29.2	29.4	29.3	29.2	30.2	30.6	31.2	29.8
2014	30.9	30.6	30.7	30.7	30.7	31.1	30.2	30.4	30.8	31.2	31.9	32.1	30.9
2015	32.4	32.5	32.8	32.2	32.3	32.3	32.9	33.3	33.4	34.0	34.1	34.8	33.1
2016	34.2	34.1	34.2	34.1	34.3	34.1	34.4	34.6	34.9	34.6	35.3	36.3	34.6
2017	35.4	35.3	35.5	35.2	35.2	35.6	36.0	35.8	36.2	36.6	37.9	38.7	36.1

Employment by Industry: Salt Lake City, UT, Selected Years, 2007–2017—*Continued*

(Numbers in thousands, not seasonally adjusted)

Industry and year	January	February	March	April	May	June	July	August	September	October	November	December	Annual average
Information													
2007	18.4	18.4	18.6	17.3	17.5	17.3	17.2	17.4	17.1	17.0	17.1	17.2	17.5
2008	16.8	17.4	17.5	17.8	18.1	18.0	17.7	17.8	17.6	17.3	17.5	17.5	17.6
2009	17.0	17.1	17.0	16.6	16.8	16.9	16.6	16.5	16.3	16.4	16.5	16.7	16.7
2010	16.0	16.2	16.6	16.7	16.5	16.5	16.6	16.2	16.4	16.4	16.9	16.9	16.5
2011	16.0	16.2	16.3	16.0	16.1	16.1	16.1	16.2	16.1	16.0	16.5	16.5	16.2
2012	15.9	16.1	16.1	18.4	19.1	19.0	17.6	17.8	17.5	17.8	18.6	18.5	17.7
2013	19.2	19.3	19.3	17.9	18.1	18.0	18.0	18.2	17.8	17.8	18.5	18.6	18.4
2014	17.9	18.2	18.3	18.0	18.1	18.2	18.1	18.6	18.1	17.8	18.0	18.1	18.1
2015	17.5	17.7	17.8	17.6	17.9	17.7	18.1	18.5	18.3	18.6	19.1	19.0	18.2
2016	18.6	19.5	18.9	18.6	18.8	19.0	19.6	20.3	19.5	19.5	19.6	19.6	19.3
2017	19.7	20.3	19.9	19.8	19.9	20.4	20.8	21.5	21.2	21.3	21.6	21.4	20.7
Financial Activities													
2007	49.1	49.8	50.0	50.2	50.5	50.6	50.6	50.5	50.2	50.4	50.5	50.8	50.3
2008	49.6	50.1	50.0	50.2	49.9	49.8	49.9	49.9	49.4	49.3	49.0	49.4	49.7
2009	48.7	48.8	48.6	48.3	48.0	47.9	47.2	47.3	46.9	46.8	46.7	47.0	47.7
2010	45.8	45.4	45.5	45.2	45.2	45.3	45.4	45.6	45.7	46.1	46.2	46.4	45.7
2011	45.5	45.7	45.8	46.0	45.9	46.2	46.2	46.4	46.3	46.3	46.4	46.6	46.1
2012	45.9	46.0	46.1	46.4	46.5	46.8	47.0	47.6	47.4	47.5	47.9	48.4	47.0
2013	47.4	47.8	47.8	48.2	48.5	49.2	49.7	50.1	49.9	50.1	50.4	50.6	49.1
2014	49.4	49.7	49.5	49.6	49.9	50.4	50.8	51.4	51.0	51.5	51.9	52.1	50.6
2015	51.9	52.3	52.4	52.4	52.8	53.1	53.5	53.6	53.6	53.9	54.1	54.4	53.2
2016	54.2	54.7	54.7	54.8	55.3	55.7	56.3	56.7	56.2	56.6	56.9	57.0	55.8
2017	56.5	56.7	56.5	56.7	57.2	57.7	57.3	57.5	57.1	57.6	58.4	58.4	57.3
Professional and Business Services													
2007	94.8	95.6	96.1	98.3	99.6	100.2	99.8	100.5	99.9	101.5	102.3	102.1	99.2
2008	98.8	99.1	99.1	99.6	100.0	99.7	99.9	100.6	99.9	99.1	97.8	97.3	99.2
2009	93.1	92.8	92.0	91.9	92.1	91.9	91.7	91.8	91.7	92.4	92.2	92.5	92.2
2010	90.0	90.5	92.4	93.2	94.2	95.1	95.9	95.1	94.5	95.6	96.0	96.7	94.1
2011	94.4	95.1	95.9	96.9	97.3	97.7	98.4	99.3	99.8	101.4	101.8	101.7	98.3
2012	99.1	100.1	100.9	101.1	102.1	103.1	103.3	104.6	104.7	106.5	107.5	107.0	103.3
2013	102.9	104.6	105.8	108.5	107.8	108.3	108.8	110.0	109.9	113.0	114.1	113.9	109.0
2014	110.6	110.5	110.9	111.9	112.3	113.3	112.8	114.4	115.0	116.4	117.0	117.7	113.6
2015	113.9	113.9	115.1	116.1	117.4	118.7	119.2	120.2	119.9	121.2	121.8	121.9	118.3
2016	118.9	119.0	119.8	120.7	121.5	122.2	124.0	124.7	124.0	124.4	124.1	122.9	122.2
2017	121.9	121.0	121.2	122.0	122.7	123.6	124.8	125.7	125.5	124.8	123.8	122.1	123.3
Education and Health Services													
2007	57.0	57.6	58.0	58.4	58.5	58.4	58.0	59.1	60.0	60.2	60.7	60.9	58.9
2008	60.5	61.5	61.6	61.6	61.6	61.4	61.1	61.7	62.6	63.7	64.4	64.5	62.2
2009	63.5	63.8	64.3	64.4	64.3	63.8	63.0	63.7	65.0	66.1	66.5	66.7	64.6
2010	65.9	66.1	66.3	66.6	66.3	66.0	65.3	65.5	66.8	67.8	67.8	67.6	66.5
2011	67.1	67.6	67.6	68.0	67.4	66.9	65.6	66.0	67.6	68.2	68.3	68.0	67.4
2012	67.7	68.1	68.1	70.7	70.6	70.3	68.4	69.2	70.3	71.2	71.9	71.9	69.9
2013	72.3	73.0	73.3	72.7	72.7	72.0	70.5	71.3	72.2	73.3	74.0	73.7	72.6
2014	72.3	72.9	73.3	73.1	73.4	72.5	71.8	73.0	73.6	74.3	75.3	75.2	73.4
2015	75.6	76.3	76.5	76.2	76.6	76.1	74.9	75.8	76.9	78.4	79.1	78.6	76.8
2016	78.2	79.1	79.3	80.0	79.6	78.9	78.7	79.6	81.1	81.7	82.5	82.1	80.1
2017	81.5	82.5	82.6	83.1	83.1	82.2	81.0	82.3	83.0	83.3	84.7	83.3	82.7
Leisure and Hospitality													
2007	48.6	49.3	49.8	49.4	48.4	49.0	48.6	48.5	48.1	47.5	48.5	49.9	48.8
2008	49.7	50.1	50.7	50.8	49.8	50.0	49.7	49.8	49.2	48.8	48.9	49.7	49.8
2009	48.7	48.6	49.2	48.9	48.2	48.2	47.7	47.8	47.3	46.7	46.9	48.0	48.0
2010	47.1	47.5	47.9	48.5	47.4	48.1	48.6	48.7	47.7	47.4	47.9	49.0	48.0
2011	48.2	48.4	49.0	49.4	48.5	48.9	48.9	49.3	48.6	47.7	48.1	49.3	48.7
2012	49.2	49.7	50.4	50.9	51.1	51.2	50.9	51.4	50.9	50.2	51.8	52.8	50.9
2013	52.1	52.7	53.6	53.8	53.1	53.8	53.8	53.8	53.2	53.0	53.9	55.2	53.5
2014	54.5	54.9	55.3	55.9	54.3	55.1	54.9	55.4	55.0	54.8	55.6	56.6	55.2
2015	55.6	56.2	57.0	57.2	56.7	57.0	57.5	58.1	57.3	56.8	57.1	58.5	57.1
2016	57.4	58.1	58.7	59.1	58.2	59.2	59.8	60.0	59.4	58.9	59.0	60.0	59.0
2017	59.2	60.1	60.7	60.8	59.9	61.0	60.3	60.8	60.4	60.6	62.1	64.3	60.9

Employment by Industry: Salt Lake City, UT, Selected Years, 2007–2017—*Continued*

(Numbers in thousands, not seasonally adjusted)

Industry and year	January	February	March	April	May	June	July	August	September	October	November	December	Annual average
Other Services													
2007	18.4	18.5	18.7	18.7	19.0	19.2	19.5	19.6	19.1	18.9	18.9	19.0	19.0
2008	18.7	18.9	19.0	19.0	19.1	19.2	19.6	20.1	19.4	18.7	18.6	18.7	19.1
2009	18.3	18.3	18.4	18.3	18.5	18.6	18.8	18.8	18.1	18.1	17.9	18.0	18.3
2010	17.9	18.0	18.3	18.0	18.1	18.1	18.4	18.4	17.9	18.0	17.9	17.8	18.1
2011	17.6	17.8	17.9	18.0	18.3	18.4	18.7	18.8	18.4	18.3	18.2	18.2	18.2
2012	18.1	18.3	18.5	18.5	18.8	18.8	19.2	19.3	19.0	19.0	19.0	19.1	18.8
2013	19.0	19.3	19.7	20.1	20.4	19.8	20.3	20.3	19.7	19.6	19.7	19.8	19.8
2014	19.7	20.0	20.2	20.4	20.4	20.7	21.1	21.1	20.7	20.5	20.6	20.5	20.5
2015	21.0	21.3	21.4	21.0	21.0	21.2	21.6	21.6	21.1	21.0	21.1	21.0	21.2
2016	20.8	21.0	21.2	21.1	21.2	21.6	21.9	22.0	21.5	21.5	21.3	21.2	21.4
2017	21.3	21.4	21.6	21.6	21.7	22.2	22.2	22.2	21.6	21.1	20.6	20.5	21.5
Government													
2007	89.9	90.1	90.1	90.5	90.2	90.8	87.3	87.8	90.5	91.1	91.4	91.7	90.1
2008	91.4	91.7	92.1	92.2	92.2	92.8	89.0	90.1	93.6	93.9	94.2	94.3	92.3
2009	93.4	93.9	93.7	94.4	94.1	94.3	90.3	91.1	94.4	94.8	94.6	94.8	93.7
2010	94.3	94.2	94.2	94.9	96.6	95.6	92.0	92.4	96.1	96.9	96.9	96.1	95.0
2011	95.2	95.3	95.4	96.3	96.4	96.5	92.7	93.2	96.4	96.1	96.7	96.9	95.6
2012	96.8	97.2	97.3	98.6	98.2	98.2	93.6	93.5	97.7	99.0	98.8	98.1	97.3
2013	97.6	98.0	97.8	99.6	100.1	100.5	95.5	95.2	100.4	102.8	102.4	102.4	99.4
2014	102.2	103.0	103.2	104.5	104.9	105.2	98.0	97.3	102.6	103.6	103.7	103.9	102.7
2015	103.1	103.9	104.6	105.3	105.8	104.8	100.1	98.9	104.5	106.5	106.1	106.4	104.2
2016	104.5	105.9	106.4	108.0	108.3	107.9	102.1	100.7	107.4	109.3	109.0	109.3	106.6
2017	107.7	108.9	109.2	110.1	110.8	110.0	102.7	102.7	108.6	110.4	110.3	110.5	108.5

Employment by Industry: Birmingham-Hoover, AL, Selected Years, 2007–2017

(Numbers in thousands, not seasonally adjusted)

Industry and year	January	February	March	April	May	June	July	August	September	October	November	December	Annual average
Total Nonfarm													
2007	532.1	534.7	538.0	534.8	537.8	540.3	535.4	537.0	538.1	538.5	541.6	543.0	537.6
2008	531.4	533.1	533.9	535.6	538.0	539.2	533.7	533.8	532.4	532.2	530.7	529.8	533.7
2009	512.1	510.4	509.0	507.2	507.5	506.1	500.6	498.6	499.0	499.4	501.5	501.2	504.4
2010	491.9	492.9	494.2	497.0	500.4	499.8	496.2	494.8	494.2	497.8	500.2	500.3	496.6
2011	489.7	492.2	495.1	497.2	498.9	501.0	498.2	498.4	501.1	500.8	504.3	505.4	498.5
2012	498.3	500.8	505.0	508.1	508.6	510.5	504.8	505.8	507.8	508.7	512.2	512.0	506.9
2013	502.8	506.4	508.5	512.0	513.9	515.5	511.3	511.9	513.8	514.6	518.3	520.1	512.4
2014	507.9	508.8	512.9	516.0	517.1	519.1	514.9	516.8	518.2	518.7	521.3	522.8	516.2
2015	512.5	515.1	516.6	520.4	523.3	524.6	522.7	523.1	523.2	525.5	528.0	528.4	522.0
2016	518.7	521.7	522.6	526.5	527.6	528.1	526.9	526.6	527.6	527.5	529.7	530.5	526.2
2017	521.5	524.9	526.7	527.6	530.4	532.5	529.9	530.7	532.1	532.1	533.0	532.4	529.5
Total Private													
2007	448.8	450.9	454.0	450.9	453.6	456.3	455.0	455.9	454.4	454.1	457.0	458.5	454.1
2008	447.4	448.6	449.2	450.8	452.9	454.1	452.2	451.8	448.4	446.7	445.3	444.1	449.3
2009	427.2	425.4	423.9	421.8	422.3	420.9	419.6	417.3	415.5	415.0	416.7	416.4	420.2
2010	407.6	408.3	409.1	411.6	412.7	413.4	413.9	413.1	410.8	413.4	415.8	415.7	412.1
2011	405.6	407.9	410.7	412.8	414.3	416.7	417.1	417.9	418.3	418.3	421.7	422.7	415.3
2012	416.3	418.1	421.9	425.2	425.7	428.2	425.9	426.7	426.8	426.5	429.8	429.5	425.1
2013	420.9	424.2	426.2	429.8	432.1	434.0	432.4	433.1	433.2	433.1	436.6	438.1	431.1
2014	426.7	427.4	431.3	434.1	434.8	436.9	435.1	436.5	436.4	436.5	438.8	440.2	434.6
2015	431.1	433.3	434.6	438.2	440.9	442.2	442.3	442.1	441.3	443.1	445.3	445.4	440.0
2016	436.4	439.1	439.9	443.5	444.5	445.0	445.1	444.5	444.4	444.2	446.0	446.6	443.3
2017	438.6	441.5	443.2	444.1	446.7	448.5	447.8	448.3	448.4	448.2	448.9	448.2	446.0
Goods Producing													
2007	81.1	81.7	82.2	81.4	81.5	82.2	81.5	81.8	81.7	81.2	80.7	80.5	81.5
2008	79.0	79.0	78.6	78.9	79.2	79.3	79.4	78.6	78.2	76.6	75.5	74.5	78.1
2009	70.4	69.3	68.6	67.0	66.9	66.0	65.9	65.3	64.9	64.0	63.9	63.9	66.3
2010	62.2	61.8	61.6	62.1	62.0	61.9	62.3	62.3	61.7	61.3	61.5	61.4	61.8
2011	60.3	60.8	61.8	61.9	62.6	63.3	62.9	63.3	63.8	63.9	64.3	64.7	62.8
2012	63.9	63.8	64.5	64.9	65.3	65.5	65.6	65.5	65.5	65.7	65.6	65.7	65.1
2013	65.2	64.8	65.6	66.0	66.3	66.5	66.4	66.6	66.4	66.4	66.3	66.9	66.1
2014	65.3	65.2	66.2	66.1	66.3	66.6	66.4	66.5	66.6	66.5	66.7	66.7	66.3
2015	66.1	66.4	66.1	65.7	66.0	66.4	66.7	66.7	66.4	66.6	66.6	66.5	66.4
2016	65.7	65.9	66.1	66.1	66.0	66.3	66.0	65.5	65.9	65.4	65.4	65.5	65.8
2017	64.7	64.8	65.4	64.9	65.7	66.1	66.1	66.3	67.2	67.0	66.3	66.4	65.9
Service-Providing													
2007	451.0	453.0	455.8	453.4	456.3	458.1	453.9	455.2	456.4	457.3	460.9	462.5	456.2
2008	452.4	454.1	455.3	456.7	458.8	459.9	454.3	455.2	454.2	455.6	455.2	455.3	455.6
2009	441.7	441.1	440.4	440.2	440.6	440.1	434.7	433.3	434.1	435.4	437.6	437.3	438.0
2010	429.7	431.1	432.6	434.9	438.4	437.9	433.9	432.5	432.5	436.5	438.7	438.9	434.8
2011	429.4	431.4	433.3	435.3	436.3	437.7	435.3	435.1	437.3	436.9	440.0	440.7	435.7
2012	434.4	437.0	440.5	443.2	443.3	445.0	439.2	440.3	442.3	443.0	446.6	446.3	441.8
2013	437.6	441.6	442.9	446.0	447.6	449.0	444.9	445.3	447.4	448.2	452.0	453.2	446.3
2014	442.6	443.6	446.7	449.9	450.8	452.5	448.5	450.3	451.6	452.2	454.6	456.1	450.0
2015	446.4	448.7	450.5	454.7	457.3	458.2	456.0	456.4	456.8	458.9	461.4	461.9	455.6
2016	453.0	455.8	456.5	460.4	461.6	461.8	460.9	461.1	461.7	462.1	464.3	465.0	460.4
2017	456.8	460.1	461.3	462.7	464.7	466.4	463.8	464.4	464.9	465.1	466.7	466.0	463.6
Mining, Logging, and Construction													
2007	36.9	37.4	37.9	37.1	37.1	37.3	37.1	37.4	37.7	37.7	37.2	37.0	37.3
2008	36.2	36.0	35.9	36.4	36.8	36.5	36.8	36.3	35.9	34.8	34.1	33.7	35.8
2009	31.4	30.9	30.9	30.0	30.1	30.1	29.9	29.4	29.2	28.0	27.9	27.8	29.6
2010	26.9	26.7	26.8	27.1	27.2	27.4	27.6	27.8	27.2	27.0	26.8	26.8	27.1
2011	25.9	26.3	27.1	27.3	27.7	28.1	27.9	28.0	28.5	28.3	28.5	28.7	27.7
2012	27.8	27.7	28.0	28.1	28.3	28.2	28.4	28.2	28.0	28.3	28.1	28.0	28.1
2013	27.6	27.1	27.9	28.0	28.2	28.2	28.3	28.4	28.0	28.0	27.7	28.1	28.0
2014	26.9	26.7	27.4	27.3	27.5	27.6	27.7	27.8	27.8	27.9	27.8	27.8	27.5
2015	27.2	27.5	27.3	27.6	28.0	28.3	28.6	28.8	28.7	28.9	28.9	28.8	28.2
2016	28.2	28.2	28.2	28.2	28.1	28.4	28.3	27.9	28.2	28.1	28.1	28.2	28.2
2017	27.5	27.5	27.8	27.6	28.3	28.6	28.6	28.8	29.4	29.7	28.9	28.6	28.4

Employment by Industry: Birmingham-Hoover, AL, Selected Years, 2007–2017—*Continued*

(Numbers in thousands, not seasonally adjusted)

Industry and year	January	February	March	April	May	June	July	August	September	October	November	December	Annual average
Manufacturing													
2007	44.2	44.3	44.3	44.3	44.4	44.9	44.4	44.4	44.0	43.5	43.5	43.5	44.1
2008	42.8	43.0	42.7	42.5	42.4	42.8	42.6	42.3	42.3	41.8	41.4	40.8	42.3
2009	39.0	38.4	37.7	37.0	36.8	35.9	36.0	35.9	35.7	36.0	36.0	36.1	36.7
2010	35.3	35.1	34.8	35.0	34.8	34.5	34.7	34.5	34.5	34.3	34.7	34.6	34.7
2011	34.4	34.5	34.7	34.6	34.9	35.2	35.0	35.3	35.3	35.6	35.8	36.0	35.1
2012	36.1	36.1	36.5	36.8	37.0	37.3	37.2	37.3	37.5	37.4	37.5	37.7	37.0
2013	37.6	37.7	37.7	38.0	38.1	38.3	38.1	38.2	38.4	38.4	38.6	38.8	38.2
2014	38.4	38.5	38.8	38.8	38.8	39.0	38.7	38.7	38.8	38.6	38.9	38.9	38.7
2015	38.9	38.9	38.8	38.1	38.0	38.1	38.1	37.9	37.7	37.7	37.7	37.7	38.1
2016	37.5	37.7	37.9	37.9	37.9	37.9	37.7	37.6	37.7	37.3	37.3	37.3	37.6
2017	37.2	37.3	37.6	37.3	37.4	37.5	37.5	37.5	37.8	37.3	37.4	37.8	37.5
Trade, Transportation, and Utilities													
2007	114.6	114.3	115.4	114.4	115.4	116.3	116.1	115.7	115.8	116.0	118.3	119.6	116.0
2008	115.6	115.0	115.4	115.1	115.1	115.2	114.8	114.9	114.3	114.1	115.1	115.8	115.0
2009	110.3	109.3	108.7	107.8	107.8	107.2	106.7	106.2	105.9	106.0	106.9	107.7	107.5
2010	104.2	104.0	104.5	104.4	105.0	105.1	105.1	105.2	104.9	106.2	107.7	108.6	105.4
2011	104.8	104.7	105.0	104.8	105.0	105.1	105.3	105.6	105.6	106.2	108.0	109.1	105.8
2012	106.2	106.1	107.1	106.8	107.4	107.4	106.9	106.8	106.6	107.2	109.6	110.4	107.4
2013	106.6	106.9	107.5	107.2	107.7	108.1	108.3	108.3	108.2	108.7	111.1	112.5	108.4
2014	108.3	107.6	108.6	108.2	108.3	108.8	108.5	108.5	108.5	108.8	111.4	112.5	109.0
2015	108.3	108.1	108.8	109.5	110.2	110.4	110.3	110.2	109.7	110.4	112.6	113.3	110.2
2016	109.6	109.6	109.8	110.1	110.5	110.3	110.0	110.0	109.7	110.0	111.7	112.7	110.3
2017	109.2	109.0	109.1	109.0	109.3	109.2	108.5	108.7	108.5	109.7	111.3	111.0	109.4
Wholesale Trade													
2007	31.4	31.6	31.8	31.4	31.4	31.7	31.5	31.5	31.6	31.6	31.7	31.8	31.6
2008	31.5	31.6	31.6	31.6	31.6	31.5	31.4	31.5	31.5	31.5	31.2	31.2	31.5
2009	30.4	30.2	30.0	29.7	29.6	29.4	29.4	29.3	29.2	29.3	28.9	28.9	29.5
2010	28.3	28.3	28.3	28.3	28.4	28.3	28.3	28.4	28.2	28.5	28.4	28.4	28.3
2011	27.9	28.1	28.0	28.2	28.2	28.1	28.4	28.4	28.5	28.7	28.7	28.9	28.3
2012	28.5	28.8	29.0	28.8	29.1	29.1	29.0	29.0	29.0	29.1	29.1	29.3	29.0
2013	29.1	29.3	29.3	29.2	29.2	29.1	29.3	29.3	29.3	29.5	29.6	29.6	29.3
2014	29.0	29.0	29.1	28.9	29.0	29.1	29.2	29.2	29.3	29.4	29.4	29.5	29.2
2015	28.8	28.9	29.0	29.0	29.1	29.0	29.1	29.1	29.0	29.1	29.2	29.2	29.0
2016	28.8	28.9	28.9	28.9	29.1	29.0	29.0	28.9	28.7	28.9	28.8	29.0	28.9
2017	28.4	28.5	28.4	28.6	28.8	28.8	28.5	28.5	28.4	28.6	28.5	28.3	28.5
Retail Trade													
2007	62.7	62.1	62.8	62.3	63.1	63.5	63.3	62.8	62.7	63.0	65.1	66.1	63.3
2008	62.9	62.3	62.7	62.2	62.2	62.4	62.0	61.8	61.3	61.4	62.8	63.5	62.3
2009	59.2	58.5	58.3	57.9	58.0	57.7	57.3	56.8	56.6	56.6	57.9	58.4	57.8
2010	55.8	55.5	56.0	55.9	56.1	56.2	55.8	55.8	55.6	56.6	58.2	59.0	56.4
2011	56.0	55.5	55.8	56.0	56.1	56.3	56.1	56.4	56.2	56.6	58.4	59.1	56.5
2012	56.3	55.7	56.1	56.1	56.5	56.5	56.1	56.0	55.7	56.4	58.8	59.3	56.6
2013	55.3	55.3	55.7	55.7	56.1	56.5	56.5	56.4	56.2	56.9	59.2	60.3	56.7
2014	56.8	56.1	56.9	56.9	56.9	57.2	56.9	56.9	56.7	57.1	59.5	60.3	57.4
2015	56.9	56.8	57.3	57.9	58.5	58.7	58.3	58.2	57.9	58.4	60.4	60.9	58.4
2016	57.7	57.7	57.8	58.3	58.5	58.4	58.1	58.1	58.0	58.3	60.1	60.6	58.5
2017	57.7	57.4	57.5	57.6	57.7	57.8	57.5	57.3	57.2	58.2	59.8	59.2	57.9
Transportation and Utilities													
2007	20.5	20.6	20.8	20.7	20.9	21.1	21.3	21.4	21.5	21.4	21.5	21.7	21.1
2008	21.2	21.1	21.1	21.3	21.3	21.3	21.4	21.6	21.5	21.2	21.1	21.1	21.3
2009	20.7	20.6	20.4	20.2	20.2	20.1	20.0	20.1	20.1	20.1	20.1	20.4	20.3
2010	20.1	20.2	20.2	20.2	20.5	20.6	21.0	21.0	21.1	21.1	21.1	21.2	20.7
2011	20.9	21.1	21.2	20.6	20.7	20.7	20.8	20.8	20.9	20.9	20.9	21.1	20.9
2012	21.4	21.6	22.0	21.9	21.8	21.8	21.8	21.8	21.9	21.7	21.7	21.8	21.8
2013	22.2	22.3	22.5	22.3	22.4	22.5	22.5	22.6	22.7	22.3	22.3	22.6	22.4
2014	22.5	22.5	22.6	22.4	22.4	22.5	22.4	22.4	22.5	22.3	22.5	22.7	22.5
2015	22.6	22.4	22.5	22.6	22.6	22.7	22.9	22.9	22.8	22.9	23.0	23.2	22.8
2016	23.1	23.0	23.1	22.9	22.9	22.9	22.9	23.0	23.0	22.8	22.8	23.1	23.0
2017	23.1	23.1	23.2	22.8	22.8	22.6	22.5	22.9	22.9	22.9	23.0	23.5	22.9

Employment by Industry: Birmingham-Hoover, AL, Selected Years, 2007–2017—*Continued*

(Numbers in thousands, not seasonally adjusted)

Industry and year	January	February	March	April	May	June	July	August	September	October	November	December	Annual average
Information													
2007	11.6	11.6	11.6	11.5	11.5	11.5	11.4	11.5	11.4	11.3	11.4	11.4	11.5
2008	11.1	11.1	11.2	11.2	11.2	11.1	11.0	11.1	10.9	10.9	10.8	10.8	11.0
2009	10.5	10.4	10.4	10.3	10.2	10.2	10.1	10.0	9.9	9.9	9.8	9.9	10.1
2010	9.8	9.7	9.7	9.5	9.5	9.6	9.4	9.4	9.3	9.3	9.3	9.3	9.5
2011	9.2	9.1	9.1	9.0	9.0	9.0	9.0	9.0	9.0	8.9	8.9	8.9	9.0
2012	8.9	8.9	9.0	8.8	8.8	8.9	8.9	8.9	8.9	8.8	8.8	8.9	8.9
2013	8.9	8.9	8.8	8.9	9.0	9.0	9.1	9.0	8.9	8.9	8.9	9.0	8.9
2014	8.8	8.7	8.7	8.6	8.6	8.5	8.3	8.3	8.2	8.3	8.4	8.4	8.5
2015	8.3	8.4	8.4	8.3	8.3	8.2	8.3	8.2	8.1	8.1	8.1	8.1	8.2
2016	8.0	8.0	8.0	8.0	7.9	8.0	7.9	7.9	7.8	7.9	8.0	7.9	7.9
2017	7.8	7.7	7.7	7.5	7.6	7.6	7.6	7.4	7.4	7.4	7.4	7.4	7.5
Financial Activities													
2007	41.7	41.8	42.0	41.0	41.2	41.5	41.4	41.4	41.5	41.5	41.7	41.9	41.6
2008	41.3	41.4	41.5	41.5	41.5	41.5	41.7	41.8	41.3	41.3	41.2	41.2	41.4
2009	40.8	40.9	40.7	40.6	40.5	40.5	40.3	40.1	39.9	39.8	39.6	39.5	40.3
2010	39.1	39.1	39.2	39.2	39.3	39.3	39.3	39.3	39.3	40.0	40.2	40.4	39.5
2011	40.0	40.1	40.0	40.2	40.1	39.7	40.1	39.9	39.8	39.8	39.9	40.0	40.0
2012	39.9	40.0	40.2	40.4	40.6	40.6	40.7	40.7	40.7	41.0	41.1	41.1	40.6
2013	40.6	40.8	40.8	41.0	41.3	41.5	41.8	42.1	42.1	42.4	42.8	42.9	41.7
2014	42.0	42.2	42.2	42.3	42.4	42.4	42.4	42.4	42.0	42.1	42.2	42.2	42.2
2015	42.1	42.1	42.2	42.2	42.3	42.3	42.4	42.4	42.2	42.3	42.3	42.3	42.3
2016	42.2	42.2	42.1	42.0	42.0	42.0	42.2	42.2	42.1	42.1	42.3	42.4	42.2
2017	42.3	42.4	42.4	42.4	42.5	42.7	42.6	42.5	42.3	41.9	41.9	42.0	42.3
Professional and Business Services													
2007	69.1	69.8	69.6	68.9	69.0	69.2	68.4	68.7	68.5	68.5	69.2	68.8	69.0
2008	67.0	67.3	66.9	67.1	67.3	67.6	66.5	66.5	66.2	66.2	66.0	65.5	66.7
2009	62.6	62.2	61.7	61.1	60.7	60.4	59.9	59.7	59.3	60.0	60.2	59.8	60.6
2010	59.5	59.8	59.9	60.7	60.4	60.0	60.9	60.6	59.9	60.6	60.3	60.1	60.2
2011	59.2	59.9	60.1	60.9	61.0	61.7	61.8	61.9	62.5	62.1	62.2	62.7	61.3
2012	61.7	62.5	63.0	64.0	63.5	64.4	64.1	64.6	64.3	64.0	63.7	63.1	63.6
2013	61.6	63.1	63.2	63.6	63.1	63.6	63.5	63.5	63.1	63.5	63.5	63.5	63.2
2014	61.5	62.2	62.5	63.5	63.5	63.7	63.6	64.6	64.5	64.8	64.3	64.3	63.6
2015	63.1	63.8	64.5	65.0	65.3	65.4	65.7	65.7	65.6	66.2	66.2	65.9	65.2
2016	64.9	65.4	65.3	66.0	66.1	66.1	66.3	66.4	65.9	66.1	66.3	66.0	65.9
2017	65.7	66.3	66.8	67.1	67.6	68.1	68.4	68.9	68.6	68.0	67.6	67.4	67.5
Education and Health Services													
2007	61.7	62.2	62.4	62.9	63.2	63.3	63.6	64.1	64.0	64.4	64.5	64.7	63.4
2008	63.8	64.3	64.5	64.5	65.0	64.9	64.9	65.0	65.1	65.7	65.1	65.0	64.8
2009	63.8	64.0	63.9	64.4	64.5	64.2	65.0	64.8	65.0	65.3	66.2	65.5	64.7
2010	64.9	65.6	65.2	65.6	65.6	65.5	65.6	65.5	65.5	65.8	66.2	65.5	65.5
2011	64.5	64.8	65.4	65.3	65.4	65.1	65.3	65.5	66.1	65.9	66.6	66.0	65.5
2012	65.8	66.1	66.4	67.0	66.4	66.7	66.2	66.9	67.7	67.4	68.3	68.3	66.9
2013	67.2	68.5	67.9	68.4	68.8	68.5	67.7	68.3	68.8	68.5	69.2	69.4	68.4
2014	67.8	68.4	68.5	69.1	68.6	68.7	68.3	68.8	69.4	69.9	69.4	69.8	68.9
2015	68.7	69.5	68.9	69.9	69.9	70.1	70.1	70.4	70.8	71.2	71.0	71.3	70.2
2016	69.9	70.8	70.4	71.2	71.1	70.9	71.3	71.7	72.8	72.9	72.5	72.9	71.5
2017	71.0	72.3	72.0	72.5	72.3	72.5	72.1	72.0	72.9	74.0	73.6	73.2	72.5
Leisure and Hospitality													
2007	42.4	42.9	43.9	43.8	44.7	45.1	45.1	45.3	44.4	44.0	43.9	44.2	44.1
2008	42.2	42.8	43.4	44.7	45.8	46.3	45.6	45.7	44.6	44.2	44.0	43.8	44.4
2009	41.4	41.9	42.4	43.2	44.1	44.3	43.5	43.3	43.4	42.7	42.8	42.8	43.0
2010	40.7	41.0	41.6	42.7	43.3	43.8	43.0	42.8	42.7	42.5	43.0	43.0	42.5
2011	40.7	41.3	42.1	43.3	43.7	45.0	44.8	45.0	44.1	44.0	44.1	43.8	43.5
2012	42.3	42.9	43.7	45.3	45.6	46.1	44.9	45.0	45.2	44.4	44.8	44.2	44.5
2013	43.1	43.5	44.5	46.7	47.8	48.2	47.1	46.8	47.3	46.6	46.7	45.8	46.2
2014	45.0	45.1	46.3	47.9	48.5	49.5	48.8	48.8	48.7	47.7	48.0	48.0	47.7
2015	46.3	46.7	47.3	48.9	50.0	50.4	49.9	49.7	49.7	49.6	49.6	49.2	48.9
2016	47.6	48.5	49.4	51.0	51.8	52.2	52.1	51.7	51.3	50.9	50.9	50.3	50.6
2017	49.1	50.0	50.8	51.6	52.4	52.9	53.0	53.0	52.0	50.7	51.1	51.4	51.5

Employment by Industry: Birmingham-Hoover, AL, Selected Years, 2007–2017—*Continued*

(Numbers in thousands, not seasonally adjusted)

Industry and year	January	February	March	April	May	June	July	August	September	October	November	December	Annual average
Other Services													
2007	26.6	26.6	26.9	27.0	27.1	27.2	27.5	27.4	27.1	27.2	27.3	27.4	27.1
2008	27.4	27.7	27.7	27.8	27.8	28.2	28.3	28.2	27.8	27.7	27.6	27.5	27.8
2009	27.4	27.4	27.5	27.4	27.6	28.1	28.2	27.9	27.2	27.3	27.3	27.3	27.6
2010	27.2	27.3	27.4	27.4	27.6	28.2	28.3	28.0	27.5	27.7	27.6	27.4	27.6
2011	26.9	27.2	27.2	27.4	27.5	27.8	27.9	27.7	27.4	27.5	27.7	27.5	27.5
2012	27.6	27.8	28.0	28.0	28.1	28.6	28.6	28.3	27.9	28.0	27.9	27.8	28.1
2013	27.7	27.7	27.9	28.0	28.1	28.6	28.5	28.5	28.4	28.1	28.1	28.1	28.1
2014	28.0	28.0	28.3	28.4	28.6	28.7	28.8	28.6	28.5	28.4	28.4	28.3	28.4
2015	28.2	28.3	28.4	28.7	28.9	29.0	28.9	28.8	28.8	28.7	28.9	28.8	28.7
2016	28.5	28.7	28.8	29.1	29.1	29.2	29.3	29.1	28.9	28.9	28.9	28.9	29.0
2017	28.8	29.0	29.0	29.1	29.3	29.4	29.5	29.5	29.5	29.5	29.7	29.4	29.3
Government													
2007	83.3	83.8	84.0	83.9	84.2	84.0	80.4	81.1	83.7	84.4	84.6	84.5	83.5
2008	84.0	84.5	84.7	84.8	85.1	85.1	81.5	82.0	84.0	85.5	85.4	85.7	84.4
2009	84.9	85.0	85.1	85.4	85.2	85.2	81.0	81.3	83.5	84.4	84.8	84.8	84.2
2010	84.3	84.6	85.1	85.4	87.7	86.4	82.3	81.7	83.4	84.4	84.4	84.6	84.5
2011	84.1	84.3	84.4	84.4	84.6	84.3	81.1	80.5	82.8	82.5	82.6	82.7	83.2
2012	82.0	82.7	83.1	82.9	82.9	82.3	78.9	79.1	81.0	82.2	82.4	82.5	81.8
2013	81.9	82.2	82.3	82.2	81.8	81.5	78.9	78.8	80.6	81.5	81.7	82.0	81.3
2014	81.2	81.4	81.6	81.9	82.3	82.2	79.8	80.3	81.8	82.2	82.5	82.6	81.7
2015	81.4	81.8	82.0	82.2	82.4	82.4	80.4	81.0	81.9	82.4	82.7	83.0	82.0
2016	82.3	82.6	82.7	83.0	83.1	83.1	81.8	82.1	83.2	83.3	83.7	83.9	82.9
2017	82.9	83.4	83.5	83.5	83.7	84.0	82.1	82.4	83.7	83.9	84.1	84.2	83.5

Employment by Industry: Buffalo-Cheektowaga-Niagara Falls, NY, Selected Years, 2007–2017

(Numbers in thousands, not seasonally adjusted)

Industry and year	January	February	March	April	May	June	July	August	September	October	November	December	Annual average
Total Nonfarm													
2007	533.0	535.6	539.3	538.9	549.0	550.4	541.0	543.9	548.4	555.4	556.9	557.0	545.7
2008	537.4	539.4	540.9	547.5	554.5	557.4	549.5	550.7	554.2	560.1	557.1	554.2	550.2
2009	530.0	530.1	531.0	533.0	538.3	539.1	534.3	534.7	537.1	543.0	543.0	540.9	536.2
2010	522.8	524.5	527.4	534.9	541.0	540.6	531.5	533.9	538.4	546.2	547.0	546.4	536.2
2011	528.5	530.7	531.6	539.6	544.0	546.5	538.4	539.5	547.8	549.9	550.5	550.3	541.4
2012	531.9	536.3	538.2	540.7	547.7	549.6	540.9	543.6	546.9	552.7	552.6	552.7	544.5
2013	533.6	536.8	539.2	542.8	549.5	551.1	544.6	546.6	551.5	558.3	558.2	557.4	547.5
2014	536.6	540.2	542.1	548.5	553.9	556.3	549.9	551.1	554.8	561.1	559.6	560.8	551.2
2015	539.4	542.5	544.3	550.7	559.0	560.9	555.7	556.5	559.5	567.3	566.4	566.9	555.8
2016	545.5	549.6	551.6	558.9	562.8	564.0	559.4	559.7	564.0	569.0	568.6	566.7	560.0
2017	549.6	553.8	555.6	558.6	565.4	567.2	562.4	563.7	567.9	573.9	575.9	572.2	563.9
Total Private													
2007	439.4	440.4	443.8	444.0	453.4	455.6	452.2	453.8	455.4	459.2	460.2	460.4	451.5
2008	443.6	443.5	444.7	450.9	457.8	461.4	458.8	459.5	459.9	462.4	459.2	456.7	454.9
2009	435.2	433.9	434.5	436.3	441.0	443.4	442.4	442.8	443.2	445.8	445.4	443.8	440.6
2010	427.6	427.7	430.1	437.8	442.0	444.0	443.4	445.4	446.9	450.0	450.1	449.7	441.2
2011	434.0	435.1	436.4	443.9	448.7	452.9	449.5	450.5	456.4	455.8	456.2	456.0	448.0
2012	440.2	442.3	444.3	447.4	454.1	457.7	453.8	456.9	457.7	460.3	459.8	459.9	452.9
2013	443.5	444.5	446.8	451.2	458.1	461.0	458.9	460.7	463.2	466.6	466.5	466.0	457.3
2014	448.3	449.7	451.2	457.7	463.7	467.4	465.0	466.1	467.3	470.8	469.0	470.7	462.2
2015	450.9	452.5	454.2	460.8	468.8	471.8	470.5	471.0	471.3	476.6	475.5	475.7	466.6
2016	456.4	458.9	460.6	468.0	471.8	474.3	473.3	473.8	474.3	477.7	477.1	474.4	470.1
2017	458.2	461.6	463.4	466.6	473.4	476.7	475.5	477.3	478.2	481.7	483.3	479.5	473.0
Goods Producing													
2007	77.7	76.5	77.3	78.2	81.0	82.4	81.6	82.3	81.6	81.1	80.5	79.0	79.9
2008	75.2	74.7	74.3	76.4	79.3	80.8	80.9	81.6	80.8	80.3	78.3	76.1	78.2
2009	70.6	69.0	68.4	69.6	70.7	70.5	70.8	71.2	70.9	70.4	69.7	67.9	70.0
2010	64.5	63.8	64.2	66.9	68.7	69.8	70.8	71.3	71.1	71.2	70.6	69.0	68.5
2011	66.7	66.4	67.0	69.4	71.2	72.9	73.4	74.1	73.5	73.1	72.4	70.5	70.9
2012	68.0	67.5	68.3	69.8	71.6	72.9	73.1	73.4	72.6	72.3	71.3	70.2	70.9
2013	67.3	66.7	67.3	68.6	71.2	72.4	72.2	73.5	73.0	73.0	72.1	70.9	70.7
2014	68.3	68.3	68.7	70.8	73.2	74.7	74.3	75.6	75.0	74.7	73.1	72.2	72.4
2015	68.6	68.2	69.0	71.1	73.8	75.0	75.6	75.5	74.9	75.4	74.7	74.1	73.0
2016	70.8	70.2	70.8	72.5	74.2	75.5	75.8	75.9	75.3	75.0	74.5	72.2	73.6
2017	70.0	69.6	69.8	72.1	73.7	75.1	74.9	75.4	75.0	74.1	73.3	71.4	72.9
Service-Providing													
2007	455.3	459.1	462.0	460.7	468.0	468.0	459.4	461.6	466.8	474.3	476.4	478.0	465.8
2008	462.2	464.7	466.6	471.1	475.2	476.6	468.6	469.1	473.4	479.8	478.8	478.1	472.0
2009	459.4	461.1	462.6	463.4	467.6	468.6	463.5	463.5	466.2	472.6	473.3	473.0	466.2
2010	458.3	460.7	463.2	468.0	472.3	470.8	460.7	462.6	467.3	475.0	476.4	477.4	467.7
2011	461.8	464.3	464.6	470.2	472.8	473.6	465.0	465.4	474.3	476.8	478.1	479.8	470.6
2012	463.9	468.8	469.9	470.9	476.1	476.7	467.8	470.2	474.3	480.4	481.3	482.5	473.6
2013	466.3	470.1	471.9	474.2	478.3	478.7	472.4	473.1	478.5	485.3	486.1	486.5	476.8
2014	468.3	471.9	473.4	477.7	480.7	481.6	475.6	475.5	479.8	486.4	486.5	488.6	478.8
2015	470.8	474.3	475.3	479.6	485.2	485.9	480.1	481.0	484.6	491.9	491.7	492.8	482.8
2016	474.7	479.4	480.8	486.4	488.6	488.5	483.6	483.8	488.7	494.0	494.1	494.5	486.4
2017	479.6	484.2	485.8	486.5	491.7	492.1	487.5	488.3	492.9	499.8	502.6	500.8	491.0
Mining, Logging, and Construction													
2007	17.6	16.3	17.2	18.3	20.8	21.9	22.1	22.4	21.7	21.6	20.8	19.6	20.0
2008	17.3	16.5	16.9	19.0	21.4	22.3	23.5	23.8	23.3	23.1	21.6	20.0	20.7
2009	17.1	16.6	17.0	18.3	19.9	20.5	21.2	21.5	20.8	20.5	19.8	17.9	19.3
2010	15.5	15.0	15.3	18.1	19.5	20.2	21.1	21.3	20.9	21.0	20.5	18.5	18.9
2011	16.5	16.1	16.7	18.6	20.3	21.4	22.2	22.5	22.2	21.8	21.0	19.1	19.9
2012	17.1	16.6	17.4	18.9	20.3	21.3	21.5	21.7	21.1	20.8	19.9	18.7	19.6
2013	16.6	16.2	16.5	17.6	20.0	20.8	21.3	21.6	21.1	21.0	20.2	18.7	19.3
2014	16.5	16.3	16.8	18.6	20.9	22.1	22.6	23.0	22.7	22.4	20.8	19.6	20.2
2015	17.2	16.6	17.1	19.1	21.6	22.3	23.1	23.2	22.9	23.1	22.4	21.5	20.8
2016	18.8	18.5	19.0	20.7	22.5	23.3	23.7	23.7	23.3	22.9	22.3	20.2	21.6
2017	18.2	17.8	18.0	20.1	21.6	22.6	23.0	23.2	22.8	22.1	21.4	19.3	20.8

Employment by Industry: Buffalo-Cheektowaga-Niagara Falls, NY, Selected Years, 2007–2017—*Continued*

(Numbers in thousands, not seasonally adjusted)

Industry and year	January	February	March	April	May	June	July	August	September	October	November	December	Annual average
Manufacturing													
2007	60.1	60.2	60.1	59.9	60.2	60.5	59.5	59.9	59.9	59.5	59.7	59.4	59.9
2008	57.9	58.2	57.4	57.4	57.9	58.5	57.4	57.8	57.5	57.2	56.7	56.1	57.5
2009	53.5	52.4	51.4	51.3	50.8	50.0	49.6	49.7	50.1	49.9	49.9	50.0	50.7
2010	49.0	48.8	48.9	48.8	49.2	49.6	49.7	50.0	50.2	50.2	50.1	50.5	49.6
2011	50.2	50.3	50.3	50.8	50.9	51.5	51.2	51.6	51.3	51.3	51.4	51.4	51.0
2012	50.9	50.9	50.9	50.9	51.3	51.6	51.6	51.7	51.5	51.5	51.4	51.5	51.3
2013	50.7	50.5	50.8	51.0	51.2	51.6	50.9	51.9	51.9	52.0	51.9	52.2	51.4
2014	51.8	52.0	51.9	52.2	52.3	52.6	51.7	52.6	52.3	52.3	52.3	52.6	52.2
2015	51.4	51.6	51.9	52.0	52.2	52.7	52.5	52.3	52.0	52.3	52.3	52.6	52.2
2016	52.0	51.7	51.8	51.8	51.7	52.2	52.1	52.2	52.0	52.1	52.2	52.0	52.0
2017	51.8	51.8	51.8	52.0	52.1	52.5	51.9	52.2	52.2	52.0	51.9	52.1	52.0
Trade, Transportation, and Utilities													
2007	102.7	100.9	101.2	100.8	102.9	104.1	102.9	103.0	104.3	104.9	107.0	108.9	103.6
2008	103.4	101.1	101.2	101.8	103.1	104.4	102.5	102.5	103.3	103.7	104.3	105.0	103.0
2009	98.4	96.9	96.6	96.1	97.6	98.4	97.7	97.7	98.2	98.8	100.4	101.2	98.2
2010	96.4	95.0	95.1	96.1	97.4	98.4	96.9	97.3	98.3	99.3	101.3	101.9	97.8
2011	97.3	95.8	96.0	97.1	98.2	99.6	98.3	99.1	99.9	100.8	103.2	104.0	99.1
2012	99.5	97.5	98.1	98.1	100.1	101.3	99.9	100.4	101.2	101.5	103.3	104.4	100.4
2013	99.2	97.5	98.0	98.2	99.8	101.0	99.9	99.9	100.9	101.5	104.0	105.6	100.5
2014	100.7	99.4	99.9	100.7	101.7	103.4	101.8	101.7	102.3	103.2	105.8	107.2	102.3
2015	102.0	100.9	100.8	101.5	103.2	104.3	103.1	102.9	103.3	104.4	106.3	107.5	103.4
2016	102.5	101.3	101.6	102.3	103.1	103.5	102.2	101.9	102.1	102.5	104.5	105.1	102.7
2017	101.0	99.2	99.7	99.6	101.2	102.1	100.6	100.7	101.3	100.4	103.4	103.9	101.1
Wholesale Trade													
2007	23.6	23.5	23.5	23.5	23.6	23.9	23.9	23.8	23.7	23.8	23.8	24.0	23.7
2008	23.4	23.2	23.2	23.1	23.1	23.2	23.2	23.0	22.7	22.6	22.5	22.4	23.0
2009	22.1	21.8	21.7	21.5	21.5	21.5	21.4	21.2	21.2	21.1	21.1	21.1	21.4
2010	20.9	20.8	20.8	21.0	21.1	21.2	21.3	21.3	21.2	21.3	21.4	21.4	21.1
2011	21.2	21.0	21.1	21.3	21.5	21.7	21.8	21.8	21.7	21.7	21.9	21.9	21.6
2012	21.6	21.6	21.6	21.6	21.7	22.0	21.9	22.1	21.9	21.9	21.8	22.0	21.8
2013	21.7	21.6	21.7	21.6	21.7	21.8	21.9	22.0	21.9	22.1	22.1	22.3	21.9
2014	22.2	22.0	22.0	22.2	22.4	22.5	22.3	22.3	22.3	22.4	22.4	22.5	22.3
2015	22.3	22.2	22.1	22.2	22.3	22.5	22.6	22.4	22.2	22.4	22.3	22.4	22.3
2016	22.1	22.0	21.9	22.0	22.1	22.0	22.0	21.8	21.5	21.6	21.7	21.8	21.9
2017	21.7	21.6	21.5	21.5	21.6	21.7	21.6	21.6	21.6	21.6	21.7	21.8	21.6
Retail Trade													
2007	61.2	59.6	59.8	59.2	60.8	61.5	61.3	61.6	61.7	62.3	64.5	65.9	61.6
2008	62.0	60.1	60.2	60.4	61.4	62.3	62.1	62.2	62.1	62.8	63.6	64.3	62.0
2009	59.7	58.6	58.6	58.4	59.6	60.4	60.2	60.6	60.7	61.3	62.9	63.5	60.4
2010	59.8	58.7	58.8	59.4	60.3	60.9	60.4	60.8	60.8	61.8	63.5	64.0	60.8
2011	60.4	59.3	59.5	60.3	60.8	61.7	61.4	62.3	62.0	62.9	65.0	65.5	61.8
2012	62.1	60.5	61.0	61.1	62.3	62.9	62.8	63.1	63.0	63.4	65.3	65.8	62.8
2013	61.7	60.3	60.6	60.9	61.9	62.8	62.5	62.5	62.3	62.7	65.0	66.1	62.4
2014	62.0	61.0	61.5	61.9	62.3	63.6	63.1	63.1	62.4	63.1	65.3	66.2	63.0
2015	62.5	61.7	61.7	62.3	63.2	63.8	63.6	63.8	63.3	64.0	65.9	66.6	63.5
2016	63.4	62.5	62.8	63.3	63.6	64.0	63.8	63.9	63.3	63.6	65.4	65.4	63.8
2017	62.4	60.9	61.4	61.6	62.4	62.9	62.2	62.6	62.0	61.2	63.8	63.5	62.2
Transportation and Utilities													
2007	17.9	17.8	17.9	18.1	18.5	18.7	17.7	17.6	18.9	18.8	18.7	19.0	18.3
2008	18.0	17.8	17.8	18.3	18.6	18.9	17.2	17.3	18.5	18.3	18.2	18.3	18.1
2009	16.6	16.5	16.3	16.2	16.5	16.5	16.1	15.9	16.3	16.4	16.4	16.6	16.4
2010	15.7	15.5	15.5	15.7	16.0	16.3	15.2	15.2	16.3	16.2	16.4	16.5	15.9
2011	15.7	15.5	15.4	15.5	15.9	16.2	15.1	15.0	16.2	16.2	16.3	16.6	15.8
2012	15.8	15.4	15.5	15.4	16.1	16.4	15.2	15.2	16.3	16.2	16.2	16.6	15.9
2013	15.8	15.6	15.7	15.7	16.2	16.4	15.5	15.4	16.7	16.7	16.9	17.2	16.2
2014	16.5	16.4	16.4	16.6	17.0	17.3	16.4	16.3	17.6	17.7	18.1	18.5	17.1
2015	17.2	17.0	17.0	17.0	17.7	18.0	16.9	16.7	17.8	18.0	18.1	18.5	17.5
2016	17.0	16.8	16.9	17.0	17.4	17.5	16.4	16.2	17.3	17.3	17.4	17.9	17.1
2017	16.9	16.7	16.8	16.5	17.2	17.5	16.8	16.5	17.7	17.6	17.9	18.6	17.2

Employment by Industry: Buffalo-Cheektowaga-Niagara Falls, NY, Selected Years, 2007–2017—*Continued*

(Numbers in thousands, not seasonally adjusted)

Industry and year	January	February	March	April	May	June	July	August	September	October	November	December	Annual average
Information													
2007	8.5	8.5	8.5	8.4	8.6	8.6	8.6	8.5	8.4	8.3	8.4	8.4	8.5
2008	8.3	8.3	8.3	8.3	8.6	8.6	8.6	8.7	8.5	8.4	8.4	8.5	8.5
2009	8.3	8.2	8.3	8.4	8.4	8.5	8.4	8.3	8.1	8.2	8.1	8.1	8.3
2010	7.9	7.8	7.9	7.7	7.7	7.8	7.9	7.9	7.8	7.8	7.8	7.7	7.8
2011	7.6	7.6	7.6	7.7	7.7	7.8	7.8	6.9	7.7	7.6	7.6	7.7	7.6
2012	7.6	7.6	7.6	7.6	7.7	7.8	7.7	7.6	7.6	7.5	7.6	7.6	7.6
2013	7.5	7.5	7.5	7.5	7.5	7.6	7.6	7.6	7.6	7.6	7.6	7.6	7.6
2014	7.6	7.6	7.6	7.6	7.6	7.7	7.6	7.6	7.6	7.6	7.6	7.6	7.6
2015	7.3	7.2	7.3	7.4	7.4	7.4	7.4	7.3	7.3	7.4	7.3	7.3	7.3
2016	7.1	7.1	7.0	7.1	6.5	7.2	7.1	7.1	7.1	7.0	7.0	7.1	7.0
2017	7.0	7.1	7.1	7.0	7.0	7.2	7.0	6.9	7.1	7.0	7.0	7.0	7.0
Financial Activities													
2007	33.3	33.4	33.6	32.9	33.0	33.5	33.5	33.4	33.0	33.3	33.4	33.9	33.4
2008	32.8	32.7	32.6	32.7	32.9	33.1	33.0	32.9	32.5	32.5	32.5	32.8	32.8
2009	31.4	31.3	31.3	31.4	31.5	31.7	31.7	31.4	31.0	31.0	30.9	31.1	31.3
2010	30.3	30.3	30.4	30.4	30.4	30.6	30.7	30.5	30.2	30.5	30.6	31.1	30.5
2011	31.1	31.1	31.2	31.5	31.1	31.4	31.4	31.7	31.5	31.4	31.5	32.2	31.4
2012	31.5	31.6	31.5	31.8	31.8	32.3	32.3	32.3	31.9	32.2	32.3	32.4	32.0
2013	31.9	31.9	32.0	31.9	31.9	32.2	32.8	32.1	31.7	32.0	32.1	32.6	32.1
2014	31.9	31.9	32.0	32.2	32.5	33.0	33.1	33.0	32.9	33.0	33.1	33.5	32.7
2015	32.9	32.9	33.0	33.3	33.7	34.0	34.3	34.4	34.1	34.2	34.4	34.6	33.8
2016	34.3	34.3	34.2	34.5	34.7	35.2	35.4	35.4	35.1	35.2	35.3	35.7	34.9
2017	36.4	36.6	36.7	36.5	36.6	37.1	37.4	37.2	36.9	37.3	36.9	37.3	36.9
Professional and Business Services													
2007	67.1	67.6	68.3	68.9	69.6	70.9	70.8	71.5	71.0	71.4	71.5	71.3	70.0
2008	69.4	70.0	70.4	72.9	73.3	74.6	74.8	74.6	73.7	73.2	72.4	71.6	72.6
2009	69.4	69.3	69.7	69.9	70.4	72.1	72.2	72.0	71.2	71.5	71.2	70.5	70.8
2010	69.2	68.9	69.4	71.6	71.7	72.5	73.5	73.5	72.8	72.6	71.5	71.5	71.6
2011	70.1	70.3	70.1	72.0	72.5	73.7	74.4	73.9	73.8	73.7	72.8	72.6	72.5
2012	71.0	71.2	71.3	72.4	72.9	74.3	74.6	74.8	73.6	74.4	73.9	73.2	73.1
2013	71.2	71.6	71.9	73.1	73.7	74.9	75.0	74.9	74.8	74.0	73.4	72.6	73.4
2014	69.9	69.7	69.2	71.0	71.9	73.4	73.7	73.3	72.7	72.9	72.1	72.3	71.8
2015	69.4	69.8	69.4	71.3	72.6	73.6	73.8	73.7	72.8	73.2	71.8	71.5	71.9
2016	69.0	69.1	69.1	70.8	71.7	72.4	72.9	72.5	71.8	72.3	71.1	70.5	71.1
2017	67.8	68.2	68.6	69.5	70.1	71.1	71.8	72.0	71.3	72.2	72.1	70.8	70.5
Education and Health Services													
2007	81.9	84.1	84.9	84.5	84.5	82.1	80.6	80.4	83.8	86.0	86.1	86.1	83.8
2008	84.1	85.7	86.3	86.6	85.7	84.0	83.0	82.6	85.8	88.2	88.5	88.6	85.8
2009	86.2	88.1	88.6	87.9	87.6	85.8	84.4	84.0	87.2	89.9	90.2	90.4	87.5
2010	87.8	89.7	90.2	90.5	90.0	87.8	85.8	85.7	88.9	91.0	91.5	91.3	89.2
2011	88.7	90.7	90.8	91.2	90.6	88.2	86.1	86.0	89.5	90.9	91.4	91.4	89.6
2012	89.2	91.7	91.5	91.4	91.1	88.1	86.4	86.7	90.3	92.4	92.5	92.9	90.4
2013	90.3	92.3	92.7	93.1	92.4	89.9	88.7	88.9	92.6	94.7	95.0	95.0	92.1
2014	91.9	94.5	94.7	94.4	93.5	91.4	89.8	89.6	92.5	94.9	94.8	95.1	93.1
2015	92.1	94.1	94.5	94.4	93.9	91.8	90.3	90.8	93.4	96.1	96.6	96.7	93.7
2016	93.5	96.2	96.5	96.7	95.9	93.4	92.2	91.9	95.5	98.4	98.9	98.6	95.6
2017	95.5	98.4	98.4	98.6	98.2	95.8	95.1	95.5	98.5	101.3	101.9	100.9	98.2
Leisure and Hospitality													
2007	45.6	46.5	46.8	47.2	50.5	50.6	50.8	51.2	50.1	50.6	49.8	49.2	49.1
2008	47.1	47.6	47.9	48.5	51.0	52.0	51.9	52.4	51.5	51.8	50.8	50.1	50.2
2009	47.5	47.5	47.8	49.0	50.8	52.4	53.2	54.2	52.9	52.0	51.0	51.0	50.8
2010	48.6	49.2	49.8	51.4	52.9	53.8	53.6	54.7	54.7	54.3	53.5	53.8	52.5
2011	49.7	50.2	50.7	51.8	54.1	55.8	54.8	55.5	57.1	55.2	54.2	54.3	53.6
2012	50.4	52.2	52.8	53.1	55.4	57.3	56.3	58.2	57.2	56.5	55.4	55.6	55.0
2013	52.5	53.4	53.7	55.1	57.6	59.0	58.7	59.6	58.6	59.3	57.8	56.9	56.9
2014	53.7	53.9	54.4	56.5	58.6	59.2	59.9	60.5	60.0	59.8	57.9	58.1	57.7
2015	54.3	55.1	55.6	57.1	59.4	60.8	61.0	61.4	60.9	60.9	59.5	58.9	58.7
2016	54.9	56.2	56.8	59.2	60.6	62.2	62.5	63.8	62.6	62.2	60.6	60.3	60.2
2017	55.8	57.7	58.2	58.3	61.6	63.1	63.3	64.2	63.1	63.6	62.0	61.5	61.0

Employment by Industry: Buffalo-Cheektowaga-Niagara Falls, NY, Selected Years, 2007–2017—*Continued*

(Numbers in thousands, not seasonally adjusted)

Industry and year	January	February	March	April	May	June	July	August	September	October	November	December	Annual average
Other Services													
2007	22.6	22.9	23.2	23.1	23.3	23.4	23.4	23.5	23.2	23.6	23.5	23.6	23.3
2008	23.3	23.4	23.7	23.7	23.9	23.9	24.1	24.2	23.8	24.3	24.0	24.0	23.9
2009	23.4	23.6	23.8	24.0	24.0	24.0	24.0	24.0	23.7	24.0	23.9	23.6	23.8
2010	22.9	23.0	23.1	23.2	23.2	23.3	24.2	24.5	23.1	23.3	23.3	23.4	23.4
2011	22.8	23.0	23.0	23.2	23.3	23.5	23.3	23.3	23.4	23.1	23.1	23.3	23.2
2012	23.0	23.0	23.2	23.2	23.5	23.7	23.5	23.5	23.3	23.5	23.5	23.6	23.4
2013	23.6	23.6	23.7	23.7	24.0	24.0	24.0	24.2	24.0	24.5	24.5	24.8	24.1
2014	24.3	24.4	24.7	24.5	24.7	24.6	24.8	24.8	24.3	24.7	24.6	24.7	24.6
2015	24.3	24.3	24.6	24.7	24.8	24.9	25.0	25.0	24.6	25.0	24.9	25.1	24.8
2016	24.3	24.5	24.6	24.9	25.1	24.9	25.2	25.3	24.8	25.1	25.2	24.9	24.9
2017	24.7	24.8	24.9	25.0	25.0	25.2	25.4	25.4	25.0	25.8	26.7	26.7	25.4
Government													
2007	93.6	95.2	95.5	94.9	95.6	94.8	88.8	90.1	93.0	96.2	96.7	96.6	94.3
2008	93.8	95.9	96.2	96.6	96.7	96.0	90.7	91.2	94.3	97.7	97.9	97.5	95.4
2009	94.8	96.2	96.5	96.7	97.3	95.7	91.9	91.9	93.9	97.2	97.6	97.1	95.6
2010	95.2	96.8	97.3	97.1	99.0	96.6	88.1	88.5	91.5	96.2	96.9	96.7	95.0
2011	94.5	95.6	95.2	95.7	95.3	93.6	88.9	89.0	91.4	94.1	94.3	94.3	93.5
2012	91.7	94.0	93.9	93.3	93.6	91.9	87.1	86.7	89.2	92.4	92.8	92.8	91.6
2013	90.1	92.3	92.4	91.6	91.4	90.1	85.7	85.9	88.3	91.7	91.7	91.4	90.2
2014	88.3	90.5	90.9	90.8	90.2	88.9	84.9	85.0	87.5	90.3	90.6	90.1	89.0
2015	88.5	90.0	90.1	89.9	90.2	89.1	85.2	85.5	88.2	90.7	90.9	91.2	89.1
2016	89.1	90.7	91.0	90.9	91.0	89.7	86.1	85.9	89.7	91.3	91.5	92.3	89.9
2017	91.4	92.2	92.2	92.0	92.0	90.5	86.9	86.4	89.7	92.2	92.6	92.7	90.9

Employment by Industry: Rochester, NY, Selected Years, 2007–2017

(Numbers in thousands, not seasonally adjusted)

Industry and year	January	February	March	April	May	June	July	August	September	October	November	December	Annual average
Total Nonfarm													
2007	509.7	512.8	514.4	516.4	524.7	526.2	516.4	515.4	520.5	527.0	527.4	527.3	519.9
2008	509.5	514.2	515.0	521.0	527.6	527.7	519.0	518.1	523.1	528.9	526.2	524.5	521.2
2009	504.4	506.2	505.6	506.0	510.8	509.1	504.6	502.7	505.5	512.8	512.0	511.8	507.6
2010	495.2	499.0	501.3	507.5	512.5	512.3	504.1	504.2	509.2	518.3	518.6	516.4	508.2
2011	499.4	504.1	506.0	515.4	517.9	519.1	511.1	511.9	519.2	525.2	525.3	525.6	515.0
2012	505.7	511.8	514.5	516.7	523.4	523.0	513.5	512.3	519.5	527.3	527.4	527.8	518.6
2013	507.3	514.9	516.1	520.3	525.8	523.6	514.1	514.2	521.9	528.9	530.2	530.2	520.6
2014	509.8	517.3	518.7	521.9	526.8	526.8	517.3	517.7	524.1	532.0	532.4	532.6	523.1
2015	513.1	519.2	520.3	526.0	531.7	532.3	523.8	523.8	528.9	539.1	539.1	538.3	528.0
2016	522.0	527.0	529.4	535.9	537.6	536.4	527.8	526.1	531.9	541.1	540.7	539.4	532.9
2017	521.7	528.9	527.5	535.9	537.9	538.0	528.4	528.2	534.9	542.2	543.0	542.9	534.1
Total Private													
2007	429.5	430.3	431.7	433.5	441.3	443.5	441.7	441.3	440.5	444.3	444.0	443.1	438.7
2008	428.8	431.3	431.8	437.2	443.5	444.3	443.0	442.8	442.1	445.1	442.0	440.0	439.3
2009	423.3	422.6	422.0	421.8	426.6	426.2	425.8	425.9	425.9	428.8	427.4	426.9	425.3
2010	412.9	414.7	417.0	423.0	426.5	427.4	428.4	429.6	429.5	434.3	433.9	431.4	425.7
2011	418.3	420.3	422.2	431.2	434.0	435.9	436.4	437.2	439.3	442.2	441.6	441.3	433.3
2012	425.7	428.7	431.3	434.2	440.1	440.8	439.6	439.2	440.7	445.4	445.1	444.5	437.9
2013	427.9	432.7	433.6	437.9	442.9	442.1	441.0	441.4	443.5	448.1	448.7	448.2	440.7
2014	431.7	436.5	438.0	441.0	446.1	446.7	445.1	445.5	446.3	452.0	451.3	450.8	444.3
2015	435.1	438.6	439.8	445.8	450.4	452.0	451.9	452.1	451.8	459.2	458.4	457.5	449.4
2016	443.3	446.8	448.8	455.7	457.0	456.7	456.3	454.7	455.2	461.0	460.2	458.3	454.5
2017	443.3	448.3	447.3	455.1	457.4	458.3	456.5	456.3	457.3	461.5	461.9	461.2	455.4
Goods Producing													
2007	92.4	91.3	91.7	92.7	94.3	95.5	95.4	95.5	94.2	93.6	92.7	91.6	93.4
2008	89.1	88.0	87.7	88.6	90.8	92.2	93.2	93.1	92.1	91.4	89.4	87.4	90.3
2009	83.7	81.9	80.8	80.6	81.7	82.2	82.9	83.5	82.0	81.5	80.2	78.5	81.6
2010	75.9	75.0	75.3	77.0	78.2	79.6	80.8	81.3	80.4	80.6	80.0	77.9	78.5
2011	76.2	75.5	75.9	77.5	79.4	81.5	82.5	82.8	81.9	81.7	80.6	79.3	79.6
2012	77.2	76.5	76.7	78.0	79.6	81.6	82.2	82.1	80.9	80.6	79.4	78.7	79.5
2013	76.3	75.3	75.4	76.8	78.6	79.8	80.5	81.0	80.0	80.0	79.2	78.0	78.4
2014	75.7	74.9	75.4	76.3	78.5	80.2	81.3	81.5	80.5	80.7	79.5	78.2	78.6
2015	76.0	75.1	75.6	77.3	79.4	80.8	81.7	81.7	80.7	81.1	80.0	78.9	79.0
2016	76.5	76.1	76.5	77.5	79.0	80.4	80.9	80.7	79.8	79.5	78.5	77.1	78.5
2017	75.1	74.9	75.1	77.1	78.4	79.6	80.4	80.7	80.0	79.8	79.6	78.2	78.2
Service-Providing													
2007	417.3	421.5	422.7	423.7	430.4	430.7	421.0	419.9	426.3	433.4	434.7	435.7	426.4
2008	420.4	426.2	427.3	432.4	436.8	435.5	425.8	425.0	431.0	437.5	436.8	437.1	431.0
2009	420.7	424.3	424.8	425.4	429.1	426.9	421.7	419.2	423.5	431.3	431.8	433.3	426.0
2010	419.3	424.0	426.0	430.5	434.3	432.7	423.3	422.9	428.8	437.7	438.6	438.5	429.7
2011	423.2	428.6	430.1	437.9	438.5	437.6	428.6	429.1	437.3	443.5	444.7	446.3	435.5
2012	428.5	435.3	437.8	438.7	443.8	441.4	431.3	430.2	438.6	446.7	448.0	449.1	439.1
2013	431.0	439.6	440.7	443.5	447.2	443.8	433.6	433.2	441.9	448.9	451.0	452.2	442.2
2014	434.1	442.4	443.3	445.6	448.3	446.6	436.0	436.2	443.6	451.3	452.9	454.4	444.6
2015	437.1	444.1	444.7	448.7	452.3	451.5	442.1	442.1	448.2	458.0	459.1	459.4	448.9
2016	445.5	450.9	452.9	458.4	458.6	456.0	446.9	445.4	452.1	461.6	462.2	462.3	454.4
2017	446.6	454.0	452.4	458.8	459.5	458.4	448.0	447.5	454.9	462.4	463.4	464.7	455.9
Mining, Logging, and Construction													
2007	16.9	15.9	16.4	17.8	19.6	20.6	20.9	21.1	20.6	20.5	20.0	19.0	19.1
2008	17.7	16.8	16.9	18.2	20.0	20.9	21.7	21.9	21.5	21.2	20.0	18.8	19.6
2009	16.3	15.6	15.5	16.6	18.3	19.3	20.1	20.4	19.6	19.2	18.4	17.1	18.0
2010	15.3	14.7	15.0	16.8	17.8	18.9	19.7	20.1	19.3	19.1	18.7	16.9	17.7
2011	15.5	15.0	15.3	16.6	18.2	19.5	20.2	20.5	20.1	19.9	19.1	18.1	18.2
2012	16.4	16.0	16.4	17.7	19.0	20.3	20.9	21.0	20.4	20.1	19.3	18.5	18.8
2013	16.9	16.5	16.6	17.6	19.6	20.5	21.1	21.2	20.6	20.6	19.8	18.8	19.2
2014	17.0	16.6	16.9	18.0	20.0	21.1	21.7	21.8	21.2	21.4	20.6	19.3	19.6
2015	17.5	16.8	17.1	18.6	20.5	21.4	21.7	21.9	21.5	21.7	20.9	19.9	20.0
2016	18.0	17.7	18.1	19.3	20.8	21.7	22.3	22.3	21.8	21.8	21.3	20.1	20.4
2017	18.6	18.2	18.5	20.4	21.6	22.2	22.9	23.1	22.5	22.2	21.7	20.4	21.0

Employment by Industry: Rochester, NY, Selected Years, 2007–2017—*Continued*

(Numbers in thousands, not seasonally adjusted)

Industry and year	January	February	March	April	May	June	July	August	September	October	November	December	Annual average
Manufacturing													
2007	75.5	75.4	75.3	74.9	74.7	74.9	74.5	74.4	73.6	73.1	72.7	72.6	74.3
2008	71.4	71.2	70.8	70.4	70.8	71.3	71.5	71.2	70.6	70.2	69.4	68.6	70.6
2009	67.4	66.3	65.3	64.0	63.4	62.9	62.8	63.1	62.4	62.3	61.8	61.4	63.6
2010	60.6	60.3	60.3	60.2	60.4	60.7	61.1	61.2	61.1	61.5	61.3	61.0	60.8
2011	60.7	60.5	60.6	60.9	61.2	62.0	62.3	62.3	61.8	61.8	61.5	61.2	61.4
2012	60.8	60.5	60.3	60.3	60.6	61.3	61.3	61.1	60.5	60.5	60.1	60.2	60.6
2013	59.4	58.8	58.8	59.2	59.0	59.3	59.4	59.8	59.4	59.4	59.4	59.2	59.3
2014	58.7	58.3	58.5	58.3	58.5	59.1	59.6	59.7	59.3	59.3	58.9	58.9	58.9
2015	58.5	58.3	58.5	58.7	58.9	59.4	60.0	59.8	59.2	59.4	59.1	59.0	59.1
2016	58.5	58.4	58.4	58.2	58.2	58.7	58.6	58.4	58.0	57.7	57.2	57.0	58.1
2017	56.5	56.7	56.6	56.7	56.8	57.4	57.5	57.6	57.5	57.6	57.9	57.8	57.2
Trade, Transportation, and Utilities													
2007	85.3	83.1	83.5	83.1	86.1	87.2	86.5	86.1	85.4	86.5	87.9	88.9	85.8
2008	85.7	83.8	83.7	84.3	85.8	86.5	85.4	85.2	84.3	85.3	85.6	86.3	85.2
2009	82.2	80.4	80.0	79.9	81.6	82.5	82.0	82.0	80.7	81.7	82.5	83.5	81.6
2010	80.5	79.3	79.6	80.6	81.9	83.2	82.2	82.5	81.6	83.1	83.7	84.6	81.9
2011	81.5	80.3	80.3	81.4	82.3	83.4	82.5	82.6	81.8	83.3	84.3	85.6	82.4
2012	82.2	80.3	80.7	80.8	83.1	84.3	83.4	83.2	82.6	83.9	85.0	85.7	82.9
2013	82.2	80.7	80.7	81.2	82.6	83.6	82.6	82.2	81.8	82.9	84.1	84.8	82.5
2014	81.8	80.8	80.5	81.3	82.7	83.7	82.6	82.7	82.2	83.1	84.2	85.1	82.6
2015	81.8	80.6	80.8	81.5	83.3	84.6	83.6	83.6	83.0	83.9	85.2	86.0	83.2
2016	82.9	81.9	81.9	82.9	83.6	84.5	83.9	83.8	83.7	84.5	85.7	86.0	83.8
2017	83.2	82.2	81.6	82.7	84.1	84.9	83.9	83.9	83.7	84.4	85.9	85.7	83.9
Wholesale Trade													
2007	17.5	17.5	17.5	17.5	17.7	17.9	18.2	18.1	17.8	17.9	17.7	17.8	17.8
2008	17.3	17.3	17.2	17.5	17.7	17.8	17.9	17.8	17.6	17.9	17.7	17.6	17.6
2009	17.2	17.0	16.8	16.7	16.9	16.9	16.9	16.8	16.6	16.6	16.4	16.5	16.8
2010	16.1	16.1	16.1	16.3	16.4	16.6	16.6	16.6	16.4	16.6	16.5	16.6	16.4
2011	16.2	16.2	16.3	16.5	16.6	16.8	16.8	16.7	16.6	17.0	16.9	16.9	16.6
2012	16.5	16.5	16.6	17.0	17.2	17.3	17.3	17.2	17.0	17.3	17.3	17.3	17.0
2013	17.2	17.1	17.1	17.2	17.3	17.4	17.4	17.3	17.3	17.2	17.1	17.2	17.2
2014	17.0	17.1	17.0	17.2	17.4	17.6	17.6	17.5	17.3	17.4	17.3	17.3	17.3
2015	17.1	17.0	17.1	17.1	17.2	17.4	17.4	17.4	17.1	17.3	17.3	17.3	17.2
2016	17.1	17.1	17.0	17.4	17.4	17.5	17.6	17.4	17.3	17.2	17.2	17.1	17.3
2017	17.1	17.1	17.1	17.3	17.5	17.6	17.4	17.4	17.4	17.4	17.5	17.5	17.4
Retail Trade													
2007	57.2	55.1	55.5	55.2	57.7	58.6	58.1	57.8	56.8	57.7	59.2	60.0	57.4
2008	57.7	55.8	55.8	56.0	57.1	57.7	57.1	57.1	56.2	56.9	57.4	58.0	56.9
2009	55.0	53.4	53.4	53.2	54.6	55.4	55.0	55.1	54.0	54.8	55.9	56.5	54.7
2010	54.4	53.3	53.6	54.3	55.3	56.3	56.0	56.3	55.1	56.3	57.0	57.7	55.5
2011	55.5	54.3	54.2	54.9	55.5	56.4	56.1	56.3	55.0	56.1	57.2	58.3	55.8
2012	55.8	54.0	54.3	54.1	55.8	56.7	56.5	56.4	55.4	56.4	57.6	57.9	55.9
2013	55.1	53.7	53.8	54.1	55.2	56.0	55.6	55.5	54.2	55.3	56.4	56.9	55.2
2014	54.5	53.5	53.3	53.9	54.9	55.7	55.2	55.5	54.5	55.2	56.3	57.0	55.0
2015	54.5	53.5	53.6	54.2	55.5	56.4	56.0	56.1	55.1	55.9	57.1	57.7	55.5
2016	55.5	54.5	54.5	55.0	55.6	56.3	56.1	56.2	55.4	56.3	57.3	57.5	55.9
2017	55.3	54.2	53.6	54.6	55.4	56.1	55.9	55.9	54.9	55.5	57.0	56.7	55.4
Transportation and Utilities													
2007	10.6	10.5	10.5	10.4	10.7	10.7	10.2	10.2	10.8	10.9	11.0	11.1	10.6
2008	10.7	10.7	10.7	10.8	11.0	11.0	10.4	10.3	10.5	10.5	10.5	10.7	10.7
2009	10.0	10.0	9.8	10.0	10.1	10.2	10.1	10.1	10.1	10.3	10.2	10.5	10.1
2010	10.0	9.9	9.9	10.0	10.2	10.3	9.6	9.6	10.1	10.2	10.2	10.3	10.0
2011	9.8	9.8	9.8	10.0	10.2	10.2	9.6	9.6	10.2	10.2	10.2	10.4	10.0
2012	9.9	9.8	9.8	9.7	10.1	10.3	9.6	9.6	10.2	10.2	10.1	10.5	10.0
2013	9.9	9.9	9.8	9.9	10.1	10.2	9.6	9.4	10.3	10.4	10.6	10.7	10.1
2014	10.3	10.2	10.2	10.2	10.4	10.4	9.8	9.7	10.4	10.5	10.6	10.8	10.3
2015	10.2	10.1	10.1	10.2	10.6	10.8	10.2	10.1	10.8	10.7	10.8	11.0	10.5
2016	10.3	10.3	10.4	10.5	10.6	10.7	10.2	10.2	11.0	11.0	11.2	11.4	10.7
2017	10.8	10.9	10.9	10.8	11.2	11.2	10.6	10.6	11.4	11.5	11.4	11.5	11.1

Employment by Industry: Rochester, NY, Selected Years, 2007–2017—*Continued*

(Numbers in thousands, not seasonally adjusted)

Industry and year	January	February	March	April	May	June	July	August	September	October	November	December	Annual average
Information													
2007	10.7	10.6	10.6	10.7	10.8	10.8	10.8	10.8	10.7	10.7	10.7	10.8	10.7
2008	10.6	10.6	10.6	10.5	10.5	10.5	10.5	10.5	10.3	10.4	10.5	10.5	10.5
2009	10.2	10.1	10.1	10.2	10.2	10.1	10.1	9.9	9.7	9.8	9.8	9.8	10.0
2010	9.6	9.5	9.5	9.4	9.5	9.5	9.6	9.6	9.4	9.4	9.4	9.3	9.5
2011	9.3	9.2	9.1	9.1	9.1	9.1	9.2	9.2	9.1	9.1	9.0	9.0	9.1
2012	8.6	8.5	8.5	8.4	8.5	8.5	8.5	8.5	8.4	8.4	8.5	8.4	8.5
2013	8.3	8.2	8.2	8.3	8.3	8.3	8.4	8.4	8.1	8.1	8.2	8.2	8.3
2014	8.2	8.2	8.2	8.1	8.1	8.2	8.4	8.3	8.2	8.4	8.4	8.5	8.3
2015	8.4	8.4	8.3	8.4	8.4	8.4	8.4	8.3	8.2	8.3	8.3	8.4	8.4
2016	8.5	8.6	8.7	8.7	8.7	8.6	8.6	8.5	8.5	8.5	8.5	8.5	8.6
2017	8.2	8.1	8.1	8.1	8.1	8.1	8.1	8.1	8.0	8.0	8.0	8.0	8.1
Financial Activities													
2007	21.8	21.7	21.7	21.7	21.7	22.2	22.6	22.6	21.6	21.6	21.6	21.7	21.9
2008	21.2	21.2	21.2	21.3	21.7	22.1	22.3	22.3	21.6	21.5	21.4	21.4	21.6
2009	20.6	20.3	20.3	20.4	20.9	21.4	21.4	21.5	21.1	20.8	20.7	20.8	20.9
2010	20.4	20.2	20.4	20.3	20.6	21.2	21.3	21.1	20.3	20.4	20.3	20.3	20.6
2011	20.3	20.3	20.4	20.7	20.9	21.6	21.9	22.0	21.3	21.3	21.2	21.4	21.1
2012	21.3	21.3	21.2	21.3	21.5	22.2	22.3	22.4	21.6	21.6	21.5	21.7	21.7
2013	21.2	21.2	21.1	21.2	21.5	22.0	22.3	22.2	21.6	21.2	21.2	21.4	21.5
2014	21.0	20.9	21.1	21.0	21.4	22.0	22.2	22.2	21.7	21.7	21.6	21.9	21.6
2015	21.6	21.6	21.7	21.7	21.9	22.3	22.3	22.3	21.8	21.8	21.9	21.9	21.9
2016	21.8	21.9	21.9	22.1	22.3	22.7	23.1	23.1	22.4	22.4	22.2	22.4	22.4
2017	21.6	21.5	21.4	21.7	21.8	22.4	22.4	22.4	21.7	21.3	21.4	21.6	21.8
Professional and Business Services													
2007	60.9	61.4	61.3	61.3	62.0	63.3	62.8	62.9	62.0	62.9	62.5	62.4	62.1
2008	61.3	61.6	61.8	63.4	63.6	64.8	64.5	65.1	64.0	64.4	63.8	63.3	63.5
2009	61.2	60.9	60.6	59.8	59.8	60.7	60.5	60.6	60.3	61.0	60.9	60.8	60.6
2010	58.9	59.3	59.5	60.3	60.3	61.8	62.6	63.1	62.1	63.3	63.2	62.4	61.4
2011	60.4	60.4	61.1	63.5	63.5	65.2	65.7	66.1	66.3	65.6	65.9	65.8	64.1
2012	64.4	64.5	64.8	66.3	66.7	67.7	67.5	67.2	66.4	67.1	67.4	66.7	66.4
2013	65.4	65.4	65.4	66.2	66.5	68.0	68.0	68.0	67.3	67.6	68.2	67.8	67.0
2014	65.6	66.2	66.5	66.4	66.8	67.6	67.5	67.3	66.7	67.1	68.0	67.8	67.0
2015	66.5	67.0	66.6	68.0	68.5	70.1	70.8	70.9	69.9	70.5	69.8	69.5	69.0
2016	68.3	68.1	68.1	69.4	69.4	69.9	69.9	69.2	68.7	69.1	69.2	68.5	69.0
2017	67.2	67.9	67.6	68.6	69.1	70.2	70.0	69.8	69.5	69.2	68.4	68.3	68.8
Education and Health Services													
2007	101.9	105.5	105.9	106.1	104.5	100.1	98.8	99.1	105.3	108.3	108.7	108.3	104.4
2008	104.0	108.6	109.0	109.3	107.7	103.4	102.0	101.7	108.4	111.1	111.8	111.6	107.4
2009	107.9	111.8	112.3	111.8	109.6	104.9	103.7	103.5	109.7	112.9	113.5	113.6	109.6
2010	109.6	113.6	114.1	114.6	112.3	107.2	106.1	105.9	112.9	115.7	116.3	116.4	112.1
2011	111.2	115.1	115.4	116.8	114.2	108.8	107.6	107.5	114.5	117.3	117.7	117.7	113.7
2012	111.5	116.9	117.5	117.2	114.8	108.9	107.8	108.0	115.8	119.0	119.6	120.0	114.8
2013	113.2	119.8	120.2	120.1	117.9	111.2	109.6	110.2	118.4	121.9	122.7	122.7	117.3
2014	117.4	123.0	123.5	123.5	120.5	115.6	113.6	114.4	120.5	124.4	124.5	124.4	120.4
2015	118.7	123.5	123.8	124.0	120.5	116.2	115.3	115.6	120.8	126.9	127.5	127.0	121.7
2016	122.2	127.0	127.3	128.5	124.9	120.4	119.2	119.2	124.5	130.0	130.4	130.4	125.3
2017	124.9	130.5	130.2	131.3	128.5	123.5	121.6	121.6	127.6	133.0	134.0	133.4	128.3
Leisure and Hospitality													
2007	37.0	37.2	37.5	38.4	42.1	44.6	45.1	44.6	41.9	41.0	40.2	39.6	40.8
2008	37.3	37.9	38.2	39.8	43.2	44.6	44.8	44.8	41.8	41.1	39.6	39.6	41.1
2009	37.7	37.4	38.0	39.2	42.7	44.3	44.9	44.8	42.6	41.2	39.8	39.8	41.0
2010	38.2	38.2	38.9	40.9	43.7	44.8	45.5	45.7	43.0	41.7	40.7	40.1	41.8
2011	39.2	39.3	39.6	41.4	43.8	45.6	46.2	46.2	43.7	43.1	42.1	41.4	42.6
2012	39.5	39.8	40.6	41.0	44.4	46.0	46.8	46.8	44.3	43.9	42.8	42.3	43.2
2013	40.5	41.2	41.7	43.1	46.2	47.7	48.1	47.8	45.5	45.4	44.0	44.0	44.6
2014	41.0	41.6	41.8	43.2	46.7	47.8	48.2	48.0	45.7	45.5	44.0	43.7	44.8
2015	41.2	41.6	42.0	43.7	47.1	48.2	48.7	48.6	46.6	45.6	44.6	44.6	45.2
2016	42.2	42.5	43.6	45.4	47.7	48.8	49.5	49.2	46.8	46.0	44.7	44.4	45.9
2017	42.2	42.4	42.5	44.5	46.2	48.2	49.0	49.0	46.1	44.9	43.6	44.9	45.3

Employment by Industry: Rochester, NY, Selected Years, 2007–2017—*Continued*

(Numbers in thousands, not seasonally adjusted)

Industry and year	January	February	March	April	May	June	July	August	September	October	November	December	Annual average
Other Services													
2007	19.5	19.5	19.5	19.5	19.8	19.8	19.7	19.7	19.4	19.7	19.7	19.8	19.6
2008	19.6	19.6	19.6	20.0	20.2	20.2	20.3	20.1	19.6	19.9	19.9	19.9	19.9
2009	19.8	19.8	19.9	19.9	20.1	20.1	20.3	20.1	19.8	19.9	20.0	20.1	20.0
2010	19.8	19.6	19.7	19.9	20.0	20.1	20.3	20.4	19.8	20.1	20.3	20.4	20.0
2011	20.2	20.2	20.4	20.8	20.8	20.7	20.8	20.8	20.7	20.8	20.8	21.1	20.7
2012	21.0	20.9	21.3	21.2	21.5	21.6	21.1	21.0	20.7	20.9	20.9	21.0	21.1
2013	20.8	20.9	20.9	21.0	21.3	21.5	21.5	21.6	20.8	21.0	21.1	21.3	21.1
2014	21.0	20.9	21.0	21.2	21.4	21.6	21.3	21.1	20.8	21.1	21.1	21.2	21.1
2015	20.9	20.8	21.0	21.2	21.3	21.4	21.1	21.1	20.8	21.1	21.1	21.2	21.1
2016	20.9	20.7	20.8	21.2	21.4	21.4	21.2	21.0	20.8	21.0	21.0	21.0	21.0
2017	20.9	20.8	20.8	21.1	21.2	21.4	21.1	20.8	20.7	20.9	21.0	21.1	21.0
Government													
2007	80.2	82.5	82.7	82.9	83.4	82.7	74.7	74.1	80.0	82.7	83.4	84.2	81.1
2008	80.7	82.9	83.2	83.8	84.1	83.4	76.0	75.3	81.0	83.8	84.2	84.5	81.9
2009	81.1	83.6	83.6	84.2	84.2	82.9	78.8	76.8	79.6	84.0	84.6	84.9	82.4
2010	82.3	84.3	84.3	84.5	86.0	84.9	75.7	74.6	79.7	84.0	84.7	85.0	82.5
2011	81.1	83.8	83.8	84.2	83.9	83.2	74.7	74.7	79.9	83.0	83.7	84.3	81.7
2012	80.0	83.1	83.2	82.5	83.3	82.2	73.9	73.1	78.8	81.9	82.3	83.3	80.6
2013	79.4	82.2	82.5	82.4	82.9	81.5	73.1	72.8	78.4	80.8	81.5	82.0	80.0
2014	78.1	80.8	80.7	80.9	80.7	80.1	72.2	72.2	77.8	80.0	81.1	81.8	78.9
2015	78.0	80.6	80.5	80.2	81.3	80.3	71.9	71.7	77.1	79.9	80.7	80.8	78.6
2016	78.7	80.2	80.6	80.2	80.6	79.7	71.5	71.4	76.7	80.1	80.5	81.1	78.4
2017	78.4	80.6	80.2	80.8	80.5	79.7	71.9	71.9	77.6	80.7	81.1	81.7	78.8

Employment by Industry: Grand Rapids-Wyoming, MI, Selected Years, 2007–2017

(Numbers in thousands, not seasonally adjusted)

Industry and year	January	February	March	April	May	June	July	August	September	October	November	December	Annual average
Total Nonfarm													
2007	480.1	482.8	485.2	489.0	494.2	495.1	484.1	488.8	493.5	492.9	494.7	493.8	489.5
2008	481.0	481.5	482.0	484.9	491.1	490.8	477.2	481.7	483.6	482.6	480.2	475.4	482.7
2009	446.2	447.8	446.1	451.8	454.3	450.1	437.7	441.4	450.6	454.5	455.1	453.0	449.1
2010	437.8	442.0	443.2	450.7	457.5	458.6	451.2	454.0	462.8	464.0	465.6	463.4	454.2
2011	452.4	454.5	457.3	465.4	470.0	470.1	466.6	468.3	476.4	476.3	479.0	479.1	468.0
2012	471.2	472.8	476.5	483.4	488.1	488.0	481.6	484.1	491.9	494.2	496.1	495.0	485.2
2013	486.7	489.7	492.2	494.5	501.3	502.8	496.9	501.5	507.7	508.9	511.1	512.6	500.5
2014	502.1	504.1	506.5	510.0	518.9	520.5	507.8	510.4	516.9	520.1	522.5	524.4	513.7
2015	513.8	516.1	518.7	523.2	530.6	531.8	525.2	524.0	533.5	537.6	539.3	541.6	528.0
2016	531.5	533.6	535.9	539.1	544.4	547.2	539.0	540.4	546.1	548.8	550.6	551.8	542.4
2017	543.3	545.3	548.0	551.1	557.4	559.8	548.3	550.2	555.5	558.9	560.9	561.5	553.4
Total Private													
2007	431.2	432.1	434.4	438.5	445.2	447.2	441.7	445.4	444.7	443.0	445.0	445.5	441.2
2008	432.0	431.4	431.7	434.7	442.1	442.5	434.7	437.6	434.7	432.3	430.2	425.5	434.1
2009	398.0	397.9	396.0	401.1	405.0	402.7	395.3	398.9	401.4	404.0	404.8	404.0	400.8
2010	390.0	392.2	393.6	400.9	408.3	410.9	408.4	411.7	414.2	414.0	415.2	414.3	406.1
2011	404.3	405.6	407.9	415.7	422.7	423.6	424.1	426.5	429.0	427.9	430.0	431.0	420.7
2012	423.1	424.3	427.9	435.2	441.1	443.5	440.3	442.7	444.3	445.7	447.3	447.4	438.6
2013	439.7	441.6	444.4	447.1	454.9	458.0	456.9	461.0	461.1	461.4	464.0	465.6	454.6
2014	455.4	456.6	458.9	462.8	473.0	475.6	467.8	470.1	470.4	472.1	474.4	477.0	467.8
2015	467.0	468.4	471.1	475.6	484.6	487.4	484.4	483.7	487.0	489.7	491.5	493.9	482.0
2016	484.6	485.8	488.0	491.4	498.0	501.4	498.0	499.2	499.1	500.5	502.0	503.4	496.0
2017	496.0	496.9	499.7	503.2	510.6	513.4	507.3	508.5	507.7	509.8	512.1	512.6	506.5
Goods Producing													
2007	122.3	121.4	121.3	123.2	124.4	125.6	123.6	125.4	124.5	123.6	123.7	123.2	123.5
2008	120.1	118.8	118.4	118.5	120.3	122.1	118.3	120.3	118.9	116.9	114.8	112.1	118.3
2009	101.3	100.5	99.2	99.4	99.3	99.5	98.5	100.9	101.0	100.1	99.2	98.6	99.8
2010	95.3	95.3	96.3	98.5	100.8	102.5	103.1	103.9	103.5	102.1	101.9	102.0	100.4
2011	100.8	101.0	101.7	103.9	106.0	107.9	108.2	109.0	108.6	108.6	108.9	109.1	106.1
2012	107.6	107.5	108.3	110.0	111.6	113.7	114.1	114.8	114.1	113.8	113.5	113.7	111.9
2013	112.5	112.6	113.5	114.6	116.9	118.9	119.4	120.1	119.5	119.4	119.8	119.8	117.3
2014	118.4	118.9	119.6	121.0	123.4	125.7	125.9	125.8	125.3	125.1	125.3	125.5	123.3
2015	123.6	124.0	124.7	126.3	128.4	130.8	131.3	131.4	130.9	131.5	131.3	131.7	128.8
2016	130.5	130.7	131.1	132.6	133.8	135.7	136.3	136.1	135.0	135.4	135.3	135.8	134.0
2017	135.1	135.3	135.8	137.5	139.0	141.3	140.9	141.2	139.9	139.9	140.0	139.9	138.8
Service-Providing													
2007	357.8	361.4	363.9	365.8	369.8	369.5	360.5	363.4	369.0	369.3	371.0	370.6	366.0
2008	360.9	362.7	363.6	366.4	370.8	368.7	358.9	361.4	364.7	365.7	365.4	363.3	364.4
2009	344.9	347.3	346.9	352.4	355.0	350.6	339.2	340.5	349.6	354.4	355.9	354.4	349.3
2010	342.5	346.7	346.9	352.2	356.7	356.1	348.1	350.1	359.3	361.9	363.7	361.4	353.8
2011	351.6	353.5	355.6	361.5	364.0	362.2	358.4	359.3	367.8	367.7	370.1	370.0	361.8
2012	363.6	365.3	368.2	373.4	376.5	374.3	367.5	369.3	377.8	380.4	382.6	381.3	373.4
2013	374.2	377.1	378.7	379.9	384.4	383.9	377.5	381.4	388.2	389.5	391.3	392.8	383.2
2014	383.7	385.2	386.9	389.0	395.5	394.8	381.9	384.6	391.6	395.0	397.2	398.9	390.4
2015	390.2	392.1	394.0	396.9	402.2	401.0	393.9	392.6	402.6	406.1	408.0	409.9	399.1
2016	401.0	402.9	404.8	406.5	410.6	411.5	402.7	404.3	411.1	413.4	415.3	416.0	408.3
2017	408.2	410.0	412.2	413.6	418.4	418.5	407.4	409.0	415.6	419.0	420.9	421.6	414.5
Mining, Logging, and Construction													
2007	20.5	19.9	20.1	21.5	22.6	23.2	23.4	23.3	23.0	22.4	22.0	21.4	21.9
2008	19.8	19.4	19.7	20.6	21.9	22.4	22.3	22.3	21.9	21.1	20.1	19.1	20.9
2009	16.7	16.4	16.3	17.4	18.2	18.4	18.7	18.5	18.1	17.8	17.1	16.4	17.5
2010	14.8	14.6	15.0	16.1	16.9	17.5	17.8	17.8	17.4	17.0	16.5	16.0	16.5
2011	14.7	14.5	14.8	15.9	17.0	17.7	18.3	18.2	17.9	17.6	17.3	16.8	16.7
2012	15.6	15.3	15.8	16.8	17.5	18.1	18.5	18.7	18.4	18.2	17.7	17.5	17.3
2013	16.6	16.4	16.7	17.3	18.7	19.5	20.0	20.2	19.9	19.8	19.5	18.9	18.6
2014	17.9	17.9	18.2	19.0	20.3	21.2	21.4	21.5	21.3	20.8	20.5	20.0	20.0
2015	18.7	18.6	19.0	20.1	21.2	22.0	22.2	22.2	21.9	21.7	21.3	20.8	20.8
2016	19.8	19.8	20.4	21.7	22.6	23.4	23.6	23.6	23.2	23.1	22.8	22.2	22.2
2017	21.4	21.4	21.8	23.0	23.9	24.9	25.0	25.0	24.4	24.6	24.6	23.8	23.7

Employment by Industry: Grand Rapids-Wyoming, MI, Selected Years, 2007–2017—*Continued*

(Numbers in thousands, not seasonally adjusted)

Industry and year	January	February	March	April	May	June	July	August	September	October	November	December	Annual average
Manufacturing													
2007	101.8	101.5	101.2	101.7	101.8	102.4	100.2	102.1	101.5	101.2	101.7	101.8	101.6
2008	100.3	99.4	98.7	97.9	98.4	99.7	96.0	98.0	97.0	95.8	94.7	93.0	97.4
2009	84.6	84.1	82.9	82.0	81.1	81.1	79.8	82.4	82.9	82.3	82.1	82.2	82.3
2010	80.5	80.7	81.3	82.4	83.9	85.0	85.3	86.1	86.1	85.1	85.4	86.0	84.0
2011	86.1	86.5	86.9	88.0	89.0	90.2	89.9	90.8	90.7	91.0	91.6	92.3	89.4
2012	92.0	92.2	92.5	93.2	94.1	95.6	95.6	96.1	95.7	95.6	95.8	96.2	94.6
2013	95.9	96.2	96.8	97.3	98.2	99.4	99.4	99.9	99.6	99.6	100.3	100.9	98.6
2014	100.5	101.0	101.4	102.0	103.1	104.5	104.5	104.3	104.0	104.3	104.8	105.5	103.3
2015	104.9	105.4	105.7	106.2	107.2	108.8	109.1	109.2	109.0	109.8	110.0	110.9	108.0
2016	110.7	110.9	110.7	110.9	111.2	112.3	112.7	112.5	111.8	112.3	112.5	113.6	111.8
2017	113.7	113.9	114.0	114.5	115.1	116.4	115.9	116.2	115.5	115.3	115.4	116.1	115.2
Trade, Transportation, and Utilities													
2007	88.7	87.7	87.9	88.8	89.9	90.4	90.2	90.0	89.7	90.0	91.2	91.5	89.7
2008	88.3	87.4	87.7	87.5	88.7	89.0	87.7	87.7	86.7	86.4	86.9	86.8	87.6
2009	82.8	81.7	81.2	82.3	83.3	83.3	82.0	81.8	81.4	82.1	82.6	82.8	82.3
2010	80.0	79.3	79.3	80.2	81.1	81.7	81.2	81.3	80.5	81.6	82.8	82.9	81.0
2011	79.8	79.4	79.5	81.3	82.1	82.5	82.6	82.6	82.2	82.5	83.7	84.1	81.9
2012	81.1	80.5	81.1	82.7	83.9	84.1	84.0	84.2	83.8	84.7	86.3	86.6	83.6
2013	84.0	83.9	84.4	85.7	87.0	87.9	87.9	88.5	87.9	88.5	89.7	90.4	87.2
2014	86.5	86.3	86.7	88.1	89.5	90.4	90.5	90.5	90.1	91.1	92.9	93.6	89.7
2015	91.4	91.0	91.4	92.9	94.3	95.1	95.2	94.8	94.3	95.2	96.5	97.5	94.1
2016	94.2	93.9	93.9	95.3	96.6	97.0	96.7	96.6	95.3	96.0	97.7	97.9	95.9
2017	95.0	94.7	95.0	96.2	97.1	97.5	97.2	96.9	95.7	96.6	97.9	97.5	96.4
Wholesale Trade													
2007	26.4	26.3	26.4	26.9	27.0	27.1	27.2	27.1	27.0	27.0	27.0	27.0	26.9
2008	26.6	26.6	26.7	26.8	27.0	27.1	26.8	26.9	26.7	26.4	26.2	26.0	26.7
2009	25.2	25.0	24.8	24.9	25.2	25.0	24.7	24.7	24.6	24.7	24.7	24.8	24.9
2010	24.3	24.3	24.4	24.6	24.8	24.9	25.0	25.0	24.6	24.6	24.7	24.8	24.7
2011	24.3	24.3	24.4	24.9	25.2	25.4	25.5	25.6	25.4	25.4	25.4	25.4	25.1
2012	25.1	25.1	25.3	25.8	26.2	26.3	26.5	26.4	26.3	26.6	26.6	26.7	26.1
2013	26.3	26.3	26.4	26.9	27.2	27.6	27.8	28.0	28.0	28.1	28.2	28.6	27.5
2014	27.2	27.4	27.5	28.3	28.7	29.0	29.1	29.0	28.7	28.7	29.0	29.1	28.5
2015	28.9	29.0	29.2	29.6	29.9	30.2	30.4	30.5	30.3	30.5	30.7	30.9	30.0
2016	30.8	30.8	30.8	31.0	31.3	31.3	31.5	31.4	31.0	31.1	31.4	31.2	31.1
2017	30.7	30.9	31.2	31.5	31.8	31.9	31.9	31.7	31.3	31.3	31.6	31.5	31.4
Retail Trade													
2007	49.2	48.3	48.3	48.6	49.4	49.6	49.4	49.4	49.2	49.6	50.7	51.1	49.4
2008	48.8	48.0	48.2	47.7	48.5	48.6	47.9	47.8	47.2	47.1	48.1	48.2	48.0
2009	45.6	44.9	44.7	45.4	45.9	46.0	45.4	45.2	45.0	45.5	46.2	46.3	45.5
2010	44.1	43.5	43.4	44.0	44.6	44.9	44.4	44.6	44.0	45.0	46.0	46.1	44.6
2011	43.8	43.4	43.3	44.3	44.8	44.9	44.8	44.8	44.5	44.8	46.0	46.3	44.6
2012	44.0	43.3	43.7	44.5	45.2	45.2	45.0	45.2	44.9	45.4	46.9	46.8	45.0
2013	44.8	44.6	45.0	45.1	46.0	46.4	46.5	46.7	46.3	46.7	47.8	48.2	46.2
2014	45.8	45.5	45.7	46.2	47.1	47.5	47.5	47.6	47.3	48.3	49.6	49.8	47.3
2015	48.0	47.6	47.8	48.6	49.6	49.9	49.6	49.4	49.0	49.6	50.6	51.1	49.2
2016	48.7	48.6	48.5	49.4	50.3	50.5	50.1	50.1	49.3	49.8	51.0	51.1	49.8
2017	49.2	48.9	48.8	49.5	49.9	50.0	49.7	49.7	49.0	49.9	50.8	50.5	49.7
Transportation and Utilities													
2007	13.1	13.1	13.2	13.3	13.5	13.7	13.6	13.5	13.5	13.4	13.5	13.4	13.4
2008	12.9	12.8	12.8	13.0	13.2	13.3	13.0	13.0	12.8	12.9	12.6	12.6	12.9
2009	12.0	11.8	11.7	12.0	12.2	12.3	11.9	11.9	11.8	11.9	11.7	11.7	11.9
2010	11.6	11.5	11.5	11.6	11.7	11.9	11.8	11.7	11.9	12.0	12.1	12.0	11.8
2011	11.7	11.7	11.8	12.1	12.1	12.2	12.3	12.2	12.3	12.3	12.3	12.4	12.1
2012	12.0	12.1	12.1	12.4	12.5	12.6	12.5	12.6	12.6	12.7	12.8	13.1	12.5
2013	12.9	13.0	13.0	13.7	13.8	13.9	13.6	13.8	13.6	13.7	13.7	13.6	13.5
2014	13.5	13.4	13.5	13.6	13.7	13.9	13.9	13.9	14.1	14.1	14.3	14.7	13.9
2015	14.5	14.4	14.4	14.7	14.8	15.0	15.2	14.9	15.0	15.1	15.2	15.5	14.9
2016	14.7	14.5	14.6	14.9	15.0	15.2	15.1	15.1	15.0	15.1	15.3	15.6	15.0
2017	15.1	14.9	15.0	15.2	15.4	15.6	15.6	15.5	15.4	15.4	15.5	15.5	15.3

Employment by Industry: Grand Rapids-Wyoming, MI, Selected Years, 2007–2017—*Continued*

(Numbers in thousands, not seasonally adjusted)

Industry and year	January	February	March	April	May	June	July	August	September	October	November	December	Annual average
Information													
2007	6.4	6.4	6.3	6.3	6.4	6.4	6.2	6.2	6.0	5.9	6.0	6.0	6.2
2008	6.0	5.9	5.7	5.8	5.9	5.9	5.9	5.9	5.8	5.8	5.8	5.8	5.9
2009	5.6	5.6	5.5	5.4	5.5	5.5	5.4	5.3	5.2	5.2	5.2	5.2	5.4
2010	5.2	5.1	5.1	5.2	5.3	5.4	5.3	5.4	5.3	5.1	5.1	5.1	5.2
2011	5.1	5.1	5.1	5.0	5.1	5.1	5.1	5.1	5.0	5.1	5.1	5.1	5.1
2012	5.1	5.0	5.0	5.0	5.1	5.1	5.2	5.2	5.1	5.1	5.1	5.1	5.1
2013	5.2	5.2	5.2	5.2	5.3	5.3	5.3	5.3	5.2	5.2	5.2	5.3	5.2
2014	5.3	5.2	5.3	5.4	5.4	5.5	5.6	5.5	5.4	5.4	5.4	5.4	5.4
2015	5.2	5.2	5.2	5.1	5.2	5.2	5.2	5.1	5.1	5.1	5.1	5.2	5.2
2016	5.1	5.1	5.1	5.3	5.4	5.4	5.4	5.4	5.3	5.3	5.4	5.5	5.3
2017	5.6	5.6	5.7	5.6	5.7	5.8	5.7	5.6	5.6	5.4	5.4	5.5	5.6
Financial Activities													
2007	22.6	22.6	22.6	23.0	23.2	23.1	23.1	22.6	22.4	22.7	22.5	22.5	22.7
2008	22.5	22.6	22.4	22.6	22.7	22.3	22.0	22.1	21.8	21.9	21.8	21.6	22.2
2009	21.1	21.2	20.9	21.4	21.4	21.4	21.2	21.3	20.7	20.9	20.8	20.7	21.1
2010	20.7	20.8	20.6	20.7	21.1	21.1	21.4	21.4	21.6	21.8	21.9	22.2	21.3
2011	21.7	21.9	21.7	22.1	22.2	22.3	22.6	22.8	22.8	22.8	23.1	23.3	22.4
2012	22.8	22.9	23.0	23.2	23.4	23.4	23.6	23.3	23.3	23.7	23.8	23.7	23.3
2013	24.0	24.2	24.2	24.3	24.5	24.6	24.4	24.4	24.4	24.3	24.4	24.3	24.3
2014	24.6	24.3	24.3	24.5	24.7	24.8	24.9	25.1	25.0	24.7	24.8	24.9	24.7
2015	24.8	24.4	24.4	24.4	24.9	24.6	24.9	25.0	24.8	24.9	25.0	25.3	24.8
2016	25.4	25.0	25.1	25.5	25.8	25.7	25.8	25.8	25.6	25.7	25.7	25.9	25.6
2017	26.1	25.9	26.0	26.0	26.3	26.6	26.3	26.0	26.0	26.0	25.5	25.9	26.1
Professional and Business Services													
2007	64.6	65.7	67.0	66.9	68.7	70.0	68.8	70.9	70.0	68.7	69.3	69.6	68.4
2008	67.1	67.3	67.1	67.3	68.4	68.0	67.6	68.3	67.6	67.9	67.4	66.1	67.5
2009	58.6	58.7	58.7	58.7	59.6	58.4	55.0	56.4	58.7	60.6	61.9	62.0	58.9
2010	57.5	59.4	59.2	62.0	63.9	64.8	62.8	64.9	68.3	68.7	69.3	68.2	64.1
2011	65.2	66.2	67.1	69.2	71.1	70.6	70.6	71.5	73.3	71.8	71.9	72.2	70.1
2012	71.8	72.2	72.8	74.7	75.6	75.6	72.8	73.5	74.5	74.8	74.7	74.1	73.9
2013	73.2	73.8	73.8	74.4	75.7	75.3	74.1	75.8	76.6	77.1	77.8	78.5	75.5
2014	76.1	76.1	75.8	77.7	80.6	79.4	72.7	74.0	74.4	76.1	76.1	76.5	76.3
2015	74.0	74.2	74.2	75.3	77.5	76.7	74.5	74.3	76.1	78.0	78.1	78.0	75.9
2016	77.0	76.8	77.5	76.5	77.2	78.1	75.6	76.4	78.8	79.5	79.4	79.3	77.7
2017	77.8	77.7	78.3	78.3	80.2	79.5	75.8	76.2	78.3	79.7	80.9	80.9	78.6
Education and Health Services													
2007	67.8	69.2	69.5	69.9	69.8	68.2	67.0	67.4	69.6	70.5	71.3	71.3	69.3
2008	69.6	70.9	71.3	71.9	72.3	70.8	69.9	69.9	71.5	72.8	73.9	73.2	71.5
2009	71.2	72.5	72.4	73.9	73.7	71.6	70.8	71.1	72.8	74.7	75.4	75.0	72.9
2010	73.2	74.2	74.3	74.2	74.1	72.6	72.5	72.6	73.3	74.5	75.1	74.5	73.8
2011	73.8	74.3	74.7	75.0	74.8	73.3	73.5	73.6	75.8	77.0	77.7	77.3	75.1
2012	75.8	77.1	77.7	78.1	78.1	76.9	76.5	77.1	79.1	80.1	80.9	80.8	78.2
2013	78.6	79.9	80.7	79.9	79.6	79.0	78.8	79.6	81.2	81.5	82.7	82.5	80.3
2014	81.4	82.7	83.2	82.1	82.4	81.6	80.6	81.3	83.3	83.4	84.3	84.9	82.6
2015	83.5	84.7	85.4	85.1	85.2	84.5	82.9	83.0	86.0	86.5	87.5	87.8	85.2
2016	85.9	87.2	87.6	87.5	88.0	87.0	86.0	86.7	88.4	88.6	89.2	89.9	87.7
2017	88.4	89.4	90.0	89.7	90.1	89.3	88.4	89.3	90.8	91.4	92.2	92.3	90.1
Leisure and Hospitality													
2007	38.4	38.8	39.2	39.7	41.9	42.4	41.7	41.9	41.7	40.8	40.1	40.3	40.6
2008	37.8	37.9	38.4	39.8	42.4	42.7	41.8	41.9	41.0	39.1	38.1	38.3	39.9
2009	36.2	36.4	36.7	38.0	40.3	40.9	40.4	40.3	40.0	38.8	38.2	38.2	38.7
2010	36.9	37.0	37.6	38.9	40.9	41.5	41.0	41.2	41.0	39.4	38.4	38.6	39.4
2011	37.5	37.5	37.9	39.1	41.1	41.7	41.4	41.6	41.3	40.2	39.8	40.0	39.9
2012	39.6	39.7	40.4	41.5	43.2	44.1	43.6	44.1	43.9	43.0	42.4	42.6	42.3
2013	41.3	41.2	41.7	42.3	45.0	45.9	45.7	46.0	45.1	44.3	43.3	43.6	43.8
2014	41.9	41.8	42.6	42.9	45.6	46.6	46.2	46.7	45.7	45.0	44.4	44.9	44.5
2015	43.4	43.8	44.5	45.1	47.6	48.6	48.6	48.6	48.1	47.0	46.5	46.6	46.5
2016	44.8	45.4	45.9	46.6	48.9	49.8	49.6	49.8	48.6	47.7	47.2	47.0	47.6
2017	46.0	46.3	46.7	47.6	49.8	50.7	50.4	50.8	49.0	48.4	47.9	48.2	48.5

Employment by Industry: Grand Rapids-Wyoming, MI, Selected Years, 2007–2017—*Continued*

(Numbers in thousands, not seasonally adjusted)

Industry and year	January	February	March	April	May	June	July	August	September	October	November	December	Annual average
Other Services													
2007	20.4	20.3	20.6	20.7	20.9	21.1	21.1	21.0	20.8	20.8	20.9	21.1	20.8
2008	20.6	20.6	20.7	21.3	21.4	21.7	21.5	21.5	21.4	21.5	21.5	21.6	21.3
2009	21.2	21.3	21.4	22.0	21.9	22.1	22.0	21.8	21.6	21.6	21.5	21.5	21.7
2010	21.2	21.1	21.2	21.2	21.1	21.3	21.1	21.0	20.7	20.8	20.7	20.8	21.0
2011	20.4	20.2	20.2	20.1	20.3	20.2	20.1	20.3	20.0	19.9	19.8	19.9	20.1
2012	19.3	19.4	19.6	20.0	20.2	20.6	20.5	20.5	20.5	20.5	20.6	20.8	20.2
2013	20.9	20.8	20.9	20.7	20.9	21.1	21.3	21.3	21.2	21.1	21.1	21.2	21.0
2014	21.2	21.3	21.4	21.1	21.4	21.6	21.4	21.2	21.2	21.3	21.2	21.3	21.3
2015	21.1	21.1	21.3	21.4	21.5	21.9	21.8	21.5	21.7	21.5	21.5	21.8	21.5
2016	21.7	21.7	21.8	22.1	22.3	22.7	22.6	22.4	22.1	22.3	22.1	22.1	22.2
2017	22.0	22.0	22.2	22.3	22.4	22.7	22.6	22.5	22.4	22.4	22.3	22.4	22.4
Government													
2007	48.9	50.7	50.8	50.5	49.0	47.9	42.4	43.4	48.8	49.9	49.7	48.3	48.4
2008	49.0	50.1	50.3	50.2	49.0	48.3	42.5	44.1	48.9	50.3	50.0	49.9	48.6
2009	48.2	49.9	50.1	50.7	49.3	47.4	42.4	42.5	49.2	50.5	50.3	49.0	48.3
2010	47.8	49.8	49.6	49.8	49.2	47.7	42.8	42.3	48.6	50.0	50.4	49.1	48.1
2011	48.1	48.9	49.4	49.7	47.3	46.5	42.5	41.8	47.4	48.4	49.0	48.1	47.3
2012	48.1	48.5	48.6	48.2	47.0	44.5	41.3	41.4	47.6	48.5	48.8	47.6	46.7
2013	47.0	48.1	47.8	47.4	46.4	44.8	40.0	40.5	46.6	47.5	47.1	47.0	45.9
2014	46.7	47.5	47.6	47.2	45.9	44.9	40.0	40.3	46.5	48.0	48.1	47.4	45.8
2015	46.8	47.7	47.6	47.6	46.0	44.4	40.8	40.3	46.5	47.9	47.8	47.7	45.9
2016	46.9	47.8	47.9	47.7	46.4	45.8	41.0	41.2	47.0	48.3	48.6	48.4	46.4
2017	47.3	48.4	48.3	47.9	46.8	46.4	41.0	41.7	47.8	49.1	48.8	48.9	46.9

Employment by Industry: Tucson, AZ, Selected Years, 2007–2017

(Numbers in thousands, not seasonally adjusted)

Industry and year	January	February	March	April	May	June	July	August	September	October	November	December	Annual average
Total Nonfarm													
2007	381.1	387.9	389.1	387.4	387.5	379.3	376.1	379.6	386.6	388.7	391.7	392.0	385.6
2008	379.2	385.2	385.1	385.6	384.5	376.1	375.1	379.6	382.4	381.6	381.3	380.6	381.4
2009	369.5	369.6	367.1	365.4	363.1	353.3	351.1	355.6	359.2	359.2	361.0	361.9	361.3
2010	352.4	356.3	355.7	357.9	358.3	346.1	342.4	348.6	351.4	354.2	357.3	359.2	353.3
2011	351.3	355.4	355.9	357.1	356.8	344.7	340.2	351.6	356.0	359.1	362.9	362.2	354.4
2012	357.4	361.2	362.6	362.7	362.2	352.3	344.4	355.3	360.9	363.6	367.2	368.1	359.8
2013	360.4	364.4	365.8	367.4	366.5	353.0	350.4	357.9	365.1	366.2	370.1	370.6	363.2
2014	363.8	366.8	366.8	368.0	366.3	356.6	353.6	357.6	366.1	369.5	373.1	374.0	365.2
2015	367.3	370.1	370.6	370.6	367.9	355.7	350.9	360.8	368.7	371.7	375.0	376.2	367.1
2016	369.3	372.3	373.3	375.7	373.0	360.5	358.3	364.2	374.5	377.9	380.7	382.2	371.8
2017	376.6	380.0	380.4	379.6	378.1	367.4	364.9	370.1	379.9	381.7	382.7	385.4	377.2
Total Private													
2007	304.3	307.8	309.3	307.8	308.8	307.8	305.2	306.2	306.0	308.0	310.4	310.9	307.7
2008	302.5	303.8	304.4	303.9	302.7	301.3	300.1	301.6	301.2	299.6	298.7	298.4	301.5
2009	289.9	288.0	286.1	283.6	282.2	280.1	278.5	279.5	279.1	278.5	280.1	281.3	282.2
2010	274.3	275.6	276.3	277.1	276.0	274.5	272.1	273.2	272.1	274.7	276.4	279.0	275.1
2011	274.3	275.6	276.5	277.5	277.7	276.2	274.3	276.7	277.2	279.3	282.6	283.9	277.7
2012	279.9	281.2	282.7	282.6	282.2	281.0	277.8	280.1	280.9	283.2	286.5	287.7	282.2
2013	282.5	284.0	285.5	286.8	286.6	284.1	282.6	285.4	286.1	286.6	290.3	290.9	286.0
2014	285.4	286.9	287.3	288.5	287.9	286.0	283.6	286.4	287.7	290.2	293.3	294.9	288.2
2015	289.7	291.0	291.4	291.3	290.0	287.9	287.0	289.5	289.8	292.4	294.5	296.1	290.9
2016	291.2	292.8	293.3	296.1	295.0	292.7	291.9	294.5	295.7	298.5	300.9	302.6	295.4
2017	299.2	300.6	300.7	299.9	299.3	298.6	296.3	298.7	300.0	300.8	301.8	304.5	300.0
Goods Producing													
2007	54.9	56.4	56.0	55.5	55.9	56.5	56.4	56.5	55.9	55.2	54.9	54.3	55.7
2008	53.6	53.3	53.2	52.5	52.4	52.8	52.6	52.4	51.6	50.4	49.3	48.3	51.9
2009	46.2	45.1	44.2	43.5	43.4	43.6	43.4	42.9	42.5	42.0	41.7	41.6	43.3
2010	40.6	40.5	40.6	40.9	41.0	41.1	41.0	41.1	40.6	40.6	40.3	40.4	40.7
2011	39.9	39.7	39.9	39.7	39.8	40.0	39.9	39.9	39.7	39.5	39.4	39.2	39.7
2012	38.9	38.8	39.1	39.1	39.3	40.0	40.1	40.2	40.0	40.2	40.5	40.7	39.7
2013	40.0	40.1	40.4	40.7	40.8	41.3	41.5	41.4	40.9	40.4	40.2	40.0	40.6
2014	39.6	39.5	39.5	39.4	39.4	39.6	39.8	40.2	39.9	39.8	39.4	39.3	39.6
2015	38.7	38.8	38.8	39.3	39.2	39.6	39.9	39.9	39.4	39.8	39.7	39.8	39.4
2016	39.2	39.4	39.3	39.6	39.7	40.0	40.3	40.4	40.1	40.4	40.5	40.6	40.0
2017	40.5	41.2	41.1	41.1	41.4	41.9	42.2	42.3	42.3	42.3	42.2	42.7	41.8
Service-Providing													
2007	326.2	331.5	333.1	331.9	331.6	322.8	319.7	323.1	330.7	333.5	336.8	337.7	329.9
2008	325.6	331.9	331.9	333.1	332.1	323.3	322.5	327.2	330.8	331.2	332.0	332.3	329.5
2009	323.3	324.5	322.9	321.9	319.7	309.7	307.7	312.7	316.7	317.2	319.3	320.3	318.0
2010	311.8	315.8	315.1	317.0	317.3	305.0	301.4	307.5	310.8	313.6	317.0	318.8	312.6
2011	311.4	315.7	316.0	317.4	317.0	304.7	300.3	311.7	316.3	319.6	323.5	323.0	314.7
2012	318.5	322.4	323.5	323.6	322.9	312.3	304.3	315.1	320.9	323.4	326.7	327.4	320.1
2013	320.4	324.3	325.4	326.7	325.7	311.7	308.9	316.5	324.2	325.8	329.9	330.6	322.5
2014	324.2	327.3	327.3	328.6	326.9	317.0	313.8	317.4	326.2	329.7	333.7	334.7	325.6
2015	328.6	331.3	331.8	331.3	328.7	316.1	311.0	320.9	329.3	331.9	335.3	336.4	327.7
2016	330.1	332.9	334.0	336.1	333.3	320.5	318.0	323.8	334.4	337.5	340.2	341.6	331.9
2017	336.1	338.8	339.3	338.5	336.7	325.5	322.7	327.8	337.6	339.4	340.5	342.7	335.5
Mining, Logging, and Construction													
2007	28.9	28.7	28.7	28.3	28.7	29.0	28.8	28.8	28.2	27.7	27.3	26.8	28.3
2008	26.0	25.8	25.8	25.3	25.2	25.4	25.4	25.3	24.7	23.8	22.8	22.0	24.8
2009	20.6	19.7	19.1	18.4	18.4	18.5	18.3	18.0	17.8	17.5	17.3	17.2	18.4
2010	16.4	16.3	16.5	16.8	16.9	17.2	17.1	17.3	17.0	17.2	17.0	17.0	16.9
2011	16.6	16.5	16.7	16.5	16.5	16.7	16.6	16.5	16.3	16.3	16.2	16.0	16.5
2012	15.7	15.5	15.8	15.9	16.1	16.7	16.8	16.9	16.8	17.0	17.3	17.5	16.5
2013	17.1	17.1	17.5	17.7	17.8	18.2	18.2	18.1	17.8	17.5	17.4	17.4	17.7
2014	17.0	17.0	17.0	17.0	16.9	17.0	17.1	17.6	17.4	17.5	17.1	16.8	17.1
2015	16.4	16.5	16.5	16.9	16.9	17.0	17.2	17.2	16.8	17.0	16.9	16.9	16.9
2016	16.4	16.5	16.4	16.5	16.6	16.7	16.6	16.6	16.6	16.8	16.9	16.9	16.6
2017	16.8	16.9	17.1	17.2	17.4	17.6	17.7	17.8	17.7	18.0	18.0	18.1	17.5

Employment by Industry: Tucson, AZ, Selected Years, 2007–2017—*Continued*

(Numbers in thousands, not seasonally adjusted)

Industry and year	January	February	March	April	May	June	July	August	September	October	November	December	Annual average
Manufacturing													
2007	26.0	27.7	27.3	27.2	27.2	27.5	27.6	27.7	27.7	27.5	27.6	27.5	27.4
2008	27.6	27.5	27.4	27.2	27.2	27.4	27.2	27.1	26.9	26.6	26.5	26.3	27.1
2009	25.6	25.4	25.1	25.1	25.0	25.1	25.1	24.9	24.7	24.5	24.4	24.4	24.9
2010	24.2	24.2	24.1	24.1	24.1	23.9	23.9	23.8	23.6	23.4	23.3	23.4	23.8
2011	23.3	23.2	23.2	23.2	23.3	23.3	23.3	23.4	23.4	23.2	23.2	23.2	23.3
2012	23.2	23.3	23.3	23.2	23.2	23.3	23.3	23.3	23.2	23.2	23.2	23.2	23.2
2013	22.9	23.0	22.9	23.0	23.0	23.1	23.3	23.3	23.1	22.9	22.8	22.6	23.0
2014	22.6	22.5	22.5	22.4	22.5	22.6	22.7	22.6	22.5	22.3	22.3	22.5	22.5
2015	22.3	22.3	22.3	22.4	22.3	22.6	22.7	22.7	22.6	22.8	22.8	22.9	22.6
2016	22.8	22.9	22.9	23.1	23.1	23.3	23.7	23.8	23.5	23.6	23.6	23.7	23.3
2017	23.7	24.3	24.0	23.9	24.0	24.3	24.5	24.5	24.6	24.3	24.2	24.6	24.2
Trade, Transportation, and Utilities													
2007	64.4	63.7	64.5	64.2	64.6	64.2	64.1	64.5	64.4	64.9	66.5	67.1	64.8
2008	64.0	63.3	63.4	62.6	62.8	62.8	62.5	63.1	62.7	62.9	63.3	63.5	63.1
2009	60.9	59.6	59.0	58.4	58.2	57.7	57.6	58.0	57.8	57.6	58.5	59.4	58.6
2010	57.3	57.0	56.9	56.9	57.0	56.9	56.7	57.0	56.4	56.7	58.3	59.0	57.2
2011	57.5	57.1	57.1	57.3	57.6	57.5	57.2	58.1	57.4	58.1	60.0	60.5	58.0
2012	58.4	57.5	57.5	57.4	57.4	57.4	56.9	57.5	57.7	58.0	59.9	60.6	58.0
2013	58.5	57.9	58.1	58.2	58.6	58.4	58.5	59.5	59.5	59.6	61.5	62.6	59.2
2014	60.3	59.9	60.1	60.1	60.1	59.9	59.6	60.3	60.2	60.6	62.4	63.3	60.6
2015	60.7	59.8	59.8	59.6	59.8	59.4	59.5	60.4	60.5	60.8	62.3	62.8	60.5
2016	60.6	59.9	59.9	60.2	60.1	59.6	59.7	60.1	59.8	60.5	62.2	63.0	60.5
2017	61.4	61.1	60.7	60.9	60.8	60.6	60.3	60.9	60.8	60.5	62.0	62.4	61.0
Wholesale Trade													
2007	9.9	9.9	10.1	10.0	10.1	10.2	10.1	10.2	10.2	10.2	10.2	10.2	10.1
2008	10.0	10.0	10.1	10.0	10.0	10.0	9.9	10.0	10.0	9.9	9.7	9.6	9.9
2009	9.3	9.1	8.8	8.8	8.7	8.7	8.7	8.7	8.7	8.7	8.6	8.6	8.8
2010	8.3	8.3	8.2	8.3	8.3	8.2	8.2	8.1	8.0	7.9	8.0	8.0	8.2
2011	7.9	8.0	8.0	7.9	8.0	7.9	8.0	7.9	8.0	8.0	8.0	8.0	8.0
2012	7.8	7.8	7.9	7.9	8.0	8.0	8.0	8.0	8.1	8.0	8.0	8.1	8.0
2013	7.9	7.9	7.9	7.9	7.9	7.9	7.8	7.9	8.0	8.0	7.9	8.0	7.9
2014	7.8	7.8	7.9	7.9	7.9	7.9	7.9	7.8	7.9	7.8	7.8	7.8	7.9
2015	7.7	7.7	7.7	7.7	7.8	7.8	7.8	7.8	7.8	7.8	7.7	7.8	7.8
2016	7.7	7.8	7.7	7.7	7.8	7.7	7.8	7.8	7.7	7.8	7.8	7.8	7.8
2017	7.7	7.8	7.7	7.7	7.7	7.7	7.7	7.7	7.7	7.6	7.6	7.6	7.7
Retail Trade													
2007	45.2	44.7	45.1	45.0	45.0	44.7	44.7	44.8	44.8	45.4	46.9	47.2	45.3
2008	44.7	44.0	44.1	43.5	43.7	43.7	43.5	43.8	43.4	43.7	44.3	44.3	43.9
2009	42.3	41.2	40.9	40.6	40.6	40.2	40.2	40.5	40.3	40.0	41.1	41.7	40.8
2010	40.1	39.7	39.6	39.6	39.6	39.6	39.3	39.7	39.2	39.5	41.0	41.4	39.9
2011	39.9	39.4	39.4	39.6	39.7	39.7	39.4	40.2	39.4	40.1	41.9	42.2	40.1
2012	40.7	39.7	39.7	39.6	39.6	39.6	39.2	39.8	39.9	40.5	42.4	42.7	40.3
2013	41.2	40.6	40.9	41.1	41.3	41.2	41.2	41.9	41.8	41.9	43.8	44.5	41.8
2014	42.8	42.3	42.4	42.5	42.4	42.2	42.0	42.7	42.4	42.8	44.5	45.1	42.8
2015	42.8	41.9	41.9	41.8	41.8	41.5	41.6	42.4	42.3	42.6	43.9	44.2	42.4
2016	42.6	42.1	42.2	42.4	42.2	41.8	41.7	42.1	41.8	42.2	43.8	44.1	42.4
2017	42.9	42.3	42.2	42.4	42.2	42.0	41.7	42.2	41.9	41.7	43.1	43.2	42.3
Transportation and Utilities													
2007	9.3	9.1	9.3	9.2	9.5	9.3	9.3	9.5	9.4	9.3	9.4	9.7	9.4
2008	9.3	9.3	9.2	9.1	9.1	9.1	9.1	9.3	9.3	9.3	9.3	9.6	9.3
2009	9.3	9.3	9.3	9.0	8.9	8.8	8.7	8.8	8.8	8.9	8.8	9.1	9.0
2010	8.9	9.0	9.1	9.0	9.1	9.1	9.2	9.2	9.2	9.3	9.3	9.6	9.2
2011	9.7	9.7	9.7	9.8	9.9	9.9	9.8	10.0	10.0	10.0	10.1	10.3	9.9
2012	9.9	10.0	9.9	9.9	9.8	9.8	9.7	9.7	9.7	9.5	9.5	9.8	9.8
2013	9.4	9.4	9.3	9.2	9.4	9.3	9.5	9.7	9.7	9.7	9.8	10.1	9.5
2014	9.7	9.8	9.8	9.7	9.8	9.8	9.7	9.8	9.9	10.0	10.1	10.4	9.9
2015	10.2	10.2	10.2	10.1	10.2	10.1	10.1	10.2	10.4	10.4	10.7	10.8	10.3
2016	10.3	10.0	10.0	10.1	10.1	10.1	10.2	10.2	10.3	10.5	10.6	11.1	10.3
2017	10.8	11.0	10.8	10.8	10.9	10.9	10.9	11.0	11.2	11.2	11.3	11.6	11.0

Employment by Industry: Tucson, AZ, Selected Years, 2007–2017—*Continued*

(Numbers in thousands, not seasonally adjusted)

Industry and year	January	February	March	April	May	June	July	August	September	October	November	December	Annual average
Information													
2007	6.5	6.4	6.4	6.3	6.3	6.0	5.9	5.9	5.9	6.0	6.0	5.9	6.1
2008	5.9	5.7	5.6	5.5	5.5	5.4	5.4	5.3	5.3	5.2	5.3	5.4	5.5
2009	5.2	5.3	5.1	5.1	5.0	4.8	4.8	4.7	4.7	4.6	4.6	4.7	4.9
2010	4.7	4.7	4.7	4.6	4.6	4.5	4.5	4.4	4.4	4.4	4.4	4.4	4.5
2011	4.3	4.5	4.3	4.3	4.4	4.3	4.4	4.5	4.4	4.4	4.5	4.5	4.4
2012	4.4	4.6	4.5	4.5	4.6	4.4	4.4	4.5	4.3	4.4	4.5	4.4	4.5
2013	4.5	4.6	4.4	4.5	4.8	4.5	4.5	4.7	4.4	4.4	4.6	4.5	4.5
2014	4.5	4.6	4.4	4.4	4.5	4.4	4.4	4.4	4.3	4.4	4.5	4.5	4.4
2015	4.4	4.6	4.4	4.5	4.4	4.4	4.4	4.6	4.4	4.5	4.8	4.8	4.5
2016	4.8	5.0	5.0	5.1	5.1	5.0	5.0	5.1	5.1	5.1	5.3	5.3	5.1
2017	5.5	5.5	5.5	5.4	5.4	5.3	5.2	5.4	5.1	5.2	5.3	5.3	5.3
Financial Activities													
2007	18.2	18.3	18.4	18.5	18.6	18.6	18.6	17.5	17.2	17.2	17.2	17.5	18.0
2008	16.6	16.7	16.8	17.0	16.9	17.1	17.1	17.1	17.0	16.6	16.6	16.9	16.9
2009	16.6	16.7	16.7	16.9	17.0	17.0	17.5	17.5	17.3	17.4	17.4	17.6	17.1
2010	17.5	17.6	17.3	17.1	17.2	17.3	17.2	17.2	17.0	17.1	17.1	17.3	17.2
2011	17.0	17.0	17.0	16.9	16.8	16.8	16.9	16.8	16.8	16.8	16.8	17.0	16.9
2012	16.8	16.9	16.6	16.6	16.7	16.8	16.8	16.9	16.9	17.1	17.1	17.3	16.9
2013	17.0	17.1	17.2	17.0	17.1	17.3	17.2	17.2	17.2	17.5	17.5	17.7	17.3
2014	17.4	17.4	17.5	17.5	17.5	17.5	17.6	17.4	17.3	17.5	17.6	17.8	17.5
2015	17.3	17.4	17.4	17.3	17.3	17.2	17.1	17.1	17.0	17.2	17.2	17.2	17.2
2016	17.1	17.1	17.1	17.0	17.0	17.1	17.1	17.2	17.3	17.4	17.5	17.6	17.2
2017	17.4	17.4	17.5	17.3	17.4	17.7	17.6	17.6	17.6	17.7	17.5	17.8	17.5
Professional and Business Services													
2007	52.1	52.7	52.9	52.6	52.5	53.1	52.5	53.5	53.5	54.2	54.5	54.2	53.2
2008	52.4	52.6	52.9	52.9	52.0	52.5	52.2	52.5	52.2	51.2	50.6	50.8	52.0
2009	49.6	48.9	48.6	47.7	47.1	47.0	46.9	46.9	46.8	46.8	47.3	47.5	47.6
2010	46.3	46.6	46.9	46.7	45.7	45.7	45.6	45.4	45.2	46.3	46.3	47.3	46.2
2011	46.0	46.4	46.7	46.7	46.4	46.6	46.3	46.5	47.5	48.4	48.8	49.4	47.1
2012	48.2	48.7	49.3	49.1	48.7	48.7	48.4	48.4	48.6	49.4	49.8	49.8	48.9
2013	49.5	49.9	50.3	50.8	50.3	49.2	48.9	49.1	49.6	49.7	50.7	50.6	49.9
2014	49.6	49.6	49.4	49.7	49.7	49.6	48.9	49.4	50.4	50.9	51.5	51.7	50.0
2015	50.9	51.1	50.7	50.5	49.8	49.4	49.6	49.8	50.5	51.0	51.4	51.6	50.5
2016	50.1	50.5	50.3	50.8	50.4	50.1	50.2	50.8	51.7	52.1	52.1	52.7	51.0
2017	52.0	51.9	51.7	51.3	50.9	51.3	51.2	51.3	51.5	52.2	51.5	52.2	51.6
Education and Health Services													
2007	53.6	54.1	54.4	54.1	54.8	54.2	54.1	54.7	55.0	56.0	56.0	56.3	54.8
2008	55.1	55.7	56.1	57.1	57.2	56.7	56.8	57.7	58.2	58.5	58.9	58.9	57.2
2009	58.5	58.8	58.8	58.4	58.6	58.1	57.9	58.5	58.7	58.8	59.0	59.2	58.6
2010	58.0	58.3	58.4	58.6	58.6	58.0	57.4	58.2	58.3	58.8	58.8	59.2	58.4
2011	58.7	59.2	59.1	59.8	59.9	59.4	59.2	60.1	60.4	60.5	60.9	61.2	59.9
2012	61.1	61.2	61.5	61.3	61.2	60.7	59.7	60.4	60.8	61.2	61.4	61.7	61.0
2013	60.6	61.1	61.3	61.5	61.4	60.8	61.0	61.9	62.1	62.2	62.6	62.6	61.6
2014	60.9	61.2	61.4	61.7	61.6	61.0	60.3	61.1	61.3	62.1	62.2	62.7	61.5
2015	61.9	62.0	62.3	62.4	62.6	61.9	62.0	62.9	63.0	63.8	63.7	64.2	62.7
2016	63.9	64.3	64.5	64.8	64.8	64.3	63.8	64.8	64.8	65.3	65.5	65.8	64.7
2017	65.1	65.5	65.6	65.3	65.2	64.7	64.0	64.8	65.2	65.3	65.6	65.6	65.2
Leisure and Hospitality													
2007	39.8	41.1	41.5	41.5	41.0	39.9	38.6	38.7	39.3	39.6	40.3	40.7	40.2
2008	40.3	41.7	41.6	41.3	41.0	39.9	38.8	39.0	39.7	40.4	40.4	40.6	40.4
2009	39.2	39.9	39.9	40.0	39.5	38.5	37.0	37.7	38.1	38.1	38.5	38.2	38.7
2010	37.4	38.4	38.9	39.5	39.1	38.0	36.8	37.1	37.5	38.0	38.4	38.7	38.2
2011	38.4	39.0	39.7	40.1	40.1	39.0	37.8	38.4	38.7	39.1	39.6	39.6	39.1
2012	39.7	40.9	41.4	41.8	41.4	40.0	38.6	39.3	39.8	40.0	40.4	40.4	40.3
2013	39.9	40.7	41.0	41.2	40.7	39.7	38.2	38.9	39.8	40.1	40.4	40.3	40.1
2014	40.6	42.1	42.3	43.1	42.4	41.1	40.0	40.6	41.3	41.7	42.3	42.1	41.6
2015	42.6	43.9	44.3	44.3	43.5	42.6	41.4	41.9	42.3	42.5	42.7	43.1	42.9
2016	42.6	43.7	44.2	45.6	44.9	43.5	42.7	43.1	43.9	44.7	44.9	44.7	44.0
2017	44.5	45.2	45.6	45.4	45.0	43.8	42.8	43.4	44.5	44.7	44.7	45.5	44.6

Employment by Industry: Tucson, AZ, Selected Years, 2007–2017—*Continued*

(Numbers in thousands, not seasonally adjusted)

Industry and year	January	February	March	April	May	June	July	August	September	October	November	December	Annual average
Other Services													
2007	14.8	15.1	15.2	15.1	15.1	15.3	15.0	14.9	14.8	14.9	15.0	14.9	15.0
2008	14.6	14.8	14.8	15.0	14.9	14.9	14.7	14.5	14.5	14.4	14.3	14.0	14.6
2009	13.7	13.7	13.8	13.6	13.4	13.4	13.4	13.3	13.2	13.2	13.1	13.1	13.4
2010	12.5	12.5	12.6	12.8	12.8	13.0	12.9	12.8	12.7	12.8	12.8	12.7	12.7
2011	12.5	12.7	12.7	12.7	12.7	12.6	12.6	12.4	12.3	12.5	12.6	12.5	12.6
2012	12.4	12.6	12.8	12.8	12.9	13.0	12.9	12.9	12.8	12.9	12.9	12.8	12.8
2013	12.5	12.6	12.8	12.9	12.9	12.9	12.8	12.7	12.6	12.7	12.8	12.6	12.7
2014	12.5	12.6	12.7	12.6	12.7	12.9	13.0	13.0	13.0	13.2	13.4	13.5	12.9
2015	13.2	13.4	13.7	13.4	13.4	13.4	13.1	12.9	12.7	12.8	12.7	12.6	13.1
2016	12.9	12.9	13.0	13.0	13.0	13.1	13.1	13.0	13.0	13.0	12.9	12.9	13.0
2017	12.8	12.8	13.0	13.2	13.2	13.3	13.0	13.0	13.0	12.9	13.0	13.0	13.0
Government													
2007	76.8	80.1	79.8	79.6	78.7	71.5	70.9	73.4	80.6	80.7	81.3	81.1	77.9
2008	76.7	81.4	80.7	81.7	81.8	74.8	75.0	78.0	81.2	82.0	82.6	82.2	79.8
2009	79.6	81.6	81.0	81.8	80.9	73.2	72.6	76.1	80.1	80.7	80.9	80.6	79.1
2010	78.1	80.7	79.4	80.8	82.3	71.6	70.3	75.4	79.3	79.5	80.9	80.2	78.2
2011	77.0	79.8	79.4	79.6	79.1	68.5	65.9	74.9	78.8	79.8	80.3	78.3	76.8
2012	77.5	80.0	79.9	80.1	80.0	71.3	66.6	75.2	80.0	80.4	80.7	80.4	77.7
2013	77.9	80.4	80.3	80.6	79.9	68.9	67.8	72.5	79.0	79.6	79.8	79.7	77.2
2014	78.4	79.9	79.5	79.5	78.4	70.6	70.0	71.2	78.4	79.3	79.8	79.1	77.0
2015	77.6	79.1	79.2	79.3	77.9	67.8	63.9	71.3	78.9	79.3	80.5	80.1	76.2
2016	78.1	79.5	80.0	79.6	78.0	67.8	66.4	69.7	78.8	79.4	79.8	79.6	76.4
2017	77.4	79.4	79.7	79.7	78.8	68.8	68.6	71.4	79.9	80.9	80.9	80.9	77.2

Employment by Industry: Tulsa, OK, Selected Years, 2007–2017

(Numbers in thousands, not seasonally adjusted)

Industry and year	January	February	March	April	May	June	July	August	September	October	November	December	Annual average
Total Nonfarm													
2007	424.2	428.2	433.8	434.4	437.5	437.7	433.2	435.0	436.5	439.9	441.2	439.3	435.1
2008	435.1	438.6	441.5	441.5	444.5	442.1	438.1	439.7	442.2	441.9	441.5	441.0	440.6
2009	428.2	427.1	427.4	424.3	424.4	421.5	413.5	413.8	414.9	417.3	418.0	416.8	420.6
2010	406.6	408.1	411.3	415.0	417.8	416.4	410.1	409.3	412.0	417.3	418.9	419.5	413.5
2011	407.7	405.2	411.8	414.7	416.0	415.7	414.3	414.3	418.1	421.9	422.8	423.9	415.5
2012	414.3	418.0	420.6	424.6	427.1	426.8	421.7	422.8	426.0	431.5	434.5	435.0	425.2
2013	423.2	425.8	428.7	431.2	433.6	433.6	430.9	432.3	434.3	437.3	438.6	438.2	432.3
2014	431.7	434.2	436.3	438.5	441.2	440.7	438.4	439.1	441.5	446.9	448.7	449.8	440.6
2015	442.5	444.3	445.1	448.1	449.1	448.0	446.0	444.4	446.4	451.5	453.7	452.9	447.7
2016	442.7	444.5	445.5	447.0	446.8	445.1	442.5	442.2	445.9	448.0	450.5	451.0	446.0
2017	437.9	441.0	445.0	445.9	447.6	448.9	445.4	446.0	450.1	456.4	460.2	460.5	448.7
Total Private													
2007	370.7	373.3	378.4	378.9	381.6	384.7	384.0	385.3	382.2	383.8	385.3	383.7	381.0
2008	380.8	382.9	385.6	385.1	387.5	388.3	387.6	388.5	385.7	383.2	382.9	382.4	385.0
2009	372.4	369.8	369.5	365.7	365.3	366.5	363.0	361.1	357.1	357.1	357.7	356.9	363.5
2010	349.6	350.0	352.4	355.5	356.7	358.4	358.8	358.4	356.1	358.7	360.1	360.8	356.3
2011	351.6	348.4	354.6	357.5	359.1	360.8	362.6	362.6	363.0	364.1	364.9	365.9	359.6
2012	358.8	360.9	362.9	367.2	369.4	372.0	371.0	371.8	370.1	373.4	376.1	376.7	369.2
2013	367.0	368.0	370.6	373.1	375.6	377.6	378.0	379.5	377.7	378.3	379.1	378.8	375.3
2014	374.4	375.1	376.9	379.4	381.8	384.2	385.1	385.4	384.1	386.9	388.3	389.8	382.6
2015	384.8	384.9	385.8	388.3	389.4	391.1	392.4	390.6	388.3	390.8	392.6	392.0	389.3
2016	384.2	384.3	385.0	387.0	387.2	388.3	388.8	388.4	387.8	389.2	391.4	391.2	387.7
2017	381.1	382.4	385.7	386.7	388.3	392.2	391.7	392.3	391.7	395.5	399.1	399.2	390.5
Goods Producing													
2007	77.8	77.8	79.1	78.6	79.4	80.6	81.4	81.9	81.0	81.8	82.1	81.8	80.3
2008	81.9	82.2	82.9	82.8	83.8	84.2	84.5	84.5	84.0	82.9	82.6	82.9	83.3
2009	81.0	79.1	77.8	75.7	74.4	74.6	73.0	72.2	71.1	70.2	69.6	69.3	74.0
2010	68.0	68.1	68.5	68.9	69.4	70.5	71.2	70.9	70.7	71.6	72.0	72.6	70.2
2011	70.7	70.0	71.7	72.5	72.8	73.7	74.1	73.9	74.3	75.0	75.3	75.5	73.3
2012	74.4	74.8	75.4	76.4	77.2	77.7	77.9	78.3	78.2	80.4	80.8	80.6	77.7
2013	78.4	78.6	79.1	79.4	79.8	80.5	80.4	80.9	80.2	80.6	80.0	79.9	79.8
2014	79.6	80.1	80.0	79.9	80.4	80.9	81.8	82.0	81.9	82.9	82.8	82.9	81.3
2015	81.7	82.1	81.4	80.8	80.2	80.3	80.2	79.4	79.0	78.7	78.4	78.3	80.0
2016	76.7	76.7	76.0	75.5	75.4	75.7	75.4	75.2	75.1	74.3	74.4	74.6	75.4
2017	72.8	73.4	73.8	73.9	74.7	76.0	75.9	76.1	76.4	77.9	78.2	78.3	75.6
Service-Providing													
2007	346.4	350.4	354.7	355.8	358.1	357.1	351.8	353.1	355.5	358.1	359.1	357.5	354.8
2008	353.2	356.4	358.6	358.7	360.7	357.9	353.6	355.2	358.2	359.0	358.9	358.1	357.4
2009	347.2	348.0	349.6	348.6	350.0	346.9	340.5	341.6	343.8	347.1	348.4	347.5	346.6
2010	338.6	340.0	342.8	346.1	348.4	345.9	338.9	338.4	341.3	345.7	346.9	346.9	343.3
2011	337.0	335.2	340.1	342.2	343.2	342.0	340.2	340.4	343.8	346.9	347.5	348.4	342.2
2012	339.9	343.2	345.2	348.2	349.9	349.1	343.8	344.5	347.8	351.1	353.7	354.4	347.6
2013	344.8	347.2	349.6	351.8	353.8	353.1	350.5	351.4	354.1	356.7	358.6	358.3	352.5
2014	352.1	354.1	356.3	358.6	360.8	359.8	356.6	357.1	359.6	364.0	365.9	366.9	359.3
2015	360.8	362.2	363.7	367.3	368.9	367.7	365.8	365.0	367.4	372.8	375.3	374.6	367.6
2016	366.0	367.8	369.5	371.5	371.4	369.4	367.1	367.0	370.8	373.7	376.1	376.4	370.6
2017	365.1	367.6	371.2	372.0	372.9	372.9	369.5	369.9	373.7	378.5	382.0	382.2	373.1
Mining, Logging, and Construction													
2007	27.0	27.0	28.0	27.7	28.0	28.9	29.1	29.4	28.9	29.4	29.5	29.2	28.5
2008	29.1	29.3	29.8	29.9	30.3	30.7	31.1	31.0	30.7	30.2	29.9	29.8	30.2
2009	29.0	28.6	28.4	27.8	27.4	27.8	27.6	27.4	26.9	26.5	26.1	26.0	27.5
2010	25.3	25.4	25.7	25.9	26.2	26.8	27.2	27.0	27.0	27.5	27.6	27.8	26.6
2011	26.2	25.6	26.7	27.0	27.1	27.4	27.3	27.2	27.3	27.6	27.5	27.4	27.0
2012	26.4	26.4	26.7	27.1	27.5	27.6	27.9	28.1	28.1	29.7	30.3	29.7	28.0
2013	27.7	27.9	28.5	29.0	29.5	30.0	29.8	30.4	30.0	30.7	30.1	29.8	29.5
2014	29.4	29.6	29.4	28.8	29.0	29.1	29.7	29.9	29.9	30.6	30.3	30.2	29.7
2015	29.5	30.0	29.7	29.8	29.7	30.1	30.3	30.1	30.0	30.2	30.0	29.9	29.9
2016	29.0	29.0	29.0	29.1	29.3	29.6	29.5	29.5	29.5	29.0	28.7	28.8	29.2
2017	27.9	28.0	28.4	28.4	28.8	29.6	29.6	29.8	30.0	30.6	30.4	30.6	29.3

Employment by Industry: Tulsa, OK, Selected Years, 2007–2017—*Continued*

(Numbers in thousands, not seasonally adjusted)

Industry and year	January	February	March	April	May	June	July	August	September	October	November	December	Annual average
Manufacturing													
2007	50.8	50.8	51.1	50.9	51.4	51.7	52.3	52.5	52.1	52.4	52.6	52.6	51.8
2008	52.8	52.9	53.1	52.9	53.5	53.5	53.4	53.5	53.3	52.7	52.7	53.1	53.1
2009	52.0	50.5	49.4	47.9	47.0	46.8	45.4	44.8	44.2	43.7	43.5	43.3	46.5
2010	42.7	42.7	42.8	43.0	43.2	43.7	44.0	43.9	43.7	44.1	44.4	44.8	43.6
2011	44.5	44.4	45.0	45.5	45.7	46.3	46.8	46.7	47.0	47.4	47.8	48.1	46.3
2012	48.0	48.4	48.7	49.3	49.7	50.1	50.0	50.2	50.1	50.7	50.5	50.9	49.7
2013	50.7	50.7	50.6	50.4	50.3	50.5	50.6	50.5	50.2	49.9	49.9	50.1	50.4
2014	50.2	50.5	50.6	51.1	51.4	51.8	52.1	52.1	52.0	52.3	52.5	52.7	51.6
2015	52.2	52.1	51.7	51.0	50.5	50.2	49.9	49.3	49.0	48.5	48.4	48.4	50.1
2016	47.7	47.7	47.0	46.4	46.1	46.1	45.9	45.7	45.6	45.3	45.7	45.8	46.3
2017	44.9	45.4	45.4	45.5	45.9	46.4	46.3	46.3	46.4	47.3	47.8	47.7	46.3
Trade, Transportation, and Utilities													
2007	83.8	83.9	85.2	84.7	85.0	85.3	84.9	84.3	84.2	85.1	86.7	86.7	85.0
2008	83.6	83.9	84.8	85.3	85.6	85.6	86.2	86.4	85.8	85.7	86.9	87.3	85.6
2009	83.6	82.8	83.1	83.6	84.0	83.9	83.0	82.8	82.2	82.6	83.8	84.3	83.3
2010	80.5	79.9	80.3	80.4	80.9	81.0	81.1	80.9	80.0	80.5	82.1	82.7	80.9
2011	79.7	78.7	79.8	80.7	81.0	81.2	81.4	81.5	81.5	81.9	83.7	84.4	81.3
2012	81.7	81.3	81.8	82.1	82.5	83.1	82.5	82.2	81.9	82.9	84.9	85.3	82.7
2013	81.1	80.7	81.2	82.0	82.5	82.8	83.0	83.3	83.2	83.6	85.4	86.4	82.9
2014	84.0	83.7	83.9	84.3	85.0	85.8	85.9	86.1	85.9	86.6	88.3	89.4	85.7
2015	86.6	86.6	86.8	87.0	87.5	88.1	87.7	87.9	87.4	90.1	92.8	93.5	88.5
2016	89.0	88.2	88.5	89.2	89.0	88.8	88.5	89.0	88.5	90.3	93.4	92.9	89.6
2017	88.1	87.2	87.2	87.3	87.4	87.7	87.9	88.0	88.2	89.6	92.2	92.6	88.6
Wholesale Trade													
2007	17.8	18.0	18.2	18.3	18.2	18.3	18.2	18.0	17.9	18.0	18.0	17.9	18.1
2008	17.7	17.7	17.7	17.5	17.4	17.4	17.5	17.4	17.3	17.1	17.1	17.0	17.4
2009	16.6	16.5	16.4	16.3	16.2	16.0	15.8	15.6	15.4	15.4	15.2	15.2	15.9
2010	15.1	15.1	15.1	15.1	15.2	15.3	15.3	15.3	15.3	15.2	15.3	15.3	15.2
2011	15.0	15.0	15.1	15.1	15.1	15.1	15.4	15.3	15.3	15.2	15.2	15.2	15.2
2012	15.0	15.1	15.2	15.3	15.4	15.5	15.3	15.4	15.5	15.6	15.5	15.5	15.4
2013	15.3	15.3	15.3	15.5	15.5	15.5	15.6	15.7	15.7	15.7	15.7	15.7	15.5
2014	15.8	15.9	15.9	15.9	15.9	16.1	16.3	16.4	16.4	16.4	16.5	16.5	16.2
2015	16.4	16.6	16.5	16.5	16.5	16.5	16.5	16.5	16.3	16.5	16.4	16.5	16.5
2016	16.5	16.5	16.4	16.5	16.4	16.4	16.5	16.5	16.5	16.4	16.5	16.6	16.5
2017	16.5	16.6	16.7	16.7	16.8	16.9	16.8	16.9	16.8	16.8	16.9	16.9	16.8
Retail Trade													
2007	44.1	43.8	44.9	44.7	45.0	45.1	44.5	44.4	44.3	44.9	46.4	46.5	44.9
2008	43.9	44.2	45.1	45.7	45.9	45.8	46.0	46.2	45.6	45.5	46.6	46.9	45.6
2009	44.8	44.3	44.8	44.9	45.5	45.6	45.1	45.2	45.0	45.3	46.7	47.0	45.4
2010	44.8	44.1	44.5	44.9	45.2	45.3	45.3	45.2	44.4	45.0	46.5	46.8	45.2
2011	44.7	43.7	44.5	45.2	45.4	45.3	45.1	45.3	45.3	45.7	47.4	47.7	45.4
2012	45.5	44.8	45.3	45.5	45.8	46.2	45.9	45.6	45.4	46.3	48.4	48.7	46.1
2013	45.5	45.1	45.6	46.0	46.5	46.8	46.8	47.0	46.9	47.4	49.1	49.9	46.9
2014	47.4	47.0	47.2	47.5	48.1	48.6	48.4	48.5	48.3	48.9	50.2	51.2	48.4
2015	48.7	48.7	48.9	49.2	49.6	50.0	49.4	49.6	49.4	50.0	51.6	52.4	49.8
2016	49.8	49.6	50.1	50.3	50.4	50.4	50.0	50.0	49.3	49.9	51.7	51.7	50.3
2017	49.1	48.5	48.4	48.5	48.4	48.6	48.7	48.4	48.0	48.8	50.5	50.9	48.9
Transportation and Utilities													
2007	21.9	22.1	22.1	21.7	21.8	21.9	22.2	21.9	22.0	22.2	22.3	22.3	22.0
2008	22.0	22.0	22.0	22.1	22.3	22.4	22.7	22.8	22.9	23.1	23.2	23.4	22.6
2009	22.2	22.0	21.9	22.4	22.3	22.3	22.1	22.0	21.8	21.9	21.9	22.1	22.1
2010	20.6	20.7	20.7	20.4	20.5	20.4	20.5	20.4	20.3	20.3	20.3	20.6	20.5
2011	20.0	20.0	20.2	20.4	20.5	20.8	20.9	20.9	20.9	21.0	21.1	21.5	20.7
2012	21.2	21.4	21.3	21.3	21.3	21.4	21.3	21.2	21.0	21.0	21.0	21.1	21.2
2013	20.3	20.3	20.3	20.5	20.5	20.5	20.6	20.6	20.6	20.5	20.6	20.8	20.5
2014	20.8	20.8	20.8	20.9	21.0	21.1	21.2	21.2	21.2	21.3	21.6	21.7	21.1
2015	21.5	21.3	21.4	21.3	21.4	21.6	21.8	21.8	21.7	23.6	24.8	24.6	22.2
2016	22.7	22.1	22.0	22.4	22.2	22.0	22.0	22.5	22.7	24.0	25.2	24.6	22.9
2017	22.5	22.1	22.1	22.1	22.2	22.2	22.4	22.7	23.4	24.0	24.8	24.8	22.9

Employment by Industry: Tulsa, OK, Selected Years, 2007–2017—*Continued*

(Numbers in thousands, not seasonally adjusted)

Industry and year	January	February	March	April	May	June	July	August	September	October	November	December	Annual average
Information													
2007	9.9	10.1	10.0	9.9	10.0	9.9	10.0	9.9	9.9	10.0	10.0	10.0	10.0
2008	9.8	9.9	9.8	10.0	10.0	10.0	10.0	9.8	9.7	9.6	9.7	9.7	9.8
2009	9.4	9.4	9.2	9.1	9.0	8.9	8.9	8.8	8.5	8.5	8.5	8.5	8.9
2010	8.4	8.3	8.3	8.7	8.7	8.5	8.7	8.5	8.4	8.3	8.3	8.4	8.5
2011	8.3	8.2	8.2	8.1	8.2	8.2	8.3	8.3	8.2	8.2	8.1	8.2	8.2
2012	8.1	8.0	8.0	7.9	7.9	7.9	8.0	7.9	7.9	7.9	7.9	7.9	7.9
2013	7.8	7.8	7.8	7.9	7.9	7.9	7.9	7.8	7.7	7.7	7.6	7.6	7.8
2014	7.5	7.4	7.5	7.4	7.3	7.4	7.4	7.3	7.1	6.9	7.0	7.2	7.3
2015	7.1	7.1	7.1	7.1	7.2	7.2	7.2	7.2	7.1	7.2	7.3	7.4	7.2
2016	7.3	7.4	7.3	7.3	7.4	7.4	7.4	7.4	7.3	7.3	7.4	7.4	7.4
2017	7.4	7.4	7.4	7.3	7.3	7.2	7.3	7.2	7.0	7.0	7.1	7.2	7.2
Financial Activities													
2007	24.9	25.1	25.3	25.0	25.0	25.1	25.2	25.1	24.9	25.0	24.8	24.8	25.0
2008	24.6	24.6	24.6	24.6	24.6	24.6	24.9	24.8	24.5	24.5	24.4	24.5	24.6
2009	24.0	23.9	23.9	24.0	24.1	24.0	24.2	23.9	23.6	23.5	23.5	23.4	23.8
2010	23.2	23.2	23.2	23.3	23.3	23.2	23.2	23.2	23.0	23.0	22.9	23.0	23.1
2011	22.7	22.6	22.6	22.6	22.5	22.6	22.6	22.6	22.5	22.6	22.6	22.7	22.6
2012	22.4	22.5	22.4	22.2	22.3	22.4	22.5	22.5	22.4	22.6	22.6	22.7	22.5
2013	22.6	22.6	22.6	22.7	22.8	22.9	23.0	23.0	22.9	23.1	23.2	23.1	22.9
2014	22.8	22.8	22.8	22.9	22.8	22.8	22.9	22.9	22.8	22.9	23.0	23.0	22.9
2015	22.9	22.9	23.0	23.0	23.1	23.1	23.5	23.4	23.3	23.4	23.3	23.3	23.2
2016	23.2	23.2	23.1	23.1	23.2	23.2	23.3	23.2	23.1	23.2	23.1	23.3	23.2
2017	22.8	22.7	22.8	22.9	22.9	23.0	23.1	23.2	23.1	23.2	23.3	23.3	23.0
Professional and Business Services													
2007	60.2	61.0	61.7	62.1	62.8	62.7	62.4	63.6	62.8	63.1	63.0	62.5	62.3
2008	63.3	64.0	64.4	64.2	64.1	63.9	63.3	63.8	63.5	62.7	62.0	60.6	63.3
2009	57.2	57.0	56.4	55.1	55.0	55.1	54.4	54.4	53.7	54.5	54.7	54.6	55.2
2010	53.6	54.0	54.4	55.3	55.1	55.3	55.2	55.1	54.9	55.7	55.1	54.6	54.9
2011	53.0	52.8	53.7	53.7	53.8	53.9	54.6	54.8	55.4	55.6	55.1	55.1	54.3
2012	53.3	54.6	54.8	55.9	56.1	56.8	56.9	57.4	57.0	57.3	57.4	56.9	56.2
2013	55.7	56.0	56.8	56.9	57.4	57.8	58.4	58.5	58.2	58.5	58.1	57.3	57.5
2014	56.8	56.9	57.6	58.3	58.8	59.2	59.0	58.7	58.4	59.9	59.6	59.3	58.5
2015	59.4	58.6	58.9	59.9	60.1	59.9	60.5	60.0	59.0	59.6	58.9	58.5	59.4
2016	57.7	57.7	57.6	58.5	58.6	59.1	59.2	58.9	59.1	59.5	58.9	58.7	58.6
2017	57.7	58.8	59.9	59.9	60.3	61.1	60.5	60.9	60.7	60.8	61.2	60.6	60.2
Education and Health Services													
2007	61.9	62.5	63.0	63.4	63.6	64.2	63.7	63.9	64.0	64.0	63.9	63.6	63.5
2008	63.8	64.2	64.4	63.4	63.7	63.6	62.8	63.0	63.2	63.1	63.2	63.2	63.5
2009	63.4	63.7	64.0	63.5	63.6	64.2	64.2	64.2	63.9	64.8	64.8	64.7	64.1
2010	64.6	64.8	65.0	65.2	65.2	65.2	65.3	65.7	65.6	66.4	66.6	66.7	65.5
2011	66.0	65.4	66.1	66.3	66.7	66.6	66.8	66.8	66.7	67.0	66.6	66.6	66.5
2012	66.1	66.1	65.9	66.6	66.8	66.8	66.5	66.9	67.1	67.4	67.6	68.0	66.8
2013	67.6	68.0	68.1	67.9	67.8	67.7	67.4	67.7	68.0	68.3	68.5	68.4	68.0
2014	67.8	68.0	68.2	68.4	68.4	68.3	68.1	68.5	68.8	69.1	69.2	69.4	68.5
2015	68.8	68.7	68.9	69.1	69.0	69.1	69.9	70.1	70.5	70.3	70.5	70.0	69.6
2016	70.2	70.4	70.6	70.3	70.0	69.8	70.2	70.4	70.8	71.3	71.1	71.2	70.5
2017	70.4	70.5	70.6	70.4	70.5	70.6	70.7	70.8	71.2	71.7	72.2	72.1	71.0
Leisure and Hospitality													
2007	35.0	35.6	36.6	36.9	37.4	37.8	37.6	37.7	36.8	36.4	36.4	36.0	36.7
2008	35.5	35.8	36.4	36.8	37.6	38.0	37.4	37.9	37.0	36.7	36.3	36.4	36.8
2009	36.2	36.4	37.5	37.6	38.0	38.3	37.7	37.4	36.9	35.9	35.7	35.1	36.9
2010	34.4	34.8	35.7	36.8	37.2	37.4	37.1	37.3	36.8	36.5	36.4	36.2	36.4
2011	34.9	34.4	36.0	37.1	37.5	37.7	37.9	38.1	37.8	37.2	36.8	36.7	36.8
2012	36.3	37.0	37.9	38.9	39.3	39.8	39.3	39.4	38.7	38.0	38.0	38.4	38.4
2013	37.2	37.6	38.4	39.3	40.3	40.4	40.4	40.9	40.3	39.5	39.3	39.2	39.4
2014	39.0	39.2	39.9	41.0	41.7	42.0	42.1	42.2	41.6	40.9	40.7	40.8	40.9
2015	40.5	41.0	41.6	43.4	44.1	44.9	44.3	44.2	43.8	43.3	43.2	42.9	43.1
2016	42.1	42.6	43.7	44.6	45.0	45.4	45.6	45.2	44.7	44.1	43.7	43.7	44.2
2017	42.5	42.8	44.2	45.3	45.4	46.3	45.9	46.0	45.2	45.3	44.9	45.1	44.9

Employment by Industry: Tulsa, OK, Selected Years, 2007–2017—*Continued*

(Numbers in thousands, not seasonally adjusted)

Industry and year	January	February	March	April	May	June	July	August	September	October	November	December	Annual average
Other Services													
2007	17.2	17.3	17.5	18.3	18.4	19.1	18.8	18.9	18.6	18.4	18.4	18.3	18.3
2008	18.3	18.3	18.3	18.0	18.1	18.4	18.5	18.3	18.0	18.0	17.8	17.8	18.2
2009	17.6	17.5	17.6	17.1	17.2	17.5	17.6	17.4	17.2	17.1	17.1	17.0	17.3
2010	16.9	16.9	17.0	16.9	16.9	17.3	17.0	16.8	16.7	16.7	16.7	16.6	16.9
2011	16.3	16.3	16.5	16.5	16.6	16.9	16.9	16.6	16.6	16.6	16.7	16.7	16.6
2012	16.5	16.6	16.7	17.2	17.3	17.5	17.4	17.2	16.9	16.9	16.9	16.9	17.0
2013	16.6	16.7	16.6	17.0	17.1	17.6	17.5	17.4	17.2	17.0	17.0	16.9	17.1
2014	16.9	17.0	17.0	17.2	17.4	17.8	17.9	17.7	17.6	17.7	17.7	17.8	17.5
2015	17.8	17.9	18.1	18.0	18.2	18.5	19.1	18.4	18.2	18.2	18.2	18.1	18.2
2016	18.0	18.1	18.2	18.5	18.6	18.9	19.2	19.1	19.2	19.2	19.4	19.4	18.8
2017	19.4	19.6	19.8	19.7	19.8	20.3	20.4	20.1	19.9	20.0	20.0	20.0	19.9
Government													
2007	53.5	54.9	55.4	55.5	55.9	53.0	49.2	49.7	54.3	56.1	55.9	55.6	54.1
2008	54.3	55.7	55.9	56.4	57.0	53.8	50.5	51.2	56.5	58.7	58.6	58.6	55.6
2009	55.8	57.3	57.9	58.6	59.1	55.0	50.5	52.7	57.8	60.2	60.3	59.9	57.1
2010	57.0	58.1	58.9	59.5	61.1	58.0	51.3	50.9	55.9	58.6	58.8	58.7	57.2
2011	56.1	56.8	57.2	57.2	56.9	54.9	51.7	51.7	55.1	57.8	57.9	58.0	55.9
2012	55.5	57.1	57.7	57.4	57.7	54.8	50.7	51.0	55.9	58.1	58.4	58.3	56.1
2013	56.2	57.8	58.1	58.1	58.0	56.0	52.9	52.8	56.6	59.0	59.5	59.4	57.0
2014	57.3	59.1	59.4	59.1	59.4	56.5	53.3	53.7	57.4	60.0	60.4	60.0	58.0
2015	57.7	59.4	59.3	59.8	59.7	56.9	53.6	53.8	58.1	60.7	61.1	60.9	58.4
2016	58.5	60.2	60.5	60.0	59.6	56.8	53.7	53.8	58.1	58.8	59.1	59.8	58.2
2017	56.8	58.6	59.3	59.2	59.3	56.7	53.7	53.7	58.4	60.9	61.1	61.3	58.3

Employment by Industry: Fresno, CA, Selected Years, 2007–2017

(Numbers in thousands, not seasonally adjusted)

Industry and year	January	February	March	April	May	June	July	August	September	October	November	December	Annual average
Total Nonfarm													
2007	308.9	312.4	315.6	317.7	318.6	318.3	316.6	318.2	318.3	316.8	316.1	315.3	316.1
2008	308.4	312.1	313.7	315.9	318.6	317.2	311.0	312.2	314.1	314.5	312.3	310.2	313.4
2009	300.2	301.2	301.8	302.3	303.1	299.4	293.4	292.8	294.8	295.5	294.8	292.5	297.7
2010	284.7	287.8	290.0	291.7	294.9	294.1	286.3	287.9	290.5	294.6	292.9	291.2	290.6
2011	285.3	289.6	292.1	293.8	294.7	292.7	289.4	289.4	292.7	293.4	292.2	290.3	291.3
2012	285.3	287.9	290.9	292.1	295.8	297.0	292.9	293.6	294.9	298.2	298.6	296.6	293.7
2013	292.7	297.2	299.9	300.8	303.1	303.9	299.8	302.3	305.0	307.2	307.8	307.2	302.2
2014	301.7	306.1	308.5	310.7	312.6	313.5	312.1	313.3	315.7	320.1	319.1	318.7	312.7
2015	313.7	317.3	320.1	322.2	324.1	325.6	323.1	324.3	328.0	332.1	331.7	331.2	324.5
2016	325.4	327.9	331.0	334.8	336.9	338.6	334.6	336.3	340.6	342.0	342.6	339.4	335.8
2017	333.2	337.4	340.3	342.9	345.4	346.2	341.4	344.0	347.4	351.4	353.2	351.2	344.5
Total Private													
2007	241.3	242.6	244.4	245.7	247.1	248.3	250.8	252.7	251.0	247.0	246.2	245.8	246.9
2008	239.4	240.4	241.0	242.6	246.0	245.5	246.0	246.9	246.0	244.2	242.0	240.8	243.4
2009	232.0	230.9	230.5	229.7	231.3	230.2	227.6	228.6	227.8	226.5	226.7	225.3	228.9
2010	218.3	218.2	219.3	221.3	224.4	225.3	224.2	226.1	226.2	227.1	226.2	225.2	223.5
2011	219.9	221.5	223.0	224.1	225.7	226.1	226.6	228.4	230.0	228.1	227.0	226.4	225.6
2012	221.8	222.6	224.7	225.7	229.4	231.3	231.3	234.0	233.3	233.4	234.2	233.0	229.6
2013	229.6	231.6	233.5	234.3	236.8	238.0	239.6	242.5	242.7	243.0	242.6	242.7	238.1
2014	237.2	239.3	240.8	242.8	244.1	245.3	248.2	251.5	251.5	253.0	251.7	251.6	246.4
2015	246.4	247.8	250.5	252.1	253.4	255.0	258.2	260.8	260.5	262.4	261.1	261.1	255.8
2016	255.3	257.0	258.8	262.0	263.7	265.4	268.5	270.6	270.3	269.9	269.7	267.4	264.9
2017	261.5	263.7	266.0	268.1	270.3	271.7	274.4	276.6	276.5	278.3	279.1	278.5	272.1
Goods Producing													
2007	48.2	48.1	48.6	48.7	49.3	49.7	52.9	53.6	51.7	48.3	46.7	45.9	49.3
2008	44.1	44.2	44.3	44.7	46.4	46.2	47.2	47.3	46.7	45.0	42.9	41.9	45.1
2009	39.8	38.8	38.8	38.5	40.0	39.2	40.2	40.9	40.0	38.0	37.2	36.3	39.0
2010	34.8	34.3	34.6	35.2	36.9	37.4	37.5	38.2	38.2	37.7	36.0	35.2	36.3
2011	33.9	34.0	34.1	34.4	35.5	36.3	36.9	37.4	37.8	36.5	34.8	34.5	35.5
2012	33.9	33.6	34.0	34.1	36.5	37.7	38.3	39.0	37.6	37.0	35.7	35.4	36.1
2013	34.6	34.5	34.8	34.9	36.0	36.9	38.1	39.0	38.6	37.7	36.4	36.3	36.5
2014	35.7	35.6	35.8	36.3	36.9	38.3	39.6	40.7	40.7	40.2	38.9	38.3	38.1
2015	37.9	38.1	39.0	39.2	39.7	41.1	42.9	43.4	43.3	42.5	40.6	40.2	40.7
2016	39.2	39.6	39.5	40.3	40.7	42.3	43.5	44.3	43.9	42.3	41.5	41.1	41.5
2017	40.0	40.8	41.6	42.1	43.5	43.6	44.5	45.0	45.5	44.9	44.1	43.9	43.3
Service-Providing													
2007	260.7	264.3	267.0	269.0	269.3	268.6	263.7	264.6	266.6	268.5	269.4	269.4	266.8
2008	264.3	267.9	269.4	271.2	272.2	271.0	263.8	264.9	267.4	269.5	269.4	268.3	268.3
2009	260.4	262.4	263.0	263.8	263.1	260.2	253.2	251.9	254.8	257.5	257.6	256.2	258.7
2010	249.9	253.5	255.4	256.5	258.0	256.7	248.8	249.7	252.3	256.9	256.9	256.0	254.2
2011	251.4	255.6	258.0	259.4	259.2	256.4	252.5	252.0	254.9	256.9	257.4	255.8	255.8
2012	251.4	254.3	256.9	258.0	259.3	259.3	254.6	254.6	257.3	261.2	262.9	261.2	257.6
2013	258.1	262.7	265.1	265.9	267.1	267.0	261.7	263.3	266.4	269.5	271.4	270.9	265.8
2014	266.0	270.5	272.7	274.4	275.7	275.2	272.5	272.6	275.0	279.9	280.2	280.4	274.6
2015	275.8	279.2	281.1	283.0	284.4	284.5	280.2	280.9	284.7	289.6	291.1	291.0	283.8
2016	286.2	288.3	291.5	294.5	296.2	296.3	291.1	292.0	296.7	299.7	301.1	298.3	294.3
2017	293.2	296.6	298.7	300.8	301.9	302.6	296.9	299.0	301.9	306.5	309.1	307.3	301.2
Mining, Logging, and Construction													
2007	21.8	21.6	22.0	21.9	21.8	22.0	21.9	21.6	20.6	20.2	19.9	19.1	21.2
2008	18.0	18.2	18.2	18.7	18.7	18.5	18.8	18.4	17.8	17.6	16.9	16.2	18.0
2009	14.8	14.3	14.5	14.3	14.4	14.3	14.3	14.1	13.7	13.1	12.9	12.2	13.9
2010	11.9	11.7	11.9	12.1	12.5	12.6	12.7	12.6	12.4	12.3	12.0	11.8	12.2
2011	11.2	11.3	11.6	11.6	11.7	11.9	12.3	12.3	12.2	11.8	11.4	11.5	11.7
2012	11.4	11.3	11.6	11.7	12.2	12.9	13.2	13.3	12.8	13.0	12.8	12.7	12.4
2013	12.4	12.4	12.8	13.0	13.5	13.8	14.1	14.2	14.0	13.7	13.6	13.5	13.4
2014	13.2	13.3	13.4	13.7	13.9	14.3	14.6	14.8	14.7	14.9	14.7	14.3	14.2
2015	14.0	14.1	14.6	15.0	15.2	15.7	16.1	16.0	15.7	15.9	15.8	15.8	15.3
2016	15.4	15.7	15.7	16.1	16.2	16.6	16.7	16.9	16.8	16.7	16.9	16.6	16.4
2017	15.8	16.3	16.9	17.2	17.5	18.0	18.2	18.1	18.3	18.2	18.1	18.0	17.6

Employment by Industry: Fresno, CA, Selected Years, 2007–2017—*Continued*

(Numbers in thousands, not seasonally adjusted)

Industry and year	January	February	March	April	May	June	July	August	September	October	November	December	Annual average
Manufacturing													
2007	26.4	26.5	26.6	26.8	27.5	27.7	31.0	32.0	31.1	28.1	26.8	26.8	28.1
2008	26.1	26.0	26.1	26.0	27.7	27.7	28.4	28.9	28.9	27.4	26.0	25.7	27.1
2009	25.0	24.5	24.3	24.2	25.6	24.9	25.9	26.8	26.3	24.9	24.3	24.1	25.1
2010	22.9	22.6	22.7	23.1	24.4	24.8	24.8	25.6	25.8	25.4	24.0	23.4	24.1
2011	22.7	22.7	22.5	22.8	23.8	24.4	24.6	25.1	25.6	24.7	23.4	23.0	23.8
2012	22.5	22.3	22.4	22.4	24.3	24.8	25.1	25.7	24.8	24.0	22.9	22.7	23.7
2013	22.2	22.1	22.0	21.9	22.5	23.1	24.0	24.8	24.6	24.0	22.8	22.8	23.1
2014	22.5	22.3	22.4	22.6	23.0	24.0	25.0	25.9	26.0	25.3	24.2	24.0	23.9
2015	23.9	24.0	24.4	24.2	24.5	25.4	26.8	27.4	27.6	26.6	24.8	24.4	25.3
2016	23.8	23.9	23.8	24.2	24.5	25.7	26.8	27.4	27.1	25.6	24.6	24.5	25.2
2017	24.2	24.5	24.7	24.9	26.0	25.6	26.3	26.9	27.2	26.7	26.0	25.9	25.7
Trade, Transportation, and Utilities													
2007	58.8	58.3	58.9	59.1	59.9	60.6	61.1	61.4	61.3	61.1	62.0	62.6	60.4
2008	58.8	58.0	58.0	57.8	59.2	59.4	59.4	59.6	59.9	59.9	60.1	60.0	59.2
2009	56.4	55.6	55.1	54.7	55.3	55.4	54.6	55.0	55.9	55.8	56.8	56.9	55.6
2010	53.7	53.3	53.3	53.8	54.1	54.8	54.8	55.6	56.1	56.7	57.8	58.0	55.2
2011	55.6	55.5	55.2	55.9	56.2	56.4	57.3	58.0	58.8	59.2	60.1	60.0	57.4
2012	56.3	55.6	55.9	56.3	57.1	57.8	58.1	58.7	59.5	59.9	61.3	61.2	58.1
2013	58.2	58.7	59.1	59.2	60.3	60.1	60.8	61.8	61.9	61.9	63.1	63.2	60.7
2014	60.3	60.3	60.6	61.0	61.2	61.5	61.8	62.2	62.6	63.2	64.1	64.7	62.0
2015	61.5	61.4	61.5	61.7	62.1	62.3	63.2	64.1	64.7	65.7	66.3	66.5	63.4
2016	63.9	63.7	63.7	64.3	65.1	65.2	65.7	66.2	66.7	67.0	68.5	67.6	65.6
2017	65.5	64.9	64.6	65.0	65.1	65.4	65.7	66.5	66.5	67.5	69.3	68.7	66.2
Wholesale Trade													
2007	12.9	13.0	13.3	13.3	13.6	14.0	14.0	14.0	13.8	13.5	13.3	13.0	13.5
2008	12.5	12.5	12.6	12.9	13.1	13.4	13.3	13.2	13.1	12.8	12.6	12.3	12.9
2009	11.9	11.8	11.7	11.7	11.8	12.1	11.9	11.9	12.0	11.9	11.9	11.6	11.9
2010	11.1	11.1	11.1	11.2	11.2	11.6	11.8	11.8	11.7	12.0	11.9	11.6	11.5
2011	12.1	12.2	12.2	12.2	12.3	12.4	12.7	12.8	12.9	12.9	12.8	12.6	12.5
2012	12.2	12.3	12.4	12.4	12.6	12.9	13.1	13.2	13.2	13.2	13.1	13.0	12.8
2013	12.9	13.1	13.2	13.4	13.8	13.8	13.8	14.0	13.8	13.8	13.7	13.6	13.6
2014	13.7	13.7	13.8	13.5	13.6	13.8	13.9	13.9	13.8	13.9	13.7	13.6	13.7
2015	13.3	13.4	13.3	13.3	13.4	13.7	14.0	14.1	14.1	14.4	14.3	14.3	13.8
2016	14.0	14.0	14.0	14.0	14.2	14.4	14.6	14.5	14.6	14.6	14.6	14.4	14.3
2017	14.3	14.1	14.1	14.1	14.2	14.5	14.6	14.6	14.5	14.8	14.8	14.6	14.4
Retail Trade													
2007	35.7	35.1	35.3	35.5	35.9	36.0	36.2	36.4	36.4	36.6	37.7	38.5	36.3
2008	35.8	35.1	35.0	35.0	35.0	34.8	34.9	35.0	35.2	35.6	36.3	36.6	35.4
2009	33.8	33.2	32.9	32.5	32.8	32.6	32.3	32.5	33.0	33.1	34.2	34.8	33.1
2010	32.4	32.0	32.0	32.2	32.3	32.4	32.2	32.6	33.1	33.4	34.4	35.0	32.8
2011	32.7	32.5	32.2	32.7	32.8	32.8	33.0	33.3	33.8	34.1	35.3	35.7	33.4
2012	33.0	32.3	32.4	32.7	33.0	33.2	33.3	33.6	34.3	34.8	36.5	36.4	33.8
2013	34.0	34.0	34.2	34.2	34.5	34.5	34.7	35.3	35.5	35.8	37.4	37.6	35.1
2014	35.2	35.0	35.3	35.9	35.9	35.9	35.8	36.0	36.4	37.0	38.3	39.0	36.3
2015	36.5	36.3	36.5	36.4	36.6	36.5	36.9	37.5	37.9	38.5	39.3	39.4	37.4
2016	37.7	37.5	37.6	37.8	38.1	38.0	38.2	38.6	38.8	39.3	40.7	40.0	38.5
2017	38.6	38.2	37.9	38.1	37.9	37.9	38.1	38.5	38.4	39.0	40.9	40.5	38.7
Transportation and Utilities													
2007	10.2	10.2	10.3	10.3	10.4	10.6	10.9	11.0	11.1	11.0	11.0	11.1	10.7
2008	10.5	10.4	10.4	9.9	11.1	11.2	11.2	11.4	11.6	11.5	11.2	11.1	11.0
2009	10.7	10.6	10.5	10.5	10.7	10.7	10.4	10.6	10.9	10.8	10.7	10.5	10.6
2010	10.2	10.2	10.2	10.4	10.6	10.8	10.8	11.2	11.3	11.3	11.5	11.4	10.8
2011	10.8	10.8	10.8	11.0	11.1	11.2	11.6	11.9	12.1	12.2	12.0	11.7	11.4
2012	11.1	11.0	11.1	11.2	11.5	11.7	11.7	11.9	12.0	11.9	11.7	11.8	11.6
2013	11.3	11.6	11.7	11.6	12.0	11.8	12.3	12.5	12.6	12.3	12.0	12.0	12.0
2014	11.4	11.6	11.5	11.6	11.7	11.8	12.1	12.3	12.4	12.3	12.1	12.1	11.9
2015	11.7	11.7	11.7	12.0	12.1	12.1	12.3	12.5	12.7	12.8	12.7	12.8	12.3
2016	12.2	12.2	12.1	12.5	12.8	12.8	12.9	13.1	13.3	13.1	13.2	13.2	12.8
2017	12.6	12.6	12.6	12.8	13.0	13.0	13.0	13.4	13.6	13.7	13.6	13.6	13.1

Employment by Industry: Fresno, CA, Selected Years, 2007–2017—*Continued*

(Numbers in thousands, not seasonally adjusted)

Industry and year	January	February	March	April	May	June	July	August	September	October	November	December	Annual average
Information													
2007	4.1	4.2	4.1	4.1	4.2	4.2	4.2	4.2	4.2	4.2	4.2	4.2	4.2
2008	4.5	4.5	4.4	4.8	4.8	4.8	4.9	4.9	4.8	4.8	4.8	4.8	4.7
2009	4.6	4.6	4.5	4.3	4.2	4.3	4.0	4.0	3.9	3.9	3.9	3.8	4.2
2010	3.8	3.7	3.7	3.5	3.5	3.5	3.6	3.5	3.5	3.5	3.5	3.5	3.6
2011	3.4	3.4	3.4	3.4	3.5	3.5	3.5	3.5	3.6	3.6	3.7	3.6	3.5
2012	3.8	3.7	3.7	3.8	3.8	3.9	3.8	3.8	3.8	3.8	3.8	3.8	3.8
2013	3.8	3.8	3.8	3.8	3.8	3.8	3.8	3.8	3.8	3.8	3.8	3.8	3.8
2014	3.8	3.8	3.8	3.8	3.8	3.8	3.9	3.9	3.9	3.9	3.9	4.0	3.9
2015	3.9	3.9	3.9	3.9	3.9	3.9	3.9	3.9	3.9	3.8	3.8	3.9	3.9
2016	3.8	3.8	3.8	3.8	3.8	3.8	3.8	3.7	3.7	3.7	3.7	3.6	3.8
2017	3.6	3.7	3.7	3.7	3.6	3.5	3.6	3.6	3.6	3.6	3.6	3.6	3.6
Financial Activities													
2007	15.3	15.4	15.4	15.5	15.5	15.6	15.4	15.3	15.3	14.9	15.0	15.0	15.3
2008	14.9	14.9	14.9	14.8	14.9	14.9	14.7	14.8	14.6	14.6	14.6	14.5	14.8
2009	14.3	14.2	14.1	14.1	13.9	13.8	13.7	13.6	13.5	13.6	13.5	13.5	13.8
2010	13.5	13.4	13.3	13.4	13.4	13.4	13.4	13.4	13.3	13.4	13.3	13.3	13.4
2011	13.2	13.2	13.2	13.2	13.1	13.1	13.0	13.0	12.8	12.6	12.6	12.6	13.0
2012	12.6	12.6	12.6	12.8	12.9	12.9	13.0	13.0	13.0	12.9	12.9	13.0	12.9
2013	12.9	12.9	12.9	13.0	12.9	12.9	13.0	12.9	12.9	12.8	12.8	12.7	12.9
2014	12.7	12.7	12.7	12.7	12.7	12.7	12.8	12.7	12.7	12.9	12.9	12.9	12.8
2015	12.8	12.8	12.9	12.9	13.0	13.0	13.2	13.2	13.2	13.2	13.2	13.1	13.0
2016	13.1	13.1	13.1	13.3	13.3	13.2	13.3	13.3	13.3	13.4	13.4	13.3	13.3
2017	13.3	13.4	13.4	13.5	13.6	13.5	13.5	13.5	13.4	13.5	13.5	13.5	13.5
Professional and Business Services													
2007	29.2	29.5	29.8	29.9	29.7	29.9	30.1	30.1	30.2	30.5	30.0	29.8	29.9
2008	30.2	30.5	30.3	30.7	30.3	30.2	31.1	31.1	31.0	30.6	30.2	30.4	30.6
2009	29.6	29.4	29.2	28.8	28.2	28.0	27.9	27.4	27.2	27.4	27.3	26.9	28.1
2010	26.0	26.2	26.6	27.2	27.2	27.1	26.8	26.8	26.3	26.6	26.6	26.3	26.6
2011	26.6	27.3	27.3	27.3	27.4	26.8	26.6	26.7	27.0	26.8	26.3	26.4	26.9
2012	26.4	26.7	27.1	26.7	26.2	26.1	26.1	26.4	26.6	27.3	28.4	27.1	26.8
2013	27.7	28.0	27.8	28.2	27.9	28.5	29.0	29.4	29.9	30.4	30.1	30.0	28.9
2014	29.0	30.1	30.2	29.8	30.3	30.1	31.3	32.1	32.3	32.9	31.8	31.6	31.0
2015	30.8	31.0	31.2	31.4	31.3	31.5	31.6	31.7	31.3	32.1	31.9	31.7	31.5
2016	31.1	31.1	31.4	31.8	31.9	31.8	32.6	32.3	32.6	32.8	32.2	31.4	31.9
2017	30.2	30.8	31.0	30.8	31.0	31.4	32.7	32.7	32.9	33.9	33.6	33.2	32.0
Education and Health Services													
2007	47.6	48.3	48.4	48.7	48.3	48.3	48.0	48.4	49.0	49.5	49.6	49.7	48.7
2008	49.1	49.9	50.3	51.0	50.9	50.6	49.9	50.2	50.3	51.1	51.4	51.6	50.5
2009	50.9	51.5	51.8	52.1	51.7	51.5	50.3	50.5	51.0	51.8	52.1	52.0	51.4
2010	51.1	51.3	51.4	52.0	51.8	51.6	51.0	51.2	51.8	52.0	52.2	52.3	51.6
2011	51.5	51.6	52.6	52.8	52.4	52.0	51.3	51.5	52.3	52.2	52.6	52.7	52.1
2012	52.2	53.2	53.6	53.6	53.5	53.2	52.5	53.1	53.6	53.7	53.7	54.0	53.3
2013	54.2	55.2	55.7	55.7	55.7	55.4	54.2	54.7	55.3	56.2	56.3	56.4	55.4
2014	55.5	55.9	56.7	57.5	56.8	56.5	56.2	56.9	57.3	58.1	58.2	58.5	57.0
2015	58.2	58.7	59.6	60.1	59.7	59.7	59.8	60.7	61.1	62.1	62.2	62.6	60.4
2016	62.0	62.9	63.9	64.4	64.1	64.1	63.8	64.5	65.0	65.4	65.6	66.0	64.3
2017	65.4	66.0	67.0	67.4	67.2	67.7	67.8	68.6	68.8	68.9	69.1	69.5	67.8
Leisure and Hospitality													
2007	27.5	27.9	28.3	28.6	28.9	29.1	28.3	28.5	28.2	27.6	27.7	27.7	28.2
2008	27.3	27.7	28.0	28.0	28.7	28.6	28.4	28.4	28.1	27.6	27.5	27.1	28.0
2009	26.2	26.5	26.6	26.9	27.5	27.5	27.2	27.1	26.3	26.0	25.9	25.9	26.6
2010	25.5	25.9	26.3	26.2	27.4	27.4	27.4	27.5	27.1	27.2	26.8	26.7	26.8
2011	26.0	26.6	27.3	27.1	27.6	27.9	27.9	28.0	27.3	26.8	26.5	26.3	27.1
2012	26.5	27.0	27.5	27.8	28.6	28.8	29.0	29.2	28.5	28.0	27.6	27.7	28.0
2013	27.5	27.6	28.4	28.5	29.2	29.6	30.0	29.9	29.3	29.3	29.1	29.3	29.0
2014	29.2	29.8	29.8	30.5	31.1	31.3	31.6	31.6	30.7	30.5	30.5	30.3	30.6
2015	30.1	30.5	31.0	31.3	32.1	32.1	32.2	32.2	31.5	31.3	31.3	31.5	31.4
2016	30.7	31.3	31.7	32.4	33.1	33.6	34.1	34.3	33.1	33.3	32.9	32.7	32.8
2017	32.2	32.6	33.1	33.9	34.4	35.0	35.1	34.9	34.0	34.2	34.1	34.4	34.0

Employment by Industry: Fresno, CA, Selected Years, 2007–2017—*Continued*

(Numbers in thousands, not seasonally adjusted)

Industry and year	January	February	March	April	May	June	July	August	September	October	November	December	Annual average
Other Services													
2007	10.6	10.9	10.9	11.1	11.3	10.9	10.8	11.2	11.1	10.9	11.0	10.9	11.0
2008	10.5	10.7	10.8	10.8	10.8	10.8	10.4	10.6	10.6	10.6	10.5	10.5	10.6
2009	10.2	10.3	10.4	10.3	10.5	10.5	9.7	10.1	10.0	10.0	10.0	10.0	10.2
2010	9.9	10.1	10.1	10.0	10.1	10.1	9.7	9.9	9.9	10.0	10.0	9.9	10.0
2011	9.7	9.9	9.9	10.0	10.0	10.1	10.1	10.3	10.4	10.4	10.4	10.3	10.1
2012	10.1	10.2	10.3	10.6	10.8	10.9	10.5	10.8	10.7	10.8	10.8	10.8	10.6
2013	10.7	10.9	11.0	11.0	11.0	10.8	10.7	11.0	11.0	10.9	11.0	11.0	10.9
2014	11.0	11.1	11.2	11.2	11.3	11.1	11.0	11.4	11.3	11.3	11.4	11.3	11.2
2015	11.2	11.4	11.4	11.6	11.6	11.4	11.4	11.6	11.6	11.7	11.7	11.6	11.5
2016	11.5	11.5	11.7	11.7	11.7	11.4	11.7	12.0	12.0	12.0	11.9	11.7	11.7
2017	11.3	11.5	11.6	11.7	11.9	11.6	11.5	11.8	11.8	11.8	11.8	11.7	11.7
Government													
2007	67.6	69.8	71.2	72.0	71.5	70.0	65.8	65.5	67.3	69.8	69.9	69.5	69.2
2008	69.0	71.7	72.7	73.3	72.6	71.7	65.0	65.3	68.1	70.3	70.3	69.4	70.0
2009	68.2	70.3	71.3	72.6	71.8	69.2	65.8	64.2	67.0	69.0	68.1	67.2	68.7
2010	66.4	69.6	70.7	70.4	70.5	68.8	62.1	61.8	64.3	67.5	66.7	66.0	67.1
2011	65.4	68.1	69.1	69.7	69.0	66.6	62.8	61.0	62.7	65.3	65.2	63.9	65.7
2012	63.5	65.3	66.2	66.4	66.4	65.7	61.6	59.6	61.6	64.8	64.4	63.6	64.1
2013	63.1	65.6	66.4	66.5	66.3	65.9	60.2	59.8	62.3	64.2	65.2	64.5	64.2
2014	64.5	66.8	67.7	67.9	68.5	68.2	63.9	61.8	64.2	67.1	67.4	67.1	66.3
2015	67.3	69.5	69.6	70.1	70.7	70.6	64.9	63.5	67.5	69.7	70.6	70.1	68.7
2016	70.1	70.9	72.2	72.8	73.2	73.2	66.1	65.7	70.3	72.1	72.9	72.0	71.0
2017	71.7	73.7	74.3	74.8	75.1	74.5	67.0	67.4	70.9	73.1	74.1	72.7	72.4

Employment by Industry: Urban Honolulu, HI, Selected Years, 2007–2017

(Numbers in thousands, not seasonally adjusted)

Industry and year	January	February	March	April	May	June	July	August	September	October	November	December	Annual average
Total Nonfarm													
2007	447.2	454.2	457.2	449.9	457.3	458.9	448.3	449.7	456.2	458.0	462.3	465.8	455.4
2008	450.9	456.6	459.0	451.6	457.3	455.5	445.7	447.2	449.4	450.1	455.7	454.3	452.8
2009	440.4	443.5	444.6	439.3	440.4	439.0	429.1	427.6	432.0	435.2	436.4	439.7	437.3
2010	427.9	432.9	434.8	434.1	437.0	433.2	428.8	425.0	433.2	438.0	442.9	445.4	434.4
2011	429.2	439.3	442.0	439.1	439.8	437.7	433.4	430.8	440.2	443.4	448.8	451.9	439.6
2012	430.7	444.7	446.8	447.5	450.3	448.3	441.2	446.1	449.3	453.4	461.3	461.2	448.4
2013	440.6	455.4	457.4	454.2	459.0	455.8	451.8	449.4	457.1	461.5	467.4	469.4	456.6
2014	456.3	460.5	463.3	461.5	464.0	460.4	454.1	455.3	461.8	465.1	471.3	470.0	462.0
2015	461.5	466.2	468.7	467.6	469.3	467.3	461.0	464.5	467.0	472.7	477.7	481.3	468.7
2016	465.0	471.9	473.8	471.4	474.4	471.1	466.7	468.5	474.8	475.2	481.1	479.1	472.8
2017	471.5	476.7	479.6	476.6	478.2	475.2	467.6	466.3	476.2	479.6	484.1	486.7	476.5
Total Private													
2007	352.6	355.4	357.7	355.4	357.7	360.9	358.2	359.8	360.6	360.2	362.9	365.5	358.9
2008	355.4	357.4	358.6	356.1	356.2	356.2	353.6	353.4	352.4	349.8	351.3	352.5	354.4
2009	342.1	343.2	342.8	337.9	337.7	338.3	335.7	335.5	336.3	336.7	336.9	339.6	338.6
2010	332.1	333.9	334.5	333.4	334.6	334.3	334.7	335.1	337.2	338.9	340.4	344.5	336.1
2011	335.2	338.8	341.0	338.4	338.4	338.7	339.8	341.3	343.9	344.2	347.9	350.5	341.5
2012	341.7	343.8	345.2	345.9	348.1	348.8	348.9	351.4	352.1	353.6	357.8	359.5	349.7
2013	351.5	354.2	355.9	355.8	356.9	357.6	359.6	359.7	360.1	361.7	366.5	368.0	359.0
2014	358.4	359.2	361.7	360.6	361.7	361.4	361.8	362.9	364.5	365.6	368.9	371.7	363.2
2015	364.0	365.5	367.6	366.7	367.6	368.4	369.4	370.0	369.7	372.7	376.9	379.5	369.8
2016	369.4	371.3	372.4	372.5	372.9	372.3	375.0	377.0	377.0	375.1	378.2	379.8	374.4
2017	374.2	375.2	378.1	375.4	376.7	376.8	376.3	377.3	378.0	379.2	382.4	384.5	377.8
Goods Producing													
2007	37.0	37.3	37.4	37.4	37.9	38.6	38.7	39.0	39.2	39.0	39.3	39.3	38.3
2008	38.4	38.6	38.7	38.2	38.0	37.8	38.0	37.9	37.7	36.9	36.9	36.5	37.8
2009	34.8	34.5	34.3	33.6	33.6	33.6	33.5	33.2	33.0	32.7	32.3	32.5	33.5
2010	32.0	31.8	31.8	31.7	31.7	31.5	31.8	31.7	31.9	32.4	32.4	32.6	31.9
2011	31.5	31.9	32.1	32.2	32.2	32.8	33.1	33.3	33.6	33.3	33.1	33.1	32.7
2012	32.4	32.3	32.3	32.2	32.2	32.6	32.8	33.0	33.4	33.5	33.7	33.5	32.8
2013	32.9	33.2	33.5	33.5	34.0	33.8	34.2	34.4	34.3	34.3	34.5	34.6	33.9
2014	33.7	34.0	34.2	34.0	34.4	34.9	35.4	35.7	35.7	36.0	35.9	35.8	35.0
2015	34.9	35.0	35.6	35.9	36.3	37.0	37.7	37.7	37.8	38.7	39.0	39.5	37.1
2016	38.8	39.4	39.7	39.5	39.8	39.9	40.2	40.2	39.7	39.1	39.0	38.9	39.5
2017	37.8	38.0	38.4	38.0	38.0	38.3	37.8	37.8	37.8	38.3	39.0	38.9	38.2
Service-Providing													
2007	410.2	416.9	419.8	412.5	419.4	420.3	409.6	410.7	417.0	419.0	423.0	426.5	417.1
2008	412.5	418.0	420.3	413.4	419.3	417.7	407.7	409.3	411.7	413.2	418.8	417.8	415.0
2009	405.6	409.0	410.3	405.7	406.8	405.4	395.6	394.4	399.0	402.5	404.1	407.2	403.8
2010	395.9	401.1	403.0	402.4	405.3	401.7	397.0	393.3	401.3	405.6	410.5	412.8	402.5
2011	397.7	407.4	409.9	406.9	407.6	404.9	400.3	397.5	406.6	410.1	415.7	418.8	407.0
2012	398.3	412.4	414.5	415.3	418.1	415.7	408.4	413.1	415.9	419.9	427.6	427.7	415.6
2013	407.7	422.2	423.9	420.7	425.0	422.0	417.6	415.0	422.8	427.2	432.9	434.8	422.7
2014	422.6	426.5	429.1	427.5	429.6	425.5	418.7	419.6	426.1	429.1	435.4	434.2	427.0
2015	426.6	431.2	433.1	431.7	433.0	430.3	423.3	426.8	429.2	434.0	438.7	441.8	431.6
2016	426.2	432.5	434.1	431.9	434.6	431.2	426.5	428.3	435.1	436.1	442.1	440.2	433.2
2017	433.7	438.7	441.2	438.6	440.2	436.9	429.8	428.5	438.4	441.3	445.1	447.8	438.4
Mining, Logging, and Construction													
2007	25.2	25.4	25.6	25.7	26.1	26.7	26.9	27.1	27.3	27.3	27.4	27.3	26.5
2008	26.6	26.8	26.8	26.4	26.1	26.0	26.2	26.1	26.0	25.5	25.4	25.0	26.1
2009	23.7	23.4	23.2	22.7	22.7	22.7	22.8	22.4	22.2	22.0	21.6	21.7	22.6
2010	21.4	21.3	21.3	21.3	21.3	21.2	21.5	21.3	21.4	21.9	21.8	21.9	21.5
2011	20.9	21.2	21.3	21.5	21.5	22.1	22.4	22.5	22.7	22.4	22.1	22.2	21.9
2012	21.6	21.5	21.6	21.6	21.7	22.0	22.2	22.3	22.6	22.7	22.8	22.6	22.1
2013	22.2	22.4	22.7	22.8	23.2	23.0	23.4	23.5	23.3	23.3	23.5	23.6	23.1
2014	22.9	23.2	23.3	23.2	23.6	23.9	24.2	24.4	24.6	24.7	24.7	24.5	23.9
2015	23.7	23.8	24.4	24.7	25.1	25.7	26.4	26.4	26.6	27.4	27.7	28.1	25.8
2016	27.7	28.1	28.4	28.2	28.5	28.5	28.8	28.7	28.3	27.7	27.7	27.5	28.2
2017	26.6	26.7	26.9	26.6	26.6	26.7	26.4	26.4	26.3	27.1	27.6	27.6	26.8

Employment by Industry: Urban Honolulu, HI, Selected Years, 2007–2017—*Continued*

(Numbers in thousands, not seasonally adjusted)

Industry and year	January	February	March	April	May	June	July	August	September	October	November	December	Annual average
Manufacturing													
2007	11.8	11.9	11.8	11.7	11.8	11.9	11.8	11.9	11.9	11.7	11.9	12.0	11.8
2008	11.8	11.8	11.9	11.8	11.9	11.8	11.8	11.8	11.7	11.4	11.5	11.5	11.7
2009	11.1	11.1	11.1	10.9	10.9	10.9	10.7	10.8	10.8	10.7	10.7	10.8	10.9
2010	10.6	10.5	10.5	10.4	10.4	10.3	10.3	10.4	10.5	10.5	10.6	10.7	10.5
2011	10.6	10.7	10.8	10.7	10.7	10.7	10.7	10.8	10.9	10.9	11.0	10.9	10.8
2012	10.8	10.8	10.7	10.6	10.5	10.6	10.6	10.7	10.8	10.8	10.9	10.9	10.7
2013	10.7	10.8	10.8	10.7	10.8	10.8	10.8	10.9	11.0	11.0	11.0	11.0	10.9
2014	10.8	10.8	10.9	10.8	10.8	11.0	11.2	11.3	11.1	11.3	11.2	11.3	11.0
2015	11.2	11.2	11.2	11.2	11.2	11.3	11.3	11.3	11.2	11.3	11.3	11.4	11.3
2016	11.1	11.3	11.3	11.3	11.3	11.4	11.4	11.5	11.4	11.4	11.3	11.4	11.3
2017	11.2	11.3	11.5	11.4	11.4	11.6	11.4	11.4	11.5	11.2	11.4	11.3	11.4
Trade, Transportation, and Utilities													
2007	86.3	85.3	85.8	85.0	85.3	85.5	85.5	85.6	85.4	85.9	88.0	89.7	86.1
2008	86.2	84.9	84.9	83.7	83.7	83.4	82.7	82.9	82.4	81.7	82.6	83.2	83.5
2009	80.6	80.0	79.4	78.3	78.3	78.5	78.2	78.1	78.3	78.4	79.7	80.9	79.1
2010	78.3	77.6	77.4	77.7	77.3	77.9	78.3	78.5	78.2	78.7	80.3	81.6	78.5
2011	79.2	78.7	78.7	78.3	78.4	78.6	78.9	79.1	79.4	80.2	82.0	83.0	79.5
2012	80.9	80.4	80.6	80.4	81.1	81.5	81.8	81.9	82.2	82.7	85.2	86.1	82.1
2013	82.8	82.6	82.9	82.6	82.7	83.2	83.3	83.5	83.2	83.5	85.6	86.7	83.6
2014	83.5	82.6	82.9	82.6	82.7	83.0	83.3	83.0	83.2	83.7	85.8	87.6	83.7
2015	84.6	84.2	84.2	83.9	83.8	84.4	84.4	84.2	84.0	84.5	86.4	87.5	84.7
2016	84.5	83.8	83.7	83.1	83.3	83.3	83.8	84.3	84.6	85.1	86.6	88.1	84.5
2017	85.5	84.4	84.4	84.0	84.2	84.6	84.9	85.4	85.5	85.4	86.5	86.8	85.1
Wholesale Trade													
2007	14.6	14.6	14.7	14.7	14.8	14.9	14.9	15.0	15.0	15.0	15.1	15.3	14.9
2008	15.0	15.0	15.1	15.1	15.1	15.1	15.1	15.1	15.1	15.0	15.0	15.0	15.1
2009	14.7	14.6	14.5	14.4	14.4	14.3	14.3	14.3	14.3	14.2	14.2	14.3	14.4
2010	14.1	14.1	14.1	14.2	14.2	14.2	14.3	14.3	14.2	14.3	14.3	14.4	14.2
2011	14.1	14.0	14.0	14.0	14.1	14.1	14.1	14.2	14.2	14.2	14.2	14.3	14.1
2012	14.1	14.1	14.1	14.0	14.1	14.2	14.2	14.3	14.3	14.3	14.3	14.4	14.2
2013	14.2	14.2	14.3	14.2	14.2	14.2	14.2	14.2	14.2	14.1	14.2	14.2	14.2
2014	14.1	14.0	14.1	14.0	14.0	14.1	14.0	14.0	14.1	14.2	14.2	14.5	14.1
2015	14.2	14.2	14.3	14.2	14.2	14.3	14.3	14.3	14.3	14.2	14.2	14.3	14.3
2016	14.1	14.0	14.0	14.0	14.0	14.1	14.1	14.2	14.2	14.2	14.2	14.4	14.1
2017	14.2	14.1	14.1	14.0	14.1	14.1	14.0	14.1	14.1	14.2	14.2	14.3	14.1
Retail Trade													
2007	47.0	46.3	46.5	45.9	46.0	46.2	46.1	46.1	46.0	46.3	48.2	49.3	46.7
2008	46.7	46.3	46.9	46.1	46.0	46.3	46.4	46.5	46.3	45.9	46.8	47.5	46.5
2009	45.7	45.2	44.8	44.1	44.0	44.3	44.2	44.1	44.5	44.8	46.0	46.9	44.9
2010	44.0	44.2	44.1	44.1	43.8	44.2	44.3	44.6	44.5	44.8	46.3	47.3	44.8
2011	45.5	45.0	45.0	44.8	44.8	44.8	45.1	45.2	45.5	46.1	47.8	48.6	45.7
2012	46.8	46.4	46.4	46.3	46.8	46.9	47.0	46.9	47.1	47.4	49.8	50.4	47.4
2013	47.8	47.4	47.5	47.2	47.2	47.4	47.5	47.6	47.3	47.5	49.5	50.3	47.9
2014	47.5	46.7	46.8	46.7	46.7	47.1	47.4	47.2	47.4	47.6	49.4	50.6	47.6
2015	48.2	47.8	47.7	47.5	47.4	47.7	47.7	47.6	47.5	48.0	49.8	50.5	48.1
2016	48.1	47.5	47.4	46.7	46.6	46.5	47.0	47.2	47.6	48.0	49.3	50.2	47.7
2017	48.2	47.2	47.2	47.0	47.1	47.2	47.6	47.7	47.6	47.2	48.3	48.1	47.5
Transportation and Utilities													
2007	24.7	24.4	24.6	24.4	24.5	24.4	24.5	24.5	24.4	24.6	24.7	25.1	24.6
2008	24.5	23.6	22.9	22.5	22.6	22.0	21.2	21.3	21.0	20.8	20.8	20.7	22.0
2009	20.2	20.2	20.1	19.8	19.9	19.9	19.7	19.7	19.5	19.4	19.5	19.7	19.8
2010	19.4	19.3	19.2	19.4	19.3	19.5	19.5	19.6	19.5	19.6	19.7	19.9	19.5
2011	19.6	19.7	19.7	19.5	19.5	19.7	19.7	19.7	19.7	19.9	20.0	20.1	19.7
2012	20.0	19.9	20.1	20.1	20.2	20.4	20.6	20.7	20.8	21.0	21.1	21.3	20.5
2013	20.8	21.0	21.1	21.2	21.3	21.6	21.6	21.7	21.7	21.9	21.9	22.2	21.5
2014	21.9	21.9	22.0	21.9	22.0	21.8	21.9	21.8	21.7	21.9	22.2	22.5	22.0
2015	22.2	22.2	22.2	22.2	22.2	22.4	22.4	22.3	22.2	22.3	22.4	22.7	22.3
2016	22.3	22.3	22.3	22.4	22.7	22.7	22.7	22.9	22.8	22.9	23.1	23.5	22.7
2017	23.1	23.1	23.1	23.0	23.0	23.3	23.3	23.6	23.8	24.0	24.0	24.4	23.5

Employment by Industry: Urban Honolulu, HI, Selected Years, 2007–2017—*Continued*

(Numbers in thousands, not seasonally adjusted)

Industry and year	January	February	March	April	May	June	July	August	September	October	November	December	Annual average
Information													
2007	8.4	8.9	8.9	8.6	9.3	9.2	8.5	9.0	8.6	8.4	8.5	8.6	8.7
2008	7.8	8.3	8.6	8.7	9.0	9.4	8.0	7.8	7.8	7.6	8.1	8.3	8.3
2009	7.4	7.9	7.7	7.7	7.3	7.4	7.0	7.2	7.3	7.6	7.3	7.3	7.4
2010	7.3	8.1	8.3	7.7	8.9	8.3	7.0	7.5	9.4	8.3	7.9	8.8	8.1
2011	6.9	7.9	8.7	6.6	6.5	6.3	6.8	6.8	6.7	6.8	7.1	7.2	7.0
2012	6.8	7.0	7.1	7.0	7.0	6.3	6.7	6.9	6.9	7.2	7.7	7.5	7.0
2013	6.9	7.0	7.1	7.0	6.6	6.5	8.2	7.0	7.3	8.0	8.3	8.5	7.4
2014	6.9	7.0	7.1	6.9	7.4	6.7	6.8	7.3	7.3	7.1	7.3	7.4	7.1
2015	7.1	7.2	7.2	7.0	6.9	6.8	7.2	7.2	7.1	7.3	8.2	8.3	7.3
2016	6.8	7.2	7.0	7.1	7.6	7.0	7.3	8.3	7.7	7.3	8.2	7.3	7.4
2017	7.5	7.7	7.8	7.7	8.4	7.5	7.6	8.6	7.7	7.6	7.8	7.7	7.8
Financial Activities													
2007	22.8	22.7	23.0	22.8	22.9	23.1	23.1	23.0	22.9	23.1	23.0	23.1	23.0
2008	22.6	22.7	22.9	22.9	22.9	22.8	22.7	22.7	22.5	22.3	22.3	22.3	22.6
2009	21.7	21.6	21.5	21.4	21.5	21.4	21.3	21.1	21.1	21.1	21.0	21.0	21.3
2010	20.6	20.7	20.7	20.6	20.6	20.5	20.7	20.6	20.6	20.6	20.5	20.7	20.6
2011	20.3	20.3	20.3	20.3	20.3	20.2	20.4	20.3	20.2	20.3	20.5	20.4	20.3
2012	20.0	20.1	20.1	20.1	20.2	20.4	20.4	20.4	20.4	20.4	20.5	20.4	20.3
2013	20.1	20.2	20.4	20.4	20.5	20.6	20.6	20.5	20.6	20.5	20.5	20.7	20.5
2014	20.5	20.5	20.8	20.7	20.7	20.8	21.0	20.9	20.8	20.9	20.9	21.1	20.8
2015	20.8	20.9	21.1	21.1	21.2	21.3	21.3	21.3	21.1	21.1	21.2	21.4	21.2
2016	21.3	21.5	21.5	21.5	21.5	21.6	21.9	21.9	21.8	21.8	21.8	21.9	21.7
2017	21.8	21.8	22.0	21.8	21.9	22.0	21.9	21.8	21.8	21.6	21.8	21.8	21.8
Professional and Business Services													
2007	59.3	59.8	60.2	59.4	59.4	60.9	60.5	60.8	61.1	61.3	61.2	61.8	60.5
2008	60.2	60.6	60.8	60.6	60.1	60.2	60.4	60.6	60.2	60.1	60.0	60.9	60.4
2009	59.3	59.3	59.4	57.9	57.5	57.6	57.1	57.0	57.0	57.8	57.4	58.1	58.0
2010	57.0	57.3	57.4	57.5	57.5	57.6	58.1	58.0	58.1	58.6	58.7	59.3	57.9
2011	59.0	60.0	60.5	60.4	60.0	60.2	60.0	60.8	61.1	60.9	61.4	62.6	60.6
2012	60.6	61.0	61.5	62.1	62.5	62.7	62.2	62.9	62.5	63.0	63.5	63.8	62.4
2013	62.9	63.6	63.9	63.8	63.6	63.8	64.3	64.5	64.5	65.3	66.1	66.1	64.4
2014	65.6	65.7	66.1	66.3	65.8	65.9	65.6	65.8	66.1	66.0	66.4	66.7	66.0
2015	65.9	66.1	66.5	66.1	65.9	66.1	66.2	65.9	65.5	66.0	66.1	66.0	66.0
2016	64.8	65.2	65.2	65.6	64.7	64.6	65.1	65.2	65.1	64.7	64.9	65.1	65.0
2017	64.3	64.5	64.9	64.5	64.3	65.1	65.1	64.9	64.8	64.6	64.7	65.6	64.8
Education and Health Services													
2007	56.3	57.3	57.6	57.6	57.8	58.2	57.2	57.0	57.8	57.8	58.1	58.1	57.6
2008	56.9	57.9	58.2	58.0	58.3	58.5	58.0	57.8	58.3	58.5	59.0	59.3	58.2
2009	58.0	58.7	59.0	58.4	58.5	58.6	57.8	57.7	58.3	58.5	58.7	59.2	58.5
2010	58.1	58.8	59.0	58.7	59.1	58.7	58.6	58.3	58.3	59.5	59.7	60.1	58.9
2011	58.1	59.5	59.6	59.5	59.8	59.1	59.2	58.9	60.0	60.1	60.8	61.0	59.6
2012	59.0	60.1	60.1	60.4	60.8	60.4	60.0	60.8	61.2	61.3	61.6	62.2	60.7
2013	60.7	61.7	62.0	62.0	62.2	62.1	61.3	61.6	62.1	61.8	62.9	62.6	61.9
2014	61.1	61.8	62.2	62.2	62.2	61.6	61.4	61.5	62.4	62.8	63.3	63.8	62.2
2015	62.9	63.9	64.4	64.4	64.5	63.9	63.5	63.8	64.6	65.0	65.3	65.8	64.3
2016	63.7	64.0	64.7	64.9	64.7	64.1	64.4	64.0	65.0	64.2	64.6	64.9	64.4
2017	64.4	64.8	65.5	65.2	65.2	64.2	63.9	63.2	64.9	65.1	65.8	66.2	64.9
Leisure and Hospitality													
2007	62.5	63.7	64.2	64.2	64.6	64.9	64.2	64.8	64.8	63.8	63.9	64.0	64.1
2008	62.8	63.4	63.3	62.8	62.9	63.1	63.0	62.9	62.5	61.7	61.4	61.1	62.6
2009	60.2	60.8	61.1	60.4	60.8	61.1	60.7	60.9	60.9	60.2	60.1	60.2	60.6
2010	58.9	59.4	59.6	59.5	59.5	59.9	60.2	60.4	60.7	60.7	60.9	61.4	60.1
2011	60.5	60.6	61.2	61.1	61.1	61.4	61.3	61.9	62.4	62.1	62.5	62.6	61.6
2012	62.0	62.6	63.1	63.3	63.7	64.4	64.6	64.9	64.9	64.9	65.0	65.5	64.1
2013	64.6	65.2	65.4	65.6	66.4	66.8	66.8	67.2	67.0	67.2	67.5	67.7	66.5
2014	66.4	66.8	67.4	67.2	67.7	67.7	67.6	67.8	68.0	68.1	68.2	68.1	67.6
2015	67.0	67.3	67.5	67.4	67.9	67.8	68.2	69.0	68.7	69.1	69.6	70.0	68.3
2016	68.6	69.2	69.5	69.6	70.1	70.6	71.1	71.9	71.8	71.7	71.7	72.3	70.7
2017	71.8	72.8	73.7	73.0	73.4	73.7	73.8	74.3	74.1	75.3	75.4	76.1	74.0

Employment by Industry: Urban Honolulu, HI, Selected Years, 2007–2017—*Continued*

(Numbers in thousands, not seasonally adjusted)

Industry and year	January	February	March	April	May	June	July	August	September	October	November	December	Annual average
Other Services													
2007	20.0	20.4	20.6	20.4	20.5	20.5	20.5	20.6	20.8	20.9	20.9	20.9	20.6
2008	20.5	21.0	21.2	21.2	21.3	21.0	20.8	20.8	21.0	21.0	21.0	20.9	21.0
2009	20.1	20.4	20.4	20.2	20.2	20.1	20.1	20.3	20.4	20.4	20.4	20.4	20.3
2010	19.9	20.2	20.3	20.0	20.0	19.9	20.0	20.1	20.0	20.1	20.0	20.0	20.0
2011	19.7	19.9	19.9	20.0	20.1	20.1	20.1	20.2	20.5	20.5	20.5	20.6	20.2
2012	20.0	20.3	20.4	20.4	20.6	20.5	20.4	20.6	20.6	20.6	20.6	20.5	20.5
2013	20.6	20.7	20.7	20.9	20.9	20.8	20.9	21.0	21.1	21.1	21.1	21.1	20.9
2014	20.7	20.8	21.0	20.7	20.8	20.8	20.7	20.9	21.0	21.0	21.1	21.2	20.9
2015	20.8	20.9	21.1	20.9	21.1	21.1	20.9	20.9	20.9	21.0	21.1	21.0	21.0
2016	20.9	21.0	21.1	21.2	21.2	21.2	21.2	21.2	21.3	21.2	21.4	21.3	21.2
2017	21.1	21.2	21.4	21.2	21.3	21.4	21.3	21.3	21.4	21.3	21.4	21.4	21.3
Government													
2007	94.6	98.8	99.5	94.5	99.6	98.0	90.1	89.9	95.6	97.8	99.4	100.3	96.5
2008	95.5	99.2	100.4	95.5	101.1	99.3	92.1	93.8	97.0	100.3	104.4	101.8	98.4
2009	98.3	100.3	101.8	101.4	102.7	100.7	93.4	92.1	95.7	98.5	99.5	100.1	98.7
2010	95.8	99.0	100.3	100.7	102.4	98.9	94.1	89.9	96.0	99.1	102.5	100.9	98.3
2011	94.0	100.5	101.0	100.7	101.4	99.0	93.6	89.5	96.3	99.2	100.9	101.4	98.1
2012	89.0	100.9	101.6	101.6	102.2	99.5	92.3	94.7	97.2	99.8	103.5	101.7	98.7
2013	89.1	101.2	101.5	98.4	102.1	98.2	92.2	89.7	97.0	99.8	100.9	101.4	97.6
2014	97.9	101.3	101.6	100.9	102.3	99.0	92.3	92.4	97.3	99.5	102.4	98.3	98.8
2015	97.5	100.7	101.1	100.9	101.7	98.9	91.6	94.5	97.3	100.0	100.8	101.8	98.9
2016	95.6	100.6	101.4	98.9	101.5	98.8	91.7	91.5	97.8	100.1	102.9	99.3	98.3
2017	97.3	101.5	101.5	101.2	101.5	98.4	91.3	89.0	98.2	100.4	101.7	102.2	98.7

Employment by Industry: Bridgeport-Stamford-Norwalk, CT, Selected Years, 2007–2017

(Numbers in thousands, not seasonally adjusted)

Industry and year	January	February	March	April	May	June	July	August	September	October	November	December	Annual average
Total Nonfarm													
2007	404.5	404.1	405.7	409.5	414.3	417.6	416.1	411.9	411.2	413.5	416.0	418.7	411.9
2008	406.6	405.4	407.7	410.1	413.3	416.4	411.0	407.0	407.6	408.4	409.0	408.9	409.3
2009	394.2	391.6	391.4	389.1	393.2	395.2	390.6	387.0	388.9	389.3	390.8	392.3	391.1
2010	378.0	376.7	379.3	385.3	393.3	395.9	395.6	391.8	390.8	392.3	393.6	396.0	389.1
2011	383.9	384.8	386.5	392.0	395.2	397.5	397.4	393.4	394.3	395.3	396.9	399.2	393.0
2012	389.8	388.9	392.5	395.1	399.4	403.6	402.0	398.5	398.2	399.4	401.4	404.1	397.7
2013	392.6	390.7	394.4	400.1	404.3	409.7	407.3	404.1	403.9	404.4	406.7	407.0	402.1
2014	395.8	394.1	397.2	403.0	407.7	410.9	409.6	407.2	406.8	408.5	411.6	412.9	405.4
2015	401.2	399.0	400.7	406.1	412.0	417.9	413.5	410.4	409.7	412.7	414.8	415.8	409.5
2016	403.4	401.9	405.0	408.0	412.5	418.0	415.7	411.6	410.5	410.8	412.0	411.7	410.1
2017	400.9	398.8	401.2	404.2	408.8	415.8	412.0	407.5	407.0	405.8	408.2	408.0	406.5
Total Private													
2007	358.9	357.8	359.4	363.2	367.1	371.7	371.0	368.6	365.7	366.9	369.0	372.0	365.9
2008	360.2	358.2	360.7	363.5	365.9	370.0	367.5	364.9	361.8	361.6	361.3	361.8	363.1
2009	348.0	345.1	344.6	343.5	346.0	348.5	347.2	344.7	343.2	343.2	344.3	346.3	345.4
2010	332.8	331.5	334.0	340.8	345.7	350.0	351.5	349.6	346.6	347.8	348.7	350.8	344.2
2011	339.6	339.9	341.6	346.7	349.6	353.3	355.9	353.2	350.3	350.7	352.1	354.3	348.9
2012	345.7	344.7	348.0	350.6	354.4	359.6	359.5	357.2	354.1	355.0	356.4	359.2	353.7
2013	348.1	346.1	349.6	355.4	359.3	364.5	364.3	362.3	359.6	359.9	361.6	362.1	357.7
2014	352.0	350.0	352.7	357.9	362.0	366.1	366.7	364.3	361.8	363.6	366.0	367.6	360.9
2015	357.2	354.8	356.2	361.2	366.7	371.7	370.4	368.0	364.8	368.2	369.7	371.1	365.0
2016	359.5	357.7	360.6	363.6	367.3	372.7	373.0	370.0	366.2	367.0	367.7	367.9	366.1
2017	357.6	354.9	357.1	360.7	364.7	371.2	370.1	366.2	363.5	362.6	364.4	364.7	363.1
Goods Producing													
2007	51.9	51.6	52.0	52.6	53.0	53.7	53.6	53.5	53.3	52.9	52.6	52.4	52.8
2008	51.2	50.6	51.0	51.7	52.3	52.5	52.1	51.9	51.8	51.1	50.6	49.8	51.4
2009	47.8	46.8	46.5	46.7	46.5	46.8	46.2	45.7	45.5	45.2	44.8	44.5	46.1
2010	42.4	42.1	42.4	43.6	44.1	44.9	45.1	45.1	44.7	44.5	44.0	43.7	43.9
2011	42.5	42.5	42.8	43.7	44.3	44.8	44.8	44.6	44.2	44.0	43.9	43.8	43.8
2012	42.5	42.5	42.4	42.6	42.9	43.6	43.5	43.4	42.8	42.8	42.8	42.7	42.9
2013	41.5	41.3	41.3	42.2	42.7	43.3	43.1	43.1	42.9	42.8	42.8	42.4	42.5
2014	41.1	40.9	40.9	41.7	42.2	42.6	42.5	42.5	42.1	42.5	42.3	41.9	41.9
2015	40.6	40.1	40.2	41.2	42.0	42.6	42.5	42.5	42.3	42.4	42.2	41.9	41.7
2016	40.7	40.5	40.7	41.5	42.0	42.5	42.6	42.5	41.9	41.9	41.8	41.4	41.7
2017	40.4	40.1	40.3	41.5	42.0	42.9	42.6	42.4	42.0	42.4	42.0	40.7	41.6
Service-Providing													
2007	352.6	352.5	353.7	356.9	361.3	363.9	362.5	358.4	357.9	360.6	363.4	366.3	359.2
2008	355.4	354.8	356.7	358.4	361.0	363.9	358.9	355.1	355.8	357.3	358.4	359.1	357.9
2009	346.4	344.8	344.9	342.4	346.7	348.4	344.4	341.3	343.4	344.1	346.0	347.8	345.1
2010	335.6	334.6	336.9	341.7	349.2	351.0	350.5	346.7	346.1	347.8	349.6	352.3	345.2
2011	341.4	342.3	343.7	348.3	350.9	352.7	352.6	348.8	350.1	351.3	353.0	355.4	349.2
2012	347.3	346.4	350.1	352.5	356.5	360.0	358.5	355.1	355.4	356.6	358.6	361.4	354.9
2013	351.1	349.4	353.1	357.9	361.6	366.4	364.2	361.0	361.0	361.6	363.9	364.6	359.7
2014	354.7	353.2	356.3	361.3	365.5	368.3	367.1	364.7	364.7	366.0	369.3	371.0	363.5
2015	360.6	358.9	360.5	364.9	370.0	375.3	371.0	367.9	367.4	370.3	372.6	373.9	367.8
2016	362.7	361.4	364.3	366.5	370.5	375.5	373.1	369.1	368.6	368.9	370.2	370.3	368.4
2017	360.5	358.7	360.9	362.7	366.8	372.9	369.4	365.1	365.0	363.4	366.2	367.3	364.9
Mining, Logging, and Construction													
2007	14.2	13.7	14.0	15.2	15.6	15.9	16.1	16.1	15.9	15.8	15.6	15.3	15.3
2008	13.9	13.7	13.9	14.8	15.2	15.3	15.3	15.3	15.1	14.6	14.2	13.6	14.6
2009	12.2	11.8	11.6	11.9	12.1	12.2	12.2	12.0	11.8	11.7	11.5	11.2	11.9
2010	9.4	9.2	9.5	10.7	11.0	11.4	11.6	11.7	11.5	11.4	11.2	10.8	10.8
2011	9.6	9.6	9.8	10.8	11.3	11.6	11.8	11.8	11.7	11.6	11.6	11.4	11.1
2012	10.4	10.3	10.5	11.2	11.5	11.8	12.0	11.9	11.7	11.6	11.6	11.5	11.3
2013	10.5	10.2	10.3	11.3	11.7	12.0	12.2	12.3	12.2	12.1	12.1	11.6	11.5
2014	10.4	10.2	10.4	11.5	12.2	12.5	12.6	12.7	12.6	12.7	12.6	12.2	11.9
2015	11.0	10.6	10.7	11.9	12.5	12.8	12.8	12.9	12.9	13.0	12.8	12.5	12.2
2016	11.4	11.1	11.4	12.3	12.7	12.9	13.0	13.0	12.8	12.8	12.7	12.2	12.4
2017	11.1	10.9	11.1	12.2	12.7	13.2	13.0	13.0	12.9	13.2	12.8	11.3	12.3

Employment by Industry: Bridgeport-Stamford-Norwalk, CT, Selected Years, 2007–2017—*Continued*

(Numbers in thousands, not seasonally adjusted)

Industry and year	January	February	March	April	May	June	July	August	September	October	November	December	Annual average
Manufacturing													
2007	37.7	37.9	38.0	37.4	37.4	37.8	37.5	37.4	37.4	37.1	37.0	37.1	37.5
2008	37.3	36.9	37.1	36.9	37.1	37.2	36.8	36.6	36.7	36.5	36.4	36.2	36.8
2009	35.6	35.0	34.9	34.8	34.4	34.6	34.0	33.7	33.7	33.5	33.3	33.3	34.2
2010	33.0	32.9	32.9	32.9	33.1	33.5	33.5	33.4	33.2	33.1	32.8	32.9	33.1
2011	32.9	32.9	33.0	32.9	33.0	33.2	33.0	32.8	32.5	32.4	32.3	32.4	32.8
2012	32.1	32.2	31.9	31.4	31.4	31.8	31.5	31.5	31.1	31.2	31.2	31.2	31.5
2013	31.0	31.1	31.0	30.9	31.0	31.3	30.9	30.8	30.7	30.7	30.7	30.8	30.9
2014	30.7	30.7	30.5	30.2	30.0	30.1	29.9	29.8	29.5	29.8	29.7	29.7	30.1
2015	29.6	29.5	29.5	29.3	29.5	29.8	29.7	29.6	29.4	29.4	29.4	29.4	29.5
2016	29.3	29.4	29.3	29.2	29.3	29.6	29.6	29.5	29.1	29.1	29.1	29.2	29.3
2017	29.3	29.2	29.2	29.3	29.3	29.7	29.6	29.4	29.1	29.2	29.2	29.4	29.3
Trade, Transportation, and Utilities													
2007	74.1	72.3	72.7	72.6	73.8	75.0	73.7	73.4	73.6	74.1	76.6	78.7	74.2
2008	75.2	73.4	73.5	73.2	73.8	74.5	73.0	72.7	73.0	72.8	74.0	75.3	73.7
2009	71.2	69.4	69.1	67.9	68.7	69.4	67.8	67.5	67.7	68.3	70.1	71.6	69.1
2010	67.7	66.5	66.7	66.9	68.5	69.6	68.6	68.4	68.4	69.3	71.1	72.8	68.7
2011	69.2	68.1	68.1	68.9	69.4	70.2	69.3	68.8	68.7	69.2	71.0	72.9	69.5
2012	70.1	68.5	68.9	68.8	69.7	70.6	69.3	69.0	69.1	69.8	71.6	72.9	69.9
2013	70.3	68.7	69.3	69.6	70.2	71.0	69.9	69.9	70.0	70.6	72.4	73.9	70.5
2014	71.0	69.6	69.8	69.9	70.5	71.3	70.1	69.8	70.1	71.0	72.9	74.3	70.9
2015	71.2	69.7	69.8	69.8	70.9	71.8	70.3	70.1	70.6	71.6	73.6	75.1	71.2
2016	71.2	70.0	70.4	70.4	71.4	71.8	70.6	70.1	70.7	71.0	72.8	74.1	71.2
2017	71.4	69.8	69.8	69.7	70.5	71.3	70.1	69.5	70.0	70.4	72.9	73.9	70.8
Wholesale Trade													
2007	14.2	14.2	14.3	14.2	14.2	14.4	14.4	14.5	14.4	14.4	14.5	14.7	14.4
2008	14.6	14.5	14.6	14.6	14.6	14.7	14.6	14.6	14.5	14.5	14.5	14.6	14.6
2009	14.2	14.1	14.0	13.7	13.6	13.7	13.6	13.5	13.4	13.4	13.2	13.3	13.6
2010	12.9	12.9	13.0	13.1	13.2	13.4	13.3	13.3	13.2	13.2	13.3	13.4	13.2
2011	13.2	13.2	13.3	13.4	13.4	13.6	13.6	13.5	13.4	13.3	13.3	13.4	13.4
2012	13.2	13.2	13.2	13.2	13.2	13.4	13.4	13.3	13.3	13.4	13.3	13.3	13.3
2013	13.3	13.2	13.3	13.3	13.4	13.5	13.5	13.5	13.4	13.5	13.5	13.6	13.4
2014	13.4	13.5	13.5	13.5	13.5	13.6	13.5	13.5	13.4	13.4	13.4	13.4	13.5
2015	13.3	13.3	13.3	13.4	13.5	13.6	13.5	13.5	13.4	13.5	13.4	13.4	13.4
2016	13.1	13.1	13.2	13.3	13.5	13.6	13.6	13.6	13.5	13.4	13.4	13.5	13.4
2017	13.3	13.3	13.4	13.3	13.3	13.6	13.7	13.7	13.6	13.6	13.8	14.0	13.6
Retail Trade													
2007	49.5	47.8	48.0	48.0	49.1	49.9	49.4	49.2	48.8	49.3	51.5	53.1	49.5
2008	50.2	48.5	48.6	48.1	48.6	49.2	48.6	48.6	48.3	48.3	49.4	50.4	48.9
2009	47.0	45.4	45.2	44.8	45.5	46.1	45.3	45.3	44.9	45.5	47.4	48.4	45.9
2010	45.6	44.4	44.5	44.8	45.9	46.6	46.4	46.2	45.6	46.5	48.0	49.2	46.1
2011	46.4	45.3	45.2	45.8	46.2	46.7	46.4	46.2	45.6	46.2	47.9	49.3	46.4
2012	47.1	45.5	45.9	45.8	46.5	47.2	46.7	46.6	46.1	46.6	48.4	49.3	46.8
2013	47.3	46.0	46.3	46.5	47.0	47.6	47.2	47.3	46.6	47.2	48.9	50.0	47.3
2014	47.7	46.3	46.5	46.7	47.2	47.9	47.5	47.3	46.9	47.7	49.3	50.3	47.6
2015	47.9	46.7	46.8	46.7	47.5	48.2	47.4	47.5	47.1	48.0	49.8	50.8	47.9
2016	48.2	47.0	47.2	47.2	47.7	48.1	47.7	47.4	47.0	47.4	48.9	49.7	47.8
2017	48.1	46.7	46.6	46.8	47.4	47.8	47.7	47.3	46.7	47.0	49.0	49.2	47.5
Transportation and Utilities													
2007	10.4	10.3	10.4	10.4	10.5	10.7	9.9	9.7	10.4	10.4	10.6	10.9	10.4
2008	10.4	10.4	10.3	10.5	10.6	10.6	9.8	9.5	10.2	10.0	10.1	10.3	10.2
2009	10.0	9.9	9.9	9.4	9.6	9.6	8.9	8.7	9.4	9.4	9.5	9.9	9.5
2010	9.2	9.2	9.2	9.0	9.4	9.6	8.9	8.9	9.6	9.6	9.8	10.2	9.4
2011	9.6	9.6	9.6	9.7	9.8	9.9	9.3	9.1	9.7	9.7	9.8	10.2	9.7
2012	9.8	9.8	9.8	9.8	10.0	10.0	9.2	9.1	9.7	9.8	9.9	10.3	9.8
2013	9.7	9.5	9.7	9.8	9.8	9.9	9.2	9.1	10.0	9.9	10.0	10.3	9.7
2014	9.9	9.8	9.8	9.7	9.8	9.8	9.1	9.0	9.8	9.9	10.2	10.6	9.8
2015	10.0	9.7	9.7	9.7	9.9	10.0	9.4	9.1	10.1	10.1	10.4	10.9	9.9
2016	9.9	9.9	10.0	9.9	10.2	10.1	9.3	9.1	10.2	10.2	10.5	10.9	10.0
2017	10.0	9.8	9.8	9.6	9.8	9.9	8.7	8.5	9.7	9.8	10.1	10.7	9.7

Employment by Industry: Bridgeport-Stamford-Norwalk, CT, Selected Years, 2007–2017—*Continued*

(Numbers in thousands, not seasonally adjusted)

Industry and year	January	February	March	April	May	June	July	August	September	October	November	December	Annual average
Information													
2007	10.7	10.8	10.9	10.7	10.9	10.8	11.1	11.2	11.4	11.1	10.5	10.6	10.9
2008	10.6	10.6	10.7	10.6	10.6	10.8	10.8	10.9	10.8	10.8	10.9	11.0	10.8
2009	11.1	11.1	11.0	10.8	10.8	10.7	10.7	10.6	10.5	10.3	10.4	10.4	10.7
2010	10.2	10.2	10.2	10.3	10.4	10.3	10.2	10.2	10.2	10.1	10.2	10.3	10.2
2011	10.2	10.2	10.2	10.2	10.2	10.3	10.5	10.5	10.3	10.3	10.4	10.6	10.3
2012	10.6	10.5	10.5	10.5	10.5	10.5	10.6	10.7	10.6	10.6	10.7	10.8	10.6
2013	10.8	11.1	11.1	11.0	11.3	11.4	11.6	11.4	11.4	11.4	11.4	11.5	11.3
2014	11.3	11.4	11.4	11.4	11.4	11.4	11.5	11.5	11.4	11.4	12.0	12.1	11.5
2015	12.0	11.9	12.0	12.1	12.0	12.2	12.2	12.2	12.2	12.2	12.2	12.3	12.1
2016	12.3	12.3	12.3	12.4	12.4	12.5	12.7	13.1	12.7	12.8	12.7	12.4	12.6
2017	12.0	12.2	12.3	12.3	12.0	12.2	12.2	12.3	12.2	12.2	12.2	12.1	12.2
Financial Activities													
2007	44.7	44.7	44.8	44.7	45.0	45.6	46.0	45.8	45.1	45.3	45.3	45.6	45.2
2008	44.9	45.1	45.3	45.1	45.1	45.7	45.5	45.6	44.8	44.7	44.6	44.7	45.1
2009	43.7	43.7	43.8	42.7	42.6	43.0	43.2	43.1	42.7	42.7	42.7	42.9	43.1
2010	42.0	42.0	42.1	42.1	42.2	42.9	43.1	43.2	42.5	42.4	42.4	42.7	42.5
2011	42.4	42.4	42.4	42.4	42.3	42.3	43.2	43.0	42.1	42.1	42.1	42.1	42.4
2012	41.7	41.6	41.6	41.5	41.6	42.2	42.3	42.0	41.4	41.5	41.4	41.5	41.7
2013	41.4	41.2	41.2	41.1	41.3	41.9	42.1	41.9	41.4	41.3	41.4	41.5	41.5
2014	40.3	40.2	40.3	40.2	40.4	41.1	41.4	41.3	40.8	40.9	41.0	41.3	40.8
2015	40.9	40.9	41.0	41.0	41.1	41.8	41.9	41.7	41.0	41.1	41.1	41.2	41.2
2016	41.0	40.8	41.0	40.8	40.8	41.2	41.4	41.1	40.5	40.6	40.7	40.6	40.9
2017	40.2	39.9	39.9	39.8	39.8	40.4	40.6	40.3	39.6	39.6	39.9	40.0	40.0
Professional and Business Services													
2007	70.1	70.0	70.2	72.0	72.5	73.2	71.9	71.8	71.4	71.9	71.9	72.0	71.6
2008	68.9	68.1	68.7	70.1	70.0	70.6	69.9	69.6	68.7	68.5	67.9	67.5	69.0
2009	65.1	64.4	64.4	64.7	64.5	65.0	64.5	64.4	64.0	64.1	63.9	64.0	64.4
2010	61.4	61.7	62.7	65.1	65.4	66.1	66.6	66.5	66.2	66.6	66.1	65.9	65.0
2011	63.7	64.5	65.0	66.4	66.8	67.2	67.8	67.5	67.1	67.3	67.3	67.1	66.5
2012	65.5	65.6	67.0	68.3	68.6	69.2	69.4	69.2	68.7	68.2	68.1	67.9	68.0
2013	65.1	65.4	65.9	67.9	68.4	69.3	69.4	69.7	68.9	68.7	68.3	67.7	67.9
2014	65.4	65.5	65.9	68.0	68.6	69.0	69.4	69.3	68.5	68.4	68.6	68.1	67.9
2015	66.0	66.0	66.0	67.9	68.6	69.1	69.3	69.4	68.4	69.7	69.7	69.2	68.3
2016	66.5	66.3	66.9	68.3	68.2	69.3	69.2	68.8	67.9	67.8	67.2	66.9	67.8
2017	63.9	63.7	64.1	65.5	65.8	66.6	65.6	65.4	64.9	64.1	63.8	63.3	64.7
Education and Health Services													
2007	59.7	61.1	60.9	61.4	60.9	60.5	60.4	59.5	60.5	61.8	62.3	62.7	61.0
2008	61.3	62.6	63.0	63.0	62.5	62.5	62.2	61.2	62.4	63.7	64.2	64.4	62.8
2009	62.8	63.6	63.5	63.4	63.6	62.7	62.8	62.2	63.3	64.2	64.6	64.9	63.5
2010	63.7	64.0	64.2	65.0	65.1	64.3	64.7	63.8	64.7	65.6	66.1	66.3	64.8
2011	65.2	65.7	65.9	66.2	66.1	65.6	65.6	64.9	65.9	66.3	66.9	67.1	66.0
2012	66.5	67.1	67.5	67.5	67.5	67.2	67.0	66.4	67.5	68.2	68.6	69.3	67.5
2013	67.6	67.7	68.4	69.3	69.3	69.0	68.4	67.5	68.6	69.4	69.9	69.4	68.7
2014	69.4	69.4	69.9	70.5	70.9	70.2	70.4	69.4	70.6	71.3	71.6	72.0	70.5
2015	71.3	71.3	71.5	71.7	72.2	71.9	71.1	70.3	70.9	72.2	72.5	72.4	71.6
2016	71.6	71.8	72.0	71.9	72.3	71.9	71.8	71.1	72.2	73.0	73.2	73.3	72.2
2017	72.7	72.9	73.1	73.2	73.7	73.3	73.5	72.5	73.8	73.9	74.8	75.3	73.6
Leisure and Hospitality													
2007	31.0	30.7	31.2	32.5	34.2	35.9	36.8	36.3	33.8	33.4	33.4	33.6	33.6
2008	31.8	31.7	32.3	33.5	35.2	36.6	36.9	36.1	34.1	33.7	32.8	32.8	34.0
2009	30.5	30.3	30.5	31.6	33.4	34.7	35.5	34.9	33.7	32.6	31.9	32.1	32.6
2010	29.9	29.6	30.2	32.1	34.0	35.5	36.5	35.7	34.0	33.4	32.8	33.1	33.1
2011	30.7	30.8	31.4	33.0	34.4	36.6	37.9	37.3	36.0	35.6	34.6	34.7	34.4
2012	32.8	32.9	34.0	35.2	37.2	39.5	40.3	39.6	37.7	37.5	36.8	37.6	36.8
2013	35.3	34.7	36.2	37.9	39.5	41.7	42.6	41.7	39.8	39.1	38.8	39.1	38.9
2014	37.1	36.7	38.0	39.6	41.2	43.4	44.0	43.2	41.5	41.2	40.6	40.8	40.6
2015	38.3	38.0	38.8	40.6	42.7	44.8	45.4	44.1	42.0	41.6	41.1	41.5	41.6
2016	39.0	38.8	40.0	40.9	42.6	45.3	46.2	45.1	42.7	42.3	41.7	41.6	42.2
2017	39.6	39.0	40.1	41.1	43.0	46.1	46.8	45.5	43.2	42.6	41.3	42.1	42.5

Employment by Industry: Bridgeport-Stamford-Norwalk, CT, Selected Years, 2007–2017—*Continued*

(Numbers in thousands, not seasonally adjusted)

Industry and year	January	February	March	April	May	June	July	August	September	October	November	December	Annual average
Other Services													
2007	16.7	16.6	16.7	16.7	16.8	17.0	17.5	17.1	16.6	16.4	16.4	16.4	16.7
2008	16.3	16.1	16.2	16.3	16.4	16.8	17.1	16.9	16.2	16.3	16.3	16.3	16.4
2009	15.8	15.8	15.8	15.7	15.9	16.2	16.5	16.3	15.8	15.8	15.9	15.9	16.0
2010	15.5	15.4	15.5	15.7	16.0	16.4	16.7	16.7	15.9	15.9	16.0	16.0	16.0
2011	15.7	15.7	15.8	15.9	16.1	16.3	16.8	16.6	16.0	15.9	15.9	16.0	16.1
2012	16.0	16.0	16.1	16.2	16.4	16.8	17.1	16.9	16.3	16.4	16.4	16.5	16.4
2013	16.1	16.0	16.2	16.4	16.6	16.9	17.2	17.1	16.6	16.6	16.6	16.6	16.6
2014	16.4	16.3	16.5	16.6	16.8	17.1	17.4	17.3	16.8	16.9	17.0	17.1	16.9
2015	16.9	16.9	16.9	16.9	17.2	17.5	17.7	17.7	17.4	17.4	17.3	17.5	17.3
2016	17.2	17.2	17.3	17.4	17.6	18.2	18.5	18.2	17.6	17.6	17.6	17.6	17.7
2017	17.4	17.3	17.5	17.6	17.9	18.4	18.7	18.3	17.8	17.4	17.5	17.3	17.8
Government													
2007	45.6	46.3	46.3	46.3	47.2	45.9	45.1	43.3	45.5	46.6	47.0	46.7	46.0
2008	46.4	47.2	47.0	46.6	47.4	46.4	43.5	42.1	45.8	46.8	47.7	47.1	46.2
2009	46.2	46.5	46.8	45.6	47.2	46.7	43.4	42.3	45.7	46.1	46.5	46.0	45.8
2010	45.2	45.2	45.3	44.5	47.6	45.9	44.1	42.2	44.2	44.5	44.9	45.2	44.9
2011	44.3	44.9	44.9	45.3	45.6	44.2	41.5	40.2	44.0	44.6	44.8	44.9	44.1
2012	44.1	44.2	44.5	44.5	45.0	44.0	42.5	41.3	44.1	44.4	45.0	44.9	44.0
2013	44.5	44.6	44.8	44.7	45.0	45.2	43.0	41.8	44.3	44.5	45.1	44.9	44.4
2014	43.8	44.1	44.5	45.1	45.7	44.8	42.9	42.9	45.0	44.9	45.6	45.3	44.6
2015	44.0	44.2	44.5	44.9	45.3	46.2	43.1	42.4	44.9	44.5	45.1	44.7	44.5
2016	43.9	44.2	44.4	44.4	45.2	45.3	42.7	41.6	44.3	43.8	44.3	43.8	44.0
2017	43.3	43.9	44.1	43.5	44.1	44.6	41.9	41.3	43.5	43.2	43.8	43.3	43.4

Employment by Industry: Worcester, MA-CT, Selected Years, 2007–2017

(Numbers in thousands, not seasonally adjusted)

Industry and year	January	February	March	April	May	June	July	August	September	October	November	December	Annual average
Total Nonfarm													
2007	265.2	266.2	267.1	269.2	272.2	274.0	266.9	266.8	270.3	273.1	274.4	273.0	269.9
2008	266.1	267.3	267.9	269.4	271.1	271.2	265.6	265.2	269.1	270.7	268.8	267.2	268.3
2009	259.5	259.3	258.5	260.4	261.4	260.4	255.6	255.4	258.7	261.2	260.8	262.4	259.5
2010	255.4	255.4	255.9	259.4	262.8	262.7	258.0	258.1	261.0	264.2	264.6	265.7	260.3
2011	259.3	260.1	261.0	264.0	265.1	264.5	262.4	260.9	265.9	268.2	269.0	268.9	264.1
2012	261.7	261.9	264.3	265.2	266.6	268.5	264.8	264.5	268.5	270.5	271.0	270.2	266.5
2013	264.6	265.2	267.2	270.6	273.0	273.6	267.2	268.3	271.4	273.6	274.6	274.7	270.3
2014	268.1	269.9	271.6	275.9	277.4	277.2	272.6	272.8	276.8	280.2	281.2	281.1	275.4
2015	272.3	273.1	275.1	278.7	281.9	281.9	276.2	276.2	279.6	283.2	284.4	285.0	279.0
2016	275.7	277.6	279.4	283.6	285.8	286.0	282.4	281.6	285.9	286.8	288.4	287.6	283.4
2017	279.8	281.6	283.4	285.7	288.0	288.8	283.5	283.7	287.9	290.7	292.2	292.2	286.5
Total Private													
2007	224.5	224.9	225.8	227.7	230.3	232.4	229.3	229.6	229.5	231.6	232.3	231.0	229.1
2008	225.2	225.7	226.1	227.7	229.1	230.1	227.7	228.0	228.4	228.9	227.0	225.7	227.5
2009	218.5	217.5	216.6	218.4	219.4	218.9	217.4	217.3	217.7	219.2	218.8	219.2	218.2
2010	213.9	213.6	214.0	217.3	219.8	220.7	220.0	220.3	220.0	222.5	222.5	223.4	219.0
2011	218.4	218.5	219.2	222.2	223.1	223.4	224.5	223.7	225.2	226.7	227.5	227.3	223.3
2012	221.1	220.5	222.4	223.8	225.1	227.2	226.9	226.7	227.1	228.6	228.6	227.7	225.5
2013	223.5	222.7	224.6	226.8	229.4	231.9	229.3	230.0	229.2	230.3	230.7	230.5	228.2
2014	226.1	226.0	227.6	231.2	233.1	235.0	234.1	234.2	233.8	236.2	236.3	236.4	232.5
2015	230.3	229.2	230.7	234.0	237.4	238.6	237.6	238.0	237.1	239.2	239.9	240.4	236.0
2016	233.6	233.6	234.8	239.2	241.3	243.1	243.1	242.6	242.5	242.8	243.1	243.0	240.2
2017	237.1	237.4	239.1	241.2	243.3	245.8	244.5	244.8	244.2	246.2	246.8	247.3	243.1
Goods Producing													
2007	43.1	42.4	42.5	43.0	43.8	44.7	44.5	44.4	44.2	44.4	44.4	43.9	43.8
2008	42.6	41.9	41.9	42.3	42.8	43.4	43.0	42.8	42.6	42.5	41.9	41.0	42.4
2009	38.8	37.7	37.0	37.3	37.6	38.0	37.7	37.7	37.6	37.5	37.4	37.1	37.6
2010	35.8	35.2	35.3	36.2	36.7	37.3	37.1	37.2	37.0	37.3	37.3	37.1	36.6
2011	35.7	35.2	35.3	36.2	37.0	37.6	38.4	38.4	38.3	38.3	38.2	38.0	37.2
2012	36.0	35.6	35.9	36.4	36.5	37.0	37.1	36.9	36.9	36.9	36.6	35.9	36.5
2013	35.0	34.8	35.0	35.5	36.2	36.9	37.1	37.1	36.9	36.6	36.4	36.1	36.1
2014	35.4	35.1	35.2	35.9	36.5	37.1	37.5	37.4	37.2	37.7	37.6	37.1	36.6
2015	36.3	35.8	36.0	37.0	37.8	38.3	38.5	38.5	38.1	38.3	38.4	38.2	37.6
2016	37.2	36.7	37.2	37.9	38.5	39.3	39.3	39.2	39.0	38.7	38.6	38.6	38.4
2017	37.2	36.6	36.9	37.7	38.4	39.2	39.3	39.5	39.0	39.2	39.3	39.3	38.5
Service-Providing													
2007	222.1	223.8	224.6	226.2	228.4	229.3	222.4	222.4	226.1	228.7	230.0	229.1	226.1
2008	223.5	225.4	226.0	227.1	228.3	227.8	222.6	222.4	226.5	228.2	226.9	226.2	225.9
2009	220.7	221.6	221.5	223.1	223.8	222.4	217.9	217.7	221.1	223.7	223.4	225.3	221.9
2010	219.6	220.2	220.6	223.2	226.1	225.4	220.9	220.9	224.0	226.9	227.3	228.6	223.6
2011	223.6	224.9	225.7	227.8	228.1	226.9	224.0	222.5	227.6	229.9	230.8	230.9	226.9
2012	225.7	226.3	228.4	228.8	230.1	231.5	227.7	227.6	231.6	233.6	234.4	234.3	230.0
2013	229.6	230.4	232.2	235.1	236.8	236.7	230.1	231.2	234.5	237.0	238.2	238.6	234.2
2014	232.7	234.8	236.4	240.0	240.9	240.1	235.1	235.4	239.6	242.5	243.6	244.0	238.8
2015	236.0	237.3	239.1	241.7	244.1	243.6	237.7	237.7	241.5	244.9	246.0	246.8	241.4
2016	238.5	240.9	242.2	245.7	247.3	246.7	243.1	242.4	246.9	248.1	249.8	249.0	245.1
2017	242.6	245.0	246.5	248.0	249.6	249.6	244.2	244.2	248.9	251.5	252.9	252.9	248.0
Mining, Logging, and Construction													
2007	9.9	9.4	9.5	10.1	10.9	11.4	11.6	11.6	11.5	11.3	11.2	10.6	10.8
2008	9.5	9.2	9.4	9.9	10.4	10.8	10.8	10.9	10.7	10.5	10.2	9.5	10.2
2009	8.3	7.9	7.7	8.4	8.8	9.1	9.2	9.3	9.2	9.1	8.9	8.5	8.7
2010	7.5	7.1	7.2	7.9	8.3	8.7	8.9	8.9	8.7	8.9	8.8	8.5	8.3
2011	7.5	7.1	7.1	8.0	8.6	9.0	9.5	9.6	9.5	9.5	9.4	9.0	8.7
2012	8.2	7.8	8.1	8.7	8.9	9.2	9.5	9.5	9.4	9.3	9.2	8.9	8.9
2013	8.2	8.0	8.1	8.7	9.3	9.8	10.0	10.0	9.8	9.6	9.4	9.0	9.2
2014	8.3	8.1	8.2	8.9	9.5	10.0	10.3	10.3	10.2	10.3	10.2	9.7	9.5
2015	8.9	8.5	8.6	9.4	10.2	10.5	10.7	10.7	10.4	10.7	10.6	10.3	10.0
2016	9.5	9.1	9.4	10.1	10.6	11.0	11.3	11.3	11.2	11.3	11.1	11.0	10.6
2017	10.0	9.5	9.7	10.4	11.0	11.5	11.8	12.0	11.7	11.7	11.7	11.5	11.0

Employment by Industry: Worcester, MA-CT, Selected Years, 2007–2017—*Continued*

(Numbers in thousands, not seasonally adjusted)

Industry and year	January	February	March	April	May	June	July	August	September	October	November	December	Annual average
Manufacturing													
2007	33.2	33.0	33.0	32.9	32.9	33.3	32.9	32.8	32.7	33.1	33.2	33.3	33.0
2008	33.1	32.7	32.5	32.4	32.4	32.6	32.2	31.9	31.9	32.0	31.7	31.5	32.2
2009	30.5	29.8	29.3	28.9	28.8	28.9	28.5	28.4	28.4	28.4	28.5	28.6	28.9
2010	28.3	28.1	28.1	28.3	28.4	28.6	28.2	28.3	28.3	28.4	28.5	28.6	28.3
2011	28.2	28.1	28.2	28.2	28.4	28.6	28.9	28.8	28.8	28.8	28.8	29.0	28.6
2012	27.8	27.8	27.8	27.7	27.6	27.8	27.6	27.4	27.5	27.6	27.4	27.0	27.6
2013	26.8	26.8	26.9	26.8	26.9	27.1	27.1	27.1	27.1	27.0	27.0	27.1	27.0
2014	27.1	27.0	27.0	27.0	27.0	27.1	27.2	27.1	27.0	27.4	27.4	27.4	27.1
2015	27.4	27.3	27.4	27.6	27.6	27.8	27.8	27.8	27.7	27.6	27.8	27.9	27.6
2016	27.7	27.6	27.8	27.8	27.9	28.3	28.0	27.9	27.8	27.4	27.5	27.6	27.8
2017	27.2	27.1	27.2	27.3	27.4	27.7	27.5	27.5	27.3	27.5	27.6	27.8	27.4
Trade, Transportation, and Utilities													
2007	50.9	50.4	50.8	50.8	51.3	51.8	50.8	50.5	50.8	51.7	52.6	52.8	51.3
2008	51.5	50.5	50.8	50.8	51.1	51.2	50.4	50.4	50.8	51.3	51.4	51.6	51.0
2009	49.2	48.2	48.1	48.1	48.4	48.7	47.5	47.3	47.6	48.2	48.7	49.2	48.3
2010	47.9	47.3	47.9	48.7	49.4	49.8	49.0	49.0	49.0	49.7	50.4	51.1	49.1
2011	49.3	48.7	48.8	49.1	49.4	49.4	48.8	48.8	49.5	50.5	51.2	51.9	49.6
2012	50.0	49.3	49.5	49.9	50.4	50.7	50.2	50.3	50.9	51.5	52.2	52.2	50.6
2013	50.5	49.9	50.2	51.0	51.8	52.5	51.4	51.5	51.8	52.3	53.4	53.8	51.7
2014	52.2	51.6	51.8	52.4	52.9	53.2	52.8	52.6	53.1	53.5	54.4	55.2	53.0
2015	52.3	51.4	51.7	52.1	52.7	53.2	52.5	52.6	52.7	53.3	54.1	54.8	52.8
2016	52.7	52.0	52.2	53.1	53.4	54.0	53.2	53.1	53.2	53.5	54.4	55.1	53.3
2017	53.5	52.7	52.8	53.1	53.5	54.2	53.5	53.5	53.6	53.9	54.5	54.9	53.6
Wholesale Trade													
2007	10.8	10.8	10.9	10.9	11.0	11.0	11.0	11.0	10.9	11.3	11.4	11.3	11.0
2008	11.3	11.3	11.5	11.5	11.7	11.7	11.7	11.8	11.7	11.9	11.8	11.8	11.6
2009	11.2	11.0	11.0	11.1	11.0	10.9	10.9	10.8	10.7	10.7	10.6	10.5	10.9
2010	10.4	10.3	10.4	10.4	10.4	10.4	10.2	10.1	9.9	10.2	10.1	10.0	10.2
2011	9.8	9.6	9.6	9.8	9.9	9.9	9.8	9.8	9.8	9.9	9.9	9.9	9.8
2012	9.9	9.9	9.9	10.1	10.1	10.2	10.3	10.3	10.3	10.5	10.5	10.3	10.2
2013	10.2	10.2	10.3	10.3	10.4	10.5	10.5	10.5	10.5	10.6	10.6	10.6	10.4
2014	10.5	10.4	10.4	10.6	10.7	10.7	10.8	10.7	10.6	10.6	10.6	10.6	10.6
2015	10.4	10.3	10.4	10.5	10.5	10.6	10.5	10.4	10.4	10.5	10.4	10.5	10.5
2016	10.3	10.2	10.3	10.4	10.4	10.5	10.5	10.5	10.5	10.5	10.5	10.4	10.4
2017	10.4	10.3	10.4	10.4	10.4	10.5	10.5	10.5	10.4	10.5	10.5	10.5	10.4
Retail Trade													
2007	29.9	29.3	29.6	29.6	29.9	30.3	29.9	29.7	29.5	30.1	30.7	30.9	30.0
2008	29.8	28.9	29.0	29.0	29.2	29.4	29.3	29.3	29.1	29.4	29.7	29.8	29.3
2009	28.5	27.8	27.7	27.7	27.9	28.3	27.7	27.7	27.5	27.9	28.4	28.9	28.0
2010	28.0	27.5	28.0	28.5	28.8	29.1	28.9	29.0	28.5	28.9	29.5	30.0	28.7
2011	29.0	28.5	28.5	28.8	28.9	29.0	28.9	28.9	29.1	29.8	30.4	30.9	29.2
2012	29.6	28.9	29.0	29.1	29.5	29.7	29.6	29.7	29.7	30.0	30.7	30.7	29.7
2013	29.5	28.9	29.0	29.6	30.2	30.5	30.0	30.1	29.9	30.3	31.1	31.3	30.0
2014	30.4	29.7	29.8	30.2	30.4	30.5	30.4	30.3	30.4	30.7	31.3	31.5	30.5
2015	30.2	29.4	29.5	29.8	30.3	30.6	30.3	30.5	30.0	30.5	31.1	31.3	30.3
2016	30.1	29.5	29.6	30.1	30.3	30.7	30.3	30.3	29.8	30.1	30.9	31.1	30.2
2017	30.1	29.5	29.5	29.8	30.1	30.5	30.2	30.3	29.9	30.0	30.5	30.7	30.1
Transportation and Utilities													
2007	10.2	10.3	10.3	10.3	10.4	10.5	9.9	9.8	10.4	10.3	10.5	10.6	10.3
2008	10.4	10.3	10.3	10.3	10.2	10.1	9.4	9.3	10.0	10.0	9.9	10.0	10.0
2009	9.5	9.4	9.4	9.3	9.5	9.5	8.9	8.8	9.4	9.6	9.7	9.8	9.4
2010	9.5	9.5	9.5	9.8	10.2	10.3	9.9	9.9	10.6	10.6	10.8	11.1	10.1
2011	10.5	10.6	10.7	10.5	10.6	10.5	10.1	10.1	10.6	10.8	10.9	11.1	10.6
2012	10.5	10.5	10.6	10.7	10.8	10.8	10.3	10.3	10.9	11.0	11.0	11.2	10.7
2013	10.8	10.8	10.9	11.1	11.2	11.5	10.9	10.9	11.4	11.4	11.7	11.9	11.2
2014	11.3	11.5	11.6	11.6	11.8	12.0	11.6	11.6	12.1	12.2	12.5	13.1	11.9
2015	11.7	11.7	11.8	11.8	11.9	12.0	11.7	11.7	12.3	12.3	12.6	13.0	12.0
2016	12.3	12.3	12.3	12.6	12.7	12.8	12.4	12.3	12.9	12.9	13.0	13.6	12.7
2017	13.0	12.9	12.9	12.9	13.0	13.2	12.8	12.7	13.3	13.4	13.5	13.7	13.1

Employment by Industry: Worcester, MA-CT, Selected Years, 2007–2017—*Continued*

(Numbers in thousands, not seasonally adjusted)

Industry and year	January	February	March	April	May	June	July	August	September	October	November	December	Annual average
Information													
2007	4.0	4.0	4.0	4.0	4.1	4.1	4.1	4.1	4.0	4.1	4.1	4.0	4.1
2008	4.1	4.1	4.1	4.2	4.2	4.2	4.1	4.1	4.0	3.7	3.7	3.7	4.0
2009	3.6	3.5	3.5	3.5	3.5	3.5	3.5	3.5	3.4	3.4	3.4	3.4	3.5
2010	3.4	3.6	3.6	3.6	3.7	3.7	3.6	3.6	3.5	3.6	3.6	3.6	3.6
2011	3.6	3.6	3.6	3.6	3.6	3.6	3.7	3.4	3.6	3.7	3.6	3.6	3.6
2012	3.6	3.6	3.6	3.6	3.7	3.7	3.7	3.8	3.7	3.6	3.7	3.7	3.7
2013	3.7	3.6	3.7	3.7	3.7	3.8	3.7	3.7	3.5	3.5	3.7	3.7	3.7
2014	3.7	3.7	3.7	3.6	3.7	3.8	3.8	3.8	3.7	3.7	3.7	3.8	3.7
2015	3.8	3.8	3.8	3.9	3.9	3.9	3.9	3.9	3.9	3.9	3.9	4.0	3.9
2016	4.0	4.0	3.9	3.9	3.7	4.0	4.0	3.9	3.8	3.8	3.7	3.7	3.9
2017	3.8	3.8	3.7	3.7	3.7	3.8	3.7	3.7	3.7	3.7	3.7	3.7	3.7
Financial Activities													
2007	15.2	15.1	15.1	15.1	15.0	15.0	15.1	15.1	14.9	14.9	14.9	14.9	15.0
2008	14.7	14.8	14.7	14.8	14.8	14.9	15.0	14.9	14.8	14.7	14.8	14.7	14.8
2009	14.8	14.8	14.8	14.7	14.7	14.9	14.8	14.8	14.7	14.7	14.7	14.7	14.8
2010	14.6	14.6	14.6	14.6	14.6	14.7	14.7	14.7	14.6	14.9	14.8	14.9	14.7
2011	14.7	14.7	14.7	14.7	14.7	14.7	14.9	14.9	14.9	15.0	15.0	15.0	14.8
2012	14.9	14.9	14.9	14.9	15.0	15.0	15.1	15.0	14.9	15.0	14.9	14.9	15.0
2013	14.8	14.8	14.8	14.8	14.8	15.0	14.9	14.9	14.8	14.8	14.8	14.8	14.8
2014	14.7	14.7	14.8	14.9	15.0	15.1	15.2	15.2	15.0	15.0	15.0	15.0	15.0
2015	14.8	14.8	14.8	14.9	15.0	15.0	15.2	15.2	14.9	15.0	14.9	14.9	15.0
2016	14.8	14.8	14.7	14.8	14.9	15.0	15.0	15.0	14.8	14.8	14.8	14.8	14.9
2017	14.7	14.7	14.6	14.7	14.8	15.0	14.9	14.8	14.6	14.6	14.5	14.7	14.7
Professional and Business Services													
2007	28.9	28.9	28.9	29.8	30.2	30.6	29.7	29.7	29.3	29.4	29.5	29.4	29.5
2008	27.9	28.0	27.9	28.4	28.6	28.9	28.6	28.8	28.6	28.3	28.0	27.9	28.3
2009	26.9	26.5	26.3	26.4	26.4	26.0	25.9	26.0	25.8	26.2	26.0	25.8	26.2
2010	25.3	24.9	25.2	25.7	26.1	26.4	26.5	26.5	26.3	26.4	26.1	26.6	26.0
2011	26.9	27.0	26.7	27.9	27.5	27.6	27.7	27.3	27.3	27.1	27.9	26.8	27.3
2012	25.8	25.4	25.8	26.1	26.0	26.5	26.4	26.5	26.0	26.3	26.2	25.9	26.1
2013	25.3	25.3	25.6	26.1	26.4	26.5	26.2	26.4	26.0	26.1	25.9	25.5	25.9
2014	25.4	25.5	25.5	26.4	26.5	26.8	26.3	26.5	26.4	26.5	26.4	26.1	26.2
2015	25.8	25.8	25.6	26.0	26.3	26.6	26.8	27.0	26.9	27.0	27.2	27.2	26.5
2016	26.1	26.4	26.4	27.5	27.8	28.1	28.4	28.4	28.3	28.4	28.4	28.2	27.7
2017	27.1	27.6	27.8	28.2	28.2	28.5	28.6	28.9	28.9	29.2	29.5	29.7	28.5
Education and Health Services													
2007	50.7	52.3	52.4	52.7	52.5	51.7	51.2	51.6	53.3	54.3	54.4	54.2	52.6
2008	53.0	54.9	55.0	54.9	54.2	53.7	53.3	53.5	55.1	56.2	56.2	56.1	54.7
2009	55.4	56.7	56.7	57.1	56.4	55.3	55.6	55.9	57.1	57.9	58.3	58.4	56.7
2010	57.3	58.6	58.4	58.2	57.8	56.8	56.9	57.1	58.6	59.4	59.8	59.7	58.2
2011	58.5	59.5	59.9	59.4	59.0	57.9	58.4	58.4	59.8	60.4	60.6	60.7	59.4
2012	60.0	61.0	61.6	61.4	61.1	60.6	60.7	60.6	61.9	62.7	63.0	63.0	61.5
2013	62.3	62.9	63.4	62.7	62.6	62.1	61.3	61.5	62.2	62.9	63.1	63.4	62.5
2014	61.9	62.9	63.6	64.1	63.8	63.2	62.8	62.9	63.8	64.8	65.0	65.0	63.7
2015	63.6	64.5	65.0	65.4	65.7	65.0	64.2	64.1	65.5	66.7	67.0	66.9	65.3
2016	65.0	65.9	66.2	66.7	66.6	65.3	65.3	65.2	66.8	67.6	67.7	67.6	66.3
2017	66.1	67.6	68.1	68.2	68.2	67.0	66.5	66.4	67.9	69.0	69.0	68.8	67.7
Leisure and Hospitality													
2007	22.1	22.2	22.5	22.7	23.7	24.5	23.8	24.1	23.3	23.2	22.7	22.2	23.1
2008	21.9	22.0	22.1	22.9	23.9	24.3	23.7	24.1	23.4	23.1	22.0	21.8	22.9
2009	21.1	21.3	21.4	22.3	23.4	23.4	23.2	23.0	22.8	22.7	21.8	22.0	22.4
2010	21.2	20.9	20.6	21.7	22.8	23.1	23.0	23.1	22.4	22.6	21.8	21.8	22.1
2011	21.2	21.2	21.4	22.4	23.0	23.5	23.4	23.4	23.0	22.9	22.2	22.4	22.5
2012	22.0	21.9	22.3	22.5	23.3	24.3	24.1	24.0	23.5	23.1	22.4	22.4	23.0
2013	22.2	21.9	22.2	23.1	23.9	24.7	24.0	24.3	23.9	24.0	23.3	23.0	23.4
2014	22.8	22.5	22.9	23.6	24.3	25.1	24.8	24.9	24.3	24.7	23.9	23.8	24.0
2015	23.4	23.0	23.5	24.3	25.4	25.7	25.3	25.5	24.6	24.4	23.8	23.8	24.4
2016	23.4	23.4	23.5	24.5	25.5	26.1	26.5	26.4	25.8	25.3	24.7	24.2	24.9
2017	24.2	23.9	24.5	24.8	25.7	26.8	26.5	26.6	25.7	25.7	25.4	25.3	25.4

Employment by Industry: Worcester, MA-CT, Selected Years, 2007–2017—*Continued*

(Numbers in thousands, not seasonally adjusted)

Industry and year	January	February	March	April	May	June	July	August	September	October	November	December	Annual average
Other Services													
2007	9.6	9.6	9.6	9.6	9.7	10.0	10.1	10.1	9.7	9.6	9.7	9.6	9.7
2008	9.5	9.5	9.6	9.4	9.5	9.5	9.6	9.4	9.1	9.1	9.0	8.9	9.3
2009	8.7	8.8	8.8	9.0	9.0	9.1	9.2	9.1	8.7	8.6	8.5	8.6	8.8
2010	8.4	8.5	8.4	8.6	8.7	8.9	9.2	9.1	8.6	8.6	8.7	8.6	8.7
2011	8.5	8.6	8.8	8.9	8.9	9.1	9.2	9.1	8.8	8.8	8.8	8.9	8.9
2012	8.8	8.8	8.8	9.0	9.1	9.4	9.6	9.6	9.3	9.5	9.6	9.7	9.3
2013	9.7	9.5	9.7	9.9	10.0	10.4	10.7	10.6	10.1	10.1	10.1	10.2	10.1
2014	10.0	10.0	10.1	10.3	10.4	10.7	10.9	10.9	10.3	10.3	10.3	10.4	10.4
2015	10.3	10.1	10.3	10.4	10.6	10.9	11.2	11.2	10.5	10.6	10.6	10.6	10.6
2016	10.4	10.4	10.7	10.8	10.9	11.3	11.4	11.4	10.8	10.7	10.8	10.8	10.9
2017	10.5	10.5	10.7	10.8	10.8	11.3	11.5	11.4	10.8	10.9	10.9	10.9	10.9
Government													
2007	40.7	41.3	41.3	41.5	41.9	41.6	37.6	37.2	40.8	41.5	42.1	42.0	40.8
2008	40.9	41.6	41.8	41.7	42.0	41.1	37.9	37.2	40.7	41.8	41.8	41.5	40.8
2009	41.0	41.8	41.9	42.0	42.0	41.5	38.2	38.1	41.0	42.0	42.0	43.2	41.2
2010	41.5	41.8	41.9	42.1	43.0	42.0	38.0	37.8	41.0	41.7	42.1	42.3	41.3
2011	40.9	41.6	41.8	41.8	42.0	41.1	37.9	37.2	40.7	41.5	41.5	41.6	40.8
2012	40.6	41.4	41.9	41.4	41.5	41.3	37.9	37.8	41.4	41.9	42.4	42.5	41.0
2013	41.1	42.5	42.6	43.8	43.6	41.7	37.9	38.3	42.2	43.3	43.9	44.2	42.1
2014	42.0	43.9	44.0	44.7	44.3	42.2	38.5	38.6	43.0	44.0	44.9	44.7	42.9
2015	42.0	43.9	44.4	44.7	44.5	43.3	38.6	38.2	42.5	44.0	44.5	44.6	42.9
2016	42.1	44.0	44.6	44.4	44.5	42.9	39.3	39.0	43.4	44.0	45.3	44.6	43.2
2017	42.7	44.2	44.3	44.5	44.7	43.0	39.0	38.9	43.7	44.5	45.4	44.9	43.3

Employment by Industry: Omaha-Council Bluffs, NE-IA, Selected Years, 2007–2017

(Numbers in thousands, not seasonally adjusted)

Industry and year	January	February	March	April	May	June	July	August	September	October	November	December	Annual average
Total Nonfarm													
2007	452.9	453.7	456.2	461.8	466.8	469.7	464.3	467.0	468.1	470.7	473.4	472.5	464.8
2008	462.5	462.9	465.3	470.2	476.0	475.7	470.5	472.5	472.3	475.5	475.3	472.7	471.0
2009	458.9	457.7	457.9	461.5	464.9	464.1	461.8	461.4	459.6	461.2	462.2	459.0	460.9
2010	448.0	447.5	451.1	458.6	463.4	464.7	461.0	462.0	458.7	464.4	465.0	464.9	459.1
2011	453.3	453.9	455.9	463.9	467.4	467.8	464.8	465.8	464.5	467.6	469.8	469.3	463.7
2012	459.6	459.7	463.5	468.7	473.2	472.6	471.3	471.2	470.2	474.0	476.7	475.9	469.7
2013	465.7	466.2	468.3	473.9	480.3	480.6	478.6	480.4	480.0	483.4	486.1	485.6	477.4
2014	474.7	476.3	478.4	482.8	487.9	487.3	484.2	486.2	485.5	489.3	491.1	492.2	484.7
2015	480.0	481.2	484.4	490.9	495.3	496.0	493.7	495.2	493.2	498.8	499.4	500.4	492.4
2016	485.9	487.0	491.4	496.9	500.7	500.6	499.7	498.9	499.9	502.4	502.0	501.9	497.3
2017	490.5	492.9	495.6	499.6	503.2	504.1	498.7	498.8	499.1	502.6	505.3	504.9	499.6
Total Private													
2007	391.7	392.1	394.7	399.6	404.2	407.7	407.6	409.3	407.2	408.3	411.0	410.9	403.7
2008	400.8	400.9	403.6	407.2	412.6	413.8	412.4	413.4	410.3	411.4	411.0	409.2	408.9
2009	395.4	393.8	394.1	396.3	399.0	399.9	398.5	398.6	395.5	395.5	396.4	394.5	396.5
2010	383.5	382.7	385.3	392.1	396.1	398.2	398.4	399.0	395.0	398.0	398.6	399.2	393.8
2011	387.9	387.9	390.5	397.1	400.4	402.6	401.7	402.0	399.9	401.1	403.1	403.4	398.1
2012	393.8	393.5	397.8	402.7	406.7	409.5	408.7	408.1	405.9	408.2	410.8	410.9	404.7
2013	400.9	400.8	403.2	408.2	413.9	415.8	415.5	417.0	415.6	417.7	420.2	420.6	412.5
2014	409.4	410.3	412.9	416.7	421.1	422.9	421.2	422.4	420.1	422.5	424.3	426.2	419.2
2015	414.3	415.1	418.6	424.1	428.0	430.5	430.1	431.0	428.2	431.9	432.3	433.7	426.5
2016	419.8	420.4	424.8	429.7	432.9	434.2	436.3	436.0	433.8	435.1	434.8	435.5	431.1
2017	424.3	426.3	429.3	432.5	435.8	437.9	436.2	436.4	433.1	435.0	437.6	438.1	433.5
Goods Producing													
2007	56.6	55.7	56.2	57.6	58.7	59.8	60.2	60.6	59.9	60.5	60.2	59.1	58.8
2008	57.5	57.3	57.9	59.4	60.6	61.2	60.9	60.9	60.4	60.2	59.4	58.1	59.5
2009	55.0	54.5	54.5	55.8	56.2	56.6	56.5	56.3	55.7	55.0	54.7	53.1	55.3
2010	50.4	49.9	50.4	52.4	52.9	53.3	53.5	53.2	52.5	52.3	52.2	51.3	52.0
2011	49.0	49.0	49.8	51.0	51.6	52.6	52.7	52.4	51.8	52.1	52.1	52.0	51.3
2012	49.9	49.5	50.6	51.7	52.5	53.3	53.6	53.5	53.4	53.6	53.7	53.5	52.4
2013	51.6	52.0	52.4	54.0	55.4	56.0	56.9	56.9	56.7	56.5	56.3	55.0	55.0
2014	53.3	53.4	53.9	56.2	56.9	57.9	58.3	58.5	58.3	58.4	58.1	57.8	56.8
2015	55.8	56.0	56.9	58.7	59.0	59.4	59.6	59.4	59.1	59.9	59.2	58.4	58.5
2016	56.2	56.1	57.5	58.9	59.5	60.2	60.6	60.6	60.2	60.2	59.8	59.0	59.1
2017	57.5	58.3	59.3	60.2	60.6	61.5	61.5	61.3	61.1	61.2	61.8	61.6	60.5
Service-Providing													
2007	396.3	398.0	400.0	404.2	408.1	409.9	404.1	406.4	408.2	410.2	413.2	413.4	406.0
2008	405.0	405.6	407.4	410.8	415.4	414.5	409.6	411.6	411.9	415.3	415.9	414.6	411.5
2009	403.9	403.2	403.4	405.7	408.7	407.5	405.3	405.1	403.9	406.2	407.5	405.9	405.5
2010	397.6	397.6	400.7	406.2	410.5	411.4	407.5	408.8	406.2	412.1	412.8	413.6	407.1
2011	404.3	404.9	406.1	412.9	415.8	415.2	412.1	413.4	412.7	415.5	417.7	417.3	412.3
2012	409.7	410.2	412.9	417.0	420.7	419.3	417.7	417.7	416.8	420.4	423.0	422.4	417.3
2013	414.1	414.2	415.9	419.9	424.9	424.6	421.7	423.5	423.3	426.9	429.8	430.6	422.5
2014	421.4	422.9	424.5	426.6	431.0	429.4	425.9	427.7	427.2	430.9	433.0	434.4	427.9
2015	424.2	425.2	427.5	432.2	436.3	436.6	434.1	435.8	434.1	438.9	440.2	442.0	433.9
2016	429.7	430.9	433.9	438.0	441.2	440.4	439.1	438.3	439.7	442.2	442.2	442.9	438.2
2017	433.0	434.6	436.3	439.4	442.6	442.6	437.2	437.5	438.0	441.4	443.5	443.3	439.1
Mining, Logging, and Construction													
2007	23.7	22.7	23.1	24.4	25.3	26.2	26.3	26.6	26.1	26.5	26.2	25.2	25.2
2008	23.6	23.4	24.0	25.5	26.5	27.0	27.0	27.1	26.8	26.5	25.9	25.1	25.7
2009	22.6	22.4	22.8	24.4	24.8	25.2	25.3	25.1	24.5	23.8	23.3	21.8	23.8
2010	19.4	19.0	19.4	21.4	21.7	22.0	22.1	22.0	21.4	21.1	21.0	20.0	20.9
2011	18.2	18.0	18.7	19.7	20.3	21.2	21.3	21.3	21.0	21.0	20.8	20.1	20.1
2012	19.0	18.6	19.5	20.6	21.3	21.8	22.0	22.1	22.0	22.4	22.2	21.9	21.1
2013	20.3	20.4	20.8	22.2	23.2	23.6	24.3	24.3	24.1	24.0	23.6	22.4	22.8
2014	21.1	21.0	21.6	23.7	24.4	25.3	25.5	25.8	25.7	25.8	25.4	25.0	24.2
2015	23.4	23.5	24.4	26.1	26.4	26.6	26.7	26.6	26.4	27.0	26.4	25.6	25.8
2016	23.8	23.7	24.9	26.2	26.8	27.5	27.9	27.9	27.6	27.5	27.3	26.3	26.5
2017	25.0	25.5	26.5	27.2	27.6	28.2	28.1	27.9	27.7	27.7	27.8	27.5	27.2

Employment by Industry: Omaha-Council Bluffs, NE-IA, Selected Years, 2007–2017—*Continued*

(Numbers in thousands, not seasonally adjusted)

Industry and year	January	February	March	April	May	June	July	August	September	October	November	December	Annual average
Manufacturing													
2007	32.9	33.0	33.1	33.2	33.4	33.6	33.9	34.0	33.8	34.0	34.0	33.9	33.6
2008	33.9	33.9	33.9	33.9	34.1	34.2	33.9	33.8	33.6	33.7	33.5	33.0	33.8
2009	32.4	32.1	31.7	31.4	31.4	31.4	31.2	31.2	31.2	31.2	31.4	31.3	31.5
2010	31.0	30.9	31.0	31.0	31.2	31.3	31.4	31.2	31.1	31.2	31.2	31.3	31.2
2011	30.8	31.0	31.1	31.3	31.3	31.4	31.4	31.1	30.8	31.1	31.3	31.9	31.2
2012	30.9	30.9	31.1	31.1	31.2	31.5	31.6	31.4	31.4	31.2	31.5	31.6	31.3
2013	31.3	31.6	31.6	31.8	32.2	32.4	32.6	32.6	32.6	32.5	32.7	32.6	32.2
2014	32.2	32.4	32.3	32.5	32.5	32.6	32.8	32.7	32.6	32.6	32.7	32.8	32.6
2015	32.4	32.5	32.5	32.6	32.6	32.8	32.9	32.8	32.7	32.9	32.8	32.8	32.7
2016	32.4	32.4	32.6	32.7	32.7	32.7	32.7	32.7	32.6	32.7	32.5	32.7	32.6
2017	32.5	32.8	32.8	33.0	33.0	33.3	33.4	33.4	33.4	33.5	34.0	34.1	33.3
Trade, Transportation, and Utilities													
2007	98.6	98.1	98.7	99.2	100.0	100.1	99.8	100.3	100.4	100.6	103.2	103.9	100.2
2008	99.4	98.5	99.0	98.7	99.9	99.6	99.0	99.4	98.9	100.1	101.8	102.6	99.7
2009	96.7	95.3	95.1	94.3	95.1	94.6	94.0	94.3	94.0	94.9	96.6	97.1	95.2
2010	92.1	91.4	92.0	93.0	94.2	93.9	93.4	93.5	92.9	94.3	96.4	98.1	93.8
2011	92.7	92.0	92.4	93.1	93.7	93.3	93.0	93.5	93.6	93.9	96.6	97.5	93.8
2012	92.9	91.8	92.4	93.0	94.0	94.2	93.5	93.3	93.4	94.6	97.5	98.6	94.1
2013	93.8	92.5	92.9	93.1	94.4	94.7	94.4	95.1	95.0	95.9	99.0	100.9	95.1
2014	95.9	95.0	95.2	95.6	96.3	96.3	95.7	96.6	96.1	97.1	99.9	102.1	96.8
2015	95.8	95.2	95.6	96.6	97.5	98.0	97.3	97.9	97.2	98.3	100.8	102.4	97.7
2016	96.2	95.6	95.7	96.7	96.8	96.6	96.7	96.8	96.4	97.0	99.2	100.3	97.0
2017	95.8	95.4	95.7	96.4	97.2	96.7	96.4	96.6	96.2	97.3	100.3	101.1	97.1
Wholesale Trade													
2007	17.7	17.7	17.8	18.0	18.0	18.3	18.3	18.3	18.4	18.4	18.5	18.6	18.2
2008	18.4	18.4	18.5	18.4	18.6	18.6	18.6	18.5	18.4	18.4	18.4	18.3	18.5
2009	18.0	17.9	17.8	17.9	17.9	18.0	18.0	17.9	17.8	17.9	17.9	17.9	17.9
2010	17.5	17.5	17.5	17.6	17.7	17.7	17.6	17.4	17.2	17.3	17.3	17.2	17.5
2011	17.0	17.0	17.0	17.0	17.1	17.1	17.1	17.0	17.2	17.1	17.2	17.1	17.1
2012	16.7	16.7	16.8	16.9	16.9	17.0	16.9	16.8	16.7	16.8	16.9	16.8	16.8
2013	16.6	16.6	16.7	16.8	17.0	17.1	17.0	16.9	16.8	16.9	17.0	17.1	16.9
2014	16.9	16.9	17.0	17.1	17.1	17.2	17.2	17.1	17.0	16.9	17.0	17.0	17.0
2015	16.4	16.4	16.5	16.7	16.9	16.9	16.8	16.9	16.7	16.8	16.9	16.9	16.7
2016	16.7	16.6	16.7	16.7	16.8	16.8	16.9	16.9	16.6	16.6	16.7	16.6	16.7
2017	16.5	16.5	16.6	16.7	16.8	16.9	16.8	16.7	16.6	16.7	16.7	16.7	16.7
Retail Trade													
2007	50.9	50.2	50.6	51.1	51.9	51.9	51.7	51.7	51.5	52.4	54.5	55.3	52.0
2008	52.1	51.1	51.2	50.9	51.3	51.2	50.8	50.7	50.2	51.0	52.6	53.6	51.4
2009	50.1	49.1	49.0	49.1	49.9	49.8	49.5	49.5	49.2	50.0	51.5	51.6	49.9
2010	48.9	48.3	48.7	49.3	50.1	50.2	49.6	49.6	49.1	50.2	51.8	52.7	49.9
2011	49.3	48.7	49.0	49.6	50.1	49.9	49.7	49.9	49.6	50.3	52.7	53.4	50.2
2012	50.0	49.0	49.4	49.8	50.5	50.6	50.2	50.0	49.9	51.1	53.3	53.8	50.6
2013	50.2	49.4	49.7	50.1	50.7	50.9	51.0	51.0	51.0	52.0	54.6	55.5	51.3
2014	52.3	51.5	51.5	52.1	52.5	52.7	52.5	52.8	52.4	53.3	55.2	56.0	52.9
2015	52.7	52.3	52.5	52.9	53.3	53.8	53.3	53.4	52.9	53.8	55.7	56.4	53.6
2016	53.3	53.0	53.0	53.7	54.0	54.1	54.4	54.3	53.9	54.6	56.4	56.9	54.3
2017	53.7	53.3	53.5	54.1	54.4	54.1	54.0	54.0	53.4	54.1	56.9	57.2	54.4
Transportation and Utilities													
2007	30.0	30.2	30.3	30.1	30.1	29.9	29.8	30.3	30.5	29.8	30.2	30.0	30.1
2008	28.9	29.0	29.3	29.4	30.0	29.8	29.6	30.2	30.3	30.7	30.8	30.7	29.9
2009	28.6	28.3	28.3	27.3	27.3	26.8	26.5	26.9	27.0	27.0	27.2	27.6	27.4
2010	25.7	25.6	25.8	26.1	26.4	26.0	26.2	26.5	26.6	26.8	27.3	28.2	26.4
2011	26.4	26.3	26.4	26.5	26.5	26.3	26.2	26.6	26.8	26.5	26.7	27.0	26.5
2012	26.2	26.1	26.2	26.3	26.6	26.6	26.4	26.5	26.8	26.7	27.3	28.0	26.6
2013	27.0	26.5	26.5	26.2	26.7	26.7	26.4	27.2	27.2	27.0	27.4	28.3	26.9
2014	26.7	26.6	26.7	26.4	26.7	26.4	26.0	26.7	26.7	26.9	27.7	29.1	26.9
2015	26.7	26.5	26.6	27.0	27.3	27.3	27.2	27.6	27.6	27.7	28.2	29.1	27.4
2016	26.2	26.0	26.0	25.8	26.0	25.7	25.4	25.6	25.9	25.8	26.1	26.8	25.9
2017	25.6	25.6	25.6	25.6	26.0	25.7	25.6	25.9	26.2	26.5	26.7	27.2	26.0

Employment by Industry: Omaha-Council Bluffs, NE-IA, Selected Years, 2007–2017—*Continued*

(Numbers in thousands, not seasonally adjusted)

Industry and year	January	February	March	April	May	June	July	August	September	October	November	December	Annual average
Information													
2007	12.3	12.4	12.4	12.5	12.6	12.7	12.7	12.7	12.6	12.6	12.6	12.6	12.6
2008	12.3	12.3	12.3	12.4	12.4	12.3	12.3	12.1	12.0	12.0	12.0	11.9	12.2
2009	11.6	11.6	11.6	11.5	11.4	11.5	11.5	11.5	11.4	11.3	11.5	11.5	11.5
2010	11.3	11.3	11.2	11.2	11.3	11.3	11.2	11.2	11.1	11.1	11.1	11.2	11.2
2011	11.2	11.2	11.1	11.1	11.1	11.2	11.4	11.4	11.3	11.3	11.4	11.4	11.3
2012	11.3	11.4	11.4	11.4	11.3	11.3	11.3	11.2	11.2	11.1	11.1	11.1	11.3
2013	11.0	11.0	11.0	11.0	11.1	11.1	11.1	11.1	11.1	11.1	11.1	11.1	11.1
2014	11.1	11.0	11.0	11.0	11.1	11.1	11.2	11.2	11.2	11.2	11.3	11.4	11.2
2015	11.3	11.4	11.4	11.5	11.6	11.7	11.7	11.8	11.6	11.7	11.8	11.9	11.6
2016	11.8	11.8	11.8	11.8	11.8	11.8	11.8	11.8	11.8	11.8	11.8	11.9	11.8
2017	11.7	11.7	11.7	11.8	11.7	11.7	11.5	11.5	11.4	11.5	11.5	11.5	11.6
Financial Activities													
2007	39.3	39.5	39.7	39.8	40.1	40.3	40.2	40.0	39.9	39.9	39.9	40.1	39.9
2008	40.2	40.5	40.7	40.5	40.8	41.0	40.9	40.7	40.6	40.7	40.6	40.8	40.7
2009	40.1	40.4	40.4	40.0	40.1	40.1	40.0	40.0	39.7	39.8	40.0	40.1	40.1
2010	40.0	40.1	40.3	40.1	40.3	40.5	40.7	40.8	40.5	40.9	40.8	40.9	40.5
2011	40.9	40.9	41.0	41.2	41.4	41.4	41.4	41.3	41.3	41.3	41.5	41.7	41.3
2012	41.3	41.2	41.3	41.5	41.6	41.6	41.8	41.8	41.7	41.8	42.0	42.1	41.6
2013	41.8	41.9	41.9	42.0	42.1	42.2	42.2	42.1	42.0	42.1	42.2	42.2	42.1
2014	42.0	42.1	42.0	41.8	41.9	42.1	42.2	42.0	41.9	42.0	42.0	42.0	42.0
2015	41.5	41.6	41.5	41.7	42.0	42.3	42.4	42.4	42.3	42.6	42.7	43.1	42.2
2016	42.9	43.0	43.2	43.3	43.3	43.5	43.8	43.7	43.5	43.5	43.5	43.6	43.4
2017	43.3	43.3	43.3	43.2	43.3	43.7	43.7	43.7	43.5	43.4	43.4	43.7	43.5
Professional and Business Services													
2007	62.0	62.7	63.2	63.9	64.3	65.1	65.4	65.3	65.3	65.4	65.9	66.6	64.6
2008	64.8	64.8	65.1	66.1	66.3	66.4	65.8	66.1	65.5	65.5	65.2	64.7	65.5
2009	63.1	62.9	62.5	63.1	63.1	63.4	63.1	63.0	62.1	62.3	62.2	62.3	62.8
2010	61.3	60.9	61.1	62.8	63.2	63.8	64.4	64.8	64.4	65.1	65.0	65.2	63.5
2011	63.3	63.4	63.7	65.3	65.3	66.0	66.8	67.0	67.0	66.6	66.6	66.3	65.6
2012	65.5	65.8	65.7	67.0	67.3	68.5	68.6	68.2	67.8	68.6	68.9	68.7	67.6
2013	67.6	67.7	67.8	69.3	69.8	70.5	70.4	70.5	70.7	72.1	72.4	73.0	70.2
2014	70.4	71.0	71.5	71.9	72.4	72.8	72.1	72.0	71.8	72.2	72.4	72.2	71.9
2015	71.7	71.9	72.5	73.7	73.8	74.4	74.3	74.1	73.8	74.4	74.2	74.2	73.6
2016	72.4	72.6	73.2	74.6	74.5	74.8	74.9	74.6	74.1	73.8	73.5	74.2	73.9
2017	72.0	72.1	72.6	72.9	72.9	73.4	73.3	72.9	72.5	72.9	72.3	72.2	72.7
Education and Health Services													
2007	63.8	64.7	64.9	65.1	65.4	65.6	65.5	66.3	66.6	67.1	67.6	67.6	65.9
2008	66.9	67.9	68.1	68.4	68.8	68.5	68.6	69.5	69.9	70.1	70.6	70.5	69.0
2009	69.8	70.2	70.1	70.3	70.2	69.7	69.7	69.9	70.5	71.1	71.4	71.2	70.3
2010	70.5	71.1	71.2	71.4	71.6	71.5	71.5	71.8	71.5	72.2	72.2	72.4	71.6
2011	72.0	72.6	72.6	73.2	73.4	73.0	72.3	72.8	73.0	74.1	74.3	74.4	73.1
2012	73.4	73.9	74.6	74.5	74.7	74.3	74.1	74.8	74.9	75.4	75.7	75.5	74.7
2013	74.5	75.1	75.1	75.1	75.3	74.8	74.3	74.7	75.0	75.4	75.6	75.5	75.0
2014	74.5	75.3	75.8	75.3	75.6	74.7	74.3	75.0	75.3	76.3	76.5	76.8	75.5
2015	75.5	75.7	76.1	76.0	76.2	75.5	76.2	76.8	77.3	78.5	78.6	78.4	76.7
2016	77.0	77.6	78.5	78.2	78.7	78.1	79.2	79.5	80.2	80.9	80.7	80.7	79.1
2017	79.2	80.0	80.4	80.1	80.6	79.8	79.5	79.9	80.1	80.6	81.0	81.0	80.2
Leisure and Hospitality													
2007	42.7	42.6	43.1	44.9	46.5	47.4	47.2	47.6	46.1	45.7	45.0	44.4	45.3
2008	43.2	43.1	43.9	45.1	46.9	48.0	48.1	48.0	46.4	45.8	44.4	43.7	45.6
2009	42.4	42.2	43.2	44.4	45.9	46.8	46.4	46.4	44.9	43.8	42.6	41.7	44.2
2010	40.7	40.8	41.8	43.7	45.0	46.1	45.9	46.0	44.6	44.7	43.5	42.7	43.8
2011	41.5	41.6	42.6	44.8	46.5	47.5	46.6	46.3	44.7	44.6	43.5	43.0	44.4
2012	42.4	42.8	44.5	46.1	47.6	48.4	48.0	47.6	45.9	45.7	44.6	44.1	45.6
2013	43.4	43.5	44.8	46.3	48.4	49.0	48.7	49.0	47.6	47.3	46.3	45.6	46.7
2014	44.9	45.2	46.0	47.2	49.1	49.9	49.5	49.3	47.7	47.6	46.3	46.2	47.4
2015	45.1	45.6	46.9	48.1	50.0	51.2	50.5	50.6	49.2	48.6	47.2	47.4	48.4
2016	45.8	46.2	47.3	49.0	50.6	51.4	51.3	51.3	49.9	50.1	48.5	48.1	49.1
2017	47.2	47.8	48.6	50.0	51.5	53.0	52.3	52.6	50.4	50.1	49.3	49.0	50.2

Employment by Industry: Omaha-Council Bluffs, NE-IA, Selected Years, 2007–2017—*Continued*

(Numbers in thousands, not seasonally adjusted)

Industry and year	January	February	March	April	May	June	July	August	September	October	November	December	Annual average
Other Services													
2007	16.4	16.4	16.5	16.6	16.6	16.7	16.6	16.5	16.4	16.5	16.6	16.6	16.5
2008	16.5	16.5	16.6	16.6	16.9	16.8	16.8	16.7	16.6	17.0	17.0	16.9	16.7
2009	16.7	16.7	16.7	16.9	17.0	17.2	17.3	17.2	17.2	17.3	17.4	17.5	17.1
2010	17.2	17.2	17.3	17.5	17.6	17.8	17.8	17.7	17.5	17.4	17.4	17.4	17.5
2011	17.3	17.2	17.3	17.4	17.4	17.6	17.5	17.3	17.2	17.2	17.1	17.1	17.3
2012	17.1	17.1	17.3	17.5	17.7	17.9	17.8	17.7	17.6	17.4	17.3	17.3	17.5
2013	17.2	17.1	17.3	17.4	17.4	17.5	17.5	17.6	17.5	17.3	17.3	17.3	17.4
2014	17.3	17.3	17.5	17.7	17.8	18.1	17.9	17.8	17.8	17.7	17.8	17.7	17.7
2015	17.6	17.7	17.7	17.8	17.9	18.0	18.1	18.0	17.7	17.9	17.8	17.9	17.8
2016	17.5	17.5	17.6	17.7	17.7	17.8	18.0	17.7	17.7	17.8	17.8	17.7	17.7
2017	17.6	17.7	17.7	17.9	18.0	18.1	18.0	17.9	17.9	18.0	18.0	18.0	17.9
Government													
2007	61.2	61.6	61.5	62.2	62.6	62.0	56.7	57.7	60.9	62.4	62.4	61.6	61.1
2008	61.7	62.0	61.7	63.0	63.4	61.9	58.1	59.1	62.0	64.1	64.3	63.5	62.1
2009	63.5	63.9	63.8	65.2	65.9	64.2	63.3	62.8	64.1	65.7	65.8	64.5	64.4
2010	64.5	64.8	65.8	66.5	67.3	66.5	62.6	63.0	63.7	66.4	66.4	65.7	65.3
2011	65.4	66.0	65.4	66.8	67.0	65.2	63.1	63.8	64.6	66.5	66.7	65.9	65.5
2012	65.8	66.2	65.7	66.0	66.5	63.1	62.6	63.1	64.3	65.8	65.9	65.0	65.0
2013	64.8	65.4	65.1	65.7	66.4	64.8	63.1	63.4	64.4	65.7	65.9	65.0	65.0
2014	65.3	66.0	65.5	66.1	66.8	64.4	63.0	63.8	65.4	66.8	66.8	66.0	65.5
2015	65.7	66.1	65.8	66.8	67.3	65.5	63.6	64.2	65.0	66.9	67.1	66.7	65.9
2016	66.1	66.6	66.6	67.2	67.8	64.4	63.4	62.9	66.1	67.3	67.2	66.4	66.2
2017	66.2	66.6	66.3	67.1	67.4	66.2	62.5	62.4	66.0	67.6	67.7	66.8	66.1

Employment by Industry: Albuquerque, NM, Selected Years, 2007–2017

(Numbers in thousands, not seasonally adjusted)

Industry and year	January	February	March	April	May	June	July	August	September	October	November	December	Annual average
Total Nonfarm													
2007	390.0	393.7	398.1	397.8	400.0	400.0	396.1	398.3	399.4	400.2	401.4	401.7	398.1
2008	392.1	394.9	396.6	398.6	400.0	398.3	396.1	398.8	400.6	399.3	395.3	392.7	396.9
2009	382.5	381.3	381.0	381.6	381.6	378.9	375.9	378.5	380.1	379.9	378.5	378.5	379.9
2010	369.4	370.5	372.0	375.6	376.1	374.9	371.1	372.2	373.5	376.0	375.8	376.5	373.6
2011	367.7	371.7	372.3	375.8	375.3	373.2	370.3	370.4	373.6	373.8	372.9	371.8	372.4
2012	364.0	367.0	369.7	371.0	371.6	368.2	366.6	368.8	372.6	377.8	377.6	376.5	371.0
2013	368.9	372.0	372.6	376.3	377.2	373.7	372.4	374.2	375.1	377.8	378.8	378.8	374.8
2014	371.1	372.9	374.0	376.5	379.5	375.4	375.6	378.0	377.9	381.5	381.9	381.5	377.2
2015	373.5	376.5	377.1	380.9	381.6	379.6	378.7	380.4	381.6	385.7	388.2	386.1	380.8
2016	379.5	383.6	383.5	387.9	388.3	385.5	385.8	387.2	389.3	388.9	390.1	390.0	386.6
2017	382.9	385.9	386.8	389.9	389.7	389.5	386.9	388.7	391.1	392.5	394.1	393.3	389.3
Total Private													
2007	312.5	314.1	317.5	317.9	320.2	321.3	319.4	320.3	318.8	318.9	319.7	320.0	318.4
2008	313.2	313.7	314.9	316.9	317.7	317.7	317.4	318.8	318.0	316.0	312.1	309.5	315.5
2009	301.2	297.9	297.1	297.6	298.2	297.2	296.7	298.0	297.1	295.6	294.3	294.0	297.1
2010	287.8	286.7	287.6	290.4	290.6	291.8	290.9	291.4	290.4	291.4	291.2	291.7	290.2
2011	285.6	287.5	287.5	291.1	291.3	290.4	290.0	289.7	290.0	289.1	288.2	286.8	288.9
2012	282.8	283.5	285.7	287.8	288.6	289.5	288.4	289.0	289.7	293.6	293.2	291.9	288.6
2013	287.6	288.4	288.8	292.7	294.1	292.2	293.0	293.8	292.0	294.3	294.8	295.1	292.2
2014	290.2	289.9	290.4	294.3	296.6	295.2	296.4	298.0	295.9	298.9	299.0	298.5	295.3
2015	293.4	294.4	294.9	299.4	300.8	300.2	300.8	301.7	300.5	303.4	304.6	303.4	299.8
2016	298.9	300.3	299.9	304.8	305.8	304.5	306.8	307.5	306.9	306.2	306.5	306.8	304.6
2017	302.8	303.2	304.2	307.4	308.1	308.8	308.4	309.6	309.2	309.1	310.4	309.5	307.6
Goods Producing													
2007	53.8	54.2	54.8	54.8	55.3	55.6	55.1	55.0	54.1	53.8	53.3	52.4	54.4
2008	51.1	51.1	51.3	51.5	51.6	52.0	51.5	51.1	50.6	49.3	48.2	47.0	50.5
2009	44.7	43.4	42.6	42.5	42.3	42.4	42.3	42.4	41.7	41.4	41.1	39.9	42.2
2010	38.9	38.4	38.3	38.8	39.1	39.4	40.0	39.8	39.6	39.3	38.9	38.5	39.1
2011	37.6	37.3	38.0	38.4	38.5	38.8	39.0	38.6	37.9	37.7	37.1	36.6	38.0
2012	36.2	36.2	36.5	36.6	37.0	37.5	37.3	37.2	36.9	37.7	37.4	37.1	37.0
2013	36.3	36.4	36.7	37.2	37.6	37.9	38.0	37.8	37.4	37.8	37.2	36.8	37.3
2014	36.3	35.9	36.0	36.3	36.8	37.0	37.4	37.5	36.9	37.4	37.1	36.9	36.8
2015	36.4	36.2	36.2	36.9	37.0	37.3	37.5	37.4	37.0	37.6	37.4	37.3	37.0
2016	36.7	36.9	36.8	37.5	37.7	37.9	38.0	37.9	37.8	37.9	37.5	37.7	37.5
2017	37.3	37.2	37.6	38.1	38.3	38.8	39.0	39.3	39.2	39.4	39.5	39.4	38.6
Service-Providing													
2007	336.2	339.5	343.3	343.0	344.7	344.4	341.0	343.3	345.3	346.4	348.1	349.3	343.7
2008	341.0	343.8	345.3	347.1	348.4	346.3	344.6	347.7	350.0	350.0	347.1	345.7	346.4
2009	337.8	337.9	338.4	339.1	339.3	336.5	333.6	336.1	338.4	338.5	337.8	338.6	337.7
2010	330.5	332.1	333.7	336.8	337.0	335.5	331.1	332.4	333.9	336.7	336.9	338.0	334.6
2011	330.1	334.4	334.3	337.4	336.8	334.4	331.3	331.8	335.7	336.1	335.8	335.2	334.4
2012	327.8	330.8	333.2	334.4	334.6	330.7	329.3	331.6	335.7	340.1	340.2	339.4	334.0
2013	332.6	335.6	335.9	339.1	339.6	335.8	334.4	336.4	337.7	340.0	341.6	342.0	337.6
2014	334.8	337.0	338.0	340.2	342.7	338.4	338.2	340.5	341.0	344.1	344.8	344.6	340.4
2015	337.1	340.3	340.9	344.0	344.6	342.3	341.2	343.0	344.6	348.1	350.8	348.8	343.8
2016	342.8	346.7	346.7	350.4	350.6	347.6	347.8	349.3	351.5	351.0	352.6	352.3	349.1
2017	345.6	348.7	349.2	351.8	351.4	350.7	347.9	349.4	351.9	353.1	354.6	353.9	350.7
Mining, Logging, and Construction													
2007	30.0	30.1	30.8	31.0	31.4	31.6	31.1	31.0	30.5	30.7	30.3	29.6	30.7
2008	28.8	28.8	29.0	29.2	29.2	29.5	29.1	28.6	28.2	27.9	27.2	26.3	28.5
2009	24.8	24.1	23.9	24.1	24.1	24.3	24.3	24.6	24.2	24.0	23.4	22.5	24.0
2010	21.6	21.1	21.0	21.3	21.4	21.7	22.2	22.1	21.8	21.6	21.3	20.9	21.5
2011	20.1	19.9	20.5	20.7	20.8	21.0	21.1	20.6	20.1	19.8	19.4	18.9	20.2
2012	18.6	18.6	18.8	18.9	19.2	19.6	19.3	19.3	19.1	19.8	19.7	19.5	19.2
2013	18.8	19.0	19.4	19.8	20.2	20.4	20.5	20.3	20.1	20.5	20.2	19.8	19.9
2014	19.5	19.4	19.5	19.8	20.2	20.4	20.8	20.8	20.4	20.9	20.8	20.6	20.3
2015	20.1	19.8	19.8	20.6	20.5	20.7	20.9	20.7	20.6	20.9	20.8	20.7	20.5
2016	20.4	20.5	20.6	21.2	21.3	21.6	22.0	21.9	21.9	22.1	21.9	22.0	21.5
2017	21.7	21.7	22.1	22.6	22.8	23.2	23.4	23.6	23.6	23.9	23.7	23.5	23.0

Employment by Industry: Albuquerque, NM, Selected Years, 2007–2017—*Continued*

(Numbers in thousands, not seasonally adjusted)

Industry and year	January	February	March	April	May	June	July	August	September	October	November	December	Annual average
Manufacturing													
2007	23.8	24.1	24.0	23.8	23.9	24.0	24.0	24.0	23.6	23.1	23.0	22.8	23.7
2008	22.3	22.3	22.3	22.3	22.4	22.5	22.4	22.5	22.4	21.4	21.0	20.7	22.0
2009	19.9	19.3	18.7	18.4	18.2	18.1	18.0	17.8	17.5	17.4	17.3	17.4	18.2
2010	17.3	17.3	17.3	17.5	17.7	17.7	17.8	17.7	17.8	17.7	17.6	17.6	17.6
2011	17.5	17.4	17.5	17.7	17.7	17.8	17.9	18.0	17.8	17.9	17.7	17.7	17.7
2012	17.6	17.6	17.7	17.7	17.8	17.9	18.0	17.9	17.8	17.9	17.7	17.6	17.8
2013	17.5	17.4	17.3	17.4	17.4	17.5	17.5	17.5	17.3	17.3	17.0	17.0	17.3
2014	16.8	16.5	16.5	16.5	16.6	16.6	16.6	16.7	16.5	16.5	16.3	16.3	16.5
2015	16.3	16.4	16.4	16.3	16.5	16.6	16.6	16.7	16.4	16.7	16.6	16.6	16.5
2016	16.3	16.4	16.2	16.3	16.4	16.3	16.0	16.0	15.9	15.8	15.6	15.7	16.1
2017	15.6	15.5	15.5	15.5	15.5	15.6	15.6	15.7	15.6	15.5	15.8	15.9	15.6
Trade, Transportation, and Utilities													
2007	68.7	68.2	68.4	68.2	69.0	68.9	68.9	69.3	69.2	69.7	71.4	72.4	69.4
2008	69.9	69.0	69.0	68.8	68.7	68.3	68.4	68.6	68.4	68.2	68.3	68.6	68.7
2009	65.3	63.8	63.6	62.8	63.2	63.0	63.1	63.2	63.3	63.6	64.3	65.0	63.7
2010	62.3	61.6	61.7	61.6	61.9	61.9	61.9	62.4	61.9	62.5	63.6	64.3	62.3
2011	61.9	61.5	61.4	62.1	62.3	61.7	61.2	61.4	61.4	61.9	63.2	63.6	62.0
2012	61.9	61.4	61.6	61.6	61.8	61.6	61.5	61.8	61.9	62.8	64.0	64.0	62.2
2013	62.0	61.5	61.4	62.0	62.1	62.0	62.6	62.9	62.4	63.2	64.7	65.3	62.7
2014	62.8	62.3	62.4	62.9	62.9	62.6	63.0	63.1	63.1	63.8	65.1	65.5	63.3
2015	63.5	63.1	63.0	63.3	63.7	63.4	63.6	63.8	63.7	64.3	65.7	66.0	63.9
2016	63.7	63.2	63.1	63.9	63.8	63.3	63.5	63.9	63.9	64.2	65.6	65.6	64.0
2017	63.5	62.7	62.6	62.7	62.7	62.6	62.7	63.1	62.9	62.9	64.5	64.9	63.2
Wholesale Trade													
2007	13.7	13.6	13.6	13.6	13.6	13.7	13.8	13.8	13.8	13.9	13.8	13.9	13.7
2008	13.8	13.6	13.5	13.5	13.5	13.4	13.5	13.4	13.2	13.1	12.9	12.8	13.4
2009	12.5	12.4	12.3	12.1	12.1	12.1	12.3	12.3	12.3	12.4	12.4	12.4	12.3
2010	12.1	12.1	12.0	12.1	12.1	12.1	12.0	12.0	11.9	11.9	11.8	11.8	12.0
2011	11.7	11.7	11.7	11.8	11.8	11.7	11.7	11.7	11.6	11.6	11.6	11.7	11.7
2012	11.6	11.7	11.8	11.8	11.9	11.9	11.9	11.9	11.8	11.9	11.9	11.9	11.8
2013	11.7	11.7	11.6	11.7	11.7	11.7	11.7	11.7	11.6	11.6	11.7	11.7	11.7
2014	11.8	11.8	11.8	12.0	12.0	11.9	12.0	11.9	11.9	11.9	11.9	11.9	11.9
2015	11.8	11.8	11.9	11.9	12.0	12.0	12.0	11.9	11.9	12.0	12.0	12.0	11.9
2016	12.0	12.0	12.0	12.1	12.0	11.9	11.9	11.9	11.9	11.8	11.8	11.8	11.9
2017	11.7	11.7	11.7	11.6	11.7	11.7	11.8	11.7	11.7	11.7	11.7	11.7	11.7
Retail Trade													
2007	44.1	43.6	43.9	43.7	44.4	44.5	44.5	44.5	44.3	44.6	46.4	47.0	44.6
2008	44.9	44.3	44.5	44.3	44.2	44.4	44.4	44.4	44.4	44.6	44.9	45.2	44.5
2009	42.4	41.2	41.2	41.0	41.2	41.4	41.5	41.5	41.6	41.6	42.4	42.9	41.7
2010	40.7	40.0	40.3	40.1	40.4	40.5	40.6	41.0	40.5	41.0	42.1	42.6	40.8
2011	40.6	40.2	40.3	40.8	41.0	40.6	40.2	40.4	40.3	40.7	42.0	42.1	40.8
2012	40.7	40.1	40.2	40.3	40.4	40.4	40.2	40.3	40.5	41.1	42.3	42.2	40.7
2013	40.5	40.1	40.1	40.6	40.7	40.7	41.2	41.4	41.0	41.8	43.2	43.5	41.2
2014	41.3	40.8	41.0	41.3	41.2	41.1	41.3	41.4	41.3	42.0	43.2	43.4	41.6
2015	41.6	41.2	41.1	41.4	41.7	41.5	41.8	42.0	41.9	42.4	43.6	43.7	42.0
2016	41.7	41.3	41.2	41.8	41.7	41.5	41.5	41.7	41.7	42.1	43.4	43.2	41.9
2017	41.6	40.9	40.8	41.0	40.9	41.0	41.0	41.2	41.0	41.0	42.5	42.7	41.3
Transportation and Utilities													
2007	10.9	11.0	10.9	10.9	11.0	10.7	10.6	11.0	11.1	11.2	11.2	11.5	11.0
2008	11.2	11.1	11.0	11.0	11.0	10.5	10.5	10.8	10.8	10.5	10.5	10.6	10.8
2009	10.4	10.2	10.1	9.7	9.9	9.5	9.3	9.4	9.4	9.6	9.5	9.7	9.7
2010	9.5	9.5	9.4	9.4	9.4	9.3	9.3	9.4	9.5	9.6	9.7	9.9	9.5
2011	9.6	9.6	9.4	9.5	9.5	9.4	9.3	9.3	9.5	9.6	9.6	9.8	9.5
2012	9.6	9.6	9.6	9.5	9.5	9.3	9.4	9.6	9.6	9.8	9.8	9.9	9.6
2013	9.8	9.7	9.7	9.7	9.7	9.6	9.7	9.8	9.8	9.8	9.8	10.1	9.8
2014	9.7	9.7	9.6	9.6	9.7	9.6	9.7	9.8	9.9	9.9	10.0	10.2	9.8
2015	10.1	10.1	10.0	10.0	10.0	9.9	9.8	9.9	9.9	9.9	10.1	10.3	10.0
2016	10.0	9.9	9.9	10.0	10.1	9.9	10.1	10.3	10.3	10.3	10.4	10.6	10.2
2017	10.2	10.1	10.1	10.1	10.1	9.9	9.9	10.2	10.2	10.2	10.3	10.5	10.2

Employment by Industry: Albuquerque, NM, Selected Years, 2007–2017—*Continued*

(Numbers in thousands, not seasonally adjusted)

Industry and year	January	February	March	April	May	June	July	August	September	October	November	December	Annual average
Information													
2007	8.8	9.1	9.4	9.4	9.5	10.2	9.3	9.3	9.3	9.5	9.5	9.5	9.4
2008	9.4	9.5	9.4	9.1	9.1	9.1	9.8	9.8	9.9	9.7	9.6	9.5	9.5
2009	8.9	8.8	8.7	9.0	8.9	9.1	9.2	9.4	9.6	9.2	9.3	9.4	9.1
2010	9.0	8.7	8.4	9.4	8.9	9.4	8.8	8.9	8.4	8.4	8.7	8.8	8.8
2011	8.6	8.6	8.6	9.2	9.5	9.2	8.7	8.1	7.8	7.9	8.0	7.8	8.5
2012	8.1	8.4	8.8	8.8	8.1	8.0	8.3	8.4	8.6	8.4	8.5	8.4	8.4
2013	8.1	8.8	8.4	8.5	8.6	8.0	7.9	7.8	7.6	7.9	8.0	7.8	8.1
2014	7.4	7.7	7.9	7.7	8.2	8.1	8.0	8.2	7.5	7.8	8.2	8.1	7.9
2015	7.4	8.0	8.2	7.9	8.3	8.0	8.1	8.7	8.3	8.1	8.4	7.7	8.1
2016	7.5	7.4	7.4	7.8	7.6	7.4	7.8	7.9	7.8	7.4	8.1	7.8	7.7
2017	7.4	7.1	7.4	7.7	7.5	7.7	7.3	7.3	7.3	7.3	7.5	7.3	7.4
Financial Activities													
2007	19.2	19.3	19.4	19.4	19.4	19.5	19.4	19.5	19.3	19.4	19.2	19.2	19.4
2008	18.9	18.9	18.8	18.9	18.8	18.8	19.0	19.0	19.0	18.8	18.5	18.5	18.8
2009	18.2	18.1	18.0	18.2	18.3	18.4	18.5	18.4	18.4	18.7	18.4	18.5	18.3
2010	18.3	18.1	18.3	18.0	17.9	18.0	18.0	17.9	17.7	17.8	17.7	17.7	18.0
2011	17.4	17.4	17.4	17.6	17.5	17.6	17.7	17.7	17.7	17.7	17.6	17.7	17.6
2012	17.5	17.6	17.7	17.6	17.7	17.7	17.8	17.8	17.7	17.9	17.8	17.8	17.7
2013	17.8	17.7	17.6	17.7	17.9	17.8	17.9	18.0	17.9	18.0	18.2	18.2	17.9
2014	17.7	17.8	17.8	17.7	17.8	17.7	18.0	17.9	17.8	18.0	17.9	17.9	17.8
2015	17.7	17.8	17.9	18.0	18.1	18.0	18.2	18.1	17.9	18.1	18.0	18.2	18.0
2016	18.1	18.2	18.2	18.4	18.4	18.3	18.3	18.4	18.3	18.4	18.4	18.4	18.3
2017	18.4	18.5	18.4	18.6	18.7	18.7	18.9	18.9	18.7	19.1	19.3	19.3	18.8
Professional and Business Services													
2007	63.6	64.4	64.9	64.7	65.1	65.7	65.8	66.5	65.6	65.2	65.2	65.4	65.2
2008	64.5	64.9	64.7	64.9	65.2	65.4	65.8	67.1	66.4	66.2	64.6	64.1	65.3
2009	62.8	62.1	61.5	61.4	61.0	60.9	60.9	61.4	60.6	59.8	59.2	59.0	60.9
2010	57.8	57.8	57.5	58.1	57.6	58.4	58.2	58.5	58.6	59.0	58.6	58.6	58.2
2011	57.3	59.3	57.7	58.0	57.8	58.1	58.2	58.3	58.7	57.7	57.3	56.7	57.9
2012	55.2	55.2	55.6	55.9	56.0	56.8	56.4	56.4	56.5	57.2	57.3	56.6	56.3
2013	56.6	56.9	56.6	57.5	57.5	57.0	57.7	57.7	57.0	57.5	57.1	57.4	57.2
2014	56.7	56.8	56.3	57.7	57.7	57.1	57.8	58.0	56.8	57.5	57.2	57.3	57.2
2015	56.3	56.4	56.3	57.0	56.8	57.1	57.7	57.6	57.3	57.9	58.0	58.1	57.2
2016	57.2	57.5	57.2	58.0	58.0	58.5	59.6	59.3	59.3	59.2	58.8	59.0	58.5
2017	58.8	59.5	59.5	60.1	59.9	60.6	61.1	61.1	61.1	60.9	61.1	60.8	60.4
Education and Health Services													
2007	48.6	48.9	49.6	49.7	49.8	48.6	48.2	48.0	48.9	49.5	49.8	49.9	49.1
2008	49.5	50.1	50.8	51.6	51.9	51.1	50.4	50.7	51.8	52.4	52.6	52.7	51.3
2009	53.1	53.5	54.1	54.1	54.3	53.0	52.5	52.9	53.9	54.0	54.2	54.2	53.7
2010	54.3	54.5	55.0	55.1	55.2	54.3	53.8	53.7	55.0	55.4	55.6	55.8	54.8
2011	55.5	55.6	55.8	55.9	55.8	54.4	54.8	54.9	56.3	56.5	56.2	56.0	55.6
2012	56.1	56.3	56.3	56.7	56.6	55.7	55.4	55.3	56.9	57.7	57.7	57.8	56.5
2013	57.5	57.7	58.0	58.3	58.3	57.1	56.1	56.8	58.0	58.4	58.6	58.6	57.8
2014	58.7	58.8	59.0	59.5	59.7	58.8	58.2	58.8	60.2	60.8	60.8	60.5	59.5
2015	60.7	61.2	61.4	62.0	62.2	61.4	60.7	61.3	62.7	63.5	63.7	63.1	62.0
2016	63.7	64.2	64.1	64.6	64.7	63.5	63.0	63.6	64.4	64.4	64.1	64.6	64.1
2017	64.3	64.7	64.5	64.9	64.8	63.7	62.8	63.5	64.2	64.8	64.4	63.8	64.2
Leisure and Hospitality													
2007	37.9	38.0	38.8	39.6	39.9	40.3	40.2	40.5	40.3	39.6	39.1	39.0	39.4
2008	37.8	37.9	38.6	39.8	40.0	40.1	39.7	39.9	39.4	38.7	37.8	37.1	38.9
2009	36.2	36.1	36.6	37.6	38.2	38.1	38.1	38.3	37.9	37.2	36.5	36.2	37.3
2010	35.5	35.9	36.7	37.7	38.3	38.1	38.0	37.9	37.4	37.1	36.5	36.4	37.1
2011	35.8	36.1	36.8	38.1	38.2	38.4	38.2	38.6	38.5	38.1	37.3	36.9	37.6
2012	36.3	36.6	37.3	38.7	39.6	39.9	39.7	40.0	39.4	39.8	38.8	38.4	38.7
2013	37.8	37.8	38.5	39.8	40.5	40.6	40.9	41.0	40.2	39.9	39.4	39.4	39.7
2014	39.1	38.9	39.3	40.8	41.8	41.9	42.0	42.4	41.8	41.8	41.0	40.7	41.0
2015	40.1	40.2	40.4	42.7	43.1	43.1	43.0	42.9	42.0	42.3	41.8	41.5	41.9
2016	40.6	41.3	41.6	42.8	43.9	43.6	44.3	44.2	43.4	42.8	42.1	41.9	42.7
2017	41.6	41.8	42.5	43.3	44.2	44.3	44.3	44.2	43.9	42.8	42.3	42.2	43.1

Employment by Industry: Albuquerque, NM, Selected Years, 2007–2017—*Continued*

(Numbers in thousands, not seasonally adjusted)

Industry and year	January	February	March	April	May	June	July	August	September	October	November	December	Annual average
Other Services													
2007	11.9	12.0	12.2	12.1	12.2	12.5	12.5	12.2	12.1	12.2	12.2	12.2	12.2
2008	12.1	12.3	12.3	12.3	12.4	12.9	12.8	12.6	12.5	12.7	12.5	12.0	12.5
2009	12.0	12.1	12.0	12.0	12.0	12.3	12.1	12.0	11.7	11.7	11.7	11.8	12.0
2010	11.7	11.7	11.7	11.7	11.7	12.3	12.2	12.3	11.8	11.9	11.6	11.6	11.9
2011	11.5	11.7	11.8	11.8	11.7	12.2	12.2	12.1	11.7	11.6	11.5	11.5	11.8
2012	11.5	11.8	11.9	11.9	11.8	12.3	12.0	12.1	11.8	12.1	11.7	11.8	11.9
2013	11.5	11.6	11.6	11.7	11.6	11.8	11.9	11.8	11.5	11.6	11.6	11.6	11.7
2014	11.5	11.7	11.7	11.7	11.7	12.0	12.0	12.1	11.8	11.8	11.7	11.6	11.8
2015	11.3	11.5	11.5	11.6	11.6	11.9	12.0	11.9	11.6	11.6	11.6	11.5	11.6
2016	11.4	11.6	11.5	11.8	11.7	12.0	12.3	12.3	12.0	11.9	11.9	11.8	11.9
2017	11.5	11.7	11.7	12.0	12.0	12.4	12.3	12.2	11.9	11.9	11.8	11.8	11.9
Government													
2007	77.5	79.6	80.6	79.9	79.8	78.7	76.7	78.0	80.6	81.3	81.7	81.7	79.7
2008	78.9	81.2	81.7	81.7	82.3	80.6	78.7	80.0	82.6	83.3	83.2	83.2	81.5
2009	81.3	83.4	83.9	84.0	83.4	81.7	79.2	80.5	83.0	84.3	84.2	84.5	82.8
2010	81.6	83.8	84.4	85.2	85.5	83.1	80.2	80.8	83.1	84.6	84.6	84.8	83.5
2011	82.1	84.2	84.8	84.7	84.0	82.8	80.3	80.7	83.6	84.7	84.7	85.0	83.5
2012	81.2	83.5	84.0	83.2	83.0	78.7	78.2	79.8	82.9	84.2	84.4	84.6	82.3
2013	81.3	83.6	83.8	83.6	83.1	81.5	79.4	80.4	83.1	83.5	84.0	83.7	82.6
2014	80.9	83.0	83.6	82.2	82.9	80.2	79.2	80.0	82.0	82.6	82.9	83.0	81.9
2015	80.1	82.1	82.2	81.5	80.8	79.4	77.9	78.7	81.1	82.3	83.6	82.7	81.0
2016	80.6	83.3	83.6	83.1	82.5	81.0	79.0	79.7	82.4	82.7	83.6	83.2	82.1
2017	80.1	82.7	82.6	82.5	81.6	80.7	78.5	79.1	81.9	83.4	83.7	83.8	81.7

Employment by Industry: Greenville-Anderson-Mauldin, SC, Selected Years, 2007–2017

(Numbers in thousands, not seasonally adjusted)

Industry and year	January	February	March	April	May	June	July	August	September	October	November	December	Annual average
Total Nonfarm													
2007	371.7	374.6	378.1	379.6	381.8	381.8	377.3	378.5	381.3	380.9	384.9	385.2	379.6
2008	378.9	380.9	382.4	381.6	384.5	381.1	375.2	376.0	378.4	376.9	376.6	372.4	378.7
2009	358.8	358.3	358.1	355.1	356.2	351.7	348.8	348.8	349.9	351.4	353.2	352.4	353.6
2010	345.0	347.1	350.0	353.6	357.9	355.9	353.3	354.7	356.3	358.6	360.5	361.1	354.5
2011	351.0	357.2	360.8	363.6	364.5	362.2	360.6	363.0	365.1	365.6	367.8	367.5	362.4
2012	360.8	363.6	366.8	367.5	370.8	369.8	364.9	367.5	370.3	370.6	374.7	375.1	368.5
2013	368.3	371.2	373.9	375.3	379.0	381.3	376.7	379.9	383.9	386.3	388.0	388.7	379.4
2014	378.6	380.3	385.2	386.8	389.5	389.4	384.3	387.7	390.7	393.8	397.1	398.6	388.5
2015	390.8	393.1	395.2	398.3	401.8	403.1	400.7	403.0	404.1	408.8	410.1	411.7	401.7
2016	401.3	404.3	406.4	409.4	410.4	409.3	407.4	409.5	410.7	412.7	415.1	415.5	409.3
2017	407.8	411.5	412.8	414.0	415.7	416.0	412.2	415.1	415.5	419.4	422.0	423.2	415.4
Total Private													
2007	316.5	319.0	322.1	323.7	325.7	326.2	324.3	325.7	325.2	324.0	327.0	327.7	323.9
2008	321.8	323.3	324.3	323.9	325.9	323.3	320.2	321.4	320.6	318.2	317.2	313.8	321.2
2009	301.2	300.4	300.0	296.8	297.9	294.3	294.1	293.8	293.0	293.6	295.1	294.4	296.2
2010	288.4	290.3	293.1	296.4	299.3	298.7	299.4	301.1	300.8	302.4	304.2	305.0	298.3
2011	295.7	301.6	305.2	307.7	308.5	307.1	307.0	309.8	309.8	309.6	311.6	311.4	307.1
2012	304.8	307.2	310.3	311.0	313.8	313.7	311.0	313.2	313.7	313.2	317.0	317.5	312.2
2013	311.0	313.7	316.0	317.2	321.1	323.7	321.7	324.5	326.4	327.9	329.7	330.3	321.9
2014	320.8	322.1	326.8	328.4	330.7	331.4	328.7	331.4	332.4	334.6	337.7	339.1	330.3
2015	332.1	333.8	335.6	338.6	341.9	343.8	343.9	345.5	344.6	348.4	349.7	351.0	342.4
2016	341.6	344.4	346.0	348.9	349.8	349.4	350.0	351.4	350.7	352.0	354.2	354.4	349.4
2017	347.7	351.1	352.0	352.9	354.4	355.4	353.9	355.8	354.3	357.4	359.8	360.8	354.6
Goods Producing													
2007	76.2	76.6	77.1	77.1	77.4	77.8	77.4	77.7	77.5	77.0	77.1	77.0	77.2
2008	76.7	76.9	76.7	76.5	76.6	76.6	75.4	75.0	74.6	73.8	72.9	72.0	75.3
2009	70.6	69.5	68.4	67.1	66.8	66.5	65.6	64.9	64.4	64.1	63.8	63.7	66.3
2010	62.0	61.6	61.8	62.2	62.7	62.9	63.0	63.0	62.9	62.8	63.0	63.4	62.6
2011	61.5	63.1	63.4	63.9	64.0	64.3	64.4	64.7	64.3	64.4	64.6	64.5	63.9
2012	64.0	64.3	64.8	64.9	65.4	65.3	65.1	65.6	65.6	66.0	66.2	66.4	65.3
2013	66.2	66.9	67.5	67.5	68.1	68.3	68.2	68.7	68.9	69.2	69.5	69.6	68.2
2014	68.8	69.0	69.7	69.9	70.5	70.9	70.3	70.7	70.6	70.6	70.9	71.2	70.3
2015	70.7	70.7	71.0	71.3	72.1	72.8	72.9	72.9	72.8	73.2	73.1	73.4	72.2
2016	73.3	73.5	73.9	74.5	75.0	75.3	76.0	76.0	75.6	75.6	76.1	76.4	75.1
2017	75.6	75.9	75.9	76.0	76.1	76.7	76.4	76.5	76.3	76.0	76.7	77.5	76.3
Service-Providing													
2007	295.5	298.0	301.0	302.5	304.4	304.0	299.9	300.8	303.8	303.9	307.8	308.2	302.5
2008	302.2	304.0	305.7	305.1	307.9	304.5	299.8	301.0	303.8	303.1	303.7	300.4	303.4
2009	288.2	288.8	289.7	288.0	289.4	285.2	283.2	283.9	285.5	287.3	289.4	288.7	287.3
2010	283.0	285.5	288.2	291.4	295.2	293.0	290.3	291.7	293.4	295.8	297.5	297.7	291.9
2011	289.5	294.1	297.4	299.7	300.5	297.9	296.2	298.3	300.8	301.2	303.2	303.0	298.5
2012	296.8	299.3	302.0	302.6	305.4	304.5	299.8	301.9	304.7	304.6	308.5	308.7	303.2
2013	302.1	304.3	306.4	307.8	310.9	312.8	308.5	311.2	315.0	317.1	318.5	319.1	311.1
2014	309.8	311.3	315.5	316.9	319.0	318.5	314.0	317.0	320.1	323.2	326.2	327.4	318.2
2015	320.1	322.4	324.2	327.0	329.7	330.3	327.8	330.1	331.3	335.6	337.0	338.3	329.5
2016	328.0	330.8	332.5	334.9	335.4	334.0	331.4	333.5	335.1	337.1	339.0	339.1	334.2
2017	332.2	335.6	336.9	338.0	339.6	339.3	335.8	338.6	339.2	343.4	345.3	345.7	339.1
Mining, Logging, and Construction													
2007	21.8	21.8	22.4	22.6	22.8	23.1	23.1	23.1	22.8	22.3	22.2	22.0	22.5
2008	21.5	21.6	21.6	21.3	21.5	21.6	20.9	20.7	20.4	20.0	19.7	19.3	20.8
2009	18.1	17.8	17.5	17.0	17.0	16.9	16.5	16.1	15.7	15.3	15.2	15.3	16.5
2010	14.5	14.3	14.4	14.7	14.9	15.0	15.0	14.8	14.7	14.6	14.6	14.7	14.7
2011	13.4	14.2	14.3	14.4	14.6	14.6	14.5	14.5	14.3	14.2	14.4	14.3	14.3
2012	14.1	14.3	14.6	14.4	14.7	14.7	14.6	14.7	14.6	14.8	14.9	14.9	14.6
2013	14.7	14.8	15.1	15.2	15.5	15.7	15.8	15.9	15.9	16.0	16.2	16.3	15.6
2014	15.7	15.7	16.1	16.1	16.3	16.5	16.1	16.4	16.3	16.3	16.5	16.6	16.2
2015	16.1	16.1	16.2	16.3	16.7	17.1	17.0	17.0	16.9	17.0	17.0	17.0	16.7
2016	17.0	17.2	17.5	17.8	18.2	18.4	18.7	18.6	18.3	18.2	18.3	18.3	18.0
2017	17.8	18.0	17.9	18.2	18.3	18.5	18.2	18.2	18.0	18.1	18.2	18.3	18.1

Employment by Industry: Greenville-Anderson-Mauldin, SC, Selected Years, 2007–2017—*Continued*

(Numbers in thousands, not seasonally adjusted)

Industry and year	January	February	March	April	May	June	July	August	September	October	November	December	Annual average
Manufacturing													
2007	54.4	54.8	54.7	54.5	54.6	54.7	54.3	54.6	54.7	54.7	54.9	55.0	54.7
2008	55.2	55.3	55.1	55.2	55.1	55.0	54.5	54.3	54.2	53.8	53.2	52.7	54.5
2009	52.5	51.7	50.9	50.1	49.8	49.6	49.1	48.8	48.7	48.8	48.6	48.4	49.8
2010	47.5	47.3	47.4	47.5	47.8	47.9	48.0	48.2	48.2	48.2	48.4	48.7	47.9
2011	48.1	48.9	49.1	49.5	49.4	49.7	49.9	50.2	50.0	50.2	50.2	50.2	49.6
2012	49.9	50.0	50.2	50.5	50.7	50.6	50.5	50.9	51.0	51.2	51.3	51.5	50.7
2013	51.5	52.1	52.4	52.3	52.6	52.8	52.4	52.8	53.0	53.2	53.3	53.3	52.6
2014	53.1	53.3	53.6	53.8	54.2	54.4	54.2	54.3	54.3	54.3	54.4	54.6	54.0
2015	54.6	54.6	54.8	55.0	55.4	55.7	55.9	55.9	55.9	56.2	56.1	56.4	55.5
2016	56.3	56.3	56.4	56.7	56.8	56.9	57.3	57.4	57.3	57.4	57.8	58.1	57.1
2017	57.8	57.9	58.0	57.8	57.8	58.2	58.2	58.3	58.3	57.9	58.5	59.2	58.2
Trade, Transportation, and Utilities													
2007	76.6	76.8	77.3	77.5	78.1	78.2	77.7	77.1	76.9	76.8	78.8	79.5	77.6
2008	77.4	77.1	77.3	75.4	75.6	75.3	75.5	75.4	75.1	74.2	74.9	75.0	75.7
2009	70.5	69.4	69.0	68.8	68.9	68.2	68.0	67.9	67.6	67.4	68.1	68.4	68.5
2010	66.2	66.2	66.6	67.4	67.9	67.9	67.8	68.0	67.7	68.7	70.0	70.5	67.9
2011	67.6	68.3	68.8	69.0	69.2	69.3	69.3	69.4	69.0	69.2	70.4	70.9	69.2
2012	68.8	68.6	69.1	69.3	69.6	69.6	69.5	69.5	69.3	69.6	71.3	71.4	69.6
2013	68.5	68.5	69.3	69.6	70.2	70.8	70.6	71.2	70.8	71.5	72.9	73.6	70.6
2014	70.2	70.1	70.5	70.8	71.3	71.9	71.5	71.9	71.7	72.8	74.3	75.3	71.9
2015	73.1	72.9	73.5	74.2	74.6	74.7	74.9	75.1	74.6	75.6	77.2	77.7	74.8
2016	74.6	74.6	74.3	74.6	75.0	74.9	75.1	75.2	75.1	75.8	77.1	78.1	75.4
2017	75.6	75.7	75.5	75.3	75.4	75.5	75.3	75.6	75.0	75.2	76.9	77.2	75.7
Wholesale Trade													
2007	17.6	17.9	17.7	17.8	17.9	18.1	18.0	17.8	17.7	17.9	18.1	18.1	17.9
2008	18.0	18.2	18.2	18.0	18.0	17.9	17.9	17.8	17.6	17.4	17.3	17.1	17.8
2009	16.7	16.4	16.3	16.2	16.1	15.9	15.9	15.9	15.8	15.9	15.8	15.7	16.1
2010	15.7	15.9	15.9	16.4	16.6	16.6	16.6	16.7	16.6	16.9	16.9	16.9	16.5
2011	16.8	17.0	17.1	17.0	17.0	17.1	17.2	17.2	17.2	17.2	17.2	17.3	17.1
2012	17.1	17.1	17.2	17.3	17.3	17.4	17.4	17.5	17.2	17.3	17.3	17.4	17.3
2013	17.1	17.2	17.2	17.3	17.5	17.6	17.5	17.7	17.5	17.6	17.7	17.7	17.5
2014	17.1	17.1	17.1	17.2	17.4	17.6	17.6	17.7	17.7	18.2	18.3	18.4	17.6
2015	18.7	18.7	18.9	19.0	19.1	19.1	19.1	19.1	19.1	19.3	19.3	19.5	19.1
2016	19.0	19.0	18.9	18.9	18.8	18.9	18.9	18.9	18.7	18.8	18.9	19.0	18.9
2017	18.6	18.6	18.6	18.5	18.5	18.7	18.6	18.6	18.4	18.4	18.4	18.4	18.5
Retail Trade													
2007	46.2	45.8	46.4	46.7	47.1	46.9	46.7	46.4	46.3	46.0	47.5	48.1	46.7
2008	46.3	45.7	45.9	44.2	44.4	44.2	44.3	44.5	44.5	44.0	44.8	45.0	44.8
2009	41.5	41.0	40.7	40.8	40.9	40.5	40.4	40.4	40.2	40.2	41.1	41.5	40.8
2010	39.7	39.5	39.9	40.1	40.4	40.4	40.3	40.4	40.2	40.8	42.0	42.5	40.5
2011	40.0	40.3	40.7	40.9	40.9	40.8	40.9	41.0	40.7	40.9	42.0	42.4	41.0
2012	40.7	40.6	40.8	40.7	41.0	40.9	40.8	40.8	40.8	40.9	42.6	42.6	41.1
2013	40.4	40.2	41.0	41.2	41.5	41.9	41.9	42.2	42.1	42.6	43.9	44.3	41.9
2014	42.0	42.0	42.3	42.2	42.4	42.8	42.5	42.7	42.5	43.1	44.5	45.1	42.8
2015	43.2	43.0	43.3	43.9	44.1	44.2	44.3	44.6	44.2	44.9	46.3	46.5	44.4
2016	44.1	44.2	43.9	44.2	44.5	44.3	44.3	44.4	44.4	44.9	46.0	46.5	44.6
2017	44.6	44.7	44.6	44.5	44.5	44.4	44.5	44.8	44.4	44.6	46.2	46.4	44.9
Transportation and Utilities													
2007	12.8	13.1	13.2	13.0	13.1	13.2	13.0	12.9	12.9	12.9	13.2	13.3	13.1
2008	13.1	13.2	13.2	13.2	13.2	13.2	13.3	13.1	13.0	12.8	12.8	12.9	13.1
2009	12.3	12.0	12.0	11.8	11.9	11.8	11.7	11.6	11.6	11.3	11.2	11.2	11.7
2010	10.8	10.8	10.8	10.9	10.9	10.9	10.9	10.9	10.9	11.0	11.1	11.1	10.9
2011	10.8	11.0	11.0	11.1	11.3	11.4	11.2	11.2	11.1	11.1	11.2	11.2	11.1
2012	11.0	10.9	11.1	11.3	11.3	11.3	11.3	11.2	11.3	11.4	11.4	11.4	11.2
2013	11.0	11.1	11.1	11.1	11.2	11.3	11.2	11.3	11.2	11.3	11.3	11.6	11.2
2014	11.1	11.0	11.1	11.4	11.5	11.5	11.4	11.5	11.5	11.5	11.5	11.8	11.4
2015	11.2	11.2	11.3	11.3	11.4	11.4	11.5	11.4	11.3	11.4	11.6	11.7	11.4
2016	11.5	11.4	11.5	11.5	11.7	11.7	11.9	11.9	12.0	12.1	12.2	12.6	11.8
2017	12.4	12.4	12.3	12.3	12.4	12.4	12.2	12.2	12.2	12.2	12.3	12.4	12.3

Employment by Industry: Greenville-Anderson-Mauldin, SC, Selected Years, 2007–2017—*Continued*

(Numbers in thousands, not seasonally adjusted)

Industry and year	January	February	March	April	May	June	July	August	September	October	November	December	Annual average
Information													
2007	6.9	7.0	7.0	7.0	7.1	7.2	7.5	7.4	7.1	7.1	7.2	7.2	7.1
2008	7.1	7.3	7.3	7.7	7.8	7.7	7.8	7.7	7.6	7.6	7.5	7.6	7.6
2009	7.2	7.4	7.5	7.3	7.3	7.3	7.5	7.1	6.9	6.8	6.8	6.8	7.2
2010	6.9	7.1	7.1	6.6	6.7	7.1	7.2	6.6	6.6	6.6	6.6	7.0	6.8
2011	7.1	7.0	7.3	7.1	6.9	7.0	6.8	6.8	6.7	7.5	7.5	7.5	7.1
2012	7.3	7.6	7.5	7.6	7.8	7.8	7.2	7.1	7.1	7.0	7.1	7.3	7.4
2013	7.3	7.4	7.3	7.3	7.4	7.3	7.4	7.2	7.2	7.2	7.1	7.1	7.3
2014	7.0	6.9	6.9	6.9	7.1	7.1	7.2	7.1	7.1	7.1	7.3	7.3	7.1
2015	7.4	7.4	7.4	7.3	7.4	7.5	7.4	7.4	7.4	7.4	7.4	7.5	7.4
2016	7.3	7.3	7.2	7.2	7.2	7.1	7.1	7.0	7.1	7.1	7.0	7.1	7.1
2017	7.2	7.2	7.2	7.3	7.3	7.3	7.4	7.4	7.3	7.4	7.4	7.4	7.3
Financial Activities													
2007	14.5	14.5	14.6	14.6	14.9	14.9	15.0	15.3	15.4	15.7	15.8	16.0	15.1
2008	16.0	16.1	16.2	16.0	16.0	15.9	15.7	16.0	15.8	15.7	15.8	15.7	15.9
2009	15.5	15.5	15.4	15.1	15.3	15.0	15.2	15.2	15.2	15.3	15.4	15.4	15.3
2010	15.1	15.2	15.2	15.2	15.3	15.2	15.1	15.1	14.9	15.2	15.3	15.2	15.2
2011	15.0	15.0	15.0	15.1	15.1	14.9	15.1	15.1	15.1	15.1	15.1	15.1	15.1
2012	14.8	14.8	15.0	14.9	15.0	15.1	15.2	15.1	15.2	15.2	15.3	15.5	15.1
2013	15.5	15.6	15.7	15.9	16.0	16.1	16.0	16.0	16.0	16.1	16.2	16.2	15.9
2014	15.7	15.7	15.9	15.9	16.0	16.2	16.3	16.4	16.3	16.3	16.4	16.6	16.1
2015	16.2	16.2	16.3	16.4	16.5	16.8	16.8	16.8	16.8	17.1	17.1	17.4	16.7
2016	17.2	17.3	17.4	17.5	17.5	17.7	17.8	18.0	18.0	18.3	18.4	18.3	17.8
2017	18.1	18.2	18.3	18.2	18.3	18.3	18.5	18.6	18.5	18.6	18.6	18.3	18.4
Professional and Business Services													
2007	55.5	56.5	57.7	58.1	58.8	59.0	58.2	58.7	58.6	58.1	58.8	58.8	58.1
2008	57.3	57.7	57.8	58.8	59.8	58.9	57.4	58.1	57.9	57.1	56.3	54.4	57.6
2009	50.8	51.0	51.2	49.3	49.4	48.6	49.8	50.0	50.4	51.8	52.9	52.2	50.6
2010	51.4	52.5	53.6	54.8	55.4	55.4	56.3	57.3	57.3	57.9	58.3	58.3	55.7
2011	56.4	58.2	59.3	60.4	60.5	60.4	61.0	62.6	63.1	62.4	62.5	62.4	60.8
2012	60.6	61.1	62.3	62.5	62.9	63.4	62.7	63.8	63.2	62.6	63.6	63.6	62.7
2013	62.0	62.8	63.3	62.9	64.1	65.4	64.4	65.3	66.4	66.7	66.9	66.6	64.7
2014	64.1	65.0	66.4	67.0	67.0	66.6	65.9	66.9	67.7	68.7	69.1	69.0	67.0
2015	67.0	67.6	67.4	68.6	69.7	70.0	70.5	70.9	71.2	71.8	71.5	71.6	69.8
2016	68.0	69.0	69.1	70.3	69.3	68.8	68.9	69.0	68.8	69.1	69.0	68.3	69.0
2017	67.2	68.1	68.1	68.4	68.7	69.3	68.8	69.2	69.4	71.3	71.6	72.0	69.3
Education and Health Services													
2007	37.3	37.5	37.6	38.1	38.1	38.0	38.2	38.6	38.7	38.2	38.2	38.1	38.1
2008	38.3	38.8	38.8	38.7	39.0	38.6	38.8	39.0	39.2	39.2	39.4	39.2	38.9
2009	38.6	38.9	39.1	39.4	39.8	39.6	39.4	39.6	39.4	39.6	39.7	39.7	39.4
2010	40.4	40.9	41.1	41.6	42.1	41.8	41.5	41.9	41.8	42.4	42.5	42.3	41.7
2011	41.5	42.3	42.5	42.0	42.1	41.9	41.5	41.6	41.6	41.4	41.6	41.6	41.8
2012	40.8	41.4	41.6	41.4	41.9	40.9	40.4	40.7	42.1	42.0	42.3	42.3	41.5
2013	41.5	42.0	42.2	42.3	42.9	42.6	42.3	42.9	43.5	43.9	44.2	44.5	42.9
2014	43.6	44.1	44.4	44.3	44.5	44.4	44.1	44.8	45.2	45.8	45.9	46.1	44.8
2015	45.1	45.8	46.1	46.3	46.4	46.6	46.0	47.1	47.1	47.6	47.9	48.0	46.7
2016	47.3	47.8	48.3	48.2	48.5	48.1	48.1	49.2	49.4	49.6	49.8	49.7	48.7
2017	48.6	49.5	49.6	49.8	49.9	49.4	49.2	50.0	50.1	50.7	50.6	50.1	49.8
Leisure and Hospitality													
2007	35.8	36.3	36.7	37.4	37.3	37.2	36.7	37.4	37.4	37.8	37.8	37.7	37.1
2008	36.3	36.5	37.1	37.6	37.7	37.1	36.7	37.2	37.2	37.6	37.3	36.9	37.1
2009	35.4	35.9	36.6	37.1	37.6	36.5	36.2	36.8	36.5	36.1	36.0	35.8	36.4
2010	34.5	34.8	35.6	36.4	36.9	36.2	36.6	37.3	37.3	36.6	36.3	36.1	36.2
2011	34.6	35.5	36.5	37.4	37.8	36.7	36.3	37.0	37.0	36.6	36.8	36.4	36.6
2012	35.1	35.6	36.4	36.6	37.4	37.8	37.2	37.8	37.6	37.1	37.4	37.2	36.9
2013	36.4	36.9	37.0	37.9	38.5	39.0	39.0	39.3	39.1	38.8	39.1	39.0	38.3
2014	38.0	37.9	39.3	39.9	40.5	40.5	39.8	40.1	40.3	39.8	40.2	40.1	39.7
2015	39.2	39.7	40.2	40.8	41.4	41.5	41.6	41.5	40.9	41.8	41.7	41.6	41.0
2016	40.2	41.0	41.8	42.5	43.2	43.3	42.8	42.8	42.4	42.3	42.6	42.3	42.3
2017	41.3	42.4	43.1	43.7	44.4	44.5	43.9	44.3	43.5	44.0	43.7	44.0	43.6

Employment by Industry: Greenville-Anderson-Mauldin, SC, Selected Years, 2007–2017—*Continued*

(Numbers in thousands, not seasonally adjusted)

Industry and year	January	February	March	April	May	June	July	August	September	October	November	December	Annual average
Other Services													
2007	13.7	13.8	14.1	13.9	14.0	13.9	13.6	13.5	13.6	13.3	13.3	13.4	13.7
2008	12.7	12.9	13.1	13.2	13.4	13.2	12.9	13.0	13.2	13.0	13.1	13.0	13.1
2009	12.6	12.8	12.8	12.7	12.8	12.6	12.4	12.3	12.6	12.5	12.4	12.4	12.6
2010	11.9	12.0	12.1	12.2	12.3	12.2	11.9	11.9	12.3	12.2	12.2	12.2	12.1
2011	12.0	12.2	12.4	12.8	12.9	12.6	12.6	12.6	13.0	13.0	13.1	13.0	12.7
2012	13.4	13.8	13.6	13.8	13.8	13.8	13.7	13.6	13.6	13.7	13.8	13.8	13.7
2013	13.6	13.6	13.7	13.8	13.9	14.0	13.8	13.9	14.5	14.5	13.8	13.7	13.9
2014	13.4	13.4	13.7	13.7	13.8	13.8	13.6	13.5	13.5	13.5	13.6	13.5	13.6
2015	13.4	13.5	13.7	13.7	13.8	13.9	13.8	13.8	13.8	13.9	13.8	13.8	13.7
2016	13.7	13.9	14.0	14.1	14.1	14.2	14.2	14.2	14.3	14.2	14.2	14.2	14.1
2017	14.1	14.1	14.3	14.2	14.3	14.4	14.4	14.2	14.2	14.2	14.3	14.3	14.3
Government													
2007	55.2	55.6	56.0	55.9	56.1	55.6	53.0	52.8	56.1	56.9	57.9	57.5	55.7
2008	57.1	57.6	58.1	57.7	58.6	57.8	55.0	54.6	57.8	58.7	59.4	58.6	57.6
2009	57.6	57.9	58.1	58.3	58.3	57.4	54.7	55.0	56.9	57.8	58.1	58.0	57.3
2010	56.6	56.8	56.9	57.2	58.6	57.2	53.9	53.6	55.5	56.2	56.3	56.1	56.2
2011	55.3	55.6	55.6	55.9	56.0	55.1	53.6	53.2	55.3	56.0	56.2	56.1	55.3
2012	56.0	56.4	56.5	56.5	57.0	56.1	53.9	54.3	56.6	57.4	57.7	57.6	56.3
2013	57.3	57.5	57.9	58.1	57.9	57.6	55.0	55.4	57.5	58.4	58.3	58.4	57.4
2014	57.8	58.2	58.4	58.4	58.8	58.0	55.6	56.3	58.3	59.2	59.4	59.5	58.2
2015	58.7	59.3	59.6	59.7	59.9	59.3	56.8	57.5	59.5	60.4	60.4	60.7	59.3
2016	59.7	59.9	60.4	60.5	60.6	59.9	57.4	58.1	60.0	60.7	60.9	61.1	59.9
2017	60.1	60.4	60.8	61.1	61.3	60.6	58.3	59.3	61.2	62.0	62.2	62.4	60.8

Employment by Industry: Bakersfield, CA, Selected Years, 2007–2017

(Numbers in thousands, not seasonally adjusted)

Industry and year	January	February	March	April	May	June	July	August	September	October	November	December	Annual average
Total Nonfarm													
2007	239.3	240.4	241.7	243.9	244.4	244.7	238.8	240.6	243.1	243.9	244.7	245.2	242.6
2008	239.8	241.6	242.4	243.9	245.0	245.6	239.9	239.5	241.3	243.6	244.4	243.0	242.5
2009	237.5	236.8	236.4	236.0	235.9	235.9	224.7	227.9	229.3	228.8	229.7	228.9	232.3
2010	225.9	226.1	229.1	233.5	233.6	233.8	224.0	227.2	230.3	232.1	233.1	234.4	230.3
2011	230.7	232.0	233.7	236.3	238.4	238.2	235.6	238.0	238.5	239.5	240.5	241.1	236.9
2012	238.6	240.7	243.4	245.6	248.0	248.9	243.5	245.0	247.0	249.5	250.6	250.4	245.9
2013	245.4	247.2	248.8	250.7	252.3	250.0	246.9	249.5	251.3	253.6	254.5	254.7	250.4
2014	250.6	252.1	254.3	256.3	258.0	255.6	252.0	255.8	258.6	259.1	261.5	261.5	256.3
2015	257.1	256.4	257.9	257.9	259.0	257.2	252.7	256.4	257.3	259.8	260.6	260.5	257.7
2016	255.8	255.8	255.3	257.0	256.2	256.0	250.0	251.3	254.3	257.1	259.2	258.3	255.5
2017	253.0	253.8	256.3	257.1	258.2	258.2	253.0	256.0	258.8	261.8	262.9	262.8	257.7
Total Private													
2007	179.8	180.8	182.0	182.1	182.8	183.0	183.3	184.2	184.5	182.6	182.9	183.3	182.6
2008	178.3	179.4	179.9	181.5	182.7	182.9	181.7	182.2	181.7	180.9	180.8	180.1	181.0
2009	175.2	173.9	173.2	172.9	173.3	172.9	170.5	171.5	169.9	168.7	168.6	167.9	171.5
2010	165.7	165.2	166.6	169.3	169.5	170.3	170.6	171.4	171.5	171.1	171.6	172.7	169.6
2011	170.2	170.9	171.9	174.6	176.6	176.6	178.8	180.3	180.4	179.5	180.1	180.8	176.7
2012	179.5	180.9	183.0	186.0	188.2	189.0	189.0	189.8	189.5	189.7	190.7	190.5	187.2
2013	186.9	187.9	189.0	191.0	193.0	192.6	192.5	194.2	193.5	194.0	194.5	194.5	192.0
2014	191.5	192.3	193.6	195.5	197.1	197.0	196.7	199.1	198.9	198.1	199.5	199.8	196.6
2015	195.9	195.1	195.8	195.5	196.2	195.9	196.4	197.3	196.1	196.4	197.2	196.9	196.2
2016	192.9	192.0	190.8	192.4	191.3	191.4	191.2	192.1	192.4	193.1	194.8	194.3	192.4
2017	189.6	189.9	191.6	192.8	194.0	193.7	194.8	195.9	196.3	197.8	198.3	198.6	194.4
Goods Producing													
2007	40.7	41.0	41.3	40.6	40.8	41.0	41.6	41.9	41.8	41.3	40.8	40.5	41.1
2008	39.6	39.6	39.5	40.1	40.3	40.9	41.0	41.0	41.2	41.0	40.6	40.7	40.5
2009	38.6	37.3	37.0	36.1	35.6	35.5	34.9	34.8	34.7	34.1	34.1	33.8	35.5
2010	33.7	33.1	33.8	34.5	35.2	35.4	35.9	36.1	36.5	36.5	36.4	36.8	35.3
2011	36.4	36.6	36.7	37.7	38.0	38.8	39.2	39.6	39.8	39.6	39.3	39.9	38.5
2012	40.3	40.9	41.5	42.3	42.6	43.2	43.8	44.1	44.2	43.8	43.8	43.1	42.8
2013	42.1	42.1	42.5	42.9	43.3	43.6	43.8	44.4	44.6	44.8	44.5	44.4	43.6
2014	44.1	44.2	44.4	45.0	45.3	45.6	45.9	46.5	46.5	46.1	45.9	45.6	45.4
2015	44.5	43.6	43.1	42.2	41.7	41.6	41.5	41.9	41.2	40.4	40.1	39.6	41.8
2016	38.5	37.8	36.8	36.3	35.9	36.1	36.5	36.7	37.2	36.7	36.8	36.6	36.8
2017	35.6	35.5	35.9	36.4	36.5	36.8	37.4	37.7	38.0	38.0	38.0	37.7	37.0
Service-Providing													
2007	198.6	199.4	200.4	203.3	203.6	203.7	197.2	198.7	201.3	202.6	203.9	204.7	201.5
2008	200.2	202.0	202.9	203.8	204.7	204.7	198.9	198.5	200.1	202.6	203.8	202.3	202.0
2009	198.9	199.5	199.4	199.9	200.3	200.4	189.8	193.1	194.6	194.7	195.6	195.1	196.8
2010	192.2	193.0	195.3	199.0	198.4	198.4	188.1	191.1	193.8	195.6	196.7	197.6	194.9
2011	194.3	195.4	197.0	198.6	200.4	199.4	196.4	198.4	198.7	199.9	201.2	201.2	198.4
2012	198.3	199.8	201.9	203.3	205.4	205.7	199.7	200.9	202.8	205.7	206.8	207.3	203.1
2013	203.3	205.1	206.3	207.8	209.0	206.4	203.1	205.1	206.7	208.8	210.0	210.3	206.8
2014	206.5	207.9	209.9	211.3	212.7	210.0	206.1	209.3	212.1	213.0	215.6	215.9	210.9
2015	212.6	212.8	214.8	215.7	217.3	215.6	211.2	214.5	216.1	219.4	220.5	220.9	216.0
2016	217.3	218.0	218.5	220.7	220.3	219.9	213.5	214.6	217.1	220.4	222.4	221.7	218.7
2017	217.4	218.3	220.4	220.7	221.7	221.4	215.6	218.3	220.8	223.8	224.9	225.1	220.7
Mining, Logging, and Construction													
2007	28.0	28.2	28.4	27.7	27.9	27.9	28.0	28.2	27.7	27.7	27.2	27.0	27.8
2008	26.2	26.2	26.1	26.5	26.6	26.9	27.3	27.2	27.1	27.2	26.8	26.8	26.7
2009	25.0	23.9	23.7	22.9	22.5	22.5	21.8	21.5	21.3	21.0	21.2	21.1	22.4
2010	21.0	20.5	21.1	21.6	22.4	22.6	22.9	23.1	23.0	23.0	23.2	23.6	22.3
2011	23.4	23.7	23.8	24.7	25.1	25.6	26.1	26.3	26.2	26.4	26.3	26.8	25.4
2012	27.5	28.0	28.5	29.2	29.5	29.8	30.1	30.3	30.0	29.9	30.0	29.4	29.4
2013	28.7	28.7	28.9	29.2	29.5	29.6	29.7	30.1	29.9	30.2	30.1	30.0	29.6
2014	29.9	30.0	30.1	30.4	30.8	30.9	31.4	31.6	31.4	31.3	31.4	31.2	30.9
2015	30.3	29.5	29.0	28.1	27.7	27.4	27.4	27.1	26.6	26.5	26.2	25.9	27.6
2016	25.1	24.4	23.4	23.0	22.7	22.7	22.9	22.9	22.9	23.0	23.3	23.2	23.3
2017	22.5	22.4	22.8	23.2	23.2	23.3	23.9	23.8	24.1	24.2	24.2	23.9	23.5

Employment by Industry: Bakersfield, CA, Selected Years, 2007–2017—*Continued*

(Numbers in thousands, not seasonally adjusted)

Industry and year	January	February	March	April	May	June	July	August	September	October	November	December	Annual average
Manufacturing													
2007	12.7	12.8	12.9	12.9	12.9	13.1	13.6	13.7	14.1	13.6	13.6	13.5	13.3
2008	13.4	13.4	13.4	13.6	13.7	14.0	13.7	13.8	14.1	13.8	13.8	13.9	13.7
2009	13.6	13.4	13.3	13.2	13.1	13.0	13.1	13.3	13.4	13.1	12.9	12.7	13.2
2010	12.7	12.6	12.7	12.9	12.8	12.8	13.0	13.0	13.5	13.5	13.2	13.2	13.0
2011	13.0	12.9	12.9	13.0	12.9	13.2	13.1	13.3	13.6	13.2	13.0	13.1	13.1
2012	12.8	12.9	13.0	13.1	13.1	13.4	13.7	13.8	14.2	13.9	13.8	13.7	13.5
2013	13.4	13.4	13.6	13.7	13.8	14.0	14.1	14.3	14.7	14.6	14.4	14.4	14.0
2014	14.2	14.2	14.3	14.6	14.5	14.7	14.5	14.9	15.1	14.8	14.5	14.4	14.6
2015	14.2	14.1	14.1	14.1	14.0	14.2	14.1	14.8	14.6	13.9	13.9	13.7	14.1
2016	13.4	13.4	13.4	13.3	13.2	13.4	13.6	13.8	14.3	13.7	13.5	13.4	13.5
2017	13.1	13.1	13.1	13.2	13.3	13.5	13.5	13.9	13.9	13.8	13.8	13.8	13.5
Trade, Transportation, and Utilities													
2007	46.3	46.0	46.4	46.6	47.1	46.9	46.7	46.8	46.8	46.7	47.5	47.9	46.8
2008	45.7	45.5	45.6	45.6	46.4	45.9	45.2	45.2	45.0	44.6	45.0	44.9	45.4
2009	43.3	43.2	42.6	42.9	43.6	42.9	43.2	43.8	42.6	42.5	42.6	42.7	43.0
2010	41.7	41.5	41.4	41.9	42.0	42.0	42.7	43.2	43.1	42.2	42.8	43.7	42.4
2011	42.5	42.2	42.2	43.1	44.0	43.7	44.5	44.8	44.6	44.2	44.8	45.2	43.8
2012	43.7	43.4	43.6	44.9	45.4	45.8	45.9	45.8	45.7	46.0	47.3	47.9	45.5
2013	46.0	45.9	46.1	47.0	47.4	47.5	47.7	48.1	47.9	47.9	49.2	49.7	47.5
2014	47.8	47.7	48.1	48.8	49.4	49.3	49.4	50.4	50.3	49.8	51.0	51.5	49.5
2015	49.6	49.4	49.7	50.2	50.6	50.5	51.1	51.2	51.0	51.4	52.3	52.3	50.8
2016	50.5	50.2	50.2	50.9	51.3	51.1	51.0	51.2	50.9	51.4	52.8	52.7	51.2
2017	50.6	50.1	50.2	50.7	51.2	51.2	51.5	52.1	51.8	52.2	53.3	53.5	51.5
Wholesale Trade													
2007	7.4	7.4	7.5	7.6	7.6	7.8	7.8	7.7	7.8	7.8	7.8	7.7	7.7
2008	7.6	7.7	7.7	7.7	7.9	7.9	7.9	8.0	8.0	7.9	7.9	7.6	7.8
2009	7.8	8.1	7.7	7.8	8.1	7.8	8.7	9.2	8.0	7.6	7.3	6.9	7.9
2010	7.1	7.1	6.8	7.3	7.3	7.7	8.5	8.7	8.8	7.5	7.4	7.4	7.6
2011	7.4	7.3	7.1	7.5	7.6	7.7	8.6	8.5	8.5	8.1	7.7	7.6	7.8
2012	7.6	7.5	7.5	8.1	8.2	8.4	8.3	8.2	8.2	8.3	8.3	8.4	8.1
2013	8.5	8.6	8.6	8.7	8.7	8.8	8.8	8.9	8.9	8.8	8.8	8.8	8.7
2014	8.8	8.9	9.0	9.1	9.1	9.1	9.0	9.1	9.0	9.0	9.0	9.0	9.0
2015	8.9	8.9	8.8	8.6	8.6	8.6	8.7	8.7	8.6	8.6	8.6	8.6	8.7
2016	8.4	8.6	8.5	8.5	8.6	8.6	8.5	8.5	8.4	8.4	8.4	8.4	8.5
2017	8.1	8.1	8.3	8.3	8.4	8.5	8.8	8.9	8.8	8.8	8.8	8.9	8.6
Retail Trade													
2007	29.4	29.0	29.1	29.2	29.2	29.0	28.8	28.9	28.8	28.6	29.7	30.1	29.2
2008	28.5	28.1	28.2	28.0	28.1	27.9	27.4	27.3	27.0	26.7	27.2	27.5	27.7
2009	26.0	25.7	25.6	25.9	26.0	25.8	25.2	25.3	25.4	25.9	26.5	27.0	25.9
2010	26.0	25.8	26.0	26.0	25.8	25.6	25.4	25.6	25.5	25.8	26.6	27.6	26.0
2011	26.5	26.3	26.5	26.8	27.1	27.0	26.9	27.0	26.8	26.9	28.0	28.4	27.0
2012	27.3	27.0	27.2	27.7	27.8	27.8	27.7	27.7	27.6	27.8	29.2	29.6	27.9
2013	28.1	27.9	28.0	28.6	28.8	28.7	28.9	29.0	28.8	29.0	30.3	30.7	28.9
2014	29.2	29.0	29.2	29.8	30.2	30.0	30.0	30.7	30.7	30.6	31.7	32.0	30.3
2015	30.6	30.5	30.8	31.2	31.5	31.5	31.6	31.7	31.6	31.9	33.0	33.1	31.6
2016	32.0	31.9	32.0	32.6	32.6	32.4	32.4	32.5	32.3	32.7	34.1	34.2	32.6
2017	32.8	32.3	32.2	32.5	32.6	32.5	32.4	32.6	32.3	32.6	33.8	33.9	32.7
Transportation and Utilities													
2007	9.5	9.6	9.8	9.8	10.3	10.1	10.1	10.2	10.2	10.3	10.0	10.1	10.0
2008	9.6	9.7	9.7	9.9	10.4	10.1	9.9	9.9	10.0	10.0	9.9	9.8	9.9
2009	9.5	9.4	9.3	9.2	9.5	9.3	9.3	9.3	9.2	9.0	8.8	8.8	9.2
2010	8.6	8.6	8.6	8.6	8.9	8.7	8.8	8.9	8.8	8.9	8.8	8.7	8.7
2011	8.6	8.6	8.6	8.8	9.3	9.0	9.0	9.3	9.3	9.2	9.1	9.2	9.0
2012	8.8	8.9	8.9	9.1	9.4	9.6	9.9	9.9	9.9	9.9	9.8	9.9	9.5
2013	9.4	9.4	9.5	9.7	9.9	10.0	10.0	10.2	10.2	10.1	10.1	10.2	9.9
2014	9.8	9.8	9.9	9.9	10.1	10.2	10.4	10.6	10.6	10.2	10.3	10.5	10.2
2015	10.1	10.0	10.1	10.4	10.5	10.4	10.8	10.8	10.8	10.9	10.7	10.6	10.5
2016	10.1	9.7	9.7	9.8	10.1	10.1	10.1	10.2	10.2	10.3	10.3	10.1	10.1
2017	9.7	9.7	9.7	9.9	10.2	10.2	10.3	10.6	10.7	10.8	10.7	10.7	10.3

Employment by Industry: Bakersfield, CA, Selected Years, 2007–2017—*Continued*

(Numbers in thousands, not seasonally adjusted)

Industry and year	January	February	March	April	May	June	July	August	September	October	November	December	Annual average
Information													
2007	2.8	2.8	2.7	2.8	2.8	2.9	2.8	2.9	2.8	2.8	2.9	2.9	2.8
2008	2.9	3.0	3.0	3.1	3.1	3.1	3.0	3.0	3.0	3.0	3.0	2.9	3.0
2009	2.8	2.8	2.8	2.8	2.8	2.8	2.8	2.7	2.7	2.7	2.7	2.7	2.8
2010	2.7	2.6	2.6	2.6	2.6	2.6	2.9	2.8	2.7	2.7	2.7	2.8	2.7
2011	2.7	2.6	2.6	2.6	2.6	2.6	2.7	2.6	2.6	2.6	2.6	2.6	2.6
2012	2.7	2.7	2.7	2.7	2.7	2.8	2.6	2.6	2.6	2.6	2.7	2.7	2.7
2013	2.7	2.6	2.6	2.6	2.6	2.6	2.5	2.5	2.5	2.4	2.5	2.4	2.5
2014	2.4	2.4	2.4	2.4	2.4	2.4	2.3	2.4	2.3	2.4	2.4	2.4	2.4
2015	2.4	2.4	2.4	2.4	2.4	2.8	2.8	3.0	3.0	2.9	2.8	2.9	2.7
2016	2.7	2.6	2.3	2.2	2.0	2.1	2.1	2.0	2.0	2.0	2.0	2.0	2.2
2017	2.0	2.0	2.0	2.0	2.0	2.0	2.0	1.9	1.9	1.9	1.9	1.9	2.0
Financial Activities													
2007	9.1	9.2	9.2	9.1	9.1	9.2	9.1	9.1	9.0	9.0	8.9	8.9	9.1
2008	8.8	8.8	8.9	9.0	9.0	8.9	8.9	8.9	8.9	8.8	8.8	8.8	8.9
2009	8.7	8.7	8.5	8.5	8.5	8.5	8.5	8.5	8.4	8.4	8.2	8.3	8.5
2010	8.2	8.3	8.3	8.3	8.4	8.3	8.2	8.1	8.1	8.0	7.9	7.9	8.2
2011	7.8	8.0	8.0	8.2	8.3	8.2	8.5	8.6	8.5	8.5	8.5	8.4	8.3
2012	8.4	8.5	8.5	8.8	9.0	8.9	8.9	8.9	8.8	8.8	8.7	8.7	8.7
2013	8.8	8.8	8.8	8.9	9.0	8.9	8.9	8.9	8.7	8.9	8.8	8.7	8.8
2014	8.7	8.6	8.7	8.7	8.8	8.7	8.7	8.6	8.6	8.8	8.6	8.7	8.7
2015	8.6	8.5	8.6	8.6	8.6	8.4	8.6	8.5	8.5	8.5	8.4	8.4	8.5
2016	8.4	8.4	8.3	8.5	8.5	8.4	8.4	8.3	8.3	8.3	8.3	8.2	8.4
2017	8.3	8.1	8.3	8.2	8.2	8.2	8.2	8.1	8.2	8.2	8.2	8.2	8.2
Professional and Business Services													
2007	26.4	26.7	26.6	26.9	26.9	26.7	26.6	26.9	27.1	25.7	25.7	25.8	26.5
2008	25.1	25.6	25.6	25.8	25.6	25.6	25.5	25.6	25.6	25.5	25.4	25.0	25.5
2009	25.1	24.5	24.5	24.4	24.3	24.5	23.9	24.2	24.2	23.7	24.2	23.8	24.3
2010	23.8	23.6	24.0	24.9	24.5	24.8	24.1	24.2	24.2	24.8	25.1	25.0	24.4
2011	25.0	25.3	25.7	25.7	25.7	25.5	26.1	26.3	26.6	26.3	26.5	26.1	25.9
2012	26.2	26.7	27.3	27.1	27.6	27.5	27.6	27.6	27.4	27.3	27.0	26.9	27.2
2013	26.5	27.1	27.1	27.0	27.3	27.2	27.0	27.2	27.0	26.9	26.4	26.3	26.9
2014	26.1	26.4	26.4	26.3	26.6	26.7	26.4	26.6	26.6	26.8	27.2	27.1	26.6
2015	26.5	26.4	26.5	26.1	26.3	26.3	26.3	26.0	25.7	26.3	26.6	26.7	26.3
2016	26.2	26.2	25.9	26.5	25.8	25.8	25.5	25.6	26.0	26.0	26.1	25.9	26.0
2017	25.4	25.6	25.9	25.5	25.6	25.3	25.7	25.8	25.9	26.2	26.3	26.8	25.8
Education and Health Services													
2007	27.5	27.9	27.9	27.8	27.6	27.7	28.1	28.1	28.3	28.4	28.5	28.7	28.0
2008	28.6	28.8	29.0	29.1	29.1	29.2	29.3	29.6	29.5	29.6	29.7	29.8	29.3
2009	29.4	29.7	29.9	29.9	30.0	30.3	29.7	30.0	29.8	30.0	29.7	29.7	29.8
2010	29.2	29.3	29.4	29.5	29.3	29.4	29.6	29.8	29.6	29.9	29.8	29.9	29.6
2011	29.5	29.6	29.7	29.9	30.1	29.9	30.1	30.4	30.6	30.5	30.5	30.8	30.1
2012	30.6	30.8	31.1	31.4	31.6	31.4	31.2	31.6	31.8	32.0	31.9	32.0	31.5
2013	31.6	32.0	32.1	32.4	32.6	32.1	32.1	32.4	32.3	32.5	32.6	32.5	32.3
2014	32.2	32.4	32.5	32.6	32.7	32.5	32.3	32.7	32.7	32.7	32.8	32.8	32.6
2015	32.5	32.7	32.9	33.3	33.5	33.5	33.2	33.7	33.7	34.0	34.1	34.1	33.4
2016	34.0	34.2	34.2	34.6	34.6	34.7	34.6	35.1	35.0	35.3	35.5	35.6	34.8
2017	35.3	35.9	36.1	36.3	36.4	36.3	36.4	36.7	36.7	37.4	37.2	37.2	36.5
Leisure and Hospitality													
2007	20.5	20.7	21.2	21.7	21.9	22.1	21.7	21.7	21.8	21.7	21.6	21.6	21.5
2008	20.9	21.2	21.4	21.8	22.0	22.1	22.0	21.9	21.5	21.2	21.2	21.0	21.5
2009	20.6	20.9	21.2	21.5	21.7	21.7	21.0	20.8	20.8	20.5	20.4	20.3	21.0
2010	19.8	20.1	20.3	20.8	20.8	21.1	20.8	20.6	20.7	20.4	20.4	20.1	20.5
2011	19.8	20.1	20.4	20.7	21.1	21.2	21.0	21.0	20.7	20.9	20.9	20.8	20.7
2012	20.6	20.8	21.2	21.6	22.0	22.2	22.0	21.9	21.7	21.8	21.9	21.9	21.6
2013	21.9	22.0	22.3	22.6	23.1	23.4	23.2	23.1	23.0	23.1	22.9	23.0	22.8
2014	22.6	22.9	23.4	23.8	24.0	24.1	24.1	24.0	24.0	23.6	23.8	24.0	23.7
2015	24.0	24.3	24.8	25.0	25.4	25.4	25.3	25.3	25.3	25.2	25.2	25.3	25.0
2016	25.2	25.2	25.5	25.8	25.7	25.8	25.6	25.3	25.2	25.4	25.4	25.4	25.5
2017	24.9	25.2	25.6	26.1	26.5	26.3	26.1	25.7	25.8	25.8	25.4	25.3	25.7

Employment by Industry: Bakersfield, CA, Selected Years, 2007–2017—*Continued*

(Numbers in thousands, not seasonally adjusted)

Industry and year	January	February	March	April	May	June	July	August	September	October	November	December	Annual average
Other Services													
2007	6.5	6.5	6.7	6.6	6.6	6.5	6.7	6.8	6.9	7.0	7.0	7.0	6.7
2008	6.7	6.9	6.9	7.0	7.2	7.2	6.8	7.0	7.0	7.2	7.1	7.0	7.0
2009	6.7	6.8	6.7	6.8	6.8	6.7	6.5	6.7	6.7	6.8	6.7	6.6	6.7
2010	6.6	6.7	6.8	6.8	6.7	6.7	6.4	6.6	6.6	6.6	6.5	6.5	6.6
2011	6.5	6.5	6.6	6.7	6.8	6.7	6.7	7.0	7.0	6.9	7.0	7.0	6.8
2012	7.0	7.1	7.1	7.2	7.3	7.2	7.0	7.3	7.3	7.4	7.4	7.3	7.2
2013	7.3	7.4	7.5	7.6	7.7	7.3	7.3	7.6	7.5	7.5	7.6	7.5	7.5
2014	7.6	7.7	7.7	7.9	7.9	7.7	7.6	7.9	7.9	7.9	7.8	7.7	7.8
2015	7.8	7.8	7.8	7.7	7.7	7.4	7.6	7.7	7.7	7.7	7.7	7.6	7.7
2016	7.4	7.4	7.6	7.6	7.5	7.4	7.5	7.9	7.8	8.0	7.9	7.9	7.7
2017	7.5	7.5	7.6	7.6	7.6	7.6	7.5	7.9	8.0	8.1	8.0	8.0	7.7
Government													
2007	59.5	59.6	59.7	61.8	61.6	61.7	55.5	56.4	58.6	61.3	61.8	61.9	60.0
2008	61.5	62.2	62.5	62.4	62.3	62.7	58.2	57.3	59.6	62.7	63.6	62.9	61.5
2009	62.3	62.9	63.2	63.1	62.6	63.0	54.2	56.4	59.4	60.1	61.1	61.0	60.8
2010	60.2	60.9	62.5	64.2	64.1	63.5	53.4	55.8	58.8	61.0	61.5	61.7	60.6
2011	60.5	61.1	61.8	61.7	61.8	61.6	56.8	57.7	58.1	60.0	60.4	60.3	60.2
2012	59.1	59.8	60.4	59.6	59.8	59.9	54.5	55.2	57.5	59.8	59.9	59.9	58.8
2013	58.5	59.3	59.8	59.7	59.3	57.4	54.4	55.3	57.8	59.6	60.0	60.2	58.4
2014	59.1	59.8	60.7	60.8	60.9	58.6	55.3	56.7	59.7	61.0	62.0	61.7	59.7
2015	61.2	61.3	62.1	62.4	62.8	61.3	56.3	59.1	61.2	63.4	63.4	63.6	61.5
2016	62.9	63.8	64.5	64.6	64.9	64.6	58.8	59.2	61.9	64.0	64.4	64.0	63.1
2017	63.4	63.9	64.7	64.3	64.2	64.5	58.2	60.1	62.5	64.0	64.6	64.2	63.2

Employment by Industry: Albany-Schenectady-Troy, NY, Selected Years, 2007–2017

(Numbers in thousands, not seasonally adjusted)

Industry and year	January	February	March	April	May	June	July	August	September	October	November	December	Annual average
Total Nonfarm													
2007	435.0	437.4	439.9	441.3	447.3	450.1	442.2	443.2	445.2	450.7	452.8	453.0	444.8
2008	438.2	441.5	442.4	447.7	453.1	454.6	447.8	447.7	447.6	452.5	452.7	450.3	448.0
2009	433.9	437.6	437.6	440.3	443.0	443.1	435.4	434.4	435.4	440.3	441.5	439.4	438.5
2010	424.4	428.3	429.6	435.9	439.5	439.0	431.2	429.7	431.7	436.0	438.3	436.4	433.3
2011	421.1	427.0	427.7	435.2	437.0	437.5	433.0	432.1	435.3	440.3	442.5	440.6	434.1
2012	428.0	433.7	434.9	441.2	445.0	445.6	437.8	438.0	440.8	447.1	450.0	447.1	440.8
2013	432.9	439.6	440.9	445.9	450.0	450.8	443.8	442.8	445.6	452.2	454.6	452.3	446.0
2014	435.6	442.7	444.2	449.2	453.0	454.2	447.5	447.2	449.2	458.6	459.2	457.1	449.8
2015	445.2	449.9	450.4	455.9	460.2	461.0	454.9	454.2	455.4	465.1	465.3	463.7	456.8
2016	450.8	457.0	458.7	465.5	465.3	467.0	462.9	462.8	464.4	473.2	472.4	471.0	464.3
2017	456.1	462.3	463.2	469.3	470.2	472.3	465.3	465.8	469.5	475.4	478.1	476.9	468.7
Total Private													
2007	328.1	328.5	331.3	332.5	337.9	340.9	339.7	340.5	339.1	341.3	343.0	342.1	337.1
2008	331.1	332.3	333.4	337.2	341.8	343.8	342.6	343.6	340.4	342.1	342.2	339.3	339.2
2009	326.6	327.5	328.0	329.2	332.0	332.9	331.1	331.6	329.6	331.2	331.8	329.5	330.1
2010	317.2	319.4	321.1	326.8	328.6	328.8	329.9	330.6	329.5	331.8	333.5	331.8	327.4
2011	320.4	323.7	324.6	330.9	332.4	333.4	334.3	334.9	335.8	337.4	339.2	337.2	332.0
2012	327.3	330.7	332.6	338.0	341.2	342.9	341.4	342.2	341.8	345.1	347.0	344.6	339.6
2013	332.2	336.1	337.8	342.9	346.4	347.7	346.6	346.8	347.2	350.6	351.8	350.0	344.7
2014	336.4	340.4	342.0	346.7	350.5	352.3	351.2	352.0	350.7	356.7	357.0	354.7	349.2
2015	345.0	347.8	348.3	353.6	357.2	359.0	358.7	359.1	356.9	362.9	363.0	361.3	356.1
2016	350.2	354.4	356.2	362.2	362.8	365.1	365.9	366.8	364.2	370.5	369.5	367.7	363.0
2017	354.5	358.8	359.7	365.2	367.0	369.5	367.9	369.2	369.7	372.6	375.0	373.4	366.9
Goods Producing													
2007	38.8	37.8	38.6	39.9	41.9	42.8	43.4	43.4	42.9	43.0	42.2	40.9	41.3
2008	38.7	37.8	38.1	39.5	41.3	42.3	42.7	42.9	42.4	42.3	41.3	39.6	40.7
2009	36.7	35.8	35.7	36.8	37.8	38.8	39.3	39.5	38.9	38.7	38.3	36.9	37.8
2010	34.7	34.0	34.4	36.1	37.0	37.9	38.0	38.2	38.5	38.1	37.7	36.8	36.8
2011	35.2	34.8	35.1	37.1	38.2	39.4	40.4	40.8	40.4	40.2	39.9	38.5	38.3
2012	37.0	36.4	37.0	39.0	40.1	41.3	41.8	42.0	41.6	41.3	40.9	40.3	39.9
2013	38.7	38.5	38.9	40.2	42.0	42.8	43.4	43.5	42.9	42.8	42.4	41.3	41.5
2014	39.5	39.0	39.3	40.9	43.2	44.4	44.8	45.3	44.7	44.7	44.4	43.6	42.8
2015	42.6	42.2	42.4	43.9	45.6	46.8	47.4	47.5	46.5	46.3	45.8	44.8	45.2
2016	43.1	42.6	43.0	44.6	46.0	46.9	47.6	47.7	47.1	47.2	46.0	45.0	45.6
2017	43.5	43.2	43.9	45.4	46.5	47.8	47.6	48.0	47.5	46.8	46.7	45.6	46.0
Service-Providing													
2007	396.2	399.6	401.3	401.4	405.4	407.3	398.8	399.8	402.3	407.7	410.6	412.1	403.5
2008	399.5	403.7	404.3	408.2	411.8	412.3	405.1	404.8	405.2	410.2	411.4	410.7	407.3
2009	397.2	401.8	401.9	403.5	405.2	404.3	396.1	394.9	396.5	401.6	403.2	402.5	400.7
2010	389.7	394.3	395.2	399.8	402.5	401.1	393.2	391.5	393.2	397.9	400.6	399.6	396.6
2011	385.9	392.2	392.6	398.1	398.8	398.1	392.6	391.3	394.9	400.1	402.6	402.1	395.8
2012	391.0	397.3	397.9	402.2	404.9	404.3	396.0	396.0	399.2	405.8	409.1	406.8	400.9
2013	394.2	401.1	402.0	405.7	408.0	408.0	400.4	399.3	402.7	409.4	412.2	411.0	404.5
2014	396.1	403.7	404.9	408.3	409.8	409.8	402.7	401.9	404.5	413.9	414.8	413.5	407.0
2015	402.6	407.7	408.0	412.0	414.6	414.2	407.5	406.7	408.9	418.8	419.5	418.9	411.6
2016	407.7	414.4	415.7	420.9	419.3	420.1	415.3	415.1	417.3	426.0	426.4	426.0	418.7
2017	412.6	419.1	419.3	423.9	423.7	424.5	417.7	417.8	422.0	428.6	431.4	431.3	422.7
Mining, Logging, and Construction													
2007	16.0	15.1	15.7	16.8	18.8	19.4	20.0	20.1	19.8	19.9	19.2	17.9	18.2
2008	16.1	15.5	15.7	17.2	18.7	19.4	20.0	20.2	19.9	19.9	19.0	17.5	18.3
2009	15.3	14.7	14.9	16.1	17.2	18.0	18.7	18.9	18.3	18.1	17.7	16.4	17.0
2010	14.5	14.0	14.3	15.9	16.7	17.4	18.1	18.4	18.1	17.6	17.0	16.2	16.5
2011	14.7	14.2	14.4	15.9	16.9	17.8	18.6	19.0	18.6	18.2	17.8	16.5	16.9
2012	15.2	14.5	14.8	16.7	17.6	18.5	18.8	18.9	18.5	18.2	17.7	17.1	17.2
2013	15.2	14.9	15.2	16.4	18.0	18.4	19.2	19.4	19.0	18.9	18.4	17.4	17.5
2014	15.9	15.6	15.8	17.2	19.3	20.0	20.3	20.7	20.3	20.3	19.9	19.0	18.7
2015	18.1	17.6	17.7	19.0	20.5	21.2	21.4	21.5	20.7	20.4	19.7	18.9	19.7
2016	17.2	16.7	17.1	18.5	19.8	20.4	20.9	21.0	20.6	20.5	19.8	18.8	19.3
2017	17.6	17.2	17.3	18.7	19.9	20.7	21.1	21.0	20.7	20.0	20.0	18.9	19.4

Employment by Industry: Albany-Schenectady-Troy, NY, Selected Years, 2007–2017—*Continued*

(Numbers in thousands, not seasonally adjusted)

Industry and year	January	February	March	April	May	June	July	August	September	October	November	December	Annual average
Manufacturing													
2007	22.8	22.7	22.9	23.1	23.1	23.4	23.4	23.3	23.1	23.1	23.0	23.0	23.1
2008	22.6	22.3	22.4	22.3	22.6	22.9	22.7	22.7	22.5	22.4	22.3	22.1	22.5
2009	21.4	21.1	20.8	20.7	20.6	20.8	20.6	20.6	20.6	20.6	20.6	20.5	20.7
2010	20.2	20.0	20.1	20.2	20.3	20.5	19.9	19.8	20.4	20.5	20.7	20.6	20.3
2011	20.5	20.6	20.7	21.2	21.3	21.6	21.8	21.8	21.8	22.0	22.1	22.0	21.5
2012	21.8	21.9	22.2	22.3	22.5	22.8	23.0	23.1	23.1	23.1	23.2	23.2	22.7
2013	23.5	23.6	23.7	23.8	24.0	24.4	24.2	24.1	23.9	23.9	24.0	23.9	23.9
2014	23.6	23.4	23.5	23.7	23.9	24.4	24.5	24.6	24.4	24.4	24.5	24.6	24.1
2015	24.5	24.6	24.7	24.9	25.1	25.6	26.0	26.0	25.8	25.9	26.1	25.9	25.4
2016	25.9	25.9	25.9	26.1	26.2	26.5	26.7	26.7	26.5	26.7	26.2	26.2	26.3
2017	25.9	26.0	26.6	26.7	26.6	27.1	26.5	27.0	26.8	26.8	26.7	26.7	26.6
Trade, Transportation, and Utilities													
2007	77.9	76.1	76.8	75.9	77.2	77.8	77.1	76.8	76.7	77.6	79.4	80.3	77.5
2008	76.4	74.9	75.0	75.2	76.1	76.8	76.1	76.2	75.8	76.5	77.4	78.5	76.2
2009	74.1	72.9	72.5	72.4	73.3	74.1	73.0	73.1	72.6	73.1	74.6	75.6	73.4
2010	71.7	70.2	70.7	71.3	71.8	72.6	72.0	72.5	71.8	72.4	73.9	75.0	72.2
2011	71.3	70.2	70.4	71.3	71.8	72.5	72.0	72.6	72.2	72.7	74.5	75.9	72.3
2012	72.6	71.4	71.5	72.2	73.3	74.0	73.5	73.6	73.1	73.9	75.7	76.3	73.4
2013	72.4	71.4	71.6	72.3	73.2	74.4	74.0	74.0	73.7	74.9	76.5	77.2	73.8
2014	73.2	72.4	72.7	73.1	73.9	74.6	74.1	74.4	74.2	76.0	76.7	77.2	74.4
2015	73.9	72.7	72.9	73.5	74.2	75.0	74.7	74.9	74.5	76.1	77.2	77.8	74.8
2016	74.8	73.7	73.8	74.2	74.8	75.6	75.5	75.7	75.5	77.1	77.5	77.7	75.5
2017	74.4	73.2	72.9	73.9	74.3	75.1	74.9	75.2	75.1	75.6	77.7	78.0	75.0
Wholesale Trade													
2007	14.7	14.6	14.8	14.7	14.7	14.8	14.6	14.5	14.2	14.2	14.1	14.1	14.5
2008	13.7	13.7	13.7	13.7	13.8	13.9	14.0	14.0	13.9	13.9	13.9	14.0	13.9
2009	13.6	13.6	13.5	13.5	13.4	13.4	13.4	13.4	13.2	13.1	13.1	13.2	13.4
2010	12.7	12.7	12.7	12.9	13.0	13.0	13.0	13.1	13.1	13.2	13.3	13.2	13.0
2011	13.1	13.1	13.1	13.3	13.3	13.3	13.3	13.4	13.2	13.1	13.2	13.2	13.2
2012	13.1	13.1	13.2	13.4	13.6	13.7	13.8	13.7	13.6	13.6	13.6	13.6	13.5
2013	13.5	13.4	13.5	13.5	13.6	13.7	13.8	13.8	13.6	13.6	13.6	13.5	13.6
2014	13.5	13.5	13.5	13.7	13.8	13.9	13.9	14.0	13.9	13.9	13.9	13.9	13.8
2015	13.9	13.9	13.9	14.0	13.9	14.0	14.1	14.0	13.8	13.8	13.9	13.8	13.9
2016	13.7	13.6	13.7	13.6	13.7	13.8	13.9	13.8	13.7	13.7	13.6	13.6	13.7
2017	13.5	13.5	13.4	13.5	13.5	13.7	13.8	13.8	13.6	13.6	13.6	13.6	13.6
Retail Trade													
2007	50.0	48.4	48.7	48.1	49.1	49.6	49.3	49.2	49.0	49.8	51.6	52.4	49.6
2008	49.6	48.2	48.2	48.3	48.8	49.3	48.8	48.9	48.3	48.8	49.7	50.6	49.0
2009	47.3	46.2	45.9	45.8	46.6	47.4	46.7	46.8	46.2	46.8	48.2	49.0	46.9
2010	46.2	44.8	45.1	45.5	45.9	46.7	46.2	46.6	45.9	46.5	47.8	48.9	46.3
2011	46.1	45.0	45.3	45.9	46.2	46.9	46.5	46.9	46.5	47.1	48.7	49.8	46.7
2012	47.3	46.2	46.2	46.7	47.5	48.0	47.5	47.7	47.1	47.9	49.7	50.0	47.7
2013	47.0	45.9	46.1	46.6	47.2	48.1	47.8	47.8	47.5	48.5	49.8	50.3	47.7
2014	47.2	46.3	46.4	46.8	47.4	48.0	47.6	47.8	47.5	49.2	49.6	49.8	47.8
2015	47.1	46.0	46.1	46.5	47.2	47.9	47.6	47.9	47.6	48.9	49.6	50.0	47.7
2016	47.7	46.8	46.7	47.4	47.7	48.2	48.1	48.3	48.1	49.5	49.7	49.7	48.2
2017	47.3	46.2	46.0	46.8	47.1	47.7	47.6	47.8	47.7	48.1	50.1	50.2	47.7
Transportation and Utilities													
2007	13.2	13.1	13.3	13.1	13.4	13.4	13.2	13.1	13.5	13.6	13.7	13.8	13.4
2008	13.1	13.0	13.1	13.2	13.5	13.6	13.3	13.3	13.6	13.8	13.8	13.9	13.4
2009	13.2	13.1	13.1	13.1	13.3	13.3	12.9	12.9	13.2	13.2	13.3	13.4	13.2
2010	12.8	12.7	12.9	12.9	12.9	12.9	12.8	12.8	12.8	12.7	12.8	12.9	12.8
2011	12.1	12.1	12.0	12.1	12.3	12.3	12.2	12.3	12.5	12.5	12.6	12.9	12.3
2012	12.2	12.1	12.1	12.1	12.2	12.3	12.2	12.2	12.4	12.4	12.4	12.7	12.3
2013	11.9	12.1	12.0	12.2	12.4	12.6	12.4	12.4	12.6	12.8	13.1	13.4	12.5
2014	12.5	12.6	12.8	12.6	12.7	12.7	12.6	12.6	12.8	12.9	13.2	13.5	12.8
2015	12.9	12.8	12.9	13.0	13.1	13.1	13.0	13.0	13.1	13.4	13.7	14.0	13.2
2016	13.4	13.3	13.4	13.2	13.4	13.6	13.5	13.6	13.7	13.9	14.2	14.4	13.6
2017	13.6	13.5	13.5	13.6	13.7	13.7	13.5	13.6	13.8	13.9	14.0	14.2	13.7

Employment by Industry: Albany-Schenectady-Troy, NY, Selected Years, 2007–2017—*Continued*

(Numbers in thousands, not seasonally adjusted)

Industry and year	January	February	March	April	May	June	July	August	September	October	November	December	Annual average
Information													
2007	10.1	10.0	10.0	9.9	10.0	10.0	10.0	10.0	9.8	9.7	9.7	9.8	9.9
2008	9.4	9.4	9.4	9.5	9.8	9.9	9.9	9.9	9.7	9.8	9.8	9.8	9.7
2009	9.8	9.7	9.6	9.6	9.6	9.7	9.6	9.6	9.4	9.2	9.3	9.3	9.5
2010	9.0	9.0	9.0	8.8	8.9	8.9	9.0	9.0	8.8	8.8	8.8	8.8	8.9
2011	8.8	8.7	8.7	8.8	8.8	8.9	9.0	8.2	8.8	8.8	8.8	8.8	8.8
2012	8.7	8.7	8.7	8.7	8.7	8.7	8.7	8.6	8.5	8.6	8.6	8.5	8.6
2013	8.5	8.5	8.5	8.6	8.5	8.5	8.5	8.6	8.5	8.5	8.6	8.7	8.5
2014	8.6	8.7	8.7	8.7	8.7	8.8	8.5	8.5	8.4	8.4	8.4	8.4	8.6
2015	8.3	8.2	8.2	8.5	8.5	8.4	8.9	8.8	8.7	8.8	8.7	8.8	8.6
2016	8.7	8.7	8.7	8.8	8.2	8.8	8.9	8.8	8.8	8.7	8.6	8.7	8.7
2017	8.5	8.6	8.6	8.5	8.5	8.6	8.5	8.4	8.4	8.4	8.4	8.4	8.5
Financial Activities													
2007	26.3	26.0	26.0	26.1	26.2	26.7	26.5	26.4	26.0	26.0	26.1	26.1	26.2
2008	25.9	25.8	25.9	25.9	26.0	26.4	26.4	26.3	25.8	25.6	25.5	25.4	25.9
2009	25.3	25.2	25.2	24.9	25.0	25.3	25.1	25.1	24.6	24.5	24.4	24.4	24.9
2010	24.3	24.2	24.3	24.3	24.3	24.7	24.8	24.7	24.3	24.5	24.4	24.6	24.5
2011	24.3	24.3	24.3	24.4	24.4	24.8	25.0	25.1	24.7	24.6	24.6	24.7	24.6
2012	24.7	24.7	24.8	24.9	24.9	25.5	25.6	25.5	25.2	25.3	25.4	25.5	25.2
2013	25.0	25.0	25.1	25.2	25.3	25.7	25.7	25.6	25.2	25.3	25.2	25.3	25.3
2014	25.2	25.1	25.1	25.0	25.2	25.7	25.9	25.7	25.4	25.5	25.4	25.5	25.4
2015	25.5	25.5	25.5	25.7	25.7	26.1	26.3	26.3	25.9	25.9	25.9	26.1	25.9
2016	25.9	25.9	26.0	26.1	26.1	26.6	26.7	26.7	26.2	26.2	26.2	26.3	26.2
2017	25.9	25.8	25.8	25.8	25.9	26.4	26.4	26.4	26.1	26.1	26.0	26.0	26.1
Professional and Business Services													
2007	51.3	51.8	52.1	52.4	52.5	54.0	54.2	54.2	53.6	53.5	53.9	54.0	53.1
2008	54.0	54.1	54.4	55.1	54.9	56.0	55.8	56.0	55.0	54.8	54.5	54.1	54.9
2009	52.9	52.3	52.6	52.3	51.7	51.8	51.6	51.2	50.9	51.2	50.8	50.5	51.7
2010	49.1	49.2	49.5	50.5	50.6	51.0	51.9	51.5	50.7	51.1	51.2	50.9	50.6
2011	50.0	50.2	50.3	51.4	51.2	51.8	52.1	51.8	51.7	51.8	52.4	51.6	51.4
2012	51.4	51.4	51.8	52.7	52.8	53.3	53.2	53.2	52.3	52.6	53.2	52.0	52.5
2013	51.8	51.8	51.9	52.9	53.0	53.6	53.5	53.2	52.8	52.3	52.3	51.8	52.6
2014	51.1	51.2	51.4	52.4	53.0	53.5	53.9	53.8	53.1	53.3	53.7	53.1	52.8
2015	53.3	53.2	53.0	53.9	54.2	55.0	54.7	54.7	53.7	54.4	54.4	54.1	54.1
2016	53.8	54.1	54.6	55.8	55.5	56.6	57.5	57.5	56.4	57.0	57.0	56.5	56.0
2017	55.3	55.4	55.3	56.1	56.3	57.1	57.2	57.5	56.2	56.9	57.0	56.8	56.4
Education and Health Services													
2007	75.3	78.0	78.1	78.2	77.7	75.9	74.9	74.5	77.7	79.4	80.3	80.1	77.5
2008	77.6	80.6	80.2	80.5	80.3	78.2	76.6	76.0	78.8	80.5	81.8	81.0	79.3
2009	78.8	82.1	82.3	82.4	81.4	79.2	77.9	77.5	80.5	82.5	83.2	82.0	80.8
2010	80.1	83.7	83.8	84.5	83.2	80.5	79.5	79.0	82.5	84.4	85.4	84.1	82.6
2011	81.4	85.4	85.4	85.9	84.7	81.9	80.5	79.9	83.6	86.1	86.5	85.4	83.9
2012	82.9	87.0	87.3	87.5	86.6	83.8	81.9	81.2	85.5	88.3	88.8	88.2	85.8
2013	85.0	89.1	89.1	89.9	88.4	84.8	83.6	83.0	87.6	90.6	91.3	90.6	87.8
2014	86.5	91.1	91.4	91.7	89.7	87.1	85.8	85.3	88.6	92.3	92.5	91.4	89.5
2015	87.8	92.0	92.1	92.2	90.6	88.5	86.8	86.2	89.7	93.3	93.6	92.5	90.4
2016	89.1	93.9	94.3	94.7	93.0	90.0	88.5	88.3	91.1	95.0	95.2	94.8	92.3
2017	90.6	95.3	95.7	96.7	94.8	92.6	90.6	90.8	95.8	98.1	98.8	97.7	94.8
Leisure and Hospitality													
2007	30.2	30.4	31.2	31.8	33.9	35.2	35.6	37.2	34.4	33.8	33.0	32.4	33.3
2008	30.7	31.2	31.9	33.1	34.9	35.7	36.5	37.7	34.6	33.9	33.1	32.2	33.8
2009	30.4	30.7	31.2	32.2	34.4	35.3	36.0	37.3	34.6	33.7	33.0	32.6	33.5
2010	30.7	31.4	31.7	33.5	34.9	35.5	36.8	37.7	35.3	34.8	34.4	33.7	34.2
2011	31.8	32.4	32.7	34.1	35.3	36.4	37.3	38.5	36.4	35.5	34.8	34.5	35.0
2012	32.5	33.5	33.6	35.1	36.9	38.3	38.7	40.2	37.8	37.2	36.5	36.0	36.4
2013	33.3	34.1	34.8	36.0	38.1	39.8	39.8	40.9	38.8	38.1	37.3	36.8	37.3
2014	34.3	34.8	35.2	36.6	38.6	40.2	39.9	40.7	38.2	38.2	37.4	37.0	37.6
2015	35.3	35.6	35.8	37.4	39.8	40.6	41.2	42.2	40.0	39.6	38.8	38.5	38.7
2016	36.2	36.9	37.2	39.1	40.4	41.8	42.3	43.4	40.6	40.5	40.2	39.8	39.9
2017	37.5	38.6	38.7	39.9	41.7	42.8	43.5	43.9	41.8	41.6	41.3	41.7	41.1

Employment by Industry: Albany-Schenectady-Troy, NY, Selected Years, 2007–2017—*Continued*

(Numbers in thousands, not seasonally adjusted)

Industry and year	January	February	March	April	May	June	July	August	September	October	November	December	Annual average
Other Services													
2007	18.2	18.4	18.5	18.3	18.5	18.5	18.0	18.0	18.0	18.3	18.4	18.5	18.3
2008	18.4	18.5	18.5	18.4	18.5	18.5	18.6	18.6	18.3	18.7	18.8	18.7	18.5
2009	18.6	18.8	18.9	18.6	18.8	18.7	18.6	18.3	18.1	18.3	18.2	18.2	18.5
2010	17.6	17.7	17.7	17.8	17.9	17.7	17.9	18.0	17.6	17.7	17.7	17.9	17.8
2011	17.6	17.7	17.7	17.9	18.0	17.7	18.0	18.0	18.0	17.7	17.7	17.8	17.8
2012	17.5	17.6	17.9	17.9	17.9	18.0	18.0	17.9	17.8	17.9	17.9	17.8	17.8
2013	17.5	17.7	17.9	17.8	17.9	18.1	18.1	18.0	17.7	18.1	18.2	18.3	17.9
2014	18.0	18.1	18.2	18.3	18.2	18.0	18.3	18.3	18.1	18.3	18.5	18.5	18.2
2015	18.3	18.4	18.4	18.5	18.6	18.6	18.7	18.5	17.9	18.5	18.6	18.7	18.5
2016	18.6	18.6	18.6	18.9	18.8	18.8	18.9	18.7	18.5	18.8	18.8	18.9	18.7
2017	18.8	18.7	18.8	18.9	19.0	19.1	19.2	19.0	18.8	19.1	19.1	19.2	19.0
Government													
2007	106.9	108.9	108.6	108.8	109.4	109.2	102.5	102.7	106.1	109.4	109.8	110.9	107.8
2008	107.1	109.2	109.0	110.5	111.3	110.8	105.2	104.1	107.2	110.4	110.5	111.0	108.9
2009	107.3	110.1	109.6	111.1	111.0	110.2	104.3	102.8	105.8	109.1	109.7	109.9	108.4
2010	107.2	108.9	108.5	109.1	110.9	110.2	101.3	99.1	102.2	104.2	104.8	104.6	105.9
2011	100.7	103.3	103.1	104.3	104.6	104.1	98.7	97.2	99.5	102.9	103.3	103.4	102.1
2012	100.7	103.0	102.3	103.2	103.8	102.7	96.4	95.8	99.0	102.0	103.0	102.5	101.2
2013	100.7	103.5	103.1	103.0	103.6	103.1	97.2	96.0	98.4	101.6	102.8	102.3	101.3
2014	99.2	102.3	102.2	102.5	102.5	101.9	96.3	95.2	98.5	101.9	102.2	102.4	100.6
2015	100.2	102.1	102.1	102.3	103.0	102.0	96.2	95.1	98.5	102.2	102.3	102.4	100.7
2016	100.6	102.6	102.5	103.3	102.5	101.9	97.0	96.0	100.2	102.7	102.9	103.3	101.3
2017	101.6	103.5	103.5	104.1	103.2	102.8	97.4	96.6	99.8	102.8	103.1	103.5	101.8

Employment by Industry: Knoxville, TN, Selected Years, 2007–2017

(Numbers in thousands, not seasonally adjusted)

Industry and year	January	February	March	April	May	June	July	August	September	October	November	December	Annual average
Total Nonfarm													
2007	364.9	365.2	368.6	370.2	371.5	371.3	369.9	374.6	374.9	373.6	376.0	376.1	371.4
2008	369.2	370.8	372.2	373.6	376.0	374.6	370.6	375.0	375.5	374.6	373.7	372.4	373.2
2009	359.6	357.7	356.5	356.6	357.4	354.9	352.4	355.2	356.9	357.6	358.7	357.9	356.8
2010	349.6	350.3	352.6	357.9	361.3	357.9	357.8	360.5	362.2	361.7	363.5	363.2	358.2
2011	355.5	358.5	361.1	364.2	365.0	363.6	361.6	366.6	368.4	367.8	369.6	368.2	364.2
2012	361.2	362.7	365.9	367.6	368.8	366.7	364.7	368.6	369.7	370.4	372.3	371.9	367.5
2013	362.5	364.6	366.7	368.9	370.0	366.1	365.1	370.2	371.5	374.6	376.1	375.9	369.4
2014	367.8	369.3	372.0	374.6	376.7	372.1	372.3	377.6	380.9	382.6	386.3	385.1	376.4
2015	376.9	376.9	378.8	383.3	385.1	381.0	381.1	386.0	389.9	392.0	393.9	393.3	384.9
2016	383.6	386.1	389.6	393.3	393.4	390.2	388.7	392.6	397.1	397.4	399.7	397.5	392.4
2017	389.3	392.3	392.7	396.3	397.1	392.3	391.5	395.6	399.2	399.6	403.0	400.1	395.8
Total Private													
2007	306.6	306.5	309.9	311.0	312.6	313.8	313.0	315.6	315.3	313.4	315.8	315.9	312.5
2008	310.1	311.1	312.6	313.8	316.3	316.9	313.3	315.1	314.4	313.2	312.4	311.0	313.4
2009	300.5	298.1	296.8	296.2	296.7	296.6	295.1	296.2	296.4	296.3	297.3	296.7	296.9
2010	289.7	289.9	292.1	296.3	298.2	299.0	299.9	301.0	301.3	300.2	301.9	301.9	297.6
2011	296.3	299.0	301.6	304.4	305.2	306.6	306.5	308.0	308.6	308.0	309.2	308.2	305.1
2012	301.7	303.1	305.9	307.5	308.6	309.2	308.3	310.6	310.6	310.1	311.7	311.4	308.2
2013	303.5	305.2	307.3	308.1	309.4	309.5	309.3	312.2	312.1	312.5	314.9	314.4	309.9
2014	308.2	308.6	311.3	313.5	315.5	315.1	315.9	319.1	320.7	321.1	323.7	324.1	316.4
2015	316.7	316.7	318.8	322.7	324.9	324.6	325.0	327.6	328.7	330.2	331.2	331.9	324.9
2016	324.5	325.4	328.4	331.8	332.5	333.5	332.7	334.3	335.9	335.5	336.7	336.3	332.3
2017	330.4	331.5	332.3	335.4	336.6	335.9	335.4	337.3	338.4	338.0	340.3	340.2	336.0
Goods Producing													
2007	61.8	61.3	62.0	62.1	62.3	62.6	62.2	62.7	62.9	62.3	62.2	61.7	62.2
2008	60.1	60.2	60.5	60.4	60.9	61.3	60.1	60.3	59.7	59.1	57.7	56.2	59.7
2009	54.0	53.1	52.5	52.5	50.7	50.4	50.0	49.9	50.2	50.4	50.1	49.5	51.0
2010	48.1	48.3	48.9	50.0	50.3	50.8	51.3	51.3	51.5	51.5	51.4	51.4	50.4
2011	50.2	50.9	51.5	51.7	51.8	52.5	52.8	53.1	53.6	54.1	53.7	52.8	52.4
2012	51.2	51.5	51.6	51.7	52.0	52.5	52.6	52.9	53.0	52.9	52.7	52.3	52.2
2013	51.1	51.7	51.8	51.6	51.7	51.8	51.8	52.1	52.0	53.0	53.0	51.8	52.0
2014	50.7	51.1	51.5	51.6	51.5	51.6	52.0	52.5	52.9	53.2	53.7	53.3	52.1
2015	51.8	51.7	51.8	52.3	52.5	52.5	53.0	53.3	54.2	54.9	54.7	54.4	53.1
2016	54.1	54.1	55.2	55.8	55.6	56.0	56.0	56.2	56.8	56.8	56.7	56.3	55.8
2017	55.6	56.0	56.2	56.4	56.8	56.7	56.8	57.0	57.2	57.4	58.3	58.5	56.9
Service-Providing													
2007	303.1	303.9	306.6	308.1	309.2	308.7	307.7	311.9	312.0	311.3	313.8	314.4	309.2
2008	309.1	310.6	311.7	313.2	315.1	313.3	310.5	314.7	315.8	315.5	316.0	316.2	313.5
2009	305.6	304.6	304.0	305.8	306.7	304.5	302.4	305.3	306.7	307.2	308.6	308.4	305.8
2010	301.5	302.0	303.7	307.9	311.0	307.1	306.5	309.2	310.7	310.2	312.1	311.8	307.8
2011	305.3	307.6	309.6	312.5	313.2	311.1	308.8	313.5	314.8	313.7	315.9	315.4	311.8
2012	310.0	311.2	314.3	315.9	316.8	314.2	312.1	315.7	316.7	317.5	319.6	319.6	315.3
2013	311.4	312.9	314.9	317.3	318.3	314.3	313.3	318.1	319.5	321.6	323.1	324.1	317.4
2014	317.1	318.2	320.5	323.0	325.2	320.5	320.3	325.1	328.0	329.4	332.6	331.8	324.3
2015	325.1	325.2	327.0	331.0	332.6	328.5	328.1	332.7	335.7	337.1	339.2	338.9	331.8
2016	329.5	332.0	334.4	337.5	337.8	334.2	332.7	336.4	340.3	340.6	343.0	341.2	336.6
2017	333.7	336.3	336.5	339.9	340.3	335.6	334.7	338.6	342.0	342.2	344.7	341.6	338.8
Mining, Logging, and Construction													
2007	19.3	19.3	19.9	20.2	20.4	20.6	20.5	20.9	21.0	20.8	20.6	20.2	20.3
2008	19.0	19.2	19.7	19.9	20.4	20.6	20.2	20.4	20.3	20.3	19.9	18.9	19.9
2009	17.4	17.2	17.3	17.0	17.3	17.5	17.5	17.4	17.5	17.6	17.4	16.8	17.3
2010	15.6	15.7	16.3	16.9	16.9	17.2	17.7	17.7	17.8	17.8	17.7	17.6	17.1
2011	16.1	16.5	17.0	17.2	17.1	17.5	17.8	18.1	18.7	19.0	18.4	17.4	17.6
2012	15.9	16.1	16.4	16.3	16.6	17.0	17.0	17.4	17.5	17.4	17.2	16.9	16.8
2013	16.0	16.5	16.6	16.6	16.8	16.8	16.8	17.1	17.2	17.9	17.8	16.9	16.9
2014	15.9	16.2	16.5	16.7	16.7	16.7	17.0	17.3	17.6	17.9	18.2	17.8	17.0
2015	16.6	16.5	16.7	17.1	17.4	17.2	17.3	17.6	18.3	19.1	18.7	18.2	17.6
2016	16.9	16.7	17.5	17.8	17.4	17.7	17.8	17.9	18.5	18.3	18.0	17.8	17.7
2017	17.1	17.4	17.7	18.0	18.3	18.3	18.2	18.4	18.6	18.6	19.1	19.3	18.3

Employment by Industry: Knoxville, TN, Selected Years, 2007–2017—*Continued*

(Numbers in thousands, not seasonally adjusted)

Industry and year	January	February	March	April	May	June	July	August	September	October	November	December	Annual average
Manufacturing													
2007	42.5	42.0	42.1	41.9	41.9	42.0	41.7	41.8	41.9	41.5	41.6	41.5	41.9
2008	41.1	41.0	40.8	40.5	40.5	40.7	39.9	39.9	39.4	38.8	37.8	37.3	39.8
2009	36.6	35.9	35.2	33.8	33.4	32.9	32.5	32.5	32.7	32.8	32.7	32.7	33.6
2010	32.5	32.6	32.6	33.1	33.4	33.6	33.6	33.6	33.7	33.7	33.7	33.8	33.3
2011	34.1	34.4	34.5	34.5	34.7	35.0	35.0	35.0	34.9	35.1	35.3	35.4	34.8
2012	35.3	35.4	35.2	35.4	35.4	35.5	35.6	35.5	35.5	35.5	35.5	35.4	35.4
2013	35.1	35.2	35.2	35.0	34.9	35.0	35.0	35.0	34.8	35.1	35.2	34.9	35.0
2014	34.8	34.9	35.0	34.9	34.8	34.9	35.0	35.2	35.3	35.3	35.5	35.5	35.1
2015	35.2	35.2	35.1	35.2	35.1	35.3	35.7	35.7	35.9	35.8	36.0	36.2	35.5
2016	37.2	37.4	37.7	38.0	38.2	38.3	38.2	38.3	38.3	38.5	38.7	38.5	38.1
2017	38.5	38.6	38.5	38.4	38.5	38.4	38.6	38.6	38.6	38.8	39.2	39.2	38.7
Trade, Transportation, and Utilities													
2007	77.6	77.1	77.9	78.3	78.7	78.5	78.1	78.7	78.7	78.8	80.6	80.9	78.7
2008	78.8	78.2	78.4	78.2	78.0	77.9	77.4	77.8	77.4	78.1	78.5	78.4	78.1
2009	74.7	73.2	72.4	72.1	71.9	72.0	71.6	71.8	71.6	71.9	72.8	73.6	72.5
2010	71.3	70.6	70.9	71.1	71.4	71.4	71.9	72.1	72.0	72.3	73.7	74.0	71.9
2011	71.5	71.3	71.8	72.4	72.7	72.9	72.9	72.9	72.9	73.3	74.9	75.5	72.9
2012	73.0	72.9	73.5	73.8	74.1	74.1	74.4	74.5	74.4	75.0	76.7	77.1	74.5
2013	74.1	74.1	74.4	74.4	74.5	74.5	74.7	74.9	74.6	75.1	76.8	77.4	75.0
2014	74.6	74.5	75.1	75.1	75.3	75.7	76.2	76.5	76.5	76.9	78.5	79.3	76.2
2015	76.4	75.6	76.2	77.0	77.4	77.5	77.7	78.4	78.4	79.0	80.4	81.4	78.0
2016	78.4	78.3	78.6	78.9	79.1	78.9	79.1	79.1	79.3	79.5	80.9	81.6	79.3
2017	78.2	77.6	77.4	77.7	77.7	77.7	77.6	78.0	78.0	77.8	79.1	79.5	78.0
Wholesale Trade													
2007	17.2	17.1	17.1	17.1	17.3	17.3	17.3	17.5	17.4	17.5	17.5	17.5	17.3
2008	17.3	17.4	17.4	17.6	17.9	17.9	17.8	17.9	18.0	18.1	17.9	17.9	17.8
2009	17.6	17.3	17.1	17.0	16.9	16.8	16.8	16.7	16.6	16.8	16.7	16.8	16.9
2010	16.7	16.6	16.7	16.5	16.5	16.5	16.4	16.2	16.2	16.1	16.0	15.9	16.4
2011	15.9	15.9	16.0	16.3	16.4	16.5	16.5	16.5	16.5	16.5	16.6	16.7	16.4
2012	16.6	16.7	16.7	16.7	16.8	16.8	16.7	16.8	16.9	16.8	16.8	16.7	16.8
2013	16.6	16.7	16.7	16.5	16.5	16.5	16.4	16.5	16.4	16.4	16.4	16.4	16.5
2014	16.3	16.4	16.4	16.3	16.4	16.3	16.2	16.4	16.5	16.4	16.5	16.6	16.4
2015	16.4	16.4	16.5	16.5	16.6	16.6	16.6	16.7	16.8	16.9	16.9	17.0	16.7
2016	16.8	16.8	16.8	16.8	16.8	16.8	16.8	16.8	16.9	16.8	16.8	16.8	16.8
2017	16.5	16.5	16.5	16.5	16.5	16.6	16.5	16.5	16.6	16.6	16.7	16.9	16.6
Retail Trade													
2007	48.7	48.2	48.9	49.4	49.5	49.3	49.1	49.3	49.4	49.5	51.1	51.4	49.5
2008	49.7	49.0	49.3	48.8	48.3	48.2	47.9	48.0	47.5	48.1	48.6	48.5	48.5
2009	46.0	45.0	44.6	44.6	44.5	44.6	44.3	44.3	44.2	44.3	45.3	45.6	44.8
2010	43.9	43.4	43.5	43.7	43.9	43.9	44.0	44.3	44.1	44.5	45.8	45.9	44.2
2011	44.0	43.6	43.9	44.1	44.2	44.4	44.4	44.3	44.2	44.7	46.1	46.4	44.5
2012	44.5	44.2	44.8	45.1	45.1	45.3	45.7	45.5	45.2	45.7	47.2	47.3	45.5
2013	45.0	44.8	45.0	45.0	45.0	45.0	45.4	45.2	44.9	45.4	47.0	47.3	45.4
2014	45.1	44.8	45.1	45.2	45.2	45.7	46.2	46.0	45.8	46.1	47.5	47.9	45.9
2015	45.6	45.0	45.4	46.1	46.2	46.4	46.6	46.9	46.7	47.2	48.4	49.0	46.6
2016	47.0	46.9	47.2	47.4	47.6	47.7	47.9	47.8	47.9	48.4	49.7	50.1	48.0
2017	48.1	47.7	47.6	48.0	47.9	48.0	47.9	47.8	47.7	47.5	48.5	48.4	47.9
Transportation and Utilities													
2007	11.7	11.8	11.9	11.8	11.9	11.9	11.7	11.9	11.9	11.8	12.0	12.0	11.9
2008	11.8	11.8	11.7	11.8	11.8	11.8	11.7	11.9	11.9	11.9	12.0	12.0	11.8
2009	11.1	10.9	10.7	10.5	10.5	10.6	10.5	10.8	10.8	10.8	10.8	11.2	10.8
2010	10.7	10.6	10.7	10.9	11.0	11.0	11.5	11.6	11.7	11.7	11.9	12.2	11.3
2011	11.6	11.8	11.9	12.0	12.1	12.0	12.0	12.1	12.2	12.1	12.2	12.4	12.0
2012	11.9	12.0	12.0	12.0	12.2	12.0	12.0	12.2	12.3	12.5	12.7	13.1	12.2
2013	12.5	12.6	12.7	12.9	13.0	13.0	12.9	13.2	13.3	13.3	13.4	13.7	13.0
2014	13.2	13.3	13.6	13.6	13.7	13.7	13.8	14.1	14.2	14.4	14.5	14.8	13.9
2015	14.4	14.2	14.3	14.4	14.6	14.5	14.5	14.8	14.9	14.9	15.1	15.4	14.7
2016	14.6	14.6	14.6	14.7	14.7	14.4	14.4	14.5	14.5	14.3	14.4	14.7	14.5
2017	13.6	13.4	13.3	13.2	13.3	13.1	13.2	13.7	13.7	13.7	13.9	14.2	13.5

Employment by Industry: Knoxville, TN, Selected Years, 2007–2017—*Continued*

(Numbers in thousands, not seasonally adjusted)

Industry and year	January	February	March	April	May	June	July	August	September	October	November	December	Annual average
Information													
2007	5.8	5.8	5.8	5.8	5.9	5.9	5.9	5.9	5.8	5.7	5.8	5.8	5.8
2008	5.8	5.8	5.8	5.8	5.9	5.9	5.8	5.7	5.7	5.8	5.8	5.8	5.8
2009	5.8	5.7	5.7	5.7	5.7	5.7	5.7	5.6	5.6	5.6	5.6	5.6	5.7
2010	5.6	5.6	5.6	5.6	5.6	5.7	5.7	5.6	5.6	5.8	5.7	5.8	5.7
2011	5.9	5.9	5.8	5.8	5.8	5.8	5.8	5.8	5.7	5.6	5.7	5.6	5.8
2012	5.6	5.7	5.6	5.7	5.7	5.7	5.8	5.7	5.6	5.7	5.7	5.7	5.7
2013	5.8	5.8	5.7	5.8	5.8	5.9	5.8	5.8	5.7	5.7	5.8	5.8	5.8
2014	5.8	5.8	5.8	5.8	5.8	5.8	5.8	5.9	5.8	5.7	5.8	5.7	5.8
2015	5.8	5.8	5.8	5.8	5.7	5.7	5.7	5.7	5.6	5.6	5.7	5.7	5.7
2016	5.6	5.7	5.7	5.7	5.7	5.7	5.8	5.7	5.7	5.7	5.7	5.7	5.7
2017	5.8	5.7	5.8	5.8	5.8	5.8	5.8	5.8	5.8	5.7	5.7	5.7	5.8
Financial Activities													
2007	18.2	18.2	18.3	18.3	18.4	18.6	18.6	18.6	18.6	18.6	18.7	18.7	18.5
2008	18.4	18.5	18.6	18.6	18.7	18.9	18.9	19.0	18.9	18.9	18.9	19.0	18.8
2009	18.4	18.5	18.3	18.3	18.3	18.1	18.0	18.0	17.9	17.8	17.8	17.8	18.1
2010	17.8	17.8	17.8	18.0	18.0	18.0	17.9	17.8	17.7	17.6	17.7	17.7	17.8
2011	17.5	17.5	17.5	17.6	17.6	17.8	17.7	17.8	17.7	17.8	17.8	17.9	17.7
2012	17.8	17.9	18.0	18.0	18.1	18.1	18.0	18.0	17.9	17.9	17.9	18.0	18.0
2013	17.7	17.6	17.9	17.9	18.0	18.1	18.1	18.1	18.1	18.0	18.0	18.1	18.0
2014	17.9	18.0	18.0	18.1	18.1	18.2	18.3	18.3	18.3	18.4	18.5	18.6	18.2
2015	18.5	18.6	18.6	18.6	18.6	18.8	18.8	18.8	18.7	18.8	18.9	19.0	18.7
2016	18.7	18.7	18.8	18.9	19.0	19.1	19.1	19.2	19.2	19.3	19.3	19.3	19.1
2017	19.2	19.2	19.2	19.4	19.4	19.5	19.5	19.6	19.5	19.6	19.5	19.5	19.4
Professional and Business Services													
2007	46.8	47.3	47.6	48.0	47.7	47.5	47.5	48.4	48.3	48.2	48.4	48.7	47.9
2008	48.3	48.7	48.6	49.4	49.4	49.3	49.3	50.2	50.8	50.9	51.1	51.3	49.8
2009	49.9	49.5	48.9	48.8	48.7	48.4	48.6	49.5	50.0	50.4	50.9	50.7	49.5
2010	50.0	50.1	50.3	52.1	52.4	51.9	52.7	53.9	53.9	54.2	54.5	54.7	52.6
2011	54.5	55.6	56.1	56.2	56.0	55.4	55.6	56.3	56.4	56.4	56.5	56.2	55.9
2012	54.9	55.1	55.7	55.7	55.8	55.4	54.7	56.1	56.1	55.4	55.6	55.4	55.5
2013	54.5	55.0	55.3	55.4	55.7	55.5	55.4	57.0	57.2	57.1	57.6	57.8	56.1
2014	57.5	57.6	58.2	59.1	59.4	58.6	58.2	59.9	60.6	60.6	60.9	61.1	59.3
2015	59.9	59.9	60.3	61.4	62.4	61.5	61.2	62.6	63.0	63.3	62.9	63.2	61.8
2016	61.1	61.4	62.2	63.1	63.4	63.4	62.8	64.0	64.2	64.3	64.3	64.4	63.2
2017	63.5	64.1	64.5	65.4	65.5	64.7	64.1	64.9	65.4	65.3	65.6	65.8	64.9
Education and Health Services													
2007	44.9	44.9	45.2	45.3	45.5	45.8	46.0	46.3	46.6	46.7	46.8	47.0	45.9
2008	46.9	47.1	47.1	47.6	47.9	47.9	47.4	47.6	47.5	47.9	48.1	48.3	47.6
2009	47.4	47.4	47.4	48.0	48.4	48.4	48.5	48.7	48.7	48.4	48.2	48.5	48.2
2010	47.9	48.1	48.4	48.6	48.7	48.8	48.6	48.8	49.2	49.0	49.2	49.2	48.7
2011	48.7	49.1	49.4	50.1	50.1	50.3	50.3	50.5	50.8	50.2	50.0	49.9	50.0
2012	49.5	49.7	49.9	49.9	50.1	50.1	50.1	50.5	50.7	50.8	50.6	50.8	50.2
2013	49.6	50.0	50.2	50.2	50.2	49.6	49.5	49.8	50.1	50.1	50.4	50.6	50.0
2014	49.7	49.8	50.0	50.0	50.6	50.4	50.4	50.9	51.4	51.7	51.7	51.9	50.7
2015	51.4	51.6	52.0	51.8	52.1	52.0	51.8	52.1	52.2	52.4	52.5	52.6	52.0
2016	52.2	52.4	52.7	52.9	53.0	52.9	52.7	53.1	53.3	53.6	53.8	53.8	53.0
2017	53.8	54.1	54.1	54.1	54.2	53.9	54.0	54.2	54.3	54.1	53.7	53.5	54.0
Leisure and Hospitality													
2007	36.4	36.7	37.8	38.1	38.8	39.3	39.2	39.6	39.0	37.7	37.9	37.7	38.2
2008	36.5	37.0	37.9	38.2	39.3	39.7	38.7	38.8	38.7	37.0	36.9	36.6	37.9
2009	35.0	35.4	36.1	36.6	37.6	37.9	37.1	37.2	37.0	36.1	36.0	35.7	36.5
2010	34.0	34.3	35.0	36.0	37.0	37.5	37.2	37.1	37.3	35.9	35.9	35.4	36.1
2011	34.6	35.2	35.9	36.9	37.5	37.8	37.4	37.6	37.8	36.9	36.7	36.4	36.7
2012	35.8	36.4	37.6	38.4	38.5	38.8	38.3	38.6	38.6	38.3	38.5	38.2	38.0
2013	36.9	37.1	37.9	38.5	39.1	39.5	39.5	39.9	39.9	39.1	38.9	38.5	38.7
2014	37.8	37.5	38.2	39.5	40.4	40.4	40.6	40.7	40.8	40.4	40.2	39.8	39.7
2015	38.6	39.1	39.7	41.2	41.5	41.8	41.9	41.9	41.8	41.4	41.3	40.7	40.9
2016	39.7	40.0	40.4	41.5	41.9	42.6	42.3	42.2	42.6	41.5	41.2	40.4	41.4
2017	39.6	40.0	40.3	41.7	42.2	42.5	42.6	42.8	43.2	43.2	43.4	42.7	42.0

Employment by Industry: Knoxville, TN, Selected Years, 2007–2017—*Continued*

(Numbers in thousands, not seasonally adjusted)

Industry and year	January	February	March	April	May	June	July	August	September	October	November	December	Annual average
Other Services													
2007	15.1	15.2	15.3	15.1	15.3	15.6	15.5	15.4	15.4	15.4	15.4	15.4	15.3
2008	15.3	15.6	15.7	15.6	16.2	16.0	15.7	15.7	15.7	15.5	15.4	15.4	15.7
2009	15.3	15.3	15.5	15.9	15.4	15.7	15.6	15.5	15.4	15.7	15.9	15.3	15.5
2010	15.0	15.1	15.2	14.9	14.8	14.9	14.6	14.4	14.1	13.9	13.8	13.7	14.5
2011	13.4	13.5	13.6	13.7	13.7	14.1	14.0	14.0	13.7	13.7	13.9	13.9	13.8
2012	13.9	13.9	14.0	14.3	14.3	14.5	14.4	14.3	14.3	14.1	14.0	13.9	14.2
2013	13.8	13.9	14.1	14.3	14.4	14.6	14.5	14.6	14.5	14.4	14.4	14.4	14.3
2014	14.2	14.3	14.5	14.3	14.4	14.4	14.4	14.4	14.4	14.2	14.4	14.4	14.4
2015	14.3	14.4	14.4	14.6	14.7	14.8	14.9	14.8	14.8	14.8	14.8	14.9	14.7
2016	14.7	14.8	14.8	15.0	14.8	14.9	14.9	14.8	14.8	14.8	14.8	14.8	14.8
2017	14.7	14.8	14.8	14.9	15.0	15.1	15.0	15.0	15.0	14.9	15.0	15.0	14.9
Government													
2007	58.3	58.7	58.7	59.2	58.9	57.5	56.9	59.0	59.6	60.2	60.2	60.2	59.0
2008	59.1	59.7	59.6	59.8	59.7	57.7	57.3	59.9	61.1	61.4	61.3	61.4	59.8
2009	59.1	59.6	59.7	60.4	60.7	58.3	57.3	59.0	60.5	61.3	61.4	61.2	59.9
2010	59.9	60.4	60.5	61.6	63.1	58.9	57.9	59.5	60.9	61.5	61.6	61.3	60.6
2011	59.2	59.5	59.5	59.8	59.8	57.0	55.1	58.6	59.8	59.8	60.4	60.0	59.0
2012	59.5	59.6	60.0	60.1	60.2	57.5	56.4	58.0	59.1	60.3	60.6	60.5	59.3
2013	59.0	59.4	59.4	60.8	60.6	56.6	55.8	58.0	59.4	62.1	61.2	61.5	59.5
2014	59.6	60.7	60.7	61.1	61.2	57.0	56.4	58.5	60.2	61.5	62.6	61.0	60.0
2015	60.2	60.2	60.0	60.6	60.2	56.4	56.1	58.4	61.2	61.8	62.7	61.4	59.9
2016	59.1	60.7	61.2	61.5	60.9	56.7	56.0	58.3	61.2	61.9	63.0	61.2	60.1
2017	58.9	60.8	60.4	60.9	60.5	56.4	56.1	58.3	60.8	61.6	62.7	59.9	59.8

Employment by Industry: McAllen-Edinburg-Mission, TX, Selected Years, 2007–2017

(Numbers in thousands, not seasonally adjusted)

Industry and year	January	February	March	April	May	June	July	August	September	October	November	December	Annual average
Total Nonfarm													
2007	209.4	210.0	211.3	213.0	212.9	212.1	207.5	211.5	212.9	217.0	219.3	220.7	213.1
2008	220.2	221.4	221.6	222.4	222.1	219.8	214.0	216.7	217.2	222.7	223.4	224.3	220.5
2009	220.1	219.4	219.3	220.4	220.6	218.0	212.9	215.0	216.3	220.4	222.0	222.3	218.9
2010	219.8	220.5	221.6	221.2	223.2	221.3	212.0	215.5	218.8	222.8	225.0	226.9	220.7
2011	224.2	225.2	226.5	227.4	228.1	226.9	220.6	224.0	225.6	226.4	230.0	231.2	226.3
2012	228.4	229.5	231.5	231.3	231.4	230.4	223.2	226.6	228.3	231.8	235.2	237.1	230.4
2013	232.3	234.5	236.1	236.4	237.3	236.7	229.5	233.8	235.1	238.1	241.8	243.8	236.3
2014	238.6	239.8	241.0	242.2	244.1	243.1	236.1	239.7	240.8	244.8	247.3	249.9	242.3
2015	245.8	247.4	248.3	248.1	250.4	249.0	242.9	245.4	246.4	248.9	251.9	253.1	248.1
2016	249.5	251.1	252.0	253.7	254.0	252.2	246.1	249.8	252.7	255.2	258.1	259.6	252.8
2017	255.9	256.2	257.7	259.0	260.0	258.9	251.1	253.7	256.1	259.8	261.9	262.8	257.8
Total Private													
2007	158.6	158.5	159.5	162.0	161.7	161.2	162.2	163.4	162.7	164.7	166.3	167.3	162.3
2008	167.3	167.7	167.7	168.8	167.8	166.7	166.5	167.2	165.1	168.3	168.0	168.6	167.5
2009	165.2	163.8	163.7	165.2	165.0	163.6	164.0	163.7	162.9	165.1	165.9	166.0	164.5
2010	164.1	164.0	164.8	164.3	166.1	165.0	163.4	165.0	166.0	167.4	168.9	171.0	165.8
2011	168.1	168.5	170.0	171.5	171.8	171.6	171.1	172.7	172.6	172.3	174.9	176.0	171.8
2012	173.6	174.1	175.7	176.1	176.0	175.6	174.0	175.8	175.3	176.7	179.4	181.1	176.1
2013	177.0	178.5	179.7	180.6	180.8	180.9	179.4	181.9	181.2	182.1	185.1	187.0	181.2
2014	181.9	182.7	183.6	185.5	186.1	186.1	185.1	187.1	186.5	188.1	190.0	192.2	186.2
2015	188.9	189.8	190.5	191.0	191.9	191.3	191.0	191.6	190.7	191.2	193.7	194.4	191.3
2016	191.5	192.3	193.0	194.3	194.0	192.9	192.5	194.4	194.7	195.6	198.2	199.1	194.4
2017	196.3	196.2	197.7	198.3	198.7	198.9	197.0	198.3	198.5	200.3	201.9	202.3	198.7
Goods Producing													
2007	19.1	19.0	19.1	19.4	19.4	19.3	19.0	19.6	19.6	19.5	19.5	19.5	19.3
2008	19.4	19.2	19.1	18.8	18.5	18.3	17.7	17.9	17.5	18.0	17.6	17.7	18.3
2009	17.0	16.7	16.4	15.8	15.7	15.5	15.3	15.3	15.1	15.3	15.1	15.1	15.7
2010	15.1	14.8	15.1	14.8	15.0	14.5	14.2	14.4	14.5	14.5	14.6	14.7	14.7
2011	14.7	14.7	14.8	14.5	14.6	14.7	14.7	14.9	15.0	15.1	15.4	15.3	14.9
2012	15.2	15.2	15.5	15.3	15.3	15.3	15.1	15.4	15.3	15.6	15.7	15.9	15.4
2013	15.6	15.8	15.9	16.0	16.0	16.1	15.9	16.2	16.0	16.2	16.3	16.4	16.0
2014	16.0	16.4	16.2	16.6	16.4	16.5	16.3	16.6	16.5	16.8	16.7	16.9	16.5
2015	16.5	16.7	16.4	16.4	16.2	16.2	15.9	15.5	15.3	15.1	15.1	15.1	15.9
2016	14.8	14.7	14.6	14.3	14.0	14.0	13.9	14.1	14.2	14.6	14.7	14.8	14.4
2017	14.9	14.9	14.9	14.8	15.0	15.2	15.3	15.4	15.3	15.5	15.6	15.7	15.2
Service-Providing													
2007	190.3	191.0	192.2	193.6	193.5	192.8	188.5	191.9	193.3	197.5	199.8	201.2	193.8
2008	200.8	202.2	202.5	203.6	203.6	201.5	196.3	198.8	199.7	204.7	205.8	206.6	202.2
2009	203.1	202.7	202.9	204.6	204.9	202.5	197.6	199.7	201.2	205.1	206.9	207.2	203.2
2010	204.7	205.7	206.5	206.4	208.2	206.8	197.8	201.1	204.3	208.3	210.4	212.2	206.0
2011	209.5	210.5	211.7	212.9	213.5	212.2	205.9	209.1	210.6	211.3	214.6	215.9	211.5
2012	213.2	214.3	216.0	216.0	216.1	215.1	208.1	211.2	213.0	216.2	219.5	221.2	215.0
2013	216.7	218.7	220.2	220.4	221.3	220.6	213.6	217.6	219.1	221.9	225.5	227.4	220.3
2014	222.6	223.4	224.8	225.6	227.7	226.6	219.8	223.1	224.3	228.0	230.6	233.0	225.8
2015	229.3	230.7	231.9	231.7	234.2	232.8	227.0	229.9	231.1	233.8	236.8	238.0	232.3
2016	234.7	236.4	237.4	239.4	240.0	238.2	232.2	235.7	238.5	240.6	243.4	244.8	238.4
2017	241.0	241.3	242.8	244.2	245.0	243.7	235.8	238.3	240.8	244.3	246.3	247.1	242.6
Mining, Logging, and Construction													
2007	11.0	11.0	11.1	11.2	11.2	11.4	11.5	11.8	11.7	11.4	11.4	11.4	11.3
2008	11.4	11.3	11.2	11.2	11.0	10.9	10.8	10.9	10.7	10.8	10.6	10.6	11.0
2009	10.3	10.1	9.8	9.7	9.5	9.3	9.3	9.1	8.9	8.9	8.8	8.8	9.4
2010	8.7	8.6	8.7	8.6	8.8	8.7	8.6	8.6	8.7	8.5	8.5	8.5	8.6
2011	8.5	8.6	8.7	8.6	8.7	8.8	8.9	9.1	9.1	9.0	9.1	9.0	8.8
2012	8.9	9.0	9.2	9.1	9.2	9.2	9.2	9.3	9.2	9.3	9.3	9.4	9.2
2013	9.0	9.1	9.3	9.5	9.6	9.8	9.7	9.9	9.8	9.8	9.8	9.9	9.6
2014	9.8	9.9	9.9	10.0	10.0	10.1	10.1	10.3	10.2	10.4	10.3	10.4	10.1
2015	10.0	9.8	9.7	9.6	9.6	9.7	9.3	9.1	9.0	8.8	8.5	8.4	9.3
2016	8.2	8.1	8.1	8.0	7.8	7.8	7.9	7.9	7.9	8.0	8.0	8.1	8.0
2017	8.1	8.1	8.2	8.2	8.4	8.6	8.7	8.8	8.6	8.6	8.6	8.6	8.5

Employment by Industry: McAllen-Edinburg-Mission, TX, Selected Years, 2007–2017—*Continued*

(Numbers in thousands, not seasonally adjusted)

Industry and year	January	February	March	April	May	June	July	August	September	October	November	December	Annual average
Manufacturing													
2007	8.1	8.0	8.0	8.2	8.2	7.9	7.5	7.8	7.9	8.1	8.1	8.1	8.0
2008	8.0	7.9	7.9	7.6	7.5	7.4	6.9	7.0	6.8	7.2	7.0	7.1	7.4
2009	6.7	6.6	6.6	6.1	6.2	6.2	6.0	6.2	6.2	6.4	6.3	6.3	6.3
2010	6.4	6.2	6.4	6.2	6.2	5.8	5.6	5.8	5.8	6.0	6.1	6.2	6.1
2011	6.2	6.1	6.1	5.9	5.9	5.9	5.8	5.8	5.9	6.1	6.3	6.3	6.0
2012	6.3	6.2	6.3	6.2	6.1	6.1	5.9	6.1	6.1	6.3	6.4	6.5	6.2
2013	6.6	6.7	6.6	6.5	6.4	6.3	6.2	6.3	6.2	6.4	6.5	6.5	6.4
2014	6.2	6.5	6.3	6.6	6.4	6.4	6.2	6.3	6.3	6.4	6.4	6.5	6.4
2015	6.5	6.9	6.7	6.8	6.6	6.5	6.6	6.4	6.3	6.3	6.6	6.7	6.6
2016	6.6	6.6	6.5	6.3	6.2	6.2	6.0	6.2	6.3	6.6	6.7	6.7	6.4
2017	6.8	6.8	6.7	6.6	6.6	6.6	6.6	6.6	6.7	6.9	7.0	7.1	6.8
Trade, Transportation, and Utilities													
2007	45.2	44.8	45.6	46.1	45.8	45.4	46.1	46.4	46.1	46.6	47.9	48.5	46.2
2008	47.6	46.8	47.1	47.3	47.0	46.8	46.9	47.2	46.5	47.2	47.6	48.2	47.2
2009	46.0	45.1	45.2	46.0	45.8	45.6	45.6	46.0	45.8	46.0	46.7	47.3	45.9
2010	45.2	44.8	45.1	45.5	45.9	45.8	45.4	46.0	45.8	46.5	47.6	48.8	46.0
2011	46.8	46.3	46.7	47.4	47.5	47.4	47.3	47.9	47.4	47.7	49.4	50.2	47.7
2012	48.6	48.2	48.8	49.0	49.0	49.3	49.4	50.1	49.5	49.8	52.0	52.6	49.7
2013	50.7	50.3	50.5	50.8	50.9	51.1	50.7	51.1	50.8	51.0	53.1	54.2	51.3
2014	51.5	51.0	51.3	52.2	52.1	52.6	52.8	52.9	52.4	52.9	54.9	55.8	52.7
2015	53.7	53.4	53.8	54.1	54.4	54.3	54.3	54.9	54.3	54.5	56.0	56.4	54.5
2016	54.5	54.0	54.2	54.8	54.7	54.5	54.7	55.0	54.4	54.7	56.6	56.8	54.9
2017	54.6	53.9	54.0	53.8	53.8	53.8	53.7	53.7	53.3	53.9	55.1	55.0	54.1
Wholesale Trade													
2007	6.5	6.6	6.9	7.2	7.1	6.9	7.0	6.9	7.0	7.3	7.3	7.3	7.0
2008	7.4	7.1	7.2	7.5	7.4	7.2	7.0	6.7	6.6	7.1	6.9	7.0	7.1
2009	6.8	6.7	6.6	7.0	6.8	6.6	6.5	6.4	6.4	6.6	6.4	6.4	6.6
2010	6.3	6.4	6.3	6.5	6.6	6.6	6.4	6.4	6.5	6.6	6.6	6.8	6.5
2011	6.6	6.6	6.8	6.9	6.9	6.8	6.7	6.7	6.8	6.7	6.8	6.9	6.8
2012	6.9	6.9	7.1	7.3	7.2	7.2	7.0	7.1	7.2	7.3	7.3	7.5	7.2
2013	7.5	7.5	7.7	7.9	7.9	7.7	7.5	7.4	7.5	7.5	7.6	7.7	7.6
2014	7.6	7.6	7.8	8.2	8.1	8.0	7.8	7.8	7.8	7.9	7.9	8.0	7.9
2015	8.1	8.1	8.2	8.4	8.4	8.3	8.2	8.3	8.3	8.3	8.3	8.3	8.3
2016	8.2	8.2	8.2	8.6	8.5	8.4	8.3	8.2	8.3	8.3	8.4	8.4	8.3
2017	8.4	8.6	8.8	8.9	8.9	8.9	8.8	8.6	8.6	8.7	8.7	8.8	8.7
Retail Trade													
2007	31.8	31.2	31.7	31.9	31.6	31.3	31.9	32.3	31.8	32.3	33.7	34.2	32.1
2008	33.2	32.7	32.8	32.6	32.3	32.3	32.7	33.3	32.7	33.2	33.8	34.2	33.0
2009	32.3	31.6	31.7	32.1	32.0	31.9	32.1	32.5	32.4	32.3	33.2	33.7	32.3
2010	32.0	31.5	31.9	32.0	32.1	32.0	32.0	32.5	32.2	32.8	33.9	34.7	32.5
2011	33.3	32.7	32.8	33.3	33.3	33.3	33.3	33.8	33.3	33.6	35.2	35.8	33.6
2012	34.2	33.6	33.9	34.0	34.0	34.2	34.5	35.0	34.6	34.8	36.9	37.2	34.7
2013	35.4	35.0	35.0	35.0	35.0	35.3	35.2	35.6	35.2	35.4	37.4	38.3	35.7
2014	35.8	35.4	35.5	35.9	35.9	36.5	36.8	36.9	36.4	36.7	38.6	39.2	36.6
2015	37.0	36.8	37.0	37.3	37.4	37.4	37.4	37.8	37.3	37.6	39.0	39.3	37.6
2016	37.8	37.3	37.5	37.7	37.7	37.6	37.8	38.1	37.4	37.9	39.6	39.7	38.0
2017	37.8	37.0	36.9	36.6	36.5	36.4	36.4	36.7	36.2	36.7	37.8	37.5	36.9
Transportation and Utilities													
2007	6.9	7.0	7.0	7.0	7.1	7.2	7.2	7.2	7.3	7.0	6.9	7.0	7.1
2008	7.0	7.0	7.1	7.2	7.3	7.3	7.2	7.2	7.2	6.9	6.9	7.0	7.1
2009	6.9	6.8	6.9	6.9	7.0	7.1	7.0	7.1	7.0	7.1	7.1	7.2	7.0
2010	6.9	6.9	6.9	7.0	7.2	7.2	7.0	7.1	7.1	7.1	7.1	7.3	7.1
2011	6.9	7.0	7.1	7.2	7.3	7.3	7.3	7.4	7.3	7.4	7.4	7.5	7.3
2012	7.5	7.7	7.8	7.7	7.8	7.9	7.9	8.0	7.7	7.7	7.8	7.9	7.8
2013	7.8	7.8	7.8	7.9	8.0	8.1	8.0	8.1	8.1	8.1	8.1	8.2	8.0
2014	8.1	8.0	8.0	8.1	8.1	8.1	8.2	8.2	8.2	8.3	8.4	8.6	8.2
2015	8.6	8.5	8.6	8.4	8.6	8.6	8.7	8.8	8.7	8.6	8.7	8.8	8.6
2016	8.5	8.5	8.5	8.5	8.5	8.5	8.6	8.7	8.7	8.5	8.6	8.7	8.6
2017	8.4	8.3	8.3	8.3	8.4	8.5	8.5	8.4	8.5	8.5	8.6	8.7	8.5

Employment by Industry: McAllen-Edinburg-Mission, TX, Selected Years, 2007–2017—*Continued*

(Numbers in thousands, not seasonally adjusted)

Industry and year	January	February	March	April	May	June	July	August	September	October	November	December	Annual average
Information													
2007	2.2	2.2	2.2	2.3	2.3	2.3	2.2	2.2	2.1	2.1	2.1	2.2	2.2
2008	2.2	2.2	2.2	2.2	2.2	2.3	2.3	2.3	2.2	2.2	2.3	2.3	2.2
2009	2.3	2.2	2.2	2.2	2.2	2.2	2.2	2.2	2.1	2.1	2.1	2.1	2.2
2010	2.1	2.0	2.0	2.0	2.1	2.0	2.0	1.9	1.9	2.0	2.0	2.0	2.0
2011	2.1	2.1	2.1	2.1	2.1	2.1	2.1	2.1	2.0	2.0	2.1	2.1	2.1
2012	2.1	2.0	2.0	2.0	2.0	2.0	2.0	2.0	1.9	2.1	2.1	2.2	2.0
2013	2.1	2.1	2.1	2.1	2.2	2.2	2.2	2.2	2.1	2.2	2.3	2.3	2.2
2014	2.2	2.2	2.2	2.2	2.2	2.2	2.2	2.2	2.1	2.2	2.3	2.3	2.2
2015	2.3	2.2	2.2	2.2	2.3	2.3	2.4	2.4	2.3	2.2	2.3	2.3	2.3
2016	2.2	2.2	2.2	2.3	2.3	2.3	2.3	2.3	2.2	2.2	2.3	2.3	2.3
2017	2.2	2.2	2.2	2.3	2.4	2.5	2.5	2.5	2.5	2.6	2.6	2.5	2.4
Financial Activities													
2007	8.8	8.8	8.8	8.9	8.9	8.9	8.9	8.9	8.9	8.9	9.0	8.9	8.9
2008	9.0	9.0	8.9	9.0	8.9	8.9	8.9	8.8	8.7	8.6	8.6	8.5	8.8
2009	8.4	8.2	8.2	8.1	8.1	8.0	8.1	8.0	7.9	8.1	8.1	8.1	8.1
2010	8.0	8.0	8.0	8.0	8.1	8.1	8.1	8.1	8.2	8.3	8.4	8.5	8.2
2011	8.4	8.4	8.5	8.5	8.5	8.6	8.6	8.6	8.6	8.6	8.6	8.7	8.6
2012	8.8	8.8	8.8	8.8	8.8	8.8	8.8	8.8	8.8	8.9	8.9	9.0	8.8
2013	8.8	8.8	8.8	8.8	8.9	8.9	8.9	9.0	8.9	9.0	9.0	9.0	8.9
2014	9.0	9.0	9.0	9.0	9.1	9.1	9.0	9.0	9.0	9.0	9.1	9.2	9.0
2015	9.0	9.0	9.0	8.9	9.0	9.0	9.0	8.9	9.0	9.0	9.0	9.1	9.0
2016	8.9	8.9	8.9	8.9	8.9	8.8	8.8	8.8	8.8	8.7	8.8	8.8	8.8
2017	8.8	8.7	8.7	8.8	8.8	8.8	8.8	8.8	8.7	8.7	8.8	8.8	8.8
Professional and Business Services													
2007	14.9	15.0	15.2	15.1	15.2	15.2	15.0	15.0	15.2	15.1	15.2	15.4	15.1
2008	15.6	15.9	15.6	15.2	15.1	15.0	15.0	15.0	14.8	15.3	15.3	15.2	15.3
2009	15.0	14.9	14.7	14.8	14.8	14.6	14.5	13.9	13.8	13.9	14.1	13.8	14.4
2010	14.0	14.2	14.0	14.0	14.0	14.1	13.9	14.0	14.1	14.3	14.4	14.7	14.1
2011	14.5	14.7	14.8	15.6	15.5	15.3	15.0	15.2	15.0	14.9	15.0	15.0	15.0
2012	15.3	15.4	15.3	15.7	15.5	15.0	15.0	15.0	15.1	15.2	14.8	14.9	15.2
2013	15.1	15.6	15.8	15.9	15.6	15.5	15.1	15.5	15.5	15.5	15.7	16.2	15.6
2014	15.5	15.7	16.0	16.1	15.9	15.7	15.3	15.7	15.6	16.1	15.5	15.8	15.7
2015	16.1	16.3	16.3	16.3	15.9	15.8	15.6	15.5	15.5	15.5	15.8	15.7	15.9
2016	15.9	16.3	16.7	16.7	16.2	16.0	16.1	16.2	16.4	16.8	16.9	16.9	16.4
2017	16.7	16.9	17.2	17.4	16.9	17.1	16.7	16.9	17.2	17.7	17.5	17.7	17.2
Education and Health Services													
2007	46.1	46.4	46.4	47.2	47.4	47.2	47.4	47.9	48.3	48.5	49.0	49.1	47.6
2008	49.3	50.2	50.2	50.9	51.1	50.6	50.9	51.1	51.4	52.3	52.6	53.0	51.1
2009	52.5	52.7	52.9	53.8	54.1	53.6	54.1	54.3	54.6	55.6	55.9	55.9	54.2
2010	55.7	55.9	56.1	55.8	56.4	56.1	55.8	56.3	57.2	57.4	57.6	57.9	56.5
2011	57.4	57.7	58.0	58.3	58.5	58.2	58.6	59.2	60.0	59.6	59.9	60.2	58.8
2012	59.4	59.9	60.1	59.9	60.0	59.6	58.6	59.2	59.5	59.8	60.2	60.4	59.7
2013	59.0	59.6	59.8	60.2	60.4	60.2	60.1	61.0	61.3	61.8	62.1	62.3	60.7
2014	61.2	61.6	61.6	61.9	62.5	62.0	62.0	62.8	63.1	63.4	63.9	64.2	62.5
2015	63.9	64.3	64.4	64.6	65.2	64.6	64.7	65.5	65.7	66.2	66.7	66.8	65.2
2016	66.2	66.9	66.8	67.8	68.2	67.4	67.0	68.2	69.0	69.0	69.4	70.0	68.0
2017	69.6	70.0	70.3	70.6	71.1	70.7	69.7	70.6	71.3	71.6	71.5	71.5	70.7
Leisure and Hospitality													
2007	17.9	17.9	17.7	18.3	18.0	18.0	18.6	18.4	17.8	18.9	18.6	18.7	18.2
2008	19.0	19.2	19.3	19.9	19.7	19.4	19.2	19.3	18.8	19.3	18.8	18.7	19.2
2009	19.0	19.0	19.1	19.3	19.1	18.8	18.9	18.8	18.6	18.9	18.8	18.8	18.9
2010	19.0	19.3	19.5	19.1	19.4	19.2	18.9	19.2	19.3	19.2	19.2	19.4	19.2
2011	19.2	19.5	20.0	20.0	19.9	20.1	19.6	19.6	19.5	19.2	19.4	19.4	19.6
2012	19.2	19.6	20.2	20.2	20.1	20.2	19.8	20.0	20.0	19.9	20.3	20.8	20.0
2013	20.5	21.0	21.5	21.4	21.3	21.3	20.9	21.3	21.2	20.9	21.1	21.2	21.1
2014	21.1	21.3	21.8	21.9	22.2	22.2	21.7	22.1	22.2	22.0	22.0	22.4	21.9
2015	21.9	22.3	22.8	22.9	23.2	23.3	23.3	23.1	23.0	23.1	23.2	23.5	23.0
2016	23.5	23.8	24.1	24.2	24.3	24.5	24.2	24.4	24.4	24.2	24.2	24.2	24.2
2017	24.2	24.3	25.0	25.2	25.3	25.3	24.9	24.9	24.8	24.8	25.3	25.6	25.0

Employment by Industry: McAllen-Edinburg-Mission, TX, Selected Years, 2007–2017—*Continued*

(Numbers in thousands, not seasonally adjusted)

Industry and year	January	February	March	April	May	June	July	August	September	October	November	December	Annual average
Other Services													
2007	4.4	4.4	4.5	4.7	4.7	4.9	5.0	5.0	4.7	5.1	5.0	5.0	4.8
2008	5.2	5.2	5.3	5.5	5.3	5.4	5.6	5.6	5.2	5.4	5.2	5.0	5.3
2009	5.0	5.0	5.0	5.2	5.2	5.3	5.3	5.2	5.0	5.2	5.1	4.9	5.1
2010	5.0	5.0	5.0	5.1	5.2	5.2	5.1	5.1	5.0	5.2	5.1	5.0	5.1
2011	5.0	5.1	5.1	5.1	5.2	5.2	5.2	5.2	5.1	5.2	5.1	5.1	5.1
2012	5.0	5.0	5.0	5.2	5.3	5.4	5.3	5.3	5.2	5.4	5.4	5.3	5.2
2013	5.2	5.3	5.3	5.4	5.5	5.6	5.6	5.6	5.4	5.5	5.5	5.4	5.4
2014	5.4	5.5	5.5	5.6	5.7	5.8	5.8	5.8	5.6	5.7	5.6	5.6	5.6
2015	5.5	5.6	5.6	5.6	5.7	5.8	5.8	5.8	5.6	5.6	5.6	5.5	5.6
2016	5.5	5.5	5.5	5.3	5.4	5.4	5.5	5.4	5.3	5.4	5.3	5.3	5.4
2017	5.3	5.3	5.4	5.4	5.4	5.5	5.4	5.5	5.4	5.5	5.5	5.5	5.4
Government													
2007	50.8	51.5	51.8	51.0	51.2	50.9	45.3	48.1	50.2	52.3	53.0	53.4	50.8
2008	52.9	53.7	53.9	53.6	54.3	53.1	47.5	49.5	52.1	54.4	55.4	55.7	53.0
2009	54.9	55.6	55.6	55.2	55.6	54.4	48.9	51.3	53.4	55.3	56.1	56.3	54.4
2010	55.7	56.5	56.8	56.9	57.1	56.3	48.6	50.5	52.8	55.4	56.1	55.9	54.9
2011	56.1	56.7	56.5	55.9	56.3	55.3	49.5	51.3	53.0	54.1	55.1	55.2	54.6
2012	54.8	55.4	55.8	55.2	55.4	54.8	49.2	50.8	53.0	55.1	55.8	56.0	54.3
2013	55.3	56.0	56.4	55.8	56.5	55.8	50.1	51.9	53.9	56.0	56.7	56.8	55.1
2014	56.7	57.1	57.4	56.7	58.0	57.0	51.0	52.6	54.3	56.7	57.3	57.7	56.0
2015	56.9	57.6	57.8	57.1	58.5	57.7	51.9	53.8	55.7	57.7	58.2	58.7	56.8
2016	58.0	58.8	59.0	59.4	60.0	59.3	53.6	55.4	58.0	59.6	59.9	60.5	58.5
2017	59.6	60.0	60.0	60.7	61.3	60.0	54.1	55.4	57.6	59.5	60.0	60.5	59.1

Employment by Industry: New Haven, CT, Selected Years, 2007–2017

(Numbers in thousands, not seasonally adjusted)

Industry and year	January	February	March	April	May	June	July	August	September	October	November	December	Annual average
Total Nonfarm													
2007	274.2	276.8	275.7	279.7	281.8	284.0	275.9	274.6	280.4	282.8	284.5	285.4	279.7
2008	277.9	280.3	278.8	280.4	282.6	282.4	273.6	271.7	277.9	279.1	281.0	280.2	278.8
2009	269.9	270.7	267.4	268.2	270.7	270.0	261.3	259.8	267.4	268.0	269.8	270.5	267.8
2010	260.4	262.4	260.8	265.1	268.9	268.3	263.8	261.4	267.3	269.1	269.5	269.3	265.5
2011	263.2	264.8	263.0	269.4	270.9	271.1	264.2	262.8	268.8	270.4	271.4	271.7	267.6
2012	266.5	269.6	268.9	273.4	275.7	276.0	268.4	266.8	273.1	274.9	276.5	277.9	272.3
2013	269.2	269.7	270.9	276.9	277.3	279.0	272.6	271.1	277.0	279.0	281.1	279.8	275.3
2014	273.6	273.9	273.4	279.1	279.3	280.6	274.8	273.0	280.3	281.1	283.4	283.7	278.0
2015	275.8	276.1	275.9	280.6	282.0	283.2	275.8	273.6	280.7	283.5	285.8	286.0	279.9
2016	276.1	278.3	280.0	283.0	284.7	286.0	278.3	276.8	284.1	285.8	287.3	288.6	282.4
2017	279.6	281.6	281.0	286.0	286.7	288.9	281.1	279.8	285.0	285.0	286.2	285.6	283.9
Total Private													
2007	237.4	239.7	238.6	242.7	244.6	246.0	243.5	242.5	244.6	245.8	246.9	247.9	243.4
2008	240.8	242.7	241.5	243.6	245.0	245.3	241.4	240.0	241.8	242.0	243.3	242.7	242.5
2009	232.9	233.5	230.3	231.4	233.2	233.5	229.8	228.9	231.6	232.3	233.2	234.4	232.1
2010	224.2	225.9	224.9	229.0	230.8	231.2	231.3	230.1	231.8	233.6	233.6	233.6	230.0
2011	227.5	228.8	227.9	233.0	234.5	235.0	232.9	232.4	234.3	235.3	236.0	236.2	232.8
2012	231.8	233.8	233.3	237.5	240.0	240.6	237.7	237.1	239.2	240.2	241.3	242.2	237.9
2013	233.9	234.5	235.5	240.3	241.1	241.8	241.0	240.7	241.8	244.1	245.3	244.6	240.4
2014	237.9	238.0	237.5	242.6	243.4	243.9	243.1	241.8	244.0	245.7	247.2	247.9	242.8
2015	240.3	239.9	239.6	244.1	245.6	246.6	244.0	242.3	244.5	247.5	249.3	249.8	244.5
2016	240.4	241.9	243.3	245.9	247.4	248.6	246.4	245.9	248.2	250.0	251.2	252.0	246.8
2017	244.3	245.3	245.0	249.7	250.7	252.6	249.9	249.2	249.9	250.0	250.8	250.0	249.0
Goods Producing													
2007	43.5	43.1	43.3	44.0	44.2	44.8	44.5	44.7	44.4	44.2	44.3	43.9	44.1
2008	43.1	42.6	42.6	42.7	43.2	43.4	43.1	42.9	42.5	42.2	42.0	41.1	42.6
2009	38.3	37.4	37.1	37.6	38.1	38.4	37.5	37.3	37.0	36.4	36.2	36.0	37.3
2010	34.2	33.7	34.0	34.7	35.4	35.7	35.8	35.9	35.8	35.3	35.1	34.9	35.0
2011	33.8	33.9	34.0	34.6	35.2	35.7	35.5	35.7	35.4	35.3	35.2	34.9	34.9
2012	34.1	34.1	34.1	34.5	35.0	35.4	35.4	35.4	35.2	34.9	34.8	34.6	34.8
2013	33.6	33.3	33.6	34.1	34.6	35.0	35.5	35.5	35.2	35.3	34.8	34.6	34.6
2014	33.5	33.3	33.4	34.3	34.8	35.2	35.7	35.6	35.4	35.2	34.8	34.6	34.7
2015	33.9	33.4	33.5	34.6	35.1	35.6	35.6	35.5	35.3	35.1	34.9	34.7	34.8
2016	33.6	33.3	33.5	34.0	34.4	34.9	35.0	35.0	34.7	34.5	34.4	34.0	34.3
2017	33.3	33.1	33.1	33.5	34.0	34.5	34.7	34.6	34.2	34.3	34.7	34.4	34.0
Service-Providing													
2007	230.7	233.7	232.4	235.7	237.6	239.2	231.4	229.9	236.0	238.6	240.2	241.5	235.6
2008	234.8	237.7	236.2	237.7	239.4	239.0	230.5	228.8	235.4	236.9	239.0	239.1	236.2
2009	231.6	233.3	230.3	230.6	232.6	231.6	223.8	222.5	230.4	231.6	233.6	234.5	230.5
2010	226.2	228.7	226.8	230.4	233.5	232.6	228.0	225.5	231.5	233.8	234.4	234.4	230.5
2011	229.4	230.9	229.0	234.8	235.7	235.4	228.7	227.1	233.4	235.1	236.2	236.8	232.7
2012	232.4	235.5	234.8	238.9	240.7	240.6	233.0	231.4	237.9	240.0	241.7	243.3	237.5
2013	235.6	236.4	237.3	242.8	242.7	244.0	237.1	235.6	241.8	243.7	246.3	245.2	240.7
2014	240.1	240.6	240.0	244.8	244.5	245.4	239.1	237.4	244.9	245.9	248.6	249.1	243.4
2015	241.9	242.7	242.4	246.0	246.9	247.6	240.2	238.1	245.4	248.4	250.9	251.3	245.2
2016	242.5	245.0	246.5	249.0	250.3	251.1	243.3	241.8	249.4	251.3	252.9	254.6	248.1
2017	246.3	248.5	247.9	252.5	252.7	254.4	246.4	245.2	250.8	250.7	251.5	251.2	249.8
Mining, Logging and Construction													
2007	11.1	10.8	11.1	11.7	12.1	12.5	12.8	12.9	12.7	12.6	12.7	12.3	12.1
2008	11.4	11.2	11.3	11.4	11.9	12.0	12.0	12.0	11.7	11.5	11.4	10.8	11.6
2009	9.5	9.1	9.1	9.6	10.1	10.3	10.2	10.2	10.1	9.7	9.6	9.3	9.7
2010	7.9	7.6	7.8	8.6	9.1	9.1	9.3	9.4	9.4	9.3	9.2	8.9	8.8
2011	8.2	8.3	8.3	8.9	9.4	9.7	9.7	9.8	9.6	9.6	9.4	9.2	9.2
2012	8.5	8.5	8.5	8.9	9.3	9.5	9.7	9.8	9.7	9.5	9.5	9.2	9.2
2013	8.4	8.1	8.4	9.1	9.5	9.8	10.2	10.3	10.2	10.0	9.8	9.5	9.4
2014	8.6	8.5	8.7	9.6	10.1	10.3	10.6	10.7	10.6	10.4	10.3	10.1	9.9
2015	9.4	9.1	9.2	10.2	10.7	11.1	11.2	11.2	11.1	11.1	11.0	10.8	10.5
2016	9.9	9.7	10.0	10.6	11.0	11.3	11.4	11.4	11.3	11.1	11.0	10.5	10.8
2017	9.8	9.7	9.7	10.2	10.6	10.9	11.0	11.0	10.9	10.9	10.9	10.4	10.5

Employment by Industry: New Haven, CT, Selected Years, 2007–2017—*Continued*

(Numbers in thousands, not seasonally adjusted)

Industry and year	January	February	March	April	May	June	July	August	September	October	November	December	Annual average
Manufacturing													
2007	32.4	32.3	32.2	32.3	32.1	32.3	31.7	31.8	31.7	31.6	31.6	31.6	32.0
2008	31.7	31.4	31.3	31.3	31.3	31.4	31.1	30.9	30.8	30.7	30.6	30.3	31.1
2009	28.8	28.3	28.0	28.0	28.0	28.1	27.3	27.1	26.9	26.7	26.6	26.7	27.5
2010	26.3	26.1	26.2	26.1	26.3	26.6	26.5	26.5	26.4	26.0	25.9	26.0	26.2
2011	25.6	25.6	25.7	25.7	25.8	26.0	25.8	25.9	25.8	25.7	25.8	25.7	25.8
2012	25.6	25.6	25.6	25.6	25.7	25.9	25.7	25.6	25.5	25.4	25.3	25.4	25.6
2013	25.2	25.2	25.2	25.0	25.1	25.2	25.3	25.2	25.0	25.3	25.0	25.1	25.2
2014	24.9	24.8	24.7	24.7	24.7	24.9	25.1	24.9	24.8	24.8	24.5	24.5	24.8
2015	24.5	24.3	24.3	24.4	24.4	24.5	24.4	24.3	24.2	24.0	23.9	23.9	24.3
2016	23.7	23.6	23.5	23.4	23.4	23.6	23.6	23.6	23.4	23.4	23.4	23.5	23.5
2017	23.5	23.4	23.4	23.3	23.4	23.6	23.7	23.6	23.3	23.4	23.8	24.0	23.5
Trade, Transportation, and Utilities													
2007	50.1	49.5	49.5	49.4	50.3	50.9	49.6	49.2	49.6	50.0	50.8	51.3	50.0
2008	50.2	49.1	49.1	49.0	49.4	49.8	48.9	48.3	48.7	48.6	49.3	49.7	49.2
2009	47.7	46.8	46.4	45.9	46.9	47.1	46.2	46.0	46.5	47.0	48.0	48.5	46.9
2010	46.1	45.3	45.4	45.2	46.3	46.7	46.2	46.3	46.1	46.7	47.6	48.3	46.4
2011	46.1	45.4	45.5	46.4	46.8	47.1	46.3	46.4	46.6	47.0	47.8	48.6	46.7
2012	47.2	46.5	46.7	46.9	47.8	48.4	47.6	47.5	47.7	48.4	49.8	50.1	47.9
2013	48.2	47.1	47.6	48.5	48.9	49.3	48.4	48.7	48.9	49.4	50.6	51.3	48.9
2014	48.8	48.2	48.4	49.0	49.6	49.8	49.3	49.3	49.5	50.1	51.5	52.1	49.6
2015	49.8	48.6	49.1	49.3	50.2	50.7	49.5	49.2	49.7	50.9	52.8	53.2	50.3
2016	50.6	49.7	50.2	50.6	51.2	51.4	50.7	50.8	51.1	52.0	53.3	53.9	51.3
2017	52.1	50.7	50.8	51.6	52.3	52.4	51.8	51.6	51.7	52.2	53.5	53.9	52.1
Wholesale Trade													
2007	11.7	11.7	11.6	11.5	11.6	11.7	11.7	11.7	11.7	11.6	11.6	11.7	11.7
2008	12.0	11.9	11.9	12.0	12.0	12.1	12.1	12.1	12.2	12.1	12.2	12.2	12.1
2009	12.0	11.9	11.7	11.6	11.6	11.6	11.6	11.5	11.6	11.5	11.5	11.5	11.6
2010	11.3	11.3	11.3	11.3	11.4	11.4	11.5	11.5	11.4	11.3	11.4	11.4	11.4
2011	11.3	11.2	11.2	11.3	11.3	11.4	11.4	11.4	11.3	11.3	11.2	11.3	11.3
2012	11.1	11.1	11.1	11.3	11.3	11.4	11.3	11.2	11.2	11.2	11.2	11.2	11.2
2013	11.0	10.9	11.0	11.2	11.2	11.2	11.2	11.2	11.1	11.1	11.1	11.1	11.1
2014	10.9	10.9	10.9	11.1	11.2	11.2	11.2	11.2	11.1	11.1	11.1	11.1	11.1
2015	11.1	11.0	11.0	11.2	11.3	11.4	11.4	11.3	11.2	11.3	11.3	11.4	11.2
2016	11.3	11.4	11.5	11.5	11.6	11.7	11.7	11.6	11.6	11.7	11.6	11.7	11.6
2017	11.6	11.5	11.5	11.7	11.8	11.8	11.7	11.6	11.6	11.6	11.7	11.9	11.7
Retail Trade													
2007	31.2	30.6	30.7	30.7	31.3	31.7	31.0	30.9	30.5	30.8	31.7	32.0	31.1
2008	30.9	29.9	29.9	29.6	30.0	30.2	29.7	29.5	29.1	29.1	29.8	30.2	29.8
2009	28.8	28.0	27.8	27.6	28.3	28.5	28.1	28.2	28.0	28.6	29.6	30.0	28.5
2010	28.2	27.4	27.5	27.4	28.0	28.3	28.2	28.3	27.8	28.4	29.2	29.7	28.2
2011	28.2	27.6	27.6	28.2	28.5	28.6	28.3	28.5	28.3	28.6	29.5	30.1	28.5
2012	29.1	28.4	28.5	28.4	29.1	29.4	28.9	28.9	28.5	29.0	30.4	30.6	29.1
2013	29.0	28.2	28.3	28.8	29.1	29.4	29.1	29.4	29.1	29.7	30.9	31.5	29.4
2014	29.5	28.9	29.0	29.2	29.6	29.8	29.8	29.8	29.5	30.0	31.3	31.8	29.9
2015	30.0	29.0	29.3	29.2	29.7	30.1	29.5	29.5	29.5	30.5	31.7	32.0	30.0
2016	30.2	29.3	29.5	29.7	30.0	30.2	30.0	30.2	29.9	30.5	31.9	32.1	30.3
2017	30.9	29.8	29.7	30.1	30.4	30.6	30.3	30.2	29.9	30.3	31.4	31.5	30.4
Transportation and Utilities													
2007	7.2	7.2	7.2	7.2	7.4	7.5	6.9	6.6	7.4	7.6	7.5	7.6	7.3
2008	7.3	7.3	7.3	7.4	7.4	7.5	7.1	6.7	7.4	7.4	7.3	7.3	7.3
2009	6.9	6.9	6.9	6.7	7.0	7.0	6.5	6.3	6.9	6.9	6.9	7.0	6.8
2010	6.6	6.6	6.6	6.5	6.9	7.0	6.5	6.5	6.9	7.0	7.0	7.2	6.8
2011	6.6	6.6	6.7	6.9	7.0	7.1	6.6	6.5	7.0	7.1	7.1	7.2	6.9
2012	7.0	7.0	7.1	7.2	7.4	7.6	7.4	7.4	8.0	8.2	8.2	8.3	7.6
2013	8.2	8.0	8.3	8.5	8.6	8.7	8.1	8.1	8.7	8.6	8.6	8.7	8.4
2014	8.4	8.4	8.5	8.7	8.8	8.8	8.3	8.3	8.9	9.0	9.1	9.2	8.7
2015	8.7	8.6	8.8	8.9	9.2	9.2	8.6	8.4	9.0	9.1	9.8	9.8	9.0
2016	9.1	9.0	9.2	9.4	9.6	9.5	9.0	9.0	9.6	9.8	9.8	10.1	9.4
2017	9.6	9.4	9.6	9.8	10.1	10.0	9.8	9.8	10.2	10.3	10.4	10.5	10.0

Employment by Industry: New Haven, CT, Selected Years, 2007–2017—*Continued*

(Numbers in thousands, not seasonally adjusted)

Industry and year	January	February	March	April	May	June	July	August	September	October	November	December	Annual average
Information													
2007	8.1	8.2	8.1	8.2	8.2	8.1	8.1	8.1	8.1	8.1	8.1	8.2	8.1
2008	8.1	8.3	8.0	7.9	7.8	7.8	7.7	7.8	7.6	7.6	7.6	7.5	7.8
2009	7.3	7.3	7.0	6.8	6.7	6.6	6.6	6.4	6.3	6.2	6.1	5.9	6.6
2010	5.7	5.6	5.5	5.3	5.3	5.2	5.1	5.1	5.0	4.9	4.9	4.9	5.2
2011	4.8	4.8	4.8	4.7	4.7	4.7	4.6	4.5	4.5	4.6	4.6	4.6	4.7
2012	4.5	4.5	4.4	4.3	4.3	4.3	4.3	4.3	4.3	4.3	4.3	4.3	4.3
2013	4.3	4.3	4.3	4.2	4.2	4.2	4.2	4.2	4.1	4.2	4.2	4.3	4.2
2014	4.3	4.2	4.1	4.1	4.1	4.1	4.2	4.1	4.0	3.7	3.7	3.7	4.0
2015	3.6	3.6	3.6	3.5	3.5	3.5	3.4	3.4	3.4	3.4	3.4	3.4	3.5
2016	3.4	3.3	3.3	3.4	3.4	3.4	3.4	3.5	3.4	3.4	3.5	3.5	3.4
2017	3.7	3.7	3.7	3.7	3.7	3.7	3.7	3.6	3.6	3.6	3.6	3.5	3.7
Financial Activities													
2007	13.8	13.8	13.7	13.7	13.8	13.9	13.8	13.7	13.4	13.4	13.3	13.4	13.6
2008	13.3	13.3	13.3	13.0	13.1	13.2	13.1	13.1	12.9	12.7	12.7	12.7	13.0
2009	12.6	12.5	12.5	12.5	12.5	12.6	12.4	12.3	12.2	12.2	12.3	12.4	12.4
2010	12.1	12.1	12.2	12.1	12.2	12.3	12.6	12.5	12.2	12.2	12.2	12.2	12.2
2011	12.3	12.3	12.3	12.2	12.2	12.3	12.3	12.3	12.0	12.0	11.8	12.0	12.2
2012	12.1	12.0	12.1	12.1	12.1	12.3	12.3	12.2	12.1	12.0	12.0	12.1	12.1
2013	12.1	12.0	12.0	12.0	12.0	12.2	12.3	12.3	12.3	12.3	12.3	12.4	12.2
2014	12.3	12.3	12.3	12.4	12.5	12.6	12.7	12.7	12.6	12.5	12.5	12.6	12.5
2015	12.5	12.4	12.4	12.5	12.6	12.7	12.7	12.7	12.6	12.6	12.5	12.5	12.6
2016	12.4	12.4	12.4	12.5	12.5	12.7	12.7	12.6	12.4	12.4	12.3	12.4	12.5
2017	12.4	12.4	12.4	12.4	12.5	12.6	12.5	12.5	12.4	12.4	12.4	12.4	12.4
Professional and Business Services													
2007	26.0	26.2	26.4	26.7	27.0	27.5	27.1	27.4	27.4	27.3	27.3	27.8	27.0
2008	27.1	27.5	27.3	27.8	27.8	28.2	26.8	26.9	26.9	26.1	25.9	26.1	27.0
2009	25.2	24.7	24.5	24.6	24.6	24.7	24.2	24.8	24.7	25.0	25.2	25.9	24.8
2010	24.8	25.4	25.2	25.9	25.8	26.4	26.5	26.5	26.2	26.3	26.3	26.4	26.0
2011	25.8	26.1	25.8	26.8	26.7	27.2	27.2	27.2	27.1	27.1	27.4	27.6	26.8
2012	27.6	27.6	27.9	28.8	28.8	28.9	28.5	28.5	28.9	28.9	29.0	29.4	28.6
2013	28.8	29.0	29.0	29.2	29.4	29.8	29.9	29.8	29.3	29.6	29.9	29.9	29.5
2014	29.0	29.2	29.1	29.6	29.8	29.9	30.0	29.7	29.5	29.9	30.2	30.5	29.7
2015	29.7	30.0	29.9	30.5	30.6	30.8	30.5	30.2	30.2	30.5	30.6	30.6	30.3
2016	29.3	29.7	29.9	30.2	30.3	30.8	30.5	30.6	30.5	30.6	30.7	31.1	30.4
2017	30.2	30.2	30.6	31.3	30.9	31.5	31.5	31.2	31.0	30.3	30.4	30.1	30.8
Education and Health Services													
2007	65.1	68.5	66.7	68.9	68.0	66.4	66.0	65.1	68.7	70.1	70.6	70.7	67.9
2008	68.2	71.0	69.6	71.1	70.3	68.6	67.9	67.2	70.3	72.4	73.6	73.2	70.3
2009	71.2	74.1	71.4	72.2	71.4	70.1	69.1	68.6	71.9	73.6	73.9	74.0	71.8
2010	72.1	74.0	72.5	74.6	73.6	71.8	71.7	70.7	74.1	76.2	75.8	75.0	73.5
2011	74.8	75.9	74.7	76.0	75.6	73.6	72.8	72.2	75.4	76.5	76.8	75.7	75.0
2012	74.9	77.5	76.0	77.3	77.6	75.7	74.4	74.0	76.7	78.0	77.8	77.9	76.5
2013	75.4	77.7	76.7	78.5	77.2	75.4	75.1	74.8	77.6	79.3	79.7	78.6	77.2
2014	77.6	78.4	77.1	79.4	77.8	76.4	75.5	75.1	78.4	79.9	80.3	80.1	78.0
2015	78.0	79.2	77.7	79.6	78.3	76.8	76.3	75.7	78.4	80.4	80.8	80.9	78.5
2016	78.1	80.1	80.0	80.4	79.4	77.9	76.9	76.4	80.0	81.1	81.4	81.3	79.4
2017	78.0	80.4	79.4	81.2	80.2	79.3	77.4	77.7	80.2	82.0	82.0	81.6	80.0
Leisure and Hospitality													
2007	19.8	19.7	20.1	20.9	22.1	23.1	23.2	23.1	22.0	21.7	21.5	21.4	21.6
2008	20.0	20.1	20.6	21.2	22.4	23.1	22.9	22.8	22.1	21.6	21.4	21.4	21.6
2009	19.9	20.0	20.6	21.1	22.3	23.1	23.1	22.9	22.3	21.5	21.1	21.2	21.6
2010	19.0	19.6	19.8	20.8	21.9	22.5	22.8	22.6	21.9	21.6	21.4	21.5	21.3
2011	19.9	20.3	20.7	21.9	23.0	23.7	23.7	23.6	23.0	22.6	22.2	22.4	22.3
2012	21.0	21.2	21.7	22.9	23.8	24.9	24.5	24.5	23.8	23.1	23.0	23.2	23.1
2013	21.2	20.8	21.8	23.2	24.1	25.1	24.9	24.8	24.0	23.6	23.3	23.0	23.3
2014	22.0	22.0	22.6	23.2	24.1	25.0	24.8	24.5	24.0	23.6	23.5	23.5	23.6
2015	22.3	22.2	22.7	23.4	24.5	25.5	25.1	24.8	24.2	23.9	23.6	23.8	23.8
2016	22.4	22.8	23.2	24.0	25.3	26.4	26.2	26.1	25.2	25.1	24.8	24.8	24.7
2017	23.8	24.0	24.1	25.1	26.1	27.4	27.2	26.9	25.8	24.4	23.4	23.3	25.1

Employment by Industry: New Haven, CT, Selected Years, 2007–2017—*Continued*

(Numbers in thousands, not seasonally adjusted)

Industry and year	January	February	March	April	May	June	July	August	September	October	November	December	Annual average
Other Services													
2007	11.0	10.7	10.8	10.9	11.0	11.3	11.2	11.2	11.0	11.0	11.0	11.2	11.0
2008	10.8	10.8	11.0	10.9	11.0	11.2	11.0	11.0	10.8	10.8	10.8	11.0	10.9
2009	10.7	10.7	10.8	10.7	10.7	10.9	10.7	10.6	10.7	10.4	10.4	10.5	10.7
2010	10.2	10.2	10.3	10.4	10.3	10.6	10.6	10.5	10.5	10.4	10.3	10.4	10.4
2011	10.0	10.1	10.1	10.4	10.3	10.7	10.5	10.5	10.3	10.2	10.2	10.4	10.3
2012	10.4	10.4	10.4	10.7	10.6	10.7	10.7	10.7	10.5	10.6	10.6	10.6	10.6
2013	10.3	10.3	10.5	10.6	10.7	10.8	10.7	10.6	10.4	10.4	10.5	10.5	10.5
2014	10.4	10.4	10.5	10.6	10.7	10.9	10.9	10.8	10.6	10.8	10.7	10.8	10.7
2015	10.5	10.5	10.7	10.7	10.8	11.0	10.9	10.8	10.7	10.7	10.7	10.7	10.7
2016	10.6	10.6	10.8	10.8	10.9	11.1	11.0	10.9	10.9	10.9	10.8	11.0	10.9
2017	10.8	10.8	10.9	10.9	11.0	11.2	11.1	11.1	11.0	10.8	10.8	10.8	10.9
Government													
2007	36.8	37.1	37.1	37.0	37.2	38.0	32.4	32.1	35.8	37.0	37.6	37.5	36.3
2008	37.1	37.6	37.3	36.8	37.6	37.1	32.2	31.7	36.1	37.1	37.7	37.5	36.3
2009	37.0	37.2	37.1	36.8	37.5	36.5	31.5	30.9	35.8	35.7	36.6	36.1	35.7
2010	36.2	36.5	35.9	36.1	38.1	37.1	32.5	31.3	35.5	35.5	35.9	35.7	35.5
2011	35.7	36.0	35.1	36.4	36.4	36.1	31.3	30.4	34.5	35.1	35.4	35.5	34.8
2012	34.7	35.8	35.6	35.9	35.7	35.4	30.7	29.7	33.9	34.7	35.2	35.7	34.4
2013	35.3	35.2	35.4	36.6	36.2	37.2	31.6	30.4	35.2	34.9	35.8	35.2	34.9
2014	35.7	35.9	35.9	36.5	35.9	36.7	31.7	31.2	36.3	35.4	36.2	35.8	35.3
2015	35.5	36.2	36.3	36.5	36.4	36.6	31.8	31.3	36.2	36.0	36.5	36.2	35.5
2016	35.7	36.4	36.7	37.1	37.3	37.4	31.9	30.9	35.9	35.8	36.1	36.6	35.7
2017	35.3	36.3	36.0	36.3	36.0	36.3	31.2	30.6	35.1	35.0	35.4	35.6	34.9

Employment by Industry: Oxnard-Thousand Oaks-Ventura, CA, Selected Years, 2007–2017

(Numbers in thousands, not seasonally adjusted)

Industry and year	January	February	March	April	May	June	July	August	September	October	November	December	Annual average
Total Nonfarm													
2007	295.8	297.5	299.4	297.8	300.2	301.7	297.7	297.6	297.9	298.7	300.2	301.3	298.8
2008	293.1	295.0	295.1	295.6	296.4	296.4	291.1	290.3	292.2	292.5	291.6	292.4	293.5
2009	284.2	282.1	280.7	280.2	280.6	279.9	272.0	272.9	273.9	275.5	277.5	278.2	278.1
2010	271.2	272.3	272.8	277.4	280.4	277.3	273.3	274.1	275.0	277.7	280.2	281.2	276.1
2011	275.1	276.0	276.2	277.9	278.3	278.4	275.1	276.0	277.6	279.8	283.1	282.7	278.0
2012	278.7	280.3	280.9	281.7	283.7	284.4	279.1	280.2	281.5	285.8	289.2	290.1	283.0
2013	285.2	287.3	287.8	287.6	289.6	288.9	285.5	287.5	288.6	292.3	296.1	297.8	289.5
2014	290.7	291.7	292.9	293.8	294.6	294.4	290.0	291.5	292.4	296.2	298.2	298.6	293.8
2015	292.4	294.2	294.7	295.5	296.2	295.7	292.4	293.7	295.8	301.0	302.8	303.8	296.5
2016	295.9	298.0	298.2	300.1	301.1	301.2	297.7	298.4	299.8	303.7	305.3	305.7	300.4
2017	298.8	300.8	301.9	303.8	305.5	305.5	301.8	303.0	304.9	305.6	308.0	307.9	304.0
Total Private													
2007	253.1	254.4	256.1	254.3	256.5	257.9	256.2	256.5	254.9	255.6	256.4	257.5	255.8
2008	249.6	251.1	251.1	251.8	252.3	252.0	250.0	250.1	250.5	249.3	247.9	248.6	250.4
2009	241.0	238.5	237.1	236.0	236.2	235.4	232.0	232.2	232.3	232.7	234.2	235.1	235.2
2010	228.6	229.1	229.5	231.5	232.9	232.3	232.0	231.7	231.7	232.9	234.5	235.7	231.9
2011	230.3	230.7	230.7	232.5	233.1	232.7	234.0	234.1	234.3	235.1	237.5	238.4	233.6
2012	234.8	235.7	236.3	237.2	238.8	239.7	238.6	239.3	239.1	242.0	244.7	245.9	239.3
2013	241.4	242.9	243.2	243.2	244.7	244.2	245.0	246.4	246.1	248.4	251.8	253.5	245.9
2014	247.0	247.4	248.5	249.2	250.0	249.8	249.5	249.6	249.1	251.1	252.6	253.2	249.8
2015	247.3	248.1	248.7	249.3	249.3	249.2	251.3	251.5	251.0	254.7	256.1	256.9	251.1
2016	249.5	251.0	250.8	253.0	253.3	253.2	254.1	254.4	254.3	256.7	257.8	258.0	253.8
2017	251.8	253.1	254.1	256.0	257.5	258.2	258.6	258.6	258.8	258.0	259.9	259.8	257.0
Goods Producing													
2007	58.0	58.2	58.6	57.9	58.7	59.0	58.3	58.3	57.5	57.3	56.7	56.1	57.9
2008	54.0	54.3	54.2	54.3	54.2	54.3	54.2	53.9	53.8	53.5	52.5	52.0	53.8
2009	50.3	48.9	48.9	48.3	47.7	47.8	46.6	46.3	45.8	45.1	44.7	44.2	47.1
2010	43.7	43.6	43.7	43.7	44.3	44.5	44.7	44.1	44.1	44.1	44.0	43.5	44.0
2011	43.1	43.1	43.1	43.2	43.2	43.2	43.4	43.4	43.3	43.2	43.3	42.8	43.2
2012	42.3	42.3	42.6	42.5	42.7	43.1	43.2	43.4	43.3	43.3	43.2	43.4	42.9
2013	43.2	43.2	43.2	43.0	43.2	43.4	43.8	44.0	44.1	44.5	44.7	44.7	43.8
2014	44.6	44.9	45.5	45.0	45.5	45.5	46.1	46.3	46.3	46.1	45.8	45.5	45.6
2015	45.2	44.9	45.6	45.2	45.2	45.6	46.2	46.4	46.0	46.2	46.0	46.1	45.7
2016	45.3	45.6	45.6	46.0	45.9	46.1	46.7	46.7	46.6	46.5	46.3	46.0	46.1
2017	45.3	45.7	46.2	46.9	47.0	47.4	47.4	47.3	47.6	47.7	47.9	47.6	47.0
Service-Providing													
2007	237.8	239.3	240.8	239.9	241.5	242.7	239.4	239.3	240.4	241.4	243.5	245.2	240.9
2008	239.1	240.7	240.9	241.3	242.2	242.1	236.9	236.4	238.4	239.0	239.1	240.4	239.7
2009	233.9	233.2	231.8	231.9	232.9	232.1	225.4	226.6	228.1	230.4	232.8	234.0	231.1
2010	227.5	228.7	229.1	233.7	236.1	232.8	228.6	230.0	230.9	233.6	236.2	237.7	232.1
2011	232.0	232.9	233.1	234.7	235.1	235.2	231.7	232.6	234.3	236.6	239.8	239.9	234.8
2012	236.4	238.0	238.3	239.2	241.0	241.3	235.9	236.8	238.2	242.5	246.0	246.7	240.0
2013	242.0	244.1	244.6	244.6	246.4	245.5	241.7	243.5	244.5	247.8	251.4	253.1	245.8
2014	246.1	246.8	247.4	248.8	249.1	248.9	243.9	245.2	246.1	250.1	252.4	253.1	248.2
2015	247.2	249.3	249.1	250.3	251.0	250.1	246.2	247.3	249.8	254.8	256.8	257.7	250.8
2016	250.6	252.4	252.6	254.1	255.2	255.1	251.0	251.7	253.2	257.2	259.0	259.7	254.3
2017	253.5	255.1	255.7	256.9	258.5	258.1	254.4	255.7	257.3	257.9	260.1	260.3	257.0
Mining, Logging, and Construction													
2007	19.4	19.6	19.8	19.6	20.2	20.8	20.5	20.7	20.1	19.9	19.4	19.0	19.9
2008	17.9	18.2	18.1	18.3	18.2	18.3	18.2	17.9	17.8	17.5	17.0	16.7	17.8
2009	15.5	14.9	15.2	15.0	14.8	14.9	14.4	14.4	14.0	13.6	13.5	13.1	14.4
2010	12.3	12.3	12.4	12.3	12.7	12.7	12.7	12.6	12.5	12.6	12.6	12.4	12.5
2011	12.4	12.3	12.3	12.5	12.5	12.5	12.7	12.8	12.6	12.8	12.8	12.6	12.6
2012	12.5	12.6	12.8	12.7	12.9	13.1	13.1	13.2	13.3	13.3	13.5	13.6	13.1
2013	13.4	13.5	13.4	13.3	13.5	13.6	13.8	13.9	14.0	14.3	14.6	14.5	13.8
2014	14.4	14.6	14.9	14.7	15.0	15.0	15.2	15.4	15.4	15.3	15.2	15.0	15.0
2015	15.0	14.8	14.9	15.0	15.0	15.3	15.6	15.6	15.2	15.2	15.3	15.2	15.2
2016	14.8	15.0	15.0	15.5	15.6	15.5	15.8	15.8	15.8	15.9	15.8	15.7	15.5
2017	15.1	15.5	15.8	16.4	16.5	16.7	16.9	17.0	17.1	17.2	17.3	17.3	16.6

Employment by Industry: Oxnard-Thousand Oaks-Ventura, CA, Selected Years, 2007–2017—*Continued*

(Numbers in thousands, not seasonally adjusted)

Industry and year	January	February	March	April	May	June	July	August	September	October	November	December	Annual average
Manufacturing													
2007	38.6	38.6	38.8	38.3	38.5	38.2	37.8	37.6	37.4	37.4	37.3	37.1	38.0
2008	36.1	36.1	36.1	36.0	36.0	36.0	36.0	36.0	36.0	36.0	35.5	35.3	35.9
2009	34.8	34.0	33.7	33.3	32.9	32.9	32.2	31.9	31.8	31.5	31.2	31.1	32.6
2010	31.4	31.3	31.3	31.4	31.6	31.8	32.0	31.5	31.6	31.5	31.4	31.1	31.5
2011	30.7	30.8	30.8	30.7	30.7	30.7	30.7	30.6	30.7	30.4	30.5	30.2	30.6
2012	29.8	29.7	29.8	29.8	29.8	30.0	30.1	30.2	30.0	30.0	29.7	29.8	29.9
2013	29.8	29.7	29.8	29.7	29.7	29.8	30.0	30.1	30.1	30.2	30.1	30.2	29.9
2014	30.2	30.3	30.6	30.3	30.5	30.5	30.9	30.9	30.9	30.8	30.6	30.5	30.6
2015	30.2	30.1	30.7	30.2	30.2	30.3	30.6	30.8	30.8	31.0	30.7	30.9	30.5
2016	30.5	30.6	30.6	30.5	30.3	30.6	30.9	30.9	30.8	30.6	30.5	30.3	30.6
2017	30.2	30.2	30.4	30.5	30.5	30.7	30.5	30.3	30.5	30.5	30.6	30.3	30.4
Trade, Transportation, and Utilities													
2007	56.4	55.8	55.9	55.5	55.8	56.5	56.7	57.1	56.7	56.6	58.3	59.8	56.0
2008	56.5	56.4	56.4	56.1	56.1	56.1	55.7	55.5	55.7	55.6	56.2	57.1	56.1
2009	54.1	53.0	52.1	51.8	52.0	51.8	51.7	51.7	51.8	52.2	53.5	54.9	52.6
2010	52.2	51.8	51.8	53.0	53.2	52.9	52.9	52.8	52.7	53.4	54.9	56.0	53.1
2011	53.5	53.0	53.0	53.7	53.7	53.9	54.2	54.3	54.0	54.4	56.6	57.4	54.3
2012	55.3	54.3	54.1	54.6	55.1	55.2	55.3	55.1	55.1	55.8	58.7	59.4	55.7
2013	56.6	56.4	56.0	56.0	56.5	56.7	56.8	56.9	56.6	57.1	60.1	61.0	57.2
2014	57.9	57.2	56.9	57.1	57.3	57.3	57.6	57.6	57.4	58.1	60.2	61.0	58.0
2015	58.2	57.8	57.4	57.4	57.6	57.7	58.4	58.3	58.0	59.2	60.9	61.5	58.5
2016	58.7	58.1	57.8	58.1	58.4	58.1	58.8	59.0	58.8	59.9	61.4	62.1	59.1
2017	59.4	58.4	58.2	59.0	59.0	58.9	59.3	59.5	59.1	59.7	61.1	61.2	59.4
Wholesale Trade													
2007	12.6	12.9	13.0	13.1	13.1	13.2	13.1	13.2	13.1	13.0	13.0	13.0	13.0
2008	12.7	12.9	12.8	12.8	12.9	12.9	12.9	12.9	12.9	12.9	12.7	12.8	12.8
2009	12.6	12.5	12.4	12.2	12.2	12.1	11.9	11.8	11.8	11.8	11.8	11.8	12.1
2010	11.8	12.0	12.1	13.0	13.0	12.7	12.5	12.3	12.0	12.1	12.3	12.2	12.3
2011	12.1	12.2	12.4	12.7	12.6	12.6	12.8	12.7	12.7	12.4	12.4	12.3	12.5
2012	12.4	12.4	12.4	12.6	12.7	12.8	12.7	12.7	12.7	12.5	12.6	12.7	12.6
2013	12.5	12.7	12.8	12.8	12.9	13.0	12.9	12.9	12.8	12.8	13.0	13.1	12.9
2014	12.9	12.9	12.9	12.9	12.9	12.8	12.7	12.7	12.6	12.7	12.7	12.8	12.8
2015	12.5	12.5	12.5	12.5	12.5	12.5	12.6	12.7	12.6	12.8	12.9	12.9	12.6
2016	12.8	12.9	12.8	12.9	13.0	13.0	13.1	13.2	13.2	13.2	13.3	13.4	13.1
2017	13.1	13.1	13.1	13.3	13.3	13.4	13.4	13.4	13.3	13.3	13.3	13.4	13.3
Retail Trade													
2007	37.9	37.0	36.9	36.6	36.7	37.1	37.4	37.7	37.4	37.4	38.9	40.2	37.6
2008	37.5	37.1	37.0	37.0	36.9	37.1	37.0	36.9	37.0	37.1	38.0	38.7	37.3
2009	35.9	35.1	34.4	34.4	34.5	34.4	34.5	34.6	34.6	35.1	36.4	37.6	35.1
2010	35.2	34.6	34.5	34.8	35.0	34.9	35.0	35.1	35.3	36.0	37.3	38.3	35.5
2011	36.1	35.5	35.3	35.6	35.6	35.8	35.8	36.0	35.8	36.5	38.5	39.3	36.3
2012	37.3	36.3	36.0	36.4	36.7	36.7	36.8	36.6	36.6	37.5	40.3	40.7	37.3
2013	38.4	37.9	37.5	37.4	37.8	37.9	38.0	38.1	37.9	38.4	41.1	41.7	38.5
2014	39.0	38.3	38.1	38.3	38.4	38.5	38.9	38.9	38.8	39.4	41.5	42.2	39.2
2015	39.8	39.3	39.0	38.9	39.1	39.2	39.7	39.6	39.5	40.5	42.0	42.5	39.9
2016	39.9	39.3	39.1	39.3	39.4	39.1	39.6	39.8	39.6	40.6	41.9	42.3	40.0
2017	40.2	39.3	39.1	39.6	39.6	39.4	39.7	39.9	39.6	40.2	41.6	41.6	40.0
Transportation and Utilities													
2007	5.9	5.9	6.0	5.8	6.0	6.2	6.2	6.2	6.2	6.2	6.4	6.6	6.1
2008	6.3	6.4	6.6	6.3	6.3	6.1	5.8	5.7	5.8	5.6	5.5	5.6	6.0
2009	5.6	5.4	5.3	5.2	5.3	5.3	5.3	5.3	5.4	5.3	5.3	5.5	5.4
2010	5.2	5.2	5.2	5.2	5.2	5.3	5.4	5.4	5.4	5.3	5.3	5.5	5.3
2011	5.3	5.3	5.3	5.4	5.5	5.5	5.6	5.6	5.5	5.5	5.7	5.8	5.5
2012	5.6	5.6	5.7	5.6	5.7	5.7	5.8	5.8	5.8	5.8	5.8	6.0	5.7
2013	5.7	5.8	5.7	5.8	5.8	5.8	5.9	5.9	5.9	5.9	6.0	6.2	5.9
2014	6.0	6.0	5.9	5.9	6.0	6.0	6.0	6.0	6.0	6.0	6.0	6.0	6.0
2015	5.9	6.0	5.9	6.0	6.0	6.0	6.1	6.0	5.9	5.9	6.0	6.1	6.0
2016	6.0	5.9	5.9	5.9	6.0	6.0	6.1	6.0	6.0	6.1	6.2	6.4	6.0
2017	6.1	6.0	6.0	6.1	6.1	6.1	6.2	6.2	6.2	6.2	6.2	6.2	6.1

Employment by Industry: Oxnard-Thousand Oaks-Ventura, CA, Selected Years, 2007–2017—*Continued*

(Numbers in thousands, not seasonally adjusted)

Industry and year	January	February	March	April	May	June	July	August	September	October	November	December	Annual average
Information													
2007	5.7	5.9	5.9	5.8	5.9	5.9	5.8	5.8	5.8	5.7	5.8	5.7	5.8
2008	5.7	5.7	5.7	5.7	5.7	5.7	5.6	5.6	5.5	5.5	5.5	5.4	5.6
2009	5.4	5.4	5.4	5.3	5.3	5.3	5.3	5.2	5.2	5.2	5.3	5.3	5.3
2010	5.2	5.2	5.2	5.2	5.2	5.2	5.2	5.2	5.1	5.0	5.0	5.0	5.1
2011	4.9	4.8	4.8	4.8	4.9	4.9	4.9	4.9	4.8	4.8	4.9	5.0	4.9
2012	5.0	5.0	5.1	5.0	5.1	5.2	5.2	5.2	5.1	5.3	5.3	5.3	5.2
2013	5.1	5.1	5.1	5.1	5.1	5.2	5.3	5.3	5.2	5.3	5.3	5.4	5.2
2014	5.4	5.4	5.4	5.4	5.4	5.5	5.4	5.3	5.2	5.2	5.2	5.3	5.3
2015	5.1	5.1	5.1	5.0	5.0	5.1	5.1	4.9	4.9	5.1	5.1	5.2	5.1
2016	4.9	4.9	4.9	4.9	5.0	5.1	5.0	5.1	5.0	4.9	5.0	5.0	5.0
2017	4.9	4.9	4.9	5.0	5.1	5.1	5.1	5.1	5.0	5.0	5.0	5.0	5.0
Financial Activities													
2007	22.7	22.7	22.8	22.8	22.9	23.1	23.0	22.8	22.6	22.7	22.1	22.1	22.7
2008	21.5	21.5	21.3	21.4	21.4	21.4	21.1	20.9	20.8	20.7	20.5	20.5	21.1
2009	20.7	20.7	20.6	20.6	20.5	20.4	20.4	20.4	20.5	20.2	20.4	20.5	20.5
2010	20.2	20.3	20.3	20.1	20.1	20.1	20.3	20.4	20.3	20.5	20.6	20.8	20.3
2011	20.6	20.6	20.8	20.7	20.7	20.7	20.7	20.3	20.1	20.0	19.6	19.9	20.4
2012	19.9	20.1	20.0	19.7	19.6	19.6	19.5	19.4	19.2	19.4	19.4	19.4	19.6
2013	19.1	19.1	19.2	18.8	18.8	18.7	18.8	18.9	18.9	18.9	18.9	18.9	18.9
2014	19.0	18.9	19.0	18.9	18.8	18.9	18.8	18.7	18.4	18.5	18.4	18.4	18.7
2015	18.0	17.8	17.8	17.9	17.9	17.6	17.8	17.7	17.6	17.7	17.6	17.5	17.7
2016	17.3	17.3	17.3	17.5	17.4	17.3	17.5	17.4	17.4	17.5	17.5	17.5	17.4
2017	17.1	17.1	17.0	16.9	17.0	16.9	16.9	16.8	16.8	16.9	17.0	16.9	16.9
Professional and Business Services													
2007	39.2	39.5	39.8	39.0	38.9	39.0	38.5	38.2	37.7	37.7	37.8	37.8	38.6
2008	37.7	38.1	38.1	38.0	38.2	38.3	38.3	38.7	38.9	38.4	38.1	38.3	38.3
2009	37.1	36.7	36.6	35.9	35.7	35.5	35.2	35.1	35.0	35.2	35.6	35.2	35.7
2010	34.1	34.2	34.5	34.2	34.2	34.4	34.3	34.4	34.2	34.3	34.2	34.5	34.3
2011	33.3	33.4	33.4	33.7	33.7	33.7	34.5	34.2	34.1	34.2	34.2	34.5	33.9
2012	34.2	34.8	35.1	35.1	35.2	35.6	35.6	35.9	35.9	36.6	36.7	36.8	35.6
2013	36.3	36.5	36.9	36.8	36.8	36.7	37.2	37.2	37.1	37.5	37.5	37.8	37.0
2014	36.3	35.8	36.2	36.2	35.8	35.8	35.9	35.7	35.6	35.9	35.7	35.8	35.9
2015	34.9	35.2	35.4	35.9	35.2	35.3	35.8	35.9	35.7	36.8	36.6	36.8	35.8
2016	35.4	35.7	35.8	36.1	36.0	36.1	35.9	35.9	35.7	36.0	36.2	36.1	35.9
2017	35.8	36.2	36.4	36.3	36.6	37.1	37.6	37.4	37.4	36.1	35.6	36.0	36.5
Education and Health Services													
2007	31.0	31.6	31.9	31.7	31.9	31.9	31.5	32.0	32.4	33.2	33.3	33.4	32.2
2008	32.8	33.6	33.4	34.0	34.2	33.7	33.1	33.7	34.5	35.0	34.9	35.2	34.0
2009	34.6	35.1	34.9	35.3	35.4	34.9	33.6	34.2	34.8	35.6	35.7	35.9	35.0
2010	34.6	35.3	35.1	36.0	36.0	35.6	34.8	35.0	35.3	35.9	36.1	36.2	35.5
2011	35.6	36.2	35.9	36.3	36.3	35.6	35.3	35.8	36.7	37.2	37.5	37.6	36.3
2012	37.3	38.0	38.0	38.3	38.4	38.0	37.1	37.6	38.1	39.0	38.9	39.4	38.2
2013	39.3	40.2	40.3	40.5	40.6	39.8	39.1	39.9	40.3	41.2	41.5	41.6	40.4
2014	40.6	41.6	41.4	42.1	42.1	41.4	40.4	40.8	41.4	42.5	42.6	42.6	41.6
2015	41.8	42.7	42.6	42.8	43.0	42.4	42.2	42.3	43.0	43.9	44.1	44.2	42.9
2016	43.3	44.3	44.1	44.6	44.5	44.3	43.6	43.8	44.3	45.5	45.3	45.4	44.4
2017	44.1	45.1	45.3	45.5	45.7	45.6	45.0	45.4	45.7	45.3	45.4	45.7	45.3
Leisure and Hospitality													
2007	30.6	31.1	31.4	31.7	32.3	32.5	32.5	32.5	32.2	32.0	32.3	32.5	32.0
2008	31.4	31.4	31.8	32.1	32.3	32.3	31.9	31.8	31.3	30.9	30.7	30.6	31.5
2009	29.5	29.4	29.3	29.5	30.2	30.4	30.2	30.1	30.0	29.9	29.7	29.8	29.8
2010	29.5	29.6	29.7	30.1	30.6	30.4	30.7	30.7	30.7	30.5	30.5	30.6	30.3
2011	30.3	30.5	30.6	31.0	31.4	31.6	31.8	32.1	32.0	31.9	31.9	31.8	31.4
2012	31.6	31.8	32.1	32.6	33.1	33.3	33.2	33.3	33.0	33.1	33.2	32.9	32.8
2013	32.4	32.9	33.0	33.4	34.1	34.1	34.2	34.4	34.1	34.1	34.0	34.3	33.8
2014	33.5	33.8	34.2	34.6	35.1	35.5	35.5	35.5	35.2	35.0	34.9	34.9	34.8
2015	34.5	35.0	35.2	35.4	35.6	35.8	36.1	36.4	36.2	36.2	36.1	36.0	35.7
2016	35.2	35.6	35.8	36.1	36.5	36.6	37.0	37.0	36.9	36.7	36.6	36.5	36.4
2017	35.8	36.1	36.5	36.9	37.4	37.6	37.7	37.5	37.6	37.7	38.3	37.9	37.3

Employment by Industry: Oxnard-Thousand Oaks-Ventura, CA, Selected Years, 2007–2017—*Continued*

(Numbers in thousands, not seasonally adjusted)

Industry and year	January	February	March	April	May	June	July	August	September	October	November	December	Annual average
Other Services													
2007	9.5	9.6	9.8	9.9	10.1	10.0	9.9	9.8	10.0	10.4	10.1	10.1	9.9
2008	10.0	10.1	10.2	10.2	10.2	10.2	10.1	10.0	10.0	9.7	9.5	9.5	10.0
2009	9.3	9.3	9.3	9.3	9.4	9.3	9.0	9.2	9.2	9.3	9.3	9.3	9.3
2010	9.1	9.1	9.2	9.2	9.3	9.2	9.1	9.1	9.3	9.2	9.2	9.1	9.2
2011	9.0	9.1	9.1	9.1	9.2	9.1	9.2	9.1	9.3	9.4	9.5	9.4	9.2
2012	9.2	9.4	9.3	9.4	9.6	9.7	9.5	9.4	9.4	9.5	9.3	9.3	9.4
2013	9.4	9.5	9.5	9.6	9.6	9.6	9.8	9.8	9.8	9.8	9.8	9.8	9.7
2014	9.7	9.8	9.9	9.9	10.0	9.9	9.8	9.7	9.6	9.8	9.8	9.7	9.8
2015	9.6	9.6	9.6	9.7	9.8	9.7	9.7	9.6	9.6	9.6	9.7	9.6	9.7
2016	9.4	9.5	9.5	9.7	9.6	9.6	9.6	9.5	9.6	9.7	9.5	9.4	9.6
2017	9.4	9.6	9.6	9.5	9.7	9.6	9.6	9.6	9.6	9.6	9.6	9.5	9.6
Government													
2007	42.7	43.1	43.3	43.5	43.7	43.8	41.5	41.1	43.0	43.1	43.8	43.8	43.0
2008	43.5	43.9	44.0	43.8	44.1	44.4	41.1	40.2	41.7	43.2	43.7	43.8	43.1
2009	43.2	43.6	43.6	44.2	44.4	44.5	40.0	40.7	41.6	42.8	43.3	43.1	42.9
2010	42.6	43.2	43.3	45.9	47.5	45.0	41.3	42.4	43.3	44.8	45.7	45.5	44.2
2011	44.8	45.3	45.5	45.4	45.2	45.7	41.1	41.9	43.3	44.7	45.6	44.3	44.4
2012	43.9	44.6	44.6	44.5	44.9	44.7	40.5	40.9	42.4	43.8	44.5	44.2	43.6
2013	43.8	44.4	44.6	44.4	44.9	44.7	40.5	41.1	42.5	43.9	44.3	44.3	43.6
2014	43.7	44.3	44.4	44.6	44.6	44.6	40.5	41.9	43.3	45.1	45.6	45.4	44.0
2015	45.1	46.1	46.0	46.2	46.9	46.5	41.1	42.2	44.8	46.3	46.7	46.9	45.4
2016	46.4	47.0	47.4	47.1	47.8	48.0	43.6	44.0	45.5	47.0	47.5	47.7	46.6
2017	47.0	47.7	47.8	47.8	48.0	47.3	43.2	44.4	46.1	47.6	48.1	48.1	46.9

Employment by Industry: El Paso, TX, Selected Years, 2007–2017

(Numbers in thousands, not seasonally adjusted)

Industry and year	January	February	March	April	May	June	July	August	September	October	November	December	Annual average
Total Nonfarm													
2007	268.7	270.2	272.4	273.1	274.6	272.2	270.0	272.1	277.8	280.8	282.5	284.7	274.9
2008	280.8	282.6	283.4	281.4	282.9	279.5	275.8	278.4	281.1	284.0	284.2	283.9	281.5
2009	278.0	277.5	277.4	277.7	277.0	275.8	271.6	272.7	276.4	278.4	279.9	280.8	276.9
2010	276.5	278.0	281.4	281.5	283.5	281.9	275.5	277.4	281.7	282.3	284.2	285.4	280.8
2011	281.2	281.6	283.1	284.2	284.4	282.7	280.6	281.9	285.7	283.0	285.4	286.8	283.4
2012	282.8	284.9	286.6	287.6	288.9	285.8	284.1	286.2	288.6	290.1	292.4	292.8	287.6
2013	287.0	289.3	290.5	291.1	292.3	289.1	287.5	290.5	293.3	294.6	297.5	297.6	291.7
2014	292.9	294.6	295.7	296.3	297.4	294.7	290.9	293.0	294.3	296.1	298.5	299.7	295.3
2015	296.1	297.9	298.8	300.2	302.0	300.9	298.1	300.2	302.4	305.4	307.5	307.6	301.4
2016	304.0	305.5	306.0	308.9	309.7	307.0	305.9	308.2	311.3	310.6	312.6	312.8	308.5
2017	309.6	311.9	312.0	313.2	314.0	310.8	307.0	309.1	312.3	314.4	316.6	316.6	312.3
Total Private													
2007	204.6	205.5	207.4	207.4	208.7	210.0	209.8	211.9	211.9	213.4	214.8	217.0	210.2
2008	213.8	214.1	214.7	215.3	216.0	215.9	215.7	218.3	215.7	216.1	216.2	215.8	215.6
2009	209.9	208.9	208.7	207.9	207.6	208.8	208.7	209.8	208.0	207.5	208.8	209.8	208.7
2010	205.9	206.6	209.7	209.8	211.1	212.7	210.5	212.0	211.2	211.4	213.0	214.1	210.7
2011	210.7	211.0	212.3	213.3	213.8	213.8	214.5	215.6	214.9	212.7	214.6	216.3	213.6
2012	212.2	214.2	215.8	217.0	218.1	218.7	218.1	220.0	219.1	219.2	221.0	221.6	217.9
2013	216.2	218.0	219.0	220.1	221.5	222.1	221.6	223.9	223.4	224.4	226.8	227.1	222.0
2014	223.5	224.7	225.8	225.9	226.9	227.1	225.4	227.1	225.3	225.8	227.7	229.0	226.2
2015	225.7	227.1	227.9	229.8	231.5	233.1	232.3	233.8	232.8	234.8	236.4	236.6	231.8
2016	233.3	234.4	234.7	237.2	237.8	237.9	238.9	240.6	239.7	238.2	240.1	240.5	237.8
2017	237.9	239.3	239.5	240.6	241.3	241.0	239.5	241.0	240.5	241.6	243.7	243.8	240.8
Goods Producing													
2007	33.8	34.0	34.3	34.5	34.6	34.9	34.8	35.5	35.6	35.8	36.0	36.0	35.0
2008	35.5	35.5	35.4	35.8	35.8	35.6	35.5	35.8	35.6	35.2	35.0	34.5	35.4
2009	33.9	33.4	32.8	32.9	32.8	32.3	32.5	33.1	32.7	32.8	32.4	32.5	32.8
2010	32.1	32.1	32.3	32.3	32.4	32.3	32.5	33.3	32.9	32.1	31.9	31.6	32.3
2011	31.2	31.1	31.3	31.3	31.4	31.2	31.1	31.9	31.6	30.7	30.7	30.5	31.2
2012	30.1	30.3	30.4	30.6	30.8	31.0	30.9	31.6	31.5	31.4	31.3	31.0	30.9
2013	30.4	30.9	30.8	30.9	31.0	31.0	30.9	31.6	31.5	31.3	31.1	30.9	31.0
2014	30.7	31.0	31.0	30.9	31.0	30.9	29.9	30.8	30.4	30.0	29.8	29.9	30.5
2015	29.7	30.2	30.3	30.6	31.1	31.1	31.1	31.4	31.6	31.8	31.6	31.6	31.0
2016	31.2	31.7	31.6	32.3	32.4	32.5	32.2	32.1	32.1	31.4	31.4	31.5	31.9
2017	31.5	32.0	32.4	32.4	32.7	32.9	32.4	32.2	32.3	32.0	32.2	32.1	32.3
Service-Providing													
2007	234.9	236.2	238.1	238.6	240.0	237.3	235.2	236.6	242.2	245.0	246.5	248.7	239.9
2008	245.3	247.1	248.0	245.6	247.1	243.9	240.3	242.6	245.5	248.8	249.2	249.4	246.1
2009	244.1	244.1	244.6	244.8	244.2	243.5	239.1	239.6	243.7	245.6	247.5	248.3	244.1
2010	244.4	245.9	249.1	249.2	251.1	249.6	243.0	244.1	248.8	250.2	252.3	253.8	248.5
2011	250.0	250.5	251.8	252.9	253.0	251.5	249.5	250.0	254.1	252.3	254.7	256.3	252.2
2012	252.7	254.6	256.2	257.0	258.1	254.8	253.2	254.6	257.1	258.7	261.1	261.8	256.7
2013	256.6	258.4	259.7	260.2	261.3	258.1	256.6	258.9	261.8	263.3	266.4	266.7	260.7
2014	262.2	263.6	264.7	265.4	266.4	263.8	261.0	262.2	263.9	266.1	268.7	269.8	264.8
2015	266.4	267.7	268.5	269.6	270.9	269.8	267.0	268.8	270.8	273.6	275.9	276.0	270.4
2016	272.8	273.8	274.4	276.6	277.3	274.5	273.7	276.1	279.2	279.2	281.2	281.3	276.7
2017	278.1	279.9	279.6	280.8	281.3	277.9	274.6	276.9	280.0	282.4	284.4	284.5	280.0
Mining, Logging, and Construction													
2007	13.4	13.7	14.1	14.3	14.4	14.7	14.6	15.1	15.2	15.6	15.8	15.8	14.7
2008	15.4	15.4	15.5	15.9	15.9	15.7	15.8	16.1	16.1	16.0	15.9	15.8	15.8
2009	15.5	15.4	15.6	15.4	15.6	15.2	15.6	15.8	15.5	15.9	15.7	15.8	15.6
2010	15.7	15.8	15.9	15.9	15.9	15.7	15.7	15.8	15.4	14.8	14.7	14.4	15.5
2011	14.2	14.0	14.1	14.0	14.0	13.7	13.8	14.1	13.9	13.2	13.2	13.0	13.8
2012	12.8	12.8	12.8	12.8	12.9	13.1	13.1	13.3	13.2	13.2	13.2	13.0	13.0
2013	12.5	12.8	12.7	12.7	12.9	13.0	13.1	13.4	13.4	13.5	13.4	13.3	13.1
2014	13.4	13.8	13.9	13.8	13.9	13.8	12.9	13.2	12.9	12.8	12.8	12.9	13.3
2015	12.8	13.1	13.2	13.5	14.0	14.0	14.1	14.3	14.5	14.7	14.6	14.6	14.0
2016	14.4	14.8	14.7	15.2	15.2	15.3	15.1	14.9	14.9	14.6	14.6	14.6	14.9
2017	14.7	15.0	15.4	15.3	15.6	15.9	15.6	15.5	15.5	15.5	15.7	15.5	15.4

Employment by Industry: El Paso, TX, Selected Years, 2007–2017—*Continued*

(Numbers in thousands, not seasonally adjusted)

Industry and year	January	February	March	April	May	June	July	August	September	October	November	December	Annual average
Manufacturing													
2007	20.4	20.3	20.2	20.2	20.2	20.2	20.2	20.4	20.4	20.2	20.2	20.2	20.3
2008	20.1	20.1	19.9	19.9	19.9	19.9	19.7	19.7	19.5	19.2	19.1	18.7	19.6
2009	18.4	18.0	17.2	17.5	17.2	17.1	16.9	17.3	17.2	16.9	16.7	16.7	17.3
2010	16.4	16.3	16.4	16.4	16.5	16.6	16.8	17.5	17.5	17.3	17.2	17.2	16.8
2011	17.0	17.1	17.2	17.3	17.4	17.5	17.3	17.8	17.7	17.5	17.5	17.5	17.4
2012	17.3	17.5	17.6	17.8	17.9	17.9	17.8	18.3	18.3	18.2	18.1	18.0	17.9
2013	17.9	18.1	18.1	18.2	18.1	18.0	17.8	18.2	18.1	17.8	17.7	17.6	18.0
2014	17.3	17.2	17.1	17.1	17.1	17.1	17.0	17.6	17.5	17.2	17.0	17.0	17.2
2015	16.9	17.1	17.1	17.1	17.1	17.1	17.0	17.1	17.1	17.1	17.0	17.0	17.1
2016	16.8	16.9	16.9	17.1	17.2	17.2	17.1	17.2	17.2	16.8	16.8	16.9	17.0
2017	16.8	17.0	17.0	17.1	17.1	17.0	16.8	16.7	16.8	16.5	16.5	16.6	16.8
Trade, Transportation, and Utilities													
2007	59.0	58.6	59.2	59.5	59.7	59.8	59.7	60.3	60.7	61.4	62.5	63.3	60.3
2008	61.0	60.2	60.3	60.0	59.9	59.9	60.0	60.6	59.8	60.1	60.5	60.7	60.3
2009	57.4	56.4	56.4	55.6	55.4	55.7	55.5	55.8	55.9	55.7	56.7	57.4	56.2
2010	55.2	55.1	55.8	56.1	56.3	56.3	56.6	56.9	56.8	57.4	58.8	59.8	56.8
2011	57.3	56.7	57.1	57.7	57.9	57.8	58.2	58.6	58.2	58.3	59.9	60.9	58.2
2012	58.7	58.3	58.6	59.4	60.0	60.2	59.7	60.1	59.7	60.0	61.9	62.4	59.9
2013	59.9	59.8	60.3	61.1	61.6	61.8	61.6	62.2	61.8	62.8	64.7	65.5	61.9
2014	63.4	62.9	63.4	63.2	63.5	63.7	63.6	63.8	63.3	63.9	65.6	66.7	63.9
2015	64.1	63.8	64.3	64.7	65.0	65.4	65.3	65.5	65.2	66.3	67.4	67.8	65.4
2016	66.0	65.6	66.1	66.6	66.7	67.0	67.3	68.4	68.0	68.4	70.3	70.3	67.6
2017	68.1	67.6	67.6	67.3	67.3	67.5	67.0	67.8	67.4	68.0	69.2	69.3	67.8
Wholesale Trade													
2007	11.0	11.0	11.1	11.3	11.3	11.4	11.3	11.4	11.4	11.5	11.5	11.6	11.3
2008	11.3	11.3	11.1	11.4	11.2	11.1	11.3	11.3	11.1	11.1	10.7	10.6	11.1
2009	10.2	10.1	10.1	9.9	9.8	9.8	9.8	9.8	9.8	9.8	9.8	9.8	9.9
2010	9.8	9.8	10.0	10.1	10.0	10.1	10.2	10.2	10.1	10.1	10.1	10.1	10.1
2011	10.0	10.0	10.1	10.1	10.2	10.2	10.4	10.4	10.4	10.3	10.2	10.3	10.2
2012	10.2	10.3	10.4	10.4	10.4	10.4	10.3	10.3	10.3	10.3	10.4	10.4	10.3
2013	10.3	10.3	10.4	10.4	10.5	10.6	10.6	10.7	10.7	10.7	10.8	10.8	10.6
2014	10.6	10.8	10.8	10.8	10.9	11.0	11.0	11.0	10.9	11.0	10.9	11.0	10.9
2015	10.9	10.9	11.0	11.1	11.1	11.2	11.2	11.2	11.2	11.2	11.2	11.3	11.1
2016	11.3	11.3	11.4	11.4	11.4	11.4	11.4	11.5	11.5	11.4	11.5	11.5	11.4
2017	11.4	11.5	11.6	11.5	11.6	11.6	11.5	11.6	11.6	11.7	11.6	11.7	11.6
Retail Trade													
2007	34.3	33.8	34.3	34.3	34.5	34.5	34.5	35.0	35.4	36.2	37.2	37.8	35.2
2008	36.1	35.3	35.6	35.0	35.0	35.2	35.2	35.6	35.3	35.5	36.3	36.6	35.6
2009	34.2	33.4	33.4	33.0	32.9	33.7	32.9	33.3	33.4	33.3	34.3	34.8	33.5
2010	33.0	32.9	33.3	33.5	33.7	33.6	33.8	34.1	34.2	34.7	36.1	37.0	34.2
2011	34.7	34.1	34.3	35.0	35.1	35.1	35.0	35.3	34.9	35.2	36.8	37.5	35.3
2012	35.7	35.1	35.2	35.9	36.3	36.4	36.0	36.3	35.9	36.2	37.9	38.4	36.3
2013	36.2	36.1	36.2	36.9	37.2	37.2	37.2	37.6	37.3	38.2	40.0	40.7	37.6
2014	38.7	38.1	38.3	38.4	38.5	38.5	38.5	38.6	38.3	38.7	40.5	41.2	38.9
2015	38.8	38.5	38.6	38.8	39.0	39.2	38.9	39.1	38.8	39.7	40.7	40.9	39.3
2016	39.0	38.5	38.7	39.1	39.2	39.4	39.6	40.6	40.1	40.7	42.4	42.3	40.0
2017	40.5	40.0	39.8	39.6	39.5	39.5	39.3	39.9	39.5	39.9	41.1	41.1	40.0
Transportation and Utilities													
2007	13.7	13.8	13.8	13.9	13.9	13.9	13.9	13.9	13.9	13.7	13.8	13.9	13.8
2008	13.6	13.6	13.6	13.6	13.7	13.6	13.5	13.7	13.4	13.5	13.5	13.5	13.6
2009	13.0	12.9	12.9	12.7	12.7	12.7	12.8	12.7	12.7	12.6	12.6	12.8	12.8
2010	12.4	12.4	12.5	12.5	12.6	12.6	12.6	12.6	12.5	12.6	12.6	12.7	12.6
2011	12.6	12.6	12.7	12.6	12.6	12.5	12.8	12.9	12.9	12.8	12.9	13.1	12.8
2012	12.8	12.9	13.0	13.1	13.3	13.4	13.4	13.5	13.5	13.5	13.6	13.6	13.3
2013	13.4	13.4	13.7	13.8	13.9	14.0	13.8	13.9	13.8	13.9	13.9	14.0	13.8
2014	14.1	14.0	14.3	14.0	14.1	14.2	14.1	14.2	14.1	14.2	14.2	14.5	14.2
2015	14.4	14.4	14.7	14.8	14.9	15.0	15.2	15.2	15.2	15.4	15.5	15.6	15.0
2016	15.7	15.8	16.0	16.1	16.1	16.2	16.3	16.3	16.4	16.3	16.4	16.5	16.2
2017	16.2	16.1	16.2	16.2	16.2	16.4	16.2	16.3	16.3	16.4	16.5	16.5	16.3

Employment by Industry: El Paso, TX, Selected Years, 2007–2017—*Continued*

(Numbers in thousands, not seasonally adjusted)

Industry and year	January	February	March	April	May	June	July	August	September	October	November	December	Annual average
Information													
2007	5.0	5.1	5.1	5.1	5.1	5.1	5.4	5.4	5.3	5.6	5.6	5.6	5.3
2008	5.8	5.8	5.8	5.7	5.9	5.9	5.6	5.6	5.5	5.5	5.5	5.5	5.7
2009	5.4	5.5	5.4	5.4	5.3	5.3	5.2	5.1	5.0	5.0	5.0	5.0	5.2
2010	5.2	5.2	5.2	5.3	5.4	5.6	5.5	5.4	5.4	5.4	5.5	5.4	5.4
2011	5.4	5.4	5.4	5.4	5.4	5.5	5.5	5.5	5.5	5.5	5.5	5.6	5.5
2012	5.7	5.7	5.8	5.7	5.8	5.8	5.9	5.9	5.9	6.0	6.0	6.1	5.9
2013	6.1	6.0	6.1	5.9	5.9	5.9	5.8	5.8	5.8	5.8	5.9	5.8	5.9
2014	5.7	5.7	5.5	5.5	5.5	5.4	5.4	5.3	5.3	5.5	5.5	5.6	5.5
2015	5.5	5.4	5.3	5.3	5.3	5.3	5.3	5.2	5.2	5.1	5.2	5.2	5.3
2016	5.1	5.0	5.0	5.1	5.1	5.1	5.1	5.1	5.0	4.9	5.0	5.0	5.0
2017	5.0	5.0	5.0	5.0	5.0	5.0	5.0	5.1	5.0	5.1	5.1	5.1	5.0
Financial Activities													
2007	11.4	11.4	11.5	11.6	11.7	11.7	11.7	11.8	11.8	11.8	11.9	12.2	11.7
2008	12.2	12.3	12.3	12.0	12.1	12.2	12.3	12.5	12.4	12.4	12.3	12.3	12.3
2009	12.2	12.2	12.2	12.2	12.1	12.0	12.0	12.0	12.0	12.0	12.0	12.0	12.1
2010	11.6	11.6	11.7	11.7	11.8	11.8	11.9	11.9	11.9	12.0	12.1	12.2	11.9
2011	12.1	12.1	12.2	12.3	12.4	12.5	12.5	12.4	12.4	12.5	12.4	12.6	12.4
2012	12.4	12.6	12.6	12.6	12.6	12.7	12.7	12.7	12.6	12.6	12.5	12.5	12.6
2013	12.3	12.3	12.3	12.4	12.4	12.4	12.1	12.1	12.1	12.1	12.1	12.1	12.2
2014	11.9	12.0	12.0	12.1	12.1	12.2	11.6	11.6	11.7	11.7	11.7	11.7	11.9
2015	11.9	12.0	12.0	12.0	12.1	12.2	12.2	12.3	12.2	12.4	12.4	12.5	12.2
2016	12.4	12.6	12.5	12.5	12.5	12.4	12.5	12.5	12.7	12.6	12.6	12.6	12.5
2017	12.5	12.6	12.6	12.6	12.6	12.5	12.6	12.7	12.7	12.7	12.8	12.8	12.6
Professional and Business Services													
2007	31.5	31.9	31.8	31.1	31.0	30.8	30.8	31.3	31.2	32.0	31.8	32.4	31.5
2008	31.7	32.0	32.0	32.1	31.8	31.7	32.2	33.5	32.7	33.2	32.9	32.8	32.4
2009	32.1	31.6	31.6	31.7	30.7	30.8	30.7	31.1	31.0	31.4	31.7	31.7	31.3
2010	31.4	31.4	32.3	31.5	31.3	30.9	31.0	31.1	31.0	31.5	31.5	31.5	31.4
2011	31.0	31.3	31.0	31.0	30.5	29.9	30.2	30.1	30.4	29.7	29.9	30.4	30.5
2012	29.9	30.1	30.5	30.5	30.1	29.8	30.0	30.3	30.3	30.5	30.4	30.6	30.3
2013	30.2	30.7	30.6	30.2	29.9	29.9	30.2	30.8	31.3	31.6	31.9	32.0	30.8
2014	31.4	31.5	31.5	31.6	31.4	31.1	31.3	31.5	31.1	31.7	31.7	31.5	31.4
2015	31.9	31.8	31.5	32.2	32.0	32.5	32.2	32.9	32.6	33.2	33.7	33.6	32.5
2016	33.5	33.4	32.9	33.4	33.0	32.7	33.6	33.7	33.8	33.5	33.5	33.9	33.4
2017	33.8	34.1	33.5	34.1	33.7	33.4	33.1	33.4	33.7	34.4	34.9	34.9	33.9
Education and Health Services													
2007	31.0	31.3	31.5	31.5	31.8	32.2	32.1	32.4	32.3	32.1	32.3	32.7	31.9
2008	32.3	32.7	32.9	32.6	32.9	32.9	32.7	33.0	33.1	33.2	33.5	33.7	33.0
2009	33.5	33.9	34.0	34.0	34.2	35.4	36.0	35.9	35.2	35.2	35.2	35.3	34.8
2010	35.2	35.2	35.7	35.9	36.1	37.7	35.8	36.0	36.2	36.3	36.4	36.7	36.1
2011	36.6	36.8	36.9	37.3	37.4	37.4	37.5	37.6	37.8	37.7	37.8	37.8	37.4
2012	37.5	38.3	38.6	38.4	38.5	38.5	38.3	38.7	38.8	39.3	39.4	39.4	38.6
2013	38.6	39.0	39.1	39.5	39.6	39.5	39.8	40.1	40.3	40.7	40.7	40.5	39.8
2014	40.3	40.9	40.9	40.9	41.1	41.0	41.0	41.2	41.1	41.5	41.8	42.0	41.1
2015	41.8	42.2	42.3	42.4	42.6	42.5	42.6	42.7	42.8	43.2	43.2	43.2	42.6
2016	43.0	43.2	43.1	43.4	43.6	43.3	43.7	44.0	44.0	44.1	44.1	44.1	43.6
2017	44.1	44.6	44.5	44.9	45.1	44.8	44.8	45.2	45.4	45.6	45.7	45.8	45.0
Leisure and Hospitality													
2007	25.6	25.8	26.5	26.6	27.1	27.4	27.1	26.9	26.8	26.6	26.4	26.5	26.6
2008	26.8	26.8	27.2	27.9	28.2	28.0	27.8	27.7	27.3	27.3	27.2	27.1	27.4
2009	26.4	26.7	27.1	27.1	28.0	27.9	27.4	27.5	27.2	26.3	26.6	26.9	27.1
2010	26.3	26.8	27.6	28.1	28.8	28.8	28.0	28.1	28.0	27.6	27.7	27.8	27.8
2011	28.0	28.3	29.1	29.1	29.6	29.9	29.9	29.8	29.5	28.9	29.0	29.1	29.2
2012	28.6	29.4	29.8	30.4	30.8	30.8	30.7	30.8	30.7	29.9	30.0	30.2	30.2
2013	29.5	29.9	30.5	30.9	31.7	31.8	31.4	31.5	31.0	30.8	30.9	31.0	30.9
2014	30.8	31.3	32.1	32.5	33.0	33.2	32.9	33.3	33.0	32.2	32.2	32.3	32.4
2015	31.5	32.2	32.7	33.3	34.1	34.4	33.9	34.2	33.8	33.4	33.5	33.3	33.4
2016	32.7	33.3	33.9	34.5	35.0	35.2	35.0	35.4	34.8	34.1	34.0	34.0	34.3
2017	33.8	34.3	34.7	35.1	35.6	35.5	35.3	35.3	34.9	34.7	34.7	34.7	34.9

Employment by Industry: El Paso, TX, Selected Years, 2007–2017—*Continued*

(Numbers in thousands, not seasonally adjusted)

Industry and year	January	February	March	April	May	June	July	August	September	October	November	December	Annual average
Other Services													
2007	7.3	7.4	7.5	7.5	7.7	8.1	8.2	8.3	8.2	8.1	8.3	8.3	7.9
2008	8.5	8.8	8.8	9.2	9.4	9.7	9.6	9.6	9.3	9.2	9.3	9.2	9.2
2009	9.0	9.2	9.2	9.0	9.1	9.4	9.4	9.3	9.0	9.1	9.2	9.0	9.2
2010	8.9	9.2	9.1	8.9	9.0	9.3	9.2	9.3	9.0	9.1	9.1	9.1	9.1
2011	9.1	9.3	9.3	9.2	9.2	9.6	9.6	9.7	9.5	9.4	9.4	9.4	9.4
2012	9.3	9.5	9.5	9.4	9.5	9.9	9.9	9.9	9.6	9.5	9.5	9.4	9.6
2013	9.2	9.4	9.3	9.2	9.4	9.8	9.8	9.8	9.6	9.3	9.5	9.3	9.5
2014	9.3	9.4	9.4	9.2	9.3	9.6	9.7	9.6	9.4	9.3	9.4	9.3	9.4
2015	9.3	9.5	9.5	9.3	9.3	9.7	9.7	9.6	9.4	9.4	9.4	9.4	9.5
2016	9.4	9.6	9.6	9.4	9.5	9.7	9.5	9.4	9.3	9.2	9.2	9.1	9.4
2017	9.1	9.1	9.2	9.2	9.3	9.4	9.3	9.3	9.1	9.1	9.1	9.1	9.2
Government													
2007	64.1	64.7	65.0	65.7	65.9	62.2	60.2	60.2	65.9	67.4	67.7	67.7	64.7
2008	67.0	68.5	68.7	66.1	66.9	63.6	60.1	60.1	65.4	67.9	68.0	68.1	65.9
2009	68.1	68.6	68.7	69.8	69.4	67.0	62.9	62.9	68.4	70.9	71.1	71.0	68.2
2010	70.6	71.4	71.7	71.7	72.4	69.2	65.0	65.4	70.5	70.9	71.2	71.3	70.1
2011	70.5	70.6	70.8	70.9	70.6	68.9	66.1	66.3	70.8	70.3	70.8	70.5	69.8
2012	70.6	70.7	70.8	70.6	70.8	67.1	66.0	66.2	69.5	70.9	71.4	71.2	69.7
2013	70.8	71.3	71.5	71.0	70.8	67.0	65.9	66.6	69.9	70.2	70.7	70.5	69.7
2014	69.4	69.9	69.9	70.4	70.5	67.6	65.5	65.9	69.0	70.3	70.8	70.7	69.2
2015	70.4	70.8	70.9	70.4	70.5	67.8	65.8	66.4	69.6	70.6	71.1	71.0	69.6
2016	70.7	71.1	71.3	71.7	71.9	69.1	67.0	67.6	71.6	72.4	72.5	72.3	70.8
2017	71.7	72.6	72.5	72.6	72.7	69.8	67.5	68.1	71.8	72.8	72.9	72.8	71.5

Employment by Industry: Allentown-Bethlehem-Easton, PA-NJ, Selected Years, 2007–2017

(Numbers in thousands, not seasonally adjusted)

Industry and year	January	February	March	April	May	June	July	August	September	October	November	December	Annual average
Total Nonfarm													
2007	336.7	337.0	341.8	343.3	348.0	350.2	342.5	342.4	346.5	350.0	349.5	349.4	344.8
2008	338.6	339.3	342.5	344.8	348.7	349.7	342.6	342.4	344.8	346.7	343.7	343.6	344.0
2009	331.0	331.0	332.5	333.4	337.9	337.4	330.3	330.1	332.9	335.5	335.8	335.2	333.6
2010	324.7	325.9	329.9	334.2	338.4	338.6	330.4	330.8	335.2	337.9	339.1	341.2	333.9
2011	328.9	331.1	334.9	340.0	343.7	345.1	338.0	338.2	343.0	344.4	345.3	346.7	339.9
2012	337.1	339.9	343.1	346.3	349.0	349.2	340.7	341.0	346.6	347.9	349.3	349.1	344.9
2013	340.5	341.4	344.1	347.9	351.3	352.4	345.0	345.8	350.4	351.8	354.1	352.8	348.1
2014	343.6	342.9	346.3	352.0	356.8	357.3	349.1	350.1	355.2	358.7	360.4	361.1	352.8
2015	349.2	349.0	351.1	355.9	361.1	360.9	355.9	356.1	360.8	365.5	367.6	368.0	358.4
2016	356.6	357.4	360.9	364.3	367.5	367.1	363.8	363.0	368.7	371.7	373.2	373.0	365.6
2017	363.0	363.7	365.3	368.7	372.6	372.7	366.7	366.5	372.4	374.5	375.0	373.0	369.5
Total Private													
2007	295.2	294.3	298.9	300.3	304.3	307.0	305.2	305.3	304.4	306.8	305.8	305.6	302.8
2008	296.6	296.0	299.0	301.3	304.9	305.6	304.2	304.0	302.2	302.7	299.3	299.3	301.3
2009	288.8	287.1	288.2	288.7	293.0	293.3	291.7	291.5	290.3	291.4	291.2	290.7	290.5
2010	282.0	281.9	285.6	289.5	292.6	293.7	292.3	293.4	293.5	295.5	296.2	298.5	291.2
2011	287.7	288.6	292.1	297.1	300.7	302.2	301.1	302.0	302.5	302.7	303.1	304.5	298.7
2012	296.1	298.1	301.3	304.2	306.4	308.0	305.3	305.9	306.5	306.5	307.8	307.3	304.5
2013	299.7	300.1	302.5	306.4	309.4	311.5	309.7	310.3	310.4	311.0	312.6	311.8	308.0
2014	303.3	302.2	305.4	310.9	315.4	316.6	314.3	314.9	315.5	318.1	319.4	320.0	313.0
2015	309.9	308.9	311.0	315.6	320.5	321.5	320.8	320.9	321.3	325.4	327.1	327.6	319.2
2016	317.4	317.3	320.5	323.8	326.8	327.5	328.2	328.1	329.2	331.5	332.6	332.3	326.3
2017	323.8	324.0	325.1	328.3	331.9	333.2	331.5	331.6	332.5	333.8	334.2	332.2	330.2
Goods Producing													
2007	55.5	54.9	55.7	56.2	57.0	57.8	57.4	57.5	57.3	57.0	56.6	55.7	56.6
2008	54.4	54.1	54.8	55.4	56.2	56.8	56.1	56.2	55.9	55.4	54.1	53.0	55.2
2009	50.9	49.8	49.6	49.6	49.7	49.7	49.6	49.2	48.7	48.2	48.1	47.4	49.2
2010	45.7	45.0	45.7	46.7	47.4	48.2	48.2	48.2	48.1	48.0	47.8	47.3	47.2
2011	45.7	45.3	46.3	47.1	47.8	48.7	48.5	48.9	48.5	47.9	47.5	47.0	47.4
2012	45.8	45.8	46.5	47.0	47.2	48.0	48.0	47.8	47.7	47.5	47.3	46.9	47.1
2013	45.8	45.5	46.0	46.8	47.5	48.0	48.1	48.2	48.1	48.3	48.1	47.6	47.3
2014	46.3	45.8	46.6	48.1	49.0	49.7	49.6	49.6	49.2	49.2	49.1	48.7	48.4
2015	47.3	46.8	47.4	48.5	49.5	49.9	50.0	50.0	49.6	50.3	50.0	49.4	49.1
2016	48.3	47.9	48.4	49.4	50.0	50.4	50.9	50.9	49.8	49.9	49.7	49.3	49.6
2017	48.1	48.3	48.9	49.7	50.4	51.1	51.1	51.1	50.7	50.3	50.2	50.1	50.0
Service-Providing													
2007	281.2	282.1	286.1	287.1	291.0	292.4	285.1	284.9	289.2	293.0	292.9	293.7	288.2
2008	284.2	285.2	287.7	289.4	292.5	292.9	286.5	286.2	288.9	291.3	289.6	290.6	288.8
2009	280.1	281.2	282.9	283.8	288.2	287.7	280.7	280.9	284.2	287.3	287.7	287.8	284.4
2010	279.0	280.9	284.2	287.5	291.0	290.4	282.2	282.6	287.1	289.9	291.3	293.9	286.7
2011	283.2	285.8	288.6	292.9	295.9	296.4	289.5	289.3	294.5	296.5	297.8	299.7	292.5
2012	291.3	294.1	296.6	299.3	301.8	301.2	292.7	293.2	298.9	300.4	302.0	302.2	297.8
2013	294.7	295.9	298.1	301.1	303.8	304.4	296.9	297.6	302.3	303.5	306.0	305.2	300.8
2014	297.3	297.1	299.7	303.9	307.8	307.6	299.5	300.5	306.0	309.5	311.3	312.4	304.4
2015	301.9	302.2	303.7	307.4	311.6	311.0	305.9	306.1	311.2	315.2	317.6	318.6	309.4
2016	308.3	309.5	312.5	314.9	317.5	316.7	312.9	312.1	318.9	321.8	323.5	323.7	316.0
2017	314.9	315.4	316.4	319.0	322.2	321.6	315.6	315.4	321.7	324.2	324.8	322.9	319.5
Mining, Logging, and Construction													
2007	15.6	14.9	15.4	16.2	17.0	17.5	17.7	17.8	17.4	17.0	16.6	15.8	16.6
2008	14.9	14.6	15.0	15.6	16.4	16.9	16.8	16.5	16.2	15.9	15.1	14.3	15.7
2009	13.0	12.6	12.8	13.3	13.6	13.6	13.6	13.4	13.1	13.0	12.7	12.1	13.1
2010	10.8	10.5	11.0	12.0	12.5	12.9	13.0	13.1	13.1	13.0	12.7	12.1	12.2
2011	10.9	10.7	11.4	12.2	12.8	13.1	13.2	13.2	13.2	13.0	12.8	12.2	12.4
2012	11.3	11.3	11.7	12.2	12.4	12.8	12.7	12.6	12.6	12.6	12.4	11.9	12.2
2013	11.1	10.9	11.4	12.1	12.7	12.9	13.0	13.1	13.3	13.4	13.1	12.5	12.5
2014	11.6	11.3	11.7	13.0	13.6	13.8	13.7	13.9	13.7	13.6	13.3	12.7	13.0
2015	11.6	11.1	11.5	12.6	13.3	13.4	13.5	13.6	13.5	14.0	13.6	13.0	12.9
2016	12.2	11.8	12.3	13.2	13.5	13.7	14.0	14.1	13.8	13.6	13.3	12.9	13.2
2017	12.0	12.1	12.5	13.1	13.7	14.0	14.1	14.2	14.0	13.9	13.7	13.4	13.4

Employment by Industry: Allentown-Bethlehem-Easton, PA-NJ, Selected Years, 2007–2017—*Continued*

(Numbers in thousands, not seasonally adjusted)

Industry and year	January	February	March	April	May	June	July	August	September	October	November	December	Annual average
Manufacturing													
2007	39.9	40.0	40.3	40.0	40.0	40.3	39.7	39.7	39.9	40.0	40.0	39.9	40.0
2008	39.5	39.5	39.8	39.8	39.8	39.9	39.3	39.7	39.7	39.5	39.0	38.7	39.5
2009	37.9	37.2	36.8	36.3	36.1	36.1	36.0	35.8	35.6	35.2	35.4	35.3	36.1
2010	34.9	34.5	34.7	34.7	34.9	35.3	35.2	35.1	35.0	35.0	35.1	35.2	35.0
2011	34.8	34.6	34.9	34.9	35.0	35.6	35.3	35.7	35.3	34.9	34.7	34.8	35.0
2012	34.5	34.5	34.8	34.8	34.8	35.2	35.3	35.2	35.1	34.9	34.9	35.0	34.9
2013	34.7	34.6	34.6	34.7	34.8	35.1	35.1	35.1	34.8	34.9	35.0	35.1	34.9
2014	34.7	34.5	34.9	35.1	35.4	35.9	35.9	35.7	35.5	35.6	35.8	36.0	35.4
2015	35.7	35.7	35.9	35.9	36.2	36.5	36.5	36.4	36.1	36.3	36.4	36.4	36.2
2016	36.1	36.1	36.1	36.2	36.5	36.7	36.9	36.8	36.0	36.3	36.4	36.4	36.4
2017	36.1	36.2	36.4	36.6	36.7	37.1	37.0	36.9	36.7	36.4	36.5	36.7	36.6
Trade, Transportation, and Utilities													
2007	70.3	68.9	69.3	69.3	70.2	70.7	70.2	70.1	69.9	71.0	72.8	73.5	70.5
2008	70.9	69.3	69.5	69.4	70.1	70.4	69.6	69.5	69.5	70.0	70.7	71.2	70.0
2009	67.9	66.8	66.5	65.9	67.0	67.3	66.6	66.4	66.4	67.3	68.2	68.7	67.1
2010	66.1	64.9	65.6	65.9	66.4	67.0	67.1	67.5	67.7	68.7	69.9	71.0	67.3
2011	68.1	67.3	67.7	68.1	68.9	69.8	69.8	70.1	70.5	71.6	73.1	74.4	70.0
2012	71.9	71.3	71.9	72.0	72.2	72.6	72.0	72.1	72.2	72.9	74.6	75.3	72.6
2013	72.5	71.6	71.7	71.9	72.5	72.8	71.8	72.3	72.3	72.9	74.4	75.3	72.7
2014	72.8	71.7	72.5	73.1	73.8	74.4	74.2	74.5	74.8	75.5	77.3	78.6	74.4
2015	75.7	74.6	75.2	75.3	76.7	77.4	77.5	77.7	77.5	78.5	80.3	81.2	77.3
2016	78.3	77.6	78.2	78.8	79.7	80.2	80.3	80.8	81.6	83.0	85.4	86.2	80.8
2017	83.3	81.9	81.6	82.2	82.8	83.3	82.7	83.1	83.8	84.6	86.3	86.6	83.5
Wholesale Trade													
2007	13.4	13.4	13.5	13.6	13.8	14.0	14.1	14.0	13.9	14.1	14.1	14.1	13.8
2008	13.8	13.8	13.8	14.0	14.1	14.2	14.3	14.2	14.0	14.0	13.9	13.8	14.0
2009	13.4	13.3	13.3	13.4	13.4	13.5	13.4	13.3	13.3	13.5	13.4	13.4	13.4
2010	13.0	12.9	13.0	13.3	13.3	13.5	13.5	13.5	13.5	13.6	13.6	13.6	13.4
2011	13.2	13.2	13.4	13.4	13.5	13.6	13.8	13.8	13.7	13.9	13.8	13.8	13.6
2012	13.7	13.7	13.8	13.9	13.8	14.0	13.8	13.7	13.7	13.6	13.5	13.5	13.7
2013	13.2	13.2	13.2	13.2	13.3	13.4	13.3	13.3	13.3	13.2	13.2	13.2	13.3
2014	13.2	13.2	13.4	13.5	13.6	13.7	13.8	13.8	13.7	13.8	13.7	13.7	13.6
2015	13.5	13.5	13.5	13.4	13.6	13.6	13.9	13.8	13.6	13.8	13.7	13.7	13.6
2016	13.5	13.5	13.6	13.8	13.9	14.0	14.0	14.0	14.0	14.2	14.2	14.4	13.9
2017	14.0	14.1	14.2	14.3	14.3	14.5	14.7	14.8	14.7	14.7	14.8	14.8	14.5
Retail Trade													
2007	41.5	40.2	40.4	40.2	40.8	41.2	41.1	41.1	40.5	41.2	42.9	43.6	41.2
2008	41.8	40.4	40.5	40.3	40.8	41.0	40.5	40.4	40.1	40.5	41.3	42.0	40.8
2009	39.5	38.8	38.6	38.2	38.9	39.3	39.1	39.1	38.5	38.9	40.0	40.5	39.1
2010	38.9	37.9	38.3	38.3	38.7	39.1	39.0	39.0	38.6	39.3	40.4	41.4	39.1
2011	39.3	38.5	38.7	38.9	39.3	39.7	39.4	39.6	39.0	39.5	40.8	41.9	39.6
2012	39.9	39.1	39.3	39.4	39.7	39.9	39.8	40.0	39.3	40.0	41.6	42.0	40.0
2013	40.1	39.3	39.3	39.4	39.8	40.1	39.7	39.9	39.5	40.0	41.2	42.0	40.0
2014	39.9	38.9	39.3	39.8	40.3	40.6	40.4	40.4	40.0	40.3	41.8	42.6	40.4
2015	40.4	39.3	39.5	39.7	40.5	41.0	40.8	40.9	40.3	40.8	42.3	42.5	40.7
2016	40.6	39.9	40.0	40.3	40.7	41.0	40.9	41.1	40.6	41.1	42.3	42.8	40.9
2017	41.1	40.2	40.1	40.4	40.6	40.9	40.4	40.4	40.0	39.9	40.5	40.4	40.4
Transportation and Utilities													
2007	15.4	15.3	15.4	15.5	15.6	15.5	15.0	15.0	15.5	15.7	15.8	15.8	15.5
2008	15.3	15.1	15.2	15.1	15.2	15.2	14.8	14.9	15.4	15.5	15.5	15.4	15.2
2009	15.0	14.7	14.6	14.3	14.7	14.5	14.1	14.0	14.6	14.9	14.8	14.8	14.6
2010	14.2	14.1	14.3	14.3	14.4	14.4	14.6	15.0	15.6	15.8	15.9	16.0	14.9
2011	15.6	15.6	15.6	15.8	16.1	16.5	16.6	16.7	17.8	18.2	18.5	18.7	16.8
2012	18.3	18.5	18.8	18.7	18.7	18.7	18.4	18.4	19.2	19.3	19.5	19.8	18.9
2013	19.2	19.1	19.2	19.3	19.4	19.3	18.8	19.1	19.5	19.7	20.0	20.1	19.4
2014	19.7	19.6	19.8	19.8	19.9	20.1	20.0	20.3	21.1	21.4	21.8	22.3	20.5
2015	21.8	21.8	22.2	22.2	22.6	22.8	22.8	23.0	23.6	23.9	24.3	25.0	23.0
2016	24.2	24.2	24.6	24.7	25.1	25.2	25.4	25.7	27.0	27.7	28.9	29.0	26.0
2017	28.2	27.6	27.3	27.5	27.9	27.9	27.6	27.9	29.1	30.0	31.0	31.4	28.6

Employment by Industry: Allentown-Bethlehem-Easton, PA-NJ, Selected Years, 2007–2017—*Continued*

(Numbers in thousands, not seasonally adjusted)

Industry and year	January	February	March	April	May	June	July	August	September	October	November	December	Annual average
Information													
2007	7.4	7.3	7.3	7.3	7.4	7.5	7.5	7.5	7.4	7.4	7.4	7.5	7.4
2008	7.4	7.4	7.4	7.5	7.6	7.5	7.5	7.4	7.3	7.3	7.1	7.2	7.4
2009	7.1	7.0	6.9	6.7	6.7	6.6	6.5	6.3	6.2	6.1	5.9	5.9	6.5
2010	5.6	5.5	5.5	5.6	5.6	5.7	5.7	5.7	5.7	5.6	5.6	5.6	5.6
2011	5.5	5.6	5.6	5.7	5.8	5.8	5.9	5.7	5.8	5.8	5.9	5.8	5.7
2012	5.7	5.8	5.9	6.0	6.0	6.1	6.0	6.1	6.1	6.0	6.1	6.1	6.0
2013	6.1	6.1	6.2	6.1	6.2	6.2	6.2	6.2	6.1	6.1	6.1	6.1	6.1
2014	6.1	6.1	6.2	6.2	6.3	6.3	6.3	6.3	6.2	6.1	6.0	6.1	6.2
2015	6.0	6.1	6.1	6.1	6.2	6.2	6.2	6.2	6.1	6.0	6.0	6.0	6.1
2016	5.9	5.9	6.0	6.1	5.9	6.1	6.1	6.0	6.0	5.8	5.7	5.6	5.9
2017	5.6	5.7	5.6	5.6	5.6	5.7	5.6	5.7	5.5	5.4	5.4	5.4	5.6
Financial Activities													
2007	16.3	16.4	16.4	16.2	16.2	16.3	16.2	16.2	16.0	16.0	15.9	15.8	16.2
2008	15.7	15.8	15.8	15.9	15.9	15.9	16.0	15.9	15.7	15.6	15.7	15.7	15.8
2009	15.5	15.6	15.5	15.6	15.7	15.8	15.8	15.7	15.6	15.6	15.6	15.6	15.6
2010	15.6	15.6	15.5	15.4	15.4	15.4	15.4	15.4	15.2	15.3	15.3	15.4	15.4
2011	15.2	15.2	15.2	15.2	15.2	15.3	15.1	15.0	15.0	15.0	15.0	15.1	15.1
2012	15.2	15.2	15.2	15.1	15.1	15.1	15.1	15.1	14.9	14.8	14.8	14.9	15.0
2013	14.9	15.0	15.0	15.1	15.1	15.2	15.2	15.1	14.9	14.8	14.8	14.8	15.0
2014	14.5	14.6	14.6	14.7	14.9	15.1	15.2	15.1	14.9	14.9	14.9	15.0	14.9
2015	15.0	14.9	15.0	14.9	15.0	15.1	15.1	15.1	14.9	14.8	14.8	14.7	14.9
2016	14.6	14.5	14.6	14.5	14.6	14.8	14.7	14.7	14.6	14.3	14.3	14.3	14.5
2017	14.1	14.2	14.3	14.2	14.2	14.5	14.5	14.5	14.3	14.3	14.4	14.4	14.3
Professional and Business Services													
2007	42.7	42.6	43.1	43.6	43.7	44.3	44.0	43.6	43.8	44.6	44.2	44.0	43.7
2008	42.2	41.5	41.9	42.6	42.7	42.7	43.2	43.2	42.7	42.9	42.4	42.7	42.6
2009	40.5	39.9	40.0	40.1	40.3	41.0	40.4	41.2	41.2	41.6	42.3	42.5	40.9
2010	41.1	40.9	41.7	42.7	42.8	43.0	42.4	42.6	42.9	44.2	45.5	47.0	43.1
2011	43.8	44.0	44.8	46.1	46.4	46.0	45.8	46.5	46.8	46.2	46.5	47.6	45.9
2012	45.3	45.2	45.4	46.1	46.1	46.4	45.8	46.0	46.5	46.7	47.1	47.5	46.2
2013	46.1	45.4	45.8	46.6	46.5	47.3	47.8	48.5	47.9	48.7	50.0	50.0	47.6
2014	48.1	47.2	47.1	48.3	48.7	49.0	48.2	48.8	49.0	49.6	51.0	51.1	48.8
2015	48.6	47.8	47.5	47.8	48.0	48.1	47.9	48.5	48.6	50.6	52.3	52.7	49.0
2016	48.8	47.9	47.8	49.2	49.2	49.6	49.8	49.9	50.6	51.7	51.8	51.8	49.8
2017	49.4	48.8	48.3	49.3	49.9	50.3	49.4	49.5	49.6	49.7	49.5	48.6	49.4
Education and Health Services													
2007	60.6	61.6	63.3	63.2	63.0	61.3	61.2	62.0	63.5	65.0	64.7	64.5	62.8
2008	62.6	64.3	65.3	65.3	64.0	62.9	62.9	63.4	64.6	65.8	66.1	65.9	64.4
2009	64.6	65.6	66.6	66.4	65.6	64.0	64.0	64.3	65.8	67.3	67.6	67.2	65.8
2010	65.0	67.5	68.2	67.8	67.8	65.9	65.4	66.0	67.3	68.2	68.4	68.2	67.1
2011	66.6	68.0	68.6	68.5	68.6	67.1	66.6	66.4	68.4	69.7	70.1	69.4	68.2
2012	67.9	70.2	71.1	71.1	70.6	69.1	68.2	68.0	70.7	71.5	71.6	71.0	70.1
2013	69.0	71.3	71.8	72.0	71.6	70.0	69.4	69.2	71.9	72.3	73.1	71.7	71.1
2014	69.9	71.6	72.2	72.8	72.5	70.6	69.8	69.4	72.3	73.9	74.2	73.7	71.9
2015	71.3	72.9	73.3	74.4	73.8	72.2	71.7	71.1	73.5	74.9	75.1	74.7	73.2
2016	72.6	74.4	75.3	75.5	74.8	72.5	72.3	71.6	74.3	75.3	75.6	74.8	74.1
2017	73.4	75.3	75.9	76.2	75.8	73.3	73.4	73.0	76.1	77.7	78.3	77.2	75.5
Leisure and Hospitality													
2007	27.6	27.8	28.7	29.4	31.5	33.7	33.2	33.0	31.3	30.8	29.2	29.4	30.5
2008	28.5	28.6	29.3	30.1	33.2	33.9	33.5	33.2	31.5	30.8	28.4	28.7	30.8
2009	27.8	27.8	28.5	29.7	33.2	34.0	34.0	33.7	32.1	31.0	29.2	29.1	30.8
2010	28.9	28.6	29.3	31.2	33.0	34.1	33.8	33.7	32.6	31.5	29.7	29.9	31.4
2011	29.0	29.4	30.0	32.3	33.8	35.0	34.9	35.1	33.5	32.5	30.9	31.0	32.3
2012	30.2	30.5	31.1	32.8	34.9	36.3	36.0	36.6	34.5	33.2	32.5	31.7	33.4
2013	31.7	31.6	32.3	34.1	36.1	37.9	37.2	36.9	35.6	34.3	32.5	32.7	34.4
2014	32.2	31.9	32.7	34.1	36.5	37.6	37.2	37.4	35.7	35.4	33.3	33.1	34.8
2015	32.5	32.4	33.0	34.8	37.3	38.6	38.4	38.4	37.4	36.5	34.8	34.9	35.8
2016	35.0	35.2	36.3	36.2	38.3	39.5	39.7	39.8	38.2	37.4	35.9	35.9	37.3
2017	35.7	35.5	36.2	36.7	38.5	40.1	40.0	40.1	38.2	37.4	35.7	35.4	37.5

Employment by Industry: Allentown-Bethlehem-Easton, PA-NJ, Selected Years, 2007–2017—*Continued*

(Numbers in thousands, not seasonally adjusted)

Industry and year	January	February	March	April	May	June	July	August	September	October	November	December	Annual average
Other Services													
2007	14.8	14.8	15.1	15.1	15.3	15.4	15.5	15.4	15.2	15.0	15.0	15.2	15.2
2008	14.9	15.0	15.0	15.1	15.2	15.5	15.4	15.2	15.0	14.9	14.8	14.9	15.1
2009	14.5	14.6	14.6	14.7	14.8	14.9	14.8	14.7	14.3	14.3	14.3	14.3	14.6
2010	14.0	13.9	14.1	14.2	14.2	14.4	14.3	14.3	14.0	14.0	14.0	14.1	14.1
2011	13.8	13.8	13.9	14.1	14.2	14.5	14.5	14.3	14.0	14.0	14.1	14.2	14.1
2012	14.1	14.1	14.2	14.1	14.3	14.4	14.2	14.2	13.9	13.9	13.8	13.9	14.1
2013	13.6	13.6	13.7	13.8	13.9	14.1	14.0	13.9	13.6	13.6	13.6	13.6	13.8
2014	13.4	13.3	13.5	13.6	13.7	13.9	13.8	13.8	13.4	13.5	13.6	13.7	13.6
2015	13.5	13.4	13.5	13.8	14.0	14.0	14.0	13.9	13.7	13.8	13.8	14.0	13.8
2016	13.9	13.9	13.9	14.1	14.3	14.4	14.4	14.4	14.1	14.1	14.2	14.4	14.2
2017	14.2	14.3	14.3	14.4	14.7	14.9	14.8	14.6	14.3	14.4	14.4	14.5	14.5
Government													
2007	41.5	42.7	42.9	43.0	43.7	43.2	37.3	37.1	42.1	43.2	43.7	43.8	42.0
2008	42.0	43.3	43.5	43.5	43.8	44.1	38.4	38.4	42.6	44.0	44.4	44.3	42.7
2009	42.2	43.9	44.3	44.7	44.9	44.1	38.6	38.6	42.6	44.1	44.6	44.5	43.1
2010	42.7	44.0	44.3	44.7	45.8	44.9	38.1	37.4	41.7	42.4	42.9	42.7	42.6
2011	41.2	42.5	42.8	42.9	43.0	42.9	36.9	36.2	40.5	41.7	42.2	42.2	41.3
2012	41.0	41.8	41.8	42.1	42.6	41.2	35.4	35.1	40.1	41.4	41.5	41.8	40.5
2013	40.8	41.3	41.6	41.5	41.9	40.9	35.3	35.5	40.0	40.8	41.5	41.0	40.2
2014	40.3	40.7	40.9	41.1	41.4	40.7	34.8	35.2	39.7	40.6	41.0	41.1	39.8
2015	39.3	40.1	40.1	40.3	40.6	39.4	35.1	35.2	39.5	40.1	40.5	40.4	39.2
2016	39.2	40.1	40.4	40.5	40.7	39.6	35.6	34.9	39.5	40.2	40.6	40.7	39.3
2017	39.2	39.7	40.2	40.4	40.7	39.5	35.2	34.9	39.9	40.7	40.8	40.8	39.3

Employment by Industry: Baton Rouge, LA, Selected Years, 2007–2017

(Numbers in thousands, not seasonally adjusted)

Industry and year	January	February	March	April	May	June	July	August	September	October	November	December	Annual average
Total Nonfarm													
2007	361.3	366.7	370.7	371.9	372.8	373.6	372.0	375.3	379.6	380.2	382.2	383.6	374.2
2008	371.1	376.1	377.5	375.6	375.5	376.1	371.3	374.1	371.1	378.9	381.9	382.5	376.0
2009	370.2	373.8	375.1	374.9	374.4	371.1	369.2	370.0	373.3	371.0	372.3	370.2	372.1
2010	359.9	362.0	364.9	364.9	366.1	365.6	361.3	364.1	365.4	368.3	368.9	368.5	365.0
2011	364.6	368.5	370.4	372.0	371.4	368.0	365.8	366.4	371.9	374.5	374.5	373.8	370.2
2012	369.0	373.9	376.1	376.8	376.7	374.5	368.2	374.2	377.6	380.1	382.2	380.7	375.8
2013	375.0	381.1	383.8	385.6	386.6	384.7	381.7	386.3	389.3	392.4	393.3	389.4	385.8
2014	383.7	388.6	391.7	393.2	396.5	393.9	392.4	397.1	401.2	405.7	403.8	402.3	395.8
2015	397.7	401.0	401.7	402.2	405.5	403.4	402.9	405.6	407.1	411.5	411.5	408.6	404.9
2016	400.1	403.8	406.2	407.2	407.3	404.7	402.8	399.5	404.4	408.2	407.4	404.2	404.7
2017	401.8	408.1	408.1	407.5	408.3	405.6	402.0	405.5	406.2	407.2	410.1	408.3	406.6
Total Private													
2007	288.8	291.5	294.8	295.1	296.8	298.0	298.8	299.4	300.4	301.8	303.2	305.2	297.8
2008	295.6	297.6	299.3	297.5	298.3	299.5	296.4	298.8	295.1	299.7	302.2	303.7	298.6
2009	293.9	294.7	295.9	296.0	296.6	294.3	294.4	295.4	294.5	291.9	293.0	291.8	294.4
2010	283.6	284.2	286.8	287.1	288.0	289.2	288.3	288.6	287.8	290.2	290.7	291.1	288.0
2011	289.7	291.5	293.7	295.0	294.6	292.9	292.8	293.9	295.1	296.9	296.7	296.6	294.1
2012	294.1	297.9	300.5	301.5	301.8	301.3	298.1	301.7	303.0	305.7	307.6	306.7	301.7
2013	303.1	307.5	310.2	312.1	313.4	312.9	313.0	315.1	315.4	318.8	319.2	316.3	313.1
2014	312.4	315.8	318.8	320.7	324.3	322.9	323.7	326.2	327.9	332.5	330.1	329.3	323.7
2015	326.5	328.2	328.8	329.5	333.1	332.2	333.9	334.3	333.5	337.5	337.0	334.6	332.4
2016	327.8	329.7	331.9	333.2	333.3	332.1	332.5	327.1	329.7	334.1	332.7	329.6	331.1
2017	328.6	333.1	332.7	332.6	333.5	332.3	331.4	332.7	331.1	332.3	334.4	332.9	332.3
Goods Producing													
2007	65.5	66.7	67.5	68.3	69.2	69.2	69.2	68.6	68.8	70.6	70.7	71.3	68.8
2008	66.2	67.0	67.5	67.3	67.7	68.2	67.1	68.3	67.8	69.0	69.5	69.9	68.0
2009	67.5	68.0	68.4	68.2	68.6	67.4	68.4	68.6	68.3	66.1	65.7	64.0	67.4
2010	63.5	63.4	63.5	62.8	62.6	63.8	64.5	64.7	64.6	64.8	64.0	64.0	63.9
2011	64.5	65.7	66.5	66.4	65.6	64.8	64.8	64.6	65.6	66.5	65.1	64.4	65.4
2012	65.1	67.1	67.8	67.5	67.4	67.1	66.4	67.8	68.8	70.1	70.4	69.3	67.9
2013	68.9	71.3	72.4	72.2	72.7	72.9	72.6	73.2	74.0	76.8	75.7	73.7	73.0
2014	73.7	75.9	77.0	76.3	77.6	77.2	78.8	80.2	82.2	84.1	80.2	78.5	78.5
2015	77.5	78.4	79.0	78.1	78.9	80.1	81.7	82.0	82.3	85.3	83.4	81.3	80.7
2016	79.3	80.3	80.8	79.7	79.9	81.6	82.3	79.6	81.0	84.6	81.9	79.7	80.9
2017	81.5	83.9	82.9	81.9	82.4	81.2	81.6	81.4	80.1	79.9	79.2	78.1	81.2
Service-Providing													
2007	295.8	300.0	303.2	303.6	303.6	304.4	302.8	306.7	310.8	309.6	311.5	312.3	305.4
2008	304.9	309.1	310.0	308.3	307.8	307.9	304.2	305.8	303.3	309.9	312.4	312.6	308.0
2009	302.7	305.8	306.7	306.7	305.8	303.7	300.8	301.4	305.0	304.9	306.6	306.2	304.7
2010	296.4	298.6	301.4	302.1	303.5	301.8	296.8	299.4	300.8	303.5	304.9	304.5	301.1
2011	300.1	302.8	303.9	305.6	305.8	303.2	301.0	301.8	306.3	308.0	309.4	309.4	304.8
2012	303.9	306.8	308.3	309.3	309.3	307.4	301.8	306.4	308.8	310.0	311.8	311.4	307.9
2013	306.1	309.8	311.4	313.4	313.9	311.8	309.1	313.1	315.3	315.6	317.6	315.7	312.7
2014	310.0	312.7	314.7	316.9	318.9	316.7	313.6	316.9	319.0	321.6	323.6	323.8	317.4
2015	320.2	322.6	322.7	324.1	326.6	323.3	321.2	323.6	324.8	326.2	328.1	327.3	324.2
2016	320.8	323.5	325.4	327.5	327.4	323.1	320.5	319.9	323.4	323.6	325.5	324.5	323.8
2017	320.3	324.2	325.2	325.6	325.9	324.4	320.4	324.1	326.1	327.3	330.9	330.2	325.4
Mining, Logging, and Construction													
2007	39.7	40.8	41.5	42.2	42.9	42.5	42.4	42.5	42.7	44.0	43.9	44.4	42.5
2008	40.4	41.0	41.5	41.3	41.6	42.1	41.1	42.3	42.0	42.9	43.4	43.6	41.9
2009	41.9	42.4	42.9	42.6	43.0	42.0	43.4	43.7	43.6	41.5	41.2	39.5	42.3
2010	38.9	38.7	38.8	38.2	37.8	38.9	39.6	39.8	39.7	39.7	38.9	38.8	39.0
2011	39.3	40.5	41.3	41.2	40.2	39.4	38.9	38.4	39.2	40.0	38.7	37.9	39.6
2012	38.9	40.9	41.3	41.0	40.7	40.1	39.5	40.9	41.9	43.2	43.4	42.3	41.2
2013	42.1	44.5	45.5	45.3	45.6	45.5	45.1	45.4	46.0	48.7	47.6	45.6	45.6
2014	45.2	47.5	48.6	47.8	49.0	48.4	49.9	51.3	53.0	54.8	50.9	49.2	49.6
2015	48.7	49.4	50.0	49.0	49.7	50.7	52.1	52.3	52.7	55.4	53.7	51.7	51.3
2016	50.1	51.0	51.7	50.6	50.8	52.4	53.0	50.3	51.6	55.1	52.5	50.3	51.6
2017	52.3	54.6	53.6	52.7	53.2	51.9	52.4	52.2	51.1	50.8	50.1	49.0	52.0

Employment by Industry: Baton Rouge, LA, Selected Years, 2007–2017—*Continued*

(Numbers in thousands, not seasonally adjusted)

Industry and year	January	February	March	April	May	June	July	August	September	October	November	December	Annual average
Manufacturing													
2007	25.8	25.9	26.0	26.1	26.3	26.7	26.8	26.1	26.1	26.6	26.8	26.9	26.3
2008	25.8	26.0	26.0	26.0	26.1	26.1	26.0	26.0	25.8	26.1	26.1	26.3	26.0
2009	25.6	25.6	25.5	25.6	25.6	25.4	25.0	24.9	24.7	24.6	24.5	24.5	25.1
2010	24.6	24.7	24.7	24.6	24.8	24.9	24.9	24.9	24.9	25.1	25.1	25.2	24.9
2011	25.2	25.2	25.2	25.2	25.4	25.4	25.9	26.2	26.4	26.5	26.4	26.5	25.8
2012	26.2	26.2	26.5	26.5	26.7	27.0	26.9	26.9	26.9	26.9	27.0	27.0	26.7
2013	26.8	26.8	26.9	26.9	27.1	27.4	27.5	27.8	28.0	28.1	28.1	28.1	27.5
2014	28.5	28.4	28.4	28.5	28.6	28.8	28.9	28.9	29.2	29.3	29.3	29.3	28.8
2015	28.8	29.0	29.0	29.1	29.2	29.4	29.6	29.7	29.6	29.9	29.7	29.6	29.4
2016	29.2	29.3	29.1	29.1	29.1	29.2	29.3	29.3	29.4	29.5	29.4	29.4	29.3
2017	29.2	29.3	29.3	29.2	29.2	29.3	29.2	29.2	29.0	29.1	29.1	29.1	29.2
Trade, Transportation, and Utilities													
2007	65.7	65.5	66.3	65.4	65.9	66.1	66.7	67.2	67.6	67.7	69.4	70.2	67.0
2008	67.7	67.1	67.7	66.7	66.8	66.9	66.8	67.3	66.4	66.8	67.9	68.8	67.2
2009	66.1	65.5	65.6	65.8	65.7	65.3	65.3	65.3	65.3	64.9	66.0	66.6	65.6
2010	64.0	63.9	64.5	64.9	65.0	64.9	64.4	64.5	64.3	65.2	66.5	67.2	64.9
2011	65.0	64.8	65.0	65.5	65.6	65.4	65.0	65.2	65.0	65.7	66.8	67.7	65.6
2012	65.8	65.8	66.4	66.5	66.7	66.4	66.0	66.3	65.8	66.8	68.7	69.1	66.7
2013	66.5	66.4	66.8	67.2	67.2	67.1	66.9	67.4	67.4	67.6	69.0	69.8	67.4
2014	67.7	67.2	67.7	67.7	67.8	67.8	67.7	67.9	67.8	68.5	70.3	71.3	68.3
2015	69.5	69.1	69.4	69.5	69.6	69.5	69.6	69.9	69.7	70.5	71.8	72.2	70.0
2016	70.3	69.9	70.3	70.2	70.2	69.4	69.8	69.4	69.5	70.3	72.0	72.6	70.3
2017	71.1	70.5	70.6	70.6	70.5	70.0	69.8	70.3	69.7	70.1	71.2	71.4	70.5
Wholesale Trade													
2007	13.2	13.2	13.3	13.2	13.3	13.5	13.7	13.8	13.8	13.8	13.9	14.0	13.6
2008	13.6	13.6	13.7	13.4	13.5	13.4	13.4	13.4	13.5	13.5	13.4	13.4	13.5
2009	13.2	13.2	13.1	13.3	13.2	13.1	12.7	12.6	12.7	12.6	12.7	12.7	12.9
2010	12.4	12.4	12.4	12.5	12.5	12.4	12.4	12.5	12.4	12.7	12.6	12.6	12.5
2011	12.7	12.7	12.7	12.8	12.9	12.9	12.9	12.9	12.9	13.0	13.0	13.0	12.9
2012	13.1	13.1	13.2	13.2	13.2	13.2	13.1	13.1	13.1	13.3	13.4	13.4	13.2
2013	13.6	13.7	13.8	13.9	13.8	13.7	13.6	13.6	13.6	13.6	13.6	13.5	13.7
2014	13.4	13.3	13.4	13.3	13.3	13.3	13.2	13.2	13.2	13.1	13.1	13.1	13.2
2015	13.2	13.2	13.3	13.2	13.2	13.2	13.2	13.2	13.1	13.3	13.3	13.3	13.2
2016	13.4	13.4	13.3	13.4	13.4	13.2	13.2	13.2	13.2	13.2	13.2	13.2	13.3
2017	13.1	13.1	13.1	13.1	13.1	13.2	13.1	13.3	13.2	13.3	13.3	13.3	13.2
Retail Trade													
2007	40.3	40.0	40.8	40.0	40.3	40.3	40.6	40.7	41.0	41.4	42.9	43.6	41.0
2008	41.5	40.9	41.4	40.8	40.7	41.0	40.9	41.1	40.2	40.9	42.1	42.9	41.2
2009	40.6	40.3	40.5	40.8	40.8	40.8	41.1	41.0	40.9	40.4	41.5	41.9	40.9
2010	40.0	39.9	40.4	40.5	40.6	40.6	40.2	40.1	40.0	40.5	41.9	42.3	40.6
2011	40.2	39.9	40.2	40.6	40.6	40.4	40.2	40.0	39.9	40.3	41.6	42.2	40.5
2012	40.5	40.5	40.9	41.0	41.0	41.0	40.9	40.8	40.5	41.3	43.0	43.2	41.2
2013	40.5	40.2	40.4	40.6	40.5	40.8	40.7	40.8	41.0	41.1	42.4	43.0	41.0
2014	40.9	40.6	40.8	40.9	40.9	41.2	41.2	41.0	41.0	41.7	43.5	44.1	41.5
2015	42.4	42.1	42.4	42.5	42.5	42.6	42.6	42.7	42.5	43.1	44.3	44.3	42.8
2016	42.8	42.7	43.1	42.9	42.8	42.9	43.0	42.5	42.5	43.5	45.0	45.7	43.3
2017	44.3	43.8	43.9	43.7	43.4	43.2	42.9	43.0	42.7	43.1	44.1	44.2	43.5
Transportation and Utilities													
2007	12.2	12.3	12.2	12.2	12.3	12.3	12.4	12.7	12.8	12.5	12.6	12.6	12.4
2008	12.6	12.6	12.6	12.5	12.6	12.5	12.5	12.8	12.7	12.4	12.4	12.5	12.6
2009	12.3	12.0	12.0	11.7	11.7	11.4	11.5	11.7	11.7	11.9	11.8	12.0	11.8
2010	11.6	11.6	11.7	11.9	11.9	11.9	11.8	11.9	11.9	12.0	12.0	12.3	11.9
2011	12.1	12.2	12.1	12.1	12.1	12.1	11.9	12.3	12.2	12.4	12.2	12.5	12.2
2012	12.2	12.2	12.3	12.3	12.5	12.2	12.0	12.4	12.2	12.2	12.3	12.5	12.3
2013	12.4	12.5	12.6	12.7	12.9	12.6	12.6	13.0	12.8	12.9	13.0	13.3	12.8
2014	13.4	13.3	13.5	13.5	13.6	13.3	13.3	13.7	13.6	13.7	13.7	14.1	13.6
2015	13.9	13.8	13.7	13.8	13.9	13.7	13.8	14.0	14.1	14.1	14.2	14.6	14.0
2016	14.1	13.8	13.9	13.9	14.0	13.3	13.6	13.7	13.8	13.6	13.8	13.7	13.8
2017	13.7	13.6	13.6	13.8	14.0	13.6	13.8	14.0	13.8	13.7	13.8	13.9	13.8

Employment by Industry: Baton Rouge, LA, Selected Years, 2007–2017—*Continued*
(Numbers in thousands, not seasonally adjusted)

Industry and year	January	February	March	April	May	June	July	August	September	October	November	December	Annual average
Information													
2007	5.5	5.5	5.5	5.7	5.8	5.6	6.0	5.9	5.8	6.6	5.9	5.8	5.8
2008	5.6	6.0	5.8	6.4	6.2	6.4	5.8	5.8	5.6	5.6	6.0	6.0	5.9
2009	5.5	5.4	5.2	5.1	5.0	4.9	4.7	4.8	4.6	4.7	4.7	4.7	4.9
2010	4.6	4.6	4.6	4.8	4.8	4.8	4.7	4.6	4.4	4.7	4.7	5.0	4.7
2011	4.8	4.9	4.8	4.9	4.8	4.8	4.8	4.9	4.8	5.0	4.9	5.0	4.9
2012	4.8	5.0	4.9	5.4	4.8	5.0	4.9	4.7	5.3	4.7	4.9	5.2	5.0
2013	5.5	5.9	6.3	6.7	6.7	6.7	7.2	6.4	5.8	5.9	6.1	5.6	6.2
2014	5.3	5.6	6.1	6.9	8.3	8.0	7.6	6.5	6.0	6.6	6.6	6.5	6.7
2015	7.0	7.2	6.1	6.9	8.0	7.5	7.7	6.9	6.2	5.6	5.7	5.8	6.7
2016	5.7	6.3	6.3	5.8	5.9	6.2	6.0	5.3	5.2	5.2	5.6	5.4	5.7
2017	4.9	5.4	5.6	6.0	6.0	5.9	5.5	5.0	4.9	5.1	5.0	4.9	5.4
Financial Activities													
2007	19.1	19.2	18.9	18.9	18.8	18.8	18.7	18.7	18.4	18.3	18.4	18.5	18.7
2008	18.2	18.2	18.3	18.1	18.1	18.2	18.0	18.0	17.8	17.9	17.8	17.8	18.0
2009	17.4	17.3	17.3	17.5	17.6	17.5	17.3	17.3	17.1	17.1	17.3	17.4	17.3
2010	17.2	17.2	17.3	17.2	17.2	17.2	16.9	16.9	16.7	16.9	16.9	17.0	17.1
2011	17.0	17.0	17.0	16.9	16.9	16.8	16.9	16.8	16.8	16.9	16.9	17.0	16.9
2012	16.9	16.9	17.0	17.0	17.0	17.0	16.9	17.1	16.9	17.1	17.3	17.3	17.0
2013	17.0	17.1	17.1	17.1	17.3	17.6	17.6	17.8	17.9	18.3	18.3	18.1	17.6
2014	17.5	17.4	17.4	17.5	17.6	17.7	18.0	18.2	18.3	18.5	18.5	18.5	17.9
2015	18.2	18.3	18.2	18.3	18.4	18.4	18.4	18.5	18.3	18.5	18.5	18.7	18.4
2016	18.5	18.5	18.5	18.5	18.8	18.7	19.0	18.9	19.0	19.0	18.9	18.8	18.8
2017	18.8	18.8	18.7	18.9	18.9	18.9	18.8	18.8	18.7	19.3	19.3	19.4	18.9
Professional and Business Services													
2007	43.8	44.2	44.9	45.1	44.4	45.0	45.4	45.8	46.3	46.7	47.0	47.3	45.5
2008	47.0	46.7	46.7	45.9	45.8	45.8	44.9	45.2	45.6	46.3	46.3	46.4	46.1
2009	44.8	44.7	44.7	44.6	44.5	44.1	43.0	43.3	42.7	42.3	42.3	42.4	43.6
2010	41.0	41.1	41.5	41.7	41.8	41.9	41.8	41.9	41.5	41.9	41.6	41.7	41.6
2011	41.6	41.9	42.3	42.8	42.6	42.4	42.2	42.8	43.3	43.0	42.7	42.8	42.5
2012	42.9	43.4	43.9	44.8	45.0	44.7	43.6	43.9	44.4	44.8	44.3	44.0	44.1
2013	44.0	44.8	45.0	45.3	44.9	44.5	44.7	45.3	45.5	45.5	45.3	44.8	45.0
2014	44.8	45.4	45.7	46.2	46.1	45.6	45.8	46.0	46.3	47.2	47.9	48.0	46.3
2015	48.2	48.7	49.0	49.1	49.4	48.7	49.1	49.4	49.0	49.2	48.9	48.2	48.9
2016	47.6	47.7	48.1	49.3	48.4	46.9	46.8	46.3	48.0	47.6	47.4	46.3	47.5
2017	45.7	46.3	46.4	46.5	46.3	46.0	46.4	46.9	46.7	47.5	48.4	47.9	46.8
Education and Health Services													
2007	42.9	43.3	43.5	44.0	44.6	44.5	44.3	44.8	44.7	44.3	44.4	44.8	44.2
2008	44.2	44.8	45.0	45.2	45.3	45.6	45.6	46.2	45.3	46.0	46.1	46.3	45.5
2009	45.7	46.2	46.4	46.7	46.6	46.3	47.4	47.5	47.8	48.5	48.6	48.6	47.2
2010	47.7	47.9	48.4	48.9	49.2	48.8	48.8	48.8	49.2	49.6	49.8	49.5	48.9
2011	49.6	49.9	50.0	49.4	49.4	49.2	49.7	49.6	50.0	50.2	50.5	50.4	49.8
2012	49.9	50.6	50.8	50.3	50.3	50.4	49.9	50.6	50.5	51.1	51.1	51.2	50.6
2013	50.9	51.3	51.3	51.5	51.7	51.3	51.3	52.3	52.3	52.5	52.8	52.5	51.8
2014	52.4	52.6	52.8	52.7	52.7	52.3	51.9	53.1	53.4	53.7	53.5	53.4	52.9
2015	53.1	53.2	53.2	53.2	53.1	52.4	52.1	52.6	52.8	53.1	53.2	53.0	52.9
2016	51.9	52.0	51.9	52.6	52.6	52.2	52.2	52.4	52.2	52.4	52.2	52.5	52.3
2017	52.4	52.8	52.9	52.9	53.0	52.9	52.2	52.7	53.0	52.9	53.5	53.3	52.9
Leisure and Hospitality													
2007	31.3	32.0	33.0	32.5	33.0	33.4	32.9	32.8	33.2	32.3	32.3	32.1	32.6
2008	31.7	32.5	32.9	33.3	33.6	33.5	33.2	33.3	32.1	32.9	33.4	33.4	33.0
2009	32.0	32.6	33.3	33.0	33.5	33.4	32.8	33.2	33.0	32.4	32.5	32.1	32.8
2010	31.0	31.3	32.2	32.4	32.9	33.1	32.7	32.8	32.8	32.4	32.6	32.1	32.4
2011	32.5	32.6	33.3	34.1	34.8	34.4	34.1	34.6	34.3	34.4	34.5	34.2	34.0
2012	33.7	33.9	34.5	34.7	35.3	35.2	35.2	36.1	36.0	35.8	35.6	35.5	35.1
2013	35.1	35.3	35.7	36.6	37.3	37.1	37.2	37.1	37.1	36.7	36.5	36.3	36.5
2014	35.5	36.0	36.4	37.6	38.2	38.3	37.8	38.1	37.8	37.4	36.8	36.9	37.2
2015	36.7	37.0	37.5	38.0	39.0	39.0	38.7	38.5	38.6	38.5	38.8	38.7	38.3
2016	37.9	38.4	39.1	40.3	40.6	40.2	39.8	38.8	38.4	38.7	38.3	38.0	39.0
2017	37.8	38.8	39.0	39.2	39.9	40.6	40.4	40.9	41.4	40.8	41.1	41.3	40.1

Employment by Industry: Baton Rouge, LA, Selected Years, 2007–2017—*Continued*

(Numbers in thousands, not seasonally adjusted)

Industry and year	January	February	March	April	May	June	July	August	September	October	November	December	Annual average
Other Services													
2007	15.0	15.1	15.2	15.2	15.1	15.4	15.6	15.6	15.6	15.3	15.1	15.2	15.3
2008	15.0	15.3	15.4	14.6	14.8	14.9	15.0	14.7	14.5	15.2	15.2	15.1	15.0
2009	14.9	15.0	15.0	15.1	15.1	15.4	15.5	15.4	15.7	15.9	15.9	16.0	15.4
2010	14.6	14.8	14.8	14.4	14.5	14.7	14.5	14.4	14.3	14.7	14.6	14.6	14.6
2011	14.7	14.7	14.8	15.0	14.9	15.1	15.3	15.4	15.3	15.2	15.3	15.1	15.1
2012	15.0	15.2	15.2	15.3	15.3	15.5	15.2	15.2	15.3	15.3	15.3	15.1	15.2
2013	15.2	15.4	15.6	15.5	15.6	15.7	15.5	15.6	15.6	15.5	15.5	15.5	15.5
2014	15.5	15.7	15.7	15.8	16.0	16.0	16.1	16.2	16.1	16.5	16.3	16.2	16.0
2015	16.3	16.3	16.4	16.4	16.7	16.6	16.6	16.5	16.6	16.8	16.7	16.7	16.6
2016	16.6	16.6	16.9	16.8	16.9	16.9	16.6	16.4	16.4	16.3	16.4	16.3	16.6
2017	16.4	16.6	16.6	16.6	16.5	16.8	16.7	16.7	16.6	16.7	16.7	16.6	16.6
Government													
2007	72.5	75.2	75.9	76.8	76.0	75.6	73.2	75.9	79.2	78.4	79.0	78.4	76.3
2008	75.5	78.5	78.2	78.1	77.2	76.6	74.9	75.3	76.0	79.2	79.7	78.8	77.3
2009	76.3	79.1	79.2	78.9	77.8	76.8	74.8	74.6	78.8	79.1	79.3	78.4	77.8
2010	76.3	77.8	78.1	77.8	78.1	76.4	73.0	75.5	77.6	78.1	78.2	77.4	77.0
2011	74.9	77.0	76.7	77.0	76.8	75.1	73.0	72.5	76.8	77.6	77.8	77.2	76.0
2012	74.9	76.0	75.6	75.3	74.9	73.2	70.1	72.5	74.6	74.4	74.6	74.0	74.2
2013	71.9	73.6	73.6	73.5	73.2	71.8	68.7	71.2	73.9	73.6	74.1	73.1	72.7
2014	71.3	72.8	72.9	72.5	72.2	71.0	68.7	70.9	73.3	73.2	73.7	73.0	72.1
2015	71.2	72.8	72.9	72.7	72.4	71.2	69.0	71.3	73.6	74.0	74.5	74.0	72.5
2016	72.3	74.1	74.3	74.0	74.0	72.6	70.3	72.4	74.7	74.1	74.7	74.6	73.5
2017	73.2	75.0	75.4	74.9	74.8	73.3	70.6	72.8	75.1	74.9	75.7	75.4	74.3

Employment by Industry: Columbia, SC, Selected Years, 2007–2017

(Numbers in thousands, not seasonally adjusted)

Industry and year	January	February	March	April	May	June	July	August	September	October	November	December	Annual average
Total Nonfarm													
2007	362.0	363.7	365.6	367.5	370.3	370.8	366.4	368.3	370.1	370.9	371.4	372.1	368.3
2008	366.6	368.1	368.6	369.0	370.7	368.1	363.1	366.1	365.6	364.3	364.6	363.6	366.5
2009	351.9	351.1	351.3	350.2	350.4	348.0	344.6	344.7	345.3	347.1	347.9	346.9	348.3
2010	342.2	343.9	345.5	347.3	349.3	347.9	343.5	344.0	345.0	348.3	349.5	348.2	346.2
2011	339.8	343.7	345.8	349.1	349.7	348.4	344.5	347.5	349.1	351.4	354.9	355.5	348.3
2012	349.7	351.7	353.9	353.9	355.9	354.6	352.5	355.0	356.4	359.4	366.5	366.3	356.3
2013	355.6	358.3	359.6	362.6	364.2	362.2	360.4	361.4	365.9	368.2	375.3	376.2	364.2
2014	367.3	366.9	371.6	373.5	375.2	372.1	370.0	373.5	375.8	380.1	385.7	386.7	374.9
2015	377.1	379.7	380.8	382.8	385.1	383.6	382.3	384.5	387.7	391.9	397.6	398.9	386.0
2016	387.1	390.5	391.1	394.0	396.3	393.5	393.3	395.0	397.4	399.0	404.1	403.3	395.4
2017	393.7	395.7	397.2	398.2	399.3	398.9	397.1	393.3	393.3	396.6	397.7	398.1	396.6
Total Private													
2007	282.2	283.7	285.3	287.5	290.0	291.7	289.3	290.1	289.9	289.7	289.5	290.2	288.3
2008	284.5	285.6	286.0	285.9	287.5	286.8	284.7	285.5	282.5	280.9	280.5	279.7	284.2
2009	269.1	267.7	267.9	266.6	267.1	266.6	264.7	264.3	263.6	264.6	265.0	264.0	265.9
2010	260.1	261.2	262.4	264.0	264.8	265.2	264.0	264.7	264.4	266.8	267.8	266.9	264.4
2011	259.3	262.5	264.3	268.1	269.3	269.2	267.8	269.5	268.9	270.7	274.0	274.8	268.2
2012	269.5	270.3	272.4	272.5	274.3	274.0	273.8	275.7	275.7	277.5	283.9	283.8	275.3
2013	274.4	275.8	276.9	280.3	282.1	282.1	282.6	284.7	285.1	286.4	292.8	294.1	283.1
2014	285.1	283.7	288.0	289.7	291.4	289.9	289.7	292.2	292.1	295.7	301.0	302.1	291.7
2015	293.0	294.7	295.6	297.3	299.8	300.3	300.3	301.4	302.4	306.5	311.8	312.8	301.3
2016	302.5	305.0	305.1	308.1	310.3	309.2	308.8	310.6	311.4	312.9	317.7	316.5	309.8
2017	308.2	309.5	310.6	311.2	312.5	312.9	311.8	308.9	307.6	310.7	312.1	311.8	310.7
Goods Producing													
2007	52.1	52.4	52.6	52.9	53.4	53.8	53.7	53.9	53.2	52.9	52.8	52.7	53.0
2008	51.6	51.2	51.0	50.4	50.5	50.9	50.6	50.5	49.9	49.1	48.9	48.4	50.3
2009	46.3	45.6	45.0	44.5	44.4	44.4	44.0	43.6	43.1	42.8	42.8	42.6	44.1
2010	42.0	42.1	42.0	41.8	41.9	42.3	42.3	41.9	41.9	42.2	42.2	42.0	42.1
2011	41.1	41.5	42.0	42.1	42.4	42.6	42.6	42.8	42.5	42.4	42.5	42.6	42.3
2012	41.9	42.1	42.5	41.9	42.2	42.5	42.7	42.7	42.6	42.8	42.9	42.7	42.5
2013	41.8	42.1	42.3	42.3	42.5	42.8	43.0	43.0	43.1	43.2	43.5	43.6	42.8
2014	43.5	43.4	43.9	44.4	44.6	44.4	44.9	44.9	45.0	45.3	45.5	45.8	44.6
2015	45.7	45.9	45.9	46.2	46.3	46.5	46.5	46.4	46.8	47.4	47.4	47.2	46.5
2016	46.6	46.8	46.8	46.7	47.0	47.5	47.9	48.3	48.3	48.3	48.7	48.8	47.6
2017	49.6	49.3	49.6	49.7	50.2	50.2	50.1	46.7	46.3	46.6	46.8	47.0	48.5
Service-Providing													
2007	309.9	311.3	313.0	314.6	316.9	317.0	312.7	314.4	316.9	318.0	318.6	319.4	315.2
2008	315.0	316.9	317.6	318.6	320.2	317.2	312.5	315.6	315.7	315.2	315.7	315.2	316.3
2009	305.6	305.5	306.3	305.7	306.0	303.6	300.6	301.1	302.2	304.3	305.1	304.3	304.2
2010	300.2	301.8	303.5	305.5	307.4	305.6	301.2	302.1	303.1	306.1	307.3	306.2	304.2
2011	298.7	302.2	303.8	307.0	307.3	305.8	301.9	304.7	306.6	309.0	312.4	312.9	306.0
2012	307.8	309.6	311.4	312.0	313.7	312.1	309.8	312.3	313.8	316.6	323.6	323.6	313.9
2013	313.8	316.2	317.3	320.3	321.7	319.4	317.4	318.4	322.8	325.0	331.8	332.6	321.4
2014	323.8	323.5	327.7	329.1	330.6	327.7	325.1	328.6	330.8	334.8	340.2	340.9	330.2
2015	331.4	333.8	334.9	336.6	338.8	337.1	335.8	338.1	340.9	344.5	350.2	351.7	339.5
2016	340.5	343.7	344.3	347.3	349.3	346.0	345.4	346.7	349.1	350.7	355.4	354.5	347.7
2017	344.1	346.4	347.6	348.5	349.1	348.7	347.0	346.6	347.0	350.0	350.9	351.1	348.1
Mining, Logging, and Construction													
2007	21.1	21.3	21.5	21.7	22.0	22.2	22.2	22.2	21.8	21.5	21.4	21.3	21.7
2008	20.4	20.4	20.3	19.7	19.8	20.1	19.9	19.9	19.6	19.1	18.9	18.6	19.7
2009	17.7	17.3	17.2	17.2	17.2	17.1	16.8	16.6	16.2	16.0	16.0	15.8	16.8
2010	15.5	15.5	15.6	15.4	15.4	15.6	15.6	15.3	15.2	15.3	15.2	15.1	15.4
2011	14.4	14.7	15.0	15.1	15.2	15.2	15.3	15.4	15.3	15.4	15.5	15.5	15.2
2012	14.9	15.0	15.3	14.8	15.1	15.3	15.5	15.6	15.6	15.6	15.7	15.7	15.3
2013	15.2	15.3	15.5	15.5	15.7	15.9	16.2	16.2	16.2	16.3	16.5	16.6	15.9
2014	16.6	16.4	16.5	16.6	16.7	16.8	17.0	17.1	17.0	17.2	17.2	17.3	16.9
2015	17.0	17.0	17.0	17.2	17.4	17.5	17.4	17.4	17.6	18.0	18.1	18.4	17.5
2016	17.6	17.9	18.1	18.2	18.5	18.8	19.1	19.4	19.6	19.7	20.1	20.1	18.9
2017	20.7	20.4	20.5	20.6	20.9	20.8	21.2	17.9	17.6	17.9	18.0	18.0	19.5

Employment by Industry: Columbia, SC, Selected Years, 2007–2017—*Continued*

(Numbers in thousands, not seasonally adjusted)

Industry and year	January	February	March	April	May	June	July	August	September	October	November	December	Annual average
Manufacturing													
2007	31.0	31.1	31.1	31.2	31.4	31.6	31.5	31.7	31.4	31.4	31.4	31.4	31.4
2008	31.2	30.8	30.7	30.7	30.7	30.8	30.7	30.6	30.3	30.0	30.0	29.8	30.5
2009	28.6	28.3	27.8	27.3	27.2	27.3	27.2	27.0	26.9	26.8	26.8	26.8	27.3
2010	26.5	26.6	26.4	26.4	26.5	26.7	26.7	26.6	26.7	26.9	27.0	26.9	26.7
2011	26.7	26.8	27.0	27.0	27.2	27.4	27.3	27.4	27.2	27.0	27.0	27.1	27.1
2012	27.0	27.1	27.2	27.1	27.1	27.2	27.2	27.1	27.0	27.2	27.2	27.0	27.1
2013	26.6	26.8	26.8	26.8	26.8	26.9	26.8	26.8	26.9	26.9	27.0	27.0	26.8
2014	26.9	27.0	27.4	27.8	27.9	27.6	27.9	27.8	28.0	28.1	28.3	28.5	27.8
2015	28.7	28.9	28.9	29.0	28.9	29.0	29.1	29.0	29.2	29.4	29.3	28.8	29.0
2016	29.0	28.9	28.7	28.5	28.5	28.7	28.8	28.9	28.7	28.6	28.6	28.7	28.7
2017	28.9	28.9	29.1	29.1	29.3	29.4	28.9	28.8	28.7	28.7	28.8	29.0	29.0
Trade, Transportation, and Utilities													
2007	68.8	68.9	69.1	69.3	69.8	69.9	69.5	69.6	69.4	69.8	70.8	71.4	69.7
2008	69.6	69.6	69.6	69.7	69.5	69.4	69.0	68.6	68.0	66.8	67.3	68.1	68.8
2009	64.6	63.6	63.2	63.1	63.4	63.3	63.2	63.1	63.0	62.9	63.7	64.5	63.5
2010	62.5	62.1	62.3	62.4	62.4	62.4	62.2	62.5	61.8	62.3	63.2	64.0	62.5
2011	61.4	61.7	61.8	62.3	62.4	62.8	62.3	62.5	62.5	62.9	64.3	64.9	62.7
2012	63.1	62.5	62.9	62.7	63.2	63.0	63.2	63.9	63.9	64.5	66.3	66.7	63.8
2013	63.9	64.0	64.3	64.5	64.9	65.2	65.7	66.1	66.2	66.9	68.1	69.1	65.7
2014	67.0	66.8	67.4	67.2	67.6	67.7	67.8	68.3	68.2	68.8	70.2	71.4	68.2
2015	68.4	68.8	68.8	69.3	70.0	70.6	71.0	71.5	71.3	72.1	73.8	74.6	70.9
2016	72.2	72.5	72.4	73.0	73.8	73.7	74.1	74.0	73.7	74.0	75.7	75.6	73.7
2017	72.9	72.5	72.7	72.4	72.7	73.1	73.3	73.9	74.0	74.5	76.6	76.5	73.8
Wholesale Trade													
2007	17.4	17.9	17.7	17.3	17.1	17.1	16.9	16.8	16.7	16.7	16.6	16.6	17.1
2008	16.8	16.9	16.7	16.8	16.9	16.8	16.7	16.3	16.0	15.9	15.8	15.9	16.5
2009	15.2	15.0	14.9	14.8	14.8	14.7	14.5	14.4	14.4	14.4	14.3	14.3	14.6
2010	14.0	14.0	14.0	14.0	13.9	13.9	13.8	13.7	13.5	13.7	13.7	13.7	13.8
2011	13.5	13.6	13.6	13.7	13.7	13.7	13.6	13.6	13.6	13.5	13.6	13.6	13.6
2012	13.7	13.8	13.8	13.7	13.9	13.9	14.1	14.1	14.0	14.0	14.0	14.0	13.9
2013	13.8	13.9	14.0	14.1	14.2	14.3	14.3	14.4	14.4	14.5	14.6	14.7	14.3
2014	14.8	14.9	15.0	14.9	14.9	14.9	15.0	15.0	15.0	14.9	14.9	15.0	14.9
2015	14.8	14.9	14.9	15.0	15.1	15.1	15.0	15.1	15.1	15.3	15.3	15.5	15.1
2016	15.4	15.6	15.6	15.7	15.8	15.7	15.7	15.6	15.7	15.5	15.6	15.6	15.6
2017	15.5	15.5	15.6	15.4	15.5	15.6	15.6	15.6	15.6	15.6	15.6	15.6	15.6
Retail Trade													
2007	39.7	39.3	39.7	40.2	40.7	40.6	40.5	40.7	40.5	40.9	41.8	42.1	40.6
2008	41.2	41.0	41.7	41.2	40.9	40.9	40.5	40.7	40.6	39.8	40.3	40.7	40.8
2009	38.7	37.9	37.8	37.9	38.1	38.1	38.1	38.7	38.1	38.0	39.0	39.5	38.3
2010	38.0	37.6	37.8	38.2	38.3	38.2	37.9	38.3	37.9	38.1	39.0	39.7	38.3
2011	37.5	37.6	37.7	38.0	38.1	38.3	38.2	38.3	38.2	38.3	39.3	39.8	38.3
2012	38.2	37.6	38.0	37.8	38.0	37.7	37.7	38.0	37.9	38.2	39.6	39.8	38.2
2013	37.8	37.7	37.9	38.2	38.4	38.4	38.6	38.9	38.8	39.4	40.2	40.7	38.8
2014	38.9	38.5	38.8	38.7	38.9	38.9	38.9	39.2	39.0	39.5	40.6	41.2	39.3
2015	39.2	39.1	39.3	39.6	39.9	40.3	40.2	40.5	40.2	41.1	42.6	43.0	40.4
2016	41.0	41.1	41.2	41.5	41.8	41.8	41.9	42.1	41.9	42.0	43.4	43.3	41.9
2017	41.6	41.3	41.4	41.5	41.6	41.7	41.3	41.4	41.0	41.4	43.0	42.3	41.6
Transportation and Utilities													
2007	11.7	11.7	11.7	11.8	12.0	12.2	12.1	12.1	12.2	12.2	12.4	12.7	12.1
2008	11.6	11.7	11.7	11.7	11.7	11.7	11.8	11.6	11.4	11.1	11.2	11.5	11.6
2009	10.7	10.7	10.5	10.4	10.5	10.5	10.6	10.5	10.5	10.5	10.4	10.7	10.5
2010	10.5	10.5	10.5	10.2	10.2	10.3	10.5	10.5	10.4	10.5	10.5	10.6	10.4
2011	10.4	10.5	10.5	10.6	10.6	10.8	10.5	10.6	10.7	11.1	11.4	11.5	10.8
2012	11.2	11.1	11.1	11.2	11.3	11.4	11.4	11.8	12.0	12.3	12.7	12.9	11.7
2013	12.3	12.4	12.4	12.2	12.3	12.5	12.8	12.8	13.0	13.0	13.3	13.7	12.7
2014	13.3	13.4	13.6	13.6	13.8	13.9	13.9	14.1	14.2	14.4	14.7	15.2	14.0
2015	14.4	14.8	14.6	14.7	15.0	15.2	15.8	15.9	16.0	15.7	15.9	16.1	15.3
2016	15.8	15.8	15.6	15.8	16.2	16.2	16.5	16.3	16.1	16.5	16.7	16.7	16.2
2017	15.8	15.7	15.7	15.5	15.6	15.8	16.4	16.9	17.4	17.5	18.0	18.6	16.6

Employment by Industry: Columbia, SC, Selected Years, 2007–2017—*Continued*

(Numbers in thousands, not seasonally adjusted)

Industry and year	January	February	March	April	May	June	July	August	September	October	November	December	Annual average
Information													
2007	6.1	6.1	6.1	6.1	6.2	6.2	6.1	6.0	6.0	6.2	6.1	6.2	6.1
2008	5.8	5.9	5.9	5.9	5.9	6.0	6.0	6.0	5.9	5.9	5.9	5.9	5.9
2009	5.9	5.8	5.9	5.8	5.8	5.8	5.7	5.7	5.7	5.7	5.7	5.6	5.8
2010	5.6	5.6	5.6	5.6	5.6	5.5	5.6	5.7	5.6	5.6	5.7	5.6	5.6
2011	5.4	5.4	5.4	5.3	5.4	5.4	5.4	5.4	5.3	5.3	5.4	5.4	5.4
2012	5.4	5.4	5.4	5.2	5.2	5.2	5.2	5.2	5.2	5.3	5.4	5.4	5.3
2013	5.5	5.8	5.8	5.9	5.6	5.4	5.5	5.5	5.5	5.6	5.7	5.7	5.6
2014	5.6	5.5	5.4	5.6	5.4	5.5	5.4	5.4	5.4	5.5	5.7	5.4	5.5
2015	5.5	5.5	5.4	5.5	5.6	5.4	5.4	5.4	5.4	5.4	5.5	5.6	5.5
2016	5.5	5.5	5.4	5.6	5.8	5.9	5.7	5.7	5.7	5.8	5.9	6.2	5.7
2017	5.6	5.9	5.9	5.7	5.9	5.6	5.4	5.3	5.3	5.3	5.4	5.4	5.6
Financial Activities													
2007	30.8	30.8	30.7	30.8	30.9	31.0	30.6	30.2	30.4	30.4	30.6	30.7	30.7
2008	30.4	30.5	30.6	30.5	30.5	30.6	30.2	30.2	30.1	30.2	30.3	30.4	30.4
2009	29.7	29.9	29.9	29.4	29.5	29.3	29.2	28.9	28.6	28.3	28.1	27.9	29.1
2010	27.7	27.7	27.6	27.3	27.3	27.3	27.0	27.0	26.8	27.0	27.0	27.0	27.2
2011	26.9	26.9	27.0	27.1	27.3	27.4	27.3	27.5	27.5	27.8	28.0	28.2	27.4
2012	28.2	28.3	28.4	28.4	28.6	28.7	28.8	28.9	29.0	29.1	29.3	29.3	28.8
2013	29.2	29.4	29.7	29.8	30.0	30.2	30.3	30.5	30.6	30.3	30.4	30.5	30.1
2014	30.1	30.1	30.1	30.1	30.2	30.2	30.1	30.2	30.2	30.1	30.1	30.2	30.1
2015	30.0	30.1	30.1	30.1	30.3	30.4	30.3	30.4	30.5	30.6	30.8	30.9	30.4
2016	30.5	30.6	30.6	30.6	30.7	30.9	30.8	31.0	31.1	31.3	31.5	31.4	30.9
2017	31.0	31.1	31.1	30.9	31.0	31.3	31.0	31.1	31.0	31.6	31.4	31.4	31.2
Professional and Business Services													
2007	42.5	42.8	43.0	43.2	43.4	43.8	43.4	44.1	44.4	44.2	43.5	43.4	43.5
2008	41.9	42.3	41.9	41.6	42.8	41.4	41.2	42.5	41.0	41.3	41.2	40.2	41.6
2009	38.3	37.7	37.9	37.6	37.4	37.4	37.0	37.3	37.1	38.8	38.9	38.4	37.8
2010	38.1	38.8	39.1	39.8	40.0	40.4	40.2	40.6	40.9	41.5	41.2	40.9	40.1
2011	40.1	41.1	41.3	42.4	42.3	42.2	42.0	42.5	42.1	42.5	43.3	44.1	42.2
2012	42.8	43.0	43.3	44.0	44.5	44.5	44.4	44.4	43.9	44.4	47.8	48.3	44.6
2013	45.0	44.0	43.8	44.8	45.2	45.2	45.2	45.6	45.7	45.9	49.9	50.8	45.9
2014	46.4	44.8	46.1	45.9	46.5	45.6	45.5	46.1	46.1	47.5	51.5	51.8	47.0
2015	47.7	47.4	47.3	47.2	47.6	47.9	47.9	47.8	48.5	51.0	53.0	54.0	48.9
2016	49.3	49.7	49.3	50.1	49.9	49.2	48.3	48.9	49.7	50.0	51.5	51.4	49.8
2017	47.8	47.8	47.9	48.2	48.4	49.1	48.7	48.0	47.6	47.5	47.8	47.6	48.0
Education and Health Services													
2007	40.0	40.4	40.6	41.3	41.7	42.1	41.7	41.5	42.0	41.8	41.8	41.7	41.4
2008	42.3	42.7	42.9	42.8	42.9	42.9	42.7	42.6	42.9	42.8	42.9	42.9	42.8
2009	41.7	42.0	42.1	42.0	42.1	41.7	41.8	41.9	42.3	42.3	42.5	42.2	42.1
2010	42.0	42.2	42.3	42.5	42.7	42.6	42.5	42.5	42.6	43.2	43.2	43.0	42.6
2011	42.2	42.8	42.8	43.9	43.8	43.5	43.3	43.0	43.3	43.6	43.7	43.4	43.3
2012	43.0	43.3	43.4	43.3	43.3	42.6	42.5	42.7	43.3	43.6	43.7	43.5	43.2
2013	42.6	43.2	43.2	43.7	44.0	43.7	43.8	44.1	44.4	44.8	45.0	45.0	44.0
2014	44.4	44.6	45.4	45.8	46.0	45.4	45.7	45.9	46.2	46.4	46.5	46.5	45.7
2015	45.9	46.4	46.6	46.7	47.2	47.0	46.9	46.8	46.9	47.0	47.4	47.3	46.8
2016	46.7	47.3	47.5	47.7	48.2	47.8	47.9	47.9	48.4	48.6	48.8	48.8	48.0
2017	48.0	48.7	48.8	48.9	48.8	48.7	48.4	48.4	48.4	50.0	49.4	49.1	48.8
Leisure and Hospitality													
2007	29.3	29.7	30.3	31.2	31.7	32.0	31.5	31.9	31.8	31.7	31.2	31.1	31.1
2008	30.0	30.5	31.0	31.9	32.3	32.6	31.9	32.0	31.8	31.8	31.1	31.0	31.5
2009	29.8	30.4	31.1	31.5	31.8	32.0	31.1	31.2	31.3	31.3	30.8	30.4	31.1
2010	29.7	30.2	30.8	31.9	32.1	31.8	31.5	31.9	32.1	32.1	32.6	31.7	31.5
2011	29.8	30.7	31.5	32.3	32.8	32.2	31.7	32.6	32.5	33.1	33.6	32.8	32.1
2012	31.4	31.9	32.5	33.0	33.2	33.1	32.7	33.6	33.5	33.5	34.1	33.4	33.0
2013	31.9	32.8	33.1	34.5	35.0	34.7	34.2	34.9	34.7	34.7	35.2	34.3	34.2
2014	33.2	33.5	34.6	35.4	35.7	35.6	35.0	35.9	35.7	36.7	36.1	35.6	35.3
2015	34.4	35.1	35.8	36.7	37.0	36.7	36.5	37.2	37.2	37.2	37.9	37.1	36.6
2016	35.7	36.6	36.9	38.2	38.7	38.0	38.0	38.7	38.4	38.7	39.3	38.1	37.9
2017	37.3	38.1	38.4	39.2	39.3	38.8	38.8	39.3	38.9	39.1	38.6	38.6	38.7

Employment by Industry: Columbia, SC, Selected Years, 2007–2017—*Continued*

(Numbers in thousands, not seasonally adjusted)

Industry and year	January	February	March	April	May	June	July	August	September	October	November	December	Annual average
Other Services													
2007	12.6	12.6	12.9	12.7	12.9	12.9	12.8	12.9	12.7	12.7	12.7	13.0	12.8
2008	12.9	12.9	13.1	13.1	13.1	13.0	13.1	13.1	12.9	13.0	12.9	12.8	13.0
2009	12.8	12.7	12.8	12.7	12.7	12.7	12.7	12.6	12.5	12.5	12.5	12.4	12.6
2010	12.5	12.5	12.7	12.7	12.8	12.9	12.7	12.6	12.7	12.9	12.7	12.7	12.7
2011	12.4	12.4	12.5	12.7	12.9	13.1	13.2	13.2	13.2	13.1	13.2	13.4	12.9
2012	13.7	13.8	14.0	14.0	14.1	14.4	14.3	14.3	14.3	14.3	14.4	14.5	14.2
2013	14.5	14.5	14.7	14.8	14.9	14.9	14.9	15.0	14.9	15.0	15.0	15.1	14.9
2014	14.9	15.0	15.1	15.3	15.4	15.5	15.3	15.5	15.3	15.4	15.4	15.4	15.3
2015	15.4	15.5	15.7	15.6	15.8	15.8	15.8	15.9	15.8	15.8	16.0	16.1	15.8
2016	16.0	16.0	16.2	16.2	16.2	16.2	16.1	16.1	16.1	16.2	16.3	16.2	16.2
2017	16.0	16.1	16.2	16.2	16.2	16.1	16.1	16.2	16.1	16.1	16.1	16.2	16.1
Government													
2007	79.8	80.0	80.3	80.0	80.3	79.1	77.1	78.2	80.2	81.2	81.9	81.9	80.0
2008	82.1	82.5	82.6	83.1	83.2	81.3	78.4	80.6	83.1	83.4	84.1	83.9	82.4
2009	82.8	83.4	83.4	83.6	83.3	81.4	79.9	80.4	81.7	82.5	82.9	82.9	82.4
2010	82.1	82.7	83.1	83.3	84.5	82.7	79.5	79.3	80.6	81.5	81.7	81.3	81.9
2011	80.5	81.2	81.5	81.0	80.4	79.2	76.7	78.0	80.2	80.7	80.9	80.7	80.1
2012	80.2	81.4	81.5	81.4	81.6	80.6	78.7	79.3	80.7	81.9	82.6	82.5	81.0
2013	81.2	82.5	82.7	82.3	82.1	80.1	77.8	76.7	80.8	81.8	82.5	82.1	81.1
2014	82.2	83.2	83.6	83.8	83.8	82.2	80.3	81.3	83.7	84.4	84.7	84.6	83.2
2015	84.1	85.0	85.2	85.5	85.3	83.3	82.0	83.1	85.3	85.4	85.8	86.1	84.7
2016	84.6	85.5	86.0	85.9	86.0	84.3	84.5	84.4	86.0	86.1	86.4	86.8	85.5
2017	85.5	86.2	86.6	87.0	86.8	86.0	85.3	84.4	85.7	85.9	85.6	86.3	85.9

Employment by Industry: North Port-Sarasota-Bradenton, FL, Selected Years, 2007–2017

(Numbers in thousands, not seasonally adjusted)

Industry and year	January	February	March	April	May	June	July	August	September	October	November	December	Annual average
Total Nonfarm													
2007	276.9	278.9	281.1	277.1	276.4	272.5	266.6	270.0	268.6	267.6	270.9	273.6	273.4
2008	268.5	271.0	272.3	266.2	264.8	259.6	254.7	256.9	255.9	253.7	254.1	255.0	261.1
2009	248.3	247.8	248.3	245.5	243.9	239.3	234.6	236.3	235.4	237.8	240.2	241.7	241.6
2010	236.2	238.0	240.0	240.1	241.7	236.5	233.1	234.9	233.6	235.1	238.4	240.4	237.3
2011	236.5	239.6	241.2	243.1	241.1	236.9	235.1	238.5	238.2	239.6	244.0	246.1	240.0
2012	243.1	245.1	248.2	247.7	246.9	242.9	240.1	242.6	243.5	246.9	252.2	253.9	246.1
2013	250.6	254.4	256.1	256.2	256.4	252.4	251.2	253.9	254.5	258.6	265.0	267.0	256.4
2014	263.1	266.3	268.9	269.0	268.7	265.1	263.9	267.5	268.3	273.8	278.6	282.0	269.6
2015	278.8	281.4	284.3	284.4	284.3	281.0	278.2	281.0	281.2	286.4	290.1	293.3	283.7
2016	290.1	293.1	295.0	294.9	293.7	289.3	289.0	291.5	292.2	296.7	300.6	302.6	294.1
2017	299.6	301.3	304.2	302.1	301.4	296.9	295.7	299.3	292.7	300.8	306.4	308.1	300.7
Total Private													
2007	248.1	249.8	251.9	247.9	247.3	246.4	240.7	241.2	239.7	238.8	241.8	244.5	244.8
2008	239.5	241.8	242.8	236.7	235.3	233.1	228.4	227.7	226.7	224.7	225.3	226.2	232.4
2009	219.7	219.1	219.4	216.2	215.0	213.5	209.1	208.8	207.6	209.8	212.1	213.7	213.7
2010	208.4	210.1	212.0	212.1	212.2	211.0	207.9	208.3	206.5	207.6	210.8	212.9	210.0
2011	209.1	212.0	213.5	215.4	213.9	212.6	211.1	211.3	211.3	212.3	216.5	218.8	213.2
2012	216.0	217.7	220.7	220.4	219.7	218.7	216.0	216.6	216.7	219.6	224.9	226.6	219.5
2013	223.5	227.1	228.7	229.0	229.4	228.3	227.2	228.1	227.9	231.3	237.4	239.5	229.8
2014	236.2	239.2	241.5	241.7	241.5	241.0	239.7	241.6	241.6	246.2	250.7	254.3	242.9
2015	251.2	253.7	256.4	256.6	256.6	256.4	253.6	254.7	254.2	258.7	262.3	265.5	256.7
2016	262.4	265.3	267.0	266.9	265.7	264.2	263.9	264.6	264.7	268.7	272.7	274.8	266.7
2017	271.7	273.2	276.0	274.4	273.3	271.8	270.5	272.5	264.6	272.5	278.4	280.2	273.3
Goods Producing													
2007	48.6	48.2	48.1	46.7	46.5	46.1	45.0	44.8	43.9	43.0	42.6	42.3	45.5
2008	41.0	40.9	40.4	39.3	39.1	39.0	38.0	37.7	37.4	36.0	35.4	35.2	38.3
2009	32.8	31.9	31.6	30.9	30.8	30.5	29.8	29.6	29.3	29.1	28.9	28.9	30.3
2010	27.8	27.8	27.7	28.0	28.3	28.6	28.6	28.7	28.6	28.4	28.3	28.4	28.3
2011	27.5	27.7	27.9	28.3	28.6	29.0	29.1	29.2	29.4	29.3	29.5	29.6	28.8
2012	29.3	29.4	29.6	29.6	29.9	30.0	29.9	30.2	30.3	30.5	30.8	30.8	30.0
2013	30.4	30.7	30.8	30.8	31.2	31.4	31.5	31.8	31.9	32.2	32.7	32.9	31.5
2014	32.8	33.0	33.2	33.6	34.1	34.3	34.5	34.8	35.3	35.4	35.5	35.8	34.4
2015	35.3	35.6	35.7	36.0	36.3	36.5	36.5	36.9	37.1	37.3	37.3	37.6	36.5
2016	37.4	37.6	37.9	38.2	38.2	38.5	38.8	38.8	39.0	39.3	39.6	40.0	38.6
2017	39.2	39.4	39.9	39.6	39.9	40.2	40.1	40.3	38.9	40.2	40.5	40.9	39.9
Service-Providing													
2007	228.3	230.7	233.0	230.4	229.9	226.4	221.6	225.2	224.7	224.6	228.3	231.3	227.9
2008	227.5	230.1	231.9	226.9	225.7	220.6	216.7	219.2	218.5	217.7	218.7	219.8	222.8
2009	215.5	215.9	216.7	214.6	213.1	208.8	204.8	206.7	206.1	208.7	211.3	212.8	211.3
2010	208.4	210.2	212.3	212.1	213.4	207.9	204.5	206.2	205.0	206.7	210.1	212.0	209.1
2011	209.0	211.9	213.3	214.8	212.5	207.9	206.0	209.3	208.8	210.3	214.5	216.5	211.2
2012	213.8	215.7	218.6	218.1	217.0	212.9	210.2	212.4	213.2	216.4	221.4	223.1	216.1
2013	220.2	223.7	225.3	225.4	225.2	221.0	219.7	222.1	222.6	226.4	232.3	234.1	224.8
2014	230.3	233.3	235.7	235.4	234.6	230.8	229.4	232.7	233.0	238.4	243.1	246.2	235.2
2015	243.5	245.8	248.6	248.4	248.0	244.5	241.7	244.1	244.1	249.1	252.8	255.7	247.2
2016	252.7	255.5	257.1	256.7	255.5	250.8	250.2	252.7	253.2	257.4	261.0	262.6	255.5
2017	260.4	261.9	264.3	262.5	261.5	256.7	255.6	259.0	253.8	260.6	265.9	267.2	260.8
Mining, Logging, and Construction													
2007	30.2	30.0	29.9	28.7	28.5	28.1	27.0	26.9	26.1	25.3	24.9	24.6	27.5
2008	23.4	23.3	23.0	22.2	22.0	22.0	21.4	21.3	21.2	20.2	19.7	19.6	21.6
2009	18.0	17.6	17.4	17.0	17.0	16.8	16.5	16.4	16.1	16.0	15.8	15.7	16.7
2010	14.9	14.9	14.9	15.0	15.2	15.5	15.5	15.6	15.5	15.3	15.2	15.1	15.2
2011	14.5	14.6	14.8	14.9	14.9	15.1	15.1	15.1	15.4	15.3	15.4	15.4	15.0
2012	14.9	15.0	15.1	15.2	15.3	15.5	15.5	15.7	15.7	16.0	16.1	16.1	15.5
2013	15.8	16.0	16.1	16.2	16.4	16.6	16.8	17.1	17.1	17.4	17.6	17.8	16.7
2014	17.7	17.8	18.1	18.4	18.7	18.9	19.1	19.3	19.6	19.7	19.6	19.7	18.9
2015	19.5	19.6	19.7	19.9	20.1	20.2	20.2	20.5	20.7	20.9	21.0	21.2	20.3
2016	20.9	21.2	21.4	21.7	21.7	21.9	22.1	22.2	22.4	22.6	22.9	23.1	22.0
2017	22.6	22.8	23.2	23.0	23.2	23.4	23.4	23.6	22.5	23.5	23.6	23.9	23.2

Employment by Industry: North Port-Sarasota-Bradenton, FL, Selected Years, 2007–2017—*Continued*

(Numbers in thousands, not seasonally adjusted)

Industry and year	January	February	March	April	May	June	July	August	September	October	November	December	Annual average
Manufacturing													
2007	18.4	18.2	18.2	18.0	18.0	18.0	18.0	17.9	17.8	17.7	17.7	17.7	18.0
2008	17.6	17.6	17.4	17.1	17.1	17.0	16.6	16.4	16.2	15.8	15.7	15.6	16.7
2009	14.8	14.3	14.2	13.9	13.8	13.7	13.3	13.2	13.2	13.1	13.1	13.2	13.7
2010	12.9	12.9	12.8	13.0	13.1	13.1	13.1	13.1	13.1	13.1	13.1	13.3	13.1
2011	13.0	13.1	13.1	13.4	13.7	13.9	14.0	14.1	14.0	14.0	14.1	14.2	13.7
2012	14.4	14.4	14.5	14.4	14.6	14.5	14.4	14.5	14.6	14.5	14.7	14.7	14.5
2013	14.6	14.7	14.7	14.6	14.8	14.8	14.7	14.7	14.8	14.8	15.1	15.1	14.8
2014	15.1	15.2	15.1	15.2	15.4	15.4	15.4	15.5	15.7	15.7	15.9	16.1	15.5
2015	15.8	16.0	16.0	16.1	16.2	16.3	16.3	16.4	16.4	16.4	16.3	16.4	16.2
2016	16.5	16.4	16.5	16.5	16.5	16.6	16.7	16.6	16.6	16.7	16.7	16.9	16.6
2017	16.6	16.6	16.7	16.6	16.7	16.8	16.7	16.7	16.4	16.7	16.9	17.0	16.7
Trade, Transportation, and Utilities													
2007	53.0	52.6	52.9	52.1	52.1	51.7	51.1	50.8	50.5	50.8	52.0	53.4	51.9
2008	51.9	51.7	51.9	50.7	50.4	49.7	48.9	48.6	48.5	48.3	48.8	49.5	49.9
2009	47.5	47.3	46.9	46.2	45.9	45.4	44.6	44.4	44.4	44.7	45.9	46.6	45.8
2010	45.2	45.4	45.6	45.7	45.5	45.2	44.5	44.7	44.5	45.1	46.4	47.4	45.4
2011	46.3	46.2	46.4	46.8	46.4	46.0	45.8	46.0	46.2	46.6	48.4	49.1	46.7
2012	48.1	48.1	48.5	48.6	48.8	48.5	47.9	47.9	48.3	49.1	50.6	51.5	48.8
2013	49.8	50.2	50.1	50.4	50.4	50.4	50.3	50.3	50.3	51.3	53.2	54.0	50.9
2014	52.0	52.3	52.5	52.7	52.6	52.5	51.8	52.3	52.3	53.1	55.1	56.2	53.0
2015	54.5	54.5	54.8	54.6	54.6	54.7	54.4	54.7	54.7	55.3	57.2	58.1	55.2
2016	56.1	56.4	56.3	56.6	56.5	56.1	55.8	56.2	56.8	57.9	59.0	59.5	56.9
2017	57.5	57.2	57.3	57.2	56.7	56.3	56.0	56.8	55.7	57.1	59.8	60.2	57.3
Wholesale Trade													
2007	8.7	8.7	8.7	8.8	8.9	8.9	8.8	8.8	8.7	8.7	8.7	8.8	8.8
2008	8.5	8.5	8.5	8.4	8.3	8.2	8.1	8.0	8.0	8.0	7.8	7.7	8.2
2009	7.4	7.4	7.3	7.3	7.2	7.3	7.2	7.2	7.2	7.2	7.1	7.2	7.3
2010	7.1	7.1	7.2	7.2	7.2	7.2	7.1	7.1	7.1	7.2	7.2	7.2	7.2
2011	7.3	7.3	7.4	7.3	7.2	7.2	7.2	7.3	7.3	7.2	7.3	7.3	7.3
2012	7.3	7.3	7.4	7.5	7.5	7.5	7.4	7.3	7.4	7.5	7.5	7.5	7.4
2013	7.4	7.5	7.6	7.6	7.6	7.7	7.6	7.6	7.6	7.8	7.8	7.8	7.6
2014	7.6	7.7	7.7	7.8	7.9	7.9	7.9	8.0	8.0	8.1	8.2	8.3	7.9
2015	8.2	8.2	8.3	8.3	8.3	8.3	8.4	8.4	8.4	8.3	8.3	8.4	8.3
2016	8.3	8.3	8.2	8.3	8.4	8.4	8.4	8.4	8.4	8.4	8.4	8.4	8.4
2017	8.4	8.4	8.4	8.6	8.6	8.6	8.5	8.5	8.4	8.4	8.5	8.6	8.5
Retail Trade													
2007	39.4	39.2	39.4	38.6	38.6	38.2	37.8	37.6	37.4	37.7	38.8	39.8	38.5
2008	39.1	38.9	39.0	38.0	37.8	37.3	36.6	36.4	36.3	36.1	36.7	37.2	37.5
2009	35.9	35.7	35.5	34.7	34.5	34.0	33.4	33.2	33.2	33.5	34.7	35.1	34.5
2010	34.1	34.2	34.3	34.4	34.2	33.9	33.4	33.5	33.3	33.9	35.0	35.7	34.2
2011	34.7	34.7	34.8	35.2	35.0	34.6	34.4	34.5	34.7	35.2	36.8	37.3	35.2
2012	36.4	36.4	36.7	36.9	37.0	36.7	36.3	36.4	36.7	37.3	38.6	39.2	37.1
2013	37.9	38.1	37.9	38.2	38.2	38.2	38.1	38.1	38.1	38.8	40.5	41.2	38.6
2014	39.7	39.9	40.1	40.2	40.0	39.8	39.2	39.5	39.5	40.2	41.9	42.6	40.2
2015	41.4	41.4	41.5	41.5	41.4	41.5	41.2	41.5	41.5	42.2	43.8	44.4	41.9
2016	42.9	43.2	43.3	43.4	43.2	42.8	42.6	43.0	43.5	44.5	45.3	45.4	43.6
2017	43.9	43.7	43.7	43.4	43.0	42.5	42.4	43.0	42.2	43.6	46.1	46.3	43.7
Transportation and Utilities													
2007	4.9	4.7	4.8	4.7	4.6	4.6	4.5	4.4	4.4	4.4	4.5	4.8	4.6
2008	4.3	4.3	4.4	4.3	4.3	4.2	4.2	4.2	4.2	4.2	4.3	4.6	4.3
2009	4.2	4.2	4.1	4.2	4.2	4.1	4.0	4.0	4.0	4.0	4.1	4.3	4.1
2010	4.0	4.1	4.1	4.1	4.1	4.1	4.0	4.1	4.1	4.0	4.2	4.5	4.1
2011	4.3	4.2	4.2	4.3	4.2	4.2	4.2	4.2	4.2	4.2	4.3	4.5	4.3
2012	4.4	4.4	4.4	4.2	4.3	4.3	4.2	4.2	4.2	4.3	4.5	4.8	4.4
2013	4.5	4.6	4.6	4.6	4.6	4.5	4.6	4.6	4.6	4.7	4.9	5.0	4.7
2014	4.7	4.7	4.7	4.7	4.7	4.8	4.7	4.8	4.8	4.8	5.0	5.3	4.8
2015	4.9	4.9	5.0	4.8	4.9	4.9	4.8	4.8	4.8	4.8	5.1	5.3	4.9
2016	4.9	4.9	4.8	4.9	4.9	4.9	4.8	4.8	4.9	5.0	5.3	5.7	5.0
2017	5.2	5.1	5.2	5.2	5.1	5.2	5.1	5.3	5.1	5.1	5.2	5.3	5.2

Employment by Industry: North Port-Sarasota-Bradenton, FL, Selected Years, 2007–2017—*Continued*

(Numbers in thousands, not seasonally adjusted)

Industry and year	January	February	March	April	May	June	July	August	September	October	November	December	Annual average
Information													
2007	4.4	4.3	4.3	4.3	4.2	4.2	4.1	4.1	4.1	4.1	4.1	4.0	4.2
2008	4.0	4.0	4.0	3.9	3.9	3.9	3.8	3.8	3.8	3.7	3.6	3.6	3.8
2009	3.6	3.6	3.5	3.5	3.4	3.5	3.4	3.4	3.4	3.4	3.4	3.4	3.5
2010	3.4	3.4	3.3	3.3	3.4	3.4	3.4	3.4	3.4	3.4	3.5	3.5	3.4
2011	3.4	3.5	3.5	3.5	3.4	3.4	3.4	3.4	3.4	3.4	3.4	3.4	3.4
2012	3.5	3.4	3.4	3.4	3.4	3.3	3.3	3.3	3.3	3.3	3.3	3.4	3.4
2013	3.3	3.3	3.4	3.4	3.4	3.4	3.4	3.4	3.3	3.3	3.3	3.3	3.4
2014	3.3	3.3	3.3	3.4	3.4	3.4	3.4	3.4	3.4	3.4	3.4	3.5	3.4
2015	3.4	3.5	3.5	3.5	3.5	3.5	3.6	3.6	3.6	3.6	3.6	3.6	3.5
2016	3.6	3.6	3.5	3.5	3.5	3.5	3.6	3.5	3.5	3.5	3.5	3.5	3.5
2017	3.5	3.4	3.5	3.5	3.5	3.5	3.5	3.4	3.3	3.4	3.4	3.4	3.4
Financial Activities													
2007	16.0	16.0	16.1	16.4	16.4	16.3	16.2	16.2	16.3	16.5	16.4	16.5	16.3
2008	16.3	16.3	16.2	15.8	15.7	15.7	15.4	15.3	15.2	15.1	15.0	15.0	15.6
2009	14.5	14.4	14.3	14.2	14.2	14.2	14.0	13.9	13.9	13.9	13.9	13.8	14.1
2010	13.6	13.6	13.6	13.7	13.6	13.6	13.7	13.7	13.6	13.7	13.8	13.9	13.7
2011	13.8	13.9	14.0	13.9	14.0	14.0	14.1	14.1	14.0	14.1	14.2	14.3	14.0
2012	14.1	14.1	14.2	14.4	14.4	14.4	14.4	14.4	14.3	14.4	14.5	14.5	14.3
2013	14.3	14.3	14.3	14.5	14.4	14.4	14.5	14.5	14.5	14.5	14.6	14.7	14.5
2014	14.3	14.4	14.4	14.4	14.4	14.4	14.5	14.5	14.5	14.7	14.7	14.7	14.5
2015	14.5	14.5	14.7	14.7	14.7	14.7	14.7	14.7	14.6	14.8	14.6	14.9	14.7
2016	14.7	14.7	14.9	14.9	14.8	14.9	14.6	14.7	14.7	14.8	14.8	14.9	14.8
2017	14.9	14.9	15.0	14.8	14.8	15.0	14.9	14.9	14.7	15.5	15.1	15.5	15.0
Professional and Business Services													
2007	35.3	36.1	36.7	35.4	35.9	36.5	34.6	35.3	35.1	33.8	34.6	35.2	35.4
2008	33.2	34.4	35.0	33.5	33.8	33.9	33.5	33.7	33.7	32.9	32.9	32.5	33.6
2009	30.8	30.9	31.3	30.4	30.6	31.2	30.2	30.3	30.3	30.6	30.6	30.8	30.7
2010	29.0	29.2	29.6	29.6	31.0	31.1	29.9	30.1	29.2	29.0	29.7	30.1	29.8
2011	28.5	29.8	29.9	31.0	30.9	31.0	30.6	30.6	30.3	30.3	31.0	31.4	30.4
2012	30.4	30.7	31.4	31.3	31.1	31.4	31.0	31.0	31.0	32.1	33.6	33.7	31.6
2013	33.1	33.9	34.5	34.6	35.2	35.2	35.0	35.3	35.4	36.1	37.1	37.4	35.2
2014	36.2	36.7	37.1	37.2	38.0	38.2	37.9	38.4	38.5	39.7	40.2	41.0	38.3
2015	39.7	40.5	40.9	41.4	42.3	42.9	41.4	41.4	41.3	42.5	43.0	43.6	41.7
2016	43.8	44.8	45.4	45.6	45.2	45.1	45.7	45.2	45.1	45.6	46.5	46.9	45.4
2017	46.0	46.6	47.4	47.2	47.0	47.4	47.5	47.9	46.6	47.5	48.4	48.2	47.3
Education and Health Services													
2007	40.8	41.6	41.5	41.3	41.3	41.3	41.0	41.3	41.6	41.7	42.0	42.2	41.5
2008	42.5	43.0	43.2	42.7	42.7	42.4	41.9	42.1	42.4	42.7	43.1	43.3	42.7
2009	43.3	43.3	43.4	43.2	43.1	42.8	42.3	42.7	42.4	43.3	43.6	43.9	43.1
2010	43.3	43.7	44.0	44.1	43.8	43.5	43.3	43.5	43.5	43.8	44.0	44.2	43.7
2011	44.1	44.5	44.7	44.8	44.7	44.3	44.1	44.3	44.4	44.7	44.9	45.3	44.6
2012	44.7	45.1	45.4	45.2	45.2	44.8	44.3	44.7	45.1	45.4	45.9	45.9	45.1
2013	45.6	46.1	46.1	46.2	46.2	45.6	45.4	45.8	46.0	46.6	47.0	47.2	46.2
2014	47.1	47.7	48.0	48.0	48.1	47.8	47.4	48.0	48.0	48.7	49.0	49.5	48.1
2015	49.3	49.6	49.8	49.8	49.9	49.7	49.5	49.9	49.9	50.7	51.0	51.3	50.0
2016	50.6	51.0	51.1	50.9	51.2	50.7	50.9	51.5	51.7	52.3	52.9	53.2	51.5
2017	52.6	53.0	52.9	52.7	52.7	52.3	52.1	52.8	52.0	52.6	52.4	52.8	52.6
Leisure and Hospitality													
2007	36.1	37.1	38.2	37.8	37.1	36.2	35.0	34.9	34.3	34.7	35.6	36.2	36.1
2008	36.0	36.7	37.2	36.5	35.5	34.6	33.4	33.2	32.6	33.1	33.9	34.6	34.8
2009	34.9	35.4	36.1	35.6	34.8	33.7	32.9	32.6	32.0	32.9	33.8	34.3	34.1
2010	34.3	35.1	36.1	35.7	34.8	34.0	33.0	32.8	32.4	32.9	33.8	34.0	34.1
2011	34.4	35.2	35.9	35.8	34.7	33.8	33.1	32.9	32.7	33.2	34.4	35.0	34.3
2012	35.4	36.3	37.5	37.1	36.2	35.6	34.7	34.6	33.8	34.3	35.6	36.0	35.6
2013	36.3	37.8	38.6	38.1	37.6	36.9	36.3	36.1	35.5	36.1	38.0	38.5	37.2
2014	38.8	39.9	41.0	40.4	39.0	38.6	38.5	38.4	37.8	39.2	40.6	41.4	39.5
2015	42.3	43.1	44.4	44.0	42.7	41.9	41.1	41.1	40.5	41.8	42.7	43.3	42.4
2016	43.1	44.0	44.6	44.0	43.1	42.3	41.6	41.8	41.0	42.4	43.4	43.8	42.9
2017	45.1	45.7	46.9	46.3	45.5	44.0	43.4	43.2	40.5	43.1	45.6	45.9	44.6

Employment by Industry: North Port-Sarasota-Bradenton, FL, Selected Years, 2007–2017—*Continued*

(Numbers in thousands, not seasonally adjusted)

Industry and year	January	February	March	April	May	June	July	August	September	October	November	December	Annual average
Other Services													
2007	13.9	13.9	14.1	13.9	13.8	14.1	13.7	13.8	13.9	14.2	14.5	14.7	14.0
2008	14.6	14.8	14.9	14.3	14.2	13.9	13.5	13.3	13.1	12.9	12.6	12.5	13.7
2009	12.3	12.3	12.3	12.2	12.2	12.2	11.9	11.9	11.9	11.9	12.0	12.0	12.1
2010	11.8	11.9	12.1	12.0	11.8	11.6	11.5	11.4	11.3	11.3	11.3	11.4	11.6
2011	11.1	11.2	11.2	11.3	11.2	11.1	10.9	10.8	10.9	10.7	10.7	10.7	11.0
2012	10.5	10.6	10.7	10.8	10.7	10.7	10.5	10.5	10.6	10.5	10.6	10.8	10.6
2013	10.7	10.8	10.9	11.0	11.0	11.0	10.8	10.9	11.0	11.2	11.5	11.5	11.0
2014	11.7	11.9	12.0	12.0	11.9	11.8	11.7	11.8	11.8	12.0	12.2	12.2	11.9
2015	12.2	12.4	12.6	12.6	12.6	12.5	12.4	12.4	12.5	12.7	12.9	13.1	12.6
2016	13.1	13.2	13.3	13.2	13.2	13.1	12.9	12.9	12.9	12.9	13.0	13.0	13.1
2017	12.9	13.0	13.1	13.1	13.2	13.1	13.0	13.2	12.9	13.1	13.2	13.3	13.1
Government													
2007	28.8	29.1	29.2	29.2	29.1	26.1	25.9	28.8	28.9	28.8	29.1	29.1	28.5
2008	29.0	29.2	29.5	29.5	29.5	26.5	26.3	29.2	29.2	29.0	28.8	28.8	28.7
2009	28.6	28.7	28.9	29.3	28.9	25.8	25.5	27.5	27.8	28.0	28.1	28.0	27.9
2010	27.8	27.9	28.0	28.0	29.5	25.5	25.2	26.6	27.1	27.5	27.6	27.5	27.4
2011	27.4	27.6	27.7	27.7	27.2	24.3	24.0	27.2	26.9	27.3	27.5	27.3	26.8
2012	27.1	27.4	27.5	27.3	27.2	24.2	24.1	26.0	26.8	27.3	27.3	27.3	26.6
2013	27.1	27.3	27.4	27.2	27.0	24.1	24.0	25.8	26.6	27.3	27.6	27.5	26.6
2014	26.9	27.1	27.4	27.3	27.2	24.1	24.2	25.9	26.7	27.6	27.9	27.7	26.7
2015	27.6	27.7	27.9	27.8	27.7	24.6	24.6	26.3	27.0	27.7	27.8	27.8	27.0
2016	27.7	27.8	28.0	28.0	28.0	25.1	25.1	26.9	27.5	28.0	27.9	27.8	27.3
2017	27.9	28.1	28.2	27.7	28.1	25.1	25.2	26.8	28.1	28.3	28.0	27.9	27.5

Employment by Industry: Dayton, OH, Selected Years, 2007–2017

(Numbers in thousands, not seasonally adjusted)

Industry and year	January	February	March	April	May	June	July	August	September	October	November	December	Annual average
Total Nonfarm													
2007	386.4	388.9	392.0	394.5	395.6	396.3	389.7	391.4	394.2	395.1	395.5	394.1	392.8
2008	384.4	385.0	383.2	385.1	386.6	387.3	382.1	383.8	384.8	383.6	381.6	379.7	383.9
2009	365.9	364.7	364.7	363.2	364.5	362.1	357.9	358.4	362.3	363.1	363.6	362.8	362.8
2010	353.7	354.3	357.2	361.1	363.2	362.1	357.7	359.1	362.5	364.8	366.4	366.3	360.7
2011	358.0	359.4	362.3	366.7	367.8	366.3	362.3	363.2	368.0	369.4	371.3	370.5	365.4
2012	363.2	365.4	367.7	369.8	371.0	372.0	365.8	367.0	369.1	369.9	372.1	372.1	368.8
2013	360.9	363.7	365.2	367.9	371.3	370.4	366.1	367.9	369.1	370.5	374.1	373.1	368.4
2014	363.3	365.2	368.2	370.9	372.9	373.7	370.8	373.4	375.0	377.4	379.5	380.3	372.6
2015	370.3	371.9	373.5	378.1	380.7	380.5	380.4	381.4	380.9	384.8	387.0	388.1	379.8
2016	377.4	380.0	382.5	384.6	385.3	384.1	385.4	385.1	386.3	387.3	389.5	389.9	384.8
2017	380.5	382.5	383.9	387.6	388.6	387.8	389.2	389.8	389.4	393.6	397.6	398.0	389.0
Total Private													
2007	324.2	326.1	328.9	331.6	332.0	333.4	329.9	331.6	332.2	332.1	333.4	333.0	330.7
2008	323.5	322.5	320.6	322.4	322.9	325.1	322.4	324.1	322.6	320.3	318.0	317.1	321.8
2009	303.2	301.5	301.1	299.5	299.3	298.1	297.3	297.7	298.7	298.2	298.9	299.4	299.4
2010	290.2	290.0	292.4	296.0	296.4	297.0	296.7	297.7	298.8	299.7	301.4	301.4	296.5
2011	294.0	294.5	297.0	301.3	301.6	301.7	300.6	301.8	304.1	304.6	306.3	307.4	301.2
2012	300.7	301.3	303.4	305.4	306.3	308.1	305.9	306.3	305.8	306.0	308.0	308.2	305.5
2013	299.4	300.3	301.7	304.6	307.4	308.4	306.6	307.8	306.3	307.5	310.7	310.3	305.9
2014	302.5	302.4	305.1	308.7	310.7	312.6	312.2	313.8	312.2	314.1	315.9	317.0	310.6
2015	309.0	308.9	310.8	314.5	318.4	318.7	319.0	319.8	318.3	321.1	323.1	324.2	317.2
2016	316.0	316.7	319.2	320.6	322.8	321.7	323.8	323.4	322.5	323.4	325.3	325.8	321.8
2017	318.6	319.1	320.4	323.9	326.6	326.8	328.1	328.8	326.8	330.3	334.0	334.9	326.5
Goods Producing													
2007	60.3	62.1	62.7	63.4	63.6	64.6	63.3	64.3	63.8	62.9	63.0	62.3	63.0
2008	60.0	59.4	57.0	57.0	57.5	60.3	59.7	60.5	59.0	58.3	56.6	55.1	58.4
2009	50.0	49.1	48.6	47.8	47.6	47.1	47.0	47.4	47.0	47.0	46.5	46.4	47.6
2010	44.4	44.1	44.7	45.8	46.5	47.3	47.7	48.1	48.0	47.7	47.8	47.5	46.6
2011	46.4	46.4	47.2	47.7	48.5	49.0	49.4	49.6	49.6	49.6	49.7	49.6	48.6
2012	48.5	48.4	48.8	49.2	49.7	50.4	50.1	50.1	50.0	49.8	49.8	49.8	49.6
2013	48.4	48.5	48.9	48.9	49.8	50.3	50.0	49.9	49.6	49.7	49.9	49.7	49.5
2014	48.5	48.7	49.3	49.7	50.6	51.4	51.4	51.8	51.6	51.6	51.6	51.5	50.6
2015	50.5	50.6	50.7	51.5	52.2	52.5	52.8	53.1	52.9	53.3	53.0	53.2	52.2
2016	52.1	52.2	52.6	52.9	53.4	53.6	54.4	54.3	54.5	54.4	54.4	54.3	53.6
2017	53.3	53.2	53.4	53.8	54.5	55.2	55.4	55.5	55.3	55.4	55.6	55.7	54.7
Service-Providing													
2007	326.1	326.8	329.3	331.1	332.0	331.7	326.4	327.1	330.4	332.2	332.5	331.8	329.8
2008	324.4	325.6	326.2	328.1	329.1	327.0	322.4	323.3	325.8	325.3	325.0	324.6	325.6
2009	315.9	315.6	316.1	315.4	316.9	315.0	310.9	311.0	315.3	316.1	317.1	316.4	315.1
2010	309.3	310.2	312.5	315.3	316.7	314.8	310.0	311.0	314.5	317.1	318.6	318.8	314.1
2011	311.6	313.0	315.1	319.0	319.3	317.3	312.9	313.6	318.4	319.8	321.6	320.9	316.9
2012	314.7	317.0	318.9	320.6	321.3	321.6	315.7	316.9	319.1	320.1	322.3	322.3	319.2
2013	312.5	315.2	316.3	319.0	321.5	320.1	316.1	318.0	319.5	320.8	324.2	323.4	318.9
2014	314.8	316.5	318.9	321.2	322.3	322.3	319.4	321.6	323.4	325.8	327.9	328.8	321.9
2015	319.8	321.3	322.8	326.6	328.5	328.0	327.6	328.3	328.0	331.5	334.0	334.9	327.6
2016	325.3	327.8	329.9	331.7	331.9	330.5	331.0	330.8	331.8	332.9	335.1	335.6	331.2
2017	327.2	329.3	330.5	333.8	334.1	332.6	333.8	334.3	334.1	338.2	342.0	342.3	334.4
Mining, Logging, and Construction													
2007	13.0	12.4	13.1	14.1	14.7	15.4	15.4	15.2	14.7	14.4	14.5	13.8	14.2
2008	12.6	12.4	12.5	13.2	13.8	14.0	14.2	14.1	13.6	13.3	12.7	12.1	13.2
2009	10.9	10.7	10.9	11.0	11.6	11.8	12.1	11.8	11.4	11.4	11.2	10.8	11.3
2010	9.7	9.3	9.8	10.5	10.7	11.2	11.5	11.4	11.2	11.0	10.9	10.4	10.6
2011	9.5	9.5	9.8	10.4	11.1	11.5	11.8	11.8	11.7	11.4	11.4	11.0	10.9
2012	10.5	10.3	10.5	10.9	11.4	11.6	11.5	11.4	11.3	11.2	11.1	10.9	11.1
2013	10.1	10.2	10.6	10.8	11.5	11.8	11.7	11.7	11.6	11.6	11.6	11.2	11.2
2014	10.4	10.4	10.9	11.2	11.9	12.3	12.5	12.5	12.3	12.2	12.0	11.8	11.7
2015	11.1	11.0	11.2	12.0	12.4	12.6	12.8	12.8	12.8	12.9	12.7	12.6	12.2
2016	11.6	11.6	11.9	12.3	12.6	12.8	12.9	12.8	12.7	12.6	12.5	12.1	12.4
2017	11.5	11.6	11.8	12.2	12.7	13.1	13.2	13.3	13.2	13.1	13.0	12.7	12.6

Employment by Industry: Dayton, OH, Selected Years, 2007–2017—*Continued*

(Numbers in thousands, not seasonally adjusted)

Industry and year	January	February	March	April	May	June	July	August	September	October	November	December	Annual average
Manufacturing													
2007	47.3	49.7	49.6	49.3	48.9	49.2	47.9	49.1	49.1	48.5	48.5	48.5	48.8
2008	47.4	47.0	44.5	43.8	43.7	46.3	45.5	46.4	45.4	45.0	43.9	43.0	45.2
2009	39.1	38.4	37.7	36.8	36.0	35.3	34.9	35.6	35.6	35.6	35.3	35.6	36.3
2010	34.7	34.8	34.9	35.3	35.8	36.1	36.2	36.7	36.8	36.7	36.9	37.1	36.0
2011	36.9	36.9	37.4	37.3	37.4	37.5	37.6	37.8	37.9	38.2	38.3	38.6	37.7
2012	38.0	38.1	38.3	38.3	38.3	38.8	38.6	38.7	38.7	38.6	38.7	38.9	38.5
2013	38.3	38.3	38.3	38.1	38.3	38.5	38.3	38.2	38.0	38.1	38.3	38.5	38.3
2014	38.1	38.3	38.4	38.5	38.7	39.1	38.9	39.3	39.3	39.4	39.6	39.7	38.9
2015	39.4	39.6	39.5	39.5	39.8	39.9	40.0	40.3	40.1	40.4	40.3	40.6	40.0
2016	40.5	40.6	40.7	40.6	40.8	40.8	41.5	41.5	41.8	41.8	41.9	42.2	41.2
2017	41.8	41.6	41.6	41.6	41.8	42.1	42.2	42.2	42.1	42.3	42.6	43.0	42.1
Trade, Transportation, and Utilities													
2007	66.3	65.5	66.3	66.9	67.1	67.2	67.0	66.6	66.5	66.7	68.1	68.7	66.9
2008	65.5	64.6	64.8	65.1	65.4	65.7	64.9	65.1	64.7	64.1	64.7	65.6	65.0
2009	62.2	61.3	61.3	61.3	61.6	61.4	60.9	60.7	60.4	60.7	61.7	62.5	61.3
2010	59.4	58.7	59.2	59.6	59.9	60.2	59.7	59.8	59.4	60.3	61.9	62.9	60.1
2011	60.1	59.3	59.7	60.5	60.9	61.1	60.9	61.1	61.1	62.1	63.7	64.7	61.3
2012	61.9	61.3	62.0	62.2	62.7	62.7	62.3	62.5	62.4	63.1	64.8	65.3	62.8
2013	62.2	61.8	62.0	62.5	63.1	63.1	63.1	63.2	62.9	63.7	65.8	66.5	63.3
2014	63.5	62.9	63.3	63.8	64.0	64.2	64.0	64.1	63.9	64.7	66.5	67.3	64.4
2015	64.7	64.4	64.5	64.9	65.7	65.7	65.5	65.5	65.0	65.7	67.2	68.1	65.6
2016	64.9	64.4	64.7	64.8	65.1	65.1	65.2	65.2	64.6	65.3	66.7	67.5	65.3
2017	64.9	64.4	64.3	64.8	65.1	65.1	65.6	65.6	64.8	65.7	67.8	68.2	65.5
Wholesale Trade													
2007	13.6	13.6	13.7	13.7	13.7	13.8	13.9	13.8	13.7	13.8	13.7	13.8	13.7
2008	13.7	13.6	13.7	13.7	13.7	13.6	13.5	13.4	13.3	13.0	12.9	12.9	13.4
2009	12.8	12.7	12.6	12.5	12.3	12.3	12.2	12.1	11.9	11.7	11.7	11.8	12.2
2010	11.7	11.7	11.7	11.7	11.7	11.8	11.8	11.8	11.7	11.8	11.7	11.8	11.7
2011	12.0	11.9	12.0	12.1	12.2	12.3	12.4	12.4	12.4	12.6	12.5	12.6	12.3
2012	12.7	12.8	12.9	12.6	12.7	12.8	12.9	12.9	12.8	12.9	12.8	12.9	12.8
2013	12.7	12.6	12.6	12.6	12.7	12.7	12.7	12.6	12.5	12.6	12.6	12.6	12.6
2014	12.6	12.6	12.6	12.7	12.8	12.9	12.8	12.8	12.8	12.8	12.9	12.9	12.8
2015	13.1	13.1	13.1	13.2	13.2	13.2	13.3	13.2	13.0	13.1	13.0	13.0	13.1
2016	12.9	12.9	12.9	12.9	12.9	13.0	13.0	12.9	12.8	12.8	12.8	12.9	12.9
2017	12.8	12.9	12.9	13.2	13.3	13.4	13.5	13.5	13.4	13.4	13.4	13.4	13.3
Retail Trade													
2007	41.3	40.5	41.1	41.7	41.8	41.7	41.4	41.1	41.1	41.3	42.8	43.2	41.6
2008	40.7	39.9	40.2	40.5	40.6	40.7	40.1	40.2	40.0	39.8	40.5	41.3	40.4
2009	38.7	37.9	38.1	38.5	39.0	39.0	38.3	38.2	38.0	38.3	39.3	39.8	38.6
2010	37.5	36.8	37.2	37.6	37.9	37.9	37.5	37.5	37.2	37.8	39.2	39.8	37.8
2011	37.4	36.8	37.1	37.7	37.9	38.0	37.7	37.8	37.7	38.6	40.2	40.8	38.1
2012	38.3	37.6	38.2	38.5	38.8	38.6	38.2	38.3	38.2	38.7	40.3	40.5	38.7
2013	38.2	37.8	38.1	38.6	39.0	38.9	38.8	38.9	38.6	39.2	40.9	41.3	39.0
2014	38.5	38.1	38.5	38.9	38.9	39.0	38.7	38.8	38.7	39.5	41.0	41.4	39.2
2015	38.7	38.5	38.6	38.9	39.4	39.5	39.2	39.3	39.0	39.5	40.9	41.5	39.4
2016	39.2	39.0	39.2	39.5	39.8	39.6	39.6	39.7	39.2	39.8	40.9	41.4	39.7
2017	39.5	38.9	38.9	39.1	39.3	39.2	39.5	39.4	38.8	39.5	41.3	41.6	39.6
Transportation and Utilities													
2007	11.4	11.4	11.5	11.5	11.6	11.7	11.7	11.7	11.7	11.6	11.6	11.7	11.6
2008	11.1	11.1	10.9	10.9	11.1	11.4	11.3	11.5	11.4	11.3	11.3	11.4	11.2
2009	10.7	10.7	10.6	10.3	10.3	10.3	10.4	10.4	10.5	10.7	10.7	10.9	10.5
2010	10.2	10.2	10.3	10.3	10.3	10.5	10.4	10.5	10.5	10.7	11.0	11.3	10.5
2011	10.7	10.6	10.6	10.7	10.8	10.8	10.8	10.9	11.0	10.9	11.0	11.3	10.8
2012	10.9	10.9	10.9	11.1	11.2	11.3	11.2	11.3	11.4	11.5	11.7	11.9	11.3
2013	11.3	11.4	11.3	11.3	11.4	11.5	11.6	11.7	11.8	11.9	12.3	12.6	11.7
2014	12.4	12.2	12.2	12.2	12.3	12.3	12.5	12.5	12.4	12.4	12.6	13.0	12.4
2015	12.9	12.8	12.8	12.8	13.1	13.0	13.0	13.0	13.0	13.1	13.3	13.6	13.0
2016	12.8	12.5	12.6	12.4	12.4	12.5	12.6	12.6	12.6	12.7	13.0	13.2	12.7
2017	12.6	12.6	12.5	12.5	12.5	12.5	12.6	12.7	12.6	12.8	13.1	13.2	12.7

Employment by Industry: Dayton, OH, Selected Years, 2007–2017—*Continued*

(Numbers in thousands, not seasonally adjusted)

Industry and year	January	February	March	April	May	June	July	August	September	October	November	December	Annual average
Information													
2007	12.1	12.1	12.0	12.1	12.2	12.2	12.1	12.1	12.0	12.0	12.1	12.1	12.1
2008	12.2	12.1	12.1	12.1	12.0	11.9	12.2	12.1	11.7	11.6	11.6	11.5	11.9
2009	11.4	11.4	11.2	10.9	10.9	10.9	10.8	10.8	10.7	10.6	10.7	10.7	10.9
2010	10.7	10.7	10.7	10.5	10.4	10.4	10.3	10.2	10.1	10.0	9.9	9.9	10.3
2011	9.8	9.8	9.8	9.8	9.7	9.8	9.8	9.7	9.7	9.5	9.4	9.3	9.7
2012	9.2	9.1	9.0	9.0	8.9	8.9	9.0	8.8	8.8	8.7	8.7	8.7	8.9
2013	8.7	8.7	8.7	8.7	8.7	8.8	8.8	8.7	8.6	8.5	8.5	8.5	8.7
2014	8.4	8.4	8.4	8.5	8.5	8.6	8.6	8.5	8.4	8.4	8.4	8.5	8.5
2015	8.4	8.4	8.4	8.5	8.5	8.6	8.6	8.6	8.5	8.5	8.5	8.5	8.5
2016	8.4	8.5	8.5	8.5	8.5	8.5	8.5	8.4	8.3	8.4	8.4	8.4	8.4
2017	8.4	8.3	8.3	8.3	8.4	8.4	8.4	8.3	8.2	8.2	8.2	8.2	8.3
Financial Activities													
2007	19.6	19.7	19.7	19.8	19.8	19.6	19.5	19.4	19.1	19.0	18.9	18.8	19.4
2008	18.7	18.4	18.3	18.2	18.1	18.0	17.8	17.7	17.4	17.2	17.1	17.1	17.8
2009	17.0	16.8	16.6	16.6	16.6	16.6	16.6	16.5	16.3	16.4	16.4	16.3	16.6
2010	16.3	16.3	16.3	16.5	16.6	16.5	16.6	16.5	16.4	16.6	16.6	16.6	16.5
2011	16.3	16.3	16.3	16.4	16.4	16.5	16.5	16.5	16.4	16.4	16.5	16.6	16.4
2012	16.4	16.4	16.5	16.7	16.7	16.8	17.0	17.0	17.0	17.0	17.1	17.1	16.8
2013	16.8	16.9	16.8	16.9	17.1	17.1	17.1	17.1	17.0	17.0	17.1	17.1	17.0
2014	16.9	17.0	17.1	17.1	17.3	17.4	17.4	17.7	17.5	17.6	17.6	17.6	17.4
2015	17.3	17.2	17.3	17.3	17.5	17.6	17.6	17.7	17.5	17.8	17.8	17.8	17.5
2016	17.5	17.6	17.6	17.7	17.7	17.8	17.9	17.8	17.8	17.9	18.0	18.2	17.8
2017	17.8	17.9	17.8	17.9	18.0	18.2	18.3	18.3	18.2	18.2	18.2	18.3	18.1
Professional and Business Services													
2007	51.0	51.2	51.3	51.5	51.4	52.1	51.7	51.8	51.8	52.3	52.0	52.0	51.7
2008	50.6	50.9	51.0	51.1	51.0	51.2	50.5	50.4	49.8	49.4	48.3	48.3	50.2
2009	46.4	45.6	45.2	45.0	44.7	45.0	45.2	45.3	45.1	44.9	45.0	45.1	45.2
2010	43.6	43.9	44.1	45.4	45.4	45.9	45.8	46.5	46.1	46.2	46.3	46.1	45.4
2011	45.6	45.7	46.2	46.9	46.6	46.9	47.0	47.5	47.4	47.3	47.3	47.7	46.8
2012	46.9	47.1	47.1	47.4	47.4	47.7	47.8	47.8	47.3	47.7	47.4	47.4	47.4
2013	46.3	46.3	46.1	47.2	47.3	47.6	47.5	48.0	47.8	48.1	48.5	48.0	47.4
2014	47.2	47.0	47.4	48.5	48.6	49.2	49.6	49.8	49.2	49.9	50.0	49.9	48.9
2015	48.3	48.1	48.7	49.8	50.6	50.9	51.3	51.1	50.8	51.4	51.5	51.2	50.3
2016	50.1	50.2	51.0	50.8	51.0	50.7	51.1	50.9	50.6	50.9	51.1	50.8	50.8
2017	49.1	49.5	49.9	50.6	50.9	51.2	51.3	51.5	50.9	51.4	51.9	51.5	50.8
Education and Health Services													
2007	64.6	65.3	65.6	65.6	64.7	63.8	63.1	63.9	66.6	67.5	67.8	68.0	65.5
2008	66.9	67.6	67.6	67.5	66.5	65.4	65.0	65.7	68.3	68.8	69.1	69.2	67.3
2009	67.6	68.6	68.7	67.9	66.9	65.7	65.4	65.6	68.5	69.1	69.2	69.1	67.7
2010	67.9	68.5	68.7	68.2	67.0	65.5	65.3	65.4	68.3	69.4	69.6	69.6	67.8
2011	68.4	69.3	69.5	69.9	68.6	66.7	65.8	66.1	69.6	70.2	70.2	70.4	68.7
2012	69.2	70.2	70.1	69.9	68.9	68.6	67.3	67.7	69.1	69.5	69.9	69.6	69.2
2013	68.0	68.9	69.1	69.3	69.0	68.3	67.8	68.4	69.1	70.0	70.5	70.0	69.0
2014	68.6	69.2	69.6	69.9	69.6	68.7	68.4	69.1	70.3	70.9	71.1	71.5	69.7
2015	70.2	70.6	70.9	70.9	71.0	69.9	69.9	70.7	71.6	72.3	73.2	73.2	71.2
2016	71.9	72.6	73.0	72.8	73.0	71.6	72.0	72.4	73.4	73.5	73.8	73.6	72.8
2017	73.0	73.4	73.6	73.7	74.1	72.6	73.1	73.5	74.7	76.3	77.2	77.6	74.4
Leisure and Hospitality													
2007	34.9	34.8	35.6	36.6	37.5	38.0	37.6	37.9	36.9	36.2	36.0	35.7	36.5
2008	34.5	34.4	34.7	36.3	37.2	37.5	37.2	37.5	36.7	36.0	35.7	35.4	36.1
2009	34.1	34.1	35.0	35.5	36.4	36.9	36.8	36.8	36.1	35.0	34.8	34.6	35.5
2010	33.4	33.3	34.0	35.3	35.9	36.5	36.6	36.6	36.0	35.1	34.9	34.6	35.2
2011	33.3	33.5	34.1	35.7	36.4	37.1	36.7	36.9	36.0	35.4	35.3	35.0	35.5
2012	34.4	34.6	35.6	36.5	37.3	38.1	37.8	37.8	36.8	35.8	35.8	35.8	36.4
2013	34.7	34.7	35.5	36.3	37.5	38.3	37.7	37.9	36.9	36.2	36.2	36.3	36.5
2014	35.5	35.3	36.0	37.2	38.2	39.1	38.9	38.9	37.6	37.3	37.1	37.1	37.4
2015	36.0	36.0	36.7	37.9	38.9	39.5	39.1	39.0	38.0	38.1	38.0	38.2	38.0
2016	37.2	37.3	37.8	39.0	39.9	40.2	40.4	40.1	39.1	38.8	38.7	38.8	38.9
2017	37.9	38.2	38.8	40.4	41.1	41.5	41.4	41.5	40.3	40.7	40.7	41.0	40.3

Employment by Industry: Dayton, OH, Selected Years, 2007–2017—*Continued*

(Numbers in thousands, not seasonally adjusted)

Industry and year	January	February	March	April	May	June	July	August	September	October	November	December	Annual average
Other Services													
2007	15.4	15.4	15.7	15.7	15.7	15.9	15.6	15.6	15.5	15.5	15.5	15.4	15.6
2008	15.1	15.1	15.1	15.1	15.2	15.1	15.1	15.1	15.0	14.9	14.9	14.9	15.1
2009	14.5	14.6	14.5	14.5	14.6	14.5	14.6	14.6	14.6	14.5	14.6	14.7	14.6
2010	14.5	14.5	14.7	14.7	14.7	14.7	14.7	14.6	14.5	14.4	14.4	14.2	14.6
2011	14.1	14.2	14.2	14.4	14.5	14.6	14.5	14.4	14.3	14.1	14.2	14.1	14.3
2012	14.2	14.2	14.3	14.5	14.7	14.9	14.6	14.6	14.4	14.4	14.5	14.5	14.5
2013	14.3	14.5	14.6	14.8	14.9	14.9	14.6	14.6	14.4	14.3	14.2	14.2	14.5
2014	13.9	13.9	14.0	14.0	13.9	14.0	13.9	13.9	13.7	13.7	13.6	13.6	13.8
2015	13.6	13.6	13.6	13.7	14.0	14.0	14.2	14.1	14.0	14.0	13.9	14.0	13.9
2016	13.9	13.9	14.0	14.1	14.2	14.2	14.3	14.3	14.2	14.2	14.2	14.2	14.1
2017	14.2	14.2	14.3	14.4	14.5	14.6	14.6	14.6	14.4	14.4	14.4	14.4	14.4
Government													
2007	62.2	62.8	63.1	62.9	63.6	62.9	59.8	59.8	62.0	63.0	62.1	61.1	62.1
2008	60.9	62.5	62.6	62.7	63.7	62.2	59.7	59.7	62.2	63.3	63.6	62.6	62.1
2009	62.7	63.2	63.6	63.7	65.2	64.0	60.6	60.7	63.6	64.9	64.7	63.4	63.4
2010	63.5	64.3	64.8	65.1	66.8	65.1	61.0	61.4	63.7	65.1	65.0	64.9	64.2
2011	64.0	64.9	65.3	65.4	66.2	64.6	61.7	61.4	63.9	64.8	65.0	63.1	64.2
2012	62.5	64.1	64.3	64.4	64.7	63.9	59.9	60.7	63.3	63.9	64.1	63.9	63.3
2013	61.5	63.4	63.5	63.3	63.9	62.0	59.5	60.1	62.8	63.0	63.4	62.8	62.4
2014	60.8	62.8	63.1	62.2	62.2	61.1	58.6	59.6	62.8	63.3	63.6	63.3	62.0
2015	61.3	63.0	62.7	63.6	62.3	61.8	61.4	61.6	62.6	63.7	63.9	63.9	62.7
2016	61.4	63.3	63.3	64.0	62.5	62.4	61.6	61.7	63.8	63.9	64.2	64.1	63.0
2017	61.9	63.4	63.5	63.7	62.0	61.0	61.1	61.0	62.6	63.3	63.6	63.1	62.5

Employment by Industry: Charleston-North Charleston, SC, Selected Years, 2007–2017

(Numbers in thousands, not seasonally adjusted)

Industry and year	January	February	March	April	May	June	July	August	September	October	November	December	Annual average
Total Nonfarm													
2007	292.1	294.6	298.3	301.2	303.5	304.4	302.0	302.5	303.3	304.7	304.5	304.5	301.3
2008	299.5	300.6	302.4	304.8	306.7	306.4	301.7	301.5	301.1	300.2	300.1	297.8	301.9
2009	287.4	286.1	287.5	288.6	289.3	289.4	284.5	284.4	284.1	284.4	284.6	283.5	286.2
2010	278.5	279.8	283.4	286.6	290.5	290.7	288.2	288.1	287.7	290.7	292.3	292.3	287.4
2011	287.9	289.5	292.2	296.5	298.7	298.5	296.7	296.3	296.9	298.0	299.3	299.5	295.8
2012	295.6	298.9	302.1	306.2	307.6	308.1	305.2	306.6	306.4	307.5	311.2	309.8	305.4
2013	303.1	305.5	307.9	311.2	313.0	314.3	313.2	314.0	313.8	315.4	317.0	317.3	312.1
2014	310.9	313.7	316.6	322.2	325.1	325.3	322.5	324.0	324.0	326.2	328.3	328.4	322.3
2015	322.5	325.5	328.9	332.2	335.8	335.6	335.4	336.7	335.0	339.2	342.0	341.6	334.2
2016	335.6	338.3	340.9	345.2	347.2	348.2	347.6	347.1	347.3	345.6	350.0	349.7	345.2
2017	345.0	348.0	350.7	352.7	355.4	356.6	356.1	355.2	352.1	355.4	357.9	355.7	353.4
Total Private													
2007	234.8	236.9	240.5	243.0	245.3	246.4	245.6	246.0	244.6	245.5	245.0	245.0	243.2
2008	240.4	241.1	242.5	244.4	246.0	246.1	243.0	242.4	240.4	239.2	238.7	236.5	241.7
2009	227.4	225.8	227.1	228.3	229.2	229.7	226.5	226.2	224.0	223.8	223.9	222.9	226.2
2010	218.2	219.1	222.3	225.0	227.3	229.8	228.3	228.3	226.8	229.0	230.3	230.5	226.2
2011	226.8	228.1	230.7	234.5	236.7	237.4	236.8	237.0	235.6	236.7	237.8	237.9	234.7
2012	234.5	237.3	240.1	243.8	245.2	246.2	244.4	245.3	243.5	244.4	245.9	246.3	243.1
2013	240.8	242.7	244.9	247.7	249.9	251.7	251.8	252.7	250.8	253.0	254.2	254.7	249.6
2014	249.3	251.3	254.1	258.7	261.6	263.3	262.0	262.3	260.7	262.4	264.1	264.4	259.5
2015	259.7	261.7	264.8	268.0	271.6	272.7	272.8	273.8	270.7	274.3	276.6	276.2	270.2
2016	270.8	273.3	275.4	279.6	281.7	283.3	283.2	283.8	282.1	280.8	285.1	284.5	280.3
2017	280.7	283.5	285.8	287.8	290.6	292.5	292.2	291.5	286.7	289.8	292.1	289.7	288.6
Goods Producing													
2007	43.3	43.6	43.9	44.3	44.5	44.7	44.7	44.6	44.4	44.8	44.6	44.5	44.3
2008	43.7	43.2	43.1	42.5	42.2	42.0	41.7	41.4	41.0	40.8	40.2	39.6	41.8
2009	37.7	37.0	37.2	36.7	36.3	36.6	35.7	36.1	36.1	35.4	35.4	35.1	36.3
2010	34.5	34.5	34.9	34.8	35.0	35.2	35.1	35.1	35.0	34.7	34.9	35.2	34.9
2011	35.0	35.1	35.4	35.7	36.2	36.6	36.6	36.6	36.6	36.5	36.7	36.7	36.1
2012	36.4	36.5	36.9	37.1	37.3	37.5	37.5	37.5	37.4	37.4	37.6	37.8	37.2
2013	37.7	38.0	38.1	38.3	38.8	39.1	39.5	39.5	39.6	39.5	39.7	40.1	39.0
2014	39.8	39.9	40.1	40.4	40.9	41.5	41.4	41.4	41.3	41.7	41.9	42.1	41.0
2015	42.1	42.7	42.5	42.4	42.9	43.5	43.7	43.7	43.7	43.9	44.2	44.1	43.3
2016	44.1	44.6	44.6	44.7	44.8	45.3	45.4	45.4	45.5	45.2	45.4	45.7	45.1
2017	45.6	46.2	46.3	46.4	46.6	46.9	47.1	46.8	46.7	46.9	47.4	47.4	46.7
Service-Providing													
2007	248.8	251.0	254.4	256.9	259.0	259.7	257.3	257.9	258.9	259.9	259.9	260.0	257.0
2008	255.8	257.4	259.3	262.3	264.5	264.4	260.0	260.1	260.1	259.4	259.9	258.2	260.1
2009	249.7	249.1	250.3	251.9	253.0	252.8	248.8	248.3	248.0	249.0	249.2	248.4	249.9
2010	244.0	245.3	248.5	251.8	255.5	255.5	253.1	253.0	252.7	256.0	257.4	257.1	252.5
2011	252.9	254.4	256.8	260.8	262.5	261.9	260.1	259.7	260.3	261.5	262.6	262.8	259.7
2012	259.2	262.4	265.2	269.1	270.3	270.6	267.7	269.1	269.0	270.1	273.6	272.0	268.2
2013	265.4	267.5	269.8	272.9	274.2	275.2	273.7	274.5	274.2	275.9	277.3	277.2	273.2
2014	271.1	273.8	276.5	281.8	284.2	283.8	281.1	282.6	282.7	284.5	286.4	286.3	281.2
2015	280.4	282.8	286.4	289.8	292.9	292.1	291.7	293.0	291.3	295.3	297.8	297.5	290.9
2016	291.5	293.7	296.3	300.5	302.4	302.9	302.2	301.7	301.8	300.4	304.6	304.0	300.2
2017	299.4	301.8	304.4	306.3	308.8	309.7	309.0	308.4	305.4	308.5	310.5	308.3	306.7
Mining, Logging, and Construction													
2007	21.6	21.8	21.8	21.9	22.0	22.1	21.9	22.2	21.9	21.7	21.5	21.2	21.8
2008	20.7	20.4	20.2	19.7	19.4	19.3	18.8	18.6	18.2	18.0	17.7	17.4	19.0
2009	16.2	15.9	16.1	15.6	15.5	15.6	15.4	15.2	15.0	14.7	14.6	14.4	15.4
2010	13.9	13.9	14.2	14.3	14.4	14.5	14.4	14.3	14.2	14.0	14.0	14.0	14.2
2011	13.8	13.8	13.9	13.9	14.2	14.3	14.1	13.9	13.8	13.6	13.6	13.4	13.9
2012	13.0	13.1	13.3	13.5	13.7	13.9	14.0	14.0	13.9	13.7	13.8	13.9	13.7
2013	14.1	14.0	14.2	14.5	14.9	15.2	15.4	15.5	15.5	15.4	15.6	15.8	15.0
2014	15.5	15.6	15.7	15.9	16.3	16.7	16.5	16.5	16.4	16.7	16.8	16.9	16.3
2015	16.7	17.0	17.2	17.2	17.5	17.9	17.9	17.9	17.8	18.1	18.4	18.4	17.7
2016	18.4	18.5	18.7	18.8	19.0	19.3	19.4	19.4	19.4	19.3	19.5	19.7	19.1
2017	19.6	19.8	20.0	20.0	20.2	20.4	20.5	20.3	20.1	20.2	20.6	20.8	20.2

Employment by Industry: Charleston-North Charleston, SC, Selected Years, 2007–2017—*Continued*

(Numbers in thousands, not seasonally adjusted)

Industry and year	January	February	March	April	May	June	July	August	September	October	November	December	Annual average
Manufacturing													
2007	21.7	21.8	22.1	22.4	22.5	22.6	22.8	22.4	22.5	23.1	23.1	23.3	22.5
2008	23.0	22.8	22.9	22.8	22.8	22.7	22.9	22.8	22.8	22.8	22.5	22.2	22.8
2009	21.5	21.1	21.1	21.1	20.8	21.0	20.3	20.9	21.1	20.7	20.8	20.7	20.9
2010	20.6	20.6	20.7	20.5	20.6	20.7	20.7	20.8	20.8	20.7	20.9	21.2	20.7
2011	21.2	21.3	21.5	21.8	22.0	22.3	22.5	22.7	22.8	22.9	23.1	23.3	22.3
2012	23.4	23.4	23.6	23.6	23.6	23.6	23.5	23.5	23.5	23.7	23.8	23.9	23.6
2013	23.6	24.0	23.9	23.8	23.9	23.9	24.1	24.0	24.1	24.1	24.1	24.3	24.0
2014	24.3	24.3	24.4	24.5	24.6	24.8	24.9	24.9	24.9	25.0	25.1	25.2	24.7
2015	25.4	25.7	25.3	25.2	25.4	25.6	25.8	25.8	25.9	25.8	25.8	25.7	25.6
2016	25.7	26.1	25.9	25.9	25.8	26.0	26.0	26.0	26.1	25.9	25.9	26.0	25.9
2017	26.0	26.4	26.3	26.4	26.4	26.5	26.6	26.5	26.6	26.7	26.8	26.6	26.5
Trade, Transportation, and Utilities													
2007	57.4	57.8	58.6	58.7	59.2	59.4	59.2	59.4	59.1	59.1	59.8	60.2	59.0
2008	57.8	57.4	57.5	57.7	57.9	57.9	57.4	57.3	56.6	57.5	58.0	57.8	57.6
2009	54.6	53.7	53.6	53.7	53.7	53.6	53.2	52.7	52.2	52.2	52.9	53.4	53.3
2010	51.6	51.6	52.4	52.5	53.1	53.8	53.8	53.7	53.4	54.3	55.3	55.9	53.5
2011	54.0	53.9	54.1	54.5	54.8	55.0	55.4	55.3	55.0	55.7	56.3	56.7	55.1
2012	55.3	55.5	56.0	56.5	56.9	57.1	57.1	57.1	56.7	57.4	58.9	59.3	57.0
2013	56.6	56.6	56.9	57.6	58.0	58.5	58.7	58.8	58.6	59.6	60.2	61.0	58.4
2014	58.6	58.5	58.6	59.4	59.9	60.8	60.2	60.2	59.8	60.2	61.5	61.9	60.0
2015	59.8	59.5	60.2	61.0	61.6	62.1	62.2	62.4	61.8	62.8	63.8	64.3	61.8
2016	62.0	62.2	62.4	63.2	63.7	63.9	63.8	63.8	63.6	63.4	65.2	65.8	63.6
2017	63.8	63.6	63.8	64.0	64.6	64.9	65.0	64.8	63.5	63.7	65.5	64.6	64.3
Wholesale Trade													
2007	9.0	9.2	9.2	9.2	9.2	9.2	9.4	9.4	9.3	9.3	9.3	9.3	9.3
2008	9.2	9.0	8.9	8.8	8.9	9.0	9.0	8.9	8.8	8.7	8.9	8.7	8.9
2009	8.3	8.2	8.2	8.2	8.2	8.0	8.1	8.1	7.9	7.9	7.9	8.0	8.1
2010	8.1	8.0	8.1	8.2	8.3	8.3	8.3	8.4	8.2	8.1	8.1	8.1	8.2
2011	8.0	8.0	8.0	8.1	8.1	8.0	8.1	8.0	7.9	7.9	7.9	7.9	8.0
2012	7.8	7.9	7.9	8.0	8.0	8.0	7.9	7.9	7.8	7.9	7.9	7.9	7.9
2013	7.7	7.7	7.8	7.9	7.9	8.0	8.0	8.0	8.0	8.0	7.9	8.0	7.9
2014	7.8	7.9	7.9	7.9	7.9	8.1	8.1	8.2	8.2	8.2	8.2	8.2	8.1
2015	8.2	8.3	8.3	8.4	8.5	8.4	8.5	8.5	8.5	8.8	8.8	8.8	8.5
2016	8.8	8.9	8.9	9.0	9.0	9.1	9.1	9.1	9.2	9.2	9.3	9.3	9.1
2017	9.3	9.4	9.4	9.4	9.5	9.6	9.6	9.7	9.5	9.5	9.5	9.5	9.5
Retail Trade													
2007	37.2	37.1	37.7	37.4	37.7	37.9	37.8	37.7	37.6	37.5	38.3	38.8	37.7
2008	36.6	36.2	36.5	36.5	36.6	36.7	36.4	36.0	35.7	35.7	36.1	36.2	36.3
2009	34.2	33.5	33.6	33.9	34.1	34.3	34.3	33.9	33.7	33.9	34.8	34.9	34.1
2010	33.4	33.3	33.7	33.7	34.2	34.6	34.5	34.3	33.9	34.6	35.0	35.0	34.2
2011	34.3	34.1	34.4	34.9	35.2	35.3	35.6	35.3	35.2	35.8	36.4	36.6	35.3
2012	34.9	34.9	35.3	35.5	35.8	36.0	36.1	36.1	35.8	36.2	37.6	37.7	36.0
2013	35.6	35.5	35.6	36.1	36.4	36.8	37.0	37.2	37.0	37.7	38.7	39.1	36.9
2014	37.0	36.9	37.3	37.7	38.0	38.5	38.4	38.2	37.9	38.1	39.4	39.8	38.1
2015	37.7	37.5	37.9	38.4	38.8	39.6	39.8	40.0	39.6	40.1	41.3	41.4	39.3
2016	39.5	39.6	39.7	40.2	40.7	40.7	40.7	40.6	40.3	40.0	41.5	41.8	40.4
2017	40.2	39.9	40.0	40.2	40.6	40.7	40.6	40.4	39.3	39.6	41.4	40.5	40.3
Transportation and Utilities													
2007	11.2	11.5	11.7	12.1	12.3	12.3	12.0	12.3	12.2	12.3	12.2	12.1	12.0
2008	12.0	12.2	12.1	12.4	12.4	12.2	12.0	12.4	12.1	13.1	13.0	12.9	12.4
2009	12.1	12.0	11.8	11.6	11.4	11.3	10.8	10.7	10.6	10.4	10.2	10.5	11.1
2010	10.1	10.3	10.6	10.6	10.6	10.9	11.0	11.0	11.3	11.6	11.6	11.9	11.0
2011	11.7	11.8	11.7	11.5	11.5	11.7	11.7	12.0	11.9	12.0	12.0	12.2	11.8
2012	12.6	12.7	12.8	13.0	13.1	13.1	13.1	13.1	13.1	13.3	13.4	13.7	13.1
2013	13.3	13.4	13.5	13.6	13.7	13.7	13.7	13.6	13.6	13.9	13.6	13.9	13.6
2014	13.8	13.7	13.4	13.8	14.0	14.2	13.7	13.8	13.7	13.9	13.9	13.9	13.8
2015	13.9	13.7	14.0	14.2	14.3	14.1	13.9	13.9	13.7	13.9	13.7	14.1	14.0
2016	13.7	13.7	13.8	14.0	14.0	14.1	14.0	14.1	14.1	14.2	14.4	14.7	14.1
2017	14.3	14.3	14.4	14.4	14.5	14.6	14.8	14.7	14.7	14.6	14.6	14.6	14.5

Employment by Industry: Charleston-North Charleston, SC, Selected Years, 2007–2017—*Continued*

(Numbers in thousands, not seasonally adjusted)

Industry and year	January	February	March	April	May	June	July	August	September	October	November	December	Annual average
Information													
2007	5.4	5.5	5.5	5.5	5.5	5.6	5.7	5.7	5.7	5.8	5.8	5.9	5.6
2008	5.6	5.6	5.6	5.5	5.6	5.7	5.7	5.7	5.6	5.4	5.4	5.5	5.6
2009	5.6	5.4	5.4	5.4	5.3	5.4	5.5	5.2	5.2	5.3	5.1	5.2	5.3
2010	5.3	5.3	5.3	5.0	4.9	5.0	4.9	5.0	4.9	4.9	4.9	5.0	5.0
2011	5.0	4.9	4.9	5.0	5.0	5.0	5.0	5.0	4.9	4.8	4.8	4.8	4.9
2012	4.8	4.9	4.8	4.8	4.8	4.9	5.0	5.0	4.9	5.0	5.1	5.2	4.9
2013	5.0	5.0	5.0	5.1	5.0	5.1	5.1	5.0	5.0	5.0	5.0	5.1	5.0
2014	5.0	5.0	5.1	5.2	5.2	5.3	5.3	5.2	5.2	5.2	5.4	5.4	5.2
2015	5.3	5.3	5.3	5.3	5.3	5.3	5.4	5.4	5.4	5.4	6.2	5.6	5.4
2016	5.5	5.5	5.8	6.3	5.6	5.6	5.6	5.6	5.5	5.6	5.7	5.8	5.7
2017	5.7	5.7	5.8	5.8	5.9	6.3	6.0	6.1	6.3	6.4	6.4	6.4	6.1
Financial Activities													
2007	12.6	12.6	12.7	12.8	12.9	13.1	13.1	13.1	12.9	12.9	12.9	13.0	12.9
2008	13.1	13.1	13.1	12.8	12.9	13.0	12.8	12.8	12.7	12.5	12.4	12.5	12.8
2009	12.1	12.0	12.0	11.9	11.8	11.9	11.7	11.7	11.5	11.6	11.5	11.5	11.8
2010	11.2	11.1	11.2	11.3	11.4	11.5	11.6	11.6	11.4	11.7	11.7	11.7	11.5
2011	11.7	11.6	11.7	11.7	11.8	11.8	11.8	11.9	12.0	12.3	12.5	12.5	11.9
2012	12.4	12.6	12.5	12.4	12.4	12.6	12.4	12.6	12.5	12.6	12.7	12.9	12.6
2013	12.5	12.7	12.7	12.7	12.9	12.8	12.9	13.1	13.0	13.2	13.3	13.3	12.9
2014	12.9	13.2	13.1	13.1	13.3	13.3	13.3	13.4	13.5	13.7	13.7	13.9	13.4
2015	14.0	14.0	14.1	14.0	14.2	14.2	14.0	14.2	14.0	14.3	14.4	14.5	14.2
2016	14.3	14.4	14.1	14.4	14.5	14.5	14.5	14.6	14.5	14.7	14.8	14.7	14.5
2017	14.7	14.7	14.9	14.8	15.0	14.9	15.0	15.0	14.9	15.0	15.0	14.9	14.9
Professional and Business Services													
2007	41.1	41.5	42.3	41.8	41.9	42.0	41.7	42.1	42.3	42.7	42.3	42.6	42.0
2008	42.5	43.3	43.8	43.7	43.8	44.0	42.6	43.1	43.2	42.5	42.5	41.7	43.1
2009	40.4	40.1	40.1	40.6	40.8	40.6	39.8	40.2	39.9	40.3	40.7	40.2	40.3
2010	39.8	40.2	40.4	41.7	41.8	42.4	41.8	42.2	41.9	42.9	43.1	42.9	41.8
2011	42.9	43.4	43.9	44.7	44.8	44.3	44.1	44.6	44.2	44.9	44.9	44.8	44.3
2012	44.6	45.6	46.1	46.9	46.8	46.6	45.3	45.8	45.9	45.8	45.7	45.8	45.9
2013	45.2	45.9	46.3	46.3	46.3	46.2	45.9	46.3	46.4	47.2	47.4	47.3	46.4
2014	46.0	47.4	48.1	48.5	48.7	48.2	48.0	48.2	48.6	48.9	49.1	49.1	48.2
2015	47.7	48.6	49.1	49.9	50.2	50.3	49.8	50.4	50.1	51.3	51.4	51.6	50.0
2016	50.3	51.1	51.5	51.9	52.2	52.2	52.7	53.2	53.0	53.0	54.2	53.3	52.4
2017	53.2	54.2	54.6	54.9	55.0	55.4	55.3	55.1	54.8	55.6	55.6	54.1	54.8
Education and Health Services													
2007	29.8	30.2	30.5	30.8	31.0	30.6	30.6	30.8	31.3	31.5	31.6	31.5	30.9
2008	31.5	31.8	31.8	32.3	32.5	32.2	32.3	32.2	32.8	32.9	33.0	32.9	32.4
2009	32.5	32.7	32.6	32.7	32.7	32.8	32.6	32.9	32.8	33.3	33.3	33.3	32.9
2010	33.0	33.1	33.5	33.4	33.4	33.4	33.3	33.5	33.9	34.4	34.7	34.9	33.7
2011	34.5	35.1	35.2	35.1	35.0	34.7	34.4	34.5	34.8	34.6	34.7	34.6	34.8
2012	34.1	34.6	34.7	34.6	34.7	34.3	34.2	34.4	34.7	35.2	35.3	35.2	34.7
2013	34.8	35.2	35.2	35.0	35.1	34.9	35.0	35.3	35.1	35.7	35.9	35.8	35.3
2014	35.8	36.0	36.2	36.5	36.6	36.6	36.4	36.7	36.7	37.3	37.4	37.4	36.6
2015	37.1	37.4	37.5	37.6	37.9	37.4	37.7	38.1	38.1	38.6	38.8	38.5	37.9
2016	38.0	38.4	38.3	38.4	38.6	38.4	38.4	38.8	39.2	39.2	39.3	39.4	38.7
2017	39.3	39.9	39.8	39.9	39.8	39.6	39.7	40.1	39.9	40.9	41.1	41.3	40.1
Leisure and Hospitality													
2007	33.5	33.7	34.8	37.1	38.4	39.1	39.0	38.8	37.6	37.5	36.9	36.2	36.9
2008	35.0	35.4	36.2	38.4	39.6	39.6	38.8	38.3	37.1	36.3	35.9	35.3	37.2
2009	33.8	34.2	35.4	36.4	37.6	37.7	37.0	36.5	35.4	34.8	34.3	33.5	35.6
2010	32.3	32.8	34.0	35.7	37.1	37.7	37.1	36.7	35.9	35.7	35.3	34.6	35.4
2011	33.4	33.7	35.1	37.2	38.3	38.9	38.2	37.9	36.8	36.6	36.4	36.2	36.6
2012	35.2	35.7	37.0	39.0	39.6	40.3	39.9	40.0	38.7	38.3	37.8	37.3	38.2
2013	36.3	36.6	37.7	39.7	40.8	41.8	41.4	41.5	40.0	39.8	39.7	39.1	39.5
2014	38.2	38.3	39.8	42.3	43.5	43.9	43.6	43.5	42.0	41.8	41.5	41.0	41.6
2015	40.2	40.7	42.5	44.1	45.6	45.9	46.0	45.7	43.9	44.3	44.0	43.7	43.9
2016	43.1	43.5	45.1	46.9	48.4	49.4	48.8	48.5	47.0	46.0	46.6	46.0	46.6
2017	44.8	45.5	46.8	48.2	49.8	50.5	50.2	49.7	46.9	47.6	47.4	47.3	47.9

Employment by Industry: Charleston-North Charleston, SC, Selected Years, 2007–2017—*Continued*

(Numbers in thousands, not seasonally adjusted)

Industry and year	January	February	March	April	May	June	July	August	September	October	November	December	Annual average
Other Services													
2007	11.7	12.0	12.2	12.0	11.9	11.9	11.6	11.5	11.3	11.2	11.1	11.1	11.6
2008	11.2	11.3	11.4	11.5	11.5	11.7	11.7	11.6	11.4	11.3	11.3	11.2	11.4
2009	10.7	10.7	10.8	10.9	11.0	11.1	11.0	10.9	10.9	10.9	10.7	10.7	10.9
2010	10.5	10.5	10.6	10.6	10.6	10.8	10.7	10.5	10.4	10.4	10.4	10.3	10.5
2011	10.3	10.4	10.4	10.6	10.8	11.1	11.3	11.2	11.3	11.3	11.5	11.6	11.0
2012	11.7	11.9	12.1	12.5	12.7	12.9	13.0	12.9	12.7	12.7	12.8	12.8	12.6
2013	12.7	12.7	13.0	13.0	13.0	13.3	13.3	13.2	13.1	13.0	13.0	13.0	13.0
2014	13.0	13.0	13.1	13.3	13.5	13.7	13.8	13.7	13.6	13.6	13.6	13.6	13.5
2015	13.5	13.5	13.6	13.7	13.9	14.0	14.0	13.9	13.7	13.7	13.8	13.9	13.8
2016	13.5	13.6	13.6	13.8	13.9	14.0	14.0	13.9	13.8	13.7	13.9	13.8	13.8
2017	13.6	13.7	13.8	13.8	13.9	14.0	13.9	13.9	13.7	13.7	13.7	13.7	13.8
Government													
2007	57.3	57.7	57.8	58.2	58.2	58.0	56.4	56.5	58.7	59.2	59.5	59.5	50.1
2008	59.1	59.5	59.9	60.4	60.7	60.3	58.7	59.1	60.7	61.0	61.4	61.3	60.2
2009	60.0	60.3	60.4	60.3	60.1	59.7	58.0	58.2	60.1	60.6	60.7	60.6	59.9
2010	60.3	60.7	61.1	61.6	63.2	60.9	59.9	59.8	60.9	61.7	62.0	61.8	61.2
2011	61.1	61.4	61.5	62.0	62.0	61.1	59.9	59.3	61.3	61.3	61.5	61.6	61.2
2012	61.1	61.6	62.0	62.4	62.4	61.9	60.8	61.3	62.9	63.1	65.3	63.5	62.4
2013	62.3	62.8	63.0	63.5	63.1	62.6	61.4	61.3	63.0	62.4	62.8	62.6	62.6
2014	61.6	62.4	62.5	63.5	63.5	62.0	60.5	61.7	63.3	63.8	64.2	64.0	62.8
2015	62.8	63.8	64.1	64.2	64.2	62.9	62.6	62.9	64.3	64.9	65.4	65.4	64.0
2016	64.8	65.0	65.5	65.6	65.5	64.9	64.4	63.3	65.2	64.8	64.9	65.2	64.9
2017	64.3	64.5	64.9	64.9	64.8	64.1	63.9	63.7	65.4	65.6	65.8	66.0	64.8

Employment by Industry: Greensboro-High Point, NC, Selected Years, 2007–2017

(Numbers in thousands, not seasonally adjusted)

Industry and year	January	February	March	April	May	June	July	August	September	October	November	December	Annual average
Total Nonfarm													
2007	365.3	366.5	370.1	370.8	372.3	370.8	363.7	369.4	370.4	373.2	373.5	373.9	370.0
2008	367.1	367.6	369.0	367.5	367.7	364.9	358.0	364.0	365.9	366.0	364.2	359.2	365.1
2009	347.6	346.5	343.4	342.6	341.7	339.8	333.0	337.5	340.1	339.5	339.2	338.2	340.8
2010	331.5	331.7	334.5	336.0	337.8	337.7	333.5	337.3	337.8	341.8	340.0	340.0	336.6
2011	333.0	335.7	337.7	340.7	341.3	338.8	333.8	338.6	341.5	342.6	343.1	342.5	339.1
2012	337.2	339.5	341.2	342.6	343.8	339.1	330.7	340.7	342.7	345.7	347.5	347.9	341.6
2013	341.0	343.1	344.4	346.4	346.8	343.7	336.5	345.6	347.6	349.8	350.3	350.5	345.5
2014	342.6	342.6	345.7	349.2	350.6	346.3	339.9	347.6	350.1	353.6	354.6	354.8	348.1
2015	348.7	350.4	351.2	355.6	356.6	353.7	346.8	354.8	356.5	359.5	360.3	360.2	354.5
2016	352.8	354.8	356.3	359.1	358.8	355.6	350.9	357.0	359.2	362.2	365.5	363.9	358.0
2017	354.8	357.6	357.5	360.4	361.1	358.9	351.7	357.9	358.9	362.0	363.9	363.2	359.0
Total Private													
2007	320.2	321.2	324.3	324.8	326.1	327.0	325.0	326.5	325.3	326.7	326.6	327.4	325.1
2008	320.6	320.7	321.7	320.0	319.8	319.6	318.0	319.9	318.4	318.2	316.2	311.7	318.7
2009	300.4	298.9	295.5	294.2	293.5	292.9	292.1	292.7	291.6	291.9	291.5	290.9	293.8
2010	284.3	284.4	286.7	287.6	288.2	290.2	291.9	292.9	291.1	294.1	292.7	293.0	289.8
2011	286.6	289.0	290.7	293.7	294.4	295.5	295.1	296.1	295.8	295.9	296.1	295.7	293.7
2012	291.7	293.5	294.8	296.0	296.8	297.1	297.1	298.1	297.4	299.0	300.5	301.4	297.0
2013	295.0	296.8	297.6	299.9	300.2	301.0	300.9	303.0	302.4	303.9	304.0	304.4	300.8
2014	297.1	297.0	299.7	302.8	303.7	303.4	304.0	305.4	305.3	308.1	308.7	309.3	303.7
2015	303.8	305.3	306.1	310.1	310.9	311.1	311.1	311.4	313.2	312.2	314.8	315.3	315.3	310.8
2016	308.6	309.9	310.7	313.9	313.3	313.5	314.8	315.4	315.2	316.5	319.3	318.5	314.1
2017	310.2	312.5	312.3	314.5	315.2	316.8	315.4	316.0	314.4	315.8	317.2	317.2	314.8
Goods Producing													
2007	81.7	81.4	81.8	81.9	81.6	81.9	81.2	81.2	80.8	81.1	80.9	81.3	81.4
2008	79.8	79.6	79.6	78.4	78.5	78.2	77.6	77.5	77.2	76.2	75.5	74.0	77.7
2009	70.6	69.4	67.7	67.2	66.2	65.9	65.4	65.3	65.1	64.4	64.0	64.1	66.3
2010	62.4	62.3	62.8	63.2	63.2	63.8	64.0	64.1	63.9	63.8	63.4	63.6	63.4
2011	62.6	63.1	63.5	64.4	64.7	65.2	65.3	65.6	65.3	64.9	64.6	64.6	64.5
2012	64.6	64.9	64.9	64.5	64.7	64.9	64.9	64.8	65.1	65.1	65.2	65.7	64.9
2013	64.7	64.4	64.8	65.3	65.5	66.2	66.2	66.2	66.4	66.6	66.4	66.5	65.8
2014	65.6	65.6	66.1	66.2	66.5	67.0	66.8	66.8	67.0	66.9	67.0	67.4	66.6
2015	66.7	67.3	67.7	68.3	68.4	68.8	69.1	69.5	69.3	69.4	69.1	69.5	68.6
2016	68.9	69.1	69.4	69.5	69.6	70.1	70.9	70.9	70.9	70.7	70.8	71.1	70.2
2017	69.8	70.6	70.8	70.7	70.7	71.0	70.8	70.7	70.4	70.4	70.7	71.1	70.6
Service-Providing													
2007	283.6	285.1	288.3	288.9	290.7	288.9	282.5	288.2	289.6	292.1	292.6	292.6	288.6
2008	287.3	288.0	289.4	289.1	289.2	286.7	280.4	286.5	288.7	289.8	288.7	285.2	287.4
2009	277.0	277.1	275.7	275.4	275.5	273.9	267.6	272.2	275.0	275.1	275.2	274.1	274.5
2010	269.1	269.4	271.7	272.8	274.6	273.9	269.5	273.2	273.9	278.0	276.6	276.4	273.3
2011	270.4	272.6	274.2	276.3	276.6	273.6	268.5	273.0	276.2	277.7	278.5	277.9	274.6
2012	272.6	274.6	276.3	278.1	279.1	274.2	265.8	275.9	277.6	280.6	282.3	282.2	276.6
2013	276.3	278.7	279.6	281.1	281.3	277.5	270.3	279.4	281.2	283.2	283.9	284.0	279.7
2014	277.0	277.0	279.6	283.0	284.1	279.3	273.1	280.8	283.1	286.7	287.6	287.4	281.6
2015	282.0	283.1	283.5	287.3	288.2	284.9	277.7	285.3	287.2	290.1	291.2	290.7	285.9
2016	283.9	285.7	286.9	289.6	289.2	285.5	280.0	286.1	288.3	291.5	294.7	292.8	287.9
2017	285.0	287.0	286.7	289.7	290.4	287.9	280.9	287.2	288.5	291.6	293.2	292.1	288.4
Mining, Logging, and Construction													
2007	18.3	18.2	18.6	18.6	18.6	18.8	18.8	18.7	18.5	18.6	18.5	18.5	18.6
2008	17.7	17.7	17.9	17.5	17.5	17.5	17.5	17.3	17.3	17.1	16.9	16.3	17.4
2009	15.1	14.8	14.5	14.4	14.1	14.1	14.0	13.9	13.7	13.3	13.1	13.1	14.0
2010	12.1	12.0	12.3	12.6	12.5	12.7	12.6	12.6	12.5	12.7	12.6	12.5	12.5
2011	11.7	12.1	12.4	12.8	12.9	13.1	13.1	13.1	13.1	12.9	12.7	12.7	12.7
2012	12.5	12.4	12.5	12.2	12.2	12.3	12.4	12.4	12.3	12.3	12.2	12.2	12.3
2013	11.9	11.9	12.2	12.4	12.5	12.7	12.8	13.0	13.0	13.0	13.0	12.9	12.6
2014	12.6	12.6	12.9	12.9	13.1	13.3	13.3	13.3	13.4	13.4	13.4	13.4	13.1
2015	12.9	13.1	13.3	13.8	13.9	14.0	14.2	14.3	14.2	14.2	13.9	14.0	13.8
2016	13.8	13.8	14.0	14.3	14.3	14.4	14.9	14.9	15.0	14.9	14.8	14.8	14.5
2017	14.3	14.7	14.9	15.0	14.9	15.2	15.2	15.1	15.1	14.9	14.9	14.9	14.9

Employment by Industry: Greensboro-High Point, NC, Selected Years, 2007–2017—*Continued*

(Numbers in thousands, not seasonally adjusted)

Industry and year	January	February	March	April	May	June	July	August	September	October	November	December	Annual average
Manufacturing													
2007	63.4	63.2	63.2	63.3	63.0	63.1	62.4	62.5	62.3	62.5	62.4	62.8	62.8
2008	62.1	61.9	61.7	60.9	61.0	60.7	60.1	60.2	59.9	59.1	58.6	57.7	60.3
2009	55.5	54.6	53.2	52.8	52.1	51.8	51.4	51.4	51.4	51.1	50.9	51.0	52.3
2010	50.3	50.3	50.5	50.6	50.7	51.1	51.4	51.5	51.4	51.1	50.8	51.1	50.9
2011	50.9	51.0	51.1	51.6	51.8	52.1	52.2	52.5	52.2	52.0	51.9	51.9	51.8
2012	52.1	52.5	52.4	52.3	52.5	52.6	52.5	52.4	52.8	52.8	53.0	53.5	52.6
2013	52.8	52.5	52.6	52.9	53.0	53.5	53.4	53.2	53.4	53.6	53.4	53.6	53.2
2014	53.0	53.0	53.2	53.3	53.4	53.7	53.5	53.5	53.6	53.5	53.6	54.0	53.4
2015	53.8	54.2	54.4	54.5	54.5	54.8	54.9	55.2	55.1	55.2	55.2	55.5	54.8
2016	55.1	55.3	55.4	55.2	55.3	55.7	56.0	56.0	55.9	55.8	56.0	56.3	55.7
2017	55.5	55.9	55.9	55.7	55.8	55.8	55.6	55.6	55.3	55.5	55.8	56.2	55.7
Trade, Transportation, and Utilities													
2007	76.1	75.7	76.5	76.3	76.8	76.6	76.5	76.9	76.7	77.0	78.0	70.0	76.8
2008	75.3	74.8	74.8	74.6	74.8	74.7	73.8	73.8	73.7	74.0	74.2	74.4	74.4
2009	70.9	70.2	70.0	69.1	69.2	68.9	68.5	68.6	68.6	68.5	69.3	69.6	69.3
2010	67.4	67.2	67.5	67.9	68.1	68.1	68.1	68.2	68.1	68.8	69.5	70.3	68.3
2011	67.9	68.1	68.3	68.7	68.9	68.8	68.8	68.8	68.7	69.0	69.9	70.5	68.9
2012	69.0	68.9	69.0	69.8	70.2	69.8	69.8	69.8	69.9	70.3	71.7	72.2	70.0
2013	69.9	70.0	70.1	70.7	70.8	70.6	70.8	71.0	70.9	72.1	72.8	73.6	71.1
2014	70.9	70.5	71.2	72.1	72.3	72.2	71.9	72.2	71.9	72.4	73.7	74.3	72.1
2015	71.8	71.7	71.9	72.8	72.5	72.6	72.4	72.9	72.9	73.9	74.7	75.8	73.0
2016	72.6	72.3	72.4	73.1	73.1	73.0	72.8	73.1	72.7	73.3	74.6	75.4	73.2
2017	73.4	72.9	72.6	73.5	73.9	74.3	74.3	74.5	74.1	74.2	75.5	76.2	74.1
Wholesale Trade													
2007	20.1	20.1	20.3	20.3	20.4	20.5	20.6	20.6	20.6	20.6	20.6	20.7	20.5
2008	20.4	20.4	20.4	20.2	20.3	20.2	20.0	19.9	19.9	19.8	19.6	19.3	20.0
2009	18.8	18.7	18.5	18.5	18.5	18.3	18.2	18.4	18.2	18.2	18.2	18.2	18.4
2010	18.0	18.0	18.2	18.2	18.2	18.1	18.1	18.2	18.0	18.0	18.0	18.0	18.1
2011	17.8	18.0	18.0	18.0	18.0	17.9	17.9	17.8	17.7	17.5	17.4	17.4	17.8
2012	17.5	17.6	17.8	18.0	18.0	18.0	18.0	18.0	18.1	18.1	18.2	18.4	18.0
2013	18.2	18.4	18.5	18.6	18.6	18.6	18.6	18.7	18.7	18.7	18.7	18.7	18.6
2014	18.5	18.5	18.7	19.1	19.2	19.0	19.0	19.0	18.9	18.7	18.7	18.8	18.8
2015	18.6	18.7	18.7	19.0	19.0	18.9	19.0	19.1	18.9	19.1	19.1	19.3	19.0
2016	19.0	19.0	19.1	19.5	19.5	19.4	19.3	19.4	19.1	19.2	19.1	19.1	19.2
2017	19.0	19.1	19.1	19.1	19.2	19.3	19.3	19.5	19.3	19.3	19.2	19.2	19.2
Retail Trade													
2007	39.6	39.3	39.7	39.6	39.9	39.7	39.5	39.6	39.4	39.7	40.6	40.9	39.8
2008	38.7	38.2	38.1	38.1	38.0	37.9	37.7	37.7	37.5	37.9	38.2	38.5	38.0
2009	36.5	36.1	36.2	35.6	35.8	35.7	35.6	35.5	35.6	35.6	36.2	36.4	35.9
2010	34.8	34.6	34.7	34.9	35.0	34.9	34.8	34.8	34.7	35.1	35.9	36.3	35.0
2011	34.6	34.5	34.7	34.9	35.1	35.1	35.1	35.2	35.0	35.4	36.4	36.8	35.2
2012	35.6	35.4	35.2	35.7	36.1	35.8	35.9	35.8	35.8	36.0	37.4	37.5	36.0
2013	35.8	35.8	35.9	36.2	36.4	36.2	36.4	36.3	36.2	37.1	38.0	38.5	36.6
2014	36.5	36.2	36.5	36.8	36.9	36.9	36.7	36.9	36.6	37.1	38.2	38.3	37.0
2015	36.7	36.5	36.6	36.9	36.9	37.1	36.9	37.2	37.2	37.8	38.8	39.3	37.3
2016	37.4	37.3	37.3	37.6	37.7	37.7	37.6	37.7	37.7	37.7	38.2	39.4	39.7	37.9
2017	37.7	37.5	37.2	37.5	37.5	37.6	37.7	37.6	37.2	37.0	38.0	37.8	37.5
Transportation and Utilities													
2007	16.4	16.3	16.5	16.4	16.5	16.4	16.4	16.7	16.7	16.7	16.8	17.3	16.6
2008	16.2	16.2	16.3	16.3	16.5	16.6	16.1	16.2	16.3	16.3	16.4	16.6	16.3
2009	15.6	15.4	15.3	15.0	14.9	14.9	14.7	14.7	14.8	14.7	14.9	15.0	15.0
2010	14.6	14.6	14.6	14.8	14.9	15.1	15.2	15.2	15.4	15.7	15.6	16.0	15.1
2011	15.5	15.6	15.6	15.8	15.8	15.8	15.8	15.8	16.0	16.1	16.1	16.3	15.9
2012	15.9	15.9	16.0	16.1	16.1	16.0	15.9	16.0	16.0	16.2	16.1	16.3	16.0
2013	15.9	15.8	15.7	15.9	15.8	15.8	15.8	16.0	16.0	16.3	16.1	16.4	16.0
2014	15.9	15.8	16.0	16.2	16.2	16.3	16.2	16.3	16.4	16.6	16.8	17.2	16.3
2015	16.5	16.5	16.6	16.9	16.6	16.6	16.5	16.6	16.8	17.0	16.8	17.2	16.7
2016	16.2	16.0	16.0	16.0	15.9	15.9	15.9	16.0	15.9	15.9	16.1	16.6	16.0
2017	16.7	16.3	16.3	16.9	17.2	17.4	17.3	17.4	17.6	17.9	18.3	19.2	17.4

Employment by Industry: Greensboro-High Point, NC, Selected Years, 2007–2017—*Continued*

(Numbers in thousands, not seasonally adjusted)

Industry and year	January	February	March	April	May	June	July	August	September	October	November	December	Annual average
Information													
2007	6.3	6.3	6.2	6.3	6.2	6.2	6.2	6.2	6.2	6.2	6.3	6.3	6.2
2008	6.2	6.1	6.2	6.2	6.2	6.3	6.2	6.1	6.0	6.0	6.2	6.2	6.2
2009	5.9	5.8	5.8	5.8	5.8	5.7	5.6	5.6	5.5	5.5	5.5	5.6	5.7
2010	5.6	5.5	5.5	5.5	5.5	5.5	5.6	5.6	5.5	5.5	5.5	5.6	5.5
2011	5.5	5.5	5.5	5.5	5.5	5.5	5.5	5.5	5.5	5.5	5.4	5.4	5.5
2012	5.4	5.5	5.4	5.4	5.4	5.4	5.4	5.3	5.3	5.3	5.3	5.3	5.4
2013	5.2	5.2	5.1	5.0	5.0	5.0	5.0	4.9	4.9	4.9	4.9	5.0	5.0
2014	4.9	4.9	4.9	4.9	4.9	5.0	5.0	5.0	5.0	5.1	5.1	5.1	5.0
2015	5.1	5.1	5.1	5.0	5.1	5.1	5.1	5.0	4.9	4.9	4.9	4.9	5.0
2016	4.9	5.0	5.0	4.8	4.8	4.8	4.9	4.9	4.8	4.8	4.8	4.8	4.9
2017	4.7	4.8	4.8	4.6	4.6	4.7	4.7	4.7	4.7	4.7	4.7	4.7	4.7
Financial Activities													
2007	22.1	22.3	22.3	22.3	22.2	22.4	22.2	22.1	22.2	22.2	22.2	22.0	22.2
2008	21.7	21.8	21.8	21.9	22.0	22.1	22.0	22.0	21.9	21.9	22.0	21.9	21.9
2009	21.5	21.4	21.2	21.2	21.2	21.2	21.0	21.0	20.9	20.9	20.8	20.6	21.1
2010	20.3	20.2	20.2	20.0	19.8	19.8	19.9	19.9	19.9	19.9	19.8	19.9	20.0
2011	19.6	19.6	19.7	19.7	19.6	19.6	19.6	19.5	19.4	19.0	18.9	18.8	19.4
2012	18.3	18.4	18.4	18.4	18.3	18.4	18.4	18.5	18.5	18.7	18.7	18.8	18.5
2013	18.3	18.4	18.4	18.4	18.4	18.5	18.3	18.4	18.1	18.1	18.2	18.2	18.3
2014	18.2	18.1	18.1	17.8	17.8	17.7	17.8	17.7	17.6	17.6	17.6	17.6	17.8
2015	17.6	17.5	17.5	17.6	17.8	18.0	18.1	18.1	18.0	18.1	18.2	18.3	17.9
2016	18.2	18.2	18.2	18.1	18.0	18.0	18.2	18.1	18.0	18.0	18.2	18.2	18.1
2017	17.9	17.9	17.7	17.6	17.6	17.6	17.6	17.5	17.5	17.5	17.5	17.5	17.6
Professional and Business Services													
2007	44.2	45.1	45.9	45.9	46.1	46.3	45.9	47.1	47.4	47.6	47.0	46.7	46.3
2008	46.1	46.2	46.6	46.5	45.7	45.4	46.0	47.5	47.5	48.0	46.0	43.8	46.3
2009	41.7	41.5	40.5	40.1	39.6	40.1	40.6	41.5	42.0	43.4	42.6	42.3	41.3
2010	42.0	42.3	42.9	42.9	42.8	43.6	44.9	45.4	45.3	46.5	45.5	45.1	44.1
2011	44.2	45.1	45.7	46.1	45.9	46.1	46.4	46.7	47.3	47.6	47.6	47.1	46.3
2012	46.6	47.0	47.7	47.5	47.1	47.1	46.6	47.2	46.8	47.4	47.6	47.6	47.2
2013	46.2	47.0	46.9	47.4	47.0	47.0	47.0	48.1	48.5	49.0	48.6	48.3	47.6
2014	47.0	47.0	47.7	48.4	48.0	47.7	48.7	49.4	50.0	51.7	51.1	51.0	49.0
2015	49.5	49.7	49.4	50.4	50.1	49.8	50.0	50.9	50.5	51.7	51.6	50.5	50.3
2016	49.0	49.4	49.1	50.1	48.7	48.7	49.5	49.6	50.3	50.8	51.7	50.6	49.8
2017	48.1	48.8	48.6	49.3	49.1	49.4	49.1	49.4	49.4	50.1	50.6	50.5	49.4
Education and Health Services													
2007	46.1	46.5	46.6	46.3	46.5	46.2	45.8	45.9	45.6	46.4	46.2	46.2	46.2
2008	45.8	46.0	46.0	46.5	46.4	46.4	46.0	46.5	46.5	47.4	47.9	47.5	46.6
2009	47.2	47.6	47.0	47.3	47.2	46.8	46.6	46.7	46.1	47.0	47.2	47.0	47.0
2010	46.4	46.3	46.5	46.5	46.5	46.3	46.3	46.5	45.9	47.1	47.0	46.9	46.5
2011	46.1	46.4	46.2	46.7	46.6	46.4	45.9	46.2	46.7	47.4	47.5	47.3	46.6
2012	46.5	47.1	47.0	47.2	47.1	46.6	47.0	47.4	48.0	48.2	48.5	48.4	47.4
2013	47.9	48.5	48.5	48.5	48.4	47.8	47.7	48.2	48.7	48.5	48.5	48.4	48.3
2014	47.3	47.7	47.6	48.0	48.0	47.4	47.3	47.5	48.2	48.6	48.8	48.6	47.9
2015	48.9	49.4	49.3	49.7	49.7	49.3	49.1	49.4	50.0	50.2	50.5	50.4	49.7
2016	49.8	50.5	50.6	51.0	50.9	50.4	50.3	50.7	50.9	51.2	51.2	51.0	50.7
2017	50.0	50.5	50.2	50.5	50.5	50.2	49.6	49.9	50.1	51.0	51.1	50.9	50.4
Leisure and Hospitality													
2007	31.0	31.2	32.1	32.6	33.4	34.0	33.6	33.7	33.1	32.6	32.6	32.5	32.7
2008	32.3	32.7	33.2	32.5	33.0	33.2	32.9	33.1	32.4	31.5	31.2	30.7	32.4
2009	29.6	29.9	30.2	30.5	31.4	31.5	31.6	31.3	30.8	29.7	29.7	29.3	30.5
2010	28.1	28.4	29.1	29.5	30.2	30.9	30.9	31.1	30.6	30.5	30.1	29.8	29.9
2011	28.8	29.3	30.0	30.7	31.3	31.8	31.5	31.8	31.0	30.6	30.3	30.0	30.6
2012	29.4	29.8	30.5	31.1	31.7	32.3	32.5	32.7	31.6	31.7	31.2	31.0	31.3
2013	30.5	30.9	31.4	32.3	32.7	33.2	33.2	33.6	32.5	32.3	32.1	32.0	32.2
2014	30.9	30.9	31.7	32.8	33.5	33.5	33.6	34.0	33.1	33.2	32.9	32.8	32.7
2015	31.8	32.2	32.8	33.8	34.7	34.9	34.4	34.8	34.3	34.1	33.9	33.5	33.8
2016	33.0	33.2	33.7	34.9	35.7	35.9	35.6	35.7	35.2	35.1	35.5	35.0	34.9
2017	34.1	34.7	35.3	35.9	36.3	36.9	36.6	36.9	36.0	35.6	34.8	34.1	35.6

Employment by Industry: Greensboro-High Point, NC, Selected Years, 2007–2017—*Continued*

(Numbers in thousands, not seasonally adjusted)

Industry and year	January	February	March	April	May	June	July	August	September	October	November	December	Annual average
Other Services													
2007	12.7	12.7	12.9	13.2	13.3	13.4	13.6	13.4	13.3	13.6	13.4	13.5	13.3
2008	13.4	13.5	13.5	13.4	13.2	13.3	13.5	13.4	13.2	13.2	13.2	13.2	13.3
2009	13.0	13.1	13.1	13.0	12.9	12.8	12.8	12.7	12.6	12.5	12.4	12.4	12.8
2010	12.1	12.2	12.2	12.1	12.1	12.2	12.2	12.1	11.9	12.0	11.9	11.8	12.1
2011	11.9	11.9	11.8	11.9	11.9	12.1	12.1	12.0	11.9	11.9	11.9	12.0	11.9
2012	11.9	11.9	11.9	12.1	12.3	12.6	12.5	12.4	12.2	12.3	12.3	12.4	12.2
2013	12.3	12.4	12.4	12.3	12.4	12.7	12.7	12.6	12.4	12.4	12.5	12.4	12.5
2014	12.3	12.3	12.4	12.6	12.7	12.9	12.9	12.8	12.5	12.6	12.5	12.5	12.6
2015	12.4	12.4	12.4	12.5	12.6	12.6	12.9	12.6	12.3	12.5	12.4	12.4	12.5
2016	12.2	12.2	12.3	12.4	12.5	12.6	12.6	12.4	12.4	12.6	12.5	12.4	12.4
2017	12.2	12.3	12.3	12.4	12.5	12.7	12.7	12.4	12.2	12.3	12.3	12.2	12.4
Government													
2007	45.1	45.3	45.8	46.0	46.2	43.8	38.7	42.9	45.1	46.5	46.9	46.5	44.9
2008	46.5	46.9	47.3	47.5	47.9	45.3	40.0	44.1	47.5	47.8	48.0	47.5	46.4
2009	47.2	47.6	47.9	48.4	48.2	46.9	40.9	44.8	48.5	47.6	47.7	47.3	46.9
2010	47.2	47.3	47.8	48.4	49.6	47.5	41.6	44.4	46.7	47.7	47.3	47.0	46.9
2011	46.4	46.7	47.0	47.0	46.9	43.3	38.7	42.5	45.7	46.7	47.0	46.8	45.4
2012	45.5	46.0	46.4	46.6	47.0	42.0	33.6	42.6	45.3	46.7	47.0	46.5	44.6
2013	46.0	46.3	46.8	46.5	46.6	42.7	35.6	42.6	45.2	45.9	46.3	46.1	44.7
2014	45.5	45.6	46.0	46.4	46.9	42.9	35.9	42.2	44.8	45.5	45.9	45.5	44.4
2015	44.9	45.1	45.1	45.5	45.7	42.6	35.7	41.6	44.3	44.7	45.0	44.9	43.8
2016	44.2	44.9	45.6	45.2	45.5	42.1	36.1	41.6	44.0	45.7	46.2	45.4	43.9
2017	44.6	45.1	45.2	45.9	45.9	42.1	36.3	41.9	44.5	46.2	46.7	46.0	44.2

APPENDIX

SEVENTY-FIVE LARGEST MSAs AND COMPONENTS
(as defined July 2015)

Core based statistical area	State/ County FIPS code	Title and Geographic Components	Core based statistical area	State/ County FIPS code	Title and Geographic Components
35620		**New York-Newark-Jersey City, NY-NJ-PA**	48201		Harris County
35620		Dutchess County-Putnam County, NY Div 20524	48291		Liberty County
	36027	Dutchess County	48339		Montgomery County
	36079	Putnam County	48473		Waller County
35620		Nassau County-Suffolk County, NY Div 35004			
	36059	Nassau County	47900		**Washington-Arlington-Alexandria, DC-VA-MD-WV**
	36103	Suffolk County	47900		Silver Spring-Frederick-Rockville, MD Div 43524
35620		Newark, NJ-PA Div 35084		24021	Frederick County
	34013	Essex County		24031	Montgomery County
	34019	Hunterdon County			Washington-Arlington-Alexandria, DC-VA-MD-WV Div
	34027	Morris County	47900		47894
	34035	Somerset County		11001	District of Columbia
	34037	Sussex County		24009	Calvert County
	34039	Union County		24017	Charles County
	42103	Pike County		24033	Prince George's County
35620		New York-Jersey City-White Plains, NY-NJ Div 35614		51013	Arlington County
	34003	Bergen County		51043	Clarke County
	34017	Hudson County		51047	Culpeper County
	34023	Middlesex County		51059	Fairfax County
	34025	Monmouth County		51061	Fauquier County
	34029	Ocean County		51107	Loudoun County
	34031	Passaic County		51153	Prince William County
	36005	Bronx County		51157	Rappahannock County
	36047	Kings County		51177	Spotsylvania County
	36061	New York County		51179	Stafford County
	36071	Orange County		51187	Warren County
	36081	Queens County		51510	Alexandria city
	36085	Richmond County		51600	Fairfax city
	36087	Rockland County		51610	Falls Church city
	36119	Westchester County		51630	Fredericksburg city
				51683	Manassas city
31080		**Los Angeles-Long Beach-Anaheim, CA**		51685	Manassas Park city
31080		Anaheim-Santa Ana-Irvine, CA Div 11244		54037	Jefferson County
	06059	Orange County			
31080		Los Angeles-Long Beach-Glendale, CA Div 31084	33100		**Miami-Fort Lauderdale-West Palm Beach, FL**
	06037	Los Angeles County			Fort Lauderdale-Pompano Beach-Deerfield Beach, FL Div
			33100		22744
16980		**Chicago-Naperville-Elgin, IL-IN-WI**		12011	Broward County
16980		Chicago-Naperville-Arlington Heights, IL Div 16974	33100		Miami-Miami Beach-Kendall, FL Div 33124
	17031	Cook County		12086	Miami-Dade County
	17043	DuPage County			West Palm Beach-Boca Raton-Delray Beach, FL Div 48424
	17063	Grundy County	33100		
	17093	Kendall County		12099	Palm Beach County
	17111	McHenry County			
	17197	Will County	37980		**Philadelphia-Camden-Wilmington, PA-NJ-DE-MD**
16980		Elgin, IL Div 20994	37980		Camden, NJ Div 15804
	17037	DeKalb County		34005	Burlington County
	17089	Kane County		34007	Camden County
16980		Gary, IN Div 23844		34015	Gloucester County
	18073	Jasper County			Montgomery County-Bucks County-Chester County, PA
	18089	Lake County	37980		Div 33874
	18111	Newton County		42017	Bucks County
	18127	Porter County		42029	Chester County
16980		Lake County-Kenosha County, IL-WI Div 29404		42091	Montgomery County
	17097	Lake County	37980		Philadelphia, PA Div 37964
	55059	Kenosha County		42045	Delaware County
				42101	Philadelphia County
19100		**Dallas-Fort Worth-Arlington, TX**	37980		Wilmington, DE-MD-NJ Div 48864
19100		Dallas-Plano-Irving, TX Div 19124		10003	New Castle County
	48085	Collin County		24015	Cecil County
	48113	Dallas County		34033	Salem County
	48121	Denton County			
	48139	Ellis County	12060		**Atlanta-Sandy Springs-Roswell, GA**
	48231	Hunt County		13013	Barrow County
	48257	Kaufman County		13015	Bartow County
	48397	Rockwall County		13035	Butts County
19100		Fort Worth-Arlington, TX Div 23104		13045	Carroll County
	48221	Hood County		13057	Cherokee County
	48251	Johnson County		13063	Clayton County
	48367	Parker County		13067	Cobb County
	48425	Somervell County		13077	Coweta County
	48439	Tarrant County		13085	Dawson County
	48497	Wise County		13089	DeKalb County
				13097	Douglas County
26420		**Houston-The Woodlands-Sugar Land, TX**		13113	Fayette County
	48015	Austin County		13117	Forsyth County
	48039	Brazoria County		13121	Fulton County
	48071	Chambers County		13135	Gwinnett County
	48157	Fort Bend County		13143	Haralson County
	48167	Galveston County		13149	Heard County
				13151	Henry County

719

Core based statistical area	State/County FIPS code	Title and Geographic Components
	13159	Jasper County
	13171	Lamar County
	13199	Meriwether County
	13211	Morgan County
	13217	Newton County
	13223	Paulding County
	13227	Pickens County
	13231	Pike County
	13247	Rockdale County
	13255	Spalding County
	13297	Walton County
14460		**Boston-Cambridge-Newton, MA-NH**
14460		Boston, MA Div 14454
	25021	Norfolk County
	25023	Plymouth County
	25025	Suffolk County
14460		Cambridge-Newton-Framingham, MA Div 15764
	25009	Essex County
	25017	Middlesex County
14460		Rockingham County-Strafford County, NH Div 40484
	33015	Rockingham County
	33017	Strafford County
38060		**Phoenix-Mesa-Scottsdale, AZ**
	04013	Maricopa County
	04021	Pinal County
41860		**San Francisco-Oakland-Hayward, CA**
41860		Oakland-Hayward-Berkeley, CA Div 36084
	06001	Alameda County
	06013	Contra Costa County
41860		San Francisco-Redwood City-South San Francisco, CA Div 41884
	06075	San Francisco County
	06081	San Mateo County
41860		San Rafael, CA Div 42034
	06041	Marin County
40140		**Riverside-San Bernardino-Ontario, CA**
	06065	Riverside County
	06071	San Bernardino County
19820		**Detroit-Warren-Dearborn, MI**
19820		Detroit-Dearborn-Livonia, MI Div 19804
	26163	Wayne County
19820		Warren-Troy-Farmington Hills, MI 47664
	26087	Lapeer County
	26093	Livingston County
	26099	Macomb County
	26125	Oakland County
	26147	St Clair County
42660		**Seattle-Tacoma-Bellevue, WA**
42660		Seattle-Bellevue-Everett, WA Div 42644
	53033	King County
	53061	Snohomish County
42660		Tacoma-Lakewood, WA Div 45104
	53053	Pierce County
33460		**Minneapolis-St Paul-Bloomington, MN**
	27003	Anoka County
	27019	Carver County
	27025	Chisago County
	27037	Dakota County
	27053	Hennepin County
	27059	Isanti County
	27079	Le Sueur County
	27095	Mille Lacs County
	27123	Ramsey County
	27139	Scott County
	27141	Sherburne County
	27143	Sibley County
	27163	Washington County
	27171	Wright County
	55093	Pierce County
	55109	St Croix County
41740		**San Diego-Carlsbad, CA**
	06073	San Diego County
45300		**Tampa-St Petersburg-Clearwater, FL**
	12053	Hernando County
	12057	Hillsborough County
	12101	Pasco County
	12103	Pinellas County

Core based statistical area	State/County FIPS code	Title and Geographic Components
19740		**Denver-Aurora-Lakewood, CO**
	08001	Adams County
	08005	Arapahoe County
	08014	Broomfield County
	08019	Clear Creek County
	08031	Denver County
	08035	Douglas County
	08039	Elbert County
	08047	Gilpin County
	08059	Jefferson County
	08093	Park County
12580		**Baltimore-Columbia-Towson, MD**
	24003	Anne Arundel County
	24005	Baltimore County
	24013	Carroll County
	24025	Harford County
	24027	Howard County
	24035	Queen Anne's County
	24510	Baltimore city
41180		**St. Louis, MO-IL**
	17005	Bond County
	17013	Calhoun County
	17027	Clinton County
	17083	Jersey County
	17117	Macoupin County
	17119	Madison County
	17133	Monroe County
	17163	St Clair County
	29071	Franklin County
	29099	Jefferson County
	29113	Lincoln County
	29183	St Charles County
	29189	St Louis County
	29219	Warren County
	29510	St Louis city
16740		**Charlotte-Concord-Gastonia, NC-SC**
	37025	Cabarrus County
	37071	Gaston County
	37097	Iredell County
	37109	Lincoln County
	37119	Mecklenburg County
	37159	Rowan County
	37179	Union County
	45023	Chester County
	45057	Lancaster County
	45091	York County
36740		**Orlando-Kissimmee-Sanford, FL Metro**
	12069	Lake County
	12095	Orange County
	12097	Osceola County
	12117	Seminole County
41700		**San Antonio-New Braunfels, TX**
	48013	Atascosa County
	48019	Bandera County
	48029	Bexar County
	48091	Comal County
	48187	Guadalupe County
	48259	Kendall County
	48325	Medina County
	48493	Wilson County
38900		**Portland-Vancouver-Hillsboro, OR-WA**
	41005	Clackamas County
	41009	Columbia County
	41051	Multnomah County
	41067	Washington County
	41071	Yamhill County
	53011	Clark County
	53059	Skamania County
38300		**Pittsburgh, PA**
	42003	Allegheny County
	42005	Armstrong County
	42007	Beaver County
	42019	Butler County
	42051	Fayette County
	42125	Washington County
	42129	Westmoreland County
40900		**Sacramento--Roseville--Arden-Arcade, CA**
	06017	El Dorado County
	06061	Placer County

Core based statistical area	State/ County FIPS code	Title and Geographic Components	Core based statistical area	State/ County FIPS code	Title and Geographic Components
	06067	Sacramento County		47081	Hickman County
	06113	Yolo County		47111	Macon County
				47119	Maury County
29820		**Las Vegas-Henderson-Paradise, NV Metro area**		47147	Robertson County
	32003	Clark County, NV		47149	Rutherford County
				47159	Smith County
17140		**Cincinnati, OH-KY-IN**		47165	Sumner County
	18029	Dearborn County		47169	Trousdale County
	18115	Ohio County		47187	Williamson County
	18161	Union County		47189	Wilson County
	21015	Boone County			
	21023	Bracken County	47260		**Virginia Beach-Norfolk-Newport News, VA-NC**
	21037	Campbell County		37053	Currituck County
	21077	Gallatin County		37073	Gates County
	21081	Grant County		51073	Gloucester County
	21117	Kenton County		51093	Isle of Wight County
	21191	Pendleton County		51095	James City County
	39015	Brown County		51115	Mathews County
	39017	Butler County		51199	York County
	39025	Clermont County		51550	Chesapeake city
	39061	Hamilton County		51650	Hampton city
	39165	Warren County		51700	Newport News city
				51710	Norfolk city
28140		**Kansas City, MO-KS**		51735	Poquoson city
	20091	Johnson County		51740	Portsmouth city
	20103	Leavenworth County		51800	Suffolk city
	20107	Linn County		51810	Virginia Beach city
	20121	Miami County		51830	Williamsburg city
	20209	Wyandotte County			
	29013	Bates County	39300		**Providence Warwick, RI-MA**
	29025	Caldwell County		25005	Bristol County
	29037	Cass County		44001	Bristol County
	29047	Clay County		44003	Kent County
	29049	Clinton County		44005	Newport County
	29095	Jackson County		44007	Providence County
	29107	Lafayette County		44009	Washington County
	29165	Platte County			
	29177	Ray County	33340		**Milwaukee-Waukesha-West Allis, WI**
				55079	Milwaukee County
12420		**Austin-Round Rock, TX**		55089	Ozaukee County
	48021	Bastrop County		55131	Washington County
	48055	Caldwell County		55133	Waukesha County
	48209	Hays County			
	48453	Travis County	27260		**Jacksonville, FL**
	48491	Williamson County		12003	Baker County
				12019	Clay County
18140		**Columbus, OH**		12031	Duval County
	39041	Delaware County		12089	Nassau County
	39045	Fairfield County		12109	St Johns County
	39049	Franklin County			
	39073	Hocking County	36420		**Oklahoma City, OK**
	39089	Licking County		40017	Canadian County
	39097	Madison County		40027	Cleveland County
	39117	Morrow County		40051	Grady County
	39127	Perry County		40081	Lincoln County
	39129	Pickaway County		40083	Logan County
	39159	Union County		40087	McClain County
				40109	Oklahoma County
17460		**Cleveland-Elyria, OH**			
	39035	Cuyahoga County	32820		**Memphis, TN-MS-AR**
	39055	Geauga County		05035	Crittenden County
	39085	Lake County		28009	Benton County
	39093	Lorain County		28033	DeSoto County
	39103	Medina County		28093	Marshall County
				28137	Tate County
26900		**Indianapolis-Carmel-Anderson, IN**		28143	Tunica County
	18011	Boone County		47047	Fayette County
	18013	Brown County		47157	Shelby County
	18057	Hamilton County		47167	Tipton County
	18059	Hancock County			
	18063	Hendricks County	39580		**Raleigh, NC**
	18081	Johnson County		37069	Franklin County
	18095	Madison County		37101	Johnston County
	18097	Marion County		37183	Wake County
	18109	Morgan County			
	18133	Putnam County	40060		**Richmond, VA**
	18145	Shelby County		51007	Amelia County
				51033	Caroline County
41940		**San Jose-Sunnyvale-Santa Clara, CA**		51036	Charles City County
	06069	San Benito County		51041	Chesterfield County
	06085	Santa Clara County		51053	Dinwiddie County
				51075	Goochland County
34980		**Nashville-Davidson--Murfreesboro--Franklin, TN**		51085	Hanover County
	47015	Cannon County		51087	Henrico County
	47021	Cheatham County		51101	King William County
	47037	Davidson County		51127	New Kent County
	47043	Dickson County		51145	Powhatan County

Core based statistical area	State/ County FIPS code	Title and Geographic Components	Core based statistical area	State/ County FIPS code	Title and Geographic Components
	51149	Prince George County	14860		Bridgeport-Stamford-Norwalk, CT
	51183	Sussex County		09001	Fairfield County
	51570	Colonial Heights city			
	51670	Hopewell city	49340		Worcester, MA-CT
	51730	Petersburg city		09015	Windham County
	51760	Richmond city		25027	Worcester County
31140		Louisville/Jefferson County, KY-IN	36540		Omaha-Council Bluffs, NE-IA
	18019	Clark County		19085	Harrison County
	18043	Floyd County		19129	Mills County
	18061	Harrison County		19155	Pottawattamie County
	18143	Scott County		31025	Cass County
	18175	Washington County		31055	Douglas County
	21029	Bullitt County		31153	Sarpy County
	21103	Henry County		31155	Saunders County
	21111	Jefferson County		31177	Washington County
	21185	Oldham County			
	21211	Shelby County	10740		Albuquerque, NM
	21215	Spencer County		35001	Bernalillo County
	21223	Trimble County		35043	Sandoval County
35380		New Orleans-Metairie, LA		35057	Torrance County
	22051	Jefferson Parish		35061	Valencia County
	22071	Orleans Parish			
	22075	Plaquemines Parish	24780		Greenville, NC
	22087	St Bernard Parish		37147	Pitt County
	22089	St Charles Parish			
	22093	St James Parish	12540		Bakersfield, CA
	22095	St John the Baptist Parish		06029	Kern County
	22103	St Tammany Parish			
25540		Hartford-West Hartford-East Hartford, CT	10580		Albany-Schenectady-Troy, NY
	09003	Hartford County		36001	Albany County
	09007	Middlesex County		36083	Rensselaer County
	09013	Tolland County		36091	Saratoga County
				36093	Schenectady County
41620		Salt Lake City, UT		36095	Schoharie County
	49035	Salt Lake County	28940		Knoxville, TN
	49045	Tooele County		47001	Anderson County
13820		Birmingham-Hoover, AL		47009	Blount County
	01007	Bibb County		47013	Campbell County
	01009	Blount County		47057	Grainger County
	01021	Chilton County		47093	Knox County
	01073	Jefferson County		47105	Loudon County
	01115	St Clair County		47129	Morgan County
	01117	Shelby County		47145	Roane County
	01127	Walker County		47173	Union County
15380		Buffalo-Cheektowaga-Niagara Falls, NY	32580		McAllen-Edinburg-Mission, TX
	36029	Erie County		48215	Hidalgo County
	36063	Niagara County			
40380		Rochester, NY	35300		New Haven-Milford, CT
	36051	Livingston County		09009	New Haven County
	36055	Monroe County			
	36069	Ontario County	37100		Oxnard-Thousand Oaks-Ventura, CA
	36073	Orleans County		06111	Ventura County
	36117	Wayne County			
	36123	Yates County	21340		El Paso, TX
24340		Grand Rapids-Wyoming, MI		48141	El Paso County
	26015	Barry County		48229	Hudspeth County
	26081	Kent County	10900		Allentown-Bethlehem-Easton, PA-NJ
	26117	Montcalm County		34041	Warren County
	26139	Ottawa County		42025	Carbon County
46060		Tucson, AZ		42077	Lehigh County
	04019	Pima County		42095	Northampton County
46140		Tulsa, OK	12940		Baton Rouge, LA
	40037	Creek County		22005	Ascension Parish
	40111	Okmulgee County		22033	East Baton Rouge Parish
	40113	Osage County		22037	East Feliciana Parish
	40117	Pawnee County		22047	Iberville Parish
	40131	Rogers County		22063	Livingston Parish
	40143	Tulsa County		22077	Pointe Coupee Parish
	40145	Wagoner County		22091	St Helena Parish
23420		Fresno, CA		22121	West Baton Rouge Parish
	06019	Fresno County		22125	West Feliciana Parish
46520		Urban Honolulu, HI	17900		Columbia, SC
	15003	Honolulu County		45017	Calhoun County
				45039	Fairfield County
				45055	Kershaw County
				45063	Lexington County
				45079	Richland County
				45081	Saluda County

Core based statistical area	State/ County FIPS code	Title and Geographic Components
35840		**North Port-Sarasota-Bradenton, FL**
	12081	Manatee County
	12115	Sarasota County
19380		**Dayton, OH**
	39057	Greene County
	39109	Miami County
	39113	Montgomery County

Core based statistical area	State/ County FIPS code	Title and Geographic Components
16700		**Charleston-North Charleston, SC**
	45015	Berkeley County
	45019	Charleston County
	45035	Dorchester County
24660		**Greensboro-High Point, NC**
	37081	Guilford County
	37151	Randolph County
	37157	Rockingham County